DIRECTORY
OF
AMERICAN
SCHOLARS

DIRECTORY
OF
AMERICAN
SCHOLARS

NINTH EDITION

VOLUME **III**

FOREIGN LANGUAGES,
LINGUISTICS, & PHILOLOGY

Rita C. Velázquez, Editor

The Gale Group

DETROIT • SAN FRANCISCO • LONDON • BOSTON • WOODBRIDGE, CT

Rita C. Velázquez, Editor

Project Associates and Contributing Editors: Michelle
Eads, Amanda Quick

Contributing Staff: Mary Alampi, Caryn Anders, Katy Balcer, Anja
Barnard, Donna Batten, Donna Craft, Andrea DeJong, Sarah DeMar, Sheila Dow, Kim
Forster, William Harmer, Kelly Hill, LySandra Hill, Sonya Hill, Crystal Holombo, Theresa
MacFarlane, Christine Maurer, Matthew Miskelly, Jacqueline Mueckenheim, Erin Nagel,
Lynn Pearce, Terry Peck, Maureen Puhl, Donna Wood.

Contributors: Chapter House, IMPS; The Electronic
Scriptorium, Ltd.

Managing Editor: Keith Jones

Manager, Technical Support Services: Theresa Rocklin
Programmer/Analyst: Jim Edwards

Manufacturing Manager: Dorothy Maki
Senior Buyer: Wendy Blurton

Product Design Manager: Cindy Baldwin
Art Director: Eric Johnson
Graphic Artist: Gary Leach

CONTENTS

PREFACE

First published in 1942 under the auspices of the American Council of Learned Societies, The Directory of American Scholars remains the foremost biographical reference to American humanities scholars. With the ninth edition, The Gale Group is continuing the tradition.

The directory is arranged for convenient use in four subject volumes: Volume I: History; Volume II: English, Speech, and Drama; Volume III: Foreign Languages, Linguistics, and Philology; Volume IV: Philosophy, Religion, and Law. Each volume of biographical listings contains a geographic index. Volume V contains an alphabetical index, a discipline index, an institutional index and a cumulative geographic index of scholars listed in the first four volumes.

The ninth edition of the Directory of American Scholars profiles more than 24,000 United States and Canadian scholars currently active in teaching, research, and publishing. The names of entrants were obtained from a variety of sources, including former entrants, academic deans, or citations in professional journals. In most cases, nominees received a questionnaire to complete, and selection for inclusion was made based on the following criteria:

1. Achievement, by reason of experience and training, of a stature in scholarly work equivalent to that associated with the doctoral degree, coupled with current activity in such work;

or

2. Achievement as evidenced by publication of scholarly works;

or

3. Attainment of a position of substantial responsibility by reason of achievement as outlined in (1) and (2).

Enhancements to the ninth edition include an index volume, simplifying the search for a particular scholar or a particular group of scholars. Indexing by discipline is sorted by primary and secondary majors, in some cases including majors that are not traditionally considered as humanities. Those individuals involved in several fields are cross-referenced into appropriate volumes.

The ninth edition of The Directory of American Scholars is produced by fully automated methods. Limitations in the printing method have made it necessary to omit most diacritics.

Individual entries can include place and year of birth, *primary discipline(s), vital statistics, education, honorary degrees, past and present professional experience, concurrent positions, *membership in international, national and regional societies, honors and awards, *research interest, *publications, and mailing address. Elements preceded by an asterisk are limited as to the number of items includes. If an entrant exceeded these limitations, the editors selected the most recent information. Biographies received in the offices of The Gale Group after the editorial deadline were included in an abbreviated manner.

The editors have made every effort to include material as accurately and completely as possible within the confines of format and scope. However, the publishers do not assume and hereby disclaim any liability to any party for any loss or damage caused by errors or omissions in the Directory of American Scholars, whether such errors or omissions result from negligence, accident, or any other cause.

Thanks are expressed to those who contributed information and submitted nominations for the new edition. Many societies provided membership lists for the research process and published announcements in their journals or newsletters, and their help is appreciated.

Comments and suggestions regarding any aspect of the ninth edition are invited and should be addressed to The Editors, Directory of American Scholars, The Gale Group, 27500 Drake Road, Farmington Hills, MI 48333-3535.

ADVISORS

David M. Fahey
Professor of History
Miami University
Miami, Ohio

Patricia Hardesty
Humanities Reference/Liaison Libraran
George Mason University
Fairfax, Virginia

Stephen Karetzky
Library Director, Associate Professor
Felician College
Lodi, New Jersey

ABBREVIATIONS

AAAS American Association for the Advancement of Science
AAUP American Association of University Professors
abnorm abnormal
acad academia, academic, academica, academie, academique, academy
accad accademia
acct account, accountant, accounting
acoust acoustical, accounstic(s)
adj adjunct, adjutant
actg acting
activ activities, activity
addn addition(s), additional
AID Agency for International Development
adjust adjust
admin administration, administrative
adminr administrator(s)
admis admissions
adv advisor(s), advisory
advan advance(d), advancement
advert advertisement, advertising
aerodyn aerodynamic(s)
aeronaut aeronautic(s), aeronautical
aesthet aesthetics
affil affiliate(s), affiliation
agr agricultural, agriculture
agt agent
AFB Air Force Base
AHA American Historical Association
akad akademi, akademia
Ala Alabama
Algem algemeen, algemen
allergol allergological, allergology
allgem allgemein, allgemeine, allgemeinen
Alta Alberta
Am America, Americain, American, Americana, Americano, Amerika, Amerikaansch, Amerikaner, Amerikanisch, Amerikansk
anal analysis, analytic, analytical
analog analogue
anat anatomic, anatomical, anatomy
ann annal(s)
anthrop anthropological, anthropology
anthropom anthropometric, anthropometrical, anthropometry
antiq antiquaire(s), antiquarian, antiquary(ies), antiquities
app appoint, appointed, appointment
appl applied
appln application
approx approximate, approximately
Apr April
apt apartment(s)

arbit arbitration
arch archiv, archiva, archive(s), archivio, archivo
archaeol archaeological, archaeology
archaol archaologie, archaologisch
archeol archeological, archeologie, archeologique, archeology
archit architectural, architecture
Arg Argentina, Argentine
Ariz Arizona
Ark Arkansas
asn association
asoc asociacion
assoc(s) associate(s), associated
asst assistant
Assyriol Assyriology
astrodyn astrodynamics
astron astronomical, astronomy
astronaut astronautical, astronautics
astronr astronomer
attend attendant, attending
atty attorney
audiol audiology
Aug August
auth author(s)
AV audiovisual
ave avenue

b born
BC British Columbia
bd board
behav behavior, behavioral, behaviour, behavioural
Bibl Biblical, Biblique
bibliog bibliografia, bibliographic, bibligraphical, bibliography(ies)
bibliogr bibliographer
bibliot biblioteca, bibliotec, bibliotek, bibliotheca, bibliothek, bibliothequeca
biog biographical, biography
biol biological, biology
bk(s) books
bldg building
blvd boulevard
bol boletim, boletin
boll bollettino
bor borough
bot botanical, botany
br branch
Brit Britain, British
Bro(s) Brother(s)
bull bulletin
bur bureau

bus business
BWI British West Indies

c children
Calif California
Can Canada, Canadian, Canadien, Canadienne
cand candidate
cartog cartografic, cartographical, cartography
cartogra cartographer
Cath Catholic, Catholique
CBS Columbia Broadcasting System
cent central
Cent Am Central America
cert certificat, certificate, certified
chap chapter
chem chermical, chemistry
chg charge
chemn chairman
Cie Compagnie
cient cientifica, cientifico
class classical
clin(s) clinic(s)
Co Companies, Company, County
coauth coauth
co-dir co-director
co-ed co-editor
co-educ co-educational
col(s) colegio, college(s), collegiate
collab collaboration, collaborative, collaborating, collaborator
Colo Colorado
Comdr Commander
com commerce, commercial
commun communication(s)
comn(s) commission(s)
comnr commissioner
comp comparative, comparee
compos composition(s)
comput computer, computing
comt committee
conf conference
cong congress
Conn Connecticut
conserv conservacion,conservation, conservatoire, conservatory
consol consolidated, consolidation
const constitution, constitutional
construct construction
consult consultant, consulting
contemp contemporary
contrib contribute, contribution
contribur contributor

conv convention
coop cooperation, cooperative
coord coordinating, coordination
coordr coordinator
corresp corresponding
Corp Corporation
coun council, counsel, counseling
counr councillor, counselor
criminol criminology
Ct Court
ctr center
cult cultra, cultural, culturale, culture
cur curator
curric curriculum
cybernet cybernetics
CZ Canal Zone
Czeck Czechoslovakia

DC District of Columbia
Dec December
Del Delaware
deleg delegate, delegations
demog demographic, demography
demonstr demonstrator
dent dental, dentistry
dep deputy
dept department
Deut Deutsch, Deutschland
develop development
diag diagnosis, diagnostic
dialectol dialectology
dig digest
dipl diploma, diploma, diplomate, diplome
dir director(s), directory
directory
Diss Abstr Dissertation Abstracts
dist district
distrib distributive
distribr distributors
div division, divorced
doc document, documentation
Dom Dominion
Dr Doctor, Drive
Drs Doctroandus

e east
ecol ecological, ecology
econ economic(s), economical, economy
ed edicion, edition, editor, editorial, edizione
educ education, educational
educr educator(s)
Egyptol Egyptology
elec electric, electrical, electricity
electrical
elem elementary
emer emeriti, emeritus
encour encouragement
encycl encyclopedia
employ employment
Eng England
environ environment, environmental
EPDA Education Professions Development Act
equip equipment
ERIC Educational Resources Information Center
ESEA Elementary & Secondary Education Act
espec especially
estab established, establishment
estud estudante, estudas, estudianet, estudio(s), estudo(s)
ethnog ethnographical, ethnography
ethnol ethnological, ethnology
Europ European
eval evaluation
evangel evangelical
eve evening
exam examination
examr examiner

except exceptional
exec executive(s)
exeg exegesis(es), exegetic, exegetical, exegetics
exhib exhibition(s)
exp experiment, experimental, experimentation
exped expedition(s)
explor exploration(s)
expos exposition
exten extension

fac faculties, faculty
facil facilities, facility
Feb February
fed federal
fedn federation
fel(s) fellow(s), fellowship(s)
filol filologia, filologico
filos filosofia, filosofico
Fla Florida
FLES Foreign Languages in the Elementary Schools
for foreign
forsch forschung, forschungen
found foundation
Fr Francais(s), French
Ft Fort

Ga Georgia
gen general, generale
geneal genealogical, genealogy
genoot genootschap
geod geodesy, geodetic
geog geografia, geografico, geographer(s), geographic, geographie, geographical, geography
geogr geographer
geol geologic, geological, geology
geophys geophysical
Ger German, Germanic, Germanisch, Germany
Ges gesellschaft
gov governing, governors
govt government
grad graduate
Gr Brit Great Britain
guid guidance
gym gymnasium

handbk(s) handbooks
Hawaii
Hisp Hispanic, Hispanico, Hispano
hist historie, historia, historial, historic, historica, historical, historique, historische, history
histol histology, histological
Hoshsch Hoshschule
hon honorable, honorary
hosp(s) hospital(s)
hq headquarters
HumRRO Human Resources Research Office
hwy highway

Ill Illinois
illum illuminating, illumination
illus illustrate, illustration
illusr illustrator
imp imperial
improv improvement
Inc Incorporated
incl include, included, includes, including
Ind Indiana
indust(s) industrial, industry(ies)
infor information
inst institut, instritute(s), institution(s), instituto
instnl institutional, institutionalized
instr instruction, instructor(s)

instruct instructional
int internacional, international, internazionale
intel intelligence
introd introduction
invest investigacion, investiganda, investigation, investigative
investr investigator
ist istituto
Ital Italia, Italian, Italiana, Italiano, Italica, Italien, Italienisch, Italienne, Italy

J Journal
Jan January
jour journal, journalism
jr junior
jurisp jurisprudence
juv juvenile(s)

Kans Kansas
Koninki koninklijk
Ky Kentucky

La Louisiana
lab laboratorie, laboratorio, laboratorium, laboratory(ies)
lang language(s)
lect lecture(s)
lectr lecturer
legis legislacion, legislatief, legislation, legislative, legislativo, legislature, legislazione
lett letter(s), lettera, letteraria, letterature, lettere
lib liberal
libr libary(ies), librerio
librn librarian(s)
lic license, lecencia
ling linguistic(s), linguistica, linguistique
lit liteary, literatur, literatura, literature, littera, literature
Ltd Limited

m married
mach machine(s), machinery
mag magazine
Man Manitoba
Mar March
Mariol Mariological, Mariology
Mass Massachusetts
mat matematica, matematiche, matematico, matematik
math mathematics, mathematical, mathematics, mathematik, mathematique(s), mathematisch
Md Maryland
mech mechanical
med medical, medicine
Mediter Mediterranean
mem member, memoirs, memorial
ment mental, mentally
metrop metropolitan
Mex Mexican, Mexicano, Mexico
mfg manufacturing
mfr manufacture, manufacturer
mgr manager(s)
mgt management
Mich Michigan
mid middle
mil military
Minn Minnesota
Miss Mississippi
mitt mitteilung
mkt market, marketing
MLA Modern Language Association of America
Mo Missouri

mod modern,moderna, moderne, moderno
monatsh monatsheft(e)
monatsschr monatsschrift
monogr monograph
Mont Montana
morphol morphologica, morphologie, morphology
mt mount, mountain(s)
munic municipal
mus museum(s)
musicol musicological, musicology

n north
nac nacional
NASA National Aeronautics & Space Administration
nat nationaal, national, nationale, nationalis, naturalized
NATO North Atlantic Treaty Organization
naz nazionale
NB New Brunswick
NC North Carolina
MCTE National Council of Teachers of English
NDak North Dakota
NDEA National Defense Education Act
NEA National Education Association
Nebr Nebraska
Ned Nederland, Nederlandsch
Nev Nevada
Neth Netherlands
Nfld Newfoundland
NH New Hampshire
NJ New Jersey
NMex New Mexico
no number
nonres nonresident
norm normal, normale
Norweg Norwegian
Nov November
NS Nova Scotia
NSW New South Wales
NT Northwest Territories
numis numismatic, numismatico, numismatique
NY New York
NZ New Zealand

occas occasional
occup occupation, occupational
Oct October
Ohio
OEEC Organization for European Economic Cooperation
off office, officer(s), official(s)
Okla Oklahoma
Ont Ontario
oper operation(s), operational, operative
ord ordnance
Ore Oregon
orgn organization, organizational
orient oriental, orientale, orientalist, orientalia
ornithol ornithological, ornithology

Pa Pennsylvania
Pac Pacific
paleontol paleontological, paleontology
PanAm Pan American
pedag pedagogia, pedagogic, pedagogical, pedagogico, pedagogoie, pedagogik, pedagogique, pedagogy
Pei Prince Edward Island
penol penological, penology
phenomenol phenomenological, phenomenologie, phenomenology
philol philologica, philological, philologie, philologisch, philology

philos philosophia, philosophic, philosophical, philosophie, philosophique, philosophisch, philosophical, philosohpy, philosozophia
photog photographic, photography
photogr photographer(s)
phys physical
pkwy parkway
pl place
polit politica, political, politicas, politico, politics,
politek, politike, politique, politsch, politisk
polytech polytechnic
pop population
Pontif Pontifical
Port Portugal, Portuguese
postgrad postgraduate
PR Puerto Rico
pract practice
prehist prehistoric
prep preparation, preparatory
pres president
Presby Presbyterian
preserv preservation
prev prevention, preventive
prin principal(s)
prob problem(s)
probtn probation
proc proceding
prod production
prof professional, professor, professorial
prog program(s), programmed, programming
proj project, projective
prom promotion
prov province, provincial
psychiat psychiatria, psychiatric, psychiatrica, psychiatrie, psychiatrique, psychiatrisch, psychiatry
psychol psychological
pt point
pub pub, publique
publ publication(s), published, publisher(s), publishing
pvt private

qm quartermaster
quad quaderni
qual qualitative, quality
quart quarterly
Que Quebec

rd road
RD Rural Delivery, Rural Free Delivery Rural Free Delivery
rec record(s), recording
rech recherche
redevelop redevelopment
ref reference
regist register, registered, registration
registr registrar
rehabil rehabilitation
rel(s) relacion, relation(s), relative, relazione
relig religion, religious
rep representative
repub republic
req requirement(s)
res research, reserve
rev review, revised, revista, revue
rhet rhetoric, rhetorical
RI Rhode Island
Rt Right
Rte Route
Russ Russian
rwy railway

s south
SAfrica South Africa
SAm South America, South American

Sask Saskatchewan
SC South Carolina
Scand Scandinavian
sch(s) school(s)
scholar scholarship
sci science(s), scientia, scientific, scientifico, scientifique, scienza
SDak South Dakota
SEATO Southeast Asia Treaty Organization
sec secondary
sect section
secy secretary
sem seminaire, seminar, seminario, seminary
sen senator, sneatorial
Sept September
ser serial, series
serv service(s)
soc social, sociedad, sociedade, societa, societas, societate, societe, societet, society(ies)
soc sci social science(s)
sociol sociological, sociology
Span Spanish
spec special
sq square
sr senior
sr sister
St Saint, Street
sta station
statist statistical, statistics
Ste Sainte, Suite
struct structural, structure(s)
subcomt subcommittee
subj subject
substa substa
super superieur, superior, superiore
suppl supplement, supplementary
supt superintendent
supv supervising, supervision
supvr supervisor
supvry supervisory
surg surgical, surgery
surv survey
Swed Swedish
Switz Switzerland
symp symposium
syst system, systematic

tech technic(s), technica, technical, technicky, techniczny, techniek, technik, technika, technikum, technique, technisch
technol technologic, technological, technologicke, technologico, technologiczny, technologie, technologika, technologique, technologisch, technology
tecnol technologia, technologica, technologico
tel telegraph(s), telephone
temp temporary
Tenn Tennessee
Terr Terrace
teol teologia, teologico
Tex Texas
textbk textbook(s)
theol theological, theologie, theologique, theologisch, theology
theoret theoretic(al)
ther therapy
trans transactions
transp transportation
transl translation, translator(s)
treas treasurer, treasury
trop tropical
TV television
twp township

u   und
UAR United Arab Republic
UK   United Kingdom
UN   United Nations
unemploy unemployment
UNESCO   United Nations Educational,
Scientific & Cultural
Organization
UNICEF   United Nations Children's Fund
univ(s) universidad, universite,
university(ies)
UNRRA   United Nations Relief &
Rehabilitation Administration
UNRWA   United Nations Relief & Works
Agency
USA United States of America
US   United States
USPHS   United States Public Health
Service

USSR Union of Soviet Socialist Republics
Utah

Va Virginia
var various
veg vegetable(s), vegetation
ver vereeniging, verein, vereingt,
vereinigung
vet veteran, veterinarian, veterinary
VI Virgin Islands
vis visiting
voc vocational
vocab   vocabulary
vol(s)   volume(s), voluntary, volunteer(s)
vchmn   vice chairman
vpres   vice president
Vt Vermont

w   west
Wash Washington
wetensch wetenschappelijk, wetenschappen
WHO World Health Organization
WI   West Indies
wid widow, widowed, widower
Wis Wisconsin
wiss wissenschaft(en), wissenschaftliche(e)
WVa West Virginia
Wyo Wyoming

yearbk   yearbook(s)
YMCA Young Men's Christian Association
YMHA Young Men's Hebrew Association
YWCA Young Women's Christian Associa-
tion
YWHA Young Women's Hebrew Association

z   zeitschrift

Biographies

A

ABBOTT, B.
PERSONAL Born 05/01/1943, Baltimore, MD, m, 1993 **DISCIPLINE** LINGUISTICS **EDUCATION** Univ Calif-Berkeley, PhD, 76. **CAREER** Prof, Ling & Philos, Mich State Univ, 76-. **MEMBERSHIPS** Ling Soc Am; Am Philos Asn; Soc Philos & Psychol; Am Asn Advancement Sci. **RESEARCH** Semantics; pragmatics; philosophy of language. **SELECTED PUBLICATIONS** Auth, Referentialiy, Specificity, Strength, and Individual Concepts, WCCFL 12, 94; auth, Thinking without English, Behavior & Philos 23, 95; auth, Doing without Partitive Constraints, in Partitives: Studies on the Syntax and Semantics of Partitive and Related Constructions, Gronigen-Amsterdam Studies in Semantics, Mouton de Gruyter, 96; auth, A Note on the Nature of Water, Mind 106, 97; auth, Models, Truth, and Semantics, Ling & Philos, 97. **CONTACT ADDRESS** Ling & Lang, Michigan State Univ, A-614 Wells Hall, East Lansing, MI, 48824-1027. **EMAIL** abbottb@pilot.msu.edu

ABBOTT, CARMETA
DISCIPLINE FRENCH LITERATURE **EDUCATION** Ohio State Univ, BA; MA; PhD. **RESEARCH** Seventeenth century theatre; eighteenth century epistolary novel; contemporary French civilization; second language pedagogy. **SELECTED PUBLICATIONS** Co-ed, Les Jumeaux martirs 1650. **CONTACT ADDRESS** Dept of French, Waterloo Univ, 200 University Ave W, Waterloo, ON, N2L 3G1. **EMAIL** ceabbott@watarts.uwaterloo.ca

ABBOUD, PETER FOUAD
PERSONAL Born 06/30/1931, Jaffa, Palestine, w, 1952, 1 child **DISCIPLINE** LINGUISTICS, ARABIC STUDIES **EDUCATION** Univ London, BS, 56; Am Univ Cairo, MA, 60; Univ Tex, Austin, PhD, 64. **CAREER** From asst instr to instr English, Am Univ Cairo, 57-61; asst prof, 64-68, assoc prof ling, 68-, prof Arabic, 84, Univ Tex, Austin; visit fac and sch, Georgetown Univ, 63, Univ of Mich, 65, 69, 70, 77, 78, 91, 94, Columbia Univ 66, Princeton Univ, 67, Univ Chicago, 94; dir, sch Arabic, Middlebury Col, 82-90; chmn, dept Mid Eastern Land and Cult, 94-98. **HONORS AND AWARDS** Am Res Ctr is Egypt fel, 71-72; Fulbright fel 75-76. **MEMBERSHIPS** Ling Soc Am; Am Orient Soc; Am Teachers Arabic; Mid E Studies Asn N Am. **RESEARCH** Classical Arabic; Arabic dialectology; and Arabic language teaching. **SELECTED PUBLICATIONS** Coauth, Beginning Cairo Arabic, Univ Tex, 65; Elementary Modern Standard Arabic, Inter-Univ Comt Near Eastern Lang, 68; auth, The Teaching of Arabic in the United States: The State of the Art, ERIC Clearinghouse for Ling, 68; coauth, Modern Standard Arabic: Intermediate Level, Ctr Near Eastern & N African Studies, Mich, 71; auth, Spoken Arabic, In: Current Trends in Linguistics, Vol VI, Mouton, 71; On Ablaut in Cairo Arabic, Afro-Asiatic Ling, 76; auth, The Verb in Northern Najdi Arabic, Bull Sch Oriental and Afr Stu, 79; auth The Classical Arabic Jussive Forms and Their Reflexes in the Modern Arabic Dialects, Zeit Deutsch Morgenlanisch Gesellschaft, 82; auth, Some Grammatical(Morphological and Syntactic-Semantic) Considerations in Arabic-English Bilingual Dictionaries, The Arabic Dictionary to Non-Arabic Speakers, Arab League Education, Cultural, and Scientific Organization, 83; coauth, Computer Assisted Instruction Program for Vocabulary and Reading Comprehension for Modern Standard Arabic, Intermediate Level, 84; auth, "The Hal Construction and the Main Verb in the Sentence," The Fergusonian Impact, Vol I, Mouton, 86; auth, "Speech and Religious Affiliation in Egypt," Studies in Honor of Edgar C. Polome, Mouton, 88; auth, A Methodology for Teaching Grammar Functionally (in Arabic),

Al-Arabiyya, 89; coauth, Come Let's Read with the Arabs, Beginning, Intermediate, Advanced Levels, Come Let's Listen with the Arabs, Beginning, Intermediate, Advanced Levels, and Come Let's Speak Fusha, Beginning, Intermediate, Advanced Levels, Sch of Arabic, Middlebury Col, 90; auth, The Teaching of Arabic in the United States: When and Whither, The Teaching of Arabic as a Foreign Language, Issues and Directions, Al-Arabiyya Monograph Series, No 2, 95. **CONTACT ADDRESS** Dept of Middle Eastern Lang and Cult, Univ of Texas, Austin, WMB 5.120, Austin, TX, 78712.

ABDELRAHIM-SOBOLEVA, VALENTINA
DISCIPLINE RUSSIAN LINGUISTICS **EDUCATION** Moscow State Univ, MA, 67; Bryn Mawr Col, PhD, 98. **CAREER** Instr, Univ Khartoum, Sudan, 72-92; teach asst, 93-95, 97, instr, summer Russian Lang Inst, 93-98, Bryn Mawr Col; instr, St Joseph's Univ, 95-97; lectr, Lincoln Univ, 98; ASST PROF, LANG & LING, LINCOLN UNIV, 98-. **CONTACT ADDRESS** 73 Cricket Ave, Apt C, Ardmore, PA, 19003. **EMAIL** soboleva@brandywine.net

ABRAHAM, JULIE L.
DISCIPLINE ENGLISH LANGUAGE AND LITERATURE **EDUCATION** Columbia Univ, PhD, 89. **CAREER** Assoc prof Eng/Women's Studies. **RESEARCH** Modern British literature; women's literature; feminist literary theory. **SELECTED PUBLICATIONS** Auth, Are Girls Necessary?: Lesbian Writing and Modern Histories. **CONTACT ADDRESS** English Dept, Emory Univ, 1380 Oxford Rd NE, Atlanta, GA, 30322-1950.

ABRAMS, JUDITH Z.
PERSONAL Born 01/27/1958, Pittsburgh, PA **DISCIPLINE** HEBREW LETTERS **EDUCATION** Oberlin Col, BA, 80; Hebrew Union Col, MAHL, 84, Baltimore Hebrew Univ, PhD, 93. **CAREER** Congreg Emanu El, asst rabbi, 85-88; Congreg Ner Shalom, rabbi, 88-91; Congreg Beth El, rabbi, 91-95; National Jewish Center for Learning and Leadership, assoc, 94-, Maqom: A Place for the Spiritually Searching, found & dir, 95-. **HONORS AND AWARDS** Herman Snyder Prize, 81; B'nai Zion Gold Medal, 82; Mother Hirsch Prize for MHL, 84; Gedaliah & Chana Cohen Prize, 93; Houston Post, Woman On the Move Award, 93; Jewish Fed of Houston, Yavneh Award, 96 **MEMBERSHIPS** CCAR , OJERPI, JIP, SBL, AAR, AJS, JWI, Hadassah, CAJE **RESEARCH** Judaism; healing; disabilities. **SELECTED PUBLICATIONS** Auth, Act of Worship: Illness, Recovery and Transcendence in Jewish Writings, coauth, JPS, 99; A Beginners Guide to the Steinsaltz Talmud, Jason Aronson Press, 98; Judaism and Disability: Portrayals in Ancient Texts from the Tanach through the Bavli, Gallaudet Univ Press, 98; Talmud for Beginners III: Living in a Non-Jewish World, Jason Aronson, 97; The Women of the Talmud, Jason Aronson, 95; Learn Talmud: How to Use the Steinsaltz English Talmud, Jason Aronson, 95; Simchat Torah: A Family Celebration, Kar Ben Copies, 95; A Family Sukkot Seder, Kar Ben Copies, 93. **CONTACT ADDRESS** Maqom: A Place for the Spiritually Searching, PO Box 31900-32, Houston, TX, 77231. **EMAIL** maqom@compassnet.com

ABRAMSON, ARTHUR SEYMOUR
PERSONAL Born 01/26/1925, Jersey City, NJ, m, 1952, 2 children **DISCIPLINE** LINGUISTICS **EDUCATION** Yeshiva Univ, AB, 49; Columbia Univ, AM, 50, PhD, 60. **CAREER** Teacher French & English pub schs, Jersey City, NJ, 50-53; lectr English to foreigners, Columbia Univ, 55-59; men res staff exp phonetics, Haskins Labs, New York, 59-63; assoc prof speech, Queens Col, NY, 63-64, prof, 65-67; head dept ling, 67-74, Prof Ling, Univ Conn, 67-, Fulbrigh teaching grant, Thailand, 53-55; lectr, NY Univ, 58-59; assoc phonetics, Columbia

Univ, 60-63; lectr speech, Hunter Col, 61-63; mem Permanent Coun for Orgn Int Cong Phonetic Sci, 71-; Am Coun Learned Soc & Ford Found fel, Southeast Asia Fel Prog, 73-74; co-ed Lang & Speech, 74-78, ed, 79- **MEMBERSHIPS** AAAS; Ling Soc Am (secy-treas, 74-78, vpres, 82); MLA; fel Acoustical Soc Am; Int Phonetic Asn. **RESEARCH** Thai language; experimental phonetics; phonology. **SELECTED PUBLICATIONS** Auth, The Vowels and Tones of Standard Thai: Acoustical Measurements and Experiments, Ind Univ, 62; coauth, A cross-language study of voicing in initial stops: Acoustical measurements, Word, 64; coauth, Distinctive features and laryngeal control, Language, 71; Voice-timing perception in Spanish word-initial stops, J Phonetics, 73; auth, Thai tones as a reference system, In: Tai Linguistics in Honor of Fang-Kuei Li, Chulalongkorn Univ, 76; Laryngeal timing in consonant distinctions, J Phonetics, 77; auth, The noncategorical perception of tone categories in Thai, In: Frontiers of Speech Communication Research, Academic Press, 79; coauth, Vowel height and the perception of consonantal nasality, J Acoust Soc Am, 81; Tone Perception Deficits in Chinese Speaking Aphasics, Brain and Lang, Vol 0047, 94. **CONTACT ADDRESS** Dept of Ling, Univ of Conn, Storrs, CT, 06268.

ABRAMSON, HENRY
DISCIPLINE JEWISH STUDIES **EDUCATION** Univ Toronto, PhD. **CAREER** Asst prof. **RESEARCH** Jewish history and culture with an emphasis on Russian and East European Jews. **SELECTED PUBLICATIONS** Auth, The Scattering of Amalek: A Model for Understanding the Ukrainian-Jewish Conflict, 94; Historiography on the Jews and the Ukrainian Revolution, Jour Ukrainian Studies, 90; A Ready Hatred: Depictions of the Jewish Woman in Medieval Antisemitic Art and Caricature, 96. **CONTACT ADDRESS** Florida Atlantic Univ, 777 Glades Rd, Boca Raton, FL, 33431. **EMAIL** habramso@fau.edu

ABU-ABSI, SAMIR
PERSONAL Born 04/04/1938, Hasbaya, Lebanon, m, 1968, 5 children **DISCIPLINE** LINGUISTICS **EDUCATION** Am Univ Beirut, BA, 63; Ind Univ, Bloomington, MA, 66, PhD(l-ing), 72. **CAREER** Instr ling, Univ Toledo, 68-72; asst prof, Am Univ, Beirut, 72-73; asst prof, 73-76, from assoc prof to prof Ling, Univ Toledo, 76-87. **MEMBERSHIPS** Ling Soc Am; Am Asn Teachers Arabic. **RESEARCH** Arabic linguistics; English linguistics; applied linguistics. **SELECTED PUBLICATIONS** Coauth, Spoken Chad Arabic, Intensive Lang Training Ctr, Ind Univ, 68; auth, Stubborn structures in Arabic-English, In: Al-Kulliyah, Am Univ Beirut, 73; A method for surveying second language teachers, Ohio Univ working papers, Applied Ling, No 6, 79; Language-in-Education in the Arab Middle East, Ann Rev Applied Ling II, 82; The Western Stereotype of Arab Women, Al-Raida, 94; Stereotypical Images of Arab Women, Phi Beta Delta International Review, 96; Innovative Second Language Education in the Middle East and North Africa, vol 4, Second Language Education, Encyclopedia of Language and Education, Kluwer Publishers, the Netherlands, 97. **CONTACT ADDRESS** English Dept, Univ of Toledo, 2801 W Bancroft St, Toledo, OH, 43606-3390. **EMAIL** sabuabs@ueft0z.utoledo.edu

ACCAD, EVELYNE
PERSONAL Born 10/06/1943, Beirut, Lebanon **DISCIPLINE** FRANCOPHONE STUDIES, AFRICAN STUDIES **EDUCATION** Anderson Col, BA, 67; Ball State Univ, MA, 68; Ind Univ, Bloomington, PhD(comp lit), 73. **CAREER** From teaching asst to instr French, Anderson Col, 65-68; teacher English & girl's counr, Int Col, Beirut, 68-70; teaching asst comp lit, Ind Univ, 71-73; asst prof, 71-80, Assoc Prof French, Univ Ill, 80- **MEMBERSHIPS** African Lit Asn (pres, 78); African Studies

1

Asn; MLA. **RESEARCH** Women in literature and society; African and Near Eastern literatures; 20th century French literature. **SELECTED PUBLICATIONS** Auth, Des Femmes, des Hommes et la Guerre: Fiction et realite au Proche-Orient, Paris: Study, 93; contribur, Bahithat: Women and Writing, v 2, 95-96; auth, Arab Women's Literary Inscriptions: A Note and Extended Bibliography, Col Lit, 95; auth, Truth Versus Loyalty, in Bell, ed, Radically Speaking: Feminism Reclaimed, Spinifex, 96; auth, Trois Chansons, in Ecritures de Femmes: Nouvelles Cartographies, Yale, 96; auth, Assia Djebar's Contribution to Arab Women's Literature: Rebellion, Maturity, Vision, World Lit Today, 96; auth, Wounding Words: A Woman's Journal in Tunisia, Heinemann, 96; auth, Saadawi's Woman at Point Zero, in, Oxford Companion to African Literature, Oxford, forthcoming; auth, Violence and Sexuality, in, Sexual Aggression: Key Research and Activism, Purdue, forthcoming; auth, Nawal El Saadawi, in, Fifty African and Caribbean Women Writers, Greenwood, forthcoming. **CONTACT ADDRESS** French Dept, Univ Ill, 707 S Mathews Ave, Urbana, IL, 61801-3625. **EMAIL** e_accad@uiuc.edu

ACHBERGER, KAREN RIPP

PERSONAL Born 04/10/1943, Madison, WI, m, 1975, 2 children **DISCIPLINE** GERMAN LITERATURE, WOMEN'S STUDIES **EDUCATION** Univ Wis-Madison, BS, 67, MA, 68, PhD(Ger lit), 75. **CAREER** Asst prof, Univ Ore, 74-79; Asst Prof Ger, St Olaf Col, 79-. **MEMBERSHIPS** MLA; Am Asn Teachers Ger; German Studies Assn; Women in Ger; Int Brecht Soc. **RESEARCH** Contemporary German women writers; Ingeborg Bachmann; postwar German opera libretto; Austrian Literature. **SELECTED PUBLICATIONS** Auth, A multidisciplinary synthesis in teaching German culture and civilization, Pac Northwest Coun Foreign Lang Proc, 76; coauth, Irmtraud Morgner's Gospel of Valeska, New Ger Critique, 78; auth, Ingeborg Bachmann's Homberg Libretto: Kleist between humanism and existentialism, Mod Austrian Lit, 79; GDR women's fiction of the 1970's: The emergence of feminism within socialism, E Cent Europe, 79; Literatur als, Libretto: Das deutsche Opernbuch seit 1945 Heidelberg, winter 80; Bachmann und die Bibel: Gomorrah als weibliche Schopfungsgeschichte, Derdunkle Schatten, Locker, Vienna, 82; co-transl (with Friedrich Achberger), Morgner, White Easter, The Duel Shoes & The Rope, Wolter, I have married again, In: German Feminism, State Univ NY Press, 84; Understanding Ingeborg Bachmann. Understanding Modern European and Latin American Literature, James Hardin, ed, Columbia: U South Carolina Press, 95; Bosartig liebevoll' den Menschen zugetan, Humor in Ingeborg Bachmanns Todesarten-Projekt, Essays zu Ingeborg Bachmanns Todesarten-Projekt, Monika Albrecht and Dirk Gottsche, eds, Munster: Konigshausen & Neumann, 98. **CONTACT ADDRESS** 1520 St Olaf Ave, Northfield, MN, 55057-1099. **EMAIL** krach@stolaf.edu

ACIMOVIC WALLACE, VESNA

PERSONAL Born 11/02/1952, Croatia, m, 1989, 1 child **DISCIPLINE** SOUTH ASIAN STUDIES, SANSKRIT-BUDDHISM **EDUCATION** Univ Calif, Berkeley, PhD, 95. **CAREER** Lectr, Stanford Univ, 93-95; vis scholar, Stanford Univ,96-97; Lectr, Univ Calif Santa Barbara, 97-. **MEMBERSHIPS** Am Acad of Rel; Am Oriental Soc; Mongolia Soc; Asn for Asian Studies. **RESEARCH** South Asian and Inner Asian Buddhism. **SELECTED PUBLICATIONS** Auth, The Buddhist Tantric Medicine in the Kalacakratantra, The Pacific World: J of the Inst of Buddhist Studies, 95; Santideva, A Guide to the Bodhisattva Way of Life (Bodhicaryvatara), 97. **CONTACT ADDRESS** Dept of Religious Studies, Univ of Calif, Santa Barbara, CA, 93106-3130. **EMAIL** vwallace@humanitas.ucsb.edu

ACKER, ROBERT

PERSONAL St. Paul, MN **DISCIPLINE** GERMAN LITERATURE & LINGUISTICS **EDUCATION** St John's Univ, Minn, BA, 68; Univ Tex, Austin, PhD, 74. **CAREER** Asst prof Ger, Univ Mo-Columbia, 74-77 & Wash State Univ, 77-78; asst prof Ger, SDak State Univ, 78-79; asst prof, 79-81, ASSOC PROF GERMAN, UNIV MONT, 82- ; ED, SELECTA: J PAC NW COUN FOR LANG, 82- . **MEMBERSHIPS** MLA; Am Asn Teachers Ger; Midwest Mod Lang Asn; Westen Asn Ger Studies; Pac Northwest Coun Foreign Lang. **RESEARCH** Twentieth century German literature; German film. **SELECTED PUBLICATIONS** Auth, Gustav Regler and Ramon Sender: A comparative study of their Mexican exile, In: Latin American Exile Writers, Univ Tex, 78; Literature about language in postwar Germany, Perspectives,; The ninth book of Parzival: A structural analysis, Proc of the Pac Northwest Coun Foreign Lang, 79; The Novels of Walser, Martin, A Critical Introduction, Colloquia Germanica, Vol 0025. 96; Koordinaten Der Liebe, World Lit Today, Vol 0069, 95; pub Ironie Vom Gluck, World Lit Today, Vol 0070, 96. **CONTACT ADDRESS** Dept of Foreign Lang, Univ of Mont, Missoula, MT, 59812-0001.

ADAMEC, LUDWIG W

PERSONAL Born 03/10/1924, Vienna, Austria, m, 1958, 1 child **DISCIPLINE** NEAR & MIDDLE EASTERN STUDIES **EDUCATION** Univ Calif, Los Angeles, BA, 60, MA, 61, PhD, 66. **CAREER** Res grant, Univ Calif, Los Angeles, 66, lectr, Near Eastern hist & Ford Found fac res grant, 66-67; asst prof Near Eastern hist & Arabic, 67-70, assoc prof, 70-72, PROF NEAR EASTERN HIST & LANG, UNIV ARIZ, 72-, DIR NEAR EASTERN CTR, 75-, Fulbright res prof, Iran, 73-74; assoc ed, Afghanistan J, 73-77; mem, bd dirs, Am Res Ctr in Egypt, 78- & Ctr Arabic Studies Abroad, 79-81; vpres, Am Inst Iranian Studies, 79-; trustee, Am Res Inst in Turkey, 79-; prof, Univ Baluchistan, Quetta, Pakistan, 81-82. **MEMBERSHIPS** Fel Mid E Studies Asn NAm; Mid E Inst. **RESEARCH** Afghanistan studies, diplomatic history, German-Afghan relations and politics; history and politics of the Islamic world; history and politics of the Near and Middle East, Iran Afghanistan, Pakistan, the Arabic world and Turkey. **SELECTED PUBLICATIONS** Auth, Afghanistan 1900-1923, A Diplomatic History, Univ Calif, 67; coauth, Afghanistan: Some New Approaches, Univ Mich, 69; ed, Historical and Political Gazetter of Afghanistan, (6 vols), 72, 73, 75, 78 & 80, Akad Drucku-u, Graz; auth, Afghanistan's Foreign Affairs in the Mid-Twentieth Century: Relations with the USSR, Germany, and Britain, Univ Ariz, 73; ed, Historical and Political Who's Who of Afghanistan, 74 & Historical Gazetteer of Iran, (4 vols), 76 & 81, Akad Druck-u, Graz. **CONTACT ADDRESS** Dept of Oriental Studies, Univ of Ariz, 1 University of Az, Tucson, AZ, 85721-0001.

ADAMS, GEORGE ROY

PERSONAL Born 11/23/1928, Lime Springs, IA, m, 1959, 3 children **DISCIPLINE** ENGLISH, LINGUISTICS **EDUCATION** Univ Okla, BA, 52, PhD, 61. **CAREER** Instr English, Boston Univ, 61-63; asst prof, Harpur Col, State Univ NY Binghamton, 63-66; assoc prof, 66-76, prof English, Univ Wis, Whitewater, 76-. **MEMBERSHIPS** MLA; Mediaeval Acad Am. **RESEARCH** Medieval literary esthetic; medieval drama; history of the English language. **SELECTED PUBLICATIONS** Auth, Paul Goodman, Twayne; Chaucer's Shipman's Tale, Explicator, 66; coauth, Good and Bad Fridays and May 3 in Chaucer, English Lang Notes, 66; Chauntecleer's Paradise Lost and Regained, Mediaeval Studies, 67. **CONTACT ADDRESS** Dept of English, Univ of Wis, 800 W Main, Whitewater, WI, 53190-1790.

ADAMS, KATHERINE L.

DISCIPLINE INTERPERSONAL COMMUNICATION **EDUCATION** Univ UT, PhD. **CAREER** Instr, Grad coordr, Calif State Univ; assoc ed, Western J of Commun; assoc ed, Women's Stud in Commun. **SELECTED PUBLICATIONS** Auth, Aubrey Fisher's Interpersonal Communication: A Pragmatic Approach Textbook, 2nd ed; authored several instructor's manuals in interpersonal and small group communication. **CONTACT ADDRESS** California State Univ, Fresno, Fresno, CA, 93740.

ADAMS, LESLIE KENNEDY

DISCIPLINE LANGUAGE **EDUCATION** Houston Baptist Univ, BA, 86, MA, 87; Tx A & M Univ, College Station, PhD, 95. **CAREER** Grad teaching asst, 87-90, Tx A & M Univ; instr to asst prof, 90-, Houston Baptist Univ. **MEMBERSHIPS** Col English Assoc; Houston World Aff Coun; Nat Coun Teachers of English; Popular Culture Assoc. **RESEARCH** Vietnam War lit & film; war lit. **SELECTED PUBLICATIONS** Auth, Father She Never Knew Still Influences Her Work, Houston Chronicle, 95. **CONTACT ADDRESS** Dept of Lang, Houston Baptist Univ, 7502 Fondren Rd, Houston, TX, 77074. **EMAIL** ladams@hbu.edu

ADAMSON, HUGH DOUGLAS

PERSONAL Born 09/30/1944, Salt Lake City, UT, m, 1969, 2 children **DISCIPLINE** LINGUISTICS, TEACHING ENGLISH AS A SECOND LANGUAGE **EDUCATION** Univ Calif, Berkeley, AB, 67; San Jose State Univ, MA, 72; Georgetown Univ, PhD(ling), 80. **CAREER** Dir English as second lang, US Peace Corps, 68; instr English as second lang, adult prog, San Jose Metro, 72-73, John Adams Adult Ctr, San Francisco Commun Col Dist, 70-71, Inst Estudies Norteamericanos, 74-75; dir English as second lang, Luther Rice Col, 76-77; prof lectr English as second lang, Am Univ, 77-78; instr English as second lang, George Washington Univ, 78-79; Asst Prof Ling, George Mason Univ, 79-, Dir, reading lab, Operation Ser, 72; coordr, Econ Inst, Univ Colo, 78; dir, English Lang Inst, George Mason Univ, 81. **MEMBERSHIPS** Ling Soc Am; Teachers English Speakers Other Lang. **RESEARCH** Variation theory; second language acquisition; first lang acquisition. **SELECTED PUBLICATIONS** Coauth, Variation theory and second language acquisiton & Variation theory and first language acquisiton, 82, Variation Omnibus. **CONTACT ADDRESS** Dept English, George Mason Univ, Fairfax, VA, 22030.

ADISA, OPAL PALMER

PERSONAL Born 11/06/1954, Kingston, Jamaica, s, 3 children **DISCIPLINE** CARIBBEAN LITERATURE; ETHNIC LITERATURE **EDUCATION** Hunter Col, Univ of NY, BA, 75; San Francisco St Univ, MA, 81; San Francisco St Univ, MA, 86; Calif Univ, Berkeley, PhD, 92. **CAREER** Assoc prof & ch Ethnic Studies, Calif Col of Arts & Crafts, 93-; coordr, Lockwood, 97-; vis prof, Stanford Univ, 95; lctr, Holy Name's Col, 94; lctr, St Mary's Col, 93; instr, San Francisco St Univ, 87, 88, 90, 92, 93; lctr, San Francisco St Univ, 81-87; poet, Oakland Museum, 86-92; instr, City Col San Francisco, 80-84. **HONORS AND AWARDS** Creative Work Fund, 98-99; Intl Woman of Year Nominee, 96-97; Canute A Brodhurst Prize, 96; Writer-in-Residence, Headlands Center for Arts, 96; instr, Univ Calif Berkeley, 96; Caribbean Writer Summer Inst Recipient, Univ Miami, 95; Calif Col Tchg Develop Grant, 95; Daily News Prize, 95; Calif Col Tchg Develop Grant, 94; Literary Women Honoree, 94; PEN Oakland/Josephine Miles Lit Award, 92; Master Folk Artist, 91-92; Bay Area Woman Writer Award, 91; Affirmative Action Dissertation-Year Fel, 90-91; Phi Beta Kappa, 91; Grad Opportunity Fel, Univ Calif Berkeley, 88-90; Grad Minority Prog Grant, Univ Calif Berkeley, 87-88; Univ Calif Berkeley Feminist Inst & Gender Study Res Grant, 87; Pushcart Prize, 87. **MEMBERSHIPS** Assoc Caribbean Women Writers & Scholars; Calif Poets in Schools; Caribbean Assoc Feminist Res & Action; Ntl Assoc Ethnic Studies; Ntl Writers Union; Soc for Study of Multi-Ethnic Lit of US; Women's Intl League for Peach & Freedom; Northern Assoc of African Amer Storytellers. **SELECTED PUBLICATIONS** Until Judgement Comes, forthcoming; The Swelling of a Womb/the Forging of a Writer, in Caribbean Writer, 98; Lying in the Tall Grasses Eating Cane, in Zyzzyva, 98; It Begins With Tears, Heinemann Pr, 97. **CONTACT ADDRESS** Dept of Ethnic Studies Prog, California Col of Arts and Crafts, Oakland, PO Box 10625, Oakland, CA, 94618. **EMAIL** Opalpro@aol.com

ADLER, SARA MARIA

PERSONAL Born 09/14/1946, Malden, MA, m, 1973, 1 child **DISCIPLINE** ITALIAN LANGUAGE & LITERATURE **EDUCATION** Smith Col, BA, 68; Harvard Univ, MA, 69, PhD(Ital lit), 76. **CAREER** Instr, 74-75, ASST PROF ITALIAN, SCRIPPS COL, 75- . **MEMBERSHIPS** Am Asn Teachers Ital; MLA; Dante Soc; Soc Ital Hist Studies. **RESEARCH** Modern Italian literature. **SELECTED PUBLICATIONS** Auth, Calvino: The Author as Fablemaker, Jose Porrua (in press); ' Amor di Virtu- A Comedy in 5 Acts, 1548, Italica, Vol 0068, 91. **CONTACT ADDRESS** Scripps Col, 1030 Columbia Ave, Claremont, CA, 91711-3948.

AFFRON, CHARLES M.

PERSONAL Born 10/16/1935, Brooklyn, NY, m, 1961, 2 children **DISCIPLINE** ROMANCE LANGUAGES **EDUCATION** Brandeis Univ, BA, 57; Yale Univ, PhD(Balzac), 63. **CAREER** From instr to asst prof French & Ital, Brandeis Univ, 62-65; from asst prof to assoc prof, 65-73, actg chmn dept, 68-69, prof French, NY Univ, 73-. **MEMBERSHIPS** MLA. **RESEARCH** Nineteenth century French novel and theatre; cinema. **SELECTED PUBLICATIONS** Auth, Patterns of Failure in La comedie humaine, Yale Univ, 66; A Stage for Poets: Studies in the Theatre of Hugo and Musset, Princeton Univ, 71; Star Acting: Gish, Garbo, Davis, Dutton, 77; Sets in Motion: Art Direction & Film Narrative, with Minella Jona Affron. **CONTACT ADDRESS** Dept of French & Ital, New York Univ, 19 University Pl, New York, NY, 10003-4556. **EMAIL** ca1e@is2.nyu.edu

AFIFI, WALID A.

DISCIPLINE INTERPERSONAL COMMUNICATION **EDUCATION** Univ Iowa, BA, 90; Univ Ariz, MA, 92; PhD, 96. **CAREER** Grad tchg asst/assoc, Univ Ariz, 90-95; asst prof, 96-. **HONORS AND AWARDS** Grad Col fel, Univ Ariz, 92; grad regist scholar Univ Ariz, 92-94; res trng fel, Univ Ariz, 95, Outstanding prof, Univ Del, 95. **MEMBERSHIPS** Mem, Speech Commun Assn, 90-; Intl Commun Assn, 90-; Intl Network on Personal Relationships, 91-; Intl Soce Stud Personal Relationships, 94-; Nat Coun on Family Rel(s), 94-. **SELECTED PUBLICATIONS** Co-auth, Media in Lebanon, Mass Media in the Middle East: A Comprehensive Reference Guide, Greenwood Publ Gp, 94; What Parents Don't Know: Taboo Topics and Topic Avoidance in Parent-Child Relationships, Parents, children, and Communication: Frontiers of Theory and Research, Lawrence Erlbaum, 95; Rethinking How to Measure Organizational Culture in the Hospital Setting: The Hospital Culture Scale, Evaluation and the Health Professions, 95; Some Things are Better Left Unsaid: Topic Avoidance in Family Relationships, Commun Quart, 95; Interpersonal Deception: XII Information Management Dimensions Underlying Deceptive and Truthful Messages, Commun Monogr(s), 96. **CONTACT ADDRESS** Dept of Commun, Univ Delaware, 162 Ctr Mall, Newark, DE, 19716.

AGES, ARNOLD

DISCIPLINE FRENCH LITERATURE **EDUCATION** Univ Carleton, BA; Ohio State Univ, MA; PhD. **RESEARCH** Enlightenment literature. **SELECTED PUBLICATIONS** Auth, The Image of Jews and Judaism in The Prelude to the French Enlightenment; pub(s) in Judeo-French area. **CONTACT ADDRESS** Dept of French, Waterloo Univ, 200 University Ave W, Waterloo, ON, N2L 3G1. **EMAIL** aages@interlog.com

AGUIRRE, ANGELA M.

DISCIPLINE SPANISH-SPANISH AMERICAN ROMANTICISM **EDUCATION** CUNY, PhD, 80. **CAREER** Prof. **HONORS AND AWARDS** Certified transl, Amer Transl Asn, ATA. **SELECTED PUBLICATIONS** Auth, Vida y cretica literaria de Enrique Pineyro, New York: Senda Nueva de Ediciones, 81; Latino Caribbean Literature, Multicultural Literature Collection, NJ: Globe Fearon, 94. **CONTACT ADDRESS** Dept of Language and Cultures, William Paterson Col, 300 Pompton Rd., Wayne, NJ, 07470.

AHEARN, EDWARD J.
PERSONAL Born 10/31/1937, New York, NY, m, 1979, 2 children **DISCIPLINE** COMPARATIVE LITERATURE & FRENCH STUDIES **EDUCATION** Manhattan Col, BA, 59; Yale Univ, PhD, 63. **CAREER** Asst prof French, 63-68, assoc prof, 68-80, Prof, 80-95, UNIV PROF, COMP LIT & FR STUDIES, BROWN UNIV, 95-; Fel, Ctr Advan Studies, Univ Ill. **HONORS AND AWARDS** Harbison Award for Gifted Teaching, Danforth Found, 70. **MEMBERSHIPS** MLA. **RESEARCH** Comparative literature of the 19th & 20th century. **SELECTED PUBLICATIONS** Auth, Rimbaud: Visions of Habitations, Univ Calif, 83; Marx & Modern Fiction, Yale, 91; Visionary Fictions: Apocalyptic Writing from Blake to the Modern Age, Yale, 96. **CONTACT ADDRESS** Dept of Comparative Lit, Brown Univ, Box E, Providence, RI, 02912-9127. **EMAIL** Edward_Ahearn@brown.edu

AHUMADA, ALFREDO
DISCIPLINE SPANISH LANGUAGE **EDUCATION** CUNY, BA, MA, Mphil, PhD. **CAREER** Eastern Stroudsburg Univ PA **HONORS AND AWARDS** Lane Cooper Dissertation Fel. **RESEARCH** The relationship between Span/Span Am Modernismo and French Symbolism; Avant-garde lit;Pre-Columbian studies. **SELECTED PUBLICATIONS** Area: Span Am lit. **CONTACT ADDRESS** East Stroudsburg Univ of Pennsylvania, 200 Prospect Street, E Stroudsburg, PA, 18301-2999.

AIKIN, JUDITH POPOVICH
PERSONAL Born 08/06/1946, Los Angeles, CA, 1 child **DISCIPLINE** GERMAN LITERATURE & LANGUAGE **EDUCATION** Univ OR, BA, 68, MA, 69; Univ CA, Berkeley, PhD, 74. **CAREER** Asst prof, 75-81, assoc prof, 81-88, prof Ger, Univ IA 88, Assoc Dean, Col Lib Arts, 89-92, Dean, Col Lib Arts, 92-97. **HONORS AND AWARDS** Am Coun Learned Soc Fel, 88-89; NEH Summer Res Fel, 88. **MEMBERSHIPS** MLA; Soc Ger Renaissance and Baroque Lit; Lyrica Soc; Lessing Soc. **RESEARCH** Seventeenth-century Ger drama, opera and song. **SELECTED PUBLICATIONS** Auth, The Mission of Rome in the Dramas of Daniel Casper von Lohenstein, Stuttgarter Arbeiten Germanistik, 76; And They Changed Their Lives from That Very Hour: Catharsis and Exemplum in the Baroque Trauerspeil, Daphnis, 81; German Baroque Drama, Twayne World Authors Series, G K Hall, 82; Genre Definition and Genre Confusion in Gryphius Double Bill: Cardenio und Celinde and Herr Peter Squentz, Colloquia Germanica, 83; Romantic comedy as Religious Allegory: The Millennial Kingdom of Caspar Stieler's Die erfreuete Unschuld, Ger Quart, 84; The Audience within the Play: Clues to Intended Audience Reaction in German Baroque Tragedies and Comedies, Daphnis, 84; Happily Ever After: An Alternative Affective Theory of Comedy and Some Plays by Birken, Gryphius and Weise, In: Absurda Comica: Studien zur deutschen Komodie des 16 und 17 Jahrhunderts, Rodopi, 88, Daphnis, 88; The Comedies of Andreas Gryphius and the Two Tpes of European Comedy, Ger Rev, 88; Das klingt sehr tragisch - Lessing's Minna von Barnhelm as Embodiment of the Genre Discussion, Lessing Yearbk, 88; Creating a Language for German Opera: The Struggle to Adapt Madrigal Versification in Seventeenth-Century Germany, Deutsche Vierteljahrsschrift, 88; The Merchant and the Moor of Venice in Lessing's Minna von Barnhelm, Mich Ger Studies, 89; Scaramutza in Germany: The Dramatic Works of Caspar Stieler, Penn State Press, 89; contr, Fertigkeit - A Milleniast Conciet in a Dedicatory Epistle by Stieler, Opitz und sein Welt: Festschrift fur George Shulz-Behrend zum 12 Februar 1988, Rodopi, 90; Narcissus and Echo: A Mythological Subtext in Harsdorffer's Operatic Allegory Seelewig (1644), Music and Letters, 91; Baroque, chpt, In: A Concise History of German Literature to 1900, Camden House, 92; Heinrich Schutz and Martin Opitz: A New Basis for German Vocal Music and Poetry, Musica e Storia, 93; Misattributed Melissa, or Let's Give David Elias Heidenreich His Due, Daphnis, 94; The Musical-Dramatic Works of David Schirmer, Daphnis, 97; What Happens When Opera Meets Drama and Vice Versa? J C Hallmann's Experiments and Their Significance, Studien zur Literature des 17 Jahrhunderts: Gedenkschrift fur Gerhard Spellerberg (1937-1996), Rodopi, 97. **CONTACT ADDRESS** Dept of Ger, Univ of IA, Iowa City, IA, 52242-1409. **EMAIL** judith-aikin@uiowa.edu

AISSEN, JUDITH
DISCIPLINE MAYAN LANGUAGE **EDUCATION** Fordham Univ, BA; Yale Univ, MA; Harvard Univ, PhD, 74. **CAREER** PROF, LING, UNIV CALIF, SANTA CRUZ. **RESEARCH** Syntax of several languages, particularly Turkish, Spanish, and most recently Tzotzil. **SELECTED PUBLICATIONS** Auth, The Syntax of Causative Constructions, Garland Publ, 79; Tzotzil Clause Structure, Dordrecht, Netherlands: D Reidel Publ Co, 87; Agreement Controllers and Tzotzil Comitatives, Language, 89; Toward a Theory of Agreement Controllers, Studies in Relational Grammar 3, Univ Chicago Press, 90; Topic and Focus in Mayan Lang, 92. **CONTACT ADDRESS** Dept of Ling, Univ Calif, 1156 High St, Santa Cruz, CA, 95064.

AKEHURST, F.R.P.
DISCIPLINE OLD FRENCH AND THE HISTORY OF FRENCH **EDUCATION** Univ Colo, PhD; Univ Minn, JD. **CAREER** Instr, Univ Minn, Twin Cities. **RESEARCH** Medieval French law. **SELECTED PUBLICATIONS** Ed, Handbook of the Troubadours, Univ Calif Press, 95; transl, "Coutumes de Beauvasis" of Philippe de Beaumanoir, Univ Pa Press, 92; published on the troubadours, the trouveres, and the fabliaux. **CONTACT ADDRESS** Univ Minn, Twin Cities, Minneapolis, MN, 55455.

AL-KASEY, TAMARA
DISCIPLINE SPANISH **EDUCATION** Univ Mass, PhD. **CAREER** Carnegie Mellon Univ. **SELECTED PUBLICATIONS** Auth, L2 acquisition of Spanish factivity, 92; A Return to the initial state in Spanish second language acquisition of Factivity, 92; Why can't Johnny learn Spanish?: A look at Spanish grammar instruction, 92. **CONTACT ADDRESS** Carnegie Mellon Univ, 5000 Forbes Ave, Pittsburgh, PA, 15213.

ALBADA-JELGERSMA, JILL ELIZABETH
PERSONAL Born 01/23/1939, Leicester, England, m, 1969, 2 children **DISCIPLINE** SPANISH, SPANISH AM LIT, CRITICAL THEORY **EDUCATION** Univ CA, Davis, PhD, 95. **CAREER** Lect, Univ of the West Indies, 88-89; lect, Univ CA, Davis, 95-97; instr, Sacramento City Col, 97-98. **MEMBERSHIPS** Modern Language Asn; Nat Coalition of Independent Scholars. **RESEARCH** Spanish Am lit, poetry, and narrative; critical and culture theory approaches; poetry and art. **SELECTED PUBLICATIONS** Auth, La autocensura y las tecnologias del ser en un poema de Antonio Cisneros, Monologo de la casta Susana, Revista se Critica Literaria Latinoamericana, Univ CA, Berkeley, 96; Antonio Cisneros and Bram Stoker: Continuities and Discontinuities, Chasqui; Revista de Literature Latinoamericana, AZ State Univ, Nov 96; review, Maria Ines Lagos, En tono mayor: relatos de formacion de protagonista femenina en Hispanoamerica, Santiago, Chile, Editorial Cuarto Propio, 96, Bul of Hispanic Studies, Univ Liverpool, UK, 98; Desire as the Abjection of the Maternal Body in the Poem Casa de Cuervos by Peruvian poet, Blanca Varela, Bul of Hispanic Studies, LXXIV 1, Jan 97; Las technologias politicas del ser en los sujetos poeticos de Nancy Morejon y Giovcanda Belli, Revista Canadiense de Estudios Hispanicos, Univ Alberta, XX1 3, spring 97; review, Frances R Aparicio and Susana Chavez-Silverman, eds, Tropicalizations: Transcultural Representations of Latinidad, Univ Press of New England, 97, Bul of Hispanic Studies, Univ of Liverpool, UK, 98; review, Ivon Gordon-Vailakis, Colibries en el exilio, Quitor, Ecuador: Editorial El Conejo, 97, Letras Femeninas, 98; review, Elia Geoffrey Kantaris, The Subversive Psyche: Contemporary Women's Narrative from Argentina and Uraguay, Clarendon Press, 95, Bul of Hispanic Studies, 98; La funcion del deseo por la mujer afroantillana en cuatro poemas de Luis Palesm Matos, Hispanic J, spring 98; 31 entries on major Caribbean Figures and Movements, Encyclopedia of Contemporary Latin American Culture, Routledge, 98; entries on Venezuelan writers Laura Antillano and Antonieta Madrid for Feminist Encyclopedia of Latin American Literature, Greenwood Press, in press; Las relaciones del poder en Cronica del Nino de Chilca, de Antonio Cisneros, Confluencia, spring 99. **CONTACT ADDRESS** 1221 Lexington Ct, El Dorado Hills, CA, 95762. **EMAIL** jill.albadajelgersma@mci2000.com

ALEXANDER, ALEY E.
DISCIPLINE FOREIGN LANGUAGES **EDUCATION** Columbia Univ, PhD, 69. **CAREER** Prof, Plumber Col. **HONORS AND AWARDS** PBK **RESEARCH** Folklore **CONTACT ADDRESS** Hunter Col, CUNY, 695 Park Ave, New York, NY, 10021. **EMAIL** aalexand@hejira.hunter.cuny.edu

ALLAIRE, JOSEPH LEO
PERSONAL Born 02/23/1929, Detroit, MI, m, 1974, 1 child **DISCIPLINE** ROMANCE LANGUAGES, FRENCH **EDUCATION** Univ Detroit, AB, 52; Wayne State Univ, MA, 57, PhD(Mod Lang), 66. **CAREER** Teacher French & Latin, pub schs, Mich, 53-62, head dept, 62-67; instr French, Wayne State Univ, 60-67; asst prof, 67-72, assoc chmn Mod Lang, 69-73, assoc prof French, Fla State Univ, 72-. **MEMBERSHIPS** Am Asn Teachers Fr; MLA; S Atlantic MLA; S Cent MLA; AAUP. **RESEARCH** French Renaissance; pre-Reformation literature; late medieval French literature, especially the 15th century. **SELECTED PUBLICATIONS** Ed, Le Miroir de l'Ame Pecheresse de Marguerite de Navarre, Wilhelm Fink, Munich, 72; auth, Foreign languages and the Founding Fathers, S Atlantic Bull, 1/77. **CONTACT ADDRESS** Dept of Mod Lang, Florida State Univ, 600 W College Ave, Tallahassee, FL, 32306-1096. **EMAIL** jallaire@fsu.edu

ALLAN, SARAH
DISCIPLINE ASIAN AND MIDDLE EASTERN LANGUAGES AND LITERATURES **EDUCATION** UCLA, BA; Univ Calif Berkeley, MA, PhD. **CAREER** Fac, Schl Oriental and African Studies, Univ London; Burlington Northern Found Prof in Chinese Studies, Dartmouth Univ. **HONORS AND AWARDS** Co-recipient, Luce Found Grant. **RESEARCH** Lang, lit, and cult of China before the Han Dynasty. **SELECTED PUBLICATIONS** Auth, The Heir and the Sage: Dynastic Legend in Early China; The Shape of the Turtle: Myth, Art and Cosmos in Early China; The Way of Water and the Sprouts of Virtue; coauth, Oracle Bone Collections in Great Britain ; Chinese Bronzes: A Selection from European Collections. **CONTACT ADDRESS** Dartmouth Col, 3529 N Main St, #207, Hanover, NH, 03755.

ALLEN, ROGER MICHAEL ASHLEY
PERSONAL Born 01/24/1942, Devon, England, m, 1972, 2 children **DISCIPLINE** ARABIC LANGUAGE AND LITERATURE **EDUCATION** Oxford Univ, BA, MA & DPhil, 68. **CAREER** Assoc prof, 73-83, PROF ARABIC LANG & LIT, UNIV PA, 83-; NAT PROFICIENCY TRAINER IN ARABIC, AM COUNCIL FOR THE TEACHING OF FOREIGN LANGS (ACTFL), 86-; DIR, HUNTSMAN PROG IN INT STUDIES & BUSINESS, UNIV PA, 93-; ed, Edebiyat, 76-91; book ed, Al-'Arabiyya, 90-95; ed bds: J of Arabic Lit, 91-96, World Lit Today, 91-, Arabic & Middle eastern Lits, 97-. **HONORS AND AWARDS** Lindback Found Award for Distinguished Teaching, Univ PA, 72; Am Res Center in Egypt fels, 70, 71, 75; Univ Helsinki Medal, 94. **MEMBERSHIPS** Am Guild of Organists, 77-; Am Coun for the Teaching of Foreign Langs (ACTFL), 88-. **RESEARCH** Second language teaching techniques, specifically Arabic; Arabic literature; translation from Near Eastern literatures. **SELECTED PUBLICATIONS** Auth, Mirrors by Mahfuz (2 parts), Muslim World, 72 & 73; coauth, God's World, Bibliotheca Islamica, 73; auth, A Study of Hadith Isa ibn Hisham, Al-Muwaylihi's View of Egyptian Society during the British Occupation, State Univ NY, 74; Al-Muwaylihi's Hadith Isa Ibn Hisham, 74, A Period of Time, 2nd rev ed, 92; Egyptian drama and fiction in the 1970s, Edebiyat, 76; contribr, Arabic literature, In: The Study of the Middle East: Research in the Humanities and Social Sciences, Wiley, 76; transl, Nagib Mahfuz, Mirrors, 77 & auth, In the Eye of the Beholder: Tales from Yusuf Idris, 78, Bibliotheca Islamica; The Arabic Novel: An Historical and Critical Survey, Syracuse Univ Press, 82; The Arabic Novel: An Historical and Critical Introduction, 82, 2nd English ed, rev and enlarged, 95; modern Arabic Lit, 87; Let's Learn Arabic, with Adel Allouche, 88; Najib Mahfuz and World Literature, in the Arabic Novel Since 1950, Mundus Arabicus vol 5, 92; The Early Arabic Novel and The Arabic Novel Outside Egypt, Chapters 5 and 6 of Modern Arabic Literature, Cambridge Hist of Arabic Lit, 92; Arabic Poetry, Arabic Poetics, Rhyme (Arabic & Persian), in New Princeton Encyclopedia of Poetry & Poetics, 93; Najib Mahfuz and the Nobel Prize: The Historical Context, in Naguib Mahfouz From Regional Fame to Global Recognition, 93; Critical Perspectives on Yusuf Idris, 94; The Short Story in Arabic and the Status of Women, in Sex and Gender in Modern Arabic Literature, 95; Higher Level Language Skills in Arabic: Parameters and Issues, in The Teaching of Arabic as a Foreign Language: Issues & Directiona, 95; Najib Mahfuz, in African Writers, 97; A Different Voice: the Novels of Ibrahim al-Kawni, in Tradition and Modernity in Arabic Literature, 97; The Development of Fictional Genres: The Novel and Short Story in Arabic, in Humanism, Culture, and Language in the Near East, 97; hadith 'Isa ibn Hisham by al-Muwaylihi, Thirty Years Later, Arab and Islamic Studies in Honor of Marsden Jones, 97; many literary articles and several translations in book form. **CONTACT ADDRESS** Dept Asian & Middle Eastern Studies, Univ PA, 847 Williams Hall, Philadelphia, PA, 19104-6305. **EMAIL** rallen@ccat.sas.upenn.edu

ALLEN, WENDY
PERSONAL VT **DISCIPLINE** LANGUAGE ACROSS THE CURRICULUM **EDUCATION** CT, BA; IN Univ, MA, PhD. **CAREER** Language, St. Olaf Col. **HONORS AND AWARDS** ACTFL's Nelson Brooks award. **SELECTED PUBLICATIONS** Coauth: Paralleles. **CONTACT ADDRESS** St Olaf Col, 1520 St Olaf Ave, Northfield, MN, 55057.

ALLGOOD, MYRALYN FRIZZELLE
PERSONAL Born 03/02/1939, Atlanta, GA, m, 1964, 1 child **DISCIPLINE** LANGUAGES **EDUCATION** Howard Col, Samford Univ, BA, 61, St AL tchr cert, 61; Univ of Alabama, MA, 63, PhD, 85. **CAREER** Chmn, dept of World Lang & Cult, 63-, Samford Univ. **CONTACT ADDRESS** Dept of World Lang & Cultures, Samford Univ, Birmingham, AL, 35229-2298. **EMAIL** mfallgoo@samford.edu

ALMEIDA, JOSE AGUSIIN
PERSONAL Born 08/28/1933, Waco, TX, m, 1964, 1 child **DISCIPLINE** SPANISH LANGUAGE & LITERATURE **EDUCATION** Baylor Univ, BA, 61; Univ Mo, Columbia, MA, 64, PhD, 67. **CAREER** Teaching asst, Univ Mo Columbia, 61-66; instr Span, Baylor Univ, 62-63; asst prof, 66-77, chmn, Latin Am studies, 79-81, Assoc Prof Lit & Span, Univ NC, Greensboro, 77-; Vis prof, Elmira Col, 67; NEH fel, 70; consult, Living Lang Method, Hampton Inst, Va, 76 & 78. **MEMBERSHIPS** MLA; Am Asn Teachers Span & Port; Asn de Cervantistas; Cervantes Soc Am; Soc Renaissance & Baroque Hisp Poetry. **RESEARCH** Poetics: literary criticism & literature, especially poetry of the Golden Age of Literature in Spain. **SELECTED PUBLICATIONS** Auth, La Critica Literaria de Fernando de Herrera, Ed Gredos, 76; coauth, Descubrir y Crear & Teacher's Guide for Descubrir y Crear, Harper & Row, 76, 3rd ed, 86; auth, Elementos picarescos en la poesia satirica del Siglo de Oro, In: La picaresca, origenes, textos y estructuras, Madrid: Fundacion Universitaria Espanola, 79; El concepto aristotelico de la imitacion en el Renacimiento de las letras espanolas: Sigo

XVI, In: Actas del Sexto Congreso Internacional de Hispanistas, Paul Malak & Son, 80; Origen de La tragedia de las equivocaciones de Xavier Villarrutia, National Symposium on Hispanic Theater, April 22-24, 1982, Univ Northern Iowa, 82; La apologia personal y la defensa teoricoliteraria disimuladas en La Dorotea, Homenaje a Alberta Porqueras Mayo, Kassel: Reichenberger, 89; Los momentos finales del primer y ultimo actos en Invitacion a la muerte de Xavier Villaurrutia, Explacion de Textos Literarios, 90-91. **CONTACT ADDRESS** Dept of Romance Langs, Univ N. Carolina, 1000 Spring Garden, Greensboro, NC, 27402-6170. **EMAIL** jalmeida@uncg.edu

ALTER, ROBERT

PERSONAL Born 04/02/1935, Bronx, NY, m, 1961, 4 children **DISCIPLINE** COMPARATIVE LITERATURE **EDUCATION** Columbia Col, BA, 57; Harvard Univ, MA, 58, PhD, 62. **CAREER** From instr to asst prof English, Columbia Univ, 62-67; assoc prof Hebrew & comp lit, 67-69, chm dept comp lit, 70-72, PROF HEBREW & COMP LIT, 69-, CLASS OF 1937 PROF, 89-, UNIV CALIF, BERKELEY. **HONORS AND AWARDS** English Instr Essay Prize, 65; Guggenheim fel, 66-67 & 78-79; Meier Segals vis lectr, Sir George Williams Univ, 68; Roland vis lectr Jewish studies, Stanford Univ, 71; Nat Endowment Humanities sr fel, 71-72; Harry Kaplan scholar in residence, Ohio State Univ, 72; contrib ed, Commentary, 73-; Buckstein vis lectr, Trent Univ, 76; Gale vis lectr, Univ Tex, Austin, 82; Nat Jewish Book Award, 82. **MEMBERSHIPS** Am Comp Lit Asn; Asn Jewish Studies; Assoc of Lit Scholars and Critics. **RESEARCH** Modern Hebrew literature; the novel; Biblical literature. **SELECTED PUBLICATIONS** Auth, Rogue's Progress: Studies in the Picaresque Novel, 64 & Field and the Nature of the Novel, 68, Harvard Univ; After the Tradition, Dutton, 69; Partial Magic: The Novel as a Self-Conscious Genre, Univ Calif, 75; ed, Modern Hebrew Literature, Behrman House, 75; auth, Defenses of the Imagination, Jewish Publ Soc, 78; A Lion for Love: A Critical Biography of Stendhal, 79 & The Art of Biblical Narrative, Basic, 82; auth, The Art of Biblical Poetry, Basic, 85; auth, The Pleasures of Reading in an Ideological Age, Simon & Schuster, 89; auth, Necessary Angels, Harvard, 91; auth, The Work of Biblical Literature, Basic, 92; auth, Hebrew and Modernity, Indiana, 94; auth, Genesis: Translation and Commentary, Norton, 96. **CONTACT ADDRESS** Dept of Comp Lit, Univ Calif Berkeley, 250 Barrows Hall, Berkeley, CA, 94720-1941.

ALTMAN, CHARLES FREDERICK

PERSONAL Born 01/09/1945, De Ridder, LA, m, 1967 **DISCIPLINE** FRENCH LITERATURE; CINEMA **EDUCATION** Duke Univ, AB & MA, 66; Yale Univ, PhD, 71. **CAREER** Fulbright-Hayes fel and lectr, Am studies, Univ Paris X, Nanterre, 70-71; asst prof French and comp lit, Bryn Mawr Col, 71-74; asst prof French, 74-77; assoc prof French and comp lit, 77-82; assoc prof Film, French and Comp Lit, Univ Iowa, 82-86; prof French & Film, 86-; fel, Cornell Univ Soc for Hum, 74-75; dir, Paris Film Ctr, 80-81; vis prof, Univ Paris III-Censier, 80-81. **HONORS AND AWARDS** Russell B Nye Prize, Jour Pop Cult, 80; French nat. Decoration, Chevalier de L'Ordre des Palmes Academiques, 84; Soc for Cinema Studies prize, 84; French film critics award for best film book publ. in 1992, 92. **MEMBERSHIPS** MLA **RESEARCH** Narrative; 12th century Western culture; Film. **SELECTED PUBLICATIONS** Two types of opposition and the structure of Latin Saints' Lives, Medievalia et Humanistica New Series, 6: 1-11; Towards a historiography of American film, Cinema Jour, 16: 1-25 & Cinema Examined, Dutton, (in press); Psychoanalysis and Cinema: The imaginary discourse, Quart Rev of Film Studies, 2: 257-72; The medieval marquee: Church portal sculpture as publicity, Jour Pop Cult, 14: 37-46; Cinema/Sound, Yale French Studies, Vol 60, 80; Genre: The musical, Routledge & Kegan Paul, London and Boston 81; D W Griffith, Spec Issue Quart Rev of Film Studies, Vol 6, No 2; The American film musical, Ind Univ Press, 88; Sound Theory/Sound Practice, Routledge, 92; The State of Sound Studies, IRIS 27, 99; Film/Genre, Ind Univ Press, (in press). **CONTACT ADDRESS** Dept of Communication Studies, Univ of Iowa, Iowa City, IA, 52242-1528.

ALVAREZ BORLAND, ISABEL

DISCIPLINE SPANISH **EDUCATION** Lycoming Col, BA; Middlebury Col, MA; Pa State Univ, PhD. **CAREER** Assoc prof. **RESEARCH** US Cuban and Latino literature; Cuban literature; Caribbean literature; contemporary Latin American narrative. **SELECTED PUBLICATIONS** Auth, Cortazar: On Critics and Interpretation, INTI 43-44, 96; Displacements and Autobiography in Cuban-American Fiction, World Lit Today 68, 94; The Task of the Historian in El general en su laberinto, Hispania 76, 93 & Interior Texts in El amor en los tiempos del colera, Hisp Rev 58, 91. **CONTACT ADDRESS** Dept of Modern Languages and Literatures, Col of the Holy Cross, 1 College St, PO Box 190A, Worcester, MA, 01610-2395. **EMAIL** ialvarez@holycross.edu

AMAR, JOSEPH P.

PERSONAL Born 12/29/1946, Grand Rapids, MI, s **DISCIPLINE** SEMITIC LANGUAGES; HISTORY **EDUCATION** The Catholic Univ of America, PhD, 88. **CAREER** PROF, UNIV NOTRE DAME, 88-, CHAIR, CLASSICS DEPT, 97-. **MEMBERSHIPS** North Amer Patristics Soc (NAPS); Middle East Studies Assoc (MESA). **RESEARCH** Cultural/linguistic interplay; Syriac language & lit; medieval Christian Arabic; Islamic history. **CONTACT ADDRESS** Dept of Classics, Univ Notre Dame, 304 O'Shaughnessy Hall, Notre Dame, IN, 46556. **EMAIL** Joseph.P.Amar.1@nd.edu

AMASON, PATRICIA

DISCIPLINE INTERPERSONAL COMMUNICATION **EDUCATION** Univ Ark, BSE, 80; Univ Ky, MA, 83; Purdue Univ, PhD, 93. **CAREER** Comm Stu, Univ Ark **SELECTED PUBLICATIONS** Coauth, Popular, rejected, and supportive preadolescents: Social cognitive and communicative characteristics, Comm Yearbook, 87; Preadolescent support networks: Social-cognitive and communicative characteristics of natural "peer counselors", Jour Thought, 87. **CONTACT ADDRESS** Univ Ark, Fayetteville, AR, 72701.

AMASTAE, JON EDWARD

PERSONAL Born 07/20/1946, Los Angeles, CA **DISCIPLINE** LINGUISTICS **EDUCATION** Univ NMex, BA, 68; Univ Ore, PhD(ling), 75. **CAREER** Asst prof English, Pan Am Univ, 75-79; Fulbright lectr ling, Univ de los Andes, Bogota, Colombia, 79-80; asst prof ling, Univ Texas, El Paso, 80-84, assoc prof 84-92, prof 92-, actg dir, lang & ling res ctr, Pan Am Univ, 76-78; chemn, dept of lang & ling, VTEP 86-93; dir, center for interamerican & border studies, 98-. **MEMBERSHIPS** Ling Soc Am; Ling Asn Can & US; Soc Caribbean Ling. **RESEARCH** Phonology; Creoles; language contact; linguistic variation. **SELECTED PUBLICATIONS** Co-ed, Contemporary Research in Romance Linguistics, John Benjamis, 95; auth, Variable Spirantigation: Constraint Weighing in Three Dialects, Hispanic Ling, 95; The Intersection of S-aspiration/deletion and spirantigation in Honduran Spanish, Lang Variation and Change, 89; Mid-Vowel Raising and its Consequences in Spanish, Ling, 82; A Note on Natural Generative Phonology and Paradigm Leveling, Ling Inquiry, 78; Dominican English Creole Phonology: An Initial Sketch, Anthrop, Ling, 79; Dominican Creole Phonology; Georgetown Univ, Papers in Lang & Ling, 79; co-ed, Spanish in the US: Sociolinguistic Aspects, Cambridge Univ Press, 82. **CONTACT ADDRESS** Dept of Lang & Ling, Univ Texas, El Paso, 500 W University Ave, El Paso, TX, 79968-0001. **EMAIL** jamastae@utep.edu

AMBROSE, Z. PHILIP

PERSONAL Born 06/09/1936, Ponca City, OK, m, 2 children **DISCIPLINE** CLASSICAL LANGUAGES **EDUCATION** Princeton Univ, PhD, 63. **CAREER** Roberts Prof Of Classical Languages And Lit, 62-, Univ Vt **HONORS AND AWARDS** Phi Beta Kappa; CANA Barlow Beach Award for Dist Serv, 85. **MEMBERSHIPS** CANE; APA; Soc for Ancient Greek Philos. **RESEARCH** Greek drama; classical tradition, J. S. Bach. **SELECTED PUBLICATIONS** Auth, The Homeric Telos, Glotta, 48, 65; auth, The Lehythian and the Anagram of Frogs 1203, AJP 89, 68; auth, Two Textual Notes on the Miks Gloriosus, CJ, 72; auth, The Etymology and Geneology of Palinusus, AJP 101, 80; auth, Weinen, Klagen, Sorgen, Fayen und die antike Redekunst, Bach Sakrbuch, 80; auth, Socrates and Prodieus in the Clouds, Essays in Ancient Greek Philos, vol 2, 83; auth, Did Women Sing in the Thesmophoriazousae?, Didascalia Sup I; transl, The Texts to Johann Sebastian Bach's Church Cantatas, Stuttgart, 84; auth, Euripides Heraclisae, Bryn Mawr, 90; auth, Ganymede in Euripides' Cyclops, N Eng Class J, 96; auth, The Complete Texts to J. S. Bach's Vocal Works, transl and commentary, 98. **CONTACT ADDRESS** Dept of Classics, Univ of Vermont, 481 Main St, Burlington, VT, 05405. **EMAIL** zambrose@zoo.uvm.edu

ANADON, JOSE

DISCIPLINE SPANISH LITERATURE **EDUCATION** Albion Col, BA, 68; Univ Mich, MA, 70, PhD, 74. **CAREER** Prof. **RESEARCH** Contemporary narrative of Latin America. **SELECTED PUBLICATIONS** Auth, Pineda y Bascunan, defensor del araucano, 77; La novela colonial de Barrenechea y Albis, 83; Historiografia literaria de America Colonial, 88. **CONTACT ADDRESS** Romance Languages and Literatures Dept, Univ of Notre Dame, Notre Dame, IN, 46556.

ANDERSEN, ELAINE

DISCIPLINE LINGUISTICS **EDUCATION** Stanford Univ, PhD, 78. **CAREER** Prof. **RESEARCH** Relationship between language & nonlinguistic cognition. **SELECTED PUBLICATIONS** Auth, Speaking with Style: The Sociolinguistic Skills of Children, London: Routledge, Kagan Paul, 90, rep 92; co-ed, Developing Commuicative Competence in a Second Language, NY: Harper & Rowe, 90, rep 91. **CONTACT ADDRESS** Dept of Linguistics, Univ Southern Calif, University Park Campus, Los Angeles, CA, 90089. **EMAIL** elaine@gizmo.usc.edu

ANDERSON, DANNY L.

PERSONAL Born 08/08/1958, Houston, TX, m, 1998 **DISCIPLINE** LATIN AMERICAN LITERATURE **EDUCATION** Univ Kansas, PhD 85, MA 82; Austin Col, BA 80. **CAREER** Univ Texas Austin, asst prof 85-88; Univ Kansas, asst prof, assoc prof, dir LAS, 88-99. **HONORS AND AWARDS** NEH Fel; U of K Diss Fel; ITT Intl Fel. **MEMBERSHIPS** MLA; Midwest MLA; LASA. **RESEARCH** Mexican literature and social history; history of reading; sociology and literature. **SELECTED PUBLICATIONS** Auth, Creating Cultural Prestige: The Case of Editorial Joaquin Moritz, 1962-1992, Latin Amer Res Rev, 96; auth, Cultural Studies and Reading Culture in twentieth Century Mexico, Indiana Jour of Hisp Lit, 95; auth, Difficult Relations Compromising Positions: Telling Involvement in Recent Mexican Narrative, Chasqui, 95; auth, Reading Social Control and the Mexican soul in: Al filo del agua, Mexican studies/Estudios Mexicanos, 95; auth, Profession and Position: Histories of the Spanish American Novel and the Academy in the United States, Siglo XX/20th Century, 94; auth, Toward a History of Post Colonial Reading, rev essay, Col Eng, 94. **CONTACT ADDRESS** Dept of Spanish and Portuguese, Univ of Kansas, Lawrence, KS, 66045. **EMAIL** djand@falcon.cc.ukans.edu

ANDERSON, DAVID G.

DISCIPLINE LANGUAGE **EDUCATION** Univ North Carolina Chapel Hill, AB, 67; MA, 74, PhD, 85, Vanderbilt Univ. **CAREER** Asst Prof, 85-87, Northeast Louisiana Univ; Asst Prof, 87-93, Assoc Prof, 93-, John Carroll Univ, Cleveland, OH. **CONTACT ADDRESS** Dept of Classical & Modern Languages & Cultures, John Carroll Univ, Cleveland, OH, 44118-4582. **EMAIL** danderson@jcu.edu

ANDERSON, KIRK

DISCIPLINE SOFTWARE APPLICATIONS FOR LANGUAGE PEDAGOGY, CIVILIZATION, 20TH-CENTURY FRE **EDUCATION** Princeton Univ, PhD. **CAREER** Fr, Wheaton Col. **RESEARCH** Relation of history to literature. **SELECTED PUBLICATIONS** Auth, Actes du colloque international de Paris: L-F Cline, Fr Rev; Literary Generations, A 'Festschrift' in honor of Edward D. Sullivan. **CONTACT ADDRESS** Dept of Fr, Wheaton Col, 26 East Main St, Norton, MA, 02766.

ANDERSON, MICHAEL JOHN

PERSONAL Born 05/30/1967, London, England, m, 1993 **DISCIPLINE** CLASSICAL LANGUAGES; LITERATURE **EDUCATION** Princeton Univ, AB, 89; Univ Oxford, DPhil, 94. **CAREER** Vis asst prof, Univ Oregon, 93/94; Mellon postdoctoral fel in humanities, Columbia Univ 94-96; asst prof, Yale Univ, 97- . **HONORS AND AWARDS** Fulbright Sch for study in Freiburg, GER, 89/90; Marshall Scholarship for study in Oxford, ENG, 90-93. **MEMBERSHIPS** APA **RESEARCH** Greek literature; Greek art. **SELECTED PUBLICATIONS** The Fall of Troy in Early Greek Poetry and Art, 97; The Sophrosyne of Persinna and the Romantic Strategy of Heliodorus' Aethiopica, Classical Philology, 97. **CONTACT ADDRESS** Dept of Classics, Yale Univ, New Haven, CT, 06520-8266. **EMAIL** michael.j.anderson@yale.edu

ANDO, CLIFFORD

DISCIPLINE CLASSICAL STUDIES **EDUCATION** Univ Mich, PhD, 96. **CAREER** Asst prof, York Univ, 96-98; asst prof, 98-. **MEMBERSHIPS** Am Philol Asn; North Am Patristics Soc. **RESEARCH** Roman history; Latin and Greek historiography. **SELECTED PUBLICATIONS** Auth, "Pagan Apologetics and Christian Intolerance in the Ages of Themistius and Augustine" in J of Early Christian Studies, 96; "Tacticus, Annales VI: Beginning and End" in Am J of Philol, 97. **CONTACT ADDRESS** Classics Dept, Univ of Southern California, Taper Hall 224, Los Angeles, CA, 90089-0352. **EMAIL** cando@usc.edu

ANDREU, ALICIA GRACIELA

PERSONAL Born 09/07/1940, Lima, Peru, m, 1980, 1 child **DISCIPLINE** SPANISH LITERATURE **EDUCATION** Chapman Col, BA, 65; Univ Wis, MA, 68; Univ Ore, PhD, 78. **CAREER** Chmn, Span & Ital Dept, 80-81, 83-84, 88-91, PROF SPAN, MIDDLEBURY COL, Dean, Spanish School, 84-86; Native instr, Nat Defense Educ Act, summer 64 & 65; Fulbright-Hays res grant, Madrid, Spain, 9/74-6/76; NEH grant, 79 & 81-82, consult, 81-; consult, D C Heath & Co, 80; Am Coun Learned Soc grant, 81; Fel, School Criticism & Theory, Northwestern Univ, summer 81; eval panelist, NEHcol teachers fels, 82-; Prog for Cultural Coop, Ministry of Culture, Spain and U S Univ, res grant, summer 96. **MEMBERSHIPS** MLA; Asoc Galdosistas; Asoc Int Hisp; Asoc Iberoamericana; Latin Am Indian Lit Asn. **RESEARCH** Nineteenth century Spanish literature; 20th century Spanish & Spanish American literature. **SELECTED PUBLICATIONS** Auth, Relacion intima entre Galdos y la literature popular, Actas del Sequndo Congreso Int Estudios Galdosianos, 78; ed, La Cruz del Olivar de Faustina Saez de Melgar, Anales Galdosianos, 80; auth, Galdos y la literatura popular, SGEL, 82; Arte y consumo Angela Grassi y El Correo de la Moda, Nuevo Hisp, winter 82; El folletin como intertexto en Tormento, AG, 82; El folletin: de Galdos a Manuel Puig, RIA, 4-9/83; Garcilaso y Bernal: Interpretations Interpreted, REH, 84; Pedo Camacho: prestidigitator del lenguaje, MLS, spring 86; Dialogo de voces en Fortunata y Jacinta, Actas del VIII Congreso de la AIH, Brown Univ, 86; Cartas de Benito Perez Galdos a Ricardo Palma, AG, 85; Miau: La escritura del poder o el poder de la escritura, AG, 86; La biblioteca de Benito Perez Galdos, KRQ, 8/88; Penito Perez Galdos: lectura y creacion, in Realismo y naturalismo en Espana en la segunda mitad del s.XIX, Antrhopos, Barcelona, 88; Garcilaso y Bernal: Interpretaciones Interpretadas, Historica, 12/88; Tormento: Un discurso de amantes, Hispania, 5/89; Juanito Santa Cruz en dialogo con el mito de don Juan, RHM, 6/89; Modelos dialogicos en la narrativa de Benito Perez Galdos, Univ de Perdue, Amsterdam, 89; Una nueva aproximacion al lenguaje de las Tradiciones Peruanas de Ricardo Palma, REH, 90; Benito Perez Galdos y el discurso americano, La Torre, 4-6/91; Tristana: El deseo y la produccion de las escritura, RLA, 91; Ramon Perez de Ayala y el mito de don Juan, ALEC, 92; Amor de Madre: Pardigma intertextual en una obra de Ricard Palma, Discurso Literario, spring 93; Maria Guerrero y el teatro de Benio Perez Galdos, in A Sesquecentennial Tribute to Galdos, JDLC, 93; Habla la ciudad: Poetica de la migracion, RCL, 8/93; Cronica de Lima, de Antonio Cisneros, o Hermelinda y la subersion de la historia, in Hispanic Culture on the Pacific Coast of the Americas: From Chilenos to Chicanos, CASU Press, 94; El crimen de la Calle de Fuencarral: Texto y context, in Narrativa Decimononica: Creacion Popular y Literatura de Consumo, Rodopi; Legitimidad linguistica y legitimidad socio-economica en un relato de Julio Ramon Ribeyro, RCLL, 94; Una re-lectura de Fabla Salvaje, de Cesar Valleyo, Contratexto, 94; Maria Guerrero: Ficcion y mito, Critica Hispanica, 95; El discurso materno en La Cruz del Olivar, de Faustina Saez de melgar, RCEH, winter 95; La critica feminista y las obras de Benio Perez Galdos y Leopoldo Alas, in Breve Historia Feminista de la literatura espanola; A day in the Bronx (short story), Array Mag, winter 95; El intertexto folletinesco en Tormento, HCLE, 3/95; Maria Guerrero: Texto y contexto en la obra dramatica de Benito Perez Galdos, in Actas del Simposio Galdos y el hispanismo norteamericano (homenaje), 2/95; El discurso matsigenka en El hablador de Mario Vargas Llosa, HJ, 96; Benito Perez Galdos, Higinia Balaguer, y El Crimen de la Calle de Fuencarral, AG, 96/97; La obra de Carmen de Icaza en la difusion de un nuevo concepto de nacion espanola, RHM; Historia y literatura en un texto de Galdos, in Actas del XII C de la AIH, England; El bildungsroman de Andrea en Nada de Carmen Laforte, RL. **CONTACT ADDRESS** Span & Ital Dept, Middlebury Col, Middlebury, VT, 05753-6001. **EMAIL** andreu@panther.middlebury.edu

ANDREWS, LARRY RAY
PERSONAL Born 08/09/1940, Greencastle, IN, m, 1961, 4 children **DISCIPLINE** ENGLISH; COMPARATIVE LITERATURE **EDUCATION** Ohio State Univ, BA, 62; Rutgers Univ, PhD(comp lit), 71. **CAREER** Instr English, Univ SC, 66-69; asst prof, 69-78, Assoc Prof English, Kent State Univ, 78-, Dean, Honors Col, 93-. **MEMBERSHIPS** Col Lang Asn. **RESEARCH** European romanticism; Russian-Western literary relations in 19th century; African American women's fiction. **SELECTED PUBLICATIONS** Auth, D V Venevitinov: A sketch of his life and works, Russ Lit Triquart, 74; Dostevskij and Hugos Le Dernier Jour d'un Condamne, Comp Lit, 77; The Spatial Imagery of Oblomovism, Neophilologus, 88; Black Sisterhood in Gloria Naylor's Novels, CLAS, 89; Hugo's Gilliatt and Leskov's Golovan: Two Eccentric Folk-Epic Heroes, Comp Lit, 94. **CONTACT ADDRESS** Honors Col, Kent State Univ, PO Box 5190, Kent, OH, 44242-0001. **EMAIL** landrews@kent.edu

ANDREWS, STEPHEN J.
PERSONAL Born 06/15/1954, Baltimore, MD, m, 1979, 4 children **DISCIPLINE** HEBRAIC AND COGNATE STUDIES **EDUCATION** Carson-Newman Col, BA, 76; Eastern Bapt Theol Sem, M Div, 79; Southeastern Bapt Theol Sem, Th M, 83; Hebrew Union Col, PhD, 95, M Phil, 98. **CAREER** Asst prof, 91-96, assoc prof, 96-98, old testament and Hebrew, Southeastern Bapt Theol Sem; prof, old testament and archaeol, Midwestern Bapt Theol Sem, 98-; dir, Morton Mus of Archaeol, Midwestern Bapt Theol Sem, 98-. **MEMBERSHIPS** Amer Oriental Soc; Inst of Bibl Res; Soc of Bibl Lit. **RESEARCH** Syro-Palestinian archaeology; Biblical Hebrew; Ancient near east. **SELECTED PUBLICATIONS** Article, Duck Tales at Nuzi: A Note on the Trussed-duck Weights Excavated at Yorgan Tepa, Studies on the Civilization and Culture of Nuzi and the Hurrians, vol 8, 241-43, CDL Press, 96; rev, Two Hundred Nuzi Texts from the Oriental Institute of the University of Chicago, Part I, Studies on the Civilization and Culture of Nuzi and The Hurrians, vol 6, Jour of the Amer Oriental Soc, 116, 269-70, 96; article, A Knowledge of Hebrew Possible to All? Old Testament Exposition and the Hebraica Veritas, Faith and Mission, 13/1, 98-114, Fall 95; rev, Analytical Key to the Old Testament, Faith and Mission, 12/1, 97-98, Fall, 94; rev, The Seven Pillories of Wisdom, Faith and Mission, 10/1, 107-110, Fall, 92; rev, An Introduction to Biblical Hebrew Syntax, Faith and Mission, 9/2, 104-6, Spring, 92; rev, The NIV Exhaustive Concordance, Faith and Mission, 9/1, 85-86, Fall, 91; contr, Mercer Dict of the Bible, Mercer Univ Press, 90. **CONTACT ADDRESS** Midwestern Baptist Theological Sem, 5001 N Oak St Trafficway, Kansas City, MO, 64118. **EMAIL** archaeology@mbts.edu

ANDRIST, DEBRA D.
DISCIPLINE SPANISH **EDUCATION** Fort Hays Kans State Univ, BA, 72; Univ Utah, MA, 79; SUNY, Buffalo, PhD, 85. **CAREER** Teach asst, Univ Utah, 78-79; adm asst, 81-82, teach asst, 79-81, instr, Intensive Eng Lang Inst, 80, 81; dir, Ctr Critical Langs, 80, SUNY, Buffalo; assoc prof, 92-96, asst, 86-92, Baylor Univ; assoc prof, 96-, CHAIR, 97-, PROF SPAN, 98-, UNIV ST THOMAS. **CONTACT ADDRESS** MACL, Univ of St. Thomas, 3800 Montrose, Houston, TX, 77006. **EMAIL** andrist@stthom.edu

ANDRONICA, JOHN LOUIS
PERSONAL Born 10/06/1942, Boston, MA, m, 1966, 2 children **DISCIPLINE** CLASSICAL LANGUAGES **EDUCATION** Col of the Holy Cross, AB, 63; Boston Col, MA, 66; Johns Hopkins Univ, PhD, 69. **CAREER** Asst prof classic lang, 69-72, dir, Wake Forest-in-Venice Prog, 71-72 & 81, assoc prof class lang, Wake Forest Univ, 72-. **MEMBERSHIPS** Am Philol Assn; Class Assn Midwest & South; Vergiliam Soc; Petronian Soc. **RESEARCH** Latin love elegy; Latin epic. **CONTACT ADDRESS** Dept of Class Lang, Wake Forest Univ, PO Box 7343, Winston Salem, NC, 27109-7343. **EMAIL** andy@wfu.edu

ANGELIS, PAUL J.
PERSONAL Born 01/28/1941, Scranton, PA, m, 1965, 3 children **DISCIPLINE** LINGUISTICS **EDUCATION** Univ Scranton, AB, 62; Georgetown Univ, PhD(ling), 68. **CAREER** Asst prof English, Col Mil Royal, 69-72; Fulbright lectr ling & English, Univ Rome, 72-73; training dir, Food & Agr Orgn UN, 73-74; from assoc to asst prof ling & English, Tex A&M Univ, 74-77; prog dir lang, Educ Test Serv, 77-81; Assoc Prof & Chmn Ling, Southern Ill Univ, 81-. **MEMBERSHIPS** Teachers English Speakers Other Lang; Nat Asn Foreign Student Affairs; Ling Soc Am. **RESEARCH** Language testing; second language acquisition; English as a foreign language. **SELECTED PUBLICATIONS** Auth, The importance and diversity of aural comprehension, Mod Lang J, 3/73; Listening comprehension and erroranalysis, AILA Proc, 74; coauth, The performance of non-native speakers of English on Toefl and verbal aptitude tests, 78 & Effects of item disclosure of Toefl performance, 12/80, Educ Testing Serv; Psycholinguistics: Two views, In: Language and Communication, Hornbeam Press, 80. **CONTACT ADDRESS** Dept of Ling, Southern Illinois Univ, Carbondale, IL, 62901-4300. **EMAIL** pangelis@siu.edu

ANKROM, JEFFREY
PERSONAL New Castle, IN **DISCIPLINE** FRENCH **EDUCATION** Ball State Univ, BA, 78 Northwestern Univ, MA, 83 Purdue Univ. **CAREER** Managing Ed and Music Ed, IN Univ Press, 97. **SELECTED PUBLICATIONS** Transl of jour articles. **CONTACT ADDRESS** Univ Press, Indiana Univ, Bloomington, 601 N. Morton St., Bloomington, IN, 47404-3797. **EMAIL** jankrom@indiana.edu

ANYINEFA, KOFFI
PERSONAL Born 11/20/1959, Badougbe-Adjome, Togo, m, 1990, 1 child **DISCIPLINE** FRENCH LITERATURE/ FRANCOPHONE LITERATURES & CULTURES **EDUCATION** Universitat Bayreuth, Germany, PhD, 89. **CAREER** Asst prof, Haverford Coll, 90-96 assoc prof, 96-present. **HONORS AND AWARDS** Alexander von Humboldt-Stiftung Fel, 97-98; NEH Summer Stipend, 97. **MEMBERSHIPS** African Literature Assn; African Studies Assn; Amer Assn of Teachers of French **RESEARCH** Francophone Lit and Culture; French Lit, colonial lit. **SELECTED PUBLICATIONS** Auth, Intertextuality in Dongala's Un fusil dans la main, un poem dans la poche, Research in African Literatures, 93; Hello and Goodbye to Negritude: Senghor, Dadie, Dongala and America, Research in African Literatures, 96; Y a bon banania: L'Afrique et le discours nationaliste dans Tombouctou de Maupassant, forthcoming in The French Review, 97; Postcolonial Postcoloniality in Henri Lopes's Le Pleurer-Rire, Research in African Literature, 98. **CONTACT ADDRESS** French Dept., Haverford Col, 370 Lancas, Haverford, PA, 19041-1392. **EMAIL** kanyinef@haverford.edu

AOUN, JOSEPH
DISCIPLINE SEMITIC LANGUAGES **EDUCATION** MIT, PhD. **CAREER** Prof, Univ Southern Calif. **RESEARCH** Distribution & interpretation of pronominal & definite descriptions. **SELECTED PUBLICATIONS** Coauth, Minimality, Reconstruction and PF- movement, Ling Inquiry 29.4, MIT Press, 98; Resumption and Last Resort to appear in J. Ouhalla and U. Shlonsky Semitic Syntax, Kluwer, 97; Epithets ms USC, 97. **CONTACT ADDRESS** Dept of Linguistics, Univ Southern Calif, University Park Campus, Los Angeles, CA, 90089. **EMAIL** aoun@hermes.usc.edu

ARAM, DOROTHY M.
DISCIPLINE COMMUNICATION DISORDERS **EDUCATION** Northwestern Univ, BS, MA; Case Western Univ, PhD. **CAREER** Com, Emerson Col. **SELECTED PUBLICATIONS** Auth, Diagnosis of Speech and Lang Disorders; Child Lang Disorders. **CONTACT ADDRESS** Emerson Col, 100 Beacon Street, Boston, MA, 02116-1596.

ARAUJO, NORMAN
PERSONAL Born 03/22/1933, New Bedford, MA **DISCIPLINE** FOREIGN LANGUAGES **EDUCATION** Harvard Col, AB, 55; Univ Aix-Marseille, cert, 55-56; Harvard Univ, MA, 57, PhD, 62. **CAREER** Asst prof French & Port, Univ MA, Amherst, 62-64; asst prof mod lang, 64-68, acting chm dept, 69-70, assoc prof Romance Lang, Boston Col, 68-; Gulbenkian Found fel, 70; Cape Verdean Govt fel, 78. **HONORS AND AWARDS** Bartolomeu Dias Prize, Acad Int Cult Portuguesa, 68. **MEMBERSHIPS** MLA; Int Conf Group Mod Port. **RESEARCH** Portuguese and French romanticism; Portuguese-African Literature. **SELECTED PUBLICATIONS** Auth, A study of Cape Verdean literature, 66; Time and Rhythm in Balzac's La Peau de Chagrin, Fr Rev, 70; The Role of Death in Becque's Les Corbeaux, Rev Langues Vivantes, 70; In Search of Eden: Lamartine's Symbols of Despair and Deliverance, Classical Folia Eds, 76; New Directions in Cape Verdean Literature?, The First Numbers of Raizes, Critical Perspectives on Lusophone African Literature, Three Continents Press, Inc, 81; Ferdinand Brunetiere, Critical Survey of Literary Theory, ed Frank Magill, vol 1, 88; Theophile Gautier, Critical Survey of Lit Theory, ed Frank Magill, vol 2, 88; Hippolyte-Adolphe Taine, Critical Survey of Lit Theory, ed Frank Magill, vol 4, 88; The Language of Business and the Business of Language in Becque's Les Corbeaux, French Rev 63, 89; Prosaic Licence and the Use of the Literary Past in Daudet's La Chevre de M. Seguin, Forum for Modern Language Studies 27: 3, 91; Petrus Borel, Dictionary of Lit Biography, ed Catharine Savage Brosman, vol 119: Nineteenth-Century French Fiction Writers: Romanticism and Realism, 1800-1860, 92. **CONTACT ADDRESS** Dept Romance Lang, Boston Col, 140 Commonwealth Ave, Chestnut Hill, MA, 02167-3800. **EMAIL** araujo@bc.edu

ARCHAMBAULT, PAUL JOSEPH
PERSONAL Born 09/17/1937, Webster, MA, m, 1965, 1 child **DISCIPLINE** FRENCH, LATIN **EDUCATION** Assumption Col, AB, 58; Yale Univ, PhD(Romance lang), 63. **CAREER** From instr to asst prof, Amherst Col, 62-68; assoc prof, 68-73, Prof French, Syracuse Univ, 73-, Amherst Col fac-trustee fel, 65-66; Nat Found on Arts & Hum jr scholar, 69. **MEMBERSHIPS** MLA; Medieval Acad Am. **RESEARCH** Mediaeval French and Latin lit; 20th century French lit. **SELECTED PUBLICATIONS** Auth, Thucydides in France: Commynes, J Hist Ideas, 1/67; Commynes and the Renaissance idea of wisdom, Humanisme et Renaissance, fall 67; Sallust in France: Thomas Basin, Papers on Lang & Lit, summer 68; Camus' Hellenic Sources (Studies in Romance Lang & Lit Ser), Univ NC, 72; Seven French Chroniclers: Witnesses to History, Syracuse Univ, 74; A Monk's Confession, Penn State Press, 96; ed, Syracuse Scholar, 79-82; Medieval romance and language, Symp, spring 81. **CONTACT ADDRESS** Dept of For Lang & Lit, Syracuse Univ, Syracuse, NY, 13244. **EMAIL** pjarcham@syr.edu

ARCHIBALD, ELIZABETH F.
DISCIPLINE MEDIEVAL; EARLY RENAISSANCE LITERATURE **EDUCATION** Univ Cambridge, MA; Yale Univ, PhD. **CAREER** Assoc prof **SELECTED PUBLICATIONS** Auth, Apollonius of Tyre: Medieval and Renaissance Themes and Variations, Boydell & Brewer, 91; co-ed, A Companion to Malory, Boydell & Brewer, 96. **CONTACT ADDRESS** Dept of English, Victoria Univ, PO Box 3070, Victoria, BC, V8W 3W1. **EMAIL** efa@uvic.ca

AREHOLE, S.
PERSONAL Born 10/19/1957, India, m, 1988, 3 children **DISCIPLINE** COMMUNICATION DISORDER **EDUCATION** Univ Texas Dallas, PhD 86. **CAREER** Univ of SW Louisiana, assoc prof, prof, 87-. **HONORS AND AWARDS** CDRC Audiology fel. **MEMBERSHIPS** ASLHA; AAS; AAA **RESEARCH** Auditory electrophysiology and Central auditory processing. **SELECTED PUBLICATIONS** Auth, Auditory evoked potentials in low-achieving gifted adolescents, coauth, Roeper Rev, forthcoming; Central auditory processing abilities of low-achieving gifted adolescents, coauth, Jour of Secondary Gifted EDU , 98; Clarification: Masking level differences with GSI-10 audiometer, Amer Jour of Audiology, 98; Identification and assessment of hearing-impaired infants and toddlers, coauth, in: F. Billeaud, ed, Communication disorders in infants and toddlers: Assessment and management. Reading MA, Andover Med Pub, 98; Objective assessment of central auditory processing disorder, Jour of Indian Speech and Hearing Assoc, 98; Cerumen management and audiology practice: Attitudes among otolaryngologists and Audiologists, coauth, Nat Stud Speech Lang and Hearing Jour, 96; A preliminary study of the relationship between long latency response and learning disorder, Brit Jour of Audiology, 95. **CONTACT ADDRESS** Dept of Communication Disorders, SW Louisiana Univ, PO Box 43170, Lafayette, LA, 70506. **EMAIL** sxa3201@usl.edu

ARENAS, FERNANDO
DISCIPLINE SPANISH AND PORTUGUESE LITERATURE **EDUCATION** N Ariz Univ, MA, 86; Univ Calif Berkeley, MA, 88; PhD, 94. **RESEARCH** Portuguese, Brazilian and Lusophone African literary and cultural studies; theoretical approaches to the study of literature and culture. **SELECTED PUBLICATIONS** Auth, Entre o lixo e a esperanza: Morangos Mofados de Caio Fernando Abreu, 90. **CONTACT ADDRESS** Spanish and Portuguese Dept, Univ of Minnesota, Twin Cities, 34 Folwell Hall, 9 Pleasant St SE, Minneapolis, MN, 55455. **EMAIL** arena002@gold.tc.umn.edu

AREND, JUTTA
DISCIPLINE GERMAN **EDUCATION** Case Western Reserve Univ, MA, 71, PhD, 72. **CAREER** Sr lectr; Ger for lang asst liaison; Ger study abroad adv; contact, Int Summer Courses, Univ Freiburg; Ger dept Fulbright adv for prog in Ger and Austria. **RESEARCH** 20th century literature; women's studies; Postmodernism; Romanticism. **SELECTED PUBLICATIONS** Auth, Man verelendet, So - oder so Patrick Suskinds Sonderlinge und ihr Verhaltnis zum Weiblichen, Ger Stud Rev 19 2, 96; Crazy Horse in Mecklenburg: Indianervisionen in Joochen Laabs Der Schattenfanger, Ger Quart 65, 92 & Dokumentation: Ingeborg Drewitz, Ger Quart 59, 86. **CONTACT ADDRESS** Dept of Modern Languages and Literatures, Col of the Holy Cross, 1 College St, Worcester, MA, 01610-2395. **EMAIL** jarend@holycross.edu

ARENS, HILTRUD
PERSONAL Born 12/08/1961, Paderbern, Germany, m, 1991, 1 child **DISCIPLINE** GERMAN LITERATURE **EDUCATION** Univ of Md, MA, 88, PhD, 97. **CAREER** VIS ASST PROF, UNIV OF MONT, 98- **HONORS AND AWARDS** Prane Awd, Univ of Md, 92; Am Fel, AAUW Ed Found, 95-96. **MEMBERSHIPS** MLA; GSA; AITG; WIG; AAUW. **RESEARCH** Contemp German lit & culture; minority lit. **SELECTED PUBLICATIONS** Auth, Kulturelle Hybriditat in der deutschen Minoritatenliteratur der achtziger Jare, Stauffenburg Verlag, 99; Libuse Monikova, Women Witers in German-Speaking Countries, Greenwood Press, 98; Industrial Revolution, Encycl of German Lit, Greenwood Press, 97; Auslandergesetz, Encycl of German Lit, Greenwood Press, 97; Erahlstrategie und Geschlechtskomponente in Bettina von Arnims Die Gunderode und Clems Brentanos Fruhlingskranze. Ein Vergleich, Internationales Jahrbuch der Bettina-von-Arnim-Gesellschaft, Saint Albin Verlag, 93. **CONTACT ADDRESS** ILL Dept, Univ of Montana, Missoula, MT, 59801. **EMAIL** harens@selway.umt.edu

ARENS, KATHERINE
PERSONAL Born 11/25/1953, Chicago, IL, s **DISCIPLINE** GERMAN STUDIES; HUMANITIES **EDUCATION** Northwestern Univ, BA, 75; Stanford Univ, AM, 75-76; Univ Vienna, 78-79; Stanford Univ, PhD, 76-80. **CAREER** Teaching fel, Stanford Univ, dept Ger studies and humanities special prog, 76-80; asst prof, 80-86, assoc prof, 86-93, prof, 93-, dept Ger lang, Univ Tex Austin. **HONORS AND AWARDS** Best article, Unterrichtspraxis, 96; Outstanding Grad Teaching award, Office of Grad Studies, Univ Tex, 97; Harry H. Ransom teaching award, Univ Tex, 91; Liberal Arts Student Coun advising award, 91; nom, Friar Centennial Teaching fel, 89, 91, 93. **MEMBERSHIPS** MLA; Amer Philos Asn; AATG; Ger Studies Asn. **RESEARCH** German idealism; Continental philosophy 1750-date; European romanticism; Literary theory; History & theory of the humanities. **SELECTED PUBLICATIONS** Article, The Linguistics of French Feminism: Semanalyse as Critical Discourse Practice, Intertexts, 2.2, 171-184, 98; article, From Caillois to The Laugh of the Medusa: Vectors of a Diagonal Science, Textual Practice, 12, no 2, 225-250, 98; article, Discourse Analysis as Critical Historiography: A Semanalyse of Mystic Speech, Rethinking History, 2, no 1, 23-50, 98; article, The Canon of Theory: Report on an Institutional Case, Comparative Lit Studies, 34, no 4, 392-413, 97; article, The Habsburg Myth: Austria in the Writing Curriculum, Unterrichtspraxis, 29, no 2, 174-87, Fall, 96; article, Wilhelm Griesinger: Psychiatry Between Philosophy and Praxis, Philos, Psychiat & Psychol, vol 3, no 3, 147-163, Sept, 96; article, Central Europe and the Nationalist Paradigm, Working Papers in Austrian Studies, Univ Minn, 96-1, Mar, 96; article, A Power-Base of Our Own: A New Case for the Historiography of the Language Sciences, Beitrage zur Geschichte der Sprachwissenschaft 6, no 1, 19-52, 96; auth, Austria and Other Margins: Reading Culture, Camden House, 96; chap, History as Knowledge: Herder, Kant, and the Human Sciences, Johann Gottfried Herder: Academic Disciplines and the Pursuit of Knowledge, Univ Va, 90; 106-19, Camden House, 96; chap, On Rereading Paul's Prinzipien der Sprachgeschichte, Multiple Perspectives on the Historical Dimensions of Language, Nodus Publ, 105-114, 96; chap, Mach und Mauthner: Der Fall eines Paradigmasechsels, Fritz Mauthner: Das Werk eines Kritischen Denkers, Bohlau, 95-109, 95; article, H. D.'s Post-Freudian Cultural Analysis: Nike versus Oedipus, Amer Imago, 52, no 4, 359-404, Winter, 95; article, Between Hypatia and Beauvoir: Philosophy as Discourse, Hypatia, 10, no 4, 46-75, Fall, 95; chap, Characterology: Weininger and Austrian Popular Science, Jew and Gender: Responses to Otto Weininger, Temple Univ Press, 121-139, 95; co-auth, Reading for Meaning: An Integrated Approach to Language Learning, Prentice-Hall, 91. **CONTACT ADDRESS** Dept. of Germanic Studies, Univ of Texas at Austin, E.P. Schoch 3.102, Austin, TX, 78712. **EMAIL** k.arenso@mail.utexas.edu

ARGYROS, ALEX
DISCIPLINE FRENCH LITERATURE **EDUCATION** Cornell Univ, PhD, 77. **CAREER** Prof. **SELECTED PUBLICATIONS** Auth, Crimes of Narration: Camus' La Chute, Editions Paratexte, 85; A Blessed Rage for Order: Deconstruction, Evolution, and Chaos, Univ Mich, 91; Narrative & Chaos, New Lit Hist, 92; Towards a View of Time as Death, Diogenes, 90. **CONTACT ADDRESS** Dept of Literature, Richardson, TX, 75083-0688. **EMAIL** aargyros@utdallas.edu

ARMENGOL, ARMANDO
DISCIPLINE SPANISH **EDUCATION** Univ Ill, PhD, 74. **CAREER** Certified Oral Proficiency tester and trainer. **RESEARCH** Latin American literature. **SELECTED PUBLICATIONS** Publ on, Latin Amer Poetry and Novel; co-ed, Palabra Nueva, ser of 3 bks on recent Chicano lit. **CONTACT ADDRESS** Dept of Languages and Linguistics, Univ of Texas, El Paso, 500 W University Ave, El Paso, TX, 79968. **EMAIL** armengol@utep.edu

ARNESON, PAT
DISCIPLINE INTERPERSONAL COMMUNICATION **EDUCATION** OH Univ, PhD, 87. **CAREER** Prof, Univ Northern CO. **MEMBERSHIPS** CO Speech Commun Asn; Western States Commun Asn; Nat Commun Asn. **RESEARCH** Interpersonal commun; qualitative research methods. **SELECTED PUBLICATIONS** Auth, Sacred Dimensions of the shaman's web. Integrative Explorations, J of Cult and Consciousness, 4(1), 97; coauth, Interpersonal communication ethics and the limits of individualism, The Electronic J of Commun/La Rev Electronique de Commun, 6(4), 96; Educational Assessment as invitation for dialogue, J of the Asn for Commun Admin, 79, 97. **CONTACT ADDRESS** Univ Northern Colorado, Greeley, CO, 80639.

ARNETT, CARLEE
PERSONAL Born 08/13/1964, Trenton, NJ, m, 1991, 2 children **DISCIPLINE** FOREIGN LANGUAGES **EDUCATION** Mt Holyoke Col, BA, 87; Univ Calif, Berkeley, MA, 91; Univ Mich, PhD, 95. **CAREER** Vis asst prof, coordr, Ohio State Univ, 97-98; asst prof, dir, Univ Ariz, 98-. **HONORS AND AWARDS** Rackham Dissertation Fel, Frank X. Braun Tchg Prize, Univ Mich, 94. **MEMBERSHIPS** Modern Lang Asn; Soc Germanic Philol; Am Asn Tchrs German. **RESEARCH** German syntax; second language acquisition; older Germanic languages. **SELECTED PUBLICATIONS** Auth, art, Perfect Auxiliary Selection in the Old Saxon Heliand, 97; auth, German Impersonal Passives, 97. **CONTACT ADDRESS** Dept of German Studies, Univ of Arizona, Box 210067, Tucson, AZ, 85721. **EMAIL** carnett@u.arizona.edu

ARONSON, HOWARD ISAAC
PERSONAL Born 03/05/1936, Chicago, IL **DISCIPLINE** LINGUISTICS **EDUCATION** Univ IL, AB, 56; IN Univ, MA, 58, PhD, 61. **CAREER** Asst prof Slavic lang, Univ Wis, 61-62; from asst prof to assoc prof ling & Slavic lang, 62-73, chmn dept ling, 72-80, Prof Ling & Slavic Lang, Univ Chicago 73-**MEMBERSHIPS** Am Asn Tchr(s) Slavic & East Europ Lang; Am Asn Advan Slavic Studies; Bulgarian Studies Group; Am Asn Southeast Europ Studies. **RESEARCH** Georgian linguistics; Bulgarian and Russian linguistics; Yiddish linguistics. **SELECTED PUBLICATIONS** Auth, The Grammatical Categories of the Indicative in the Contemporary Bulgarian Literary Language, In: To Honor Roman Jakobson, 67 & Bulgarian Inflectional Morphophonology, 68, Mouton; Towards a Semantic Analysis of Case and Subject in Georgian, Lingua, 70; Grammatical Subject in Old Georgian, Bedi Kartlisa, 76; Interrelationships Between Aspect and Mood in Bulgarian, Folia Slavica, 77; English as an Active Language, Lingua, 77; Georgian: A first-year reading grammar, Slavica, 82; Form, Function, and the 'perfective' in Bulgarian, In: The Scope of Slavic Aspect, Slavica, 85; Modern Georgian, In: The Indigenous Languages of the Caucasus, Caravan, 91. **CONTACT ADDRESS** Dept of Slavic Lang & Lit, Univ of Chicago, 1130 E 59th St, Chicago, IL, 60637-1539. **EMAIL** hia5@midway.uchicago.edu

ARROYO, CIRIACO
DISCIPLINE HISPANIC STUDIES AND COMPARATIVE LITERATURE **EDUCATION** Pontifical Univ Salamanca, MA; Univ Munich, PhD. **CAREER** Emerson Hinchliff prof; Hon Doc in Humane Letters, St Joseph's Univ. **RESEARCH** European novel; dichotomy reason decision; concepts of literature, reading, and writing. **SELECTED PUBLICATIONS** Auth, El alma de Espana, Cien anos de inseguridad, Oviedo, Ediciones Nobel, 96; Las humanidades en la era tecnologica, 98. **CONTACT ADDRESS** Dept of Romance Studies, Cornell Univ, 285 Goldwin Smith Hall, Ithaca, NY, 14853. **EMAIL** cma6@cornell.edu

ASCARI, ROSALIA COLOMBO
DISCIPLINE ITALIAN LANGUAGE AND LITERATURE **EDUCATION** Universita Bocconi; PhD. **CAREER** Prof, Sweet Briar Col . **RESEARCH** 19th and 20th century Italian lit; Occhipinti. **SELECTED PUBLICATIONS** Auth, articles and reviews in Annali d'Italianistica; coauth, L'Analyse du texte. **CONTACT ADDRESS** Sweet Briar Col, Sweet Briar, VA, 24595. **EMAIL** ascari@sbc.edu

ASHLEY, LEONARD R.N.
PERSONAL Born 12/05/1928, Miami, FL **DISCIPLINE** ENGLISH, LINGUISTICS **EDUCATION** McGill Univ, BA, 49, MA, 50; Princeton Univ, AM, 53, PhD, 56. **CAREER** Instr, 53-55, Univ Utah; instr, 55-56, Royal Can Air Force, London; 2nd asst to air hist, 56-58; instr, 58-61, Univ Rochester; from instr to assoc prof, 61-72, prof, 72-, prof emeritus, 95-, Brooklyn Col; res grants, Univ Utah, 55 & Univ Rochester, 60; lectr, 61-, New Sch Social Res; Brooklyn Col fac res grant, 68; contrib ed, Papertexts, Simon & Schuster & Washington Sq Press; consult, Harper & Row & Oxford Univ Press; exec bd, Amer Name Soc; ed bd, 65-, names reviewer, Bibliotheone d' Humanisme et Renaissance, Geneva; co-ed, 97, 99, Amer Soc of Geolinguistics. **HONORS AND AWARDS** Shakespeare Gold Medal, 49; hon, LHD, 98. **MEMBERSHIPS** MLA; Am Name Soc (pres, 79, 87); Int Conf Gen Semantics; NY Acad of Sci; Intl Linguistics Assn; Amer Soc of Geolinguistics, pres, 85, 91-. **RESEARCH** English drama; English language, especially onomastics and geolinguistics; English nondramatic literature. **SELECTED PUBLICATIONS** Auth, The Complete Book of Superstition, Prophecy, and Luck, Barricade Bks, 95; auth, The Complete Book of Magic and Witchcraft, Barricade Bks, 95; auth, The Complete Book of Devils and Demons, Barricade Bks, 96; auth, The Complete Book of Devil's Disciples, Barricade Bks, 96; auth, The Complete Book of Spells, Curses and Magical Recipes, Barricade Bks, 92; auth, The Complete Book of Vampires, Barricade Bks, 98; auth, The Complete Book of Ghosts and Poltergeists, 99; auth, George Alfred Henty and the Victorian Mind, Internet Scholar pub, 98; auth, Turkey: Names and Naming Practices, Internet Scholar pub, 98. **CONTACT ADDRESS** Dept of English, Brooklyn Col, CUNY, Brooklyn, NY, 11210.

ASHLIMAN, D.L.
PERSONAL Born 01/01/1938, Idaho Falls, ID, m, 1960, 3 children **DISCIPLINE** GERMAN **EDUCATION** Rutgers, PhD, 69; Univ of UT, BA, 63 **CAREER** Assoc Prof, 77-86, Chair, 94-97, Univ of Pittsburgh; Visit Prof, 92, 96, 97, 98, Univ of Augsburg, Ger **HONORS AND AWARDS** Academ Dean, Semester at Sea, 94 **RESEARCH** Indo-European folktales **SELECTED PUBLICATIONS** Auth, Voices from the Past: The Cycle of Life in Indo-European Folktales, Kendall/Hunt Publishing Co., 95; A Guide to Folktales in the English Language, Greenwood Press, 87 **CONTACT ADDRESS** German Dept, Univ of Pittsburgh, Pittsburgh, PA, 15260. **EMAIL** dash+@pitt.edu

ASTOUR, MICHAEL CZERNICHOW
PERSONAL Born 12/17/1916, Kharkov, Russia, m, 1952 **DISCIPLINE** ANCIENT HISTORY, SEMITIC STUDIES **EDUCATION** Univ Paris, Lic es Lett, 37; Brandeis Univ, PhD(Mediter studies), 62. **CAREER** Asst prof Europ lang, Brandeis Univ, 60-65, Mediter studies, 63-65; assoc prof, 65-69, PROF ANCIENT HIST, SOUTHERN IL UNIV, EDWARDSVILLE, 69-, Vis prof, Univ NC, Chapel Hill, 69-70; Am Philos Soc grant, 72; assoc fel, Am Res Inst, Turkey, 72. **MEMBERSHIPS** Corresp mem Inst Antiq & Christianity; Am Name Soc; AHA; Am Orient Soc; Soc Bibl Lit. **RESEARCH** History, geography and civilization of the ancient Near East; western Semitic lit and mythology; Greco-Semitic connections. **SELECTED PUBLICATIONS** Auth, Place Names, In: Ras Shamra Parallels, vol 2, Pont Bibl Inst, Rome, 75; Continuite et changement dans la toponymie de la Syrie du Nord, In: La Toponymie Antique, Univ Strasbourg & E J Brill, Leiden, 77; Tall-Al-Hamidya, vol 2, with S. Eichler and M. Wafler, and D. Warburton, J of the Am Oriental Soc, vol 113, 93; The Hurrians, with G. Wilhelm, J of Near Eastern Studies, vol 53, 94; The Cities of Seleukid Syria, with J. D. Granger, J of the Am Oriental Soc, vol 114, 94; Place-Names from the Elba Tablets (Italian), with A. Archi, P. Piacentini, and F. Pomponio, J of the Am Oriental Soc, vol 117, 97. **CONTACT ADDRESS** Dept of Hist Studies, Southern IL Univ, Edwardsville, IL, 62026.

ATHANASSAKIS, APOSTOLOS N.
DISCIPLINE CLASSICAL LINGUISTICS, GREEK POETRY **EDUCATION** Univ Pa, PhD, 65. **CAREER** PROF, CLASS LING, UNIV CALIF, SANTA BARBARA. **SELECTED PUBLICATIONS** Transl, introd, text, Via Sancti Pachomii, Scholars' Press, 75; Transl, introd, comment, The Homeric Hymns, Johns Hopkins Univ Press, 76; Transl, text, The Orphic Hymns, Scholar's Press, 77; Transl, introd, Hesiod: Theogony, Works and Days, Shield, Johns Hopkins Univ Press, 88; ed, Essays on Hesiod, Vol I, Ramus 21, 92; Essays on Hesiod, Vol II, Ramus 21, 93. **CONTACT ADDRESS** Dept of Classics, Univ Calif, Santa Barbara, CA, 93106-7150. **EMAIL** gmangold@humanitas.ucsb.edu

ATKINSON, COLIN B.
DISCIPLINE ENGLISH LANGUAGE; LITERATURE **EDUCATION** McGill, BEng; Sir George Williams, BA; Columbia, MA; NY Univ, PhD, 71. **CAREER** Assoc prof. **RESEARCH** Victorian period; women's studies; the drama. **SELECTED PUBLICATIONS** Pub (s), Sydney Owenson, Lady Morgan; Maria Edgeworth; attitudes to death in nineteeth-century American parlour songs; and the place of Thomas Bentley and Anne Wheathill in the devotional tradition of women in Renaissance England. **CONTACT ADDRESS** Dept of English Language and Literature, Univ of Windsor, 401 Sunset Ave, Windsor, ON, N9B 3P4. **EMAIL** p68@uwindsor.ca

ATLAS, JAY DAVID
PERSONAL Born 02/01/1945, Houston, TX **DISCIPLINE** PHILOSOPHY & LINGUISTICS **EDUCATION** Amherst Col, AB, 66; Princeton Univ, PhD, 76. **CAREER** Asst prof, 76-80, assoc prof Philos, 81-88, prof philos, Pomona Col, 89-,

Mem common rm, Wolfson Col, Oxford, 78 & 80; vis fel, Princeton Univ, 79; sr assoc, JurEcon, Inc, 81-; res assoc, Inst Advan Study School Hist, Princeton, NJ, 82-84, 86; vis lectr, Dept Philos, Univ Hong Kong, 86; vis prof, Dept Philos, UCLA, 89-95; vis prof, Dept Dutch Ling, Univ Groningen, The Netherlands, spring 95; vis scholar, Max Planck Inst for Psycolinguistics, nijmegen, The Netherlands, 97. **MEMBERSHIPS** Am Philos Asn; Asn Symbolic Logic. **RESEARCH** Philos of lang; metaphysics; linguistics and lit theory. **SELECTED PUBLICATIONS** Auth, Frege's polymorphous concept of presupposition and its role in theory of meaning, Semantikos, 1: 29-44; Presupposition: A sematico-pragmatic account, Pragmatics Microfiche, 1.4, D13-G9, 75; Negation, ambiguity, and presupposition, Ling & Philos, 1: 321-336; On presupposing, Mind, 87: 396-411; Reference, meaning, and translation, Philos Books, 21: 129-140; coauth, It-clefts, informativeness, and logical form: Radical pragmatics, In: Radical Pragmatics, Acad Press, 81; auth, Is not logical?, Proc 11th Int Symposium on Multiple-Valued Logic, Inst Elec & Electronics Engrs, 81; Comparative adjectives and adverbials of degree, Ling & Philos, 84; Whate are negative existence statements about?, Ling & Philos, 88; Philosophy without Ambiguity: A Logico-Linguistic Essay, Clarendon Press, Oxford, 89; Only noun phrases, pseudo-negative generalized quantitatives, negative plarity items, and monotanacity, J Semantics, 96. **CONTACT ADDRESS** Dept Philos, Pomona Col, 333 N College Way, Claremont, CA, 91711-6319. **EMAIL** jatlas@pomona.edu

ATTRIDGE, DEREK
DISCIPLINE ENGLISH LANGUAGE AND LITERATURE **EDUCATION** Natal Univ, BA; Cambridge Univ, BA; PhD. **CAREER** Dist vis prof English. **RESEARCH** British and Irish modernism; poetic form and performance; literary theory; South African writing. **SELECTED PUBLICATIONS** Auth, Poetic Rhythm: An Introduction, Cambridge, 95; auth, Peculiar Language: Literature as Difference from the Renaissance to James Joyce Cornell, 88; The Rhythms of English Poetry Longman, 82; Well-weighed Syllables: Elizabethan Verse in Classical Metres , Cambridge, 74; ed, Acts of Literature by Jacques Derrida, Routledge, 92; The Cambridge Companion to James Joyce, Cambridge, 90; co-ed, Writing South Africa: Literature, Apartheid, and Democracy, Cambridge, 98; Post-structuralist Joyce: Essays from the French, Cambridge, 84; The Linguistics of Writing: Arguments between Literature and Language, Routledge, 88; Post-structuralism and the Question of History, Cambridge, 87. **CONTACT ADDRESS** Dept of English, Rutgers Univ, 510 George St, Murray Hall, New Brunswick, NJ, 08901-1167.

AUBERY, PIERRE
PERSONAL Born 08/08/1920, Mt. St. Aignan, m, 1950, 1 child **DISCIPLINE** FRENCH LANGUAGE & LITERATURE **EDUCATION** Lycee du Havre, BA, 39; Univ Toulouse, LicLet, 44; D Univ, Paris, 55. **CAREER** Journaliste Parlementaire, Paris, 47-52; instr romance lang, Duke Univ, 53-57; asst prof French, Mt Holyoke Col, 57-61; vis prof, Univ Alta, 61-62; assoc prof, 62-67, PROF FRENCH, STATE UNIV NY, BUFFALO, 67-, Guggenheim fel, 64-65; pres, Buffalo Br, Alliance Francaise, NY, 65-68; civilization ed, Fr Rev, 67-74; consult French lit, Encycl Judaica; rev ed, Comtemp Fr Civilization, 76-. **MEMBERSHIPS** Soc Ecrivains Normands; Am Asn Teachers Fr; Am Soc 18th Century Studies. **RESEARCH** Jewish literature; romantic Religions and social consciousness; a sociological approach to literature and literary criticism. **SELECTED PUBLICATIONS** Auth, Milieux juifs de la France contemporaine, PLON, 62; coauth, Juifs et Canadiens, Ed du Jours, Montreal, 67; auth, Pour une lecture ouvriere de la litterature, Ed Syndicalistes, 69; Mecislas Golbert, Intellectual Biography, Minard, 78. **CONTACT ADDRESS** Dept of Mod Lang, State Univ of NY, Buffalo, NY, 14260.

AUGER, JULIE
DISCIPLINE FRENCH LITERATURE **EDUCATION** Univ Pa, PhD, 94. **CAREER** Asst prof. **RESEARCH** Sociolinguistics; morphosyntax; Quebec Colloquial French; spoken French in general and other Gallo Romance dialects. **SELECTED PUBLICATIONS** Auth, pubs on subject doubling, subject pronomica, morphosyntactic variation, and hypercorrection. **CONTACT ADDRESS** Dept of French and Italian, Indiana Univ, Bloomington, 300 N Jordan Ave, Bloomington, IN, 47405.

AULD, LOUIS
DISCIPLINE FRENCH LANGUAGE AND LITERATURE **EDUCATION** Oberlin Col, BA; Univ Calif Los Angeles, MA; Bryn Mawr Col, PhD, 68. **CAREER** Fac, Kenyon Col, Smith Col, and Duke Univ; admstr, Yale Schl Music; dir, Lang Lrng Ctr, Central Conn State Univ. **HONORS AND AWARDS** Founder, LYRICA Soc; ed, Ars LYRICA. **MEMBERSHIPS** LYRICA. **RESEARCH** 17th century French literature, with special emphasis on word-music relations. **SELECTED PUBLICATIONS** Auth, studies of Moliere's comedy-ballets, the literary origins of French opera, early French art song, and the court ballet. **CONTACT ADDRESS** Central Connecticut State Univ, 1615 Stanley St, New Britain, CT, 06050.

AUSTIN, PAUL MURRAY
PERSONAL Born 05/17/1941, China, m, 1964, 3 children **DISCIPLINE** RUSSIAN LANGUAGE & LITERATURE **EDUCATION** Univ Toronto, BA, 63, PhD(Russ lit), 70; Cornell Univ, MA, 64. **CAREER** Lectr Russ, Brock Univ, 67-68; lectr, 68-70, asst prof, 70-75, ASSOC PROF RUSS, MCGILL UNIV, 75-, CHMN DEPT, 81-. **MEMBERSHIPS** Can Asn Slavists; Am Asn Advan Slavic Studies; Am Asn Teachers Slavic & E Europ Lang. **RESEARCH** Soviet linguistic policy; Russian romanticism; Soviet Turkic linguistic policy. **SELECTED PUBLICATIONS** Auth, The Etymology of King in Soviet Turkic Languages, Can J Ling, 67; An Interview with Ilya Ehrenburg, Soviet Studies, 69; Russian Loan Words in the Proposed Reform of Soviet Turkic Alphabets, Gen Ling, 73; Russian Loans in Uzbek, Nat Papers, 74; Russian Views of Lowry, Can Lit, 74; La litterature quebecoise d'apresgue-re vue de Moscou, Rev de L'Univ d'Ottawa, 74; The Development of Modern Literary Uzbek: Some Historical Analogies, Can Slavonic Papers, 75; Petr Kudrjasev: Russia's First Romantic Ethnographer, Studies Romanticism, 76; Boris Pasternak, A Literary Biography, Vol 1, 1890-1928, with C. Barnes, Canadian Slavonic Papers-Revue Canadienne Des Slavistes, Vol 34, 92. **CONTACT ADDRESS** Dept of Russ & Slavic Studies, McGill Univ, 1001 Sherbrooke St, Montreal, PQ, H3A 2T5.

AUSTIN, TIMOTHY ROBERT
PERSONAL Born 05/22/1952, Tonbridge, England, m, 1995, 4 children **DISCIPLINE** STYLISTICS, LINGUISTICS **EDUCATION** Oxford Univ, England, MA, 73; Univ Mass, PhD, 77. **CAREER** Asst prof Eng, 77-83, dir, interdisciplinary prog ling studies, 81-85, assoc prof, 83-94, prof, 94, dept chemn, 96-, Loyola Univ Chi. **MEMBERSHIPS** MLA; Midwest Mod Lang Assn. **RESEARCH** Linguistic analysis of literary style; English early romantic poets; history of the English language. **SELECTED PUBLICATIONS** Auth, Language Crafted: To Linguistic Theory of Poetic Syntax, Bloomington: Indiana UP, 84; auth, Poetic Voices: Discourse Linguistics and the Poetic Text, Tuocaloosa: University of Alabama Press, 94; auth, Confronting the Ancestral Voices: Some Thoughts on Assessment, ADE Bulletin, 97. **CONTACT ADDRESS** Dept of English, Loyola Univ, Chicago, 6525 N Sheridan Rd, Chicago, IL, 60626-5385. **EMAIL** taustin@luc.edu

AVELAR, IDELBER
DISCIPLINE SPANISH LITERATURE **EDUCATION** Univ NC, MA; Duke Univ, PhD. **CAREER** Asst prof, Univ Ill Urbana Champaign. **RESEARCH** Latin American literature and intelectual histories; critical theory. **SELECTED PUBLICATIONS** Auth, Alegoria y postdictadura: Notas sobre la memoria del mercado, 97; Marx en inminencia y urgencia (o la hipotesis de una espectrologia deconstructiva), 95; El espectro en la temporalidad de lo mesi nico: Derrida y Jameson a proposito de la firma Marx, 95; Conficciones y la retorica del nombre propio: Autobiografia y politica en Juvenilia, de Miguel Can La Torre, 95; A Morta, de Oswald de Andrade: A Emergencia de uma Mimesis Paradoxal no Teatro Brasileiro, Latin Am Theatre Rev, 95; Bares desiertos y calles sin nombre: Literatura y experiencia en tiempos sombrios, Rev de Critica Cult, 94. **CONTACT ADDRESS** Spanish, Italian, and Portuguese Dept, Univ Ill Urbana Champaign, 52 E Gregory Dr, Champaign, IL, 61820. **EMAIL** iavelar@uiuc.edu

AVERY, GEORGE COSTAS
PERSONAL Born 07/27/1926, Philadelphia, PA, m, 1951, 2 children **DISCIPLINE** GERMAN LANGUAGE AND LITERATURE **EDUCATION** Univ PA, AB, 51, AM, 55, PhD, 59. **CAREER** From instr to asst prof Ger lang & lit, St Joseph's Col, PA, 55-60; from instr to asst prof, 60-67, assoc prof Ger, 67-71, PROF GER, SWARTHMORE COL, 71-, Lectr, Swarthmore Col, 59-60; Fulbright-Hays res grant, Ger, 65-66. **MEMBERSHIPS** MLA; Am Asn Teachers Ger. **RESEARCH** German literature since 1900; Herwarth Walden and Der Sturm; German romanticism. **SELECTED PUBLICATIONS** Auth, A poet beyond the pale: some notes on the shorter works of Robert Walser, Mod Lang Quart, 6/63; Die Darstellung des Kunstlers bei Franz Kafka, Weltfreunde, Prague, 67; Das Ende der Kunst Zur Robert Walser's Spatprosa, Schweizer Monatsch, 6/68; Inquiry and Testament: A Study of the Novels and Short Prose of Robert Walser, Univ PA, 68; Freud and the Child Woman-The Memoirs of Fritz Wittels, with E. Timms, Germanic Rev, Vol 71, 96; Kraus, Karl Stoessl, Otto-Correspondence 1902-1925 (German), with G. J. Carr, Germanic Rev, Vol 72, 97. **CONTACT ADDRESS** Dept of Language, Swarthmore Col, Swarthmore, PA, 19081.

AVINS, CAROL JOAN
PERSONAL Born 05/09/1950, New York, NY **DISCIPLINE** RUSSIAN & COMPARATIVE LITERATURE **EDUCATION** Univ PA, BA, 70; Yale Univ, PhD(Slavic lang & lit), 74. **CAREER** Asst prof, 74-80, ASSOC PROF RUSSIAN LANG & LIT & COMP LIT, NORTHWESTERN UNIV, 80-. **MEMBERSHIPS** MLA; Am Asn Teachers Slavic & East Europ Lang; Am Asn Advan Slavic Studies; AAUP; Am Coun Teachers Russ. **RESEARCH** Twentieth century Russian literature; 20th century comparative literature. **SELECTED PUBLICATIONS** Auth, Border Crossings: The West and Russian Identity in Soviet Literature, 1917-1934, Univ CA Press; Kinship and Concealment in 'Red Cavalry' and Babel 1920 Diary, Slavic Rev, Vol 53, 94. **CONTACT ADDRESS** Dept of Slavic Lang & Lit, Northwestern Univ, Evanston, IL, 60201.

AXELROD, MARK R.
PERSONAL Born 03/31/1946, Philadelphia, PA, m, 2 children **DISCIPLINE** COMPARATIVE LITERATURE **EDUCATION** Indiana Univ, BA, 69, MA, 77; Univ Minn, PhD, 88. **CAREER** Tutor, Edinburgh Univ, 89-90; asst prof, Chapman Univ, 90-. **HONORS AND AWARDS** Ind Univ Experimental Fiction Writing Award, 76; Allaince Francaise Nat Lit Essay Award, 74, 75, 76; Camargo Fel in Fiction Writing, 82, 86; Western Ill Univ Nat Playwriting Award, 84; Nat Teleplay Award, Univ Wis Screenwriters Forum, 90; McGinnis Award, Univ Iowa, Best Short Story 1990, Iowa Review, 90; Bronze Award for Screenwriting, Festival Int de Video do Algarve, 90; Silver Seal Award for Screenwriting, London Int Film & Video Festival, 91; Award in Screenwriting, Scottish Asn Filmmakers, 93; recipient of numerous grants and fellowships. **MEMBERSHIPS** New Novel Asn; MLA; Am Comp Lit Asn; Samuel Beckett Soc; Int Comp Lit Asn. **RESEARCH** Film; Latin American fiction. **SELECTED PUBLICATIONS** Auth, Neville Chamberlain's Chimera or Nine Metaphors of Vision, Membrane Press, 78; auth, The Politics of Style in the Fiction of Balzac, Beckett & Cort zar, Macmillan Publ/St. Martin's Press, 92; auth, Bombay California, Pac Writers Press, 94; auth, Cardboard Castles, Pac Writers Press, 96; auth, Cloud Castles, Pac Writers Press (forthcoming 98); auth, The Poetics of Novels: Fiction & Its Execution, Macmillan Publ (forthcoming 98); author of numerous articles and other publications. **CONTACT ADDRESS** Dept English, Chapman Univ, Orange, CA, 92866.

AXELROD, MELISSA
DISCIPLINE NATIVE AMERICAN LANGUAGES, MORPHOSYNTAX, SEMANTICS, MORPHOLOGY, SOCIOLINGUI **EDUCATION** Univ Colo, PhD. **CAREER** Instr, Univ NMex. **RESEARCH** Native American languages; morphosyntax. **SELECTED PUBLICATIONS** Auth, Incorporation in Koyukon Athabaskan, IJAL 56, 90; The Semantics of Time: Aspectual Categorization in Koyukon Athabaskan, Univ NEbr Press, 93; coauth, Han Zaadlitlee. Koyukon Language Curriculum, YKSD, 83; coauth, Active voice and middle diathesis: A cross-linguistic perspective, in Fox, B and P Hopper, eds, Voice: Form and Function, John Benjamins, 94; coed, Sitsiy Yugh Noholnik Ts'in'. As My Gradfather Told It: Traditional Stories from the Koyukuk, YKSD and ANLC, 83. **CONTACT ADDRESS** Univ NMex, Albuquerque, NM, 87131. **EMAIL** axelrod@unm.edu

AZEVEDO, MILTON M.
PERSONAL Born 04/27/1942, Ouro Fino, Brazil **DISCIPLINE** LINGUISTICS **EDUCATION** Cornell Univ, MA, 71, PhD, 73. **CAREER** Lecturer, Univ Ill, Fall 72; Asst Prof, 72-76; Univ Calif, Berkeley, Asst Prof, 76, Assoc Prof, 83, Prof, 90; Vis Prof, Univ Colo, 75-76, Univ Minn, 77-78; Dir, Univ Calif & Univ Ill Barcelona Stud Ctr, 96-98. **MEMBERSHIPS** Am Asn Teachers Span & Port; N Am Catalan Soc. **RESEARCH** Literary linguistics; translation theory. **SELECTED PUBLICATIONS** Auth, O Subjuntivo em Portugues: Um Estudo Transformacional, Petropolis, 76; auth, Passive Sentences in English and Portugese, Georgetown Univ Press; 80; auth, A Contrastive Phonology of Portugese and English, Georgetown Univ Press, 81; co-auth, A Practical Guide to Teaching of Spanish, 2nd ed, Nat Textbook Co, 88; Introduccion a la linguistica espanola, Prentice Hall, 92; La parla i el text, Llieda, Spain, 96; Lecturas periodisticas, 5th ed, DC Health, 96; co-ed, Catalan Review, 9:3, 95. **CONTACT ADDRESS** Univ Calif, Berkeley, Berkeley, CA, 94720.

AZZI, MARIE-DENISE BOROS
PERSONAL Born 11/25/1938, Paris, France, w, 1968, 2 children **DISCIPLINE** FRENCH **EDUCATION** Univ Calif Los Angeles, PhD, 64 **CAREER** Prof, Rutgers Univ **MEMBERSHIPS** AAUP; PMLA; BAAG; Sarte Stud Int; NEMLA. **SELECTED PUBLICATIONS** Auth, La problematique de l'ecriture dans Les Faux-Monnayeurs d'Andre Gide, Les Lettres Modernes, 90; The Immoralist, in Cyclopedia of Literary Characters, Salem Press, 90; The Infernal Machine, in Cyclopedia of Literary Characters, Salem Press, 90; Lafcadio's Adventures, in Cyclopedia of Literary Characters, Salem Press, 90; Vautrin et Protos: une etude intertextuelle, Modern Lang Stud, 93. **CONTACT ADDRESS** 79 Kingsberry Dr, Somerset, NJ, 08873. **EMAIL** borosazz@rci.rutgers.edu

B

BABBY, LEONARD HARVEY
PERSONAL Born 07/29/1939, New York, NY **DISCIPLINE** SLAVIC & GENERAL LINGUISTICS **EDUCATION** Brooklyn Col, BA, 62; Harvard Univ, MA, 65, PhD(Slavic ling), 70. **CAREER** Asst prof Slavic ling, Princeton Univ, 69-71; asst prof, 71-79, PROF SLAVIC LING, CORNELL UNIV, 80-. **MEMBERSHIPS** Ling Soc Am. **RESEARCH** Russian syntax and the Russian language in general; Slavic syntax. **SELECT-**

ED PUBLICATIONS Auth, The deep structure of adjectives and the participles in Russian, Language, 73; A note on agreement in Russian, Glossa, 73; Towards a formal theory of parts of speech, Readings in Slavic Transformational Syntax, 74; A Transformational Grammar of Russian Adjectives, Mouton, The Hague, 74; Nominalization, Passivization and Causativization-Evidence from Russian, Welt Der Slaven-Halbjahresschrift Fur Slavistik, Vol 42, 97. **CONTACT ADDRESS** Dept of Mod Lang & Ling, Cornell Univ, Morrill Hall, Ithaca, NY, 14850.

BABCOCK, ARTHUR EDWARD
PERSONAL Born 05/15/1946, Chicago, IL, m, 1972 **DISCIPLINE** FRENCH LANGUAGE & LITERATURE **EDUCATION** Univ MI, AB, 68, MA, 69, PhD(French), 74. **CAREER** Asst prof, 74-80, PROF FRENCH, UNIV SOUTHERN CA, 80-. **MEMBERSHIPS** AAUP; Am Asn Teachers French; MLA; Philol Asn Pac Coast. **RESEARCH** Twentieth-century French literature; Andre Gide. **SELECTED PUBLICATIONS** Auth, La Symphonic pastorale as self-conscious fiction, French Forum, 1/78; Perspective narrative dans Les Thibault, Ky Romance Quart, fall 79; Portraits of Artists: Reflexivity in Gidean Fiction, 1902-1946, York, 81; Past-Imperfect-French Intellectuals, 1944-1956, with T. Judt, French Review, Vol 67, 94. **CONTACT ADDRESS** Dept of French & Ital, Univ of Southern CA, Los Angeles, CA, 90007.

BACH, EMMON
DISCIPLINE LINGUISTICS **EDUCATION** Univ Chicago, PhD, 59. **CAREER** Prof emer. **SELECTED PUBLICATIONS** Auth, In Defense of Passive, Ling Philos, 81; On Time, Tense, and Aspect: An Essay in English Metaphysics, Acad, 81; Some Generalizations of Categorial Grammars, Foris, 84; Informal Lectures on Formal Semantics, SUNY, 89; co-ed, The Algebra of Events, Ling Philos, 88. **CONTACT ADDRESS** Linguistics Dept, Univ of Massachusetts, Amherst, S College 133, Amherst, MA, 01003. **EMAIL** bach@unbc.edu

BACHMAN, CHARLES ROGER
PERSONAL Born 10/15/1936, Oskaloosa, IA, d, 3 children **DISCIPLINE** COMPARATIVE LITERATURE **EDUCATION** Baylor Univ, BA, 61; Ind Univ, PhD, 65. **CAREER** From asst prof to assoc prof, 65-78, prof Eng, 78-, State Univ NY Col Buffalo; Lectr drama, Univ Queensland, Australia, 74-76. **RESEARCH** Modern and contemporary drama; fiction; Native American Literature. **SELECTED PUBLICATIONS** Art, Communion and conflict in Hardy and Hauptmann, Revue des Langues Vivantes, autumn 68; art, Life into art: Gerhart Hauptmann and Michael Kramer, Ger Quart, 5/69; art, Albee's A Delicate Balance: Parable as nightmare, Revue des Langues Vivantes, spring 70; art, Defusion of menace in the plays of Sam Shepard, Mod Drama, 12/76 & Contemp Lit Criticism, Vol 17, 80. **CONTACT ADDRESS** Dept of English, SUNY, Buffalo, 1300 Elmwood Ave, Buffalo, NY, 14222-1095.

BACON, HELEN HAZARD
PERSONAL Born 03/09/1919, Berkeley, CA **DISCIPLINE** CLASSICAL LANGUAGES & LITERATURE **EDUCATION** Bryn Mawr Col, BA, 40, PhD(classics), 55. **CAREER** Instr Greek & English, Bryn Mawr Col, 46-48, instr Greek, 48-49; instr classics, Woman's Col, 51-52; from instr to assoc prof, Smith Col, 53-61; assoc prof, 61-65, PROF CLASSICS, BARNARD COL, COLUMBIA UNIV, 65-, Mem, Col Bd Latin Comt, 61-64; Am Asn Univ Women Founders fel, 63-64; mem fac, Bread Loaf Sch English, Vt, summers 66, 68, 73 & 75; scholar-in-residence, Am Acad in Rome, 68-69; Blegen Distinguished vis res prof, Vassar, fall 79; consult Latin lang & scholar, Comt Physicians Overseeing Translation of 16th Century Latin Medieval Text, 73-. **HONORS AND AWARDS** DLitt, Middlebury Col, 70. **MEMBERSHIPS** Am Philol Asn; Archaeol Inst Am. **RESEARCH** Greek tragedy; Plato; ancient romances. **SELECTED PUBLICATIONS** Auth, Socrates crowned, Va Quart Rev, 59; Barbarians in Greek Tragedy, Yale Univ, 61; The Shield of Eteocles, Arion, 64; Woman's Two Faces: Sophocles' View of Woman's Relation to the Tragedy of Oedipus and His Family, Sci & Psychoanal, 66; co-transl, Aeschylus' Seven against Thebes, Oxford Univ, 73; auth, In- and Out-door Schoolings Robert Frost and the Classics, Am Scholar, 74; For Girls: From Birches to Wild Grapes, Yale Rev, 77; Aeschylus and Early Tragedy, In: Ancient Writers: Greece, Scribner's, 82; The Chorus in Greek Life and Drama, Arion-A Journal of Humanities and the Classics, Vol 3, 95. **CONTACT ADDRESS** Dept of Greek & Latin, Barnard Col, New York, NY, 10027.

BACON, THOMAS IVEY
PERSONAL Born 08/15/1940, Lubbock, TX, m, 1968, 1 child **DISCIPLINE** GERMAN LANGUAGE & LITERATURE, SCHOLARLY & LITERARY TRANSLATIONS **EDUCATION** TX Tech Univ, BA, 63; Univ TX, Austin, MA, 67, PhD(Ger), 70. **CAREER** Asst prof, Furman Univ, 69-74; Assoc Prof Ger & Chmn Dept, TX Tech Univ, 74-. **MEMBERSHIPS** Am Asn Teachers Ger; MLA; Western Asn Ger Studies; Am Literary Translr Asn. **RESEARCH** German theater; German expressionism; Dadaism. **SELECTED PUBLICATIONS** Translr, Gerald Bisiner, Fragmente Zum Ich, 72 & Herbert Heckmann, Ubuville, The City of the Grand Egg, 73, Dimension; auth, Two from Germany, Furman Studies, 74; translr, Gerald Bisinger, Free and Alone and Other Poems, Dimension, 75; auth, Martin Luther and the Drama, Ed Rodopi, Amsterdam, 76; translr, Martin Roda Becher, No Luck with Women, Dimension, 78; Understanding Max Frisch, with W. Koepke, German Studies Rev, Vol 16, 93. **CONTACT ADDRESS** Dept of Germanic & Slavic Lang, TX Tech Univ, PO Box 4579, Lubbock, TX, 79409.

BAER, JOACHIM THEODOR
PERSONAL Born 11/11/1933, Essen, Germany, 2 children **DISCIPLINE** FOREIGN LANGUAGES **EDUCATION** Ind Univ, AB, 57; Harvard Univ, PhD, 63. **CAREER** Asst prof Russ, Vanderbilt Univ, 62-66; asst prof Slavic lang & lit & Jonathan Dickinson Bicentennial preceptor, Princeton Univ, 66-71; asst prof Russ & Polish lang & lit, NY Univ, 71-73; assoc prof Slavic lang & lit, 73-76, prof, Univ NC, Greensboro, 76-, NDEA-Fulbright Hays award, Poland, 65-66 & res scholar, Inst Lit Studies, Polish Acad Sci, 69-70; Ger Acad Exchange Serv res awards, 74 & 78. **HONORS AND AWARDS** Distinguished Service Award, Polish Am Club, 93; Phi Beta Kappa, Ind Univ, 57. **MEMBERSHIPS** Am Asn Advan Slavic Studies; Am Asn Teachers Slavic & East Europ Lang; Int Asn Slavic Lang & Lit; AAUP; Schopenhauer Ges. **RESEARCH** Nineteenth and early 20th century Russian literature; late 19th and early 20th century Polish literature; Russian and Polish. **SELECTED PUBLICATIONS** Auth, Dal' und Leskov als Vertreter des Kunstlerischen Philologismus, Z Slavische Philol, Vol XXXVII, No 1; Nietzsche's Influence in the Early Work of Waclaw Berent, Scando-Slavica, 71; Philologism and Conservatism in Nineteenth-Century Russian Literature, Slavic Studies, Hokkaido Univ, 72; Vladimir Ivanovic Dal' as a Belletrist, Mouton, The Hague, 72; co-ed, Mnemozina: Studia Litteraria Russica in Honorem Vsevolod Setchkarev, Fink, Munich, 74; auth, Waclaw Berent, His Life and Work, Institutum Historicum Polonicum, Rome, 74, Ex Antemurale, XVIII: 75-239; Arthur Schopenhauer und die russische Literatur des spaten 19 und fruhen 20 Jahrhundert, Sagner, Munich, 80; Schopenhauer und Afanasij Fet, 61 Schopenhauer Jahrbuch fur das Jahr 1980, KrAm, Frankfurt, 80. **CONTACT ADDRESS** Dept of Ger & Russ, Univ of No Carolina, 1000 Spring Garden, Greensboro, NC, 27412-0001. **EMAIL** jtbaer@fagan.uncg.edu

BAGBY, LEWIS
PERSONAL Born 07/24/1944, Brooklyn, NY, m, 1967, 2 children **DISCIPLINE** RUSSIAN LITERATURE **EDUCATION** Pomona Col, BA, 66; Stanford Univ, MA, 69; Univ Mich, Ann Arbor, PhD(Slavic lang & lit), 72. **CAREER** From Instr to Assoc Prof, 70-85, Prof Russ Lang & Lit, Univ Wyo, 85-, Dir, Int Programs, 95-, Dir, Wyoming-Saratov Initiative, 91-. **HONORS AND AWARDS** John P. Ellbogen Meritorious Classroom Teaching, 85; Hon Doctorate, Saratov State Univ, 98; recipient of many other contracts and grants. **MEMBERSHIPS** Rocky Mountain Mod Lang Asn; Am Asn of Teachers of Slavic and E Europ Lang; Am Asn for the Advancement of Slavic Studies. **RESEARCH** Prose fiction of Aleksandr Bestuzhev-Marlinjkij; Russian romantic prose fiction; transition from Russian romanticism to realisim. **SELECTED PUBLICATIONS** Auth, Pedagogical Devices in Third Year Russian Composition, Russ Lang J, spring 74; Contribr, Human values, quantification and literary evolution, In: The Architecture of Reading, Ohio State Univ, 76; auth, Narrative Double-Voicing in Lermontov's A Hero of Our Time, Slavic & East Europ J, 78; transl, The Test, Bestuzev-Marlinksij's tale, Russian Romantic Prose: An Anthology, 79; auth, A Concurrence of Psychological and Narrative Structures: Anamnesis in Valentin Rasputin's Upstream, Downstream, Can Slavonic Papers, fall 80; Aleksandr Bestuzev-Marlinskij's Roman i Ol'ga: Generation and degeneration, Slavic & East Europ J, winter 81; Mikhail Bakhtin's Discourse Typologies: Theoretical and Practical Considerations, Slavic Rev, spring 82; Bestuzev-Marlinskij's Mulla Nur: A Muddled Myth to Rekindle Romance, Russ Lit, spring 82; auth, Alexander Bestuzhev-Marlinsky and Russian Byronism, Penn State Univ Press, 95; A Hero of Our Time: An AATSEEL Critical Companion, NW Univ Press, forthcoming 99; author of numerous other journal articles, chapters in books, encyclopedias, and dictionaries. **CONTACT ADDRESS** Dept of Mod & Class Lang, Univ of Wyo, PO Box 3603, Laramie, WY, 82071-3603. **EMAIL** lbagby@uwyo.edu

BAGNALL, ROGER SHALER
PERSONAL Born 08/19/1947, Seattle, WA, m, 1969, 2 children **DISCIPLINE** GREEK PAPYROLOGY, ANCIENT HISTORY. **EDUCATION** Yale Univ, BA, 68; Univ Toronto, MA, 69, PHD(class studies), 72. **CAREER** Asst prof classics, Fla State Univ, 72-74; asst prof Greek & Latin, 74-79, assoc prof to prof Classics & Hist, Columbia Univ, 74-; mem bd, Scholars Press, 77-85; pres, Egyptological Sem of NY, 81-83; vis prof, Univ Florence, 81. **HONORS AND AWARDS** Am Coun Learned Soc grant-in-aid, 75; Am Coun Learned Soc study fel, 76-77; Am Philos Soc grant-in-aid, 80; Guggenheim fel, 90-91; Fel, Am Numismatic Soc; Assoc Academie Royale des Sciences; des Lettres et des Beaux-Arts de Relgique. **MEMBERSHIPS** Am Soc Papyrologists (secy-treas, 74-79); Am Philol Asn (secy-treas, 79-85); Asn pour les Etudes Grecques; Egypt Exploration Soc; Asn Ancient Historians. **RESEARCH** Greek papyri; social and economic history of the late Roman Egypt; Hellenistic social and economic history. **SELECTED PUBLICATIONS** Coauth, Ostraka in the Royal Ontario Museum (2 vols), Samuel Stevens, Toronto, 71-76; auth, Ptolemaic Foreign Correspondence in Tebtunis Papyrus 8, J Egyptian Archaeol, 75; The Administration of the Ptolemaic Possessions, Brill, Leiden, 76; coauth, Ostraka in Amsterdam Collections, Terra, Zutphen, 76; auth, The Florida Ostraka: Documents from the Roman Army in Upper Egypt, Duke Univ, 76; Bullion Purchases and Landholding in the Fourth Century, Chronique d'Egypt, 77; coauth, The Chronological Systems of Byzantine Egypt, Terra, Zutphen, 78; Columbia Papyri VII, Scholars Press, 78; auth, Egypt in Late Antiquity, Princeton, 93; coauth, Demography of Roman Egypt, Cambridge, 94; auth, Reading Papyri, Writing Ancient History, Routledge, 95. **CONTACT ADDRESS** Columbia Univ, 1130 Amsterdam Ave, Rm 606, New York, NY, 10027-6900. **EMAIL** baguall@columbia.edu

BAGULEY, DAVID
PERSONAL Born 04/28/1940, Leicester, England **DISCIPLINE** FRENCH LITERATURE **EDUCATION** Univ Nottingham, BA, 63; Univ Leicester, MA, 66; Univ Nancy, DUniv, 69. **CAREER** Asst English, Univ Nantes, 66-67; lectr French, Univ Leicester, 67-68; from lectr to assoc prof, 68-77, PROF FRENCH, UNIV WESTERN ONT, 77-. **MEMBERSHIPS** MLA; Soc Fr Studies. **RESEARCH** French literature of the 19th century; the naturalist novel; literary criticism. **SELECTED PUBLICATIONS** Auth, Fecondite d'Emile Zola: Roman a These, Evangile, Mythe, 73 & Bibliographie de la Critique sur Emile Zola, 1864-1970, 76, Univ Toronto; Emile Zola-An Intellectual in the Dreyfus Affair (French), French Rev, Vol 66, 93; Emile Zola Revisited, with W. J. Berg and L. K. Martin, French Forum, Vol 19, 94; Literature and Rationality-Ideas of Agency in Theory and Fiction, with P. Livingston, French Studies, Vol 49, 95; Emile Zola-'Nana', A Critical Edition (French), C. Becker, ed, Revue d'Histoire Litteraire de la France, Vol 95, 95; Correspondence, Vol 9, October 1897-September 1899 Laffaire Dreyfus (French), with E. Zola and B. H. Bakker, Nineteenth-Century French Studies, Vol 23, 95; Emile Zola-Correspondence, Vol 10-October 1899 to September 1902 (French), with O. Morgan and J. A. Walker, eds, B. H. Bakker, ed dir, H. Mitterand, Lit Advisor, Nineteenth-Century French Studies, Vol 24, 96; Zola-A Life, with F. Brown, French Forum, Vol 21, 96; The Poetics of Maupassant (French), with M. Bury, French rev, Vol 69, 96; Politics and Narratives of Birth-Gynocolonization from Rousseau to Zola, with C. A., Mossman, French Rev, Vol 69, 96; Alexandre Dumas, The 'Vicomte de Bragelonne' (French), with D. Coward, French Studies, Vol 51, 97; Emile Zola Centenary Colloquium 1893-1993, London, 23-25 September 1993, with P. Pollard, Modrn Language Rev, Vol 92, 97. **CONTACT ADDRESS** Dept of French, Univ of Western Ont, London, ON, N6A 5B8.

BAHR, EHRHARD
PERSONAL Born 08/21/1932, Kiel, Germany **DISCIPLINE** GERMAN LITERATURE **EDUCATION** Univ KS, MS, 58; Univ CA, Berkeley, PhD(Ger), 68. **CAREER** Acting asst prof, 66-68, from asst prof to assoc prof, 68-72, PROF GER, UNIV CA, LOS ANGELES, 72-, CHMN DEPT GERMANIC LANG, 81-. **HONORS AND AWARDS** UCLA Distinguished Teaching Award, 70. **MEMBERSHIPS** MLA; Am Asn Teachers Ger; Am Soc 18th Century Studies; Am Lessing Soc; Heinrich Heine Soc. **RESEARCH** Eighteenth century German literature; German classicism; modern German literature. **SELECTED PUBLICATIONS** Auth, Kafka and the Prague spring, Mosaic, summer 70; Georg Lukacs, Colloquium, 71 (also in English & French translr); Die Ironie im Spatwerk Goethese, Erich Schmidt, Berlin, 72; Goethes Wanderjahre as an experimental novel, Mosaic, spring 72; Ernst Bloch, Colloquium, Berlin, 74; ed, Kant, Was ist Aufklarung, Reclam, Stuttgart, 74; auth, The pursuit of happiness in the political writings of Lessing and Kant, In: Studies on Voltaire and the Eighteenth Century, 151: 167-184, 76; Personenwechselung in Goethes Westostlichem Divan, Chronik des Wiener Goethevereins, 73: 117-125; Nelly Sachs, H C Beck, 80; ed, Goethe, Wilhelm Meisters Lehrjahre, Reclam, Stuttgart, 82; World War II and the Exiles-A Literary Response (German and English), with H. F. Pfranner, German Studies Rev, Vol 17, 94; Goethe-Seeing and Believing (German), with I. Graham, Colloquia Germanica, Vol 27, 94; Adversaries of Goethe in His Later Years-Writes Associated with the Young-German School, Nationalists, and Orthodox Christians, Goethe Jahrbuch, Vol 112, 95; Goethe Mignon and Her Sisters-Interpretations and Reception (German), with G. Hoffmeister, German Studies Rev, Vol 19, 96; Critical Approaches to Goethe Classical Dramas-'Iphigenie', 'Torquato Tasso', and Die 'Naturliche Tochter', with I. Wagner, German Studies Rev, Vol 20, 97. **CONTACT ADDRESS** Dept of Germanic Lang, Univ of CA, 405 Hilgard Ave, Los Angeles, CA, 90024. **EMAIL** bahr@humnet.ucla.edu

BAILEY, PHILLIP
DISCIPLINE FRENCH **EDUCATION** Saint John's Univ, BA, 85; Univ Va, MA, 87, PhD, 93. **CAREER** Asst prof, Univ Central Ark, 93- . **RESEARCH** Nineteenth and twentieth-century French literature; problems of narrative technic; study of foreign language anxiety and learning styles. **SELECTED PUBLICATIONS** Auth, Proust's Self Reader: The Pursuit of Literature as Privileged Communication, Summa Publ, 97. **CONTACT ADDRESS** Univ Central Ark, 201 Donaghey Ave, Conway, AR, 72035-0001.

BAKER, JOSEPH O.
PERSONAL Born 12/26/1938, Murray, UT, m, 1961, 3 children **DISCIPLINE** GERMAN LANGUAGE & LITERATURE **CAREER** Asst prof, 67-73, Assoc Prof Ger, Brigham Young Univ, 73-, Dir Study Abroad, 74-86. **HONORS AND AWARDS** Fulbright Scholar, Germany, Summer, 88. **MEMBERSHIPS** MLA; Rocky Mountain Mod Lang Asn; Heinrich von Kleist Gesellschaft; AATG; ICEE Board of Directors, 83-87. **RESEARCH** Heinrich von Kleist; German poetic realism. **SELECTED PUBLICATIONS** Ethics of Life and Death with H J Kleist; Im Noneugarten, Anthology of German Women's Writing (1850-1907) w/Michelle Stott; German Cultural History, Multimedia, independent study course. **CONTACT ADDRESS** Brigham Young Univ, 4094 Jkhb, Provo, UT, 84602-0002. **EMAIL** Joseph_baker@BYU.edu

BAKER, MARY JORDAN
PERSONAL Chicago, IL **DISCIPLINE** FRENCH RENAISSANCE LITERATURE **EDUCATION** Stanford Univ, AB, 61; Univ VA, MA, 64; Harvard Univ, PhD(Romance lang), 69. **CAREER** Instr French, DePauw Univ, 64-65; asst prof, 68-75, ASSOC PROF FRENCH, UNIV TX, AUSTIN, 75-. **MEMBERSHIPS** Am Asn Teachers Fr; Renaissance Soc Am; Mod Humanities Res Asn. **SELECTED PUBLICATIONS** Auth, Didacticism and the Heptameron: the Misinterpretation of the Tenth Tale as an Exemplum, Fr Rev, 12/71; Fiammetta and the Angiosses douloureuses qui procedent d'amours, Symposium, winter 73; France's First Sentimental Novel and Novels of Chivalry, Bibliot Humanisme et Renaissance, 1/74; The sonnets of Louise Labe: a reappraisal, Neophilologus, 76; The Role of the Moral Lesson in Heptameron, Fr Studies, 1/77; coauth, Panache Litteraire, Harper & Row, 78; Metadiegetic Narrative in the 'Heptameron', Studies in the Literary Imagination, Vol 25, 92; The Disnarrated in Les 'Cent Nouvelles Nouvelles' & Events That Do Not Happen But Could Have, Orbis Literarum, Vol 50, 95. **CONTACT ADDRESS** 2301 Windsor Rd, Austin, TX, 78703.

BAKER, SUSAN READ
PERSONAL Born 12/15/1942, El Dorado, AR **DISCIPLINE** FRENCH LITERATURE **EDUCATION** Univ TX Austin, BA, 64; Harvard Univ, MA, 65, PhD(French), 70. **CAREER** Asst prof, Harvard Univ, 70-76; ASSOC PROF FRENCH, UNIV FL, 76-. **MEMBERSHIPS** MLA; North Am Soc 17th Century Fr Lit; Am Asn Teaching Fr; Am Soc 18th Century Studies; SAtlantic Mod Lang Asn. **RESEARCH** Comedy in 17th-18th centuries; 17th century French moralists; 17th century philosophy and history of ideas. **SELECTED PUBLICATIONS** Auth, La Rochefoucauld and the Art of the Self-Portrait, Romanic Rev, 1/74; Tragic Vision in Racine's Iphigenie and Euripides' Iphigenia in Aulis, Degre Second, 7/77; La Rochefoucauld and Jacques Esprit, Rev Hist Lit Fr, Vol 78, No 2; Collaboration et Originalite--Chez la Rochefoucauld, Univ FL Press, 80; Sentimental feminism in Marivaux's La Colonie, In: To Hold a Mirror to Nature, 82; Sun-King-The Ascendancy of French-Culture During the Reign of Louis-XIV, with D. L. Rubin, French Rev, Vol 66, 93; Pierre Corneille-Poetics and Political Drama Under Louis-XIII, with D. Clarke, Modern Philol, Vol 92, 94; 'Port Royal Insolite', Critical Edition of 'Recueil De Choses Diverses' (French), with J. Lesaulnier, French Rev, Vol 68, 95. **CONTACT ADDRESS** Dept of Romance Lang & Lit, Univ of FL, P O Box 117405, Gainesville, FL, 32611-7405.

BALAKIAN, ANNA
PERSONAL Born 07/14/1916, Constantinople, Turkey, m, 1945, 2 children **DISCIPLINE** FRENCH LITERATURE **EDUCATION** Hunter Col, AB, 36; Columbia Univ, AM, 38, PhD, 43. **CAREER** Teacher high sch, Hunter Col, 37-43; from instr to asst prof French lit, Syracuse Univ, 43-44; from adj asst prof French to assoc prof foreign lang educ, 55-64, PROF FRENCH & COMP LIT, WASH SQ COL, NY UNIV, 64-, Res assoc, MLA, 59-60; vis prof, City Univ New York, 67-68; Guggenheim fel, 69-70; Nat Endowment for Humanities grant, 72-74; dir, Symbolism (vol), In: Comp Hist of Lit in Europ Lang; vis prof comp lit, State Univ NY Stony Brook, 75-76; consult, Nat Endowment for Humanities, 78-79. **HONORS AND AWARDS** Distinguished Scholar Award, Hofstra Univ, 75., LHD, New Haven Univ, 77. **MEMBERSHIPS** MLA; Am Asn Teachers Fr (vpres, 68-71); Am Comp Lit Asn (pres, 77-8); Pen Club; Auth Guild. **RESEARCH** Modern French literature; research in the international repercussions of the surrealist and symbolist movements; origin and development of surrealism in literature. **SELECTED PUBLICATIONS** Auth, Literary Origins of Surrealism, Columbia Univ, 47; Span transl, Zig-Zag, Chile, 57; Surrealism: The Road to the Absolute, Noonday, 59; Andre Breton as philosopher, Yale Fr Studies, summer 64; The Symbolist Movement: A Critical Appraisal, Random, 67, rev ed, 77; Andre Breton, Magus of Surrealism, Oxford Univ, 71, Span ed, Monte Avila, Venezuela, 76; Introductory Essay to Anais Nin Reader, Swallow, 73; Mallarme et la Liberte, Europe, 4/76; Ren Char: In search of the Violet Man, World Lit Today, summer 77; The Problem of Literary History-A Response, Neohelicon, Vol 20, 93; Canon Harassment, Can Rev of Comparative Lit, Vol 20, 93; Theorizing Comparison-The Pyramid of Similitude and Difference, World Lit Today, Vol 69, 95; Litterature/Lits-et-Ratures/Erutarettil, A Retrospective on an Avant-Garde Journal, Forum for Modern Language Studies, Vol 32, 96; Reminiscences and Reflections on Andre Breton, Esprit Createur, Vol 36, 96. **CONTACT ADDRESS** Dept of Comp Lit, New York Univ, New York, NY, 10003.

BALASUBRAMANIAN, RADHA
DISCIPLINE RUSSIAN LITERATURE **EDUCATION** Ind Univ, PhD. **CAREER** Asst prof Russ, Univ Nebr, Lincoln. **RESEARCH** The influences of India on Russian literature and vice-versa. **SELECTED PUBLICATIONS** Published articles on works by Dostoevsky, Korolenko, Sholokhov, Sologub, and on teaching Russian to foreigners. **CONTACT ADDRESS** Univ Nebr, Lincoln, Lincoln, NE, 68588-0417.

BALDERSTON, DANIEL
DISCIPLINE LANGUAGES **EDUCATION** Univ California-Berkeley, AB, 74; MA, 78, PhD, 81, Princeton Univ. **CAREER** Asst Prof, Earlham Col, 80-82; Asst Prof, Wittenburg Univ, 82-83; Asst/Assoc/Full Prof, Tulane Univ, 83-98; Prof, Univ Iowa 99-. **CONTACT ADDRESS** Dept of Spanish, Univ of Iowa, Iowa City, IA, 52242. **EMAIL** daniel_balderston@uiowa.edu

BALDWIN, THOMAS PRATT
PERSONAL Born 02/25/1941, Rome, GA, 4 children **DISCIPLINE** GERMAN LITERATURE **EDUCATION** Univ Heidelberg, Zertifikat, 63; Univ Wis-Madison, MA, 67, PhD, 72. **CAREER** From instr to asst prof, 68-74, assoc prof, 74-79, prof Ger, 80-, Western KY Univ; consult, Nat Endowment Humanities, 78-. **HONORS AND AWARDS** NDEA Fellow **MEMBERSHIPS** Am Assn Teachers Ger; Soc for German Am Studies, Ky Coun on Teaching of Foreign Lang **RESEARCH** Austrian literature; pedagogy. **SELECTED PUBLICATIONS** Auth, The Public Image of Germans in Louisville and Jefferson County, Kentucky: 1840-1872, Yearbook of German-American Studies 29, 94. **CONTACT ADDRESS** Dept of Foreign Lang, Western Kentucky Univ, 1 Big Red Way St, Bowling Green, KY, 42101-3576. **EMAIL** thomas.baldwin@wku.edu

BALL, D.
PERSONAL Born 02/27/1937, New York, NY, m, 1967, 2 children **DISCIPLINE** COMPARATIVE LITERATURE **EDUCATION** Brandeis Col, BA, 59; Licesa es lettres, Sorbonne, 65; docteur en lit generale et compare, Univ de Paris IV, Sorbonne, 72. **CAREER** Lectr, Smith Col, 69-72; asst prof, 72-74, assoc prof, 76, prof, 80-, fr & comparative lit, Smith Col. **HONORS AND AWARDS** Seaglione prize for literary transl, MLA, 76. **MEMBERSHIPS** ALTA. **RESEARCH** Translation of poetry; Writing under occupation, 1940-44. **SELECTED PUBLICATIONS** Auth, Des Poux et des hommes: La Solution finale dans les quotidiens en 1942, Les Temps Modernes, 97; auth, Acclaiming Adair: Against a Certain Tendency in Translation Theory, Transl Rev, 96; auth, Underground Laughter (1940-1944), Literature and War, Editions Rodopi, 90; co-auth, Moliere's Dom Juan: Form, Meaning, Audience, Mod Philol, 83; rev, Dickens in French, Dickens Studies, fall, 83; article, Is Tenure a Threat to Academic Freedom?, Can Asn of Univ Teachers, 81; auth, On Translating Goethe's Faust, The Ger Rev, 80; auth, Turgenev's Dialectic, The Mass Rev, 79; auth, La Definition ironique, Rev de Lit Comparee, 76; auth, Vers une theorie de l'ironie: perspectives sur Swift, Etudes Anglaises, 76; co-auth, Listening to an Angolan Revolutionary, The New Republic, 62. **CONTACT ADDRESS** Smith Col, Northampton, MA, 01063. **EMAIL** dball@sophia.smith.edu

BANERJEE, MARIA NEMCOVA
PERSONAL Born 11/22/1937, Prague, Czechoslovakia, m, 1961 **DISCIPLINE** RUSSIAN & COMPARATIVE LITERATURE **EDUCATION** Univ Paris, Baccalaureat, 55; Univ Montreal, MA, 57; Harvard Univ, PhD(Slavic), 62. **CAREER** Tutor Russ lit, Harvard Univ, 61-62; asst prof, Brown Univ, 62-64; from vis lectr to asst prof, 64-72, assoc prof, 72-79, PROF RUSS LIT, SMITH COL, 79-, Vis lectr, Wellesley Col, 63-64; Int Res & Exchanges Bd scr scholar, Int Russ Lit, Leningrad, 73-74. **MEMBERSHIPS** Am Asn Advan Slavic Studies; Czech Soc Arts & Sci Am. **RESEARCH** Nineteenth and 20th century Russian and European literatures, especially Dostoevsky and symbolism; Pushkin; Russian and European realism in the novel. **SELECTED PUBLICATIONS** Auth, Rozanov on Dostoevsky, Slavic East Europ J, winter 71; The Metamorphosis of an Icon, Female Studies, Vol IX, 75; Pushkin's The Bronze Horseman: An Agonistic Vision, Mod Lang Studies, 78; The Narrator and His Masks in Viacheslew Ivanov's Povest' o Suetomire Tsareviche, Can-Am Slavic Studies, 78; Vitezslov Nezval's Progue with Fingers of Rain: A Surrealistic Image, Slavic and East Europ J, 79; The American Revolver: An Essay on Dostoevsky's The Devils, Mod Fiction Studies, 81; Pavel Yavor and the Pathos of Exile, In: Far From You, Toronto, 81; Metapoesis-The Russian Tradition from Pushkin to Chekhov, with M. C. Finke, Russian Rev, Vol 55, 96. **CONTACT ADDRESS** Dept of Russ, Smith Col, Northampton, MA, 01061.

BANGERTER, LOWELL A.
DISCIPLINE GERMAN **EDUCATION** Univ IL, PhD, 70. **CAREER** Prof; Univ WY, 70-; served as dir, UW Hum Semester, dept grad adv & dept head. **HONORS AND AWARDS** WY Coun for the Hum fel, 78; UW res grant, 80. **RESEARCH** 18th century Ger lit; mod Austrian and East Ger lit. **SELECTED PUBLICATIONS** Auth, 7 bk(s) & numerous articles; publ, Engl transl of several works of 20th-century Austrian lit. **CONTACT ADDRESS** Dept of Mod and Class Lang(s), Univ WY, PO Box 3964, Laramie, WY, 82071-3964. **EMAIL** BANG@UWYO.EDU

BANNON, CYNTHIA J.
DISCIPLINE CLASSICAL STUDIES **EDUCATION** Harvard Univ, BA, 84; Univ Mich, PhD, 91. **CAREER** Asst prof. **RESEARCH** Roman law; Latin prose style and grammar; rhetoric; history. **SELECTED PUBLICATIONS** Auth, The Brothers of Romulus, Princeton, 97. **CONTACT ADDRESS** Dept of Classical Studies, Indiana Univ, Bloomington, 300 N Jordan Ave, Bloomington, IN, 47405.

BANTA, FRANK GRAHAM
PERSONAL Born 05/31/1918, Franklin, IN **DISCIPLINE** GERMAN LINGUISTICS **EDUCATION** IN Univ, AB, 39; Univ MD, MA, 41; Univ Berne, PhD, 51. **CAREER** Instr foreign lang, Univ MD, 39-44; from instr to assoc prof Ger, Univ IL, Urbana, 51-64, chmn dept 55-64; assoc prof, 64-70, PROF GER LING, IN UNIV, BLOOMIMGTON, 70-, Dir, Arts & Sci Teaching Resources Ctr, Ind Univ, 75-77. **MEMBERSHIPS** MLA; Ling Soc Am; Am Asn Teachers Ger (vpres, 71-73); Indoger Ges. **RESEARCH** Middle High German; Germanic and Indo-European linguistics. **SELECTED PUBLICATIONS** Auth, Berthold von Regensburg, In: Die deutsche Literatur des Mittelalters: Verfasserlexikon, 78; The Grammar of Early-New-High-German, Contributions to Phonetics and Morphology, Vol 6, The Declension of Adjectives (German), with H. J. Solms and K P. Wegera, J of English and Germanic Philol, Vol 92, 93; Dictionary of the Middle High German Language Used in Official Documents, Fascicles 3-8 (German), with B. Kirchstein, U. Schulze, S. Ohly and P. Schmitt, J of English and Germanic Philol, Vol 94, 95; Consonant Strength in Upper German Dialects, with K. G. Goblirsch, J of English and Germanic Philol, Vol 95, 96. **CONTACT ADDRESS** Dept of Ger Lang, Indiana Univ, Bloomington, Bloomington, IN, 47401.

BANZIGER, HANS
PERSONAL Born 01/15/1917, Romanshorn, Switzerland, m, 1943, 3 children **DISCIPLINE** GERMAN LITERATURE **EDUCATION** Univ Zurich, Dr Phil(Ger lit), 42. **CAREER** Teacher Ger, County Sch, Trogen, Switz, 43-67; docent Ger lit, Col Indust & Social Educ, St Gallen, Switz, 53-67, pvt docent, 65-67; assoc prof, 67-70, chmn dept, 71-72, prof, 71-82, EMER PROF GER, BRYN MAWR COL, 71-. **MEMBERSHIPS** MLA; Am Asn Teachers Ger; Int Ger Asn; Swiss Authors Soc; Swiss Pen. **SELECTED PUBLICATIONS** Auth, Frisch und Durrenmatt, 60, 7th ed, 76 & Zwischen Protest & Traditionsbewusstsein: On M Frisch, 75, Francke, Bern; contribr, Glucksfischer und Auswanderer: On Jakob Schaffner, Schweizer Monatshefte, 75; Widerstand gegen Modestromungen: on R Henz, Festschrift Rudolf Henz, 77; Das namenlose Tier und sein Territorium: On Kafka, Deutsche Vierteljahresschrift, 79; Verzweiflung unf Auferstehungen auf dem Todesbett, Deutsche Vierteljahresschrift, 80; Durrenmatt in Ungarn, Schweizer Monatshefte, 81; Schloss-Haus-Bau, Studien zu einem Motivkomplex, Francke, Bern/Munchen, 82; Max Frisch, with W. Koepke, Colloquia Germanica, Vol 25, 92. **CONTACT ADDRESS** Dept of Ger, Bryn Mawr Col, Bryn Mawr, PA, 19010.

BAR-LEWAW, ITZHAK I.
PERSONAL Born 02/09/1922, Nriow, Poland **DISCIPLINE** SPANISH LITERATURE **EDUCATION** Hebrew Univ, MA, 53; Nat Univ Mexico, PhD, 59. **CAREER** Lectr, Hebrew Univ, 53-55; lectr, Univ Chile, 60; lectr, Univ Ecuador, 62; asst prof, Univ Kansas, 61-63; asst prof, Univ Florida, 63-64; assoc prof, Univ Sask, 64-67; PROF, YORK UNIV, 67-. **MEMBERSHIPS** Int Asn Hispanists **SELECTED PUBLICATIONS** Auth, Gabriel de la Concepcion Valdes, 59; auth, Placido, Vida y Obra, 60; auth, Temas Literarios Iberoamericanos, 61; auth, Introduccion Critico-biografica a Jose Vasconcelos, 65; auth, Jose Vasconcelos, Vida y Obra, 66; auth, La Revista "Timon" y Jose Vasconcelos, 71; auth, La Obra Periodestica de Jose Vasconcelos, 2 vols, 91, vol 3, 92; coauth, Pedro de Toledo, El primer traductor espanol del More Nebujim, 66. **CONTACT ADDRESS** Winters Col, York Univ, 4700 Keele St, Downsview, ON, M3J 1P3.

BARABTARLO, GENNADY
PERSONAL Born 02/15/1949, Moscow, Soviet Union, m, 1968, 1 child **DISCIPLINE** RUSSIAN LITERATURE & LINGUISTICS **EDUCATION** Univ Moscow, Diploma in Russian Letters (equivalent to MA), 72; Univ Ill, PhD, 85. **CAREER** Sr res fel, 72-75, vice-provost for res, The Pushkin Lit Museum, 76-78; res & teaching asst, Univ Ill, Champaign-Urbana, 80-84; from asst prof to assoc prof, 85-94, prof Russ lit, 94-, Dept Chair, 95-, Univ Mo. **RESEARCH** Pushkin; Nabokov. **SELECTED PUBLICATIONS** Auth, Phantom of Fact: Nabokov's Pnin, Ardis, 89; co-ed, A Small Alpine Form: Nabokov's Short Stories, Garland Publ, 92; auth, Aerial View: Essays on Nabokov's Art and Metaphysics, Peter Lang, 93; ed, What a Pity: Solzhenitsyn's Short Stories, Duckworth, 96; author of numerous articles and other publications. **CONTACT ADDRESS** Univ Missouri, 451 GCB, Columbia, MO, 65211. **EMAIL** gragl@showme.missouri.edu

BARAN, HENRYK
DISCIPLINE LANGUAGES, LITERATURES, AND CULTURES **EDUCATION** Harvard Univ, PhD. **CAREER** Prof, Univ Albany, State Univ NY. **RESEARCH** 19th and 20th Century Russian Literature, with a special emphasis on modernism and the avant-garde; poetics and theory of literature, semiotics, folklore and literature, Polish literature. **SELECTED PUBLICATIONS** Managing ed, Elementa: A Journal of Slavic Studies and Comparative Semiotics, Harwood Acad Publ. **CONTACT ADDRESS** Dept of Languages, Literatures, and Cultures, Univ at Albany, SUNY, Humanities 235, Albany, NY, 12222. **EMAIL** hebaran@ibm.net

BARBE, KATHARINA
PERSONAL Berlin, Germany, m, 1990, 2 children **DISCIPLINE** LINGUISTICS **EDUCATION** Univ Houston, BA, 84; Rice Univ, MA, 88, PhD, 89. **CAREER** Instr, 89-90, asst prof, 90-96, assoc prof, 96- , Northern Ill Univ, 89-. **HONORS AND AWARDS** DAAD Scholar, 80-81; NEH, 93. **MEMBERSHIPS** AATG; ICTFL; GFDS. **RESEARCH** Linguistic pragmatics; translation theory; SLA. **SELECTED PUBLICATIONS** Auth, Isn't it ironic that..., Jour Pragmatics, 93; Begin in German, Teaching Ideas: A Collection of Successful Classroom Strategies, Cherry Hill, 93; Reading in the intermediate classroom: Der Rattenfanger von Hameln, Teaching German, 94; The translation of loans: Anglicisms in German, Perspectives: Studies in Translatology, 94; The dichotomy literal and free translation, META: Transl Jour; Dubbing in the Translation Classroom, Perspectives: Studies in Translatology, 96; Bewerbung um eine Praktikantenstelle im Ausland, Unterrichtsmaterialien zur Vorbereitung auf die Prufung Zertifikat Deutsch fur den Beruf, 98. **CONTACT ADDRESS** Dept of Foreign Languages & Literature, No Illinois Univ, De Kalb, IL, 60115. **EMAIL** kbarbe@niu.edu

BARBER, ELIZABETH J. WAYLAND
PERSONAL Born 12/02/1940, Pasadena, CA, m, 1965 **DISCIPLINE** ARCHAEOLOGY, LINGUISTICS **EDUCATION** Bryn Mawr Col, BA, 62; Yale Univ, PhD, 68. **CAREER** Res assoc, Princeton Univ, 68-89; LECTR TO FULL PROF, OCCIDENTAL COL, 70-. **HONORS AND AWARDS** NEH Grants, 72, 74, & 93; J Guggenheim Memorial Fel, 79-80; Wenner-Gren ACLS Haynes grants; book prizes from Amer Hist Asn, 93, Costume Soc, 92 & 95. **MEMBERSHIPS** Archaeol Inst of Am; Linguistic Soc of Am; Textile Soc of Am; Costume Soc of Am; LACUS; CIETA. **RESEARCH** Prehistoric archaeology and languages of Southern & Eastern Europe; decipherment; ancient textiles, costumes, & rituals. **SELECTED PUBLICATIONS** Auth, The Mummies of Urumchi, W.W. Norton, 99; auth, Women's Work-The First 20,000 Years, W.W. Norton, 94; auth, Prehistoric Textiles, Princeton Univ Press, 91; auth, Archaeological Decipherment, Princeton Univ Press, 74; auth, On the Origins of the Vily/Rusalki, Varia on the Indo-European Past, 97; auth, Minoan Women and the Challenge of Weaving for Home, Trade, and Shrine, Texnh: Craftsmen, Craftswomen and Craftsmanship in the Aegean Bronze Age, 97; auth, Textiles of the Neolithic through Iron Ages, The Oxford Encycl of Archaeol in the Near East, 97; auth, On the Antiquity of East European Bridal Clothing, Dress, 94; auth, The Peplos of Athena, Goddess and Polis: The Panathenaic Festival in Ancient Athens, Princeton, 92. **CONTACT ADDRESS** 1126 N. Chester Ave., Pasadena, CA, 91104. **EMAIL** barber@oxy.edu

BARBER, PAUL THOMAS
PERSONAL Born 07/16/1941, Santa Barbara, CA, m, 1965 **DISCIPLINE** GERMAN **EDUCATION** Univ of Calif at Santa Barbara, BA, 63; Yale Univ, PhD, 68. **CAREER** Instr, 67-68, asst prof, Princeton Univ, 68-70; FOWLER MUSEUM OF CULTURAL HIST, UCLA, RES ASSOC, 90-. **RESEARCH** Folklore; oral literature; rhetoric. **SELECTED PUBLICATIONS** Auth, Vampires, Burial and Death: Folklore and Reality, Yale Univ Press, 88; auth, Staking Claims: Vampires of Folklore and Legend, Skeptical Inquirer, 96; auth, Mummification in the Tarim Basin, J of Indo-European Studies, 95; auth, The Real Vampire, Nat Hist, 95; auth, Cremation, J of Indo-European Studies, 90; auth, Forensic Pathology and the European Vampire, J of Folklore Res, 87. **CONTACT ADDRESS** 1126 N. Chester Ave., Pasadena, CA, 91104.

BARCHILON, JACQUES
PERSONAL Born 04/08/1923, Casablanca, Morocco, m, 1960, 2 children **DISCIPLINE** ROMANCE LANGUAGES, THE FAIRY TALE **EDUCATION** Univ Rochester, AB, 50; Harvard Univ, AM, 51, PhD, 56. **CAREER** Teaching fel, Harvard Univ, 52-55; instr, Smith Col, 55-56; instr, Brown Univ, 56-69; instr, 59-65, assoc prof, 65-71, PROF FRENCH, UNIV CO, BOULDER, 71-, Chmn, French & Ital Dept, 81-, Res grants, Coun Res & Creative Work, Univ Colo, 61, 63, 64, 76, 77, 79 & 80 & Am Philos Soc, 63, 64, 71 & 80; fac fel, Univ CO, 64; exchange prof French & comp lit, Ctr Univ Savole, Chambery, France, 78-79. **MEMBERSHIPS** MLA; Am Asn Teachers French; NAm Soc for 17th Century French Lit. **RESEARCH** French literature; the fairy tale; Charles Perrault. **SELECTED PUBLICATIONS** Auth & ed, Perrault's Tales of Mother Goose, Peirpont Morgan, 56; co-ed, The Authentic Mother Goose, Swallow, 60; auth, Charles Perrault, Dix-septieme Siecle, 62; Esprit et Humor chez Perrault, Studi Francesi, 67; Le Conte merveilleux francais, Champion, 75; A Concordance to Charles Perrault's Tales, Prose and Verse (2 vols), Norwood, 77-79, chap, In: La Coherence Ingerieure, Hean-Michel Place, 77; Contes de Perrault, Slatkine Reprints, 80; Charles Perrault, A Critical Biography, G K Hall, 81; 20th-Century Renewal of Interest in the 16th-Century 'Roman De Perceforest', Lettres Romanes, Vol 46, 92. **CONTACT ADDRESS** Dept of French & Ital, Univ of CO, Boulder, CO, 80309.

BARLOW, JOHN DENISON
PERSONAL Born 09/28/1934, Brooklyn, NY, m, 1970, 3 children **DISCIPLINE** GERMAN LITERATURE, FILM, PHILANTHROPY & LITERATURE **EDUCATION** NY Univ, BA, 58, MA, 61, PhD, 67. **CAREER** Instr Ger, Univ Col, NY Univ, 61-67; asst prof, 67-72, assoc prof Ger, 72-81, prof German, 81-98, dir, 82-84, prof English, 91-98, assoc dean lib arts, 84-87, act dean Lib Arts, 88-98, dean Emeritus, prof Emeritus English & German, 98-, Ind Univ-Purdue Univ, Indianapolis; Ottendorfer mem fel, 66-67; Danforth assoc, 70-. **MEMBERSHIPS** MLA; Am Assn Teachers Ger. **RESEARCH** Twentieth century literature; film. **SELECTED PUBLICATIONS** Auth, German Expressionist Film, Twayne, 82; translator, Jean Amery, On Aging, 94. **CONTACT ADDRESS** Dept of German, Indiana Univ-Purdue Univ, Indianapolis, 1100 W Michigan St, Indianapolis, IN, 46202-2880. **EMAIL** jbarlow@iupui.edu

BARNES, BETSY
DISCIPLINE FRENCH LINGUISTICS **EDUCATION** Ind Univ, PhD. **CAREER** Instr, Univ Minn, Twin Cities. **SELECTED PUBLICATIONS** Auth, The Pragmatics of Left Detachment in Spoken Standard French, Benjamin's, 85; coauth, Deux Mondes, 2nd ed, McGraw-Hill, 93. **CONTACT ADDRESS** Univ Minn, Twin Cities, Minneapolis, MN, 55455.

BARNES, JIM WEAVER
PERSONAL Born 12/22/1933, Summerfield, OK **DISCIPLINE** COMPARATIVE LITERATURE, CREATIVE WRITING **EDUCATION** Southeast Oklahoma State Univ, BA, 64; Univ Ark, Fayetteville, MA, 66, PhD, 72. **CAREER** Instr English, Northeastern Okla State Col, 65-68; prof comp lit, 70-, ed, The Chariton Review, Truman State Univ, 76-; Nat Endowment for the Arts creative writing fel, 78; Rockefeller Found Bellagio Fel, 90; Sr Fulbright to Switerland, 93-94; Akaademie Schloss Solitude Fel, 98. **HONORS AND AWARDS** Transl Prize Summons and Sign, Columbia Univ, 80; The Am Book Award, 98. **MEMBERSHIPS** Coord Coun of Lit Mags; MLA. **RESEARCH** Twentieth century fiction and poetry; creative writing. **SELECTED PUBLICATIONS** Auth, On Native Ground, University of Oklahoma Press, 97; auth, Paris, University of Illinois Press, 97. **CONTACT ADDRESS** Div of Lang & Lit, Northeast Missouri State Univ, 100 E Normal St, Kirksville, MO, 63501-4221. **EMAIL** jbarnes@truman.edu

BARNOUW, DAGMAR
DISCIPLINE GERMAN **EDUCATION** Yale Univ, PhD. **CAREER** Prof, Univ Southern Calif. **SELECTED PUBLICATIONS** Auth, Weimar Intellectuals & the Threat of Modernity, 88; Visible Spaces: Hannah Arendt & the German-Jewish Experience, 90; Critical Realism: History, Photography & the Work of Siegfried Kracauer, 94; Deutschland 1945: Ansichten von Krieg und Gewalt; Germany 1945: Photography, History and Memory, 96; Anthropologische Dichtungen: Elias Canetti, 96. **CONTACT ADDRESS** Col Letters, Arts & Sciences, Univ Southern Calif, University Park Campus, Los Angeles, CA, 90089. **EMAIL** barnouw@hermes.usc.edu

BARNSTONE, WILLIS
PERSONAL Born 11/13/1927, Lewiston, ME, m, 1949, 3 children **DISCIPLINE** SPANISH & COMPARATIVE LITERATURE **EDUCATION** Bowdoin Col, BA, 48; Columbia Univ, MA, 56; Yale Univ, PhD, 60. **CAREER** Teacher French & English, Anavrita Acad, Greece, 49-50; instr French, Univ MD Overseas Prog, Perigueux, France, 55-56; from instr to asst prof Span, Wesleyan Univ, 58-62; assoc prof Span & comp lit, 62-66, prof Span & Port, 66-68, prof E Asian studies, 73-76, Prof Comp Lit, IN Univ, Bloomington, 66-, Prof Latin Am Studies, 76-, Guggenheim fel, Spain, 61-62; Am Coun Learned Soc Studies fel, 68-69; vis prof, Univ CA, Riverside, 68-69 & Inst Prof, Buenos Aires, 75-; Fulbright teaching fel, Argentina, 75; Nat Endowment for Humanities sr res fel, 79-80. **HONORS AND AWARDS** Cecil Hemley Mem Award, 68; Lucille Medwick Award, 78, Poetry Soc Am; Gustav Davidson Mem Award, 80., DLitt, Bowdoin Col, 81. **MEMBERSHIPS** MLA. **RESEARCH** Spanish; ancient Greek; English, Greek and Spanish poetry; theory and practice of translation. **SELECTED PUBLICATIONS** Auth, New Faces of China, IN Univ, 73; Egypt: Love, Death and Magic, Rev, 75; My Voice Because of You, State Univ NY, 76; China Poems, Univ MO, 76; Portugal: Poet Kings and the Sea, Sat Evening Post, 77; Real and Imaginary History in Borges and Cavafy, Comp Lit, 77; Billy and Meursault: A Failure of the Senses, Tex Quart, 78; Antonio Machado: a Theory of Method in His Dream, Landscape and Awakening, Revista Hisp Mod, 78; Memoir About a Metaphysical and Mystical Poet & Deciphering the Borges Persona Through the Essays and the Poetry, Critica Hispanica, Vol 15, 93; Translation Theory With a Semiotic Slant, Semiotica, Vol 102, 94; 'Federico in August', Partisan Rev, Vol 61, 94; 'Sunflower', Chicago Rev, Vol 42, 96; 'Into the Sun', Chicago Rev, Vol 42, 96. **CONTACT ADDRESS** Dept of Comp Lit, Indiana Univ, Bloomington, Bloomington, IN, 47401.

BAROLINI, TEODOLINDA
PERSONAL Born 12/19/1951, Syracuse, NY, w, 1980, 1 child **DISCIPLINE** ITALIAN LITERATURE **EDUCATION** Sarah Lawrence Col, BA, 72; Columbia Univ, MA, 73, PhD, 78. **CAREER** Asst prof Italian, Univ Calif, Berkeley, 78-83; assoc prof, 83-89, full prof, 89-92, Italian, NY Univ; prof and chemn Dept of Italian, Columbia Univ, 92- . **HONORS AND AWARDS** AAUW fel, 77; ACLS fel, 86; NEH fel, 86; Marraro Prize of MLA, 86; John Nicholas Brown Prize, Medieval Acad, 88; Guggenheim fel, 98. **MEMBERSHIPS** Dante Soc; Medieval Acad; Renaissance Soc of Am; Am Asn of Tchrs of Italian; MLA. **RESEARCH** Medieval and early Renaissance Italian literature, especially lyric tradition through Petrarch; Dante; Petrarch; Boccaccio. **SELECTED PUBLICATIONS** Auth, Dante's Poets: Textuality and Truth in the Comedy, Princeton, 84; auth, The Undivine Comedy: Detheologizing Dante, Princeton, 92; auth, Minos' Tail: The Labor of Devising Hell (Inferno 5.1-24), Romantic Rev, 96; auth, Guittone's Ora parra, Dante's Doglia me reca, and the Commedia's Anatomy of Desire, in, Baranski, ed, Seminario Dantesco Internazionale/International Dante Seminar, Le Lettere, 97. **CONTACT ADDRESS** Dept of Italian, Columbia Univ, 502 Hamilton Hall, New York, NY, 10027. **EMAIL** tb27@columbia.edu

BARON, FRANK
DISCIPLINE GERMAN LITERATURE **EDUCATION** Univ IL, BA; IN Univ, MA; Univ CA-Berkeley, PhD. **CAREER** Prof, 70, Univ KS. **HONORS AND AWARDS** Grants, Alexander von Humboldt found; NEH; Nat Sci Found; Fulbright Found; Ger Acad Exchange (DAAD); Univ KS Hall Ctr., Dir, Max Kade Ctr for Ger-Am Stud. **RESEARCH** Ger Renaissance and Reformation lit hist. **SELECTED PUBLICATIONS** Auth, bk(s) and articles on var aspects of the Europ Faust tradition and on the works of Rainer Maria Rilke, Thomas Mann, Hermann Hesse, and Albert Bloch; co-auth, bk about Hungary and Auschwitz. **CONTACT ADDRESS** Dept of Ger Lang and Lit, Univ Kansas, Admin Building, Lawrence, KS, 66045. **EMAIL** fbaron@kuhub.cc.ukans.edu

BARON, JAMES
PERSONAL Born 11/21/1942 **DISCIPLINE** CLASSICAL STUDIES **EDUCATION** Catholic Univ Am, AB, 64; Univ Minn, MA, 67, PhD, 72. **CAREER** Tchg asst, 66-69; tchg assoc, 69-70, Univ Minn; asst prof, Macalester Col, St Paul, Minn, 70-71; asst prof, Concordia Col, Moorehead, Minn, 70-71; asst prof, Col William and Mary in Va, 71-76; assoc prof, 76- & ept ch, 83-89 & 91-92. **RESEARCH** Augustan poetry; classical tradition in film; Scandinavian literature. **SELECTED PUBLICATIONS** Auth, Drag Humor in Aristophanes Comedies, Class Asn Mid W and S, 90; Direct Address to the Audience in the Films of Ingmar Bergman: A Classical Device Radically Transformed, Inaugural Meeting Int Soc for the Class Tradition, Boston, 91; The Orpheus Myth in the Early Films of Ingmar Bergman, CAMWS Southern Sect Meeting, Richmond, 92; Horatii Carmina I.37.17-20: Citus Venator: Homo aut Canis, Class Asn Mid W and S, Atlanta Georgia, 94; Bergman's Cries and Whispers, a Masterpiece of Classical Architecture, Soc Advancement for Scand Study, Davenport, 94; Alliteration and Other Sound Effects in Seneca's Tragedies, Class Asn Mid W and S, Southern Section, Chapel Hill, NC, 94; Willa Cather's Alexandra Bergson: Aeneas on the Nebraska Prairie, Class Asn Mid W and S, Omaha, 95 & A Child of Soil Reads Catullus, Horace, and Vergil, Amer Philol Asn, San Diego, 95; rev, Persona: the Transcendent Image, Scand Stud, vol 60, 98. **CONTACT ADDRESS** Dept of Classical Studies, Col of William and Mary, Morton Hall, PO Box 8795, Williamsburg, VA, 23187-8795. **EMAIL** jrbaro@facstaff.wm.edu

BARON, JOHN H.
PERSONAL Born 05/07/1936, Milwaukee, WI, m, 1973, 3 children **DISCIPLINE** SPANISH, FRENCH **EDUCATION** Brandies Univ, PhD, 67; Harvard Univ, MA, 59, BA, 58 **CAREER** Prof, 69-, Tulane Univ **MEMBERSHIPS** Am Musicol Soc **RESEARCH** Jewish music; New Orleans Music **SELECTED PUBLICATIONS** Auth, Ballet des Fees de forest de Saint Germain, New York: Dance Perspectives No. 62, 75; A History of Chamber Music, Stuyvesant, NY, Pendragon Press, 98; Coauth, The Remarkable mrs. Beach, Warren, MI: Harmonie Park Press, 94 **CONTACT ADDRESS** Dept of Music, Tulane Univ, New Orleans, LA, 70118-5683. **EMAIL** caccini@mailhost.tcs.tulane.edu

BARR, JEANINE R.
PERSONAL Born 05/15/1941, Toledo, OH, m, 1981 **DISCIPLINE** SPEECH COMMUNICATON, RHETORIC AND PUBLIC ADDRESS, HEALTH COMMUN, INTERPERSONAL COMMUN **EDUCATION** OH Univ, BFA, 63; Mesme of OH, MA, 67; Univ MD, PhD, 94. **CAREER** Instr, SUNY, Albany; asst prof to assoc prof, York Col of PA, 70-. **HONORS AND AWARDS** NIH grant, summer 80. **MEMBERSHIPS** Nat Commun Asn; Pi Kappa Delta. **RESEARCH** Communica-

tion in recovery from addiction; forensics. **SELECTED PUBLICATIONS** Co-auth, Communication in Recovery; misc articles on addiction, recovery, and forensics. **CONTACT ADDRESS** York Col, Pennsylvania, 206D MAC Center, York, PA, 17403. **EMAIL** jbarr@eagle.ycp.edu

BARRACK, CHARLES MICHAEL
PERSONAL Born 01/06/1938, Los Angeles, CA **DISCIPLINE** GERMANIC LINGUISTICS, GERMAN LITERATURE **EDUCATION** San Diego State Col, BA, 61; Univ WA, MA, 66, PhD(Ger ling), 69. **CAREER** Actg asst prof Ger, 68-69, asst prof, 69-74, assoc Prof Germanics, Univ WA, 74-. **MEMBERSHIPS** Ling Soc Am. **RESEARCH** Historical linguistics; epistemology. **SELECTED PUBLICATIONS** Coauth, The Tragic Background to Lessing's Minna von Barnhelm, Bessing Yearbk, 70; auth, Conscience in Heinrich von Ofterdingen: Novalis' Metaphysic of the Poet, Ger Rev, 71; Mephistopheles: 'Ein Teil von jener Kraft/Die stets das Bose will und stets das Gute Schafft, Seminar, 71; Nietzsche's Dionysus and Apollo: Gods in Transition, Nietzsche-Studien, spring 74; A Diachronic Phonology from Proto-Germanic to Old English Stressing West-Saxon Conditions, Mouton, The Hague, 74; Muspilli: A Dilemma in Restructuring, Folia Ling, 75; Lexical Diffusion and the High German Consonant Shift, 76 & The High German Consonant Shift: Polygenetic or Monogenetic? (in press), Lingua; Ablaut and Reduplication in the Germanic Verb, with F. Vancoetsem, Zeitschrift Fur Dialektologie Und Linguistic, Vol 62, 95. **CONTACT ADDRESS** Dept of Germanics, Univ of Washington, Seattle, WA, 98195.

BARRICELLI, JEAN-PIERRE
PERSONAL Born 06/05/1924, Cleveland, OH **DISCIPLINE** ROMANCE LANGUAGES, COMPARATIVE LITERATURE **EDUCATION** Harvard Univ, BA, 47, MA, 48, PhD(Romance lang & lit), 53. **CAREER** From instr to asst prof Romance lang & lit, Brandeis Univ, 53-63; assoc prof, 63-66, chmn dept French & Ital, 65-68, chmn, Dept Comp Lit, 66-75, chmn, Dept Lit & Lang, 76-81, Prof Romance Lang & Comp Lit, Univ CA, Riverside, 66-, Conductor, Cafarelli Opera Co, Cleveland, OH & Waltham Symphony Orchestra, MA, 54-59; dir, Wien Int Scholar Prog, Brandeis Univ, 58-63; Fulbright lectr, Norweg Sch Bus Admin & Univ Bergen, Norway, 62-63; ed, Ital Quart, 72-76 & Heloconian, 75- **HONORS AND AWARDS** Humanities Inst Award, Univ CA, 68-69; Distinguished Teaching Award, Univ CA, Riverside, 75. **MEMBERSHIPS** Am Comp Lit Asn; MLA; Dante Soc; Balzac Soc; Am Asn Advan Humanities. **RESEARCH** European Romanticism; Renaissance; literature and music. **SELECTED PUBLICATIONS** Coauth, Ernest Chausson, Univ OK, 55; auth, Balzac and Beethoven: The Growth of a Concept, Mod Lang Quart, 12/64; Demonic Souls: Three Essays on Balzac, Edda, Oslo, 64; Sogno and Sueno: Dante and Calderon, Comp Lit Studies, 72; A Manzoni, Twayne, 76; Machiavelli's Prince, Barron's, 75; Chekhov's Great Plays, Columbia & NY Univ, 81; co-ed & coauth, Interrelations of Literature, MLA, 82; Michelangelo Finito & Reformational Spirit in Contemporary Renaissance Painting, Sculpture and Architecture-In the Self, The Later Sonnets, and the Last Pieta, New Literary Hist, Vol 24, 93. **CONTACT ADDRESS** Dept of Lit & Lang, Univ of CA, Riverside, CA, 92521.

BARRICK, WILLIAM D.
PERSONAL Born 01/05/1946, Hayden, CO, m, 1966, 4 children **DISCIPLINE** OLD TESTAMENT, HEBREW **EDUCATION** Denver Baptist Bible Col, Ba, 68; San Francisco Baptist Theol Sem, MDiv 71, ThM, 72; Grace Theol Sem, ThD, 81. **CAREER** Prof, Denver Baptist Theol Sem, 72-78; exegetical consult for Bible transl, Chittagong, Bangladesh, 81-96; assoc prof, 97-98, prof, 98- , The Master's Sem, Sun Valley, Calif. **HONORS AND AWARDS** Denver Baptist Bible Col alumnus of the year, 80. **MEMBERSHIPS** Evangel Theol Soc; Soc of Bibl Lit; Natl Asn of Profs of Hebrew. **RESEARCH** Hebrew; Old Testament textual criticism; Leviticus; Job; Bible translation. **SELECTED PUBLICATIONS** Auth, William Carey: Memorable Man, Respected Personality, in Weber, ed, Mahan Sadhak William Carey, Bangladesh: Literature Division, 93, in Bengali; auth, the FACTS of Witnessing to People Outside Our Culture, Gospel Herald and the Sunday Sch Times, 94; auth, In the Folds of God's Garment, in 100 Meditations for Advent and Christmas, Upper Room Books, 94; consult, Holy New Testament, Bangladesh Bible Soc, 96; auth, 1 Samuel 1-17 Introduction and Mesages, Living Life, 97; auth, 1 Samuel 18-31 Messages, Living Life, 97; auth, 2 Samuel 1-14 Introduction and Messages, Living Life, 97; auth, 2 Samuel 14-24 Messages, Living Life, 97; auth, Hosea Introduction and Messages, Living Life, 97; auth, 1 Kings 1-4.28 Introduction and Messages and Proverbs 3:21-4:27 Messages, Living Life, 98; auth, Ancient Manuscripts and Biblical exposition, Master's Sem J, 98; auth, Isaiah 53 and 1 Kings 4:29-10:29 and Proverbs 5:1-23 Messages, Living Life, 98; auth, 1 Kings 19:1-22:53 and Proverbs 8:1-36 Messages, Living Life, 98; auth, Daniel 1:1-4:27 Introduction and Messages and Proverbs 10:22-12:8 Messages, Living Life, 98; auth, Daniel 4:28-12:13 and Proverbs 12:9-13:16 Messages, Living Life, 98; consult, Book of Psalms, Bangladesh Bible Soc, 98; consult, Pentateuch, Bangladesh Bible Soc, 98; consult, Holy Bible, Bangladesh Bible Soc, 98. **CONTACT ADDRESS** The Master's Sem, 13248 Roscoe Blvd, Sun Valley, CA, 91352. **EMAIL** bbarrick@mastersem.edu

BART, BENJAMIN FRANKLIN
PERSONAL Born 12/21/1917, Chicago, IL, m, 1942, 3 children **DISCIPLINE** ROMANCE LANGUAGES **EDUCATION** Harvard Univ, AB, 38, AM, 46, PhD, 47. **CAREER** Instr Romance lang, Harvard, 47; asst prof, Pomona Col, 47-50; asst prof, Univ MI, 50-56; from assoc prof to prof, Syracuse Univ, 56-67; PROF FRENCH, UNIV PITTSBURGH, 67-, Dir Comp Lit Prog, 74-, Ford Found fel, 52-53; Am Coun Learned Socs grants-in-aid, 60, 61, & 63; Am Philol Soc grant, 74; Camargo Found fel, 81; Nat Endowment for Humanities fel, 81. **MEMBERSHIPS** Am Asn Teachers Fr; MLA. **RESEARCH** French 19th century literature; the teaching of French. **SELECTED PUBLICATIONS** Auth, Flaubert's Landscape Descriptions, Univ MI, 56; Madame Bovary and the Critics, Scribner's, 66; Flaubert, Syracuse Univ, 67; The Legendary Sources of Flaubert's Saint Julien, Univ Toronto, 77; Naturalist Fiction-The Entropic Vision, with D. Baguley, French Forum, Vol 17, 92. **CONTACT ADDRESS** Dept of French, Univ of Pittsburgh, Pittsburgh, PA, 15260.

BARTLETT, CYNTHIA L.
DISCIPLINE ADULT NEUROGENIC COMMUNICATION DISORDERS **EDUCATION** IN Univ, BA, MA; Univ Pittsburgh, PhD. **CAREER** Com, Emerson Col. **SELECTED PUBLICATIONS** Areas: commun disorders in AIDS and commun with people with AIDS in AIDS; recovery in stroke related aphasia. **CONTACT ADDRESS** Emerson Col, 100 Beacon Street, Boston, MA, 02116-1596.

BARTSCH, SHADI
PERSONAL Born 03/17/1966, London, England, m, 1996 **DISCIPLINE** LATIN LITERATURE OF THE EARLY EMPIRE, CULTURAL THEORY AND INTERPRETATION, HISTORY OF CLASSICAL RHETORIC, THE ANCIENT NOVEL. **EDUCATION** Princeton Univ, BA (summa cum laude), 87; Harvard Univ, in PhD prog, 87-89, then as exchange scholar at the Univ CA, Berkeley, 88-89; Univ CA, Berkeley, MA, Latin, 89, PhD (Classics), 92. **CAREER** Acting asst prof, Classics and Rhetoric, Univ CA, Berkeley, 91-92, asst prof, 92-95, assoc prof, 95-98; vis assoc prof, Classics, Univ Chicago, Jan-June, 98, prof, Classics and the Committee on the History of Culture, Univ Chicago, July 98-; ed bd, Representations, 97-98; ed bd, Classical Philology, 98-. **HONORS AND AWARDS** Mellon fel in the Humanities, Harvard Univ, 87-89; Berkeley fel, Univ CA, Berkeley, 89-91; Richardson Prize for Trans into Latin, Univ CA, Berkeley, 90; Honorary P S Allen Junior Res fel, Corpus Christi, Oxford, 90; Humanities Res fel, Univ CA, Berkeley, 95-96; George Walsh Memorial Lecturer, Univ Chicago, 98. **MEMBERSHIPS** APA; adv committee for APA 1998; adv committee for ICAN 2000; co-ordinator, Workshop on Ancient Societies, Univ Chicago, 98-99. **SELECTED PUBLICATIONS** Auth, Decoding the Ancient Novel: The Reader and the Role of Description in Heliodorus and Achilles Tatius, Princeton Univ Press, 89; Actors in the Audience: Theatricality and Doublespeak from Nero to Hadrian, Harvard Univ Press, 94; Ideology in Cold Blood: A Reading of Lubcan's Civil War, Harvard Univ Press, 98; review, V Rudich, Dissidence and Literature under Nero: The Prince of Rhetoricization, in the Times Literary Supp, March 27, 98; Ars and the Man: The Politics of Art in Vergil's Aeneid, Classical Philology, forthcoming 98; Saints, Stoics, Specularity: A Genealogy of the Exemplum in the Latin West, forthcoming in Zeitschrift fur Antike und Christentum, 99; The Philosopher as Narcissus: Knowing Oneself in Classical Antiquity, forthcoming in Robert S Nelson, ed, Seeing as Others Saw: Visuality Before and Beyond the Renaissance, Cambridge Univ Press, 99; ed with Tom Sloan, Oxford Encyclopedia of Rhetoric, Oxford Univ Press, forthcoming; auth, The Cult of the Trope: Hermeneutics and the Classics in the Middle Ages, Princeton Univ Press, forthcoming; The Mirror of Philosophy: Specularity, Sexuality, and Self-Knowledge in the Roman Empire, forthcoming; numerous other articles, reviews, papers, and publications. **CONTACT ADDRESS** Dept of Classics, Univ of Chicago, 1010 E 59th St, Chicago, IL, 60637. **EMAIL** sbartsch@midway.uchicago.edu

BASHIR, ANTHONY S.
DISCIPLINE ADULT NEUROGENIC COMMUNICATION DISORDERS **EDUCATION** Northwestern Univ, BS, MS, PhD. **CAREER** Com, Emerson Col. **HONORS AND AWARDS** Fel, Am Speech-Lang-Hearing Asn. **SELECTED PUBLICATIONS** Areas: Learning Disabilities and Lang Disorders. **CONTACT ADDRESS** Emerson Col, 100 Beacon Street, Boston, MA, 02116-1596.

BASHIRI, IRAJ
PERSONAL Born 07/31/1940, Behbahan, Iran, m, 1968, 3 children **DISCIPLINE** MODERN IRANIAN LINGUISTICS & LITERATURE **EDUCATION** Pahlavi Univ, BA, 63; Univ MI, Ann Arbor, MA, 68, PhD, 72. **CAREER** Lectr Eng, Pahlavi Univ & Brit Coun, 63-64; instr, Imp Iranian Air Forces, 65; lectr Persian, Univ MI, 67-72; vis asst prof Iranian studies & Turkish, 72-73, asst prof, 73-78, Assoc Prof Iranian Studies & Turkish, Univ MN, Minneapolis, 78-96, Assoc Chmn, Dept South Asian Studies, 81-83, Acting chmn, Dept south Asian Studies, 83-84; Acting Chmn, Dept Russ & East Europ Studies, 89-91, assoc Chmn, Dept Russ & Europ Studies, 87-89; IREX Research Res scholar Tajikistan, 93-94; Chmn, Dept Slavis & Central Asian Lang & Lit, 97-98. **HONORS AND AWARDS** Col Lang Asn Distinguished tchr award, 80. **MEMBERSHIPS** Soc Iranian Studies; Mid EStudies Asn NAm. **RESEARCH** Iranian linguistics and lit. **SELECTED PUBLICATIONS** Auth, Persian for beginners, 72 & To be as the origin of syntax: A Persian framework, 73, Bibliotheca Islamica; Hedayat's Ivory Tower: Structural Analysis of The Blind Owl, Manor House, 74; Hafiz' Shirazi Turk: A structuralist point of view, Muslim World, 7 & 10/79; Hafiz and the sufic Ghazal, Studies in Islam, 1/79; Persian for Beginners: Pronunciation and Writing, 9/80, tape manual with notes on grammar, 11/80, reading texts, 7/81, Persian Syntax, 81, Burgess Publ Co; Introduntion Biography Plot Summary and Notes in English and Persian, Mazda of Tajikistan, Dushnabe, 94; Kamal Khujandi: Epoch and Its Importance in the History of Central Asian Civilization, Tehran-Dushanbe, 96; The History of a National Catastrophe, Rahim Masov (trans 96); The Saminds and the Revival of the Civiliation of the Iranian Peoples, Acad of Sci Tajikistan, Dushanbe, 96. **CONTACT ADDRESS** Inst of Lang Asian and Slavic Lang and Lit, Univ of MN, 192 Klaeber Ct, 320 16 Ave SE, Minneapolis, MN, 55455. **EMAIL** bashi001@maroon.tc.umn.edu

BATES, MARGARET JANE
PERSONAL Born 01/27/1918, New York, NY **DISCIPLINE** SPANISH, PORTUGUESE **EDUCATION** Hunter Col, AB, 38; Columbia Univ, MLA, 40; Cath Univ Am, PhD, 45. **CAREER** Mem interdept comt orgn of libr in Peru & Brazil, US Dept of State, 41-44; from asst prof to assoc prof Romance lang, 44-55; vdir, Inst Ibero-Am studies, 50-55; Prof Romance Lang, Cath Univ Am, 44-, Dir, Inst Ibero-Am Studies, 55-, Ford fac fel, 53-54. **MEMBERSHIPS** MLA, Am Asn Tchrs Span & Port. **RESEARCH** Spanish and Portuguese linguistics and lit; discretion in the works of Cervantes; Gregorio de Mattos, poet of 17th century Brazil. **SELECTED PUBLICATIONS** Ed, Las Poesias Completas de Gabriela Mistral, Aguilar, Madrid, 58, 2nd ed, 62, 3rd ed 66. **CONTACT ADDRESS** 5914 Carlton Lane, Bethesda, MD, 20016.

BATES, SCOTT
PERSONAL Born 06/13/1923, Evanston, IL, m, 1948, 4 children **DISCIPLINE** FRENCH, FILM **EDUCATION** Carleton Col, BA, 47; Univ WI, MA, 48, PhD(French), 54. **CAREER** Asst prof, 54-64, Prof French Lang & Lit, Univ of The South, 64-, Ed, Ecol Papers, 70-72. **MEMBERSHIPS** MLA. **RESEARCH** Modern French poetry; modern English and American poetry. **SELECTED PUBLICATIONS** Auth, Guillaume Apollinaire, Twayne, 67; ed, Poems of War Resistance, Grossman, 69; Petit glossaire des mots libres d'Apollinaire, Sewane, 75; The ABC of Radical Ecology, Highlander, 82; To Fix the Press & Efforts of the Hutchins-Commission to Define the Duties of a Free Press in the 1940's, Am Heritage, Vol 45, 94; 'Pizza', Sewanee Rev, Vol 103, 95; And Then There Was Usenet & The Beginnings of One of the Most Popular Features of Todays Internet, Am Heritage, Vol 46, 95; The Ancient-History of the Internet, Am Heritage, Vol 46, 95. **CONTACT ADDRESS** Dept of Lang & Lit, Univ of the South, Sewanee, TN, 37375.

BATTS, MICHAEL S.
PERSONAL Born 08/02/1929, Mitcham, England **DISCIPLINE** GERMANIC STUDIES **EDUCATION** Univ London, BA, 53, DLitt, 73; Univ Freiburg, DPhil, 57; Univ Toronto, MLS, 74. **CAREER** PROF EMER GERMANIC STUD, UNIV BRITISH COLUMBIA. **MEMBERSHIPS** Can Asn Univ Tchrs Ger; Mod Hum Res Asn. **SELECTED PUBLICATIONS** Auth, The Bibliography of German Literature: A Historical and Critical Survey, 78; auth, A History of Histories of German Literature: Prolegomena, 87; auth, A History of Histories of German Literature 1835-1914, 93; coauth, Scandinavian Literature in English Translation 1928-77, 78; ed, Echoes and Influences of German Romanticism, 87. **CONTACT ADDRESS** Germanic Stud, Univ of British Columbia, 1873 East Mall, Vancouver, BC, V6T 1Z1. **EMAIL** msb@unixg.ubc.ca

BAUER, GEORGE HOWARD
PERSONAL Born 12/31/1933, Cortez, CO, m, 1962, 2 children **DISCIPLINE** FRENCH LANGUAGE & LITERATURE **EDUCATION** Univ CO, BA, 55; IN Univ, MA, 60, PhD(Fr), 67. **CAREER** Instr French, Dartmouth Col, 61-63; lectr, Northwestern Univ, Evanston, 63-64, instr Romance lang, 64-67, asst prof French, 67-70; asst prof, Univ MN, Minneapolis, 70-73, assoc prof Ital & French, 73-77, acting chmn dept comp lit, 73-74; Chmn, Dept French & Ital, Univ Southern CA, 77-, Am Coun Learned Socs study fel, 68-69; distinguished vis prof humanities, Univ WY, 76-77. **MEMBERSHIPS** Am Asn Teachers Fr; MLA; Col Art Asn Am; Asn Studies Dada & Surrealism; Am Comp Lit Asn. **RESEARCH** Twentieth century French literature; relation between art and literature; comparative literature. **SELECTED PUBLICATIONS** Auth, Interview as Autobiography: Jean Paul Sartre, L'Esprit Createur, 77; Caligula: Portrait de l'artiste ou rien, Revue des Lettres Modernes, 75; Duchamp, Delay, Overlay in Mid-America, Uomo di lettere/Lhomme, 78; Letre/Barthes XYZ Game, New York Literary Forum, 78; Satre, In: Critical Bibliography of French Literature, 79; Eatins, The Other, In: Homosexualities and French Literature, Cornell Univ, 79; Peinture et engagement, In: Sartre et les

Arts, Obliques, Paris, 81; Sartre, In: Cabeen Critical Bibliography of French Literature, 79. **CONTACT ADDRESS** Dept of French and Ital, Univ of Southern CA, Los Angeles, CA, 90089.

BAUERLEIN, MARK
DISCIPLINE ENGLISH LANGUAGE AND LITERATURE **EDUCATION** Univ Calif Los Angles, PhD, 88. **CAREER** Prof **RESEARCH** 19th-century American literature; critical theory. **SELECTED PUBLICATIONS** Auth, Literary Criticism: An Autopsy; The Pragmatic Mind: Explorations in the Psychology of Belief; Whitman and the American Idiom. **CONTACT ADDRESS** English Dept, Emory Univ, 1380 Oxford Rd NE, Atlanta, GA, 30322-1950.

BAUMGARTEN, JOSEPH M.
PERSONAL Born 09/07/1928, Vienna, Austria, m, 1954, 6 children **DISCIPLINE** ORIENTAL STUDIES **EDUCATION** Brooklyn Col, BA, 50; Mesifta Torah Vodaat, dipl, 50; John Hopkins Univ, PhD(Orient studies), 53. **CAREER** PROF RABBINIC LIT, BALTIMORE HEBREW COL, 53-, Vis prof, Univ MD, 62-63, 76-77, Towson State Col, 70-71 & Univ of the Negev, Israel, 72-73. **MEMBERSHIPS** Soc Bibl Lit; Am Orient Soc; Rabbinical Coun Am. **RESEARCH** Jewish law and sects in time of the second temple; Qumran (Dead Sea Scrolls) literature. **SELECTED PUBLICATIONS** Auth, Unwritten Law in Pre-Rabbinic Period, J Study Judaism, 72; Exclusion of Netinim and Proselytes in 4 Q fl, Revue de Qumran, 72; Does TLH in Temple Scroll Refer to Crucifixion, J Biblical Lit, 72; Studies in Qumran Law, Brill-Leiden, 77; Heavenly Tribunal and the Personification of Sedeq, In: Aufstieg Und Niedergng Der Romishen Welt, 79; Pharisaic-Sadducean Controversies About Purity and the Qumran Texts, 80 & Exclusions from the Temple: Proselytes and Agrippa I, 82, J Jewish Studies; A New Qumran Substitute for the Divine Name and Mishnah-Sukkah 4.5 & A 2nd Temple Variant in a Berakhah Formula From 4Q266, An Investigation of a Disguise or a Substitution, Jewish Quart Rev, Vol 83, 92; Jewish Law From Jesus to the Mishnah, with E. P. Sanders, Jewish Quart Rev, Vol 83, 93; Hoo-Hakol You Are All or AunSIC-Hoo-Hakol & Scribal Error or a Peculiar Variant of the Divine Name Form the Qumran Damascus Document-A Reply to M. Kister, Jewish Quart Rev, Vol 84, 94; Zab-Impurity in Qumran and Rabbinic Law & The Significance of Levitical Purity in the Religious Life of the Jews of the 2nd Temple Period, J of Jewish Studies, Vol 45, 94; The Red Cow Purification Rites in Qumran Texts & An Evaluation of the Significance of the Para-Ritual Tebul-Yom-Fragments in Light of Tannaitic Sources, J of Jewish Studies, Vol 46, 95; Qumran Cave 4, Vol 5, Miqsat-Maase-Ha-Torah, with E. Qimron and J. Strugnell, J of the Am Oriental Soc, Vol 116, 96; Qumran Prayer and Religious Poetry, with B. Nitzan, J of Semitic Studies, Vol 41, 96; The Religious Laws of the Qumran Community, Annales-Histoire Sciences Sociales, Vol 51, 96. **CONTACT ADDRESS** Baltimore Hebrew Univ, 3200 Labyrinth Rd, Baltimore, MD, 21215.

BAUMGARTNER, INGEBORG HOGH
PERSONAL Born 01/29/1936, Oberstuben, Czechoslovakia, m, 1967, 1 child **DISCIPLINE** GERMAN LITERATURE **EDUCATION** Univ Mich, AB, 58, PhD(Ger), 70; Univ Wis, AM, 59. **CAREER** Instr Ger, Loyola Univ Chicago, 65-66; Prof Ger, Albion Col, 66- **MEMBERSHIPS** MLA; Am Asn Teachers Ger. **RESEARCH** German drama; 19th and 20th century German literature; Thomas Mann. **SELECTED PUBLICATIONS** Auth, Ambiguity in Buchner's Woyzeck, Mich Ger Studies, fall 75; coauth, A one-semester introduction to literary interpretation, Die Unterrichtspraxis, spring 77. **CONTACT ADDRESS** Dept of Foreign Lang, Albion Col, 611 E Porter St, Albion, MI, 49224-1831. **EMAIL** ibaumgartner@albion.edu

BAUML, FRANZ H.
PERSONAL Born 06/12/1926, Vienna, Austria, m, 1958 **DISCIPLINE** LANGUAGES **EDUCATION** Univ Berkeley, BA, 53, MA, 55, PhD(Ger), 57. **CAREER** From instr to assoc prof, 57-65, Prof Ger, Univ CA, Los Angeles, 65-, Am Coun Learned Soc res grant-in-aid, 59. **MEMBERSHIPS** MLA; Mediaeval Acad Am. **RESEARCH** Mediaeval German literature. **SELECTED PUBLICATIONS** Auth, Rhetorical Devices and Structure in the Ackermann aus Bohmen, Univ CA, 60; Zur mundlichen Uberlieferung des Nibelungenliedes, Deut Vierteljahrsschrift, 67; Kudrun: Die Handschrift, W de Gruyter Berlin, 69; Medieval Civilization in Germany: 800-1273, Thames & Hudson, London, 69; coauth, Weiteres zur mundlichen Uberlieferung des Nibelungenliedes, Deut Vierteljahrsschrift, 72; A Dictionary of Gestures, Scarecrow, 75; A Concordance to the Nibelungenlied, Maney & Son, Leeds, 76; Varieties and Consequences of Medieval Literacy and Illiteracy, Speculum, 80; Vocalism-Old English Poetry Between Orality and Literacy (German), with U. Schaefer, Poetica-Zeitschrift Fur Sprach-Und Literaturwissenschaft, Vol 27, 95. **CONTACT ADDRESS** Dept of Ger Lang, Univ of CA, Los Angeles, CA, 90024.

BAUSCHINGER, SIGRID ELISABETH
PERSONAL Born 11/02/1934, Frankfurt, Germany **DISCIPLINE** MODERN GERMAN LITERATURE **EDUCATION** Univ Frankfurt, Dr Phil, 60. **CAREER** Instr Ger, Oberlin Col, 62-64; asst prof, 64-68; asst prof, 68-71, assoc prof, 71-79, head dept, 76-79, Prof Ger, Univ Mass, Amherst, 79. **HONORS AND AWARDS** Franz Rosenzweig Res Center for Ger-Jewish Lit and Cult Hist fel, 93; Am Asn Tchr(s) Ger hon mem, 95. **MEMBERSHIPS** MLA **RESEARCH** Twentieth century Ger lit; lit of exile; Ger-Jewish lit. **SELECTED PUBLICATIONS** Contribr, Psychologie in der Literaturwissenschaft, Lothar Stiehm, Heidelberg, 71 & Gedichte der Menschheitsdammerung, Albin Fink, Munchen, 71; coauth, Elementary German, Van Nostrand Rineholt, 71; coauth & co-ed, Amerika in der Deutschen Literatur, Reclam, 75; auth, Else Lasker-Schuler, Ihr Werk und ihre Zeit, Lothar Stiehm, Heidelberg, 80; co-ed, Amherster Kolloquien zur Deutschen Literatur, 81; auth, Die Posaune der Reform, Francke, Bern, 89; ed, Ich habe ekieas zu sagen, Annette Kolb 1860-1867, Diederichs, Munchen, 93. **CONTACT ADDRESS** Dept of Ger, Univ of Massachusetts, Herter Hall, Amherst, MA, 01003-0002. **EMAIL** bauschin@german.umass.edu

BAYLESS, OVID LYNDAL
PERSONAL Born 07/20/1931, Duncan, OK, m, 1953, 3 children **DISCIPLINE** SPEECH; COMMUNICATION **EDUCATION** Baylor Univ, BA, 53, MA, 59; Univ Denver, PhD(speech), 65. **CAREER** Instr, broadcasting workshop, Baylor Univ, 59; instr English, US Air Force Acad, 62 63, asst prof tech writing & speech, 65-67, assoc prof advan compos & speech, 67-74, deputy dir instr technol, 68-74; PROF SPEECH COMMUN & CHMN DEPT SPEECH COMMUN & DRAMATIC ARTS, ARK STATE UNIV, 74- **MEMBERSHIPS** Speech Commun Asn; Am Forensic Asn; Int Commun Asn; Broadcast Educ Asn. **RESEARCH** Group problem-solving; persuasion; broadcasting. **SELECTED PUBLICATIONS** Auth, The American forces Vietnam network, J Broadcasting, 69; The oral history program, 69 & Television as a demonstration tool, 69, Educ TV. **CONTACT ADDRESS** Arkansas State Univ, PO Drawer 396, State University, AR, 72467-0369.

BAZIN, NANCY TOPPING
PERSONAL Born 11/05/1934, Pittsburgh, PA, m, 1992, 6 children **DISCIPLINE** FRENCH AND ENGLISH **EDUCATION** Ohio Wesleyan Univ, BA, 56; Middlebury Grad School of French, MA, 58; Stanford Univ, PhD, 69 **CAREER** Eminent Scholar, Old Dominion Univ, 96-; prof, Old Dominion Univ, 84-; assoc prof, Old Dominion Univ, 78-84; Chair, Dept Eng, Old Dominion Univ, 85-89; dir, Women's Studies, Old Dominion Univ, 78-85 **HONORS AND AWARDS** Winner, 2nd Annual Charles O and Elisabeth C Burgess Faculty Res Creativity Award, 96; Resident Fel, Center for the Humanities of the Virginia Foundation for the Humanities and Public Policy, 95; Outstanding Faculty Award, State Council Higher Education Virginia, 94; Ball Brothers Res Found Fel, 94; Phi Kappa Phi, 88; Sigma Tau Delta, 88; Phi Beta Kappa, 55; Mortar Board, 55; Kappa Delta Pi, 56 **MEMBERSHIPS** Modern Lang Assoc; African Lit Assoc; Ntl Women's Studies Assoc; Virginia Woolf Soc; Doris Lessing Soc **RESEARCH** 20th Century Writers **SELECTED PUBLICATIONS** Auth, Virginia Woolf and the Androgynous Vision, Rutgers, 73; auth, Conversations with Nadine Gordimer, Univ Miss, 90; auth, "Venturing into Feminist Consciousness: Two Protagonists from the Fiction of Buchi Emecheta and Bessie Head," Critical Perspectives on Buchi Emecheta, 96 **CONTACT ADDRESS** 4005 Gosnold Ave, Norfolk, VA, 23508-2917. **EMAIL** ntbazin@aol.com

BEARD, ROBERT EARL
PERSONAL Born 02/26/1938, Fayetteville, NC, m, 1960, 2 children **DISCIPLINE** SLAVIC LINGUISTICS **EDUCATION** Univ NC, AB, 59; Univ Mich, MA, 61, PhD(Slavic ling), 66; Moscow State Univ, cert Russ, 69. **CAREER** Lectr Russ lang, Univ Mich, 64-65; asst prof Russ & ling, 65-73, Assoc Prof Russ & Ling, Bucknell Univ, 73-, Dir Prog, 65-, Int Res & Exchanges Bd, exchange scholar, 76; Fulbright exchange scholar, Univ Beograd, Yugoslavia, 76-77. **MEMBERSHIPS** Ling Soc Am; Am Asn Teachers Slavic & East Europ Lang; Am Asn Advan Slavic Studies; Int Ling Asn; Am Asn Southeast Europ Studies. **RESEARCH** Teaching of Russian; generative grammar; lexicology. **SELECTED PUBLICATIONS** Auth, Dynamic glossing, Slavic East Europ J, 19: 49-57; Semantically based model ..., Language, 52: 108-20; Once more on ed-adjectives, J Ling, 12: 155-7; Material adjectives, Linguistics, 190: 5-34; On the extent of irregularity, Lingua, 42: 305-41; Derivations within derivations, VIII Int Cong Slavists, Zagreb-Ljubljana, 9/78; The Indo-European Lexicon, North-Holland Publishing Co, 81; auth, Bibliography of Morphology, 88; auth, Lexeme-Morpheme Bas Morphology, SUNY, 95. **CONTACT ADDRESS** Bucknell Univ, Lewisburg, PA, 17837-2029. **EMAIL** rbeard@bucknell.edu

BEARDSLEY, THEODORE S., JR.
PERSONAL Born 08/26/1930, East St. Louis, IL, m, 1955, 3 children **DISCIPLINE** SPANISH; FRENCH **EDUCATION** Southern Ill Univ, BS, 52; Wash Univ, MA, 54; Univ Penn, PhD, 61. **CAREER** Asst prof, Univ Wisc, 62-65; dir, Hisp Soc of Amer, 65-; pres, Hisp Soc of Amer, 95-; adjunct prof, Eckerd Col, 97-. **HONORS AND AWARDS** Fulbright award, France, 52-53, Ecuador, 74; corresponding mem, Real Acad Espanola, 70; mem, Acad Norteamericana de la lengua espanola, 76. **MEMBERSHIPS** Intl Ling Asn. **RESEARCH** Bibliography; Hispano-Classical tradition; Celestina; Spanish in the U.S.; Hispanic music. **SELECTED PUBLICATIONS** CD-ROM, Early Celestina Electronic Texts and Concordance, 97; CD, Enric Madriquera: Caribbean Music 1920-1941, 94; auth, Cervantes on Stage in the United States, Hisp Rev, 54, 86; auth, Spanish in the United States, WORD, 33, 82; auth, Elogio de la Bibliofilia, 74; auth, Hispano-Classical Translations: 1482-1699, 70. **CONTACT ADDRESS** Hispanic Society of America, 613 W 155th St, New York, NY, 10032.

BEASLEY, FAITH E.
PERSONAL Born 03/18/1958, Springfield, OH, m, 1994, 1 child **DISCIPLINE** FRENCH **EDUCATION** Mount Holyoke Col, BA, 80; Princeton Univ, MA, PhD, 86. **CAREER** Asst prof, 86-91, assoc prof, 91- , Dartmouth Col; vis assoc prof, Univ Michigan, 95-96; vis assoc prof, Am Grad Sch of Int Mgt, 96-97. **MEMBERSHIPS** MLA; NASSCFL; SE-17. **RESEARCH** Women writers; history and literature, seventeenth century France; memoirs; development of literary criticism; salons. **SELECTED PUBLICATIONS** Auth, Revising Memory: Women's Fiction and Memoirs in Seventeenth-Century France, Rutgers, 90; auth, Un Mariage Critique: Zayde et De L'Origine des Romans, XVIIieme Siecle, 93; auth, The Voices of Shadows: Lafayette's Zayde, in, Goldsmith, ed, Going Public: Women and Publishing in Early Modern France, Cornell, 95; auth, Moliere's Precious Women in Context, in Gaines, ed, Approaches to Teaching Moliere, MLA, 95; co-ed, Approaches to Teaching The Princess of Cleves, MLA, 98; auth, Villedieu and Her Public, in Lalande, ed, A Labor of Love: Critical Reflections on the Writing of Mme de Villedieu, Greenwood, forthcoming; auth, Roger Chartier, in Kritzman, ed, Columbia History of Twentieth-Century French Thought, Columbia, forthcoming; contribur, Sartori, ed, The Feminist Companion to French Literature, Greenwood, forthcoming. **CONTACT ADDRESS** Dept of French and Italian, Dartmouth Col, Hanover, NH, 03755. **EMAIL** Faith.Beasley@dartmouth.edu

BEATTY, MICHAEL
DISCIPLINE INTERPERSONAL AND ORGANIZATIONAL COMMUNICATION **EDUCATION** Univ MO, BS; Cent MO State Univ, MA; OH State Univ, PhD. **CAREER** Comm, Cleveland St Univ. **SELECTED PUBLICATIONS** Co-auth, Personality and Communication: Trait Perspectives, Hampton Press, 97; Trait Verbal Aggressiveness and the Appropriateness and Effectiveness of Fathers' Interaction Plans, Commun Quart, 96; auth, Thinking Quantitatively, An Integrated Approach to Communication Theory and Research, Hillsdale, NJ: Erlbaum, 96. **CONTACT ADDRESS** Commun Dept, Cleveland State Univ, 83 E 24th St, Cleveland, OH, 44115. **EMAIL** m.beatty@csuohio.edu

BEATY, JEROME
DISCIPLINE ENGLISH LANGUAGE AND LITERATURE **EDUCATION** Univ Ill, PhD, 56. **CAREER** Prof **RESEARCH** Victorian literature; poetics; the theory of the novel. **SELECTED PUBLICATIONS** Auth, Misreading Jane Eyre: A Postformalist Paradigm; coauth, Poetry: From Statement to Meaning; "Middlemarch" from Notebook to Novel; ed, Norton Introduction to the Short Novel; Norton Introduction to Fiction; Norton Introduction to Literature; New Worlds of Literature; Villette; Middlemarch. **CONTACT ADDRESS** English Dept, Emory Univ, 1380 Oxford Rd NE, Atlanta, GA, 30322-1950.

BEAUDRY, AGNES PORTER
PERSONAL Born 12/09/1932, Charleston, WV, m, 1973 **DISCIPLINE** FRENCH LITERATURE **EDUCATION** Marshall Univ, AB, 54; Case Western Reserve Univ, MA, 58; Univ Ill, Urbana, PhD(French), 68. **CAREER** Teacher French, Fairfax Hall, Waynesboro, Va, 55-57; teacher, Mansfield High Sch, Ohio, 58-59; instr, Ft Hays State Col, 59-60; instr Muskingum Col, 60-62; asst, Univ Ill, Urbana, 63-65, instr, 65-67; asst prof, 67-72, assoc prof, 72-80, Prof French, Depauw Univ, 80-. **MEMBERSHIPS** Am Asn Teachers Fr; Simone de Beauvoir Soc; Women in Fr **RESEARCH** Marcel Proust; 20th-century French memoirs; Marguerite Duras. **SELECTED PUBLICATIONS** Auth, "Proust's Final Montesquieu Pastiche," Marcel Proust, A Critical Panorama, Univ Ill, 73; The Treatment of Time in Proust's Pastiches, Fr Rev, spring 74; Memoirs in Critical Bibliography of French Literature, XX Century, Syracuse Univ Press, 80; Detruire, dit-ellc: Destruction or deconstruction, Int Fiction Rev, 81; auth, "A Neophyte in Literary Semiotics," American Journal of Semiotics, 82; assoc ed, Simone de Beauvoir Studies, 97-98, 98-99. **CONTACT ADDRESS** Dept of Modern Lang, DePauw Univ, 313 S Locust St, Greencastle, IN, 46135-1736. **EMAIL** abeaudry@depauw.edu

BEAUMONT, DANIEL E.
PERSONAL Seattle, WA **DISCIPLINE** NEAR EASTERN STUDIES **EDUCATION** Univ Wash, BA, 75, MA, 86; Princeton Univ, PhD, 91 **CAREER** Tchg asst, 88-89; lectr, 91-92, Princeton Univ; ASST PROF OF ARABIC, UNIV ROCHESTER, 92- . **HONORS AND AWARDS** Fulbright grant, 89; Princeton fel, 90; and numerous fellowships and grants. **MEMBERSHIPS** MESA. **RESEARCH** Literature; Narrative; Psychoanalysis. **SELECTED PUBLICATIONS** Auth, A Mighty and Never Ending Affair, Jour Arabic Lit, 93; The Trickster and Rhetoric in the Maqamat, Edebiyat, 94; Parody and Lying in Medieval Islam: Jahiz's Book of Misers, Studia Islamica, 94; Hard-boiled: Narrative Discourse in Early Muslim Traditions,

Studia Islamica, 96; The Modality of Narrative, Jour Am Acad Relig, 97; In the Second Degree: Fictional Technique in Tanukhi's Al-Faraj ba'd ash-shidda, Jour Arabic & Mid E Lit, 98; King, Queen, Master, Slave: The Master/Slave Dialectic and The One Thousand and One Nights, Neophilologus, 98; Peut-on tuer avec des noyaux de dattes?: Intertextuality and Dream-work in The Thousand and One Nights and Genesis, Comp Lit, 98. **CONTACT ADDRESS** Dept Relig & Classics, Univ of Rochester, Rochester, NY, 14627. **EMAIL** dano@troi.cc.rochester.edu

BEAUVOIS, MARGARET H.
DISCIPLINE ROMANCE LITERATURE **EDUCATION** Univ Tex, PhD. **CAREER** Asst prof. **SELECTED PUBLICATIONS** Auth, pubs on subject of computer-mediated communication. **CONTACT ADDRESS** Dept of Romance Languages, Knoxville, TN, 37996.

BEBOUT, LINDA J.
DISCIPLINE ENGLISH LANGUAGE; LITERATURE **EDUCATION** Central, BA; San Francisco State Univ, MSc; Cornell, PhD, 77. **CAREER** Asst prof **RESEARCH** Teaching of second-language vocabulary and the usage of gender-related terms in popular culture, such as in song lyrics. **SELECTED PUBLICATIONS** Pub (s), usage of gender-related words in English; language; language disorders and cross cultural attitudes toward them & teaching and learning English as a Second Language. **CONTACT ADDRESS** Dept of English Language and Literature, Univ of Windsor, 401 Sunset Ave, Windsor, ON, N9B 3P4. **EMAIL** ljb@uwindsor.ca

BECK, SIGRID
DISCIPLINE LINGUISTICS **EDUCATION** Univ Tuebingen, PhD. **CAREER** Asst prof, Univ Conn. **RESEARCH** Semantics, syntax-semantics interface. **SELECTED PUBLICATIONS** Auth, Quantified Structures as Barriers for LF-Movement, Natural Lang Semantics 4, 96; Negative Islands and Reconstruction In Extraction and Extraposition in German, Amsterdam: John Benjamins, 95. **CONTACT ADDRESS** Dept of Linguistics, Univ of Connecticut, 1266 Storrs Rd, Storrs, CT, 06269-1085. **EMAIL** sbeck@sp.uconn.edu

BECKER, ALTON LEWIS
PERSONAL Born 04/06/1932, Monroe, MI, m, 1953, 3 children **DISCIPLINE** LINGUISTICS **EDUCATION** Univ MI, BA, 54, PhD(ling), 66; Univ CT, MA, 56. **CAREER** Instr English, Univ CT, 54-56 & Ripon Col, 56-58; Fulbright teacher, Kambawsa Col, Burma, 58-61; instr, 61-64, instr English & Thai, 64-65, instr English, 65-68, from asst prof to assoc prof ling, 68-74, PROF LING & ANTHROP, UNIV MI, ANN ARBOR, 74-, Assoc mem exec comt, Ctr S & Southeast Asian Studies, Univ MI, 63-, dir, 72-75; mem Ctr Res on Lang & Lang Behav, 65-; Ford Found vis prof ling, Inst Keguruan dan Ilmu Pendidikan, Malang, Java, 69-71; mem, Inst for Advan Study, Princetown, 81-82. **MEMBERSHIPS** Ling Soc Am; Burma Res Soc. **RESEARCH** Formal description of discourse; history and structure of Southeast Asian languages. **SELECTED PUBLICATIONS** Auth, Journey Through the Night: Some Reflections on Burmese Traditional Theatre Drama Rev, winter 70; coauth, Rhetoric: Discovery and Change, Harcourt, 71; A Linguistic Image of Nature: The Burmese Numerative Classifier System, Int J Sociol of Lang, 75; co-ed, The Imagination of Reality, Ablex, 79; auth, Text-building, Epistemology and Aesthetics in Javanese Shadow Theatre, 79; coauth, Person in Kawi, Oceanic Ling, 176; auth, The Figure a Sentence Makes, Syntax & Semantics, 12/79; On Emerson on Language, Georgetown Univ, 82; On Arnheim on Language, J of Aesthetic Education, Vol 27, 93. **CONTACT ADDRESS** Dept of Ling, Univ of MI, Ann Arbor, MI, 48104.

BECKER, EDWARD
DISCIPLINE ANALYTIC PHILOSOPHY AND PHILOSOPHY OF LANGUAGE **EDUCATION** Johns Hopkins Univ, PhD, 70. **CAREER** Assoc prof, Univ Nebr, Lincoln. **RESEARCH** Quine. **SELECTED PUBLICATIONS** Quine and the Problem of Significance, Proc of the 7th Int Wittgenstein Symp, 83; Holistic Behaviorism, Proc of the 9th Int Wittgenstein Symp, 85. **CONTACT ADDRESS** Univ Nebr, Lincoln, Lincoln, NE, 68588-0417.

BECKER, LUCILLE FRACKMAN
PERSONAL Born 02/04/1929, New York, NY, m, 1954, 4 children **DISCIPLINE** FRENCH LANGUAGE & LITERATURE **EDUCATION** Barnard Col, BA, 49; Univ Aix-Marseille, Dipl Etudes Francaises, 50; Columbia Univ, MA, 54, PhD(French), 58. **CAREER** Instr French, Columbia Univ, 54-58 & Rutgers Univ, 58-68; assoc prof, 68-76, PROF FRENCH & CHMN DEPT, DREW UNIV, 77-. **MEMBERSHIPS** MLA; AAUP; Am Asn Teachers Fr. **RESEARCH** Twentieth century French literature; 19th century French literature; French novel. **SELECTED PUBLICATIONS** Auth, Pessimism and Nihilism in the Plays of Henry de Montherlant, Yale Fr Studies, spring-summer 62; coauth, The Versification Techniques of Louis Aragon, Fr Rev, 5/65; co-ed, Le Maitre de Santiago, Heath, 65; auth, Henry de Montherlant: A Critical Biography, Southern IL Univ, 70; Louis Aragon, Twayne, 71; Henry de Montherlant, In: Colliers Encycl, 73; Henry de Montherlant and Suicide, Romance Notes, winter 75; Georges Simenon, G K Hall, 77; Louis Aragon, In: Encyclopedia World Literature in 20th Century, Ungar, 81; 'Divine', with F. Mallet-joris, World Lit Today, Vol 67, 93; A 'Nous Deux, Satan', with P. Boulle, World Lit Today, Vol 67, 93; 'Alienor', with Z. Oldenbourg, World Lit Today, Vol 68, 94; Georges Simenon (French), with P. Assouline, World Lit Today, Vol 68, 94. **CONTACT ADDRESS** Dept of French, Drew Univ, Madison, NJ, 07940.

BEDINI, SILVIO A.
PERSONAL Born 01/17/1917, Ridgefield, CT, m, 1951, 2 children **DISCIPLINE** COMPARATIVE LITERATURE **EDUCATION** Columbia Univ, 35-42; Univ Bridgeport, LLd 70. **CAREER** Smithsonian Inst Nat Museum Hist Tech, curator, 61-65, asst dir, 65-72, dep dir, 72-77; Smithsonian Inst, keeper of the rare books, 77-82, Hist emeritus, 82-. **HONORS AND AWARDS** Abbot Payson Usher Awd; Paul Bunge Awd; J T Fraser Prize of Excellence. **MEMBERSHIPS** APA; SAH; AAS; WAS. **RESEARCH** Historical research in history of horology and history science; scientific instruments; early Amer Science. **SELECTED PUBLICATIONS** Auth, The Pope's Elephant, Manchester Eng, Carcanet Press, 97; The Mace and the Gavel: Symbols of Authority in America, Philadelphia, Amer Philo Soc, 97; Science and Instruments in 17th Century Italy, Alsershot Eng, Ashgate Pub, 94; The Trail of Time: Time Measurement With Incense in East Asia, Cambridge, Cambridge Univ Press, 94; Thomas Jefferson Statesman of Science, NY, Macmillan Pub, 90. **CONTACT ADDRESS** Smithsonian Inst, 4303 47th St N W, Washington, DC, 20016-2449. **EMAIL** sbedini@compuserve.com

BEECHER, MAUREEN URSENBACH
PERSONAL Born 03/19/1935, Calgary, AB, Canada **DISCIPLINE** COMPARATIVE LITERATURE, WESTERN HISTORY **EDUCATION** Brigham Young Univ, BSc, 58; Univ UT, MA, 66, PhD(comp lit), 73. **CAREER** Res historian & ed western hist, Church of Jesus Christ Latter-Day Saints, 72-80; ASSOC PROF ENGLISH & RES HISTORIAN, BRIGHAM YOUNG UNIV, PROVO, UT, 80-. **HONORS AND AWARDS** John Whitmer Hist Asn Award, 78. **MEMBERSHIPS** AHA; Western Hist Asn; Mormon Hist Asn; Asn for Mormon Lett. **RESEARCH** History of women in America; history of Mormon women; literature of the Mormon movement. **SELECTED PUBLICATIONS** Auth, Three Women and the Life of the Mind, UT Hist Quart, winter 75; Letters From the Frontier: Commerce, Nauvoo and Salt Lake City, J of Mormon Hist, 75; Past and Present: Some Thoughts on Being a Mormon Woman, Sunstone, 76; Under the Sunbonnets: Mormon Women with Faces, BYU Studies, summer 76; contribr, The Oft-crossed Border: Canadians in Utah, In: The Peoples of Utah, Utah State His Soc, 76; contribr, Eliza R Snow, In: Mormon Sisters, Emmeline, 77; auth, The Eliza Enigma: The Life and Legend of Eliza R Snow, Dialogue: J Mormon Thought, reprinted in, Sister Saints, spring 78; contribr, Women in Twentieth Century Utah, In: Utah's History, Brigham Young Univ, 78; Tryed and Purified as Gold & 19th-Century Reminiscences and Diaries of Latter-Day Saints-Mormon Womens Lives, Brigham Young Univ Studies, Vol 34, 94; On Being Mormon in Canada and Canadian in Utah-Personal Essay, Brigham Young Univ Studies, Vol 36, 97. **CONTACT ADDRESS** Brigham Young Univ, Provo, UT, 84602.

BEENE, LYNNDIANNE
DISCIPLINE LANGUAGE AND RHETORIC, PROFESSIONAL WRITING, AND CONTEMPORARY FICTION **EDUCATION** Univ Kans, PhD. **CAREER** Instr, Univ NMex. **RESEARCH** Contemporary grammar models. **SELECTED PUBLICATIONS** Auth, The Riverside Handbook, 92. **CONTACT ADDRESS** Univ NMex, Albuquerque, NM, 87131.

BEER, JEANETTE MARY AYRES
PERSONAL Wellington, New Zealand, 2 children **DISCIPLINE** MEDIEVAL FRENCH, LINGUISTICS **EDUCATION** Victoria Univ, Wellington, BA, 54, MA, 55; Oxford Univ, BA, 58, MA, 62; Columbia Univ, PhD(French), 67. **CAREER** Asst lectr French, Victoria Univ, Wellington, 56; lectr English & French, Univ Montpellier, 58-59; lectr French, Otago Univ, 62-64; instr, Barnard Col, 66-68; from assoc prof to prof, Fordham Univ, 68-80, dir medieval studies, 72-80, prof French, 77-80; prof, Purdue Univ & Chmn Dept, 80-, Actg assoc dean, Thomas More Col, 72-73. **HONORS AND AWARDS** Fel, St. Anne's Col, Nat Endowment Humanities prog grant, 75-; mem, Nat Bd Consult, Nat Endowment Humanities, 77-; Nat Endowment Humanities res fel; fel, Ctr for Humanisic Stu; Purdue Res Fnd Res Gra; Phi Kappa Phi; Dean's Incentive Awd; Am Cnl of Learned Soc Travel Gra; Am Philops Soc Gra. **MEMBERSHIPS** Am Asn of Tchr of French; Anglo-Norman Text Sco; Columbia Univ Medieval Sem; Col Univ Grad Faculties Alumni; Int Arthurian Soc; Int Courtly Lit Soc; Lady Margaret Hall; Medieval Acad of Am; Mod Lang Asn of Am; Sr Mem of Oxford Univ; Soc Guilhem IX; Soc Rencesvals **RESEARCH** Medieval French literature, especially historians; linguistic and stylistic aspects of Old French; comparative literature. **SELECTED PUBLICATIONS** Auth, Villehardouin-Epic Historian, Droz, Geneva, 68; Villehardouin and the oral narrative, Studies Philol, 7/70; Explication de texte of a surrealist poem by Paul Eluard, Teaching Lang Through Lit, 5/71; A medieval Cato-virtus or virtue?, Speculum, 1/72; French Nationalism Under Philip Augustus-an Unexpected Source, Mosaic, winter, 74; Durative Traces in the Comencier-plus-infinitive Formula of Thirteenth Century French, Romance Philol, 74; A medieval Caesar, Droz, Geneva, 76; Stylistic Heterogeneity in the Middle Ages, In: Jean Misrahi Memorial Volume, Fr Lit Publ Co, 77; Narrative Conventions of Truth in the Middle Ages, Geneva, 81; Medieval Fables--Marie de France, AH & AW Reed, Ltd, UK & Australia, 80; transl, Medieval Fables--Marie de France, Dodd, 83; auth, Narrative Conventions of Truth in the Middle Ages, Droz, 81; trans, Master Richard's Bestiary of Love and Response, Penny Royal, 81, 86; auth, Early Prose in France, Medieval Inst, 92; ed, Translation Theory and Practice in the Middle Ages, Medieval Inst, 97; co-ed, Translation and the Transmission of Culture between 1300 and 1600, Medieval Inst, 95; co-ed, Romance Languages Annual, Vols III, IV, V, VI, and VII, Purdue Res Fnd, 92-96; **CONTACT ADDRESS** Dept of Foreign Lang & Lit, Purdue Univ, West Lafayette, IN, 47907-1968. **EMAIL** beer@purdue.edu

BEHLER, ERNST
PERSONAL Born 09/04/1928, Essen, West Germany, m, 1967, 1 child **DISCIPLINE** GERMANICS, COMPARATIVE LITERATURE **EDUCATION** Univ Munich, PhD, 51. **CAREER** Docent philos, Univ Bonn, 61-63; assoc prof Germanics, WA Univ, 64-65, prof Ger & comp lit, 65-66; chmn Humanities Coun, 73-78, PROF GER & COMP LIT, UNIV WA, 66-, Co-Dir Humanities Prog & Chmn Comp Lit, 76-, Guggenheim Found fel, 67 & 75-76; Am Coun Learned Soc fel, 70-71. **MEMBERSHIPS** MLA; Comite d'honneur de la Societe des Etudes Staeliennes; hon mem, Ovidianum Societas, Bucharest; Am Comp Lit Asn. **RESEARCH** Romanticism; history of ideas and critism. **SELECTED PUBLICATIONS** Coauth, Critical Edition of F Schlegel's Works (35 vols), 58 & auth, Die Ewigkeit der Welt, 65, Schoeningh, Paderborn; Friedrich Schlegel, Rowohlt, Hamburg, 66; Madame de Stael a Weimar, Studi Francesi, 69; Techniques of Irony in Light of the Romantic Theory, Rice Univ Studies, 72; Klassische Ironie, Romantische Ironie, Tragische Ironie, Wiss Buchgesellschaft, Darmstadt, 72; Die Geschichte des Bewusstseins, Hegel-Studies, 72; Nietzsche's Challenge to Romantic Humanism, Can Rev Comp Lit, 5/78; The Reception of Calderon Among the German Romantics, Studies in Romanticism, 81; Historicism and Sense of Modernity in Herder 'Auch Eine Philosophie Der Geschichte Zur Bildung Der Menschheit', Etudes Germaniques, Vol 49, 94. **CONTACT ADDRESS** Univ WA, Seattle, WA, 98195.

BEHNKE, KERSTIN
DISCIPLINE GERMAN **EDUCATION** Stanford Univ, PhD. **CAREER** Asst prof, Northwestern Univ; appointed founding dir, Northwestern's Office Study Abroad. **HONORS AND AWARDS** Distinguished lectr, Charles Deering McCormick Univ, 95-96. Fac Honor Roll Dept of German, Northwestern Univ. **RESEARCH** Philosophy and aesthetics of representation from Descartes through German Idealism to Postmodernism. **SELECTED PUBLICATIONS** Auth, Romantische Arabesken: Lineatur ohne Figur und Grund zwischen Ornament-Schrift und Text, Gewebe, in: Schrift, Fink Verlag, 93; Representation, Krise der, in: Historisches W"rterbuch der Philosophie, Schwabe & Co, 92; educ documentaries, Drehort: Neubrandenburg; AZUBI; Drehort: Bern; Faces of a City. **CONTACT ADDRESS** Dept of German, Northwestern Univ, 1801 Hinman, Evanston, IL, 60208. **EMAIL** kbehnke@nwu.edu

BEIZER, JANET L.
PERSONAL Born 04/09/1952, New York, NY, 1 child **DISCIPLINE** FRENCH LITERATURE **EDUCATION** Cornell Univ, BA, 74; Yale Univ, PhD(French), 81. **CAREER** Asst prof, 81-88, assoc prof, 88-95, dir, undergrad studies/distinguished majors/study abroad, 89-90, chair, grad studies comm, 92-94, dir grad studies, 94-95, PROF FRENCH, UNIV VA, 95-. **HONORS AND AWARDS** Phi Beta Kappa, Phi Kappa Phi, 74; Fulbright Fellowship, Paris, 74-75; Univ VA Fac summer research grants, 82, 85, 86, 89, 90, 92, 93, 95, 97; NEH summer research grant, 88, 98; NEH travel grant, 91; MLA Aldo and Jeanne Scaglione Prize for French and Francophone Studies, 95 (for Ventriloquized Bodies); Nat Humanities Center Fellow, 98-99. **MEMBERSHIPS** MLA. **RESEARCH** Nineteenth century narrative, psychoanalysis and literature. **SELECTED PUBLICATIONS** Transl, Maria Paganini, Intertextuality and the Strategy of Desire: Melancolique Villegistare de Madame de Breyues, Yale French Studies, 79; Family Plots: Balzac's Narrative Generations, Yale Univ Press, 86; Reading Women: The Novel in the Text of Hysteria, Compar(a)ison 1, 93; Emma's Daughter: Femininity, Maternity, and 'Mothersickness' in Madame Bovary, in From Exile to Vagrancy: Home and its Dislocations in Nineteenth-Century France, ed Suzanne Nash, SUNY Press, 93; Les Lettres de Flaubert a Louise Colet, Une Physiologie du style, in L'Oeuvre de l'oeuvre: Etudes sur la correspondance de Flaubert, ed Raymonde Debray Genette & Jacques Neefs, Presses Universitaires de Vincennes, 93; Rewriting Ophelia: Fluidity, Madness and Voice in Louise Colet's La Servante, in Embodied Voices: Representing Female Vocality in Western Culture, ed Nancy Jones and Leslie Dunn, Cambridge Univ Press, 94; Ventriloquized Bodies: Narratives of

Hysteria in Nineteenth-Century France, Cornell Univ Press, 94; Mirrors and Fatherhood in Le Pere Goriot, in Pere Goriot, Norton Critical Edition, ed Peter Brooks, Norton, 98; Critical Introduction to Rachilde in The Decadent Reader, ed Asti Hustvedt, Zone Books (forthcoming 98); You Can't Judge a Book By It's Cover: Old Goriot and Modernism, in Approaches to Teaching Balzac's Ols Goriot, ed Michal Ginsberg, MLA (forthcoming). **CONTACT ADDRESS** Dept of French, Univ of Virginia, 302 Cabell Hall, Charlottesville, VA, 22903-3125. **EMAIL** jlb@virginia.edu

BEKKER, HUGO
PERSONAL Born 02/12/1925, Netherlands, m, 1952, 2 children **DISCIPLINE** GERMAN **EDUCATION** Univ Mich, MA, 56, PhD, 58. **CAREER** Asst prof Ger, Univ Ore, 58-61, res grant, 60; assoc prof, 61-66, Prof Ger, Ohio State Univ, 66-, Vis prof, Univ British Columbia, 71. **MEMBERSHIPS** Am Asn Teachers Ger; MLA; Renaissance Soc Am. **RESEARCH** Poetry. **SELECTED PUBLICATIONS** Auth, The Nibelungenlied: A Literary Analysis, Univ Toronto, 71; Andreas Gryphius: Poet Between Epochs, Lang Verlag, Bern, 73; Friedrich von Hausen: Inquiries into His Poetry, Univ NC, 77; The Poetry of Albrecht von Johansdorf, Univ Calif, Davis, 78; Gottfried von Strassburgs Tristan: Journey through the Realm of Eros, Camden House, 87. **CONTACT ADDRESS** Dept of Ger, Ohio State Univ, 1841 Millikin Rd, Columbus, OH, 43210-1229.

BELKNAP, ROBERT LAMONT
PERSONAL Born 12/23/1929, New York, NY, m, 1997, 3 children **DISCIPLINE** RUSSIAN LITERATURE **EDUCATION** Princeton Univ, AB, 51; Columbia Univ, MA, 54, PhD, 60. **CAREER** From instr to assoc prof Russ lang & lit, 57-69, assoc dean student affairs, Columbia Col, 68-69, chmn dept Slavic lang, 70-76, actg dean, 76-77, dir, Columbia Russ Inst, 77-80, Prof Russ, Columbia Univ, 69-. **HONORS AND AWARDS** Inter-Univ Comt Travel Grants study grant, Leningrad, 63; Am Coun Learned Soc & IREX fel study in Moscow, 66-67; NEH, Kennan Inst, Bellagio Ctr, and Guggenheim fellowships. **MEMBERSHIPS** Am Asn Advan Slavic Studies. **RESEARCH** Nineteenth century Russian novel. **SELECTED PUBLICATIONS** Auth, The Structure of The Brothers Karamazov, Mouton, The Hague, 67, Northwestern, 89, St. Petersburg, Acad Proj, 97; coauth, Tradition and Innovation, General Education and the Reintegration of the University, Columbia, NY, 78; auth, The Genesis of the Brothers Karamazov, Northwestern, 90. **CONTACT ADDRESS** Dept of Slavic Lang, Columbia Univ, 2960 Broadway, New York, NY, 10027-6900. **EMAIL** rb 12@columbia.edu

BELL, STEVEN
DISCIPLINE MODERN SPANISH AMERICAN LITERATURE **EDUCATION** Univ Kans, BA, 77; Univ Ky, MA, 79; Univ Kans, PhD, 84. **CAREER** English and Lit, Univ Ark. **SELECTED PUBLICATIONS** Ed & coauth, Critical Theory, Cultural Politics, 93. **CONTACT ADDRESS** Univ Ark, Fayetteville, AR, 72701.

BELL-VILLADA, GENE HAROLD
PERSONAL Born 12/05/1941, Port-au-Prince, Haiti, m, 1975 **DISCIPLINE** SPANISH, COMPARITIVE LITERATURE **EDUCATION** Univ Ariz, BA, 63; Univ Calif, Berkeley, MA, 67; Harvard Univ, PhD(Romance lang), 74. **CAREER** Instr Span, State Univ NY, Binghamton, 71-73; lectr, Yale Univ, 73-74; from asst to prof Span, Williams Col, 75-, Nat Endowment for Humanities fel, 7-12/79; Am Philos Soc grant, 82; res dir, Hamilton Col, prog in Madrid, 86-87; chmn Romance Lang, 93-95, 97-. **MEMBERSHIPS** MLA; Am Asn Teachers Span & Port; Latin Am Studies Asn. **RESEARCH** Spanish-American Comparative literature; Latin-American studies; sociology of literature. **SELECTED PUBLICATIONS** Auth, Borges and His Fiction: A Guide to His Mind and Art, Univ NC Press, 81; Names and narrative pattern, In: One Hundred Years of Solitude, Latin Am Lit Rev, spring-summer 81; Garcia Marquez: The Man and His Work, UNC Press, 90; Art for Art's Sake and Literary Life, Univ of Nebraska Press, 96. **CONTACT ADDRESS** Dept of Romance Lang, Williams Col, 995 Main St, Williamstown, MA, 01267-2600. **EMAIL** Gene.H.Bell-Villada@Williams.edu

BELLAMY, JAMES ANDREW
PERSONAL Born 08/12/1925, Evansville, IN **DISCIPLINE** ARABIC **EDUCATION** Centre Col, Ky, AB, 46; Univ Pa, PhD(Orient studies), 56. **CAREER** Interim lectr Arabic, Univ Pa, 56-57; asst prof, Wayne State Univ, 58-59; lectr, 59-60, from asst prof to assoc prof, 60-68, PROF ARABIC, UNIV MICH, ANN ARBOR, 68-, Assoc ed, J Am Orient Soc, 70-75; Am Coun Learned Soc fel. **MEMBERSHIPS** Mid East Inst; MLA; Mid Eastern Stud Asn N Am. **RESEARCH** Arabic literature. **SELECTED PUBLICATIONS** Auth, Fa Ummuhu Hawiyah, A Note on Surah 101 9, J Amer Oriental Soc, Vol 0112, 92; Some Proposed Emendations to the Text of the Koran, J Amer Oriental Soc, Vol 0113, 93; Qanaa --Contentment in Arabic Literature, A Study of the 'Kitab Al Qanaa Wa T Ta Affuf' By Ibnabiddunya, J Amer Oriental Soc, Vol 0114, 94; Ibnbaskuwal M 578 1183--'Kitab Al-Mustagitin Bi-Ilah', J Amer Oriental Soc, Vol 0114, 94; Ibnalabbar, Politician and Valencian Arab Writer 1199-1260--Proceedings of the Int Conf Ibnalabbar and His Times, Held in Onda, 1989, J Amer Oriental Soc; The Development of the Arabic Scripts From the Nabatean Era to the 1st Islamic Century According to Dated Texts, J Amer Oriental Soc, Vol 0115, 95; An Introduction to Koranic and Classical Arabic in An Elementary Grammar of the Language, J Amer Oriental Soc, Vol 0116, 96. **CONTACT ADDRESS** Univ Michigan, Ann Arbor, MI, 48109.

BELTON, JOHN
DISCIPLINE ENGLISH LANGUAGE AND LITERATURE **EDUCATION** Columbia Univ, BA; Harvard Univ, MA; PhD. **CAREER** Prof **RESEARCH** Film theory; cultural studies. **SELECTED PUBLICATIONS** Auth, Widescreen Cinema; auth, America Cinema/American Culture. **CONTACT ADDRESS** Dept of English, Rutgers Univ, 510 George St, Murray Hall, New Brunswick, NJ, 08901-1167.

BELTRAN, LUIS
PERSONAL Born 09/06/1932, Salmanca, Spain, m, 1962, 2 children **DISCIPLINE** COMPARATIVE LITERATURE **EDUCATION** Univ Salamanca, LLB, 54, lic philos, 56; Univ Mich, MA, 61, PhD(comp lit), 66. **CAREER** From asst prof to assoc prof, 66-77, Prof Comp Lit, Span & Port, Ind Univ, Bloomington, 77- **MEMBERSHIPS** Mediaeval Acad Am; MLA. **RESEARCH** Comparative medieval literature; Spanish poetry. **SELECTED PUBLICATIONS** Auth, Hacia la Tierra Alfaguara, Madrid, 70; The poet, the king and the cardinal virtues in Juan de Mena's Laberinto, Speculum, 71; La Vieille's past, Romanische Forsch, 72; Anaya mi Esperanza, Alfaguara, Madrid, 73; El Fruto de su Vientre, Samo, Mex, 73; Razones de Buen Amor: Oposiones y Convergencias en el Libro del Arcipreste de Hita, Castalia, Madrid, 77. **CONTACT ADDRESS** Dept of Compt Lit, Indiana Univ, Bloomington, Bloomington, IN, 47401.

BENDA, GISELA
PERSONAL Born 10/05/1941, Brandenburg-Havel, Germany **DISCIPLINE** GERMAN LANGUAGE & LITERATURE **EDUCATION** Univ Munster, BA, 62; Marquette Univ, MA, 64; Northwestern Univ, PhD(Ger), 67. **CAREER** Asst prof, 67-72, ASSOC PROF GER, MARQUETTE UNIV, 72-. **MEMBERSHIPS** Am Asn Teachers Ger; MLA; AAUP. **RESEARCH** Works of Heinrich Heine, Friedrich Nietzsche, Rainer Maria Rilke and Franz Kafka. **SELECTED PUBLICATIONS** Auth, The Jewish Reception of Heine,Heinrich, Ger Quart, Vol 0067, 94; The Jewish Reception of Heine, Heinrich, Ger Quart, Vol 0067, 94; Nietzsche Philosophy of Art, Ger Quart, Vol 0067, 94. **CONTACT ADDRESS** Dept of Ger, Marquette Univ, Milwaukee, WI, 53233.

BENDER, BYRON WILBUR
PERSONAL Born 08/14/1929, Roaring Spring, PA, m, 1950, 5 children **DISCIPLINE** LINGUISTICS **EDUCATION** Goshen Col, BA, 49; Ind Univ, MA, 50, PhD(ling), 63. **CAREER** Asst prof anthrop & ling, Goshen Col, 59-62; English prog supvr, Trust Territory of Pac Islands, 62-64; assoc prof English Lang Inst, 64-65, assoc prof to prof Ling, 65-, chm dept Ling, 69-95, Univ Hawaii, Manoa, US Peace Corps grant, Pac & Asian Ling inst for develop pedag materials on Marshallese lang, 66-67; consult Maori educ, NZ Coun Educ Res, 68-69; dir, Ling Inst of Ling Soc Am, 77. **MEMBERSHIPS** Ling Soc Am; Polynesian Soc. **RESEARCH** Language acquisition; Micronesian languages; Austronesian linguistics. **SELECTED PUBLICATIONS** Auth, Marshallese Phonology, Oceanic Ling, 68; Spoken Marshallese, Univ Hawaii, 69; contribr, Current Trends in Linguistics: Linguistics in Oceania, Mouton, The Hague, 71; auth, Linguistic factors in Maori education, NZ Coun Educ Res, 71; Parallelisms in the Morphophonemics of Several Micronesian Languages, Oceanic Ling, 73; coauth, A Ulithian Grammar, Australian Nat Univ, 73; Marshallese-English Dictionary, Univ Hawaii, 76; contribr, Studies in Pacific Languages and Cultures in Honour of Bruce Biggs, 81. **CONTACT ADDRESS** Dept of Ling, Univ of Hawaii Manoa, 1890 E West Rd, Honolulu, HI, 96822-2318. **EMAIL** bender@hawaii.edu

BENDER, ERNEST
PERSONAL Born 01/02/1919, Buenos Aires, Argentina **DISCIPLINE** INDOLOGY **EDUCATION** Temple Univ, AB, 41; Univ Pa, PhD(Orient studies), 47. **CAREER** Indo-Aryan linguist, 46-50, asst prof, 50-58, from res assoc prof to assoc prof Indo-Aryan lang & lit, 58-67, PROF INO-ARYAN LANG & LIT, UNIV PA, 67-, Am Coun Learned Soc fel, 47-48; Rockefeller Found fel, 47-48; Am Philos Soc grant, 50; Guggenheim Found fel, 55-56; assoc ed, J Am Orient Soc, 58-63, actg chief ed, 64-, coordr, Coun Sanskrit Stud, 78-; consult, Nat Endowment for Humanities, 68-69 & 72-, sr fel, 72-73; consult, Inst Advan Stud World Relig, 71-, travel grant, 72; fel, Bhandarkar Orient Res Inst, India, 72-; consult, NDEA; consult & contribr, Merriam Webster, Encycl Britannica & Grolier. **MEMBERSHIPS** Ling Soc Am; Ling Soc India; Asn Asian Stud; fel Royal Asiatic Soc; Int Asn Sanskrit Stud. **RESEARCH** Indo-Aryan languages and literature; language and social structure; medieval Indian illustrated manuscripts and texts. **SELECTED PUBLICATIONS** Auth, The Trials and Tribulations of A Text Kalyan 'Dhanyavilasa', J of the Amer Oriental Soc, Vol 0115, 95. **CONTACT ADDRESS** Univ of Pa, 820 Williams Hall CU, Philadelphia, PA, 19104.

BENDER, MARVIN LIONEL
PERSONAL Born 08/18/1934, Mechanicsburg, PA, m, 1956, 2 children **DISCIPLINE** LINGUISTICS, ANTHROPOLOGY **EDUCATION** Dartmouth Col, BA, 56, MA, 58; Univ Tex, Austing, PhD(ling), 68. **CAREER** Master math, Adisadel Col, Cape Coast, Ghana, 59-60; res assoc, Educ Res Coun, Greater Cleveland, 60-62; asst prof math, Haile Selassie Univ, 62-65; proj specialist ling, Ford Found 68-69; asst prof math, Haile Selassie Univ, 69-70; vis asst prof ling, Stanford Univ, 70-71; asst prof, 71-76, ASSOC PROF ANTHROP, SOUTHERN ILL UNIV, CARBONDALE, 76-, Ford Found consult, EAfrica, 69-70; prin investr, NSF grant, 73-75; ed, Nilo-Sahelian Newsletter. **MEMBERSHIPS** Ling Soc Am; fel Am Anthrop Asn; Am Fed Teachers. **RESEARCH** Comparative and historial linguistics; descriptive and theoretical linguistics; Afroasiatic and Ethiopian languages; Nilo-Sahelian languages. **SELECTED PUBLICATIONS** Auth, Nubians and the Nubian Language in Contemporary Egypt in A Case of Cultural and Linguistic Contact, J of Pidgin and Creole Lang(s), Vol 0008, 93; Nominal and Verbal Plurality in Chadic, Word--J of the Int Ling Assoc, Vol 0044, 93; Toward A Typology of European Languages, Word-J of the Int Ling Assoc, Vol 0044, 93; A Concise Introduction to Syntactic Theory the Government Binding Approach, Word--J of the Int Ling Assoc, Vol 0045, 94; Language and Soc in Africa in the Theory and Practice of Sociolinguistics, Word-J of the Int Ling Assoc, Vol 0046, 95; English-Kanuri Dictionary in English, Kanuri, Word-J of the Int Ling Assoc, Vol 0047, 96; Loan Verbs in Maltese - A Descriptive and Comparative Study, J of Pidgin and Creole Lang(s), Vol 0012, 97. **CONTACT ADDRESS** Dept Foreign Languages & Liter, Southern Ill Univ, Carbondale, IL, 62901.

BENDER, TODD K.
PERSONAL Born 01/08/1936, Stark County, OH, m, 1958, 2 children **DISCIPLINE** ENGLISH, CLASSICAL LANGUAGES **EDUCATION** Kenyon Col, BA, 58; Stanford Univ, PhD(class lang & English), 62. **CAREER** Instr English, Stanford Univ, 61-62; instr, Dartmouth Col, 62-63; asst prof, Univ Va, 63-65; assoc prof, 65-73, PROF ENGLISH, UNIV WIS, MADISON, 73-, Am Coun Learned Soc grant-in-aid, Oxford Univ, 63 & fel, Bibliot Nat, Paris, 65-66; Am Philos Soc grant, Paris, 69; vis prof, World Campus Prog, 73; Fulbright lectr, Univ Athens, Greece, 78-79. **MEMBERSHIPS** MLA. **RESEARCH** Nineteenth century English and European literature; Homeric Greek; computational linguistics. **SELECTED PUBLICATIONS** Auth, Conrad,Joseph and the Fictions of Skepticism, Anq--A Quart J of Short Articles Notes and Rev(s), Vol 0006, 93; Conrad Existentialism, Anq--A Quart J of Short Articles Notes and Rev(s), Vol 0006, 93; Hopkins in A Literary Biography, 19th-Century Lit, Vol 0049, 94; Representing Modernist Texts in Editing As Interpretation, Engl Lang Notes, Vol 0031, 94; The Invention of the West in Conrad, Joseph and the Double-Mapping of Europe and Empire, Clio--A J of Lit Hist and the Philos of Hist, Vol 0025, 96; Hopkins Against Hist, Clio--A J of Lite Hist and the Philos of Hist, Vol 0026, 97. **CONTACT ADDRESS** Dept of English, Univ of Wis, Madison, WI, 53706.

BENICHOU, PAUL
PERSONAL Born 09/19/1908, Tlemcen, Algeria, m, 1929, 1 child **DISCIPLINE** FRENCH LITERATURE **EDUCATION** Univ Paris, Sorbonne, Lic es Let, 27; Ecole Normale Superieure, Univ Paris, Agrege des Let, 30, Dr es Lett, 71. **CAREER** Prof lettres, Lycee Janson de Sailly, Paris, 37-40; prof French lit, Inst Francais, Buenos Aires, 43-49; prof lettres, Lycee Condorcet, Paris, 49-58; PROF FRENCH LIT, HARVARD UNIV, 59-79. **MEMBERSHIPS** Soc d'Hist Litteraire de la France; Am Acad Arts & Sci. **RESEARCH** French literature; Spanish literature, especially the romancero. **SELECTED PUBLICATIONS** Auth, The Correspondence of Vigny,Alfred,De, Vol 2 August 1830-September 1835, Revue D Histoire Lit De La Fr, Vol 0092, 92. **CONTACT ADDRESS** 79 rue N-D des Camps, Paris, ., 75006.

BENOUIS, MUSTAPHA KEMAL
PERSONAL Born 05/24/1936, Descartes, Algeria, m, 1961, 3 children **DISCIPLINE** FRENCH LANGUAGE & LITERATURE **EDUCATION** Univ Toulouse, CELG, 60, Lic es Lett, 63, Dipl Etudes Super, 64; Univ Ill, Urbana, PhD(French), 71. **CAREER** Prof hist geog, Course Brossolette, Ain Temouchent, Algeria, 56-57; lectr French, Campbell Col, Belfast, 61-62; prof English, Lycee d'Etat de Mazamet, France, 64-65; teaching asst French, Univ Ill, Urbana, 65-68, instr, 68-69; from instr to asst prof, Univ Tenn, Knoxville, 69-72; asst prof, 72-76, assoc prof & chmn div, 76-81, Prof French & Chmn Europ Lang & Lit, Univ Hawaii, Manoa, 81-, Assoc ed, Fr Contemp Civilization, 75-; Nat Endowment for Humanities fel, Inst Contemporary Fr Cult, 81. **MEMBERSHIPS** AAUP; Am Asn Teachers Fr; Am Transl Asn; Centre d'Etudes des Litteratures d'Expression Francaise. **RESEARCH** French Renaissance; French civilization, stylistics. **SELECTED PUBLICATIONS** Auth, The Thorny Business of Name Genre in Some Special Cases, Fr Rev, Vol 0067, 94. **CONTACT ADDRESS** Dept of European Lang & Lit, Univ of Hawaii Manoa, 1890 E West Rd, Honolulu, HI, 96822-2362.

BENSKY, ROGER DANIEL
DISCIPLINE FRENCH LITERATURE **EDUCATION** Univ Western Australia, BA, MA; Univ Paris, PhD. **CAREER** Eng Dept, Georgetown Univ **RESEARCH** Modern theater; mysticism. **SELECTED PUBLICATIONS** Auth, pubs on symbolism, thematic of puppetry and contemporary dramatists. **CONTACT ADDRESS** French Dept, Georgetown Univ, 37th and O St, Washington, DC, 20057.

BENSON, DOUGLAS KEITH
PERSONAL Born 06/08/1944, Marysville, CA, m, 1965, 2 children **DISCIPLINE** SPANISH LITERATURE & CULTURE **EDUCATION** NMex State Univ, BA, 66; Univ NMex, MA, 68, PhD(Spanish lit), 73. **CAREER** Chmn mod lang, Hastings Col, 69-80; asst prof, 80-82, Assoc Prof Spanish Lang & Lit, Kans State Univ, 82-. **MEMBERSHIPS** Am Asn Teachers of Span & Port. **RESEARCH** Contemporary Spanish poetry (1950-1970); teaching culture in language classrooms; Spanish Amer literature and culture. **SELECTED PUBLICATIONS** Auth, Novisimos, Post Novisimos and Classics, the Poetry of the 80s in Spain, Anales De La Literatura Espanola Contemporanea, Vol 0018, 93; Stud in 20th-Century Literature, Anales De La Lit Espanola Contemporanea, Vol 0018, 93; 'Album in Versos De Juventud', Hispania--A J Devoted to the Tchg of Span and Port, Vol 0077, 94; 'Album - Versos De Juventud', Hispania--A J Devoted to the Tchg of Span and Porte, Vol 0077, 94; The Photograph of A Shadow, the Generation of Poets of the 1950s, Anales De La Lit Espanola Contemporanea, Vol 0020, 95; The Poetics of Self Consciousness in 20th-Century Spanish Poetry, Anales De La Lit Espanola Contemporanea, Vol 0020, 95; Album in Verse For Young People, Hispania--A J Devoted to the Tchg of Span and Port, Vol 0079, 96; Rhythm in Guillen,Jorge 'Cantico', Anales De La Lit Espanola Contemporanea, Vol 0021, 96; Album in Verse For Young-People, Hispania--A J Devoted to the Tchg of Span and Port, Vol 0079, 96. **CONTACT ADDRESS** Kansas State Univ, 233 Harvey Dr, Manhattan, KS, 66506.

BENSON, MORTON
PERSONAL Born 12/13/1924, Newark, NJ, m, 1955 **DISCIPLINE** FOREIGN LANGUAGES, LEXICOGRAPHY **EDUCATION** NY Univ, BA, 47; Univ Grenoble, Cert, 48; Univ Pa, PhD(Russ), 54. **CAREER** Asst prof Russ & Ger, Ohio Univ, 54-60; PROF SLAVIC LANG, UNIV PA, 60-, Vis lectr Princeton Univ, 64 & Columbia Univ, 65; mem joint comt East Europ, Am Coun Learned Soc, 71-73. **MEMBERSHIPS** MLA; Am Asn Teachers Slavic & East Europ Lang (pres, 64); Ling Soc Am. **RESEARCH** Russian; Serbocroatian; Slavic linguistics. **SELECTED PUBLICATIONS** Auth, On Russian Names, Russ Ling(s), Vol 0016, 92; A Notes on Russian Orthography, Slavic and E Europ J, Vol 0037, 93; A Supplementary Russian English Dictionary, Slavic and E Europ J, Vol 0037, 93; Encounters With Fugard the 'Blood Knot' in Native of the Karoo, 20th Century Lit, Vol 0039, 93; A Notes on Russian Orthography, Slavic and E Europ J, Vol 0037, 93; Pikes-Peak Vision in the Broadmoor Art Academy, 1919-1945, NMex Hist Rev, Vol 0068, 93; Schoenberg Private Program For the 'String Quartet in D Minor, Op.7', J Musicol, Vol 0011, 93; A Supplementary Russian English Dictionary, Slavic and E Europ J, Vol 0037, 93; Eisenhower, Dwight, D. and the West, J West, Vol 0034, 95; Defining Dictionary of the Russian Language, Slavic and E Europ J, Vol 0039, 95; Defining Dictionary of the Russian Language - Slavic and E Europ J, Vol 0039, 95; Rs-A Concordance to the Dictionaries of Modern Russian, Russ Ling(s), Vol 0019, 95; Art, Hist and Politics in the Former Yugoslavia in An Interview With Benson,Michael, Cineaste, Vol 0022, 96; Retracing Major Long, Stephen ,H. 1820 Expedition in the Itinerary and Botany, Montana-Mag of Western Hist, Vol 0047, 97; Tear Gas and Etiquette A Report on Censorship and Fear at the Seoul Documentary Film and-Video Festival Special Reference to Hinton/Gordon the 'Gate of Heavenly Peace', Sight and Sound, Vol 0007, 97; Market Stalinism Experiences at the 2nd Annual Seoul Documentary Film and Video Festival, Sight and Sound, Vol 0007, 97. **CONTACT ADDRESS** Dept of Slavic Lang, Univ of Pennsylvania, Philadelphia, PA, 19104.

BENSON, RENATE
PERSONAL Germany **DISCIPLINE** GERMAN STUDIES **EDUCATION** Univ Cologne, 61-62; Univ Montreal, LL, 65; McGill Univ, PhD, 70. **CAREER** Lectr to PROF, GERMAN STUDIES, UNIV GUELPH, 67-. **HONORS AND AWARDS** Distinguished Prof Award, Col Arts, 90. **MEMBERSHIPS** MLA; CAUTG; OATG; Hum Asn. **SELECTED PUBLICATIONS** Auth, Erich Kastner, Studien zu seinem Werk, 73; auth, Aspects of Love in Anne Hebert's Short Stories, in J Can Fiction, 79; auth, German Expressionist Drama: Ernst Toller and Georg Kaiser, 84. **CONTACT ADDRESS** Dept of German Studies, Univ Guelph, Guelph, ON, N1G 2W1. **EMAIL** rbenson@langlit.arts.uoguelph.ca

BENTLEY, ERIC
PERSONAL Born 09/14/1916, England, m, 2 children **DISCIPLINE** DRAMA, COMPARATIVE LITERATURE **EDUCATION** Oxford Univ, BA, 38, BLitt, 39; Yale Univ, PhD, 41. **CAREER** Matthews prof dramatic lit, Columbia Univ, 54-69; CORNELL PROF THEATRE, STATE UNIV NY BUFFALO, 77-82, Guggenheim fel, 48-49 & 67-68; Charles Eliot Norton prof poetry, Harvard Univ, 60-61; ed, Works of Brecht, Grove Press, 60-67; Ford Found artist in residence, Berlin, 64-65. **HONORS AND AWARDS** Longview Award, 60; George Nathan Prize, 67; Obie, 78; inducted into the Theatre Hall of Fame, New York, 98., DFA, Univ Wis, 75; DLitt, Univ East Anglia, UK, 79. **MEMBERSHIPS** Fel Am Acad Arts & Sci; PEN Club; Am Acad of Arts and Letters; **RESEARCH** Literary record albums; poetry and songs. **SELECTED PUBLICATIONS** Auth, The Life of the Drama, 64; The Theatre of Commitment, 67; Theatre of War, 72; The Recantation, 72; Are You Now Or Have You Ever Been, 72; Rallying Cries, Three Plays, New Repub Bks, 77; Lord Alfred's Lover (play), Can Theatre ,Rev, 78; The Brecht Commentaries, Grove Press, 81; auth, The Kleist Variations, 81; auth, Monstrous Martyrdoms, 85; auth, Bentley on Brecht, 98. **CONTACT ADDRESS** 194 Riverside Dr, Ste 4E, New York, NY, 10025-7259.

BEREAUD, JACQUES
DISCIPLINE FRENCH **EDUCATION** l'Universite de Lille, PhD, 64. **CAREER** Prof; fac, Cornell Univ, 66-; chemn dept, 81-84 and actg ch, 91-92; dir Educo, Cornell-Duke prog in Paris, 92-93; coordr, Lang Prog, 66-; dir, Undergrad Stud, 84-. **RESEARCH** Pedagogy of foreign language teaching; contemporary French culture and civilization. **SELECTED PUBLICATIONS** Auth, Nouveaux points de vue, by J. Noblitt, DC Heath, 78; Un memoire inedit de Defauconpret Revue du Nord Lille, 65; La traduction en France a l'epoque romantique Comparative Litterature Studies, 71; La chanson francaise depuis mai 1968, Fr Rev, 88; coauth, Appreciations du francais moderne, an advanced integrated French text, Holt, Rinehart and Winston, 72. **CONTACT ADDRESS** Dept of Romance Studies, Cornell Univ, 283 Goldwin Smith Hall, Ithaca, NY, 14853. **EMAIL** jb73@cornell.edu

BERGEN, ROBERT D.
PERSONAL Born 05/18/1954, Lawrence, KS, m, 1979, 1 child **DISCIPLINE** OLD TESTAMENT, BIBLICAL HEBREW **EDUCATION** Hardin Simmons Univ, BA, 76; Southwestern Baptist Theol Sem, Mdiv, 79, PhD, 86. **CAREER** Assoc Prof of OT and Biblical Lang, 86-98, Hannibal-LaGrange Coll. **MEMBERSHIPS** SBL, ETS, Inst of Biblical Res. **RESEARCH** Discourse Linguistics. **SELECTED PUBLICATIONS** Auth, 1,2 Samuel, New American Commentary, vol 7, 96; 1,2, Samuel, Shepherd's Notes, 98; Ed of Biblical Hebrew and Discourse Linguistics, 94. **CONTACT ADDRESS** Hannibal-LaGrange Col, 2800 Palmyra Rd, Hannibal, MO, 63401. **EMAIL** bbergen@hlg.edu

BERGHAHN, KLAUS L
PERSONAL Born 08/05/1937, Dusseldorf, West Germany, m, 1967, 1 child **DISCIPLINE** GERMAN LITERATURE **EDUCATION** Univ Munster, Staatsexamen, 63, PhD (Ger), 67. **CAREER** Tutor Ger, Univ Munster, 64-67; from asst prof to assoc prof, 67-73, Prof GER, Univ WIS-MADISON, 73-, Vis prof, Inst Res Humanities, 72-73, Romnes fel, Univ Wis-Madison, 75. **MEMBERSHIPS** Schiller Soc; MLA; Am Lessing Soc; Am Asn Teachers Ger. **RESEARCH** German literature since 1750, literary theory and criticism, methodology and history of Germanistik. **SELECTED PUBLICATIONS** Auth, Nation and Nationalism in Schiller Essay Deutsche Grosse and his Drama Wilhelm Tell, Zeitschrift Germ, Vol 0005, 95; Destructional Forms of Absolutized Moral Teachings in the Early Works of Schiller, Friedrich, Zeitschrift Germ, Vol 0005, 95; Life Signs--Aphorisms and Marginalia, Germ Quart, Vol 0067, 94. **CONTACT ADDRESS** 4118 Hiawatha Dr, Madison, WI, 52711.

BERGMANN, FRANK
PERSONAL Born 01/20/1941, Markneukirchen, Germany, m, 4 children **DISCIPLINE** AMERICAN & COMPARATIVE LITERATURE **EDUCATION** Univ AR, MA, 66; Eberhard-Karls-Universitaet Tuebingen, GER, DPhil(Am lit), 69. **CAREER** Instr lang, KS Wesleyan Univ, 65-66; Wiss asst Am lit, Am Studies Dept at Tuebingen, WGer, 66-68 & Univ Frankfurt, WGer, 68-69; asst prof English & Ger, 69-73, chm div humanities, 73-76, assoc prof, 73-79, prof English & Ger, Utica Col, Syracuse Univ, 79-, assoc dean for humanities, 91-96, assoc dean for arts and sciences, 96-, acting dean of the fac, 98; mem, vis comt mod foreign lang & lit, Lehigh Univ, 74-78; member, fac ed comm, Syracuse Univ Press, 94-98; series ed, New York Classics reprints, Syracuse Univ Press, 86-; member, nat screening comm for Fulbright graduate study awards to Germany, 95-96. **HONORS AND AWARDS** Valedictorian, Ravensburg, 61; Fulbright scholarship to Hamilton Col, 61-62; Dr Phil, Magna Cum Laude, 69; Distinguished Teaching Award, Utica Col, 85; Clark Res Award, Utica Col, 94. **MEMBERSHIPS** AAHE; ALSC; Cooper Soc; Arthur Miller Soc; MLA; NYSHA. **RESEARCH** American literature 1861-1914; literature of upstate New York; fairy tales and literary fantasy. **SELECTED PUBLICATIONS** Auth, The Worthy Gentleman of Democracy: John William De Forest and the American Dream, Carl Winter Univ, Heidelberg, Ger, 71; Robert Grant, Twayne Publ, 82; ed and auth, Upstate Literature: Essays in Memory of Thomas F O'Donnell, Syracuse Univ Press, 85 (John Ben Snow manuscript prize; certificate of merit, Regional Conference of Hist Agencies, NY State). **CONTACT ADDRESS** Div Arts and Sciences, Utica Col of Syracuse Univ, 1600 Burrstone Rd, Utica, NY, 13502-4892. **EMAIL** fbergmann@utica.ucsu.edu

BERGREN, ANN L.T.
DISCIPLINE CLASSICAL PHILOLOGY **EDUCATION** Wellesley Col, BA, 61-65; Univ Iowa, MA, 65-68; Harvard Univ, PhD, 68-73. **CAREER** Tchg fel, Harvard Univ, 71; instr, Wellesley Col, 72; asst prof, Princeton Univ, 72-79; summer vis asst prof, Univ Iowa, 73; vis asst prof, Stanford Univ, 76; vis prof, Harvard Univ, 93; adj prof, South Calif Inst of Arch, 87-; PROF, CLASS, UCLA, 79-. **HONORS AND AWARDS** Fel(s), Ctr Hellenic Stud, 76-77; Amer Coun of Learned Soc, 84; Chicago Inst for Arch and Urbanism, 89-90; Hum Res Inst, Univ Calif-Irvine, 91; Hon(s) Collegium Fac Recognition award, 86; distinguished tchg award, Univ Calif, LA, 88; award for excellence in the tchg of classics, Amer Philol Assn, 88., Ed bd(s), Amer Philol Assn, 80-84; Helios, Jour of the Class Assn of the Southwestern US, 79-82; Univ Calif Publ in Class Stud, 83-88. **RESEARCH** Architecture. **SELECTED PUBLICATIONS** Auth, "Letter to Jennifer Bloomer on Architecture and the Feminine," ANY Architecture New York, "Architecture and the Feminine: Mop-Up Work," 94; "The (Re)Marriage of Penelope and Odysseus," Architecture Gender Philosophy, Assemblage, A Critical Jour of Arch and Design Cult 21, 93. **CONTACT ADDRESS** Dept of Classics, Univ Calif, PO Box 951436, Los Angeles, CA, 90095-1436.

BERGSTROM, ANNA
PERSONAL Born 03/25/1961, Sweden **DISCIPLINE** FRENCH, FRENCH EDUCATION, SPANISH **EDUCATION** Univ Wis-Madison, BA, 83, MA, 86; Penn State Univ, PhD, 95. **CAREER** Vis lectr, Dept Fr & Ital, Ind Univ, 93-95; ASST PROF, DEPT FOR LANG, LIT, UNIV DEL, 95-. **HONORS AND AWARDS** Mortar Board Outstanding Prof Award Distinction, 98 **MEMBERSHIPS** Am Asn Appl Ling, Europ Second Lang Acquisition, Am Asn Teachers of Fr, Del Coun on the Teaching of For Lang. **RESEARCH** Appl ling, second lang acquisition, acquisition of temporality. **SELECTED PUBLICATIONS** Auth, L'influence des distinctions aspectuelles sur l'acquisition des temps en francais langue etrangere," Acquisition et Interaction en Langue Etrangere, No. 9; coauth, "Tense and Aspect in SLA and FLL: Learner Narratives in English (SL) and French (FL)," Can Modern Lang Rev, No. 52; review, "Semantique de la temporalite en fracais," The French Reivew, Apr 98. **CONTACT ADDRESS** Dept For Lang & Lit, Univ of Delaware, 326 Smith Hall, Newark, DE, 19716. **EMAIL** bergstro@udel.edu

BERKELEY, ISTVAN S.N.
DISCIPLINE COGNITIVE SCIENCE **EDUCATION** Univ Leeds, England, BA, 87; Univ Alberta, Can, MA, 90, PhD, 97. **CAREER** Inst, Athabasca Univ, 95; res asst, Univ Alberta, 94-96; lectr, 96-97; ASST PROF, UNIV SOUTHWESTERN LA, 97-. **CONTACT ADDRESS** Univ of Southwestern Louisiana, PO Box 43770, Lafayette, LA, 70504. **EMAIL** istvan@usl.edu

BERKLEY, CONSTANCE E. GRESHAM
PERSONAL Born 11/12/1931, Washington, DC **DISCIPLINE** AFRICAN LITERATURE, ISLAMIC LITERATURE **EDUCATION** Columbia University, BA, 1971, MA, 1972; New York University, Dept of Near Eastern Language & Literature, PhD, 1979. **CAREER** Fordham University, Black Drama, 1971-72; Vassar College, literature lecturer, 1972-75; Ramapo College, African literature, 1976; Fordham University, asst professor, African/Afro-American & Islamic literature, starting 1979; Vassar College, Studies Program, lecturer of Africana Studies, currently. **HONORS AND AWARDS** One of the founders of the Sudan Studies Assn, 1981; Editor of the SSA Newsletter; Specialist in the literature of the famous Sudanese writer, Tayeb Salih; Invited participant in special tribute to Tayeb Salih at Asilah's 17th Season in Asilah Morocco, 1994; Fulbright Lecturer at Ahfad Univ for Women, Omdurman, Sudan, 1990 **MEMBERSHIPS** Harlem Writer's Guild, 1961-; NEC Dramatists Workshop Affiliate, 1969-; New York State Council of the Arts, lecturer; Intl Poetry Society; Assn Study Afro-American Life & History; Middle Eastern Studies Assn; bd dir, Natl Council of Soviet American Friendship, 1968; African Literature Assn; New York African Studies Assn; contributing editor, American Dialog, 1967; guest lecturer, "Islam in Africa," CBS/NYU Sunrise Semester Program, "1400 Years of Islam," 1980; guest lecturer, New School for Social Research, 1980-81. **SELECTED PUBLICATIONS** Poetry published in several anthologies; auth, Black American Writers Past & Present; auth, Biography of Living Black Writers, Fisk University; numerous articles concerning Sudanese literature. **CONTACT ADDRESS** Program in Africana Studies, Vassar Col, 124 Raymond Ave, Poughkeepsie, NY, 12601-6121.

BERKMAN, LEONARD
PERSONAL Born 07/21/1938, New York, NY, m, 1962, 2 children **DISCIPLINE** THEATRE, SPEECH **EDUCATION** Columbia Univ, BA, 60; Yale Univ, MFA, 63, DFA(Playwriting, Dramatic Lit & Criticism), 70. **CAREER** Instr English, Univ Tex, El Paso, 63-64; instr Playwriting, Univ Mass, 68-69; asst prof Theatre & Speech, 69-78, assoc prof Theatre, Smith Col, 78-83; prof, 83-94; Anne Hesseltine Hoyt prof of Theatre, 94. **HONORS AND AWARDS** Smith College Disting Teacher Award, 92; Charis Medal for Teaching, 94. **MEMBERSHIPS** Am Theatre Asn. **RESEARCH** Nineteenth and 20th century European drama; American drama; Afro-American and African

drama; Latino and Latin American Drama; Canadian Drama; Australian Drama. **SELECTED PUBLICATIONS** Auth, Four books on rock, Mass Rev, Spring 71; Really, Now (play), Publ Broadcasting Syst, 71; Two Demon Plays, Can Broadcasting Corp, 73; Off-off-off Broadway, in Massachusetts, Magic Dust, Winter 78; Viola! Rape in Technicolor, Smith, 2/78; Jane Addams Mem Theatre, Chicago, 3/78; Til the Beatles reunite, WTTT, 3/79; Sleeping Through the End of the World: The Plays and Poems of Rochelle Owens, Parnaussus, Spring 82; I Won't Go See A Play Called A Parent's Worst Nightmare, NY Stage & Film Co, Poughkeepsie, NY, 95; Quits, NYU Experimental Theatre Wing, NYC, 98. **CONTACT ADDRESS** Dept Theatre, Smith Col, 98 Green St, Northampton, MA, 01063-0001. **EMAIL** lberkman@sophia.smith.edu

BERKVAM, MICHAEL
DISCIPLINE FRENCH LITERATURE **EDUCATION** Univ Wis, PhD, 73. **CAREER** Assoc prof. **SELECTED PUBLICATIONS** Auth, Correspondence and Collected Papers of Pierre Michel Hennin, 79; pubs on Proust, Sartre; co-auth, Eighteenth-Century Cities: A Panorama. **CONTACT ADDRESS** Dept of French and Italian, Indiana Univ, Bloomington, 300 N Jordan Ave, Bloomington, IN, 47405.

BERLIN, CHARLES
PERSONAL Born 03/17/1936, Boston, MA, m, 1965, 2 children **DISCIPLINE** HEBRAIC AND JUDAIC LITERATURE **EDUCATION** Hebrew Teachers Col, BJEd, 56, MHL, 59; Harvard Univ, AB, 58, AM, 59, PhD, 63; Simmons Col, MS, 64. **CAREER** Lectr mod Hebrew, 62-65, LEE M FRIEDMAN BIBLIOGR IN JUDAICA, COL LIBR, HARVARD UNIV, 62-, Consult, Univ Fla Libr, 73, Univ Tex Libr, 74, New York Pub Libr, 75 and Emory Univ Libr, 76. **MEMBERSHIPS** Asn Jewish Libr (vpres, 67-68, pres, 68-69); Asn Jewish Studies (treas, 70-72, exec secy, 72-). **RESEARCH** Bibliography of Hebraica and Judaica; Jewish history. **SELECTED PUBLICATIONS** Auth, Digital Imaging at the Harvard Library--The Judaica Divisions Israeli Poster Image Database, Harvard Libr Bull, Vol 0005, 94. **CONTACT ADDRESS** Harvard Col Libr, Harvard Univ, Cambridge, MA, 02138.

BERLIN, NETTA
DISCIPLINE LATIN AND GREEK LANGUAGE AND LITERATURE **EDUCATION** Wellesley Col, BA, 84; Univ MI, MA, 88, PhD, 93. **CAREER** Asst prof, 93-, Tulane Univ. **RESEARCH** Epic poetry, mythology, ancient literary criticism. **SELECTED PUBLICATIONS** Auth, War and Remembrance: Aeneid 12.554-60, and Aeneas' Memory of Troy, Amer Jour Philol 119, 98. **CONTACT ADDRESS** Dept of Class Stud, Tulane Univ, 6823 St Charles Ave, New Orleans, LA, 70118. **EMAIL** nberlin@mailhost.tcs.tulane.edu

BERNARDO, ALDO SISTO
PERSONAL Born 05/17/1920, Italy, m, 1942, 3 children **DISCIPLINE** ROMANCE PHILOLOGY **EDUCATION** Brown Univ, AM, 47; Harvard Univ, PhD (Romance philol), 50. **CAREER** Instr French and Ital, Triple Cities Col, Syracuse, 49-50; from asst prof to assoc prof Romance lang, State Univ NY Binghamton, 50-58, prof Ital, 58-73, chmn humanities div, 59-73, co-dir ctr medieval and early Renaissance studies, 66-73; pres, Verrazzano Col, 73-75; PROF ITAL AND COMP LIT, STATE UNIV NY BINGHAMTON, 75-, Fulbright res grant, Rome, 55-56; Am Coun Learned Soc res grant, 58; Guggenheim fel, 64-65; mem nat screening comt, Fulbright-Hays Act, Italy and Greece, 66-67; chmn univ awards comt, Res Found State Univ NY, 68-; sr fel, Ctr Medieval and Early Renaissance Studies, State Univ NY Binghamton, 75-; DISTINGUISHED SERV PROF, 79-; Nat Endowment for Humanities transl grant, 79-80. **MEMBERSHIPS** MLA; Am Asn Teachers Ital; Mediaeval Acad Am; Dante Soc Am. **RESEARCH** Computer-aided translations; Petrarch; mediaeval esthetics. **SELECTED PUBLICATIONS** Auth, Petrarch Remedies for Fortune Fair and Foul, Renaissance Quart, Vol 0046, 93. **CONTACT ADDRESS** Dept of Romance Lang, State Univ NY, Binghamton, NY, 13901.

BERND, CLIFFORD ALBRECHT
PERSONAL Born 05/14/1929, Bronxville, NY, m, 1972, 2 children **DISCIPLINE** GERMAN LITERATURE **EDUCATION** NY Univ, BA, 50; Univ Md, MFS, 52; Univ Heidelberg, PhD , 58. **CAREER** From instr to asst prof Ger, Princeton Univ, 58-64; assoc prof, 64-68, chmn dept, 65-76, PROF GER, UNIV CALIF, DAVIS, 68-, German Foreign Off Exchange fel, 54-56; mem, Int Fed Mod Lang and Lit; rev ed, German Quart, 64-68; Am Philos Soc Grant, 65; Humanities Inst awards, Univ Calif, 66 and 71; Fulbright res scholar, Kiel, Ger, 68-69; Fritz Thyssen Found fel, 72; vis fel Ger lit, Univ Leicester, 77. **MEMBERSHIPS** Schiller Ges; Goethe Ges; Kleist Ges; Holderlin Ges; corresp mem Storm Ges. **RESEARCH** German literature of the 17th, 18th and 19th centuries. **SELECTED PUBLICATIONS** Auth, Storm,Theodor and Groth, Klaus Correspondence, J Eng Ger Philol, Vol 0092, 93; Grillparzer, Franz--A Century of Criticism, J Eng Ger Philol, Vol 0096, 97; Grillparzer, Franz--A Central Figure in the Awakening of a New Austrian Consciousness in the 19th Century, Mod Austrian Lit, Vol 0028, 95; Phases of Grillparzer Scholarship in America, 1821-1971, Mod Austrian Lit, Vol 0028, 95. **CONTACT ADDRESS** Dept of Ger, Univ of Calif, Davis, CA, 95616-5200.

BERNIER, PAUL
DISCIPLINE COGNITIVE SCIENCE AND PHILOSOPHY OF MIND **EDUCATION** Univ Montreal, PhD. **CAREER** Prof. **RESEARCH** Philosophy of language. **SELECTED PUBLICATIONS** Pub(s), in Mind and Lang; Quebec Stud; Philos of Sci. **CONTACT ADDRESS** Dept of Philos, Concordia Univ, Montreal, 1455 de Maisonneuve W, Montreal, PQ, H3G 1M8. **EMAIL** pbernie@vax2.concordia.ca

BERNINGHAUSEN, JOHN
DISCIPLINE CHINESE **EDUCATION** Univ Minn, BA, 65; Stanford Univ, MA, 68, PhD, 80. **CAREER** Charles A. Dana prof & dept chem; spec lang training, Mandarin Training Ctr, Taipei, 63; CIC Far Eastern Lang Inst, Ohio State Univ, 65; Inter-Univ Prog, Taipei, 65-66; CIC Far Eastern Lang Inst, Ind Univ, 69; Inter-Univ Prog, Taipei, 70-71; dean, Middlebury Chinese Sch, 88-94; chem, Div For Lang, Middlebury Col, 91-94; actg dir, Lang Sch, Middlebury Col, 90-91; chem, Div For Lang, Middlebury Col, 81-86; co-founder & 1st chem, interdisciplinary major in East Asian Stud, 79-84; established a Chinese lang prog, Middlebury Col, 76-; dir, Chinese Lang Prog, Univ Vermont, 73-76, founded the UVM Chinese Prog, full-time instr; Engl Lang Tchr, Extramural Prog, Chinese Unive Hong Kong, 71-72. **MEMBERSHIPS** Asn Asian Stud; Chinese Lang Teachers Asn & Nat Asn Scholars. **SELECTED PUBLICATIONS** Auth, A Great Leap Backward, Middlebury Col Mag, 89; Modern Chinese Short Stories, ITEMS, joure Soc Sci Res and Coun, 83; coauth, Chinese Breakthrough, Cheng and Tsui Co, Boston, 95; transl, Literature and Life, Stanford UP, 96; 3 dissident 1979 short stories, Locks, Cats, & Fire, under the title of Three Professors, 84; We Must Still Prepare for a Long and Determined Struggle, A 1949 speech in commemoration of the 30th anniversary of the May Fourth Movement by Mao Dun, in Lit in Revolutionary China, 80. **CONTACT ADDRESS** Dept of Chinese, Middlebury Col, Middlebury, VT, 05753.

BERNSTEIN, ECKHARD RICHARD
PERSONAL Born 08/05/1938, Grimma, Germany, m, 1965, 2 children **DISCIPLINE** GERMAN & COMPARATIVE LITERATURE **EDUCATION** Univ Marburg, Staatsexamen, 65, Assessorexamen, 68; Case Western Reserve Univ, PhD(comp lit), 71. **CAREER** Instr English lit, Youngstown Univ, 65-66; instr Ger lit, Lake Erie Col, 66-67; teaching asst English & Latin, Kirchain Sch, Ger, 67-68; from instr to asst prof, 70-74, assoc prof, 74-81, prof Ger Lit, Col of the Holy Cross, 81-. **MEMBERSHIPS** Am Asn Teachers Ger; Renaissance Soc of Am; Pirckheimer Gesellschaft; Gutenberg Gesellschaft. **RESEARCH** German Renaissance and Baroque literature; reception of antiquity; East German literature; German resistance to Hitler. **SELECTED PUBLICATIONS** Auth, Thomas Murner's Latin: Some Notes on the First German Aeneid, Class Folia, 72; Die Erste Deutsche Aeneis, Anton Hain, Meisenhaim, Ger, 74; From Struwwelpeter to Rotfuchs: Suggestions for Using Children's Books in Culture Classes, Unterrichtspraxis, 76; Daniel Symonis Aneis - ubersetzung, Daphnis, 78; Die Literatur des Fruhhumanismus, Metzler Verlag, Stuttgart, 78; German Humanism, Twayne Publ, 83; Ulrich von Hutten, 88; Hans Sachs, 94. **CONTACT ADDRESS** Dept of Mod Langs, Col of the Holy Cross, 1 College St, Worcester, MA, 01610-2322. **EMAIL** ebernste@holycross.edu

BERRONG, RICHARD MICHAEL
PERSONAL Born 09/20/1951, Milwaukee, WI **DISCIPLINE** SIXTEENTH CENTURY FRENCH LITERATURE **EDUCATION** Univ Va, BA, 73; Stanford Univ, MA, 74; Cornell Univ, PhD (French), 77. **CAREER** ASST PROF FRENCH, UNIV LOUISVILLE, 77- **RESEARCH** Sixteenth century French literature. **SELECTED PUBLICATIONS** Auth, Turandot as Political Fable--Puccini Last Opera, Opera Quart, Vol 0011, 95; Reading the Readers of the Gargantua--A Debate on the Nature and Purpose of Literature, Studi Francesi, Vol 0038, 94. **CONTACT ADDRESS** Dept of Mod Lang, Univ Louisville, Louisville, KY, 40208.

BERRY, MARGARET
PERSONAL Greensboro, NC **DISCIPLINE** ENGLISH, SOUTH ASIAN STUDIES **EDUCATION** St Joseph Col, BA, 44; Cath Univ, Am, MA, 50; St Johns Univ, NY, PhD (English), 56; Univ Pa, MA, 68. **CAREER** From instr to assoc prof English, St Joseph Col, 54-65; ASSOC PROF ENGLISH, JOHN CARROLL UNIV, 65-, Ford Found Asian studies grant, 63-64; NDEA fel S Asia studies, 67-68; Danforth assoc, 72; vis res scholar, Univ Mysore, fall 73; vis lectr, Univ Madurai, fall 73; fac fel, John Carroll Univ, 73. **MEMBERSHIPS** Asn Asian Studies; AAUP. **RESEARCH** Literary criticism of the English Catholic revival; Indian fiction in English. **SELECTED PUBLICATIONS** Auth, Western Plainchant--A Handbook, Mus Times, Vol 0135, 94; Childe and Australia--Archaeology, Politics and Ideas, Australian Hist Stud, Vol 0027, 96; The Service Books of the Royal Abbey of Saint Denis--Images of Ritual and Music in the Middle Ages, J Theol Stud, Vol 0047, 96. **CONTACT ADDRESS** Dept of English, John Carroll Univ, 20700 N Park Blvd, Cleveland, OH, 44118.

BERTELSEN, DALE A.
DISCIPLINE SPEECH COMMUNICATION **EDUCATION** Penn State Univ, MA, 85; PhD, 89. **CAREER** Asst prof, 88-93, assoc prof, 93-96, PROF, 96-, BLOOMSBURG UNIV; Emerging Scholar Award, 93, a nd Distinguished Serv Award, 96, from Kenneth Burke Soc; E L Hunt Scholar Award, 97; Distinguished tchg fel, 97, and Distinguished Serv Award, 98 from E Commun Asn. **MEMBERSHIPS** Nat Commun Asn; E Commun Asn; Speech Commun Asn of PA; Sppech Commun Asn of PR; Kenneth Burke Soc. **RESEARCH** Media criticism; Rhetorical criticism. **SELECTED PUBLICATIONS** Auth Media Form and Government: Democracy as an Archetypal Image in the Electronic Age, Commun Quart, 92; Kenneth Burke's Conception of Reality: The Process of Transformation and its Implic ations for Thetorical Criticism, Extensions of the Burkeian System, Univ Alabama Press, 93; Sophistry, Epistemology, and the Media Context, Philos and Rhetoric, 93; coauth Analyzing Media: Communication Technologies as Symbolic and Cognitive Systems, Guilford Publ, 96. **CONTACT ADDRESS** Dept of Commun Studies & Theatre Arts, Bloomsburg Univ of Pennsylvania, 400 E 2nd St, Bloomsburg, PA, 17815-1301. **EMAIL** dberte@planetx.bloomu.edu

BERTHOFF, ANN EVANS
PERSONAL Born 02/13/1924, New York, NY, m, 1949, 2 children **DISCIPLINE** ENGLISH, LINGUISTICS **EDUCATION** Cornell Col, Iowa, AB, 45; Radcliffe Col, AM, 48. **CAREER** Instr English, Bradford Jr Col, 48-51, Bryn Mawr Col, 51-62 and Haverford Col, 63-65; lectr, Swarthmore Col, 65-67; assoc prof, 70-78, PROF ENGLISH, UNIV MASS, BOSTON, 78-, Mem, NCTE Comn on Compos, 78-81; consult, WNET/ Channel 13, 79- and Bread Loaf Sch English, 80; dir, Nat Endowment for Humanities Summer Sem, 80. **MEMBERSHIPS** NCTE; Conf Col Compos and Commun; Col English Asn; New England Col English Asn (pres, 77-78); MLA. **RESEARCH** English pedagogy; philosophy of language; Renaissance poetry. **SELECTED PUBLICATIONS** Auth, Problem Dissolving by Triadic Means, Coll Eng, Vol 0058, 96; Percy, Walker Castaway Essays, Sewanee Rev, Vol 0102, 94; Spiritual Sites of Composing--Introductory Remarks, Coll Compos Commun, Vol 0045, 94; Assigning Places--The Function of Introductory Composition as a Cultural Discourse, Coll Eng, Vol 0056, 94; Royce Mature Ethics, Rel Lit, Vol 0025, 93; Santayana, Pragmatism and the Spiritual Life, Rel Lit, Vol 0025, 93; Sign, Textuality, World, Rel Lit, Vol 0025, 93. **CONTACT ADDRESS** 14 Thoreau St, Concord, MA, 01742.

BERTRAND DE MUNOZ, MARYSE
PERSONAL Montreal, PQ, Canada **DISCIPLINE** SPANISH LITERATURE **EDUCATION** MA (litterature espagnole), 59; LL (litterature et langues modernes) 59; Dipl del Inst de Cultura Hispanica, 60; Univ Paris, PhD, 62. **CAREER** PROF TITULAIRE DE LITTERATURE, ESPAGNOLE, UNIV MONTREAL. **MEMBERSHIPS** Asn Can Hispanists (pres, 94-96); Am Asn Tchrs Span Port; Asn Espanola de Semiotica; Asn Int Hispanistas; Asn Int Semiotica; Asn docteurs Univ Paris; Asn diplomes Univ Montreal. **SELECTED PUBLICATIONS** Auth, La guerra civile espagnole et la litterature francaise, 72; auth, La guerra civil espanola en la novela, 82, 87; auth, La comena de Camelo Jose Cela, 89; auth, La novela europea y americana y la guerra civil espanola, 94; auth, La guerra civil espanola y la literatura francesca, 95. **CONTACT ADDRESS** Dept of literature, Univ of Montreal, CP 6128, Succ Centre Ville, Montreal, PQ, H3C 3J7.

BERWALD, JEAN-PIERRE
DISCIPLINE FRENCH LITERATURE **EDUCATION** OH State Univ, PhD. **CAREER** Tchr, Univ MA Amherst. **SELECTED PUBLICATIONS** Auth, Au Courant: Teaching French with the Mass Media. **CONTACT ADDRESS** Dept of French and Italian Studies, Univ Massachusetts Amherst, Mass Ave, Amherst, MA, 01003. **EMAIL** berwald@fritaI.umass.edu

BESSETTE, GERARD
PERSONAL Born 02/25/1920, Sabrevois, Canada **DISCIPLINE** FRENCH **EDUCATION** External Classique St Croix, BA, 41; Univ Montreal, MA, 46, LittD, 50, Univ Ottawa, 82. **CAREER** From instr to asst prof French, Univ Sask, 46-51; asst prof, Duquesne Univ, 51-60; from asst prof to assoc prof, 60-79, PROF FRENCH, QUEEN'S UNIV, ONT, 79-, Can rep, poetry sect, Olympic Games, 48. **HONORS AND AWARDS** Prix Litteraire de la Prov de Que, 65; Prix du Gov General, 66 and 72; Prix Athanase David, 80. **MEMBERSHIPS** Royal Soc Can; Sov Ecrivains Can. **RESEARCH** French and French Canadian literature. **SELECTED PUBLICATIONS** Auth, The Conversion, Queens Quart, Vol 0100, 93. **CONTACT ADDRESS** Dept of French, Queens Col, CUNY, Kingston, ON, K7L 3N6.

BEST, JANICE
DISCIPLINE FRENCH LITERATURE **EDUCATION** Univ Strasbourg, PhD. **CAREER** Prof. **MEMBERSHIPS** APFUCC **RESEARCH** Nineteenth century literature **SELECTED PUBLICATIONS** Auth, Adaptation et experimentation: essai sur la methode experimentale d'Emile Zola, Jose Corti, 86; Lieux de rencontre et d'intrigue; Moralite, politique et dialogisme. **CONTACT ADDRESS** Acadia Univ, Wolfville, NS, B0P 1XO. **EMAIL** janice.best@acadiau.ca

BEST, OTTO FERDINAND
PERSONAL Born 07/28/1929, Steinheim, Germany, m, 4 children **DISCIPLINE** GERMAN LITERATURE **EDUCATION** Univ Munich, PhD, 63. **CAREER** Asst, Col Hippolyte Fontaine, DiJon, France, 52-53; ed, Insel Verlag, S Fischer Verlag, Verlag Kiepenheuer and Witscher, R Piper and Co, 54-68; lectr Ger philol, Univ Munich, 65-68; prof Ger, Univ NDak, 68-69; assoc prof, 69-71, PROF GER, UNIX MD, COLLEGE PARK, 71- **MEMBERSHIPS** MLA; AAUP; Am Asn Teachers Ger; Lessing Soc. **RESEARCH** European literature of the 18th century; European literature of the 20th century; European philosophy. **SELECTED PUBLICATIONS** Auth, The Fin De Siecle Culture of Adolescence, J Engl Germ Philol, Vol 0095, 96. **CONTACT ADDRESS** Dept of Ger and Slavic Lang and Lit, Univ of Md, College Park, MD, 20742-0001.

BETHIN, CHRISTINA Y.
DISCIPLINE SLAVIC LINGUISTICS **EDUCATION** Univ Roch, BA, 72; Univ Ill, Urbana-Champaign, MA, 74, PhD, 78. **CAREER** Lectr, Univ Va, 78-79; asst, 79-85, assoc 85-95, chair, dept Ger, Slav langs & lits, 94-97, PROF, 95-, SUNY, STONY BROOK. **CONTACT ADDRESS** Dept of Linguistics, SUNY, Stony Brook, Stony Brook, NY, 11794-4376.

BETLYON, JOHN WILSON
PERSONAL Born 06/05/1949, York, PA, m, 9 children **DISCIPLINE** NEAR EASTERN LANGUAGES AND CIVILIZATIONS **EDUCATION** Bucknell Univ, AB (cum laude), 71; Harvard Univ, MTS, 73, PhD, 78. **CAREER** Asst prof, Relig, NC Wesleyan Col, 78-80; Campus minister, Lycoming Col, 80-81; Chaplain & assoc prof, Relig, Smith Col, 81-89; Chaplain, US Army, 89-92; Chaplain & assoc prof, Univ North FL & Jacksonville Univ, 92-95; lect, PA State Univ, 95-. **MEMBERSHIPS** SBL; ASOR. **RESEARCH** Persian Period history and religion. **SELECTED PUBLICATIONS** Auth, Coins, Commerce, and Politics: Coins from the Limes Arabicus Project, 1976-1985, in The Roman Frontier in Central Jordan: Interim Report of the Limes Arabicus Project, 1980-1985, S Thomas Parker, ed, British Archaeological Reports Int Series 340, part ii, Oxford British Archaeological Reports, 87; Archaeological Evidence of Military Operations in Southern Judah during the Early Hellenistic Period, The Biblical Archaeologist, 91; Canaanite Myth and the Early Coinage of the Phonecian City-States, in Ancient Economy in Mythology: East and West, Morris Silver, ed, Rowman & Littlefield, 91; Coinage, in Anchor Bible Dictionary, vol 1, D N Freedman, ed, Doubleday, 92; Money, in HarperCollins Bible Dictionary, rev ed, P J Achtemeier, ed, Harper, 96; many other publications. **CONTACT ADDRESS** 1243 Haymaker Rd, State College, PA, 16801. **EMAIL** jwb14@psu.edu

BETZ, DOROTHY
DISCIPLINE FRENCH LITERATURE **EDUCATION** Cornell Univ, MA, PhD. **CAREER** Prof. **RESEARCH** Nineteenth century French poetry. **SELECTED PUBLICATIONS** Auth, Chateaubriand's Itineraire and the Profits of Tourism; Vicor Hugo, Juliette Drouet and an Unpublished Anniversary Letter from 1851; Baudelaire, Swinburne and the Legacy of Greece. **CONTACT ADDRESS** French Dept, Georgetown Univ, 37th and O St, Washington, DC, 20057.

BETZ, FREDERICK
PERSONAL Born 06/29/1943, New York, NY, m, 1970 **DISCIPLINE** GERMAN LANGUAGE & LITERATURE **EDUCATION** Columbia Univ, BA, 64; Ind Univ, MA, 67, PhD(Ger Comp Lit), 73. **CAREER** Instr Ger, Univ Ill, Chicago Circle, 69-72; asst prof, Univ Maine, Orono, 74-78; asst prof, 78-80, from assoc prof to prof, 80-86 Ger, Southern Ill Univ, Carbondale. **HONORS AND AWARDS** SIU Library Delta Award 90 for scholarly contribs to Ger Lit. **MEMBERSHIPS** MLA; Am Asn Teachers Ger; Mencken Society, Sinclair Lewis Society. **RESEARCH** Theodor Fontane; 19th century realism and naturalism, novel and novelle; reception study and literary sociology. **SELECTED PUBLICATIONS** Auth, Fontane's VdS in the AAZ: Gutzkow or Roquette?, Modern Lag Notes, 72; Die Zwanglose Gesellschaft: Freundeskreis um Fontane, Jahrbuch f brandenburgische Landesgeschichte, 76; Authorship & source of song & subtitle in Fontane's FJT, German Quart, 76; Strindberg or Stauffer?: The Mann's Misquotation of Fontane, Germanic Notes, 79; contribr, DerZug nach dem Western: Aspects of Paul Lindau's Novel, Sherwood Nottingham, 79; Fontanes Irrungen, Wirrungen: zeitgenossische Rezeption, Nymphenburger Munich, 80; ed, Erlauterungen und Dokumente zu Fontanes Irrungen, Wirrungen, Reclam Stuttgart, 79; Theodor Fontane, L'Adultera, Reclam Stuttgart, 82; Heinrich Mann's Der Untertan, 93. **CONTACT ADDRESS** Dept of Foreign Lang & Lit, Southern Illinois Univ, Carbondale, IL, 62901. **EMAIL** fbtz@aol.com

BEVERLEY DRIVER, EDDY
PERSONAL m **DISCIPLINE** GERMAN **EDUCATION** Col Wooster, BA, 58-62; Ind Univ, MA, 62-64; Freie Univ, Berlin, 64-66; Ind Univ, PhD, 66-69. **CAREER** Instr, Middlebury Col, 69-70; dir, Middlebury Col Grad Sch, 71-72; asst prof, Middlebury Col, 70-73; ch, dept ger and russ, 74-76; asst prof, Dickinson Col, 73-77; dir, Ctr Pa Consitorium, 78-83; instr, Dickinson, Franklin and Marshall, Gettysburg, Wilson col(s), 77-83; assoc prof, 83-94; ch, ger dept, 94-97; prof, 94-97. **MEMBERSHIPS** Mem, Soc Advan Scand Study; Am Scand Found; Am Assn Tchr(s) Ger. **SELECTED PUBLICATIONS** Auth, Brecht in Dialogue with Karin Michaelis, James K. Lyon and Hans-Peter Breuer, Univ Del Press, London: AUP, 95; Herta Muller: Art Transcends Boundaries, Provincetown Arts, 13, 97-98; rev(s), Herta Muller, The Land of Green Plums, Metropolitan Bk(s), 96; Herlinde Nitsch Ayers, Rollenkonflikte im Werk von Hebbel, Ibsen und Strindberg, 97. **CONTACT ADDRESS** Dept of Ger, Dickinson Col, PO Box 1773, Carlisle, PA, 17013-2896.

BEVINGTON, GARY LOYD
PERSONAL Born 02/03/1944, Ft Madison, IA, 2 children **DISCIPLINE** LINGUISTICS **EDUCATION** Middlebury Col, AB, 66, MA, 67; Univ Mass, Amherst, PhD, 70. **CAREER** Asst prof ling, Univ Mass Amherst, 70-71; asst prof, 71-75, assoc prof, 75-80, prof ling, Northeastern Ill Univ, 80-99, prof emer, Ling and International/Intercultural Studies, 99-; Humboldt Res fel & lectr, Univ Munich, 75; Fulbright Sr. Lectr, Univ Jena, Ger, 91; schol-in-residence, The Newberry Libr, 97-. **MEMBERSHIPS** Ling Soc Am. **RESEARCH** Albanian language; phonological theory; Balkan linguistics; American Indian linguistics. **SELECTED PUBLICATIONS** Auth, Albanian Phonology, Harrassowitz, 74; Die albanische betonung im lichte der generativen phonologie, Akten Int Albanologischen Kolloquiums Innsbruck 1972 Gednachtnis Norbert Jokl, 77; A Note on Stress Reduction in Albanian, CLS Bk Squibs, 77; Relativization in Albanian Dialects, Folia Slavica, 79; On Classifying Albanian Verbs, Papers for the V Congress of Southeast European Studies, 84; Maya for Travelers and Students: A Guide to Language and Culture in Yucatan, Univ Tex Press, 95; Where Do Words Come From? An Introduction to Etymology, Kendall-Hunt, 95; English Language and Indians, the Encyclopedia of North American Indians, Houghton-Mufflin, 96. **CONTACT ADDRESS** 1310 Main St, Evanston, IL, 60202-4625. **EMAIL** G-Bevington@neiu.edu

BEYNEN, GIJSBERTUS KOOLEMANS
PERSONAL Born 06/12/1935, Surabaya, Indonesia **DISCIPLINE** LANGUAGES; LINGUISTICS **EDUCATION** Candidate Degree in Law and Slavic Languages, 57 and 59, Leiden Univ; State Univ New York Col at Geneseo, MS, 74; Stanford Univ, PhD, 67. **CAREER** Asst Prof, 63-66, Emporia State Univ; Asst Prof, 66-69, Fordham Univ; Asst Prof, 69-73, Univ Rochester, NY; Interviewer, 83, Univ Chicago and Natl Opinion Research Ctr; Visiting Asst Prof, 83, Kent State Univ; Parttime Asst Prof, 85-88, Ohio Wesleyan Univ; Assoc Prof, 74-88, Univ Libraries, Ohio State Univ; Prof and Chr Designate, 88-91, Univ South Africa; Temp Asst Prof, 92-94, Iowa State Univ; Librarian, 97-98, Newton Correctional Facility; Adjunct Faculty Mem, 98-, Mercy Col of Health Sciences. **HONORS AND AWARDS** UNESCO Scholarship at Novi Sad Univ, 59; UNESCO Scholarship at Warsaw Univ, 61; IREX Exchange Fel at LMSU, 71-72; IREX Summer Grant for Study in Bulgaria, 76; Natl Endowment for the Humanities Translation Grant, 81-82; Midwest Universities Consortium for Intl Activities Exchange Scholarship at LMSU, 81-82; Summer Teachers Exchange Scholarship at Lomonosov Moscow State Univ (LMSU). **MEMBERSHIPS** Assoc of College and Research Libraries **RESEARCH** Shota Rustaveli; Bantu linguistics; folklore **SELECTED PUBLICATIONS** Auth, The Symbolism of the Leopard in the Vepxist'q'aosani, The Annual of the Society for the Study of Caucasia, 90; Vampires, Cannibals, and Foreign Devils: The Structure of Xenophobia in Bulgarian Folklore, The Southern African Journal for Folklore Studies, 91; A Bulgarian Legend in Relation to the Oedipus Tales, Balcanistica, 92; The National Bibliographies of the Turkic Republics of the Soviet Union, Government Information Quarterly, 98. **CONTACT ADDRESS** 3320 Valdez Dr., Des Moines, IA, 50310-4944.

BICKERTON, DEREK
PERSONAL Born 03/25/1926, Bebington, England, m, 3 children **DISCIPLINE** LINGUISTICS **EDUCATION** Cambridge Univ, BA, 49, MA, 68, PhD (ling), 76; Univ Leeds, dipl ling, 67. **CAREER** Lectr English, Univ Col Cape Coast, 64-66; sr lectr ling, Univ Guyana, 67-71; lectr, Univ Lancaster, 71-72; assoc prof, 72-76, PROF LING, UNIV HAWAII, MANOA, 76-, Prin investr, Nonstandard Hawaiian English Proj, 73-75 and Origins Creole Syntax Proj, 75-78. **MEMBERSHIPS** Caribbean Ling Soc. **RESEARCH** Linguistic variation; pidgin and Creole languages; language universals. **SELECTED PUBLICATIONS** Auth, The Origins of Saramaccan Syntax--A Reply to Mcwhorter, John Substratal Influence in Saramaccan Serial Verb Constructions, J Pidgin Creole Langs, Vol 0009, 94; Will the Real Hawaii Pidgin Stand up, J Pidgin Creole Langs, Vol 0009, 94; Nautical Pidgin and Dilliard, J Pidgin Creole Langs, Vol 0011, 96; The Acquisition of Mauritian Creole, J Pidgin Creole Langs, Vol 0011, 96; The Biology of Language, J Pidgin Creole Langs, Vol 0012, 97; Sato, Charlene, Junko--June 25, 1951 to January 28, 1996, J Pidgin Creole Langs, Vol 0011, 96. **CONTACT ADDRESS** Dept of Ling, Univ Hawaii, Manoa, HI, 96822.

BIEN, GLORIA
PERSONAL Born 12/24/1940, Lanchow, China, m, 1979 **DISCIPLINE** LANGUAGE, LITERATURE **EDUCATION** Univ Calif, Berkeley, BA, 62, MA, 65; Univ Wash, Seattle, PhD, 75. **CAREER** Vis asst prof, 77-78, Indian Univ; asst prof, 74-80, Conn Col, N London CT; vis asst prof, 81-82, Univ Oregon; asst prof, 82-85, assoc prof, 85-, Colgate Univ. **RESEARCH** Chinese-French literary relations **CONTACT ADDRESS** Dept East Asian Lang & Lit, Colgate Univ, Hamilton, NY, 13346. **EMAIL** gbien@center.colgate.edu

BIGGS, N.
PERSONAL Born 03/09/1964, St. Louis, MO, m, 1991, 3 children **DISCIPLINE** FOREIGN LANGUAGE **EDUCATION** Harvard Univ, BA, 86; Univ Calif Los Angeles, MA, PhD, 89-95. **CAREER** Chair, dept of foreign lang, Houghton Col. **MEMBERSHIPS** MLA **RESEARCH** Linguistics; French & Italian lit. **CONTACT ADDRESS** 8927 Upper St, Rushford, NY, 14777. **EMAIL** ubiggs@houghton.edu

BIGGS, ROBERT DALE
PERSONAL Born 06/13/1934, Pasco, WA **DISCIPLINE** ASSYRIOLOGY **EDUCATION** Eastern Wash State Col, BA, 56, Johns Hopkins Univ, PhD(Assyriol), 62. **CAREER** Res assoc Assyriol, Orient Inst, 63-64, from asst prof to assoc prof, 64-72, Prof Assyriol, Univ Chicago, 72-, Fel, Baghdad Sch, Am Schs Orient Res, 62-63; assoc ed, Assyrian Dictionary, 64-; ed, J Near Eastern Studies, 71- **MEMBERSHIPS** Am Orient Soc; Archaeol Inst Am. **RESEARCH** Babylonian and Assyrian languages; Sumerian language. **SELECTED PUBLICATIONS** Auth, The Abu Salabikh tablets: A preliminary survey, J Cuneiform Studies, 66; Semitic names in the Fara Period, Orientalia, 67; SA ZI GA: Ancient Mesopotamian Potency Incantations, J J Augustin, 67; An esoteric Babylonian commentary, Rev Assyriologie, 68; coauth, Cuneiform Texts from Nippur: The Eighth and Ninth Seasons, Univ Chicago, 69; auth, Inscriptions from al-Hiba-Lagash: The First and Second Seasons, 76 & co-ed, Seals and Sealing in the Ancient Near East, 77, Undena, Malibu; coauth, Nippur II: The North Temple and Sounding E, Univ Chicago, 78. **CONTACT ADDRESS** Orient Inst, Univ of Chicago, 1155 E 58th St, Chicago, IL, 60637-1540. **EMAIL** r-biggs@uchicago.edu

BIJLEFELD, WILLEM A.
PERSONAL Born 05/08/1925, Tobelo, Indonesia, m, 1950, 4 children **DISCIPLINE** ISLAMIC STUDIES, HISTORY OF RELIGIONS **EDUCATION** Univ Groningen, BD, 46, Drs Theol, 50; Univ Utrecht, Dr Theol, 59. **CAREER** Chaplain to overseas studies, Univ Leiden, 50-55; consult, Islam in Africa Proj, Northern Nigeria, 59-64; asst prof Arabic and Islamic studies, Univ Ibadan, 64-66; assoc prof, 66-68, acad dean, 69-74, PROF ISLAMICS, HARTFORD SEM FOUND, 68-, Dir, Duncan Black Macdonald Ctr, 74-, Dir, Pierre Benignus Studies Ctr, Islam in Africa Proj, Ibadan, 64-66; ed, Muslim World, 67- **MEMBERSHIPS** Deut Ges Relig-u Missionswiss; fel Mid E Studies Asn. **RESEARCH** Qur'anic studies; history of the discipline of history of religions; Muslim-Christian relations, past and present. **SELECTED PUBLICATIONS** Auth, A Century of Arabic and Islamic Studies at Hartford Seminary, Muslim World, Vol 0083, 93. **CONTACT ADDRESS** D B Macdonald Ctr, Hartford Sem, 110 Sherman St, Hartford, CT, 06105.

BILLIAMS, LYNN BARSTIS
DISCIPLINE COMPARATIVE LITERATURE **EDUCATION** Univ of IL, PhD, 74; SUNY-Albany, MLS, 76 **CAREER** Librn III, 89-, Auburn Univ; Assoc Prof, 76-89, Volun St Comnty col **HONORS AND AWARDS** AL Libr Asn Col and Univ Div awd for outstand contrib to prof lit **MEMBERSHIPS** Am Libr Asn; AL Hist Asn; AL Libr Asn **RESEARCH** AL art colonies **SELECTED PUBLICATIONS** Auth, Printmaking as a Bozart of the South, 1914-1947, Southern Quarterly, 98; American Printmakers, 1880-1945: An Index to Reproductions and Biocritical Information, Scarecrow, 93 **CONTACT ADDRESS** Dept of Humanities, Auburn Univ, Auburn, AL, 36849-5606. **EMAIL** willily@mail.auburn.edu

BILLICK, DAVID JOSEPH
PERSONAL Born 05/19/1947, Toledo, OH, m, 1973 **DISCIPLINE** SPANISH LITERATURE BIBLIOGRAPHY **EDUCATION** Univ Toledo, BA, 69, MA, 71; Univ Iowa, PhD (Span), 76. **CAREER** Instr, Univ Iowa, 76-77; asst prof Span, Rutgers Univ, 77-80; Assoc Ed, Hispania, 76-, LIBR ASST, UNIV MICH, 81- **MEMBERSHIPS** Am Asn Teachers Span and Port; MLA; Nat Womens Studies Asn; Am Libr Asn. **RESEARCH** Women in Hispanic literature; Jose de Espronceda; 19th century Spanish literature. **SELECTED PUBLICATIONS** Auth, Bibliography of Publications on the Comedia 1991-1992, Bull Comediantes, Vol 0044, 92. **CONTACT ADDRESS** Grad Libr Ref Dept, Univ of Mich, Ann Arbor, MI, 48109.

BILLS, GARLAND D.
DISCIPLINE LINGUISTICS **EDUCATION** Univ Tex, Austin, PhD. **CAREER** Instr, Univ NMex. **MEMBERSHIPS** Exec dir, Ling Asn of Southwest. **RESEARCH** Sociolinguistics; syntax-semantics. **SELECTED PUBLICATIONS** Auth, Lan-

guage shift, linguistic variation, and teaching Spanish to native speakers in the United States, in La ensenanza del espanol a hispanohablantes: Praxis y teorea, ed, M.C. Colombi and F.X. Alarcon, D C Heath, 96; coauth, The geography of language shift: Distance from the Mexican border and Spanish language claiming in the southwestern U. S., Int J of Sociol of Lang, 114, 95; The many faces of language maintenance: Spanish language claiming in five southwestern states, in Spanish in four continents: Studies in language contact and bilingualism, ed, Carmen Silva-Corvalan, Georgetown UP, 95. **CONTACT ADDRESS** Univ NMex, Albuquerque, NM, 87131. **EMAIL** gbills@unm.edu

BING, JANET MUELLER
PERSONAL Born 01/18/1937, Oak Park, IL, m, 1964, 1 child **DISCIPLINE** LINGUISTICS **EDUCATION** Coe Coll, BA, 59; Stanfor Univ, MA, 60; Univ Mass, Amherst, PhD (ling), 79. **CAREER** Assoc dir appl ling, Sch Int Training, 70-74; instr ling, Univ NH, 79-80; asst prof, Univ Minn, 81-82; ASST PROF LING, OLD DOMINION UNIV, 82-, Consult, Inter-Link Assocs, 81- **MEMBERSHIPS** Ling Soc Am; Teachers English to Speakers Other Lang. **RESEARCH** Theoretical linguistics; applied linguistics; first language acquisition. **SELECTED PUBLICATIONS** Auth, English Sound Structure, Lang, Vol 0073, 97. **CONTACT ADDRESS** 39 Moore St, Princeton, NJ, 08540.

BINGHAM, JOHN L.
DISCIPLINE SPANISH **EDUCATION** Vanderbilt Univ, BA, 41, MA, 47. **CAREER** Taft teaching fel, Univ Cincinnati, 41; asst, Univ Calif, Los Angeles, 47-50; from instr to asst prof Span and French, 50-62, asst dean, Col Arts and Sci, 55-65, assoc dean, 65-80, ASSOC PROF SPAN, VANDERBILT UNIV, 62- **MEMBERSHIPS** SAtlantic Mod Lang Asn; Conf Acad Deans Southern States. **RESEARCH** Nineteenth and 20th century Spanish literature. **SELECTED PUBLICATIONS** Auth, Thomas,Earl, W.--We Remember, Hisp J Devoted Tchg Span Port, Vol 0076, 93. **CONTACT ADDRESS** Col of Arts and Sci, Vanderbilt Univ, Nashville, TN, 37240.

BIRCHER, MARTIN
PERSONAL Born 06/03/1938, Zurich, Switzerland **DISCIPLINE** GERMAN LITERATURE **EDUCATION** Univ Zurich, DrPhil, 65. **CAREER** Asst prof, 68-71, Assoc Prof Ger, McGill Univ, 71-, Schweizer Nationalfonds fel, 65-68; lectr, Univ Zurich, 71-; Guggenheim fel, NY, 71-72; fel, Janggen-Pohn-Stiftung, St Gallen, 72-73 and Privatdozenten-Stiftung, Univ Zurich, 72-73; res fel, Alexander von Humboldt Found, 76-77; ed, Wolfenbutteler Barock-Nachrichten, Hamburg, 78-; RES DIR 17TH CENTURY, HERZOG AUGUST BIBLIOTHEK WOLFENBUTTEL, 78- **MEMBERSHIPS** Shakespeare Ges Wes; Int Asn Ger Studies; Swiss-Ger Acad Soc; Int Asn Studies Ger Baroque Lit. **RESEARCH** German literature, 16th to 18th centuries; Swiss Literature; Shakespeare. **SELECTED PUBLICATIONS** Auth, Arcadia in Helvetia, Euphorion Zeitschrift Literaturgeschichte, Vol 0089, 95; Gryphius, Anderas Autographs, Daphnis Zeitschrift Mittlere Deut Lit, Vol 0023, 94. **CONTACT ADDRESS** Dept of German, McGill Univ, Montreal, ON, 101 PQ H3A 2T5.

BIRGE, BETTINE
DISCIPLINE EAST ASIAN LANGUAGES AND CULTURES **EDUCATION** Columbia Univ, PhD, 92. **CAREER** Asst prof, Univ Southern Calif. **RESEARCH** Pre-modern Chinese civilization; Chinese thought and cultural history. **SELECTED PUBLICATIONS** Auth, Chu Hsi and Women's Education. **CONTACT ADDRESS** East Asian Studies Center, Univ Southern Calif, University Park Campus, Los Angeles, CA, 90089.

BIRNBAUM, HENRIK
PERSONAL Born 12/13/1925, Breslau, Germany, m, 1965, 2 children **DISCIPLINE** SLAVIC LANGUAGES AND LITERATURES **EDUCATION** Univ Stockholm, Phil Cand, 49, Phil Mag, 52, Phil Lic, 54, PhD, 58. **CAREER** Asst Slavic lang, Russ Inst, Univ Stockholm, 47-53, asst prof, univ, 58-61; instr Russ, Ger and Swedish, High Schs and Jr Cols, Stockholm, 53-58; assoc Prof Slavic lang, 61-64, dir Ctr Russ and E Europ Studies, 68-78, PROF SLAVIC LANG, UNIV CALIF, LOS ANGELES, 64-, Vis lectr, Harvard Univ, 60; consult, Rand Corp, Santa Monica, 62-66; prof Slavic, Baltic and Balkan ling, Univ Munich, 72-73. **MEMBERSHIPS** Am Asn Advan Slavic Studies; Ling Soc Am; corres mem Swedish Royal Acad Lett; Am Med Acad; Asn Scand Slavists. **RESEARCH** Comparative and historical Slavic linguistics; mediaeval and Renaissance Slavic literature and history. **SELECTED PUBLICATIONS** Auth, The Location of the Moravian State - Revisited, Byzantinoslavica, Vol 0054, 93; The Legacy of Genghis-Khan and Other Essays on Russia Identity, Welt Der Slaven-Halbjahresschrift Fur Slavistik, Vol 0038, 93; Jakobson the Futurist, Russ Rev, Vol 0053, 94; An Introduction to the Morphological Concept on Slavic Accentology, Slavic and E Europ Jour, Vol 0038, 94; An Introduction to the Morphological Concept on Slavic Accentology, Slavic and E Europ J, Vol 0038, 94; The Linguistic Sign Reconsidered in Arbitrariness, Iconicity, Motivation, Elementa-Jour Slavic Studies Comp Cult Semiotics, Vol 0002, 95; Slavic Studies at the 11th International Slavists Congress in Bratislava, Slavic Rev, Vol 0054, 95; The Linguistic Sign Reconsidered - Arbitrariness, Iconicity, Motivation, Elementa-J of Slavic Stud and Comp Cult Semiotics, Vol 0002, 95; On the Widely-Traveled Methodius and the Location of Old Moravia, Hopefully For the Last Time in Critical Observations on a Recent Publication of Kronsteiner, Byzantinoslavica, Vol 0057, 96; Guro, Elena, Sodergran, Edith, and the Karelian Isthmus, Russ Lit, Vol 0040, 1996; 'Molenie Danila Zatocnika' and Its Genre--The 'Supplication of Daniel the Exile,' Poetic Forms in Old Russian Literature, Zeitschrift Fur Slawistik, Vol 0042, 97; The Dawn of Slavic - An introduction to Slavic Philology, Welt Der Slaven-Halbjahresschrift Fur Slavistik, Vol 0042, 97; Linguistic interrelations in Early Rus, and East Slavs 9th-Century to 11th-Century, Slavic Rev, Vol 0056, 97; The Slavs - Origins of Their Name, History of Migration to Europe and the Beginnings of Russian History From a Historico-Onomastic Perspective, Slavic Rev, Vol 0056, 97. **CONTACT ADDRESS** Dept of Slavic Lang, Univ Calif, Los Angeles, CA, 90024.

BIRNER, BETTY
DISCIPLINE LINGUISTICS **EDUCATION** Northwestern Univ, PhD, 92. **CAREER** Postdoctoral fel, Inst Res Cognitive Sci, IRCS, Univ Pa **RESEARCH** The linguistic realization of inferrable information in discourse; general discourse functions served by classes of syntactic constructions; cross-linguistic correlations between syntax and discourse functions. **SELECTED PUBLICATIONS** Coauth, book on the discourse functions of marked syntactic constructions in English, Benjamins. **CONTACT ADDRESS** Dept of Linguistics, Northwestern Univ, 1801 Hinman, Evanston, IL, 60208. **EMAIL** betty@linc.cis.upenn.edu

BISHOP, MICHAEL
PERSONAL Born 04/19/1938, London, England **DISCIPLINE** MODERN FRENCH LITERATURE **EDUCATION** Univ Manchester, BA, 59; Univ Man, MA, 68; Univ Kent, PhD(French lit), 77. **CAREER** Asst master mod lang, King's Sch, Cheshire, England, 60-63; chmn mod & class lang, Sisler High Sch, Winnipeg, Can, 63-66 & 67-69; chmn French lit & lang, George Stephenson Sch, Newcastle, England, 69-70; asst prof, 70-79, ASSOC PROF FRENCH LIT & LANG, DALHOUSIE UNIV, 80-, Mem, Manitoba Comt Develop Univ Entrance Oral Tests, 67-69; assoc ed, Dalhousie French Studies, Dalhousie Univ, 78-80 & Ethos, 81-; actg ed, Dalhousie French Studies, Dalhousie Univ, 80- **MEMBERSHIPS** Soc Fr Studies; Am Asn Teachers Fr. **RESEARCH** Nineteenth and 20th century French literature; contemporary French literature, especially poetry; French art. **SELECTED PUBLICATIONS** Auth, Le Chemin Sous La Mer, World Lit today, Vol 0067, 93; Questioning Jabes,Edmond, Dalhousie Review, Vol 0072, 93; A Year in Poetry - 92 - From Bonnefoy and Dubouchet to Zins and Khouryghata, and Beyond, Fr Rev, Vol 0066, 93; Debut Et Fin De La Neige, Fr Rev, Vol 0066, 93; Axiales, World Lit today, Vol 0067, 93; Poemes Pour Un Texte 1970-1991, Fr Rev, Vol 0066, 93; 20th-Century French Avant-Garde Poetry, 1907-1990, Fr Forum, Vol 0018, 93; C Etait Un Paysage, World Lit today, Vol 0067, 93; Sans Lieu Sinon Lattente, World Lit today, Vol 0067, 93; Un Recit, World Lit today, Vol 0067, 93; Dans La Chaleur Vacante and Ou Le Soleil, World Lit today, Vol 0067, 93; Pages, World Lit today, Vol 0067, 93; Petits Elements De Physique Amoureuse, World Lit today, Vol 0067, 93; Le Chemin Sous La Mer, World Lit today, Vol 0067, 93; Cingles, World Lit today, Vol 0067, 93; Les Portes D En Bas, World Lit today, Vol 0067, 93; L Arbre Et La Glycine, World Lit today, Vol 0067, 93; Verses, Fr Rev, Vol 0067, 94; Trouver La Source, World Lit today, Vol 0068, 94; L Or Du Commun, World Lit today, Vol 0068, 94; Elegiades, World Lit today, Vol 0068, 94; Maintenant, World Lit today, Vol 0068, 94; Aux Heures Dafflu-ence, World Lit today, Vol 0068, 94; Distance De Fuite, World Lit today, Vol 0068, 94; Suite Pour Une Enfance, Fr Rev, Vol 0067, 94; Connaissance De La Mort, World Lit today, Vol 0068, 94; Katana, World Lit today, Vol 0068, 94; The Year in Poetry - From Guillevic, Deguy and Jaccottet to Tellermann, Etienne and Baude, Fr Rev, Vol 0068, 94; Le Passager, World Lit today, Vol 0068, 94; Grand Jour, World Lit today, Vol 0069, 95; instants Pour La Seconde Vie, World Lit today, Vol 0069, 95; Apres Beaucoup D Annees, World Lit today, Vol 0069, 95; The Year in French Poetry, 94 - From Cesaire and Glissant to Broda and Bancquart, Fr Rev, Vol 0068, 95; D Un Pas Suspendu, World Lit today, Vol 0069, 95; Cristal Et Fumee, World Lit today, Vol 0069, 95; Mesure Du Pire, World Lit today, Vol 0069, 95; Mon Anthologie, World Lit today, Vol 0069, 95; La Vie Errante, World Lit today, Vol 0069, 95; Writings For the Newspaper - Reviews From 1951-1970, World Lit today, Vol 0069, 95; Les Vies Simultanees, World Lit today, Vol 0069, 95; Mesure Du Pire, Fr Rev, Vol 0069, 95; On Silence, World Lit today, Vol 0070, 96; The Contemporary Novel in France, Dalhousie Review, Vol 0075, 96; A Ce Qui Nen Finit Pas, World Lit today, Vol 0070, 96; Enigmatiques, World Lit today, Vol 0070, 96; The Poesie-Eclatee of Char,Rene, Fr Rev, Vol 0070, 96; The theater of the Poem - Regarding Albiach,Anne,Marie, World Lit today, Vol 0070, 96; Ocean, World Lit today, Vol 0070, 96; Strophes Pour Une Agape, World Lit today, Vol 0070, 96; Frenaud,andre Glosses On La Sorciere De Rome, World Lit today, Vol 0070, 96; Du Silence, World Lit today, Vol 0070, 96; The Year in Poetry - From Frenaud, Stetie and Deguy to Chedid, Han and Esteban, Fr Rev, Vol 0069, 96; La Terre Agee, World Lit today, Vol 0071, 97; The Year in Poetry - From Dupin, Guillevic and Marteau to Dohollau, Commere and Atlan, Fr Rev, Vol 0070, 97. **CONTACT ADDRESS** Dept French, Dalhousie Univ, Halifax, NS, B3H 4H8.

BITTRICH, LOUIS EDWARD
PERSONAL Born 11/04/1937, Omaha, NE, m, 1961, 2 children **DISCIPLINE** COMPARATIVE LITERATURE, THEATRE **EDUCATION** Gustavus Adolphus Col, BA, 59; Bowling Green State Univ, MA, 60; Univ NC, PhD (comp lit), 67; Southwest Texas State Univ, MA, 85. **CAREER** Instr English & dir theatre, Tex Lutheran Col, 60-62; instr English, Gustavus Adolphus Col, 62-63; asst prof, Winthrop Col, 65-66; asst prof, Gustavus Adolphus Col, 66-67; assoc prof, 67-79, prof English, 79-, chemn dept, 67-95, prof theatre, 95, chemn dept, Texas Lutheran Col; Exchange prof humanities, Winthrop Col, 65-66. **HONORS AND AWARDS** Ford Found fel, 65. **MEMBERSHIPS** MLA. **RESEARCH** Modern Roman elegies; contemporary mythology; Romantic poetry. **SELECTED PUBLICATIONS** Auth, Alchemy vindicated in our age, Cresset, 4/72. **CONTACT ADDRESS** Dept of Theatre, Texas Lutheran Univ, 1000 W Court St, Seguin, TX, 78155-5978. **EMAIL** bittrich@txlutheran.edu

BIXLER, JACQUELINE
PERSONAL Born 05/21/1953, Cleveland, OH, m, 1977, 3 children **DISCIPLINE** LATIN AMERICAN LITERATURE, CULTURE & HISTORY **EDUCATION** Ohio Univ, BA, 75; KS Univ, PhD, 80 **CAREER** Prof, 80-, VA Tech **HONORS AND AWARDS** Alumni Tch Awd, 94; Diggs Tch Schol Awd, 92 **MEMBERSHIPS** MLA; AATSP; Sigma Delta Pi **RESEARCH** Latin Am theatre **SELECTED PUBLICATIONS** Auth, Convention and Transgression: The Theatre of Emilio Carballido, Bucknell U niv Press, 97 **CONTACT ADDRESS** Dept of Foreign Lang, Virginia Tech, Blacksburg, VA, 24061-0225. **EMAIL** jbixler@vt.edu

BJERKE, ROBERT ALAN
PERSONAL Born 12/23/1939, Eau Claire, WI **DISCIPLINE** GERMANIC LANGUAGES **EDUCATION** Univ Wis, BA, 61, MA, 62, PhD(Ger), 66; Univ Minn-Minneapolis, MA, 73. **CAREER** Asst prof Norweg, St Olaf Col, 66-71; librn, Univ Wis Ctr-Manitowoc County, 73-. **RESEARCH** Genealogy; Norwegian language and literature; bibliography. **SELECTED PUBLICATIONS** Auth, A Contrastive Study of Old German and Old Norwegian Kinship Terms, Ind Univ, 69; Fifteen Modern Norwegian Stories: An Intermediate Norwegian Reader, St Olaf Col, 71; Utvandringen fra Nannestad til Amika, In: Nannestad Bygdebok, Vol 4; Manitowoc-skogen: A Biographical and Genealogical Directory of the Residents of Norwegian Birth and Descent in Manitowoc and Kewaunee Counties in Wisconsin from the First Settlement to 1900, Manitowoc WI, Dobbs, 94. **CONTACT ADDRESS** Univ of Wisconsin, 705 Viebahn St, Manitowoc, WI, 54220-6699. **EMAIL** rbjerke@uwc.edu

BJORK, ROBERT ERIC
PERSONAL Born 02/19/1949, Virgina, MN **DISCIPLINE** MEDIEVAL AND SCANDINAVIAN LITERATURE **EDUCATION** Pomona Col, BA, 71; Univ Calif, Los Angeles, MA, 75, PhD(English), 79. **CAREER** ADJ LECTR ENGLISH AND MED, UNIV CALIF, LOS ANGELES, 79-, Tech ed, J Community Health, 79-82; prin ed, Univ Calif, Los Angeles, Clinicl Scholars Prog, Sch Med, 80- **HONORS AND AWARDS** Elmer Friman Award, Health Sci Commun Asn, 82. **MEMBERSHIPS** MLA; Medieval Acad Am; Am Lit Transl Asn; Am Scand Found; Am Med Writers Asn. **RESEARCH** Old English poetry; modern Swedish literature; biomedical writing. **SELECTED PUBLICATIONS** Auth, Anglo-Saxon Litanies of the Saints, Albion, Vol 0024, 92; The Saxon 'Genesis' - An Edition of the West Saxon 'Genesis B' and the Old-Saxon Vatican 'Genesis,' Mich Ger Stud, Vol 0018, 92; Speech as Gift in 'Beowulf,' and Joining Methods of Style and Rhetorical Analysis With Medieval theories of Language, Speculum-J of Medieval Stud, Vol 0069, 94; A Grammar of Old-English, Vol 1 - Phonology, Speculum-J of Medieval Stud, Vol 0069, 94; A Sudden Liberating Thought, Scand Stud, Vol 0067, 95; Thorkelin,Grimur,Jonsson Preface to the First Edition of 'Beowulf,' 1815/, Scand Stud, Vol 0068, 96; In the Foreground - 'Beowulf,' Speculum-J of Medieval Stud, Vol 0071, 96; The Translators invisibility - A History of Translation, J of Eng and Ger Philol, Vol 0096, 97. **CONTACT ADDRESS** 18212 Nordhoff St, Northridge, CA, 91325.

BLACK, MARGARETTA
PERSONAL Born 10/26/1933, Chicago, IL **DISCIPLINE** FRENCH LANGUAGE & LITERATURE **EDUCATION** Marian Col, BA, 61; Case Western Reserve Univ, MA, 66; Univ Wis-Madison, PhD, 72. **CAREER** Elem tchr, Ind, 54-62; teacher French & hist, 62-65, Acad Immaculate Conception, Oldenburg; instr French, 66-69, asst prof, 71-80, dean acad affairs, 74-87, prof French 82-, chemn dept for lang, 91-, Marian Col, Ind. **MEMBERSHIPS** Am Assn Teachers French, Am Conf on Teaching For Lang, Central States Conf on Teaching For Lang; Ind For Lang Teachers Assn. **RESEARCH** The French novel since 1950; French cultural history--Middle Ages and Renaissance; French film and cinematography, standards in ed and as-

sessment measures, interview. **CONTACT ADDRESS** 3200 Cold Springs Rd, Indianapolis, IN, 46222-1997. **EMAIL** marga@marian.edu

BLACK, NANCY BREMILLER
PERSONAL Born 11/12/1941, Norristown, PA, m, 1964, 2 children **DISCIPLINE** ENGLISH; COMPARATIVE LITERATURE **EDUCATION** Vassar Col, BA, 63; Univ Pa, MA, 64; Columbia Univ, PhD(English), 71. **CAREER** Lectr English, City Col New York, 71-72; from instr to Assoc Prof, 72-95, PROF ENGLISH, BROOKLYN COL, 95-. **HONORS AND AWARDS** Shaughnessy scholar, 81-82. **MEMBERSHIPS** MLA; Mediaeval Acad Am. **RESEARCH** Medieval comparative literature. **SELECTED PUBLICATIONS** Co-ed, White on Red: Images of the American Indian, Kennikat, 76; ed and transl, The Perilious Cemetary, Garland, 94. **CONTACT ADDRESS** Dept of English, Brooklyn Col, CUNY, 2900 Bedford Ave, Brooklyn, NY, 11210-2813.

BLACKWELL, MARILYN JOHNS
PERSONAL Born 08/01/1948, Cincinnati, OH, m, 1980 **DISCIPLINE** SCANDINAVIAN LITERATURE, FILM **EDUCATION** Univ Wis, BA, 70; Univ Wash, MA, 73, PhD(Scand lit), 76. **CAREER** Lectr, Univ BC, 75-77; ASST PROF, UNIV VA, 77-, Mellon fac fel, Harvard Univ, 81-82. **MEMBERSHIPS** Soc Advan Scand Studies; MLA. **RESEARCH** Comparative literature. **SELECTED PUBLICATIONS** Auth, Dinesen,Isak - The Engendering of Narrative, Scand Stud, Vol 0065, 93; The Play and Mirrors - a Study of the Film Aesthetic of Bergman,Ingmar, Scand Stud, Vol 0066, 94; Swedish - a Comprehensive Grammar, Mod Lang J, Vol 0078, 94; Ideology and Specularity in Enquist, Per, Olov 'Tribadernas Natt,' Scand Stud, Vol 0067, 95; Strindberg Post-Inferno Plays, Scand Stud, Vol 0067, 95; Between Stage and Screen - Bergman,Ingmar Directs, Scand Stud, Vol 0068, 96; The Silence, in Bergman,Ingmar - Disruption and Disavowal in The Movement Beyond Gender, Scandinavica, Vol 0035, 96. **CONTACT ADDRESS** Dept Ger, Univ Va, Charlottesville, VA, 22903.

BLACKWOOD-COLLIER, MARY
DISCIPLINE FRENCH LITERATURE **EDUCATION** Univ de Paris-Sorbonne, PhD, 90. **CAREER** Instr, Ventura Col, 75-78; diction coach, Mus Acad W, 76-84; instr, Santa Barbara Commun Col, 76-84; assoc prof, 81-. **HONORS AND AWARDS** Tchr yr, 92. **SELECTED PUBLICATIONS** Auth, Carmen: Femme fatale or Modern Myth? Merimee's and Bizet's Image of Rebellion, W Va Univ Philol Papers, vol 41, 95; La Carmen essentielle et sa realisation au spectacle, Peter Lang Publ, 94; co-auth, Christian Readings for the Classroom, NAACFLLF Proceedings Jour 1, 91. **CONTACT ADDRESS** Dept of Fr, Westmont Col, 955 La Paz Rd, Santa Barbara, CA, 93108-1099.

BLAIR, JOHN
DISCIPLINE GERMAN LITERATURE **EDUCATION** Univ Ind Bloomington, PhD. **RESEARCH** Eighteenth century German literature. **SELECTED PUBLICATIONS** Auth, Transgressive Currents in Goethe's Wilhelm Meister's Apprenticeship. **CONTACT ADDRESS** Dept Foreign Languages and Literature, State Univ of West Georgia, Carrollton, GA, 30118. **EMAIL** jblair@westga.edu

BLAIR, JOHN T.
DISCIPLINE GERMAN **EDUCATION** Hendrix Col, BA, 81; Univ Ind, MA, 84, PhD, 94. **CAREER** Prof. **MEMBERSHIPS** Goethe Soc N Am; MLA; Asn Tchr German. **RESEARCH** Kafka literary sociology; Freud; Shakespeare. **SELECTED PUBLICATIONS** Auth, The Vulgar Clown in Wilhelm Meister's Apprenticeship: A Cultural Perspective and its Impact on Interpretation. **CONTACT ADDRESS** Dept of Foreign Languages, State Univ W Ga, Carrollton, GA, 30118. **EMAIL** jblair@westga.edu

BLAKE, NANCY
DISCIPLINE COMPARATIVE LITERATURE **EDUCATION** Univ Paris, PhD, 80. **CAREER** Prof, Univ IL Urbana Champaign. **RESEARCH** 19th and 20th century Europ and Am lit; painting and film; Modernism and Post-Modernism; interdisciplinary research; psychoanalytic theory; women's studies; transl. **SELECTED PUBLICATIONS** Auth, Ezra Pound et l'imagisme; Henry James: Ecriture et absence; Gertrude Stein; John Barth; Emily Dickinson: L'amour de loin; pubs on literature; Lacanian Theory. **CONTACT ADDRESS** Comp Lit Dept, Univ Illinois Urbana Champaign, E Gregory Drive, PO Box 52, Champaign, IL, 61820.

BLANEY, BENJAMIN
PERSONAL Born 09/06/1940, Newton, MA, m, 1969, 3 children **DISCIPLINE** GERMANIC LINGUISTICS **EDUCATION** Colby Col, AB, 62; Middlebury Col, MA, 64; Univ Colo, Boulder, PhD, 72. **CAREER** Teacher Ger & English, Woodbridge Jr High Sch, NJ, 62-63; instr Ger, Mich Technol Univ, 64-67; asst prof, assoc prof, 83-93, prof Ger, 93-, Miss State Univ, 72-. **HONORS AND AWARDS** Paideia Award Serv, 89; Burlington N Excellence Tchg Award, 90; John Grisham Master Tchr Award, 97; Distinguished Serv Award, 97. **MEMBERSHIPS** Am Asn Teachers Ger; Soc Advan Scand Studies; Int Saga Soc; Soc Ger Philol. **RESEARCH** Historical linguistics; medieval Ger literature; Old Norse literature. **SELECTED PUBLICATIONS** Auth Berserkr, Medieval Scandinavia: An Encyclopedia, Garland, 93; Western European Dissertations on Hispanic and Luso-Brasilian Languages and Literatures: A Retrospective Index, Clearing House Lang Lit, 95. **CONTACT ADDRESS** Dept of For Lang, Mississippi State Univ, Drawer Fl, Misssippi State, MS, 39762-5720. **EMAIL** bb1@ra.msstate.edu

BLATT, STEPHEN J.
DISCIPLINE INTERPERSONAL COMMUNICATION **EDUCATION** Morehead State Univ, BA, 64; Ohio Univ, MA, 67; PhD, 70. **CAREER** Assoc prof, 71-. **RESEARCH** The use of small groups in classroom management strategies. **SELECTED PUBLICATIONS** Publ, Midwestern Edu Researcher, 95; Rev of Higher Edu, 96. **CONTACT ADDRESS** Dept of Commun, Univ Dayton, 300 Col Park, Dayton, OH, 75062. **EMAIL** Sblatt@Udayton.edu

BLAU, HERBERT
PERSONAL Born 05/03/1926, Brooklyn, NY, m, 1981, 4 children **DISCIPLINE** ENGLISH; COMPARATIVE LITERATURE **EDUCATION** NY Univ, BchE, 47; Stanford Univ, MA, 49, PhD, 54. **CAREER** From asst prof to prof, San Francisco State Univ, 50-65; co-found and co-dir, The Actor's Workshop of San Francisco, 52-65; co-dir, Repertory Theater of Lincoln Ctr, NY, 65-67; prof, City Univ of NY, 67-68; provost and dean, School of Theater and Dance, Calif Inst of the Arts, 68-71; found and artistic dir, KRAKEN theatre, 71-81; prof of the Arts and dir of Inter-Arts Prog, Oberlin Col, 72-74; dean, div of Arts and Hums, Univ of Md, 74-76; prof, Univ of Md, 76-78; prof, Univ of Wis, 78-84; disting. prof, Univ of Wis, 84- ; ed and adv bds, Performing Arts J, Discourse, Theater J, Assaph, World Encycl of Contemp Theatre, Mod Int Drama, Jour of Beckett Studies, Contemp Dramatists, The Drama Rev, Arts in Soc. **HONORS AND AWARDS** Ford Found fel, 59; President's Disting. Serv Award, 65; Guggenheim fels, 62, 77; Camargo Found fel, 84; George Nathan Award for Dramatic Criticism; Sen fel for Independant Study/Res, Nat Endowment for Hums, 84; Nat Endowment for Hums grant, 90; The Kenyon Rev prize for literary excellence, 93. **SELECTED PUBLICATIONS** Auth, The Impossible Theater: A Manifesto, 64; Blooded Thought: Occasions of Theater, 82; Take Up the Bodies: Theater at the Vanishing Point, 82; The Eye of Prey: Subversions of the Postmodern, 87; The Audience, 90; Universals of Performance; or, Amortizing Play, By Means of Performance: Intercult Studies of Theater and Ritual, ed R. Schechner and W. Appel, 90; The Oversight of Ceaseless Eyes, Around the Absurd: Essays on Modern and Postmodern Drama, ed E. Brater and R. Cohn, 91; Quaquaquaqua: The Babel of Beckett, The World of Beckett, ed J. Smith, Psychiatry and Humanities, vol 12, 91; The Surpassing Body, The Drama Rev 35.2, 91; Ready-made Desire, Confronting Tennessee Williams? A Streetcar Named Desire: Essays in Critical Pluralism, ed P.C. Kolin, 92; Nothing in Itself: Complexions of Fashion, 92; The Prospect Before Us, Discourse 14.2, 92; Ideology, Performance, and the Illusions of Demystification, Crit Theory and Performance, ed J.G. Reinelt and J. Roach, 92; Spacing Out in the American Theater, The Kenyon Rev 14.2, 93; A Valediction: Chills and Fever, Mourning, and the Vanities of the Sublime, Performing Arts Jour 16.1, 94; Rhetorics of the Body: Do You Smell a Fault?, Cult Artifacts and the Production of Meaning: The Page, the Image and the Body, ed. M. Ezell and K. O'Brien O'Keefe, 94; Fantasia and Simulacra: Subtext of a Syllabus for the Arts in America, The Kenyon Rev 16.2, 94; Flat-Out Vision, Fugitive Images: From Photography to Video, ed P. Petro, 95; coed, Performance Issue(s): Happenings, Body, Spectacle, Discourse 14.2, 92. **CONTACT ADDRESS** Dept of English, Univ of Wisconsin, Milwaukee, PO Box 413, Milwaukee, WI, 53201.

BLEZNICK, DONALD WILLIAM
PERSONAL Born 12/24/1924, New York, NY, m, 1952, 2 children **DISCIPLINE** ROMANCE LANGUAGES **EDUCATION** City Col New York BA, 46; Nat Univ Mex, MA, 48; Columbia Univ, PhD (Span lit), 54. **CAREER** Instr Romance lang, Ohio State Univ, 49-55; from asst prof to prof, Pa State Univ, 55-67; dept hd, 67-72; PROF, UNIV CINCINNATI, 67-; assoc ed, Hispania, 63-74; ed, 74-. **HONORS AND AWARDS** Knight's Cross of the Order of Civil Merit, King Juan Carlos I of Spain, 77; Rieveschl Award, 80., Am Philos Soc grant, 64. **MEMBERSHIPS** MLA; Am Assn Tchr Span & Port; Renaissance Soc Am; Midwest Mod Lang Assn; Comediantes. **RESEARCH** Political theory of Spain's Golden Age and its influence on literature; history of the Spanish essay; Spanish Golden Age literature. **SELECTED PUBLICATIONS** Auth, Altamirano, Ignacio, Manuel-in Memoriam, Hispania--Jour Devoted Tchg Span Port, vol 0076, 93; Remembering Mead, Hispania--Jour Devoted Tchg Span Port, vol 0079, 96. **CONTACT ADDRESS** Dept Romance Lang, Univ Cincinnati, Cincinnati, OH, 45221.

BLISS, FRANCIS ROYSTER
PERSONAL Born 06/07/1919, Big Stone Gap, VA, m, 1943, 3 children **DISCIPLINE** LATIN, GREEK **EDUCATION** Bowdoin Col, AB, 40; Univ NC, PhD(Latin), 51. **CAREER** From instr to asst prof classics, Colby Col, 48-55; assoc prof, Western Reserve Univ, 55-66; assoc prof classics, UNIV VT, 66-70, PROF, 70-79. **MEMBERSHIPS** Class Asn Mid W & S; Class Asn New England; Soc Ancient Greek Philos; Vergilian Soc; Am Philol Asn. **RESEARCH** Literary imitation, cultural history. **SELECTED PUBLICATIONS** Auth, Roman law and Romand citizenship, Law in a Troubled World, W Reserve Univ, 59; The Plancus ode, Trans & Proc Am Philol Assn, 60; A rogues' gallery, Class Outlook, 63; Unity of Odyssey Eight, Bucknell Rev, 68. **CONTACT ADDRESS** RFD 1, Box 240, New Vineyard, ME, 04956.

BLOCK, HASKELL M.
PERSONAL Born 06/13/1923, Chicago, IL **DISCIPLINE** COMPARATIVE LITERATURE **EDUCATION** Univ Chicago, AB, 44; Harvard Univ, AM, 47; Univ Paris, D Univ, 49. **CAREER** Tchg Fel, Harvard Univ, 48-49; instr, Queens Col, NY, 49-52; from asst prof to assoc prof comp lit, Univ Wis, 52-61; prof, Brooklyn Col & Grad Sch, City Univ New York, 61-75; prof, State Univ NY Binghamton, 75-; vis prof English, Univ Dusseldorf, 72-73; chmn exec comt, Eastern Comp Lit Conf, 76-; H Fletcher Brown prof comp lit, Univ Del, 77-78; vis prof comp lit, Univ Antwerp, 81. **HONORS AND AWARDS** Fulbright res scholar, Univ Cologne, 56-57 & Univ Paris, 68-69; fel, Colloquium Comp Lit, NY Univ, 70-., Consult ed, Random House, NY, 61-; mem selection comt Western Europe, Foreign Area Fel Prog, 65-68; exec officer, Doctoral Prog Comp Lit, City Univ New York, 68-71; ASSOC, SEM THEORY OF LIT, COLUMBIA UNIV, 70-; mem selection comt, Camargo Found, 71-. **MEMBERSHIPS** Inst Comp Lit asn (secy, 58-64); Am Comp Lit Asn (secy, 60-65, vpres. 71-74, pres, 74-77); MLA; Dante Soc Am; Soc Fr Studies. **RESEARCH** Modern drama and novel, symbolist movement. **SELECTED PUBLICATIONS** Auth, An Anthology Of Belgian Symbolist Poets--World Lit Today, Vol 0067, 93. **CONTACT ADDRESS** Dept of Comp Lit, State Univ NY, Binghamton, NY, 13901.

BLODGETT, EDWARD D.
PERSONAL Born 02/26/1935, Philadelphia, PA **DISCIPLINE** COMPARATIVE LITERATURE **EDUCATION** Amherst Col, BA, 56; Univ Minn, MA, 61; Rutgers Univ, PhD, 69. **CAREER** Res master Eng, Girard Col, 58; tchg asst, Univ Minn, 58-61; instr Fre, Inst Am Univ, Aix-en-Provence, 62-63; instr, Eng & classics, Rutgers Univ & Douglas Col, 63-66; asst to assoc prof, 66-74, prof 75-94, chair, comp lit & film stud, 75-85, 91-93, UNIV PROF COMPARATIVE LITERATURE, UNIV ALTA, 94-; vis prof, Univ Sherbrooke, 79; vis prof, Freie Univ Berlin, 88; assoc ed, Can Rev Comp Lit, 74-; exec coun, Calgary Inst Hum, 77-88. **HONORS AND AWARDS** Delta Phi Lambda; Lambda Alpha Phi; fel, Royal Soc Can; Gov Gen Award Eng lang poetry. **SELECTED PUBLICATIONS** Auth, Taking Away the Names, 75; auth, Sounding, 77; auth, Beast Gate, 80; auth, Configuration, 82; auth, Arche/Elegies, 83; auth, Musical Offering, 86; auth, Alice Munro, 88; auth, Da Capo, 90; auth, Apostrophes: Woman at a Piano, 96; transl, Flamenca, 95; co-transl, The Love Songs of the Carmina Burana, 87. **CONTACT ADDRESS** Dept of Comp Lit, Univ of Alberta, Edmonton, AB, T6G 2E6.

BLUE, WILLIAM ROBERT
PERSONAL Born 04/02/1943, Shreveport, LA, m, 1970 **DISCIPLINE** SPANISH LITERATURE **EDUCATION** Univ Calif, Davis, AB, 65, MA, 67; Penn State Univ, PhD(Span), 71. **CAREER** Asst prof, 70-74, ASSOC PROF SPAN, UNIV KANS, 74-, Exec Comt 16th and 17th Century Span Drama, MLA, 78-83. **MEMBERSHIPS** MLA; Am Asn Teachers Span & Port; Comediantes. **RESEARCH** Spanish Golden Age theater and literature. **SELECTED PUBLICATIONS** Auth, Heavenly Bodies--The Realms of la 'Estrella De Sevilla', Rev Estudios Hispanicos, Vol 0031, 97. **CONTACT ADDRESS** Dept of Span & Port, Univ of Kans, Lawrence, KS, 66044.

BLUMBERG, SHERRY H.
DISCIPLINE JEWISH EDUCATION **EDUCATION** Hebrew Union Col, PhD, 91. **CAREER** Assoc prof, Univ Southern Calif. **RESEARCH** Curriculum; teacher training; educating for religious experience. **SELECTED PUBLICATIONS** Auth, electronic publ, Teaching Children about God. **CONTACT ADDRESS** Hebrew Union College-Jewish Institute Of Religion, Univ Southern Calif, University Park Campus, Los Angeles, CA, 90089.

BLUMENTHAL, BERNHARDT GEORGE
PERSONAL Born 03/08/1937, Philadelphia, PA, m, 1965, 4 children **DISCIPLINE** GERMAN **EDUCATION** La Salle Col, BA, 59; Northwestern Univ, MA, 61; Princeton Univ, PhD(Ger), 65. **CAREER** Assoc prof, 63-73, prof Ger, La Salle Col, 73-, chemn dept foreign lang & lit, 69-. **MEMBERSHIPS** Am Asn Teachers Ger. **RESEARCH** German and comparative literatures, especially modern. **SELECTED PUBLICATIONS** Auth, Gertrud Kolmar: Love's Service to the Earth, 9/69 & The Play Element in the Poetry of Else Lasker-Schuler, 9/70, Ger Quart; the Poetry Class, Unterrichtspraxis, fall 71; Paula Ludwig's Poetry: Themes of Love and Death, Ger Quart, 11/71; The Writings of Regina Ullmann, Seminar, 3/73; Original Ger-

man Lyric Poetry in Lyrical Germanica, 9/74 & Ger Am Studies, 5/77; Imagery in Christine Busta's Writing, Seminar, 5/77; Fragen im Herbst, Jeder fur sich allein and Kultursteine, Impressum, vol 8, no 7/8. 94; Fragen im Herbst, Das Boot, vol 32, no 127, 94; Jeder fur sich allein and Kultursteine, Trans-Lit, vol 3, no 2, 94; Culture Stones, Queries in the Fall, and Alone with Ourselves, Int J of Transpersonal Studies, vol 14, nos 1/2, 95; Uriel Birnbaum: Forgotten Angel of the Sun, Modern Austrian Lit, vol 29, no 1, 96; Wenn du gehst, Das Boot, vol 34, no 134, 96; Fragen im Herbst, Wiedergefunden, Wenn du gehst, Trans-Lit, vol 5, no 2, 96; When You Go, Through Sun and Shower, ed Chris Tyler, Owings Mills, MD: Watermark Press, 97; Review of Birgit R Erdle's Antlitz--Mord--Gesetz: Figuren des Anderen bei Gertrud Kolmar und Emmanuel Levinas, Monashefte, vol 89, no 2, summer 97; Sprich leise, Trans-Lit, vol 7, no 1, 98. **CONTACT ADDRESS** Dept of Foreign Lang, LaSalle Univ, 1900 W Olney Ave, Philadelphia, PA, 19141-1199. **EMAIL** blumenth@lasalle.edu

BLUMSTEIN, SHEILA ELLEN
PERSONAL Born 03/10/1944, New York, NY **DISCIPLINE** LINGUISTICS, PSYCHOLINGUISTICS **EDUCATION** Univ Rochester, AB, 65; Harvard Univ, PhD(ling), 70. **CAREER** Asst prof, 70-76, ASSOC PROF LING, BROWN UNIV, 76-, Res assoc, Aphasia Res Ctr, Sch Med, Boston Univ, 70-; vis scientist, Mass Inst Technol Res Lab Electronics, 74 & 77-78, consult, 74-; fel, Guggenheim Found, 77-78 & Radcliffe Inst, 77-78; mem, Commun Sci Study Sect, NIH, 76-; bd gov, Acad Aphasia, 78- **MEMBERSHIPS** Acad Aphasia; Ling Soc Am; Acoustical Soc Am. **RESEARCH** Aphasia; speech perception. **SELECTED PUBLICATIONS** Auth, A Perspective on the Neurobiology Of Language, Brain And Lang, Vol 0060, 97; The Influence of Language on the Acoustic Properties of Phonetic Features--A Study of the Feature Strident in Ewe and English, Phonetica, Vol 0051, 94; The Foreign Accent Syndrome--A Reconsideration, Brain and Lang, Vol 0054, 96; The Role of Lexical Status on the Phonetic Categorization of Speech in Aphasia, Brain and Language, Vol 0046, 94; Effects of Speaking Rate on the Vowel Length Distinction in Korean, Jour of Phonetics, Vol 0021, 93; Effects of Speaking Rate on Voice-Onset Time in Thai, French, and English, Jour of Phonetics, Vol 0025, 97. **CONTACT ADDRESS** Dept of Ling, Brown Univ, 1 Prospect St, Box E, Providence, RI, 02912-9127.

BLY, PETER ANTHONY
PERSONAL Born 07/31/1944, King's Lynn, England, m, 1968, 2 children **DISCIPLINE** SPANISH LITERATURE **EDUCATION** Univ London, England, BA, 66, MA, 67, PhD(Span), 78. **CAREER** Asst prof, Dalhousie Univ, 68-71; ASSOC PROF SPAN, QUEEN'S UNIV, ONT, 71- **HONORS AND AWARDS** Best Article Award, Can Asn Hispanists, 78, 79 & 80. **MEMBERSHIPS** Can Asn Hispanists (pres, 81-84); Int Asn Hispanists; Int Galdo's Asn; Am Asn Teachers Span & Port; Brit Asn Hispanists. **RESEARCH** works of Benito Perez Galdos; modern Spanish novel; medieval Spanish literature. **SELECTED PUBLICATIONS** Auth, Fortunata and Jacinta, Mod Lang Rev, Vol 0090, 95; Galdos and the Ideology of Domesticity in Spain, Bulletin of Hisp Stud, Vol 0071, 94; Romanos and the Pleasures of the Imagination, Critica Hisp, Vol 0018, 96; The Mask of Erotic Financial Language in 3 Social Novels by Perezgaldos,Benito, Rev Lit, Vol 0058, 96; The Loss of Virginity of 3 Galdosian Heroines--Tormento, Fortunata And Tristana, Insula-Rev de Letras Y Ciencias Humanas, Vol 0048, 93. **CONTACT ADDRESS** Dept of Span & Ital, Queen's Univ, Kingston, ON, K7L 3N6.

BOATENG, FAUSTINE
DISCIPLINE FRENCH LANGUAGE AND LITERATURE **EDUCATION** Universite de Besancon, BA; Howard Univ, PhD. **CAREER** Asst prof. **MEMBERSHIPS** ALA; CLA. **RESEARCH** French African and Caribbean literature; works by Francophone African women writers. **SELECTED PUBLICATIONS** Auth, Asante--The Heritage Library of African Peoples; Rosen, 96. **CONTACT ADDRESS** Clark Atlanta Univ, 223 James P Brawley Dr, SW, Atlanta, GA, 30314.

BOCHIN, HAL WILLIAM
PERSONAL Born 02/23/1942, Cleveland, OH, m, 1975, 1 child **DISCIPLINE** SPEECH COMMUNICATION **EDUCATION** John Carroll Univ, BA, 64; Univ WI-Madison, MA, 67; IN Univ, Bloomington, PhD(speech), 70. **CAREER** Asst prof, 69-75, assoc prof, 75-77, PROF SPEECH COMMUN & DIR FORENSICS, CA STATE UNIV, FRESNO, 78-. **HONORS AND AWARDS** Meritorious Performance Awards, 88, 90; Outstanding Prof, 97. **MEMBERSHIPS** Am Forensics Asn; Nat Commun Asn. **RESEARCH** History of American public address; argumentation; rhetorical criticism. **SELECTED PUBLICATIONS** Auth, Caleb B Smith's opposition to the Mexican War, Ind Mag Hist, 6/73; Controlling Land Use: Issues & Evidence, Alan, 75; contribr, American broadcasting: A source book on the history of radio and TV, Hastings House, 75; coauth, The San Francisco simulation, Commun Educ, 3/77; auth, Law Enforcement: Issues & Evidence, Alan, 77; coauth, with Michael A. Weatherson, Hiram Johnson: A Bio-Bibliography, Greenwood Press, 88; auth, Richard Nixon: Rhetorical Strategist, Greenwood Press, 90; President Nixon's First Inaugural Address, in Halford Ryan, ed, The Inaugural Addresses of Twentieth Century American Presidents, Praeger, 93; Richard Milhous Nixon, in Halford Ryan, ed, U. S. Presidents as Orators, Greenwood Press, 95; coauth, with Michael A. Weatherson, Hiram Johnson: Political Revivalist, Univ Press of Am, 95; auth, Marcus Moziah Garvey, in Richard Leeman, ed, African-American Orators: A Bio-Critical Sourcebook, Greenwood, 96; President Clinton's First Inaugural Address, in Lloyd Rohler, ed, Great Speeches for Criticism and Analysis, Alistair Press, 97. **CONTACT ADDRESS** Dept of Commun, California State Univ, Fresno, 5201 N Maple, Fresno, CA, 93740-9739. **EMAIL** halb@csufresno.edu

BODDE, DERK
PERSONAL Born 03/09/1909, Brant Rock, MA **DISCIPLINE** EAST ASIAN STUDIES **EDUCATION** Harvard Univ, AB, 30; Univ Leyden, Neth, PhD, 38. **CAREER** Lectr Chinese, 38, from asst prof to prof, 38-75, EMER PROF CHINESE, UNIV PA, 75-, Specialist on China, Off Strategic Serv & Off War Info, 42-45; Fulbright res fel, Peking, China, 48-49; Guggenheim fel, 70-71; Nat Endowment for Humanities fel, Cambridge, Eng, 74-75; Dr Sun Yat-sen distinguished vis prof China studies, Georgetown Univ, 81. **MEMBERSHIPS** Am Orient Soc (pres, 68-69); Asn Asian Studies; Am Acad Arts & Sci; Am Philos Soc. **RESEARCH** Chinese philosophy, history and law; Chinese popular religion. **SELECTED PUBLICATIONS** Auth, Sanctioned Violence in Early-China, Jour of the Amer Oriental Soc, Vol 0112, 92. **CONTACT ADDRESS** Univ Penn, 29 W Phil-Ellena St, Philadelphia, PA, 19119.

BODINE, JAY F.
DISCIPLINE GERMAN LITERATURE **EDUCATION** Princeton Univ, PhD. **CAREER** Assoc prof. **RESEARCH** Computer applications in language; literary theory; study of socio-political reality in literature. **SELECTED PUBLICATIONS** Auth, pubs on Karl Kraus, Heinrich Heine, Ludwig Wittgenstein, Walter Benjamin, Manes Sperber, and Max Frisch. **CONTACT ADDRESS** Foreign Languages and Literature Dept, Colorado State Univ, Fort Collins, CO, 80523. **EMAIL** jbodine@vines.colostate.edu

BOEHNE, PATRICIA JEANNE
PERSONAL Born 02/04/1940, Neuilly, France, m, 1960, 2 children **DISCIPLINE** MEDIEVAL HISPANO-ARABIC & CATALAN LITERATURE **EDUCATION** Ind Univ, Bloomington, BA, 61, MA, 62, PhD, 69. **CAREER** Instr Span & French, Bradley Univ, 63-65; asst prof Span, Franklin & Marshall Col, 68-70; assoc prof Romance lang, 70-75; Prof Romance Lang, Eastern Col, 75-, Chmn Lang Dept, 74-, Humanist evaluator Hisp, Pub Comt for Humanities Pa, 77-. **HONORS AND AWARDS** Phi Sigma Iota; Sigma Delta Pi; Kappa Delta Pi; Am Philos Soc Mellon fel, Vatican microfilm libr; Linbock Award, 87. **MEMBERSHIPS** NAm Catalan Soc; MLA; Renaissance Soc Am; Am Asn Teachers Span & Port. **RESEARCH** Catalan Neoplatonism. **SELECTED PUBLICATIONS** Auth, Dream and Fantasy in Early Catalan Prose, Hisp, Barcelona, 75; transl, Introduction to Catalan Literature, Ind Univ 77; Catalan Studies, Hispam, Barcelona, 77; J V Foix, Twayne, 80; The Renaissance Catalan Novel, Twayne. **CONTACT ADDRESS** Dept of Lang, Eastern Col, 1300 Eagle Rd, Saint Davids, PA, 19087-3696. **EMAIL** pboehne@eastern.edu

BOENING, JOHN
PERSONAL Born 06/15/1942, New York, NY, m, 1 child **DISCIPLINE** COMPARATIVE LITERATURE **EDUCATION** Pace Col, BA, 64; Univ Md, MA, 66; Ind Univ, PhD(comp lit), 71. **CAREER** Teaching asst English, Univ Md, 64-66; univ fel, Ind Univ, 66-68; from instr to assoc prof, 69-75; Dir Comp Lit Prog, Univ Toledo; prof English Comp Lit, 80; chmn dept, 91-97; div rep, MLA Delegate Assembly, 80-82, 85-88; CEAO Chairs Caucus, 95-97; vis scholar Univ Saarbruecken, 97. **HONORS AND AWARDS** Univ fel Indiana Univ; Delta Phi Alpha; Phi Kappa Phi; Arts & Sciences Exceptional Merit Award, Univ Toledo. **MEMBERSHIPS** MLA; Am Soc Aesthet; Am Comp Lit Asn; Am Soc Eighteenth-Century Studies; Am Lit Translators Assn; Am Lit Translators Assn; Int Comp Lit Asn, Am Lit Translators Assn; Int Herder Soc. **RESEARCH** Literature and the visual arts; Anglo-German literary relations; modern poetry. **SELECTED PUBLICATIONS** Auth, Literature, language frontiers, and cultural thanatology, Proc VII Int Cong Aesthet, 73; auth, Some recent theories of reception and influence: Their implications for the study of international literary relations, Prov VIII Cong Int comp Lit Asn, 76; ed, The Reception of Classical German Literature in England, 1760-1860: A Documentary History from Contemporary Periodicals (10 vols), Garland, NY, 77; auth, Too German, and not German enough: Lessing's reputation in England, Lessing Yearbk, 81; The Sezession Movement as a verbal fiction, Proc IX Cong Int Comp Lit Asn, 81; Pioneers and Precedents: The Rise of the Critic and the Reception of German Literature in England, Int Archiv Sozialgeschichte Deutschen Lit, 82; Comparative Lit, Incommensurability and Cultural Misreading, in Cultural Dialogue and Misreading, ec Mabel Lee and Yue Daiyun, Beijing, Beijing Univ Press and Sydney, Univ of Sydney World Lit Series, 97; More patchwork than Pastiche: Longfellow's Golden Legend and Goethe's Faust, in Parodia, Pastiche, Mimetismo, ed P Mildonian, Rome, Editore Bulzoni, 97, others. **CONTACT ADDRESS** 2801 W Bancroft St, Toledo, OH, 43606-3390. **EMAIL** jboenin@uoft02.utoledo.edu

BOERNER, PETER
PERSONAL Born 03/10/1926, Tartu, Estonia, m, 1959, 3 children **DISCIPLINE** COMPARATIVE LITERATURE, GERMAN LITERATURE **EDUCATION** Univ Frankfurt, DrPhil, 54. **CAREER** Prog asst, Radio Frankfurt, 48-49; fel, Col Europe, Bruges, Belgium, 54-55; cur, Goethe Mus, Dusseldorf, 55-58; asst prof Ger, Stanford Univ & res dir, Stanford Overseas Studies Ctr, Beutelsbach, Ger, 58-61; from asst prof to assoc prof Ger, Univ Wis, 61-64; assoc prof, State Univ NY Buffalo, 64-66; prof comp lit, Univ Wis-Madison, 66-71, PROF COMP LIT, GER & W EUROP STUDIES, IND UNIV, BLOOMINGTON, 71-, Vis prof, Univ Mich, 67, Middlebury Col, 68 & Yale Univ, 78; Guggenheim fel, 70-71; fel, Herzog August Bibliothek, Wolfenbuttel, WGer, 76-77; fel, Zentrum fur interdisziplinare Forschung, Bielefeld, WGer, 80-81. **MEMBERSHIPS** Goethe Ges; Int Ver Ger Sprach-u Literaturwiss; Am Soc 18th Century Studies; Am Comp Lit Asn; Soc Etudes Staeliennes. **RESEARCH** International literary relations; 18th century and romanticism. **SELECTED PUBLICATIONS** Auth, The German Idea--4 English Writers And The Reception Of German Thought, Ger Quart, Vol 0068, 95; West-Ostlicher Divan-Ger, Jour Engl and Ger Philol, Vol 0096, 97. **CONTACT ADDRESS** Indiana Univ, Bloomington, 1213 E First St, Bloomington, IN, 47401.

BOFMAN, THEODORA HELENE
PERSONAL Born 11/19/1947, Chicago, IL, 2 children **DISCIPLINE** SOUTHEAST ASIAN LANGUAGE & LITERATURE **EDUCATION** Univ MI, BA, 69, PhD, 78; Yale Univ, MA, 71. **CAREER** Lectr ling & Eng, Ben Gurion Univ, 78-80; from Instr to Prof Linguistics, Northeastern IL Univ, Chicago, 81. **RESEARCH** Thai lit & linguistics; lang acquisition. **SELECTED PUBLICATIONS** Auth, Poetics of the Ramakian, Northern IL Univ. **CONTACT ADDRESS** Dept Linguistics, Northeastern Illinois Univ, 5500 N St Louis Ave, Chicago, IL, 60625-4625. **EMAIL** t-boffman@neiu.edu

BOGEN, JOSEPH E.
PERSONAL Born 07/13/1926, Cincinnati, OH, m, 1955, 2 children **DISCIPLINE** NEUROSURGERY **EDUCATION** Whittier Col, AB, 49; Univ S Calif, MD, 56; **CAREER** Asst surg, Cornell Med Sch, 57; Res fel Neurophysiol, Calif Inst Tech, 58; res assoc Neurophysiol, 59, asst neurology, 63 Loma Linda Univ; asst clin prof neurosurg, Calif coll Med, 64; Consult Neurosurg, Calif Inst Tech, 68-80; Assoc clin prof, Univ S Calif, 73-77, Clin prof, 77- ; adj prof, Univ Calif Los Angeles, 84- ; vis prof, Calif Inst Tech, 95-99. **HONORS AND AWARDS** Natl Res Council fel, 58-59; diplomate, Am Bd of Neurological Surg, 66; fel Am Coll Surg, 68. **MEMBERSHIPS** Sigma Xi; AAAS; Los Angeles Soc Neurol Sci; So Calif Neurosurg Soc; Am Acad Neurol; Am Assoc Neurol Surg; Am Coll Surgeons; Soc for Neurosci; Behavioral Neurol Soc; Western Pain Soc; Am Pain Soc; Int Neuropsychol Soc; Acad of Aphasia. **RESEARCH** Postural reflexology; cerebral localization; surgery for epilepsy; neuropsychology and behavioral neurology. **SELECTED PUBLICATIONS** Auth, Comments on Dysgenic Cortex, in Neurosurgery, 95; auth, Disconnection Syndrome, in Blackwell Dictionary of Neuropsychology, Blackwell, 96; auth, Does Cognition in the Disconnected Right Hemisphere Require Right Hemisphere Possession of Language?, in Brain and Lang, 97; auth, The Neurosurgeon's Interest in the Corpus Callosum, in A History of Neurosurgery, Am Assoc Neurol Surg, 97; auth, Split-brains: Interhemispheric Exchange as a Source of Creativity, in Encyclopedia of Creativity, in press; auth, My Developing Understanding of Roger Wolcott Sperry's Philosophy, Neuropsychologia, in press; coauth, Encyclopedia of Neuroscience, in press. **CONTACT ADDRESS** PO Box 50566, Pasadena, CA, 91115. **EMAIL** jbogen@cns.caltech.edu

BOHN, WILLIARD
PERSONAL Born 12/02/1939, Oakland, CA **DISCIPLINE** FRENCH AND COMPARATIVE LITERATURE **EDUCATION** Univ Calif, Berkeley, BA, 64, MA, 67, PhD(French), 73. **CAREER** Asst prof French & comp lit, Brandeis Univ, 72-75; res assoc comp lit, Univ Calif, Berkeley, 75-79; ASST PROF FRENCH, ILL STATE UNIV, 79-, Am Coun Learned Soc grant-in-aid, 77-78. **MEMBERSHIPS** Am Comp Lit Asn; MLA; Asn Int Amis Guillaume Apollinaire; Asn Studies Dada & Surrealism. **RESEARCH** Guillaume Apollinaire; 20th century French poetry; literature and art. **SELECTED PUBLICATIONS** Auth, Where Dream Becomes Reality--Reflections on Breton,Andre and Surrealism/, Esprit Createur, Vol 0036, 96; Literary Futurism--Aspects of the 1st Avant-Garde, Comp Lit, Vol 0045, 93; Pound,Ezra And The Symbolist Inheritance, Comp Lit, Vol 0047, 95; Madness and Modernism, Insanity in the Light of Modern-Art, Literature, and Thought--Philos and Literature, Vol 0017, 93; Severini,Gino And Futurist Ideography--Danzatrice Mare, Mln-Mod Lang Notes, Vol 0109, 94; Artistic Relations--Literature and the Visual-Arts in 19th-Century France, Comp Lit Stud, Vol 0033, 96; Family Secrets and the Psychoanalysis of Narrative, Philos and Lit, Vol 0017, 93; Severini,Gino And Futurist Ideography--Danzatrice Mare, Mln-Mod Lang Notes, Vol 0109, 94; Collaborative Form-Stud in the Relations of the Arts, Comp Lit, Vol 0046, 94; Visual Poetry in Catalonia, Rusinol,Santiago, Forum for Mod Lang Stud, Vol 0032, 96. **CONTACT ADDRESS** Dept of French, Illinois State Univ, Normal, IL, 61761.

BOND, GERALD ALBERT
PERSONAL Born 03/15/1944, Rochester, NY, m, 1966, 2 children **DISCIPLINE** FRENCH AND GERMAN LANGUAGE, MEDIEVAL HISTORY **EDUCATION** William Col, BA, 65; Tufts Univ, MA, 66; Yale Univ, PhD(Medieval studies), 73. **CAREER** Instr Ger, 70-73, asst prof French & Ger, 73-78, ASSOC PROF FRENCH & GERMAN, 78- **HONORS AND AWARDS** Younger humanist fel, Mellon Found, 76; Camargo Found fel, 77. **MEMBERSHIPS** Medieval Acad; MLA; Int Courtly Lit Soc. **RESEARCH** Medieval lyric poetry; courtly love; game and literature. **SELECTED PUBLICATIONS** Auth, The Game of Love, Troubadour Wordplay, Romance Philol, Vol 0048, 94; The Envy of Angels--Cathedral Schools and Social Ideas in Medieval Europe, Speculum- Jour Medieval Stud, Vol 0071, 96. **CONTACT ADDRESS** Dept of Foreign Lang Lit & Ling, Univ of Rochester, Rochester, NY, 14627.

BOND, ZINNY SANS
PERSONAL Born 09/01/1940, Riga, Latvia **DISCIPLINE** LINGUISTICS **EDUCATION** Univ Akron, BA, 62; Ohio State Univ, MA, 67, PhD(ling), 71. **CAREER** Asst prof ling, Univ Alta, 71-73; asst prof, 74-80, ASSOC PROF HEARING & SPEECH SCI, OHIO UNIV, 80-, Consult, Wright-Pattersen Air Force Base, 74-77. **MEMBERSHIPS** Ling Soc Am; Acoust Soc Am; Am Speech & Hearing Asn; Asn Advan Baltic Studies. **RESEARCH** Phonetics; phonology; speech perception. **SELECTED PUBLICATIONS** Auth, The Elusive Illusive Syllable, Phonetica, Vol 0050, 93; Latvian-English English-Latvian Dictionary, Mod Lang Jour, Vol 0078, 94. **CONTACT ADDRESS** Dept of Hcaring & Speech Sci, Ohio Univ, Athens, OH, 45707.

BONDANELLA, PETER
DISCIPLINE ITALIAN LITERATURE **EDUCATION** Univ Oregon, PhD, 70. **CAREER** Prof. **MEMBERSHIPS** Am Asn Italian Studies. **RESEARCH** Renaissance and contemporary literature; comparative literature and literary theory; Italian cinema. **SELECTED PUBLICATIONS** Auth, Machiavelli and the Art of Renaissance History; Francesco Guicciardini; The Dictionary of Italian Literature; The Eternal City: Images of Rome in the Modern World; Federico Fellini: Essays in Criticism; Italian Cinema: From Neorealism to the Present; Perspectives on Federico Fellini; The Films of Roberto Rossellini; Umberto Eco and the Open Work. **CONTACT ADDRESS** Dept of French and Italian, Indiana Univ, Bloomington, 300 N Jordan Ave, Bloomington, IN, 47405.

BONEBAKKER, SEEGER A.
PERSONAL Born 09/21/1923, Wisch, Netherlands, m, 1953 **DISCIPLINE** ARABIC LANGUAGE AND LITERATURE **EDUCATION** State Univ Leiden, Drs, 51, PhD (Semitic lang), 56. **CAREER** Mem acad staff, State Univ Leiden, 49-60; from asst prof to assoc prof, Arabic studies, Columbia Univ, 60-69; PROF ARABIC, UNIV CALIF, LOS ANGELES, 69-, Dir, Concordance et Indices Tradition Musulmane, Union Acad Int, 59-60; Columbia Univ Coun Res Humanities grant, Neth, 63; Nat Found Arts and Humanities sr fel, 67-68; regents fac fel, Univ Calif, 72-73 and 75-76; prin investr, Onomasticon Arabicum Proj, Univ Calif, Los Angeles, 76-; Corresp, Royal Nether Acad Arts and Sci, Amsterdam, 80. **MEMBERSHIPS** Am Orient Soc. **RESEARCH** Medieval Arabic literature and biography; history of medieval Arabic rhetoric and philology. **SELECTED PUBLICATIONS** Auth, Research on Arabisms in Italian with Particular Attention to Sicily, Romance Philol, Vol 0047, 94; Research on Arabisms in Italian with Particular Attention to Sicily, Romance Philol, Vol 0047, 94. **CONTACT ADDRESS** Dept of Near East Lang and Cult, Univ of Calif, Los Angeles, CA, 90024.

BONFINI, MARIE ROSEANNE IHM
PERSONAL Born 11/21/1935, Philadelphia, PA **DISCIPLINE** FRENCH LANGUAGE & LITERATURE, COMPARATIVE LITERATURE **EDUCATION** Immaculata Col, AB, 58; Univ Paris, dipl French studies, 62; Fordham Univ, MA, 64; Univ Rochester, PhD(French/comp lit), 69. **CAREER** Sec teacher, Norfolk Cath High Sch, Va, 62-65; acad dean, 71-78, Prof French, Immaculata Col, 68-; Coordr, Inst Res, 82-92, pres, 92-; Res grant, Univ Rochester in Paris, 67; Fulbright reviewer, State Pa Selection Comt, 74; Nat Endowment for Humanities res grant, 78; Lilly grant medieval studies, 80; Nat Endowment for Humanities grant, Harvard Univ, 83; Harvard Univ Inst for Presidents, 93. **HONORS AND AWARDS** West Catholic High School Hall of Fame, Pheta, 98. **MEMBERSHIPS** Am Asn Teachers Fr. **RESEARCH** Middle Ages and French literature; creative leisure; play theory and comparative literature. **CONTACT ADDRESS** Immaculata Col, Immaculata, PA, 19345-0654.

BONGIE, LAURENCE
PERSONAL Born 12/15/1929, Turtleford, SK, Canada **DISCIPLINE** FRENCH **EDUCATION** Univ BC, BA, 50; Univ Paris, PhD, 52. **CAREER** Lectr, 53, instr 54-56, asst prof, 56-61, assoc prof, 61-66, prof & dept head, 66-92, PROF EMER FRENCH, UNIV BC, 92-. **HONORS AND AWARDS** Hum Res Coun fel, 55-56; Can Coun sr fel, 63-64, 75-76; Soc Sci & Hum fel, 82-83; Killam sr fel, 82-83; sr Killam res prize, 87; Officier de l'Ordre des Palmes Academiques. **MEMBERSHIPS** Fre, Int, Am & Can Soc's 18th Century Stud; Soc Acad Freedom & Scholar; BC Soc Transls & Interps. **RESEARCH** 18th century studies **SELECTED PUBLICATIONS** Auth, David Hume: Prophet of the Counter-Revolution, 65; auth, Diderot's Femme Savante, 77; auth, Condillac, Les Monades, 80, Fre transl, 94; auth, The Love of a Prince: Charles Edward Stuart in France 1745-1748, 86. **CONTACT ADDRESS** Dept of French, Univ of British Columbia, Vancouver, BC, V6T 1Z1.

BOON, JEAN-PIERRE
DISCIPLINE FRENCH LITERATURE **EDUCATION** Columbia Univ, PhD. **CAREER** Dept Frenc, Univ Kan **RESEARCH** French film. **SELECTED PUBLICATIONS** Publ(s), on Montaigne, Baudelaire. **CONTACT ADDRESS** Dept of French and Italian, Univ Kansas, Admin Building, Lawrence, KS, 66045.

BORCHARDT, FRANK L.
PERSONAL Born 11/16/1938, New York, NY **DISCIPLINE** GERMAN **EDUCATION** St Peter's Col, AB, 60; Johns Hopkins Univ, MA, 62, PhD (Ger), 65. **CAREER** Asst prof Ger, Northwestern Univ, 65-68; asst prof Ger and comp lit, Queens Col, NY, 68-71; ASSOC PROF GER, DUKE UNIV, 71-, Chmn Dept, 82-, Fulbright res fel, Univ Wurzburg, 71-72; Am Coun Learned Socs fel, 78-79. **MEMBERSHIPS** Renaissance Soc Am; Medieval Acad Am; Am Asn Teachers Ger. **RESEARCH** Renaissance; Middle Ages; modern German drama. **SELECTED PUBLICATIONS** Auth, Boehme--An Intellectual Biography of the 17th Century Philosopher and Mystic, Ger Quart, Vol 0067, 94; Hellwig, Johann--A Descriptive Bibliography, Sixteenth Century J, Vol 0027, 96. **CONTACT ADDRESS** Dept of Ger, Duke Univ, Durham, NC, 27706.

BORDEAU, CATHERINE
DISCIPLINE FRENCH **EDUCATION** Univ MI, Ann Arbor, BA, MA, PhD. **CAREER** Asst prof, Lyon Col. **RESEARCH** 19th century French lit; gender studies. **SELECTED PUBLICATIONS** Auth, The Gendering of the Creator, in Jeering Dreamers: Essays on L'Eve Future, Atlanta, 96. **CONTACT ADDRESS** Dept of For Lang, Lyon Col, 300 Highland Rd, PO Box 2317, Batesville, AR, 72503. **EMAIL** cbordeau@lyon.edu

BORER, HAGIT
DISCIPLINE SYNTAX, MORPHOLOGY, LANGUAGE ACQUISITION **EDUCATION** MIT, PhD. **CAREER** Prof, Univ Southern Calif. **RESEARCH** Comparative syntax; interaction between syntax & morphology; language acquisition. **SELECTED PUBLICATIONS** Auth, Parametric Syntax: Case Studies in Semitic &Romance Languages, Foris Publ, Dordrecht, 84; Restrictive Relatives in Modern Hebrew, Natural Lang & Ling Theory 2, 84; I-Subjects, Ling Inquiry 17 3, 86; Anaphoric AGR, in The PRO Drop Parameter, Reidel, Dordrecht, 89; The Causative- Alternative: A Case Study in Parallel Morphology, J Ling Rev, 92; The Ups & Downs of Hebrew Verb Movement, Natural Lang and Ling Theory 13, 95; coauth, The Maturation of Syntax, in Parameter Setting, Reidel, Dordrecht, 87. **CONTACT ADDRESS** Dept of Linguistics, Univ Southern Calif, University Park Campus, Los Angeles, CA, 90089. **EMAIL** borer@almaak.usc.edu

BORGESON, PAUL W.
DISCIPLINE SPANISH LITERATURE **EDUCATION** Vanderbilt Univ, PhD, 77. **CAREER** Assoc prof, Univ Ill Urbana Champaign. **RESEARCH** Spanish American Literature; poetry of the 1960s to date; ideology and poetics; popular language; aesthetic tradition. **SELECTED PUBLICATIONS** Auth, Hacia el hombre nuevo: Poesia y pensamiento de Ernesto Cardenal, 84; Los talleres del tiempo: Verso escogido, 92; La lucha permanente: Arte y sociedad en La Espiga Amotinada, 94; Lengua viva, 98. **CONTACT ADDRESS** Spanish, Italian, and Portuguese Dept, Univ Ill Urbana Champaign, 52 E Gregory Dr, Champaign, IL, 61820. **EMAIL** borgeson@uiuc.edu

BORMANN, DENNIS ROBERT
PERSONAL Born 11/07/1935, Mitchell, SD, m, 1962, 2 children **DISCIPLINE** SPEECH COMMUNICATION, GERMAN **EDUCATION** Univ SDak, 57; Univ Iowa, MA, 59, PhD (speech, drama), 68. **CAREER** Asst prof Speech, Mankato State Col, 64-66; from instr to assoc prof, 66-77, interim chmn speech, 75-77, PROF SPEECH, UNIV NEBR-LINCOLN, 77-, Woods fac res fel, Univ Marburg, 73; comn int and intercultural speech commun, Speech Commun As, 77-79. **MEMBERSHIPS** Speech Commun Asn; AAUP. **RESEARCH** Rhetorical theory; German rhetoric and poetic; public address. **SELECTED PUBLICATIONS** Auth, The 6th Canon--Belletristic Rhetorical Theory and Its French Antecedents, Philos Rhet, Vol 0029, 96. **CONTACT ADDRESS** Dept of Speech Cummun, Univ of Nebraska, Lincoln, P O Box 880329, Lincoln, NE, 68588-0329.

BORMANSHINOV, ARASH
PERSONAL Born 12/05/1922, Belgrade, Yugoslavia, m, 1959, 5 children **DISCIPLINE** SLAVIC LINGUISTICS **EDUCATION** Univ Pa, AM, 56, PhD, 58. **CAREER** Asst prof Russ and Ger, Rensselaer Polytech Inst, 58-59; asst prof Russ, Rutgers Univ, 59-60; asst prof Slavic lang and lit, Princeton Univ, 60-66; asst prof Slavic ling, NY Univ, 66-68 and City Col New York, 68-80. John Hay Whitney Found fel, 56-57; lectr Russ, Mohawk Educ TV, Albany, NY, 58-59; Am Coun Learned Soc res grants, Uralic and Altaic Lang, 59-63; Inter-Univ Comt travel grant, 60; consult educ TV, NY Univ, 61; Doris Duke travel grant, 62; fac res grant, NY Univ, 67-68; vis prof, New Sch Soc Res, 68; assoc prof Russ, Univ Okla, 69; VIS PROF, YESHIVA UNIV, 71- **MEMBERSHIPS** MLA; Am Orient Soc; Am Asn Teachers Slavic and East Europ Lang; Mongolia Soc; Asn Asian Studies. **RESEARCH** South Slavic linguistics; Yugoslav literature; Kalmyk-Oirat studies. **SELECTED PUBLICATIONS** Auth, A Secret Kalmyk Mission to Tibet in 1904, Cent Asiatic J, Vol 0036, 92. **CONTACT ADDRESS** 6811 Gairlock Pl, Lanham, MD, 20801.

BOSKOVIC, ZELJKO
PERSONAL Born 11/27/1964, Tuzla, Bosnia and Herzegovina, s **DISCIPLINE** LINGUISTICS **EDUCATION** Sarajevo Univ, BA, 88; W Va Univ, MA, 91; Univ Conn, MA, 93, PhD, 95. **CAREER** Asst Prof, Univ Conn, 95-. **HONORS AND AWARDS** Roma Jacobson fel, Univ Conn, 91-93; NSF grant, 95-96; Hasan Brkic Award, Sarajevo Univ, 87, 88. **RESEARCH** Linguistics; syntax **SELECTED PUBLICATIONS** Auth, Categorial Status of Null Operator Relatives and Finite Declarative Complements, Lang Res, 94; D-Structure, Theta-Criterion, and Movement into Theta-Positions, Ling Anal, 94; Case Properties of Clauses and the Greed Principle, Studia Ling, 95; coauth Comprehension of Non-Lexical Categories in Agrammatism, Jour Psycholinguistic Res, 95; auth Participle Movement and Second Position Cliticization in Serbo-Croatian, Lingua, 95; Selection and the Categorial Status of Infinitival Complements, Natural Lang & Linguistic Theory, 96; Coordination, Object Shift, and V-movement, Linguistic Inquiry, 97; Superiority Effects with Multiple Wh-Fronting in Servo-Croatian, Lingua, 97; On Certain Violations of the Superiority Condition, Agro, and Economy of Derivation, Jour Linguistics, 97; Pseudoclefts, Studia Linguistics, 97; The Syntax of Nonfinite Complementation: An Economy Approach, Mit Press, 97; Formal Approaches to Slavic Linguistics: The Connecticut Meeting, Mich Slavic Publ, 97; Scrambling and Last Resort, Linguistic Inquiry, 98. **CONTACT ADDRESS** Linguistics Dept, Univ of Conn, Storrs, CT, 06269. **EMAIL** boskovic@uconnum.uconn.edu

BOTTERILL, STEVEN
PERSONAL Born 02/10/1958, Shoreham, United Kingdom **DISCIPLINE** ITALIAN, LITERATURE, MEDIEVAL STUDIES **EDUCATION** Cambridge Univ, BA, 80, MA, 84, PhD, 84 **CAREER** Res Fel, 83-86, Queens' col; Asst Prof, 86-92, Assoc Prof, 92-, UC Berkeley **MEMBERSHIPS** AAIS, AATI, ALSC, NAS **RESEARCH** Dante **SELECTED PUBLICATIONS** Auth, Dante and the Mystical Tradition: Bernard of Clairvaux in the Commedia, Cambridge UP, 94 **CONTACT ADDRESS** Italian Studies, Univ of California, Berkeley, Berkeley, CA, 94720-2620. **EMAIL** Stevenb@uclink4.berkeley.edu

BOTZENHART-VIEHE, VERENA
DISCIPLINE EUROPEAN HISTORY, GREEK SOCIETY, WESTERN CIVILIZATION **EDUCATION** Univ Tulsa, BA, 74; Univ Calif, Santa Barbara, MA, 75, PhD, 80. **CAREER** 1977-78 Pres, Hist Grad Stud Assn, Univ Calif, 77-78; tchg asst, Univ Calif, 75-78; adjunct prof, Youngstown State Univ, 86-90; assist prof, 90; fac consult, Princeton, 94-; assoc prof, 96-. **HONORS AND AWARDS** Sullins award, Univ Tulsa, 74; grant, Sem Fur Politische Bildung in Munich, 88-93; fac develop grant, Univ Chicago, 91; Silver memorial scholar, 89; President's grant, Univ Calif, 83. **MEMBERSHIPS** Mem, President's Admissions Task Force. **SELECTED PUBLICATIONS** Auth, George Bancroft, Notable U.S. Ambassadors 1775-1995: A Biographical Dictionary, Greenwood Press, 96. Andrew White, Notable U.S. Ambassadors 1775-1995: A Biographical Dictionary, Greenwood Press, 96; rev(s), Origins of a Spontaneous Revolution: East Germany, 1989, by Karl Dieter Opp, Peter Voss, and Christiane Gern, History, Rev of New Bk(s), 96; The End of an Era? Europe 1945-1990s, by Antonio Varsori, Hist Rev of New Bk(s), 96; The Cold War-A History, by Martin Walker, Hist Rev of New Bk(s), 95; James B. Conant: Harvard to Hiroshima and the Making of the Nuclear Age, by James G. Hershberg, The Historian, 94; Chester Bowles: New Dealer in the Cold War, by Howard B Schaffer, Hist Rev(s) of New Bk(s), 94. **CONTACT ADDRESS** Rel, Hist, Philos, Classics Dept, Westminister Col, New Wilmington, PA, 16172-0001. **EMAIL** verenabv@westminster.edu

BOUDREAU, HAROLD LAVERNE
PERSONAL Born 03/15/1928, Ashkum, IL, m, 1955, 1 child **DISCIPLINE** MODERN SPANISH LITERATURE **EDUCATION** Univ Ill, Champaign, BA, 48, MA, 50; Univ Wis-Madison, PhD (Span), 66. **CAREER** From instr to prof Span, 58-69, chmn dept Span and Port, 71-77, PROF SPAN, UNIV MASS, AMHERST, 69-, Consult, Nat Endowment Humanities, 76-78. **MEMBERSHIPS** MLA; Am Asn Teachers Span and Port. **RESEARCH** Modern Spanish novel and poetry; critical theory. **SELECTED PUBLICATIONS** Auth, A Sesquicenten-

nial Tribute to Galdos 1843-1993, Rev Estud Hisp, Vol 0031, 97. **CONTACT ADDRESS** Dept of Span and Port, Univ of Mass, Amherst, MA, 01003.

BOULTON, MAUREEN
DISCIPLINE FRENCH LITERATURE **EDUCATION** Col of New Rocjelle, BA, 70; Univ Pa, MA, 72, PhD, 76; Oxford Univ, Mlitt, 80. **CAREER** Prof. **RESEARCH** Textual criticism; manuscript studies; relations between lyric poetry and medieval romance. **SELECTED PUBLICATIONS** Auth, The Song in the Story, 93; ed, Old French Evangile de l'Enfance. **CONTACT ADDRESS** Romance Languages and Literatures Dept, Univ of Notre Dame, 221 Decio Hall, Notre Dame, IN, 46556. **EMAIL** maureen.b.boulton.1@nd.edu

BOVE, CAROL MASTRANGELO
DISCIPLINE FRENCH LANGUAGE, LITERATURE, AND CULTURE **CAREER** Prof. **RESEARCH** Contemporary literature and theory; film; and women's studies; Julia Kristeva. **SELECTED PUBLICATIONS** Publ, Twentieth Century French fiction, theory, and film; ed, Claude Richard's study of American literature, Univ Pa Press. **CONTACT ADDRESS** Dept of Mod Lang, Westminister Col, New Wilmington, PA, 16172-0001. **EMAIL** cbove@westminster.edu

BOWEN, BARBARA C.
DISCIPLINE FRENCH **EDUCATION** Oxford, BA, 58, MA, 62; Univ Paris, Doc, 62. **CAREER** Instr, 62-63, asst, 63-66, assoc, 66-73, prof, 73-87, Univ Ill; PROF FR, COMP LIT, VANDERBILT, 87-. **CONTACT ADDRESS** 1818 Cedar Ln, Nashville, TN, 37212.

BOWMAN, FRANK PAUL
PERSONAL Born 06/12/1927, Portland, OR **DISCIPLINE** FRENCH LITERATURE **EDUCATION** Reed Col, BA, 49; Yale Univ, MA, 52, PhD(French), 55. **CAREER** Asst prof French, Univ Calif, 54-62; assoc prof, Reed Col, 62-63; assoc prof, 63-65, PROF FRENCH, UNIV PA, 65-, Guggenheim fel, 68-69; vis prof French, Univ Paris, 73-75; Nat Endowment Humanities fel, 78-79. **MEMBERSHIPS** MLA; Mod Humanities Res Asn; Int Asn Fr Studies; Soc Etudes Romantiques. **RESEARCH** French romanticism; autobiography. **SELECTED PUBLICATIONS** Auth, Voyage en Egypte--French, French Forum, Vol 0018, 93; French Historians and Romanticism, Romantisme, Vol 0025, 95; Exile and Glory--From the Family Novel to Literary Identity in the Works of Chateaubriand-French, French Forum, Vol 0020, 95; Renan,Ernest--Histoire Des Origines Du Christianisme, Rev Hist Lit de la France, Vol 0096, 96; French Autobiography, Devices and Desires, French Forum, Vol 0020, 95; Poetics of the New History, Fr Rev, Vol 0068, 95; Krudener,Madame,De 1764-1824--Romanticism and the Holy-Alliance, Romantisme, Vol 0024, 94; Stael,Germaine,De Delphine Vol 2, the Avant-Texte, Contribution to a Study of Genetic Criticism, Romantisme, Vol 0024, 94. **CONTACT ADDRESS** Dept of Romance Lang, Univ of Pa, Philadelphia, PA, 19174.

BOWSKY, MARTHA WELBORN
PERSONAL Born 07/17/1950, High Point, NC, m, 1986, 2 children **DISCIPLINE** CLASSICAL STUDIES **EDUCATION** Univ of Michigan, Ann Arbor, PhD, 83; Univ of NC, Chapel Hill, MA, 74, BA, 72. **CAREER** Asst, Assoc, Prof, 84-, Univ of the Pacific Coast; Vis Asst Prof, 83-84, Univ of Cal, Davis. **HONORS AND AWARDS** Who's Who Among Amer Tchr; Amer Philos Soc; HEH Trave to Collections; Amer Philos Soc. **MEMBERSHIPS** Assoc Intl d'Epigraphie Grecque et Latine; Amer Philological Assoc; Archaeol Inst Amer; Assoc of Ancient Hist; CA Classical Assoc. **RESEARCH** Epigraphy; Ancient Hist; Women's Gender Stud. **SELECTED PUBLICATIONS** Auth, An Atticizing Stele from Western Crete, Zeitschrift fur Papyrologie und Epigraphik 118, 97; Knossos and Campania: the Critical Connection, Preliminary Publication of the Eleventh International Congress of Greek and Latin Epigraphy, 97; Roman Crete: No Provincial Backwater, Proceedings of the Seventh International Cretological Congress, Rethymnon, Crete, 95; Eight Inscriptions from Roman Crete, Zeitschrift fur Papyrologie und Epigraphik, 95; Cretan Connections: The Transformation of Hierapytna, Cretan Studies, 95; Portrait of a Polis: Lato pros Kamara in the Late Second Century B.C., Hesperia, 89. **CONTACT ADDRESS** 824 Burr St, Davis, CA. **EMAIL** MWBowsky@vmsl.cc.uop.edu

BOYCE, ELIZABETH
DISCIPLINE SPANISH **CAREER** Prof; Houston Baptist Univ, 7 yrs; sponsor, Span Club; fac assoc, Rex Fleming Readers; Med Prof Interview Comt. **HONORS AND AWARDS** Fac Woman of the Yr, 96 & Opal Goolsby Outstanding tchg awd, 94. **RESEARCH** Spanish literature before 1700. **SELECTED PUBLICATIONS** Coauth, groundbreaking bk poetry written by women in Spain in the 16th and 17th centuries. **CONTACT ADDRESS** Language Dept, Houston Baptist Univ, 7502 Fondren Rd, Houston, TX, 77074. **EMAIL** BoyceES@aol.com

BOYD, BARBARA WEIDEN
PERSONAL Born 03/31/1952, Bronx, NY, m, 1980, 1 child **DISCIPLINE** CLASSICAL STUDIES **EDUCATION** Manhattanville Col, BA, 74; Univ Mich, MA, 76. PhD, 80. **CAREER** Asst prof to prof, Bowdoin Col, 80- . **HONORS AND AWARDS** NEH Fel, 87-88. **MEMBERSHIPS** Am Philol Asn; Vergilian Soc; Class Asn of the Midwest & South; Class Assn of New England. **RESEARCH** Latin poetry, Vergil and Ovid; Augustan Rome; Republican Roman literature and society. **SELECTED PUBLICATIONS** Auth, Cydonea mala: Virgilian Word-Play and Allusion, in Harvard Studies in Class Philol, 83; auth, Tarpeia's Tomb: A Note on Propertius 4.4, in Am J of Philol, 84; auth, Parva seges satis est: The Landscape of Tibullan Elegy in 1.1. and 1.10, in Transactions of the Am Philol Asn, 84; auth, the Death of Corinna's Parrot Reconsidered: Poetry and Ovid's Amores, in the Class J, 87; auth, Propertius on the Banks of the Eurotas, in Class Q, 87; auth, Virtus Effeminata and Sallust's Sempronia, in Transactions of the Am Philol Asn, 97; auth, Non Hortamine Longo: An Ovidian "Correction of Virgil, in Am J of Philol, 90; auth, Vergil's Camilla and the Traditions of Catalogue and Ecphrasis, in Am J of Philol, 92; auth, Non enarrabile textum: Ecphrastic Trespass and Narrative Ambiguity in the Aeneid, in Vergilius, 95; auth, Bibliography for Ovid's Amores and Metamorphoses, in Teacher's Guide to Advanced Placement Courses in Latin, 95; auth, Changes in the 1999 Advanced Placement Examinations in Latin (Vergil and Latin Literature), in Class Outlook, 97; auth, Ovid's Literary Loves: Influence and Innovation in the Amores, Univ Michigan Pr, 97; auth, Pallas and Turnus: Selections from Vergil, Aeneid Books 10 and 12, Bolchazy-Carducci, 98. **CONTACT ADDRESS** Dept of Classics, Bowdoin Col, Brunswick, ME, 04011. **EMAIL** bboyd@bowdoin.edu

BRADFORD, CAROLE A.
PERSONAL Born 03/14/1937, Hammond, IN **DISCIPLINE** SPANISH & FRENCH **EDUCATION** Univ Tenn, BA, 58, MA, 59; Vanderbilt Univ, PhD(Span), 72. **CAREER** Instr romance lang, Univ Tenn, 59-66; instr, 70-72, Asst Prof Romance Lang, Bowling Green State Univ, 72-, Fel, Nat Endowment Humanities, NY Univ, 78-79. **MEMBERSHIPS** MLA; Am Asn Teachers Span & Port; Am Asn Univ Prof. **RESEARCH** Spanish 20th century poetry; Spanish 19th century novel. **SELECTED PUBLICATIONS** Auth, Gilalbert, Juan, Voice In Exile, Anales De La Literatura Espanola Contemporanea, vol 0018, 93. **CONTACT ADDRESS** Dept of Romance Lang, Bowling Green State Univ, Bowling Green, OH, 43403.

BRADFORD, CLINTON W.
PERSONAL Born 11/05/1909, Grapevine, AR, w, 1946, 2 children **DISCIPLINE** SPEECH COMMUNICATION **EDUCATION** Univ Arkansas, BA, 38; State Univ Iowa, MA, 41; Louisiana State Univ, PhD, 51. **CAREER** Prof Speech Commun, Louisiana State Univ, 51-73. **RESEARCH** Researching and writing histories of Bradford family and Warbritton family. **SELECTED PUBLICATIONS** Auth, Ministry for Retired Persons, Reily Memorial Univ Church, 87. **CONTACT ADDRESS** 212 Amherst Ave, Baton Rouge, LA, 70808-4603.

BRADLEY, KEITH RICHARD
PERSONAL Born 04/30/1946, Oldswinford, England, m, 1976, 3 children **DISCIPLINE** ANCIENT HISTORY, CLASSICAL LANGUAGES **EDUCATION** Sheffield Univ, BA, 67, MA, 68; Oxford Univ, BLitt, 75. **CAREER** Asst prof, Johns Hopkins Univ, 72-77; vis asst prof, Stanford Univ, 77-80; ASST PROF CLASSICS & ANCIENT HIST, UNIV VICTORIA, 80- **MEMBERSHIPS** Soc Prom Roman Studies; Am Philol Asn; Am Asn Ancient Historians; Class Asn Can. **RESEARCH** Roman social history; Roman historiography. **SELECTED PUBLICATIONS** Auth, Slaves And Freedmen in Roman Society Under the Empire--A Selection of Texts With Translations--German, Greek And Latin, vol 0068, 96; Suetonius, 'Lives Of Galba, Otho And Vitellius', Latomus, vol 0055, 96. **CONTACT ADDRESS** Dept of Classics, Univ of Victoria, Victoria, BC, V8W 2Y2.

BRADY, PATRICK S.
DISCIPLINE FRENCH LITERATURE **EDUCATION** Sorbonne Univ, DUP, 60. **CAREER** Prof. **SELECTED PUBLICATIONS** Auth, pubs on catastrophe theory, chaos theory, and complexity theory. **CONTACT ADDRESS** Dept of Romance Languages, Knoxville, TN, 37996.

BRADY, ROBERT M.
DISCIPLINE INTERPERSONAL COMMUNICATION **EDUCATION** Univ Mich, PhD. **CAREER** Comm Stu, Univ Ark **HONORS AND AWARDS** Fulbright Cols Outstanding Adv Award., Vice-chair. **SELECTED PUBLICATIONS** Articles, Jour Business Comm; Comm Monographs; Western Jour Comm; Jour Language Soc Psychol; Soc Behavior Personality. **CONTACT ADDRESS** Univ Ark, Fayetteville, AR, 72701.

BRAESTER, YOMI
PERSONAL Born 06/24/1964, Israel, m, 1998 **DISCIPLINE** COMPARATIVE LITERATURE, EAST ASIAN STUDIES **EDUCATION** Hebrew Univ, BA, 85, MA, 91; Yale Univ, MA, 92, PhD, 97. **CAREER** Post-doc fel, CCS, Univ Calif, Berkeley, 97-98; ASST PROF, COMP LIT, UNIV GA, 98-; dir, Chinese Lang Prog, Univ Ga, 98-. **HONORS AND AWARDS** Pacific Cult Fnd Res Grant; China Times Cultural Fnd Award. **MEMBERSHIPS** MLA, AAS. **RESEARCH** Comparative lit, E Asian stud **SELECTED PUBLICATIONS** Auth, "Shanghai's Economy of the Spectacle: The Shanghai Race Club in Liu Na'ou's and Mu Shiying's Stories," Modern Chinese Lit, 9:1, 95; "The Cruelty in Writing: Lu Xun's 'Diary of a Madman' and Authorial Complicity," Literature and Cruelty: Proceedings of the Sixth Annual Graduate Conference in French Francophone and Comparative Literature, 96; "Modern Identity and Karmic Retribution in Clara Law's Reincarnations of Golden Lotus," Asian Cinema 10, 98. **CONTACT ADDRESS** 133 Ashley Cir, Apt 3, Athens, GA, 30605. **EMAIL** yomi@arches.uga.edu

BRANSFORD WILSON, JR, JOE
DISCIPLINE SOUTH ASIAN STUDIES, RELIGIOUS STUDIES **EDUCATION** Univ Wis, Madison, BA, MA; Univ Va, PhD. **CAREER** Assoc prof Philos and Relig, asst ch and chair-elect, dept Philos and Relig, Univ NC, Wilmington. **RESEARCH** Yogacara School of Buddhism. **SELECTED PUBLICATIONS** Auth, Translating Buddhism from Tibetan: An Introduction to the Language of Literary Tibetan and the Study of Philosophy in Tibetan, Snow Lion, 92; Problems and Methods in the Translation of Buddhist Texts from Tibetan, in Buddhist Translations: Problems and Perspectives, Tibet House, 95; Tibetan Commentaries on Indian Shastras, in Jose Cabezon and Roger Jackson, eds, Tibetan Literature: Studies in Genre, Snow Lion, 96; Persons, Minds, and Actions: Indo-Tibetan Analyses of the Person in Anglo-American Perspective, in Ninian Smart and B Srinivasa Murthy, eds, East-West Encounters in Philosophy and Religion, Popular Prakashan, 96; The Monk as Bodhisattva: a Tibetan Integration of Buddhist Moral Points of View, J of Relig Ethics 24.2, 96. **CONTACT ADDRESS** Univ N. Carolina, Wilmington, Bear Hall, Wilmington, NC, 28403-3297. **EMAIL** wilsonj@uncwil.edu

BRASCH, WALTER MILTON
PERSONAL Born 03/02/1945, San Diego, CA, m, 1983 **DISCIPLINE** LANGUAGE & CULTURE **EDUCATION** San Diego State Col, AB, 66; Ball State Univ, MA, 69; Ohio Univ, PhD, 74. **CAREER** Reporter-ed daily newspapers, Calif, Ind, Iowa & Ohio, 65-71; exec producer-writer, MID Productions, 71-74; asst prof jour, Temple Univ, 74-76; PROF JOUR, BLOOMSBURG UNIV, 80-; Writer-producer, United Screen Artists & United TV Productions, 65-66 & 75-81; writer, Maushake Advert, 65-66 & 76-80; corresp ed, Jour Hist, 75-; consult, Major Makers Video Productions, 76-80; writer, Weitzman polit pub rels; consult ed, Int J Creole Studies, 77-; copywriter/media advisor, Jackson-Walsh Advertising, L.A., 73-81; writer-consult, K-Squared Productions, 95-. **HONORS AND AWARDS** Meritorious Achievement Medal, U.S. Coast Guard, 77; Flotilla Commanders Award, 78; Creative Teaching Award, Bloomsburg Univ, 81; Creative Arts Award, 83; Director's Award, Soc Professional Journalists, 92; Nat Freedom of Infor Award, 94; Points of Excellence winner/alumni, San Diego State Univ, Col Arts & Letters, 97; Scribendum Libros honor (honoris causa), Alpha Kappa Delta. **MEMBERSHIPS** Soc Prof Journalists; United Auto Workers/Nat Writers Union; Newspaper Guild; Nat Soc Newspaper Columnists; Penn Press Club; Penn Women's Press Asn. **RESEARCH** Media history; media and society; journalism. **SELECTED PUBLICATIONS** Auth, Enquiring Minds and Space Aliens, Mayfly, 96; Sex and the Single Beer Can: For Casinos, 6-Hour Visitors Make a Full House, In: Mosaic I, McGraw-Hill, 96; Joel Chandler Harris, Uncle Remus, and the American Social Conscience, In: The Eye of the Reporter, Western Ill Press, 96; Probing the Media and American Culture, Mayfly, 97; The American Muckraker: Investigating America's Social Conscience, In: American Cities and Suburbs: An Encyclopedia, Garland, 98; Brer Rabbit, Uncle Remus, and the Cornfield Journalist: The Tale of Joel Chandler Harris, 98; author of a biweekly syndicated newspaper column, Spectrum Features Syndicate; weekly syndicated radio show, United Broadcasting Network. **CONTACT ADDRESS** Dept Jour, Bloomsburg Univ of Pennsylvania, 400 E 2nd St, Bloomsburg, PA, 17815-1399. **EMAIL** brasch@planetx.bloomu.edu

BRAULT, GERARD JOSEPH
PERSONAL Born 11/07/1929, Chicopee Falls, MA, m, 1954, 3 children **DISCIPLINE** FRENCH LITERATURE **EDUCATION** Assumption Col, Mass, AB, 50; Laval Univ, AM, 52; Univ Pa, PhD(Romance lang), 58. **CAREER** Teaching fel Univ, Pa. 54-56; instr French, Bowdoin Col, 57-59, asst prof Romance lang, 59-61; assoc prof, Univ Pa, 61-65, vdean grad sch arts & sci, 62-65; head dept, Prof French, Pa State Univ, University Park, 65-, Fulbright fel, Strasbourg, France, 56-57 & res scholar, 68-69; NDEA Lang Res Sect res contracts, 60 & 63; Am Coun Learned Soc travel grants, 60, 66, 70, 73, 76 & grant-in-aid, 63; Am Philos Soc grants-in-aid, 60, 66 & 72; Guggenheim fel, 68-69; fel Inst Arts & Humanistic Studies, Pa State Univ, 76-; bd mem, Medieval Ctr, Univ Lille III, 77-, **HONORS AND AWARDS** Ordre des Palmes Acad, 65, Officier, 75; Officer, Ordre Nat du Merite, 80., DLitt, Assumption Col, Mass, 76. **MEMBERSHIPS** MLA; Int Arthurian Soc; fel Mediaeval Acad Am; Am Asn Teachers Fr; fel Heraldy Soc

London. **RESEARCH** Medieval French literature, especially Song of Roland; medieval heraldic terminology; New England French language and culture. **SELECTED PUBLICATIONS** Auth, Birth and Development of the Chanson-De-Geste in Europe, J Medieval Studies, vol 0070, 95; Maria and Her Mother, Conflict and Continuity in 'Maria Chapdelaine', Quarterly J Modern Lit, vol 0050, 96; Paris, Gaston and the 'Histoire Poetique De Charlemagne', Studi Francesi, vol 0040, 96; The Complete Romances of Chretien-De-Troyes--Staines, French Rev, vol 0068, 95; The Subject of Violence--The 'Song Of Roland' and the Birth of the State--Haidu, French Forum, vol 0021, 96. **CONTACT ADDRESS** Pennsylvania State Univ, 402 Burrowes Bldg, University Park, PA, 16802.

BRAUN, ERNST
PERSONAL Born 12/16/1921, Breslau, Germany, m, 1956, 2 children **DISCIPLINE** GERMAN LITERATURE **EDUCATION** Univ Wis, BA, 47, MA, 48, PhD, 60. **CAREER** Instr German, Univ Tenn, 49-53; asst prof German & comp lit, Queens Col, NC, 55-57, assoc prof & chmn dept foreign lang, 57-59; asst prof German, Bowling Green State Univ, 60-61, chmn dept German & Russian, 61-62; assoc prof German, 62-64, Prof German, Univ Mo-Columbia, 64-, Chmn Dept German & Slavic Studies, 62-68, 76-, **MEMBERSHIPS** MLA; Midwest Mod Lang Asn; Am Asn Teachers Ger. **RESEARCH** German literature; comparative literature. **SELECTED PUBLICATIONS** Auth, Silences Roar, the Life and Drama of Erdman, New Theatre Quarterly, vol 0009, 93. **CONTACT ADDRESS** Dept of Germanic & Slavic Lang, Univ of Mo, Columbia, MO, 65201.

BRAUN, THEODORE EDWARD DANIEL
PERSONAL Born 04/18/1933, Brooklyn, NY, m, 1965, 1 child **DISCIPLINE** FRENCH LITERATURE & LANGUAGE **EDUCATION** St John's Univ, NY, BA, 55; Univ Calif, Berkeley, MA, 61, PhD(Romance lang & lit), 65. **CAREER** Teacher High Sch, NY, 54-55; asst English, Lycee Emile-Loubet, France, 55-56; from asst prof to assoc prof French, Univ Wis-Milwaukee, 64-70; Prof French, Univ Del, 70-, Frank L Weil Inst Studies Relig & Humanities, 67; Nat Endowment Humanities grant, 74; pres, Univ Fac Sen, 76-77; Ctr Advan Study, Univ Del, 81-82. **MEMBERSHIPS** MLA; Am Soc 18th Century Studies; Am Asn Teachers Fr; AAUP; E Cent Am Soc 18th Century Studies. **RESEARCH** Voltaire; 18th century French and comparative literature. **SELECTED PUBLICATIONS** Auth, Theater, Opera, and Audience in Revolutionary Paris--Analysis and Repertory, Comp Drama, vol 0030, 96; Eclecticism and Coherences of the Enlightenment--Miscellany Offered to Ehrard, French Rev, vol 0068, 94. **CONTACT ADDRESS** Dept of Lang & Lit, Univ of Del, Newark, DE, 19711.

BRAUN, WILHELM
PERSONAL Born 06/29/1921, Vienna, Austria **DISCIPLINE** GERMAN LITERATURE **EDUCATION** Univ Toronto, BA, 49, MA, 50, PhD, 53. **CAREER** Lectr Ger, Univ Toronto, 51-53; asst prof, Morehouse Col, 53-56; from instr to assoc prof, 56-66, Prof Ger Lit, Univ Rochester, 66-, Mem, Vorstand Int Robert Musil Gesellschaft, 76. **MEMBERSHIPS** MLA; Am Asn Teachers Ger. **RESEARCH** Modern German literature; Robert Musil. **SELECTED PUBLICATIONS** Auth, Muthel, Johann, Gottfried Concerti for Keyboard Instruments and Strings, Musikforschung, vol 0047, 94; 'Praeludia Ad Ludum Comicum De Aminta Et Silvia' in the 1630 Collection of Dramas 'Liebeskampff'--The Issue of Its Authorship, Daphnis-Zeitschrift Fur Mittlere Deutsche Literatur, vol 0022, 93; Dedekind, Constantin, Christian Die 'Aelbianische Musen-Lust', Musikforschung, vol 0048, 95. **CONTACT ADDRESS** Dept of For & Comp Lit, Univ of Rochester, 500 Joseph C Wilson, Rochester, NY, 14627-9000.

BREE, GERMAINE
PERSONAL Born 10/02/1907, Lasalle, France **DISCIPLINE** FRENCH LITERATURE **EDUCATION** Univ Paris, Lic es Lett, 30, dipl, 31, Agrege, 32. **CAREER** Teacher, Oran, Algeria, 32-36; from lectr to prof French lit, Bryn Mawr Col, 36-52; chmn dept French, Wash Sq Col, NY Univ, 53-60, head dept Romance lang, Grad Sch Arts & Sci, 54-60; Vilas prof French, inst Res Humanities, Univ Wis-Madison, 60-73; KENAN PROF HUMANITIES, WAKE FOREST UNIV, 73-, Vis prof French, Wellesley Col, 59 & Am Univ Cairo, Egypt, 70; Fulbright prof, Univ London, Eng, 65-66; mem Fleming Comn Doctoral Coun, State Educ Dept, State Univ NY, 72, chmn French Rating Comt doctoral prog; mem adv bd, Am Coun Learned Soc & Nat Foun Arts & Humanities. **HONORS AND AWARDS** Chevalier, Legion of Honor, 58., LittD, Smith Col, 60, Mt Holyoke Col, 63, Allegheny Col, 63, Duke Univ, 64, Oberlin Col, 66, Dickinson Col, 68, Rutgers Univ, 69, Wake Forest Univ, 69, Brown Univ, 71, Univ Wis-Milwaukee, 73, NY Univ, 75, Univ Mass, Amherst, 76 & Kalamazoo Col, 77; LHD, Wilson Col, 60, Colby Col, 64, Univ Mich, 70 & Davis-Elkins Col, 72; LLD, Middlebury Col, 65. **MEMBERSHIPS** MLA (vpres to pres, 73-75); Am Philos Soc; Am Asn Teachers Fr; AAUP; PEN Club. **RESEARCH** Contemporary French literature. **SELECTED PUBLICATIONS** Auth, from One Period to Another in Poetics of Passage--a Tribute to Tisonbraun, Micheline, Esprit Createur, Vol 0034, 94; Morot-Sir, Edouard and the Literary Text in Theory and the Pleasure of the Text, Romance Notes, Vol 0035, 95; Morot, Sir Edouard and the Literary Text in Theory and the Pleasure of the Text, Romance Notes, Vol 0035, 95; in One's Heart of Hearts and the Crossing of the Century in Sarraute,Nathalie L'usage De La Parole' and 'Tu Ne Taimes Pas', Esprit Createur, Vol 0036, 96; Two Scholars Reflect on their Careers in the Making of a University Professor, USA-1936-84, PMLA Pub(s) MLA Am, Vol 0109, 94. **CONTACT ADDRESS** Dept of French, Wake Forest Univ, Winston-Salem, NC, 27109.

BREINES, JOSEPH
DISCIPLINE FRENCH **EDUCATION** Yale Univ, PhD, 94. **CAREER** ADJ ASST PROF FRENCH, BOSTON COL, 95-. **CONTACT ADDRESS** 24 Groveland St, Auburndale, MA, 02466. **EMAIL** breinesj@bc.edu

BREND, RUTH MARGARET
PERSONAL Winnipeg, MB, Canada **DISCIPLINE** LINGUISTICS **EDUCATION** Univ Man, BA, 46, dipl social work, 47; Univ Mich, MA, 60, PhD(ling), 64. **CAREER** Social worker, Dept of Health & Pub Welfare, Man, 49-51; transl & linguist, Wycliffe Bible Transl, Mex, 53-57; res assoc ling, Univ Mich, 57-64; lectr, 64-66, from asst prof to assoc prof, 66-76, PROF LING, MICH STATE UNIV, 76-, Teaching asst phonology, Summer inst Ling, Univ Ikla, 54-66; consult, ling workshop, Ecuador & Peru, 60-61; lectr ling, San Marcos Univ, Lima, 61; ed, Lang Learning, 64-66; res assoc, Univ Mich, 64-; vis lectr ling, Monash Univ, Australia, 68; Fulbright prof, Norway, 75-76. **MEMBERSHIPS** Ling Soc Am; int Soc Phonetic Sci. **RESEARCH** General linguistic theory; structure and analysis of unwritten languages; general linguistic, grammatical and phonological description, especially from the tagmemic viewpoint. **SELECTED PUBLICATIONS** Auth, A University Course in English Grammar, Word-J int Ling Asn, Vol 0045, 94; Batad-Ifugao Dictionary in With Ethnographic Notes, Word, Vol 0048, 97. **CONTACT ADDRESS** Dept of Ling, Michigan State Univ, 3363 Burbank Dr, Ann Arbor, MI, 48105.

BRENNAN, VIRGINIA M.
PERSONAL Born 12/14/1958, Manhasset, NY **DISCIPLINE** LANGUAGE **EDUCATION** Yale Univ, BA, 80; Columbia Teacher's Col, MA, 85; Univ Ma Amherst, Phd, 93. **CAREER** Swarthmore Col, 90-94; Vanderbilt Univ, 94- . **RESEARCH** Semantics, lang acquisition, pragmatics. **SELECTED PUBLICATIONS** Auth, Specific Situations II, in Proceedings: Formal Grammar Conference at ESSLLI VIII, ESSLI, 96; Quantificational Modals, Linguistic Inquiry, 97; The Relativization of Modals, Proceedings of the Eleventh Amsterdam Colloquium, 97; Conversational Backgrounds and Topics, Cornell Univ Press, 98; rev, Mood at the Interface, GLOT Int, forthcoming. **CONTACT ADDRESS** Vanderbilt Univ, Box 1567-B, Nashville, TN, 37235. **EMAIL** virginia.m.brennan.1@vanderbilt.edu

BREVART, FRANCIS B.
PERSONAL Born 10/17/1945, Casablanca, Morocco, m, 1979, 1 child **DISCIPLINE** GERMAN **EDUCATION** McGill Univ, BS, 66, MA, 70, PhD(comp lit), 75. **CAREER** Lectr Ger lang, Loyola Col, Montreal, 70-71; lectr Ger & French lang, Loyola Col, Montreal & Vanier Col, 71-72; asst prof Ger lit Mid Ages, Univ Munich, 75-77 & Univ Munster, 77-81; ASST PROF GER LIT MID AGES, UNIV PA, 81- **RESEARCH** Astronomical-astrological German literature manuscripts; epigonic heroic German literature: Dietrich epics; the theme of the Enfances. **SELECTED PUBLICATIONS** Auth, Dreams and Herbs in Studies on the 'Circa instans' Manuscript of Petronell and on Medieval German Dream Books, Zeitschrift Fur Deutsches Altertum Und Deutsche Literatur, Vol 0121, 92; The Lorscher Arzneibuch in A Medicinal Compendium from the 8th-Century--Codex-Bambergensis Medicinalis 1--Text, Translation, and Technical Glossary, Isis, Vol 0085, 94; The Lorscher-Arzneibuch in A Medicinal Compendium from the 8th-Century--Codex-Bambergensis Medicinalis 1--Text, Translation, and Technical Glossary, Isis, Vol 0085, 94; The Methods and Problems of Text-Editing For Medieval German Literature, Speculum-J Medieval Stud, Vol 0070, 95; The Organization of Knowledge in Medical Manuscripts, Zeitschrift Fur Deutsches Altertum Und Deutsche Lit, Vol 0124, 95; The Methods and Problems of Text-Editing For Medieval German Literature, Speculum--J Medieval Stud, Vol 0070, 95. **CONTACT ADDRESS** Univ Penn, 255 S 36th St, Philadelphia, PA, 19104-3805.

BREWER, JOHN T.
PERSONAL Born 03/01/1938, Palo Alto, CA **DISCIPLINE** GERMAN **EDUCATION** Pomona Col, BA, 59; Univ Tex, PhD(Ger lang), 62. **CAREER** From instr to asst prof Ger, Univ Calif, Riverside, 62-67; asst prof, 68-71, ASSOC PROF GER, WASH STATE UNIV, 71-, Publ dir, PNCFL, 77-81. **MEMBERSHIPS** MLA; Am Asn Teachers Ger; Western Asn Ger Studies. **RESEARCH** 18th century German literature; Romanticism. **SELECTED PUBLICATIONS** Auth, Lessing 'Nathan the Wise' and the Critics--1779-1991, Seminar--J Germanic Stud, Vol 0032, 96. **CONTACT ADDRESS** Dept of Foreign Lang & Lit, Wash State Univ, Pullman, WA, 99164.

BREWER, MARIA MINICH
PERSONAL Budapest, Hungary **DISCIPLINE** FRENCH LITERATURE **EDUCATION** Univ Witwatersrand, Johannesburg, BA, 66; State Univ NY Buffalo, MA, 70; Yale Univ, PhD(French), 77. **CAREER** Instr, Ohio State Univ, 77-78; asst prof, 78-85, assoc prof, Univ Minn, 86-. **MEMBERSHIPS** MLA, MMLA, IAPL **RESEARCH** 20th century French literature, culture, theater; narrative, theater studies, gender, literary and cultural theory **SELECTED PUBLICATIONS** Auth, An Energetics of Reading: The Intertextual in Claude Simon, The Romanic Rev, 82; auth, A Loosening of Tongues: From Narrative Economy to Women Writing, MLN, 84; auth, Recasting Oedipus: Narrative and the Discourse od Myth in Claude Simon, Stanford Fre Rev, 85; auth, Performing Theory, Theater J, 85; auth, Surviving Fictions: Gender and Difference in Postmodern and Postnuclear Nattative, Discourse, 87; auth, Samuel Beckett: Postmodern Narrative and the Nuclear Telos, Boundary 2, 86-87; auth, Parodies, repliques, ecritures, Revue des Sciences Humaines, 90; auth(Re)inventions referentielles et culturelles chez Claude Simon: les images les instants les voix les fragments du temps du monde, Revue des Lettres Modernes, 94; auth, Claude Simon: Narrativities Without Narrative, Univ Neb, 95. **CONTACT ADDRESS** Dept of French & Ital, Univ of Minn, 9 Pleasant St S E, Minneapolis, MN, 55455-0194. **EMAIL** brewe003@tc.umn.edu

BRIND'AMOUR, LUCIE
DISCIPLINE LATE MEDIEVAL AND 16TH CENTURY, AND QUEBEC LITERATURE **EDUCATION** Univ Montreal, PhD, 77. **CAREER** Assoc prof, La State Univ. **SELECTED PUBLICATIONS** Auth, Rhetorique et th?atralite, in Studi mediolatnini e volgari, 75-76; L'archeologie du signe, 83; La tradition de l'amour courtois, in A Comparative History of Literatures in European Languages, 88. **CONTACT ADDRESS** Dept of Fr Grad Stud, Louisiana State Univ, Baton Rouge, LA, 70803.

BRINNER, WILLIAM MICHAEL
PERSONAL Born 10/06/1924, Alameda, CA, m, 1951, 3 children **DISCIPLINE** PHILOLOGY, ISLAMIC HISTORY **EDUCATION** Univ Calif, Berkeley, AB, 48, MA, 50, PhD, 56. **CAREER** From instr to assoc prof, 56-64, chmn dept & dir Near Eastern Lang & Area Ctr, 65-70, dir Ctr Arabic Studies Abroad, 67-70, PROF NEAR EASTERN LANG, UNIV CALIF, BERKELEY, 64-, Lectr Arabic, Ctr Mid Eastern Studies, Harvard Univ, 61; Am Coun Learned Soc-Soc Sci Res Coun grant Near Eastern studies, 61-62; mem, Am Res Ctr Egypt, 68-70; consult, US off Educ, 65-68; Guggenheim fel, 65-66; mem joint comt Near & Mid E, Am Coun Learned Soc-Soc Sci Res Coun, 66-70 & chmn, 69-70; mem exec comt, Am inst Iranian Studies, 68; Fulbright-Hays fac res award, 70-71 & sr consult, Comt int Exchange Persons, 72-73; dir, Univ Calif Studies Ctr, Jerusalem, 73-75. **MEMBERSHIPS** Am Orient Soc (pres, 76-77); Mediaeval Acad Am; Mid E Studies Asn N Am (pres, 69-70); Am Asn Teachers Arabic (pres, 68-69); Am Prof for Peace Mid E (vpres, 77-). **RESEARCH** Arabic language and literature; Islamic history. **SELECTED PUBLICATIONS** Auth, Textual Sources for the Study of Islam, J Amer Acad Relig, Vol 0060, 92; The Origins of Modern Jewish Studies and the Founding of the Hebrew-University--introduction, Judaism, Vol 0045, 96; Demonizing the Queen of Sheba in Boundaries of Gender and Culture in Postbiblical Judaism and Medieval Islam, J Amer Oriental Soc, Vol 0116, 96. **CONTACT ADDRESS** Dept of Near Eastern Studies, Univ of Cal, 1229 Dwinelle Hall, Berkeley, CA, 94720.

BRISTER, LOUIS EDWIN
PERSONAL Born 07/14/1938, El Dorado, AR, d, 3 children **DISCIPLINE** GERMAN LANGUAGE & LITERATURE **EDUCATION** Miss State Univ, BA, 62; Univ Tex, Austin, MA, 66, PhD, 68. **CAREER** From instr to asst prof Ger, 66-71, chmn dept mod lang, 71-78, assoc prof, 71-79, Prof Ger, Southwest Tex State Univ, 79-. **MEMBERSHIPS** SWestern Coun Latin Am Studies; Soc Ger-Am Studies; Tex State Hist Asn; SCentral Mod Lang Asn. **RESEARCH** German-Americana. **SELECTED PUBLICATIONS** Auth, William von Rosenberg's Kritik: A History of the Society for the Protection of German Immigrants in Texas, Southwestern Hist Quart, 81-82; Eduard Harkort: Ein Freiheitskampfer in Mexiko und Texas, Beitrage zur Geschichte Dortmunds und der Grafschaft Mark, 82; In Mexican Prisons: The Journal of Eduard Harkort, 1832-1834, 86; Witness to Revolution: Herman Ehrenberg's Memoir of the Texas Revolution (forthcoming 99); author of several articles. **CONTACT ADDRESS** Dept of Mod Lang, Southwest Tex State Univ, 601 University Dr, San Marcos, TX, 78666-4685. **EMAIL** lb21@swt.edu

BRIZIO, FLAVIA
DISCIPLINE ITALIAN LITERATURE **EDUCATION** Univ Wash, PhD, 88. **CAREER** Assoc prof. **SELECTED PUBLICATIONS** Auth, pubs on contemporary literary theory, postmodernism, women writers, fictional autobiography, the use of memory, metafiction, and intertextuality. **CONTACT ADDRESS** Dept of Romance Languages, Knoxville, TN, 37996.

BRODMAN, MARIAN
DISCIPLINE FRENCH **EDUCATION** Rosemont Col, BA, 67; Bryn Mawr Col, MA, 69, PhD, 77. **CAREER** Asst prof, Lehigh Univ; instr, Univ Ark; assoc prof, Univ Central Ark, 86-. **MEMBERSHIPS** Ark Foreign Lang Tchr Asn; AATF (Arkansas Chapter) Awards Comt Chair, Central States Conf Tchg Foreign Lang. **CONTACT ADDRESS** Univ Central Ark, 201 Donaghey Ave, Conway, AR, 72035-0001. **EMAIL** marianb@mail.uca.edu

BRODSKY, PATRICIA POLLOCK
PERSONAL Born 06/22/1941, Douds, IA, m, 1968 **DISCIPLINE** COMPARATIVE LITERATURE, GERMAN **EDUCATION** State Univ Iowa, BA, 64; Univ Calif, Berkeley, MA, 66, PhD(comp lit), 72. **CAREER** Asst prof, 74-80, assoc prof, 74-80, PROF GER & RUSS, UNIV MO-KANSAS CITY, 86-; Univ Mo-Kans City fac res grants, 75,77, 94; res, travel grants to Ger, Switz, Poland, 79,84,88,93; Fulbright res award, 84; Univ Kans City Trustees Grant, 86; NEH Trav to Collections grant, 88; NEH summer stipen, 92; DAAD summer study grant, 94; Univ Mo Res Board grant, 96; res assoc, Russ & East Europ Ctr, Univ Ill, Urbana, 76-97. **HONORS AND AWARDS** Weldon Spring Hum Fel, 84; N T Veatch Award Disting Res & Creative Activity, 93. **MEMBERSHIPS** MLA; Am Comp Lit Asn; Int Comp Lit Asn; Am Asn Teachers Slavic & East Europ Lang; Am Asn Teachers Ger; Am Counc Teachers Russ; Rilke-Ges. **RESEARCH** 20th cent lit; antifascism, ethnic stereotyping in lit; borderland cultures; workers' culture, Ger-Slav relations; Rainer Maria Rilke. **SELECTED PUBLICATIONS** Auth, Unkenrufe, World Lit Today, Vol 0067, 93; Babel, Bobrowski, Bienek and the Role of the Cultural intermediary, Germano-Slavica, Vol 0008, 93; The Last Years of Soviet Russian Literature in Prose Fiction 1975-1991, World Lit Today, Vol 0068, 94; Atomic Ghost in Poets Respond to the Nuclear Age, World Lit Today, Vol 0069, 95; The Black Cook As Mater-Gloriosa in Grass 'Faust' Parodies in Die 'Blechtrommel', Colloquia Germanica, Vol 0029, 96; Dressed Like a Soldier Kant, Hermann, Muller, Armin in World-War-II in Central-Europe in 2 Gdr Novels/, Symp--Quart J in Modern Lit(s), Vol 0049, 96; The Black Cook As Mater-Gloriosa in Grass 'Faust' Parodies in Die 'Blechtrommel', Colloquia Germanica, Vol 0029, 96. **CONTACT ADDRESS** Dept of Foreign Lang, Univ of MO, Kansas City, 218 Scofield Hall, 5100 Rockhill Rd, Kansas City, MO, 64110-2499. **EMAIL** dbrodsky@igc.apc.org

BRODY, JULES
PERSONAL Born 03/06/1928, New York, NY, m, 1953, 3 children **DISCIPLINE** FRENCH **EDUCATION** Cornell Univ, AB, 48; Columbia Univ, AM, 49, PhD(French), 56. **CAREER** Lectr French, Columbia Univ, 50-53, from instr to assoc prof, 53-63; prof French & chmn dept foreign & comp lit, Univ Rochester, 63-68; prof romance lang & assoc dean fac, Queens Col, NY, 68-75; PROF ROMANCE LANG & LIT, HARVARD UNIV, 75-, Chmn Dept, 80-, Guggenheim fel & Fulbright res fel, 61-62. **MEMBERSHIPS** Soc Fr Studies; Soc Studies 17th Century; MLA; Am Asn Teachers Fr. **RESEARCH** French literature of the 17th century; classical tradition in France; Montaigne. **SELECTED PUBLICATIONS** Auth, Referential Practice in Language and Lived Space Among the Maya, Lang in Soc, Vol 0022, 93; Itza Maya Texts--With A Grammatical Overview, Colonial Latin Amer Hist Rev, Vol 0004, 95; Ozumacin Chinantec Texts, Lang, Vol 0073, 97. **CONTACT ADDRESS** Dept Geography & Anthropology, Louisiana State Univ, Baton Rouge, LA, 70803.

BROOKS, PETER PRESTON
PERSONAL Born 04/19/1938, New York, NY, 3 children **DISCIPLINE** FRENCH & COMPARATIVE LITERATURE **EDUCATION** Harvard Univ, AB, 59, MA, 62, PhD, 65. **CAREER** From instr to assoc prof French, 65-75, dir lit major, 74-80, prof French & comp lit, 75-80, dir Div Humanities Ctr, 79-82, chmn, Dept Fr, 83-88, CHESTER D TRIPP PROF HUMANITIES, YALE UNIV, 80-, Dir Whitney Humanities Ctr, 80-91, 97-, Dir, Dept Comp Lit, 91-97, lectr, Law School, spring 89-90, 92-93, 95-96 & 97-98; Morse fell 67-68; Am Coun Learned Soc grant-in-aid, 67 & 72; contrib ed, Partisan Rev, 72-; Guggenheim fel, 73-74; mem adv comt, Pac Mod Lang Asn, 76-80; Am Counc Learned Soc fel, 79-80; chmn, ed bd, Yale J Criticism, 87-; NEH res fel, 88-89; vis prof, Summer Inst in Lit, Univ Texas, Austin, 78 & 79; Professore a contratto, Universita di Bologna, 5/90; exec coun, MLA, 94-97; School Criticism & Theory, Dartmouth Col, summer 94; ad bd, Stanford Humanities Ctr, 96 **HONORS AND AWARDS** Decorated Officier des Palmes Academiques, 86; Am Acad Arts & Sci, 91; Doctor Honoris Causa, Ecole Normale Superieure, Paris, 97., MAH, Yale Univ, 75. **MEMBERSHIPS** MLA; Acad of Lit Studies. **RESEARCH** Romanticism; theory and analysis of narrative; psychoanalysis and literary criticism. **SELECTED PUBLICATIONS** Auth, The Novel of Worldliness, Princeton Univ, 69; Nouvelle critique et critique nouvelle aux Etats-Unis, Nouvelle Rev Francaise, 9/69; ed, The Child's Part, Beacon, 72; co-ed, Man and His Fictions, Harcourt, 73; auth, The Melodramatic Imagination, Yale Univ, 76, reprint, Columbia Univ, 85; reprint with new intro, Yale Univ, 95; Freud's masterplot, Yale Fr Studies, 78; co-ed, Jean Genet: A Collection of Critical Essays, Prentice-Hall, 78; Repetition, repression, and return: Great Expectations and the study of plot, New lit Hist, 80; Reading for the Plot, Alfred A Knopf, 84; reprint Vintage Books, 85; reprint Harvard Univ, 92; Body Work, Harvard Univ Press, 93, Korean transl, 97; Psychoanalysis and Storytelling, Blackwell, 94; co-ed, Law's Stories, Yale Univ Press, 96; co-ed, Honore de Balzac, Pere Goriot, W W Norton, 98. **CONTACT ADDRESS** Whitney Humanities Ctr, Yale Univ, P O Box 208298, New Haven, CT, 06520-8298. **EMAIL** pbrooks@minerva.cis.yale.edu

BROWN, FREDERICK
PERSONAL Born 12/23/1934, New York, NY **DISCIPLINE** FRENCH **EDUCATION** Yale Univ, BA, 56, PhD, 60. **CAREER** Asst instr French, 59-60; from instr to asst prof, Univ Tex, 60-63; asst prof French & gen lit, State Univ NY Binghamton, 63-65; prof off French desk, African-Am inst, 64-65; from asst prof to assoc prof French, 65-72, PROF FRENCH, STATE UNIV NY STONY BROOK, 72-, Guggenheim fel, 70-71. **MEMBERSHIPS** MLA **RESEARCH** Modern French literature. **SELECTED PUBLICATIONS** Auth, An essay on surrealism, Tex Quart, 62; On Louis Aragon: Silence and history, Southern Rev, 67; An Impersonation of Angels: A Biography of Jean Cacteau, Viking, 68; co-transl, the Essays of Paul Valery, Bollingen Ser, Vol XI, Princeton Univ, 70; auth, Pere-Lachaise: Elysium as Real Estate, Viking, 73. **CONTACT ADDRESS** Dept of Romance Lang, Univ of NY, Stony Brook, NY, 11790.

BROWN, JAMES LORIN
PERSONAL Born 09/26/1920, Hanford, CA **DISCIPLINE** FRENCH **EDUCATION** Univ Calif, Berkeley, PhD, 52. **CAREER** From asst prof to assoc prof, 63-73, PROF FRENCH, CALIF STATE UNIV, CHICO, 73-. **SELECTED PUBLICATIONS** Auth, Reference to Cunegonde in 1756, Mod Lang Notes, 11/53; Note sur Pataques, 9/54 & Contribution a L'histoire du nom parade, 4/59, Fr Mod. **CONTACT ADDRESS** Dept of Foreign Lang, California State Univ, Chico, First & Normal St, Chico, CA, 95926.

BROWN, JAMES W.
PERSONAL Born 08/28/1934, Anderson, IN, m, 1957, 3 children **DISCIPLINE** SPANISH **EDUCATION** Ind Univ, BS, 56, MA, 61, PhD(Span), 67. **CAREER** Teacher, High Sch, Fla, 58-60; asst prof, 64-67, assoc prof, 68-71, PROF SPAN, BALL STATE UNIV, 71-, Vis asst prof & resident dir, Ind Univ Jr Year in Peru, 67. **MEMBERSHIPS** MLA; Am Coun Teaching Foreign Lang; Am Asn Teachers Span & Port. **RESEARCH** Spanish American novel; foreign language teaching methods and curriculum design. **SELECTED PUBLICATIONS** Ed, Tomochic, Porrua, Mexico City, 68; auth, El hermano asno from Fioretti through Freud, Symposium, winter 71; coauth, A testing of the audio active voice reflector in the foreign language classroom, Mod Lang J, 3/72; Gazapo: Modelo para Armar, Nueva Narrativa Hispanoam, 9/73; auth, Expatriate syndrome: Mario Vargas Llosa on Peruvian racism, Essays Lit, spring 76; Heriberto Frias, Twayne, 78; And the Revolution Began, Romance Literary Studies: Homage to Harvey L Johnson, 79; Vargas Llosa's Recent Novels and Expatriate Syndrome, In: Requiem For the Boom, Montclair Symposium Proceedings, 80. **CONTACT ADDRESS** Dept of Foreign Lang, Ball State Univ, Muncie, IN, 47306.

BROWN, JOHN LACKEY
PERSONAL Born 04/29/1914, Ilion, NY, m, 1941, 2 children **DISCIPLINE** COMPARATIVE LITERATURE, FRENCH **EDUCATION** Hamilton Col, BA, 35; Cath Univ Am, MA, 36, PhD(French, Medieval Latin), 39. **CAREER** Asst prof French, Cath Univ Am, 39-42; asst chief publ sect, Off War Info, 42-43; correspondent Sunday ed, NY Times, Paris, 45-48; cult attache, US Embassies, Paris, Brussels, Rome, Mexico City, 48-68; Prof Comp Lit, Cath Univ Am, 68-, **HONORS AND AWARDS** Awarded Grand Prix de la Critique, 54; mem, Cath Comn on Intellectual & Cult Affairs, 60-; fel, Ctr Advan Studies, Wesleyan Univ, 62-63; vis prof French & English, Univ Louisville, 66-67; prof Am lit & civilization, Inst Anglo-Am Studies, Nat Univ Mex, 66-68; lectr, Cath Inst Paris, 69, Univs Laval, McGill, Montreal & Toronto, 70; dir gen Am Bicentennial Exposition in Paris and Warsaw, 75; vpres, Int Asn Lit Critics, 73-; sr Fulbright prof Am Lit, Univ Lisbon, 79-80; Newstadt Prize, 82; Doctor honoris causa, Univ Queretaro, 84; Am correspondent J des Poetes. **MEMBERSHIPS** MLA; Am Studies Asn; Am Comp Lit Asn; Mediaeval Acad Am; Dante Soc. **RESEARCH** European, especially Franco, American literary relations in the 19th and 20th centuries; Europe avantgarde movements of the 20th century; the problem of expatriation in American literature. **SELECTED PUBLICATIONS** Auth, The Methodus of Jean Bodin: A Critical Study, Cath Univ Am, 39; contribr, chap on France, In: Public Opinion and Foreign Policy, Harper, 49; auth, Panorama de la Litterature Contemporaine Aux Etats-Unis, 54 & 2nd ed, 72, Hemingway, 61, Gallimard, Paris, Il Gigantesco Teatro, Opera Nuove, Rome, 63; Dialogos Transatlanticos, Limusa Wiley, Mexico, 66; Valery Larbaud, Twayne, 81; Verse Shards, Proteus, 82. **CONTACT ADDRESS** 3024 Tilden St NW, Washington, DC, 20008.

BROWN, JOHN MADISON
PERSONAL Born 04/28/1934, Long Beach, CA, m, 1964, 3 children **DISCIPLINE** GERMAN **EDUCATION** Yale Univ, AB, 56; Johns Hopkins Univ, MA, 63, PhD(Ger), 69. **CAREER** Exchange asst English, Robert Koch Schule, Berlin, 60-61; teaching asst Ger, Johns Hopkins Univ, 62-66; from instr to asst prof, Bucknell Univ, 66-70; asst prof, Washington Univ, St Louis, 70-75; asst prof, 75-77, ASSOC PROF GER, VA MILITARY INST, 77-. **MEMBERSHIPS** Am Teachers Ger; MLA; SAtlantic Mod Lang Asn; Am Asn Univ Prof. **RESEARCH** German literature; German culture; American-German intellectual relations. **SELECTED PUBLICATIONS** Auth, Toward a perspective for the Indian element in Hermann Hesse's Siddhartha, Ger Quart, 3/76; Thomas Jefferson and things German-preliminary findings, Report, 78. **CONTACT ADDRESS** Dept of Mod Lang, Va Millitary Inst, Lexington, VA, 24450.

BROWN, MICHAEL G.
PERSONAL Born 03/31/1938, Scranton, PA **DISCIPLINE** HUMANITIES & HEBREW **EDUCATION** Harvard Col, BA, 60; Columbia Univ, MA, 63; Jewish Theol Sem, MHL, 66, rabbi, 68; State Univ NY Buffalo, PhD, 76. **CAREER** PROF HUMANTIIES & HEBREW, YORK UNIV, 68-, dir, Ctr Jewish Stud, 95-; chair Can stud, vis assoc prof, Hebrew Univ (Jerusalem), 80-82; vis assoc prof, Univ Toronto, 83-84; vis assoc prof, Univ Calif San Diego, 85, 88; fel, Am-Holy Land stud proj, 85-87. **HONORS AND AWARDS** DD (Hon), Jewish Theol Sem, 94 **MEMBERSHIPS** Dir, Asn Hebrew Schs; dir, Can Jewish Hist Soc; Can Sem Zionist Thought; Asn Jewish Stud; Rabbinical Assembly; Toronto Bd Rabbis. **SELECTED PUBLICATIONS** Auth, Jew or Juif? Jews, French Canadians, and Anglo-Canadians 1759-1914, 87; auth, The Israeli-American Connection: Its Roots in the Yishuv 1914-1945, 96; ed, Approaches to Antisemitism: Context and Curriculum, 94. **CONTACT ADDRESS** Dept of Humanities, York Univ, 4700 Keele St N, North York, ON, M3J 1P3.

BROWN, ROBERT
DISCIPLINE DISTANCE LEARNING **EDUCATION** Univ Md, PhD, 77. **CAREER** Okla St Univ. **HONORS AND AWARDS** Best Collection Essays Technical Scientific Comm; Frank R. Smith Award Outstanding Jour Article., Dean, Arts & Sciences **SELECTED PUBLICATIONS** Coauth, Technical Writing for Non-Native Speakers of English; Auth, Harcourt-Brace, 95; Team Conferences: Full Collaboration in the Report Writing Process," in A Publications Management: Essays for Professional Communicators; Rethinking the Approach to Communication Training, Technical Communication, 94. **CONTACT ADDRESS** Oklahoma State Univ, 101 Whitehurst Hall, Stillwater, OK, 74078.

BROWN, ROYAL SCOTT
PERSONAL Born 06/20/1940, Raleigh, NC, m, 1964, 2 children **DISCIPLINE** CONTEMPORARY FRENCH LITERATURE **EDUCATION** Pa State Univ, BA, 62; Middlebury Col, MA, 63; Columbia Univ, PhD(French), 75. **CAREER** Grad assoc French, Ind Univ, 63-64; lectr romance lang, Queens Col, 64-70; dir, City Univ NY, Prog Study Abroad, Nancy, France, 70-72; lectr, 72-75, asst prof, 75-81, ASSOC PROF ROMANCE LANG, QUEENS COL, 82-, vis assoc prof, NY Univ, summers 81 & 82. **MEMBERSHIPS** MLA. **RESEARCH** Interdisciplinary studies; cinema; contemporary French literature. **SELECTED PUBLICATIONS** Auth, Film-Music - The Good, the Bad, and the Ugly/, Cineaste, Vol 21, 1995; 'Alphaville' - Godard,JL/, Cineaste, Vol 22, 1996; 'Seven'/, Cineaste, Vol 22, 1996; La 'Ceremonie' - Chabrol,C/, Cineaste, Vol 22, 1997; In Defense of Video Screenings/, Cineaste, Vol 22, 1997; Back from Among the Dead - The Restoration of Hitchcock,Alfred 'Vertigo'/, Cineaste, Vol 23, 1997. **CONTACT ADDRESS** Dept of Romance Lang, Queens Col, CUNY, 6530 Kissena Blvd, Flushing, NY, 11367-1597.

BROWN, STEVEN M.
PERSONAL Philadelphia, PA **DISCIPLINE** JEWISH EDUCATION AND STUDIES **EDUCATION** Jewish Theol Sem Am, BA, BHL; Columbia Univ, MA, EdD. **CAREER** Prin, Cent Hebrew HS Long Island, NY; head tchr to headmaster, N Brch Solomon Schechter Day School, 80-96; educ dir, Adath Jeshurun, Elkins Park, Pa; dir, Melton Res Ctr Jewish Educ, 96; dean William Davidson Grad Schl Jewish Educ, Jewish Theol Sem Am. **HONORS AND AWARDS** Jewish educ workshops, Israel and Argentina; exec bd, Jewish Educ Assembly; pres, Solomon Schechter Day Schl Principals Coun; bd dir, Jewish Comm Rel Coun Philadelphia; bd dir, Adath Jeshurun. **MEMBERSHIPS** Asn Supervision and Curr Devel; Jewish Fed Greater Philadelphia. **SELECTED PUBLICATIONS** Auth, L'Ela--L'Ela: Higher and Higher--Making Jewish Prayer Part of Us; Reclaiming Our Legacy.* Marbeh Torah, Marbeh Chaim-The More Torah, The More Life; Willing, Leaming, and Striving, A Course for Teaching Jewish Youth Based on Emet Ve-Emunah; Approaches to the Numinous, Learn Torah With. Dr Brown. **CONTACT ADDRESS** Jewish Theol Sem of America, 3080 Broadway, New York, NY, 10027. **EMAIL** stbrown@jtsa.edu

BROWNE, MAUREEN
PERSONAL Born 12/28/1921, Louisville, KY **DISCIPLINE** FOREIGN LANGUAGES **EDUCATION** Nazareth Col, Ky, AB, 54; Fordham Univ, MA & PhD, 58. **CAREER** Fulbright scholar, Univ Paris, 58-59; PROF ROMANCE LANG &

CHMN DEPT, BRESCIA COL, KY, 59-, Col consult, Foreign Lang Asn of Archdiocese of Louisville, 63-64. **MEMBERSHIPS** Am Asn Teachers Fr; Am Asn Teachers Span & Port. **RESEARCH** Medieval French literature; history of the 14th century as seen in the work of Eustache Deschamps. **SELECTED PUBLICATIONS** Auth, A Blake Source for VonHolst/, Blake-An Illustrated Quart, Vol 29, 1996. **CONTACT ADDRESS** Dept of Mod Lang, Brescia Col, Owensboro, KY, 42301.

BROWNING, BARTON W.
PERSONAL Born 08/22/1940, Springfield, IL, m, 1964, 2 children **DISCIPLINE** GERMAN LITERATURE **EDUCATION** Wesleyan Univ, BA, 62; Univ Calif, Berkeley, MA, 65, PhD(-Ger), 70. **CAREER** Asst prof, 69-76, ASSOC PROF GER, PA STATE UNIV, UNIVERSITY PARK, 76-. **MEMBERSHIPS** Am Asn Teachers Ger; MLA; Am Soc Ger Lit 16th & 17th Centuries; Int Arbeitskreis Deutsche Barock-Lit; fel, Herzog August Bibliot Wolfenbuttel. **RESEARCH** German Baroque literature; 19th century German literature; European Renaissance and Baroque literature. **SELECTED PUBLICATIONS** Auth, Stifter's Nachsommer and the fourth commandment, Colloquia Germanica, 73; Cooper's influence on Stifter: Fact or scholarly fiction?, Mod Lang Notes, 74; Ein Kleiner Hofmannswaldau fund in Pennsylvanien, Wolfenbuttler Barock-Nachrichten, 75; Joseph Roth's Lengende vom heiligen Trinker: Essence and Elirir, Protest-Form-Tradition, 79; Grillparzer ein 'Bruderzwist im Hauser Habsburg' and the Historical Braunschweig,Heinrich,Julius,von/, Mod Austrian Lit, Vol 28, 1995; **CONTACT ADDRESS** Dept of Ger, Pennsylvania State Univ, University Park, PA, 16802-1014.

BRUCE, JAMES C.
PERSONAL Born 07/15/1929, Washington, DC, d **DISCIPLINE** GERMAN **EDUCATION** Howard U, AB 1952, MA 1968; Univ Of Chicago, PhD 1963. **CAREER** SC State Coll, German instructor, 1956-57; Univ of Chicago, German instructor, 1961-64, asst prof of German, 1964-69, assoc prof German, 1969-89, assoc prof emeritus, 1989-; Soka Univ, Japan, prof of English, 1989-. **HONORS AND AWARDS** Fulbright Fellowship Univ of Frankfurt am Main, Germany 1960-61; Inland Steel Fac Fellowship Univ of Chicago 1965. **MEMBERSHIPS** Mem Mod Lang Assn Of Am; sec Am Assn of Tchrs of German 1974; Midwest Mod Lang Assn; Literarische Gesellschaft Chicago; mem IL Commn Human Rel 1971-73. **CONTACT ADDRESS** Dept of Eng Lit, Soka Univ, 1-236 Tangi-cho Hachioji, Tokyo, ., 192.

BRUEGGEMANN, AMINIA M.
DISCIPLINE GERMAN **EDUCATION** Univ Mich, PhD, 93. **CAREER** Languages, Old Dominion Univ. **SELECTED PUBLICATIONS** Auth, Brueggemann, Aminia & Hubert Rast. Assoziationen: Arbeitsbuch. 2nd Year German Language Program, Communicative Approach; Hill, 91; Brueggemann, Aminia. Chronotopos Amerika bei Max Frisch, Peter Handke, Gunter Kunert und Martin Walser, Peter Lang, 96. **CONTACT ADDRESS** Old Dominion Univ, 4100 Powhatan Ave, Norfolk, VA, 23058. **EMAIL** AMB100F@hamlet.bal.odu.edu

BRULOTTE, GAETAN
PERSONAL Born 04/08/1945, Quebec, PQ, Canada, d **DISCIPLINE** FRENCH LITERATURE; 20TH CENTURY **EDUCATION** Sorbonne & Univ of Paris, PhD. **CAREER** Prof French, Univ S Fla, 88-; vis prof, Univ Quebec, 89-90; vis prof, Sorbonne-Paris, 94; vis prof, Univ Grenoble, 93. **HONORS AND AWARDS** Phi Kappa Phi Artist/Scholar of the Year **MEMBERSHIPS** MLA; Fr Writer's Soc; Quebec Writer's Union **RESEARCH** French & Francophone Studies; Creative Writing; Comparative Literature. **SELECTED PUBLICATIONS** Oeuvres de chair, Figures du discours erotique, Presses de l'Universite, 98; Les Cahiers de Limentinus, Lecturs fin de siecle, XYZ, 98; Epreuves, Lemeac, 99; L'Univers de Jean Paul Lemieux, Fides, 96; Ce Qui nous tient (1989 Literary Grand Prize of Trois-Rivieres), Lemeac, 88. **CONTACT ADDRESS** Dept of Modern Languages, Univ of So Florida, 606 Colebrook Court, Lutz, FL, 33569. **EMAIL** brulotte@chuma1.cas.usf.edu

BRUMFIELD, WILLIAM CRAFT
PERSONAL Born 06/28/1944, Charlotte, NC **DISCIPLINE** RUSSIAN LITERATURE & ART HISTORY **EDUCATION** Tulane Univ, BA, 66; Univ Calif, Berkeley, MA, 68, PhD(Slavic lang), 73 **CAREER** Vis lectr Russ lit, Univ Wis-Madison, 73-74; asst prof Russ lit, Harvard Univ, 74-79; ASST PROF RUSS LIT, TULANE UNIV, 81-, Res dir, ACTR Moscow, 79-80. **MEMBERSHIPS** Am Asn Advan Slavic Studies; Am Asn Teachers Slavic East Europ Lang; MLA. **RESEARCH** Ideology in the Russian novel of the 1860's; Dostoevsky and the French Enlightenment; Russian architectural history. **SELECTED PUBLICATIONS** Auth, Sleptsov redvius, Calif Slavic Studies, 76; Bazarov and Rjazanov: The romantic archetype in Russian nihilism, Slavic East Europ J, winter 77; Petersburg: the imperial design, 11/78, Harvard Mag; Therese philosophe and Dostoevsky's Great Sinner, Comp Lit, summer 80; Ukrainian Churches: Kiev and Chernihiv, Harvard Ukrainian Fund, 81; The Soviet Union: Post-war architecture and planning, Bull Atomic Scientists, 3/82; Le-Corbusier and the Mystique of the USSR - Theories and Projects for Moscow 1928-1936 - Cohen,JL/, Am Hist Rev, Vol 98, 1993; Architecture and Ideology in Eastern-Europe during the Stalin Era - An Aspect of Cold-War History - Aman,A/, Slavic Rev, Vol 53, 1994; Moscow and Leningrad, A Topographical Guide to Russian Cultural History, Vol 1, Buildings and Builders, Vol 2, Writers, Painters, Musicians and their Gathering Places - Ward,CA/, Slavic Rev, Vol 54, 1995; The Church-of-Christ-the-Savior in Moscow - Russian - Kirichenko,El/, Slavic Rev, Vol 55, 1996; A History of St. Petersburg - French - Berelowitch,W, Medvedkova,o/, Slavic Rev, Vol 56, 1997; The Development of Medieval Church Architecture in the Vologda Region of the Russian North/, Architect Hist, Vol 40, 1997. **CONTACT ADDRESS** Dept of Ger & Slavic Lang, Tulane Univ, 6823 St Charles Ave, New Orleans, LA, 70118-5698.

BRUNEAU, MARIE FLORINE
PERSONAL Born 05/18/1943, Casablanca, Morocco, m, 1989 **DISCIPLINE** LANGUAGES **EDUCATION** Univ Calif-Berkeley, BA, 73, MA, 75, PhD, 80. **CAREER** Tchg asst, 73-77, Instr, 79-80, Univ Cal-Berkeley; asst prof French, 80-86, assoc prof French, 86-96, PROF FRENCH, 96- , UNIV S CALIF; vis assoc prof, Univ Chicago, 88. **HONORS AND AWARDS** Taft lectr at Cinc Conf Romance Lang, 91; NEH 89-90; numerous honors, awards, and grants. **MEMBERSHIPS** MLA; 17th Century Fr Lit Soc; Phi Beta Kappa. **RESEARCH** 17th Century literature; Mystical theology; Gender studies. **SELECTED PUBLICATIONS** Auth, Racine, jansenisme et modernite, Jose Corti, 86; Psychoalysis and its Abject: What Lurks Behind the Fear of 'Mother" Studies in Psychoanalytic Theory, 92; L'Amour maternel comme alibi a la production de l'ecriture chez Marie de l'Incarnation, Etudes Litteraires, 94; Female Mystics and the Modern World. Marie de l'Incarnation (1599-1672) Madame Guyon (1648-1717) SUNY Press, 98; Dans les oubliettes de Versailles: Liberte intellectuelle, tolerance et poursuite du bonheur dans la pensee guyonnienne, Le Labyrinthe de Versailles: Parcours critique de Moliere a Malebranche, Rodopi, 98; Guyon, Jeanne Marie Bouvier de la Motte, Encyclo of Women and World Relig, Macmillan, 98. **CONTACT ADDRESS** Dept of French & Italian, Univ Southern California, Los Angeles, CA, 90089-0359. **EMAIL** bruneau@usc.edu

BRUNER, JEFFREY
PERSONAL Born 03/20/1960, Holdenville, OK **DISCIPLINE** SPANISH LITERATURE AND CULTURE **EDUCATION** OK Baptist Univ, BA, 83; Rutgers Univ, MA, 86, PhD, 90. **CAREER** Asst Prof, Assoc Prof, 90 to 96-, West Virginia Univ; Asst Prof, 88-90, Trenton State College. **MEMBERSHIPS** MLA; NMLA; SCLA. **RESEARCH** Historical Novel, Narratology, Lit and other Arts, Cultural Studies. **SELECTED PUBLICATIONS** Auth, El Valle de los Caidos, La historia de Espana seguin Goya Vasari y Rojas, Bogota, Bogota Cen Univ, 98; Pre-Texts and Con-Texts: Poeta en Nueva York Viaje a la luna and the Theater of Federico Garcia Lorca, MIFLC Rev, 94; The Lie that Reveals Truth: Art as/and History in Carlos Rojas' El Valle de loa Caidos, Hispanofila, 94; Glorias y miserias de la dramaturgia de Maria Manuela Reina, Estreno: Cuadernos del Teatro Espanol Contemporaneo, 93; Visual Art as Narrative Discourse: The Ekphrastic Dimension of Carmen Laforet's Nada, Anales de la Literatura Espanola, Contemporanea, 93. **CONTACT ADDRESS** Dept of Foreign Languages, West Virginia Univ, Box 6298, Morgantown, WV, 26506-6298. **EMAIL** jbruner@wvu.edu

BRUNER, M. LANE
PERSONAL Born 07/25/1958, Kansas City, MO, m, 1984 **DISCIPLINE** SPEECH COMMUNICATION/RHETORICAL AND CRITICAL THEORY **EDUCATION** CA State Univ, Northridge, BA, 91; Louisiana State Univ, MA, 93; Univ Washington, PhD, 97. **CAREER** Asst prof of communication, Babson Coll. **HONORS AND AWARDS** Wilma Grimes Memorial Teaching Award in Performance Studies, 94; MacFarlane Scholarship, Outstanding Humanities Graduate Student, 96. **MEMBERSHIPS** International Communication Assn; Natl Communication Assn; The Assn for the Study of Nationalities; Amer Soc for Hist of Rhetoric **RESEARCH** Rhetorical theory; collective identity construction and political memory; political theory; nationalism; critical theory. **SELECTED PUBLICATIONS** Auth, Producing Identities: Gender Problematization and Feminist Argumentation, Argumentation and Advocacy, Spring 96; Towards a Poststructural Rehetorical Critical Praxis: Foucault, Limit Work and Jenninger's Kristallnacht Address, Rhetorica, Spring 96; From Etnic of Nationalism to Strategic Multiculturalism: Shifting Strategies of Remembrance in the Quebecois Secessionist Movement, Javnost, fall 97; Strategies of Remembrance in Pre-Unification West Germany, Quarterly Journal of Speech, 98. **CONTACT ADDRESS** History & Society Div, Babson Col, Babson Park, MA, 02157. **EMAIL** bruner@babson.edu

BRUNSDALE, MITZI MALLARIAN
PERSONAL Born 05/16/1939, Fargo, ND, m, 1961, 3 children **DISCIPLINE** ENGLISH, COMPARATIVE LITERATURE **EDUCATION** NDak State Univ, BS, 59, IMS, 61; Univ NDak, PhD(English), 76. **CAREER** Asst prof, 76-78, assoc prof English, Mayville State Col, 78-,prof, 83-, bk critic, Houston Post, Tex, 70-89; grant rev panelist, Nat Endowment for Humanities, 77-; chair, Humanities Coun, 80-, bk critic, The Armchair Detective, 96-, bk critic, Publishers Weekly, 96-. **RESEARCH** Early 20th century British literature; early 20th century European comparative literature; D H Lawrence. **SELECTED PUBLICATIONS** Auth, Lawrence and the Myth of Brynhild, Western Humanities Rev, autumn 77; The Effect of Mrs Rudolf Dircks' Translation of Schopenhauer's The Metaphysics of Love on D H Lawrence's Early Fiction, Rocky Mountain Rev Lang & Lit, spring 78; D H Lawrence and Raymond Otis: Brothers of Blood, NMex Humanities Rev, winter 78-79; The German Effect on D H Lawrence and his Works, 1885-1912, P L Verlag, Berne, 79; Alexander Solzhenitsy, In: The Encyclopedia of Short Fiction, 81, Boris Pasternak, In: The Encyclopedia of Short Fiction, 81 & D H Lawrence, In: A Critical Survey of Poetry (in prep), Salem Press; D H Lawrence's David: Drama as a Vehicle for Religious Prophecy, In: Themes in Drama V, Cambridge Univ Press, 82; Toward the Greater Day: Rilke, Lawrence, and Immortalilty, Comp Lit Sudies, 82; Sigrid Undset: Ch... of Norway, Oxford: Berg, 88; Dorothy L. Sayers: Solving the Mystery of Wickedness, Oxford: Berg, 90; James Joyce: The Short Fiction, NY: Twayne, 93; James Herriot, NY: Twayne, 96. **CONTACT ADDRESS** Mayville State Col, 330 3rd St NE, Mayville, ND, 58257-1299.

BRUSH, CRAIG BALCOMBE
PERSONAL Born 05/28/1930, Manhattan, NY **DISCIPLINE** FRENCH **EDUCATION** Princeton Univ, AB, 51; Columbia Univ, MA, 55, PhD, 63 **CAREER** Instr French, Choate Sch, 51-54; from instr to asst prof, Columbia Univ, 55-66; asst prof, City Col New York, 66-70; assoc prof, 70-73, chmn dept mod lang, 73-79, PROF FRENCH, FORDHAM UNIV, 73- **MEMBERSHIPS** MLA; Soc Amis Montaigne; Renaissance Soc Am **RESEARCH** French literature in the 16th and 18th centuries **SELECTED PUBLICATIONS** Auth, Montaigne and Bayle, Nijhoff, The Hague, 66; coauth, Bayle: Historical and Critical Dictionary, Bobbs, 67; ed, Selected writings of Pierre Gassendi, Johnson Reprint, 73; Montaigne and Religious Freedom - The Dawn of Pluralism - Smith,MC/, Fr Forum, Vol 17, 1992; Pascal and Disbelief - Catechesis and Conversion in the 'Pensees' - Wetsel,D/, Theol Studies, Vol 57, 1996; Montaigne among the Moderns - Receptions of the 'Essais' - Marchi,DM/, Fr Forum, Vol 21, 1996. **CONTACT ADDRESS** 411 W 115th St, New York, NY, 10025.

BRUSHWOOD, JOHN STUBBS
PERSONAL Born 01/23/1920, Glenns, VA, m, 1945, 2 children **DISCIPLINE** SPANISH AMERICAN LITERATURE **EDUCATION** Randolph-Macon Col, BA, 40; Univ Va, MA, 42; Columbia Univ, PhD, 50 **CAREER** Instr Romance lang, Va Polytech Inst, 42-44; from instr to prof Span, Univ Mo, 46-67, chmn dept Romance lang, 53-57 & 58-59; ROY A ROBERTS PROF LATIN AM LIT, UNIV KANS, 67-, Fund Advan Educ fel, 51-52; Am Philos Soc grant, 57; Am Coun Learned Soc grant, 61; Soc Sci Res Coun grant, 71; Nat Endowment for Humanities, summer 76; Bellagio scholar in residence, 78. **HONORS AND AWARDS** DLitt, Randolph-Macon Col, 81 **MEMBERSHIPS** Midwest Mod Lang Asn (pres, 62-63); MLA; Am Asn Teachers Span & Port; Inst Int Lit Iberoam. **RESEARCH** Mexican literature; Spanish American novel **SELECTED PUBLICATIONS** Auth, Mexico in Its Novel: A Nation's Search for Identity, Univ Tex, 66; Enrique Gonzales Martinez, Twayne, 69; Los Ricos en la Prosa Mexicans, Diogenes, 70; Mexico en su Novela, Fondo Cult Economics, 73; The Spanish American Novel: A Twentieth Century Survey, Univ Tex, 75; Genteel Barbarism: New Readings of Nineteenth Century Spanish American Novels, Univ Nebr, 81; cotransl, The Precipice (Galindo), Univ Tex, 69; Don Goyo (Aguilera-Malta), Humana, 80; An 'Ark for the Next Millennium' - Pacheco,JE/, Am Bk Rev, Vol 16, 1994; Azuela, los 'De Abajo' - Griffin,C/, Hispanic Rev, Vol 63, 1995; The Intellectual, the Artist, and the Reader/, PMLA-Publ Mod Lang Asn Am, Vol 112, 1997; Rio,Angel,Del and the Literature of Ideas/, Hispania, Vol 80, 1997. **CONTACT ADDRESS** 2813 Maine Ct, Lawrence, KS, 66044.

BUCHER, GERARD C.
DISCIPLINE COMPARATIVE LITERATURE **EDUCATION** Ecole des Hautes Etudes, PhD. **CAREER** Prof, SUNY Buffalo. **RESEARCH** The rel between relig and fiction and among anthrop and philos; critical theory; and philos; M. Heidegger; J. Derrida; R. Girard. **SELECTED PUBLICATIONS** Auth, La vision et l'enigme, Elements pour une analytique du logos, ed. du Cerf, 89; Le testament poetique, 94; articles on literature by Bernanos, Mallarme, Rimbaud, Robbe-Grillet; articles on semiotics and religion (Judaism and Christianity). **CONTACT ADDRESS** Dept Comp Lit, SUNY Buffalo, 639 Clemens Hall, Buffalo, NY, 14260.

BUCKSTEAD, RICHARD C.
PERSONAL Born 03/17/1929, Viborg, SD, m, 1956, 4 children **DISCIPLINE** AMERICAN LITERATURE, ASIAN LITERATURE **EDUCATION** Yankton Col, BA, 50; Univ SDak, MA, 56; State Univ Iowa, PhD(English), 59. **CAREER** Instr English, Augustana Col, SDak, 57-58; asst prof, Southeast Mo State Col, 58-61; asst dean, 64-67, dir Asian studies, 71-73, asst prof to assoc prof, 61-80, prof English, St Olaf Col, 80-, Assoc Cols Midwest grant Asian studies, 67-68; vis prof, Chulalong-

korn Univ Bangkok, 67-68. **MEMBERSHIPS** Asn Asian Studies. **RESEARCH** The novels of Yukio Mishima; Japanese prose; Chinese poetry. **SELECTED PUBLICATIONS** Auth, Kawabata and the Divided Self, China Printing, Taipei, 72; The meaning of symbol in Kawabata's Thousand Cranes, Tamkang Rev, Taipei, 11/72; The search for a symbol in Kawabata's Snow Country, 6/73 & The role of nature in Mishima's The Sound of Waves, 2/77, Asian Profile, Hong Kong; A conversation with a Master Luthier, The Strad, Kent, 5/77. **CONTACT ADDRESS** Dept of English, St Olaf Col, 1520 St Olaf Ave, Northfield, MN, 55057-1099. **EMAIL** buckster@stolaf.edu

BULLARD, JOHN MOORE
PERSONAL Born 05/06/1932, Winston-Salem, NC **DISCIPLINE** BIBLICAL STUDIES; ENGLISH LANGUAGE AND LITERATURE **EDUCATION** AB, 53, AM, 55, UNC- Chapel Hill; Mdiv, 57, PhD, 62, Yale Univ. **CAREER** Asst in Instruction, Yale Univ, 57-62; Asst Prof, 61-65, Assoc Prof, 65-70, Albert C. Outler Prof, 70-, Chmn, Dept of Religion, 63-, Wofford Col. **HONORS AND AWARDS** James Graduate Fel at Yale, 57-62; Dana Fel, Emory Univ, 89-90. **MEMBERSHIPS** Amer Acad of Religion; Soc of Biblical Lit; South Carolina Acad of Religion; New Bach Soc; Moravian Music Fdn. **RESEARCH** The Hymn as Literary form from ancient Sumerians to the Hebrew Psalter and beyond. **CONTACT ADDRESS** Dept of Religion, Wofford Col, 429 N. Church St., Spartanburg, SC, 29303. **EMAIL** bullardjm@wofford.edu

BULLARO, GRACE RUSSO
DISCIPLINE COMPARATIVE LITERATURE **EDUCATION** CUNY, City Col NY, BA, 71; SUNY, Stony Brook, MA, 91, PhD, 93. **CAREER** Adj asst prof, SUNY, Nassau Community Col, 90-; adj asst prof, CUNY, Lehman Col, 91-. **CONTACT ADDRESS** English Dept, Lehman Col, CUNY, 250 Bedford Park W, Bronx, NY, 10468. **EMAIL** Gracerbullaro@MSN.com

BUMP, JEROME FRANCIS ANTHONY
PERSONAL Born 06/13/1943, Pine River, MN, 2 children **DISCIPLINE** ENGLISH LITERATURE, COMPARATIVE STUDIES **EDUCATION** Univ Minn, Minneapolis, BA, 65; Univ Calif, Berkeley, MA, 66, PhD(English), 72 **CAREER** Asst prof, 70-76, assoc prof, 76-85, PROF ENGLISH, UNIV TEX, AUSTIN, 85-. **HONORS AND AWARDS** Nat Endowment for Humanities fel, 74. **MEMBERSHIPS** NCTE; Int Hopkins Asn **RESEARCH** Emotional intelligence; creativity; Victorian literature. **SELECTED PUBLICATIONS** Auth, 1 bk, 1 ed, 35 articles, 9 chap, 2 ed letters, 1 bibliogr, 14 rev essays, 21 rev & 71 papers. **CONTACT ADDRESS** Dept of English, Univ of Tex, Austin, TX, 78712-1164. **EMAIL** bump@mail.utexas.edu

BURCH, FRANCIS FLOYD
PERSONAL Born 05/15/1932, Baltimore, MD **DISCIPLINE** COMPARATIVE LITERATURE, THEOLOGY **EDUCATION** Fordham Univ, AB, 56, MA, 58; Woodstock Col, PhL, 57, STL, 64; Univ Paris, Dr, 67. **CAREER** Teacher English & French, Gonzaga High Sch, Washington, DC, 57-60; ordained priest, Roman Catholic, 63; from asst prof to assoc prof, 67-76, trustee, 71-76, asst acad dean, 72-74, prof English, St Joseph's Univ, PA, 76-, Scholar-in-residence English, Millersville State Col, 78. **HONORS AND AWARDS** Alpha Epsilon Delta; Alpha Sigma Nu; Merit Awards for teaching SJU, 80, 83. **MEMBERSHIPS** Int Soc Neoplatonic Studies; MLA; AAUP; Renaissance English Text Soc. **RESEARCH** Ironic, Conversational poetry 1850 to the present, French and Anglo-American; the neoplatonic tradition in literature and religion; Tristan Corbiere. **SELECTED PUBLICATIONS** Auth, Corbiere and Verlaine's Romances sans paroles, Mod Lang Rev, 58; Clement Mansfield Ingleby on Poe's Raven, Am Lit, 63; Soirees bretonnes: The first published verse of Alexis and Edouard Corbiere, Romance Notes, 70; Tristan Corbiere: L'originalite des amours jaunes et leur influence sur T S Eliot, Nizet, Paris, 70; co-ed, Tristan Corbiere: Oeuvres completes, Gallimard, Paris, 70; auth, Sur Tristan Corbiere: Lettres inedites adressees au poete et premieres critiques le concernant, Nizet, Paris, 75; Introd & transl, The Path to Transcendence: From Philosophy to Mysticism in Saint Augustine, Pittsburgh Theol Monogr Series, No 37, 81; The Iconography of Tristan Corbiere: A Manifold or Miscellaneous Self, Studies in Comparative Literature, 91; A Letter from Laurence Housman concerning A E Housman's Poetry, Notes and Queries, 92; RH Benson, Dictionary of Literary Biography, 95. **CONTACT ADDRESS** St. Joseph's Col, 5600 City Ave, Philadelphia, PA, 19131-1376.

BURGIN, DIANA LEWIS
PERSONAL Born 08/04/1943, Boston, MA **DISCIPLINE** SLAVIC LANGUAGES & LITERATURES **EDUCATION** Awarthmore Col, BA, 65; Harvard Univ, MA, 67, PhD(Slavic), 73. **CAREER** Teaching fel Russ, Harvard Univ, 70-71; from instr to asst prof, Wellesley Col, 71-75; asst prof, 75-80, ASSOC PROF RUSS, UNIV MASS, BOSTON, 80-, Corresp, Quincy Patriot Ledger, 72-; assoc Russ lit, Russ Res Ctr, Harvard Univ, 73-; vis lectr Russ, Cambridge Ctr Adult Educ, 74-75. **MEMBERSHIPS** MLA; Am Asn Advan Slavic Studies. **RESEARCH** Nineteenth and 20th century Russian literature; Solzhenitsyn; Dostoevsky. **SELECTED PUBLICATIONS** Contribr, The Mystery of The Queen of Spades: A new interpretation, Mnemozina, 74; auth, The fate of modern man: Ideas of fate, justice and happiness in Solzhenitsyn's Cancer Ward, Soviet Studies, 74; Rzevsky's Solzhenitsyn: Creator and Heroic Deed, Western Humanities Rev, 78; Bulgakov's early tragedy of the scientist-creator: An interpretation of Heart of a Dog, Slavic & East Europ J, 78; co-transl, The Invisible Book, Ardis, 78; Art in the Light of Conscience - 8 Essays on Poetry by Tsvetaeva,Marina - Tsvetaeva,M/, Russ Rev, Vol 53, 1994; Mother-Nature Versus the Amazons - Tsvetaeva,Marina and Female Same-Sex Love/, J Hist Sexuality, Vol 6, 1995. **CONTACT ADDRESS** Dept of Russ, Univ of Mass, Boston, MA, 02125.

BURGOS, FERNANDO
PERSONAL Osorno, Chile, 2 children **DISCIPLINE** SPANISH-AMERICAN LITERATURE **EDUCATION** Univ Chile, BA, 70; Univ FL, PhD(Span-Am lit), 81. **CAREER** Asst prof Span Am lit, Univ Chile, 71-76; graduate asst, 76-80, res asst Span Am lit, Ctr Latin Am Studies, Univ FL, 78-80; Span instr, Middlebury Col, summer 80 & 81; asst prof Span & Span Am Lit, 81-87, assoc prof, 87-96, prof, Univ Memphis, 96-. **HONORS AND AWARDS** Recognition of Outstanding Contrib to the Univ FL, May 81; SPUR Award, 87, 94; fel, vis Scholars Prog, 88; Center for Latin Am and Caribean Studies, Univ IL-Urbana-Champaign, summer 88; Univ Memphis, fac development leave, spring 89; exec comm, Univ IL/Univ Chicago Joint Center for Latim-Am Studies, summer 92; Univ Memphis, Recognition for Outstanding Res Activities. **MEMBERSHIPS** Asociacion Int de Hispanistas (AIH). **RESEARCH** Spanish-American literature, 19th and 20th centuries; Spanish-American Modernity. **SELECTED PUBLICATIONS** Auth, Sarduy: Una escritura en movimento, La Chispa 81 Selected Proc, 81; Conexiones: Barrolo y modernnidad, Escritura, 1-6/81; La novela moderna hispanoamericana: un ensayo sobre el concepto literario de modernidad; Madrid: Origenes, 85, 2nd ed, 90; ed, Prosa hispanica de vanguardia, Madrid: Origenes, 86; ed, Los ochenta mundos de Cortazar: ensayos, Madrid: Edi-6, 87; ed, Las voces del karai: estudios sobre Augusto Roa Bastos, Madrid: Edelsa, 88; Antologia del cuento hispanoamericano, Mexico: Editorial Porrua, 91; ed, Esteban Echeverria, El matadero, Ensayos Esteticos y Prosa Varia de Esteban Echeverria (Critical Ed), Hanover, NH: Ediciones del Norte, 92; Vertientes de la modernidad hispanoamericana, Caracas: Monte Avila Editores, 95; Cuentos de Hispanoamerica en el siglo veinte, 3 vols, Madrid: Castalia, 97; and thirty-five articles in professional journals and books, published in Chile, Argentina, Mexico, Germany, Puerto Rico; the US, Spain, and Venezuela. **CONTACT ADDRESS** Dept of Foreign Langs, Univ Memphis, Campus Box 5264, Memphis, TN, 38152-0001. **EMAIL** fburgos@cc.memphis.edu

BURGOS, FERNANDO
PERSONAL Osorno, Chile, 2 children **DISCIPLINE** SPANISH-AMERICAN LITERATURE **EDUCATION** Univ Chile, BA, 70; Univ Fla, PhD, 81. **CAREER** Asst prof Span Am lit, Univ Chile, 71-76; instr Span, Univ Fla, 76-80, res asst Span Am lit, Ctr Latin Am Studies, 78-80; asst prof, 81-87, assoc prof, 87-96, prof, Memphis State Univ, 96-. **HONORS AND AWARDS** Sup Perf in Univ Res Awd. **MEMBERSHIPS** Assoc Int de Hispanistas **RESEARCH** Spanish-American literature, 19th and 20th centuries; Spanish-American Modernity. **SELECTED PUBLICATIONS** Auth, La novela moderna hispanoamericana: un ensayo sobre el concepto litario de modernidad, Origenes, 85, 90; auth, Prosa hispanica de vanguardia, Origenes, 86; auth, Los ochenta mundos de Cortazar: ensayos, Edi-6, 87; auth, Las voces del karai: estudios sobre Augusto Roa Bastos, Edelsa, 88; auth, Antologia del cuento hispanoamericano, Porrua, 91; auth, Esteban Echeverria El matadero, Ensayos Esteticos y Prosa Varia de Esteban Echeverria, Edicions del Norte, 92; auth, Vertientes de la modernidad hispanoamericana, Monte Avila Editores, 95; auth Cuentos de Hispanoamerica en el siglo viente, Castalia, 97. **CONTACT ADDRESS** Dept of Foreign Lang, Memphis State Univ, Campus Box 526430, Memphis, TN, 381526430. **EMAIL** fburgos@cc.memphis.edu

BURKE, JAMES F.
PERSONAL Born 08/26/1939, Little Rock, AR, m, 1964, 2 children **DISCIPLINE** MEDIEVAL SPANISH LANGUAGE & LITERATURE **EDUCATION** Univ Ark, BA, 61; Univ NC, MA, 63, PhD(Span), 66. **CAREER** Instr Span, Univ NC, 65-66; from asst prof to assoc prof, 66-76, PROF SPAN, UNIV TORONTO, 76-. **MEMBERSHIPS** Mediaeval Acad Am; Am Asn Teachers Span & Port; Can Asn Hispanists. **RESEARCH** Hispano-Arabic language and literature. **SELECTED PUBLICATIONS** Auth, History and Vision: Figural Structure of El Caballero Zifar, Tamesis, 72; Four comings of Christ in Berceo's Santa Oria, Speculum, 73; The Estrella De Sevella and saturnine melancholy, Bull Hispanis Tudies, 74; Juan Ruiz, serranas, and the rites of spring, J Medieval & Renaissance Studies, 75; The Insouciant Reader and the Failure of Memory in 'Celestina'/, Critica Hispanica, Vol 15, 1993; The 3rd Chronicle of Alfonso-X - La 'Gran Conquista de Ultramar' - Spanish - Gonzalez,C/, Mod Lang Rev, Vol 89, 1994; The 'Poema del Cid' and the 'Poema de Fernan Gonzalez' - The Transformation of an Epic Tradition - Bailey,M/, Hisp Rev, Vol 62, 1994. **CONTACT ADDRESS** Dept of Ital & Hispanic Studies, Univ of Toronto, Toronto, ON, M5S 1A1.

BURLESON, BRANT R.
DISCIPLINE INTERPERSONAL COMMUNICATION **EDUCATION** Ill, PhD, 82. **CAREER** Prof, Purdue Univ. **RESEARCH** Social support; comforting; communication and emotion; philosophy of science. **SELECTED PUBLICATIONS** Auth, Comforting messages; Significance, approaches, and effects, Commun of Soc Support, 94; Thoughts about talk in romantic relationships; Similarity makes for attraction (and happiness, too), Commun Quart, 94; Personal relationships as a skilled accomplishment, Jour of Soc and Personal Relationships, 95; Men's and women's evaluations of communication skills in personal relationships: When sex differences make a difference-and when they don't, J of Soc and Personal Relationships, 96; The socialization of emotional support skills in childhood, Handbook of Soc Support and the Family, 96. **CONTACT ADDRESS** Dept of Commun, Purdue Univ, 1080 Schleman Hall, West Lafayette, IN, 47907-1080. **EMAIL** xwxf@vm.cc.purdue.edu

BURLING, ROBBINS
PERSONAL Born 04/08/1926, Minneapolis, MN, m, 1951, 3 children **DISCIPLINE** ANTHROPOLOGY & LINGUISTICS **EDUCATION** Yale Univ, BA, 50; Harvard Univ, PhD, 58. **CAREER** From instr to asst prof anthrop, Univ Pa, 57-63; assoc prof, 63-67, Prof Anthrop & Ling, Univ Mich, Ann Arbor, 67-; Fulbright Found lectr, Rangoon, Burma, 59-60; fel, Ctr Advan Studies Behav Sci, 63-64; Guggenheim Found fel, 71-72; vis prof, Univ Gothenburg, Sweden, 79-80; Fulbright Found Lectr, Skillong, India, 96-97. **MEMBERSHIPS** Am Anthrop Asn; Ling Soc Am; Asn Asian Studies. **RESEARCH** Anthropology; linguistics. **SELECTED PUBLICATIONS** Auth, Rengsanggri, Family and Kinship in a Garo Village, Univ Pa, 63; Hill Farms and Padi Fields, Prentice-Hall, 65; Man's Many Voices, 70 & English in Black and White, 73, Holt; The Passage of Power, Acad Press, 74; Sounding Right, Newbury House, 82; Learning a Field Language, Univ Mich Press, 84; Patterns of Language, Acad Press, 92; The Strong Women of Modhupur Dhaka, Univ Press Ltd, 97. **CONTACT ADDRESS** Dept of Anthrop, Univ of Mich, 500 S State St, Ann Arbor, MI, 48109-1382. **EMAIL** rburling@umich.edu

BURNETT, DAVID GRAHAM
PERSONAL Born 11/28/1944, Detroit, MI, m, 1970, 2 children **DISCIPLINE** FRENCH LITERATURE, HUMANITIES **EDUCATION** Princeton Univ, BA, 66; Ind Univ, MA, 68, PhD(French), 73. **CAREER** Lectr Am civilization, Univ Pau, France, 69-70; lectr French, Ind Univ, 72-73, vis asst prof, 73-76, asst dean arts & sci, 73-76, asst prof continuing studies, 76-80; MEM FAC, DEPT FRENCH, NC STATE UNIV, 80-. **MEMBERSHIPS** Am Asn Higher Educ; MLA; Nat Univ Exten Asn; Am Asn Advan Humanities. **RESEARCH** Nineteenth and 20th century French literature; educational philosophy; humanities policy. **SELECTED PUBLICATIONS** Auth, The Living Learning Center of Indiana University, In: Development and Experiement in College Teaching, 74; Thematic function of sexual identity in Gautier's Comedie de la mort, Nottingham Fr Studies, 77; The theme of ocean exploration in the Poetry of Theophile Gautier, Exploration, 77; Movement and stasis in The Flies by Jean-Paul Sartre, Perspectives, 78. **CONTACT ADDRESS** Dept of French, No Carolina State Univ, Raleigh, NC, 27650.

BURRES, KENNETH LEE
PERSONAL Born 08/12/1934, Topeka, KS, m, 1956, 3 children **DISCIPLINE** BIBLICAL STUDIES, LINGUISTICS **EDUCATION** Baker Univ, AB, 56; Garrett Theol Sem, BD, 60; Northwestern Univ, MA, 61, PhD, 70. **CAREER** Pastor, United Methodist Church, Gary, IN, 64-67; asst prof, 67-71, assoc prof Relig, 71-93, PROF, CENT METHODIST COL, 93-, CHAIR, DEPT OF PHILOS & RELIG, 97-. **MEMBERSHIPS** Soc Bibl Lit; Am Academy of Relig. **RESEARCH** Linguistic analysis of New Testament Greek; New Testament theology; early Christian history. **SELECTED PUBLICATIONS** Auth, Prolegomena to a new biblical lexicography, Soc Bibl Lit Sem Papers, 71. **CONTACT ADDRESS** Dept of Relig, Central Methodist Col, 411 Central Methodist Sq, Fayette, MO, 65248-1198. **EMAIL** ckburres@mcmsys.com

BURTON, JOAN
PERSONAL Columbia, MO, m **DISCIPLINE** CLASSICAL STUDIES **EDUCATION** BA, 75, MA, 78, CPhil, 83, PhD, 88, Univ Calif, Berkeley. **CAREER** Actg instr, tchg assoc, classics, Univ Calif, Berkeley, 79-86; actg instr, classics, Univ Calif, Santa Cruz, 88; asst prof, 88-94, assoc prof, 94-, classics, chemn and assoc prof, comp lit, 98-, Trinity Univ. **HONORS AND AWARDS** Phi Beta Kappa, 74; dept citation class lang, 75; chancellor's fel, classics, 77-78, 80-81; John Rogers Fac Fel, 90-92. **MEMBERSHIPS** APA; Byzantine Stud Conf; Women's Class Caucus. **RESEARCH** Greek and Roman literature and culture; women's studies. **SELECTED PUBLICATIONS** Auth, The Function of the Symposium Theme in Theocritus' Idyll, Greek Roman, and Byzantine Stud, 92; auth, Why the Ancient Greeks Were Obsessed with Heroes and the Ancient Egyptians Were Not, Class Bull, 93; auth, Theocritus' Urban Mimes: Mobility, Gender and Patronage, Univ Calif, 95; auth, Women's Commensality in the Ancient Greek World, Greece and Rome, 98. **CONTACT ADDRESS** Dept of Classical Studies, Trinity Univ, 715 Stadium Dr, San Antonio, TX, 78212-7200.

BUSI, FREDERICK
DISCIPLINE FRENCH LITERATURE **EDUCATION** CT Univ, PhD. **CAREER** Prof, Univ MA Amherst. **RESEARCH** Lit and the hist of ideas in 19th and 20th century France; fantastic lit; anti-Semitic lit. **SELECTED PUBLICATIONS** Auth, pubs on SuarSs, Beckett, Dumont, and La Pens. **CONTACT ADDRESS** Dept of French and Italian Studies, Univ Massachusetts Amherst, Mass Ave, Amherst, MA, 01003.

BUTLER, KATHARINE G.
DISCIPLINE COMMUNICATION SCIENCES AND DISORDERS **EDUCATION** MI State Univ, PhD, 67. **CAREER** Res prof CCC-SLP. **HONORS AND AWARDS** Pres, Am Speech-Lang-Hearing Assoc, 96-. **RESEARCH** Lang acquisition and disorders; children's discourse acquisition, narrative mode of thought, and lang processing in the early years (0 to 5) among school aged children from culturally diverse populations. **SELECTED PUBLICATIONS** Ed, Language and Stuttering in Children: Perspectives on an Interrelationship, Topics Lang Disorders, 95; The New Narrative Landscape: Interface between Ability and Disability, Topics Lang Disorders, 95; Assessment Across Disorders: Perspectives, Practices, and Procedures, Aspen, 94. **CONTACT ADDRESS** Syracuse Univ, Syracuse, NY, 13244.

BUTLER, THOMAS J.
PERSONAL Born 05/15/1929, Detroit, MI, m, 1954, 3 children **DISCIPLINE** SLAVIC LANGUAGES & LITERATURE **EDUCATION** Harvard Univ, AB, 51, MA, 55, PhD(Slavic lang & lit), 63. **CAREER** Teaching fel Russ, Harvard Univ, 58-60; asst prof, Tufts Univ, 62-67; asst prof slavic lang, Univ Wis-Madison, 68-71, assoc prof, 71-79; vis lectr, 79-80, MEM FAC, RUSS RES CTR, HARVARD UNIV, 80-, Coun Learned Soc res grant, 72; Am Philos Soc travel grant, Yugoslavia, 73; Fulbright fel, Univ Belgrade, 67-68, 81-82 & Univ Sarajevo, 77-78; rev ed, Slavic & E Eruop J, 70-71; mem rev staff, Books Abroad, 71-. **MEMBERSHIPS** Am Asn Teachers Alavic & E Europ Lang; Int Conf Bulgarian Studies; MLA; Am Asn S Slavic Studies (secy-treas, 73-75). **RESEARCH** South Slavic and Russian languages and literatures; Slavic cultural history; preparation of a bilingual anthology of Serbo-Croatian texts. **SELECTED PUBLICATIONS** Auth, The Origins of the War for a Serbian Language and Orthography, Harvard Univ, 70; The linguistic heterogeneity of Njegos's Gorski Vijenac, Proc Pac Northwest Conf Foreign Lang, 72; Njegos's early poem on a Russian theme, Mnemozina, 74; Literary style and poetic function in Mesa Selimovic's The Dervish and Death, Slavonic & E Europ Rev, winter 75 & Savremenik, 5/75; Yugoslavia's Slavic languages: A historical perspective, Rev Nat Lit, spring 75; The language of Serbian and Croatian medieval tales, Slavic Ling & Lang, Teaching Slavica, 76; ed, Bulgaria Past and Present, AAAS, 76; Monumenta Serbocroatica: A Bilingual Anthology of Serbian and Croatian Texts, Mich Slavic Publ, 80; The Bulgarians in the 17th-Century - Slavic Orthodox Society and Culture under Ottoman Rule - Hupchick,DP/, Slavonic and East Europ Rev, Vol 72, 1994. **CONTACT ADDRESS** 32 Vernon St, Nahant, MA, 01908.

BYBEE, JOAN L.
PERSONAL Born 02/11/1945, New Orleans, LA, m, 1 child **DISCIPLINE** LINGUISTICS **EDUCATION** Univ TX, Austin, BA (Spanish & English), 66; San Diego State Univ, MA (linguistics), 70; Univ CA, Los Angeles, PhD (linguistics), 73. **CAREER** Asst prof, 73-78, assoc prof, Linguistics, 78-85, prof Linguistics, SUNY at Buffalo, 85-89; assoc dean, 92-93, prof Linguistics, Univ NM, 89-. **HONORS AND AWARDS** Distinguished Alumni Award from the Col of arts and Letters of San Diego State Univ, 76; Guggenheim fel, 87-88; Regent's Prof, Univ NM, 96-. **MEMBERSHIPS** Linguistic Soc of Am; Asn for Linguistic Typology. **RESEARCH** Phonology; morphology; grammaticization; language change; language universals. **SELECTED PUBLICATIONS** Auth, (as Joan B Hooper) An Introduction to Natural Generative Phonology, Academic Press, 76; Morphology: a Study of the Relation Between Meaning and Form, Amsterdam: John Benjamins, 85; co-auth with Revere Perkins and William Pagliuca, The Evolution of Grammar: Tense, Aspect and Modality in the Language of the World, Univ Chicago Press, 94; ed with Suzanne Fleischman, Modality in Grammar and Discourse, John Benjamins, 95; ed with John Haiman and Sandra Thompson, Essays on Language Function and Language Type, John Benjamins; co-auth with Jean Newman, Are Affixes More Natural Than Stem Changes?, Linguistics, 95; auth, Regular Morphology and the Lexicon, Language and Cognitive Processes, 95; Diachronicand Typological Properties of Morphology and Their Implications for Representation, in Laurie Feldman, ed, Morphological Aspects of Language Processing, Lawrence Erlbaum Assocs, 95; The Semantic Development of Past Tense Modals in English, in Joan Bybee and Suzanne Fleischman, eds, Modality in Grammar and Discourse, John Benjamins, 95; co-auth with Suzanne Fleischman, Issues in Mood and Modality, introductory essay for the volume, in Bybee and Fleischman, eds, Modality in Grammar and Discourse, John Benjamins, 95; Productivity, Regularity and Fusion: How Language Use Affects the Lexicon, in Rajendra Singh, ed, Trubetzkoy's Orphan, Mouton De Gruyter, 96; auth, Semantic Aspects of Morphological Typology, in Bybee, John Haiman and Sandra Thompson, eds, Essays on Language Function and Language Type, John Benjamins, 97. **CONTACT ADDRESS** Dept of Linguistics, Univ of New Mexico, Humanities 526, Albequerque, NM, 87131-1196. **EMAIL** jbybee@unm.edu

BYERS, LORI
DISCIPLINE ORGANIZATIONAL COMMUNICATION **EDUCATION** PhD. **CAREER** Spalding Univ **SELECTED PUBLICATIONS** Auth chapter: Pearson and Nelson's text Understanding and Sharing: An Introduction to Speech Communication. **CONTACT ADDRESS** Spalding Univ, 851 S. Fourth St., Louisville, KY, 40203-2188.

BYRE, CALVIN S.
PERSONAL Born 11/22/1947, Appleton, MN, m, 1972 **DISCIPLINE** CLASSICAL LANGUAGES AND LITERATURES **EDUCATION** Univ Minn, BA, 69; Univ Chicago, PhD, 76; Rosary Col, MALS, 85. **CAREER** Asst prof/head of ref, Roosevelt Univ, 86-90; asst prof of bibliog and adjunct asst prof of classics, Univ Okla, 90-96; assoc prof of bibliog and adjunct assoc prof of classics, Univ Okla, 96-. **HONORS AND AWARDS** Phi Beta Kappa; Robert V. Cram Memorial Scholar in Classics, Univ Minn; Ford four-year fel, Univ Chicago. **MEMBERSHIPS** Amer Philol Asn; Classical Asn of the Middle West and South. **RESEARCH** Greek epic; Literary criticism. **SELECTED PUBLICATIONS** Auth, Suspense in the Phaeacian Episode of Apollonius' Argonautica, Ill Class Studes, 22, 65-73, 97; auth, On the Departure from Pagasae and the Passage of the Plactae in Apollonius/ Argonautica, Mus Helveticum, 54, 106-114, 97; auth, The Killing of Apsyrtus in Apollonious Rhodius' Argonautica, Phoenix, 50, 3-16, 96; auth, Distant Encounters: The Prometheus and Phaethon Episodes in Apollonius' Argonautica, Amer Jour of Philol, 117, 275-283, 96; auth, The Rhetoric of Description in Odyssey, 9.116-41, Odysseus and the Goat Island, Class Jour, 89, 357-367, 94; auth, On the Description of the Harbor of Phorkys and the Cave of the Nymphs, Odyssey, 13.96-112, Amer Jour of Philol, 115, 1-13, 94; auth, Narration, Description, and Theme in the Shield of Achilles, Class Jour, 88, 33-42, 92; auth, The Narrator's Addresses to the Narratee in Apollonius Rhodius' Argonautica, Transactions of the Amer Philos Asn, 121, 215-227, 91; auth, Penelope and the Suitors before Odysseus: Odyssey, 18.158-303, Amer Jour of Philol, 109, 159-173, 88; auth, Per aspera (et arborem) ad astra. Ramifications of the Allegory of Arete in Quintus Smyrnaeus Posthomerica, 5, 49-68, Hermes, 110, 184-195, 82. **CONTACT ADDRESS** 1727 Bryant Cir., Norman, OK, 73026. **EMAIL** cbyre@ou.edu

C

CABLE, THOMAS MONROE
PERSONAL Born 06/17/1942, Conroe, TX, m, 1 child **DISCIPLINE** ENGLISH LANGUAGE & LINGUISTICS **EDUCATION** Yale Univ, BA, 64; Univ TX, PhD, 69. **CAREER** Asst prof Eng, Univ IL, Urbana-Champaign, 69-72; assoc prof Eng, 72-79, prof eng, Univ TX, Austin, 79, Blumberg Centennial Prof Eng, 84; Am Coun Learned Socs fel, 76-77; Fulbright, France, 80, 92. **HONORS AND AWARDS** TX Excellence Tchg Award, Col of Lib Arts, 90. **MEMBERSHIPS** MLA; Medieval Acad Am; Ling Soc Am. **RESEARCH** Hist of Eng prosody; hist of the Eng lang; Old and Middle Eng lit. **SELECTED PUBLICATIONS** Auth, The Meter and Melody of Beowulf, Univ Ill, 74; coauth, A History of the English Language, Prentice-Hall, 3rd ed, 78, 4th ed, 93; The English Alliterative Tradition, Univ Penn, 91; A Companion to Baugh and Cable's History of the English Language, 2nd ed, Prentice-Hall, 93. **CONTACT ADDRESS** Dept of Eng, Univ of Texas, Austin, TX, 78712-1164. **EMAIL** tcable@mail.utexas.edu

CACHIA, PIERRE J.E.
PERSONAL Born 04/30/1921, Fayyum, Egypt, m, 1992, 3 children **DISCIPLINE** MODERN ARABIC LITERATURE **EDUCATION** Am Univ Cairo, BA, 42; Univ of Edinburgh, PhD, 51. **CAREER** Tchr, Am Univ Cairo, 46-48; lectr, sen lectr, reader, Univ of Edinburgh, 50-75; prof, Columbia Univ, 75-91. **HONORS AND AWARDS** Woodrow Wilson fel, 91-92. **MEMBERSHIPS** Am Oriental Soc; Middle East Studies Asn; Brit Soc for Middle Eastern Studies; Union Europeenee D'Islamisants Et Arabisants. **RESEARCH** Modern Arab Lit; Egyptian Folk Lit. **SELECTED PUBLICATIONS** Auth, Taha Husayn: His Place in the Egyptian Literary Renaissance, 56; Popular Narrative Ballads of Modern Egypt, 89; An Overview of Modern Arabic Literature, 90; The Arch Rhetorician of the Schemer's Skimmer: a Handbook of late Arabic badi, 98; coauth, History of Islamic Spain, 65, coed, Jour of Arabic Literature and its Supplements, 1970-1996. **CONTACT ADDRESS** Columbia Univ, 608 Kent Hall, New York, NY, 10027.

CADELY, JEAN ROBERT JOSEPH
DISCIPLINE FRENCH LITERATURE **EDUCATION** Quebec Univ, PhD. **CAREER** Asst prof. **MEMBERSHIPS** MLA; Ling Soc Am; Can Ling Asn. **SELECTED PUBLICATIONS** Auth, Elision et Agglutination en Creole Haitien: Le cas des Pronoms Personels: Etudes Creoles, 95; Representations syllabiques et distribution des diphtongues en creole hartien, 88. **CONTACT ADDRESS** Dept of Modern Languages, Florida State Univ, 11200 SW 8th St, Miami, FL, 33174.

CAILLER, BERNADETTE ANNE
PERSONAL Born 06/08/1941, Poitiers, France, w **DISCIPLINE** AFRICAN & CARIBBEAN LITERATURE **EDUCATION** Univ Poitiers, Lic es Lett, 61, Dipl d Etudes Superieures, 64; Univ Paris, Capes, 68; Cornell Univ, MA, 67, PhD(comp lit), 74. **CAREER** Asst prof, 74-79, Assoc Prof French, Univ Fla, 79- **MEMBERSHIPS** African Lit Assn; Conseil Int d'Etudes Francophones; African Stu Assn; Int Comp Lit Assn. **RESEARCH** Edouard Glissant; Negritude and post Negritude in relation to Emmanuel Levinas' philosophy; literature in a civil war context. **SELECTED PUBLICATIONS** Auth, Proposition poetique, Ine lecture de l'oeuvre d'Aime Cesaire, Naaman, 76, 2nd ed, Nouvelles du Sud, 94; authConquerants de la nuit nue: Edouard Glissant et l'H(h)istorie antillaise, Etudes Litteriares Francaises, vol 45, Gunter Narr Verlag, 88; co-ed, Toward Defining the African Aesthetic, Three Continents Press, 82; auth, If the Dead could only speak! Reflections on Texts by Niger, Hughes, an dFodeba, The Surreptious Speech: Presence Africaine and the Politics of Otherness, 1947-1987, Univ Chicago, 92; auth, Creolization versus Francophonie. Language, Identity and Culture in the Works of Edouard Glissant, L'Heritage de Caliban, 92; auth, The Impossible Ecstasy: an Analysis of Valentin Y. Mudimbe's Dechirures, Research in African Literatures, 93; auth, Hiterlerisme et enterprise coloniale 2: le cas Damas, French Cultural Studies, 94; auth, Si Marie-Madeleine se racontait:analyse d'une figure de Feux, Roman, Historie et Mythe dans l'oeuvre de Narguerite Yourcenar, SIEY, 95; auth, La transgression creatrice d'Andree Chedid: Nefertiti ou le reve d'Akhnaton, Les memoires d'un scribe, Litteratures autobiographiques de la Francophonie, C.E.L.F.A., 96; auth, Interface between Fiction and Autobiography: From Shaba 2 to Les Corps glorieux, Canad Jour of African Stu, Vol 30, No 3, 96. **CONTACT ADDRESS** Dept of Romance Lang and Lit, Univ Fla, PO Box 117405, Gainesville, FL, 32611-7405. **EMAIL** cailler@rll.ufl.edu

CALABRESE, ANDREA
DISCIPLINE LINGUISTICS **EDUCATION** Mass Inst Tech, PhD. **CAREER** Assoc prof, Univ Conn. **RESEARCH** Phonological theory, Romance linguistics, historical linguistics. **SELECTED PUBLICATIONS** Auth, A Constraint-Based Theory of Phonological Markedness and Simplification Procedures, Ling Inquiry 26, 96; Sievers' Law in Gothic: A Synchronic Analysis and Some Speculations on its Historical Development, Ling Rev 11, 94; The Sentential Complementation of Salentino, In Syntactic Theory and Italian Dialects, Torino: Rosenberg Selliers, 93; Palatalization Processes in the History of Romance Languages: A Theoretical Study, In Linguistic Perspectives on the Romance Languages, Current Issues in Ling Theory 103, Amsterdam: Johns Benjamins, 93. **CONTACT ADDRESS** Dept of Linguistics, Univ of Connecticut, 1266 Storrs Rd, Storrs, CT, 06269. **EMAIL** calabres@uconnvm.uconn.edu

CALDWELL, LARRY
DISCIPLINE LINGUISTICS, ENGLISH LANGUAGE **EDUCATION** Univ Nebr, PhD. **CAREER** Former dir, wrtg. **RESEARCH** Norse myth, saga, and legend. **SELECTED PUBLICATIONS** Articles, English Quart; Extrapolation. **CONTACT ADDRESS** Dept of Eng, Univ Evansville, 1800 Lincoln Ave, Evansville, IN, 47714. **EMAIL** lc4@evansville.edu.

CALLAGHAN, CATHERINE A.
PERSONAL Born 10/30/1931, Berkeley, CA **DISCIPLINE** LINGUISTICS **EDUCATION** Univ Calif, Berkeley, BA, 54, PhD(ling), 63. **CAREER** Sci linguist, Smithsonia Inst, 62; asst prof ling, Univ Hawaii, 64; asst prof, 65-69, ASSOC PROF LING, OHIO STATE UNIV, 69-, Am Asn Univ Women fel, 64-65; NSF grant res Calif Indian lang, 66-80. **MEMBERSHIPS** AAAS; Ling Soc Am. **RESEARCH** Reconstruction of proto languages; anthropological linguistics; occult. **SELECTED PUBLICATIONS** Auth, Proto-Miwok Numerals, Intl Jour Amer Ling, Vol 0060, 94. **CONTACT ADDRESS** Dept of Ling, Ohio State Univ, Columbus, OH, 43210.

CALLAN, RICHARD JEROME
PERSONAL Born 01/04/1932, Mt Vernon, NY, m, 1954 **DISCIPLINE** ROMANCE LANGUAGES **EDUCATION** Iona Col, AB, 57; Fordham Univ, MA, 59; St Louis Univ, PhD(-Span), 65. **CAREER** Instr Span, St Michael's Col, Vt, 60-63; assoc prof, St Louis Univ, 65-69; ASSOC PROF SPAN AM LIT, UNIV NH, 69- **MEMBERSHIPS** MLA; Am Asn Teachers Span & Port; Inst Int Lit Iberoam; Midwest Mod Lang Asn. **RESEARCH** Spanish American literature; archetypal approach to literature; Meso-American mythology. **SELECTED PUBLICATIONS** Auth, Archetypes in Stories by Arevalomartinez, Rafael, Critica Hispanica, Vol 0017, 95. **CONTACT ADDRESS** Dept of Ancient & Mod Lang, Univ of NH, Durham, NH, 03824.

CAMAYD FREIXAS, ERIK
DISCIPLINE SPANISH LITERATURE **EDUCATION** Tufts Univ, BA, 80; Harvard Univ, MA, PhD. **CAREER** Lang instr, Tufts Univ, 80; tchg fel, Harvard Univ, 84-86; asst prof, Marquette Univ, 94-97; asst prof, Fla Int Univ, 97-. **MEMBERSHIPS** MLA; Latin Am Studies Asn; Am Studies Asn. **SELECTED PUBLICATIONS** Auth, Heteroglosia y parodia

historiografica en Cien alos de soledad, 96; Reflections on Magical Realism: A Return to Legitimacy, The Legitimacy of Return, 96; 'Alturas de Macchu Picchu': Forma y sentido en su retorica elegiaca, 95; Teoria y sentido del realismo m gico, 95; co-auth, Encyclopedia of Contemporary Latin American and Caribbean Cultures, Routledge, 97; Benet's Readers' Encyclopedia, 96. **CONTACT ADDRESS** Dept of Modern Languages, Florida State Univ, 11200 SW 8th St, Miami, FL, 33174. **EMAIL** camayde@fiu.edu

CAMERON, ALAN
PERSONAL Born 03/13/1938, Windsor, England, m, 1961, 2 children **DISCIPLINE** CLASSICAL PHILOLOGY, BYZANTINE STUDIES **EDUCATION** Oxford Univ, BA, 61, MA, 64. **CAREER** Lectr Latin, Univ Glasgow, 61-64, Bedord Col, Univ London, 64-71 & Kings Col, 72-76; ANTHON PROF LATIN, COLUMBIA UNIV, 77- **HONORS AND AWARDS** N H Baynes Prize, London Univ, 67; J Conington Prize, Oxford Univ, 68; fel, British Acad, 75. **MEMBERSHIPS** Soc Roman Studies; Am Philol Asn; fel Am Acad Arts & Sci. **RESEARCH** Latin literature; Roman history; Byzantine history and literature. **SELECTED PUBLICATIONS** Auth, Gender in Performance--The Presentation of Difference in the Performing Arts, Theatre Res Intl, Vol 0019, 94; Just Another Fucking Mystery at Sea, Meanjin, Vol 0055, 96; The Life of Stephen, Saint of the Monastery of Mar-Saba-Italian-Leontius-Of-Damascus, Heythrop Jour-Quart Rev Philos And Theol, Vol 0035, 94; Egypt in Late-Antiquity, NY Rev Of Bk(s), Vol 0042, 95; The Roman Near-East, 31-Bc-337-Ad, NY Rev Bk(s), Vol 0042, 95; The Byzantine Church--Between Power and Spirit 313-1204-French, Rev Belge Philol Et D Hist, Vol 0072, 94; On the Date of John-Of-Gaza, Class Quart, Vol 0043, 93; Byzantines and Jews- Some Recent Work on Early Byzantium, Byzantine and Modern Greek Studies, Vol 0020, 96; Transforming Womens Work--New-England Lives in the Industrial-Revolution, Labor Hist, Vol 0036, 95; Themistius and the Imperial Court-Oratory, Civic Duty, and Paideia from Constantius to Theodosius, Amer Hist Rev, Vol 0102, 97; Genre and Style in Callimachus, Transactions Amer Philol Assn, Vol 0122, 92; The Origenist Controversy--The Cultural Construction of an Early-Christian Debate, Scottish Jour Theol, Vol 0050, 97; Ancient Anagrams/, American Journal Of Philology, Vol 0116, 1995; Holy City, Holy Places--Christian Attitudes to Jerusalem and the Holy-Land in the 4th-Century, Heythrop Jour-Quart Rev Philos and Theol, Vol 0034, 93. **CONTACT ADDRESS** Columbia Univ, 2960 Broadway, New York, NY, 10027-6900.

CAMPANA, PHILLIP JOSEPH
PERSONAL Born 04/10/1941, Jersey City, NJ, 2 children **DISCIPLINE** GERMAN **CAREER** Assoc prof, 70-74, PROF GER, TENN TECHNOL UNIV, 74-, Chmn Dept, 70-, Mem evaluation team foreign lang, Southern Asn Cols & Schs, 72-; assoc ed, Schatzkammer, 80-; chmn, Tenn Bd Regents Task Force on Improv Qual in Teacher Educ. **HONORS AND AWARDS** Outstanding Fac Award, Tenn Technol Univ, 76. **MEMBERSHIPS** MLA; AAUP; Am Coun Teaching Foreign Lang; Am Asn Teachers Ger. **RESEARCH** German Romanticism; Heinrich Boell; German novel. **SELECTED PUBLICATIONS** Auth, Syracuse Language Systems--Tripleplay-Plus-German, Mod Lang Jour, Vol 0080, 96. **CONTACT ADDRESS** Dept of Foreign Lang, Tenn Technol Univ, Cookeville, TN, 38501.

CAMPBELL, LEE
DISCIPLINE COMPOSITION, PROFESSIONAL WRITING, AND LINGUISTICS **EDUCATION** Ill State Univ, BA, 81, MA, 83; Purdue Univ, PhD, 90. **CAREER** Asst prof Eng, 95-, adv, Eng to speakers of other lang endorsement, 95-, web site mgr, dept Eng, 97-, ed, fac Handbk, Valdosta State Univ, 95-; asst prof Eng, Henderson State Univ, 92-95; Asst prof Eng, Marquette U niv, 90-92. **MEMBERSHIPS** Nat Coun of Tchr of Eng; Conf on Col Compos and Commun; Mod Lang Asn; S Atlantic Mod Lang Asn; Soc for Tech Commun; Southeastern Conf on Ling; Rhet Soc of Am; Phi Kappa Phi. **RESEARCH** Applied linguistic theory; argumentation and rhetorical theory. **SELECTED PUBLICATIONS** Auth, 'It is as if a green bough were laid across the page': Thoreau on Eloquence, in Rhet Soc Quart, 90; An Applied Relevance Theory of the Making and Understanding of Rhetorical Arguments, in Lang and Commun, 92; Argument,in Encycl of Eng Stud and Lang Arts, 95. **CONTACT ADDRESS** Dept of Eng, Valdosta State Univ, 1500 N. Patterson St, Valdosta, GA, 31698. **EMAIL** jlcampbe@valdosta.edu

CAMPION, EDMUND J.
DISCIPLINE FRENCH LITERATURE **EDUCATION** Yale Univ, PhD, 76. **CAREER** Prof. **SELECTED PUBLICATIONS** Auth, Montaigne, Rabelais, and Marot as Readers of Erasmus, 95; pubs on Erasmus and French literary works from the early modern period. **CONTACT ADDRESS** Dept of Romance Languages, Knoxville, TN, 37996.

CAMPOS, JAVIER F.
DISCIPLINE MODERN LANGUAGES AND LITERATURE **EDUCATION** Universidad de Concepcion, Pedagogia en Espanol; Univ MN, PhD **CAREER** Fac, Universidad de Concepcion, OH State Univ, CA State Univ Chico, and Marshall Univ; assoc prof, Fairfield Univ, current. **HONORS AND AWARDS** Letras de Oro, Univ Miami and Span govt, 91. **SELECTED PUBLICATIONS** Auth, Las Ultimas Fotografeas, 81; La Ciudad en Llamas, 86' Las Cartas Olvidadas del Astronauta, 92. **CONTACT ADDRESS** Fairfield Univ, 1073 N Benson Rd, Fairfield, CT, 06430.

CAMURATI, MIREYA BEATRIZ
PERSONAL Born 08/17/1934, Buenos Aires **DISCIPLINE** SPANISH AMERICAN LITERATURE **EDUCATION** Univ Buenos Aires, Prof en Letras, 59; Univ Pittsburgh, PhD(Span Am lit), 70. **CAREER** Instr Span lang & lit, Univ Buenos Aires, 59-65, asst prof Span Am lit, 65-68; asst prof Span, IN Univ Northwest, 70-73; asst prof, 73-75, assoc prof Span Am lit, 75-80, Prof Spain AM Lit, State Univ NY Buffalo, 80-, prof Span Am lit, Univ Salvador, 64-68. **MEMBERSHIPS** MLA; Am Asn Teachers Span & Port; Inst Int Lit Iberoam; Int Asn Hispanists. **RESEARCH** Spanish American avant garde poetry; Spanish American modernismo; contemporary Spanish American novel. **SELECTED PUBLICATIONS** Auth, Funcion literaria del cuento intercalado en D Segundo Sombra, La vorangine y Cataclaro, Rev Iberoam, 4-6/71; Blest Gana, Lukacs, y la novela historical Cuadernos Americanos, 11-12/74; Un capitulo de versificacion modernista: El poema de clausulas ritmicas, Bull Hispanique, 9-12/74; Una ojeada a la poesia concreta en Hispanoamerica: Dos precursores, y escasos epigonos, Cuadernos Hispanoamericanos, 2/76; La fabula en Hispanoamerica, Universidad Nacional Autonoma de Mexico, 78; Bifurcacion, multiplicacion, ficcion, Hispanofila, 1/79; Poesia y poetica de Vincente Huidobro, Fernando Garcia Cambeiro, Buenos Aires, 80; Enfoques, D C Heath, 80; Bioy Casares y el Alegre Trabajo de la Inteligencia, Buenos Aires: Corregidor, 90. **CONTACT ADDRESS** Dept of Mod Lang & Lit, State Univ of NY, P O Box 604620, Buffalo, NY, 14260-4620.

CANCEL, ROBERT
PERSONAL Born 07/16/1950, Brooklyn, NY, m, 1973, 2 children **DISCIPLINE** AFRICAN LITERATURE **EDUCATION** State Univ NY New Paltz, BS, 72; Univ Wis-Madison, MA, 77, PhD(African lang & lit), 81. **CAREER** Ed films, African Media Ctr, Mich State Univ, 78-80; ASST PROF AFRICAN & COMP LIT, DEPT LIT, UNIV CALIF, SAN DIEGO, 80- **MEMBERSHIPS** African Lit Asn; MLA. **RESEARCH** African oral narrative traditions, especially from the Tabwa people of Zambia; oral narrative traditions from the New World (Caribbean and the Americas); African and Caribbean written literatures in English, Spanish and Bantu languages **SELECTED PUBLICATIONS** Auth, Black-African Cinema, Res African Lit, Vol 0026, 95; Gordimer, Nadine Meets Ngugi-Wa-Thiongo--Text into Film in Oral-History, Res African Lit, Vol 0026, 95. **CONTACT ADDRESS** Dept of Lit D-007, Univ Calif, San Diego, La Jolla, CA, 92039.

CAP, JEAN-PIERRE
PERSONAL Born 06/02/1934, Longueil-Ste-Marie, France, m, 1962, 2 children **DISCIPLINE** FRENCH LANGUAGE & LITERATURE **EDUCATION** Temple Univ, BA, 57, MA, 60; Univ Pa, MA, 60; Rutgers Univ, PhD, 66. **CAREER** Instr French, Skidmore Col, 61-62; from instr to asst prof, Univ Md, 62-68; assoc prof, 68-78, prof, 78-94, OLIVER EDWIN WILLIAMS PROF, FOR LANG & LIT, LAFAYETTE COL, 94-; Assoc ed, Claudel Studies, 67-80, co-ed, 83; Humanities enrichment grant, 73-74; Nat Hist Publ & Records Comn grant, 85. **HONORS AND AWARDS** Palmes Academiques, 80, officer 95. **MEMBERSHIPS** Am Asn Teachers Fr; AAUP; Soc Fr Prof Am; Claudel Soc; Am Comp Lit Asn; AAA Gide;UVAN; Shevchenko Scientific Soc (bd); Am Soc Fr Acad Palms & others. **RESEARCH** The novel; 20th century French literature; literary criticism; European history. **SELECTED PUBLICATIONS** Auth, Techniques et themes dans l'oeuvre de jean Schulmberger, 71; ed, Jacques Riviere-Jean Schlumberger: Corresp 1909-1995, 80; Decadence of Freedom, Jacques Riviere's Perception of Russian mentality, 84; ed, Henri-Gheon-Jacques Riviere: Corresp 1910-1924, 88; co-ed, Charles DuBos-Jacques Riviere: Corresp 1913-1925 & Charles DuBos-Isabelle Riviere: Corresp 1925-1935, 90; ed, Rozenie ou les Moscovites, 93; articles on Alain-Fournier, Claudel, Conrad, Desjardins, Dostoevsky, Gheon, Gide, Lafayette, Martin du Gard, Mistral, Peguy, Proust, Riviere, Schlumberger & others. **CONTACT ADDRESS** Dept of Lang, Lafayette Col, Easton, PA, 18042-1798.

CAPELES, MERVIN
DISCIPLINE SPANISH LANGUAGE AND LITERATURE **EDUCATION** SUNY Buffalo, PhD. **CAREER** Asst prof. **MEMBERSHIPS** CLA; MLA. **RESEARCH** Spanish language, literature, civilization and culture; literary criticism. **SELECTED PUBLICATIONS** Auth, El cuento fantastico en Puerto Rico y Cuba, Reichenberg, 95; Mejunje; Bajo la luna erotica del CaribQ. **CONTACT ADDRESS** Clark Atlanta Univ, 223 James P Brawley Dr, SW, Atlanta, GA, 30314.

CAPTAIN, YVONNE
DISCIPLINE ROMANCE LANGUAGES; LITERATURE **EDUCATION** Pitzer Col, BA, 73, Stanford Univ, PhD, 84. **CAREER** Asst prof to assoc prof, George Washington Univ, 84- ; pres, Phi Beta Delta Honors Soc, 97-99. **HONORS AND AWARDS** Dorothy Danforth-Compton Dissertation Fel, 83; Fel, Sch of Criticism & Theory, 86; Post-Doctoral Fel, 87; Eulalia Bernard Award, 98; Maurice East Award, Outstanding Leadership, 98; Phi Beta Delta Recognition Award, 98. **MEMBERSHIPS** Phi Beta Delta Honors Soc for Int Scholars; Soc for Values in Higher Educ. **SELECTED PUBLICATIONS** Auth, The Culture of Fiction in the Works of Manuel Zapata Olivella, Univ of Mo Press, 93; El espiritu de la risa en el cuento de Ana Lydia Vega, Revista Iberoamericana, 93; Writing for the Future: Afro-Hispanicm in a Global, Critical Contest, Afro-Hispanic Rev, 94; The Poetics of the Quotidian in the Works of Nancy Morejon, in Singular Like a Bird, Howard Univ Press, 99; Manuel Zapata Olivella, in Encarta Africana, 99. **CONTACT ADDRESS** Dept of Romance Lang & Lit, George Washington Univ, Washington, DC, 20052. **EMAIL** ycaptain@gwu.edu; http://gwis2.circ.gwu.edu/üycaptain

CARDONA, GEORGE
PERSONAL Born 06/03/1936, New York, NY, m, 1958, 2 children **DISCIPLINE** INDOARYAN AND INDO-EUROPEAN LINGUISTICS **EDUCATION** NY Univ, BA, 56; Yale Univ, MA, 58, PhD, 60. **CAREER** Asst prof Indo-Aryan lang, 60-65, assoc prof ling, 65-67, PROF LING, UNIV PA, 67-, US Off Educ grant, 62-64, publ grant, 65; Am Inst Indian Studies fac res grant, 65-66; vis prof, Orient Inst, Baroda, 1/66; vis lectr, Swarthmore Col, spring 67. **MEMBERSHIPS** Ling Soc Am; Am Orient Soc; Am Philol Asn; Ling Soc Europe. **RESEARCH** Indo-Aryan and Indo-European linguistics. **SELECTED PUBLICATIONS** Auth, The Indo-Aryan Languages, Jour Ling, Vol 0028, 92; The Philosophy of the Grammarians, Jour Amer Oriental Soc, Vol 0113, 93. **CONTACT ADDRESS** Dept of Ling, Univ of Pa, 255 S 36th St, Philadelphia, PA, 19104-3805.

CARGAS, HARRY JAMES
PERSONAL Born 06/18/1932, Hamtramck, MI, m, 1957, 6 children **DISCIPLINE** WORLD & AMERICAN LITERATURE AND RELIGION **EDUCATION** Univ Mich, Ann Arbor, BA, 57, MA, 58; St Louis Univ, PhD(English), 68. **CAREER** Teacher English, St David's Sch, NY, 58-60 & Montclair Acad, NJ, 60-61; ed-in-chief, Cath Bk Reporter, New York, 61-62 & Queen's Work Mag, St Louis, Mo, 63-64; dir, Orientation English Foreign Students, St Louis Univ, 64-69; assoc prof & chmn dept, 69-80, PROF LIT, LANG & RELIG, WEBSTER COL, 80-, Mem bk rev prog, Mo Pub Radio, 75- **MEMBERSHIPS** PEN; Amnesty Int; Nat Inst on Holocaust. **RESEARCH** The Holocaust; contemporary world literature; process theology. **SELECTED PUBLICATIONS** Auth, Ace of Freedoms--Merton, Thomas Christ, Cithara-Essays Judeo-Christian Tradition, Vol 0033, 93. **CONTACT ADDRESS** Dept of English, Webster Col, 470 E Lockwood Ave, Saint Louis, MO, 63119-3194.

CARLIN, CLAIRE L.
DISCIPLINE SEVENTEENTH-CENTURY FRENCH LITERATURE **EDUCATION** Univ Calif, Sanata Barbara, PhD. **RESEARCH** Feminist theory. **SELECTED PUBLICATIONS** Auth, The Woman as Heavy: Female Villains in the Theater of Pierre Corneille, Fr Rev 59, 86; Corneille's Trois Discours: A Reader's Guide, Orbis Litterarum 45, 90; Philip Butler's Baroque: A Feminist Re-Birth, L'Esprit Createur, 93. **CONTACT ADDRESS** Dept of French, Victoria Univ, PO Box 3045 STN CSC, Victoria, BC, V8W 3P4. **EMAIL** ccarlin@uvic.ca

CARLTON, CHARLES MERRITT
PERSONAL Born 12/12/1928, m, 1957, 3 children **DISCIPLINE** FRENCH LANGUAGE, ROMANCE LINGUISTICS **EDUCATION** Univ Vt, AB, 50; Middlebury Col, MA, 51; Univ Mich, PhD, 63. **CAREER** Teaching asst French, Univ Mich, 54-58; teaching asst English as foreign lang, English Lang Inst, 57-58; instr French, Mich State Univ, 58-62; asst prof French & gen ling, Univ Mo, 62-66; from asst to assoc prof, 66-77, prof French & Romance Ling, Univ Rochester, 77-; vis prof, NDEA French Inst, Univ Vt, 64; ed, Comp Romance Ling Newslett, 70-71; lectr English as foreign lang, Babes-Bolyai Univ, Cluj, Romania, 71-72; consult, Nat Endowment for Humanities, Title VI, Dept of Educ, 74-; vis prof, Univ Ky, Cluj program, 77; co-ed, Miorita, 77-89. **HONORS AND AWARDS** Nat Sci Found Award, 65; Nat Defense For Lang Award, 70; Fulbright-Hays Awards, Romania, 74, 78 & 82, Brazil, 86; Int Res & Exchanges Bd Award, Romania, 82, 91. **MEMBERSHIPS** AAA; Soc Romanian Studies. **RESEARCH** Romanian language; Romance linguistics. **SELECTED PUBLICATIONS** Auth, What is so Imperative? Revue Roumaine de Linguistique, 92; auth,Romanian and Its Place in "the Romania" Revue Roumaine de Linguistique, 93-95; auth, Romanian Rural Life & Lexical Differentiation: Latin/non-Latin, Romanian Civilization, 95-96; ed, Papers from the Fourth World Congress for Soviet and East European Studies, Harrogate, 1990, London, 96; auth, Romanian Poetry in English Translation: An Annotated Bibliography & Census (1740-1996), Center for Romanian Studies, 97. **CONTACT ADDRESS** 3 Thornfield Way, Fairport, NY, 14450. **EMAIL** carlton@ling.rochester.edu

CARMICHAEL, CARL W.
DISCIPLINE COMMUNICATION, COMMUNICATION ASPECTS OF AGING, SOCIAL LINGUISTICS **EDUCATION** Univ IA, PhD. **CAREER** Instr, CA State Univ. **RESEARCH** Critical thinking. **SELECTED PUBLICATIONS** Wrote a chapter on aging in a bk on Intercultural Commun. **CONTACT ADDRESS** California State Univ, Fresno, Fresno, CA, 93740.

CARNICKE, SHARON MARIE
DISCIPLINE RUSSIAN/THEATRE ARTS **EDUCATION** Moscow Univ, cert, 70; Barnard Col, AB, 71; NY Univ, MA, 73; Columbia Univ, MPhil, 77, PhD, 79. **CAREER** Adj asst prof, Sch Visual Arts, 80-83; adj asst prof, 84-86, vis asst prof, 86-87; asst prof, 87-92, ASSOC PROF, 87-, UNIV SOUTHERN CALIF. **CONTACT ADDRESS** Sch Theatre, Drama Cte, Univ of So California, Los Angeles, CA, 90089-0791. **EMAIL** carnicke@usc.edu

CARR, RICHARD ALAN
PERSONAL Born 07/15/1938, Maplewood, NJ **DISCIPLINE** FRENCH **EDUCATION** Princeton Univ, AB, 60, MA, 63, PhD(French), 69. **CAREER** Instr, 64-69, asst prof, 69-75, ASSOC PROF FRENCH, IN UNIV, 75-. **MEMBERSHIPS** MLA; Am Asn Teachers Fr; Soc Francaise Seiziemistes. **RESEARCH** French Renaissance literature; Renaissance narrative. **SELECTED PUBLICATIONS** Ed, Histoires tragiques, Champion, Paris, 77; auth, Pierre Boaistuau's Histoires Tragiques: A Study of Narrative, Univ NC, 79; V. Habanc, Nouvelles Histoies tant tragiques que comiques, Droz, 89; B. Poissenot, Nouvelles Histoires tragiques, Geneva, Droz, 96; Marconville, De la bonte et mauvaistie des femmes, Paris, Champion, 98. **CONTACT ADDRESS** Dept French, Indiana Univ, Bloomington, Bloomington, IN, 47405. **EMAIL** carrr@indiana.edu

CARRE, MARIE-ROSE
DISCIPLINE FRENCH LITERATURE **EDUCATION** Univ Paris, PhD. **CAREER** Prof, Univ MA Amherst. **RESEARCH** 17th century lit and hist of ideas; 20th century surrealism; poetry. **SELECTED PUBLICATIONS** Auth, Le Bourgeois parisien de 1640 peint par lui-meme. **CONTACT ADDRESS** Dept of French and Italian Studies, Univ Massachusetts Amherst, Mass Ave, Amherst, MA, 01003.

CARROLL, CARLETON WARREN
PERSONAL Born 10/20/1939, Rochester, NY **DISCIPLINE** FRENCH LANGUAGE **EDUCATION** Ohio State Univ, BA, 61; Univ Wis-Madison, MA, 65, PhD(French), 68. **CAREER** Asst prof French & Ital, Univ Wis-Madison & Univ Wis-Exten, 67-74, chmn dept, 69-74; asst prof, 74-78, assoc prof French, 78-94, Ore State Univ, 94-. **HONORS AND AWARDS** Chevalier de l'Ordre des Palmes Academique, 92. **MEMBERSHIPS** Am Asn Teachers Fr; Int Arthurian Soc; Soc Rencesvals; AAUP, Int Courtly Lit Soc. **RESEARCH** Medieval French literature; medieval Provencal literature; interlinguistics. **SELECTED PUBLICATIONS** Co-ed, Chretien de Troyes' Yvain, ou le Chevalier au Lion, Appleton, 68; auth, A Comparative Structural Analysis of Arnaut Daniel's Lo ferm voler and Peire Vidal's Mout m'es bon e bel, Neophilologus, 70; coauth, On the Generalization of the Sestina, Delta, 75; auth, Medieval Romance Paleography-a Brief Introduction, In: Medieval Manuscripts and Textual Criticism, Univ NC, 76; co-transl, Chretien de Troyes, Ywain, the Knight of the Lion, Frederick Ungar, 77,92; ed and trans, Chretien de Troyes' Erec et Enide, Garland, 87; co-trans, Chretien de troyes, Arthurian Romances, Penguin, 91; A Reappraisal of the Relationship Between Two Manuscripts of Erec et Enide, Nottingham French Studies 30.2: 34-42, autumn 91; Un Fragment inedit d'Erec et Enide et sa place la tradition manuscrite, Scriptorium: Revue Internationale des Etudes Relatives aux Manuscrits/Int review of Manuscript Studies 46.2:242-50 + pl. 20 (photographs), 92; co-trans, Lancelot, In Lancelot-Grail: The Old French Arthurian Vulgate and Post-Vulgate in Translation, Garland, 93, 95; Quelques Observations sur les reflets de la cour d'Henri II dans l'oeuvre de Chretien de Troyes, Cahiers de Civilisation Medievale, 37: 33-39, 94; Cite or Vile? A Lexical Problem in the Lancelot-Grail Cycle, The Lancelot-Grail Cycle: Text and Transformations, 139-51, ed, William W. Kibler, Austin: Univ of Tx Press, 94; Text and Image: The Case of Erec et Enide, Word and Image in Arthurian Literature, ed Keith Busby, New York: Garland Publishing, 96, 58-78. **CONTACT ADDRESS** Dept of Foreign Lang & Lit, Oregon State Univ, 210 Kidder Hall, Corvallis, OR, 97331-4603. **EMAIL** ccarroll@orst.edu

CARROLL, DAVID
DISCIPLINE FRENCH LANGUAGE **EDUCATION** The Johns Hopkins Univ, PhD. **CAREER** PROF/CH, FR, UNIV CALIF, IRVINE. **SELECTED PUBLICATIONS** Auth, The Subject in Question: The Languages of Theory and the Strategies of Fiction; Paraesthetics: Foucault, Lyotard, Derrida; French Literary Fascism: Nationalism, Anti-Semitism, and the Ideology of Culture; pub(s), and articles on lit theory. **CONTACT ADDRESS** Dept of Fr and Ital, Univ Calif, Irvine, CA, 92697.

CARROLL, LINDA LOUISE
PERSONAL Born 06/10/1949, Seattle, WA, m, 1997 **DISCIPLINE** ITALIAN, LINGUISTICS **EDUCATION** Princeton Univ, AB, 71; Harvard Univ, MA, 72, PhD , 77. **CAREER** Vis instr, 75-76, instr, 76-77, asst prof Ital, Gonzaga Univ, 76-81; Adj asst prof ling, Whitworth Col, 77-79; chmn dept Mod Lang, Gonzaga Univ, 78-81; asst prof, 81-87, assoc prof, 87-92, grad fac, 89-, prof Ital, Tulane Univ, 92-, women's studies fac assoc 94-; adj assoc prof Ital, Syracuse Univ, spring 86; Newcomb fel, 94. **HONORS AND AWARDS** Gonzaga Res Counc res grant, 79; Fulbright Comn res scholar, 84; NEH Travel to Collections award, 85; Delmas Found res fel, 85; Newberry Library Short-Term Resident fel, 86; Am Philos Soc res grant, 89; Gladys Krieble Delmas Found res grant, 90. **MEMBERSHIPS** Am Asn Ital Studies; Am Asn Tchr(s) Ital/Am Asnc Ital Studies; AAUP; Dante Soc Am; Int Soc Dialectology and Geolinguistics; Ling Asnc Canada and U S; MLA; Pacific Northwest Coun Foreign Lang; Philol Asn Pacific Coast; Renaissance Soc Am; Sixteenth Century Soc; Soc for Renaissance Studies; South Central Mod Lang Asn; WA Asn For Lang Tchr(s). **RESEARCH** Italian historical linguistics; Italian Renaissance theater; phonology. **SELECTED PUBLICATIONS** Auth, Language and Dialect in Ruzante and Goldoni, Longo, 81; Linguistic Variation and Social Protest in the Plays of Ruzante, Allegorica, 83; Carnival Themes in the Plays of Ruzante, Ital Culture, 84; Linguistic Correlates of Emotion in Ruzante, In: The Eleventh LACUS Forum 1984 (Robert A Hall Jr, ed), Hornbeam Press, 85; Carnival Rites as Vehicles of Protest in Renaissance Venice, Sixteenth Century Jour, 85; Cycles in Life and in Literature: The Case of Ruzante, Jour Asn Teachers Ital, 86; Authorial Defense in Boccaccio and Ruzante: From Liminal to Liminoid, Romance Quart, 87; Ruzante's Early Adaptations from More and Erasmus, Italica, 89; Who's on Top?: Gender as Societal Power Configuration in Italian Renaissance Drama, Sixteenth Century Jour, 89; Angelo Beolco tra comico e serio, In: Il Convegno Internazionale de Studi sul Ruzante (Giovanni Calendoli and Giuseppe Velluci, ed), Corbo e Fiore, 89; Angelo Beolco (Il Ruzante), Twayne, 90, incl Twayne's World Authors on CD-ROM, 97; Giorgione's Tempest: Astrology is in the Eyes of the Beholder, In: Reconsidering the Renaissance Papers from the Twenty-First Annual Conference (Mario Di Cesare, ed), Medieval and Renaissance Texts and Studies, 92; The Peasant as Imperialist: An Unpublished Canzone in Ruzantine Style, Italica, 93; Un Paradiso Senza Dio nella Padova del Rinasciemento, In: III Convegno Internazionale di Studi sul Ruzante (Giovanni Calendoli, ed), Societa Cooperative Tipografica, 93; A Non-theistic Paradise in Renaissance Padua, Sixteenth Century Jour, 93; Machiavelli's Veronese Prostitute?: Venetia Figurata, In: Gender Rhetorics: Postures of Dominance and Submission in History (Richard C Trexler, ed), Medieval and Renaissance Texts and Studies, 94; The Spirit in the Body: Pysical and Psycological Influence on Holy Anorexia in the Case of Maria Janis, American Society of Church History Papers, Theological Res Exchange Network, 95; Holy Anorexia Revisited: The Reputation of Fasting in the Case of Maria Janis, The Psychohistory Rev, 98; transl, How To (and How Not To) Get Married in Sixteenth Venice (Patricia H Labalme and Laura Sanguineti White), Renaissance Quart, forthcoming; Il Contadino e il Filoimperialismo: Una Canzone Inedita in Stile Ruzantiano, In: IV Convegno Internazionale di Studi sul Ruzante (Giovanni Calendoli, ed), Societa Cooperativa Tipografica, forthcoming; Bernardo Dovizi, Il Bibbiena, In: Encyclopedia of the Renaissance (Paul F Grendler, ed), Scribner's. **CONTACT ADDRESS** Dept of Fr & Ital, Tulane Univ, 6823 St Charles Ave, New Orleans, LA, 70118-5698. **EMAIL** lincar@mailhost.tcs.tulane.edu

CARRUBBA, ROBERT W.
DISCIPLINE LATIN LITERATURE, NEO-LATIN STUDIES **EDUCATION** Princeton, PhD. **CAREER** VP, Acad Aff; prof, Fordham Univ. **SELECTED PUBLICATIONS** Auth, The Epodes of Horace: A Study in Poetic Arrangemen, 69; Englebert Kaempfer's Exotic Pleasures: Fascicle III, Curious Scientific and Medical Observations, 96. **CONTACT ADDRESS** Dept of Class Lang and Lit, Fordham Univ, 113 W 60th St, New York, NY, 10023.

CARSON, KATHARINE WHITMAN
PERSONAL Born 10/26/1923, Bistol, TN **DISCIPLINE** FRENCH LITERATURE **EDUCATION** Barnard Col, AB, 45; Columbia Univ, MA, 65, PhD(French), 71. **CAREER** Instr French, Rutgers Univ, 68-71 & lectr, 71-72; ASST PROF FRENCH, BARUCH COL, 73-78; Res Assoc, US Arab Chamber of Commerce, NY, 81-, Consult educ div, Simon & Schuster, 72-73; consult-evaluator, New York Bd Educ, 74-75; consult-evaluator, NY Bd Educ, 74-75; bibliog-consult, H P Kraus Rare Bks, 79-80; vis assoc prof, Yeshiva Univ, 80 & Fairleign Dickinson Univ, 79-81. **MEMBERSHIPS** AAUP; MLA, Am Asn Teachers Fr. **RESEARCH** Eighteenth century French novel. **SELECTED PUBLICATIONS** Auth, Des Hommes Illustres, World Lit Today, Vol 0069, 95; Genevieve et Attila, World Lit Today, Vol 0068, 94. **CONTACT ADDRESS** 435 W 119 St, New York, NY, 10027.

CARTER, ALBERT HOWARD
DISCIPLINE COMPARATIVE LITERATURE **EDUCATION** Univ Chicago, BA; Univ Iowa, MA, PhD. **CAREER** Prof. **HONORS AND AWARDS** Distinguished Tchr Awd. **MEMBERSHIPS** Soc Values Higher Edu; Am Soc Bioethics Humanities. **SELECTED PUBLICATIONS** Auth, Italo Calvino: Metamorphoses of Fantasy; First Cut: A Season In The Human Anatomy Lab, Picador, 97. **CONTACT ADDRESS** Eckerd Col, 54th Ave S, PO Box 4200, St Petersburg, FL, 33711.

CARTER, WILLIAM CAUSEY
PERSONAL Born 03/28/1941, Jesup, GA, m, 1967, 3 children **DISCIPLINE** FRENCH LANGUAGE AND LITERATURE **EDUCATION** Univ Ga, BA, 63, MA, 67; Ind Univ, PhD(French), 71. **CAREER** Asst prof French, Ohio Univ, 71-74; asst prof, 74-78, PROF FRENCH, UNIV ALA, BIRMINGHAM, 78- **MEMBERSHIPS** MLA; SAtlantic Mod Lang Asn. **RESEARCH** Nineteenth and twentieth century French literature. **SELECTED PUBLICATIONS** Auth, Time and Sense--Proust and the Experience of Literature, Modernism-Modernity, Vol 0004, 97; The Correspondence of Proust, Marcel, Vol 19, Fr Rev, Vol 0069, 95; Metaphoric Narration--Paranarrative Dimensions Ii a la Recherche du Temps Perdu, Fr Rev, Vol 0067, 93; Metaphoric Narration--Paranarrative Dimensions in a la Recherche du Temps Perdue, Fr Rev, Vol 0067, 94; Proust, Philosophy of the Novel, Stud in the Novel, Vol 0026, 94; Proust Between 2 Centuries, Stud in the Novel, Vol 0027, 95. **CONTACT ADDRESS** 604 Warwick Rd, Birmingham, AL, 35209.

CARUTH, CATHY
DISCIPLINE ENGLISH LANGUAGE AND LITERATURE **EDUCATION** Yale Univ, PhD, 88. **CAREER** Prof Eng/Dir comp lit prog. **RESEARCH** English and German Romanticism; trauma theory; psychoanalytic theory. **SELECTED PUBLICATIONS** Auth, Unclaimed Experience: Trauma, Narrative and History; co-ed/intro, Critical Encounters: Reference and Responsibility in Deconstructive Writing; Trauma: Explorations in Memory; Empirical Truths and Critical Fictions: Locke Wordsworth, Kant, Freud. **CONTACT ADDRESS** English Dept, Emory Univ, 1380 Oxford Rd NE, Atlanta, GA, 30322-1950.

CASA, FRANK PAUL
PERSONAL Born 11/18/1932, San Lucido, Italy, m, 1957, 2 children **DISCIPLINE** ROMANCE LANGUAGES **EDUCATION** Univ Ill, BA, 55, MA, 56; Univ Mich, PhD(Span), 63. **CAREER** From instr to asst prof Romance lang, Harvard Univ, 63-69; assoc prof, 69-76, PROF UNIV MICH, ANN ARBOR, 76-, CHMN DEPT, 73-, Guggenheim fel, 67-68; chief-reader, Educ Testing Serv, 78- **MEMBERSHIPS** MLA **SELECTED PUBLICATIONS** Auth, Fatal Union, Pluralistic Approach to the Spanish Wife-Murder Comedias, Bulletin of the Comediantes, Vol 0044, 92; Rojaszorrilla, Francisco, De and Moreto, Agustin-Analysis, Hisp Rev, Vol 0065, 97. **CONTACT ADDRESS** 1410 Hill St, Ann Arbor, MI, 48104.

CASAGRANDE, JEAN
PERSONAL Born 08/19/1938, Oran, Algeria, m, 1963, 2 children **DISCIPLINE** FRENCH LANGUAGE AND LINGUISTICS **EDUCATION** Univ SFla, BA, 63; Ind Univ, MA, 64, PhD(Fr), 68. **CAREER** Lectr French & Ital, Ind Univ, 66-68, asst prof, 68; asst, 68-73, Assoc PROF FRENCH & LING, UNIV FLA, 73-, Vis prof, Ling Soc Am Summer Inst, 72 & co-dir, 75; Nat Endowment for Humanities fel, 72-73. **MEMBERSHIPS** Ling Soc Am; Am Asn Teachers Fr; Southeast Conf Ling (pres, 74-75); Int Soc Phonetic Sci. **RESEARCH** French language, syntax and semantics; linguistic theory. **SELECTED PUBLICATIONS** Auth, The Canon in a Structure Course--The Case of French, Romance Quart, Vol 0041, 94. **CONTACT ADDRESS** 1732 NW Seventh Ave, Gainesville, FL, 32603.

CASCARDI, ANTHONY JOSEPH
PERSONAL Born 12/29/1953, New York, NY, m, 1978 **DISCIPLINE** COMPARATIVE LITERATURE **EDUCATION** Princeton Univ, BA, 75; Harvard Univ, MA, 77, PhD(Romance lang), 80. **CAREER** ASST PROF COMP LIT, UNIV CALIF, BERKELEY, 80-, Soc Fel in the Humanities fel, Columbia Univ, 82-. **MEMBERSHIPS** MLA. **RESEARCH** Skepticism and knowledge in the novels of Cervantes, Dostoyevsky and Flaubert. **SELECTED PUBLICATIONS** Auth, A Pragmatist Philosophy of Life in Ortegaygasset, Philos and Lit, Vol 0019, 95; The Subjects of Modernity, Mod Lang Quart, Vol 0054, 93; Ethics and Aesthetics in Conrad, Joseph, W Hum Rev, Vol 0049, 95; The Meaning of Literature, Mod Lang Quart, Vol 0054, 93; The Subject as Action--Transformation and Totality in Narrative Aesthetics, Mod Fiction Stud, Vol 0040, 94; Genres in Dialogue--Plato and the Construct of Philosophy, Philos and Lit, Vol 0020, 96. **CONTACT ADDRESS** Dept of Comp, Univ Calif, Calif Berkeley, CA, 94704.

CASE, FREDRICK I.
PERSONAL Born 09/19/1939, Georgetown, Guyana **DISCIPLINE** FRENCH **EDUCATION** Univ Hull, BA, 65; Univ Leicester, MA, 68; Univ Lille, DUn, 70. **CAREER** Sch tchr, Eng & France, 60-68; lectr to assoc prof, 68-80, coordr African stud prog, 78-80, PROF FRENCH, UNIV TORONTO, 80-, assoc ch grad stud Fr, 84-85, ch Fr, 85-90, prin, New Col, 91-96, dir, Ca-

ribbean stud prog, 95-96. **SELECTED PUBLICATIONS** Auth, Aime Cesaire; Bibliographie, 73; auth, La Cite Ideale dans Travail d'Emile Zola, 74; auth, Racism and National Consciousness, 79; auth, The Crisis of Identity: Studies in the Guadeloupean and Martiniquan Novel, 85. **CONTACT ADDRESS** New Col, Univ Toronto, Toronto, ON, M5S 1A1.

CASE, THOMAS EDWARD
PERSONAL Born 02/27/1934, Minneapolis, MN, m, 1960, 1 child **DISCIPLINE** SPANISH **EDUCATION** Col St Thomas, BA, 56; State Univ Iowa, MA, 58, PhD(Span), 62. **CAREER** Asst, State Univ Iowa, 56-61; from asst prof to assoc prof, 61-69, PROF SPAN, SAN DIEGO STATE UNIV, 69-, Fulbright lect grant, Bogota, 65; resident dir, Calif Univ Int Progs, Univ Madrid, Spain, 74-75. **MEMBERSHIPS** Am Asn Teachers Span & Port; Philol Asn Pac Coast; Pac Coast Coun Latin Am Studies. **RESEARCH** Latin American novel; Golden Age literature. **SELECTED PUBLICATIONS** Auth, Al Acecho, World Lit Today, Vol 0070, 96; Esta Maldita Lujuria, World Lit Today, Vol 0067, 93; Parody, Gender and Dress in Lope-De-Vega La Doncella Teodor, Bulletin Comediantes, Vol 0046, 94; Margins of Fiction--Poetics of Latin-American Narrative-Span, World Lit Today, Vol 0067, 93; Respiracion Artificial, World Lit Today, Vol 0068, 94; Ferre,Rosario-A Search for Identity, World Lit Today, Vol 0070, 96; Lope and the Moriscos, Bulletin Comediantes, Vol 0044, 92; Language and Orthodoxy in La Farsa del Sacramento Llamada de Los Lenguajes, Bulletin Comediantes, Vol 0048, 96. **CONTACT ADDRESS** Dept of Span, San Diego State Univ, 5500 Campanile Dr, San Diego, CA, 92182-0002.

CASERTA, ERNESTO GIUSEPPE
PERSONAL Born 03/19/1937, Montenero, Italy, m, 1968, 2 children **DISCIPLINE** ITALIAN LITERATURE **EDUCATION** Gannon Col, BA, 60; Tulane Univ, MA, 63; Harvard Univ, PhD(Ital), 69. **CAREER** From instr to asst prof Ital, Boston Univ, 67-70; asst prof, 70-80, ASSOC PROF ITAL, DUKE UNIV, 80-, Am Philos Soc grant, 76-77. **MEMBERSHIPS** Dante Soc Am; Am Asn Teachers Ital; SAtlantic Mod Lang Asn. **RESEARCH** Nineteenth and twentieth century Italian literature, aesthetics and criticism. **SELECTED PUBLICATIONS** Auth, Croce and Gentile a Century Later--Essays, Unpublished Texts and a Bibliographic Appendix 1980-1993, Forum Italicum, Vol 0029, 95; Realism--Verga and the Minor Italian Realists, Forum Italicum, Vol 0028, 94; With the Cards on the Table-- Works by Manzoni,Alessandro and other Critical and Philological Works on Italian Culture in America, Forum Italicum, Vol 0028, 94. **CONTACT ADDRESS** Dept of Romance Lang, Duke Univ, Durham, NC, 27706.

CASMIR, FRED L.
PERSONAL Born 12/30/1928, Berlin, Germany, m, 1986, 2 children **DISCIPLINE** SPEECH AND COMMUNICATION **EDUCATION** David Lipscomb Col, BA, 50; Ohio State Univ, MA, 55, PhD, 61. **CAREER** Part-time Fac, East Los Angeles Col, 73-74; Part-time Fac to Assoc Prof, San Fernando Valley State Col, 61-73; Instr to Prof Commun, 56-94, Distinguished Prof, Pepperdine Univ, 94-. **HONORS AND AWARDS** Outstanding Teacher, Pepperdine Univ, 73; Second-place winner, national papers contest, Nat Asn Educ Broadcasters, 81; Teacher of the Year, Alumni Asn, Pepperdine Univ, 85; PRSSA, Outstanding Fac Advisor, 86; Outstanding Sr Interculturalist, Soc Intercultural Educ, Training and Res, Int, 87; Assoc, Sears-Roebuck Found Grant and Assoc Project for Asian Studies, Fac Development, Pepperdine Univ, 90-91; Fel, Irvine Found Grant, 93; recipient of several research grants from Pepperdine University and others. **MEMBERSHIPS** Nat Commun Asn; Pi Kappa Delta; Ger Speech Asn; Int Commun Asn; World Commun Asn; Western Speech Commun Asn. **SELECTED PUBLICATIONS** Ed, Building communication theories: A socio-cultural approach, Lawrence Erlbaum Assoc, 94; Communication in Eastern Europe: The role of history, culture and media in contemporary conflict, Lawrence Erlbaum Assoc, 95; auth, Foundations for the study of intercultural communication based on a third culture building model, Int J Intercultural Relations (in press); ed, Ethics in Intercultural and International Communication, Lawrence Erlbaum Assoc (in press); author and editor of numerous other articles and publications. **CONTACT ADDRESS** Seaver Col, Pepperdine Univ, 24255 Pacific Coast Hwy, Malibu, CA, 90263. **EMAIL** fcasmir@pepperdine.edu

CASSELL, ANTHONY K.
PERSONAL Born 03/31/1941, Reading, England **DISCIPLINE** ITALIAN & MEDIEVAL LITERATURE **EDUCATION** Univ Toronto, BA, 63; Johns Hopkins Univ, PhD, 69. **CAREER** Asst prof, 71-76, assoc prof Italian, prof Italian & comp literature, 86, Univ IL, Urbana, 76-, assoc ed, Italian Culture & Dante Studies; Dante Soc Am Coun, 80-84, 90-94; Guggenheim Fel, 85. **HONORS AND AWARDS** Outstanding Book Award, Choice, 76. **MEMBERSHIPS** Am Asn Teachers Ital; Dante Soc Am; Am Boccaccio Asn; MLA; Mediaeval Acad Am; Am Asn Italian Studies; Ren Soc Am. **RESEARCH** Boccaccio; Danta; Petrarca. **SELECTED PUBLICATIONS** Auth, The crow of the fable and the Corbaccio, Mod Lang Notes, 70; The Corbaccio and the secundus tradition, Comp Lit, 73; Boccaccio's Corbaccio, 75; Moral and structural conflict in the Corbaccio, Mod Lang Notes, 75; ed & translr, the Corbaccio, Univ Ill, 75; auth, Pride failure and conversion in Inferno I, Dante Studies, 76; Farinata and the image of the Arca, Yale Ital Studies, 77; The Tomb, the Tower and the Pit, Italica, 79; The Lesson of Ulysses, Dante Studies, 81; Pier della Vigna: History and Iconography, Dante, Petrarch and Others, 82; Ulisseana: A Bibliography on Dante's Ulysses until 1980, Italian Cult, 81; auth, Dante's Fearful Art of Justice, Univ Toronto, 84; ed Diana's Hunt Caccia di Diana: Boccaccio's First Fiction, Univ Pa, 91; Lectura Dantis Americana, Inferno I, Univ Pa, 89; ed, The Corbaccio or the Labyrinth of Love, Pegasus Press, 93. **CONTACT ADDRESS** Dept Spanish, Italian & Portugues, Univ Illinois, 707S Mathews Ave, Urbana, IL, 61801-3625. **EMAIL** acassell@uiuc.edu

CASSIDY, FREDERIC GOMES
PERSONAL Born 10/10/1907, Jamaica, WI, m, 1931, 4 children **DISCIPLINE** ENGLISH AND AMERICAN LANGUAGE **EDUCATION** Oberlin Col, AB, 30, Am, 32; Univ Mich, PhD, 38. **CAREER** Teaching fel English, Univ Mich, 34-35 & 36-38, instr, 38-39; lectr English lang, Univ Strasbourg, France, 35-36; from instr to assoc prof, 42-49, PROF ENGLISH, UNIV WIS-MADISON, 49-, Dir English Lang Surv, 48-, Res asst & ed, Early Mod English Dict, 31-35 & 36-37, Mid English Dict, 51; field worker, Ling Atlas of US & Can, Ohio & Wis, 39-41; Fulbright res scholar, 51-52 & 58-59; consult, Dialect Surv Brit Caribbean, 54-; first hon fel, Univ Col West Indies, 58-59; vis prof English lit, Stanford Univ, 63-64; consult, Funk & Wagnalls, 64-70; dir & ed, Dict Am Regional English, 65-. **HONORS AND AWARDS** Silver Musgrave Medal, Inst Jamaica, 62; Centenary Medal, 80. **MEMBERSHIPS** Ling Soc Am; Am Dialect Soc (pres, 55-57); MLA; Mediaeval Acad Am; Soc Caribbean Ling (pres, 72-76); Am Name Soc (pres, 80). **RESEARCH** Pidgin and Creole languages; English lexicography. **SELECTED PUBLICATIONS** Auth, Pigeons in Cahoots--Etymology of the Words Cahoots and Cahooter, Amer Speech, Vol 0068, 93; 50 Years Among the New Words--A Dictionary of Neologisms, 1941-1991, Lang, Vol 0069, 93; Short Note on Creole Orthography, Jour Pidgin and Creole Lang(s), Vol 0008, 93; Malcolm--An Essay on a Friend, Verbatim, Vol 0019, 93; Dialect Studies in Britain, Jour Intl Ling Assn, Vol 0046, 95; More on Jesus-H-Christ--American English Curse-Words, Amer Speech, Vol 0070, 95. **CONTACT ADDRESS** Univ Wis, 6123 Helen White Hall, Madison, WI, 53706.

CASSIRER, THOMAS
PERSONAL Born 04/28/1923, Rome, Italy, m, 1948, 1 child **DISCIPLINE** FRENCH AND AFRICAN LITERATURE **EDUCATION** McGill Univ, BA, 45; Yale Univ, PhD(Fr & comp lit), 53. **CAREER** Asst prof French, Smith Col, 60-65; assoc prof, 65-69, PROF FRENCH & AFRICAN LIT, UNIV MASS, AMHERST, 69-. **MEMBERSHIPS** MLA; Am Asn Teachers Fr; African Studies Asn. **RESEARCH** Eighteenth century French literature; modern African literature. **SELECTED PUBLICATIONS** Auth, Francophone Theater of Senegal-Ger, Res African Lit, Vol 0024, 93. **CONTACT ADDRESS** Dept of French & Italian, Univ of Mass, Amherst, MA, 01002.

CASTANEDA, JAMES AGUSTIN
PERSONAL Born 04/02/1933, Brooklyn, NY **DISCIPLINE** SPANISH LITERATURE **EDUCATION** Drew Univ, AB, 54; Yale Univ, MA, 55, PhD, 58; Univ Paris, cert, 57. **CAREER** From asst prof to assoc prof Span & French, Hanover Col, 58-61; from asst prof to assoc prof, 61-67, chmn dept classics, Ital, Port, Russ & Span, 64-72, PROF SPAN, RICE UNIV, 67-, Danforth fel, 54-58 & teaching fel, 58-; vis lectr, Univ NC, 62-63, dir Year-at-Lyon, 67-68 & vis prof, 68; pres, Inst Hisp Cult Houston, 72; miembro titular, Inst Cult Hisp Madrid, 72-; mem bd dirs, L'Alliance Francaise Houston, 72-74; vis prof Span, Mt Holyoke Col, 76-77. **MEMBERSHIPS** MLA; Renaissance Soc; Soc Values Higher Educ; Am Asn Teachers Fr; Am Asn Teachers Span & Port. **RESEARCH** Golden Age drama of Spain; French literature. **SELECTED PUBLICATIONS** Auth, After Its Kind, Approaches to the Comedia, Bulletin Comediantes, Vol 0045, 93; Rojaszorrilla, Francisco, De and Moreto, Agustin--Analysis, Bulletin Hisp Stud, Vol 0072, 95; Remembering Mead, Hispania-A Jour Devoted to the Tchg Span and Portuguese, Vol 0079, 96; Sorpesas-Spanish, Mod Lang Jour, Vol 0078, 94; Understanding Metaphor in Literature, Mod Lang Jour, Vol 0080, 96; Modern Spanish Prose with a Selection of Poetry, Mod Lang Jour, Vol 0081, 97; Texto-Y-Vida--Introduction tTo Spanish-American Literature, Mod Lang Jour, Vol 0078, 94. **CONTACT ADDRESS** Dept of Span Portuguese & Classics, Rice Univ, Houston, TX, 77001.

CASTEEN, JOHN
PERSONAL Born 12/11/1943, Portsmouth, VA, 1 child **DISCIPLINE** OLD ENGLISH LITERATURE, HISTORY OF THE ENGLISH LANGUAGE **EDUCATION** Univ Va, BA, 65, MA, 66, PhD(English), 70. **CAREER** Asst to dean, Co of Arts & Sci, Univ Va, 69-70; asst prof English, Univ Calif, Berkeley, 70-75; asst prof, 75-77, ASSOC PROF ENGLISH, UNIV VA, 77-, DEAN OF ADMIS, 75- **RESEARCH** Patristics; early American literature. **SELECTED PUBLICATIONS** Auth, Poem for Mary Magdalene, Shenandoah, Vol 0046, 96. **CONTACT ADDRESS** Dept of English, Univ of Va, Charlottesville, VA, 22901.

CASTELLANOS, ISABEL
DISCIPLINE SPANISH LITERATURE **EDUCATION** Georgetown Univ, PhD. **CAREER** Prof. **RESEARCH** Afro Cuban and Afro Colombian culture; works of Lydia Cabrera; Spanish American sociolinguistics. **SELECTED PUBLICATIONS** Auth, Patak: A Collection of Afro-Cuban Myths, 96; co-auth, Cultura Afrocubana, 94. **CONTACT ADDRESS** Dept of Modern Languages, Florida State Univ, 11200 SW 8th St, Miami, FL, 33174. **EMAIL** castella@servms.fiu.edu

CASTELLS, RICARDO
DISCIPLINE SPANISH LITERATURE **EDUCATION** Duke Univ, PhD, 91. **CAREER** Asst prof. **RESEARCH** Renaissance and Baroque Spanish literature. **SELECTED PUBLICATIONS** Auth, El caballero de Olmedo de Lope de Vega: 'Aojado estes', 95; Damas y caballeria: la mujer guerrera y la prensa neoyorquina durante la guerra de independencia cubana, 95; From Crenica to Comedia: Catholic Evangelization and Indigenous Oral Traditions in the Inca Garcilaso and Calderen, 94; The Hidden Intertext in Alejo Carpentier's Los pasos perdidos, 94. **CONTACT ADDRESS** Dept of Modern Languages, Florida State Univ, 11200 SW 8th St, Miami, FL, 33174.

CASTRICANO, JODEY
DISCIPLINE CULTURAL STUDIES **EDUCATION** Simon Fraser, BA, MA; British Columbia, PhD. **CAREER** Asst Prof **SELECTED PUBLICATIONS** Auth, If a Building Is a Senctence, So Is A Body: Kathy Acker's Empire of the Senseless and Postcolonial Gothic; Rude Awakenings--or, What happens When a Lesbian Reads the Hieroglyphics of Sleep in Djuna Barnes Nightwood; West Coast Line, 94. **CONTACT ADDRESS** Dept of English, Wilfrid Laurier Univ, 75 University Ave W, Waterloo, ON, N2L 3C5. **EMAIL** jcastric@mach1.wlu.ca

CASTRO, AMANDA
DISCIPLINE SPANISH LITERATURE **EDUCATION** Univ Pittsburgh, PhD, 91. **CAREER** Asst prof. **RESEARCH** Spanish language and linguistics; poetry. **SELECTED PUBLICATIONS** Auth, Celebracion de mujeres, 93. **CONTACT ADDRESS** Foreign Languages and Literature Dept, Colorado State Univ, Fort Collins, CO, 80523. **EMAIL** acastro@vines.colostate.edu

CASTRO LEE, CECILIA
DISCIPLINE SPANISH LITERATURE **EDUCATION** Emory Univ, PhD. **SELECTED PUBLICATIONS** Auth, pubs on Spanish and Latin-American writers; ed, The Literature of Democratic Spain: 1975-1992; co-ed, On Men and Monsters. **CONTACT ADDRESS** Dept Foreign Languages and Literature, State Univ of West Georgia, Carrollton, GA, 30118.

CATHEY, JAMES E.
DISCIPLINE LINGUISTICS **EDUCATION** Oregon State Univ, BS, 62; Univ Wash, MA, 64, PhD, 67. **CAREER** Prof. **RESEARCH** Germanic synchronic and historical phonology; Finnish phonology. **SELECTED PUBLICATIONS** Auth, 501 Hebrew Verbs, Hauppauge, 96; Ivrit yisre'elit kesafa shemit: gene'alogya vetipologya, 95; Hasegoliyyim-gzira qavit 'o mesoreget?, 95; Direct instruction of grammatical structure to students of Hebrew as a foreign language, 95; On the formation of diminutives in Modern Hebrew morphology, Hebrew Studies, 94. **CONTACT ADDRESS** Linguistics Dept, Univ of Massachusetts, Amherst, 720 Massachusetts Ave, Amherst, MA, 01003. **EMAIL** cathey@german.umass.edu

CAUFIELD, CARLOTA
DISCIPLINE HISPANIC STUDIES **EDUCATION** Univ Havana, Cuba, MA, 79; San Francisco State Univ, MA, 86; Tulane Univ, New Orleans, PhD, 92. **CAREER** Asst prof; Mills Col, 92-. **RESEARCH** Eboli poetry; 20th century Spanish and Latin American poetry; contemporary literature of Spain and Latin America; Hispanic cultures; Hispanic writers in the US; feminist critical theories. **SELECTED PUBLICATIONS** Auth, A las puertas del papel con amoroso fuego, Torremozas, Madrid, 96; ed, Literary and Cultural Journeys: Selected Letters to Arturo Torres-Rioseco, Ctr for the Bk, Oakland, 95; Book of XXXIX Steps, a poetry game of discovery and imagination, Hyperbk for the Macintosh, 5 Diskettes, Mobile, Alabama: Intelibks, 95; Estrofas de papel, barro y tinta, Cafe Central, Barcelona, 95; Visual Games for Words & Sounds. Hyperpoems for the Macintosh, Diskette. Intelibks, San Francisco, 93; bk column, Resenas, 92-95, Tiempo Latino; bk rev(s) for, lit mag Lateral, Barcelona, 95-; contribur to anthologies, Diez jovenes poetas que inspiran en espanol, INTI, 90; Looking for Home, Women Writing about Exile, Milkweed Ed(s), 90; Bridges to Cuba, Michigan Quart Rev, 94; These are not Sweet Girls, Poetry by Latin Amer Women, White Pine Press, 94; Poesea cubana: la isla entera, Betania, 95; Poesea hispano-caribena escrita en Estados Unidos, Fundacion Federico Garcea Lorca, 95 & Poeseda, An Anthology of AIDS Poetry from the US, Latin Am and Spain, Ollantay Press, 95; contribur of poetry to, Haight Ashbury Lit J; Luz en arte y literatura; Lyra, Linden Lane Mage; Mich Quart Rev; Poetry San Francisco: Termino Mag; Tex Rev; Visions & Walrus; contribur essays to, ANQ; Poet's Market; Revista Iberoamericana; Middlebury Col Rev;

Chasqui; La Torre; Alba de America; El gato tuerto & Bohemia. **CONTACT ADDRESS** Dept of Hispanic Studies, Mills Col, 5000 MacArthur Blvd, Oakland, CA, 94613-1301. **EMAIL** amach@ella.mills.edu

CAUJOLLE, CLAUDE

DISCIPLINE FRENCH LINGUISTICS AND PHONOLOGY **EDUCATION** PA State Univ, PhD. **CAREER** Instr, Hollins Col, 72. **RESEARCH** Tchg of French grammar. **SELECTED PUBLICATIONS** Auth, Plaisir de Lire; See Me Read. **CONTACT ADDRESS** Hollins Col, Roanoke, VA, 24020.

CAUVIN, JEAN-PIERRE BERNARD

PERSONAL Born 02/25/1936, Casablanca, Morocco, m, 1963, 2 children **DISCIPLINE** FRENCH LANGUAGE & LITERATURE **EDUCATION** Princeton Univ, BA, 57, PhD, 68. **CAREER** Lectr, Harvard Univ, 63-66; asst prof, Princeton Univ, 66-72; Assoc Prof French, Univ TX Austin, 72-85, Prof 85-, Chmn, 85-94, Consult French lit, Col Entrance Exam Bd, 76-90; Chief reader, AP Program French, 92-96. **HONORS AND AWARDS** Officier de l'ordre des Palmes Academiques, 93. **MEMBERSHIPS** MLA; SCent Mod Lang Asn; Am Asn Tchr(s) Fr; Soc Professeurs Fr Am. **RESEARCH** Nineteenth and twentieth century French poetry; Surrealism. **SELECTED PUBLICATIONS** Auth, Henri Bosco et la Poetique du Sacre, Klincksieck, Paris, 74; contribr, Le reel et l'imaginaire dans l'oeuvre de Henri Bosco, Jose Corti, Paris, 76; Poems of Andre Breton: A Bilingual Anthology (with M.A. Caws), Univ of Tex Press, 82; Co-ed, Panache Litteraire: Textes du monde francophone, 3rd ed, Heinle & Heinle, 94. **CONTACT ADDRESS** Dept of Fr & Ital, Univ of Texas, Austin, TX, 78712-1197. **EMAIL** jpcauvin@mail.utexas.edu

CAVALLARI, HECTOR MARIO

DISCIPLINE HISPANIC STUDIES **EDUCATION** San Francisco State Univ, BA, 69; Univ Calif at Irvine, MA, 72, PhD, 72. **CAREER** Prof; Mills Col, 86-. **RESEARCH** Contemporary Latin American literature; Hispanic cultures; literary criticism; critical theory, Hispanic cinema. **SELECTED PUBLICATIONS** Auth, La practica de la escritura. Concepcion, Chile: Ediciones LAR, 90; Leopoldo Marechal: El espacio de los signos. Xalapa, Mexico: Univ Vercruzana, 82; Antigona Velez: Justicialismo y obra dramatica, Gestos 10 20, 95; coauth, Escritura y desfetichizacion: En torno a El perseguidor, de Julio Cortazar, Revista de Critica Literaria Latinoamericana XXII, 96; bk contrib, Textualidadm modelacion, descentramiento: Notas sobre el proceso critico, In El puente de las palabras, Wash, EUA: Interamer/OEA, 94; Leopoldo marechal: ideologia, escritura, compromiso, In Ensaos de literatura europea e hispanoamericana, San Sebastian: Editorial de la Univ del Pais Vasco, 90; Liliana Heker: (d)enunciar el orden, In Commemorative Ser, Essays in Honor of Seymour Menton, Riverside: Univ Calif, 91; nJulio Cortazar: Todos los juegos el juego, In Los ochenta mundos de Julio Cortazar, Madrid: Edi-6, 87; El agape de la escritura, In Homenaje a Leopoldo marechal, Buenos Aires: Corregidor, Articles: La tramoya de la escritura en La invencion de Morel, de Adolfo Bioy Casares, Bull Hisp Stud, Liverpool, UK 74, 97; La literatura latinoamericana: Busqueda problematica de una voz propia, Alba de Am 14, 96. **CONTACT ADDRESS** Dept of Hispanic Studies, Mills Col, 5000 MacArthur Blvd, Oakland, CA, 94613-1301.

CAVALLO, JOANN

PERSONAL Born 05/21/1959, Summit, NJ **DISCIPLINE** ITALIAN **EDUCATION** Rutgers Univ, BA, 81; Yale Univ, MA, 84, PhD, 87. **CAREER** Assoc prof of Ital, Columbia Univ, 93- ; DIR, COLUMBIA UNIV SUMMER PROG IN SCANDIANO (ITALY), 95-. **HONORS AND AWARDS** Nat Ital Am Found Schol, 86; Columbia Univ Coun for Res in the Humanities, 89-90. **MEMBERSHIPS** Renaissance Soc of Amer **RESEARCH** Italian Renaissance literature and history **SELECTED PUBLICATIONS** auth, Boiardo's "Orlando Innamorato": An Ethics of Desire, 93; L'Orlando Furioso nella critica angloamericana 1986-1991, Lettere italiane, 93; "Purgatorio 24", Dante's Divine Comedy: Introductory Readings II: Purgatorio, 93; Elsa Morante and the Adventures of Caterina, Forum Italicaum, 94; Paradiso 2, Dante's "Paradiso": Introductory Readings, 95; Fortune and Romance: Boiardo in America, 98; L'Orlando Innamorato come speculum principis, Il Boiardo e il mondo Estense nel Quattrocento: Atti del convegno internazionale di studi, Scandiano-Modena-Reggio Emilia-Ferrara, 98. **CONTACT ADDRESS** Columbia Univ, New York, NY, 10027. **EMAIL** jac3@columbia.edu

CAVANAGH, SHEILA T.

DISCIPLINE ENGLISH LANGUAGE AND LITERATURE **EDUCATION** Brown Univ, PhD, 88. **CAREER** Assoc prof **RESEARCH** Renaissance literature; Shakespeare; literary criticism; feminist theory. **SELECTED PUBLICATIONS** Auth, Wanton Eyes and Chaste Desires: Female Sexuality in The Faerie Queene. **CONTACT ADDRESS** English Dept, Emory Univ, 1380 Oxford Rd NE, Atlanta, GA, 30322-1950.

CAVIGIOLI, RITA C.

PERSONAL Born 01/10/1954, Turin, Italy, s **DISCIPLINE** ITALIAN LITERATURE **EDUCATION** Univ Turin, Laurea, 78; Univ Wash, MA, 80; UCLA, PhD, 93. **CAREER** Tchr, Univ Wash, 78-80, Italian Leceo, 80-85, 89-96, UCLA, 85-87, 87-88, Univ Mo, 96-99; tchg asst consult, UCLA, 87. **HONORS AND AWARDS** Laurea cum laude, 78; Tchg Fel, 85-88, Res Assistantship Grant, 89, UCLA; British Council Scholar, 93, Univ E Anglia; EEC, 93, Glasgow-Turin. **MEMBERSHIPS** Modern Lang Asn; Am Asn Italian Stud; Am Asn Tchrs Italian; Am Italian Hist Asn; Immigration Hist Res Ctr. **RESEARCH** 19th/20th century literature; Italian language and culture; women's literature; autobiographical writing; pedagogical literature; migration narratives. **SELECTED PUBLICATIONS** Auth, By Airmail. Testo di letture e civilta inglese e americana, 90; auth, art, Introduction to Comic Language in the EFL Classroom. A Resource Pack for Teacher Trainers, 94; auth, La fatica di iniziare il libro. Problemi di autorita nel diario di Sibilla Aleramo, 95; auth, art, L'America va alle elementari. Tra cultura e immaginario, 96; auth, art, Tutto sta che l'insegnante abbia cuore e intelligenza: esercizio letterario ricerca pedagogica e professionalita femminile in un diario scolastico dell'Italia postunitaria, 98. **CONTACT ADDRESS** Dept of Romance Languages, Univ of Missouri, Columbia, Columbia, MO, 65211. **EMAIL** langrita@showme.missouri.edu

CAWS, MARY ANN

PERSONAL Born 09/10/1933, Wilmington, NC, m, 1952, 2 children **DISCIPLINE** FRENCH LITERATURE **EDUCATION** Bryn Mawr Col, BA, 54; Yale Univ, MA, 56; Univ Kans, PhD(French lit), 62. **CAREER** Vis asst prof French, Univ Kans, 64; from asst prof to assoc prof, 66-74, PROF ROMANCE LANG, HUNTER COL & GRAD CTR, CITY UNIV NEW YORK, 74-, Exec Off Comp Lit Phd Prog, 76-, Asst ed, French Rev, 70-; Guggenheim fel, 72-73; Fulbright-Hays sr travel res scholar, 72-73; ed, Dada/Surrealism, 72-; ed, Le Siecle eclate, 74; mem adv bd Western Europe, Fulbright-Hays Rcs Prog, 77-; Nat Endowment for Humanities fel, 79-80. **HONORS AND AWARDS** Ordre des Palmes Acad Lit Studies, French Govt, 77. **MEMBERSHIPS** MLA; Asn Studies Dada & Surrealism (treas, 68-70, pres, 71-73); Am Asn Teachers Fr; Am Comp Lit Asn. **RESEARCH** Contemporary poetry; Dada and surrealism; poetics and literary theory. **SELECTED PUBLICATIONS** Auth, Bonnefoy, Yves, Sostenuto--On Sustaining the Long Poem, Esprit Createur, Vol 0036, 96; Decentering the Invitation, to Take the Trip--A New Look at Baudelaire,Charles Invitation Au Voyage, Esprit Createur, Vol 0034, 94; Reverdy, Pierre Dehors, Europe-Rev Lit Mensuelle, Vol 0072, 94; The Imagination of Reference--Meditating the Linguistic Condition, Fr Rev, Vol 0067, 94; Poetry, Passion and the Holocaust, Romance Notes, Vol 0035, 95; Arts of Impoverishment-- Beckett, Rothko, Resnais, Comp Lit Stud, Vol 0033, 96; Forum-The Personal in Scholarship--Problems with Personal Criticism, Pmla-Pub Mod Lang Assn Am, Vol 0111, 96; Poetry as Plenitude, Esprit Createur, Vol 0036, 96; Earth Writing in the Novelistic Work of Aragon, Fr Rev, Vol 0069, 96; What Can a Woman Do For the Late James,Henry, Raritan-Quart Rev, Vol 0014, 94; Rage Begins at Home--Tones of Voice in a Text Designed to Arouse and Authorize Anger, Mass Rev, Vol 0034, 93; Ruskin Race and Ours, the Dramatic Style, Browning Inst Stud, Vol 0018, 90. **CONTACT ADDRESS** Grad Ctr City, Univ of New York, 33 W 42nd, New York, NY, 10036.

CAZENAVE, ODILE

DISCIPLINE FRANCOPHONE LITERATURE **EDUCATION** Pa State Univ, PhD, 88. **CAREER** Assoc prof. **SELECTED PUBLICATIONS** Auth, pubs on African and Caribbean women writers. **CONTACT ADDRESS** Dept of Romance Languages, Knoxville, TN, 37996.

CENIZA, SHERRY

DISCIPLINE AMERICAN LANGUAGE **EDUCATION** Univ IA, PhD, 90. **CAREER** Assoc prof, TX Tech Univ. **SELECTED PUBLICATIONS** Publ(s) in the following areas: Walt Whitman, 19th Century women activists and writers, the essay as a literary genre, feminist criticism, and multiculturalism. **CONTACT ADDRESS** Texas Tech Univ, Lubbock, TX, 79409-5015. **EMAIL** ditsc@ttacs.ttu.edu

CERF, STEVEN ROY

PERSONAL Born 10/09/1945, New York, NY **DISCIPLINE** GERMAN, COMPARATIVE LITERATURE **EDUCATION** Queens Col, City Univ New York, BA, 66; Yale Univ, MPh, 71, PhD(Ger), 75. **CAREER** Teaching asst Ger, Yale Univ, 69-70, instr, 70-71; instr, 71-75, asst prof, 75-82, ASSOC PROF GER, BOWDOIN COL, 82-, Nat Endowment Humanities fel in residence for col teachers, Ind Univ, 78-79. **MEMBERSHIPS** MLA; Am Asn Teachers Ger; Northeast Mod Lang Asn; Arthur Schnitzler Res Asn; Thomas Mann Ges. **RESEARCH** Thomas Mann; Hugo von Hofmannsthal; Georg Brandes. **SELECTED PUBLICATIONS** Auth, In a New Light--Wagner Buhnenweihfestpiel-Wagner, Wieland 1951 Parsifal Introduced the Postwar Bayreuth Style, Opera News, Vol 0059, 95; Against Fascism--Exile-Literature as History, Colloquia Ger, Vol 0027, 94; Hofmannsthal or the Geometry of the Subject--Psychostructural and Iconographic Studies of the Prose Works, Colloquia Ger, Vol 0025, 92; Music and German Literature--Their Relationship Since the Middle-Ages, Colloquia Ger, Vol 0026, 93; Opera and the Culture of Fascism, Opera News, Vol 0061, 97; Wagner, Richard and the Anti-Semitic Imagination, Ger Quart, Vol 0069, 96; Taming Hansel und Gretel for Opera--Background to Humperdinck Composition-Too Grimm for Words, Opera News, Vol 0061, 96; False Dawn--Wagnerian Problemdichtung-How Hans-Sachs Warning at the End of Die 'Meistersinger' Echoes Through German History, Opera News, Vol 0057, 93; The Films of Wenders, Wim--Cinema as Vision and Desire, German Quart, Vol 0067, 94; Against Fascism--Exile-Literature as History, Colloquia Ger, Vol 0027, 94; Rheingold's Curse--Tracing This Wagner Works Troubled Early Performance History, Opera News, Vol 0061, 97; Undertones of Insurrection--Music, Politics, and the Social Sphere in the Modern German Narrative, Jour English and Ger Philol, Vol 0094, 95; The Problematic Bourgeois-20th-Century Criticism on Mann,Thomas Buddenbrooks and The Magic Mountain, Colloquia Ger, Vol 0028, 95. **CONTACT ADDRESS** Dept of Ger, Bowdoin Col, 7700 College Station, Brunswick, ME, 04011-8477.

CHACE, WILLIAM M.

DISCIPLINE ENGLISH LANGUAGE AND LITERATURE **EDUCATION** Univ Calif Berkeley, PhD, 68. **CAREER** Prof Eng/pres Emory Univ. **RESEARCH** Modern British and American literature. **SELECTED PUBLICATIONS** Auth, The Political Identities of Ezra Pound and T. S. Eliot; Lionel Trilling: Criticism and Politics; ed, Justice denied: The Black Man in White America; James Joyce: A Collection of Critical Essays. **CONTACT ADDRESS** English Dept, Emory Univ, 1380 Oxford Rd NE, Atlanta, GA, 30322-1950.

CHAFFEE-SORACE, DIANE

DISCIPLINE SPANISH **EDUCATION** Wells Col, BA, 73; Duke Univ, MA, 75, PhD, 79. **CAREER** Teach asst, Duke Univ, 75-77; lectr, SUNY, Stony Brook, 77- 80; asst prof, Univ Va, 80-82; lectr, Washington Univ, 82-85; asst prof, 86-90, assoc prof, 91-, chair, dept mod langs & lits, 97-, Loyola Col; **CONTACT ADDRESS** Dept of Mod Langs, Lit, Loyola Col, 4501 N Charles St, Baltimore, MD, 21210-2699.

CHAIKA, ELAINE OSTRACH

PERSONAL Born 12/20/1934, Milford, Mass, m, 1960, 3 children **DISCIPLINE** LINGUISTICS **EDUCATION** RI Col, BEd, 60; Brown Univ, MAT, 65, PhD(ling), 72 **CAREER** Teacher, Mill Sch, Eastbrook, Maine, 54-55, Veteran's High Sch, Warwick, RI, 60-61 & George S West Jr High Sch, Providence, RI, 61-62; instr English, Bryant Col, 66-67; asst prof, 71-74, assoc prof, 75-78, Prof Ling, Providence Col, 78-, Nat Endowment for Humanities fel, 82. **MEMBERSHIPS** Am Dialect Soc; Ling Soc Am; MLA. **RESEARCH** Schizophrenic language; deviant linguistic productions; sociolinguistics. **SELECTED PUBLICATIONS** Grammars and Teaching, Col English, 78, reprinted, In: Readings in Applied English Linguistics, 82; Response to Bowden, Col English, 40: 370-374; Jargons and Language Change, Anthropological Ling, 2/80; How Shall a discourse be understood, Discourse Proc, 4: 71-87; Review of Zeleman Making Sense of it, Col Commun & Compos, 2/81; Language: The Social Mirror, Newbury House, 10/82; A unified explanation for the deverse structural deviations in the speech of adult schizophrenics, J Commun Disorders, 15: 167-189; auth, Understanding Psychotic Speech: Understanding Psychotic Speech, Chas C. Thomas, 94; auth, Language: the Social Mirror, Heinle & Heinle, 94; auth, On analysing schizophrenic soeech: what model should we use?, Speech and Language Disorders in Psychiatry, Gaskell, 94; auth, Intention, attention, and schizophrenic speech, Commun and the Mentally Ill Patient, Jessica Kingsley Pub, 97. **CONTACT ADDRESS** Dept Ling, Providence Col, 549 River Ave, Providence, RI, 02918-0002. **EMAIL** echaika@providence.edu

CHAITIN, GILBERT D.

DISCIPLINE FRENCH LITERATURE **EDUCATION** Princeton Univ, PhD, 69. **CAREER** Prof. **RESEARCH** Psychoanalytic theory of narrative; Lacan's teachings about the relation of subjectivity to language; psychoanalytic notions of identity in relation to language and culture. **SELECTED PUBLICATIONS** Auth, Rhetoric and Culture in Lacan, 96; pubs on Chretien de Troyes, Dostoyevski, Zola, Stendhal, Hugo, Renan, Camus, Lacan, comparative literature, literature and psychoanalysis; co-ed, Romantic Revolutions, 90. **CONTACT ADDRESS** Dept of French and Italian, Indiana Univ, Bloomington, 300 N Jordan Ave, Bloomington, IN, 47405.

CHAMBERLIN, V.A.

PERSONAL Born 07/18/1924, Topeka, KS, m, 1955, 2 children **DISCIPLINE** SPANISH LITERATURE **EDUCATION** Wasburh Univ Topeka, AB, 49; Univ Kans, MA, 53; PhD, 57. **CAREER** Fredonia High School kans, 49-51; Pembroke Country Day School Kans City, 51-53; instr, Univ Calif Los Angeles, 57-59; asst to assoc prof, Okla State Univ, 59-63; assoc prof, 63-68; prof, Univ Kans, 68-96. **MEMBERSHIPS** MLA; Am Asn of Tchr of Spanish and Portuguese. **RESEARCH** Perez Galdos; 19th Century Spanish Literature; Hispano-Russian literary relations; Color Symbolism; Anaimal Imagery; Humor. **SELECTED PUBLICATIONS** Auth, Two Character-Creating Servants: Nina in Gomez de la Avellaneda's El Artista barqueeero and Benina in Galdo's Misericordia, in Romance Quart, 94; Erotic Equine Imagery: a Time-Honored Communicative Metaphor in Spanish Literature, in Studies in Honor of Gilberto Paolini, 96. **CONTACT ADDRESS** Dept of Spanish and Portuguese, Univ of Kans, Lawrence, KS, 66045. **EMAIL** vachamb@falcon.cc.ukans.edu

CHAMBERS, J.K.
PERSONAL Born 07/12/1938, Grimsby, ON, Canada **DISCIPLINE** LINGUISTICS **EDUCATION** Univ Windsor, BA, 61; Queen's Univ, MA, 63; Univ Alta, PhD, 70. **CAREER** Asst prof, 70-75, assoc prof, 75-82, PROF LINGUISTICS, UNIV TORONTO, 82-; vis fel Univ Reading(Eng), 76-77, 83-84, 90-91; Hong Kong Univ 97. **SELECTED PUBLICATIONS** Auth, Sociolinguistic Theory: Language Variation and Its Social Significance 95; coauth, A Very Small Rebellion 77; Dialectology 80, 2nd ed, 98; ed, Canadian English 75; The Languages of Canada 79; co-ed, Dialects of English 91. **CONTACT ADDRESS** Dept of Linguistics, Univ of Toronto, Toronto, ON, M5S 3H1. **EMAIL** chambers@chass.utoronto.ca

CHAMBERS, MORTIMER HARDIN
PERSONAL Born 01/09/1927, Saginaw, MI, m, 1973, 3 children **DISCIPLINE** CLASSICAL PHILOLOGY **EDUCATION** Harvard, AB, 49, PhD, 54; Oxford, MA, 55. **CAREER** Instr, classics, Harvard, 54-55; asst prof, history and Greek, Univ Chicago, 55-58; asst prof, assoc prof, prof History, UCLA, 58-. **HONORS AND AWARDS** Rhodes Scholarship; Fulbright Scholarship. **MEMBERSHIPS** Am Hist Asn; Am Philol Asn. **RESEARCH** Greek history; history of classical scholarship. **SELECTED PUBLICATIONS** Auth, Aristotle's History of Athenian Democracy, with J Day, Berkeley-Los Angeles, 62; Polybius, selections trans, ed, E Badian, New York, 66; The Western Experience, with four coauthors, New York, 74, ed 7, 98; Aristotelis Athenaion Politeia, Leipzig, 86, ed 2, 94; Georg Busolt, His Career in His Letters, Leiden, 90; Aristotle, Staat der Athener, Berlin-Darmstadt, 90; George Grote's History of Greece, in: George Grote Reconsidered, Hildescheim, 96; Athen's Alliance with Egesta in the Year of Antiphon, with R Galluci-P Spanos, Zeitschrift fur Papyrologie und Epigraphik 83, 90; The Reception of Gibbon in the New World, in: Imperium Romanum, Festschrift for Karl Christ, Stuttgart, 98. **CONTACT ADDRESS** Dept of History, Univ of California, Los Angeles, Los Angeles, CA, 90024-1473. **EMAIL** chambers@history.ucla.edu

CHANDLER, DANIEL ROSS
PERSONAL Born 07/22/1937, Wellston, OK **DISCIPLINE** SPEECH COMMUNICATION, RELIGION **EDUCATION** Univ Okla, BS, 59; Purdue Univ, MA, 65; Garrett Theol Sem, BD, 68; Ohio Univ, PhD(commun), 69. **CAREER** Asst prof speech, Cent Mich Univ, 69-70, State Univ NY, New Paltz, 70-71 & City Univ New York, 71-75; ASST PROF COMMUN, RUTGERS UNIV, NEW BRUNSWICK, 76-, Asst pastor, Peoples Church of Chicago, 65-66; mem denominational affairs comt, Community Church of New York, 72-, John Haynes Scholar comt, 72-; vis fel, Princeton Univ, 74-75, 77, 79-80; res fel, Yale Univ, 74-75, 77 & 78; Marland fel, Union Theol Sem Columbia Univ, 75-76; vis scholar, New Sch for Social Res, 76-77. **MEMBERSHIPS** Nat Coalition Against Censorship; Speech Commun Asn; Speech Commun Asn Eastern States; Relig Speech Commun Asn; Acad Freedom Clearinghouse. **RESEARCH** Liberal religious movement in America; communication of mass movements; history and philosophy of freedom of speech. **SELECTED PUBLICATIONS** Auth, The Dawn of Religious Pluralism--Voices From the Worlds-Parliament-Of-Religions, 1893, Rel Hum, Vol 0027, 93; A Celebration of Humanism and Freethought, Rel Hum, Vol 0029, 95; Crimes of Perception--An Encyclopedia of Heresies and Heretics, Rel Hum, Vol 0029, 95; The American Radical, Rel Hum, Vol 0029, 95; 50 Days of Solitude, Rel Hum, Vol 0029, 95; Blavatsky, Madame Baboon, Rel Hum, Vol 0029, 95; Solitude--A Philosophical Encounter, Rel Hum, Vol 0029, 95; The Secularization of the Academy, Rel Hum, Vol 0028, 94; A Nation of Victims--The Decay of te American Character, Rel Hum, Vol 0028, 94; Pilgrimage Of Hope--100-Years of Global Interfaith Dialog, Rel Hum, Vol 0027, 93; A Fire in the Mind--The Life of Campbell, Joseph, Rel Hum, Vol 0027, 93; The Minds Sky--Human Intelligence in a Cosmic Context, Rel Hum, Vol 0027, 93; Holy Fire, Rel Hum, 0029, 95; An Aristocracy of Everyone--The Politics of Education and the Future of Education, Rel Hum, Vol 0028, 94; Paine, Thomas--Apostle of Freedom, Rel Hum, Vol 0029, 95; A Brief-History of American Culture, Rel Hum, Vol 0029, 95; American Religious Humanism, Rel Hum, Vol 0030, 96; America Alternative Religions, Rel Hum, Vol 0029, 95; Mapping American Culture, Rel Hum, Vol 0029, 95; Dewey,John--An Intellectual Portrait, Rel Hum, Vol 0029, 95; Same-Sex Unions in Premodern Europe, Rel Hum, Vol 0029, 95; Selling God--American Religion in the Marketplace of Culture, Rel Hum, Vol 0028, 94; The Evolution of Progress--The End of Economic-Growth and the Beginnings of Human Transformation, Rel Hum, Vol 0028, 94; Visions Of A Better World, Rel Hum, Vol 0028, 94; The Lambda Directory of Religion and Spirituality--Sources of Spiritual Support for Gay Men and Lesbians, Rel Hum, Vol 0029, 95; Cosmos Crumbling--American Reform and the Religious Imagination, Rel Hum, Vol 0028, 94; The Worlds-Parliament-of-Religions --The East/West Encounter, Chicago, 1893, Rel Hum, Vol 0029, 95; One Nation Under God--Religion in Contemporary American Society, Rel Hum, Vol 0028, 94; Notes From a Wayfarer--The Autobiography of Thielicke, Helmut, Rel Hum, Vol 0029, 95. **CONTACT ADDRESS** Dept of Commun, Rutgers Univ, New Brunswick, NJ, 08903.

CHANDLER, STANLEY BERNARD
PERSONAL Born 05/31/1921, Canterbury, England, m, 1954, 2 children **DISCIPLINE** ROMANCE LANGUAGES **EDUCATION** Univ London, BA, 47, PhD(Ital), 53. **CAREER** Asst lectr Ital, Univ Col, Univ London, 48-50; lectr, Aberdeen Univ, 50-57; assoc prof, 57-63, PROF ITAL, UNIV TORONTO, 63-, Chmn Dept Ital Studies, 73- **MEMBERSHIPS** MLA; Am Asn Teachers Ital; Dante Soc Am; Can Soc Ital Studies; Int Asn Ital Lang & Lit (int vpres, 73-82). **RESEARCH** Italian Romanticism; the works and thought of Alessandro Manzoni; Italian literature and society in the 19th century. **SELECTED PUBLICATIONS** Auth, Youth According to the Romantics and to Leopardi, Romance Quart, Vol 0041, 94; Women as Seen by Italian Writers of the Romantic Period, Otto-Novecento, Vol 0019, 95; Blue-Skies and Escapes-From-Reality in Verga, Giovanni Oeuvre, Otto-Novecento, Vol 0018, 94; La Miraculosa-Aqua--A Reading of le Porretane, Quaderni D Italianistica, Vol 0013, 92; Realism and the Role of the Author According to Verga,Giuseppe--Theory of the Novel in the Second Half of the 19th-Century, Critica Letteraria, Vol 0020, 92; Permanent Human Characteristics According to the RomanticsaAnd to Manzoni, Quaderni D Italianistica, Vol 0014, 93. **CONTACT ADDRESS** Dept of Ital Studies Fac of Arts & Sci, Univ of Toronto, Toronto, ON, M5S 1A1.

CHANDLER MCENTYRE, MARILYN
DISCIPLINE COMPARATIVE LITERATURE **EDUCATION** Princeton Univ, Phd, 84. **CAREER** Assoc prof, Mills Col, 84-94; vis prof, Princeton theol Sem, 95; asst prof, Trenton State Col, 94-96; assoc prof, Westmont Col, 96-. **HONORS AND AWARDS** Whiting fel, Princeton Univ, 84; Arnold Graves award outstanding tchg award, ACLS, 88; outstanding tchg award, Northen Calif, 89., Dean's nomination, National prof yr awards, 91. **RESEARCH** Literature and medicine. **SELECTED PUBLICATIONS** Auth, Mercy that Burns: Violence and Vision in Flannery O'Connor's Fiction, Theology Today, 96; Cripple Time, Academic Medicine, 96; rev, In the Beauty of the Lilies, by John Updike, Princeton Theol Bulletin, 96; Who Cares?: Stories of Healing in Community, Literature and Medicine, 96; A Virtuous Woman, Contemp Lit Criticism, Gale Press, 96; Fishing on the Arid Plain: Reflections on Teaching The Waste Land, The Waste Land, Univ Calcutta Press, 96; My Brother's Keeper: The Cain and Abel Motif in 'Of Mice and Men, Univ Tenn Press, 96; Natural Wisdom: Steinbeck's Men of Nature as Prophets and Peacemakers, Steinbeck and the Environment, Univ Ala Press, 96; Salt: The Spirit and Spunk of Flannery O'Connor, Theology Today, 96; Beyond Chicken Soup: Food Fads and Folk Medicine, Mid-Atlantic Almanack, 95. **CONTACT ADDRESS** Dept of Rel, Westmont Col, 955 La Paz Rd, Santa Barbara, CA, 93108-1099.

CHANDOLA, ANOOP CHANDRA
PERSONAL Born 12/24/1937, Pauri, India, m, 1963, 1 child **DISCIPLINE** LINGUISTICS **EDUCATION** Univ Allahabad, BA, 54; Univ Lucknow, MA, 56; Univ Calif, Berkeley, MA, 61; Univ Chicago, PhD(ling), 66. **CAREER** Tutor Hindi, Sardar Vallabhbhai Vidyapeeth, 56-57, lectr, 57-58; lectr, Univ Baroda, 58-59; from asst prof to assoc prof , 63-71, prof , Univ Ariz, 71-. **HONORS AND AWARDS** Outstanding Faculty Award in Humanities, from AAFSAA, 91. **MEMBERSHIPS** American Anthropological Asn; Ling Soc Am; Asn Asian Studies; Ling Soc India. **RESEARCH** Linguistic theory and method; Hindi language and literature; Hinduism, music and linguistics. **SELECTED PUBLICATIONS** Some Systems of Musical Scales and Linguistic Principles, Semiotica, 70; A Systematic Translation of Hindi-Urdu into English, Univ Ariz Press, 70; An Evolutionary Approach to Sentence Formation, Linguistics, 75; Folk Drumming in the Himalayas, 77 & Situation to Sentence, 79, AMS; The Way to True Worship, Univ Press of Am, 91; Contactics, Univ Press of Am, 92. **CONTACT ADDRESS** Dept of East Asian Studies, Univ of Ariz, Tucson, AZ, 85721-0001. **EMAIL** chandola@u.arizona.edu

CHANG, CECILIA
DISCIPLINE CHINESE **EDUCATION** Fu-jen Catholic Univ, BA; Univ Calif, Angeles, MA; Univ Mass, EDD. **CAREER** Lectr, Williams Col, 89-; vis lectr, Princeton Univ, 87 & Univ Mich, 88; head instr, Middlebury Chinese Summer Sch, 87-93; Princeton in Beijing Chinese Summer Prog, 94. **RESEARCH** Chinese language pedagogy; applied linguistics. **SELECTED PUBLICATIONS** Auth, Computer workbook for Intermediate Reader in Modern Chinese, Princeton UP, 96. **CONTACT ADDRESS** Center for Foreign Languages, Literatures and Cult, Williams Col, Williamstown, MA, 01267. **EMAIL** Cecilia.Chang@williams.edu

CHATHAM, JAMES RAY
PERSONAL Born 11/11/1931, Caryville, FL, m, 1961, 1 child **DISCIPLINE** SPANISH PHILOLOGY **EDUCATION** Fla State Univ, BA, 53, MA, 56, PhD, 60. **CAREER** Instr mod lang, Miss State Univ, 57-59; assoc prof mod lang, 60-63, assoc prof Romance lang, Univ Ala, 63-64; PROF FOREIGN LANG & HEAD DEPT, MISS STATE UNIV, 64-, NDEA fel, Univ Tex, 62; mem bd dir, Am Coun Teaching Foreign Lang, 67-68. **MEMBERSHIPS** SAtlantic Mod Lang Asn; Am Asn Teachers Span & Port; Mediaeval Acad Am. **RESEARCH** Mediaeval Spanish language and literature; Golden Age drama. **SELECTED PUBLICATIONS** Auth, Remembering Mead, Hispania-Jour Devoted to the Tchg Span and Port, Vol 0079, 96. **CONTACT ADDRESS** Drawer FL, Mississippi State Univ, Mississippi State, MS, 39762.

CHAUDERLOT, FABIENNE SOPHIE
PERSONAL Born 08/11/1960, Marseilles, France **DISCIPLINE** FRENCH **EDUCATION** Fac.des Sciences Humame, MA, 83; Inst d' Adminstration des Entreprises, MBA, 85; San Diego State Univ, MA, 89; Univ Calif San Diego, PhD, 95. **CAREER** Lectr, Univ Calif, Riverside, 95-96; asst prof, Univ Puerto Rico, 96-97; asst prof, Wayne State Univ, 97-. **HONORS AND AWARDS** Grant, 97-98, Wayne State Univ., Instructional Excellence Award, San Diego Commun Col District, 88-89, 90-91. **MEMBERSHIPS** MLA; IAPL. **RESEARCH** 18TH Century French philosophy and literature; post structuralist french philosophy and theory. **CONTACT ADDRESS** Dept of Romance Languages, Wayne State Univ, 487 Manoogian, Detroit, MI, 48202. **EMAIL** f.chauderlot@wayne.edu

CHAVY, PAUL
PERSONAL Born 07/19/1914, Saint-Florent, France, m, 1938, 2 children **DISCIPLINE** FRENCH LANGUAGE AND LITERATURE **EDUCATION** Univ Paris, Agrege des Let, 42. **CAREER** Head dept, 48-69, prof, 48-80, EMER PROF FRENCH, DALHOUSIE UNIV, 80-, Officier de l'Instruction Publique, 56; Chevalier, Legion d'Honneur, 65. **MEMBERSHIPS** Can Comp Lit Asn (pres, 71-73). **RESEARCH** History of translations. **SELECTED PUBLICATIONS** Auth, Poetry as a Mirror--Imitation and Awareness of Self in the Pleiade Latin Poetry-Fr, Renaissance and Reformation, Vol 0020, 96; Genesis and Cosmogony in Western Medieval Pre-Scientific Literature, Can Rev Comp Lit-Rev Can de Lit Comparee, Vol 0023, 96. **CONTACT ADDRESS** Dept of French Studies, Dalhousie Univ, Halifax, NS, B3H 3J5.

CHELKOWSKI, PETER JAN
PERSONAL Born 07/10/1933, Lubliniec, Poland, m, 1961, 2 children **DISCIPLINE** NEAR EASTERN LANGUAGES AND LITERATURES **EDUCATION** Jagiellonian Univ, MA, 58; Univ Tehran, PhD(lit), 68. **CAREER** Assoc prof Near Eastern Lang & Lit, 68-75, prof Persian and Iranian studies & chmn near eastern lang & lit, dir ctr near eastern studies, 75-78, PROF NEAR EASTERN STUDIES, NY UNIV, 78- **MEMBERSHIPS** Mid Eastern Studies Asn; Am Orient Soc; Coun Nat Lit. **RESEARCH** Persian religious drama; Persian literature; theatre, drama and literature in the Near East. **SELECTED PUBLICATIONS** Auth, Community Process and the Performance of Muharram Observances in Trinidad--Tdr-The Drama Review-Jour Performance Stud, Vol 0038, 94. **CONTACT ADDRESS** Kevorkian Ctr for Near Eastern Studies, New York Univ, 50 Washington Sq South, New York, NY, 10003.

CHEN, JINGSONG
PERSONAL Born 04/07/1959, Jiangsu, China, m, 1988, 2 children **DISCIPLINE** CHINESE LITERATURE AND LANGUAGE **EDUCATION** The Jangzou Normal Coll China, BA, 81; Acad of China Arts Beijing, MA, 84; Univ Calif Riversid e, PhD, 92. **CAREER** Res, The Acad of Chinese Arts, 84-86; CT interpreter, 89-; lectr, Univ Calif Riverside, 92-. **HONORS AND AWARDS** Outstanding Tchg Asst, Univ Calif Riverside, 92; First Prize Chinese Prose Contest Chicago, 97; Interpreter of the Year, New World Lang Service Riverside, 97. **MEMBERSHIPS** Asian Study Asn; Calif Interpreter Asn. **RESEARCH** Comparative Drama; Dramatic Theories and Criticism. **SELECTED PUBLICATIONS** Auth, Qingshan Shaonian Shi, 97; numerous articles in Chinese and English. **CONTACT ADDRESS** Dept of Literature and Languages, Univ of Calif, Riverside, CA, 92521. **EMAIL** Jingsong.Chen@ucr.edu

CHEN, LILLY
DISCIPLINE LINGUISTICS, CHINESE LANGUAGE **EDUCATION** Nat Taiwan Univ, BA; Univ IL, Champaign-Urbana, MA, PhD. **CAREER** Hon vis lectr, Hebei Agr Univ, 83, 84; lectr, Rice Univ. **HONORS AND AWARDS** Shu Juan Award, Nat Taiwan Univ; Fulbright scholar. **RESEARCH** The great Chinese novel Hung-lou meng (Dream of the Red Chamber). **SELECTED PUBLICATIONS** Publ work includes articles in the J of Chinese Ling and the J of Decorative Art, as well as the publ(s) of the Chicago Ling Soc, the Berkeley Ling Soc. **CONTACT ADDRESS** Rice Univ, PO Box 1892, Houston, TX, 77251-1892. **EMAIL** lchen@rice.edu

CHEN, SHIH-SHIN
PERSONAL Born 08/03/1957, Taiwan, m **DISCIPLINE** SPEECH COMMUNICATION, ORGANIZATIONAL ORGANIZATION **EDUCATION** Univ MD, College Park, PhD, 93. **CAREER** Assoc prof, Nat Taipei Col of Nursing. **HONORS AND AWARDS** ICA Convention,(Washington, DC), org comm div, top three paper, 93. **MEMBERSHIPS** ICA; NCA. **RESEARCH** Org culture; org comm. **SELECTED PUBLI-**

CATIONS Co-auth, with E Fink, A Galileo Analysis of Organizational Climate, Human Communication Res, 21 (4), 95. **CONTACT ADDRESS** National Taipei Col of Nursing, 89, Nei-Chiang St, Wanhua, .. **EMAIL** shihshin@ntcn.ntcn.edu.tw

CHENEY, DONALD
PERSONAL Born 07/14/1932, Lowell, MA, m, 1956, 2 children **DISCIPLINE** ENGLISH, COMPARATIVE LITERATURE **EDUCATION** Yale Univ, BA, 54, MA, 57, PhD, 61. **CAREER** From instr to asst prof English, Yale Univ, 60-67; assoc prof, 67-75, PROF ENGLISH, UNIV MASS, AMHERST, 75-, Morse fel, Yale Univ, 64-65; corresp ed, Spenser Newslett, 70-78, ed, 74-78; co-ed, Spenser Encycl, 79- **MEMBERSHIPS** MLA; Renaissance Soc Am; Spenser Soc; Milton Soc Am; ACLA. **RESEARCH** Renaissance poetry and drama. **SELECTED PUBLICATIONS** Auth, Gazing on Secret Sights--Spenser, Classical Imitation, and the Decorum of Vision, Jour Eng and Ger Philol, Vol 0092, 93. **CONTACT ADDRESS** Dept of English, Univ of Mass, Amherst, MA, 01003-0002.

CHERMAK, GAIL D.
DISCIPLINE CCC- AUDIOLOGY **EDUCATION** State Univ NY, BA, 72; Ohio State Univ, BA, 73, PhD, 75. **CAREER** Interim Dean, Col Liberal Arts, Wash State Univ, 97-; prof and ch, Wash State Univ, 90-97; assoc prof, Wash State Univ, 82-90; asst prof, Wash State Univ, 77-82; asst prof, Southern Ill Univ, 75-77. **RESEARCH** Central auditory processing disorders, international rehabilitation development. **SELECTED PUBLICATIONS** Auth, Central Auditory Testing, In Handbook of Pediatric Audiology, Wash, DC:Gallaudet, 96; coauth, Central Auditory Processing Disorders: New Perspectives, San Diego: Singular Publ Group, 97; Observations on the Use of the SCAN Administered in a School Setting to Identify Central Auditory Processing Disorders in Children, Lang,Speech, and Hearing Services in Sch 28, 97; Central Auditory Processing: Current Status of Research and Implications for Clinical Practice, Amer J Audiology 5 2, 96; The Effectiveness of an Interactive Hearing Conservation Program for Elementary School Children, Lang, Speech, and Heraing Services in Sch 27 1, 96; Study Compares Screening Tests of Central Auditory Processing, Hearing J, 48 5, 95; Three Commonly Asked Questions About Central Auditoroy Processing Disorders: Management, Amer J Audiology 4 1, 95; Evidence for Development of Distinction of Voice Onset Time in a Child With Left-Hemisphere Lesion, Perceptual and Motor Skills 81, 95; Three Commonly Asked Questions About Central Auditory Processing Disorders: Assessment, Amer J Audiology, 3 3, 94. **CONTACT ADDRESS** Dept of Speech and Hearing Sciences, Washington State Univ, 201 Daggy Hall, Pullman, WA, 99164-2420. **EMAIL** chermak@wsu.edu

CHERNETSKY, VITALY
DISCIPLINE SLAVIC LANGUAGES **EDUCATION** Moscow State Univ, BA, 89; Univ Pa, MA, 93, PhD, 96. **CAREER** Asst prof. **RESEARCH** Twentieth-century Ukrainian, Russian and East European literature; film and visual arts, and sexuality in Slavic and East European Cultures. **SELECTED PUBLICATIONS** Auth, Late Soviet Culture: A Parallax for Postmodernism, 94; Epigonoi, or Transformations of Writing in the Texts of Valerija Narbikova and Nina Iskrenko, 94; Opening the Floodgates: The New Ukrainian Writing, 97; Travels through Heterotopia: The Textual Realms of Patrick Modiano's Rue des Boutiques Obscures and Mikhail Kuraev's Kapitan Dikshtein, 98. **CONTACT ADDRESS** Dept of Slavic Languages, Columbia Col, New York, 2960 Broadway, New York, NY, 10027-6902. **EMAIL** vac10@columbia.edu

CHERRY, CHARLES MAURICE
PERSONAL Born 09/16/1944, SC, m, 1973, 2 children **DISCIPLINE** SPANISH GOLDEN-AGE LITERATURE **EDUCATION** Furman Univ, BA, 65; Univ SC, MA, 69; Northwestern Univ, PhD, 80. **CAREER** Teacher Spanish, George Washington High Sch, VA, 65-67 & Camden High Sch, SC, 67-69; instr, Furman Univ, 69-71; teaching asst, Northwestern Univ, 71-73; teacher, Niles North High Sch, IL, 73-74; instr, 74-80, asst prof, 80-84, assoc prof, 84-90, PROF SPANISH, FURMAN UNIV, 90-. **HONORS AND AWARDS** Cervantes Award, NEH Seminar, Election to Phi Sigma Iota, Sigma Delta Pi, Kappa Delta Pi. **MEMBERSHIPS** MLA; Am Coun Teaching Foreign Lang; Am Asn Teachers Spanish & Portuguese; SCOLT (exec bd); South Eastern Coun on Latin Am Studies. **RESEARCH** Spanish drama of the golden age; foreign language pedagogy; twentieth-century Spanish poetry; cross-cultural studies. **SELECTED PUBLICATIONS** Ed, A History of the South Carolina Chapter of the American Association of Teachers of Spanish and Portuguese, Furman Univ, 81; auth, Jose Hierro, Twentieth Century Spanish Poets, vol 108 of Dictionary of Literary Biography, 91; 15 entries on fifteenth- and sixteenth-century Spanish poets and dramatists in Dictionary of Literature of the Iberian Peninsula, 2 vols, London and Westport, CT: Gale, 93; auth, Claudio Rodriguez, Twentieth Century Spanish Poets, vol 134 of Dictionary of Literary Biography, 94. **CONTACT ADDRESS** Dept Mod Langs and Lits, Furman Univ, 3300 Poinsett Hwy, Greenville, SC, 29613-0002. **EMAIL** maurice.cherry@furman.edu

CHEUNG, DOMINIC C.N.
DISCIPLINE EAST ASIAN LANGUAGES ,COMPARATIVE LITERATURE **EDUCATION** Univ Wash, PhD, 73. **CAREER** Prof, Univ Southern Calif. **RESEARCH** Modern Chinese fiction & poetry; Asian literature. **SELECTED PUBLICATIONS** Auth, From William Shakespeare to Ueda Akinari; The Isle Full of Noises: Modern Chinese Poetry from Taiwan. **CONTACT ADDRESS** East Asian Studies Center, Univ Southern Calif, University Park Campus, Los Angeles, CA, 90089.

CHEW, KRISTINA
PERSONAL Born 12/10/1968, Oakland, CA, m, 1995, 1 child **DISCIPLINE** COMPARATIVE LITERATURE **EDUCATION** Yale Univ, PhD, 95. **CAREER** Vis asst prof, Williams Col, 94-95; Vis scholar, St. Louis Univ, 96-98; asst prof, 98-. **MEMBERSHIPS** Am Philol Asn; Class Asn of the Middle West and South; Am Class League; MLA. **RESEARCH** Roman poetry; Greek philosophy; Classical tradition; Translation; Classics and multiculturalism. **SELECTED PUBLICATIONS** Auth, "What Does 'E Pluribus Unum' Mean?: Teaching Classics and Multicultural Literature Together," in The Class J, 97. **CONTACT ADDRESS** Dept of Modern & Classical Languages, Univ of St. Thomas, Mail Drop 4296, St. Paul, MN, 55105.

CHIAMPI, JAMES T.
DISCIPLINE ITALIAN LANGUAGE **EDUCATION** Yale Univ, PhD. **CAREER** ASSOC PROF, ITAL, UNIV CALIF, IRVINE. **SELECTED PUBLICATIONS** Auth, Shadowy Prefaces: Conversion and Writing in the 'Divine Comedy'; pub(s), articles on Dante and the lit of the Ital Renaissance. **CONTACT ADDRESS** Dept of Fr and Ital, Univ Calif, Irvine, CA, 92697.

CHICK, EDSON MARLAND
PERSONAL Born 05/29/1924, Boston, MA, m, 1953, 4 children **DISCIPLINE** GERMAN **EDUCATION** Brown Univ, AB, 45; Princeton Univ, PhD(Ger), 53. **CAREER** Instr Ger, Princeton Univ, 51; asst prof, Wesleyan Univ, 52-57 & Univ Calif, Riverside, 57-60; assoc prof, State Univ NY, Binghamton, 61-64; from assoc prof to prof, Dartmouth Col, 64-72; Prof Ger, Williams Col, 72-92, Fulbright res grant, Hamburg, 60-6 1; mem comt examrs, Ger Col Entrance Exam Bd Advan Placement Prog, 71-74; Fulbright res grant, Berlin, 78-79. **MEMBERSHIPS** MLA; Am Asn Tchrs Ger; Mod Hum Res Asn. **RESEARCH** Twentieth century; satire; censorship. **SELECTED PUBLICATIONS** Auth, Ernst Barlach, Twayne, 67; Voices in discord: Some observations on Die Judenbuche, Ger Quart, 69; Dances of Death, Welekind, Brecht, Durrenmatt, and the Satiric Trdition, Camden House, 84. **CONTACT ADDRESS** RRI, Box 51, Proctorsville, VT, 05153.

CHING, JULIA
PERSONAL Shanghai, China **DISCIPLINE** RELIGION/ CHINESE CULTURE **EDUCATION** Col New Rochelle, NY, BA, 58; Catholic Univ America, MA, 61; Australian Nat Univ, PhD, 72; St. Andrews Col, NC, LHD, 93. **CAREER** Lectr, Australian Nat Univ, 71-74; assoc prof, Columbia Univ, 74-75; assoc prof, Yale Univ, 75-78; assoc prof, 78-81, PROF, VICTORIA COL, UNIV TORONTO 94-. **MEMBERSHIPS** Chinese Cult Ctr Greater Toronto; Royal Soc Can; Can Pugwash Gp. **SELECTED PUBLICATIONS** Auth, Probing China's Soul, 90; auth, Chinese Religions, 93. **CONTACT ADDRESS** Victoria Col, Univ Toronto, Toronto, ON, M5S 1K9. **EMAIL** jching@chass.utoronto.ca

CHING, MARVIN K.L.
DISCIPLINE LINGUISTIC PERSPECTIVES ON LITERATURE **EDUCATION** FL State Univ, PhD. **CAREER** Engl, Univ Neb. **SELECTED PUBLICATIONS** Ed, SECOL Rev. **CONTACT ADDRESS** Univ NE, NE.

CHINOSOLE, Null
PERSONAL Born 07/14/1942, New York, NY **DISCIPLINE** COMPARATIVE LITERATURE **EDUCATION** Univ Oregon, PhD, 86. **CAREER** San Franciso State Univ, acting dean Third Wld Stud, 70, asst prof 69-70; Nkrumah Teachers' College Zambia, chmn eng dept 71-73; San Franciso State Univ, chmn womens stud 88-90, assoc prof 90-. **HONORS AND AWARDS** Operation Crossroads; res 6th Pan African Congress. **MEMBERSHIPS** Black Women Stirring the Waters. **RESEARCH** African Diaspora Literary Studies; Black Women's Lit. **SELECTED PUBLICATIONS** Auth, Skeins of Self and Skin, in: Autobiographical Writing of the African Diaspora, Peter Lang, 99, forthcoming; Schooling the Generations in the Politics of Prison, ed, New Earth Press, 95. **CONTACT ADDRESS** Dept of Womens Studies, San Francisco State Univ, 1600 Holloway Ave, San Francisco, CA, 94132. **EMAIL** chinosole@athena.sfsu.edu

CHISHOLM, DAVID
PERSONAL Born 08/30/1940, New Rochelle, NY, m, 1971, 2 children **DISCIPLINE** GERMAN LANGUAGE & LITERATURE **EDUCATION** Oberlin Col, BA, 62; Univ Chicago, MA, 65; Ind Univ, PhD, 71. **CAREER** Lectr Ger, Ind Univ, 70-71; postdoctoral fel, Univ Cincinnati, 71-72; asst prof, Univ Ill, Urbana, 72-73; asst prof, 73-76, assoc prof German, 77-, Univ Ariz; Am Coun Learned Societies grant-in-aid, 73-74; Alexander-Von-Humboldt Found res grant, 79-80 & 81-82; Fulbright selection comt, Bonn, Ger, 81; Fulbright travel grant, 81-82. **HONORS AND AWARDS** Nominated for Innovative Teaching Award, 97; faculty development grant to integrate CD, laserdisc and DVD technology into General Education course on Music and German Literature, 97; Alexander von Humboldt Grant, Marbach, Berlin and Leipzig, 97; Fulbright Grant, German Stud Sem, 98. **MEMBERSHIPS** MLA; Am Asn Teachers Ger; Soc Advan of Scand Studies; Asn Lit & Ling Computing; Leasing Soc. **RESEARCH** German lyric and dramatic verse; linguistic and computational approaches to literature; German-Scandinavian comparative literature. **SELECTED PUBLICATIONS** Auth, German Cabaret Songs in the Weimar Republic, Dimensions, van Acken, 93; coauth, Base Tag Set for Verse, Guidelines for Electronic Text Encoding and Interchange, Text Encoding Initiative, 94; auth, Lexicality and the Versification of Johann Heinrigh Voss: Observations on Prosodic Feature Analysis, Insights in Germanic Linguistics, de Gruyter, 95; coauth, Encoding Verse Texts, Computers and the Hum, 95; auth, Pøst-Renaissance German: Computer-Aided Approaches, Lit and Ling Computing, 95; auth, Prosodic Aspects of German Hexameter Verse, Poetics Today, 95; auth, Early Literary Cabaret and Modernism in Berlin, Politics in German Literature, Camden House, 97. **CONTACT ADDRESS** Dept of German, Univ of Ariz, PO Box 210067, Tucson, AZ, 85721-0067.

CHITORAN, IOANAA
DISCIPLINE LINGUISTICS AND FRENCH **EDUCATION** Cornell Univ, PhD, 97. **CAREER** Asst prof, Dartmouth Col. **RESEARCH** Romance linguistics; phonology--the interface between phonology and phonetics, between phonology and morphology. **SELECTED PUBLICATIONS** Auth, Prominence vs. Rhythm: The Predictability of Stress in Romanian Zagona in Grammatical Theory and Romance Languages, John Benjamins, 96; Les langues romanes: deux ou trois genres?, Les langues naeo-latines, 92. **CONTACT ADDRESS** Dartmouth Col, 3529 N Main St, #207, Hanover, NH, 03755. **EMAIL** ioana.chitoran@dartmouth.edu

CHITTENDEN, JEAN STAHL
PERSONAL Born 03/30/1924, Davenport, IA, d, 1 child **DISCIPLINE** ROMANCE LANGUAGES **EDUCATION** Univ Ariz, BA, 44; Univ Ill, MA, 48; Univ Tex, Austin, PhD(romance lang), 64. **CAREER** Instr Span & English, Elmhurst Col, 49-52; instr Span, Univ Tex, Austin, 59-64; from asst prof to assoc prof, 64-74, PROF SPAN, TRINITY UNIV, 74-, CHMN DEPT FOREIGN LANG, 70-, Consult, Dallas Independent Sch Dist, 62, Tex Educ Agency, 62 & MLA, 62-64; reader, Advan Placement Exam, Educ Testing Serv, 72, 74, 75, 77, 78 & 79; exec comt, Asn Dept For Lang, 78-80. **MEMBERSHIPS** MLA; Am Asn Teachers Span & Port; Am Coun Teaching Foreign Lang; AAUP; Asn Depts Foreign Lang. **RESEARCH** Golden Age drama; contemporary Spanish novel. **SELECTED PUBLICATIONS** Auth, Calderondelabarca, Pedro the 1st Version of la Vida Es Sueno, Hispania-Jour Devoted to the Tchg of Span and Port, Vol 0076, 93; The School of Calderon--Study and Investigation, Rev de Estudios Hispan, Vol 0028, 94; The Prince in the Tower, Hispania-Jour Devoted to the Tchg of Span and Port, Vol 0077, 94; The Theater of Claramonte and la Estrella De Sevilla, Hispania-Jour Devoted to the Tchg of Span and Port, Vol 0077, 94; Tirso-De-Molina, el Burlador de Sevilla and Convidado de Piedra, Hispania-Jour Devoted to the Tchg of Span and Port, Vol 0076, 93; Bancescandamo,Francisco, Como Se Curan Los Celos and Orlando Furioso, Hispania-Jour Devoted to the Tchg of Span and Port, Vol 0076, 93; The Golden-Age Comedia--Text, Theory and Performance, Hispania-Jour Devoted to the Tchg of Span and Port, Vol 0079, 96; The Art of Autobiography in Cuba in the 19th-Century, Hispania-Jour Devoted to the Tchg of Span and Port, Vol 0079, 96; Remembering Mead, Hispania-Jour Devoted to the Tchg of Span and Port, Vol 0079, 96; Quine Mal Anda En Mal Acaba, Hispania-Jour Devoted to the Tchg of Span and Port, Vol 0078, 95; El Conde Partinuples, Hispania-Jour Devoted to the Tchg of Span and Port, Vol 0078, 95; The Art of Autobiography in Cuba in the 19th-Century, Hispania-Jour Devoted to the Tchg of Span and Port, Vol 0079, 96. **CONTACT ADDRESS** Dept of For Lang, Trinity Univ, San Antonio, TX, 78284.

CHOMSKY, NOAM
PERSONAL Born 12/07/1928, Philadelphia, PA, m, 1949, 3 children **DISCIPLINE** LINGUISTICS **EDUCATION** Univ Penn, BA 49, MA 51, PhD 55. **CAREER** Mass Inst Tech, asst prof, prof, Ferrin P Ward Prof, inst prof, 55-76. **HONORS AND AWARDS** Kyoto Prize; Dist Sci Cont Awd; Helmholtz Awd. **MEMBERSHIPS** NAS; AAAS. **RESEARCH** Linguistics; Philosophy; Intl Affairs. **SELECTED PUBLICATIONS** Auth, The Minimalist Program, 95; Year 501, 93. **CONTACT ADDRESS** Room E39-219, Massachusetts Inst of Tech, 77 Massachusetts Dr, Cambridge, MA, 02139. **EMAIL** chomsky@MIT.edu

CHOPYK, DAN BOHDAN
PERSONAL Born 01/02/1925, Ukraine, m, 1956, 4 children **DISCIPLINE** RUSSIAN LANGUAGE **EDUCATION** Univ Birmingham, BCom, 53; Univ Colo, Boulder, MA, 62; Ukrainian Free Univ, BLaw, 63, PhD(philol), 70. **CAREER** PROF LANG, UNIV UT, 69- **MEMBERSHIPS** Am Asn Advan Slavic Studies; Rocky Mountain Asn Slavic Studies (pres, 79-80); Am Popular Cult Asn; Ukrainian Hist Asn. **RESEARCH** Slavic phonology and morphophonemics; 17th and 18th century East Slavic literature; Slavic folklore and civilization. **SELECTED PUBLICATIONS** Auth, Between Reason and Irrationality--The Prose of Pidmohylnyj, Valerijan, World Lit Today, Vol 0069, 95. **CONTACT ADDRESS** Dept of Lang, Univ of Utah, Salt Lake City, UT, 84112.

CHOW, KAI WING
DISCIPLINE EAST ASIAN STUDIES **EDUCATION** Univ Calif Davis, PhD. **CAREER** Assoc prof. Univ Ill Urbana Champaign. **RESEARCH** Intellectual cultural history of Ming Ch'ing China; social history of popular religions and intellectual developments in sixteenth and seventeenth centuries. **SELECTED PUBLICATIONS** Auth, Ritual, Cosmology, and Ontology: Chang Tsai's (1020-1077) Moral Philosophy and Neo-Confucian Ethics, Philos E W, 93; The Rise of Confucian Ritualism in Late Imperial China: Ethics, Classics and Lineage Discourse, Stanford, 94. **CONTACT ADDRESS** Dept East Asian Languages and Cultures, Univ Ill Urbana Champaign, 52 E Gregory Dr, Champaign, IL, 61820. **EMAIL** k-chow@uiuc.edu

CHRIST, MATTHEW R.
DISCIPLINE CLASSICAL STUDIES **EDUCATION** Carleton Col, BA, 82; Princeton Univ, PhD, 87. **CAREER** Asst prof. **RESEARCH** Greek Historiography; Athenian rhetoric and law; Athenian social history. **SELECTED PUBLICATIONS** Auth, Herodotean Kings and Historical Inquiry, 94; Liturgy Avoidance and Antidosis in Classical Athens, 90. **CONTACT ADDRESS** Dept of Classical Studies, Indiana Univ, Bloomington, 300 N Jordan Ave, Bloomington, IN, 47405.

CHRISTIANSEN, HOPE
DISCIPLINE MODERN SPANISH AMERICAN LITERATURE **EDUCATION** Kans State Univ, BA, 79, MA, 81; Univ Kans, PhD, 90. **CAREER** English and Lit, Univ Ark. **HONORS AND AWARDS** Fulbright Col Master Tchr Award. **SELECTED PUBLICATIONS** Area: nineteenth-century literature and the novel in all periods. **CONTACT ADDRESS** Univ Ark, Fayetteville, AR, 72701.

CHRISTIANSON, PAUL
DISCIPLINE ENGLISH LANGUAGE AND LITERATURE **EDUCATION** St Olaf, BA, 55; State Univ Iowa, MA, 56; Wash Univ, PhD, 64. **CAREER** Mildred Foss Thompson prof. **SELECTED PUBLICATIONS** Auth, books on medieval cult and lit. **CONTACT ADDRESS** Dept of Eng, Col of Wooster, Wooster, OH, 44691.

CHRZANOWSKI, JOSEPH
PERSONAL Born 09/02/1941, Providence, RI **DISCIPLINE** SPANISH AND LATIN AMERICAN LITERATURE **EDUCATION** Fairfield Univ, BA, 66; Pa State Univ, MA, 67, PhD(Span), 71. **CAREER** Assoc prof, 69-80, PROF SPAN, CALIF STATE UNIV, LOS ANGELES, 80- **MEMBERSHIPS** Am Asn Teachers Span & Port; Latin Am Studies Asn; Int Inst Latin-Am Lit; MLA; Philol Asn Pac Coast. **RESEARCH** Latin American novel, theatre and short story. **SELECTED PUBLICATIONS** Auth, Gringo Viejo, the Labyrinth of Solitude-Revisited, Intl Fiction Revw, Vol 0019, 92; A Tribute to Earle, Peter,G., Hisp Rev, Vol 0061, 93. **CONTACT ADDRESS** Dept of Foreign Lang & Lit, California State Univ, Los Angeles, 5151 Rancho Castilla, Los Angeles, CA, 90032-4202.

CHU, CHAUNCEY CHENG-HSI
PERSONAL Born 11/21/1930, Chang-shu, China, m, 1966, 2 children **DISCIPLINE** LINGUISTICS **EDUCATION** Taiwan Normal Univ, BA, 53, MA, 59; Univ TX, Austin, MA, 64, PhD(ling), 70. **CAREER** Instr English, Taiwan Normal Univ, 59-64, asst prof English & ling, 64-67; asst prof ling & Chinese, 69-74, assoc prof Chinese & Ling, 74-84, prof, Univ FL, 85-; dir, prog in Ling, 79-82. **HONORS AND AWARDS** Distinguished Teaching Award, Univ FL, 75. **MEMBERSHIPS** Ling Asn Can & US; Ling Soc Am. **RESEARCH** Historical syntax, functional & discourse grammar. **SELECTED PUBLICATIONS** Auth, A Contrastive Phonology of Mandarin Chinese and American English, Taiwan Normal Univ, 65; Linguistics: Theory, Application & Chinese Syntax, 79; A Ref Grammar of Mandarin Chinese for Speakers of English, Peter Lang, 83; Historical Syntax: Theory and Application to Chinese, Crane, 87; A Discourse Grammar of Mandarin Chinese, Peter Lang, 98; and over 60 journal articles and book chapters. **CONTACT ADDRESS** Dept of African & Asian Langs, Univ FL, 470 Grinter Hall, Gainesville, FL, 32611-5565. **EMAIL** chauncey@aall.ufl.edu

CHUNG, SANDRA
DISCIPLINE AUSTRONESIAN LINGUISTICS **EDUCATION** Radcliffe Col, AB; Harvard Univ, PhD, 76. **CAREER** PROF, LING, UNIV CALIF, SANTA CRUZ. **RESEARCH** Chamorro syntax. **SELECTED PUBLICATIONS** "VP's and Verb Movement," Chamorro, Natural Language and Linguistic Theory, 90; "Functional Heads and Proper Government in Chamorro," Lingua, 91; "Wh-Agreement and "'Referentiality'," Chamorro, Linguistic Inquiry, 94. **CONTACT ADDRESS** Dept of Ling, Univ Calif, 1156 High St, Santa Cruz, CA, 95064.

CHURCH, DAN M.
DISCIPLINE TWENTIETH-CENTURY THEATER AND FILM, TECHNOLOGY AND LANGUAGE ACQUISITION **EDUCATION** Wake Forest Col, BA, 61; Middlebury Col, MA, 62; Univ Wis, PhD, 68. **CAREER** Asst prof Fr, Antioch Col, 65-67; asst prof, 67-70; assoc prof, 70-; dir, Vanderbilt-in-Fr, 74-76; dir, Workshop on the Quest Authoring Syst, 86; dir, Mellon Regional fac develop sem, 86; dir, lang lab, Vanderbilt Univ, 88-96. **MEMBERSHIPS** Comput Assisted Lang Instr Consortium; chemn, Courseware Develop Spec Interest Gp. **SELECTED PUBLICATIONS** Auth, Interactive Audio for Foreign-Language Learning, Lit & Ling Comp, V, 2; AndrQ Barsacq, Gaston Baty, and Roger Planchon, Theatrical Directors: A Biographical Dictionary, Greenwood Press, 94; rev, GramDef French, CALICO J, 98. **CONTACT ADDRESS** Vanderbilt Univ, Nashville, TN, 37203-1727. **EMAIL** barrettt@ctrvax.vanderbilt.edu 3

CHVANY, CATHERINE VAKAR
PERSONAL Born 04/26/1927, Paris, France, m, 1948, 3 children **DISCIPLINE** SLAVIC LANGUAGES AND LITERATURES **EDUCATION** Radcliffe Col, BA, 63; Harvard Univ, PhD(Slavic lang & lit), 70. **CAREER** Instr Russ, Wellesley Col, 66-67; instr, 67-70, lectr, 70-71, asst prof, 71-74, ASSOC PROF RUSS, MASS INST TECHNOL, 74-, Fel, Harvard Russ Res Ctr, 79- **HONORS AND AWARDS** Lilly Postdoctoral Teaching Award fel, Mass Inst Technol, 75-76. **MEMBERSHIPS** Am Asn Advan Slavic Studies; Ling Soc Am; Am Asn Teachers Slavic & EEurop Lang. **RESEARCH** Syntax; Russian language teaching; Bulgarian. **SELECTED PUBLICATIONS** Auth, Lipson, Alexander--Contributions for Him and by Him, Slavic and E Europ Jour, Vol 0039, 95 Mental Grammar - Russian Aspect And Related Issues - Durstandersen,P/, Slavic and E Europ Jour, Vol 0038, 94; New Vistas in Grammar--Invariance and Variation, Word-Jour Intl Ling Assn, Vol 0047, 96; Interrogative Pronouns and Question--Words in Modern Bulgarian--Bulgarian, Slavic and E Europ Jour, Vol 0037, 93. **CONTACT ADDRESS** Dept of Russian, Room 14N 216 Mass Inst Technol, 77 Massachusetts Ave, Cambridge, MA, 02139.

CICCARELLI, ANDREA
DISCIPLINE ITALIAN LITERATURE **EDUCATION** Columbia Univ, PhD, 90. **CAREER** Assoc prof. **RESEARCH** Nineteenth and twentieth century poetry, narrative and theatre; literary criticism and theory; current Italian literature and culture. **SELECTED PUBLICATIONS** Auth, Manzoni: la coscienza della letteratura; pubs on Romanticism. **CONTACT ADDRESS** Dept of French and Italian, Indiana Univ, Bloomington, 300 N Jordan Ave, Bloomington, IN, 47405.

CIHOLAS, KARIN NORDENHAUG
PERSONAL Roanoke, VA, m, 1962, 2 children **DISCIPLINE** COMPARATIVE LITERATURE, FRENCH **EDUCATION** Univ Richmond, BA, 62; Univ NC, Chapel Hill, MA, 70, PhD, 72. **CAREER** Instr Comp Lit, Univ NC, Chapel Hill, 72-73; Instr Mod Lang, Campbell Col, 72-74; from Asst Prof to Assoc Prof Mod Lang, 74-94, Van Winkle Prof Lang, Centre Col, 94-, Chmn, Hum Div, 79-83, Assoc Dean of Col, 83-92, Dir Int Prog, 89-92, Chmn Humanities Div, 95-98. **HONORS AND AWARDS** Mod Lang Award, Univ Richmond, 62; Phi Beta Kappa, 62; AAUW Dissertation Fel, 71; Mellon Grants, 81, 86; NEH Distinguished Prof, 94; KY Arts Coun Grant, 97. **MEMBERSHIPS** MLA. **RESEARCH** Andr Gide; Thomas Mann; 20th century lit. **SELECTED PUBLICATIONS** Auth, Gide'a Art of the Fugue: A Thematic Analysis of Les Faux-Monnayeurs, Univ NC Press, 74; author of numerous short stories, plays, and poems. **CONTACT ADDRESS** Centre Col, 600 W Walnut St, Danville, KY, 40422-0000. **EMAIL** Ciholas@centre.edu

CINTAS, PIERRE FRANCOIS DIEGO
PERSONAL Born 02/19/1929, Sfax, Tunisia, 2 children **DISCIPLINE** GENERAL & FRENCH LINGUISTICS **EDUCATION** Univ CO, MA, 62; IN Univ, PhD(French ling), 69. **CAREER** Teacher French & Latin, VT Acad, 59-60; teaching asst French, Univ CO, 60-62; lectr phonetics, Univ Grenoble, 62-63; teaching asst French, IN Univ, 63-65; lectr, Harvard Univ, 65-70; asst prof French & ling, Univ VA, 70-76; asst prof French & educ, Dalhousie Univ, 76-78; asst prof French, 78-82, ASSOC PROF FRENCH, PA STATE UNIV, 82-; Bibliogr ling, Mod Lang Asn Int Bibliog, 69-80; assoc ed, Bibliog of Am Coun Teaching Foreign Lang, 76-82; instr, French Sch, Middlebury Col, 77-86. **HONORS AND AWARDS** Chevalier des Palmes Academiques. **MEMBERSHIPS** Am Asn Teachers Fr; MLA; Am Coun Teaching Foreign Lang; Int Phonetic Asn; Am Assoc for Applied Linguistics. **RESEARCH** French syntax; applied linguistics; lexicology; computer assisted instruction. **SELECTED PUBLICATIONS** Auth, Self Evaluation and a Sense of Responsibility, Fr Rev, 68; Teacher Evaluation, AAUP Bull, 71; Mechant Poete vs Poete Mechant, In: Papers in Linguistics and Phonetics to the Memory of Pierre Delattre, 72; Apprentissage et Maitrise du langage, Bull FIPF, 74; coauth, Aspect in English and German in a Semantically Based Model, Views on Lang, 75; Language Acquisition, 1977 Northeast Conf Reports, 77; auth, Aspect, aktionsart and lexicalization, In: Contrastive Linguistics, Hochschul Verlag, Stuttgart, 78; Sans Bornes, Holt, Rinehart & Winston, 90; Elements of French Grammar, software interactive program, PA State, 96. **CONTACT ADDRESS** Pennsylvania State Univ, 1600 Woodland Rd, Abington, PA, 19001-3990. **EMAIL** pfc1@psu.edu

CIPLIJAUSKAITE, BIRUTE
PERSONAL Born 04/11/1929, Kaunas, Lithuania **DISCIPLINE** ROMANCE LANGUAGES **EDUCATION** Lycee Lithuanien, Tubingen, Ger, BA, 47; Univ Montreal, MA, 56; Bryn Mawr Col, PhD(Span lit), 60. **CAREER** From instr Span to prof, 60-73, JOHN BASCOM PROF SPAN, UNIV WIS MADISON, 73-, Univ Wis res grants, 62, 66, 68 & 71; Guggenheim fel, 67-68; fel, Inst Res Humanities, Madison, 71-72; consult to pres, State Univ NY Stony Brook, 76-78. **MEMBERSHIPS** Inst Res Humanities; Am Asn Teachers Span & Port; Inst Lithuanian Studies; Asn Int Hispanistas. **RESEARCH** Spanish poetry, contemporary and Golden Age; 19th and 20th century novel; Lithuanian literature, 19th to 20th centuries. **SELECTED PUBLICATIONS** Auth, Rosas De Fuego--Spanish, World Lit Today, Vol 0071, 97; Quevedo and the Generation-of-27 1927-1936--Spanish, World Lit Today, Vol 0067, 93; Campoalange, Maria, My Childhood and its World--Spanish, Hisp Rev, Vol 0061, 93; Dialogos de Afrodita En Tres Tiempos, World Lit Today, Vol 0068, 94; Astonishing World--The Selected Poems of Gonzalez, Angel 1956-1986, World Lit Today, Vol 0068, 94; Arbres En La Musique, World Lit Today, Vol 0069, 95; El Ojo De Dios, Insula-Rev de Letras y Ciencias Humanas, Vol 0048, 93; No Temeras, World Lit Today, Vol 0069, 95; Del Vacio Y Sus Dones, World Lit Today, Vol 0068, 94; Towards a Serene Affirmation, the New Trends of Feminist Poetry, Rev de Estudios Hispanicos, Vol 0029, 95; Garcialorca, Federico and the Culture of Male Homosexuality--Lorca, Dali, Cernuda, Gilalbert, Prados and the Quiet Voice of Homosexual Love--Spanish, Hisp Rev, Vol 0062, 94; Salinas, Pedro, Guillen, Jorge, Correspondence %+1923-1951--Spanish, Hisp Rev, Vol 0062, 94; Sacar-De-Ti-Tu-Mejor-Tu--Ferratermora,Jose, Summarized, Hispania-Jour Devoted to the Tchg of Span and Port, Vol 0080, 97; Glosove Na Zheni--Anthology of Contemporary Spanish Poetry in Translation--Bulgarian, World Lit Today, Vol 0071, 97; Atencia, Maria, Victoria, Poetry--Bulgarian, Spanish, World Lit Today, Vol 0071, 97; La Tia Agueda--Spanish, World Lit Today, Vol 0070, 96; Tiempos Del Cantar Poetry 1976-1993--Spanish, World Lit Today, Vol 0070, 96; Spanish Avant-Garde Poetry 1918-1936--Spanish, World Lit Today, Vol 0070, 96; El Sol, la Sombra, en el Instante, World Lit Today, Vol 0069, 95; The Farce--Spanish Women Playwrights Between 1918 and 1936--Spanish, World Lit Today, Vol 0068, 94; Miradas Sobre El Agua, World Lit Today, Vol 0068, 94; Alada Mia--Anthology 1978-1994--Spanish, World Lit Today, Vol 0071, 97. **CONTACT ADDRESS** Dept of Span, Univ of Wis, Madison, WI, 53706.

CISAR, MARY
PERSONAL IL, m, 2 children **DISCIPLINE** EIGHTEENTH-CENTURY FRENCH LITERATURE **EDUCATION** Kalamazoo Col; Brown Univ, MA, PhD. **CAREER** French, St. Olaf Col. **SELECTED PUBLICATIONS** Area: Mennonite women's autobiography. **CONTACT ADDRESS** St Olaf Col, 1520 St Olaf Ave, Northfield, MN, 55057.

CISMARU, ALFRED
PERSONAL Born 10/26/1929, Paris, France, m, 1957, 2 children **DISCIPLINE** FRENCH LITERATURE **EDUCATION** Fordham Univ, BS, 56; NY Univ, MA, 58, PhD, 60. **HONORS AND AWARDS** MLA; Am Asn Teachers Fr., Instr French & Span, Brooklyn Col, 58-59; from assoc prof to prof French, St Michael's Col (Vt), 59-70, chmn dept lang, 59-70, fac res fund awards, 62-68; PROF CLASS & ROMANCE LANG, TEX TECH UNIV, 70-. **MEMBERSHIPS** French literature of the 18th century; contemporary French literature. **RESEARCH** Auth, Marguerite Duras, Twayne, 71; Boris Vian, G K Hall, 73; Marivaux and Moliere: A Comparison, Tex Tech Press, 77. **SELECTED PUBLICATIONS** Auth, Anti-Semitism in France, Midwest Quart-Jour Contemp Thought, Vol 0034, 93; What is the Enlightenment--French, Fr Rev, Vol 0067, 94; Kant Philosophy and the Enlightenment, Fr Rev, Vol 0068, 95; The Cultural Origins of the French-Revolution, Fr Rev, Vol 0066, 93; Sagan, Francoise--The Superficial Classic, World Lit Today, Vol 0067, 93. **CONTACT ADDRESS** Texas Tech Univ, Lubbock, TX, 79409.

CIVIL, MIGUEL
PERSONAL Born 05/07/1926, Sabadell, Spain, 2 children **DISCIPLINE** ASSYRIOLOGY, LINGUISTICS **EDUCATION** Univ Paris, PhD, 58. **CAREER** Res assoc Assyriol,

Univ Pa, 58-63; from asst prof to assoc prof Near Eastern Lang & civilizations & ling, 63-70, Prof Near Eastern Lang & Civilizations & Ling, Univ Chicago, 70-, Mem ed bd, Chicago Assyrian Dict, 67-; dir d'etudes associe etranger, Sorbonne, 68-70; ed, Materials for the Sumerian Lexicon, 68- **MEMBERSHIPS** Am Orient Soc; Am Sch Orient Res. **RESEARCH** Sumerian grammar and literature; anthropology of Mesopotamia; lexicography. **SELECTED PUBLICATIONS** Auth, Prescriptions medicales Sumeriennes, Rev D'Assyriol, 60; The message of Lu-dingirra, J Near Eastern Studies, 64; Notes on Sumerian lexicography, J Cuneiform Studies, 66; coauth, Vol IX, Materials for the Sumerian Lexicon, 67 & auth, Vol XIII-XIV, 71, Pontificio Inst Biblico, Rome. **CONTACT ADDRESS** Oriental Institute Univ, Univ of Chicago, 1155 E 58th St, Chicago, IL, 60637-1540.

CLADER, LINDA
PERSONAL Born 02/11/1946, Evanston, IL, m, 1991 **DISCIPLINE** CLASSICAL PHILOLOGY; HOMILETICS **EDUCATION** Carleton Col, AB, 68; Harvard Univ, AM, 70, PhD, 73; Church Divinity School of Pacific, M Div, 88. **CAREER** Instr to full prof Classical languages, Carleton Col, 72-90; asst to assoc prof, homiletics, Church Divinity School Pacific, 91-. **HONORS AND AWARDS** Phi Beta Kappa, 68. **MEMBERSHIPS** AAR/SBL; Acad Homiletics **RESEARCH** Liturgical preaching; Myth; Homer. **SELECTED PUBLICATIONS** Auth, Preaching the Liturgical Narratives: The Easter Vigil and the Language of Myth, Worship, 98. **CONTACT ADDRESS** Church Divinity Sch of the Pacific, 2451 Ridge Rd, Berkeley, CA, 94709. **EMAIL** Lclader@cdsp.edu

CLAMURRO, WILLIAM
DISCIPLINE SPANISH LITERATURE **EDUCATION** Amherst Col, BA, 67; Univ Wash, MA, 68, PhD, 75. **CAREER** Adj instr, Montclair State Col, 77-78; asst prof, Univ Md, 78-86; assoc prof, 86-92; prof, Denison Univ, 92-97; prof, Emporia State Univ, 97-. **MEMBERSHIPS** Asn Int Hispanistas; Cervantes Soc Am; AATSP; Asn Int Siglo de Oro; MLA. **SELECTED PUBLICATIONS** Auth, Language and Ideology in the Prose of Quevedo, 91; Manuel Puig y la construccion de la lectura postmoderna, Univ Iowa, 94; Madness and Narrative Form in Estragos que causa el vicio, 95. **CONTACT ADDRESS** Div of Foreign Languages, Emporia State Univ, 1200 Commercial St, Emporia, KS, 66801-5087. **EMAIL** clamurrw@esumail.emporia.edu

CLARK, BASIL ALFRED
PERSONAL Born 07/19/1939, Prospect, ME, m, 1966, 2 children **DISCIPLINE** ENGLISH LITERATURE & LANGUAGE **EDUCATION** Bowdoin Col, AB, 60; Univ ME, MA, 69; OH State Univ, PhD, 75. **CAREER** From Asst Prof to Assoc Prof, 75-85, prof eng, Saginaw Valley State Univ, 85. **MEMBERSHIPS** MLA; NCTE. **RESEARCH** Medieval Brit lit. **SELECTED PUBLICATIONS** Heike Monogatari and Beowulf: A Comparative Study, Bull Shikoku Women's Univ 9.2, 90. **CONTACT ADDRESS** Saginaw Valley State Univ, 7400 Bay Rd, University Center, MI, 48710-0001. **EMAIL** baclark@svsu.edu

CLARK, EVE VIVIENNE
PERSONAL Born 07/26/1942, Camberley, England, m, 1967 **DISCIPLINE** LINGUISTICS, PSYCHOLINGUISTICS **EDUCATION** Univ Edinburgh, MA, 65, dipl, 66, PhD(ling), 69. **CAREER** Res assoc lang, 69-70, lectr, 70-71, asst prof ling, 71-77, ASSOC PROF LING, STANFORD UNIV, 77-, NSF grant, Stanford Univ, 71-75, 75-79 & 80-83; Spencer Found grant, 79-80 & 80-83; fel, Ctr Adv Study Behavioral Sci, 79-80. **MEMBERSHIPS** Ling Soc Am; Soc Res Child Develop; Int Asn Study Child Lang. **RESEARCH** Language acquisition; semantics; word-formation. **SELECTED PUBLICATIONS** Auth, Reference States and Reversals--Undoing Actions with Verbs, Jour Child Lang, Vol 0022, 95. **CONTACT ADDRESS** Dept of Ling, Stanford Univ, Stanford, CA, 94305-1926.

CLARK, HUGH R.
DISCIPLINE HISTORY AND EAST ASIAN STUDIES **EDUCATION** Univ Pa, PhD. **CAREER** Prof Hist and E Asian Stud, ch, dept Hist, Ursinus Col. **HONORS AND AWARDS** Laughlin Prof Achievement Award, Ursinus Col; grant, Chiang Ching-kuo Found, NEH, Comt for Scholarly Res in China. **RESEARCH** Middle period Chinese history. **SELECTED PUBLICATIONS** Auth, Community, Trade, and Networks: Southern Fujian Province from the 3rd to the 13th Centuries. **CONTACT ADDRESS** Ursinus Col, Collegeville, PA, 19426-1000.

CLARK, JOHN RICHARD
PERSONAL Born 06/11/1947, Dayton, OH, m, 1 child **DISCIPLINE** CLASSICAL LANGUAGES, MEDIEVAL LATIN **EDUCATION** Univ Cincinnati, BA, 69; Cornell Univ, MA, 71, PhD, 74. **CAREER** Asst prof, Univ Pa, 75-79; Asst Prof, 80-86, Assoc Prof Class, Medieval & Palaeography, Fordham Univ, 86-. **MEMBERSHIPS** Am Philol Asn; Medieval Acad Am. **RESEARCH** Marsilio Ficino's De vita(1489); medieval Latin love lyric; Plautus. **SELECTED PUBLICATIONS** Auth, Structure and symmetry in the Bacchides of Plautus, Transactions of the Am Philol Asn, 76; Two ghost editions of Marsilio Ficino's De vita, Papers of the Bibliog Soc of Am, 79; Teaching Medieval Latin, Class J, 79; Word play in Plautus' Amphitruo, Class Philol, 80; Marsilio Ficino among the alchemists, Class Bull, 83; coauth, Marsilio Ficino: Three Books on Life: A Critical Edition and Translation with Introduction & Notes, SUNY, 89; auth, Platonianus es, non Plautinianus (Jerome Ep. 22.30), CW, 84; The Traditional Figure of Dina and Abeland's First Planetus, Proceeds of PMR Conf, 82; Roger Bacon and the Composition of Marsilio Ficino's De vita longa, J Warburg & Courtauld Inst, 86; Love & Learning in the Metamorphosis Golye Episcopi, MJ, 86. **CONTACT ADDRESS** Dept of Class, Fordham Univ, 441 E Fordham Rd, Bronx, NY, 10458-5191. **EMAIL** clark@murray.fordham.edu

CLARK, MARY MORRIS
PERSONAL Born 12/28/1941, Tuscaloosa, AL, 3 children **DISCIPLINE** LINGUISTICS, AFRICAN LANGUAGES **EDUCATION** Univ NH, BA, 62; Univ Mass, PhD(ling), 78. **CAREER** Teacher English, math & sci, US Peace Corps, Nigeria, 64-65; instr, Sch for Int Training, 75-78; ASST PROF LING, ENGLISH DEPT, UNIV NH, 78- **MEMBERSHIPS** Ling Soc Am; African Ling Soc; North Eastern Ling Soc; Teachers of English to Speakers of Other Lang; NCTE. **RESEARCH** The use of tone and intonation in languages; the interaction of phonology with other parts of the grammar; applications of linguistics in language teaching. **SELECTED PUBLICATIONS** Auth, Classification of Adults for Family Studies of Developmental Language Disorders, Jour Speech and Hearing Res, Vol 0039, 96; Guilty if Charged--A Response to the Bernstein, Richard Account of the Silva, Donald Case at the University-of-New-Hampshire--An Exchange, NY Rev Bk(s), Vol 0041, 94. **CONTACT ADDRESS** English Dept, Univ of NH, 125 Technology Dr, Durham, NH, 03824-4724.

CLARK, THOMAS L.
DISCIPLINE ENGLISH LINGUISTICS **EDUCATION** Univ Utah, BA, 64, MA, 66; Ohio Univ, PhD, 70. **CAREER** Prof, Univ Nev, Las Vegas. **HONORS AND AWARDS** William Morris Award, 87, App Barrick Res Prof, Univ Nev, Las Vegas, 90. **MEMBERSHIPS** Ed bd, NCTE, 80-93; bd of gov, Am Name Soc, 85-88; vice pres, 83-85, pres, Am Dialect Soc, 85-87; exec bd, Am Coun of Learned Soc, 88-92. **SELECTED PUBLICATIONS** Auth, Expanding the Scope: Volume II of DARE is Only Part of the Story, Am Speech, vol 69, 94; Western Lore and Language: A Dictionary for Enthusiasts of the West, Univ Utah Press, 96. **CONTACT ADDRESS** Dept of Eng, Univ Nev, Las Vegas, Las Vegas, NV, 89154-5011. **EMAIL** tlc@nevada.edu

CLARKE, ERNEST GEORGE
PERSONAL Born 06/16/1927, Varna, ON, Canada, m, 1951, 4 children **DISCIPLINE** NEAR EASTERN STUDIES **EDUCATION** Univ Toronto, BA, 49, BD, 52, MA, 53; Univ Leiden, DLitt(Aramaic), 62. **CAREER** Lectr Old Testament, Queen's Theol Col, Kingston, 56-58, prof, 58-61; assoc prof, 61-64, chmn dept, 70-75, PROF NEAR EASTERN STUDIES, VICTORIA COL, UNIV TORONTO, 64-, Mem, Br Sch Archaeol; Can Conn leave fel, 69-70; vis fel, Univ Col, Cambridge, 69-70; gov, gov counc, Univ Toronto, 79- **MEMBERSHIPS** Am Orient Soc; Soc Bibl Lit; Can Soc Bibl Studies (pres, 67-68). **RESEARCH** Preparation of a computer generated keyword in context concordance to Targum pseudo-Jonathan to the Pentateuch. **SELECTED PUBLICATIONS** Auth, An Aramaic Bibliography, Pt 1--Old, Official, and Biblical Aramaic, Cath Biblical Quart, Vol 0056, 94. **CONTACT ADDRESS** Dept of Near Eastern Studies, Univ of Toronto, Toronto, ON, M5S 1A1.

CLARKE, MURRAY
DISCIPLINE COGNITIVE SCIENCE AND PHILOSOPHY OF SCIENCE **EDUCATION** W Ontario Univ, PhD. **CAREER** Prof; ch. **RESEARCH** Implications of evolutionary psychology, empirical psychology. **SELECTED PUBLICATIONS** Auth, Doxastic Voluntarism and Forced Belief, Philos Stud Volume 50, 86; Epistemic Norms and Evolutionary Success, Synthese, Volume 85, 86; Natural Selection and Indexical Representation, Logic and Philosophy of Science in Quebec, Volume II, Boston Stud in the Philos of Sci, 96; "Darwinian Algorithms and Indexical Representation," Philos of Sci, Volume 63, Number 1, 96. **CONTACT ADDRESS** Dept of Philos, Concordia Univ, Montreal, 1455 de Maisonneuve W, Montreal, PQ, H3G 1M8. **EMAIL** eud@vax2.concordia.ca

CLAS, ANDRE
PERSONAL Born 06/01/1933, Laning, France **DISCIPLINE** LINGUISTICS **EDUCATION** Univ Strasbourg, BA, 53; Univ Montreal, MA, 60; Univ Tubingen, DPh, 67. **CAREER** Lectr to assoc prof, 63-76, dept ch, 72-81, PROF LINGUISTICS, UNIV MONTREAL, 76-; ed, META (Translator's J), 68-. **MEMBERSHIPS** Soc de la linguistique romane; Can Ling Soc. **SELECTED PUBLICATIONS** Auth, Phonetique appliquee, 67; auth, Le francais, langue des affaires, 69; auth, Richesses et particularites du francais ecrit au Quebec, 79, 82; auth, Guide de la correspondance, 80; auth, Sons et langage, 83; auth, Visages du francais, Varietes lexicales de l'espace francophone, 90; auth, Compact Worterbuch der exakten Naturwissenschaften und der Technik Band II Deutsch-Franzosisch, Band I Francais-Allemand, 91, 95; auth, L'environnement traductionnel, 92; auth, La Traductique, 93; auth, TATAO: Recherches de pointe et applications immediates, 95; auth, Introduction a la lexicologie explicative et combinatoire, 95. **CONTACT ADDRESS** Dept of Linguistics, Univ Montreal, CP 6128, Succ Centre-ville, Montreal, PQ, H3C 3J7.

CLASSEN, ALBRECHT
PERSONAL Born 04/23/1956, Germany, m, 1984, 1 child **DISCIPLINE** FOREIGN LANGUAGES **EDUCATION** Univ Marburg, MA, 82; Univ Va, PhD, 86. **CAREER** From asst prof to assoc prof to prof, 87-, Univ Ariz. **HONORS AND AWARDS** Edgar-Shannon-Award, 86, Univ Va; El Paso Natural Gas Found Fac Achievement Award, 95; Univ Tchr Grant, 99, Rotary Int., Pres, AATG, 97-98; Pres, AATG, 92-98. **MEMBERSHIPS** MLA; SEMA; Oswald von Wolkenstein Gesellschaft; Rocky Mountain MLA; ICLS. **RESEARCH** Medieval and early modern German literature and history. **SELECTED PUBLICATIONS** Auth, The German Volksbuch. A Critical History of a Late-Medieval Genre, 95; auth, Tristania, Vol. XVI, 95; auth, Tristania, Vol. XVII, 96; auth, Diu Klage, Mittelhochdeutsch-neuhochdeutsch. Einleitung Ubersetzung, Kommentar und Anmerkungen, 97; auth, Trisania, Vol. XVII, 98. **CONTACT ADDRESS** 2413 E 4th St, Tucson, AZ, 85719. **EMAIL** aclassen@u.arizona.edu

CLAUSING, GERHARD
PERSONAL Born 02/16/1943, Germany, m, 1989 **DISCIPLINE** GERMAN LINGUISTICS **EDUCATION** Univ of Calif at Berkeley, AB, 66, MA, 68, PhD, 74. **CAREER** Instr to asst prof, Univ of Minn, 72-76; ASST PROF 76-79, ASSOC PROF, 79-93, FULL PROF, 93-, CHAIR, UNIV OF SOUTHERN CALIF, 90-. **HONORS AND AWARDS** Equipment and res grants, Univ of Southern Calif, 89-94; Sigerson Found, 87; IBM Socrates Grant, 86-88; Goethe Inst Grants, 81 & 84. **MEMBERSHIPS** MLA; AATG. **RESEARCH** German and applied linguistics; cultural studies; drama. **SELECTED PUBLICATIONS** Auth, Ubergange. Sprechen-Berichten-Diskutieren. Genre-Based Conversation in German, Heinle and Heinle, 94; Speaking German Naturally (video tape), Donn Sigerson Found, 87; coauth, Interaktion. A Text-Based Intermediate German Course, Houghton Miffline, 90; Deutsch naturlich! A Communication-Oriented First Course, Houghton Mifflin, 86; Zur Situation der deutschen Sprache in Kalifornien, Deutsch als Muttersprache in den Vereinigten Staaten, Teil 2, Steiner, 85. **CONTACT ADDRESS** Dept of German, Univ of Southern California, Los Angeles, CA, 90089-0351. **EMAIL** clausing@usc.edu

CLAUSSEN, ERNEST NEAL
PERSONAL Born 08/15/1933, Petersburg, IL, m, 1961, 2 children **DISCIPLINE** SPEECH COMMUNICATION **EDUCATION** Ill State Univ, BS, 55; Southern Ill Univ, Carbondale, MA, 59, PhD(speech), 63. **CAREER** Instr speech & econ, Mendota High Sch, Ill, 55-56; asst prof speech, Colo State Col, 59-61; from asst prof to assoc prof, 63-71, assoc dean col lib arts & sci, 69-71, prof Speech, Bradley Univ, 71-. **HONORS AND AWARDS** The Harvard Award, 89; Sanford Award; 97 fror the Illinois Speech and Theatre Assoc. **MEMBERSHIPS** Speech Commun Asn; Rhetoric Soc Am. **RESEARCH** Rhetorical theory; rhetorical criticism; public communication. **SELECTED PUBLICATIONS** Auth, John Sharp Williams: Pacesetter for democratic keynoters, Southern Speech, 65; Hendrick B Wright and the nocturnal committee, Pa Mag Hist & Biog, 65; He kept us out of war: Martin H Glynn's keynote, Quart J Speech, 66; co-ed (with Karl R Wallace), John Lawson's Lectures Concerning Oratory, Southern Ill Univ Press, 72; Alben Barkley's rhetorical victory in 1948, Southern Speech Commun J, fall 79. **CONTACT ADDRESS** Dept of Speech Commun, Bradley Univ, 1501 W Bradley Ave, Peoria, IL, 61625-0002. **EMAIL** claussen@bradley.edu

CLAYMAN, DEE LESSER
PERSONAL New York **DISCIPLINE** CLASSICAL PHILOLOGY **EDUCATION** Wellesley Col, BA, 67; Univ Pa, MA, 69, PhD(classics), 72. **CAREER** Asst prof classics, Brooklyn Col, 72-77, assoc prof, 78-81, PROF CLASSICS, BROOKLYN COL & GRAD CTR, CITY UNIV NEW YORK, 82-, Grants-in-aid, Am Philos Soc, 75 & Am Coun Learned Soc, 78. **MEMBERSHIPS** Am Philol Asn; Asn Lit & Ling Computing; Asn Computational Linguistics. **RESEARCH** Greek poetry; computer-assisted stylometry; history of literary criticism. **SELECTED PUBLICATIONS** Auth, Trends and Issues in Quantitative Stylistics, Transactions of the Amer Philol Assn, Vol 0122, 92. **CONTACT ADDRESS** Dept of Classics, Brooklyn Col, CUNY, Brooklyn, NY, 11210.

CLAYTON, JOHN DOUGLAS
PERSONAL Born 12/14/1943, Cheshire, England, m, 1968, 2 children **DISCIPLINE** RUSSIAN LITERATURE **EDUCATION** Univ Cambridge, BA, 65; Univ Ill, Urbana, AM, 67, PhD(Russ), 71. **CAREER** Asst prof Slavic studies, 71-76, ASSOC PROF MOD LAND & LIT, UNIV OTTAWA, 76-. **MEMBERSHIPS** Can Asn Slavists; Am Asn Teachers Slavic & East Europ Lang; Am Asn Advan Slavic Studies; Asn Can Theatre History. **RESEARCH** Alexander Pushkin; 20th centu-

ry Russian theatre. **SELECTED PUBLICATIONS** Auth, Chekhov--A Life in Letters, Slavic Rev, Vol 0055, 96; Larionov, Mikhail and the Russian Avant-Garde, Russ Rev, Vol 0054, 95; Chekhov, Anton--The Sense and the Nonsense, Slavic Rev, Vol 0054, 95; Russian Lexemes Prav- and Slav, Semantic Analysis of Pushkin, A.S. Boris Godunov, Russ Lit, Vol 0038, 95; Laboratory of Dreams--The Russian Avant-Garde and Cultural Experiment, Russ Rev, Vol 0056, 97; Povesti Belkina and the Commedia-Dellarte, Russ Lit, Vol 0040, 96; Izver-Revel--Russian Poetry--Poetic Etymology and the Wellsprings of Creativity, Essays in Poetics, Vol 0022, 97; The Theatrical Instinct--Evreinov, Nikolai and the Russian Theater of the Early-20th-Century, Can Slavonic Papers-Rev Can des Slavistes, Vol 0034, 92. **CONTACT ADDRESS** Dept of Mod Lang & Lit, Univ of Ottawa, Ottawa, ON, K1N 6N5.

CLAYTON, TOM
PERSONAL Born 12/15/1932, New Ulm, MN, w, 1955, 4 children **DISCIPLINE** ENGLISH, CLASS & NEAR EASTERN STUDIES **EDUCATION** Univ Minn, BA, 54; Oxford Univ, DPhil, 60. **CAREER** Instr English, Yale Univ, 60-62; asst prof, Univ Calif, Los Angeles, 62-67, assoc prof, 67-68; assoc prof, 68-70, PROF ENGLISH, UNIV MINN, MINNEAPOLIS, 70-, PROF CLASS & NEAR EASTERN STUDIES, 80-, CHMN, CLASS CIVILIZATION PROG, 82-, MORSE-ALUMNI DISTINGUISHED TEACHING PROF ENGL & CLASSICAL STUDIES, 93-; Am Coun Learned Soc grant, 62-63; fel, Inst for Humanities, Univ Calif, 66-67; assoc, Danforth Assoc Prog, 72-77; Guggenheim fel, 78-79; Bush fel, Univ Minn, 85; NEH award, Div Res Tools, 88. **HONORS AND AWARDS** Rhodes Scholar, Minn and Wadham, 54; Distinguished Teaching Award, Col Lib Arts, Univ Minn, 71; Morse-Alumni Award, Outstanding contrib undergrad educ, Univ Minn 82. **MEMBERSHIPS** Asn of Am Rhodes Scholars; Asn Literary Scholars and Critics; Renaissance English Text Soc; Int Shakespeare Asn; Shakespeare Asn Am. **RESEARCH** Shakespeare; literary criticism; earlier 17th Century English literature. **SELECTED PUBLICATIONS** Ed & auth, The Shakespearean Addition in the Books of Sir Thomas Moore, Ctr Shakespeare Studies, 69; ed & auth, The Non-Dramatic Works of Sir John Suckling, Clarendon, 71; ed & auth, Cavalier Poets, Oxford Univ, 78; auth, Is this the promis'd end?, Revision in the role of the King himself, in The Division of the Kingdom, Clarendon, 83; The texts and publishing vicissitudes of Peter Nichol's Passion Play, in The Library, 87; ed & auth, The Hamlet First Published (Q1, 1603), Univ Del, 92; That's she that was myself: Not-so-famous last words and some ends of Othello, Shakespeare Survey, 94; So our virtues lie in the interpretation of the time: Shakespeare's Coriolanus and Coriolanus, and Some Questions of Value, Ben Johnson J, 94; Who has no children in Macbeth?, in Festschrift for Marvin Rosenbert, Univ Del, 98 (forthcoming); So quick bright things come to confusion, or what else was A Midsummer's Night Dream about?, in Festschrift for Jay L Halio, in prep. **CONTACT ADDRESS** Dept of English, Univ of Minn, 207 Church St SE, Minneapolis, MN, 55455-0134. **EMAIL** tsc@unm.edu

CLEMENTE, ALICE RODRIGUES
PERSONAL Born 07/28/1934, Pawtucket, RI **DISCIPLINE** SPANISH AND PORTUGUESE **EDUCATION** Brown Univ, AB, 56, MA, 59, PhD(Span), 67. **CAREER** Instr Span, Randolph-Macon Woman's Col, 59-61 & Wheaton Col, 64; from instr to asst prof, 64-71, assoc prof, 64-80, PROF SPAN & PORT, SMITH COL, 80-. **MEMBERSHIPS** Asoc Int Hispanistas. **RESEARCH** Gil Vicente; Portuguese novel; Jesuits in the Orient. **SELECTED PUBLICATIONS** Auth, Goncalves, A Instrucao dos Amantes, World Lit Today, Vol 0067, 93; Rui--An Early Portuguese Jurist and the Status of Women, Mln-Modern Lang Notes, Vol 0108, 93; La Escala de los Mapas, World Lit Today, Vol 0068, 94; O Chao Salgado, World Lit Today, Vol 0068, 94; Vals Negro, World Lit Today, Vol 0069, 95; Womens Literature in Contemporary Brazil--Portuguese, World Lit Today, Vol 0069, 95; Si al Atardecer Llegara el Mensajero, World Lit Today, Vol 0070, 96; Lo Raro es Vivir--Spanish, World Lit Today, Vol 0071, 97; Women, Literature and Culture in the Portuguese--Speaking World, World Lit Today, Vol 0071, 97. **CONTACT ADDRESS** Dept of Hispanic Studies, Smith Col, Northampton, MA, 01060.

CLENDENEN, E. RAY
PERSONAL Born 03/09/1949, Dallas, TX, m, 1971, 2 children **DISCIPLINE** TEXTLINGUISTICS **EDUCATION** Rice Univ, BA, 71; Dallas Theol Sem, ThM, 75; Dropsie Univ, MA, 82; Univ Texas at Arlington, PhD, 89. **CAREER** Prof of Old Testament, Criswell Col, 82-96; ed, academic books, Broadman & Holman Publ, 92- . **MEMBERSHIPS** Soc of Bibl Lit; Evangel Theol Soc; Inst of Bibl Res; Natl Asn of Prof of Hebrew. **RESEARCH** Textlinguistics, Biblical Hebrew. **SELECTED PUBLICATIONS** Auth, The Structure of Malachi: A Textlinguistic Study, Criswell Theol Rev, 87; auth, Discourse Strategies in Jeremiah 10, J of Bibl Lit, 88; auth, Life in God's Land: An Outline of the Theology of Deuteronomy, in Patterson, ed, The Church at the Dawn of the 21st Century, Criswell, 89; auth, articles in Dockery, ed, The Holman Bible Handbook, Broadman, 92; ed, Old Testament, Believer's Study Bible, Nelson, 91; auth, Old Testament Prophets as Hortatory: Examples from Malachi, J of Textlinguistics and Transl, 93; auth, Postholes, Postmodernism, and the Prophets, in Dockery, ed, The Challenges of Postmodernism, Bridgepoint, 94; auth, Religious Background for the Old Testament, in Dockery, ed, Foundations for Biblical Interpretation, Sloan, Broadman, and Holman, 94; auth, Interpreting the Minor Prophets for Preaching, Faith and Mission, 95; auth, The Minor Prophets, in Dockery, ed, The Holman Concise Commentary, 98; gen ed, 19 vols, The New American Commentary, 98. **CONTACT ADDRESS** Broadman & Holman Publishers, 127 9th Ave N, MSN 164, Nashville, TN, 37234. **EMAIL** rclende@lifeway.com

CLINTON, JEROME WRIGHT
PERSONAL Born 07/14/1937, San Jose, CA, m, 1966, 2 children **DISCIPLINE** PERSIAN LITERATURE **EDUCATION** Stanford Univ, AB, 59; Univ Pa, MA, 62; Univ Mich, MA, 67, PhD(Persian lit), 71. **CAREER** Instr Persian lang & lit, Univ Minn, 70-72; dir, Tehran Ctr, Am Inst Iranian Studies, 72-74; ASST PROF PERSIAN LANG & LIT, PRINCETON UNIV, 74-, Assoc ed, Iranian Studies, 71-76. **MEMBERSHIPS** Soc Iranian Studies; Mideast Studies Asn. **RESEARCH** Persian literature of the 20-12th centuries; contemporary Persian poetry and prose. **SELECTED PUBLICATIONS** Auth, Persian Literature--A Biobibliographical Survey Begun by the Late Storey,C.A., Vol 4, Pt 2, Poetry C.Ad1100-to-1225, Bulletin Sch Oriental and African Stud-Univ London, Vol 0059, 96. **CONTACT ADDRESS** Princeton Univ, 110 Jones Hall, Princeton, NJ, 08540.

CLIVIO, GIANRENZO PIETRO
PERSONAL Born 01/18/1942, Turin, Italy **DISCIPLINE** LINGUISTICS, LITERATURE **EDUCATION** Univ Torino, Italy, BA, 62; Brandeis Univ, MA, 64; Harvard Univ, PhD (ling), 67. **CAREER** From asst prof to assoc prof, 68-77, PROF ITAL, UNIV TORONTO, 77-, Pres, Can Ctr Ital Cult & Educ, 77-81; pres, Nat Cong Ital Canadians, Ont Region, 80-; assoc ed, Can J Ital Studies, 81-; ed, Il Forneri, Bull Can Soc Ital Ling, 81- **MEMBERSHIPS** Am Asn Teachers Ital; Ling Asn US & Can; Int Soc Phonetic Sci; Can Soc Ital Ling (pres, 81-). **RESEARCH** Romance linguistics; sociolinguistics; Italian literature. **SELECTED PUBLICATIONS** Auth, Observations on Poetic Texts by Borelli, Vittorio, Amedeo and On Settecento Piedemontese, Studi Piemontesi, Vol 0023, 94. **CONTACT ADDRESS** Dept of Ital Studies, Univ of Toronto, Toronto, ON, M5S 1A1.

CLOGAN, PAUL MAURICE
PERSONAL Born 07/09/1934, Boston, MA, 3 children **DISCIPLINE** ENGLISH, COMPARATIVE LITERATURE **EDUCATION** Boston Col, AB, 56, MA, 57; St Michael's Col, PhL, 58; Univ Ill, PhD, 61. **CAREER** From instr to asst prof English, Duke Univ, 61-65; assoc prof English & comp lit, Case Western Reserve Univ, 65-72; adj prof, Cleveland State Univ, 71-72; prof English, Univ N TX, 72-. **HONORS AND AWARDS** Duke Found grant, 62-63; Am Coun Learned Soc fels, 62-64 & 71-72; sr Fulbright-Hays res fels, Italy, 65-66, Scuola Vaticana di Paleografia e Diplomatica, 66-67 & France, 78; Fulbright-Hays res fel; vis lectr, Univ Pisa, 65; Am Philos Soc grants, 65-67 & 69-70; US/UK cult exchange vis lectr, Univ Keele, 66; Bollingen Found & Prix de Rome fels, 66-67; fel, Am Acad Rome, 67; ed, Medievalia et Humanistica, 68-; mem steering comt, Asn Ctr Medieval & Renaissance Studies; Nat Endowment for Humanities fel, 70-71; vis mem, Inst Advan Study, NJ, 70 & 77; Univ N Tx; fac res grants, 72-75 & 80-81; vis lectr, Univ Tours, 78; MLA Mdeieval Exec Comt, 80-86; Deleg Assembly, 81-86; John Nicholas Brown Prize Comt, 81-83; Medieval Acad Am nominating comt, 75-76. **MEMBERSHIPS** MLA; Medieval Acad Am; Mod Humanities Res Asn; Ling Soc Am; Int Asn Univ Prof of English. **RESEARCH** Medieval literature and culture; history of the English language; literary theory. **SELECTED PUBLICATIONS** Auth, Chaucer and the Thebaid Scholia, Studies Philol, 64; Chaucer's use of the Thebaid, English Miscellany, 67; The medieval Achilleid, E J Brill, 68; The figural style and meaning of the second nun's prologue and tale, Medievalia et Humanistica, 72; coauth, Medieval hagiography and romance, 75; auth, Medieval poetics, 76, The narrative style and meaning of the man of law's tale, 77 & coauth, Transformation and continuity, 77, Cambridge Univ; Literary genres in a medieval textbook, Medievalia et Humanistica, 82; coauth Byzantine and Western Studies, 84; Fourteenth and Fifteenth Centuries, 86; The Early Renaissance, 87; Literary Theory, 88; Spectrum, 92; Columbian Qunicentenary, 92; Renaissance and Discovery, 93; Breaching the Boundaries, 94; Convergences, 94; Diversity, 95; Historical Inquiries, 97; Transitions, 98. **CONTACT ADDRESS** Univ of No Texas, PO Box 5074, Wayland, MA, 01778-6074. **EMAIL** pclogan@ibm.net

CLOUSER, ROBIN A.
DISCIPLINE GERMAN LITERATURE **EDUCATION** Ursinus Col, AB, 63; Univ Pa, AM, 65; Univ Kans, PhD, 71. **CAREER** Asst instr, Univ Pa, 64-65; tchg asst, 65-69, dir, elem Ger prog, 67-68, assoc dean, Nunemaker Col, Univ Kansas, 72-73; alumni secy, 74-75, ch, dept Germ Lang, 75-82, asst to assoc prof, 74-89, prof, 89-, ch, dept, Mod Lang, Ursinus Col, 96-. **HONORS AND AWARDS** NEH res fel, Eberhardt-Karls Univ, Bundesrepublik Deut; APS res fel, Deut Demokratische Republik, 82; res fel, Am Philos Soc, Goethe und Schiller Archiv and Nat Bibliothek der deutschen Klassik, Weimar, Ger, 91; dir, Ursinus summer res and internships in Germany prog, Eberhardt-Karls Univ, Ger, 96; Andrew W Mellon grant, Lafayette & Ursinus Col, 97-2000. **SELECTED PUBLICATIONS** Auth, 'Sosias tritt mit einer Laterne auf': Messenger to Myth in Kleist's Amphitryon, Ger Rev, 50, 75; Romeo und Julia auf dem Dorfe: Keller's Variations upon Shakespeare, J of Eng and Ger Philol, 77, 78; Ideas of Utopia in Goethe's Novelle, publ of Eng Goethe Soc, 49, 79; The Spiritual Malaise of a Modern Hercules: Hauptmann's Bahnwarter Thiel, Ger Rev, 55, 80; Heroism in Kleist's Das Erdbeben in Chili, Ger Rev, 58, 83; The Pilgrim of Consciousness: Hauptmann's Syncretistic Fairy Tale, Hauptmann- Forschung, Neue Beitrage / Hauptmann Research, New Directions, eds, Peter Sprengel, Philip Mellen, Peter Lang, 86; Gerhart Hauptmann, 1862-1946, Res Guide: Drama, Res Publ, 86; Love and Social Contracts: Goethe's Unterhaltungen deutscher Ausgewanderten, in Germanic Series in America, ed, Katherina Mommsen, Peter Lang, 91. **CONTACT ADDRESS** Dept of Mod Lang, Ursinus Col, Olin Hall, Collegeville, PA, 19426. **EMAIL** rclouser@acad.ursinus.edu

CLOUTIER, CECILE
PERSONAL Born 06/13/1930, Quebec, PQ, Canada, m, 1966, 1 child **DISCIPLINE** FRENCH **EDUCATION** Laval Univ, BA, 51, LL, 53, DES, 54; La Sorbonne, PhD, 62; McMaster Univ, MPH, 81; Univ Toronto, MTH, 82; Univ Tours, DPs, 83. **CAREER** Prof, Univ Ottawa, 58-64; prof, 64-95, PROF EMER FRENCH, UNIV TORONTO, 95-; guest prof, Laval Univ; guest prof, Queen's Univ; guest prof, Univ Napoli. **HONORS AND AWARDS** Gov Gen Award poetry, 86; res award, Univ Toronto, 87; Univ Peking Medal, 93; Medaille de la Societe des Poetes francais, 94. **MEMBERSHIPS** PEN; Asn des ecrivains de langue francaise; Union des ecrivains; Soc des ecrivains can; Asn lit can et que. **SELECTED PUBLICATIONS** Auth, Mains de sable, 60; auth, Cuivre et soies, 64; auth, Paupieres, 70; auth, Chaleuils, 79; auth, Pres, 83; auth, Perihelie, 90; auth, Ostraka, 94; auth, Bagues, 96. **CONTACT ADDRESS** Dept of French, Univ Toronto, 7 King's Col Cir, Toronto, ON, M5S 1A1.

CLUBB, LOUISE GEORGE
PERSONAL Born 07/22/1930, New York, NY, m, 1954 **DISCIPLINE** COMPARATIVE LITERATURE **EDUCATION** George Washington Univ, AB, 52, MA, 56; Columbia Univ, PhD(comp lit), 63. **CAREER** Instr English, Univ Md, 56-57 & fall 60, instr English & comp lit, 61-62; asst prof English & comp lit, George Washington Univ, 62-64, vis asst prof Ital & comp lit, 64-65, assoc prof, 66-70, PROF ITAL & COMP LIT, UNIV CALIF, BERKELEY, 70-, Guggenheim fel, 65-66; res fel, Univ Calif, Berkeley, 73; mem nat screening comt, Inst Int Educ, 72; Am Philos Soc grant, 72-73; Am Conn Learned Soc fel, 77. **MEMBERSHIPS** Dante Soc Am; Renaissance Soc Am; Am Asn Advan Humanities; Am Comp Lit Asn; Am Asn Teacher Ital. **RESEARCH** Chivalric epic; Renaissance literature; Renaissance drama in England, Italy, Spain and France. **SELECTED PUBLICATIONS** Auth, Can We Speak of Erudite Comedy at the Time of Shakespeare--A Discussion of the Theories of Clubb, Louise, George and Her Response, Lettere Italiane, Vol 0044, 92; Un Repertorio di Una Compagnia della Commedia Dellarte-- Note On Ms-180 of the Spencer Collection of the New-York-Public-Library, Lettere Italiane, Vol 0047, 95. **CONTACT ADDRESS** Dept of Comp Lit, Univ of Calif, Berkeley, CA, 94720.

COADY, JAMES MARTIN
PERSONAL Born 08/14/1941, Kokomo, IN, m, 1966, 1 child **DISCIPLINE** LINGUISTICS **EDUCATION** St Meinrad Col, BA, 63; Ind Univ, Bloomington, IN, 67, PhD(ling), 73. **CAREER** Teacher hist, Bennett High Sch, Marion, Ind, 63-64; instr English, Am Univ Beirut, 67-69; Assoc Prof Ling, Ohio Univ, 71-, Chmn Dept, 80- **MEMBERSHIPS** Ling Soc Am; Teacher English to Speakers Other Lang; Int Reading Asn; Am Asn Applied Ling. **RESEARCH** Reading; vocabulary acquisition; teaching English to speakers of other languages. **SELECTED PUBLICATIONS** Auth, Autonomous Learning of Vocabulary through Extensive Reading, Univ Toulouse (France), 94; author of several articles in, and co-editor of: Second-Language Vocabulary Acquisition: A Rationale for Pedagogy, Cambridge Univ Press, 97; auth, The Development of Lexis in Writing, In: Vom Gelenkten zum Freien Schreiben im Fremdsprachen-Unterricht, Peter Lang Press, 97; author of numerous other articles. **CONTACT ADDRESS** Dept of Ling, Ohio Univ, Athens, OH, 45701-2979. **EMAIL** coady@ohiou.edu

COATES, CARROL F.
DISCIPLINE FRENCH LANGUAGE AND LITERATURE **EDUCATION** Univ OK, BA; MA; Yale Univ, PhD. **CAREER** Fac, SUNY Binghamton. **HONORS AND AWARDS** Ed, Jour Haitian Studies; assoc ed, Callaloo--A Journal of African-American, Caribbean, and African Arts and Letters. **RESEARCH** Poetic structuration of metrical discourse (17th and 19th-century French literature); semiotics of theater (Quebec theater); francophone lit, with concentration on Haitian lit, cult, hist; grammatical and stylistic analysis. **SELECTED PUBLICATIONS** Ed, Transl from Francophone Literature of North Africa, West Africa, and the Caribbean in CARAF Bks series, UP VA. **CONTACT ADDRESS** SUNY Binghamton, PO Box 6000, Binghamton, NY, 13902-6000. **EMAIL** ccoates@binghamton.edu

COBB, EULALIA BENEJAM
PERSONAL Born 10/03/1944, Barcelona, Spain, m, 1967, 2 children **DISCIPLINE** FRENCH, SPANISH **EDUCATION** Birmingham-Southern Col, BA, 66; Univ NC, MA, 68; Univ Ala, PhD(Romance lang), 72. **CAREER** Instr French & Span, Univ Ala, 71-72; instr French, Stillman Col, 72-73; inst assoc, Inst Higher Educ, Univ Ala, 73-74; ASSOC PROF FRENCH, WESTERN MD COL, 74-, Affirmative action officer, Western Md Col, 77-78; writer, 81- **MEMBERSHIPS** AAUP; Southeastern Mod Lang Asn. **RESEARCH** Jean Anouilh; surrealism; French women writers. **SELECTED PUBLICATIONS** Auth, A Necessary Rigor--The Implications of Multiculturalism for Academic-Standards, Proteus, Vol 0010, 93. **CONTACT ADDRESS** Dept of Foreign Lang, Western Maryland Col, Westminster, MD, 21157.

COBBS, ALFRED LEON
PERSONAL Born 09/12/1943, Pamplin, VA **DISCIPLINE** GERMAN LANGUAGE & LITERATURE **EDUCATION** Berea Col, BA, 66; Univ Mo, Columbia, MA, 68; Univ Cincinnati, PhD(German), 74. **CAREER** Instr, Univ Cincinnati, 69-73; asst prof, Univ Va, 73-79; asst prof German, Wayne State Univ, 79-; asst prof, Wayne State Univ, 79-84; assoc prof, 84-. **HONORS AND AWARDS** Fulbright Summer Seminars, Federal Republic of Germany, 74, 83; President's Award for Excellence in Teaching, Wayne State Univ, 84. **MEMBERSHIPS** MLA; Am Asn Teachers German;literature of minorities in Germany; foreign language pedagogy. **RESEARCH** German-American literary relations; modern German literature; imagology in literature. **SELECTED PUBLICATIONS** Auth, Teaching Kafka's Verwandlung on the intermediate level, Unterrichtspraxis, 80; Image of the Black in German literature, The Harold Jantz Collection, Duke Univ Ctr Int Studies, 81; contribr, Articles on Ulrich von Hutten & several lesser-known writers, Deutsches Literatur-Lexikon, 81; auth, The Image of America in Postwar German Literature: Reflections and Perceptions, Peter Lang Verlag, 82. **CONTACT ADDRESS** Dept of Romance & Germanic Lang, Wayne State Univ, 451 Manoogian, Detroit, MI, 48202-3919. **EMAIL** a.cobbs@wayne.edu

COBLIN, WELDON SOUTH
PERSONAL Born 02/26/1944, Lexington, KY, m, 1970, 2 children **DISCIPLINE** CHINESE AND SINO-TIBETAN LINGUISTICS **EDUCATION** Univ Wash, BA, 67, PhD(Chinese), 72. **CAREER** Teaching assoc, Univ Wash, 72-73; asst prof, 73-78, ASSOC PROF CHINESE, UNIV IOWA, 78-, Chmn Dept Asian Lang & Lit, 81- **MEMBERSHIPS** Am Orient Soc; Ling Soc Am; Asn Asian Studies, Soc Study Early China. **RESEARCH** Chinese historical linguistics; Tibetan historical linguistics. **SELECTED PUBLICATIONS** Auth, A New Approach to Chinese Historical Linguistics, Jour Amer Oriental Soc, Vol 0115, 95; Marginalia on 2 Translations of the Qieyun Preface, Jour Chinese Ling, Vol 0024, 96; 2 Notes on the London Long-Scroll, Bulletin Sch Oriental and African Stud-Univ London, Vol 0058, 95; Northwest Reflections on the Yunjing, Toung Pao, Vol 0082, 96; Proto-Chinese and Sino-Tibetan, Jour Chinese Ling, Vol 0024, 96. **CONTACT ADDRESS** Dept of Asian Lang & Lit, Univ of Iowa, Iowa City, IA, 52240.

COCOZZELLA, PETER
PERSONAL Born 11/20/1937, Monacilioni, Italy, m, 1964, 1 child **DISCIPLINE** SPANISH LANGUAGE AND LITERATURE **EDUCATION** R Regis Col (Colo), AB, 59; St Louis Univ, PhD(Span), 66. **CAREER** Teacher high sch, Colo, 59-60; from instr to asst prof Span, Univ Mo-St Louis, 65-67; asst prof, Dartmouth Col, 67-70; asst prof, 70-73, ASSOC PROF SPAN, STATE UNIV NY, BINGHAMTON, 73- **MEMBERSHIPS** MLA; Am Asn Teachers Span & Port; NAmer Catalan Soc. **RESEARCH** Castilian and Catalan literatures of the 15th century. **SELECTED PUBLICATIONS** Auth, Les Hores Bruixes, World Lit Today, Vol 0069, 95; Diary 1979-1980, World Lit Today, Vol 0069, 95; Elsa Scheider--Spanish, Estreno-Cuadernos del Teatro Espanol Contemporaneo, Vol 0019, 93; Ipotesi di Giustizia nel Principato di A, World Lit Today, Vol 0067, 93; Oe, Oe, Oe--Spanish, Estreno-Cuadernos del Teatro Espanol Contemporaneo, Vol 0023, 97; Tocant a Ma..., World Lit Today, Vol 0068, 94; Complete Works, Vol 5--Catalan, World Lit Today, Vol 0067, 93; Si Prega di Non Disturbare--Italian, World Lit Today, Vol 0070, 96; La Revoca, World Lit Today, Vol 0067, 93; Pel Bell Nord Glacat--Catalan, World Lit Today, Vol 0070, 96; Il Cigno, World Lit Today, Vol 0069, 95; Attesa sul Mare, World Lit Today, Vol 0070, 96; Les Illes Grogues, World Lit Today, Vol 0070, 96. **CONTACT ADDRESS** Dept of Romance Lang, State Univ NY, Binghamton, NY, 13901.

COELHO, CARL
DISCIPLINE NEUROLOGIC BASES OF SPEECH AND LANGUAGE **EDUCATION** Mich State Univ, BA, 74; Univ Ariz, MS, 76; Univ Conn, PhD, 82. **CAREER** Asst prof, Univ Conn. **RESEARCH** Neurologic disorders of speech and language in adults. **SELECTED PUBLICATIONS** Auth, Discourse Deficits Following Traumatic Brain Injury: A Critical Review of the Recent Literature, Aphasiology, 95; coauth, The Assessment of Limb Apraxia: An Investigation of Task Effects and Their Cause, Brain and Cognition, 96; Treatment Efficacy for Cognitive-Communication Disorders Resulting from Traumatic Brain Injury in Adults, J Speech and Hearing Res, 96; Application of Semantic Feature Analysis as a Treatment for Aphasic Dysnomia, Amer J Speech-Lang Pathology, 95; Impairments of Discourse Abilities and Executive Functions in Traumatically Brain Injured Adults, Brain Injury, 95. **CONTACT ADDRESS** Dept of Communication Sci, Univ of Connecticut, 850 Bolton Rd, Storrs, CT, 06269-1085. **EMAIL** coelho@uconnvm.uconn.edu

COFFEY, JEROME EDWARD
PERSONAL Born 08/04/1940, Elmira, NY, m, 1964, 2 children **DISCIPLINE** ENGLISH LANGUAGE AND LINGUISTICS **EDUCATION** Canisius Col, AB, 62; State Univ NY, Buffalo, MA, 65, PhD(English lang), 68. **CAREER** Asst prof English, Western Ill Univ, 66-68 & State Univ NY Col, Brockport, 68-72; ASSOC PROF ENGLISH, MONT STATE UNIV, 72-. **MEMBERSHIPS** MLA; Ling Soc Am. **RESEARCH** Oral poetry in Old and Middle English; the Faeroese language and bardic poetry. **SELECTED PUBLICATIONS** Auth, Barbara, Scandinavian Stud, Vol 0066, 94; The Scholar and the Web--Electronic Resources for the Scandinavian Scholar on the World-Wide-Web, Scandinavian Stud, Vol 0067, 95. **CONTACT ADDRESS** Dept of English, Montana State Univ, Bozeman, MT, 59715.

COFFTA, DAVID J.
DISCIPLINE CLASSICAL PHILOLOGY **EDUCATION** Adjunct assoc prof, Canisius Col. **MEMBERSHIPS** APA; CAMWS. **SELECTED PUBLICATIONS** Auth, Programmatic Synthesis in Horace, Odes 3 13 in Collection Latomus, forthcoming; Programme and Persona in Horace Odes 1 5, in Eranos, forthcoming. **CONTACT ADDRESS** Classics Dept, Canisius Col, 2001 Main St, Buffalo, NY, 14208. **EMAIL** cofftad@canisius.edu

COHEN, ALVIN PHILIP
PERSONAL Born 12/12/1937, Los Angeles, CA, 2 children **DISCIPLINE** CHINESE PHILOLOGY & CULTURAL HISTORY **EDUCATION** Univ Calif, Berkeley, BS, 60, MA, 66, PhD(Orient Lang), 71. **CAREER** Lectr Orient Lang, Univ Calif, Davis, 70-71; asst prof, 71-77, assoc prof Chinese, Univ Mass, Amherst 77-83; actg bibliogr Orient Collection, Univ Mass, Amherst, 71-. **HONORS AND AWARDS** Fulbright-Hays Fel, 68-69; China and Inner Asia Council of the Assoc for Asian Studies grant, 95-97. **MEMBERSHIPS** Am Orient Soc; Chinese Lang Teachers Asn; Soc Study Chinese Relig; Assn for Asian Studies. **RESEARCH** Chinese historiography; Chinese folk religion. **SELECTED PUBLICATIONS** Auth, A bibliography of writings contributory to the study of Chinese folk religion, J Am Acad Relig, 75; Grammar Notes for Introductory Classical Chinese, Chinese Materials Ctr, 75, 2nd ed, 80; Humorous anecdotes in Chinese historical texts & Notes on a Chinese workingclass bookshelf, J Am Orient Soc, 76; Coercing the rain deities in ancient China, Hist Relig, 78; ed, Selected Works of Peter A Boodberg, Univ Calif, Berkeley, 79; Legend, Lore and Religion in China, Chinese Materials Ctr, 79. **CONTACT ADDRESS** Asian Lang Dept, Univ of Massachusetts, Amherst, MA, 01003-0002.

COHEN, WALTER ISAAC
PERSONAL Born 10/21/1949, New York, NY, 3 children **DISCIPLINE** COMPARATIVE LITERATURE **EDUCATION** Stanford Univ, BA, 71; Univ Calif, Berkeley, MA, 74, PhD(comp lit), 80. **CAREER** Prof Comp Lit, Cornell Univ, 92-; dean grad school, Cornell Univ, 93-; vprovost & dean grad school, 98-. **HONORS AND AWARDS** Clark Distinguished Teaching Award, Cornell, 86; Mellon Professorship In Teaching, 88-90. **MEMBERSHIPS** MLA; Marxist Lit Group. **RESEARCH** History of European Lit. **SELECTED PUBLICATIONS** Auth, Drama of a Nation: Public Theater in Renaissance England and Spain, Cornell Univ Press, 85; ed, The Norton Shakespeare, Norton, 97. **CONTACT ADDRESS** Grad Sch, Cornell Univ, 384 Gladwell Hall, Ithaca, NY, 14853-6201. **EMAIL** wic1@cornell.edu

COHN, DORRIT
PERSONAL Born 08/09/1924, Vienna, Austria, 2 children **DISCIPLINE** GERMAN AND COMPARATIVE LITERATURE **EDUCATION** Radcliffe Col, BA, 45, MA, 46; Stanford Univ, PhD(Ger), 64. **CAREER** From asst prof to prof Ger, Ind Univ, Bloomington, 64-71; actg chmn, Ger Dept, 77-78, PROF GER, HARVARD UNIV, 71-, Guggenheim Found fel, 70-71; mem adv comt, PMLA, 75-79; chmn div 20th century Ger lit, MLA, 76-77; mem ed adv bd, German Quart, 78-; vis sr fel, Coun of Humanities, Princeton Univ, 82- **MEMBERSHIPS** Am Asn Teachers Ger; Am Comp Lit Asn; MLA; Acad Lit Studies. **RESEARCH** Modern novel; 19th and 20th century German literature; narrative theory. **SELECTED PUBLICATIONS** Auth, Kafka and Hofmannsthal, Mod Austrian Lit, Vol 0030, 97; Ein-Eigentlich-Traumerischer-Doppelsinn--Mann,Thomas-Telling Timelessness in der Zauberberg, Germanisch-Romanische Monatsschrift, Vol 0044, 94; Optics and Power in the Novel--Seltzer,Mark and Bender,James and Their Critical-Studies of the Panopticon, New Lit Hist, Vol 0026, 95; Freud Case-Histories and the Question of Fictionality, Oxford Ger Stud, Vol 0025, 96; To See or Not to See--Invisibility, Clairvoyance, and Revisions of History in Invisible Man and la Casa de los Espiritus, Comp Lit Stud, Vol 0033, 96; Reply to Bender,John and Seltzer,Mark, New Lit Hist, Vol 0026, 95. **CONTACT ADDRESS** Dept of Germanic Lang, Harvard Univ, Boylston Hall, Cambridge, MA, 02138.

COHN, ROBERT G.
PERSONAL Born 09/05/1921, Richmond, VA, m, 1947, 2 children **DISCIPLINE** FRENCH **EDUCATION** Univ Va, BA, 43; Yale Univ, MA, 47, PhD, 49. **CAREER** Founding ed, Yale French Studies, 48-49, instr French, Yale Univ, 49-50; Fulbright fel, 50-51; asst prof French, Swarthmore Col, 52-54 & Vassar Col, 54-57; assoc prof, 59-64, PROF FRENCH, STANFORD UNIV, 64-, Guggenheim fel, 56-57; in charge confs French, Univ NY, 54-57; fels, Am Coun Learned Soc & Nat Endowment for Humanities, 69-70; assoc ed, Stanford Fr Rev & Stanford French & Italian Studies. **MEMBERSHIPS** MLA. **RESEARCH** French poetry; 19th and 20th century French literature. **SELECTED PUBLICATIONS** Auth, Mallarme Prolongation--A Reply to Furbank,P.N., NY Rev Bk(s), Vol 0042, 95; Mallarme Wake, New Lit Hist, Vol 0026, 95. **CONTACT ADDRESS** Dept of French & Ital, Stanford Univ, Stanford, CA, 94305.

COLANERI, JOHN NUNZIO
PERSONAL Born 01/08/1930, New York, NY, m, 1967, 1 child **DISCIPLINE** ITALIAN **EDUCATION** City Col New York, BA, 52; Columbia Univ, MA, 54, PhD(Ital), 68. **CAREER** Prof Ital & Chmn Dept Mod Lang, Iona Col, 59-, Part-time lectr Ital, Col New Rochelle, 61- **MEMBERSHIPS** Ital Teachers Asn (pres, 69-71); Am Asn Teachers Span & Port. **SELECTED PUBLICATIONS** Auth, Fra Cristoforon and L'innominato: Two of a kind?, J NY State Fed Foreign Lang Teachers, 5/68; translr, Giovannitti, the United Nations silver anniversary, Thought, summer 70; auth, Reflection of a man: Guido Cavalcanti, Paideuma, winter 72; Edition of Lezzioni d'amore, Fink, Munich, 73; co-ed (with G Lipton), Italian English--English Italian Bilingual Dict, 80, 2nd ed, 82; Italian-English/English-Italian Bilingual Dictionary, 89, Barrons, 2nd ed, revised, 98; 501 Italian Verbs, Barrons, 92; auth, The Immigrant Mother, Ital Am Rev, 93. **CONTACT ADDRESS** Dept of Mod Lang, Iona Col, 715 North Ave, New Rochelle, NY, 10801-1890.

COLBY-HALL, ALICE MARY
PERSONAL Born 02/25/1932, Portland, ME, m, 1976 **DISCIPLINE** MEDIEVAL FRENCH LITERATURE **EDUCATION** Colby Col, BA, 53; Middlebury Col, MA, 54; Columbia Univ, PhD, 62. **CAREER** Teacher high sch, Maine, 54-55; teacher French, Gould Acad, Bethel, Maine, 55-57; lectr, Columbia Univ, 59-60; from instr to assoc prof Romance Studies, 62-75, Prof Romance Studies, Cornell Univ, 75-. **HONORS AND AWARDS** Fulbright grant, 53-54; NEH Fel, 84-85; recipient, Medaille des Amis d'Orange, 85; Chevalier des Arts et Lettre, French Govt, 97. **MEMBERSHIPS** Mediaeval Acad Am; MLA; Soc Rencesvals; Int Arthurian Soc; Acad de Vaucluse; Les Amis d'Orange; Soc Guilhem IX. **RESEARCH** Chretien de Troyes; the style of medieval French literary texts; William cycle epics. **SELECTED PUBLICATIONS** Auth, The Portrait in 12th Century French Literature: An Example of the Stylistic Originality of Chretien de Troyes, Droz, 65; In Search of the Lost Epics of the Lower Rhone Valley, Olifant, 80/81; Frustration and Fulfillment: The Double Ending of the Bel Inconnu, Yale Fr Studies, 84; William of Orange in the Canso de la Crosada, Magister Regis: Studies in Honor of Robert Earl Kaske, 86; L'Heraldique au service de la linguistique: le cas du cor nier de Guillaume, Au carrefour des routes d'Europe: la chanson de geste, 87; Guillaume d'Orange sur un noveau sceau medieval de l'abbaye de Gellone et la vache pie de Chateauneuf-de-Gadagne, Etudes sur l'Herault, 93. **CONTACT ADDRESS** Dept of Romance Studies, Cornell Univ, Goldwin Smith Hall, Ithaca, NY, 14853-3201. **EMAIL** amc12@cornell.edu

COLE, PETER
PERSONAL Born 08/01/1941, Miami Beach, FL, m, 1958, 2 children **DISCIPLINE** LINGUISTICS, LANGUAGE TEACHING **EDUCATION** Bard Col, AB, 62; Southern Ill Univ, Carbondale, MA, 71; Univ Ill, Urbana, PhD(ling), 73. **CAREER** Instr English, Haifa Univ, Haifa, 67-68 & Southern Ill Univ, Carbondale, 69-73; asst prof, 73-80, ASSOC PROF LING, UNIV ILL, URBANA-CHAMPAIGN, 80- **MEMBERSHIPS** Linguistic Soc Am. **RESEARCH** Syntax and foreign language instruction; semantics; Hebrew and Quechua. **SELECTED PUBLICATIONS** Auth, The Art of the Indigenous, Queens Quart, Vol 0101, 94; Defending the Bottom Line--Hurst,Robert and Patitucci, John Talk to Down-Beat, Down Beat, Vol 0062, 95; The Yellow-Jackets--We Gave Up Writing for Airplay, Down Beat, Vol 0064, 97; Redman,Joshua--So, You Wanna Be a Jazz Star, Down Beat, Vol 0060, 93; Hip-Hop Herbie--Hancock, Herbie Latest Work-In-Progress Dis Is Da Drum, Down Beat, Vol 0061, 94; Miller, Marcus--Solo Status, Down Beat, Vol 0061, 94; Duke,George--Radio Formats Be Damned, Down Beat, Vol 0062, 95; Marienthal, Eric, Down Beat, Vol 0060, 93. **CONTACT ADDRESS** Dept of Ling, Univ of Ill at Urbana-Champaign, Urbana, IL, 61801.

COLECCHIA, FRANCES
PERSONAL Pittsburgh, PA **DISCIPLINE** MODERN LANGUAGES **EDUCATION** Duquesne Univ, BEd, 47; Univ Pittsburgh, MLitt, 49, PhD, 54. **CAREER** Dir lang lab prog, 60-72, PROF SPAN, DUQUESNE UNIV, 47-, CHMN MOD LANG DEPT, 77-, Assoc ed, Estudios, 51-55; V Cicto Int fel, Cent Univ Eduador, 62; Fulbright lectr grant, Colombia, 63-64; vis prof Span novel, Mt Mercy Col, 68; ed, Nalld Sec Sch Dir Pa, 69; guest lectr Latin Am lit, Educ Prof Develop Assistance Inst, ECarolina Univ, 69; grant, US Off Educ Inst, Crisis: Women in Higher Educ, 71; assoc ed, Garcia Lorca Rev, 73-; coordr res prog, Women Ethnicity and Mental Health, 75-77. **HONORS AND AWARDS** Am-Ital Women of Achievement Award, 69. **MEMBERSHIPS** MLA; Inst Int Lit Iberoam; Am Asn Univ Women; Nat Coun Admin Women Educ; Am Asn Teachers Span & Port. **RESEARCH** Latin American theatre; theatre of Garcia Lorca; contemporary Latin American literature of protest. **SELECTED PUBLICATIONS** Auth, Blood Wedding, Yerma, and the House of Bernarda Alba, Garcialorca Tragic Trilogy, Estreno-Cuadernos del Teatro Espanol Contemporaneo, Vol 0019, 93; The History of the Commedia-Dellarte in Modern Hispanic Literature with Special Attention to the Work of Garcia-Lorca, Estreno-Cuadernos del Teatro Espanol Contemporaneo, Vol 0023, 97; Love Customs in 18th-Century Spain, Critica Hispanica, Vol 0017, 95; The Answer la Respuesta--English, Spanish, Critica Hispanica, Vol 0018, 96; An Introduction to Spanish-Amer Lit 3rd-Edition, Critica Hispanica, Vol 0018, 96; The State of Theater in Spain--Spanish , Estreno-Cuadernos del Teatro Espanol Contemporaneo, Vol 0023, 97; Celestinas Brood, Continuities of the Baroque in Spanish and Latin-American Literatures, Critica Hispanica, Vol 0016, 94; Funeral En Teruel, Modern Evocations of an Ancient Legend--A Compatarive Study Between Tirso-De-Molina, Hartzenbush and Monteshuidobro, Critica Hispanica, Vol 0016, 94; Lorca Drawings and Poem, Critica Hispanica, Vol 0018, 96; A Selected Bibliography of Studies on Garcia Lorca,Federico la Casa de Bernarda Alba 1985-1994, Estreno-Cuadernos del Teatro Espanol Contemporaneo, Vol 0021, 95; Federico--Una Historia Distinta, Estreno-Cuadernos del Teatro Espanol Contemporaneo, Vol 0021, 95; An Introduction to Spanish-Amer Lit 3rd-Edition, Critica Hispanica, Vol 0018, 96; Writing, Private Space--Laforet, Matute, Moix, Tusquets, Riera and Roig by Themselves--Spanish, Critica Hispanica, Vol 0015, 93. **CONTACT ADDRESS** Dept of Mod Lang, Duquesne Univ, Pittsburgh, PA, 15219.

COLILLI, PAUL
DISCIPLINE ITALIAN LITERATURE **EDUCATION** Univ Toronto, PhD. **RESEARCH** Renaissance; modern-to-contemporary lit. **SELECTED PUBLICATIONS** Auth, Signs of the Hermetic Imagination, 94; auth, La poetica dell'aletheia nell'Africa del Petrarca, 93; auth, Poliziano's Science of Tropes, 89; auth, Petrarch's Allegories of Writing, 88. **CONTACT ADDRESS** Dept of Foreign Languages, Laurentian Univ, 935 Ramsey Lake Rd, Sudbury, ON, P3E 2C6.

COLKER, MARVIN L.
PERSONAL Born 03/19/1927, Pittsburgh, PA, m, 1959, 1 child **DISCIPLINE** LATIN **EDUCATION** Univ Pitts, BA summa cum laude, 48; Harvard Univ, PhD 51. **CAREER** Univ Virginia, inst, asst prof, assoc prof, prof, ch dept classics, prof emeritus, 53 to 98-. **HONORS AND AWARDS** Sheldon Fel Harvard; Litt D hon Trinity Col; Guggenheim Fel; Fulbright Fel; BSA Fel; Phi Beta Kappa. **MEMBERSHIPS** MAA; MARC; MLA; CAMW&S. **RESEARCH** Medieval latin; latin palaeography; cataloguing of medieval manuscripts. **SELECTED PUBLICATIONS** Auth, Latin poems from Paris Codex B N lat 8433, Medievalia et Humanistica, 58; De nobilitate animi, Mediaeval Studies, 61; Richard of Saint Victor and the anonymous of Bridlington, Traditio, 62; Analecta Dublinensia, Mediaeval Acad Am, 75; A Hagiographic polemic, Mediaeval Studies, 77; Galteri De Castellione Alexandreis, Antenore, 78; Trinity College Dublin Library: Descriptive Catalogue of the Medieval and Renaissance Latin Manuscripts, 2 vols, 91. **CONTACT ADDRESS** Dept of Classics, Virginia Univ, 105 Westminster Rd, Charlottesville, VA, 22901. **EMAIL** mlcolker@cstone.net

COLLINS, DEREK B.
PERSONAL Born 08/24/1965, Washington, DC, m, 1990, 2 children **DISCIPLINE** COMPARATIVE LIT/CLASSICS; FOLKLORE & MYTHOLOGY **EDUCATION** Univ CA, Los Angeles, MA, 91; Harvard Univ, PhD, 97. **CAREER** ASST PROF CLASSICS, UNIV TEXAS AT AUSTIN, 97-. **HONORS AND AWARDS** Nat Academy of Sciences, Ford Found, Doctoral Dissertation fel, 9/96--6/97. **MEMBERSHIPS** Am Philos Asn; Classical Asn of the Middle West and South; Am Folklore Soc. **RESEARCH** Greek lit; comparative lit (German); witchcraft. **SELECTED PUBLICATIONS** Trans, Greek selections in the Appendix to Claude Calame, The Craft of Poetic Speech in Ancient Greece, Cornell Univ Press, 95; auth, The Myth and Ritual of Ezili Freda in Hurston's Their Eyes Were Watching God, Western Folklore 55, 96; trans with J. Orion, Claude Calame, Young Women's Choruses in Ancient Greece: Their Morphology, Religious Role, and Social Functions, Lanham, MD, Rowman & Littlefield Pubs, 97; auth, Fatum, in the Dictionaire International des Termes Litteraitres, gen ed, Jean-Marie Grassin, A. Francke-Berne, Saur-Vg Pub, Berne, Munich, Paris, New York, 97; On the Aesthetics of the Deceiving Self in Nietzsche, Pindar, and Theognis, Nietzsche-Studien 26, 97; Review of Jacob Rabinowitz, The Rotting Goddess: The Origin of the Witch in Classical Antiquity, Scholia 7 (ns), 16, 98; Immortal Armor: The Concept of Alke in Archaic Greek Poetry, Lanham, MD, Rowman & Littlefield Pubs, 98; Hesiod and the Divine Voice of the Muses, Arethusa, forthcoming, 99. **CONTACT ADDRESS** Dept of Classics, Univ Texas at Austin, 123 Waggener Hall, Austin, TX, 78712-1181. **EMAIL** dbcollins@mail.utexas.edu

COLLINS, K.K.
PERSONAL Born 09/15/1947, Union City, TN, m, 1970, 1 child **DISCIPLINE** ENGLISH LANGUAGE AND LITERATURE **EDUCATION** Col William & Mary, AB, 69; Vanderbilt Univ, PhD(English), 76. **CAREER** Lectr, 76-77, asst prof, 77-82, ASSOC PROF ENGLISH, SOUTHERN ILL UNIV, CARBONDALE, 82- **HONORS AND AWARDS** Fel, Woodrow Wilson Diss, Nat Endowment Hum Summer, Mellon Sem; Sch of Criticism and Theory Sch; Am Philos Soc grant. **MEMBERSHIPS** MLA; Mod Humanities Res Asn; Dickens Soc. **RESEARCH** Nineteenth-century English literature; literature and philosophy; literature and science. **SELECTED PUBLICATIONS** Auth, Lewes,G.H.--A Life, Nineteenth Century Prose, Vol 0020, 93; auth, Thomas Woolner and The Oxford and Cambridge Magazine, Notes and Quotes, 83; auth, The British and Foreign Rev, Brit Lit Mags, 84; coauth, Lewes at Colonus: An early Victorian view of translation from the Greek, mod Lang Rev, 87; auth, Reading George Eliot reading Lewes's obituaries, Mod Philol, 87. **CONTACT ADDRESS** Dept of English, Southern Ill Univ, Carbondale, IL, 62901-4300. **EMAIL** kkcoll@siu.edu

COLOMBAT, ANDRE P.
DISCIPLINE FRENCH **EDUCATION** Universite Lyon II, Fr, MA ; Washington Univ, PhD. **CAREER** Assoc prof. **RESEARCH** Bilingual writers, Beckett, Green, Bianciotti, Semprun, Huidobro, del Castillo, Wiesel, Feyderman, Agosin, Chavez; contemporary philosophy and criticism, Deleuze, French film and the Holocaust; Modern France and francophone literature. **SELECTED PUBLICATIONS** Auth, The Holocaust In French Film, 93; Deleuze et la litterature, 90. **CONTACT ADDRESS** Dept of Foreign Languages, Loyola Col, 4501 N Charles St, Baltimore, MD, 21210. **EMAIL** apc@loyola.edu

COMPAGNON, ANTOINE
PERSONAL Born 07/20/1950, Brussels, Belgium, s **DISCIPLINE** FRENCH LITERATURE **EDUCATION** Ancien eleve de l'Ecole polytechnique, Paris, 73; Ingenieur des Ponts et Chaussees, Paris, 75; Licence de Lettres modernes, Univ Paris, 7, 72, maitrise, 73, doctorat de troisieme cycle, 77; Docteur es Lettres, 85. **CAREER** Attache de recherche, Ctr Nat de la Recherche Sci, Paris, 75-78; Maitre de conferences, Ecole polytechnique, Paris, 78-80; prof, Inst Fr du Royaume-Uni, London, 80-81; maitre-asst, Univ Rouen, 81-84; maitre de conferences, Univ Rouen, 84-85; prof of french, Columbia Univ, 85-91; prof, Univ du Mans, 89-90; Blanche W. Knopf prof of french and comparative lit, Columbia Univ, 91-; chair, dept of french and romance philol, 92-94; prof, Univ de Paris IV-Sorbonne, 94-. **HONORS AND AWARDS** Pensionnaire de la Fondation Thiers, Paris, 75-78; fel, John Simon Guggenheim Memorial Found, 88; visiting fel, All Souls Col, Oxford, 94; Chevalier des Palmes acad, 95; fel, Amer Acad of Arts and Sci, 97. **SELECTED PUBLICATIONS** Auth, Le Demon de la theorie. Litterature et sens commun, Paris, Editions du Seuil, 98; auth, Connaissez-vous Brunetiere? Enquete sur un antidreyfusard et ses amis, Paris, Editions du Seuil, 97; auth, Chat en poche: Montaigne et l'allegorie, Paris, Editions du Seuil, 93; article, Les Classiques decoiffes, Critique, 615-616, 98; article, Charles Baudelaire, Les Fleurs du mal, Paris, L'Ecole des lettres, Editions du Seuil, 93; co-auth, L'Esprit de l'Europe, Paris, Flammarion, 3 vol, 93. **CONTACT ADDRESS** Columbia Univ, 513 Philosophy Hall, New York, NY, 10027. **EMAIL** amc6@columbia.edu

COMPITELLO, MALCOLM ALAN
PERSONAL Born 02/09/1946, Brooklyn, NY, m, 1977, 1 child **DISCIPLINE** SPANISH LANGUAGE AND LITERATURE **EDUCATION** St John's Univ, BA, 68, MA, 70; Ind Univ, PhD(Span), 77. **CAREER** Asst prof, 77-81, ASSOC PROF SPAN, MICH STATE UNIV, 81-, Ed, The Am Hisp, 75- & An Annual Bibliog Post-Civil-War Span Fiction, 77-; vis prof, Span Sch, Middlebury Col, 80. **MEMBERSHIPS** Am Asn Teachers Span; MLA. **RESEARCH** Contemporary Spanish literature; literary sociology; contemporary Spanish cultural history. **SELECTED PUBLICATIONS** Auth, Reflections on the Act of Narrating, Benet, Vargasllosa and Dacunha,Euclides, Insula-Revista de Letras y Ciencias Humanas, Vol 0048, 93. **CONTACT ADDRESS** Dept Romance Lang, Michigan State Univ, East Lansing, MI, 48824.

CONANT, JONATHAN BRENDAN
PERSONAL Born 12/16/1941, Hartford, CT, m, 1964, 1 child **DISCIPLINE** GERMANIC PHILOLOGY, PEDAGOGY **EDUCATION** Yale Univ, AB, 64, MPhil, 68, PhD(Ger), 69. **CAREER** Asst prof Ger, Brown Univ, 69-75, vis assoc prof, Univ Minn, Minneapolis, 75-77, ASSOC PROF FOREIGN LANG & LIT, UNIV MINN, DULUTH, 77-, Assoc ed, Unterrichtspraxis, 77- **MEMBERSHIPS** Am Asn Teachers Ger. **RESEARCH** Old Icelandic poetry; runology and foreign language pedagogy. **SELECTED PUBLICATIONS** Auth, The Rhythms of Drottkvaett and Other Old Icelandic Meters, Lang, Vol 0070, 94. **CONTACT ADDRESS** Dept of Foreign Lang & Lit, Univ of Minn, 10 University Dr, Duluth, MN, 55812-2496.

CONAWAY BONDANELLA, JULIA
DISCIPLINE ITALIAN LITERATURE **EDUCATION** Univ Oregon, PhD, 73. **CAREER** Assoc prof. **HONORS AND AWARDS** Tchg Awd. **MEMBERSHIPS** Am Asn Italian Studies; Nat Collegiate Honors Coun. **RESEARCH** Medieval and Renaissance literature; comparative literature; history of ideas; Petrarchism. **SELECTED PUBLICATIONS** Auth, Petrarch's Visions and Their Renaissance Analogs; The Dictionary of Italian Literature; The Italian Renaissance Reader; Giorgio Vasari's The Lives of the Artists. **CONTACT ADDRESS** Dept of French and Italian, Indiana Univ, Bloomington, 300 N Jordan Ave, Bloomington, IN, 47405.

CONNER, MAURICE WAYNE
PERSONAL Born 08/20/1938, Houston, TX, m, 1966 **DISCIPLINE** GERMANIC LANGUAGE & LITERATURE **EDUCATION** Univ Tex-Arlington, BA, 64; Univ Nebr-Lincoln, MA, 66, PhD(Ger), 73. **CAREER** Instr English as second lang, Stuttgarter Fremdsprachenschule, 63-64; instr Ger, Univ Wis-Green Bay, 66-68; instr, 71-73, asst prof, 73-76, assoc prof, 76-81, asst dean, Col Arts & Sci, 79-80, vchair, Dept Foreign Lang, 81-82, prof Ger, Univ Nebr, Omaha, 81-, lab dir, Univ Wis-Green Bay, 66-68; co-ed, Schatzkammer der deutschen Sprachlehre, 75-77; consult, Central States Conf Teaching Foreign Lang, 81-82. **HONORS AND AWARDS** Fellow, Center for Great Plains Study, 95; Certificate of Merit, Am Asn of Teachers of Ger, 88; Excellence in Teaching Award, Univ of Nebr at Omaha, 84; Outstanding Ger Teacher in Nebr, 82; Who's Who in Am Education; Who's Who among America's Teachers. **MEMBERSHIPS** MLA; Am Asn Teachers Ger; Soc for Ger-Am Studies; Am Asn of Univ Profs; Ger-Texan Heritage Soc. **RESEARCH** Austrian literature; German-Americana; foreign language pedagogy. **SELECTED PUBLICATIONS** Coauth, A German Dialect Spoken in South Dakota: Swiss-Volhynian, Ger-Am Studies, 74; Language Camp Guidelines, Die Unterrichtspraxis, 74; auth, New Curricular Connections, In: The Language Connection: From the Classroom to the World, 77; From Switzerland to South Dakota: A Two Century Journey, Schatzkammer, 79; Schnitzler's Sterben and Durrenmatt's Der Meteor: Two Responses to the Prospect of Death, Ger Notes, 80; ed, New Frontiers in Foreign Language Education, 80 & A Global Approach to Foreign Language Education, 81, Nat Textbk Co; auth, Teaching Global Perspectives, Mod Lang J, 81; Thinking Styles in Foreign Language Learning, Improving College and Univ Teaching, 83; German-American Reminiscences of Early Life in Austin County, Texas, Yearbook of Ger-Am Studies, 93; Anti-German Ku Klux Klan Activity in a Texas Community, Schlatzkammer, 97. **CONTACT ADDRESS** Dept Foreign Lang, Univ Nebr, 6001 Dodge St, Omaha, NE, 68182-0002. **EMAIL** mconner@unomaha.edu

CONNER, PATRICK WAYNE
PERSONAL Born 07/31/1946, Marion Station, MD, m, 1968, 1 child **DISCIPLINE** MEDIEVAL LITERATURE, ENGLISH AND GERMANIC PHILOLOGY **EDUCATION** Univ Md, BA, 68, MA, 70, PhD(English), 75. **CAREER** Instr English, Univ Md, 70-74, instr & adv, 74-76; lectr ling, Goucher Col, 75-76; ASST PROF ENGLISH, WVA UNIV, 76-. **MEMBERSHIPS** MLA; AAUP; Early English Text Soc; Southeastern Medieval Asn. **RESEARCH** Old English literature; oral-formulaic studies; diachronic linguistics. **SELECTED PUBLICATIONS** Auth, Computing Methodologies and New Horizons in Medieval Research-French, Speculum-Jour Medieval Stud, Vol 0071, 96; Hypertext in the Last Days of the Book, Bulletin John Rylands Univ Lib Manchester, Vol 0074, 92; Computing Methodologies and New Horizons in Medieval Research--French, Speculum-Jour Medieval Stud, Vol 0071, 96. **CONTACT ADDRESS** Dept of English, West Virginia Univ, P O Box 6296, Morgantown, WV, 26506-6296.

CONNOLLY, JULIAN WELCH
PERSONAL Born 10/19/1949, Newburyport, MA, m, 1991 **DISCIPLINE** LANGUAGES & LITERATURE **EDUCATION** Harvard Col, AB, 72; Harvard Univ, AM, 74, PhD(Slavic lang & lit), 77. **CAREER** Asst Prof Slavic Lang & Lit, Univ Va, 77- **MEMBERSHIPS** Am Asn Advan Slavic Studies; Am Asn Teachers Slavic & E Europ Lang; MLA. **RESEARCH** Symbolism; early Soviet prose; Nabokov. **SELECTED PUBLICATIONS** Auth, The role of duality in Sologub's Tvorimaja Legenda, Die Welt der Slaven, 74-75; A modernist's palette: Color in the prose fiction of Eugenij Zamjatin, Russ Lang J, 79; Bunin's Petlistye Ushi: The Deformation of a Byronic Rebel, Can-Am Slavic Studies, 80; Desire and renunciation: Buddhist elements in the prose of Ivan Bunin, Can Slavonic Papers, 81; The function of literary allusion in Nabokov's Despair, Slavic and East Europ J, 82; Ivan Bunin, G K Hall & Co, 82; Nabovov's Earl, Fiction: Patterns of Self and Other, Cambridge: Cambridge Univ Press, 92; Nabovov's "Invitation to a Behead-

ing": A Critical Companion, Evanston: Northwestern Univ Press, 97. **CONTACT ADDRESS** Dept Slavic Lang & Lit, Univ Va, 109 Cabell Hall, Charlottesville, VA, 22903-3125. **EMAIL** jwc4w@virginia.edu

CONNOR, WALTER ROBERT
PERSONAL Born 07/30/1934, Worcester, MA, m, 1968, 2 children **DISCIPLINE** CLASSICAL STUDIES **EDUCATION** Hamilton Coll, BA, 56; Princeton Univ, PhD, 61. **CAREER** Instr, 60-63, Univ MI; jr fel, 63-64, Ctr Hellenic Studies; asst prof, 64-70, assoc prof, 70-72, prof, 72-89, Princeton Univ; prof, 89-present, Duke Univ; pres and dir, 89-present, Natl Humanities Ctr. **HONORS AND AWARDS** Phi Beta Kappa, Woodrow Wilson, Danforth, ACLS, and NEH fels; Fulbright fel, Univ Coll, Oxford, 56-57, Howard Behrman Award for Distinguished Achievement in Humanities, 86; LHD, Hamilton and Knox Colleges; Fel, Amer Acad Arts Sciences and Amer Phil Soc.. **MEMBERSHIPS** Howard Behrman Awar for Distinguished Achievement in the Humanities, 86; LHD Hamilton Coll, 91; fel, Amer Acad of Artist Sciences, 92-; LHD Knox Coll, 93; fel, American Philosphical Soc, 96-. **RESEARCH** Ancient Greek hist and lit **SELECTED PUBLICATIONS** Auth, The New Politicians of Fifth Century Athens, 71, reissued 92; Thucydides, 87; coauth, The Life and Miracles of Saint Luke of Steiris, 94; Theses and His City, Religion and Power in the Ancient Greek World, 96; Festival and Democracy, Democratie athenienne et Cultrue, 96. **CONTACT ADDRESS** National Humanities Ctr, 7 Alexander Dr, Res Triangle Pk, NC, 27709. **EMAIL** connor@ga.unc.edu

CONRAD, CHARLES R.
DISCIPLINE ORGANIZATIONAL COMMUNICATION, RHETORICAL THEORY **EDUCATION** Univ Kansas, PhD. **CAREER** Prof, Texas A&M Univ. **HONORS AND AWARDS** Southern Commun Journal's Outstanding Article Awd; Distinguished Tchg Awd, Asn Former Stud at Texas A&M Univ. **SELECTED PUBLICATIONS** Auth, Strategic Organizational Communication; ed, The Ethical Nexus; assoc ed, Quart J Speech. **CONTACT ADDRESS** Dept of Speech Communication, Texas A&M Univ, College Station, TX, 77843-4234. **EMAIL** csnidow@tamu.edu

CONRAD, JOSEPH LAWRENCE
PERSONAL Born 06/26/1933, Kansas City, MO, m, 1955, 3 children **DISCIPLINE** RUSSIAN LANGUAGE AND LITERATURE **EDUCATION** Univ Kans, BA, 55; Univ Tex, PhD, 61. **CAREER** From instr to asst prof, Ger & Russ, Fla State Univ, 59-62; asst prof, Univ Tex, 62-66; chmn dept Slavic lang, 66-75, PROF RUSS LANG & LIT, UNIV KANS, 66-, Int Res & Exchanges Bd scholar, Moscow Univ, spring 74; Fulbright res scholar, Zagreb, Yugoslavia, 81. **MEMBERSHIPS** Am Asn Advan Slavic Studies; Am Asn Teachers Slavic & E Europ Lang; Am Asn S Slavic Studies; Am Asn Southeast Europ Studies. **SELECTED PUBLICATIONS** Auth, Practical Sorcery--Incantations, Charms-Russian, Slavic and E Europ Jour, Vol 0037, 93; Folk Remedies in the Angara Region--Russian, Slavic and E Europ Jour, Vol 0037, 93. **CONTACT ADDRESS** Dept of Slavic Lang, Univ of Kans, Lawrence, KS, 66044.

CONROY, PETER VINCENT
PERSONAL Born 04/09/1944, New York, NY, m, 1967 **DISCIPLINE** FRENCH **EDUCATION** Queens Col, BA, 65, MA, 67; Univ of Wis, PhD, 70. **CAREER** ASST PROF, 70-74, ASSOC PROF, 74-86, PROF, 86-, UNIV OF ILL AT CHICAGO. **MEMBERSHIPS** MLA; ASECS: AATF. **RESEARCH** 18th Century novel; Montesquieu; J.J. Rousseau. **CONTACT ADDRESS** Dept of Spanish & French, M/L 315, Univ of Ill, 601 S Morgan, Chicago, IL, 60607-7117.

CONTRERAS, HELES
PERSONAL Born 08/01/1933, Victoria, Chile, m, 1955, 5 children **DISCIPLINE** SPANISH LINGUISTICS AND SYNTACTIC THEORY **EDUCATION** Concepcion Univ, Profesor de Estado, 57; Ind Univ, MA, 59, PhD(ling), 61. **CAREER** Prof ling, Concepcion Univ, 61-64; vis asst prof ling & Romance lang, 64-65, asst prof, 65-67, assoc prof, 67-79, PROF LING & ROMANCE LANG, UNIV WASH, 79-. **RESEARCH** Spanish grammar. **SELECTED PUBLICATIONS** Auth, On Null Operator Structures, Natural Lang and Ling Theory, Vol 0011, 93; On the Position of Subjects, Syntax and Semantics, Vol 0025, 91. **CONTACT ADDRESS** Dept of Ling, Univ of Wash, Seattle, WA, 98105.

CONTRERAS, RAOUL
DISCIPLINE LATINO STUDIES **EDUCATION** Univ Ca, PhD, 92. **CAREER** Asst prof. **RESEARCH** Chicano studies; Latino studies; race ethnic studies; political science. **SELECTED PUBLICATIONS** Auth, Principles and Foundations of Chicano Studies: Chicano Organization on University Campuses in California, Univ Houston, 92; Chicano Movement Chicano Studies: Social Science and Self-conscious Ideology: Perspectives in Mexican American Studies-Mexican Americans in the 1990's, 97. **CONTACT ADDRESS** Dept of Minority Studies, Indiana Univ, Northwest, 3400 Broadway, Gary, IN, 46408.

CONVERSE, HYLA STUNTZ
PERSONAL Born 10/31/1920, Lahore, Pakistan, m, 1951, 2 children **DISCIPLINE** HISTORY OF RELIGIONS, SOUTH ASIAN LITERATURE **EDUCATION** Smith Col, BA, 43; Union Theol Sem, BD, 49; Columbia Univ, PhD(hist of relig), 71. **CAREER** Relief & rehab worker, Eglise Reforme France, 45-48; dir student work, Judson Mem Church, New York, 52-55; dir lit & study, Nat Student Christian Fed, 57-63; asst prof Asian relig & humanities, 68-78, chmn humanities fac, 73-78, assoc prof, 78-80, PROF ASIAN RELIG & HUMANITIES, OKLA STATE UNIV, 80-, Fulbright res fel, India, 74-75; Am Inst Pakistan Studies fel, 78-79. **MEMBERSHIPS** Am Orient Soc; Bhandarkar Oriental Res Inst. **RESEARCH** Religions of South Asia; literature of South Asia; arts of South Asia. **SELECTED PUBLICATIONS** Auth, An Ancient Sudra Account of the Origins of Castes, Jour Amer Oriental Soc, Vol 0114, 94. **CONTACT ADDRESS** Dept Relig Studies, Oklahoma State Univ, Stillwater, OK, 74074.

CONWELL, DAVID
PERSONAL Born 01/13/1959, Philadelphia, PA, m, 1992, 2 children **DISCIPLINE** CLASSICAL STUDIES **EDUCATION** Trinity Col, BA, 82; Univ Pa, PhD, 92. **CAREER** Instr, Baylor School, 95-. **HONORS AND AWARDS** NEH Teacher Exchange Fel, 97. **MEMBERSHIPS** Archaeol Inst of Am; Am Philol Asn; Classical Asn of the Midwest and South. **RESEARCH** Archaeology of Cyprus, Greece, and Italy; Ancient fortifications; Art history. **SELECTED PUBLICATIONS** Auth, "The White Poros Wall on the Athenian Pnyx: Character and Context," in The Pnyx in the Hist of Athens, 96; "Rediscovering the Athenian Long Walls," in Am School of Class Studies Newsletter, 95; "Topography and Toponyms between Athens and Piraeus," in J of Ancient Topography, 93. **CONTACT ADDRESS** 1112 Crown Point Rd W, Signal Mountain, TN, 37377.

COOEY, PAULA M.
PERSONAL Hays, KS, m, 1 child **DISCIPLINE** RELIGION, THEOLOGY AND COMPARATIVE LITERATURE **EDUCATION** Univ Ga, BA, philos, 68; Harvard Divinity Sch, MTS, 74; Harvard Univ, grad sch of arts & sci, PhD, 81. **CAREER** Visiting instr, Conn Col, 9/79-9/80; instr part-time, relig, Univ Mass, Harbor Campus, 9/80-1/81; asst prof, relig, Trinity Univ, 9/81-7/87; assoc prof, relig, Trinity Univ, 8/87-8/93; prof, relig, Trinity Univ, 8/93-. **HONORS AND AWARDS** Co-dir, Southwest Regional Amer Acad of Relig workshop on teaching for jr facul, 94-96; Sears-Roebuck Found award for excellence in teaching & campus leadership, 91; Trinity Univ nom for CASE award, 88. **MEMBERSHIPS** Amer Acad of Relig; Soc for Buddhist-Christian Studies; Soc for the Sci Study of Relig; Amer Asn of Univ Prof. **RESEARCH** Death and dying from a feminist perspective. **SELECTED PUBLICATIONS** Auth, Family, Freedom, and Faith: Building Community Today, Westminster John Knox Press, ix-131, 96; auth, Religious Imagination and the Body: A Feminist Analysis, Oxford Univ Press, vii-184, 94; article, Bad Women: The Limitations of Theory and Theology, Horizons in Feminist Theology, Fortress, 97; article, Kenosis, Popular Religiosity, Religious Pluralism, Dict of Feminist Theol, John Knox Westminster Press, 96; article, Re-Membering the Body: A Theological Resource for Resisting Domestic Violence, Theol & Sexuality, 3, 27-47, 95; article, Mapping the Body through Religious Symbolism: The Life and Work of Frida Kahlo as Case Study, Imagining Faith: Essays in Honor of Richard R. Niebuhr, Scholars Press, 105-125, 95; article, Backlash, Jour of Feminist Studies, 10, 1, 109-111, 94. **CONTACT ADDRESS** Dept. of Religion, Trinity Univ, 715 Stadium Dr., San Antonio, TX, 78212-7200. **EMAIL** pcooey@trinity.edu

COOK, EUNG-DO
PERSONAL Born 02/03/1935, Seosan, Korea, m, 1964, 2 children **DISCIPLINE** LINGUISTICS **EDUCATION** Chungang Univ, Korea, BA, 59, MA, 61; Univ Hawaii, MA, 65; Univ Alta, PhD(ling), 68. **CAREER** Lectr English, Chungang Univ, Korea, 61-63; asst prof ling, York Univ, 68-69; from asst prof to assoc prof, 69-75, PROF LING, UNIV CALGARY, 75-, Head Dept, 76-, Can Coun res grant, 69-71; Killam sr res scholar, 72-73; vis scholar, Brit Columbia Prov Mus, 75-76; Can Coun leave fel, 75-76; Killam res fel, 79. **MEMBERSHIPS** Ling Soc Am; Can Ling Asn; Ling Asn Gt Brit. **RESEARCH** Generative grammar; Athabaskan languages; Korean. **SELECTED PUBLICATIONS** Auth, Polysemy, Homophony, and Morphemic Identity of Chipewyan--Spoken in the Northwest-Territories of Western Canada, Folia Ling, Vol 0026, 92; Phonetic and Phonological Features of Approximants in Athabaskan and Eskimo, Phonetica, Vol 0050, 93; New Occasions Teach New Duties, Modern Medical Discoveries and Ethical Decisions, Expository Times, Vol 0106, 94; Athapaskan--A Polysynthetic Language Family from the Western Half of the Northwest-Territories and Its Very Complex Morphological Verb Composition-A Structural Overview, Meta, Vol 0038, 93; Language Death-- Factual and Theoretical Explorations with Special Reference to East-Africa, Word-Jour Intl Ling Assn, Vol 0046, 95; Against Moraic Licensing in Bella-Coola, Ling Inquiry, Vol 0025, 94; Blackfoot Dictionary of Stems, Roots And Affixes, Intl Jour Amer Ling, Vol 0060, 94; Chilcotin Flattening and Autosegmental Phonology, Lingua, Vol 0091, 93; Syllable, Tone, and Verb Paradigms--Studies in Chinese Linguistics, Word-Jour Intl Ling Assn, Vol 0044, 93. **CONTACT ADDRESS** Dept of Ling, Univ of Calgary, Calgary, AB, T2N 1N4.

COOK, ROBERT FRANCIS
PERSONAL Born 10/24/1944, Atlanta, GA **DISCIPLINE** MEDIEVAL FRENCH LANGUAGE & LITERATURE **EDUCATION** King Col, AB, 65; Vanderbilt Univ, MA, 68, PhD(French), 70; Univ Pittsburgh, MS, 75. **CAREER** Asst prof French, Univ Pittsburgh, 69-75; assoc Prof French, 75-91, FULL PROF, UNIV VA, 91-. **MEMBERSHIPS** MLA; Am Asn Teachers Fr; Mediaeval Acad Am; Int Arthurian Soc; Soc Rencesvals. **RESEARCH** The chansons de geste; textual criticism. **SELECTED PUBLICATIONS** Auth, Les manuscrits de Baudouin de Sebourc, Romania, 70; ed, Le batard de Bouillon, chanson de geste, Droz-Minard, 72; coauth, Le deuxieme Cycle de la Croisade, Droz, 72; auth, Foreign language study and intellectual power, ADFL Bull, 5/77; coauth, The Legendary Sources of Flaubert's Saint Julien l'Hospitalier, Univ Toronto, 77; coauth, Chanson d'Antioche, Chanson de geste, 80; Aucassin et Nicolete, a Critical Bibliography, 82; The Sense of the Song of Roland, 87. **CONTACT ADDRESS** Dept of French, Univ of Virginia, 302 Cabell Hall, Charlottesville, VA, 22903. **EMAIL** rfc@virginia.edu

COOK, SUSAN L.
PERSONAL Born 12/22/1949, Toledo, OH, s, 2 children **DISCIPLINE** HUMAN COMMUNICATIONS **EDUCATION** Univ Denver, PhD, 97. **CAREER** Adj Fac, Metro State Col of Denver, 93-; Asst Prof, James Madison Univ, 87-98; Asst Prof, Gonzaga Univ, 98-. **HONORS AND AWARDS** Cum laude (BA); All Am Schol (Master's Prog); Phi Kappa Gamma. **MEMBERSHIPS** NCA; ICA; STC; ATTW; ABC. **RESEARCH** Cognition and communication; technology and cognition. **SELECTED PUBLICATIONS** Coauth, The Failure to Communicate: Restructuring Telecommunications Based Services and our Perceptions about Them, Int Telecommunications Union: Telecom 95 - Technol Su Summit, 95; auth, The Psychological and Sociological Characteristics of E-mail, Regional Conf As Asn Bus Communicators, 96; Reflecting Upon the Rhetorical Concept of Inventio and Poster's Mode of Information, Regional Conf Int Commun Asn, 97; Coming Home to Orality: Oral Residue in an Online Dialogue Across Time, Regional Conf Nat Commun Asn, 97; Lessons We Have Learned About Persuasion: Hitler's Ten Steps for Persuading, Regional Conf Nat Commun Asn, 98. **CONTACT ADDRESS** 3915 W. Randolph Rd., #5, Spokane, WA, 99224.

COOLEY, ROBERT E.
PERSONAL m, 2 children **DISCIPLINE** HEBREW STUDIES **EDUCATION** Wheaton Col, BA; Wheaton Col Grad Sch, MA; NY Univ, PhD. **CAREER** Asst to the pres, Dropsie Univ; acad dean, Evangel Col; prof, Southwest Mo State Univ; dir, Ctr Archaeol Res, Southwest Mo State Univ; pres, 81-97; chancellor, Gordon-Conwell Theol Sem, 97-. **HONORS AND AWARDS** Ch bd dir(s), World Relief Corp; pres, Assn Theol Sch(s), US, Can; bd dir(s), InTrust mag; pres, In Trust, Inc. **SELECTED PUBLICATIONS** Sr ed, Christianity Today. **CONTACT ADDRESS** Gordon-Conwell Theol Sem, 130 Essex St, South Hamilton, MA, 01982.

COONS, DIX SCOTT
PERSONAL Born 07/11/1930, Mesa, AZ, m, 1956, 5 children **DISCIPLINE** SPANISH; LATIN AMERICAN LITERATURE **EDUCATION** Brigham Young Univ, BA, 55, MA, 57; Univ Tex, PhD(Span), 64. **CAREER** Asst Span, Univ Tex, 56-57; asst, St Stephen's Episcopal Sch, 57-63; from instr to asst prof, Brown Univ, 63-66; asst prof, 66-68, Assoc Prof Span, RI Col, 68-. **MEMBERSHIPS** Am Asn Teachers Span & Port. **RESEARCH** Latin-American novel and short story; modernismo; Mexican novel. **CONTACT ADDRESS** Dept of Span, Rhode Island Col, 600 Mt Pleasant, Providence, RI, 02908-1924.

COOPER, CRAIG
DISCIPLINE GREEK; ROMAN **EDUCATION** Univ Alberta, BA, 83; Univ Brit Columbia, MA, 85, PhD, 92. **CAREER** Asst prof **RESEARCH** Greek historiography; Athenian law; Athenian orators and rhetoric. **SELECTED PUBLICATIONS** Auth, Hyperides and the Trial of Phryne, Phoenix 49, 95. **CONTACT ADDRESS** Dept of Classics, Univ of Winnipeg, 515 Portage Ave, Winnipeg, MB, R3B 2E9. **EMAIL** craig.cooper@uwinnipeg.ca

COOPER, DANIELLE CHAVY
PERSONAL Born 12/11/1921, Paris, France, m, 1947, 1 child **DISCIPLINE** FOREIGN LANGUAGES **EDUCATION** Univ Paris, BA, 39, MA, 41, PhD(Am lit), 42; Univ Southern Calif, PhD, 63. **CAREER** Teacher English & Span, Sec Schs, France, 42-44; asst French, Whalley Range High Sch & Univ Manchester, 45-46; Marcelle Parde teaching fel, Bryn Mawr Col, 46-47; lang coordr, Isabelle Buckley Schs, Los Angeles, Calif, 55-56; instr French & Ger, Immaculate Heart Col, 57-60, asst prof French, 60-63; lectr, Univ Colo, 63-65; from assoc prof to prof, Keuka Col, 65-70, chmn dept mod lang, 65-70; chmn div lang & civilizations, 71-73, chmn dept lang & humanities, 75-77, PROF FRENCH, MONTEREY INST INT STUDIES, INSTR

FRENCH, FR FOUND CALIF, LOS ANGELES, 56-58; bd reviewer, Bks Abroad/World Lit Today, 58-; instr, Univ Southern Calif, 58; mem, Alliance Francaise. **HONORS AND AWARDS** Chevalier, Ordre des Palmes Academiques, 72. **MEMBERSHIPS** Am Asn Teachers Fr; MLA; African Studies Asn; Am Name Soc; Philol Asn Pac Coast. **RESEARCH** French phonetics; African and Caribbean literature of French expression; translation theory and practice. **SELECTED PUBLICATIONS** Auth, Le Voile de Draupadi, World Lit Today, Vol 0068, 94; L Expedition, World Lit Today, Vol 0067, 93; La Voyeuse Interdite, World Lit Today, Vol 0067, 93; La Fin des Pierres et des Ages, World Lit Today, Vol 0067, 93; La Nuit Cyclone, World Lit Today, Vol 0067, 93; L 'Amour au Temps des Solitudes, World Lit Today, Vol 0067, 93; L Ange Aveugle, World Lit Today, Vol 0067, 93; Poing Mort, World Lit Today, Vol 0067, 93; Le Grand Ghapal, World Lit Today, Vol 0067, 93; La Fille du Gobernator, World Lit Today, Vol 0069, 95; Terrenoire, World Lit Today, Vol 0068, 94; Homme Rompu, World Lit Today, Vol 0068, 94; Thoreau Walden--The Pond in Winter, Explicator, Vol 0051, 93; La Fontaine des Innocents, World Lit Today, Vol 0067, 93; L Inventaire, World Lit Today, Vol 0069, 95; La Montagne Des Signaux, World Lit Today, Vol 0069, 95; Inquisition, World Lit Today, Vol 0068, 94; Un Attieke Pour Elgass, World Lit Today, Vol 0068, 94; Un Fils Dorage, World Lit Today, Vol 0067, 93. **CONTACT ADDRESS** Monterey Inst of Foreign Studies, PO Box 1978, Monterey, CA, 93940.

COOPER, HENRY RONALD, JR.
DISCIPLINE SLAVIC LANGUAGES AND LITERATURES **EDUCATION** City Col of New York, BA (summa cum laude, Russian Lit), 67; Columbia Univ, MA (Russian Lit), 69; Russian Inst, Columbia Univ, Cetificate, 69; Columbia Univ, PhD (Slavic Lit), 74. **CAREER** US Dept of State, escort-interpreter, Serbian and Croatian, 84-; asst tour guide, Lipson Travel, Inc, USSR and East Europe, 68; counter-intelligence special agent, US Army, 69-71; preceptor in Slavic, 73, res asst, 73-74; asst prof, Northwestern Univ, 74-81; asst prof, 81-84, assoc prof, 84-91, prof, IN Univ, 91-, prof and chair, Slavic Dept, 91-, acting dean, Int Prog, 91-92; dir, summer workshop in Soviet & East European Langs, IN Univ, 86, 87; dir, Russian and East European Inst, 86-91. **HONORS AND AWARDS** Phi Beta Kappa; Pi Delta Phi; Grad Honors in Slavic, CCNY, 66-67; Prize for Papers in Problems of Slovene Culture, 76-77; Order of the Yugoslav Flag with Gold Star, 89; Zahvala (Acknowledgement), Govt of the Republic of Slovenia, 92; John W Ryan Award for Int Service, IN Univ, 94; corresponding member, Slovene Academy of Sciences and Arts, 95. **MEMBERSHIPS** Asn of Literary Scholars and Critics; Am Asn for the Advancement of Slavic Studies; Am Asn of Teachers of Slavic and East European Langs; Soc for Slovene Studies; North Am Serbian Studies Asn; Am Asn for Southeast European Studies; The Fellowship of SS Alban and Sergius; Bulgarian Studies Asn; Early Slavic Lit Asn. **RESEARCH** Slavic lits (especially Old Russian, South Slavic), Slavic Bible translations. **SELECTED PUBLICATIONS** Auth, Marin Drzic and France Preseren, in Vasa D Mihailovich, ed, South Slavic Writers before World War II (Dictionary of Literary Biography, vol 147, Bruccoli, Clark, and Layman, 95; Translating the Freising Manuscripts to Reflect Assumptions about Their Literary and Historical Context, in Janos Kos, et al, Zbornik Britinski spomeniki, ZRC/SAZU, Institut za slovensko literaturo in literarne vede, 96; Intro, Death and the Dervish, English trans by Bogdan Radic and Stephen Dickey, Northwestern Univ Press, 96; The Translation of the Bible Into Slavic Languages: Biblical Citations in the Vitas of Cyril and Methodius, Slavica Tergestina, Trieste, Italy, 5, 97; Kajetan Kovic in Vasa D Mihailovich, ed, South Slavic Writers after World War II (Dictionary of Literary Biography, vol 181), Bruccoli, Clark, Layman, 97; The Origins of the Church Slavonic Version: An Alternative Hypothesis, Proceedings, Int Symposium on the Interpretation of the Bible, Slovene Academy of Sciences and Arts, Ljubljana, Slovenia, 86; The Tense Situation of Slavic: Past, Present, and Future, ADFL Bul, 98; four translations, 28 other publications. **CONTACT ADDRESS** Dept of Slavic Languages and Literatures, Indiana Univ, Bloomington, Ballantine Hall 502, Bloomington, IN, 47405-6616. **EMAIL** Cooper@Indiana.edu

COOPER, JERROLD STEPHEN
PERSONAL Born 11/24/1942, Chicago, IL, 3 children **DISCIPLINE** ASSYRIOLOGY **EDUCATION** Univ Calif, Berkeley, AB, 63, AM, 64; Univ Chicago, PhD(Assyriol), 69. **CAREER** Asst prof, 68-74, assoc prof, 74-79, prof Near Eastern Studies, Johns Hopkins Univ, 79-, Co-ed, J Cuneiform Studies, 72-89. **MEMBERSHIPS** Am Orient Soc; Am Schools of Oriental Res. **SELECTED PUBLICATIONS** Auth, The Return of Ninurta to Nippur, Pontif Bibl Inst, 78; Symmetry and repetion in Akkadian narrative, J Am Orient Soc, 78; Apodotic death and the historicity of historical omens, Mesopotamia, Vol 8, 80; Studies in Mesopotamian Lapidary Inscription, Vol I & II, J Cuneiform Studies & Rev'd Assyriologie, 80; The Curse of the Agade, Johns Hopkins Press, 82; ed, Mesopotamian Civilizations, 87-; auth, Reconstructing History from Ancient Sources: The Lagash-Umma Border Conflict, Malibu, Udena Publ, 87; auth, Sumerian and Akkadian royal Inscriptions Vol.1: Presargonic Inscriptions, New Haven, Am Oriental Soc, 86; co-ed, The Study of the Ancient Near East in the 21st Century: The WF Albright Centenary Conference, Eisenbrauns, 96; auth, Paradigm and Propaganda: The Dynasty of Akkade in the 21st Century BC, Akkad, the First World Empire: Structure, Ideology, Traditions, ed. M. Liverani, 11-23, 93; Magic and M(is)use: Poetic Promiscuity in Mesopotamian Ritual, Mesopotamian Poetic Language: Sumerian and Akkadian, Styx Publ, 47-57, 96. **CONTACT ADDRESS** Dept of Near Eastern Studies, Johns Hopkins Univ, 3400 N Charles St, Baltimore, MD, 21218-2680. **EMAIL** anzu@jhu.edu

COOPER, VINCENT O'MAHONY
PERSONAL Born 12/03/1947, Basseterre, St. Kitts, m, 1975, 2 children **DISCIPLINE** LINGUISTICS, ENGLISH **EDUCATION** Univ Bordeaux, dipl, 67; Col VI, BA, 72; Princeton Univ, MA, 74, PhD, 79. **CAREER** Adj instr socioling, Hunter Col, City Univ New York, 76; Instr English, Col of the VI, 77-, from Asst Prof to Prof English/Ling, Univ VI, 79-. **HONORS AND AWARDS** ACLS Res Grant, 75; Fulbright Schol to Belize, 86; Martin Luther King-Rosa Parks, Cesar Chavez State Award for Outstanding Schol, Mich State Univ, 90; Cornel Univ Int Schol Award, 93; Cornell Univ Res Workshop Grant, Sept 18-20, 97. **RESEARCH** Sociolinguistics; Caribbean Creole languages; Caribbean literatures. **SELECTED PUBLICATIONS** Coauth, Three Islands (poetry), Univ VI, 87; Tremors (poetry), UVI, 89; auth, Mahogani and other poems, In: Kunapipi, Univ Haarhus Press, 93; The Poetry of Althea Romeo-Mark, In: Routledge Encyclopedia of Post Colonial Literatures, 94; Language and Gender in the Kalinago Amerindian Community of St. Croix, In: The Indigenous People of the Carribean, Univ Fl Press, 97; An Anthology of PanCarribean Poetry: With Selections in Translation from French, Spanish, and Dutch and Their Related Vernaculars, Harbrace Col Publ, 97 (in progress). **CONTACT ADDRESS** Dept of English, Univ of the Virgin Islands, 2 John Brewers Bay, St. Thomas, VI, 00802-9990. **EMAIL** vcooper@uvi.edu

COPJEC, JOAN
DISCIPLINE COMPARATIVE LITERATURE **EDUCATION** Univ WI, MA; NY Univ, PhD. **CAREER** Prof/Dir Ctr Study Psychoanalysis and Cult. **RESEARCH** Comp lit; cinema; lit criticism. **SELECTED PUBLICATIONS** Auth, Read My Desire: Lacan Against the Historicists, MIT, 94; ed, Jacques Lacan: Television, Norton, 90; Shades of Noir, Verso, 93; Radical Evil, Verso, 93; Supposing the Subject, Verso, 94. **CONTACT ADDRESS** Dept Comp Lit, SUNY Buffalo, 639 Clemens Hall, Buffalo, NY, 14260.

COPPOLA, CARLO
PERSONAL Born 10/01/1938, Wooster, OH, m, 1981, 2 children **DISCIPLINE** COMPARATIVE LITERATURE, LINGUISTICS **EDUCATION** John Carroll Univ, BS, 60; Univ Chicago, MA, 61, PhD(comp lit), 75. **CAREER** Lectr Hindi & Urdu ling, 68-70, asst prof, 70-75, assoc prof, 75-82, PROF HINDI & URDU LING, OAKLAND UNIV, 82-, Chmn Area Studies Prog, 76-, SAsian bibliogr, Publ MLA, 71-76; ed, J SAsian Lit, 63-; asst ed, J Asian Studies, 78- **MEMBERSHIPS** Asn Asian Studies; Philol Asn Pac Coast; N Indian Studies Asn (pres, 75-78); MLA; SAsia Lit Asn. **RESEARCH** Modern Hindi; Urdu literature; Indian writing in English; Marxist aesthetics. **SELECTED PUBLICATIONS** Auth, Husband, Lover, Holy Man, an Intercultural Comedy, World Lit Today, Vol 0067, 93; Footsteps, World Lit Today, Vol 0070, 96; The State Witness, World Lit Today, Vol 0069, 95; Sensuous Horizons--The Stories and Plays, World Lit Today, Vol 0071, 97; The Novel in Javanese--Aspects of Its Social and Literary Character, World Lit Today, Vol 0067, 93; Contemporary Urdu Short-Stories--An Anthology, World Lit Today, Vol 0066, 92. **CONTACT ADDRESS** Dept of Mod Lang & Lit, Oakland Univ, Rochester, MI, 48063.

CORBEILL, ANTHONY
DISCIPLINE CLASSICAL LANGUAGES AND LITERATURE **EDUCATION** Univ MI, AB, 83; Univ CA, Berkeley, MA, 85, PhD, 90. **CAREER** Assoc prof, Univ KS. **HONORS AND AWARDS** APA fel, Thesaurus Linguae Latinae, Ger, 90-91; Rome Prize fel, Am Acad Rome, 94-95., Adv coun, AAR; contrib, TOCS-IN. **MEMBERSHIPS** Mem, Am Philol Assn; CAMWS; Am Class League; Soc of Fellows Am Acad Rome; outsanding acad book, Controlling Laughter. Polit Humor in the Late Roman Republic, Princeton, 97. **RESEARCH** Latin lit and Roman cult hist. **SELECTED PUBLICATIONS** Auth, Controlling Laughter. Political Humor in the Late Roman Republic, Princeton, 96; Deviant Diners in Roman Political Invective, Roman Sexualities, Princeton, 98. **CONTACT ADDRESS** Dept of Class, Univ Kansas, Admin Building, Lawrence, KS, 66045.

CORBETT, JANICE
DISCIPLINE ENGLISH LANGUAGE AND LITERATURE **EDUCATION** B.A. Eastern College, M.S.(Comm), PhD (Eng), Temple Univ **CAREER** Fac, Delaware Valley Col, 96-. **HONORS AND AWARDS** Fellow, Rome Sem Art and Ideology; NEH fellow, UCLA., Pub rel ed, staff writer, and dir. **RESEARCH** Eng wrting and compos. **SELECTED PUBLICATIONS** Auth, academic publ(s) in Perf Arts Jour, Tech Comms Jour, and JAISA. **CONTACT ADDRESS** Delaware Valley Col, 700 E Butler Ave, Doylestown, PA, 18901-2697. **EMAIL** CorbettJ@devalcol.edu

CORBETT, NOEL L.
PERSONAL Born 11/23/1938, Bowmanville, ON, Canada, m, 1963 **DISCIPLINE** FRENCH LANGUAGE AND LINGUISTICS **EDUCATION** Univ Toronto, BA, 60, MA, 63, PhD(French), 67. **CAREER** Teaching asst French, Victoria Col, Univ Toronto, 62-66, lectr, 66-67; asst prof, 67-72, prog coordr fac educ, 77-81, ASSOC PROF FRENCH, YORK UNIV, 72-, Can Coun res fel, 69-70, 73-74 & 81-82; Can Secy of State grant, 72; fac fel, York Univ, 79-80. **MEMBERSHIPS** MLA; Ling Soc Am; Soc Ling Romane; Can Asn Univ Teachers; Can Ling Asn. **RESEARCH** Diachronic study of French and Romance languages; medieval French language and literature; synchronic structure of French and Canadian French. **SELECTED PUBLICATIONS** Auth, Tense and Narrativity--From Medieval Performance to Modern Fiction, Romance Philol, Vol 0046, 92. **CONTACT ADDRESS** Dept of French Studies, York Univ, 4700 Keele St, Downsview, ON, M3J 1P3.

CORGAN, MARGARET M.
PERSONAL Born 08/24/1936, Wilkes-Barre, PA **DISCIPLINE** FRENCH LANGUAGE & LITERATURE **EDUCATION** Marymount Col, NY, BA, 58; Univ Rennes, dipl French Lang & Lit, 59; Fordham Univ, MA, 62, PhD(French), 67. **CAREER** Instr French, Col Misericordia, 59-61; asst, Fordham Univ, 61-63; instr, St John's Univ, NY, 64-65; from asst prof to assoc prof, 65-74, prof French, King's Col, PA, 74-, chmn Dept Foreign Lang & Lit, 77-. **HONORS AND AWARDS** Fulbright Scholar, Univ of Paris, 63-64; French Government Grantee, Chambre de Commerce et d'Industrie, Paris, Summer, 82; Herve Le Blanc Distinguished Service Prof, King's Coll, 92-97; National French Contest Admin of the Year, 92. **MEMBERSHIPS** Am Asn Teachers Fr; Am Coun Teaching For Lang; Am Asn Univ Women. **RESEARCH** Twentieth century French literature; bibliography of twentieth century French authors; translation. **CONTACT ADDRESS** Dept of Foreign Lang & Lit, King's Col, 133 N River St, Wilkes Barre, PA, 18711-0801. **EMAIL** mmcorgan@rs01.kings.edu

CORMIER, R.J.
PERSONAL Born 11/23/1938, Bridgeport, CT, m, 1960, 2 children **DISCIPLINE** LANGUAGE AND LINGUISTICS **CAREER** Tchg asst Fr, Stanford Univ, 60-62; tchg fel, instr, Fr, Harvard Univ, 63-67; instr, Fr, Tufts Univ, 65-67; asst prof, Fr, Univ Virginia, 67-72; assoc prof Fr, chemn dept, Fr and Ital, 73-75, prof, 79, Temple Univ, 72-84; prof of Fr, Hum, and Eng, 84-94, adj prof Eng, 94-95, Wilson Col; vis prof Fr, 96- , Longwood Col. **HONORS AND AWARDS** Fac summer res grant, 68, 69, 71; Am Coun Learned Soc travel grants, 75, 76, 80; Chevalier des Palmes Academiques, 77; DLitt, Univ Bridgeport, 80; Fulbright Senior Res Fel, 83-84; NEH grant, 86. **MEMBERSHIPS** Am Asn of Tchrs of Fr; Am Council on the Tchg of For Lang; Anglo- Norman Texts Soc; Int Arthurian Soc; Medieval Acad of Am; MLA; Popular Cult Asn; Vergillian Soc. **RESEARCH** Medieval comparative literature, French, Latin, and Celtic. **SELECTED PUBLICATIONS** Auth, Classical Continuity and Transposition in Two Medieval Adaptations of the Aeneid, Symposium, 94; auth, Taming the Warrior: Responding to the Charge of Sexual Deviance in Twelfth-Century Vernacular Romance, in Maddox, ed, Literary Aspects of Courtly Culture, Brewer, 94; auth, Metaphor and Sign in Beowulf: The H(e)art in Heorot, Lang and Style, 94; auth, Sylvia's Tame Stag: Classical Continuity, Transposition, and Intertextuality in Two 12th Century Adaptations of Virgil's Aeneid, Eos, 93; auth, The Antlers of Silvia's Stag: A Note on the Chronology of the Aeneid, The Classical World, 93; auth, Ovid, Influence of, and, Virgil, Influence of, in Kibler, ed, Medieval France: An Encyclopedia, Garland, 95; auth, Jean Frappier in Damico, ed, Dictionary of Medieval Scholarship, vol 2, Garland, 96; auth, Inventing the Vernacular in the Gutters of Virgil's Aeneid: From Marginal Dirt to Seminal Romance, Esprit Createur, 98; auth, Amazons, and, Dueling, in Duncan, ed, Encycl of Sport in American Culture, East Tenn, forthcoming. **CONTACT ADDRESS** 1403 Johnston Dr, Farmville, VA, 23901. **EMAIL** rcormier@longwood.lwc.edu

CORNGOLD, STANLEY ALAN
PERSONAL Born 06/11/1934, Brooklyn, NY, 1 child **DISCIPLINE** GERMAN AND COMPARATIVE LITERATURE **EDUCATION** Columbia Univ, AB, 57; Cornell Univ, MA, 63, PhD(comp lit), 69. **CAREER** Instr English, Univ Md, Europ div, 59-62; teaching asst, Cornell Univ, 63-64, teaching asst French, 64-65; from lectr to asst prof Ger, 66-72, assoc prof, 72-79, assoc prof Ger & comp lit, 79-81, Prof Ger & Comp Lit, Princeton Univ, 81- . **HONORS AND AWARDS** Nat Endowment for Humanities fel, 73-74; Guggenheim fel, 77-78; Acad of Lit Stud, 83-88; listed, Who's Who in America; Fulbright Res Fel, 86-87; pres, Kafka Soc of Am, 87-88; Princeton Univ grant-in-aid, 90-97; consult for German Lit, Guggenheim Found, 92- ;publ comt, MLA, 93-95; invited mem, Heidelberg Club Int, 95- ; fac assoc, Int School of Theory in the Hum at Santiago de Compostela, 96- ; bd of dir, Literature da Quieli, 98. **MEMBERSHIPS** MLA; PEN Club; Am Comparative Lit Asn. **RESEARCH** European Romanticism; modern German literature; modern poetics. **SELECTED PUBLICATIONS** Auth, The Commentators' Despair: The Interpretation of Kafka's Metamorphosis, Assoc Faculty Press, 73; auth, The Fate of the Self: German Writers and French Theory, Columbia, 86; auth, Franz Kafka: The Necessity of Form, Cornell, 88;

coauth, Borrowed Lives, SUNY Albany, 91; auth, Complex Pleasure: Forms of Feeling in German Literature, Stanford, 98. **CONTACT ADDRESS** Dept of Germanic Languages & Literatures, Princeton Univ, Princeton, NJ, 08544-5264. **EMAIL** corngold@princeton.edu

CORRE, ALAN DAVID

PERSONAL Born 05/02/1931, London, England, m, 1957, 4 children **DISCIPLINE** SEMITIC STUDIES, LINGUISTICS **EDUCATION** Univ London, BA, 51; Univ Manchester, MA, 53; Univ Pa, PhD(ling), 62. **CAREER** Minister, Congregation Mikveh Israel, Pa, 55-63; from asst prof to assoc prof, 63-68, PROF HEBREW STUDIES, UNIV WIS-MILWAUKEE, 68-, Chmn Dept, 80-, Nat Endowment for Humanities younger scholar fel, Univ Col, Univ London, 67-68. **HONORS AND AWARDS** Res in Humanities Prize, Wis Acad Sci, Arts & Lett, 66; Standard Oil of Ind Award for teaching excellence, 73. **MEMBERSHIPS** Ling Soc Am; Am Orient Soc. **RESEARCH** Semitic linguistics; Sefardic studies; Judeo-Arabic studies. **SELECTED PUBLICATIONS** Auth, A Lexicon of the Hebrew and Aramaic Elements in Modern Judezmo, Jour Amer Oriental Soc, Vol 0115, 95. **CONTACT ADDRESS** Dept of Hebrew Studies, Univ of Wis-Milwaukee, Milwaukee, WI, 53201.

CORTES, JULIO

PERSONAL Born 01/23/1924, Bilboa, Spain, m, 1967, 1 child **DISCIPLINE** ARABIC LANGUAGE **EDUCATION** Univ Madrid, Dr(Semitic philol), 65. **CAREER** Dir, Centro Cult Hispanico, Damascus, Syria, 56-60, 62-67; vis lectr, 67-68, assoc prof, 68-80, PROF ARABIC & SPAN, UNIV NC, CHAPEL HILL, 80-, Consult, Suppl to Oxford English Dict, 69- **HONORS AND AWARDS** Oficial, Orden Merito Civil, Spain, 59. **MEMBERSHIPS** Am Orient Soc; Am Asn Teachers Arabic; Am Asn Teachers Span & Port; MLA; Union Europeenne d'Arabisants et d'Islamisants. **RESEARCH** Arabic lexicography; Quranic Arabic. **SELECTED PUBLICATIONS** Auth, You Are Not Good at Making Songs My Boy--Judgments on Trenet,Charles, Europe-Rev Lit Mensuelle, Vol 0074, 96. **CONTACT ADDRESS** Dept of Romance Lang, Univ of NC, Chapel Hill, NC, 27514.

CORY, MARK

DISCIPLINE TWENTIETH CENTURY GERMAN LITERATURE **EDUCATION** Dartmouth Col, BA, 63; Indiana Univ, MA, 68, PhD, 71. **CAREER** English and Lit, Univ Ark. **HONORS AND AWARDS** Dir, Humanities. **SELECTED PUBLICATIONS** Area: German experimental radio playss. **CONTACT ADDRESS** Univ Ark, Fayetteville, AR, 72701.

COSTELLO, JOHN ROBERT

PERSONAL Born 09/12/1942, New York, NY, m, 1967 **DISCIPLINE** LINGUISTICS **EDUCATION** Wagner Col, BA, 64; NY Univ, MA, 66, PhD(Ger ling), 68. **CAREER** Instr Ger, Univ Col, 67-68, asst prof, 68-72, ASSOC PROF LING, WASHINGTON SQ COL, NY UNIV, 73-, Consult, Universe Bks & Lexik Houser Publ. **MEMBERSHIPS** Ling Soc Am; Int Ling Asn (pres, 81-82); Soc Ger-Am Studies. **RESEARCH** Historical linguistics; linguistic reconstruction; language acquisition. **SELECTED PUBLICATIONS** Auth, Theory and Data in Phonological Reconstruction--Whence and Whither, Word-Jour Intl Ling Assn, Vol 0046, 95; The 50th Anniversary of the Linguistic Circle of New-York, Now Known as the International Linguistic Association Ila, Word-Jour Intl Ling Assn, Vol 0045, 94; Aspects of the History of Linguistics, the 50th Anniversary of Word-Introduction, Word-Jour Intl Ling Assn, Vol 0046, 95; The Anatomy of Antiliberalism, Mich Law Rev, Vol 0092, 92. **CONTACT ADDRESS** Dept of Ling, New York Univ, 719 Broadway, New York, NY, 10003-6806.

COTNAM, JACQUES

PERSONAL Born 07/20/1941, m, 1964, 1 child **DISCIPLINE** FRENCH-CANADIAN LITERATURE **EDUCATION** Laval Univ, BA & BPh, 62, Lic es Lett, 64, Dipl Etudes Super, 66, D es L, 78. **CAREER** From lectr to asst prof, 64-72, ASSOC PROF FRENCH LIT, YORK UNIV, 72-, Lectr, MLA, 69 & Col de France, Paris, 70; lectr at var foreign univs, 73-; vis prof, Univ de Guenoble III, 80-82. **MEMBERSHIPS** Amis Andre Gide; Can Asn Comp Lit; Can Asn Univ Teachers; Asn Can Univ Teachers Fr. **RESEARCH** Influence of nationalism on literature; Andre Gide and English and American literatures; cosmopolitism and the French symbolist movement. **SELECTED PUBLICATIONS** Auth, Books and Reading in Quebec 1800-1850-French, Univ Toronto Quart, Vol 0062, 92; The Gazette Litteraire of Montreal 1778-1779--Our 1st Work of Fiction, Voix and Images, Vol 0020, 95. **CONTACT ADDRESS** Dept of French Lit, York Univ, 4700 Keele St, Downsview, ON, M3J 1P3.

COTTRELL, ROBERT DUANE

PERSONAL Born 02/20/1930, Farmersburg, IA, m, 1965, 2 children **DISCIPLINE** FRENCH LITERATURE **EDUCATION** Columbia Univ, BS, 57; Yale Univ, PhD(Romance lang), 61. **CAREER** From instr to asst prof Romance lang, Northwestern Univ, 60-65; asst prof, Amherst Col, 65-68; assoc prof, 68-71, chmn dept, 74-78, PROF ROMANCE LANG, OHIO STATE UNIV, 71-, Vis prof, Univ Pittsburgh, 72. **MEMBERSHIPS** MLA; Am Asn Teachers Fr; Mod Humanities Res Asn; Soc Amis Montaigne. **RESEARCH** French Renaissance literature. **SELECTED PUBLICATIONS** Auth, Bourdeille,Pierre,De, Lord of Brantome--French, Sixteenth Century Jour, Vol 0027, 96; Italian Citations in the Essais by Montaigne--French, Fr Rev, Vol 0066, 93; A Sceve Celebration--Delie 1544-1994, Esprit Createur, Vol 0036, 96; Bilingual Montaigne--The Latin of the Essais--French, Fr Rev, Vol 0066, 93; The Dialogue in Early-Modern France, 1547-1630--Art and Argument, Sixteenth Century Jour, Vol 0026, 95; Marot,Clement Complete Poetical Works, Vol 2-French, Fr Forum, Vol 0020, 95; Biblical Inspiration in the Work of Marguerite-De-Navarre--Poetry, Theater-French, Fr Forum, Vol 0018, 93; Solitude--A Philosophical Encounter, Philos and Lit, Vol 0019, 95; Calvin and the Dynamics of Speech--Study of Reformed Rhetoric-French, Fr Rev, Vol 0068, 95; Delie as Other--Toward a Poetics of Desire in Sceve Delie, Esprit Createur, Vol 0036, 96; Montaigne and the Art of the Prologue in the 16th-Century--French, Fr Rev, Vol 0067, 94. **CONTACT ADDRESS** Dept of Romance Lang, Ohio State Univ, 1841 Millikin Rd, Columbus, OH, 43210-1229.

COUGHLIN, EDWARD V.

PERSONAL Born 03/02/1932, Norwood, MA, m, 1989, 2 children **DISCIPLINE** ROMANCE LANGUAGES **EDUCATION** Col Holy Cross, BA, 54; Boston Col, MA, 55; Univ Mich, PhD, 65. **CAREER** Asst prof, 64-74, assoc prof, 74-81, Prof Span Lit, Univ Cincinnati, 81- **MEMBERSHIPS** Am Asn Teachers Span & Port; Am Soc 18th Century Studies; Ctr Estud del Siglo XVIII. **RESEARCH** Eighteenth and 19th century Spanish literature. **SELECTED PUBLICATIONS** Coauth, Bibliografia selecta y critica de Octavio Paz, Univ San Luis Potosi, 73; ed, Habides de Ignacio Lopez de Ayala, Ed Hisp, 74; co-ed, Homenaje a Octavio Paz, Univ San Luis Potosi, 76; auth, Adelardo Lopez de Ayala, Twayne, 77; ed, Tres obras ineditas de Ramon de la Cruz, Puvill, 79; coauth, Cambios: La cultura hisp nica, Heinle & Heinle, 83; transl, Poems of Roberto Sosa, Span Publ, 84; ed, Ten Unedited Plays of Ramon de la Cruz, Hispanofila, 87; Nicasio Alvarez de Cienfuegos, Twayne, 88. **CONTACT ADDRESS** Dept of Romance Lang, Univ of Cincinnati, PO Box 210377, Cincinnati, OH, 45221-0377. **EMAIL** coughlev@email.uc.edu

COURTEAU, JOANNA

PERSONAL Born 04/15/1939, Lwow, Poland, 2 children **DISCIPLINE** SPANISH, PORTUGUESE **EDUCATION** Univ Minn, Minneapolis, BA, 60; Univ Wis-Madison, MA, 62, PhD, 70. **CAREER** Instr Span, Sullins Col, 63-65; asst prof, Univ Ark, Fayetteville, 67-71; asst prof Span & Port, 71-76, assoc prof, Foreign lang & lit, 76-80, Prof Span & Port, Iowa State Univ, 76-; Vis prof, Warsaw Univ, Poland, 79; Assoc ed, Hispania, 93-99. **HONORS AND AWARDS** NDEA fel, 60-65; Ford fel, 66-67; ICA grant, 79; Galbenbian Found grant 88; Wilton Park award, 97. **MEMBERSHIPS** AAUP (comt, 91-93, exec counc 94-97, govt relation comt, 95-97); AATSP (exec comt, 92-95); AIL (exec comt, 84-90); APSA (pres, 96-98, exec comt, 98-01, founding mem, 93-96). **RESEARCH** Modernist Brazilian novel; modernist peninsular poetry; XIX Spanish poetry; feminist literature. **SELECTED PUBLICATIONS** More than fifty articles & book chpt; co-ed vol on Hispanic Women's writing in the XIX Century and an encycl on Hispanic poetry. **CONTACT ADDRESS** Foreign Lang & Lit Dept, Iowa State Univ, Ames, IA, 50011-0002. **EMAIL** courteau@iastate.edu

COURTRIGHT, JOHN A.

PERSONAL Born 11/18/1948, m **DISCIPLINE** INTERPERSONAL COMMUNICATION **EDUCATION** Univ Iowa, BA, 71; MA, 73; PhD, 76. **CAREER** Res asst, Univ Iowa, 72-74; tchg asst, Univ Iowa, 74-76; instr, grad course in comp assisted statistical anal, Univ Iowa, 76; asst prof, Cleveland State Univ, 76-80; assoc prof, Cleveland State Univ, 80-85; asst dir, Comp Ctr, Cleveland State Univ, 83-86; prof, Cleveland State Univ, 85-86; prof, 86-; exec ed, Arts & Sci Newsletter, 92-96; ch, 86-. **HONORS AND AWARDS** Award, Speech Commun Assn, 91; grant, 95; grant, UNIDEL Found, 97., Assoc ed, mem, ed bd, Commun Res Rpt, 96-99; ed referee, Commun Rpt, 96; assoc ed, mem ed bd, Commun Quart, 96-99; Jour Commun, 96-99; Commun Edu, 96-99. **RESEARCH** Multimedia presentation; statistics and environmental design. **SELECTED PUBLICATIONS** Co-auth, Commun Research Methods. Glenview, Scott, Foresman, 84; Inertial Forces and the Implementation of a Socio-Technical Systems Approach: A Commun Study, Org Sci, 95; Thinking Rationally About Nonprobability, Jour of Broadcasting and Electronic Media, 96; Communicating Online: A Guide to the Internet, Mayfield Publ Co, 98; The Mayfield Quick Guide to the Internet: For Communincations Students, Mayfield Publ Co, 98. **CONTACT ADDRESS** Dept of Commun, Univ Delaware, 162 Ctr Mall, Newark, DE, 19716.

COWART, WAYNE

DISCIPLINE LINGUISTICS **EDUCATION** City Univ NY, PhD, 83. **CAREER** Assoc prof, 89-. **RESEARCH** Psychology and biology of language; philosophy of mind. **SELECTED PUBLICATIONS** Auth, Experimental Syntax: Applying objective methods to sentence judgments, Sage, 97; pubs in Lang, Perceptual and Motor Skills, Memory and Cognition, Cognition, The Jour of Psycholinguistic Research, and The Jour of Verbal Lrng and Verbal Behav. **CONTACT ADDRESS** Dept of Linguistics, Southern Maine Univ, 37 Col Ave, Gorham, MN, 04038-1083. **EMAIL** usmadm@maine.maine.edu

COWEN, ROY C.

PERSONAL Born 08/02/1930, Kansas City, MO, w, 1956, 1 child **DISCIPLINE** GERMAN **EDUCATION** Yale Univ, BA, 52; Univ Gottingen, Germany, PhD, 61. **CAREER** Instr to asst prof to assoc prof to prof, 60-, Univ Mich. **HONORS AND AWARDS** John Williams Award, 67; Sr Fel NEH, 72-73; Bundesverdienstkreuz 1 Klasse (Sr Off Cross), 85., Chair, Univ Mich, 79-85; ed, Michigan Germanic Studies, 86-. **MEMBERSHIPS** AATG; ALCS; Grabbe-Gesellschaft; Grillparzer-Gesellschaft: Forum Vormarz Forschung; IVG; Hauptmann-Gwsellschaft. **RESEARCH** German literature **SELECTED PUBLICATIONS** Auth, Naturalismus: Kommentar zu einer Epoche, Munich, 81; auth, Hauptmann Kommentar zum nichtdramatischen Werk, Munich, 81; auth, Der Poetische Realismus: Kommentar zu einer Epoche, Munich, 85; auth, Das deutsche Drama im 19, Jahrhundert, Stuttgart, 88; auth, Christian Dietrich Grabbe, Dramatiker ungeloster Widerspruche, Bielefeld, 98. **CONTACT ADDRESS** Dept of Germanic Lang & Lit, Univ Mich, Ann Arbor, MI, 48109-1275. **EMAIL** rcowen@umich.edu

COX, GARY D.

PERSONAL MI, m, 1993, 3 children **DISCIPLINE** SLAVIC STUDIES **EDUCATION** Earlham Col, BA, 69; Ind Univ, MA, 73; Columbia Univ, PhD, 78. **CAREER** Asst prof, Univ Mo/ Columbia Inst, 76-81; asst/assoc prof, Southern Methodist Univ, 81- . **HONORS AND AWARDS** Phi Beta Kappa; SMU Authors' Award, 92. **MEMBERSHIPS** Am Asoc of Teachers of Slavic/Eastern Europ Lang; Am Asoc for Advan of Slavic Studies; Human Behavior and Evolution Soc. **RESEARCH** Russian literature and culture; Dostoevsky; evolution of cultural systems. **SELECTED PUBLICATIONS** Tyrant and Victim in Dostoevsky, 84; auth, Crime and Punishment: A Mind to Murder, 90. **CONTACT ADDRESS** Foreign Langs & Lits, Russian Area, SMU, Dallas, TX, 75275. **EMAIL** gcox@post.smu.edu

COX, JERRY LYNN

PERSONAL Born 04/14/1945, Wichita, KS, m, 1973, 2 children **DISCIPLINE** GERMAN, APPLIED LINGUISTICS **EDUCATION** Wichita State Univ, BA, 68; Univ Colo Boulder, MA, 72; Ind Univ Bloomington, MS, 75, PhD(Ger ling), 77. **CAREER** Instr, 76-77, ASST PROF GER AND ENGLISH AS A SECOND LANG, FURMAN UNIV, 77- DIR LANG LAB, 76-, Fulbright fel ling, Univ Hamburg, 72-73. **MEMBERSHIPS** Am Asn Teachers Ger; Ling Soc Am; Teachers English to Speakers of Other Lang; Am Asn Appl Ling; Am Coun Foreign Lang Teachers. **RESEARCH** Foreign language methodology; applied linguistics-language acquisition; comparative Germanic linguistics. **SELECTED PUBLICATIONS** Auth, Modern German Grammar, Mod Lang Jour, Vol 0081, 97; Modern German Grammar Workbook, Mod Lang Jour, Vol 0081, 97; Collins Cobuild Key Words in the Media, Mod Lang Jour, Vol 0080, 96. **CONTACT ADDRESS** Dept of Mod Foreign Lang, Furman Univ, 3300 Poinsett Hwy, Greenville, SC, 29613-0002.

COZEA, ANGELA

DISCIPLINE FRENCH LITERATURE **EDUCATION** Univ Calgary, BA; Univ Montreal, MA; PhD. **RESEARCH** Modern presentations of the concepts of perspective and style in the literary, visual, clinical discourses; figures of encounter between the ethical and the aesthetic in German and French philosophy; limits of experience-conceptualising history, practising rememoration after Shoah. **SELECTED PUBLICATIONS** Auth, La fidelite aux choses: pour une perspective benjaminienne, 96. **CONTACT ADDRESS** Dept of French, Western Ontario Univ, London, ON, N6A 5B8.

CRABTREE, LOREN WILLIAM

PERSONAL Born 09/02/1940, Aberdeen, SD, m, 1961, 3 children **DISCIPLINE** HISTORY; ASIAN STUDIES **EDUCATION** Univ Minn, BA, 61, MA, 65, PhD(hist), 69. **CAREER** Instr hist, Bethel Col, St Paul, Minn, 65-67; from instr to assoc prof, 67-85, PROF HIST, COLO STATE UNIV, 85-, Dean, Col Liberal Arts, 91-97, Provost, 97-. **HONORS AND AWARDS** Nat Endowment for Humanities Younger Humanist fel, 73-74. **MEMBERSHIPS** Asn Asian Studies; AHA; Asia Soc; Conf Faith & Hist; Western Soc Sci Asn. **RESEARCH** Chinese history, 1900-1937; rural development in Asia; Christian missions in China and India. **SELECTED PUBLICATIONS** Auth, The papers of the National Federation of Settlements, Soc Serv Rev, 66; Communism and the Chinese cultural tradition, Int Quart, 68; coauth, Descriptive Inventories of Collections in the Social Welfare Archives Center, Greenwood, 70; From Mohensodaro to Mao: Perspectives on reaching Asian civilization, Hist Teacher, 73; auth, New perspectives on Sino-American relations, 73 & coauth, Interpreting Asia to Americans, 74, Rocky Mountain Soc Sci J; auth, Seeing red in China: Missouri Synod missionaries and the Chinese Revolution, 1913-30, Selected Papers on Asia, 76; coauth, The Lion and the Dragon: An Introduction to the Civilizations of India and China, J Weston Walch, 79. **CONTACT ADDRESS** Off of the Provost, Colorado State Univ, Fort Collins, CO, 80523-0001. **EMAIL** 1crabtree@vines.colostate.edu

CRAIG, CHARLOTTE MARIE
PERSONAL Born 01/14/1929, Ostrava, Czechoslovakia, m, 1954 **DISCIPLINE** GERMAN LANGUAGE AND LITERATURE **EDUCATION** Univ Puget Sound, BA & teaching cert, 57; Univ Ariz, MA, 60; Rutgers Univ, PhD(Ger), 64. **CAREER** Teacher English & hist, Alaska Pub Schs, 57-59; asst prof Ger, Univ Kans, 64-68; lectr, George Washington Univ, 68-69; prof & chairperson Ger & comp lit, Schiller Col, Heidelberg, Ger, 69-73; PROF GER, KUTZTOWN STATE COL, 74-, Watkins fac fel Ger lit, Univ Kans, 65. **MEMBERSHIPS** MLA; Asn Teachers Ger; Am Soc 18th Century Studies; Northeastern Am Soc 18th Century Studies. **RESEARCH** Eighteenth century German literature; 18th century comparative literature. **SELECTED PUBLICATIONS** Auth, Laocoons Body and the Aesthetics of Pain--Winckelmann, Lessing, Moritz, Goethe, Germ Notes and Rev(s), Vol 0025, 94; Journey to Oblivion--The End of the East European Yiddish and German Worlds in the Mirror of Literature, Germ Notes and Rev(s), Vol 0025, 94; Enzensberger,Hans,Magnus Political Crumbs, Germ Notes and Rev(s), Vol 0025, 94; Schiller and the Issue of Armed Conflict, Germ Notes and Rev(s), Vol 0027, 96; Shakespeare Observed--Studies in Performance on Stage and Screen, Germ Notes and Rev(s), Vol 0025, 94; Peter Schlemihl, Germ Notes and Rev(s), Vol 0026, 95; A Concise History of German Literature to 1900, Germ Notes and Rev(s), Vol 0026, 95; Journey to Oblivion--The End of the East European Yiddish and German Worlds in the Mirror of Literature, Germ Notes and Rev(s), Vol 0025, 94; The German Nachspiel in the 18th-Century, Germ Notes and Rev(s), Vol 0024, 93; Musarion and Other Rococo Tales by Wieland, Christoph, Martin, Germ Notes and Rev(s), Vol 0024, 93; The Further Adventures of the Baron-Munchhausen, Germ Notes and Rev(s), Vol 0024, 93. **CONTACT ADDRESS** Kutztown Univ, Pennsylvania, Kutztown, PA, 19530.

CRAIG, CHRISTOPHER P.
DISCIPLINE CLASSICAL STUDIES **EDUCATION** Oberlin Col, BA, 74; Univ NC, PhD, 79. **CAREER** Instr, Stockley Inst, 83-84; Tchg fel, Univ NC, 78-79; instr, Univ Ca, 79-80; asst prof, 80-86; assoc prof, 86-. **HONORS AND AWARDS** Dir, Vergilian Soc Am, 85-93. **MEMBERSHIPS** Am Philol Asn; Archaeol Inst Am; Class Asn Middle W and S; Am Class League; Vergilian Soc Am; Tennessee Lang Tchr Asn; Tennessee Class Asn; Int Soc Hist Rhet; Am Soc Hist Rhet; Speech Commun Asn. **RESEARCH** Classical rhetoric and oratory; Cicero. **SELECTED PUBLICATIONS** Auth, Cicero's Strategy of Embarrassment in the Speech for Plancius, Am Jour Philol, 90; Form as Argument in Cicero's Speeches, Scholars, 93; Three Simple Questions for Teaching Cicero's First Catilinarian Oration, Class Jour, 93; Teaching Cicero's Speech for Caelius: What Enquiring Minds Want to Know, Class Jour, 95. **CONTACT ADDRESS** Dept of Classics, Knoxville, TN, 37996. **EMAIL** ccraig@utk.edu

CRAIG, VIRGINIA ROBERTSON
PERSONAL Born 10/16/1935, Ft Worth, TX, m, 1954, 1 child **DISCIPLINE** SPANISH LANGUAGE; LITERATURE **EDUCATION** Bethel Col, Tenn, BA, 56; Univ Mo-Columbia, PhD, 68. **CAREER** Chairperson dept mod foreign lang, 76-80; asst prof Span, Ind Univ, Ft Wayne, 69-; Ind Univ grant-in-aid, 70-71; dir, Ind Univ Overseas Study Prog, Madrid, 77-78. **HONORS AND AWARDS** Distinguished Tchg Award, Ind Univ, 75. **MEMBERSHIPS** MLA; Am Asn Tchrs Span & Port; Comediantes. **RESEARCH** Seventeenth century Spanish drama; Spanish civilization and culture. **SELECTED PUBLICATIONS** Contribur, Manual of Hispanic Bibliography, Univ Wash, 70; Annotated Analytical Bibliography of Tirso de Molina Studies, 1627-1977, Univ Mo, 79. **CONTACT ADDRESS** Dept of Mod Foreign Langs, Indiana Univ-Purdue Univ, Fort Wayne, 2101 Coliseum Blvd E, Fort Wayne, IN, 46805-1445. **EMAIL** craig@IPFW.edu

CRANE, SUSAN
DISCIPLINE ENGLISH LANGUAGE AND LITERATURE **EDUCATION** Univ Wisconsin, BA: Univ Calif Berkeley, MA; PhD. **CAREER** Prof **RESEARCH** Gender; cultural history; Medieval English and French literature. **SELECTED PUBLICATIONS** Auth, Insular Romance; auth, Gender and Romance in Chaucer's Canterbury Tales . **CONTACT ADDRESS** Dept of English, Rutgers Univ, 510 George St, Murray Hall, New Brunswick, NJ, 08901-1167.

CRANNELL, KENNETH C.
PERSONAL Born 04/05/1934, Lynn, MS, m, 1960, 2 children **DISCIPLINE** ORAL INTERPRETATION **EDUCATION** Emerson Col, BA, 55, MA, 57; Northwestern Univ, PhD, 70. **CAREER** From instr to assoc prof, 57-69, PROF SPEECH & COMM STUDIES & CHMN DIV ORAL INTERPRETATION, EMERSON COL, 69-, Asst, Northwestern Univ, 61-62, instr interpretation, 64-65; speech consult, St John's Sem, 67-68; vis instr homiletics, Pope John XXIII Sem, 70-78; consult, Harvard Divinity Sch, 73; Consul, Crannell Consulting. **MEMBERSHIPS** Speech Commun Asn; Eastern States Commun Asn; New Eng Speech Asn; Eastern Commun Asn. **RESEARCH** Prosody; oral performance; modern poetry. **SELECTED PUBLICATIONS** Coauth, Oral interpretation: graduate programs, Speech Teacher, 72; contribr, Oral interpretation bibliography, NC Speech J, 73; auth, A prosodic analysis of The Hill Wife, Rodophi, Studies Interpretation, Vol II; auth, Voice and Articulation, 4th ed, Wadsworth. **CONTACT ADDRESS** Div of Oral Interpretation, Emerson Col, 100 Beacon St, Boston, MA, 02116-1596. **EMAIL** kcrhapsode@aol.com

CRANSTON, EDWIN AUGUSTUS
PERSONAL Born 10/18/1932, Pittsfield, MA, m, 1960 **DISCIPLINE** JAPANESE LITERATURE **EDUCATION** Univ Ariz, BA, 54; Stanford Univ, MA, 63, PhD(Japanese lit), 66. **CAREER** Instr Japanese, 65-66, from asst prof to assoc prof, 66-72, prof Japanese Lit, Harvard Univ, 72-, Fulbright-Hays res grant, 69-70. **HONORS AND AWARDS** MA, Harvard Univ, 72. **MEMBERSHIPS** Am Asn Asian Studies; Asn Teachers Japanese. **RESEARCH** Heian literature; Man'yoshu; poetry of Izumi Shikibu. **SELECTED PUBLICATIONS** Auth, The Izumi Shikibu Diary: A Romance of the Heian Court, Harvard Univ, 69; The poetry of Izumi Shikibu, Monumenta Nipponica, 70; Water-plant imagery in the Man'yoshu, Harvard J Asiatic Studies, 71; Murasaki's Art of fiction, Japan Quart, 4-6/71; coauth, Nihon Koten Bungei: The Courtly Tradition in Japanese Art and Literature, Kodansha Int, Tokyo, 73; auth, Young Akiko: The Literary Debut of Yosano Akiko (1878-1942), Lit East & West, 74; The Dark Path: Images of Longing in Japanese Love Poetry, Harvard J Asiatic Studies, 75; contribr, Toward a Reconsideration of Makurakotoba: An Analysis of Preposited Figurative Elements in a Choka by Hitomaro, In: Man'yoshu Kenkyu, Hanawa Shobo, Vol V, 76; A Waka Anthology, Vol I: The Gem-Glistening Cup, Stanford Univ, 93. **CONTACT ADDRESS** Dept of E Asian Lang & Civilizations, Harvard Univ, 2 Divinity Ave., Cambridge, MA, 02138-2020.

CRAWFORD, DAN
DISCIPLINE EPISTEMOLOGY, COGNITIVE SCIENCE, AND PHILOSOPHY OF RELIGION **EDUCATION** Univ Pittsburgh, PhD, 72. **CAREER** Vis prof, Univ Nebr, Lincoln. **SELECTED PUBLICATIONS** Published in the areas of knowledge and perception, the cosmological argument, Augustine, and W. Sellars. **CONTACT ADDRESS** Univ Nebr, Lincoln, Lincoln, NE, 68588-0417.

CRAWFORD, RONALD LEE
PERSONAL Born 03/28/1939, Warren, OH, m, 1973, 2 children **DISCIPLINE** GERMAN LITERATURE **EDUCATION** Heidelberg Col, BS, 61; Kent State Univ, MA, 67; Rutgers Univ, PhD(Ger), 74. **CAREER** Temp instr, Hiram Col, 61-63; from instr to asst prof, 66-77, ASSOC PROF GER, KENT STATE UNIV, 77-, Nat Endowment for Humanities, summer, 80. **MEMBERSHIPS** Am Asn Teachers Ger. **RESEARCH** Classical German literature; Schiller. **SELECTED PUBLICATIONS** Auth, All or Nothing--The Axis and the Holocaust 1941-1943, Germ Notes and Rev(s), Vol 0025, 94. **CONTACT ADDRESS** 1615 Bobwhite Trail, Stow, OH, 44224.

CRAWFORD, SIDNIE WHITE
PERSONAL Born 01/08/1960, Greenwich, CT, m, 1994 **DISCIPLINE** NEAR EASTERN LANGUAGES AND CIVILIZATIONS **EDUCATION** Harvard Univ, PhD, 88; Harvard Divinity School, MTS, 84; Trinity Coll, BA, 81. **CAREER** Assoc Prof of Hebrew Bible, 97-; Chmn of Classics, Univ of Nebraska; Asst, Assoc Prof of Rel Studies, 89-97, Albright Coll; Asst Prof of Rel, 88-89, St Olaf Coll. **HONORS AND AWARDS** United Methodist Church Award for Exemplary Tchg' Jacob Albright Award; Faculty Member of the Year; Cert of Distinction in Tchg; Abraham Joshua Herschel Prize for Rel Stud. **MEMBERSHIPS** SBL, ASOR, AIA. **RESEARCH** Second Temple Judaism, Dead Sea Scrolls, Hebrew Bible Textual Criticism. **SELECTED PUBLICATIONS** Co-auth, 4Qdeuteronomya, c, d, f, g, I, n, o, p, Discoveries in the Judaean Desert XIV, Oxford Univ, 95; coauth, 4Qreworked Pentateuch: 4Q364-367, Discoveries in the Judaean Desert XIII, Oxford Univ, 94; auth, A Response to Elizabeth Owen's "4Qdeut": A Pre-Samaritan Manuscript, Dead Sea Discoveries 5, 98; Has Esther been Found at Quamran?, 4Qproto-Esther and the Esther Corpus, Revue ke Qumran 17, 96; Amram, Testament of, "Angelic Liturgy" and eighteen other entries in Dictionary of Biblical Judaism, NY, Macmillan, 95. **CONTACT ADDRESS** Univ of Nebr, 236 Andrews Hall, Lincoln, NE, 68588. **EMAIL** scrawfor@ulinfo.url.edu

CRECELIUS, KATHRYN JUNE
PERSONAL New Rochelle, NY **DISCIPLINE** FRENCH LITERATURE **EDUCATION** Bryn Mawr Col, BA, 73; Yale Univ, MA, 74, PhD(French), 78. **CAREER** ASST PROF FRENCH, MASS INST TECHNOL, 78- **MEMBERSHIPS** Am Asn Teachers French; Friends George Sand; MLA; Northeast Mod Lang Asn. **RESEARCH** George Sand; French novel; French-Canadian novel. **SELECTED PUBLICATIONS** Auth, Merimee--Colomba and Carmen, Nineteenth-Century Fr Stud, Vol 0022, 94; Sand,George and Idealism, Esprit Createur, Vol 0034, 94; Sand, George--Life and Works in Text and Pictures-German, Nineteenth-Century Fr Stud, Vol 0022, 93; Ich-Liebe-Also-Bin-Ich--Sand, George Life and Works--German, Nineteenth-Century Fr Stud, Vol 0022, 93. **CONTACT ADDRESS** For Lang and Lit Mass Inst Technol, Cambridge, MA, 02139.

CREEL, BRYANT L.
DISCIPLINE SPANISH LITERATURE **EDUCATION** Univ Ca, PhD, 78. **CAREER** Assoc prof. **SELECTED PUBLICATIONS** Auth, pubs on sixteenth and seventeenth century Peninsular prose and poetry, and contemporary Portuguese. **CONTACT ADDRESS** Dept of Romance Languages, Knoxville, TN, 37996.

CRISPIN, JOHN
PERSONAL Born 05/03/1936, Tienen, Belgium, m, 1966, 1 child **DISCIPLINE** SPANISH LANGUAGE AND CONTEMPORARY LITERATURE **EDUCATION** Univ St Thomas, Tex, BA, 60; Univ Wis-Madison, MA, 62, PhD(Span & French), 67. **CAREER** Prof Exp: From instr to asst prof, 65-71, ASSOC PROF SPAN, VANDERBILT UNIV, 71-, CHMN SPAN-PORTT, 79-. **MEMBERSHIPS** MLA; Am Asn Teachers Span & Port. **RESEARCH** Contemporary poetry and novel; intellectual history; comparative literature. **SELECTED PUBLICATIONS** Auth, La Noche le es Propicia, World Lit Today, Vol 0067, 93; La Voz a Ti Debida, Razon de Amor, Largo Lamento--Spanish, Rev de Estudios Hispanicos, Vol 0030, 96; El Tiempo y Yo, o el Mundo a la Espalda, World Lit Today, Vol 0067, 93; Spanish Poetry of the 20th-Century--Modernity and Beyond, World Lit Today, Vol 0069, 95; Correspondence 1923-1951--Spanish, World Lit Today, Vol 0066, 92; El Ojo de la Aguja, World Lit Today, Vol 0068, 94; The Canon--Reflections on Literary and Theatrical Reception Perezdeayala, Ramon Versus Benavente, Jacinto---Spanish, World Lit Today, Vol 0068, 94; Audience and Authority in the Modernist Theater of Garcialorca, Federico, World Lit Today, Vol 0071, 97; El Don de la Simiente, World Lit Today, Vol 0068, 94; Montages and Fragments--An Approach to Avant-Garde Spanish Narrative--Spanish, World Lit Today, Vol 0070, 96; Alberti,Rafael on Ibiza--6 Weeks in the Summer Of 1936--Spanish, World Lit Today, Vol 0070, 96; Reflections on Lorca Private Mythology, Once Five Years Pass and the Rural Plays, Rev Estudios Hispanicos, Vol 0029, 95; The Aesthetic Code of Valleinclan,Ramon,Del, World Lit Today, Vol 0069, 95. **CONTACT ADDRESS** Dept of Span & Port, Vanderbilt Univ, Box 1518-B, Nashville, TN, 37203.

CRIST, LARRY S.
PERSONAL Born 01/16/1934, Harrisburg, PA, m, 1961, 3 children **DISCIPLINE** FRENCH **EDUCATION** Western Md Col, BA, 55; Princeton Univ, MA, 59, PhD(French), 63. **CAREER** Lectr French, Queens Col, NY, 61-63; from asst prof to assoc prof, 63-75, PROF FRENCH, VANDERBILT UNIV, 75-, Chmn Dept French & Ital, 80-. **MEMBERSHIPS** Am Asn Teachers Fr; Mediaeval Acad Am; MLA; AAUP; Soc Rencesvals. **RESEARCH** Medieval French cycle of the Crusade; semiotics of medieval French literature. **SELECTED PUBLICATIONS** Auth, Metrical Arts of the Early Chanson-De-Geste--Essays on the Musicality of the Narrative--French, Speculum-Jour Medieval Stud, Vol 0071, 96; Authority and Autonomy in Lentree Despagne, Speculum-Journal Medieval Stud, Vol 0071, 96; Family Relationships in Epic Poetry--Research on 12th-Century French Chansons-De-Geste and Romances--German, Speculum-Jour Medieval Stud, Vol 0068, 93; Medieval Narrative and Narratology--Subjects and Objects of Desire, Cithara-Essays in the Judeo-Christian Tradition, Vol 0033, 93; Kings, Heroes and Family Groups--Research on the Chanson-De-Geste in the 13th-Century and 14th-Century and the Formation of Cycles--German, Speculum-Jour Medieval Stud, Vol 0068, 93; Perceval or the Conte Du Graal--French, Romance Philol, Vol 0050, 97. **CONTACT ADDRESS** Dept of French, Vanderbilt Univ, Box 1598 Sta B, Nashville, TN, 37235.

CRO, STELIO
PERSONAL Born 04/07/1936, Rome, Italy, m, 1973 **DISCIPLINE** ITALIAN, SPANISH **EDUCATION** Univ Buenos Aires, Lic en Let, 63; Univ Venice, DLing e Lett Straniere(-Span), 66. **CAREER** Assoc prof Ital, Univ Buenos Aires, 67-69; asst prof Ital & Span, Fla State Univ, 69-72; from asst prof to assoc prof, 72-78, HEAD DEPT, MCMASTER UNIV, 76-, PROF ITAL, 78-. **MEMBERSHIPS** MLA; Am Asn Teachers Span & Port; Am Asn Teachers Ital. **RESEARCH** Italian 19th century literature; Spanish 19th and 20th century literature; Cervantes. **SELECTED PUBLICATIONS** Auth, Parabola, Forum Italicum, Vol 0030, 96; Pienezza, Forum Italicum, Vol 0030, 96; Paternita, Forum Italicum, Vol 0030, 96; La Scoperta di Amleto, Forum Italicum, Vol 0030, 96; Mattinata, Gradiva, Vol 0006, 94; Filmetti, Gradiva, Vol 0006, 94. **CONTACT ADDRESS** Dept of Romance Lang, McMaster Univ, 1280 Main St W, Hamilton, ON, L8S 4M2.

CROFT, LEE B.
PERSONAL Born 09/19/1946, Cut Bank, MT, m, 1981, 4 children **DISCIPLINE** FOREIGN LANGUAGES **EDUCATION** Ariz State Univ, BS, 68; Univ Ariz, MA, 70; Cornell Univ, PhD, 73. **CAREER** From asst prof to assoc prof to prof, 73-, Ariz State Univ. **HONORS AND AWARDS** Dean's Distinguised Tchg Award, 78, ASU CLAS; Distinguised Fac Achievement Award, 85, Bulington Northern Found; Joe Malik Jr Ariz Slavic Stud Award, 93; Alpha Mu Gamma Honorary Stud Mentorship Award, 95., Dept coordr, 75-, dir of critical lang inst, 91-98, Ariz State Univ. **MEMBERSHIPS** AATSEEL; AAASS;

RMMLA; ACTR. **RESEARCH** Linguistic iconicity; poetry translation; mnemonotactics. **SELECTED PUBLICATIONS** Auth, art, Triplicity and Textual Iconicity: Russian Literature Through a Triangular Prism, 95. **CONTACT ADDRESS** Arizona State Univ, Tempe, DLL-0202, Tempe, AZ, 85287-0201. **EMAIL** lee.croft@asu.edu

CRONE, ANNA LISA
PERSONAL Born 06/09/1946, Brooklyn, NY, 1 child **DISCIPLINE** RUSSIAN LITERATURE, LITERARY THEORY **EDUCATION** Educ: Goucher Col, BA, 67; Harvard Univ, MA, 69, PhD, 75. **CAREER** Instr, Goucher Col & Johns Hopkins Univ, 71-74; Prof Russ, Univ Chicago, 77-, Senator, 91-94, Founder, Slavic Forum; Fel, Radcliffe Inst Independent Study, 76-77; mem ed bd, Russ Lang J. **HONORS AND AWARDS** Quantrell Award for Excellence in Teaching, 85; Honorary Doctorate, Goucher Col, 88; Honorary Sr Res Fel, Inst Slavonic and Eastern Europ Studies, Univ London, 98-99. **MEMBERSHIPS** Am Asn Teachers Slavic & Eastern Europ Lang; MLA; Phi Beta Kappa. **RESEARCH** Late nineteenth and early twentieth-century Russian; literature and religious thought; Russian poetry and poetics. **SELECTED PUBLICATIONS** Auth, The disintegration of the mystical body: The church in Balzac and Rozanov, Die Welt der Slawen, 78; Unnamuno and Dostoevskij: Some thoughts on atheistic humanitarianism, Hispanofila, 78; Blok as Don Juan in Axmatora's Poems bez geoja & Gnosticism in Bely's Fotile Letaer, 82, Russ Lang J; Axmatora's Imitation of Annenskij, Wiener Slawistiches Jahrbueh, 81; Difference in Saussure and Derrida, Neophilologus, 78; Rozanov and the End of Literature, JAL Verlag, 78; Pasternak's Pushkinien Variations, Die Weit der Slawen, 79; The Presence of Mandelstham in the Dedication to Poema bez geroja, Russ Lit, 82; co-ed, New Studies in Russian Language & Literature, Slavic Press, 86; author of numerous articles on Russian literature of Silver Age and other topics. **CONTACT ADDRESS** Dept of Slavic Lang, Univ of Chicago, 1130 E 59th St, Chicago, IL, 60637-1539. **EMAIL** acrone@midway.uchicago.edu

CROSBY, DONALD H.
PERSONAL Born 04/03/1927, New York, NY, m, 1973, 4 children **DISCIPLINE** GERMANIC STUDIES **EDUCATION** NY Univ, AB, 51; Princeton Univ, AM, 53, PhD, 55. **CAREER** Instr Ger, Princeton Univ, 54-55; asst prof, Union Col, NY, 55-56; from instr to asst prof, Ind Univ, Bloomington, 58-63; vis assoc prof Ger lang, Queens Col, NY, 64-65; from assoc prof to prof, Univ Kans, 65-70; PROF GER LANG, UNIV CONN, 70-, Consult, US Dept Defense, 56-61; Am Coun Learned Soc studies fel, 63-64; vis prof, Dartmouth Col, 70; Fulbright fel, Univ Munich, 78. **MEMBERSHIPS** Am Asn Teachers Ger; Heinrich von Kleist Ges. **RESEARCH** Literature of the Goethezeit; Heinrich von Kleist; musical-literary relations. **SELECTED PUBLICATIONS** Auth, Kleist on Stage, 1804-1987, Jour Eng and Ger Philol, Vol 0094, 95. **CONTACT ADDRESS** Dept of Ger Lang, Univ of Conn, Storrs, CT, 06268.

CROSSGROVE, WILLIAM CHARLES
PERSONAL Born 06/06/1938, Archbold, OH, m, 1965, 2 children **DISCIPLINE** GERMAN, MEDIEVAL STUDIES **EDUCATION** Ohio Univ, AB, 59; Univ Tex, PhD(Ger ling), 62. **CAREER** From Instr to Assoc Prof, 62-80, Prof Ger, Brown Univ, 80-, Chmn Dept, 73-76 & 85-88; Res assoc ling, Univ Kiel, 65-66; vis prof, Columbia Univ, 70; **HONORS AND AWARDS** Alexander von Humboldt-Stiftung res fel, 70-71, 80, 98. **MEMBERSHIPS** Am Asn Teachers Ger; Mediaeval Acad Am; Am Asn Hist Sci. **RESEARCH** Comparative Germanic grammar; Middle High German literature; medieval technical literature. **SELECTED PUBLICATIONS** Auth, German Reader Erste Stufe, Heath, 78, 3rd ed, 92; Die deutsche Sachliteratur des Mittelalters, Lang, 94; co-ed, Vernacularization of Science, Technology, and Medicine in Late Medieval Europe. Special issue of Early Science and Medicine, 98. **CONTACT ADDRESS** Dept of Ger, Brown Univ, Providence, RI, 02912-1979.

CROWHURST, MEGAN J.
DISCIPLINE LINGUISTICS **EDUCATION** Univ BC, BA, 85; Univ Ariz, MA, 89, PhD, 91. **CAREER** Assoc, 91-93, lectr, 92-93, Univ Tex, Austin; asst prof, Yale Univ, 93-94; ASST PROF, LINGUISTICS, UNIV NC, CHAPEL HILL, 94-. **CONTACT ADDRESS** Dept of Linguistics, Univ of No Carolina, Chapel Hill, CB 3155, Chapel Hill, NC, 27599-3155.

CROWLEY, JOSEPH P.
PERSONAL Born 02/27/1946, South Bend, IN, m, 1972, 5 children **DISCIPLINE** LANGUAGE **EDUCATION** Univ Toronto, BA, 69; Univ NC Chapel Hill, PhD, 80. **CAREER** Asst prof, 80-98, assoc prof, 98-, Auburn Univ, Montgomery. **RESEARCH** Old Engl lang; glosses & additions to prayer bks; MS Royal 2 A xx; name stud **CONTACT ADDRESS** Dept of English, Auburn Univ, Montgomery, PO Box 244023, Montgomery, AL, 36124. **EMAIL** jcrowley@edla.aum.edu

CROWNER, DAVID L.
DISCIPLINE LANGUAGE **EDUCATION** Pacific Lutheran Univ, BA, 61; Rutgers Univ, PhD, 67. **CAREER** Instr, Hartwick Col, 64-67; Asst Prof to Prof of German, 67-, Gettysburg Col. **CONTACT ADDRESS** Gettysburg Col, Box 398, Gettysburg, PA, 17325. **EMAIL** crowner@gettysburg.edu

CUENCA, JOSE RAMON ARALUCE
DISCIPLINE SPANISH LITERATURE **EDUCATION** Fla State Univ, PhD. **CAREER** Assoc prof, Univ Southern Calif. **SELECTED PUBLICATIONS** Auth, El libro de los estados: Don Juan Manuel y la sociedad de su tiempo and Sintaxis de la paremia en el Arcipreste de Talavera. **CONTACT ADDRESS** Dept of Spanish and Portuguese, Univ Southern Calif, University Park Campus, Los Angeles, CA, 90089. **EMAIL** araluce@usc.edu

CULATTA, BARBARA
DISCIPLINE COMMUNICATIVE DISORDERS **EDUCATION** Univ Pittsburgh, PhD. **CAREER** Prof; post-doctoral fel, Johns Hopkins Univ. **MEMBERSHIPS** Partners of the Am prog. **SELECTED PUBLICATIONS** Publ on, using play and story enactments in intervention contexts highlight these clinical practices; relationship between perceptual and linguistic deficits; lang difficulties in children with Spina Bifida & intervention practices within classroom contexts. **CONTACT ADDRESS** Dept of Communicative Disorders, Univ of RI, 8 Ranger Rd, Ste. 1, 116 Adams , Kingston, RI, 02881-0807. **EMAIL** barb@uriacc.uri.edu

CULBERTSON, DIANA
PERSONAL Born 09/18/1930, Atlanta, GA **DISCIPLINE** COMPARATIVE LITERATURE, RELIGION **EDUCATION** Siena Heights Col, BA, 52: John Carroll Univ, MA, 58; Univ NC, Chapel Hill, PhD(comp lit), 71; Aquinas Inst Theol, Iowa, MA, 80. **CAREER** Lectr world lit, St John Col Cleveland, 63-65; instr English, Univ NC, Chapel Hill, 70-71; asst prof, 71-76, ASSOC PROF COMP LIT, KENT STATE UNIV, 76-, Danforth Found fel, 76. **MEMBERSHIPS** MLA; Am Acad Relig; Am Comp Lit Asn; Cath Theol Soc Am. **RESEARCH** Comparative literature; religion; theology. **SELECTED PUBLICATIONS** Auth, Aint-Nobody-Clean, the Liturgy of Violence in Glory--Self-Sacrificing Racial Violence in Zwick, Edward Film, Rel and Lit, Vol 0025, 93; Inscribing the Other, So Hum Rev, Vol 0028, 94; The Jews Body, So Hum Rev, Vol 0028, 94. **CONTACT ADDRESS** Dept of English, Kent State Univ, PO Box 5190, Kent, OH, 44242-0001.

CULHAM, PHYLLIS
PERSONAL Born 06/22/1948, Junction City, KS, m, 1969, 1 child **DISCIPLINE** ANCIENT HISTORY, CLASSICAL LITERATURE **EDUCATION** Univ Kans, BA, 70; State Univ NY Buffalo, MA, 72, PhD, 76. **CAREER** Lectr classics, Univ Calif, Irvine, 75-77; asst prof hist, Univ Ill, Chicago, 77-79; from Asst Prof to Assoc Prof, 79-91, prof hist, US Naval Acad, 91-. **HONORS AND AWARDS** NEH Curriculum Grant, 94. **MEMBERSHIPS** Asn Ancient Historians; Am Philol Asn. **RESEARCH** Roman bureaucratic history; Latin epigraphy. **SELECTED PUBLICATIONS** Auth, Classics: A Discipline and Profession in Crisis, 89; Seneca's on Favors, 95. **CONTACT ADDRESS** Dept of Hist, US Naval Acad, Annapolis, MD, 21402. **EMAIL** culham@nadn.navy.mil

CULL, JOHN T.
DISCIPLINE SPANISH **EDUCATION** Parkland Jr Col, Champaign and Univ Ill at Urbana-Champaign, BA, 75; Univ Ill at Urbana-Champaign, MA, 78, PhD, 84. **CAREER** Assoc prof. **RESEARCH** European emblem literature; Grupo de investigacion sobre literatura Emblematica Espanola; a compendium of Illustrated Spanish emblems; Spanish golden age comedia; Spanish golden age prose; medieval Spanish medicine; Spanish sentimental fiction. **SELECTED PUBLICATIONS** Auth, Hablan poco y dicen mucho: The Function of Discovery Scenes in the Drama of Tirso de Molina, Mod Lange Rev 91 3, 96; Purging Humor(s): Medical and Scatalogical Imagery in Tirso de Molina, Bull of the Comediantes 47 2, 95; Emblems in the Secular Drama of Calderon: A Review Article, Romance Quart 41 2, 94. **CONTACT ADDRESS** Dept of Modern Languages and Literatures, Col of the Holy Cross, 1 College St, PO Box 113A, Worcester, MA, 01610-2395. **EMAIL** jcull@holycross.edu

CULTER, SUZANNE
DISCIPLINE EAST ASIAN STUDIES **EDUCATION** Univ Hawaii, PhD. **CAREER** Asst prof. **RESEARCH** Sociology of Japan **SELECTED PUBLICATIONS** Auth, Industry Restructuring and Family Migration Decisions: A Community Study in Japan, 94; auth, Coal Industry Decline in Japan: Community and Household Response, JAI, 92. **CONTACT ADDRESS** East Asian Studies Dept, McGill Univ, 845 Sherbrooke St, Montreal, PQ, H3A 2T5.

CUMMINS, FRED
PERSONAL m, 1 child **DISCIPLINE** LINGUISTICS **EDUCATION** Trinity Col Dublin, BA, 91; Ind Univ, MA, 96, PhD, 97. **CAREER** Postdoctoral res, 97-; tchg, 97-98; led working sessions Rhythm Study Group, Ind Univ, 96; res asst to Dr Robert Port, 92-95; assoc instr, 95; crse instr; assoc instr, 96; invited sem, Dept Colloquium, Northwestern Univ, 97. **HONORS AND AWARDS** Cognitive Sci Dissertation awd, Ind Univ, 98; Mellon postdoctoral fel, Northwestern Univ, 97; Res Incentive Dissertation yr fel awd, Ind Univ, 96; Cognitive Scie Summer res awd, Ind Univ, 96 Best Student Paper in Speech Communication, Acoust Soc Am, St Louis, Mo, 95; Cognitive Sci Summer res awd, Ind Univ, 95; Connectionist Models Summer Sch Fel, Univ Colo, 93; Cognitive Sci Summer Res Awd, Ind Univ, 93; Cognitive Sci Fel, Ind Univ, 91. **MEMBERSHIPS** Acoust Soc Am; Cognitive Sci Soc; Cognitive Sci Soc Ireland; Irish Res Sci Asn. **RESEARCH** Temporal patterning in speech production and perception; speech rhythm; motor control and the coordination of skilled action; dynamic modeling within cognitive science; the relationship nbetween phonetics and phonology; biological and physiological influences on prosody; cross-linguistic variation in prosodic structure; dysfluencies and ataxias; speech rate. **SELECTED PUBLICATIONS** Coauth, Rhythmic Coordination in English Speech: An Experimental Study, PhD thesis, Ind Univ, Also Technical Report 198, Ind Univ Cognitive Sci Prog, 97; Rhythmic constraints on English stress timing, Proceedings of the Fourth International Conference on Spoken Language Processing, Alfred duPont Inst, Wilmington, Delaware, 96; Rhythmic Commonalities Between Hand Gestures and Speech, Proceedings of the 18th Annual Conf of the Cognitive Sci Soc, Lawrence Erlbaum Assoc, 96; A Dynamic Approach to Rhythm in Language: Toward a Temporal Phonology, Proceedings of the Chicago Ling Soc, Dept Ling, Univ Chicago, 96; Self-Entrainment in Animal Behavior and Human Speech, Online Proceedings of the 1996 Midwest Artificial Intelligence and Cognitive Sci Conf, 96. **CONTACT ADDRESS** Dept of Linguistics, Northwestern Univ, 1801 Hinman, Evanston, IL, 60208. **EMAIL** f-cummins@nwu.edu

CUNLIFFE, WILLIAM GORDON
PERSONAL Born 03/25/1929, Southport, England, m, 1957, 2 children **DISCIPLINE** GERMAN **EDUCATION** Univ London, BA, 53; Univ Hamburg, PhD(Ger), 63. **CAREER** Lektor transl & interpretation, Univ Saarlandes, 55-60; lectr Ger, Univ Bradford, 60-62; asst prof, 62-68, ASSOC PROF GER, UNIV WIS-MADISON, 68- **MEMBERSHIPS** MLA **RESEARCH** Medieval and modern German literature; modern English and American literature. **SELECTED PUBLICATIONS** Auth, Fact and Fiction--German History and Literature 1848-1924, Seminar- Jour Ger Stud, Vol 0029, 93. **CONTACT ADDRESS** Dept of Ger, Univ of Wis, Madison, WI, 53706.

CURLEY, MICHAEL JOSEPH
PERSONAL Born 12/23/1942, Hempstead, NY, 2 children **DISCIPLINE** MEDIEVAL LITERATURE, LATIN **EDUCATION** Fairfield Univ, BA, 64; Harvard Univ, MA, 65; Univ Chicago, PhD, 72. **CAREER** Prof Eng, dir Honors Prog, Univ Puget Sound, 71-; NEH fel classics, Univ Tex, Austin, 77-78; Am Coun Learned Soc fel Celtic, Harvard Univ, 79-80; Graves fel Celtic, Univ Wales, Aberystwyth, 82-83. **MEMBERSHIPS** Medieval Acad Am; Medieval Assn of Pac. **RESEARCH** Latin literature; palaeography; Celtic. **SELECTED PUBLICATIONS** Auth & trans, Maarie de France, Purgatory of Saint Patrick, Binghamton: Center for Medieval and Renaissance Texts, 93; auth, Geoffrey of Monmouth, New York: Macmillan, 94. **CONTACT ADDRESS** Honor's Program, Univ of Puget Sound, 1500 N Warner St, Tacoma, WA, 98416-0005. **EMAIL** curley@ups.edu

CURRAN, MARK JOSEPH
PERSONAL Born 08/30/1941, Abilene, KS, m, 1969 **DISCIPLINE** SPANISH, PORTUGUESE **EDUCATION** Rockhurst Col, BSBA, 63; St Louis Univ, PhD(Span & Latin Am studies), 68. **CAREER** Asst prof, 68-73, ASSOC PROF SPAN & PORT, ARIZ STATE UNIV, 73- **MEMBERSHIPS** Am Asn Teachers Span & Port; Pac Coast Coun Latin Am Studies; Am Folklore Soc. **RESEARCH** Folklore and popular culture of Brazil; Latin American civilization; northeastern literature of Brazil. **SELECTED PUBLICATIONS** Auth, Brazil Literatura-De-Cordel String-Literature--Poetic Chronicle and Popular History, Stud Latin Amer Pop Cult, Vol 0015, 96. **CONTACT ADDRESS** Dept of Foreign Lang, Arizona State Univ, Tempe, Tempe, AZ, 85281.

CURRY, CORRADA
DISCIPLINE ITALIAN LITERATURE AND CULTURE **EDUCATION** La State Univ, PhD, 85. **CAREER** Asst prof, La State Univ. **SELECTED PUBLICATIONS** Auth, Immagini letterarie e arti figurative, in Can J of Ital Stud, 93; Ritorno in Sicilia (poems), in Voices in Ital Am, 96; Description and Meaning in Three Novels by Gustave Flaubert, 96. **CONTACT ADDRESS** Dept of Fr Grad Stud, Louisiana State Univ, Baton Rouge, LA, 70803.

CURSCHMANN, MICHAEL
PERSONAL Born 01/11/1936, Cologne, Germany, m, 1961, 1 child **DISCIPLINE** GERMAN STUDIES **EDUCATION** Univ Munich, PhD, 62. **CAREER** From asst prof to full prof, Princeton Univ, 63- ; vis prof Univ Munich, 85-86; vis prof Univ Tribourg, 96; vis prof Univ Tubingen, 99. **HONORS AND AWARDS** Guggenheim fel, 70-71; corresp mem, Inst for Ger Stud, Univ London, 92- ; corresp mem, Bavarian Acad Sci, 97- . **MEMBERSHIPS** Medieval Acad of Am. **RESEARCH** European Middle Ages to 1600; verbal and visual arts. **SELECTED PUBLICATIONS** Coauth, Der Berner und der Riese Sigenot aug Wildenstein, PBB, 94; auth, Constantine-Heraclius: German Texts and Picture Cycles, in Aronberg-Lavin, ed, Piero della Francesca and His Legacy, Washington,

95; auth, Hofische Laienkultur zwischen Mundlichkeit und Schrift-lichkeit: Das Zeugnis Lamberts von Ardres, in Muller, ed, Auffuhrung und Schrift in Mittelalter und fruher Neuzeit, Stuttgart, 96; auth, Vom Wandel im bildlichen Umgang mit literarischen Gegenstanden: Rodenegg, Wildenstein und das Flaarsche Haus in Stein am Rhein, Fribourg, 97; auth, Wolfgang Stammler und die Folgen: Wort und Bild als interdisziplinares Forschungsthema in internationalem Rahmen, in, Lutz, ed, Das Mittelalter und die Germanisten, Zur neueren Methodengeschichte der germanischen Philologie, Freiburg, 98. **CONTACT ADDRESS** 134 Sycamore Rd, Princeton, NJ, 08540. **EMAIL** micur@princeton.edu

CURTIS, ALEXANDER ROSS
PERSONAL Born 08/06/1931, Tredegar, Wales, m, 1964 **DISCIPLINE** ROMANCE LANGUAGES **EDUCATION** Univ Wales, BA, 53, MA, 57; Univ Paris, DUniv(French), 66. **CAREER** From instr to asst prof, 57-70, acad secy, 66-70, assoc chmn dept, 70-71, ASSOC PROF FRENCH, UNIV TORONTO, 70-. **MEMBERSHIPS** Asn Can Univ Teachers Fr; Can Asn Appl Ling. **RESEARCH** Seventeenth century French theatre; comparative stylistics. **SELECTED PUBLICATIONS** Auth, Politics, Women, Power, Elements for a Theory of the Captive--Study on the Theater of Racine, Jean--French, Univ Toronto Quart, Vol 0063, 93. **CONTACT ADDRESS** Dept of French Univ Col, Univ of Toronto, Toronto, ON, M5S 1A1.

CURTIS, JAMES MALCOLM
PERSONAL Born 04/16/1940, Florence, AL, m, 1962, 1 child **DISCIPLINE** RUSSIAN LITERATURE **EDUCATION** Vanderbilt Univ, BA, 62; Columbia Univ, MA, 64, PhD(Russ), 68. **CAREER** Actg asst prof Russ, Univ Calif, Berkeley, 66-68; asst prof, 68-72, assoc prof, 72-78, PROF RUSS, UNIV MO-COLUMBIA 79-, Am Coun Learned Soc fel, 76-77. **MEMBERSHIPS** Am Asn Teachers Slavic & E Europ Lang; Am Asn Advan Slavic Studies. **RESEARCH** Tolstoy; Dostoevsky; critical theory. **SELECTED PUBLICATIONS** Auth, The Recurrence of Fate--Theater and Memory in 20th-Century Russia, Slavic Rev, Vol 0054, 95; Chekhov Plays--An Opening Into Eternity, Slavic and E Europ Jour, Vol 0040, 96; Russian Art and Architecture in the 19th-Century, Photographs of Barshchevsky,I.F., Slavic Rev, Vol 0055, 96; Hidden Treasures--Russian and Soviet Impressionism, 1930-1970s, Slavic Rev, Vol 0054, 95; Swan Lake--A Classic Ballet Revisited On Its Centenary--Historian Brings 20th-Century Insight to Bear on the Creation of a 19th-Century, Dance Mag, Vol 0069, 95; Chekhov Plays--An Opening Into Eternity, Slavic and E Europ Jour, Vol 0040, 96; The Dutch Connection in Russian Literature--Notes on Some Implications of Alpers, Svetlana the Art of Describing, Russ Lit, Vol 0038, 95; Art of the Soviets--Painting, Sculpture and Architecture in a One-Party State, 1917-1922, Slavic Rev, Vol 0053, 94. **CONTACT ADDRESS** Dept of Ger & Slavic Studies, Univ of Mo, Columbia, MO, 65201.

CUTTER, WILLIAM
PERSONAL Born 02/09/1937, St. Louis, MO, m, 1970 **DISCIPLINE** MODERN HEBREW LITERATURE, EDUCATION **EDUCATION** Yale Univ, AB, 59; Hebrew Union Col, Ohio, MA, 65; Univ Calif, Los Angeles, PhD(Near Eastern lit), 71. **CAREER** From instr to asst prof Hebrew lit, 65-71, asst dean col, 65-69, dir sch educ, sch Judaic studies, 69-76, assoc prof, 71-76, PROF HEBREW LIT EDUC, HEBREW UNION COL, CALIF, 76- **MEMBERSHIPS** Cent Conf Am Rabbis; AAUP; Asn Jewish Studies; Nat Asn Temple Educr; Nat Comn Jewish Educ. **RESEARCH** Hebrew literature between 1880 and 1940; contemporary Jewish religious education; American Jewish fiction. **SELECTED PUBLICATIONS** Auth, Hebrew and Modernity, Mod Judaism, Vol 0015, 95; Reading for Ethics - Renouncing Simplicity, Rel Edu, Vol 0088, 93. **CONTACT ADDRESS** Sch of Educ, Hebrew Union Col, Los Angeles, CA, 90007.

CYPESS, SANDRA MESSINGER
PERSONAL Born 01/05/1943, Brooklyn, NY, m, 1964, 2 children **DISCIPLINE** SPANISH, PORTUGUESE **EDUCATION** Brooklyn Col, AB, 63; Cornell Univ, MA, 65; Univ Ill, Urbana, PhD(Span), 68. **CAREER** Asst prof Span, Duke Univ, 67-70; assoc prof, Point Park Col, 70-75; asst prof, Carnegie-Mellon Univ, 75-76; asst prof, 76-80, ASSOC PROF SPAN, STATE UNIV NY BINGHAMTON, 80-, Vis assoc prof, Univ Haifa. **MEMBERSHIPS** MLA; Am Asn Teachers Span & Port; Northeast Mod Lang Asn. **RESEARCH** Latin American drama; narrative technique; feminist criticism. **SELECTED PUBLICATIONS** Auth, Violent Acts, a Study of Contemporary Latin-American Theater, Mod Drama, Vol 0037, 94; The Revealed Genres in Los Empenos de una Casa by Juana-Ines-De-La-Cruz, Hispamerica-Rev Lit, Vol 0022, 93. **CONTACT ADDRESS** Dept of Romance Lang, State Univ NY, Binghamton, NY, 13901.

CZERWINSKI, EDWARD J.
PERSONAL Born 06/06/1929, Erie, PA **DISCIPLINE** SLAVIC DRAMA AND THEATRE, COMPARATIVE LITERATURE **EDUCATION** Grove City Col, BA, 51; Pa State Univ, MA, 55; Univ Wis, MA, 64, PhD(Russ, Polish), 65. **CAREER** Instr English, Ga Tech, 57-59; asst prof English & drama, McNeese State Col, 59-60: assoc prof Russ & Polish lit, Univ Pittsburgh, 65-66; assoc prof Slavics & chmn dept, State Univ NY, Buffalo & Millard Fillmore Eve Div, 66-67; assoc prof Russ & Polish, Univ Kans, 67-70; PROF RUSS & COMP LIT, STATE UNIV NY STONY BROOK, 70-, Chmn Comt Acad Exchange With Poland, 73-, Special ed & mem ed bd, Comp Drama; ed, Slavic & EEurop Theatre J. **HONORS AND AWARDS** Distinguished Teaching Award, NY State Asn Foreign Lang Teachers, 75. **MEMBERSHIPS** MLA; Am Asn Teachers Slavic & EEurop Lang; Int Fedn Mod Lang & Lit; AAUP; Am Asn Advan Slavic Studies. **SELECTED PUBLICATIONS** Auth, The Year of the Frog, World Lit Today, Vol 0068, 94; Milosz,Czeslaw-- A Stockholm Conference September 9-11, 1991, Slavic and E Europ Jour, Vol 0038, 94; Literature and Tolerance--Views from Prague, World Lit Today, Vol 0069, 95; Still Alive--An Autobiographical Essay, World Lit Today, Vol 0068, 94; Mr Cogito, World Lit Today, Vol 0069, 95; The Memory of the Body--Essays on Theater and Death, World Lit Today, Vol 0067, 93; The Bride of Texas, World Lit Today, Vol 0070, 96; Contemporary East European Poetry--An Anthology, World Lit Today, Vol 0068, 94; The Mature Laurel--Essays on Modern Polish Poetry, Slavic and East Europ Jour, Vol 0037, 93; The Jingle Bell Principle, World Lit Today, Vol 0067, 93; The Poets Work--An Introduction to Milosz,Czeslaw, Slavic and E Europ Jour, Vol 0037, 93; A Journey Through Other Spaces--Essays and Manifestos, 1944-1990, World Lit Today, Vol 0068, 94; 20th-Century European Drama, World Lit Today, Vol 0068, 94; The Achievement of Skvorecky,Josef, World Lit Today, Vol 0069, 95; Spoiling Cannibals Fun--Polish Poetry of the Last 2 Decades of Communist Rule, Slavic and E Europ Jour, Vol 0037, 93; Goodbye, Samizdat--20 Years of Czechoslovak Underground Writing, World Lit Today, Vol 0067, 93. **CONTACT ADDRESS** Dept of Ger & Slavic Lang, State Univ of NY, Stony Brook, NY, 11790.

D

D'ANDREA, ANTONIO
PERSONAL Born 11/22/1916, Messina, Italy **DISCIPLINE** ITALIAN **EDUCATION** Univ Pisa, Dottorato in Filosofia, 39. **CAREER** Assoc prof to prof, 56-86, ch Ital, 64-76, PROF EMER ITALIAN, McGILL UNIV, 86-; dir, Ital Cultur Inst Montreal, 62-64. **HONORS AND AWARDS** Stella della Solidarieta italiana; Grande Ufficiale, Ordine al Merito della Repubblica (Ital); Queen's Silver Jubilee Medal; Royal Soc Can. **MEMBERSHIPS** Can Mediter Int; Can Soc Ital Stud; Asn Profs Ital Que; Can Soc Renaissance Stud. **SELECTED PUBLICATIONS** Auth, Il nome della storia, 82; auth, Strutture inquiete, 93; co-ed, Discours contre Machiavel, 74; co-ed, Yearbook of Italian Studies, 71-75. **CONTACT ADDRESS** Dept of Ital, McGill Univ, 1001 Sherbrooke St W, Montreal, PQ, H3A 1G5.

D'ARMS, JOHN H.
PERSONAL Born 11/27/1934, Poughkeepsie, NY, m, 1961, 2 children **DISCIPLINE** CLASSICAL PHILOLOGY **EDUCATION** Princeton Univ, AB, 56; New College, Oxford, BA (Literae Humaniores), 59; Harvard Univ, PhD (Classical Philol), 65. **CAREER** Chmn, dept classical studies, Univ MI, 72-75, 76-77, 80-85; dir, Am Academy in Rome and A W Mellon Prof, School of Classical Studies, 77-80; dean, Horace H Rackham School of Graduate Studies, Univ MI, 85-95, prof history, 86-97, Vice Provost for Academic Affairs, 90-95, G F Else Prof Humanities, Univ MI, 95-97; adjunct prof Classics and History, Columbia Univ, 97-; pres, AM Coun of Learned Societies, 97-. **HONORS AND AWARDS** Phi Beta Kappa, Princeton Univ, 56; Princeton Univ, Keasbey Scholar, 56; Honorary Woodrow Wilson fel, 56; Fulbright fel, Univ Rome, 61-62; Am Coun Learned Societies fel, 71-72; fel, John Simon Guggenheim Memorial Found, 75-76; vis member, School of Historical Studies, Inst for Advanced Study, Princeton, 75-76; corresponding member, German Archaeological Inst, Rome, 80-; Distinguished Faculty Achievement Award, Univ MI, 82; fel, Am Academy of Arts and Sciences, 92-; Centennial Medal, Am Academy in Rome, 95; Presidential Medal for Outstanding Service, Univ MI, 95; member, Am Philos Soc, 98; Docteur Honoris Causa (honorary), Univ Montreal, 98. **MEMBERSHIPS** Archaeolog Inst of Am; Am Hist Asn; Soc for the Promotion of Roman Studies (England); Am Philol Asn. **RESEARCH** Roman social, cultural, and economic history; Roman historiography; Latin epigraphy; Roman art, architecture, and archaeology; Latin prose and poetry. **SELECTED PUBLICATIONS** Auth, Romans on the Bay of Naples: A Social and Cultural Study of the Villas and their Owners from 150 BC to AD 400, Harvard Univ Press, 70; co-ed with E C Kopff, Roman Seaborne Commerce: Studies in Archaeology and History (Memoirs of the Am Academy in Rome), 80; auth, Commerce and Social Standing in Ancient Rome, Harvard Univ Press, 81; Control, Companionship, and Clientela: some Social Functions of the Roman Communal Meal, Echos du Monde Classique, N S 3, 84; The Roman Convivium and the Idea of Equality, in O Murray, ed, Sympotica: A Symposium on the Symposium, Claredon Press, Oxford, 90; Slaves at Roman Convivia, in W J Slater, ed, Dining in a Classical Context, Univ MI Press, 91; Heavy Drinking and Drunkenness in the Roman World: Questions for Historians, in O Murray, ed, In Vino Veritas, British School at Rome, 95; Funding Trends in the Academic Humanities, 1970-1995: Reflections on the Stability of the System, in A Kernan, ed, What's Happened to the Humanities, Princeton Univ Press, 97. **CONTACT ADDRESS** American Council of Learned Societies, 228 E 45th St, New York, NY, 10017-3398.

DAIGLE-WILLIAMSON, MARSHA A.
PERSONAL Born 06/16/1946, St. John, ME, m, 1992 **DISCIPLINE** FOREIGN LANGUAGES **EDUCATION** Col New Rochelle, BA, 66; Univ Wisc, MA, 67; Univ Mich, PhD, 84. **CAREER** Tchg Fel, 67-72, adj lectr, 85, Univ Mich; Instr, Washtenaw Commun Col, 84-85; Instr, Oakland Commun Col, 85-89; From asst prof to assoc prof to prof to chemn, 85-. **HONORS AND AWARDS** Tchg Fel, Univ Mich, 67-72; Fac Merit Award, 87, Excellence in Tchg Award, 88, 90, 93, Spring Arbor Col; Sabbatical Stud on Dante, Rome, Italy, 95-96. **MEMBERSHIPS** Pi Delta Phi, Kappa Gamma Pi; Sigma Tau Delta; Mich Acad Science, Arts and Letters. **RESEARCH** Dante; CS Lewis; renaissance **SELECTED PUBLICATIONS** Ed, Ann Arbor Wedding Consultant; auth, art, Dante's Divine Comedy and CS Lewis's Narnia Chronicles, 86; auth, entry, Francis Bason: The New Atlantis, 95; auth, entry, Andrew Marvell: Bermudas, 98; auth, art, Tradition and Lewis's Individual Talent, 98. **CONTACT ADDRESS** 3030 Roundtree Blvd, Ypsilanti, MI, 48197. **EMAIL** marshadw@admin.arbor.edu

DAILEY, JOSEPH
DISCIPLINE ORGANIZATIONAL AND INTERPERSONAL COMMUNICATION **EDUCATION** Marquette Univ, MA; Univ Ill, PhD. **CAREER** Law, Caroll Col. **SELECTED PUBLICATIONS** Auth, The Reluctant Candidate: Dwight Eisenhower in 1951. **CONTACT ADDRESS** Carroll Col, Wisconsin, 100 N East Ave, Waukesha, WI, 53186.

DAINARD, JAMES A.
PERSONAL Born 05/26/1930, Golden, BC, Canada **DISCIPLINE** FRENCH **EDUCATION** Univ BC, BA, 51, MA, 61, BLS, 62; Univ Alta, PhD, 67. **CAREER** Instr to asst prof, Romance lang, Univ Alta, 63-68; asst prof to prof, 68-95, PROF EMER FRENCH, UNIV TORONTO, 95-. **SELECTED PUBLICATIONS** Ed, Editing Correspondence, 79; contrib ed, Correspondance generale d'Helvetius, vols 1-4, 81-; gen ed, La Correspondance de Madame de Graffigny, vols 1-5, 85-. **CONTACT ADDRESS** Univ Col, Univ Toronto, Toronto, ON, M5S 3H7.

DAMIANI, BRUNO MARIO
PERSONAL Born 04/15/1942, Pola, Italy **DISCIPLINE** SPANISH, ITALIAN **EDUCATION** Ohio State Univ, BA, 63, MA, 64; Johns Hopkins Univ, PHD(romance lang & lit), 67. **CAREER** Asst prof, 67-69, ASSOC PROF ROMANCE LANG & LIT, CATH UNIV AM, 69-, Consult Title VII & prog qual consult, Task Group C, Dept Health, Educ & Welfare, 72; prog off, Nat Endowment for Humanities, 76. **MEMBERSHIPS** Asoc Int Hispanistas; MLA; Am Asn Teachers Span & Port. **RESEARCH** Medieval, Renaissance and Baroque periods; Spanish Renaissance literature; Spanish and Italian medieval literature. **SELECTED PUBLICATIONS** Auth, Garcilaso-De-La-Vega and the Italian Renaissance, Hispania-Jour Devoted Tchg Span and Port, Vol 0079, 96; La Amistad Pagada--Spanish, Bulletin Hisp Stud, Vol 0072, 95; Writing Women in Late-Medieval and Early-Modern Spain-- The Mothers of Teresa-Of-Avila, Cath Hist Rev, Vol 0082, 96; Introduction to Cervantes--Italian, Hisp Rev, Vol 0061, 93; Cervantes, Presenting the Disintegrated World in the Form of a Novel--Spanish, Hisp Rev, Vol 0064, 96; Espinel,Vicente, History and Critical Anthology, Vol 1-2-Spanish, Hisp Rev, Vol 0064, 96. **CONTACT ADDRESS** Dept of Mod Long, Catholic Univ of America, Washington, DC, 20017.

DAMROSCH, DAVID N.
PERSONAL Born 04/13/1953, Bar Harbor, ME, m, 1974, 3 children **DISCIPLINE** COMPARITIVE AND ENGLISH LITERATURE **EDUCATION** Yale Univ, BA, 75, PhD(comp lit), 80. **CAREER** Speechwriter & ed, Off Special Asst to the Pres for Health, White House, Washington, DC, 79; asst prof, 80-; prof comp lit, Columbia Univ, 87-. **MEMBERSHIPS** MLA; Am Comp Lit Asn. **RESEARCH** The novel; epic and romance; scripture. **SELECTED PUBLICATIONS** Auth, The Narrative Covenant, 87; We Scholars, 95; ed, The Longman Anthology of British Literature, 98. **CONTACT ADDRESS** Dept of English & Comp Lit, Columbia Univ, 2960 Broadway, New York, NY, 10027-6900. **EMAIL** dnd2@columbia.edu

DANA, MARIE IMMACULEE
PERSONAL Born 10/28/1931, Albany, NY **DISCIPLINE** FRENCH LANGUAGE & LITERATURE **EDUCATION** Rosemont Col, BA, 53; McGill Univ, MA, 62; Fulbright, 63-64; Univ Pa, PhD(French), 68. **CAREER** Teacher, St Agnes Sch, 53-54; teacher French, Latin & hist, Our Lady of Mercy Acad, 55-60 & St Peter High Sch, 60-63; instr, 54-63, asst prof, 67-73, assoc prof French, Carlow Col, 73-, chemn dept lang 67-, chemn, dept educ, 75-, prof, 92-, vice pres acad affairs, 92-, travel grant, Bibliotheque Nationale, Paris, 66; consult, Duquesne-Carlow Pupil-Personnel Serv Prog; Acad Am Coun Educ Admin fel, 74; consult, Pa Dept Educ, 77-; Adv bd mem,

Project 81, 78-. **MEMBERSHIPS** MLA; Am Coun Teaching For Lang. **RESEARCH** Twentieth century French literature. **SELECTED PUBLICATIONS** Auth, Lope de Vega in the work of Moliere, Hispanofila (in press). **CONTACT ADDRESS** Dept of Acad Affairs, Carlow Col, 3333 Fifth Ave, Pittsburgh, PA, 15213-3165. **EMAIL** midanarsm@carlow.edu

DANESI, MARCEL
PERSONAL Born 10/01/1946, Lucca, Italy **DISCIPLINE** ITALIAN STUD **EDUCATION** Univ Toronto, BA, 69, MA, 71, PhD, 74; Royal Conserv, ARCT, 83. **CAREER** Vis prof, Rutgers Univ, 72-74; PROF ITALIAN STUD, VICTORIA COL, UNIV TORONTO, 74-, dir, prog semiotics & commun theory; vis prof, Catholic Univ Milan, 91; permanent vis prof, Univ Lugano, 95-. **SELECTED PUBLICATIONS** Auth, Vico, Metaphor and the Origin of Language, 93; auth, Cool: The Signs and Meanings of Adolescence, 94; auth, Messages and Meanings: Introduction to Semiotics, 94; auth, Giambattista Vico and the Cognitive Science Enterprise, 95; auth, Increase Your Puzzle IQ, 97; coauth, Applied Psycholinguistics, 85; co-ed, Ital Asn Applied Ling, 90-. **CONTACT ADDRESS** Victoria Col, Univ of Toronto, NF 217, Toronto, ON, M5S 1K7.

DANIELS, MARILYN
DISCIPLINE LANGUAGES **EDUCATION** NYU, PhD, 89; Wm Paterson Col, MA, 80, BA, 79 **CAREER** Assoc Prof, 96-, Asst prof, 90-96, PA St Univ; Asst Prof, 89-90, Cent CT St Univ; Asst Prof, 87-88, Univ of Charleston **HONORS AND AWARDS** Matthews Awd for Excel in Res, 97; Campus Advisory Board Tch Awd, 96 **RESEARCH** Sign language **SELECTED PUBLICATIONS** Auth, Benedictine Roots in the Development of Deaf Education, Listening with the Heart, Bergin and Garvey, 97; The Dance in Christianity: A History of Religious Dance Through the Ages, Paulist Press, 81 **CONTACT ADDRESS** Pennsylvania State Univ, Dunmore, PA, 18512-1699. **EMAIL** mxd34@psu.edu

DANKER, FREDERICK W.
PERSONAL Born 07/12/1920, Frankenmuth, MI, m, 1948, 2 children **DISCIPLINE** NEW TESTAMENT THEOLOGY, LIGUISTICS **EDUCATION** Concordia Sem, BA, 42, BD, 50; Univ Chicago, PhD, 63. **CAREER** From asst prof to prof New Testament exec theol, 54-74; PROF NEW TESTAMENT EXEC THEOL, CHRIST SEM-SEMINEX, 74-. **MEMBERSHIPS** Am Philol Asn; Soc Bibl Lit; Am Soc Papyrologists; Societas Novi Testamenti Studiorum; Cath Bibl Asn. **RESEARCH** Greek tragedy; Greek and Latin Epigraphy; Greek Lexicography. **SELECTED PUBLICATIONS** Auth, Apollonios-Of-Tyana in New-Testament Exegesis--Research Report and Continuing Discussion--German, Cath Bibl Quart, Vol 0058, 96; The Preface to Luke Gospel--Literary Convention and Social-Context in Luke-I,1-4 and Acts-I,1, Cath Bibl Quart, Vol 0057, 95; Paul the Accused--His Portrait in the Acts of the Apostles, Cath Bibl Quart, Vol 0058, 96; A Translator Freedom--Modern English Bibles and Their Language, Cath Bibl Quart, Vol 0057, 95. **CONTACT ADDRESS** 6928 Plateau Ave, St Louis, MO, 63139.

DANLY, ROBERT LYONS
PERSONAL Born 01/03/1947, Hinsdale, IL **DISCIPLINE** JAPANESE LITERATURE **EDUCATION** Yale Univ, BA, 69, MA, 71, PhD(Japanese lit), 80. **CAREER** Asst prof, 79-82, Assoc Prof Japanese Lit, Univ Mich, 82-, Reader, Nat Endowment for Humanities, 80-81; consult, The Kenyon Rev, 81-; mem, exec comt, PROG COMP LIT, UNIV MICH, 81-, CTR JAPANESE STUDIES, 82- **HONORS AND AWARDS** The Am Bk Award for Translation, 82. **MEMBERSHIPS** Asn Asian Studies; Asn Teachers Japanese; MLA; Pen; Am Lit Transl Asn. **RESEARCH** Premodern Japanese fiction of the 17th and 18th centuries; Japanese novel of the early modern period, 1868-1930. **SELECTED PUBLICATIONS** Auth, Ihara,Saikaku and Opening Night in the Capital, Lit Rev, Vol 0039, 96. **CONTACT ADDRESS** Dept Far Eastern Lang & Lit, Univ Mich, 105 S State St, Ann Arbor, MI, 48109-1285.

DARST, DAVID HIGH
PERSONAL Born 06/08/1943, Greensboro, NC, m, 1969, 2 children **DISCIPLINE** GOLDEN AGE SPANISH LITERATURE **EDUCATION** Univ of the South, AB, 65; Univ NC, Chapel Hill, MA, 67; Univ Ky, PhD, 70. **CAREER** Asst prof, 70-76, assoc prof span, 76-81, asst dir humanities, 78-81, full prof Spanish & assoc dir humanities, Fla State Univ, 81-, Nat Endowment for Humantities grants, 74, 78 & 81-82. **RESEARCH** Renaissance and baroque; humanities. **SELECTED PUBLICATIONS** Auth, The comic art of Tirso de Molina, Estudios de Hispanofila, The two worlds of La Ninfa del Cielo, Hisp Res & The thematic design of El Condemado por Desconfiado, Kentucky Romance Quart, 74; Tirso de Molina's The Trickster of Seville: A Critical Commentary, Simon & Schuster, 76; Lope de Vega y Cervantes o la modernidad literaria, Arbor, Madrid, 77; Juan Buscan, Twayne, 78; Andrenio's perception of reality and the structure of El Criticon, Hispania, 77; Witchcraft in Spain: The testimony of Martin de Castanega's Treatise on Superstition and Witchcraft, Proc Am Philos Soc, 79. **CONTACT ADDRESS** Dept of Mod Lang, Florida State Univ, 600 W College Ave, Tallahassee, FL, 32306-1096. **EMAIL** ddarst@mailer.fsu.edu

DASSONVILLE, MICHEL
PERSONAL Born 12/27/1927, Lille, France, m, 1949, 3 children **DISCIPLINE** FRENCH LITERATURE **EDUCATION** Univ Lille, BA, 46, Lic es Let, 48; Univ Sacre-Coeur, MA, 51; Laval Univ, DLet, 53. **CAREER** Asst prof French lit, Laval Univ, 53-58; charge de cours, Cath Inst Paris, 58-60; from vis asst prof to assoc prof, 60-63, PROF FRENCH LIT, UNIV TEX, AUSTIN, 63-, Res grants, French Govt, 53 & 58 & Can Arts Coun, 57; Casgrain Prize, 58, Minnie Stevens Piper prof, 65; cult secy, Alliance Francaise, Paris, 58-60; pres, Alliance Francaise, Austin, Tex, 63-67. **HONORS AND AWARDS** Chevalier des Palmes Academiques, French Govt, 76. **MEMBERSHIPS** S Cent Mod Lang Asn. **RESEARCH** Sixteenth century French literature. **SELECTED PUBLICATIONS** Auth, Sceve,Maurice and Christian Thought--French, Zeitschrift fur Franzosische Sprache und Literatur, Vol 0106, 96. **CONTACT ADDRESS** Univ of Tex, Sutton Hall 215, Austin, TX, 78712.

DAUSTER, FRANK NICHOLAS
PERSONAL Born 02/05/1925, Irvington, NJ, m, 1949, 2 children **DISCIPLINE** SPANISH **EDUCATION** Rutgers Univ, AB, 49, MA, 50; Yale Univ, PhD(Span), 53. **CAREER** From instr to asst prof Romance lang, Wesleyan Univ, 50-55; from asst prof to assoc prof, 55-61, Prof Romance Lang, 61-97, PROF EMERITUS, RUTGERS UNIV, NEW BRUNSWICK, 97. **MEMBERSHIPS** MLA; Am Asn Teachers Span & Port; Inst Int Lit Iberoam. **RESEARCH** Contemporary Latin America, particularly the theater and poetry. **SELECTED PUBLICATIONS** Auth, Breve Historia de la Poesia Mexicana, 56, Ensayos sobre Poesia Mcxicana, 63 & Breve Historia del Teatre Hispanoamericano, Siglox XIX-XX, 66, 2nd ed, 73, Studium; co-ed, Literatura de Hispanoamericana, Harcourt, 70; auth, Xavier Villaurrutia, Twayne, 71; co-ed, En un acto, Van Nostrand, 74; Ensayos sobre Teatro Hispanoamericana, Sepsetentas, 75; co-ed, 9 dramaturgos hispanamericanos, Ginol, 79, 2d ed, 98. **CONTACT ADDRESS** 159 Lakeside Dr N, Piscataway, NJ, 08854.

DAVIAU, DONALD G.
PERSONAL Born 09/30/1927, Medway, MA, m, 1950 **DISCIPLINE** GERMAN **EDUCATION** Clark Univ, BA, 50; Univ Calif, MA, 52, PhD, 55. **CAREER** From instr to assoc prof Ger, 55-75, chmn dept Ger & Russ, 69-75, prof German, Univ Calif, Riverside, 75-, ed, Mod Austrian Lit, 71-. **HONORS AND AWARDS** Ehrenkreuz fur Wissenschaft und Kunst, Austrian Govt, 77. **MEMBERSHIPS** MLA; Am Asn Teachers Ger; Int Arthur Schnitzler Res Asn (pres, 78-); Hugo von Hofmannsthal Gesellschaft; Am Coun for Study Austrian Lit (pres, 80-). **RESEARCH** Modern Austrian and German literature. **SELECTED PUBLICATIONS** Co-ed, The Correspondence of Arthur Schnitzler and Raoul Auernheimer, Univ NC, 72; coauth, The Correspondence of Hugo von Hofmannsthal and Raoul Auernheimer, Mod Austrian Lit, 74; coauth, The Ariadne auf Naxos of Hugo von Hoftmannsthal and Richard Strauss, Univ NC, 76; Hermann Bahr and decadence, Mod Austrian Lit, 77; auth, The Letters of Arthur Schnitzler to Hermann Bahr, Univ NC, 78; Das junge und das jungste Wien, In: Osterreichische Gegenwart, Francke Verlag, 80; Hermann Bahr and the secessionist art movement in Vienna, In: The Turn of the Century, Bouvier Verlag, 81; Das Exilerlebnis, 82; coed, The Correspondence of Stefan Zweig with Raoul Auernheimer and Richard Beer-Hofmann, 83; Der Mann von Ubermorgen, 84; ed, Stefan Zweig/Paul Zech. Briefe 1910-1942, 84 & 87; Hermann Bahr, 85; coed, Exil: Wirkung und Wertung, 85; ed, Major Figures of Comtemporary Austrian Literature, 87; ed, Major Figures of Modern Austrian Literature, 88; coed, Austrian Fiction Writers 1875-1913, 89; coed, Austrian Fiction Writers after 1914, 89; ed, Major Figures of Turn-of-the-Century Austrian Literature, 91; ed, Austrian Writers and the Anschluss, 91; ed, Osterreichische Tagebuchschriftsteller, 94; ed, Major Figures of the Austrian Inteerwar Years 1918-1938, 95; ed, Jura Soyfer and His Time, 95; coed, Geschichte der osterreichischen Literatur, 97; ed, Major Figures of Nineteenth-Century Austrian Literature, 98. **CONTACT ADDRESS** Dept of Literature & Language, Univ of California, Riverside, 900 University Ave, Riverside, CA, 92521-0001. **EMAIL** donald.daviau@ucr.edu

DAVIDHEISER, JAMES CHARLES
PERSONAL Reading, PA, 1 child **DISCIPLINE** FOREIGN LANGUAGE, LITERATURE **EDUCATION** La Salle Col, BA, 63; Univ Pittsburgh, MA & PhD(Ger lang & lit), 72. **CAREER** Instr English, Univ Mainz, 67-68; instr Ger, Univ Pittsburgh, 68-69; asst prof Ger lang & lit, Univ Del, 69-76, fac res grant, 73; ASSOC PROF GER & CHMN DEPT, UNIV OF THE SOUTH, 76-, Fulbright grant, 77; Exxon Found grant, 81. **MEMBERSHIPS** Am Asn Teachers Ger; Lessing Soc; Southern Comp Lit Asn. **RESEARCH** Modern German literature; comparative literature; 18th century literature. **SELECTED PUBLICATIONS** Auth, Grammar Groups in the Student-Centered Classroom, For Lang Annals, Vol 0029, 96; Intermediate Conversation and Composition Courses--What Makes Them Successful, For Lang Annals, Vol 0028, 95. **CONTACT ADDRESS** Dept of Ger, Univ of the South, Sewanee, TN, 37375.

DAVIDSON, HUGH MACCULLOUGH
PERSONAL Born 01/21/1918, Lanett, AL, m, 1951, 1 child **DISCIPLINE** ROMANCE LANGUAGES **EDUCATION** Univ Chicago, AB, 38, PhD, 46. **CAREER** From instr to asst prof French, Univ Chicago, 46-53, asst dean col, 49-52, chmn col French staff, 51-53; asst prof Romance lang, Dartmouth Col, 53-56, prof, 56-62, chmn dept, 57-59; prof French, Ohio State Univ, 62-76; mem fac, 76-79, PROF FRENCH, UNIV VA, 79-, Carnegie fel, Univ Chicago, 48-49; Fulbright res scholar, France, 59-60; Nat Found Arts & Humanities sr fel, 67-68; mem ed comt, PMLA, 68-73. **HONORS AND AWARDS** MA, Dartmouth Col, 56. **MEMBERSHIPS** Am Asn Teachers Fr; MLA; Int Asn Fr Studies. **RESEARCH** Seventeenth and 18th century French literature; methods of literary study and criticism; literature and philosophy. **SELECTED PUBLICATIONS** Auth, Playing with Truth--Language and the Human Condition in Pascal Pensees, Fr Forum, Vol 0020, 95. **CONTACT ADDRESS** Dept of French, Univ of Va, Charlottesville, VA, 22903.

DAVIDSON, JOHN E.
PERSONAL Born 09/27/1960, Knoxville, TN **DISCIPLINE** FOREIGN LANGUAGES; LITERATURE **EDUCATION** Univ South, BA, 82; Univ Iowa, MA, 90; Cornell Univ, PhD, 93. **CAREER** Asst prof, USU, 93-. **HONORS AND AWARDS** Fulbright Scholar; NEH Summer Grant. **MEMBERSHIPS** AATG; MLA; GSA. **RESEARCH** Film; literature; cultural theory. **SELECTED PUBLICATIONS** Auth, art, Hegemony and Cinematic Strategy, 96; auth, art, In der Fuhrer's Face: Undermining Reflections in and on Winfried Bonengel's Beruf Neonazi, 97; auth, art, Overcoming the Germany's Past(s) in Film since the Wende, 97; auth, Deterritorializing the New German Cinema, 98; auth, art, Working for the Man, Whoever That May Be: The Vocation of Wolfgang Liebeneiner, 99. **CONTACT ADDRESS** Ohio State Univ, 314 Cunz Hall, Columbus, OH, 43210-1229. **EMAIL** davidson.92@osu.edu

DAVIS, DALE W.
DISCIPLINE COMPARATIVE LITERATURE AND VICTORIAN LITERATURE **EDUCATION** Univ OK, PhD, 68. **CAREER** Assoc prof Eng, mem, grad fac, instr, Hum Stud, mem, Univ Honors Coun, dir, Bachelor of Gen Stud degree prog, TX Tech Univ. **RESEARCH** Interdisciplinary educ. **SELECTED PUBLICATIONS** Publ articles on Victorian lit, pedag, lit theory, and criticism, and co-auth a standard two-volume textbook on interdisciplinary hum--The Humanities in Western Culture (8th Edition). **CONTACT ADDRESS** Texas Tech Univ, Lubbock, TX, 79409-5015. **EMAIL** ditdd@ttacs.ttu.edu

DAVIS, GAROLD N.
PERSONAL Born 10/14/1932, Downey, ID, m, 1954, 5 children **DISCIPLINE** GERMAN AND COMPARATIVE LITERATURE **EDUCATION** Brigham Young Univ, BA, 58, MA, 59; Johns Hopkins Univ, PhD(Ger lit), 62. **CAREER** Instr Ger, Univ Pa, 62-63; asst prof, Southern Ore Col, 63-66; asst prof Ger & comp lit, Univ Colo, 66-68; PROF GER, BRIGHAM YOUNG UNIV, 68-, Assoc Dean, Col Humanities, 80-. **MEMBERSHIPS** MLA **RESEARCH** Anglo-German literary relations; Romanticism; Austrian Heimat literature. **SELECTED PUBLICATIONS** Auth, When Truth Was Treason--German Youth Against Hitler, Brigham Young Univ Stud, Vol 0036, 97 Behind the Iron-Curtain, Recollections of Latter-Day-Saints Mormon in East-Germany, 1945-1989, Brigham Young Univ Stud, Vol 0035, 95. **CONTACT ADDRESS** Dept of Ger Lang, Brigham Young Univ, 4094 Jkhb, Provo, UT, 84602-0002.

DAVIS, JAMES
DISCIPLINE READING IN A FOREIGN LANGUAGE **EDUCATION** Ouachita Univ, BA; Univ Chicago, MA, Sch Int Training, MA, Univ Miss, PhD. **CAREER** English and Lit, Univ Ark. **SELECTED PUBLICATIONS** Rev ed, Language Learning. **CONTACT ADDRESS** Univ Ark, Fayetteville, AR, 72701.

DAVIS, KENNETH G.
PERSONAL Born 09/16/1957, Louisville, KY **DISCIPLINE** PASTORAL THEOLOGY, CROSS-CULTURAL COMMUNICATION **EDUCATION** St. Louis Univ, BA, cum laude, 80; Washington Theol Union, MA, 85; Pacific Sch of Theol, DMin, 91. **CAREER** Deaconate in Honduras, 85-86; found dir, Hispanic ministry, 86-88; assoc pastor, St. Paul the Apostle Church, San Pablo, CA, 88-91; staff, intl office RENEW, 91-94; found dir, DMin, Oblate Sch Theol, 94-97; asst prof, Mundelein Sem, 97- . **MEMBERSHIPS** ACHTUS; Amer Acad Rel; Asn DMin Eduuc; CORHIM; Inst de Litugia Hispana; Nat Org Catechesis for Hispanics; Nalt Catholic Coun Hispanic Ministry. **RESEARCH** Religious faith of US Hispanics. **SELECTED PUBLICATIONS** Auth, Child Abuse in the Hispanic Community: A Christian Perspective, Apuntes, 12(3), Fall, 92, 127-136; Auth, Cuando El Tomar Ya No Es Gozar, LA, Franciscan Comm Press, 93; What's New in Hispanic Ministry, Overheard, Fall 93; auth, Primero Dios, Susquehanna UP, 94; Following the Yellow Brick Road: Rahner Reasons Through Petitionary Prayer, Living Light, 30(4), Summer, 94, 25-30; The Hispanic Shift: Continuity Rather than Conversion, in An

Enduring Flame: Studies on Latino Popular Religiosity, NY, Bildner Ctr W Hemispheric Studs, 94, 205-210; The Hispanic Shift: Continuity Rather Than Conversion, Jour Hispanic/Latino Theol, 1(3), May 94, 68-79; Preaching in Spanish as a Second Language, in Perspectivas, Kansas City, Sheed and Ward, 95; Presiding in Spanish as a Second Language, AIM, Wint 95, 22-24; Encuentros, in New Catholic Encycl, vol 19, Wash DC, Catholic UP, 95; Afterward, in Discovering Latino Religion, NY, The Bildner Ctr W Hemispheric Studs, 95; Selected Pastoral Resources, in Perspectivas, Kansas City, Sheed and Ward, 95; Las Bodas de Plata de Una Lluvia de Oro, Revista Latinoamericana de Teologia, 12(37), April, 96, 79-91; coauth, The Attraction and Retention of Hispanics to Doctor of Ministry Programs, Theol Ed, 33(1), Autumn, 96, 75-82; Presiding in Spanish as a Second Language, in Misa, Mesa y Musa, Schiller Park, IL, J.S. Paluch Co, 97; Misa, Mesa y Musa, Schiller Park, IL, J. S. Paluch, 97; From Anecdote to Analysis: A Case for Applied Research in the Ministry, Pastoral Phychol, 46(2), 97, 99-106; La Catequesis ante la Experiencia Rligiosa, Catequetica, 1, 97, 3-8; Introduction, Listening: Jour of Rel and Cult 32(3), Fall, 97, 147-151; Challenges to the Pastoral Care of Central Americans in the United States, Apuntes 17(2), Summer 97, 45-56, A New Catholic Reformation? Chicago Studs, 36(3), Dec 97, 216-223; Petitionary Prayer: What the Masters Have to Say, Spiritual Life, Summer 97, 91-99; A Survey of Contemporary US Hispanic Catholic Theology, Theol Dig, 44(3), fall 97, 203-212; co-ed, Listening: Journal of Religion and Culture, vol 32, no 3, Fall, 97; co-ed, Chicago Studies, vol 36, no 3, Dec, 97; co-ed, Theol Today, vol 54, no 4, Jan, 98; Visions and Dreams, Theol Today, 54(4), Jan 98, 451-452. **CONTACT ADDRESS** Dept of Theology, Mundelein Sem, 1000 E Maple Ave, Mundelein, IL, 60060. **EMAIL** kenonel@interaccess.com

DAVIS, STUART
PERSONAL Born 06/23/1957, San Francisco, CA **DISCIPLINE** LINGUISTICS **EDUCATION** UCLA, BA, 79; Univ AZ, PhD, 85. **CAREER** Asst prof, 89-95, assoc prof of Linguistics, IN Univ, 95-. **MEMBERSHIPS** Linguistics Soc of America. **RESEARCH** Phonology; semitic languages. **SELECTED PUBLICATIONS** Auth, Topics in Syllable Geometry, in the series, Outstanding Dissertations in Linguistics, Garland Press, 88; with Donna Jo Napoli, A Prosodic Template in Historical Change: The Passage of the Latin Second Conjugation into Romance, Rosenberg and Sellier: Turin, 94; Emphasis Spread in Arabic and Grounded Phonology, Linguistic Inquiry, 95; with Michael Hammond, On the Status of On-Glides in American English, Phonology, 95; with Donna Jo Napoli, On Root Structure and the Destiny of the Latin Second Conjugation, Folia Linguistica Historica, 95; with Jin-Seong Lee, Korean Patial Reduplication Reconsidered, Lingua, 96; with Bushra Zawaydeh, Output Configurations in Phonology: Epenthesis and Syncope in Cairene Arabic, in S Davis, ed, Optimal Viewpoints: The IN Univ Ling Club, 97; ed, Optimal Viewpoints, IN Univ Linguistics Club, 97; auth, On the Moraic Representation of Underlying Geminates: Evidence from Prosodic Morphology, in H van der Hulst, R Kager, and W Zonneveld, eds, The Prosody-Morphology Interface, Cambridge Univ Press, forthcoming; Syllable Contact in Optimality Theory, Korea J of Ling, forthcoming; numerous other publications. **CONTACT ADDRESS** Dept of Linguistics, Indiana Univ, Bloomington, Bloomington, IN, 47405. **EMAIL** davis@indiana.edu

DAVISON, ALAN R.
DISCIPLINE SPANISH LITERATURE **EDUCATION** Univ Utah, BA, 81, PhD, 91; Univ Ca, MA, 85. **CAREER** Assoc prof. **SELECTED PUBLICATIONS** Auth, The Adventures of Captain Harvey, Odyssey Shield, 97; El corno emplumado/The Plumed Horn: A Voice of the Sixties Textos Toledanos, 94. **CONTACT ADDRESS** Westminster Col Salt Lake City, 1840 S 1300 E, Salt Lake City, UT, 84105. **EMAIL** a-daviso@wcslc.edu

DAVISON, JEAN MARGARET
PERSONAL Born 04/19/1922, Glens Falls, NY **DISCIPLINE** CLASSICAL LANGUAGES, ANCIENT HISTORY **EDUCATION** Univ Vt, AB, 44; Yale Univ, AM, 50, PhD(class archaeol), 57; Univ Ital Stranieri, Perugia, dipl, 60. **CAREER** Cryptanalyst, US Dept War, 44-45; foreign serv clerk, US Dept State, Athens, 45-46 & Vienna, 47-49; instr ancient hist, Latin, Greek & Greek art, 55-59, from asst prof to prof, 59-72, ROBERTS PROF CLASS LANG & LIT, UNIV VT, 72-, Am Philos Asn res grant, 67-68; mem managing comt, Am Sch Class Studies, Athens, 65, mem exec comt, 73, vis prof, 74-75. **MEMBERSHIPS** Archaeol Inst Am; Vergilian Soc Am; Class Asn New England; Am Sch Orient Res; Asn Field Archaeol. **RESEARCH** Greek Archaeology; Homeric studies; pre-Roman Italy. **SELECTED PUBLICATIONS** Auth, Vitruvius on Acoustical Vases in Greek and Roman Theaters, Amer Jour Archaeol, Vol 0100, 96. **CONTACT ADDRESS** Dept of Classics, Univ of Vt, Burlington, VT, 05401.

DAVISON, ROSENA
PERSONAL United Kingdom **DISCIPLINE** FRENCH **EDUCATION** McGill Univ, BA, 71, MA, 74, PhD, 81. **CAREER** Asst prof, 92-90, ASSOC PROF FRENCH, SIMON FRASER UNIV, 90-, dept ch, 91-94. **MEMBERSHIPS** MLA; Asn interdisciplinaire de recherche sur l'epistolaire; Can Soc Eighteenth Century Stud; Am Soc Eighteenth Century Stud; Asn des profs de francais aux univ et col can. **SELECTED PUBLICATIONS** Auth, Diderot et Galiani: etude d'une amitie philosophique, 85; auth, Diderot, Galiani, et Vico: un itineraire philosophique (Diderot Studies, 88); auth, Mme d'Epinay's Contribution to Girls' Education, in Women Intellectuals of the French Eighteenth Century, 94; co-ed, Man and Nature, vol 8, 90. **CONTACT ADDRESS** Dept of French, Simon Fraser Univ, Burnaby, BC, V5A 1S6. **EMAIL** rdavison@sfu.can

DAWSON, ROBERT LEWIS
PERSONAL Born 07/26/1943, Buenos Aires, Arg **DISCIPLINE** FRENCH LITERATURE, PORTUGUESE **EDUCATION** Trinity Col, BA, 65; Yale Univ, MPhil, 68, PhD(French), 72. **CAREER** Actg asst prof French & Ital, Univ Santa Clara, Calif, 70-72; asst prof, Rol lins Col, Fla, 73-75; asst prof, 75-78, Assoc Prof French, Univ Texas, Austin, 79-, Fel, La Fondation Camargo, Cassis, France, 72-73. **MEMBERSHIPS** Am Soc 18th Century Studies; Soc d-etude dix-huitieme siecle. **RESEARCH** Eighteenth-century French literature. **SELECTED PUBLICATIONS** Auth, Baculard d'Arnaud: life & prose fiction, Studies on Voltaire & 18th Century, 76; ed, International Directory of 18th Century Research and Scholars, Int Soc 18th Century Studies, 79; Additions to the Bibliographies of 17th and 18th Century French Prose Fiction, Voltaire Found, 88; auth, The French booktrade and the Pemission Sample of 1777, Studies in Voltaire, 92. **CONTACT ADDRESS** Dept of French & Ital, Univ of Tex, Austin, TX, 78712-1026.

DAWSON BOYD, CANDY
PERSONAL Born 08/08/1946, Chicago, IL, d **DISCIPLINE** LANGUAGE ARTS **EDUCATION** Northeastern Illinois State University, BA, 1967; University of California, Berkeley, CA, MA, 1978, PhD, 1982. **CAREER** Overton Elementary School, Chicago, IL, teacher, 1968-71; Longfellow School, Berkeley, CA, teacher, 1971-73; University of California, Berkeley, CA, extension instructor in language arts, 1972-79; St Mary's College of California, Moraga, CA, extension instructor in language arts, 1972-79; Berkeley Unified School District, Berkeley, CA, district teacher trainer in reading and communication skills, 1973-76; ST MARY'S COLLEGE OF CALIFORNIA, MORAGA, CA, lecturer to assistant professor, 1976-83, chair of reading leadership elementary education, and teacher effectiveness programs, 1976-87, tenured associate professor, 1983-91, professor, 1991-94; MASTERS PROGRAMS IN READING & SPECIAL EDUC, CHAIR, 1994-. **HONORS AND AWARDS** First Distinguished Professor of the Year, St Mary's College, 1992; author, Circle of Gold, Scholastic, 1984; Coretta Scott King Award Honor Book for Circle of Gold, American Library Association, 1985; Outstanding Bay Area Woman, Delta Sigma Theta, 1986; **MEMBERSHIPS** Member, St Mary's College Rank and Tenure Committee, 1984-87; member, multiple subjects waiver programs committee, review committee, State of California Commission on Teacher Credentialing, 1985-, advisory committee for multiple subject credential with an early childhood emphasis, State of California Commission on Teacher Credentialing, 1986-87. **SELECTED PUBLICATIONS** Author, Breadsticks and Blessing Places, Macmillan, 1985, published in paperback as Forever Friends, Viking, 1986; author, Charlie Pippin, Macmillan, 1987; author, Chevrolet Saturdays, Macmillan, 1993; author, Fall Secrets, Puffin, 1994; A Different Beat, 1994; author, Daddy, Daddy, Be There, Philomel, 1995; Spotlight on Literature Program, McGraw-Hill, 1995. **CONTACT ADDRESS** Sch of Education, St. Mary's Col of California, Box 4350, Moraga, CA, 94575.

DE BARY, WM. THEODORE
PERSONAL Born 08/09/1919, NY, m, 1942, 4 children **DISCIPLINE** EAST ASIAN STUDIES **EDUCATION** Columbia Col, BA 41; Columbia Univ, MA 48, PhD 53. **CAREER** Columbia Univ, Special Serv Prof 90-; Heyman Cen Humanities, dir 81-; John Mitchell Mason Prof 79-90; exe vp 71-78; pres assoc Asian Stud 69-70; chemn univ sen 69-70; Carpenter Prof Oriental stud 66-78; chmn dept E Asian lang and cult 60-66; dir E Asian lang 60-72; chemn comm Oriental stud 53-61. **HONORS AND AWARDS** Hon Doc of Letters and Humane Letters, Col Univ, St Lawrence Univ, Loyola Univ; Order of the Rising Sun; Pres Townsend Harris Medal; John Jay Award; Alexander Hamilton Medal; Lionel Trilling Book Awd; Mark Van Doren Prize; Great Teacher Awd; Awd for Excell Grad Fac Alum; Frank Tannenbaum Mem Awd; Guggenheim Fel; Watumull Prize; Fishburn Prize. **MEMBERSHIPS** Founder or co-founder of, Heyman Cen for Humanities; The Society of Fellows in the Humanities; The Society of Senior Scholars; The Univ Lectures; Trilling Seminars; The Univ Seminars in Asian Thought and Religion and Neo-Confucian Studies; Alumni Colloquia in the Humanities. **RESEARCH** Confucianism; Civil society; Human rights. **SELECTED PUBLICATIONS** Auth, Asian Values and Human Rights, Harvard Univ Press, 98; Confucianism and Human Rights, Columbia Univ Press, 97; Sources of Korean Tradition, CUP, 97; Waiting for the Dawn: A Plan for the Prince, CUP, 93; auth or coauth. **CONTACT ADDRESS** Dept of Special Service, Columbia Univ, 502 Kent Hall, NYC, NY, 10027-3918. **EMAIL** wtd1@columbia.edu

DE LEY, HERBERT C.
PERSONAL Born 11/24/1936, Altadena, CA, m, 1990, 1 child **DISCIPLINE** FRENCH **EDUCATION** Yale Univ, PhD, 63. **CAREER** Vis assoc prof French, Univ Cal-Riverside, 67-68, Univ Chicago, 69, UCLA, 76-77; prof of French, Univ Ill-Urbana, 77-; Chevalier, Palmas Academies, 93. **MEMBERSHIPS** MLA; NASSCFL. **RESEARCH** La Fontaine; Brantome; Saint Simon. **SELECTED PUBLICATIONS** Auth Marcel Proust et le duc de Saint-Simon, Univ Ill Press, 66; Saint-Simon Memorialist, Univ Ill Press, 75; The Movement of Thought, Univ Ill Press, 85; Le jeu classique, Jeu et theorie des jeux au Grand Siecle, Tubingen, 88; Fixing up Reality, La Fontaine and Levi-Strauss, Tubingen, 96. **CONTACT ADDRESS** Dept of French, Univ Ill, Urbana, IL, 61801. **EMAIL** h_deley@uiuc.edu

DE LOOZE, LAURENCE
DISCIPLINE FRENCH LITERATURE **EDUCATION** Univ Oregon, BA; Univ Toronto, MA; PhD. **RESEARCH** Medieval and Renaissance culture/literature; theories of autobiography and textuality, film; role of the poet; gender issues; metaphor and analogy. **SELECTED PUBLICATIONS** Auth, The Pseudo-Autobiography of the Fourteenth Century, 97; pub(s) on autobiography and subjectivity, film, Gustav Mahler, medieval literature and medievalism, Racine, and Wallace Stevens. **CONTACT ADDRESS** Dept of Modern Languages, Western Ontario Univ, London, ON, N6A 5B8.

DE RAFOLS, WIFREDO
DISCIPLINE SPANISH LITERATURE, CULTURE, AND LITERARY THEORY **EDUCATION** Johns Hopkins Univ, MA; Univ Calif, Davis, PhD. **CAREER** Assoc prof Span, dir, grad stud, Univ Nev, Reno. **RESEARCH** Hermeneutics; artificial reading. **SELECTED PUBLICATIONS** Published widely within his area of specialization -- 19th- and 20th-century Spanish literature; his publications examine works by Zorrilla, Perez Galdos, Valle-Inclan, and Jimenez. **CONTACT ADDRESS** Univ Nev, Reno, Reno, NV, 89557. **EMAIL** fdrafols@unr.edu

DEAN, DENNIS RICHARD
PERSONAL Born 05/29/1938, Belvidere, IL, m, 1968 **DISCIPLINE** ENGLISH, HISTORY OF SCIENCE **EDUCATION** Stanford Univ, AB, 60, AM, 62; Univ Wis-Madison, PhD(English), 68. **CAREER** Instr English, Kenosha Ctr, Univ Wis, 67-68; asst prof, 68-73, assoc prof English, 73-82, PROF ENGLISH & HUMANITIES, UNIV WIS-PARKSIDE, 82-, Fulbright award, Korea, 77; NSF grant, New Zealand, 82. **MEMBERSHIPS** AAUP; Hist Sci Soc; Keats-Shelley Asn. **RESEARCH** Literature and science; British romantics; history of science, especially geology. **SELECTED PUBLICATIONS** Auth, The San-Francisco Earthquake of 1906, Annals of Sci, Vol 0050, 93. **CONTACT ADDRESS** Humanities Div, Univ of Wis-Parkside, Kenosha, WI, 53140.

DEAN, KENNETH
DISCIPLINE EAST ASIAN STUDIES **EDUCATION** Stanford Univ, PhD. **CAREER** Assoc prof. **RESEARCH** Taoist studies; popular culture; Chinese lit. **SELECTED PUBLICATIONS** Auth, Comic Inversion and Cosmic Renewal in the Ritual Theater of Putian: The God of Theater in Southeast China, 94; auth, Irrigation and Individuation: Cults of Water Deities along the Putian Plains, 94; auth, Taoist Ritual and Popular Cults of Southeast China, Princeton, 93. **CONTACT ADDRESS** East Asian Studies Dept, McGill Univ, 845 Sherbrooke St, Montreal, PQ, H3A 2T5.

DEBICKI, ANDREW PETER
PERSONAL Born 06/28/1934, Warsaw, Poland, m, 2 children **DISCIPLINE** SPANISH **EDUCATION** Yale Univ, BA, 55, PhD, 60. **CAREER** Instr Span, Trinity Col, Conn, 57-60; asst prof, Grinnell Col, 60-62, from assoc prof to prof Span, 62-68; prof, 68-76, DISTINGUISHED PROF SPAN, 76-, Vice-Chancellor, Res & Grad Studies, 94-96, DEAN, GRADUATE SCHOOL, 93-, DEAN, GRADUATE SCHOOL & INT PROGS, UNIV KS, 96-; Fulbright grant, 66; fels, Am Coun Learned Soc, 66-67, Guggenheim, 71-72, 80 & Nat Humanities Ctr, 80, 92-93; NEH, 92-93; Bellagio, 93. **HONORS AND AWARDS** Prize, Hispania, 71; Teaching Award, Univ KS, 72; Balfour Jeffrey Res Award, Univ KS, 83. **MEMBERSHIPS** MLA; Am Asn Teachers Span & Port. **RESEARCH** Spanish and Latin American contemporary poetry; poetics and literary theory. **SELECTED PUBLICATIONS** Auth, La poesia de Jose Gorostiza, Andrea, Mex, 62; Estudios sobre poesia espanola: La generacion de 1924-1925, Gredos, Madrid, 68 & 81; Damaso Alonso, Twayne, 70 & Catedra, Madrid, 74; La poesia de Jorge Guillen, 73 & Poetas hispanoamericanos contemporaneos, 76, Gredos, Madrid; ed, Pedro Salinas, Taurus, Madrid, 76; Antologia de la poesia mexicana moderna, Tamesis, London, 77; Poetry of Discovery: The Spanish Generation of 1956-71, Kentucky, 82; Angel Gonzalez, Jucar, 89; Spanish Poetry of the Twentieth Century, KY, 94, Gredos, 97. **CONTACT ADDRESS** The Graduate School, Univ of Kansas, Lawrence, KS, 66045-0001. **EMAIL** adebicki@ukans.edu

DEBRECZENY, PAUL
PERSONAL Born 02/16/1932, Budapest, Hungary, m, 1959, 2 children **DISCIPLINE** RUSSIAN LITERATURE **EDUCATION** Eotvos Univ, Hungary, BA, 53, BA, 55; Univ London, PhD(Russ), 60. **CAREER** Res asst Russ lit, Inst Lit Hist, Hungarian Acad Sci, 55-56; trans ed, Pergamon Press, Oxford, England, 59-60; asst prof Russ & chm dept, Tulane Univ, 60-66, assoc prof, 66-67; assoc prof, 67-74, chm dept, 74-79, prof Russ, 74-83, alumni distinguished prof Russ and Comp Lit, 83-, Univ NC, Chapel Hill. **HONORS AND AWARDS** Int Res & Exchanges Bd res fel, 73 & 82; Nat Endowment for Humanities fel, 78 & 79. **MEMBERSHIPS** Am Asn Teachers Slavic & EEurop Lang (vpres, 78-79); Am Asn Advan Slavic Studies; MLA; Southern Conf Slavic Studies (pres, 77). **RESEARCH** Nineteenth century Russian literature; comparative literature; sociology of literature. **SELECTED PUBLICATIONS** Auth, Niklolay Gogol and His Contemporary Critics, Am Philos Soc, 66; co-ed, Literature and National Identity: 19th Century Russian Critical Essays, Univ Nebr, 70; ed, 2 special issues devoted to Pushkin, Can-Am Slavic Studies, summer 76 & spring 77; co-ed, Chekhov's Art of Writing: A Collection of Critical Essays, Slavica Publ, 77; trans & ed, Alexander Pushkin: Complete Prose Fiction, 83 & auth, The Other Pushkin: A Study of Alexander Pushkin's Prose Fiction, 83, Stanford Univ Press; auth, Temptations of the Past, historical novel, Hermitage Publ, 82; co-ed, Russian Narrative and Visual Arts: Varieties of Seeing, 94; auth, Social Functions of Literature: Alexander Pushkin and Russian Culture, 97. **CONTACT ADDRESS** Dept of Slavic Lang, Univ N. Carolina, Chapel Hill, NC, 27599-3165.

DECK, ALLAN F.
PERSONAL Born 04/19/1945, Los Angeles, CA, s **DISCIPLINE** THEOLOGY; LATIN AMERICAN STUDIES **EDUCATION** St Louis Univ, BA, 69, PhD, 74; Jesuit Sch of Theol at Berkeley, MDiv, 76; Gregorian Univ, STD, 88. **CAREER** Admin, Our Lady of Guadalupe Church, 76-79; Dir, Hispanic Ministry, Diocese of Orange, 79-85; Asst Prof of Theology, Jesuit Sch of Theol, 87-92; Assoc Prof of Theol, Loyola Marymt Univ, 92-96; Exec Dir, Loyola Inst for Spirituality, 97-. **HONORS AND AWARDS** Catholic Press Asn 1st Place Award Pro Book Category, 89. **MEMBERSHIPS** Acad of Catholic Hispanic Theol of the US, (co-founder & 1st pres); Nat Catholic Counc for Hisp Ministry, (co-founder & 1st pres). **RESEARCH** Hispanic religious expressions & spirituality. **SELECTED PUBLICATIONS** Auth, Francisco Javier Alegre: A Study in Mexican Literary Criticism, Historical Inst of the Soc of Jesus, 76; auth, The Second Wave, Paulist Press, 89; auth, Perspectivas: Hispanic Ministry, Sheed & Ward, 95; Hispanic Catholic Culture in the US, Univ Notre Dame Press, 94. **CONTACT ADDRESS** 480 S Batavia St, Orange, CA, 92868. **EMAIL** deck8@juno.com

DECOSTA-WILLIS, MIRIAM
PERSONAL Born 11/01/1934, Florence, Alabama, w, 1972 **DISCIPLINE** SPANISH **EDUCATION** Wellesley Coll, BA 1956; Johns Hopkins Univ, MA 1960, PhD 1967. **CAREER** Owen Coll, instructor 1960-66; Memphis State Univ, assoc prof of Spanish 1966-70; Howard Univ, assoc prof of Spanish 1970-74, prof & chmn of dept 1974-76; LeMoyne-Owen Coll, prof, Romance Languages, prof of Spanish & dir of DuBois program, 1979-88. **HONORS AND AWARDS** Phi Beta Kappa 1956; Johns Hopkins Fellowship 1965. **MEMBERSHIPS** Mem, Coll Language Assn; bd of dirs, MSU Center for Rsch on Women; chair TN Humanities Council; bd Federation of State Humanities Councils; editorial bd Sage & Afro-Hispanic Review; life mem NAACP; chmn, Exec bd/mem, TN Humanities Council, 1981-87; chmn & founding mem, Memphis Black Writers' Workshop, 1980-. **SELECTED PUBLICATIONS** Ed, Blacks in Hispanic Literature Kennikat Pr 1977; articles in CLAJ, Journal of Negro History, Black World Negro History Bulletin, Revista Interamericana, Caribbean Quart; Sage Afro-Hispanic Review; Outstanding Faculty Mem of the Year, LeMoyne-Owen Coll, 1982; Homespun Images: An Anthology of Black Memphis Writers & Artists, 1988; editor, The Memphis Diary of Ida B Wells, Beacon Press, 1994. **CONTACT ADDRESS** Visiting Commonwealth Prof of Spanish, George Mason Univ, Dept of Foreign Languages & Literature, Fairfax, VA, 22030.

DEE, JAMES HOWARD
PERSONAL Born 12/30/1943, Albany, NY, m, 1969 **DISCIPLINE** CLASSICAL LANGUAGES AND LITERATURE **EDUCATION** Univ Rochester, BA, 66; Univ Tex Austin, PhD(classics), 72. **CAREER** Asst prof, 72-79, ASSOC PROF CLASSICS, UNIV ILL CHICAGO CIRCLE, 79-, Chairperson Classics, 82-, Nat Endowment for Humanities residential fel, 77-78. **MEMBERSHIPS** Am Philol Asn; Class Asn Middle West & South; Vergilian Soc. **RESEARCH** Augustan Latin poetry; stylistic qualities in Greek and Latin epic; Roman moral and humanistic values. **SELECTED PUBLICATIONS** Auth, Greek and Egyptian Mythologies, Class Bulletin, Vol 0071, 95; The Scepter and the Spear--Studies on Forms of Repetition in the Homeric Poems, Class World, Vol 0090, 97; A Repertory of English Words with Classical Suffixes .4., Class Jour, Vol 0089, 94; The Interpretation of Order--A Study in the Poetics of Homeric Repetition, Class World, Vol 0090, 97; A Repertory of English Words with Classical Suffixes .3., Class Jour, Vol 0088, 93. **CONTACT ADDRESS** Dept of Classics, Univ of Ill, Chicago Circle, Chicago, IL, 60680.

DEFRANCIS, JOHN
PERSONAL Born 08/31/1911, Bridgeport, CT, m, 1938, 1 child **DISCIPLINE** CHINESE **EDUCATION** Yale Univ, BA, 33; Columbia Univ, MA, 41, PhD(Chinese), 48. **CAREER** Asst prof Chinese, Seton Hall Univ, 62-66; prof, 66-76, EMER PROF CHINESE, UNIV HAWAII, MANOA, 76-, Assoc ed, J Am Orient Soc, 50-55; Am Philos Soc grant, 51-52; Soc Sci Res Conn & Am Coun Learned Soc grants Chinese math, 59-63; US Off Educ grants, 62-67. **MEMBERSHIPS** Chinese Lang Teachers Asn; MLA; Am Orient Soc. **SELECTED PUBLICATIONS** Auth, Chinese Script and the Diversity of Writing Systems, Linguistics, Vol 0032, 94; Graphemic Indeterminacy in Writing Systems, Word-Jour Intl Ling Assn, Vol 0047, 96; How Efficient is the Chinese Writing System, Visible Lang, Vol 0030, 96. **CONTACT ADDRESS** Univ of Hawaii, at Manoa, Honolulu, HI, 96822.

DEGRAFF, AMY
DISCIPLINE FRENCH CIVILIZATION,FRENCH CONVERSATION, FRENCH LITERATURE OF THE 17TH AND **EDUCATION** Sorbonne, Univ Paris, Diplome d'Etudes Superieures; Univ Va, PhD. **CAREER** Assoc prof Fr, ch, dept Romance Lang, Randolph-Macon Col. **RESEARCH** Psychological criticism in film and literature; the 17th century French fairy tale **SELECTED PUBLICATIONS** Auth, The Tower and the Well: A Psychological Interpretation of the Fairy Tales of Mme d'Aulnoy; From Glass Slipper to Glass Ceiling, or 'Cinderella', the Endurance of a Fairy Tale, Merveilles et Contes. **CONTACT ADDRESS** Dept of Romance Lang, Randolph-Macon Col, Ashland, VA, 23005-5505. **EMAIL** adegraff@rmc.edu 42

DEHON, CLAIRE L.
PERSONAL Born 12/17/1941, Uccle, Belgium **DISCIPLINE** FRENCH **EDUCATION** Inst Hist I'Art, Brussels, MA, 64; Univ KS, MA, 69, PhD, 73. **CAREER** From Asst Prof to Assoc Prof, 72-89, Prof French, KS State Univ, 89. **HONORS AND AWARDS** Nat Endowment for Hum fel, 81-82; Phi Beta Kappa. **MEMBERSHIPS** Am Asn Tchr(s) Fr; African Lit Asn; ALSC; KFLA; MAAAS. **RESEARCH** Novels in French in Black Africa. **SELECTED PUBLICATIONS** Auth, Le theatre d'Emile Verhaeren: quelques interpretations, Le Flambeau, 75; Allegory in E Verhaeren plays, Philol Quart, 7/78; La Dame du photographe: sa structure, son sens, Rev Pacifique, fall 78; Corinne: une artiste heroine de roman, 19th Cent Fr Studies, 80; Colette and Art Nouveau, Colette, the Woman, the Writer, 81; De Nouvelles Valeurs dous le roman camerounais, Presence Francophone 26, 85; Les Influences de la litterature Kreditiomelle sur le roman camerounais, Neohelium 16.2, 89; Le roman camerounais d'expression Francaise, SUMMA, 89; Le Roman en Afrique noire francophone, French Rev 68.6, 95; Women in Black African Novels in French, NWSA 8.1, 96. **CONTACT ADDRESS** Dept of Mod Lang, Kansas State Univ, 104 Eisenhower Hall, Manhattan, KS, 66506-2800. **EMAIL** dehoncl@ksu.edu

DEHORATIUS, EDMUND F.
PERSONAL Philadelphia, PA **DISCIPLINE** CLASSICAL LANGUAGES **EDUCATION** Duke Univ, BA, 95. **CAREER** Tchr, Bancroft Sch, 95- , dept chemn, 89- . **HONORS AND AWARDS** MA For Lang Asn, David Taggart Clancy Prize, Chester Middlesworth Award, Duke Univ. **MEMBERSHIPS** APA, Class Asn New England; Medieval Acad Am; Renaissance Soc Am. **RESEARCH** Classical tradition; paleography; Latin literature; pedagogy. **CONTACT ADDRESS** 5 Einhorn Rd, #3, Worcester, MA, 01609-2207. **EMAIL** edehorat@bancroft.pvt.k12.ma.us

DEINERT, HERBERT
PERSONAL Born 12/13/1930, Germany, m, 1957, 2 children **DISCIPLINE** GERMAN LITERATURE **EDUCATION** Yale Univ, PhD(Ger lit), 60. **CAREER** Asst prof Ger lit, Univ Ga, 59-61 & Duke Univ, 61-65; chmn dept, 68-74, PROF GER LIT, CORNELL UNIV, 74-, Consult, Nat Endowment for Humanities, 74-78. **MEMBERSHIPS** MLA; Am Asn Teachers Ger. **RESEARCH** Baroque; 19th century realism; the 20th century. **SELECTED PUBLICATIONS** Auth, Colonialism and the Postcolonial Condition, Pmla-Pub(s) Mod Lang Assn Am, Vol 0110, 95; Crazy Ideas--Heilbrun Method in Madness--Comment, Opera News, Vol 0058, 94; Boehme--An Intellectual Biography of the 17th-Century Philosopher And Mystic, Jour Eng and Ger Philol, Vol 0093, 94; Dithyrambists of the Fall--Gnosticism in Modern Aesthetics and Philosophy--German, Jour Eng and Ger Philol, Vol 0095, 96. **CONTACT ADDRESS** Dept of Ger Lit, Cornell Univ, Ithaca, NY, 14853.

DEKEYSER, R.M.
DISCIPLINE EDUCATION **EDUCATION** Stanford Univ, PhD, (Education), 86. **CAREER** Vis asst prof, 88-91, asst prof, 91-97, assoc prof, Linguistics Dept, Univ Pittsburgh, 97-. **HONORS AND AWARDS** ACTFL Emma Birkmailer Award for doctoral dissertation res on foreign lang ed, 87; Mellon Fel, Inst for Advance Studies Prog, administered by the Nat Foreign Lang Center, 97. **MEMBERSHIPS** AAAL; TESOL. **RESEARCH** Second lang acquisition; cognitive psychology. **SELECTED PUBLICATIONS** Auth, The Effect of Error Correction on Grammar Knowledge and Oral Proficiency, The Modern Language J, 77, 93; How Implicit Can Adult Second Language Learning Be?, AILA Rev, 11, 94; Learning Second Language Grammar Rules: An Experiment with a Miniature Linguistic System, Studies in Second Language Acquisition, 17, 95; The Differential Role of Comprehension and Production Practice, Language Learning, 46, 96; Beyond Explicit Rule Learning: Automatizing Second Language Morphosyntax, Studies in Second Language Acquisition, 19, 97; Beyond Focus on Form: Cognitive Prespectives on Learning and Practicing Second Language Grammar, in C Doughty & J Williams, eds, Focus on Form in Classroom Language Acquisition, Cambridge Univ Press, 98. **CONTACT ADDRESS** Dept of Linguistics, Univ of Pittsburgh, Pittsburgh, PA, 15260.

DEKOVEN, MARIANNE
DISCIPLINE ENGLISH LANGUAGE AND LITERATURE **EDUCATION** Radcliffe Univ, BA; Stanford, PhD. **CAREER** Prof. **RESEARCH** Feminist theory and criticism; modernism and postmodernism; cultural history. **SELECTED PUBLICATIONS** Auth, A Different Language: Gertrude Stein's Experimental Writing; auth, Rich and Strange: Gender, History, Modernism. **CONTACT ADDRESS** Dept of English, Rutgers Univ, 510 George St, Murray Hall, New Brunswick, NJ, 08901-1167. **EMAIL** dekoven@rci.rutgers.edu

DEKYDTSPOTTER, LAURENT
DISCIPLINE FRENCH LITERATURE **EDUCATION** Cornell Univ, PhD, 95. **CAREER** Asst prof. **SELECTED PUBLICATIONS** Auth, The Syntax and Semantics of the French Ne Que Construction, 93; Nested Variable and Locality, 92; The Syntax of Predicate Clefts, 91. **CONTACT ADDRESS** Dept of French and Italian, Indiana Univ, Bloomington, 300 N Jordan Ave, Bloomington, IN, 47405.

DEL CARO, ADRIAN
PERSONAL Born 12/29/1952, Eveleth, MN, m, 1985, 1 child **DISCIPLINE** FOREIGN LANGUAGES **EDUCATION** Univ Minn, MA, 77, PhD, 79. **CAREER** Lect, Univ Calif, Riverside, 79-80; from asst prof to assoc prof to prof, 80-92, La State Univ; prof, chemn, Univ Colo, Boulder, 92-. **HONORS AND AWARDS** Graduate School Dissertation Fel, 87-79, PhD with Distinction, 79. **MEMBERSHIPS** Am Asn Tchrs German; Modern Lang Asn; N Am Henie Soc; N Am Nietzsche Soc; German Stud Asn; Am Asn Univ Profs. **RESEARCH** Late 18th, 19th, 20th, century literature and thought; literature and philosophy; poetry. **SELECTED PUBLICATIONS** Auth, Nietzsche contra Nietzsche: Creativity and the Anti-Romantic, 89; auth, Holderlin: The Poetics of Being, 91; auth, Hugo von Hofmannsthal: Poets and the Language of Life, 93; auth, The Early Poetry of Paul Celan: In the beginning was the word, 97; auth, art, Nietzsche, Sacher-Masoch, and the Whip, 98. **CONTACT ADDRESS** 886 W Chestnut Cir, Louisville, CO, 80027. **EMAIL** adrian.delcaro@colorado.edu

DEL VALLE, JOSE
DISCIPLINE SPANISH AND PORTUGUESE **EDUCATION** SUNY at Buffalo, MA, 90; Georgetown Univ, PhD, 94. **CAREER** Asst prof, Miami Univ **RESEARCH** Spanish historical linguistics; history of Hispanic linguistics; minority languages. **SELECTED PUBLICATIONS** Auth, El trueque s/x en espanol antiguo: Aproximaciones teoricas, Tubingen, Germany: Max Niemeyer, 96; Modern linguistics in Menendez Pidal, In Multiple Perspectives on the Historical Dimension of Language, Munster, Germany: Nodus, 96; La historificacion de la linguestica historica: Los oregenes de Ramon Menendez Pidal, Historiographia Ling 24, 97. **CONTACT ADDRESS** Dept of Spanish and Portugise, Miami Univ, Oxford, OH, 45056. **EMAIL** delvalj@miavx1.muohio.edu

DELGADO, LUISA ELENA
DISCIPLINE SPANISH LITERATURE **EDUCATION** Univ Calif Santa Barbara, PhD, 89. **CAREER** Assoc prof, Univ Ill Urbana Champaign. **RESEARCH** Modern and contemporary Spanish literature; Spanish culture and film; literary theory. **SELECTED PUBLICATIONS** Auth, El interes del relato: Estrategias narrativas en la serie de Torquemada, Anales Galdosianos, 90; El derecho de revision: La de Bringas y el discurso de la alienacion femenina, Romance Lang Annual, 92; Palabras contra palabras: el lenguaje de la historia en Tirano Banderas, Anthropos, 92; Mas estragos que las revoluciones: detallando lo feminino en La de Bringas, Rev Hispanica Moderna, 95; Cambiando de genero: lenguaje e identidad en dos textos galdosianos, Insula, 95; Pliegos de (des)cargo: las paradojas discursivas de La incognita, 96. **CONTACT ADDRESS** Spanish, Italian, and Portuguese Dept, Univ Ill Urbana Champaign, 52 E Gregory Dr, Champaign, IL, 61820. **EMAIL** ldelgado@uiuc.edu

DELISLE, JEAN
PERSONAL Born 04/13/1947, Hull, PQ, Canada **DISCIPLINE** TRANSLATION STUDIES/HISTORY **EDUCATION** Laval Univ, BA, 68; Univ Montreal, LTrad, 71, MTrad, 75; Sorbonne Nouvelle (Paris), DTrad, 78. **CAREER** PROF, SCH TRNASLATION & INTERPRETATION, UNIV OTTAWA, 74-. **HONORS AND AWARDS** Can Coun schol, 76. **MEMBERSHIPS** Soc traducteurs Que, 72-92; Union ecrivains que, 87-94; Can Asn Transl Stud, 87- (pres 91-93); pres, Comt

Hist Transl, 90-. **SELECTED PUBLICATIONS** Auth, L'Analyse du discours comme methode de traduction, 80; auth, Les Obsedes textuels, 83; auth, Au coeur du trialogue canadien/ Bridging the Language Solitudes, 84; auth, La Traduction au Canada/Translation in Canada 1534-1984, 87; auth, The Language Alchemists, 90; auth, La Traduction raisonee, 93; coauth, Bibliographic Guide for Translators, Writers and Terminologists, 79; coauth, International Directory of Historians of Translation, 3rd ed 96; ed, L'enseignement de l'interpretation et de la traduction: de la theorie a la pedagogie, 81; ed, Les Traducteurs dans l'histoire, 95; ed, Translators Through History, 95. **CONTACT ADDRESS** Sch Transl & Interp, Univ Ottawa, Ottawa, ON, K1N 6N5. **EMAIL** jdelisle@aix1.uottawa.ca

DELLA NEVA, JOANN
DISCIPLINE FRENCH LITERATURE **EDUCATION** Brwyn Mawr Col, AB, 76; Univ Penn, MA, 78; Princeton Univ, MA, 80, PhD, 82. **CAREER** Assoc prof. **RESEARCH** Renaissance literature. **SELECTED PUBLICATIONS** Auth, pubs on Marot, Sceve, Du Bellay, Ronsard, and Renaissance imitation theory. **CONTACT ADDRESS** Romance Languages and Literatures Dept, Univ of Notre Dame, Notre Dame, IN, 46556.

DELLEPIANE, ANGELA B.
PERSONAL Born 05/13/1926, Rio Cuarto, Argentina, m, 1962 **DISCIPLINE** SPANISH AMERICAN LITERATURE **EDUCATION** Univ Buenos Aires, MA, 48, PhD(Romance philol), 52. **CAREER** Prof Latin, Teacher's Col, Buenos Aires, 48-57; asst prof Span lit, Fordham Univ, 61-63; from asst prof to assoc prof philol, phonetics & Span lit, 63-72, Prof Span Am Lit, City Col New York, 73-; PROF SPAN AM LIT, GRAD CTR, CITY UNIV NEW YORK, 69-, Consult & panelist, Fel Div, Nat Endowment for Humanities, 77-79; vis prof, Univ Ky, 78. **MEMBERSHIPS** Int Inst Ibero-Am Lit; Asn Int de Hispanistas; Am Asn Teachers Span & Port; Latin Am Studies Asn. **RESEARCH** Spanish American narrative; Gauchesca literature; structural stylistics. **SELECTED PUBLICATIONS** Auth, A Tribute to Earle, Peter,G., Hisp Rev, Vol 0061, 93. **CONTACT ADDRESS** Span Doctoral Frog Grad Ctr, Univ of New York, 33 W 42nd St, New York, NY, 10036.

DEMBOWSKI, PETER FLORIAN
PERSONAL Born 12/23/1925, Warsaw, Poland, m, 1954, 3 children **DISCIPLINE** ROMANCE PHILOLOGY **EDUCATION** Univ BC, BA, 52; Univ Paris, DUniv, 54; Univ Calif, Berkeley, PhD, 60. **CAREER** Instr French & Russ, Univ BC, 54-56; from asst prof to assoc prof French, Univ Toronto, 60-66; assoc prof French & ling, 66-69, dean students, Div Humanities, 68-70, PROF FRENCH, UNIV CHICAGO, 69-, CHMN DEPT ROMANCE LANG & LIT, 76-, Guggenheim fel, 70-71; resident master, Smell & Hitchcock Halls, Univ Chicago, 73-79; vis mem, Sch Hist Studies, Inst Advanced Study, Princeton, 79-80. **HONORS AND AWARDS** Chevalier, Acad Palms, France, 81. **MEMBERSHIPS** MLA; Soc Ling Romane; Mediaeval Acad Am. **RESEARCH** Linguistics; medieval French literature; Old French hagiography. **SELECTED PUBLICATIONS** Auth, Medieval French Martyrologia Passionaries--French, Speculum-Jour Medieval Stud, Vol 0069, 94; The Short Lyric Poems of Froissart, Jean--Fixed Forms and the Expression of the Courtly-Ideal, Speculum-Jour Medieval Stud, Vol 0070, 95; The Medieval Saints Lives--Spiritual Renewal and Old French Literature, Romance Philol, Vol 0049, 96; The Lady as Saint--A Collection of French Hagiographic Romances of the 13th-Century, Romance Philol, Vol 0047, 94; The Legendier Apostolique Anglo-Normand--French, Speculum-Jour Medieval Stud, Vol 0068, 93; Studies on Old-French Verse Legends 10th-Century to the 13th-Century--The Legend as a Genre Along with the Chanson-De-Geste and the Romance--German, Romance Philol, Vol 0047, 93; The French Tradition of Textual Philology and Its Relevance to the Editing of Medieval Texts, Mod Phil, Vol 0090, 93; The Vie Saint Gregore--A 14th-Century Norman Poem-French, Speculum-Journal Medieval Stud, Vol 0068, 93; The Legendier Apostolique Anglo-Normand-French, Speculum- Jour Medieval Stud, Vol 0068, 93;: Lexical Iteration--A Study on the Usage of a Stylistic Figure in 11 French Romances from the 12th and 13th Centuries-French, Romance Philol, Vol 0048, 94; Towards a Synthesis--Essays on the New Philology, Romance Philol, Vol 0049, 96; The Literary Importance of Froissart, Jean Romance Meliador--Truth Within Fiction, Etudes Francaises, Vol 0032, 96. **CONTACT ADDRESS** Dept of Romance Lang, Univ of Chicago, Chicago, IL, 60637.

DEMERS, RICHARD ARTHUR
PERSONAL Born 09/10/1941, Portland, OR, 2 children **DISCIPLINE** LINGUISTICS **EDUCATION** Ore State Univ, BA, 63; Univ Wash, MA, 65, PhD(Ger), 68. **CAREER** Asst prof ling, Univ Mass, Amherst, 68-73, assoc prof, 74-75; assoc prof, 75-80, PROF LING, UNIV ARIZ, 80-, Fel, Mass Inst Technol, 71-72; reader squibs & arts, Ling Inquiry & mem bd ed, Ling Anal, 74- **MEMBERSHIPS** Ling Soc Am. **RESEARCH** Lummi (structure, syntax, grammar) 1972 to present; Old Icelandic phonology 1973 to present; native American languages of Arizona 1975 to present. **SELECTED PUBLICATIONS** Auth, Predicates and Pronominal Arguments in Straits Salish, Lang, Vol 0070, 94. **CONTACT ADDRESS** Dept of Ling Math, Univ of Ariz, P O Box 210028, Tucson, AZ, 85721-0028.

DENDLE, BRIAN JOHN
PERSONAL Born 03/30/1936, Oxford, England, m, 1962, 2 children **DISCIPLINE** ROMANCE LANGUAGES **EDUCATION** Oxford Univ, BA, 58, MA, 62; Princeton Univ, MA, 64, PhD(Romance lang), 66. **CAREER** Instr French, Kenyon Col, 61-63; instr Span, Princeton Univ, 66; asst prof, Univ Mich, 66-69; assoc prof, Univ Ala, 69-71; assoc prof, 71-78, PROF SPAN, UNIV KY, 78- **MEMBERSHIPS** MLA; Int Inst Spain. **RESEARCH** Galdos; Spanish Romanticism; Spanish novel on the 19th century. **SELECTED PUBLICATIONS** Auth, On the Origin of the Phrase La Virgen-De-Los-Ultimos-Amores--Espronceda Debt to Chateaubriand, Bulletin Hisp, Vol 0097, 95; Solar Imagery in 3 Novels of Espina,Concha, Anales de la Literatura Espanola Contemporanea, Vol 0022, 97; The Suplemento-Literario of La-Verdad 1923-1926--Spanish, Hisp Rev, Vol 0061, 93; Galdos and the Visit of President Loubet, 1905, Bulletin Hisp, Vol 0095, 93; Las Ruinas de mi Convento, A Romantic Novel by Patxot, Fernando 1851, Critica Hisp, Vol 0018, 96; History and Fiction in Galdos Narratives, Rev Estudios Hispanicos, Vol 0028, 94; Marianela, the Discovery of a New World and the Limitations of Science, Insula-Rev de Letras y Ciencias Humanas, Vol 0048, 93. **CONTACT ADDRESS** Dept of Span & Ital, Univ of Ky, 500 S Limestone St, Lexington, KY, 40506-0003.

DENHAM, SCOTT
DISCIPLINE GERMAN LANGUAGE & LITERATURE **EDUCATION** Univ of Chicago, BA, 84; Harvard Univ, AM, 89, PhD, 90. **CAREER** Tutor, teaching fel, instr, Harvard Univ, 85-90; assoc prof, Davidson Col, 90-. **HONORS AND AWARDS** B.Blume Prize for acad excellence, 84-86; Danforth Ctr for Teaching and Learning Cert of Distinction in Teaching, 85-89; William R. Kenan Fund Grant, Harvard Univ, 89; Davidson Col fac summer res grant, 91; Nat Endowment for the Hums Summer Stipend, 92; Salzburg Sem Fel, 93; Southern Reg. Educ Bd., Small Grants Prog, 94; Am Coun on Germany Fel, 95; DAAD grants, 95, 96; Davidson Col fac res grants, 96, 97, 98; Davidson Col Mellon Found Grant, 98; DAAD Summer Study Visit Scholar, 98. **MEMBERSHIPS** MLA; German Studies Asn; Soc of Architectural Hists; Kafka Soc of Am; Arnold-Zweig Gesellschaft; Am Coun on Germany; Am Asn of Teachers of German. **SELECTED PUBLICATIONS** Auth, Die juengste Juengerei: Is Ernst Juenger Finding a Place in the German Pantheon?, in German Politics & Society 22, 91; Georg Trakl's 'Grodek', in Masterplots II: Poetry, 92; Franz Kafka in the GDR, 1949-1989, in J of the Kafka Soc of Am 16/1, 92; Visions of War: The Ideology and Imagery of War Fictions in German Literature Before and After the Great War, 92; Some Current Views of German Modernism, in German Politics and Society 28, 93; Schindler's List in Germany and Austria: A Reception Study, in German Politics and Society 13.1, 95; The American Council on Germany Seventeenth German-American Young Leaders Conference 1995, Am Coun on Germany Occasional Paper, 96; All Quiet on the Western Front, in Masterplots: Twentieth Anniversary Revised Second Ed, 97; coauth, Moerderische Mentalitaet? Die doppelte Goldhagen-Rezeption in den USA, Evangelische Kommentare 5, 97; ed, A Sourcebook of German Studies Courses, 94; coed, A User's Guide to German Cultural Studies, 97. **CONTACT ADDRESS** Dept of German, Russian & Japanese, Davidson Col, Davidson, NC, 28036-1719. **EMAIL** scdenham@davidson.edu

DENNIS, HARRY JOE
PERSONAL Born 01/16/1940, Cisco, TX, m, 1962, 1 child **DISCIPLINE** SPANISH AND PORTUGUESE LANGUAGES AND LITERATURES **EDUCATION** Univ Ariz, BA, 62, MA, 65; PhD(Span & Port), 70. **CAREER** Instr Span, Tex Col Arts & Indust, 65-66; instr English for foreign studies, English Lang Inst, Univ Ariz, summers 64-69; vis prof Span, Univ Nev, Las Vegas, 69-70; ASST PROF SPAN & PORT, CALIF STATE UNIV, SACRAMENTO, 70-, Assoc mem bd, Luso Am Educ Found, San Francisco, 72-; dir, Calif State Univ Syst Prog, Guanajuato, Mex, 75-77 & Spain, 81; assoc ed, Los Ensayistas; managing ed, Explicacion de textos literario. **MEMBERSHIPS** Am Asn Teachers Span & Port. **RESEARCH** Contemporary Latin American prose fiction; Brazilian literature of the 20th century. **SELECTED PUBLICATIONS** Auth, Juegos de la Edad Tierna, Explicacion de Textos Literarios, Vol 0023, 94. **CONTACT ADDRESS** Dept of Span & Port, California State Univ, Sacramento, 6000 J St, Sacramento, CA, 95819-2694.

DENOMME, ROBERT T.
PERSONAL Born 05/17/1930, Fitchburg, MA **DISCIPLINE** FRENCH **EDUCATION** Assumption Col, AB, 52; Boston Univ, MA, 53; Univ Paris, dipl, 59; Columbia Univ, PhD, 62. **CAREER** Instr French & Span, St Joseph's Col, Pa, 56-60; from instr to asst prof French, Univ Va, 60-64; asst prof, Univ Chicago, 64-66; assoc prof, 66-70, PROF FRENCH LIT, UNIV VA, 70-, CHMN DEPT FRENCH, 77-, Reader French lang & lit, Educ Testing Serv, 71-77; mem adv bd, Nineteenth-Century French studies, 72-; Am Philos Soc grant, 75; vis prof Fr, Univ Orleans, France, 78. **MEMBERSHIPS** MLA; Am Asn Teachers Fr; SAtlantic Mod Lang Asn. **RESEARCH** Romanticism; realism and symbolism; 19th century French literature. **SELECTED PUBLICATIONS** Auth, Madame Bovary, Fr Rev, Vol 0067, 94; A Critical Bibliography of French Literature, Vol 5, the 19th-Century, Fr Forum, Vol 0020, 95; Contemplation and Dream--Hugo,Victor, Poet of Intimateness-French, Fr Rev, Vol 0068, 94; Complete Poetic Works, Vol 3, Odes--French, Nineteenth-Century Fr Stud, Vol 0024, 95; Oeuvres-Poetiques-Completes, Vol 4, Les Exiles, Amethystes--French, Nineteenth-Century Fr Stud, Vol 0023, 95. **CONTACT ADDRESS** Dept of French, Univ of Va, 302 Cabell Hall, Charlottesville, VA, 22903.

DENT, GINA
DISCIPLINE AFRICAN DIASPORIC LITERATURE **EDUCATION** Univ Calif, BA, 89; Columbia, PhD, 97. **CAREER** English and Lit, Columbia Univ **SELECTED PUBLICATIONS** Ed, Black Popular Culture, 92. **CONTACT ADDRESS** Columbia Univ, 2960 Broadway, New York, NY, 10027-6902.

DER-HOUSSIKIAN, HAIG
PERSONAL Born 08/16/1938, Cairo, Egypt, m, 1961 **DISCIPLINE** LINGUISTICS **EDUCATION** Am Univ Beirut, BA, 61, MA, 62; Univ Tex Austin, PhD, 69. **CAREER** Instr English, Brit Lebanese Training Col, Beirut, 60-62; asst prof Swahili & ling, 67-70, assoc prof foreign lang & ling, 70-77, acting dir ling, Univ, 71-72, dir, Ctr African Studies, 73-79, PROF FOREIGN LANG & LING, UNIV FLA, 77-, Chair, Dept African & Asian Lang & Lit, 82-91; Res assoc, Univ, Dar es Salaam, 66. **HONORS AND AWARDS** Fulbright-Hays res award, EAfrica, 66-67; sr Fulbright lectr, Univ Luanda, Angola, 72-73, Univ Benin, Togo, 79-80 & 81 & Univ Ouagadougou, Upper Volta, 81; Acad specialist grant, vis prof, Univ Marien Ngouabi, Barazzaville, Congo 5-8/88; invited vis prof, Dept of African Langs & Lits, Univ Zimbabwe, harare, Zimbabwe, 89. **MEMBERSHIPS** Ling Soc Am; African Studies Asn. **RESEARCH** Bantu linguistics; Swahili and Arabic dialectology; syntax and semantics. **SELECTED PUBLICATIONS** Auth, Linguistic assimilation in an urban center of the Kenya Coast, J African Lang, 68; The semantic content of class in Bantu and its syntactic significance, Linguistics, 70; Educated urban Swahili, J Lang Asn EAfrica, 71; The evidence for a Niger-Congo hypothesis, Cahiers d'Etudes Africaines, 72; A Bibliography of African Linguistics, Ling Res, Inc, 72; co-ed, Language and Linguistic Problems in Africa, Hornbeam, 77; Tem Grammar Handbook, Tem: Communication and Culture, Tem: Special Skills, Peace Corps Lang Handbk Series, 80. **CONTACT ADDRESS** Ctr for African Studies, Univ of Fla, PO Box 14105 Univ Station, Gainesville, FL, 32604. **EMAIL** haig@aall.ufl.edu

DERBYSHIRE, WILLIAM W.
PERSONAL Born 12/30/1936, Philadelphia, PA, 3 children **DISCIPLINE** RUSSIAN AND SLAVIC LINGUISTICS **EDUCATION** Univ Pa, BA, 58, MA, 59, PhD (Slavic ling), 64. **CAREER** Asst instr Russ lang, Univ Pa, 59-61; asst prof Russ lang and lit, Lycoming Col, 61-63; from asst prof to assoc prof, State Univ NY Binghamton, 64-59, chmn dept, 67-69; assoc prof Russ and Slavic ling, 69-76, chmn, Dept Slavic Lang and Lit, 69-80, PROF SLAVIC LING, RUTGERS UNIV, 76-, Fulbright res fel, Inst Ling, Univ Zagreb, 72-73; mem exec coun, Soc for Slovene Studes, 77-. **MEMBERSHIPS** Am Asn Teachers Slavic and East Europ Lang; MLA; AAUP; Am Asn Advan Slavic Studies; Soc for Slovene Studies. **RESEARCH** Russian lexicology and lexicography; homonymy in Slavic languages; Slovene language. **SELECTED PUBLICATIONS** Auth, The Beginnings of the Scientific Study of Minor Slavic Languages--The Correspondence Between Baudouindecourtenay, Jan and Oblak, Vatroslav, Slavic Rev, Vol 53, 94; A Complete English Slovene Dictionary--Slovene and English, Slavic East European J, Vol 40, 96; Slovene English Dictionary--Slovene and English, Slavic East European J, Vol 40, 96. **CONTACT ADDRESS** Dept of Slavic Lang and Lit, Rutgers Univ, New Brunswick, NJ, 08903.

DERRYBERRY, BOB R.
PERSONAL Born 07/19/1937, Wardville, OK, m, 1958, 2 children **DISCIPLINE** SPEECH COMMUNICATION **EDUCATION** East Central State Univ Okla, BA, 60; East Central State Univ, MT, 62; Univ Ark, MA, 66; Univ Mo, PhD, 73 **CAREER** Instr, Southwest Baptist Col, 61-69; instr, Univ Mo, 69-70; assoc prof, Southwest Baptist Univ, 70-78; prof & chair, Ouachita Baptist Univ, 78-81; senior prof, dept chair, dir Forensics, Southwest Baptist Univ, 81- **HONORS AND AWARDS** Mo Gov Award Excellence in Teaching, 92, 97; Ed Board, Southern Jrn Forensics, 97-98; Keynote Address Presenter, Pi Kappa Delta Ntl Convention Develop Conf, 93; Loren Reid Serv Award, 92; E.R. Nichols Award Outstanding Forensics Educator, Pi Kappa Delta, 90 **MEMBERSHIPS** Speech & Theatre Assoc Missouri President, 90; Pi Kappa Delta Ntl Forensic Fraternity; **SELECTED PUBLICATIONS** Auth, "Linking department and forensics directing in the small college," Speech Communication Assoc Annual Meeting, ERIC, 96; auth, "Future considerations for multidimensional forensic programs," Speech Theatre Assoc Mo Jrnl, 96; auth, "Understanding and utilizing academic freedom in the religious affiliated university," Speech Communication Assoc Annual Meeting, ERIC, 95 **CONTACT ADDRESS** 341 S Chicago Place, Bolivar, MO, 65613.

DERSOFI, NANCY
PERSONAL Boston, MA **DISCIPLINE** ITALIAN, COMPARATIVE LITERATURE **EDUCATION** Radcliffe Col, AB, 57; Harvard Univ, AM, 59, PhD(comp lit), 66. **CAREER** Asst prof Ital, Conn Col, 66-68 & Queens Col, 68-71; asst prof, 72-80, assoc Prof Ital, Bryn Mawr Col, 80-, Sibley fel Greek, 65-66; I Tatti fel Ital, Harvard Univ, 76-77; prof Comp Lit, 89-. **MEMBERSHIPS** MLA; Renaissance Soc Am; Am Assoc of Teachers of Italian; Am Assoc of Italian Studies. **RESEARCH** Renaissance theater; early modern actresses. **SELECTED PUBLICATIONS** Auth, Arcadia and the Stage: An Introduction to the Dramatic Art of Angelo Beolco, Called Ruzante, Jose Porrua Turanzas, 78; Ruzente L'Auconitana The Woman from Ancena, trans with intro ed notes, Univ of Calif Press, Berkeley, 94. **CONTACT ADDRESS** Bryn Mawr Col, 101 N Merion Ave, Bryn Mawr, PA, 19010-2899. **EMAIL** ndersofi@brynmawr.edu

DESAUTELS, JACQUES
PERSONAL Born 01/18/1937, Iberville, PQ, Canada **DISCIPLINE** GREEK LANGUAGE & CIVILIZATION **EDUCATION** Univ Montreal, BA, 56; Col l'Immaculee-Conception, BPh, 61; Univ Laval, LL, 64; Univ d'Aix-Marseille, DoctL, 66. **CAREER** PROF DE LANGUE, DE LITTERATURE ET DE CIVILISATION GRECQUES, UNIV LAVAL, 67-, vice-recteur, 77-82, doyen, fac des lettres, 95-. **SELECTED PUBLICATIONS** Auth, Dieux et mythes de la Grece ancienne, 88; auth, Le Quatrieme Roi mage, 93; auth, La dame de Chypre, 96. **CONTACT ADDRESS** Fac lettres, Univ Laval, Pavillon de Koninck, Quebec, PQ, G1K 7P4.

DESAUTELS, JACQUES
PERSONAL Born 01/18/1937, Iberville, PQ, Canada **DISCIPLINE** GREEK LANGUAGE & CIVILIZATION **EDUCATION** Univ Montreal, BA, 56; Col de l'Immaculee-Conception, BPh, 61; Univ Laval, LL, 64; Univ d'Aix-Marseille, DoctL, 66. **CAREER** PROF DE LANGUE, DE LITTERATURE ET DE CIVILISATION GRECQUES, UNIV LAVAL, 67-, vice-recteur, 77-82, doyen, fac des lettres, 95-. **SELECTED PUBLICATIONS** Auth, Dieux et mythes de la Grece ancienne, 88; auth, Le Quatrieme Roi mage, 93; auth, La dame de Chypre, 96. **CONTACT ADDRESS** Fac des lettres, Laval Univ, Pavillon de Koninck, Quebec, PQ, G1K 7P4. **EMAIL** Jacques.Desautels@fl.ulaval.ca

DESROCHES, RICHARD HENRY
PERSONAL Born 10/17/1927, Worcester, MA, d, 2 children **DISCIPLINE** ROMANCE LANGUAGES **EDUCATION** Clark Univ, AB, 47; Yale Univ, PhD, 62. **CAREER** Master French, Span & Latin, Tabor Acad, Marion, Mass, 49-51; asst, Yale Univ, 53-57; from instr to asst prof Romance lang, 57-69, asst fir, NDEA French Inst, Tours, France, 62-68, instr, 63-65, 67-68, acting chmn dept Romance lang, Univ, 73-74, Assoc Prof Romance Lang, Univ Ore, 69-98, Master Span, Hamden Hall Country Day Sch, Conn, 56-57. **MEMBERSHIPS** Am Asn Tchr(s) Fr; Philol Asn Pac Coast. **RESEARCH** Eighteenth century French novel. **SELECTED PUBLICATIONS** Coauth, Guide for French, Curric Publ, Portland Pub Sch, Ore, 62; auth, An eighteenth century philosopher's literary protest against slavery, Proc Pac Northwest Conf Foreign Lang, 4/64; Preromantic melancholy and the philosophical mind, Pac Coast Philol, 4/68; Reality behind the myth in Giraudoux's La Guerre de Troie n'aura pas lieu, Rev Langues Vivantes, 6/68. **CONTACT ADDRESS** Dept of Romance Lang, Univ of OR, Eugene, OR, 97403-1205. **EMAIL** rdesroch@oregon.uoregon.edu

DEWEESE, PAMELA
DISCIPLINE SPANISH LANGUAGE AND LITERATURE **EDUCATION** Univ NC Greensboro, BA; Univ NC Chapel Hill, MA; PhD. **CAREER** Asst prof, Sweet Briar Col. **RESEARCH** Mod Span lit; comp lit. **SELECTED PUBLICATIONS** Auth, articles and papers on the works of contemp Span novelist, Luis Goytisolo. **CONTACT ADDRESS** Sweet Briar Col, Sweet Briar, VA, 24595.

DI MAIO, IRENE STOCKSIEKER
DISCIPLINE GERMAN LANGUAGE, LITERATURE AND CULTURE/HISTORY, AND FILM **EDUCATION** La State Univ, PhD, 76. **CAREER** Assoc prof Ger, A&S fac senate, univ fac senate, A&S CAPPE comt, ch, Women's and Gender stud, Delta Phi Alpha, La State Univ. **RESEARCH** Eighteenth to twentieth century German literature with focus on the nineteenth century. **SELECTED PUBLICATIONS** Auth, The Multiple Perspective in Wilhelm Raabe's Third-Person Narratives of the Braunschweig Period, J. Benjamins, 81; Reclamations of the French Revolution: Fanny Lewald's Literary Response to the Nachmaumlrz in Der Seehof, Geist und Gesellschaft. zur Rezeption der Franzoumlsiszhen Revolution, ed Eitel Timm, Munich Fink, 90; Borders of Culture: The Native American in Friedrich Gerst&aumlcker's North American Narratives, in Yearbk of Ger Am Stud 28, 93. **CONTACT ADDRESS** Dept of For Lang and Lit, Louisiana State Univ, 124 C Prescott Hall, Baton Rouge, LA, 70803.

DI NAPOLI, THOMAS JOHN
DISCIPLINE MODERN GERMAN LITERATURE, GERMAN LANGUAGE **EDUCATION** Univ Tex, Austin, PhD, 71. **CAREER** Assoc prof Ger, undergrad adv, La State Univ. **RESEARCH** East German studies; German children's literature. **SELECTED PUBLICATIONS** Auth, Thirty Years of Children's Literature in the German Democratic Republic, in Ger Stud Rev, No 2, 84; The Children's Literature of Peter Hacks, Peter Lang Publ, 87. **CONTACT ADDRESS** Dept of For Lang and Lit, Louisiana State Univ, 220A Prescott Hall, Baton Rouge, LA, 70803. **EMAIL** dinapoli@homer.forlang.lsu.edu

DIAZ, LOMBERTO
PERSONAL Born 04/16/1914, Pinar del Rio, Cuba, m, 1940, 2 children **DISCIPLINE** SPANISH AND SPANISH AMERICAN LITERATURE **EDUCATION** Univ Havana, Dr, 38, Dr and Master, 44; Ind State Univ, Terre Haute, BA, 65, MA, 66; Fla State Univ, PhD (philos), 69. **CAREER** Prof polit sci, Interam Ctr Econ and Soc Studies, Dominican Repub, 63; instr Span, Ind State Univ, Terre Haute, 65-66; assoc prof, Northeastern Mo State Col, 66-67; instr, Fla State Univ, 67-69; assoc prof, 69-73, dir summer prog, 71, 72 and 74, prof, 73-80, EMER PROF SPAN, IND STATE UNIV, EVANSVILLE, 80-, Vis prof, Inst Filologia Hispanica, Saltillo, Mex, 71, Univ San Luis Potosi, 72. **MEMBERSHIPS** Am Asn Teachers Span and Port; Circulo Cult Panam; MLA; AAUP. **RESEARCH** Latin American studies. **SELECTED PUBLICATIONS** Auth, To Gullon,Ricardo in From His Students, Critica Hispanica, Vol 18, 1996. **CONTACT ADDRESS** Dept of Foreign Lang, Indiana State Univ, 8600 University Blvd, Evansville, IN, 47712.

DIAZ, ROBERTO IGNACIO
DISCIPLINE SPANISH AMERICAN LITERATURE **EDUCATION** Harvard Univ, PhD. **CAREER** Asst prof, Univ Southern Calif. **RESEARCH** Literary-historical study of Spanish American writing in English and French. **SELECTED PUBLICATIONS** Publ on, 19th and 20th century Spanish American literature. **CONTACT ADDRESS** Dept of Spanish and Portuguese, Univ Southern Calif, University Park Campus, Los Angeles, CA, 90089. **EMAIL** rdiaz@bcf.usc.edu

DIAZ-DUQUE, OZZIE FRANCIS
PERSONAL Born 09/17/1951, Guanajay, Cuba **DISCIPLINE** ROMANCE LANGUAGES & LITERATURES **EDUCATION** Queens Col, City Univ New York, BA, 73; Univ Iowa, MA, 75, PhD, 80. **CAREER** Instr Span, 73-82, Asst Prof Span & Port, Univ Iowa, 82-, Med interpreter Am sign lang, Hosps & Clinics, Univ Iowa, 80-; consult & lectr, Col Nursing, Univ Iowa, 77, lectr, Col Med, 74- **HONORS AND AWARDS** Haney Medal, NY City Student Art League, 71; Sigma Delta Pi, Nat Hisp Honor Soc, 72; Magna Cum Laude, Queens Col, CUNY, 73; Outstanding Schol, Univ Iowa, 80; Certificate of Merit, Lyons Club, Iowa City, 83; Volunteer of the Year, State of Iowa Gubernatorial Award, JCAC, 87; Certificate of Merit, Bureau of Business Practice, 89; U.S. Surgeon General's Certificate of Merit, 93; Staff Excellence Award, Univ Iowa, 93. **MEMBERSHIPS** MLA; Am Med Writers Asn; Am Transl Asn. **RESEARCH** Foreign language teaching techniques; communication in medical settings; vocal music and literature. **SELECTED PUBLICATIONS** Auth, Manual de Transplante de Hidago, Transplant Unit, Dept Surgery, Univ Iowa Hospitals and Clinics, 96; Why don't I?, Iowa Rev, 9/96; Selections of poetry, Lambda Publ, 12/96; ed and consult, Spanish for Medical Personnel, Jarvis and Lebredo, Houghton Mifflin, 96; auth, Trauma Cerebral: Manual de informacion, Dept Neurology, Univ Iowa Hospitals and Clinics, 97; coauth, Interpreting in Health Care Settings, New Physician Mag, 2/97; Poetry and essay in Looking Queer: An Anthology, Hawthorne Press, 98; author of numerous other articles. **CONTACT ADDRESS** Dept Span & Port, Univ Iowa, 111 Phillips Hall, Iowa City, IA, 52242. **EMAIL** odduque@blue.weeg.uiowa.edu

DICK, ERNST S.
DISCIPLINE GERMANIC PHILOLOGY, MEDIEVAL LITERATURE **EDUCATION** Univ Munster, PhD. **CAREER** Instr, Univ VA; affil, Johns Hopkins Univ, Univ MT, Univ WI; prof, 68. **RESEARCH** Germanic word studies and medieval Ger lit. **SELECTED PUBLICATIONS** Publ(s), etymological and semantic study on central terms of Germanic relig and cult; co-ed bk(s), and numerous articles on medieval Ger lit, Germanic philol, reception studies, and folklore; auth, articles on Annette von Droste-Hulshoff and Friedrich Durrenmatt. **CONTACT ADDRESS** Dept of Ger Lang and Lit, Univ Kansas, Admin Building, Lawrence, KS, 66045. **EMAIL** esdick@kuhub.cc.ukans.edu

DICKERSON, GREGORY WEIMER
PERSONAL Born 03/08/1937, Hanover, NH, m, 1967, 2 children **DISCIPLINE** CLASSICAL LANGUAGES & LITERATURE **EDUCATION** Harvard Univ, AB, 59; Princeton Univ, MA, 65, PhD, 72. **CAREER** Teaching fel classics, Phillips Acad, Andover, Mass, 59-60; secy, Am Sch Class Studies, Athens, 63-64; instr, Gilman Sch, Baltimore, 64-66; instr classics, 67-70, asst prof Greek, 70-76, assoc prof Greek, Bryn Mawr Col, 76-. **MEMBERSHIPS** Am Phil Asn. **RESEARCH** Greek drama. **SELECTED PUBLICATIONS** Auth, Aristophanes' Ranae 862: A note on the anatomy of Euripidean Tragedy, Harvard Studies Class Philol, 74; coauth, Sophocles' Women of Trachis, Oxford Univ, 78. **CONTACT ADDRESS** Dept of Greek, Bryn Mawr Col, 101 N Merion Ave, Bryn Mawr, PA, 19010-2899. **EMAIL** gdickers@brynmawr.edu

DICKIE, MATTHEW WALLACE
PERSONAL Born 11/20/1941, Edinburgh, Scotland **DISCIPLINE** CLASSICAL PHILOLOGY **EDUCATION** Univ Edinburgh, MA, 64; Univ Toronto, PhD (Greek), 72. **CAREER** Instr classics, Swarthmore Col, 67-68; asst prof, 72-78, ASSOC PROF CLASSICS, UNIV ILL, CHICAGO CIRCLE, 78-, Chmn Dept, 80-. **RESEARCH** Early Greek poetry; Greek ethics; Greek history. **SELECTED PUBLICATIONS** Auth, A Knidian Phallic Vase From Corinth, Hesperia, Vol 62, 93; A New Epigram by Poseidippus on an Irritable Dead Cretan, Bullf Am Society Papyrologists, Vol 32, 95; Baskania, Probaskania and Prosbaskania, Glotta Zeitschrift Griechische Lateinische Sprache, Vol 71, 93; Hermeias on Plato Phaedrus 238d and Synesius Dion 14.2, Am J Philol, Vol 114, 93; A New Epigram by Poseidippus on an Irritable Dead Cretan, Bull Am Soc Papyrologists, Vol 32, 95; Dioscorus and the Impotence of Envy, Bull Am Soc Papyrologists, Vol 30, 93; **CONTACT ADDRESS** Dept of Classics, Univ of Ill, Chicago Circle, Box 4348, Chicago, IL, 60680.

DIETRICH, CRAIG
PERSONAL Born 08/15/1937, Butte, MT **DISCIPLINE** CHINESE SOCIAL AND ECONOMIC HISTORY **EDUCATION** Univ Chicago, AB, 61, PhD (Chinese hist), 70. **CAREER** Asst prof Chinese hist, Univ Minn, 66-67; from instr to asst prof, 68-73; ASSOC PROF CHINESE HIST, UNIV MAINE, PORTLAND-GORHAM, 73-, Instr Chinese hist, Bowdoin Col, 68-70, asst prof, 71-73; Am Coun Learned Soc res grant Chinese civilization, 73-74. **MEMBERSHIPS** Asn Asian Studies. **RESEARCH** Late traditional Chinese economic organization; 17th century Chinese-European intellectual contacts. **SELECTED PUBLICATIONS** Auth, Les Opera Parfumes, Aspects of Orientalism in 19th Century French Opera, Theatre Research International, Vol 22, 97. **CONTACT ADDRESS** Dept of Hist, Univ of Maine at Portland-Gorham, Portland, ME, 04103.

DIETZ, DONALD T.
PERSONAL Born 09/09/1939, Chicago, IL, m, 1963, 6 children **DISCIPLINE** SPANISH **EDUCATION** Univ Notre Dame, BA, 61; Univ Ariz, PhD (Span), 68. **CAREER** Instr Span, Univ Dayton, 65-66; from asst prof to assoc prof and admin asst to chmn dept, Ball State Univ, 66-72; prof Span and chmn dept mod lang, Univ Louisville, 72-76; Prof Span and Chairperson Dept, Tex Tech Univ, 76-. **MEMBERSHIPS** Am Asn Teachers Span and Port; MLA. **RESEARCH** The Autos Sacramentales; Spanish Renaissance. **SELECTED PUBLICATIONS** Auth, Baroque Art and Sacramental Drama, Calderon No Hay Instante Sin Milagro, Bull Comediantes, Vol 46, 94. **CONTACT ADDRESS** Dept of Span, Tex Tech Univ, Lubbock, TX, 79413.

DIJKSTRA, BRAM
PERSONAL Born 07/05/1938, Tandjung Pandan, Indonesia, m, 1964 **DISCIPLINE** AMERICAN & COMPARATIVE LITERATURE **EDUCATION** Ohio State Univ, BA, 61, MA, 62; Univ Calif, Berkeley, PhD, 67. **CAREER** From actg instr to asst prof, 66-73, assoc prof, 73-85, prof Am & comp lit, Univ Calif, San Diego, 85-. **RESEARCH** Visual arts and literature; sociology of literature; literature and ideology. **SELECTED PUBLICATIONS** Auth, Faces in Skin, Oyez, 65; The Hieroglyphics of a New Speech; Cubism, Stieglitz and the early Poetry of William Carlos Williams, Princeton, 69; contribr, Encounters: Essays in Literature and the Visual Arts, Studio Vista, London, 71; Un Reve Americain: Norman Mailer et l'esthetique de la domination, Temps Mod, Paris 4/72; The androgyne in nineteenth-century art and literature, Comp Lit, winter 74; Painting and ideology: Picasso and Guernica, Praxis, 76; ed, William Carlos Williams on Art and Artists, New Directions, 78; Nicht-repressive rhythmische Strukturen in einigen Formen afro-amerikanischer und westindischer Musik, Die Zeichen, Fischer Verlag, Frankfurt, 81; auth Idols of Perversity: Fantasies of Feminine Evil in Fin-de-siecle Culture. Oxford Univ, 86; Defoe and Economics: The Fortunes of ROXANA in the History of Interpretation, MacMillan, 87; The High Cost of Parasols: Images of Women in Impressionist Art, California Light, Chronicle Books, 90; America and Georgia O'Keefe, Georgia O'Keefe, The New York Years, A A Knopf, 91; Early Modernism in Southern California: Provincialism or Eccentricity Modernist Art 1900-1950, Univ Calif, 96; Evil Sisters: The Threat of Female Sexuality and the Cult of Manhood, A A Knopf, 96; Georgia O'Keefe and the Eros of Place, Princeton Univ, 98. **CONTACT ADDRESS** Dept Lit, Univ Calif San Diego, 9500 Gilman Dr., La Jolla, CA, 92093-5003.

DILLER, GEORGE THEODORE
PERSONAL Born 01/01/1940, Hanover, NH, m, 1961, 3 children **DISCIPLINE** MEDIEVAL FRENCH **EDUCATION** Princeton Univ, AB, 61; Middlebury Col, MA, 63; Stanford Univ, PhD (French), 68. **CAREER** Instr French, Brandeis Univ, 66-68; asst prof, 68-73, ASSOC PROF FRENCH, UNIV

FLA, 73-. **MEMBERSHIPS** Soc Anciens Textes Francais; SAtlantic Mod Lang Asn; Repertoire Int Medievistes. **RESEARCH** Medieval French historians, especially Froissart; Romans antiques. **SELECTED PUBLICATIONS** Auth, Froissart, Historiography, The University Curriculum and Isabeau of Bavaria, Romance Quart, Vol 41, 94. **CONTACT ADDRESS** Dept of RLL, Univ of Fla, P O Box 117405, Gainesville, FL, 32611-7405.

DIMARIA, SALVATORE
DISCIPLINE ITALIAN LITERATURE **EDUCATION** Univ Wis, PhD, 78. **CAREER** Assoc prof. **RESEARCH** Dramatic theater in the Italian Renaissance. **SELECTED PUBLICATIONS** Auth, pubs on dramaturgical innovations, semiotics of theater, Machiavelli, and Ariosto. **CONTACT ADDRESS** Dept of Romance Languages, Knoxville, TN, 37996.

DIMIC, MILAN VELIMIR
PERSONAL Born 03/15/1933, Belgrade, Yugoslavia, m, 1959, 2 children **DISCIPLINE** COMPARATIVE AND GERMAN LITERATURE **EDUCATION** Univ Belgrade, MA, 56; Univ Vienna, dipl, 56. **CAREER** Instr Ger, Serbian Acad Sci and Inst Exp Phonetics, 56-57; asst prof comp lit, Univ Belgrade, 57-62; from asst prof to assoc prof, 66-72, chmn dept comp lit, 69-75 and 81, PROF GERMAN AND COMP LIT, UNIV ALTA, 72-, Chmn Comp Lit Prog, 67-, Res asst, Inst Theory of Lit and Aesthet, Belgrade, 60-62; mem, Can Coun Acad Panel, 74-78, chmn 76-78; ED, CAN REV COMP LIT, UNIV ALTA PRESS AND UNIV TORONTO PRESS, 74-. **MEMBERSHIPS** MLA; Asn Can Univ Teachers Ger; Can Asn Slavists; Am Comp Lit Asn; Can Comp Lit Asn. **RESEARCH** Romanticism; folklore; methods in literary scholarship. **SELECTED PUBLICATIONS** Auth, Greene, E. J. H.--In-Memoriam, Can Rev Comp Lit-Rev Can Litt Comp, Vol 22, 95; Why Study Canonization, Can Rev Compa Lit Rev Can Litt Com, Vol 20, 93; 20 Years of The Canadian Review of Comparative Literature, Can Rev Compa Lit Rev Can Litt Com Vol 20, 93; Canons and Canonization, from Theory to Practice, Can Rev Compa Lit Rev Can Litt Com, Vol 20, 93; The New Editorship and the Future of the Canadian Review Of Comparative Literature Revue Canadienne De Litterature Comparee, Can Rev Compa Lit Rev Can Litt Com, Vol 23, 96; Re VisionS of Canadian Literature--Introduction, Can Rev Compa Lit Rev Can Litt Com, Vol 20, 93. **CONTACT ADDRESS** Dept of Comp Lit, Univ of Alta, Edmonton, AB, T6G 2E6.

DIMLER, GEORGE RICHARD
PERSONAL Born 10/21/1931, Baltimore, MD **DISCIPLINE** GERMAN LANGUAGE & LITERATURE **EDUCATION** Fordham Univ, AB, 56, MA, 60; Woodstock Col, STB, 62, STL, 64; Middlebury Col, MA, 66; Univ Calif, Los Angeles, PhD(Germanic lang), 70. **CAREER** Instr Ger, Marquette Univ, 62-; Asst prof, Loyola Col, Md, 70-71; assoc prof, 72-81, PROF LANG, FORDHAM UNIV, 82-; NDEA fel, 67-70; Nat Endowment for Humanities grant, 74; Am Coun of Learned Socs fel, 75; Ger Acad Exchange Serv fel, 76-77 & 78-79; Herzog August bibliothek, Wolfenbuttek Stipendium, 79. **MEMBERSHIPS** Am Asn Teachers Ger; MLA; Mid Atlantic Lang Asn; Goethe Soc Am (treas, 72); Renaissance Soc Am **RESEARCH** German baroque literature, Jesuit drama; Jesuit emblematics. **SELECTED PUBLICATIONS** Auth, Friedrich Spee's Trutznachtigall, Herbert Lang, Bern, 73; The genesis and development of Spee's love imagery in the Trutznachtigall, Germanic Rev, 73; Don Quixote and Simplicius Simplicissimus: Study in alienation, Thought, 74; Gottfried Von Strassburg's Tristan, Amsterdamer Beitrage, 75; The egg as emblem: Genesis and structure of a Jesuit emblem book, Studies in Iconography, 76; A bibliographical survey of Jesuit emblem books in Early Jesuit colleges, Archivum Hist Soc Jesu, 76; Friedrich Spees Trutznachtigall, Univ Press Am, 81; Imago Primi Saeculi: The secular tradition and the Jesuit emblem book, Thought, 81; Jesuit Series, Corpus Librorum Emblematum, vol 1, McGill-Queens Press, 97. **CONTACT ADDRESS** Fordham Univ, 501 E Fordham Rd, Bronx, NY, 10458-5191. **EMAIL** dimler@murray.fordham.edu

DINNEEN, DAVID A.
DISCIPLINE LINGUISTICS, AND ROMANCE PHILOLOGY **EDUCATION** Harvard Univ, PhD. **CAREER** Prof; dept ch, Univ KS. **HONORS AND AWARDS** Coord, basic lang prog. **RESEARCH** For lang pedag. **SELECTED PUBLICATIONS** Co-auth, a first-yr textbk in French, Chapeau! **CONTACT ADDRESS** Dept of French and Italian, Univ Kansas, Admin Building, Lawrence, KS, 66045. **EMAIL** dad@ukans.edu

DIONNE, RENE
PERSONAL Born 01/29/1929, Saint-Philippe-de-Neri, PQ, Canada **DISCIPLINE** LETTRES FRANCAISES **EDUCATION** Univ Laval, BA, 50; Univ Montreal, MA, 55, LL, 60; L'Immaculee-Conception Montreal, LPh, 58; Univ Sherbrooke, DL, 74. **CAREER** Prof, Col Saint-Ignace, 54-56, 58-59; prof, Col Sainte-Marie, 65-69; prof, Univ Montreal, 67-69; prof, Univ Sherbrooke, 69-70; PROF LETTRES FRANcAISES, UNIV OTTAWA, 70-, dir dept, 75-78; prof invite, Univ Kiel, 88; prof associe, Univ Moncton, 89-95. **HONORS AND AWARDS** Prix de l'Ambassade suisse, 60; Prix litteraire de La Press, 79; Prix litteraire Champlain, 80; LittD(hon), York Univ, 95. **RESEARCH** French-Canadian literature. **SELECTED PUBLICATIONS** Auth, Antoine Gerin-Lajoie, homme de lettres, 78; auth, La Patrie litteraire 1760-1895, 78; auth, Bibliographie de la litterature outaouaise et franco-ontarienne, 78, 81; auth, Repertoire des professeurs et chercheurs, 78, 80; auth, La Litterature canadienne de langue francaise, 88; auth, Anthologie de la poesie franco-ontarienne, des origines a nos jours, 91; auth, La Litterature regionale aux confins de l'histoire et de la geographie, 93; auth, Histoire de la litterature franco-ontarienne, des origines a nos jours, tome 1, 97; auth, Anthologie de la litterature franco-ontarinenne, des origines a nos jours, tome 1, 97; coauth, L'Age de l'interrogation 1937-1952, 80, 94; coauth, Bibliographie de la critique de la litterature quebecoise et canadienne-francaise dans les revues canadiennes 88, 91, 92, 94; ed, Propos litteraires, 73; ed, Propos sur la litterature outaouaise et franco-ontarienne, 4 tomes, 78-83; ed, Situation de l'edition et de la recherche, 78; ed, Quatre Siecles d'identite canadienne, 83; ed, Le Quebecois et sa litterature, 84. **CONTACT ADDRESS** Dept of Lettres Francaises, Univ of Ottawa, Ottawa, ON, K1N 6N5.

DITSKY, JOHN M.
DISCIPLINE ENGLISH LANGUAGE; LITERATURE **EDUCATION** Detroit, PhB, MA; NY Univ, PhD, 67. **CAREER** Prof **SELECTED PUBLICATIONS** Auth, essays on East of Eden; John Steinbeck: Life, Work and Criticism; The Onstage Christ; The Grapes of Wrath; Friend & Lover; poetry ed, The Windsor Rev. **CONTACT ADDRESS** Dept of English Language and Literature, Univ of Windsor, 401 Sunset Ave, Windsor, ON, N9B 3P4.

DOAK, KEVIN M.
DISCIPLINE EAST ASIAN STUDIES **EDUCATION** Univ Chicago, PhD, 89. **CAREER** Assoc prof, Univ Ill Urbana Champaign. **RESEARCH** Modern Japanese cultural & intellectual history; nationalism; romanticism as social ideology. **SELECTED PUBLICATIONS** Auth, Dreams of Difference: The Japan Romantic School and the Crisis of Modernity, Univ Calif, 94; Nationalism as Dialectics: Ethnicity, Moralism, and the State in Early Twentieth Century Japan, Univ Hawaii, 94; Ethnic Nationalism and Romanticism in Early Twentieth-Century Japan, J Japanese Studies, 96. **CONTACT ADDRESS** Dept East Asian Languages and Cultures, Univ Ill Urbana Champaign, 52 E Gregory Dr, Champaign, IL, 61820. **EMAIL** k-doak@uiuc.edu

DOBSEVAGE, ALVIN P
PERSONAL Born 11/29/1922, New York, NY, m, 1949, 3 children **DISCIPLINE** PHILOSOPHY, FOREIGN LANGUAGE **EDUCATION** City Col New York, BA, 42; Harvard Univ, MA, 48; Columbia Univ, MPhilos, 52; Cent Conn State Univ, MA, 82. **CAREER** Instr philos, Brooklyn Col, 51-53; vconsul info off, US Info Serv, Salisbury, Rhodesia, 55-58; teacher Latin, Wilton High Sch, Conn, 58-65; asst prof, 65-82, ASSOC PROF FRENCH, LATIN AND LING, WESTERN CONN STATE COL, 82-, CHMN DEPT MOD LANG, 81-, Adj asst prof Latin, Saturday Sch Lang, NY Univ, 60-68; adj asst prof philos, Danbury State Col, 60-; lectr, Univ Conn, Stamford Br, 63-64; ed, Hermes Americanus; Nat Endowment for Humanities grant, Am Acad Rome, 82. **HONORS AND AWARDS** Letter of Commendation from Off Personnel, Dept of Army for Work as Mem Haines Bd Study Group, 40, regarding civil affairs, Psychol Oper, 67. **MEMBERSHIPS** Am Philos Asn; Am Philol Asn; Mediaeval Acad Am; Class Asn New England; MLA. **RESEARCH** Gaston Bachelard's theory of imagination; aesthetics and metaphysics; teaching French and Latin. **SELECTED PUBLICATIONS** Auth, The Metamorphoses of Apuleius--On Making an Ass of Oneself, Class W, Vol 89, 96. **CONTACT ADDRESS** 45 Dodgingtown Rd, Bethel, CT, 06801.

DOCKERY, CHARLES D.
DISCIPLINE FRENCH LANGUAGE **EDUCATION** Earlham Col, BA, 61; IA Univ, PhD, 74. **CAREER** Prof, Davidson Col, 74. **HONORS AND AWARDS** 2 Mellon grants., Res dir Montpellier study abroad prog, Davidson Col. **RESEARCH** Cult and lit of Quebec; the Francophone short story; tchg vocab and grammar through traditional and contemp songs; transl theory; multimedia courseware develop. **SELECTED PUBLICATIONS** Coauth, software program devel at Middlebury to teach French phonetics. **CONTACT ADDRESS** Davidson Col, 102 N Main St, PO Box 1719, Davidson, NC, 28036.

DOCTER, MARY K.
DISCIPLINE HISPANIC LANGUAGES AND LITERATURES **EDUCATION** Univ Calif, LA, PhD, 91. **CAREER** Assistant Professor of Spanish, Westmont College, 1992-present Assistant Professor, Department of Hispanic Studies, Scripps College, Claremont, 1988-92 Bilingual Instructor, Colegio Eton, Mexico City, Mexico, 1981-82 **HONORS AND AWARDS** UCLA Distinguished Teaching Award, 1986-87 **RESEARCH** 20th cent Latin Am lit; romance ling. **SELECTED PUBLICATIONS** Auth, La Piedra y la masa: Un analisis comparativo de dos textos de Vallejo, Hispania 72:1, 89. **CONTACT ADDRESS** Dept of Eng, Westmont Col, 955 La Paz Rd, Santa Barbara, CA, 93108-1099.

DOERKSEN, VICTOR GERARD
PERSONAL Born 01/09/1934, Winnipeg, MB, Canada, m, 1960, 2 children **DISCIPLINE** GERMAN LITERATURE AND CRITICISM **EDUCATION** Univ Man, BA, 58, MA, 60; Univ Zurich, DPhil(Ger), 64. **CAREER** Asst prof Ger, Univ NB, 60-61; lectr, 61-62 and 64-65, from asst prof to assoc prof, 66-74, PROF GER, UNIV COL, UNIV MAN, 74-, HEAD DEPT, 68-, Can Coun res grant, 67-. **MEMBERSHIPS** Asn Can Univ Teachers Ger; Int Germanistenverband. **RESEARCH** Nineteenth century German literature; literary criticism. **SELECTED PUBLICATIONS** Auth, Reflections on Realism--Paradox, Norm, and Ideology in 19th Century German Prose, Seminar J Ger Stud, Vol 30, 94. **CONTACT ADDRESS** Dept of Ger, Univ of Man, Winnipeg, MB, R3T 2N2.

DOHERTY, KAREN A.
DISCIPLINE COMMUNICATION SCIENCES AND DISORDERS **EDUCATION** Univ WI Madison, PhD, 94. **CAREER** Asst prof CCC-A, Syracuse Univ. **RESEARCH** Speech perception in the hearing-impaired; psychoacoustics and amplification. **SELECTED PUBLICATIONS** Coauth, Spectral Weights for Overall Discrimination in Listeners with Sensorineural Hearing Loss, Jour Acoustical Soc Am, 96; Psychometric Functions for the Discrimination of Spectral Variance, Jour Acoustical Soc Am, 96; Use of a Correlational Method to Estimate a Listener's Weighting Function for Speech, Jour Acoustical Soc Am, 96. **CONTACT ADDRESS** Syracuse Univ, Syracuse, NY, 13244.

DOHERTY, LILLIAN E.
DISCIPLINE GREEK AND LATIN LITERATURE **EDUCATION** St Mary's Col, BA; Univ Notre Dame, MA; Univ Chicago, PhD. **CAREER** Instr, George Mason Univ; Howard Univ; asst prof, 87; assoc prof, 93-. **HONORS AND AWARDS** Affil, women's stud prog; comp lit prog. **SELECTED PUBLICATIONS** Auth, Tyro in Odyssey 11: Closed and Open Readings, Helios, 92; Gender and Internal Audiences in the Odyssey, Amer Jour of Philol, 92; Siren Songs: Gender, Audiences, and Narrators in the Odyssey, Univ Mich Press, 95; Sirens, Muses and Female Narrators in the Odyssey, The Distaff Side: Representing the Female in Homer's Odyssey, Oxford UP, 95 y **CONTACT ADDRESS** Dept of Class, Univ MD, 4229 Art-Sociology Building, College Park, MD, 20742-1335. **EMAIL** LL21@umail.umd.edu

DOLEZEL, LUBOMIR
PERSONAL Born 10/03/1922, Lesnice, Czechoslovakia **DISCIPLINE** SLAVIC & COMPARATIVE LITERATURE **EDUCATION** Charles Univ Prague, grad, 49; Czeck Acad Sci, PhD, 58. **CAREER** High sch tchr, Czeck, 49-54; res fel, Czeck Acad Sci, 58-68; assoc prof, Charles Univ Prague, 61-68; vis prof, Univ Mich, 65-68; vis prof, 68-71, prof, 71-88, ch dept, 80-83, PROF EMER SLAVIC & COMPARATIVE LIT, UNIV TORONTO, 88-; vis prof, Univ Amsterdam, 76; vis prof, Univ Munich, 77. **HONORS AND AWARDS** Can Coun leave fel, 77-78; Connaught sr fel, 83-84; Mem Medal Resistance; fel, Royal Soc Can. **MEMBERSHIPS** Toronto Semiotic Cir; Can Comp Lit Asn; Asn Czeck Writers. **SELECTED PUBLICATIONS** Auth, On the Style of Modern Czech Prose Fiction, 60; auth, Dictionary of Standard Czech, vol 1, 60; coauth, Narrative Modes in Czech Literature, 73; coauth, Occidental Poetics: Tradition and progress, 90; ed, Information Theory and Linguistics, 64; co-ed, Statistics and Style, 69; co-ed, Heterocosmica: Fiction and Possible Worlds, 98. **CONTACT ADDRESS** Univ of Toronto, Robarts Libr, 14th Fl, Toronto, ON, M5S 1A1.

DOLEZVELOVA-VELINGEROVA, MILENA
PERSONAL Prague, Czechoslovakia **DISCIPLINE** CHINESE LANGUAGE & LITERATURE **EDUCATION** Charles Univ, Prague, MA, 55; Oriental Inst, Prague, PhD, 65. **CAREER** Res assoc, Oriental Inst, Czeck Acad Sci, 54-68; res assoc, Inst Lit, Chinese Acad Sci, Beijing, 58-59; res assoc, Ctr Chinese Studs, Univ Mich, 67-68; assoc prof, 69-75, PROF, UNIV TORONTO 75-. **HONORS AND AWARDS** Sr. Res Vis Fel, Corpus Christi Col, Cambridge Univ, 84-85; Res Scholar, The Rockfeller Found Stud & Conf Ctr, Bellagio, Italy, 85; vis scholar, Harvard Univ, 90-91. **MEMBERSHIPS** Asn Asian Studs; Toronto Semiotic Circle; Can Asn Comparative Lit. **SELECTED PUBLICATIONS** Coauth/transl, The Ballad of the Hidden Dragon, 71; coauth, The Chinese Novel at the Turn of the Century, 80; coauth/ed, A Selective Guide to Chinese Literature 1900-1949, 88; coauth/ed, Poetics East and West, 89. **CONTACT ADDRESS** Dept of East Asian Studies, Univ of Toronto, Toronto, ON, M5S 1S3.

DOMARADZKI, THEODORE F.
PERSONAL Born 10/27/1910, Warsaw, Poland **DISCIPLINE** COMPARATIVE CIVILIZATIONS **EDUCATION** Acad Polit Sci (Warsaw), Polit Sci Dipl, 36; Univ Warsaw, MA (Hist), 39; Univ Rome, LittD (Slavic Philol), 41. **CAREER** Lectr, Univ Rome, 41-47; dir, prof & founder, dept Slavic stud, Ctr Polish & Slavic Res, Univ Montreal, 48-76; PROF & DIR, INST COMPARATIVE CIVILIZATIONS OF MONTREAL, 76-. **HONORS AND AWARDS** Order Can; Order Polonia Restituta; Papal Order St Gregory Great; Order St Sava; Ordo Constantini Magni; Sovereign Order St John Jerusalem; Polish Golden Cross Merit; Medal Polish Educ Merit. **MEMBER-**

SHIPS Can Asn Slavists; Can Soc Comp Stud Civilizations; Can Int Acad Hum Soc Sci; Que Ethnic Press Asn; PEN; Soc ecrivains Can; Inst Ital Cultur. **SELECTED PUBLICATIONS** Auth, Norwid poet of Christianity, 84; auth, Entre le romantisme et le symbolisme: C. Baudelaire et C. Norwid, in Les Cahiers de Varsovie, 86; auth, C.K. Norwid in Canada, 89; auth, Personalite ethniques au Quebec, 91; ed, Slavic & East Europ Stud, 56-76; ed, Slavic Publ/Publ Slaves, 73-. **CONTACT ADDRESS** Inst Comp Civilizations of Montreal, PO Box 759, Succ Outremont, Montreal, PQ, H2V 4N9.

DONAHUE, JOHN F.
DISCIPLINE CLASSICAL STUDIES **EDUCATION** Col Holy Cross, AB, 80; Univ NC at Chapel Hill, MA, 90, PhD, 96. **CAREER** Adj instr; Col William and Mary, 97; adj asst prof, Williamsburg, Va; tchg asst, Med Word Formation and Entymology, 94 & Latin, 91-93, Univ NC at Chapel Hill; Fay Sch, 86-88; UNC res ast, L'Annee Philiologique, 89-91, 94; Latin tutor, 91-93; fact checker, Amer Nat Biog, Oxford UP, 95-. **HONORS AND AWARDS** UNC Grad Sch Dissertation fel, 95; UNC Grad Sch Dept Class Travel Awd(s), 94 & Kappa Delta Pi Honor Soc, Colombia Univ, 84. **MEMBERSHIPS** Amer Philol Asn; Asn Int d'Epigraphie Grecque et Latine; Class Asn Mid W and S. **RESEARCH** Roman social history; Ancient dining; Latin inscriptions. **SELECTED PUBLICATIONS** Auth, Feasts and Females: Sex Roles, Public Recognition and Community Banquets in the Western Roman Empire, Class Asn Mid W and S, Nashville, 96; Public Banqueting in the Roman Empire: Issues for Consideration, Class Asn Mid W and S, Southern Section, Chapel Hill, 94 & Distributions of Bread During the Later Roman Empire: Some Chronological Problems, Class Asn Mid W and S, Atlanta, 94. **CONTACT ADDRESS** Dept of Classical Studies, Col of William and Mary, Morton Hall, PO Box 8795, Williamsburg, VA, 23187-8795. **EMAIL** jfdona@facstaff.wm.edu

DONAHUE, THOMAS JOHN
PERSONAL Born 01/09/1943, Philadelphia, PA, 2 children **DISCIPLINE** FRENCH LITERATURE, THEATRE **EDUCATION** Univ Pa, AM, 67 PhD, 73. **CAREER** Asst prof, 65-80, Assoc Prof, 80-91, prof, 91-, St Joseph's Univ. **HONORS AND AWARDS** Scholarship of the Alliance Francaise de Philadelphie, 64-65; fel Camargo Found, 78; Award for Tchg, Award for Scholarship, St Joseph's Univ. **MEMBERSHIPS** Am Asn of Tchrs of French; Alliance Francaise de Philadelphie. **RESEARCH** Auth, 20th-Century French theater; French theater history; theater semiotics. **SELECTED PUBLICATIONS** The Theater of Fernando Arrabal, New York Univ Press, 80; auth, Structures of Meaning: A Semiotic Approach to the Play Text, Fairleigh Dickinson. **CONTACT ADDRESS** Dept of French, St. Joseph's Univ, 5600 City Ave, Philadelphia, PA, 19131-1376. **EMAIL** tdonahue@sju.edu

DONALDSON, PETER SAMUEL
PERSONAL Born 11/21/1942, New York, NY, m, 1965, 3 children **DISCIPLINE** ENGLISH, HISTORY **EDUCATION** Columbia Univ, AB, 64, PhD (English), 74; Cambridge Univ, BA, 66, MA, 70. **CAREER** Preceptor English, Columbia Col, 67-68; from instr to asst prof, 69-78, assoc, 78-88, PROF LIT, MASS INST TECHNOL, 88-, Amm Fetter Friedlaender Prof Hum, 93-98, dept Hhead, 89-, dir, Shakespeare Elect Arch, 92-; Lectr comp lit, City Col New York, 67-69; Old Dom fel lit, Mass Inst Technol, 73; Nat Endowment for Humanities fel, 75; Am Counc Learned Soc fel, 82. **HONORS AND AWARDS** Fel, Royal Hist Soc, (UK), 79-. **MEMBERSHIPS** MLA; SAA. **RESEARCH** Rensaissance thought and letters: Machiavellian political tradition; Shakespeare in film and digital media. **SELECTED PUBLICATIONS** Auth, Staging the Gaze--Postmodernism, Psychoanalysis and Shakespearean Comedy, Renaissance Quart, Vol 47, 94; auth, Machiavelli and Mystery of State, Cambridge Univ Press, 88; auth, Shakespearean Films/Shakespearean Directors, Urwin Hyman, 90. **CONTACT ADDRESS** Massachussetts Inst Tech, 77 Massachusetts Ave, Cambridge, MA, 02139-4307. **EMAIL** psdlit@mit.edu

DORENLOT, FRANCOISE
PERSONAL Born 03/28/1934, Paris, France **DISCIPLINE** FRENCH LANGUAGE AND LITERATURE **EDUCATION** Univ Aix-Marseille, Lic en Droit, 55; Univ Paris, Lic es Let, 57: Univ Cincinnati, MA, 58; Univ Calif, Los Angeles, PhD (French), 66. **CAREER** Lectr French, McGill Univ, 61-65; lectr, 65-66, from instr to asst prof, 66-72, Assoc Prof French, City Col New York, 72-. **SELECTED PUBLICATIONS** Auth, THE MISSING CENTER OR NIHILISM AND LITERATURE - PAPERS WRITTEN IN HONOR OF TISON-BRAUN,MICHELINE/, ESPRIT CREATEUR, Vol 34, 1994 **CONTACT ADDRESS** Dept of Romance Lang City, City Col, CUNY, New York, NY, 10031.

DORIAN, NANCY CURRIER
PERSONAL Born 11/05/1936, New Brunswick, NJ **DISCIPLINE** LINGUISTICS, GERMANIC AND CELTIC LANGUAGES **EDUCATION** Conn Col, BA, 58; Univ Mich, MA, 61, PhD (ling), 65. **CAREER** Lectr, 65-66, from asst prof to assoc prof, 66-78, prof ling, Ger and anthrop, 78-79, William R Kenan, Jr, Prof Ling, Bryn Mawr Col, 80-. **MEMBERSHIPS** Ling Soc Am; Int Ling Asn; Celtic Studies Asn; Scottish Oral Hist Group. **RESEARCH** Linguistic change; language death; Scottish Gaelic and Pennsylvania Dutch. **SELECTED PUBLICATIONS** Auth, A Response to Ladefoged Other View of Endangered Languages, Lang, Vol 69, 93; An Introduction to the Ecology of Written Language, Lang, Vol 71, 95; Multilingualism, Lang, Vol 72, 96; Language Selection and Switching in Strasbourg, Lang, Vol 69, 93; Language Conflict and Language Planning, Language in Society, Vol 25, 96; Sustaining Local Literacies, Lang Soc, Vol 24, 95; 1st Language Attrition, Lang, Vol 68, 92; Language of the Islenos--Vestigial Spanish in Louisiana, Romance Philol, Vol 47, 94; Foundations of Bilingual Education and Bilingualism, Lings, Vol 32, 94; Sociolinguistics--A Sociological Critique, Lang, Vol 70, 94; Varieties of Variation in a Very Small Place--Social Homogeneity, Prestige Norms, and Linguistic Variation, Lang, Vol 70, 94; Endangered Languages, Lang, Vol 70, 94; Purism Vs Compromise in Language Revitalization and Language Revival, Lang Soc, Vol 23, 94. **CONTACT ADDRESS** Dept of Ger and Anthrop, Bryn Mawr Col, Bryn Mawr, PA, 19010.

DORON, PINCHAS
PERSONAL Born 07/05/1933, Poland, m, 1969, 5 children **DISCIPLINE** HEBREW LANGUAGE, BIBLE **EDUCATION** Hebrew Univ, Jerusalem, BA, 62, MA, 64; NY Univ, PhD (Hebrew studies), 75. **CAREER** Instr Hebrew and Talmud, Jewish Theol Sem, 64-65; lectr Hebrew, Hunter Col, 65-66; ASST PROF HEBREW, QUEENS COL, 66-, Instr, The Ulpan Ctr, 69-70. **MEMBERSHIPS** Asn Jewish Studies; Nat Asn Professors Hebrew. **RESEARCH** Biblical research; Hebrew language and literature; medieval Hebrew literature. **SELECTED PUBLICATIONS** Auth, Labor, Crafts and Commerce in Ancient Israel, Cath Biblical Quart, Vol 57, 95; New Evidence for the Pentateuch Text in the Aleppo Codex, Cath Biblical Quart, Vol 56, 94. **CONTACT ADDRESS** 730 E 7th St, Brooklyn, NY, 11218.

DORSEY, JAMES
DISCIPLINE ASIAN AND MIDDLE EASTERN LANGUAGES AND LITERATURES **EDUCATION** Colgate Univ, BA; IN Univ, MA; Univ WA, PhD. **CAREER** Asst prof, Dartmouth Col. **RESEARCH** Mod Japanese lit, criticism, and intellectual hist; class Japanese drama and lit theory. **SELECTED PUBLICATIONS** Trans, Japanese fiction. **CONTACT ADDRESS** Dartmouth Col, 3529 N Main St, #207, Hanover, NH, 03755.

DORSINVILLE, MAX
PERSONAL Born 01/30/1943, Port-au-Prince, Haiti, m, 1964, 1 child **DISCIPLINE** ENGLISH, COMPARATIVE LITERATURE **EDUCATION** Univ Sherbrooke, BA, 66, MA, 68; City Univ New York, PhD (comp lit), 72. **CAREER** Lectr, 70-72, asst prof, 72-75, dir, Ctr for French-Can Studies, 75-80, ASSOC PROF ENGLISH, MCGILL UNIV, 75-, Can Coun fel, 77-78. **MEMBERSHIPS** Can Comp Lit Asn (treas, 75-77); Asn Can Univ Teachers English. **RESEARCH** Twentieth century American novel; comparative Canadian literature; comparative African literature. **SELECTED PUBLICATIONS** Auth, Haiti--Its Literature and Way of Life, Can Rev Comparative Lit Rev Canadienne Litterature Comparee, Vol 21, 94. **CONTACT ADDRESS** Dept of English, McGill Univ, 853 Sherbrooke W, Montreal, PQ, H3A 2T6.

DOSWALD, HERMAN K.
PERSONAL Born 03/24/1932, Oakland, CA, m, 1956, 2 children **DISCIPLINE** GERMAN **EDUCATION** Univ Calif, Berkeley, AB, 55; Univ Wash, MA, 59, PhD, 65. **CAREER** Instr Ger, Oberlin Col, 59-60, Univ Wash, 60-61, Seattle Univ, 61-62; actg asst prof, Univ Kans, 64-65, asst prof, 65-67; from asst prof to assoc prof, Fresno State Col, 67-72; prof Ger and chmn dept Ger and Slavic lang and lit, Kent State Univ, 72-79; Prof Ger and Head Dept Foreign Lang and Lit, Va Polytech Inst and State Univ, 79-. **MEMBERSHIPS** Int Vereinigung fur Germanische Sprach-und Literaturwissenschaft. **RESEARCH** Hugo von Hofmannsthal; modern German literature; East German literature. **SELECTED PUBLICATIONS** Auth, Ich Nenne Das Wahrheitserfindung--Kipphardt, Heinar and His Concept of Documentary Theater as Historiography, Ger Stud Rev, Vol 18, 95; The Comedy--A Theatrical Mission--Foundations and Interpretations, Ger Stud Rev, Vol 18, 95. **CONTACT ADDRESS** Dept of Foreign Lang and Lit, Va Polytech Inst and State Univ, Blacksburg, VA, 24061.

DOUBLES, MALCOLM CARROLL
PERSONAL Born 08/14/1932, Richmond, VA, m, 1956, 3 children **DISCIPLINE** RELIGION, PHILOLOGY **EDUCATION** Davidson Col, BA, 53; Union Theol Sem, Va, BD, 57; Univ St Andrews, PhD, 62. **CAREER** Pastor, Lebanon & Castlewood Presby Churches, VA, 60-65; asst prof Old Testament, St Andrews Presby Col, 65-69, mem Christianity & cult team, 65-74, chmn freshman Christianity & cult team, 67-71, assoc prof relig, 69-76, dean students, 74-76; prof Relig & Dean Col, 76-97, DISTINGUISHED PROF INTL STUDIES, COKER COL, 97-; Fulbright fel, Pakistan, 84, P R China, 88; NEH younger humanist fel, 71-72; managing ed, St Andrews Rev, 72-76; managing ed, Prog for Comput & Publ Targumic Lit, 74-. **MEMBERSHIPS** Soc Bibl Lit; Int Orgn for Study Old Testament; Asn Targumic Studies 2E **RESEARCH** Aramaic language and literature, with particular reference to Targumic studies; linguistics, with particular reference to Hebrew and Greek; New Testament background, with particular reference to Jewish history. **SELECTED PUBLICATIONS** Auth, Toward the publication of the Palestinian Targum(s), Vetus Testamentum, Vol XV, No 1; Indications of antiquity in the Fragment Targum, in In Memoriam Paul Kahle, Topelmann, 68; contrib, The History of the Jews in the Time of Christ, T&T Clark & Sons, 73. **CONTACT ADDRESS** Coker Col, 300 E College Ave, Hartsville, SC, 29550-3797. **EMAIL** mdoubles@aol.com

DOUBROVSKY, SERGE
PERSONAL Born 05/22/1928, Paris, France, m, 1955, 2 children **DISCIPLINE** FRENCH **EDUCATION** Sorbonne, Lic philos, 49, Lic English, 51, Dd'Etat(Fr lit), 64; Nat Ministry Educ, France, Agrege, 54. **CAREER** Instr French, Harvard Univ, 55-57; asst prof, Brandeis Univ, 57-61; from assoc prof to prof, Smith Col, 61-66; PROF FRENCH, NY UNIV, 66-, Guggenheim fels, 65-66, 68-69. **MEMBERSHIPS** MLA. **RESEARCH** Seventeenth century literature; contemporary criticism and fiction. **SELECTED PUBLICATIONS** Auth, Excerpts From Le Livre Brise, Genre Forms of Discourse and Culture, Vol 26, 93; The Fact is That Writing is a Profoundly Immoral Act--An Interview with Doubrovsky, Serge, Genre Forms Discourse Cult, Vol 26, 93; Autobiography Truth Psychoanalysis Reprinted from Autobiographics, Pg 68-79, 88; Genre Forms Discourse Cult, Vol 26, 93. **CONTACT ADDRESS** Dept of French, New York Univ, 19 University Pl, New York, NY, 10003-4556.

DOUDOROFF, MICHAEL JOHN
PERSONAL Born 04/26/1939, Carmel, CA, m, 1963, 1 child **DISCIPLINE** SPANISH LANGUAGE & LITERATURE **EDUCATION** Stanford Univ, AB, 61, MA, 65, PhD(Span), 69. **CAREER** From acting asst prof to asst prof, 65-76, assoc prof, 76-88, PROF SPAN, UNIV KS, 88-. **MEMBERSHIPS** MLA; Am Asn Teachers Span & Port; Latin Am Studies Asn; AAUP; MMLA; IILI. **RESEARCH** Hispanic folklore; Spanish American literature; Venezuelan poetry. **SELECTED PUBLICATIONS** Auth, Tensions and triangles in Al Filo del Agua, Hispania, 74; El auto de los reyes magos en tradicion reciente, Rev Dialectologia y Tradiciones Populares, 74; Coordinate design in a Chilean Nueva Novels, Latin Am Lit Rev, 75; Lectura de La boba y el Buda, In: Aproximaciones a G Alvarez Gardeazabal, Bogota, Plaza Y Janes, 77; N S Momaday y la novela indigenista en ingles, Texto Critico, 79; Moros y Cristianos in Zacatecas, Lawrence, Amadeo Concha, 81; Lesbia y liron, SFQ, 78; Ruben Dario y las primas de Euterpe, in RD Azul y Prosas profanas, ed, Debicki & Doudoroff, Madrid, Alhambra, 85; Jose Emilio Pacheco: an Overview of the Poetry, Hispania, 89, rev and trans in Verani, La hoguera y el viento, MEX, UNAM/Era, 93; Prologo, Juan Liscano, Nuevo mundo Orinoco, Caracas, Monte Avila, 93; ed, Romulo Gallegos, Canaima, Pittsburgh UP, 96; translations of works by Juan Liscano, Santa Lopez, Jose Balza, Rafael Castillo Zapata. **CONTACT ADDRESS** Dept of Span & Port, Univ of Kansas, 3062 Wescoe, Lawrence, KS, 66045-2166. **EMAIL** mdoudoroff@ukans.edu

DOUGHERTY, RAY CORDELL
PERSONAL Born 09/18/1940, Brooklyn, NY, m, 1982, 3 children **DISCIPLINE** LINGUISTICS, PHILOSOPHY OF LANGUAGE **EDUCATION** Dartmouth Col, BA, 62, MS, 64; Mass Inst Technol, PhD, 68. **CAREER** Res assoc ling, Mass Inst Technol, 68-69; asst prof, 69-72, Assoc Pr of Ling, NY Univ, 72-; Fulbright prof ling, Univ Salzburg, Austria, 76-77. **MEMBERSHIPS** Ling Soc Am; Philos Sci Asn. **RESEARCH** Grammar; semantics; history of science. **SELECTED PUBLICATIONS** Auth, A grammar of coordination: I,II, Language, 12/70; coauth, Appositive NP constructions, 1/72 & auth, A surveey of linguistic methods, 11/73, Found Lang. **CONTACT ADDRESS** Dept of Ling, New York Univ, 719 Broadway, New York, NY, 10003-6806. **EMAIL** doughert@acfz.nyu.edu

DOUGLASS, R. THOMAS
PERSONAL Born 06/24/1932, Morristown, NY, m, 1981 **DISCIPLINE** SPANISH, LINGUISTICS **EDUCATION** George Washington Univ, BA, 54; Univ Pa, PhD (Romance ling), 64. **CAREER** Teacher high sch, NY, 58-62; from asst prof to assoc prof Span and ling, Millersville State Col, 63-67; assoc prof French, Span and ling and head dept foreign lang, Simpson Col, 67-70; ASSOC PROF SPAN, UNIV IOWA, 70-, Vis lectr ling, St Joseph's Col, Pa, 64-66; textbk consult, Xerox Col Publ, 72-73; CO-ED, IOWA FOREIGN LANG BULL, 72-; lang arts consult, Scott, Foresman and Co, 73; TEXTBK CONSULT, HOLT-RINEHART, RANDOM HOUSE AND PRENTICE-HALL, 76-. **MEMBERSHIPS** Am Asn Teachers Span and Port; Am Coun Teaching Foreign Lang. **RESEARCH** Spanish spelling; historical Spanish grammar; teaching methods in foreign languages. **SELECTED PUBLICATIONS** Auth, Y Tu, Que Dices, Mod Lang J, Vol 77, 93. **CONTACT ADDRESS** Univ Of Iowa, 218 Schaeffer Hall, Iowa City, IA, 52242.

DOUTHWAITE, JULIA V.
DISCIPLINE FRENCH LITERATURE **EDUCATION** Univ Wash, BA, 81, MA, 84; Princeton Univ, MA, 86, PhD, 90. **CAREER** Assoc prof. **RESEARCH** Prose fiction; voyage literature; enlightenment philosophy and history; feminist criticism;

comparative studies. **SELECTED PUBLICATIONS** Auth, Exotic Women: Literary Heroines and Cultural Strategies in Ancien Regime France, 92; Between Monster and Model, Eighteenth C Life, 97. **CONTACT ADDRESS** Romance Languages and Literatures Dept, Univ of Notre Dame, Notre Dame, IN, 46556.

DOW, JAMES RAYMOND
PERSONAL Born 01/02/1936, D'Lo, MS **DISCIPLINE** GERMAN FOLKLORE **EDUCATION** MS Col, BA, 57; Univ IA, MA, 61, PhD(Ger), 66. **CAREER** Instr Ger, Univ IA, 64-66; asst prof, Univ WY, 66-70; asst prof, 71-74, assoc prof, 74-80, prof Ger, IA State Univ, 80-. **RESEARCH** Hermann Hesse's Marchen; Romantic Kunstmarchen; American-German folkloristic studies. **SELECTED PUBLICATIONS** Co-ed, Internationale Volkskundliche Bibliographie, 82; German Volkskunde; Nazification of an Academic Discipline; Volkische Wissenschaft. **CONTACT ADDRESS** Dept of Foreign Lang and Lit, Iowa State Univ, Ames, IA, 50011-0002. **EMAIL** jrdow@iastate.edu

DOWELL, PETER W.
DISCIPLINE ENGLISH LANGUAGE AND LITERATURE **EDUCATION** Univ Minn, PhD, 65. **CAREER** Assoc prof/ assoc dean Emory Col. **RESEARCH** 20th century American literature; American poetry and poetics; American studies. **SELECTED PUBLICATIONS** Ed, "Ich Kuss Die Hand:" The Letters of H L Mencken to Gretchen Hood. **CONTACT ADDRESS** English Dept, Emory Univ, 1380 Oxford Rd NE, Atlanta, GA, 30322-1950.

DOWLING, JOHN CLARKSON
PERSONAL Born 11/14/1920, Strawn, TX, m, 1949 **DISCIPLINE** SPANISH **EDUCATION** Univ Colo, BA, 41; Univ Wis, MA, 43, PhD (Span), 50. **CAREER** Markham traveling fel from Univ Wis, Spain, 50-51; instr Span and Port, Univ Wis, 51-53; prof foreign lang and head dept, Tex Tech Col, 53-63; prof Span and Port and chmn dept, Ind Univ, Bloomington, 63-72; prof span and head dept Romance lang, 72-79, ALUMNI FOUND DISTINGUISHED PROF ROMANCE LANG, UNIV GA, 80-, DEAN GRAD SCH, 79-, GUGGENHEIM FEL, 59-60; Am Philos Soc grants, 71, 74 and 81; dir, Nat Endowment for Humanities Sem Col Teachers, 77. **HONORS AND AWARDS** Award, Acad Alfonson X el SAbio, Spain, 55. **MEMBERSHIPS** MLA; Am Asn Teachers Span and Port; Asoc Int Hispanistas; Am Soc 18th Century Studies; Hispanic Soc Am. **RESEARCH** Spanish Golden Age prose; 18th and 19th century Spanish literature; modern Spanish drama. **SELECTED PUBLICATIONS** Auth, The Merchant From Cadiz, The Don Roque of Moratin, Dieciocho Hisp Enlightenment, Vol 16, 93. **CONTACT ADDRESS** Dept of Romance Lang, Univ of Ga, Athens, GA, 30620.

DOWLING, WILLIAM C.
DISCIPLINE ENGLISH LANGUAGE AND LITERATURE **EDUCATION** Dartmouth Univ, BA; Harvard Univ, PhD. **CAREER** Prof. **MEMBERSHIPS** SHEAR; Henry Sweet Soc; ALSC. **RESEARCH** 18th-Century English literature; American literature of the Revolution and early republic; semantic theory and philosophy of language. **SELECTED PUBLICATIONS** Auth, The Critic's Hornbook, The Boswellian Hero, Language and Logos in Boswell's Life of Johnson, Jameson/ Althusser/ Marx, Poetry and Ideology in Revolutionary Connecticut, The Epistolary Moment: the Poetics of the Eighteenth-Century Verse Epistle, Literary Federalism in the Age of Jefferson **CONTACT ADDRESS** Dept of English, Rutgers Univ, 510 George St, Murray Hall, New Brunswick, NJ, 08901-1167. **EMAIL** wcdowling@aol.com

DOWNING, PAMELA A.
PERSONAL Born 12/25/1948, Rockford, IL, m, 1990, 2 children **DISCIPLINE** LINGUISTICS **EDUCATION** Univ Calif Berkeley, PhD, 84. **CAREER** Visiting lectr, Univ Calif Santa Barbara, 85-86; visiting asst prof, UCLA, 84-85, 86-87; visiting lectr, San Diego State Univ, 83-84; visiting prof, Seijo Univ, Tokyo, Japan, summer, 96; assoc prof, Univ Wisc Milwaukee, 87-. **MEMBERSHIPS** Ling Soc of Amer; Intl Pragmatics Asn. **RESEARCH** Functional syntax & semantics; Discourse analysis; Sociolinguistics; Japanese. **SELECTED PUBLICATIONS** Auth, Proper names as a referential option in English conversation, Studies in Anaphora, Amsterdam, John Benjamins, 95-143, 96; auth, Numeral Classifier Systems: the case of Japanese, Amsterdam, John Benjamins, 96; auth, Word order in discourse: by way of introduction, Word Order in Discourse, Amsterdam, John Benjamins, 1-27, 95; co-ed, Word Order in Discourse, Amsterdam, John Benjamins, 95; auth, Pragmatic and semantic constraints on numeral quantifier float in Japanese, Jour of Ling, 29, 1, 65-93, 93; co-ed, The Linguistics of Literacy, Amsterdam, John Benjamins, 92; auth, The use of wa as a cohesion marker in Japanese oral narratives, Perspectives on Topicalization: the case of Japanese wa, Amsterdam, John Benjamins, 3-56, 87; auth, The anaphoric use of numeral classifiers in Japanese, Noun Classification and Categorization, Amsterdam, John Benjamins, 345-75, 86; auth, The relation between word formation and meaning, Quaderni di Semantica, 5, 67-75, 84; auth, Factors influencing lexical choice in narrative, The Pear Stories: cognitive, cultural and lexical aspects of nar-

rative production, Norwood, NJ, Ablex, 89-126, 80; auth, On the creation and use of English compound nouns, Lang, 53, 810-842, 77. **CONTACT ADDRESS** Univ of Wisconsin Milwaukee, PO Box 413, Milwaukee, WI, 53201. **EMAIL** downing@uwm.edu

DOYLE, ESTHER M.
PERSONAL Born 03/21/1910, Boston, MA **DISCIPLINE** ENGLISH, SPEECH **EDUCATION** Emerson Col, BLI, 35; Boston Univ, MA, 40; Northwestern Univ, PhD, 64. **CAREER** Tchr elem schs, Mass 29-37; oral English supvr & teacher, high schs, NY, 37-44; hosp recreation worker, Mil Welfare Serv, Am Red Cross, 44-45; from instr to prof English, 45-71, chmn dept, 67-75, Dana prof, 71-75, emer prof eng, 75-, Juniata Col; lectr, 60-61, Bethany Bible Sem; partic, Nat Humanities Series Progs, 69-73; vis prof, 71, Univ Ariz. **MEMBERSHIPS** Speech Commun Assn; AAUP. **RESEARCH** Verse drama. **SELECTED PUBLICATIONS** Co-ed, Studies in Interpretation, Vol I, 72 & Vol II, Amsterdam, 77. **CONTACT ADDRESS** Dept of English, Juniata Col, Huntingdon, PA, 16652.

DOYLE, RUTH LESTHA
PERSONAL Born 12/13/1944, Doylestown, PA **DISCIPLINE** FRENCH LANGUAGE AND LITERATURE **EDUCATION** Univ NC, Chapel Hill, AB, 66, MA, 68, PhD (Romance lang and lit), 76. **CAREER** Asst prof French, Elon Col, 67-71; asst prof French and head dept, Univ Charleston, 72-75; ASST PROF FRENCH AND ITAL, CENT MO STATE UNIV, 76-. **MEMBERSHIPS** Am Asn Teachers French; MLA. **RESEARCH** French romanticism; computer aided instruction in modern languages; Italian language. **SELECTED PUBLICATIONS** Auth, Teletexte Perspective Sur La France Aujourdhui, Fr Rev, Vol 68, 94; Cultural Diversity at the Heart of Bull, Fr Rev, Vol 68, 94; Cultural Diversity--Germans, French and Americans, French Review, Vol 68, 94. **CONTACT ADDRESS** Dept of Mod Lang Cent Mo, State Univ, Warrensburg, MO, 64093-8888.

DRAKE, DANA BLACKMAR
PERSONAL Born 12/18/1926, Macon, GA **DISCIPLINE** ROMANCE LANGUAGES, LAW **EDUCATION** Davidson Col, AB, 48; Univ Va, LLB, 51; NY Univ, LLM, 52; Middlebury Col, MA, 66; Univ NC, Chapel Hill, PhD (Span), 67. **CAREER** Jr Partner, Young and Hollis, Columbus, Ga, 52-55; attorney, Joint Comt Taxation, 55-59; asst mgr real estate, Trust Dept, Citizens Southern Nat Bank, 59-62; instr Span, Univ NC, Chapel Hill, 62-67; asst prof, 67-71, assoc prof, 71-82, PROF SPAN, VA POLYTECH INST AND STATE UNIV, 82-. **MEMBERSHIPS** Am Asn Teachers Span and Port; MLA; Cervantes Soc Am. **RESEARCH** Cervantes. **SELECTED PUBLICATIONS** Auth, Rossetti Goblin Market, Explicator, Vol 51, 92; Ibsen A Doll House, Explicator, Vol 53, 94. **CONTACT ADDRESS** 210 University Club, Blacksburg, VA, 24060.

DRESSLER, HERMIGILD
PERSONAL Born 02/03/1908, Belleville, IL **DISCIPLINE** CLASSICAL PHILOLOGY **EDUCATION** Cath Univ Am, AM, 38, PhD, 47. **CAREER** Registr, Quincy Col, 47-50, prof class lang and chmn div humanities, 50-53; from asst prof to assoc prof Greek and Latin, Cath Univ Am, 53-73, chmn dept, 71-73; PROF GREEK AND LATIN, QUINCY COL, 73-, ED DIR, FATHERS OF THE CHURCH, 75-. **MEMBERSHIPS** Ling Soc Am; Am Philol Asn; N Am Patristic Soc. **RESEARCH** Translations of papal documents; medieval Latin. **SELECTED PUBLICATIONS** Auth, Goethe Studies on the Analogy Between Color and Sound and its Validation by Modern Research, Goethe Jahrbuch, Vol 107, 90; The Principle of Polarity in Goethe Explanations of the Problem of The Major Minor Relationship as Anticipation of The Polaristic Position in Harmonic Theory, Goethe Jahrbuch, Vol 109, 92. **CONTACT ADDRESS** Dept of Greek and Latin, Quincy Col, 1831 College Ave, Quincy, IL, 62301.

DREW, SHIRLEY K.
DISCIPLINE ORGANIZATIONAL COMMUNICATION **EDUCATION** Bowling Green State Univ, BA, MA, PhD. **CAREER** Assoc prof. **RESEARCH** Relationship disengagement. **SELECTED PUBLICATIONS** Publ, health commun, personal narratives. **CONTACT ADDRESS** Dept of Commun, Pittsburg State Univ, 1701 S Broadway St, Pittsburg, KS, 66762.

DRINKA, BRIDGET
DISCIPLINE INDO-EUROPEAN HISTORICAL LINGUISTICS **EDUCATION** Univ IL at Champaign-Urbana, BA; Georgetown Univ, MS; Univ TX at Austin, PhD. **CAREER** Asst prof; taught at, L'Istituto Am in Florence, Italy; Am Univ; Univ TX at Austin & Univ MO at Kansas City; adv, Sigma Tau Delta. **HONORS AND AWARDS** Fac Develop Leave awd; Fac Res Awd, UTSA, 93; special Facu Res Grant, 94; Fulbright-Hays Gp Proj Grant; Personal Enrichment Grant, UTSA. **RESEARCH** Hist of Eng; principles of linguistics; hist and sociolinguistics; linguistic methods of analyzing lit. **SELECTED PUBLICATIONS** Auth, The sigmatic aorist in Indo-European, J of Indo-Europ Stud, 95; publ in, Indogermanische Forschungen, Word, J of Indo-Europ Stud. **CONTACT ADDRESS** Col of Fine Arts and Hum, Univ Texas at San Antonio, 6900 N Loop 1604 W, San Antonio, TX, 78249. **EMAIL** bdrinka@lonestar.utsa.edu

DRUXES, HELGA
DISCIPLINE GERMAN **EDUCATION** Brown Univ, MA, 85, Ph, 87. **CAREER** Assoc prof, Williams Col, 87-. **RESEARCH** Contemporary Germany after 1945; 19th-century Realist Novel; Contemporary German Women Writers; Critical Theory; French Feminist Theory; Women's Studies; Comparative Literature French, American, British; Identity Psychology; Cultural Studies. **SELECTED PUBLICATIONS** Auth, Queerbeet: An Intermediate German Reader, Peter Lang, 88; The Feminization of Dr Faustus: Female Identity Quests from Stendhal to Morgner, Pa State Univ Press, 93; Remembering as Revision: Fictionalizing Nazism in Postwar Germany, MLN 94; Resisting Bodies: The Negotiation of Female Agency in Twentieth-Century Women's Fiction, Wayne State Univ Press, 96. **CONTACT ADDRESS** Center for Foreign Languages, Literatures and Cult, Williams Col, Williamstown, MA, 01267. **EMAIL** Helga.Druxes@williams.edu

DRYDEN, M.
PERSONAL Born 01/11/1946, San Antonio, TX, d, 1 child **DISCIPLINE** FOREIGN LANGUAGE EDUCATION; ENGLISH EDUCATION; ENGLISH **EDUCATION** Univ Tex-Austin, BA, 80, MA, 92. **CAREER** Instr, Austin Commun Col; refugee ESL coordinator, 97- . **HONORS AND AWARDS** Phi Zeta Kappa teaching excellence, 93. **MEMBERSHIPS** TESOL **RESEARCH** Adult education ESL; refugee ESL. **SELECTED PUBLICATIONS** Auth, Teaching Language Teachers to be More Collaborative: The Second Language Learner Course at the University of Texas at Austin, MLA J, 97. **CONTACT ADDRESS** Dept of Adult Educ, Austin Comm Col, Austin, TX, 78741. **EMAIL** mdryden@mail.utexas.edu

DRYER, MATTHEW S.
PERSONAL Born 04/27/1950, Toronto, ON, Canada, m, 1979 **DISCIPLINE** LINGUISTICS **EDUCATION** Univ Toronto, BA, 72, MSc, 73; Univ Mich, AM, 75, PhD (ling). 79. **CAREER** Vis asst prof ling, Univ Windsor, 78-79; sessional instr, Univ Calgary, 79; VIS ASST PROF LING, UNIV ALTA, 80-. **RESEARCH** Typology and universals; syntactic theory. **SELECTED PUBLICATIONS** Auth, Languages of the World--Classical Ethiopic, Language, Vol 71, 95; A Grammar of Tauya, Can J Ling Revue Canadienne De Linguistique, Vol 39, 94; A Grammar of Lezgian, Can J Ling Revue Canadienne De Linguistique, Vol 41, 96; A Grammar of Supyire, Can J Lin Revue Canadienne De Linguistique, Vol 41, 96; Barasano Syntax--Jones, W, Jones ,P, Word J Int Ling Assn, Vol 45, 94; On The 6 Way Word Order Typology, Studs Lang, Vol 21, 97; Languages of The World--Gunin-Kwini, Lang, Vol 71, 95; Languages of the World - Mbalanhu - Fourie,Dj/, Language, Vol 71, 95; Languages Of The World--Cantonese, Lang, Vol 71, 95; Focus, Pragmatic Presupposition, and Activated Propositions, J Pragmatics, Vol 26, 96. **CONTACT ADDRESS** Dept of Ling, Univ Alta, Edmonton, AB, T6G 2E7.

DUBE, PIERRE
PERSONAL Born 08/23/1943, Toronto, ON, Canada, m, 2 children **DISCIPLINE** FRENCH LITERATURE **EDUCATION** Univ Toronto, BA; MA; Ohio State Univ, PhD. **CAREER** Prof **RESEARCH** Early Romantic writers. **SELECTED PUBLICATIONS** Auth, Bibliographie de la critique sur Francois-Rene de Chateaubriand; Les Aventures du dernier Abencerage: Past and Present; co-ed, Pascal's Pensees and Lettres provinciales. **CONTACT ADDRESS** Dept of French, Waterloo Univ, 200 University Ave W, Waterloo, ON, N2L 3G1. **EMAIL** phdube@watarts.uwaterloo.ca

DUBOIS, BETTY LOU
PERSONAL Born 12/13/1927, Oklahoma City, OK **DISCIPLINE** APPLIED LINGUISTICS, ENGLISH AS FOREIGN LANGUAGE **EDUCATION** Univ Okla, BA, 49, MA, 54; Univ NMex, PhD (ling and lang pedag), 72. **CAREER** Asst prof, 73-76, assoc prof, 76-80, PROF SPEECH, NMEX STATE UNIV, 80-, Consult, Southwest Multicult Ethnic Study Ctr, Univ Tex, El Paso, 73-; head ed comt, Papers in Southwest English, Trinity Univ, 76-. **MEMBERSHIPS** Ling Asn of Can and US; Int Asn Appl Ling; Int Asn Study Child Lang; Ling Asn of Southwest; Teachers English to Speakers Other Lang. **RESEARCH** Elementary school language arts; nonstandard southwest English; sex-linked communicative behavior. **SELECTED PUBLICATIONS** Auth, Constructing and Reconstructing Gender--The Links Among Communication, Language, and Gender, Lang Soc, Vol 22, 93. **CONTACT ADDRESS** New Mexico State Univ, Box 3W, University Park, NM, 88003.

DUBRUCK, EDELGARD E.
PERSONAL Born 11/01/1925, Breslau, Germany, m, 1957, 1 child **DISCIPLINE** FOREIGN LANGUAGES **EDUCATION** Univ Mich, MA, 55, PhD (Romance lang and lit). 62. **CAREER** Vis lectr French, Oakland Univ, 62-65; from asst prof to assoc prof, 65-75, PROF FRENCH, MARYGROVE COL, 75-, CHMN DEPT FOREIGN LANG, 73-, US Govt scholar, Mich State Univ, 51-52; vis lectr, Kalamazoo Col, 61. **MEMBERSHIPS** MLA. **RESEARCH** Humor and humorous intent in French literature of the Middle Ages; French poetry of the Baroque. **SELECTED PUBLICATIONS** Auth, Weasel and Werewolf, Typological Studies on Romance Literature of the

Middle Ages and the Renaissance, Romance Philology, Vol 47, 93. **CONTACT ADDRESS** Dept of Foreign Lang, Marygrove Col, Detroit, MI, 48221.

DUCKERT, AUDREY ROSALIND
PERSONAL Born 03/28/1927, Cottage Grove, WI **DISCIPLINE** ENGLISH PHILOLOGY & LINGUISTICS **EDUCATION** Univ WI, BS, 48, MA, 49; Radcliffe Col, PhD, 59. **CAREER** Res asst, WI Eng Lang Surv, Univ WI, 48-52; ed asst, G&C Merriam Co, Mass, 53-56; from instr to assoc prof, 59-72, Prof Eng, Univ MA, Amherst, 72-, Assoc ed & columnist, Names, Am Name Soc, 61-65; mem adv bd, Ling Atlas US & Can, 64- & Dict Am Regional English, 65-; vis res assoc, Univ Wis-Madison, 66-67; consult, Oxford Eng Dict, Suppl II, 68-; Am Coun Learned Soc sr fel, 73-74; vis prof Eng, Emory Univ, 78; adj ed, Dict Am Regional Eng, 81. **MEMBERSHIPS** Am Dialect Soc (pres, 74); Am Name Soc (pres, 71); Mediaeval Acad Am; Mod Hum Res Asn, Gt Brit; Ling Soc Am. **RESEARCH** Lexicography; medieval lang and lit; dialectology. **SELECTED PUBLICATIONS** Coauth, A Method for Collecting Dialect, Am Dialect Soc, 53; auth, The linguistic atlas of New England revisited, Publ Am Dialect Soc, 4/63; co-ed, Handbook of the Linguistic Geography of New England, AMS, 72; Lexicography in English, NY Acad Sci Annal, 73; auth, Tbe second time around: Methods in dialect revisiting, Am Speech, 74; The winds of change, In: James B McMillan: (festschrift), Essays in Linguistics by His Friends and Colleagues, Univ AL, 77;adj ed, Dictionary of American Regional Ehglish, 80. **CONTACT ADDRESS** Dept of Eng, Univ of Massachusetts, Amherst, MA, 01003-0002.

DUDLEY, EDWARD J.
PERSONAL Born 07/18/1926, St. Paul, MN, m, 1959, 2 children **DISCIPLINE** SPANISH, ENGLISH **EDUCATION** Univ MN, Minneapolis, BA, 49, MA, 51, PhD, 63. **CAREER** Tchr, Am Sch, Managua, Nicaragua, 54-55; instr Span, St John's Univ, MN, 56-60; asst prof, UCLA, 63-70; chmn & prof Hisp lang & lit & dir comp lit prog, Univ Pittsburgh, 70-74; chmn dept Span, Ital & Port, 74-77, chmn dept French & Dept Ger & Slavic, 76-77, Prof Span & Comp Lit, State Univ NY Buffalo, 74-, Chmn Dept Mod Lang & Lit, 77-, Consult, Nat Bd Consult, Nat Endowment for Hum, 76. **MEMBERSHIPS** MLA; Mediaeval Acad Am; Asn Int Hispanistas; Cervantes Soc Am; Conrad Soc Am. **RESEARCH** Cervantes; early prose fiction; comp lit. **SELECTED PUBLICATIONS** Auth, Three patterns of imagery in Conrad's Heart of Darkness, Rev des Langues Vivantes, 65; coauth, El cuento, Holt, 66; auth, Court and country: The fusion of two images of love in Juan Rodriguez's El siervo libre de amor, PMLA, 67; Don Quixote as magus: The rhetoric of interpolation, Bull Hisp Studies, 72; co-ed, The Wild Man Within: An Image in Western Thought from the Renaissance to Romanticism, Univ Pittsburgh, 72; co-ed, 2nd ed, El cuento, Holt, 84; co-ed, American Attitudes toward Foreign Languages and Foreign Cultures, Bouvier, Bonn, 83; auth, The Endless Text: Don Quijote and The Hermeneutics of Romance, SUNY Press, 97; various other articles and essays on Cervantes. **CONTACT ADDRESS** Dept of Mod Lang & Lit, State Univ of NY, PO Box 604620, Buffalo, NY, 14260-4620. **EMAIL** edudley@acsu.buffalo.edu

DUGGAN, HOYT NOLAN
PERSONAL Born 04/05/1938, Atlanta, TX, m, 1962, 1 child **DISCIPLINE** MEDIEVAL LANGUAGES & LITERATURE **EDUCATION** Centenary Col La, BA, 60; Pembroke Col, BA, 63; Oxford Univ, MA, 68; Princeton Univ, PhD(English), 69. **CAREER** From assist to prof english, Univ VA, 68-; Nat Endowment for Humanities fel, 73-74. **HONORS AND AWARDS** Fel, 93-94, assoc Fel, Inst for Advanced Technology in the Humanities, 94; NEH Fel, 73-74; Sesquicentennial Fel, 73-74; NEH Summer Fel, 70; Charles G. Osgood Fel, 68-69; Rhodes Scholar, 60-63. **MEMBERSHIPS** Chemn, Mediaeval Acad Am, 94-; MLA; Early English Text Soc; Soc Study Medieval Lang & Lit; Dir, Soc for Early English and Norse Electronic Texts, 93-; Envoi; Labyrinth; CLH-L. **RESEARCH** Critical edition of the Middle English Wars of Alexander; Ovidian commentaries in the Middle Ages; Middle English alliterative poetry. **SELECTED PUBLICATIONS** Co-ed, Piers Plowman: Corpus Christi College, Oxford MS 201, Univ Mich Press and SEENET, 98; auth, Creating an Electronic Archive of Piers Plowman, Pub of the Inst for Advanced Tech in the Humanities, Res Reports, Second Series, 94; The Role and Distribution of -ly Adverbs in Middle English Alliterative Verse, Loyal Letters: Studies on Mediaeval Alliterative Poetry and Prose, 94; Libertine scribes and maidenly editors: Meditations on textual criticism and metrics, English Historical Metrics, 96; Meter, Stanza, Vocabulary, Dialect, A Companion to the Gawain-Poet, 97; Some Unrevolutionary Aspects of Computer Editing, The Literary Text in the Digital Age, 96. **CONTACT ADDRESS** Dept of English, Univ of Virginia, Bryan Hall, Charlottesville, VA, 22903. **EMAIL** hnd@virginia.edu

DUGGAN, JOSEPH JOHN
PERSONAL Born 09/08/1938, Philadelphia, PA, m, 1981, 3 children **DISCIPLINE** MEDIEVAL LITERATURE, PHILOLOGY **EDUCATION** Fordham Univ, AB, 60; Ohio State Univ, PhD(Romance lang), 64. **CAREER** Instr French, 64-65, asst prof, 65-66, asst prof, French & comp lit, 66-71, assoc prof, 71-78, prof French, Comp Lit & Romance Philol, Univ Calif, Berkeley, 78-, assoc dean, Graduate Div, 89-; Nat Humanities Found younger scholar fel, 68-69; Guggenheim fel, 79-80; ed, Romance Philol, 82-87. **HONORS AND AWARDS** Mythopoesis: Literatura, totalidad, ideologia. Ofrecido a Joseph J. Duggan por su distinguida aportacion a los estudios literarios, Anthropos, 92. **MEMBERSHIPS** Mediaeval Acad Am; Soc Rencesvals. **RESEARCH** Medieval French and Spanish literatures; Romance philology. **SELECTED PUBLICATIONS** Auth, Formulas in the Couronnement de Louis, Romania, 66; Yvain's good name: The unity of Chretien de Troyes Chevalier au Lion, Orbis Litterarum, 69; A Concordance to the Chanson de Roland, Ohio State Univ Press, 70; The Song of Roland: Formulaic Style and Poetic Craft, Univ Calif Press, 73; ed & contribr, Oral Literature: Seven Essays, Scottish Acad Press, 75; auth, Ambiguity in Twelfth and Thirteenth-Century French and Provencal Literature: A Problem or a Value?, In: Studies in Honor of John Misrahi, Fr Lit Publ, 77; The Generation of the Episode of Baligant, Romance Philol, 77; A Guide to Studies on the Chanson de Roland, Grant & Cutler, 77; auth, A New Fragment of Les Enfances Vivien, Univ Calif Press, 85; auth, Medieval Epic as Popular Historiography: Appropriation of Historical Knowledge in the Vernacular Epic, In: Grundriss der romanischen Literatureu des Mittelalters, vol 2, Carl Winter, 86; auth, The Cantar de mio Cid: Poetic Creation in its Economic and Social Contexts, Cambridge Univ Press, 89; auth, L' episode d'Aupais dans Girart de Roussillou, In: Reading Around the Epic, King's Col, London. 98. **CONTACT ADDRESS** Dept of Comp Lit, Univ of Calif, 4118 Dwinelle Hall, Berkeley, CA, 94720-2510. **EMAIL** roland@socrates.berkeley.edu

DUKAS, VYTAS
PERSONAL Born 02/14/1923, Lithuania, m, 1957, 2 children **DISCIPLINE** SLAVIC LANGUAGES **EDUCATION** Univ Mich, BA, 54, MA, 55 and 56, PhD (comp lit), 65. **CAREER** Asst prof Russ and Ger, 59-66, assoc prof Russ, 66-69, chmn dept Russ and Ger, 68-71, PROF RUSS, SAN DIEGO STATE UNIV, 69-. **MEMBERSHIPS** Am Asn Teachers Ger; Am Asn Teachers Slavic and East Europ Lang. **RESEARCH** Russian literature; Soviet poetry; Russian and German comparative literature. **SELECTED PUBLICATIONS** Auth, Dvoistvennye Otnosheniya, Izlyublennye Rasskazy, World Lit Today, Vol 68, 94; Absonia, World Lit Today, Vol 70, 96; Apverstas Pasaulis, World Lit Today, Vol 70, 96; In Anyones Tongue, World Lit Today, Vol 68, 94; 2 Utopian Plays--Komediantai, Idioto Pasaka, World Lit Today, Vol 69, 95; Ketvirtoji Siena, World Lit Today, Vol 71, 97; Drabuzeliais Baltais, World Lit Today, Vol 69, 95; Kramola, World Lit Today, Vol 67, 93. **CONTACT ADDRESS** Dept of Ger and Russ, San Diego State Univ, San Diego, CA, 92182.

DULAI, SURJIT SINGH
PERSONAL Born 11/06/1930, Danubyu, Burma, m, 1965, 2 children **DISCIPLINE** COMPARATIVE LITERATURE, SOUTH ASIAN STUDIES **EDUCATION** Panjab Univ, BA, 50, MA, 54; Mich State Univ, PhD, 65. **CAREER** Lectr English, Urdu, Panjab Univ, 54-59; headmaster, G N High Sch, Partab, Pura, 59-60; asst English & comp lit, Mich State Univ, 62-67, fel, 64-65; asst prof English, Long Island Univ, 65-66; asst prof humanities, 66-70, assoc prof humanities & Asian studies, 70-74, prof English, 74-, Mich State Univ; co-ed, J SAsian Lit, 69-. **HONORS AND AWARDS** Fulbright-Hays fel, Off Health, Educ, Welfare, 70-71; Rockefeller Found award, 76; Mich State Univ Excellence in Diversity Award, 95. **MEMBERSHIPS** Asn Asian Studies; Can Asn SAsian Studies; MLA; Popular Cult Asn; Asn Gen & Lib Studies. **RESEARCH** Interdisciplinary humanities; Indian & comparative literature; Anglo-Indian literature. **SELECTED PUBLICATIONS** Co-ed, Punjab in Perspective, 91; coauth, Contemporary Poets, St James Press, 95; co-ed, World Literature and Thought, 4 v, v1, 96, v2, 97. **CONTACT ADDRESS** Dept of English, Michigan State Univ, 201 Morrill Hall, East Lansing, MI, 48824-1036. **EMAIL** dulai@pilot.msu.edu

DUMAS, BETHANY K.
PERSONAL Born 04/01/1937, Corpus Christi, TX, s **DISCIPLINE** LINGUISTIC **EDUCATION** Lamar Univ, BA, 55-59; Univ Ark, MA, PhD, 59-71. **CAREER** Instr, Aug 64-May 66, MO State Univ; asst prof, Aug 66- June 73, Southern Univ (Baton Rouge); asst prof, visiting assoc prof, Aug 73-74, Summer 75, English Trinity Univ; adjunct prof, 93, Univ TN, Knoxville, Spring 93; professional lectr, fall 97, Georgetown Univ; assoc prof, Aug 74- , Univ TN, Knoxville. **HONORS AND AWARDS** Univ TN Intl Travel Grant, 96; Univ TN English Dept Hodges Travel/Research Grants 93, 97, 98. **MEMBERSHIPS** South Atlantic Amer Dialect Soc (vice president, 80, president, 81), 73-present; Linguistic Soc of Amer, 74-present; Amer Dialect Soc (Executive Committee, 81-84; Assn for Computational Linguistics, 85-88; Amer Bar Assn, 84, 90, 98- ; Law and Soc Assn, 90-94, 96- ; Intl Assn of Forensic Linguists (Membership Secetary, 93-94), 93- . **SELECTED PUBLICATIONS** Auth, Warning Labels on the Locite RC/609 Containers and the Material Safety Data Sheets on Loctite RC/609, Language in Action: New Studies of Language in Society, Hampton, 97; auth,English in the American Midwest, review of Hearland English: Variation and Transition in the American Midwest, 97; auth, Linguistic Ambiguity in Non-Statutory Language: Problems in The Search Warrant in the Matter of 7505 Derris Drive, Forensic Linguistics: The Intl Journal of Language and the Law, 98; auth,Southern Mountain English: The Language of The Ozarks and Southern Appalachia, a chapter in Living English, Praeger, July 99. **CONTACT ADDRESS** Dept of English, Univ TN, 301 McClung Tower, Knoxville, TN, 37996-0430. **EMAIL** dumasb@utk.edu

DUNAWAY, JOHN MARSON
PERSONAL Born 06/24/1945, Washington, GA, m, 1966, 2 children **DISCIPLINE** FRENCH LANGUAGE AND LITERATURE **EDUCATION** Emory Univ, BA, 67; Duke Univ, MA, 71, PhD (French), 72. **CAREER** Asst prof, 72-77, chmn, Dept Mod Foreign Lang, 76-79, ASSOC PROF FRENCH, MERCER UNIV, 77-. **HONORS AND AWARDS** Don Quixote Award, Valdosta State Col, 76. **MEMBERSHIPS** Am Asn Teachers Fr; SAtlantic Mod Lang Asn. **RESEARCH** Twentieth century French literature, philosophy, and religious thought. **SELECTED PUBLICATIONS** Auth, Mauriac, Francois Revisited, Fr Rev, Vol 70, 96; Diner Dadie, Fr Rev, Vol 66, 93. **CONTACT ADDRESS** Dept of Mod Foreign Lang, Mercer Univ, 1400 Coleman Ave, Box G, Macon, GA, 31207-0003.

DUNCAN, BRUCE
PERSONAL Born 02/17/1942, Bryn Mawr, PA, m, 1964, 2 children **DISCIPLINE** GERMAN LITERATURE, GERMAN LINGUISTICS **EDUCATION** Williams Col, BA, 64; Cornell Univ, MA, 66, PhD, 69. **CAREER** Asst prof, 69-75, assoc prof, 75-81, Prof Ger, Dartmouth Col, 81-, assoc dean of fac hum, 89-93, Vis prof Ger, Univ Cincinnati. **HONORS AND AWARDS** Woodrow Wilson Fel, 64; DAAD Fel, 66-67; Am Coun Learned Socs Grant-in-Aid Fel, 76; DAAD Res Travel Fel, 93. **MEMBERSHIPS** Am Asn Tchr(s) Ger; Intern Arnim Soc. **RESEARCH** Eighteenth century Ger lit; Ger Romanticism; second lang acquisition. **SELECTED PUBLICATIONS** Auth, Hand, heart, and language in Minna von Barnhelm, 72 & The Marchese's story in Wilhelm Meisters Lehrjahre, 72, Seminar; A Cool Medium as social corrective: J M R Lenz's Concept of Comedy, Colloquia Ger, 75; Some correspondences between Arnim's Majoratsherren and Fichte's Concept of the Ich, Monatshefte, 76; The Comic Structure of Lenz's Soldaten, Mod Lang Notes (Ger issue), 76; Ich Pflanzel Gerstenberg's Ugolino and the mid-life crisis, Ger Rev, 78; The implied reader in Lessing's Theory of Comedy, Lessing Yearbk, 78; Fate and Coincidence in Arnim's Seltsames Begegnen und Wiedersehen, 79, Seminar; Die Versohnung in der Sommerfrische. Eine ungedruckte Erzahlung Achim von Arnims, Aurora, 80; Emilia Galotti lag auf dem Tisch aufgeschlagen: Werther as (Mis-)Reader, Goethe Yearbook 82; An Worte labt sich trefflich glauben. Die Sprache der Luise Millerin, In: Friedrich Schiller: Kunst Humanitat und Politik in der spaten Aufklarung, Max Niemeyer Verlag, 82; Werther's Reflections on the Tenth of May, In: Exile and Enlightenment: Studies in Honor of Guy Stern on His 65th Birthday, Wayne State Univ Press, 87; Werke von und uber Achim von Arnim seit Volker Hoffmanns Die Arnim-Forschung 1945-1972, In: Neue Tendenzen der Arnim-Forschung, Edition, Biographie, Interpretation, mit unbekannten Dokumenten, Lang, 90; Some Common Themes in Sturm und Drang Reception, In: Momentum Dramaticum: Aufsatze zu Ehren von Eckehard Catholy aus Analab seines 75: Geburtstages, Univ Waterloo Press, 90, Ontario; Co-auth (with Otmar Foelsche) Doch ein Begriff mub bei dem Worte sein: Teaching Literature with an Electronically Annotated Text, Die Unterrichtspraxis, 95; Achim von Arnim's Novellas of 1812, Mellen, 97; Lovers, Patricides and Raging Fools: Aspects of Sturm und Drang Drama, Camden, 99. **CONTACT ADDRESS** Dept of Ger, Dartmouth Col, 6084 Dartmouth Hall, Hanover, NH, 03755-3511. **EMAIL** Bruce.Duncan@dartmouth.edu

DUNHAM, VERA S
PERSONAL Born 12/13/1912, Moscow, Russia, m, 1942, 1 child **DISCIPLINE** SLAVIC LANGUAGES AND LITERATURE **EDUCATION** Univ Erlangen, PhD (slavic philol), 35; Univ Brussels, lic-lettres, 38. **CAREER** Prof, Wayne State Univ, 61-75; PROF, QUEENS COL, CITY UNIV NEW YORK, 75-, Res analyst, Off Strategic Serv, Washington, DC, 44-45; assoc ed, Common Cause, Univ Chicago, 46-47; res consult, Inst Int Social Res, Princeton Univ, 59-60; vis prof, Slavic Dept, Univ Mich, 65 and Columbia Univ, 67. **MEMBERSHIPS** Am Asn Avan Slavic Studies; Am Asn Teachers Slavic and Eastern Europ, Lang. **RESEARCH** A Literary study of the worker and the Soviet system--the 1960's and 1970's. **SELECTED PUBLICATIONS** Auth, Literary Politics in the Soviet Ukraine, 1917-1934, Russ Hist Histoire Russe, Vol 21, 94. **CONTACT ADDRESS** 15 Stephens Path, Port Jefferson, NY, 11777.

DUNN, F.M.
PERSONAL Born 10/15/1955, Aberdeen, Scotland, m, 1986, 2 children **DISCIPLINE** CLASSICAL LITERATURE **EDUCATION** Yale Univ, BA, 76, MA, 80, PhD, 85. **CAREER** Asst Prof, Assoc Prof, 93 to 96-, UC Santa Barbara; Asst Prof, 86-93, Northwestern Univ; vis Instr, 85-86, N Carolina State Univ. **HONORS AND AWARDS** Human Res Awd; Jr Fac Fel; NEH Fel; ACLS Fel. **MEMBERSHIPS** APA **RESEARCH** Greek Drama; Narrative Theory; Latin Poetry. **SELECTED PUBLICATIONS** Auth, Tragedy's End: Closure and Innovation in Euripidean Drama, Oxford Univ Press, 96;

coed, Beginnings in Classical Literature, Yale Clas Stud, Cambridge Univ Press, 92; coed, Classical Closure: Reading the End in Greek and Latin Literature, Princeton Univ Press, 97; auth, Orestes and the Urn, Mnemosyne, 98; Ends and Means in Euripides' Hercules, Classical Closure, 97; Rhetorical Approaches to Horace's Odes, Arethusa, 95; Euripides and the Rites of Hera Akraia, Greek Roman and Byzantine Stud, 94. **CONTACT ADDRESS** Dept of Classics, Univ Calif Santa Barbara, Santa Barbara, CA, 93106. **EMAIL** fdunn@humanitas.ucsb.edu

DUNN, PETER NORMAN
PERSONAL Born 03/23/1926, London, England, m, 1953, 6 children **DISCIPLINE** ROMANCE LANGUAGES **EDUCATION** Univ London, BA, 47, MA, 49, DLitt, 73. **CAREER** Asst lectr Span, Aberdeen Univ, 49-50, lectr, 50-66; prof Span lit, Univ Rochester, 66-77; PROF ROMANCE LANG, WESLEYAN UNIV, 77-, Examr Span, Scottish Univs Entrance Bit, 51-60; Joint Matriculation Bd, Northern Univ, England, 60-66; vis prof Span, Western Reserve Univ, 64-65. **MEMBERSHIPS** MLA; Asn Hispanists Gt Brit; Cervantes Soc Am; Internation Asn Hispanists. **RESEARCH** Spanish literature; medieval, Renaissance and 17th century. **SELECTED PUBLICATIONS** Auth, Discourse Analysis as Sociocriticism, the Spanish Golden Age, Hisp Rev, Vol 63, 95; Language, Text, Subject--A Critique of Hispanism, J Hisp Philol, Vol 17, 92; The Picaresque--A Symposium on the Rogues Tale, Hisp Rev, Vol 63, 95; Framing the Story, Framing the Reader, Modern Lan Rev, Vol 91, 96; The Concept of Genre and Picaresque Literature, Bull Hisp Stud, Vol 72, 95 Shaping Experience, Narrative Strategies In Cervantes, Mln Modern Lang Notes, Vol 109, 94; Refiguring the Hero, From Peasant to Noble in Lope De Vega and Calderon, Bull Hisp Stud, Vol 70, 93; Tragicomedy and Novelistic Discourse in Celestina, Comp Lit, Vol 45, 93. **CONTACT ADDRESS** Dept of Romance Lang, Wesleyan Univ, Middletown, CT, 06457.

DUNN, SUSAN
PERSONAL Born 07/19/1945, New York, NY **DISCIPLINE** FRENCH LITERATURE **EDUCATION** Smith Col, BA, 66; Harvard Univ, PhD, 73. **CAREER** Teaching fel Romance tang, Harvard Univ, 67-70, instr French, 70-73; PROF FRENCH, WILLIAMS COL, 73-; Instr French, Wellesley Col, 71-73; NEH fel in residence, Princeton Univ, 75-76; fel, Camargo Found, 81; NEH, 90 & 97. **MEMBERSHIPS** MLA **RESEARCH** French and American Revolutions **SELECTED PUBLICATIONS** Auth, Nerval et le roman historique, Minard, Paris, 81; The Deaths of Louis XVI, Princeton Univ Press, 94; co-auth, The Lion, the Fox, and the President, Harvard Mag, 95; ed, Diversity and Citizenship, Rowman and Littlefield, 96; Sister Revolutions, French Lightning, American Light, Farrar, Strauss, Giroux, 99; Revolutionary Men of Letters and the Pursuit of Radical Change, William & Mary Quart, 53; co-auth, Revolutionary Myths in France and America, Partisan Rev, 58. **CONTACT ADDRESS** Dept of Romance Lang, Williams Col, Stetson Hall, Williamstown, MA, 01267-2600. **EMAIL** sdunn@williams.edu

DUPUY, BEATRICE
DISCIPLINE SECOND AND FOREIGN LANGUAGE ACQUISITION, ATTRITION, COURSE DESIGN, BILINGUA **EDUCATION** Univ Southern Calif, PhD, 94. **CAREER** Asst prof, La State Univ. **SELECTED PUBLICATIONS** Auth, Incidental Vocabulary Acquisition in French, in Appl Lang Lrng, 93; L'acquisition du language chez l'enfant aveugle, in Cahiers du Ctr Technique Nat d'Etudes et de Recheches sur les Handicaps et les Inadaptions, 95; Premi(res conversations entre des m(res et leurs jeunes enfants aveugles, in Aspects sociaux et cognitifs de la conversation chez l'enfant et l'adult, 95. **CONTACT ADDRESS** Dept of Fr Grad Stud, Louisiana State Univ, Baton Rouge, LA, 70803.

DUQUETTE, JEAN-PIERRE
PERSONAL Born 06/27/1939, Valleyfield, PQ, Canada **DISCIPLINE** FRENCH LITERATURE **EDUCATION** Univ Montreal, LL, 63; Doctorat de 3e cycle Lettres modernes, Paris X, 1969. **CAREER** Asst to assoc prof, 69-85, PROF FRENCH, McGILL UNIV, 85-, dept ch, 85-96. **SELECTED PUBLICATIONS** Auth, Flaubert ou l'architecture du vide, 72; auth, Germaine Guevremont: une route, une maison, 73; auth, Fernand Leduc, 80; auth, Colette, l'amour de l'amour, 84; ed, Centenaire de Jean Cocteau, 90; ed, L'Espace du regard, 94. **CONTACT ADDRESS** Dept of French, McGill Univ, 3460 McTavish St, Montreal, PQ, H3A 1X9. **EMAIL** jpduquet@leacock.lan.mcgill.ca

DURAND, FRANK
PERSONAL Born 05/12/1932, Brooklyn, NY, m, 1955, 2 children **DISCIPLINE** SPANISH LITERATURE AND LANGUAGE **EDUCATION** NY Univ, BA, 53; Northwestern Univ, MA, 54, Univ Mich, PhD, 62; Brown Univ, MA, 65. **CAREER** Teaching asst Span, Northwestern Univ, 53-54; teaching fel, Univ Mich, 56-60; asst prof, 60-65, assoc prof Span lit, 65-72, PROF HISP STUDIES AND CHMN DEPT HISP AND ITAL STUDIES, BROWN UNIV, 72-, Howard Found Fel, 68-69. **MEMBERSHIPS** MLA; Am Asn Teachers Span and Port. **RESEARCH** Nineteenth and 20th century Spanish literature; literary criticism; Latin American novel. **SELECTED PUBLICATIONS** Auth, The Striking Illusion--Proust and Dostoievski, A Comparison of Fictional Aesthetics, Revue D Histoire Litteraire De La France, Vol 96, 96. **CONTACT ADDRESS** Dept of Hisp and Ital Studies, Brown Univ, Providence, RI, 02912.

DURER, CHRISTOPHER
PERSONAL Born 09/15/1928, Warsaw, Poland, m, 1967, 1 child **DISCIPLINE** ENGLISH, COMPARATIVE LITERATURE **EDUCATION** Chicago Teachers Col, BEd, 61; Univ Calif, Berkeley, MA, 63, PhD (comp lit), 69. **CAREER** Instr humanities, Univ Mo, Rolla, 63-64; instr comp lit, San Francisco State Col, 65-67, Univ Calif, Berkeley, 68-69; asst prof English, 69-73, ASSOC PROF ENGLISH and MOD LANG, UNIV WYO, 73-. **MEMBERSHIPS** MLA; Am Comp Lit Asn; Int Comp Lit Asn; Am Soc 18th Century Studies. **RESEARCH** Comparative theory and history; English 18th century literature; 20th century drama. **SELECTED PUBLICATIONS** Auth, Musical Metamorphoses--Forms and History of Arrangement, Musik und Kirche, Vol 63, 93; The International Glen Gould Festival in Groningen , Musica, Vol 47, 93; Report on the 17th Edition of the Tage Alter Musik Held in Herne, December 1992, Musica, Vol 47, 93; Kagel Die Erschopfung Der Welt, Musica, Vol 48, 94; Freyer Distanzen, Musica, Vol 48, 94; 100 Years of Opera in Essen 1893-1993, Musica, Vol 47, 93; Fortner in Seinem Garten Liebt Don Perlimplin Belisa, Musica, Vol 48, 94; Geister Der ModerneReport on a Recent Concert Series in Recklinghausen March 7-14, 1993, Musica, Vol 47, 93; Hummel Gorbatschow, Musica, Vol 48, 94; Freyer Flugel Schlage, Musica, Vol 48, 94. **CONTACT ADDRESS** Dept of English, Univ of Wyo, Laramie, WY, 82070.

DURHAM, CAROLYN ANN
PERSONAL Born 02/13/1947, Plainview, NE **DISCIPLINE** FRENCH LANGUAGE AND LITERATURE **EDUCATION** Wellesley Col, BA, 69; Univ Chicago, MA, 72, PhD, 76. **CAREER** Lectr French, Univ Chicago, 76; asst prof, 76-80, Assoc Prof French, Col Wooster, 81. Nat Endowment for Hum seminar, The Problematics of L'Ecriture Feminine, summer 79. **MEMBERSHIPS** MLA; Nat Women's Studies Asn. **RESEARCH** Twentieth-century novel; feminist lit criticism; film. **SELECTED PUBLICATIONS** Auth, The contradictory become coherent: La Religieuse and Paul et Virginic, Eighteenth Century: Theory & Interpretation, spring 82; L'Art Romanesque de Raymond Roussel, French Literature Publications, Inc, 82; Noman, Everywomen: Claudine Hermann's Les Voleuses de Langue, Bucknell Rev: Lit, Arts & Ideology 82; The Contexture of Feminism: Marie Cardinal and Multicultural Literacy, univ IL press, 91; auth, At the Crossroads of Gender and Culture: Where Feminism and Sexism in The mod lang jrnl, 95. **CONTACT ADDRESS** Dept of French, Col of Wooster, 1189 Beall Ave, Wooster, OH, 44691-2363. **EMAIL** cdurham@acs.wooster.edu

DURHAM, KEN R.
PERSONAL Born 03/21/1948, m, 1973, 2 children **DISCIPLINE** RELIGION AND COMMUNICATION **EDUCATION** David Lipscomb Col, BA, 70; La State Univ, MA, 72, PhD, 74; post doc grad work Austin Presbyterian theol sem, Abilene Christian Univ. **CAREER** Instr, Inst Christian Studies, 77-78; vis fac, 88; lectr, Okla Christian Univ, 91; David Lipscomb Univ, 89; adjunct fac, Harding Univ Grad Sch Rel, 89; contrib ed, 21st Century Christian, 93-; vis fac, 97-. **SELECTED PUBLICATIONS** Auth, Speaking From the Heart: Richer Relationships Through Communication, Sweet Publ, 86; Jesus, Our Mentor and Model, Baker Bk House, 87; co-auth, Becoming Persons of Integrity, Baker Bk House, 88; Anchors For the Asking, Baker Bk House, 89. **CONTACT ADDRESS** Dept of Relig, Pepperdine Univ, 24255 Pacific Coast Hwy, Malibu, CA, 90263. **EMAIL** kdurham@pepperdine.edu

DURHAM, SCOT
DISCIPLINE FRENCH **EDUCATION** Yale Univ, PhD. **CAREER** Asst prof; lect, Univ de Paris IV, Sorbonne; Univ Ca, Riverside; Univ Pa; SUNY, Binghamton; Stanford Univ; Miami Univ; Le College Int de Philos. **RESEARCH** 20th century literature; Foucault & Deleuze. **SELECTED PUBLICATIONS** Auth, The Deaths of Jean Genet, and Introduction: In the Language of the Enemy, Yale Fr Studies, 97; Genet's Shadow Theatre: Memory and Utopian Phantasy in Un captif amoureux, L'Esprit Createur, 95; From Magritte to Klossowski: The Simulacrum between Painting and Narrative, 93; Technology of Death and Its Limits: Baudrillard, Ballard, and the Simulation Model, Rethinking Technol, 93; ed, Jean Genet, Yale Fr Studies, special issue. **CONTACT ADDRESS** Dept of French, Northwestern Univ, 1801 Hinman, Evanston, IL, 60208.

DURMELAT, SYLVIE
DISCIPLINE FRENCH AND FRANCOPHONE 20TH CENTURY LITERATURES AND CULTURES, "BEUR" NARRAT **EDUCATION** Univ Mich, PhD, 95. **CAREER** Asst prof, La State Univ. **SELECTED PUBLICATIONS** Auth, Faux et d? de langue dans les romans d'Azouz Begag, in Francophone Plurielle, 95; L'apprentissage de l'ecriture dans Geogette! de Farida Belghoul, L'ecriture d?centr?e dans le roman contemporain en France, 96. **CONTACT ADDRESS** Dept of Fr Grad Stud, Louisiana State Univ, Baton Rouge, LA, 70803.

DURR, VOLKER
DISCIPLINE GERMAN **EDUCATION** Princeton Univ, PhD. **CAREER** Assoc prof, Northwestern Univ. **RESEARCH** A monograph on Rilke. **SELECTED PUBLICATIONS** Auth, essays and articles on, poetry; fiction; relation of history to literature; interaction of literature and philosophy; Lessing; Goethe; Bettina von Arnim; Nietzsche: Literature and Values; Coping with the Past; a monograph on Flaubert's Sallamb. **CONTACT ADDRESS** Dept of German, Northwestern Univ, 1801 Hinman, Evanston, IL, 60208. **EMAIL** v-durr@nwu.edu

DUSSIAS, PAOLA E.
DISCIPLINE SPANISH LITERATURE **EDUCATION** Univ Ariz, PhD. **CAREER** Asst prof, Univ Ill Urbana Champaign. **RESEARCH** Constraints on Spanish/English codeswitching; sentence processing in bilinguals. **SELECTED PUBLICATIONS** Auth, Sentence Matching and the Functional Head Constraint in Spanish/English Codeswitching, Spanish Applied Ling, 97. **CONTACT ADDRESS** Spanish, Italian, and Portuguese Dept, Univ Ill Urbana Champaign, 52 E Gregory Dr, Champaign, IL, 61820. **EMAIL** dussias@uiuc.edu

DUST, PATRICK
DISCIPLINE TWENTIETH-CENTURY SPANISH LITERATURE **EDUCATION** Univ Chicago, PhD. **CAREER** Literature, Carleton Univ. **MEMBERSHIPS** Auth, Ortega y Gasset and the Question of Modernity. **CONTACT ADDRESS** Carleton Col, 100 S College St., Northfield, MN, 55057-4016.

DUVAL, JOHN
DISCIPLINE TRANSLATION THEORY AND PRACTICE **EDUCATION** Univ Ark, MFA, PhD. **CAREER** English and Lit, Univ Ark. **HONORS AND AWARDS** Dir, Prog Literary Translation. **SELECTED PUBLICATIONS** Auth, Cuckolds, Clerics, and Countrymen: Medieval French Fabliaux, 82; Transl, Long Blues in A Minor, 88; Tales of Trilussa by Carlo Salustri, 90; The Discovery of America by Cesare Pascarella, 91; Auth, Fabliaux, Fair and Foul, 92. **CONTACT ADDRESS** Univ Ark, Fayetteville, AR, 72701.

DVORAK, PAUL FRANCIS
PERSONAL Born 05/26/1946, Queens, NY, m, 1969, 2 children **DISCIPLINE** GERMAN LANGUAGE & LITERATURE **EDUCATION** La Salle Col, BA, 68; Univ Md, MA, 70, PhD(Ger), 73. **CAREER** Instr, Univ Md, 70-74; asst prof Ger, Va Commonwealth Univ, 74-, res grant, Va Commonwealth Univ, 78-79, 82-83, 93-94; Fulbright grant, Summer, 81. **HONORS AND AWARDS** Faculty Research Grant, Virginia Commonwealth University, 93-94; Faculty Development Grant, College of H&S, VCU, 95. **MEMBERSHIPS** Am Asn Teachers Ger; Am Coun Teaching of Foreign Lang; Am Coun Study Austrian Lit; Am Transl Assn. **RESEARCH** Post-War German literature; Austrian literature; foreign language pedagogy. **SELECTED PUBLICATIONS** Auth, Adapting personalized questions to second-year foreign language courses, Die Unterrichtspraxis, 75; transit, Ezekiel, humanizing the slave laws in Israel, hope in the OT, letter to the Romans, In: Interpreter's Dictionary of the Bible, Suppl, Abingdon, 76; auth, Communication, small groups and the interview in the foreign language classroom, For Lang Annals, 78; Notation for nouns continued, Die Unterrichtspraxis, 81; Joachim Unseld, Franz Kafka, A Writer's Life, (Translation from the German of Franz Kafka, Ein Schrifstellerleben), Riverside: Ariadne Press, 94; Robert Schneider, Dirt, (Translation from the German of Franz Kafka. Ein Schrifstellerleben), Riverside: Ariadne Press, 96. **CONTACT ADDRESS** Dept of Foreign Lang, Virginia Commonwealth Univ, Box 2021, Richmond, VA, 23284. **EMAIL** pdvorak@atlas.vcu.edu

DWORKIN Y MENDEZ, KENYA C.
DISCIPLINE SPANISH **EDUCATION** Univ Hawaii, PhD. **CAREER** Languages, Carnegie Mellon Univ. **SELECTED PUBLICATIONS** Coauth, Manifestaciones del habla afrocubana: La literatura como fuente dialectal, Jour Iberian & Latin Am Studies, 90; Rigoberta Menchu: 'Los indegenas no nos quedamos como bichos aislados, inmunes, desde hace 500 anos. No, nosotros hemos sido protagonistas de la Historia', Nuevo Texto Cretico 93; Rigoberta Menchu: Con quien nos identicamos?, Jour Iberian & Latin Am Studies 3, 92. **CONTACT ADDRESS** Carnegie Mellon Univ, 5000 Forbes Ave, Pittsburgh, PA, 15213.

DYCK, MARTIN
PERSONAL Born 01/16/1927, Gruenfeld, Ukraine, 4 children **DISCIPLINE** GERMAN LITERATURE, LITERATURE AND MATHEMATICS **EDUCATION** Univ Man, BA, 53, MA, 54; Univ Cincinnati, PhD, 56. **CAREER** Asst prof Ger and Russ, Mass Inst Technol, 56-58; from asst prof to prof Ger, Univ Mich, 58-65; PROF GER AND HUMANITIES, MASS INST TECHNOL, 65-, Guggenheim and Am Coun Learned Soc fels, 61-62; Am Philos Soc award, 69; assoc ed, Hist Mathematica, 72-76. **MEMBERSHIPS** MLA; Hist Sci Soc; Int Soc Ger Lang and Lit; AAUP; Lessing Soc Am. **RESEARCH** German literature of the 18th and 20th centuries, especially Goethe, Novalis, Schiller and Kafka; theory of poetry, major fiction, and comedy; foundations of literature and mathematics.

SELECTED PUBLICATIONS Auth, The Age of Goethe Today--Critical Reexamination and Literary Reflection, Ger Stud Rev, Vol 15, 92; Performing Schiller--The Critics Speak, 1946-1985, Ger Stud Rev, Vol 15, 92. **CONTACT ADDRESS** Ger Lit Sect, Massachusetts Inst of Tech, PO Box 281, Cambridge, MA, 02238.

DYE, ROBERT ELLIS
PERSONAL Born 03/21/1936, m, 1959, 3 children **DISCIPLINE** GERMAN LANGUAGE AND LITERATURE **EDUCATION** Univ Utah, BA, 60; Rutgers Univ, MA, 63, PhD (Ger), 66. **CAREER** Teaching asst Ger, Univ Utah, 59-60; teaching asst, Rutgers Col, Rutgers Univ, 61-62, instr, 63-64; instr, Douglass Col, 64-66; asst prof, 66-71, ASSOC PROF, 71-79, PROF GER, MACALESTER COL, 79-, Chmn Dept Ger and Russ, 77 **MEMBERSHIPS** MLA; Goethe-Gesellschaft. **RESEARCH** Goethe; literature and religion. **SELECTED PUBLICATIONS** Auth, Women, Water, and the Males Deliquescence, In Goeth, Ger Notes Rev, Vol 24, 93. **CONTACT ADDRESS** Dept of Ger Lang and Lit, Macalester Col, 1600 Grand Ave, St Paul, MN, 55105.

E

EARHART, HARRY BYRON
PERSONAL Born 01/07/1935, Aledo, IL, m, 1956, 3 children **DISCIPLINE** HISTORY OF RELIGIOUS, ASIAN STUDIES **EDUCATION** Univ Chicago, BD and MA, 60, PhD, 65. **CAREER** Asst prof relig, Vanderbilt Univ, 65-66; from asst prof to assoc prof, 66-69, PROF RELIG, WESTERN MICH UNIV, 75-, Fac res fels, 68 and 73; Fulbright res grant and prof relig, Int Summer Sch Asian Studies, Ewha Womans Univ, Korea, 73; adv Far Eastern relig, Encycl Britannica; ed, Relig Studies Rev, 75-80. **MEMBERSHIPS** Am Acad Relig; Asn Asian Studies; Am Soc Study Relig. **RESEARCH** History of Japanese religion; Japanese new religions; new religious movements. **SELECTED PUBLICATIONS** Auth, Women and Millenarian Protest in Meiji Japan--Deguchi, Nao and Omotokyo, Monumenta Nipponica, Vol 48, 93. **CONTACT ADDRESS** Dept of Relig, Western Michigan Univ, Kalamazoo, MI, 49001.

EARLE, PETER G.
PERSONAL Born 05/31/1923, Yonkers, NY, m, 1949, 3 children **DISCIPLINE** SPANISH AND LATIN AMERICAN LITERATURE **EDUCATION** Mexico City Col, BA, 49, MA, 51; Univ Kans, PhD, 59. **CAREER** Instr Span, Princeton Univ, 56-59; asst prof, Wesleyan Univ, 59-63; assoc prof, 63-69, PROF SPAN, UNIV PA, 69-, Assoc ed, Hisp Rev, 64-73, ed, 73-; adv ed, Latin Am Lit Rev, 72-. **MEMBERSHIPS** Am Asn Teachers Span and Port; MLA; Mod Humanities Res Asn; Inst Int Lit Iberoamericana. **RESEARCH** Modern Spanish literature; modern Latin American literature. **SELECTED PUBLICATIONS** Auth, Mexican Narrative from Los De Abajo to Noticias Del Imperio, Hisp Rev, Vol 63, 95; Rereading the Spanish American Essay--Translations of 19th and 20th Century Womens Essays, Hisp Rev, Vol 65, 97; The Elusive Self--Archetypal Approaches to the Novels of Unamuno, Miguel,De, Hisp Rev, Vol 62, 94. **CONTACT ADDRESS** Dept of Romance Lang, Univ of Pa, Philadelphia, PA, 19174.

EASTMAN, CAROL M.
PERSONAL Born 09/27/1941, Boston, MA **DISCIPLINE** LINGUISTICS, ANTHROPOLOGY **EDUCATION** Univ Mass, BA, 63; Univ Wis, PhD (ling), 67 **CAREER** Asst prof anthrop and ling, 67-73, assoc prof, 73-79, PROF ANTHROP, UNIV WASH, 79-, Vis prof, Univ Nairobi, 79-80; ADJ PROF LING AND WOMEN STUDIES, UNIV WASH, 79-. **MEMBERSHIPS** Ling Soc Am; fel African Studies Asn; Am Anthrop Asn; Current Anthrop. **RESEARCH** Bantu linguistics and literature; Northwest Indian languages; language and culture. **SELECTED PUBLICATIONS** Auth, To the Charlottes--Dawson, George 1878 Survey of the Queen Charlotte Islands, W Hist Quart, Vol 25, 94. **CONTACT ADDRESS** Dept of Anthrop, Univ Wash, Seattle, WA, 98195.

ECONOMOU, ELLY HELEN
PERSONAL Thessaloniki, Greece **DISCIPLINE** BIBLICAL AND MODERN LANGUAGES **EDUCATION** Pac Union Col, BA, 66; Andrews Univ, MA, 67; Univ Strasbourg, France, PhD, 75. **CAREER** Instr French, 67-70, instr French & Greek, 70-72, Prof Bibl Lang & Relig, Andrews Univ, 72-77. **MEMBERSHIPS** Soc Bibl Lit; MLA; Int Platform Asn; Am Class League. **RESEARCH** Ecumenical studies; religion, the Greek Orthodox church, patristic lit; papyrology. **SELECTED PUBLICATIONS** Auth, Beloved Enemy, Pac Press Publ Asn, 68; numerous articles in Youth's Beakon & Children's Friend, 51-72. **CONTACT ADDRESS** Dept of Relig, Andrews Univ, 100 US Hwy 31, Berrien Springs, MI, 49104-0001.

EDGEWORTH, ROBERT J.
DISCIPLINE LATIN AND GREEK LANGUAGE AND LITERATURE **EDUCATION** Univ Mich, PhD. **CAREER** Prof Classics, actg chemn, dept For Lang and Lit, La State Univ, 88-89, 92, 94. **RESEARCH** Classical epic and epistolography. **SELECTED PUBLICATIONS** Auth, The Ivory Gate and the Threshold of Apollo, in Classica et Mediaevalia 37, 86; The Colors of the Aeneid, Peter Lang, 92. **CONTACT ADDRESS** Dept of For Lang and Lit, Louisiana State Univ, 145A Prescott Hall, Baton Rouge, LA, 70803.

EDWARDS, ANTHONY S.G.
PERSONAL Born 07/04/1942, Scarborough, England, m, 1975, 2 children **DISCIPLINE** MEDIEVAL; EARLY RENAISSANCE LITERATURE **EDUCATION** Univ Reading, BA; Univ McMaster, MA; Univ London, PhD. **CAREER** Vis prof, Univ Washington, 88; prof. **HONORS AND AWARDS** Can Coun Leave fel, 76-77; Leave fel, SSHRCC, 83-84; Guggenheim fel, 88-89. **MEMBERSHIPS** Mem, Chaucer Variorum; Yale Edition of the Works of St. Thomas More. **RESEARCH** Bibliography and textual criticism. **SELECTED PUBLICATIONS** Ed, George Cavendish's Metrical Visions, Univ SC, 80; Middle English Prose: A Critical Guide to Major Authors and Genres, Rutgers UP, 84; auth, John Skelton: The Critical Heritage, Routledge, 81; Stephen Hawes, Twayne, 83; MS Pepys 2006: A Facsimile, Pilgrim Bk(s), 86; co-ed, Middle English Prose: Essays on Bibliographical Problems, Garland, 81; coauth, An Index of Printed Middle English Prose, Garland, 85; contrib, Readings in Middle English Romance, Cambridge, 94. **CONTACT ADDRESS** Dept of English, Victoria Univ, PO Box 3070, Victoria, BC, V8W 3W1.

EDWARDS, GRACE TONEY
DISCIPLINE APPALACHIAN LITERATURE, APPALACHIAN FOLKLORE, AMERICAN LITERATURE, COMPOSIT **EDUCATION** Appalachian State Univ, BS, MA; Univ VA, PhD. **CAREER** Prof, dir, Appalachian Reg Stud Ctr, ch, Appalachian Stud prog, Radford Univ. **SELECTED PUBLICATIONS** Auth, Emma Belle Miles: Feminist Crusader in Appalachia, in the anthology Appalachia Inside Out; Our Mother's Voices: Narratives of Generational Transformation, in the J of Appalachian Stud. **CONTACT ADDRESS** Radford Univ, Radford, VA, 24142. **EMAIL** gedwards@runet.edu

EDWARDS, MARY LOUISE
DISCIPLINE COMMUNICATION SCIENCES AND DISORDERS **EDUCATION** Stanford Univ, 79. **CAREER** Prof CCC-SLP, Syracuse Univ. **RESEARCH** The nature, develop and remediation of disordered phonology in children; clinical applications of phonological theory; long-range outcomes for phonologically disordered preschoolers. **SELECTED PUBLICATIONS** Auth, Developmental Phonology in Human Communication and its Disorders, York, 95; Phonological Process Analysis in Children's Phonology Disorders: Pathways and Patterns, Am Speech-Lang-Hearing Assn, 94; Phonological Processes: Definitions, Uses and Limitations in Child Phonology: Perception and Production (Encyclopedia of Language and Linguistics), Pergamon, 94. **CONTACT ADDRESS** Syracuse Univ, Syracuse, NY, 13244.

EDWARDS, VIVIANE
PERSONAL Charlo, NB, Canada **DISCIPLINE** SECOND LANGUAGE EDUCATION **EDUCATION** Univ NB, BA, 63, BEd, 66, MEd, 85. **CAREER** Coord, Second Lang Svcs, Prov NB, 72-85; PROF EDUC, UNIV NEW BRUNSWICK 85-, dir Second-Lang Educ Ctr 85-. **HONORS AND AWARDS** Merit Award, Univ New Brunswick, 90. **MEMBERSHIPS** Can Asn Immersion Tchrs; Can Asn Second-Lang Tchrs. **SELECTED PUBLICATIONS** Auth, French Immersion Process, Product and Perspective in Can Mod Lang Rev, 92; auth, Touch of ... Class! in Can Mod Lang Rev, 94. **CONTACT ADDRESS** Second-Language Educ Centre, Univ New Brunswick, Fredericton, NB, E3B 6E3. **EMAIL** vedwards@unb.ca

EEKMAN, THOMAS
PERSONAL Born 05/20/1923, Middelharnis, Netherlands, m, 1946, 4 children **DISCIPLINE** SLAVIC LITERATURES **EDUCATION** Univ Amsterdam, MA, 46, PhD (Slavic lang), 51. **CAREER** Docent S Slavic lang and lit, Univ Amsterdam, 55-66; vis prof, 60-61, res grants, 66-78, PROF SLAVIC LANG, UNIV CALIF, LOS ANGELES, 66-, Vis prof Russ lit, Univ Hamburg, 72-73 and Aarhus Univ, 73; Am Coun Learned Soc res grants, 72-73, 73-74 and 78-; Univ Calif Humanities Inst res grant, 73; co-ed, Calif Slavic Studies, 73-. **HONORS AND AWARDS** Order of Yugoslav Flag, Yugoslav Govt, 65; Martinus Nijhoff Award, Netherlands, 81. **MEMBERSHIPS** Philol Asn Pac Coast; Am Asn S Europ Studies; W Slavic Asn; Asn Int des Lang et Litt Slaves. **RESEARCH** Nineteenth and 20th century Russian literature; comparative Slavic literature; poetics. **SELECTED PUBLICATIONS** Auth, Studies on the Skaz of Leskov, N .S. and Mihailovic, Dragoslav, Slavic Rev, Vol 55, 96; Slavic Drama; The Question of Innovation--Donskov, A, Sokoloski, R, Weretelnyk, R, Slavic Rev, Vol 52, 93; Modern Trends in Serbian and Croatian Poetry--Vinaver, Stanislav and Ujevic, Tin, Russ Lit, Vol 40, 96. **CONTACT ADDRESS** Dept of Slavic Lang, Univ of Calif, 405 Hilgard Ave, Los Angeles, CA, 90024.

EGEA, ESTEBAN R.
DISCIPLINE SPANISH AND FRENCH LITERATURE **EDUCATION** Harvard Univ, PhD, 74. **CAREER** Assoc prof. **RESEARCH** Linguistics; English as a second language. **SELECTED PUBLICATIONS** Auth, Los adverbios terminados en mente en el espanol contemporaneo, Inst Caro y Cuervo, 80; Using a Computer-generated Concordance to Analyze and Document Stylistic Devices in Robert Pinget's Fable, Comput Humanities, 77. **CONTACT ADDRESS** Dept of Literature, Richardson, TX, 75083-0688. **EMAIL** egea@utdallas.edu

EGERT, EUGENE
PERSONAL Born 12/29/1935, Rudnik, Poland, m, 1961, 2 children **DISCIPLINE** GERMANIC LANGUAGES **EDUCATION** Univ BC, 58, MA, 61; Univ Tex, PhD (Ger), 77. **CAREER** Instr Ger, Univ Wash, 64-67; from asst prof to assoc prof, 67-77, PROF GER, UNIV ALTA, 77-, **MEMBERSHIPS** Am Asn Teachers Ger; Asn Can Univ Teachers Ger; Mediaeval Acad Am. **RESEARCH** Early Middle High German literature; Middle High German lyric; Middle High German courtly epic. **SELECTED PUBLICATIONS** Auth, The Presentation and Function of Artistic Elements in Gottfried Von Strassburg Tristan, Seminar J Ger Stud, Vol 30, 94. **CONTACT ADDRESS** Dept of Ger Lang, Univ of Alta, Edmonton, AB, T6G 2G2.

EHRE, MILTON
PERSONAL Born 04/15/1933, New York, NY, m, 1963, 2 children **DISCIPLINE** RUSSIAN LITERATURE, GENERAL HUMANITIES **EDUCATION** City Col New York, BA, 55; Columbia Univ, MA, 66, PhD, 70. **CAREER** Asst prof, 67-72, assoc prof, 72-81, prof Russ & humanities, Univ Chicago, 81-. **HONORS AND AWARDS** Am Coun Learned Soc grant, 70-71; Guggenheim fel, 75-76. **MEMBERSHIPS** Am Assn Advan Slavic Studies; Am Assn Teachers Slavic & East Europ Lang. **RESEARCH** Russian literature of the 19th & 20th century; Russian prose fiction; Russian drama. **SELECTED PUBLICATIONS** Auth, Fedor Sologub's The Petty Demon: Erotica, Time and Decadence, The Silver Age, London: MacMillan, 92; auth, Meaning in Oblomov, Ivan A. Goncarov: Leben, Werk und Wirkung, Cologne: Bohlau, 95; auth, Ivan Goncharov's A Usual Story and the Precipice, Alexander Ostrovsky's Forest, Alexander Pushkis's Boris Godunov, Guide to Russian Literature, London: Fitzroy, 97, auth, Issac Babel, Boston: Twayne, 86, CD-ROM version, New York, Macmillan, 97; **CONTACT ADDRESS** Dept of Slavic, Univ of Chicago, 1130 E 59th St, Chicago, IL, 60637-1539. **EMAIL** m-ehre@uchicago.edu

EHRET, CHRISTOPHER
PERSONAL Born 07/27/1941, San Francisco, CA, m, 1963, 2 children **DISCIPLINE** AFRICAN HISTORY, HISTORICAL LINGUISTICS **EDUCATION** Univ Redlands, BA, 63; Northwestern Univ, Evanston, MA and cert African studies, 66, PhD (African hist), 69. **CAREER** Asst prof, 68-72, assoc prof, 72-78, PROF AFRICAN HIST, UNIV CALIF, LOS ANGELES, 78-, Ford Found grant African relig hist, 71-74; Fulbright grant, 82. **MEMBERSHIPS** Kenya Hist Soc; Hist Soc Tanzania. **RESEARCH** Development and use of linguistic evidence in historical reconstruction; eastern and southern African history; Nilotic and Cushitic historical linquistics. **SELECTED PUBLICATIONS** Auth, Kingship and State--The Buganda Dynasty, J Interdisciplinary Hist, Vol 28, 97. **CONTACT ADDRESS** Dept of Hist, Univ of Calif, Los Angeles, CA, 90024.

EHRLICH, LINDA C.
DISCIPLINE JAPANESE AND COMPARATIVE LITERATURE **EDUCATION** Univ Hawaii, PhD, 89. **CAREER** English, Case Western Reserve Univ. **SELECTED PUBLICATIONS** Coed, Cinematic Landscapes, an anthology of articles on the interface between the visual arts and the cinemas of China and Japan, Univ Tex Press, 94. **CONTACT ADDRESS** Case Western Reserve Univ, 10900 Euclid Ave, Cleveland, OH, 44106. **EMAIL** lce2@po.cwru.edu

EICHMANN, RAYMOND
DISCIPLINE MEDIEVAL FRENCH FABLIAUX AND DRAMA **EDUCATION** Univ Ark, BA, 65; Univ Ark, MA, 67, Univ Ky, PhD, 73. **CAREER** English and Lit, Univ Ark. **HONORS AND AWARDS** Chair, dept; Chair, European Studies prog. **SELECTED PUBLICATIONS** Area: medieval French fabliaux. **CONTACT ADDRESS** Univ Ark, Fayetteville, AR, 72701.

EICHNER, HANS
PERSONAL Born 10/30/1921, Vienna, Austria **DISCIPLINE** GERMAN LANGUAGE AND LITERATURE **EDUCATION** Univ London, BA, 44, BA(Hons), 46, PhD, 49; Queen's Univ, LLD, 74. **CAREER** Asst lectr, Bedford Col (London), 48-50; asst prof to prof, Queen's Univ, 50-67; prof, 67-88, ch grad dept Ger, 67-72, ch Ger, 75-84, PROF EMER GERMAN, UNIV TORONTO, 88-; hon prof hum, Univ Calgary, 78; adj prof, Queen's Univ, 90-. **HONORS AND AWARDS** Fel, Royal Soc Can, 67. **MEMBERSHIPS** Can Asn Univ Tchrs Ger. **SELECTED PUBLICATIONS** Auth, Thomas Mann, 53, 2nd rev ed 61; auth, Reading German for Scientists, 59; auth, Four German Authors: Mann-Rilke-Kafka-Brecht, 64; auth, Friedrich Schlegel, 70; auth, Deutsche Literatur im klassisch-

romantischen Zeitalter 1795-1805, 1 Teil, 90; ed, Friedrich Schlegel: Literary Notebooks 1797-1801, 57, 2nd (Ger) ed, 80; ed, Kritische Friedrich Schlegel-Ausgabe, vols 2-6, vol 16, 58-81; ed, 'Romantic' and its Cognates: The European History of a Word, 72; ed, Der Artushof und andere Erzahlungen (Eichendorff), 91; ed, Ausgewahlte Schriften, 94; gen ed, Canadian Studies in German Language and Literature. **CONTACT ADDRESS** Box 41, Rockwood, ON, N0B 2K0.

ELAM, HELEN REGUEIRO
PERSONAL Born 09/18/1943, Montevideo, Uruguay **DISCIPLINE** COMPARATIVE LITERATURE **EDUCATION** Brandeis Univ, BA, 64; Brown Univ, PhD (comp lit), 69. **CAREER** Asst prof English and comp lit, Columbia Univ, 69-75; asst prof English, Yale Univ, 75-77; ASSOC PROF ENGLISH, STATE UNIV NY ALBANY, 77-, Chamberlain fel, Columbia Univ, 74; Soc for Humanities jr fel, Cornell Univ, 73-74. **MEMBERSHIPS** MLA; Am Comp Lit Asn. **RESEARCH** Nineteenth and 20th century English, American, French, German and Greek poetry; literary criticism and literary theory; 19th and 20th century novel. **SELECTED PUBLICATIONS** Auth, Introduction--Romantic Poets and Their Critics, The Case of Hartman, Geoffrey, H, Stud Romanticism, Vol 35, 96. **CONTACT ADDRESS** Dept of English, State Univ of NY, 1400 Washington Ave, Albany, NY, 12222-1000.

ELARDO, RONALD JOSEPH
PERSONAL Born 08/25/1948, Buffalo, NY, m, 1972, 3 children **DISCIPLINE** GERMAN LANGUAGE & LITERATURE **EDUCATION** State Univ NY Buffalo, BA, 70; Purdue Univ, MA, 72; Univ Mich, PhD(Ger lang & lit), 79. **CAREER** Teaching asst Ger, Purdue Univ, 70-72; lectr, Univ Mich, 79-80 & Oakland Univ, 80-81; ASST PROF GER & ENGLISH, ADRIAN COL, 81-. **MEMBERSHIPS** MLA; Am Asn Teachers Ger **RESEARCH** The writings of Friedrich Wilhelm Joseph von Schelling; German romantic fairy tales; Alchemy and the medieval German epics. **SELECTED PUBLICATIONS** Auth, Lanzelet, alchemy and individuation, Symp, summer 80; E T A Hoffmann's Klein Zaches, the Trickster, Sem, 9/80; E T A Hoffman's Nussknacker und Mausekonig: The mousequeen in the tragedy of the hero, Ger Rev, winter 80; The maw as infernal medium in Ritter Gluck and Die Bergwerke zu Falun, New Ger Studies, spring 81. **CONTACT ADDRESS** Dept of Foreign Lang, Adrian Col, 110 S Madison St, Adrian, MI, 49221-2575. **EMAIL** r.elardo@adrian.adrian.edu

ELBAZ, ANDRE ELIE
PERSONAL Born 03/19/1937, Fez, Morocco, 2 children **DISCIPLINE** FRENCH AND COMPARATIVE LITERATURE **EDUCATION** Univ Bordeaux, Lic es Lett, 62; Sorbonne, DUniv(lit), 69. **CAREER** Teacher French, Universal Israelite Alliance, Meknes, Morocco, 56-61; prof English, UNESCO Emergency Prog, Niamey, Niger, 61-63; lectr French, Western Wash State Col, 63-65; assoc prof, 65-80, PROF FRENCH, CARLETON UNIV, 80-, Mem bd dirs, Can Serv Overseas Students and Trainees, 66-68; Can Coun and Humanities Res Coun Can grants, 69-78; fac consult, Acad Coun World Inst Sephardic Studies, 73-; guest lectr Sephardic Studies, Yeshiva Univ, 73-; researcher folk lit, Can Ctr Folk Cult Studies, Nat Museum Man, Ottawa, 76-78; Can Coun leave fel, 78-69. **HONORS AND AWARDS** Numerous Res Awards from Can Coun and Carleton Univ. **MEMBERSHIPS** Int Comp Lit Asn; Can Asn Folklore Studies; World Union Jewish Studies; Acad Coun World Inst Sephardic Studies; Int Res Prog Zola and Naturalism. **RESEARCH** French literataure and the Dreyfus affair; French and North American Jewish literature; Sephardic popular literature. **SELECTED PUBLICATIONS** Auth, Hassine, David, Ben--The Education of a Poet and Talmid Hakham Synagogue Official From Meknes at the Beginning of the 18th Century, Revue Etudes Juives, Vol 155, 96. **CONTACT ADDRESS** Dept of French, Carleton Univ, 1125 Colonel By Dr, Ottawa, ON, K1S 5B6.

ELDER, ARLENE ADAMS
PERSONAL Born 05/11/1940, Los Angeles, CA, 1 child **DISCIPLINE** AFRICAN, ETHNIC AMERICAN, & AUSTRALIAN-ABORIGINAL LITERATURE **EDUCATION** Immaculate Heart Col, AB, 61; Univ Denver, MA, 62; Univ Chicago, PhD(English), 70. **CAREER** Instr English, Emmanuel Col, 62-65; lectr, 70-71, asst prof, 71-76, assoc prof, 76-90, prof English & comp lit, Univ Cincinnati, 91-, affiliated with the Center for Women's Studies Certificate program; vis Fulbright lectr lit, Univ Nairobi, Kenya, 76-77. **MEMBERSHIPS** MLA, member exec coun, division of African lit, 95-2000; Soc Study Multi-Ethnic Lit US; AAUP; member, exec coun, African Lit Asn, 94-2000. **RESEARCH** African lit; ethnic Americans; Australian-Aboriginal lit. **SELECTED PUBLICATIONS** Auth, The Hindered Hand: Cultural Implications of Early African-American Fiction, Greenwood, 79; and many essays on African, African-Am, and women's literature. **CONTACT ADDRESS** Dept of English, Univ of Cincinnati, PO Box 210069, Cincinnati, OH, 45221-0069. **EMAIL** elder2@fuse.net

ELDREDGE, LAURENCE MILTON
PERSONAL Born 05/21/1931, Melrose, MA, m, 1979, 2 children **DISCIPLINE** MIDDLE ENGLISH AND MEDIEVAL LATIN LITERATURE **EDUCATION** Colgate Univ, AB, 53; Columbia Univ, MA, 59, PhD (English), 63. **CAREER** From instr to asst prof lit, Antioch Col, 62-69; assoc prof, 69-72, PROF ENGLISH, UNIV OTTAWA, 72-. **MEMBERSHIPS** Medieval Acad Am; Asn Can Univ Teachers English; Early English Text Soc; New Wyclif Soc; New Chaucer Soc. **RESEARCH** Fourteenth century poetry; 14th century philosophy, 14th and 15th century culture. **SELECTED PUBLICATIONS** Auth, Sciences and the Self in Medieval Poetry--Alan-Of Lille Anticlaudianus and Gower, John Confessio Amantis, Mod Lang Rev, Vol 92, 97; 9 Medieval Latin Plays, Medium Aevum, Vol 64, 95; Sciences and the Self in Medieval Poetry--Alan of Lille Anticlaudianus and Gower, John Confessio Amantis, Mod Lang Rev, Vol 92, 97; The Textual Tradition of Benvenutus Grassus De Arte Probatissima Oculorum, Studi Medievali, Vol 34, 93; The Rise and Decline of the Scholastic Quaestio Disputata with Emphasis on its Use in the Teaching of Medicine and Science, Medium Aevum, Vol 63, 94; A History of Anglo Latin Literature 1066-1422, Medium Aevum, Vol 63, 94; The Latin and German Etymachia, Medium Aevum, Vol 66, 97. **CONTACT ADDRESS** Dept of English, Univ of Ottawa, Ottawa, ON, K1N 6N5.

ELFE, WOLFGANG DIETER
PERSONAL Born 12/02/1939, Berlin, Germany, m, 1964, 2 children **DISCIPLINE** MODERN GERMAN LITERATURE **EDUCATION** Philipps-Univ, Marburg, WGer, BA, 64; Univ Mass, MA, 66, PhD (Ger), 70. **CAREER** Instr, Williams Col, 66-68; from instr to asst prof, State Univ NY Albany, 68-73; asst prof, 73-76, ASSOC PROF GER, UNIV SC, 76-, Dir, State Univ NY-Prog in Wuzburg, WGer, 72-73. **MEMBERSHIPS** MLA; SAtlantic Mod Lang Asn; Am Asn Teachers Ger; Soc Exile Lit (exec secy, 78-). **RESEARCH** German exile literature; German expressionism; literature of East Germany. **SELECTED PUBLICATIONS** Auth, Remarks on the Needed Reform of German Studies in the United States, Southern Hum Rev, Vol 28, 94; German Socialist Literature 1860-1914--Predicaments of Criticism, Southern Hum Rev, Vol 28, 94; Major Figures of Austrian Literature--The Interwar Years 1918-1938, Ger Quart, Vol 70, 97. **CONTACT ADDRESS** Univ of SC, Columbia, SC, 29210.

ELKINS, MICHAEL R.
PERSONAL Born 02/03/1959, Knoxville, TN, s **DISCIPLINE** SPEECH COMMUNICATION **EDUCATION** Univ of Tenn-Knoxville, BS, 8/82, MA, 12/85; South Ill Univ-Carbondale, PhD, Speech Communication, 8/97. **CAREER** Teaching asst, Univ of Tenn-Knoxville, 83-85; lecturer, Tex A&M Univ, 86-89; course/coord/visiting instr/lecturer, Texas A&I Univ, 89-92; instructor, 97-, asst prof & ch, 97-, Tex A&M Univ, 95-97. **HONORS AND AWARDS** South Ill Univ Dept of Speech Commun Thomas J Pace, Jr, Outstanding Teacher Award, 95., Ch, Dept of Commun & Theatre Arts, Tex A&M Univ Kingsville, 97. **MEMBERSHIPS** Nat Commun Assoc; Cent Speech Commun Assoc; Southern States Commun Assoc; Tex Speech Commun Assoc; Int Soc for Gen Semantics; Pac & Asian Commun Assoc; Commun Educ Assoc; Am Assoc of Univ Women; Phi Kappa Phi; Golden Key; Kappa Delta Pi; Phi Delta Kappa; Pi Kappa Delta; Gamma Beta Pi; Alpha Zeta. **RESEARCH** Communication. **SELECTED PUBLICATIONS** Auth, Communication apprehension, teacher preparation, and at-risk students: Revealing South Texas secondary school teacher perceptions, Tex Speech Commun J, vol 20, 3-10, 95; auth, I will fear no audience: General semantics to the rescue, J of the Ill Speech & Theatre Assoc, vol 47, 41-43, 96; co-auth, Perceptions of cultural differences from international faculty in selected colleges and universities in South Texas, Tex Speech Commun J, vol 21, 3-12, 97; co-auth, The Texas Speech Commun J: A twenty year retrospective, Tex Speech Commun J, vol 23, 73-77, 98; Cultural issues in the workplace, J of the Ill Speech & Theatre Assoc. **CONTACT ADDRESS** Dept of Commun & Theatre Arts, Tex A&M, Kingsville, Campus Box 178, Kingsville, TX, 78363. **EMAIL** kfmre00@tamuk.edu

ELLIOTT, MICHAEL
DISCIPLINE ENGLISH LANGUAGE AND LITERATURE **EDUCATION** Amherst Col, BA, 92; Columbia Univ, PhD, 98. **CAREER** Asst prof **RESEARCH** 19th and 20th century American literature, Native American literature, and cultural studies; ties between literature and social science in the history of ideas about "race" and "culture" in the United States. **SELECTED PUBLICATIONS** Auth, pubs about Native American literature in arts/revs for Am Quart, Early Am Lit, Studies Am Indian Lits, and Biography. **CONTACT ADDRESS** English Dept, Emory Univ, 1380 Oxford Rd NE, Atlanta, GA, 30322-1950.

ELLIS, KEITH A.A.
PERSONAL Born 04/05/1935, Jamaica **DISCIPLINE** HISPANIC LITERATURE **EDUCATION** Univ Toronto, BA, 58; Univ Wash, MA, 61, PhD, 62. **CAREER** PROF SPANISH & PORTUGUESE, UNIV TORONTO, 62-. **HONORS AND AWARDS** Fel, Royal Soc Can; Can Hispanists' Prize Best Bk. **MEMBERSHIPS** MLA; Can Asn Hispanists; Can Asn Latin Am Stud; Jamaican Can Asn; Can-Cuban Friendship Asn. **SELECTED PUBLICATIONS** Auth, El arte narrativo de Francisco Ayala, 64; auth, Critical Approaches to Ruben Dareo, 74; auth, Tres ensayos sobre Nicolas Guillen, 80; auth, Cuba's Nicolas Guillen: Poetry and Ideology, 84; auth, Nicolas Guillen: poesia y ideologea, 87; auth, Nicolas Guillen (1902-1989): A Life of Poetic Service, 91; coauth, Mirrors of War, 85; coauth, La poesia de Emilio Ballagas, 90; ed, La cabeza del cordero de Francisco Ayala, 70; co-ed, El ensayo y la cretica literaria en Iberoamerica, 70; co-ed, Encyclopedia of Spanish American Literature, 90. **CONTACT ADDRESS** Dept of Spanish & Portuguese, Univ of Toronto, Toronto, ON, M5S 1A1.

ELLIS, MARION LEROY
PERSONAL Born 03/27/1928, Georgetown, SC **DISCIPLINE** FRENCH **EDUCATION** Univ SC, AB, 38, MA, 50; Univ Aix-Marseille, Dr Univ, 55. **CAREER** Asst prof English, Va Polytech Inst, 57-60; prof French and chmn dept lang, Erskine Col, 60-61; assoc prof French and Span, Va Polytech Inst, 61-64; assoc prof French, Lewis and Clark Col, 65-68 and N Tex State Univ, 68-69; prof foreign lang and head dept, 69-79, PROF ENGLISH SECOND LANG AND FOREIGN LANG, LAMAR UNIV, 79-, Acad leader, Exp in Int Living, 64-65. **HONORS AND AWARDS** Chevalier, Palmes Academiques, 67, Officier, 77. **MEMBERSHIPS** Am Asn Teachers Fr. **RESEARCH** Acadian culture in Southeast Texas; contemporary French theater; history of the Russian colony in the department of Alpes-Maritimes, France. **SELECTED PUBLICATIONS** Auth, Rapports, A Textbook, Fr Rev, Vol 67, 94. **CONTACT ADDRESS** Dept Foreign Lang, Lamar Univ, Beaumont, TX, 77710.

ELLIS, ROBERT
PERSONAL Born 07/08/1955, Fort Worth, TX, m, 1989, 2 children **DISCIPLINE** OLD TESTAMENT AND BIBLICAL HEBREW **EDUCATION** Hardin Simmons Univ, BS, 77; Southwest Baptist Theol Sem, MD, 81; PhD, 88. **CAREER** Instr, Hardin-Simmons Univ, 84-86; asst prof, Southwest Baptist Theol Sem, 86-96; prof, Hardin-Simmons Univ, 98-. **HONORS AND AWARDS** Distinguished Alumnus of Logsdon School of Theol. **MEMBERSHIPS** Nat Asn of baptist Porf of Rel; Soc of Bibl Lit. **RESEARCH** Old Testament Prophets and Wisdom Literature; Biblical Hebrew. **SELECTED PUBLICATIONS** Auth, Divine Gift and Human Response: An Old Testament Model for Stewardship, Southwestern J of Theol, 95; Are There Any Cows of Bashan on Seminary Hill?, Southwestern J of Theol, 95; article in New Int Dictionary of Old Testament Theol and Exegesis, 97; The Theological Boundaries of Inclusion and Exclusion in the Book of Joshua, Rev and Expositor, 98. **CONTACT ADDRESS** Box 16235, Abilene, TX, 79698-6235. **EMAIL** rellis@hsutx.edu

ELLRICH, ROBERT JOHN
PERSONAL Born 01/15/1931, Bridgeport, CT **DISCIPLINE** FRENCH LITERATURE **EDUCATION** Harvard Univ, BA, 52, MA, 53, PhD, 60. **CAREER** From instr to asst prof Romance lang, Princeton Univ, 59-64, coordr French sect, NDEA Inst, 63; asst prof, 64-69, dir, arts and sci honors prog, 77-80, ASSOC PROF FRENCH AND COMP LIT, UNIV WASH, 69-, Princeton Univ Coun Humanities res fel, 63-64. **MEMBERSHIPS** MLA; Int Asn Fr Studies; Am Soc 18th Century Studies. **RESEARCH** French literature of the 17th and 18th centuries; development of the novel; Dante. **SELECTED PUBLICATIONS** Auth, Rousseau Occasional Autobiographies, Fr Forum, Vol 19, 94; Rousseau Dialogues--An Interpretive Essay, Fr Forum, Vol 17, 92. **CONTACT ADDRESS** Dept of Romance Lang GN-60, Univ of Wash, Seattle, WA, 98195.

ELSON, MARK JEFFREY
DISCIPLINE SLAVIC AND GENERAL LINGUISTICS **EDUCATION** Univ Mich, Ann Arbor, BA, 68; Harvard Univ, MA, 72, PhD (ling), 73. **CAREER** Asst prof Russ, Amherst Cot, 73-74; asst prof, 75-81, ASSOC PROF SLAVIC LANG AND LIT, UNIV VA, CHARLOTTESVILLE, 81-. **MEMBERSHIPS** Ling Soc Am; Am Asn Teachers Slavic and E Europ Lang; Southeastern Conf Ling; MLA. **SELECTED PUBLICATIONS** Auth, A Latin Source for the Conditional Auxiliary in Romanian, Zeitschrift Rom Philol, Vol 108, 92; The Accentual Patterns of the Slavic Languages, Slavic East Europ J, Vol 38, 94; A Latin Source for the Conditional Auxiliary in Romanian, Zeitschrift Rom Philol, Vol 108, 92; Labyrinth of Life--A Video Based Advanced Polish Language Course, Mod Lan J, Vol 78, 94; Catalan, Lan, Vol 70, 94; The Accentual Patterns of the Slavic Languages, Slavic East Europ J, Vol 38, 94; Collocational Stress in Contemporary Standard Macedonian, Slavic East Europ J, Vol 37, 93; Beginners Polish, Mod Lan J, Vol 80, 96; Vocabulary of Soviet Society and Culture--Selected Guide to Russian Words, Idioms, and Expressions of the Post Stalin Era, 1953-1991, Mod Lang J, Vol 77, 93. **CONTACT ADDRESS** Univ of Va, 1 Cabell Hall, Charlottesville, VA, 22903-3125.

ELSTUN, ESTHER NIES
PERSONAL Born 02/22/1935, Berkshire Heights, PA, m, 1956, 1 child **DISCIPLINE** GERMANIC LANGUAGES & LITERATURES **EDUCATION** Colo Col, BA, 60; Rice Univ, MA, 64, PhD(Ger), 69. **CAREER** Instr Ger, Colo Col, 60-61; from asst prof to assoc prof Ger, 68-76, chm dept foreign lang, 71-76, prof Ger, George Mason Univ, 76- ; consult, State Coun for Higher Ed in Va, 71-72, 77, Va Dept of Educ, 79, US Dept of Educ, 80-81; pres, Va Coun for Study Abroad, 81-82, Va

Hum Conf, 89-90; dir, George Mason Univ/Univ Wuerzburg exchange prog, 90- . **HONORS AND AWARDS** Phi Beta Kappa; Delta Phi Alpha. **MEMBERSHIPS** MLA; Am Asn Teachers Ger; AAUP. **RESEARCH** Twentieth-century German literature; the Young Vienna Circle; post-war and contemporary novel in German. **SELECTED PUBLICATIONS** Auth, Richard Beer-Hofmann: His Life and Work, Pa State, 83; ed, Human Rights: A Cross-Disciplinary Symposium, Va Tech Center for Programs in the Humanities, 90. **CONTACT ADDRESS** Dept of Modern & Classical Languages, George Mason Univ, 4400 University Dr, Fairfax, VA, 22030-4444.

ELWOOD, WILLIAM N.
PERSONAL Born 09/21/1962, East Orange, NJ, d **DISCIPLINE** HUMAN COMMUNICATION **EDUCATION** Purdue Univ, PhD, 92. **CAREER** Asst prof, Dept Commun, Auburn Univ, 92-94; res assoc, Affiliated Systems Corp, 94-96; adj asst prof, Sch of Public Health, Univ Tex; 96-, sr res scientist, Behavioral Research Group, 96-. **HONORS AND AWARDS** Best Book, Nat Commun Asn, 96. **MEMBERSHIPS** Int AIDS Soc; Am Public Health Asn; Nat Commun Asn. **RESEARCH** Drug abuse; HIV prevention; communication rules. **SELECTED PUBLICATIONS** Auth, Rhetoric in the War on Drugs: The Triumphs and Tragedies of Public Relations, Praeger Publ, 94; ed, Public Relations Inquiry as Rhetorical Criticism: Case Studies of Corporate Discourse and Social Influence, Praeger Series in Political Communication, Best Book Award, 95; auth, Power in the Blood: A Handbook on AIDS, Politics, and Communication, Lawrence Earlbaum Assoc, 98; assoc Amer ed, AIDS Care: Psychological and Socio-medical Aspects of AIDS/HIV, 97-; author of numerous articles. **CONTACT ADDRESS** 402 Yuam Ave., Apt. 1, Houston, TX, 77006-3433. **EMAIL** wnelwood@earthlink.net

EMBLETON, SHEILA
PERSONAL Ottawa, ON, Canada **DISCIPLINE** LANGUAGE/LITERATURE/LINGUISTICS **EDUCATION** Univ Toronto, BS, 75, MS, 76, PhD, 81. **CAREER** Lectr, 80-81, asst prof, Grad Prog Interdisciplinary Studs, 83-84, asst prof , 82-84, ASSOC PROF LANGS, LIT & LING, YORK UNIV 84-, assoc dean, Fac Arts, 94-97. **HONORS AND AWARDS** Queen Elizabeth II Scholar, 79-80; Gov Gen Gold Medal, 75; Dr. Harold C. Parsons Scholar, 72-73; Archibald Young Scholar, 73-74. **MEMBERSHIPS** Can Soc Stud Names; Finno-Ugic Stud Asn; Int Soc Hist Ling Asn; Ling Soc Am; Int Coun Onomastic Sci; Can Friends Finland. **SELECTED PUBLICATIONS** Auth, Statistics in Historical Linguistics, 86; auth, Lexicostatistics Applied to the Germanic, Romance, and Wakashan Families, in Word, 85; auth, Mathematical Methods of Genetic Classification, in Sprung From Some Common Source: Investigations into the Prehistory of Languages, 91. **CONTACT ADDRESS** Dept of Language, Literature & Linguistics, York Univ, North York, ON, M3J 1P3. **EMAIL** embleton@yorku.ca

EMENEAU, MURRAY BARNSON
PERSONAL Born 02/28/1904, Lunenburg, Canada, m, 1940 **DISCIPLINE** SANSKRIT, LINGUISTICS **EDUCATION** Dalhousie Univ, BA, 23; Oxford Univ, BA, 26, MA, 35; Yale Univ, PhD, 31. **CAREER** Instr classics, Yale Univ, 26-31, researcher, 31-40; from asst prof to prof Sanskrit, gen ling and fac res lectr, 40-71, EMER PROF SANSKRIT AND GEN LING, UNIV CALIF, BERKELEY, 71-, Guggenheim fel, 49 and 56. **HONORS AND AWARDS** LHD, Univ Chicago, 68; LLD, Dalhousie Univ, 70. **MEMBERSHIPS** Am Orient Soc (pres, 53-54); Ling Soc Am (vpres, 48, pres, 49); hon fel Royal Asiatic Soc; Int An Tamil Res (vpres, 66-); hon mem Ling Soc India. **SELECTED PUBLICATIONS** Auth, Dravidian Linguistics--An Introduction, J Am Orient Soc, Vol 113, 93; Tamil Expressives with Initial Voiced Stops, Bulletin of the School of Oriental and African Studies University of London, Vol 56, 93; The Palatalizing Rule in Tamil Malayalam and Telugu, J Am Orient Soc, Vol 115, 95. **CONTACT ADDRESS** Dept of Ling, Univ of Calif, Berkeley, CA, 94720.

EMMA, RONALD DAVID
PERSONAL Born 07/21/1920, London, England, m, 1948, 1 child **DISCIPLINE** ENGLISH, PHILOLOGY **EDUCATION** City Col New York, BBA, 41; Duke Univ, MA, 51, PhD, 60. **CAREER** Instr English, Col William & Mary, 54-60; asst prof, Cent Mich Univ, 60-61; from asst prof to assoc prof, Southern Conn State Col, 61-66; prof English, Windham Col, 66-78, chmn dept English, 66-70, chmn div humanitites, 66-74; ASST PROF ACCT, ALBERTUS MAGNUS COL, 81-, Asst, Duke Univ, 52-53; Col William & Mary res grants-in-aid, 58 & 59; vis lectr English, Univ Mass, 76-77; consult ed, English Literary Renaissance. **MEMBERSHIPS** MLA; Milton Soc Am; Yeats Soc; Int Asn Philos & Lit; Am Acct Asn. **RESEARCH** Grammar and style in Milton; Milton and 17th century poetry; contemporary Irish poetry. **SELECTED PUBLICATIONS** Auth, Milton's Grammar, Mouton The Hague, 63; co-ed, Language and Style in Milton, Ungar, 67 & Seventeenth-Century English Poetry, Lippincott, 69; The exordium and Paradise Lost, S Atlantic Quart, autumn 72; Milton's grammar, In: Milton Encyclopedia, Vol II; Poetry (a variety), in var Jours, US & Abroad. **CONTACT ADDRESS** 61 Elizabeth St, West Haven, CT, 06516.

EMPLAINCOURT, EDMOND ARTHUR
PERSONAL Born 08/02/1943, Roux, Belgium, m, 1975, 2 children **DISCIPLINE** ROMANCE PHILOLOGY **EDUCATION** Col William & Mary, BA, 69; Univ Ala, MA, 72, PhD(French), 75. **CAREER** From Asst Prof to Assoc Prof, 75-92, Prof French, Miss State Univ, 92-, Head, Dept For Lang, 97-. **HONORS AND AWARDS** Outstanding Honors Fac, 95. **MEMBERSHIPS** Soc Rencesvals. **RESEARCH** Epic, especially Old French; textual criticism. **SELECTED PUBLICATIONS** Auth, CR. of Jean-Marie d'Heur Sur la date, la composition et la destination de La Chanson de la croisade albigeoise, M langes offerts Charles Rostaing, Olifant 4, 78; Lettres in dites de Marie-Angelique Arnauld des religieuses, Yearbook of the Am Philos Soc, 80; La Geste du Chevalier au Cygne, vol 9 of The Old French Crusade Cycle, Univ Ala Press, 89; Sur la destination de La Chanson du Chevalier au Cygne, Olifant 17, 92; CR. of Douglas A. Kibbee, for to Speke French Trewely: The French Language in England, 1000-1600, Modern Lang Note 77, 93; author and coauthor of numerous other articles. **CONTACT ADDRESS** Dept of Foreign Lang, Mississippi State Univ, P O Box Fl, Mississippi State Univ, MS, 39762-5720. **EMAIL** eaempl@ra.msstate.edu

ENG, DAVID L.
DISCIPLINE ASIAN AMERICAN LITERATURE **EDUCATION** Columbia, AB, 90; Berkeley, MA, 90, PhD, 95. **CAREER** English and Lit, Columbia Univ **HONORS AND AWARDS** Mellon Found grant., President's Postdoctoral Fel. **SELECTED PUBLICATIONS** Coed, Queer in Asian America, Temple University Press, 98. **CONTACT ADDRESS** Columbia Univ, 2960 Broadway, New York, NY, 10027-6902.

ENGBERG, NORMA J.
DISCIPLINE MEDIEVAL LITERATURE, OLD ENGLISH, LATIN **EDUCATION** George Washington Univ, BA, 61; Univ Fla, MA, 63; Univ Pa, Philadelphia, PhD, 69. **CAREER** Instr, George Washington Univ, 64-67; asst prof, Calif State Col, 68; asst prof, 69-75, assoc prof, 75-, dir, grad stud, 76-83, pres, past pres, Phi Kappa Phi, 79-81, ch, grad coun, Univ Nev, Las Vegas, 81-83. **MEMBERSHIPS** UNLV corp rep, Am Assn Univ Women, 82-84. **RESEARCH** Translations from Latin. **SELECTED PUBLICATIONS** Auth, Exposing Readers of Beowulf-in-Translation to the Original Poem's Phonology, Morphology, and Syntax, Old Eng Newsl; vol15, no 2, 82; Mod-Maegen Balance in Elene, The Battle of Maldon and The Wanderer, Neuphilologische Mitteilungen, vol 85, no 2, 84; PE100-408 Anglo Saxon Language, PE1075-1400 History, and PR1490-1799 Anglo-Saxon Literature, in 3rd ed of Books for College Libraries, Virginia Clark, ed, Am Libr Asn, 88. **CONTACT ADDRESS** Dept of Eng, Univ Nev, Las Vegas, 4505 Maryland Pky, PO Box 455011, Las Vegas, NV, 89154-5011. **EMAIL** adamsc@nevada.edu

ENGELBERG, EDWARD
PERSONAL Born 01/21/1929, Germany, m, 1950, 3 children **DISCIPLINE** COMPARATIVE LITERATURE AND ENGLISH **EDUCATION** Brooklyn Col, BA, 51; Univ Ore, MA, 52; Univ Wis, PhD, 57. **CAREER** From instr to assoc prof English, Univ Mich, 57-65; assoc prof, 65-67, chmn, Comp Lit Prog, 65-72, chmn, Dept Romance and Comp Lit, 71-75, chmn, Joint Prog Lit Studies, 71-75, PROF COMP LIT, BRANDEIS UNIV, 67-, Nat Endowment for Humanities sr fel, 75; fac rep, Bd Trustees, Brandeis Univ, 76-78, mem, Acad Planning Comt, 75-78; mem, exec comt, Eastern Comp Lit Conf. **MEMBERSHIPS** MLA; Am Comp Lit Asn; AAUP. **RESEARCH** Romanticism and literary history; modern poetry; English-German relations. **SELECTED PUBLICATIONS** Auth, Running to Paradise, Yeats Poetic Art, Eng Lit Transition 1880-1920, Vol 38, 95; Collected Letters, Vol 6, Beitrage Geschichte Arbeiterbewegung, Vol 36, 94. **CONTACT ADDRESS** Dept of Romance and Lit Comp, Brandeis Univ, Waltham, MA, 02154.

ENGELHARDT, KLAUS HEINRICH
PERSONAL Born 11/17/1936, Wurzburg, Germany, m, 1967, 2 children **DISCIPLINE** FRENCH LITERATURE **EDUCATION** Univ Munich, Staatsexamen, 62, PhD(Romance lang), 68. **CAREER** Teaching asst Ger, Lycee Descartes, Tours, France, 60-61; asst prof French, Univ Munich, 65-69; asst prof French & Ger, 69-74, acting chmn dept foreign lang, 70-71, assoc prof, 74-82, prof French & Ger, Lewis & Clark Col, 82-. **MEMBERSHIPS** MLA; AAUP; Am Asn Teachers Fr. **RESEARCH** French novel; French theatre; Occitan culture. **SELECTED PUBLICATIONS** Auth, Contributions on French literature, In: Kindler Literatur Lexikon, Munich, 64-73; Le Langage des yeux dans la Chartreuse de Parme de Stendhal, Stendhal Club, Grenoble, 7/72; Une Source Roumaine du Tueur Sans Gages d'Eugene Ionesco, Neueren Sprachen, Ger, 1/72; coauth, Daten der Franzosischen Literatur, dtv, Munchen, 79. **CONTACT ADDRESS** Dept of Foreign Lang, Lewis & Clark Col, 0615 SW Palatine Hill Rd, Portland, OR, 97219-7879. **EMAIL** klaus@lclark.edu

ENNS, PETER
PERSONAL Born 01/02/1961, Passaic, NJ, m, 1984, 3 children **DISCIPLINE** NEAR EASTERN LANGUAGE AND CIVILIZATIONS **EDUCATION** Messiah Col, BA, 82; Harvard, MA, 93; Harvard, PhD, 94 **CAREER** Assoc prof Old Testament, Westminister Theolog Seminary, 94- **MEMBERSHIPS** Soc Bibl Lit; Inst Bibl Res; Evangelical Theolog Soc **RESEARCH** Early Jewish Biblical Interpretation; Old Testament Theology; New Testament's use of the Old Testament; Wisdom Literature **SELECTED PUBLICATIONS** Exodus, Zondevan, forthcoming; ed, The New Testament's Use of the Old in Its Historical-Hermeneutical Milieu, Zondervan, forthcoming; auth, Exodus Retold: Ancient Exegesis of the Departure from Egypt in Wis 10:15-21 and 19:1-9, Scholars Press, 97 **CONTACT ADDRESS** Westminister Theol Sem, PO Box 27009, Philadelphia, PA, 19118.

EPPLE, JUAN ARMANDO
PERSONAL Born 04/26/1946, Osorno, Chile, m, 1967, 1 child **DISCIPLINE** SPANISH AMERICAN LITERATURE **EDUCATION** Austral Univ Chile, BA, 71; Harvard Univ, MA, 77, PhD (romance lang), 80. **CAREER** Asst prof lit theory, Austral Univ Chile, 72-74; instr Span, Ohio State Univ, 79-80; ASST PROF ROMANCE LANG, UNIV ORE, 80-. **MEMBERSHIPS** MLA; Inst Internac Lit Iberoamericana; Midwest Mod Lang Asn; Pac Coast Coun Latin Am Studies. **RESEARCH** Chicano literature; Latin American literary historiography. **SELECTED PUBLICATIONS** Auth, Interview with Padurafuentes, Leonardo, Hisp Revista Lit Vol 24, 95; De Repente Los Lugares Desaparecen, Revista Iberoamericana, Vol 60, 94; Postmodernism--A Poet from the 3rd World, A Conversation with Manns, Patricio, Confluencia Revista Hispanica Critiques Journals 3. Simpson 7, Revista De La Sociedad De Escritores De Chile, Chasqui Revista Literatura Latinoamericana, Vol 25, 96; The Voices of Poniatowska, Elena--An Interview, Confluencia Revista Hisp Cult Y Lit, Vol 5, 90; With Manns, Patricio, Confluencia Revista Hisp Cult Y Literatura, Vol 8, 92; Feminine Voices, Interview With Navarro, Heddy, Confluencia Revista Hisp Cult Y Lit, Vol 7, 91; Writing as Palimpsest, Actas Del Alto Bio Bio and the Chilean Indigenist Canon, Mester, Vol 21, 92; An Approach to Chilean Testimonial Literature, Revista Iberoamericana, Vol 60, 94; Transcribing the River of Dreams, An Interview with Zurita, Raul, Revista Iberoamericana, Vol 60, 94; The Voices of Poniatowska, Elena--An Interview, Confluencia Revista Hisp Cult Y Lit, Vol 5, 90; The Grupo Trilce and Chilean Poetic Promotion in the Sixties, Revista De Critica Literaria Latinoamericana, Vol 23, 97. **CONTACT ADDRESS** Dept Romance Lang, Univ Ore, Eugene, OR, 94703.

EPSTEIN, EDMUND LLOYD
PERSONAL Born 10/15/1931, New York, NY, m, 1965, 3 children **DISCIPLINE** ENGLISH, LINGUISTICS **EDUCATION** Queens Col, NY, BA, 51; Yale Univ, MA, 53; Columbia Univ, PhD(English), 67. **CAREER** Ed dict, various publ, 53-55; instr English, Univ Buffalo, 55-57; ed trade-and-text-bks, B P Putnam's Sons, 57-63 & Farrar, Straus & Giroux, 63-65; from assoc prof to prof English, Southern Ill Univ, Carbondale, 65-74; prof English, Queens Col City Univ New York 74-; Ed-in-chief, James Joyce Rev, 57-61; consult, James Joyce Quart, 63-; ed-in-chief, Lang & Style, 68-; vis scholar, Univ Col, Univ London, 71-72; prof English,Grad Ctr., City Univ New York, 81-; exchange prof , Univ Paris, 82, 95. **HONORS AND AWARDS** Excellence in Teaching Award, Standard Oil Found, Ind, 71, nominated Distinguished Prof of English, 97; nominated for Award for Excellence in Teaching, 97. **MEMBERSHIPS** MLA; Ling Soc Am; Mediaeval Acad Am. **RESEARCH** Modern British literature; linguistics, the analysis of style, structural semantics, the analysis of meaning. **SELECTED PUBLICATIONS** Coauth, Linguistics and English prosody, Studies Ling, 58; Interpretation of Finnegans Wake, James Joyce Quart, summer 66; auth, The Ordeal of Stephen Dedalus: Conflict of the Generations in James Joyce's A Portrait of the Art as a Young Man, Southern Ill Univ, 71; Language and Style, Methuen, London, 78; auth Women's Language and Style: Studies in Contemporary Language #1, Queens Col, 78; auth A Starchamber Quiry: a Joyce Centennial Publication, 1882-1982, Methuen, London, 82; auth Joyce Centenary Essays, Southern Ill Univ, 1983; auth Mythic Worlds, Modern Worlds: the Writings of Joseph Campbell on James Joyce, Harper-Collins, 93; auth The Language of African Literature, Africa World Press, 98. **CONTACT ADDRESS** Dept of English, Queens Col, CUNY, 6530 Kissena Blvd, Flushing, NY, 11367-1597. **EMAIL** epstein@qcvaxa.acc.qc.edu

EPSTEIN, RICHARD
DISCIPLINE LINGUISTICS **EDUCATION** UCLA, San Diego, PhD. **CAREER** Instr, Rutgers, State Univ NJ, Camden Col of Arts and Sci. **RESEARCH** Semantics; pragmatics; Kumeyaay, a native American language. **SELECTED PUBLICATIONS** Auth, Some Uses of the Demonstrative Clitic pu in Jamul Diegueo, Hokan-Penutian Lang Workshop, 91; The Development of the Definite Article in French, Perspectives on Grammaticalization, John Benjamins, 94; L'article dQfini en anciens frantais: l'expression de la subjectivitQ, Langue Fr, 95; Le temps dans la linguistique cognitive, ModQles ling 95; Viewpoint and the Definite Article in Conceptual Structure, Discourse and Language, Cambridge, 96. **CONTACT ADDRESS** Rutgers, State Univ NJ, Camden Col of Arts and Sci, New Brunswick, NJ, 08903-2101. **EMAIL** repstein@camden.rutgers.edu

ERICKSON, DANIELE NATHAN
PERSONAL Born 07/30/1958, Sioux Falls, SD **DISCIPLINE** LATIN, GREEK **EDUCATION** Concordia Coll Moorhead Minn, BA, 81; Tex Tech Univ, MA, 85; Syracuse Univ, PhD, 90. **CAREER** Instr, Newport High School, 82-86; instr, The Louisiana School LA,86-93; asst prof, Univ NDak, 98-. **HONORS AND AWARDS** Grad magna cum laude, Concordia Coll, 81; Who's Who Among America's Teachers, 94. **MEMBERSHIPS** Am Philol Asn; Am Council on the Teaching of Foreign Lang; Am Classical League. **RESEARCH** Teaching of Latin and Greek; Roman History. **SELECTED PUBLICATIONS** Introduction, translation and notes, Eutropius' Compendium of Roman History, 90. **CONTACT ADDRESS** 310 Walnut St, Apt #2, Grand Forks, ND, 58201. **EMAIL** danieric@badlands.nodak.edu

ERICKSON, GERALD M.
PERSONAL Born 09/23/1927, Amery, WI, m, 1951, 3 children **DISCIPLINE** CLASSICAL LANGUAGES **EDUCATION** Univ Minn, BS, 54, MA, 56, PhD (classics), 68. **CAREER** Teacher, Edina-Morningside Pub Schs, 56-65 and 66-67; vis lectr Latin, 65-66, asst prof Latin and Greek, 67-70, ASSOC PROF CLASSICS, UNIV MINN, MINNEAPOLIS, 70-, Consult classics, Am Coun Teaching Foreign Lang Annual Bibliog Foreign Lang Teaching, 69-; reader, Col Entrance Exam Bd, Advan Placement, 75-76, chief reader designate, 77, chief reader, 78. **MEMBERSHIPS** Am Class League; Class Asn Mid W and S; Am Philol Asn. **RESEARCH** Language teaching, methods and materials; madness and deviant behavior in Greece and Rome; computer based instruction for teaching vocabulary development, technical terminology and ancient Greek. **SELECTED PUBLICATIONS** Auth, Reading Classical Latin--The 2nd Year, Mod Lan J, Vol 77, 93. **CONTACT ADDRESS** Dept of Classics, Univ of Minn, 310 Folwell Hall, Minneapolis, MN, 55455.

ERICKSON, JOHN DAVID
PERSONAL Born 01/09/1934, Aitkin, MN, m, 1959, 2 children **DISCIPLINE** COMTEMPORARY FRENCH AND COMPARATIVE LITERATURE **EDUCATION** Univ Minn, BA, 58, MA, 61, PhD (French), 63; Harvard Univ, MA, 59. **CAREER** From instr to asst prof French and comp lit, Univ Iowa, 63-65; assoc prof French lit, Univ Kans, 65-70; vis prof French and Am lit, Mohammed V Univ, Morocco, 70-72; prof French lit, Univ Kans, 72-80; PROF AND CHMN FRENCH, LA STATE UNIV, 80-, Founder and cd, L'Esprit Createur, 61-; Fulbright lectr to Morocco, 70-72; vis prof Univ Damascus, 76; Adv bd, Oeuvres et critiques and French lit pubs Fulbright, 61, 70-72 and 81; Mellon fel, spring, 79; Nat Endowment for Humanities, summer, 79. **MEMBERSHIPS** MLA; Am Asn Teachers Fr; Asn Univ Teachers Gr Brit; Soc Fr Studies, Gt Brit; Soc Fr Prof Am. **RESEARCH** Contemporary literature; modern novel; modern criticism. **SELECTED PUBLICATIONS** Auth, Veiled Women and Veiled Narrative in Benjelloun, Tahar The Sandchild, Boundary 2 Int J Lit Cult, Vol 20, 93. **CONTACT ADDRESS** Dept of French and Italian, Louisiana State Univ, Baton Rouge, LA, 70808.

ERLICH, VICTOR
PERSONAL Born 11/22/1914, Petrograd, Russia, m, 1940, 2 children **DISCIPLINE** SLAVIC LANGUAGES AND LITERATURES **EDUCATION** Free Polish Univ, MA, 37; Columbia Univ, PhD, 51. **CAREER** Asst lit ed, New Life, Warsaw, 37-39; rcs writer, Yiddish Encycl, 42-43; from asst prof to prof Slavic Lang and lit, Univ Wash, 48-62; BENSINGER PROF RUSS LIT, YALE UNIV, 62-, Rockefeller fel, 49; Ford fel, 53-54; Fulbright lectr, 57-58; Guggenheim fel, 57-58, 64 and 76-77; Nat Endowment Humanities sr fel, 68-69. **HONORS AND AWARDS** MA, Yale Univ, 63. **MEMBERSHIPS** MLA; Am Asn Advan Slavic Studies (vpres, 73-77). **RESEARCH** Methodology of literary scholarship; modern Russian poetry; Soviet criticism **SELECTED PUBLICATIONS** Auth, Art and Reality, A Note on Babel, Issak Metaliterary Narratives, Can Slavonic Papers Revue Canadienne Slavistes, Vol 36, 94; Exploring Gogol, Slavic Rev, Vol 54, 95. **CONTACT ADDRESS** Dept of Slavic Lang and Lit, Yale Univ, New Haven, CT, 06520.

ERMOLAEV, HERMAN
PERSONAL Born 11/14/1924, Tomsk, Russia **DISCIPLINE** SOVIET AND RUSSIAN LITERATURE **EDUCATION** Stanford Univ, BA, 51; Univ Calif, Berkeley, MA, 54, PhD (Slavic lang and lit), 59. **CAREER** Instr Russ, Army Lang Sch, 55; from instr to assoc prof, Russ and Soviet lit, 59-70, McCosh fel, 67-68, Prof Russ and Soviet Lit, Princeton Univ, 70-. **MEMBERSHIPS** Am Asn Advan Slavic Studies; Am Asn Teachers Slavic and E Europ Lang (pres, 71-73); Asn Russ Am Scholars USA. **RESEARCH** Sholokhov; Soviet censorship; Solzhenitsyn. **SELECTED PUBLICATIONS** Auth, Barratt, Andrew Review of Gorki, Maxim Untimely Thoughts--A Comment, Slavic East Europ J, Vol 41, 97. **CONTACT ADDRESS** Dept of Slavic Lang and Lit, Princeton Univ, Princeton, NJ, 08540.

ERTL, WOLFGANG
PERSONAL Born 05/27/1946, Sangerhausen, Germany, m, 1969 **DISCIPLINE** GERMANIC LANGUAGES AND LITERATURE **EDUCATION** Univ Marburg, Ger, BA, 69; Univ NH, MA, 70; Univ Pa, PhD (Ger lang and lit), 75. **CAREER** Lectr, Univ Pa, 74-76; asst prof, Swarthmore Col, 76-77; ASST PROF GER, UNIV IOWA, 77-, Univ Iowa Old Gold summer fel, 79, 81 and 82. **MEMBERSHIPS** MLA; Am Asn Teachers Ger; Western Asn Ger Studies; Goethe Soc NAm; Int Brecht Soc. **RESEARCH** Twentieth century German literature; literature of the German Democratic Republic; modern poetry. **SELECTED PUBLICATIONS** Auth, Eichendorff Scholarly Reception--A Survey, Ger Stud Rev, Vol 20, 97; Sonnenhang Nachtspur, Ger Rev, Vol 70, 95; Poetic Process, Ger Stud Rev, Vol 20, 97. **CONTACT ADDRESS** Dept of Ger, Univ of Iowa, 103 Schaeffer Hall, Iowa City, IA, 52242-1409.

ESCOBAR, ANNA MARIA
DISCIPLINE SPANISH LITERATURE **EDUCATION** State Univ NY, MA; PhD, 86. **CAREER** Assoc prof, Univ Ill Urbana Champaign. **RESEARCH** Spanish variation; language contact theory; Andean sociolinguistics. **SELECTED PUBLICATIONS** Auth, Los bilingues y el castellano en el Peru, Inst de Estudios Peruanos, 90; Evidential uses in the Spanish of Quechua speakers in Peru, SW J Ling, 94; From time to modality in Spanish in Contact with Quechua, Hisp Ling, 97; Contrastive and innovative uses of the present perfect and the preterite in Spanish in contact with Quechua, Hispania, 97; co-auth, Practical Review of Spanish Grammar, Univ Ill, 98. **CONTACT ADDRESS** Spanish, Italian, and Portuguese Dept, Univ Ill Urbana Champaign, 52 E Gregory Dr, Champaign, IL, 61820. **EMAIL** aescobar@uiuc.edu

ESSIF, LES
DISCIPLINE FRENCH LITERATURE **EDUCATION** Brown Univ, PhD, 91. **CAREER** Asst prof. **RESEARCH** Dramatic and performance theories concerning contemporary French theatre; foreign language performance pedagogy; twentieth century critical theory. **SELECTED PUBLICATIONS** Auth, pubs on semiotics of theatrical space in post 1950 theatre. **CONTACT ADDRESS** Dept of Romance Languages, Knoxville, TN, 37996.

ESTEVEZ, VICTOR A.
PERSONAL Born 08/23/1938, Jersey City, NJ, d, 2 children **DISCIPLINE** CLASSICAL STUDIES **EDUCATION** Fordham Univ at Shrub Oak, BA, 63; Fordham Prep Sch in Bronx, MA, 65; Wis Univ, PhD, 74. **CAREER** Assoc prof; Univ Mo, 75-; past dir, Undergrad Stud; dir, TA's and the elementary Latin prog; written 3 crs, Univ Independent Study; comt & panels, Status of Women, Acad Appeals, Minority Aff, Student Publ, Curric, Campus Writing Bd, Univ Grievance Panel; adv, Gay and Lesbian Alliance; 2 yrs, Columbia Human Rights Comn, on bd dir, Commun Nurseries Inc, KOPN, The Mid-Mis souri AIDS Proj, Gay/Lesbian Telephone Helpline, Columbia Cares: Fundraising for AIDS in Mid-Missouri, the Missouri Task Force for Lesbian and Gay Concerns, ch 1 yr & Nat Gay and Lesbian Task Force; fac, Fordham Prep Sch in Bronx, 63-66; fac, Catholic Univ, Wash, 66-68; full-time fac, Howard & part-time,Trinity Co, 68-69; assoc dir, Carnegie Data Bank Proj, Nat Catholic Educ Asn, 69-70; full-time fac, Univ Houston & part-time, Rice Univ, 74; tenured in, 81; vis prof, Leicester Univ, UK, 85-86. **HONORS AND AWARDS** Laus publica & cash prize, Certamen Capitolinum XXIV, 74; distinguised crse awd, Nat Univ Cont Educ Asn; Mid-Mo Chap, ACLU, Civil Libertarian Yr awd, 93. **RESEARCH** Hellenistic poetry; Augustan poetry. **SELECTED PUBLICATIONS** Auth, Chloe and the Fawn: The Structure of Odes I 23, Helios 7, 79-80; Aeneid II and the Helen and Venus Episodes, Classical J 76, 81; Quem tu, Melpomene: The Poet's Lowered Voice C. IV 3, Emer 50, 82; Oculos ad moenia torsit: On Aeneid 4. 220, Class Philol 77, 82 & Oratio Panegyrica in Fridericum Rudolphum Solmsen. **CONTACT ADDRESS** Dept of Classical Studies, Univ of Missouri-Columbia, 309 University Hall, Columbia, MO, 65211. **EMAIL** clstudve@showme.missouri.edu

ETZKORN, GIRARD J.
PERSONAL Born 09/18/1927, Kirkwood, MO **DISCIPLINE** PHILOSOPHY, FRENCH **EDUCATION** Quincy Col, BA, 53; St Joseph Sem, Ill, STB, 57; Cath Univ Louvain, PhD (philos), 61. **CAREER** From instr to assoc prof philosophy, Quincy Col, 61-71; assoc prof, Southern Ill Univ, CArbondale, 71-72; RES PROF CRITICAL ED OF WILLIAM OCKHAM, FRANCISCAN INST, 73-, Am Philos Soc grant, 65-66. **MEMBERSHIPS** Int Soc Study Medieval Philos; Am Philos Asn; AAUP. **RESEARCH** Critical editions of medieval manuscripts; French and German phenomenology and existentialism; translating of French philosopher Michel Henry. **SELECTED PUBLICATIONS** Auth, William De La Mare, Scriptum in Secundum Librum Sententiarum, Speculum J Medieval Stud, Vol 72, 97; Bonaventure Sermons de Diversis, Speculum J Medieval Stud, Vol 70, 95. **CONTACT ADDRESS** Franciscan Inst, St Bonaventure, NY, 14778.

EVANS, HARRY B.
DISCIPLINE LATIN POETRY, ROMAN TOPOGRAPHY **EDUCATION** NC Univ, PhD. **CAREER** Prof, Fordham Univ. **SELECTED PUBLICATIONS** Auth, Publica Carmina: Ovid's Books from Exile, 83; Water Distribution in Ancient Rome: The Evidence of Frontinus, 94. **CONTACT ADDRESS** Dept of Class Lang and Lit, Fordham Univ, 113 W 60th St, New York, NY, 10023.

EVANS, MARTHA NOEL
PERSONAL Born 02/21/1939, Philadelphia, PA, m, 1964, 2 children **DISCIPLINE** FRENCH LITERATURE **EDUCATION** Wellesley Col, BA, 60; Yale Univ, PhD (Fr lang and Lit), 67. **CAREER** Instr French, Peace Corps, 62 and 63;; from instr to asst prof, 65-69, asst prof, 74-76, ASSOC PROF FRENCH, MARY BALDWIN COL, 76-. **MEMBERSHIPS** AAUP; Am Asn Teachers Fr; SAtlantic Mod Lang Asn. **RESEARCH** Pre-romantic French literature; nineteenth-century French novel; psychoanalysis, Lacan. **SELECTED PUBLICATIONS** Auth, Incriminations--Guilty Women Telling Stories, Mod Philol, Vol 94, 97; Incriminations--Guilty Women Telling Stories, Mod Philol, Vol 94, 97. **CONTACT ADDRESS** Dept of French, Mary Baldwin Col, Staunton, VA, 24401.

EXNER, RICHARD
PERSONAL Born 05/13/1929, Niedersachswerfen, Germany, m, 1955, 2 children **DISCIPLINE** GERMAN AND COMPARATIVE LITERATURE **EDUCATION** Univ Southern Calif, AB, 51, PhD (Ger), 57. **CAREER** Instr Ger, Univ Rochester, 55-56; from instr to asst prof, Princeton Univ, 56-60; assoc prof, Oberlin Col, 60-65, PROF GER, UNIV CALIF, SANTA BARBARA, 65-, Fulbright sr res award and Guggenheim fel, 67-68; vis prof humanities, Mass Inst Technol, 69-70; MEM COMT ADVAN PLACEMENT IN GER, COL ENTRANCE EXAM BD, 72-, chief reader Ger lit, 76-77; vis prof Ger lit, Stanford Univ, 73-74; mem, Bavarian Acad Fine Arts, 79; vis prof, Univ de Nice, 80. **MEMBERSHIPS** Am Coun Studies Austrian Lit (vpres, 72-); MLA; Inst Compt Lit Asn; Thomas Mann Ges; Am Literary Translr Asn. **RESEARCH** Lyric poetry; German and comparative literature of the 19th and 20th centuries. **SELECTED PUBLICATIONS** Auth, High Time, Lit Rev, Vol 37, 94; Mann, Thomas Diaries, 1949-1950, World Literature Today, Vol 67, 93; Amost a Conversation, Kenyon Review, Vol 18, 96; Born, Lit Rev, Vol 36, 93; The Magician, A Life of the German Writer Mann, Thomas, Vol 2, Years of Suspense, 1919 and 1933, World Literature Today, Vol 67, 93; Mann, Thomas, Diaries 1953-1955, World Lit Today, Vol 71, 97; Mann, Thomas--A Biography, World Lit Today, Vol 70, 96; The Onset of Winter, Lit Rev, Vol 36, 93; Our Time, Kenyon Rev, Vol 18, 96; Mann, Thomas, Meyer, Agnes, E., Correspondence 1937-1955, World Lit Today, Vol 68, 94. **CONTACT ADDRESS** Dept of Ger and Slavic Lang, Univ of Calif, Santa Barbara, CA, 93106.

EYKMAN, CHRISTOPH WOLFGANG
PERSONAL Born 12/06/1937, Frankfurt, Germany **DISCIPLINE** GERMAN LITERATURE **EDUCATION** Univ Bonn, PhD, 64. **CAREER** Asst prof Ger, Antioch Col, 64-68; asst prof, 68-72, Assoc Prof Ger, 72-82, prof Ger, Boston Col, 82. **MEMBERSHIPS** MLA. **RESEARCH** Comp lit; 20th century Ger lit; theory of lit. **SELECTED PUBLICATIONS** Auth, Die Funktion des Hasslichen in der Lyrik G Heyms, G Trakls und G Benns, Bouvier, Bonn, 65; Der Verlust der Geschichte in der Deutschen Literatur des 20 Jahrhunderts, Neophilologus, 70; Geschichtspessimismus in der Deutschen Literatur des 20, Jahrhunderts, Francke, Berne, 70; Zur Sozialphilosophie des deutschen Expressionismus, Z Deut Philol, 72; Denk-und Stilformen des Deutschen Expressionismus, Francke, Berne, 73; Phanomenologie der Interpretation, Francke, Berne, Munich, 77; Schreiben als Erfahrung, Bouvier, Bonn, 85; Der Intellektuelle in der Westeuropaischen und Amerikanischen Romanliteratur ab 1945, hitzeroth, Marburg, 92; Asthetische Erfahrung in der Lebenswelt des Westeuropaischen und Amerikanischen Romans, Francke, Tubingen and Basel, 97; numerous articles on German and Austrian Exile Literature. **CONTACT ADDRESS** Dept of Ger Studies, Boston Col, 140 Commonwealth Ave, Chestnut Hill, MA, 02167-3800.

F

FABIAN, HANS JOACHIM
PERSONAL Born 08/01/1926, Elbing, Germany, m, 1951, 2 children **DISCIPLINE** GERMAN **EDUCATION** Syracuse Univ, BA, 50, MA, 52, MSLS, 54; Ohio State Univ, PhD (Ger lit), 63. **CAREER** Dir libr, Wilmington Col, 54-61; asst Ger, Ohio State Univ, 61-62, asst prof libr admin, 63-64; instr Ger, Ohio Univ, 62-63; dir jr year abroad, 68-69, ASST PROF GER, UNIV MICH, ANN ARBOR, 64-, Rackham fel, 67. **MEMBERSHIPS** Am Asn Teachers Ger; MLA. **RESEARCH** German expressionism; Georg Kaiser. **SELECTED PUBLICATIONS** Auth, Eine Halbtagsstelle in Pompeji, World Lit Today, Vol 68, 94; Kolberg, Hist J Film Radio TV Vol 14, 94; Tree, Rock, Concrete--Journey Between Heaven and Hell, World Lit Today, Vol 70, 96; Herr Paul, World Lit Today, Vol 68, 94; Der Gesandte, World Lit Today, Vol 66, 92; Die Satellitenstadt, World Lit Today, Vol 67, 93. **CONTACT ADDRESS** Dept of Ger, Univ Mich, Ann Arbor, MI, 48104.

FAGLES, ROBERT
PERSONAL Born 09/11/1933, Philadelphia, PA, m, 1956, 2 children **DISCIPLINE** COMPARATIVE LITERATURE, ENGLISH **EDUCATION** Amherst Col, AB, 55; Yale Univ, MA, 56, PhD (English), 59. **CAREER** Instr English, Yale Univ, 59-

60; from instr to asst prof, 60-65, assoc prof English and comp lit, 65-70, dir prog comp lit, 65-76, PROF ENGLISH and COMPLIT, PRINCETON UNIV, 70-. **RESEARCH** The epic tradition; Greek tragedy; Greek, Latin and English lyric poetry. **SELECTED PUBLICATIONS** Auth, Rain, Steam, and Speed, Sewanee Rev, Vol 101, 93; The Pair Oared Shell, Sewanee Rev, Vol 101, 93. **CONTACT ADDRESS** Dept of English and Comp Lit, Princeton Univ, Princeton, NJ, 08540.

FAGUNDO, ANA MARIA
PERSONAL Born 03/13/1938, Santa Cruz de Tenerife, Spain **DISCIPLINE** COMPARATIVE LITERATURE, SPANISH AND ENGLISH LITERATURE **EDUCATION** Univ Redlands, BA, 62; Univ Wash, MA, 64, PhD (comp lit), 67. **CAREER** Asst prof Span lit, 67-76, ASSOC PROF CONTEMP SPAN LIT, UNIV CALIF, RIVERSIDE, 76-, Ed-in-Chief, Alaluz. **HONORS AND AWARDS** Carabela de Oro poetry prize. **MEMBERSHIPS** Am Asn Teachers Span and Port; Sociedad Colegial de Escritores. **RESEARCH** Contemporary Spanish poetry; contemporary American poetry. **SELECTED PUBLICATIONS** Auth, Cantico or a Tribute to Mother, Insula Revista De Letras Y Ciencias Humanas, Vol 48, 93. **CONTACT ADDRESS** Dept of Span, Univ Calif, Riverside, CA, 92502.

FAIGLEY, LESTER
PERSONAL Charleston, WV, m, 1969, 2 children **DISCIPLINE** ENGLISH; LINGUISTICS **EDUCATION** Univ Wash, PhD, 76. **CAREER** Prof English, Univ Tex at Austin, 79-; Dir, Div of Rhet & Composition. **HONORS AND AWARDS** MLA Mina P Shaughnessy Prize, 92; Conf of Col Composition & Commun Outstanding Book Award, 94. **MEMBERSHIPS** Conf of Col Composition & Commun; Modern Language Asn; Rhet Soc of Am. **RESEARCH** Rhetorical theory; impacts of technology on writing; visual rhetoric. **SELECTED PUBLICATIONS** Auth, Fragments of Rationality: Postmodernity and the Subject of Composition, Univ Pittsburgh Press, 92; auth, Yours for the Revolution (probably Pepsi, but never mind), J of Adv Composition, 14, 593-596, 94; co-auth, Going Electric: Creating Multiple Site for Innovation in a Writing Program, Resituating Writing: Constructing and Administering Writing Programs, Boynton/Cook, 46-58, 95; co-auth, Discursive Strategies for Social Change: An Alternative Rhetoric of Argument, Rhet Rev, 14, 142-72; 95; auth, Literacy After the Revolution, Col Composition & Commun, 48, 30-43, 97. **CONTACT ADDRESS** Div of Rhet & Composition, Univ Tex at Austin, Austin, TX, 78712-1122. **EMAIL** faigley@uts.cc.utexas.edu

FAIRLEY, IRENE R.
PERSONAL Born 01/02/1940, Brooklyn, NY **DISCIPLINE** LINGUISTICS, ENGLISH **EDUCATION** Queens Col, NY, AB, 60; Harvard Univ, MA, 61, PhD (ling), 71. **CAREER** From instr to asst prof English, C W Post Col, Long Island Univ, 68-73; asst prof English and ling, 73-76, ASSOC PROF ENGLISH, NORTHEASTERN UNIV, 76-, Am Coun Learned Soc grant-in-aid, 77-78; Guggenheim fel, 79-80. **MEMBERSHIPS** Ling Soc Am; MLA; Semiotic Soc Am; Millay Colony for Arts. **RESEARCH** Linguistic approaches to literature, stylistics, poetics. **SELECTED PUBLICATIONS** Auth, Millay, Edna, Stvincent Gendered Language and Form, Sonnets from an Ungrafted Tree, Style, Vol 29, 95. **CONTACT ADDRESS** 34 Winn St, Belmont, MA, 02178.

FALK, JULIA SABLESKI
PERSONAL Born 09/21/1941, Englewood, NJ, m, 1967, 1 child **DISCIPLINE** LINGUISTICS **EDUCATION** Georgetown Univ, BS, 63; Univ WA, MA, 64, PhD, 68. **CAREER** From instr to assoc prof, 66-78, Prof Ling, MI tate Univ, 78-, Assoc Dean Col Arts & Lett, 79-86, Sr researcher educ, Inst Res on Teaching, 76-77; vis prof, Univ Hong Kong, 95. **HONORS AND AWARDS** Woodrow Wilson fel, 63; Nat Defense Educ Act Title IV fel, 63-66; Nat Sci Found fel, 65; MI State Univ Paul Varg Alumni Award, 93. **MEMBERSHIPS** Ling Soc Am; North Am Assoc Hist Lang. **RESEARCH** Hist of linguistics; linguistics and educ. **SELECTED PUBLICATIONS** Auth, Equational clauses in Bengali, Language, 65; A Generative Phonology of a Spanish Dialect, 65 & Nominalizations in Spanish, 68, Univ Wash; auth, Linguistics and Language, Wiley, 1st ed, 73, 2nd ed, 78; Language and linguistics: Bases for a curriculum, In: Language in Education, Ctr Appl Ling, 78; Lang acquisition and the teaching and learning of writing, Col English, 79; coauth, Speaking Black English and reading, J Negro Educ, 82; Otto Jespersen, Leonard Bloomfield, and American Strucal Linguistics, Language, 92; To Be Human: A History of the Study of Language, In: Language: Readings in Language and Culture, St Martins Press, 5th ed, 94, 6th ed, 95; co-auth, The Saleski Family and the Founding of the LSA Linguistics Institutes, Historiographia Linguistica, 94; The Women Foundation Members of the Linguistic Society of America, Language 94; Portraits of Women Linguistics: Louise Pound, Edith Claflin, Adelaide Hahn, In: History of Linguistics 1993: Papers from the Sixth International Conference on the History of the Language Sciences, John Benjamins Publ, 95; Roman Jakobson and the History of Saussurean Concepts in North American Linguistics, Historiographia Linguistica, 95; Words without Grammar: Linguists and the International Auxiliary Language Movement in the United States, Lang & Commun, 95; co-auth, Further Notes on Reinhold E Saleski, Historiographia Linguistica, 96; Territoriality, Relationships, and Reputation: The Case of Gladys A Reichard, Southwest Jour Ling, 97; The American Shift from Historical to Non-Historical Linguistics, Language and Commun, 98. **CONTACT ADDRESS** Dept of Ling, Michigan State Univ, A615 Wells Hall, East Lansing, MI, 48824-1027. **EMAIL** jsfalk@pilot.msu.edu

FALKNER, THOMAS M.
DISCIPLINE GREEK AND LATIN LITERATURE **EDUCATION** LeMoyne Univ, AB, 69; SUNY, MA, 71, PhD, 75. **CAREER** Vis scholar Cambridge Univ, 96-97; prof; ch-. **HONORS AND AWARDS** Six different grants, NEH; fel in residence., Dit, Wooster-in-Greece prog, 84. **SELECTED PUBLICATIONS** Co-ed, Old Age in Greek and Latin Literature; auth, Euripides' Orestes, The Poetics of Old Age in Greek Epic, Lyric, and Tragedy; articles on Greek and Latin poetry, articles on Sophoclean tragedy. **CONTACT ADDRESS** Dept of Classics, Col of Wooster, Wooster, OH, 44691. **EMAIL** tfalkner@acs.wooster.edu

FALLON, JEAN
DISCIPLINE 16TH CENTURY FRENCH LITERATURE, 19TH CENTURY POETRY **EDUCATION** Univ VA, PhD. **CAREER** Instr, Hollins Col, 90. **RESEARCH** French lyric poets of the 16th century. **SELECTED PUBLICATIONS** Auth, Voice and Vision in Ronsard's Les Sonnets pour Helene. **CONTACT ADDRESS** Hollins Col, Roanoke, VA, 24020.

FANGER, DONALD LEE
PERSONAL Born 12/06/1929, Cleveland, OH, m, 1955, 3 children **DISCIPLINE** RUSSIAN & COMPARATIVE LITERATURE **EDUCATION** Univ CA, Berkeley, BA, 51, MA, 54; Harvard Univ, PhD, 62. **CAREER** Instr Russ lang & lit, Brown Univ, 60-62; from asst prof to assoc prof Russ lang & lit & dir Slavic Div, Stanford Univ, 66-68; chmn slavic dept, 73-82, Prof Slavic & Comp Lit, Harvard Univ, 68-98, Harry Levin Research Prof of Lit, 98-, Mem nat adv comt, Inter-Univ Comt Travel Grants, 67-68; Am Coun Learned Soc res grant, 68-69; mem prog comt, Int Res & Exchanges Bd, 69-73; Guggenheim fel, 75-76; fel, Am Acad Arts & Sci, 80-; res fel, Rockefeller Found Ctr Advan Study, Bellagio, summer 81. **HONORS AND AWARDS** Christian Gauss Award, Phi Beta Kappa, 80. **MEMBERSHIPS** MLA; Am Asn Tchr(s) Slavic & East Europ Lang; Am Comp Lit Asn, Am Acad of Arts & Sci. **RESEARCH** Develop of the Russ novel. **SELECTED PUBLICATIONS** Auth, Dostoevsky today, Survey, 4/61; Romanticism and comparative literature, Comp Lit, spring 62; ed, Brown Univ Slavic Reprint Series, 61-66; auth, Dostoevsky and Romantic Realism, Harvard Univ, 65 & Univ Chicago, 67; The Peasant in 19th Century Russia, Stanford Univ, 68; The Creation of Nikolai Gogol, Harvard Univ, 79. **CONTACT ADDRESS** Dept of Slavic Lang & Lit, Harvard Univ, Boylston Hall, Cambridge, MA, 02138-3800. **EMAIL** fanger@fas.harvard.edu

FANT, J. CLAYTON
DISCIPLINE CLASSICAL STUDIES **EDUCATION** Williams Coll, BA, 69; Univ of Mich, PhD, 76. **CAREER** Asst Prof, 76-79, Wellesley Coll; Instr, 79-81, St Stephen's School Rome; vis Asst Prof, 81-83, Univ of Mich; Asst Prof, Assoc Prof, 84-, Univ of Akron. **HONORS AND AWARDS** Amer Acad Rome Fel. **MEMBERSHIPS** AIA, APA, ASMOSIA, Vergilian Society. **RESEARCH** Roman Archaeology **SELECTED PUBLICATIONS** Auth, Cavum Antrum Phrygiae, The Organization and Operations of the Roman Imperial Marble Quarries at Docimium, BAR Intl Series, 89; Ancient Marble Quarrying and Trade, BAR Intl Series, 88; Ideology Gift and Trade, A Distribution Model for the Roman Imperial Marbles, in: The Inscribed Economy, Production and Distribution in the Roman Empire in the Light of Instrumentum Domesticum, ed W V Harris & S Panciera, JRA, 93; The Imperial Marble Yard at Portus, in: Ancient Stones, Quarrying Trade and Provenance. Interdisciplinary Studies on Stones and Stone Technology in Europe and Near East from the Prehistoric to the Early Christian Period, ed, M Waelkens, N Herz & L Moens, 92. **CONTACT ADDRESS** Dept of Classics, Univ of Akron, 326 Olin, Akron, OH, 44325-1910. **EMAIL** cfant@uakron.edu

FARBER, GERALD HOWARD
PERSONAL Born 03/21/1935, El Paso, TX, m, 1967, 4 children **DISCIPLINE** COMPARATIVE LITERATURE, ENGLISH & AMERICAN LITERATURE **EDUCATION** Univ CA, Los Angeles, BA, 58; CA State Univ, Los Angeles, MA, 62; Occidental Col, PhD, 70. **CAREER** Lectr English, 62-65, asst prof, CA State Univ, Los Angeles, 66-68; from lectr to asst prof, 68-74, assoc prof, 74-81, PROF COMP LIT, SAN DIEGO STATE UNIV, 81-; Maitre assistant associe, 74 & maitre de conferences associe, 77, Univ Paris VII. **RESEARCH** Aesthetics; the teaching of literature; comedy; eighteenth-century European lit; Marcel Proust. **SELECTED PUBLICATIONS** Auth, The Student as Nigger, 70 & The University of Tomorrowland, 72, Simon & Schuster; A Field Guide to the Aesthetic Experience, Foreworks Press, 82; The Third Circle: On Education and Distance Learning, Sociological Perspectives, vol 41, no 4, 98; Aesthetic Resonance: Beyond the Sign in Literature, Reader: Essays in Reader-Oriented Theory, Criticism, and Pedagogy, no 32, fall, 94; Golden Grove Unweaving (and not a moment too soon), Fiction International, no 27, 94; Learning How To Teach: A Progress Report, College English, vol 52, no 2, Feb 90. **CONTACT ADDRESS** Dept of English and Comp Lit, San Diego State Univ, San Diego, CA, 92182-8140. **EMAIL** jfarber@mail.sdsu.edu

FARBER, JAY JOEL
PERSONAL Born 11/06/1932, Philadelphia, PA, m, 1952, 2 children **DISCIPLINE** CLASSICAL LANGUAGES AND LITERATURES **EDUCATION** Univ Chicago, BA, 52, MA, 54; Yale Univ, PhD (Greek and ancient hist), 59. **CAREER** Instr classics, Univ Chicago, 57-60; asst prof, Rutgers Univ, 60-63; assoc prof, 63-70, chmn dept, 63-79, PROF CLASSICS, FRANKLIN AND MARSHALL COL, 70-, Rutgers Univ Res Coun grants, 61 and 62; vis res assoc, Ctr Int Studies, Princeton Univ, 62-63; examnr, comt advan placement classics, Col Entrance Exam Bd, 71-74. **MEMBERSHIPS** Am Philol Asn; Am Soc Papyrologists; Class Asn Atlantic States. **RESEARCH** Greek myth; Greek tragedy; Greek political theory. **SELECTED PUBLICATIONS** Auth, The Documents from the Bar Kokhba Period in the Cave of Letters--Greek Papyri, Aramaic and Nabatean Signatures and Subscriptions, J Am Orient Soc, Vol 115, 95; Ancient Greek Alive, Classical World, Vol 89, 96. **CONTACT ADDRESS** Dept of Classics, Franklin and Marshall Col, Lancaster, PA, 17604.

FARINA, LUCIANO FERNANDO
PERSONAL Born 01/03/1943, Milan, Italy, m, 1982 **DISCIPLINE** ITALIAN, COMPUTATIONAL LINGUISTICS **EDUCATION** Catholic Univ, BST, 70; Ohio State Univ, MA, 72, PhD (Romance Ling), 77. **CAREER** Teach asst, 70-76, instr, 76-77, ASST PROF ITAL, OHIO STATE UNIV, 77- AND DIR ITAL LANG PROG, 76-, RES DIR COMPUTER APPLN ITAL, INSTRUCT AND RES COMPUTER CTR, OHIO STATE UNIV, 75-, DIR INDIVIDUALIZED LANG INSTR, 77-; res guest, Vocabolario Dialetti Svizzera Italiana, Lugano, Switz, summer 76 and consult, 79; consult, Archivio Storico Ticinese, Bellinzona, Switzerland, 80, ASSESSORATO CULT, REGIONE LOMBARDIA, MILANO, ITALY, 80 AND PYRAMID SERV CORP, COLUMBUS, OHIO, 80-. **MEMBERSHIPS** Asn Comput Ling; Asn Ling and Lit Comput; Soc Ling Ital; MLA; Am Asn Applied Ling. **RESEARCH** Lexicography; dialectology; pedagogy. **SELECTED PUBLICATIONS** Auth, Bravo,Italian Grammar for Foreigners--Course In Italian Language And Civilization, Mod Lang J, Vol 77, 93. **CONTACT ADDRESS** Dept Romance Lang, Ohio State Univ, 1841 Millikin Rd, Columbus, OH, 43210-1229.

FARKAS, DONKA F.
DISCIPLINE ROMANCE LANGUAGES **EDUCATION** Univ Bucharest, Romania, BA; Univ Chicago, PhD, 81. **CAREER** PROF, LANG, UNIV CALIF, SANTA CRUZ. **RESEARCH** Semantics of complementation, quantifier scope and modality. **SELECTED PUBLICATIONS** Auth, Intensional Descriptions and the Romance Subjunctive Mood, Garland Publ, 85; On Obligatory Control, Ling and Philos, 88; Two Cases of Underspecification in Morphology, Ling Inquiry, 90; On the Semantics of Subjunctive Complements, Romance Lang and Mod Ling Theory, John Benjamins Publ, 92. **CONTACT ADDRESS** Dept of Ling, Univ Calif, 1156 High St, Santa Cruz, CA, 95064.

FARNHAM, ANTHONY EDWARD
PERSONAL Born 07/02/1930, Oakland, CA, m, 1957, 2 children **DISCIPLINE** ENGLISH, PHILOLOGY **EDUCATION** Univ Calif, Berkeley, AB, 51; Harvard Univ, MA, 57, PhD(English), 64. **CAREER** From instr to assoc prof, 61-72, PROF ENGLISH, MT HOLYOKE COL, 72-, Vis asst prof, Amherst Col, 64-65; lectr, Smith Col, 65-66; vis asst prof, Univ Calif, Berkeley, 66-67. **MEMBERSHIPS** Mediaeval Acad Am; MLA; Am Cath Hist Asn; Asn Literary Scholars & Critics; Dante Soc Am; New Chaucer Soc; Phi Beta Kappa **RESEARCH** Old and Middle English language and literature; history of the English language. **SELECTED PUBLICATIONS** Ed, A Sourcebook in the History of English, Holt, Rinehart & Winston, 69; auth, Statement and Search in the Confessio Amantis, Mediaevalia, 93. **CONTACT ADDRESS** Dept of English, Mount Holyoke Col, 50 College St, South Hadley, MA, 01075-1461.

FAULHABER, CHARLES BAILEY
PERSONAL Born 09/18/1941, East Cleveland, OH, m, 1971 **DISCIPLINE** MEDIEVAL SPANISH LITERATURE **EDUCATION** Yale Univ, BA, 63, MPhil & PhD, 69; Univ WI-Madison, MA, 66. **CAREER** Actg instr Span, Yale Univ, 68-69; from Asst Prof to Assoc Prof, 69-80, Prof Span, Univ CA, Berkeley, 80-, Chmn, Dept Span & Port, 89-94, James D. Hart Dir, The Bancroft Libr, 95-; ed, The Romance Philol, 82-, ed-in-chief, 86-87; assoc ed, Hispania, 95-98. **HONORS AND AWARDS** Prin investr, Hispanic Soc Am, Nat Endowment for Hum, 76 & 78-80; Guggenheim fel, 82-83; mem, Hisp Soc Am, 83; Ministerio de Asuntos Exteriores de Espana, beca de investigacion, 89, 95; NEH grants, 89-91, 91-93, 94-95; Quincentenary Postdoctoral Fel, Spain, 91. **MEMBERSHIPS** MLA; Assoc Int Hispanistas; Medieval Acad Am; Am Acad Res Hist Medieval Spain; Am Asn Tchr(s) Span & Port; AAUP; Asn

Hisp Lit Medieval; Asn Computers and the Hum; Medieval Asn Pacific. **RESEARCH** Medieval rhetoric; computers and hum. **SELECTED PUBLICATIONS** Coauth, Normas para BOOST, Hisp Seminary of Medieval Studies, Ltd, 86; auth, Libros y bibliotecas en la Espana medieval. Una bibliografia de fuentes impresas, Research Bibliographies and Checklists, Grant & Cutler, 87; Medieval Manuscripts in the Library of the Hispanic Society of America. Documents and Letters, The Hisp Soc Am, 93; Necrology: Ruth House Webber (1918-1997), La Coronica 25.2, 97; Sobre la cultura ibrica medieval: Las lenguas vern culas y la traduccion, Actas del VI Congreso Internacional de la Asociacion Hisp nica de Literatura Medieval, Univ Alcal , 97; author numerous other articles and publ. **CONTACT ADDRESS** The Bancroft Library, Univ of California, Berkeley, CA, 94720-6000. **EMAIL** cfaulhab@library.berkeley.edu

FAUROT, JEANNETTE L.

PERSONAL Born 03/01/1943, St. Lambert, PQ, Canada **DISCIPLINE** CHINESE LITERATURE, CHINESE LANGUAGE **EDUCATION** Harvard Univ, BA, 64; Univ Calif, Berkeley, MA, 67, PhD, 72. **CAREER** From instr to asst prof, 71-77, Assoc Prof Chinese, 77-92, prof Chinese, Univ TX Austin, 92. **MEMBERSHIPS** Asn Asian Studies; Chinese Lang Teachers Asn; Southwest Conf Asian Studies. **RESEARCH** Mod Chinese fiction; early Chinese thought; Tang and Sung poetry. **SELECTED PUBLICATIONS** Ed, Chinese Fiction From Taiwan: Critical Perspectives, Indiana Univ Press, 80; Ancient Chengdu, Chinese Materials Center, 92; Gateway to the Chinese Classics, China Books & Periodicals, 95; Asian-Pacific Folktales and Legends, Touchstone, 95. **CONTACT ADDRESS** Dept of Asian Studies, Univ of Texas, Austin, TX, 78712-1026.

FEAL, CARLOS

PERSONAL Born 03/06/1935, La Coruna, Spain **DISCIPLINE** ROMANCE LANGUAGES, SPANISH **EDUCATION** Univ Madrid, PhD(Romance lang), 63. **CAREER** Lectr Span, Univ Lyon, 60-61 & Univ Nantes, 63-66; asst prof, Univ Mich, Ann Arbor, 66-69; assoc prof, 69-75, prof Span, State Univ NY Buffalo, 75-, fac res fels, Univ Mich, 69 & State Univ NY, 70, 74 & 79. **MEMBERSHIPS** MLA; Am Asn Teachers Span & Port. **RESEARCH** Modern Spanish literature; Golden Age Drama. **SELECTED PUBLICATIONS** Auth, La poesia de Pedro Salinas, Gredos, Madrid, 65; Eros y Lorca, Edhasa, Barcelona, 73; coauth, Unamuno: El Otro y Don Juan, Planeta, Madrid, 76; Honory adulterio en Realidad, Anales Galdosianos, 77; Conflicting Names, Conflicting Laws: Zorrila's Don Juan Tenorio, Pac Mod Lang Asn, 5/81; Vivir en los pronombres: Sobre el amor en Pedro Salinas, Journal of Hispanic Research, 2/93-94; coauth Painting on the Page: Interartistic Approaches to Modern Hispanic Texts, SUNY Press, Albany, 95. **CONTACT ADDRESS** Dept of Mod Lang & Lit, SUNY, Buffalo, PO Box 604620, Buffalo, NY, 14260-4620.

FEAL, GISELE C.

PERSONAL Born 07/05/1939, Froges, France, 2 children **DISCIPLINE** SPANISH, FRENCH **EDUCATION** Univ Grenoble, France, Lic es Lett, 62; Sorbonne, Agreg l'Univ, 65; Unich Mich, PhD(French), 72. **CAREER** Prof Span, Nantes, France, 65-66; asst prof French, Eastern Mich Univ, 67-68; lectr French, Univ Mich, 68-69; Prof French & Span, State Univ Col Buffalo, 73-, Dir, NY State Span Hon Soc; fel, Res Found, State Univ NY. **MEMBERSHIPS** MLA; Am Asn Teachers Fr; Am Asn Teachers Span. **RESEARCH** Psychoanalytically oriented criticism of Spanish and French literature. **SELECTED PUBLICATIONS** Auth, La Mythologie matriarcale chez Claudel, Montherlant, Gommelyuck, Ionesco et Genet, Peter Lang, New York, 93; Le Theatre onirique d'Eugene Ionesco, Un itineraire psychologique (in press). **CONTACT ADDRESS** Dept of Foreign Lang, SUNY, Buffalo, 1300 Elmwood Ave, Buffalo, NY, 14222-1095. **EMAIL** Fealgc@snybufaa.cs.snybuf.ede

FEAL, ROSEMARY GEISDORFER

PERSONAL Born 09/07/1955, NY **DISCIPLINE** SPANISH **EDUCATION** Instituto Belga Guatemalteco, Bachillerato en Letras, 72; Univ Paul Valery, Diplome d'Etudes Francaises, 76; Allegheny Col, BA (magna cum laude), 77; State Univ of NY at Buffalo, PhD (with distinction), 84. **CAREER** Lectr, Canisius Col, 82-86; Mellon Postdoctoral Tchg Fel, 86-87, asst prof of Spanish, 87-90, assoc Prof of Spanish, 90-96, prof of Spanish, 96-98, Fac Assoc, Inst for Res and Ed on Women and Gender, Univ of Rochester, 99-. **HONORS AND AWARDS** Grad School Fel, 80, Excellence in Tchg Awd, Univ at Buffalo, 80; Mellon postdoctoral Fel, 86-87, Bridging Fel with Art Hist, 89, Outstanding Woman Awd, Univ of Rochester, 98; grant for publication, Ministerio de Cultura, 94; resident fel, Humanities Inst, Univ at Stony Brook, 97. **MEMBERSHIPS** MLA; Feministas Unidas; Asociacion Internacional de Hispanistas; Asociacion de Literatura Hispanica Femenina; Latin Am Studies Asn; Afro-Latin Am Res Asn. **RESEARCH** Latin American Lit with specialization in: Afro-Hispanic Lit; contemporary novel; women's writing; autobiographical studies; feminist theory; queer theory. **SELECTED PUBLICATIONS** Auth, Novel Lives: The Fictional Autobiographies of Guillermo Cabrera Infante and Mario Vargas Llosa, Univ of NC Studies in the Romance Languages and Lits, 86; The Double Bind: Feminism and Afro-Hispanism, Afro-Hispanic Rev, 91; Feminist Interventions in the Race for Theory: Neither Black Nor White, Afro-Hispanic Rev, 91; Latin American Feminist Criticism and the Realm of the Real, Letras Femeninas, 94; coauth, Painting on the Page: Interartistic Approaches to Modern Hispanic Texts, State Univ of NY Press, 95. **CONTACT ADDRESS** Dept of Modern Lang and Lit, SUNY, Buffalo, 910 Clemens Hall, Buffalo, NY, 14260. **EMAIL** feal@acsu.buffalo.edu

FEDERMAN, RAYMOND

PERSONAL Born 05/15/1928, Paris, France, m, 1960, 1 child **DISCIPLINE** ENGLISH, COMPARATIVE LITERATURE **EDUCATION** Columbia Univ, BS, 57; Univ Calif, MA, 59, PhD, 63. **CAREER** Tchg asst French, Univ CA, Los Angeles, 57-59; lectr, Univ CA, Santa Barbara, 59-62, asst prof, 62-64; from Assoc Prof to Prof French, 64-68, Prof English & Comp Lit, 73-90, Distinguished Prof Eng and Comp Lit, State Univ NY-Buffalo, 90-, Melodia E. Jones Ch of Lit, 94-; mem bd consult, Coord Coun Lit Mags, 73-76. **HONORS AND AWARDS** Guggenheim fel, 66-67; Frances Steloff Fiction Prize, 71; Panache Exp Fiction Prize, 72; Fulbright Fel, Israel, 82-83; NEH Fel/Fiction, 86; Am Bk Award, 86; DAAD Fel, Berlin, 89-90. **MEMBERSHIPS** PEN Am; MLA; Am Comp Lit Asn; Am Asn Tchr(s) Fr. **RESEARCH** Twentieth century French lit; contemp fiction; creative writing. **SELECTED PUBLICATIONS** Auth, Double or nothing (novel), 71 & ed, Surfiction (essays on modern fiction), 75, Swallow; auth, Amer Eldorado (novel), Ed Stock, 74; Take it or leave it (novel), Fiction Collective, 76; Me too (poems), Westcoast Rev, 76; co-ed, Cahier de L'herne: Samuel Beckett, Eds L'Herne Paris-France, 77; auth, Imagination as plagiarism, New Lit Hist, 77; The voice in the closet (fiction), Tri-Quart, 77; The Two Fold Vilration (novel), Ind Univ Press, 82; Smiles on Washington Square, 85; To Whom it May Concern, 90; CRITIFICTION, 94; La Fourrure de una Taute Rachel, 96. **CONTACT ADDRESS** Dept of Eng, State Univ NY, PO Box 604610, Buffalo, NY, 14260-4610. **EMAIL** moinous@aol.com

FEIN, DAVID ALAN

PERSONAL Born 05/15/1949, Cambridge, MA, m, 1971, 2 children **DISCIPLINE** FRENCH **EDUCATION** Brown Univ, BA, 71; Cornell Univ, PhD (French), 76. **CAREER** Asst prof, 77-81, ASSOC PROF FRENCH, UNIV NC, GREENSBORO, 82-. **MEMBERSHIPS** Am Asn Teachers French; SAtlantic Mod Lang Asn; Southeastern Medieval Asn. **RESEARCH** Medieval French lyric poetry; 15th-century French literature. **SELECTED PUBLICATIONS** Auth, Villon Yesterday and Today--Papers from the Colloquium Honoring the 500th Anniversary of the Printing of Villon Testament, Fr Stud, Vol 48, 94; Vos Qui Les Biaus Mos Entendez, Audience Collusion in 12th Century French Narrative, Neophilologus, Vol 77, 93; Complete Poetry French, Fr Rev, Vol 67, 94; Le Latin Sivrai--Problematic Aspects of Narrative Authority in 12th Century French Literature, Fr Rev, Vol 66, 93. **CONTACT ADDRESS** Dept of Romance Lang, Univ of NC, 1000 Spring Garden, Greensboro, NC, 27412-0001.

FELDMAN, HEIDI M.

PERSONAL Born 02/24/1949, Philadelphia, PA, 2 children **DISCIPLINE** DEVELOPMENTAL PSYCHOLOGY; MEDICINE **EDUCATION** Univ Calif, MD, 79; Univ Penn, PhD, 75. **CAREER** Asst prof, Univ Pittsburgh, 84-90; dir, Child Develop Unit, Children's Hospital of Pittsburgh, 84-93; interim dir, Dept Communication Disorders, Children's Hospital of Pittsburgh, 86-87; dir, Down Syndrome Center, Children's Hospital of Pittsburgh, 89-91; assoc prof Pediatrics, Univ of Pittsburgh School of Medicine, 90-; division chief, General Acad Pediatrics, Children's Hospital of Pittsburgh, 93-; secondary appt, Dept Communication Science & Disorders, School of Health & Rehabilitation Sciences, Univ Pittsburgh, 96-. **HONORS AND AWARDS** Phi Beta Kappa, 70; Miles S Murphy Award for Distinction in Psychology, 70; Mortar Board Senior Women's Honor Soc, Univ Pa, 69-70; Ntl Sci Found Fel, 72-75; Frank-Arendsee-Feldman Found for Medical Res and Scholar, 78; Soc for Pediatric Res Member, 92-96; Soc Pediatric Res Senior Member, 96-. **MEMBERSHIPS** Amer Women's Med Assoc, 82-85; Mass Med Soc, 82-83; Boston Inst for Parents, Infants, and Children, 83-84; Fac Assoc School of Med, Univ Pittsburgh, 84-; Soc Developmental-Behavioral Pediatrics, 85-; Soc Res in Child Dev, 85-; Amer Acad Pediatrics, 86-. **SELECTED PUBLICATIONS** A playroom observation procedure to assess children with mental retardation and ADHD, Jour Abnormal Child Psychol, 98; Caring for children with special needs, Contemporary Pediatrics, 98; Teaching pediatric residents about early intervention and special education, Jour Developmental & Behavioral Pediatrics, 97. **CONTACT ADDRESS** Dept. of Communication Science and Disorders, Univ of Pittsburgh, 3705 Fifth, Pittsburgh, PA, 15213. **EMAIL** feldmanh@pop.pitt.edu

FELDSTEIN, RONALD FRED

PERSONAL Born 08/15/1947, Newark, NJ, m, 1975, 2 children **DISCIPLINE** SLAVIC LINGUISTICS, RUSSIAN **EDUCATION** Princeton Univ, MA, 69, PhD (Slavic lang), 73. **CAREER** Instr Russian and ling, State Univ NY, Binghamton, 69-73, asst prof, 73-76, dir, Critical Lang Prog, 74-76; asst prof, 76-80, ASSOC PROF SLAVIC LING, IND UNIV, 80-, Co-dir Slavic workshop, Ind Univ, Bloomington, 78-81. **MEMBERSHIPS** Am Asn Teachers of Slavic and East Europ Lang. **RESEARCH** Slavic accentology; Slavic historical phonology; contemporary Slavic phonology. **SELECTED PUBLICATIONS** Auth, On Church Slavonic Accentuation--The Accentuation of a Russian Church Slavonic Gospel Manuscripts from the 15th Century, Slavic East Europ J, Vol 37, 93. **CONTACT ADDRESS** 603 Plymouth Rd, Bloomington, IN, 47401.

FELLBAUM, CHRISTIANE

DISCIPLINE FRENCH, GERMAN **EDUCATION** Northeastern Univ, BA; Princeton Univ, PhD. **CAREER** Res staff, Princeton Univ, 87-; vis scholar, LADL, Univ Paris, 86-88; assoc prof, 80-. **MEMBERSHIPS** Mem, ed bd ling jour(s). **SELECTED PUBLICATIONS** Auth, articles, Intl Jour Lexicography, Revue Quebecoise de Linguistique, Revue Linguistique de Vincennes, The Psychol Rev. **CONTACT ADDRESS** Dept of Art and Sci, Westfield State Col, 577 Western Ave., Westfield, MA, 01085.

FENVES, PETER

DISCIPLINE GERMAN **EDUCATION** Johns Hopkins Univ, PhD. **CAREER** Prof German, Northwestern Univ. **SELECTED PUBLICATIONS** Auth, A Peculiar Fate: Metaphysics and World-History in Kant; Chatter: Language and History in Kierkegaard; ed, Raising the Tone of Philosophy: Late Essays by Kant, Transformative Critique by Derrida; essays and articles on, Marx; Kant; George Eliot; Nietzsche; Adorno; Benjamin; Jan-Luc Nancy; Kierkegaard; Kleist; H"lderlin. **CONTACT ADDRESS** Dept of German, Northwestern Univ, 1801 Hinman, Evanston, IL, 60208. **EMAIL** p-fenves@nwu.edu

FERGUSON, MARGARET WILLIAMS

PERSONAL Born 12/28/1948, Columbus, OH **DISCIPLINE** ENGLISH LITERATURE, COMPARATIVE LITERATURE **EDUCATION** Cornell Univ, BA, 69; Yale Univ, MPhil, 72, PhD (comp lit), 74. **CAREER** ASST PROF ENGLISH, YALE UNIV, 74-, Morse fel, Yale Univ, 77-78. **MEMBERSHIPS** MLA; Shakespeare Asn Am. **RESEARCH** Renaissance literature; literary theory. **SELECTED PUBLICATIONS** Auth, Dangerous Familiars--Representations of Domestic Crime in England, 1550-1700, Mod Philol, Vol 94, 96. **CONTACT ADDRESS** Dept of English, Yale Univ, New Haven, CT, 06520.

FERGUSON, WILLIAM ROTCH

PERSONAL Born 02/14/1943, Fall River, MA, m, 1983 **DISCIPLINE** ROMANCE LANGUAGES,SPANISH **EDUCATION** Harvard Univ, BA, 65, MA, 70, PhD, 75. **CAREER** Clark Univ, Worcester, Assoc Prof Spanish, 83, Asst Prof, 79-83, Vis Prof, 77-79; Adjunct Prof Eng, 89, Univ PA, Philadelphia, Vis Lectr Spanish Renaissance Lit, 86-87; Assoc Ed, 86-87, Hispanic Review; Asst Prof Spanish, 75-77, Inst Spanish, 71-75, Univ Boston. **HONORS AND AWARDS** Don Membership, Phi Beta Kappa; Clark Chapter, Sigma Delta Pi, (Spanish Natl Hon Soc), 87. **MEMBERSHIPS** AAUP; MLA; NEMLA; Intl Inst in Spain; Assoc Intl del Siglo de Oro. **RESEARCH** Spanish Lit, espec Golden Age and 20th Century; Latin Am Lit; Creative Writing in Eng. **SELECTED PUBLICATIONS** De lo suave a lo aspero: Notas sobre las estetica de Herrera, Revista de Estudios Hispanicos, Universidad de Puerto Ricom, Rio Piedran, 81; I Was Not Always A Magician, Mississippi Review, Hattiesburg, MS, 80; Space Invaders, Fictin NY vol 6 no 3, 81; Aubade, Cnato, Andover, MA, vol 3, no 2, 80; On The Beach, Harvard Advocate, civ, 1, 70; Poem For Mirko In Which He Appears Near the End, Sumac, 69. **CONTACT ADDRESS** Clark Univ, Estabrook 302, Worcester, MA, 01610. **EMAIL** wferguson@clarku.edu

FERNANDES, JAMES

PERSONAL Born 01/18/1947, Lihue, HI, m, 1988, 3 children **DISCIPLINE** SPEECH COMMUNICATION **EDUCATION** Univ Michigan, PhD, 80. **CAREER** Prof, commun, 75-, dir univ outreach, 95-96, Gallaudet Univ; adj prof, Univ Hawaii, 87-95; dir, Gallaudet Univ Pacific Reg Ctr, Univ Hawaii, 87-95. **HONORS AND AWARDS** Phi Beta Kappa, 69; pres award, Gallaudet Univ, 86; Nat Assoc of the Deaf, Golden Hand Award, 95. **MEMBERSHIPS** Nat Assoc of the Deaf; Nat Commun Assoc; ADARA. **RESEARCH** Deaf American public address; communication pedagogy with deaf students. **SELECTED PUBLICATIONS** Coauth, Guide to Better Hearing: A Resource Manual, City of Honolulu/GTE, 94; coauth, Signs of Eloquence: Selections from Deaf American Public Address, in, Readings in the Language, Culture, History, and Arts of Deaf People: Selected Papers from the Deaf Way Conference, Gallaudet, 94; auth, Communication Cops and Language Police, in Garretson, ed, Deafness: Life and Culture II, National Association of the Deaf, 95; auth, Partners in Education, Gallaudet Today, 96; auth, Creative Problem Solving--From Top to Bottom, Speech Commun Tchr, 98. **CONTACT ADDRESS** Dept of Communication Arts, Gallaudet Univ, 800 Florida Ave NE, Washington, DC, 20002. **EMAIL** JFernandes@gallua.gallaudet.edu

FERNANDEZCIFUENTES, L.

PERSONAL Born 07/31/1945, Leon, Spain, m, 1995, 2 children **DISCIPLINE** HISPANIC LITERATURES **EDUCA-**

TION Madrid Univ, MA, 70; Princeton Univ, PhD, 76. **CAREER** Asst prof, 76-83, assoc prof, 83-88, Princeton Univ; prof, Harvard Univ, 88-. **RESEARCH** Hispanic literatures. **SELECTED PUBLICATIONS** Ed, Los majos de Cadiz, Cadiz, 98; ed, Don Juan Tenorio, Barcelona, 93; auth, Garcia Lorca en el teatro: la norma y la diferencia, Zaragoza, 83; auth, Teoria y mercado de la novela en Espana, Madrid, 83. **CONTACT ADDRESS** Harvard Univ, 516 Boylston Hall, Cambridge, MA, 02138. **EMAIL** cifuent@fas.harvard.edu

FERRAN, OFELIA
DISCIPLINE SPANISH AND PORTUGUESE LITERATURE **EDUCATION** Syracuse Univ, BA, 88; Cornell Univ, PhD, 97. **RESEARCH** Contemporary Spanish peninsular literature; contemporary Spanish women writers; exile literature; narrative constructions and representations of memory; autobiography. **SELECTED PUBLICATIONS** Auth, 'Cuatro anos en Pares', de Victoria Kent: la 'doble voz' en la escritura femenina del exilio, 98; La escritura y la historia: Entrevista con Paloma Deaz-Mas, 9 de diciembre, 1995, 97; 'Una palabra, ya sabes: un cadaver': la poetica del trauma en Paul Celan, 95; Ekfrasis y Exilio: dos versiones de 'un amor interrumpido', 94. **CONTACT ADDRESS** Spanish and Portuguese Dept, Univ of Minnesota, Twin Cities, 34 Folwell Hall, 9 Pleasant St SE, Minneapolis, MN, 55455. **EMAIL** ferra007@tc.umn.edu

FERRANTE, JOAN M.
PERSONAL Born 11/11/1936, Jersey City, NJ **DISCIPLINE** COMPARATIVE MEDIEVAL LITERATURE **EDUCATION** Barnard Col, Columbia Univ, BA, 58; Columbia Univ, MA, 59 PhD(comp medieval lit), 63. **CAREER** From asst prof to assoc prof, 66-74, dir, Casa Italiana, 78-80, PROF ENGLISH & COMP LIT, COLUMBIA UNIV, 74-, Am Coun Learned Soc fel, 69-70; Adv Bd, Speculum, Medieval Acad Am, 75-78; Consult Ed, Records of Civilization, Columbia Univ Press, 75-; Nat Endowment for Humanities fel, 80-81. **MEMBERSHIPS** Mediaeval Acad Am; Renaissance Soc Am; Dante Soc Am (vpres, 79-82); Int Arthurian Soc. **RESEARCH** Medieval romance and allegory; Dante; Provencal poetry. **SELECTED PUBLICATIONS** Coauth, introd to & transl, The Lais of Marie de France, Dutton, 78; auth, Narrative patterns in the Decameron, Romance Philol, 78; Florence and Rome, the Two Cities of Man, In: Divine Comedy, Acta, Binghampton Conf Early Renaissance, 78; Ab joi mou lo vers e'l comens, The Interpretation of the Medieval Lyric, Macmillan, 79; Artist Figures in the Tristan Stories, Tristania, 79; Some thoughts on the application of modern critical methods to medieval literature, Yrbk Comp & Gen Lit, 28; The education of women in the middle ages in theory, fact and fantasy, In: Beyond Their Sex, Learned Women of the European Past, NY Univ, 80; Cortes' Amor in Medieval Texts, Speculum, 80. **CONTACT ADDRESS** Dept of English & Comp Lit, 2960 Broadway, New York, NY, 10027-6900.

FETZER, GLENN W.
PERSONAL Born 09/20/1955, Woodbury, NJ, m, 1985 **DISCIPLINE** FRENCH **EDUCATION** CUNY Grad Sch, PhD, 88. **CAREER** Asst de langue anglaise, Lycee Jacques Decours, Paris, 85-86; inst, King's Col, 84-85, 86-87; asst prof, assoc prof, chemn, Calvin Col, 87- . **MEMBERSHIPS** Am Assoc Tchrs Fr; Int Assoc Philos and Lit. **RESEARCH** Contemporary French poetry. **SELECTED PUBLICATIONS** Auth, Immutability and Change in the Poetics of Emmanuel Hocquard, in Romance Lang Annual, 93; auth, Dream Imagery and the Dialectics of Consciousness in Andre du Boucher's et la nuit, in LitteRealite, 94; auth, Memory, Absence, and the Consciousness of Self in the Novels of Mehdi Charef, in CLA J, 95; auth, Avenement de la parole: Illusion et Realite Chez Anne Teyssieras et Celine Zins, in Thirty Voices in the Feminine, Rodopi, 96; auth, Andre du Bouchet: Imaging the Real, Seeing the Unseeable, in, Nottingham, in Fr Stud, 96; auth, Finding One's Way: Poetry and the Mind's Eye in the Work of Celine Zins, in Romance Notes, 98; auth, Le Shakespeare d'Emmanuel Hocquard, in ALFA, 97/98; auth, French Poetry of Our Time: Crisis and Response, in Literature and the Renewal of the Public Sphere, Macmillan, 98; auth, Palimpsests of the Real in Recent French Poetry, Rodopi, 99. **CONTACT ADDRESS** Dept of French, Calvin Col, 3201 Burton St SE, Grand Rapids, MI, 49546. **EMAIL** fetzer@calvin.edu

FETZER, JOHN FRANCIS
PERSONAL m, 2 children **DISCIPLINE** GERMAN **EDUCATION** NY Univ, AB, 53; Columbia Univ, MA, 57; Univ Calif, Berkeley, PhD(Ger), 65. **CAREER** Instr Ger, Northwestern Univ, 62-65; from asst prof to assoc prof, 65-76, PROF GER LANG & LIT, EMERITUS, UNIV CA, DAVIS, 76-93; Chmn, Dept Ger & Russ, 81-84, 96-97, Am Philos Soc & Humanities Inst fels, 69-70; vis prof: Dartmouth, 76, Univ Exeter, 89-90; retired, 93. **HONORS AND AWARDS** Fulbright, 54, 80, 89; Am Phil Soc & Humanities Inst fels, 69-70; Guggenheim 80-81. **MEMBERSHIPS** MLA; Am Asn Teachers Ger; Ger Studies Asn. **RESEARCH** German Romanticism; relationships between music and literature; modern German lit. **SELECTED PUBLICATIONS** Auth, Ritter Gluck's Ungluck: The crisis of creativity in the Age of Epigone, 71, Ger Quart; Schatten ohne Frau: Marginalia on a Werther motif, Ger Rev, 71; The scales of injustice: Comments on Heinrich Boll's Die Waage der Baleks, Ger Quart, 72; Recent trends in Clemens Brentano research (1968-1970), Lit Wiss Jahrbuch, 72; Romantic Orpheus: Profiles of Clemens Brentano, Univ Calif, 74; Paul Elbogen, In: Deutsche Exilliteratur I, Francke, 76; coauth, Bibliographie der Buchrezensionen fur deutsche Literatur, Univ Microfilms, 77; Clemens Brentano, Twayne, 81; On the Threshold of German Romanticism, in Englishand German Romanticism, winter 85; Ludwig Tieck, in European Writers: The Romantic Century, Scribner's, 85; From the Blue Flower to the True Blue, Anna Seghers' Variations on a Romantic Theme from her Exile Years in Mexico, in Literarische Wege zwischen den Kontinenten, Niemeyer, 85; Jakob: Guardian of the Musical Threshold, in Franz Grillparzer: Der Arme Spielmann, Wayne State, 88; Annette Kolb, in Deutschsprachige Exilliteratur seit 1933, Francke, 89; Romantic Irony, in European Romanticism: Literary Cross-Currents, Modes, and Models, Wayne State, 89; Music, Love, Death, and Doctor Faustus, Camden, 90; Mediation as Medication for the Romantic Malady?, in Romantik--eine lebendige Krnakheit, Rodopi, 91; Music on the Threshold of German Romanticism, in The Romantic Tradition, Univ Press, 92; Visconti's Cinematic version of Death in Venice, in Approaches to Teaching Mann's Death in Venice and Other Short Stories, MLA, 92; Die musikalische Muse und Annette Kolb, in Ich habe etwas zu sagen: Annette Kolb 1870-1967, Diederichs, 93; Mignon's Minions: ambroise Thomas' opera Mignon, in Goethe's Mignon und ihre Schwestern, Lang, 93; Das Drama der Romantik/Die romantische Lyrik, in Romantik-Handbuch, Jahrbuch des Freien Deutschen Hochstifts, 95; Changing Perspectives of Thomas Mann's Doctor Faustus: Criticism 1947-1992, Camden, 96. **CONTACT ADDRESS** Dept of Ger & Russ, Univ of California, Davis, CA, 95616-8606. **EMAIL** jffetzer@ucdavis.edu

FICHTNER, EDWARD G.
PERSONAL Born 00/00/1931 **DISCIPLINE** GERMANIC PHILOLOGY, GERMAN LINGUISTICS **EDUCATION** Univ Ill, AB, 57; Ind Univ, MA, 60; Univ Pa, PhD (Ger), 66. **CAREER** Instr Ger, St Joseph's Col, Pa, 62-63 and Columbia Univ, 63-67; from asst prof to assoc prof, 67-77, PROF GER, 78-, MEM DOCTORAL FAC GER LANG, GRAD CTR, QUEENS COL, CITY UNIV NEW YORK, 73-, Managing ed, Word, 80. **MEMBERSHIPS** MLA; Ling Soc Am; Int Ling Asn. **RESEARCH** Structure of modern German; medieval German literature; medieval Scandinavian language and literature. **SELECTED PUBLICATIONS** Auth, Cleft Sentences in English, A Comprehensive View, Word J Int Ling Assoc, Vol 44, 93. **CONTACT ADDRESS** Dept of Germantic and Slavic Langs, Queens Col, CUNY, 6530 Kissena Blvd, Flushing, NY, 11367.

FIDO, FRANCO
PERSONAL Born 07/15/1931, Venice, Italy, m, 1958, 2 children **DISCIPLINE** ITALIAN AND COMPARATIVE LITERATURE **EDUCATION** Univ Pisa, DLett(Ital lit), 53; Ital govt, Lib Doc, 69; Brown Univ, MA, 71. **CAREER** French govt fel, Sorbonne, 53-54; lectr Ital, Faculte des Lett, Dijon, 54-58; instr, Univ Calif, Berkeley, 58-61; lectr, Faculte des Lett, Grenoble, 61-63; from asst prof to prof Ital, Univ Calif, Los Angeles, 63-69, chmn dept, 66-69; prof, Brown Univ, 69-78; R Pierotti prof Ital lit, Stanford Univ, 78-79; UNIV PROF, BROWN UNIV, 79-. **MEMBERSHIPS** MLA; Am Asn Teachers Ital; Dante Soc Am; Am Soc 18th Century Studies. **RESEARCH** Italian literature and theatre from the 18th to the 20th century; Boccaccio; Italian Renaissance, especially Machiavelli. **SELECTED PUBLICATIONS** Auth, Goldoni, Carlo and Voltaire, Revue D Histoire Du Theatre, Vol 45, 93; The Philosophes, America and the Indians, Rivista Di Letterature Moderne E Comparate, Vol 48, 95; Aspects of Baretti, Giuseppe, Marcantonio English Works--Didactics and So Called Nonsense, Invective and Theater, Rivista Di Letterature Moderne E Comparate, Vol 46, 93. **CONTACT ADDRESS** Dept of Hisp and Ital Studies, Brown Univ, Providence, RI, 02512.

FIEDLER, THEODORE
PERSONAL Born 10/01/1942, Altenburg, MO, m, 1963, 1 child **DISCIPLINE** GERMAN, LANGUAGE AND LITERATURE **EDUCATION** Washington Univ, AB, 64, MA(Ger) and MA(comp lit), 66; Univ Tubingen, PhD (Ger), 69. **CAREER** Asst prof, Univ Calif, Irvine, 68-75; assoc prof, Univ Tex, San Antonio, 76-77; ASSOC PROF GER, UNIV KY, 77-, Fulbright fel, 66-68; Am Philos Soc grant-in-aid, 73. **MEMBERSHIPS** MLA; Int Brecht Soc; Semiotic Soc Am. **RESEARCH** Twentieth century German literature and literary theory; poetics; film. **SELECTED PUBLICATIONS** Auth, Continuity and New Beginning Colloquia Germanica Past and Present, Colloquia Germanica, Vol 26, 93. **CONTACT ADDRESS** Dept of Ger, Univ of Ky, 500 S Limestone St, Lexington, KY, 40506-0003.

FIELD, NORMA
DISCIPLINE PREMODERN JAPANESE POETRY AND PROSE **EDUCATION** IN Univ, MA, 74; Princeton Univ, PhD, 83. **CAREER** Lit, Univ Mich. **SELECTED PUBLICATIONS** Auth, And Then, La State Univ press & Tokyo Univ Press, 78, The Splendor of Longing in the Tale of Genji, Princeton Univ Press, 78; In the Realm of a Dying Emperor, Pantheon, 93. **CONTACT ADDRESS** Univ MI, 515 E. Jefferson St, Ann Arbor, MI, 48109-1316.

FIFER, ELIZABETH
PERSONAL Born 08/05/1944, Pittsburgh, PA, m, 1970, 1 child **DISCIPLINE** COMPARATIVE LITERATURE, ENGLISH **EDUCATION** Univ MI, Ann Arbor, BA, 65, MA, 66, PhD, 69. **CAREER** Lectr hum, Res Col, Univ MI, 69-72; asst prof, 73-80, Assoc Prof Eng, Lehigh Univ, 80-, prof eng, Lehigh Univ. **MEMBERSHIPS** MLA; Asn Theater Res. **RESEARCH** Gertrude Stein; Contemp lit; Contemp drama; Contemp fiction (U S & World). **SELECTED PUBLICATIONS** Auth, The Confessions of Italo Sveno, Contemp Lit, 73: Sexstereo Typing in Geography & Plays, Univ Mich Papers Women's Studies, 75; Tragedy into Melodrama, Lex et Scientia, 77; The Interior Theater of Gertrude Stein, Signs, 78; Rescued Readings: Reconstruction of Gertrude Stein's Difficult Texts, Wayne State Univ, 92. **CONTACT ADDRESS** Dept of Eng, Lehigh Univ, 35 Sayre Dr, Bethlehem, PA, 18015-3076. **EMAIL** EF00@lehigh.edu

FIGUEIRA, DOROTHY
DISCIPLINE COMPARATIVE LITERATURE **EDUCATION** Univ Chicago, PhD, 85. **CAREER** Asst prof, Univ IL Urbana Champaign. **RESEARCH** Europ rel with the cult of India; Indo-Europ mythology; lit and relig; transl theory; comp drama and epic. **SELECTED PUBLICATIONS** Auth, Translating the Orient; Exoticism: A Doctrine of Decadence; publ(s) on the reception and construct of Indian class texts and cult in Europ thought of the 18th, 19th and 20th centuries. **CONTACT ADDRESS** Comp Lit Dept, Univ Illinois Urbana Champaign, E Gregory Drive, PO Box 52, Champaign, IL, 61820.

FIGUEREDO, DANILO H.
DISCIPLINE LATIN AMERICAN LITERATURE, LIBRARY SCIENCE, COMPARATIVE LITERATURE **EDUCATION** Montclair State Univ, BA, 76; Rutgers Univ, MLS, 78; New York Univ, MA, 88. **CAREER** Asst prof lit, Montclair State Univ, dir, bilingual prog, Lat Am bibliog, asst ch map div, Newark Pub Libr; LIBR DIR, BLOOMFIELD COL, 90-; exec dir NJ Libr Assoc. **CONTACT ADDRESS** Library, Bloomfield Col, Bloomfield, NJ, 07003. **EMAIL** Danilo_Figueredo@Bloomfield.edu

FIGURITO, JOSEPH
PERSONAL Born 11/24/1922, Gaeta, Italy, m, 1956 **DISCIPLINE** ROMANCE LANGUAGES, PHILOLOGY **EDUCATION** Boston Col, AB, 47; Middlebury Col, MA, 49, DML, 53; Univ Rome, cert, 52. **CAREER** Instr French, 47-48, instr Romance lang, 48-54, asst prof, 55-68, actg chmn dept, 71, Assoc Prof Mod Lang, Boston Col, 68-88, prof emeritus, 88-; Asst prof, exten, Harvard Univ, 57-68 & assoc prof, 68-81. **HONORS AND AWARDS** Silver Medal of Cult, Italy, 62; Knight, Order of Merit, Italy, 68; French Honor Society, Pi Delta Phi, Honorary mem, 97. **MEMBERSHIPS** Asn of Alumni & Friends of Ital Sch of Middlebury Col (pres 60-62); MLA; Am Asn Tchr(s) Ital (pres New Engl chap 62-64); Dante Soc Am (council mem 64-66); Mediaeval Acad Am; Honorary mem Harvard Univ Exten Alumni Asn, 81. **RESEARCH** Dante, Boccaccio, Petrarch and Leopardi; Lit and opera; 17th century French lit. **SELECTED PUBLICATIONS** Auth, A Student Guide to the Divina Commedia, Eaton, 59; L'Ultimo Baluardo dei Borboni nel Risorgimento, Italica, 9/61; contribr, A Concordance to Dante's Divine Comedy, Harvard Univ, 65; auth, Dante, Divine Comedy, Bk Notes, Barnes & Noble, 69; Leopardi Ribelle, In: Leopardi e l'Ottocento, Acts of II International Congress of Studies on Leopardi, Olschki, Florence, 70; Leopardi e Macchiavelli, In: Leopardi e la Letteratura Italiana dal Duecento al Trecento, Acts of IV Int Cong of Studies on Leopardi, Olschki, Florence, 78; Leopardi e Frontone, In: Leopardi e il Mondo Antico, Acts of the V Int Cong of Studies on Leopardi, Olschki, Florence, 82; Opinioni Politico-Religiose di Leopardi, In: Il Pensiero Storico e Politico di Giamcomo Leopardi, Acts of VI Int Cong of Studies on Leopardi, Olschki, Florence, 89; La Vita e le Opere di Don Salvatore Buonomo, In: Gaeta e Dintorni, Collana, Nova et Vetera, No 3, Gaeta, 91. **CONTACT ADDRESS** Dept of Romance Lang & Lit, Boston Col, 110 Sycamore St, Roslindale, MA, 02131-2606.

FILER, MALVA ESTHER
PERSONAL Born 02/25/1933, Arg, m, 1964, 2 children **DISCIPLINE** SPANISH AMERICAN LITERATURE **EDUCATION** Univ Buenos Aires, BA, 58; Columbia Univ, PhD(-philos), 66. **CAREER** Lectr Span, 63-66, instr, 66-68, asst prof, 69-72, Assoc Prof Span, Brooklyn Col, 73- **MEMBERSHIPS** MLA; Inst Int Lit Iberoam; Assoc Int de Hispanistas **RESEARCH** Contemporary Spanish American literature. **SELECTED PUBLICATIONS** Coauth, Voces de Hispanoamerica: Antologia literia, 88, 96; auth, Salvador Elizondo and Servero Sarduy: Two Borgesian Writers, Borges and his Successors, Univ of MO, 90; auth, Los perros del paraiso y la nueva novela historica, En este aire y Iuz de America: Homenaje a Alfredo A. Roggiano, Inst Unt de Lit Iberoam, 90; auth, La vision de America en la obra de Abel Posse, La novel argentina de los aflos 80; Vervuert Verlag, 91; auth, Cesar Aira y su aprcrifa historia de los caciques cura, VII Congreso Nacional de Literatura Argentina, Univ Nacional de Tueuman, 93; auth, Los nuevos narradores de la Conquista, Reflejos, Vol 1, No 2, 93; auth, Maluco: re-escritura de los relatos de la expedicion de Mafallanes, Actas Irvine, 92; auth, La historia apocrifa en las novelas

de los postmodernistas rioplatenses, Alba de America, 12:22-23, 94; auth, Hispanoamerica en la obra de Jose Maria Merino, Actas XXIX Congreso del Instituto Internacionnal del Literatura Iberoamericana, Univ Barcelona, 94. **CONTACT ADDRESS** Dept of Mod Lang, Brooklyn Col, CUNY, 2900 Bedford Ave, Brooklyn, NY, 11210-2889. **EMAIL** mfiler@email.gc.cuny.edu

FILIPS-JUSWIGG, KATHERINA P.
PERSONAL Poltava, USSR, 1 child **DISCIPLINE** RUSSIAN LITERATURE; EUROPEAN LITERATURE **EDUCATION** Pedag Inst, Vinnitsa, USSR, BA, 41; Univ Montreal, MA, 55, PhD, 61. **CAREER** Asst prof Russ & Ukrainian lang & lit, Univ Alta, 61-62; assoc prof Russ lang, lit & cult, Ore State Univ, 62-67; assoc prof, 67-71; chmn dept Slavic lang, 68-74; prof Russ lang, lit & cult, Univ Wis-Milwaukee, 71, consult Russ lit, Slavic & EEurop Jour, 78. **HONORS AND AWARDS** Nat Joe Malik Serv Award, Am Asn Tchrs Slavic & European lang, 87. **MEMBERSHIPS** MLA; Am Asn Tchrs Slavic & Europ Lang; Am Asn Advan Slavic Studies; Asn Russ-Am Scholars US; Int Dostoevsky Soc; Int PEN Club; Am Mikhail Bulgakov Society. **RESEARCH** Russ & European novel. **SELECTED PUBLICATIONS** Auth, Russian words in the German post-war memoirs, Slavic & EEurop Jour, 64; Names of poets in the poetry of Georgij Ivanov, Names, 67; Innokentij Volodin in Solzhenitsyn'sne First Circle..., Trans Asn Russ-Am Scholars, 74; New chapters for Solzenicyn's V Kruge Pervom ..., Russ Lang Jour, 75; ed, Boris Singermann (Moskau), Brechts' Zur Aesthetik der Montage, Dreigroschenoper, Brecht-Jahrbuch 1976, 76; auth, Nemtsy o Russkikh (Russians in German Memoirs), Slavica (Volga Bks), 76; Russkaja religioznaia zizn' . . . , 76 & Anglo-American books on L N Tolstoy: A critical bibliography for the 70's, 78, Trans Asn Russ-Am Scholars; Paradigmy metafory krehcheniia v Mastere I Margarite Bulgakova, Trans Asn Russ-Am Scholars, 85; Novyj Zhurnal 164, Kontinent, 87; Ivan Elagin in Memoriam, Novyj Zhurnal 165, 87; Bulgakov?s Master I Margarita: Metaphor and Method, ed Munir Sendich, Studies in Slavic Literatures and Culture, 88; rev., ed V. Sechkarev, Otkliki. Sbornik statej pamjati N.N. Uljanova, 88; Igrajushchij chelovek Ju. Ivaska, Novyi Shurnal 171, 88; ed Katharina Wilson, three articles (Aleksadra Tolstaya, Rina Levinson, Eugenia Dimer), Encyclopedia of Continental Women Writers, 91; Mikhail Bulgakov's Master and Margarita and Oscar Wilde's Salome: Motif Pattern and Allusions, Trans Asn Russ-Am Scholars, 91; (A Biographical Note and Complete Bibliography of Prof. Z.O.Yurieff), Trans Asn Russ-Am Scholars, 92-93; ed M. Ledkovskaia, A. Tolstaya, Dictionary of Russian Women Writers, 94; Dolgopolov - Professor, Scholar, Literary Critic, Novyj Zhurnal, 95; ed E. Etkind, Am Doctoral Diss on Derzhavin, Symposium Dedicated to Gavriil Derzhavin, 95; Pamiati I.V. Chinnova, Trans Asn Russ-Am Scholars, 96-97; auth, Ukazatel; (four indexes) for M. Chudakova's Zhizneopisanie Mikhaila Bulgakova, Russkij Aktsent, 97. **CONTACT ADDRESS** Dept of Foreign Languages and Linguistics, Univ of Wisconsin, Milwaukee, PO Box 413, Milwaukee, WI, 53201-0413. **EMAIL** kfj@csd.uwm.edu

FINCH, PATRICIA S.
DISCIPLINE SPANISH LANGUAGE AND LITERATURE **EDUCATION** Bowling Green State Univ, BA, MA; Catholic Univ Am, PhD. **CAREER** Fac, 91-; assoc prof and chr Span Dept. **RESEARCH** Don Quijote in Western Art and Thought; preparing Spanish-language edition of La Celestina. **SELECTED PUBLICATIONS** Auth, published articles on La Celestina, Don Quijote, magic and witchcraft in medieval and Golden Age Spain. **CONTACT ADDRESS** Centre Col, 600 W Walnut St, Danville, KY, 40422. **EMAIL** finch@centre.edu

FINCO, ALDO
PERSONAL Born 01/05/1921, Asiago, Italy, m, 1958, 2 children **DISCIPLINE** FOREIGN LANGUAGES **EDUCATION** Collegio Colombo, BA, 49; Boston Univ, BA, 55; Middlebury Col, MA, 63, DML, 67. **CAREER** Teacher French & Latin, Millis High Schs, Mass, 55-60; lectr Ital, Univ NH, 60-64; asst prof Ital, Univ Iowa, 65-68; assoc prof, 68-76, Prof Romance Lang, Tex Tech Univ, 76-; Teacher, French, Berwick Acad, Maine, 60-64. **MEMBERSHIPS** Am Asn Teachers Ital; Cent States Mod Lang Asn; Inst Ital Cult. **RESEARCH** Italian trecento and ottocento. **SELECTED PUBLICATIONS** Auth, La voce degli esseri nelle liriche di Antonio Fogazzaro, Studies by mem SCent Mod Lang Asn, 69; L'arte di Antonio Fogazzaro, 70 & Letture Italiane per conversazione, 71; Grafica Toscana, Firenze, Italy; Appunti, Tex Tech Univ, 72; Una Donna Fogazzariana: Iole Moschini, Studies by mem SCent Mod Lang Asn, 73; L'umorismo di Antonio Fogazzaro, Romance Notes, 73; Dante and the Laurel Crown, Studies by the Members of SCMLA, winter 76; The Italian-Americans: Their Contribution in the Field of Literature, in Proceedings of the Comparative Literature Symposiu, Tex Tech Univ, 78; Dino Buzzati's Un caso clinico and Boris Vian's Les Batisseurs d'empire, Francia, 82; Buzzati's poetic solitude, Studies by the Members of SCMLA, 83; Buzzati fumettista e Pittore, Romance Notes, 89; Buzzati e la musica, Rivista di Studi Italiani, 93; Primo Levi: Lo spettro di Auschwitz, Rivista di Studi Italiani, 94; Mario Rigoni Stern: la voce della montagna, Asiago, ieri, oggi, domani. **CONTACT ADDRESS** Dept of Class & Romance Lang, Texas Tech Univ, Lubbock, TX, 79409-0001.

FINDLEY, CARTER VAUGHN
PERSONAL Born 05/12/1941, Atlanta, GA, m, 1968, 2 children **DISCIPLINE** HISTORY; MIDDLE EASTERN STUDIES **EDUCATION** Yale Col, BA, 63; Harvard Univ, PhD, 69. **CAREER** Asst prof, 72-79, assoc prof hist, Ohio State Univ, 79-, Soc Sci Res Coun fel, 76-77, 79, 86-87, Inst Adv Study, 81-82; Fulbright-Hays Sr Res Fel, 94 & 98; vis prof, Ecole des Hautes en Sci Soc, Paris, 94; vis lect Dept Hist, Bilkent Univ, Ankara, 97. **HONORS AND AWARDS** OH Acad Publ Award and M Fuat Koprulu Book Prize Turkish Stud Assoc. **MEMBERSHIPS** Fel MidE Inst; fel MidE Studies Asn NAm; AHA; Am Oriental Soc; Comite Int pour les Etudes Pre-Ottomanes et Ottomanes; Oh Acad Hist; Turkish Stud Assoc (pres 90-92, vpres, 98-00, pres-elect, 00-02); Economic Soc Hist Found Turkey; World Hist Assoc. **RESEARCH** Ottoman history; Turkish studies; world history. **SELECTED PUBLICATIONS** Auth, Bureaucratic Reform in the Ottoman Empire: The Sublime Porte, 1789-1922, Princeton Univ, 80; Ottoman Civil Officialdom: A Social History, Princeton Univ, 89; Economic Bases of Revolution and Repression in the Late Ottoman Empire, Comparative Studies in Society and History, 86; La soumise, la subversive: Fatma Aliye, romanciere et feministe, Turcica, 95; Ebu Bekir Ratib's Vienna Embassy Narrative: Discovering Austria or Propagandizing for Reform in Istanbul, Wiener Zeitschrift fur die Kunde des Morgenlandes, 95; An Ottoman Occidentalist in Europe, 89: Ahmed Midhat Meets Madame Gulnar, 1889; Am Hist Rev, 98; coauth Twentieth-Century World, Houghton Mifflin, 98. **CONTACT ADDRESS** Dept Hist, Ohio State Univ, 230 W 17th Ave, Columbus, OH, 43210-1361. **EMAIL** findley.1@osu.edu

FINE, ELIZABETH C.
PERSONAL Born 12/20/1948, Cincinnati, OH, m, 1977 **DISCIPLINE** ORAL INTERPRETATION OF LITERATURE **EDUCATION** Univ Tex, Austin, BS, 71, PhD (commun), 78; Univ Calif, Berkeley, MA, 73. **CAREER** Teaching asst rhetoric, Univ Calif, Berkeley, 72-73; teaching asst speech, Univ Tex, Austin, 74-77; lectr and asst prof speech, Univ Ill, Urbana, 77-79; ASST PROF HUMANITIES and COMMUN, VA POLYTECH INST and STATE UNIV, 79-. **MEMBERSHIPS** Speech Commun Asn; Am Folklore Asn; Southern Speech Commun Asn. **RESEARCH** Ethnography of speaking; aesthetics of verbal act. **SELECTED PUBLICATIONS** Auth, The Politics of Public Memory--Tourism, History, and Ethnicity in Monterey, California, Semiotica, Vol 111, 96. **CONTACT ADDRESS** Dept of Commun, Studies Va Polytech Inst and State Univ, Blacksburg, VA, 24060.

FINE, ELLEN SYDNEY
PERSONAL Born 09/30/1939, New York, NY, d **DISCIPLINE** FRENCH LITERATURE AND LANGUAGE **EDUCATION** Smith Col, BA, 61; Univ Calif, Berkeley, MA, 64; NY Univ, PhD (French), 79. **CAREER** Researcher dept doc, French Embassy Press and Info Serv, 63-64; asst prof, 64-80, ASSOC PROF FRENCH, KINGSBOROUGH COMMUNITY COL, 80-, Vis lectr, Jack P Eisner Inst Holocaust Studies of the City Univ New York, 81-82. **MEMBERSHIPS** MLA; Northeastern Mod Lang Asn; Am Asn Teachers Fr. **RESEARCH** Holocaust studies; Elie Wiesel. **SELECTED PUBLICATIONS** Auth, Discourse of Jewish Identity in 20th Century France, Philos Lit, Vol 19, 95. **CONTACT ADDRESS** 130 E 18th St, New York, NY, 10003.

FINEGAN, EDWARD J.
DISCIPLINE LINGUISTICS LAW **EDUCATION** Iona Col, BS; Ohio Univ, MA; Univ Mich, MA; Ohio Univ, PhD. **CAREER** Prof; post-doc, Univ Southern Calif; Ohio State Univ, Ling Inst & Harvard Law Sch; Liberal Arts fel, Harvard Law Sch. **MEMBERSHIPS** Past dir, Amer Lang Inst/Nat Iranian Radio and Tv. **RESEARCH** Legal writing. **SELECTED PUBLICATIONS** Auth, Language: Its Structure and Use; coauth, Looking at Languages. **CONTACT ADDRESS** School of Law, Univ Southern Calif, University Park Campus, Los Angeles, CA, 90089.

FINELLO, DOMINICK LOUIS
PERSONAL Born 03/17/1944 **DISCIPLINE** SPANISH RENAISSANCE & BAROQUE LITERATURE **EDUCATION** Brooklyn Col, BA, 65; Univ IL, Urbana-Champaign, MA, 67, PhD(Span), 72. **CAREER** Asst prof, 71-75, assoc prof, 75-87, prof span, Rider Univ, 88-. **MEMBERSHIPS** Inst Asn Hispanists; Cervantes Soc Am; Am Asn Teachers Span & Port; MLA. **RESEARCH** Cervantes; 16th century Spanish literature; southern European Renaissance. **SELECTED PUBLICATIONS** Auth, Temas y formas de la literature espanola, Revista Filol Espanola, 75; Cervantes y lo pastoril a nueva luz, Anales Cervantinos, 77; co-ed with R Rodriguez, La cornada by Alfonso Sastre, with notes and intro, Ed Abra, 78; auth, The Galatea: Theory and practice of the pastoral novel, In: Cervantes, his World and his Art, Fordham Univ, 78; Una olvidada defensa de la poesia del s 16, Anuario de Letras, 78; En la Sierra Morena--Actas del 6th Cong Int de Hisp, Toronto, 77; Don Quijote's Profession and Mark Van Doren's Profession, Actac del I Cong Int Sobre Cervantes, Madrid, 81; An Analytical and Biographical Guide to Criticism on Don Quijote (1790-1893), with Dana Drake, Newark, DE: Juan de la Cuesta-Hispanic Monographs, 87; Pastoral Themes and Forms in Cervantes's Fiction, Lewisburg, PA: Bucknell Univ Press, 94; Cervantes: Essays on Social and Literary Polemics, London: Boydell & Brewer, Tamesis, 98. **CONTACT ADDRESS** Dept Foreign Lang, Rider Univ, 2083 Lawrenceville, Lawrenceville, NJ, 08648-3099. **EMAIL** finello@rider.edu

FINK, BEATRICE
PERSONAL Born 09/13/1933, Vienna, Austria, m, 1955, 3 children **DISCIPLINE** FRENCH LITERATURE, HISTORY OF IDEAS **EDUCATION** Bryn Mawr Col, BA, 53; Yale Univ, MA, 56; Univ Pittsburgh, PhD (French), 66. **CAREER** From instr to asst prof French, 64-72, ASSOC PROF FRENCH, UNIV MD, COLLEGE PART, 72-, Am Philos Soc res grant, 81. **MEMBERSHIPS** MLA; Am Soc 18th Century Studies; Soc Fr Etude XVIIIe Siecle; Int Soc 18th Century Studies (secy, 79-); Asn Benjamin Constant. **RESEARCH** Benjamin Constant; food in 18th century French literature; Sade and utopian thought. **SELECTED PUBLICATIONS** Auth The Big Book of Secrets--Book Peddling in the 17th and 18th Centuries, Fr Rev, Vol 70, 96; Gynographs--French Novels by Women of the Late 18th Century, French Forum, Vol 19, 94; Love Apples, Fr Rev, Vol 67, 94; Portraits, Memoirs, Recollections, Fr Rev, Vol 67, 93; Constant, Benjamin, Oeuvres Completes--General Correspondence I 1774-1792, Fr Rev, Vol 69, 95. **CONTACT ADDRESS** 6111 Madawaska Rd, Bethesda, MD, 20816.

FINK, KARL J.
PERSONAL Born 11/12/1942, Delmont, SD, m, 1964, 3 children **DISCIPLINE** GERMAN LANGUAGE & LITERATURE **EDUCATION** Wartburg Col, BA, 64; Univ Ariz, MA, 66; Univ Ill, PhD(Ger), 74. **CAREER** Asst prof Ger, Univ Ill, 74-77, Southern Ill Univ, 77-78 & Univ Ky, 78-82; assoc prof Ger & chmn dept, St Olaf Col, 82-87, 95-97; dir, Ill-Austria Exchange Prog, Univ Ill, 74-77; Minnesota German Festival, coordinator, 98. **HONORS AND AWARDS** Grawemeyer Award, Univ Louisville, 79. **MEMBERSHIPS** MLA; Am Asn Teachers Ger; Am Soc Eighteenth Century Studies; Goethe Soc NAm; Int Herder Soceity; History of Science Society. **RESEARCH** Goethe studies; 18th century science; foreign language methodology. **SELECTED PUBLICATIONS** Auth, Learning to read German: A search for relevant models, Studies in Lang Learning, 77; The ecospace concept for the bicultural classroom abroad, Int Educ, 79; contribr, The meta-language of Goethe's history of color theory, In: The Quest for the New Science, Southern Ill Univ Press, 79; auth, Atomism: A counterpoint tradition in Goethe's writings, Eighteenth Century Studies, 80; contribr, Herder's theory of origins: From poly to palingenesis, In: Herder: Innovator through the Ages, Bouvier Press, 81; auth, Herder's stages of life as forms in geometric progression, Eighteenth Century Life, 81; Goethe's West-Ostlicher Divan: Orientalism restructured, Int J Mid East Studies, 82; Dualisten, Trinitarier, Solitarier: Formen der Autoritat in Goethes Geschichte der Farbenlehre, Goethe-Jahrbuch, 82; Goethe as Critic of Literature, American University Press, 84; co-ed Goethe's History of Science, Cambridge, 91; The Eighteenth Century German Book Review, Winter, 95; Goethe Shides in North American, Eighteenth-Century Life, 96; The Politics of Heners' Pluralism, The European Legacy, 96. **CONTACT ADDRESS** St. Olaf Col, 1520 St Olaf Ave, Northfield, MN, 55057-1099. **EMAIL** kjfink@stolaf.edu

FINK, ROBERT J.
PERSONAL Born 02/17/1931, Rochester, NY, m, 1974, 1 child **DISCIPLINE** FRENCH RENAISSANCE, CINEMA **EDUCATION** Univ Toronto, BA, 54, MA, 58; Univ Chicago, PhD (Romance lang), 71. **CAREER** From instr to asst prof French, St Michael's Col, Univ Toronto, 65-73; arts officer, Can Coun, 73-77; assoc prof, St Francis Xavier Univ, 78-80; assoc prof, Mt Allison Univ, 80-81; PROF FRENCH, ACADIA UNIV, 81-. **MEMBERSHIPS** MLA; Renaissance Soc Am; Can Soc Renaissance Studies. **RESEARCH** French Renaissance humanism; French-Canadian novel and cinema. **SELECTED PUBLICATIONS** Auth, The National Wildlife Refuges--Theory, Practice, and Prospect, Harvard Environmental Law Rev, Vol 18, 94. **CONTACT ADDRESS** Dept of Mod Lang, Acadia Univ, Wolfville, NS.

FIORDO, RICHARD A.
PERSONAL Born 11/02/1945, Chicago, IL, d, 1 child **DISCIPLINE** ENGLISH, SPEECH, COMMUNICATION **EDUCATION** Northern Ill, BA, 67; San Francisco State Univ, MA, 70; Univ Ill, PhD, 74 **CAREER** Instr, E Stroudsberg State Univ, 75; assoc prof, Univ Calgary, 75-95; assoc prof, Eureka Col, 95-97; prof, Univ N Dak, 97- **HONORS AND AWARDS** Distinguished Service **MEMBERSHIPS** Ntl Communication Assoc; Assoc Education in Jour & Mass Communication **RESEARCH** Human Relations; Public Relations; Cultural Commentary **SELECTED PUBLICATIONS** "Truth and Justice in Mass Media Reporting and Commentary: More Than One Master in American Adversarial Contests," Proceedings of the International Society for the Study of Argumentation, 98 **CONTACT ADDRESS** School of Communication, Univ North Dakota, PO Box 7169, Grand Forks, ND, 58203. **EMAIL** fiordo@prairie.nodak.edu

FIORE, ROBERT L.
PERSONAL Born 08/02/1935, New York, NY, m, 1986, 2 children **DISCIPLINE** ROMANCE LANGUAGES **EDUCATION** Iona Col, BA, 61; Middlebury Col, MA, 62; Univ NC, Chapel Hill, PhD(Romance lang), 67. **CAREER** Instr Span, Univ NC, Greensboro, 62-67; asst to assoc prof, 67-75, PROF, MICH STATE UNIV, 76-, Assistant Dean, Col of Arts & Letters, 80-86. **HONORS AND AWARDS** Honors in Italian, Iona Col, 61; Cultura Hispanica Scholarship, 62; Paul Varg Col of Arts & Letters Alumni Teacher's Award, 94. **MEMBERSHIPS** Am Asn Teachers Span & Port; Comediantes; MLA. **RESEARCH** Spanish. **SELECTED PUBLICATIONS** Auth, Towards a Bibliography on Jorge Luis Borges (1923-69), In: The Calderon de la Barca Studies 1951 69, Univ Toronto, 71; El gran teatro del mundo: An ethical Interpretation, Hisp Rev, 72; Drama and Ethos: Natural-Law Ethics in Spanish Golden Age Theater, Univ KY, 75; Desire and Disillusionment in Lazarillo de Tormes, Studies Lang & Lit, 76; The Interaction of Motives and Mores in La Verdad Sospechosa, Hispanofila, 77; Lazarillo de Tormes: Estructura narrative de una novela picaresca, In: Actas del 1 Congr Int Sobre la Picaresca, 78; Lazarillo de Tormes and Midnight Cowboy: The Picaresque Model and Myth, In: Studies in Honor of Everett W Hesse, 81; Lazarillo de Tormes, Twayne, 84; co-ed, Studies in Honor of William C. McCrary, Univ of NE Press, 86; La Jezebel de Tirso: Reina astuta, muer que manda en casa, Critica Hispanica 8, 86; Alarcon's El dueno de las estrallas:Hero and Pharmakos, Hispanic Rev, 61, 93; Fuenteovejuna: Philosophical Views on the State and Revolution, Hispanic Essays in Honor of Frank P. Casa, 97; Lazarillo de Tormes: The Sceptic Histor and the Poetics of Silence, Critica Hispanica, 19, 97; ed, Critica Hispanica, 19, 97. **CONTACT ADDRESS** Dept of Romance Lang, Michigan State Univ, 161 Old Horticulture, East Lansing, MI, 48824-1112. **EMAIL** fiore@pilot.msu.edu

FIRCHOW, EVELYN SCHERABON
PERSONAL Vienna, Austria, m, 1969, 2 children **DISCIPLINE** GERMANIC LANGUAGES & LITERATURES **EDUCATION** Univ Tex, Austin, BA, 56; Univ Man, MA, 57; Harvard Univ, PhD, 63. **CAREER** Teacher math, Balmoral Hall Sch, Winnipeg, Man, 53-55; teaching fel, German, Harvard Univ, 57-58, 61-62; lectr, Univ Md Br Munich, 61; from instr to asst prof Ger, Univ Wis-Madison, 62-65; assoc prof Ger philol, 65-69, acting chair, Ger Philol prog, Univ Minn, 77 & 84, PROF GER & GER PHILOL, UNIV MINN, MINNEAPOLIS, 69-; NDEA-Fulbright-Hays fac fel, Univ Iceland, 67-68; vis prof Ger philol, Univ Fla, 73; Inst Advan Studies res fel, Univ Edinburgh, 73; Alexander von Humboldt-Stiftung res fel, 60-61, 77, 81, 85, 90, 93; vis scholar res grant, Austria, 77; Fulbright res prof, Univ Iceland, 80; NEH fel, independent study & res, 80-81; vis res prof, Nat Cheng Kung Univ, Tainan, Taiwan, 82-83; vis prof, Jilin Univ, Chang Chun, Chna, 87; vis prof, Univ Graz, Austria, 89 & 91; vis prof, Univ Vienna, Austria, 95; vis prof, Univ Bonn, Germany, 96. **HONORS AND AWARDS** Correspondin mem, Center for Multilingualism, Brussels, Belgium, 86; Am Inst Indian Studies, fel, India, 88; Bush fel, Univ Minn, 89-90; Thor Thors fel, Univ Iceland, 94; Fac fel, Univ Minn, summer 95 & 96; McKnight fel, Univ Minn, summer, 95 & 96; De consolatione philologiaei: A Festschrift in Honor of Evelyn Scherabon Firchow, forthcoming. **MEMBERSHIPS** AAUP; ICLA; ACLA; ALLC; Alexander von Humboldt Asn of Am; Fulbright Alumni Asn; Oswald von Wolkenstein Gesellschaft; Mediavistern-Verband Deutschlands; Asn Literary Scholars & Critics. **RESEARCH** Germanic philology; medieval studies; linguistics. **SELECTED PUBLICATIONS** Co-ed, Taylor Starck-Festschrift, 64, Studies by Einar Haugen, 72 & Studies for Einar Haugen, 72, Mouton, The Hague; co-transl & ed, Einhard: Vita Karoli Magni, The Life of Charlemagne: The Latin Text with a New English Translation, introduction, notes and illustrations, Univ Miami, 72 and Biblioteca Germanica 3/85; co-ed, Was Deutsche Lesen: Modern German Short Stories, McGraw, 73; Deutung und Bedeutung, Mouton, The Hague, 73; ed & transl, Modern Icelandic Short Stories, 74 & East German Short Stories, 79, Twayne; transl, Einhard: Das Leben Karls, des Grossen, Reclam, 3rd ed, 97; co-ed (with K Grimstad), The Old Icelandic Elucidarius, Reykjavik, 87; The Old Norse Elucidarius: Original Text and English Translation,Camden House, 92; Notker der Deutsche von St Gallen: De interpretatione, Boethius Bearbeitung von Aristoteles Schrift peri hermeneias, Konkordanze, Wortlisten und Abruck des Textes nach dem Codex Sangallensis 818, de Gruyter, 95; Notker der Deutsche von St Gallen: Categoriae, Boethius Bearbeitung von Aristoteles Schrift kategorial, Konkordanzen, Wortlisten und Abdruck der Texte nach den Codices Sangallensis 818 und 825, Walter de Gruyter, 96; reprint, Einhard: Vita Caroli magni, Das Leben Karls des Grofsen, 3rd rev ed, Philipp Reclam, 97; Alois Brandstetter: The Abbey, Ariadne Press, 98; Notker der Deutsche von St Gallen: Martianus Capellas De nuptiis Philologiae et Mercurii, Textabdruck, Konkordanzen und Wortlisten nach dem Codex Sangallensis 872, forthcoming, 98. **CONTACT ADDRESS** Dept of Ger, Scand & Dutch, Univ Minn, 9 Pleasant St SE, Minneapolis, MN, 55455-0194. **EMAIL** Firch001@tc.umn.edu

FIRESTONE, RUTH H.
PERSONAL Born 08/19/1936, Baltimore, MD, m, 1970, 2 children **DISCIPLINE** GERMAN **EDUCATION** Univ PA, BA, 59; Univ Colo, MA, 65, PhD, 72. **CAREER** Asst prof German, Otterbein Col, 69-70; from asst to assoc prof German, 73-86, dept chair, Germanic and Slavic Stud, Univ Mo, Columbia; PROF GERMAN, CHAIR, DEPT MOD LANGS, FORT HAYS STATE UNIV, 86-. **HONORS AND AWARDS** Shumway Prize German, Univ Pa, 59; Baur-van Sweringen Award German, Univ Colo, 66;2d prize, Univ Chicago, dept Germanic Lang Lit Folklore Prize Comp, 72; Fulbright for Col Teachers of German Civ, 77; Purple Chalk for teaching, Univ Mo, 84; NEH Summer Seminar, "Beowolf and the Reception of Germanic Antiquity," Harvard Univ, 93., Delta Phi Alpha, Phi Sigma Iota, Phi Kappa Phi. **MEMBERSHIPS** Mod Lang Asn; Am Asn of Teachers of German; Medieval Acad. **RESEARCH** Medieval German Literature; heroic narrative; Arthurian narrative. **SELECTED PUBLICATIONS** Auth, Queen Helche the Good: Model for Noblewomen," Women as Protagonists and Poets in the German Middle Ages: Feminist Approaches to the Study of Middle High German Literature, 91; auth, "Boethian Influence on Gottfried's Tristan: A preliminary Assessment,"in Tristan-Tristant: Melanges en l'honneur de Danielle Buschinger, 96. **CONTACT ADDRESS** Dept Modern Languages, Fort Hays State Univ, 600 Park St, Hays, KS, 67601-4099. **EMAIL** rfiresto@tiger.fhsu.edu

FISCHLER, ALEXANDER
PERSONAL Born 12/28/1931, Reichenberg, Czechoslovakia, m, 1958, 2 children **DISCIPLINE** COMPARATIVE LITERATURE **EDUCATION** Univ Wash, BA, 54, PhD (compt lit), 61. **CAREER** Teaching asst and assoc, Univ Wash, 52-56, assoc 57-59; teaching asst, Ind Univ, 56-57; from instr to asst prof English, Whitman Col, 59-62; asst prof foreign lang, Univ Ore, 62-64; asst prof, 64-66, ASSOC PROF FRENCH AND COMP LIT, STATE UNIV NY BINGHAMTON, 66-. **MEMBERSHIPS** Am Comp Lit Asn; MLA, Am Asn Teachers Fr. **RESEARCH** English-French literature, 19th and 20th centuries. **SELECTED PUBLICATIONS** Auth, From Weydon Priors to Tower Green, Elh Eng Lit Hist, Vol 63, 96; Purloined Posterity, The Reforms and Reputation of Madame Vestris Mathews, Lucia, Elizabeth, Bartolozzi, Womens Stud Interdisciplinary J, Vol 24, 95; Verdi Rigoletto, Opera News, Vol 61, 96; Lines Which Circles Do Contain--Circles, the Cross, and Donne Dialectic Scheme of Salvation, Papers on Language and Literature, Vol 30, 94; Sullivan Hms Pinafore, Opera Quart, Vol 13, 97; Oberon and Odium, Opera Quart, Vol 12, 95; Gilbert and Donizetti, Opera Quart, Vol 11, 95; Sullivan the Pirates of Penzance, Opera Quart, Vol 13, 97. **CONTACT ADDRESS** Dept of Romance Lang and Lit, State Univ of NY, Binghamton, NY, 13901.

FISHER, JAMES RANDOLPH
PERSONAL Born 11/05/1906, Norfolk, VA **DISCIPLINE** ENGLISH LANGUAGE AND LITERATURE **EDUCATION** Howard Univ, AB, 31, AM, 33. **CAREER** Chmn dept lang and lit, Rust Col, 35-38; Allen Univ, 40-43; sophomore English, Tenn State Col, 45-47; prof, 47-72, chmn sophomore English, 48-74, chmn dept lang and lit, prof, 72-74, EMER PROF ENGLISH, SAVANNAH STATE COL, 74-. **MEMBERSHIPS** MLA; Mod Humanities Res Asn; Int Asn Univ Prof English; Col English Asn; Milton Soc Am. **SELECTED PUBLICATIONS** Auth, British Physicians, Medical Science, and the Cattle Plague, 1865-66, Bulletin of the History of Medicine, Vol 67, 93; Not Quite a Profession--The Aspirations of Veterinary Surgeons in England in the Mid 19th Century, Hist Rsch, Vol 66, 93. **CONTACT ADDRESS** Dept of English, Savannah State Col, Box 20434, Savannah, GA, 31404.

FISHER, JOHN C.
PERSONAL Born 11/27/1927, Mendon, NY, m, 1956, 2 children **DISCIPLINE** LINGUISTICS, LITERATURE **EDUCATION** Champlain Col, BA, 53; Univ Mich, AM, 54, EdD(English lang and lit), 62. **CAREER** From instr to assoc prof, 57-62, dir summer instr, 62-68, chmn dept, 72-74, PROF ENGLISH, STATE UNIV NY COL, OSWEGO, 63-, Vis lectr, English Lang Inst, Univ Mich, 57-61; instr, State Univ NY, Ford Found Indonesia Proj, 62-63; Fulbright lectr, Univ Rome, 63-64; dir, NEA Inst English, 65; coordr, BA Ling Prog, State Univ NY Col, Oswego, 66-73; exec secy, NY State English Coun, 68-70, fel, 70; vis prof, ling, Univ Hawaii, Hilo, 70; vis prof, English, Inter-Am Univ PR, 70. **MEMBERSHIPS** MLA; NCTE. **RESEARCH** Nineteenth century British literature; linguistics, especially in literary criticism; English as a foreign language. **SELECTED PUBLICATIONS** Auth, Reinventing a Livelihood--How United States Labor Laws, Labor Management Cooperation Initiatives, and Privatization Influence Public Sector Labor Markets, Harvard J Legislation, Vol 34, 97. **CONTACT ADDRESS** Perry Hill RD 3, Oswego, NY, 13126.

FISHMAN, JOSHUA AARON
PERSONAL Born 07/18/1926, Philadelphia, PA, m, 1951, 3 children **DISCIPLINE** SOCIOLINGUISTICS **EDUCATION** Univ Pa, BA and MS, 48; Columbia Univ, PhD (social psychol), 53. **CAREER** Res assoc social psychol, Jewish Educ Comt New York, 50-54; res assoc and res dir, Col Entrance Exam Bd, 55-58; assoc prof psychol and Human rels, Univ Pa, 58-60; prof psychol and sociol, 60-66, Distinguished Univ Res Prof Soc Sci, Yeshiva Univ, Soc Sci Res Coun fel, 54-55; fels, Ctr Advan Study Behav Sci, 63-64, Inst for Advan Study, NJ, 75-76 and Nat Inst Educ, 76-77; consult, Ministry Finance, Repub Ireland, 65-; sur sr specialist, East-West Ctr, Univ Hawaii, 68-69; ed, INT J SOCIOL LANG, 74-. **HONORS AND AWARDS** PedD, Yeshiva Univ, 68. **MEMBERSHIPS** Am Psychol Asn; Am Sociol Asn; Am Anthrop Asn; Ling Soc Am; Yivo Inst Jewish Res. **RESEARCH** Sociology of language; bilingual education; applied linguistics. **SELECTED PUBLICATIONS** Auth, Haugen, Einar, Lan, Vol 71, 95; Speaking of Diversity--Language and Ethnicity in 20th Century America, J Am Ethnic Hist, Vol 13, 94; Linguistic Imperialism, Mod Lan J, Vol 77, 93. **CONTACT ADDRESS** Soc Sci Div, Yeshiva Univ, 500 W 185th St, New York, NY, 10033.

FITCH, BRIAN T.
PERSONAL Born 11/19/1935, London, England **DISCIPLINE** FRENCH **EDUCATION** Kings Col, Univ Durham, BA, 58; Univ Strasbourg, Dr de l'U, 62. **CAREER** Asst lectr, Manchester Univ, 62-65; vis assoc prof, 65-66, head Fr, 71-75, assoc ch grad stud Fr, 77-81, UNIV PROF, 89-, GERALD LARKIN PROF FRENCH, TRINITY COL, UNIV TORONTO, 96-; vis sr res fel, Merton Col, Oxford, 70; vis prof, Bar-Ilan Univ, Israel, 83; vis prof, Montpellier Univ, 93. **HONORS AND AWARDS** Can Coun leave fel, 70-71, 76-77, 82-83; Connaught sr fel, 88-89. **MEMBERSHIPS** MLA; Can Asn Univ Tchrs; Can Comp Lit Asn. **SELECTED PUBLICATIONS** Auth, The Narcissistic Text: A Reading of Camus Fiction, 82; auth, Monde a l'envers/texte reversible: la fiction de Bataille, 82; auth, Beckett and Babel: an Investigation into the Status of the Bilingual Work, 88; auth, Reflections in the Mind's Eye: Reference and its Problematization in Twentieth Century French Fiction, 91; auth, Lire les recits de Maurice Blanchot, 92; auth, 'The Fall': A Matter of Guilt, 95; ed, Configuration critique de Julien Green, 64; ed, Ecrivains de la Modernite, 81; founding ed, Albert Camus J, 68-87; founding co-ed, Texte, 82-. **CONTACT ADDRESS** Trinity Col, Univ of Toronto, Toronto, ON, M5S 1H8.

FITCH, J.G.
DISCIPLINE GREEK; ROMAN DRAMA **EDUCATION** Cornell Univ, BA, 63, Cert Edu, 66, MA, 67, PhD, 74. **CAREER** Prof, 73-; ch. **HONORS AND AWARDS** Pres, Class Assn of Vancouver Island, 82-83; coun mem, Class Assn of Can, 84-86; prog ch, Class Assn of Can, 90. **MEMBERSHIPS** Mem, Amer Philol Assn; Soc for Lit and Sci. **RESEARCH** Senecan tragedy; didactic poetry. **SELECTED PUBLICATIONS** Auth, Seneca's Hercules Furens, Cornell UP, 87; Seneca's Anapaests, Scholars Press, 88; Sense-Pauses and Relative Dating in Seneca, Sophocles and Shakespeare, Amer Jour of Philol 102, 81; coauth, Theory and Context of the Didactic Poem, Florilegium 5, 83. **CONTACT ADDRESS** Dept of Greek and Roman Studies, Victoria Univ, PO Box 1700 STN CSC, Victoria, BC, V8W 2Y2. **EMAIL** fitch@uvvm.uvic.ca

FITZ, BREWSTER
DISCIPLINE COMPARATIVE LITERATURE **EDUCATION** Yale, PhD, 73. **CAREER** Engl, Okla St Univ. **RESEARCH** Non-Western World Literature, Multi-cultural Literatures, Native American Literature and Critical Theory. **SELECTED PUBLICATIONS** Auth, Rapture in Liminality: Leslie Marmon Silko's 'Yellow Woman', Univ Tex, El Paso, 96; Some Theoretical Reflexions in Leslie Marmon Silko's Gloss on 'Coyote and Lark', 96; Dialogistic Witchery in 'Tony's Story', 97; Undermining Narrative Stereotypes in Simon Ortiz's 'The Killing of a State Cop', 97. **CONTACT ADDRESS** Oklahoma State Univ, 101 Whitehurst Hall, Stillwater, OK, 74078.

FITZ, EARL EUGENE
PERSONAL Born 03/07/1946, Marshalltown, IA, m, 1973, 1 child **DISCIPLINE** LUSO-BRAZILIAN STUDIES **EDUCATION** Univ Iowa, BA, 68, MA, 70; City Univ New York, MA, 73, PhD (comp lit), 77. **CAREER** Vis lectr Span and Port, Univ Mich, Ann Arbor, 76-77; asst prof, Dickinson Col, 77-78; ASST PROF LUSO-BRAZILIAN STUDIES AND SPAN AM LIT, PA STATE UNIV, 78-. **MEMBERSHIPS** MLA; Am Asn Teachers Span and Port; Am Translr Asn; Midwest Mod Lang Asn. **RESEARCH** Spanish Am Lit and culture; comparative literature. **SELECTED PUBLICATIONS** Auth, Exotic Nations--Literature and Cultural Identity in the United States and Brazil, 1830-1930, Comp Lit Stud, Vol 33, 96; Book of the 4th World, Comp Lit Stud, Vol 32, 95; Metafiction in Latin American Narrative, Mester, Vol 26, 97. **CONTACT ADDRESS** Dept of Span Ital and Port, Pennsylvania State Univ, 352 Burrowes Bldg, University Park, PA, 16802-6203.

FITZGERALD, ALOYSIUS
PERSONAL Born 07/03/1932, New York, NY **DISCIPLINE** SEMITIC LANGUAGES **EDUCATION** Cath Univ Am, BA, 54, STL, 61; Manhattan Col, MA, 58; Pontif Bibl Inst, Rome, SSL, 64. **CAREER** Asst prof theol, Manhattan Col, 67-69; asst prof, 69-80, ASSOC PROF SEMITIC LANG, CATH UNIV AM, 80-, Chmn Dept, 72-. **RESEARCH** Northwest Semitic philology. **SELECTED PUBLICATIONS** Auth, In Hora Mortis--Evolution of the Christian Pastoral on Death in the 4th and 5th Centuries in Western World, Cath Hist Rev, Vol 82, 96. **CONTACT ADDRESS** Dept of Semitic Lang, Catholic Univ of America, Washington, DC, 20064.

FIZER, JOHN
PERSONAL Born 06/13/1925, Ukraine, m, 1957, 4 children **DISCIPLINE** SLAVIC AND COMPARATIVE LITERATURE **EDUCATION** Columbia Univ, MA, 52, PhD, 60. **CAREER** Analyst & interviewer, Harvard Univ, 51; asst prof Russ, Univ Notre Dame, 54-60; Prof Slavic & Comp Lit, Rutgers Univ, New Brunswick, 60-; Academician of the Natl Acad of Sciences of Ukraine, Hon prof of the Natl Univ of Kiev-Mohyla Acad, Kiev Unkraine. **MEMBERSHIPS** AATSEEL **RESEARCH** Lit aesthetics and theory; aesthetics; psychol. **SELECTED PUBLICATIONS** Auth, Philosophy in the Soviet Union: A Survey of the Mid-Sixties, De Reydel, Dordrecht, 67; Conceptual affinities and differences between A A Potebnja's theory of internal form and Roman Ingarden's stratum of aspects, In: American Contributions to the Seventh International Congress of Slavists, Mouton, The Hague, 73; The concept of strata in Roman Ingarden's theory of literary structure, In: The Personality of the Critic, Pa State Univ, 73; Some correlations in the aesthetics of A A Potebnja and Benedetto Croce, In: Sumbolae in Honorarem Georgii Y Shevelov, Logos, Munich, 73; Ingarden's prhases, Bergson's durree reele and William James' stream: metaphoric variants or mutually exclusive concepts on the theme of time, In: Analecta Husserliana, Dortrecht, 76; Psychologism and Psychoaesthetico: A Historical and Critical View of Their Relations, John Benjamin's BV, Amsterdam, 81; Psychologism and Psychoaesthetics: A Historical View of Their Relations, Amsterdam: John Benjamin B.V. 81; Psychologizm i psychoestetyka, Warsaw: PWN, 91; Alexander A. Potebja's Psycholinguistic Theory of Literature: A Metacritical Inquiry, Harvard Univ Press, 86. **CONTACT ADDRESS** Dept of Slavic Lang & Lit, Rutgers Univ, PO Box 5062, New Brunswick, NJ, 08903-5062. **EMAIL** fizer@rci.rutgersledu

FLECK, JERE
PERSONAL Born 03/02/1935, New York, NY, m, 1966 **DISCIPLINE** GERMANIC LINGUISTICS **EDUCATION** Univ Munich, Dr Phi l(Ger philol), 66. **CAREER** Asst prof Ger lang, Univ Cincinnati, 66-67 and Vanderbilt Univ, 67-70; asst prof, 70-73, ASSOC PROF GER LANG, UNIV MD, COLLEGE PARK, 73-. **MEMBERSHIPS** Pedagog Sem Ger Philol; MLA; Am Asn Teachers Ger; SAtlantic Mod Lang Asn; Mongolia Soc. **RESEARCH** Pre-Christian Germanic religion and cultural history; Germanic, Indo-European and general historic linguistics; language pedagogics and methodology. **SELECTED PUBLICATIONS** Auth, Knowing Engineers--Response, Soc Stud Sci, Vol 24, 94. **CONTACT ADDRESS** Dept of Ger and Slavic Lang, Univ Md Col, College Park, MD, 20742-0001.

FLEISCHMAN, SUZANNE
PERSONAL Born 10/25/1948, Chicago, IL **DISCIPLINE** LINGUISTICS, MEDIEVAL LITERATURE **EDUCATION** Univ Mich, BA, 69; Univ Lisbon, cert Port, 70; Univ Calif, Berkeley, MA, 71, PhD, 75. **CAREER** Instr Span, Mills Col, 74-75; asst prof, 78-79, lectr, 75-79, assoc prof French, 80-, prof, 86-, Univ Calif, Berkeley. **HONORS AND AWARDS** Am Coun Learned Socs fel, 77; Nat Endowment for Humanities, summer grant, 78; Guggenheim fel, 81-82. **MEMBERSHIPS** Ling Soc Am; MLA; Int Pragmatic Asn; Int Soc for Hist Ling. **RESEARCH** Problems of language growth and culture; language and gender; language and medicine. **SELECTED PUBLICATIONS** Auth, Cultural and Linguistic Factors in Word Formation: An Integrated Approach to the Development of the Suffix -age, California, 77; auth, The Future in Thought and Language: Diachronic Evidence from Romance, Cambridge, 82; auth, Tense and Narrativity: From Medieval Performance to Modern Fiction, Texas, 90; co-ed and contribur, Modality in Grammar and Discourse, John Benjamins, 95; auth, "Methodologies and Ideologies in Historical Grammar: A Case-Study from Old French," in Bloch, ed, Medievalism and the Modernist Temper, Johns Jopkins, 96; auth, "Medieval Vernaculars and the Myth of Monoglossia: A Conspiracy of Linguistics and Philology," in Literary History and the Challenge of Philology: The Legacy of Erich Auerbach, Stanford, 96; auth, The Battle of Feminism and Bon Usage: Instituting Nonsexist Usage in French, French Rev, 97; auth, "Gender, The Personal, and the Voice of Scholarship," Signs: A J of Women and Culture, 98; auth, A Linguist Reflects on Illness and Disease, Journal of Medical Hum, 99; auth, "Language and Medicine," in Handbook of Discourse Analysis, Blackwell, forthcoming. **CONTACT ADDRESS** French Dept, Univ of California, Berkeley, 4125 Dwinelle Hall, Berkeley, CA, 94720-2580. **EMAIL** suzanne@socrates.berkeley.edu

FLEMING, RAYMOND RICHARD
PERSONAL Born 02/27/1945, Cleveland, Ohio, m, 1969 **DISCIPLINE** ITALIAN **EDUCATION** Univ of Notre Dame, IN, BA, 1967; Univ of Florence, Italy, 1967-68; Harvard Univ, Cambridge MA, 1968-69, PhD, 1976. **CAREER** Univ of Notre Dame, Notre Dame IN, instructor, 1969-72; Univ of CA, San Diego CA, asst prof, 1973-80; Miami Univ, Oxford OH, assoc prof of Italian and asst dean of graduate school, 1980-, assoc dean of graduate school, 1985-87; PA State Univ, Univ Park PA, prof of com lit and Italian, currently. **HONORS AND AWARDS** Ford Foundation Fellowships, 1966, 1972; Fulbright Grant to Florence Italy, 1967; Woodrow Wilson Fellowship to Harvard Univ, 1968; Ingram-Merrill Poetry Award, 1971; Alexander Von Humboldt Fellowship to Germany, 1978; American Philosophical Society Research Grant, 1982; author of Diplomatic Relations (book), 1982; author of Keats, Leopardi, and Holderlin (book), 1987; Natl Endowment for the Humanities, grant, 1989, endowed professorship, 1991. **MEMBERSHIPS** Dante Society of Amer, Amer Council of Learned Societies. **SELECTED PUBLICATIONS** Author of Ice and Honey (book), 1979. **CONTACT ADDRESS** Professor of Comparative Literature and Italian, Pennsylvania State Univ, 433 N Burrowes Building, University Park, PA, 16802.

FLETCHER, ROBERT E.
PERSONAL Born 12/12/1938, Detroit, MI, m **DISCIPLINE** LAW, FILM **EDUCATION** Fisk Univ, attended 1956-59; Wayne State Univ, BA 1961; Natl Educ TV Film Training Sch, attended 1970; Comm Film Workshop Council TV News Cinematography Prog 1971; Natl Acad of TV Arts & Sci/Third World Cinema Prod Inc 1976-77; New York University School of Law, JD, 1990. **CAREER** No Student Movement Harlem, field organizer 1963-64; SNCC Jackson MS, Selma AL Atlanta GA, photographer field coord editorial & air dir 1964-68; freelance photographer journalist & film maker 1968-; Brooklyn Coll, adj prof dept of film studies 1975-76; "Vote for Your Life", prod/dir 1977; "Weatherization, What's It all About?"; Video & TV Prod, summer 1977; WPIX-TV, bi-weekly talk show; "A Nation in View", co-producer; Cravath, Swaine & Moore, attorney, 1991-. **HONORS AND AWARDS** Cinematographer dir "A Luta Continva" 1971; documentary film on liberation struggle in Mozambique "O Povo Organizado" 1975; panelist "Voices of the Civil Rights Movement" Smithsonian Inst 1980. **MEMBERSHIPS** Mem Intl Photographers of the Motion Picture Indus; chmn bd dir Rod Rodgers Dance Co 1973-; photographs pub in Ebony, Essence, Black Enterprises, Tuesday, Life, Redbook, NY Mag; author of publ in MS. **CONTACT ADDRESS** Cravath, Swaine & Moore, 825 Eighth Ave, New York, NY, 10019-7415.

FLEURANT, KEN
PERSONAL m, 2 children **DISCIPLINE** FRENCH LITERATURE **EDUCATION** Holy Cross Col, BA; Princeton Univ, MA, PhD. **CAREER** Adv French prog. **RESEARCH** French and Francophone cultural studies; cultural and political history of Quebec; European Renaissance and Enlightenment studies; all aspects of French literature. **SELECTED PUBLICATIONS** Auth, pubs on contemporary literature. **CONTACT ADDRESS** Dept of French, Univ of Wisconsin, Green Bay, 2420 Nicolet Dr, Green Bay, WI, 54311-7001. **EMAIL** fleurank@uwgb.edu

FLIER, MICHAEL S.
PERSONAL Los Angeles, CA, s **DISCIPLINE** SLAVIC LANGUAGES & LITERATURE **EDUCATION** Univ of Calif at Berkeley, BA, 62, MA, 64, PhD, 68. **CAREER** Vis acting asst prof of Slavic Languages and Lit, Univ of Calif at Berkeley, 68; asst prof of Slavic Languages, 68-73, assoc prof of Slavic Languages, 73-79, prof of Slavic Languages and Lit, Univ of Calif at Los Angeles, 79-91; vis prof of Slavic Languages, Columbia Univ, 88; Vis prof of Slavic Languages and Lit, 89, Oleksandr Potebnja Prof of Ukrainian Philology, Harvard Univ, 91-. **HONORS AND AWARDS** Travel grant, Inter-University Comt on Travel Grants, Moscow State Univ, 66-67; travel grant, Int Res and Exchanges Board, Moscow State Univ & Charles Univ, 71; summer fel for jr fac, UCLA, 77; travel grant, Int Res and Exchanges Board, Russian Language Inst of the Acad of Sci of the U.S.S.R., 78; summer col inst fel, Col of Letters and Sci, UCLA, 84; study grant, Kennan Inst for Advanced Russian Studies, 85; President's Fel in the Humanities, Univ of Calif, 90; John Simon Guggenheim Memorial Found Fel, 90-91; IREX Grant, 96. **MEMBERSHIPS** Am Asn for Teachers of Slavic and East European Languages; Am Asn for the Advancement of Slavic Studies; Linguistic Soc of Am. **SELECTED PUBLICATIONS** Co-ed, Medieval Russian Culture II, Univ of Calif Press, 94; For SK: In Celebration of the Life and Career of Simon Karlinsky, Berkeley Slavic Specialties, 94; The Language and Verse of Russia. In Honor of Dean S. Worth on his Sixty-fifth Birthday, Vostochnaya Literatura Pub, 95; ed, Ukrainian Philology and Linguistics, 94. **CONTACT ADDRESS** Dept of Slavic Languages and Literatures, Harvard Univ, Barker Center, 12 Quincy St., Cambridge, MA, 02138. **EMAIL** flier@fas.harvard.edu

FLORY, STEWART GILMAN
PERSONAL Born 10/28/1941, New York, NY, m, 1970 **DISCIPLINE** CLASSICAL LANGUAGES & LITERATURES **EDUCATION** Yale Univ, BA, 64, MA, 67, MPhil, 68, PhD(classics), 69. **CAREER** Asst prof classics, Amherst Col, 69-77; Chmn Dept Classics, Gustavus Adolphus Col, 79-, Am Sch Class Studies fel, Athens, 74-75 & sr assoc, 82-83; Nat Endowment for Humanities fel, Rome, summer, 80 & foreign col teachers, 82-83. **MEMBERSHIPS** Am Philol Asn; Archaeol Inst Am. **RESEARCH** Herodotus; Homer; Plato. **SELECTED PUBLICATIONS** Auth, The Personality of Herodotus, Arion, 69; Laughter, tears and wisdom in Herodotus, Am J Philol, 78; Medea's right hand, Tapa, 78; Who read Herodotus' histories, Am J Philol, Vol 101. **CONTACT ADDRESS** 800 W College Ave, Saint Peter, MN, 56082-1498. **EMAIL** sflory@gac.edu

FLOWERS, RONALD BRUCE
PERSONAL Born 01/11/1935, Tulsa, OK, m, 1959, 3 children **DISCIPLINE** RELIGION, AMERICAN CHURCH HISTORY **EDUCATION** Tex Christian Univ, BA, 57; Vanderbilt Univ, BD, 60, STM, 61; Univ Iowa, PhD(relig, Am church hist), 67. **CAREER** Asst prof, 66-72, assoc prof relig, Tex Christian Univ, 72-83, prof 84-. **HONORS AND AWARDS** Danforth assoc, 71-; Weatherly Prof of Religion, 98. **MEMBERSHIPS** Disciples of Christ Hist Soc; Am Acad of Relig. **RESEARCH** The history of religion in America; church and state relationships in America. **SELECTED PUBLICATIONS** Auth, An Introduction to Church-State Relationships, Encounter, summer 71; Piety in Public Places, Christianity & Crisis, 11/71; A Selected Bibliography on Religion and Public Education, J Church & State, autumn 72; The Supreme Court's Three Tests of the Establishment Clause, Religion in Life, spring 76; coauth, Toward Benevolent Neutrality: Church, State, and the Supreme Court, Baylor Univ, 77, rev ed, 82, 5th rev ed, 84; Freedom of Religion Versus Civil Authority in Matters of Health, Ann Am Acad Pol Soc Sci, 11/79; The Supreme Courts Interpretation of the Free Exercise Clause, Relig Life, fall 80; The 1960's: A Decisive Decade in American Church-State Relationships, Encounter, summer 82;auth, Religion in Strange Times: The 1960's and 1970's, 84; co auth, The Naturalization of Rosika Schwimmer, Journal of Church and State, spring 90; auth, In Praise of Conscience: Marie Averil Bland, Angelican and Episcopal History, March 93; Government Accomodation of Religious-Based Conscientious Objection, Seton Hall Law Rev, 93; That Godless Court?: Supreme Court Decisions on Church-State relationships, 94. **CONTACT ADDRESS** Dept of Relig, Tex Christian Univ, Box 298100, Fort Worth, TX, 76129-0002. **EMAIL** r.flowers@tcu.edu

FOGEL, HERBERT
PERSONAL Born 04/24/1931, New York, NY **DISCIPLINE** ROMANCE LANGUAGES **EDUCATION** NY Univ, BA, 52, MA, 55, PhD (Romance lang), 63. **CAREER** Instr French, NY Univ, 56-59; instr, Queens Col, NY, 60-61; from instr to asst prof, 61-67, ASSOC PROF FRENCH, LONG ISLAND UNIV, 67, Fulbright fel, Sorbonne, 59-60. **MEMBERSHIPS** MLA; Am Asn Teachers Fr. **SELECTED PUBLICATIONS** Auth, The Complete Discography of Mitropoulos, Dimitri, Association for Recorded Sound Collections J, Vol 23, 92; Rosbaud, Hans--A Biobibliography, Assoc Rec Sound Collect J, Vol 24, 93; The Devils Music Master--Furtwangler, Wilhelm, Assoc Rec Sound Collec J, Vol 24, 93. **CONTACT ADDRESS** Dept of Mod Lang, Long Island Univ, Brooklyn, NY, 11201.

FOLEY, MARY KATHLEEN
DISCIPLINE ASIAN THEATER **EDUCATION** Rosemont Col, BA, 69; Univ Bochum, W Germany, Fulbright cert, 70; Univ Mass, Amherst, MA, 75; Univ Hawaii, PhD, 79. **CAREER** Asst to assoc to PROF, UNIV CALIF, 80-, PROVOST PORTER COL, 89-, UNIV CALIF, SANTA CRUZ. **CONTACT ADDRESS** Porter Col, Univ of California, Santa Cruz, 301 Heller Dr, Santa Cruz, CA, 95064.

FONG, GRACE
DISCIPLINE EAST ASIAN STUDIES **EDUCATION** Univ British Columbia, PhD. **CAREER** Assoc prof. **RESEARCH** Classical Chinese poetry; literary theory and criticism; gender and representation; Chinese film. **SELECTED PUBLICATIONS** Art, Inscribing Desire: Zhu Yizun's Love Lyrics in Jingzhi ju qinqu, Harvard Jour Asiatic Studies, 94; auth, The Early Literary Traditions, 94; auth, Wu Wenying and the Art of Southern Song Ci Poetry, Princeton, 87. **CONTACT ADDRESS** East Asian Studies Dept, McGill Univ, 845 Sherbrooke St, Montreal, PQ, H3A 2T5.

FONTANELLA, LEE
PERSONAL Born 07/23/1941, Stafford Springs, CT, m, 1974, 1 child **DISCIPLINE** HISPANIC STUDIES, COMPARATIVE LITERATURE. **EDUCATION** Williams Col, BA, 63; New York Univ, MA, 66; Princeton Univ, MA, 68, PhD (Romance lang and lit), 71. **CAREER** Instr Span, Williams Col, 63-64; asst prof, 70-76, ASSOC PROF SPAN, UNIV TEX, AUSTIN, 76-, Coun Int Exchange Scholars fel, 77-78. **MEMBERSHIPS** SCent Mod Lang Asn; SCent Soc 18th Century Studies; Am Asn Teachers Span and Port; MLA; Am Soc 18th Century Studies. **RESEARCH** Spanish romantic literature and essay; comparative literature; 19th century popular science and photohistory. **SELECTED PUBLICATIONS** Auth, New Italian, Forum Ital, Vol 28,94; From Tusiani to Tusiani--Notes on Poetry in Italian and English with Special Reference to the Works of Tusiani, Joseph, Otto Novecento, Vol 19, 95; Sospensioni Forum Ital, Vol 30, 96; Dibiasio, Rodolfo Between Self Reflection and Cosmological Tension--Concerning Patmos, Forum Italicum, Vol 29, 95; Dialect Idiolect in Serrao, Achille Poetry, Otto Novecento, Vol 17, 93; Don Juan in New York, Gradiva, Vol 6, 97; Sospensioni, Forum Italicum, Vol 30, 96; Paulhan, Jean and Ungaretti, Giuseppe--Correspondence 1921-1968, Forum Italicum, Vol 28, 94; Attesa Sul Mare, Forum Ital, Vol 29, 95; New Italian Poets, Forum Ital, Vol 28, 94; Doplicher, Fabio--Selected Poems, Forum Ital, Vol 28, 94; Previously Unpublished Poems of Breton, Andre with Italian Translations, Gradiva, Vol 6, 96; Doplicher, Fabio--Selected Poems, Forum Ital, Vol 28, 94; Attesa Sul Mare, Forum Ital, Vol 29,

95; Image of the Frozen Lake, Gradiva, Vol 5, 93; Down Below, Gradiva, Vol 5, 93; In the Rereading, Gradiva, Vol 5, 93; Interno Esterno, Forum Ital, Vol 28, 94; Page and Awakening, Gradiva, Vol 5, 93; I Think of an Elephant, Gradiva, Vol 5, 93; Paper Curtain, Gradiva, Vol 5, 93; Valesio, Paolo, Gradiva, Vol 5, 93; Words for Emma, Gradiva, Vol 5, 93; To my Father, Gradiva, Vol 5, 93; Fr Rm, Gradiva, Vol 5, 93; In the Nightime, Gradiva, Vol 5, 93; On a Straight Path Gradiva, Vol 5, 93; Responses to the Questionnaire Concerning Italian Poets and their Poetry in the United States, Gradiva, Vol 5, 93; The Roman de Tristan By Thomas, Studi Francesi, Vol 38, 94; Sulla Rotta Di Magellano, Forum Ital, Vol 31, 97; Dibiasio, Rodolfo Between Self Reflection and Cosmological Tension--Concerning Patmos, Forum Italic, Vol 29, 95; Interno Esterno, Forum Italicum, Vol 28, 94; The Poetry of Betti, Ugo, Critica Letteraria, Vol 20, 92; Paulhan, Jean and Ungaretti, Giuseppe--Correspondence 1921-1968, Forum Ital, Vol 28, 94. **CONTACT ADDRESS** Dept of Span and Port, Univ of Tex, Batts Hall, Austin, TX, 78712.

FORCADAS, ALBERTO M.
PERSONAL Born 11/25/1935, Barcelona, Spain, m, 1966 **DISCIPLINE** ROMANCE LANGUAGES **EDUCATION** Univ Ga, BBA, 62; Univ Mo-Columbia, MA, 64, PhD (Span), 66. **CAREER** Asst prof, 66-70, assoc prof, 70-79, PROF SPAN AND CATALAN, UNIV ALTA, 80-, Univ Alta res grant-in-aid, 67-68; Can Coun res grant Catalan-English dict, 68-69. **MEMBERSHIPS** MLA; Am Asn Teachers Span and Port; Can Asn Hispanists; Can Asn Latin Am Studies; Assoc Int Llenqua and Lit Catalanes. **RESEARCH** Golden Age literature, especially theatre; Catalan language and literature; Ruben Dario and modernism. **SELECTED PUBLICATIONS** Auth, Maror, les Regles del Genere--W Lit Today, Vol 70, 96; Poetic Works, Vol 3, 1980-1990, W Lit Today, Vol 68, 94; Materia Dels Astres, W Lit Today, Vol 67, 93; El Pati, W Lit Today, Vol 67, 93; Mascarada, W Lit Today, Vol 71, 97; La Veu Melodiosa, W Lit Today, Vol 69, 95; Ronda Naval Sota La Boira, W Lit Today, Vol 69, 95; Short Novels, Vol 6, 1978-1982, W Lit Today, Vol 67, 93; The Intertextual Presence of the Propalladia by Torresnaharro in the Prologue and Tratado I of the Lazarillo de Tormes, Revista de Literatura, Vol 56, 94; Opera al Paradis, W Lit Today, Vol 68, 94; Tot Es Caduc, W Lit Today, Vol 68, 94; Espriu, Salvador The Years of Initiation 1929-1943, W Lit Today, Vol 69, 95; The Hour of the Nations, World Lit Today, Vol 69, 95; The Garden Across the Border--Rodoreda, Merce Fiction, W Lit Today, Vol 69, 95; Perfils Cruels, W Lit Today, Vol 70, 96; Amor De Cans, W Lit Today, Vol 70, 96. **CONTACT ADDRESS** Dept of Romance Lang, Univ of Alta, Arts Bldg, Edmonton, AB, T6G 2E1.

FORD, ALVIN EARLE
PERSONAL Born 11/07/1937, Edmonton, AB, Canada **DISCIPLINE** FRENCH LITERATURE **EDUCATION** Univ BC, BA, 59, MA, 62; Univ Pa, PhD, 71. **CAREER** Instr French, Univ Sask, Regina, 62-65; lectr, 68-71, asst prof, 71-76, assoc prof, 76-81, prof French, 81-, Calif State Univ, Northridge. **MEMBERSHIPS** Am Assn Teachers Fr; Am Soc 18th Century Studies Res. **RESEARCH** Medieval apocrypha; enlightenment. **SELECTED PUBLICATIONS** Auth, L'evangile de Nicodeme: Les Versions Courtes en Ancien Francais et en Prose, Droz, Geneva, 73; auth, La vengeance de Nostre-Seigneur: The old French prose versions, Vol I: The version of Japheth, Pontifical Inst Mediaeval Studies, 82; co-ed, Paradigms in Medieval Thought: Applications in Medieval Disciplines, Mellon, Lewiston, 90; auth, La Vengeance de Nostre-Seigneur, vol 2, Pontifical Institute of Medieval Studies, 93. **CONTACT ADDRESS** Dept of Foreign Lang & Lit, California State Univ, Northridge, 18111 Nordhoff St, Northridge, CA, 91330-8200.

FORD, JAMES
DISCIPLINE LANGUAGE AWARENESS **EDUCATION** Henderson State Univ, BSE, 62; Univ Central Ark, MSE, 67, Univ Ark, MA, 68; Ohio State Univ, PhD, 74. **CAREER** English and Lit, Univ Ark. **HONORS AND AWARDS** Acting Chair, Dept; Chair, dept, 77-86. **SELECTED PUBLICATIONS** Areas: language attitudes, and foreign language acquisition/learning. **CONTACT ADDRESS** Univ Ark, Fayetteville, AR, 72701.

FORD, JAMES FRANCIS
PERSONAL Born 02/15/1937, Russell County, AL, m, 1972, 4 children **DISCIPLINE** FOREIGN LANGUAGE EDUCATION, SPANISH **EDUCATION** Henderson State Univ, BSE, 62; Univ Cent Ark, MSE, 67; Univ Ark, MA, 68; Ohio State Univ, PhD (for lang educ), 74. **CAREER** Instr Spanish methods, Ark State Univ, 68-69 and Univ Ark, 69-70; asst prof Spanish methods, Okla State Univ, 72-74; asst prof, 74-77, ASSOC PROF SPANISH AND CHMN DEPT FOR LANG, 77-, Bd of dir, Cent State Conf Teaching For Lang, 76-80. **MEMBERSHIPS** MLA; Am Coun Teaching For Lang; Am Asn Teachers Span and Port; Teachers English Speakers Other Lang. **RESEARCH** Language acquisition; sociolinguistics; teacher training. **SELECTED PUBLICATIONS** Auth, Intermediate Spanish, Mod Lan J, Vol 79, 95; Facetas--Conversation and Writing, Mod Lan J, Vol 78, 94; Personajes, Mod Lan J, Vol 77, 93; Claro--Impressions and Ideas, Mod Lan J, Vol 79, 95; Intermediate Spanish--Civilization and Culture, 5th Edition, Mod Lan J, Vol 79, 95; Intermediate Spanis Conversation Review, 5th Edition, Mod Lan J, Vol 79, 95; Claro--Tapescript, Mod Lan J, Vol 79 95; Intermediate Spanish Lit Art, 5th Eition Spanish, Mod Lan J, Vol 79, 95; Facetas--Reader, Mod Lan J, Vol 78, 94; Intermediate Spanish--Laboratory Manual and Creative Exercises, Mod Lan J, Vol 79, 95. **CONTACT ADDRESS** Dept For Lang, Univ Ark, Fayetteville, AR, 72701-1202.

FORD, RICHARD R.
DISCIPLINE SPANISH **EDUCATION** Univ Chicago, PhD, 73. **CAREER** Past ch, UTEP's Dept Lang and Ling; past dir, Univ Honors Prog; coord and tchr, UTEP's Translation & Interpretation prog; accredited by the Amer Translator's Asn for transl from Span-Engl and Engl-Span. **RESEARCH** Spanish American literature and translation. **SELECTED PUBLICATIONS** Publ on Span Amer lit, in Revista de Occidente, Revista Iberoamericana, Cuadernos Americanos, and Romance Notes; transl, Colors on Desert Walls: The Murals of El Paso, Tex Western Press, 97. **CONTACT ADDRESS** Dept of Languages and Linguistics, Univ of Texas, El Paso, 500 W University Ave, El Paso, TX, 79968. **EMAIL** rford@utep.edu

FOREST, JEAN
PERSONAL Born 03/03/1942, Montreal, PQ, Canada **DISCIPLINE** FRENCH LITERATURE **EDUCATION** Laurentian Univ, BA, 63; Laval Univ, MA, 66, PhD (French lit), 71. **CAREER** Assoc Prof French Lit, Univ Sherbrooke, 70-. **RESEARCH** French 19th century prose and poetry; modern criticism. **SELECTED PUBLICATIONS** Auth, Holy Foolishness, Parabola Myth Tradition Search Meaning, Vol 19, 94. **CONTACT ADDRESS** 2990 Rue Savard, Sherbrooke, PQ, JIK 1S4.

FORMAN, MICHAEL LAWRENCE
PERSONAL Born 06/30/1940, Kansas City, MO, m, 1963, 4 children **DISCIPLINE** LIMGUISTICS, ANTHROPOLOGY **EDUCATION** John Carroll Univ, AB, 61; Cornell Univ, PhD, 72. **CAREER** Asst researcher, Pac & Asian Ling Inst, 68-69, acting asst prof, 69-72, asst prof, 72-73, chmn Southeast Asian studies, 77-80, Assoc Prof Ling, Univ Hawaii, Manoa, 73-, Second Language Acquisition faculty; assoc ed, Oceanic Ling; co-ed, The Carrier Pidgeon, 93-96; contribr, Biography: An Interdisciplinary Quart. **HONORS AND AWARDS** Nat Endowment for Humanities study fel, 74-75; Soc Sci Res Inst, 80-82, 93-95; Excellence in Teaching Award, Univ Hawaii Board of Regents, 84, Univ Hawaii Col Lang, Ling, & Lit, 84; Robert W. Clapton Award for Distinguished Community Service, 86. **MEMBERSHIPS** Am Anthrop Asn; Ling Soc Am; Ling Soc Philippines. **RESEARCH** Child language acquisition; pidginization and creolization; Philippine descriptive linguistics. **SELECTED PUBLICATIONS** Auth Kapampangan Grammar Notes, 71 & Kapampangan Dictionary, 71, Univ Hawaii; coauth, Riddles: Expressive models of interrogation, Ethnology, Vol X , Nov 4 & In: Directions in Sociolinguistic Holt, 72; ed, World Englishes 2000, Univ Hawaii Press, 97. **CONTACT ADDRESS** Dept of Ling, Univ of Hawaii Manoa, 1890 E West Rd, Honolulu, HI, 96822-2318. **EMAIL** forman@hawaii.edu

FORSTER, MERLIN HENRY
PERSONAL Born 02/24/1928, Delta, UT, m, 1952, 5 children **DISCIPLINE** SPANISH AND PORTUGUESE **EDUCATION** Brigham Young Univ, BA, 56; Univ Ill, MA, 57, PhD, 60. **CAREER** Instr Romance lang, Univ Tex, 60-61, asst prof, 61-62; from asst prof to assoc prof, Univ Ill, Urbana-Champaign, 62-69, prof, 69-78, dir, Ctr Latin Am Studies, 72-78; PROF SPAN AND PORT AND CHMN DEPT, UNIV TEX, AUSTIN, 79-, Soc Sci Res Coun res grant, 65-66; Fulbright-Hays res fel, Arg, Uruguay, Chile, Brazil and Peru, 71; res assoc, Ctr Advan Study, Univ Ill, 76. **MEMBERSHIPS** Am Asn Teachers Span and Port; Latin Am Studies Asn; Inst Int Lit Iberoam (pres, 79-81). **RESEARCH** Spanish American poetry and drama; Mexican literature; Brazilian and Portuguese literature. **SELECTED PUBLICATIONS** Auth, The Concept of Ars Poetica in the Poetry of Rojas, Gonzalo, Chasqui Revista Lit Latinoamericana, Vol 22, 93. **CONTACT ADDRESS** Dept of Span and Port, Univ Tex, Austin, TX, 78712.

FORSYTH, PHYLLIS
PERSONAL Brookline, MA **DISCIPLINE** CLASSICAL STUDIES/HISTORY/FINE ART **EDUCATION** Mount Holyoke Col, BA, 66; Univ Toronto, MA, 67, PhD, 72. **CAREER** Tchr Fel, Univ Toronto, 67-69: PROF, UNIV WATERLOO 69-, founding ch, dept class studs, 79-88, acting ch 94-. **HONORS AND AWARDS** Distinguished Tchr Awd. **MEMBERSHIPS** Ont Class Asn; Can Fedn Hum; Archeol Inst Am; Can Mediter Inst. **RESEARCH** Latin literature; Aegean Bronze Age; effect of natural disasters on the ancient world. **SELECTED PUBLICATIONS** Auth, Atlantis: The Making of Myth, 80; ed, Labyrinth: A Classical Magazine for Secondary Schs, 73-84, 88-94. **CONTACT ADDRESS** Dept of Classical Studies, Univ Waterloo, 200 University Ave W, Waterloo, ON, N2L 3G1. **EMAIL** forsyth@watarts.uwaterloo.ca

FOSTER, BENJAMIN READ
PERSONAL Born 11/15/1945, Bryn Mawr, PA, m, 1975, 2 children **DISCIPLINE** ASSYRIOLOGY **EDUCATION** Princeton Univ, BA, 68; Yale Univ, MA, MPhil, 74, PhD, 75. **CAREER** Instr Arabic, 73-75, asst prof Assyriol, 75-81, Assoc Prof Assyriol, Yale Univ, 81-86, prof, 86-; chmn dept Near East lang, 89-98. **HONORS AND AWARDS** Amer Res Inst in Turkey fel, 77, 79; Mellan Fel; NEH Translation Grant, 83-84. **MEMBERSHIPS** Am Orient Soc. **RESEARCH** Soc and economic hist of early Mesopotamia; Akkadian lit. **SELECTED PUBLICATIONS** Umma in the Sargonic Period, Memoirs of Conn Acad of Arts & Sci, No 20, 82; Administration and Use of Institutional Land in Sargonic Sumer, Copenhagen Studies in Assyriology, No 9, 82; coauth, Sargonic Tablets from Telloh in the Istanbul Archeological Museum, Babylonian Sect, Univ Mus, Philadelphia, 82; auth, Before the Muses An Anthology of Akkadian Literature, 93; auth, From Distant Days Myths Tales and Poetry of Ancient Mesopotauria, 95; auth, Un Araboen el Neuro Mindo 1668-1683, 89, (Argentina). **CONTACT ADDRESS** Sterling Mem Libr, Rm 318, Yale Univ, PO Box 208236, New Haven, CT, 06520-8236. **EMAIL** benjamin.foster@yale.edu

FOSTER, DAVID WILLIAM
PERSONAL Born 09/11/1940, Seattle, WA, m, 1966, 1 child **DISCIPLINE** ROMANCE LANGUAGES **EDUCATION** Univ Wash, BA, 61, MA, 63, PhD, 64. **CAREER** Tchng asst, 61-64, Univ Wash; vis instr, 62, Fresno St Col; vis asst prof, 64, Vanderbilt Univ; asst prof, 64-66, Univ Missouri; asst prof, assoc prof, prof, 66-, Arizona St Univ. **CONTACT ADDRESS** 928 West Palm Lane, Phoenix, AZ, 85007-1535. **EMAIL** david.foster@asu.edu

FOUCHEREAUX, JEAN
DISCIPLINE FRENCH LITERATURE **EDUCATION** Univ Iowa, MA, PhD. **CAREER** Assoc prof. **SELECTED PUBLICATIONS** Auth, pubs on francophone studies in North America and implementation of new teaching strategies through technology. **CONTACT ADDRESS** Department of Foreign Languages and Classics, 37 Col Ave, Gorham, MN, 04038-1083. **EMAIL** jeanf@usm.maine.edu

FOURNIER, HANNAH
DISCIPLINE FRENCH LITERATURE **EDUCATION** Univ Toronto, BA; Univ Western Ontario, MA; PhD. **RESEARCH** Sixteenth century renaissance; reformation literature; history of French women writers. **SELECTED PUBLICATIONS** Auth, pub(s) on Marie de Gournay and Marguerite de Navarre; co-ed, Les Jumeaux martirs 1650. **CONTACT ADDRESS** Dept of French, Waterloo Univ, 200 University Ave W, Waterloo, ON, N2L 3G1. **EMAIL** hsfourer@watarts.uwaterloo.ca

FOURNY, DIANE
DISCIPLINE SEVENTEENTH- AND EIGHTEENTH-CENTURY FRENCH LITERATURE **EDUCATION** Stanford Univ, PhD. **CAREER** Assoc prof, Univ KS. **HONORS AND AWARDS** H Bernerd Fink distinguished Tchg award. **RESEARCH** Psychoanalytic and anthrop approaches to lit. **SELECTED PUBLICATIONS** Auth, articles on Corneille, Diderot, and Rousseau. **CONTACT ADDRESS** Dept of French and Italian, Univ Kansas, Admin Building, Lawrence, KS, 66045. **EMAIL** kufacts@ukans.edu

FOWKES, ROBERT ALLEN
PERSONAL Born 04/07/1913, Harrison, NY **DISCIPLINE** LINGUISTICS **EDUCATION** NY Univ, AB, 34, AM, 35; Columbia Univ, PhD, 47. **CAREER** Asst Ger, NY Univ, 35-36; asst, Columbia Univ, 37-38, from instr to prof, 38-73, chmn dept Ger lang, 57-68; prof and chmn dept Ger lang, 73-78, EMER PROF LING AND GER, NY UNIV, 78-, Lectr Celtic lang, Univ Pa, 67. **MEMBERSHIPS** Ling Soc Am; MLA; Int Ling Asn. **RESEARCH** Germanic Indo-European and comparative linguistics; Welsh and other Celtic languages; Welsh etymological dictionary. **SELECTED PUBLICATIONS** Auth, Spirit Pond Runestones--A Study in Linguistics, Verbatim, Vol 22, 96; Eyebrows and Lowbrows, Verbatim, Vol 19, 93; The International Linguistic Association, A Subjective History, Word J Int Ling Assoc, Vol 45, 94. **CONTACT ADDRESS** 632 Van Cortland Park Ave, Yonkers, NY, 10705.

FOWLER, CAROLYN A.
DISCIPLINE FRENCH LITERATURE **EDUCATION** Univ Pa, PhD. **CAREER** Prof. **RESEARCH** Haitian culture and literature; Cameroonian literature; French heritage of Madagascar; African American literature; literature and culture as reflected in literary and general interest periodicals. **SELECTED PUBLICATIONS** Auth, pubs on Haitian authors, and African American aesthetics. **CONTACT ADDRESS** Foreign Languages and Literature Dept, Colorado State Univ, Fort Collins, CO, 80523. **EMAIL** cfowler@vines.colostate.edu

FOWLER, SHELLI
DISCIPLINE COMPARATIVE AMERICAN CULTURES. **EDUCATION** Univ Tex at Austin, PhD. **CAREER** Asst prof, Washington State Univ. **RESEARCH** African American literature, critical pedagogy; ethnic and cultural studies. **SELECTED PUBLICATIONS** Coauth, Site Visits: Itineraries for Writers, Houghton Mifflin. **CONTACT ADDRESS** Dept of English, Washington State Univ, 1 SE Stadium Way, PO Box 645020, Pullman, WA, 99164-5020. **EMAIL** fowlers@wsu.edu

FOWLIE, WALLACE
PERSONAL Born 11/08/1908, Brookline, MA **DISCIPLINE** FRENCH LITERATURE **EDUCATION** Harvard Univ, AB, 30, AM, 33, PhD, 36. **CAREER** Master French, Taft Sch, 30-31; instr, Harvard Univ, 31-35; prof French and Ital lit, Bennington Col, 35-41; asst prof French, Yale Univ, 41-46; assoc prof, Univ Chicago, 46-50; prof and head dept, Bennington Col, 50-62; prof, Univ Colo, 62-64; JAMES B DUKE PROF FRENCH, DUKE UNIV, 64-, Guggenheim fel, 48-49; adv ed, Poetry Mag, 50-. **HONORS AND AWARDS** Vursell Award, Am Acad and Inst Arts and Lett, 80. **MEMBERSHIPS** MLA; Am Asn Teachers Fr. **RESEARCH** Rimbaud; clowns and angels; Jacob's night. **SELECTED PUBLICATIONS** Auth, Sand, George and Idealism, Sewanee Rev, Vol 102, 94; My France--Politics, Culture, Myth, Sewanee Rev, Vol 101, 93; Imagining Paris--Exile, Writing, and American Identity, Sewanee Rev, Vol 101, 93; The Work of Fire, Sewanee Rev, Vol 104, 96; Proust and the Sense of Time, Sewanee Rev, Vol 102, 94; Post Scripts--The Writers Workshop, Sewanee Rev, Vol 103, 95; A Throw of the Dice--The Life of Mallarme, Stephane, Sewanee Rev, Vol 103, 95; Mosaic, Sewanee Rev, Vol 104, 96; The Inferno of Dante--A New Verse Translation, Sewanee Rev, Vol 103, 95; The Cubist Poets In Paris--An Anthology, Sewanee Rev, Vol 103, 95; Whos Afraid of Claudel, Paul--Reflections on 2 Translations of Partage de Midi, Claudel Stud, Vol 20, 93; The Portable Dante, Sewanee Rev, Vol 102, 94; Rimbaud in Abyssinia, Sewanee Rev, Vol 101, 93. **CONTACT ADDRESS** Dept of Fr, Duke Univ, Durham, NC, 27706.

FOX, DIANA
PERSONAL Born 04/10/1951, Seattle, WA **DISCIPLINE** SPANISH LITERATURE **EDUCATION** Univ Ore, BA, 75; Duke Univ, MA, 77, PhD (Romance lang), 79. **CAREER** Lectr Span, Duke Univ, 79-80; ASST PROF SPAN AND HUMANITIES, COLUMBIA UNIV, 80-, Am Coun Learned Soc fel, 83; res assoc, Univ Calif, Berkeley, 83. **MEMBERSHIPS** MLA; Am Asn Teachers Span and Port. **RESEARCH** Spanish Golden Age theater, especially political aspects of Calderon; narrative theory of Cervantes; medieval Spanish literature. **SELECTED PUBLICATIONS** Auth, The Prince in the Tower, Perceptions of La Vida Es Sueno, Mln Mod Lan Notes, Vol 110, 95; Parallel Lives--Spanish and English National Drama 1580-1680, Comp Lit Stud, Vol 30, 93; The Prince in the Tower, Perceptions of La Vida Es Sueno, Mln Mod Lan Notes, Vol 110, 95; An Ideological Reading of Calderon, El Medico de Su Honra, Bull Comediantes, Vol 45, 93; Fatal Union, A Pluralistic Approach to the Spanish Wife Murder Comedias, Bull Hisp Stud, Vol 70, 93. **CONTACT ADDRESS** 560 Riverside Dr No 10-A, New York, NY, 10027.

FOX, EDWARD INMAN
PERSONAL Born 08/22/1933, Nashville, TN **DISCIPLINE** FOREIGN LANGUAGES **EDUCATION** Vanderbilt Univ, BA, 54, MA, 58; Princeton Univ, MA, 59, PhD, 60. **CAREER** Asst prof Span, Vanderbilt Univ, 60-64, assoc prof, 64-66; assoc prof Romance lang Univ Mass, 66-67; Prof Hispanic studies and chmn dept, Vassar Col, 67-71, John Guy Vassar prof mod lang, 71-74, dean fac, 71-72, dir long range educ planning, 72-73; pres, Knox Col, Ill, 74-82; PROF SPAN AND PORT, NORTHWESTERN UNIV, 82-, Vis prof, Escuela Verano, Mex, 58-60 and 62; Am Philos Soc grants, 63 and 68; Fulbright res grant, Spain, 65-66; mem exec and nominating comt, Spanish IV, MLA, 65-68, secy, Spanish V, 67, chmn, 68; delivered lect, Spain and Brit Isles, 66,74 and 77, US, 67-68 and 77-82; vis prof Romance lang, Wesleyan Univ, 71; Miguel de Unamuno prof, Univ Salamanca, 73; chmn, Great Lakes District Rhodes Scholarship Comt, 79-81; mem exec comt, Spanish V, MLA, 80-84; Nat Endowment Humanities fel, 82-83. **MEMBERSHIPS** Asoc Int Hispanistas; MLA. **RESEARCH** Nineteenth and twentieth century Spanish literature and intellectual history. **SELECTED PUBLICATIONS** Auth, Crossfire, Philosophy and the Novel in Spain, 1900-1934, Mln Mod Lan Notes, Vol 110, 95; Hispanic Studies in Honor of Ribbans, Geoffrey, Bull Hisp Stud, Vol 70, 93; Crossfire, Philosophy and the Novel in Spain, 1900-1934, Mln Mod Lan Notes, Vol 110, 95; Azorin in the Postwar, Aesthetics and Psychology of Old Age and Solitude, Insula Revista de Letras Y Ciencias Humanas, Vol 48, 93. **CONTACT ADDRESS** Northwestern Univ, Evanston, IL, 60201.

FOX, LINDA CHODOSH
PERSONAL Born 05/20/1943, Charlottesville, VA, m, 1967, 2 children **DISCIPLINE** FOREIGN LANGUAGE **EDUCATION** Douglass Col, BA, 65; Ind Univ, Bloomington, MA 67; Univ Wis-Madison, PhD(Span), 74. **CAREER** Lectr, 71-74, asst prof Span, Ind Univ-Purdue Univ, Fort Wayne, 74-95; assoc prof Span, 96-; dir of Women's Studies, 82-88; 95, newsletter ed, Feministas Unidas: A coalition of feminist scholars in Span, Span-Am, Luso-Brazilian, Afro-Port & Chicano-Riqueno Studies; 81-96. **HONORS AND AWARDS** Phi Beta Kappa, 65; Sigma Delta Pi Honorary, 65; Outstanding Teacher Award Indiana U-Purdue U, Fort Wayne, 96; Best Teachers in America; 98. **MEMBERSHIPS** MLA; Am Asn Teachers Span & Port; Assoc Lit Hisp Femenina; Feministas Unidas. **RESEARCH** Power in the family and beyond: Dona Perfecta and Bernarda Alba as manipulators of their destinies; characterization of women in Hispanic literature. **SELECTED PUBLICATIONS** Auth, Vision of Cain and Abel in Spain's generation of 1898, CLA J, 6/78; Las lagrimas y la tristeza en el Lazarillo de Tormes, Revista Estudios Hisp, 10/79; Making Bonds, Breaking Bonds: The Mother-Daughter Relationship in Chicana Poetry 1975-1985, in En homenaje a Victoria Urbano, ed, Adelaida Lopez de Martinez, Madrid: Editorial Fundamentos, 93; From Chants to Borders to Communion: Pat Mora's Journey to Nepantla, Bilingual Review, Revista Bilingue, Sept-Dec, 96. **CONTACT ADDRESS** Dept of Mod Foreign Lang, Indiana Univ-Purdue Univ, Fort Wayne, 2101 Coliseum Blvd E, Ft. Wayne, IN, 46805-1499. **EMAIL** fox@epfw.edu

FRADIN, JOSEPH I.
DISCIPLINE COMPARATIVE LITERATURE **EDUCATION** Columbia Univ, BA; PhD. **CAREER** Fac, Columbia Univ; fac, Cornell Univer; prof, SUNY Buffalo, present. **RESEARCH** Novels of Dickens; writing and violence; art and the ethical. **SELECTED PUBLICATIONS** Auth, articles in a number of jour(s) including PMLA, 19th century fiction; TX studies in lang(s) and lit, and Conradiana. **CONTACT ADDRESS** Dept Comp Lit, SUNY Buffalo, 639 Clemens Hall, Buffalo, NY, 14260.

FRAJZYNGIER, ZYGMUNT
PERSONAL Born 04/03/1938, Radom, Poland, m, 1971, 2 children **DISCIPLINE** LINGUISTICS, AFRICAN LANGUAGES AND LINGUISTICS **EDUCATION** Univ Warsaw, MA, 63, PhD (philol), 68; Univ Ghana, MA, 65. **CAREER** Doktorant African lang, Univ Warsaw, 65-68, adjunct, 68-69; asst prof, 70-76, assoc prof, 76-82, PROF LING, UNIV COLO, 82-, Sr lectr, Bayero Col, Ahmadu Bello Univ, Kano, Nigeria, 74-75. **MEMBERSHIPS** Ling Soc Am. **RESEARCH** Semantics; syntax. **SELECTED PUBLICATIONS** Auth, A Dictionary of Migama--Migama French and French-Migama Sara, Chad With a Grammatical Introduction, Bull Sch Orient African Stud Univ London, Vol 57, 94; Chadic Lexical Roots--Vol I, Tenetative Reconstruction, Grading, Distribution and Comments, Vol II, Documentation, Bull School Orient African Stud Univ London, Vol 59, 96; A Dictionary of the Tangale Language Kaltungo, Northern Nigeria, with a Grammatical Introduction, Bull Sch Orient African Stud UnivLondon, Vol 57, 94; A Grammar of Lango, Stud Lan, Vol 18, 94; Language Death--Factual and Theoretical Explorations with Special Reference to East Africa, Stud Lan, Vol 19, 95. **CONTACT ADDRESS** Dept Ling, Univ Colo, Box 295, Box 295, Boulder, CO, 80309-0295.

FRAKES, JEROLD C.
PERSONAL Born 11/02/1953, Peoria, IL, s, 2 children **DISCIPLINE** COMPARATIVE LITERATURE, LATIN, GREEK **EDUCATION** Univ of MN, PhD, 82 **CAREER** Asst Prof, 82-87, USC; Guest Prof, 87-, Mittellatein Univ; Prof, 88-93, USC; Prof, 93-97, Prof, 97-, USC **HONORS AND AWARDS** Fulbright, 79 **RESEARCH** Yiddish **SELECTED PUBLICATIONS** Auth, The Fate of Fortune in the Early Middle Ages: The Boethian Tradition, Leiden: E.J. Brill, 87; Brides and Doom: Gender, Property and Power in Medieval German Women's Epic, Philadelphia: Univ of Pennsylvania Press, 94 **CONTACT ADDRESS** Univ of So California, Los Angeles, CA, 90089. **EMAIL** frakes@usc.edu

FRANCESCHETTI, ANTONIO
PERSONAL Born 10/13/1939, Padova, Italy, m, 1965, 3 children **DISCIPLINE** ITALIAN **EDUCATION** Univ Padova, Dr Lett, 63; Columbia Univ, PhD (Ital), 68. **CAREER** Lectr Ital, Univ Reading, 64; lectr, Barnard Col, Columbia Univ, 64-66, from instr to asst prof, 66-69; asst prof, 69-71, assoc prof, 71-80, PROF ITAL, SCARBOROUGH COL, UNIV TORONTO, 80-, Can deleg, Asn Int Studi Ling and Lett Ital, 76-; rep Ital, Humanities Res Coun Can, 77-. **MEMBERSHIPS** MLA; Am Asn Teachers Ital; Asn Int Studi Ling and Lett Ital; Soc Dante Alighieri. **RESEARCH** Chivalric literature in the Middle Ages and the Renaissance; 18th century poetics and poetry. **SELECTED PUBLICATIONS** Auth, The Origins of the Bel Gherardino, Quaderni D Italianistica, Vol 13, 92; Proclaiming a Classic--The Canonization of Orlando Furioso, Renaissance and Reformation, Vol 19, 95; Uneasy Structures--Theoretical Premises and Historical and Literary Verifications, Quaderni D Italianistica, Vol 16, 95; Cervantes and Ariosto, Quaderni D Italianistica, Vol 14, 93; Boiardo, Matteo, Maria--A Bibliographical Catalog, Quaderni D Italianistica, Vol 15, 94. **CONTACT ADDRESS** Div of Humanities Scarborough Col, Univ of Toronto, West Hill, ON, M5S 1A1.

FRANCIS, WINTHROP NELSON
PERSONAL Born 10/23/1910, Philadelphia, PA, m, 1939, 3 children **DISCIPLINE** LINGUISTICS **EDUCATION** Harvard Univ, AB, 31; Univ Pa, AM, 35, PhD, 37. **CAREER** From instr to prof English, Franklin and Marshall Col, 37-62; prof, 62-76, chmn dept ling, 68-75, EMER PROF LING AND ENGLISH, BROWN UNIV, 76-, Fulbright res scholar, Univ Leeds, 56-57; Nat Endowment for Humanities sr fel, 72-73; vis sr lectr, Univ Trondheim, Norway, 76-77. **MEMBERSHIPS** MLA; NCTE; Ling Soc Am; Am Dialect Soc; Int Ling Asn. **RESEARCH** English language; dialectology; mechanolinguistics. **SELECTED PUBLICATIONS** Auth, The Oxford Companion to the English Language, Language in Society, Vol 22, 93; The Science of Words, Language, Vol 73, 97; Automating the Lexicon--Research and Practice in a Multilingual Environment, Lan, Vol 73, 97; English in Britain and Overseas--Origins and Developments, Lan Soc, Vol 25, 96; Historical Linguistics 1993, Lan, Vol 73, 97; New Directions in English Language Corpora--Methodology, Results, Software Developments, Lan, Vol 70, 94. **CONTACT ADDRESS** Brown Univ, Box E, Providence, RI, 02912.

FRANCKE, KUNO
DISCIPLINE GERMAN ART AND CULTURE **EDUCATION** Univ Heidelberg, Tex, MA; Univ G_ttingen, PhD. **CAREER** Prof; fac, Harvard Univ, 68-; taught at, Univ Calif, Berkeley & Univ Toronto; mem, Sidney Sussex Col, Cambridge & former fel, Inst Advanced Stud in the Humanities, Edinburgh; Humanities Res Ctr, Canberra & Wolfenbnttel Res Ctr; corr fel, Brit Inst Ger Stud. **RESEARCH** Literary and cultural history of the several German-speaking countries in its social context. **SELECTED PUBLICATIONS** Auth, B. Traven: The Life Behind the Legends, a biog of the auth of Treasure of the Sierra Madre; The Last Frontier: Imagining Other Worlds, from the Scientific Revolution to Modern Science Fiction; Last Words: Variations on a Theme of Cultural History; Die Entdeckung des Ich; Trails in No-Man's Land & The Gender of Death. **CONTACT ADDRESS** Dept of Germanic Languages and Literature, Harvard Univ, 8 Garden St, Cambridge, MA, 02138.

FRANCO, CHARLES
PERSONAL Born 12/09/1941, Italy, m, 1978, 2 children **DISCIPLINE** ITALIAN LITERATURE **EDUCATION** Rutgers Univ, PhD, 77. **CAREER** Assoc prof, chemn dept, SUNY Stony Brook. **MEMBERSHIPS** AATI. **RESEARCH** Medieval Italian literature. **SELECTED PUBLICATIONS** Auth, Dante: Summa Medievalis. **CONTACT ADDRESS** Dept of European Languages, SUNY, Stony Brook, Stony Brook, NY, 11794-3359. **EMAIL** cfranco@notes.cc.sunysb.edu

FRANK, ELFRIEDA
PERSONAL Born 02/06/1916, Vienna, Austria **DISCIPLINE** LATIN **EDUCATION** Univ Milan, LittD, 38; Bryn Mawr Col, MA, 41; Univ Va, PhD (classics), 51. **CAREER** Asst prof classics, Cornell Col, 53-56; from asst prof to assoc prof, Tex Tech Univ, 56-61; from asst prof to assoc prof, 61-70, Prof Classics, Univ New Orleans, 70-. **MEMBERSHIPS** Am Philol Asn; Class Asn Mid W and S. **RESEARCH** Latin philology; Latin epic poetry; Ovid. **SELECTED PUBLICATIONS** Auth, The Ordinary Seaman, NY Rev Of Bks, Vol 44, 97. **CONTACT ADDRESS** Dept of Foreign Lang, Univ New Orleans, New Orleans, LA, 70122.

FRANK, FRANCINE
PERSONAL Born 04/18/1931, New York, NY, d **DISCIPLINE** LINGUISTICS SPANISH **EDUCATION** NY Univ, BA, 52; Cornell Univ, MA, 53; Univ IL, Urbana, PhD, 55. **CAREER** Instr Span, Univ IL, Urbana, 55-57; asst lang training supvr, Inter-govt Comt Europ Migration, 59-66; asst prof, 66-80, asst dean, Col Arts & Sci, 73-74, coordr, curric & interdisciplinary studies, div Humanities, 75-77, assoc prof Span & Ling, State Univ NY Albany, 80-87, dir Ling, 73-85, Consult Span proficiency exam, NY State Educ Dept, 70-80; Fulbright sr lectr appl ling, Rome, Italy, 71-72; lectr, English Lang, US Embassy, Yugoslavia, 71-72; mem, Regents External Degree Bachelors Comt, NY State, 73-84; Fulbright sr lectr ling & English as a second lang, Buenos Aires, Argentina, 80; vis prof, Sohia Univ, Bulgeria, 94; assoc Dean Col of Humanities & Fine Arts, 85-86, Dean Col of Hum & Fine Arts, 86-93, prof Linguistics and Women's Studies, 87-97, dir Ling & Cognitive Science, 94-97, dir Center for the Arts and Humanities, 94-97, PROF EMERITA, SUNY, 97. **HONORS AND AWARDS** Research fel, Univ Awards Prog, SUNY Research Found, summer 82; Presidential Award for Excellence in Academic Service, SUNYA, 86; Making Waves Award for Community Service and Commitment to Feminist Goals, Albany Area Chapter, Nat Org for Women (NOW), 89; Book Language, Gender, and Professional Writing selected by Choice as an Outstanding Academic Book for 89-90; Bread and Roses Award for extraordinary contributions on behalf of gender equity, from the Council of Women's Groups at the Univ at Albany, 92; Evan R. Collins Award in recognition of distinguished service and devotion to the Univ at Albany by members of the faculty, 93; co-dir, Ford Found three-year Grant for Internationalizing Women's Studies, 95-98; Named Professor Emerita, Univ at Albany, SUNY, 97. **MEMBERSHIPS** Int Ling Asn; Ling Soc Am; MLA; Fulbright Alumni Asn; Linguistic Assoc of CAN and the US (LACUS); Nat Women's Studies Asn; Societas Linguistica Europaea. **RESEARCH** Spanish linguistics, especially syntax; pidgin and creole languages; sociolinguistics, especially language and gender. **SELECTED PUBLICATIONS** Auth, Taxemic redundancy in Spanish, In: Structural Studies on Spanish Themes, Acta Salmanticensia, Filos y Letras, Salamanca, Vol XII, No 3; The training of an English teacher, Lingua & Nuova Didattica, 9/72; Language and education in the Leeward Netherlands Antilles, Caribbean Studies, 1/74; Women's language in America: Myth and reality, In: Women's Language and Style, Studies in Contemporary Language, No 1, Akron, 78; co-ed, Colloquium on Spanish and Luso-Brazilian Linguistics, Georgetown Univ Press, 79; coauth, Language and the Sexes,

SUNY Press, 84;auth, Language Planning and Sexual Equality: Guidelines for Non-Sexist Usage, in Sprachwandel und feministische Sprachpolitik: Internationale Perspektiven, Westdeutscher Verlag, 85; El genero gramatical y los cambios sociales, Espanol actual 43, 85; El Sexo como Factor Sociolinguistico: Algunas Consideraciores Teoricas y Metodologicas, Actas del V Congrso Internacional de la Asociacion de Linguistica y Filologia de la America Latina (ALFAL), Caracas, 86; coauth, Language, Gender, and Professional Writing: Theoretical Approaches and Guidelines for Nonsexist Usage, The Modern Language Asn, 89; Planificacion linguistica y cambio social, Seminario de Estudios sobre la Mujer (proceedings of the joint 86 Seminar in Women's Studies, SUNY/Univ Costa Rica), San Jose, Costa Rica, Ministry of Culture, 89; A Dean's Perspective on Women in Academe, The Cornell Lectures: Women in the Linguistics Profession, Comm on the Status of Women in Linguistics, Linguistic Soc of Am, 90; Japanese trans of Language and the Sexes, Kansai Univ Press, 95. **CONTACT ADDRESS** Dept of Women's Studies, Rm 55341, State Univ of NY at Albany, 1400 Washington Ave, Albany, NY, 12222-1000. **EMAIL** fwf@cnsvax.albany.edu

FRANK, RICHARD MACDONOUGH
PERSONAL Born 12/04/1927, Louisville, KY, m, 1950, 4 children **DISCIPLINE** SEMITIC STUDIES, ARABIC **EDUCATION** Cath Univ Am, AB, 53. **CAREER** From instr to assoc prof Semitic and Egyptian lang, 55-73, PROF SEMITIC AND EGYPTIAN LANG AND LIT, CATH UNIV AM, 73-. **MEMBERSHIPS** Am Orient Soc; Cath Bibl Asn Am. **RESEARCH** Islamic philosophy and theology. **SELECTED PUBLICATIONS** Auth, The Physical Theory of Kalam--Atoms, Space and Void in Basrian Mutazili Cosmology, J Am Orient Soc, Vol 116, 96; Dona Lambra and Family Conflict in the Legend of the Siete Infantes De Lara Found in the Chronicles and Old Romances, Confluencia Revista Hisp Cult Y Lit, Vol 5, 90; Theology and Society in the 2nd Century and the 3rd Century of the Hijra--A History of Religious Thought in Early Islam, J Am Orient Soc, Vol 114, 94; Dona Lambra and Family Conflict in the Legend of the Siete Infantes de Lara Found in the Chronicles and Old Romances, Confluencia Revista Hisp Cult Y Lit, Vol 5, 90. **CONTACT ADDRESS** Dept of Semitic Lang, Catholic Univ of America, Washington, DC, 20017.

FRANK, YAKIRA H
PERSONAL Born 11/15/1923, New York, NY, m, 1945, 2 children **DISCIPLINE** LINGUISTICS **EDUCATION** Honter Col, AB, 43; Univ Pa, MA, 45; Univ Mich, PhD, 49. **CAREER** From instr to assoc prof, 62-74, PROF ENGLISH and DIR STAMFORD CAMPUS, UNIV CONN, 74-, Am Coun Learned Soc fel, 49; lectr, Hunter Col, 51-55 and 58 and Univ Conn, Stanmford, 61-62; mem bd, Conn Humanities Coun, 77-. **MEMBERSHIPS** Ling Soc Am; NCTE; MLA; Teachers English as Second Lang. **RESEARCH** Stylistics; dialect geography; bilingualism. **SELECTED PUBLICATIONS** Auth, Oxford Yiddish, Vol 3--Studies in Yiddish Language, Literature and Folklore, J Jewish Stud, Vol 47, 96. **CONTACT ADDRESS** Univ of Conn Stamford Campus Scofieldtown Rd, Stamford, CT, 06903.

FRANKE, WILLIAM
DISCIPLINE COMPARATIVE LITERATURE **EDUCATION** Williams Col, BA, 78; Oxford Univ, MA, 80, Univ Calif, Berkeley, MA, 88; Stanford Univ, PhD, 91. **CAREER** Adj fac, 84-86, Columbia Col; assoc prof, 91-, Vanderbilt Univ. **RESEARCH** Dante, Phil of lit, Poetry & Poetics, theory **CONTACT ADDRESS** Program in Comparative Literature, Vanderbilt Univ, Box 1709 - Station B, Nashville, TN, 37235.

FRANKEL, MARGHERITA
PERSONAL Sao Paulo, Brazil, m, 1963 **DISCIPLINE** ITALIAN AND FRENCH LITERATURE **EDUCATION** Brooklyn Col, BA, 68; NY Univ, PhD (French), 73. **CAREER** Asst prof, 73-76, ASSOC PROF ITAL, NY UNIV, 76-. **HONORS AND AWARDS** Gustav O Arlt Award in Humanities, Nat Coun Grad Schs, 75. **MEMBERSHIPS** Dante Soc Am; MLA; Renaissance Soc Am; Mediaeval Acad Am; Am Comp Lit Asn. **RESEARCH** Dante; Renaissance literature; Vico. **SELECTED PUBLICATIONS** Auth, Public and Private Concerns, Index Censorship, Vol 24, 95; Mikve and Philosophy of Halakha, Tradition J Orthodox Jewish Thought, Vol 31, 97. **CONTACT ADDRESS** Dept of French and Ital, New York Univ, 19 University Pl, New York, NY, 10003.

FRANKLIN, URSULA
PERSONAL Born 06/03/1929, Widdersberg, Germany, m, 1949 **DISCIPLINE** FRENCH LANGUAGE AND LITERATURE **EDUCATION** Mich State Univ, BA, 64, MA, 66, PhD (French), 71. **CAREER** Instr French, Mich State Univ, 70-71; asst prof, 71-74, assoc prof, 74-80, Prof French, Grand Valley State Col, 80-, Am Coun Learned Soc fel, 78-69. **MEMBERSHIPS** MLA; Am Asn Teachers Fr; Am Coun Teaching Foreign Lang; AAUP. **RESEARCH** Stephane Mallarme; French symbolism; prose peom in French literature. **SELECTED PUBLICATIONS** Auth, Valery and Poe--A Literary Legacy, Fr Rev, Vol 67, 93; Valery, Paul--Music, Mysticism, Mathematics, Mod Lan Rev, Vol 90, 95; Mallarme, the Arts and theory, 19th Century Fr Stud, Vol 25, 96; The Crisis of French Symbolism, Mod Philol, Vol 91, 93; Laforgue, Jules and Poetic Innovation, 19th Century Fr Stud, Vol 22, 94; The Crisis of French Symbolism, Mod Philol, Vol 91, 93; Valery, Paul Charmes, Mod Lan Rev Vol 91, 96; The Poetics of yhe Occasion--Mallarme and the Poetry of Circumstance, Fr Rev, Vol 68, 95; Valery, Paul--Music, Mysticism, Mathematics, Mod Lan Rev, Vol 90, 95; Valery, Paul Charmes, Mod Lan Rev, Vol 91, 96. **CONTACT ADDRESS** Dept of French, Grand Valley State Univ, Allendale, MI, 49401.

FRANKS, J. RICHARD
DISCIPLINE CCC-AUDIOLOGY **EDUCATION** Brigham Young Univ, BA, 52, MA, 59; Mich State Univ, PhD, 64. **CAREER** Prof, Washington State Univ. **SELECTED PUBLICATIONS** Auth, A Training Program for Native Americans in Communication Disorders, Amer Speech-Lang-Hearing Asn, 88 & Testing Auditory Selective Attention, Wash Speech and Hearing Asn, 88. **CONTACT ADDRESS** Dept of Speech and Hearing Sciences, Washington State Univ, 201 Daggy Hall, Pullman, WA, 99164-2420. **EMAIL** franks@wsu.edu

FRANKS, STEVEN
PERSONAL Born 05/18/1955, London, England, m, 1985, 3 children **DISCIPLINE** LINGUISTICS **EDUCATION** Princeton, AB, 77; UCLA, MA, 79; Cornell, PhD, 85. **CAREER** Lang analyst, US Dept of Defense, 84-87; asst prof, 87-94, assoc prof, IN Univ, 94-, chmn, Linguistics Dept, 98-. **HONORS AND AWARDS** Fulbright, 77-78; NSF Graf fel; Prize for an Outstanding Work of Linguisitics Scholarship, AATSEEL, Dec 96; short-term guest professorship, Univ CT, 96-97. **MEMBERSHIPS** Ling Soc of Am; Am Asn of Teachers of Slavic and East European Lang. **RESEARCH** Syntactic theory and analysis; Slavic linguistics; Clitics. **SELECTED PUBLICATIONS** Auth, Parameters of Slavic Morphosyntax, Oxford Univ Press, 95; Asymmetries in the Scope of Russian Negation, with S Brown, J of Slavic Ling, 3-2, 95; Reflections: Building Bridges, J of Slavic Ling,4-1, 96; Knowledge of Binding in Normal and SLI Children, with P Connell, J of Child Lang, 23-2, 96; Licensing and Identification of Null Subjects in Slavic, in Formal Approaches to Slavic Linguistics: The College Park Meeting, ed by J Toman, with M Lindseth, 96; Grammar as a Mental Organ: A Survey of the GB Perspective, with C Rudin, Int J of Slavic Ling and Poetics, 96; Empty Subjects and Voice-Altering Mporphemes in Slavic, Int J of Slavic Ling and Poetics, 96; Formal Approaches to Slavic Linguistics: The Indiana Meeting, Michigan Slavic Materials, ed by M Lindseth and S Franks, 97; The Syntax of Pleonastic Negation in Russian, in Formal Apoproaches to Slavic Linguistics: The Cornell University Meeting, ed, by W Browne, et al, with S Brown, 97; South Slavic Clitic Placement is Still Syntactic, Penn Working Papers in Linguistics, 4-2, 97; Review, Formale Slavistik, ed, by U Junghanns & G Zybatow, J of Slavic Ling, 5-2, 97; Formal Approaches to Slavic Linguistics: The Connecticut Meeting, ed with Z Boskovic and W Snyder, Michigan Slavic Materials, 98; Parameters of Slavic Morphosyntax Revisited: A Minimalist Retrospective, in Formal Approaches to Slavic Linguistics: The Connecticut Meeting, ed by Z Boskovic, et al, 98; The Syntax of Adverbial Participles in Russian Revisited, with L Babby, Slavic and East European J 42-3, 98; numerous other publications, with several forthcoming. **CONTACT ADDRESS** Dept of Linguistics, Indiana Univ, Bloomington, Memorial Hall, Bloomington, IN, 47401. **EMAIL** FRANKS@Indiana.Edu

FRANZ, THOMAS RUDY
PERSONAL Born 04/07/1942, South Milwaukee, WI, 4 children **DISCIPLINE** SPANISH LITERATURE **EDUCATION** Carroll Col, BA, 64; Univ Kans, MA, 67, PhD(Span), 70. **CAREER** Instr Span & English, Plymouth Wis Pub Schs, 65-66; asst prof, 70-75, assoc prof, 75-80, PROF MOD LANG, OHIO UNIV, 80-, Ohio Univ Res Inst res grant, 74. **MEMBERSHIPS** MLA; Midwest Mod Lang Asn; Am Asn Teachers Span & Port **RESEARCH** Miguel de Unamuno; 19th and 20th century Spanish novel; comparative literature. **SELECTED PUBLICATIONS** Auth, The figure of the civil guard in the novels of Camilo Jose Cela, Occas Papers Lang, Lit & Ling, 12/71; Ancient rites and the structure of Unamuno's Amor y Pedagogia, Romance Notes, 12/71; Humor in Unamuno's Paz en la Guerra, Horizontes, 4/72; Cela's La familia del heroe, the nouveau roman, and the creative act, Mod Lang Notes, 3/73; Menendez y Pelayo as Antolin S Paparrigopulos of Unamuno's Niebla, Papers Lang & Lit, spring 73; El sentido de humor y adquisicion de autoconciencia en Niebla, Cuadernos Catedra Miguel de Unamuno, 73; The philosophical bases of Fulgencio Entrambosmares in Amor y Pedagogia, Hispania, 9/77; Remaking Reality in Galdos, Strathmore Press, 82. **CONTACT ADDRESS** Dept of Mod Lang, Ohio Univ, Athens, OH, 45701-2979. **EMAIL** franz@oak.cats.ohiou.edu

FRASER, HOWARD MICHAEL
PERSONAL Born 11/11/1943, New York, NY, m, 1967, 1 child **DISCIPLINE** SPANISH AM LIT **EDUCATION** Columbia Univ, BA, 64; Univ NMex, MA, 66, PhD (Span), 70; Harvard Univ, AM, 67. **CAREER** Res asst Span, Hisp Inst US, 63-64; grad asst, Univ NMex, 64-66, instr English, col educ, 67; teaching asst Port, 69-70, instr Span, 70; lab asst Englsih, Southwestern Coop Educ Lab, 68; asst prof Span, Univ Wis-Madison, 70-74; asst prof, 74-77, ASSOC PROF MOD LANG, COL WILLIAM AND MARY, 77-, Reader Span, Columbia Col, 63-64; instr Span, Peace Corps Training Ctr, NMex, 65-66 and Ithaca, NY, 66. **MEMBERSHIPS** MLA; Am Asn Teachers Span and Port; AAUP; Midwest Mod Lang Asn; Inst Int Lit Iberoam. **RESEARCH** Modernist fiction in Spanish America; Spanish American theatre. **SELECTED PUBLICATIONS** Auth, Apocalyptic Vision and Modernisms Dismantling of Scientific Discourse--Lugones Yzur, Hispania J Devoted Teaching of Span Portug, Vol 79, 96; Apocalyptic Vision and Modernisms Dismantling of Scientific Discourse--Lugones Yzur, Hispania J Devoted Teaching Port, Vol 79, 96; Using Spanish Synonyms, Mod Lan J, Vol 79, 95. **CONTACT ADDRESS** Dept of Mod Lang, Col of William and Mary, Williamsburg, VA, 23185.

FRASER, THEODORE
DISCIPLINE FRENCH **EDUCATION** Fordham Univ, AB, 56; Brown Univ, MA, 63, PhD, 67. **CAREER** Prof. **RESEARCH** Modern religious themes/structures in fiction and film; 20th-Century French literature and civilization; French Intellectuals from WWII to the present; 19th-century French Literature. **SELECTED PUBLICATIONS** Auth, The Modern Catholic Novel in Europe, NY: Twayne/Macmillan, 94; The French Essay, NY: Twayne, 86 & The Moralist Tradition in France, Wash/NY: Assoc Fac Press, 82; Le Duchat, 1st ed of Rabelais, Geneva: Droz, 71. **CONTACT ADDRESS** Dept of Modern Languages and Literatures, Col of the Holy Cross, 1 College St, PO Box 145A, Worcester, MA, 01610-2395. **EMAIL** tfraser@holycross.edu

FRAUTSCHI, RICHARD LANE
PERSONAL Born 11/14/1926, Rockford, IL, m, 1973, 4 children **DISCIPLINE** FRENCH **EDUCATION** Univ Wis, AB, 49; Harvard Univ, AM, 53, PhD, 58. **CAREER** Instr French, Smith Col, 54-58; from asst prof to prof, Univ NC, Chapel Hill, 58-70; Prof French & Head Dept, 70-89, prof, 89-90, PROF EMERITUS, 96-, PA STATE UNIV; Am Coun Learned Soc grant, 68; vis prof French, St Augustine's Col, NC, 60-70; mem advan placement comt French, Col Entrance Exam Bd, 70-76, consult, 76-88. **HONORS AND AWARDS** Nat Sci Found-Pa State Univ grant, 71; Am Philos Soc Grant, 72; Int Res & Exchanges Bd grant, Soviet Union, 75; Int Res & Exchange Bd grant, Poland & Czech Rep, 80-81; Camargo Found grant, 81; res fel, Macquarie Univ, Australia, 82; NEH grants, 91-95 **MEMBERSHIPS** MLA; Am Asn Teachers Fr; Soc Fr Etude XVIIIe Siecle; Am Soc 18th Century Studies; Asn Computing Machinery. **RESEARCH** French literature of the 16th and 18th centuries; quantitative stylistics; pedagogy. **SELECTED PUBLICATIONS** Coauth, Pour et Contre, Manuel de Conversations Graduees, Dodd, 72 & 2nd ed, Harper, 78; auth, The authorship of certain unsigned articles in the Encyclopedie, Computer Studies Humanities & V erbal Behav, 70; Styles de roman et styles de censure dan la 2de moitie du 18e siecle, Studies on Voltaire, 72; A project for computer-assisted analysis of French prose fiction, 1751-1800, In: The Computer and Literary Studies, Edinburgh Univ, 73; coauth, Bibliographie due Genre Romanesque Francais, 1751-1800, Mansell, 77; A Model for Chi-Square Analysis of Regression Vocabularyy in H de Crenne's Les Angoysses douloureuses, Comput & Humanities, 79; Le comportement verbal du narrateur dans Gil Bias: Quelques observations quantitatives, Studies Voltaire, 81; Le jeu des axes de narration dans Les Liaisons dangereuses: Etude de focalisation enonciative, Marche Romane, 82; coauth, Bibliographie du genre romanesque, 1700-1800, Oxford: Voltaire Fdn, forthcoming. **CONTACT ADDRESS** Dept of French, Pennsylvania State Univ, University Park, PA, 16802. **EMAIL** jaa2@psu.edu

FRAZIER, LYN
DISCIPLINE LINGUISTICS **EDUCATION** Univ Wis, BA, 74; Univ Conn, PhD, 78. **CAREER** Prof. **RESEARCH** Syntax; relation between theories of grammar and theories of the mental representation and processing of language. **SELECTED PUBLICATIONS** Auth, Syntactic Complexity, Cambridge, 85; Syntactic Processing: Evidence from Dutch, Natural Lang Ling Theory, 87; Focus in relative clause construal, MIT, 96; co-auth, Filler-Driven Parsing: A Study of Gap-Filling in Dutch, J Memory Lang, 89; Argument Structure and Associate Preferences, Cognition, 95; Constraint satisfaction as a theory of sentence processing, J Psycholinguistic Res, 95. **CONTACT ADDRESS** Linguistics Dept, Univ of Massachusetts, Amherst, S College 225, Amherst, MA, 01003.

FREEAR ROBERTS, HELEN
DISCIPLINE SPANISH LITERATURE **EDUCATION** Univ New Hampshire, BS; Univ Conn, MA, PhD. **CAREER** Vis asst prof. **RESEARCH** Contemporary Spanish drama. **SELECTED PUBLICATIONS** Auth, Deconstruction and Enigma in 'Numa una leyenda' (rev), 96. **CONTACT ADDRESS** Spanish Dept, Col of the Holy Cross, Worcester, MA, 01610-2395.

FREED, BARBARA
DISCIPLINE FRENCH AND SECOND LANGUAGE ACQUISITION **EDUCATION** Univ Pa, PhD. **CAREER** Languages, Carnegie Mellon Univ. **SELECTED PUBLICATIONS** Auth, The Linguistic Consequences of Study Abroad Experiences. In preparation for the "Studies in Bilingualism Se-

ries.". John Benjamins Publ Co; Foreign Language Acquisition Research and The Classroom, Lexington, MA: D. C. Heath & Co, 91; The Foreign Language Requirement in Teaching Languages at College: Curriculum and Content, NTC Publ Gp, 92; Language Learning in a Study Abroad Context: The Effects of Interactive and Non-Interactive Out-of Class Contact on Grammatical Achievement and Oral Proficiency, 90. **CONTACT ADDRESS** Carnegie Mellon Univ, 5000 Forbes Ave, Pittsburgh, PA, 15213.

FREEDMAN, DAVID NOEL
PERSONAL Born 05/12/1922, New York, NY, m, 1944, 4 children **DISCIPLINE** SEMITIC LANGUAGES AND LITERATURE **EDUCATION** Univ Calif, Los Angeles, AB, 39; Princeton theol Sem, ThB, 44; Johns Hopkins Univ, PhD, 48. **CAREER** Instr, Johns Hopkins Univ, 47-48; asst prof Hebrew and Old Testament lit, Western Theol Sem, 48-51, prof, 51-60; prof, Pittsburgh Theol Sem, 60-61, James Anderson Kelso prof, 61-64; prof, Grad Theol Union Berkeley, 64-71; prof, San Francisco Theol Sem, 64-70, Gray prof, 70-71, actg dean fact 66-67, dean, 67-71; PROF NEAR EAST STUDIES AND DIR STUDIES RELIG, UNIV MICH, ANN ARBOR, 71-, Assoc ed, J Bibl Lit, Soc Bibl Lit, 52-54, ed, 55-59; guest prof, McCormick Theol Sem, 59; Guggenheim fel, 58-59; lectr, Uppsala Univ, 59 and Int Cong old Testament Scholars, Bonn, Ger, 62; Am Asn Theol Sem fel, 63-64; dir, Ashdod Excavation Proj, 62-64; co-ed, Anchor Bible Ser, Doubleday, 64-71, ed, 71-; William Copley Winslow lectr archaeol and Bible, 66; Danforth vis prof, Int Christian Univ, Tokyo, 67; Am Coun Learned Soc grant-in-aid, 68; dir, Am Sch Orient Res, Jerusalem, 69-70 and 76-77; vis prof, Hebrew Univ, Jerusalem, 76-77, Macquarie Univ, Sydney, Australia, 80, Univ Queensland, Brisbane, Australia and Texas Christion Univ, 81, Brigham Univ, Utah, 81-82. **HONORS AND AWARDS** DLitt, Univ of the Pac, 73; DSc, Davis and Elkins Col, 74. **MEMBERSHIPS** Soc Bibl Lit; Am Orient Soc; Am Schs Orient Res (vpres, 70-); Cath Bibl Asn Am; Bibl Colloquium (secy-treas 65-). **SELECTED PUBLICATIONS** Auth, Psalm Cxix--Matrix, Form, and Setting, Cath Biblical Quart, Vol 55, 93. **CONTACT ADDRESS** Prog on Studies in Relig, Univ of Mich, 1053 LSandA Bldg, Ann Arbor, MI, 48104.

FREEMAN, BRYANT C.
DISCIPLINE SEVENTEENTH-CENTURY FRENCH LITERATURE **EDUCATION** Yale Univ, PhD. **CAREER** Prof, Univ KS . **SELECTED PUBLICATIONS** Auth, Concordance du Theatre et des Poesies de Jean Racine; pub(s), twelve bk(s) in the course of Haitian studies. **CONTACT ADDRESS** Dept of French an Italian, Univ Kansas, Admin Building, Lawrence, KS, 66045. **EMAIL** kufacts@ukans.edu

FREEMAN, DAVID
DISCIPLINE LINGUISTICS **EDUCATION** Dartmouth Col, BA; Stanford Univ, MA; Univ AZ, MA, PhD. **CAREER** Prof; dir, Lang Devel and TESOL. Programs, **MEMBERSHIPS** Mem, Nat Conf Res Lang and Lit; Ctr Expansion of Lang and Thinking; Mod Lang Assn; Intl Reading Assn; CA Reading Assn; Tchr(s) Eng to Speakers of Other Lang; CA TESOL; Nat Coun Tchr(s) Eng; Nat Assn Bilingual Edu; CA Assn Bilingual Edu. **SELECTED PUBLICATIONS** Co-auth, Whole Language for Second Language Learners, N.H.: Heinemann, 92; Between Worlds: Access to Second Language Acquisition, Heinemann, 94; Teaching Reading and Writing in the Spanish/English Bilingual Classroom, Heinemann, 97. **CONTACT ADDRESS** Div Lang, Lit and Cult, Fresno Pacific Col, 1717 S Chestnut, Fresno, CA, 93702.

FREEMAN, DONALD CARY
PERSONAL Born 03/19/1938, Boston, MA, m, 1970, 2 children **DISCIPLINE** ENGLISH LINGUISTICS **EDUCATION** Middlebury Col, AB, 59; Brown Univ, AM, 61; Univ Conn, PhD (English), 65. **CAREER** Asst prof Eng, Univ Calif, Santa Barbara, 65-68; from asst prof to assoc prof Eng and ling, Univ Mass Amherst, 68-71, prof ling, 71-76, assoc dean fac humanities and fine arts, 72-74; chmn, Comt Ling, 76-80, PROF ENGLISH, TEMPLE UNIV, 76-, Nat Sci Found res fel ling, Mass Inst Technol, 67-68; vis prof English, Univ Lancaster, 71-72; dir, Ling Inst, Ling Soc Am, 74; mem, Grad Fel Rev Panel, Nat Res Coun, 75-77 and 79; vis prof gen ling, Univ Regensburg, Fed Repub Ger, 78 and Tech Univ Berlin, 80. **MEMBERSHIPS** MLA; Ling Soc Am; NCTE. **RESEARCH** English stylistics; metrics; the teaching of English. **SELECTED PUBLICATIONS** Auth, Catch@Ing* the Nearest Way--Macbeth and Cognitive Metaphor, J Pragmatics, Vol 24, 95. **CONTACT ADDRESS** Dept of English, Temple Univ, Philadelphia, PA, 19122.

FREEMAN, THOMAS PARRY
PERSONAL Born 05/22/1944, Chicago, Ill, m, 5 children **DISCIPLINE** GERMAN LITERATURE, HUMANITIES **EDUCATION** Haverford Col, AB, 65; Stanford Univ, MA, 66, PhD(Ger & humanities), 70. **CAREER** Teaching asst Ger, Stanford Univ, 67-68; instr Ger & humanities, Columbia Univ, 68-71; asst prof Ger, State Univ NY, Brockport, 71-75, assoc prof, 75-81; Assoc Prof Ger, Beloit Col, 81-, Mem fac literature, New Sch Social Res, spring 71; Ger Acad Exchange Serv fel, 72; **HONORS AND AWARDS** State Univ NY Res Found grants-in-aid, 72-73 & 74-75; Mellon fel, Ger, Univ Pittsburgh, 76-77; Alexander von Humboldt fel, 79-80, 96; Cullister Fnd Grants; Hewlett-Mellon Grants, NEH Summer fels; Sr Fulbright Res fels; **MEMBERSHIPS** Midwest MLA; Fulbright Alum Asn; Alexander von Humboldt Asn Am.Am Asn Prof Yiddish; MLA. **RESEARCH** Modern German literature; German exile literature; Holocaust studies. **SELECTED PUBLICATIONS** Auth, El uso del sueno en la poesia de Benn y Mallarme, Folia Humanistica, 9/69; The lotus and the tigress--symbols of mediation in Hans Henny Jahnn's Perrudja, Genre, summer 74; co-ed, Hans Henny Jahnn--Gesammelte Werke 7 Banden, Hoffmann und Campe, 74; auth, Zu Hans Henny Jahnns Leben, und Werk, Freie Akademie der Kunste in Hamburg, 80; Hans Henny Jahnn, 80 & Hans Erick Nossack, 80, Columbia Dict of Modern European Literature, Columbia Univ Press; Mythische Strukturen in Hans Henny Jahnns Perrudja, text und Kritik, 1/80; Hans Henny Jahnns Schweizerr Aufenthalt, Akten des VI Internationalen Germanistenkongresses, Peter Lanf, 80; auth, The Cowboy and the Astronaut - The American Image in German Periodical Advertisements, Jou of Popular Culture, 72; auth, Heinrich Hoffman's Der Struwelpeter, Violence in German Children's Literature, Jour of Popular Cult, 77; auth, Zu Pastor Ephraim Magnus, Programsheft Staatstheater Kassel, 79/80; auth, Umstrittener Dichter Hans Henny Jahn, Kultur fur alle, Hamburger Kulturbegorde, 84; auth, Haupttendenzen der Jahn-Forschung Ein Oberblick, Archaische Moderne der Dichter, Architekt und Orgelbauer Hans Henny Jahn, Metzher & Poeschel, 96; auth, Deutschland als multikulturelle Gesellschaft Stimmen der Minderheiten in der neuren literatir, Fremdverstehen in Sprache, literature und medien, Peter Lang, 97; auth, Jewish Identity and the Holocaust in Robert Schindel's Geburtig, Modern Austrian Literatur, 97; auth, Kurt Tucholsky, Yale Companion to Jewish Writing and Thought in German Culture, 1096-1996, Yale Univ, 97. **CONTACT ADDRESS** Dept of Mod Lang, Beloit Col, 700 College St, Beloit, WI, 53511-5595. **EMAIL** freemant@beloit.edu

FREEMAN, YVONNE
DISCIPLINE BILINGUAL EDUCATION **EDUCATION** Taft Col, AA; Univ CA-Santa Barbara, BA; Stanford Univ, MA; Univ AZ, MA, PhD. **CAREER** Prof; div hd, Fresno Pacific Col. **HONORS AND AWARDS** Bd dir(s), Whole Lang Umbrella. **MEMBERSHIPS** Mem, Nat Conf Res Lang and Lit; Ctr Expansion of Lang and Thinking; Mod Lang Assn; Intl Reading Assn; CA Reading Assn; Tchr(s) Eng to Speakers of Other Lang; CA TESOL; Nat Coun Tchr(s) Eng; Nat Assn Bilingual Edu; CA Assn Bilingual Edu. **RESEARCH** Effective practices for tchg Eng to lang minority students. **SELECTED PUBLICATIONS** Co-auth, Report Card on Basal Readers, Richard C Owen, 88; Whole Language for Second Language Learners, N.H.: Heinemann, 92; Between Worlds: Access to Second Language Acquisition, Heinemann, 94; Teaching Reading and Writing in the Spanish/English Bilingual Classroom, Heinemann, 97. **CONTACT ADDRESS** Div Lang, Lit and Cult, Fresno Pacific Col, 1717 S Chestnut, Fresno, CA, 93702. **EMAIL** yfreeman@fresno.edu

FREIS, CATHERINE R.
DISCIPLINE GREEK AND LATIN LANGUAGES AND LITERATURES **EDUCATION** Univ Calif, PhD. **CAREER** Dept ch & dir, Core Curric. **HONORS AND AWARDS** Amer Philol Asn awd & Millsaps Cole Distinguished prof awd. **SELECTED PUBLICATIONS** Publ on, drama and language pedagogy. **CONTACT ADDRESS** Dept of Classics, Millsaps Col, 1701 N State St, Jackson, MS, 39210. **EMAIL** freiscr@okra.millsaps.edu

FREIS, RICHARD
DISCIPLINE GREEK AND LATIN LANGUAGES AND LITERATURES **EDUCATION** Univ Calif, PhD. **CAREER** Dept Classics, Millsaps Col **HONORS AND AWARDS** Amer Philol Asn awd & Millsaps Col Distinguished prof awd. **RESEARCH** Greek philosophy; religious studies and comparative literature. **SELECTED PUBLICATIONS** Publ on, class and mod lit & publ poet. **CONTACT ADDRESS** Dept of Classics, Millsaps Col, 1701 N State St, Jackson, MS, 39210. **EMAIL** freissr@okra.millsaps.edu

FRENCH, HAROLD WENDELL
PERSONAL Born 01/14/1930, Wichita, KS, m, 3 children **DISCIPLINE** ASIAN RELIGIOUS TRADITIONS, PSYCHOLOGY OF RELIGION **EDUCATION** York Col, Nebr, BA, 52; United Sem Dayton, MDiv; Boston Univ, STM; McMaster Univ, PhD (relig hist India), 72. **CAREER** Asst prof Asian relig tradition, St Andrews Col, NC; Assoc Prof Asian Relig Tradition, Univ SC, 72-. **HONORS AND AWARDS** Amoco Teacher of Year, Univ SC, 77. **MEMBERSHIPS** Am Acad Relig; Asn Asian Studies; World Coun Relig. **RESEARCH** The Ramakrishna movement and the West; modern Indian religious movements; death perspectives. **SELECTED PUBLICATIONS** Auth, Maurice, F. D. and Unitarianism, Victorian Stud, Vol 37, 94. **CONTACT ADDRESS** Dept of Relig Studies, Univ of SC, Columbia, SC, 29208.

FRENCH, PAULETTE
PERSONAL Born 06/16/1941, Laconia, NH **DISCIPLINE** COMPARATIVE LITERATURE, FRENCH **EDUCATION** Colby Col, BA, 63; Univ Paris at the Sorbonne, cert prof francais, 64; Univ Md, College Park, MA, 67; Univ Colo, Boulder, PhD (comp lit), 71. **CAREER** Instr French and Span, Bowie State Col, 65-66; assoc French, Univ Colo, Boulder, 67-69; asst prof Romance lang, Univ Maine, Orono, 69-72, asst to vpres, 72-73; asst vchancellor acad affairs, Univ Calif, Irvine, 73-76; ASSOC PROF FRENCH AND COMP LIT AND CHMN LANG AND CLASSICS, UNIV MAINE, 76-, Conf interpreter, US State Dept, Washington, DC, 64-66; instr English as foreign lang, Econ Opportunity COmn, San Jose, Calif, 66-67; Am Coun Educ fel, 73-74. **HONORS AND AWARDS** Prix Litteraire Hachette et Larousse laureate, 63-64. **MEMBERSHIPS** Medieval Acad Am; Am Asn Teacher Fr; MLA; AAUP; Nat Asn Women Deans and Counr. **RESEARCH** Moliere; Medieval lyric poetry; academic administration. **SELECTED PUBLICATIONS** Auth, Moving Pictures, Still Words, Poetry Rev, Vol 83, 93; Malle, Louis--In Memoriam, Sight Sound, Vol 6, 96; No End in Sight , Index Censorship, Vol 24, 95; Fieldwork, 95 6, J Egyptian Archaeol, Vol 82, 96. **CONTACT ADDRESS** Dept of Lang and Classics, Univ of Maine, Orono, ME, 04473.

FRESCO, ALAIN D.
DISCIPLINE FRENCH LITERATURE **EDUCATION** Univ Delaware, BA, 69; Univ Ind, PhD, 81. **CAREER** Asst prof, Univ Ill Urbana Champaign. **SELECTED PUBLICATIONS** Auth, 'Les Vies Africaines': A Series of Popular Literature Today, 82. **CONTACT ADDRESS** French Dept, Univ Ill Urbana Champaign, 52 E Gregory Dr, Champaign, IL, 61820. **EMAIL** a-fresco@uiuc.edu

FRESCO, KAREN
DISCIPLINE FRENCH LITERATURE **EDUCATION** Carleton Col, BA, 69; Univ Ind, PhD, 83. **CAREER** Assoc prof, Univ Ill Urbana Champaign. **MEMBERSHIPS** International Arthurian Society;International Courtly Literature Society;Medieval Academy of America;Medieval Association of the Midwest;Modern Language Association **SELECTED PUBLICATIONS** Auth, The Troubadour Lyric: A Psychocritical Reading (rev), Manchester Univ, 90; ed, Le Bel Inconnu, Garland; Les Posies de Gillebert de Berneville, Droz, 88. **CONTACT ADDRESS** French Dept, Univ Ill Urbana Champaign, 52 E Gregory Dr, Champaign, IL, 61820. **EMAIL** k-fresco@uiuc.edu

FREY, HERSCHEL J.
PERSONAL Born 12/27/1935, Waco, TX, m, 1964 **DISCIPLINE** SPANISH LINGUISTICS, APPLIED LINGUISTICS **EDUCATION** Tex Christian Univ, BA, 57; Univ Wis, MA, 58; Univ NC, PhD (Romance lang), 63. **CAREER** Instr Spanish, Univ NC, 62-63; asst prof Spanish ling, Univ Wash, 63-66; asst prof, Univ Calif, Los Angeles, 66-69; ASSOC PROF SPANISH LING, UNIV PITTSGURGH, 70-, Chmn Spanish I, Mod Lang Asn Am, 68; Fulbright lectr ling, Buenos Aires, Arg, 69-70. **MEMBERSHIPS** MLA; Am Asn Teachers Span and Port; Am Coun Teaching Foreign Lang. **RESEARCH** Linguistics, especially Spanish; Spanish applied linguistics. **SELECTED PUBLICATIONS** Auth, Observations on the Border of Text, Mln Mod Lan Notes, Vol 109, 94. **CONTACT ADDRESS** Dept of Hisp Studies, Univ of Pittsburgh, 1309 Cathedral/Learn, Pittsburgh, PA, 15260-0001.

FREY, JOHN ANDREW
PERSONAL Born 08/29/1929, Cincinnati, OH **DISCIPLINE** ROMANCE LANGUAGES **EDUCATION** Univ Cincinnati, BA, 51, MA, 52; Cath Univ Am, PhD (Romance lang), 57. **CAREER** Assoc prof French, 60-70, chmn dept, 66-69, Prof Romance Lang and Lit, George Washington Univ, 70-. **RESEARCH** Nineteenth century French literature; stylistics. **SELECTED PUBLICATIONS** Auth, Rimbaud 1891-91, Fr Rev, Vol 70, 96; Les Illuminations--A Different Reader, Fr Rev, Vol 70, 96; Mallarme--The Poetics of theater and Writing, Fr Rev, Vol 70, 96; Performance in the Texts of Mallarme, Fr Rev, Vol 68, 94; Desire for the Virgin--The Herodiade According to Mallarme, Fr Rev, Vol 68, 95. **CONTACT ADDRESS** Dept of Romance Lang and Lit, George Washington Univ, Washington, DC, 20006.

FRICKEY, PIERRETTE M.
DISCIPLINE FRENCH LITERATURE **EDUCATION** Augusta Col, BA; Univ SC, MA, PhD. **RESEARCH** Twentieth century French literature; literature of the Caribbean. **SELECTED PUBLICATIONS** Auth, pubs on Caribbean theater, French poet Aragon, and Jean Rhys. **CONTACT ADDRESS** Dept Foreign Languages and Literature, State Univ of West Georgia, Carrollton, GA, 30118.

FRIEDBERG, MAURICE
PERSONAL Born 12/03/1929, Rzeszow, Poland, m, 1956, 2 children **DISCIPLINE** SLAVIC LANGUAGES & LITERATURE **EDUCATION** Brooklyn Col, BSc, 51; Russian Inst, cert & Columbia Univ, AM, 53, PhD (Slavic Lang & Lit), 58. **CAREER** Lectr Russ, Hunter Col, 55-58, from instr to asst prof, 58-62, assoc prof & in charge Russ Div, 62-65; prof Slavic Lang & Lit, Ind Univ, Bloomington, 66-75, dir Russ & E Europ Inst, 67-71; prof Russ Lit & head Dept Slavic Lang & Lit, Univ Ill, Urbana, 75-; Center for Adv Study, prof, 95-; assoc, Russ

Res Ctr, Harvard Univ, 53; lectr, Brooklyn Col, 54, 62, & Middlebury Col, 60, 61; vis asst prof Russ Lit, Columbia Univ, 61-62; travel grant, St Antony's Col, Oxford Univ, 62; inst study USSR, Munich, Ger, 63, 68; Fulbright vis prof, Hebrew Univ, Israel, 65-66; mem fel comt, Nat Endowment for Humanities, 70: mem bd dirs, Int Res & Exchanges Bd, 70-73; Guggenheim fel, 71 & 81-82; juror, Nat Bk Award, 73. **MEMBERSHIPS** MLA; Am Asn Advan Slavic Studies; Am Asn Teachers Slavic & East Europ Lang; corresp mem Polish Inst Arts & Sci, US. **RESEARCH** Soviet and 19th century Russian literature; Polish literature. **SELECTED PUBLICATIONS** Auth, Russian Classics in Soviet Jackets, Columbia Univ, 62: The Party and the Poet in the USSR, NY Univ, 63; ed, A Bilingual Collection of Russian Short Stories, Vols I & II, 64 & 65, Random House; auth, The Jew in Post-Stalin Soviet Literature, B'nai B'rith, 70: A Imagem do Judeu na Literatura Sovietica Pos-Stalinista, Ed Grijalbo, Sao Paulo, 71; co-ed & contribr, Encyclopedia Judaica (16 vols), Macmillan, 71-72: ed, Leon Trotsky, The Young Lenin, Doubleday, 72; A Decade of Euphoria: Western Literature in Post-Stalin Russia 1954-64, Ind Univ, 77; Literary Translation in Russia, Penn State Univ, 97. **CONTACT ADDRESS** Dept of Slavic Lang & Lit, Univ of Illinois, Urbana-Champaign, 707 S Mathews Ave, Urbana, IL, 61801-3625. **EMAIL** friedbrg@uiue.edu

FRIEDMAN, EDWARD HERBERT

PERSONAL Born 01/19/1948, Richmond, VA, m, 1974 **DISCIPLINE** SPANISH LITERATURE **EDUCATION** Univ Va, BA, 70; Johns Hopkins Univ, MA, 71, PhD (Romance lang), 74. **CAREER** Asst prof, Kalamazoo Col, 74-77, asst prof, 77-80, Assoc Prof Span, Ariz State Univ, 80-. **MEMBERSHIPS** MLA, Rocky Mountain Mod Lang Asn: Rocky Mountain Medieval and Renaissance Asn Am Asn Teachers Span and Port. **SELECTED PUBLICATIONS** Auth, Representing the Other--Race, Text, and Gender in Spanish and Spanish American Narrative, Mod Lan Rev, Vol 88, 93; Autobiography as Burla in the Guzman De Alfarache, Hispania J Devoted Teaching Span Portug, Vol 76, 93; Language, Text, Subtext--A Critique of Hispanism, Hispania J Devoted Teaching Span Portug, Vol 77, 94;Through the Shattering Glass, Cervantes and the Self Made World, Mod Philol, Vol 93, 95; Spanish Picaresque Fiction, A New Literary History, Revista Estudios Hisp, Vol 28, 94; Don Quijotes Sally into Tthe World of Opera, Hispania J Devoted Teaching Span Portug, Vol 78, 95; Autobiography as Burla in the Guzman de Alfarache, Hispania J Devoted Teaching Span Portug, Vol 76, 93; Cervantine Journeys, Hispania J Devoted Teaching Spanm Portug, Vol 76, 93; Spanish Eloquence in Art, Hispaniam J Devoted Teaching Span Portug, Vol 79, 96; Pastoral Themes and Forms in Cervantes Fiction, Hispania J Devoted Teaching Span Portug, Vol 80, 97; The Novelist as Playwright, Cervantes and the Entremes Nuevo, Hispania J Devoted Teaching Span Portug, Vol 77, 94; Reading Redressed--Or the Media Circuits of Don Quijote, Confluencia Revista Hisp Cult Y Lit, Vol 9, 94; Don Quijotes Sally into the World of Opera, Hispania J Devoted to the Teaching of Span Portug, Vol 78, 95; Spanish Eloquence in Art, Hispania J Devoted to the Teaching of Spanish and Portuguese, Vol 79, 96; Pastoral Themes and Forms in Cervantes Fiction, Hispania J Devoted Teaching of Span and Portug, Vol 80, 97; Cervantes and the Turks--Historical Reality Versus Literary Fiction In La Gran Sultana and El Amante Liberal, Hispania J Devoted Teaching Span Portug, Vol 77, 94; Historia Lastimera Del Principe Erasto, Hispania J Devoted Teaching Span Portug, Vol 80, 97CoSMic Chaos Exploring Los Trabajos De Persiles Y Sigismunda Williamsen, Ar, Hispania J Devoted Teaching Span Portug, Vol 79, 96; Through the Shattering Glass, Cervantes and the Self Made World, Mod Philol, Vol 93, 95; The Allegoric Theater of Barrios, Miguel,De Levi,Daniel, Hispania J Devoted To The Teaching Of Spanish And Portuguese, Vol 80, 97 The Novelist As Playwright, Cervantes And the Entremes-Nuevo - Reed,Ca/, Hispania-A J Devoted To The Teaching Of Spanish And Portuguese, Vol 77, 94 Miracles, Duels, And Cide-Hamete Moorish Dissent - Hahn,J/, Hispania-A J Devoted To The Teaching Of Spanish And Portuguese, Vol 77, 94; The Distortion of Logic and Polyphony in Quevedo Prose Writings, Hispania J Devoted Teaching Span Portug, Vol 78, 95. **CONTACT ADDRESS** Dept of Foreign Lang, Arizona State Univ, Tempe, Tempe, AZ, 85281.

FRIEDMAN, EVA MARY

PERSONAL Born 10/21/1926, Berlin, Germany, m **DISCIPLINE** GERMAN **EDUCATION** Hunter Col, BA, 49; Johns Hopkins Univ, MA, 51, PhD(German), 54. **CAREER** Instr mod lang, Cedar Crest Col, 52-53; from instr to assoc prof, 53-73, dir Ger prog, 73-74, PROF GER, ADELPHI UNIV, 73-. **HONORS AND AWARDS** Senner Prize, 49. **MEMBERSHIPS** MLA; Am Asn Teachers Ger. **RESEARCH** Nineteenth century German literature; foreign languages in the elementary school; Theodor Storm; business German program development. **SELECTED PUBLICATIONS** Auth, Rainer Maria Rilkes Aufzeichmumgen des Malte Laurids Brigge oder das Problem der menschlichen Existenz; T The child in German literature: From marionette through symbol to reality, winter 69 & The generation gap 100 years ago: The father-son conflict in Theodor Storm's novellen, winter 74, Univ Dayton Rev; Existence and alienation in Rainer Maria Rilke's Notebooks of Malte Laurids Brigge, Univ Dayton Rev, 81; Amerikaspiegelung in Theodor Storm's Novelle, Botjer Basch, In: Schriften Der Theodor Storm Gesellschaft, 83; Lessing's Nathan der Weise and Ronetti Roman's Manesse: A Comparison in Lessing and the Enlightenment, ed Alexej Ugrinsky, Greenwood Press, 86. **CONTACT ADDRESS** Dept of Lang & Int Studies, Adelphi Univ, 1 South Ave, Garden City, NY, 11530-4299. **EMAIL** Friedman@ADLIBV.adelphi.edu

FRIEDMAN, MELVIN JACK

PERSONAL Born 03/07/1928, Brooklyn, NY, m, 1958, 2 children **DISCIPLINE** ENGLISH, COMPARATIVE LITERATURE **EDUCATION** Bard Col, AB, 49; Columbia Univ, AM, 52; Yale Univ, PhD (comp lit), 54. **CAREER** Assoc ed, French Studies, Yale Univ, 51-53; assoc prof comp lit, Univ Md, 62-66; PROF COMP LIT, UNIV WIS-MILWAUKEE, 66-, Vis sr fel, Univ EAnglia, 72; mem fel comt, Nat Endowment for Humanities, 73-74; Fulbright sr lectr, Univ Antwerp, 76. **MEMBERSHIPS** MLA; PEN. **RESEARCH** Twentieth century novel; 20th century literary criticism. **SELECTED PUBLICATIONS** Auth, 3 Views Of Modernism, Mississippi Quart, Vol 46, 93; Wandering and Home, Beckett Metaphysical Narrative, Contemporary Lit, Vol 36, 95; The Beckett Studies Reader, Contemporary Literature, Vol 36, 95; Beckett Dying Words, Contemporary Lit, Vol 36, 95; Nobodys Home, Speech, Self, and Place in American Fiction from Hawthorne to Delillo, Novel Forum Fiction, Vol 28, 95; Cabell, James, Branch and Richmond In Virginia, Am Lit, Vol 66, 94; Innovation in Beckett, Samuel Fiction, Contemporary Lit, Vol 36, 95; Accidents of Influence, Writing as a Woman and a Jew in America, Int Fiction Rev, Vol 20, 93. **CONTACT ADDRESS** Dept of Comp Lit, Univ of Wis, Milwaukee, WI, 53201.

FRIEDMAN, RICHARD ELLIOTT

DISCIPLINE BIBLE, NEAR EASTERN LANGUAGES AND LITERATURES **EDUCATION** Harvard Univ, ThD, 78. **CAREER** Assoc Prof Bible, Univ Calif, San Diego, 76-. **RESEARCH** Literary and historical research in bible. **SELECTED PUBLICATIONS** Auth, The Refiners Fire--The Making of Mormon Cosmology, 1644-1844, J Interdisciplinary Hist, Vol 27, 96; Religion in a Revolutionary Age, Pennsylvania Mag Hist Biog, Vol 121, 97; Law and Ideology in Monarchic Israel, J Am Orient Soc, Vol 114, 94. **CONTACT ADDRESS** Dept of Lit C-005, Univ of Calif, 9500 Gilman Dr, La Jolla, CA, 92093-5003.

FRIEDRICH, PAUL

PERSONAL Born 10/22/1927, m, 1974, 6 children **DISCIPLINE** LINGUISTICS, ANTHROPOLOGY, POETRY **EDUCATION** Harvard Univ, BA, 50, MA, 51; Yale Univ, PhD, 57. **CAREER** Res assoc, Russ Res Ctr, 49-50; asst prof anthrop, Harvard Univ, 57-58; asst prof jr ling, Deccan Col, India, 58-59; asst prof anthrop, Univ Pa, 59-62; assoc prof, 62-67, prof anthrop & ling, Univ Chicago, 67-; prof anthrop, ling & soc thought, 92. **MEMBERSHIPS** Ling See Am; Amer Anthro Assoc; Amer Acad Arts & Sci . **RESEARCH** Homeric Greek; Russian; Mexican languages on cultures. **SELECTED PUBLICATIONS** Auth, Russia and Eurasia, Encyclopedic 1 World, Cultures, 94; auth, Music in Russian Poetry, Lang, 98. **CONTACT ADDRESS** Dept of Anthrop, Univ of Chicago, 1126 E 59th St, Chicago, IL, 60637-1539.

FRIEDRICHSMEYER, ERHARD MARTIN

PERSONAL Born 08/09/1933, Rugby, ND, 3 children **DISCIPLINE** GERMAN **EDUCATION** Lakeland Col, BA, 58; Univ WI, MA, 59; Univ MN, PhD, 64. **CAREER** Instr Ger, Concordia Col, Moorhead, MN, 59-60; instr, Univ MN, 61-63; asst prof, Univ WI-Milwaukee, 63-66; from asst prof to assoc prof, 66-70, Prof Ger, McMicken Col, Univ Cincinnati, 70. **HONORS AND AWARDS** UC Distinguished Tchg Award. **RESEARCH** Nineteenth and Twentieth century Ger lit. **SELECTED PUBLICATIONS** Auth, Schnitzler's Der Grune Kakadu, Z Deutsche Philol, 69; The Dogmatism of Pain-Grass' Local Anaesthetic, Dimension, 71; The Bertram Episode in Hesse's Glass Bead Game, Ger Rev, 74; Hagiography and Humor in Hesse's Glass Bead Game, In: Hermann Hesse Heute, Bouvier, Bonn, 80; Die satirische Kurzprosa Heinrich Bolls, Univ NC Press, 81; The Swan Song of a Male Chauvinist, In: Of The Fisherman and His Wife: Gunter Grass, The Flounder in Critical Perspective, AMS Press, 82; Adrian Leverbuhn: Thomas Mann's Lachender Faust; Colloquia Germanica, 1/2, 84; Gunter Grass's The Rat: Making Room for Doomsday, South Atlantic Rev, 89; Hermat, Utopie und Sprachsuche in Boll's Frauen von Flusslandscharft, In: Geschichte und Melancholia, 95. **CONTACT ADDRESS** Dept of Ger Lang & Lit, Univ of Cincinnati, P O Box 210372, Cincinnati, OH, 45221-0372.

FRIER, BRUCE WOODWARD

PERSONAL Born 08/31/1943, Chicago, IL **DISCIPLINE** CLASSICAL STUDIES, HISTORY OF LAW **EDUCATION** Trinity Col, Conn, BA, 64; Princeton Univ, PhD, 70. **CAREER** Lectr Latin, Bryn Mawr Col, 68-69; Prof Class Studies, Univ Mich, 69-, Prof Law, Univ Mich, 81-. **HONORS AND AWARDS** Goodwin Award of Merit, 83; Guggenheim Fel, 84-85. **MEMBERSHIPS** Am Philol Asn. **RESEARCH** Roman legal history; Roman social and economic history; ancient demography. **SELECTED PUBLICATIONS** Auth, Libr Annales Pontificum Maximorum: The Origins of the Annalistic Tradition, Am Acad Rome, 79; Landlords and Tenants in Imperial Rome, Princeton Univ, 80; The Rise of the Roman Jurists, Princeton Univ, 85; Casebook on the Roman Law of Delicts, Schol Press, 89; The Demography of Roman Egypt, Cambridge Univ, 94. **CONTACT ADDRESS** Dept of Class Studies, Univ of Mich, 625 S State St, Ann Arbor, MI, 48109-1003. **EMAIL** bwfrier@umich.edu

FRISCHER, BERNARD

DISCIPLINE CLASSICAL STUDIES **EDUCATION** Wesleyan Univ, BA, 71; Univ Heidelberg, PhD, 75; FAAR, 76. **CAREER** Asst prof, 76-80; assoc prof, 80-91; ch, 84-88; dir, UCLA Hum Comp Facility, 87-88; dir, Univ Calif Edu Abroad Prog, Italy, 88-90; dir, Univ Calif Edu Abroad Prog, UCLA Campus Off, 92-98; PROF, CLASSICS, UCLA, 91-; vis prof, Univ Bologna, 93; vis prof, Univ Pa, 94; resident class stud, Amer Acad Rome, 96; sec, Acad Sen Univ Calif, 94-96; dir, UCLA Rome Reborn proj, 96; dor.UCLA Cult Virtual Reality lab, 98; dept repr, Legis Assembly, 93-. **HONORS AND AWARDS** Woodrow Wilson fel, 71; jr fel, Mich Soc Fel(S), 71-74; Rome Prize fel, 74-76; ACLS fel, 81-82, 96-97; Paul Mellon sr fel, Ctr Adv Stud in the Visual Arts, Nat Gallery, Wash DC, 96-98., Ch, Cmte to Rev the Summer Sch Roman Topography and Archaeol, Amer Acad Rome, 83; ch, Software Cmte, Amer Philol Assn, 88. **MEMBERSHIPS** Mem, Amer Philol Assoc, 71-; Archaeol Inst Am, 76-; Adv Cmte, Amer Acad Rome, 76-; ed bd, Class Antiquity, 81-87; adv cmte, proj Perseus, 87-93; Classics Selection Cmte, Fullbright Exchange Commission, 84-88. **SELECTED PUBLICATIONS** Auth, "Horace and the End of Renaissance Humanism in Italy: Quarrels, Religious Correctness, Nationalism and Academic Protectionism," Arethusa 28, 95; "La Villa dei Papiri: Modello per la Villa Sabina di Orazio?," Cronache Ercolanesi 25, 95; "Horazens Sabinum: Dichtung und Wahrheit," Romische Lebenskunst, 96; "Rezeptionsgeschichte and Interpretation: The Quarrel of Antonio Riccoboni and Nicolo Cologno about the Structure of Horace's Ars Poetica," Zeitgenosse Horaz, Der Dichter und seine Leser seit zwei Jahrtausenden, 96; co-auth, Sentence Length and Word-type at Sentence Beginning and End: Reliable Authorship Discriminators for Latin Prose, New Stud on the Authorship of the Hist Augusta, Res Hum Comp 5, Oxford Univ Press, 96; How To Do Things With Words/Stop: Two Studies on the Historia Augusta and Cicero's Orations, Papers from the Seventh Intl Colloquium on Latin Lings, Jerusalem, Innsbrucker Beitrage zur Sprachwissenschaft 96. **CONTACT ADDRESS** Dept of Classics, Univ Calif, 405 Hilgard Ave., Los Angeles, CA, 90095-1417. **EMAIL** frischer49@aol.com

FROMKIN, VICTORIA A

PERSONAL Born 05/16/1923, Passaic, NJ, m, 1948, 1 child **DISCIPLINE** LINGUISTICS, EXPERIMENTAL PHONETICS **EDUCATION** Univ Calif, Berkeley, AB, 44, MA, 63, PhD (ling), 65. **CAREER** Asst prof English, Calif State Univ, 65; asst prof speech, 66-67, asst prof ling, 67-69, actg dir phonetics lab, 68-69, chmn dept, 72-76, PROF LING, UNIV CALIF, LOS ANGELES, 69-, DEAN GRAD DIV, 79-, Nat Insts Health grant, 63-; asst prof lang sem, Calif State Col Los Angeles, spring 65; Off Naval Res contract, 66-; mem ling panel, Nat Sci Found, 76-78: ling deleg, Nat Acad Sci, China, 74; vis prof, Univ Stockholm, 77. **MEMBERSHIPS** Fel Acoust Soc Am; Ling Soc Am; Int Phonetic Asn; Asn Machine Transl and Computational Ling; Am Assoc Applied Ling. **RESEARCH** Electromyographics studies of speech **SELECTED PUBLICATIONS** Auth, Linguistic Representational and Processing Analyses of Agrammatism--Introduction, Brain and Language, Vol 50, 95p; The Mind of a Savant Language Learning and Modularity, Lingua, Vol 99, 96; Some Thoughts about the Brain Mind Language Interface, Lingua, Vol 100, 97; Comprehension and Acceptability Judgments in Agrammatism--Disruptions in the Syntax of Referential Dependency, Brain Lan, Vol 45, 93; Jakobson, Roman--A Linguists View of Aphasia, Brain Lan, Vol 47, 94. **CONTACT ADDRESS** Dept of Ling, Univ Calif, Los Angeles, CA, 90024.

FROSE, VICTOR

PERSONAL Born 06/09/1940, Neuendorf, Ukraine **DISCIPLINE** LANGUAGE EDUCATION **EDUCATION** Univ BC, BEd, 67; Western Wash State Col, MEd, 67; Univ Minn, PhD, 77. **CAREER** Asst prof to prof, Univ Man, 70-79; PROF LANGUAGE EDUCATION, UNIV BRITISH COLUMBIA, 86-, dept head, 86-96. **SELECTED PUBLICATIONS** Auth/co-ed, An Experience-Based Approach to Language and Reading, 77; auth/co-ed, Research in the Language Arts, 81; auth/co-ed, Whole-Language, 90, 94; auth/co-ed, A Language Approach to Reading, 91; auth/co-ed, Language Across the Curriculum, 97; co-ed, Eng Quart, 85-91. **CONTACT ADDRESS** Dept of Lang Educ, Univ of British Columbia, Vancouver, BC, V6T 1Z4.

FROW, JOHN

DISCIPLINE CULTURAL STUDIES **EDUCATION** PhD. **CAREER** Prof English, Univ Queensland; dep dir, Australian Key Ctr Cult and Media Policy. **RESEARCH** Literary theory. **SELECTED PUBLICATIONS** Auth, Cultural Studies and Cultural Value, pending.

FRYDMAN, ANNE

PERSONAL Born 05/27/1947, New York, NY, m, 1982 **DISCIPLINE** RUSSIAN AND COMPARATIVE LITERATURE **EDUCATION** Sarah Lawrence Col, BA, 68; Columbia Univ,

MA, 69, PhD (Russ lit), 78. **CAREER** Kenan fel humanities, Soc Fels in Humanities, Columbia Univ, 77-79; vis asst prof, State Univ NY, Purchase, 79-82; VIS ASST PROF RUSS LIT, STATE UNIV NY, PURCHASE, 79-, Preceptor Slavic lang, Columbia Univ, 73-76, vis lectr, 79; vis lectr Slavic lang and lit, Princeton Univ, 80; consult, Theatre Dept, State Univ NY, Purchase, 80; vis asst prof Slav lang, Princeton, 80-81. **MEMBERSHIPS** Int Chekhov Soc (exec secy, 80-82); Am Asn Advan Slavic Studies. **RESEARCH** Anton Chekhov's short stories, form and vision; the prose of Isaac Babel. **SELECTED PUBLICATIONS** Auth, Pirozhkova Memoir of Babel--Introduction, Can Slavonic Papers Rev Can Slavistes, Vol 36, 94. **CONTACT ADDRESS** 425 Riverside Dr Apt 7J, New York, NY, 10025.

FRYE, RICHARD NELSON
PERSONAL Born 01/10/1920, Birmingham, AL, 4 children **DISCIPLINE** IRANIAN **EDUCATION** Univ Ill, AB, 39; Harvard Univ, Am, 40, PhD, 46. **CAREER** Exec secy Near East comt, 48-50, Am Coun Learned Soc; from asst prof to assoc prof Mid Eastern studies, 51-57, assoc dir, 55-57, Mid East Ctr, Aga Khan Prof Iranian, 57, Harvard Univ; asst ed, 50-58, Speculum; vis lectr Iranian archaeol, 66-67, Hermitage Mus; corresp fel, 66-, Ger Archaeol Inst; dir, 69-74, Asia Inst, Pahlavi Univ, Iran; ed bull & monogr ser, 69-74; consult, 76-, Pahlavi Libr, Tehran. **HONORS AND AWARDS** Hon PhD, 92, Univ Tajikistan. **MEMBERSHIPS** Hon mem Zorastrian Assn of NAm; Am Orient Soc (vice pres, 66); Nat Assn Armenian Studies & Res,founder. **RESEARCH** Iranian studies; middle Persian and central Asian history; archaeology. **SELECTED PUBLICATIONS** Auth, The Heritage of Iran, London, 62; auth, The History of Ancient Iran, Beck Munich, 83; auth, The Heritage of Central Asia, Wiener, Princeton, 96; auth, The Histories of Nishapur, Harvard Univ, 65; auth, Bukhara the Medieval Achievement, Univ Okla, 65; auth, Persia, London, 68; ed, Middle Iranian inscriptions from Dura Europas, Corpus Inscriptionium Iranicarum, Lund Humphries, London, 68; auth, Sasanian Seals in the Collection of Mohsen Foroughi, Lund Humphries, London, 72; auth, Excavations of Qasr-i Abu Nasr, Harvard Univ, 73; auth, Neue Methodologie in der Iranistik, Harrasowitz, Wiesbaden, 74; auth, Opera Minora, Asia Inst, Shiraz, 76-77. **CONTACT ADDRESS** Harvard Univ, 6 Divinity Ave, Cambridge, MA, 02138. **EMAIL** frye@fas.harvard.edu

FRYER, T. BRUCE
PERSONAL Born 01/21/1941, Philadelphia, PA, m, 1964, 2 children **DISCIPLINE** FOREIGN LANGUAGES **EDUCATION** Muhlenberg Col, BA, 62; Middlebury Col, MA, 66; Univ Tex, Austin, PhD (foreign lang educ), 70. **CAREER** Teacher Span, Spring-Ford Area Schs, 62-67, head dept foreign lang, 64-67; teaching assoc Span educ, Univ Tex, Austin, 67-70; asst prof, 70-74, ASSOC PROF SPAN, UNIV SC, 74-, COORDR, DIV SPAN AND PORT, 75-, MEM BD DIRS, SOUTHERN CONF LANG TEACHING, 76-. **MEMBERSHIPS** Am Asn Teachers Span and Port; Am Asn Teachers Fr; Am Coun Teaching Foreign Lang; Teaching English Speakers Other Lang. **RESEARCH** Foreign language teaching methodology; international business. **SELECTED PUBLICATIONS** Auth, Beyond Borders--Profiles in International Education, Mod Lan J, Vol 80, 96; Foreign Language Curricular Needs of Students Preparing for an Internship Abroad, Mod Lan J, Vol 77, 93; Understanding Global Cultures--Metaphorical Journeys Through 17 Countries, Mod Lan J, Vol 81, 97. **CONTACT ADDRESS** Dept of Foreign Lang and Lit, Univ SC, Columbia, SC, 29208.

FUCHS, ESTHER
PERSONAL Tel Aviv, Israel **DISCIPLINE** HEBREW LITERATURE **EDUCATION** Brandeis Univ, PhD, 80. **CAREER** Univ Texas, asst prof, 80-85; Univ Arizona Tucson, assoc prof, 85-. **MEMBERSHIPS** AJS, SBL, NAPH. **RESEARCH** Women in Biblical literature; women in modern Hebrew literature; S.Y. Agnon. **SELECTED PUBLICATIONS** Auth, Israeli Mythogynies: Women in Contemporary Hebrew Fiction, Albany: SUNY Press, 87. **CONTACT ADDRESS** Dept of Judaic Studies, Univ of Arizona, Franklin Bldg 305, Tucson, AZ, 85721. **EMAIL** fuchs@u.arizona.edu

FUEGI, JOHN B.
PERSONAL Born 05/09/1936, London, England, 2 children **DISCIPLINE** COMPARATIVE LITERATURE **EDUCATION** Pomona Col, BA, 61; Univ Southern Calif, PhD(comp lit), 67. **CAREER** Lectr Am lit, Free Univ Berlin, 66-67; from asst prof to prof comp lit, Univ Wis, Milwaukee, 67-76; Prof Ger, Slavic & Comp Lit & Dir Comp Lit, Univ MD, 76-86. **HONORS AND AWARDS** Vis fel, Wesleyan Ctr for Humanities, 69; Am Coun Learned Soc sr res fel in East Europ Studies, 73-74; Univ Wis, Milwaukee sr res fel in 20th century studies, 73-74; co-ed, Brecht Jahrbuch, 73-89; Rockefeller Found award, 82-83; Kurt Weill Found fel, 84, 85; Guggenheim fel, 84-85; PBS award for Beckett Directs Beckett, 88-89; Maryland Hum Coun award, 97-98. **MEMBERSHIPS** MLA; Am Comp Lit Asn; Int Comp Lit Asn; Am Asn Teachers Ger; AAUP. **RESEARCH** Relationship of German, Russian and English literatures; the drama, especially Shakespeare and Brecht; E. Hauptmann; Derlah; M. Steffin; Virginia Woolf; Hildegard von Bingen; the relationship of literature and film. **SELECTED PUBLICATIONS** Auth, producer & dir, The Wall (film), Acme Films, 61; auth, The Essential Brecht, Univ Calif, Studies Comp Lit, 72; ed, Brecht Today: Yearbook of International Brecht Society, 71-79 & 82-89; auth, Explorations in no man's land: Shakespeare's poetry as theatrical film, Shakespeare Quart, 72; The Form and the Pressure: Shakespeare's Haunting of Bertolt Brecht, Mod Drama, 72; Moliere and Brecht: The Authorship of Brecht's Don Juan, Comp Lit Studies, 74; auth, Bertolt Brecht: Chaos According to Plan, Cambridge, 87; producer, dir & auth, Red Ruth, Nordisk Film, 90 and The War Within: A Portrait of Virginia Woolf; auth, Brecht and Company, Grove, 94; auth, Brecht et Cie, Fayard, 95; auth, Brecht und Co, Eva Hamburg, 97. **CONTACT ADDRESS** 2701 Curry Dr, Adelphi, MD, 20783.

FULCO, WILLIAM J.
PERSONAL Born 02/24/1936, Los Angeles, CA, s **DISCIPLINE** NEAR EASTERN LANGUAGES & LITERATURE **EDUCATION** Univ Santa Clara, AB, 59; Univ Santa Clara, MA, PhL, 60; STM, STL, 67; Yale Univ, PhD, 70. **CAREER** Ntl Endowment for Humanities Prof Ancient Mediterranean Studies, Loyola Marymount Univ, 98-; Organizer & Host Loyola Marymount Univ Intl Conf in Near Eastern Archaeology, 96-98; correspondent, Annotazioni Numismatiche, 91-; assoc ed, Cath Bibl Quart; Corp Representative of Univ S Calif to Amer Schools of Oriental Res; co-dir, Univ S Calif & Jordanian Dept of Antiquities joint archaeological excavation, Jordan, 90; adjunct prof Archaeology, Univ S Calif, 89-98; participant, Dept of Antiquities, Jordan, Amman Citadel Project; lctr, Univ Judaism, 84-90; lctr Theolog Dept, Loyola Marymount Univ, 84-97. **HONORS AND AWARDS** Mortar Board (Pi Sigma Alpha), Univ S Calif, Faculty of the Month, 95; Megiddo Expedition Israel, 94-. **MEMBERSHIPS** Cath Bibl Assoc Archaeology Committee, 96-; Amer Numismatic Assoc; Amer Numismatic Soc; Amer Oriental Soc; Amer Schools of Oriental Res; Cath Bibl Assoc Amer; Ntl Assoc Afroasiatic Linguistics; Numismatic Soc India; Soc Bibl Lit. **RESEARCH** Linguistics; Archaeologty **SELECTED PUBLICATIONS** Coauth, Tyre: The Shrine of Apollo, Coins & Stamped Handles, 96; Searching for Revelations at Megiddo, in Loyola Marymount Univ VISTAS, 96; coauth, Coins from the Excavations at Tell Nimrin, in Amer Jour of Numismatics, 95-96. **CONTACT ADDRESS** Department of Classics, Loyola Univ, 6525 N Sheridan Rd, PO Box 45041, Los Angeles, CA, 90045-0041. **EMAIL** fulco@usc.edu

FULLER, CLARENCE
PERSONAL Born 01/17/1927, Foxboro, MA **DISCIPLINE** FOREIGN LANGUAGES **EDUCATION** Brown Univ, AB, 50; Middlebury Col, MA, 51. **CAREER** Lectr French, Sch Gen Studies, Columbia Univ, 55-56, instr, Columbia Col, 59-61; asst prof, 61-65, Assoc Prof French and Span, Bloomfield Col, 65-. **RESEARCH** Phonetics; French. **SELECTED PUBLICATIONS** Auth, Instructions for the Desert, Stand Mag, Vol 37, 96. **CONTACT ADDRESS** Dept of Lang, Bloomfield Col, Bloomfield, NJ, 07003.

FULLER, HOMER WOODROW
PERSONAL Born 08/14/1916, Dawn, MO, m, 1942, 2 children **DISCIPLINE** MODERN GERMAN LITERATURE **EDUCATION** Emory Univ, AB, 38; Univ Wis, Am, 40, PhD, 52. **CAREER** Teaching fel Ger, Univ NC, 40-41; instr, Emory Univ, 41-45; grad asst, Univ Wis, 45-47; assoc prof Ger lang, 47-73, PROF GER, UNIV TENN, KNOXVILLE, 73-, Fulbright res scholar, Vienna and Fund Advan Educ fel, 55-56. **MEMBERSHIPS** MLA; SAtlantic Mod Lang Asn. **RESEARCH** Nineteenth century German literature; the German novelle; Theodor Storm's easthetic theories. **SELECTED PUBLICATIONS** Auth, The Schooner Pilgrims Progress, A Voyage Around The World 1932-1934, Am Neptune, Vol 56, 96. **CONTACT ADDRESS** Dept of Ger and Slavic Lang, Univ of Tenn, Knoxville, TN, 37916.

FULLER, LAWRENCE BENEDICT
PERSONAL Born 07/27/1936, Orange, NJ, m, 1971, 2 children **DISCIPLINE** ENGLISH, HISTORY **EDUCATION** Dartmouth Col, AB, 58; Columbia Univ, MA, 63; Pennsylvania State Univ, MA, 83; Johns Hopkins Univ, PhD(Educ), 74. **CAREER** Assoc prof English, Bloomsburg Univ, 71-. **HONORS AND AWARDS** Phi Betta Kappa; Phi Kappa Phi; Fulbright Scholar, Norway, 93-94. **MEMBERSHIPS** Hist Educ Soc; NCTE. **RESEARCH** History of education; literature for adolescents; methods of teaching secondary English. **SELECTED PUBLICATIONS** Auth, A sense of our own history, Independent Sch Bull, 12/71; Private secondary education: the search for a new model, 1880-1915, Foundational Studies, Spring 75; Research papers in English methods classes: introduction to varieties of opinion, English Educ, Summer 76; William M Sloane: A biographical study of turn of the century attitudes toward American education, Foundational Studies, Fall 78; Literature for adolescents: The early days, The ALAN Rev, Spring 79; Students' rights of expression: The decade since Tinker, English J, 12/79; Literature for adolescents: A historical perspective, English Educ, 2/80; Media Education: Where Have We Been? Where Are We Going?, English Education, February, 96. **CONTACT ADDRESS** Dept of English, Bloomsburg Univ of Pennsylvania, 400 E 2nd St, Bloomsburg, PA, 17815-1399. **EMAIL** lfuller@planetx.bloomu.edu

FULLER, M.A.
DISCIPLINE CHINESE LITERATURE **EDUCATION** Yale, BA, 74, PhD, 82. **CAREER** Asst prof, Harvard, 84-90; asst prof, 92-93, assoc prof, Univ CA, Irvine, 93-. **RESEARCH** Classical Chinese poetry; literary theory. **SELECTED PUBLICATIONS** Auth, Road to East Slope: the Development of Su Shi's Poetic Voice, Stanford, 90. **CONTACT ADDRESS** Univ of California, Irvine, Irvine, CA, 92717. **EMAIL** mafuller@uci.edu

FULLERTON, GERALD LEE
PERSONAL Born 08/03/1941, San Francisco, CA **DISCIPLINE** GERMANIC LINGUISTICS **EDUCATION** Stanford Univ, AB, 63, MA, 65; Univ Mich, Ann Arbor, PhD(Ger), 71. **CAREER** Instr Ger, Meramec Community Col, 64-66; instr, Drake Univ, 66-68; asst prof, State Univ NY Buffalo, 71-75; asst prof, Univ Tex San Antonio, 76-77; Asst Prof Ger, Univ Minn, Twin Cities, 77- **MEMBERSHIPS** Ling Soc Am. **RESEARCH** Comparative Germanic grammar; syntax of modern Ger. **SELECTED PUBLICATIONS** Auth, The source of the Gothic fourth weak conjugation, Language, 71; The development of obstruents in four Germanic endings, 74 & Grimm's law and WGmc 2sg verb endings -s, 75, Linguistics; Historical Germanic Verb Morphology, Walter de Grunter, Berlin, 77; On teaching the subjective use of modal auxiliaries, Die Unterrichtspraxis, 77; Subjective modals, assessment adverbs and source phrases, In: Studies in Descriptive German Grammar, Julius Groos, Heidelberg, 82; auth, The Gothic Genitive Plural: An Analysis of Morphological Structure, Michigan Germanic Stud, 83; auth, The Germanic Weak Nonpresent Formations, Beitrage zur Geschichte der Deutschen Sprache und Literatur, 89; auth, Reduplication and the Prosody of Ancient Germanic, Beitrage zur Geschichte der Deutschen Sprache und Literatur, 91; auth, PIE Syllabification and Germanic Nominal Inflection, in, On Germanic Linguistics, de Gruyter, 92. **CONTACT ADDRESS** Dept of German, Univ of Minn, 9 Pleasant St S E, Minneapolis, MN, 55455-0194. **EMAIL** fulle001@tc.umn.edu

FURNESS, EDNA LUE
PERSONAL Born 01/26/1906, Knox Co, NE **DISCIPLINE** ENGLISH & SPANISH **EDUCATION** Univ CO, AB & BE, 28, MA, 39, EdD, 51. **CAREER** Teacher, High Schs, CO, 28-33 & WY, 33-39; instr Span, Pueblo Col, 42-45; instr English & mod lang, Casper Col, WY, 45-47; from asst prof to prof English & foreign lang educ, Univ WY, 47-61; prof English & Span, 61-72, EMER PROF LANG & LIT, WY STATE UNIV, 72-; Instr, Univ CO, 50-51; fac res grant, Univ WY, 57; Coe fel Am studies, Coe Found, 59; Delta Kappa Gamma res grant, 60-61; US Off Educ res grant, 66-67, humanities res grant, 71-72. **HONORS AND AWARDS** Haiku Award, Washington Poets Asn, 80. **MEMBERSHIPS** NEA; Int Platform Asn; Nat Coun Teachers English. **RESEARCH** Comparative literature; translation; children's literature. **SELECTED PUBLICATIONS** Coauth, New Dimensions in the Teaching of English, Pruett, 67; auth, Trends in Literature on Teaching the Language Arts, contribr, Teaching of Listening, Scarecrow, 71, Linguistics in the Elementary School Classroom, Macmillan, 71 & Language Arts in the Elementary School, Lippincott, 72; auth, Mediterranean magic, 74 & Spelling is Serious Stuff, 78, Delta Kappa Gamma Bull; contribr, Educational Assessment of Learning Problems, 78; Assessment and Correction of Language Arts Difficulties, 80; Spelling for the Millions, 66; Guide to Better English Spelling, 91. **CONTACT ADDRESS** 725 S Alton Way Windsor Gardens-6B, Denver, CO, 80231.

FURST, LILIAM RENEE
PERSONAL Born 06/30/1931, Vienna, Austria **DISCIPLINE** COMPARATIVE LITERATURE, GERMAN **EDUCATION** Univ Manchester, BA, 52; Univ Cambridge, PhD (Ger), 57; Ital Govt dipl, 65. **CAREER** From asst prof to assoc prof Ger, Queen's Univ Belfast, 55-66; assoc prof and head dept comp lit, Univ Manchester, 66-71; vis prof comp lit and Ger, Dartmouth Col, 71-72; prof comp lit and romance lang and dir grad prog, Univ Ore, 72-75; PROF COMP LIT, UNIV TEX, DALLAS, 75-, Am Coun Learned Soc res fel, 74-75; hon res assoc comp lit, Harvard Univ, 74-75; Mather vis prof English and foreign lang, Case Western Reserve Univ, 78-79; vis prof Ger, Stanford Univ, 81-82; Guggenheim fel, 82-83; Marta Sutton Weeks fel, Stanford Humanities Ctr, 82-83. **MEMBERSHIPS** MLA; Mod Humanities Res Asn; Am Comp Lit Asn; Int Comp Lit Asn; Western Asn Ger Studies. **RESEARCH** European Romanticism; aspects of narration, 1770-1970; women's studies. **SELECTED PUBLICATIONS** Auth, The Critical Mythology of Irony, Comp Lit Stud, Vol 31, 94; Poetic Madness and the Romantic Imagination, 19th Century Lit, Vol 52, 97; Struggling for Medical Reform in Middlemarch,19th Century Literature, Vol 48, 93; The Ambiguity of Taste--Freedom and Food in European Romanticism, Arcadia, Vol 31, 96; Realism and Hypertrophy 19th Century Fr Stud, Vol 22, 93; The Resistance of Reference, Linguistics, Philosophy, and the Literary Text, Comp Lit Stud, Vol 30, 93; Vital Signs--Medical Realism in 19thCentury Fiction, Comp Lit Studies, Vol 30, 93; Rereading, Comp Lit Stud, Vol 32, 95. **CONTACT ADDRESS** 7654 Royal Lane, Dallas, TX, 75230.

G

GABBARD, KRIN
PERSONAL Born 01/29/1948, Charleston, IL, m, 1973 **DISCIPLINE** COMPARATIVE LITERATURE **EDUCATION** Univ Chicago, BA, 70; IN Univ, PhD, 79. **CAREER** Asst prof, Classics and Modern Lang, Univ SD, 77-79; asst prof, English, Stephens Col, 79-81; asst prof, 81-87, assoc prof, 87-97, prof, Comparative Lit, SUNY Stony Brook, 98-. **MEMBERSHIPS** Soc for Cinema Studies; ACLA; MLA; Sonneck Soc. **RESEARCH** Jazz; film hist and theory; psychoanalysis. **SELECTED PUBLICATIONS** Auth, The Circulation of Sado-Masochistic Desire in the Lolita Texts, J of Film and Video, 94, repeated in Psyart: A Hyperlink J for Psychological Study of the Arts (http://www.clas.ufl.edu/ipsa/journal/articles/gabbar01.htm); ed, Representing Jazz, Duke Univ Press, 95; ed, Jazz Among the Discourses, Duke Univ Press, 95; auth, Psychoanalysis and Film Study in the 1990s, The Am Psychoanalyst 29 4, 96; Jammin' at the Margins: Jazz and the American Cinema, Univ Chicago Press, 96; Louis Armstrong and His Audiences, Jazz: A Century of Change, ed Lewis Porter, Schirmer, 97; The Ethnic Oedipus: The Jazz Singer and Its Remakes, Play It Again, Sam: Retakes on Remakes, ed Andrew Horton and Stuart Y McDougal, Univ CA Press, 98; Borrowing Black Masculinity: The Role of Johnny Hartman in The Bridges of Madison County, in Soundtrack Available: Essays on Film and Popular Music, ed Arthur Knight and Pamela Robertson, Duke Univ Press, 99; Kansas City Dreamin': Robert Altman's Jazz History Lesson, to appear in Music and Cinema, ed James Buhler, Caryl Flinn, and David Neumeyer, Wesleyan Univ Press, 99; Psychiatry and the Cinema, with Glen O Gabbard, MD, 1st ed, 86, rev and expanded, AM Psychiatric Press, 99; Stanley Kubrick and the Art Cinema, to appear in an anthology on A Clockwork Orange, Cambridge Univ Press. **CONTACT ADDRESS** Dept of Comparative Lit, SUNY, Stony Brook, Stony Brook, NY, 11794. **EMAIL** kgabbard@notes.cc.sunysb.edu

GABRIELE, JOHN P.
DISCIPLINE SPANISH LITERATURE **EDUCATION** Univ Conn, BA, 75, MA, 77; Univ NC, PhD, 81; Univ de Salamanca, Spain. **CAREER** Prof. **RESEARCH** Nineteenth and Twentieth-Century Spanish Theatre **SELECTED PUBLICATIONS** Auth, Suma valleinclaniana, Anthropos, 92; De lo particular a lo universal: El teatro espanol del siglo XX y su contexto, Vervuert Verlag, 94; Projections of the Unconscious Self in Buero's Theatre, Neophilologus 78, 94; Mapping the Boundaries of Gender: Men, Women and Space in La casa de Bernarda Alba, Hisp Jour, 94; Teatro espanol de urgencia. El caso de Manuel Martinez Mediero, El teatro espanol contemporaneo, Autores y tendencias, Edition Reichenberger, 95; Writing the Body in Lorca's Rural Trilogy: Toward a Dramatization of Feminine Self-Consciousness, La Chispa, 95: Selected Proceedings, Tulane Univ, 95; Estrategias feministas en el teatro breve de Carmen Resino, Letras Femeninas 21, 95; Gender in the Mirror: A Feminist Perspective on the Esperpento de la hija del capitan, Revista Hisp Mod, 95; Towards a Feminist Reality of Women's Prison Literature: Lidia Falcon's En el infierno: ser mujer en las carceles de Espana, Monogr Rev/Revista Monografica: Hisp Prison Lit 11, 95; Towards a Radical Feminist Stage Rhetoric in the Short Plays of Lidia Falcon, Symposium, 97; La est tica de la crueldad en el teatro antropofagico de Manuel Martinez Mediero, Perspectivas sobre la cultura hispanica: XV aniversario de una colaboracion interuniversitaria, Serv de Publ-Univ de Cordoba, 97; From Assimilation to Liberation: Reassessing In s's Role in Jos¤ Zorrilla's Don Juan Tenorio, Letras Peninsulares, 97; El teatro como arte de la existencia consciente: El hombre de oro de Juan Mayorga, Gestos 24, 97; Politics and the Discourse of Violence in Manuel Martinez Mediero's Lisistrata, La Chispa 97: Selected Proc, Tulane Univ, 97; Dialogo con Jos¤ Maria Rodriguez Mendez, cronista teatral, Iberoamericana 21.2, 97; El teatro breve de Lidia Falcon, Editorial Fundamentos, 97. **CONTACT ADDRESS** Dept of Span, Col of Wooster, Wooster, OH, 44691. **EMAIL** jgabriele@acs.wooster.edu

GAEFFKE, PETER
PERSONAL Born 12/06/1927, Breslau, m, 1958, 2 children **DISCIPLINE** INDOLOGY, COMPARATIVE LITERATURE **EDUCATION** Univ Mainz, WGer, MA, 51, PhD(Indoeurop ling), 52. **CAREER** Prof Hindi, Univ Utrecht, Netherlands, 64-75; PROF INDIAN LIT, UNIV PA, 75-. **HONORS AND AWARDS** MA, Univ Pa, 75. **MEMBERSHIPS** Ger Orient Soc; Dutch Orient Soc; Am Orient Soc; Am Asn Comp Lit. **RESEARCH** Medieval and modern literatures in Hindi, Urdu and Bengal. **SELECTED PUBLICATIONS** Auth, The Indian Narrative--Perspectives and Patterns, J Am Orient Soc, Vol 0115, 95; The 'Songs' of Dadu, J Am Orient Soc, Vol 0116, 96; Philology and Confrontation--Hacker,Paul on Traditional and Modern Vedanta, J Am Orient Soc, Vol 0117, 97. **CONTACT ADDRESS** S Asia Regional Studies Dept, Univ of Pa, Philadelphia, PA, 19174.

GAGLIARDI, FRANK M.
DISCIPLINE CLASSICAL LANGUAGES **EDUCATION** Carleton Col, BA, 72; Univ Mich, PhD, 76. **CAREER** Prof & dir, Oakley Ctr for the Humanities & Soc Sci. **RESEARCH** Greek Tragedy; archaic Greek literature and culture, especially Homer and lyric poetry; critical theory, especially gender studies and anthropological approaches to Greek culture; Roman comedy. **SELECTED PUBLICATIONS** Publ on, Horace Odes 1.5; Sophocles' Philoctetes. **CONTACT ADDRESS** Classics Dept, Williams Col, Stetson Hall, Williamstown, MA, 01267. **EMAIL** mhoppin@williams.edu

GAINES, JAMES FREDERICK
PERSONAL Born 05/31/1949, Somerville, MA, m, 1975 **DISCIPLINE** FRENCH LITERATURE **EDUCATION** Mich State Univ, BA, 71; Univ Pa, MA, 75, PhD(Fr), 77. **CAREER** Asst prof, 77-80, ASSOC PROF FRENCH, SOUHTEASTERN LA UNIV, 80-, Coordr, Univ Hon Prog, Southeastern La Univ, 80-. **MEMBERSHIPS** NAm Soc 17th Century Fr Lit; MLA; Am Asn Teachers Fr. **RESEARCH** Moliere; history and sociology of literature, especially comic theatre; ideologies of French seventeenth century literature. **SELECTED PUBLICATIONS** Auth, Moliere 'Tartuffe,' Theatre J, Vol 0044, 92; Moliere 'George Dandin,' Theatre J, Vol 0044, 92; Valincour, G S--the Limits of Honnetete, Fr Rev, Vol 0066, 93; Costume and Fashion in the Plays of Moliere, Jean, Baptiste, Poquelin--A 17th-Century Perspective, Fr Rev, Vol 0067, 94; Tragedy at the Time of Henri-II and Charles-IX, Bibliotheque D Humanisme Et Renaissance, Vol 0057, 95; Moliere and Marx--Prospects For A New Century, Esprit Createur, Vol 0036, 96; The Awakening of Feelings and the Paradox of Conscience in L'ecole-Des-Femmes' in Play By Moliere, Fr Rev, Vol 0070, 97. **CONTACT ADDRESS** Southeastern La Univ, 500 Western Ave, PO Box 724, Hammond, LA, 70402-0001.

GAIR, JAMES WELLS
PERSONAL Born 12/27/1927, Buffalo, NY, w, 1950, 2 children **DISCIPLINE** LINGUISTICS **EDUCATION** Univ Buffalo, BA, 49, MA, 56; Cornell Univ, PhD(ling), 63. **CAREER** Instr English, Univ Buffalo, 49-51; instr gen educ, State Univ NY Utica, 51-54; instr commun & lit, Univ Buffalo, 54-57, lectr gen stud & asst to dean, Col Arts & Sci, 57-58; res asst NDEA Sinhalese proj, 61-62, from asst prof to assoc prof, 62-74, dir NDEA SAsia Ctr, 67-69, Prof Ling, Cornell Univ, 74-, Instr, Can Ling Inst, Univ Alta, 62-66. **HONORS AND AWARDS** Fulbright-Hays res grant, Ceylon, 64-65 & 69-70, lectr award, Sri Lanka, 76-77. **MEMBERSHIPS** Ling Soc Am; Asn Asian Studies; Ling Soc India; Royal Asiatic Soc, Ceylon; D Litt, Kelaniya Univ, 1993. **RESEARCH** South Asian languages and linguistics; English linguistics. **SELECTED PUBLICATIONS** Auth, The alphabet, Collier's Encyclopedia, 66; coauth, Colloquial Sinhalese, Cornell Univ SAsia Prog, 68; auth, Colloquial Sinhalese Clause Structures, Mouton, 70; Sinhalese digiossia, Anthrop Ling, Vol X, No 8; coauth, Literary Sinhala, Cornell Univ SAsia Prog, 74; coauth, Spoken Sri Lanka (Jaffna) Tamil, Univ Ceylon (in press); auth, Papers in South Asian Linguistics: Sinhala and South Asian Language, Oxford Univ Press, 98; coauth, A New Course in Reading Pali, Motilal Baharsilass, Delhi, 98. **CONTACT ADDRESS** Dept of Modern Lang & Ling, Cornell Univ, 203 Morrill Hall, Ithaca, NY, 14853-4701. **EMAIL** jwg2@cornell.edu

GAISSER, JULIA HAIG
PERSONAL Born 01/12/1941, Cripple Creek, CO, m, 1964, 1 child **DISCIPLINE** CLASSICAL PHILOLOGY **EDUCATION** Brown Univ, AB, 62; Harvard Univ, AM, 66; Edinburgh Univ, PhD, 66. **CAREER** Asst prof classics, Newton Col, 66-69, Swarthmore Col, 70-72 & Brooklyn Col, 73-75; Assoc Prof, 75-84, Prof Latin, Bryn Mawr Col, 84-. **HONORS AND AWARDS** NEH Sr Fel, 85-86, 93-94; ACLS Fel, 89-90; MBE, 90; Res, Bellagio Study & Conf Ctr, Bellagio, Italy, 94; Vis Schol, Phi Beta Kappa, 96-97. **MEMBERSHIPS** Class Asn Atlantic States; Am Philol Asn; Renaissance Soc. **RESEARCH** Greek epic; Latin poetry; classical tradition. **SELECTED PUBLICATIONS** Auth, A structural analysis of the digressions in the Iliad and the Odyssey, Harvard Studies Class Philol, 68; Adaptation of traditional material in the Glaucus-Diomedes episode, Trans Am Philol Soc, 69; Structure and tone in Tibullus 1 6, Am J Philol, 71; Tibullus 1 7: A tribute to Messalla, Class Philol, 71; Noun-epithet combinations in the Homeric hymn to Demeter, Trans Am Philol Soc, 74; coauth, Partons in antiquity, Am J Physics, 77; auth, Mythological Exempla in Propertius 1 2 and, Am J Philol, 77; Tibullus 2 3 and Vergil's Tenth Eclogue, Trans Am Philol, 77; Catullus and his Renaissance Readers, Oxford, 93. **CONTACT ADDRESS** Dept of Latin, Bryn Mawr Col, 101 N Merion Ave, Bryn Mawr, PA, 19010-2899. **EMAIL** jgaisser@brynmawr.edu

GALAND, RENE
PERSONAL Born 01/27/1923, France **DISCIPLINE** FRENCH **EDUCATION** Univ Rennes, Lic es Let, 44; Yale Univ, PhD(French), 52. **CAREER** Instr French, Yale Univ, 49-51; from asst prof to assoc prof, 51-63; chmn dept, 68-72, PROF FRENCH, WELLESLEY COL, 63-, Asst ed, Fr Rev, 67-74; reviewer Breton Lit, World Lit Today, 78- **HONORS AND AWARDS** Chevalier, Palmes Academiques, French Govt, 71; Xavier de Langlais Prize for Breton Literature, 79. **MEMBERSHIPS** Am Asn Teachers Fr; Soc Fr Prof Am; Soc Inter-Celtic Arts & Cult. **RESEARCH** Nineteenth and twentieth century French literature; Breton language and literature. **SELECTED PUBLICATIONS** Auth, Ar Vougou, World Lit Today, Vol 0067, 93; Arvoriz, World Lit Today, Vol 0067, 93; Eus Un Amzer Zo Bet, World Lit Today, Vol 0067, 93; Did Giraudoux Know Stead, William, T., RLC-Rev De Litterature Comparee, Vol 0067, 93; The Monster of the Feuillantines and Hugo, Adele Recollections of Her Father--A Hugolian Enigma, Rev D Histoire Litteraire De La Fr, Vol 0094, 94. **CONTACT ADDRESS** Wellesley Col, Box 45, Wellesley, MA, 02181.

GALCHINSKY, MICHAEL
PERSONAL Born 10/20/1965, Denver, CO **DISCIPLINE** LANGUAGES **EDUCATION** Northwestern Univ, BA, 87; Univ Calif, PhD, 94. **CAREER** Asst prof, Ga St Univ, 98-. **HONORS AND AWARDS** Northwestern Univ Engl Dept Award, Best Sr Creative Writing Major, 87; Phi Beta Kappa, 87; East Bay Jewish Federation Linkages to Israel Grant for Study in Israel, 89,91,92; Mellon Found Grant, 90; UC Berkeley Outstanding Grad Student Instr Award, 90; UC Berkeley Humanities Grad Res Grant, London, 91; Mellon Found Dissertation Fel, 91-92; UC Berkeley Chancellor's Dissertation Fel, 92-93; Millsaps Fac Develop Summer Grants, 95, 97; Commendation for Svc, Millsaps Personnel Comm, 96-97; Amer Coun of Learned Societies Grant, Travel to an Int Conf, 96; Commendations, Teaching & Prof Develop, Millsaps Personnel Comm, 94-95, 95-96; Vis Skirball Fel, Oxford Centre, Hebrew & Jewish Stud, Oxford Univ, 98. **MEMBERSHIPS** Modern Lang Assoc; S Atlantic Modern Lang Assoc; Assoc for Jewish Stud; S Central Modern Lang Assoc. **RESEARCH** Victorian novels & poetry; hist of literary criticism & theory; Amer lit & popular culture; poetics & creative writing; nineteenth century British stud; Jewish cultural stud, women's literary hist; hist & theory of the novel. **SELECTED PUBLICATIONS** Auth, The Origin of the Modern Jewish Woman Writer: Romance and Reform in Victorian England, Wayne St Univ Press, Detroit, 96; coauth; Insider/Outsider: American Jews and Multiculturalism, Berkeley: Univ of Calif Press, 98; art, introduction, Insider/Outsider: American Jews and Multiculturalism, Berkeley: Univ of Calif Press, 98; auth, Permanently Blacked: Julia Frankau's Jewish Race, Victorian Lit & Culture, 99. **CONTACT ADDRESS** Georgia State Univ, Univ Plaza, Atlanta, GA, 30303. **EMAIL** mgalchinsky@gsu.edu

GALLAGHER, EDWARD J.
PERSONAL Born 10/09/1943, Philadelphia, PA, m, 1977 **DISCIPLINE** FOREIGN LANGUAGE **EDUCATION** La Salle Univ, AB, 65; Brown Univ, AM, 67, PhD, 72. **CAREER** Asst prof, Wash Univ, 72-74; asst prof, Rosemont Col, 74-75; vis asst prof, Wash Univ, St Louis, 75-77; from asst prof to assoc prof to prof, 77-, Wheaton Col. **RESEARCH** Medieval french literature; the French Novel. **SELECTED PUBLICATIONS** Auth, art, Bedier and the Tristan Legend: The Case of the Bride Quest Episodes, 96; auth, art, Last Writes: Extreme Unction and Flaubert's Madame Bovary, 97; auth, art, Undiscovered Countries: The Role of Some Minor Characters in Flaubert's Madame Bovary, 97; auth, art, Narrative Uncertainty in Flaubert's Madame Bovary, 98; auth, art, The Eucharist in Flaubert's Madame Bovary and Mauriac's Therese Desqueyroux, 98. **CONTACT ADDRESS** Dept of French, Wheaton Col, Norton, MA, 02766. **EMAIL** egallagh@wheatonma.edu

GALLAHER, EDWARD J.
DISCIPLINE MEDIEVAL AND RENAISSANCE FRENCH LITERATURE **EDUCATION** Brown Univ, PhD. **CAREER** Prof; ch. **RESEARCH** Socio-Religious Life of Late Medieval France; The Modern French Novel. **SELECTED PUBLICATIONS** Ed, La Passion Nostre Seigneur; publ articles on Tristan legend, Visio Lazari, Roman de Silence, Rousseau, Flaubert, Mauriac; publ in: Tristania, Romance Notes, New Zealand, Jour of Fr Stud, Fr Stud Bulletin, Neuphilologische Mitteilunge. **CONTACT ADDRESS** Dept of Fr, Wheaton Col, 26 East Main St, Norton, MA, 02766.

GALLANT, CHRISTEL
PERSONAL Troisdorf, Germany **DISCIPLINE** LANGUAGES/TRANSLATION **EDUCATION** Univ Neuchatel (Switz) LL, 69, DL, 78. **CAREER** Instr, 64, prof adj, 69, prof agregee, 78, PROF TITULAIRE, DIR DEP DE TRADUCTION ET DES LANGUES, UNIV MONCTON, 85-, dir du dep, 93-96. **HONORS AND AWARDS** SSHRCC grant. **SELECTED PUBLICATIONS** Auth, L'Acadie, le berceau de la traduction officielle au Canada, in Cultures de Canada francais, 2, 85; auth, L'influence des religions catholique et protestante sur la traduction des textes sacres a l'intention des Micmacs dans les provinces Maritimes: du livre de prieres de l'abbe Maillaird (1717-1762) a la traduction des Evangiles par Silar Tertius Rand (1810-1899), in TTR-Etudes sur le texte et ses transformations, 3(2), 90; auth, Paul Mascarene, in Circuit, automne, 95. **CONTACT ADDRESS** Dep de traduction et des langues, Univ Moncton, Moncton, NB, E1A 3E9. **EMAIL** gallanc@umoncton.ca

GALLATI, ERNST
PERSONAL Born 10/12/1934, Switzerland **DISCIPLINE** GERMAN AND COMPARATIVE LITERATURE **EDUCATION** Engelberg Col, Switz, BA, 54; Univ Zurich, MA, 58; McGill Univ, PhD(ger lit), 66. **CAREER** Tenure Ger, French and hist, Schinznach High Sch, Switz, 59-62; teaching asst Ger,

MCGill Univ, 62-64; asst prof, San Diego State Univ, 64-67; lectr, Col Geneva, Switz, 67-70; asst prof 70-75, ASSOC PROF GERMAN, MCGILL UNIV, 75-, Can Coun res fel, 73-74; vis prof, Univ Montreal, 72-73. **MEMBERSHIPS** Swiss Teachers Soc, Swiss Asn Univ Prof Ger; MLA; Can Asn Univ Teachers Ger. **RESEARCH** German and French literature 1815-1850; German poetry 18th to 20th century. **SELECTED PUBLICATIONS** Auth, Haller, Albrecht, Von Fame as a Poet--A History of Reception, Colloquia Germanica, Vol 0025, 92. **CONTACT ADDRESS** Dept of Ger, McGill Univ, PO Box 6070, Montreal, PQ, H3A 2T6.

GALLI, BARBARA E.
PERSONAL Born 12/01/1949, Montreal, PQ, Canada, d **DISCIPLINE** GERMANIC LANGUAGES; LITERATURE **EDUCATION** Carleton Univ Ottawa, BA 73; Univ Toronto, MA 76; McGill Univ, PhD 90. **CAREER** Univ Alabama, Aaron Aronov Ch 97-. **MEMBERSHIPS** AAR; AJS; ALA; MLA **RESEARCH** The thought of Franz Rosenzweig. **SELECTED PUBLICATIONS** Auth, Franz Rosenzweig and Jehuda Halevi: Translating Translation Translators, McGill-Queen's Univ Press, 95; God Man and the World: Lectures and Essays, trans and ed, Syracuse Univ Press, 98; Franz Rosenzweig and the New Thinking, trans and ed, Afterward by Alan Udoff, SUP, 98; Orientation in the Modern World: Franz Rosenzweig's Writings in a Cultural Vein, trans and ed, SUP, forthcoming, March 99. **CONTACT ADDRESS** Dept of Religious Studies, Univ of Alabama, 212 Manly Hall, Tuscaloosa, AL, 35487-0264. **EMAIL** bgalli@woodsquad.as.ua.edu

GALLUCCI, JOHN
DISCIPLINE RENAISSANCE AND CLASSICAL FRENCH LITERATURE **EDUCATION** BS License es lettres, BS, Strasbourg, 79; Maitrise Avignon, 83; Yale Univ, MA, 82, PhD, 88. **CAREER** Instr, Yale Univ; Actg ch, Comm Acad Advising, 97; ch, Working Comm on FLAC, 92-96; assoc prof-. **HONORS AND AWARDS** Picker fel; fel, Am Coun Learned Soc., Co-organizer, weekend colloquium on for lang tchg, 93. **SELECTED PUBLICATIONS** Auth, Entre copie et autographe: le texte des Pensees de Pascal, Travaux de Litterature; Pascal, Henry Adams and American Modernity, De la morale a l'economie politique; Politique et ecriture: la 'disposition' pascalienne comme principe de liberte, Justice et force: politiques au temps de Pascal; Poetic Pascal, or the Pensees as an Infinite Text, Dalhousie Fr Studies; Pascal and Kenneth Burke: An Argument for a 'Logological' Reading of the Pensees, Fr Seventeenth-Century Lit; Faith and Language: Allegories of Interpretation in Pascal, Fr Forum; Pascal poeta-theologus, Fr Seventeenth-Century Lit; rev(s), The Fr Rev, Papers on Fr Seventeenth-Century Lit; transl, Yale Fr Studies. **CONTACT ADDRESS** Dept of Philos and Relig, Colgate Univ, 13 Oak Drive, Hamilton, NY, 13346. **EMAIL** jgallucci@center.colgate.edu

GALPERIN, WILLIAM
DISCIPLINE ENGLISH LANGUAGE AND LITERATURE **EDUCATION** Univ Chicago, BA; Brown Univ, MA, PhD. **CAREER** Prof. **RESEARCH** Late 18th-century and early 19th-century British poetry and fiction; literary and cultural theory; film studies. **SELECTED PUBLICATIONS** Auth, Revision and Authority in Wordsworth; auth, The Return of the Visible in British Romanticism. **CONTACT ADDRESS** Dept of English, Rutgers Univ, 510 George St, Murray Hall, New Brunswick, NJ, 08901-1167. **EMAIL** whg1@ix.netcom.com

GALTON, HERBERT
PERSONAL Born 10/01/1917, Vienna, Austria, m, 2 children **DISCIPLINE** SLAVIC LANGUAGES **EDUCATION** Univ London, PhD(Slavic ling), 51. **CAREER** Sr monitor, Brit Broadcasting Corp Monitoring Serv, Reading, Eng, 56-62; translr-ed, US Dept State Foreign Broadcast Info Serv, US Embassy, Vienna, 56-62; from asst prof to assoc prof, 62-69, PROF SLAVIC LANG, UNIV KANS, 69-, Inter-univ comt travel grants exchange scholar, Bulgaria, 65, Czech, 67-68 and Yugoslavia, 70-71. **MEMBERSHIPS** Am Asn Advan Slavic Studies; Am Asn Teachers Slavic & EEurop Lang. **RESEARCH** Comparative Slavic syntax and phonology-synchronic and diachronic; functional morphology; philosophy. **SELECTED PUBLICATIONS** Auth, On the Possibility of Reciprocal Influence between Altaic and Proto-Slavic, Wiener Slavistisches Jahrbuch, Vol 0038, 92; Did Proto-Bulgarian Influence Old-Bulgarian, Zeitschrift Fur Slawistik, Vol 0039, 94; Neither Universals nor Preferences--The Genesis fo Slavic, Folia Linguistica Historica, Vol 0017, 96. **CONTACT ADDRESS** Dept of Slavic Lang, Univ of Kans, Lawrence, KS, 66044.

GALVAN, DELIA V.
PERSONAL Mexico City, Mexico **DISCIPLINE** LITERATURE AND CIVILIZATION OF SPANISH AMERICA **EDUCATION** Univ Cincinnati, BA, MA, PhD. **CAREER** Instr, Bucknell Univ; John Carroll Univ; assoc prof, 91-. **SELECTED PUBLICATIONS** Publ, Spanish American Women Writers of Fiction. **CONTACT ADDRESS** Dept of For Lang, Cleveland State Univ, 83 E 24th St, Cleveland, OH, 44115.

GANIM, JOHN MICHAEL
PERSONAL Born 02/18/1945, Weehawken, NJ **DISCIPLINE** ENGLISH, LINGUISTICS **EDUCATION** Rutgers Univ, BA, 67; IN Univ, MA, 69, PhD, 74. **CAREER** From asst prof to assoc prof, 74-88, prof eng, Univ CA, Riverside, 88, ch Eng Dept, 96. **HONORS AND AWARDS** Jr Fac Award, Ctr Medieval and Renaissance Studies, 77. **MEMBERSHIPS** MLA; Medieval Acad Am; Medieval Asn Pacific. **RESEARCH** Middle Eng lit; Chaucer; Old Eng lit. **SELECTED PUBLICATIONS** Auth, Disorientation, style and consciousness in Sir Gawain and the Green Knight, PMLA, 76; Tone and Time in Chaucer's Troilus, ELH, 76; Style and Consciousness in Middle English Narrative, Princeton Univ Press; Bakhtin, Chaucer, Carnival, Lent, Studies in the Age of Chaucer, 87; Chaucer, Boccaccio and the Problme of Popularity, In: Assays, Pittsburgh Univ Press, 87; Carnival Voices in the clerk's Envoy, Chaucer Rev, 87; Chaucer and the Noise of the People; Exemplaria, spring 90; Chaucerian Theatricality, Princeton Univ Press, 90; Forms of Talk in the Canterbury Tales, Poetica, 91; The Literary Uses of New History, In: The Idea of Medieval Literature: New Essays on Chaucer and Medieval Culture in Honor of Donald R Howard (James M Dean and Christian K Zacher, ed); Univ Del Press, 92; Chaucerian Ritual and Patriarchal Romance, Chaucer Yearbook, 92; Literary Anthropology at the Turn of the Centuries: E K Chambers' The Mediaeval Stage, Envoi, 93; The Devil's Writing Lesson, In: Oral Poetics in Middle English Poetry (Mark Amodio, ed), Garland, 94; Medieval Literature as Monster: The Grotesque Before and After Bakhtin, Exemplaria, 95; Recent Studies on Literature, Architecture, and Urbanism, MLQ, 9/95; The Myth of Medieval Romance, In: Medievalism and the Modernist Temper (R Howard Bloch and Stephen G Nichols, ed), Johns Hopkins Univ Press, 96; Double Entry in the Shipman's Tale: Chaucer and Book keeping Before Pacioli, Chaucer Rev, 96. **CONTACT ADDRESS** Dept of Eng, Univ of California, 900 University Ave, Riverside, CA, 92521-0001. **EMAIL** john.ganim@ucr.edu

GAO, Q.
PERSONAL Born 03/28/1955, Lanzhou, China, m, 2 children **DISCIPLINE** CHINESE GRAMMAR **EDUCATION** Ohio State Univ. PhD 98. **CAREER** Ohio State Univ, tchr assoc; Wright State Univ, adj fac instr. **MEMBERSHIPS** LSA **RESEARCH** Syntactic Structure; Sentence Structure; Argument Structure; Chinese Grammar. **SELECTED PUBLICATIONS** Auth, Chinese NP Structure, Linguistics, 94; auth, Resulting Verb Compounds and BA Construction in Chinese, Jour of Chinese Linguistics, 96. **CONTACT ADDRESS** Dept of Linguistics, Ohio State Univ, 2590 Lorain Ct, Columbus, OH, 43210. **EMAIL** Gao@osu.edu

GARAUD, CHRISTIAN
DISCIPLINE FRENCH LITERATURE **EDUCATION** Univ Poitiers, PhD. **CAREER** Prof, Univ MA Amherst. **RESEARCH** 17th century lit; French cult studies autobiography; play and lit. **SELECTED PUBLICATIONS** Auth, pubs on Segalen, Paulhan, Aury, and Ernaux. **CONTACT ADDRESS** Dept of French and Italian Studies, Univ Massachusetts Amherst, Mass Ave, Amherst, MA, 01003. **EMAIL** cgaraud@frital.umass.edu

GARBER, ZEV WARREN
PERSONAL Born 03/01/1941, Bronx, NY, m, 1975, 4 children **DISCIPLINE** JEWISH STUDIES HEBREW **EDUCATION** Hunter Col, BA, 62; Univ Southern Calif, MA, 70. **CAREER** Teaching asst relig, 64-68, teaching asst hist, 67-68, Univ Southern Calif; from instr to asst prof, 70-73, assoc prof Hebrew, 73-79, prof Jewish Studies, 79-, Los Angeles Valley Col; lectr Judaica, Univ Judaism, 65-; Mem Found Jewish Cult fel, 70-71; lectr Jewish studies, Univ Calif, Riverside, 71-72; asst prof Hebrew, Calif State Univ, 72-; consult Rabbinics, Relig Studies Rev J, 78-80; ed, Iggeret, 82-. **MEMBERSHIPS** Nat Assn Prof Hebrew, Soc Bibl Lit; Am Acad Relig; Am Orient Soc; Assn Jewish Studies. **RESEARCH** Holocaust, Biblica, Hebraica, Judaica **SELECTED PUBLICATIONS** Auth, Perspectives on Zionism, Shofar 94; auth, What Kind of God? UPA, 95; auth, Peace In Deed, Scholars, 98; auth, Academic Approaches to Teaching Jewish Studies, UPA, 99. **CONTACT ADDRESS** Dept of Jewish Studies, Los Angeles Valley Col, 5800 Fulton Ave, Van Nuys, CA, 91401-4062. **EMAIL** zevgarber@juno.com

GARDAPHE, FRED L.
PERSONAL Born 09/07/1952, Chicago, IL, m, 1982 **DISCIPLINE** ENGLISH; CULTURAL STUDIES **EDUCATION** Univ of Wis at Madison, 76; Univ of Chicago, AM, 82; Univ of Ill Chicago, PhD, 93. **CAREER** Prof of English and Ed Studies, Columbia Col, 80-98; Prof of Italian/American Studies, SUNY Srony Brook, 98-. **HONORS AND AWARDS** Fac Development Grant, Columbia Col, 86; Dept of English Award, Univ of Chicago, 82; William F. Vilas Scholar, Univ of Wis, 75; Res fel, Immigration Hist Res Center, Minn, 86; Vis prof, Univ Sassari, Italy, 98; Road Scholar, Ill Humanities Counc, 96-98. **MEMBERSHIPS** Nat Book Critics Cr; MLA; Soc of Midland Authors; Midwast MLA; Soc for the Study of Multi-Ethnic Lit of the United States; Am Asn of Italian Studies; Nat Writers Union; Am Italian Hist Asn; Ill Ethnic Coalition. **RESEARCH** Italian/American culture; ethnic American cultures; immigration. **SELECTED PUBLICATIONS** Coauth, (Ex)tending or Escaping a Tradition: Don DeLillo and Italian/American Literature, Beyond the Margin, Farleigh Dickinson Univ Press, 98; (In)visibility: Cultural Representation in the Criticism of Frank Lentricchia, Differentia, 94; auth, Fascism and Italian/American Writers, Romance Languages Annual, Purdue Univ Press, 93; In Search of Italian/American Writers, Italian Am, 97; Here are the Italian/American Writers, Canadian J of Italian Studies, 96; Breaking and Entering: An Italian American's Literary Odyssey, Forkroads, 95, Beyond The Godfather, 97. **CONTACT ADDRESS** Dept of English/European Studies, State Univ of NY Stony Brook, Stony Brook, NY, 11794-3359. **EMAIL** fgar@aol.com

GARFINKEL, ALAN
PERSONAL Born 09/06/1941, Chicago, IL, m, 1965, 2 children **DISCIPLINE** SPANISH **EDUCATION** Univ Ill, Urbana, BA, 63, MA, 64; Ohio State Univ, PhD(educ), 68. **CAREER** Teacher Span, Waukegan Twp High Sch, Ill, 64-66; asst prof foreign lang educ, Okla State Univ, 69-72; asst prof, 72-74, ASSOC PROF FOREIGN LANG EDUC, PURDUE UNIV, WEST LAFAYETTE, 72-, Asst Dir, Div Sponsored Prog, 81, ED NOTES and NEWS, MOD LANG J, 74-. **MEMBERSHIPS** Am Coun Teaching Foreign Lang; MLA; Nat Soc Studies Educ; Am Asn Teachers Span & Port. **RESEARCH** Language teaching methodology and curriculum; language teacher education; continuing education. **SELECTED PUBLICATIONS** Auth, Fuentes--Lectura-y-Redaccion, Mod Lang J, Vol 0081, 97; Fuentes--Conversacion-y-Gramatica, Mod Lang J, Vol 0081, 97. **CONTACT ADDRESS** FLL/SC, Purdue Univ, West Lafayette, IN, 47907-1968.

GARIANO, CARMELO
PERSONAL Born 03/04/1922, Nicosia, m, 1953, 2 children **DISCIPLINE** FOREIGN LANGUAGES **EDUCATION** Univ Catania, Italy, DLet, 46; Univ Buenos Aires, Arg, Prof en Let, 51, Lic en Let, 53; De Paul Univ, MA, 56; Univ Chicago, PhD(-Spanish), 64. **CAREER** Lectr Latin Am lit, Univ Buenos Aires, 51-52, aesthet and stylistics, 52-53; instr Span, Univ Detroit, 57-60; asst prof, Roosevelt Univ, 60-62; asst prof, 62-68, PROF ROMANCE LANG, CALIF STATE UNIV, NORTHRIDGE, 68, Assoc prof classics, Nat Univ Litoral, Arg, 51-53; mem, Nat Fed Mod Lang Teachers Asn, 59-. **MEMBERSHIPS** MLA; Am Asn Teachers Span & Port. **RESEARCH** Diachronic linguistics; Spanish medieval literature; medieval and Renaissance studies. **SELECTED PUBLICATIONS** Auth, A List of 1st-Verses of Spanish Poems (16th-Century 17th-Century), Hispania-A J Devoted to the Teaching of Spanish and Portuguese, Vol 0078, 95. **CONTACT ADDRESS** Dept of Foreign Lang, California State Univ, Northridge, 18111 Nordhoff St, Northridge, CA, 91324.

GARNETT, MARY ANNE
DISCIPLINE 19TH CENTURY FRENCH LITERATURE **EDUCATION** Wisc State Univ, BA, 70; Univ Wisc, MA, 71, PhD, 80. **CAREER** English and Lit, Univ Ark **SELECTED PUBLICATIONS** Ed, Women in French Newsletter. **CONTACT ADDRESS** Univ Ark Little Rock, 2801 S University Ave., Little Rock, AR, 72204-1099. **EMAIL** magarnett@ualr.edu

GARR, W. RANDALL
PERSONAL Born 12/21/1954, Norwalk, CT **DISCIPLINE** SEMITIC LANGUAGES **EDUCATION** Vassar Col, AB, 77; Yale Univ, MA, 79, MPhil, 80, PhD(Near East lit), 82. **CAREER** LECTR NORTHWEST SEMITIC LANG, UNIV PA, 82-. **MEMBERSHIPS** Am Orient Soc; Soc Bibl Lit; Am Schs Orient Res; Ling Soc Am; Asn Jewish Studies. **RESEARCH** History of the Hebrew language; comparative semitics; history of Syria-Palestine. **SELECTED PUBLICATIONS** Auth, The Grammar and Interpretation of Exodus-Vi,3 and An Analysis of the Literary Construction of the Divine Names El-Shaddai and Yahweh Within the Context of the Priestly (P) Document, J Biblical Lit, Vol 0111, 92. **CONTACT ADDRESS** Dept of Orient Studies, Univ of Pa, Philadelphia, PA, 19104.

GARRETSON, DEBORAH
DISCIPLINE RUSSIAN LANGUAGE **EDUCATION** NY Univ, PhD. **CAREER** Assoc prof, Dartmouth Col. **HONORS AND AWARDS** Interp, INF and the START I and START II treaties, as well as at the US-USSR summit meetings, 85-. **RESEARCH** Second lang acquisition **SELECTED PUBLICATIONS** Auth, numerous articles on var aspects of 2nd lang acquisition ranging from the psycholinguistics of reading in a second lang to cult frameworks for Second Language Methodology. **CONTACT ADDRESS** Russ Dept, Dartmouth Col, 44 N College St, Hanover, NH, 03755-1801. **EMAIL** deborah.garretson@dartmouth.edu

GASCHE, RODOLPHE
DISCIPLINE COMPARATIVE LITERATURE **EDUCATION** Freie Universitat, MA; PhD **CAREER** Fac, Freie Universitat; fac, Johns Hopkins Univ; fac, SUNY Buffalo. **RESEARCH** 19th- and 20th-century French lit; critical theory and its rel to continental philos since early romanticism. **SELECTED PUBLICATIONS** Auth, Die hybride Wissenschaft, Met-

zler, 73; System und Metaphorik in der Philosophie von Georges Bataille, Lang, 78; The Tain of the Mirror: Derrida and the Philosophy of Reflection, Harvard, 86; Interventions of Difference: On Jacques Derrida, Harvard, 94; trans, works by Derrida and Lacan into German. **CONTACT ADDRESS** Dept Comp Lit, SUNY Buffalo, 639 Clemens Hall, Buffalo, NY, 14260. **EMAIL** gasche@acsu.buffalo.edu

GASPERETTI, DAVID
DISCIPLINE RUSSIAN LITERATURE **EDUCATION** Lawrence Univ, BA, 76; Univ Calif, Los Angeles, MA, 78, PhD, 85. **CAREER** Vis asst prof, Univ Tulsa, 83-85; asst prof, Univ Tulsa, 85- 89; asst prof, 89-96, ASSOC PROF RUSSIAN, UNIV NOTRE DAME, 96-. **CONTACT ADDRESS** Dept of German & Russian Lang, Lit, Univ of Notre Dame, Notre Dame, IN, 46556.

GAVRONSKY, SERGE
PERSONAL Born 08/16/1932, Paris, France, m, 1960, 1 child **DISCIPLINE** ROMANCE LANGUAGES **EDUCATION** Columbia Univ, BA, 54, MA, 55, PhD, 65. **CAREER** From lectr to assoc prof, 60-75, prof French & chmn dept, 75-, Barnard Col, Columbia Univ; Sterling Currier grant, Columbia Univ & NEH pilot grant, 78; John Simon Guggenheim Found fel, Camargo Found fel, French Govt grant & Mellon Fac grant, 79; NEH implementation grant, 82; vis, 83, Natl Human Ctr; judge, 90, Acad Amer Poets's Harold Morton Landon Prize in Transl; NY St Coun on Arts, transl grant, 91; judge, Jeanne Scaglione Prize in transl, MLA, 98. **HONORS AND AWARDS** Chevalier, 81, Officier, 91, Chevalier, 98, dans l'Ordre des Palmes Academiques, French Govt; Whitney Olin Professor of French, 94. **MEMBERSHIPS** Pen Club. **SELECTED PUBLICATIONS** Auth, Louis Zukofsky, l'Homme/poete, transl De A 1 A 7 Ulysse fin de Siecle, 94; auth, Toward a New Poetics: Contemporary Writing in France, Univ Calif Press, 94; auth, Joyce Mansour Cris/Screams, trans Post-Apollo Press, 95; auth, Parlons de lui, poems, pierre Annette, 95; auth, Reduction du Tryptique, poemes, Philippe Millereau, 96; auth, Six Contemporary French Women Poets, S Ill Univ Press, 97; auth, Mallarme Spectal ou Zukofsky au travail, La Main Courante, 98. **CONTACT ADDRESS** Dept of French, Barnard Col, 3009 Broadway, New York, NY, 10027-6598. **EMAIL** sgavronsky@barnard.columbia.edu

GAY-CROSIER, RAYMOND
PERSONAL Born 08/30/1937, Basel, Switzerland, m, 1963, 1 child **DISCIPLINE** FRENCH LITERATURE **EDUCATION** Univ Berne, PhD(Romance), 65. **CAREER** Asst Ger lit, Stanislas, Lycee Louis-le-Grand, Paris, 60-61; prof French & philos, Lycee de Berthoud, Switz, 62-66; asst prof French, Trent Univ, 66-67; assoc prof, 67-73, grad coordr, 70-80, fac develop grant, 73-74, Prof French, Univ Fla, 73-, Chmn, 80-93; Chair, Ed Bd, Humanities Monograph Series, Presses of the Univ Fla, 77-92; Gen Ed, Ars interpretandi series, Peter Lang, 86-; Asst Ed, The Fr Rev, 86-; Ed-in-chief of the Camus series, Revue des Lettres Modernes, 87-; For Books Ed, S Atl Rev, 90-93. **HONORS AND AWARDS** Am Coun Learned Soc grant, 82; Chevalier, 87, Officier, 93, Palmes Acad¤miques Pres, SAMLA, 93-94. **MEMBERSHIPS** MLA; Am Asn Teachers Fr. **RESEARCH** Twentieth-century French literature, criticism and history of ideas. **SELECTED PUBLICATIONS** Auth, Les envers d'un ¤chec, Etude sur le th¤¤tre d'Albert Camus, Paris, Minard, 67; contribr & ed, Albert Camus, 70, Sherbrooke, Celef, 70; Religious Elements in the Secular Lyrics of the Troubadours, NC Univ Press, 71; ed, Albert Camus series, Revue des Lettres Modernes, Vol 7, 74, Vol 9, 78, Vol 11, 82, Vol 12, 85, Vol 13, 89, Vol 14, 91, Vol 15, 94, Vol 16, 95, Vol 17, 96; Albert Camus, Darmstadt, Wissenschaftliche Buchgesellschaft, 76; contribr & ed, Albert Camus 1980, Univ Fla, 80; International Camus Criticism, Critical Bibliography of French Literature, Syracuse Univ, 80; ed and contribr, Albert Camus: oeuvre ferm¤e, oeuvre ouvert?, Gallimard, 84; La navette entre l'exil et le royaume: le voyage comme apprentissage du d¤senchantement chez Albert Camus, Lendemains XXI:81, 96; Points de rencontre et points de choc. D¤sir transformateur et violence g¤n¤atrice: Claude Simon et l'acte de lecture, In: Point de recontre: le roman, Oslo, Res Coun of Norway, Kult Skriftserie, no 37, vol II, 96; Lyrisme et ironie: le cas du Premier Homme, Camus et le lyrisme, SEDES, 97; author of numerous other journal articles and book chapters since 1980. **CONTACT ADDRESS** Dept of Romance Lang & Lit, Univ of Florida, P O Box 117405, Gainesville, FL, 32611-7405. **EMAIL** gaycros@rll.ufl.edu

GAYLORD, INEZ K.
DISCIPLINE FRENCH LANGUAGE AND LITERATURE **EDUCATION** Wellesley Col, BA; Univ Chicago, MA, PhD. **CAREER** Prof. **RESEARCH** Twentieth-century novel. **SELECTED PUBLICATIONS** Auth, numerous articles on fiction and film. **CONTACT ADDRESS** Dept of French, Col of Wooster, Wooster, OH, 44691.

GEARHART, SUZZANE
DISCIPLINE FRENCH LANGUAGE **EDUCATION** Johns Hopkins Univ, PhD. **CAREER** PROF, FR, UNIV CALIF, IRVINE **SELECTED PUBLICATIONS** Auth, The Open Boundary of History and Fiction; The Interrupted Dialectic: Philosophy, Psychoanalysis, and Their Tragic Other; pub(s), articles on Fr lit, hist, philos, and psychoanalysis. **CONTACT ADDRESS** Dept of Fr and Ital, Univ Calif, Irvine, CA, 92697.

GEARY, JOHN STEVEN
PERSONAL Born 08/18/1948, Oakland, CA, m, 1978 **DISCIPLINE** MEDIEVAL LITERATURE, ROMANCE PHILOLOGY **EDUCATION** Univ Calif, Berkeley, AB, 70, MA, 72, Ph-D(Romance philol), 79. **CAREER** ASST PROF SPANISH LIT, UNIV COLO, BOULDER, 79-. **MEMBERSHIPS** MLA; Am Asn Teachers of Spanish & Portuguese. **RESEARCH** Medieval Spanish epic poetry; Medieval Catalan poetry; comparative Romance linguistics. **SELECTED PUBLICATIONS** Auth, La Gran Conquista de Ultramar--Biblioteca-Nacional-MS-1187, Romance Philol, Vol 0046, 92; Seneca and 'Celestina,' Romance Philol, Vol 0047, 93; Villasandino and His Lyric Voice, Romance Philol, Vol 0046, 93; The Pitas-Payas Episode of the 'Libro De Buen Amor'--Its Structure and Comic Climax, Romance Philol, Vol 0049, 96. **CONTACT ADDRESS** Dept of Spanish Lit, Univ of Colo, Box 278, Boulder, CO, 80309-0278.

GEIST, JOSEPH E.
DISCIPLINE ENGLISH LANGUAGE AND LITERATURE **EDUCATION** Univ Kan, PhD. **CAREER** Prof and chr, Div English, For Langs, Comm-Theater Arts, and Art. **RESEARCH** American literature; contemporary theatre; and cinematic studies. **SELECTED PUBLICATIONS** Auth, articles on T.S. Eliot, the Liberal Arts, 20th Century Film and Drama. **CONTACT ADDRESS** Central Methodist Col, 411 Central Methodist Sq, Fayette, MO, 65248.

GELBER, LYNNE LEVICK
PERSONAL Born 02/06/1939, Philadelphia, PA, m, 1959, 2 children **DISCIPLINE** FRENCH& COMPARATIVE LITERATURE **EDUCATION** Bryn Mawr Col, AB, 60, MA, 62; Univ Colo, Boulder, PhD, 71. **CAREER** From instr to asst prof, 68-77, assoc prof, 77-81, prof French, Skidmore Col, 81-, coordr, Skidmore Jr Yr Abroad, 80-, chairperson, Dept Foreign Lang & Lit, 79-, adj prof, Union Grad Sch, 72-75. **HONORS AND AWARDS** Nat Endowment for Humanities teaching fel, Princeton Univ, 75-76. **MEMBERSHIPS** Paul Claudel Soc; MLA; AM Asn Teachers Fr; AAUP; Am Asn Univ Women. **RESEARCH** Modern French literature; French poetry; women in French literature. **SELECTED PUBLICATIONS** Auth, The art criticism of Paul Claudel, Claudel Newslett, 2/72; Camille Claudel's art and influence, Claudel Studies, fall 72; Women in France since the revolution, Empire State Col, spring 73; Claudel on Rodin: Sweet vengeance and bitter memory, Claudel Studies, spring 76; ed, Dialogues with the Unseen and the Unknown: Essays in Honor of Andre Malraux, 78; In/ Stability: The Shape and Space of Claudel's Art Criticism, UMI Res Press, 80. **CONTACT ADDRESS** Dept For Language & Literature, Skidmore Col, 815 N Broadway, Saratoga Springs, NY, 12866-1698. **EMAIL** lgelber@skidmore.edu

GELFAND, ELISSA DEBORAH
PERSONAL Born 01/26/1949, New York, NY, 1 child **DISCIPLINE** FRENCH STUDIES, WOMEN'S STUDIES **EDUCATION** Barnard Col, BA, 69; Brown Univ, MA, 72, PhD, 75. **CAREER** Prof Eng, Ecole Active Bilingue, Paris, 73-75; asst prof, 75-81, assoc prof, 81-88, Prof French, Mount Holyoke Col, 88-, Dir, Women's Studies Prog, 82-84, 98-, Instr French, Alliance Ft Providence, RI, 71-73; instr English, Int House, Paris, 73; Andrew W Mellon fel interdisciplinary res, 79. **MEMBERSHIPS** Ed bd, Women in French Studies; Am Asn Tchr(s) Ft; MLA; Northeast Mod Lang Asn; Nat Women's Studies Asn; Women's Caucus Mod Lang. **RESEARCH** Feminist theory, women's and gender studies; prison lit. **SELECTED PUBLICATIONS** Auth, Alberline Sarrazin: A control case for femininity in form, Fr Rev, 12/77; A response to the void: Madame Roland's memoires particuliers and her imprisonment, Romance Notes, 79; translr, texts by B Broult, F Pachirier & D Pogg, In: New French Feminisms, Univ MA Press, 80; auth, Women prison writers in France: Twice criminal, Mod Lang Studies, 80-81; Imprisoned women: Toward a socio-literary feminist analysis, Yale Fr Studie, 81; Imagination in Confinement: Women Writers from French Prisons, Cornell Univ Press, 83; coauth, French Feminist Criticism: An Annotated Bibliography, Garland Press, 85 **CONTACT ADDRESS** Dept of French, Mount Holyoke Col, 50 College St, South Hadley, MA, 01075-1461. **EMAIL** egelfand@mtholyoke.edu

GELLRICH, MICHELLE
DISCIPLINE GREEK LITERATURE AND PHILOSOPHY, LITERARY THEORY, DRAMA **EDUCATION** Univ Calif, Berkeley, PhD, 82. **CAREER** Assoc prof, La State Univ. **HONORS AND AWARDS** Lily Found tchg grant, 84; ACLS fel, 86; LSU summer fac res stipend, 92; Alpha Lambda Delta, 96. **RESEARCH** Greek literature and philosophy; classical rhetoric. **SELECTED PUBLICATIONS** Auth, Tragedy and Theory: The Problem of Conflict Since Aristotle, 88; Aristotle's Poetics and the Problem of Tragic Conflict, Ramus, 94; Aristotle's Rhetoric: Theory, Truth, and Metarhetoric, Cabinet of the Muses, 90; Socratic Magic: Enchantment, Irony, and Persuasion in Some Dialogues of Plato, in Class World, 94. **CONTACT ADDRESS** Dept of Eng, Louisiana State Univ, 223E Allen Hall, Baton Rouge, LA, 70803.

GEMUNDEN, GERD
DISCIPLINE GERMAN AND COMPARATIVE LITERATURE **EDUCATION** Univ OR, PhD, 88. **CAREER** Assoc prof, Dartmouth Col. **RESEARCH** Contemp Ger lit and film, lit theory, and travel lit. **SELECTED PUBLICATIONS** Auth, comp study of speechless subj(s) around 1800; publ(s) about writers and filmmakers R. W. Fassbinder, Peter Handke, Heiner Muller, and Wim Wenders. **CONTACT ADDRESS** Dartmouth Col, 3529 N Main St, #207, Hanover, NH, 03755.

GENDZIER, STEPHEN J.
PERSONAL Born 07/14/1930, New York, NY, m, 1958, 4 children **DISCIPLINE** FRENCH LITERATURE **EDUCATION** Oberling Col, BA, 52; Columbia Univ, MA, 53, PhD, 59. **CAREER** Instr, 56-60, Columbia Univ; asst prof, 60-62, Mass Inst Technol; asst prof, 62-66, assoc prof, 66-, co-chmn, romance & comp lit, 97-, Brandeis Univ. **MEMBERSHIPS** Am Assn Tchrs Fr; MLA; Soc Fr Etude XVIIIe Siecle. **RESEARCH** The French enlightenment; the English and French novel of the eighteenth century. **SELECTED PUBLICATIONS** Auth, L'Interpretation de la figure humaine chez Diderot et chez Balzac, L'Annee Balzacienne, 62; art, Balzac's Changing Attitudes Toward Diderot, Fr Studies, 4/65; auth, Denis Diderot: The Encyclopedia, Harper, 69; auth, Diderot and the Jews, Diderot Studis, 73. **CONTACT ADDRESS** 36 Hayes Ave, Lexington, MA, 02173. **EMAIL** gendzier@binah.cc.brandeis.edu

GENNO, CHARLES N.
PERSONAL Born 11/19/1934, Toronto, ON, Canada **DISCIPLINE** GERMAN **EDUCATION** Univ Toronto, BA, 57, MA, 59, PhD, 61. **CAREER** Alexander von Humboldt res fel (Ger), 60-61; asst to assoc prof, 63-87, PROF GERMAN, UNIV TORONTO, 87-, dept ch, 89-94; vis prof, Univ BC, 67; guest prof, Univ Trier (Germany), 73. **SELECTED PUBLICATIONS** Auth, Structured Language Practice and Grammatical Review, 2nd ed, 90; auth, German for Advanced Intermediates, 3rd ed, 92; ed, The First World War in German Narrative Prose, 80. **CONTACT ADDRESS** German Dept, Univ of Toronto, 97 St George St, Toronto, ON, M5S 1A1.

GENTRY, F.G.
PERSONAL Born 06/08/1942, Boston, MA, m, 1972 **DISCIPLINE** GERMAN AND ENGLISH **EDUCATION** Boston Col, BS, Ger and Eng, 63; Indiana Univ, MA, Ger, 66, PhD, Ger, 73. **CAREER** Instr, SUNY-Albany, 69-74; asst prof, SUNY-Albany, 74-75; asst prof, Univ Wis Madison, 75-80; assoc prof, Univ Wis Madison, 80-84; guest prof, Lehrstuhl Schupp, Univ Freiburg, 84; prof, Univ Wis Madison, 84-91; prof, Penn State Univ, 91-. **HONORS AND AWARDS** Alpha & Omega, Boston Col Sch of Educ Honor Soc, 62; Alpha Sigma Nu, Nat Jesuit Honor Soc, 62; Delta Phi Alpha, Nat Ger Honor Soc, 64, pres, Beta Chap, 68; Campion Distinguished Alumnus Award, Boston Col, 77; Seal of the Univ Freiburg, 85; fel, Vilas assoc, Univ Wis Madison, 86-88; Alexander von Humboldt-Stiftung fel, 78, 79, summer 82; Inst for Res in the Humanities, 77; Indiana Univ-Kiel Univ Exchange fel, 64. **MEMBERSHIPS** Alexander-von-Humboldt Assoc of Amer; Amer Assoc of Tchrs of Ger; Fulbright Assoc; Ger Studies Assoc; Gesellschaft fur interkulturelle Germnaistik; Intl Arthurian Soc; Intl Courtly Lit Soc; Intl Vereinigung fur Ger Sprachund Lit; Mediavisten-Verband; Medieval Acad of Amer; Mod Lang Asn; Oswald-von-Wolkenstein-Gesellschaft; Wolfram-von-Eschenbach-Gesellschaft. **RESEARCH** Medieval literature and culture. **SELECTED PUBLICATIONS** Co-ed, with James K. Walter, Heroic Epic, The Ger Libr, vol 1, NY, 95; Bibliographie zur fruhmittelhochdeutschen, Dichtung, Berlin, 92; ed, German Medievalism, Studies in Medievalism 3/4, Cambridge, 91; ed, Gottfried von Strasburg, The Ger Libr, vol 3, NY, 88; articles, Owe armiu phaffheite: Heinrich von Melk's Views on Clerical Life, Medieval Purity and Piety: Essays on Medieval Clerical Celibacy and Religious Reform, NY, Garland, 337-52, 98; Kaiserchronik, Dict of Lit Bio: Ger Writers and Works of the Early Middle Ages, 800-1170, vol 148, NY/ London, Gale Res, 202-207,95; Notker von Zwiefalten, Dict of Lit Bio: Ger Writers and Works of the Early Middle Ages 800-1170, vol 148, NY/London, Gale Res, 106-109, 95; Der Arme Hartmann, Dict of Lit Bio: Ger Writers and Works of the Early Middle Ages, 800-1170, vol 148, NY/London, Gale Res, 10-13, 95; Silent that Others Might Speak: Notes on the Ackermann aus Bohmen, Ger Quart, 67, 484-492, 94. **CONTACT ADDRESS** Pennsylvania State Univ, 305 Burrowes Bldg., University Park, PA, 16802. **EMAIL** fggi@psu.edu

GEORGE, EDWARD V.
PERSONAL Born 12/10/1937, Buffalo, NY, m, 1968 **DISCIPLINE** CLASSICAL LANGUAGES **EDUCATION** Niagara Univ, BA, 59; Canisius Col, MS, 62; Univ Wis, MA, 62, PhD(-Classics), 66. **CAREER** Asst prof classics, Univ Tex, Austin, 66-71; assoc prof, 71-78, PROF CLASSICS, TEX TECH UNIV, 78-. **MEMBERSHIPS** Am Philol Asn; Class Asn Midwest & South; Class Asn Southwestern US; Vergilian Soc Am; Am Class League (vpres, 80-82). **RESEARCH** Augustan Latin and Hellenistic Greek poetry; teaching classical humanities; Renaissance Latin Lit. **SELECTED PUBLICATIONS** Auth, Stoics and Neostoics--Rubens and the Circle of Lipsius, Class World, Vol 0087, 94; The Antiquarians and the Myth of Antiq-

uity--the Origins of Rome in Renaissance Thought, Class World, Vol 0090, 96; Andreas and the Ambiguity of Courtly Love, 16th Century J, Vol 0027, 96; Valerius-Maximus and the Rhetoric of the New Nobility, Class World, Vol 0089, 96. **CONTACT ADDRESS** 2007 28th St, Lubbock, TX, 79411.

GEORGE, EMERY EDWARD
PERSONAL Born 05/08/1933, Budapest, Hungary **DISCIPLINE** GERMANIC LANGUAGES, EAST EUROPEAN STUDIES **EDUCATION** Univ Mich, BA, 55, MA, 59, PhD(-Ger), 64. **CAREER** Instr Ger, Univ Mich, 62-64; from instr to asst prof, Univ Ill, Urbana, 64-66; from asst prof to assoc prof, 66-75, off res admin res grant, 67-68, PROF GER LANG and LIT, UNIV MICH, ANN ARBOR, 75-, Assoc ed Russ lit, Triquarterly, 73-; found ed, Mich Ger Studies, 75-76; FEL, INT ACAD POETS, ENGLAND, 76-; Int Res and Exchanges Bd fel, 81. **HONORS AND AWARDS** Hopwood Award in Poetry, 60. **MEMBERSHIPS** MLA; AM Soc Aesthet; Holderlin Ges; Poetry Soc Am; Int Poetry Soc. **RESEARCH** German literature of the Age of Goethe; English literature; Russian and Hungarian literataure. **SELECTED PUBLICATIONS** Auth, The Problem of Christ in the Works of Holderlin, Friedrich, J Eng and Ger Philol, Vol 0093, 94; The Lyrical Element in Poetry--Norm and Ethos of the Genre in the Works of Holderlin, Brentano, Eichendorff, Rilke, and Benn, Colloquia Germanica, Vol 0027, 94; Holderlin Later Poetic Fragments--'Unendlicher Deutung Voll,' J Eng and Ger Philol, Vol 0094, 95; The 4th-Tone: Holderlin as a Philosopher and a Poet, J Eng and Ger Philol, Vol 0094, 95; Holderlin Later Poetic Fragments--'Unendlicher Deutung Voll,' J Eng and Ger Philol, Vol 0094, 95; Holderin 'Poems and Fragments,' J Eng and Ger Philol, Vol 0095, 96; The Poet as Thinker--Holderlin in France, J Eng and Ger Philol, Vol 0095, 96; Critical Approaches to Goethe Classical Dramas 'Iphigenie', 'Torquato Tasso', and Die 'Naturliche Tochter,' J Eng and Ger Philol, Vol 0096, 97. **CONTACT ADDRESS** Dept of Ger, Univ of Mich, Ann Arbor, MI, 48109.

GEORGE, HERMON, JR.
PERSONAL Born 11/22/1945, Tampa, Florida, d **DISCIPLINE** SPANISH **EDUCATION** Wilkes College, Wilkes-Barre, PA, BA, 1967; Middlebury College, Middlebury, VT, MA, 1968; University of California, Irvine, CA, PhD, 1979. **CAREER** Wartburg College, Waverly, IA, instructor of Spanish, 1968-70; Fisk University, Nashville, TN, instructor of Spanish, 1970-71; Spelman College, Atlanta, GA, instructor of Spanish, 1971-73; California State University, Fresno, CA, assistant professor of ethnic studies, 1978-81; SUNY College, New Paltz, NY, assistant professor, Black Studies, 1981-85; University of Northern Colorado, Greeley, CO, associate professor and coordinator, 1985-91; professor, 1991-. **MEMBERSHIPS** Member-at-large, executive board, National Council for Black Studies, 1980-87; reviewer, Social Science Journal, 1980-81, 1985-; reviewer, Science & Society, 1987-; regional editor, Western Journal of Black Studies, 1991-96; member, National Conference of Black Political Scientists, 1988-89. **SELECTED PUBLICATIONS** The Black Scholar, advising & contributing editor, 1994; Western Social Science Assn, exec council, 1993-96; The Social Science Journal, assoc editor, 1994-95; Contemporary Authors, V 126, 1989;American Race Relations Theory, Lanham MD, Univ Press of America, 1984; "Black Power in Office: The Limits of Electoral Reform", reprinted in Talmadge Anderson Ed, Black Studies: Theory, Method, and Critical Perspectives 1990; Fellowship, NEH, Summer Institute on African-American Culture, 1987; Faculty Excellence Award, Univ of Northern Colorado, 1987; "Clarence Thomas: 'Loyal Foot Soldier' for Reaganism"; Court of Appeal: The Black Community Speaks Out on the Racial and Sexual Politics of Thomas vs Hill, 1992. **CONTACT ADDRESS** Dept of Africana Studies, Univ of Northern Colorado, Greeley, CO, 80639. **EMAIL** hhgeorg@bentley.unco.edu

GEORGE, KEARNS
DISCIPLINE ENGLISH LANGUAGE AND LITERATURE **EDUCATION** Yale Univ, BA; Columbia Univ, MA; Boston Univ, PhD. **CAREER** Prof. **RESEARCH** Modernism; literature and philosophy; literary theory. **SELECTED PUBLICATIONS** Auth, Ezra Pound: The Cantos. **CONTACT ADDRESS** Dept of English, Rutgers Univ, 510 George St, Murray Hall, New Brunswick, NJ, 08901-1167. **EMAIL** gwkearns@aol.com

GEORGES, ROBERT A.
PERSONAL Born 05/01/1933, Sewickley, PA, m, 1956, 1 child **DISCIPLINE** FOLKLORE, LINGUISTICS **EDUCATION** Ind State Col, BS, 54; Univ Pa, MA, 61; Ind Univ, PhD, 64. **CAREER** Teacher English, Bound Brook High Sch, NJ, 54-56; Southern Regional High Sch, Manahawkin, 58-60; from instr to asst prof English, Univ Kans, 63-66; from asst prof to assoc prof English and folklore, 66-76, vchmn, Folklore and Mythology Group, 67-68, chmn 68-76, PROF ENGLISH and FOLKLORE, UNIV CALIF, LOS ANGELES, 76-, Guggenheim fel, 69-70. **MEMBERSHIPS** MLA; Ling Soc Am; Am Folklore Soc. **RESEARCH** Narrating process; narrative analysis; conceptual foundations of folklore and mythology studies. **SELECTED PUBLICATIONS** Auth, The Concept of Repertoire in Folkloristics, Western Folklore, Vol 0053, 94; Research Ethics--Cases and Materials, J Folklore Res, Vol 0034, 97; The Centrality in Folkloristics of Motif and Tale Type, J Folklore Res, Vol 0034, 97. **CONTACT ADDRESS** Folklore and Mythology Studies Univ of Calif Los, Los Angeles, CA, 90024.

GERATO, ERASMO GABRIELE
PERSONAL Born 03/24/1943, Formia, Italy, 1 child **DISCIPLINE** ITALIAN & FRENCH LANGUAGE & LITERATURE **EDUCATION** City Univ New York, BS, 66; Univ Wis, MA, 68, PhD(Ital-French), 74. **CAREER** Teaching asst Ital, Univ Calif, Los Angeles, 66-67 & Univ Wis, 67-70; asst prof, 70-77, assoc prof Ital-French, Fla State Univ, 77-, Cofrs Univ Scholar, 74-75. **HONORS AND AWARDS** Ward Medal, City Univ New York, 66; Fullbright Scholarship, 71; Pi Delta Phi-National French Honor Society; The Dante Society Univ S. Florida (life membership); Director of International Linkage Institutes 80-Present (State of Florida); French Academic Palms, 93 (Chevalier); Promotion, French Academic Palms, 98 (Officer). **MEMBERSHIPS** Am Assoc of Teachers of Fr; Am Assoc of Teachers of Ital; Am Soc of Fr Acad Palms. **RESEARCH** Italian and French language, literature and linguistics. **SELECTED PUBLICATIONS** Auth, A Critical Study of the Life and Works of Alessandro Poerio, Casa Editrice C Maccari, 75; Thematic fragments in Alessandro Poerio's poetry, La Parola del Popolo, 5/75; La Chartreuse de Parme: A study of its origins A discussion of several possible sources, La Stagione, 1/76; Reality of illusion and illusion of reality in Leopardi's Zibaldone, SAtlantic Bull, 5/76; Un capolavoro della lett italiana del 600: La Reina de Scotia--Studio critico della sua lingua e stile, Neuphilolische Mitteilungen, 6/76; Vittorio Alfieri, the artist and his creation: An exposition of Alfieri's personal nature as reflected in his protagonists, Rocky Mt Rev, 81; Guido Gustavo Gozzano: A Literary Interpretation, Madrid: Jose Porrua Turanzas, 83; Salvatore Quasimodo Nobel Laureates in Literature. Ed. R. Pribic, New York, Garlando, 90, 341-344. **CONTACT ADDRESS** Dept of Mod Lang, Florida State Univ, University Center, Room A5529, Tallahassee, FL, 32306-2510. **EMAIL** egerato@mailer.fsu.edu

GERBER, BARBARA LESLIE
PERSONAL Born 10/29/1941, New York, NY **DISCIPLINE** COMPARATIVE LITERATURE, FRENCH **EDUCATION** Brooklyn Col, BA, 62; Univ Wis-Madison, MA, 65, PhD, 68. **CAREER** Asst prof French, St Lawrence Univ, 68-73; asst prof, 73-77, assoc prof, 77-81, prof comp lit, 82-, Brooklyn Col; Dir, St Lawrence Jr Year in France, 71-72; dir, Spec Baccalaureats Degree Prog Adults, 79-86; dir Master of Arts in Liberal Studies, 82-97; dir, Comparative Lit Prog, Brooklyn Col, CUNY. **MEMBERSHIPS** AAUP; MLA; Am Comp Lit Asn. **RESEARCH** Twentieth century French novel and theatre. **SELECTED PUBLICATIONS** Contrib, Twentieth Century French Fiction, Rutgers Univ, 75; coauth, Dictionary of Modern French Idioms, Garland, 77; transl, Color of Time, Zone Press, 80. **CONTACT ADDRESS** 2901 Bedford Ave, Brooklyn, NY, 11210. **EMAIL** bgerber@brooklyn.cuny.edu

GERDES, NEIL W.
PERSONAL Born 10/19/1943, Maline, IL, 2 children **DISCIPLINE** LIBRARIAN; SPIRITUALITY **EDUCATION** Univ Ill, AB, 65; Harvard Univ, BD, 68; Columbia Univ, MA, 71; Univ Chicago, MA, 75; Univ St Mary of the Lake, Dmin, 94. **CAREER** Instr, Tuskegee Institute, 69-71; libr asst, Augustana Col, 72-73; libr prof, Meadville Theol Sch, 73-; libr, program dir, Chicago Cluster Theol Sch, 77-80; dir, Hammond Libr, 80-; prof, Chicago Theol Sem, 80-. **HONORS AND AWARDS** Ordained to ministry Unitarian Universalist Assn, 1975. **MEMBERSHIPS** ALA; Am Theol Libr Asn; Chicago Area Theol Libr Asn; Unitarian Universalist Mins Asn; Assn Liberal Religious Scholars; Phi Beta Kappa. **RESEARCH** Spirituality, liberal religious history. **CONTACT ADDRESS** Meadville/Lombard Theol Sch, 5701 S Woodlawn Ave, Chicago, IL, 60637-1602. **EMAIL** ngerdes@meadville.edu

GERICKE, PHILIP OTTO
PERSONAL Born 12/24/1936, Ukiah, CA, 4 children **DISCIPLINE** ROMANCE LANGUAGES & LITERATURE **EDUCATION** Univ Calif, Riverside, BA, 58; Univ Calif, Berkeley, MA, 60, PhD, 65. **CAREER** Assoc Span, Univ Calif, Riverside, 62-63, lectr, 63-64; asst prof foreign lang, San Fernando Valley State Col, 64-66; asst prof, 66-71, assoc prof, 71-78, assoc dean, grad div, 75-81, PROF SPAN, UNIV CALIF, RIVERSIDE, 78-94, PROF EMER, 94-. **MEMBERSHIPS** MLA; Am Asn Teachers Span & Port; PAMLA; Asn Intl de Hispanists. **RESEARCH** Spanish literature of the Middle Ages and early Renaissance. **SELECTED PUBLICATIONS** Coauth, El Vencimjento del mundo, tratado ascetico del siglo XV: edicion, Hispanofila, 64; auth, El Invencionario de Alfonso de Toledo, Rev Arch, Bibliot & Mus, 1-12/67; The narrative structure of the Laberinto de fortuna, Romance Philol, 5/68; ed & transl, Manuel C Rojo's Historical Notes on Lower California, Dawson's 72; The turtledove in four sixteenth-century versions of Fontefrida, El Romancero, Hoy, 79; On the structure of the Libro de Buen Amor: A question of method, Ky Romance Quart, 2/81; Apostillas a Sacone de la prision y romances relacionados actas del congresso Romanuro-Caucimero, UCLA, 84; Porrua Turanzai, 87; ed, Alfonso de Toledo's Invencionario, Hispanic Sem of Medieval Studies, 92. **CONTACT ADDRESS** Dept of Lit & Lang, Univ of Calif, 900 University Ave, Riverside, CA, 92521-0001. **EMAIL** philip.gericke@ucr.edu

GERIG, WESLEY LEE
PERSONAL Born 09/17/1930, Ft Wayne, IN, m, 1952, 4 children **DISCIPLINE** RELIGION, HEBREW, THEOLOGY **EDUCATION** Ft Wayne Bible Col, AB, 51; Fuller Theol Sem, M div, 54, ThM, 56; Univ Iowa, PhD(relig), 65. **CAREER** From instr to assoc prof Bible & theol, 57-69, acad dean, 71-73, Prof Bible & Theol, Ft Wayne Bible Col, 69-91, Chmn Dept Bibl Studies, 62-91; Taylor Univ, 92-;Instr Bibl lang & dir admis, prof Bibl & theol; Winona Lake Sch Theol, 64-. **MEMBERSHIPS** Evangel Theol Soc; Am Acad Relig. **RESEARCH** The Hebrew-Gentile relations in the Old Testament; the social ethics of the Apostolic Fathers; Koine Greek. **CONTACT ADDRESS** Div Bibl Studies, Taylor Univ, Ft. Wayne, 1025 W Rudisill Blvd, Fort Wayne, IN, 46807-2197. **EMAIL** wsgerig@tayloru.edu

GERLACH, U. HENRY
PERSONAL Born 06/29/1938, Berlin, Germany, m, 1965, 4 children **DISCIPLINE** GERMAN LITERATURE **EDUCATION** Univ Utah, BA, 64; Cornell Univ, MA, 66, PhD (Ger Lit), 68. **CAREER** Asst prof Ger Lang, Cornell Univ, 64-68; asst prof, 68-74, assoc Prof Ger Lang & Lit & Foreign Lang Methodoloty, Univ Ill, Urbana, 74-87, Alexander von Humboldt-Stiftung Dozentenstipendiat, 74-75. **HONORS AND AWARDS** Knight's Cross for Science and Art (Austria). **MEMBERSHIPS** MLA; Am Asn Teachers Ger; Am Coun Teaching Foreign Lang; Hebbel-Ges. **RESEARCH** Nineteenth century German drama; literary history; foreign language methodology. **SELECTED PUBLICATIONS** Auth, Hebbel as a Critic of His Own Works, A Kummerle, 72; Hebbel-Bibliographie 1910-1970, 73, Friedrich Hebbel: Briefe, 75 & Briefe von und an F Hebbel, 78, C Winter; contribr, Motiv des unterdrueckten Gewissen in Hochwaelders Heiligem Experiment, In: Hebbel-Jahrbuch, Oesterreich in Geschichte und Lit, 80; C F Meyer-Biibliographie, 94. **CONTACT ADDRESS** Univ of Illinois, Urbana-Champaign, 707 S Mathews Ave, Urbana, IL, 61801-3625. **EMAIL** ugerlach@uiuc.edu

GERLI, EDMONDO MICHAEL
PERSONAL Born 09/11/1946, San Jose, Costa Rica, m, 1966, 1 child **DISCIPLINE** SPANISH LANGUAGE AND LITERATURE **EDUCATION** Univ Calif, Los Angeles, BA, 68, PhD(Hisp lang & lit), 72; Middlebury Col, Madrid, MA, 69. **CAREER** Asst prof, 72-77, assoc prof, 77-81, PROF SPAN, GEORGETOWN UNIV, 81-, Co-ed, Hispano-Italic Studies, 76. **HONORS AND AWARDS** Williams Prize, Hispanic Rev, 81. **MEMBERSHIPS** MLA; SAtlantic Mod Lang Asn; Am Acad Res Historians Medieval Spain; Am Asn Teachers Span & Port; Asoc Int Hispanistas. **RESEARCH** Medieval Spanish literature; Renaissance Spanish literature. **SELECTED PUBLICATIONS** Auth, Columbus and the Shape of the Word, Authority and Experience in the 'Relacion' of the 3rd-Voyage, J Hisp Philol, Vol 0016, 92; Kinship and Polity in the 'Poema De Mio Cid,' Rev De Estudios Hispanicos, Vol 0028, 94; 'Tirant Lo Blanch,' A Novel of History and Fiction, Hisp Rev, Vol 0062, 94; Complicitous Laughter, Hilarity and Seduction in 'Celestina,' Hisp Rev, Vol 0063, 95; Montoro , Anton, De and the Wages of Eloquence--Poverty, Patronage and Poetry in 15th-Century Castile, Romance Philol, Vol 0048, 95. **CONTACT ADDRESS** Sch Lang and Ling, Georgetown Univ, Washington, DC, 20007.

GERMAIN, CLAUDE
PERSONAL Born 06/27/1941, St. Tite, PQ, Canada **DISCIPLINE** LINGUISTICS **EDUCATION** Univ Montreal, LL, 65, CAPES, 67, MA, 68; Univ Aix-Marseille (France), PhD(Ling), 70; Univ Ottawa, PhD(Philos), 89. **CAREER** Tchr, Royal Mil Col, St-Jean, 65-67; prof ling, Univ Ottawa, 70-79; prof educ, Univ Montreal, 79-87; CH LINGUISTICS, UNIV QUEBEC MONTREAL, 87-. **HONORS AND AWARDS** Can Mod Lang Rev Best Article Award, 85; Ghyslaine Coutu-Vaillancourt Award, 85. **SELECTED PUBLICATIONS** Auth, Le Point sur l'approche communicative, 91, 2nd ed 93; auth, Evolution de l'enseignement des langues: 5000 ans d'histoire, 93; coauth, L'evaluation de la communication ecrite au primaire, 2 vols, 85; ed, Le point sur la grammaire en didactique des langues, 95; ed, Les eleves sourds: Style cognitif et education bilinguel/biculturelle, 95. **CONTACT ADDRESS** Lnguistics Dept, Univ of Quebec Montreal, CP 8888, Succ Centre-ville, Montreal, PQ, H3C 3P8.

GERMAIN, EDWARD B.
PERSONAL Born 12/30/1937, Saginaw, MI, m, 1 child **DISCIPLINE** ENGLISH LANGUAGE; ENGLISH LITERATURE **EDUCATION** Univ Mich, PhD, 69. **CAREER** Instr, US Naval Reserve, 63-65; instr, Eastern Mich Univ, 64-66; teaching fel, Univ Mich Ann Arbor, 66-69; asst prof, eng, Pomona Col, 69-75; lectr, Wayne State Univ, 76; assoc prof, humanities, Nathaniel Hawthorne Col, 76-79; instr, eng, Rennes, France, 82-83; instr, eng, Phillips Acad, 79-. **HONORS AND AWARDS** Sabbatical grant, 97-98; Who's Who Among American Teachers, 96; appointment, sch yr abroad, France, 82-83; Keenan grant for writing, Phillips Acad, 82; sabbatical fel, Pomona Col, 75-76; fac res grant, Pomona Col, 70, 71, 75; Avery Hopwood award for creative writing, Univ Mich, 68; Phi Kappa Phi, 65. **MEMBERSHIPS** Intl James Joyce. **SELECTED PUBLICATIONS** Auth, The Annotated Sisters, teaching web

site, http://www.andover.edu/english/joyce, 98; auth, Jane Kenyon, Ron Padgett, Lee Harwood, Robert Dana, Charles Henri Ford, Contemporary Poets of the English Language, St. James Press, London, revised, 96; ed, Surrealist Poetry in English, Penguin Books Ltd, London, 78; ed, Shadows of the Sun: the Diaries of Harry Crosby, Black Sparrow Press, Santa Barbara, Calif, 77; ed, Flag of Ecstasy: Selected Poems of Charles Henri Ford, Black Sparrow Press, 72. **CONTACT ADDRESS** PO Box 278, Dublin, NH, 03444. **EMAIL** egermain@andover.edu

GERRARD, CHARLOTTE
DISCIPLINE FRENCH LITERATURE **EDUCATION** Univ Pittsburgh, PhD, 66. **CAREER** Assoc prof. **RESEARCH** Philosophy of Camus and Sartre. **SELECTED PUBLICATIONS** Auth, Montherlant and Suicide, 77; pubs on Camus, Vian, Montherlant, Maulnier, Sartre, Ionesco, Ribemont-Dessaignes and antitheism in drama. **CONTACT ADDRESS** Dept of French and Italian, Indiana Univ, Bloomington, 300 N Jordan Ave, Bloomington, IN, 47405.

GESELL, GERALDINE C.
DISCIPLINE CLASSICAL STUDIES **EDUCATION** Vassar Col, BA, 53; Univ Okla, MA, 55; Univ NC, PhD, 72. **CAREER** Asst prof, 72-79; assoc prof, 79-85; prof, 85-. **MEMBERSHIPS** Advis Counc Am Acad Rome; Archaeol Inst Am; Class Asn Mid W and S; Tennessee Class Asn. **SELECTED PUBLICATIONS** Auth, Town, Palace, and House Cult in Minoan Crete, 85; pubs on Minoan relig and ritual artifacts, preliminary reports of the Kavousi Excavations and pottery technol. **CONTACT ADDRESS** Dept of Classics, Knoxville, TN, 37996. **EMAIL** ggesell@utk.edu

GESNER, B. EDWARD
PERSONAL Born 09/22/1942, Middleton, NS, Canada, m, 1971, 3 children **DISCIPLINE** DIALECTOLOGY, APPLIED LINGUISTICS **EDUCATION** Univ King's Col, BA Hons, 63; Dalhousie Univ, MA, 67; Univ Toulouse II, Dr 3 cycle ling, 77. **CAREER** Teacher French, Queen Elizabeth High Sch, 65-66; lectr, 67-69, asst prof, 69-80, ASSOC PROF FRENCH, DALHOUSIE UNIV, 80-, Res assoc, Int Ctr Res Biling, Laval Univ, 80-81. **MEMBERSHIPS** Am Asn Teachers Fr. **RESEARCH** Acadian morphology and syntax; pedagogy of French as second language. **SELECTED PUBLICATIONS** Auth, Ecrivons--Strategies for Writing in French as a 2nd-Language, Can Mod Lang Rev-Revue Canadienne Des Langues Vivantes, Vol 0049, 93; Invitation--Contexts, Culture and Communication, 4th ed, Can Mod Lang Rev-Revue Canadienne Des Langues Vivantes, Vol 0051, 95. **CONTACT ADDRESS** French Dept, Dalhousie Univ, Halifax, NS, B3H 3J5.

GIBALDI, JOSEPH
PERSONAL Born 08/20/1942, Brooklyn, NY, m, 1962, 2 children **DISCIPLINE** ENGLISH, COMPARATIVE LITERATURE **EDUCATION** City Col New York, BA, 65; City Univ New York, MA, 67; NY Univ, PhD(comp lit), 73. **CAREER** Instr English, Brooklyn Col, 71-73; asst prof comp lit, Univ Ga, 73-76; ASSOC DIR, BK PUBL AND RES PROG, MOD LANG ASN AM, 76-, Southeastern Inst Medieval and Renaissance Studies fel, 76; adj prof English, Fairleigh Dickinson Univ, 77- **MEMBERSHIPS** MLA; Am Comp Lit Asn; Renaissance Soc; New Chaucer Soc. **RESEARCH** Medieval and Renaissance literature; interdisciplinary studies; professional subjects. **SELECTED PUBLICATIONS** Auth, Don-Giovanni, Myths of Seduction and Betrayal, Philos and Lit, Vol 0017, 93. **CONTACT ADDRESS** Modern Language Association, 62 Fifth Av, New York, NY, 10011.

GIBBS, VIRGINIA
DISCIPLINE SPANISH **EDUCATION** Univ Wis, BA; NY Univ, MA; Univ Minn, PhD. **CAREER** Assoc prof. **HONORS AND AWARDS** Co-founder & member bd dir, Northeast Iowa People for Animal Welfare, PAW. **SELECTED PUBLICATIONS** Auth, Las Sonatas du Valle-Indan, Madrid. **CONTACT ADDRESS** Dept of Modern Languages, Luther Col, 700 College Dr, Decorah, IA, 52101. **EMAIL** gibbsvir@luther.edu

GIBIAN, GEORGE
PERSONAL Born 01/29/1924, Prague, Czechoslovakia, 5 children **DISCIPLINE** RUSSIAN, COMPARATIVE LITERATURE **EDUCATION** Univ Pittsburgh, AB, 43; Sch Adv Int Studies, AM, 47; Harvard Univ, PhD, 51. **CAREER** Instr English, Smith Col, 51-53, from asst prof to assoc prof English & Russ, 53-61; prof, 61-76, chemn dept, 63-73 & 80-82, chemn comt Soviet Studies, 66-70 & 81-82, Goldwin Smith Prof Russ and Comp Lit, Cornell Univ, 76-, Assoc prof Slavic lit, Univ Calif, Berkeley, fall 59; Guggenheim fel, 60; Fulbright res fel, Paris, fall 60; exchange prof, Soviet Acad Sci, Leningrad, 65-66; exec secy, Masaryk Publ Trust, 67-; joint comt Slavic studies, Am Coun Learned Soc & Soc Sci Res Coun, 67-68; sr assoc, Russ Inst, Columbia Univ, 69-70; Nat Endowment Humanities sr grant, 74. **MEMBERSHIPS** Am Asn Advan Slavic Studies; Am Asn Teachers Slavic & East Europ Lang. **RESEARCH** The novel; Russ contemporary literature. **SELECTED PUBLICATIONS** Auth, Tolstoy and Shakespeare, Mouton, The Hague, 57; Interval of Freedom: Soviet Literature during the Thaw, Univ Minn, 60; ed, Crime and Punishment, Norton, 89; coauth Masaryk, Spirit of Russia, Allen & Unwin, London, 67; Anna Karenina, Norton, 95; ed & translr, Russia's Lost Literature of the Absurd, 71 & co-ed & contribr, Russian Modernism, 76, Cornell Univ; The Man with the Black Coat: Russian Literature of the Absurd, Northwestern Univ Press, 97; The Poetry of Jaroslav Seifert, Catbird Press, 98. **CONTACT ADDRESS** Dept of Russ Lit, Cornell Univ, 236 Goldwin Smith Hall, Ithaca, NY, 14853-3201. **EMAIL** GG30@cornell.edu

GIBSON, MELISSA K.
PERSONAL Born 09/18/1969, Erie, PA, s **DISCIPLINE** ORGANIZATIONAL COMMUNICATION **EDUCATION** Edinboro Univ, BA, 92; Ohio Univ, MA, 95, PhD, 97. **CAREER** Asst Prof, Western Mich Univ, 97-. **HONORS AND AWARDS** Res Fel, 96-97; Central States Commun Asn Outstanding New Teacher Award, 98; Top Paper, Orgn Commun Div, Nat Commun Asn, 98. **MEMBERSHIPS** Nat Commun Asn; Central States Commun; Am Soc Training & Development; Int Commun Asn. **RESEARCH** Organizational communication; applied communication theory; training and development; nonprofit organizations. **CONTACT ADDRESS** Western Michigan Univ, 215 Sprau Tower, Kalamazoo, MI, 49008. **EMAIL** melissa.gibson@wmich.edu

GIBSON, TODD
DISCIPLINE TIBETAN STUDIES **EDUCATION** Ind Univ, PhD, 91 **CAREER** Inst, 91-pres, Antioch Univ; Inst, 94-96, Teikyo Univ; Inst, 97, Denver Univ **MEMBERSHIPS** Am Acad of Relig **RESEARCH** Inner Asian and Tibetan History; Culture; Relig **SELECTED PUBLICATIONS** Auth, Two Figures in the Early Great Perfection," in Tibet Jrnl, 99; "Notes on the History of the Shamanic in Tibet and Inner Asia," Numen 44, 97 **CONTACT ADDRESS** 31646 Broadmoor, Evergreen, CO, 80439.

GIEBER, ROBERT L.
PERSONAL Born 01/22/1944, Clifton, KS **DISCIPLINE** FRENCH LANGUAGE AND LITERATURE **EDUCATION** Kans State Teachers Col, BEd, 65; Univ Iowa, MA, 66; Univ Nebr, PhD, 71. **CAREER** Instr French, Ft Hays State Col, 66-69; Prof French, Simpson Col, 71-, Chmn Dept, 74-, Nat Endowment Humanities res grant, 75. **MEMBERSHIPS** Am Asn Teachers French; Mediaeval Acad Am. **RESEARCH** Medieval hagiography; medieval & Renaissance civilization. **SELECTED PUBLICATIONS** Ed, A critical edition of La Vie Saint-Jehan-Baptiste, an old French poem of the early 14th century, Z Romanische Philol, 78; An English-French Glossary of Educational Terminology, Univ Press Am, 81; Poetic elements of rhythm in the ballades, Rondeaux and Virelais of Guillaume de Machaut, Romantic Rev, 82. **CONTACT ADDRESS** Dept of Foreign Lang, Simpson Col, 701 N C St, Indianola, IA, 50125-1297. **EMAIL** gieber@simpson.edu

GIES, DAVID THATCHER
PERSONAL Born 08/18/1945, Pittsburgh, PA, m, 1994 **DISCIPLINE** SPANISH LITERATURE **EDUCATION** PA State Univ, BA, 67; Univ Pittsburgh, MA, 70, PhD(Span), 72. **CAREER** Assoc prof, St Bonaventure Univ, 70-79; vis lect, Univ Birmingham, England, 78; assoc prof Span, 79-91, COMMONWEALTH PROF SPAN, UNIV VA, 92-, chair, dept span, 83-90, 92-95; ed, Dieciocho: Hispanic Enlightenment. **HONORS AND AWARDS** John Simon Guggenheim fel, 83-84; NEH Sr fels. **MEMBERSHIPS** MLA; Am Asn Teachers Span & Port; Assoc Int de Hispanistas. **RESEARCH** Spanish Enlightenment and Romanticism. **SELECTED PUBLICATIONS** Auth, Agustin Duran: A Biography and Literary Appreciation, Tamesis, London, 75; Nicolas Fernandez de Moratin, Twayne, 79; Theatre and Politics in Nineteenth-Century Spain, Cambridge, 88; The Theatre in Nineteenth-Century Spain, Cambridge, 94; ed, Grimaldi, La pata de cabra, Rome, Bulzoni, 86; ed, Romanticismo, Madrid, Taurus, 89; ed, Historia y critica de la literatura espanola, siglo XVIII, Barcelona, Critica, 92; ed, Zorrilla Don Juan Tenorio, Madrid, Casalia, 94; ed, Moratin La petimetra, Madrid, Castalia, 95; ed, Cambridge Companion to Modern Spanish Culture, Cambridge, 98; seventy-five scholarly articles and 100+ book reviews. **CONTACT ADDRESS** Dept Span, Univ Virginia, 115 Wilson Hall, Charlottesville, VA, 22903-3125. **EMAIL** dtg@virginia.edu

GIGNAC, FRANCIS THOMAS
PERSONAL Born 02/24/1933, Detroit, MI **DISCIPLINE** PHILOLOGY, THEOLOGY **EDUCATION** Loyola Univ, Ill, AB, 55, MA, 57, MA, 68; Oxford Univ, DPhil(Greek), 64. **CAREER** Instr Greek, Loyola Univ, Ill, 65-67; from asst prof to assoc prof Theol, Fordham Univ, 68-74; assoc prof Bibl Studies & chmn dept, Cath Univ Am, 74-, NSF travel grant, 67. **MEMBERSHIPS** Cath Bibl Asn; Am Philol Asn; Am Soc Papyrologists. **RESEARCH** The language of the non-literary Greek papyri; the language of the Greek New Testament; textual criticism. **SELECTED PUBLICATIONS** Auth, The language of the non-literary Greek papyri, Am Studies Papyrology, 70; The text of Acts in Chrysostom's homilies, Traditio, 70; The pronunciation of Greek stops in the papyri, Trans & Proc Am Philol Asn, 70; An Introductory New Testament Greek Course, Loyola Univ, 73; A Grammar of the Greek Papyri of the Roman and Byzantine Periods (2 vols), Cisalpino-La Goliardica, Milan, 76 & 81. **CONTACT ADDRESS** Dept of Biblical Studies, Catholic Univ of America, 620 Michigan Ave NE, Washington, DC, 20064-0002. **EMAIL** gignac@cua.edu

GILBERT, HARVEY R.
DISCIPLINE COMMUNICATION SCIENCES **EDUCATION** Univ Wis, PhD, 69. **CAREER** Prof , Univ Conn; dept ch. **RESEARCH** Normal and disordered voice, cleft palate and speech physiology. **SELECTED PUBLICATIONS** Coauth, Perceptions of Tonal Changes in Normal Laryngeal, Esophageal, and Artificial Laryngeal Male Cantonese Speakers, Folia Phoniatrica et Logopaedica, 64-70, 1998; Acoustic, Aerodynamic, Physiologic, and Perceptual Properties of Modal and Vocal Fry Registers. Acoustical Society of America, 2649-2658, 1998; Formant Frequency Development: 15-36 months, J Voice 3, 97; Formant Frequency and Bandwidth Development in Infants and Toddlers, Folia Phoniatrica et Logopaedica 49, 97; Some Aerodynamic Characteristics of Acute Laryngitic Voice, J Voice 3, 97; Vocal Fundamental Frequency Characteristics of Infant Hunger Cries: Birth to 12 months, Int J Pediatric Otorhinolaryngology 34, 96. **CONTACT ADDRESS** Dept of Communication Sci, Univ of Connecticut, 850 Bolton Rd, Storrs, CT, 06269-1085. **EMAIL** harveyg@uconnvm.uconn.edu/

GILES, MARY E.
PERSONAL Born 09/18/1934, Missoula, MT, m, 1953, 2 children **DISCIPLINE** SPANISH LITERATURE, HUMANITIES **EDUCATION** Univ Idaho, BA, 55; State Univ Wash, MA, 57; Univ Calif, Berkeley, PhD, 61. **CAREER** Teaching asst, State Univ Wash, 55-57 and Univ Calif, Berkeley, 58-61; from instr to asst prof foreign lang, Calif State Col Hayward, 61-64; from asst prof to assoc prof Span, 64-71, PROF HUMANITIES, UNIV SACRAMENTO, 71-, Part-time instr, Univ Idaho, 56-57; ed, Studia Mystica, 78- **MEMBERSHIPS** Philol Asn Pac Coast; Am Asn Teachers Span & Port; MLA; Asn Advan Humanities. **RESEARCH** Nineteenth century and contemporary Spanish novel. **SELECTED PUBLICATIONS** Auth, God Speaks in the Night--The Life, Times and Teaching of John-of-the-Cross, Studia Mystica, Vol 0015, 92; Heresy and Mysticism in 16th-Century Spain--The Alumbrados, Theol Stud, Vol 0055, 94. **CONTACT ADDRESS** Dept of Humanities, California State Univ, Sacramento, Sacramento, CA, 95818.

GILLETTE STURM, FRED
DISCIPLINE PHILOSOPHY OF ART AND AESTHETICS, LATIN AMERICAN AND IBERIAN PHILOSOPHY, CH **EDUCATION** Allegheny Col, AB, 46; Union Theological Seminary, MDiv, 48; Rochester, AM, 50; Columbia Univ, PhD, 61; Vanderbilt, cert, 49; Tunghai, cert, 63. **CAREER** Prof, Univ NMex. **MEMBERSHIPS** Int Ctr for Asian Stud; Royal Asiatic Soc; Int Sinological Comt; co-dir; REs Gp for Chinese & Comp Aesthet; Int Soc for Chinese Philos; Ctr de Estudos Luso-Brasileiros; Acad Brasileira de Filosofia; pres, Soc for Iberian and Lat Am Thought. **SELECTED PUBLICATIONS** Auth, American Indians: Time in Outlook and Language, in Encycl of Time, Garland, 95; Radhakrishnan's Philosophy of Art, in New Essays in the Philosophy of Sarvepalli Radhakrishnan,Indian Bk Ctr, 95; Philosophy and the Intellectual Tradition, in Latin America: Its Problems and Its Promise, 3rd ed, Boulder & London, 97; Brazil, Philosophy, in Encycl of Philos, Routledge, 98. **CONTACT ADDRESS** Univ NMex, Albuquerque, NM, 87131.

GILMAN, DONALD
PERSONAL Born 02/24/1945, Newport News, VA **DISCIPLINE** FRENCH, COMPARATIVE LITERATURE **EDUCATION** Univ NC, Chapel Hill, AB, 67, PhD(French, comp lit), 76; Univ Harvard, AM, 70. **CAREER** Instr French, Christopher Newport Col, Col William & Mary, 67-70; asst prof, 74-79, assoc prof French & Humanities 79-87; prof 87-; vis prof, Univ de Nancy II, 1997-98; Pres, Medieval Asn Midwest, 96-97. **HONORS AND AWARDS** Grants, Government of PQ and Canadian Embassy, 91-92; Travel Grants, CNRS (France), 91, Learned Societies of Canada, 91, Univ Toronto, 88, Univ Cent. MI, 83 & 81, Univ BC, 81; National Endowment for the Humanities, 89 & 80; Newwberry Library, Chicago, 83-84. **MEMBERSHIPS** Renaissance Soc Am; Medieval Asn Midwest, pres, 96-97; Midwest Mod Lang Asn; 16th-century Studies. **RESEARCH** 16th-century French lit; Renaissance lit in France and Italy; history of literary criticism, from Plato to French structuralism. **SELECTED PUBLICATIONS** Ed., Everyman and Company: Essays on the Theme and Structure of European Moral Play, 89; co-ed, Louis Le Caron, Dialogues, 86; auth, Petrarch's Sophonisba: Seduction, Sacrifice, and Patriarchal Politics in Sex and Gender in Medieval Renaissance Lit: The Latin Tradition, 97; auth, Theories of Dialogue, in The Dialogue in Early Modern France, 1547-1630: Art and Argumentation, 93; auth, Ronsard's concept of the Poete Humain, Bibliotheque d'Humanisme et Renaissance; 83, plus numerous other articles. **CONTACT ADDRESS** Dept of Modern Languages and Classics, Ball State Univ, 2000 W University, Muncie, IN, 47306-0465. **EMAIL** dwgilman@bsuvc.bsu.edu

GILMORE, ROGER H.
DISCIPLINE FRENCH LITERATURE **EDUCATION** Univ Nebr, PhD. **CAREER** Assoc prof. **SELECTED PUBLICA-**

TIONS Auth, pubs on second language acquisition, second language pedagogy, and teaching methodologies. **CONTACT ADDRESS** Foreign Languages and Literature Dept, Colorado State Univ, Fort Collins, CO, 80523. **EMAIL** rgilmore@vines.colostate.edu

GILROY, JAMES PAUL
PERSONAL Born 08/30/1947, Worcester, MA **DISCIPLINE** FRENCH LITERATURE, ROMANCE LANGUAGES, HUMANITIES **EDUCATION** Col Holy Cross, BA, 68; Princeton Univ, MA, 70, PhD, 72. **CAREER** Asst prof, 72-79, assoc prof, 79-90, PROF FRENCH, UNIV DENVER, 90-. **HONORS AND AWARDS** Knight Acad Palms, France, 92; Univ Scholar/Teacher of the Year, Univ Denver, 92; Top Honors Prof Award, 95, 96, 97 & 98. **MEMBERSHIPS** Rocky Mountain Mod Lang Asn; Soc Prof Fr Am; Am Asn Teachers Fr; Les Amis Lang Francaise; Philol Asn Pac Coast. **RESEARCH** Romanticism and Pre-Romanticism; French fiction of 18th and 19th centuries; French Enlightenment; non-metropolitan French literature. **SELECTED PUBLICATIONS** Auth, The Theme of Etre and Paraitre in the Works of Agrippa d'Aubigne, Bull Rocky Mountain Mod Lang Asn, 73; Theatricality in the Universe of Balzac's Le Pere Goriot, Degre 2nd, 77; Prevostian themes in the Suite de Manon Lescaut, in Enlightenment Essays, 77; Peace and the Pursuit of Happiness in the French Utopian Novel, in Studies on Voltaire and the Eighteenth Century, Voltaire Found, 79; The Romantic Manon and Des Grieux, Naaman, Sherbrooke, 80; The theme of the woman in Balzac's La Cousine Bette, Rocky Mountain Rev, 80; Structures epiques et liturgiques dans Maria Chapdelaine, Bull Societe des Professeurs Francais en Amerique, 81; ed, Francophone literatures of the New World, Vol II, in Occasional Papers, 82; Prevost's Le Doyen de Killerine: The Career of an Imperfect Mentor, Studies on Voltaire, 84; The Pursuit of the Real in Rina Lasnier's Presence de l'absence, in Traditionalism, Nationalism, and Feminism: Women Writers of Quebec, Greenwood Press, 85; Rabelais, the Good Doctor: Health and Sanity in the Quart Livre, European Studies J, 85; Prevost Theophe: A Liberated Heroine in Search of Herself, French Rev, 87; Food, Cooking and Eating in Proust's A la recherche du temps perdu, Twentieth Century Lit, 87; Variations of the Theme of Mentor in the Later Abbe Prevost, Studies on Voltaire, 89; Prevost's Mentors: The Master-Pupil Relationship in the Major Novels of the Abbe Prevost, Studia Humanitatis, 90; Erik Satie and Le Piege de Meduse, Ars Musica Denver, 89; Educators of Kings and Commoners in the Abbe Prevost's Semi-Fictional Works, Nottingham French Studies, 90; Self-Educated Women in the Novels of Abbe Prevost, Studies on Voltaire, 92; Teaching a Literature Course on the French Revolution, French Rev, 93. **CONTACT ADDRESS** Dept of Langs & Lits, Univ of Denver, 2040 S Race St, Denver, CO, 80210-4308.

GIMENEZ, ANTONIO
DISCIPLINE ROMANCE LANGUAGES **EDUCATION** Ohio State Univ, MA; PhD, 73. **CAREER** Prof, Williams Col, 74-; dir in residence, Hamilton Col Acad Yr in Spain, 77-78, 82-83, 91-92; ch, Romance Lang dept, Williams Col, 84-88, 95-97. **HONORS AND AWARDS** NEH fel, Univ Pittsburgh, 75; NEH fel, Cornell Univ, 81. **RESEARCH** Contemporary Spanish narrative; 19th-century travel literature on and about Spain; 20th-century history and civilization of Spain. **SELECTED PUBLICATIONS** Co-ed, From Dante to Garcea Marquez: Studies in Romance Literatures and Linguistics, Williams Col, 87; Los espanoles y la guerra, an ed with introduction, transl and notes of Richard Ford's, An Historical Enquiry into the Unchangeable Character of a War in Spain, Madrid: Editorial Tayo, 90; George Borrow and the Spanish Press, Proceedings of the George Borrow in Wales Conf, Toronto, 90; Cosas de los ingleses! La Espana vivida y sonada en la Correspondencia entre George Borrow and Richard Ford, Madrid: Editorial Complutense, 97. **CONTACT ADDRESS** Center for Foreign Languages, Literatures and Cult, Williams Col, Williamstown, MA, 01267. **EMAIL** Antonio.Gimenez@williams.edu

GINSBERG, ELLEN SUTOR
PERSONAL Born 04/18/1935, South Bend, IN, m, 1962 **DISCIPLINE** FRENCH LANGUAGE & LITERATURE **EDUCATION** Northwest Univ, BA, 55, MA, 56; Univ Chicago, PhD, 63; Univ Vienna, cert Ger, 63. **CAREER** Lectr Eng, Ecole Norm Super de Jeunes Filles, France, 61-62, asst prof, 65-69; vis asst prof, Univ MD, 71-72; asst prof, 72-80, Assoc Prof French, Cath Univ AM, 81-, Chmn Dept of Mod Lang, 94-95. **MEMBERSHIPS** MLA; SAtlantic Mod Lang Asn; Northeast Mod Lang Asn; Renaissance Soc Am; Southeast Renaissance Conf. **RESEARCH** French lit of the Renaissance; comp lit of the Renaissance; drama; poetry. **SELECTED PUBLICATIONS** Ed, Le Cesar de Jacques Grevin: Edition Critique, Droz, Geneva, 71; auth, The Legacy of Muret's Julius Caesar, Acta Conventus Nen-Latini Lovaniensis, Wilhelm Fink, Munich, 73; coauth, Fictional material and philosophic method, Mod Lang Studies, fall, 73; auth, Genre theory in the French Renaissance, French Lit Ser Vol IV, 77; Joachim du Bellay's Latin poem Patriae Desiderium and his vernacular poetry, In: Acta Conventus Neo-Latini Turonensis, Vrin, Paris, 80; The Amores of Joachim Du Bellay: A Neo-Latin Cycle of Love Poems, Acta Conventus Neo-Latini Bono, Nensis, MRT,, Binghamton, 85; Peregrinations of the Kiss: Thematic Relationships between Neo-Latin and French Poetry in the Sixteenth Century, Acta Conventus Neo-Latini Sanctandreani, MRTS, Binghamton, 86; Marc-Antoine de Muret: A Re-Evaluation, Acta Conventus Neo-Latini Guelpherbytani, MRTS, Binghamton, 88; Translation, Imitation, Transofrmation: Du Bellay as Self Translator, Acta Conventus neoo-Latini Hafnienis, MRTS, Binghamton, 94. **CONTACT ADDRESS** Dept of Mod Lang, Catholic Univ of America, 620 Michigan Ave N E, Washington, DC, 20064-0002. **EMAIL** ginsberg@cua.edu

GINSBURG, MICHAL P.
DISCIPLINE FRENCH **EDUCATION** Yale Univ, PhD. **CAREER** Prof and ch, Northwestern Univ; co-dir, Interdisciplinary Group on Fr Culture Soc; co-organizor, Narrative Int Conf; past fel, Wissenschaftskolleg, Berlin; former dir, Program in Comparative Lit and Theory; ed bd, Comp Lit Studies. **HONORS AND AWARDS** Lect, Am Comp Lit Asn conf; Int Soc for the Study European Ideas ,Utrecht; Dickens conf, Dijon. **RESEARCH** 19th-century novel in France and England; contemporary theory. **SELECTED PUBLICATIONS** Auth, Flaubert Writing: A Study of Narrative Strategies, Stanford Univ Press, 86; Economics of Change: Form and Trans- formation in the Nineteenth-Century Novel, Stanford Univ Press, 96; Framing Narrative, Poetics Today, 97; La Tentation du biographique, Gustave Flaubert: Intersections. **CONTACT ADDRESS** Dept of French, Northwestern Univ, 1801 Hinman, Evanston, IL, 60208.

GIRO, JORGE A.
PERSONAL Born 10/21/1933, Havana, Cuba, m, 1961, 2 children **DISCIPLINE** LANGUAGE **EDUCATION** Jose Marti Univ, LLB/PhD, 57; Ind State Univ, BA, 63, MS, 64. **CAREER** Full prof to chemn, Towson Univ, 66-. **CONTACT ADDRESS** Towson Univ, Towson, MD, 21252. **EMAIL** jgiro@towson.edu

GITTLEMAN, SOL
PERSONAL Born 06/05/1934, Hoboken, NJ, m, 1956, 3 children **DISCIPLINE** GERMAN, COMPARATIVE LITERATURE **EDUCATION** Drew Univ, MA, 55; Columbia Univ, AB, 56; Univ Mich, 61. **CAREER** From instr to asst prof Ger, Univ Mich, 59-64; from asst prof to assoc prof & chemn dept, 64-72, Prof Ger, Tufts Univ, 72-, Consult & reviewer, Choice, 63-; assoc ed, J Int Arthur Schnitzler Soc, 64-. **HONORS AND AWARDS** Harbison Award for Gifted Teaching, Danforth Found, 71; honorary degrees, Dr. Humane Letters, Hebrew College, 95 & 96. **MEMBERSHIPS** Am Asn Teachers Ger; MLA. **RESEARCH** Anglo-German literary relations in 19th century; German expressionism; works of Frank Wedekind. **SELECTED PUBLICATIONS** Auth, John Hay as a critic, Victorian Newsletter, autumn 63; Image of America in Wedekind, Ger Quart, 3/66; Wedekind and Brecht: A literary relationship, Mod Drama, 2/68; Frank Wedekind, Twayne, 68; Sholom Aleichem: A Non-Critical Introduction to His Works, Mouton, 74; Thomas Mann and the Jews: A final word, Dayton Univ Rev, spring 76; Sternheim and Wedekind, Ger Quart, 1/76; Shtetl to Suberbia: The Family In Jewish Literary Imagination, Beacon, 78. **CONTACT ADDRESS** Off of the Provost, Tufts Univ, Medford, MA, 02155. **EMAIL** SGittleman@infonet.tufts.edu

GLADE, HENRY
PERSONAL Born 10/08/1920, Germany, m, 1958 **DISCIPLINE** GERMAN, RUSSIAN **EDUCATION** Elizabethtown Col, AB, 42; Univ Pa, MA, 48, PhD(Ger), 58. **CAREER** Prof mod lang, Hershey Jr Col, 50-53; instr Ger, Bates Col, 53-54; asst prof French and Ger, 54-55, assoc prof Ger, 55-62, PROF GER and RUSS, MANCHESTER COL, 62-, CHMN DEPT MOD LANG, 67-, Sr Fulbright fel and Int Res and Exchanges Bd grant, sr exchange scholar, Gorky Inst World Lit, 70-71; Am Philos Soc grant res Moscow, 72; vis prof, Slavisches Inst der Univ zu Koln, 79-80. **MEMBERSHIPS** MLA; Am Asn Teachers Slavic & Europ Lang; Am Asn Teachers Ger. **RESEARCH** Modern German drama; Soviet-German literary relations. **SELECTED PUBLICATIONS** Auth, Der Engel Schwieg, World Lit Today, Vol 0068, 94; Gegen Die Laufrichtung, World Lit Today, Vol 0069, 1995; The Russian-German Literary Exchange in the Postcommunist Era, 1992-1995, Germano-Slavica, Vol 0009, 96; Hope is Like a Wild Animal--Correspondence 1945-1953, World Lit Today, Vol 0070, 96. **CONTACT ADDRESS** Manchester Col, Box 36, North Manchester, IN, 46962.

GLADNEY, FRANK Y.
PERSONAL Born 01/20/1936, Mt. Vernon, NY, m, 1958, 3 children **DISCIPLINE** SLAVIC LANGUAGES **EDUCATION** Harvard Univ, AB, 57, AM, 59, PhD(Slavic Lang & Lit), 66. **CAREER** Assoc Prof Slavic Lang, Univ Ill, Urbana-Champaign, 63-, Ed Slavic & E Europ J, 7O-75. **MEMBERSHIPS** Am Asn Teachers Slavic & E Europ Lang; Am Asn Advan Slavic Studies; Ling Soc Am. **RESEARCH** Russian, Polish and Czech grammar. **SELECTED PUBLICATIONS** Auth, Fel, Ctr Advan Studies, Univ Ill, 73; Nat Endowment for Humanities younger humanist fel, 73-74; Camargo Found fel, 77; distinguished vis prof, Eastern Ill Univ, Summer, 81; Item and process in Russian verbal inflection, In: American Contributions to the VIII International Congress of Slavists, 78; Fel, Ctr Advan Studies, Univ Ill, 73; Nat Endowment for Humanities younger humanist fel, 73-74; Camargo Found fel, 77; distinguished vis prof, Eastern Ill Univ, Summer, 81. **CONTACT ADDRESS** Dept of Slavic Lang & Lit, Univ of Illinois, Urbana-Champaign, 707 S Mathews Ave, Urbana, IL, 61801-3625. **EMAIL** gladney@uiuc.edu

GLASS, ERLIS
PERSONAL Born 12/24/1941, Philadelphia, PA, m, 1961, 2 children **DISCIPLINE** GERMANIC LANGUAGES AND LITERATURES **EDUCATION** Radcliffe Col, BA, 63; Harvard Univ, MA, 64; Bryn Mawr Col, PhD(Ger), 73. **CAREER** Asst prof Ger, 66-76, dir, Continuing Educ, 76-78, ASSOC PROF GER, ROSEMONT COL, 76-, Chmn, Placement Info Ctr, Am Asn Teachers Ger, 74- 76; vis prof, Ursinus Col, 79-81. **MEMBERSHIPS** Am Asn Teachers Ger (treas, 75-77); Northeast Mod Lang Asn. **RESEARCH** Expressionist drama; comparative Romanticism; age of Goethe. **SELECTED PUBLICATIONS** Auth, Athenaum, a Yearbook of Romanticism, Vol 1, Ger Quart, Vol 0065, 92; According to the Measure of My Powers of Comprehension--Articles and Essays, World Lit Today, Vol 0067, 93; Treibeis, World Lit Today, Vol 0067, 93; Der 'Mann Meiner Traume,' World Lit Today, Vol 0067, 93; Holderlin--The Poetics of Being, Ger Stud Rev, Vol 0016, 93; The Woman as Survivor--The Evolution of the Female Figure in the Works of Boll, Heinrich, Ger Quart, Vol 0067, 94; Behind the Mask--Kierkegaard Pseudonymic Treatment of Lessing in the 'Concluding Unscientific Postscript,' Ger Quart, Vol 0068, 95; Die 'Schone Frau,' World Lit Today, Vol 0069, 95; Die 'Glaserne Stadt,' World Lit Today, Vol 0069, 95; Jean-Paul, Ger Stud Rev, Vol 0018, 95; Die 'Novizin,' World Lit Today, Vol 0070, 96. **CONTACT ADDRESS** Rosemont Col, Montgomery Ave, Rosemont, PA, 19010.

GLEASON, MICHAEL
DISCIPLINE LATIN **EDUCATION** Brown Univ, PhD. **CAREER** Dept Classics, Millsaps Col **SELECTED PUBLICATIONS** Publ on, medieval Latin. **CONTACT ADDRESS** Dept of Classics, Millsaps Col, 1701 N State St, Jackson, MS, 39210. **EMAIL** gleasm@okra.millsaps.edu

GLEAVES, ROBERT MILNOR
PERSONAL Born 03/18/1938, Nashville, TN, m, 1964, 2 children **DISCIPLINE** SPANISH LANGUAGE, SPANISH AMERICAN LITERATURE **EDUCATION** David Lipscomb Col, BA, 60; Vanderbilt Univ, MA, 63, PhD(Span), 68. **CAREER** From instr to asst prof Span, Univ SFla, 65-69; asst prof, 69-72, ASSOC PROF SPAN, UNIV NC, CHARLOTTE, 72-. **MEMBERSHIPS** Am Asn Teachers Span & Port; Int Inst Iberoam Lit; SAtlantic Mod Lang Asn. **RESEARCH** Contemporary Spanish-American prose fiction; Spanish-American poetry. **SELECTED PUBLICATIONS** Auth, The Reaffirmation of Analogy, an Introduction to Carreraandrade, Jorge Metaphoric System, Confluencia-Rev Hispanica de Cult y Lit, Vol 0010, 94. **CONTACT ADDRESS** Dept of Foreign Lang, Univ of NC, 9201 University City, Charlotte, NC, 28223-0002.

GLENN, JERRY
PERSONAL Born 09/05/1938, Little Rock, AR **DISCIPLINE** GERMAN **EDUCATION** Yale Univ, BA, 60; Univ Tex, MA, 62, PhD(Ger), 64. **CAREER** Asst prof Ger, Univ Wis-Milwaukee, 64-67; from asst prof to assoc prof, 67-72, dir hon prog, 77-79, PROF GER, UNIV CINCINNATI, 72-, HEAD DEPT, 80-. **MEMBERSHIPS** MLA; Am Asn Teachers Ger; Am Lessing Soc (secy-treas, 68-74); Am Lit Transl Asn; Mid-E Hons Asn (pres, 79-80). **RESEARCH** German lyric, literature and classics. **SELECTED PUBLICATIONS** Auth, Von Der Krummung Des Raumes, World Lit Today, Vol 0066, 92; Coping with the Past--Germany and Austria after 1945, Colloquia Germanica, Vol 0025, 92; Historical and Critical Edition of Works, Poetry and Prose, Vol 7, 'Atemwende', Pt 1, Text, Pt 2, Apparatus, Ger Quart, Vol 0065, 92; Collected Autobiographical Writings--Almost a Lifestory, World Lit Today, Vol 0067, 93; Kaschnitz, Marie, Luise--A Biography, World Lit Today, Vol 0067, 93; Atlantische Brucke, World Lit Today, Vol 0067, 93; Wortgrund Noch--Lyrics and Prose, World Lit Today, Vol 0067, 93; Ein Sprung Im Schweigen--Poems and Cycles, World Lit Today, Vol 0067, 93; Auslander, Rose--Materials on Her Life and Works, World Lit Today, Vol 0067, 93; Der Aufstand Der Requisiten, World Lit Today, Vol 0067, 93; Collected Essays--Home in the Language, World Lit Today, Vol 0067, 93; Jahrtausend-Furbitte, Poesie Der Fakten 6, World Lit Today, Vol 0067, 93; Das Mogliche Ist Ungeheuer--Selected Poems, World Lit Today, Vol 0068, 94; Celan, Paul, Sachs, Nelly Correspondence, World Lit Today, Vol 0068, 94; Foxtrot Im Erfurter Stadion, World Lit Today, Vol 0068, 94; The Classical-World Today, Ger Quart, Vol 0067, 94; Holocaust Visions--Surrealism and Existentialism in the Poetry of Celan, Paul, Colloquia Germanica, Vol 0028, 95; Lichtfall, World Lit Today, Vol 0069, 95; Where There Is Freedom--Interviews 1977-1993, World Lit Today, Vol 0069, 95; Word Traces--Readings of Celan, Paul, Colloquia Germanica, Vol 0028, 95; Poems 1953-1991, World Lit Today, Vol 0069, 95; Encounters with Celan, Paul--Reminiscences and Interpretations, Mod Austrian Lit, Vol 0028, 95; Die Wirklichkeit Erfindet Mich--Lyrical Works 1948-1993, World Lit Today, Vol 0069, 95; Wir-Wissen-Ja-Nicht-Was-Gilt--Interpretations of 20th-Century German Poetry, Ger Rev, Vol 0070, 95; Breath-turn, Mod Austrian Lit, Vol 0029, 96; Israels Letzter Psalm--

Poems, Mod Austrian Lit, Vol 0029, 96; Writing Is Travel Without Luggage--Information about Myself, World Lit Today, Vol 0070, 96; Celan, Paul--Poet, Survivor, Jew, Mod Austrian Lit, Vol 0029, 96; Pathways to Celan, Paul--A History of Critical Responses as a Chorus of Discordant Voices, World Lit Today, Vol 0071, 97; Die Zunge Als Lohn--Poems 1991-1995, World Lit Today, Vol 0071, 97. **CONTACT ADDRESS** Dept of Ger, Univ of Cincinnati, P O Box 210372, Cincinnati, OH, 45221-0372.

GLENN, KATHLEEN MARY
PERSONAL Born 06/12/1936, Exeter, CA **DISCIPLINE** SPANISH LITERATURE **EDUCATION** Stanford Univ, BA, 57, MA, 61, PhD(Span), 70; Univ Madrid, dipl Hisp studies, 59. **CAREER** Instr, Univ Victoria, 64-66; instr, Col San Mateo, 67-69; asst prof, Univ Santa Clara, 69-73 and Kans State Univ, 73-74; ASSOC PROF SPAN, WAKE FOREST UNIV, 74-, ASSOC ED, ANALES DE LA LITERATURE ESPANOLA CONTEMPORARIES, 76-. **MEMBERSHIPS** MLA; Am Asn Teachers Span & Port; S Cent Mod Lang Asn; SAtlantic Mod Lang Asn; Asn Lit Femenina Hisp. **RESEARCH** Twentieth century Spanish novel; 20th century Spanish theater. **SELECTED PUBLICATIONS** Auth, Corazon Tan Blanco, Hispania-J Devoted to Tchg of Span and Port, Vol 0076, 93; Fiction and Seduction--The Fantastic Trilogy of Torrenteballester, Hisp Rev, Vol 0061, 93; Women-Writers of Contemporary Spain--Exiles in the Homeland, Anales De La Lit Espanola Contemporanea, Vol 0018, 93; Nubosidad Variable, Hispania-J Devoted to Tchg of Span and Port, Vol 0076, 93; A Conversation with Fernandezcubas, Cristina, Anales De La Lit Espanola Contemporanea, Vol 0018, 93; New Andalusian Narrative--A Reading of Its Texts, Hispania-J Devoted to Tchg of Span and Port, Vol 0076, 93; Voices of Their Own--Contemporary Spanish Narrative By Women, Hisp Rev, Vol 0062, 94; Bella Y Oscura, Hispania-J Devoted to Tchg of Span and Port, Vol 0077, 94; Postmodern Parody and Culinary-Narrative Art in Esquivel,Laura 'Como Agua Para Chocolate,' Chasqui-Rev De Lit Latinoamericana, Vol 0023, 94; La Agonia De Proserpina, Hispania-J Devoted to Tchg of Span and Port, Vol 0077, 94; La Parabola De Carmen La Reina, Hispania-J Devoted to Tchg of Span and Port, Vol 0077, 94; Apology to Apostrophe--Autobiography and the Rhetoric of Self-Representation in Spain, Rev De Estudios Hispanicos, Vol 0028, 94; El Columpio, Hispania-J Devoted to Tchg of Span and Port, Vol 0078, 95; Cuentos Del Barrio Del Refugio, Anales De La Lit Espanola Contemporanea, Vol 0020, 95; Con Agatha En Estambul, Hispania-J Devoted to Tchg of Span and Port, Vol 0078, 95; La Reina De Las Nieves, Anales De La Lit Espanola Contemporanea, Vol 0021, 96; Short Feminist History of Spanish Literature (in Spanish), Vol 1, Feminist Theory, Discourses and Difference--Feminist Focus on Spanish Literature, Hisp Rev, Vol 0064, 96; Manana En La Batalla Piensa En Mi, Hispania-J Devoted to Tchg of Span and Port, Vol 0079, 96; La Duda Y Otros Apuntes Para Escribir Una Coleccion De Relatos, Hispania-J Devoted to Tchg of Span and Port, Vol 0079, 96; Adversarios Admirables, Hispania-J Devoted to Tchg of Span and Port, Vol 0080, 97; The Invention of the Grupo-Leones--An Essay and Interviews, Hispania-J Devoted to Tchg of Span and Port, Vol 0080, 97; En El Ultimo Azul, Anales De La Lit Espanola Contemporanea, Vol 0022, 97; Lo Raro Es Vivir, Anales De La Lit Espanola Contemporanea, Vol 0022, 97. **CONTACT ADDRESS** Dept of Romance Lang, Wake Forest Univ, Winston-Salem, NC, 27109.

GLENN, PIERCE
PERSONAL Born 09/10/1940, San Diego, CA, s **DISCIPLINE** ROMANCE LANGUAGES **EDUCATION** UCLA, PhD, 77 **CAREER** Asst prof, UVA, 78-84; assoc prof, MU, 85-. **HONORS AND AWARDS** Golden Key Honor Soc, Georgetown Univ; Scholar, Johns Hopkins Bologna Ctr. **MEMBERSHIPS** MLA; AAIS; AATI. **RESEARCH** Italian Baroque. **SELECTED PUBLICATIONS** Auth, art, What is Tragic About Torrismondo, 91; auth, art, Tecniche teatrali ne I promessi sposi, 95; auth, art, A bacchic dithyramb in the Ottocento?, 95; auth, Alessandro Manzoni and the Aesthetics of the Lombard Seicento: Finding the arts in the narrative of I promessi sposi, 98. **CONTACT ADDRESS** Dept of Romance Languages, Univ of Missouri, A/S 123, Columbia, MO, 65211. **EMAIL** pierceg@missouri.edu

GLINERT, LEWIS
DISCIPLINE ASIAN AND MIDDLE EASTERN LANGUAGES AND LITERATURES **EDUCATION** Oxford Univ, BA; Univ London, PhD. **CAREER** Fac Schl Oriental and African Studies, Univ London; vis assoc prof Hebrew, Univ Chicago; asst prof Linguistics, Haifa and Bar-Ilan Univ; prof, Dartmouth Col. **HONORS AND AWARDS** Int Adv Bd, Israel Ctr Lang Policy. **RESEARCH** Cult and linguistics of Israeli and Jewish soc in lang policy and in tech and safety discourse. **SELECTED PUBLICATIONS** Auth, The Grammar of Modern Hebrew; The Joys of Hebrew; Hebrew in Ashkenaz: A Language in Exile; Mamme Dear: A Turn-of-the-Century Collection of Model Yiddish Letters; Product Safety Information and Language Policy in an Advanced Third World Economy; We Never Changed our Language: Attitudes of Hasidic Educators to Yiddish Language Acquisition; BBC documentaries: Tongue of Tongues: The Rebirth of Hebrew and Golem: The Making of a Modern Myth. **CONTACT ADDRESS** Dartmouth Col, 3529 N Main St, #207, Hanover, NH, 03755.

GLOWACKI, KEVIN T.
DISCIPLINE CLASSICAL STUDIES **EDUCATION** Loyola Univ, BA, 83, MA, 85; Bryn Mawr Col, MA, 87, PhD, 91. **CAREER** Asst prof. **RESEARCH** Greek art and archaeology; Greek sculpture; topography & monuments of Athens; Aegean Bronze & Iron Ages; mythological representation in art. **SELECTED PUBLICATIONS** Auth, A New Fragment of the Erechtheion Frieze, Hesperia, 95; The Acropolis of Athens before 566 B.C, Univ Pa, 97. **CONTACT ADDRESS** Dept of Classical Studies, Indiana Univ, Bloomington, 300 N Jordan Ave, Bloomington, IN, 47405.

GLOWKA, ARTHUR WAYNE
PERSONAL Born 03/18/1952, Weimar, TX, m, 1992, 2 children **DISCIPLINE** MEDIEVAL LITERATURE, ENGLISH LINGUISTICS **EDUCATION** Univ Tex, BA, 73, MA, 75; Univ Del, PhD(English), 80. **CAREER** Prof English, Ga Col and State Univ, 80-. **MEMBERSHIPS** S Atlantic Mod Lang Asn; New Chaucer Soc; Am Dialect Soc. **RESEARCH** Prosody; history of the English language; neology; medieval literature. **SELECTED PUBLICATIONS** Auth, Yachtjacking, Boatnapping, or Getting Seajacked by Ship-jackers, Am Speech 62, 87; A Simplified Model of Language Variation and Change: A History of the Bot People, Glowka and Lance; A Guide to Chaucer's Meter, Univ Press of Am, 91; co-ed, Language Variation in North American English: Research and Teaching, MLA, 93; auth, The Poetics of Layamon's Brut, In: Text and Tradition in Layamon's Brut, Arthurian Studies 33, 94; Lawman and the Sabellian Heresy, Int J for the Semiotics of Law 8.24, 95; Layamon's Heathens and the Medieval Grapevine, In: Literacy and Orality in Early Middle English Literature, ScriptOralia 83, 96; coauth, Among the New Words, Am Speech 72, Fall and Winter 97. **CONTACT ADDRESS** Dept of English & Speech, Georgia Col, PO Box 490, Milledgeville, GA, 31061-0490. **EMAIL** wglowka@mail.gac.peachnet.edu

GOBERT, DAVID LAWRENCE
PERSONAL Born 10/18/1932, Decatur, IL, m, 1956, 5 children **DISCIPLINE** FRENCH LANGUAGE AND LITERATURE **EDUCATION** Millikin Univ, BA, 54; State Univ Iowa, MA, 56, PhD(Fr), 60. **CAREER** Asst prof French and Span, Coe Col, 58-61, assoc prof French, 62-65, actg chmn dept foreign lang, 64-65; assoc prof, 65-70, asst dean, col lib arts and sci, 68-70, assoc dean humanities, 71-74, PROF FRENCH, SOUTHERN ILL UNIV, 71-, Admin intern, Am Coun Educ, Syracuse Univ, 69-70; French reader, Educ Testing Serv, 77-78. **MEMBERSHIPS** Am Asn Teachers Fr. **RESEARCH** Eighteenth century French literature; French novel; applied French linguistics. **SELECTED PUBLICATIONS** Auth, Business and Marketing--Readings and Vocabulary in French, Mod Lang J, Vol 0077, 93; A-La-Rencontre-Des-Mots--Method of Analysis and Acquisition, Mod Lang J, Vol 0079, 95; Modal Value of the Future and Conditional Tenses and Their Uses in Contemporary French, Fr Rev, Vol 0068, 95. **CONTACT ADDRESS** Dept of Foreign Lang, Southern Ill Univ, Faner Hall, Carbondale, IL, 62901.

GODIN, JEAN CLEO
PERSONAL Born 08/13/1936, Petit-Rocher, NB, Canada, m, 1963, 4 children **DISCIPLINE** FRENCH AND QUEBEC LITERATURE **EDUCATION** Boston Col, BA, 61; Univ Montreal, Lic es Lett, 64; Aix-Marseille, D Univ, 66. **CAREER** Chmn dept French studies, 74-77, PROF LIT, UNIV MONTREAL, 66-, Mem jury Coun Arts, Gov Gen Prize, 71-73. **MEMBERSHIPS** Asn Can Univ Teachers Fr; MLA; Can Lit Asn; Asn Can Theatre Hist. **RESEARCH** French novel of the 19th and 20th centuries; theatre Quebecois. **SELECTED PUBLICATIONS** Auth, Nelligan--Poems and Textes-Dasile, 1900-1941, Vol 2, Rev d Histoire de l Amerique Fr, Vol 0046, 92; Nelligan--Complete Poems, 1896-1941, Vol 1, Rev d Histoire de l Amerique Fr, Vol 0046, 92; Nelligan, Emile--Handwritten Poems, Rev d Histoire de l Amerique Fr, Vol 0046, 92; Nelligan Amoureux, Rev d Histoire de l Amerique Fr, Vol 0046, 92; The Library of Grandbois, Alain, Etudes Fr, Vol 0029, 93; Introduction--Grandbois, Alain, A Writer Who Due to His Ability to Reach Inside His Readers, Is Popular the World Over, Etudes Fr, Vol 0030, 94; The Autobiographical Novel and Ethnicity in African Literature, Etudes Fr, Vol 0031, 95. **CONTACT ADDRESS** Dept of French Studies, Univ of Montreal, CP 6128, Montreal, PQ, H3C 3J7.

GOEDICKE, HANS
PERSONAL Born 08/07/1926, Vienna, Austria **DISCIPLINE** EGYPTOLOGY **EDUCATION** Univ Vienna, PhD, 49. **CAREER** Res Assoc Egyptol, Brown Univ, 52-56; lectr, 60-62, from asst prof to assoc prof, 62-68, prof, 68-79, CHMN NEAR EASTERN STUDIES, JONHS HOPKINS UNIV, 79-, Howard fel, 56-57; tech asst, Unesco-Centre doc l'ancienne Egypte, Cairo, 57-58; asst, Univ Gottingen, 58-60; Am Philos Soc grant, 66; John Simon Guggenheim Mem fel, 66-67; mem, Am Res Ctr Egypt; dir archaeol exped, Giza, Egypt, 72 and 74 and Tell el Rataba, 77, 78 and 81; corresp mem, Ger Archaeol Inst, 74. **MEMBERSHIPS** Egypt Explor Soc, London. **RESEARCH** Egyptian historical and administrative inscriptions. **SELECTED PUBLICATIONS** Auth, Thoughts About the Papyrus-Westcar, Zeitschrift fur Agyptische Sprache und Altertumskunde, Vol 0120, 93; The Story of Sinuhe, J Near Eastern Stud, Vol 0052, 93; The God Sopdu, J Near Eastern Stud, Vol 0053, 94; Religion in Ancient-Egypt--Gods, Myths, and Personal Practice, J Near Eastern Stud, Vol 0054, 95; The Thutmosis-I Inscription Near Tomas, J Near Eastern Stud, Vol 0055, 96. **CONTACT ADDRESS** Dept of Near Eastern Studies, Johns Hopkins Univ, 3400 N Charles St, Baltimore, MD, 21218.

GOETZ, THOMAS HENRY
PERSONAL Born 02/09/1936, Philadelphia, PA, m, 1970, 1 child **DISCIPLINE** FRENCH LITERATURE **EDUCATION** La Salle Col, BA, 61; Syracuse Univ, MA, 63, PhD, 67. **CAREER** Asst prof French, Ill Wesleyan Univ, 66-67; from asst prof to prof, 67-91, Distinguished Service prof French, State Univ NY Col Fredonia, 91-, chmn, Dept Foreign Lang & Lit, 79-89; ed, Nineteenth-Century Fr Studies, 72-; consult, La Bd Regents, 82. **HONORS AND AWARDS** Chevalier, Ordre des Palmes Academiques, 81; NEH fel, 77, 79, 84, 87, 88; Chevalier, 81, Officier, 89, Ordre des Palmes Academiques; NY State UUP Excellence Award. **MEMBERSHIPS** MLA; Am Asn Teachers Fr; Soc Etudes Romantiques; Asn de l'Ordre des Palmes Academiques; Am Soc de l'Ordre des Palmes Academiques. **RESEARCH** Nineteenth-century French literature; Hippolyte Taine. **SELECTED PUBLICATIONS** Auth, Taine and the Fine Arts, Ed Playor, 73; Poetry and Civilization: An Essay on the Humanities and the Human Condition, in Studies in the Humanities, Indiana Univ, Pa, 6/73; A Partially Unpublished Taine Letter, Romance Notes, 73; Poe and Taine: A Neglected French Critic, Poe Studies, 73; transl, The Defeat of the Armouchiquois Savages, Nat Museum of Man Mercury Ser, Can, 75; Paul Bourget's Le Disciple and the Text-Reader Relationship, Fr Rev, 78; auth, Edmond Louis Antoine and Jules Alfred Huot de Goncourt, in European Writers, The Romantic Century, Charles Scriber's, 85; The Uses of Translation: French Literature in 19th Century America, Laurels, 86; ed, articles on 19th-century French authors for the World Book Encycl, 89-90; auth, section on Goncourt brothers, in A Critical Bibliography of French Literature, Syracuse Univ Press, 94. **CONTACT ADDRESS** State Univ of New York Col, 1 Suny at Fredonia, Fredonia, NY, 14063-1143. **EMAIL** goetz@ait.fredonia.edu

GOETZ-STANKIEWICZ, MARKETA
PERSONAL Born 02/15/1927, Liberec, Czechoslovakia **DISCIPLINE** GERMANIC STUDIES **EDUCATION** Univ Toronto, BA, 54, MA, 55, PhD, 57. **CAREER** Instr to prof, 57-92, dept head, 80-85, PROF EMER GERMANIC STUD, UNIV BRITISH COLUMBIA, 92-. **HONORS AND AWARDS** UBC Cert Merit Excellence Tchg, 72, 92; Ordo Libri Bohemici, 88; Boeschenstein Medal, Can Asn Univ Tchrs Ger, 92; Hlavka Medal, Czech Acad Sci, 92. **MEMBERSHIPS** Ed bd, Seminar, 65-70; ed comt, Can Rev Comp Lit, 75-. **SELECTED PUBLICATIONS** Auth, The Silenced Theatre: Czech Playwrights Without A Stage, 79; ed, The Filter of Translation, 80; ed, Drama Contemporary: Czechoslovakia, 85; ed, The Vanek Plays: Four Authors, One Character, 87; ed, Good-Bye, Samizdat: Twenty years of Czechoslovak Underground Writing, 92; co-ed, Essays on German Literature in Honour of G. Joyce Hallamore, 68. **CONTACT ADDRESS** Dept of Germanic Stud, Univ of British Columbia, Vancouver, BC, V6T 1Z1.

GOHEEN, JUTTA
PERSONAL Born 06/29/1935, Zwickau, Germany, m, 1965 **DISCIPLINE** GERMAN **EDUCATION** Padagogische Hochsch Potsdam, Staatsexamen, 56, PhD(Ger), 57; Univ Bonn, Staatsexamen(English), 61. **CAREER** Asst Ger, Padagogische Hochsch Potsdam, 56-58; lectr, McMaster Univ, 63-64, asst prof, 64-65; asst prof, 65-68, assoc prof, 68-81, PROF GER, CARLETON UNIV, 81-. **RESEARCH** Medieval literature: linguistic stylistics; language as means of manipulation. **SELECTED PUBLICATIONS** Auth, Sexuality and Obscenity--A Literary-Psychological Study of Medieval and Renaissance Epics, Ger Stud Rev, Vol 0015, 1992; Womens Issues in German Literature Since 1945, Jahrbuch fur Int Germanistik, Vol 0024, 92; Mothers, Daughters, Women--Femininity in Literature, Jahrbuch fur Int Germanistik, Vol 0027, 95; On Nightingales and the Mundane--Poetry on Poetry in Minnesang and Self-Reflective Songs, Speculum-J Medieval Stud, Vol 0072, 97. **CONTACT ADDRESS** Dept of Ger, Carleton Univ, 1125 Colonel By Dr, Ottawa, ON, K1S 5B6.

GOIC, CEDOMIL
PERSONAL Born 03/03/1928, Antofagasta, Chile, m, 1956, 5 children **DISCIPLINE** SPANISH AMERICAN AND CHILEAN LITERATURE **EDUCATION** Univ Chile, Santiago, Profesorde Estado, 53, Dr en Filos(Romance philol), 65. **CAREER** Prof, Dept Span, Univ Chile, 55-76; PROF SPAN AM LIT, DEPT ROMANCE LANG, UNIV MICH, 76-, Vis prof Span Am lit, Dept Romance Lang, Univ Tex, Austin, 65-67 and Dept Span and Port, Univ Wis, 67-68; res evaluator humanities, Nat Comn Sci Invest, 71 and Cath Univ Chile, 75. **MEMBERSHIPS** Int Inst Iberoam Lit; MLA; Asoc Int Hispanistas. **RESEARCH** Spanish American novel; Spanish American poetry; Spanish American colonial literature. **SELECTED PUBLICATIONS** Auth, Huidobro, Vicente, an Analysis of the Poems El 'Espejo de Agua' and 'Ano Nuevo,' Rev Iberoamericana, Vol 0060, 94. **CONTACT ADDRESS** Dept of Romance Lang, Univ of Mich Ann, 812 E Washington St, Ann Arbor, MI, 48109-1275.

GOLAB, ZBIGNIEW
PERSONAL Born 03/16/1923, Nowy Targ, Poland, m, 1947, 1 child **DISCIPLINE** SLAVIC LINGUISTICS **EDUCATION** Wroclaw Univ, MA, 47; Jagiellonian Univ, PhD(Slavic ling), 58. **CAREER** Adj asst prof Slavic ling, Slavic Inst, Polish Acad Arts and Sci, 55-61; assoc prof, 61-67, PROF SLAVIC LING, UNIV CHICAGO, 67-, Yugoslav Comt Cult Exchange with Foreign Countries studies fel, 58; Fulbright-Hays res fel, Yugoslavia, 68: **MEMBERSHIPS** Am Asn Teachers Slavic & East Europ Lang; Polish Inst Arts & Sci Am; Macedonian Acad Arts & Sci, Skopje, Yugoslavia. **RESEARCH** Comparative Slavic linguistics; Slavic-Balkan linguistics; Polish syntax. **SELECTED PUBLICATIONS** Auth, Slavic Chelovek (Homo) against the Background of Proto-Slavic Terminology, J Indo-Europ Stud, Vol 0023, 95. **CONTACT ADDRESS** Dept Slavic, Univ of Chicago, 1130 E 59th St, Chicago, IL, 60637.

GOLB, NORMAN
PERSONAL Born 01/15/1928, Chicago, IL, m, 1949, 3 children **DISCIPLINE** JEWISH HISTORY, HEBREW AND JUDEO-ARABIC STUDIES **EDUCATION** Roosevelt Col, BA, 48; Johns Hopkins Univ, PhD, 54. **CAREER** Warburg res fel Judaeo-Arabic studies, Hebrew Univ, Jerusalem, 55-57; vis lectr Semitic lang, Univ Wis, 57-58; from instr to asst prof Mediaeval Jewish studies, Hebrew Union Col, 58-63; from asst prof to prof Hebrew and Judeo-Arabiic Studies, Univ Chicago, 63-88, Rosenberger Prof Jewish Hist and Civilization, 88-. **HONORS AND AWARDS** Adler res fel, Dropsie Col, 54-55; Am Philos Soc grants-in-aid, 59, 63 & 67; Am Coun Learned Soc grants-in-aid, 63 & 65; Guggenheim Mem Found fels, 64-65 & 66-67; voting mem, Orient Inst, 64-; vis fel, Clare Hall, Cambridge Univ, 70; Nat Endowment for Humanities grant, 70-72; Grand Medal of Honor of the City of Rouen, 85; Docteur Honoris Causa (Histoire), Univ of Rouen, 87; Medal of Haute Normandie, 87. **MEMBERSHIPS** Fel Am Acad Jewish Res; life mem, Clare Hall, Cambridge Univ, 80-; Soc de l'Histoire de France, 87-; Founder and vice-pres, Soc for Judeo-Arabic Studies, 84-. **RESEARCH** Jewish History, Hebrew and Judeo-Arabic Studies. **SELECTED PUBLICATIONS** Auth, A Judaeo-Arabic Court Document of Syracuse, AD 1020, J Near Eastern Studies, 73; The Problem of Origin and Identification of the Dead Sea Scrolls, Proc Am Philos Soc, 80; Nature et destination du monument hebraique decouvert a Rouen, Proc Am Acad Jewish Res, 81; coauth (with Omeljan Pritsak), Khazarian Hebrew Documents of the Tenth Century, Cornell Univ Press, 82, trans to Russ, 97; auth, Les Juifs de Rouen au Moyen Age, Presses Univ de Rouen, 85; Who Wrote the Dead Sea Scrolls?, Scribner, 95, translated in Ger, Dutch, Port, Fr, Japanese; The Jews of Medieval Normandy, Cambridge Univ Press, 98; ed, Judeo-Arabic Studies, Harwood Acad Press, 97. **CONTACT ADDRESS** Univ of Chicago, 1155 E 58th St, Chicago, IL, 60637-1540. **EMAIL** n.golb@uchicago.edu

GOLDBERG, RITA MARIA
PERSONAL Born 10/01/1933, New York, NY **DISCIPLINE** SPANISH **EDUCATION** Queens Col, NY, BA, 54; Middlebury Col, MA, 55; Brown Univ, PhD, 68. **CAREER** Lectr Span, Queens Col, NY, 56-57; from asst prof to prof, 57-71, Harriet Lewis prof mod lang, 71-75, chmn dept, 72-75, Charles A Dana Prof Mod Lang & Lit, St Lawrence Univ, 75-; Danforth Found grants, 60-61 & 63-64; Assoc Newman Alumni, NY fel, 63; chmn Regional Conf Am Prog in Spain, 71-72, 75-76 & 79-81. **HONORS AND AWARDS** Phi Betta Kappa; Sigma Delta Pi. **MEMBERSHIPS** MLA; Am Asn Teachers Span & Port; AAUP; ACT FL; NYSFLT. **RESEARCH** Romance; 17th century poetry and music; modern novel and theatre. **SELECTED PUBLICATIONS** Auth, Una nueva version manuscrita del romance de Lope De pechos sobre uan torre, Hisp Rev, 67; Un modo de subsistencia del romancero nuevo: romances de Gongora y Lope de Vega en bailes del Siglo de Oro, Bull Hisp, 70; Don Fernando Cortes, III Marques de Valle: su boda con dona Mencia de la Cerda y el inventario de bienes de 1602, 70 & Mas datos sobre Don Pedro Cortes, IV Marques del Valle de Oaxaca, 71, Bull Nat Arch Gen, Mex; La Familia de Calderon y la Calle de la Nao o Henao, ABC, Madrid, 9/74; The Impossible Dream of Integration, in Fornells and Cynthia: Ruiz-Fornells; The United States and the Spanish World, SGEL, Madrid, 79. **CONTACT ADDRESS** Dept of Mod Lang & Lit, St Lawrence Univ, Canton, NY, 13617-1499. **EMAIL** rgol@music.stlawu.edu

GOLSTON, CHRIS
PERSONAL Born 02/03/1961, Fort Hood, TX, m, 1990, 2 children **DISCIPLINE** LINGUISTICS **EDUCATION** Univ Calif - Los Angeles, PhD, 91. **CAREER** Teacher, San Francisco Chinese Parents Comt Sch, 83-84; Teacher, Maybeck High Sch, 84-86; Vis External Lectr, Univ Ariz, 91-92; Vis Asst Prof, Stanford Univ, 92-93; Vis Asst Prof, UCLA, 94; Asst Prof Linguistics, Calif State Univ Fresno, 96-. **MEMBERSHIPS** Ling Soc Am. **RESEARCH** Phonology; Morphology; meter. **SELECTED PUBLICATIONS** Co-auth, The Hopi Coyote Story as Narrative: The Problem of Evaluation, J Pragmatics, 87; Zero morphology and constraint interaction: subtraction and epenthesis in German dialects, Yearbook of Morphology, Marburg Univ, 95; The phonology of Classical Arabic meter, Linguistics, Stockholm Univ, 97; Idre germansk vers kvantifierande, Meter Medel, Stockholm Univ, 98; The structure of the German root, Phonology and Morphology of the Germanic Languages, Niemeyer, 98; auth, Syntax outranks phonology: evidence from Ancient Greek, Phonology, 95; Prosodic constraints on roots and words, In: Studia Grammatica: Interfaces in Phonology, Akademie Verlag, 96; Direct Optimality Theory: representation as pure markedness, Lang, 96. **CONTACT ADDRESS** Linguistics Dept, California State Univ, Fresno, PO Box 92, Fresno, CA, 93740-0001. **EMAIL** chrisg@csufresno.edu

GOLUMBIA, DAVID
PERSONAL Born 06/22/1963, Detroit, MI **DISCIPLINE** ENGLISH LANGUAGE AND LITERATURE **EDUCATION** Oberlin Col, BA, 95; Univ of Pennsylvania, PhD, 98. **CAREER** Independent scholar **MEMBERSHIPS** Modern Lang Assoc; Amer Phil Assoc; Linguistic Soc of Amer. **RESEARCH** Cultural studies; deconstruction; analytic philosophy (contemporary); linguistics (contemporary) as subjects for cultural studies; print and other media history **SELECTED PUBLICATIONS** Auth, Toward an Ethics of Cultural Acts: The Jamesian Dialectic in Broken Wings, the Henry James Review, 94; Black and White World: Race, Ideology, and Utopia in Triton and Star Trek, Cultural Critique 32, 95-96; Resisting the World: Philip K. Dick, Cultural Studies, and Metaphysical Realism, Science Fiction Studies 23:1, 96; Hypercapital, Postmodern Culture 7:1, 96; Rethinking Philosophy in the Third Wave of Feminism, Hypatia: A Journal of Feminist Philosophy, 97; Quines Ambivalence, Cultural Critique 38, 97-98; Feminism and Mental Representation: Analytic Philosophy, Cultural Studies, and Narrow Content, Is Feminist Philsophy Philosophy?, 99. **CONTACT ADDRESS** 502 Seminary Row, Apt 62, New York, NY, 10027. **EMAIL** dgolumbi@sas.uenn.edu

GONTRUM, PETER B.
PERSONAL Born 02/13/1932, m, 1956, 3 children **DISCIPLINE** GERMAN & COMPARITIVE LITERATURE **EDUCATION** Haverford Col, BA, 54; Princeton Univ, MA, 56; Univ Munich, PhD, 58. **CAREER** Instr Ger, Univ Chicago, 58-61; from asst prof to assoc prof, 61-72, prof Ger, Univ Ore, 72-, head Dept Ger Lang & Lit, 78-84; prof Emeritus, 98; Am Philos Soc grant, 60, 65-66; Am Coun Learned Soc grant & Alexander von Humboldt fel, 65-66; Alexander von Humboldt fel, 71 & 79; mem Nat Fulbright Selection Comn, 71-73; Fulbright lectr, Univ Mannheim, 74. **MEMBERSHIPS** Am Asn Teachers Ger; MLA; Philol Asn Pac Coast; Am Comp Lit Asn; Int Comp Lit Asn. **RESEARCH** Rilke; modern German literature; Hesse, Brecht, Durrenmatt and Frisch. **SELECTED PUBLICATIONS** Auth, Natur und Dingsymbolik als Ausdruck de Inneren Welt Hermann Hesses, Univ Munich, 58; The legend of Rip van Winkle in Max Frisch's Stiller, Studies Swiss Lit, 71; Max Firsch and the theatre of Bertolt Brecht, German Life and Letters, 1/80. **CONTACT ADDRESS** Dept of German Language & Lit, Univ of Oregon, Eugene, OR, 97403-1205.

GONZALEZ, ALFONSO
PERSONAL Born 01/07/1938, Mexico City, Mexico, m, 1963, 3 children **DISCIPLINE** MEXICAN LITERATURE, SPANISH LANGUAGE **EDUCATION** Univ Kans, BA, 67, MA, 68, PhD(Span), 71. **CAREER** Asst prof Span, Ohio Univ, 71-75; prof Span, 82-83, Calif State Univ Los Angeles, 78-, Ohio Univ res inst grants Mex Cult, 72-73 & 73-74; vis prof Lat Am Lit, Univ Southern Calif, 75-76. **HONORS AND AWARDS** MPPP Award for Spring 87-Summer 88, CSULA; Lottery Funds Award, Spring 94, 87, CSULA; PPSI Award, CSULA. **MEMBERSHIPS** Am Asn Teachers Span & Port; MLA; Philol Asn Pac Coast; Pac Coast Coun Latin Am Studies. **RESEARCH** Latin American literature; Latin American studies. **SELECTED PUBLICATIONS** Auth, El novumundismo en la prosa de ficcion de Altamirano, Palabra & Hombre, 10-12/72; Onomasticas and creativity in Dona Barbara and Pedro Paramo, Names, 3/73; Narrative techniques in twentieth-century Spanish American novomundismo, Grad Studies Latin Am, Fall 73; Elementos del Quijote en la caracterizacion de La Voragine, Romance Notes, 74; Elementos hispanicos y clasicos en la caracterizacion de La Voragine, Cuadernos Am, 5-6/75; introd to chap on Julieta Campos, In: Mujeres en la Literature, Fleischer Ed, Mex, 78; Indice de la Cultura en Mexico (1962-1971), Univ Microfilms Int, 78; Entrando en la posmodernidad, Mexico: UNAM, 98. **CONTACT ADDRESS** 5151 Rancho Castilla, Los Angeles, CA, 90032-4202. **EMAIL** alfonso.Gonzalez@worldnet.atl.net

GONZALEZ, BERNARDO ANTONIO
PERSONAL Born 06/20/1950, San Pedro, CA, m, 1976, 2 children **DISCIPLINE** MODERN SPANISH LITERATURE **EDUCATION** Univ Calif, Berkeley, AB, 72, MA, 74, PhD(Romance lang and lit), 79. **CAREER** ASST PROF SPAN, WESLEYAN UNIV, 79-. **MEMBERSHIPS** MLA; Am Asn Teachers of Span and Portuguese; Northeastern MLA. **RESEARCH** Contemporary Spanish fiction; theory of the novel. **SELECTED PUBLICATIONS** Auth, Cuando Acabe la Guerra, Anales de la Lit Espanola Contemporanea, Vol 0018, 93; Theater in Spain, Between Tradition and Avant-Garde, Rev de Estudios Hispanicos, Vol 0027, 93; Ultima Batalla En El Pardo, Estreno-Cuadernos del Teatro Espanol Contemporaneo, Vol 0020, 94; Popular National Theater--On the Theory and Practice of Rodriguezmendez, Jose, Maria, Estreno-Cuadernos del Teatro Espanol Contemporaneo, Vol 0020, 94; The Theory of Theater Criticism During the 2nd-Republic, the Case of Chabas, Juan, Anales de la Lit Espanola Contemporanea, Vol 0020, 95; Yo Fui Actor Cuando Franco, Manana, Aqui, A la Misma Hora, Estreno-Cuadernos del Teatro Espanol Contemporaneo, Vol 0021, 95; Puigserver, Fabia, Man of Theater, Estreno-Cuadernos del Teatro Espanol Contemporaneo, Vol 0021, 95; Olmo, Lauro El 'Perchero' (1953)--Playwrighting in the Social, Economic and Political Contexts of the Times, Estreno-Cuadernos del Teatro Espanol Contemporaneo, Vol 0022, 96; Spanish Alternative Theater Today, Estreno-Cuadernos del Teatro Espanol Contemporaneo, Vol 0022, 96; Reflections on Theatrical Politics, Estreno-Cuadernos del Teatro Espanol Contemporaneo, Vol 0023, 97. **CONTACT ADDRESS** Dept of Romance Lang, Wesleyan Univ, Middletown, CT, 06457.

GONZALEZ, ELOY
DISCIPLINE MEDIEVAL AND GOLDEN AGE SPANISH LITERATURE **EDUCATION** Ohio State Univ, PhD, 74. **CAREER** Assoc prof, Wash State Univ 81-. **RESEARCH** Medieval and golden age Spanish literature. **SELECTED PUBLICATIONS** Auth, Metafora y simetria en el prologo del Abencerraje, Explicacion de textos literarios 5, 76; Carnival on the Stage: Cefalo y Pocris, a comedia burlesca, Bull Comediantes 30, 78; La muerte, entierro y honras de Chrespina Marauzmana, gata de Juan Chrespo, de Bernardino de Albornoz Edition of the poem, with a prologue and notes, Revista de lit 51, 89, publ Consejo Superior de Investigaciones Cientificas, Madrid, Spain; Las batallas en el Amadis de Gaula, Selecta, J Pacific Northwest Coun on For Lang 10, 89 & Tipologia literaria de los personajes en el Amadis de Gaula, Nueva Revista de Filologia Hisp 39, 91; coauth, Montalvo's Recantation, Revisited, Bull Hisp Stud 55, 78. **CONTACT ADDRESS** Dept of Foreign Languages and Literatures, Washington State Univ, 1 SE Stadium Way, Pullman, WA, 99164. **EMAIL** eloygonz@wsunix.wsu.edu

GOODE, WILLIAM OSBORNE
PERSONAL Born 06/22/1939, Chase City, VA, m, 1972, 3 children **DISCIPLINE** FRENCH LITERATURE **EDUCATION** Washington and Lee Univ, BA, 60; Duke Univ, MA, 63, PhD(French), 68. **CAREER** Asst prof French, Univ Md, 67-68 and Univ Pa, 68-73; asst prof, 74-78, ASSOC PROF FRENCH, UNIV NC, GREENSBORO, 78-, ADVERT MGR, THE FR REV, 80-. **MEMBERSHIPS** MLA; Am Asn Teachers Fr; S Atlantic Mod Lang Asn; AAUP. **RESEARCH** Seventeenth century French literature; classical theater; tragedy. **SELECTED PUBLICATIONS** Auth, Dissonant Harmonies--Drama and Ideology in 5 Neglected Plays of Corneille, Pierre, Fr Forum, Vol 0017, 92; Moliere and Plurality--Decomposition of the Classicist Self, Fr Rev, Vol 0066, 93; Subjectivity and Subjugation in 17th-Century Drama and Prose--The Family Romance of French Classicism, Fr Forum, Vol 0019, 94. **CONTACT ADDRESS** Dept of Romance Lang, Univ of NC, 1000 Spring Garden, Greensboro, NC, 27412-0001.

GOODMAN, DAVID G.
DISCIPLINE LANGUAGES; ASIAN CULTURE **EDUCATION** Yale Univ, BA, 69; Cornell Univ, PhD, 82. **CAREER** Visiting Asst Prof, Univ Kansas, 81-82; Asst Prof, 82-86, Assoc Prof, 86-90, Prof, 90-, Univ Illinois. **CONTACT ADDRESS** Dept of East Asian Languages and Cultures, Univ of Illinois, Urbana-Champaign, 608 S Matthews Ave, Urbana, IL, 61801. **EMAIL** dgoodman@uiuc.edu

GOODSON, ALFRED CLEMENT
PERSONAL Born 11/30/1946, Houston, TX **DISCIPLINE** COMPARATIVE LITERATURE, ENGLISH **EDUCATION** Rice Univ, BA, 68; State Univ NY Buffalo, PhD(comp lit), 73. **CAREER** Asst prof, 72-77, ASSOC PROF ENGLISH, MICH STATE UNIV, 77-, Alexander von Humboldt Stiftung res grant, Deutsches Seminar, Tubingen, 79. **RESEARCH** Romantic poetics; critical theory; myth. **SELECTED PUBLICATIONS** Auth, Frankenstein in the Age of Prozac: Artistic Creativity, Depression, Modern Medicine, Lit and Med, Vol 0015, 96. **CONTACT ADDRESS** 403 Kensington Rd, East Lansing, MI, 48823.

GOPNIK, MYRNA
PERSONAL Born 06/21/1935, Philadelphia, PA, m, 1954, 6 children **DISCIPLINE** LINGUISTICS, SEMIOTICS **EDUCATION** Univ Pa, BA, 62, MA, 64, PhD(ling), 68. **CAREER** Instr hist and philos sci, Phila Col Arts, 67-68; invited lectr info sci, Drexel Inst Technol, 68; res, assoc auto transl, Univ Montreal, 68-69; ASSOC PROF LING, MCGILL UNIV, 69-. **MEMBERSHIPS** Ling Soc Am; Can Ling Asn; Ling Asn Can & US; Can Asn Hist & Philos Sci; MLA. **RESEARCH** Linguistic metatheory; textlingusitics; semiotics. **SELECTED PUBLICATIONS** Auth, Impairments of Tense in a Familial Language Disorder, J Neurolinguistics, Vol 0008, 94; Compensatory Strategies in Genetic Dysphasia--Declarative Memory, J Neurolinguistics, Vol 0010, 97; Neuroanatomical Correlates of Familial Language Impairment--A Preliminary-Report, J Neurolinguistics, Vol 0010, 97; Genetic Dysphasia--Introduction, J Neurolinguistics, Vol 0010, 97; What Underlies Inflectional Error Patterns in Genetic Dysphasia, J Neurolinguistics, Vol 0010, 97. **CONTACT ADDRESS** Dept of Ling, McGill Univ, 1001 Sherbrooke, St Montreal, PQ, H3A 1G5.

GORDON, ALEXANDER LOBBAN
PERSONAL Born 04/12/1935, Grantown-on-Spey, Scotland **DISCIPLINE** FRENCH **EDUCATION** Aberdeen Univ, MA, 58; Sorbonne, DUniv (French), 65. **CAREER** Asst English, Univ Rennes, 58-59; from lectr to asst prof French, 61-70, ASSOC PROF FRENCH, UNIV MAN, 70-. **MEMBERSHIPS** MLA; Int Soc Hist Rhetoric. **RESEARCH** French poetry of the 16th century; modern French poetry. **SELECTED PUBLICATIONS** Auth, Concordance of the Works of Rabelais, Francois, Bibliotheque d Humanisme et Renaissance, Vol 0055, 93; Dialectic and Knowledge in la 'Sepmaine' of Dubartas, Fr Forum, Vol 0019, 94; Rhetoric-Rhetoriqueurs-Rederijkers, Proceedings of The Colloquium, Amsterdam, November 10-13, 1993, Rhetorica-J Hist of Rhet, Vol 0014, 96; Emblematic Structures in French Renaissance Culture, Fr Forum, Vol 0022, 97. **CONTACT ADDRESS** Dept of French and Span, Unif of Man, Winnipeg, MB, R3T 2M8.

GORDON, LYNN
DISCIPLINE LINGUISTICS AND TESOL **EDUCATION** Univ Calif, Los Angeles, PhD. **CAREER** Assoc prof, Washington State Univ. **SELECTED PUBLICATIONS** Auth, Maricopa Morphology and Syntax, 86. **CONTACT ADDRESS** Dept of English, Washington State Univ, 1 SE Stadium Way, PO Box 645020, Pullman, WA, 99164-5020. **EMAIL** gordonl@wsunix.wsu.edu

GORMAN, JOHN
PERSONAL Born 08/28/1938, Hoboken, NJ **DISCIPLINE** GERMAN **EDUCATION** Manhattan Col, BA, 60; Johns Hopkins Univ, MA, 61, PhD(Ger), 67. **CAREER** Asst prof foreign lang, Lamar State Col, 65-66 and Univ Miami, 67-74; WRITER, 74-. **RESEARCH** German-Spanish literary relations; comparative literature. **SELECTED PUBLICATIONS** Auth, Lost in the City, Am Bk Rev, Vol 0015, 93. **CONTACT ADDRESS** 4713 NW 7th St, Miami, FL, 33126.

GORUP, RADMILA J.
DISCIPLINE SLAVIC LANGUAGES **EDUCATION** Univ Belgrade, BA; St John's University, MA; Columbia Univ, PhD. **CAREER** Prof. **RESEARCH** Theoretical linguistics; sociolinguistics; South Slavic cultures; Serbian literature. **SELECTED PUBLICATIONS** Auth, Semantic Organization of the Serbocroatian Verb, 87; Women in Andric's Writing, 95; History as Human Construct: Radoslav Petkovic's Sudbina i Komentari, Serbian Studies, 96. **CONTACT ADDRESS** Dept of Slavic Languages, Columbia Col, New York, 2960 Broadway, New York, NY, 10027-6902. **EMAIL** rjg26@columbia.edu

GOSS, NOBLE T.
PERSONAL Born 08/11/1944, Heppner, OR, m, 1973, 4 children **DISCIPLINE** FOREIGN LANGUAGES **EDUCATION** Pepperdine Col, BA, 66; Portland State Univ, MA, 73; Univ Ore, MA, 79, PhD, 87. **CAREER** Res asst, Univ Ore, 84-96; instr, Lane Commun Col, 84-96; ASST PROF, HARDING UNIV, 96-. **HONORS AND AWARDS** Dissertation, The Theme of Chastity in Ariosto and Spenser, 87. **MEMBERSHIPS** AATSP; AFLTA. **RESEARCH** Golden age, Spain, drama & poetry; Renaissance Epic; FL teaching methodology. **CONTACT ADDRESS** Dept of Foreign Languages, Harding Univ, Box 12263, Searcy, AR, 72143. **EMAIL** ngoss@harding.edu

GOUVERNEUR, GRAY HENRY
DISCIPLINE COMPARATIVE RELIGION, ART HISTORY **EDUCATION** Sarah Lawrence, BA, 65; Univ Mich, MA, 80; doctoral work, Univ Kent, Canterbury. **CAREER** Teach, Fordham Univ, Dalton Sch, 66-68; teach, Azhar Acad, Cairo Am Col, 70-78; lect, Cambridge Univ, 88; instr, Bellarmine Col, 91-92; instr, Center Col, 93; DIR, FOUNDER PUB HOUSES: ISLAMIC TEXTS SOC, QUINTA ESSENTIA, FOUNSVITAE, 80-. **CONTACT ADDRESS** 49 Mockingbird Valley Dr, Louisville, KY, 40207. **EMAIL** grayh101@aol.com

GRAF, ERIC
DISCIPLINE SPANISH LANGUAGE AND LITERATURE **EDUCATION** Univ VA, PhD, 96. **CAREER** Span, Smith Col **SELECTED PUBLICATIONS** Auth, Forcing the Poetic Voice: Garcilaso de la Vega's Sonnet XXIX as a Deconstruction of the Renaissance Idea of Harmony, MLN 109 2, 94; May I Have This Dance Unveiling Vicente Aleixandre's El vals, Romanic Rev 85 2, 94; Escritor/Excretor: Cervantes's 'Humanism' on Philip II's Tomb, Cervantes 19 1, 99. **CONTACT ADDRESS** Dept of Span and Portuguese, Smith Col, Northampton, MA, 01063. **EMAIL** egraf@sophia.smith.edu

GRAGG, GENE BALFORD
PERSONAL Born 08/24/1938, Amsterdam, NY, m, 1969, 2 children **DISCIPLINE** LINGUISTICS, SUMEROLOGY **EDUCATION** Loyola Univ, Chicago, BA, 60; West Baden Col, Lic Phil, 62; Univ Chicago, PhD, 66. **CAREER** Res assoc Sumerian, Univ Amsterdam, 67-69; from Asst Prof to Assoc Prof, 69-82, Prof, Univ Chicago, 82-, Chmn 79-85; Dir, Oriental Inst, 97-. **MEMBERSHIPS** Ling Soc Am; Am Orient Soc. **RESEARCH** Historical linguistics; Sumerian; Cushitic. **SELECTED PUBLICATIONS** Auth, The Sumerian Dimensional Infixes, Butzon, 73; Oromo, of Wallagga, In: Non-Semitoc Languages of Ethiopia, 75; Dictionary of Oromo, 82; Achaemenid Royal Inscriptions (elec), 97. **CONTACT ADDRESS** Oriental Inst, Univ of Chicago, 1155 E 58th St, Chicago, IL, 60637-1540. **EMAIL** g-gragg@uchicago.edu

GRAHAM, WILLIAM A.
PERSONAL Born 08/16/1943, Raleigh, NC, m, 1983, 1 child **DISCIPLINE** ISLAMIC STUDIES, HISTORY OF RELIGIONS **EDUCATION** Univ NC, Chapel Hill, Comp Lit, AB, 66; Harvard Univ; AM, 70, PhD, 73, Comp Rel and Islamics. **CAREER** Lectr, Asst Prof, 73-, Harvard Univ; Assoc Prof, Sr Lectr, Prof, Hist of Rel and Islamic Stud, M of Currier House, 91-; Chr, 87-90, Dir, Center for Middle Eastern Stud, 90-96, Chr, Dept of Near Eastern Lang and Civilization, 97-, Harvard Admin Posts. **HONORS AND AWARDS** Danforth; Woodrow Wilson Grad Fellowship; ACLS, Hist Rel Books Award; J.S. Guggenheim Fellowship. **MEMBERSHIPS** Amer Soc for the Stud of Rel; Middle East Stud Assoc; Amer Oriental Soc; Amer Acad of Rel. **RESEARCH** History of Religion; Scripture, Pilgrimage; Islamic Studies, Qur'an, Rituals, Traditionalism **SELECTED PUBLICATIONS** Auth, Divine Word and Prophetic Word in Early Islam, Mouton, 78; Beyond the Written Word, Cambridge Univ, 87; coauth, The Heritage of World Civilizations, Practice Hall, 4th ed, 97. **CONTACT ADDRESS** Currier House, Harvard Univ, 64 Linnaean St, Cambridge, MA, 02138. **EMAIL** wgraham@fas.harvard.edu

GRANT, RAYMOND JAMES SHEPHERD
PERSONAL Born 05/26/1942, Aberdeen, Scotland, m, 1973 **DISCIPLINE** LANGUAGE AND LITERATURE **EDUCATION** Univ Aberdeen, MA, 64; Cambridge Univ, PhD(English), 71. **CAREER** Asst prof, 67-74, assoc prof, 74-80, PROF ENGLISH, UNIV ALTA, 80-. **RESEARCH** Anglo-Saxon verse; homilies; texts transcribed in the 16th and 17th centuries. **SELECTED PUBLICATIONS** Auth, A Copied Tremulous Worcester Gloss at Corpus: Cambridge Manuscript-41 from Corpus-Christi-College Library Containing Bede 'Historia Ecclesiastica,' Neuphilologische Mitteilungen, Vol 0097, 96; The Pedlar-Poet and the Prince of Editors--Mcfarlan, James and Dickens, Charles, Dickensian, Vol 0093, 97. **CONTACT ADDRESS** Dept of English, Univ of Alta, Edmonton, AB, T6G 2E5.

GRANT, RICHARD BABSON
PERSONAL Born 01/18/1925, Boston, MA **DISCIPLINE** FRENCH **EDUCATION** Harvard Univ, PhD(Romance lang), 52. **CAREER** From instr to prof Romance lang, Duke Univ, 52-71; PROF FRENCH, UNIV TEX, AUSTIN, 71-. **MEMBERSHIPS** MLA; Am Asn Teachers Fr. **RESEARCH** French naturalism; French romanticism. **SELECTED PUBLICATIONS** Auth, Contemplation and Dreams--Hugo, Victor, Poet of Intimacy, 19th-Century Fr Stud, Vol 0022, 93; Hugo, Victor Le 'Rhin' and the Search for Identity, 19th-Century Fr Stud, Vol 0023, 95. **CONTACT ADDRESS** Dept of French and Ital, Univ of Tex, Austin, TX, 78712.

GRAY, EUGENE FRANCIS
PERSONAL Born 04/22/1936, Flint, MI, m, 1964, 2 children **DISCIPLINE** FRENCH LITERATURE **EDUCATION** Univ Mich, Ann Arbor, BSE, 60, MA, 62, PhD, 68. **CAREER** Instr lang & phys sci, Detroit Inst Technol, 62-67; asst prof, 67-71, acting chmn dept, 71-72, assoc prof, 71-81, prof French, Mich State Univ, 81-, dir, lang learning ctr, 91. **MEMBERSHIPS** Am Assn Teachers Fr; CALICO. **RESEARCH** Nineteenth century French novel; French literary style; history of science. **SELECTED PUBLICATIONS** Auth, Gustave Flaubert, in A Critical Bibliography of Nineteenth-Century French Literature, 94; ed Madame Bovary: A Collection of Essays, 95. **CONTACT ADDRESS** Dept of Romance Lang, Michigan State Univ, 161 Old Horticulture, East Lansing, MI, 48824-1112. **EMAIL** graye@pilot.msu.edu

GRAY, FLOYD FRANCIS
PERSONAL Born 08/12/1926, Meadville, PA **DISCIPLINE** FRENCH **EDUCATION** Syracuse Univ, BA, 50; Inst Phonetique, Univ Paris, 51, Ecole Prof Francais a l'Etranger, cert, 51; Univ Wis, MA, 52, PhD, 56. **CAREER** Asst English, Lycee Henri-Martin, Saint-Quentin, 50-51; instr French, Univ Wis, 55-56; from instr to assoc prof, 56-65, univ fel, 58, prof French, Univ Mich, Ann Arbor, 65-; vis prof 16th century French lit, Univ Calif, Santa Barbara, 70-71; managing ed, Mich Romance Studies. **HONORS AND AWARDS** Palmes Academiques, French Govt, 75. **MEMBERSHIPS** Am Asn Teachers Fr; Soc ALmis Montaigne; MLA. **RESEARCH** French 16th and 17th century literature, especially Montaigne; Du Bellay; Rabelais. **SELECTED PUBLICATIONS** Auth, Le Style de Montaigne, Nizet, Paris, 58; Albert Thibaudet's Montaigne, Gallimard, Paris, 63; ed & transl, Gargantua and Pantagruel, 66 & auth, Anthologie de la Poesie francaise du XVIe siecle, 67, Appleton; Rabelais et l'ecriture, Nizet, Paris, 74; La Poetique de Du Bellay, 78 &; ed, Textes et Intertextes, Etudes sur le XVIe siecle pour Alfred Glauser, 79, Nizet, Paris; Poetiques: Theorie et critique litteraires, Mich Romance Studies, Vol 1, 80; auth, La Balance de Montaigne, Nizet, Paris, 82; La BruySre amateur de caractSres, Nizet, 86; Montaigne bilingue, Champion, Paris, 91; Rabelais et le comique du discontinu, Champion, 94; ed, Rabelais, Gargantua, Champion, 95; auth, Rabelais, Pantagruel, Champion, 97. **CONTACT ADDRESS** Dept of Romance Lang, Univ of Mich, 812 E Washington St, Ann Arbor, MI, 48109-1275. **EMAIL** FGray@umich.edu

GRAY, MARGARET
DISCIPLINE FRENCH LITERATURE **EDUCATION** Yale Univ, PhD, 86. **CAREER** Assoc prof. **RESEARCH** Narrative dynamics and their relation to historical, cultural and theoretical frameworks. **SELECTED PUBLICATIONS** Auth, Postmodern Proust, 92; articles on Proust, George Sand, Beckett, and Toussaint. **CONTACT ADDRESS** Dept of French and Italian, Indiana Univ, Bloomington, 300 N Jordan Ave, Bloomington, IN, 47405.

GRAY, RICHARD T.
DISCIPLINE GERMAN **EDUCATION** Univ NC, Greensboro, BA, 74; Univ Cincinnati, MA, 76; Univ Va, PhD, 81. **CAREER** Asst prof, Univ Va, 81-82; vis asst prof, Reed Col, 82-84; asst prof, 84-88, assoc, 88-91, Mills Col; assoc prof, 91-93, PROF GER, UNIV WASH. **CONTACT ADDRESS** Dept of Germanics, Univ of Washington, Box 35310, Seattle, WA, 98195-3130. **EMAIL** woyzeck@u.washington.edu

GRAYSON, ALBERT K.
PERSONAL Born 04/01/1935, Windsor, ON, Canada **DISCIPLINE** NEAR EASTERN STUDIES **EDUCATION** Univ Toronto, BA, 55, MA, 58; Univ Vienna, 59-60; Johns Hopkins Univ, PhD, 62. **CAREER** Res asst, Orient Inst Univ Chicago, 62-63; asst prof hist, Temple Univ, 63-64; asst prof to assoc prof, 64-72, PROF NEAR EASTERN STUD, UNIV TORONTO, 72-. **HONORS AND AWARDS** Can Coun pre-doctoral fel, 59-61; Samuel S Fels Fund fel, 61-62; SSHRCC ed grant, 81-2001. **MEMBERSHIPS** Soc Mesopotamian Stud; Brit Sch Archaeol Iraq; Fondation Assyriologique Georges Dossin; Rencontre Assyriologique Int; Am Orient Soc. **SELECTED PUBLICATIONS** Auth, Assyrian and Babylonian Chronicles-Texts from Cuneiform Sources V, 75,; auth, Assyrian Royal Inscriptions I, 72, II 76; auth, Babylonian Historical-Literary texts - Toronto Semitic Texts and Studies III, 75; coauth, Papyrus and Tablet, 73; coauth, Royal Inscriptions on Clay Cones from Ashur Now in Istanbul, 84; coauth, Assyrian Rulers of the Third and Second Millenia BC - Royal Inscriptions of Mesopotamia: Assyrian Perids I, 87; coauth, Assyrian Rulers of the Early First Millenium BC I-II - Royal Inscriptions of Mesopotamia: Assyrian Periods II-III, 91, 96; coauth, Cambirdge Ancient History III, 92. **CONTACT ADDRESS** Near Eastern Stud, Univ of Toronto, 4 Bancroft Ave, Toronto, ON, M5S 1A1.

GREEN, ANNE
DISCIPLINE GERMAN LANGUAGE AND CULTURE **EDUCATION** Univ Ill, PhD. **CAREER** Languages, Carnegie Mellon Univ. **MEMBERSHIPS** Study Abroad Scholarships Comt; Lang Learning Resource Lab Advisory Comt; Western Pa Am Asn Tchrs German. **SELECTED PUBLICATIONS** Coauth, The Most Noble Diet: Food Selection and Ethics, New York: Diet Ethics, 94; Adapting Games for the Foreign Language Classroom, 94; Mod Lang Undergrad Handbook, 95; Games for the German Classroom, 95. **CONTACT ADDRESS** Carnegie Mellon Univ, 5000 Forbes Ave, Pittsburgh, PA, 15213.

GREEN, GEORGIA MARKS
PERSONAL Born 04/16/1944, Atlanta, GA **DISCIPLINE** LINGUISTICS **EDUCATION** Univ Chicago, BA, 66, MA, 69, PhD(ling), 71. **CAREER** Asst prof, 71-73, ASSOC PROF LING, UNIV ILL, URBANA, 73-, Fels, Ctr Advan Study, Univ Ill, 70-71 and 78-79. **MEMBERSHIPS** MLA; Ling Soc Am. **RESEARCH** Syntax; semantics; pragmatics. **SELECTED PUBLICATIONS** Auth, The Language of Judges, Yale Law J, Vol 0103, 94; Auxiliary Inversions and the Notion Default Specification, J Ling, Vol 0032, 96. **CONTACT ADDRESS** Dept of Ling, Univ Ill, 707 S Mathews Ave, Urbana, IL, 61801-3625.

GREEN, LISA
DISCIPLINE LINGUISTICS **EDUCATION** Grambling State Univ, BS, 85; Univ Ky, MA, 87; Univ Mass, PhD, 93. **CAREER** Asst prof. **RESEARCH** Syntactic theory; African-American English syntax and semantics. **SELECTED PUBLICATIONS** Auth, Verb Phrase patterns in Black English and Creole (rev), J Pidgin Creole Lang, 94; A Unified Account of Auxiliaries in African American English, CLS, 94. **CONTACT ADDRESS** Linguistics Dept, Univ of Massachusetts, Amherst, S College 317, Amherst, MA, 01003. **EMAIL** lgreen@linguist.umass.edu

GREEN, VIRGINIA M.
DISCIPLINE FRENCH **EDUCATION** B.A., University of Puget Sound; Ph.D., Duke University. **CAREER** Asst prof; dir Assessment. **SELECTED PUBLICATIONS** Publ, sev articles on French Renaissance lit. **CONTACT ADDRESS** Dept of Eng, Phillips Univ, 100 S University Ave, PO Box 10, Enid, OK, 73701-6439. **EMAIL** vmgreen@enid.com

GREENBAUM, MICHAEL B.
PERSONAL NJ, m, 4 children **DISCIPLINE** JEWISH EDUCATION AND STUDIES **EDUCATION** Univ Miami, BS; Jewish Theol Sem, MA; Columbia Univ, PhD, 94. **CAREER** Asst prof, vice chancellor, and CEO, Jewish Theol Sem. **HONORS AND AWARDS** Secy, Nat Ramah Comm; secy, Joint Ret Bd Conser Mvmt; secy, Morningside Area Alliance; evaluator, Nat Comm Accrediting; evaluator, Mid States Asn Cols and Schls. **MEMBERSHIPS** E Asn Col and Univ Bus Officers. **RESEARCH** Louis Finkelstein. **SELECTED PUBLICATIONS** Auth, The Finkelstein Years, Tradition Renewed: A History of The Jewish Theological Seminary, 97. **CONTACT ADDRESS** Jewish Theol Sem of America, 3080 Broadway, New York, NY, 10027. **EMAIL** migreenbaum@jtsa.edu

GREENBERG, MARC L.
PERSONAL Born 11/09/1961, Los Angeles, CA, m, 1988, 2 children **DISCIPLINE** LANGUAGE; LITERATURE **EDUCATION** Univ Calif Los Angeles, BA, 83, PhD, 90; Univ Chicago, MA, 84. **CAREER** Asst prof to assoc prof, Univ Ks, 90-. **HONORS AND AWARDS** Zahvala, Republic of Slovenia, 92, NEH Res Fel, 93; Fulbright-hays Fel, 88-89. **MEMBERSHIPS** Soc of Slovene Stud, Amer Assoc of Teachers of Slavic & E Eur Lang; SE Eur Stud Assoc; Amer Assoc for the Adv of Slavic Stud. **RESEARCH** Hist Slavic & Indo-Eur ling; dialectology. **SELECTED PUBLICATIONS** Auth, Archaisms and Innovations in the Dialect of Sredisce; In Slavic Stud, 95; The vowel system of the Sredisce dialect based on the descriptions of Karel Ozvald, Rodopi, 96; The Sociolinguistics of Sloven, intro, Mouton de Gruyter, 97; auth, Sound Repetition and Metaphorical Structure in the Igor' Tale, Slavic, 98; Is Slavic ceta an Indo-European Archaism? In J of Slavic Ling & Poetics, 99. **CONTACT ADDRESS** Dept Slavic Lang & Lit, Univ Ks, 2134 Wescoe Hall, Lawrence, KS, 66045-2174. **EMAIL** m-greenberg@ukans.edu

GREENBERG, MOSHE
PERSONAL Born 07/10/1928, Philadelphia, PA, m, 1949, 3 children **DISCIPLINE** SEMITICS **EDUCATION** Univ Pa, AB, 49, PhD(Orient studies), 54; Jewish Theol Sem Am, MHL, 54. **CAREER** Asst prof Hebrew, Univ Pa, 54-58, assoc prof, 58-61, prof Bibl studies, 61-65, Ellis prof Hebrew, 65-70; PROF BIBLE, HEBREW UNIV JERUSALEM, 70-, Ed, monogr ser, J Bibl Lit, 60-66; fel, Guggenheim Found, 61; vis lectr, Hebrew Univ, Jerusalem, 61; vis lectr, Swarthmore Col, 63; vis prof Bible, Jewish Theol Sem Am, 64-70; mem, Bible Transl Comt, Jewish Publ Soc Am, 66-; Danforth Found Harbison award, 68; acad adv Bible curriculum, Israel ministry educ, 72-. **MEMBERSHIPS** Am Orient Soc; Soc Bible Lit; Bible Colloquium; fel Am Acad Jewish Res. **RESEARCH** Biblical philology and religion. **SELECTED PUBLICATIONS** Auth, Prayer in the Hebrew Bible--The Drama of Divine-Human Dialogue, J Am Orient Soc, Vol 0115, 95; The Law of the Temple in Ezekiel-40-48, Israel Explor J, Vol 0046, 96. **CONTACT ADDRESS** Dept of Bible Hebrew, Univ of Jerusalem, Jerusalem, ..

GREENBERG, NATHAN ABRAHAM
PERSONAL Born 08/23/1928, Boston, MA, m, 1952, 3 children **DISCIPLINE** CLASSICAL PHILOLOGY **EDUCATION** Hebrew Teachers Col, Boston, BJEd, 48; Harvard Univ, AB, 50, AM, 52, PhD, 55. **CAREER** From instr to assoc prof, 56-69, assoc dean humanities, 67-68, chmn dept, 70-76, PROF CLASSICS, OBERLIN COL, 69-, Fulbright scholar, Italy, 55-56; Rockefeller Found study grant, 62-63; Am Coun Learned Soc study grant, 68; Fulbright sr res fel, Belgium, 69-70; vis fel, Wolfson Col, Oxford Univ, 76-77; Am Coun Learned Soc res fel, 76-77. **MEMBERSHIPS** AAUP; Am Philol Asn; Archaeol Inst Am; Vergilian Soc. **RESEARCH** Ancient poetics; political philosophy; computer use in literary study. **SELECTED PUBLICATIONS** Auth, The Attitude of Agamemnon: Homer, 'Iliad', Book-1, Class World, Vol 0086, 93. **CONTACT ADDRESS** Dept of Classics, Oberlin Col, King Bldg, Oberlin, OH, 44074.

GREENBERG, WENDY
PERSONAL Born 12/31/1951, Philadelphia, PA **DISCIPLINE** FRENCH, COMPARATIVE LITERATURE **EDUCATION** Columbia Univ, BA, 73, MA, 74, PhD(Fr), 79. **CAREER** Preceptor, Columbia Univ, 74-77; ASST PROF FRENCH, PA STATE UNIV, FOGELSVILLE, 79-, Nat Endowment for Humanities fel, Harvard Univ, 81. **MEMBERSHIPS** MLA; Am Asn Teachers Fr; Alliance Francaise. **RESEARCH** Theory of metaphor; Victor Hugo; 19th century French romanticism. **SELECTED PUBLICATIONS** Auth, Sous Letoile Du Chien, Fr Rev, Vol 0066, 93; The Educational Legacy of Romanticism, Fr Rev, Vol 0066, 93; Modernity and Revolution in Late-19th-Century France, Fr Rev, Vol 0067, 94; Rereading Lamartine Today, Fr Rev, Vol 0068, 95; Allons-Nous Etre Heureux, Fr Rev, Vol 0070, 97. **CONTACT ADDRESS** Pennsylvania State Univ, Univ Pk, PA, 16802.

GREENE, ROBERT WILLIAM
PERSONAL Born 01/03/1933, Boston, MA, m, 1959, 2 children **DISCIPLINE** ROMANCE LANGUAGES **EDUCATION** Boston Col, AB, 54; Middlebury Col, MA, 58; Univ Pa, PhD(Romance lang), 63. **CAREER** From instr French to asst prof, Univ Calif, Berkeley, 63-69; assoc prof, Univ Iowa, 69-74; vis prof, 74-75, PROF FRENCH, STATE UNIV NY, ALBANY, 75-, Am Coun Learned Soc grant-in-aid, 73; Am Philos Soc grant, 75; Nat Endowment for Humanities res fel, 80-81. **MEMBERSHIPS** MLA; Am Asn Teachers Fr; Northeastern Mod Lang Asn. **RESEARCH** Modern French poetry and fiction. **SELECTED PUBLICATIONS** Auth, Lost Beyond Telling--Representations of Death and Absence in Modern French Poetry, Fr Forum, Vol 0017, 92; The Presence of the Image--Bonnefoy, Yves Critique of 9 Painters and Sculptors, Fr Forum, Vol 0021, 96; When Apollinaire, Malraux and Bonnefoy Write about Art, Esprit Createur, Vol 0036, 96. **CONTACT ADDRESS** Dept of French, State Univ of NY, Albany, NY, 12222.

GREENFIELD, JONAS CARL
PERSONAL Born 10/30/1926, New York, NY, m, 1950, 3 children **DISCIPLINE** HEBREW AND SEMITIC LANGUAGES **EDUCATION** City Col New York, BSS, 49; Yale Univ, MA, 51, PhD(Near Eastern lang), 56. **CAREER** Instr Semitics, Brandeis Univ, 54-56; from asst prof to assoc prof Hebrew, Univ Calif, Los Angeles, 56-65; prof, Univ Calif, Berkeley, 65-71; PROF ANCIENT SEMITIC LANG, HEBREW UNIV JERUSALEM 71-, Lectr grad sch, Univ Judaism, 57-68; Guggenheim fel and Fulbright travel fel, 63-64; Am Coun Learned Soc/Soc Sci Res Coun fel, 68-69; Fulbright-Hays fel, 68-69; trustee, W F Albright Inst Archaeol Res, 69-; mem transl comt, Psalms, Jewish Publ Soc, 73; vis prof, Brandeis Univ, 74-75; ED, ISRAEL EXPLORATION J, 76-. **MEMBERSHIPS** Am Orient Soc; Soc Bible Lit; Am Acad Jewish Res; Am Schs Orient Res; Ling Soc Am. **RESEARCH** Semitic philology; Iranian studies; history and culture of ancient Near East. **SELECTED PUBLICATIONS** Auth, Kerets Dream, Dhrt and Hdrt: the Importance of the Dream in the Keret Epic from Ugarit, Bull of Sch of Orient and African Stud-Univ London, Vol 0057, 94; Babathas Ketubba, Israel Explor J, Vol 0044, 94; The Prayer of Levi: Reconstruction of the Aramaic (4qtlevi-A) and the Greek (Athos, Cod.39, No.3108) Manuscripts, An Inspection of the Characteristics, Translation, Possible Reconstruction of and Commentary on the Document, J Biblical Lit; Untitled--Reply, Va Mag of Hist and Biogr, Vol 0103, 95; Let Us Cross-over the River--the Final Illness of Jackson, Stonewall, Va Mag of Hist and Biogr, Vol 0103, 95. **CONTACT ADDRESS** Dept of Semitic Lang, Hebrew Univ, Jerusalem, ..

GREENFIELD, SUMNER M.
PERSONAL Born 12/13/1921, Boston, MA, m, 1946, 2 children **DISCIPLINE** SPANISH **EDUCATION** Boston Col, AB, 44; Boston Univ, AM, 47; Harvard Univ, AM, 51, PhD(Romance lang), 57. **CAREER** From instr to assoc prof, 51-67, PROF SPAN, UNIV MASS, AMHERTS, 67-. **MEMBERSHIPS** MLA; Am Asn Teachers Span & Port; New England Coun Latin Am Studies. **RESEARCH** Twentieth century Spanish literature; the modernist movement. **SELECTED PUBLICATIONS** Auth, The Funambulesque Muse, the Poetics of Carnivalization in Valleinclan--Spanish, Hisp Rev, Vol 0061, 93; Theater in Spain Between the Tradition and the Avant-Garde (1918-1939), Anales de la Lit Espanola Contemporanea, Vol 0019, 94; Valleinclan and the Theater, Innovation in la 'Cabeza Del Dragon', El 'Embrujado' and la 'Marquesa Rosalinda,' Anales de la Lit Espanola Contemporanea, Vol 0020, 95; Valle-Inclan and the Theater--Innovation in la 'Cabeza Del Dragon', El 'Embrujado', and la 'Marquesa Rosalinda,' Anales de la Lit Espanola Contemporanea, Vol 0021, 96; Nada, Anales de la Lit Espanola Contemporanea, Vol 0021, 96. **CONTACT ADDRESS** Dept of Span and Port, Univ of Mass, Amherst, MA, 01003.

GREGORY, ELMER RICHARD
PERSONAL Born 09/25/1938, Baytown, TX, m, 1967, 1 child **DISCIPLINE** ENGLISH, COMPARATIVE LITERATURE **EDUCATION** Univ Tex, Austin, BA, 60; Rice Univ, MA, 61; Univ Ore, PhD(comp lit), 65. **CAREER** Asst prof English, Univ Ga, 65-67; from asst prof to assoc prof, 67-77, PROF ENGLISH, UNIV TOLEDO, 77-. **MEMBERSHIPS** Conf Christianity and Lit; Milton Soc Am; MLA. **RESEARCH** John Milton; 17th century British literature; detective stories. **SELECTED PUBLICATIONS** Auth, Milton and Tradition, Milton Stud, Vol 0029, 92; Moore, Marianne 'Poetry,' Explicator, Vol 0052, 93; Milton Protestant Sonnet Lady--Revisions in the Donna-Angelicata Tradition, Comp Lit Stud, Vol 0033, 96. **CONTACT ADDRESS** Dept of English, Univ of Toledo, Toledo, OH, 43606.

GRENOBLE, LENORE A.
DISCIPLINE RUSSIAN LANGUAGE AND LITERATURE **EDUCATION** Univ CA Berkeley, PhD, 86. **CAREER** Assoc prof and chr, Prog Ling and Cog Sci. **RESEARCH** Semantics and discourse analysis; Slavic and Tungusic lang(s); deixis; verbal categories; lang endangerment. **SELECTED PUBLICATIONS** Auth, Deixis and Information Packaging in Russian Discourse, Pragmatics and Beyond, Cambridge UP; Deixis, thematic structure and participant tracking in Russian discourse, Papers 2nd Int Conf Deixis, 96; coauth, The Role of Deictics in Discourse Coherence: French voici/voila and Russian vot/von, Jour Pragmatics, 96; Endangered Languages: Current Issues and Future Prospects, Int Jour Soc Lang, 96; ed, Essays in the Art and Theory of Translation, Edwin Mellen, 97. **CONTACT ADDRESS** Dartmouth Col, 44 N College St, #208, Hanover, NH, 03755-1801. **EMAIL** lenore.grenoble@dartmouth.edu

GREPPIN, JOHN AIRD COUTTS
PERSONAL Born 04/02/1937, Rochester, NY, m, 2 children **DISCIPLINE** LINGUISTICS **EDUCATION** Univ Rochester, AB, 61; Univ Wash, MA, 66; Univ Calif, Los Angeles, PhD, 72. **CAREER** Asst prof, Univ Fla, 71-72; asst prof, Cleveland State Univ, 75-80; assoc prof, 80-83; full prof, 83-; vis prof, Philipp's Univ, 93. **HONORS AND AWARDS** Russell Mumford Tuttle Award for Proficiency in Greek, Univ Rochester, 61; Silver medal, Melchiatarist Congregation, Venice, Italy; recipient of numerous IREX grants, NEH fellowships, and other grants., ACLS fel, 65; NEH fel, 66, 67, 69, 78; IREX grant, 79; AGBU Alex Manoogian grant, 79-95. **MEMBERSHIPS** Am Philol Asn; Am Oriental Soc; Soc Armenian Studies. **RESEARCH** Classical and Middle Armenian Philology; Classics; Indo-European linguistics. **SELECTED PUBLICATIONS** Auth, A Medieval Arabic-Armenian Pharmaceutical Dictionary, Vienna, Mechitaristen-Buch-druckerei, Studien zur armenischen Geschichte XVI, 97; co-ed, Studies in Honor of Jaan Puhvel, Part I: Ancient Languages and Philology, J Indo-Europ Studies Monograph No 20, Inst for the Study of Man, 97; Studies in Honor of Jaan Puhvel, Part II: Mythology and Religion, J Indo-Europ Studies Monograph No 21, Inst for the Study of Man, 97; auth, The Diffusion of Greek Medicine into the Middle East and the Caucasus, Curzon Press (forthcoming 99); author and editor of numerous other books and articles. **CONTACT ADDRESS** Program in Ling, Cleveland State Univ, 1983 E 24th St, Cleveland, OH, 44115-2440. **EMAIL** j.greppin@csuohio.edu

GRIBBLE, CHARLES EDWARD
PERSONAL Born 11/10/1936, Lansing, MI **DISCIPLINE** SLAVIC LANGUAGES **EDUCATION** Univ MI, BA, 57; Harvard Univ, AM, 58, PhD, 67. **CAREER** From lectr to asst prof Russ, Brandeis Univ, 61-68; asst prof Slavic, Ind Univ, Bloomington, 68-75, asst chmn dept Slavic lang & lit & dir Slavic Workshop, 68-70; assoc prof, 75-88, Prof Slavic Lang, OH State Univ, 88-, chmn dept, 90-96; Pres, Slavica Publ, 68-97; Slavic area fel, 72; partic sr scholar exchange to USSR, Int Res & Exchanges Bd, 72. **HONORS AND AWARDS** Phi Beta Kappa; Phi Kappa Phi; Phi Eta Sigma; Boynton Sch, 56-57 **MEMBERSHIPS** Ling Soc Am; Am Asn Tchr Slavic & East Europ Lang; Am Asn Advan Slavic Studies; Am Asn Southeast Europ Studies; Ling Soc Europe; MLA. **RESEARCH** Hist and struct of Russ; comp Slavic linguistics; South Slavic lang(s). **SELECTED PUBLICATIONS** Ed, Studies Presented to Professor Roman Jakobson by His Students, 68, auth, Russian Root List with a Sketch of Russian Word Formation, 73, Medieval Slavic Texts, vol I, 73 & A Short Dictionary of 18th Century Russian, 76, Slavica. **CONTACT ADDRESS** Dept of Slavic Lang, Ohio State Univ, 1841 Millikin Rd, Columbus, OH, 43210-1229. **EMAIL** gribble3@osu.edu

GRIFFEN, TOBY DAVID
PERSONAL Born 05/12/1946, Washington, DC **DISCIPLINE** LINGUISTICS, GERMAN **EDUCATION** The Citadel, BA, 68; Univ Va, MA, 69; Univ Fla, PhD(ling). **CAREER** Asst prof Ger, Wichita State Univ, 75-77; ASST PROF GER, SOUTHERN ILL UNIV, EDWARDSVILLE, 77-, Res scholar award, Southern Ill Univ, Edwardsville, 78. **MEMBERSHIPS** Ling Asn Can and US; Int Ling Asn; Int Soc Phonetic Sci; Am Asn Teachers Ger. **RESEARCH** Nonsegmental model of phonology; Germanic/Indo-European sound shifting; methodology of teaching pronunciation. **SELECTED PUBLICATIONS** Auth, Germano-European and the Phonetic Plausibility Theory, Word-J Int Ling Asn, Vol 0044, 93. **CONTACT ADDRESS** Dept Foreign Lang, Southern Ill Univ, 6 Hairpin Dr, Edwardsville, IL, 62026-0001.

GRIFFIN, DAVID ALEXANDER
PERSONAL Born 01/25/1919, Buffalo, NY, m, 1942, 5 children **DISCIPLINE** ROMANCE LANGUAGES **EDUCATION** Univ Chicago, AB, 47, AM, 49, PhD(Span), 56. **CAREER** Instr Romance lang, Oberlin Col, 52-56; vis asst prof Span, Newcomb Col, Tulane Univ, 56-57; asst prof mod lang, Univ Okla, 57-59; sci linguist and asst head dept Southwestern Europ and Latin Am lang, Foreign Serv Inst, US Dept State, 59-61; assoc prof Romance lang, 61-74, acting chmn dept, 71-72, PROF ROMANCE LANG, OHIO STATE UNIV, 74-, CHMN DEPT, 72-. **MEMBERSHIPS** Ling Soc Am; Int Ling Asn; Ling Soc Europe. **RESEARCH** General linguistics; Romance linguistics; Spanish dialectology. **SELECTED PUBLICATIONS** Auth, On the Origin of Spanish Eres, Hisp Rev, Vol 0062, 94. **CONTACT ADDRESS** Dept of Romance Lang, Ohio State Univ, 190 N Oval Dr, Columbus, OH, 43210.

GRIFFIN, JOHN R.
PERSONAL Born 03/31/1938 **DISCIPLINE** ENGLISH, HISTORY **EDUCATION** Xavier Univ, BS, 59, AM, 61; Univ Paris, cert, 60; Univ Ottawa, PhD(English), 63; Trinity Col, Dublin, PhD(hist), 72. **CAREER** Vis prof Am lit, Univ Torino, 59-60; from asst prof to assoc prof, 63-73, PROF ENGLISH LIT, SOUTHERN COLO STATE COL, 73-, Ital Govt fel, Ciriolo Italiano, Italy, 68; consult, Choice Mag, 73-74. **MEM-**

BERSHIPS MLA; Rocky Mountain Mod Lang Asn. RESEARCH Medieval, Renaissance and Victorian periods. SELECTED PUBLICATIONS Auth, Newman after 100-Years, Church Hist, Vol 0062, 93; Before Infallibility--Liberal Catholicism in Biedermeier Vienna, Church Hist, Vol 0062, 93; Thrown among Strangers--Newman,John,Henry in Ireland, Cath Hist Rev, Vol 0079, 93; Newman and Heresy--The Anglican Years, Church Hist, Vol 0064, 95; The Great-Dissent--Newman, John, Henry and the Liberal Heresy, Church Hist, Vol 0064, 95; Newman, John, Henry--Sermons 1824-1843, Church Hist, Vol 0065, 96; Newman, John, Henry--Selected Sermons, Church Hist, Vol 0065, 96; 2 Cardinals--Newman, J. H., Mercier, D. J., Church Hist, Vol 0066, 97, The Letters and Diaries of Newman, John, Henry, Vol 7--Editing the 'British Critic', January 1839 to December 1840, Church Hist, Vol 0066, 97. CONTACT ADDRESS Univ Southern Colo, Pueblo, CO, 81001.

GRIGGS, JOHN W.
PERSONAL Born 10/05/1948, Three Rivers, MI, d **DISCIPLINE** FOREIGN LANGUAGE **EDUCATION** Ariz State Univ, BA, 70, MA, 71, PhD, 83. **CAREER** Chemn, 71-, Glendale Comm Col. **MEMBERSHIPS** AATSP **RESEARCH** Spanish civil war; modern Spanish poetry, drama, novel. **CONTACT ADDRESS** Glendale Comm Col, Arizona, 600 W Olive Ave, Glendale, AZ, 85302. **EMAIL** griggs@gc.maricopa.edu

GRIMSTAD, KAAREN
DISCIPLINE OLD ICELANDIC LANGUAGE AND LITERATURE **EDUCATION** Harvard Univ, PhD. **CAREER** Assoc prof, Univ Minn, Twin Cities. **RESEARCH** Children's literature. **SELECTED PUBLICATIONS** Auth, Text Editing as Dialogue, Ger Stud in Honor of Anatoly Liberman, Nowele 31/32, Odense UP, 97; coauth, Munu vit ekki at thve aettask: A Closer Look at Dialogues in Hrafnkels saga, Arkiv for nordisk filologi 111, 96. **CONTACT ADDRESS** Dept of Ger, Scand & Dutch, Univ Minn, Twin Cities, 231 Folwel, Minneapolis, MN, 55455. **EMAIL** grims001@tc.umn.edu

GRISE, YOLANDE
PERSONAL Born 08/05/1944, Montreal, PQ, Canada **DISCIPLINE** FRENCH LITERATURE **EDUCATION** Univ Montreal, BA, 64, BPed, 65; Univ Laval, LL, 71; Univ Sorbonne, ML, 72, DL 3e cycle, 77. **CAREER** Prof hist, Univ Laval, 78-79; prof adj, 80, prof agregee, 83, PROF LITTERATURE, LETTRES FRANCAISES, UNIV OTTAWA, 80-, prof titulaire, 90. **HONORS AND AWARDS** Boursiere, Govt Que, 71-72, 72-75; Conseil des arts du Can, 72-75. **MEMBERSHIPS** Soc des etudes latines (Paris); l'Union des ecrivains quebecois; l'Assoc des etudes canadiennes; l'Assoc des litt can et quebecoise. **SELECTED PUBLICATIONS** Auth, Le suicide dans la Rome antique, 82; auth, Textes litteraires de l'Ontario francais, 82; auth, Le Monde des dieux, 85; auth, Les arts visuels en Ontario francais, 90; coauth, RSVP! Clefs en main/RSVP! Keys to the Future, 91; co-dir, Melanges de litterature canadienne-francaise et quebecoise offerts a Rejean Robidoux, 92; co-dir, Emile Nelligan, Cinquante ans apres sa mort, 93; ed, Les Etats generaux de la recherche sur la francophonie a l'exterieur du Quebec, 95. **CONTACT ADDRESS** Dep des lettres francaises, Univ Ottawa, Ottawa, ON, K1N 6N5.

GRITTNER, FRANK MERTON
PERSONAL Born 02/12/1927, Ashland, WI, m, 1949, 5 children **DISCIPLINE** FOREIGN LANGUAGES **EDUCATION** Northland Col, BA, 50; Univ Wis, MA, 52, PhD(foreign lang educ), 72. **CAREER** Teacher Ger, Fond du Lac Pub Schs, Wis, 52-56; teacher Ger and Span, Madison Pub Schs, 56-60; STATE SUPVR FOREIGN LANG, WIS DEPT PUB INSTR, 60-, Comt mem, MLA studies of effectiveness of NDEA Title XI Foreign Lang Summer Inst Prog, 67; ed, Cent States Conf Teaching Foreign Lang publ, 68-74; educ auditor, Milwaukee Biling Prog, and State Off Educ ESEA Title VII grant, 69-72. **MEMBERSHIPS** Am Coun Teaching Foreign Lang (pres, 75); Am Asn Teachers Ger (pres, 84); Cent States Conf Teaching Foreign Lang; Asn Dept Foreign Lang (secy, 65-68); Nat Coun State Supvr Foreign Lang (pres, 64-65). **RESEARCH** History of foreign language acquisition. **SELECTED PUBLICATIONS** Auth, In a Class by Itself--Focus on Instruction, For Lang Ann, Vol 0026, 93; Curriculum Renewal in School Foreign-Language Learning, Mod Lang J, Vol 0077, 93; In a Class by Itself--Focus on Instruction, For Lang Ann, Vol 0027, 94; In a Class by Itself--Focus on Instruction, For Lang Ann, Vol 0028, 95; Toward a Definition of Learning-Disabled (LD) as Applied to the Foreign-Language Student, For Lang Ann, Vol 0028, 95; Strategies and Techniques in Foreign-Language Teaching--Introduction, For Lang Ann, Vol 0029, 96; In a Class by Itself--Focus on Instruction, For Lang Ann, Vol 0029, 96; Introduction to this Special Edition on Culture, For Lang Ann, Vol 0029, 96; Focus on Illustration, For Lang Ann, Vol 0030, 97. **CONTACT ADDRESS** Dept Pub Instr, PO Box 7841, Madison, WI, 53707.

GROCH, JOHN R.
DISCIPLINE COMPUTER-MEDIATED COMMUNICATION **EDUCATION** PhD **CAREER** Coordr, Commun Stud in Continuing Educ. **RESEARCH** Film; mass cult; postmodernism. **SELECTED PUBLICATIONS** Written on, popularity of The Wizard of Oz & comic authorship in the films of the Marx Brothers. **CONTACT ADDRESS** Commun Dept, Chatham Col, Woodland Rd., Pittsburgh, PA, 15232.

GROSS, DAVID STUART
PERSONAL Born 02/22/1942, Mineola, NY, m, 1971, 1 child **DISCIPLINE** ENGLISH, COMPARATIVE LITERATURE **EDUCATION** Wesleyan Univ, BA, 65; Univ Iowa, MA, 69, PhD(comp lit), 73. **CAREER** Asst prof English, Winona State Col, 71-73; ASST PROF ENGLISH, UNIV OKLA, 73-. **MEMBERSHIPS** MLA; Soc Amis Flaubert. **RESEARCH** The novel; literature and society; Marxist theory. **SELECTED PUBLICATIONS** Auth, Minor Prophecies--The Literary Essay in the Culture Wars, World Lit Today, Vol 0067, 93; Rethinking Theory--A Critique of Contemporary Literary-Theory and an Alternative Account, World Lit Today, Vol 0067, 93; Cultural Criticism, Literary-Theory, Poststructuralism, World Lit Today, Vol 0068, 94; The Idea of the Postmodern--A History, World Lit Today, Vol 0069, 95; Public-Access--Literary-Theory and American Cultural Politics, World Lit Today, Vol 0069, 95; The Institution of Theory, World Lit Today, Vol 0069, 95. **CONTACT ADDRESS** Dept of English, Univ of Okla, Norman, OK, 73069.

GROSS, SABINE
PERSONAL Born 09/11/1957, Frankfurt, Germany **DISCIPLINE** GERMAN LITERATURE **EDUCATION** Univ Calif - Santa Barbara, PhD, 91. **CAREER** Asst Prof, 92-97, Assoc Prof, Univ Wis - Madison, 97-. **MEMBERSHIPS** MLA; AATG; Women in Ger; IVG; IAPL; Int Soc Study of Time. **RESEARCH** 20th-century German literature; literary theory; reader response & narratology; theater; film; study of time. **SELECTED PUBLICATIONS** Auth, Lese-Zeichen: Kognition, Medium und Materialitut im Leseprozea, Wissenschaftliche Buchgesellschaft, 94; Narrative Time and the Reader, Semiotics Around the World: Synthesis in Diversity. IASS Congress Proceedings, Mouton de Gruyter, 97; The World Turned Image: Reading Pattern Poems, Poetics Today, Spring 97; Cognitive Readings or the Disappearance of Literature in the Mind, Poetics Today, Summer 97; ed, Monatshefte, Winter 97; author of numerous other articles and book chapters. **CONTACT ADDRESS** Univ Wisconsin Madison, 1220 Linden Dr., Madison, WI, 53706.

GROSSFELD, BERNARD
PERSONAL Born 06/13/1933, Vienna, Austria, m, 1964, 3 children **DISCIPLINE** HEBREW LANGUAGE AND LITERATURE **EDUCATION** Univ Calif, Los Angeles, BA, 59, Berkeley, MA, 62; Johns Hopkins Univ, PhD(Near Eastern studies), 68. **CAREER** Chaplain, US Air Force, 62-64; grad student Near Eastern studies, Johns Hopkins Univ, 64-68; asst prof, 69-73, chmn dept, 70-73, assoc prof, 73-80, PROF HEBREW AND ARAMAIC, UNIV WIS-MILWAUKEE, 80-, Chmn Dept, 76-. **MEMBERSHIPS** Soc Biblical Lit; Am Orient Soc; Asn Jewish Studies; Asn Targumic Studies; Nat Asn Prof Hebrew. **RESEARCH** Targum, Aramaic Bible translation; Bible language and literature; Rabbinic language and literature. **SELECTED PUBLICATIONS** Auth, A Grammar of the Palestinian Targum Fragments from the Cairo-Genizah, J Biblical Lit, Vol 0111, 92; The Dialect of the Ahiqar Proverbs, J Biblical Lit, Vol 0113, 94; Studies in the Targum to the 12 Prophets--From Nahum to Malachi, J Am Orient Soc, Vol 0116, 96. **CONTACT ADDRESS** Dept of Hebrew Studies, Univ of Wis, Curtin Hall 904, Milwaukee, WI, 53201.

GROSSI, VERONICA
DISCIPLINE ROMANCE LANGUAGES **EDUCATION** Univ Tex, Austin, MA, 90, PhD, 96. **CAREER** Lectr, Univ Tex, Austin, 96-99; asst prof, Univ NC, Greensboro, 97. **CONTACT ADDRESS** Dept of Romance Langs, Univ of No Carolina, Greensboro, 321 McIver Bldg, PO Box 26170, Greensboro, NC, 27402-6170. **EMAIL** vgrossi@uncg.edu

GROSSMAN, JOAN DELANEY
PERSONAL Born 12/12/1928, Dubuque, IA **DISCIPLINE** SLAVIC LANGUAGES **EDUCATION** Clarke Col, AB, 52; Columbia Univ, MA, 62; Harvard Univ, PhD(Slavic lang & lit), 67. **CAREER** Asst prof Russ, Mundelein Col, 67-68; asst prof, 68-80, ASSOC PROF SLAVIC LANG AND LIT, UNIV CALIF, BERKELEY, 80-, Consult, US-USSR summer lang teachers enchange, Int Res and Exchanges Bd, 69-72; Am Coun Learned Soc fel, 71-72; Guggenheim fel, 78-79. **MEMBERSHIPS** Am Asn Advan Slavic Studies; Western Slavic Asn; Mod Lang Asn. **RESEARCH** Russian literary and cultural trends at the end of the 19th and the early 20th century; Russian novel. **SELECTED PUBLICATIONS** Auth, The Perception of English Literature in Russia--Investigations and Materials, Russ Rev, Vol 0055, 96. **CONTACT ADDRESS** Dept of Slavic Lang, Univ of Calif, 366 Le Conte Hall, Berkeley, CA, 94720-7301.

GROSSMAN, KATHRYN MARIE
PERSONAL Born 12/06/1945, New York, NY **DISCIPLINE** FRENCH LITERATURE, UTOPIAN STUDIES **EDUCATION** Bryn Mawr Col, AB, 67; Yale Univ, MPhil, 70, PhD(Romance lang), 73. **CAREER** Asst prof, 73-80, ASSOC PROF FRENCH LANG AND LIT, PA STATE UNIV, 81-, ACTG ASST DEAN, COL LIB ARTS, 82-. **MEMBERSHIPS** MLA; Am Asn Teachers Fr; Am Coun Teaching Foreign Lang; Soc Utopian Studies; Am Asn Advan Humanities. **RESEARCH** Victor Hugo (prose fiction); romanticism; utopias. **SELECTED PUBLICATIONS** Auth, The Mysteries of Paris and London, 19th-Century Fr Stud, Vol 0024, 95. **CONTACT ADDRESS** Pennsylvania State Univ, University Pk, PA, 16802.

GROSSVOGEL, DAVID I.
PERSONAL Born 06/19/1925, San Francisco, CA, d, 2 children **DISCIPLINE** FRENCH, ROMANCE STUDIES **EDUCATION** Univ Calif, BA, 49; Univ Grenoble, cert, 50; Columbia Univ, MA, 51, PhD(French), 54. **CAREER** Instr French lang & lit, Columbia Univ, 53-56; vis lectr, Harvard Univ, 56-57, asst prof Romance lit, 57-60; assoc prof Romance Studies, 60-64, prof, 64-70, GOLDWIN SMITH PROF COMP LIT & ROMANCE STUDIES, CORNELL UNIV, 70-; Fulbright fel, Paris, 59-60; Guggenheim fel, 63-64; found & ed, Diacritics, 71-. **MEMBERSHIPS** MLA **RESEARCH** Criticism; cinema; modern European literature. **SELECTED PUBLICATIONS** Auth, Self-Conscious Stage, Columbia Univ; Anouilh's Antigone, Integral Ed, 58; Four Playwrights and a Postscript, Cornell Univ, 62; Sagan's Bonjour Tristesse, Integral Ed, 64; Limits of the Novel, Cornell Univ, 68; co-ed, Divided We Stand: Reflections on the Crisis at Cornell, Doubleday, 70; Mystery and Its Ficitons: From Oedipus to Agatha Christie, Johns Hopkins Univ, 79; Dear Ann Landers, Contemporary Books, 87; coauth, Changing Channels: America in T V Guide, Univ Ill Press, 92. **CONTACT ADDRESS** Dept of Romance Studies, Cornell Univ, 203 Morrill Hall, Ithaca, NY, 14853-4701. **EMAIL** dig3@cornell.edu

GROSZ, ELIZABETH
DISCIPLINE COMPARATIVE LITERATURE **CAREER** Fac dept philos, Monash Univ; Julian Park Prof Comp Lit, 99. **SELECTED PUBLICATIONS** Auth, Crossing Boundaries: Feminisms and the Critique of Knowledges, 88; Jacques Lacan: A Feminist Introduction, 90; Sexual Subversions: Three French Feminists, 89; Sexy Bodies: The Strange Carnalities of Feminism, 95; Space, Time and Perversion: Essays on the Politics of Bodies, 95; Volatile Bodies: Toward a Corporeal Feminism, 94. **CONTACT ADDRESS** Dept Comp Lit, SUNY Buffalo, 639 Clemens Hall, Buffalo, NY, 14260. **EMAIL** egrosz@acsu.buffalo.edu

GROTANS, ANNA A.
PERSONAL Born 03/23/1962, Minneapolis, MN **DISCIPLINE** FOREIGN LANGUAGE **EDUCATION** Univ Minn, BA, 84, PhD, 92; Univ Toronto, MA, 85. **CAREER** Asst prof, Brigham Young Univ, 92-93; asst prof, Ohio State Univ, 93-. **HONORS AND AWARDS** DAAD, 88-89; Tchg Fulbright, 89-90; NEH Summer Stipen, 97; Fulbright Jr Res, 97-98. **MEMBERSHIPS** Medieval Acad; AATG; MLA; AABS. **RESEARCH** Medieval German studies; Paleography. **SELECTED PUBLICATIONS** Coauth, art, Pride and Prejudice: Notker Labeo and his Editors, 94; coauth, art, The Altdeutsche Textbibliothek Notker Labeo Edition, 95; coauth, The St. Gall Tractate: A Classroom Guide to Rhetorical Syntax, 95; auth, art, Notker's De rhetorica in Early Modern Bavaria, 96; auth, art, Sih tir selbo lector: Lexical and Graphic Cues for Reading in Tenth-Century St. Gall, 97. **CONTACT ADDRESS** Dept of German, Ohio State Univ, 314 Cunz Hall, Columbus, OH, 43210-1229. **EMAIL** grotans.1@osu.edu

GROTON, ANNE H.
PERSONAL Born 04/08/1954, Oak Park, IL **DISCIPLINE** CLASSICAL STUDIES **EDUCATION** Wellesley Coll, AB, 76; Univ of Michigan, MA. 77, PhD 82. **CAREER** Asst Prof, Assoc Prof to Prof, 81-, St Olaf Coll. **HONORS AND AWARDS** Award for Excellence in the Tchg of Class, Amer Philos Assoc. **MEMBERSHIPS** Amer Philos Assoc; Class Assoc Middle West and South; Class Assoc of Minnesota; Amer Soc Papyrologists; Vergilian Soc. **RESEARCH** Ancient Greek and Roman Drama, especially comedy. **SELECTED PUBLICATIONS** Auth, From Alpha to Omega: A Beginning Course in Classical Greek, Focus Publishing, 95. **CONTACT ADDRESS** Dept Classics, St Olaf Coll, 1520 St Olaf Ave, Northfield, MN, 55057-1098. **EMAIL** groton@stolaf.edu

GRUBISIC, VINKO
PERSONAL Born 04/05/1943, Posuski Gradac, Bosnia and Herzegovina **DISCIPLINE** SLAVIC LITERATURE **EDUCATION** Aix En Provence Univ, PhD, 74. **SELECTED PUBLICATIONS** Auth, O Hrvatskom Jeziku, Ziral, 75; Grafija hrvatske lapidarne cirilice, 78; Bibliography of the Croatian Language, Norval, 87; Elementary Croatian I, Zagreb, 94; Druzenje s tijelom, Napredak, 95; Elementary Croatian II, Zagreb, 96; coauth, Illustrated Dictionary for Children, Zagreb, 89. **CONTACT ADDRESS** Dept of German and Slavic Literature, Waterloo Univ, 200 University Ave W, Waterloo, ON, N2L 3G1. **EMAIL** vggrubis@artshh.watstar.uwaterloo.ca

GRUNER, CHARLES R.
PERSONAL Born 11/06/1931, Pinckneyville, IL, m, 1958, 2 children **DISCIPLINE** SPEECH COMMUNICATION **EDU-**

CATION Southern Ill Univ, BS, 55, MA, 56; The Ohio State Univ, PhD, 63. **CAREER** Grad asst in Speech Dept, 55-56, res asst & res assoc, Southern Ill Univ, 63-64; teacher of speech, Webster Groves High School, 56-57; instr, 57-60, asst prof, St. Lawrence Univ, 60-64; asst prof, 64-66, assoc prof, Univ of Neb, 66-69; Ed, GA Speecj Commun J, 75-77, Assoc Prof, 69-74, Prof, Univ of GA, 74-. **HONORS AND AWARDS** Eagle Scout, 46-. **MEMBERSHIPS** Int Soc for General Semantics; Southern Speech Commun Asn; Ga Speech Asn; Am Inst of Parliamentarians; Workshop Libr on World Humor; Int Soc for Humor Studies. **SELECTED PUBLICATIONS** Auth, The Game of Humor: A Comprehensive Theory of Why We Laugh, Transaction Pub, 97; Parliamentary Procedure as the Major Part of a Course in Problem-Solving, Parliamentary J, 94; Appreciation and Understanding of Satire: Another Quasi-Experiment, Psychol Reports, 96; The Teachin/Research Symbiosis: A Two-Way Street, ERIC Clearinghouse on Reading, English, and Commun, 95; Satire as Persusion, ERIC Document ED, microfische; coauth, Evaluative Responses to Jokes in Informative Speech With and Without Laughter by an Audience: A Partial Replication, Psychol Reports, 94; Semantic Differential Measurements of Connotations of Verbal Terms and Their Doublespeak Facsimiles in Sentence Context, Psychol Reports, 95. **CONTACT ADDRESS** Dept of Speech Communication, Univ of Georgia, Athens, GA, 30602. **EMAIL** cgruner@uga

GRUNFELD, MIHAI
DISCIPLINE LATIN AMERICAN LITERATURE **EDUCATION** Univ Toronto, Can, BA; Univ Mich, Arbor, MA; Univ Calif, PhD. **CAREER** Act in, Latin Amer stud prog & Int stud prog **RESEARCH** Modern Latin American poetry, especially the Avant-Garde, representation of indigenous culture in Latin America.. **CONTACT ADDRESS** Dept of Hispanic Studies, Vassar Col, Mail Drop 451, Poughkeepsie, NY, 12604-0451. **EMAIL** grunfeld@vassar.edu

GRUZINSKA, ALEKSANDRA
PERSONAL Poznan, Poland **DISCIPLINE** FRENCH LANGUAGE AND LITERATURE **EDUCATION** State Univ NY, Buffalo, BA, 64, MA, 66; Pa State Univ, PhD(French), 73. **CAREER** Instr, Rosary Hill Col, 65-68; instr, Sweet Briar Col, 71-73; ASST PROF FRENCH, ARIZ STATE UNIV, 73-. **MEMBERSHIPS** MLA; AAUP **RESEARCH** E M Cioran; the French short story in the nineteenth century; Octave Mirbeau. **SELECTED PUBLICATIONS** Auth, Mirabeau, Octave--Proceedings from the International-Colloquium-Of-Angers from September 19 To September 22, 1991, 19th-Century Fr Stud, Vol 0022, 94; Mirbeau, Octave--'Amours Cocasses', 'Noces Parisiennes,' 19th-Century Fr Stud, Vol 0024, 96; Mirbeau Fictions, 19th-Century Fr Stud, Vol 0025, 97; Petits Poemes Parisiens, 19th-Century Fr Stud, Vol 0025, 97. **CONTACT ADDRESS** Dept of Foreign Lang, Arizona State Univ, Tempe, Tempe, AZ, 85281.

GUALTIERI, ANTONIO ROBERTO
PERSONAL Born 03/08/1931, Toronto, ON, Canada, m, 1955, 4 children **DISCIPLINE** COMPARATIVE RELIGION, PHILOSOPHY OF RELIGION **EDUCATION** McGill Univ, BA, 60, BD, 61, STM, 63, PhD(hist of relig), 69. **CAREER** Minister, United Church of Can, 56-64; instr relig, Vassar Col, 65-66, lectr relig and chaplain, 66-67; asst prof, 67-70, assoc prof, 70-81, PROF RELIG, CARLETON UNIV, 81-, Can Coun res grant, India study, 72-73. **MEMBERSHIPS** Can Soc Studies Relig; Can Theol Soc; Am Acad Relig. **RESEARCH** Methodology and epistemology in religion; religious indigenization and syncretism; religious ethics. **SELECTED PUBLICATIONS** Auth, Religious Cosmologies as Justifications of Moralities, Stud in Relig-Sci Religieuses, Vol 0022, 93; Founders and Apostates: Radical Contradictions between Soteriological Programs of the Founders of Great Religious Traditions and the Transformative Intentions of Devotees, J Am Acad of Relig, Vol 0061, 93. **CONTACT ADDRESS** Dept of Religion, Carleton Univ, 1125 Colonel By Dr, Ottawa, ON, K1S 5B6.

GUERRO, MARIA C.M. DE
PERSONAL Born 05/26/1950, Rosario, Argentina, m, 1974, 2 children **DISCIPLINE** ENGLISH AND LINGUISTICS **EDUCATION** Univ of Miss, MA, 73; Inter-Am Univ of Puerto Rico, EdD, 90. **CAREER** LECTR, 80-81, INSTR, 81-86, ASST PROF OF ENGLISH AND LINGUISTICS, 86-90, ASSOC PROF OF ENGLISH AND LINGUISTICS, 91-96, PROF OF ENGLISH AND LINGUISTICS, INTER AM UNIV METRO, 96-. **HONORS AND AWARDS** Scholars for the Dream Travel Awd, 95; Dr. Ilia Morales Awd for Acad Excellence, Inter Am Univ Doctoral prog, 91; fulbright scholar, Univ of Miss, 72-74. **MEMBERSHIPS** Am Asn of Applied Linguistics; Teachers of English to Speakers of Other Languages Int (TESOL); TESOL Puerto Rico; Int Reading Asn. **RESEARCH** Second language learning and tchg; socio-cultural theory. **SELECTED PUBLICATIONS** Coauth, Assessing the impact of peer revision on L2 writing, Applied Linguistics, 98; Peer revision in L2 classroom: Social-Cognitive activities, mediating strategies, and aspects of social behavior, J of Second Lang Writing, 96; Social-cognitive dimensions of interaction in L2 Peer Revision, Modern Lang J, 94; auth, Forma nd functions of inner speeech in adult second language learning, Vygotskian Approaches to Second Lang Rese, Ablex Press, 94; The din phenomenon: Mental rehearsal in the second language, Foreign Lang Annals, 87. **CONTACT ADDRESS** English Dept, Inter American Univ of Puerto Rico, PO Box 191293, San Juan, PR, 00919-1293. **EMAIL** mguerre@inter.edu

GUETTI, JAMES L.
DISCIPLINE ENGLISH LANGUAGE AND LITERATURE **EDUCATION** Amherst Univ, BA; MA; Cornell, PhD. **CAREER** Prof. **RESEARCH** Philosophy of language; critical theory; modern literature. **SELECTED PUBLICATIONS** Auth, Wittgenstein and the Grammar of Literary Experience; auth, The Limits of Metaphor; Word-Magic. **CONTACT ADDRESS** Dept of English, Rutgers Univ, 510 George St, Murray Hall, New Brunswick, NJ, 08901-1167.

GUIEU, JEAN-MAX
PERSONAL Born 10/24/1943, Marseille, France **DISCIPLINE** FRENCH LITERATURE **EDUCATION** Univ Aix en Provence, Lic es Lett, 67, Maitrise de lett, 68; Univ Md, PhD(-French), 75. **CAREER** Instr ling and phonetics, Univ Aix en Provence, 67-68; instr French, Univ Md, 68-73; prof, Lycee Francais Int Wash, 73-76; ASST PROF FRENCH, SCH FOREIGN SERV, GEORGETOWN UNIV, 76-, Collabr res comt, Complete Corresp of Emile Zola, 75-. **MEMBERSHIPS** Am Asn Teachers Fr. **RESEARCH** Emile Zola's lyric dramas; literature and politics. **SELECTED PUBLICATIONS** Auth, 'Mireio' and 'Mireille'--Mistral Poem and Gounod Opera, Opera Quart, Vol 0010, 93; Bruneau, Alfred and Zola, Emile--Naturalism on the Lyric Stage, Opera Quart, Vol 0010, 94. **CONTACT ADDRESS** Dept of French Sch Foreign Serv, Georgetown Univ, Washington, DC, 20067.

GUITAR, BARRY
DISCIPLINE COMMUNCATION SCIENCES **EDUCATION** Univ Wis, PhD, 74. **CAREER** Dept Comm, Vermont Univ **SELECTED PUBLICATIONS** Auth, Stuttering: An integrated approach to its nature and treatment, Williams & Wilkins, 98; coauth, Onset timing in selected labial muscles in stutterers and non stutterers, Jour Speech Hearing Res, 88; The tonic stretch reflexes in lip, tongue, and jaw muscles, Brain Res, 79; Stuttering therapy: The relation between attitude change and long-term outcome, Jour Speech Hearing Disorders, 78. **CONTACT ADDRESS** Dept of Communication Sciences, Vermont Univ, 360 Waterman Bldg, Burlington, VT, 05405. **EMAIL** bguitar@zoo.uvm.edu

GUITART, JORGE MIGUEL
PERSONAL Born 09/15/1937, Havana, Cuba, m, 1969, 2 children **DISCIPLINE** SPANISH, LINGUISTICS **EDUCATION** George Washington Univ, BA, 67; Georgetown Univ, MS, 70, PhD, 73. **CAREER** Tchg fel, Georgetown Univ, 69-71, instr Span, 71-73; asst prof, 73-77, assoc prof 77-82, prof span ling, State Univ NY at Buffalo, 82-, Dir Span Lang Instr, 74-89, Dir State Univ NY at Buffalo/Univ of Salamanca summer prog, 75-76, Dir, Span Undergraduate Studies, 95-, adj prof learning instr, 96-; vis prof, Univ Pittsburgh, summer 89-96; vis prof, Universidad nacional Federico Villarreal, Peru, summer 97, 98; vis prof, PA State Univ, fall 96. **MEMBERSHIPS** Ling Soc Am; MLA; Am Asn Tchr(s) Span & Port. **RESEARCH** Span linguistic theory; Caribbean Span dialectology. **SELECTED PUBLICATIONS** Auth, Markedness and a Cuban Dialect of Spanish, Georgetown Univ, 76; Aspects of Spanish aspect: A new look at the imperfect/preterit distinction, In: Contemp Studies in Romance Ling, 78; Conservative vs radical dialects of Spanish: Implications for language instruction, Bilingual Rev, 78; Aspectos del consonantismo habanero: Reexamen descriptive, Bol de la Academia Puertorriquena de la Lengua Espanola, 78; co-ed, La estructura fonica de la lengua castellana, Anagrama, 80; auth, on loanword phonology as distinctive feature phonology in Cuban Spanish, In: Linguistics Symposium on Romance Languages, Georgetown Univ, Vol 9, 81; Sobre la silaba como entidad fonematica en los dialectos del Caribe Hispanico, Thesaurus, 81; coauth, Dialectologia Hispanoamericana, Almar, 82; On the Contribution of Spanish language variation studies to contemporary linguistic theory, In: Spanish in the U S Setting: Beyond the Southwest, Nat Clearinghouse for Bilingual Educ, 83; Fonologia, In: Introduccion a la linguistica actual, Edditoiral Playor, madrid, 83; Syntax, semantics, and pragmatics of the subjunctive in Spanish noun clauses, Hisp Jour, 84; The resolution of phonological ambiguity in a simulated English-Spanish borrowing situation, In: Proceedings of the 13th Linguistic Symposium on Romance Languages, John Benjamin, 85; co-ed, Fonologia del espanol del Caribe, Fundaction La Casa de Bello, 86; auth, Sobre el uso del subjuntivo espanol en dos dialectos caribenos, Thesaurus, 87; The case of a syntax-dependent post lexical module in Spanish phonology, In: Advances in Romance Linguistics, Foris, 88; co-auth, Dialectologia Hispanoamerica, 2nd ed, Colegio de Espana, 88; co-auth, Fundamentos de linguistica hispanica, Editorial Playor, Madrid, 88; auth, Perception of English vowels by Hispanic children of limited English proficiency, In: Research Issues and Problems in United States Spanish: Latin America and Southwestern Varieties, Pan Am Univ, 88; Concatenation/stratum phonology (nee Lexical Phonology) and a Dominican dialect of Spanish, In: American Spanish Pronunciation:Theoretical and Applied Perspectives, Georgetown Univ Press, 89; On Spanish cleft sentences, In: Proceedings of the Seventeenth Annual Symposium on the Linguistics of Romance Languages, John Benjamin, 89; co-auth, Somos asi, EMC Publ, 89; auth, Aspectos pragmaticos del modo en los complementos de predicados de conocimiento y de adquisicion de conocimiento en espanol, In: Indicativo y subjunctivo, Taurus Universitaria, 90; On the Pragmatics of Spanish Mood, In: Knowledge and Acquisition-of Knowledge Predicates, Discourse-Pragmatic Approaches to Categories of the Verb: The Evidence from Romance, Routledge, 91; co-auth, Personajes, Houghton Mifflin Co, 92; auth, Foreigner's Notebook, Shuffaloff, 93; Simbolism fonico en un poema de Cesar Vallejo, In: El puente de las palabras: Homenaje a David Lagmanovich, Org Am States, 94; The NP-based, class/member analysis of mood choice in Spanish relative clauses, In: Papers in Second Language Teaching and Linguistics in Honor of Tracy D Terrell, McGraw Hill, 95; Spanish in contact with itself and the phonological characterization of conservative and radical styles, In: Spanish in Contact, Cascadilla Press, 96; Film Blanc, Meow Press, 96; co-ed, Identity, Community, and Pluralism in American Life, Oxford Univ Press, 97; auth, Nociones de psicolinguistica, Departamento de Linguistica y Literatura de la Universidad Nacional Federico Villarroel, Peru, 97; Variability, multilectalism, and the organization of phonology in Caribbean Spanish, In: Issues in Phonology and Morphology of the Major Iberian Languages, Georgetown Univ Press, 97. **CONTACT ADDRESS** Dept Mod Lang & Lit, State Univ NY, 910 Clemens Hall, Buffalo, NY, 14260-4620. **EMAIL** guitart@acsu.buffalo.edu

GULSOY, J.
PERSONAL Born 08/15/1925, Ordu, Turkey, m, 1959, 2 children **DISCIPLINE** ROMANCE LANGUAGES, HISPANIC LINGUISTICS **EDUCATION** Univ BC, BA, 53; Univ Toronto, MA, 55; Univ Chicago, PhD, 61. **CAREER** From instr to assoc prof, 58-70, PROF SPAN, UNIV TORONTO, 70-, Can Coun grant, 67-68. **MEMBERSHIPS** Am Asn Teachers Span & Port; Soc Ling Romane; Medieval Acad Am. **RESEARCH** Lexicographical compilations; Catalan and Spanish linguistics; Hispanic dialectology. **SELECTED PUBLICATIONS** Auth, The Minorcans of Florida--History, Language and Culture, Romance Philol, Vol 0046, 92. **CONTACT ADDRESS** Dept of Hispanic Studies, Univ of Toronto, Toronto, ON, M5S 1A1.

GUMPEL, LISELOTTE
PERSONAL Berlin, Germany **DISCIPLINE** HUMANITIES, GERMAN **EDUCATION** San Francisco State Col, BA, 64; Stanford Univ, MA, 66, PhD, 71. **CAREER** From Asst Prof, to Prof Ger Lang & Lit, 68-98, Prof Emeritus, Univ Minn, Morris, 98-. **HONORS AND AWARDS** NEH Fel, 72; Helen Cam res fel, 77-78. **MEMBERSHIPS** MLA (life member); AAUP; Am Asn Teachers Ger; GIG; IVG; Women in Ger. **RESEARCH** German literature; semantics; esthetics. **SELECTED PUBLICATIONS** Auth, The essence of reality as a construct of language, Found Lang, 3/74; The structure of idioms: A phenomenological approach, Semiotica, J Int Asn Semiotic Studies, 12-1/74; Metaphor as nominalized meaning: A phenomenological analysis of the lyrical genre, Jarhbuch Int Germanistik, 76; Concrete Poetry from East and West Germany: The Language of Exemplarism and Experimentalism, Yale Univ, 76; Metaphor Reexamined: A Non-Aristotelian Perspective, Ind Univ, 85; Meaning and Metaphor: The World in Verbal Translation, Schmidt-Verlag and Stanford Univ (forthcoming); author of numerous other articles. **CONTACT ADDRESS** 111 Marquette Ave S, # 1008, Minneapolis, MN, 55401.

GUMPERZ, JOHN J.
DISCIPLINE LINGUISTICS, ANTHROPOLOGY **EDUCATION** Univ Cincinnati, BA, 47; Univ Mich, PhD(Ger ling), 54. **CAREER** Instr ling, Cornell Univ, 52-54; from instr to assoc prof S Asian lang and ling, 56-67, PROF ANTHROP, UNIV CALIF, BERKELEY, 67-, Ford Found fel ling, India, 54-56; mem comt socioling, Soc Sci Res Coun, 66-73; Trainers of Teachers of Teachers comt, Berkeley sch bd, 69-71. **MEMBERSHIPS** Ling Soc Am; Am Anthrop Asn; Ling Soc India; AAAS. **RESEARCH** Sociolinguistics; linguistics and cognitive anthropology; applied linguistics. **SELECTED PUBLICATIONS** Auth, Treacherous Words--Gender and Power in Academic Assessment, Folia Linguistica, Vol 0030, 96. **CONTACT ADDRESS** Dept of Anthrop, Univ of Calif, 232 Kroeber Hall, Berkeley, CA, 94720.

GUNDEL, J.K.
PERSONAL Born 07/16/1942, Krakou, Poland, m, 1964, 1 child **DISCIPLINE** LINGUISTICS **EDUCATION** Univ Texas, PhD, 74. **CAREER** Vis asst prof, Univ Hawaii, 78-80; asst prof, 80-87, assoc prof, 87-92, prof, linguis, 92-, Univ Minn. **MEMBERSHIPS** Linguistic Soc Amer **RESEARCH** Semantics; pragmatics; syntax; lang processing; lang & cognition. **SELECTED PUBLICATIONS** Coauth, Cognitive Status and Form of Referring Expressions in Discourse, Language 69.2, 93; art, Shared Knowledge, Encycl of Lang & Ling, Pergamon Press, 93; art, Focus and Natural Language Processing vol 3 Discourse, Working Papers of the Inst for Logic & Ling, IBM Deutschland Info-syst GMbH Heidleberg, 94; art, Understanding Reference: Where Communication and Cognition Meet, Form & Function in Lang, Odense Univ press, 95; co-ed, Reference and Referent Accessibility, John Benjamins & Co,

96; coauth, Prosodic Tune and Information Structure, Proceed 1995 Ann Conf of the Can Ling Soc, Toronto Working Papers in Ling, 95; art, Relevance Theory Meets the Givenness Heirarchy: an Account Of Inferrables, Reference and Referent Accessibility, John Benjamins & Co, 96; art, Pragmatic Function And Linguistic Form, J Korean Ling 21.1, 97; coauth, Relevance, Referring Expressions and the Givenness Hierarchy, Proceed Workshop On Relevance Theory, Univ Herfordshire, 97; art, Shared Knowledge, Concise Encycl of The Phil of Lang, Oxford Elsevier Science Ltd, 97; coauth, What Brings A Higher-Order Entity Into Focus of Attention?, Proceed Workshop on Anaphora 35th Ann Mtg Assoc Of Computational Ling, 97; art, Centering Theory And The Givenness Hierarchy: A Proposed Synthesis, Centering Theory In Discourse, Oxford Univ Press, 98. **CONTACT ADDRESS** Dept of Linguistics, Univ of Minnesota, 192 Klaeber Ct, 320 16th Ave SE, Minneapolis, MN, 55455. **EMAIL** gunde00@maroon.tc.umn.edu

GUNTERMANN, GAIL
PERSONAL Born 10/09/1938, Miles City, MT **DISCIPLINE** SPANISH, FOREIGN LANGUAGE EDUCATION **EDUCATION** Univ Mont, BA, 60, Univ NMex, MA, 69; Ohio State Univ, PhD(foreign lang educ), 77. **CAREER** Teacher Span, Whitefish Schs, Mont, 60-62 and Albany Union High Sch, Ore, 62-65; lang coordr and instr Span, Brockport State Col, New York, 69-71; lang coordr, Avarice, SA, El Salvador, 74-76; methods instr and supvr student teachers Span and French, Fredonia State Col, New York, 77; ASST PROF SPAN AND METHODS, ARIZ STATE UNIV, 77-. **MEMBERSHIPS** Am Coun Teaching Foreign Lang; Am Asn Teachers Span & Port; MLA. **RESEARCH** Error analysis and perception. **SELECTED PUBLICATIONS** Auth, En-Contacto--A 1st Course in Spanish, 4th ed, Mod Lang J, Vol 0077, 93; Education for the Intercultural Experience, Mod Lang J, Vol 0079, 95; Language Education for Intercultural Communication, Mod Lang J, Vol 0080, 96. **CONTACT ADDRESS** Dept of Foreign Lang, Arizona State Univ, Tempe, Tempe, AZ, 85287.

GUPTA, BRIJEN KISHORE
PERSONAL Born 09/17/1929, Ferozpur, India, m, 1957, 3 children **DISCIPLINE** HISTORY, SOUTH ASIAN STUDIES **EDUCATION** Dayanand Col, India, BA, 52; Yale Univ, MA, 54; Univ Chicago, PhD, 58. **CAREER** Lectr hist & govt, 58-60, Southern Ill Univ; lectr Asian studies, 60-63, Victoria Univ, NZ; asst prof hist, 63-67, assoc prof, 67-69, Brooklyn Col; prof, 69-76, Univ Rochester; prof, 70-76, State Univ NY Col Brockport; sr fel & dir, res & develop, coun int & pub affairs, 76-; vis fel, 61-62, Inst Advan Studies, Australian Nat Univ; Carnegie Soc Sci Res Fund grant, NZ, 61-62; Am Philos Soc grant, 66-67; vis prof, Columbia Univ, 68-69; Swedenberg Found res grant, 71-72; Tarak Nath Das-Ram Mahun Roy lectr, Yale Univ, 75; NEH lectr, Univ Wis-Madison, 76; consult, UN Ctr Transnational Corps, 80-82. **MEMBERSHIPS** AHA; Assn Asian Studies; Indo-Brit Hist Soc. Overbrook fel, Yale Univ, 53-54; Found World Govt fel, 54-55; Univ & Asia Found fel, Univ Chicago,55-58; Rapporteur, Strategy for Peace Conf, Stanley Found, 77; NSF res grant, 78-80; Assn Asian Studies grant, 80-81 **RESEARCH** Indian science policy; comparative intellectual history; urban studies. **SELECTED PUBLICATIONS** Auth, Sirajuddaullah and the East India Company, 1756-57, E J Brill, 62 & 66; coauth, Indian and American Labor Legislations and Practices: A Comparative Analysis, Asia Publ House, 66; auth, India in English Fiction, 1800-1970, Scarecrow-Grolier, 73; art, The Working Class in Modern India, New Polit, 11/73; art, The Ethical System in Sankara and Swedenborg, Indian J Theol, 12/73; coauth, Learning About India: An Annotated Guide for the Nonspecialists, Univ NY Albany, 77; Small Business Development in the Inner City Area of Rochester, 2 vols, NY Coun on Int & Pub Affairs, 78; art, The Political Economy of North-South Relations: Studies in the Transfer of US Science and Technology, Nat Tech Info Serv, 81; auth, India, Amer Bibliographical Center and Clio Press, 84. **CONTACT ADDRESS** 226 Idlewood Rd, Rochester, NY, 14618.

GURA, TIMOTHY
PERSONAL Born 09/03/1947, Peoria, IL, s **DISCIPLINE** INTERPRETATION **EDUCATION** Northwestern Univ, BS, 69, PhD, 74; Univ Mich, AM, 71. **CAREER** Prof Speech Commun and Dept Chair, Brooklyn Col, City Univ New York, 84-. **HONORS AND AWARDS** Tow Award. **MEMBERSHIPS** NCA. **RESEARCH** Performance of literature; shakespeare; teaching. **SELECTED PUBLICATIONS** Coauth, Oral Interpretation, 10th ed, 2000. **CONTACT ADDRESS** 275 W. 12th St., New York, NY, 10014. **EMAIL** tgura@brooklyn.cuny.edu

GUSTAFSON, RICHARD FOLKE
PERSONAL Born 06/17/1934, Hartford, CT **DISCIPLINE** RUSSIAN LANGUAGE AND LITERATURE **EDUCATION** Yale Univ, AB, 56; Columbia Univ, PhD, 63. **CAREER** Instr Russ, Brown Univ, 60-62; from lectr to asst prof, Yale Univ, 62-65; assoc prof, 65-72, Prof Russ, Barnard Col, Columbia Univ, 72-, Chmn Dept, 65-. **MEMBERSHIPS** MLA; Am Asn Advan Slavic Studies; Am Asn Teachers Slavic & East Europ Lang. **RESEARCH** Russian poetry; 19th-century fiction; Tolstoy; and Russian religion and philosophy. **SELECTED PUBLICATIONS** Auth, The Upas Tree: Pushkin and Erasmus Darwin, PMLA, 1/60; auth, Tjutcev's Imagery and What It Tells Us, 6/60 & The Suffering Usurper: Gogol's Diary of a Madman, 3/65, Slavic & East Europ J; The Imagination of Spring: The Poetry of Afanasy Fet, Yale Univ, 66; auth, Leo Tolstoy, Resident and Stranger: A Study in Fiction and Theology, Princeton Univ, 86. **CONTACT ADDRESS** Dept of Russ Barnard Col, Columbia Univ, 3009 Broadway, New York, NY, 10027-6598. **EMAIL** rgustafson@barnard.columbia.edu

GUTHKE, KARL SIEGFRIED
PERSONAL Born 02/17/1933, Lingen, Germany, m, 1965, 1 child **DISCIPLINE** GERMAN LITERATURE **EDUCATION** Univ Tex, MA, 53; Univ Gottingen, PhD, 56. **CAREER** From instr to prof Ger lit, Univ Calif, Berkeley, 56-65; prof Ger, Univ Toronto, 65-68; PROF GER, HARVARD UNIV, 68-, Am Philos Soc grant-in-aid, 61-62; vis prof, Univ Colo, 63 and Univ Mass, 67; Guggenheim fel, 65; Am Coun Learned Soc fel, 72-73. **HONORS AND AWARDS** Walter C Cabot Prize, Harvard Univ, 77., MA, Harvard Univ, 68. **MEMBERSHIPS** MLA; Am Lessing Soc (pres, 71-72); Acad Lit Studies; Lessing Akad Schiller Ges. **RESEARCH** Anglo-German literary relations; 18th century German literature; Gerhart Hauptmann. **SELECTED PUBLICATIONS** Auth, Traven, B.--A Vision of Mexico, German Quarterly, Vol 0066, 93; Das Leben-Vom-Ende-Her, the Last Words in a Biography: Literary Biography as a Genre, Euphorion-Zeitschrift fur Literaturgeschichte, Vol 0087, 93; Der 'Sarg Auf Dem Bus', a Short Story Sometimes Attributed to Traven, B., Actually Written by His Wife Lujan, Rosa, Elena, Germanisch-Romanische Monatsschrift, Vol 0044, 94; Traven 'Macario' between Indian Folklore and the Fairy-Tales of the Brothers Grimm, Zeitschrift fur Deutsche Philologie, Vol 0114, 95; Between Dream and Reality--The Uniquely Austrian in Literature, German Quart, Vol 0068, 95; Traven,B. and His English-Speaking Readers--New Material from Traven Correspondence with Chatto-and-Windus and Babb, Sanora, Zeitschrift fur Germanistik, Vol 0006, 96; Nietzsche Collapse: Forsternietzsche, Elisabeth--The View from Paraguay, Harvard Libr Bull, Vol 0007, 96. **CONTACT ADDRESS** Dept of Ger, Harvard Univ, Boylston Hall, Cambridge, MA, 02138-3800.

GUTHRIE, ELIZABETH M.
DISCIPLINE FRENCH LANGUGE **EDUCATION** Univ Ill, PhD. **CAREER** DIR, FR LANG PROG, LECTR, UNIV CALIF, IRVINE. **SELECTED PUBLICATIONS** Auth, "Classroom Discourse and Linguistic Intake"; "Intake, Communication, and Second-Language Teaching." **CONTACT ADDRESS** Dept of Fr and Ital, Univ Calif, Irvine, CA, 92697.

GUTIERREZ, JESUS
PERSONAL Born 10/31/1928, Santander, Spain **DISCIPLINE** SPANISH LANGUAGE AND LITERATURE **EDUCATION** Univ Comillas, PhBach, 49; Inst Cath, Paris, Dipl, 59; Fordham Univ, MA, 63; Hunter Col, MA, 70; City Univ New York, PhD(Span and Span Am), 73. **CAREER** Asst prof Span lang and lit, Col Guizar Valencia, 52-57; instr sociol and Span, Marymount Manhattan Col, 65-68; lectr Span, Queens Col, NY, 70-73, asst prof, 73-74; asst prof, Hofstra Univ, 74-76; vis prof, Wellesley Col, 76-77; assoc prof, Douglass Col, Rutgers Univ, 77-78 and York Col, City Univ New York, 78-81; ASSOC PROF SPAN GOLDEN AGE, WAYNE STATE UNIV, 81-, Examr NY Reg Interviewing Comt Teacher Exchange Prof, Europe and Latin Am, 66-68; consult, Bilingual Educ Prog Girl Scouts Am, 73-75. **MEMBERSHIPS** MLA; Asoc Int Hispanistas; Am Asn Teachers Span & Port; Soc Menendez Pelayo. **RESEARCH** Spanish literature and thought of the Renaissance and Golden Age; the 18th century. **SELECTED PUBLICATIONS** Auth, Denina, Carlo and His Defense of Spain: Introduction, Dieciocho-Hisp Enlightenment, Vol 0015, 92. **CONTACT ADDRESS** Dept of Span Lang and Lit, Wayne State Univ, Detroit, MI, 48202.

GUTIERREZ-VEGA, ZENAIDA
PERSONAL Born 06/23/1924, Union del Reyes, Cuba **DISCIPLINE** SPANISH, SPANISH AMERICAN LITERATURE **EDUCATION** Inst Sec Educ, Matanzas, Cuba, BA, 45; Univ Havana, PhD(Span lit), 50; Univ Madrid, PhD(Romance philol), 66. **CAREER** Prof Span & lit, Inst Sec Educ Velado, Havana, 52-62; prof, Univ Las Villas, Cuba, 59-62; asst prof Span & Span Am lit, Univ Mo, St Louis, 67-68; asst prof, State Univ NY Col Oswego, 68-72; Prof Span, Hunter Col, 72-; Mem, Ministry Educ, Cuba, 56-57; mem, Inst Hisp Cult, Madrid, 62-66. **HONORS AND AWARDS** Lit Prize, Inst Hisp Cult, Madrid, 66; Summa cum Laude, 66; fel, Inst de Cultura Hispanica, 62-67; PSC-CUNY grants, 84, 85, 87. **MEMBERSHIPS** MLA; Am Asn Teachers Span & Port. **RESEARCH** Hispanic American literature; poets, essayists, novelists of the twentieth century of Spain and Latin America. **SELECTED PUBLICATIONS** Auth, Jose Maria Chacon y Calvo, Hispanista Cubano, Ediciones Cultura Hispanica, 69; auth, Epistolario Alfonso Reyes-Jose Ma. Chacon, Fundacion Universitaria Espanola, 76; auth, Estudio Bibliografico de Jose Ma. Chacon, Fundacion Universitaria Espanola, 82; auth, Fernando Ortiz en sus Cartas a Jose Ma. Chacon, Fundacion Universitaria Espanola, 82; auth, Corresponsales Espanoles de Jose Ma. Chacon, Fundacion Universitaria Espanola, 86; auth, Carmen Conde: de Viva Voz, Senda Nueva de Ediciones, 92. **CONTACT ADDRESS** 220 E 63rd St, Apt 4L, New York, NY, 10021.

GUTWIRTH, MADELYN
PERSONAL Born 01/04/1926, Brooklyn, NY, m, 1948, 3 children **DISCIPLINE** FRENCH LITERATURE, WOMEN'S STUDIES **EDUCATION** Brooklyn Col, BA, 47; Bryn Mawr Col, MA, 49, PhD(French), 58. **CAREER** Instr French, Haverford Col, 50-51; assoc prof, 66-69, PROF FRENCH, WEST CHESTER STATE COL, 69-, FAC Coordr, Arts and Sci, 79-, Vis lectr French, Univ Pa, 67-68; Am Count Learned Soc fel, 71-72. **MEMBERSHIPS** MLA; Northeast Mod Lang Asn (pres, 73-74); Am Soc 18th Century Studies; Soc d'Etudes Staeliennes; AAUP. **RESEARCH** Madame de Stael; Romanticism; the 18th century. **SELECTED PUBLICATIONS** Auth, Changing the Past: French 18th-Century Studies--A Feminist Challenge, 18th-Century Stud, Vol 0028, 94. **CONTACT ADDRESS** Dept of Foreign Lang, West Chester Univ, West Chester, PA, 19380.

GYEKENYESI GATTO, KATHERINE
PERSONAL Born 11/27/1945, Braunau, Austria, m, 1968, 4 children **DISCIPLINE** LANGUAGES **EDUCATION** John Carroll Univ, AB, 67; Case Western Reserve Univ, MA, 71, PhD, 75. **CAREER** Asst prof, 75-80, assoc prof, 80-92, prof, 92-, chmn 90-97, actng dir, univ honors prog, 88-89, John Carroll Univ. **RESEARCH** Medieval Spanish lit; Hispanic film; Hungarian lit; Hispanic & Hungarian women writers; Hungarian film. **CONTACT ADDRESS** Classical & Modern Languages and Cultures, John Carroll Univ, University Hts, OH, 44118. **EMAIL** gatto@jcu.edu

H

HABERL, FRANZ P.
PERSONAL Born 03/08/1935, Nurnberg, Germany, d **DISCIPLINE** GERMAN LANGUAGE AND LITERATURE **EDUCATION** Ursinus Col, BA, 59; Cornell Univ, MA, 61, PhD(-Ger & comp lit), 64. **CAREER** Instr Ger, Ohio Univ, 62-63; from instr to asst prof, C W Post Col, Long Island Univ, 63-65; asst prof, Univ Md, 65-66; asst prof, Brooklyn Col, 66-69; assoc prof and chmn dept, Mt Allison Univ, 69-73; PROF GER, DAWSON COL, 73-. **MEMBERSHIPS** MLA; Can Asn Univ Teachers Ger. **RESEARCH** German literature especially the Age of Goethe; modern drama and modern novel. **SELECTED PUBLICATIONS** Auth, Midas Oder die Schwarze Leinwand, World Lit Today, Vol 0066, 92; Dreck, World Lit Today, Vol 0067, 93; Der Traum des Konditors, World Lit Today, Vol 0067, 93; Dramas, Vol 3, World Lit Today, Vol 0069, 95; Das Kliff, World Lit Today, Vol 0070, 96; Inselgeschichten, World Lit Today, Vol 0070, 96. **CONTACT ADDRESS** Dept of Mod Lang, Dawson Col, 535 Viger Ave, Montreal, PQ, H2L 2P3.

HABERLAND, PAUL MALLORY
PERSONAL Born 09/24/1935, Milwaukee, Wis, m, 1962, 2 children **DISCIPLINE** GERMAN LITERATURE & LANGUAGE **EDUCATION** Haverford Col, BA, 57; Johns Hopkins Univ, MA, 60, PhD(Ger), 69. **CAREER** Actg asst prof Ger, Univ Calif, Riverside, 64-66; from instr to asst prof, Lawrence Univ, 66-72; lectr English, Univ Gottingen, Ger, 72-73; assoc prof, 74-79, Prof Ger, Western Carolina Univ, 79-, Head Dept Mod Lang, 81-90. **HONORS AND AWARDS** Fulbright scholar, US, Austria, Germany; Am Philos Soc res grant; Austrian Govt res grant. **MEMBERSHIPS** MLA; Am Asn Teachers Ger; SAtlantic Mod Lang Asn. **RESEARCH** Eighteenth century German literary criticism; 19th century German literature; 20th century Austrian literature. **SELECTED PUBLICATIONS** Auth, The Development of Comic Theory in Germany during the Eighteenth Century, Goppinger Arbeiten Ger Alfred Kummerle, 71; The reception of German literature in Baltimore's literary magazines 1800-1875, Ger-Am Studies, 74; Number symbolism: The father-daughter relationship in E T A Hoffmann's Rat Krespel, 75 & A Fabian's view of Goethe--an unpublished letter from Sidney Webb to Beatrice Potter, 76, Lang Quart; Duality, the artist, and Wolfgang Bauer, Mod Austrian Lit, 78; The role of art in the writings of Barbara Frischmuth, Mod Austrian Lit, 81; auth, Literary Censorship in Austria since 1945, Germanic Rev, 65, No. 2, 90; auth, Amerika als das Andere - Das Amerikabild in den Schriften von Wolfgang Bauer und Gerhard Roth, Akten des VIII. Int Germisten-Kongresses, Band 9, 91. **CONTACT ADDRESS** Dept of Mod Foreign Lang, Western Carolina Univ, Cullowhee, NC, 28723.

HABERLY, DAVID T.
PERSONAL Born 12/11/1942, Tucson, AZ, m, 1963, 2 children **DISCIPLINE** ROMANCE LANGUAGES **EDUCATION** Harvard Univ, AB, 63, AM, 64, PhD(Romance lang), 66. **CAREER** From instr to asst prof romance lang, Harvard Univ, 66-73; chmn, Dept Span, Ital and Port, 73-78, ASSOC PROF PORT, UNIV VA, 73-. **MEMBERSHIPS** MLA; Am Asn Teachers Span & Port. **RESEARCH** Brazilian and Portuguese literature; Spanish American and North American literature. **SELECTED PUBLICATIONS** Auth, Trail of Miracles--Stories from a Pilgrimage in Northeast Brazil, Hisp Rev, Vol 0061, 93. **CONTACT ADDRESS** Dept of Span Ital and Port, Univ of Va, 1 Cabell Hall, Charlottesville, VA, 22903-3125.

HABOUSH, JA-HYUN KIM
DISCIPLINE EAST ASIAN STUDIES **EDUCATION** Univ Columbia, PhD, 78. **CAREER** Prof, Univ Ill Urbana Champaign. **RESEARCH** Cultural and intellectual history and literature of late Choson and early modern Korea; gender and women's narratives. **SELECTED PUBLICATIONS** Auth, A Heritage of Kings: One Man's Monarchy in the Confucian World, Columbia Univ, 88; Filial Emotions and Filial Values: Changing Patterns in the Discourse of Filiality in Late Choson Korea, Harvard J Asiatic Studies, 95; The Memoirs of Lady Hyeggong: The Autobiographical Writings of a Crown Princess of Eighteenth Century Korea, Univ Calif, 96. **CONTACT ADDRESS** Dept East Asian Languages and Cultures, Univ Ill Urbana Champaign, 52 E Gregory Dr, Champaign, IL, 61820. **EMAIL** jhaboush@uiuc.edu

HADLEY, MICHAEL LLEWELLYN
PERSONAL Born 04/06/1936, Campbell River, BC, Canada, m, 1959, 4 children **DISCIPLINE** GERMAN LANGUAGE AND LITERATURE **EDUCATION** Univ BC, BA, 59; Univ Man, MA, 64; Queen's Univ, Ont, PhD(Ger), 71. **CAREER** Foreign Serv officer, Can Govt, 59-62; lectr Ger, St John's Col, Univ Man, 62-64; asst prof, Univ Winnipeg, 65-70; asst prof, 70-73, chmn dept, 74-80, ASSOC PROF GER LANG AND LIT, UNIV VICTORIA, 74-, Chmn, External Rels Comt, Humanities Res Coun Can, 78-. **MEMBERSHIPS** Can Asn Univ Teachers Ger (vpres, 76-78, pres, 78-80); Am Asn 18th Century Studies; Can Asn 18th Century Studies; Am Lessing Soc; Maritime Defense Asn Can. **RESEARCH** Eighteenth-century literature; Deutsche Schauerromantik; U-Boat warfare in Canadian waters. **SELECTED PUBLICATIONS** Auth, Understanding Remarque, Erich, Maria, Seminar-J Ger Stud, Vol 0029, 93; Understanding Bernhard, Thomas, Seminar-J Ger Stud, Vol 0029, 93; Understanding Canetti, Elias, Seminar-J Ger Stud, Vol 0029, 93; The Longest Battle--The Royal-Canadian-Navy in the Atlantic, 1939-1945, Am Neptune, Vol 0054, 94; The Kaisers Pirates--German Surface Raiders in World-War-I, Mariners Mirror, Vol 0081, 95; The Defeat of the U-Boats--The Battle of the Atlantic, Am Neptune, Vol 0055, 95; Graf-Spees Raiders--Challenge to the Royal-Navy, 1914-1915, Mariners Mirror, Vol 0082, 96. **CONTACT ADDRESS** Dept of Ger Lang and Lit, Univ of Victoria, Victoria, BC, V8W 2Y2.

HAFTER, MONROE Z.
PERSONAL Born 06/28/1926, New York, NY, m, 1957, 2 children **DISCIPLINE** SPANISH LITERATURE **EDUCATION** Harvard Univ, PhD, 56. **CAREER** Teaching fel Span, Harvard Univ, 51-56; from instr to asst prof Romanic lang, Williams Col, 56-60; from asst prof to assoc prof, 60-67, PROF SPAN, UNIV MICH, ANN ARBOR, 67-, Am Philos Soc grant, 58; Williams Col Class of 1900 Fund grant, 58; grant, Rackham Sch Grad Studies, Univ Mich, Ann Arbor, 62; Fulbright and Guggenheim Found res grants, 67-68. **MEMBERSHIPS** MLA; Am Soc 18th Century Studies. **RESEARCH** Transition in Spanish literature from Golden Age to nineteenth century; moralist literature, satire and novel. **SELECTED PUBLICATIONS** Auth, Santos, Francisco el 'Rey Gallo' and 'Discursos de la Hormiga,' Bull of Hisp Stud, Vol 0070, 93; 2 Perspectives on Self in Spanish Autobiography (1743-1845), Dieciocho-Hisp Enlightenment, Vol 0016, 93; The Account Books of The Corrales-de-Comedias of Madrid, 1706-1719--Study and Documents, Bull of Hisp Stud, Vol 0071, 94; Noches Lugubres, Hisp Rev, Vol 0062, 94. **CONTACT ADDRESS** Dept of Romance Lang, Univ of Mich, Ann Arbor, MI, 48109.

HAGENS, JAN LUBER
DISCIPLINE GERMAN LITERATURE **EDUCATION** Univ Va, MA, 83; Univ Tubingen, staatsexamen, 88; Princeton Univ, MA, 90, PhD, 93. **CAREER** Asst prof, Carleton Col, 93-95; asst prof, Eckerd Col, 95- 97; ASST PROF GER, UNIV NOTRE DAME, 97-. **CONTACT ADDRESS** Dept of German & Russian, Univ of Notre Dame, 318 O'Shaughnessy Hall, Notre Dame, IN, 46556. **EMAIL** jan.l.hagens.2@nd.edu

HAGIWARA, TAKAO
DISCIPLINE JAPANESE AND COMPARATIVE LITERATURE **EDUCATION** Sophia Univ, BA, 71;Univ British Columbia, MA, 79, PhD, 86. **CAREER** English, Case Western Reserve Univ. **SELECTED PUBLICATIONS** Auth, The Idea of Innocence in Kenji Miyazawa,Tokyo: Meijishoin, 88; Coed, The Mother in Japanese Literature,Tokyo: Shinyosha, 97. **CONTACT ADDRESS** Case Western Reserve Univ, 10900 Euclid Ave, Cleveland, OH, 44106. **EMAIL** txh13@po.cwru.edu

HAHM, DAVID EDGAR
PERSONAL Born 09/30/1938, Milwaukee, WI, m, 1964, 4 children **DISCIPLINE** CLASSICAL LANGUAGES, ANCIENT PHILOSOPHY, INTELLECTUAL HISTORY **EDUCATION** Northwestern Col, Wis, BA, 60; Univ Wis-Madison, MA, 62, PhD(classics), 66. **CAREER** Asst prof class lang, Univ Mo-Columbia, 66-69; from asst prof to assoc prof class, 69-78, PROF CLASSICS, OHIO STATE UNIV, 78-, Fel, Ctr Hellenic Studies, Wash, DC, 68-69. **MEMBERSHIPS** Am Philol Asn; Am Philos Asn; Hist Sci Soc; Class Asn Midwest & South. **SELECTED PUBLICATIONS** Auth, The Nature of Man in Early Stoic Philosophy, Phoenix-J Class Asn of Can, Vol 0045, 91; The Chain of Change--A Study of Aristotles Physics, Pt 7, Isis, Vol 0084, 93. **CONTACT ADDRESS** Dept of Greek & Latin, Ohio State Univ, 230 N Oval Mall, Columbus, OH, 43210-1335. **EMAIL** hahm.1@osu.edu

HAHN, HANNELORE
DISCIPLINE SPANISH **EDUCATION** San Jose State Univ, BA, MA; Columbia Univ, PhD. **CAREER** Asst prof, Col St. Elizabeth. **RESEARCH** Kafka's influence on Latin Am writers; Cuban writers in exile; Orlando Saa Thomas Mann's influence on Latin Am writers; transl tech. **SELECTED PUBLICATIONS** Auth, Las novelas de J Leyra, 97; Los Balseros de la libertad de J Leyva, WPU, 97; Tierrade Extranos de J A Albertini, Pensamiento, 97; Reacion to U Hegi's book:Tearing the Silence, CSE, 97; Las novelas de J. Leyva, Youngstown State Univ, 97; El desafio existential en la obra de Josefina Leyva, Circulo de Cultura, WPU, 97; El Tiempo Inagotado de Irene Marquina de J Leyva, Simposio en la Univ de Bariloche, Argentina, 97; Las novelas de J Leyva, Circulo de Escritores y Poetas de Nueva York, 97; rev, El Tiempo Inagotado de Irene Marquina de J Leyva, Pensamiento, Fla, 97; Los balseros de la libertad de Josefina Leyva, Pensamiento, Fla, 1997 & El veranito de , Circulo de Cult, 97; article on, Los Balseros de la Libertad de J Leyva, Pensamiento Lit Mag, 97; Los Balseros de la libertad de Josefina Leyva, Pensamiento, 97. **CONTACT ADDRESS** Dept of For Lang, Col of Saint Elizabeth, 2 Convent Rd., Morristown, NJ, 07960. **EMAIL** hahn@liza.st-elizabeth.edu

HAHN, OSCAR
PERSONAL Born 07/05/1938, Iquique, Chile, m, 1971, 1 child **DISCIPLINE** SPANISH AMERICAN POETRY, LITERARY THEORY **EDUCATION** Univ Chile, Profesor Span, 63; Univ Iowa, MA, 72; Univ Md, PhD(Span), 77. **CAREER** Prof Hisp lit, Univ Chile Arica, 65-73; instr, Univ Md, 74-77; asst prof Span Am poetry, 77-79, ASSOC PROF SPAN AM LIT, UNIV IOWA, 79-, Hon fel writing, Int Writing Prog, Univ Iowa, 72; contrib ed Span Am poetry, Handbook of Latin American Studies, Libr Cong, 77-. **MEMBERSHIPS** MLA; Inst Lit Iberoam. **RESEARCH** Spanish American literature; literary theory. **SELECTED PUBLICATIONS** Auth, 20th-Century Chilean Literature, Rev Iberoamericana, Vol 0060, 94; Huidobro, Vicente, from the Mechanic Kingdom to the Apocalypse, Rev Iberoamericana, Vol 0060, 94. **CONTACT ADDRESS** Dept of Span, Univ of Iowa, Iowa City, IA, 52240.

HAHN, THOMAS GEORGE O'HARA
PERSONAL Born 04/26/1946, New York, NY, 2 children **DISCIPLINE** ENGLISH LITERATURE & LANGUAGE **EDUCATION** Fordham Univ, AB, 68; Univ Calif Los Angeles, MA & PhD(English), 74. **CAREER** Asst prof, 73-80, assoc prof, 80-96, prof, Univ Rochester, 96, dir, Writing Prog, 76-81, dir, medieval sds ctr, 75-76, 83-84, 87-88, ch, cluster on premodern sds, 89-, dir grad sds Eng, 82-83, 96-97, , assoc, Susan B. Anthony Ctr for Women's Sds, 85-, gen ed, Chaucer Bibliographies, 84, gov brd, Robbins Lib, 87. **HONORS AND AWARDS** NEH Sum fel, ACLS fel, Vis mem, Wolfson Col, Cambridge; Ford Foun Tchg, PI, for NEH Prog Gra; E P Curtis Awd for Tchg Excel; Reach Teams Awd for Curricular Innov. **MEMBERSHIPS** Mediaeval Acad Am; MLA; New Chaucer Soc; Early English Text Soc; Index Mid English Prose. **RESEARCH** Old and Middle English language and literature; Medieval studies. **SELECTED PUBLICATIONS** Auth, Urian Oakes's Elegie and Puritan poetics, Am Lit, 73; General literary criticism--years work in Old English studies, Old English Newslett, 75 & 81; The audience in the medieval dramatic performance, Res Opportunities in Renaissance Drama, 77; I gentili e l'uom nasce a la riva de l'Indo, L'Alighierei, 77; The Indian tradition of the Middle Ages, Viator, 78; Primitivism and savagery in English discovery narratives of sixteenth century, J Medieval & Renaissance Studies, 78; ed, Me Letter of Alexander to Aristotle, Medieval Studies, 79; Upright Lives: Documents Concerning the Natural Virtue and Wisdom of the Indians, 81; coauth, Text and Context: Chaucer's Friar Tale; auth, Studies in the Age of Chaucer, 83; auth, Teaching the Resistant Woman: The Wife if Bath and the Academy, Exemplaria, 92; auth, The Performance of Gender in the Prioress, The Chaucer Yearbook, 92; auth, Traditional Religion, Social History, and Literary Study, Assays, 96; auth, Old Wives' Tales and Masculine Intuition, Retelling Stories, Lupack & Hahn, 97; auth, Early Middle English, Cambridge Hist of the Middle English Lit, Wallace, 98. **CONTACT ADDRESS** Dept of English, Univ of Rochester, 500 Joseph C Wilson, Rochester, NY, 14627-9000. **EMAIL** thhn@db3.cc.rochester.edu

HAIDT, REBECCA
PERSONAL Born 10/26/1961, New York, NY **DISCIPLINE** SPANISH **EDUCATION** Washington Univ, AB, 83, AM, 89, PhD, 92. **CAREER** ASST PROF OF SPANISH, 92-98, ASSOC PROF OF SPANISH, OHIO STATE UNIV, 98-. **HONORS AND AWARDS** Fulbright fel for independent res, 84-85; DAAD Direktstipendium, 87-88. **MEMBERSHIPS** ASECS; MLA; Iber-American Soc for Eighteenth-Century studies. **RESEARCH** Eighteenth-Century Spain; enlightenment; gender; cultural studies. **SELECTED PUBLICATIONS** Auth, Embodying Enlightenment: Knowing the Body in Eighteenth-Century Spanish Lit and Culture, St. Martin's Press, 98; How Should Medicine Know the Body?: Feijoo's El medico de si mismo, Dieciocho, 96; Los besos de amor and La maja desnuda: The Fascination of the Senses in the Ilustracion, Revista de Estudios Hispanicos, 95; Fray Gerundio and Luxury: The Rococo Aesthetics of Feminized Form, Dieciocho, 94. **CONTACT ADDRESS** Dept of Spanish & Portuguese, Ohio State Univ, Columbus, OH, 43210. **EMAIL** haidt.1@osu.edu

HAIDU, PETER
PERSONAL Born 03/07/1931, Paris, France, 2 children **DISCIPLINE** FRENCH **EDUCATION** Univ Chicago, BA, 52; Columbia Univ, MA, 59, PhD(French), 66. **CAREER** From instr to asst prof French, Columbia Univ, 61-68; from asst prof to assoc prof, Yale Univ, 68-72; assoc prof, Univ Va, 72-74; PROF FRENCH AND SCH HUMANITIES, UNIV ILL, 74-, Morse fel, Yale Univ, 70-71; Nat Endowment for Humanities fel, 77-78; Camargo Found fel, 77-78. **RESEARCH** Semiotics; French and medieval literature; theory of literature. **SELECTED PUBLICATIONS** Auth, The Art of Medieval French Romance, Mod Lang Quart, Vol 0054, 93. **CONTACT ADDRESS** Dept of French, Univ of Ill, Urbana, IL, 61801.

HAILE, GETATCHEW
PERSONAL Born 04/19/1931, m, 1964, 4 children **DISCIPLINE** LINGUISTICS, RELIGION **EDUCATION** Am Univ Cairo, BA, 57; Coptic Theol Col Cairo, BD, 57; Univ Tubingen, PhD(semitic philol), 62. **CAREER** Lectr, Amharic, Ge'ez and Arabic, HSI Univ, Ethiopia, 62-64, asst prof Amharic, Ge'ez and Arabic and chmn dept Ethiopian lang, 64-69; exchange scholar ling, Univ Calif, Los Angeles, 69-70; vis prof African studies, Okla State Univ, 70-71; assoc prof Amharic, Ge'ez and Arabic, HSI Univ, Ethiopia, 71-75; CATALOGUER, HILL MONASTIC MANUSCRIPT LIBR, ST JOHN'S UNIV, MINN, 76-, Contrib ed, Northeast African Studies, Mich State Univ. **RESEARCH** Ge'ez literature; Amharic grammar. **SELECTED PUBLICATIONS** Auth, From Emperor Selassie, Haile to Polotsky, H. J.--An Ethiopian and Semitic Miscellany, J Royal Asiatic Soc, Vol 0006, 96. **CONTACT ADDRESS** Hill Monastic Ms Libr, St John's Univ, Collegeville, MN, 56321.

HAILE, HARRY G.
PERSONAL Born 07/31/1931, TX, m, 1952, 3 children **DISCIPLINE** GERMAN LITERATURE **EDUCATION** Univ Ark, BA, 52, MA, 54; Univ Ill, PhD, 57. **CAREER** Instr Ger, Univ Pa, 56-57; from asst prof to assoc prof, Univ Houston, 57-63; assoc prof, 63-65, chmn dept, 64-67, head dept, 67-73, assoc mem, Ctr Advan Studies, 69-70, PROF GER, UNIV ILL, URBANA, 65-, Am Coun Learned Soc grant, 60; Deut Forschungsgemeinschaft grant, 62-63; vis prof Ger, Univ Mich, 78. **MEMBERSHIPS** MLA; Am Asn Teachers Ger; Goethe Soc; Wiener Goethe Verein. **RESEARCH** Humanities education and higher education in the United States; pre-industrial German literature; Martin Luther biography. **SELECTED PUBLICATIONS** Auth, The Faust Motif as a National Symbol in Benet, Stephen, Vincent and Mann, Thomas, Zeitschrift fur Deut Philol, Vol 0111, 92; Weimar and Milan--The Exchange between Goethe and Manzoni in Letters and Documents, Ger Quart, Vol 0066, 93; A Concise History of German Literature to 1900, Ger Quart, Vol 0066, 93. **CONTACT ADDRESS** 1001 W White St, Champaign, IL, 61820.

HAKUTANI, YOSHINOBU
PERSONAL Born 03/27/1935, Osaka, Japan, m, 1967, 2 children **DISCIPLINE** AMERICAN LITERATURE, LINGUISTICS **EDUCATION** Hiroshima Univ, Japan, BA, 57; Univ Minn, Minneapolis, MA, 59; Pa State Univ, PhD(English), 65. **CAREER** Instr English, SDak State Univ, 59-61; asst prof, Calif State Univ, Northridge, 65-68; asst prof, 68-71, assoc prof, 71-80, PROF ENGLISH, KENT STATE UNIV, 80-, Res fel, Kent State Univ, 71-72. **MEMBERSHIPS** MLA; Ling Soc Am; Conf Col Compos & Commun; English Lit Asn Japan **RESEARCH** Japanese literature. **SELECTED PUBLICATIONS** Co-ed, The World of Japanese Fiction, Dutton, 73; co-ed, American Literary Naturalism: A Reassessment, Carl Winter, 75; auth, Young Dreiser: A Critical Study, Assoc Uiv Press, 80; ed, Critical Essays on Richard Wright, Hall, 82; ed, Selected Magazine Articles of Theodore Dreiser: Life and Art in the American 1890s, Assoc Univ Press, 85-87; ed, Selected English Writings of Youne Noguchi: An East-West Literary Assimilation, Assoc Univ Press, 90-92; co-ed, The City in African-American Literature, Assoc Univ Press, 95; auth, Richard Wright and Racial Discourse, Univ Mo Press, 96; co-ed, Haiku: This Other World by Richard Wright, Arcade/Little Brown, 98. **CONTACT ADDRESS** Dept of English, Kent State Univ, PO Box 5190, Kent, OH, 44242-0001. **EMAIL** yhakutan@kent.edu

HALE, MARK
DISCIPLINE LINGUISTICS **EDUCATION** Univ Mich, BA, 76; Ind Univ, MA, 80; Harvard Univ, PhD, 87. **CAREER** Assoce prof, Concordia Univ, 94-; visiting prof, Cornell Univ, 97; vis prof, Harvard Summer Sch, 95, 96; visiting prof, Univ Wien, 95; assoc prof, Harvard Univ, 90-94; vis prof, Univ Wien, 91; asst prof, Harvard Univ, 87-90; tchg fel, Harvard Univ, 82-86; tchg asst, Ind Univ, 79-80. **HONORS AND AWARDS** FRDP Res grant, 94-97; Whiting fel, Harvard Univ,

86-87; Fulbright Stud grant, Univ Regensburg, Ger, 85-1986; grad stud fel, Ind Univ, 78-79; class distinction and univ hon(s), Univ Mich, 76; Harry Helfman Fund Alumni scholar, Univ Mich, 75. **SELECTED PUBLICATIONS** Co-ed, Harvard Working Papers in Linguistics, Volume 2, Harvard Univ, 93; rev, Review of D. Lightfoot, How to Set Parameters, Lang 70, 94; Commentary on Epstein, Flynn and Martohardjono, Second language acquisition: theoretical and experimental issues in contemporary research, Behavioural and Brain Sciences, 96; Deriving Wackernagel's Law: prosodic and syntactic factors determining clitic placement in the language of the Rigveda, Approaching Second: second position clitics and related phenomena, CSLI, Stanford Univ, 96; Regular Syntactic Change, Interdisciplinary Syntax, Basil Blackwell, 97; The Role of Prosody in the Study of Archaic Indo-Iranian Syntax, Festschrift for Calvert Watkins, Innsbrucker Beitraege zur Sprachwissenschaft, 97; coauth, The Phonology-Syntax Interface in Rotuman, Proc of the Third Meeting of the Austronesian Formal Ling Assn, UCLA, 97. **CONTACT ADDRESS** Dept of Classics, Mod Lang and Ling, Concordia Univ, Montreal, 1455 de Maisonneuve W, Montreal, PQ, H3G 1M8. **EMAIL** hale1@alcor.concordia.ca

HALE, THOMAS ALBERT

PERSONAL Born 01/05/1942, Boston, MA, m, 1968, 1 child **DISCIPLINE** AFRICAN AND FRENCH LITERATURE **EDUCATION** Tufts Univ, BA, 64, MA, 68; Univ Rochester, PhD(French), 74. **CAREER** Agr co-op asst, Peace Corps, Union Nigerienne de Credit et de Cooperation, 64-66; admin asst, NDEA French Inst, Tufts Univ, 67; ASSOC PROF FRENCH AND COMP LIT, PA STATE UNIV, 73-, Co-ed, Cahiers Cesairiens, 74- and African Lit Asn Newsletter, 74-78; Fulbright sr lectr, Univ de Niamey, Niger, 80-81. **MEMBERSHIPS** MLA; African Lit Asn (secy-treas, 74-79, press, 81-82); Am Asn Teachers French; African Studies Asn; Am Comp Lit Asn. **RESEARCH** Caribbean literature; French literature outside France. **SELECTED PUBLICATIONS** Auth, The Negritude Poets--An Anthology of Translations from the French, Res in African Lit, Vol 0023, 92; A Comment Regarding Gadjigo,Samba Review of Scribe, Griots and Novelist, Res in African Lit, Vol 0023, 92; Griottes--Female Voices from West-Africa, Res in African Lit, Vol 0025, 94; African Novels and the Question of Orality, Res in African Lit, Vol 0025, 94; Oral Poetry--Its Nature, Significance and Social-Context, Res in African Lit, Vol 0026, 95; Status and Identity in West-Africa--Nyamakalaw of Mande, Res in African Lit, Vol 0027, 96; Misrepresenting and Misreading the 'Epic of Askia Mohammed,' Res in African Lit, Vol 0027, 96. **CONTACT ADDRESS** French Dept, Pennsylvania State Univ, 434 N Burrowes Bldg, University Park, PA, 16802-6204.

HALEY, MICHAEL

DISCIPLINE LINGUISTICS **EDUCATION** Fla State Univ, PhD. **CAREER** Univ Alaska. **SELECTED PUBLICATIONS** Coauth, Noam Chomsky, Twayne, 94; The Semeiosis of Poetic Metaphor, Indiana Univ Press, 89; Managing ed, Peirce Seminar Papers: Essays in Semiotic Analysis, 93, 94, 97, 98.. **CONTACT ADDRESS** Univ Alaska Anchorage, 3211 Providence Dr., Anchorage, AK, 99508.

HALFORD, PETER W.

PERSONAL Essex County, m, 3 children **DISCIPLINE** FRENCH LANGUAGE; LITERATURE **EDUCATION** Univ Windsor, BA, MA; l'Universite des Sciences Humaines in Strasbourg, Fr, PhD. **CAREER** Couns; prof. **HONORS AND AWARDS** Excellence in univ tchg, Ont Coun Univ Fac Assoc, 83. **RESEARCH** 300 year history of the French language of our area. **SELECTED PUBLICATIONS** Auth, Le Francais des Canadiens a la veille de la Conquete. **CONTACT ADDRESS** Dept of French Language and Literature, Univ of Windsor, 401 Sunset Ave, Windsor, ON, N9B 3P4. **EMAIL** dadotoo@uwindsor.ca

HALL, LINDA

DISCIPLINE MODERN LATIN AMERICA, MODERN MEXICO **EDUCATION** Columbia Univ, PhD, 76. **CAREER** Prof, dir, Lat Am Stud prog, Univ NMex. **HONORS AND AWARDS** Phi Alpha Theta; NEH; Ctr for US Mex Stud, Univ Calif, San Diego, Huntington Libr; Fulbright. **MEMBERSHIPS** Am Hist Asn. **RESEARCH** Modern Mexico; US Latin relations. **SELECTED PUBLICATIONS** Auth, Alvaro Obregon: Power and Revolution in Mexico, 81; Oil, Banks, and Politics: The United States and Post-Revolutionary Mexico, 95; coauth, Revolution on the Border: The United States and Mexico, 1910-1920, 88. **CONTACT ADDRESS** Univ NMex, Albuquerque, NM, 87131.

HALLE, MORRIS

PERSONAL Born 07/23/1923, Liepaja, Latvia, m, 1955, 3 children **DISCIPLINE** MODERN LANGUAGES, LINGUISTICS **EDUCATION** Univ Chicago, MA, 48; Harvard Univ, PhD(Slavic lang & lit), 55. **CAREER** Teaching fel Russ & Ger, Univ Chicago, 47-48; teaching fel Russ, Harvard Univ, 49-51; from asst prof to prof, 51-76 Ferrari P Ward prof, 76-81, Inst Prof Mod Lang & Ling, Mass Inst Technol, 81-96, Prof Emeritus, 96-. **HONORS AND AWARDS** Guggenheim fel, 60-61; fel, Ctr Advan Studies Behav, 60-61; J.R. Killian Jr Fac Achievement Award lectr, 78-79; Sci prize of Union de Assurances de Paris, 91; DSC (hon), Branders, 89; DHL (hon), Univ Chicago, 92. **MEMBERSHIPS** Fel Am Acad Arts & Sci; Ling Soc Am (vpres, 73, pres, 74); Nat Acad of Sci. **RESEARCH** Phonetics; general linguistics; Slavic languages and linguistics. **SELECTED PUBLICATIONS** Auth, The Sound Pattern of Russian, Mouton, The Hague, 59; coauth, Preliminaries to Speech Analysis, MIT Press, 63; The Sound Pattern of English, Harper, 68; auth, The accentuation of Russian words, Language, 4, 9/73; coauth, An Essay on Stress, MIT Press, 87; auth, On Stress and Accent, Indo-Euro Lang, 7, 3/97. **CONTACT ADDRESS** Massachusetts Inst of Tech, E39-218, Cambridge, MA, 02139-4307. **EMAIL** halle@mit.edu

HALLECK, GENE B.

DISCIPLINE TESL/PSYCHOLINGUISTICS **EDUCATION** Penn State Univ, PhD, 90. **CAREER** Assoc Prof, eng Dept, OK State Univ. **MEMBERSHIPS** TESOL; AAAL; ILTA; ACTFL. **RESEARCH** Oral Proficiency **SELECTED PUBLICATIONS** Auth, Interrater reliability of the OPI: Using academic trainee raters, Foreign Lang Annals, 96; Assessing oral proficiency: A comparison of holist and objective measures, Modern Lang J, 95; coauth, Testing language and teaching skills of international teaching assistants: The limits of contemporary strategies, TESOL Qtly, 95; coauth, Solving the plagiary puzzle: Role plays for intl students, TESOL J, 95; coauth, Probing above the ceiling in oral interviews: What's up there?, in: Current developments and alternatives in language assessment, eds, S Hunta, V Kohonen, L Kurki-Suonio, S Luoma, Jyvaskyla, U of Jyvaskyla, 97; coauth, The OPI as speech event: Native and non-native speaker's questions, in: Language proficiency interviews, eds, Richard Young, Agnes He, Benjamins, 98; coauth, Let them eat cake! Or how to avoid losing your head in cross-cultural conversations, in: Lang Prof Interviews, eds, Richard Young, Agnes He, Benjamins, 98; rev, Traveling through idioms: An exercise guide to the world of Amer idioms, Kadden, Modern Lang J, 98. **CONTACT ADDRESS** TESL Program, Oklahoma State Univ, 205 Marrill Hall, Stillwater, OK, 74078.

HALLEN, CYNTHIA L.

DISCIPLINE LINGUISTICS & PHILOLOGY **EDUCATION** Univ Arizona, PhD, 91. **CAREER** Assoc prof, 7 yrs, Brigham Young Univ **RESEARCH** Dickinson, Lexicography, philology, translation poetry. **CONTACT ADDRESS** Linguistics Dept, Brigham Young Univ, 2140 JKHB, Provo, UT, 84602-6278. **EMAIL** cynthia_hallen@byu.edu

HALLER, HERMANN WALTER

PERSONAL Born 06/02/1945, Aarau, Switzerland **DISCIPLINE** ITALIAN LINGUISTICS, ROMANCE PHILOLOGY **EDUCATION** Univ Bern, SWI, PhD, 71. **CAREER** Sci asst Romance philol, Univ Bern, 70-72; instr, 73-74, asst prof, 74-80, asst prof, Prog Comp Lit, 78-80, assoc prof Romance Lang, 80-88, PROF ROMANCE LANG, GRAD CTR, QUEENS COL, CITY UNIV NEW YORK, 89-; vis prof, NY Univ, 80, Brown Univ, 80-81, Johns Hopkins Univ, 93, Middleburg Col, 94, Univ of Treut, ITA, 96. **HONORS AND AWARDS** International Dino Compana Prize, 91; Fellow, NEH, 94-95. **MEMBERSHIPS** MLA; Am Asn Teachers Ital; Int Ling Asn; Ling Soc Am. **RESEARCH** Early Italian texts; history of Italian language; Italian stylistics; Italian dialectology; dialect literature. **SELECTED PUBLICATIONS** Auth, Der Deiktische Gebrauch des Demonstrativums im Altitalienischen, Lang, Bern, 73; ed & auth, Il Panfilo veneziano, Edizione critica, Olschki, Firenze, 82; The Hidden Italy. A Bilingual Edition of Italian Dialect Poetry, Detroit, Wayne State Univ Press, 86; Una lingua perduta e ritrovata: l'italiano degli italo-americani, Firenze, La Nuova Italia, 93; Literature in Dialect, Dialect in Literature: A Sociolinguistic Perspective, J of the Institute of Romance Studies, Supp 1, London, 96; Italian, Joshua A. Fishman and Ofelia Garcia, eds, in The Multilingual Apple. Languages in New York City, Berlin-New York: Mouton De Gruyter, 97; The Dialects Abroad, Martin Maiden and Mair Parry, eds, in The Dialects of Italy, London-New York: Routledge, 97. **CONTACT ADDRESS** European Languages and Literature, Queens Col, CUNY, 6530 Kissena Blvd, Flushing, NY, 11367-1597.

HALLETT, JUDITH P.

PERSONAL Born 04/04/1944, Chicago, IL, m, 1966, 2 children **DISCIPLINE** CLASSICAL PHILOLOGY **EDUCATION** Wellesley Univ, BA, 66; Harvard Univ, MA, 67, PhD, 71. **CAREER** Lectr and Vis Asst Prof, Clark Univ, 72-74; Asst Prof, Boston Univ, 74-82; Asst Prof Mellon Found, Brandeis Univ, 82-83; Assoc Prof, 83-93, Prof, Univ Md, 93-, Dept Chair, 96-. **HONORS AND AWARDS** Blegen Vis Schol, Vassar Col, 80; NEH Fel Col Teachers, 86-87; Distinguished Scholar-Teacher, Univ Md, 92-93. **MEMBERSHIPS** Am Philol Asn; Classical Asn Atlantic States; Phi Beta Kappa; Am Asn Univ Prof; Women's Classical Caucus. **RESEARCH** Latin language and literature; Roman culture; women, sexuality, and the family in classical antiquity; the classical tradition. **SELECTED PUBLICATIONS** Auth, Fathers and Daughters in Roman Society: Women and the Elite Family, Princeton Univ Press, 84; Feminist Theory, Historical Periods, Literary Canons and the Study of Greco-Roman Antiquity, Feminist Theory and the Classics, 93; Martial's Sulpicia and Propertius, Women in Classical Antiquity: Essays in Honor of Joy K. King, Oak Park, 93; ed and contribr, Six ¤North Americanl Women Classicists, special issue of Classical World, Nov/Dec 96-Jan/Feb 97; co-ed and contribr, The Personal Voice in Classical Scholarship, Routledge, 96; Roman Sexualities, Princeton, 97; author of numerous articles and other publications. **CONTACT ADDRESS** Classics Dept, Univ of Maryland, College Park, MD, 20742. **EMAIL** jh10@umail.umd.edu

HALLOCK, ANN HAYES

PERSONAL Born 05/13/1941, Los Angeles, CA **DISCIPLINE** ITALIAN LITERATURE **EDUCATION** Stanford Univ, BA, 63; Middlebury Col, MA, 66; Harvard Univ, PhD(Romance lang & lit), 74. **CAREER** Asst prof Ital lang & lit, Univ Calif, Rkiverside, 71-72; asst prof, 72-80, Assoc Prof Ital Lang & Lit, Tulane Univ, 80-, Consult, Nat Bilingual/Bicultural Resource Ctr Southern US, 75-77 & Nat Endowment for Humanities, 76-. **HONORS AND AWARDS** Cultural Achievement Award, Greater New Orleans Ital Cult Soc, 77; Cavaliere Ufficiale nell'Ordine di Merito, Repub of Italy, 77. **MEMBERSHIPS** Dante Soc; MLA; Am Asn Teachers Ital; SCent Mod Lang Asn; SAtlantic Mod Lang Asn. **RESEARCH** Dante and Italian literature from 13th to 14th centuries; poetry of Michelangelo. **SELECTED PUBLICATIONS** Auth, Dante's Selva Oscura and other obscure Selvas, Forum Italicum, 3/72; The pre-eminent role of Babilonia in Petrarch's Theme of the Two Cities, Italica, 77; Ugo Foscolo and the critics of Michelangelo's Rime, SAtlantic Bull, 11/77; Ensuring an Italian Renaissance, Asn Dept Foreign Lang Bull, 3/78; Michelangelo the Poet, Page-Ficklin, 78; Explication of Michelangelo's obscure pastoral poem, Rom Notes, spring 79; The origin of Michelangelo's poetic expression, Ital Quart, summer 80; Fantasticheria: Verga's declaration of transition, Ital Cult, 3/82. **CONTACT ADDRESS** Dept of French & Ital, Tulane Univ, 6823 St. Charles Ave, New Orleans, LA, 70118-5698.

HALLORAN, STEPHEN MICHAEL

PERSONAL Born 02/08/1939, Cohoes, NY, m, 1965, 2 children **DISCIPLINE** ENGLISH, SPEECH **EDUCATION** Holy Cross Col, BS, 60; Rensselaer Polytech Inst, PhD(commun & rhetoric), 73. **CAREER** English teacher, Hoosic Valley Cent Sch, 63-67; from instr to asst prof, 69-78, ASSOC PROF COMMUN, RENSSELAER POLYTECH INST, 78- **MEMBERSHIPS** NCTE; Coun Col Compos & Commun; Speech Commun Asn; Rhetoric Soc Am; Int Soc Hist of Rhetoric. **RESEARCH** Rhetorical criticism; theory of composition. **SELECTED PUBLICATIONS** Auth, History as Rhetoric--Style, Narrative, and Persuasion--Carpenter, Rhetorica-J Hist Rhet, vol 0015, 97. **CONTACT ADDRESS** Dept of Lang, Rensselaer Polytech Inst, Troy, NY, 12181.

HALLSTEIN, CHRISTIAN W.

DISCIPLINE GERMAN **EDUCATION** Pa State Univ, PhD. **CAREER** Languages, Carnegie Mellon Univ. **SELECTED PUBLICATIONS** Auth, Four Short Stories by Arnold Krieger, Studio Schaffen und Forschen, 93; Interactive Grammar Practice in a Communicative Context, Mod Lang Dept. Duquesne Univ; A New Look at Interactive Computer-Aided Language Learning, Jour Computing Small Cols, 90; Information Access and Interactive Learning: Two Modes of Computer-Aided Language Instruction, Coauth, Prospectives In Foreign Language Teaching, Youngstown State Univ, 89. **CONTACT ADDRESS** Carnegie Mellon Univ, 5000 Forbes Ave, Pittsburgh, PA, 15213.

HALPERN, CYNTHIA L.

PERSONAL Born 05/11/1952, Rochester, NY, m, 1973, 3 children **DISCIPLINE** SPANISH **EDUCATION** Bryn Mawr Col, PhD, 91. **CAREER** Assoc prof, Cabrini Col, 94-. **HONORS AND AWARDS** Tchr Year; Linback Award for Dist Tchg, Cabrini Col, 98. **MEMBERSHIPS** AATSP; PASE; MLA **RESEARCH** Golden age theater. **SELECTED PUBLICATIONS** Auth, The Political Theater of Early Seventeenth Century Spain, with Special Reference to Juan Ruiz de Alarcon. **CONTACT ADDRESS** Cabrini Col, 610 King of Prussia Rd, Radnor, PA, 19087. **EMAIL** cynthia.halpern@cabrini.edu

HALPERN, CYNTHIA LEONE

PERSONAL Born 05/11/1952, Rochester, NY, m, 1973, 3 children **DISCIPLINE** SPANISH GOLDEN AGE THEATER **EDUCATION** Bryn Mawr Col, PhD, 91. **CAREER** Assoc Prof, 7 yrs, CHMN, ROMANCE LANG & LIT, CABRINI COL, 1994-. **HONORS AND AWARDS** Linback Award for Excellence in Teaching; Philadelphia Area Spanish Educators, Spanish Teacher of the Year, 97. **MEMBERSHIPS** PASE, AATSP, MLAPV, CTFL. **RESEARCH** Theater of Juan Ruiz de Alavcon **SELECTED PUBLICATIONS** Auth, Political Theater of Early Seventeenth-Century Spain, with Special Reference to Juan Ruiz de Alavcon. **CONTACT ADDRESS** 510 Oak Grove Rd., Radnor, PA, 19087. **EMAIL** cynthia.halpern@cabrini.edu

HALPORN, JAMES WERNER

PERSONAL Born 01/04/1929, New York, NY, m, 1951, 2 children **DISCIPLINE** GREEK, LATIN **EDUCATION** Columbia Univ, AB, 49, MA, 50; Cornell Univ, PhD(Greek, Latin), 53. **CAREER** Instr Greek & Latin, Columbia Col, 54-58; vis lectr classics, Carleton Univ, 58-59; vis asst prof, Univ Mo, 59-60; asst prof, 60-64, assoc prof, 64-68, Prof Class Studies & Comp Lit, Ind Univ, Bloomington, 68-, Fulbright fel, Univ Vienna, 53-54; rep adv coun, Am Acad Rome, 62-, mem class jury Rome Prize fels, 70-71; Am Coun Learned Soc/Int Bus Mach Corp fel, 66-67; chmn region IX, Woodrow Wilson Nat Fel Found, 69-; vis prof classics & comp lit, Univ Calif, Berkeley, 71-72; mem comt on placement, Am Philol Asn, 80-83; vis scholar classics, Harvard Univ, 81-82 **MEMBERSHIPS** Am Philol Asn; NAm Patristic Soc; Class Asn Gt Brit; Soc Promotion Roman Studies; Soc Promotion Hellenic Studies. **RESEARCH** Late Latin literature; Latin palaeography; Greek and Latin metrics. **SELECTED PUBLICATIONS** Auth, Pause and Effect--An Introduction to the History of Punctuation on the West, J Medieval Studies, Vol 0069, 94; Early Printed Editions of Cassiodorus 'De Anima', Traditio-Studies Ancient Medieval Hist Thought Relig, Vol 0051, 96; Liutprand-Of-Cremona and the Freising-Codex, Munich-Clm-6388, J Medieval Studies, Vol 0070, 95. **CONTACT ADDRESS** 702 Ballantine Rd, Bloomington, IN, 47401.

HALSEY, MARTHA T.
PERSONAL Richmond, VA **DISCIPLINE** ROMANCE LANGUAGES **EDUCATION** Goucher Col, AB, 54; State Univ Iowa, MA, 56; Ohio State Univ, PhD(Span), 64. **CAREER** Instr Span & French, Iowa State Univ, 56-59; asst instr Span, Ohio State Univ, 59-64; asst prof, 64-70, assoc prof, 70-79, Prof Span, PA State Univ, University Park, 79-, Ed assoc, Mod Int Drama, Ky Romance Quart & Estreno. **MEMBERSHIPS** Am Asn Teachers Span & Port; MLA; Northeast Mod Lang Am; S Atlantic Mod Lang Asn. **RESEARCH** Nineteenth and twentieth century Spanish literature. **SELECTED PUBLICATIONS** Auth, An International Seminar on Arniches, Carlos And His Work, Estreno-Cuadernos Del Teatro Espanol Contemporaneo, Vol 0020, 94; 'Puesto Ya El Pie En El Estribo' Debuts At Melilla, Rodriguezmendez, Jose, Maria Does Cervantes, Estreno-Cuadernos Del Teatro Espanol Contemporaneo, Vol 0023, 97; A Seminar on Theater and Its Teaching, Estreno-Cuadernos Del Teatro Espanol Contemporaneo, Vol 0020, 94; Homage to Buerovallejo, Antonio In The Ateneo, Estreno-Cuadernos Del Teatro Espanol Contemporaneo, Vol 0023, 97; Revival of Recuerda, Martin Las 'Arrecogias' In Valencia, Estreno-Cuadernos Del Teatro Espanol Contemporaneo, Vol 0023, 97; Olmo, Lauro--In-Memoriam, Estreno-Cuadernos Del Teatro Espanol Contemporaneo, Vol 0022, 96. **CONTACT ADDRESS** Dept of Span, Pennsylvania State Univ, University Park, PA, 16802.

HALTON, THOMAS
PERSONAL Born 02/06/1925, Cavan, Ireland **DISCIPLINE** GREEK, LATIN **EDUCATION** Maynooth Col, Ireland, BA, 46, STB, 49; Univ Col, Dublin, MA, 58; Cath Univ Am, PhD, 63. **CAREER** Assoc prof, 60-75, Prof Greek & Latin, Cath Univ AM, 75- **MEMBERSHIPS** Early Christian Greek **SELECTED PUBLICATIONS** Auth, The Martyrdom of Pionios-French, Cath Hist Rev, Vol 0081, 95; John-Chrysostom, The Homilies on the Statues--An Introduction, Cath Hist Rev, Vol 0080, 94. **CONTACT ADDRESS** Dept of Greek & Latin Cath, Catholic Univ of America, 620 Michigan Ave N E, Washington, DC, 20064-0002.

HAMALIAN, LEO
PERSONAL Born 01/13/1920, New York, NY, m, 1943, 3 children **DISCIPLINE** ENGLISH, COMPARATIVE LITERATURE **EDUCATION** Cornell Univ, BS, 42; Columbia Univ, MA, 47, PhD(English), 54. **CAREER** Instr English, New York Univ, 47-54; from instr to assoc prof, 54-67, PROF ENGLISH LIT, CITY COL NEW YORK, 67-, DIR, GRAD CREATIVE WRITING, 72-, Smith-Mundt grant, Syria, 62-64; Am Studies Sem fel, Columbia Univ, 68-; dean, Calif Inst of Arts, 70-72; mem, bd dir, Tuum Est Drug Rehabil Ctr, Venice, 71-; Fulbright lectr, Univ Tehran, 74-75 & Univ Hamburg, 80; ed, Ararat. **MEMBERSHIPS** MLA; NCTE; Am Studies Asn; English Union; PEN Club. **RESEARCH** T S Eliot; D H Lawrence; comparative continental literature. **SELECTED PUBLICATIONS** Auth, Wright, Richard and Racial Discourse, Am Lit, Vol 0069, 97. **CONTACT ADDRESS** Dept of English, City Col, CUNY, New York, NY, 10031.

HAMEL, MARY
DISCIPLINE ANCIENT AND MEDIEVAL EUROPEAN LITERATURE, CHAUCER, AND THE ENGLISH LANGUAGE **EDUCATION** Pa State Univ, PhD. **CAREER** Dept Eng, Mt. Saint Mary's Col **SELECTED PUBLICATIONS** Publ, a bk and articles on, Middle Engl lit; assoc ed, scholarly jour Chaucer Rev. **CONTACT ADDRESS** Dept of English, Mount Saint Mary's Col, 16300 Old Emmitsburg Rd, Emmitsburg, MD, 21727-7799. **EMAIL** hamel@msmary.edu

HAMILTON, JAMES FRANCIS
PERSONAL Born 12/09/1939, Cleveland, OH, m, 1963, 2 children **DISCIPLINE** FRENCH LITERATURE & LANGUAGE **EDUCATION** Kent State Univ, BSEd, 62; Ohio State Univ, MA, 65, PhD(Romance lang), 70. **CAREER** Teacher French, Lincoln High Sch, Cleveland, Ohio, 62-63; instr & asst supvr, Ohio State Univ, 63-69; asst prof, Denison Univ, 69-70; asst prof, 70-76, assoc prof, 76-81, Prof French, Univ Cincinnati, 81-, Taft fac grant, 72. **MEMBERSHIPS** Am Asn Teachers Fr; MLA; Soc Fr Etude VIIIe Siecle; Am Soc Eighteenth Century Studies. **RESEARCH** Rousseau and romanticism; Montesquieu to Zola. **SELECTED PUBLICATIONS** Auth, The Recovery of Psychic Center in Daudet Les 'Lettres De Mon Moulin', 19th C French Studies, Vol 0024, 95; Dickens A 'Tale Of Two Cities', Explicator, Vol 0053, 95; Terrorizing the Feminine in Hugo, Dickens, And France, J Modern Lit, Vol 0048, 94; The Heros Journey to Niagara in Chateaubriand and Heredia, French And Cuban Exiles, Romance Quarterly, Vol 0041, 94. **CONTACT ADDRESS** Dept of Romance Lang, Univ of Cincinnati, P O Box 210377, Cincinnati, OH, 45221-0377.

HAMILTON, JOHN DANIEL BURGOYNE
PERSONAL Born 10/19/1939, Los Angeles, CA **DISCIPLINE** CLASSICAL LANGUAGES, GREEK MYTHOLOGY & RELIGION **EDUCATION** St Louis Univ, AB, 63; AM, 64; Weston Col, Cambridge, MS, MDiv, 69; Univ MN, PhD, 73. **CAREER** Instr classics, Univ Santa Clara, 65-66; asst prof, 72-76, assoc prof Classics, 77-, GRAD STUDIES ADV, CLASSICS, COL OF THE HOLY CROSS, 89-. **MEMBERSHIPS** Am Philol Asn; Class Asn New England; Class Asn Midwest & South; Soc Promotion Hellenic Studies; Class Asn Gt Brit. **RESEARCH** Greek epic and drama; mythology; Roman satire. **SELECTED PUBLICATIONS** Auth, Justin's Apology 66: A review of scholarship, 72 & The church and the language of mystery, 77, Ephemerides Theol Lovanienses; transl (with B Nagy), L Gernet, The Anthropology of Ancient Greece, Johns Hopkins, 81; Antigone: Kinship, Justice and the Womb, in Myth and the Pelis, Cornell, 91; At Sea with Myth: A Bibliography for Charting a Course, NE Clas J, Dec 89; contrib, articles in The World Book Encyclopedia, 93. **CONTACT ADDRESS** Dept of Calssics, Col of the Holy Cross, 1 College St, Worcester, MA, 01610-2395. **EMAIL** jhamilto@holycross.edu

HAMILTON, RICHARD
PERSONAL Born 12/19/1943, Bryn Mawr, PA, m, 1965, 2 children **DISCIPLINE** GREEK LITERATURE **EDUCATION** Harvard Col, AB, 65; Univ Mich, PhD(class), 71. **CAREER** From Asst Prof to Assoc Prof, 71-88, Prof Greek, Bryn Mawr Col, 88-. **MEMBERSHIPS** Am Philol Asn. **RESEARCH** Greek literature; Greek religion. **SELECTED PUBLICATIONS** Auth, Epinikion: General Form in the Odes of Pindar, Mouton, The Hague, 74; The Architecture of Hesiod's Theogany and Works and Days, Hopkins, 89; Choes and Anthesteria, Mich, 92; Treasure Map, Mich (forthcoming 98). **CONTACT ADDRESS** Dept of Greek, Bryn Mawr Col, 101 N Merion Ave, Bryn Mawr, PA, 19010-2899. **EMAIL** rhamilto@brynmawr.edu

HAMLIN, FRANK RODWAY
PERSONAL Born 04/10/1935, Wolverhampton, England, m, 1968, 2 children **DISCIPLINE** ROMANCE LINGUISTICS **EDUCATION** Univ Birmingham, BA, 57, PhD(French), 59 Cambridge Univ, MA, 61. **CAREER** Lectr mediaeval French, Queen's Univ, Belfast, 60-61; res fel French, Gonville & Caius Col, Cambridge, 61-63; asst prof, 63-68, assoc prof, 68-78, Prof French, Univ BC, 78-, Can Coun fel, 68-69, 76-77 & 82-83. **MEMBERSHIPS** Soc Ling Romane; Soc Fr Onomastique; English Place-Name Soc; Can Soc Study Names; Am Name Soc. **RESEARCH** Toponymy, especially of Southern France; Old Provencal language and literature. **SELECTED PUBLICATIONS** Auth, The Adventure of Languages in the West--Their Origins, Their History, Their Geography, J Int Ling Asn, Vol 0047, 96; A History of Indo-European Verb Morphology, J Int Ling Asn, Vol 0046, 95. **CONTACT ADDRESS** Dept of French, Univ of BC, Vancouver, BC, V6T 1W5.

HAMMERMEISTER, KAI
PERSONAL Born 07/15/1967, Guttingen, Germany **DISCIPLINE** FOREIGN LANGUAGES **EDUCATION** Univ Tubingen, 88-90; Univ Va, MA, 92, PhD, 95. **CAREER** Instr, Univ Va, 95-96; asst prof, Ohio State Univ, 98-. **MEMBERSHIPS** MLA **RESEARCH** German intellectual history; literary theory; aerthetics; Hermeneutics. **SELECTED PUBLICATIONS** Auth, art, Inventing History: Toward a Gay Holocaust Literature, 96; auth, art, Pragmatismus als Anti-Asthetik, 96; auth, art, Literature between Social Change and the Valuation of Tradition, 99; auth, Hans-Georg Gadamer, 99. **CONTACT ADDRESS** Dept of Germanic Languages and Literatures, Ohio State Univ, 1841 Millikin Rd, 314 Cunz Hall, Columbus, OH, 43210. **EMAIL** hammermeister.2@osu.edu

HAMP, ERIC PRATT
PERSONAL Born 11/16/1920, London, England, m, 1951 **DISCIPLINE** LINGUISTICS **EDUCATION** Amherst Col, BA, 42; Harvard Univ, MA, 48, PhD(ling), 54. **CAREER** Chief lend-lease, Govt Union SAfrica, 42-46; from instr to assoc prof, 50-62, chmn, Dept Ling, 66-69, Prof Indo-Europ Ling, Univ Chicago, 62-, Prof Behav Sci, 71-, Prof Slavic Lang, 80-, Dir, Ctr Balkan & Slavic Studies, 65-, Vis lectr, Univ Mich, 53, Univ Wash, 62, Europe, 65-67 & 73-78 & US cult exchange lectr, Univ Bucharest, USSR, 75 & 76; Fulbright res scholar, Greece, 55-56 & Fulbright-Hays fel, Copenhagen Univ, 66-67; mem staff, Gaelic Dialect Surv, Edinburgh, 56-58; secy comt lang prog, Am Coun Learned Soc, 59-63, chmn, 63-69; Am Coon Learned Soc-Soc Sci Res Coun grant Albanian res, Greece & Yugoslavia, 60-61; mem, Nat Sci Found Sem Comput Ling, Rand Corp, 63; mem, Comt Automatic Lang Processing, Nat Acad Sci-Nat Res Coun, 64- & Comt Ling Info, Ctr Appl Ling, 64-68; vis prof, Ind Univ, 64, Univ Belgrade, 64 & 67, Univ Ill, 68 & Univ Salzburg, 79 & 82; mem, Comt Hist & Theory Ling, Ind Univ Press, 65-73, Adv Comt East Europ Coun Int Exchange Scholars, 66-78, Comt Lang & Lit, Ctr Neo-Hellenic Studies, 67-78, US Nat Comn, UNESCO, 72-78 & Phillips Fund Comt, Am Philos Soc, 77-; chmn, Comt Ill Place-Name Surv, 66-; consult, US Off Educ, 66-72, Harper & Row, 71-, Nat Endowment for Humanities, 76-82, Nat Sci Found Subcomt Linguistics, 77-79 & Am Printing House for Blind, 77-; adv, Encycl Britannica, 69-; assoc ed, Int J Am Ling, 69-; vis scholar, Inst Arts & Humanistic Studies, Pa State Univ, 69; Guggenheim fel, 73-74. **HONORS AND AWARDS** Ling Soc Am Collitz prof, Univ Tex, 60; Vernam Hull lectr Celtic studies, Harvard Univ, 71; Innaugural lectr, Ctr Celtic Studies, Aberystwyth, 79., LHD, Amherst Col, 72. **MEMBERSHIPS** Fel Am Acad Arts & Sci; Am Philos Soc; Ling Soc Am (vpres, 63 & 70, pres, 71); MLA; fel Am Anthrop Asn. **RESEARCH** General linguistics; Indo-European language and culture; Celtic, Balkan and Amerindian languages. **SELECTED PUBLICATIONS** Auth, The Typology of Indo-European, J Indo-European Studies, Vol 0022, 94; On the Indo-European Origins of the Retroflexes in Sanskrit, J Am Oriental Soc, Vol 0116, 96; Tascio--A Comment on a Recent Article by Bernardostempel, Zeitschrift Fur Celtische Philologie, Vol 0046, 94; The Death of the Irish Language--A Qualified Obituary, Modern Philol, Vol 0091, 93; On Northern-European Maro--Versus Mori--In Celtic, Zeitschrift Fur Celtische Philologie, Vol 0046, 94. **CONTACT ADDRESS** Dept of Ling, Univ of Chicago, Chicago, IL, 60637.

HAN, MIEKO
DISCIPLINE EAST ASIAN LANGUAGES **EDUCATION** Univ Tex, PhD, 61. **CAREER** Prof, Univ Southern Calif. **RESEARCH** Japanese language; linguistics and phonetic study of Asian languages. **SELECTED PUBLICATIONS** Auth, Living in Japan: Intermediate Conversational Japanese; Acoustic Manifestations of Mora Timing in Japanese. **CONTACT ADDRESS** East Asian Studies Center, Univ Southern Calif, University Park Campus, Los Angeles, CA, 90089.

HANAN, PATRICK DEWES
PERSONAL Born 01/04/1927, New Zealand, m, 1951, 1 child **DISCIPLINE** CHINESE LITERATURE **EDUCATION** Univ NZ, BA, 48, MA, 49; Univ London, BA, 53, PhD, 60. **CAREER** Lectr Chinese, Sch Orient & African Studies, Univ London, 54-63; from assoc prof to prof, Stanford Univ, 63-68; prof Chinese lit, 68-89, Victor S. Thomas Prof of Chinese Lit, 89-98, Victor S Thomas Res Prof of Chinese Lit, 98-, Harvard Univ. **HONORS AND AWARDS** Guggenheim fel, 77; fel, Am Acad of Arts & Sci, 77-; Levenson Award of Asn Asian Stud, 90; Concurrent Prof of Nanjimg Univ, 95-. **MEMBERSHIPS** Asn Asian Studies; Am Orient Soc. **RESEARCH** Chinese literature. **SELECTED PUBLICATIONS** Auth, The Chinese Short Story, 73; auth, The Chinese Vernacular Story, 81; auth, The Invention of Li Yu, 88; transl, The Carnal Prayer Mat, 90; auth, A Tower for the Summer Heat, 92; transl, The Sea of Regret, 95; transl, The Money Demons, 98. **CONTACT ADDRESS** Dept of Far Eastern Lang, Harvard Univ, 2 Divinity Ave, Cambridge, MA, 02138-2020. **EMAIL** hanan@fas.harvard.edu

HANKAMER, JORGE
PERSONAL Born 09/12/1940, Alvin, TX **DISCIPLINE** LINGUISTICS **EDUCATION** Rice Univ, BA, 62, MA, 66; Yale Univ, PhD(Ling), 71. **CAREER** Fel Ling, Mass Inst Technol, 71-73; asst prof, Tufts Univ, 72-73; asst prof, Harvard Univ, 73-78, assoc prof Ling, 78-80; from assoc prof to prof Ling, Univ Calif, Santa Cruz, 80-83; ed, Ling Inquiry, Squibs & Discussions, 75-77 & Dissertations in Ling ser, Garland Publ Co, 75-; vis asst prof Ling, Bogazici Univ, Istanbul, 76-77; assoc ed, Language, 81-; assoc vice chancellor, Planning and Programs, UCSC, 90-95; dean of Humanities, 95-. **MEMBERSHIPS** Ling Soc Am; New Eng Ling Soc. **RESEARCH** Syntax and semantics of natural language; Turkish syntax. **SELECTED PUBLICATIONS** Auth, Unacceptable ambiguity, 73 & coauth, Deep and surface anaphora, 76, Ling Inquiry; auth, On the interpretation of anaphoric expressions, Georgetown Univ Round Table, 76; Multiple analysis, In: Mechanisms of Syntactic Change, 77; coauth, Ambiguity, Encycl Einandi, 78. **CONTACT ADDRESS** Cowell Commons, Univ of California, Santa Cruz, 1156 High St, Santa Cruz, CA, 95064-0001.

HANLIN, TODD
PERSONAL Born 11/09/1941, Buchanan, MI, m, 1969, 2 children **DISCIPLINE** CONTEMPORARY DRAMA AND PROSE OF THE GERMAN-SPEAKING COUNTRIES **EDUCATION** Wabash Col, BA, 64, Univ Kans, MA, 67; Bryn Mawr Col, PhD, 75. **CAREER** English and Lit, Univ Ark. **HONORS AND AWARDS** Outstanding Tchr Award; Fulbright grant. **SELECTED PUBLICATIONS** Area: Franz Kafka. **CONTACT ADDRESS** Univ Ark, Fayetteville, AR, 72701.

HANNA, BLAKE THOMPSON
PERSONAL Born 08/02/1927, Boston, MA, m, 1950, 3 children **DISCIPLINE** LINGUISTICS, MODERN LANGUAGES **EDUCATION** Bowdoin Col, BA, 48; Univ Montreal, MA, 53, PhD(French), 64. **CAREER** Instr English, Col Stanislas, Montreal, 53-57; from asst prof to assoc prof, 57-69, Prof Ling, Univ Montreal, 69-, Can Coun res grant, 66. **MEMBERSHIPS** MLA; Soc Transl & Interpreters Can (vpres, 67-68); Soc Fr Etude XVIIIe Siecle; Am Soc 18th Century Studies; Can Soc 18th Century Studies. **RESEARCH** Translating and interpreting; 18th century French literature; teaching English as a second language. **SELECTED PUBLICATIONS** Auth, How to Write a Precis, Meta, Vol 0038, 93; Comparative Stylistics of French and English, A Methodology for Translation, Meta, Vol 0041, 96. **CONTACT ADDRESS** Sch of Transl, Univ Montreal, PO Box 6128 Br, Montreal, PQ, H3C 3J7.

HANREZ, MARC
PERSONAL Born 08/15/1934, Brussels, Belgium, 3 children **DISCIPLINE** ROMANCE LANGUAGES **EDUCATION** Free Univ Brussels, Lic en Philos et Lett & Agrege, 58; Univ Paris, VII, Dr 3e Cycle, 73. **CAREER** Asst prof Romance lang, Univ Mass, Amherst, 67-70; assoc prof, 70-76, Prof French, Univ Wis-Madison, 76-, Guggenheim fel, 72-73. **RESEARCH** Contemporary French literature, especially Abellio, Celine, Drieu la Rochelle, Malraux, Proust; the war fiction, ideology and fine arts. **SELECTED PUBLICATIONS** Auth, Celine, Gallimard, Paris, 61, 69; ed, Les Ecrivains et la Guerre d'Espagne, Dossiers H, Paris, 75; auth, Sous les signes d'Abellio, L'Age d'Homme, Lausanne, 76; ed, Drieu la Rochelle, Cahiers de l'Herne, Paris, 82; auth, La Grande Chose Americaine, Cadex Editions, 92. **CONTACT ADDRESS** Dept of French & Ital, Univ of Wis, 1220 Linden Drive, Madison, WI, 53706-1557.

HANSEN, THOMAS S.
DISCIPLINE ELEMENTARY AND INTERMEDIATE LANGUAGE COURSES **EDUCATION** Tufts Univ, AB, 69, AM, 71; Harvard Univ, PhD, 77. **CAREER** Lang, Wellesley Col. **HONORS AND AWARDS** Ch the Admin Law Comt the Judicial Council, a mem the KS Bar Asn J Board Ed(s) and serves as Counsel to the Topeka Metropolitan Transit Authority. **CONTACT ADDRESS** Wellesley Col, 106 Central, Wellesley, MA.

HANSEN, WILLIAM F.
PERSONAL Born 06/22/1941, Fresno, CA, m, 1994, 1 child **DISCIPLINE** CLASSICAL STUDIES, FOLKLORE **EDUCATION** Univ Calif, Berkeley, BA, 65, PhD, 70. **CAREER** From asst prof to assoc prof, Class Stud & Fel of the Folklore Inst, 70-85, prof, 85-92, prof Class Stud & Folklore, 92- , assoc dean fac, 86-92, chemn, Class Stud, 97- co-dir Program in Mythology Stud, 98- , Indiana Univ, Bloomington. **HONORS AND AWARDS** Phi Beta Kappa, 65; NEH Younger Hum Fel, 72-73; Am Coun Learned Soc fel, 77-78, 92. **MEMBERSHIPS** Am Philol Asn; Class Asn of the Middle West and South; Am Folklore Soc; Calif Folklore Soc; Hoosier Folklore Soc; Int Soc for Folk-Narrative Res; Int Soc for Contemp Legend Res. **RESEARCH** Mythology; folklore; early Greek epic; early fiction. **SELECTED PUBLICATIONS** Auth, The Theft of the Thunderweapon: A Greek Myth in Its International Context, Classica et Mediaevalia, 95; auth, Abraham and the Grateful Dead Man, in Bendix, ed, Folklore Interpreted: Essays in Honor of Alan Dundes, Garland, 95; auth, The Protagonist on the Pyre: Herodotean Legend and Modern Folktale, Fabula, 96; auth, Phlegon of Tralles' Book of Marvels, Univ Exeter, 96; auth, Homer and the Folktale, in Morris, ed, A New Companion to Homer, Brill, 97; auth, Idealization as a Process in Ancient Greek Story-Formation, Symbolae Osloenses, 97; auth, Mythology and Folktale Typology: Chronicle of a Failed Scholarly Revolution, J of Folklore Res, 97; ed, Anthology of Ancient Greek Popular Literature, Indiana, 98. **CONTACT ADDRESS** Classical Studies Dept, Indiana Univ, Bloomington, 1020 E Kirkwood Ave, Bloomington, IN, 47405-7103. **EMAIL** hansen@indiana.edu

HANSON, KLAUS D.
DISCIPLINE GERMAN **EDUCATION** Univ IL, PhD, 72. **CAREER** Prof; Univ WY, 73-; taught in, Ger & Japan; supvr, UW's stud exchange-Univ Oldenburg; dept head, 84-89; dir, lang lab. **RESEARCH** Contemp Ger theater and cult; pedag; Renaissance and Baroque lit. **SELECTED PUBLICATIONS** Publ, bk, articles, on Ger theater and Baroque poetry. **CONTACT ADDRESS** Dept of Mod and Class Lang(s), Univ WY, PO Box 3964, Laramie, WY, 82071-3964. **EMAIL** HANSON@UWYO.EDU

HARDER, BERNHARD D.
DISCIPLINE ENGLISH LANGUAGE; LITERATURE **EDUCATION** BC, BA, MA; NC Univ, PhD, 70. **CAREER** Assoc prof. **RESEARCH** International and Aboriginal literatures. **SELECTED PUBLICATIONS** Co-ed, Oxford UP ed of On the Properties of Things: John Trevisa's Translation of Bartholomaeus Anglicus De Proprietatibus Rerum: A Critical Text, 3 vols; pub (s), relationships between lang and soc and on Medieval and int lit. **CONTACT ADDRESS** Dept of English Language and Literature, Univ of Windsor, 401 Sunset Ave, Windsor, ON, N9B 3P4. **EMAIL** harder@uwindsor.ca

HARDIN, JAMES NEAL
PERSONAL Born 02/17/1939, Nashville, TN **DISCIPLINE** GERMAN & COMPARATIVE LITERATURE **EDUCATION** Washington & Lee Univ, AB, 60; Univ NC, Chapel Hill, MA, 64, PhD(Ger & comp lit), 67. **CAREER** Asst Ger, Univ NC, 62-67; from asst prof to assoc prof, 69-73, Ger Acad Exchange Serv grant, 73, Prof Ger, Univ SC, 73-, Fulbright fel, 60-61; Alexander von Humboldt fel, 74-75. **MEMBERSHIPS** MLA; SAtlantic Mod Lang Asn; Am Asn Tchrs Ger; Am Soc Ger Lit 16th & 17th Centuries. **RESEARCH** Sixteenth and 17th century Ger lit; Ger Baroque novel; descriptive bibl. **SELECTED PUBLICATIONS** Auth, Theme of salvation in the novels of Hermann Broch, PMLA, 70; George B Shaw's Saint Joan, Diesterweg, 74; Hermann Broch's theories of mass psychology, Ger Quart, 74; Johann Beers Parodie Printz Adimantus, Jahrbuch int Ger, 75; Descriptive bibliography and the works of Johann Beer, Wolfenbutteler Barocknachrichten, 77; ed, Der verliebte Oesterreicher von Johann Beer, Lang, Bern, 78; auth, Eine Beschreibende Bibliographie der Werke Johann Beers, Francke Verlag, 78; Johann Beer, Twayne Series, 79; co-ed, Figures of German Literature in Dictionary of Literacy, 93-97, ed, Camden House in Print, Boydell and Brewer, 98-. **CONTACT ADDRESS** Dept of Ger and Slavic, Univ of SC, Columbia, SC, 29208. **EMAIL** camdenhouse@compuserve.com

HARDING, GEORGE E.
PERSONAL Born 08/11/1950, Birmingham, AL, m, 1974, 2 children **DISCIPLINE** GERMANIC LANGUAGES & LITERATURE **EDUCATION** Birmingham-Southern Col, BA, 72; Miss State Univ, MA, 74; Univ Tenn, Knoxville, PhD, 85. **CAREER** Teacher, Knoxville City Schs, 81-86; Instr, for lang, Univ Kentucky Community Col, 86-87; from asst to ASSOC PROF, GERMAN, FRANCIS MARION UNIV, 87-. **HONORS AND AWARDS** Gerti Wunderlich Award, 80; Delta Phi Alpha, 71; Phi Delta Phi, 74; Phi Kappa Phi, 79. **MEMBERSHIPS** S Atlantic Mod Lang Asn; Philogical Asn Carolinas. **RESEARCH** Medieval literature **SELECTED PUBLICATIONS** Ed, The Gast of Gy, 95; ed, Golf: The Thinking Game, 95; auth, rev of The Pilgrimage Motif in the Works of the Medieval German Author Hartmann von Aue, Arturiana, 97 **CONTACT ADDRESS** Francis Marion Univ, CEMC 113, Florence, SC, 29501. **EMAIL** gharding@fmarion.edu

HARE, JOHN
PERSONAL m, 2 children **DISCIPLINE** CLASSICAL PHILOSOPHY **EDUCATION** Princeton Univ, PhD, 75 **CAREER** Staff Assoc, House Foreign Affairs Comm, Washington DC, 82-83; Amer Philos Assn Congressional fel, 81-82; vis fel, Hum, Medical Col Penn, 78-81; vis asst prof, Univ Mich, 75; Instr, 74, asst prof, 75-81, assoc prof, 81-87, prof 87, Lehigh Univ; prof, Calvin Col, 89. **HONORS AND AWARDS** Inst Adv Christian Stud (IFACS) Bk prize, 97; Pew Evangelical fel, 91-92; Jr Lindback awd for disting tchg, 81; Elected Hon Mem Phi Beta Kappa, 79. **MEMBERSHIPS** APA; APA Congressional fel selection comm, 83-89; Mem NY Aristotle Group, 75-81; Prog Comm APA Central Div, 96-97. **SELECTED PUBLICATIONS** Auth, The Apology as an Inverted Parody of Rhetoric, Arethusa, 14.2, Fall, 81, 205-216; Ethics and International Affairs, London, MacMillan, 82; Plato's Euthyphro, Bryn Mawr, 81, 2nd ed, 85; The Unfinished Business of the Peace Process in the Middle East, Report of Congressional Study Mission to Europe and the Middle East, Nov 82, House Foreign Affairs Comm, 97th Congress, 2nd Session; The Hospice Movement and the Acceptance of Death, Hospice USA, ed Austin H. Kutscher, New York, Columbia UP, 83, 9-17; Threats and Intentions, Evangelical Perspective on the Catholic Bishops' Pastoral Letter, ed Dean Curry, Grand Rapids, Eerdmans, 84, 139-157; Philosophy in the Legislative Process, Intl Jour Applied Ethics, 2, 2, Fall 84, 81-88; Credibility and Bluff, in Nuclear Weapons and the Future of Humanity, Totowa, Rowman and Allanheld, 86, 191-199; Nuclear Deterrence as Bluff, in Political Realism and International Morality: Ethics in the Nuclear Age, Boulder, Westview Press, 87, 144-152; Aristotelian Justice and the Pull to Consensus, in Intl Jour Applied Ethics, 3,3, Spring 89, 37-49; Commentary on Timothy J. Brennan, Academic Disciplines and Representative Advocacy, Bus and Prof Ethics Jour, 6, 1, 88, 56-62; Il Movemento Hospice e L'accettazione della Morte, Progressi Clinici: Medicina, 3, 3, 88, 137-140; Eleutheriotes in Aristotle's Ethics, in Ancient Philos, Spring, 88, 19-32; The Moral Argument for the Existence of God, and The Claims of Religious Experience, in Evidence for Faith, Richardson, Probe, 90, 231-252, and 253-273; Jackie Kennedy and the Seven Dwarfs, in Dialogue, April/May, 91, 23, 6, 20-31; The Atonement: How Does Christ Bridge the Gap, in The Banner, April 13, 92, 4-6; Government, Ethics in, in Encycl of Ethics, 92, 412-416, rev 97; Puffing up the Capacity, Jour Philos Res, XIX, 94, 75-88; Commercial Contracts and the Moral Contract, in Christian Scholar's Rev, XXIII, 3, 94, 259-266; The Invitation, poem, Dialogue, March/April 95, 8; The Atonement, Perspectives, May 95, 16-18; The History of Christian Ethics, in New Dictionary of Christian Ethics and Pastoral Theology, ed David Kingon, InterVarsity Press, 95, 33-42; The Unhappiest Man, in Kierkegaard's Either/Or, International Kierkegaard Commentary, Mercer Press, 95, 91-108; Kantian Ethics, International Politics and the Enlargement of the Foedus Pacificum, in Sovereignty at the Crossroads, Rowman, 96, 71-92; The Moral Gap, Oxford, Clarendon Press, 96; Atonement, Justification, and Santification, in A Companion to the Philosophy of Religion, Blackwell, 97, 549-555; Augustine, Kant and the Moral Gap, The augustinian Tradition, ed Gareth Matthews, U of California P, 97, 220-230; Why Bertrand Russell was not a Christian, Bk (s) and Cult, May/June, 98, 26-28. **CONTACT ADDRESS** Univ of Notre Dame, Flanner 1112, Notre Dame, IN, 46556. **EMAIL** hare.2@nd.edu

HARLOW, L.L.
PERSONAL Born 06/10/1949, Batesville, IN, m, 1973, 1 child **DISCIPLINE** LANGUAGE **EDUCATION** Ball St Univ, BA, 71; Purdue Univ, MAT, 78, PhD, 82. **CAREER** Tchr, 71-72, Port Huron Schl Corp; Tchr, 74-76, Tippecanoe Schl Corp; Tchng Asst, 76-82, Purdue Univ; Asst Prof, 82-85, Atlantic Christian Col; Asst Prof, 91, Assoc Prof, 91-, Assoc Dean, 97-, Ohio St Univ. **HONORS AND AWARDS** Fondation Franco-Americaine, Voyage d'etudes, 94; MLA/NEH Awd, Middlebury Col, 91; Univ Res Grant, 90; Intl Trvl Grant, College of Humanities, 87, 92, 96; Grant-in-Aid, 86; David Ross Fel, 81, 79; Phi Delta Kappa Ed Hon; Phi Kappa Phi Honor Soc; Pi Delta Phi French Hon. **MEMBERSHIPS** Amer Coun on the Tchng of Foreign Lang; Amer Assoc of Tchrs of French; Amer Assoc of Univ Supv Coor and Dir of Foreign Lan Prog; Ohio Foreign Lang Tchrs Assoc. **RESEARCH** Foreign Language Pedagogy; TA Training; Sociopragmatics. **SELECTED PUBLICATIONS** CoAuth, Bravo Culture et Litterature, Heinle & Heinle, 93; CoAuth, Bravo Communication et Grammaire, Heinle & Heinle, 93 & 94; Bravo Communication, Grammaire, Culture et Litterature, Heinle & Heinle, 98; CoAuth, Collaborative Partnerships for Articullatin Asking the Right Questions, For Lang Ann, 96; CoAuth, Politeness Strategies in French and English Implications for Second Language Acquisition, Speech Acts Across Cultures, 95; Priorities for Intermediate-Level Language Instruction, Mod Lang Jour, 94; The Effects of the Yellow Highlighter - Second Language Learner Strategies and Their Effectiveness A Research Update, Canadian Mod lang Rev, 88. **CONTACT ADDRESS** Ohio State Univ, College of Humanities, 230 N Oval, Columbus, OH, 43210. **EMAIL** harlow.1@osu.edu

HARMS, ROBERT THOMAS
PERSONAL Born 04/12/1932, Peoria, IL, m, 1956, 4 children **DISCIPLINE** LINGUISTICS **EDUCATION** Univ Chicago, AB, 52, AM, 56, PhD, 60. **CAREER** From instr to asst prof Russ & ling, 58-65, assoc prof ling & Slavic lang, 65-67, actg chmn, 72-73, chmn dept, 73-77, prof ling, Univ Tex, Austin, 67-, Grant, Inter-Univ Comt Travel Grants, Leningrad State Univ, USSR, 62-63, res grant, Hungarian Acad Sci, Budapest & Univ Szeged, 67-68; Fulbright res scholar, Univ Helsinki, 68; res grant, USSR Acad of Sci, Tallinn & Syktyvkar, 78. **MEMBERSHIPS** Ling Soc Am. **RESEARCH** Phonology; historical linguistics; Uralic linguistics. **SELECTED PUBLICATIONS** Auth, Estonian Grammar, 62 & Finnish Structural Sketch, 64, Uralic & Altaic Ser, Ind Univ; The Measurement of Phonological Economy, Language, 66; Introduction to Phonological Theory, Prentice-Hall, 68; coauth, How do Languages Get Crazy Rules, In: Linguistic Change and Generative Theory, Ind Univ, 72; auth, Uralic languages, In: Encycl Britannica, 74. **CONTACT ADDRESS** Dept of Ling, Univ of Tex, Austin, TX, 78712-1026. **EMAIL** harms@mail.utexas.edu

HARPER, SANDRA NADINE
PERSONAL Born 06/28/1938, Fostoria, OH, m, 1959 **DISCIPLINE** ROMANCE LANGUAGES **EDUCATION** Ohio State Univ, BS, 59, MA, 65, PhD(Span theater), 68. **CAREER** Teacher pub schs, Ohio, 59-62; instr, 68-69, asst prof, 69-79, Assoc Prof Romance Lamg, Ohio Wesleyan Univ, 79-, Chairperson, 80-, Mellon grant, Ohio Wesleyan Univ, 72-73, 76 & 80. **MEMBERSHIPS** MLA; Am Asn Teachers Span & Port; AAUP. **RESEARCH** Contemporary Spanish theater, especially Alfonso Sastre; developing real communication in the foreign language classroom; the works of Rosario Castellanos. **SELECTED PUBLICATIONS** Auth, Buerovallejo, Antonio In His Mirrors, Estreno-Cuadernos Del Teatro Espanol Contemporaneo, Vol 0023, 97; Reina, Maria Manuela 'Reflejos Con Cenizas'--A Conflation Of Generations, Estreno-Cuadernos Del Teatro Espanol Contemporaneo, Vol 0023, 97; La 'Truhana'--Gala,, Estreno-Cuadernos Del Teatro Espanol Contemporaneo, Vol 0021, 95. **CONTACT ADDRESS** Dept of Romance Lang, Ohio Wesleyan Univ, 61 S Sandusky St, Delaware, OH, 43015-2398.

HARPINE, WILLIAM
PERSONAL Born 09/15/1951, Washington, DC, m, 1977, 3 children **DISCIPLINE** SPEECH COMMUNICATION **EDUCATION** Coll of William and Mary, BA, 73; Northern IL Univ, MA, 74; Univ IL at Urbana-Champaign, PhD, 82. **CAREER** Temporary instr, 75-76, IA State Univ; asst prof, 79-82, Coll of William & Mary; prof, 82-present, Univ Akron. **MEMBERSHIPS** Natl Communication Assn; Amer Soc for the Hist of Rhetoric **RESEARCH** 19th century Amer public speaking; rhetoric theory. **SELECTED PUBLICATIONS** Auth, The Appeal to Tradition: Cultural Evolution and Logical Soundness, Informal Logic, 93; Stock Issues and Theories of Ethics, Southern Journal of Forensics, 96; Epideictic and Ethos in the Amarna Letters: The Withholding of Argument, Rhetoric Society Quarterly, 98. **CONTACT ADDRESS** Sch of Communication, Univ Akron, 108 Kolbe Hall, Akron, OH, 44325-1003.

HARPOLD, TERRY
DISCIPLINE LITERATURE, COMMUNICATION, AND CULTURE **EDUCATION** Univ Pa, PhD, 94. **CAREER** Asst prof, mem, Ctr for New Media Educ and Res, & Graphics, Visualization, & Usability Ctr, Ga Inst of Technol. **RESEARCH** Postmodern culture and literature. **SELECTED PUBLICATIONS** Publications include discussions of hypertextual narrative form and its graphical representations, the "inverted landscapes" of author J.G. Ballard, and the obscured political economies of cartographic depictions of the Internet. **CONTACT ADDRESS** Sch of Lit, Commun & Cult, Georgia Inst of Tech, Skiles Cla, Atlanta, GA, 30332. **EMAIL** terry.harpold@lcc.gatech.edu

HARRINGTON, KAREN A.
DISCIPLINE FRENCH LITERATURE **EDUCATION** Ca State Univ, BA, 73, MA, 78; Univ Ca, PhD, 86. **CAREER** Tchg asst, 80-83; tchg fel, Univ Ca, 83-84; instr, Valley Jr Col, 82-86; asst prof, 86-94; assoc prof, 94-. **HONORS AND AWARDS** Outstanding Tchg Awd. **MEMBERSHIPS** MLA; Tennessee For Lang Tchr Asn; Am Coun Tchg For Lang. **SELECTED PUBLICATIONS** Fragmentation and Irony in Les Fleurs du Mal, 92; Tirman, Alvin, and Karen Harrington; French Dominance at the Forefront of Modern Mathematics, 92; Harrington, Karen, and Josette Penso, 96. **CONTACT ADDRESS** Dept of Foreign Language, East Tennesee State Univ, PO Box 70717, Johnson City, TN, 37614-0717. **EMAIL** harringk@etsu.edu

HARRIS, ALICE C.
PERSONAL Born 11/23/1947, Columbus, GA, m, 1976, 2 children **DISCIPLINE** LINGUISTICS **EDUCATION** Randolph Macon Woman's Col, AB, 69; Univ Essex, MA, 72; Harvard Univ, PhD, 76. **CAREER** From res asst prof to assoc prof to prof to chemn, 79-, Vanderbilt Univ. **HONORS AND AWARDS** Phi Beta Kappa, 87; Leonard Bloomfield Book Award, 98; Earl Sutherland Prize, 98; Vis Erskine Fel, 99., Society Study of Caucasia, 90-98; Vanderbilt Univ Fac Senate, 91-94, Secretary, 93-94. **MEMBERSHIPS** Int Society for Hist Linguistics; Linguistics Society of Am; Society for the Study of Caucasia; Modern Language Assoc. **RESEARCH** Diachronic syntax and morphology; language universals; languages of the Caucasus. **SELECTED PUBLICATIONS** Auth, Georgian Syntax: A Study in Relational Grammar, 81; auth, Diachronic Syntax: The Cartvelian Case, 85; auth, article, Ergative-to-Accusative Shift in Agreement: Tabassaran, 94; coauth, Historical Syntax in Cross-Linguistic Perspective, 95; auth, article, Extension in Diachronic Syntax and Morphology, 96. **CONTACT ADDRESS** Linguistics Program, Vanderbilt Univ, Nashville, TN, 37212. **EMAIL** harrisac@ctrvax.vanderbilt.edu

HARRIS, DANIEL A.
DISCIPLINE ENGLISH LANGUAGE AND LITERATURE **EDUCATION** Yale Univ, BA; MA; PhD. **CAREER** Prof. **RESEARCH** Jewish studies; Victorian poetry; modern and contemporary poetry; graduate student pedagogy. **SELECTED PUBLICATIONS** Auth, Yeats: Coole Park and Ballylee; auth, Inspirations Unbidden: the 'Terrible Sonnets' of Gerard Manley Hopkins. **CONTACT ADDRESS** Dept of English, Rutgers Univ, 510 George St, Murray Hall, New Brunswick, NJ, 08901-1167. **EMAIL** dharris@aol.com

HARRIS, FREDERICK JOHN
PERSONAL Born 07/29/1943, New York, NY **DISCIPLINE** FRENCH, COMPARATIVE LITERATURE **EDUCATION** Fordham Univ, BA, 65; Columbia Univ, MA, 66, PhD, 69. **CAREER** Asst prof, 70-79, asoc prof, 79-84, prof, French & Comp lit, 84-, chmn div humanities, 79-85, chmn dept modern lang & lit, 95-, Fordham Univ. **MEMBERSHIPS** MLA; Am Assn Teachers Fr; Soc des Amis d'Andre Gide; Intl Comparative Lit Assn; Amer Comparative Lit Assn; Bd of Adv, Krieg und Literatur/hav and Literature. **RESEARCH** Twentieth century French literature; 19th century French literature; 20th century comparative literature. **SELECTED PUBLICATIONS** Auth, Andre Gide and Romain Rolland: Two Men Divided, Rutgers Univ, 73; auth, The Dehack to the Debarquement: World War II France on the Stage, Modern War on Stage & on Screen, Der Moderne Krieg aut der Buhne; auth, Andre Gide et la guerre: Deux apercus, Fr Rev, 74; auth, Tonio Kroger: An explication de texte, Teaching Language Through Literature, 73; auth, Annotated Bibliographical Listings on Gide and the Novel, A Critical Bibliog of French Lit, Syracuse Univ Press, 80; auth, Encounters with Darkness, French and German Writers on World War II, Oxford Univ Press, 83; auth, Celine in Germany, yearbk of Comparative & Gen Lit, XXXVIII, 89. **CONTACT ADDRESS** Fordham Univ, Lincoln Ctr Campus, New York, NY, 10023.

HARRIS, JANE GARY
PERSONAL New York, NY, 2 children **DISCIPLINE** SLAVIC LANGUAGE & LITERATURE **EDUCATION** Stanford Univ, BA, 59; Columbia Univ, MA & PhD, 69. **CAREER** Instr, Univ Pittsburgh, 67-69; asst prof, Indiana Univ, Bloomington, 73-74; assoc prof & chairperson dept Slavic lang & lit, full prof Russian lang, lit, & cult, Univ Pittsburgh, 75-, corresp ed, Canadian-American Slavic Studies, 73-; dir summer sem, Nat Endowment for Humanities, 81 & 83; acad dean, Semester at Sea, 84 **HONORS AND AWARDS** Nat Bk Award, 80. **MEMBERSHIPS** AAAS; MLA; Am Asn Teachers Slavic & East Europ Lang, Pres 95-97; Am Soc Eighteenth Century Studies; Asn Dept Foreign Lang; CIEE. **SELECTED PUBLICATIONS** Auth, History of a feminine image: Towards an analysis of Boris Pasternak's esthetic vision, Russian Lit Triquart, 74; transl, Osip Mandelstam's poetry, The Silver Age of Russian Culture, Ardis, 75; Osip Mandelstam's prose fiction, Russian Lit Triquart, 75; Osip Mandelstam's critical essays, Modern Russian Poets on Poetry, Ardis, 76; auth, An inquiry into the use of autobiography as a stylistic determinant of the modernist aspect of Osip Mandelstam's literary prose, American Contributions to the VIIIth International Congress of Slavists, Slavica Publ, 78; Osip Mandelstam: The Complete Critical Prose and Letters, Ardis, 79 & 97, 3rd ed; G R Derzhavin: The Poetic Imagination in Evolution (in prep); Osip Mandelstam, G K Hall, 88; ed, American Contributions to the Xth International Congress of Slavists, Slavica Publ, 88; Autobiographical Statements: Essays on the Autobiographical Mode in Twentieth-Century Russian Literature, Princeton Univ, 90; Lydia Ginzburg: In Memorium, Essays, C-ASS, 94. **CONTACT ADDRESS** Dept of Slavic Languages & Literaature, Univ Pittsburgh, 1417 C/L, Pittsburgh, PA, 15260. **EMAIL** jgh@pitt.edu

HARRISON, ANN TUKEY
PERSONAL Born 04/19/1938, Geneva, NY **DISCIPLINE** ROMANCE LANGUAGES, LINGUISTICS **EDUCATION** Mich State Univ, BA, 57; Univ Mich, MA, 58, PhD(Romance ling), 62. **CAREER** Teaching asst French, Univ Mich, 57-61; instr, Univ Wis, 61-63, asst prof French & ling, 63-65; from asst prof to assoc prof Romance lang, 65-73, Prof French, Mich State Univ, 73- **HONORS AND AWARDS** Ruth Dean Annual Lectr, Mt Holyoke Col, 76. **MEMBERSHIPS** MLA; AAUP; Medieval Acad; Am Asn Teachers French. **RESEARCH** French medieval language and literature; French linguistics. **SELECTED PUBLICATIONS** Auth, 'Ballades Et Rondeaux', French Rev, Vol 0067, 94; The 'Romance of the Rose' and its Medieval Readers--Interpretation, Reception, Manuscript Transmission, French Rev, Vol 0068, 95. **CONTACT ADDRESS** 277 Maplewood Dr, Lansing, MI, 48823.

HARRISON, JAMES W.
PERSONAL Born 05/31/1945, Lebanon, PA, m, 1971, 5 children **DISCIPLINE** GERMAN **EDUCATION** Univ of North Carolina at Chapel Hill, PhD, 76. **CAREER** Prof of German and humanities, Southern Utah Univ, 76-98. **HONORS AND AWARDS** Distinguished Faculty Dir; Thunderbird Prof of the Year; Outstanding Educator of the Year; mem of Speakers Bureau for Utah Endowment for the Humanities; Fulbright Fel; Distinguished Faculty Lecture Award; Distinguished Educator Award. **MEMBERSHIPS** Arizona Ctr for Medieveal and Renaissance Studies. **RESEARCH** German High Middle Ages. **SELECTED PUBLICATIONS** Auth, "Hartmann's 'Der Arme Heinrich': A Precartesian View of Medicine", in Selecta 13, 92; auth, "Schopenhauer, Wagner, and the 'Ring'", Selecta 14, 93; auth, A Concise History of the West, Stipes, 93; coauth, Hartmann von aue. 'Der Arme Heinrich', Stipes, 93. **CONTACT ADDRESS** Department of Language and Literature, Southern Utah Univ, 351 W. Center St., Cedar City, UT, 84702. **EMAIL** harrison@suu.edu

HART, GAIL K.
DISCIPLINE GERMAN LANGUAGE **EDUCATION** SUNY, BA, 72; Univ Rochester, MA, 77; Univ Va, MA, 79, PhD, 83. **CAREER** Instr, Yale Univ, 84-87; Reed Col, 87-90; ASSOC DEAN, HUM FOR UNDERGRAD STUD, PROF, GERMAN, UNIV CALIF, IRVINE, 90-. **SELECTED PUBLICATIONS** Auth, Readers and their Fictions in the Novels and Novellas of Gottfried Keller, Univ NC Stud Germ Lang and Lit, 89; Tragedy in Paradise: Family and Gender Politics in German Bourgeois Tragedy 1750-1850, Camden House, 96; Verleiblichungen: Literatur- und kulturgeschichtliche Studien uber Strategien, Formen und Funktionen der Verleiblichung in Texten von der Fruhzeit bis zum Cyberspace, St. Ingbert: Rohrig Universitatsverlag, 96. **CONTACT ADDRESS** Dept of Ger, Univ Calif, Irvine, CA, 92697. **EMAIL** gkhart@uci.edu

HART, JOHN AUGUSTINE
PERSONAL New Haven, CT **DISCIPLINE** EUROPEAN FICTION IN TRANSLATION **EDUCATION** Yale Univ, PhD. **CAREER** Lit, Carnegie Mellon Univ. **MEMBERSHIPS** Area: Shakespeare. **CONTACT ADDRESS** Carnegie Mellon Univ, 5000 Forbes Ave, Pittsburgh, PA, 15213.

HART, PATRICIA
DISCIPLINE SPANISH LITERATURE **EDUCATION** Univ NC, Chapel Hill, PhD. **CAREER** Assoc prof Span, Purdue Univ. **RESEARCH** 20th century Hispanic fiction; women in Hispanic fiction; Detective fiction; Catalan. **SELECTED PUBLICATIONS** Auth, The Spanish Sleuth, Fairleigh Dickinson Univ Press, 87; Narrative Magic in the Fiction of Isabel Allende, Fairleigh Dickinson Univ Press, 89; More Heaven and Less Mud: The Precedence of Catalan Unity Over Feminism in Francesc Betriu's Filmic Vision of MercS Rodoreda's La Plaoa del Diamant, The Garden Across the Border: MercS Rodoreda's Fiction, Susquehanna Univ Press, 94; Magic Feminism in The Stories of Eva Luna, by Isabel Allende, in Feminism/Postmodernism/Multiculturalism, Assoc Univ Press, 94; The Deconstruction of the Soldadera in Laura Esquivel's Como agua para chocolate, Cincinnati Romance Rev, Vol XIV, 95; Visual Strategies in Gabriel Retes' Film, El bulto, Portland State Univ Press, 95; Can a Good Feminist Sit Through Kika? Rape, Recovery, and Submission Fantasies in the Films of Pedro Almodovar, Anuario de Cine y Lit en Espanol, Vol III, 97; co-ed, Romance Lang Annual, Vol VI, 94; Vol VII, 95; Vol VIII, 96. **CONTACT ADDRESS** Dept of For Lang and Lit, Purdue Univ, 1080 Schleman Hall, West Lafayette, IN, 47907-1080. **EMAIL** hartp@omni.cc.purdue.edu

HART, PIERRE ROMAINE
PERSONAL Born 05/06/1935, Baraboo, WI, m, 1958, 2 children **DISCIPLINE** RUSSIAN LITERATURE **EDUCATION** Antioch Col, BA, 57; Univ Wis-Madison, MS, 60, MA, 66, PhD(Russ lit), 68. **CAREER** Asst prof Russ, State Univ NY Buffalo, 67-72, assoc prof, 72-79; Prof Russ, LA State Univ, 80-, Am Coun Educ fel, 78-79. **MEMBERSHIPS** Am Asn Teachers Slavic & E Europ Lang. **RESEARCH** Russian 18th century poetry; symbolist prose; fictional representations of childhood. **SELECTED PUBLICATIONS** Auth, Metaphor, Metonymy and Myth in the 'Petty Demon', Slavic East Europ J, Vol 0041, 97; Metaphor, Metonymy and Myth in the 'Petty Demon', Slavic East Europ J, Vol 0041, 97; Narrative Oscillation in Gogol 'Nevsky Prospect', Studies Short Fiction, Vol 0031, 94. **CONTACT ADDRESS** Dept of Class, Ger & Slavic Lang, Louisiana State Univ, Baton Rouge, LA, 70808.

HART, THOMAS ROY
PERSONAL Born 01/10/1925, Raleigh, NC, m, 1945, 2 children **DISCIPLINE** ROMANCE LANGUAGES & LITERATURE **EDUCATION** Yale Univ, BA, 48, PhD, 52. **CAREER** Instr Span, Amherst Col, 52-53; instr Romance lang, Harvard Univ, 53-55; asst prof, Johns Hopkins Univ, 55-60; assoc prof, Emory Univ, 60-64; Prof Romance Lang, Univ Ore, 64-, Fulbright res grants, Univ Montpellier, 50-51 & Univ Madrid, 66-67; ed, Comp Lit, 72- **MEMBERSHIPS** Assoc Int Hispanistas. **RESEARCH** Spanish literature of the Middle Ages and Golden Age; Portuguese literature. **SELECTED PUBLICATIONS** Auth, Is Literary-History Possible, Comp Lit, Vol 0045, 93; Epic and Empire, Politics and Generic From Virgil to Milton, Comp Lit, Vol 0046, 94; The Ethics of Reading in Manuscript Culture--Glossing The 'Libro De Buen Amor', Philos Lit, Vol 0018, 94; The Carnival Stage--Vicentine Comedy Within the Serio-Comic Mode, Modern Lang Rev, Vol 0090, 95; The Carnival Stage--Vicentine Comedy Within the Serio-Comic Mode, Modern Lang Rev, Vol 0090, 95; Andreas and the Ambiguity of Courtly Love, Comp Lit, Vol 0048, 96; History and Warfare in Renaissance Epic, Comp Lit, Vol 0049, 97. **CONTACT ADDRESS** Dept of Romance Lang, Univ of Ore, Eugene, OR, 97403.

HARTH, ERICA
PERSONAL New York, NY, m, 1984 **DISCIPLINE** FRENCH LITERATURE **EDUCATION** Barnard Col, BA, 59; Columbia Univ, MA, 62, PhD, 68. **CAREER** Instr French, NY Univ, 64-66; from instr to asst prof, Columbia Univ, 67-71; lect, Tel-Aviv Univ, Israel, 71-72; asst prof, 72-75, assoc prof, 75-85, prof French & Comp Lit, 85-92, PROF HUMANITIES & WOMEN'S STUDIES, BRANDEIS UNIV, 92-; Fel, NEH, 70, 89-90, Am Coun Learned Socs, 78, ACLS, 89-90 & Bunting Inst, 89-90. **MEMBERSHIPS** MLA. **RESEARCH** Seventeenth century French literature; sociology of literature. **SELECTED PUBLICATIONS** Auth, Cyrano de Bergerac and the Polemics of modernity, Columbia Univ, 70; The tragic moment in Athalie, Mod Lang Quart, 12/72; Exorcising the beast: Attempts at rationality in French classicism, MLA Publ, 1/73; Classical innateness, Yale Fr Studies, 6/73; The creative alienation of the writer: Sartre, Camus and Simone de Beauvoir, Mosiac, spring 75; Classical disproportion: La Bruyere's Caracteres, L'Esprit Createur, spring-summer 75; Sur des vers de Virgile (III, 5): Antinomy and totality in Montaigne, Fr Forum, 1/77; Ideology and Culture in Seventeenth-Century France, Cornell Univ Press, 83; Cartesian Women: Versions and Subversions of Rational Discourse in the Old Regime, 92. **CONTACT ADDRESS** Dept of Romance & Comp Lit, Brandeis Univ, ROCL - MS024, Waltham, MA, 02215-2700. **EMAIL** harth@binah.cc.brandeis.edu

HARTMAN, C.
PERSONAL Born 11/26/1946, Phoenixville, PA, m, 1978, 1 child **DISCIPLINE** CHINESE LITERATURE **EDUCATION** Indian Univ, BA, 67; Indiana Univ, MA, 70; Indiana Univ, PhD, 75 **CAREER** Asst prof, Ntl Taiwan Univ, 77-79; asst prof, Univ Wis, 79-80; asst prof, St Univ NY Albany, 80-85; assoc prof, St Univ NY Albany, 85-93; prof, St Univ NY Albany, 93- **HONORS AND AWARDS** Assoc Asian Studies; Joseph Levenson Prize **MEMBERSHIPS** Assoc Asian Studies **RESEARCH** Literature; History; T'ang and Sung Dynasty **SELECTED PUBLICATIONS** Han Yu and the T'ang Search for Unity, Princeton Univ Pr, 86; The Indiana Companion to Traditional Chinese Literature, Ind Univ Pr, 86; "The Making of a Villian: Ch'in Kuei and Tao-hsueh," Harvard Jrnl Asiatic Studies, 98 **CONTACT ADDRESS** Dept E Asian Studies, Univ Albany, Albany, NY, 12222. **EMAIL** Hartman@cnsvax.albany.edu

HARTMAN, JAMES WALTER
PERSONAL Born 01/28/1939, Newark, OH **DISCIPLINE** ENGLISH LANGUAGE, LINGUISTICS **EDUCATION** OH Univ, BA, 61; Univ MI, MA, 62, PhD, 66. **CAREER** Instr Eng, Eastern IL Univ, 63-64; asst prof Eng & ling, OH Univ, 66-67; asst prof Eng lang, Univ WI-Madison, 67-70; Assoc Prof, 70-85, Prof Eng & Ling, Univ KS, 85-, Asst dir, Dict Am Regional Eng, 67-70; Assoc Ed, 70-; Assoc Ed, Am Speech, 72-97; Ed Publ, Am Dialect Soc, 76-95. **MEMBERSHIPS** Am Dialect Soc; NCTE. **RESEARCH** Dialectology; sociolinguistics; lexicography; Am Eng pronunciation. **SELECTED PUBLICATIONS** Auth, Phonological Variation in the United States, In: Dictionary of American Regional English, Vol I, 85; Some Possible Changes in the Pronunciation of Young Americans (maybe), Am Speech 59.3, 84; ed, Cambridge International Dictionary of English, Cambridge Univ Press, 96; co-ed, English Pronouns Dictionary, 15th, Cambridge Univ Press, 97. **CONTACT ADDRESS** Dept of Eng Wescoe Hall, Univ of Kansas, Lawrence, KS, 66045-0001. **EMAIL** jwhartma@eagle.cc.ukans.edu

HARTMAN, STEVEN LEE
PERSONAL Born 05/04/1946, Lexington, VA **DISCIPLINE** SPANISH LINGUISTICS **EDUCATION** Univ Wis, BA, 66, MA, 68, PhD(Span), 71. **CAREER** Asst Prof Span, Southern Ill Univ Carbondale, 71-, Vis prof, Univ Veracruzana, Mexico, 73. **MEMBERSHIPS** Am Asn Teachers Span & Port; MLA; Ling Soc Am; Asn Comput Ling. **RESEARCH** Historical linguistics; generative phonology; computational linguistics. **SELECTED PUBLICATIONS** Auth, A Comprehensive Spanish Grammar, Modern Lang J, Vol 0080, 96. **CONTACT ADDRESS** Dept of Foreign Lang & Lit, Southern Ill Univ, Carbondale, IL, 62832.

HARVEY, CAROL
PERSONAL Born 04/18/1941, Heckmondwike, United Kingdom, m, 1964, 2 children **DISCIPLINE** FRENCH **EDUCATION** Univ Edinburgh, MA, 63, PhD, 69; Univ Caen, LL, 64. **CAREER** Lectr, Univ Caen, 63-64; ed asst lexicography, WM Collins, Glasgow, 66-69; asst prof, 70-76, assoc prof, 76-84, PROF FRENCH, UNIV WINNIPEG, 84-; vis fel, Corpus Christi Col, Cambridge, 89; vis prof, Univ Perpignan (France), 91-92. **HONORS AND AWARDS** Chevalier, Ordre des Palmes Acad, France. **MEMBERSHIPS** Int Courtly Lit Soc; Can Soc Medievalists; Medieval Acad Am; MLA. **SELECTED PUBLICATIONS** Auth, Intertextuality in the Anglo-Norman Lyric, in J Rocky Mt Medieval Renaissance Asn, 89; auth, Gabrielle Roy: institutrice: reportage et texte narratif, in Cahiers franco-canadiens de l'Ouest, 91; auth, Le cycle manitobain de Gabrielle Roy, 93; auth, Georges Bugnet et Gabrielle Roy: paysages litteraires de l'Ouest canadien, in LitteRealite, 94; auth, La litterature au feminin, 95. **CONTACT ADDRESS** French Dept, Univ Winnipeg, 515 Portage Ave, Winnipeg, MB, R3B 2E9.

HARVEY, MARIA-LUISA ALVAREZ
PERSONAL Torreon, Mexico, 1 child **DISCIPLINE** TWENTIETH CENTURY SPANISH LITERATURE **EDUCATION** TX Western Col, BA, 65; Univ TX, El Paso, MA, 66; Univ AZ, PhD, 69; Jackson State Col, M Sci in Ed, 72; post-doctoral work, Harvard Univ, summers 72 and 73. **CAREER** Teaching assoc Span, Univ Ariz, 69; asst prof & head dept mod lang, Col Artesia, 69-70; assoc prof, 70-74, prof Span, 74-80, Prof Mod Foreign & Dir, Hons Prog, DEAN OF W. B. DUBOIS HONORS COL AND PROF OF MFL, JACKSON STATE UNIV, 81-. **HONORS AND AWARDS** Phi Beta Kappa; Danforth Assoc, Teacher of the Year, 78; Outstanding Educator Award, 90 (during the Salute to Prominent Women in MS). **MEMBERSHIPS** Nat Collegiate Hons Coun; Southern Regional Honors Council. **RESEARCH** Twentieth century Spanish poetry; bilingual education; human development. **SELECTED PUBLICATIONS** Auth, Cielo y tierra en la poesia lirica de Manuel Altolaguirre, Univ & Col Press Miss, 72; Where is the critical period of development for the disadvantaged, fall-winter, 73 & Is teaching selection the answer, fall, 74, IL Schs J; Teach Spanish to Black students? Make it relevant! Make it Black!, J Negro Educ, summer 74; A good teacher and an eclectic approach: The hopeful answer to successful reading instruction, fall 74 & Teach them reading while you teach them Spanish ... or French ... or any other subject, summer 75, Reading Horizons; One egg has the subject, another has the predicate: A Spanish (or English) teaching game, Elem English, 4/75; Lorca's Yerma: Frigid ... or mismatched?, Col Lang Asn J, 6/80; Minorities and Women and Honors Education, in P. G. Friedman, R. C. Jenkins-Friedman, eds, Fostering Academic Excellence Through Honors Programs, New Directions for Teaching and Learning, No 25, San Francisco, Jossey-Bass, March 86; I Like to Examine Insects: An Honors Program Comes of Age, The College Bd Rev, summer 87; An Honors Program Approach to the Making of Professionals, The Gifted Child Today, May/June 90. **CONTACT ADDRESS** W. B. DuBois Honors Col, Jackson State Univ, 1400 Lynch St, Jackson, MS, 39217-0001.

HARVEY, ROBERT
DISCIPLINE COMPARATIVE LITERATURE **EDUCATION** Univ Ca, BA, 72; Univ Paris, DUEL, 72, DEA, 84; San Francisco State Univ, MA, 75; Univ Ca, PhD, 88. **CAREER** Asst prof, 88-94; assoc prof, 94-. **HONORS AND AWARDS** Merit Awd Tchg, 90. **MEMBERSHIPS** Am Asn Tchr French; Asn des Amis de Pontigny-Cerisy; Can Soc Hermeneutics Postmodern Thought; Int Asn Philos Lit; MRAP; MLA; Sartre Soc; Soc Cinema Studies. **SELECTED PUBLICATIONS** Auth, Search for a Father: Sartre, Paternity and the Question of Ethics, Univ Mich, 91; Notebooks for an Ethics (rev), 94; Le Nouvel Ordre ecologique, (rev), 94; Force Fields: Between Intellectual History and Cultural Critique (rev), 94; co-auth, Marguerite Duras: A Bio-Bibliography, Greenwood, 97; ed, Toward the Postmodern, Humanities, 93. **CONTACT ADDRESS** English Dept, SUNY Stony Brook, Stony Brook, NY, 11794. **EMAIL** rharvey@ccmail.sunysb.edu

HASHIMOTO, I.Y.
DISCIPLINE LANGUAGE AND WRITING **EDUCATION** Stanford Univ, BA, 67; Univ Wis, MA, 69; Univ Mich, PhD, 78. **CAREER** Instr, Univ Mich; Idaho State Univ; prof, 83-. **HONORS AND AWARDS** Dir, Whitman Col Wrtg Ctr; exec comm, Conf Col Compos and Commun. **RESEARCH** Academic writing, modern non-fiction prose. **SELECTED PUBLICATIONS** Auth, Thirteen Weeks: A Guide to Tchg Col Writing. **CONTACT ADDRESS** Dept of Eng, Whitman Col, 345 Boyer Ave, Walla Walla, WA, 99362-2038. **EMAIL** hashimiy@whitman.edu

HASLAM, GERALD WILLIAM
PERSONAL Born 03/18/1937, Bakersfield, CA, m, 1961, 5 children **DISCIPLINE** AMERICAN LITERATURE, LINGUISTICS **EDUCATION** San Francisco State Col, AB, 63, MA, 65; Union Grad Sch, PhD, 80. **CAREER** Teaching asst English, Wash State Univ, 65-66; instr, San Francisco State Col, 66-67; from asst prof to assoc prof, 67-71, PROF ENGLISH, SONOMA STATE UNIV, 71-, Gen Semantics Found res grant, 66; invitational scholar, Polish Acad Sci, Warsaw, 66; mem nat acad adv bd, Multi-Cult Inst, 67-; dir, Okie Studies Proj & Arch, Sonoma State Col, 76-; ed, Lit Hist Am West, Nat Endowment for Humanities, 79- **HONORS AND AWARDS** Arizona Quart Award, 69. **MEMBERSHIPS** Col Lang Asn; Western Am Lit Asn; Multi-Ethnic Lit of US. **RESEARCH** The West in American literature; non-white American writers; American dialects. **SELECTED PUBLICATIONS** Auth, High Lonesome, the American Culture of Country-Music, Western Am Lit, Vol 0031, 96; Drink Cultura-Chicanismo, Western Am Lit, Vol 0028, 94. **CONTACT ADDRESS** Dept of English, Sonoma State Univ, Rohnert Park, CA, 94928.

HASLETT, BETTY J.
DISCIPLINE SPEECH COMMUNICATION **EDUCATION** Univ Wis, MA, 68; Univ Minn, BA, 67; PhD, 71. **CAREER** Asst prof, 71-76; asoc prof, 76-86; prof, 87-; dept grad comm, 78-; ch, Univ Promotion & Tenure Comm, 92; dir, woman's stud prog, 96-. **HONORS AND AWARDS** Mortar Bd Award for tchg excellence, 84; UDRF grant, 87; dean's grant, 92., Reviewer, Jour Family Rel(s), 91; Commun Monogr(s), 90, 92 - 95; Jour Broadcasting and Electronic Media, 92, 93; Jour Lang and Soc Psychol, 87, 92, 96; Jour Commun, 86; Commun Yrbk, 95; Mayfield Press, 95; assoc ed, Commun Monogr(s), 86, 88; Human Commun Res, 82 86, 92-95; Commun Quart, 85, 87; Mgt Commun, 96-. **MEMBERSHIPS** Mem, Intl Commun Assn; Speech Commun Assn, E Commun Assn. **SELECTED PUBLICATIONS** Auth, Commentary, Communication and Sex-Role Socialization, Garland Press, 93; Mary Anne Fitzpatrick, Women in Communication, Greenwood Press, 96; co-auth, Micro Inequities: Up Close and Personal, Subtle Discrimination: Principles and Practices, Sage, 97; **CONTACT ADDRESS** Dept of Commun, Univ Delaware, 162 Ctr Mall, Newark, DE, 19716.

HASSELBACH, INGRID TIESLER
PERSONAL Rabishau, Germany, m, 1972 **DISCIPLINE** GERMAN LITERATURE **EDUCATION** Goethe Univ, GER, Staatsexamen; Tulane Univ, PhD, 78. **CAREER** Asst prof German, FL State Univ, 65-73; LECTR GERMAN, LOYOLA UNIV, 75-; LECTR GERMAN, TULANE UNIV, 78-. **MEMBERSHIPS** Mod Foreign Lang Asn. **RESEARCH** Modern German literature (Gunter Grass); women in German literature of the 19th century; medieval German literature. **SELECTED PUBLICATIONS** Auth, Gunter Grass Katz u Maus Interpretation, Oldenbourg Verlag Munchen, 2nd ed, 71. **CONTACT ADDRESS** 6363 St Charles Ave, New Orleans, LA, 70118-6195.

HASSELBACH, KARL HEINZ
PERSONAL Giessen, Germany **DISCIPLINE** GERMAN LANGUAGES & LITERATURE **EDUCATION** Univ Marburg, DPhil(Ger), 71. **CAREER** Actg asst prof, Fla State Univ, 65-72; asst prof, 72-74, Assoc Prof Ger, Tulane Univ, 74- **MEMBERSHIPS** AAUP; MLA; Am Asn Teachers Ger. **RESEARCH** Nineteenth century German literature; German dialectology; modern German novel. **SELECTED PUBLICATIONS** Auth, The Secret of Identity, Ernst Junger, Der 'Arbeiter' in Light of Thomas Mann, 'Doktor Faustus', Deutsche Vierteljahrsschrift Fur Literaturwissenschaft Und Geistesgeschichte, Vol 0069, 95. **CONTACT ADDRESS** Dept Ger & Slavic Lang, Tulane Univ, 6823 St Charles Ave, New Orleans, LA, 70118-5698.

HAST, M.H.
PERSONAL Born 05/28/1931, New York, NY, m, 1953, 2 children **DISCIPLINE** SPEECH SCIENCE **EDUCATION** Brooklyn College, BA, 53; Univ S Cal, MA, 57; Ohio State Univ, PhD, 61. **CAREER** Assoc Prof, Prof, 69 to 74-, Northwestern Univ Med Sch; Instr, post grad fel, Asst Prof, 61-69, Univ Iowa. **HONORS AND AWARDS** Gould intl Awd; NATO SR fel; NEH; NIH. **MEMBERSHIPS** AAAS; RSM; LSL; AACA; APS; AAHM. **SELECTED PUBLICATIONS** Auth, Anatomy of the Larynx, in: Otolaryngology, ed GM English, NY, Harper and Row Pub, 95; coauth, Andreas Vesalius on the teeth/: An annotated translation from De Humani Corporis Fabrica, Clinical Anatomy, 95; coauth, Hyoid structure laryngeal anatomy and vocalization in felids, Mammalia, Carnivora, Felide, 94; coauth, Andreas Vesalius on the larynx and hiod bone: An annotated translation from the 1543 and 1555 editions of De Humani Corporis Fabrica, Med History, 93. **CONTACT ADDRESS** Dept of Otolaryngology, Northwestern Univ, 303 E Chicago Ave, Chicago, IL, 60611. **EMAIL** m-hast@nwu.edu

HATASA, KAZUMI
DISCIPLINE JAPANESE LANGUAGE **EDUCATION** Waseda Univ, BA, 80; Univ Ill, Urbana-Champaign, MA, 85; Univ Ill, Urbana-Champaign, PhD, 89. **CAREER** Asst, ESL lang lab, Univ Ill, Urbana-Champaign, 82-83; instr, Middlebury Col, 83, 84, 86, 88, tchg asst, Univ Ill, Urbana-Champaign, 83-85; res asst, Univ Ill, 85-88; prof, Middlebury Col, 86; asst prof Japanese, 88-94, dir, For Lang Media Ctr, 93-, assoc prof Japanese, 94-, dir, Ctr for Technol-Enhanced Lang Lrng and Instr, Purdue Univ, 97-. **HONORS AND AWARDS** Global Initiative grant, Purdue Univ, 94; fel, Japan Found, 96., Mem, Bd of Dir of Asn of Tchr of Japanese. **MEMBERSHIPS** Mem, Asn for Asian Stud; Asn of Tchr of Japanese; Can Asn of Tchr of Japanese; Nihongo Kyoiku Gakkai; Comput Assisted Lang Lrng and Instr Consortium; Int Asn of Lang Lab. **RESEARCH** Technology enhanced language learning and instruction; Japanese language. **SELECTED PUBLICATIONS** Auth, Nihongo kyoshi no tameno computer literacy, Gekkan Nihongo , ALC Press, 96; Computer Literacy for Japanese Language Professionals-What do we need to know about applications of the computer?, in Progress in Japanese Linguistics and Pedagogy: A Collection in Honor of Professor Akira Miura, ed by Hubbard, Sakamoto & Davis, ALC Press, 97; coauth, Making Electronic Communication Possible in Japanese on the Internet, in Tele-collaboration in foreign languages: proceedings of the Hawaii Symposium 95,Univ Hawaii Second Lang Tchg and Curric Ctr, 96; co-ed, Bridging Gaps Proceedings of the Sixth Annual Lake Erie Teachers of Japanese Conference, LETJC, 94. **CONTACT ADDRESS** Dept of For Lang and Lit, Purdue Univ, 1080 Schleman Hall, West Lafayette, IN, 47907-1080. **EMAIL** khatasa@purdue.edu

HATHAWAY, ROBERT L.
DISCIPLINE SPANISH LITERATURE OF THE XVI AND XVII CENTURIES **EDUCATION** Williams Col, BA, 53; Georgetown Univ, MS, 57; Brown Univ, MA, 63, PhD, 69. **CAREER** Prof, Colgate Univ, emer. **HONORS AND AWARDS** NEW fel in residence, Harvard Univ, 76-77. **SELECTED PUBLICATIONS** Auth, Not Necessarily Cervantes: Readings of the Quixote, Juan de la Cuesta-Hispanic Monogr, 95; ed, The "Villancicos" from The "Cancionero" of Pedro Manuel Jimenez de Urrea, and Ximenez de Urrea, Penitencia de amor, Exeter Univ Press 76, 90; articles and rev(s), Anales Cervantinos, Boletin de la Biblioteca Menendez Pelayo, Bulletin of the Comediantes, Celestinesca, Cervantes, Hisp Rev, Jour of Hisp Philol, Nueva Revista de Filologea Hispanica. **CONTACT ADDRESS** Dept of Romance Lang, Colgate Univ, 13 Oak Drive, Hamilton, NY, 13346.

HATTON, ROBERT WAYLAND
PERSONAL Born 02/05/1934, Columbus, OH, m, 1954, 3 children **DISCIPLINE** ROMANCE LANGUAGES **EDUCATION** Capital Univ, AB, 57; Middlebury Col, AM, 59. **CAREER** Teacher pub schs, Ohio, 58-60; Binat Cult Ctr Grantee, US Info Agency, Colombia, 60-62; instr Span, Ohio Wesleyan Univ, 62-63; from asst prof to assoc prof, 63-70, prof mod lang, Capital Univ, 70-, escort interpreter, US Dept State, 66-70. **MEMBERSHIPS** Am Asn Teachers Span & Port; Taurine Bibliophiles Am; Am Coun Teaching Foreign Lang; Midwest Asn Lang Studies. **RESEARCH** Editing of student texts. **SELECTED PUBLICATIONS** Co-ed, La gloria de Don Ramiro, Heath, 66; ed, Hombre hispanico, C E Merrill, 70; Los clarines del miedo, Xerox, 71; coauth, The Bullfight: A Teaching and Study Guide, Advan Press Am, 74; ed, Just a Little Bit of the Civil War as seen by W J Smith, Co M, 2nd OVC, Ohio Hist, Parts I & II, summer-autumn 75; coauth, A Day at the Bullfight: A Viable Alternative to the Language Fair, Foreign Lang Ann, 2/77; auth, The Sideline Show, NAWDAC J, fall 78; Louis Bromfield Revisited, Ohioana Quart, summer 80. **CONTACT ADDRESS** Dept of Mod Lang, Capital Univ, 2199 E Main St, Columbus, OH, 43209-2394.

HAUSER, WILLIAM BARRY
PERSONAL Born 05/02/1939, Washington, DC, m, 1973, 3 children **DISCIPLINE** JAPANESE, ASIAN AMERICAN, & ASIAN HISTORY **EDUCATION** Univ Chicago, SB, 60; Yale Univ, MA, 62, PhD(hist), 69. **CAREER** Lectr hist, Univ Mich,

Ann Arbor, 67-69, asst prof, 70-74; asst prof, 74-77, assoc prof, 77-83, PROF HIST, UNIV ROCHESTER, 83-, CHMN DEPT, 79-85, Nat Endowment for Humanities younger humanist fel, 71-72; Japan Found fel, 76; Mellon Found Fac fel, Univ Rochester, 77; Nat Endowment Humanities fel, 82-83. **MEMBERSHIPS** Asn Asian Studies. **RESEARCH** Economic and social change in Tokugawa Japan; Japanese local history; Asian women's history; Asian Am hist, lit. **SELECTED PUBLICATIONS** Auth, Kinsei Osaka ni okeru shogyo kiko no henshitsu katei--Osaka wata tonya no baai, Shakai Keizai Shigaku, 70; Economic Institutional Change in Tokugawa Japan--Osaka and Kinai Cotton Trade, Cambridge Univ, 74; The diffusion of cotton processing and trade in the Kinai region in Tokugawa, Japan, J Asian Studies, Vol XXXIII, 74; The Early Development of Osaka and Rule by Status, Miyamoto Mataji sensei koki kinen ronbunshu, Kindai Keizai no rekishiteki kiban, 77; Osaka: A commercial city in Tokugawa Japan, Urbanism Past & Present (transl, Sasaki Gin'ya, Sengoku Daimyo Rule and Commerce), 78; Japan Before Tokugawa: Political Consolidation and Economic Growth, 1500-1650, Princeton Univ, 81; Burghers, In: Japan Handbuch, Wiesbaden: Frank Steiner Verlag, 81; auth, Woman and War: The Japanese Film Image, in Recreating Japanese Women, 1600-1945, Univ Calif, 91; auth, Why so Few? Female Household Heads in Early Modern Osaka, J Fam Hist, II, 4, 86; auth, Fires on the Plain: The Human Costs of the Pacific War, in Reforming Japanese Cinema, Univ Tnchana, 92; auth, Tokugawa Japan, in Asian in Western and World History, ME Sharpe, 97. **CONTACT ADDRESS** Dept of Hist, Univ of Rochester, 500 Joseph C Wilson, Rochester, NY, 14627-9000.

HAVILAND, BEVERLY
DISCIPLINE COMPARATIVE LITERATURE **EDUCATION** Sarah Lawrence Col, BA, 74; Princeton Univ, MA, 75, PhD, PhD. **CAREER** Adj asst prof, Occidental Col, 89; asst prof, 84-92; assoc prof, Vassar Col, 92-96; assoc prof, 96-. **SELECTED PUBLICATIONS** Auth, Henry James's Last Romance: Making Sense of the Past and the American Scene, Cambridge, 97; Passing from Paranoia to Plagiarism: The Abject Authorship of Nella Larsen, Modern Fiction Studies, 97; The Return of the Alien: Henry James on the Lower East Side 1904, Henry James Rev, 95; 'Psychic Mulattos': The Ambiguity of Race, Common Knowledge, 94; Waste Makes Taste: Thorstein Veblen, Henry James, and the Sense of the Past, Int Jour Polit, Culture, Soc, 94. **CONTACT ADDRESS** Dept of Comparative Studies, SUNY Stony Brook, Stony Brook, NY, 11794. **EMAIL** beverly.haviland@sunysb.edu

HAWKINS, JOHN A.
DISCIPLINE SYNTAX, SEMANTICS, HISTORICAL LINGUISTICS AND PSYCHOLINGUISTICS **EDUCATION** Cambridge Univ, PhD. **CAREER** Prof, Univ Southern Calif. **RESEARCH** Syntax & semantics; historical linguistics; psycholinguistics. **SELECTED PUBLICATIONS** Auth, Definiteness &Indefiniteness, 78; Word Order Universals, 83; Comparative Typology of English and German, 86; ed, Explaining Language Universals, 88. **CONTACT ADDRESS** Dept of Linguistics, Univ Southern Calif, University Park Campus, Los Angeles, CA, 90089. **EMAIL** hawkins@.usc.edu

HAWKINS, KATE
DISCIPLINE SPEECH COMMUNICATION **EDUCATION** Univ Tex, PhD. **CAREER** Dir undergrad stud, Tex Tech Univ; assoc prof, asso dir, Elliot Sch Commun. **HONORS AND AWARDS** Awards tchg excellence, Wichita state Univ. **SELECTED PUBLICATIONS** Publ, areas of gender and power in language and leadership in small group communication. **CONTACT ADDRESS** Dept of Commun, Wichita State Univ, 1845 Fairmont, Wichita, KS, 67260-0062. **EMAIL** hawkins@elliott.es.twsu.edu

HAWKINS, RALPH K.
PERSONAL Born 06/24/1969, Yuma, AZ, m, 1990, 1 child **DISCIPLINE** BIBLICAL LANGUAGES **EDUCATION** David Lipscomb Univ, BA, 90, MA, 95; Univ of the South, DMin, 98. **HONORS AND AWARDS** Endow for Bibl Res, 97. **MEMBERSHIPS** Am Schools of Orient Res; Cath Bib Asn; Soc of Bibl Lit. **RESEARCH** Archaeology; Historiography of ancient Israel. **SELECTED PUBLICATIONS** Auth, A Heritage in Crisis. **CONTACT ADDRESS** 275 North Carolina Ave, Sewanee, TN, 37355. **EMAIL** Hawkirk9@sewanee.edu

HAWLEY, JOHN STRATTON
DISCIPLINE COMPARATIVE RELIGION **EDUCATION** Amherst Col, AB, 63; Union Theol Sem, MDiv, 66; Harvard Univ, PhD, 77; Univ Delhi, 72; Univ Wis, 71; Hebrew Univ, 66-67. **CAREER** Inst, St. George's Sch, Jerusalem, 67-68; asst prof, Bowdoin Col, 77-78; vis assoc prof, Grad Theol Union, 82; from asst to assoc to prof, Asian Langs & Lit, Univ Wash, 78-85; dir, Southern Asian Inst, Columbia Univ, 89-95; dir, Nat Resource Ctr S Asia, Columbia Univ, 89-97; PROF REL, BARNARD COL, COLUMBIA UNIV, PRESENTLY. **CONTACT ADDRESS** Barnard Col, New York, NY, 10027. **EMAIL** jsh3@columbia.edu

HAYDAR, ADNAN
DISCIPLINE MODERN AND CLASSICAL ARABIC LITERATURE **EDUCATION** Am Univ Beirut, BA, 63, MA, 68; Univ Calif, PhD, 77. **CAREER** English and Lit, Univ Ark. **HONORS AND AWARDS** Dir, King Fahd Middle East Studies Prog; Ed, Syracuse Univ Press. **SELECTED PUBLICATIONS** Area: modern Arabic literature. **CONTACT ADDRESS** Univ Ark, Fayetteville, AR, 72701.

HAYDEN, GEORGE A.
DISCIPLINE EAST ASIAN LANGUAGES **EDUCATION** Stanford Univ, PhD, 72. **CAREER** Assoc prof, Univ Southern Calif. **RESEARCH** Classical Chinese language; pre-modern Chinese literature. **SELECTED PUBLICATIONS** Auth, Crime and Punishment in Medieval Chinese Drama: Three Judge Pao Plays. **CONTACT ADDRESS** East Asian Studies Center, Univ Southern Calif, University Park Campus, Los Angeles, CA, 90089.

HAYNE, DAVID MACKNESS
PERSONAL Born 08/12/1921, Toronto, ON, Canada, m, 1955 **DISCIPLINE** FRENCH **EDUCATION** Univ Toronto, BA, 42; Univ Ottawa, MA, 44, PhD, 45. **CAREER** From lectr to assoc prof, 45-61, registr univ col, 56-61, Prof French, Univ Toronto, 61-, Mem, Nat Res Coun Can, 42-43; Dir Mil Intel, Dept Nat Defence, 43-45; gen ed, Dictionary Can Biog, 65-69; assoc ed, Univ Toronto Quart, 65-76. **MEMBERSHIPS** Fel Royal Soc Can; Asn Can Univ Teachers Fr; Bibliog Soc Can; Can Ling Asn; Can Comp Lit Asn. **RESEARCH** French-Canadian literature; 17th century French literature. **SELECTED PUBLICATIONS** Auth, Challenges, Projects, Texts--Canadian Editing, Univ Toronto Quarterly, Vol 0066, 97; Jean Rivard or The Art of Success--Ideology and Utopia in the Works of Gerinlajoie, Voix & Images, Vol 0017, 92; Lorne Pierce and Quebec Literature, Voix & Images, Vol 0017, 92; French-Canadian Authors--A Bibliography of Their Works and of English-Language Criticism, Univ Toronto Quarterly, Vol 0063, 93. **CONTACT ADDRESS** Univ of Toronto, Rm 143, Toronto, ON, M5S 1A1.

HAYWOOD, RICHARD MOWBRAY
PERSONAL Born 04/28/1933, Baltimore, MD, m, 1965, 2 children **DISCIPLINE** RUSSIAN & EAST EUROPEAN HISTORY **EDUCATION** NY Univ, BA, 54; Oxford Univ, MA, 60; Columbia Univ, PhD(Russ hist), 66. **CAREER** From asst prof to assoc prof Russ hist, Eastern Mich Univ, 65-69; ASSOC PROF RUSS & E EUROP HIST, PURDUE UNIV, WEST LAFAYETTE, 69-, Nat Endowment for Humanities younger scholar fel, 69. **HONORS AND AWARDS** Nat Endow Humanities younger scholar fel, 69; Fulbright-Hays fac res abroad prog, 83; IREX sr scholar fel, 83; IREX short term res scholar, 90. **MEMBERSHIPS** Am Asn Advan Slavic Studies **RESEARCH** Nineteenth century Russia; Russian transportation **SELECTED PUBLICATIONS** Auth, The Beginnings of Railway Development in Russia in the Reign of Nicholas I, 1835-1842, Duke Univ, 69; The Question of Standard Gauge for Russian Railways, 1836-1860, 3/69 & The Ruler Legend: Tsar Nicholas I and the Route of the St Petersburg-Moscow Railway, 1842-1843, 12/78, Slavic Rev; The Winter Palace in St Petersburg: Destruction by Fire and Reconstruction, December 1837-March 1839, Jahrbucher fur Geschichte Osteuropas, No 2, 79; The Development of Steamboats on the Volga River and its Tributaries, 1817-1856, Res in Econ Hist, Vol 6, 81; Russia Enters the Railway Age, 1842-1855, East European Monographs, Columbia Univ, 98. **CONTACT ADDRESS** Dept of Hist, Purdue Univ, West Lafayette, IN, 47907-1968.

HAZEL, HARRY CHARLES
PERSONAL Born 05/28/1936, Seattle, WA, m, 1965, 6 children **DISCIPLINE** SPEECH COMMUNICATION **EDUCATION** Gonzaga Univ, AB, 60; Univ Wash, MA, 66; Wash State Univ, PhD(speech), 72. **CAREER** Instr speech, Yakima Valley Col, 66-70; asst prof speech, 71-76, dir summer sessions & continuing educ, 73-75, prof Commun Arts Dept, Gonzaga Univ, 76-, dean Sch Continuing Educ, 75-. **MEMBERSHIPS** Speech Commun Asn. **RESEARCH** Medieval communication theory and public address; American political campaigns; homiletics. **SELECTED PUBLICATIONS** Auth, The Bonaventuran Ars Concionandi, Western Speech, fall 72 & In: S Bonaventura 1274-1974, Vol II, Col St Bonaventure, Rome, 73; Harry Truman: Practical Persuader, Today's Speech, spring, 74; Images of War, Guilt, and Redemption in the First Crusade Speech of Urban II, Commun Quart, spring 78; Blending Speech, English and Logic, Commun, spring 81; The Art of Talking to Yourself and Others, Kansas City: Sheed and Ward, 87; Savonarola: The Disputatious Preacher, Journal of the Northwest Communication Asn, spring 87; The Power of Persuation, Kansas City: Sheed and Ward, 89; Power and Constraint in the Rhetoric of Catherine of Siena, Journal of the NW Comm Asn, spring 91; Public Speaking Handbook: A Liberal Arts Perspective, co-auth by John Caputo, Dubuque, Iowa: Kendall/Hunt, 94; Interpersonal Communication: Competency Through Critical Thinking, co-auth by John Caputo and Colleen McMahon, Boston: Allyn & Bacon, 94. **CONTACT ADDRESS** Dept Commun Arts, Gonzaga Univ, 502 E Boone Ave, Spokane, WA, 99258-0001. **EMAIL** hazel@calvin.gonzaga.edu

HEALEY, WILLIAM C.
DISCIPLINE COMMUNICATIVE DISORDERS **EDUCATION** Univ Mo, PhD, 63. **CAREER** Ch, dept Spec Educ, Univ Nev, Las Vegas. **SELECTED PUBLICATIONS** Auth, Monitoring and mainstreaming amplification units for the children: The need for standard practices, NSSHLA J, 18, 91; Inclusion in childhood services: Ethics and endocratic oughtness, in Hayes, L, Hayes, G, Moore, S, & Ghezzi, P, Ethics and Developmental Disabilities, Context Press, 94; What administrators want from special education teachers, CEC Today, 95. **CONTACT ADDRESS** Dept of Spec Educ, Univ Nev, Las Vegas, 4505 Maryland Pky, Las Vegas, NV, 89154-3014. **EMAIL** healey@nevada.edu

HECHT, LEO
PERSONAL Born 03/16/1927, Vienna, Austria, m, 1954, 1 child **DISCIPLINE** RUSSIAN LANGUAGE & LITERATURE **EDUCATION** Columbia Univ, BS, 60, MA, 61 PhD(Slavic langs), 73. **CAREER** Instr polit sci, US Govt Sch, Dept Defense, 56-60; instr Ger, Univ Md, 69-70; assoc prof Russ & chmn dept foreign lang & lit, 72-80, Chmn Russ Studies, George Mason Univ, 80-, Fulbright fel to Moscow Univ, 82; ed, Newsnotes on Soviet & E Europ Drama & Theatre. **MEMBERSHIPS** Am Asn Teachers Slavic & E Europ Lang; MLA. **RESEARCH** Russian cultural history; contemporary Soviet affairs. **SELECTED PUBLICATIONS** Auth, Vladimir Vysotskii--Hamlet With a Guitar, Slavic East Europ J, Vol 0037, 93. **CONTACT ADDRESS** Dept of Foreign Lang & Lit, George Mason Univ, 4400 University Dr, Fairfax, VA, 22030-4444.

HEDRICK, DONALD KEITH
PERSONAL Born 02/26/1947, Kansas City, MO, m, 1969, 2 children **DISCIPLINE** ENGLISH LANGUAGES AND LITERATURE **EDUCATION** Univ Kans, AB, 69; Cornell Univ, MA, 72, PhD(English), 74. **CAREER** Instr, Univ New Orleans, 73-76; ASST PROF ENGLISH, KANS STATE UNIV, 76-, Res grants, Kans State Univ, 77-78. **MEMBERSHIPS** MLA; Shakespeare Asn Am. **RESEARCH** Shakespearean drama; contemporary theories of literature and style; philosophy of language. **SELECTED PUBLICATIONS** Auth, Crossing the Postmodern Divide, Philos Lit, Vol 0018, 94. **CONTACT ADDRESS** Dept of English, Kansas State Univ, 106 Denison Hall, Manhattan, KS, 66506-0701.

HEGEL, ROBERT EARL
PERSONAL Born 01/09/1943, Goodrich, MI, 4 children **DISCIPLINE** CHINESE LITERATURE **EDUCATION** Mich State Univ, BA, 65; Columbia Univ, MA, 67, PhD, 73. **CAREER** From instr to asst prof Asian studies & ling, Case Western Reserve Univ, 72-74; asst prof, 75-79, assoc prof, 79-88, PROF CHINESE, WASH UNIV, ST LOUIS, 88-. **HONORS AND AWARDS** ACLS grants, 77, 78 & 87; Wash Univ Distinguished Fac Award, 89. **MEMBERSHIPS** Asn Asian Studies; MLA; Chinese Lang Teachers Asn. **RESEARCH** Chinese vernacular fiction and drama; Chinese print culture. **SELECTED PUBLICATIONS** Contribr, Sui T'ang yen-i and the aesthetics of the seventeenth century Suchow elite, in Chinese Narrative, 77; contribr, Maturation and conflicting values, in Critical Essays on Chinese Fiction, 80; auth, The Novel in Seventeenth Century China, 81, co-ed, Expressions of Self in Chinese Literature, 85; contribr, Distinguishing levels of audiences, In; Popular Culture in Late Imperial China, 85; contribr, Political integration in Ru Zhijuan's Lilies, in Reading the Modern Chinese Story, 88; contrbr, Unpredictability & meaning in Ming-Qing literaati novels, in Paradoxes of Traditional Chinese Literature, 94; auth, Traditional Chinese fiction: The state of the field, J Asian Studies, 94; auth, Reading Illustrated Fiction in Late Imperial China, 98. **CONTACT ADDRESS** Dept Asian & Near Eastern Langs, Wash Univ, Box 1111, 1 Brooking, St. Louis, MO, 63130-4899. **EMAIL** rhegel@artsci.wustl.edu

HEIDEN, BRUCE A.
PERSONAL Born 09/04/1951, Brooklyn, NY, d, 2 children **DISCIPLINE** CLASSICAL PHILOLOGY **EDUCATION** Columbia, BA, 72; Cornell, PhD, 84. **CAREER** Asst prof, 84-80, assoc prof, 90-, Ohio State Univ, 84-. **MEMBERSHIPS** Amer Philol Asn; Brit Class Asn; Class Asn of Midwst & S **RESEARCH** Homer; Greek drama; Cognitive science. **SELECTED PUBLICATIONS** Rev, Journal of Hellenic Studies, 93; auth, Sic te servato: An Interpretation of Propertius 1.21, Class Philol, 95; The Three Movements of the Iliad, Greek, Roman, and Byzantine Studies, 96; The Ordeals of Homeric Song, Arethusa, 97; The Simile of the Fugitive Homicide: Analogy, Foiling and Allusion, Am Jour Philol, 98; The Placement of Book-Divisions in the Iliad, Jour Hellenic Studies, 98. **CONTACT ADDRESS** Dept of Greek & Latin, Ohio State Univ, Columbus, OH, 43210. **EMAIL** heiden.1@osu.edu

HEIDENREICH, ROSMARIN
DISCIPLINE GERMAN/ENGLISH/LITERATURE **EDUCATION** Moorehead State Univ, BA, 64; Univ Man, MA, 66; Univ Toronto, PhD, 83. **CAREER** Prof, Schiller Univ, Ger, 68-69; prof, Univ Tubingen, Ger, 69; prof, Univ Freiburg, Ger, 69-74; PROF ENGLISH & TRANSLATION, ST. BONIFACE COL, UNIV MANITOBA, 83-. **HONORS AND AWARDS** Can Coun Doctoral Fel, 76-79. **MEMBERSHIPS** Can Asn

Comp Lit; Can Asn Transl Studs. **SELECTED PUBLICATIONS** Auth, The Postwar Novel in Canada: Narrative Patterns and Reader Response, 89; auth, Recent Trends in Franco-Manitoban Fiction and Poetry, in Prairie Fire, 11, 90; auth, Causer l'amour dans le Far-West du Canada, in Poetiques de la Francophonie, 96. **CONTACT ADDRESS** Dept of English, St. Boniface Col, Winnipeg, MB.

HEIDSIECK, ARNOLD
PERSONAL Born 02/20/1937, Leipzig, Germany **DISCIPLINE** GERMAN **EDUCATION** Free Univ, PhD, 66. **CAREER** PROF OF GERMAN, UNIV OF SOUTHERN CALIF. **RESEARCH** German and comparative intellectual history. **SELECTED PUBLICATIONS** Auth, Das Groteske und das Absurde im modernen Drama, Kohlhammer, 69; Adam Smith's Influence on Lessing's View of Man and Society, Lessing Yearbook, 83; Lessing, Locke und die anglikanische Theologie, Lessing und die Toleranz, Wayne State Univ Press, 86; The Intellectual Contexts of Kafka's Fictions: Philosophy, Law, Relig, Camden House, 94. **CONTACT ADDRESS** 11 23rd Ave, Venice, CA, 90291. **EMAIL** heidsiec@mizar.usc.edu

HEIN, NORVIN
PERSONAL Born 08/19/1914, East Canton, OH, m, 1951, 3 children **DISCIPLINE** COMPARATIVE RELIGION **EDUCATION** Col Wooster, BA, 37; Yale Univ, BD, 46, PhD(relig), 51. **CAREER** Instr Eng, Ewing Christian Col, Univ Allahabad, 39-43; from instr to assoc prof, 50-76, Prof Comp Relig, Yale Univ, 76-, Dir Grad Studies, 78-, Fulbright res grant, India, 64-65; consult & panelist, Nat Endowment for Hum, 77-Emer Prof, Yale Univ. **MEMBERSHIPS** Am Orient Soc; Asn Asian Studies; Royal Asiatic Soc; Am Soc Study Relig (vpres, 72-75, pres, 75-78); Am Acad Relig. **RESEARCH** Hinduism, hist of relig; Indian hist. **SELECTED PUBLICATIONS** Auth, The Miracle Plays of Mathura, Yale Univ & Oxford Univ, 72; Hinduism, In: Reader's Guide to the Great Religions, Free Press, 65, 2nd rev & enlarged ed, 77; Caitanya's ecstasies and the theology of the name, In: Hinduism: New Essays in the History of Religion, E J Brill, 76; contribr, Die Religion in Geschichte und Gegenwart, Hinduism in Religions of the World, St. Martin's Press, 83, 3rd ed, 93. **CONTACT ADDRESS** 6 Tuttle Rd Bethany, New Haven, CT, 06525. **EMAIL** morvin.hein@yale.edu

HEINEMANN, EDWARD ARTHUR
PERSONAL Born 09/16/1941, New York, NY, m, 1964, 2 children **DISCIPLINE** FRENCH **EDUCATION** Hamilton Col, AB, 63; Princeton Univ, MA, 66, PhD(French), 70. **CAREER** From lectr to asst prof, 66-74, Assoc Prof French, Univ Toronto, 74- **MEMBERSHIPS** MLA; Soc Rencesvals; Medieval Acad Am. **RESEARCH** Chanson de geste; history of the French language. **SELECTED PUBLICATIONS** Auth, La 'Prise Dorange' or the Courtly Parody of an Epic, Romance Philol, Vol 0046, 93; Oral Formulas and Narrative Motifs in the Old French Epic Tradition--Definition and Utilization, J Medieval Studies, Vol 0069, 94. **CONTACT ADDRESS** Dept of French, Univ of Toronto, Toronto, ON, M5S 1A1.

HEINEN, HUBERT
PERSONAL Born 03/05/1937, Houston, TX, m, 1959, 3 children **DISCIPLINE** GERMAN LANGUAGE & LITERATURE **EDUCATION** Univ Tex, BA, 58, PhD(Ger), 64. **CAREER** Instr Ger, Univ Pa, 63-64; from asst prof to assoc prof, Univ Pittsburgh, 64-69; Assoc Prof Ger, Univ Tex, Austin, 69- **MEMBERSHIPS** MLA; Am Asn Teachers Ger; SCent Mod Lang Asn; Medieval Acad Am. **RESEARCH** Middle and Early New High German language and literature; German-American cultural history. **SELECTED PUBLICATIONS** Auth, Reinmar Studies--A Commentary on the So-Called Pseudo-Lieder of Reinmar, Speculum, Vol 0069, 94; Songs of Love and Lust--An Examination of the German Lyrics of the Minnesong of the Late 12th-Century and Early 13th-Century, Speculum, Vol 0067, 92; A Revision of Karl Bartsch Die 'Schweizer Minnesanger', Speculum, Vol 0067, 92; Egypt and the Nile Valley, Vol 1, From the Beginning to the End of the Old Empire, 12000-2000, Historische Zeitschrift, Vol 0260, 95. **CONTACT ADDRESS** Dept of Ger Lang, Univ of Tex, 0 Univ of Texas, Austin, TX, 78712-1026.

HEINRICH, AMY VLADECK
PERSONAL Born 06/05/1945, New York, NY, m, 1965, 2 children **DISCIPLINE** JAPANESE & COMPARATIVE LITERATURE **EDUCATION** Columbia Univ, BA, 67, MA, 76, PhD(Japanese lit), 80. **CAREER** Lectr East Asian Studies, Columbia Univ, 80-, Res assoc, East Asian Inst, Columbia Univ, 80-81; consult, Nat Humanities Fac, 80-81. **MEMBERSHIPS** Asn Asian Studies; Am Comp Lit Asn. **RESEARCH** Modern Japanese poetry; women's literature: Japanese & English; comparative literature: Japanese, Chinese, English. **SELECTED PUBLICATIONS** Auth, The Poems of Chuya Nakahara/, World Lit Today, Vol 0069, 95; Contemporary Japanese Womens Poetry, Vol 2, 'Other Side River', World Lit Today, Vol 0070, 96; 'Cage Of Fireflies'--Modern Japanese Haiku, World Lit Today, Vol 0068, 94; Images of Japanese Women--A Westerners View, World Lit Today, Vol 0067, 93; The Poetry and Poetics of Junzaburo Nishiwaki--Modernism in Translation, World Lit Today, Vol 0069, 95. **CONTACT ADDRESS** Columbia Univ, 250 W Broadway, New York, NY, 10013.

HEINZE, RUTH-INGE
PERSONAL Born 11/04/1919, Berlin, West Germany **DISCIPLINE** RELIGION, ASIAN FOLKLORE **EDUCATION** Univ Calif, Berkeley, BA, 69, MA, 71, PhD(Asian studies), 74. **CAREER** Ed text bks, Follett Publ Co, Chicago, 55-56; lectr anthrop, Exten Course, Berlin, 63-73; producer, Radio Broadcast Berlin, 63-68; lectr English, Univ Chiang Mai, Thailand, 72; Res Assoc, Ctr South & Southeast Asia Studies, Univ Calif, Berkeley, 73-, Am Inst Indian Studies travel grant, 75; lectr Southeast Asia, Univ San Francisco, 75-76; Fulbright res fel, Inst Southeast Asian Studies, Singapore, 78-79; dir & ed newslett, Asian Folklore Studies Group; nat dir, Independent Scholars Asia, 81- **MEMBERSHIPS** Asn for Asian Studies; Asian Folklore Studies Group; Independent Scholars Asia; Int Asn Study Asian Med. **RESEARCH** Historical and functional analysis of religious practices in South and Southeast Asia; psychological anthropology; translation of foreign texts. **SELECTED PUBLICATIONS** Auth, The Rock Art of Utah, Am Indian Culture Res J, Vol 0019, 95. **CONTACT ADDRESS** Ctr for South & Southeast Asia Studies, Univ of Calif, 260 Stephens Hall, Berkeley, CA, 94720.

HEIPLE, DANIEL L
PERSONAL Born 12/22/1942, Oregon City, OR, d, 1 child **DISCIPLINE** SPANISH LITERATURE, COMPARATIVE LITERATURE **EDUCATION** Univ Ore, BA, 66; NY Univ, MA, 71; Univ Tex, Austin, PhD(Spanish), 77. **CAREER** Asst Prof Spanish, Tulane Univ, 77- **RESEARCH** Spanish golden age literature, music and art; medieval courtly love tradition. **SELECTED PUBLICATIONS** Auth, The Two-Of-Coins, and Unheeded Omen in El 'Buscon', Critica Hisp, Vol 0015, 93; Political Posturing on the Jewish Question by Lope-De-Vega And Fariaesousa, Hisp Rev, Vol 0062, 94. **CONTACT ADDRESS** Spanish Dept, Tulane Univ, 6823 St Charles Ave, New Orleans, LA, 70118-5698.

HELBLING, ROBERT E.
PERSONAL Born 05/06/1923, Lucerne, Switzerland, m, 1956 **DISCIPLINE** GERMAN & FRENCH LITERATURE **EDUCATION** Univ Utah, MA, 49; Stanford Univ, PhD, 59. **CAREER** Instr Ger & French, Univ Utah, 50-53; asst, Stanford Univ, 53-55; from instr to assoc prof, 55-66, traveling scholar, 61 & 63, honrs dir, 64-66, chmn dept lang, 65-77, Prof Ger & French, Univ Utah, 66- **MEMBERSHIPS** MLA; Asn Depts Foreign Lang (pres, 74). **RESEARCH** Modern German and French literature, especially existentialist literature; Heinrich von Kleist. **SELECTED PUBLICATIONS** Auth, Theater, Theory, Speculation--Walter Benjamin and the Scenes of Modernity, German Studies Rev, Vol 0016, 93. **CONTACT ADDRESS** Dept of Lang, Univ of Utah, Orson Spencer Hall, Salt Lake City, UT, 84112-8916.

HELLENBRAND, HAROLD
DISCIPLINE EARLY AMERICAN LITERATURE, WORLD LITERATURES **EDUCATION** Stanford Univ, PhD. **CAREER** Prof, Dean, Col Liberal Arts, Univ Minn, Duluth. **SELECTED PUBLICATIONS** Auth, The Unfinished Revolution: Education and Politics in the Thought of Thomas Jefferson, Univ Del Press, 89. **CONTACT ADDRESS** Dept of Eng, Univ Minn, Duluth, Duluth, MN, 55812-2496.

HELLERSTEIN, NINA SALANT
PERSONAL Born 03/29/1946, New York, NY, m, 1970, 2 children **DISCIPLINE** MODERN FRENCH LITERATURE, FRENCH CIVILIZATION **EDUCATION** Brown Univ, BA, 68; Univ Chicago, MA, 69, PhD(Fr), 74. **CAREER** Adj asst prof Fr, Bernard Baruch Col, 74-75; vis asst prof, Vassar Col, 75-76; instr, Rosary Col & Roosevelt Univ, 76-78; asst prof to prof French, Univ Ga, 78-; dept head Romance Langs, Univ Ga, 92-93. **MEMBERSHIPS** S Atlantic Mod Lang Asn; MLA; Paul Claudel Soc; Soc Paul Claudel; Asn des Amis de la Fondation St John Perse; Am Asn of Teachers of French; NE Mod Lang Asn; Women in French; Pi Delta Phi (honorary); Simone de Beauvoir soc; Consiel International des Etudes Francophones. **RESEARCH** Paul Claudel; Modern French poetry; Simone de Beauvoir; Marguerite Duras; French and Francophone women's writing. **SELECTED PUBLICATIONS** Auth, Social, Sexual and Intellectual Revolt in the Works of Avante-Garde Dramatist Agnes Eschene, Women in Fr Studies, July 93; Le Poete et ses Interlocuteurs dans les Cing Grandes Odes, In: Paul Claudel: Les Odes, Les Editions Albion Press, 94; Narrative Innovation and the Construction of Self in Marguerite Audoux's Marie-Claire, Fr Rev, Dec 95; L'Ecriture des Conversations dans le Loir-et-Cher de Paul Claudel, In: Ecritures claudliennes: Actes du Colloque de Besancon, May 94; Food and the Female Existentialist Body, In: L'Invite, Fr Forum 22, 97; Phenomenology and Ekphrasis in Claudel's Connaissance de l'Est, Nottingham Fr Studies 36, 97. **CONTACT ADDRESS** Dept of Romance Lang, Univ Ga, Athens, GA, 30602-1815. **EMAIL** hellerst@arches.uga.edu

HELM, JAMES JOEL
PERSONAL Born 12/17/1937, Chicago, IL, m, 1960, 2 children **DISCIPLINE** CLASSICAL STUDIES **EDUCATION** Elmhurst Col, BA, 59; Union Theol Sem, MDiv, 63; Univ Mich, Ann Arbor, MA, 65, PhD(class studies), 68. **CAREER** Instr class studies, Univ Mich, Ann Arbor, 66-68; asst prof, 68-74, chmn dept, 76-82, Assoc Prof Classics, Oberlin Col, 74-, Vis assoc prof classics, Scripps Col, 78-79. **MEMBERSHIPS** Am Philol Asn; Archaeol Inst Am; Class Asn Mid West & South. **RESEARCH** Greek paleography; computer applications in classical studies; poetry of Catullus. **SELECTED PUBLICATIONS** Auth, Koros--From Satisfaction to Greed, Classical World, Vol 0087, 93. **CONTACT ADDRESS** Dept of Classics, Oberlin Col, 135 W Lorain St, Oberlin, OH, 44074-1076.

HELMETAG, CHARLES HUGH
PERSONAL Born 04/07/1935, Camden, NJ, m, 1959, 2 children **DISCIPLINE** GERMAN **EDUCATION** Univ Pa, BA, 57; Univ Ky, MA, 59; Princeton Univ, PhD(Ger), 68. **CAREER** Instr, Ger Purdue Univ, 60-62; asst prof, 64-75, assoc prof, 75-80, Prof Ger, Villanova Univ, 80-, Chmn Dept Mod Lang, 73-, **MEMBERSHIPS** Am Asn Teachers Ger; MLA; AAUP; Northeast Mod Lang Asn. **RESEARCH** Nineteenth and 20th century German literature; German film. **SELECTED PUBLICATIONS** Auth, Recapturing the 1950s in Schlondorff,Volker Film Adaptation of 'Homo Faber', Germanic Notes Rev, Vol 0027, 96. **CONTACT ADDRESS** Dept of Mod Lang & Lit, Villanova Univ, 845 E Lancaster Ave, Villanova, PA, 19085.

HEMMINGWAY, BEULAH S.
PERSONAL Born 03/11/1943, Clarksdale, Mississippi, m **DISCIPLINE** LANGUAGES **EDUCATION** Coahoma Jr Coll, 1962; Alcorn State Univ, BS 1964; NC Central Univ, MA 1965; FL State Univ, PhD 1981. **CAREER** Southern University, teacher, 1965-66; Voorhees College, teacher, 1966-67; Benedict College, teacher, 1967-72; Florida A&M University, associate professor, language & literature, beginning 1972, professor, currently. **HONORS AND AWARDS** Florida A&M University, Teacher of the Year, 1987-88, Meritorious Service Award, 15-19 years, 1988; Teaching Incentive Award Program (TIP), Winner, 1993. **MEMBERSHIPS** Natl Council of Teachers of English; College Language Association; FL College, English Teachers, Undergrad Council for the College of Arts & Science 1982-; Role & Scope Committee 1976; Library Resource Comm 1977; Curriculum Comm for Lang & Lit; Southern Association of Colleges & Schools Editing Committee; Homecoming Committee 1983; chairperson Poetry Festival 1975-82; advisor Lambda Iota Tau 1975-82; search comm for vp academic affairs FL A&M Univ 1982; Coll Level Acad Skills Test Task Force; reader for scoring state-wide essays holistically; board of directors LeMoyne Art Foundation 1980-82; Mothers March of Dimes 1982-; vice pres Natl Council of Negro Women 1982-; Jack & Jill of America 1979-81; prog chairperson 112th anniv Bethel Baptist Church; Tallahassee Urban League; NAACP; panelist FL Division of Cultural Affairs 1986; American Popular Culture Assn 1988; Drifters Inc 1989. **SELECTED PUBLICATIONS** Author, publications include: "Critics Assessment of Faulkners Black Characters FL A&M Univ" 1978; "A Comparative Pilot Study by Sex & Race of the Use of Slang" Soc for Gen Syst Rsch 1978; "Abyss-Gwendolyn Brooks Women" FL A&M Univ Bulletin; read paper 45th Annual Convention of Coll Lang Assoc 1985 "Can Computer Managed Grammar Make a Difference That Makes a Difference?"; Author Chapter 4, "Through the Prism of Africanity: A Preliminary Investigation of Zora Neale Hurston's Mules and Men," presented paper at American Popular Culture Assn 1989; "Through the Prism of Africanity," Zora in Florida, 1991; seminar: "Black Women Writers," 1983; workshop: "Teaching English Composition," Bay County English Teachers, Panama City, Florida; numerous other publications. **CONTACT ADDRESS** Professor, Florida A&M Univ, Tallahassee, FL, 32307.

HENRY, ERIC PUTNAM
PERSONAL Born 03/15/1943, Greensboro, NC, m, 1976, 2 children **DISCIPLINE** CHINESE LITERATURE & HISTORY **EDUCATION** Amherst Col, BA, 72; Yale Univ, Mph, 76, PhD, 79. **CAREER** Vis asst prof Chinese lang & lit, Dartmouth Col, 80-82; LECTR CHINESE LANG, UNIV NC, 82- . **MEMBERSHIPS** Asn Asian Studies; Warring States Project. **RESEARCH** Chinese drama and fiction; Chinese legendary history; Chinese social history. **SELECTED PUBLICATIONS** Auth, Chinese Amusement: The Lively Plays of Li Yu, Shoe String Press, 80. **CONTACT ADDRESS** Asian Studies Curric, Univ N. Carolina, Campus Box 3267, Chapel Hill, NC, 27514. **EMAIL** henryhme@bellsouth.net

HENRY, FREEMAN GEORGE
PERSONAL Born 09/08/1942, Pontiac, MI, 1 child **DISCIPLINE** FRENCH LITERATURE **EDUCATION** Ashland Col, BA, 64; Wash State Univ, MA, 66; Univ Colo, PhD(French), 73. **CAREER** Asst English, Lycee Janson de Sailly, Paris, 67-68; from instr to asst prof French, Univ Ga, 70-77; asst prof, 77-80, Assoc Prof French, Univ SC, 80-, Grad Dir, 82-, Assoc ed, Fr Lit Ser, 79- **MEMBERSHIPS** MLA; Am Asn Teachers Fr; SAtlantic Mod Lang Asn. **RESEARCH** Nineteenth century French literature; French poetry and theatre. **SELECTED PUBLICATIONS** Auth, Translating Slavery--Gender and Race in French Womens Writing, 1783-1823, Nineteenth Century French Studies, Vol 0024, 95; A Case of Questionable Motives, Nineteenth Century French Studies, Vol 0022, 94. **CONTACT ADDRESS** Dept of Foreign Lang & Lit, Univ of SC, Columbia, SC, 29208.

HENS, GREGOR
PERSONAL Born 11/25/1965, Cologne, Germany **DISCIPLINE** FOREIGN LANGUAGES **EDUCATION** Univ Mo-Columbia, MA, 91; Univ Calif, Berkeley, PhD, 95. **CAREER** Asst prof, Ohio State Univ, 95-. **MEMBERSHIPS** MLA; LSA; Soc Germanic Philol. **RESEARCH** Germanic linguistics (syntax, semantics, pragmatics); contemporary German/Austrian literature. **SELECTED PUBLICATIONS** Auth, art, The Definition of a Grammatical Category: Gothic Absolute Constructions, 95; auth, art, (jm) einen Brief schreiben: Zur Valenz in der Konstruktionsgrammatik, 96; auth, art, Constructional Semantics in Germany: The Dative of Inaction, 97; auth, art, What Drives Herbeck? Schizophrenia, Immediacy, and the Poetic Process, 99, auth, Thomas Bernhards Triligie der Kunste: Der Untergeher, Holzfallen, Alte Meister, 99. **CONTACT ADDRESS** 314 Cunz Hall, Columbus, OH, 43210-1229. **EMAIL** hens.1@osu.edu

HENSEY, FREDERICK GERALD
PERSONAL Born 10/30/1931, Albany, NY, m, 1956, 2 children **DISCIPLINE** LINGUISTICS, ROMANCE LANGUAGES **EDUCATION** Univ Am, MEX, BA, 56; Univ TX, Austin, PhD, 67. **CAREER** Teaching asst English, Univ Nacional Autonoma, MEX, 60-62; vis prof ling, Pontificia Cath Univ, Brazil, 65; ASSOC PROF TO FULL PROF SPAN & PORT, UNIV TX, AUSTIN, 66-; Vis prof ling, Vanderbilt Univ, Nashville, 68, Tulane Univ, New Orleans, 69, Univ los Andes, Bogota, 77, Universidad Autonoma de Guadalajara, MEX, 93, 96; Fulbright Comn sr lectr, Colombia, 77; Univ Mobile, Latin Am Campus, San Marcos, Nicaragua, 98. **MEMBERSHIPS** Am Asn Teachers Span & Port; Ling Soc Am; Asoc Latinoam Ling Filol; Universala Esperanto Asocio; North Am Catalan Soc; Am Translators Asn; Nat Asn of Judiciary Translators and Interpreters; Am Soc of Interpreters; Asn de Linguistica y Filologia de la America Latina. **RESEARCH** Sociological linguistics; general Romance linguistics; translation. **SELECTED PUBLICATIONS** Coauth, Modern Portuguese: A Project of the Modern Language Association (and Accompanying Teacher's Guide), Random House & Knopf, 70; auth, Portuguese inflectional morphology, Lang Quart, 71; The Sociolinguistics of the Brazilian Uruguayan Border, Mouton, 72; Portuguese Vowel Alternations in Casagrande and Saciuk: Generative Studies in Romance Linguistics, Newbury House, 72; Grammatical variation in Southwestern United States Spanish, Linguistics, The Hague, 73; Toward a grammatical analysis of Southwestern Spanish, In: Studies in Southwestern Bilingualism, Newbury House, 76; coauth, Three Essays on Linguistic Diversity in the Spanish-Speaking World, Mouton, 76; co-ed, Contemporary Studies in Romance Linguistics, Georgetown Univ, 77. **CONTACT ADDRESS** Dept of Span & Port, Univ Texas, Austin, TX, 78712-1026. **EMAIL** f.hensey@mail.utexas.edu

HENSLEY, CARL WAYNE
PERSONAL Born 02/25/1936, Bristol, VA **DISCIPLINE** SPEECH COMMUNICATION **EDUCATION** Milligan Col, BA, 58; Christian Theol Sem, MDiv, 63; Butler Univ, MA, 66; Univ MN, PhD, 72. **CAREER** Minister, Christian Church, IN, 58-66; prof preaching, MN Bible Col, 66-73; aux prof, Bethel Theol Sem, 72-78; prof & chmn dept commun, Bethel Col, 73, Consult, 77, mediator, 86. **MEMBERSHIPS** Speech Commun Asn; Int Asn Bus Communicators; Relig Speech Commun Asn; Cent States Speech Asn; Disciples of Christ Hist Soc. **RESEARCH** Hist and criticism of public address; intellectual hist of Am relig movement; 19th century revivalism; conflict mgmt. **SELECTED PUBLICATIONS** Auth, Harry S Truman: Fundamental Americanism in foreign policy speechmaking, Southern Speech Commun J, 75; Rhetorical vision and the Persuasion of a historical movement, Quart J of Speech, 75; Alexander Campbell and the second coming of Christ: A footnote to history, Discipliana, 76; Illustration: The sermonic workhorse, New Pulpit Digest, 77; That board meeting at Corinth, Princeton Sem Bull, 79; Rhetoric and reality in the Restoration movement, Mission J, 82. **CONTACT ADDRESS** 3900 Bethel Dr, Saint Paul, MN, 55112-6999. **EMAIL** whensly@bethel.edu

HENTON, CAROLINE G.
DISCIPLINE PHONETICS **EDUCATION** Univ E Anglia, England, BA, 76; Royal Soc Arts, MA, 78; Univ Oxford, MPhil, 82; Univ Ozford, PhD, 85. **CAREER** Dir, Lang Dev, Voice Proc Corp, 95-96; Dir, DECtalk Ling Dev, Digital Equip Corp, 96-96; consult, Claris Corp, Digital Equip Corp, 97-98; VPRES, STRATEGIC TECH, FONIX CORP, 98-. **CONTACT ADDRESS** 200 W Cliff Dr #18, Santa Cruz, CA, 95060. **EMAIL** henton@ling.ucsc.edu

HERENDEEN, WYMAN H.
DISCIPLINE ENGLISH LANGUAGE; LITERATURE **EDUCATION** Brown, BA, MA; Toronto Univ, PhD, 84. **CAREER** Prof; dept head. **HONORS AND AWARDS** Choice best acad bk designation. **RESEARCH** Cultural studies; history of ideas; persistence of the classical tradition. **SELECTED PUBLICATIONS** Auth, From Landscape to Literature: The River and the Myth of Geography; co-ed, Ben Jonson's 1616 Folio. **CONTACT ADDRESS** Dept of English Language and Literature, Univ of Windsor, 401 Sunset Ave, Windsor, ON, N9B 3P4. **EMAIL** whh@uwindsor.ca

HERIQUE, EMMANUEL
DISCIPLINE FRENCH LITERATURE; LINGUISTICS **EDUCATION** Univ Nancy II, PhD. **RESEARCH** Irregularities in language; phonetics and phonology; linguistic readings of literary texts. **SELECTED PUBLICATIONS** Auth, A Case Study of the Emergence and Evolution of an Interjection in the French Language, Proc of the Fourteenth Intl Cong of Ling, Akademie-Verlag, 87. **CONTACT ADDRESS** Dept of French, Victoria Univ, PO Box 3045 STN CSC, Victoria, BC, V8W 3P4. **EMAIL** herique@uvic.ca

HERMAND, JOST
PERSONAL Born 04/11/1930, Kassel, Germany, m, 1956 **DISCIPLINE** MODERN GERMAN LITERATURE **EDUCATION** Univ Marburg, PhD, 55. **CAREER** From asst prof to prof Ger, 58-67, Vilas Res Prof, Univ Wis-Madison, 67-, Am Coun Learned Soc fel, 65-66; vis prof, Harvard Univ, 67, Univ Tex, Austin, 70, Free Univ WBerlin, 77 & 94, Univ Bremen, 78, Univ Giessen, 81, Univ Marburg, 81; Univ Essen, 86, Univ Kassel, 88; Univ Freiberg, 89; Univ Potsdam, 93; Univ Oldenburg, 94; Univ Munich, 98. **MEMBERSHIPS** MLA; Int Brecht Soc; Heine Soc. **RESEARCH** Cultural and intellectual history of Germany between 1870-1914; Heinrich Heine; literature after 1945. **SELECTED PUBLICATIONS** Auth, Literaturwissenschaft und Kunstwissenschaft, Metzler, Stuttgart, 65; Stilkunst um 1900, Akademie, Berlin, 67; Synthetisches Interpretieren, Nymphenburger, Munich, 68; Pop International, Athenaum, Frankfurt, 71; ed, Heine's Reisebilder, Hoffmann & Campe, Hamburg, 73; auth, Streitobjekt Heine, Athenaum, Frankfurt, 75; Orte Irgendwo Formen utopischen Denkens, Athenaum, Koenigstein, 81; Konkretes Hoeren. Zum Inhalt der Instrumentalmusik, Argument, Berlin, 81; Kulturgeschichte der Bundesrepublik Deutschland, Nymphenburges, Munich, 86-88; Adolph Menzel, Rowohlt, Hamburg, 85; Arnold Zweig, Rowohlt, Hamburg, 90; Ueber Heinrich Heine, Lang, Frankfurd, 91; Grne Utopien in Deutschland, Fischer, Frankfurd, 91; Old Dreams of a New Reich, Indiana, 91; Geschichte der Germanistik, Rowohlt, Hamburg, 94; Judentum und deutsche Kultur, Boehlau, Cologne, 96; A Hitler Youth in Poland, Northwestern, Evanston, 97; Die deutschen Dichterbnde, Boehlau, Cologne, 98. **CONTACT ADDRESS** Dept of Ger, Univ of Wis, 1220 Linden Drive, Madison, WI, 53706-1557.

HERMANN, E.C.
PERSONAL Born 10/13/1930, Argentina, m, 1956, 3 children **DISCIPLINE** SPANISH LITERATURE **EDUCATION** Univ BsAs Argentina, MS 57; Occidental Col, MA honors 77, life tchg cred 78. **CAREER** Sweet Briar Col, vis asst prof 89-96, vis assoc prof, 98-; Randolph-Macon Woman's Col, act assoc prof 96-97; Lynchburg Col asst prof, assoc prof, 88 to 98-; Col of William and Mary, asst prof 87-88; High Point Acad, prof 84-87; Flintridge Sacred Heart Acad, lang Dept ch 78-83; Occidental Col, inst 76-78; Northwestern Univ, lectr 68-72. **HONORS AND AWARDS** Jessie Ball duPont Sem Participant; James A Huston Excel Sch Awd Nom; LCVA Fac Gnts. **MEMBERSHIPS** AATSP; NEMLA; MACLAS; AHI; LASA; MIFLIC. **RESEARCH** Literary works produced by contemporary Argentine Women writers. **SELECTED PUBLICATIONS** Auth, Contemporary Argentinean Women Writers, co-ed, Univ Press Florida, 98; Viajes en la palabra y en la imagen, ed, Buenos Aries, Ediciones de Arte Gaglianone, 96; Escritoras Argentinas Contemporaneas, co-ed, U of Texas, Stud in Contemporary Spanish-Amer, NY, Peter Lang, 93; La utopia de escribir, Alina Diaconu Los devorados, Alba de Amer, 96; Exilios internos: El viage en cinco escritoras argentinas, coauth, Hispanic Jour, 94; Francisca Lopez, Mito y discurso ed la novela femenina de posguerra en Espana, ed, Hispanic Jour, forthcoming; Anibal Gonzalez, ed, Jour and the Development of Spanish Amer Narrative, Revista Iberoamerica, 96; Doris Meyer, Interpreting the Spanish American Essay, Chasqui, 95; Teresa Mendez-Faith, Breve diccionario de la literature paraguaya, Hispanic Jour, 95. **CONTACT ADDRESS** Dept of Spanish, Lunchburg Col, 3172 Woodcreek Dr, Charlottesville, VA, 22911. **EMAIL** herman@sbc.edu

HERMANSEN, MARCIA
PERSONAL Montreal, PQ, Canada **DISCIPLINE** ARABIC AND ISLAMIC STUDIES **EDUCATION** Univ Waterloo, BA, 72; Univ Chicago, PhD, 82. **CAREER** Lectr, 79-80, Queen's Univ, Ontario; Visiting Prof, 85-86, McGill Univ, Montreal; Religious Studies, 82-97, San Diego State Univ; Assoc Prof, 97-, Loyola Univ. **HONORS AND AWARDS** Amer Research Ctr in Cairo Award for Post-Doctoral Research, 86; Fulbright, US Dept of Educ Faculty Research Abroad Award, Pakistan, 89-90; Fulbright Lectureship in Islamic Studies, Malaysia, 94; San Diego Historical Soc, Award for Best paper on San Diego Religious History, 94; Fel, Inst for the Advanced Study of Religion, Univ Chicago Divinity School, 95; Sr Fel, Rutgers Univ Ctr for Historical Analysis, 96-97; Performance Salary Step Increase Award (PSSI), San Diego State Univ, 96-97. **MEMBERSHIPS** Chr, Study of Islam Sect, Amer Acad of Religion; Amer Acad of Religion; Middle East Studies Assoc. **RESEARCH** Arabic and Islamic Studies; history of religions **SELECTED PUBLICATIONS** Auth, The Muslim Community of San Diego, Muslim Communities in America, 94; Shah Wali Allah of Delhi's Hujjat Allah al-Baligha (The Conclusive Argument from God), 96; The Study of Visions in Islam, Religion 27, 97; Mystical Visions as Good to Think: Examples from Pre-Modern South Asian Sufi Thought, Religion 27, 97; Religion and Literature in Muslim South Asia, Muslim World, 97; In the Garden of American Sufi Movements: Hybrids and Perennials, New Trends and Developments in the World of Islam, 97; Women, Men, and Gender in Islam, The Muslim Almanac: A Reference Work on the History, Faith, Culture, and Peoples of Islam, 96. **CONTACT ADDRESS** Theology Dept, Loyola Univ, 6525 N Sheridan Rd, Crown Ctr., Chicago, IL, 60626. **EMAIL** mherman@orion.luc.edu

HERNADI, PAUL
DISCIPLINE COMPARATIVE LITERATURE **EDUCATION** Univ Vienna, PhD, Hist of Theater, 63; Yale Univ, PhD, Compar Lit, 67. **CAREER** PROF, ENG, UNIV CALIF, SANTA BARBARA. **RESEARCH** Lit theory; Hist of crit; Europ drama. **SELECTED PUBLICATIONS** Auth, Beyond Genre: New Directions, Literature Classification, Cornell Univ Press, 72; Interpreting Events: Tragicomedies of History on the Modern Stage, Cornell Univ Press, 85; Cultural Transactions: Nature, Self, Society, Cornell Univ Press, 95; ed, What is Literature? and What is Criticism?, Ind Univ, 78, 81; The Horizon of Literature, Univ Nebr Press, 82; The Rhetoric of Interpretation and the Interpretation of Rhetoric, Duke Univ Press, 89. **CONTACT ADDRESS** Dept of Eng, Univ Calif, Santa Barbara, CA, 93106-7150. **EMAIL** hernadip@humanitas.ucsb.edu

HERNANDEZ, JUAN
DISCIPLINE LATIN AMERICAN LITERATURE **EDUCATION** Tex Christ Univ, PhD, 81. **CAREER** Assoc prof. **RESEARCH** Translation studies; 20th century Latin American and U.S. American literature; poetry writing. **SELECTED PUBLICATIONS** Auth, Poetas de los Angeles, Univ de Guanajuato, 92; Poetry from Chile: 26 New Voices, Ca State Univ, 93; 21 Voces de Humo y Rafaga: Poesea de Jalisco, Ca State Univ, 94; Poesea contemporanea de los Angeles, Univ de Guadalajara, 94; Vida sin fin, confusiones de Pocho y otros poemas/ Endless Life, Pocho Confusions and other poems, Guadalajara, 94. **CONTACT ADDRESS** Dept of Literature, Richardson, TX, 75083-0688. **EMAIL** juan@utdallas.edu

HERNANDEZ PECORARO, ROSILIE
DISCIPLINE SPANISH LITERATURE **EDUCATION** Boston Univ, BA, 90; Univ Calif Irvine, MA, 94; PhD, 98. **CAREER** Asst prof, Univ Ill Urbana Champaign. **RESEARCH** Peninsular literature; Golden Age narrative, poetry, and theatre; literary and critical theory. **SELECTED PUBLICATIONS** Auth, The Absence of the Absence of Women: Cervantes's Don Quixote and the Explosion of the Pastoral Tradition, 98. **CONTACT ADDRESS** Spanish, Italian, and Portuguese Dept, Univ Ill Urbana Champaign, 52 E Gregory Dr, Champaign, IL, 61820. **EMAIL** rhernan@uiuc.edu

HERRERO, JAVIER
PERSONAL Born 08/12/1926, Murcia, Spain, m, 1962, 3 children **DISCIPLINE** ROMANCE LANGUAGES **EDUCATION** Univ Madrid, LLB, 49, BA, 51, PhD(philos), 56. **CAREER** Asst philos, Univ Madrid, 54-55; asst Span, Univ Edinburgh, 56-60, lectr, 60-66; assoc prof, Duke Univ, 66-67, prof, 67-68; prof, Univ Pittsburgh, 68-74, Mellon prof, 74-79; William R Kenan Jr Prof Span, Univ Va, 79-, Univ Edinburgh res grant, 62; Sir Ernest Cassel res grant, 65; Guggenheim fel, 68; Am Philos Soc grant, 73; Nat Endowment for Humanities grant, 73. **MEMBERSHIPS** MLA; SAtlantic Mod Lang Asn; Asoc Int Hispanistas. **RESEARCH** Spanish and comparative literature, 17th to 20th centuries; literary criticism. **SELECTED PUBLICATIONS** Auth, The Jewish Dragon, Apocalypse, Intolerance and Magic, Critica Hisp, Vol 0015, 93. **CONTACT ADDRESS** Dept of Span, Univ of Va, 1 Cabell Hall, Charlottesville, VA, 22903-3125.

HERRON, ROBERT DEUPREE
PERSONAL Born 06/29/1935, Roanoke, VA, m, 1964, 3 children **DISCIPLINE** SPANISH, PORTUGUESE **EDUCATION** Univ Richmond, BA, 57; Univ Wis, MA, 59, MA, 63, PhD Span, 68. **CAREER** Instr Span & Port, Miami Univ, 63-68; asst prof Port, Univ NMex, 68-73, actg dir, Lang & Area Ctr Latin Am, 69-70; assoc prof Span & Port, 73-76, chmn dept, 73-82, prof Mod Lang, St Louis Univ, 76-, dir, Andean Studies & Res Ctr, Univ NMex in Quito, Ecuador, 71-72; prof emeritus Mod Lang, St Louis Univ. **MEMBERSHIPS** MLA; Am Asn Teachers Span & Port; Midwest Mod Lang Asn. **RESEARCH** Brazilian and Portugues prose fiction of 19th and 20th centuries; Spanish American literature; Chicano literature. **SELECTED PUBLICATIONS** Auth, Lima Barreto's Isias Caminha as a psychological novel, Luso-Brazilian Rev, Winter 71; Personajes y paises en Adalberto Ortiz, Suplemento Dominical, El Comercio, Quito, Ecuador, 4/72; O tema da amizade em O amanuense Belmiro, de Cyro dos Anjos, Suplemento lit, Minas Gerais, Belo Horizonte, Brazil, 9/72; Three Fables: Translations from A Dor da Bruxa e outras Fabulas by Robert Reis, Vol VI, Webster Rev, Spring 81. **CONTACT ADDRESS** Dept of Mod & Class Lang, St. Louis Univ, 221 N Grand Blvd, St. Louis, MO, 63103-2097.

HERTLING, GUNTER H.
PERSONAL Born 06/14/1930, Pasadena, CA, m, 1953, 2 children **DISCIPLINE** GERMAN **EDUCATION** Univ Calif, Berkeley, BA, MA, PhD(Ger), 61. **CAREER** Assoc Ger, Univ Calif, Berkeley, 60-61; from instr to assoc prof, 61-74, Grad Sch res Fund grant, 65, sen, fac senate, 72-74, Prof Germanic, Univ Wash, 74- **HONORS AND AWARDS** Osterreichische Gesil Lit, Vienna, 80. **MEMBERSHIPS** MLA; Am Asn Teachers Ger; Philol Asn Pac Coast; Stifter-Gesellschaft. **RESEARCH** Eighteenth and 19th century German literature, literary theories, aesthetics and culture. **SELECTED PUBLICATIONS** Auth, 'Martin Salander'--Politics and Poetry of Gottfried Keller, Novel of the Grunderzeit, German Quarterly, Vol 0069, 96. **CONTACT ADDRESS** Dept of Germanics, Univ of Wash, Seattle, WA, 98195.

HERZ, JULIUS MICHAEL
PERSONAL Born 02/04/1926, Vienna, Austria **DISCIPLINE** GERMAN **EDUCATION** Univ Vienna, PhD(Ger); Vanderbilt Univ, MA, 58. **CAREER** Teacher, Austria, 49-50; instr English, Austro-Am Inst Educ, 52, Western civilization, Ithaca Col, 55-56 & Ger & French, Univ Maine, 56-57; asst prof, 57-75, Assoc Prof Ger, Temple Univ, 75- **MEMBERSHIPS** MLA; AAUP; Int Arthur Schnitzler Res Asn. **RESEARCH** German and Austrian literature; bibliography; German-American studies. **SELECTED PUBLICATIONS** Auth, Ein Lese-Und-Bilderbuch-Von-Menschen--Unpublished Letters of Thomas Mann, Alfred Knopf, and Loweporter, 1929-1934, Seminar, Vol 0030, 94; Lenau--His Life, Work and Influence, Modern Austrian Lit, Vol 0027, 94. **CONTACT ADDRESS** Dept of Ger & Slavic Lang, Temple Univ, Philadelphia, PA, 19122.

HERZFELD, ANITA
PERSONAL Buenos Aires, Argentina **DISCIPLINE** LINGUISTICS, ENGLISH AS A SECOND LANGUAGE, LATIN AMERICAN STUDIES **EDUCATION** Teacher's Col, Arg, BSc, 53, BA, 61; Univ Kans, MA, 65, MPhil, 74, PhD, 78. **CAREER** Asst coordr lang develop, KU Cent Am & Ford Found Prog, 63-67; chmn, English Dept, Univ Buenos Aires, 67-68; dir jr yr abroad & prof ling, Univ Kans at Univ Costa Rica, 68-70 & 75; foreign study adv & asst to dean col, 71-74, instr ling, 71-75, Fulbright Adv & Dir, Off Study Abroad, 75-85, Univ Kans, 76-, Lectr ling, NDEA Summer Insts, 62-64; dir jr yr in Ger, Univ Erlangen-Nurnberg, 73; Fulbright fac develop res grant, Panama, 79; Fulbright specialists grant, Ger, 79; Admin internship, Off Acad Abb Ku, 80-; Tinker grant, Cent Am, 82; Exec Dir Cent Am Scholar Prog, Georgetown Univ 85-89; Dir Undergrad Adv , Ctr Lat Am Studies, 90-, assoc prof Ctr Lat Am Studies, 90-, Univ Ks. **HONORS AND AWARDS** Outstanding Intl Woman Award, Women's Hall Fame, Intrauniv Vis Prof Grant, Univ Ks; Phi Beta Delta, found mem. **MEMBERSHIPS** Soc Caribbean Ling; Ling Soc Am; Nat Asn Foreign Student Affairs; Coun Int Educ Exchange; Latin Am Studies Asn; Soc Pidgins & Creoles; Fulbright Asn; Circulo Linguistico, Ricardo J Alfaro, Univ Panama; Asoc de Linguistica y Filologia de la Am Latina; SSILA. **RESEARCH** Caribbean Creoles; higher education in the Americas; Costa Rican theater; Language & identify; indigenous languages of the Americas; language and society in Latin America; Creoles of Costa Rica, Panama and Honduras. **SELECTED PUBLICATIONS** Co-ed, Metodologia de la Evaluacion Universitaria: Teoria y practica, Univ Kans, 69; coauth, Notas y Ejercicios de Composicion, Prentice Hall, 69; transl, Mary Lester, Un viaje a traves de Honduras, Educa, 71; co-ed, Planificacion, Coordinacion, Autonomia, Innovaciones: Perspectivas Latinoamericanas, Univ Kans, 72; coauth, El Teatro de Hoy en Costa Rica, Ed Costa Rica, 73; co-ed, La Universidad y los Universitarios: Carrera docente, investigacion, estudios postgraduos, Univ Kans, 74; auth, Towards the description of Creoles, Proceedings of the Mid-Am Ling Conf, Univ Minn, 76; Second language Acrolect replacement, Working Papers in Linguistics, Univ Kans, 77; Cohesion in Limonese Creole: in Search of a Methodology, Proceedings of the 1992 Mid-America Linguistics Conference, Univ Mo-Columbia, 93; Limonese Creole: Cohesion in Stories and Conversations, Proceedings of the XV International Congress of Linguists, Sainte-Foy, 93; El espanol de Limon, Variacion Lexica del Espanol del Mundo, Univ Tokio, 94; The Meeting of Three Worlds: the Linguistic Outcomes of African and European Encounters in the Americas, Five Hundred Years after Columbus: Proceedings of the 47 International Congress of Americanists, Middle Am Res Inst, Tulane Univ, 94; Language and Identify: the Black Minority of Costa Rica, Revista de Filologia y Linguistica, Univ de Costa Rica, 95; The Teasing Strategy in Limonese Creole, in Proceedings of the Mid-America Linguistics Conference, Univ Ks, 96; Rev Banana Fallout: Class, Color and Culture among the West Indians in Costa Rica, J Pidgins & Creole Languages, John Benjamins Publ Co, 96; Limonese Creole Proverbs and Sayings, Revista de Filologia y Linguistica de la Univ de Costa Rica, 97; Varilex 1997, Variacion lexica del espanol del mundo, The Spanish of Costa Rica, Univ Tokyo, 97; Marcadores del discurso criollo liminense de Costa Rica, in Actas del Congreso Internacional de la Asociacion de Linguistica y Filologia de la America Latina, Univ Nac Autonoma de Mexico, 96. **CONTACT ADDRESS** Ctr of Latin American Studies, Univ Ks, 107 Lippincott Hall, Lawrence, KS, 66045. **EMAIL** herzfeld@ukans.edu

HESTER, RALPH M.
PERSONAL Born 12/22/1931, Fort Worth, TX, m, 1966, 2 children **DISCIPLINE** ROMANCE LANGUAGES & LITERATURE **EDUCATION** Univ Calif, Los Angeles, BA, 54, MA, 56, PhD(Romance lang), 63. **CAREER** Asst French, Univ Calif, Los Angeles, 54-56, assoc, 56-57, asst 58-59, assoc, 59-60, lectr, 61-63; from asst prof to assoc prof, 63-78, Prof French, Stanford Univ, 78-, Chmn, Dept Fr & Ital, 79- **MEMBERSHIPS** MLA; Am Asn Teachers Ft; Renaissance Soc Am. **RESEARCH** French Renaissance literature; methodology in teaching of French. **SELECTED PUBLICATIONS** Auth, Lapidary Inscriptions--Renaissance Essays for Donald Stone, French Forum, Vol 0018, 93. **CONTACT ADDRESS** Dept Ft & Ital, Stanford Univ, Stanford, CA, 94305-1926.

HEWITT, ANDREW
DISCIPLINE COMPARATIVE LITERATURE **EDUCATION** Sidney Sussex Col, BA; MA; Cornell Univ, PhD. **CAREER** Assoc prof, SUNY Buffalo. **RESEARCH** Critical theory and the dialogue between French and Ger intellectual; cult traditions in the 20th century; the relationship of mass cult to the historical avant-garde; aesthetic constructions of gender and sexuality; mod dance. **SELECTED PUBLICATIONS** Auth, Fascist Modernism; Political Inversions. **CONTACT ADDRESS** Dept Comp Lit, SUNY Buffalo, 639 Clemens Hall, Buffalo, NY, 14260. **EMAIL** ahewitt@acsu.buffalo.edu

HEWSON, JOHN
PERSONAL Born 12/19/1930, Tugby, England, m, 1954, 3 children **DISCIPLINE** LINGUISTICS **EDUCATION** Univ Col, London, BA, 52; Inst Educ, London, PGCE, 53; Univ Laval, MA(Fre), 58, MA(ling), 60, DUn, 64. **CAREER** Asst to assoc prof Fr, 60-68, prof ling, 68-, HENRIETTA HARVEY PROF LINGUISTICS, MEMORIAL UNIV NFLD, 97-. **HONORS AND AWARDS** Fel, Royal Soc Can. **MEMBERSHIPS** Can Ling Asn; Ling Soc Am; Ling Asn Great Brit; Philol Soc; Soc Linguistique Romane. **SELECTED PUBLICATIONS** Auth, Oral French Pattern Practice, 63; auth, La Pratique du francais, 65; auth, Article and Noun in English, 72; auth, The Beothuk Vocabularies, 78; auth, A Computer-Generated Dictionary of Proto-Algonquian, 93; auth, The Cognitive System of the French Verb, 97; coauth, Fundamentals for a Science of Language, 84; coauth, The Micmac Grammar of Father Pacifique, 90; coauth, Tense and Aspect in Indo-European Languages, 97. **CONTACT ADDRESS** Dept of Linguistics, Memorial Univ of Newfoundland, St. John's, NF, A1B 3X9.

HIGGINBOTHAM, VIRGINIA
PERSONAL Born 11/06/1935, Dallas, TX **DISCIPLINE** ROMANCE LANGUAGES, CONTEMPORARY SPANISH LITERATURE **EDUCATION** Southern Methodist Univ, BA, 57, MA, 62; Tulane Univ, PhD, 66. **CAREER** Teaching asst Span, Southern Methodist Univ, 60-62 & Tulane Univ, 62-66; asst prof, 66-73, Assoc Prof Span & Port, Univ Tex, Austin, 73-. **MEMBERSHIPS** Am Asn Teachers Span & Port; MLA. **RESEARCH** Contemporary Spanish literature. **SELECTED PUBLICATIONS** Auth, The Comic Spirit of Federico Garcia Lorca, Univ Tex, 74; Luis Bunuel, Twayne, 79; Spanish Film Under Franco, Univ Tex, 88; Spirit of the Beehive, Flicks Books, 98. **CONTACT ADDRESS** Dept of Span & Port, Univ of Tex, Austin, TX, 78712-1026. **EMAIL** vhigginbotham@mail.utexas.edu

HIGGINS, LYNN ANTHONY
PERSONAL Born 07/21/1947, Ann Arbor, MI **DISCIPLINE** FRENCH LANGUAGE & LITERATURE **EDUCATION** Oberlin Col, BA, 69; Univ MN, Minneapolis, MA, 73, PhD, 76. **CAREER** Vis lectr French, Hamline Univ, fall 73; Grad tchg asst and assoc, Univ MN, Minneapolis, 70-76; Vis lectr Comp Lit, Univ of Pittsburgh, fall 83; from Asst Prof French to Prof, 76-, Ch, French & Ital Dept, 93-, Dartmouth Col, Nat Endowment for Hum fel, 79 & Camargo fel, 81; Vis scholar and lectr, Vt and NH Coun for Hum Lit Series, 80. **HONORS AND AWARDS** Choice Outstanding Acad Bk Award, 96; MLA Jeanne and Aldo Scaglione Prize, Best Bk in French and Francophone Studies, 97; Dir Am Scholars; Who's Who of Am Women. **MEMBERSHIPS** MLA; Nat Women's Studies Asn; Asn for French Cult Studies; New Novel Asn. **RESEARCH** French novel; lit theory; women and autobiog. **SELECTED PUBLICATIONS** Auth, Nouvelle nouvelle autobiography: Monique Wittig's Le Corps Lesbien, Sub-Stance, 77; coauth, Conversation w Christiane Rochefort, Esprit Createur, 79; Godard and Rochefort: Two or three things about prostitution, Fr Rev, 75; auth, Typographical eros: Reading Ricardou in the third demension, Yale Fr Studies, 79; Literature a la lettre: Ricardou and the poetics of Anagram, Romanic Rev, 82; Barthes' imaginary voyages, Studies in Twentieth Century Lit, 82; Parables of theory: Jean Ricardou's metafiction, Summa Publ, 84; Ed, contr, History and Literature, Studies in Twentieth Century Lit, fall 85; Co-ed, contr, Screen/Memory: Rape and its alibis in Last Year at Marienbad, In: Rape and Representation, Columbia Univ Press, 91; If looks could kill: Louis Malle's portraits of collaboration, In: Fascism, Aesthetics, and Culture (Richard J Golsan, ed), Univ Press New England, 92; Sexual fantasies and war memories: Claude Simon's Narratology, In: Gendering War Talk (Miriam Cooke & Angela Woollacott, ed), Princeton Univ Press, 93; Gender and war narrative in La Route des Flandres, In: Claude Simon (Celia Britton, ed), Longman, 93; Pagnol and the paradoxes of Frenchness, In: Identity Papers: Scenes of Contested Nationhood in Twentieth-Century France (Tom Conley & Steven Ungar, ed), Univ Minn Press, 96; New Novel, New Wave, New Politics: Fiction and the Representation of History in Post War France, Univ Nebr Press, 96; Le Langage, l'etrangete et les formes de l'histoire dans La Route Des Flandres de Claude Simon, In: Lectures de La Route des Flandres (Francine Dugast-Portes & Michele Touret, ed), Presses Univ de Rennes; The Barbie affair and the trial of memory, In: Fascism's Return: Scandal, Revision and Ideology since 1980 (Richard J Golsan, ed), Univ Nebr Press, 98. **CONTACT ADDRESS** Dept of Romance Lang & Lit, Dartmouth Col, 6087 Dartmouth Hall, Hanover, NH, 03755-3511. **EMAIL** lynn.higgins@dartmouth.edu

HIGGINS, ROGER F.
DISCIPLINE LINGUISTICS **EDUCATION** Cambridge Univ, BA, 63; Yale Univ, MPhil, 69; Univ Mass, PhD, 73. **CAREER** Asst prof. **RESEARCH** Historical syntax of English. **SELECTED PUBLICATIONS** Auth, The Pseudo-cleft Construction in English, Garland, 79; On J. Emonds's Analysis of Extraposition, Seminar, 73. **CONTACT ADDRESS** Linguistics Dept, Univ of Massachusetts, Amherst, S College 124, Amherst, MA, 01003.

HIGONNET, MARGARET RANDOLPH
PERSONAL Born 10/02/1941, New Orleans, LA, m, 1974 **DISCIPLINE** COMPARATIVE LITERATURE, ENGLISH **EDUCATION** Bryn Mawr Col, BA, 63; Yale Univ, PhD(comp lit), 70. **CAREER** Instr English, George Washington Univ, 67-68; asst prof, 70-75, assoc prof, 75-81, PROF ENGLISH, UNIV CONN, 81-, CHMN, COMP LIT PROG, 78-, Fulbright prof, 81. **MEMBERSHIPS** MLA; English Inst (secy, 76-80); Am Comp Lit Asn. **RESEARCH** Jean Paul Richter; literary theory; Romanticism. **SELECTED PUBLICATIONS** Auth, Forum--Interdisciplinarity in Literary-Studies--Perspectives from Particular Fields, MLA Pubs, Vol 0111, 96; Academic Anorexia--Some Gendered Questions About Comparative Literature, Comp Lit, Vol 0049, 97. **CONTACT ADDRESS** Dept of English, Univ of Conn, Storrs, CT, 06268.

HILGAR, MARIE-FRANCE
PERSONAL Born 06/19/1933, St. Palais, France, m, 1954, 4 children **DISCIPLINE** FRENCH LITERATURE **EDUCATION** Indiana Univ Pa, BA, 63; San Francisco State Col, MA, 66; Univ Calif, Davis, PhD(French), 71. **CAREER** Prof French, Peace Corps, 66; lectr, San Francisco State Col, 67; Prof French, Univ Nev, Las Vegas, 71-, Nat chmn, N Am Soc for 17th Century Fr Lit, 77; ed, Tape Hiss, Nev Foreign Lang Newslett, 77-; conf chmn, Pacific Northwest Conf Foreign Lang, 79. **MEMBERSHIPS** MLA; Int Asn Fr Studies; Asn Caracterologie; Am Soc 17th Century; Soc Fr Etude XVIIe Siecle. **RESEARCH** French theater of the 17th century; women authors; Madame Deshoulieres. **SELECTED PUBLICATIONS** Auth, Weber 'Tartuffe', Australian J French Studies, Vol 0033, 96; A Reference Grammar of Modern French, Modern Lang J, Vol 0081, 97; Moliere in His Era, French Rev, Vol 0068, 95; Polemics and Strategy in the 'Dom Juan' of Moliere, French Rev, Vol 0067, 94; Literate Women and the French-Revolution of 1789, French Rev, Vol 0070, 97. **CONTACT ADDRESS** Dept of Foreign Lang, Univ of Nev, P O Box 455047, Las Vegas, NV, 89154-5047.

HILL, L. BROOKS
PERSONAL Born 10/21/1943, Grenada, MS, m, 1961, 2 children **DISCIPLINE** SPEECH COMMUNICATION **EDUCATION** Univ of Memphis, BA, 64; Univ of Ala, MA, 65; Univ of Ill, PhD, 68. **CAREER** Prof, Univ of Okla, 68-88; prof & ch, Trinity Univ, 88-. **HONORS AND AWARDS** Phi Kappa Phi; local teaching awards. **MEMBERSHIPS** Natl Commun Assoc; Int Assoc for Intercultural Commun Studs (pres); Int Commun Assoc. **RESEARCH** Intercultural commun. **SELECTED PUBLICATIONS** Co-auth, The Needs of the International Student, Teaching and Directing the Basic Communication Course, Kendall/Hunt, 263-270, 93; co-auth, various articles in Organization and Behavior in Cross-Cultural Settings, Sanshusha, 193-218, 219-242, 289-312, 94; co-auth, articles in Cross-Cultural Communication and Aging in America, Erlbuam, 5-23, 1143-161, 97. **CONTACT ADDRESS** Dept of Speech & Drama, Trinity Univ, 715 Stadium Dr, San Antonio, TX, 78212. **EMAIL** lhill@trinity.edu

HILL, STEVEN PHILLIPS
PERSONAL Born 04/25/1936, Estherville, IA **DISCIPLINE** SLAVIC LANGUAGES & LITERATURES **EDUCATION** Stanford Univ, BA, 57; Univ Mich, Ann Arbor, MA, 58, PhD, 65. **CAREER** From instr to asst prof, 61-69, Assoc Prof Russ, Univ Ill, Urbana, 69-. **MEMBERSHIPS** Am Asn Teachers Slavic & EEurop Lang; Soc Cinema Studies; Early Slavic Studies Asn; Am Asn for Advance Slavic Studies. **RESEARCH** Russian film history; East European film history; Russian 20th century drama. **SELECTED PUBLICATIONS** Auth, Kuleshov--prophet without honor?, Film Cult, spring 67; The Soviet film today, Film Quart, summer 67; coauth, Russian drama after Chekhov: A guide to English translations, 1900-1969, Theatre Doc, fall 69; A quantitative view of Soviet cine-

ma, Cinema J, spring 72; Ilia Frez and Russian children's films, Film Cult, 74; The N-Factor and Russian Prepositions, Mouton, The Hague, 77; auth, Strange case of the vanishing epigraphs, in Eisenstein's Battleship Potemkin, Avon, 78; Career survey of Capra, Lubitsch, Sternberg, and Wyler, in Master Space--Film Imanges, Greenwood, 92. **CONTACT ADDRESS** Dept of Slavic, Univ of Ill, Slavic, 3092 FLB, 707 S Math, Urbana, IL, 61801-3625.

HILLEN, GERD
PERSONAL Born 10/18/1935, Ehren, Germany, m, 1965, 1 child **DISCIPLINE** GERMAN LITERATURE **EDUCATION** Stanford Univ, PhD(Ger), 68. **CAREER** Asst prof, 65-71, assoc prof & chmn dept, 71-77, Prof Ger, Univ Calif, Berkeley, 77- **MEMBERSHIPS** Lessing Soc; Philol Asn Pac Coast; MLA; Int Arbeitskreis fur Barockliterature. **RESEARCH** Seventeenth and 18th century German literature. **SELECTED PUBLICATIONS** Auth, Lessing 'Philotas'--Aesthetic Experiment with Intended Satirical Effect--A Contribution to the Study Of Sources and the History of Text and Influence, Daphnis-Zeitschrift Fur Mittlere Deutsche Literatur, Vol 0021, 92. **CONTACT ADDRESS** Dept of Ger, Univ Calif, 5315 Dwinelle Hall, Berkeley, CA, 94720-3244.

HILLERS, DELBERT ROY
PERSONAL Born 11/07/1932, Chester, SD, m, 1958, 2 children **DISCIPLINE** OLD TESTAMENT, SEMITIC LANGUAGES **CAREER** Instr Hebrew, Concordia Sr Col, 58-60; from asst prof to assoc prof Hebrew & Old Testament, 63-70, Prof Semitic Lang, Johns Hopkins Univ, 70-, Ann prof, Am Sch Orient Res, Jerusalem, 68-69; Am Philos Soc grant, 68-69. **MEMBERSHIPS** Soc Bibl Lit; Am Orient Soc. **RESEARCH** Northwest Semitic languages; Old Testament. **SELECTED PUBLICATIONS** Auth, Textbook Of Aramaic Documents From Ancient-Egypt, Cath Biblical Quarterly, Vol 0057, 95. **CONTACT ADDRESS** Dept of Near Eastern Studies, Johns Hopkins Univ, 3400 N Charles St, Baltimore, MD, 21218.

HILTON, RONALD
PERSONAL Born 07/31/1911, Torquay, England, m, 1939, 1 child **DISCIPLINE** INTERNATIONAL RELATIONS, ROMANCE LANGUAGES **EDUCATION** Oxford Univ, BA, 33, MA, 36, Univ Perugia, Italy, dipl, 36. **CAREER** Dir, Comite Hispano-Ingles Libr, Madrid, 36; asst prof mod lang, Univ BC, 39-41; assoc prof Romanic langs, 42-49, dir Hisp Am & Luso-Brazilian studies, 44-64, PROF ROMANIC LANG, STANFORD UNIV, 49-, EXEC DIR CALIF INST INT STUDIES, 64-, Ed, Who's Who in Latin Am, 43-; assoc ed, Southern Republic's Who's Who in Am, 43-; ed, Hisp Am Report, 48-64; hon prof, Univ San Marcos, Peru, vis prof, Univ Brazil & lectr, Latin Am Repub, 49; cult dir, KGEI, Univ of Air, 53-56; consult, Stanford Res Inst, 64-70; ed, World Affairs Report, 70-; vis prof, Fr univs, 70 & Acad Sci, USSR, 71; vis fel, Japanese univs, 73. **MEMBERSHIPS** MLA; Am Asn Teachers Span & Port; Hisp Soc Am. **RESEARCH** East-West relations; Soviet foreign policy; cultural history of the West. **SELECTED PUBLICATIONS** Auth, Tribute to the Espinosas-on the Celebration of Aurelio Espinosa 90th Birthday, Hispania, Vol 0080, 97. **CONTACT ADDRESS** Stanford Univ, 766 Santa Ynez, Stanford, CA, 94305.

HINDERER, WALTER
PERSONAL Born 09/03/1934, Ulm, Germany, m, 1966 **DISCIPLINE** GERMAN LITERATURE/PHILOSOPHY **EDUCATION** Abitur, Kepler Gymnasium, Ulm, 54; Univ Tubingen, German & Eng Lit, European History & Phil, 54-55; Univ Munich, 55-60, PhD, 60. **CAREER** Dir, Acad Div, 61-66, R. Piper & Co (publ), Munich, 61-66; asst prof, German, 66-69, Penn St Univ; assoc prof, German, 69-71, Univ CO; vis prof, 70-71, Stanford Univ; prof, German, 71-78, Univ MD; prof, German, 78-, Princeton Univ. **HONORS AND AWARDS** Fel, Inst for Res in Humanities, Univ WI, 76-77; DAAD Res Grant, 84; Fel, Inst for Advanced Study Berlin, 85-86; Fel, Franz Rosenzweig Res Center, 95, Hebrew Univ; Order of Merit of the Fed Rep of Germany, 95; Alexander von Humboldt Award, 98. **MEMBERSHIPS** Intl Vereinigung fur Germanische Sprach und Lit; Modern Language Asn; AATG; Schiller-Gesellschaft; Buchner-Gesellschaft; Heine-Gesellschaft; Gesellschaft fur Interkulturelle Germanistik. **RESEARCH** German & European lit of the 18th, 19th, and 20th centuries; concepts and ideas of German drama; political poetry; politics and lit; German soc and cult history; rhetoric and oratory; lit theory; poetics and aesthetics; history of criticism. **SELECTED PUBLICATIONS** Auth, Arbeit an der Gegenwart. Zur deutschen Literatur nach 1945, Wurzburg: Verlag Konigshausen und Neumann, 94; ed, Brechts Dramen, Intrepretationen, Verlag Philipp Reclam jun, 95; ed, Kleists Dramen Literaturstudium, Interpretationen, Verlag Philipp Reclam jun, 97; ed, Codierungen von Liebe in der Kinstperiode, Verlag Konigshausen & Neumann, 97; auth, Von der Idee des Menschen, Uber Friedrich Schiller, Verlag Konigshausen & Neumann, 98; ed, Kleists Erzahlungen, Literaturstudium, Interpretationen, Reclam Verlag, 98; auth, Die Rhetorik der Parabel. Zu ihrem asthetischen Funktionszuusammenhang und Funktionswechsel bei Friedrich Schiller, Fabel und Parabel Kulturgeschichtliche Prozesse im 18, Jahrhundert. 94; auth, Die Depotenzierung der Vernunft: Kompensationsmuster im praromantischen und romantischen Diskurs, Romantiches Erzahlen, Verlag Konigshausen & Neumann, 95; auth, Den Dichtern geht es wie dem Araukaner, Anmerkungen zu Gunter Kunerts Poetik, Kunert Werkstatt, Materialien und Studien zu Gunter Kunerts literarischem Werk, Aisthesis Verlag, 95; auth, Das Rocheln der Mona Lisa. Aspeckt von Ernst Jandels Lyrik im Kontext der sechziger Jahre, Text & Kriktik. Zeitschrift fur Literatur, 96; auth, Die Entmundigung der Mundigkeit. Zum Paradigmawechsel eines anthropologischen Konzepts im philosophischen und literarischen Diskurs der Kinstperiode, Lit und Erfahrungswandel 1789-1930, Intl Corvey-Symposiums 9 & 12, 93; auth, Im babylonischen Turm, oder: Steine aus dem Glashaus, Amerikas Kampf um den Kanon und um kulturelle Einheit, Neue Rundschau. Der postkoloniale Blick. Eine neue Weltliteratur?, Jahrgang 96; auth, Das Reich der Schatten In Interpretationen. Gedichte von Friedrich Schiller, Stuttgart Philipp Reclam Verlag, 96; auth, Torquato Tasso, Goethe-Handbuch Vol II, JB Metzler Verlag, 96; auth, Literatur als Anweisung zum Fremdverstehen, Deutsch und fur Asien, IDV-Regionaltagung Asien - Beijing, 94, Intl Cul Pub, 96; ed, Zur Liebesauffassung der Kinstperiode, Codierungen von Liebe in der Kinstperiode, Verlag Konigshausen & Neumann, 97; ed, Liebessemantik als Provokation, Codierunger von Liebe in der Kunstperiode, Verlag Konigshausen & Neumann, 97; ed, Prinz Friedrich von Homburg. Zweideutige Vorfalle, Kleists Dramen, Literaturstudium, Interpretationen, Verlag Philipp Reclam jun, 97; auth, Literarisch-Asthetische Auftakte zur Romantischen Musik, Jahrbuch der deutschen Schillergesellschaft, 1997, Alfred Kroner Verlag, 97; auth, Das Killektivindividuum Nation im deutschen Kiontext. Zu seinem Bedeutungswandel im vor-und nachrevolutionaren Diskurs, Volk-Nation-Europa. Zur Romantisierung und Entromantisierung politischer Begriffe, Verlag Konigshausen & Neumann, 98; ed, Die heilige Cacilie oder die Gewalt der Musik, Kleists Erzahlungen. Literaturstudium, Interpretationen, Reclam Verlag, 98. **CONTACT ADDRESS** Dept of Germanic Lang and Lit, Princeton Univ, 230 E Pyne, Princeton, NJ, 08544-5264. **EMAIL** Hinderer@Princeton.edu

HINDS, LEONARD
DISCIPLINE FRENCH LITERATURE **EDUCATION** Emory Univ, PhD, 95. **CAREER** Asst prof. **RESEARCH** French narrative prose; philosophical prose; literary theory. **SELECTED PUBLICATIONS** Auth, pubs on Montaigne, Charles Sorel, and Madeleine de Scudery. **CONTACT ADDRESS** Dept of French and Italian, Indiana Univ, Bloomington, 300 N Jordan Ave, Bloomington, IN, 47405.

HINTZ, SUZANNE S.
DISCIPLINE SPANISH, LITERATURE **EDUCATION** Purdue Univ, BA, 67; Univ of VA, Med, 78; Geo Mason Univ, MA, 91; Cath Univ of Am, PhD, 93 **CAREER** Prof, 93-98, Germanna Comnty col; Div Chair, 98-, Northrn VA Cmnty Col **HONORS AND AWARDS** Embassy of Spain awd, 91; DeFerrari Sch, 90-93; Lee-Hatzfeld Sch, 90-92 **MEMBERSHIPS** MLA, SAMLA, LASA, MACLAS, AATSP **RESEARCH** Catalan lit **SELECTED PUBLICATIONS** Auth, Una bibliografia de obras escritas por y sobre rosario Ferre 1970-1994, Literal books, 98; Essays in Honor of Josep M. Sola-Sole: Linguistic and Literary Relations of Catalan and Castilian, Peter Lang, 96 **CONTACT ADDRESS** No Virginia Comm Col, Woodbridge, VA, 22191. **EMAIL** shintz@nv.cc.va.us

HINZE, KLAUS-PETER WILHELM
PERSONAL Born 09/06/1936, Berlin, Germany, m, 1967, 2 children **DISCIPLINE** GERMAN & COMPARATIVE LITERATURE **EDUCATION** Frere Univ Berlin, Staatsexamen, 65; Wash Univ, MA & PhD, 69. **CAREER** Asst prof Ger, Case Western Reserve Univ, 67-71; assoc prof, 71-78, Prof Ger & Comp Lit, Cleveland State Univ, 78-, Asst Dean Arts & Sci, 80-, Lit agent, Kreisselmeier Publ, Munich, 76-; scholar, Austrian govt, 76, W Ger Govt, 77, Akad Wiss, 78 & Stiller Soc, 79. **HONORS AND AWARDS** Scholar, Austrian govt, 76. **MEMBERSHIPS** MLA; Am Asn Teachers Ger; Int Arthur Schnitzler Res Asn; Goethe Soc; Wiener Goethe-Soc. **RESEARCH** Goethe; German 20th century literature. **SELECTED PUBLICATIONS** Auth, Goethes Spiegelungstechnik im Bereich seiner Erzahlungen, Orbis Litterarum, 70; Goethes Dialogerzahlung Die Guten Weiber, Neophilologus, 71; Neue Aspekte zum Kafka-Bild, Mod Austrian Lit, 71; Kom Strukt Goethes Erzahl, Boehlau, Cologne, 75; Ernst Weiss Bibliographie, Engel, Hamburg, 77; ed, Der Andere Augenzeuge: Ich der Augenzeuge, Heyme, Munich, 79; auth, Die Gruppe 1925, Dvjs, Der Zweite Augenzeuge, GRM, 81. **CONTACT ADDRESS** Dept of Mod Lang, Cleveland State Univ, 1983 E 24th St, Cleveland, OH, 44115-2440.

HIRSCH, MARIANNE
PERSONAL Born 09/23/1949, Timisoara, Romania, 3 children **DISCIPLINE** COMPARATIVE LITERATURE, FRENCH **EDUCATION** Brown Univ, BA, & MA, 70, PhD, 75. **CAREER** Vis instr French, Dartmouth Col, 74-75, asst prof, 75-77; Mellon asst prof humanities, Vanderbilt Univ, 77-78; asst prof French & Comp Lit, 78-82, assoc prof French & Cmp Lit, 82-89, PROF, 89-; PARENTS DISTINGUISHED RESEARCH PROF, DARTMOUTH COL, 95-99. **HONORS AND AWARDS** Magna Cum Laude, 70; Phi Beta Kappa, 70; Fulbright Fellowship (declined), 70; DAAD Fellowship (declined), 70; NDEA Title IV Fellowship, 71-72; AAUW Dissertation Fellowship, 73-74; Dartmouth Col Jr Faculty Fellowship, 79; Faculty Development Grant, Wellesley Center for Research on Women, 80; Stanford Humanities Center Fellowship (declined), 84-85; Dartmouth Col Sr Faculty Grant, 85; Mary Ingraham Bunting Institute Fellowship, 84-85; Mellon Course Development Award, 86; Mellon Humanities Institute on Gender and War, Dartmouth Col,.90; Nat Humanities Center Fel, 92-93; Rockefeller Foundation Bellagio Residence Fel, 95; Mellon Humanities Institute, Cultural Memory and the Present, Dartmouth Col, 96; Distinguished Graduate School Alumna Award, Brown Univ, 96. **MEMBERSHIPS** MLA; NE Mod Lang Asn; Am Comp Lit Asn; Am Asn Teachers French; Southern Comp Lit Asn. **RESEARCH** Contemporary fiction; hist and theory of narrative; women's studies. **SELECTED PUBLICATIONS** Auth, An Interview with Michel Butor, Contemp Lit, summer 78; coauth, A Conversation with Christiane Rochefort, L'Esprit Createur, summer 79; Godard and Rochefort: Two or Three Things About Prostitution, French Rev; auth, Beyond the Single Vision: Henry James, Michel Buton, Uwe Johson (Choice Outstanding academic book of the year), Summa Pub Co, 81; The Novel of Formation as Genre: Between Great Expectations and Lost Illusions, Genre, 79; Michel Buton: The Decentralized Vision, Contemp Lit, summer 81; Mothers and Daughters: A Review Essay, Signs, fall 81; A Mother's Discourse: Incorporation and Repetition in La Princesse de Cleves, Yale Fr Studies, Vol 62, 81; auth, The Mother/Daughter Plot: Narrative, Psychoanalysis, Feminism (Choice Outstanding academic book of the year), IN Univ Press, 89; Family Frames: Photography, Narrative and Postmemory, Harvard Univ Press, 97; auth of several articles and ed of five volumes. **CONTACT ADDRESS** Dept French & Italian, Dartmouth Col, 6087 Dartmouth Hall, Hanover, NH, 03755-3511. **EMAIL** marianne.hirsch@dartmouth.edu

HIRSCHBACH, FRANK DONALD
PERSONAL Born 05/13/1921, Berlin, Germany **DISCIPLINE** FOREIGN LANGUAGES **EDUCATION** Southern Conn State Col, BA, 46; Yale Univ, MA, 49, PhD, 52. **CAREER** Instr Ger, Yale Univ, 52-57; asst prof, Clark Univ, 57-58; from asst prof to assoc prof, 58-66, Prof Ger, Univ Minn, Minneapolis, 66-, Dir Honors Div, Col Lib Arts, 71-, Chmn Dept, 82-, Morse fel, 54-55; Ger Acad Exchange Serv grant, 74-75; Int Res & Exchanges Bd res fel, 79. **MEMBERSHIPS** MLA; Am Asn Teachers Ger. **RESEARCH** Modern German literature; literature of German Democratic Republic. **SELECTED PUBLICATIONS** Auth, Nazi Germany and the American Germanists--A Study of Periodicals, 1930-1946, Germanic Notes Rev, Vol 0028, 97; Anna Seghers in Exile--Essays, Texts, Documents, Germanic Notes Rev, Vol 0026, 95. **CONTACT ADDRESS** Dept of Ger, Univ of Minn, Minneapolis, MN, 55455.

HIRTLE, WALTER HEAL
PERSONAL Born 08/23/1927, Lunenburg, NS, Canada, m, 1959, 4 children **DISCIPLINE** LINGUISTICS **EDUCATION** Univ BC, BA, 48; Dalhousie Univ, MA, 50; Laval Univ, MA, 59, PhD(ling), 63. **CAREER** From asst prof to assoc prof, 59-69, Prof English Ling, Laval Univ 69- **MEMBERSHIPS** Can Ling Asn; Can Asn Appl Ling; Ling Asn Can-US. **RESEARCH** English grammar; psychomechanics of language; Guillaumean linguistics. **SELECTED PUBLICATIONS** Auth, Syntax-Autonomous or Meaning Motivated, Can J Ling, Vol 0039, 94; The Simple Form Again--An Analysis of Direction-Giving and Related Uses, J Pragmatics, Vol 0024, 95. **CONTACT ADDRESS** Dept of Lang & Ling, Laval Univ, Quebec, PQ, G1K 7P4.

HIZ, HENRY
PERSONAL Born 10/08/1917, Leningrad, Russia, m, 1943 **DISCIPLINE** LINGUISTICS, PHILOSOPHY **EDUCATION** Free Univ Brussels, lic en philos, 46; Harvard Univ, PhD(philos), 48. **CAREER** Asst philos, Underground Univ Warsaw, 40-44; adj math, Univ Warsaw, 49-50; asst prof, Univ Utah, 52-54 & Pa State Univ, 55-60, assoc prof, 60-64, Prof Ling, Univ Pa, 64-, Vis lectr, Univ Pa, 51, 53, 54 & 58-59; investr, NSF Tranformation & Discourse Analysis Proj, 58-; vis prof philos, NY Univ, 69- 71 & Jagiellonian Univ, 77; vis fel philos, Clare Hall, Cambridge, Eng, 76-77; Guggenheim fel ling, 76-77. **MEMBERSHIPS** Ling Soc Am; Semiotic Sco Am (pres, 75-76); Am Philos Asn. **RESEARCH** Formal grammars; mathematical logic; philosophy of art. **SELECTED PUBLICATIONS** Auth, Zellig Harris, 23-October-1909 May-22-1992, In-Memoriam, Proceedings Am Philos Soc, Vol 0138, 94. **CONTACT ADDRESS** Dept of Ling, Univ of Pa, Philadelphia, PA, 19174.

HODDER, ALAN
DISCIPLINE COMPARATIVE RELIGION **EDUCATION** Harvard Col, BA; Harvard Divinity Sch, MTS; Harvard Univ, MA, PhD. **CAREER** Assoc prof, dir, undergrad educ in Comp Stud of Relig, Harvard Univ; vis assoc prof, Hampshire Col. **SELECTED PUBLICATIONS** Publ include studies of Puritan pulpit rhetoric, orientalism, American transcendentalism, and the Bengal renaissance. **CONTACT ADDRESS** Hampshire Col, Amherst, MA, 01002.

HODDIE, JAMES HENRY
PERSONAL Born 01/16/1936, Attleboro, MA, m, 1965, 2 children **DISCIPLINE** ROMANCE LANGUAGES **EDUCATION** Boston Univ, AB, 58; Univ Wis, MA, 59; Brown Univ, PhD, 65. **CAREER** From instr to asst prof Span, Univ Pittsburgh, 62-65; asst prof, Yale Univ, 65-67; from Asst Prof to Assoc Prof, 67-92, Prof Spanish, Col Lib Arts, Boston Univ, 92-. **HONORS AND AWARDS** Schol on Augustus Howe Buck Educ Fund, Boston Univ, 54-58; Kemper K. Knapp Fel, Univ Wisc, 58-59; Univ Fel, Brown Univ, 60-62; Phi Beta Kappa, Mass Epsilon, 57; Phi Sigma Iota, Omega Chapter, 58; Phi Beta Delta, Boston Univ, 90. **MEMBERSHIPS** Asn Int de Hispanistas. **RESEARCH** Spanish biography in the 20th century, especially Maranon and Gomez de la Serna; Spanish novel. **SELECTED PUBLICATIONS** Auth, Vivencias Hispanicas: Cuentos del Siglo XX, Harcourt Brace Jovanovich, Inc, 88; Jose Echegaray, El gran Galeoto, Introduction, edition and notes, Letras Hispanicas, Ediciones Catedra, 89; La unidad y universalidad en la ficcion modernists de Gabriel Miro, Origenes, 92; author of numerous articles and papers. **CONTACT ADDRESS** Dept of Lang, Boston Univ, 718 Commonwealth Ave, Boston, MA, 02215-2423. **EMAIL** jhhoddie@bu.edu

HODGES, CAROLYN RICHARDSON
PERSONAL Born 11/25/1947, Roebling, New Jersey, m, 1972 **DISCIPLINE** GERMAN **EDUCATION** Beaver College, BA, 1969; University of Chicago, MA, 1971, PhD, 1974. **CAREER** Central YMCA Community College, instructor of German, 1970-72; Kennedy-King Jr College, assistant professor of humanities, 1975-82; Univ of Tennessee, Knoxville, assistant professor of German, 1982-88, associate professor of German, 1988-. **HONORS AND AWARDS** Chancellor's Citation for Extraordinary Service, Univ of Tennessee, 1987; Merrill Research Award, College of Education, Univ of Tennessee-Knoxville, 1990, 1992; Outstanding Advising, College of Liberal Arts, 1991; Dissertation Year Award, Ford Foundation, 1973-74; Trustee Fellowship, Univ of Chicago, 1969-73; Faculty Travel Award, Univ of Tennessee, 1983. **MEMBERSHIPS** Secretary/treasurer, Southern Comparative Literature Assn, 1990-; vice-president, Tennessee American Assn of Teachers of German, 1987-89; board member, Tennessee Foreign Language Teacher Assn, 1989-92; editorial reviewer, Soundings an Interdisciplinary Journal, 1985-91; member, Tennessee Collaborative Council on Foreign Language, 1986-. **CONTACT ADDRESS** Univ of Tennessee, Knoxville, 701 McClung Tower, Knoxville, TN, 37996-0470.

HODGES, JOHN O.
PERSONAL Born 01/26/1944, Greenwood, Mississippi, m, 1972 **DISCIPLINE** MODERN LANGUAGES **EDUCATION** University of Nantes, France, certificate, 1966-67; Morehouse College, Atlanta, GA, BA, 1968; Atlanta University, Atlanta, GA, MA, 1971; University of Chicago, Chicago, IL, MA, 1972, PhD, 1980. **CAREER** Morehouse College, Atlanta, GA, director of language laboratory, 1969-70; Barat College, Lake Forest, IL, director of Afro-American studies, 1972-75, assistant professor of English, 1972-75; University of Chicago, Chicago, IL, assistant dean of university students, 1980-82; University of Tennessee, Knoxville, TN, associate professor, 1988-, acting head of department rel studies, 1989-90. **HONORS AND AWARDS** Merrill Overseas Fellow, Morehouse, 1966-67; Rockefeller Fellow, Rockefeller Foundation, 1970-71; Ford Fellow, Ford Foundation, 1976-78; NEH Fellow, National Endowment for Humanities, 1984. **MEMBERSHIPS** Member, American Academy of Religion, 1982-; member, Modern Language Association, 1981-; member, College Language Association, 1982-; member, South Atlantic Modern Language Assn, 1983; annual dinner committee, Urban League, Langston Hughes Society, 1984-. **CONTACT ADDRESS** Department of Religion, Univ of Tennessee, 501 McClung Tower, Knoxville, TN, 37914.

HOEFERT, SIGFRID
PERSONAL Born 08/14/1925, Poland, m, 1954, 3 children **DISCIPLINE** GERMAN **EDUCATION** Univ Toronto, BA, 58, MA, 60, PhD(Ger), 63. **CAREER** Lectr, 61-63, from asst prof to assoc prof, 63-69, Prof Ger, Univ Waterloo, 69-, Soc Sci & Humanities Res Coun Can awards & fac res grants. **MEMBERSHIPS** Am Asn Teachers Ger; Can Asn Univ Teachers Ger; Can Comp Lit Asn Int Ver Ger Sprach-u Literaturwiss; MLA. **RESEARCH** Naturalism; literature of the German Democratic Republic. **SELECTED PUBLICATIONS** Auth, Poets During the Stagnation Period--Studies on Georg Buchner Reception in East-Germany, Zeitschrift Germanistik, Vol 0004, 94; Approaches to Georg Buchner--An International-Colloquium Held at the Akademie-Der-Wissenschaften in East-Berlin, 1988, Zeitschrift Germanistik, Vol 0004, 94; Understanding Gerhart Hauptmann, Seminar, Vol 0030, 94; Literature in Various Media-- Gerhart Hauptmann Tragicomedy Die 'Ratten' and its Adaptations For Film, Radio, and Television, Seminar, Vol 0030, 94; From Critical and Capitalist Realism--Modern German Literature from the Soviet/Russian Viewpoint, Germano-Slavica, Vol 0009, 96; German-Language Books Published by Moscow and St-Petersburg Publishing Houses 1731-1991, Germano-Slavica, Vol 0009, 96; Diaries, 1906-1913--With the Travel-Diary of the Journey to Greece and Turkey, 1907, Seminar, Vol 0032, 96. **CONTACT ADDRESS** Dept of Ger & Russ, Univ of Waterloo, Waterloo, ON, N2L 3G1.

HOENIGSWALD, HENRY M.
PERSONAL Born 04/17/1915, Breslau, Germany **DISCIPLINE** LINGUISTICS **EDUCATION** Univ Florence, D Litt, 36. **CAREER** Mem staff, Inst Studies Etruschi, 36-38; lectr ling, Yale Univ, 39-42, res asst, 45-46; lectr phonetics & ling, Hartford Sem Found, 42-43, instr, 45-46; in charge army specialized training in Hindustani, Univ Pa, 43-44; mem staff, foreign serv inst, US Dept State, 46-47; assoc prof classic lang, Univ Tex, 47-48; assoc prof, 48-59, chmn dept, 63-70, Prof Ling, Univ PA, 59-, Am Coun Learned Soc fel, 42-43, 44-45; lectr, Hunter Col, 42-43 & 46; Guggenheim fel, 50-51; vis assoc prof, Georgetown Univ, 52-53 & 54; assoc ed, J Am Orient Soc, 52-54, ed, 54-58; sr linguist, Deccan Col, India, 55; Newberry Libr fel, 56; chmn Am comt, SAsian Lang, 56; vis assoc prof, Princeton Univ, 59-60; vis prof, Yale Univ, 61-62; Nat Sci Found sr fel, Ctr Advan Study Behav Sci, 62-63; mem comt lang prog, Am Coun Learned Soc, 63-70; mem univ sem, Columbia Univ, 64-; mem corp vis comt, Mass Inst Technol, 68-74; Fulbright lectr, Oxford Univ, 76-77; fel, St John's Col, Oxford, 76-77; chmn, overseers comt to vis Dept of Ling, Harvard Univ, 78- **HONORS AND AWARDS** LHD, Swarthmore Col, 81. **MEMBERSHIPS** Ling Soc Am (pres, 58); Am Orient Soc (pres, 66-67); Am Philos Soc; Am Acad Arts & Sci; Philol Soc. **RESEARCH** History of linguistics; Indo-European comparative linguistics; theory of change and reconstruction. **SELECTED PUBLICATIONS** Auth, On Verbal Accentuation in the Rg-Veda, J Am Oriental Soc, Vol 0114, 94; The Bopp-Symposium 1992 at the Humboldt-Universitat Berlin--Proceedings of the Conference Held in Commemoration of Franz Bopp, Bicentennial, March 24-26, 1992, Historiographia Ling, Vol 0022, 95; A Paradigm Lost--The Linguistic Theory of Mikolaj Kruszewski, Slavic Rev, Vol 0054, 95. **CONTACT ADDRESS** Univ of Pa, 618 Williams Hall, Philadelphia, PA, 19104.

HOFFMANN, KLAUS D.
DISCIPLINE GERMAN LITERATURE **EDUCATION** Univ Iowa, PhD. **CAREER** Assoc prof. **RESEARCH** Study of the heritage of Germans from Russia. **CONTACT ADDRESS** Foreign Languages and Literature Dept, Colorado State Univ, Fort Collins, CO, 80523. **EMAIL** khoffmann@vines.colostate.edu

HOFFMEISTER, GERHART
PERSONAL Born 12/17/1936, Giessen, Germany, m, 1966, 1 child **DISCIPLINE** GERMAN & COMPARATIVE LITERATURE **EDUCATION** Univ Md, College Park, PhD(Ger), 70. **CAREER** Referendar English & Ger, Cologne Sch Syst, 64-66; instr Ger, Univ Md, 66-70; asst prof, Univ Wis-Milwaukee, 70-74; assoc prof, Wayne State Univ, 74-75; assoc prof, 75-79, Prof Ger, Univ Calif, Santa Barbara, 79-, Am Philos Soc grant, 75. **MEMBERSHIPS** MLA; Am Asn Teachers Ger; Philol Asn Pac Coast. **RESEARCH** German baroque; German-Hispanic relations; European romanticism. **SELECTED PUBLICATIONS** Auth, The Influence of Italian Humanism on the German Literature Before 1600, German Quarterly, Vol 0067, 94; Early Romanticism--Epoch, Work, Influence, German Quarterly, Vol 0067, 94; Italian-European Cultural Ties During the Baroque Period, German Quarterly, Vol 0065, 92. **CONTACT ADDRESS** Dept of Ger & Slavic Lang, Univ of Calif, 552 University Rd, Santa Barbara, CA, 93106-0001.

HOFFMEISTER, WERNER
DISCIPLINE GERMAN AND COMPARATIVE LITERATURE **EDUCATION** Brown Univ, PhD, 62. **CAREER** Emeritus Prof Ger and Comp Lit. **RESEARCH** Ger and comparative lit of the 19th and 20th centuries, particularly prose fiction. **SELECTED PUBLICATIONS** Auth, publ(s) about Fontane, Kleist, Grass, Thomas Mann, Musil, and Ger-Am lit rel(s). **CONTACT ADDRESS** Dartmouth Col, 3529 N Main St, #207, Hanover, NH, 03755.

HOGELAND, L.M.
PERSONAL Born 08/16/1959, Glendale, CA, s **DISCIPLINE** MODERN THOUGHT AND LITERATURE **EDUCATION** Stanford Univ, AB, 81; PhD, 92. **CAREER** Assoc Prof English & Women's Studies, Univ Cincinnati. **RESEARCH** American women writers; Feminist criticism and theory. **SELECTED PUBLICATIONS** Auth, Fear of Feminism, MS, 94; Feminism and Its Fictions: The Consciousness-Raising Novel and the Womens Liberation Movement; Univ Penn Press, 98. **CONTACT ADDRESS** Univ Cincinnati, PO Box 0069, Cincinnati, OH, 45221-0069. **EMAIL** Lisa.Hogeland@UC.edu

HOHENDAHL, PETER U.
PERSONAL Born 03/17/1936, Hamburg, Germany, m, 2 children **DISCIPLINE** GERMAN STUDIES **EDUCATION** Univ Hamburg, PhD, 64. **CAREER** Asst prof Ger, PA State Univ, 65-68; assoc prof, WA Univ, 68-69, prof, 70-77, chmn dept, 70-77; Prof Ger & Comp Lit, Cornell Univ, 77-, Chmn Dept, 81-86; Jacob Gould Shurman Prof Ger & Comp Lit, 85-; Merton vis prof, Free Univ Berlin, 76; Distinguished vis prof, OH state Univ, 87. **HONORS AND AWARDS** Choice Outstanding Acad Bk Award, 96. **MEMBERSHIPS** MLA; Am Asn Tchr(s) Ger; Ger studies Asn; Namer Heine soc; AHA. **RESEARCH** Theory of lit; 18th and 19th century Europ lit; mod Ger lit. **SELECTED PUBLICATIONS** Auth, Literaturkritik und Offentlichkeit, Piper, 74; auth, Der europaische Roman der Empfindsamikeit, Athenaion, 77; Der Europaische Roman der Empfindsamkeit, 77; The Institution of Criticism, Cornell Univ Press, 82; Building a National Literature, The Case of Germany, 1830-1870, 89; Reappraisals: Shifting Alignments in Postwar Critical Theory, 91; Geschichte Opposition Subersion: Studien zur Literatur des 19 Jahrhunderts, 93; Prismatic Thought: Theodore W. Adorno, 95. **CONTACT ADDRESS** Dept of Ger Studies, Cornell Univ, 193 Goldwin Smith Hall, Ithaca, NY, 14853-3201. **EMAIL** puhl@cornell.edu

HOJI, HAJIME
DISCIPLINE LINGUISTICS AND EAST ASIAN LANGUAGES AND CULTURES **EDUCATION** Univ Wash, PhD, 85. **CAREER** Assoc prof, Univ Southern Calif. **RESEARCH** East Asian linguistics. **SELECTED PUBLICATIONS** Auth, Anaphora and Japanese Syntax; Japanese/Korean linguistics. **CONTACT ADDRESS** East Asian Studies Center, Univ Southern Calif, University Park Campus, Los Angeles, CA, 90089.

HOLLAND, NORMAN
DISCIPLINE HISPANO-AMERICAN LITERATURES **EDUCATION** Johns Hopkins Univ, PhD. **CAREER** Assoc prof, Hampshire Col. **SELECTED PUBLICATIONS** Writes on Latin Am and Latino lit and cult. **CONTACT ADDRESS** Hampshire Col, Amherst, MA, 01002.

HOLLANDER, ROBERT
PERSONAL Born 07/31/1933, Manhattan, NY, m, 1964, 2 children **DISCIPLINE** ENGLISH, COMPARATIVE LITERATURE **EDUCATION** Princeton AB, 55; Columbia PhD, 62. **CAREER** Col Sch, NYC, teacher, latin eng, 55-57; Colum Col, instr eng, 58-62; Princeton, lectur euro lit, dept RLL, 62; Princeton, prof euro lit, depots RLL and CL, 75-98; Butler Col, Master, 91-95, chmn comp lit, 94-98; Fellowships, Guggenheim, Fulbright, NEH 2, Rockefeller Found, Bellagio; Founding Memb of Intl Dante Seminar, pres, 92-2000; Mem, Bd trust, Collegiate Sch NYC, 90-96, 98-2001; Vs prof, Univ Florence, 88; Nat Humanities Cen, Mem, Bd trust, 81-, Chmn Comm on Schol Affairs, 87-88, Vice Chmn and VP of the center, 87-88, Chmn Bd, 88-91; Emer Stat, 91-. **HONORS AND AWARDS** The Howard T Behrman Award, Princ, 86; Gold Medal of the Cty Florence, behalf of Dante, 88; John Witherspoon Award in Humanities, NJ Comm, 88; Bronze Medal of the Cty of Tours, 93; Hon Cit of Certaldo, behalf of Boccaccio, 97. **MEMBERSHIPS** Dante Soc Am; Soc Dante Italiana; Am Boccaccio Asn. **RESEARCH** Dante; Boccaccio; late Medieval Europe **SELECTED PUBLICATIONS** Allegory in Dante's Commedia, Prin, 69; Boccaccio's Two Venuses, Colum, 77; Studies in Dante, Longo, 80; Il Virgilio dantesco, Oschki, 83; Boccaccio's Last Fiction, Il Corbaccio, Penn, 88; Dante's Letter to Cangrande, Mich, 93; Boccaccio's Dante and the Shaping Force of Satire, Mich, 97. **CONTACT ADDRESS** Princeton Univ, Dept Romance Languages, Princeton, NJ, 0854. **EMAIL** bobh@phoenix.princeton.edu

HOLLERBACH, WOLF
PERSONAL Born 11/30/1935, Cologne, Germany, m, 1962, 3 children **DISCIPLINE** ROMANCE LANGUAGES **EDUCATION** Univ Bonn, State dipl (French, English), 62; Univ Rennes, PhD(stylistics), 61. **CAREER** Asst Ger, Lycee Garcons, Rennes, 59-60; lectr French, Univ Bonn, 62; lectr Ger, Ger Acad Exchange & prof French, Univ Cuenca, Ecuador, 62-65; dir lang dept, univ, 63-65; asst prof French, 65-67, assoc prof French & Span, 67-73, Prof French & Span, Univ Alaska, Fairbanks, 73-, Vis prof lit theory, Univ Hamburg, 76-77. **MEMBERSHIPS** Am Asn Teachers Fr; Am Asn Teachers Span & Port; Philol Asn Pac Coast; Am Coun Teaching Foreign Lang. **RESEARCH** Literary theory; structural analysis of literary texts; structural approach to French syntax. **SELECTED PUBLICATIONS** Auth, The 'Syntax of Contemporary French'--Response, French Rev, Vol 0069, 96. **CONTACT ADDRESS** Dept of French & Span, Univ of Alaska, Fairbanks, AK, 99701.

HOLLIS, SUSAN T.
PERSONAL Born 03/17/1939, Boston, MA, d, 2 children **DISCIPLINE** RELIGION; ANCIENT NEAR EASTERN LANGUAGES & CIVILIZATIONS **EDUCATION** Harvard, PhD, 82 **CAREER** Prof, Union Inst Los Angeles, 91-93; dean & prof, Sierra Nevada Col, 93-95; center dir & assoc dean, Central NY Center, State Univ of NY, Empire State Col, 96- **HONORS AND AWARDS** Teaching Excellence, Harvard Col; Who's Who in the West, East, America, World, Women **MEMBERSHIPS** Amer Res Egypt; Amer Acad Relig; Soc Bibl Lit; Int Assoc Egyptologist; Amer Folklore Soc **RESEARCH** Ancient Egypt; Ancient Israel; Egyptian Relations; Folklore **SELECTED PUBLICATIONS** Ed, Ancient Egyptian Hymns, Prayers, and Songs. An Anthology of Ancient Egyptian Lyric Poetry, Scholar's Press, 95; co-ed & contributor, Feminist Theory and the Study of Folklore, Univ Ill, 93; auth, "Otiose Deities and the Ancient Egyptian Pantheon," Jrnl Amer Res Center in Egypt, 98 **CONTACT ADDRESS** SUNY Empire State Col, 219 Walton St, Syracuse, NY, 13202-1226. **EMAIL** susan_hollis@sln.esc.edu

HOLMBERG, I.E.
DISCIPLINE GREEK LITERATURE **EDUCATION** Univ Vermont, BA, 80; Yale Univ, PhD, 90. **CAREER** Asst prof, 91. **RESEARCH** Homer and early Greek poetry; critical theory. **SELECTED PUBLICATIONS** Auth, The Sign of Metis, Arethusa, 97; The Odyssey and Female Subjectivity, Helios, 95; Euripides' Helen: Most Noble and Most Chaste, AJP 116, 95. **CONTACT ADDRESS** Dept of Greek and Roman Studies, Victoria Univ, PO Box 1700 STN CSC, Victoria, BC, V8W 2Y2. **EMAIL** ingrid@uvic.ca

HOLMLUND, CHRISTINE
DISCIPLINE FRENCH LITERATURE **EDUCATION** Univ Wis, PhD, 84. **CAREER** Assoc prof. **RESEARCH** Film studies; women's studies; critical theory. **SELECTED PUBLICATIONS** Auth, pubs on mainstream and experimental films from Canada, France, the U.S., Austria, Sweden, Costa Rica, and Ecuador, and French feminist theory. **CONTACT ADDRESS** Dept of Romance Languages, Knoxville, TN, 37996.

HOLSCHUH, ALBRECHT
PERSONAL Born 02/28/1937, Voklingen, Germany, m, 1968, 5 children **DISCIPLINE** GERMANIC STUDIES **EDUCATION** Princeton Univ, AM, 61, PhD(Ger), 64. **CAREER** Instr Ger, Princeton Univ, 62-64; asst prof, 64-68, Assoc Prof Ger, Ind Univ Bloomington, 68-, Chmn Dept, 78-, Am Coun Learned Soc fel, 81. **MEMBERSHIPS** MLA; Am Asn Teachers Ger; Midwest Mod Lang Asn; Am Coun Teaching Foreign Lang; AAUP. **RESEARCH** Twentieth century German literature. **SELECTED PUBLICATIONS** Forum--Relevance, Philology and Baackmann Essay on Bachmann 'Undine Geht', German Quarterly, Vol 0068, 95. **CONTACT ADDRESS** Dept of Ger Studies, Indiana Univ, Bloomington, 1 Indiana University, Bloomington, IN, 47405.

HOLTZ, AVRAHAM
PERSONAL Born 05/26/1934, New York, NY, m, 4 children **DISCIPLINE** MODERN HEBREW LITERATUERE **EDUCATION** Brooklyn Col, BA, 55; Jewish Theol Sem Am, MHL, 59, DHL, 62. **CAREER** Dean acad develop, 72-80, Prof Mod Hebrew Lit, Jewish Theol Sem Am, 73-. **HONORS AND AWARDS** Nat End of the Hum. **SELECTED PUBLICATIONS** Ed, The Holy City: Jews on Jerusalem, Norton/Viking, 71; auth, Isaac Dov Berkowitz: Voice of the Uprooted, Cornell Univ, 73; auth, B'Olam Hanah shava shel Hazal Marot U-Meqorot: Mahadura; auth, Mueret u-meuyeret shel Hakhnasat Kallah le-Shmuel Yosef Agnon. **CONTACT ADDRESS** Jewish Theol Sem of America, 3080 Broadway, New York, NY, 10027-4649.

HOLTZ, BARRY
PERSONAL Boston, MA **DISCIPLINE** JEWISH EDUCATION AND STUDIES **EDUCATION** Tufts Univ, BA; Brandeis Univ, PhD. **CAREER** Vis prof, Hebrew Univ; co-dir, Melton Res Ctr; assoc prof, Jewish Theol Sem; lect, 92nd Street Y, New York. **SELECTED PUBLICATIONS** Auth, Back to the Sources: Reading the Classic Jewish Texts, Simon and Schuster 84; Finding Our Way: Jewish Texts and the Lives we Lead Today, Schocken, 90; The Schocken Guide to Jewish Books, 92; coauth, Your Word is Fire: The Hasidic Masters on Contemplative Prayer, Jewish Lights Press. **CONTACT ADDRESS** Jewish Theol Sem of America, 3080 Broadway, New York, NY, 10027. **EMAIL** baholtz@jtsa.edu

HOLUB, RENATE
PERSONAL Born 10/06/1946, Germany, 7 children **DISCIPLINE** ITALIAN, GERMAN, PHILOSOPHY, SOCIAL THEORY **EDUCATION** Univ Wisc, PhD, 83. **CAREER** Univ Cal-Berkeley. **MEMBERSHIPS** Am Philos Asn; Am Sociol Asn. **RESEARCH** Social theory; European studies. **CONTACT ADDRESS** Univ Calif Berkeley, 317 Campbell Hall, Berkeley, CA, 94720. **EMAIL** rholub@socrates.berkeley.edu

HOLUB, ROBERT C.
PERSONAL Born 08/22/1949, Neptune, NJ **DISCIPLINE** GERMAN LITERATURE, LITERARY THEORY **EDUCATION** Univ Pa, BA, 71; Univ Wis-Madison, MA, 73, MA, 76, PhD(German), 79. **CAREER** Teaching asst, Univ Wis-Madison, 72-78; Asst Prof German, Univ Caliv, Berkeley, 79-. **MEMBERSHIPS** MLA; Am Asn Teachers of German; Heinrich Heine Soc. **RESEARCH** Literary theory; oppositional literature in Germany from 1750 to present; literature of the German restoration period (1815-1848), especially Heinrich Heine. **SELECTED PUBLICATIONS** Auth, Nietzsche and the Feminine, German Quarterly, Vol 0068, 95; The German Left--Red, Green and Beyond, German Studies Rev, Vol 0017, 94; The Extra-Moral-- Friedrich Nietzsche, Simone Weil, Heinrich Von Kleist, Franz Kafka, Colloquia Germanica, Vol 0029, 96; Nietzsche and Metaphor, Colloquia Germanica, Vol 0029, 96; Reappraisals, Shifting Alignments in Postwar Critical-Theory, Comp Lit, Vol 0047, 95; Poisoned Arrows--Theory and Literature in the Modern-Age, Germanic Rev, Vol 0070, 95; Nietzsche, Feminism and Political-Theory, German Quarterly, Vol 0068, 95; Toward a Theory of Radical Origin--Essays on Modern German Thought, German Quarterly, Vol 0070, 97; The Ambiguity of Taste--Freedom and Food in European Romanticism, J English Germanic Philol, Vol 0096, 97. **CONTACT ADDRESS** Dept German, Univ Calif, 5315 Dwinelle Hall, Berkeley, CA, 94720-3244.

HONEYCUTT, JAMES M.
DISCIPLINE DEPARTMENT OF SPEECH COMMUNICATION **EDUCATION** Univ Ill, PhD. **CAREER** Assoc prof, La State Univ. **RESEARCH** Relational conflict; marital interaction. **SELECTED PUBLICATIONS** Published over a dozen studies in intrapersonal communication processes in terms of covert dialogues or imagined interactions. **CONTACT ADDRESS** Dept of Speech Commun, Louisiana State Univ, Baton Rouge, LA, 70803.

HOOLEY, DANIEL M.
DISCIPLINE LATIN AND GREEK LITERATURE **EDUCATION** Minn Univ, MA, PhD, Class, PhD, Engl. **CAREER** Assoc prof; Univ Mo, 92-; actv, Honors Col Humanities sequence; taught at, Allegheny Col, Carleton Col & Princeton Univ. **RESEARCH** Satire; later Latin; Classical tradition; translation studies. **SELECTED PUBLICATIONS** Auth, The Classics in Paraphrase: Ezra Pound and Modern Translators of Latin Poetry & The Knotted Thong: Structures of Imitation in Persius. **CONTACT ADDRESS** Dept of Classical Studies, Univ of Missouri-Columbia, 309 University Hall, Columbia, MO, 65211. **EMAIL** clstuddh@showme.missouri.edu

HOOVER, DAVID LOWELL
PERSONAL Born 02/10/1949, Goshen, IN, m, 1974, 1 child **DISCIPLINE** MEDIEVAL LITERATURE, LINGUISTICS **EDUCATION** Manchester Col, BA, 71; Ind Univ, MA, 74, PhD(English lang), 80. **CAREER** Instr English, Ind Cent Univ, 80-81; ASST PROF ENGLISH, NY UNIV, 81- **MEMBERSHIPS** MLA. **RESEARCH** Medieval language and literature; metrics; stylistics. **SELECTED PUBLICATIONS** Auth, Theory, Fact, and Grammar, 2 Approaches to Old-English Meter, Modern Philol, Vol 0092, 94. **CONTACT ADDRESS** English Dept, New York Univ, 19 University Pl, New York, NY, 10003-4556.

HOOVER, MARJORIE LAWSON
PERSONAL Born 02/01/1910, New York, NY **DISCIPLINE** GERMAN & RUSSIAN LITERATURE **EDUCATION** Smith Col, AB, 30; Univ Bonn, PhD, 34; Yale Univ, MA, 62. **CAREER** Instr Ger, St Xavier Col, 35-36 & Swarthmore Col, 36-38; from instr to lectr, Oberlin Col, 38-53, lectr, 55-59, from assoc prof to prof Ger & Russ, 59-76; Retired. Campbell prof Ger & Russ, Wells Col, 77. **MEMBERSHIPS** MLA; Am Asn Teachers Slavic & E Europ Lang; Am Asn Advan Slavic Studies; Int Brech Soc. **RESEARCH** Contemporary German literature; Russian theater. **SELECTED PUBLICATIONS** Auth, Das 'Gleichgewicht Des Lichts Der Tages Und Der Nachtsterne', World Lit Today, Vol 0068, 94. **CONTACT ADDRESS** 704 Washington St Apt 2A, New York, NY, 10014.

HOPKINS, LEROY TAFT, JR.
PERSONAL Born 08/19/1942, Lancaster, PA **DISCIPLINE** ENGLISH, GERMAN **EDUCATION** Millersville St Coll, BA 1966; Harvard U, PhD 1974. **CAREER** Millersville State Coll, asst prof of German 1979-; Urban League of Lancaster Co Inc, acting exec dir 1979, asso dir 1976-79; Hedwig-Heyle-Schule (W Germany), instr English 1974-76; NE Univ, instructor German 1971-72. **HONORS AND AWARDS** Received Travelling Fellowship Harvard Univ 1969-70; Study/Visit Grant for Research, German Academic Exchange Service, 1989; Member of Honor Society, Phi Kappa Phi, 1991. **MEMBERSHIPS** Adv Com on Black History PA Hist & Mus Commn 1979-; com person City of Lancasters Overall Econ Devel Prog; Bd Mem Lancastger Co Library/Lancaster Neighborhood Hlth Ctr 1977-; chmn PA Delegation to White House Conf on Libraries 1978-79; 1st vice pres, Lancaster Historical Society, 1989-; mem, Pennsylvania Humanities Council, 1988-. **CONTACT ADDRESS** Dept of For Lang, Millersville Univ, Millersville, PA, 17551.

HOPPER, PAUL
DISCIPLINE ENGLISH AND LINGUISTICS **EDUCATION** Univ Tex, PhD. **CAREER** Lit, Carnegie Mellon Univ. **HONORS AND AWARDS** Ed, Jour Lang Scis; 's Language, Collitz Prof LSA's Linguistics Inst, Fulbright Fel; Guggenheim Fel. **MEMBERSHIPS** MLAl; Ling Soc Am. **SELECTED PUBLICATIONS** Coauth, Grammaticalization, Cambridge, 93. **CONTACT ADDRESS** Carnegie Mellon Univ, 5000 Forbes Ave, Pittsburgh, PA, 15213.

HORAN, ELIZABETH R.
PERSONAL Born 07/06/1956, Boston, MA, m, 1980, 1 child **DISCIPLINE** LITERATURE IN ENGLISH, SPANISH, LATIN, AND ITALIAN **EDUCATION** Barnard Col, BA 78; Univ Calif-Santa Cruz, MA, 84, PhD, 88. **CAREER** Lectr, Wheelock Col, 87-88; Vis Asst Prof, Tufts Univ, 88-89; Asst Prof, 89-95, Assoc Prof, Ariz State Univ, 95-. **HONORS AND AWARDS** Fulbright Schol, 85-87, 95-96; Gabriela Mistral Award, Org Am States, 90. **MEMBERSHIPS** MLA; ACLA; Letras Feministas; Emily Dickinson Int Soc. **RESEARCH** US & Latin American women writers; translations; biography. **SELECTED PUBLICATIONS** Co-transl, Happiness, White Pine Press, 93; auth, Gabriela Mistral, an Artist and Her People, Org Am States, 94; To Market: The Dickinson Copyright Wars, Emily Dickinson J, 96; Santa Maestra Muerta: Body and Nation in Portraits of Gabriela Mistral, Taller de Letras, 97; Reading the Book of Memory, Always from Somewhere Else: A Memoir of My Jewish Father, The Feminist Press at CUNY, 98; author of numerous other articles and publications. **CONTACT ADDRESS** English Dept, Arizona State Univ, Tempe, Tempe, AZ, 85287-0302. **EMAIL** elizabeth.horan@asu.edu

HORN, PIERRE LAURENCE
PERSONAL Born 11/13/1942, Paris, France, m, 1968 **DISCIPLINE** FRENCH, COMPARATIVE LITERATURE **EDUCATION** Brooklyn Col, City Univ New York, BA, 64; Columbia Univ, MA, 65, PhD, 74. **CAREER** Instr French, Columbia Univ, 68-69; asst prof, Clark Univ, 69-75; asst prof, 75-78, assoc prof French, 78-84, PROF, WRIGHT STATE UNIV, 84-; Contract escort & interpreter, US Dept State, 64-68; mem, bd dirs, Am Soc Interpreters, 72-77. **HONORS AND AWARDS** Chevalier de l'Ordre des Palmes academiques, French Govt, 78; Col of Liberal Arts, Wright State Univ, Merit Award for Outstanding Teaching, 82; WSU Bd of Trustees Award for Faculty Excellence, 88; WSU Presidential Award for Outstanding Faculty Member, 89; Braye Golding Distinguished Prof of Research, 92-95. **MEMBERSHIPS** MLA; Am Asn Teachers Fr; Am Soc Interpreters; Popular Cult Asn. **RESEARCH** Nineteenth-century French literature; 20th century French literature; comparative novel. **SELECTED PUBLICATIONS** Auth, On a Whitman quotation in Les Caves du Vatican, Fr-Am Rev, winter 76; Un correspondent oublie de Victor Hugo: George J Harney, Revue Hist Lit France, 3-4/77; Isabelle: a detective novel by Andre Gide, Romance Notes, fall 77; Reflections on Mme de Renal's first name, Nineteenth-Century Fr Studies, fall-winter 77; L'episode des banquiers dans Cesar Birotteau et Jerome Paturot, L'Annee Balzacienne, 78; Marguerite Yourcenar's Le Labyrinthe du Monde: A Modern Autobiography In: The Writer and the Past, ed, Donald L. Jennermann, IN State Univ Press, 81; Victor Hugo's Theatrical Royalties during his Exile Years, Theatre Res Int, spring 82; co-ed, The Image of the Prostitute in Modern Literature, NY: Frederic Ungar Pubs, 84; auth, Marguerite Yourcenar, Boston: Twayne Pubs, 85; Louis XIV, NY: Chelsea House, 86; Lafayette, NY: Chelsea House, 89; ed, Handbook of French Popular Culture, Westport, CT: Greenwood Press, 91; auth, Modern Jewish Writers of France, Lewisburg, NY: Edwin Mellon Press, 97; Dictionary of French Cinema, Westport, CT: Greenwood Press, forthcoming; and numerous articles appearing in the following publications: The World Encyclopedia of Cartoons, Phenix, French-Am Rev, Modern Lang J, English Lang Notes, Cyclopedia of Literary Characters II, Contemp Graphic Artists, Cyclopedia of World Authors II, Great Lives from History: Twentieth Century, Identities and Issues in Literature (and several other publications). **CONTACT ADDRESS** Wright State Univ, 3640 Colonel Glenn, Dayton, OH, 45435-0001. **EMAIL** phorn@wright.edu

HORSLEY, RITTA JO
PERSONAL 2 children **DISCIPLINE** GERMAN LANGUAGE & LITERATURE **EDUCATION** Radcliffe Col, AB, 62; Harvard Univ, MA, 64, PhD(Ger lang & lit), 70. **CAREER** Asst prof Ger, 69-76, assoc dean spec prog & interdisciplinary studies, Col Arts & Sci, 76-77, assoc prof Ger, Univ Mass, Boston, 76-. **HONORS AND AWARDS** Fulbright Senior Professor; DAAD Study. **MEMBERSHIPS** Am Asn Teachers Ger; MLA; Women in Ger. **RESEARCH** Age of Goethe; 20th century German fiction; women in literature; European Witch Persecutions; Lesbian Studies. **SELECTED PUBLICATIONS** Articles concerning Irmgard Keun, Iugeborg Bachmaun, and European Witch Persecutions. **CONTACT ADDRESS** Dept of Mod Lang, Univ of Massachusetts, Boston, 100 Morrissey Blvd, Boston, MA, 02125-3393. **EMAIL** horsley@umbsky.cc.umb.edu

HORWATH, PETER
PERSONAL Born 06/27/1929, Petrovgrad, Yugoslavia, 3 children **DISCIPLINE** GERMAN **EDUCATION** Ind Univ, Bloomington, BA, 52, MA, 53; Univ Mich, PhD, 59. **CAREER** Ind Univ, 52-53; Holy Cross Col, 55-59; Univ Ariz, 60-63; E Washington State Univ, 67; Prescott Col, 68-73; Prof, 67, assoc prof, 73, chair, 84-92, coord German, 92, Arizona State Univ. **CONTACT ADDRESS** Dept of Langs, Lit, Arizona State Univ, Tempe, Tempe, AZ, 85287-0202.

HORWEGE, RONALD EUGENE
PERSONAL Born 03/05/1944, St. Francis, KS, m, 1970, 2 children **DISCIPLINE** GERMANIC LINGUISTICS **EDUCATION** Univ Kans, BA, 66; Ind Univ, Bloomington, MA, 68, PhD, 71. **CAREER** Asst prof, 71-79, Assoc Prof Ger, Sweet Briar Col, 79-; Chmn, Dept Mod Lang, 81-, Guest lectr, Cent Va Community Col, 72-; Fulbright Sem on Ger Cult fel, 76; Sweet Briar Col res grant, 77-78, 81 & 82; Danish teacher, Gen Electric Plant, Lynchburg, 78-79; consult, NEH grant, 79. **MEMBERSHIPS** Am Asn Teachers Ger; Am Coun for Study Austrian Lit. **RESEARCH** Early New High German; German literature and German nationalism; Old Icelandic. **SELECTED PUBLICATIONS** Auth, Marquard von Lindau: De nabuchodonosor, Jahrbuch fur internationale Germanistik, 76, 79. **CONTACT ADDRESS** Dept of Mod Lang, Sweet Briar Col, Box 35, Sweet Briar, VA, 24595-1056. **EMAIL** horwege@sbc.edu

HOTTELL, RUTH A.
DISCIPLINE FRENCH **EDUCATION** Western Ky Univ, BA, 74; Univ Louisville, MA, 81; Univ Ill, PhD, 87. **CAREER** Assoc prof French. **SELECTED PUBLICATIONS** Auth, A Poetics of Pain: Evelyne Accad's Critical and Fictional World, World Lit Today, 97; Chanter son pays-La Rue Cases-Negres d'Euzhan Palcy, Martinique, 97; The Diabolic Dialogic: Les Diaboliques by Henri-Georges Clouzot, Lit Film Quarterly, 96; The Delusory Denouement and other Narrative Strategies in Maupassant's Fantastic Tales, Romanic Rev, 94; The Time of Ecofeminism, Humanities, 94; co-auth, The Pedantic Eye/I: Feminist Theory and Pedagogy, State Univ NY, 97. **CONTACT ADDRESS** Foreign Languages Dept, Univ of Toledo, Univ Hall 5210, Toledo, OH, 43606. **EMAIL** fac2995@uoft01.utoledo.edu

HOUNG, CAROLINE C.
DISCIPLINE LINGUISTICS, CHINESE LANGUAGE **EDUCATION** Chengchi Univ, Taiwan, BA, 75; Occidental Col, MA; Univ TX, Austin, PhD, 87. **CAREER** Instr, Univ TX, Austin; instr, Univ Houston; instr, Soochow Univ, Taiwan; instr, Nat Ocean Univ, Taiwan; instr, Fort Bend Independent Sch Dist; Prof, Rice Univ. **SELECTED PUBLICATIONS** Auth, Popular Chinese Expressions in American English; Communicating in Chinese Workbook. **CONTACT ADDRESS** Rice Univ, PO Box 1892, Houston, TX, 77251-1892. **EMAIL** houng@ruf.rice.edu

HOUSTON, MONA T.
DISCIPLINE FRENCH LITERATURE **EDUCATION** Yale Univ, PhD, 64. **CAREER** Assoc prof. **RESEARCH** History of theater. **SELECTED PUBLICATIONS** Auth, pubs on Villiers de l'Isle-Adam, Sartre, and Pasinetti; co-auth, Harper's Grammar of French; co-ed, Mauriac's Genitirix 66; French Symbolist Poetry: An Anthology, 80. **CONTACT ADDRESS** Dept of French and Italian, Indiana Univ, Bloomington, 300 N Jordan Ave, Bloomington, IN, 47405.

HOWARD, JOAN E.
PERSONAL Born 08/25/1951, Augusta, ME, 1 child **DISCIPLINE** MODERN LANGUAGE **EDUCATION** Univ New Hamp, BA, 73; Univ RI, MA, 76; Univ Conn, PhD, 87. **CAREER** Dir, 91-, Word Works; Instr, Asst Prof, 81-89, Univ New Hamp. **HONORS AND AWARDS** Ludwig Vogelstein Foun Fel; Florence Gould Foun Gnt; NH Dept Cult Affs; UNH Cen Hum; AAUW Diss Fel; CRIC Gnt; Phi Kappa Phi; Pi Sigma, Alpha. **MEMBERSHIPS** MLA; WSP; WBC. **RESEARCH** Marguerite Yourcenar **SELECTED PUBLICATIONS** Trans, Carson McCullers: A young Girl's Heart, by Josyane Savigneau, Boston, Houghton Mifflin, in press; coed, Les Visages de la mort dans l' oeuve de Marguerite Yourcenar, Tours FR, SIEY, 93; trans, Marguerite Yourcenar: Inventing a Life, by Josyane Savigneau, Chicago, U of Chicago Press, 93; auth, From Violence to Vision: Sacrifice in the Works of Marguerite Yourcenar, Carbondale, S IL U Press, 92. **CONTACT ADDRESS** Word Works, 78 Congress St, Portsmouth, NH, 03801-4018. **EMAIL** wrdwks@nh.ultranet.com

HOWARD, LLOYD H.
PERSONAL Born 12/08/1951, Los Angeles, CA **DISCIPLINE** ITALIAN/MEDIEVAL STUD **EDUCATION** Univ BC, BA, 73; Johns Hopkins Univ, MA, 75, PhD, 76. **CAREER** Instr to asst prof, 76-90, prof, State Univ NY Oswego, 90-; ch, dept Hispanic & Ital stud, 89-94, DIR MEDIEVAL STUD PROG, UNIV VICTORIA, 96-99. **HONORS AND AWARDS** Gilman fel, SSHRCC grants. **MEMBERSHIPS** Can Soc Ital Stud (adv bd). **SELECTED PUBLICATIONS** Ed bd, Quaderni d'italianistica; ed bd, Can J Ital Stud. **CONTACT ADDRESS** Medieval Stud Prog, Univ of Victoria, PO Box 3045, Victoria, BC, V8W 3P4.

HOWELL, RICHARD WESLEY
PERSONAL Born 09/06/1926, Berkeley, CA, m, 1948, 4 children **DISCIPLINE** ANTHROPOLOGY, LINGUISTICS **EDUCATION** Univ Calif, Berkeley, AB, 49, PhD,(anthrop), 67; Univ Hawaii, MA, 51. **CAREER** Asst prof anthrop, Richmond Col, NY, 67-69; assoc prof sociol, Univ Sask, 69-70; Assoc Prof Anthrop, Univ Hawaii At Hilo, 70-, Vis assoc prof E Asian Lang, Univ Hawaii, Manoa, 75-76; vis assoc prof ling, Int Christian Univ, Tokyo, 76-77. **MEMBERSHIPS** Am Anthrop Asn; Southern Anthrop Asn. **RESEARCH** Japanese ethnology; sociolinguistics; social conflict. **SELECTED PUBLICATIONS** Auth, Following the Brush--An American Encounter with Classical Japanese Culture, J Asian Hist, Vol 0029, 95. **CONTACT ADDRESS** Dept of Anthrop, Univ Hawaii at Hilo, Hilo, HI, 96720.

HOYT, GILES REID
PERSONAL Born 07/28/1943, Binghamton, NY, m, 1965, 1 child **DISCIPLINE** GERMAN LITERATURE **EDUCATION** Harpur Col, BA, 65; State Univ NY, Binghamton, MA, 68; Univ Ill, PhD(Ger), 73. **CAREER** Instr English, Jamestown Community Col, 71-73; lectr Ger, Univ Wis-Milwaukee, 74-75; asst prof, 76-81, Assoc, 81-93, PROF GER, ASSOC DEAN, IND UNIV-PURDUE UNIV, INDIANAPOLIS, 93-; NEH grant-in-residence Ger, Univ Cincinnati, 75-76. **MEMBERSHIPS** Am Asn Teachers Ger; MLA; Int Arbeitskreis Barockliteratur; Midwest Mod Lang Asn, Asn Intl Educators; Soc Ger-Am Stud. **RESEARCH** Seventeenth cent Ger lit; Ger novel; immigration hist. **SELECTED PUBLICATIONS** Auth, Johann Hellwig--A Descriptive Bibliography, German Quarterly, Vol 0069, 96; Sebastian Brant, the 'Ship Of Fools' in Critical Perspective, 1800-1901, German Studies Rev, Vol 0020, 97; Wolfgang Hildesheimer and His Critics, Seminar, Vol 0032, 96; Physics, Classics, and the Bible--Elements of the Secular and the Sacred in Heinrich Barthold Brockes 'Irdisches Vergnugen In Gott', 1721, German Quarterly, Vol 0066, 93; Previously Unknown Poetry of Sigmund-Von-Birken, German Quarterly, Vol 0067, 94. **CONTACT ADDRESS** Off Intl Affairs, Indiana Univ-Purdue Univ, Indianapolis, 620 Union Dr, Indianapolis, IN, 46202. **EMAIL** hoyt@iupui.edu

HSIEH, HSIN-I
PERSONAL Taiwan **DISCIPLINE** LINGUISTICS, CHINESE **EDUCATION** Taiwan Univ, BA, 63, MA, 6; Univ Calif, Berkeley, PhD(ling), 71. **CAREER** Asst prof Chinese, Univ Detroit, 70-71; asst res linguist, Univ Calif, Berkeley, 72; asst prof, 72-76, from assoc prof to prof Chinese, Univ Hawaii 76-83. **MEMBERSHIPS** Ling Soc Am; Assoc Asian Stud. **RESEARCH** Application of logic and mathematics to linguistics; Chinese linguistics; philosophy of language. **SELECTED PUBLICATIONS** Auth, The psychological reality of Taiwanese tone Sandhi rules, In: Papers from the Sixth Regional Meeting of Chicago Ling Soc, 70; coauth, The time variable in phonological change, J Ling, 7 1:1-13, 71; auth, Lexical diffusion: Evidence from child language acquisition, Glossa, 6 1:89-104, 72 & In: The Lexicon in Phonological Change, Mouton, 77; A new method of dialect subgrouping, J Chinese Ling, 1 1:64-92, 73 & In: The Lexicon in Phonological Change, Mouton, 77; Time as a cause of phonological irregularities, Lingua, 33 3: 253-264, 74; contribr, How generative is phonology?, In: The Transformational-Generative Paradigm and Modern Linguistic Theory, John Benjamins, Amsterdam, 75; auth, On the unreality of some phonological rules, Lingua, 38 1:1-19, 76; Set theory as a meta-language for natural languages, Papers in Ling, 13 3: 529-542, 80. **CONTACT ADDRESS** Dept East Asian Lang, Univ of Hawaii, 1890 E West Rd, Honolulu, HI, 96822-2318. **EMAIL** hhsieh@hawaii

HSIEH, YVONNE Y.
DISCIPLINE 20TH-CENTURY FRENCH LITERATURE **EDUCATION** Univ Stanford, PhD. **RESEARCH** East-West literary relations; exoticism in French Literature. **SELECTED PUBLICATIONS** Auth, Segalen's Literary Encounter with China: Chinese Moulds, Western Thoughts, U of Toronto P, 88; From Occupation to Revolution: China Through the Eyes of Loti, Claudel, Segalen and Malraux (1895-1933), Summa Publ, Inc Birmingham, 96. **CONTACT ADDRESS** Dept of French, Victoria Univ, PO Box 3045 STN CSC, Victoria, BC, V8W 3P4. **EMAIL** yhsieh@uvic.ca

HUALDE, JOSE IGNACIO
DISCIPLINE SPANISH LITERATURE **EDUCATION** Univ Southern Calif, MA, 85; PhD, 88. **CAREER** Assoc prof, Univ Ill Urbana Champaign. **SELECTED PUBLICATIONS** Auth, Euskararen azenteurak, Univ Basque Country, 97; Catalan. Descriptive Grammars Series, Routledge, 92; Basque Phonology, Routledge, 91; A gap filled: Postpostinitial accent in Azkoitia Basque, Ling, 98; Accentuation and empty vowels in Ondarroa Basque: Against the concept of phonological derivation, Lingua, 96; co-auth, The Basque Dialect of Lekeitio, Univ Basque Country, 94; A Phonological Study of the Basque Dialect of Getxo, Hualde & Xabier Bilbao, 92; co-ed, Towards a History of the Basque Language, John Benjamins, 95; Generative Studies in Basque Linguistics, Benjamins, 93. **CONTACT ADDRESS** Spanish, Italian, and Portuguese Dept, Univ Ill Urbana Champaign, 52 E Gregory Dr, Champaign, IL, 61820. **EMAIL** j-hualde@uiuc.edu

HUANG, J.
PERSONAL Born 06/04/1948, Taiwan, m, 1977, 2 children **DISCIPLINE** LINGUISTICS **EDUCATION** PhD, 82, MIT. **CAREER** Prof, 83-85, Natl Tsing-Hua Univ; Prof, 85-90, Cornell Univ; Prof, 90-, Univ California-Irvine. **HONORS AND AWARDS** Guggenheim Fel, 89; Fel, Ctr for Advanced Study in the Behavioral Sciences, 97-98. **MEMBERSHIPS** Linguistics Soc of Amer. **RESEARCH** Linguistic theory; syntax **CONTACT ADDRESS** Dept of Linguistics, Univ of California-Irvine, 3151 SSPA, Irvine, CA, 92697-5100. **EMAIL** jhuang@uci.edu

HUBBARD, CAROL P.
PERSONAL Born 12/24/1958, Champaign, IL **DISCIPLINE** SPEECH-LANGUAGE PATHOLOGY **EDUCATION** Univ Ill, BS, 81; MS, 82; Univ Wash, Seattle, 92. **CAREER** Unit speech clinician, Farmer City-Mansfield Pub Sch, 82-84; speech-language pathologist, Burnham Hosp, 84-86; teaching assoc/res asst, Univ Wash, Seattle, 86-92; res assoc, Univ Ill, 93; ASST PROF, UNIV WIS-MILWAUKEE, 93- . **SELECTED PUBLICATIONS** auth with D. Prins, Syllabic Stress and the Occurrence of Stuttering, Jour of Speech and Hearing Res, 91; with D. Prins, Constancy of Interstress Intervals in the Fluent Speech of People Who Stutter During Adaptation Trials, Jour of Speech and Hearing Res, 92; with D. Prins, Word Familiarity, Syllabic Stress Pattern, and Stuttering. Jour of Speech and Hearing Res, 94; Reliability of Judgments of Stuttering and Disfluency in Young Children's Speech. Jour of Commun Disorders, 98; Stuttering, Stressed Syllables, and Word Onsets. Jour of Speech, Language, and Hearing Res, 98. **CONTACT ADDRESS** Dept Comm Sci and Disorders, Univ Wis, PO Box 413, Milwaukee, WI, 53201. **EMAIL** chubbard@uwm.edu

HUBER, THOMAS
PERSONAL Born 03/23/1937, Berlin, Germany, m, 1988, 2 children **DISCIPLINE** GERMAN LANGUAGE AND LITERATURE **EDUCATION** Univ VT, MA, 62; Princeton Univ, MA, 64, PhD, 65. **CAREER** Instr Ger, Univ Vt, 61-62 & Princeton Univ, 64-65; lectr philol, Univ Bergen, Norway, 65-66; from asst prof to assoc prof Ger, 66-77, dir studies, Sch Ger, 66-67, 69-70 & 72-73, 87-88, 91-92, 96-97; Prof Ger, Middlebury Col, 77-, Dean, Sch Ger & Chmn Dept, 73-91, Consult int educ, Inst Int Educ, 67-68; bd men, Coun Int Educ Exchange, 76-81. **HONORS AND AWARDS** Ger-Am Friendship Award, 85. **MEMBERSHIPS** MLA; AATC. **RESEARCH** Period of enlightenment in Germany; contemp Ger novel; popular Europ fiction. **SELECTED PUBLICATIONS** Auth, Studien zur Theorie des Ubersetzens, Hain: Meisenheim, 67; US Programs in Germany: Problems and Perspectives, IIE, New York; coauth, Modern German, Harcourt Brace Jovanovich, 71, 2nd ed, 78; auth, Studium in den USA, 74 & Studium in den USA--a case study, 74, aspekte, Frankfurt; coauth, Thomas Mann's Tonio Kroger, Harcourt Brace Jovanovich, 78. **CONTACT ADDRESS** Dept Ger, Middlebury Col, Middlebury, VT, 05753-6001. **EMAIL** thomas_huber@flannet.middlebury.edu

HUBERT, JUDD D.
DISCIPLINE FRENCH LANGUAGE **EDUCATION** Columbia Univ, PhD. **CAREER** PROF EMER, FR, UNIV CALIF, IRVINE. **SELECTED PUBLICATIONS** Auth, Essai d'exegese racinienne; Moliere and the Comedy of the Intellect. **CONTACT ADDRESS** Dept of Fr and Ital, Univ Calif, Irvine, CA, 92697.

HUBERT, MARIE LOUISE
PERSONAL Born 06/25/1914, New York, NY **DISCIPLINE** FRENCH **EDUCATION** St Joseph's Col NY, AB, 36; Columbia Univ, AM, 39; Yale Univ, PhD(French), 50. **CAREER** Pres, 56-71, prof French, Albertus Magnus Col, 42-, dir Inst Res, 72-, pres, Conn Coun Higher Educ, 65-67. **HONORS AND AWARDS** LLD, Albertus Magnus Col, 72. **MEMBERSHIPS** Am Asn Teachers Fr; Asn for Inst Res. **SELECTED PUBLICATIONS** Auth, Pascal's Unfinished Apology, Yale Univ & Presses Univs de France, 52; coauth, Pascal, In: The Seventeenth Century, Vol 4, A Critical Bibliography of French Literature, Syracuse Univ, 62; contribr, New Structures of Campus Power, Jossey-Bass, 78. **CONTACT ADDRESS** Dir Inst Res, Albertus Magnus Col, 700 Prospect St, New Haven, CT, 06511-1189.

HUBERT, RENEE RIESE
PERSONAL Born 07/02/1916, Wiesbaden, Germany, m, 1950 **DISCIPLINE** FRENCH, COMPARATIVE LITERATURE **EDUCATION** Univ Lyon, BedL, 36; Columbia Univ, MA, 45, PhD, 51. **CAREER** Instr French & German, Wilson Col, 45-47; instr French, Columbia Univ, 48-49; mem fac, Sarah Lawrence Col, 49-53; instr, Harvard Univ, 53-55; asst prof, Suffolk Univ, 55-56; asst prof French & German, San Fernando Valley State Col, 58-62, assoc prof French & chmn dept foreign lang, 62-65; assoc prof French, Univ Ill, Urbana, 65-66, prof, 66-67; Prof French & Comp Lit, Univ Calif, Irvine, 67-, Guggenheim fel, 64-65; Nat Endowment for Humanities, 79. **MEMBERSHIPS** MLA; Am Asn Teachers Fr; Int Fed Mod Lang & Lit; Int Asn Studies Fr. **RESEARCH** Modern Poetry; relation of literature and fine arts; surrealism. **SELECTED PUBLICATIONS** Auth, Apollinaire and the Faceless-Man--The Creation and Evolution of a Modern Motif, French Forum, Vol 0017, 92; Picasso and Apollinaire--The Metamorphoses of Memory, 1905-1973, French Forum, Vol 0022, 97. **CONTACT ADDRESS** Dept of French & Comp Lit, Univ of Calif, Irvine, CA, 92664.

HUFFINES, MARION LOIS
PERSONAL Born 10/01/1945, Chester, PA **DISCIPLINE** GERMAN, SOCIOLINGUISTICS **EDUCATION** Maryville Col, TN, BA, 67; Ind Univ, Bloominton, MA, 69, PhD, 71. **CAREER** Prof Ger & Ling, Bucknell Univ, 71-, assoc vice pres, acade affairs; Nat Endowment for Humanities fel, 80. **MEMBERSHIPS** AAHE **RESEARCH** Sociolinguistics; Am dialects; PA Ger. **SELECTED PUBLICATIONS** Auth, Sixteenth century printers and standardization of new high German, J English & Ger Philol, 74; OE aglaeca: Magic and moral decline of monsters and men, Semasia, 74; The original manuscript of Ulrich Schmidt: Chivalry and Peasantry of the Late Middle Ages, Gordon, 77; English in contact with Pennsylvania German, Ger Quart, 53: 352-366; Pennsylvania German: Maintenance and shift, Int 3 Soc Lang, 25: 43-57; over 40 articles on the Language and Culture of the Pennsylvania Germans. **CONTACT ADDRESS** Academic Affairs, Bucknell Univ, Lewisburg, PA, 17837-2029.

HUFFMAN, CLAIRE
PERSONAL New York, NY **DISCIPLINE** ITALIAN, COMPARATIVE LITERATURE **EDUCATION** Barnard Col, BA, 66; Harvard Univ, MA, 67, PhD, 72. **CAREER** Instr, Harvard Univ, 70-71; instr, 71-72, asst prof, 72-77, assoc prof, 77-81, prof modern lang & lit, 82-, Brooklyn Col; NEH fel, mod poetry, 74-75; City Univ New York fac res grant, Anglo-Ital poetry, 74, 78, 89, 91, 92, 96; Andrew Mellon fel humanities, twentieth century lit, Harvard Univ, 77-78; vis fac fel, Brooklyn Col, 77-78. **MEMBERSHIPS** MLA; Dante Soc Am. **RESEARCH** Eugenio Montale; modern poetics, 1870-1970; Renaissance literature in Europe; comparative literature; twentieth century theater; translation. **SELECTED PUBLICATIONS** Art, Montale, Eliot and the poetic object, Ital Quart, 80; auth, Montale and the Occasions of Poetry, Princeton Univ Press, 82; auth, Montale for the English Speaking, Leopardi, 87; auth, preface to Satura by Eugenio Montale, Norton, 98. **CONTACT ADDRESS** PO Box 326, Stony Brook, NY, 11790.

HUGHES, WILLIAM NOLIN
PERSONAL Born 05/21/1918, Raymond, WA, m, 1953, 3 children **DISCIPLINE** GERMAN **EDUCATION** Univ Wash, BA, 41; Northwestern Univ, MA, 52, PhD(Ger lit), 55. **CAREER** Personnel supvr, Boeing Aircraft Co, Seattle, Wash, 41-46; asst to labor adv, Allied Comn for Austria, 46-49; asst, Econ Coop Admin Mission to Austria, 49-50; instr, Univ Mich, 55-60; asst prof, Columbia Univ, 60-63; assoc prof, 63-66, chnmn dept 65-75, asst dean, Col Arts & Sci, 75-80, Prof Ger, Mich State Univ, 66-. Ed, Ger Lit Sect, MLA Intern Bibliog, 81- **MEMBERSHIPS** MLA; Am Asn Teachers Ger; Thomas Mann Gesellschaft. **RESEARCH** Modern literature; German literature of the 17th century. **SELECTED PUBLICATIONS** Auth, Structures of Oral Narrative--Parasyntactic and Sentential Analyses on the Example of English Jokes, Word, Vol 0046, 95. **CONTACT ADDRESS** 513 Ardson Rd, East Lansing, MI, 48823.

HULL, ALEXANDER
PERSONAL Born 07/17/1928, Portland, OR, m, 1952 **DISCIPLINE** FRENCH **EDUCATION** Univ Wash, BA, 45, MA, 47, PhD(Romance ling), 55. **CAREER** From instr to asst Prof French, Univ Mass, 54-60; vis asst prof, Univ Mich, 60; assoc prof, St John's Col, Man, 60-62; asst prof, 62-66, Assoc Prof Romance Lang, Duke Univ, 66-, Fulbright grant, France, 49-50. **MEMBERSHIPS** MLA; Am Asn Teachers Fr; Ling Soc Am; Asn Can Studies in US; Am Coun Teaching For Lang. **RESEARCH** North American French dialects; history of the French language; applied linguistics. **SELECTED PUBLICATIONS** Auth, Linguistic and Ethnographic Atlas of Reunion Island, J Pidgin Creole Lang, Vol 0009, 94; Teaching of Mother-Tongues--Current Issues in Different Parts of the World, French Rev, Vol 0067, 93; The Creoles, French Rev, Vol 0069, 96; Tense and Aspect in Seychelles Creole--Values and Interferences, French Rev, Vol 0068, 95; French in the Francophone World, French Rev, Vol 0069, 96. **CONTACT ADDRESS** Dept of Romance Lang, Duke Univ, Durham, NC, 27706.

HUMPHRIES, JOHN J.
PERSONAL Born 08/24/1955, Tuscaloosa, AL, m, 1998 **DISCIPLINE** FRENCH & COMPARATIVE LITERATURE **EDUCATION** Duke Univ, hist & romance lang, AB, 77; Yale Univ, fr & comp lit, MA, 78, M Phil, 80, PhD, 81. **CAREER** Chemn, dept of fr & ital, 97-, assoc chemn, dept of fr, 93-95, dir of grad studies in fr, 85-90, mem, steering comt for prog in comp lit, 94-, prof, fr, eng, and comp lit, 82-, La State Univ. **HONORS AND AWARDS** Nat Endow for the Humanities fel, 95-96; LSU Found Distinguished Facul award, 93; principal scholar, LEH Summer Seminar for high sch teachers, 88; co-dir, proj on Intertextuality and Civilization in the Americas, merit scholar, Duke Univ, 73-77; Acad of Amer Poets prize, 77; Distinction in Romance Lit, Duke Univ, 77; Phi Beta Kappa, Duke Univ; Univ fel, Yale Univ; Phi Kappa Phi, 85; nom, SC Rev and The Mass Rev; General Electric awards for Younger Writers, 86; Distinguished Short Stories Published award, 87; Thomas York Mem award for short fiction, 88; nom, Southwest Rev, CCLM/General Electric awards for younger writers, 89; Manship Summer res grant; Artist's fel in creative writing, La Div of the Arts, 92; Summer res stipend, LSU Coun on Res, 84, 87; Amer Coun of Learned Soc grant-in-aid, 86; Nat Endow for the Humanities travel to collections grant, 86; Lyndhurst Found regrant, 86. **MEMBERSHIPS** MLA. **RESEARCH** Nineteenth and twentieth century French lit; Asian studies; Am lit; Literary theory and comparative lit. **SELECTED PUBLICATIONS** Auth, The Meaning Behind Miyoshi's Lament: A Response to Masao Miyoshi's Reply to Japan in Theory, New Lit Hist, 97; auth, The Idea of Japan, New Lit Hist, 97; auth, The Karmic Text: A Buddhist Reading of Jacques Derrida and Paul de Man Rading Walter Benjamin's The Task of the Translator, Univ of Toronto Quart, 97; co-ed, Poetics of the Americas: New Perspectives on Intertextuality and Civilization, LSU Press, 97; auth, The Discourse of Southerness, or How We Can Know There Will Be Such a Thing as the South and Southern Literary Culture in the Twenty-First Century, The Future of Southern Letters, Oxford Univ Press, 96; co-ed, The Future of Southern Letters, Oxford Univ Press, 96; auth, A Bestiary (poems), Blue Pond Press, 95; auth, The Perry and Harris Treaties and the Invention of Modern Japan, Tamkang Rev, 95; auth, Images of the Floating World: The Idea of Japan, Antioch Rev, 95; auth, Proust and the Bonsai Tree, a Comparative Discussion of Eastern and Western Theories of Art, Southwest Rev, 94. **CONTACT ADDRESS** Dept. of French and Italian/Dept. of English/ Prog, Louisiana State Univ, 205 Prescott Hall, Baton Rouge, LA, 70803-5309. **EMAIL** jhumphries125@msn.com

HUMPHRIES, TOM
DISCIPLINE CROSS CULTURAL COMMUNICATION **EDUCATION** Union Grad Sch, Cross-Cult Commun and Lang Learning, PhD, 77. **CAREER** LECTR, UNIV CALIF, SAN DIEGO. **SELECTED PUBLICATIONS** Co-auth, Deaf in America: Voices from a Culture, Harvard, 88; Deaf Culture and Cultures, Multicultural Issues in Deafness, Longman, 93; auth, Of Deaf Mutes, the Strange, and the Modern Deaf Self, Culturally Affirmative Psychotherapy with Deaf Persons, Erlbaum, 95. **CONTACT ADDRESS** Dept of Commun, Univ Calif, San Diego, 9500 Gilman Dr, La Jolla, CA, 92093. **EMAIL** thumphri@weber.ucsd.edu

HUNT, IRMGARD E.
DISCIPLINE GERMAN LITERATURE **EDUCATION** Univ Wash, PhD. **CAREER** Prof. **RESEARCH** German philosophical traditions; socio-political and utopian aspects of the literatures of German speaking countries; women's literature. **SELECTED PUBLICATIONS** Auth, pubs on Gunter Grass, Christa Wolf, Walter Hollerer, Ingeborg Bachmann, Urs Jaeggi, and a motif history of war and peace in German literature. **CONTACT ADDRESS** Foreign Languages and Literature Dept, Colorado State Univ, Fort Collins, CO, 80523. **EMAIL** ihunt@vines.colostate.edu

HUNTER, LINDA
DISCIPLINE AFRICAN LITERATURE **EDUCATION** Univ Ind, BA, 70, MA, 72, PhD, 76. **CAREER** Dept African Lang, Wisc Univ **RESEARCH** Hausa language, linguistics, and literature; language in society; stylistics. **SELECTED PUBLICATIONS** Auth, Transformation in African Verbal Art: Voice, Speech, Language, Jour Am Folklore, 96; Uvulectomy-the making of a ritual, S African Jour al of Med, 95. **CONTACT ADDRESS** Dept of African Languages and Literature, Univ of Wisconsin, Madison, 500 Lincoln Drive, Madison, WI, 53706. **EMAIL** hunter@lss.wisc.edu

HUPPAUF, BERND
PERSONAL Born 10/19/1942, Waldenburg, Poland, m, 3 children **DISCIPLINE** GERMAN, LITERATURE **EDUCATION** Univ of Tubingen, Ger, PhD, 70 **CAREER** Prof, 74-93, Univ of NSW; Prof, 94-, NYU **RESEARCH** Cult Theory **SELECTED PUBLICATIONS** Auth, Methodendiskussion, 95; War, Violence and the Modern Condition, 97; Unzeitgemasses uber den Krieg: Ernst Junger, Von Boll bis Buchheim, 97 **CONTACT ADDRESS** New York, NY, 10003. **EMAIL** bh4@is2.nyu.edu

HURST, MARY JANE
DISCIPLINE LINGUISTICS **EDUCATION** Univ MD, PhD, 86. **CAREER** Assoc prof, TX Tech Univ. **MEMBERSHIPS** Ch, SCMLA's Women's Caucus; vice-pres/pres-elect, Ling Asn of the Southwest. **RESEARCH** Lang in lit. **SELECTED PUBLICATIONS** Auth, The Voice of the Child in American Literature: Linguistic Approaches to Fictional Child Language, Univ KY Press, 90; tech ed, HTLV-1 and the Nervous System, Liss, 89. **CONTACT ADDRESS** Texas Tech Univ, Lubbock, TX, 79409-5015. **EMAIL** ditmg@ttacs.ttu.edu

HUSSAIN, AMIR
PERSONAL Born 10/31/1965, Llyalpur, Pakistan, w, 1989 **DISCIPLINE** ISLAMIC STUDIES **EDUCATION** Univ Col, Univ of Toronto, BSc, 87; MA, 90; PhD, 89. **CAREER** Asst prof, 97-; instr, McMaster Univ, 94-97, Univ of Waterloo, 94-97; Lectr Humanities, Univ of Toronto, 94-95; teaching asst, Univ of Toronto, 89-95. **HONORS AND AWARDS** Arbor Award, Univ of Toronto, 98, Doctoral Fellowship, Soc Sci and Humanities Res Coun of Can 91-93; Reuben Wells Leonard Mem Scholar, 83-87 **MEMBERSHIPS** Amer Acad of Religion; Can Soc for the Study of Religion; Middle East Studies Asn **RESEARCH** Islamic Studies; Religion and literature; Christianity. **SELECTED PUBLICATIONS** Coauth, Trying to Profess Religion Globally: North, South, East and West, 98; auth, The Concept of Law in Islam, 97; auth, Salman Rushdie and The Satanic Verses, 97; coauth, Islam, 94; **CONTACT ADDRESS** Dept of Religious Studies, California State Univ, Northridge, Northridge, CA, 91330-8316. **EMAIL** amir.hussain@csun.edu

HUTCHEON, LINDA
PERSONAL Toronto, ON, Canada **DISCIPLINE** ENGLISH/COMPARATIVE LITERATURE **EDUCATION** Cornell Univ, MA, 71; Univ Toronto, BA, 69, PhD, 75. **CAREER** Asst prof, 76-82, assoc prof, 82-85, prof, McMaster Univ, 85-88; PROF ENGLISH, UNIV TORONTO, 88-. **HONORS AND AWARDS** Woodrow Wilson Fel, 69-79; Killam Postdoc fel, 78-79; John P. Robarts Ch Can Studs, 88-89; Guggenheim Fel, 92-93. **MEMBERSHIPS** MLA; Int Comp Lit Asn; Can Comp Lit Asn; Toronto Semiotic Circle; Ctr Italian Can Studs; Asn Can Col Univs Tchrs Eng. **SELECTED PUBLICATIONS** Auth, Narcissistic Narrative: The Metafictional Paradox, 80; auth, The Canadian Postmodern: A Study of Contemporary English-Canadian Fiction, 88; auth, Irony's Edge: The Theory and Politics of Irony, 95; coauth, Opera: Desire, Disease, Death, 96. **CONTACT ADDRESS** Dept of English, Univ Toronto, Toronto, ON, M5S 1A1.

HUTTON, LEWIS J.
PERSONAL Born 07/26/1921, New York, NY, m, 1948, 4 children **DISCIPLINE** ROMANCE LANGUAGES, RELIGION **EDUCATION** Columbia Univ, AB, 42, MA, 46; Princeton Theol Sem, BD, 44; Princeton Univ, MA, 48, PhD(Romance lang, Span), 50; Union Theol Sem, STM, 50. **CAREER** Instr Span, Princeton Univ, 45-48; instr, NY Univ, 48-49; minister, First Presby Church, Gowanda, NY, 51-55; sr minister, Capitol Hill Presby Church, Wash, DC, 55-62; sr minister, First Presby Church, Kirksville, Mo, 62-64; from asst prof to assoc prof Span, Drake Univ, 64-66; assoc prof, 66-72, Prof Span, Univ RI, 72-, Assoc Span, George Washington Univ, 57-62. **MEMBERSHIPS** MLA; Am Asn Teachers Span & Port; Am Soc Church Hist; Soc Bibl Lit. **RESEARCH** Sixteenth and seventeenth century Spanish literature; contemporary intellectual thought; sixteenth century ecclesiastical history. **SELECTED PUBLICATIONS** Auth, Cervantes and the Burlesque Sonnet, Sixteenth Century J, Vol 0024, 93. **CONTACT ADDRESS** Dept of Span, Univ of RI, Kingston, RI, 02881.

HYE, ALLEN EDWARD
PERSONAL Born 12/01/1944, New Brunswick, NJ, m, 1967, 2 children **DISCIPLINE** GERMAN & SCANDINAVIAN LITERATURE **EDUCATION** Franklin & Marshall Col, BA, 66; Middlebury Col, MA, 67; Univ CT, PhD(Ger), 72. **CAREER** Instr Ger, Franklin & Marshall Col, 72-73; asst prof, Lehigh Univ, 73-78; assoc prof Ger, Wright State Univ, 78-95, prof Ger, Wright State Univ, 95-. **MEMBERSHIPS** Am Asn Teachers Ger; Soc Advan Scand Studies; German Studies Asn. **RESEARCH** Modern German drama; modern Danish drama; science and literature. **SELECTED PUBLICATIONS** Auth, Modernes Deutschland im Brennpunkt, W W Norton, 78; Shoeless Joe and the American Dream, The Markham Rev, 15, 86; An American Apocalypse: Religious Parody in The Iowa Baseball Confederacy, Aethlon 6.2, 89; The Baseball Messiah: Christy Mathewson and the Celebrant, Aethlon 7.1, 90; Fantasy + Involvement = Thought: Kjeld Abell's Conception of Theater, Scandinavian Studies 63, 90; Se alting i spejle: The Mirror and Other Key Symbols in the Plays of Kjeld Abell, Univ of Dayton Rev, 23,2, 95; The Moral Dilema of the Scientist in Modern Drama, Edwin Meller Press, 96. **CONTACT ADDRESS** Dept of Mod Lang, Wright State Univ, 3640 Colonel Glenn, Dayton, OH, 45435-0002. **EMAIL** ahye@wright.edu

HYER, PAUL V.
PERSONAL Born 06/02/1926, Ogden, UT, m, 1948, 8 children **DISCIPLINE** ASIAN HISTORY, CULTURE **EDUCATION** Brigham Young Univ, BA, 51; Univ Calif, Berkeley, MA, 53, PhD, 60. **CAREER** Asst prof to prof, 58-66, Coordr, Asian Studies Prog, 61-67, Prof hist & Asian Studies, Brigham Young Univ, 66-; res, Toyo Bunko on Mongolia & China border lands, 63-64, Academia Sinica, 66-67; vis prof, Chengchi Univ, 71-72; ed, Mongolia Soc Bull, 69-; vis prof, Inner Mongolia Univ, 81. **HONORS AND AWARDS** Maeser Award for Excellence in Res. **MEMBERSHIPS** Asn of Asian Studies; Mongolia Soc; Int Altaistic Conf. **RESEARCH** Modern Mongolian & Tibetan history; Japanese expansion. **SELECTED PUBLICATIONS** Ed, Papers of the CIC Far Eastern Language Institute, Univ of Mich, 63; The Cultural Revolution in Inner Mongolia, China Quart, 68; articles in: Encycl Americana, 70; Hu Shih: The Diplomacy of Gentle Persuasions, The Diplomats in Crisis, Am Bibliog Ctr, 74; The Mongolian Nation Within the People's Republic of China, Case Studies on Human Rights and Fundamental Freedoms, The Hague, 75; The Chin-tan-tao Movement: A Chinese Revolt in Mongolia, Altaica, Helsinki, 77; Mongolian Stereotypes and Images, J Mongolian Studies, 78; Mongolia's Culture and Society, Praeger's Westview, 79. **CONTACT ADDRESS** Kennedy Center for Int Studies, Brigham Young Univ, HRCB, Provo, UT, 84602-0002. **EMAIL** pnkhyer@aol.com

HYERS, M. CONRAD
PERSONAL Born 07/31/1933, Philadelphia, PA, m, 1955, 3 children **DISCIPLINE** COMPARATIVE MYTHOLOGY & HISTORY OF RELIGIONS **EDUCATION** Carson-Newman Col, BA, 54; Eastern Theol Sem, BD, 58; Princeton Theol Sem, ThM, 59, PhD(phenomenol relig), 65. **CAREER** From instr to assoc prof hist relig, Beloit Col, 65-77; assoc prof, 77-81, PROF HIST RELIG, GUSTAVUS ADOLPHUS COL, 81-97, PROF EMER 97-. **HONORS AND AWARDS** Humanities develop grant, 69; Assoc Col Midwest non-Western studies fel, East-West Ctr, 70; Nat Found Humanities fel, 70-71; Fund Studies Great Relig fel, 71; Nat Found Humanities res fel, 75-76. **MEMBERSHIPS** Am Acad Relig **RESEARCH** A phenomenological study of the mythological motifs of Paradise Lost, fall and degeneration; a phenomenological study of the nature and function of comedy and humor in relation to the sacred; interfaith relations. **SELECTED PUBLICATIONS** Auth, Holy Laughter: Essays on Religion in the Comic Perspective, Sea-

bury, 69; The Dialectic of the Sacred and the Comic, Cross Currents, winter 69; The Ancient Ch'an Master as Clown Figure and Comic Midwife, Philos East & West, winter, 69-70; The Comic Perspective in Zen Literature and Art, Eastern Buddhist, 72; Zen and the Comic Spirit, Rider, London, 73; The Chickadees: A Contemporary Zen Fable, Westminster, 74; The Comic Vision and the Christian Faith, Pilgrim, 81; The Meaning of Creation: Genesis and Modern Science, John Knox, 84; And God Created Laughter, The Bible as Divine Comedy, John Knox, 86; Once-Born, Twice-Born Zen, The Soto and Rinzai Schools of Japan, Hollowbrook, 89; The Laughing Buddha, Hollowbrook, 90; The Spirituality of Comedy, Comic Heroism in a Tragic World, Transaction Publ, 96. **CONTACT ADDRESS** 2162 Harbor View Drive, Dunedin, FL, 34698.

I

IANNACE, GAETANO ANTONIO
PERSONAL Born 11/00/1927, m, 1962, 1 child **DISCIPLINE** ITALIAN LANGUAGE & LITERATURE, HUMANITIES **EDUCATION** NY Univ, BA, 56, MA, 62, PhD(Ital), 64. **CAREER** Instr Ital, NY Univ, 60-64, asst prof, 64-67; assoc prof, 67-71, PROF ITAL & HUMANITIES, CENT CONN STATE COL, 71-, Instr, Fordham Univ, 65-66; adj asst prof, Pace Col, 65-66; instr French, Mt Vernon Adult Educ High Sch, 65-67. **MEMBERSHIPS** MLA; Am Asn Teachers Ital; Ital Hist Soc Am. **RESEARCH** Twentieth century Italian novel; Dante-Joyce, an interdisciplinary approach; 20th century European theater. **SELECTED PUBLICATIONS** Auth, Terra e Cielo, Forum Italicum, Vol 0029, 95. **CONTACT ADDRESS** Dept of Mod Lang, Central Connecticut State Univ, New Britain, CT, 06050.

IANNUCCI, AMILCARE ALFREDO
PERSONAL Born 03/13/1946, Casalvieri, Italy, m, 1970 **DISCIPLINE** ITALIAN LITERATURE **EDUCATION** Univ Toronto, BA, 70; Harvard Univ, AM, 72, PhD(Ital lit), 77. **CAREER** From instr to asst prof, 73-78, ASSOC PROF ITAL, UNIV TORONTO, 78-. **MEMBERSHIPS** Mediaeval Acad Am; Dante Soc Am; Can Soc Ital Studies; Can Soc Renaissance Studies; Humanities Asn Can. **RESEARCH** Dante; Medieval and Renaissance Italian literature. **SELECTED PUBLICATIONS** Auth, The 'Gospel of Nicodemus' in Medieval Italian Literature, Quaderni D Italianistica, Vol 0014, 93. **CONTACT ADDRESS** Univ Toronto, 38 Marianfeld, Toronto, ON, M6B 3W1.

IBSEN, KRISTINE L.
DISCIPLINE SPANISH LITERATURE **EDUCATION** Calif State Univ, BA, 83; Univ Calif Los Angeles, MA, 84, PhD, 91. **CAREER** Assoc prof. **RESEARCH** Spanish American literature. **SELECTED PUBLICATIONS** Auth, pubs on Sor JuanA Ines de la Cruz, Julio Cortazar and Pablo Neruda. **CONTACT ADDRESS** Romance Languages and Literatures Dept, Univ of Notre Dame, Notre Dame, IN, 46556.

IGEL, REGINA
PERSONAL Born 04/26/1942, Sao Paulo, Brazil **DISCIPLINE** PORTUGUESE **EDUCATION** Univ Sao Paulo, BA, 64; Univ Iowa, MA, 70; Univ N Mex, PhD(Port), 73. **CAREER** Instr Port, Univ Iowa, 68-70 & Univ N Mex, 70-73; asst prof, 73-77, Assoc PROF PORT, UNIV MD, 78-. **MEMBERSHIPS** MLA; Am Asn Teachers Span & Port (secy, 76); Mid-Atlantic Asn Port High Sch (vpres, 75). **RESEARCH** Brazilian literature of the 19th and 20th centuries. **SELECTED PUBLICATIONS** Auth, The Sugarcane Plantation in the Poetry of Cabraldemeloneto, Joao, World Lit Today, Vol 0066, 92. **CONTACT ADDRESS** Dept of Span & Port, Univ of Md, College Park, MD, 20742.

IGGERS, WILMA ABELES
PERSONAL Born 03/23/1921, Mirkov, Czechoslovakia, m, 1948, 3 children **DISCIPLINE** MODERN GERMAN & CZECH LITERATURES **EDUCATION** McMaster Univ, BA, 42; Univ Chicago, AM, 43, PhD, 52. **CAREER** Instr French & Ger, Univ NB, 46; asst prof mod lang, Philander Smith Col, 50-55; asst prof Ger, Dillard Univ & Tulane Univ, 57-63; asst prof, Loyola Univ, Ill, 63-65; from asst prof to assoc prof Ger, 65-75, actg chmn mod lang, 76-77, PROF GER, CANISIUS COL, 75-. **HONORS AND AWARDS** DAAD Award, Ger Acad Exchange Serv, 78. **MEMBERSHIPS** MLA; AAUP; Mod Humanities Res Asn; Czech Soc Arts & Sci in US; Soc Hist Czech Jews. **RESEARCH** Cultural History of the Jews in Boehmia and Moravia; recent Czech literature; Karl Kraus. **SELECTED PUBLICATIONS** Auth, A History of Habsburg Jews, 1670-1988, Jewish Quart Rev, Vol 0084, 94; I Am Snowing, the Confessions of a Woman of Prague, World Lit Today, Vol 0068, 94; Land der Vater und Verrater, World Lit Today, Vol 0070, 96. **CONTACT ADDRESS** Dept of Mod Lang, Canisius Col, 2001 Main St, Buffalo, NY, 14208.

IGNASHEV, DIANE M. NEMEC
PERSONAL Born 09/15/1951, Chicago, IL, w, 1974 **DISCIPLINE** SLAVIC LANGUAGES AND LITERATURE **EDUCATION** Univ Chicago, Dept of Slavic Langs and Lit, PhD, 84. **CAREER** PROF, DEPT OF GERMAN AND RUSSIAN, CARLETON COLL, NORTHFIELD, MN. **MEMBERSHIPS** AAASS; AATSEEL. **RESEARCH** Russian theater; women's studies; Russian film/visual art. **CONTACT ADDRESS** Dept of German and Russian, Carleton Col, Northfield, MN, 55057. **EMAIL** dignasche@carleton.edu

ILIE, PAUL
DISCIPLINE SPANISH AND COMPARATIVE LITERATURE **EDUCATION** Brown Univ, PhD. **CAREER** Prof, Univ Southern Calif. **RESEARCH** Hispano-French relations. **SELECTED PUBLICATIONS** Auth, the Age of Minerva trilogy, 2 vol; publ on, Voltaire; Goya; Span Romantic poets; Unamuno; Cela; Surrealism, the Literature of Exile & Post-Spanish Civil war; fiction. **CONTACT ADDRESS** Col Letters, Arts & Sciences, Univ Southern Calif, University Park Campus, Los Angeles, CA, 90089. **EMAIL** pilie@usc.edu

ILIESCU, NICOLAE
PERSONAL Born 05/21/1919, Romania, m, 1953, 2 children **DISCIPLINE** LANGUAGES **EDUCATION** Univ Padua, Dr in Lett, 47; Harvard Univ, PhD, 58. **CAREER** From instr to asst prof Italian, 58-63, assoc prof, 63-68, PROF ROMANCE LANG & LIT, HARVARD UNIV, 68-, UNESCO grant, Fiesole, Italy, 50-51; Guggenheim fel, Rome, 61-62. **MEMBERSHIPS** MLA; Renaissance Soc Am; Mediaeval Acad Am; Dante Soc Am; Am Asn Teachers Ital. **RESEARCH** Nineteenth century Italian literature; medieval Italian literature and Dante; Renaissance Italian literature, especially Petrarch. **SELECTED PUBLICATIONS** Auth, Da Manzoni a Nievo (considerazioni sul romanzo ital), 59 & Il Canzoniere petrarchesco e Sant Agostine, 62, Soc Acad Romena, Rome. **CONTACT ADDRESS** Harvard Univ, Cambridge, MA, 02138.

ILLIANO, ANTONIO
PERSONAL Born 04/21/1934, Monte di Procida, Italy, m, 1962, 1 child **DISCIPLINE** ROMANCE LANGUAGE & LITERATURES **EDUCATION** Univ Naples, DottL, 58; Univ Calif, Berkeley, PhD(Romance lang & lit), 66. **CAREER** Asst Ital, Univ Ill, 59-60 & Univ Calif, Berkeley, 60-63; assoc, Univ Calif, Santa Barbara, 63-66; asst prof Romance lang, Univ Tex, Austin, 66-68, res & acad excellence prog fel, 66; vis asst prof Romance Lang, Univ Ore, 68-69; asst prof, 69-71, assoc prof, 71-82, Prof Romance Lang, Univ NC, Chapel Hill, 82-, Pogue leave, Univ NC, Chapel Hill, 77; mem fac, Ital Sch, Middlebury Col, summer 81, Univ Ga Cortona Prog, summer, 82. **MEMBERSHIPS** MLA; Am Asn Teachers Ital; Dante Soc Am. **RESEARCH** Medieval and modern literature. **SELECTED PUBLICATIONS** Auth, Per una definizione della vena cosmogonica di Calvino, Italica, fall 72; Italian without a master, Mark Twain J, 74; Metapsichica e Letteratura in Pirandello, 82; auth, Per l'esegesi del Corbaccio, 91; auth, Morfologia dello narrazione manzoniano, 93; auth, Sulle sponde del Prepurgaturio, 97; auth, From Boccaccio to Pirandello, 97. **CONTACT ADDRESS** Dept of Romance Lang, Univ of NC, Chapel Hill, NC, 27514. **EMAIL** ailliano@email.unc.edu

IMAMURA, SHIGEO
PERSONAL Born 08/14/1922, San Jose, CA, m, 1963 **DISCIPLINE** LINGUISTICS, ENGLISH AS A SECOND LANGUAGE **EDUCATION** Matsuyama Univ Commerce, Dipl, 43; Univ Mich, Ann Arbor, BA, 53, MA, 64. **CAREER** Teacher supvr English as second lang, Ehime State Bd Educ, Japan, 49-55; asst prof, Ehime Univ, Japan, 55-61, assoc dir English teaching inst, 56-61; asst prof English as second lang, Mich State Univ, 61-62; asst prof, Ehime Univ, 62-63; asst prof, 63-64, dir English lang ctr, 64-73, ASSOC PROF ENGLISH AS A SECOND LANG, MICH STATE UNIV, 66-, Dir Spec Progs, English Lang Ctr, 78-, Dir, Konan-Ill Ctr, Kobe, Japan, 77-78. **MEMBERSHIPS** Nat Asn Foreign Student Affairs; Asn Teachers English as Second Lang; Teachers English to Speakers Other Lang. **RESEARCH** Pronunciation and grammar in teaching English as a second language; teaching Japanese as a second language, especially grammar; inter-cultural understanding. **SELECTED PUBLICATIONS** Coauth, Readings from Samuel Clemens, 69 & Readings on American Society, 69, Blaisdell; auth, Basic knowledge for Studies in the United States, Kenkyusha, Tokyo, 72; Teaching of English in the Middle East and Indonesia, 72 & Cultural interference in language learning, 73, English Lang Educ Coun Bull, Tokyo; International Understanding and the Teaching of English, Lang Educ Coun Tokyo, 74. **CONTACT ADDRESS** English Lang Ctr, Michigan State Univ, East Lansing, MI, 48824.

IMBERT, PATRICK L.
PERSONAL Born 02/04/1948, Paris, France **DISCIPLINE** FRENCH LITERATURE **EDUCATION** Institut catholique de Paris, Licence, 69; Univ Ottawa, MA, 70, PhD, 74. **CAREER** Asst prof, McMaster Univ, 74-75; asst prof, 75, PROF LETTRES FRANCAISES, UNIV OTTAWA, 84-. **MEMBERSHIPS** Societe de Philosophie de l'Outaouais; Int Asn Semiotic; Can Semiotic Asn; Can Comp Lit Asn; Asn Can Que Lit. **SELECTED PUBLICATIONS** Auth, Roman quebecois contemporain et cliches, 83; auth, L'Objectivite de la Presse, 89; auth, Les discours du Nouveau Monde au Canada francais et en Amerique latinel/Los discursos del Nuevo Mundo en el Canada francofono y en America latina, 95. **CONTACT ADDRESS** Univ of Ottawa, Ottawa, ON.

IMHOFF, BRIAN
DISCIPLINE SPANISH **EDUCATION** Pa State Univ, BA, 84; Univ Ill, Urbana-Champaign, MA, 88, PhD, 96. **CAREER** Asst prof, Texas A & M Univ, 97-. **HONORS AND AWARDS** Texas A & M Univ, Prog to Enhance Schol and Creative Activities, Off of the VP for Res, 88; Texas A & M Univ, Undergrad Res Opportunities Prog, Dept Mod and Classical Lang, 97; FLAS Title VI Summer Fel for For Lang Study, Brazilian Portuguese, 88; Univ Ill List of Excellent Teachers, 85, 88; Univ Scholars Prog of Penn State Univ, 82-84; Phi Sigma Iota, Beta Chap, 83. **MEMBERSHIPS** MLA, 91-; Amer Asn Tchrs Span and Portuguese, 95-; Ling Asn Southwest, 96-; Medieval Acad Amer, 97-; Southeast Conf on Ling, 98-; South Atlantic Mod Lang Asn, 98-. **SELECTED PUBLICATIONS** Auth, On the Chronology and Recession of the Old Spanish -ie Imperfect, La coronica 26 2, 98; Bibliography of Spanish Linguistics, Comp Romance Ling Newsl 41 2, 92 & Bibliography of Spanish Linguistics, Comp Romance Ling Newsl 40 2, 91; coauth, Bibliography of Spanish Linguistics, Comp Romance Ling Newsl 39 2, 90. **CONTACT ADDRESS** Dept of Modern and Classical Languages, Texas A&M Univ, College Station, TX, 77843-4238. **EMAIL** b-imhoff@tamu.edu

IMPEY, OLGA TUDORICA
PERSONAL Born 09/25/1937, Constanta, Romania, m, 1967, 2 children **DISCIPLINE** SPANISH MEDIEVAL & RENAISSANCE LITERATURE **EDUCATION** Univ Bucharest, BA, 61; Univ Ky, PhD(Span), 72. **CAREER** Asst prof Span & romance ling, Univ Bucharest, 61-67; teaching asst, Univ Ky, 68-72; instr, Princeton Univ, 72-74; asst prof, 75-80, Assoc Prof Span, Ind Univ, 80-, Lectr Span & Romance ling, Princeton Univ, 74-75. **MEMBERSHIPS** MLA; Midwest Mod Lang Asn; Asociacion Internacional de los Hispanistas; Soc Romanian Studies. **RESEARCH** Spanish and European medieval prose and poetry; Spanish Renaissance poetry; rhetoric and stylistics (theory and practice). **SELECTED PUBLICATIONS** Auth, The Severed Word, Ovid 'Heroides' and the Novela-Sentimental, Modern Philol, Vol 0091, 93. **CONTACT ADDRESS** Indiana Univ, Bloomington, 1033 Hawthorne, Bloomington, IN, 47401.

INGBER, ALIX
DISCIPLINE SPANISH **EDUCATION** Brooklyn College CUNY, BA; Univ IL, MA; CUNY, PhD. **CAREER** Prof, Sweet Briar Col. **RESEARCH** Golden Age Span lit and transl; computer assisted instruction in Span. **SELECTED PUBLICATIONS** Auth, El bien mas alto, A Reconsideration of Lope de Vega's Honor Plays, Univ Presses FL; articles on Span and Latin Am lit; original programs for computer-assisted instruction in Span. **CONTACT ADDRESS** Sweet Briar Col, Sweet Briar, VA, 24595. **EMAIL** ingber@sbc.edu

INGEMANN, FRANCES
PERSONAL Born 10/25/1927, Trenton, NJ **DISCIPLINE** LINGUISTICS **EDUCATION** Montclair State Univ, BA, 49; Columbia Univ, MA, 50; Ind Univ, PhD, 56. **CAREER** Instr English, Univ PR, 50-52; instr, Columbia Univ, 50, 51, 56; linguist, Haskins Labs, 56-57; asst prof English, 57-61, assoc prof English & ling, 61-66, prof ling, 66-, Univ Kans; lectr phonetics, Univ Edinburgh, 59-60. **MEMBERSHIPS** Ling Soc Am; Acoust Soc Am; Am Assn Phonetic Sci. **RESEARCH** Acoustic phonetics; New Guinea languages; Liberian languages. **SELECTED PUBLICATIONS** Coauth, Studies in Cheremis, the Supernatural; Eastern Cheremis Manual, Ind Univ, 61. **CONTACT ADDRESS** Dept of Ling, Univ of Kansas, Lawrence, KS, 66045-2140. **EMAIL** fing@ukans.edu

INGEMANSON, BIRGITTA
DISCIPLINE RUSSIAN LITERATURE AND CONTEMPORARY CIVILIZATION **EDUCATION** Princeton Univ, PhD. **CAREER** Assoc prof, Washington State Univ. **RESEARCH** Russian literature, culture, and history. **CONTACT ADDRESS** Dept of Foreign Languages and Literatures, Washington State Univ, 1 SE Stadium Way, Pullman, WA, 99164. **EMAIL** wsunis@wsu.edu

INGHAM, NORMAN WILLIAM
PERSONAL Born 12/31/1934, Holyoke, MA **DISCIPLINE** SLAVIC LANGUAGES & LITERATURES **EDUCATION** Middlebury Col, AB, 57; Univ Mich, MA, 59; Harvard Univ, PhD(Slavic), 63. **CAREER** Inter-Univ Comt Travel Grants study & res grant, Charles Univ, Prague, 63-64; asst prof Slavic lang & lit, Ind Univ, 64-65; asst prof, Harvard Univ, 65-71; Assoc Prof & Chemn, Dept Slavic Lang & Lit, Univ Chicago, 71-, Chemn Comt on Slavic & East Europ Studies, 82-91; dir, Center for East Europ and Russ/Eurasian Studies, 91-96; vis fel, Dumbarton Oaks Ctr Byzantine Studies, 72-73. **MEMBERSHIPS** Am Asn Teachers Slavic & East Europ Lang; Am Asn Advan Slavic Studies; Czech Soc Arts & Sci. **RESEARCH** Medieval Russian and Slavic literature. **SELECTED PUBLICATIONS** Auth, The Limits of Secular Biography in Med-Slavic Literature, Particularly Old Russian, In: American Contributions to the Sixth International Congress of Slavists, Mouton, The Hague, 68; The Sovereign as Martyr, East and West, Slavic & East Europ J, 73; E T A Hoffman's Reception in Russia, Jal, 74; co-ed, Mnemozina: Studia Litteraria Russica in Honorem Vsevolod Setchkarev, Wilhelm Fink, 74; auth, Irony

in Povest' o Gore: Zlocastii, Slavic & East Europ J, 80; The Martyred Prince and the Question of Slavic Cultural Continuity in the Early Middle Ages, Calif Slavic Studies, 82; ed, The Church and Religious Culture in Old Russ, Canadian-Am Slavic Studies, 91; Early East-Slavic Lit as Sociocultural Fact, California Slavic Studies, 19, 94. **CONTACT ADDRESS** Dept of Slavic Lang & Lit, Univ of Chicago, 1130 E 59th St, Chicago, IL, 60637-1539.

INGWERSEN, NIELS
PERSONAL Born 05/18/1935, Horsens, Denmark, m, 1961 **DISCIPLINE** SCANDINAVIAN LITERATURE **EDUCATION** Copenhagen Univ, Cand Mag, 63. **CAREER** Adj Danish lit & lang, Hellerup Seminaruim, Denmark, 64-65; from asst prof to assoc prof, 65-73, PROF SCAND LIT, UNIV WIS-MADISON, 73-, Res assoc, Odense Univ, Denmark, 71-72; assoc ed, Scand Studies, 71-; vis prof, Aarhus Univ, Denmark, 78-79. **MEMBERSHIPS** Soc Advan Scand Studies (pres, 69-71); Dansklaerer-foreningen; MLA. **RESEARCH** Danish novel; Danish prose of 1890's; theory of the novel. **SELECTED PUBLICATIONS** Auth, Sandemoses Ryg, World Lit Today, Vol 0067, 93; Ubekraeftede Forlydender, World Lit Today, Vol 0067, 93; Mellem ar og Dag, World Lit Today, Vol 0068, 94; Krigen, World Lit Today, Vol 0068, 94; The Rags--Studies on Common Danish-Norwegian Literature After 1814, Scand Stud, Vol 0067, 95; The Need for Narrative--The Folktale as Response to History, Scand Stud, Vol 0067, 95; Literary-Criticism, a Selection, Scanddinica, Vol 0034, 95; Peddling My Wares, J Engl and Germanic Philol, Vol 0096, 97. **CONTACT ADDRESS** Dept of Scand Studies, Univ of Wis, 1302 Van Hise Hall, Madison, WI, 53706.

INSLER, STANLEY
PERSONAL Born 06/23/1937, New York, NY **DISCIPLINE** INDO-IRANIAN LINGUISTICS **EDUCATION** Columbia Col, AB, 57; Yale Univ, PhD, 63. **CAREER** From instr to asst prof, 63-70, assoc prof, 70-80, prof Sanskrit & chemn dept, grad sch, Yale Univ, 80-, Morse fel, 67-68. **MEMBERSHIPS** Am Orient Soc; Ling Soc Am; fel Royal Asiatic Soc; Deut Morganlaandische Ges. **RESEARCH** History of Sanskrit language; comparative Indo-Iranian linguistics; Zoroastrianism. **SELECTED PUBLICATIONS** Auth, The Indra Hymns of the Rg-Veda, J Amer Oriental Soc, Vol 0113, 93; The Question Sentences in the Rg-Veda, J Amer Oriental Soc, Vol 0113, 93; Asura in Early Vedic Religion, J Amer Oriental Soc, Vol 0113, 93. **CONTACT ADDRESS** Dept of Eastern & Southern Asian Lang, Yale Univ, PO Box 208236, New Haven, CT, 06520-8236.

IRRIZARRY, E.
PERSONAL Born 11/13/1937, Paterson, NJ, m, 1963, 3 children **DISCIPLINE** HISPANIC LITERATURE **EDUCATION** Montclair State Univ, BA, 59; Rutgers Univ, MA, 63; The George Washington Univ, PhD,70. **CAREER** Tchr, Glane Rock High School, 58-60; Ramapo Reg High School, 60-63; instr, Univ Puerto Rico, 63-66; Howard Univ, 66-68; The George Washington Univ, 68-70; prof, Georgetown Univ, 70-; Ed, Hispania, 93-. **HONORS AND AWARDS** N Am Acad of the Spanish Lang; Royal Spanish Acad; Cross of the Order of Alphonse the Sage; Prize for Lit, Inst of Puerto Rico; Distinguished Service Award, Foreign Lang Educators of NJ, 93. **MEMBERSHIPS** Am Asn of Tchrs of Spanish and Portuguese; Sigma Delta Pi Honorary Spanish Frat; Council of Editors of Learned Journals. **RESEARCH** Hispanic Literature; Computer analysis of literature; Literature and art. **SELECTED PUBLICATIONS** Auth, Dos Poetas de Huelva en America: Juan Ramon Jimenez, cronista, Odon Betanzos Palacios, juglar, 96; Informatica y literatura, 97. **CONTACT ADDRESS** 1600 N Oak St, #1615, Arlington, VA, 22209. **EMAIL** irizarre@gusun.georgetown.edu

IRSFELD, JOHN HENRY
PERSONAL Born 12/02/1937, Bemidji, MN, m, 1965, 1 child **DISCIPLINE** ENGLISH & AMERICAN LITERATURE & LANGUAGE **EDUCATION** Univ Tex, Austin, BA, 59, MA, 66, PhD(English), 69. **CAREER** From asst prof to assoc prof, 69-77, prof English & chemn dept, Univ Nevada, Las Vegas, 77-. **HONORS AND AWARDS** Barrick Scholar Award, Univ Nev, Las Vegas, 85-86; Nev Governor's Arts Award for Excellence in the Arts, 94. **MEMBERSHIPS** Nev Hum Comt, 81-87; NEH bd, 88, 89, 90, 92. **RESEARCH** Twentieth century English and American literature; poetry and poetics; fiction. **SELECTED PUBLICATIONS** Auth, Stop, rewind, and play (story), SDak Rev, 3/74; Ambivalence hardy fire (short story), Kans Quart, summer 74; The right thing: What it is, and how Theodore Roethke achieved it, Sparrow, 75; Coming Through (novel), 75 & Little Kingdoms (novel), 76, Putnam; The horse fountain (short story), Kans Quart, winter 76; Have you knocked on Cleopatra? (short story), 12/76 & The tourist (short story), 11/76, Las Vegas; auth, Rats Alley, 87. **CONTACT ADDRESS** Dept of English, Univ of Nev, PO Box 455011, Las Vegas, NV, 89154-5011. **EMAIL** irsfeld@nevada.edu

IRVIN, DEBORAH M.
DISCIPLINE BEHAVIORAL DISORDERS, SPECIAL EDUCATION **EDUCATION** Temple Univ, BA; Univ Nebr, Omaha, MS; Univ Nebr, Lincoln, PhD. **CAREER** Career

counr, career placement serv, 88-91, instr, 91-95, asst prof, Univ Nebr, Omaha, 95-. **RESEARCH** Illegal and legal chemical substance use among adolescent populations. **SELECTED PUBLICATIONS** Auth, Substance Abuse in Adolescents: Implications for At-risk Youth, Spec Serv in Sch, 1. **CONTACT ADDRESS** Univ Nebr, Omaha, 60th & Dodge Sts, Kayser Hal, Omaha, NE, 68182-0054.

ISAAC, EPHRAIM
PERSONAL Born 05/29/1936, Nedjio, Ethiopia, m **DISCIPLINE** HISTORY, PHILOLOGY **EDUCATION** Concordia Coll, BA 1958; Harvard Univ Div School, BD 1963; Harvard Univ, PhD 1969. **CAREER** Harvard Univ, instr 1968-69, lecturer 1969-71, assoc prof 1971-77; Hebrew Univ, visiting prof 1977-79; Inst for Advanced Study Princeton, fellow 1979-80; Princeton Theol Sem/Hunter Coll, visiting prof 1980-81; Bard Coll, visiting prof 1981-83; Lehigh Univ, visiting prof of religion Princeton Univ, visiting prof, 1983-85; Institute of Semitic Studies, dir 1985. **HONORS AND AWARDS** Second Prize Ethiopian HS Matric Award 1954; Ethiopian Natl Prize for literacy (Humanity) 1967; Outstanding Educators of Amer 1972; Fellow Endowment for the Humanities 1979; NEH Rsch Grant 1976-77; Harvard Univ Faculty Fund Rsch Grants; Concordia Coll Scholarships 1956-58; Univ Coll of Addis Ababa Fellowship 1954-56. **MEMBERSHIPS** Dir general Natl Literacy Campaign of Ethiopia 1966-72; bd mem Amer Assn for Ethiopian Jews 1973-; pres Ethiopian Student Assn in North Amer 1959-62; vice chmn Ethiopian Famine Relief Comm 1984-; bd mem African Studies Heritage Assoc 1969-73; chmn Comm for Ethiopian Literacy 1963-68; treas Harvard Graduate Student Assoc 1962-65; chorale dir Harvard Graduate Chorale 1962-64. **SELECTED PUBLICATIONS** Ethiopic Book of Enoch, Doubleday, 1983; A History of Religions in Africa, Oxford. **CONTACT ADDRESS** Inst of Semitic Studies, 9 Grover Ave, Princeton, NJ, 08540-3601.

ISANG, S. AKPAN
PERSONAL Itak, Nigeria, 3 children **DISCIPLINE** ORGANIZATIONAL COMMUNICATION **EDUCATION** Howard Univ, PhD 96. **CAREER** Nyack College, asst prof, 97-. **HONORS AND AWARDS** Aids Short Story Awd; Aids Video Awd **MEMBERSHIPS** ICA; IMA; IPA **RESEARCH** Audience influence on media; mentoring in organization **SELECTED PUBLICATIONS** Auth, Mentoring as Interpersonal Communication: An Application of a Mentoring Model to a Black Cultural Environment. **CONTACT ADDRESS** Dept of Communication, Nyack Col, 1 South Blvd, Nyack, NY, 10960-3698. **EMAIL** isang@nyack.edu

ISBELL, JOHN C.
DISCIPLINE FRENCH LITERATURE **EDUCATION** Cambridge Univ, PhD, 90. **CAREER** Asst prof. **RESEARCH** French Revolution; development of European Romanticism. **SELECTED PUBLICATIONS** Auth, The Birth of European Romanticism: Truth and Propaganda in Stael's De l'Allemagne, Cambridge, 94; Madame de Stael: Ecrits retrouves, 95; A Romantic Civilization 1776-1848, 96; Mme de Stael, OEuvres de jeunesse, 97. **CONTACT ADDRESS** Dept of French and Italian, Indiana Univ, Bloomington, 300 N Jordan Ave, Bloomington, IN, 47405.

ISHAM, WILLIAM P.
PERSONAL Born 05/30/1955 **DISCIPLINE** LINGUISTICS **EDUCATION** Univ of Kans, BA, 79; Gallaudet Univ, MA, 82; Northeastern Univ, PhD, 91. **CAREER** Staff interpreter, 83-85, acting coord, 85, Gallaudet Interpreting Service, Gllaudet Univ; freelance Amer sign lang/English interpreter, 85-86; teaching asst, Dept of Psychology, 86-90, isntr, 91-92, Northeastern Univ; ASST PROF, DEPT OF LINGUISTICS, UNIV OF NMex, 93-. **HONORS AND AWARDS** Grant-In-Aid, Univ of NMex, 98; Int Travel Grant, Am Coun of Learned Soc, 94; Post-Doctoral fel, Fyssen Found, Univ of Paris, 91-92 & 92-93; Biomedical Sci Support Comt, Northeastern Univ, 87-90. **MEMBERSHIPS** Community Task Force on Interpreting in Legal Settings, Community Outreach Prog for the Deaf; Nmex Am Sign Lang Teachers Asn; Interpreting: Int J of Res and Practice in Interpreting; Seminar on Interpreting Res, Aarhus Business School; Registry of Interpreters for the Deaf, Inc; Nat Asn of the Deaf; Conf of Interpreter Trainers. **RESEARCH** Translation studies; American sign language and the deaf community; language and cognition; inferential statistics. **SELECTED PUBLICATIONS** Auth, Interpreting Property Concepts, At the Turn of the Century: The AVLIC 98 Conf Papers, AVLIC Inc, in press; auth, Phonological Interference in Interpreters of Spoken-Languages: An Issue of Storage or Process?, Language Processing and Interpreting: Interdisciplinary Perspectives, in press; auth, On the Relevance of Signed Languages to Research in Interpretation, Target, 95; auth, Memory for Sentence Form after Simultaneous Interpretation: Evidence Both for and against Deverbalization, Bridging the Gap: Empirical Research in Simultaneous Interpretation, 94; auth, Signed Language Interpreting, Routledge Encyc of Translation Studies, 98; auth, Memory for Form after Simultaneous Interpretation: Comparisons of Language, Modality, and Process, Proceedings of the Thirteenth Nat Conv of the Registry of Interpreters for the Deaf, RID Pub, 95; Pride and Pluralism, TBC News, 93; coauth, A Common Conceptual Code in Bilinguals: Evidence

from Simultaneous Interpretation, Sign Language Studies, 94; coauth, Blackness, Deafness, IQ and g, Intelligence, 93; coauth, Simultaneous Interpretation and the Recall of Source-language Sentences, Language and Cognitive Processes, 93. **CONTACT ADDRESS** Dept of Linguistics, Univ of New Mexico, Humanities 526, Albuquerque, NM, 87131-1196. **EMAIL** ISHAM@unm.edu

ISHIKAWA, MINAKO
DISCIPLINE JAPANESE **EDUCATION** Georgetown Univ, PhD, 93. **CAREER** Asst prof. **RESEARCH** Sociolinguistics; discourse analysis; language acquisition. **SELECTED PUBLICATIONS** Auth, Iconicity in Discourse: The Case of Repetition, Text, 91. **CONTACT ADDRESS** Center for Foreign Languages, Literatures and Cult, Williams Col, Williamstown, MA, 01267. **EMAIL** Minako.Ishikawa@williams.edu

ISHIMATSU, GINETTE
PERSONAL Born 05/30/1958, San Jose, CA **DISCIPLINE** SOUTH ASIAN STUDIES **EDUCATION** Univ Calif, Berkeley, BA, 79, MA, 85, PhD, 94. **CAREER** Vis asst prof, relig stud, Whittier Col, 93-94; fac dir, South India Term Abroad, Madurai, India, 97; asst prof, Asian relig, Univ Denver, 98-. **MEMBERSHIPS** AAR; JAAR. **RESEARCH** South Indian Hindu temples and temple rituals; Saiva Siddhanta; Siva. **SELECTED PUBLICATIONS** Auth, Book Notes, Relig Stud Rev, 93-94; auth, rev, Home of Dancing Sivan: The Traditions of the Hindu Temple in Citamparam by Paul Younger, Critical Rev of Books in Relig, 96; auth, The Making of Tamil Saiva Siddhanta, Contrib to Indian Sociol, 99. **CONTACT ADDRESS** Dept of Religious Studies, Univ of Denver, 2150 S Race St, Denver, CO, 80208. **EMAIL** gishimat@du.edu

ISHMAN, SYBIL R.
PERSONAL Born 07/25/1946, Durham, NC, m **DISCIPLINE** FOREIGN LANGUAGES **EDUCATION** Univ of NC (Greensboro), BA 1968; NC Central Univ, MA 1971; Univ of NC (Chapel Hill), PhD 1980. **CAREER** NC Central Univ, grad asst 1969-71, instr 1970-72; NC State Univ, assist prof 1980-. **MEMBERSHIPS** Mem Am Assn Univ Women; Modern Lang Assn; Natl Counc of Tchrs of English; mem TESOL; Natl Smart Set Durham Chpt. **CONTACT ADDRESS** No Carolina State Univ, 281 Tompkins Hall, Raleigh, NC, 27695.

ISSACHAROFF, MICHAEL
PERSONAL Born 10/06/1942, Hove, England **DISCIPLINE** FRENCH **EDUCATION** Univ London, BA, 63; Univ Strasbourg, DUn, 67. **CAREER** Asst prof, Univ Chicago, 68-71; vis assoc prof, Wash Univ, 71-72; assoc prof, 72-78, PROF FRENCH, UNIV WESTERN ONT, 78-; vis prof, Univ Jerusalem, 81; vis prof, Johns Hopkins Univ, 83-84; vis prof, Univ Caen, 88-90; vis prof, Univ Paris 7, 90-91. **HONORS AND AWARDS** Fel, Royal Soc Can; fel, Royal Soc Arts. **MEMBERSHIPS** NY Acad Sci; MLA. **SELECTED PUBLICATIONS** Auth, J-K Huysmans devant la critique en France, 70; auth, L'Espace et la nouvelle, 76; auth, Le spectacle du discours, 85; auth, Discourse as Performance, 89; auth, Lieux comiques ou le temple de Janus, 90; coauth, Pensamiento y lenguaje, 94; coauth, De la pensee au langage, 95; ed, Langages de Flaubert, 77; ed, Sartre et la mise en signe, 82; ed, On Referring in Literature, 87; ed, Performing Texts, 87. **CONTACT ADDRESS** 57 rue Auguste Lancon, Paris, ., 75013.

ITO, JUNKO
DISCIPLINE THEORETICAL PHONOLOGY **EDUCATION** ICU, Tokyo, BA, MA; Univ Mass-Amherst, PhD, 86. **CAREER** PROF, LING, UNIV CALIF, SANTA CRUZ. **RESEARCH** Structure of the phonological lexicon; Prosodic morphology and phonology. **SELECTED PUBLICATIONS** Auth, A Prosodic Theory of Epenthesis, Natural Lang and Ling Theory, 89; Melodic Dissimilation in Ainu, Ling Inquiry, 84; Licensed segments and safe paths, Can Jour of Ling, 93. **CONTACT ADDRESS** Dept of Ling, Univ Calif, 1156 High St, Santa Cruz, CA, 95064.

IVANOV, VYACHESLAV V.
DISCIPLINE BALTIC, INDO-EUROPEAN LINGUISTICS **EDUCATION** Moscow State Univ, Eng Philology, 51, Hittite, Indo-Euroepan Grammar, PhD, 54; Univ Vilnius, Doct, Baltic, Indo-European Ling, 80. **CAREER** PROF, SLAVIC LANGS, LITS, UNIV CALIF, LOS ANGELES, 91-; prof, Stanford Univ, 90-91; RES FEL, INST SALVIC & BALKAN STUD, RUSSIAN ACAD SCIS, MOSCOW, 89-; DIR, INST WORLD CULTURE and PROF, PHILOS, MOSCOW STATE UNIV, 92-; dir, All-Union Libr For Lit, Moscow, 89-93; chair, dept structural typology, Inst Salvic, Balkan Studies, Acad Scis USSR, 63-69; prof, Archival & Hist Inst, Moscow, 88-89; chair, Res Grp Computer Trans, Inst Computer Tech & Exact Mechanics, Acad Scis USSR, 59-61; asst prof, Lab Comput Trans, State Pedagogical Inst For Langs, Moscoq, 59-61. **CONTACT ADDRESS** Dept of Slavic Langs, Lit, Univ of California, Los Angeles, 115 Kinsey Hall, Box 951502, Los Angeles, CA, 90095-1502. **EMAIL** ivanov@ucla.edu

IWAMOTO, YOSHIO
PERSONAL Born 11/25/1931, New Westminster, BC, Canada **DISCIPLINE** MODERN JAPANESE LITERATURE **EDUCATION** Univ Mich, BA, 58, MA, 59, PhD(Japanese lit), 64. **CAREER** Asst prof Japanese lang & lit, Univ Mich, 64-68; asst prof, Univ Ill, 68-69; ASSOC PROF JAPANESE & COMP LIT, IND UNIV, BLOOMINGTON, 69-, Vis assoc prof Japanese lit, Univ Hawaii, 71. **MEMBERSHIPS** Asn Asian Studies; Am Orient Soc; MLA; Asn Teachers Japanese. **RESEARCH** Modern Japanese novel; politics and literature in modern Japan; Japanese-Western literary relations. **SELECTED PUBLICATIONS** Auth, Shoshaman a Tale of Corporate Japan, World Lit Today, Vol 0066, 92; Legacies and Ambiguities--Postwar Fiction and Culture in West-Germany and Japan, Modern Fiction Stud, Vol 0038, 92; Katasumi No Hito-Tachi, World Lit Today, Vol 0067, 93; Boku Ga Honto Ni Wakakatta Koro, World Lit Today, Vol 0067, 93; A Voice From Postmodern Japan, World Lit Today, Vol 0067, 93; Ryuiki E- I-Fuesong, World Lit Today, Vol 0067, 93; History of the Showa Spirit, World Lit Today, Vol 0068, 94; 3 Plays, World Lit Today, Vol 0068, 94; Sennichi No Ruri, World Lit Today, Vol 0068, 94; Dance Dance Dance, World Lit Today, Vol 0068, 94; Haha Naru Nagi toChichi Naru Shike, World Lit Today, Vol 0069, 95; Writing Ground-Zero--Japanese Literature and the Atomic-Bomb, World Lit Today, Vol 0069, 95; Ichigo-Batake Yo Eien Ni, World Lit Today, Vol 0069, 95; Between the Eagle and the Sun--Traces of Japan, World Lit Today, Vol 0070, 96; Hiroshima Notes, World Lit Today, Vol 0070, 96; Abe, Kobo, 'Kangaroo Notebook, World Lit Today, Vol 0071, 97. **CONTACT ADDRESS** Dept of EAsian Lang & Lit, Indiana Univ, Bloomington, Goodbody Hall, Bloomington, IN, 47401.

J

JACKENDOFF, RAY SAUL
PERSONAL Born 01/23/1945, Chicago, IL, 2 children **DISCIPLINE** LINGUISTICS **EDUCATION** Swarthmore Col, BA, 65; MA Inst Technol, PhD(ling), 69. **CAREER** Lectr ling, Univ CA, Los Angeles, 69-70; asst prof, 71-73, assoc prof, 73-78, prof ling, Brandeis Univ, 78-; Special ling, Rand Corp, 69-70; Guggenheim fel, 93-94; fel, Center for Advanced Studies in Behavioral Science, 83-84. **HONORS AND AWARDS** Gustave Arlt Humanities Award, 75. **MEMBERSHIPS** Ling Soc Am; Soc for Philos and Psychol (pres, 90-91). **RESEARCH** Semantics; syntactic theory; musical cognition; consciousness. **SELECTED PUBLICATIONS** Auth, Semantic Interpretation in Generative Grammar, 72, X-Bar Syntax, 75, coauth (with Fred Lerdahl), A Generative Theory of Tonal Music, 82 & Semantics and Cognition, Mass Inst Technoll Press, 83; Consciousness and the Computational Mind, 87; Semantic Structures, 90; Languages of the Mind, 92; Architecture of the Language Faculty, 97; Patterns in the Mind, Basic Books, 94. **CONTACT ADDRESS** Volen Center, Brandeis Univ, 415 South St, Waltham, MA, 02254.

JACKMAN, JARRELL C.
PERSONAL Born 12/05/1943, Kenosha, WI, m, 1998, 1 child **DISCIPLINE** GERMAN AND AMERICAN STUDIES **EDUCATION** UCLA, BA, 66; Cal State Univ, MA, 69; Univ Cal, SB, PhD, 77. **CAREER** Exec Dir, 81-, Santa Barbara Trust for Hist Preservations. **HONORS AND AWARDS** Fulbright Fel; U of Cal Fel; DAAD; Spanish Min Cult Res Gnt. **MEMBERSHIPS** CMSA; SBDO; SBHA; SCIF; SMRC; CHS. **RESEARCH** German History and Literature; Spanish Colonial History. **SELECTED PUBLICATIONS** Coed, Santa Barbara Presido Area 1840-present, Univ California, Santa Barbara CA, 93; Presidos of the Big Bend Area, by James E Ivey, in: Public Historian, 92; Felipe de Goicoechea: Santa Barbara Presidio Commandante, in: The Spanish Beginnings in CA, UCSB, 90, pub, Anson Luman Press, Santa Barb, 93. **CONTACT ADDRESS** 5060B Calle Real, Santa Barbara, CA, 93111. **EMAIL** sbthp@rain.org

JACKSON, ELIZABETH R.
PERSONAL Born 05/13/1926, Boston, MA, m, 1970, 2 children **DISCIPLINE** FRENCH LITERATURE **EDUCATION** Reed Col, BA, 47; Univ Toulouse, cert philos, 51; Wellesley Col, MA, 59; Univ Paris, DUniv(French lit), 63. **CAREER** Statist asst, Nat Bur Econ Res, 47-48; teacher, Putney Sch, 48-49; tutor French, Goddard Col, 53-55; vis lectr, Knox Col, 63-65; assoc, humanities & French, Univ Calif, San Diego, 65-66; chmn, Dept French & Ital, 75-80, PROF FRENCH, SAN DIEGO STATE UNIV, 69-, Fr Govt grant & Fulbright travel grant, 60-62; Am Philos Soc grant-in-aid, 63; grant, Centre national de la recherche scientifique, 65. **MEMBERSHIPS** MLA; Am Asn Teachers Fr; Asn Studies Dada & Surrealism. **RESEARCH** Modern French poetry; Chenier; modern French novel. **SELECTED PUBLICATIONS** Auth, The Picture, the Poem, the Book--Michaux, Henri 3-Dimensional Creation, Harvard Libr Bull, Vol 0006, 95; Perse, Saintjohn and the Arts, Fr Rev, Vol 0068, 95. **CONTACT ADDRESS** Dept of French & Ital, San Diego State Univ, San Diego, CA, 92182.

JACKSON, KENNETH DAVID
PERSONAL Born 07/21/1944, Henderson, TX **DISCIPLINE** LUSO-BRAZILIAN LITERATURE, COMPARATIVE LITERATURE **EDUCATION** Univ Ill, BA, 66; Univ Wis, MA, 67, PhD(Span & Port), 73. **CAREER** Instr English, Ill Wesleyan Univ, 68-70; teaching asst Port, Univ Wis, Madison, 70-71; asst prof, Univ NMex, 73-74; asst prof, 74-79, ASSOC PROF PORT & SPAN, UNIV TEX, AUSTIN, 80-, Gulbenkian Found fel, 76; Am Inst Indian Studies fel, 82. **MEMBERSHIPS** Am Asn Teachers Span & Port; Royal Asiatic Soc; SCent Mod Lang Asn; Pac Northwest Conf Foreign Lang. **RESEARCH** Contemporary Brazilian literature; Portuguese literature; Portuguese oral & folk traditions in Asia. **SELECTED PUBLICATIONS** Auth, Tales From the Mountain, World Lit Today, Vol 0067, 93. **CONTACT ADDRESS** Dept of Span & Port, Univ of Tex, Austin, TX, 78712.

JACKSON, KENT PHILLIPS
PERSONAL Born 08/09/1949, Salt Lake City, UT, m, 1975, 5 children **DISCIPLINE** ANCIENT NEAR EASTERN LANGUAGES **EDUCATION** Brigham Young Univ, BA, 74; Univ Mich, MA, 76, PhD(Near Eastern studies), 80. **CAREER** Teaching asst world hist, Brigham Young Univ, 74-75; ed, Am Schs Orient Res, 76-80; ASST PROF ANCIENT SCRIPTURE, BRIGHAM YOUNG UNIV, 80-, Teaching asst world relig, Univ Mich, 78; Old Testament area dir, Brigham Young Univ, 82- **MEMBERSHIPS** Mormon Scripture Soc; Soc Bibl Lit; Am Schs Orient Res. **RESEARCH** Canaanite inscriptions; West Semitic personal names; Biblical history. **SELECTED PUBLICATIONS** Auth, Revolutionaries in the First-Century + Zealots, Rebellion, and the 1st Jewish Revolt Against the Roman-Empire, Brigham Young Univ Stud, Vol 0036, 97. **CONTACT ADDRESS** Dept of Anicent Scriptures, Brigham Young Univ, Joseph Smith Bldg, Provo, UT, 84602-0002.

JACKSON, ROBERT LOUIS
PERSONAL Born 11/10/1923, New York, NY, m, 1951, 2 children **DISCIPLINE** SLAVIC LANGUAGES AND LITERATURES **EDUCATION** Cornell Univ, BA, 44; Columbia Univ, MA, 49; Univ Calif, PhD(Slavic Lang & Lit), 56. **CAREER** Asst prof Russ Lang & Lit, 59-62, assoc prof, 62-67, prof Russ Lit, Yale Univ, 67-, chmn, B E Bensinger Prof Slavic Languages and Literatures, 91. **HONORS AND AWARDS** Honorary Doctor's Degree, Moscow State Univ; 94; Am Assoc of Teachers of Slavic and East European Languages, 94; Prize for Outstanding Work in the field of Slavic Languages and Literature for Dialogues with Dostoevsky: The Overwhelming Questions, Stanford Univ Press, 93, 94. **MEMBERSHIPS** MLA; Am Asn Teachers Slavic & E Europ Lang; Am Asn Advan Slavic Studies; Int Dosteovsky Soc (vpres, 71-); NAm Dostoevsky Soc (pres, 70-). **RESEARCH** Interaction of aesthetic and philosophical thought in the 19th century Russian literature; chance and fate in 19th century literature; tragedy and the Brothers Karamazov. **SELECTED PUBLICATIONS** Auth, Dostoevsky's Quest for Form: A Study of His Philosophy of Art, Yale Univ, 66; The Testament of F M Dostoevsky, Russ Lit, 73; Miltonic Imagery and Design in Pushkin's Mozart and Salieri: The Russian Satan, Am Contributions to Seventh Int Congr Slavists, 73; auth, introd & ed, Crime and Punishment, a collection of critical essays, In: Twentieth Century Interpretations, Prentice-Hall, 74; Dialogues with Dostoevsky, The Overshelming Questions, Stanford Univ Press, 93. **CONTACT ADDRESS** Dept of Slavic Languages, Yale Univ, PO Box 208236, New Haven, CT, 06520-8236.

JACKSON, WILLIAM EDWARD
PERSONAL Born 12/01/1936, Creedmoor, NC, m, 1961, 3 children **DISCIPLINE** GERMAN LANGUAGE & LITERATURE **EDUCATION** NC Col, BA, 58; NY Univ, MA, 61; Univ Pa, PhD(Ger), 72. **CAREER** Lectr Ger, City Col New York, 61-64; acting instr, 70-71, from instr to asst prof, 71-75, assoc prof Ger, Yale Univ, 75-80; prog officer, Gen Res Prog, Nat Endowment for Humanities, 80-81; ASSOC PROF GER & ASSOC DIR, CARTER G WOODSON INST, UNIV VA, 81-. **MEMBERSHIPS** Am Asn Teachers Ger; MLA; Medieval Acad Am. **RESEARCH** Medieval German language; medieval German literature; medieval Austrian culture. **SELECTED PUBLICATIONS** Auth, Reinmar Studies--A Commentary on the So-Called Spurious Poems of Reinmar Der Alte, J Engl and Germanic Philol, Vol 0092, 93; The Crusade Motif in the Poetry of Reinmar Der Alte, Germanisch-Romanische Monatsschrift, Vol 0043, 93; Reinmar Studies--A Commentary on the So-Called Spurious Poems of Reinmar Der Alte, J Engl and Germanic Philol, Vol 0092, 93. **CONTACT ADDRESS** Dept of Ger Lang, Univ of Va, Charlottesville, VA, 22903.

JACOBS, CAROL F.
DISCIPLINE COMPARATIVE LITERATURE **EDUCATION** Cornell Univ, MA; Johns Hopkins Univ, PhD. **CAREER** Prof, SUNY Buffalo. **RESEARCH** Lit theory as it appears in Eng, French, and Ger lits in the 18th, 19th, and 20th centuries; critical theory of the same periods. **SELECTED PUBLICATIONS** Auth, The Dissimulating Harmony on Nietzsche, Rilke, Artaud, and Benjamin, Johns Hopkins UP, 78; Uncontainable Romanticism: Shelley, Bronte, Kleist, Johns Hopkins, 89; Telling Time on Lessing, Ford Madox Ford, Wordsworth, Rilke, de Man, Benjamin, and Levi-Strauss, Johns Hopkins, 93. **CONTACT ADDRESS** Dept Comp Lit, SUNY Buffalo, 639 Clemens Hall, Buffalo, NY, 14260.

JACOBS, RODERICK ARNOLD
PERSONAL Born 05/29/1934, London, England, m, 1962, 2 children **DISCIPLINE** DIACHRONIC LINGUISTICS, STYLISTICS, DISCOURSE **EDUCATION** Univ London, BA, 56; Harvard Univ, EdM, 62; Univ Ca, San Diego, MA, 70, PhD, 72. **CAREER** Teacher English & French, Pub Schs, London, England, New Brunswick, Can & Newton, Mass, 56-64; curric supvr English & reading, Tuxedo Pub Schs, NY, 64-66; assoc prof lit, State Univ NY Col Oneonta, 66-68; res fel ling, Univ Calif, San Diego, 68-72; teacher & researcher Amerindian lang & cult, Pala Indian Band Calif, 72-73; prof ling & English lang, Univ Hawaii, Manoe, 73-, consult, Peace Corps Training Div, 70-71; consult bilingual educ, Trust Territory Micronesia, 78-; dir bilingual studies, Dept English Second Lang, 77-79, ch dept English Second Lang, 94-, Univ Hawaii, Manoa, 77-. **MEMBERSHIPS** Ling Soc Am; NCTE; TESOL. **RESEARCH** Syntactic change; discourse analysis; stylistics; cognitive linguistics. **SELECTED PUBLICATIONS** Co-ed, Vanity Fair, 64 & Wuthering Heights, 65, Harper; coauth, English Transformational Grammar, Ginn-Blaisdell, 68; auth, On Transformational Grammar, NCTE, 69; coauth, Transformations, Style, and Meaning, 71 & auth, Studies in Language, 73, Xerox; Syntactic Change, Univ Calif, 75; English Syntax, Oxford, 95. **CONTACT ADDRESS** Dept of Ling, Univ Hi Manoa, 1890 E West Rd, Honolulu, HI, 96822-2318. **EMAIL** rjacobs@hawaii.edu

JACOBSEN, THORKILD
PERSONAL Born 06/07/1904, Copenhagen, Denmark, m, 1966, 4 children **DISCIPLINE** ASSYRIOLOGY **EDUCATION** Univ Copenhagen, MA, 27, Dr Phil(Assyriol), 39; Univ Chicago, PhD(Syriac), 29. **CAREER** Field Assyriologist, Orient Inst, Univ Chicago, 29-37, res assoc Assyriol, 37-42, from asst prof to prof soc insts, 42-62, chmn dept Near Eastern lang & lit & dir Orient Inst, 46-48, dean div humanities, 48-51; PROF ASSYRIOL, HARVARD UNIV, 63-74. Haskell lectr, Oberlin Col, 52; Am Coun Learned Soc lectr hist relig, 66-67; Guggenheim fel, 68-69. **HONORS AND AWARDS** MA, Harvard Univ, 63. **MEMBERSHIPS** Am Philos Soc; Am Acad Arts & Sci; corresp mem Royal Danish Acad Arts & Sci, Brit Acad; Am Soc Studies Relig. **RESEARCH** Ancient Mesopotamian languages; archaeology; civilization. **SELECTED PUBLICATIONS** Auth, The Historian and the Sumerian Gods, J Amer Oriental SOC, Vol 0114, 94. **CONTACT ADDRESS** E Washington Rd, Bradford, NH, 03221.

JACOBSON, HOWARD
PERSONAL Born 08/21/1940, Bronx, NY, m, 1965, 4 children **DISCIPLINE** CLASSICAL LITERATURE **EDUCATION** Columbia Col, NY, BA, 62; Univ Chicago, AM, 63; Columbia Univ, PhD, 67. **CAREER** Instr Greek & Latin, Columbia Univ, 66-68; from Asst Prof to Assoc Prof, 68-80, Prof Classics, Univ Ill, Urbana, 80-; Lady Davis Vis Prof, Hebrew Univ, Jerusalem, Winter 83. **HONORS AND AWARDS** C.J. Goodwin Award of Merit, 85. **MEMBERSHIPS** Am Philol Asn. **RESEARCH** Latin literature; Hellenistic Judaism; comparative literature. **CONTACT ADDRESS** Dept of Classics, Univ of Ill, 707 S Mathews Ave, Urbana, IL, 61801-3625.

JACOBSON, RODOLFO
PERSONAL m, 1944, 4 children **DISCIPLINE** LINGUISTICS, BILINGUAL EDUCATION **EDUCATION** Univ Panama, AB, 52; Univ Mich, MA, 64, PhD(ling), 66. **CAREER** Teacher, Escuela Prof, Panama, 52-62; instr English as foreign lang, English Lang Inst, Univ Mich, 65, lectr, 65-66; assoc prof English, State Univ NY Col Cortland, 66-69, prof English & dir English socioling prog, 69-74; PROF LING, UNIV TEX, SAN ANTONIO, 74-, Consult, Ministry Educ, Panama, 60-62; lectr, Am Univ Beirut & Am Univ Cairo, 73; consult, United Independent Sch Dist, Laredo, Tex, 75-79; dir, Title VIII Training fel, demonstration proj, 77-; interpreter & examr, Adm US Courts, Washington, DC, 80-81. **MEMBERSHIPS** Teachers English to Speakers Other Lang; Nat Asn Bilingual Educ; Int Sociol Asn; Ling Asn Southwest; Am Educ Res Asn. **RESEARCH** Sociolinguistics; Spanish language varieties and use; methods in bilingual instruction. **SELECTED PUBLICATIONS** Auth, Incorporating sociolinguistic norms into an EFL program, TESOL Quart, 76; La reinvindicacion de parole, Estudios Filol, 76; The social implications of intrasentential codeswitching, in: Chicano Scholarship (the New Scholar), 77; Anticipatory embedding and imaginary content, in: Swallow VI Proc, 78; Semantic compounding in the speech of Mexican American bilinguals, in: Bilingualism & Bilingual Educ, 79; Beyond ESL: The teaching of content other than language arts in bilingual education, Southwest Educ Development Lab, Austin, Tex, 79; Can bilingual teaching techniques reflect bilingual community behavior?, in: Bilingual Educ and Public Policy, Ypsilanti, Mich, 79; Can and should the Laredo experiment be duplicated elsewhere?, in: NABE Proc, 81. **CONTACT ADDRESS** 14222 Golden Woods, San Antonio, TX, 78285.

JACOBY, SALLY
DISCIPLINE LINGUISTICS **EDUCATION** Northwestern Univ, BS, 69; Tel Aviv Univ, BA, 78; Univ Birmingham, UK, MA, 86; UCLA, PhD, 98. **CAREER** Instr, Tel Aviv Univ, 77-88; adj asst prof, Soka Univ, 95-96; asst prof, Dept of Commun, Univ New Hampshire, 96- . **MEMBERSHIPS** AAAL; AAUP; AILA; CIOS; ICA; NCA. **RESEARCH** Language and social

interaction; conversation analysis; situated interpersonal communication; ethnographic and discourse analytic approaches to communicative competence; language and discourse socialization; multi-modal communication; ethnography of communication; expert-novice interaction; Hebrew conversation. **SELECTED PUBLICATIONS** Co-auth, Interpretive journeys: How Physicists Talk and Travel Through Graphic Space, in Configurations, 94; ed, sp issue, and co-auth, Co-Construction, Res on Lang and Soc Interaction, 95; co-auth, A Genre-based Developmental Writing course for Undergraduate ESL Science Majors, in Academic Writing in a Second Language: Essays on Research and Pedagogy, Ablex, 95; auth, When I Come Down I'm in the Domain State: Grammar and Graphic Representation in the Interpretive Activity of Physicists, in Ochs, co-ed, Interaction and Grammar, Cambridge, 96; auth, Down to the Wire: The Cultural Clock of Physicists and the Discourse of Consensus, Lang and Soc, 97; auth, Saying What Wasn't Said: Negative Observation as a Linguistic Resource for the Interactional Construction of performance feedback, in The Language of Turn and Sequence, Oxford, 98. **CONTACT ADDRESS** Dept of Communication, Univ New Hampshire, 20 College Rd, Durham, NH, 03824-3586. **EMAIL** swj@hopper.unh.edu

JAHN, GARY ROBERT
PERSONAL Born 09/29/1943, Minneapolis, MN, m, 1984, 5 children **DISCIPLINE** RUSSIAN LITERATURE **EDUCATION** Univ Minn, BA, 65; Univ Wis, MA, 68, PhD, 72. **CAREER** Asst prof Russ lang & lit, St Olaf Col, 71-72 & State Univ NY, Buffalo, 72-77; from Asst Prof to Assoc Prof, 77-98, Prof Russ Lang & Lit, Univ Minn, 98-. **MEMBERSHIPS** Am Asn Teachers Slavic & East Europ Lang; Am Asn Advan Slavic Studies. **RESEARCH** Nineteenth century Russian literature, in particular the prose fiction of the second half of the 19th century; the life and work of L N Tolstoy. **SELECTED PUBLICATIONS** Auth, A structural analysis of Leo Tolstoy's God Sees the Truth, But Waits, Studies Short Fiction, 75; The aesthetic theory of Leo Tolstoy's What Is Art?, J Aesthet & Art Criticism,, 75; Thematic development in Fathers and Sons, Col Lit, 77; L N Tolstoj's Narodnye rasskazy, Russ Lang J, 77; L N Tolstoj's Vision of the power of death and How Much Land Does a Man Need?, 78 & The image of the railroad in Anna Karenina, 81, Slavic & East Europ J; The unity of Anna Karenina, Russ Rev, 82; Tolstoj and Kant, in New Perspectives on 19th Century Russian Prose, Slavica Press, 82; The Death of Ivan Leich: An Interpretation, Macmillan, 93. **CONTACT ADDRESS** Dept of Slavic & Central Asian Lang, Univ of Minn, 318 16th Ave SE, Minneapolis, MN, 55455-0280. **EMAIL** gjahn@tc.umn.edu

JAINI, PADMANABH S.
PERSONAL Born 10/23/1923, Mangalore, India, m, 1956, 1 child **DISCIPLINE** LINGUISTICS, SOUTH & SOUTHEAST ASIAN RELIGIONS **EDUCATION** HPT Col, India, BA, 47; BJ Inst Res, Ahmedabad, MA, 49; Vidyodaya Pirivena, Ceylon, Tripitakacarya, 51; Univ London, PhD (Sanskrit Lit) 59. **CAREER** Lectr Sanskrit & Pali, Benaras Hindu Univ, 52-56; Pali & Buddhist Sanskrit, Univ London, 56-64, reader, 65-67; vis lectr Buddhism, Univ Mich, Ann Arbor, 64-65, prof Indic Lang, 67-72; prof Buddhism, Univ Calif, Berkeley, 72-94; prof Emeritus, grad school, 94. **RESEARCH** Pali and Buddhist Sanskrit language and literature; Abhidharma studies; comparative study of Indian religions. **SELECTED PUBLICATIONS** Ed, Abhidharmadipa, K P Jayawal Inst, 52; auth, On the theory of two Vasubandhus, 58 & The Vaibhasika theory of words, 59, Bull Sch Orient & African Studies, Univ London, ed, Milinda-Tika, Pali Text Soc London, 61; auth, The story of Sudhana and Manohara, 66, Aloka of Haribhadra and the Saratama of Ratnakarasanti: A comparative study of the two commentaries of the Astasahasrika, 72 & Jina Rsabha as an avatara of Visnu, 77, Bull Sch Orient & African Studies, Univ London; The Jaina Path of Purification, Univ Calif, 78; Gender and Salvation: Jaina Debates on the Spiritual Liberation of Women, foreword by R Goldman, xxiv, Preface 4, Univ of Berkeley Press, Berkeley, 91. **CONTACT ADDRESS** Dept of South and Southeast Asian Lang & Lit, Univ of California, Berkeley, 7303 Dwinelle Hall, Berkeley, CA, 94720-0001.

JAMES, DOROTHY
DISCIPLINE GERMAN **EDUCATION** Univ London, UK, PhD. **CAREER** Prof, Hunter Col, 78-; ch, Ger Dept, 13 yrs; fac, Grad Sch, CUNY; trained tester, oral proficiency on the ACTFL model, 83 & trainer, testing, 85; past dir, NEH funded Hunter Col proj to institute a proficiency-based curric in an urban univ; proj dir, NEH funded Proj, CUNY: A Model Curric in Ger, 94-97. **HONORS AND AWARDS** NYSAFLT awd, 89; Northeast Conf awd, 93; ADFL awd, 94. **MEMBERSHIPS** Pres, Asn Departments For Languages, 90; interim dir, For Languages at the MLA & ed, ADFL Bull, 90-91; ch, MLA Adv Comt For Languages and Literatures, 95-96. **SELECTED PUBLICATIONS** Auth, Raimund and Vienna, Cambridge UP, 70 & Georg Bnchner's Dantons Tod, Mod Humanities Res Asn, 82; ed, Patterns of Change, German Drama and the European Tradition, Peter Lang, 90. **CONTACT ADDRESS** Dept of German, Hunter Col, CUNY, 695 Park Ave, New York, NY, 10021.

JAMME, ALBERT W.F.
PERSONAL Born 06/27/1916, Senzeille, Belgium **DISCIPLINE** ENGLISH, FRENCH **EDUCATION** Cath Univ Louvain, DTheol, 47, DOr, 52; Pontif Bibl Comm, Rome, Lic, 48. **CAREER** Res Prof Semitics, Cath Univ Am, 55-, Epigraphical adv, Govt Saudi Arabia, 68-69. **MEMBERSHIPS** Cath Bibl Asn Am; Am Orient Soc. **RESEARCH** Pre-Islamic Arabian sci. **SELECTED PUBLICATIONS** Auth, Pieces Epigraphiques de Heid bin Aqil, la Necropole de Timna, (Hagr Kohlan), Biblio Mus, Louvain, 52; La Kynastie de Sarahbiil Yakuf et la documentation epigraphique sud-arabe, Ned Hist Archaeol Inst, Istanbul, 61; Sabaean inscriptions from Mahram Bilquis (Marib), Johns Hopkins Univ, 62; Miscellanees d'ancient arabe, I-XX, Washington, 71-98; Carnegie Museum 1974-1975 Yemen Expedition, Carnegie Natural Hist Spec Publ No 2, Pittsburgh, 76. **CONTACT ADDRESS** Dept of Semitics, Catholic Univ of America, 620 Michigan Ave N E, Washington, DC, 20064-0002.

JANKOFSKY, KLAUS P.
DISCIPLINE MEDIEVAL AND COMPARATIVE LITERATURE, HISTORICAL LINGUISTICS, SHAKESPEARE **EDUCATION** Univ Saarlandes, Ger, Dr phil. **CAREER** Prof, hd, dept Eng, Univ Minn, Duluth. **RESEARCH** Death and dying in literature and historical documents. **SELECTED PUBLICATIONS** Auth, John Ciardi's Medievalism." Medievalism in North America, ed, Kathleen Verduin, Bury St. Edmunds, D S Brewer, Cambridge, 94; ed, The South English Legendary: A Critical Assessment, Francke, 92. **CONTACT ADDRESS** Dept of Eng, Univ Minn, Duluth, Duluth, MN, 55812-2496.

JANZEN, HENRY DAVID
DISCIPLINE ENGLISH LANGUAGE; LITERATURE **EDUCATION** Assumption Univ, BA; Univ Windsor, MA; Wayne State Univ, PhD, 70. **CAREER** Prof **RESEARCH** Renaissance literature; editing and textual criticism. **SELECTED PUBLICATIONS** Pub (s), Heywood, Middleton, Milton & Shakespeare; prepared ed 2 manuscript plays, Thomas Heywood's The Escapes of Jupiter and Francis Jaques's The Queen of Corsica. **CONTACT ADDRESS** Dept of English Language and Literature, Univ of Windsor, 401 Sunset Ave, Windsor, ON, N9B 3P4. **EMAIL** janzen4@uwindsor.ca

JARA, RENE
DISCIPLINE SPANISH AND PORTUGUESE LITERATURE **EDUCATION** Univ Cath Valparaiso, BA, 61; Ariz State Univ, PhD, 79. **RESEARCH** Seventeenth century Spanish American narratives and poetry; colonial writing in Spanish America; colonial heritage in the New Latin American novel. **SELECTED PUBLICATIONS** Auth, Los pliegues del silencio, 96; Amerindian Images and the Legacy of Columbus, Univ Minn, 92; co-auth, Perfil historiografico de una literatura colonial, 92. **CONTACT ADDRESS** Spanish and Portuguese Dept, Univ of Minnesota, Twin Cities, 34 Folwell Hall, 9 Pleasant St SE, Minneapolis, MN, 55455.

JAROW, E.H.
DISCIPLINE RELIGIONS OF INDIA, COMPARATIVE LITERATURE **EDUCATION** Columbia Univ, PhD, 91 **CAREER** ASST PROF, REL STUD, VASSAR COL, 94-. **CONTACT ADDRESS** Dept of Relig, Vassar Col, Poughkeepsie, NY, 12604. **EMAIL** ehjarow@vassar.edu

JARVI, RAYMOND
PERSONAL Born 11/10/1942, Seattle, WA **DISCIPLINE** MODERN SWEDISH LITERATURE, SWEDISH THEATRE **EDUCATION** Univ Wash, BA, 64, MA, 66, PhD(drama arts), 70. **CAREER** Instr Scand, Univ Wash, 68-70, asst prof, 70-78; ASSOC PROF SWEDISH, NORTH PARK COL, 79-. **MEMBERSHIPS** Soc Advan Scand Studies; Swed Pioneer Hist Soc. **RESEARCH** August Strindberg; Swedish literature, 1890-1914; Swedish-American place-names. **SELECTED PUBLICATIONS** Auth, Gustav-Iii and the Swedish Stage--Opera, Theater, and Other Foibles--Essays in Honor of Astrand, Hans, Scand Stud, Vol 0066, 94; Gustav-Iii and the Swedish Stage--Opera, Theater, and Other Foibles--Essays in Honor of Astrand, Hans, Scand Stud, Vol 0066, 94; Soderberg, Hjalmar on Strindberg, August--The Perspective of a Theater Critic and the Influence of a Dramatist, Scand Stud, Vol 0068, 96; Soderberg, Hjalmar on Strindberg, August--The Perspective of a Theater Critic and the Influence of a Dramatist, Scand Stud, Vol 0068, 96. **CONTACT ADDRESS** No Park Col, 5125 N Spaulding, Chicago, IL, 60625.

JARVIS, DONALD KARL
PERSONAL Born 04/06/1939, Ithaca, NY, m, 1965, 6 children **DISCIPLINE** FOREIGN LANGUAGE EDUCATION **EDUCATION** Brigham Young Univ, BA, 64; Ohio State Univ, PhD, 70. **CAREER** Teacher foreign lang, Beaver Pub Schs, 65-66; teacher Russ, Salt Lake City Pub Schs, 66-67; assoc prof, 70-80, chmn dept Asian & Slavic lang, 76-79, prof Russ, Brigham Young Univ, 80-; assoc dir Gen Educ, 81-; coodr, Lang Teaching Res, 81-; Ed, Newslett, Am Assn Teachers Slavic & E Europ Lang, 72-74. **MEMBERSHIPS** Am Assn Teachers Slavic & E Europ Lang; Am Coun Teaching Russ. **RESEARCH** Language teaching; Russian linguistics; Russian culture. **SELECTED PUBLICATIONS** Auth, Teaching foreign etiquette in the foreign language class: Student involvement techniques, Foreign Lang Ann, 5/75; coauth, Russian Language Study in 1975: A Status Report, MLA, 76; art, The Langugage Connection: From the Classroom to the World, Nat Textbk, 77; ed, Techniques for increasing Slavic program enrollments: A collection of success stories, Am Assn Teachers Slavic & E Europ Lang, 78; auth, Krazvitiiu kommunikativinoi sposobnosti uchashchixsia (obsor amerikanskix eksperimentov i metodov) Russkii iazyk za rubezhom, 1/78; coauth, Viewpoints: A Listening and Conversation Course in Russian, Brigham Young Univ Press, 79; art, A study of the effect of parallel translations on second language reading and syntax acquisition, Mod Lang J, 82; co-ed, Russian Language Teaching, Slavica, 82. **CONTACT ADDRESS** Dept of Germanic & Slavic Lang, Brigham Young Univ, 4094 Jkhb, Provo, UT, 84602-0002.

JARVIS, GILBERT ANDREW
PERSONAL Born 02/13/1941, Boston, MA, m, 1963, 2 children **DISCIPLINE** FOREIGN & SECOND LANGUAGE EDUCATION **EDUCATION** St Norbert Col, BA, 63; Purdue Univ, West Lafayette, MA, 66, PhD(foreign lang educ), 70. **CAREER** Teacher French & English, Mineral Point High Sch, Wis, 63-65; instr French & educ, Purdue Univ, 65-70; from asst prof to assoc prof, 70-76, prof Foreign & Second Lang Educ, Ohio State Univ, 76-, chmn Humanities Educ, 80-86, chmn, Educational studies, 87-95, dir, English as a Second Language Programs, 95-. **HONORS AND AWARDS** NY State Nat Foreign Language Leadership Award, 81. **MEMBERSHIPS** Am Coun Teaching Foreign Lang; Am Educ Res Asn. **RESEARCH** Foreign language learning and curricula development and measurement. **SELECTED PUBLICATIONS** Ed, Review of Foreign Language Education, Nat Texbk, Vols V, VI, VII & VIII, 73, 74, 75 & 76; coauth, Connaitre et se Connaitre, 76, Passeport pour la France & Vivent les Differences, 77, Invitation, 79, 84, 88, 93, , Et Vous, 83, 86, 90 & Nous Tous, 83, 86, 90, Holt; Invitation Essentials, 91, 95. **CONTACT ADDRESS** English as a Second Language Programs, Ohio State Univ, 1961 Tuttle Park Pl, Columbus, OH, 43210-1285. **EMAIL** Jarvis.3@osu.edu

JEANNET, ANGELA MARIA
PERSONAL Born 08/08/1931, Pergine, Italy, 5 children **DISCIPLINE** FRENCH **EDUCATION** Univ Florence, DLet, 54. **CAREER** Teaching asst, Lycee Fenelon, Lille, France, 52-54; instr Ital & French, Univ Colo, 56-62; asst prof Romance lang, Pa State Univ, 62-67; asst prof French, 67-71, ASSOC PROF ITAL & FRENCH, FRANKLIN & MARSHALL COL, 71-, Danforth assoc. **MEMBERSHIPS** AAUP; MLA; Am Asn Teachers Ital; Asn Ital Studies. **RESEARCH** Contemporary literature; women's studies. **SELECTED PUBLICATIONS** Auth, Writing in Dante Cult of Truth From Borges toBoccaccio, Comparative Lit Stud, Vol 0033, 96. **CONTACT ADDRESS** Dept of French & Ital, Franklin and Marshall Col, Lancaster, PA, 17604.

JEHLIN, MYRA
DISCIPLINE ENGLISH LANGUAGE AND LITERATURE **EDUCATION** CUNY, BA; Univ Calif Berkeley, MA; PhD. **CAREER** Prof. **RESEARCH** Transatlantic cultural relations; literature and history. **SELECTED PUBLICATIONS** Auth, American Incarnation: The Individual, the Nation, and the Continent; auth, The English Literatures of America; ed, Papers of Empire. **CONTACT ADDRESS** Dept of English, Rutgers Univ, 510 George St, Murray Hall, New Brunswick, NJ, 08901-1167. **EMAIL** jehlen@rci.rutgers.edu

JELINSKI, JACK BERNARD
PERSONAL Born 10/01/1943, Wisconsin Rapids, WI, m, 1968, 2 children **DISCIPLINE** SPANISH LITERATURE **EDUCATION** Univ Wis-Madison, BA, 67, PhD(Span), 74; Ind Univ, Bloomington, MA, 69. **CAREER** Teaching assoc Span, Ind Univ, Bloomington, 68-69; lectr, Univ Wis-Madison, 71-72; asst prof, 73-77, ASSOC PROF SPAN & HEAD DEPT MOD LANG, MONT STATE UNIV, 77-, Prog consult lang & ethnic studies, Nat Endowment Humanities, 78-79, reviewer/panelist, Div Res Prog. **MEMBERSHIPS** Am Asn Teachers Span & Port; MLA; AAUP. **RESEARCH** Twentieth-century novel; literary criticism. **SELECTED PUBLICATIONS** Auth, The Language We Inherited--A Bilingual Course in Spanish, 2nd-Ed, Hispania-J Devoted to the tchg of Span and Port, Vol 0076, 93; The Language We Inherited--A Bilingual Course in Spanish, 2nd Ed, Spanish and English, Hispania-J Devoted to the tchg of Span and Port, Vol 0076, 93; From Simple Sentences toCompound Sentences--An Advanced Course Span Grammar, Hispania-J Devoted to the tchg Span and Port, Vol 0077, 94; From Simple Sentences toCompound Sentences--An Advanced Course of Spanish Grammar, Hispania-J Devoted to the tchg of Span and Port, Vol 0077, 94; Composicion-Practica, Textbk, Hispania-J Devoted to the tchg of Span and Port, Vol 0078, 95; Tu-Diras, Introduction toSpanish-Language and Culture, Hispania-J Devoted to the tchg of Span and Port, Vol 0078, 95; Composicion-Practica, Textbk, Hispania-J Devoted to the tchg of Span and Port, Vol 0078, 95; Approaches toQuestions on the Learning and Acquisition of Spanish as a Foreign-Language or 2nd-Language, Hispania-J Devoted to the tchg of

Span and Port, Vol 0078, 95; Mario as Biblical Analog in Delibes,Miguel 'Cinco Horas Con Mario', Cla J-Col Lang Asn, Vol 0038, 95. **CONTACT ADDRESS** Dept of Mod Lang, Montana State Univ, Bozeman, MT, 59715.

JENKINS, FRED W.
PERSONAL Born 04/13/1957, Cincinnati, OH, m, 1992 **DISCIPLINE** CLASSICAL PHILOLOGY **EDUCATION** Univ Cincinnati, BA, 79; Univ Ill Urbana-Champaign, AM, 81, PhD, 85, MS, libr & info sci, 86. **CAREER** Catalog spec and asst prof, 87-96, coord & head collection mgt and assoc prof, 96-, Univ Dayton Libr. **HONORS AND AWARDS** Phi Beta Kapp, 78; Acad Libr Asn of Oh Res grant, 93, 97; Choice Outstanding Acad Book, 96; Oh Libr Found Res award, 97. **MEMBERSHIPS** Amer Soc of Papyrologists; Amer Libr Asn. **RESEARCH** Later Latin literature; Papyrology; History & bibliography of classical studies. **SELECTED PUBLICATIONS** Co-auth, Reorganizing Collection Development and Acquisitions in a Medium-sized Academic Library, Libr Acquisitions: Practice and Theory, 22.3, 287-293, fall, 98; auth, Classical Studies, Mag for Libr, 9th ed, 356-362, 97; co-auth, Internet Resources for Classical Studies, Col & Res Libr News, 58.4, 255-259, apr, 97; auth, A Ptolemaic Account, Bull of the Amer Soc of Papyrologists, 33, 21-23, 96; auth, Classical Studies: A Guide to the Reference Literature, Libr Unlimited, 96; auth, A Coptic Account from the Michigan Collection, Archiv fur Papyrusforschung, 41.2, 191-193, 95; auth, A Fourth-Century Receipt from the Michigan Collection, Bull of the Amer Soc of Papyrologists, 31.3-4, 137-139, 94. **CONTACT ADDRESS** Univ of Dayton, 105F Roesch Library, Dayton, OH, 45469-1360. **EMAIL** jenkins@data.lib.udayton.edu

JENKINS, FREDERIC MAGILL
PERSONAL Born 01/28/1930, Oakland, CA, m, 1956, 2 children **DISCIPLINE** CONTEMPORARY FRENCH, LINGUISTICS **EDUCATION** Swarthmore Col, BA, 52; Univ Calif, Berkeley, MA, 57, PhD(ling), 63. **CAREER** Asst prof French, San Diego State Col, 61-64; asst prof, 64-67, resident dir, Study Abroad Prog in France, 74-75, ASSOC PROF FRENCH & LING, UNIV ILL, 67-, Ling bibliogr, Am Coun Teaching Foreign Lang, 71-74. **MEMBERSHIPS** Am Asn Teachers Fr; Am Coun Teaching Foreign Lang; Can Ling Asn. **RESEARCH** Contemporary French linguistics; normative French grammar. **SELECTED PUBLICATIONS** Auth, Larousse French-English/English-French Dictionary, Fr Rev, Vol 0069, 96; Systematic Grammar of the French-Language, Fr Rev, Vol 0069, 96; The Oxford-Hachette French Dictionary, Fr Rev, Vol 0069, 96. **CONTACT ADDRESS** Dept of French, Univ of Ill, Champaign, IL, 61820.

JENNINGS, LAWRENCE CHARLES
PERSONAL Born 11/10/1912, Exeter, MO, m, 1938, 3 children **DISCIPLINE** ENGLISH LITERATURE, ENGLISH LANGUAGE **EDUCATION** Southwest Mo State Col, BS, 34; Nazarene Theol Sem, BD, 48; Northwestern Mo State Col, MS, 60; Univ Okla, EdD(English), 71. **CAREER** Teacher English, Midway High Sch, Mo, 35-41; prin, Butterfield High Sch, 41-43; teacher bus, Maryville High Sch, 54-55; asst prof English, Can Nazarene Col, 55-63; from asst prof to assoc prof English, 64-69, chmn, div lang, lit & speech, 76-78, prof, 69-79, head dept, 72-79, EMER PROF ENGLISH, BETHANY NAZARENE COL, 79-. **MEMBERSHIPS** S cent Mod Lang Asn; S Cent Renaissance Conf; Southwest Lit Asn. **RESEARCH** Image of the professor in English literature from Carlyle to Snow; literary figures of the Mississippi River South. **CONTACT ADDRESS** Dept of English, Bethany Nazarene Col, Bethany, OK, 73008.

JENNINGS, LEE B.
PERSONAL Born 05/03/1927, Willard, OH, m, 1974 **DISCIPLINE** GERMAN **EDUCATION** Ohio State Univ, BA, 49; Univ Ill, Urbana, MA, 51, PhD(Ger), 55. **CAREER** Instr Ger, Univ Colo, 56; instr Harvard Univ, 56-57; from instr to asst prof, Univ Calif Los Angeles, 57-62; assoc prof, Univ Tex, 62-68; PROF GER, UNIV ILL, CHICAGO CIRCLE, 68-, Alexander von Humboldt Found res fel, Munich & Marbach, Ger, 65-67; Ger Acad Exchange Serv res fel, fall 73; Nat Endowment for Humanities grant, 82. **MEMBERSHIPS** MLA Am Asn Teachers Ger. **RESEARCH** German 19th century literature; psychology and literature; the absurd and the grotesque in literature. **SELECTED PUBLICATIONS** Auth, Bending the Frame in the German Cyclical Narrative--Arnim, Achim, Von Der 'Wintergarten' and Hoffmann,E.T.A. Die 'Serapionsbruder', Seminar- J Ger Stud, Vol 0029, 93; Keller, Gottfried 'Sieben Legenden'--A Description of His Narrative Writing, Colloquia Germanica, Vol 0027, 94; Keller, Gottfried 'Sieben Legenden'--A Description of His Narrative Writing, Colloquia Germanica, Vol 0027, 94; Life, A Death--Grillparzer Der 'Traum Ein Leben', Modern Austrian Lit, Vol 0028, 95; Uhland,Ludwig and the Critics, Seminar-J Ger Stud, Vol 0032, 96; Eichendorff Scholarly Reception--a Survey, Colloquia Germanica, Vol 0029, 96; Eichendorff Scholarly Reception--a Survey, Colloquia Germanica, Vol 0029, 96. **CONTACT ADDRESS** Dept of Ger, Univ of Ill, Chicago Circle, Box 4348, Chicago, IL, 60680.

JENSEN, FREDE
PERSONAL Born 02/17/1926, Auning, Denmark **DISCIPLINE** FRENCH & PROVENCAL PHILOLOGY **EDUCATION** Univ Copenhagen, MA, 53; Univ Salamanca, dipl, 55; Univ Calif, Los Angeles, PhD, 61. **CAREER** Asst prof French, Univ Alta, Calgary, 61-64, Univ Calif, Los Angeles, 64-67; assoc prof, 67-73, PROF FRENCH, UNIV COLO, BOULDER, 73-, Mem ed bd, Semasia, 73- **MEMBERSHIPS** MLA; Rocky Mountain Mod Lang Asn; Centre Guillaume IX, Assoc Int d'Etudes Occitanes (pres, 81-). **RESEARCH** Old Provencal morphology, phonology and syntax; troubadour poetry. **SELECTED PUBLICATIONS** Auth, On the Provenance of Spanish Blanco and Portuguese Branco, Romance Notes, Vol 0033, 92; Lexicon for Romance Linguistics, Vol 5, 2--Occitan and Catalan, Romance Philol, Vol 0047, 93; The Relative-Interrogative Pronoun in Old-French, Cahiers De Civilisation Medievale, Vol 0036, 93; On a Few Archaic Features in Duecento Tuscan, Romance Notes, Vol 0034, 94; Arbuteus and the Ty-Cluster in Romance, Romance Philology, Vol 0048, 94; Etymology, Engl Lang Notes, Vol 0034, 96. **CONTACT ADDRESS** Dept of French, Univ of Colo, Box 238, Boulder, CO, 80309-0238.

JENSEN, J. VERNON
PERSONAL Born 09/29/1922, Scandia, MN, m, 1954, 2 children **DISCIPLINE** SPEECH COMMUNICATION **EDUCATION** Augsburg Col, BA, 47; Univ Minn, MA, 48, PhD(speech, hist), 59. **CAREER** Instr speech & hist, Augsburg Col, 48-51; teaching asst hist, 51-53, instr commun, 53-59, from asst prof to assoc prof speech & commun, 59-67, dir, Commun Prog, 70-73, PROF SPEECH & COMMUN, UNIV MINN, MINNEAPOLIS, 67-, Fulbright lectr, State Training Col Teachers, Rangoon, Burma, 61-62. **MEMBERSHIPS** Speech Commun Asn; Am Asn Advan Humanities; Am Forensic Asn; Hist Sci Soc. **RESEARCH** Rhetorical criticism; British and Commonwealth public speaking; Thomas Henry Huxley as a communicator. **SELECTED PUBLICATIONS** Auth, Huxley, Thomas, Henry Address at the Opening of the Johns-Hopkins-University in September 1876, Notes and Records of the Royal Soc of London, Vol 0047, 93; Sir Raleigh, Walter Speech From the Scaffold--A Translation of the 1619 Dutch Ed, and Comparison With English Texts, Rhetorica-J Hist Rhetoric, Vol 0015, 97. **CONTACT ADDRESS** Dept of Speech Commun, Univ of Minn, Minneapolis, MN, 55455.

JENSEN, JOHN BARRY
PERSONAL Born 12/30/1943, Provo, UT, m, 1969, 4 children **DISCIPLINE** PORTUGUESE, LINGUISTICS **EDUCATION** Brigham Young Univ, BA, 65; Harvard Univ, AM, 68, PhD(Port & ling), 71. **CAREER** Vol educr, Peace Corps, Brazil, 65-67; asst prof Port, Univ Va, 70-78; ASSOC PROF MOD LANG, FLA INT UNIV, 78-, CHAIRPERSON, 80-, Nat Endowment for Humanities younger humanist fel, 74-75; vis lectr Span & Port, State Univ NY Albany, 77-78; Fulbright lectr, Columbia, 81. **MEMBERSHIPS** Am Asn Teachers Span & Port; Ling Soc Am; Am Coun Teaching Foreign Lang; Southeast Coun Ling; Asn Brasileira Ling. **RESEARCH** Portuguese and Brazilian sociolinguistics; Spanish linguistics; applied linguistics. **SELECTED PUBLICATIONS** Auth, Writing Portuguese Electronically--Spontaneous Spelling Reform, Hispania-J Devoted to the tchg Span and Port, Vol 0078, 95; Writing Portuguese Electronically--Spontaneous Spelling Reform, Hispania-J Devoted to the tchg Span and Port, Vol 0078, 95. **CONTACT ADDRESS** Dept of Mod Lang, Florida Intl Univ, 1 F I U South Campus, Miami, FL, 33199-0001.

JENSEN, JOHN T.
PERSONAL Born 06/23/1944, Philadelphia, PA, m, 1972 **DISCIPLINE** PHONOLOGY, ENGLISH LINGUISTICS **EDUCATION** Univ Pa, BA, 66; McGill Univ, PhD, 72. **CAREER** Mem fac, Univ Colo, Boulder, 73-76; MEM FAC, UNIV OTTAWA, 76-, NIH fel, Mass Inst Technol, 72-73; ed, Cahiers Linguistiques d'Ottawa, 76-82. **MEMBERSHIPS** Ling Soc Am; Can Ling Asn. **RESEARCH** Syntax; morphology. **SELECTED PUBLICATIONS** Auth, English Phonology--An Introduction, Can J Ling-Revue Canadienne De Linguistique, Vol 0039, 94. **CONTACT ADDRESS** Dept of Ling, Univ of Ottawa, Ottawa, ON, K1N 6N5.

JENSEN, THEODORE WAYNE
PERSONAL Born 08/31/1944, Sacramento, CA, 3 children **DISCIPLINE** HISPANIC LANGUAGES & LITERATURE **EDUCATION** Univ Mont, BA, 66, MA, 70; State Univ NY Buffalo, PhD(Hisp Lang & Lit) 76. **CAREER** Instr, State Univ NY Buffalo, 70-74; lectr, Canisius Col, 72-73; prof Span, Montana State Univ-Billings, 74-, Nat Endowment for Humanities fel, Duke Univ, Summer, 76; Am Coun Learned Soc res grant, 78. **HONORS AND AWARDS** Men of Achievement; Outstanding Young Men of America; National Directory of Latin Americanists; Billings Latino Club's Chris Rosas Award. **MEMBERSHIPS** Inst Int Lit Iberoamericana; Am Asn Teachers Span & Port. **RESEARCH** Spanish American modernismo; contemporary short fiction of Latin America; Spanish Theatre of the Golden Age; Board of Dir, Pacific Northwest Council For Languages; Assoc of Language Teachers. **SELECTED PUBLICATIONS** El pitagorismo en Las fuerzas extranas de Lugones, In: Fantasia y Realismo Magico en Iberoamerica, Mich State Univ, 75; Modernista Pythagorean literature: The symbolist inspiration, In: Waiting For Pegasus: Studies of the Presence of Symbolism and Decadence in Hispanic Letters, West Ill Univ, 79; The Phoenix and folly in Lope's La noche de San Juan, Forum for Mod Lang Studies, 80; Christian-Pythagorean dualism in Nervo's El donador de almas, Ky Romance Quart, 81; Ruben Dario's final profession of Pythagorean Faith, Latin Am Lit Rev, 82; Contexto Fantastico en el realismo de Omnibus, Revista Iberoamericana, 82; El jardin encantado y las vislumbres del oro: La disimulada fantasia apolinea en los primeros cuentos de Dario, Anales de literatura hispanoamericana, 92. **CONTACT ADDRESS** Dept of Foreign Lang & Lit, Montana State Univ, Billings, 1500 N 30th St, Billings, MT, 59101-0298. **EMAIL** fl_jensen@vixen.emcmt.edu

JEREZ FARRAN, CARLOS
DISCIPLINE SPANISH LITERATURE **EDUCATION** Univ Sheffield, BA, 80; Univ Mass, MA, 83, PhD, 87. **CAREER** Assoc prof. **RESEARCH** Peninsular Spanish literature of the 19th and 20th centuries. **SELECTED PUBLICATIONS** Auth, pubs on Garcia Lorca, Valle-Inclan, Delibes, Matute, and Martin-Santos. **CONTACT ADDRESS** Romance Languages and Literatures Dept, Univ of Notre Dame, Notre Dame, IN, 46556.

JEWERS, CAROLINE
DISCIPLINE COMPARATIVE MEDIEVAL LITERATURE **EDUCATION** Univ OR, PhD. **CAREER** Asst prof, Univ KS. **RESEARCH** Renaissance and critical theory. **SELECTED PUBLICATIONS** Auth, articles on women troubadours, medieval romance, and the poet Eustache Deschamps. **CONTACT ADDRESS** Dept of French and Italian, Univ Kansas, Admin Building, Lawrence, KS, 66045. **EMAIL** cjewers@falcon.cc.ukans.edu

JEWSBURY, GEORGE FREDERICK
PERSONAL Born 11/26/1941, Colchester, IL, m, 1964, 3 children **DISCIPLINE** RUSSIAN & EAST EUROPEAN HISTORY **EDUCATION** Mankato State Col, BA, 62; Univ Wash, MA, 65, PhD(hist), 70; Univ Bucharest, dipl Romanian studies, 68. **CAREER** From instr to asst prof, 67-76, ASSOC PROF HIST, OKLA STATE UNIV, 76-, Fulbright teaching fel, Univ Nancy, 71-72. **MEMBERSHIPS** Am Asn Advan Slavic Studies; Fulbright Alumni Asn; Am Asn southeastern Europ Studies. **RESEARCH** Russian activities in the Danubian principalities; Russia in the nineteenth century; French Emigres in Russia. **SELECTED PUBLICATIONS** Auth, Nicholas-I and the Russian Intervention in Hungary, Russ Hist, Vol 0020, 93; Russia Balkan Entanglements 1806-1914, Russ Hist, Vol 0020, 93; Revolution and Genocide--On the Origins of the Armenian Genocide and the Holocaust, Historian, Vol 0055, 93; Alexander-I, Int Hist Rev, Vol 0017, 95; Conflict and Chaos in Eastern-Europe, Amer Hist Rev, Vol 0101, 96; Culture and History in Eastern-Europe, Amer Hist Rev, Vol 0101, 96. **CONTACT ADDRESS** Dept of Hist, Oklahoma State Univ, Stillwater, OK, 74078.

JIMENEZ, FRANCISCO
PERSONAL Born 06/29/1943, Jalisco, Mexico, m, 1968, 3 children **DISCIPLINE** LATIN AMERICAN LITERATURE **EDUCATION** Santa Clara Univ, BA, 66; Columbia Univ, MA, 69, PhD(Latin Am lit), 72. **CAREER** Precepter Span & Port, Columbia Univ, 69-70, assoc, fall 70, instr 71-72, asst prof, spring 73; from Asst Prof to Prof, 73-86, Sanfilippo Prof Mod Lang & Lit, Santa Clara Univ, 86-, Chmn Dept, 97-, Dir Arts & Humanities, 81-, VPres Acad Affairs, 90-94; Mem, Western Asn Schs & Cols Accrediting Comn, 89-95; Mem, Bd Far West Labs for Educ Res and Develop, 88-91; consult & mem, WNET-TV Nat Adv Comt proj, 75-77; vchmn, Calif State Comn Teacher Prep & Lic, 76-77, chmn, 77-79; West Coast ed, Bilingual Rev. **HONORS AND AWARDS** Ariz Quart Ann Award, Univ Ariz, 73; Pres Special Recognition Award for Fac, 78; Mem, Bd Trustees, Santa Clara Univ, 81-87; Mem, Bd Trustees, Archbishop Mitty High Sch, 95-98; James Barnes Farmer Distinguished Guest Prof, Miami Univ, Ohio, 96-97; John and Patricia Beatty Award, Calif Libr Asn, for: The Circuit; Americas Award, for: The Circuit, 97; **MEMBERSHIPS** MLA; Am Asn Teachers Span & Port; Hispanic Inst US; Pac Coast Coun Latin Am Studies; Nat Chicano Counc Higher Educ. **RESEARCH** Mexican literature; Chicano literature; Latin American literature. **SELECTED PUBLICATIONS** Contribr, Encycl of World Literature in the 20th Century, Vol IV, Ungar, 75; coauth, Viva la Lengua?, 75 & Spanish Here and Now, 78, Harcourt; ed, Identification and Analysis of Chicano Literature, 78 & co-ed, Hispanics in the United States: An Anthology of Creative Literature, 80, Bilingual Press; Mosaico de la vida: Prosa chicana, cubana y puertorriqueña, Harcourt, 81; co-ed, Hispanics in the United States: An Anthology of Creative Literature, Vol II, Bilingual Press, 82; contribr, Dict of Mexican American History, Greenwood Press, 82; auth, Poverty and Social Justice, Bilingual Press, 87; The Circuit: Stories from the Life of a Migrant Child, Univ NMex Press, 97; La Mariposa, Houghton Mifflin, 98. **CONTACT ADDRESS** Dept of Mod Lang, Santa Clara Univ, 500 El Camino Real, Santa Clara, CA, 95053-0001. **EMAIL** fjimenez@mailer.scu.edu

JIN, XUEFEI
DISCIPLINE ENGLISH LANGUAGE AND LITERATURE **EDUCATION** Brandeis Univ, PhD, 93. **CAREER** Asst prof **RESEARCH** Creative writing; poetry. **SELECTED PUBLICATIONS** Auth, Between Silences; Facing Shadows; Oceans of Words. **CONTACT ADDRESS** English Dept, Emory Univ, 1380 Oxford Rd NE, Atlanta, GA, 30322-1950.

JOCHNOWITZ, GEORGE
PERSONAL Born 08/01/1937, Brooklyn, NY, m, 1962, 2 children **DISCIPLINE** LINGUISTICS, ROMANCE LANGUAGES **EDUCATION** Columbia Univ, AB, 58, MA, 60, PhD(ling), 67. **CAREER** Instr French & Ital, Temple Univ, 61-63; instr French, NY Univ, 63-65; lectr Romance lang, Queens Col, NY, 65-68; asst prof ling, 68-72, ASSOC PROF LING, COL STATEN ISLAND, CITY UNIV NEW YORK, 72-, Nat Sci Found grant, 68-69; vis lectr Yiddish, Yale Univ, 72-73. **MEMBERSHIPS** Ling Soc Am; MLA; Soc Ling Romane; Am Dialect Soc. **RESEARCH** French dialects; Judeo-Italian dialects. **SELECTED PUBLICATIONS** Auth, A Judeo-Italian Translation of the Book of Jonah, Romance Philol, Vol 0048, 95. **CONTACT ADDRESS** Col of Staten Island, CUNY, Staten Isl, NY, 10301.

JOFEN, JEAN
PERSONAL Born 11/13/1922, Vienna, Austria, m, 1944, 4 children **DISCIPLINE** GERMAN LITERATURE **EDUCATION** Brooklyn Col, BA, 43; Brown Univ, Ma, 45; Columbia Univ, PhD, 53; Yeshiva Univ, MS, 60, cert psychol, 62. **CAREER** Assoc prof Ger, Stern Col for Women, Yeshiva Univ, 53-60; chmn dept, 60-78, Prof Ger & Slavic Lang, Baruch Col, 60-, Chmn Dept Mod Lang, 77- . **HONORS AND AWARDS** Littaure res fel, 63-64; univ scholar spec fund, 65-66; univ res fel, 68; Am Asn Univ Women fel, 68-69; Ford Found grant, 70; Population Coun grant, 71-72; Nat Endowment for Humanities fel, 74., Organized first int cong The Marlowe Soc of Am, Sheffield, England, 83. **MEMBERSHIPS** MLA; Am Psychol Asn; Col Yiddish Asn; Marlowe Soc Am (pres, 75-); Am Asn Yiddish Prof (vpres). **RESEARCH** Yiddish linguistics and general philology; literature and psychology. **SELECTED PUBLICATIONS** Auth, Yiddish for Beginners, 55 & A Linguistics Atlas of Eastern European Yiddish, 60, Edwards Bros; A Freudian interpretation of Freud's Moses, Brit Ivrit Olamit, 74; The Yiddish idiom and proverb as mirror of Jewish cultural values Mosaic; Traces of the book of Esther in the works of Shakespeare, Studies Cult Life of Jews in England, Vol V, 75; Yiddish Literature for Beginners 75, coauth, Hebrew for Beginners, 76 & Chinese for Beginners, 77, Edwards Bros; Das letzte Geheimnis, Francke Verlag, Bern, 72; auth, The Jewish Mystic in Kafke; ed, Elizabethan COncordance Series, A concordance to the works of Christopher Marlow, The Shakespeare Apocrypha, 81; auht, The First American Attempt to Produce a Yiddish Language Atlas, in Language and Communication, Vol 18, 88; auth, Kafka and the Rebbe of Gur, in MJS Annual VII, 90. **CONTACT ADDRESS** 1684 52nd St, Brooklyn, NY, 11204.

JOHN, DAVID GETHIN
PERSONAL Born 03/24/1947, Wales, m, 1972, 3 children **DISCIPLINE** GERMAN LITERATURE & LANGUAGE **EDUCATION** Univ Toronto, BA, 67, MA, 70, PhD(Ger), 75. **CAREER** ASST PROF GER, UNIV WATERLOO, 74-. **MEMBERSHIPS** Can Asn Univ Teachers Ger; Can Soc 18th Century Studies; Am Soc 18th Century Studies; Lessing Soc; Deutsche Ges fur die Erforschung des 18 Jahreshundert. **RESEARCH** German theatre, especially 18th century; German language pedagogy. **SELECTED PUBLICATIONS** Auth, A New Ending for Goethe 'Stella', Goethe Jahrbuch, Vol 0111, 94; Biermann, Wolf, Seminar-J Ger Stud, Vol 0030, 94; A Concise History of German Literature to1900, Seminar-J Ger Stud, Vol 0030, 94; Koch, Heinrich, Gottfried, Research Lost and Found, Germanic Notes and Rev(S), Vol 0027, 96; Bibliogrphia Dramatica Et Dramaticorum-Annotated Bibliography of 18th-Century Dramas Published and Performed on Former German Imperial Territory Together With Their Adaptions, Translations, and Reception Up Until the Present Tim, Seminar-J Ge. **CONTACT ADDRESS** Dept of Ger, Univ of Waterloo, Waterloo, ON, N2L 3G1.

JOHN-STEINER, VERA P.
DISCIPLINE PSYCHOLINGUISTICS, COGNITIVE PSYCHOLOGY, BILINGUALISM **EDUCATION** Univ Chicago, PhD. **CAREER** Instr, Univ NMex. **RESEARCH** Productive and creative thinking; cross-cultural education. **SELECTED PUBLICATIONS** Auth, Cognitive pluralism in a sociocultural context, Mind, Cult and Activ: Int J, 2, 95; Women's collaborative interactions, in D I Slobin, J Gerhardt, A Kyratzis, & J Guo, eds, Social interaction, social context, and language: Essays in honor of Susan Ervin-Tripp, Lawrence Erlbaum Assoc, 96; Notebooks of the mind, 2nd ed, Oxford UP, 97; coauth, The implications of "First language acquisition as a guide for theories of learning and pedagogy" in a pluralistic world, Ling and Educ, 7, 95; Sociocultural approaches to learning and development: A Vygotskian framework, Educ Psychologist, 31, 96. **CONTACT ADDRESS** Univ NMex, Albuquerque, NM, 87131. **EMAIL** vygotsky@unm.edu

JOHNSON, ANITA L.
DISCIPLINE CONTEMPORARY SPANISH THEATER, POST CIVIL WAR SPANISH NOVEL **EDUCATION** BA, Carlow Col, 74; Middlebury Col, MA, 76; Univ WI-Madison, PhD, 88. **CAREER** Act dir, Vassar Wesleyan Colgate prog, Spain, 88-89, 95; ed, Esterno, 96-; assoc prof. **HONORS AND AWARDS** Grant,program for coop, Span Ministry Cult and Am Univ(s), 90; travel grant, Am Coun Learned Soc, 90. **SELECTED PUBLICATIONS** Publ, articles on Garcia Lorca, Domingos Miras, Alfonso Sastre, Concha Romero, the contemporary Span stage, Anales de La Lit Espanola Contemporanea, Gestos, Estreno, Critica Hisp, Confluencias. **CONTACT ADDRESS** Dept of Romance Lang, Colgate Univ, 13 Oak Drive, Hamilton, NY, 13346. **EMAIL** ajohnson@center.colgate.edu

JOHNSON, CARROLL B.
PERSONAL Born 01/09/1938, Los Angeles, CA **DISCIPLINE** SPANISH LITERATURE **EDUCATION** Univ Calif, Los Angeles, BA, 60, MA, 61; Harvard Univ, PhD(Romance lang), 66. **CAREER** Acting asst prof, 64-66, from asst prof to assoc prof, 66-75, vchmn dept, 72-75, chmn dept Span & Port, 75-81, PROF SPAN, UNIV CALIF, LOS ANGELES, 75-. **MEMBERSHIPS** MLA; Renaissance Soc Am; Cervantes Soc Am; Asn Int Hisp. **RESEARCH** Seventeenth century Spanish prose fiction; 16th century Spanish drama; literature and psychoanalysis. **SELECTED PUBLICATIONS** Auth, Molho, Maurice + Obituary, Hispania-J Devoted to the tchg Span and Port, Vol 0079, 96; Economies and Lineages in La 'Gitanilla' + The Contrast Between Gypsies and Aristocrats in the Cervantine Text, Mester, Vol 0025, 96; From One Subject to the Next--Social Criticism and Psychoanalysis, Mester, Vol 0026, 97. **CONTACT ADDRESS** Dept of Span & Port, Univ of Calif, Los Angeles, CA, 90024.

JOHNSON, DONALD BARTON
PERSONAL Born 06/15/1933, Indianapolis, IN, m, 1975 **DISCIPLINE** RUSSIAN LITERATURE **EDUCATION** Ind Univ, BA, 54; Univ Calif, Berkeley, MA, 58; Univ Calif, Los Angeles, PhD(Slavic ling), 66. **CAREER** Asst prof Russ & Slavic ling, Ohio State Univ, 65-66; asst prof, 66-72, assoc prof, 72-80, PROF RUSS & SLAVIC LING, UNIV CALIF, SANTA BARBARA, 80-, Consult, Rand Corp, 67-69; Inter-Univ Comt Travel Grants grant, Bulgaria & Russia, 68-69; prof & actg chmn dept Russ, Monash Univ, Australia, 75-76. **MEMBERSHIPS** Am Asn Teachers Slavic & E Europ Lang; Am Asn Advan Slavic Studies; Philol Asn Pac Coast; MLA. **RESEARCH** Literary structuralism; Nabokov; Russian modernism. **SELECTED PUBLICATIONS** Auth, Conversations in Exile--Russian Writers Abroad, Slavic and E Europ J, Vol 0037, 93; L 'Inconnue De La Seine' and the Naiads of Nabokov, Vladimir, Europe-Revue Litteraire Mensuelle, Vol 0073, 95; Madness, Death and Disease in the Fiction of Nabokov, Vladimir, Slavonic and E Europ Rev, Vol 0074, 96. **CONTACT ADDRESS** Dept of Ger & Russ, Univ of Calif, Santa Barbara, CA, 93106.

JOHNSON, JEANNE M.
DISCIPLINE SPEECH-LANGUAGE PATHOLOGY **EDUCATION** Western Wash State Col, Bellingham, BA, 73; Western Wash Univ, Bellingham, MA, 78; Southern Ill Univ at Carbondale, PhD, 86. **CAREER** Actg dept ch, Wash State Univ, 96 and 97-98; Assoc prof, Grad Fac, Dept Speech & Hearing Sci, Wash State Univ, 93-; Adj assoc prof, Dept Commun Disorders, Eastern Wash Univ, 95; Asst prof, Grad Fac, Dept Speech & Hearing Sci, Wash State Univ, 87-93. **HONORS AND AWARDS** William F. Mullen Excellence in Teaching Award, College of Liberal Arts, Wash State Univ, 95; Tenure and Promotion to Assoc Prof, 93; Phi Kappa Phi Honor Soc, 86-; App to Grad Fac, Wash State Univ, 89; Doc Fel Award, Southern Ill Univ, 85-86; Delta Kappa Gamma Honor Soc, 80-83. **MEMBERSHIPS** Amer Speech-Lange-Hearing Asn; Wash State Speech and Hearing Asn; National Coun for Exceptional Children; Int Soc for Infant Stud; Soc for Res in Child Develop. **RESEARCH** Language development of children with prenatal drug exposure, augmentative communication, communication of individuals with severe, multiple disabilities, parent-child interaction, american sign language development and conversation. **SELECTED PUBLICATIONS** Coauth, Standardized Test Performance of Children with a History of Prenatal Exposure to Multiple Drugs/Cocaine, J Commun Disorders 30, 97 & Augmenting Basic Communication in Natural Contexts, Baltimore: Paul H. Brookes, 96. **CONTACT ADDRESS** Dept of Speech and Hearing Sciences, Washington State Univ, 201 Daggy Hall, Pullman, WA, 99164-2420. **EMAIL** wsunis@wsu.edu

JOHNSON, JULIE GREER
PERSONAL Born 09/06/1945, Hartford, CT **DISCIPLINE** SPANISH AMERICAN LITERATURE **EDUCATION** Memphis State Univ, BA, 67; Ind Univ, MA, 70, PhD(Span lit), 75. **CAREER** From instr to asst prof Span, Univ NC, Asheville, 74-77; ASST PROF SPAN, UNIV GA, 77-. **MEMBERSHIPS** MLA; Am Asn Teachers Span & Port; Latin Am Studies Asn; SAtlantic Mod Lang Asn; Am Soc 18th Century Studies. **RESEARCH** Colonial Spanish American literature. **SELECTED PUBLICATIONS** Auth, Spanish Chronicles of the Indies, 16th-Century, Hispania-J Devoted to the tchg Span and Port, Vol 0078, 95; 'Alteraciones Del Dariel', An Epic Poem By Paramoycepeda, Juan, Francisco, Hispania-J Devoted to the tchg Span and Port, Vol 0078, 95; Word From New-Spain--The Spiritual Autobiography of Maria-De-San-Jose, Madre 1656-1719, Hispania-J Devoted to the tchg Span and Port, Vol 0078, 95; Spanish Chronicles of the Indies, 16th-Century, Hispania-J Devoted to the tchg Span and Port, Vol 0078, 95. **CONTACT ADDRESS** Dept Romance Lang, Univ of Ga, Athens, GA, 30602.

JOHNSON, KYLE B.
DISCIPLINE LINGUISTICS **EDUCATION** Univ Calif Irvine, BA, 81; Univ Mass, PhD, 85. **CAREER** Assoc prof. **RESEARCH** Syntactic theory; comparative Germanic data. **SELECTED PUBLICATIONS** Auth, When Verb Phrases Go Missing, 97; In Search of the Middle Field, 96; Object Positions, Nat Lang Ling Theory, 94; co-auth, On the Acquisition of Word Order in Nominals, 96; Lowering and Mid-Size Clauses, 97. **CONTACT ADDRESS** Linguistics Dept, Univ of Massachusetts, Amherst, S College 122, Amherst, MA, 01003. **EMAIL** kbj@linguist.umass.edu

JOHNSON, LEONARD WILKIE
PERSONAL Born 09/01/1931, Oakland, CA **DISCIPLINE** FOREIGN LANGUAGES **EDUCATION** Dartmouth Col, AB, 53; Harvard Univ, AM, 55, PhD(Romance lang & lit), 62. **CAREER** Acting instr French, 61-62, from instr to asst prof, 62-71, ASSOC PROF FRENCH, UNIV CALIF, BERKELEY, 71-, Asst dir, studies ctr, Univ Calif in Bordeaux, France, 63-65. **MEMBERSHIPS** MLA; Am Asn Teachers Fr; Renaissance Soc Am. **RESEARCH** Neo-Platonism in French literature, especially 16th and 17th centuries; emblem literature. **SELECTED PUBLICATIONS** Auth, Princes or Princes + France--15th-Century Politics and Poetry, Fr Rev, Vol 0068, 95. **CONTACT ADDRESS** Dept of French, Univ of Calif, 4125 Dwinelle Hall, Berkeley, CA, 94720-2581.

JOHNSON, MAYUMI YUKI
DISCIPLINE JAPANESE LINGUISTICS **EDUCATION** Univ MS, PhD. **CAREER** Lit, Univ Mich. **SELECTED PUBLICATIONS** Auth, Suggestopedia and Japanese Language Teaching, ICU JPN Educ Res Ctr Bull, 90, A Proposal: Classroom Activities Taking into Account Mood and Memory, Middlebury Confer Japanese Linguistics & Lang Tchng, 90; One Aspect of Japanese Modality: The Usage of 'So,' 'Yo,' and 'Rashii', ICU Lang Res Bull, 90. **CONTACT ADDRESS** Univ MI, 515 E. Jefferson St, Ann Arbor, MI, 48109-1316.

JOHNSTON, JOHN
DISCIPLINE ENGLISH LANGUAGE AND LITERATURE **EDUCATION** Columbia Univ, PhD, 84. **CAREER** Prof **RESEARCH** Modern fiction; British and American Poetry; critical theory. **SELECTED PUBLICATIONS** Auth, Carnival of Repetition; trans, On the Line; co-trans, In the Shadow of the Silent Majorities. **CONTACT ADDRESS** English Dept, Emory Univ, 1380 Oxford Rd NE, Atlanta, GA, 30322-1950.

JOHNSTON, OTTO WILLIAM
PERSONAL Born 02/26/1942, Staten Island, NY, m, 1966, 1 child **DISCIPLINE** GERMANIC LANGUAGES & LITERATURES, PHILOLOGY **EDUCATION** Wagner Col, BA, 63; Columbia Univ, MA, 66; Princeton Univ, PhD(Ger lang & lit), 69. **CAREER** Instr English & Ger, Berlitz Sch Lang, 61-62; Instr Ger, Columbia Univ, 63-64; PROF GER, UNIV FLA, 69-, Chmn Dept Ger & Slavic Lang & Lit, 79-, Alexander von Humboldt fel, 74 & 82; Exxon Impact grant, 78. **MEMBERSHIPS** MLA; Am Asn Teachers Ger; Am Coun Teachers Foreign Lang; S Atlantic Mod Lang Asn. **RESEARCH** Nineteenth century German literature; literary sociology; philology. **SELECTED PUBLICATIONS** Auth, Nestroy and the Critics, Colloquia Germanica, Vol 0029, 96; Narration as Natural Relationship--Die 'Wahlverwandschaften'--The Problem of the Portrayability of Nature and Society Since Goethe Plan for a So-Called Novel about the Universe, Ger Quart, Vol 0069, 96; Nestroy and the Critics, Colloquia Germanica, Vol 0029, 96. **CONTACT ADDRESS** Dept Ger & Slavic Lang & Lit, Univ of Fla, P O Box 117430, Gainesville, FL, 32611-7430.

JOHNSTON, PATRICIA ANN
PERSONAL Chicago, IL **DISCIPLINE** CLASSICAL LANGUAGES **EDUCATION** Univ Calif, Los Angeles, AB, 67; Univ Calif, Berkeley, MA, 72, PhD(classics), 75. **CAREER** Asst prof, 75-82, ASSOC PROF CLASSICS, BRANDEIS UNIV, 82-, Vis asst prof, Univ Southern Calif, 78-79. **MEMBERSHIPS** Am Philol Asn; Class Asn New England; Vergilian Soc. **RESEARCH** Latin language and literature; Greek language and literature. **SELECTED PUBLICATIONS** Auth, Love and Laserspicium in Catullus 7, Classical Philol, Vol 0088, 93; The Roman Theater and its Audience, Classical Philol, Vol 0088, 93. **CONTACT ADDRESS** Dept Class & Oriental Studies, Brandeis Univ, Waltham, MA, 02254.

JOHNSTON, STANLEY HOWARD
PERSONAL Born 04/28/1946, Cleveland, OH, m, 1976 **DISCIPLINE** ENGLISH LANGUAGE AND LITERATURE: ARCHIVES AND ACADEMIC LIBRARIES FOR THE LI **EDU-**

CATION BA, Columbia Univ, 68; MA, 70, PhD, 77, Univ Western Ontario; MSLS Case Western Reserve Univ, 79. **CAREER** Tchg Asst, Dept English, Univ Western Ontario, 71-72; Asst ed, Spenser Newsletter, Univ Western Ontario, 84-90; Bibliog The Cleveland Herbals Proj Hist Div Cleveland Hea Sci Library, 90-; Cur of Rare Books, the Holden Arboretum. **HONORS AND AWARDS** Phi Beta Mu. **MEMBERSHIPS** The Bibilo Soc, Bibilo Soc Of Am, Council on Bot and Horticulture Libraries, Am Library Assoc(Rare Gooks and Manuscript Div), Soc for the Hist of Natural Hist. **RESEARCH** Analytical and Descritptive Biblio; Book and Printing Hist, Bot and Horticultural Hist; Medical Hist; Hist of Bot Illus. **SELECTED PUBLICATIONS** A Study of the Career and Literary Publications of Richard Pynson, Dissertation, UWO 1977; The Cleveland Herbal, Botanical and Horticultural Collections, Kent State Univ Press, 92; Cleveland's Treasures of Botanical Literature, Orange Frazer Press, 98; Inter column in CBHL Newsletter, 95. **CONTACT ADDRESS** Holden Arboretum, 9500 Sperry Rd, Mentor, OH, 44060. **EMAIL** stanley177@aol.com

JONAS, KLAUS WERNER
PERSONAL Born 06/22/1920, Stettin, Germany, m, 1945 **DISCIPLINE** GERMAN LANGUAGE & LITERATURE **EDUCATION** Rutgers Univ, MLS, 55; Univ Munster, PhD, 55. **CAREER** Instr Ger, Douglass Col, Rutgers Univ, 50-55; librn Ger lit, Yale Univ Libr, 55-57; from asst prof to assoc prof, 57-65, chmn dept, 59-61, PROF GER, UNIV PITTSBURGH, 65-, MLA res grants, 56 & 60; Caroline Newton grant, Yale Univ, 57; Am Coun Learned Soc res grant, 58; cur Thomas Mann Arch, Deut Akad Wiss Berlin, 60-; Bollingen Found res grants, 61 & 63; Charles E Merrill Found fac fel, 63; Ford Found fels, 66 & 67; Guggenheim Mem Found fel, 73-74. **MEMBERSHIPS** MLA; Rilke Soc; Am Asn Teachers Ger; Bibliog Soc Am; Int Ver Ger Sprach-u Literaturwiss. **RESEARCH** Modern German literature and culture; bibliography; Anglo-German literary relations. **SELECTED PUBLICATIONS** Auth, Universitatsbibliothek-Dusseldorf--Catalog of the Mann, Thomas Collection, J Engl and Ger Philol, Vol 0092, 93; Universitatsbibliothek-Dusseldorf--Catalog of the Mann,Thomas Collection, J Engl and Gerc Philol, Vol 0092, 93; Universitatsbibliothek-Dusseldorf--Catalog of the Thomas-Mann-Collection, Colloquia Germanica, Vol 0026, 93; Mann, Thomas Bibliography--The Works, J Engl and Ger Philol, Vol 0094, 95; German-Language Exile Literature Since 1933, Vol 4, US Bibliographies--Writers, Publishers and Literary Scholars, J Engl and Ger Philol, Vol 0095, 96. **CONTACT ADDRESS** Dept of Ger Lang & Lit, Univ of Pittsburgh, Pittsburgh, PA, 15260.

JONASSAINT, JEAN
DISCIPLINE FRENCH **EDUCATION** Universite du Quebec a Montreal, BA, 77, MA, 81, PhD, 90 **CAREER** Sr lectr, Universite du Quebec a Montreal, 79-96; asst prof to Andrew W. mellow asst prof, Duke Univ, 96- . **HONORS AND AWARDS** Andrew W. Mellow Asst prof; Etudes ethniques canadiennes, ministere du Patrimoine canadien, res grant; Fonds FCAC, PhD grant; Canada Arts Coun/Explorations res grant. **MEMBERSHIPS** Amer Comparative Lit Assoc; Consiel int d' etudes francophones; Modern Lang Assoc of Amer; S Atlantic Modern Lang Assoc of Amer. **RESEARCH** Francophone lit; theory & hist of lit; comparative lit; postnational lit & lit prod in immigration, creative writing & publ. **SELECTED PUBLICATIONS** Auth, Migration et etudes litteraires, J of Canadian Stud, 96; Des recits haitiens au Quebec, Neue Romania, 97; Le Nomade enracine, in Rene Depestre, Le Metier a metisser, Paris, Stock, 98; Haitian Literary Production in the United States, 1948-1986, in American Literatures and Languages, Harvard Engl Stud, 99; Les Romans de tradition haitienne: des recits tragiques, 99. **CONTACT ADDRESS** Dept of Romance Stud, Duke Univ, Box 90257, Durham, NC, 27708.

JONES, CHRISTOPHER M.
DISCIPLINE FRENCH **EDUCATION** Univ Mass, PhD. **CAREER** Languages, Carnegie Mellon Univ. **HONORS AND AWARDS** Dir, Lang Learning Resource Ctr. **SELECTED PUBLICATIONS** Auth, Portes Ouvertes: an interactive multimedia approach to first-year French; Coauth, Fort Worth: Holt Rinehart and Winston, 97. Language-related Technology: Notes from Carnegie Mellon, Pa Lang Forum, 96; The Oral Language Archive: A Digital Audio Database for Foreign Language Study, CALL Journal, 96; The passe-blanc: Boris Vian and the New French Literary Establishment, Cincinnati Romance Rev,94. **CONTACT ADDRESS** Carnegie Mellon Univ, 5000 Forbes Ave, Pittsburgh, PA, 15213.

JONES, LARRY BERT
PERSONAL Born 11/11/1953, Kansas City, MO, m, 1977, 1 child **DISCIPLINE** LINGUISTICS **EDUCATION** Brown Univ, AB, 76; Univ Tex, Arlington, MA, 78, PhD(ling), 80. **CAREER** TRANSL & CONSULT, SUMMER INST LING, INDONESIA BR, 77-, Vis consult, Summer Inst Ling, Mex Br, 77; vis consult & lectr, Summer Inst Ling, Philippine Br, 81-82; vis lectr, Nat Ctr Indonesian Lang, Jakarta Indonesia, 82. **MEMBERSHIPS** Ling Asn Can & US. **RESEARCH** Prag and the context of speech as it relates to linguistic and translation theory; Papuan languages; discourse analysis. **SELECTED PUBLICATIONS** Coauth, Levels of significant information in discourse, Mid-Am Linquistics Conf Okla, Univ Okla, 79; A discourse particle in Cajonos Zapotec & Multiple levels of information in discourse, in: Discourse Studies in Mesoamerican Languages, Summer Inst Lings, summer 79; auth, Pragmatic information in the fourth Gospel, Summer Inst Ling, Dallas, 79; Pragmatic influences on English written discourse, in: The Sixth Lacus Forum 1979, Hornbeam Press, 80; Pragmatic Aspect of English Text Sucture, Summer Inst Ling, 82; coauth, Verb morphology and discourse structure in Mesoamerican languages, in: Paper in Text Ling, Buske Press, 82. **CONTACT ADDRESS** 1009 J St, La Porte, IN, 46350.

JONES, MARGARET E.W.
PERSONAL Born 02/04/1938, New York, NY, m, 1964 **DISCIPLINE** SPANISH **EDUCATION** State Univ NY Albany, BA, 59; Univ Wis, MA, 61, PhD(contemp Span), 63. **CAREER** Asst prof Span, Salem Col, 63-64; from asst prof to assoc prof, NC Col Durham, 64-67; from asst prof to assoc prof, 67-75, assoc dean grad sch, 77-79, PROF SPAN, UNIV KY, 75-. **MEMBERSHIPS** Am Asn Univ Women; Women's Caucus Mod Lang; MLA; Am Asn Teachers Span & Port. **RESEARCH** Modern and contemporary Spanish literature. **SELECTED PUBLICATIONS** Auth, Literature, the Arts, and Democracy--Spain in the 80s, Revista De Estudios Hispanicos, Vol 0026, 92; 'Atila', Hispania-J Devoted to the tchg Span and Port, Vol 0076, 93; El 'Hilo De Seda', Hispania-J Devoted to the tchg Span and Port, Vol 0076, 93; Voices of Their Own, Contemporary Spanish Narrative By Women, Bull Hisp Stud, Vol 0072, 95. **CONTACT ADDRESS** Dept of Span, Univ of Ky, 500 S Limestone St, Lexington, KY, 40506-0003.

JONES, NICHOLAS FRANCIS
PERSONAL Born 08/22/1946, Lynwood, CA, m, 1971, 2 children **DISCIPLINE** ANCIENT HISTORY, CLASSICAL PHILOLOGY **EDUCATION** Univ Southern Calif, BA, 68; Univ Calif, Berkeley, MA, 72, PhD(classics), 75. **CAREER** Instr, 75-76, asst prof 76-81, assoc, 82-97, PROF CLASSICS, UNIV PITTSBURGH, 97-, Am Coun Learned Soc res fel hist, 78-79. **MEMBERSHIPS** Am Philol Asn; Archaeol Inst Am; Asn Ancient Historians. **RESEARCH** Greek and Roman hist; classical philol. **SELECTED PUBLICATIONS** Auth, Public Organization in Ancient Greece, Am Philos Soc, 87; auth, Ancient Greece: State and Society, Prentice Hall, 97; auth, The Associations of Classical Athens. The Response to Democracy, Oxford Univ Press, 99. **CONTACT ADDRESS** Dept of Classics, Univ Pittsburgh, 1518 CL, Pittsburgh, PA, 15260-0001. **EMAIL** NFJ2+@Pitt.edu

JONES, RANDALL LEE
PERSONAL Born 02/21/1939, Cedar City, UT, m, 1962, 5 children **DISCIPLINE** LINGUISTICS, GERMANIC LANGUAGES **EDUCATION** Brigham Young Univ, BA, 63, MA, 65; Princeton Univ, MA, 66, PhD, 70. **CAREER** Asst prof ling, Cornell Univ, 68-72; ling consult, Cent Intel Agency Lang Sch, 72-74; asst prof ling, Cornell Univ, 74-78; assoc prof, 78-82, prof Ger, 82-, dean, Coll of Hum, Brigham Young Univ, 91-97; **MEMBERSHIPS** Ling Soc Am; MLA; Assn Comput Ling; Am Assn Teachers Ger; Am Coun Teaching Foreign Lang. **RESEARCH** German syntax; language testing. **SELECTED PUBLICATIONS** Art, TICCIT and CLIPS: The Early Years, 84-97, Thirty Yars of Computer Assisted Language Instruction, Festschrift for John R. Russell, CALICO Monograph Series 3, Durham, NC: CALICO, 95. **CONTACT ADDRESS** Dept of German, Brigham Young Univ, 3078 Jkhb, Provo, UT, 84602-0002. **EMAIL** randall_jones@byu.edu3

JONES, ROBERT ALSTON
PERSONAL Born 10/10/1938, Charleston, SC, m, 1961, 3 children **DISCIPLINE** MODERN GERMAN LITERATURE **EDUCATION** Duke Univ, AB, 60; Univ Tex, MA, 62, PhD(Ger), 66. **CAREER** Asst Prof Ger, Tufts Univ, 65-66; from Asst Prof to Assoc Prof, 66-98, Prof Ger, Univ Wis, Milwaukee, 98-; Assoc Dean for Research, Grad Sch, 90. **HONORS AND AWARDS** Alexander von Humbolt Found res fel, Ger, 77-78; DAAD, Univ of Turbingen, 62-63. **MEMBERSHIPS** Brecht Soc; Am Asn Teachers Ger; Kafka Soc; MLA. **RESEARCH** Elementary language instruction; German literature, especially of the modern period; modern German drama. **SELECTED PUBLICATIONS** Auth, Art and Entertainment: Jenian Literature and the Circus, 1890-1933, 85; coauth, Frank Wedekcud: A Bibliographic Handbook, 96. **CONTACT ADDRESS** Dept of Ger, Univ of Wis, PO Box 413, Milwaukee, WI, 53201-0413. **EMAIL** rajones@uwm.edu

JONES, TOBIN H.
PERSONAL Born 04/13/1939, Minneapolis, MN, m, 1962 **DISCIPLINE** FRENCH LITERATURE **EDUCATION** Univ Minn, Minneapolis, BA, 62, MA, 65, PhD(French), 69. **CAREER** Assoc prof. **RESEARCH** Development of the French novel; contemporary poetry; literary theory and criticism; French cultural studies. **SELECTED PUBLICATIONS** Auth, pubs on French novels and the aesthetics of narrative fiction of the eighteenth, nineteenth, and twentieth centuries. **CONTACT ADDRESS** Foreign Languages and Literature Dept, Colorado State Univ, Fort Collins, CO, 80523. **EMAIL** thjones@vines.colostate.edu

JONES, WARD
DISCIPLINE CLASSICAL STUDIES **EDUCATION** Univ Richmond, BA, 52; Univ NC at Chapel Hill, MA, 57, PhD, 59. **CAREER** Instr, Ohio State Univ, 59-61; assoc prof, 61-67; prof, 67- & Chancellor prof, 68-, Col William and Mary; vis assoc prof, Tufts Univ in Naples, Italy, 65-66 & Univ NC, 66. **HONORS AND AWARDS** Ovatio awd, Class Asn Mid W and S, New Orleans, 88; Listed in Whols Who in Am, 85-; VP, 65-66 & pres, 66-67, Class Asn Va; sec-treas, 66-68 & pres, 80-82, Class Asn Mid W and S, Southern Sect; exec comt, Class Asn Mid W and S, 79-82; mng ed, Class J, 70-80; nominating comt, Class Asn Mid W and S; dir, 70-, VP, 78-80 & pres, 80-, Mediter Soc Am; VP, 86-88 & Marshal, 90-92, Alpha Chap of Phi Beta Kappa & pres, Alpha Delta Gamma, Hon Medieval and Renaissance Fraternity, 94-95; fel Inst Advanced Study in Arts and Humanities, Univ Minn, 67 - $300,00; fel Southeastern Inst Medieval and Renaissance Stud, Duke Univ & Univ NC, 66 - $600,00; 67 -600,00; 68 - $600.00 & 69-70 - $14,000,00; fac res assignments, William and Mary, 78 & 92-93. **RESEARCH** Vergil; Legend of the Sack of Troy; early history of the College of William and Mary. **SELECTED PUBLICATIONS** Auth, A New Latin Quitrent Poem of the College of William & Mary, Va Mag Hist and Biog, vol 96, 88; The So-Called Silvestris Commentary on the Aeneid and Two Other Interpretations, Speculum, 89 & A Latin Munusculum among the Papers of Francis Nicholson, Bodleian Libr Record, 93; coauth, The Commentary on the First Six Books of the Aeneid of Vergil Commonly Attributed to Bernardus Silvestris, Univ Nebr Press, 77 & An Aeneid Commentary of Mixed Type: the Glosses in MSS Harley 4946 and Ambrosianus Glll inf, The Pontifical Inst Mediaeval Stud, Toronto, 96; co-ed, Solomon Henning's Chronicle of Courland and Livonia, Baltic Stud Ctr, Madison, 92; rev, Schreiber and Maresca, Commentary on the First Six Books of Vergilis Aeneid by Bernardus Silvestris, in Vergilius, 80. **CONTACT ADDRESS** Dept of Classical Studies, Col of William and Mary, Morton Hall, Williamsburg, VA, 23187-8795. **EMAIL** jwjone@facstaff.wm.edu

JORDAN, GREGORY D.
PERSONAL Born 12/09/1951, Jackson, MS, m, 1973, 3 children **DISCIPLINE** HEBRAIC, COGNATE STUDIES **EDUCATION** Belhaven Col, BA, 73; Trinity Evangel Div Sch, MA, 77; Hebrew Union Col-Jewish Inst of Relig, PhD, 86. **CAREER** Chr, 84-89, Bible & Relig Dept, King Col; mem, Bd of dir, 85-87, Inst of Holy Land Stud; Chr of the Hum div, 87-89, v pres, acad affairs/dean Fac, 90-97, actng dean, Admis, 96-97, provost & actng pres, 96-97, pres, 97-, King Col. **HONORS AND AWARDS** Paul Harris Award, Bristol Rotary Club; Erna and Julius Krouch Scholar, Hebrew Union Col; Joseph and Helen Regenstein Fel, Hebrew Union Col; S H Scheur Fel, Hebrew Union Col; Isle Hitchman Fel, Hebrew Union Col; Tchng Award, King Col. **MEMBERSHIPS** Soc of Bibl Lit; Am Soc of Oriental Res; Inst for Bibl Res. **RESEARCH** Near Eastern history. **CONTACT ADDRESS** President, King Col, 1350 King College Rd, Bristol, TN, 37620-2699. **EMAIL** gdjordan@king.edu

JORGENSEN, BETH E.
PERSONAL Born 10/11/1953, Staten Island, NY, m, 1975, 2 children **DISCIPLINE** SPANISH **EDUCATION** Oberlin Col, BA, 75; Univ Wisc - Madison, MA, 78, PhD, 86. **CAREER** Lectr, 82-83, Univ Wisc - Madison; asst prof, 86-93, assoc prof, 93-, chmn, dept of Modern Lang & Cult, 94-98, assoc prof, 98-, Univ Rochester. **CONTACT ADDRESS** Modern Languages & Cultures, Univ of Rochester, PO Box 270082, Rochester, NY, 14627. **EMAIL** bjgn@uhurn.cc.rochester.edu

JORGENSEN, PETER ALVIN
PERSONAL Born 07/31/1941, Jersey City, NJ, m, 1970, 2 children **DISCIPLINE** GERMANIC PHILOLOGY, GERMAN **EDUCATION** Princeton Univ, AB, 63; Harvard Univ, MA, 71, PhD(Ger philol), 72. **CAREER** Asst prof Ger philol, Univ Calif, Riverside, 71-76; ASSOC PROF GER PHILOL, UNIV GA, 76-. **MEMBERSHIPS** Soc Advan Scand Stuides; MLA; Mediaeval Acad Am; Medieval Asn Pac Coast; SAtlantic Mod Lang Asn. **RESEARCH** Old Norse manuscripts and paleography; saga forgeries; Old English and Old Norse folklore. **SELECTED PUBLICATIONS** Auth, Ten Icelandic exempla and their Middle English Source, Opuscula, 70; The Icelandic translations from Middle English, in: Studies for Einar Haugen, Mouton, the Hague, 72; Four Aeventyri, Opuscula, 75; The two-troll variant of the Bear's Son folktale in Halfdanar Saga Bronufostra and Grims Saga Lodinkinna, Arv, J Scand Folklore, 75; Hafgeirs Saga Flateyings: An eighteenth-century forgery, J English & Ger Philol, 77; St Julian and Basilissa in Medieval Iceland, Jakob Benediktsson Festschrift, 77; Beowulf's Swimming Contest with Breca: Old Norse Parallels, Folklore, 78; The gift of the useless weapon in Beowulf and the Icelandic sagas, Arkiv Nordisk Filol, 79; Thiostolfs Saga Hamramma: The case for forgery, Gripla, 79. **CONTACT ADDRESS** Dept of Ger & Salvic Lang, Univ of Ga, Athens, GA, 30602.

JOSEPH, BRIAN DANIEL
PERSONAL Born 11/22/1951, New York, NY, m, 1975, 1 child **DISCIPLINE** LINGUISTICS, INDO-EUROPEAN STUDIES **EDUCATION** Yale Univ, AB, 73; Harvard Univ,

AM, 76, PhD(ling), 78. **CAREER** Lectr, Univ Alta, 78-79; ASST PROF LING, OHIO STATE UNIV, 79. Izaak Walton Killam fel, Univ Alta, 78-79. **MEMBERSHIPS** Ling Soc Am; Can Ling Asn; Mod Greek Studies Asn; Am Asn Teachers Slavic & East Europ Lang; Am Asn Southeast Europ Studies. **RESEARCH** Indo-European linguistics; relational grammar and the syntax of Modern Greek; Balkan linguistics. **SELECTED PUBLICATIONS** Auth, The Morphosyntax of the Modern Greek Verb as Morphology and Not Syntax--Discussion, Ling Inquiry, Vol 0024, 93; Compendium of the Worlds Languages, Vol 1, Abaza to Lusatian, Vol 2, Maasai toZuni, Modern Lang J, Vol 0078, 94. **CONTACT ADDRESS** Dept Ling, Ohio State Univ, Columbus, OH, 43210.

JOSEPHS, ALLEN
PERSONAL Born 11/20/1942, Charlotte, NC, 3 children **DISCIPLINE** MODERN SPANISH LITERATURE, MODERN LITERATURES **EDUCATION** Univ NC, Chapel Hill, BA, 65; NY Univ, MA, 66; Rutgers Univ, PhD(Span), 73. **CAREER** Asst prof, 69-76, assoc prof, 76-79, PROF SPAN, UNIV W FLA, 79-, Consult, Westinghouse Elec Corp, Spain, 74-75; Nat Endowment for Arts fel, 79-80. **MEMBERSHIPS** MLA; SAtlantic Mod Lang Asn; Am Asn Teachers Span & Port. **RESEARCH** The work of Federico Garcia Lorca; Spanish culture and civilization; Hemingway and other writers on Spain. **SELECTED PUBLICATIONS** Auth, The Face in the Mirror--Hemingway Writers, Amer Lit, Vol 0067, 95. **CONTACT ADDRESS** Dept Foreign Lang, Univ W Fla, Pensacola, FL, 32514.

JOSEPHS, HERBERT
PERSONAL Born 11/11/1932, New York, NY, m, 1958, 1 child **DISCIPLINE** ROMANCE LANGUAGES **EDUCATION** Brooklyn Col, BA, 53; Fordham Univ, MA, 57; Princeton Univ, MA, 59, PhD, 63. **CAREER** Asst instr, Princeton Univ, 57-59; Instr French, Amherst Col, 60-62; from instr to assoc prof, 62-72, PROF FRENCH LIT, 72- , Mich State Univ, 72-, Nat Endowment for Humanities, summer grant, 75 & 81; Am Coun Learned Soc grant-in-aid, 76; Mich State Univ Found Res Grant, 81, 84, 86; Mich Coun Hum Bicentennial Celebration Fr Revolution. **HONORS AND AWARDS** Paul Varg Award Tchg & Scholar: Col Arts & Lett, Mich State Univ, 90; Mich Prof Yr-CASE Award, 93; Apollo Award, 95. **MEMBERSHIPS** AAUP; Am Soc 18th Century Studies; MLA. **RESEARCH** Literature of the French Enlightenment; Denis Diderot; French novel of the Enlightenment. **SELECTED PUBLICATIONS** Auth, Manon Lescaut: A rhetoric of intellectual evasion, Romanic Rev, 10/68; Le Neveu de Rameau: Diderot's Dialogue of Language and Gesture, Ohio State Univ, 69; Metaphor and discovery in Diderot's Lettre sur les Sourds et Muets, Ky Romance Quart, Vol XX, No 2; La Religieuse: The dark cave of the Libertine soul, Mod Lang Notes, 76; The Marquis de Sade and women: Exorcising the awe of the sacred, Studies in Burke & His Time, 77; Diderot's Eloge de Richardson: A Paradox on Praising, In: Essays on the Age of Enlightment in Honor of Ira 0 Wade, Droz, 77; At the frontiers of the real: Forms and shadows of Diderot's narrative art, Forum, XVI, 78; Le paysan parvenu: Satire and the fiction of innocence, Fr Forum, Vol V, 80; ed Diderot, Digression and Disperion: A Bicentennial Tribute, Fr Forum Publ, 84; Diderot and teh Dramatization of Philosophical Thought, Skill and Education: Reflection and Experience, Springer-Verlag, 92; Une Guerre a l'Opera, De la Litterature Francaise, Bordas, 93; rev Crisis beneath the Tears: Identitiy and Ideology: Diderot, Sade and the Serious Genre, EMF: Stud in Early Fr, Signs of the Early Modern, 96; Manon, Marguerite, Violetta: On Angelism in Literature and Opera Ars Lyrica, 97. **CONTACT ADDRESS** Dept of Romance & Class Lang, Michigan State Univ, 161 Old Horticulture, East Lansing, MI, 48824-1112. **EMAIL** josephsh@pilot.msu.edu

JOST, DOMINIK
PERSONAL Born 07/26/1922, Lucerne, Switzerland, m, 1953 **DISCIPLINE** GERMAN LITERATURE **EDUCATION** Univ Fribourg, PhD(Ger lit), 46. **CAREER** Prof Ger lang & lit, Kantonssch St Gallen, Switz, 53-67; assoc prof Ger lit, Univ Rochester, 67-69; PROF GER LANG & LIT, ST GALLEN COL ECON & SOC SCI, 70-, Vis prof, McGill Univ, 69-70; mem bd, Erasmus, Int Bull Comtemp Scholar, 72-. **MEMBERSHIPS** Akademische Ges Schweizerischer Germanisten; Asn Suisse Litt Gen St Comp. **RESEARCH** Ludwig Derleth, 1870-1948; German literature since 1890; Goethe. **SELECTED PUBLICATIONS** Auth, Stefan George und seine Elite, Speer, Zurich, 49; Ludwig Derleth, Kohlhammer, Stuttgart, 65; Literarischer Jugendstil, Metzler, Stuttgart, 69 & 80; ed, Ludwig Derleth: Das Werk (6 vols), Hinder & Deelmann, Behhnhausen/Gladenbach, 71-72; auth, Henry D Thoreau in Switzerland, in: Thoreau Abroad, Shoe String, 71; Deutsche Klassi: Goethes Romische Elegien, Verlag Dokumentation, Munich, 74 & 78; Die Dichtung Ludwig Derleths Einfuhrung in Das Werk, Hinder & Deelmann, Bellnhausen, 75; Die Wirklichkeit des Dichters, Ed Interfrom, Zurich, 77. **CONTACT ADDRESS** Schneebergstr 27 9000 St, Gallen, ..

JOUBERT, ANDRE
PERSONAL Born 07/01/1924, Lyon, France **DISCIPLINE** FRENCH **EDUCATION** Sorbonne, Lic, 46, dipl, 47, cert, 56. **CAREER** Lectr, French-German Inst, Ludwigsburg, 56-57, Tech Univ, Hannover, 58; lects, 58-59, from asst profto assoc prof, 59-72, PROF FRENCH, UNIV MAN, 72-. **RESEARCH** Contemporary French novel; literary criticism in France; philosophy of time. **SELECTED PUBLICATIONS** Auth, Colette et Cheri, Ed Nizet, Paris, 72. **CONTACT ADDRESS** Dept of French, Univ of Man, Winnipeg, MB, R3T 2N2.

JOYCE, DOUGALS A.
PERSONAL Born 07/20/1922, Carbonear, NF, Canada, m, 1960 **DISCIPLINE** GERMANIC LANGUAGES **EDUCATION** McGill Univ, BA, 43; Harvard Univ, AM, 44, PhD, 52. **CAREER** Lectr, Ger, 50-54, from asst prof to assoc prof, 54-67, PROF GER & HEAD DEPT, TRINITY COL, UNIV TORONTO, 67-, Founding mem & asst ed, Seminar: J Ger Studies, 64-; Can Coun grant, 73-74. **MEMBERSHIPS** MLA; Asn Can Univ Teachers Ger (secy, 60-62); Hofmannsthal Soc. **RESEARCH** Literary criticism of the post-romantic period in Germany; German drama of the nineteenth century; Hugo von Hofmannsthal. **SELECTED PUBLICATIONS** Auth, Hofmannsthal, Hugo, Von--Poets and the Language of Life, Seminar-J Ger Stud, Vol 0030, 94. **CONTACT ADDRESS** Dept of Ger Trinity Col, Univ of Toronto, Toronto, ON, M5S 1H8.

JUFFS, ALAN
PERSONAL Born 09/28/1959, London, England **DISCIPLINE** LINGUISTICS **EDUCATION** Univ London, UK, BA (Combined honors in French and German), 82; Univ Durham, UK, MA, (Applied Linguistics), 85; McGill Univ, Montreal, PhD (Linguistics), 94. **CAREER** Lect, Hunan Agricultural Col, Hunan, P R of China, 82-84; asst prof, Int Univ of Japan, Grad School of Int Relations, 85-89; asst prof, 93-98, assoc prof, Dept of Linguistics, Univ of Pittsburgh, 98-. **MEMBERSHIPS** Am Asn of Applied Ling; Ling Soc of Am. **RESEARCH** Second lang acquistition; lang processing; semantics; syntax; lang pedagogy. **SELECTED PUBLICATIONS** Auth, An Introduction to Communicative Methodology in English Teaching, Hunan Provincial Service Foreign Languages Asn, 84; Learnability and the Lexicon: Theories and Second Language Acquisition Research (Language Acquisition and Language Disorders, vol 12), John Benjamins, 96; Garden Paths and Error Data in Second Language Sentence Processing, with Michael Harrington, Language Learning, 46, 96; Parameters in the Lexicon, Language Variation, and Language Development, in A Stringfellow, D Cahana-Amitay, E Hughes, & A Zukowski, eds, Proceedings of the 20th Annual Boston Univ Conference on Language Development, vol 1, Cascadilla Press, 96; Semantics-Syntax Correspondences in Second Language Aquisition, Second Language Res, 12, 96; Constraints on Wh-Movement in Two Different Contexts of Non-Native Language Acquisition: Competence and Processing, with Lydia White, in S Flynn, G Martohardjono, & W O'Neill, eds, The Generative Study of Second Language Acquisition, Lawrence Erlbaum Assocs, 97; Individual Processing Performance in Second Language Acquisition Research, Second Lang Res, 14, 98; The Acquisition of Semantics-Syntax Correspondences and Verb Frequencies in ESL Materials, Language Teaching Res, 2, 98; Main Verb vs Reduced Relative Clause Ambiguity Resolution in Second Language Sentence Processing, Lang Learning, 48, 98; numerous other articles. **CONTACT ADDRESS** Dept of Linguistics, Univ of Pittsburgh, 2816 CL, Pittsburgh, PA, 15260. **EMAIL** juff+@pitt.edu

JULIEN, HELENE
DISCIPLINE 20TH CENTURY FRENCH LITERATURE **EDUCATION** Ecole Normale Superieure, DEA., Maitrise Universite de Paris IV-Sorbonne; Princeton Univ, MA, PhD. **CAREER** Asst prof, Colgate Univ. **HONORS AND AWARDS** Intl travel and res grant, AR State Univ, 94; McMahon grant, Princeton Univ, 91; grant, Fulton-McMahon Fund, 89; Armstrong fel, Princeton Univ, 88-92; French government scholar, Ecole Normale Superieure, 84-89, Nominated, prof yr award, AR State Univ, 96. **SELECTED PUBLICATIONS** Auth, L'Orphee meurtrier des Cahiers: regard sur la poetique de Valery, Bulletin des Etudes Valeryennes; Catherine Pozzi, Feminist Companion to Fr Lit; Les Cahiers de Valery 1920-1928: problemes de genre et de statut, Rocky Mountain Rev; 1920: une annee de reflexion poetique dans les Cahiers, Paul Valery: Vers anciens et poietique des Cahiers. **CONTACT ADDRESS** Dept of Romance Lang, Colgate Univ, 13 Oak Drive, Hamilton, NY, 13346.

JUN, SUN-AH
PERSONAL Born 11/06/1958, South Korea, m, 1986, 1 child **DISCIPLINE** LINGUISTICS **EDUCATION** Oh State Univ, PhD, 93. **CAREER** Asst prof, dept of ling, Univ Calif Los Angeles, 93-. **MEMBERSHIPS** Ling Soc of Amer; Acoust Soc of Amer. **RESEARCH** Phonetics and Phonology. **SELECTED PUBLICATIONS** Co-auth, Rate Effects on French Intonation: Phonetic Realization and Prosodic Organization, Jour of Phonetics, 98; auth, The Phonetics and Phonology of Korean Prosody: intonational phonology and prosodic structure, Garland, 96; co-auth, A Prosodic analysis of three types of wh-phrases in Korean, Lang and Speech, 96; auth, Asymmetrical prosodic effects on the laryngeal gesture in Korean, Phonology and phonetic evidence: Papers in Laboratory Phonology, Cambridge, 95; co-auth, Distribution of Devoiced High Vowels in Korean, Proceedings of the Intl Conf on Spoken Lang Processing, 94. **CONTACT ADDRESS** Dept. of Linguistics, UCLouisiana, 3125 Campbell Hall, 405 Hilgar, Los Angeles, CA, 90095-1543. **EMAIL** jun@humnet.ucla.edu

JUNTUNE, THOMAS WILLIAM
PERSONAL Born 05/27/1940, Astoria, OR, m, 1968, 2 children **DISCIPLINE** GERMANIC LINGUISTICS **EDUCATION** Stanford Univ, AB, 63, MA, 64; Princeton Univ, MA, 66, PhD(ling), 68. **CAREER** Asst prof, 67-71, assoc prof, 71-80, Prof Ger, Mich State Univ, 80-, Res grant, Alexander von Humboldt Found, Ger, 74-75; 89-90; resident dir jr yr, Freiburg, Ger, 82-83. **MEMBERSHIPS** MLA; Ling Soc Am; Am Asn Teachers Ger; Sem Germanic Philol; Soc Advan Scand Studies. **RESEARCH** Germanic syntax; Germanic phonology; old Icelandic; Germanic-Finnousric Language content. **SELECTED PUBLICATIONS** Auth, The informational value of Germanic loanwords into Finnish, Amsterdamer Beitrage zur alteren Germanistik, 73; Reflexivization and reflexive verbs in old Icelandic, Nordic Lang & Mod Ling, Vol 3, 78; Using parallel Bible translations in teaching the history of the German language, Yrbk Sem Germanic Philol, 80; Subject and Reflexure in Old Icelandic in Recent Developments in Germaic Linguistics, CILT, 93, 92; Languages and Peoples in Contrast; Early Germanic & Early Finnu in The Germanic Mosaic: Cultural and Linguistic Diversity in Society, 94. **CONTACT ADDRESS** Dept of Ling & Lang, Michigan State Univ, A615 Wells Hall, East Lansing, MI, 48824-1020. **EMAIL** juntune@pilot.msu.edu

JURADO, JOSE
PERSONAL Born 12/22/1925, Madrid, Spain, m, 1961, 1 child **DISCIPLINE** SPANISH LITERATURE **EDUCATION** Univ Madrid, Bachiller, 49, lic, 56, Dr(philos & lett), 63. **CAREER** Asst Latin philol, Univ Madrid, 58-59; prof Span philol & lit, Univ Caldas, Colombia, 60-62; vis asst prof, Univ Chicago, 62-63; asst prof, Univ Va, 63-64; from asst prof to assoc prof, 64-73, PROF SPAN LIT, CARLETON UNIV, 73-, Can Coun grant, 67. **MEMBERSHIPS** Am Asn Teachers Span & Port. **RESEARCH** Eighteenth century and Old Spanish literature. **SELECTED PUBLICATIONS** Auth, On the Lesson Yelos/Yergos From the 'Libro De Buen Amor', Boll De La Real Acad Espanola, Vol 0074, 94; A Critical-Study of the Word Feste in Ruiz, Juan 'Libro De Buen Amor', Revista De Filologia Espanola, Vol 0075, 95; John of the Cross--'Cantico Espiritual, Poesias, Codice Inedito De Marchena Del Cb-Mch--, Revista De Filologia Espanola, Vol 0077, 97. **CONTACT ADDRESS** Dept of Span, Carleton Univ, 1125 Colonel By Dr, Ottawa, ON, K1S 5B6.

JURKEVICH, GAYANA
PERSONAL Montreal, PQ, Canada **DISCIPLINE** SPANISH **EDUCATION** Mount Holyoke Col, AB, 74; Univ Minn, MA, 77; NYU, MPhil, 85; NYU, PhD, 87. **CAREER** Teaching assoc, Univ Minn, 75-77; personnel mgt, US Dept of State, 77-81; actress, adm coord, GALA, Teatro Hispano, Inc, 77-81; instr, The Key Sch, 86-87; instr, Anne Arundel Comm Col, 86-87; adjunct asst prof, Baruch Col/CUNY, 87-88; sub asst prof, Baruch Col/CUNY, 88-89; asst prof, Baruch Col/CUNY, 89-92; assoc prof, Baruch Col/CUNY, 93-98. **HONORS AND AWARDS** Fel, Mount Holyoke Col; fel, Univ Minn; fel, NYU. **MEMBERSHIPS** Phi Kappa Phi; MLA; AATSP. **SELECTED PUBLICATIONS** Auth, The Elusive Self: Archetypal Approaches to the Novels of Miguel de Unamuno, Univ Mo, 91; auth, Defining Castile in Literature and Art: Institucionismo, The Generation of 1898, and the Origins of Modern Spanish Landscape,Revista Hispanica Moderna, 47, 94; auth, A Poetics of Time and Space: Ekphrasis and the Modern Vision in Azorin and Velazquez, MLN, 110.2, 95; auth, Azorin's Magic Circle: The Subversion of Time and Space in Dona Ines, Bull of Hisp Studies, LXXIII, 96; auth Azorin's Painted Lady: Maria Fontan and the Economics of Ekphrasis in La Chispa '97. Selected Proceedings of the Eighteenth Louisiana Conference of Hisp Lang and Lit, Tulane UP, 97. **CONTACT ADDRESS** Dept of Modern Languages, Baruch Col, CUNY, 17 Lexington Ave, Box G-1224, New York, NY, 10010.

K

KABAKOFF, JACOB
PERSONAL Born 03/20/1918, New York, NY, m, 1944, 3 children **DISCIPLINE** HEBREW LANGUAGE & LITERATURE **EDUCATION** Yeshiva Univ, BA, 38; Jewish Theol Sem, MHL, 44, DHL, 58. **CAREER** Asst rabbi, Har Zion Temple, Philadelphia, 44-46; rabbi, B'nai Israel of Olney, 44-48; educ dir, Flatbush Jewish Ctr, 48-50; mem ed staff, Encycl Hebraica, Jerusalem, 50-52; prof Hebrew & dean, Cleveland Col Jewish Studies, 52-68; assoc prof Hebrew, 68-72, PROF HEBREW, LEHMAN COL, 72-, Am Philos Soc grant, 67; Mem Found Jewish Cult grant, 67-68; ed, Jewish Bk Annual, Jewish Bk Coun, 77-; Asn Prof of Hebrew (pres, 74-76). **HONORS AND AWARDS** DD, Jewish Theol Sem, 72. **MEMBERSHIPS** Am Acad Jewish Res; Am Jewish Hist Soc; World Union Jewish Studies; Nat Orgn Hebrew Cult (vpres, 77-). **RESEARCH** Current Israeli literature; American Hebrew litera-

tary and cultural history. **SELECTED PUBLICATIONS** Auth, Some East European Letters on Emigration--Rethinking the American Jewish Experience, Amer Jewish Arch, Vol 0045, 93. **CONTACT ADDRESS** Div Hebraic & Judaic Studies, Lehman Col, CUNY, Bronx, NY, 10468.

KACANDES, IRENE
DISCIPLINE GERMAN LANGUAGE **EDUCATION** Harvard Univ, PhD, 91. **CAREER** Fac, Univ Tex; Asst prof, Dartmouth Col. **RESEARCH** Goethe, Kleist, Grass, and Christa Wolf; narrative theory; 20th-century cult studies. **SELECTED PUBLICATIONS** Auth, publ(s) about orality and literacy, feminist linguistics, and the Holocaust. **CONTACT ADDRESS** Dartmouth Col, 3529 N Main St, #207, Hanover, NH, 03755.

KACHRU, BRAJ BEHARI
PERSONAL Born 05/15/1932, Srinagar, India, m, 1965, 1 child **DISCIPLINE** NON-NATIVE ENGLISHES, SOCIOLINGUISTICS **EDUCATION** Jammu & Kashmir Univ, BA, 52; Allahabad Univ, MA, 55; Edinburgh Univ, dipl, 59, PhD(ling), 61. **CAREER** Lectr ling, Lucknow Univ, 62-63; res assoc, 63-64, from asst prof to assoc prof, 64-70, head dept, 69-79, PROF LING, UNIV ILL, URBANA, 70-, Coordr, Div Applied Ling, 74-, Mem SAsia lang comt, Comt Instnl Coop, 65-; consult, Dict English Lang, Random House, 66; Am Inst Indian Studies fac fel, 67-68; chmn comt varieties English, Asn Commonwealth Lit & Lang Studies, 68; assoc Ctr Advan Studies, Univ Ill, 71-72; ed, Papers on SAsian Ling, 73; consult, Ford Found, 74 & 75; mem lang comt, SAsia Regional Coun, 77-; dir, Ling Inst Ling Soc Am, 78; chmn, Int Conf SAsian Lang & Ling, 80-**MEMBERSHIPS** Philol Soc, Eng; Ling Soc Am, Ling Soc India; Ling Asn Can & US. **RESEARCH** South Asian English and linguistics; Kashmiri language and literature; varieties of English. **SELECTED PUBLICATIONS** Auth, Englishes--Studies in Varieties of English 1984-1988, J Pidgin and Creole Lang, Vol 0008, 93; Multilingualism in India, Lang in Soc, Vol 0024, 95; World Englishes, Agony and Ecstasy + The Universalization of English, J Aesth Educ, Vol 0030, 96; A Macro Sociolinguistic Analysis of Language Vitality--Geolinguistic Profiles and Scenarios of Language Contact in India, Lang in Soc, Vol 0025, 96. **CONTACT ADDRESS** Dept of Ling, Univ of Ill, 707 S Mathews Ave, Urbana, IL, 61801-3625.

KACHRU, YAMUNA
PERSONAL Born 03/05/1933, Purulia, India, m, 1965, 2 children **DISCIPLINE** LINGUISTICS **EDUCATION** Bihar Univ, BA, 53; Patna Univ, MA, 55; Univ London, PhD, 65. **CAREER** Lectr Hindi, Ranchi Women's Col, India, 56-58; lectr, Sch Orient & African Studies, Univ London, 59-65; asst res prof ling, 65-66, asst prof ling & Eng, 67-68, assoc prof ling, Eng & Hindi, 68-71, Prof Ling & Eng as Second Lang, Univ IL, Urbana, 71-94, Prof Ling, 94-98; Act Dir, Div Eng as an Int lang, Univ IL, 84-85, 85-89; Rockefeller fel, Deccan Col, 58-59; Am Inst Indian Studies fac fels, 67-68, 71-72 & 85-86; assoc, Ctr Advan Study, Univ IL, 75. **HONORS AND AWARDS** Two Gold Medals, Panta Univ, 55; Distinction in Ling, Deccan Col, 58-59; Assoc, Center for Advan Study, Univ IL, 75; Grants from Res Bd, Univ IL, Am Coun Learned Soc & Smithsonian Found; mem, ed bd, World Englishes Blackwell, Oxford) and Eng in Asia, Nat Inst Educ, Singapore. **MEMBERSHIPS** Ling Soc Am; Am Asn Appl Ling; Lling Soc India. **RESEARCH** Generative grammars of South Asian languages; pragmatics; contrastive rhetoric; Second Lang acquisition; world Eng. **SELECTED PUBLICATIONS** Auth, An Intro to Hindi Syntax, Univ Ill, 66; ed, Studies in Linguistics Sciences, Special Issues on Hindi Linguistics, 71; Topics in a Transformational Grammar of Hindi (in Hindi), Agra, Central Inst of Hindi, 74; On the semantics of the causative construction in Hindi-Urdu, In: The Grammar of Causative Constructions, Syntax and Semantics set VI, Acad Press, 76; On relative clause formation in Hindi-Urdu, Ling, 78; Aspects of Hindi Grammar, Manohar Publ, India, 80; ed, Dimensions of South Asian Linguistics, fall 81; Cross-cultural texts, discourse strategies and discourse interpretation, In: Discourse Across Cultures: Strategies in World Englishes, Prentice-Hall, 87; Ergativity, Subjecthood and Topicality in Hindu-Urdu, In: Studies on Ergativity (spec vol Lingua), North-Holland Elsevier, The Netherlands, 87; Hindi-Urdu, In: World's Major Languages, Croom-Helm, 87; ed, Special Issue on Pedagogical Grammars of English: Approaches and Resources, winter 87; Writers in Hindi and English, In: Contrastive Rhetoric: Theory and Case Studies, Written Commun Annual, vol 3, Sage Publ, 88; Cognitivie and cultural styles in second language acquisition, Annual Rev Applied Ling, 88; co-ed, Pragmatics and Language Learning, monogr 1-V, 90-94; Social meaning and creativity in Indian English speech acts, In: Language, Communication and Social Meaning, Georgetown Univ Monogr Series on Lang and Ling, 92; Self, identity and creativity: Women writers in India, In: Self as Person in Asian Theory and Practice, SUNY Press, Albany, 94; Lexcial components of cultural contact: Speech act verbs in Hindi-English dictionaries, In: Cultures, Ideologies, and the Dctionary: Studies in Honor of Ladislav Zgusta, Max Niemeyer Verlag, 95; co-ed, Language, Gender, and Power, 95; Culture and argumentative writing in world Englishes, In; World Englishes 2000, Univ Hawaii Press, 97. **CONTACT ADDRESS** Dept of Ling, Univ of Illinois, 707 S Mathews Ave, Urbana, IL, 61801-3625. **EMAIL** ykachur@staff.uiuc.edu

KAGA, MARIKO
DISCIPLINE JAPANESE LANGUAGE **EDUCATION** Kobe Kaisei Women's Col, BA; Univ Ill, MA, PhD.Columbia Univ, PhD. **CAREER** Japanese, Carleton Col **SELECTED PUBLICATIONS** Auth, Exercise in Japanese Counters. **CONTACT ADDRESS** Carleton Col, 100 S College St., Northfield, MN, 55057-4016.

KAHANE, HENRY
PERSONAL Born 11/02/1902, Berlin, Germany, m, 1931, 2 children **DISCIPLINE** GENERAL & ROMANCE LINGUISTICS **EDUCATION** Univ Berlin, PhD, 30 **CAREER** Asst, Univ Berlin, 32; lectr, Univ Florence, 35-38; teaching fel comp lit, Univ Southern Calif, 39-41; from instr to assoc prof, Span & ling, 41-49, dir univ prog ling, 60-62, acting dir Ctr Advan Studies, 71-72, Prof Span & Ling, Univ Ill, Urbana, 49-, CTR Advan Studies, 68-, Guggenheim fels, 55-56,62-63; mem, Am Sch Class Studies, Athens; assoc ed, Romance Philol; consult spec proj, Nat Found for Humanities. **HONORS AND AWARDS** Silver Award, Acad Athens, 76., DLitt, Univ Ill, 77. **MEMBERSHIPS** MLA; Ling Soc Am; Int Arthurian Soc; Am Name Soc; Wolfram von Eschenbach Gesellschaft. **RESEARCH** Mediterranean linguistics; cultural linguistics; Hellenistic survivals in Western culture. **SELECTED PUBLICATIONS** Auth, Justinian Credo in Western Medieval Literature, Byzantinische Zeitschrift, Vol 0084, 92; The Romance Jargons in Romania, Word-J Int Ling Asn, Vol 0044, 93. **CONTACT ADDRESS** Dept of Ling, Univ of Ill, Champaign, IL, 61820.

KAHF, MOHJA
DISCIPLINE COMPARATIVE LITERATURE **EDUCATION** Rutgers Univ, PhD. **CAREER** English and Lit, Univ Ark. **SELECTED PUBLICATIONS** Auth, Nusaiba's Scar, Islamic Horizons, 94. **CONTACT ADDRESS** Univ Ark, Fayetteville, AR, 72701.

KAI-WING, CHOW
DISCIPLINE CHINESE STUDIES **EDUCATION** Hong Kong Baptist Univ, diploma; New Asia Inst Adv Chinese Stud, MA; Univ Calif, Davis, PhD. **CAREER** Asst prof, Univ Ill, 88-94, ASSOC PROF, 94-, Champaign- Urbana; ASSOC CURATOR, SPURLOCK MUS, UNIV ILL, 98-. **CONTACT ADDRESS** Univ of Illinois, Urbana-Champaign, 608 S Mathews Ave, Urbana, IL, 61801. **EMAIL** k-chow1@uiuc.edu

KAILING, JOEL
PERSONAL Atlanta, GA, m, 4 children **DISCIPLINE** SPEECH, INTERCULTURAL COMMUNICATION **EDUCATION** Univ Ky, PhD. **CAREER** Assoc prof, Lee Univ, 94-. **MEMBERSHIPS** Lee Comm Club; Lee Univ Vindagua, Missions Alive. **SELECTED PUBLICATIONS** Inside, Outside, Upside Down, Int Rev Missions, 88; A New Solution to the African Christian Problem; Missiology, 94. **CONTACT ADDRESS** Lee Univ, 1120 N. Ocoee St, Cleveland, TN, 37320-3450. **EMAIL** jkailing@leeuniversity.edu

KAISER, DANIEL HUGH
PERSONAL Born 07/20/1945, Philadelphia, PA, m, 1968, 2 children **DISCIPLINE** RUSSIAN & FAMILY HISTORY **EDUCATION** Wheaton Col, Ill, AB, 67; Univ Chicago, AM, 70, PhD(Russ hist), 77. **CAREER** Instr hist, King's Col, NY, 68-71; asst prof, Trinity Col, Ill, 71-73; vis asst prof, Russ hist, Univ Chicago, 77-78; asst prof hist, Univ Chicago, 77-78; asst prof hist, Grinnell Iowa Coll, 79-84; assoc prof, 84-86; prof hist, 86-; Joseph F Rosenfield prof social studies, 84-; chemn dept hist, 89-90, 96-98; Lectr & tour dir, Smithsonian Inst tours to USSR, 76-. **HONORS AND AWARDS** Mem adv bd Soviet Studies in History, 79-85; editl bd Slavic Rev, 96; Fel Nat Endowment Humanities, 79, 92-93, John Simon Guggenheim Meml Found, 86; Fulbright-Hays Fac Research Abroad Found, 86. **MEMBERSHIPS** AHA; Am Assn Advan Slavic Studies; Early Slavic Studies Assn, vp, 95-97; Slavonic and East European Medieval Studies Group, UK; Study Group on 18th Century Russia, UK; 18th Century Russian Studies Assn. **RESEARCH** Russian and comparative law; Russian and comparative family history; Historical climatology. **SELECTED PUBLICATIONS** Trans ed, The Laws of Rus Tenth to Fifteenth Centuries, Charles Schlacks Jr, Publisher, 92; co-ed, with Gary Marker, Reinterpreting Russian History 860-1860s, 94; The Growth of the Law in Medieval Russia, Princeton Univ Press, 80; Muscovite Law, 1300-1500, Dict Middle Ages (in press). **CONTACT ADDRESS** Dept of History, Grinnell Col, PO Box B, Grinnell, IA, 50112-0805. **EMAIL** kaiser@ac.grin.edu

KALAIDJIAN, WALTER
DISCIPLINE ENGLISH LANGUAGE AND LITERATURE **EDUCATION** Univ Ill Urbana-Champaign, PhD, 92. **CAREER** Prof **RESEARCH** 20th-century American literature and culture. **SELECTED PUBLICATIONS** Auth, American Culture Between the Wars: Revisionary Modernism and Postmodern Critique; Languages of Liberation: The Social Text in Contemporary American Poetry; Understanding Theodore Roethke. **CONTACT ADDRESS** English Dept, Emory Univ, 1380 Oxford Rd NE, Atlanta, GA, 30322-1950.

KALBOUSS, GEORGE
PERSONAL Born 06/21/1939, New York, NY, m, 1962, 2 children **DISCIPLINE** RUSSIAN LANGUAGE & LITERATURE, DRAMA **EDUCATION** Columbia Univ, AB, 60, AM, 61; NY Univ, PhD(Slavic lang), 68. **CAREER** Vis instr Russ, Dartmouth Col, 66; instr, Purdue Univ, 66-67; asst prof, Dartmouth Col, 67-73, asst dean, 68-73; assoc prof Slavic Lang & Lit, Ohio State Univ, 73-. **HONORS AND AWARDS** Distinguished Teaching Award, Ohio State Univ, 77. **MEMBERSHIPS** Am Asn Teachers Slavic & E Europ Lang; Am Asn Advan Slavic Studies. **RESEARCH** Works of Fiodor Sologub; poetry and prose of Russian symbolism; computer-assisted instruction. **SELECTED PUBLICATIONS** Auth, From Mystery to Fantasy: An Attempt to Categorize the Plays of the Russian Symbolists, Canadian American Slavic Studies, Winter 1974; On 'Armenian Riddles' and Their Offspring 'Radio Erevan', Slavic and East European J, Fall 1977; Andrei Bely and the Modernist Movement in Russian Drama, In: "Andrey Bely: A Critical Review" (ed. Gerald Janacek), Univ of Kentucky Press, 78; The Many Faces Behind the Masks of Zoloto v Iazuri, In: "Andrey Bely Centenary Papers" (ed. Boris Christa), Hakkert, 80; The Plays of the Russian Symbolists, E. Lansing, Russian Language J, 82; Sologub and Myth, Slavic and East European J, Winter 83; Echoes of Nietzsche in the works of Fedor Sologub, "Nietzsche in Russia" (ed. Bernice Rosenthal), Princeton Univ Press, 86; Rhyming Patterns in Griboedov's "Gore ot Uma", Slavic and East European J, Spring 95; Russian Culture, Simon and Schuster, 98. **CONTACT ADDRESS** Dept of Slavic Lang & Lit, Ohio State Univ, 1841 Millikin Rd, Columbus, OH, 43210-1229. **EMAIL** kalbouss.1@osu.edu

KAMENISH, PAULA K.
DISCIPLINE WORLD LITERATURE, EUROPEAN LITERATURE, DRAMA, NOVELLA, AND NOVEL **EDUCATION** Ctr Col Ky, BA; Univ NC, Chapel Hill, MA, PhD. **CAREER** Assoc prof, Univ NC, Wilmington. **RESEARCH** German and French theatre of the 20th century; Dada movement. **SELECTED PUBLICATIONS** Published articles on Shakespeare, French Canadian author Roch Carrier, and various modern dramatists. **CONTACT ADDRESS** Univ N. Carolina, Wilmington, Morton Hall, Wilmington, NC, 28403-3297. **EMAIL** kamenishp@uncwil.edu

KAMLA, THOMAS A.
DISCIPLINE MEDIEVAL GERMAN LITERATURE, 18TH-20TH CENTURY GERMAN LITERATURE, GERMAN LAN **EDUCATION** St John's Univ, Univ of MN, BA, 61; Univ WI, MA, 69, PhD, 73. **CAREER** Univ Scranton, 78-; Univ NE, 76-78; Carnegie Mellon Univ, 72-76. **RESEARCH** 19th-20th century Ger lit; psychoanalytic criticism; turn of the century; expressionism; exile lit. **SELECTED PUBLICATIONS** Auth, scholarly bk:Confrontation with Exile: Studies in the German Novel; articles,19th and 20th century Ger authors. **CONTACT ADDRESS** Dept of For Lang(s) and Lit(s), Univ of Scranton, Scranton, PA, 18510. **EMAIL** Kamlatl@tiger.uofs.edu

KAMUF, PEGGY
DISCIPLINE FRENCH AND COMPARATIVE LITERATURE **EDUCATION** Cornell Univ, PhD. **CAREER** Prof, Univ Southern Calf; Visiting Professor at the Centre d'Etudes Feminines, Universite de Paris VIII and from 1991-96; Directeur de Programme at the College International de Philosophie in Paris. **RESEARCH** Translation theory; philosophy and literature; 18th-century aesthetics; post-structuralist literary and feminist theory. **SELECTED PUBLICATIONS** Auth, Fictions of Feminine Desire: Disclosures of Heloise, 82; Signature Pieces: On The Institution of Authorship, 88; ed, A Derrida Reader: Between the Blinds, 91. **CONTACT ADDRESS** Col Letters, Arts & Sciences, Univ Southern Calif, University Park Campus, Los Angeles, CA, 90089. **EMAIL** kamuf@.usc.edu

KANE, LESLIE
DISCIPLINE COMPARATIVE LITERATURE **EDUCATION** Brooklyn Col, BA; Fairleigh Dickinson Univ, MA; NY Univ, PhD. **CAREER** Pres, David Mamet Soc; ed, David Mamet Newsletter; former VP, Harold Pinter Soc. **RESEARCH** Stage and screenplays of David Mamet and the drama of Harold Pinter. **SELECTED PUBLICATIONS** Publ, lit jour(s); The Language of Silence: On the Unspoken and the Unspeakable in Modern Drama; David Mamet: A Casebook; Israel Horovitz: Critical Essays. **CONTACT ADDRESS** Dept of Engl, Westfield State Col, 577 Western Ave., Westfield, MA, 01085.

KANELLOS, NICOLAS
DISCIPLINE LANGUAGE, LITERATURE **EDUCATION** Univ Autonoma Mex, Mex Lit & Cult, 64-65; Farleigh Dickinson Univ, BA, Span, 66; Univ Tex, MA, Roman Lang, 68; Univ Lisboa Portugal, Portuguese Lit & Cult, 69070; Univ Tex, PhD, Span & Portuguese, 74. **CAREER** PROF, UNIV HOUSTON, 80-. **SELECTED PUBLICATIONS** America's Hispanic People: Their Images Through History, 97; edr, Biographical Dictionary of Hispanic Literature in the United States, Greenwood Press, 89; Mexican-American Theater Legacy and Reality, Lat Am Rev Press, 87; Hispanic-American Almanac: A Reference Work on Hispanics in the United States, Gale Res, 93, Hispanic Firsts, Gale Res, 97.. **CONTACT ADDRESS** Dept Hisp & Class Lang, Univ Houston, Houston, TX, 77204-3128.

KANES, MARTIN
PERSONAL Born 09/21/1927, Philadelphia, PA, m, 1953 **DISCIPLINE** ROMANCE LANGUAGES **EDUCATION** Univ Paris, Dr(comp lit), 53; Univ Pa, PhD, 59. **CAREER** Instr Romance lang, Univ Pa, 53-59; asst prof French, Univ Calif, Davis, 59-66; assoc prof French lit, Univ Calif, Santa Cruz, 66-71, PROF FR & COMP LIT, 71-79. Fels, Guggenheim & Fulbright, 65-66. **MEMBERSHIPS** MLA. **RESEARCH** French and comparative literature of the 19th century; Zola; Balzac. **SELECTED PUBLICATIONS** Auth, Balzac Against Balzac, Fr Forum, Vol 0018, 93; Paris at the Time of Balzac and in the 'Comedie Humaine'--City and Society, 19th-Century Fr Stud, Vol 0022, 93. **CONTACT ADDRESS** State Univ NY, Albany, NY, 12222.

KANEVSKAYA, MARINA
PERSONAL Born 04/18/1956, Moscow, Russia, m, 1986, 1 child **DISCIPLINE** RUSSIAN LITERATURE **EDUCATION** Moscow State Univ, MA, 79; Indiana Univ, PhD, 97. **CAREER** Asst instr, 89, 90, 93, 94, 96, 97, 98, Summer Workshop Slavic E Europ Lang Ind Univ; res asst, 89, asst instr, 90, 93-95, Dept Slavic Lang & Lit, Ind Univ; tchr, 91, 92, Summer Lang School, Beloit Col; lectr, Dept Slavic Lang, Univ Texas Austin, 90-92; lectr, Depauw Univ, 97; lectr, Georgetown Univ, 97-98; lectr, George Wash Univ, 98; ASST PROF, UNIV MONTANA, 98- . **HONORS AND AWARDS** Grad Stud Res Awd, Ind Univ, 94; Mellon grant, 93, 94, 96; Am Assoc of Univ Women Educ Found, Car Devel Grant, 95-96; IREX predissertation res grant (Moscow) 96; Salaroglio Mod For Lang Scholar, 96. **MEMBERSHIPS** Am Asn Advan Russian Studies; Am Asn Tchrs Russian & E Europ Langs. **RESEARCH** 19th & 20th Century Russian literature. **SELECTED PUBLICATIONS** Auth, Nikolai Pavlovich Antsiferov-Teacher of Human Science, E/W Educ, 93; Petty Demon by Fedor Sologub as a Travesty, Selected Stories by Fedor Sologub, Zapizdat Publ, 94; A Corrupted Quotation as a Key to a New Meaning: Chekhov on Gogol, Gogolevskii sbornik, Obrazovanie, 94; Moscow as a Host of Pushkin's Celebrations of 1880, Grad Essays on Slavic Lang & Lit, Univ Ctr Russian & E Europ Stud, 95; A Diary of a Writer from Tioplyi Stan: The Beautifulness of Life by Evgenii Popov, NW Univ Press, 98; Pushkin as a 'Universal' Poet: Varnhagen von Ense and Dostoevsky, Proceedings of the 1966 Cent Slavic Conf, Univ Missouri-Columbia, 98; Icon in the Structure of Dostoevsky's Notes from the House of the Dead, Znamia, 98; The Semiotic Validity of the Mirror Image in Vladimir Nabokov's Despair, Proceedings of Vladimir Nabokov's Centennial Festival, Cornell Univ Press, 99. **CONTACT ADDRESS** Dept For Lang, Univ of Montana, Missoula, MT, 59812. **EMAIL** MKANEV@selway.umt.edu

KAPLAN, EDWARD HAROLD
PERSONAL Born 01/09/1936, New York, NY, m, 1957, 2 children **DISCIPLINE** CHINESE HISTORY & LANGUAGE **EDUCATION** Georgetown Univ, BS, 60; Univ Iowa, MA, 63, PhD, 70. **CAREER** Instr hist, Univ Del, 64-68; from lectr to asst prof, 68-74, assoc prof hist, Western Wash Univ 74- **MEMBERSHIPS** Asn Asian Studies; Am Orient Soc; AHA. **RESEARCH** Sung history; Chinese economic history. **SELECTED PUBLICATIONS** Transl & ed, Maxims for the Well Governed Household, Occasional Papers No 1, Prog EAsian Studies, 71 & An Economic History of China, by Chou Chin-sheng, Occasional Papers No 7, 74, Western Wash Univ; A Monetary History of China, East Asian Res Aids and Translations, no 5, Western Wash Univ Ctr East Asian Studies, 94. **CONTACT ADDRESS** Dept of Hist, Western Washington Univ, M/S 9056, Bellingham, WA, 98225-5996. **EMAIL** kaplan@cc.wwu.edu

KAPLAN, EDWARD KIVIE
PERSONAL Born 03/04/1942, Boston, MA, m, 1968, 3 children **DISCIPLINE** FRENCH & COMPARATIVE LITERATURE **EDUCATION** Brown Univ, BA, 64; Columbia Univ, MA, 66, PhD, 70. **CAREER** Instr French, Barnard Col, Columbia Univ, 67- 71; asst prof, Amherst Col, 71-78; asst prof, prof French & comparative literature, Brandeis Univ, 78-; res assoc Tauber Inst Study Europ Jewry; NEH fel, 85-86. **HONORS AND AWARDS** Lewis Galantiere Prize, 90. **MEMBERSHIPS** MLA; Am Asn Teachers Fr; Soc Etud Romantiques; Soc Values Higher Educ; Assoc Jewish Stud. **RESEARCH** 19th century French literature; Michelet; Baudelaire; Bonnefoy; Heschel. **SELECTED PUBLICATIONS** Auth, Gaston Bachelard's Philosophy of Imagination, Philos & Phenomenol Res, 9/72; Language and reality in A J Heschel's Philosophy of Religion, J Am Acad Relig, 3/73; Les Deux sexes de l'esprit: Michelet phenomenologue de l'imagination ..., Europe, 12/73; Michelet's Poetic Vision: A Romantic Philosophy of Nature, Man, and Woman, Univ Mass, 77; Mysticism and despair in Abraham J Heschel's religious thought, J Relig, 1/77; Michelet's revolutionary symbolism: From Hermencutics in politics, 4/77 & The courage of Baudelaire and Rimbuad: The anxiety of faith, 12/78, Fr Rev; ed Baudelaire and the Vicissitudes of Venus: Ethical Irony in Fleurs du Mal, The Shaping of Text: Style, Imagery, and Structure in French Literature, Bucknell Univ, 93; Sacred versus Symbolic Religion: Abraham Joshua Heschel and Martin Buber, Mod Judaism, 94; auth Holiness in Words: Abraham Joshua Heschel's Poetics of Piety, SUNY, 96; Abraham Heschel, Yale Companion to Jewish Writing and Thought in Germany, 1096-1996, Yale Univ, 97; The Voices of Marceline Desbordes-Valmore: Deference, Self-Assertion, Accountability, Fr Forum, 97; La Spiritualite de Michelet: Une nouvelle religion republicaine, Litterature et Nation Michelet et la question sociale, Univ Fr Rabelais, 97; auth Abraham Joshua Heschel, Prophetic Witness, Yale Univ, 98; Recovering the Origins, ADFL Bull, 98; Ecstasy and Insight: Baudelaire's Fruitful Tensions, Romance Quart, 98; L'Internet de Michelet: Evolution, Immortalite, Fragilite du Moi, Europe, 98. **CONTACT ADDRESS** Dept Romance & Comp Lit, Brandeis Univ, MS-024, Waltham, MA, 02254-2700. **EMAIL** edwkaplan@brandeis.edu

KAPLAN, ELIZABETH ANN
DISCIPLINE COMPARATIVE LITERATURE **EDUCATION** Univ Birmingham, BA, 58; Rutgers Univ, PhD, 70. **CAREER** Prof, 87-. **SELECTED PUBLICATIONS** Auth, Fritz Lang: A Guide to References and Resources, Hall, 81; Women and Film: Both Sides of the Camera, 90; co-auth, Talking About the Cinema, 74; co-ed, Late Imperial Culture, 95. **CONTACT ADDRESS** English Dept, SUNY Stony Brook, Stony Brook, NY, 11794. **EMAIL** eakaplan@ccmail.sunysb.edu

KAPLAN, GREGORY
DISCIPLINE SPANISH LITERATURE **EDUCATION** Univ Pa, PhD, 94. **CAREER** Asst prof. **SELECTED PUBLICATIONS** Auth, pubs on different aspects of converso literature. **CONTACT ADDRESS** Dept of Romance Languages, Knoxville, TN, 37996.

KAPLAN, JAMES MAURICE
PERSONAL Born 03/16/1943, Worcester, MA **DISCIPLINE** FRENCH LITERATURE **EDUCATION** Univ Mass, Amherst, BA, 64; Univ Calif, Berkeley, PhD(French), 71. **CAREER** Teaching asst French, Univ Calif, Berkeley, 65-66, 67-69; asst English, Lycee Bellevue, Toulouse, France, 66-67; escortinterpreter French & Swed, US Dept State, 72-76; asst prof, 76-80, ASSOC PROF FRENCH, MOOREHEAD STATE COL, 80-, Fulbright fel, 66-67; Swed Govt fel, 69-70; Nat Endowment for Humanities grants, 78 & 81; resident dir, St Cloud State Univ prog in France, 81. **MEMBERSHIPS** MLA. **RESEARCH** French 18th century poetry; French 18th century opera; Jungian literary analysis. **SELECTED PUBLICATIONS** Auth, Gustav III, the Public Child--The Rhetorical and Political Education of a Prince, Scand Stud, Vol 0066, 94. **CONTACT ADDRESS** Dept of Foreign Lang, Moorhead State Univ, Moorhead, MN, 56560.

KAPLAN, JANE PAYNE
PERSONAL Born 10/03/1937, Richmond, VA, m, 1964, 2 children **DISCIPLINE** FRENCH LANGUAGE & LITERATURE, LINGUISTICS **EDUCATION** Univ NC, Chapel Hill, BA, 59; La State Univ, Baton Rouge, PhD(Romance philol), 70. **CAREER** Lectr French, Yale Univ, 64-65; instr, Southern Conn State Col, 65-67; asst prof, Quinnipiac Col, 69-70; asst prof French & ling, 71-74, from assoc Prof to Prof French, Ithaca Col, 74-83. **HONORS AND AWARDS** Danforth Associate; Fulbright, 63-64; Dana Teaching Fel for excellence in teaching, 84-85; Oracle Society, faculty inductee, 89; Sears-Roebuck Teaching Excellence & Campus Leadership Award, 90. **MEMBERSHIPS** AATF; Soc Etudes XVIIe Siecle. **RESEARCH** Eighteenth century literature; seventeenth century theater; semiotics. **SELECTED PUBLICATIONS** Auth, Complexity of character and the overlapping of a single personality in Cocteau's Les Enfants Terribles, Australian J Fr Studies, XII: 89-104; A visual and temporal decoding of the pragmatic structure of Jaques le fataliste, Semiotica, 36: 1-25; Diderot, In: Encyclopedic Dictionary of Semiotics, 87; Food as a Structural Catalyst in Lesage's Gil Blas, Food & Foodways, vol 2, 88; The Role of the Active Listener, The French Review, Feb, 88. **CONTACT ADDRESS** Dept of Modern Lang, Ithaca Col, 953 Danby Rd, Ithaca, NY, 14850-7002. **EMAIL** kaplan@ithaca.edu

KAPLAN, ROBERT B.
DISCIPLINE WRITTEN DISCOURSE, LINGUISTIC POLICY **EDUCATION** USC, PhD. **CAREER** Prof emer, Univ Southern Calif. **RESEARCH** Analysis of written discourse; role of language in national development. **SELECTED PUBLICATIONS** Coauth, Writing across languages: Analysis of L2 Texts, Reading, MA: Addison Wesley, 87. **CONTACT ADDRESS** Dept of Linguistics, Univ Southern Calif, University Park Campus, Los Angeles, CA, 90089. **EMAIL** kaplan@usc.edu

KARCH, DIETER
PERSONAL Born 11/29/1927, Ludwigshafen/Rhine, Germany, m, 1959 **DISCIPLINE** GERMANIC LINGUISTICS, GENERAL LINGUISTICS **EDUCATION** Univ of Washington, MA, 64, PhD(Ger Philol), 67. **CAREER** From instr to assoc prof Ger, 66-76, Prof Mod Lang, Univ Nebr, 76-, Woodsfac fel, Univ Marburg, 71-72; sr fac res, IDS Mannheim, 77. **MEMBERSHIPS** MLA; Am Asn Teachers Ger. **RESEARCH** Dialectology; Standard German; Colloquial German. **SELECTED PUBLICATIONS** Auth, Gimmeldingen Krs Neustadt an der Weinstrasse/Mutterstadt Krs Ludwigshafen am Rhein Phonai 13, 73, Mannheim-Umgangssprache Phonai 16, 75 & Zur Morphologie vorderpfalzischer Dialekte Phonai Beiheft 3, 75, Niemeyer, Tubingen; Siedlungspfalzisch im Kreis Waterloo, Ontario Kanada Phonai 18, 77 & Braunschweig-Veltenhof Pfalzische Sprachinsel in Ostfalischen Phonai 20, 78, Niemeyer, Tubingen; Neuburg am Rhein Eine alemannische Sprachinsel in der sudlichen Vorderpfalz, Univ Nebr, 78; Jockgrim Krs Germersheim/Niederhorbach Krs Landau-Bad Berrgzabern Niemeyer Tubingen Phonai 22, 80; Phonemidistribution Dargestellt an rheinhessischen Ortsmundarten DDG 107 I/II Elwert, Marburg. **CONTACT ADDRESS** Dept of Mod Lang & Lit, Univ of Nebr, PO Box 880315, Lincoln, NE, 68588-0315. **EMAIL** dkarch@unlinfo.unl.edu

KARLINSKY, SIMON
PERSONAL Born 09/22/1924, Harbin, Manchuria **DISCIPLINE** SLAVIC LANGUAGES & LITERATURES **EDUCATION** Univ Calif, Berkeley, BA, 60, PhD(Slavic), 64; Harvard Univ, MA, 61. **CAREER** Acting asst prof, 63-64, from asst prof to assoc prof, 64-67, chmn dept, 67-69, PROF SLAVIC LANG & LIT, UNIV CALIF, BERKELEY, 67-, Vis assoc prof, Harvard Univ, 66; Guggenheim Mem Found fel, 69-70 & 77-78. **MEMBERSHIPS** MLA; Am Asn Advan Slavic Studies; Am Asn Teachers Slavic & East Europ Lang; Philol Asn Pac Coast. **RESEARCH** Modern Russian literature; comparative literature. **SELECTED PUBLICATIONS** Auth, Tsvetaeva,Marina Through the Eyes of her Contemporaries, Russ Rev, Vol 0054, 95; Talmud Translations, Tradition-J Orthodox Jewish Thought, Vol 0029, 95; Karlinsky Review of Gorchakov Book on Tsvetaeva, Marina--A Rejoinder, Russ Rev, Vol 0055, 96. **CONTACT ADDRESS** Dept of Slavic Lang & Lit, Univ of Calif, 5416 Dwinelle Hall, Berkeley, CA, 94720.

KARSEN, SONJA PETRA
PERSONAL Born 04/11/1919, Berlin, Germany **DISCIPLINE** SPANISH **EDUCATION** Carleton Col, BA, 39; Bryn Mawr Col, MA, 41; Columbia Univ, PhD, 50. **CAREER** Instr Span, Lake Erie Col, 43-45; instr mod lang, Univ PR, 45-46; instr Span, Syracuse Univ, 47-50; instr, Brooklyn Col, 50-51; personal asst to dept dir-gen, 51-52, UNESCO, Paris; Latin Am desk, prog div tech assistance dept, 52-54, mem tech assistance mission, Costa Rica, 54; asst prof mod lang, Sweet Briar Col, 55-57; assoc prof Span, 57-61, chmn dept Romance lang, 57-65, fac res lectr 63, chmn dept mod lang, 65-79, prof Span, 61-87, prof emerita, 87-, Skidmore Col; contribr ed, Bks Abroad, 65-67; Fulbright lectr, Free Univ Berlin, 68; mem, Fulbright North-East Regional Screening Comt, 70-71, chmn 71 & 74. **HONORS AND AWARDS** Chevalier, Palmes Academiques, 63; Foreign Language Leadership Award, New York State Asn Foreign Lang Teachers, 73; Nat Distinguished Leadership Award, NY State Asn Lang Teachers, 79; elected to Phi Sigma Iota, 79; Spanish Heritage Award, 81; Alumni Achievement Award, Carleton Col, 82; NY State Asn For Lang Tchrs Capitol District For Lang, Distinguished Service Award, 87; elected hon mem, Sigma Delta Pi; International Woman of the year, 91-92, Int Biog Ctr, Cambridge Eng. **MEMBERSHIPS** MLA; Am Asn Teachers Span & Port; Nat Asn Self-Instr Lang Prog (treas, 73-77, vpres, 81-82); Am Asn Univ Women; Asn Int Hispanistas. **RESEARCH** Spanish American literature; Latin American literature and culture; translation. **SELECTED PUBLICATIONS** Auth, Jaime Torres Bodet, Twayne, 71; auth, Essays on Iberoamerican Literature and History, Peter Lang, 88; ed, Papers on Foreign Languages, Literature and Culture, 1982-87, New York State Association of Foreign Language Teachers, 88; transl, Leopoldo Zea, The Role of the Americas in History, Rowman and Littlefield, 92; auth, Bericht uber den Vater: Fritz Karsen (1885-1951), Overall Verlag, 93. **CONTACT ADDRESS** 1755 York Ave, Apt 37A, New York, NY, 10128-6875.

KARTTUNEN, FRANCES
PERSONAL Born 04/16/1942, Boston, MA, m, 1983, 2 children **DISCIPLINE** LINGUISTICS **EDUCATION** Radcliffe Col/Harvard Univ, AB, 64; Ind Univ, MA, 68, PhD, 70. **CAREER** Sr Univ Res Scientist, Univ Tex, 78-. **RESEARCH** Language contact and language change; the social dimensions of language and culture contact; language learning in children and adults; descriptive linguistics; non-Indo-European languages, especially Mesoamerican and Finno-Ugric languages. **SELECTED PUBLICATIONS** Auth, Between Worlds: Guides, Interpreters, and Survivors, Rutgers Univ Press, 94; coauth, Language Death, Language Genesis, and World History, J World Hist 95; auth, Rethinking Malinche, Indian Women of Early Mexico, Univ Okla Press, 97; Raising the Alarm for Endangered Languages, Univ Helsinki Quart, 97; What I Might Have Been: Ella Simon (1902-1981), Arvot, analyysi, tulkinta ¤studies in honor of Professor Seikko Eskolal, Finnish Hist Soc, 97; Indigenous Writing as a Vehicle of Postconquest Continuity and Change in Mesoamerica, Native Traditions in the Postonquest World, Dumbarton Oaks, 98. **CONTACT ADDRESS** Univ Texas, 303 Garrison Hall, Austin, TX, 78712. **EMAIL** fkarttunen@mail.utexas.edu

KASKE, ROBERT EARL
PERSONAL Born 06/01/1921, Cincinnati, OH, m, 1958, 1 child **DISCIPLINE** ENGLISH, COMPARATIVE LINGUISTICS **EDUCATION** Xavier Univ, Ohio, AB, 42; Univ NC,

MA, 47, PhD(English & comp ling), 50. **CAREER** Instr English, Mediaeval lit & comp ling, Wash Univ, 50-52, asst prof, 52-57; asst prof Mediaeval lit, Pa State Univ, 57-58; assoc prof, Univ NC, 58-61; prof, Univ Ill, 61-64; prof, 64-75, AVALON FOUND PROF HUMANITIES, CORNELL UNIV, 75-, Guggenheim fel, 62-63 & 77-78; assoc mem, Ctr Advan Studies, Univ Ill, 62-63; Soc for Humanities fel, Cornell Univ, 72-73; chief ed, Traditio, 75-; Nat Endowment for Humanities res materials grant, 77; Southeastern Inst Medieval & Renaissance Studies sr fel, 79. **MEMBERSHIPS** Acad Lit Studies; MLA; fel Mediaeval Acad Am; Dante Soc Am; Int Asn Univ Prof English. **RESEARCH** Old and Middle English language and literature; Medieval Biblical exegesis and mythography; Dante. **SELECTED PUBLICATIONS** Auth, Amnon and Thamar on a Misericord in Hereford-Cathedral + The Decorative, Iconographic and Religious Significance of Medieval Centerpieces and Supporters, Remarks on Their Enigmatic Aspects, Traditio-Studies in Ancient and Medieval History Thought and Rel. **CONTACT ADDRESS** Dept of English, Cornell Univ, Ithaca, NY, 14853.

KASPER, LORETTA F.
PERSONAL Born 02/14/1951, Brooklyn, NY, m, 1973 **DISCIPLINE** COGNITIVE PHYCHOLOGY **EDUCATION** Brooklyn Col, BA, 72, MA, 75; Col Staten Island, BA, 80; Rutgers Univ, MS, 82, PhD, 85. **CAREER** Lectr, coordr, 83-88, Wagner Col; adj instr, Kean Col, New Jersey, 87-88; instr, adj asst prof, 87-92, Col Staten Island, from asst prof to assoc prof, 92-, Kingsborough Commun Col, CUNY. **HONORS AND AWARDS** New York State Regents Scholar, 68-72; Phi Beta Kappa, 72; Nat Honor Soc, 80; Rutgers Univ Fel, 82-83; Col Staten Island Alumni Hall of Fame, 88; Merit Award Excellence Tchg, 89, Col Staten Island; Who's Who East, 94; PSC-CUNY-26 Grant, 95-96; Kingsborough Commun Col Grant, 96; PSC-CUNY-27 Grant, 96-97; CUNY Fac Development Colloquium Grant, 97; PSC-CUNY-29 Grant, 98-99. **MEMBERSHIPS** CUNY Asn Readers Educators; CUNY ESL Council; Int Consortium: NCTE; Int Reading Asn; Nat Council Tchrs English; NJ TESOL-BE, Inc; NYS TESOL; TESOL Int. **RESEARCH** Content-Based ESL instruction; technology in ESL instruction; metacognitive factors in second language acquisition; reading and writing as integrated skills. **SELECTED PUBLICATIONS** Auth, art, Writing, metacognition, and computer technology, 97; auth, Teaching English Through the Disciplines: Psychology, 97; auth, Interdisciplinary English, 98; auth, art, ESL writing and the principle of nonjudgmental awareness: Rationale and implementation, 98; auth, art, Interdisciplinary English and the Internet: Technology meets content in the ESL course, 98. **CONTACT ADDRESS** 27 Toddy Ave, Staten Island, NY, 10314. **EMAIL** drlfk@aol.com

KASTER, ROBERT A.
PERSONAL Born 02/06/1948, New York, NY, m, 1969, 2 children **DISCIPLINE** LATIN LANGUGE AND LITERATURE. **EDUCATION** Dartmouth Coll, AB, 69; Harvard Univ, MA, 71; PhD, 75. **CAREER** Harvard Univ: Tchg Fel, 72-73; Instr, Colby Col, 73-74; asst prof, 75-82, assoc prof, 82-89, prof, 89-97 Univ Chicago; prof, Princeton Univ; 97- **HONORS AND AWARDS** Nat Endowment Hum Fel, 80-81; John Simon Guggenheim Memorial Found Fel, 91-92; Charles J. Goodwin Award of Merit, 91., Pres, Am Philol Asn, 96; Avalon Found Distinguished Service Prof, 96-97. **MEMBERSHIPS** Am Philol Asn; Asn Ancient Historians; Women's Class Caucus. **RESEARCH** Origins of Rome; Greek: Plato; Euripides; Sophocles. **SELECTED PUBLICATIONS** Auth, Guardians of Language: The Grammarian and Society in Late Antiquity, TheTransformation of the Classical Heritage, /vik 11, Berkeley-Univ Calif Press, 88; Studies on the Text of Suetonius De Grammaticis et Rhetoribus, The American Philological Association: American Classical Studies, Scholars Press, 92; Suetonius: De Grammaticis et Rhetoribus, Clarendon Press, 95. **CONTACT ADDRESS** Princeton Univ, 1 Nassau Hall, Princeton, NJ, 08544. **EMAIL** kaster@princeton.edu

KATARZYNA, OLGA B.
DISCIPLINE SPANISH **EDUCATION** Univ Warsaw, MA, 90; Univ Chicago, PhD, 98. **CAREER** Vis asst prof, Williams Col, 98-99. **HONORS AND AWARDS** Univ Warsaw Merit fel, 87-90; Nat Jour Students' Awd, 85. **RESEARCH** Contemporary Spanish Literature and Culture; Romanticism in Europe and Latin America; 19th and 20th Century Hispanic Literature; Medieval Spanish Literature and History; Spanish Language and Culture. **SELECTED PUBLICATIONS** Auth, Indifference and Catastrophe: Spanish Short Story on the Threshold of the 21st Century, XXII Congreso de Letras Hispanicas, 96. **CONTACT ADDRESS** Center for Foreign Languages, Literatures and Cult, Williams Col, Williamstown, MA, 01267. **EMAIL** Katarzyna.O.Beilin@williams.edu

KATASSE, CONNY
DISCIPLINE ENGLISH AS A GLOBAL LANGUAGE **EDUCATION** Union Inst, PhD. **CAREER** Univ Alaska. **SELECTED PUBLICATIONS** Area: Deaf children and English in Perspectives in Education and Deafness. **CONTACT ADDRESS** Univ Alaska Anchorage, 3211 Providence Dr., Anchorage, AK, 99508.

KATH, RUTH R.
DISCIPLINE GERMAN **EDUCATION** Syracuse Univ, BA; Univ Conn, MA; Univ Iowa, PhD. **CAREER** Prof, Luther Col, 79-; listed in, World's Who's Who of Women, Who's Who Among Amer Women, Who's Who in the Midwest; 1969 and 1970, instr, Lindau Sailing Sch, Ger, 69 & 70; Fulbright sr awd, 85; **HONORS AND AWARDS** Oral Proficiency Testing Workshop--German scholar, Iowa Dept Edu, 86; 1988-1991, charter member, Iowa Governor's Commn on For Lang & Int Edu; pres, Iowa Chap, 83-85., Proj, Monuments to Jewish Tradition in Berlin, E Ger, 90; co-founded, Distinguished Ecumenical Lect Ser, 93. **MEMBERSHIPS** Delta Phi Alpha, Nat Ger Honorary Soc, 70-; Amer Asn Tchr(s) Ger, 75-; Iowa For Lang Asn, 74-. **SELECTED PUBLICATIONS** Auth, The Correspondence of Gerhard Marcks and Marguerite Mildenhain, 1970-1981:A Mingling of Souls, Iowa State Univ Press & Luther Col Press, 91; Children in the Poetry of Bertolt Brecht: Images of Young People and Examples for Youthful Audiences, Bern Switzerland, Peter Lang Verlag, 82. **CONTACT ADDRESS** Dept of Modern Languages, Luther Col, 700 College Dr, Decorah, IA, 52101. **EMAIL** kathruth@luther.edu

KATRITZKY, LINDE
PERSONAL Born 07/28/1928, Ansbach, Germany, m, 1952, 4 children **DISCIPLINE** GERMAN **EDUCATION** Univ of Munich, Staatsexamen in Hist, German and English, 47-52; Univ FL, MA, 82-84, PhD, 84-88. **CAREER** Graduat Teaching Asst, 82-84, Lectr, 84-88, Adjunct Assoc Prof, 88-94, Adjunct Prof, 1995-present, Univ FL. **MEMBERSHIPS** Honor Soc of Phi Kappa Phi; Lichtenberg-Gesellschaft; Howe Soc of the Univ FL; President's Council, Univ FL (distinguished member); Soc for German-Amer Studies; MLA (Modern Language Assn); Amer Soc for Eighteen-Century Studies; Amer Assn of Teachers of German Studies; Johann-Karl-Gesellschaft in Sonderhausen, Germany; Mid Western Section ASECS; South Eastern Section of ASECS. **RESEARCH** German and English eighteeth-century culture; literature and science; Samuel Johnson, The Letters of Junius; Georg Christoph Lichtenberg; Nachtwachen. Von Bonaventura. **SELECTED PUBLICATIONS** Lichtenbergs Gedankensystem: Denkanleitung fur Jedermann, The Enlightenment, German Interdisciplinary Studies, 95; Johnson and The Letters of Junius: New Perspectives on an Old Enigma, Ars Interpretandi/The Art, 96; A guide to Bonaventura's Nightwatches, in press. **CONTACT ADDRESS** Dept German & Slav languages, Univ FL, 1221 S.W. 21st Ave., Gainesville, FL, 32611.

KATZ, MARILYN A.
DISCIPLINE CLASSICAL LANGUAGES **EDUCATION** Columbia Univ, BA, 66, Yale Univ, MA, 68, PhD, 75. **CAREER** Trinity Col, Hartford, CT, 66; Lectr Trinity Col, Hartford, CT, 67, 68; Vis Instr, Wesleyan Univ, Middletown, CT, 70-71; Tchng Intern, Brooklyn Col, CUNY, 72-73, P/T Instr; 73-75, F/T Instr; 75, Instr, Sarah Lawrence Col, 75, 76; Vis Instr, Columbia Col, Columbia Univ, 75-77; Asst Prof; 76, 77, Asst Prof, Vis Lectr, Yale Col, Guest Fel, Morse Col, 80, Wesleyan Univ, Asst Prof, 78-83; Assoc Prof, 83-90; Prof 90-. **HONORS AND AWARDS** Yale Univ fel, 68; Mary Cady Tew Profize, 68; Samuel K. Bushnell Fel, 69-70; Elizabeth & A. Varvick Stout Fel, 71-72; Biddle Travel Sch, 73; Mem, Sch Hist, Studies, Inst Adv Study, 77-78; ACLS Fel Recent Ph.D.'s, 78; Nat Endowment Hum, 79, 80, 89, 90-91; Fac fel, Ctr Hum, 82; Elected mem, Am Philol Asn, 84-87, 87-90; Nat Endowment Hum, 87; Chair, Am Philol Asn, 89-90; Guggenheim Found, 93. **MEMBERSHIPS** Am Philological Asn, 67; Women's Classical Caucus, 72; Columbia Univ Seminar on Women and Society, 74; Am Asn Univ Prof, 79; Mod Lang Asn, 79, Columbia Univ Sem Clas Civilization, 83; Gardiner Seminar, 86; Soc Biblical Lit, 86; Yale Univ Judaic Studies Fac Seminar, 86. **SELECTED PUBLICATIONS** Sexuality and the Body in Ancient Greece, Metis. Revue d'anthropologie du monde grec ancient 4.1, 89, 155 - 79; Profoblems Sacrifice in Ancient Cultures, In The Bible in the Light Cuneiform Literature. Scripture in Context III, Edwin Mellen Profess, 90; Patriarchy and Inheritance in Greek and Biblical Antiquity: The Epiclerate and the Levirate. Profoceedings the Xth World Congress Jewish Studies, Magnes Profess, 90; Penelope's Renown: Meaning and Indeterminacy in Homer's Odyssey. Profinceton, New Jersey: Profinceton Univ Profess, 91; Review Suzanne Dixon, The Roman Mother, New England Clas Newsl & Jour 17, 90; Review Robert Garland, The Greek Way Life, The Classical Outlook 69, 91-92; Bouphonia and Goring Ox: Homicide, Animal Sacrifice, and Judicial Profocess, invited contribution to refereed volume, Nomodeiktes: Greek Studies in Honor Martin Ostwald, Univ Mich Profess, 92; Did the Greeks Believe in Their Myths? An Essay on the Constitutive Imagination History and Theory 31, 92; Ox Slaughter and Goring Oxen: Homicide, Animal Sacrifice, and Judicial Profocess, Yale Jour Law & Hum, 92; Politics and Pomegranates, in Essays on the Homeric Hymn to Demeter, Profinceton Univ Profess, 93; Ideology and 'the Status Women' in Ancient Greece, History and Theory Beiheft 31: History and Feminist Theory, 92; Homecoming and Hospitality: Recognition and the Construction Identity in the Odyssey,' in Epic and Epoch, Texas Tech Univ Pess, 94; The Character Tragedy: Women and the Greek Imagination, Arethusa 27.1, 94; Ideology and 'the Status Women' in Ancient Greece, in Feminists Revision History, Rutgers Univ Profess, 93; Ideology and 'the Status Women' in Ancient Greece, in Women in Antiquity: New Assessments, Routledge, 95. **CONTACT ADDRESS** Wesleyan Univ, Middletown, CT, 06459. **EMAIL** mkatz@wesleyan.edu

KATZ, MICHAEL RAY
PERSONAL Born 12/09/1944, New York, NY **DISCIPLINE** RUSSIAN LANGUAGE AND LITERATURE **EDUCATION** Williams Col, BA, 66; Oxford Univ, BA, MA and DPhil(Russ), 72. **CAREER** Asst prof, 72-78, chmn prog comp lit, 77-78, ASSOC PROF RUSS, WILLIAMS COL, 78-, CHMN DEPT GER and RUSS, 80-, Vis scholar, Univ Calif, Berkeley, 75-76. **MEMBERSHIPS** Am Asn Advan Slavic Studies; Am Asn Teachers Slavic and E Europ Lang. **RESEARCH** Russian romantic poetry; dreams in Russian fiction; Russian intellectual history. **SELECTED PUBLICATIONS** The Brothers Karamazov--Worlds of the Novel, Slavic Rev Vol 53, 94; Holy Foolishness--Dostojevski Novels and the Poetics of Cultural-Critique, Slavic and E Europ J, Vol 38, 94 **CONTACT ADDRESS** Dept of Russ, Univ Texas, Arlington, TX, 76019.

KAUFFMAN, JANET
DISCIPLINE VISUAL/MIXED TEXTS **EDUCATION** PhD. **CAREER** E Mich Univ **SELECTED PUBLICATIONS** Auth, Award The Weather Book, Tex Tech Univ Press, 81; World a Woman Could Walk, Knopf, 83; Collaborators, Knopf, 86; Where the World Is, Montparnasse Press, 88; Obscene Gestures for Women, Knopf, 89; The Body in Four Parts, Graywolf, 94; Characters on the Loose, Graywolf, 97. **CONTACT ADDRESS** Eastern Michigan Univ, Ypsilanti, MI, 48197.

KAUFMAN, STEPHEN ALLAN
PERSONAL Born 09/11/1945, Minneapolis, MN, m, 1972, 2 children **DISCIPLINE** ANCIENT NEAR EASTERN LANGUAGES, OLD TESTAMENT **EDUCATION** Univ Minn, BA, 62; Yale Univ, PhD(Near Eastern lang and lit), 70. **CAREER** Asst prof North-West semitics, Univ Chicago, 71-76; assoc prof, 76-81, PROF BIBLE and COGNATE LIT, HEBREW UNION COL, 81-, Vis sr lectr, Haifa Univ, Israel, 74-76; ED, SOC BIBL LIT, ARAMAIC SERIES, 79- **MEMBERSHIPS** Am Oriental Soc; Soc Bibl Lit. **RESEARCH** Aramaic studies; humanities micro computing. **SELECTED PUBLICATIONS** The Causative Stem in Ugaritic and the Causative Form in Semitic--A Morphologic-Semantic Analysis of the S-Stem and Disputed Non-Sibilant Causative Stems in Ugaritic, J Am Oriental Soc, Vol 113, 93; Old Aramaic Grammar of Texts from 7th-8th Century BC, J Am Oriental Soc, Vol 115, 95; A Scholars; Dictionary of Jewish Palestinian Aramaic--An Article Rev of Sokoloff, Michael Dictionary, J Am Oriental Soc, Vol 114, 94; The Dead Sea Scrolls on Microfiche--A Comprehensive Facsimile Edition of the Texts from the Judean Desert, Vol 3, Inventory List of Photographs, J Am Oriental Soc, Vol 116, 96; The Function of the Niphal in Biblical Hebrew in Relationship to Other Passive-Reflexive Verbal-Systems and to the Pual and Hophal in Particular--Siebesma,Pa, Cath Bibl Quart, Vol 56, 94; Living Waters--Scandinavian orientalistic Studies Presented to Lokkegaard,Frede on His 75th Birthday, January 27th, 1990, J Am Oriental Soc, Vol 113, 93; The Dead-Sea-Scrolls on Microfiche--A Comprehensive Facsimile Edition of the Texts from the Judean Desert, Vol 2, Companion Volume, J Am Oriental Soc, Vol 116, 96; The Dead-Sea-Scrolls Catalog--Documents, Photographs, and Museum Inventory Numbers, J Am Oriental Soc, Vol 116, 96. **CONTACT ADDRESS** Dept Bible and Cognate Lit, Hebrew Union Col, Cincinnati, OH, 45220.

KAULBACH, ERNEST NORMAN
PERSONAL Born 01/03/1935, Bridgeport, CT, m, 1970, 2 children **DISCIPLINE** MEDIEVAL STUDIES AND PHILOSOPHY **EDUCATION** St Mary's Univ, AB, 57, STL, 61; Fairfield Univ, MA, 61; Cornell Univ, PhD(medieval studies), 70. **CAREER** Instr English, St Joseph's Col, 61-62; instr English and theol, St Mary's Col, 63-66; vis assoc prof English, classics and philos, 70-73, ASSOC PROF ENGLISH and CLASSICS, UNIV TEX, AUSTIN, 73- **MEMBERSHIPS** Mediaeval Acad Am; Dante Soc Am. **RESEARCH** Medieval philosophy, literature and theology. **SELECTED PUBLICATIONS** Culture And The King--The Social Implications Of The Arthurian Legend, J Engl Ger Philol, Vol 95, 96. **CONTACT ADDRESS** Dept of English, Univ of Tex, 0 Univ of Texas, Austin, TX, 78712-1026.

KAYE, ALAN STEWART
PERSONAL Born 03/02/1944, Los Angeles, CA, m, 1972, 2 children **DISCIPLINE** LINGUISTICS, NEAR EASTERN STUDIES **EDUCATION** Univ Calif, Los Angeles, BA, 65; Univ Calif, Berkeley, MA, 68, PhD(ling), 71. **CAREER** Asst prof, Univ Colo, 68-71; asst prof, 71-74, assoc prof and chmn ling, 74-78, Prof and Dir, Lab Phonetic Res, CALIF STATE UNIV, FULLERTON, 78-, Nat Endowment Humanities grant, 73-74; Am Philos Soc grant, 73-74 and 75-76; Fulbright res grant, 78-79; instr, Pepperdine Univ, 74-76; CONSULT, ROCKWELL INT, 76-; INSTR, UNIV CALIF, IRVINE, 77- **MEMBERSHIPS** Philos Asn Pac Coast; Am Orient Soc; Ling Soc Am; Can Ling Asn; Mid East Studies Asn NAm. **RESEARCH** Arabic dialectology; Semitic linguistics; field linguistics (Africa, S Asia). **SELECTED PUBLICATIONS** Perspectives on Arabic Linguistics, Mod Lang J, Vol 81, 97; A

Syntax of Sanani Arabic, J Am Oriental Soc, Vol 117, 97; Pronouncing Arabic, J Am Oriental Soc, Vol 116, 96; Lectures in English and Arabic Sociolinguistics, Vol 73, 97; The Wonder of Words--Introduction to Linguistics, Word-J Int Ling Assn, Vol 45, 94; New Light on Boswell--Critical and Hist Essays on the Occasion of the Bicentenary of the 'Life of Johnson,' Biography-An Interdisciplinary Quart, Vol 16, 93; Biblical Hebrew--An Introductory Grammar, J Am Oriental Soc, Vol 116, 96; Essays on Hebrew, J Am Oriental Soc, Vol 116, 96; Focusschrift in Honor of Fishman, Joshua, A. on the Occasion of His 65th Birthday, Vol 1, Bilingual Education, Vol 2, Language Ethnicity, Vol 3, Language Planning, Can J Ling-Revue Canadienne De Ling; Language in the News--Discourse and Ideology in the Press, Can J Ling-Revue Canadienne De Linguistique, Vol 38, 93; Levantine Arabic for Non-Natives--A Proficiency-oriented Approach, Mod Lang J, Vol 79, 95; The Search for the Perfect Language, Can J Ling-Revue Canadienne De Linguistique, Vol 41, 96; The State of Language, J Int Linguistic Assn, Vol 45, 94; On Language--Selected-Writings of Greenberg, Joseph, H., Can J Ling-Revue Canadienne De Linguistique, Vol 39, 94; Reconstructing Proto-Afroasiatic Proto-Afrasian--Vowels, Tone, Consonants, and Vocabulary, Can J Ling-Revue Canadienne De Linguistique, Vol 41, 96; Early Arabic Grammatical Theory, Heterogeneity and Standardization, Word-J Int Linguistic Assn, Vol 45, 94; Theoretical and Practical Phonetics, Word-J Int Linguistic Assn, Vol 45, 94; Repetition in Arabic Discourse, Paradigms, Syntagms, and the Ecology of Language, Word-J Int Linguistic Assn, Vol 45, 94; Chadian Arabic, J Semitic Studies, Vol 42, 97; The Life and Mind of Jones, , Biog-An Interdisciplinary Quart, Vol 16, 93; Dictionary of Postclassical Yemeni Arabic, J Am Oriental Soc, Vol 112, 92; Reconstructing Languages and Cultures in the Series Trends in Linguistics Studies and Monographs 58, Can J Ling-Revue Canadienne De Linguistique, Vol 40, 95; Interlinguistics--Aspects of the Science of Planned Languages, Can J Ling-Revue Canadienne De Linguistique, Vol 39, 94; Modern Arabic--Structures, Functions and Varieties, Lang, Vol 73, 97; New Departures in Linguistics, J Int Linguistic Assn, Vol 47, 96; The Arabic Dialect of Qift Upper Egypt--Grammar and Classified Vocabulary, J Am Oriental Soc, Vol 116, 96; The Arabic Language in Am, Lang Soc, Vol 22, 93; Arabic Sociolinguistics--Issues and Perspectives, Lang Soc, Vol 25, 96; A Basic Vocabulary of the Bedouin Arabic Dialect of the Jbali Tribe Southern Sinai, J Am Oriental Soc, Vol 114, 94; Strophic Poetry--Proceedings of the 1st Int Congress on Arabic, Hebrew and Romance Strophic Poetry Held in Madrid in December, 1989, Bulletin of the School of Oriental and African Studies-University; Visible Speech--The Diverse Oneness of Writing Systems, Word-J Int Linguistic Assn, Vol 44, 93; An Index of Nigerian Languages, Word-J Int Linguistic Assn, Vol 47, 96; The Lang of News Media, Can J Ling-Revue Canadienne De Linguistique, Vol 39, 94; English Across Cultures--Cultures Across English, Can J Ling-Revue Canadienne De Linguistique, Vol 39, 94; North-Am Contributions to the Hist of Linguistics--Studies in the Hist of the Language Sciences, Can J Ling-Revue Canadienne De Linguistique, Vol 38, 93; Toward A Typology of European Langs, Can J Ling-Revue Canadienne De Linguistique, Vol 38, 93; Hamito-Semitic Etymological Dictionary--Materials for A Reconstruction, Bull Schl Oriental African Studies-Unive London, Vol 60, 97; Language Change and National Integration--Rural Migrants in Khartoum J Am Oriental Soc, Vol 114, 94; Sem-Kham-Yafet--Proceedings of the 7th Hamito-Semitic-indo-European Conference Milan, June 1, 93, J Am Oriental Soc, Vol 117, 97; Linguistics and Biblical Hebrew, J Am Oriental Soc, Vol 114, 94. **CONTACT ADDRESS** Dept of Ling, California State Univ, Fullerton, 800 N State College Blvd, Fullerton, CA, 92634.

KAZAZIS, KOSTAS
PERSONAL Born 07/15/1934, Athens, Greece, m, 1958, 2 children **DISCIPLINE** BALKAN LINGUISTICS **EDUCATION** Univ Lausanne, Lic es Sci Polit, 57; Univ Kans, MA, 59; Ind Univ, PhD(ling), 65. **CAREER** Instr ling, Univ Ill, Urbana, 64-65; from asst prof to assoc prof, 65-77, PROF LING, UNIV CHICAGO, 77-, NDEA grant, 67-68. **MEMBERSHIPS** Ling Soc Am; Mod Greek Studies Asn; Soc Romanian Studies; Soc Albanian LStudies; Am Asn Southeast Europ Studies. **RESEARCH** Languages in contact; bilingualism; sociolinguistics. **SELECTED PUBLICATIONS** Discover Romanian--An Introduction to the Language and Culture, Mod Lang J, Vol 80, 96. **CONTACT ADDRESS** Dept of Ling, Univ of Chicago, 1010 E 59th St, Chicago, IL, 60637-1512.

KE, C.R.
PERSONAL Born 09/23/1954, China, m, 1982, 1 child **DISCIPLINE** LINGUISTICS **EDUCATION** Indiana Univ Bloom, PhD 92. **CAREER** Univ Iowa, asst prof, Chinese lang co-or, 93-. **MEMBERSHIPS** AAAL; ACTFL; CLTA **RESEARCH** Second language acquisition; Chinese language and pedagogy; Experimental psycholinguistics; language assessment; curriculum and teacher development. **SELECTED PUBLICATIONS** Auth, Effects of strategies on the learning of Chinese characters among foreign language students, Jour of the Chin Lang Teach Assoc, 98; Effects of language background on the learning of Chinese characters among foreign language students, Foreign Lang Annals, 98; An Inquiry into the Reading Strategies of Intermediate and Advanced Learners of Chinese as a Foreign Language, coauth, Jour of the CLTA, 97; An empirical study on the relationship between Chinese character recognition and production, Modern Lang Jour, 96; A Gating Experiment with Chinese, Lang Teach and Ling Stud, 95; Aspects of Accuracy in a Proficiency-Oriented Program, ADFL Bulletin, 95. **CONTACT ADDRESS** Dept of Asian Languages and Literature, Univ of Iowa, 659 Phillips Hall, Iowa City, IA, 52242. **EMAIL** chuanren-ke@uiowa.edu

KEATEN, JAMES A.
DISCIPLINE INTERCULTURAL COMMUNICATION **EDUCATION** PA State Univ, PhD, 70. **CAREER** Prof, Univ Northern CO. **MEMBERSHIPS** Speech Commun Asn; Western States Commun Asn; Japanese Psychol Asn. **RESEARCH** Commun apprehension; cross-cultural commun. **SELECTED PUBLICATIONS** Coauth, Teaching people to speak well: Training and remediation of communication reticence, Hampton Publ Co, 95; Komyunikeishon fuan to wa nanika? ¤A definition of communication apprehension and related constructsl, Hokuriku Daiguku Kiyo, 20, 96; Development of an instrument to measure reticence, Commun Quart, 45, 97; Communication apprehension in Japan: Grade school through secondary school, Int J of Intercultural Rel, 21, 97; Assessing the cross-cultural validity of the Personal Report of Communication Apprehension scale (PRCA-24), Japanese Psychol Res, 40, 98; Fundamentals of communication: An intercultural perspective, Kawashima Shotem, 98. **CONTACT ADDRESS** Univ Northern Colorado, Greeley, CO, 80639. **EMAIL** jkeaten@bentley.unco.edu

KECK, CHRISTIANE ELISABETH
PERSONAL Born 07/19/1940, Jena, Germany **DISCIPLINE** GERMANIC LANGUAGES & LITERATURE **EDUCATION** Col New Rochelle, AB, 61; Columbia Univ, MA, 62; Univ Tex, Austin, PhD(Ger), 66. **CAREER** Prof Ger and Head, Dept For Lang and Lit, Purdue Univ, West Lafayette, 92-; Assoc Dir, Ctr for Int Bus Educ and Res, 92-. **HONORS AND AWARDS** Amoco Award for Outstanding Univ Teaching, 84; Federal Cross of Merit, Ger, 89; Goethe Medaille, 92; Ind Ger Teacher of the Year, 98. **MEMBERSHIPS** MLA; Am Asn Teachers Ger; Am Comp Lit Asn; ADFL. **RESEARCH** Italian Renaissance as an influence on German literature; 19th century German drama and novelle; the European historical novel; business German; women in literature. **SELECTED PUBLICATIONS** Auth, Renaissance and Romanticism: Tieck's Conception of Cultural Decline as Portrayed in his Vittoria Accorombona, In: Ser, German Studies in America, Vol 20, 76; Handbook on Business German; ed, Global Business Languages. **CONTACT ADDRESS** Dept of Foreign Lang & Lit, Purdue Univ, West Lafayette, IN, 47907-1968. **EMAIL** ckeck@purdue.edu

KEEL, WILLIAM D.
DISCIPLINE GERMAN DIALECTOLOGY, GERMANIC PHILOLOGY **EDUCATION** IN Univ, PhD, 77. **CAREER** Instr, Inst fur deutsche sprache, Mannheim; prof; ch, 90-. **HONORS AND AWARDS** Ger-Am collab res grants, Am Coun Learned Soc(s); Ger Acad Exchange Serv, (DAAD)., Ed, Yrbk of Ger-Am Stud, 86; exec comm, Soc Ger-Am Stud; exec comm KS Assn of tchr(s) Ger, 94-97. **MEMBERSHIPS** Mem, Speakers' Bureau Kans Hum Coun. **RESEARCH** Volga Ger settlements and dialects in KS. **SELECTED PUBLICATIONS** Co-ed, German Emigration from Bukovina to the Americas, Univ Munch, 96; auth, articles treating Hannoverian Low German, German-Bohemian and Mennonite Low German dialects in KS and Mo as well as the settlement history of Pa Germans in KS. **CONTACT ADDRESS** Dept of Ger Lang and Lit, Univ Kansas, Admin Building, Lawrence, KS, 66045. **EMAIL** wkeel@falcon.cc.ukans.edu

KEENAN, JOHN
DISCIPLINE ASIAN RELIGIONS **EDUCATION** Charles Borromeo Sem, AB; Univ Pa, MA; Univ Wis, PhD. **CAREER** Prof; Middlebury Col, 86-. **HONORS AND AWARDS** Frederick Streng awd. **SELECTED PUBLICATIONS** Auth, The Gospel of Mark: A Mahayana Reading; How Master Mou Removes our Doubts: A Reader Response Study of the Mou-Tzu-Li-hou-lunm & The Meaning of Christ: A Mahayana Theology. **CONTACT ADDRESS** Dept of Religion, Middlebury Col, Middlebury, VT, 05753.

KEENER, FREDERICK M.
PERSONAL Born 12/28/1937, New York, NY, m, 1961, 2 children **DISCIPLINE** ENGLISH, COMPARATIVE LITERATURE **EDUCATION** St John's Univ, NY, AB, 59; Columbia Univ, MA, 60, PhD(English), 65. **CAREER** From instr to asst prof English, St John's Univ, NY, 61-66; from asst prof to assoc prof, Columbia Univ, 66-72, dean summer session, 72-74; from assoc prof to prof, 74-78; PROF ENGLISH, HOFSTRA UNIV, 78-, Lectr, Hunter Col, 66; Nat Endowment for Humanities res fel, 76-77; vis prof, Columbia Univ, 81. **MEMBERSHIPS** MLA; Conf Brit Studies; Am Soc 18th Century Studies. **RESEARCH** Eighteenth century British literature; 18th century comparative literature. **SELECTED PUBLICATIONS** Critical Essays on Pope, Alexander, Scriblerian and the Kit-Cats, Vol 27, 95. **CONTACT ADDRESS** Dept of English, Hofstra Univ, 1000 Fulton Ave, Hempstead, NY, 11550-1091.

KEFFER, JR., CHARLES K.
DISCIPLINE FRENCH LANGUAGE AND LITERATURE **EDUCATION** Univ NC Wilmington, BA; Univ NC Chapel Hill, MA and PhD. **CAREER** Fac, 79-; prof. **HONORS AND AWARDS** Rookie of Yr Awd, Centre Col; David Hughes Mem Awd Excel Tchg, Centre Col, 88., Dir res study-abroad prog, Centre Col;Fulbright Exch Tchr, Ger. **RESEARCH** French language and literature. **SELECTED PUBLICATIONS** Auth, scholarly articles on Michel de Montaigne. **CONTACT ADDRESS** Centre Col, 600 W Walnut St, Danville, KY, 40422. **EMAIL** keffer@centre.edu

KELLER, GARY D.
PERSONAL Born 01/01/1943, San Diego, CA, m, 1967, 1 child **DISCIPLINE** SPANISH-ENGLISH BILINGUALISM, CHICANO LITERATURE **EDUCATION** Univ of the Ams, BA, 63; Columbia Univ, MA, 67, PhD(Span), 71; New Sch Social Res, MA, 72. **CAREER** Instr Span, Pace Col, 67-69; instr, Columbia Col, Columbia Univ, 69-70; asst prof, City Col New York, 70-74; assoc prof, Dept Foreign Lang and Humanities, York Col, City Univ New York, 74-78, chmn dept, 74-76; prof, William Paterson Col NJ, 78-79; DEAN, GRAD SCH, EASTERN MICH UNIV, 79-, Vis asst prof, NY Univ, 73 and 77; adj prof, Teachers Col, Columbia Univ, 77-79. **MEMBERSHIPS** MLA; Ling Soc Am; Int Ling Asn. **RESEARCH** Spanish-English bilingualism; higher education administration. **SELECTED PUBLICATIONS** Tijuana--Stories On The Border, Revista De Estudios Hispanicos, Vol 30, 96. **CONTACT ADDRESS** Grad Dean Eastern, Eastern Michigan Univ, Ypsilanti, MI, 48197.

KELLER, HANS-ERICH
PERSONAL Born 08/08/1922, Balsthal, Switzerland, m, 2 children **DISCIPLINE** MEDIEVAL FRENCH LITERATURE, HISTORY OF ROMANCE LANGUAGES **EDUCATION** Univ Basel, Mittellehrerexamen, 47, Oberlehrerexamen, 50, Doktorexamen(French, Ital), 52, Privatdozent, 58. **CAREER** Privatdozent French medieval lit, Univ Basel, 58-59 and French ling, 60-61; substitute prof, Univ Innsbruck, 59-60; vis prof French and Romance ling, Univ Mich, Ann Arbor, 61-63; prof French and Occitan ling and dir inst, Univ Utrecht, 63-69; PROF FRENCH LANG and MEDIEVAL LIT, OHIO STATE UNIV, 69- **MEMBERSHIPS** Soc Ling Romane; MLA; Soc Rencesvals Etude Epopees Romanes (pres, Dutch Nat Br, 64-69); Int Arthurian Soc; Int Courtly Lit Soc. **RESEARCH** French and Occitan dialectology; Rolandian matter; Arthuriana. **SELECTED PUBLICATIONS** Edition of Martin, Francois, Raymond Collection of Ancient and Modern Poetry from Languedoc, in the Dialect of Montpellier Continuation and End, Revue Des Langues Romanes, Vol 97, 93; Collection of Metaphors and Figurative Comparisons from Medieval Occitan and French Verse, Vol 1, Part 1--Literary Comparisons, Nature, Inanimate Nature, Vol 2, Part 2--Nature, the Living World, Vol 3--Man, Man and the Ext, Cahiers De Civilisation; Edition of Martin, Francois Raymond Collection of Ancient and Modern Poetry from Languedoc, in the Dialect of Montpellier Continuation and End, Revue Des Langues Romanes, Vol 97, 93; The 'Pseudo-Turpin' as a Source for the 'Novellino,' Zeitschrift fur Romanische Philologie, Vol 109, 93; Peoples and Languages of France, Mod Lang J, Vol 81, 97; The 'Song of Roland,' Cahiers De Civilisation Medievale, Vol 37, 94. **CONTACT ADDRESS** 1594 Essex Rd, Columbus, OH, 43221.

KELLER, HOWARD HUGHES
PERSONAL Born 09/05/1941, Brooklyn, NY, m, 1969 **DISCIPLINE** THEORETICAL LINGUISTICS, RUSSIAN LITERATURE **EDUCATION** Fordham Univ, AB, 63; Georgetown Univ, PhD(Russ), 67. **CAREER** Asst prof ling, Southern Ill Univ, Carbondale, 66-67; Fulbright lectr, Univ Sofia, 67-68; assoc prof, 70-80, PROF RUSS, MURRAY STATE UNIV, 80-, BK REV ED, SLAVIC AND EAST EUROP J, 78-; Nat Endowment for Humananities fel, 78; Presidential res fel, Murray State Univ, 79; ED, SLAVIC and EAST EUROP J, 80-; Nat Endowment for Humanities fel, 81. **MEMBERSHIPS** Am Asn Teachers Slavic and East Europ Lang; Ling Soc Am; Am Asn Advan Slavic Studies; Am Asn Teachers Ger; Ling Soc Am. **RESEARCH** Slavic and Germanic word formation; language teaching methodology; language and the brain. **SELECTED PUBLICATIONS** Russian-English Online Dictionary, Superdic-3.01, Mod Lang J, Vol 80, 96. **CONTACT ADDRESS** Dept of Foreign Lang, Murray State Univ, Murray, KY, 42071.

KELLER, JOHN ESTEN
PERSONAL Born 09/27/1917, Lexington, KY **DISCIPLINE** ROMANCE LANGUAGES **EDUCATION** Univ Ky, AB, 40, AM, 42; Univ NC, PhD, 46. **CAREER** Insts, Univ NC, 43-46; asst prof, Univ Ky, 46-47; from asst prof to assoc prof, Univ Tenn, 47-50; from asst prof to prof Romance lang, Univ NC, Chapel Hill, 50-67, exec secy curric in folklore, 63-67; assoc dean, Col Arts and Sci, 67-72, PROF SPAN and CHMN DEPT SPAN and ITAL, UNIV KY, 67- **HONORS AND AWARDS** UK Sang Award Outstanding Contribr to Grad Educ, 73. **MEMBERSHIPS** MLA; Mediaeval Acad Am; Am Asn Teachers Span and Port; SAtlantic Mod Lang Asn (pres, 67-68); corresp mem Hisp Soc Am. **RESEARCH** Roman philology; Old Spanish literature; iconography of brief medieval Spanish narrative. **SELECTED PUBLICATIONS** The Learned King--

The Reign of Alfonso-X of Castile, Hispania-A J Devoted Tchg Span Port, Vol 77, 94; The 'Libro De Alexandre,' Medieval Epic and Silver Latin, Romance Quart, Vol 42, 95. **CONTACT ADDRESS** Dept of Span and Ital, Univ of Ky, Lexington, KY, 40506.

KELLETT, PETE
DISCIPLINE ORGANIZATIONAL COMMUNICATION **EDUCATION** Sheffield City Polytech, Eng, BA, 83; Southern IL Univ, Carbondale, MA, 85, PhD, 90. **CAREER** Asst prof, Univ NC, Greensboro; consult, Piedmont Triad area of NC. **MEMBERSHIPS** Speech Commun Asn; Int Commun Asn. **RESEARCH** Organizational commun; organizational change management. **SELECTED PUBLICATIONS** Author of approximately 20 book chapters, journal articles, and convention papers in organizational commun and related areas. **CONTACT ADDRESS** Univ N. Carolina, Greensboro, 102 Fergus, Greensboro, NC, 27412-5001. **EMAIL** Kellettp@iris.uncg.edu

KELLEY, KATHLEEN ALITA
PERSONAL Born 11/19/1932, Bradford, England, m, 1970, 2 children **DISCIPLINE** LATIN AMERICAN LITERATURE **EDUCATION** Univ Ariz, PhD, 92. **CAREER** Asst prof, 92-98, assoc prof, Span & Fr, Pa State Univ, 98-. **HONORS AND AWARDS** Tinker Found Grant, 87; NEH grant, 93. **MEMBERSHIPS** Int Soc Humor Studies; MLA; Am Transl Asn; Am Lit Transl Asn; Latin Am Indian Lit Asn; Latin Am Studies Asn. **RESEARCH** Translation theory; humor. **SELECTED PUBLICATIONS** Auth, Jose Maria Arguedas and the Tenets of Neo-Modernity: the Andean Novelist's Challenge to a Zeitgeist, in Beyond Indigenous Voices: LAILA/ALILA 11th International Symposium on Latin American Indian Literatures, Labyrinthos Press, 96; auth, The Clapham Omnibus: Translating the Comic Text, in Translation and Meaning, Part 3: Proceedings of the Maastricht Session of the 2nd International Maastricht-Lodz Duo Colloquium, UPM, 96; co-transl, Path Through the Cane Fields, White Adder Press, 97; auth, The Persistence of Center: Jose Maria Arguedas and the Challenge to the Postmodern Outlook, in Jose Maria Arguedas: Reconsiderations for Latin American Cultural Studies, Latin American Series No. 29, Ohio Univ Ctr for Int Studies, 98; translator and author of numerous articles and other publications. **CONTACT ADDRESS** MP-215, Malvern, PA, 19355. **EMAIL** kak7@psu.edu

KELLEY, MICHAEL ROBERT
PERSONAL Born 08/20/1940, Washington, DC, 1 child **DISCIPLINE** ENGLISH LITERATURE, LINGUISTICS **EDUCATION** Cath Univ Am, BA, 62, MFA, 65, PhD(English), 70. **CAREER** Asst prof, 70-75, assoc prof, 75-80, prof English, George Mason Univ, 80-, Contrib ed, Mod Humanities Res Asn Bibliog, 75-. **MEMBERSHIPS** MLA; Mediaeval Acad Am. **RESEARCH** Medieval English drama; Chaucer; literary aesthetics. **SELECTED PUBLICATIONS** Auth, Fifteenth Century Flamboyant Style and the Castle of Perseverance, Comp Drama, spring 72; English for Foreign Speakers--a Television Solution, AV instr, 11/72; Flamboyant Drama, Southern Ill Univ, 78. **CONTACT ADDRESS** Dept of English, George Mason Univ, 4400 University Dr, Fairfax, VA, 22030-4444. **EMAIL** mkelley@gmu.edu

KELLING, HANS-WILHELM L.
PERSONAL Born 08/15/1932, Schwerin, Germany, m, 1958, 3 children **DISCIPLINE** GERMAN LANGUAGE & LITERATURE **EDUCATION** Brigham Young Univ, BA, 58; Stanford Univ, MA, 60, Ph, 67. **CAREER** Teaching asst Ger, Brigham Young Univ, 57-58; asst, Stanford Univ, 58-61; from asst prof to assoc prof, 62-72, chmn, Dept Germanic Lang, 77-82, Prof Ger, Brigham Young Univ, 72-, Chmn Dept Germanic & Slavic Lang, 82- **MEMBERSHIPS** MLA; Rocky Mountain Mod Lang Asn; Am Asn Teachers Ger. **RESEARCH** German literature of the classical period; cultural history. **SELECTED PUBLICATIONS** Coauth, Deutsche Aufsatzhilfe, Brigham Young Univ, 67 & 68; auth, Bettina von Arnim--a study in Goethe idolatry, Bull Rocky Mountain Mod Lang Asn, 6/69; The idolatry of poetic genius, Yearbk English Goethe Soc, 70; The Idolatry of Poetic Genius in German Goethe Criticism Herbert Lang, Berne, 70; coauth, Deutscwhie Man's Sagt und Schreibt, 72 & auth, Deutsche Kulturgeschichte, 73; Holt; Goethe the Dichterprophet, Ger Life & Lett, 73. **CONTACT ADDRESS** Brigham Young Univ, 2007A JKHB, Provo, UT, 84602-0002. **EMAIL** hans-wilhelm_kelling@byu.edu

KELLMAN, STEVEN G.
PERSONAL Born 11/15/1947, Brooklyn, NY **DISCIPLINE** COMPARATIVE LIT **EDUCATION** Univ Cal, Berk, PhD, 72, MA, 69; State Univ NY, Bing, BA, 67. **CAREER** Ashbel Smith Prof, comp lit, Univ TX San Antonio, 95-, Prof comp lit, 85-, Assoc prof, 80-85, Asst prof, 76-80, Vis prof, 82; Univ Irvine, Vis lectu, 75-76; Tel Aviv Univ, Lectu, 73-75; Bemdji State Col, Asst prof, 72-73. **HONORS AND AWARDS** H L Mencken Awd, 86; John E Sawyer fel, Longfellow Inst Harv, 97; NEH 96; Fulbright Sr lectr, 80; Partners of the Amers, Peru, 88-95; Fulbright-Hays study grant to China, 95; UTSA, Amoco Awd, teaching, 85. **MEMBERSHIPS** Modern Lang Asn; Am Comp Lit Asn; Nat Bk Critics Circ; PEN Am Cen. **RESEARCH** Fiction; film; lit crit; nonfiction. **SELECTED PUBLICATIONS** Ed, Masterplots II: American Fiction Series, rev ed, Pasadena CA, Salem, 99; Ed with Irving Malin, Into the Tunnel: Essay's On William Gass's Novel and Leslie Fielder and American Culture, Newark, Univ Del Press, 99 and 98; Ed, Perspectives on Raging Bull, NY, G K Hall, 94; The Plague: Fiction and Resistance, Bost, Twayne, 93. **CONTACT ADDRESS** Div of Foreign Languages, Univ Texas, San Antonio, San Antonio, TX, 78249-0644. **EMAIL** kellman@lonestar.utsa.edu

KELLY, DAVID H.
PERSONAL Born 09/23/1929, Philadelphia, PA, 3 children **DISCIPLINE** CLASSICAL LINGUISTICS **EDUCATION** Cath Univ Am, BA, 52; Univ PA, MA, 54, PhD, 58. **CAREER** From asst prof to assoc prof class & ling, La Salle Univ, 61-70, chmn dept for lang, 67-69, dean arts & sci, 69-70; Prof Class, Montclair State Col, 70. **HONORS AND AWARDS** MSU Distinguished Tchr, 98. **MEMBERSHIPS** Am Philol Asn; Class Asn Atlantic States (pres, 77-78). **RESEARCH** Lang tchg methodology; class hum; syntax of Greek and Latin. **SELECTED PUBLICATIONS** Auth, Distinctive feature analysis in Latin phonology, Am J Philol, 67; Transformations in the Latin nominal phrase, Class Philol, 68; Tense in the Latin independent operative, Glotta, 72; Latin the tool subject, Class Outlook, 73; Revolution in classical studies, Class J, 73; Egyptians and Ethiopians: Color, race, and racism, Class Outlook, 91; Case: Grammar and terminology, Class World, 93. **CONTACT ADDRESS** Dept of Class, Montclair State Univ, 1 Normal Ave, Montclair, NJ, 07043-1699. **EMAIL** kellyd@mail.montclair.edu

KELLY, LOUIS G.
DISCIPLINE LINGUISTICS **EDUCATION** Univ Laval, PhD. **CAREER** Prof, Univ Ottawa. **RESEARCH** Translation theory; history of linguistics; sociolinguistics. **SELECTED PUBLICATIONS** Auth, Twenty-five Centuries of Language Teaching, Newbury House, 69; Quaestiones Alberti de modis significandi: A Critical Edition, Benjamins, 77; The True Interpreter: A History of Translation Theory in the West, Blackwells, 79; Prorsus Taliter. The Latin Text of Kipling's Just So Stories, Centaur Bk(s), 85; A Critical Edition of Basil Valentine, His Triumphant Chariot of Antimony. London, Garland Publishing, 90. **CONTACT ADDRESS** Dept of Linguistics, Univ Ottawa, 70 Laurier Ave, PO Box 450, Ottawa, ON, K1N 6N5.

KELLY, VAN
DISCIPLINE FRENCH LITERATURE **EDUCATION** Univ NC, Chapel Hill, PhD. **CAREER** Assoc prof, Univ KS. **RESEARCH** French moralists and mod poetry. **SELECTED PUBLICATIONS** Auth, Pascalian Fictions: Antagonism and Absent Agency in the Wager and Other Pensees, Summa, 92; co-ed, Epic and Epoch: Essays on the History and Interpretation of a Genre, Tex Tech UP, 84. **CONTACT ADDRESS** Dept of French and Italian, Univ Kansas, Admin Building, Lawrence, KS, 66045. **EMAIL** kufacts@ukans.edu

KEMP, HENRIETTA J.
DISCIPLINE GERMAN, HISTORY, LIBRARY SCIENCE **EDUCATION** Univ Iowa, BA, 66; Univ Pittsburgh, MLS, 71. **CAREER** LIBR, 81-, SUPERV, FINE ARTS COLLECT, 89-, LUTHER COL. **CONTACT ADDRESS** Library, Luther Col, 700 College Dr, Decorah, IA, 52101. **EMAIL** kempjane@luther.edu

KENKEL, KONRAD
DISCIPLINE GERMAN LANGUAGE **EDUCATION** IN Univ, PhD, 75. **CAREER** Dir, Middlebury Ger Summer Schl; Assoc prof, Darmouth Col. **HONORS AND AWARDS** Bundesverdienstkreuz, Fed Repub Ger, 96. **RESEARCH** Ger lit and art from the turn of the century through the Weimar Repub. **SELECTED PUBLICATIONS** Auth, comp studies about the treatment of myth; publ(s) about Gryphius, Hofmannsthal, Gustav Mahler, and var postwar Ger auth(s). **CONTACT ADDRESS** Dartmouth Col, 3529 N Main St, #207, Hanover, NH, 03755.

KENNEDY, CHRIS
DISCIPLINE LINGUISTICS **EDUCATION** Univ Calif Santa Cruz, PhD. **CAREER** Prof, Northwestern Univ. **RESEARCH** Syntax; semantics; syntax-semantics interface; adjectives and comparatives; anaphora and ellipsis; natural language processing. **SELECTED PUBLICATIONS** Auth, Cross-polar anomaly and the ontology of degrees, 98; Antecedent contained deletion and the syntax of quantification, Ling Inquiry, 97; Verb phrase deletion and 'Nonparasitic' Gaps, Ling Inquiry, 97; coauth, Attributive comparatives and bound ellipsis, Ling Res Center Report LRC-97-03, Univ Calif, Santa Cruz, 97; An indexical account of certain ambiguities, Proceedings of ESCOL '95, Ithaca, Cornell LingClub, 96; Comparatives, indices, and scope, Proceedings of FLSM VI. Bloomington: Ind Univ Ling Club, 95; Morphological alignment and head projection: Towards a nonderivational account of stress in Dakota, Phonology at Santa Cruz 3, Ling Res Center, Univ Calif, Santa Cruz, 95; Argument contained ellipsis, Ling Res Center, Report LRC-94-03, Univ Calif, Santa Cruz, 94. **CONTACT ADDRESS** Dept of Linguistics, Northwestern Univ, 1801 Hinman, Evanston, IL, 60208.

KENNEDY, WILLIAM JOHN
PERSONAL Born 04/26/1942, Brooklyn, NY, m, 1967, 2 children **DISCIPLINE** RENAISSANCE & COMPARATIVE LITERATURE **EDUCATION** Manhattan Col, BA, 63; Yale Univ, PhD(comp lit), 69. **CAREER** Instr Eng, Fairleigh Dickinson Univ, 67-70; asst prof comp lit, 70-76, assoc prof, 76-82, Prof comp lit, Cornell Univ, 82-, Vis assoc prof comp lit, NY Univ, 82. **HONORS AND AWARDS** Guggenheim fel 87-88; Villa Serbelloni, 98. **MEMBERSHIPS** MLA; Am Comp Lit Asn; Renaissance Soc Am. **RESEARCH** Lit theory; rhetorical criticism; lyric poetry. **SELECTED PUBLICATIONS** Auth, Rhetorical Norms in Renaissance Literature, Yale Univ Press, 78; Jacopo Sannazaro, VNIV New England Press, 83; Authorizing Petrarch, Cornell Univ Press, 94. **CONTACT ADDRESS** Comp Lit Dept, Cornell Univ, Ithaca, NY, 14850. **EMAIL** WJK3@cornell.edu

KENNEDY-DAY, KIKI
PERSONAL Chicago, IL, m, 1988 **DISCIPLINE** NEAR EASTERN LANGUAGES AND LITERATURE-ARABIC (ISLAMIC PHILOSOPHY) **EDUCATION** NY Univ, PhD, 96. **CAREER** St John's Univ Jamaica; Adj Asst Prof, Hofstra Univ NY, 98-. **MEMBERSHIPS** APA. **RESEARCH** Islamic Philosophy; Ibn Sina. **SELECTED PUBLICATIONS** Auth, articles about Al-Kindi, Aristotelianism in Islamic Philos, Routledge Encycl of Islamic Philos, 98. **CONTACT ADDRESS** Fort Washington Ave, 4A, New York, NY, 10033.

KEPNES, STEVEN D.
PERSONAL Born 05/21/1952, Boston, MA, m **DISCIPLINE** JEWISH STUDIES **EDUCATION** Hobart and William Smith Colleges, BA, 74; Univ Chicago, Divinity, MA, 76; Univ Chicago, PhD (Modern Jewish thought and relig and psychol studies), 83; study abroad, Hebrew Univ of Jerusalem, 83, 85, 87, 93-95. **CAREER** Assoc prof, Dept of Philos and Relig and Dir of Jewish Studies, Colgate Univ Hamilton, NY, 93-; ed, Judaism section, Religious Studies Rev, 94-; ed, Biblical Hermeneutics, Textural Reasoning, 96-. **HONORS AND AWARDS** Phi Beta Kappa, 74; Sheuer fel in Jewish Studies, Univ Chicago, 79-80; Lakritz grant in Buber Scholarship, 85, 88; Mellon Found fel, 86-88; Memorial Found for Jewish Culture, 86-87; Am Academy of Relig Res grant, 87-88; Colgate Univ Major Res grant, 93-94; Hartman Inst Fel, Jerusalem, 93-95. **MEMBERSHIPS** AJS; AAR. **RESEARCH** German Jewish thought; hermaneutics. **SELECTED PUBLICATIONS** Co-ed with David Tracy, The Challenge of Psychology to Faith, Concilium, vol 156, Seabury, 82(published in eight languages); auth, The Text as Thou: Martin Buber's Dialogical Hermaneutics and Narrative Theology, IN Univ Press, 92; The Dialogic Self, The Endangered Self, Don Capps and Richard Fenn, eds, Princeton Theol Sem, 92; Introduction, Martin Buber, Toward a New German Translation of the Scriptures, trans by Alan Swensen, ed by Steven Kepnes, Post-Critical Biblical Interpretation, Peter Ochs, ed, Fortress Press, 93; Martin Buber's Dialogical Biblical Hermaneutics, Protestans Szemle (Hungarian), 17:2, 92; Budapest, also in Literary Criticism and Biblical Hermeneutics (Hungarian and English), Tibor Fabiny, ed, Szged: Attlia Jozsef Univ Press, 93; Martin Buber's Dialogical Biblical Hermaneutics, Martin Buber and the Human Sciences, Maurice Friedman, ed, SUNY, 96; ed, Interpreting Judaism in a Postmodern Age, NY Univ Press, 96; auth, Postmodern Interpretations of Judaism: Deconstructive Approaches, Interpreting Judaism in a Postmodern Age, Steven Kepnes, ed, NY Univ Press, 96; co-auth with Peter Ochs and Robert Gibbs, Reasoning After Revelation: Dialogues in Postmodern Jewish Philosophy, Westview, 98; auth, Surviving Holocaust Judaism, Modern Judaism, forthcoming. **CONTACT ADDRESS** Dept of Philos and Relig, Colgate Univ, Hamilton, NY, 13346-1398. **EMAIL** skepnes@center.colgate.edu

KERR, LUCILLE
DISCIPLINE SPANISH AND PORTUGUESE **EDUCATION** Yale Univ, PhD. **CAREER** Prof, Univ Southern Calif. **RESEARCH** Modern fiction and the critical theory of narrative; texts from the Spanish American tradition. **SELECTED PUBLICATIONS** Auth, Suspended Fictions: Reading Novels by Manuel Puig & Reclaiming the Author: Figures & Fictions from Spanish America. **CONTACT ADDRESS** Col Letters, Arts & Sciences, Univ Southern Calif, University Park Campus, Los Angeles, CA, 90089. **EMAIL** lkerr@bcf.usc.edu

KESLER, LINC
DISCIPLINE LINGUISTICS **EDUCATION** Yale Univ, BA, 71; Univ Toronto, MA, 72, PhD, 81. **CAREER** Engl, Oregon St Univ. **RESEARCH** Semiotics; renaissance & 17th century Brit, native Am & Asian lit. **SELECTED PUBLICATIONS** Auth, The Idealization of Women in the Renaissance: Morphology and Change in Three Poetic Texts, Mosaic, 90; Fate and Narrative Sturcture in Lermontov's A Hero of Our Time, Texas Studies in Language & Literature, 90; Ben Jonson Johns Hopkins Guide to Literary Theory and Criticism, 93. **CONTACT ADDRESS** Oregon State Univ, Corvallis, OR, 97331-4501. **EMAIL** lkesler@orst.edu

KESSLER, ANN VERONA
PERSONAL Born 01/28/1928, Aberdeen, SD **DISCIPLINE** MODERN & CHURCH HISTORY **EDUCATION** Mt Marty

Col, BA, 53; Creighton Univ, MA, 57; Univ Notre Dame, PhD, 63. **CAREER** Teacher elem schs, 47-49, 57-59 & Mt Marty High Sch, 52-56; from instr to assoc prof, 62-73, acad dean, 63-65, head dept hist, 68-77, Prof Hist, Mt Marty Col, 73-98, Professor Emeritus, 98-; mem, Am Benedictine Acad, 67-98; mem, Fulbright Scholar Selection Comt, 77, 79. **HONORS AND AWARDS** Teaching Excellence and Campus Leadership Award, Sears-Roebuck Found, 91. **MEMBERSHIPS** Am Acad Polit & Soc Sci; AHA; Am Polit Sci Asn. **RESEARCH** Fate of religious orders in France since the revolution; modern church-state controversies; monastic history and biography of Benedictines. **SELECTED PUBLICATIONS** Auth, French Benedictines under stress, fall 66 & Political legacy to the religions in France: Laic laws of the Third Republic, 12/69, Am Benedictine Rev; Post-Revolution Restoration of French Monasticism, SDak Soc Sci Asn J, fall 77; Founded on Courage, Inspired with Vision: Mt Marty Col, In: From Idea to Institution, 89; First Catholic Bishop of Dakota: Martin Marty, In: South Dakota Leaders, 89; Benedictine Men and Women of Courage, 96. **CONTACT ADDRESS** Mount Marty Col, 1105 W 8th St, Yankton, SD, 57078-3724. **EMAIL** akessler@rs6.mtmc.edu

KETROW, SANDRA M.

PERSONAL Born 05/20/1949, Indianapolis, IN **DISCIPLINE** SPEECH COMMUNICATION **EDUCATION** AB, 71, MS, 78, PhD, 82, Ind Univ. **CAREER** Teacher, eng, Lawrenceburg High Sch, 76-78; assoc instr/ed asst, dept of speech comm, Ind Univ & Central States Speech Jour, 78-81; asst prof & dir of pub speaking, dept of speech, Univ Fla, 81-84; visiting asst & adjunct prof, dept of speech, Butler Univ, 84-86; asst prof, 86-92, assoc prof, 92-98, prof & dir of grad prog, 98-, dept of speech comm, Univ RI. **HONORS AND AWARDS** Fel, Teaching & Tech, Univ RI, 97-98; World Who's Who of Women, 95-; Who's Who of Intl Women, 94-; Who's Who of Bus & Professional Women, 93-; Who's Who of Amer Women, 93-. **MEMBERSHIPS** Nat Comm Asn; Intl Comm Asn; Eastern Comm Asn. **RESEARCH** Nonverbal communication; Argumentation in groups. **SELECTED PUBLICATIONS** Co-auth, Processes and Outcomes Related to Non-Rational Argument in Societal Groups, Argument in a Time of Change: Proceedings of the Tenth AFA/SCA Argumentation Conference, 103-109, Nat Comm Asn, 98; co-auth, Social Anxiety and Performance in an Interpersonal Perception Task, Psychological Reports, 81, 991-996, 97; co-auth, Improving Decision Quality in the Small Group: The Role of the Reminder, Small Group Communication, 404-410, 97; auth, Is it Homophobia, Heterosexism, Sexism, or Can I Pass?, Lesbians in Academia: Degrees of Freedom, 106-112, NY, Routledge, 97; co-auth, Improving Decision Making in the Group: Arguing with Constructive Intent, Proceedings of the Ninth AFA/SCA Argumentation Conference, Speech Comm Asn, 95; co-auth, Improving Decision Quality in the Small Group: The Role of the Reminder, Small Group Research, 26, 4, 521-541, 95; co-auth, Using Argumentative Functions to Improve Decision Quality in the Small Group, Argument and the Postmodern Challenge: Proceedings of the Eighth AFA/SCA Argumentation Conference, 218-225, Speech Comm Asn, 93. **CONTACT ADDRESS** Dept. of Communication Studies, Univ of Rhode Island, 60 Upper College Rd., Suite 1, Kingston, RI, 02881-0812. **EMAIL** ketrow@uriacc.uri.edu

KEUMSIL, KIM YOON

DISCIPLINE LINGUISTICS **EDUCATION** Univ Paris III-Sorbonne, PhD, 84. **CAREER** Prof & dir, Bilingual-ESL Grad prog. **RESEARCH** Machine-mediated discourse and ethnolinguistic identity. **SELECTED PUBLICATIONS** Publ in the areas of, sociolinguistics, psycholinguistics, second language acquisition, and pragmatics. **CONTACT ADDRESS** Dept of Language and Cultures, William Paterson Col, 300 Pompton Rd., Wayne, NJ, 07470.

KEVRA, SUSAN

PERSONAL Born 03/26/1963, New Brunswick, NJ, m, 1991 **DISCIPLINE** FRENCH **EDUCATION** Oberlin Col, BA, 85; Univ of Mich, MA, 88; Univ of Mass at Amherst, PhD, 98. **CAREER** Vis prof, Marlboro Col. **HONORS AND AWARDS** Women in French Graduate Student Essay Prize, 94; Phi Kappa Phi Honor Soc, 92; Micheline Dufau Prize for Excellence in Tchg French, 92. **MEMBERSHIPS** MLA; Am Coun for Quebec Studies; Women in French; Conseil Int d'etudes francophones. **RESEARCH** Quebec Lit; women's studies. **SELECTED PUBLICATIONS** Auth, Indigestible Stew and Holy Piss: The politics of Food in Rodolphe Girard's marie Calumet, Quebec Studies, Vol 27, 99; Of Pigs and Princesses: Corporeal Currency in the Meat Market: Themes of Consumption in Les Trois petits cochons, Women in French Studies Vol 2, 94. **CONTACT ADDRESS** Marlboro Col, Marlboro, VT, 05346. **EMAIL** skevra@marlboro.edu

KIBBEE, DOUGLAS

DISCIPLINE FRENCH LITERATURE **EDUCATION** Colgate Univ, BA, 71; Univ Ind, MA, 75; PhD, 79 **CAREER** Prof, Univ Ill Urbana Champaign. **RESEARCH** History of French language; lexicography; politics of language; history of linguistics. **SELECTED PUBLICATIONS** Auth, For to Speke French Trewely The French Language in England, 1000-1600: Its Status, Description and Instruction, John Benjamins, 91; Emigrant Languages and Acculturation: The Case of Anglo-French, Rasmus Rask Quarterly, 95; The 'New Historiography', the History of French and 'Le Bon Usage'in Nicot's Dictionary (1606), 95; co-ed, New Analysis of Romance Languages: Proceedings of the Eighteenth Linguistic Symposium on Romance Languages, John Benjamins. **CONTACT ADDRESS** French Dept, Univ Ill Urbana Champaign, 52 E Gregory Dr, Champaign, IL, 61820. **EMAIL** dkibbee@uiuc.edu

KIBLER, LOUIS WAYNE

PERSONAL Born 07/23/1939, Clifton Forge, VA, m, 1960, 3 children **DISCIPLINE** ITALIAN, FRENCH **EDUCATION** Ind Univ, BA, 61, PhD(French), 65. **CAREER** Asst prof Ital & French, Ind Univ, Bloomington, 65-72; assoc prof mod lang, Sweet Brair Col, 72-74; assoc prof Ital, Wayne State Univ, 74-**MEMBERSHIPS** Am Asn Teachers Ital; AAIS; AAUP. **RESEARCH** Twentieth century Italian and French prose and theater; medieval Italian theater. **SELECTED PUBLICATIONS** Coauth, Giorno per Giorno, Macmillian, 71; auth, Imagery as expression; Moravia's Indifferenti, Italica, fall 72; Reality and Realism of Moravia, Ital Quart, summer 73; Imagery in Georges Bataille's Le Bleuduciel, Fr Rev, spring 74; Patterns of time, In: Pavese's La luna e ifalo, Forum Italicum, fall 78; Moravia and Guttuso: A la recherche de la realite perdue, Italica, summer 79; ed, Ezio d'Errico's Theater of the Absurd: Three Plays, Fairleigh Dickinson Univ Press, 91; auth, Myth and Meaning in D'Annunzio's La figlia di Iorio, Annali d'Italianistica, 87; Moravia as Journalist, Homage to Moravia, Forum Italicum, 93. **CONTACT ADDRESS** Dept of Romance, Wayne State Univ, 487 Manoogian Hall, Detroit, MI, 48202-3919. **EMAIL** l.kibler@wayne.edu

KIEFFER, BRUCE

DISCIPLINE GERMAN **EDUCATION** Columbia Univ, BA, 73; Princeton Univ, PhD, 79. **CAREER** Prof, Williams Col, 78-; dir, Ctr For Lang, Lit & Cult, 86-90. **HONORS AND AWARDS** NEH res fel, 82-83. **RESEARCH** German literature and thought 1750-1900; American and German comparative political history. **SELECTED PUBLICATIONS** Auth, The Storm and Stress of Language: Linguistic Catastrophe in the Early Works of Goethe, Lenz, Klinger and Schiller, 86. **CONTACT ADDRESS** Center for Foreign Languages, Literatures and Cult, Williams Col, Williamstown, MA, 01267. **EMAIL** Bruce.Kieffer@williams.edu

KILLIAM, MARIE-THERESE

DISCIPLINE FRENCH LANGUAGE AND LITERATURE **EDUCATION** Mt Holyoke Col, BA; Columbia Univ, MA; PhD. **CAREER** Assoc prof, Sweet Briar Col. **RESEARCH** 20th century lit and mod literary criticism. **SELECTED PUBLICATIONS** Auth, The Art Criticism of Paul Claudel; coauth, L'Analyse du texte; articles on modern French writers and on French cinema. **CONTACT ADDRESS** Sweet Briar Col, Sweet Briar, VA, 24595. **EMAIL** metzidakis@sbc.edu

KIM, NAM-KIL

DISCIPLINE EAST ASIAN LANGUAGES AND CULTURES **EDUCATION** Univ Wash, PhD, 74. **CAREER** Assoc prof & dir, Korean Stud Inst, Univ Southern Calif. **RESEARCH** Chinese, Japanese and Korean linguistics. **SELECTED PUBLICATIONS** Auth, Intermediate Modern Korean; The Use of keyss in Korean. **CONTACT ADDRESS** East Asian Studies Center, Univ Southern Calif, University Park Campus, Los Angeles, CA, 90089.

KING, KATHERINE CALLEN

PERSONAL Born 10/27/1942, OR, s, 2 children **DISCIPLINE** COMPARATIVE LIT **EDUCATION** Vassar Col, Poughkeepsie, AB, 67; Columbia Univ NY, MA, 69; Princeton, PhD, 78. **CAREER** John Jay Col, NY, lectr, 70-72; Univ Southern Cal, classics dept, 80; asst prof, 78-85, assoc prof, 85-, UCLA, comp lit, ch, 96-. **HONORS AND AWARDS** UCLA distg teach awd; Annual facul recog awd; Mortarbd facul of the quarter. **MEMBERSHIPS** ACLA; ICLA. **RESEARCH** Classical tradition; epic; gender stud; Cultural Stud. **SELECTED PUBLICATIONS** Achilles: Paradigms of the War Hero from Homer to the Middle Ages, Univ Cal Press, 87; paperbk ed, Univ Cal Press, 94; Homer, ed, classical heritage series, Garland Press, 94; Hybrid Genre? Leslie Marmon Silko's Epic Almanac? Forthcoming in: The Postcolonial Cond of Hybridity, ed Najib Mokhtari, Univ Ibn Tofail Faculte des Lettres et des Sciences Humaines, Kenitra Morocco, 98; many numerous articles. **CONTACT ADDRESS** Chair, Comparative Lit, Univ California, 212 Royce Hall, Los Angeles, CA, 90095-1536. **EMAIL** king@humnet.ucla.edu

KING, PAUL E.

PERSONAL Born 10/07/1955, Fort Stockton, TX, m, 1977, 2 children **DISCIPLINE** SPEECH COMMUNICATION **EDUCATION** Univ North Tx, PhD, 85. **CAREER** ASSOC PROF, TX CHRISTIAN UNIV, 85-. **HONORS AND AWARDS** Fine Arts & Commun Col Teaching Award; Pi Kappa Delta; Pi Gamma Mu. **MEMBERSHIPS** ICA; SCA; SSCA. **RESEARCH** Information processing; interpersonal influence. **SELECTED PUBLICATIONS** Auth, Surviving an appointment as department chair, J of the Asn for Commun Admin, 97; coauth, Mindfulness, mindlessness, and communication instruction, Commun Ed, 98; A case study of the Weberian leadership of Joseph Smith, The J of Commun and Religion, 98; Compliance-gaining strategies, communication satisfaction, and willingness to comply, Commun Reports, 94; Contagion theory and the communication of public speaking anxiety, Commun Ed, 94. **CONTACT ADDRESS** Speech Commun Dept, Texas Christian Univ, Box 298000, Ft. Worth, TX, 76129.

KINGSTON, JOHN

DISCIPLINE LINGUISTICS **EDUCATION** Univ Chicago, BA, 76, MA, 77; Univ Calif Berkeley, PhD, 85. **CAREER** Assoc prof. **RESEARCH** Relationship of phonetic theory; methods to phonology. **SELECTED PUBLICATIONS** Auth, Articulatory Binding, Cambridge, 90; Integrating Articulations in the Perception of Vowel Height, Phonetica, 91; co-auth, The Inadequacy of Underspecification, NE Ling Soc, 89; Resonance Versus Source Characteristics in Perceiving Spectral Continuity between Vowels and Consonants, Univ Wis; Phonetic Knowledge, Language, 94. **CONTACT ADDRESS** Linguistics Dept, Univ of Massachusetts, Amherst, S College 321, Amherst, MA, 01003. **EMAIL** jkingston@linguist.umass.edu

KINGSTONE, BASIL D.

DISCIPLINE TRANSLATION ENGLISH-FRENCH; FRENCH-ENGLISH **EDUCATION** Oxford, BA, MA, DPhil; Ottawa, MA. **CAREER** Prof & ch French prog; ed, Can Jour Neth Stud & Newsl the Can Asn for the Advancement of Neth Stud and the Can Asn for Transl Stud. **RESEARCH** Netherlandic Dutch and Flemish studies; Andre Gide. **SELECTED PUBLICATIONS** Transl, Quebec short stories into English & Mijn vriend Andre Gide into French. **CONTACT ADDRESS** Dept of French Language and Literature, Univ of Windsor, 401 Sunset Ave, Windsor, ON, N9B 3P4. **EMAIL** bkingst@uwindsor.ca

KINKADE, RICHARD PAISLEY

PERSONAL Born 01/07/1939, Los Angeles, CA, m, 1962, 5 children **DISCIPLINE** ROMANCE LANGUAGES **EDUCATION** Yale Univ, BA, 60, PhD(Span), 65. **CAREER** Instr Span, Yale Univ, 60-62, 63-65; from asst prof to assoc prof Romance Lang, Univ Ariz, 65-71; prof Romance Lang & chmn dept, Emory Univ, 71-74; prof Romance Lang & head dept Romance & Class Lang, Univ Conn, 77-82; prof Span & dean, fac of Humanities, Univ Ariz, 82-87, bus mgr, La Coronica, 72-76; consult, Div Educ, Nat Endowment for Humanities, 76-77, res grant, 78-79; reviewer Jacob K Javits Fel Prog, US Dept of Ed, 97. **MEMBERSHIPS** MLA; Mediaeval Acad Am; SAtlantic Mod Lang Asn; Asn Int Hispanistas; Am Asn Teachers Span & Port. **RESEARCH** Medieval Spanish language and literature. **SELECTED PUBLICATIONS** Auth, The historical date of the coplas and the death of Jorge Manrique, Speculum, 3/70; A new Latin source for Berceo's Milagros: MS 110 of Madrid's Biblioteca Nacional, Romance Philol, 11/71; Sancho IV: puente literario entre Alfonso el Sabio y Juan Manual, PMLA, 10/72; Arabic mysticism and the Libro de buen amor, In: Estudios literarios de hispanistas norteamericanos dedicados a H Hatzfeld, 74; La evidencia para el influjo de los antiguos immrama irlandeses en la literature cspanola medieval, Actas del V Cong Int de Hispanistas, 78; Mito y realidad en el mundo medieval espanol, In: John Esten Keller Festschrift, 80; Iconography and literature: King Alfonso's most personal appearance in the Cantigas de Santa Maria, Miracle 209, Hispania (in prep); coauth (with John E Keller), Iconography and Narrative Art in Medieval Spanish Fiction, Univ Press Ky, 84. **CONTACT ADDRESS** Dept of Spanish and Portuguese, Univ of Arizona, Tucson, AZ, 85721-0067. **EMAIL** rpk@u.arizona.edu

KIPA, ALBERT ALEXANDER

PERSONAL Born 09/10/1939, Kiev, Ukraine, m, 1966, 2 children **DISCIPLINE** GERMAN & SLAVIC LITERATURE **EDUCATION** City Col NY, BA, 62; Univ Pa, AM, 64, PhD(Ger), 72. **CAREER** Vis lectr English, Univ Freiburg, 64-65; from instr to prof Ger & Russ, 66-96, J & F Seeger Prof of Comp Lit, Muhlenberg Col, 96-, head, Dept For Lang and Lit, 89-93, 97-; Mem Nat Adv Coun, Ethnic Heritage Studies, US Dept Educ, 80-82. **HONORS AND AWARDS** NEH study grant, 78; Lindback Found Award for Distinquished Teaching, 80; sr Fulbright fel, Germany, 81; Cert of Merit, Am Asn Teachers Ger & Goethe Inst, 87; Citation for Outstanding Service in For Lang Educ, PA Dept Educ, 91; IREX grant, to Ukraine, 95. **MEMBERSHIPS** AAUP; Am Asn Teachers Ger; Am Asn Teachers Slavic & EEurop Lang; PA State Mod Lang Asn (pres, 90-92). **RESEARCH** Germano-Slavic literary relations; translation theory and practise. **SELECTED PUBLICATIONS** Auth, Gerhart Hauptmann in Russia: First notices, Mod Lang Notes, 10/73; Gerhart Hauptmann in Russia: 1880-1917, Helmut Buske, 74; K D Bal'mont and Gerhart Hauptmann, In: Views and Reviews of Modern German Literature, Delp, 74; Ivan Franko's view of Gerhart Hauptmann, In: Probleme der Komparatistik und Interpretation, 77 & co-ed, Probleme der Komparatistik und Interpretation, 77, Bouvier; Aufnahme--Weitergabe: Literarische Impulse um Lessing und Goethe, Helmut Buske, 82; auth, The Poet as Translator: Paulo Hrabous'kyj and Goethe's Faust, In: Aufnahrue-Weiter-gabe..., 82; Lesja

Ukrainka and Gerhart Hauptmann: Anatomy of an Admiration, In: Hauptmann Research. New Directions, Peter Lang, 86; Das Hauptmannbild Lesja Ukrainkas und seine Rolle in ihrem Schaffen, In: Lesia Ukrainka und die europaische Literatur, B"hlau Verlag, 94; coauth, Goethe's Weimar and the Slavic Realm: The Ukrainian Dimension, In: A Reassessment of Weimar Classicism, Edwin Mellon Press, 96. **CONTACT ADDRESS** Dept of Foreign Lang, Muhlenberg Col, 2400 W Chew St, Allentown, PA, 18104-5586. **EMAIL** kipa@muhlenberg.edu

KIRBY, JOHN T.
PERSONAL Born 05/09/1955, New Haven, CT, 2 children **DISCIPLINE** CLASSICS & COMPARATIVE LITERATURE **EDUCATION** Choate Sch, diploma, 73; Univ NC Chapel Hill, AB, 77; Univ NC Chapel Hill, MA, 81; Univ NC Chapel Hill, PhD, 85. **CAREER** Asst prof, class lang and lit, Smith Col, 85-87; founding chair, prog in class studies, Purdue Univ, 88-94; chair, prog in comparative lit, Purdue Univ, 94-. **HONORS AND AWARDS** Phi Eta Sigma, 74; Phi Beta Kappa, 76; Morehead Scholar, Univ NC, 73-77; Univ Res Asst, Univ NC, 80-81; Classics Teaching fel, Univ NC, 83-84; Software develop grant, ACIS Found of IBM, 85; Robert E. Frane Memorial Scholar, 85; Morris House fel, Smith Col, 86; Facul Teaching Award nominee, Smith Col, 86; Libr Scholars grant prog award, Purdue Univ, 87; Facul teaching award nominee, Smith Col, 87, 88; XL Summer facul grant, Purdue Res Found, 88; Univ Outstanding Undergraduate Teaching Award nominee, Purdue Univ, 88; XL summer facul grant, Purdue Res Found, 90; XL Intl Travel grant, Purdue Res Found, 91; res leave, dept foreign lang and lit, Purdue Univ, spring, 91; NEH fel, Univ Iowa, fall, 91; fel, Ctr for Humanistic Studies, Purdue Univ, spring, 93; Scholar-in-residence, Choate Rosemary Hall, fall, 93; Sch of Liberal Arts Outstanding Teaching award, Purdue Univ, 93; Amer Philol Asn award for Excellence in the Teaching of the Classics, 96; Twentieth Century award for achievement, Intl Bio Ctr, 97., Man of the Year, Am Biog Inst, 96; International Man of the Year, Int Biog Ctr, 96-97; listed in Int Dir of Distinguished Leadership, 7th Ed, 97; listed in Int Who's Who of Intellectuals, 12th Ed, 97. **MEMBERSHIPS** Mod Lang Asn; Amer Comparative Lit Asn; Amer Philol Asn; Calif Class Asn; Class Asn of the Middle West and South; Amer Soc for the Hist of Rhetoric. **RESEARCH** Classical Greek and Latin literature; Classical rhetoric and poetics; Literary theory. **SELECTED PUBLICATIONS** Auth, The Rhetoric of Cicero's Pro Cluentio, 90; ed, The Comparative Reader: A Handlist of Basic Reading in Comparative Literature, 98; jour articles, Amer Jour of Philol, 118, 517-554, 97; Philos and Rhetoric, 30, 190-202, 97; Voices in Italian Amer, 7, 207-211, 96; Ill Class Studies, 20, 77-81, 95; Voices in Italian Amer, 6, 71-76, 95; book chap, Ciceronian Rhetoric: Theory and Practice, 13-31, Roman Eloquence: Rhetoric in Society and Literature, 97; Classical Greek Origins of Western Aesthetic Theory, 29-45, 96; The Great Triangle in Early Greek Rhetoric and Poetics, 3-15, 94; The Neo-Latin Verse of Joseph Tusiani, 180-204, Joseph Tusiani: Poet, Translator, Humanist, 94; auth, Secret of the Muses Retold: Classical Influences on Itlaian Authors of the Twentieth Century, Chicago: University of Chicago Press, in press; ed, Landmark Essays on Ciceronian Rhetoric, Davis CA: Hermagoras Press/Erlbaum, in press. **CONTACT ADDRESS** Dept of For Lang and Lit, Purdue Univ, 1080 Schleman Hall, W. Lafayette, IN, 47907-1354. **EMAIL** corax@purdue.edu

KIRKPATRICK, SUSAN
PERSONAL Born 01/16/1942, Newcastle, WY, 1 child **DISCIPLINE** SPANISH LITERATURE, FEMINIST CRITICISM **EDUCATION** Univ Wyo, BA, 63; Cambridge Univ, MA, 65; Harvard Univ, PhD(comp lit), 72. **CAREER** Instr Span, Brandeis Univ, 70-71; asst prof Span Lit, 71-78, from assoc to prof Span Lit, Univ Calif, San Diego, 78-88. **HONORS AND AWARDS** Guggenheim Fellowship, 86-87. **MEMBERSHIPS** MLA; Int Asn Hispanists; Exec Council 93-96. **RESEARCH** Spanish nineteenth century literature; romanticism. **SELECTED PUBLICATIONS** Auth, From Octavia Santino to El yermo de las almas, Rev Hispanica Mod, Vol 37, 72-73; Tirano Banderas y la estructura de la historian Nueva Rev Filologia Hispanica, Vol 24, 76; Spanish romaniticism and the liberal project: The crisis of Larra, Studies Romanticism, Vol 16, 77; Larra: El laberinto inextricable de un romantics liberal, Gredos, Madrid, 77; The Ideology of Costumbrismo, Ideologies & Lit, Vol 2, No 7; On the threshold of the realist novel: Fernan Caballero, Publ Mod Lang Asn (in prep); Fantasy, Seduction and the Woman Reader: Rosalia de Castro's Novels, in The Politics/Poetics of Gender, ed Lou Charnon-Deutsch and Jo Labanyi; New York, Oxford Univ Press, 95. **CONTACT ADDRESS** Lit Dept, Univ of California, 9500 Gilman Dr, La Jolla, CA, 92093-5003. **EMAIL** skirkpatrick@ucsd.edu

KIRKWOOD, GORDON MACDONALD
PERSONAL Born 05/07/1916, Toronto, ON, Canada, m, 1940, 2 children **DISCIPLINE** CLASSICAL PHILOLOGY **EDUCATION** Univ Toronto, AB, 38; Cornell Univ, AM, 39; Johns Hopkins Univ, PhD(Greek), 42. **CAREER** Latin master, Lower Can Col, 45-46; from instr to prof, 46-73, chmn dept, 63-72, Frederic J Whiton Prof Classics, Cornell Univ 73-, Ford fel, 53-54; Guggenheim fel, 56-57; Am Coun Learned Soc fel, 62-63; co-ed, Cornell Studies in Class Philol; Nat Endowment for Hum fel, 77. **MEMBERSHIPS** Am Philol Asn; Class Asn Atlantic States; AAUP. **RESEARCH** Greek lit. **SELECTED PUBLICATIONS** Auth, A Study of Sophoclean Drama, Cornell Univ, 58; A Short Guide to Classical Mythology, Holt, 60; Early Greek Monody, 74 & ed, Poetry and Poetics, Studies in Honor of James Hutton, 75, Cornell Univ; Selections from Pindar, Am Philol Asn, 82. **CONTACT ADDRESS** Dept of Classics, Cornell Univ, Ithaca, NY, 14850. **EMAIL** GMK4@Cornell.edu

KISSLING, PAUL J.
PERSONAL Born 08/03/1957, Toledo, OH, m, 1979, 2 children **DISCIPLINE** BIBLICAL LANGUAGES **EDUCATION** Univ of Sheffield, PhD, 91. **CAREER** Great Lakes Christian Col MI, prof, 91-; Co-editor, Col Press, NIV Old Testament Commentary. **MEMBERSHIPS** SBL, IBR **RESEARCH** Hebrew narrative research **SELECTED PUBLICATIONS** Auth, Reliable Characters in the Primary History, in: JSOTSup, 96. **CONTACT ADDRESS** Dept of Old Testament, Great Lakes Christian Col, 4808 Omar Dr, Lansing, MI, 48917. **EMAIL** pjk@voyager.net

KITCHELL, KENNETH F.
PERSONAL Born 10/24/1947, Brockton, MA, m, 1970, 1 child **DISCIPLINE** CLASSICAL STUDIES **EDUCATION** Coll of Holy Cross, BA, 69; Loyola Univ Chicago, MA, 73; PhD, 76. **CAREER** Loyola Univ, 74; Quigley Preparatory Sem S Chicago, 74-76; Cath High School Baton Rouge, 80-81; Am School of Class Studies Athens Greece, 89; co-dir, Program in Greece Vergilian Soc of Am, 90; instr, 76-78; asst prof, 83-94, assoc prof, 94-97, prof, LA State Univ, 97-; vis prof, Univ Mass, 98-99. **HONORS AND AWARDS** Amoco Found award for Outstanding Undergraduate Techg, 80; Am Philol Asn Award for excellence in Tchg of Classics, 83; LSU Student Govt Asn Fac Award, 91; Robert L Amborski Distinguished Honors Prof Award, 93; Ovatio, Clasical Asn of the Middle W and S, 94; Summer Scholar Centre for Hellenic Studies Wash DC, 97; Lsu Alumni Asn Distinguished Fac Award, 97; Who's Who in the South and Southwest; Who's Who of Emerging Leaders in America; Men of Achievement; Dictionary of International Biography; Who's Who in American Education. **MEMBERSHIPS** Am Philol Asn; Archaeol Inst Am; Am Class League; Asn of Ancient Hist; Class Asn of the Middle west and S; Class Asn of New England, Joint Asn of Class Tchrs; Mass Foreign Lang Asn; Class Asn of Mass; Class Asn of the Pacific Northwest Am Council on the Tchg of Foreign Lang. **RESEARCH** Latin and Greek Pedagogy; Crete. **SELECTED PUBLICATIONS** Entering the Stadiun, Approaches to Ancient Greek Athletics, Class Bull, 98;coauth, A Trilogy on the Herpetology of Linnaeus's Systema Naturae X, Smithsonian Herpetological Service, 94; Albertus Magnus De Animalibus: A Medieval Summa Zoologica, 98. **CONTACT ADDRESS** The Dept of Classics, Univ of Mass, 520 Herter Hall, Amherst, MA, 01003. **EMAIL** kkitchel@classics.umass.edu

KLAUSENBURGER, JURGEN
PERSONAL Born 07/22/1942, Reghin, Romania, m, 1967, 3 children **DISCIPLINE** ROMANCE LINGUISTICS **EDUCATION** Univ Mich, Ann Arbor, BA, 64, MA, 66, PhD(Romance ling), 69. **CAREER** Asst prof, 69-75, assoc prof, 75-81, PROF FRENCH AND ROMANCE LING, UNIV WASH, 81-. **MEMBERSHIPS** Ling Soc Am. **RESEARCH** Historical Romance linguistics; French phonology; phonological theory. **SELECTED PUBLICATIONS** Auth, Derivational Morphology and Lexical, Romance Philol, Vol 0046, 92; Introduction to Natural Morphology, Romance Philol, Vol 0046, 93; Morphology And Mind in a Unified Approach to Explanation in Linguistics, Can J Ling-Rev Can Ling, Vol 0039, 94; Analyticity and Syntheticity in a Diachronic Perspective with Special Reference to Romance Languages, Can J Ling-Rev Can Ling, Vol 0039, 94, Grammaticalization in a Conceptual Framework, Can J Ling-Rev Can Ling, Vol 0039, 94; Germanic and Romance in Belgium and Luxembourg, Fr Rev, Vol 0067, 94; A Morphous Morphology, Can J Ling-Rev Can Ling, Vol 0040, 95; New Developments in French Grammar and Grammar Research, Fr Rev, Vol 0069, 96. **CONTACT ADDRESS** Dept of Romance Lang, Univ of Wash, Seattle, WA, 98195.

KLEE, CAROL
DISCIPLINE SPANISH AND PORTUGUESE LITERATURE **EDUCATION** Wooster Col, BA, 75; Univ Tex Austin, MA, 80; PhD, 84. **RESEARCH** Bilingualism; sociolinguistics; language contact; second language acquisition. **SELECTED PUBLICATIONS** Co-auth, The expression of past reference in Spanish narratives of Spanish/Quechua bilingual speakers, Georgetown Univ, 95; Spanish OV/VO word order variation in Spanish/Quechua bilingual speakers, Georgetown Univ, 95; ed, Faces in a crowd: The individual learner in multisection courses, 94. **CONTACT ADDRESS** Spanish and Portuguese Dept, Univ of Minnesota, Twin Cities, 34 Folwell Hall, 9 Pleasant St SE, Minneapolis, MN, 55455. **EMAIL** Carol.A.Klee-1@tc.umn.edu

KLEIN, ANNE
DISCIPLINE RELIGIOUS STUDIES, TIBETAN BUDDHISM, CLASSICAL TIBETAN LANGUAGE **EDUCATION** Univ VA, PhD, 81. **CAREER** Prof, ch, dept Relig Stud, Rice Univ. **HONORS AND AWARDS** Fulbright dissertation res fel, India and Nepal, 80; NEH summer grant, 94; NEH transl grant, 94. **SELECTED PUBLICATIONS** Auth, Knowing, Naming, and Negation: A Sourcebook on Tibetan Sautrantika; Knowledge and Liberation; Path to the Middle: Oral Madhyamika Philosophy in Tibet: The Spoken Scholarship of Kensur Yeshey Tupden; Meeting the Great Bliss Queen:Buddhists, Feminists, and the Art of the Self, Beacon Press, 94. **CONTACT ADDRESS** Rice Univ, PO Box 1892, Houston, TX, 77251-1892. **EMAIL** klein-A@rice.edu

KLEIN, DENNIS ALLAN
PERSONAL Born 10/19/1943, New York, NY, 1 child **DISCIPLINE** SPANISH **EDUCATION** Univ Kans, BSEd, 65, MA, 67; Univ Mass, PhD, 73. **CAREER** Asst prof, Southwest Mo State Univ, 73-75; vis instr, Univ Mo-Rolla, 75-76; asst prof, 76-78, assoc prof, 78-83, prof, 83-, Span, Univ S Dak, Bibliog, MLA; Nat Endowment for Humanities summer fel, 79, 84, 93, 94, 95; Exxon Foreign Lang Workshop, 81. **MEMBERSHIPS** MLA **RESEARCH** Spanish drama; bibliography; comparative drama. **SELECTED PUBLICATIONS** Auth, Asi que pasen cinco anos: A Search for Sexual Identity, J Span Studies: 20th Century, 75; The Old Women in the Theatre of Garcia Lorca, 75 & Christological Imagery in Lorca's Yerma, 78, Garcia Lorca Rev; coauth, Garcia Lorca: A Selectively Annotated Bibliography of Criticism, Vol I, 79 & Vol II (in press), Garland; auth, Peter Shaffer, Twayne, 79, Rev Ed. 93; "Literary Onomastics in Peter Shaffer's Shrivings and Equus," Lit Onomastic Studies, 80; Peter and Anthony Shaffer: A Reference Guide, G K Hall, 82; auth, "Amadeus: The Third Part of Peter Shaffer's Dramatic Trilogy," Modern Language Studies, 83; auth, Blood Wedding, Yerma, and the House of Bernarda Alba: Federico Garcia Lorca's Tragic Trilogy, Twayne, 91. **CONTACT ADDRESS** Dept of Modern Lang, Univ of So Dakota, 414 E Clark St, Vermillion, SD, 57069-2390. **EMAIL** dklein@sunflowr.usd.edu

KLEINHENZ, CHRISTOPHER
PERSONAL Born 12/29/1941, Indianapolis, IN, m, 1964, 2 children **DISCIPLINE** ITALIAN LITERATURE, PHILOLOGY **EDUCATION** Ind Univ, Bloomington, AB, 64, MA, 66, PhD(Ital), 69. **CAREER** From instr to asst prof Ital, Univ Wis-Madison, 68-70; vis asst prof Ital, Ind Univ, Bloomington & resident dir foreign studies prog, Bologna, Italy, 70-71; asst prof, 71-75, assoc prof, 75-80, prof Ital & chmn Medievl Studies, Univ Wis-Madison, 80-; vice-pres, Am Asn of Teachers of Italian, 93-98; counr, Dante Soc of Am, 85-91; pres, Am Boccaccio Asn, 93-; ch, Comm on Centers and Regional Asns (CARA) of the Medieval Acad of Am, 93-98; pres, Medieval Asn of the Midwest, 84-85; Exec comm, Medieval and Renaissance Italian Literature, MLA, 86-90; member, Delegate Assembly, Modern Language Asn, 91-93. **HONORS AND AWARDS** Fulbright Fellowship to Italy, 64-65; Fellow, Institute for Research in the Humanities. 74-75; dir, Development Grant, NEH, 76-79; co-dir, research Tools Grant, NEH, 80-84; Vilas Assoc, Univ of Wisconsin, 85-87; Newberry Library/NEH Fellowship, 88-89. **MEMBERSHIPS** MLA; Medieval Acad Am; Dante Soc Am; Int Arthurian Soc; Am Asn Teachers Ital. **RESEARCH** Medieval Italian literature; Romance philology; textual criticism. **SELECTED PUBLICATIONS** Ed, Medieval Manuscripts and Textual Criticism, 76; co-ed, Medieval Studies in North America, 82; auth, The Early Italian Sonnet, 86; co-ed, Saint Augustine, the Bishop: A Book of Essays, 94; numerous articles and chapters in: Dante Studies, Italica, Forum Italicum, Filologia e critica, Alighieri, Traditio, Romance Philology, Aevum, Studi e problemi di critica testuale, Lectura Dantis, Thought, Journal of Medieval and Renaissance Studies, Quaderni d'italianistica, Annali d'Italianistica, Romance Quart, and others; ed, Dante Studies, 89-; book review ed, Italica, 84-93; mem, ed board, Medieval Acad Reprints for Teaching, 78-93, ch, 81-93; Bibliographer, Studi e problemi di critica testuale, 70-; Dante Soc of Am, 84-; Am Boccaccio Asn, 83-; and BIGLLI, 94- . **CONTACT ADDRESS** Dept of Fr & Ital, Univ of Wis, 1220 Linden Drive, Madison, WI, 53706-1557. **EMAIL** kleinhenz@lss.wisc.edu

KLIBBE, LAWRENCE H.
PERSONAL Born 10/07/1923, Utica, NY, m, 1952, 2 children **DISCIPLINE** ROMANCE LANGUAGES **EDUCATION** Syracuse Univ, AB, 49, MA, 51, PhD, 54. **CAREER** From instr to assoc prof mod lang, Le Moyne Col, 53-59; assoc prof, St Johns Univ, NY, 59-65, dept rep, Brooklyn Ctr, 60-65; ASSOC PROF SPAN, NY UNIV, 65-. **MEMBERSHIPS** Am Asn Teachers Span and Port. **RESEARCH** Spanish 19th and 20th century literature; United State-Spanish literary relations. **SELECTED PUBLICATIONS** Auth, The 1st Performances of Garcia Lorca, Federico Plays 1920-1945, Estreno-Cuadernos del Teatro Espanol Contemporaneo, Vol 0020, 94. **CONTACT ADDRESS** Dept of Span, New York Univ, 19 University Pl, New York, NY, 10003.

KLIGERMAN, JACK
PERSONAL Born 08/28/1938, Atlantic City, NJ, m, 1960, 2 children **DISCIPLINE** ENGLISH, PHOTOGRAPHY, LINGUISTICS **EDUCATION** Syracuse Univ, BA, 60, MA, 62; Univ Calif, Berkeley, PhD, 67. **CAREER** Asst prof, 67-75, assoc prof, 75-88, prof English, 89-, dept chemn, 97-, Lehman Col; Va Ctr for Creative Arts residency, summer 82. **MEM-**

BERSHIPS John Burroughs Memorial Asn. **RESEARCH** Photography; American and English literature; stylistics. **SELECTED PUBLICATIONS** Auth, Photography as a Celebration of Nature, The Structurist, 80; auth, Photography and Technology, The Structurist, 82; auth, Photographic Exhibitions: Paris in the Nineties, Godwin-Ternbach Museum, Queens Col. **CONTACT ADDRESS** Dept of English, Lehman Col, CUNY, Bronx, NY, 10468.

KLIMA, EDWARD STEPHENS
PERSONAL Born 06/21/1931, Cleveland, OH, m, 1968 **DISCIPLINE** LINGUISTICS, THEORY OF LANGUAGE **EDUCATION** Dartmouth Col, BA, 53; Harvard Univ, MA, 55, PhD (ling), 65. **CAREER** From instr to assoc prof ling, Mass Inst Technol, 57-67; PROF LING, UNIV CALIF, SAN DIEGO, 67-; Consult, Bolt, Beranek and Newman, 65-66 and lang acquisition proj, Harvard Univ, 65-67; Nat Sci Found fel, 66-67; Partic, Edinburgh Conf Psycholing, 66 and Ciba Found Conf, London, Eng, 68. **MEMBERSHIPS** Ling Soc Am; Int Ling Asn. **RESEARCH** Linguistics; psycholinguistics; historical linguistics. **SELECTED PUBLICATIONS** Auth, Right-Hemisphere Damage Aphasia in American Sign Language, Brain Lang, Vol 0060, 97. **CONTACT ADDRESS** Dept of Ling, Univ of Calif, San Diego, PO Box 109, La Jolla, CA, 92093.

KLINE, JOHN A.
PERSONAL Born 07/24/1939, Marshalltown, IA, m, 1974, 5 children **DISCIPLINE** SPEECH COMMUNICATION **EDUCATION** Iowa St Univ, BS, 67; Univ of Iowa, MS, 68, PhD, 70; Federal Executive Inst, Sr Exec, 86. **CAREER** Tchr, 66-67, Iowa St Univ; Grad NDEA/Res Fel, 67-70 Univ of Iowa; Asst Prof, Dir, 70-71, Fundamentals of Speech Com, Univ of New Mexico; Asst Prof, Dir, 71-75, Grad Stud, Univ of Missouri-Columbia; Assoc Prof, Dean, Communication, 75-82, Prof, Dir, Academic Affairs, 82-92, Provost, 92-, United States Air Univ. **HONORS AND AWARDS** Undergrad Scholar Fel, Iowa St Univ, 65-67; NDEA Fel, Univ of Iowa, 67-70; Central States Speech Assoc Outstanding Tchr, 72; Phi Kappa Phi Honor Soc, 76; Fed Employee of the Year Montgomery AL, 79; Awd for Meritous Civilian Svc, 84; Whos Who in America 45th Ed, 88; Decoratin for Exceptional Civilian Svc, 88. **MEMBERSHIPS** Natl Comm Assoc; Phi Delta Kappa; Amer Coun on Ed **SELECTED PUBLICATIONS** Art, Indicators of Good Marriages, Home Life, 93; auth, Parlez Pour Quon Vous Ecoute (French Trans Speaking Effectively), 93; auth, Listening Effectively, Air Univ Press, 96. **CONTACT ADDRESS** USAF Air Univ, 55 LeMay Plaza South, Maxwell AFB, AL, 36112-6335. **EMAIL** jkline@hq.au.af.mil

KLINE, THOMAS JEFFERSON
PERSONAL Born 07/16/1942, Washington, DC, 2 children **DISCIPLINE** FRENCH LITERATURE **EDUCATION** Oberlin Col, BA, 64; Columbia Univ, MA, 66, PhD(French), 69. **CAREER** Instr French, Columbia Univ, 68-69, asst prof, 70; asst prof, 70-72, assoc provost, Fac Arts & Lett, 76-79, mem prof comp lit, 78-79, assoc prof, State Univ NY, Buffalo, 72-79; Prof French & Chmn Mod Lang & Lit, Boston Univ, 79-, Adj prof, Univ Grenoble, 72-73. **MEMBERSHIPS** Malraux Soc; Northeast Mod Lang Asn; AATF. **RESEARCH** Modern French novel; contemporary European drama and film. **SELECTED PUBLICATIONS** Auth, Andre Malraux and the Metamorphosis of Death, Columbia Univ, 73; Bertolucci's Dream Loom: A Psychoanalytic Study of Cinema, Univ Mass Press, 87; ed, The Film and the Book, L'Esprit Createur, summer 90; auth, Screening the Text: Intertextuality in New Wave French Cinema, Johns Hopkins, 92; I film di Bernardo Bertolucci, Gremese, Rome, 93; author of numerous articles on Andre Malraux, Paul Claudel, Jean Giraudoux, and others. **CONTACT ADDRESS** Dept Mod For Lang & Lit, Boston Univ, 718 Commonwealth Ave, Boston, MA, 02215-2423. **EMAIL** jkline@bu.edu

KLOPP, CHARLES
PERSONAL Born 04/14/1937, Palatine, IL, m, 1962, 3 children **DISCIPLINE** ITALIAN LITERATURE **EDUCATION** Princeton Univ, AB, 59; Harvard Univ, MA, 65, PhD(Ital lit), 70. **CAREER** Instr English, Robert Col, Istanbul, 59-64; teaching fel humanities, Harvard Univ, 65-67; lectr Ital, Stanford Univ, 68-69; asst prof Ital, Princeton Univ, 69-76; asst prof, 76-80, ASSOC PROF ITAL, OHIO STATE UNIV, 80-. **MEMBERSHIPS** Am Asn Teachers Ital; Midwest Mod Lang Asn; MLA; Am Asn Univ Prof Ital. **RESEARCH** Modern Italian literature. **SELECTED PUBLICATIONS** Auth, Concordance For Dannunzio, Gabriele Isotteo and Elegie Romane, Italica, Vol 0069, 92; Il Principio Di Verita, World Lit Today, Vol 0067, 93; Letters To Abba, Marta in The Unpublished Correspondence of Pirandello, Luigi and His Actress, Italica, Vol 0070, 93; Le Persone Normali, World Lit Today, Vol 0067, 93; Requiem, Un Allucinazione, World Lit Today, Vol 0067, 93; Calende Greche, Ricordi Duna Vita Imaginaria, World Lit Today, Vol 0067, 93; La Variante Di Luneburg World Lit Today, Vol 0068, 94; Le Citta Del Dottor Malaguti, World Lit Today, Vol 0069, 95; Il Guerrin Meschino, Frammento Di Un Opra Dei Pupi, World Lit Today, Vol 0069, 95; Due Nomi Per Charlie, World Lit Today, Vol 0070, 96; L Infinito, Forse, World Lit Today, Vol 0070, 96; Viaggio In Italia Del Dottor Dapertutto, Attraverso Vizi E Virtu Degli Intellettuali, World Lit Today, Vol 0071, 97; Anima Amante, World Lit Today, Vol 0071, 97; Alonso E I Visionari, World Lit Today, Vol 0071, 97. **CONTACT ADDRESS** Dept of Romance Lang and Lit, Ohio State Univ, 1841 Millikin Rd, Columbus, OH, 43210-1229.

KLOSTERMAIER, KLAUS KONRAD
PERSONAL Born 06/14/1933, Munich, Germany, m, 1971, 3 children **DISCIPLINE** COMPARATIVE RELIGION **EDUCATION** Pontif Gregorian Univ Rome, B Phil, 54, Lic Phil, 55, Dr Phil, 61; Univ Bombay, PhD(ancient Indian hist and cult), 69. **CAREER** Res guide philos, Inst Orient Philos, Agra Univ, 62-64; vis prof Indian Anthrop, Tata Inst Soc Sci, Bombay-Chembur, 64-65; dir, Inst Indian Cult, Bombay Bandra, 65-70; from asst prof to assoc prof World relig, 70-73, PROF WORLD RELIG, UNIV MAN, 73-; S L Swamikannu Pillai lectr, Univ Madras, 68-69; mem bd dirs, Shastri Indo-Can Inst, Montreal-New Delhi, 72-75. **MEMBERSHIPS** Asn Asian Studies; Am Orient Soc; Can Soc Studies Relig; Int Soc Psychol Relig; Ger Soc Missions Sci. **RESEARCH** Interreligious dialogue; Indian philosophies and religions; Judian art. **SELECTED PUBLICATIONS** Transl, The Infancy of Krsna in Critical Edition of the Harivamsa Couture, J Am Orient Soc, Vol 0113, 93; Buddhism Reevaluated by Prominent 20th-Century Hindus, J Dharma, Vol 0020, 95; Studying the Sikhs in Issues for North America, Studies Relig-Scis Religieuses, Vol 0024, 95; The Hermeneutic Center in An Investigation of Interpretive Methodologies in The Study of Theology Through Dialogue and a Transcultural Understanding of Religion, J Ecumenical Studies, Vol 0034, 97; Religious Studies as World Theology J Ecumenical Studies, Vol 0034, 97; Interreligious Dialogue Between Tradition and Modernity, J Ecumenical Studies, Vol 0034, 97. **CONTACT ADDRESS** Dept of Relig, Univ of Man, Ft Garry Campus, Winnipeg, MB, R3T 2N2.

KNAPP, BETTINA
PERSONAL New York, NY, m, 1949, 2 children **DISCIPLINE** FRENCH LITERATURE **EDUCATION** Columbia Univ, BA, 47, MA, 49, PhD, 55. **CAREER** Lectr French lit, Columbia Univ, 52-59; assoc prof, Hunter Col, 60-73; PROF ROMANCE LANG, HUNTER COL and GRAD CTR CITY, UNIV NY, 73-; Guggenheim fel, Am Philos Soc grant; ed adv, Drama and Theatre, Nineteenth Century Fr Studies and 20th Century. **HONORS AND AWARDS** Shuster Award; Palmes Academiques, French Govt; Alliance Francaise medal. **RESEARCH** French theatre, poetry, novel; comparative mythology and literature. **SELECTED PUBLICATIONS** Auth, The Archetypal Woman Fulfilled and Ancient Egyptian Religion in Isis, Harmony of Flesh, Spirit, Logos, Quart J Mod Lit, Vol 0050, 96. **CONTACT ADDRESS** Dept of Fr, Hunter Col, CUNY, 695 Park Ave, New York, NY, 10021.

KNAPP, RICHARD GILBERT
PERSONAL Born 11/24/1940, Litchfield, CT **DISCIPLINE** FRENCH LITERATURE & LANGUAGE **EDUCATION** Wesleyan Univ, BA, 62; Columbia Univ, MA, 64, PhD(Fr), 69. **CAREER** From inst to asst prof French, Lafayette Col, 67-71; asst prof, 71-74, assoc prof, PROF FRENCH, MARS HILL COL, 74-. **MEMBERSHIPS** AAUP; MLA; Am Coun Teaching Foreign Lang; Am Soc 18th Century Studies; Am Asn Teachers Fr **RESEARCH** Voltaire; Diderot; history of ideas. **SELECTED PUBLICATIONS** Auth, The fortunes of Poe's Essay on Man in 18th century France, Vol 82, In: Studies on Voltaire and the Eighteenth Century, Inst et Musee Voltaire, Geneva, 71. **CONTACT ADDRESS** Dept of Mod Foreign Lang, Mars Hill Col, Mars Hill, NC, 28754. **EMAIL** rknapp@mhc.edu

KNELLER, JOHN WILLIAM
PERSONAL Born 10/15/1916, Oldham, England, m, 1943, 1 child **DISCIPLINE** FRENCH LITERATURE **EDUCATION** Clark Univ, BA, 38; Yale Univ, MA, 48, PhD, 50. **CAREER** From instr to prof French, Oberlin Col, 50-69, chm dept Romance lang, 58-65, provost, 65-69; prof mod lang & pres, 69-79 emer pres, Brooklyn Col, 79-; prof Humanities & Arts, Hunter Col & Grad Ctr, City Univ New York, 79-, **HONORS AND AWARDS** Managing ed, Fr Rev, 62-65, ed, 65-68; trustee, Clark Univ, 68-74 & Brooklyn Inst Arts & Sci, 71-79; Chevalier, Ordre Palmes Academiques, 72, officer, 82; chm, subcomt enrollment goals & projections, NY State Educ Comn Adv Coun on Higher Educ & mem adv coun., LittD, Clark Univ, 70. **MEMBERSHIPS** MLA; Am Asn Teachers Fr. **RESEARCH** J J Rousseau; 19th century French literature; music and literature. **SELECTED PUBLICATIONS** Coauth, The Poet and His Moira, El Disdichado, PMLA, 60; Introduction a la Poesie Francaise, Ginn, 62; Initiation au Francais, Macmillan, 63; auth, The Changing College, Oberling Alumni Mag, 66; Translation and Transformation: New Roles for Research, Proc MLA Conf, 72; Newer Clothes for Emperors, Centerpoint, fall 74; The Terrifying Pips of Reality, Fr Rev, 3/78. **CONTACT ADDRESS** PhD Prog Fr Grad Ctr City, Univ New York, 33 W 42nd St, New York, NY, 10036.

KNIGHT, ALAN EDGAR
PERSONAL Born 09/07/1931, Plant City, FL, 2 children **DISCIPLINE** FRENCH AND COMPARATIVE LITERATURE **EDUCATION** Fla State Univ, BA, 58; Fordham Univ, MA, 60; Yale Univ, PhD(French), 65. **CAREER** Acting instr French lang and lit, Yale Univ, 63-64; asst prof French lit, 64-70, ASSOC PROF FRENCH AND COMP LIT, PA STATE UNIV, UNIVERSITY PARK, 70-; Assoc ed, Treteaux. **MEMBERSHIPS** MLA; Mediaeval Acad Am; Soc Int lEtude Theatre. **RESEARCH** Medieval drama; literary theory; literature and society. **SELECTED PUBLICATIONS** Auth, 2 Morality Plays Written at the End of The Middle-Ages and During the Religious-Wars, Fr Rev, Vol 0066, 93; La Passion Isabeau in An Edition of Paris, Bibliotheque-Nationale-Ms-Fr-966, J Medieval Studies, Vol 0068, 93; Le Livre De La Deablerie, Fr Rev, Vol 0068, 94; Rhetoric and the Origins of Medieval Drama J Medieval Studies, Vol 0070, 95; Rhetoric And The Origins of Medieval Drama - Enders,J, Speculum-A J Medieval Studies, Vol 0070, 95; Faded Pageant, The End of the Mystery-Plays In Lille, J The Midwest Mod Lang Asn, Vol 0029, 96; 15th-Century Farce, Fr Rev, Vol 0069, 96; The Biblical Drama of Medieval Europe, J Medieval Studies, Vol 0072, 97. **CONTACT ADDRESS** Dept of French, Pennsylvania State Univ, 316 Burrowes, University Park, PA, 16802.

KNOWLTON, EDGAR C., JR.
DISCIPLINE ROMANCE LANGUAGES, SPANISH, LINGUISTICS **EDUCATION** Harvard, AB, 41, AM, 42; Stanford, PhD, 59. **CAREER** Instr to PROF EMERITUS, EUROPEAN LANG, UNIV HAWAII, MANOA, 48. **CONTACT ADDRESS** Dept European Langs, Univ of Hawaii, Honolulu, 1890 East-West Rd, Honolulu, HI, 96822.

KNOX, BERNARD MACGREGOR WALKER
PERSONAL Born 11/24/1914, Bradford, England, m, 1 child **DISCIPLINE** CLASSICAL PHILOLOGY **EDUCATION** Cambridge Univ, BA, 36; Yale Univ, PhD, 48, LHD, 83. **CAREER** Instr Classics, Yale Univ, 47-48; asst prof & fel, Branford Col,48-54, from assoc prof to prof, 54-60; Dir, Ctr Hellenic Studies, Washington DC 61-85, Guggenheim fel, 56-57; Sather lectr, Univ Calif, Berkeley, 63; chmn, Soc Preserv Greek Heritage, 77-; Martin lectr, Oberlin Col, 81; West lectr, Stanford Univ, 84; Nellie Wallace lectr, Oxford Univ, 75; Spielvogel-Diamonstein award PEN, 90; Frankel priize, NEH, 90; NEH Jefferson lectr, 92. **HONORS AND AWARDS** Award for Lit, Nat Inst Arts & Lett, 67; George Jean Nathan Award for Dramatic Criticism, Mfrs Hanover Trust, 78., MA, Harvard Univ, 61; LittD, Princeton Univ, 64; DHL, George Washington Univ, 77; Georgetown Univ, LHD, 88; LHD (HON) Univ Mich, 85. **MEMBERSHIPS** Am Philol Soc; Am Archaeol Inst; AAAS; Am Philol Asn (pres 80). **RESEARCH** Greek tragedy; Latin and Greek literature. **SELECTED PUBLICATIONS** Auth, Oedipus at Thebes, Yale Univ, S7; The Heroic Temper, Univ Calif, 64; Word and action: Essays on the ancient theater, Johns Hopkins Press, 79; asst ed & contribr, Cambridge History of Classical Literature, Vol I (in press); coauth (with Robert Foyles), The Theban plays of Sophocles, Viking Press (in prep); Essays Ancient and Modern, 89; The Oldest Dead White European Males, 93; Backing into the Future, 94 **CONTACT ADDRESS** 13013 Scarlet Oak Dr, Darnestown, MD, 20878-3551.

KNOX, EDWARD CHAPMAN
PERSONAL Born 10/05/1939, Meriden, CT, m, 1965 **DISCIPLINE** ROMANCE LANGUAGES **EDUCATION** Wesleyan Univ, BA, 61; Yale Univ, PhD(French), 66. **CAREER** Asst prof Romance lang, Case Western Reserve Univ, 66-69; asst prof French, 69-74, dean French sch, 73, assoc prof, 74-79, PROF FRENCH, MIDDLEBURY COL, 80-; DEAN FRENCH SCH, 76-. **MEMBERSHIPS** MLA; Am Asn Teachers Fr; Am Coun Teaching Foreign Lang. **RESEARCH** Literary style. **SELECTED PUBLICATIONS** Auth, Culture Studies in the Teaching of French in Reply, Fr Rev, Vol 0069, 95. **CONTACT ADDRESS** Dept of French, Middlebury Col, Middlebury, VT, 05753-6001.

KNUST, HERBERT
DISCIPLINE COMPARATIVE LITERATURE **EDUCATION** PA State Univ, PhD, 61. **CAREER** Prof, Univ IL Urbana Champaign . **RESEARCH** 19th-and 20th-century Ger lit; drama; literary thematics; Am-Ger rel(s); lit and the other arts. **SELECTED PUBLICATIONS** Auth, Wagner, the King and The Waste Land; Theatrical Drawings and Watercolors (rev); Leben des Galilei (rev); ed, Montage, Satire and Cultism: Germany between the Wars; George Grosz: Briefe 1913-59; pubs on T.S. Eliot, Camus, Brecht, Frisch, Grosz, Hofmannsthal, Kastner, Piscator, Tucholsky, satire, the Everyman theme, the Faust theme, and sci in lit. **CONTACT ADDRESS** Comp Lit Dept, Univ Illinois Urbana Champaign, E Gregory Drive, PO Box 52, Champaign, IL, 61820.

KNUTSON, HAROLD CHRISTIAN
PERSONAL Born 12/18/1928, Minneapolis, MN, m, 1967 **DISCIPLINE** FRENCH **EDUCATION** Univ Minn, AB, 49, MA, 52; Univ Calif, Berkeley, PhD(Romance lit), 62. **CAREER** Teaching asst, Univ Minn, 51-52 and Univ Calif, Berkeley, 55-59; from instr to assoc prof, 60-75, asst dean, fac arts, 69-72 and assoc dean, 77-82, PROF FRENCH, UNIV BC, 75-; Can Coun Leave fel, 72-73; Social Sci and Humanities Res Coun Can leave fel, 79-80. **MEMBERSHIPS** Asn Can Univ Teachers Fr; MLA; NAm Soc 17th Century Fr Lit; Can Comparative Lit Asn. **RESEARCH** French drama of the 17th centu-

ry; comedy; criticism. **SELECTED PUBLICATIONS** Auth, An Enemy of the People and Ibsen, Henrik in Ibsen Reluctant Comedy, Comparative Drama, Vol 0027, 93; Forms of Address in Ibsen Ghosts, Scandinavica, Vol 0033, 94; Moliere, Don Juan, Essays in Theatre-Etudes Theatrales, Vol 0014, 96. **CONTACT ADDRESS** Dept of French, Univ of BC, Vancouver, BC, V6T 1W5.

KOC, RICHARD
DISCIPLINE GERMAN LITERATURE **EDUCATION** SD State Univ, BA; Stanford Univ, MA, PhD. **CAREER** Prof. **RESEARCH** German drama; history of German cabaret and variet; German film, literature and music; psychological approaches to literature. **SELECTED PUBLICATIONS** Auth, pubs on Goethe, Schiller and Thomas Mann. **CONTACT ADDRESS** German Dept, Columbia Col, New York, 14 E Cache La Poudre St, Colorado Springs, CO, 80903. **EMAIL** rkoc@cc.colorado.edu

KOCH, ERNST
PERSONAL Born 10/20/1906, Berlin, Germany, m, 1946, 2 children **DISCIPLINE** GERMANIC LANGUAGES AND LITERATURES **EDUCATION** Pa State Univ, AB, 28, AM, 31; NY Univ, PhD(Ger), 34. **CAREER** Teacher, Jr High Sch, NJ, 28-29; instr Ger, Pa State Univ, 29-31; from instr to asst prof, NY Univ, 33-46; from asst prof to prof, 46-73, chmn dept, 52-56, assoc dean students, 67-68, asst dean acad adjustments, 68-73, EMER PROF GER, BROOKLYN COL, 73-; Consult, Ger, col text dept, Am Bk Col, 47-52. **MEMBERSHIPS** MLA **RESEARCH** Eighteenth century German literature, especially Schiller and Lessing; Scandinavian literature, especially Ibsen; problems of administration in higher education. **SELECTED PUBLICATIONS** Auth Wann Ich Einmal Sol Scheiden in Text Version of a Gerhardt, Paul Song Stanza, Musik Und Kirche, Vol 0064, 94; The Appointment of Pastors in the German, Gothic Villages of the Duchy of Saxony-Gotha, At the End of the 16th Century and the Beginning of the 17th Century, Archiv fur Reformationsgeschichte-Archive for Reformation, Hist, Vol 0085, 94; 17th Century Ideas Concerning This Life and the Next in Report on A Colloquium Held at the Heinrich-Schutz-Haus in Bad-Kostritzthuringen, February 95, Musik Und Kirche, Vol 0065, 95; Mughal Painters and Their Work in a Biographical Survey and Comprehensive Catalog, Am Orient Soc, Vol 0116, 96. **CONTACT ADDRESS** 780 E 32nd St, Brooklyn, NY, 11210.

KOCH, KENNETH
PERSONAL Born 02/27/1925, Cincinnati, OH, m, 1957, 1 child **DISCIPLINE** ENGLISH, COMPARATIVE LITERATURE **EDUCATION** Harvard Univ, AB, 48; Columbia Univ, MA, 53, PhD, 59. **CAREER** Asst, Univ Calif, Berkeley, 51; from instr to assoc prof, 59-71, PROF ENGLISH and COMP LIT, COLUMBIA UNIV, 71-; Guggenheim fel, 61; Fulbright grant, 78, 82. **HONORS AND AWARDS** Harbison Award, Danforth Found, 70. **RESEARCH** Twentieth century American poetry; modern European literature. **SELECTED PUBLICATIONS** Auth, The Villino, Raritan-a Quart Rev, Vol 0012, 93; One Train May Hide Another, NY Rev Books, 93; One Train May Hide Another, Parabola-Myth Tradition and the Search for Meaning, Vol 0019, 94; Introduction to the Green Lake is Awake, Selected Poems, Am Poetry Rev, Vol 0023, 94; A Heroine of the Greek Resistance, Am Poetry Rev, Vol 0023, 94; A New Guide, Am Poetry Rev, Vol 0023, 94; Your Genius Made Me Shiver, Am Poetry Rev, Vol 0025, 96; An Interview With Koch, enneth, Am Poetry Rev, Vol 0025, 96; The True Life, Am Poetry Rev, Vol 0025, 96; How in Her Pirogue She Glides, Am Poetry Rev, Vol 0025, 96; What Makes This Statue Noble Seeming, Am Poetry Rev, Vol 0025, 96; Au Coconut School, Am Poetry Rev, Vol 0025, 96; Allegheny Menaces, Am Poetry Rev, Vol 0025, 96; Might I Be the First, Am Poetry Rev, Vol 0025, 96; In Ancient Times, Am Poetry Rev, Vol 0025, 96; Vous Etes Plus Beaux Que Vous Ne Pensiez, Poetry, Vol 0168, 96; Diving Along, Am Poetry Rev, Vol 0025, 96; Lets Pour, Am Poetry Rev, Vol 0025, 96; They Say Prince Hamlets Found a Southern Island, Am Poetry Rev, Vol 0025, 96; Mediterranean Suns, Am Poetry Rev, Vol 0025, 96; Africa Paese Notturno, Am Poetry Rev, Vol 0025, 96; Let Us Praise The Elephant, Am Poetry Rev, Vol 0025, 96. **CONTACT ADDRESS** Dept of English, Columbia Univ, New York, NY, 10027.

KOCH, PHILIP
PERSONAL Born 12/31/1927, New York, NY, m, 1952, 2 children **DISCIPLINE** ROMANCE LANGUAGES **EDUCATION** Harvard Univ, AB, 49, AM, 51, PhD(French and Ital), 55. **CAREER** Instr French lang, Phillips Exeter Acad, 49; instr French lang, Northwestern Univ, 55-56; from instr to asst prof French, Bryn Mawr Col, 56-61; from asst prof to assoc prof, 61-66, chmn dept French and Ital, 66-72, PROF FRENCH, UNIV PITTSBURGH, 66-; Reader advan placement French, Educ Testing Serv, 60-65; consult French, Regents Doc Eval Proj, NY State, 75-76 and Masters Rev Proj, City Univ New York, 82. **MEMBERSHIPS** Am Asn Teachers Fr; NAnt Soc 17th Century Fr Lit; Am Soc 18th Century Studies; Societe Francaise dEtude du XVIIIe Siecle. **RESEARCH** French literature of the 17th and 18th centuries; modern Italian literature; influence of the Commedia dellarte on French comedy. **SELECTED PUBLICATIONS** Auth, Pub Cornelian Theater in the Metadramatic Dimension, Fr. Rev, Vol 0067, 93; Is There Such a Thing as Translation, Viewpoint of Structural Linguistics, Zeitschrift Romanische Philol, Vol 0109, 93; Tesniere, Lucien Dependency Grammar, An International-Colloquium Held in Mont-Saint-Aignan, Zeitschrift Semiotik, Vol 0015, 93; Speech, Character and Reference in the Drama of Racine, Jean in French, Fr Rev, Vol 0068, 94; Speech in Situational Context in Theory and Practice in the Analysis of Spontaneous Language Usage, Zeitschrift Franzosische Sprache Lit, Vol 0104, 94; Language Change and Expressive Orality, Lili-Zeitschrift Literaturwissenschaft Linguistik, Vol 0026, 96; Historical Semantics and Cognition, A Symposium Held in Berlin, September 96, Zeitschrift Semiotik, Vol 0018, 96; Semantics of the Prototype in Semasiology or Onomasiology, Zeitschrift Franzosische Sprache Lit, Vol 0106, 96. **CONTACT ADDRESS** Dept of Fr and Ital, Univ of Pittsburgh, Pittsburgh, PA, 15260.

KODA, KEIKO
DISCIPLINE JAPANESE AND SECOND LANGUAGE ACQUISITION **EDUCATION** Univ Ill, PhD. **CAREER** Languages, Carnegie Mellon Univ. **SELECTED PUBLICATIONS** Auth, Second language reading research: Problems and possibilities. Applied Psycholinguistics, 94; Development of L2 word recognition, 94; Cognitive consequences of L1 and L2 orthographies, 95; L2 Word Recognition Research: A Critical Rev, Mod Lang Jour , 96, Cross-linguistic transfer of orthographic knowledge, 97; Cambridge Univ Press. **CONTACT ADDRESS** Carnegie Mellon Univ, 5000 Forbes Ave, Pittsburgh, PA, 15213.

KOEKKOEK, BYRON J.
PERSONAL Born 05/19/1924, MI, m, 1955, 2 children **DISCIPLINE** GERMANIC AND GERMAN LINGUISTICS **EDUCATION** Olivet Col, BA, 49; Univ Mich, MA, 50; Univ Vienna, PhD, 53. **CAREER** From instr to assoc prof, 53-65, chmn dept Germanic and Slavic, 71-76, PROF GER, STATE UNIV NY, BUFFALO, 65-; CORRESP OVERSEAS MEM; INST FUR DEUTSCHE SPRACHE, MANNHEIM, GER, 69-. **MEMBERSHIPS** MLA; Ling Soc Am; Ling Asn Can and US; Am Asn Teachers Ger. **RESEARCH** Germanic and German linguistics. **SELECTED PUBLICATIONS** Auth, The Dictionary of German in German, Engl Ger Philol, Vol 0092, 93; Principles of German Orthography in German, Vol 0070, 94; Learning and Teaching Grammar in Unit I in German, Mod Lang J, Vol 0078, 94; Language as Organism in Metaphors, A Key to Grimm, Jacob, Concept of Language in German, J Engl Ger Philol, Vol 0094, 95. **CONTACT ADDRESS** Dept of Mod Lang and Lit, State Univ NY, Buffalo, NY, 14260.

KOENEN, LUDWIG
PERSONAL Born 04/05/1931, Cologne, Germany, m, 1955, 4 children **DISCIPLINE** CLASSICAL PHILOLOGY, PAPYROLOGY **EDUCATION** Univ Cologne, Dr(class philol), 57, Drhabil(class philol), 69. **CAREER** From asst prof to assoc prof and from cur to chief cur class philol and papyrology, Univ Cologne, 56-75; PROF PAPYROLOGY, UNIV MICH, ANN ARBOR, 75-; Res study papyri Cairo, Univ Cologne, 62-65; field dir papyri, Photog Arch Egyptian Mus, Cairo Int Asn Papyrologists, 69, 71, 73 and 76; corresp mem, Ger Archaeol Inst, 75. **MEMBERSHIPS** Am Philol Asn; Am Soc Papyrologists (vpres, 78-80, pres, 81-); Int Asn Papyrologists. **RESEARCH** Classical philology; papyrology; patristics. **SELECTED PUBLICATIONS** Auth, Phoenix From the Ashes in the Burnt Archive from Petra, Mich Quart Rev, Vol 0035, 96. **CONTACT ADDRESS** 1312 Culver, Ann Arbor, MI, 48103.

KOENIG, JEAN-PAUL FRANCOIS XAVIER
PERSONAL Born 03/12/1933, Tananarive, Madagascar, m, 1961, 3 children **DISCIPLINE** FRENCH, AFRICAN LITERATURE **EDUCATION** Univ NC, Chapel Hill, MA, 67; Universite de Toulouse, France, Doctorat (compt lit), 73. **CAREER** From Instr to Asst Prof, 67-91, Assoc Prof French, Univ NC, Greensboro, 91-. **HONORS AND AWARDS** Elected mem of the Malagasy Acad, 90. **MEMBERSHIPS** SAtlantic Mod Lang Asn. **RESEARCH** Malagasy literature. **SELECTED PUBLICATIONS** Auth, L'influence de la Litterature Francaise dans l'oeuvre de Jacques Rabemananjara, 12/77 & L'histoire Malgache dans l'oeuvre de Jacques Rabemananjara, 5/78, Univ Sherbrooke. **CONTACT ADDRESS** Dept of Romance Lang, Univ of N. Carolina, 1000 Spring Garden, Greensboro, NC, 27412-0001. **EMAIL** koenigj@fagan.uncg.edu

KOEPKE, WULF
PERSONAL Born 09/24/1928, Luebeck, Germany, m, 1953, 4 children **DISCIPLINE** GERMAN LANGUAGE AND LITERATURE **EDUCATION** Univ Freiburg, PhD(Ger lit), 55. **CAREER** Lectr Ger, Univ Malaya, 55-59; head div, Goethe-Inst, Munich, 59-65; assoc prof Ger, Univ Ill, Chicago, 65-68; assoc prof, Rice Univ, 68-71; assoc prof, 71-73, PROF GER, TEX AM UNIV, 73-. **MEMBERSHIPS** MLA; Jean-Paul-Ges; Lessing Soc; Am Soc 18th Century Studies; Western Asn Ger Studies. **RESEARCH** Eighteenth century and 20th century German literature; the structure of the German language; German culture and civilization. **SELECTED PUBLICATIONS** Auth, Secret Councils Versus Secret-Societies in an Unknown Chapter From the Classical Romantic History of Weimar in German, Eighteenth Century Studies, Vol 0027, 93; Correspondence With Friends 1933-1958, Ger Studies Rev, Vol 0016, 93; Goethe Wilhelm Meisters Travels in Translation of the 1st Edition, Ger Studies Rev, Vol 0016, 93; Paul,Jean Siebenkas in the 1796 Facsimile Edition With Accompanying Variants From the 1818 Edition and Previously Unpublished Preliminary, Sketches to Both Editions, Ger Studies Rev, Vol 0016, 93; German-Jewish History of the 19th and 20th Century, Ger Studies Rev, Vol 0016, 93; In the Beginning was Auschwitz, Anti-Semitism and Philosemitism in Postwar Germany in German, Ger Studies Rev, Vol 0016, 93; The Languages of Paradise Race, Religion, and Philology in the 19th Century, Mod Philol, Vol 0092, 94; Division and Self-Enlightenment in Wieland, Christoph, Martin Agathon Project in German, J Engl Ger Philol, Vol 0093, 94; The Gruppe-47 in the History of the Federal Republic of Germany in German, Ger Quart, Vol 0067, 94; Division and Self-Enlightenment in Wieland, Christoph, Martin Agathon Project, J Engl Ger Philol, Vol 0093, 94; The Lyric Element in Poetry, Norm and Ethos of the Genre in Holderlin, Brentano, Eichendorff, Rilke, Benn, J Germanic Studies, Vol 0030, 94; 2-Faced Reality, Magic Realism and Nonfascist Literature in German, Ger Quart, Vol 0068, 95; Laocoon Body and the Aesthetics of Pain in Winckelmann Lessing Herdermoritz, Goethe Colloquia Germanica, Vol 0028, 95; Historicity and the Present in Festschrift for Irmscher, Hans, Dietrich on His 65th Birthday, Ger Studies Rev, Vol 0018, 95; Literature and Third-Reich, Ger Studies Rev, Vol 0019, 96; The Retention of Language After Emigration, In Israel in the 1920s, Part 1, Transcripts and Audio Documents, Ger Studies Rev, Vol 0019, 96; 187071-198990 in German Unifications and the Change of Literary Discourse, Ger Studies Rev, Vol 0019, 96; A Purified Modernism -in Mann, Heinrich Untertan and Political Publications on Continuity of German History Between the Kaiserreich and Third-Reich in German, J Germanic Studies, Vol 0033, 97; Reading Jean-Paul in an Attempt at His Poetic Anthropology of the Self, Ger Studies Rev, Vol 0020, 97. **CONTACT ADDRESS** Dept of Mod Lang, Tex AM Col, Station, TX, 77843.

KOERNER, ERNST F.K.
PERSONAL Born 02/05/1939, Mlewiec, Poland **DISCIPLINE** LINGUISTICS **EDUCATION** Univ Gottingen, 62-63; Freie Univ Berlin, 63-64, BPhil, 65; Univ Edinburgh, 64-65; Justus Liebig Univ Giessen, 66-68, MA, 68; Simon Fraser Univ, PhD, 71; DScPhil(hon), Univ Sofia, Bulgaria, 94. **CAREER** Assoc prof, 76-88, PROF GENERAL LINGUISTICS, UNIV OTTAWA, 88-. **HONORS AND AWARDS** Can Coun scholar, 68; Diploma & Bronze Medal, Lille, Fr, 81; Medal Acad Merit, Nicholas Copernicus Univ, Poland, 95; fel, Royal Soc Can, 97; fel, Royal Soc Arts, London, 98. **SELECTED PUBLICATIONS** Auth, Saussurean Studies, 88; auth, Practicing Linguistic Historiography: Selected Essays, 89; auth, Professing Linguistic Historiography, 95; subj ed hist ling, Encyclopedia of Language and Linguistics, 10 vols, 94; chief ed, Historiographia Linguistica, 73-; chief ed, Diachronica, 84-. **CONTACT ADDRESS** Dept of Ling, Univ of Ottawa, Ottawa, ON, K1N 6N5.

KOESTER, RUDOLF ALFRED
PERSONAL Born 03/16/1936, m, 1973 **DISCIPLINE** GERMANIC LANGUAGES & LITERATURES **EDUCATION** Univ CA, Los Angeles, BA, 58, MA, 59; Harvard Univ, PhD, 64. **CAREER** Acting instr Ger, Univ CA, Los Angeles, 62-64, asst prof, 64-69; assoc prof, 69-76, Prof Ger, Univ NV, Las Vegas, 76. **HONORS AND AWARDS** UNLV Found Outstanding Grad Fac Award, 93. **MEMBERSHIPS** Rocky Mountain Mod Lang Asn; Int Ver Ger Sprach-u Literaturwiss; Am Asn Tchr(s) Ger. **RESEARCH** Nineteenth and 20th century Ger lit. **SELECTED PUBLICATIONS** Auth of numerous studies on Kleist, Fontane, Thomas Mann, Hesse, Georg Kaiser, Hofmannsthal, Hauptmann and others in Monatshefte, Ger Rev, Ger Life & Lett, Rev des Langues Vivantes, Orbis Litterarum, Ger Quart & Librarium; Hermann Hesse, Metzler, Stuttgart, 75; Die Hesse-Rezeption in den USA, In: Hermann Hesses weltweite Wirkung-Internationale Rezeptionsgeschichte, Suhrkamp, Frankfurt/Main, 77; Joseph Roth, Colloquium Verlag, Berlin, 82; Hermann Broch, Colloquium Verlag, Berlin, 87; Jakob Wassermann, Morgenbuch Verlag, Berlin, 96. **CONTACT ADDRESS** Dept of For Lang, Univ of NV, PO Box 455047, Las Vegas, NV, 89154-5047.

KOGAN, VIVIAN
PERSONAL Cairo, Egypt, m, 1969, 2 children **DISCIPLINE** ROMANCE LANGUAGES **EDUCATION** Grinnell Col, AB, 62; Brown Univ, AM, 66, PhD(French), 72. **CAREER** Instr, 69-71, Asst Prof French, Dartmouth Col, 71-. **MEMBERSHIPS** MLA. **RESEARCH** The contemporary French novel; 19th century fiction. **SELECTED PUBLICATIONS** Auth, Signs and signals in La Chartreuse de Parme, 19th Century Fr Studies, 11/73; Le jeu de la regle et du hasard, Fr Rev, 12/75; L'emploi du temps, l'emploi des temps, Teaching Lang Through Lit, 4/76; Raymond Queneau: A critical bibliography, In: A Critical Bibliography of French Literature; The Flowers of Fiction: Time and Space in Raymond Queneau's Les Flurs Bliues, French Forum, 82; Le Jules d'Athenais, Roman, 88; Michelet et les di erences, Lectures de la di erence sexuelle, de Femmes, 90. **CONTACT ADDRESS** Dept of French, Dartmouth Col, 6087 Dartmouth Hall, Hanover, NH, 03755-3511. **EMAIL** viviankogan@dartmouth.edu

KOHL, STEPHEN WILLIAM
PERSONAL Born 04/23/1944, Grand Island, NE, m, 1989, 1 child **DISCIPLINE** JAPANESE LANGUAGE & LITERATURE **EDUCATION** Univ Wash, BA, 67, PhD(Japanese), 74. **CAREER** Instr, 72-74, asst prof, 74-79, assoc prof Japanese Lang & Lit, Univ Ore, 79-, dir, Ore Japan Study Ctr, Waseda Univ, 74-75, 88-89; chmn, Asian Studies Prog, Univ Ore, 78-80, dept chmn, East Asian Lang, 81-87. **MEMBERSHIPS** Asn Asian Studies; Asn Teachers Japanese; Am Orient Soc; Japan Soc; Philol Asn Pac Coast. **RESEARCH** Contemporary Japanese literature; Japanese-Americans in the Northwest; translation. **SELECTED PUBLICATIONS** Coauth, The White Birch School of Japanese Literature, Asian Studies Prog, Univ Ore, 75; auth, Shiga Naoya and the literature of experience, Monumenta Nipponica, Vol 32, No 2; coauth, The Three Crabs, Japan Quart, Vol XXV, No 3; auth, I for the Mysterious, Dread Japan: The quest of Ronald McDonald, The East, 78; An Early Account of Japanese life in the Pacific Northwest, Pac Northwest Quart, 79; The Cliff's Edge, 80 & Withered Fields, 82, Midwest Publ Int; Strangers in a Strange Land: Japanese Castaways and the Opening of Japan, Pac Northwest Quart, 82; auth, The Saint of Mt. Koya and the Song of the Troubadour, Takakuwa Bujutsu, 90; Wind and Stone, Stonebridge Press, 92. **CONTACT ADDRESS** Dept of East Asian Lang, Univ of Ore, Eugene, OR, 97403-1205. **EMAIL** kohl@oregon.uoregon.edu

KOIKE, DALE A.
DISCIPLINE ROMANCE LINGUISTICS **EDUCATION** Univ New Mexico, PhD 81. **CAREER** Univ Tex, assoc prof 85-; N Carolina State Univ, asst prof 82-85; Univ Cal SB, lectr 80-82. **MEMBERSHIPS** AATSR; ACTFL. **RESEARCH** Spanish and Portuguese pragmatics; Discourse analysis; Second language acquisition. **SELECTED PUBLICATIONS** Auth, Language and Social Relationship in Brazilian Portuguese: The Pragmatics of Politeness, Austin TX, Univ of TX Press, 92; auth, Romance Linguistics: The Portuguese Context, coed, Westport CT, Bergin and Garvey, 92; auth, Christina Makara Biron and Dale A Koike, Puntos de vista: Converscacion, Boston, Heinle & Heinle, 94; auth, Vamos ao Brasil: Exploratory Portuguese Language and Culture for Middle School Students, coauth, Newburyport MA, Focus Pub, forthcoming; Transfer of Pragmatic Competence and Suggestions in Spanish Foreign Language Learning, Susan Gass, Joyce Neu, eds, Speech Acts Across Cultures, Berlin, Mouton de Gruyter, 95; auth, Perspectives on Second Language Acquisition from Spanish, co-ed, Austin TX, Cen for Lang Edu Studies, 98; auth, Function of the Adverbial ya in Spanish Narrative Discourse, Jour of Pragmatics, 96; Negation in Spanish and English Suggestions and Requests: Mitigating Effects?, Jour of Pragmatics, 94. **CONTACT ADDRESS** Dept of Spanish and Portuguese, Texas Univ, Austin, TX, 78712. **EMAIL** d.koike@mail.utexas.edu

KOLBERT, JACK
PERSONAL Born 04/25/1927, Perth Amboy, NJ, m, 1949, 2 children **DISCIPLINE** ROMANCE LANGUAGES **EDUCATION** Univ Southern Calif, AB, 48, AM, 49; Columbia Univ, PhD(French lit), 57. **CAREER** Lectr French, Columbia Univ, 53; Ford Found instr French and Span, Wesleyan Univ, 54-55; from asst prof to prof Romance lang, Univ Pittsburgh, 55-65, chmn dept Romance lang and lit, 59-65; prof French lit, Univ NMex, 65-77; pres higher educ, Monterey Inst Foreign Studies, 77-80; DIR DEVELOP, CALIF ACAD SCI, 80-; Fulbright res fel, 63-64; MEM BIBLIOG and RES COMT, MLA, 65-; mem Comn Foreign Lang, State NMex, 66-77; Hidalgo de Nobleza, Sec of State, NMex, 67-77; vis prof Romance lang, Pomona Col, 70-71; hon consult, French Repub, NMex, 70-77; pres city coun, City of Albuquerque, 74-77; HON FRENCH CONSULT, CENT CALIF, 78-; ADJ PROF, UNIV SAN FRANCISCO and WORLD COL WEST, 80-. **HONORS AND AWARDS** Officier, Palmes Academiques, 65. **MEMBERSHIPS** MLA; Am Asn Teachers Fr. **RESEARCH** Andre Maurois; modern French literature; French literary criticism. **SELECTED PUBLICATIONS** Auth, The Silence of the Sea Le Silence De La Mer, Fr Rev, Vol 0067, 93; Celebration Talmudique, Fr Rev, Vol 0067, 93; Vol De Nuit and Terre Des Hommes, Fr Rev, Vol 0067, 93; The Popular-Front and Central-Europe in the Dilemmas of French Impotence, 1918-1940 Fr Rev, Vol 0067, 94; Quinze Ans in French, Fr Rev, Vol 0068, 95; The Plague in Fiction and Resistance, Fr Rev, Vol 0069, 95; Les Mots in Vercors, Fr Rev, Vol 0069, 96; Tous Les Fleuves Vont A La Mer, Fr Rev, Vol 0069, 96; Wiesel,Elie in Memory Pilgrim in French, Fr Rev, Vol 0069, 96; Silence in the Novels of Wiesel,Elie, Fr Rev, Vol 0070, 97. **CONTACT ADDRESS** Develop and Membership, California Acad of Science, San Francisco, CA, 94118.

KOLONOSKY, WALTER F.
PERSONAL Born 01/16/1938, Danville, PA, m, 1963, 2 children **DISCIPLINE** RUSSIAN LANGUAGE AND LITERATURE **EDUCATION** Lycoming Col, BA, 63; Univ Pa, MA, 65; Univ Kans, PhD(Russian), 72. **CAREER** Instr Russ and French, Kans State Col, 65-67; asst prof Russ lang and lit, Pa State Univ, 70-73; ASSOC PROF RUSS LANG and LIT, KANS STATE UNIV, 73-; ASSOC ED, STUDIES IN 20TH CENTURY LIT, 76-; DIR, OFF STUDY ABROAD, KANS STATE UNIV, 77-; exchange prof, Int Res and Exchanges Bd, summer 78; Fulbright adv, Kans State Univ, 78-. **MEMBERSHIPS** AM Asn Teachers Slavic and East Europ Lang; Nat Asn For Student Affairs. **RESEARCH** Twentieth century Russian literature; comparative literature; Russian folklore. **SELECTED PUBLICATIONS** Auth, Encounters With Pasternak in Russian, Slavic E European J, Vol 0037, 93; Double-Talk in Sinyavskii,Andrei Dissertation, Slavic E European J, Vol 0039, 95; Tertz,Abram and the Poetics of Crime, Slavic E European J, Vol 0041, 97. **CONTACT ADDRESS** 514 Wickham Rd, Manhattan, KS, 66502.

KOM, AMBROISE
DISCIPLINE FRANCOPHONE STUDIES **EDUCATION** Universite de la Sorbonne Nouvelle, Paris III, PhD, 81. **CAREER** Eleanor Howard O'Leary prof. **RESEARCH** Literary production and its institutions; Colonial education and creativity; Francophonie; Imperialism and African cultures. **SELECTED PUBLICATIONS** Auth, Education et democratie en Afrique, le temps des illusions, Paris: l'Harmattan, 96; Le Cas Chester Himes, Paris: Nouvelles du Sud, 94; George Lamming et le destin des Caraibes, Montreal: Didier, 86; Le Harlem de Chester Himes, Sherbrooke: Naaman, 78; et al, Dictionnaire des oeuvres litteraires de langue francaise en Afrique au Sud du sahara, vol 2, 79-89, San Francisco, Bethesda, London: Int Scholars Publ, 96; Dictionnaire des oeuvres litteraires de langue francaise en Afrique au Sud du Sahara, Vol 1, des Origines a 78, San Francisco, Bethesda, London: Int Scholars Publ, 96; Mongo Beti, 40 ans d'ecriture, 60 ans de dissidence, Presence Francophone 42, 93 & Litteratures africaines, Paris: Silex, 87. **CONTACT ADDRESS** Dept of Modern Languages and Literatures, Col of the Holy Cross, 1 College St, PO Box 46A, Worcester, MA, 01610-2395. **EMAIL** akom@holycross.edu

KOMAR, KATHLEEN LENORE
PERSONAL Born 10/11/1949, Joliet, IL **DISCIPLINE** MODERN GERMAN AND ENGLISH LITERATURE **EDUCATION** Univ Chicago, BA, 71; Princeton Univ, MA, 75, PhD(-comp lit), 77. **CAREER** Asst Prof Ger Lang and Comp Lit, Univ Calif, Los Angeles, 77, Am Coun Learned Soc grant, 78. **MEMBERSHIPS** MLA; Am Comp Lit Asn; Philol Asn Pac Coast; Western Asn Ger Studies. **RESEARCH** Fragmented, multilinear narratives in the early 20th century: German and American; the poetry of Rainer Maria Rilkc and Wallace Stevens; the works of Hermann Broch. **SELECTED PUBLICATIONS** Auth, Through the Lens of the Reader in Explorations of European Narrative, J Ger Studies, Vol 0029, 93; Naturalism in the European Novel in New Critical Perspectives, Mod Fiction Studies, Vol 0039, 93; Countercurrents on the Primacy of Texts in Literary-Criticism, J Ger Studies, Vol 0030, 94; Lesarten in New Methodologies and Old Texts, J Ger Studies, Vol 0030, 94; Why There are so Few Men in My Comparative Literature Courses on Women-Writers, Womens Studies, Interdisciplinary J, Vol 0023, 94; Klytemnestra In Germany in Revisions of a Female Archetype by Reinig, Christa and Bruckner,Christine, Ger Rev, Vol 0069, 94; Es-War-Mord in Schroeter Film Malina in the Murder of Bachmann, Ingeborg at the Hands of an Alter-Ego, Mod Austrian Lit, Vol 0027, 94; The Kunstmarchen of Hofmannsthal, Musil, And Doblin in German, Mod Austrian Lit, Vol 0027, 94; The State of Comparative Literature in Theory and Practice 94, World Lit Today, Vol 0069, 95; The Beginning of Terror in a Psychological-Study of Rilke, Rainer, Maria Life and Work, J Engl Ger Philol, Vol 0094, 95 Comparative Literature in Introduction to Comparative Literature as an Academic Discipline in German, Germanisch-Romanische Monatsschrift, Vol 0045, 96; Experimental Setups in the Experimental Relationship Between Literature and Reality in Musil, Robert Drei Frauen, Mod Austrian Lit, Vol 0030, 97. **CONTACT ADDRESS** Dept of Ger Lang, Univ of Calif, Los Angeles, CA, 90024.

KOONTZ, CHRISTIAN
DISCIPLINE ENGLISH LITERATURE, LINGUISTICS **EDUCATION** Mercyhurst Col, BA; Cath Univ Amer, MA, PhD. **CAREER** Prof, 80-. **RESEARCH** Writing to learn, heal, and create. **SELECTED PUBLICATIONS** Auth, Cultivating Multiple Intelligences through the Living Journal. **CONTACT ADDRESS** Dept of Eng, Univ Detroit Mercy, 4001 W McNichols Rd, PO BOX 19900, Detroit, MI, 48219-0900. **EMAIL** KOONTZC2@udmercy.edu

KOOREMAN, THOMAS EDWARD
PERSONAL Born 02/07/1936, St. Louis, MO, m, 1967, 2 children **DISCIPLINE** SPANISH, SPANISH AMERICAN LITERATURE **EDUCATION** Northeast Mo State Univ, BS, 59; Univ Mo, Columbia, MAT, 66, PhD(Span), 70. **CAREER** Asst prof, 70-74, assoc prof, 74-82, PROF SPAN, BUTLER UNIC, 82-. **MEMBERSHIPS** Am Asn Teachers Span and Port; Inst Int Lit Iberoam; Am Coun Teaching Foreign Lang; AAUP. **RESEARCH** Spanish American literature; Nineteenth century Spanish literature; foreign-language methodology. **SELECTED PUBLICATIONS** Auth, Poetic Vision and the Creation of Character in El Coronel No Tiene Quien Le Escriba, Romance Notes, Vol 0033, 93; The Culture of Fiction in the Works of Zapataolivella, Manuel, Romance Quart, Vol 0042, 95. **CONTACT ADDRESS** Dept of Mod Foreign Lang, Butler Univ, 4600 Sunset Ave, Indianapolis, IN, 46208-3443.

KOPFF, EDWARD CHRISTIAN
PERSONAL Born 11/22/1946, Brooklyn, NY **DISCIPLINE** GREEK, LATIN **EDUCATION** Haverford Col, BA, 68; Univ NC, Chapel Hill, PhD(classics), 74. **CAREER** Asst dir classics, Intercol Ctr Class Studies, Rome, Italy 72-73; asst prof, 73-76, Assoc Prof Classics, Univ Colo, Boulder, 76, BK REV ED, CLASS J, 77-; Nat Endowment for the Humanities fel, Am Acad Rome, 78-79; AM ED, QUADERAI DI STORIS, 82-. **MEMBERSHIPS** Am Philol Asn; Asn Ancient Historians; Class Asn Midwest and South. **RESEARCH** Transmission of ancient literature; Greek palaeography; ancient drama. **SELECTED PUBLICATIONS** Auth, Sophocles in Trachiniae in Greek and English, Editor, Am J Philol, Vol 0114, 93; Sophocles in Fabulae in Greek and English, Am J Philol, Vol 0114, 93. **CONTACT ADDRESS** Dept of Classics, Univ of Colo, Box 248, Boulder, CO, 80309-0248.

KOPP, RICHARD L.
PERSONAL Born 06/23/1934, New York, NY, m, 1958, 2 children **DISCIPLINE** ROMANCE LANGUAGES **EDUCATION** Queens Col, BA, 55; State Univ Iowa, MA, 57; NY Univ, PhD(French), 67. **CAREER** From instr to asst prof French, Col of the Holy Cross, 59-69; asst prof, 69-74, chmn dept, 73, assoc prof, 74-78, prof Mod Lang, Fairleigh Dickinson Univ, 78, Ford Found grant, 69; fac res grant, Fairleigh Dickinson Univ, 72-73. **HONORS AND AWARDS** Founders Day Award, NY Univ, 68. **MEMBERSHIPS** MLA; Soc Amis Marcel Proust; Asn Study Higher Educ; Am Asn Higher Educ. **RESEARCH** Proust; Gide; Svevo. **SELECTED PUBLICATIONS** Auth, Proust's Elstir and the meaning of social success, Laurel Rev, Fall 70; Marcel Proust as a Social Critic, Fairleigh Dickinson Univ, 71; The presentation of the artist in Proust and Svevo, Univ SFla Lang Quart, Winter 76; contribr, Critical Bibliography of French Literature, 79; The Moralist Tradition in France, Asn Fac Press, 82. **CONTACT ADDRESS** Dept of Mod Lang, Fairleigh Dickinson Univ, 285 Madison Ave, Madison, NJ, 07940-1099.

KOPPISCH, MICHAEL SEIBERT
PERSONAL Born 07/12/1942, Baltimore, MD, m, 1973 **DISCIPLINE** FRENCH **EDUCATION** Johns Hopkins Univ, BA, 64, MA, 67, PhD(French), 70. **CAREER** Instr French, Northwestern Univ, 67-70; asst prof, 70-76, assoc prof, 76-81, PROF FRENCH, MICH STATE UNIV, 81-. **MEMBERSHIPS** MLA; Am Asn Teachers Fr; North Am Soc 17th Century Fr Lit. **RESEARCH** Seventeenth century French literature; European novel. **SELECTED PUBLICATIONS** Auth, Til Death Do Them Part, Love, Greed, and Rivalry in Moliere L Avare, Esprit Createur, Vol 0036, 96; Essays on Le Tartuffe in French, Esprit Createur, Vol 0036, 96; Falsehood Disguised, Unmasking the Truth in Larochefoucauld, Fr Forum, Vol 0021, 96. **CONTACT ADDRESS** Dept of Romance Lang, Michigan State Univ, East Lansing, MI, 48823.

KORTEPETER, CARL MAX
PERSONAL Born 05/27/1928, Indianapolis, IN, m, 1957, 7 children **DISCIPLINE** HISTORY, NEAR EASTERN LANGUAGES **EDUCATION** Harvard Univ, BA, 50, McGill Univ, MA, 54; Univ London, PhD(hist), 62; Rytgers Univ, M.Sc., 89. **CAREER** Instr sci, Robert Col, Istanbul, 50-53; Prof, Russ hist, U.S. Army, 54-56;lectr Islamic studies, Univ Toronto, 61-64, from asst prof to assoc prof, 64-67; Sr fel, Am Res Inst, Turkey, 66-67, bd mem & secy, 69-71; vis prof, Princeton Univ, 71-72; dir, Princeton Mid E Syst, 76-; Am Res Ctr Egypt sr fel, 78; Assoc prof hist & near eastern lang, NY Univ, 67-96. **MEMBERSHIPS** MidEast Instr; Turkish Studies Asn; Am Res Ctr Egypt; MidEast Studies Asn. **RESEARCH** Turko-Slavic contacts; institutions of the Islamic Ottoman state; the US and Soviet rel(s) in the Middle East. **SELECTED PUBLICATIONS** Auth, Ottoman Imperial Policy and the Economy of the Black Sea Region, J Am Orient Soc, 66; The Islamic-Ottoman Social Structure: The Quest for a Model of Ottoman History, In: Near East Round Table I: Turkish History and Politics, NY Univ, 69; ed, Literature and Society: The Modern Near East, 71 & auth, Ottoman Imperialism during the Reformation: Europe and the Caucasus, 72, NY Univ; auth, The origins and Nature of Turkish power, Fakueltesi Tarih Arastirmalari Dergisi, Ankara Univ, 72, The Ottoman Turks: Nomad Kingdon to Worl Empire, 91; Co-auth, The Human Experience, Columbus, 85; Co-ed, The Transformation of Turkish Culture: The Ataturk Legacy, Princeton, 86; ed, Literature and Society: The Modern Middle East, 73; Oil and Economic Geography, 93. **CONTACT ADDRESS** Kevorkian Ctr Near Eastern Studies, New York Univ, Washington Sq, New York, NY, 10003. **EMAIL** cmaxadk@aol.com

KOSTA, BARBARA
DISCIPLINE FOREIGN LANGUAGES **EDUCATION** Univ Calif, Berkeley, 89. **CAREER** Assoc Prof, Univ Ariz, 95-. **HONORS AND AWARDS** German Acad Exchange, 96; Fulbright Res Fel, 96-97. **MEMBERSHIPS** Women in German; Women's Caucus of the Modern Lang; Modern Lang Asn; German Stud Asn; Assoc Am Tchrs German. **RESEARCH** German cinema; autobiography; weemae republic and contemporary German literature. **SELECTED PUBLICATIONS** Coauth, Auf deutsch: Arbeitsbuch, 90; coauth, Auf deutsch: Instructor's Manual and Testing Program, 90; coauth, Auf

deutsch: First Year German Textbook, 90; auth, art, Employed Bodies: The Female Servant in Works by Marieluise Fleiser, 92; auth, Recasting Autobiography: Women's Counterfictions in Contemporary German Literature, 94. **CONTACT ADDRESS** Dept of German Studies, Univ of Arizona, Tucson, AZ, 85721.

KOVACH, THOMAS A.
PERSONAL Born 10/22/1949, Providence, RI, m, 1999, 3 children **DISCIPLINE** COMPARATIVE LITERATURE **EDUCATION** Columbia Univ, BA, 71; Princeton Univ, PhD, 78. **CAREER** Asst prof, assoc prof, Univ Utah, 78-85; dept chemn, assoc prof, Univ Ala, 90-94; dept head, assoc prof, Univ Ariz, 94-. **HONORS AND AWARDS** Fulbright-hays Grad Fel, 74-75; Fulbright-Hays Grant, 83; Phi Beta Kappa., Grad Col Fel, Princeton Univ, 71-74; Deutscher Verein Prize, Columbia Univ, 71. **MEMBERSHIPS** MLA; German Stud Asn; Am Asn Tchrs German. **RESEARCH** Rilke; Hofmannsthal; German-Jewish writers. **SELECTED PUBLICATIONS** Auth, Hofmannsthal and Symbolism: Art and Life in the Work of a Modern Poet, 85; auth, art, Rilkes Wendung zur Musik: Das Gedicht Besturz mich, Musik, 86; auth, art, Sidelights, 90; auth, art, Traditionalist Modernism or Modernist Traditionalism: The Case of Hugo von Hofmannsthal, 93; auth, art, Rilke's 'Die Insel Der Sirenen and the Music of Silence, 98. **CONTACT ADDRESS** Dept of German Studies, Univ of Arizona, Tucson, AZ, 85721-0067. **EMAIL** tkovach@u.arizona.edu

KOVARSKY, DANA
DISCIPLINE COMMUNICATIVE DISORDERS **EDUCATION** Univ TX at Austin, PhD, 89. **CAREER** Asst prof; post doctoral fel, Univ KS in Lawrence. **RESEARCH** Lang and soc interaction in clinical contexts, including sch(s) and med settings. **SELECTED PUBLICATIONS** Publ on, interactional patterning of adult-centered and child-centered lang therapy; conflict talk in rural Appalachian day care ctr(s); gp lang therapy practices among adults with traumatic brain injury; ethnog of commun disorders & lange use in contexts of schooling. **CONTACT ADDRESS** Dept of Communicative Disorders, Univ of RI, 8 Ranger Rd, Ste. 1, 108 Adams , Kingston, RI, 02881-0807. **EMAIL** dkovars@uriacc.uri.edu

KOZMA, JANICE M.
PERSONAL Born 12/20/1945, Wyandotte, MI **DISCIPLINE** ITALIAN LANGUAGE & LITERATURE **EDUCATION** Univ Florence, dipl/cert Ital, 65; Univ MI, Ann Arbor, BA, 68, MA, 70, PhD, 73. **CAREER** Vis asst prof Ital, Univ KY, Lexington, 73-74; adj prof, FL Int Univ, 74-75; asst prof, 77-80, Assoc Prof Ital, Univ KS, 80-, Tchg fels, Univ MI, 68-73. **HONORS AND AWARDS** Cavaliere dello Stato: Knight of the Order of Merit of the Italian Republic. **MEMBERSHIPS** MLA; Am Asn Tchr(s) Ital; Am Asn Univ Profs Ital; Midwest Mod Lang Asn. **RESEARCH** Italy's post-war neo-realistic novels; narrative techniques. **SELECTED PUBLICATIONS** Auth, Carosello: A Cultural Reader, Holt, Rinehart & Winston, 78, 2nd ed, 82; Vasco Pratolini, In: Columbia Dictionary of Modern European Literature, Columbia Univ Press, 2nd ed, 80; Pratolini's Il Quartiere: The metaphor, Ky Romance Quart, XXIX: 37-45; Metaphor in Pratolini's novels: Il Quartiere and Cronache Di Poveri Amanti, Romance Notes, XX: 1-6; Scholl, Bianco, V, 60--Glod, A Quattr' Occhi, Italica, 57: 215; Functions of Metaphor in Pratolini's Cronache Di Pover Anianti: Maciste and the Signora, Ital Cult, 81; Omen and Image: Presage and Sacrifice in Moravia's La Ciociara, Italica, 84; The Racconti romani and the Nuovi racconti romani: Moravia's Romani de Roma, Papers in Romance, 85; The Architecture of Imagery in Alberto Moravia's Fiction, Univ NC Press, 93; Say it with Flowers: Imagistic Represenations of Women in Alberto Moravia's Prose, Italica, 93; Francesca Duranit, In: Dictionary of Literary Biography, 95; Bio-Fictive Conversations and the Uncentered Woman in Francesca Duranti's Novels, The Italianist, 96; Pratolini, Vasco, Il Quartiere, Harcourt Brace, 96; Grow Up! Grazia Deledda's Adult-Adolescent Males of Arrested Maturation, Annali d'italianistica, 97. **CONTACT ADDRESS** Dept of French & Ital, Univ of Kansas, Lawrence, KS, 66045-0001.

KRA, PAULINE
PERSONAL Born 07/30/1934, Lodz, Poland, m, 1955, 2 children **DISCIPLINE** FRENCH LITERATURE **EDUCATION** Barnard Col, BA, 55, Columbia Univ, MA, 63, PhD, 68; Queens Col CUNY, MA , 90. **CAREER** Lectr French, Queens Col, 64-65; vis lectr, Rutgers Univ, 3/68; asst prof, 68-74, assoc prof, 74-82, Prof French, Yeshiva Univ, 82. **HONORS AND AWARDS** Phi Beta Kappa, 55. **MEMBERSHIPS** Am Soc for 18th Century Studies; Northeast Am Soc for 18th Century Studies; Am Asn Tchr(s) French; MLA. **RESEARCH** Montesquieu; computer appl to lit anal; conceptual struct. **SELECTED PUBLICATIONS** Auth, The invisible chain of the Lettres persanes, Studies on Voltaire and the 18th Century, 63; Religion in Montesquieu's Lettres persanes, Institut et Musee Voltaire, 70; Note on the derivation of names in Voltaire's Zadig, Romance Notes, 75; The Role of the Harem, In: Imitations of Montesquieu's Lettres persanes, Studies on Voltaire and the Eighteenth Century, 79; L'Enchaninement des chapitres de l'Espirt des lois, Studi Francesi, 82; Jean de La Bruyere, In: European Writers (George Stade, ed), NY, 84; Montesquieu and Women, In: French Women and the Age of Enlightenment (Samia I Spencer, ed), Bloomington, 84; The Politics of National Character, In: Studies on Voltaire and the 18th Century, 89; Multiplicity of voices in the Lettres persanes, Revue belge de philologie et d'histoire, 92; Montesquieu's Lettres persanes and George Lyttelton's Letters from a Persian in England, Transactions of the Eighth Int Cong on the Enlightenement, Studies on Voltaire and the 18th Century, 92; In Search of National Character, ARTFL Proj Newsletter, 94-95; les Chaines argumentatives dans l'Espirit des lois, La fortune de Montesquieu: Montesquieu Ecrivain, Bordeaux, 95; The Name Rica and the Veil in Montesquieu's Lettres persanes, Studi Francesi, 98. **CONTACT ADDRESS** Dept of French, Yeshiva Univ, 245 Lexington Ave, New York, NY, 10016-4699. **EMAIL** kra@ymail.yu.edu

KRABBE, JUDITH
DISCIPLINE GREEK AND LATIN AND SANSKRIT LANGUAGES AND LITERATURES **EDUCATION** Cath Univ, PhD. **CAREER** Dept Classics, Millsaps Col **SELECTED PUBLICATIONS** Auth, The Metamorphoses of Apuleius; coauth, An Introduction to Sanskrit. **CONTACT ADDRESS** Dept of Classics, Millsaps Col, 1701 N State St, Jackson, MS, 39210. **EMAIL** krabbjk@orka.millsaps.edu

KRAMER, KARL D.
PERSONAL Born 01/19/1934, Seattle, WA, m, 1955, 1 child **DISCIPLINE** RUSSIAN LANGUAGES AND LITERATURE **EDUCATION** Univ Wash, AB, 55, MA, 57, PhD(comp lit), 64. **CAREER** From instr to asst prof Russ, Northwestern Univ, 61-65; asst prof Slavic lang and lit, Univ Mich, Ann Arbor, 65-70; ASSOC PROF SLAVIC LANG and LIT, UNIV WASH, 70-. **MEMBERSHIPS** MLA; Am Asn Advan Slavic Studies; Am Asn Teachers Slavic and EEurop Lang. **RESEARCH** Nineteenth century Russian literature; Soviet literature. **SELECTED PUBLICATIONS** Auth, Chekhov for the Stage in The Sea Gull, Uncle Vanya, The Three Sisters, The Cherry Orchard, Slavic E European J, Vol 0038, 94. **CONTACT ADDRESS** Dept of Slavic Lang and Lit, Univ of Wash, Seattle, WA, 98105.

KRAMER, PHYLLIS S.
PERSONAL New York, NY, 4 children **DISCIPLINE** JEWISH STUDIES **EDUCATION** Hunter Coll, BA, 61; Syracuse Univ, MA, 63; McGill Univ Montreal, PhD, 94. **CAREER** Chaplain, Marianopolis Coll Montreal, 78-96; vis prof, Univ Haifa Israel, 95; vis prfo, Univ Tel Aviv Israel, 97-98. **HONORS AND AWARDS** Jewish Studies Shloimr Wiseman Book Prize, McGill Univ, 90. **MEMBERSHIPS** AAR; SBL. **RESEARCH** Women in Hebrew Scripture. **SELECTED PUBLICATIONS** Auth, Biblical Women That Come in Pairs: The Use of Pairs as a Literary device in the Hebrew Bible, Genesis, 98; The Dismissal of Hager in Five Art Work of the 16th and 17th Centuries, Genesis. **CONTACT ADDRESS** 6848 Palmetto Circle South, Apt #1215, Boca Raton, FL, 33433.

KRATZ, BERND
PERSONAL Born 01/25/1935, Saarbruecken, Germany **DISCIPLINE** GERMANIC LINGUISTICS, MEDIEVAL GERMAN LITERATURE **EDUCATION** Univ Marburg, Staatsexamen, 62, PhD(Ger, French, Span), 63. **CAREER** Wiss asst Ger, Univ Marburg, 63-66; assoc prof, 67-74, PROF GER, UNIV KY, 74-; ED, COLLOQUIA GERMANICA, FRANCKE, BERN, 76-. **MEMBERSHIPS** MLA **RESEARCH** Germanic linguistics; Medieval German literature. **SELECTED PUBLICATIONS** Auth, Literature as a Legitimization of Power in Studies on the Function of German-Language Poetry in the 13th Century Kingdom of Bohemia,Speculum-A, J Medieval Studies, Vol 0068, 93. **CONTACT ADDRESS** Dept of Ger Lang and Lit, Univ of Ky, 500 S Limestone St, Lexington, KY, 40506-0003.

KRATZ, HENRY
PERSONAL Born 03/23/1922, Albany, NY, m, 1951, 1 child **DISCIPLINE** GERMANIC LANGUAGES **EDUCATION** NY State Col Teachers, BA, 42; Ohio State Univ, MA, 46, PhD, 49. **CAREER** Asst Ger, Ohio State Univ, 45-48, instr, 48-49; instr, Univ Mich, 49-53; instr, Univ Mass, 53-55; asst ed, G and C Merriam Co, 55-60; from asst prof to assoc prof Ger, Univ Ore, 60-65; PROF GER, UNIV TENN, KNIXVILLE, 65-; HEAD DEPT GER and SLAVIC LANG, 72-. **MEMBERSHIPS** Soc Advan Scand Studies; Am Name Soc. **RESEARCH** Middle High and Old High German; Old Norse. **SELECTED PUBLICATIONS** Auth, Wolfram Von Eschenbach Parzival in Lefevere, Colloquia Germanica, Vol 0026, 93; German and Latin Fables of the Early Modern Age, Vol 1, Selected Texts, Vol 2, The Fundamentals of the History of Fable During the Early Modern Age, Commentaries on Authors and Collections, Colloquia Germanica, Vol 0026, 93; Felustadur Timans, World Lit Today, Vol 0067, 93; Spillvirkjar, World Lit Today, Vol 0067, 93; World Lit Today, Vol 0067, 93; Kvikasilfur, World Lit Today, Vol 0070, 96; Wolfram Von Eschenbach, Colloquia Germanica, Vol 0026, 93; Dalk Gaan Niks Verlore Nie, World Lit Today, Vol 0067, 93; Fyrirgefning Syndanna, World Lit Today, Vol 0067, 93; Travel and Worldly Experience in Medieval German Literature in Papers Read at the 11th Anglo-German Colloquium, 11-15 September 1989 at the University of Liverpool, Colloquia Germanica, Vol 0026, 93; Hafborg, World Lit Today, Vol 0069, 95; Englar Alheimsins, World Lit Today, Vol 0069, 95; Hengiflugid, World Lit Today, Vol 0069, 95; Falsarinn, World Lit Today, Vol 0069, 95; Tvilysi, Myndir A Syningu, World Lit Today, Vol 0070, 96; Hvildarlaus Ferd Inni Drauminn, World Lit Today, Vol 0071, 97. **CONTACT ADDRESS** Dept of Ger and Slavic Lang, Univ of Tenn, Knoxville, TN, 37916.

KRATZER, ANGLELIKA
DISCIPLINE LINGUISTICS **EDUCATION** Univ Konstanz, BA, 73, PhD, 79. **CAREER** Prof. **RESEARCH** Formal semantics; syntax-semantics interface. **SELECTED PUBLICATIONS** Auth, Stage Level and Individual Level Predicates, Univ Chicago, 95; Severing the External Argument from its Verb, Kluwer, 96; Scope or Pseudoscope? Are there Wide Scope Indefinites?, Kluwer, 98. **CONTACT ADDRESS** Linguistics Dept, Univ of Massachusetts, Amherst, Amherst, MA, 01003. **EMAIL** kratzer@linguist.umass.edu

KRAUSE, MAUREEN THERESE
PERSONAL Evanston, IL **DISCIPLINE** GERMAN **EDUCATION** Northwestern Univ, BA, 69; Ohio State Univ, MA, 70, PhD(Ger), 80. **CAREER** Instr Ger, Ohio State Univ, 80-81; ASST PROF GER, ROSE-HULMAN INST TECHNOL, 81-. **MEMBERSHIPS** MLA; Am Asn Teachers Ger; E T A Hoffmann Ges; Am Coun Teaching Foreign Lang. **RESEARCH** German romanticism, novel theory, pedagogy. **SELECTED PUBLICATIONS** Auth, Paragraphs on Translation, Mod Lang J, Vol 0078, 94; Durrenmatt, Friedrich, German Quart, Vol 0068, 95. **CONTACT ADDRESS** Div of Humanities, Rose-Hulman Inst of Technol, Terre Haute, IN, 47803.

KRAUSS, MICHAEL
PERSONAL Born 08/15/1934, Cleveland, OH, m, 1962, 4 children **DISCIPLINE** LINGUISTICS **EDUCATION** Harvard Univ PhD 59. **CAREER** Univ Alaska Fairbanks, prof 60-, dir of Native Lang Cen, 72-. **HONORS AND AWARDS** NSF; NEH **MEMBERSHIPS** LSA; SSILA **RESEARCH** Alaskan Eyak Languages, Eskim-Aleut, endangered languages, Celtic Scandinavian. **SELECTED PUBLICATIONS** Auth, Alaska Native Languages: Past, Present and Future, 80; In Honor of Eyak, 82; The World's languages in Crisis, 92. **CONTACT ADDRESS** Alaska Native Language Center, Univ of Alaska, Fairbanks, Fairbanks, AK, 99775. **EMAIL** fyanlp@aurorr.alaska.edu

KRAWCZENIUK, JOSEPH V.
PERSONAL Born 10/07/1924, Tarnopol, Ukraine, m, 1957, 4 children **DISCIPLINE** GERMAN, RUSSIAN **EDUCATION** Univ Munich, PhD(Ger), 51; Columbia Univ, MSLS, 60. **CAREER** Cataloguer, Butler Libr, Columbia Univ, 60-62; from asst prof to assoc prof mod lang, 62-72, Prof Ger, King's Col, PA, 72-. **MEMBERSHIPS** MLA; Shevchenko Sci Soc. **RESEARCH** Comparative literature; bibliography; problems of ecumenism. **SELECTED PUBLICATIONS** Auth, The giant from St George's Hill: Metropolitan Andrew Sheptytzky, Redeemer's Voice, Can, 63; The cult of Sts Cyril and Methodius in Ukraine, Lohos, Can, 64; Ucrainica in foreign languages, Asn Ukrainian Writers Almanach, 65; Ivan Franko and his foreign friends, 68 & Gerhart Hauptmann's works in Ukrainian: A bibliographic review, 78, Shevchenko Sci Soc Proc; transl, Taras Schevchenko's works, America, 79; auth, Reverend John Volansky, First Ukrainian Priest in the US, Lohos, Can, 81; Henrik Ibsen and Ukrainian literature, Ukrainian Nat Asn Almanach, 81; Rev John Wolansky in Brazil, Almanac of the Ukr Natl Assn, 94; First Ukrainian Diplomatic Mission in American, Almanac of the Ukr Fratl Assn, 94. **CONTACT ADDRESS** King's Col, 133 N River St, Box 1513, Wilkes Barre, PA, 18711-0801. **EMAIL** jvkrawcz@gw02.Kings.edu

KREISS, PAUL THEODORE
PERSONAL Born 05/11/1926, Riedisheim, France, m, 1942, 10 children **DISCIPLINE** FRENCH, GERMAN **EDUCATION** Concordia Teachers Col, Ill, BSEd, 52; Boston Univ, MEd, 57; Northwestern Univ, PhD(French), 68. **CAREER** Teacher-prin elem sch, Mass, 52-56; teacher elem sch, Mo, 56-60; from instr to asst prof French & Ger, 60-73, assoc prof French, Concordia Teachers Col, Ill, 73-, ed Foreign Lang Sect, Instruct Mat Guide for Lutheran Elem Schs, 68-; mem, Lutheran Curric Resource Comt, 68-. **MEMBERSHIPS** Am Asn Teachers Fr; Am Coun Teaching Foreign Lang. **RESEARCH** French literature of the 17th and 18th centuries; teaching foreign language in the elementary schools. **SELECTED PUBLICATIONS** Auth, Foreign languages in elementary schools, Lutheran Educ, 6/61; Fleshpots or Angels Food, Motif, Fall 62. **CONTACT ADDRESS** Dept of Foreign Lang, Concordia Univ, Illinois, 7400 Augusta St, River Forest, IL, 60305-1499.

KRETSCHMAR, WILLIAM A., JR.
PERSONAL Born 09/13/1953, Ann Arbor, MI, m, 1976, 2 children **DISCIPLINE** ENGLISH; LINGUISTICS **EDUCATION** Univ Chicago, PhD 80; Yale Univ, MA 76; Univ Mich, BA high honors 71-75. **CAREER** Univ Georgia, asst prof, assoc prof, prof, 86 to 95-; Univ Wis, asst prof, 82-86. **MEMBERSHIPS** ADS; MLA; LSA. **RESEARCH** Language varia-

tion; dialectology; medieval lit. **SELECTED PUBLICATIONS** Auth, Concise Dictionary of Pronunciation, co-ed, Oxford, Oxford Univ Press, 98; auth, American English for the 21st Century, in: Englishes Around the World, ed, Edgar Schneider, Amsterdam, John Benjamins, 97; auth, Dimensions in Variation in American English Vocabulary, English World-Wide, 96; auth, Foundations in American English,, in: Focus on the USA, ed, Edgar Schneider, Phil, John Benjamins, 96; auth, Quantitative Areal Analysis of Dialect Features, Lang Variation and Change, 96; auth, Intro to Quantitative Analysis of Linguistic Survey Data, w/E Schneider, Thousand Oaks CA, Sage, 96; auth, Handbook of the Linguistic Atlas of the Middle and South Atlantic States, co-ed, Chicago, Univ Chicago Press, 93. **CONTACT ADDRESS** Dept of English, Univ of Georgia, Athens, GA, 30602. **EMAIL** billk@atlas.uga.edu

KREVANS, NITA
DISCIPLINE COMPARATIVE LITERATURE, CLASSICS **EDUCATION** Yale Col, BA, 75; Cambridge Univ, BA, 77; Princeton Univ, PhD; 84. **CAREER** Assoc prof, Univ Minn, Twin Cities. **RESEARCH** Hellenistic and Latin lyric. **SELECTED PUBLICATIONS** Auth, Print and the Tudor Poets, in Reconsidering the Renaissance, ed, M A Di Cesare, Medieval and Renaissance Texts and Studies, 93, Binghamton, 92; Ilia's Dream: Ennius, Virgil, and the Mythology of Seduction, HSCP 95, 93; Fighting against Antimachus: the 'Lyde' and the 'Aetia' Reconsidered, in Hellenistica Groningana. 1. Callimachus, eds, M A Harder, R F Regtuit, and G C Wakker, Groningen, 93; Medea as Foundation-heroine, in Medea, eds, Clauss and Johnston, Princeton UP, 97. **CONTACT ADDRESS** Dept of Class and Near Eastern Stud, Univ Minn, Twin Cities, Minneapolis, MN, 55455. **EMAIL** Nita.Krevans-1@tc.umn.edu

KROIS, JOHN MICHAEL
PERSONAL Born 11/24/1943, Cincinnati, OH **DISCIPLINE** PHILOSOPHY, GERMAN **EDUCATION** Ohio Univ, BA, 68, MA, 70; Pa State Univ, PhD(philos), 75. **CAREER** Asst prof philos, Tech Univ of Braunschweig, 75-77; res fel, Inst Study Philos and Humanism, Munich, 77-79; ASST PROF PHILOS, UNIV TRIER, 80-. **MEMBERSHIPS** Charles S Peirce Soc; Hegel Soc Am; Ger Soc Semiotic Studies; Am Philos Asn; Semiotic Soc Am. **RESEARCH** Natural law theory; history of philosophy; philosophy of history. **SELECTED PUBLICATIONS** Auth, Verene and Cassirer in On New Beginnings, Clio-A, J Lit Hist Philos Hist, Vol 0023, 94; A Note About Philosophy and History in the Place of Cassirer Erkenntnisproblem, Sci Context, Vol 0009, 96. **CONTACT ADDRESS** Dept of Philos, Univ of Trier, Trier, ., 5500.

KROLL, PAUL WILLIAM
PERSONAL Born 04/24/1948, Detroit, MI **DISCIPLINE** CHINESE MEDIEVAL LITERATURE **EDUCATION** Univ Mich, BA, 70, MA, 73, PhD(Chinese lit). 76. **CAREER** Lectr Chinese, Univ Mich, 75-76; asst prof, Univ Va, 76-79; asst prof, 79-82, Assoc PROF CHINESE, UNIV COLO, BOULDER, 82-; REV ED, CHINESE LIT: ESSAYS, ARTICLES and REV, 79-; ASSOC ED, SOC STUDY CHINESE RELIG BULL, 79-; vis asst prof Chinese, Univ Calif, Berkeley, fall, 81. **MEMBERSHIPS** Am Orient Soc; Medieval Acad Am; Asn Asian Studies; Tang Studies Soc; Soc Study Chinese Relig. **RESEARCH** Medieval Chinese literature and religion, especially of the Tang dynasty. **SELECTED PUBLICATIONS** Auth, Us and Them and Address at the Sesquicentennial Anniversary Meeting of the American-Oriental-Society March 31, 92, J Am Orient Soc, Vol 0113, 93; On Far Roaming and Interpretation With New Translation and Commentary of a Taoist-Themed Poem from the Chu Tzu Anthology of Chinese Lyrics, J Am Orient Soc, Vol 0116, 96; Buddhism in Chinese Society in An Economic History From the 5th Century to the 10th Century, J Am Orient Soc, Vol 0116, 96; The Trail of Time in Time Management With Incense in East-Asia, J Am Orient Soc, Vol 0116, 96; China Bibliography in A Research Guide to Reference Works About China Past and Present, J Am Orient Soc, Vol 0116, 96; The Problem of Meaning in Early Chinese Ritual Bronzes, J Am Orient Soc, Vol 0116, 96; From Benares to Beijing in Essays on Buddhism and Chinese Religion in Honor of Prof Jan, Yun, J Am Orient Soc, Vol 0116, 96; Boundaries in China, J Am Orient Soc, Vol 0116, 96; Time and Space in Chinese Culture, J Am Orient Soc, Vol 0116, 96; The Cloudy Mirror in Tension and Conflict in The Writings of Qian, J Am Orient Soc, Vol 0117, 97; Taoism Under the Tang in Religion and Empire During the Golden Age of Chinese, J Am Orient Soc, Vol 0117, 97; Libro Dei Monti E Dei Mari, Shanhai Jing in Cosmography and Mythology in Ancient China, J Am Orient Soc, Vol 0117, 97. **CONTACT ADDRESS** Dept of Orient Langs and Lits, Univ of Colo, Box 279, Boulder, CO, 80309-0279.

KRONEGGER, MARIA ELISABETH
PERSONAL Born 09/23/1932, Graz, Austria **DISCIPLINE** MODERN LANGUAGES **EDUCATION** Sorbonne, dipl, 54; Univ Kans, ME, 57; Fla State Univ, PhD, 60; Univ Graz, MA, 60. **CAREER** Asst prof French, Ger, English lit, Rosenberg Col, Switz, 61-62; asst prof French lit and humanities, Hollins Col, 62-64; PROF FRENCH and COMP LIT, MICH STATE UNIV, 64-; Chmn and adv, Nat Screening Comt for Grants Grad Study Abroad, Inst Int Educ, Fulbright Hays and other

progs, 71-77. **HONORS AND AWARDS** Certificate Distinguished Serv, Int Int Educ, 77. **MEMBERSHIPS** MLA; Int Comp Lit Asn; Soc Fr Prof Am; AAUP; Chinese Comp Lit Asn. **RESEARCH** Baroque literature and the other arts; impressionist literature and the other arts; phenomenology and structuralism. **CONTACT ADDRESS** Dept of Romance Lang, Michigan State Univ, Wells Hall 502, East Lansing, MI, 48823.

KRONIK, JOHN WILLIAM
PERSONAL Born 05/18/1931, Vienna, Austria, m, 1955, 2 children **DISCIPLINE** SPANISH LANGUAGE & LITERATURE **EDUCATION** Queens Col, NY, BA, 52; Univ WI, MA, 53, PhD(Span). 60. **CAREER** Asst prof Romance lang, Hamilton Col, 58-63; from asst prof to assoc prof Span, Univ IL, 63-66; assoc prof, 66-71, dir grad studies, 70-73, Prof Romance Studies, Cornell Univ, 71-; Fulbright fel, Madrid, 60-61; mem, nat screening comt for Spain & Portugal, Inst Int Educ, 62-64, chmn, 63-64; adv ed Span, Appleton-Century-Crofts, 62-75; vis lectr, Columbia Univ, 68; assoc ed, Hispania, 70-81; Am Philos Soc res grant, 70; mem Grad Rec Exam Comt Examiners 72-83, chmn, 78-83; Corporator, Int Inst in Spain, 72-; vis prof, Syracuse Univ, 72, Bryn Mawr Col, Madrid, 73, Purdue Univ, 78, Middlebury Col Grad Sch Span, 79, 80, 86, 91, Brigham Young Univ, 82, Univ of CO, 89, Univ of CA-Berkeley, 91, Univ of CA-Irvine, 94, UCLA, 99; Consult, NAT Endowment for Humanities, 73-; ed assoc, Ky Romance Quart, 74-97; mem adv comt, PMLA, 77-81, ed bd, 83-85, ed, 86-92; acting ed, Estreno, 78-79; ed, Anales Galdosianos, 85-90, hon ed, 91-; Rockefeller res residency, Italy, 75; dir, Nat Endowment for Humanities Summer Seminar for Teachers, 83, 87, 92; ACLS grant, 83; Guggenheim fel, 83-84; US-Span Joint Comt Grant, 87-88; Consul, Guggenheim Found, 87-, NAT Humanities Center, 89-; Christian Gauss Award Comt, 94-96. **HONORS AND AWARDS** DHL, IL Col, 79; Distinguished Retiring Ed, Coun of Eds of Learned Journals, 92., DHL, IL Col, 79. **MEMBERSHIPS** MLA; Am Asn Teachers Span & Port; Int Asoc Hispanists; Int Galdos Assoc (pres, 81-85). **RESEARCH** Hispanic literature of the 19th and 20th centuries; Franco-Spanish literary relations; Latin Am drama; critical theory. **SELECTED PUBLICATIONS** Co-ed, La familia de Pascual Duarte, Appleton, 61; Emilia Pardo Bazan and the Phenomenom of French Decadentism, PMLA, Oct 66; La farsa y el teatro espanol de preguerra, Hispanofila-Castalia, 71; Buero Vallejo's El tragaluz and Man's Existence in History, Hisp Rev, spring 73; Usigili's El Gesticulador and the Fiction of Truth, Latin Am Theatre Rev, fall 77; Galdos and the Grotesque, Anejo, Anales Galdosianos, 78; Galdosian reflections: Feijoo and the Fabrication of Fortunata, Mod Lang Notes, spring 82; co-ed, Textos y Contextos de Galdos, Castalia, 94; coauth, Creacion de Una Realidad Ficticia: Las Novelas de Torquemada, Castalia, 97; co-ed, Intertextual pursuits: Literary Mediations in Modern Spanish Narrative, Bucknell, 98. **CONTACT ADDRESS** Dept of Romance Studies, Cornell Univ, 283 Goldwin Smith Hall, Ithaca, NY, 14853-3201. **EMAIL** jwk4@cornell.edu

KROTKOFF, GEORG
PERSONAL Born 05/21/1925, Vienna, Austria, m, 1952 **DISCIPLINE** ARABIC PHILOLOGY **EDUCATION** Univ Vienna, PhD, 50 **CAREER** Lectr Ger, Ain Shams Univ, Cairo, 51-55; from lectr to asst prof, Univ Baghdad, 55-59; asst prof Arabic, Orient Sem, 60-66, ASSOC PROF ARABIC, JOHNS HOPKINS UNIV, 66-. **MEMBERSHIPS** Am Orient Soc; Am Asn Teachers Arabic; MidE Studies Asn NAm. **RESEARCH** Arabic philology and linguistics; dialects of Arabic and modern Aramaic. **SELECTED PUBLICATIONS** Auth, The Neo-Aramaic Dialect of the Village Hertevin Siirt, J Am Orient Soc, Vol 0113, 93; Christian Arabic of Baghdad, J Am Orient Soc, Vol 0116, 96. **CONTACT ADDRESS** Dept of Near Eastern Studies, Johns Hopkins Univ, 3400 N Charles St, Baltimore, MD, 21218.

KRUGER, CAROLE A.
PERSONAL m, 2 children **DISCIPLINE** FRENCH LANGUAGE AND LITERATURE **EDUCATION** Univ NC Greensboro, BA, 79; MA, 83; Duke Univ, PhD, 91. **CAREER** Assoc prof, Davidson Col, 87-; res dir Jr Yr Abroad prog, 93-94. **HONORS AND AWARDS** Dir self-directional progs, Davidson Col; ed, Women in French. **RESEARCH** 19th century French novel and theater; soc and polit discourse in mid-century France; lit and cult of Quebec; female autobiography, humor, and Colette. **SELECTED PUBLICATIONS** Auth, publ articles on var aspects of Colette's works, on Benonte Groult and the contemp novel in France, and an interview of Elisabeth Badinter. **CONTACT ADDRESS** Davidson Col, 102 N Main St, PO Box 1719, Davidson, NC, 28036.

KRZYZANOWSKI, JERZY ROMAN
PERSONAL Born 12/10/1922, Lublin, Poland, m, 1948, 3 children **DISCIPLINE** SLAVIC LANGUAGES **EDUCATION** Univ Warsaw, Phil Mag, 59; Univ Mich, PhD(comp lit), 65. **CAREER** Vis lectr Polish, Univ Calif, 59-60; lectr, Univ Mich, 60-63; asst prof Slavic, Univ Colo, 63-64; assoc prof, Univ Kans, 64-67; assoc prof, 67-70, PROF SLAVIC, OHIO STATE UNIV, 70-. **MEMBERSHIPS** Am Asn Advan Slavic Studies; Asn Advan Polish Studies (pres, 77-79); Polish Inst Arts and Sci Am; North Am Study Ctr Polish Affairs. **RESEARCH** Polish literature; Russian literature; comparative lit-

erature. **SELECTED PUBLICATIONS** Auth, Jedzmy, Wracajmy, World Lit Today, Vol 0067, 93; The Commission, World Lit Today, Vol 0068, 94; The World of the Polish Borderland in the Works of Odojewski, Wlodzimierz, Pamietnik Literacki, Vol 0085, 94; Beyond Metafiction in Self-Consciousness in Soviet Literature, World Lit Today, Vol 0068, 94; Sleeper at Harvest, World Lit Today, Vol 0069, 95; Modernism and Revolution in Russian Literature in Transition, World Lit Today, Vol 0069, 95; Parables from the Past in The Prose Fiction of Aitmatov, Chingiz, World Lit Today, Vol 0069, 95; Trans-Atlantyk, World Lit Today, Vol 0069, 95; Invisible Allies, World Lit Today, Vol 0070, 96; Self Portrait with Woman, World Lit Today, Vol 0070, 96; Muza-Donowa in A Celebration of Pirie, Donald Contribution to Polish Studies, Slavic E European J, Vol 0041, 97; The Winters Hero, World Lit Today, Vol 0071, 97. **CONTACT ADDRESS** Dept of Slavic Lang and Lit, Ohio State Univ, Columbus, OH, 43210.

KUBIAK, DAVID PAYNE
PERSONAL Born 08/13/1950, Milwaukee, WI, s **DISCIPLINE** PHILOLOGY **EDUCATION** Loyola Univ, BA, 72; Harvard Univ, AM, 74; PhD, 79. **CAREER** Prof Classics, Wabash Col, 97-; assoc prof Classics, Wabash Col, 85-97; asst prof Classics, Wabash Col, 79-85; instr Latin, Buckingham, Browne and Nichols School, 78-79; asst Senior Tutor, Kirkland House, Harvard Col, 77-79; Tchg Fel Classics, Harvard Univ, 73-79. **HONORS AND AWARDS** NEH Summer Seminar Member, Amer Acad in Rome, 91; McLain-McTurnan-Arnold Res Scholar, Wabash Col, 89; Bowdoin Prize in Latin Composition, Harvard Univ, 77; Competitive Grant, Harvard Classics Dept, 76. **MEMBERSHIPS** Amer Philoi Assoc; Classics Assoc of Middle West & South; Ind Classical Conf; Vergilian Soc. **RESEARCH** Late Republican and Augustan Roman Poetry; Early Christian Poetry **SELECTED PUBLICATIONS** Lucan IX, in Bryn Mawr Classical Commentary Series, 85; Epic and Comedy in Prudentius' Humn to St. Eulalia (Peristephanon 3), Philogus, forthcoming; Memories of An Aesthete: A Conversation with Sir Harold Acton, Modern Age, forthcoming; "Ciceros, Vergil, and the Rejection of Friendship in Marcel Proust's A la recherche du temps perdu," Classical & Mod Lit, 97. **CONTACT ADDRESS** Dept of Classics, Wabash Col, Crawfordsville, IN, 47933. **EMAIL** kubiakd@wabash.edu

KUBLER, CORNELIUS C.
DISCIPLINE CHINESE **EDUCATION** Cornell Univ, BA, 72, MA, 75; Nat Taiwan Univ, MA, 78; Cornell, PhD, 81. **CAREER** Principal, Am Inst Taiwan, 81-87; chair, dept Asian, African Langs, For Svc Inst, 88-91; PROF CHINESE, CHAIR DEPT ASIAN STUD, WILLIAMS COL, 91-. **HONORS AND AWARDS** Superior Hon Awd, Amer Inst in Taiwan, 87; Dept of State Outstanding Performance Awd, 88, 89, 90; Asn for Asian Studies grant, 92; Mellon fel, Inst Adv Stud, Nat for Lang Ctr, 93; Fulbright res-lecturing Awd to Taiwan, 96-97. **RESEARCH** Chinese language pedagogy; Chinese linguistics, particular dialectology; language contact. **SELECTED PUBLICATIONS** Auth, Desiderata for a Basic Chinese Language Textbook, Chinesisch Unterricht, 92; Teaching Advanced Conversation and Comprehension Through Xiangsheng, J Chinese Lang Tchr(s) Asn, 93; Performing Comic Dialogs, Far Eastern Publ(s), Yale Univ Press, 95; NFLC Guide for Basic Chinese Language Programs, Task Force Chair, Ohio State, 97; Study Abroad as an Integral Part of the Chinese Language Curriculum, J Chinese Lang Tchr(s) Asn, 97; A Framework for Basic Chinese Language Programs, J Chinese Lang Tchr(s) Asn, 97; Recommendations of the US National Task Force on Basic Chinese, Chinesisch Unterricht, 97; coauth, Read Chinese Signs, Boston, 93. **CONTACT ADDRESS** Dept of Asian Stud, Williams Col, Williamstown, MA, 01267. **EMAIL** cornelius.c.kubler@williams.edu

KUCERA, HENRY
PERSONAL Born 02/15/1925, Czechoslovakia, m, 1951, 2 children **DISCIPLINE** SLAVIC LANGUAGES & LINGUISTICS **EDUCATION** Charles Univ, Prague, MA, Harvard Univ, PhD(Slavic lang); 52; Brown Univ, MA, 58. **CAREER** Asst prof for lang, Univ FL, 52-55; asst prof mod lang, 55-58, assoc prof, 58-63, Prof Slavic Lang, Ling & Cognitive Sci, 63-, prof cognitive sci, 81-90, Fred M Seed prof ling and cognitive scis, 82-, Brown Univ; Ford fel, 60-61; Guggenheim Found fel, 60-61; Howard Found fel, 60-61, mem admin bd, 78-; Int Bus Machines Corp res assoc, Mass Inst Technol, 60-63; mem, Am Comt Slavists, 65-68; vis prof, Univ MI, 67; consult, ling panel, Am Heritage Dictionary, 67-69; Nat Endowment for Hum sr fel, 68-69; vis prof, Univ CA, Berkeley, 69; Am Coun Learned Soc fel, 69-70; res assoc, Harvard Univ, 77-79. **HONORS AND AWARDS** Phi Beta Kappa; DSc, hon, Bucknell Univ, 84; PhD, hon, Masaryk Univ, Brno, Czech, 90. **MEMBERSHIPS** Ling Soc Am; MLA; Asn for Comput Ling; Am Asn Tchrs Slavic & East Europ Lang; Cognitive Sci Soc; Czech Soc Arts and Sci in Am; Prague Ling Circle. **RESEARCH** General and Slavic linguistics; computers in linguistic research; language and cognition. **SELECTED PUBLICATIONS** Auth, The Phonology of Czech, Mouton, The Hague, 61; coauth, Computational Analysis of Present-Day AmEnglish, Brown Univ, 67; A Comparative Quantitative Phonology of Russian, Czech, and German, Am Elsevier, 68; ed, American Contributions to the 6th International Congress of Slavists, Mouton, The Hague, 68; auth, Computers in Linguistics and in Literary Studies, Brown

Univ, 69; coauth, Time in Language, Univ Mich, 75; Frequency Analysis of English Usage, Houghton Mifflin Co, 82. **CONTACT ADDRESS** Dept of Slavic Lang, Brown Univ, PO Box E, Providence, RI, 02901-1674. **EMAIL** Henry_Kucera@brown.edu

KUDSZUS, WINFRIED
PERSONAL Born 09/10/1941, Dillingen, Germany **DISCIPLINE** GERMAN LITERATURE **EDUCATION** Univ Calif, Berkeley, MA, 66, PhD(Ger), 68. **CAREER** From actg asst prof to asst prof Ger, Stanford Univ, 67-68; asst prof, Univ Calif, Berkeley, 68-70; res fel humanities, Soc Humanities, Cornell Univ, 69-70; assoc prof Ger, Univ Calif, Berkeley, 70-74; vis prof, Univ Tubingen, Ger, 71-72; PROF GER, UNIV CALIF, BERKELEY, 74-; Vis res prof lit theory and psychiat, Univ Mainz, Ger, 75-76; spec appt lit theory and psychoanal, Univ Frankfurt, Ger, 76. **MEMBERSHIPS** Int Soc Lit Studies and Psychiat; MLA; Holderlin-Gesellschaft. **RESEARCH** German literature 18th-20th centuries; literar and cultural theory; literature and psychology. **SELECTED PUBLICATIONS** Auth, Poetic Process, Ger Quart, Vol 0070, 97. **CONTACT ADDRESS** Dept of Ger, Univ of Calif, 5315 Dwinelle Hall, Berkeley, CA, 94720-3244.

KUENZLI, RUDOLF ERNST
PERSONAL Born 07/28/1942, Switzerland, m, 1968, 2 children **DISCIPLINE** ENGLISH LITERATURE, COMPARATIVE LITERATURE **EDUCATION** Univ Wis-Madison, MA-(English), 68, MA(Ger), 69, PhD(comp lit), 71. **CAREER** Asst prof 70-76, assoc prof, 76-82, Prof English and Comp Lit, Univ Iowa, 82-; Res fel English and comp lit, Univ Iowa, 76; fel, Sch Criticism and Theory, Univ Calif, 78; DIR, DADA ARCH RES CTR, 78-; Inst Res Humanities fel, 79-80; chmn program comp lit, Univ Paul Valery, 80-83; vis prof, Montpellier, France, 81-82. **MEMBERSHIPS** MLA; Midwestern Mod Lang Asn; Comp Lit Asn; Asn Study Lit and Philos; Asn Study Dada and Surrealism. **RESEARCH** Avant-garde; Nietzsche; philosophies of language. **SELECTED PUBLICATIONS** Auth, Identities and Introduction, J Midwest Mod Lang Asn, Vol 0028, 95. **CONTACT ADDRESS** Dept of Lit, Univ of Iowa, 308 English Phil Bld, Iowa City, IA, 52242-1492.

KUEPPER, KARL JOSEF
PERSONAL Born 08/08/1935, Cologne, Germany, m, 1963, 2 children **DISCIPLINE** GERMAN LINGUISTICS **EDUCATION** Univ Cologne, MA, 62, MEd, 64; Univ Muenster, DPhil, 70. **CAREER** From asst prof to assoc prof, Univ NB, 65-78, prof, 78-79, actg assoc dean arts, 75-76 and 77-78; DEAN OF FAC, BISHOPS UNIV, 80-. **MEMBERSHIPS** Can Asn Univ Teachers Ger; Can Ling Asn; Can Asn Advan Netherlandic Studies; Can Asn Applied Ling. **RESEARCH** Historical German linguistics; contrastive and applied linguistics. **SELECTED PUBLICATIONS** Auth, Pretext and Subtext in Reflections on Form and Function of German Late Medieval Texts Containing Reports of Urban Events, Zeitschrift Deutsche Philol, Vol 0116, 97. **CONTACT ADDRESS** Dean's Office, Bishop's Univ, Lennoxville, PQ, J1M 1Z7.

KUHN-OSIOUS, ECKHARD
DISCIPLINE GERMAN **EDUCATION** Univ Colo at Boulder, PhD. **CAREER** Assoc prof; past ch, AATG Testing Comn; dir, Hunter summer prog, Ger. **RESEARCH** 18th-century enlightenment literature; Goethe, and the 20th century up to the present. **SELECTED PUBLICATIONS** Main auth, 3-vol series of introductory textbk(s), used and/or tested at various col in CUNY; publ on, lit and pedagogical topics. **CONTACT ADDRESS** Dept of German, Hunter Col, CUNY, 695 Park Ave, New York, NY, 10021.

KUIZENGA, DONNA
PERSONAL Born 01/30/1947, Princeton, NJ **DISCIPLINE** FRENCH LANGUAGE AND LITERATURE **EDUCATION** Adelphi Univ, AB, 68; City Univ New York, PhD(French), 74. **CAREER** Instr French, Adelphi Univ, 69-71; asst prof, 74-79, ASSOC PROF FRENCH, UNIV MO-COLUMBIA, 79-; Vis assoc prof Fr, Univ Wis-Madison, 79-80. **MEMBERSHIPS** MLA; Am Asn Teachers French; NAm Soc Study Seventeenth Century French Lit; Asn Int Etudes Fr; AAUP. **RESEARCH** Seventeenth-century French literature; womens studies. **SELECTED PUBLICATIONS** Auth, Et In Arcadia Ego in Essais on the Pastoral Novel, Fr Rev, Vol 0066, 93; Le Prince Deguise, La Mort De Cesar, Fr Rev, Vol 0068, 95; Gherardi, Evariste Italian Theater, Vol 1, Fr Rev, Vol 0069, 96; Bolduc, Benoit Andromede Delivree, Intermede Anonyme 1623, Fr Rev, Vol 0069, 96. **CONTACT ADDRESS** Dept of Romance Lang, Univ of Mo, Columbia, MO, 65211.

KUMPF, MICHAEL
DISCIPLINE LANGUAGE **EDUCATION** Luthe Col, BA, 68; MA, 72, PhD, 74, Ohio State Univ. **CAREER** Prof, Classics, 75-98, Chr, Foreign Lang and Lit, 81-84 and 98-, Valparaiso Univ; **CONTACT ADDRESS** Dept of Foreign Languages and Literature, Valparaiso Univ, Valparaiso, IN, 46383. **EMAIL** michael.kumpf@valpo.edu

KUNO, SUSUMU
PERSONAL Born 08/11/1933, Tokyo, Japan, m, 1967, 2 children **DISCIPLINE** LINGUISTICS **EDUCATION** Univ Tokyo, AB, 56, AM, 58; Harvard Univ, PhD, 64. **CAREER** From instr to assoc prof, 64-69, Prof Ling, 69-, Chmn Dept, 72-77, 78-91, Harvard Univ. **HONORS AND AWARDS** Guggenheim fel, 77-78; Hon Doc, Univ Paris VII, 97. **MEMBERSHIPS** Asn Comput Mach; Asn Comput Ling (pres, 67); Ling Soc Am. **RESEARCH** Generative grammar; functional syntax; Japanese and English syntax; computational linguistics; discourse analysis. **SELECTED PUBLICATIONS** Auth, Computer Analysis of Natural Languages, Proc Symp Applied Math, 67; auth, "Locatives in Existential Sentences," Linguistic Inquiry, 72; auth, "Functional Sentence Perspective," Linguistic Inquiry, 72; auth, The Structure of the Japanese Language, MIT, 73; coauth, Functional Syntax and GB Theory, U Chicago, 93. **CONTACT ADDRESS** Dept of Ling, Harvard Univ, 315 Boylston Hall, Cambridge, MA, 02138-3800. **EMAIL** kuno@fas.harvard.edu

KURMAN, GEORGE
PERSONAL Born 06/10/1942, Tallinn, Estonia, m, 1965, 4 children **DISCIPLINE** COMPARATIVE AND ESTONIAN LITERATURE **EDUCATION** Cornell Univ, BA, 62; Columbia Univ, MA, 66; Ind Univ, PhD(comp lit), 69. **CAREER** Transl Estonian epic poetry, UNESCO, 69-70; from asst prof to assoc prof, 70-80, PROF ENGLISH and COMP LIT, WESTERN ILL UNIV, 80-; Int Res and Exchanges Bd fel, Estonian lit, 72-73. **MEMBERSHIPS** Asn Advan Baltic Studies; corresp mem Inst Estonian Lang and Lit. **SELECTED PUBLICATIONS** Auth, Conrad Heart of Darkness as Pretext for Barth Night Sea Journey in the Colonists Passage Upstream, Intl Fiction Rev, Vol 0020, 93; Tabamatus, World Lit Today, Vol 0068, 94. **CONTACT ADDRESS** Dept of English, Western Illinois Univ, Macomb, IL, 61455.

KURTH, WILLIAM CHARLES
PERSONAL Born 10/23/1932, Waterloo, IA, m, 1958, 3 children **DISCIPLINE** LATIN, GREEK **EDUCATION** Univ Northern Iowa, AB, 53; Univ Tex, MA, 59; Univ NC, PhD, 65. **CAREER** Tchr, 55-56, high Sch, Wis; instr Latin, 57-59, Baylor Univ; from instr to asst prof classics, 62-67, Univ Ill; assoc prof, 67-73, chmn dept, 67-76, prof classics, 73-, Luther Col, Iowa; consult programmed Latin, 67, Macalester Col; NEH fel, Univ Tex, 77-78. **MEMBERSHIPS** Am Philol Assn; Am Class League; Class Assn Mid W & S. **RESEARCH** Aulus Gellius; the minor Latin rhetoricians. **CONTACT ADDRESS** Dept of Classics, Luther Col, 700 College Dr, Decorah, IA, 52101-1045. **EMAIL** kurthwmc@luther.edu

KUSCH, MANFRED
PERSONAL Born 10/11/1941, Germany **DISCIPLINE** FRENCH LITERATURE, COMPARATIVE LITERATURE **EDUCATION** Univ Gottingen, Ger, MA, 66; Univ Calif, Berkeley, PhD(comp lit), 73. **CAREER** Asst prof, 71-80, ASSOC PROF FRENCH, UNIV CLAIF, DAVIS, 80-. **MEMBERSHIPS** MLA; Am Soc 18th Century Studies; Philol Asn Pac Coast. **RESEARCH** French novel of the 18th century; theory of the novel; comparative literature. **SELECTED PUBLICATIONS** Auth, Mental Machinery in The Origins and Consequences of Psychological Ideas .1. 1600-1850, Brit J Hist Sci, Vol 0027, 94; Recluse, Interlocutor, Interrogator in Natural and Social Order in Turn of the Century, Psychological Research Schools, Isis, Vol 0086, 95; The Inner Side of Nature in Fechner, Gustav, Theodor, Scientific and Philosophical World View, Brit J Hist Sci, Vol 0028, 95; Piaget Before Piaget in, Brit J Hist Sci, Vol 0028, 95; Automating Air Pumps in An Empirical and Conceptual Analysis, Technol Cult, Vol 0036, 95; We Have Never Been Modern in, Brit J Hist Sci, Vol 0028, 95; Constructing the Subject in Historical Origins of Psychological Research, Brit J Hist Sci, Vol 0028, 95; The Jung Cult in Origins of a Charismatic Movement, Brit J Hist Sci, Vol 0028, 95; Gestalt Psychology in German Culture, 1890-1967 in Holism and The Quest for Objectivity, Brit J Hist Sci, Vol 0029, 96; Rethinking Objectivity, Brit J Hist Sci, Vol 0029, 96; Metaphors in the History of Psychology, Brit J Hist Sci, Vol 0030, 97; The Sociophilosophy of Folk Psychology, Studies Hist Philos Sci, Vol 0028, 97. **CONTACT ADDRESS** Dept of French and Ital, Univ of Calif, Davis, CA, 95616.

KUSHNER, EVA
PERSONAL Born 06/18/1929, Prague, Czechoslovakia **DISCIPLINE** COMPARATIVE LITERATURE **EDUCATION** McGill Univ, BA, 48, MA, 50, PhD, 56. **CAREER** Lectr philos, Sir George Williams Univ, 52-53; lectr Fr, McGill Univ, 52-55; lectr, Univ Col, London, 58-59; lectr to prof Fr & comp lit, Carleton Univ, 61-76; prof Fr & comp lit, McGill Univ, 76-87; prof, 87-94, PROF EMER, UNIV TORONTO, 94-, SR FELLOW, COMPARATIVE LITERATURE, 97-. **SELECTED PUBLICATIONS** Auth, Patrice de la Tour du Pin, 61; auth, Le mythe d'Orphee dans la litterature francaise contemporaine, 61; auth, Chants de Boheme, 63; auth, Saint-Denys Garneau, 67; auth, Francois Mauriac, 72; ed, Renewals in the Theory of Literary History, 84; ed, La problematique du sujet chez Montaigne, 95; ed, Constraints to Freedom of Scholarship and Science, 96; co-ed, Proceedings of the VIIth Congress of the Int Comp Lit Asn. **CONTACT ADDRESS** Victoria Univ, Univ of Toronto, 73 Queen's Park Cr, Pratt 322, Toronto, ON, M5S 1K7.

KUSMER, ROBERT L.
PERSONAL Cleveland, OH **DISCIPLINE** FOREIGN LANGUAGE **EDUCATION** Cleveland State Univ, BA, 72; Northwestern Univ, PhD, 83; Kent State Univ, MLS, 88. **CAREER** Cataloger, 90-92; head Tech Serv, 92-96, Mentor Public Libr; cataloger, Univ Notre Dame, 97-. **HONORS AND AWARDS** Beta Phi Mu, 89; Sidney L. Jackson Memorial Award, Kent State Univ, 89; DAAD, 79-80. **MEMBERSHIPS** ALA, ACRL; ALCTS **RESEARCH** Librarianship; German literature in English; philosophy; theology; general humanities. **CONTACT ADDRESS** Theodore M. Hesburg Library, Univ of Notre Dame, Notre Dame, IN, 46556. **EMAIL** kusmer.1@nd.edu

KUSSI, PETER
DISCIPLINE SLAVIC LANGUAGES **EDUCATION** Queens Col, BS; Univ Wis, MS; Columbia Univ, PhD. **CAREER** Prof. **RESEARCH** Czech literature; comparative literature; theory of translation. **SELECTED PUBLICATIONS** Ed, Toward the Radical Center; ed, A Karel Capek Reader; Writing on the Wall, An Anthology of Czech Literature. **CONTACT ADDRESS** Dept of Slavic Languages, Columbia Col, New York, 2960 Broadway, New York, NY, 10027-6902. **EMAIL** pk10@columbia.edu

KUSTANOVICH, KONSTANTIN
PERSONAL Born 08/22/1945, Soviet Union, m, 1992, 1 child **DISCIPLINE** RUSSIAN LITERATURE **EDUCATION** Columbia Univ, PhD, 86. **CAREER** Asst prof, Lafayette Col, 86-87; asst prof, Vanderbilt Univ, 87-94; assoc prof, 94- ; dean, Russian Sch Norwich Univ, 92-97. **MEMBERSHIPS** AATSEEL, AAAASS. **RESEARCH** Russian literature; Russian culture; theory of literature and culture. **SELECTED PUBLICATIONS** Auth, The Two Worlds in Jurij Zivago's Poem Zimnjaja noc, Russian Lit, 92; auth, The Naturalistic Tendency in Contemporary Soviet Fiction: Thematics, Poetics, Functions, New Directions in Soviet Literature, 92; auth, The Artist and the Tyrant: Vasily Aksenov's Works in the Brezhnev Era, 92; auth, Erotic Glasnost: Sexuality in Recent Russian Literature, World Lit Today, 93; Venichka Erofeev's Grief and Solitude: Existentialist Motifs in the Poema, Venedikt Erofeev's Moscow-Petushki: Critical Perspectives, 97. **CONTACT ADDRESS** Vanderbilt Univ, Box 1525, Nashville, TN, 37235. **EMAIL** kustakv@ctrvax.vanderbilt.edu

KUXDORF, MANFRED
PERSONAL Born 07/04/1933, Cologne, Germany, m, 1963, 2 children **DISCIPLINE** GERMAN LITERATURE **EDUCATION** Univ Waterloo, BA, 63, MA, 65; Univ Alta, PhD(Ger), 69. **CAREER** Assoc chmn dept Ger lang, 74-75, ASSOC PROF GER, UNIV WATERLOO, 74-; Humanities Res Coun Can publ grant, 71; Can Coun res grants, 71, 72 and leave fel, 75-76; vis prof, Univ Mannheim, 72-73; Ger Acad Exchange Serv stipend, 72-73; ASSOC ED, GERMAN-SLAVICA, 73-. **MEMBERSHIPS** Can Asn Univ Teachers Ger; Int Arthur Schnitzler Res Asn; MLA; Int Vereinigung fur Germanistische Sprach - u Literaturwissenschaft. **RESEARCH** Modern German literature, especially expressionism. **SELECTED PUBLICATIONS** Auth, Love in Expressionism in A Study of Poetry Published in the Js Die Aktion and Der Sturm from 1910-1914, J Ger Studies, Vol 0029, 93. **CONTACT ADDRESS** Dept Ger and Slavic Lang and Lit, Univ Waterloo, Waterloo, ON, N2L 3G1.

KUZNIAR, A.A.
PERSONAL Born 10/31/1956, Hamilton, ON, Canada, s **DISCIPLINE** GERMAN LITERATURE **EDUCATION** Princeton Univ, PhD, 83. **CAREER** Assoc Prof, Univ NC, 83- . **HONORS AND AWARDS** Humboldt Fel, 97-98. **SELECTED PUBLICATIONS** Auth, Deyaled Endings: Nomencalture in Novais and Hoelderlin, 83; ed, Outing Goethe and His Age, 96. **CONTACT ADDRESS** German Dept., Univ N. Carolina, CB #3160, Chapel Hill, NC, 27599-3160.

KYLE HIGGINS, AMANDA
DISCIPLINE GENERAL AND SPECIAL EDUCATION; LEARNING DISABILITIES **EDUCATION** Univ NMex, BA, 73, MA, 78, PhD, 88. **CAREER** Coordr, spec educ undergrad prog, spec educ grad generalist prog, Univ Nev, Las Vegas. **SELECTED PUBLICATIONS** Coauth, Hypermedia text-only information support for students with learning disabilities and remedial students, J of Learning Disabilities, 29, 96; Creating individualized computer assisted instruction for students with autism utilizing multimedia authoring software, Focus on Autism and Other Devel Disabilities, 11,96. **CONTACT ADDRESS** Dept of Spec Educ, Univ Nev, Las Vegas, 4505 Maryland Pky, Las Vegas, NV, 89154-3014. **EMAIL** higgins@nevada.edu

KYM, ANNETTE
DISCIPLINE GERMAN **EDUCATION** Univ Cincinnati, PhD. **CAREER** Assoc prof, Hunter Col; Grad Sch & Univ Ctr, CUNY; Hunter Col, 85-; coordr, basic lang sequence; supvr, adj fac & mentor, grad stud doing tchg practica at Hunter Col; past tchr, distance learning crse over interactive tv, Hunter and Brooklyn Col; expert tester for, Prnfung Wirtschaftsdeutsch Int.

HONORS AND AWARDS Distinguished Tchr Awd, NY State Asn of For Lang Teachers. **SELECTED PUBLICATIONS** Auth, bk on Hesse's Role As A Critic & on pedagogical topics. **CONTACT ADDRESS** Dept of German, Hunter Col, CUNY, 695 Park Ave, New York, NY, 10021.

L

L'ALLIER, LOUIS
PERSONAL Born 02/27/1961, PQ, Canada **DISCIPLINE** CLASSICAL STUDIES **EDUCATION** Univ Ottawa, MA, 89; Laval Univ, PhD, 96. **CAREER** Lectr, Laval Univ, 96-. **MEMBERSHIPS** Am Philol Asn; Class Asn of Can; Soc des Etudes Anciennes du Quebec. **RESEARCH** Ancient Greek literature. **SELECTED PUBLICATIONS** Auth, "Le Heros Xenophontique et les Femmes," 98; "Le Domaine de Scillonte; Xenophon et l'Exemple Perse," 98; "Xenophon's Park at Scillua: Some Ancient and Modern Views on Nature," 97. **CONTACT ADDRESS** 24 Benedict St, Hull, PQ, J8Y 5G1. **EMAIL** l.lallier@sympatico.ca

LABORDE, ALICE M.
DISCIPLINE FRENCH LITERATURE **EDUCATION** UCLA, PhD. **CAREER** PROF EMER, FR, UNIV CALIF, IRVINE. **SELECTED PUBLICATIONS** Auth, Diderot et Madame de Puisieux; Le Mariage du Marquis de Sade. **CONTACT ADDRESS** Dept of Fr and Ital, Univ Calif, Irvine, CA, 92697.

LABRADOR, JOSE J.
PERSONAL Born 04/08/1941, Castejon, Spain, m, 1966, 1 child **DISCIPLINE** SPANISH LANGUAGE & LITERATURE **EDUCATION** Univ Madrid, BA, 61; Case Western Reserve Univ, MA, 68, PhD, 71. **CAREER** From instr to assoc prof, 69-88, prof Span, Cleveland State Univ, 88-; vis prof, Middlebury Col, Summer 76. **HONORS AND AWARDS** CSU Distinguished Fac Award for Res and Schol, 97. **MEMBERSHIPS** Mediaeval Soc Am; Midwest Mod Lang Asn. **RESEARCH** Spanish medieval literature and history; European literature and history; Medieval philosophy. **SELECTED PUBLICATIONS** Co-ed, Cancionera de poeseas varias. Manuscrito 3902 de la Bibbliboteca Nacional de Madrid, in Coleccion Cancioneros Castellanos, vol 2, Cleveland State Univ, 89; Estudios en homenaje a Enrique Ruiz-Fornells, ALDEEU, 90; Poeseas del Maestro Leon y de Fray Melchor de la Serna y otros, in Codice numero 961 de la Biblioteca Real de Madrid, Cleveland State Univ, 91; coauth, Tabla de los principios de la poeseas espanola, in Siglos XVI-XVII, Cleveland State Univ, 93; co-ed, Cancionera de poeseas varias, in Manuscrito No. 1587 de la Biblioteca Real de Madrid, Visor Libros, Madrid, 94; Cancionero sevillano de Nueva York, Univ Sevilla, 96; coauth, Manuscrito Fuentelsol (Madrid, Palacio II-973). Con poemas de Fray Luis de Leon, Fray Melchor de la Serna, Hurtado de Mendoza, Linan, Gongora, Lope y otros, in Seguido ahora de un apendice con las poeseas del fraile benito Fray Melchor de la Serna, Cleveland State Univ, 97; co-ed, Romancero de Palacio, Univ Penn, Visor Libros, Madrid, 98; author of numerous journal articles and book contributions. **CONTACT ADDRESS** Dept of Modern Lang, Cleveland State Univ, 1983 E 24th St, Cleveland, OH, 44115-2440. **EMAIL** J.labrador@popmail.csuohio.edu

LACKEY, ROBERT SAM
DISCIPLINE LANGUAGE ARTS AND DISTANCE LEARNING **EDUCATION** Univ Tulsa, PhD, 70. **CAREER** Southwest Tex State Univ **MEMBERSHIPS** Channel One, Chapbook, Okla Eng Jour. **SELECTED PUBLICATIONS** Area: poetry. **CONTACT ADDRESS** Southwestern OK State Univ, 100 Campus Dr, Weatherford, OK, 73096. **EMAIL** lackeys@swosu.edu

LACY, NORRIS J.
PERSONAL Born 03/08/1940, Hopkinsville, KY **DISCIPLINE** FRENCH **EDUCATION** Murray St Univ, AB, 62; Ind Univ, MA, 63, PhD, 67. **CAREER** Lectr, 65-66, Ind Univ; asst prof, 66-70, assoc prof, 70-75, prof, 76-88, Univ Kansas; vis assoc prof, 75-76, UCLA; prof, 88-98, Wash Univ, St Louis; Edwin Erle Sparks Prof, 98-, Penna St Univ. **RESEARCH** Arthurian lit, medieval romance, fabliaux **CONTACT ADDRESS** Dept of French, Pennsylvania State Univ, University Park, PA, 16802. **EMAIL** njl2@psu.edu

LADD, BARBARA
DISCIPLINE ENGLISH LANGUAGE AND LITERATURE **EDUCATION** Univ NC Greensboro, MFA, 81; Univ Tex Austin, MA, 85; Univ NC Chapel Hill, PhD, 90. **CAREER** Prof **RESEARCH** Late nineteenth- and twentieth-century southern literature especially with history and literary texts; applications of New Historicism to the writing of literary histories, to the inscription of race, ethnicity, and gender in conceptions of the literary; classification and mis-classification of literature in terms of nation and region. **SELECTED PUBLICATIONS** Auth, Nationalism and the Color Line in the Work of George W. Cable, Mark Twain, and William Faulkner, LSU, 96; essays and reviews in Am Lit, Miss Quart, So Quart, and So Atlantic Rev. **CONTACT ADDRESS** English Dept, Emory Univ, 1380 Oxford Rd NE, Atlanta, GA, 30322-1950. **EMAIL** bladd@emory.edu

LADEFOGED, PETER
PERSONAL Born 09/17/1925, Sutton, England, m, 1953, 3 children **DISCIPLINE** LINGUISTICS, ENGLISH **EDUCATION** Univ Edinburgh, MA, 51, PhD, 59. **CAREER** Lectr phonetics, Univ Edinburgh, 53-61; W African Lang Surv fel, 61-62; from asst prof to assoc prof English, 62-65, PROF LING, UNIV CALIF, LOS ANGELES, 65-, Team leader, Uganda Lang Surv, 68. **MEMBERSHIPS** Acoust Soc Am; Int Phonetic Asn; Int Asn Voice Identification; Am Speech and Hearing Asn; Ling Soc Am (pres). **RESEARCH** Experimental phonetics; African languages; phonology. **SELECTED PUBLICATIONS** Auth, Another View of Endangered Languages, Lang, Vol 0068, 92; Clicks and Their Accompaniments, J Phonetics, Vol 0022, 94; The Status of Phonetic Rarities, Lang, Vol 0072, 96; Phonetic Structures of Banawa, an Endangered Language, Phonetica, Vol 0054, 97; Abercrombie, David and the Changing Field of Phonetics, J Phonetics, Vol 0025, 97. **CONTACT ADDRESS** Dept of Ling, Univ of Calif, Los Angeles, CA, 90024.

LADUSAW, WILLIAM A.
DISCIPLINE LINGUISTICS **EDUCATION** Univ Ky, BA; Univ Tex, Austin, PhD, 79. **CAREER** PROF, DEPT CH, UNIV CALIF, SANTA CRUZ. **RESEARCH** Syntax and semantics of negation, negative concord, and negative polarity items. **SELECTED PUBLICATIONS** Auth, Polarity Sensitivity as Inherent Scope Relations, Garland Publ, 80; "Logical Form and Conditions on Grammaticality," Ling and Philos, 82; "A Proposed Distinction between Levels and Strata," Ling in the Morning Calm, The Linguistic Society of Korea, 87; coauth, Towards a Non-grammatical Account of Thematic Roles, Thematic Relations, Acad Press, 88. **CONTACT ADDRESS** Dept of Ling, Univ Calif, 1156 High St, Santa Cruz, CA, 95064.

LAFAYETTE, ROBERT
DISCIPLINE LANGUAGE LEARNING AND TEACHING, APPLIED LINGUISTICS **EDUCATION** Ohio State Univ, PhD, 71. **CAREER** Prof, La State Univ. **SELECTED PUBLICATIONS** Auth, The Culture Revolution in Foreign Language Teaching, 75; Conna?tre la France, 83; L'enseignement du fran(ais aux Etats-Unis, 88; La Francophonie: R?flexions sur la culture et la civilization, 93. **CONTACT ADDRESS** Dept of Fr Grad Stud, Louisiana State Univ, Baton Rouge, LA, 70803.

LAFLEUR, RICHARD ALLEN
PERSONAL Born 09/22/1945, Newburyport, MA, m, 1967, 3 children **DISCIPLINE** CLASSICAL STUDIES **EDUCATION** Univ Va, BA, 68, MA, 70; Duke Univ, PhD, 73. **CAREER** Asst prof, 72-77, ASSOC PROF CLASSICS, UNIV GA, 77-, Head Dept, 80-, Ed, Class Outlook, 79-; chmn, comt Prom Latin, 79-81, exec comt, 79-83, S sect secy-treas, 78-; Class Asn Midwest & South. **HONORS AND AWARDS** Am Philol Asn Award, Excellence in Teaching Classics, 84; Classical Asn Midwest & South, Ovatio, 85; Am Classical League, pres, 84-86, hon pres for life, 86-; Univ GA, Bronze Medallion, Public Service, 88; For Lang Asn Ga, Teacher of the Year, 88; Ga Governors Award, Humanities, 89. **MEMBERSHIPS** Am Class League; Am Philol Asn; Archaeol Inst Am; Class Asn Mid W & S; Vergilian Soc. **RESEARCH** Juvenal; Roman satire; Latin pedagogy. **SELECTED PUBLICATIONS** Auth, The Teaching of latin in American Schools, Scholars Press, 87; Latin Poetry for the Beginning Student, Longman, 87; Wheelock's Latin, Harper Collins, 95; Love and Transformation: An Ovid Reader, Scott Foresman-Addison Wesley 98; Latin for the 21st Century: From Concept to Classroom, Scott Foresman-Addison Wesley, 98. **CONTACT ADDRESS** Dept Classics, Univ of Ga, Athens, GA, 30602-0001. **EMAIL** rlafleur@parallel.park.uga.edu

LAFONTANT, JULIEN J.
PERSONAL Port-au-Prince, Haiti, m **DISCIPLINE** FOREIGN LANGUAGES **EDUCATION** SUNY Binghamton, MA (distinction) 1974, PhD 1976. **CAREER** Exec Mansion Morovia Liberia, translator 1961-63; Ivory Coast Embassy Monrovia Liberia, translator 1963-66; Cuttington Coll Suakoko Liberia, asst prof 1966-72; SUNY Binghamton, teaching asst 1972-76; Univ of NE Lincoln, asst prof 1976-77; Acting Chair Black Studies UNO, asst prof 1977-78; Univ of NE, assoc prof 1978-82, full prof French Chair Black Studies UNO 1983-85; full prof French and Black Studies 1986-. **HONORS AND AWARDS** Great Teacher Awd Univ of NE Omaha 1982. **SELECTED PUBLICATIONS** book on Montesquieu; book entitled Understanding A Culture; several articles dealing with the Black exper in general and the French encounter with Blacks. **CONTACT ADDRESS** Dept of Foreign Languages, Univ of Nebraska-Omaha, Omaha, NE, 68182-0001.

LAGO, MARY MCCLELLAND
PERSONAL Born 11/04/1919, Pittsburgh, PA, m, 1944, 2 children **DISCIPLINE** MODERN ENGLISH AND BENGALI LITERATURE **EDUCATION** Bucknell Univ, BA, 40; Univ Mo-Columbia, MA, 65, PhD(English), 69. **CAREER** Instr, 64-70, lectr, 70-75, res grants, 71-74, assoc prof, 75-78, PROF ENGLISH, UNIV MO-COLUMBIA, 78-, Am Philos Soc res grants, 67, 68 and 70; Am Coun Learned Soc/Ford Found Joint SAsia Prog grant, 72-73; Nat Endowment for Humanities grant, 80-83. **HONORS AND AWARDS** DLitt, Bucknell Univ, 81. **MEMBERSHIPS** MLA; Midwest Mod Lang Asn; Asn Asian Studies; Soc of Authors, London; Virginia Woolf Soc. **RESEARCH** Modern Indian literature; late 19th and early 20th century English literature and art history. **SELECTED PUBLICATIONS** Auth, A 'River Called Titash', World Lit Today, Vol 0069, 95. **CONTACT ADDRESS** Dept of English, Univ Missouri, Columbia, MO, 65201.

LAIRET, DOLORES PERSON
PERSONAL Born 12/27/1935, Cleveland, OH, w **DISCIPLINE** FOREIGN LANGUAGES **EDUCATION** Wheaton Coll, AB 1957; Middlebury Coll, AM 1958; Univ of Paris; Case Western Reserve U, PhD 1972. **CAREER** Cleveland State Univ, assoc prof 1972-77, instructor 1971-72, lecturer 1969-71; City of Cleveland, sr personnel asst 1969-71; Western Reserve Univ, teaching fellow lecturer 1965-67; John Marshall HS, French teacher 1963-65; Fox Lane Sch Bedford NY, Educator 1960-62; Southern Univ Baton Rouge, instructor 1959. **HONORS AND AWARDS** Recipient of various Fellowships. **MEMBERSHIPS** Mem Am Assn of Tchrs of French 1971-; Am Assn of Univ Prof 1971; Am Council on Tching of Foreign Lang 1972-; NE Modern Lang Assn 1974-; African Lit Assn; Music Critics Assn; OH Mod Lang Tchrs Assn; past sec & pres Cleveland Chap Tots & Teens Inc 1963-73; mem of bd Glenville Health Assn 1974-; mem Champs Inc 1964-; Am Spec Lctr for US Dept of State in Niger Mali Upper Volta Senegal & Togo. **SELECTED PUBLICATIONS** The Francophone African Novel Perspectives for Critical Eval; Presence Africaine; various articles on Jazz Cleveland Press Showtime. **CONTACT ADDRESS** E 24 St & Euclid Ave, Cleveland, OH, 44115.

LAKER, JOSEPH ALPHONSE
PERSONAL Born 03/17/1941, Indianapolis, IN **DISCIPLINE** HISTORY, JAPANESE STUDIES **EDUCATION** Marian Col, BA, 63; IN Univ, MA, 67, PhD, 75. **CAREER** Instr hist, St Olaf Col, 67-70; asst prof, 74-80, assoc prof, 80-94, PROF HIST, WHEELING COL, 94-; NEH Summer Seminar, Brown Univ, 79; Fulbright/Hays Summer Seminar, Korea, 87; co-dir, NEH Summer Inst for High Sch Tchr(s), summer 95. **MEMBERSHIPS** Asn Asian Studies; Econ Hist Asn; Bus Hist Asn. **RESEARCH** The develop of the Japan beer industry; mod Japan economic and soc hist; Japan Colonialism. **SELECTED PUBLICATIONS** Encyclopedia of World War II, Cord Publ, 78; Oligopoly at home and expansion abroad: The develop of the Japan beer industry, 1907-1937, Proc Second Int Symp Asian Studies, 80; coauth, Tchr Outreach in Japanese Studies, Educ About Asia, fall 96. **CONTACT ADDRESS** Wheeling Jesuit Col, 316 Washington Ave, Wheeling, WV, 26003-6243. **EMAIL** lakerj@wju.edu

LALLY, TIM DOUGLAS PATRICK
PERSONAL Born 11/11/1942, Los Angeles, CA, m, 1973, 1 child **DISCIPLINE** OLD & MIDDLE ENGLISH LANGUAGE & LITERATURE **EDUCATION** Harvard Col, AB, 68; State Univ NY, Stony Brook, MA, 72, PhD(English), 80. **CAREER** Instr, Bowling Green State Univ, 76-80; Asst Prof, 80-84, Assoc Prof English, Univ South Ala, 84-98, retired, 98-; Ed, J Advan Compos, 80-86. **MEMBERSHIPS** MLA; Medieval Acad Am; NCTE; Conf on Col Compos & Commun; Early English Text Soc. **RESEARCH** Medieval English poetry and drama; teaching of advanced composition. **SELECTED PUBLICATIONS** Auth, The nature of innovation in writing instruction, English Lang Arts Bull, 78; Thought and feeling in the Old English Wanderer, In Geardagum III, 79; The Gothic aesthetic of the Middle English St Erkenwald, Ball State Univ Forum, 79; The intellectual content of freshman English, English Lang Arts Bull, 80; Synchronic vs diachronic popular culture studies and the Old English elegy, In: 5000 Years of Popular Cult Before Printing, Bowling Green Univ Press, 80. **CONTACT ADDRESS** Dept English, Univ South Ala, Mobile, AL, 36688-0002. **EMAIL** tlally@jaguar1.usouthal.edu

LAMARRE, THOMAS
DISCIPLINE EAST ASIAN STUDIES **EDUCATION** Univ Chicago, PhD. **CAREER** Asst prof. **RESEARCH** Cultural and intellectual Japanese history. **SELECTED PUBLICATIONS** Auth, Writing Doubled Over Broken: Provisional Names, Acrostic Poems and the Perpetual Contest of Doubles in Heian Japan, 94; rev, Karatani K'jin, The Origins of Modern Japanese Literature, 94. sGEN **CONTACT ADDRESS** East Asian Studies Dept, McGill Univ, 845 Sherbrooke St, Montreal, PQ, H3A 2T5.

LAMOUREUX, NORMAND J.
DISCIPLINE FRENCH **EDUCATION** Boston Col, MA, 60, BA, 57; Ind Univ, PhD, 67. **CAREER** Prof & ch dept lang & lit, Col of Holy Cross. **RESEARCH** French language and pedagogy. **SELECTED PUBLICATIONS** Auth, Tout Ensemble, Fort Worth: Holt, Rinehart and Winston, 96; Ensemble: Grammaire, 5th ed, Fort Worth: Holt, Rinehart and Winston, 94; En-

semble: Litterature, 5th ed, Fort Worth: Holt, Rinehart and Winston, 94; Ensemble: Culture et Societe, 5th ed, Fort Worth: Holt, Rinehart and Winston, 94 & Ensemble: Histoire, Fort Worth: Holt, Rinehart and Winston, 92. **CONTACT ADDRESS** Dept of Modern Languages and Literatures, Col of the Holy Cross, 1 College St, PO Box 182A, Worcester, MA, 01610-2395. **EMAIL** nlamoure@holycross.edu

LANCE, DONALD M.
PERSONAL Born 07/10/1931, Gainesville, TX, s **DISCIPLINE** ENGLISH LINGISTICS **EDUCATION** Texas A&M Col, BA, 52; Univ Tx-Austin, MA, 62; PhD, 68. **CAREER** High sch teacher, English & Spanish, 57-64; grad instr, Univ Tx-Austin, 64-67; asst prof, Texas A&M Univ, 67-89; asst prof, Univ Mo - Columbia, 69-94; assoc prof, 72-78; prof, 78-94; prof emeritus, 94- . **HONORS AND AWARDS** Strathmore's Who's Who, 98. **MEMBERSHIPS** Ling Soc of Am; Am Dial Soc; Amer Name Soc; MLA; Mo Folklore Soc; Coun of Geog Names Authorities. **RESEARCH** Phonology; syntax; pedagogical linguistics, discourse. **SELECTED PUBLICATIONS** auth, Pronunciation in The Century Dictionary, Dictionaries, 96; auth, Regional Vocabulary in Missouri, Language Variety in the South, 97; auth, Discourse, Information, and Syntax, Papers from the 1997 Mid-America Linguistics Conference, 97; auth with Martha D. Patton, Sequential Chains of Connections: A Linguistic Analyis of Written Expository Discourse, Papers from the 1997 Mid-America Linguistics Conference; auth, Regional Variation in Subjective Dialect Divisions in the United States, A Handbook of Perceptual Dialectology. **CONTACT ADDRESS** 2208-F Bushnell Dr., Columbia, MO, 65201. **EMAIL** engdl@showme.missouri.edu

LANE, CHRISTOPHER
DISCIPLINE ENGLISH LANGUAGE AND LITERATURE **EDUCATION** Univ London, PhD. **CAREER** Fac, Univ Wisc Milwaukee; Mellon Fel Hum, Univ Penn, 95-96; assoc prof, 88-. **RESEARCH** Victorian literature; British colonial fiction; critical theory. **SELECTED PUBLICATIONS** Auth, The Ruling Passion, Duke UP, 95; The Burdens of Intimacy, Univ Chicago, 98; ed, The Psychoanalysis of Race, Columbia UP, 98. **CONTACT ADDRESS** English Dept, Emory Univ, 1380 Oxford Rd NE, Atlanta, GA, 30322-1950.

LANG, MABEL LOUISE
PERSONAL Born 11/12/1917, Utica, NY **DISCIPLINE** CLASSICAL PHILOLOGY **EDUCATION** Cornell Univ, AB, 39, Bryn Mawr Col, AM, 40, PhD, 43. **CAREER** From instr to assoc prof class philol, 43-59, actg dean, 58-59 & 60-61, Prof Greek to PROF EMERITUS, Bryn Mawr Col, 59-, Fulbright res grant, Greece, 59-60; chmn comt admis & fels, Am Sch Class Studies, Athens, 67-72, chmn managing comt, 75-80; Blegen Distinguished Vis Res prof, Vassar Col, 76-77; Martin lectr, Oberlin Col, 82. **HONORS AND AWARDS** LittD, Holy Cross Col, 75, Colgate Univ, 78. **MEMBERSHIPS** Archaeol Inst Am; Am Philol Asn; Am Philos Soc. **RESEARCH** Greek history, literature and epigraphy. **SELECTED PUBLICATIONS** Auth, Pylos tablets, 1957-1962, Am J Archaeol, 58-63; The Athenian Citizen, 60 & Weights and Measures of the Athenian Agora, 64, Am Sch Class Studies, Athens; The palace of Nestor, Vol II, in The Frescoes, Princeton Univ, 68; The Athenian Agora, XXI, Graffiti and Dipinti, 76 & Socrates in the Agora, 78, Am Sch Class Studies, Athens; auth, Herodotean Narrative and Discourse, Harvard Univ Press, 84; auth, The Athenian Agora, Ostraca, 90. **CONTACT ADDRESS** Dept of Greek, Bryn Mawr Col, Bryn Mawr, PA, 19010. **EMAIL** mlang@brynmawr.edu

LANGACKER, RONALD WAYNE
PERSONAL Born 12/27/1942, Fond du Lac, WI, m, 1966 **DISCIPLINE** LINGUISTICS **EDUCATION** Univ Ill, AB, 63, AM, 64, PhD(ling), 66. **CAREER** From asst prof to assoc prof, 66-76, PROF LING, UNIV CALIF, SAN DIEGO, 76-, Assoc ed, Language 71-77; Nat Endowment for Humanities sr fel, 73-74; Guggenheim fel, 78-79. **MEMBERSHIPS** Ling Soc Am; AAUP. **RESEARCH** Linguistic theory; Uto-Aztecan languages. **SELECTED PUBLICATIONS** Auth, Raising and Transparency, Lang, Vol 0071, 95; Constituency, Dependency, and Conceptual Grouping + Cognitive Grammar, Cognitive Ling, Vol 0008, 97. **CONTACT ADDRESS** Dept of Ling, Univ of Calif, San Diego, 9500 Gilman Dr, La Jolla, CA, 92093.

LANGE, HORST
DISCIPLINE GERMAN LANGUAGE, LITERATURE, AND CULTURE **EDUCATION** Univ Tubingen, MA; Univ Va, PhD. **CAREER** Asst prof Ger, Univ Nev, Reno. **RESEARCH** 18th- and early 19th-century German literature. **SELECTED PUBLICATIONS** Published a book on Kant and articles on Frege and Goethe. **CONTACT ADDRESS** Univ Nev, Reno, Reno, NV, 89557. **EMAIL** lange@unr.edu

LANGENDOEN, DONALD TERENCE
PERSONAL Born 06/07/1939, Paterson, NJ, m, 1984, 1 child **DISCIPLINE** LINGUISTICS, ENGLISH **EDUCATION** Mass Inst Technol, BS, 61, PhD, 64. **CAREER** From asst prof to assoc prof ling, OH State Univ, 64-69; Prof Eng, Brooklyn Col, City Univ New York, 69-88, Prof Ling, Grad CTR, 71- Vis assoc prof, Rockefeller Univ, 68-69; sr Fulbright lectr, Rijksuniv Utrecht, The Neth, 77; vis scientist IBM TJ Watson Res Ctr, York Town Heights, 86-87; Univ of AZ, 88-, head linguistics dept 88-97, vis prof, Univ of Hong Kong, 98. **HONORS AND AWARDS** Fel NY Acad Sci, NYC 77, Named Ptnr in Edn, Bd of Edn, NYC 82. **MEMBERSHIPS** Ling Soc Am; Asn Comput Ling. AAAS, chair 99-; Asn for Linguistic and Lit Computing. **RESEARCH** Eng syntax; linguistic theory; psycholinguistics. **SELECTED PUBLICATIONS** Auth, The London School of Linguistics, 68; The Study of Syntax, 69, Essentials of English Grammar, 70 & coed, Studies in Linguistic Semantics, 71, Holt; coed, An Integrated Theory of Linguistic Ability, Crowell, 76, co-auth, The Vastness of Natural Languages, Blackwell, 84; ed, Linguistics Abstracts, 97-, co-ed, Optimality Theory: An Overview, Blackwell, 97. **CONTACT ADDRESS** Dept of Linguistics, Univ of AZ, PO Box 210028, Tucson, AZ, 85721. **EMAIL** langendt@arizona.edu

LANGLEY, STEPHEN G.
PERSONAL Born 12/25/1938, Gardner, MA **DISCIPLINE** THEATRE, SPEECH **EDUCATION** Emerson Col, BA, 60, MA, 61; Univ Ill, Urbana, PhD, 65. **CAREER** Lectr speech, 63-65, from instr to assoc prof, 65-76, bus mgr, Theatre Div, 66, gem mgr, Ctr Performing Arts, 68-75, prof theatre, Brooklyn Col, 76-, dir div Performing Arts Mgt, 75-, grad dept chp, Theatre Dept, 78-. **MEMBERSHIPS** Dramatists Guild; Am Theatre Asn. **RESEARCH** Puritanism and the American drama; performing arts administration. **SELECTED PUBLICATIONS** Auth, Theatre management in America: Principle and practice, and producers on producing, Drama Bk Specialists, 73, rev ed, 80. **CONTACT ADDRESS** Performing Arts Ctr, Brooklyn Col, CUNY, 2901 Bedford Ave, Brooklyn, NY, 11210-2813.

LANGLOIS, WALTER G.
DISCIPLINE FRENCH **EDUCATION** Yale Univ, PhD, 55. **CAREER** Emer prof; prof Fr, 74-. **RESEARCH** 20th century French lit and espec Andre Malraux. **SELECTED PUBLICATIONS** Publ on, Andre Malraux. **CONTACT ADDRESS** Dept of Mod and Class Lang(s), Univ WY, PO Box 3964, Laramie, WY, 82071-3964. **EMAIL** JMONTZ@UWYO.EDU

LANGSTON, DWIGHT E.
DISCIPLINE GERMAN **EDUCATION** Furman Univ, BA, 86; Tulane Univ, PhD, 73. **CAREER** Instr, Lingua-Schule Germany; Instr, Wesleyan Coll; Asst prof to assoc prof, Univ Central Ark, 86- . **HONORS AND AWARDS** Fulbright Sch. **MEMBERSHIPS** Am Asn Tchrs German. **CONTACT ADDRESS** Univ Central Ark, 201 Donaghey Ave, Conway, AR, 72035-0001.

LANSING, RICHARD HEWSON
PERSONAL Born 05/14/1943, Rochester, NY, m, 1972 **DISCIPLINE** ITALIAN & COMPARATIVE LITERATURE **EDUCATION** Columbia Col, NY, AB, 65; Univ Calif, Berkeley, MA, 67, PhD(comp lit), 72. **CAREER** Teaching asst Ital, Univ Calif, Berkeley, 67-69, assoc, 69-70, actg instr comp lit, 70-71; asst prof, 72-78, Assoc Prof Ital & Comp Lit & Chemn Dept Comp Lit, Brandeis Univ, 78-, Mabelle McLeod Lewis mem fund grant, 72. **MEMBERSHIPS** MLA; Dante Soc Am; Mediaeval Acad Am; Am Asn Univ Prof Ital; Am Asn Teachers Ital. **RESEARCH** Dante; comparative medieval literature; epic and romance. **SELECTED PUBLICATIONS** Auth, Two similes: The shipwrecked swimmer and Elijah's ascent, Romance Philol, 74; Submerged meanings in Dante's similes, Dante Studies, 76; Stylistic and structural duality in Manzoni's I Promessi Sposi, Italica, 75; From Image to Idea: A Study of the Simile in Dante's Commedia, Longo, Ravenna, 77; The structure of meaning in Lampedusa's Il Gattopardo, PMLA, 5/78; Dante's unfolding vision, approaches to teaching Dante's divine comedy, MLA, 82. **CONTACT ADDRESS** Dept of Romance & Comp Lit, Brandeis Univ, 415 South St, Waltham, MA, 02154-2700.

LAPAIRE, PIERRE J.
PERSONAL Born 01/07/1954, Boulogne, France, m, 1997, 2 children **DISCIPLINE** FRENCH LANGUAGE **EDUCATION** Univ Perpionan, Fr, BA, 76, MA, 77; Univ No Carolina, Chapel Hill, MA, 80, PhD, 84. **CAREER** Asst prof, High Point Col, 83-85; asst prof, 85-90, assoc prof, 90-94, prof, 94-, Univ No Carolina, Chapel Hill. **MEMBERSHIPS** MLA; STMLA; Camput Stud Asn; AATF. **RESEARCH** Stylistics; Camus; twentieth century French drama; Djian; Montherlant. **SELECTED PUBLICATIONS** Auth, Aspects de la dualite du discours Montherlantien, Dalhousie Fr Stud, 93; auth, Elements de la binarite stylistique chez Camus: Un Style polarise, Fr Rev, 93; auth, Montherlant et la parole: Etude d'un language dramatique, Summa, 93; auth, Racine, Corneille, Flaubert, Balzac, Camus, in, Reference Guide to World Literature, St James, 95; auth, L'esthetique binaire de Baudelaire: A Une Passante et la beaute fugitive, Romance Notes, 95; auth, Heliotropies, Caracteres, 95. **CONTACT ADDRESS** Dept of Foreign Languages and Literatures, Univ of No Carolina, 601 S College Rd, Wilmington, NC, 28403-3297. **EMAIL** lapairep@uncwil.edu

LAPIERRE, ANDRE
DISCIPLINE FRENCH AND FRENCH CANADIAN LINGUISTICS **EDUCATION** Univ Ottawa, BA, 64, MA, 68; Univ Strasbourg, PhD(ling), 72. **CAREER** Lectr French, 66-69, asst prof ling, 72-82, ASSOC PROF LING, UNIV OTTAWA, 82- Book rev ed, Onomastica, 81-. **MEMBERSHIPS** Can Soc Study Names (pres, 82-); Am Name Soc; Can Ling Asn. **RESEARCH** North American French place-names; French and French Canadian lexicology and dialectology. **SELECTED PUBLICATIONS** Auth, Quelques aspects quantitatifs de la conjugaison en francais contemporain, Le francais moderne, 74; Situation du francais ontarien, Protee, 79; L'orthographe de la langue maternelle: le cas des Franco-Ontariens, Can Mod Lang J, 79; Le Manuel de l'abbe Thomas Maguire et la langue quebecoise au XIXe siecle, Rev hist Am francaise, 81; Toponymie francaise en Ontario, Etudes vivantes, Montreal, 81; ed, L'Ontario francais du sud-ouest: temoignages oraux, Univ Ottawa Press, 82. **CONTACT ADDRESS** Dept of Ling, Univ of Ottawa, Ottawa, ON, K1N 6N5.

LARDINOIS, ANDRE P.M.H.
DISCIPLINE ARCHAIC GREEK POETRY, GREEK TRAGEDY, GREEK AND ROMAN MYTHOLOGY **EDUCATION** Free Univ, Neth, BA, 84, MA, 88; Princeton Univ, MA, 91, PhD, 95. **CAREER** Asst prof, Univ Minn, Twin Cities. **RESEARCH** Voices of women in Greek literature and society. **SELECTED PUBLICATIONS** Auth, Lesbian Sappho and Sappho of Lesbos, in J N Bremmer, ed, From Sappho to de Sade: Moments in the History of Sexuality, London-NY, 89; Greek Myths for Athenian Rituals: Religion and Politics in Aeschylus' Eumenidesand Sophocles' Oedipus Coloneus, GRBS 33/4, 92; Subject and Circumstance in Sappho's Poetry, TAPA 124, 94; Wisdom in Context: The Use of Gnomic Statements in Archaic Greek Poetry, PhD Diss, Princeton Univ, 95; Who Sang Sappho's Songs?, in E Greene, ed, Reading Sappho: Contemporary Approaches, Berkeley, 96; Modern Paroemiology and the Use of Gnomai in Homer's Iliad, CP 92, 97; coauth, Tragic Ambiguity: Anthropology, Philosophy and Sophocles' Antigone, Leiden, 87. **CONTACT ADDRESS** Dept of Class & Near Eastern Stud, Univ Minn, Twin Cities, Minneapolis, MN, 55455. **EMAIL** lardi001@tc.umn.edu

LARIVIERE, RICHARD WILFRED
PERSONAL Born 01/27/1950, Chicago, IL, m, 1971, 1 child **DISCIPLINE** INDIAN STUDIES **EDUCATION** Univ IA, BA, 72; Univ PA, PhD(Sanskrit), 78. **CAREER** Vis lectr Sanskrit, Univ PA, 78-79; vis asst prof, Univ IA, 80-81; asst prof, 82-85, prof Sanskrit, 86-89, Ralph B Thomas Regents Prof, Univ Tx, Austin, 90-, assoc vice-pres for int progs, Univ TX, 95-; Fel, Fulbright-Hays, 76-77, Am Inst Indian Studies, 76-77 & 80, Soc Sci Res Coun, 79 & Nat Endowment for Humanities, 79-83; panelist, National Endowment for Humanities, 80; bd of dirs, HCL/Perot Systems, NU, Amsterdam, 95-. **HONORS AND AWARDS** CESMEO Prize, 89; Gonda Lect, Royal Dutch Academy, 94; Prof-College de France, Paris, 96-97; Am Coun of Learned Socs delegate to int academic union, Paris, 95-. **MEMBERSHIPS** Am Orient Soc; Asn Asian Studies; Royal Asiatic Soc; Bhandarkar Orient Res Inst; Asiatic Soc Bengel. **RESEARCH** Classical Indian culture and philosophy; classical and modern Hindu law; history of religions. **SELECTED PUBLICATIONS** Auth, The Indian Supreme Court and the Freedom of Religion, J Const & Parliamentary Studies, 75; A Note on the Kosadivya, Adyar Libr Bull, 76; Madhyamamimamsa--The Sankarsakanda, Wiener fur die Kunde Sudasiens, 81; Ordeals in India and Europe, J Am Orient Soc, 81; The Divy tattva of Raghunandana Bhattacarya: Ordeals in Hindu Law, Manohar, New Delhi, 81; The Judicial Wager in Hindu Law, Ann Bhandarkar Orient Res Inst, 81; Asedha and Akrosa--Arrest in the Sarasvativilasa, Festschrift J D M Derret, 82; A Compilation of Pitamaha Verses Found in Two Manuscripts from Nepal, Studien zur Indologie & Iranistik, 85. **CONTACT ADDRESS** Dept Orient & African Lang & Lit, Univ Texas, Main 101, Austin, TX, 78712. **EMAIL** rwl@uts.cc.utexas.edu

LARSEN, KEVIN
DISCIPLINE SPANISH **EDUCATION** Harvard Univ, PhD, 83. **CAREER** Assoc prof; Univ WY, 89-. **RESEARCH** 19th-century Peninsular Spanish lit. **SELECTED PUBLICATIONS** Auth, bk on, Gabriel Miro, 92. **CONTACT ADDRESS** Dept of Mod and Class Lang(s), Univ WY, PO Box 3964, Laramie, WY, 82071-3964. **EMAIL** KLARSEN@UWYO.EDU

LASNIK, HOWARD
PERSONAL Born 07/03/1945, Washington, DC, m, 1973, 1 child **DISCIPLINE** LINGUISTICS **EDUCATION** Carnegie Inst of Tech, BS, 67; Harvard Univ, MA, 69; Mass Inst of Tech, PhD, 72. **CAREER** Prof, Univ Conn, 81-; assoc prof, Univ Conn, 76-81; asst prof, Univ Conn, 72-76. **HONORS AND AWARDS** Phi Kappa Phi; Di Delta Epsilon; Woodrow Wilson Fel; Harvard Grad Prize Fel; NIH Trainee; NSF Grad Fel; Univ Conn Res Grant, 75, 86, 87, 88; Sloan Found Vis Scientist, Univ Calif Irvine, 78-79; Postdoctorate Fel, Mass Inst of Tech, 84-85; Ntl Sci Found Res Grant, 95-96; Univ Conn Alumni Assoc Fac Award, 88. **MEMBERSHIPS** Generative Linguists of the Old World; N Eastern Linguistic Soc; Linguistic Soc Amer; Languages & Linguistics Ed Brd; Rivista di Linguistics Advisory

Brd; Lincom Studies in Theoretical Linguistics Advisory Brd. **RESEARCH** Syntactic Theory; Logical Form; Learnability **SELECTED PUBLICATIONS** Auth, Minimalist Analysis, Blackwell, forthcoming; auth, Chains of arguments, Working Minimalism, MIT Pr, forthcoming; auth, A gap in an ellipsis paradigm: Some theoretical implications, Linguistic Analysis, forthcoming. **CONTACT ADDRESS** Dept Linguistics, U-145, Univ of Connecticut, 341 Mansfield Rd, Storrs, CT, 06269-1145. **EMAIL** lasnik@uconnvm.uconn.edu

LATEINER, DONALD
PERSONAL Born 06/01/1944, New Rochelle, NY, m, 1 child **DISCIPLINE** CLASSICAL STUDIES, ANCIENT HISTORY **EDUCATION** Univ Chicago, BA, 65; Cornell Univ, MA, 67; Stanford Univ, MA, 70, PhD(classics), 72. **CAREER** Lectr hist, San Francisco State Col, 68-69; acting asst prof classics, Stanford Univ, 71-72; asst prof class studies, Univ PA, 72-79; asst prof, 79-82, Assoc Prof Humanities-Classics, 82-85, prof, 85-92, JOHN WRIGHT PROF GREEK & HUMANITIES, OH WESLEYAN UNIV, 93-. **HONORS AND AWARDS** Am School of Classical Studies @ Athens, Seymour fel, 69-70; Center for Hellenic Studies, Washington, D.C., vis Sr Scholar, 99. **MEMBERSHIPS** Am Philol Asn; Am Asn Ancient Historians; Archaeol Inst Am; Friends Ancient Hist. **RESEARCH** Greek epic; nonverbal behaviors in ancient lit; Greek historiography; Latin elegy; Greek oratory. **SELECTED PUBLICATIONS** Auth, The Speech of Teutiaplus, Greek, Roman & Byzantine Studies, 75; Tissaphernes and the Phoenician fleet, Trans Am Philol Asn, 76; Obscenity in Catullus, Ramus, 77; No Laughing Matter: A Lterary Tactic in Herodotus, Trans Am Philol Asn, 77; An Analysis of Lysias' Defense Speeches, Rivista Storica dell' Antichita, 81; The Historical Method of Herodotus, Tornto, 89; The Failure of the Ionian Revolt, Historia, 82; Mimetic Syntax: Metaphor from World Order, Am J of Philol, 90; Sardonic Smile, Nonverbal Behavior in Homeric Epic, Ann Arbor, 95. **CONTACT ADDRESS** Dept of Humanities-Classics, Ohio Wesleyan Univ, 61 S Sandusky St, Delaware, OH, 43015-2398. **EMAIL** dglatein@cc.owu.edu

LATIMER, DAN RAYMOND
PERSONAL Born 07/15/1944, San Angelo, TX, m, 1970, 1 child **DISCIPLINE** COMPARATIVE LITERATURE, ENGLISH STUDIES **EDUCATION** Univ Tex, Austin, BA, 66; Univ Mich, Ann Arbor, MA, 67, PhD(comp lit), 72. **CAREER** Asst prof, 72-78, ASSOC PROF ENGLISH, AUBURN UNIV, 78-; RES AND WRITING, 82-, Asst Ed, Southern Humanities Rev. **MEMBERSHIPS** MLA; Am Comp Lit Asn; Southern Comp Lit Asn. **RESEARCH** Symbolism; modern criticism; Goethe. **SELECTED PUBLICATIONS** Auth, Editors Comment + A Narrative Can Have a Powerful Rhetorical Appeal, Southern Humanities Rev, Vol 0028, 94; Editors Comment + National Epics, Southern Humanities Rev, Vol 0030, 96; Editors Comment + an Approach to the Work of Gauchet, Marcel, Southern Humanities Rev, Vol 0031, 97. **CONTACT ADDRESS** Dept of English, Auburn Univ, University, AL, 36849.

LATTA, ALAN DENNIS
PERSONAL Born 06/28/1940, Wichita, KS, m, 1962, 1 child **DISCIPLINE** GERMAN LANGUAGE AND LITERATURE **EDUCATION** Univ Kans, AB, 62; Yale Univ, MA, 65, PhD(Ger), 69. **CAREER** From lectr to asst prof, 67-76, ASSOC PROF GER, TRINITY COL, UNIV TORONTO, 76-. **MEMBERSHIPS** MLA; Can Asn Univ Teachers Ger. **RESEARCH** Thomas Mann; German literature since 1945; novel. **SELECTED PUBLICATIONS** Auth, The Reception of Mann, Thomas die 'Betrogene' + With an Accompanying Bibliography .2. the Scholarly Reception, Internationales Archiv fur Sozialgeschichte Der Deutschen Literatur, Vol 0018, 93; Approaches to Teaching Mann 'Death in Venice' and Other Short Fiction, Seminar-J Ger Stud, Vol 0030, 94; Mann, Thomas Der 'Tod in Venedig'--a Developmental History as a Reflection of Philosophical Systems, Seminar-J Ger Stud, Vol 0033, 97. **CONTACT ADDRESS** Dept of Ger, Univ of Toronto, 97 St George St, Toronto, ON, M5S 1A1.

LATTA, SUSAN M.
DISCIPLINE ENGLISH LITERATURE AND LINGUISTICS **EDUCATION** Ind State Univ, BA, MA; Purdue Univ, PhD. **CAREER** Dir, wrtg prog; asst prof, 96-. **RESEARCH** Participatory action research and computer assisted instruction. **SELECTED PUBLICATIONS** Pub(s), essays on mass media in the classroom, student self-assessment, and critical research methodologies. **CONTACT ADDRESS** Dept of Eng, Univ Detroit Mercy, 4001 W McNichols Rd, PO BOX 19900, Detroit, MI, 48219-0900. **EMAIL** LATTAS7@udmercy.edu

LAUBENTHAL, PENNE J.
PERSONAL Born 08/02/1944, Athens, AL, m, 1961, 2 children **DISCIPLINE** ENGLISH, SPEECH **EDUCATION** Athens Col, Ala, BA, 65, MAT, 68; George Peabody Col, PhD(English), 72. **CAREER** Tutor & instr, 65-68, from asst prof to assoc prof, 68-72, PROF ENGLISH, ATHENS COL, ALA, 72-, CHAIRPERSON HUMANITIES DEPT, 80-. **HONORS AND AWARDS** Outstanding Committment to Teaching, 91; NEH Fel, 80, 88, 97. **MEMBERSHIPS** MLA; AAUP; SAtlantic Mod Lang Asn; Speech Commun Asn. **RESEARCH** Modern drama; comparative literature; modern French literature. **SELECTED PUBLICATIONS** Auth, A Humanist Looks at the Mind-Body Connection, J Med Asn Ga, 11/94; Biography of C. Eric Lincoln, In: A Bibliographical Guide to Alabama Literature; author of poetry published in Poet magazine and Elk River Review; reviews published in Myhtosphere and J Poetry Therapy. **CONTACT ADDRESS** Dept of English, Athens State Col, 300 N Beaty St, Athens, AL, 35611-1999. **EMAIL** laubepj@athens.edu

LAUER, JANICE M
PERSONAL Detroit, MI **DISCIPLINE** RHETORIC, LINGUISTICS **EDUCATION** Marygrove Col, BA, 54; St Louis Univ, MA, 61; Univ Mich, EdD(English rhetoric), 67. **CAREER** PROF ENGLISH, MARYGROVE COL, 62-; DIR WRITING PROG ENGLISH, UNIV DETROIT, 72-, Bd dirs, Rhetoric Soc Am, 78-78; dir writing, Cranbrook Writers Conf, 76-. **MEMBERSHIPS** Rhetoric Soc Am; Conf Col Compos and Commun; NCTE. **RESEARCH** Heuristics; creative process; rhetoric. **SELECTED PUBLICATIONS** Auth, Memorial Tribute to Berlin, James, A., 1942-1994, Coll Engl, Vol 0056, 94. **CONTACT ADDRESS** Dept of English, Univ of Detroit, Detroit, MI, 48221.

LAURENTI, JOSEPH L.
PERSONAL Born 12/10/1931, Hesperange, Luxembourg **DISCIPLINE** FOREIGN LANGUAGES **EDUCATION** Univ Ill, AB, 58, MA, 59; Univ Mo, PhD(Span), 62. **CAREER** Instr Span, Univ Mo, 59-62; asst prof Span, Ital and Ger, 62-66, PROF SPAN AND ITAL, ILL STATE UNIV, 66-, US corresp, Quad Ibero-Am; consult, PMLA. **MEMBERSHIPS** Am Asn Teachers Span and Port. **RESEARCH** Modern Italian literature; Spanish Golden Age. **SELECTED PUBLICATIONS** Auth, The Collection of theological and Legal Works by Maimonides-Moses Ben Maimon--Contained in the University of Illinois Urbana Libr--Editions from the 16th-Century and 17th Century, Sefarad, Vol 0054, 94; Course in Applied Spanish Grammar--Morphosyntaxis, Mod Lang J, Vol 0079, 95. **CONTACT ADDRESS** Dept of Span, Illinois State Univ, Normal, IL, 61761.

LAVALVA, ROSEMARIE
DISCIPLINE ITALIAN LANGUAGE AND LITERATURE **EDUCATION** Rutgers Univ, PhD. **CAREER** Prof/Dir grad studies. **RESEARCH** Romantic and late Romantic lit; the transition to "modernism": Pascoli, D'Annunzio, Pirandello, and Svevo; philosophical, anthropological, and psychoanalytical views of early 20th century thinkers in rel to the lit text. **SELECTED PUBLICATIONS** Auth, I Sacrifici Humani, 91. **CONTACT ADDRESS** SUNY Binghamton, PO Box 6000, Binghamton, NY, 13902-6000. **EMAIL** rlavalva@binghamton.edu

LAVERY, GERARD B.
PERSONAL Born 02/03/1933, Brooklyn, NY **DISCIPLINE** CLASSICAL LANGUAGES **EDUCATION** Fordham Univ, AB, 55, MA, 56, PhD(classics), 65. **CAREER** Asst prof, 61-72, ASSOC PROF CLASS LANG, COL OF THE HOLY CROSS, 72-, Batchelor Ford fac fel, 69. **MEMBERSHIPS** Am Philol Asn; AAUP. **RESEARCH** Plutarch; Roman history and politics; Lucretius. **SELECTED PUBLICATIONS** Auth, Plutarch 'Lucullus' and the Living Bond of Biog, Class J, Vol 0089, 94; Never Seen in Public--Seneca and the Limits of Cosmopolitanism, Latomus, Vol 0056, 97. **CONTACT ADDRESS** Col of the Holy Cross, Box 89 A, Worcester, MA, 01610.

LAWALL, SARAH NESBIT
PERSONAL Wellesley, MA, m, 1957, 2 children **DISCIPLINE** COMPARATIVE LITERATURE, FRENCH **EDUCATION** Oberlin Col, AB, Phi Betta Kappa, 56; Yale Univ, PhD(comp lit), 61. **CAREER** From asst prof to assoc prof French, 66-74, actg chmn dept comp lit, 69, chmn dept, 74-78, prof Comp Lit, Univ Mass, Amherst, 74-, adj prof French, 78-,gen ed, Norton World Masterpieces, 98-. **HONORS AND AWARDS** Director, NEH Institute ("The Theory and Teaching of World Literature"): six-week summer session, 87; grant 9/1/86-6/30/88. **MEMBERSHIPS** Am Comp Lit Asn; Int Comp Lit Assoc, MLA; AAUP; Am Asn Teachers Fr; Int Soc Comp Study Civilizations. **RESEARCH** Theory and practice of world literature; the surrealist tradition; phenomenological literary theory. **SELECTED PUBLICATIONS** Auth, Critics of Consciousness: The Existential Structures of Literature, Harvard Univ, 68; Ponge and the Poetry of Self-Knowledge, Contemp Lit, 70; Poetry from Dada to Tel Quel, Wayne State Univ, 74; coauth, Decouverte de l'essai, Harcourt, 74; auth, A style of silence: Two Readings of Yves Bonnefoy's Poetry, Contemp Lit, 75; The Poem as Utopia, Fr Forum, 76; Poetry Taking Place, World Lit Today, 79; The Time and Space of Translation, Pac Quart, 80; Euripides' Hippolytus, Introduction, Translation and Commentary by Gilbert and Sarah Lawall, Bristol Classical Press, 86; Rene Wellek and Modern Literary Criticism, Comparative Lit, 40, 1, winter 88; Richard Moulton: Literature and Cultural Studies in 1911, Yearbook of Comparative and Gen Lit, 39, 90-91; Bonnefoy's Pierre ecrite: Progressive Ambiguity as The Many in the One, in The Ladder of High Designs: Structure and Interpretation of the French Lyric Sequence, ed by Doranne Fenoalta and David Lee Rubin, Iniv Va Press, 91; Naguib Mahfouz and the Nobel Prize: A World of Expectations, in Naguib Mahfouz, ed by Michael Beard and Adnan Haydar, Syracuse Univ Press, 93; World Literature in Context, in Global Perspectives on Teaching Literature, ed by Sandra Lott, NCTE, 93; Preface and "Reading World Literature" in Reading World Literature: Theory, History, Practice: edited and with an introduction by Sarah Lawall, Austin:Univ Tx P, 94; Richard Moulton and World Literature from the English Point of View, in No Small World, New Quests, New Canons, New Directions in Theory and Pedagogy of World Literature, ed Michael Carroll, National Council of Teachers of English, 96; Introduction and Rene Welleck and Perspectivism in Rene Welleck, ed Sarah Lawall, Yearbook of Comp and Gen Lit, 44, 96. **CONTACT ADDRESS** Dept of Comp Lit, Univ of Mass, Amherst, MA, 01003-0002. **EMAIL** lawall@complit.umass.edu

LAWLER, JAMES RONALD
PERSONAL Born 08/15/1929, Melbourne, Australia, m, 1954, 2 children **DISCIPLINE** FRENCH LITERATURE **EDUCATION** Univ Melbourne, BA, 50, MA, 52; Univ Paris, DUniv, 54. **CAREER** Lectr French, Univ Queensland, 55-56; sr lectr, Univ Melbourne, 57-62; prof and head dept, Univ Western Australia, 63-71; prof and chmn dept, Univ Calif, Los Angeles, 71-74; McCulloch prof, Dalhousie Univ, 74-79; PROF FRENCH, UNIV CHICAGO, 79-, Brit Coun interchange scholar, 67; Australian Acad Humanities fel, 70-; Guggenheim Found fel, 74; asst ed, Fr Rev, 74-; ed, Dalhousie French Studies, 79; vis fel, Australian Nat Univ, 81. **HONORS AND AWARDS** Officier, Palmes Academiques, 70. **MEMBERSHIPS** MLA; Am Asn Teachers Fr; Asn Can Univ Prof Fr; Int Asn Fr Studies (vpres, 74-). **RESEARCH** Modern French poetry; poetics; 20th century novel. **SELECTED PUBLICATIONS** Auth, The Poetry of Baudelaire and French Poetry, 1838-1852, Fr Rev, Vol 0069, 96; Aux Mots Patients Et Sauveurs + Another Look at the Poetry of Bonnefoy, Yves, Esprit Createur, Vol 0036, 96. **CONTACT ADDRESS** Univ Chicago, Chicago, IL, 60637.

LAWRENCE, SAMUEL G.
DISCIPLINE INTERPERSONAL AND INTERCULTURAL COMMUNICATION **EDUCATION** PhD. **CAREER** Univ Albany - SUNY **SELECTED PUBLICATIONS** Auth, Normalizing stigmatized practices: Achieving co-membership by 'doing being ordinary, Res Lang & Soc Interaction, 96. **CONTACT ADDRESS** Univ Albany-SUNY, 1400 Washington Ave, Albany, NY, 12222. **EMAIL** jedwards@csc.albany.edu

LAWSON, DARREN P.
PERSONAL Born 08/18/1964, Asheboro, NC, m, 1988, 1 child **DISCIPLINE** ORGANIZATIONAL COMMUNICATION **EDUCATION** Bob Jones Univ, BA, 86, MA, 88; Univ Kans, PhD, 96. **CAREER** Fac, Bob Jones Univ, 88-93; Grad Teaching Asst, Univ Kans, 93-96; Assoc Dean, 96-97, Dean, Sch Fine Arts, Bob Jones Univ, 97-. **HONORS AND AWARDS** Am Legion Award, 86; Employee Merit Award, Bob Jones Univ, 93; Distinguished Technical Commun Award, SC Chapter Soc Tech Commun, 93; Departmental Award for Teaching Excellence, Univ Kans, 95; Outstanding Grad Teaching Asst Award, Univ Kans, 96; Employee Merit Award, Bob Jones Univ, 97; Pac Bell Knowledge Network Learning Application Award, 97; Education World Best of the Month Award, Virtual Presentation Asst website, 97. **MEMBERSHIPS** Nat Commun Asn; Int Commun Asn. **RESEARCH** Organizational assimilation; communication technology; training and development. **SELECTED PUBLICATIONS** Coauth, The Relationship Between Prisonization and Social Skills Among Prison Inmates, The Prison J, 96; auth, Netiquette: Understanding and Using Electronic Mail, Handbook of Business Communication, 97; Electronic Mail: Attributes, Guidelines, and Educational Applications, Balance 17, 98. **CONTACT ADDRESS** School of Fine Arts, Bob Jones Univ, Greenville, SC, 29614. **EMAIL** dplawson@bju.edu

LAZARUS, C.L.
PERSONAL Born 07/30/1956, Chicago, IL **DISCIPLINE** SPEECH PATHOLOGY **EDUCATION** Northwestern Univ, PhD 97. **CAREER** Northwestern Univ, assoc dir, voice speech lang serv, 80 to 98-. **MEMBERSHIPS** ASHA; ISHA; CASLA; Dysphagia Res Soc. **RESEARCH** Swallowing disorders, head neck cancer patients; management of swallowing disorders. **SELECTED PUBLICATIONS** Auth, Communication problems in individuals with head and neck cancer, in: L. Cherney ed, Topics in Geri Rehab, in press; Swallowing disorders in head neck patients treated with radiotherapy and adjuvant chemotherapy, coauth, Laryngoscope, 96; Comments on effects of cold touch and chemical stimulation of the anterior faucial pillar on human swallowing, ed, Dysphagia, 96; Effects of a sour bolus on oropharyngeal swallow measures in patients with neurogenic dysphagia, coauth, Jour of Speech and Hearing Research, 95; Swallow recovery in an oral cancer patient following surgery radiotherapy and hyperthermia , coauth, Head and Neck, 94. **CONTACT ADDRESS** Dept of Medicine, Northwestern univ, 303 E Chicago Ave, Chicago, IL, 60611. **EMAIL** claz@nwu.edu

LE HIR, MARIE-PIERRE
DISCIPLINE FRENCH AND COMPARATIVE LITERATURE **EDUCATION** Freie Universitat, MA, 79; Univ Iowa, PhD, 86. **CAREER** English, Case Western Reserve Univ.

HONORS AND AWARDS Dir, French Studies Prog. **RESEARCH** Linguistics **SELECTED PUBLICATIONS** Auth, book Le Romantisme aux Encheres: Ducange, Pixere court, Hugo Benjamins, 92; Bridging National Fields: XIXth-Century Scholarship in French and American Perspectives. Nineteenth-Century French Studies 24, 95-96, Defining French Cultural Studies, Jour Midwest Mod Lang Asn, 96; The Societe des Gens de Lettres and French Socialism: Association as Resistance to the Industrialization and Censorship of the Press. Nineteenth-Century French Studies 24, 96; Imagining the discipline: beyond Frenchness and Francophilia, Contemporary French Civilization 21, 97; French Cultural Studies in the United States: a Case Study in French Cultural Studies, Jour Contemporary French Studies, 97. **CONTACT ADDRESS** Case Western Reserve Univ, 10900 Euclid Ave, Cleveland, OH, 44106.

LE MOINE, ROGER
PERSONAL Born 11/06/1933, La Malbaie, PQ, Canada **DISCIPLINE** LETTRES FRANCAISES **EDUCATION** Univ Ottawa, BA, 57; Univ Laval, MA, 72, DES, 64, DL, 70. **CAREER** PROF TITULAIRE, LETTRES FRANCAISES, UNIV OTTAWA. **HONORS AND AWARDS** Prix Champlain, 68; mem, Soc royale Can, 93. **MEMBERSHIPS** Soc des Dix. **SELECTED PUBLICATIONS** Auth, Joseph Marmette, sa vie, son oeuvre, 68; auth, L'Amerique et les poetes francais de la Renaissance, 72; auth, Napoleon Bourassa, l'homme et l'artiste, 74; auth, Un Quebecois bien tranquille, 85; auth, Deux loges montrealaises du Grand Orient de France, 91. **CONTACT ADDRESS** Dep lettres francaises, Univ Ottawa, CP 450, Succ A, Ottawa, ON, K1N 6N5.

LEACH, ELEANOR W.
DISCIPLINE CLASSICAL STUDIES **EDUCATION** Bryn Mawr Col, BA, 59; Yale Univ, PhD, 63. **CAREER** Prof. **RESEARCH** Latin texts. **SELECTED PUBLICATIONS** Auth, Absence and Desire in Cicero's De Amicitia, CW, 93; Oecus on Ibycus: Investigating the Vocabulary of the Roman House, Oxbow, 97. **CONTACT ADDRESS** Dept of Classical Studies, Indiana Univ, Bloomington, 300 N Jordan Ave, Bloomington, IN, 47405.

LEAL, LUIS
PERSONAL Born 09/17/1907, Linares, Mexico, m, 1936, 2 children **DISCIPLINE** SPANISH **EDUCATION** Northwestern Univ, BA, 40; Univ Chicago, AM, 41, PhD, 50. **CAREER** Instr Span, Univ Chicago, 42-43, 46-48, asst prof, 48-52; assoc prof mod lang, Univ Miss, 52-56; assoc prof, Emory Univ, 56-59; assoc prof, 59-62, prof, 62-76, Emer Prof Span, Univ Ill, Urbana, 76-, Vis prof, Univ Ariz, 55-56, Univ Calif, Santa Barbara, 76-77 and Univ Calif, Los Angeles, 77-78; ACTG DIR, CTR FOR CHICANO STUDIES, UNIV CALIF, SANTA BARBARA, 80-. **MEMBERSHIPS** Am Asn Teachers Span and Port; MLA. **RESEARCH** Spanish American literature, especially the short story; Mexican literature; Chicano literature. **SELECTED PUBLICATIONS** Auth, Rulfo, Juan--From Paramo to Hope--a Critical-Reading of his Work, Hisp Rev, Vol 0061, 93; No Frontiers--the Process of Desmythification in the Works of North American and Mexican Authors, Mexican Stud-Estudios Mexicanos, Vol 0009, 93; El 'Corrido De Joaquin Murrieta' + the Murrieta,Joaquin Corrido--Origin and Popularity, Mexican Stud-Estudios Mexicanos, Vol 0011, 95. **CONTACT ADDRESS** Univ Calif, Santa Barbara, CA, 93106.

LEBANO, EDOARDO A.
DISCIPLINE ITALIAN LITERATURE **EDUCATION** Cath Univ Am, PhD, 66. **CAREER** Prof. **RESEARCH** Renaissance epic; nineteenth century narrative; advanced language and Italian American studies. **SELECTED PUBLICATIONS** Auth, pubs on teaching of Italian in United States. **CONTACT ADDRESS** Dept of French and Italian, Indiana Univ, Bloomington, 300 N Jordan Ave, Bloomington, IN, 47405.

LEBLANC, WILMER JAMES
PERSONAL Born 11/01/1928, Abbeville, LA, m, 1961, 3 children **DISCIPLINE** LINGUISTICS **EDUCATION** Univ Southwestern La, BA, 52; State Univ IA, MA, 54. **CAREER** From instr to assoc prof Span, Loras Col, 54-67, chmn dept mod for lang, 64-67; jr instr Span, Univ VA, 68-70; asst prof, Madison Col VA, 70-71; instr, Univ VA, 71-72; asst prof French & Eng, 72-75, Assoc Prof Eng, For Lang and Speech, Paul D Camp Community Col, 75. **MEMBERSHIPS** Am Asn Tchr(s) Span & Port; Am Asn Tchrs Fr. **RESEARCH** Hist of the Span lang; Golden Age, Span Am and contemp Span drama. **CONTACT ADDRESS** Div of Commun, Paul D. Camp Comm Col, Franklin, VA, 23851. **EMAIL** jleblanc@pc.cc.va.us

LEBOFSKY, DENNIS STANLEY
PERSONAL Born 10/28/1940, Philadelphia, PA, m, 1965, 5 children **DISCIPLINE** LINGUISTICS; ENGLISH **EDUCATION** Temple Univ, BA, 61; Princeton Univ, MA, 65, PhD(ling), 70. **CAREER** From Instr to Asst Prof, 65-84, Assoc Prof English, Temple Univ, 84-. **RESEARCH** Philadelphia English. **CONTACT ADDRESS** Dept of English, Temple Univ, 1114 W Berks St, Philadelphia, PA, 19122-6029. **EMAIL** dlebofsk@nimbus.temple.edu

LEDERER, HERBERT
PERSONAL Born 06/09/1921, Vienna, Austria, m, 1948, 2 children **DISCIPLINE** GERMAN **EDUCATION** Brooklyn Col, BA, 48; Univ Chicago, MA, 49, PhD(Ger), 53. **CAREER** Instr Ger, Univ Chicago, 49-52; asst prof, Wabash Col, 52-53 assoc prof and chmn dept, 53-57; assoc prof, Ohio Univ, 57-61 and Queens Col NY, 61-69; head, Dept Ger and Slavic Lang, 69-79, PROF GER, UNIV CONN, 69-, Mem staff, Ger Summer Sch, Middlebury Col, 53-69; chief reader Ger Advan Placement, Educ Testing Serv, 64-67; chmn Ger comt, Col Entrance Exam Bd, 67-; Leo Baeck Soc Am Coun Learned Soc res grant, 68-69; vpres, Nat Fed Mod Lang Teachers Asn, 71, pres, 72; pres, Am Coun Study Austrian Lit, 72-80, Asn Depts Foreign Lang, 78. **HONORS AND AWARDS** Austrian Cross of Honor for Arts and Letters, First Class, 76. **MEMBERSHIPS** Am Asn Teachers Ger; MLA; Int Arthur Schnitzler Res Asn; AAUP; Am Coun Studies Austrian Lit. **RESEARCH** Modern German literature, especially Schnitzler and the young Vienna school; contemporary theater; linguistics and teaching methodology. **SELECTED PUBLICATIONS** Auth, Nestroy, Johann 1801-1862--World Vision and Dramatic Writings, Colloquia Germanica, Vol 0025, 92; Schnitzler, Arthur and Beerhofmann, Richard--Correspondence, 1891-1931, J Engl and Ger Philol, Vol 0094, 95. **CONTACT ADDRESS** Dept of Ger and Slavic Lang, Univ of Conn, Storrs, CT, 06268.

LEDFORD-MILLER, LINDA
DISCIPLINE SPANISH **EDUCATION** Univ CA, Irvine, BA, 78; Univ TX at Austin, MA, 83, PhD, 88; PA State Univ, MA, 86. **CAREER** Dept For Lang & Lit, Univ Scranton **HONORS AND AWARDS** Fulbright lectureship,San Carlos Univ, Guatemala City, 90; Fulbright-Hayes fel, Brazil, 79-80. **MEMBERSHIPS** Am Asn of Tchrs Span and Port; Latin Am Stud Asn; MACLAS Brazilian Stud Asn; Northeast Asn Luso-Brazilianists; AAUP; Soc for Am Travel Writing. **SELECTED PUBLICATIONS** Auth, Voice to the Visited: Indigenous Presence in the Guatemala Travel Writings of the Abbot Brasseur de Bourboug and Alfred Valois, Monographic Review/Revista Monografica: Hispanic Travel Lit, XII, 96; French Travelers to Guatemala in The Nineteenth Century, Lit and Travel, Amsterdam and Atlanta: Rodopi, 93; The Perverse Passions of Dalton Trevisan, Lit and the Bible, Amsterdam and Atlanta: Rodopi, 93; Shoes for Little Peter: Narrative Technique in Trevisan's Not at All Exemplary Novella, Pedrinho, Brasil/Brazil, 4, 90; Francis Erskine Calderon de la Barca, 3000 word essay for Dictionary of Lit Biog 184, Amer Travel Writers 1776-1864, Columbia, Bruccoli Clark Layman, 97; Demetrio Aguilera Malta, 1000 word ref essay, Cyclopedia of World Authors, 3rd rev ed, Englecliff, Salem Press, 97; Mary Helen Ponce, 1000 word ref essay, Cyclopedia of World Authors, 3rd rev ed, Englecliff, Salem Press, 97; Richard Rodriguez, 1000 word ref essay for Cyclopedia of World Authors, 3rd rev ed, Englecliff, Salem Press, 97; Jose Donoso, rev of previous text and new bibliog essays, Cyclopedia of World Authors, 3rd rev ed, Englecliff, Salem Press, 97; Jose Lins do Rego, rev of previous text and new bibliog essays, Cyclopedia of World Authors, 3rd rev ed, Englecliff, Salem Press, 97; If the River Was Whiskey by T. Coraghessan Boyle, 1500 word ref essay for Masterplots II, Short Story, Suppl, Pasadena, Salem Press, 96; Midnight Mass by Machado de Assis, 1500 word ref essay for Masterplots II, Short Story, Suppl, Pasadena, Salem Press, 96 & Ecco by Ronald Sukenick, 1500 word ref essay for Masterplots II, Short Story, Suppl, Pasadena, Salem Press, 96; rev(s), Com Brazilian Portuguese for Spanish Speakers, Hispania, 77 2, 94 & Espanol para hoy: en el mundoy la communidad, Hispania, 77 1, 94; transl, Benedito Nunes, Narrativo ... muitas vozes, translated as, Narration in Many Voices, Rev Contemp Lit XV.3, 95. **CONTACT ADDRESS** Dept of For Lang(s) and Lit(s), Univ of Scranton, Scranton, PA, 18510. **EMAIL** LedfordLl@uofs.edu

LEE, ALVIN A
PERSONAL Born 09/30/1930, Woodville, ON, Canada, m, 1957, 5 children **DISCIPLINE** ENGLISH LANGUAGE AND LITERATURE **EDUCATION** Univ Toronto, BA, 53, MA, 58, PhD, 61; Victoria Univ, BD, 57. **CAREER** From asst prof to assoc prof, 60-70, dean grad studies, 71-73, PROF ENGLISH, MCMASTER UNIV, 70-, VPRES ACAD, 74-, Can Coun sr fel, 66-67. **MEMBERSHIPS** Mediaeval Acad Am; MLA; Asn Can Univ Teachers English. **RESEARCH** Old English poetry; contemporary Canadian poetry. **SELECTED PUBLICATIONS** Auth, Good Hall and Earth Dragon, 'Beowulf' and the 1st-Phase Language, Engl Stud in Can, Vol 0019, 93; Taking Life Seriously, a Study of the Argument of the 'Nichomachean Ethics', Engl Stud in Can, Vol 0022, 96. **CONTACT ADDRESS** Dept of English, McMaster Univ, 1280 Main St W, Hamilton, ON, L8S 4L8.

LEE, CHARLES NICHOLAS
PERSONAL Born 07/27/1933, Washington, DC, m, 1956, 4 children **DISCIPLINE** RUSSIAN LITERATURE **EDUCATION** Univ Md, BA, 55, MA, 58; Harvard Univ, PhD Russ, 64. **CAREER** Instr French, Ger & Russ, Univ Md, 56-60; asst prof Ger & Russ, Bucknell Univ, 63-65; from asst prof to assoc prof, 65-74, chmn, Dept Slavic Lang & Lit, 67-69, prof Russ, Univ Colo, Boulder, 74-, chmn, Dept Slavic Lang & Lit, 80-, NDEA summer fel, 65; Am Coun Learned Soc humanities fel, 75-76. **MEMBERSHIPS** Am Asn Advan Slavic Studies; Am Asn Teachers Slavic & E Europ Lang. **RESEARCH** Russian prose of the 20th century emigration; Tolstoy in Russian & Western literature; A I Solzhenitsyn. **SELECTED PUBLICATIONS** Auth, The philosophical tales of M A Aldanov, Slavic & East Europ J, 71; Mark Aleksandrovic Aldanov: Zizn'i tvorcestvo, Russkaja lit v emigracii, 72; Dreams and daydreams in the early fiction of L N Tolstoy, Am Contrib Seventh Int Congr Slavists, 73; The short stories of M A Aldanov, In: Mnemozina; studia litteraria in honorem Vsevolod Setchkarev, 74; Man and the land in the fiction of Solzhenitsyn, Rocky Mountain Soc Sci J, 74; Mark Aldanov, In: Mod Encycl Russ & Soviet Lit, 77; Ecological ethics in the fiction of L N Tolstoj, Am Contrib Eighth Int Congr Slavists, 78; Mark Aldanov: Russian, Jewry and the World, Midstream, 81; Darwin, Degeneracy, & Regeneration in Cexov's Fiction, in Russian Language J, 97; M A Aldanov, in Reference Guide to Russian Literature, 98. **CONTACT ADDRESS** Dept of Germanic & Slavic Lang & Lit., Univ of Colorado, Box 276, Boulder, CO, 80309-0276. **EMAIL** leecn@spot.colorado.edu

LEE, JOSEPH PATRICK
PERSONAL Born 11/30/1942, Leitchfield, KY, m, 1972 **DISCIPLINE** FRENCH LANGUAGE & LITERATURE **EDUCATION** Brescia Col, BA, 63; Fordham Univ, PhD, 71. **CAREER** Asst prof French, Brescia Col, 67-71 & Univ Ga, 71-78; acad dean & assoc prof French, Belmont Abbey Col, 78-81;PROVOST & SR VPRES ACAD AFFAIRS & PROF FRENCH, BARRY UNIV, 81-; Am Philos Soc res grant, 74. **HONORS AND AWARDS** Woodrow Wilson Fellow, 63-64; Danforth Fellow, 63-67; Fulbright Fellow, 66-67. **MEMBERSHIPS** MLA; Am Asn Teachers Fr; Am Soc 18tb Century Studies; Soc Fr Etude XVIIIe Siecle; S Atlantic Mod Lang Asn. **RESEARCH** Eighteenth century French literature; Voltaire; Anglo-French literary relations. **SELECTED PUBLICATIONS** Contrib, The Complete Works of Voltaire, Voltaire Found, 68; Dictionnaire des journalistes de langue francaise (1600-1789), Univ Grenoble, 76; auth, Voltaire and Cesar de Missy, Studies Voltaire & 18th Century, 76; Le Sermon philosophique: A Voltairean creation, Studies Lang & Lit, Eastern Ky Univ, 76; Voltaire and Massillon: Affinities of the heart, Fr Rev, 77; The Textual History of Voltaire's Sermon des cinquante, Studies on Voltaire & 18th Century, 92; contrib, Dictionaire de Voltaire, 94; Voltaire et ses combats, 97; La Philosophie clandestine a l'age classique, 97; auth, The Genesis and Publication of Voltaire's Sermon du rabbin Akib, Studies in Voltaire & 18th Century, 97. **CONTACT ADDRESS** Sr VPres for Acad Affairs, Barry Univ, 11300 NE 2nd Ave, Miami, FL, 33161-6695. **EMAIL** jplee@mail.barry.edu

LEE, SONIA M.
PERSONAL Born 01/25/1938, Paris, France, m, 1958, 3 children **DISCIPLINE** FRENCH LITERATURE **EDUCATION** Univ Wis, BS, 64, MA, 66; Univ Mass, PhD(French lit), 74. **CAREER** Instr French, Univ Mass, 67-72; instr French, Univ PR, 72-73; asst prof to prof, Trinity College, 73-; coordr of African Concentration and African Minor, Trinity Col, 92-. **HONORS AND AWARDS** Summer Melon Grant to work on Women Writers of Francophone Can, 78; Summer Melon Grant to work on a new course on African Lit, 84; Summer Women's Studies Grant, Ford Foundation, to prepare a new course in French and Women's studies: French Women Writers and Women Writers in French, 87; NEH Summer Fellowship to study Modern Critical Theory in French Narrative with Prof Rigolot, Princeton Univ, 88. **MEMBERSHIPS** Am Asn Teachers Fr; Soc Study Multi-Ethnic Lit US; Secy of the Francophone African Lit Sect, NEMLA Conv, 75, 81; Elected Pres of the Francophone African Lit Sect, NEMLA Conv, 76; Chercheur Assoc- Centre d'Etudes Afro-Americaines and Tiers Monde Anglophone, 87; Advisor to the Institut National de Recherche Pedagogque for the French Ministry of Educ, 87; Elected Pres of Francophone Lit Sect, Mid-hudson MLA Conf, 88; Coop Prof in Hall High School: Project on the French Revolution, 88-89; co-chair of two panels: Les Nouvelles critures Africaines, ALA meeting, NY, 90. **RESEARCH** Women writers of French speaking world. **SELECTED PUBLICATIONS** Auth, The Awakening of the Self in the Heroines of Sembene Ousmane, Critique, 12/75; The Image of the Woman in the African Folktale from the Sub-Saharan Francophone Area, Yale Fr Studies, 76; Franco-American Literature of New England: Two Significant Writers, Multi-Ethnic Lit US, 78; A selective bibliography of three prominent African authors, In: Critical Bibliography of French Literature of the 20th Century, Syracuse Univ, 79; A Critical Essay on Camara Laye, Twayne; Camara Laye, Chantre Malink, in: Hommage Camara Laye, Arts et Lettres, Magazine culturel du Soleil, 82; Camara Laye, Twayne's Series, G.K. Hall Publ, 83; Le Theme du bonheur chez les romancieres de l'Afrique occidentale, Presence Francophone, Univ Sherbrooke, no 29, 87; Changes in the Mother Image in West African fiction, Neohelicon, June 88; Entretiens avec Aminata Sow Fall, ALA Bull, Fall 88; Conversations with Miriam Tlali, ALA Bull, Summer 91; auth, Les Romancieres du continent noir, Hatier, 94; Daughters of Hagar: Daughters of Muhammad, The Marabout and the Muse (ed. Kenneth Harrow), Heinemann, 96; African Women Writers, and The Francophone Novels in West Africa, Encyclopedia of Sub-Saharan Africa (ed. John Middleton), Charles Scribner's Sons, Summer 97. **CONTACT ADDRESS** Trinity Col, 300 Summit St, Box 1355, Hartford, CT, 06106-3186. **EMAIL** sonia.lee@trincoll.edu

LEE, TA-LING
PERSONAL Born 01/24/1934, Nanking, China, m, 1958, 1 child **DISCIPLINE** CHINESE & AMERICAN HISTORY **EDUCATION** Chung Hsing Univ, Taiwan, BA, 58; NY Univ, MA, 61, PhD(hist), 67 **CAREER** News ed, Chinese Info Serv, NY, 58-67; transl Chinese & English, UN, 67-68; asst prof hist, Youngstown State Univ, 68 & 69; asst prof, 69-73, assoc prof, 73-78, PROF HIST, SOUTHERN CONN STATE UNIV, 78-; Vis fac fel, Yale Univ, 78 & 80 **MEMBERSHIPS** AHA; Asn Asian Studies; Am Asn Chinese Studies **RESEARCH** Chinese Revolution of 1911; cultural revolution in China; modern Chinese politcs **SELECTED PUBLICATIONS** Co-auth, Failure of a Democracy Movement, Univ Md Sch Law, 91; contrib, Historical Dictionary of Revolutionary China, 1839-1976, Greenwood Press, 92; co-auth, A Quantitative Analysis of Judicial Practice and Human Rights in the People's Republic of China, East Asia Res Ins, 92; co-auth, Tiananmen Aftermath, Univ Md Sch Law, 92; Chinese Intellectuals after Tiananmen, in: Forces of Change in Contemporary China, Univ SC Press, 93; co-auth, The Bamboo Gulag, Univ Md Sch Law, 94; American Policy Toward China and Japan: The East Asian giants, in: American in the Twenty-first Century: Opportunities and Challenges, Prentice-Hall, 96; co-auth, To Cope with a Bad Global Image: Human Rights in the People's Republic of China, 1993-1994, Univ Press Am, 97. **CONTACT ADDRESS** Dept of Hist, Southern Conn State Univ, 501 Crescent St, New Haven, CT, 06515-1330.

LEEBER, VICTOR F.
PERSONAL Born 02/18/1922, Elkins, WV **DISCIPLINE** ROMANCE LANGUAGES **EDUCATION** Boston Col, AB, 46, MA, 47; Weston Col, STL, 54; Univ Madrid, PhD(Span), 57. **CAREER** From instr to assoc prof, 47-66, Prof Mod Lang, Fairfield Univ, 66-, Chmn Dept, 57- **MEMBERSHIPS** MLA; Am Asn Cols Teacher Educ; Am Asn Teachers Span & Port. **RESEARCH** Golden Age Spanish literature; neoclassical Mexican literature; Romance philology. **SELECTED PUBLICATIONS** Auth, Perfiles Literarios, Holt, 63; El P Abad y su obra Poetica, Porrua, Spain, 65. **CONTACT ADDRESS** Dept of Mod Lang, Fairfield Univ, 1073 N Benson Rd, Fairfield, CT, 06430-5195.

LEER, NORMAN ROBERT
PERSONAL Born 02/25/1937, Chicago, IL **DISCIPLINE** ENGLISH, COMPARATIVE LITERATURE **EDUCATION** Grinnell Col, AB, 58; Ind Univ, MA, 60, PhD(English), 64. **CAREER** Instr English, State Univ NY Stony Brook, 63-65; asst prof, Beloit Col, 65-67; assoc prof Roosevelt Univ, 67-72, assoc prof, 72-78, prof English, 78-, mem bd, Urban Life Ctr, 72-; coordr, Educ Network, Asn Humanistic Psychol, 72-74 & Midwest Regional Newslett, 78-; Fulbright lectr English, Odense Univ, Denmark, 74-75; lectr, Center for Older Adults, Fourth Presbyterian Church of Chicago, 96-. **HONORS AND AWARDS** Phi Beta Kappa, Grinnell College, 58; Poetry Prize, All Nations Poetry Contest, Triton Col, 76, 77, 78, 79 & 81; Burlington Northern Award, Roosevelt Univ (for teaching and scholarship), 86; Illinois Significant Poet's Award, 90; Samuel Ortrowski Award, Roosevelt Univ (for best creative work), 98. **RESEARCH** Modern literature in the light of existential philosophy and humanistic psychology; writing poetry; application of some of the techniques of humanistic psychology to college teaching. **SELECTED PUBLICATIONS** Auth, Escape and Confrontation in the Stories of Philip Roth, Christian Scholar, summer 66; The Limited Hero in the Novels of Ford Madox Ford, Mich State Univ, 67; The Double Theme in Malamud's Assistant: Dostoevsky with Irony, Mosaic, spring 71; Innovation and power struggles: An Experiential Deadlock, J Humanistic Psychol, winter 73; To Doris Lessing: Inside the Apocalypse, Oyez Rev, spring 75; Riding Commas to the Moon: Teaching Maleness and Imagination, New Directions in Teaching, winter 78; Slightly Crumpled Survival Flower (poems), Spoon River Poetry Press, 85; I Dream My Father in a Stone (poems), Mellen Poetry Press, 91; Second Lining (poems), Mellen Poetry Press, 97; Over 100 individual poems in Spoon River Quart, Willow Review, Rhino, Oyez Review, The Wolf Head Quart, Poetry Digest, and American Poets and Poetry. **CONTACT ADDRESS** Dept of English, Roosevelt Univ, 430 S Michigan Ave, Chicago, IL, 60605-1394.

LEFFEL, KATHERINE
DISCIPLINE ENGLISH LINGUISTICS AND SYNTACTIC THEORY **EDUCATION** Univ FL, PhD, 88. **CAREER** Dept Eng, Univ Ala **HONORS AND AWARDS** Dir, eng dept ling prog. **SELECTED PUBLICATIONS** Auth, Views on Phrase Structure, Kluwer Academic Press. **CONTACT ADDRESS** Univ AL, 1400 University Blvd, Birmingham, AL, 35294-1150.

LEHISTE, ILSE
PERSONAL Born 01/31/1922, Tallinn, Estonia **DISCIPLINE** LINGUISTICS **EDUCATION** Univ Hamburg, PhD, 48; Univ Mich, PhD(ling), 59. **CAREER** Mem fac, Univ Hamburg, 48-49; assoc prof Ger philol, Kans Wesleyan Univ, 50-51; assoc prof mod lang, Detroit Inst Technol, 51-56; res assoc acoustic phonetics, Commun Sci Lab, Univ Mich, 57-63; assoc prof ling and Slavic lang and lit, 63-65, chmn dept, 65-71, PROF LING, OHIO STATE UNIV, 65-, Nat Sci Found res grants, 61-63 and 63-65; guest prof, Univ Cologne, 65; Guggenheim fel, 69 and 75-76; guest prof ling, Univ Vienna, Austria, 74; Ctr Advan Study Behav Sci fel, 75-76; guest prof, Univ Tokyo, 80. **HONORS AND AWARDS** Distinguished Res Award, Ohio State Univ, 80., DU, Univ Essex, Eng, 77, Univ Lund, Sweden, 82. **MEMBERSHIPS** Fel Acoust Soc Am; Ling Soc Am; Ling Soc Europe; Int Soc Phonetic Sci. **RESEARCH** Acoustic phonetics; perception of spoken language; historical phonology. **SELECTED PUBLICATIONS** Auth, Perception of Prominence by Estonian and English Listeners, Lang and Speech, Vol 0035, 92; Bilingualism, Lang, Vol 0068, 92; Lost Prosodic Oppositions--a Study of Contrastive Duration in Estonian Funeral Laments, Lang and Speech, Vol 0037, 94; Introduction to Phonetics, J Phonetics, Vol 0022, 94. **CONTACT ADDRESS** Dept of Ling, Ohio State Univ, 222 Oxley Hall, 1712 Neil, Columbus, OH, 43210.

LEHMANN, WINFRED PHILIPP
PERSONAL Born 06/23/1916, Surprise, NE, m, 1940, 2 children **DISCIPLINE** LINGUISTICS AND GERMANIC PHILOLOGY **EDUCATION** Northwestern Col, AB, 36; Univ Wis, AM, 38, PhD(Ger philol), 41. **CAREER** From instr to asst prof, Wash Univ, 46-49; from assoc prof to prof Ger, 49-63, ASHBEL SMITH PROF LING AND GER LANG, UNIV TEX, AUSTIN, 63-, Fulbright fel, Norway, 50-51; dir Georgetown Univ English Lang Prog, Ankara, Turkey, 55-56; Guggenheim fel, 72-73; mem bd dirs, Am Coun Learned Soc, 72- and Inst Deut Sprache, 73-; chmn, Ling Deleg to Peoples Repub China, 74. **HONORS AND AWARDS** Brothers Grimm Prize, Philipps-Univ, Marburg, Ger, 75; Nehru Mem Lectr, 81. **MEMBERSHIPS** Ling Soc Am (pres, 73); MLA; Ling Soc Paris; Indogermanische Gesellschaft; foreign mem, Royal Acad Sci, Denmark. **RESEARCH** Indo-European linguistics; general linguistics. **SELECTED PUBLICATIONS** Auth, Old-English and its Closest Relative--a Survey of the Earliest Ger Languages, Mich Ger Stud, Vol 0017, 91; Perspectives on Indo European Language, Culture and Religion--Studies in Honor of Polome, Edgar, C, J Indo Europ Stud, Vol 0021, 93; Comment on the 'Typology of Indo-European' by Pulleyblank, Edwin, G., J Indo-Europ Stud, Vol 0021, 93; Studies in Brythonic Word Order, Zeitschrift fur Celtische Philologie, Vol 0046, 94; Proto Indo European--a Multiangular View .4. a Tentative Version of the Calcutta Fragment of Proto Indo European, J Indo Europ Stud, Vol 0022, 94; Poetic Principles in the South Asian Literary Tradition Interrelatedness of Grammar, Prosody and Other Elements of Language, College Lit, Vol 0023, 96; Medieval Dialectology, Zeitschrift fur Dialektologie Und Linguistik, Vol 0064, 97. **CONTACT ADDRESS** Univ Tex, 3800 Eck Lane, Austin, TX, 78712.

LEHNERT, HERBERT HERMANN
PERSONAL Born 01/19/1925, Lnebeck, Germany, m, 1952, 2 children **DISCIPLINE** GERMAN **EDUCATION** Christian Albrechts Universitat, PhD, 52. **CAREER** Instr, Secondary Schools in Schleswig Holstein, Germany, 51-57; Lectr in German, Univ of Western Ontario, 57-58; instr, NY Univ, summer 58; lectr in German, 58-59, asst prof to prof of German, Rice Univ, 59-68; prof of German, Univ of Kans, 68-69; vis prof of German, Harvard Univ, 70; PROF OF GERMAN, 69-94, PROF EMERITURS RECALLED, RES PROF OF GERMAN, UNIV OF CALIF AT IRVINE, 95-. **HONORS AND AWARDS** Thomas Mann Medaille of the Deutsche Thomas Mann Gesellschaft, 98; NEH Fel, 73 & 77; NEH seminar for col teachers, 81; Guggenheim Fel, 78. **MEMBERSHIPS** MLA; AATG. **RESEARCH** German lit, especially in the 20th-Century. **SELECTED PUBLICATIONS** Auth, Thomas Mann: Fiktion, Mythos, Religion, Kohlhammer, 65 & 68; Struktur und Sprachagie, Kohlhammer, 66 & 72; coauth, Nihilismus der Menschenfreundlichkeit: Thomas Manns Wandlung und sein Essay Goethe und Tolstoi, Klostermann, 91; co-ed, Thomas Mann's Doctor Faustus: A Novel at the Margin of Modernism, Camden House, 91. **CONTACT ADDRESS** Dept of German, Univ of California, Irvine, Irvine, CA, 92697. **EMAIL** hlehnert@uci.edu

LEHOUCK, EMILE
PERSONAL Born 06/25/1935, Brussels, Belgium, m, 1962, 1 child **DISCIPLINE** ROMANCE LANGUAGES FRENCH LITERATURE **EDUCATION** Free Univ Brussels, Lic en philol romane and Agrege, 57, PhD, 65. **CAREER** Aspirant, Belgian Nat Found Sci Res, 61-66; asst prof, Univ Congo, 66-67; asst prof, 67-72, assoc prof, 72-79, PROF FRENCH, UNIV COL, UNIV TORONTO, 80-. **RESEARCH** Charles Fourier and the French literature; the romantic theatre. **SELECTED PUBLICATIONS** Auth, Leaving Without Leaving--the Account of Travel Literature in the 19th-Century, Univ Toronto Quart, Vol 0063, 93. **CONTACT ADDRESS** Dept of French Univ Col, Univ of Toronto, Toronto, ON, M5S 1A1.

LEICHTY, ERLE VERDUN
PERSONAL Born 08/07/1933, Alpena, MI, m, 1963 **DISCIPLINE** ASSYRIOLOGY **EDUCATION** Univ Mich, BA, 55, MA, 57; Univ Chicago, PhD(Assyriol), 60. **CAREER** From res asst to res assoc Assyriol, Orient Inst, Univ Chicago, 60-63; from asst prof to assoc prof ancient hist, Univ Minn, 63-68; assoc prof Assyriol, 68-71, prof Assyriol, Univ Pa, 71-97, Clark Research prof of Assyriol, Univ Pa, 98-, Cur Akkadian Lang & Lit, Univ Mus, 68-95, Guggenheim fel, 64-65; ed, Expedition, 70-73 & J Cuneiform Studies, 72-91; ed, Occasional Publications of the Babylonian Fund, 76-; ed, for the Ancient Near East, The Am Hist Asn's Guide to Historical Literature, Oxford, 95; Curator of Tablet collections, Univ Museum, Univ Pa, 96-. **HONORS AND AWARDS** Fel, Am Numismatic Soc, 56; alternate Fulbright to England, 62-63; Fulbright to England, 63-64 (declined); annual prof of the Baghdad Schools of the American Schools of Oriental Research, 63-64 (declined); fel of the Guggenheim Foundation, 64-65; trustee, Institute of Semitic Studies, Princeton, NJ, 85-90. **MEMBERSHIPS** Am Orient Soc; Archaeol Inst Am; Am Schs Orient Res; Assoc of Current Anthropology; British School of Archaeology in Iraq. **RESEARCH** Ancient Near Eastern history. **SELECTED PUBLICATIONS** Auth, A Bibliography of the Kuyunjik Collection of the British Museum, Trustees Brit Mus, 64; The Omen Series Shumma Izbu, J J Augustin, 69; A Remarkable Forger, 70 & Demons and Population Control, 71, Expedition; Two Late Commentaries, Arch fur Orientforsch, 73; The Fourth Tablet of Erimhaus, Alter Orient und Altes Testament, 75; Literary Notes, Essays on the Ancient Near East in Memory of J. J. Finkelstein, 77; A Collection of Recipes for Dyeing, Alter Orient und Altes Testament-Sonderreihe 203, 79; The Curator's Write: The Summerian Dictionary, Expedition 24, 82; An Inscription of Ashur-etel-ilani, Journal of the American Oriental Soc, 83; Bel-epush and Tammaritu, Anatolian Studies 33, 83; A Legal Text from the Reign of Tiglath-Pileser III, American Oriental Series 67, 87; Omens from Doorknobs, Journal of Cuneiform Studies 39, 87; Catalogue of Babylonian Tablets in the British Museum, vol 6, London, 86, vol 7, London, 87, vol 8, London, 88; Ashurbanipal's Library at Ninevah, Syro-Mesopotamian Studies Bulletin, 88; Making Dictionaries, Humanities 9/3, 88; Guaranteed to Cure, A Scientific Ilumanist, Studies in Memory of Abraham Sachs, 89; Feet of Clay, Dumue2-dub-ba-a, Studies in Honor of Ake W. Sjoberg, 89; Esarhaddon's 'Letter to the Gods," Ah, Assyria..., Studies in Assyrian History and Ancient Near Eastern Historiography presented to Hayim Tadmor, Scripta Hierosolymitana 33, 90; A Tamitu from Nippur, Lingering Over Words, Studies in Ancient Near Eastern Literature in Honor of William L. Moran, 90; Sheep Lungs, The Tablet and Scroll, Near Eastern Studies in Honor of William W.Hallo, 93; Ritual, Sacrifice, and Divination in Mesopotamia, Ritual and Sacrifice in the Ancient Near East, OLA 55, 93; The Origins of Scholarship, Die Rolle der Astronomie in den Kulturen Mesopotamiens, Grazer Morgenlandishe Studies 3, 93; The Distribution of Agricultural Tools in Mesopotamia, Sulma IV, 93; Esarhaddon, King of Assyria, Civilizations of the Ancient Near East, 2, 95; Section 5: Ancient Near East, Guide to Historical Literature, 95; Angurinnu, Weiner Zeitschrift fur die Kunde des Morgenlandes 86, 96; Divination, Magic, and Astrology, Assyria 1995, 97; qabutu, sahu, and me-gati, Oelsner Fs, in press; An Old Babylonian Chronicle, Cagni Mem Vol, in press; The Fifth Tablet of Summa Izbu, CTMMA 2, in press. **CONTACT ADDRESS** Dept Orient Studies, Univ Pa, 255 S 36th St, Philadelphia, PA, 19104-3805.

LEIGHTON, LAUREN GRAY
PERSONAL Born 06/21/1934, Virginia, MN, m, 1960, 2 children **DISCIPLINE** RUSSIAN LITERATURE, ROMANTICISM **EDUCATION** Univ Wis-Madison, BA, 60; Ind Univ, MA, 62; Univ Wis-Madison, PhD(Slavic lang), 68. **CAREER** Instr Russian, Mercer Univ, 62-63; instr, Grinnell Col, 63-64; asst prof Slavic, Univ Va, 67-72; assoc prof, Northern Ill Univ, 72-78; PROF SLAVIC, UNIV ILL, CHICAGO CIRCLE, 78-, US-USSR Acad Exchange, IREX-USSR Ministry Higher Educ, 70 and IREX-USSR Acad Sci, 77; ed, Slavic and East Europ J, 75-78. **MEMBERSHIPS** MLA; Asn Advan Slavic Studies; Am Asn Univ Prof, Am Asn Teachers Slavic and East Europ Lang. **RESEARCH** Russian romanticism; Pushkin; modern Russian fiction. **SELECTED PUBLICATIONS** Auth, Schiller and Zhukovskii--Aesthetic Theory in Poetic Translation, Slavic and E Europ J, Vol 0037, 93; Translation and Plagiarism, Pushkin and Thomas, D.M., Slavic and E Europ J, Vol 0038, 94; Speculative Freemasonry and the Enlightenment--a Study of the Craft in London, Paris, Prague and Vienna, Slavonic and East Europ Rev, Vol 0073, 95; A History of Russian Translation Fiction--Old Russia 18th-Century, Vol 1, Prose, Slavic Rev, Vol 0055, 96; The Lyric Poetry of Pushkin Time--the Elegiac School, Slavic and E Europ J, Vol 0040, 96. **CONTACT ADDRESS** Dept of Slavic Lang and Lit, Univ of Ill, Chicago Circle, Chicago, IL, 60680.

LEKI, ILONA
PERSONAL Born 12/24/1947, Dieburg, Germany **DISCIPLINE** FRENCH LITERATURE, ENGLISH AS A SECOND LANGUAGE **EDUCATION** Univ Ill, AB, 68, AM, 70, PhD(French), 75. **CAREER** Instr English, Knox County Adult Educ, 74-76; instr, 76-80, ASST PROF ENGLISH, UNIV TENN, 80-, Translr French, US Govt Joint Publ Res, 74-; sr ed fac publ, Univ Tenn, 75-77; asst prof French, Knoxville Col, 75-77. **MEMBERSHIPS** MLA;SAtlantic Mod Lang Asn; Am Asn Teachers Fr; Southern Comp Lit Asn; Alliance Francaise (treas, 77-78). **RESEARCH** French New Novel, particularly novels of Alain Robbe-Grillet; prose works of Henri Michaux; second language acquisition. **SELECTED PUBLICATIONS** Auth, Assessing 2nd-Language Writing in Academic Contexts, Coll Composition and Commun, Vol 0044, 93; Students Perceptions of Eap Writing Instruction and Writing Needs Across the Disci-

plines, Tesol Quart, Vol 0028, 94; Coping Strategies of Esl Students in Writing Tasks Across the Curriculum, Tesol Quart, Vol 0029, 95; Completely Different Worlds--Eap and the Writing Experiences of Esl Students in University Courses, Tesol Quart, Vol 0031, 97. **CONTACT ADDRESS** Univ Tennessee, 502 Longview Rd Apt E, Knoxville, TN, 37996.

LELAND, CHARLES WALLACE
PERSONAL Born 03/22/1928, Culver, IN **DISCIPLINE** ENGLISH LITERATURE, SCANDANAVIAN DRAMA **EDUCATION** Oberlin Col, AB, 50; Oxford Univ, BA, 53, MA, 56; Univ Toronto, STB, 58. **CAREER** Lectr English, 59-62, asst prof, 62-69, ASSOC PROF ENGLISH, UNIV TORONTO, 69-, Roman Cath priest, Congregation of St Basil, 59-. **MEMBERSHIPS** Asn Advan Scand Studies Can; Ibsen Soc Am; Soc Advan Scand Study. **RESEARCH** Ibsen; Strindberg; literature of the English Renaissance. **SELECTED PUBLICATIONS** Auth, Catiline and the Burial Mound, Mod Drama, Vol 0038, 95. **CONTACT ADDRESS** St Michael's Col Univ of Toronto, Toronto, ON, M5S 1J4.

LEMASTER, JIMMIE R.
PERSONAL Born 03/29/1934, Pike County, OH, m, 1966, 3 children **DISCIPLINE** ENGLISH LANGUAGE AND LITERATURE **EDUCATION** Defiance Col, BS, 59; Bowling Green State Univ, 62, PhD(English), 70. **CAREER** Teacher English, Stryker High Sch, 59-61; teacher, Bryan High Sch, 61-62; prof and chmn dept, Lang and Lit, Defiance Col, 62-77; Dir Am Studies Prog, Baylor Univ, 77-, Ed, Tex Writers Newsletter, 79-80; lectr Am lit, Second Foreign Lang Inst, Peking, 80-81; EXECUTIVE SECY, SOUTHWEST CONF HUMANITIES CONSORTIUM, 81-. **HONORS AND AWARDS** Publs Award, South and West, Inc, 70; Ohio Poet of Year, 76; Dean of Col Award Acad Excellence, 77. **MEMBERSHIPS** MLA; Aaup; Am Studies Asn; SCent Mod Lang Asn; Conf Col Teachers English. **RESEARCH** Twentieth century American literature; Jesse Stuart. **SELECTED PUBLICATIONS** Auth, A Chinese London Connection + A Conversation With Zhang, Bao, Anq-Quart J Short Articles Notes And Rev(s), Vol 0010, 97. **CONTACT ADDRESS** Am Studies Prog, Baylor Univ, Waco, TX, 76798.

LEMOINE, FANNIE J.
DISCIPLINE CLASSICAL STUDIES **EDUCATION** Bryn Mawr Univ, PhD, 68. **CAREER** Dept Classics, Wisc Univ **RESEARCH** Latin literature; medieval studies; science fiction. **SELECTED PUBLICATIONS** Auth, Martianus Capella: A Literary Re-Evaluation; pubs on medieval topics and Latin teaching issues. **CONTACT ADDRESS** Dept of Classics, Univ of Wisconsin, Madison, 500 Lincoln Drive, Madison, WI, 53706. **EMAIL** lemoine@macc.wisc.edu

LENZ, JOHN RICHARD
PERSONAL Born 07/03/1957, New York, NY, m, 1994, 1 child **DISCIPLINE** CLASSICAL STUDIES **EDUCATION** Columbia Univ, PhD, 93. **CAREER** 90-91, Union College; 91-94, Chmn 94-, Drew Univ. **HONORS AND AWARDS** Fulbright Travel Grant, Greece, 88-89. **MEMBERSHIPS** Bertrand Russell Society, Pres; NJ Classical Assoc, VP. **RESEARCH** Bertrand Russell, ancient Greece. **CONTACT ADDRESS** Dept of Classics, Drew Univ, Madison, NJ, 07940. **EMAIL** jlenz@drew.edu

LEON, PEDRO
PERSONAL Born 03/12/1926, Ligre, France, m, 1949, 1 child **DISCIPLINE** PHONETICS, LINGUISTICS **EDUCATION** Univ Paris, Lic es Lett, 51; Univ Besancon, DUniv, 60; Sorbonne, Dr es Lett, 72. **CAREER** Asst prof, Inst Phonetics, Sorbonne, 50-58; asst prof French, Ohio State Univ, 58-60, dir lang lab, Ctr Appl Ling and maitre asst, Fac Lett, Univ Besancon, 60-63, assoc prof French, 63-64; assoc prof, 64-65, PROF FRENCH AND DIR EXP PHONETICS LAB, UNIV TORONTO, 65-, Can Coun res grants, 65-66, 69-71 and 73-74. **HONORS AND AWARDS** Palmes academiques, 77., Dr, Univ de Nancy, 82. **MEMBERSHIPS** MLA; Inst Soc Phonetic Sci; Speech Commun Asn; Fr-Can Asn Advan Sci; Can Ling Asn. **RESEARCH** Canadian French; phonostylistics; prosody. **SELECTED PUBLICATIONS** Auth, Savoir-Dire, a Course in Phonetics and Pronunciation, Fr Rev, Vol 0066, 93; How to Pronounce French Words From Rhythms to Sounds, Fr Rev, Vol 0066, 93; an Introduction to French Pronunciation, Fr Rev, Vol 0066, 93; Codignola, Tristano an Important Component of the Liberal Socialist Movement, Ponte, Vol 0049, 93; Phonostylistics--Response to Martinet, Andre, Ling, Vol 0031, 95. **CONTACT ADDRESS** Exp Phonetics Lab, Univ of Toronto, 39 Queen's Park Crescent E, Toronto, ON, M5S 1A1.

LEON, PIERRE R.A.
PERSONAL Born 03/12/1926, Ligre, France **DISCIPLINE** PHONETICS **EDUCATION** Sorbonne, LL, 52, DL, 72; Univ Besancon, DUn, 60. **CAREER** Asst prof, Sorbonne, 50-58; asst prof, Ohio State, 58-60, 63-64; dir, ctr appl ling, Univ Besancon, 60-63; prof, founder & dir, Exp Phonetics Lab, Univ Toronto, 65-91. **HONORS AND AWARDS** Prix de l'acad francaise, 66; Commandeur palmes acad, 94. **MEMBERSHIPS** Soc Ling Paris; Ling Soc Can; Int Soc Phonetic Sci; Soc des auteurs de l'Ontario. **SELECTED PUBLICATIONS** Auth, Prononciation du francais standard, 66, 72, 77, 86; auth, Le dialogue, 85; auth, Chants de la Toundra, 85; auth, Le conte, 87; auth, Structure du francais moderne, 89; auth, Phonetisme et prononciations du francais, 90; auth, Precis de phonostylistique, 93. **CONTACT ADDRESS** 150 Farnham Ave, #504, Toronto, ON, M4V 1H5.

LERNER, ANNE LAPIDUS
PERSONAL m, 1 child **DISCIPLINE** JEWISH LITERATURE AND WOMEN'S STUDIES **EDUCATION** Harvard Univ, AB, 64, MA, 65, PhD, 77. **CAREER** Prof; dean, List College; vice chancellor, Jewish Theol Sem, 69. **HONORS AND AWARDS** Co-dir, Gender and Text Conf, 90; ed, prog adv, MA prog in Jewish Women's Studies, Jewish Theol Sem Am; dir, Ctr Conv to Judaism; ed bd, Women's League Outlook, Hadassah, Judaism, and Lilith. **RESEARCH** Study of modern Jewish literature particularly modern poetry; the reinterpretation of texts by modern writers; and the position of women in Judaism. **SELECTED PUBLICATIONS** Auth, Who Has Not Made Me a Man: The Movement for Equal Rights for Women in American Judaism; Passing the Love of Women: A Study of Gide's Saul' and its Biblical Roots; ed, Gender and Text: Feminist Approaches To Modern Hebrew and Yiddish Literature, Harvard Univ Press. **CONTACT ADDRESS** Jewish Theol Sem of America, 3080 Broadway, New York, NY, 10027. **EMAIL** anlerner@jtsa.edu

LERNER, ISAIAS
PERSONAL Born 03/13/1932, Buenos Aires, Argentina, m, 1967, 1 child **DISCIPLINE** SPANISH LITERATURE **EDUCATION** Univ Buenos Aires, professor, 59; Univ Ill, Urbana-Champaign, PhD(Span), 69. **CAREER** Instr Latin and Span, Univ Buenos Aires, 60-66; asst prof Span lit, Univ Ill, Urbanna-Champaign, 69-71; assoc prof, 71-79, PROF SPAN LIT AND CHMN DEPT, HERBERT H LEHMAN COL, CUNY, 79-, PROF LETTERS, 80-, Guggenheim fel Span lit, 77-78; fel, Herbert H Lehman Col, 77-78. **HONORS AND AWARDS** Premio Extraordinario Augusto Malaret, Real Acad Espanola, 73. **MEMBERSHIPS** MLA; Am Asn Teachers Span and Port. **RESEARCH** Spanish literature of the XVI and XVII century; history of the Spanish language; XVIII century Spanish lexicography. **SELECTED PUBLICATIONS** Auth, Rhetorics and Narration in Mexia, Pero, 'Historia Imperial', Bull Hisp Stud, Vol 0070, 93. **CONTACT ADDRESS** Herbert H. Lehman Col, CUNY, New York, NY, 10021.

LESIKIN, JOAN
DISCIPLINE ENGLISH TO SPEAKERS OF OTHER LANGUAGES **EDUCATION** Rutgers Univ, MFA, 70; Columbia Univ, PhD, 95. **CAREER** Asst prof & act dir, Acad ESL prog. **RESEARCH** Areas of sociology of education and research methodologies related to educational texts. **SELECTED PUBLICATIONS** Publ on res interest. **CONTACT ADDRESS** Dept of Language and Cultures, William Paterson Col, 300 Pompton Rd., Wayne, NJ, 07470.

LESKO, LEONARD HENRY
PERSONAL Born 08/14/1938, Chicago, IL, m, 1966 **DISCIPLINE** EGYPTOLOGY **EDUCATION** Loyola Univ Chicago, AB, 61, MA, 64; Univ Chicago, PhD(Egyptol), 69. **CAREER** Instr Latin and Greek, Quigley Prep Sem S, Chicago, 61-64; res asst, Orient Inst, Univ Chicago, 64-65; actg instr Egyptology, Univ Calif, Berkeley, 66-67, actg asst prof, 67-69, from asst prof to assoc prof, 69-72, dir, Near Eastern Studies Ctr, 73-75, chmn dept Near Eastern studies, 75-77 and 79-81, prof, 77-82, chmn prog ancient hist and archaeol, 78-79; WILBUR PROF EGYPTOLOGY AND CHMN DEPT, BROWN UNIV, 82-, Nat Endowment for Humanities younger humantist fel, 70-71; collab ed Coffin texts, Orient Inst, Univ Chicago, 71-; Am Coun Learned Soc award, 73-74; Nat Endowment for Humanities proj grant, 75-79. **HONORS AND AWARDS** FIAT Fac fel, Turin, 90; NEH Hum Inst, 94-95; RI Comt Hum Grant, 98. **MEMBERSHIPS** Egypt Explor Soc; Am Orient Soc; Am Res Ctr Egypt; Fondation Egyptol Reine Elisabeth, Brussels; Int Asn Egyptologists. **RESEARCH** Ancient Egyptian religious literature; Egyptian history and language. **SELECTED PUBLICATIONS** Auth, High Tech Projects for Research and Distribution, Zeitschrift fur Agyptische Sprache Und Altertumskunde, Vol 0121, 94; Voyage to Lower and Upper Egypt, Amer J Archaeol, Vol 0098, 94; Black Athena--the Afroasiatic Roots of Classical Civilization .2. the Archaeological and Documentary Evidence, J Interdisciplinary Hist, Vol 0024, 94; Popular Religion in Egypt During the New-Kingdom, J Near Eastern Stud, Vol 0054, 95; A Dictionary of Late Egyptian, 5 vols, Berkeley & Providence, 82- 90; auth, Egyptological Studies in Honor of Richard A Parker, Hanora & London, 86; co-auth, Religion in Ancient Egypt, Ithaca, 91; ed, Pharoah's Workers: The Villagers of Deir al-Madina, Ithaca, 94; co-ed, Exodus: Egyptian Evidence, Winona Lake, 97; ed, Ancient Egyptian and Mediterranean Studies in Memory of William A Wood, Providence, 98. **CONTACT ADDRESS** Dept of Egyptology, Brown Univ, Box 1899, Providence, RI, 02912. **EMAIL** LLosko@Brownvm.Brown.edu

LESKO BAKER, DEBORAH
DISCIPLINE FRENCH LITERATURE **EDUCATION** Yale Univ, PhD. **CAREER** Assoc prof, 89-. **RESEARCH** Renaissance literature. **SELECTED PUBLICATIONS** Auth, Narcissus and the Lover, Stanford, 87; The Subject of Desire, Purdue, 96; pubs on Petrarch, Joachim DuBellay, Louise Lab, rhetorical and mythical structures in texts by Flaubert and Marguerite Duras. **CONTACT ADDRESS** French Dept, Georgetown Univ, 37th and O St, Washington, DC, 20057.

LESMAN, ANN ST CLAIR
DISCIPLINE SPANISH **EDUCATION** Rollins Col, BA; Duke Univ, Med; Univ MD, MA, PhD. **CAREER** Prof & prog coordr; pres, For Lang Asn of VA, 89-91; Fulbright-Hayes sponsored gp proj, Mexico, 96. **HONORS AND AWARDS** Outstanding fac mem & received the campus Alumni Fedn Fac of the Yr Awd, 96; Awd for Excellence in For Lang Educ, For Lang Asn of VA, 80. **SELECTED PUBLICATIONS** Publ on, tchg of conversational skills. **CONTACT ADDRESS** Dept of Span, Shenandoah Univ, 1460 University Dr., Winchester, VA, 22601.

LESSL, THOMAS M.
PERSONAL Born 10/11/1954, Milwaukee, WI, m, 1976, 2 children **DISCIPLINE** DEPT SPEECH COMMUN **EDUCATION** Univ Tex, Austin. **CAREER** ASSOC PROF, SPEECH COMMUN, UNIV GA, 85-. **MEMBERSHIPS** Nat Commun Asn **RESEARCH** Rhetoric of Science **SELECTED PUBLICATIONS** "Toward a Definition of Religious Communication: Scientific and Religious Uses of Evolution, Jour Commun & Relig, 93; "Naturalizing Science: Two Episodes in The Evolution of a Rhetoric of Scientism," West Jour of Commun, 96; "The Social Implications of Genre: A Burkean Interpretation Aristotle," Speaker & Gavel, 97; "Conceptualizing Rhetoric Through Analogy. The speech Commun Tchr, 97; "Heresy, Orthodoxy, and the Politics of Science," Quart Jour of Speech, 98. **CONTACT ADDRESS** Dept Speech Commun, Univ Ga, Athens, GA, 30602. **EMAIL** tlessl@arches.uga.edu

LESTER, ROBERT CARLTON
PERSONAL Born 02/01/1933, Lead, SD, m, 1954, 3 children **DISCIPLINE** COMPARATIVE RELIGION **EDUCATION** Mont State Univ, BA, 55; Yale Univ, BD, 58, MA, 59, PhD(comp relig), 63. **CAREER** From asst prof to assoc prof philos and relig, Am Univ, DC, 62-70; assoc prof, 70-72, PROF RELIG STUDIES, UNIV COLO, BOULDER, 72-, Vis lectr, Foreign Serv Inst, US Dept State, 67-; vis prof Asian studies, Cornell Univ, 68-69; Fulbright-Hays sr res fel, India, 74-75. **MEMBERSHIPS** Asn Asian Studies; Am Acad Relig; fel Soc Relig Higher Educ. **RESEARCH** Buddhism in Southeast Asia; Hinduism; South Indian Vaishnavism. **SELECTED PUBLICATIONS** Auth, The Sattada Srivaisnavas, J Amer Oriental Soc, Vol 0114, 1994 **CONTACT ADDRESS** Relig Studies, Univ of Colo, Boulder, CO, 80309. **EMAIL** Robert.Lester@Colorado.edu

LETTS, JANET TAYLOR
PERSONAL Born 09/19/1930, Ho-Ho-Kus, NJ **DISCIPLINE** FRENCH LITERATURE **EDUCATION** Swarthmore Col, BA, 52; Univ Strasbourg, dipl, 55; Yale Univ, PhD, 62. **CAREER** Instr French, Wellesley Col, 59-60; from instr to assoc prof, 67-76, PROF FRENCH, WHEATON COL MASS, 76-, Chmn Dept, 66-, Mem adv comt, Jr Year in France, Sweet Briar Col. **MEMBERSHIPS** MLA; Int Asn Fr Studies; Soc Fr Hist Studies. **RESEARCH** Seventeenth century French literature. **SELECTED PUBLICATIONS** Auth, L 'Enfant Meduse', Fr Rev, Vol 0066, 93; L 'Homme De La Passerelle', Fr Rev, Vol 0068, 95; Les 'Catalinaires', Fr Rev, Vol 0070, 97. **CONTACT ADDRESS** Dept of French, Wheaton Col, Norton, MA, 02766.

LEUNG, KAI-CHEONG
PERSONAL Born 06/19/1936, Hong Kong, m, 1968, 2 children **DISCIPLINE** CHINESE LANGUAGE AND CULTURE **EDUCATION** Hong Kong Univ, BA and MA, 63; Leeds Univ, Dipl, 66; Int Phonetic Asn, Cert, 66; Univ Calif, Berkeley, PhD(Orient lang), 74. **CAREER** Lectr English and educ, Grantham Col Educ, 64-69; lectr, English and extra-mural studies, Chinese Univ Hong Kong, 67-69; asst prof Chinese, 73-79, ASSOC PROF CHINESE, SAN JOSE STATE UNIV, 79-, Consult, Asian-Am Bilingual Ctr, Berkeley, 80-81. **MEMBERSHIPS** Int Phonetic Asn; Asn Asian Studies; Philol Asn PACIFIC Coast; Chinese Lang Teachers Asn. **RESEARCH** Chinese drama; East-West literary relations; pedagogy. **SELECTED PUBLICATIONS** Auth, Turbulence, World Lit Today, Vol 0067, 93; 'Masks and Crocodile'--a Contemporary Chinese Poet and his Poetry, World Lit Today, Vol 0067, 93; The Transparent Eye--Reflections on Translation, Chinese Literature and Comparative Poetics, World Lit Today, Vol 0068, 94; The Short Stories of Chen Ruoxi Translated From the Original Chinese--a Writer at the Crossroads, World Lit Today, Vol 0068, 94; The 'Remote Country of Women', World Lit Today, Vol 0069, 95; The 'Butchers Wife' and Other Stories, World Lit Today, Vol 0070, 96. **CONTACT ADDRESS** Dept of Foreign Lang, San Jose State Univ, San Jose, CA, 95192.

LEVARIE SMARR, JANET
DISCIPLINE COMPARATIVE LITERATURE **EDUCATION** Princeton Univ, PhD, 75. **CAREER** Prof, Univ IL Urbana Champaign . **RESEARCH** Early Renaissance in rel to the Class and the Middle Ages; Vergil and Petrarch; Ovid, Dante and Boccaccio; women writers in the Renaissance. **SELECTED PUBLICATIONS** Auth, Italian Renaissance Tales; Boccaccio and Fiammetta: The Narrator as Lover; Boccaccio's Eclogues; ed, Historical Criticism and the Challenge of Theory; publ(s) on Renaissance poetry, plot theory, Chaucer, Spenser, Anacreontics, and Renaissance women writers. **CONTACT ADDRESS** Comp Lit Dept, Univ Illinois Urbana Champaign, E Gregory Drive, PO Box 52, Champaign, IL, 61820.

LEVENDUSKI, CRISTINE
DISCIPLINE ENGLISH LANGUAGE AND LITERATURE **EDUCATION** Univ Minn, PhD, 89. **CAREER** Assoc prof/dir grad studies. **RESEARCH** American studies; early American literature. **SELECTED PUBLICATIONS** Auth, Peculiar Power: A Quaker Woman Preacher in 18th Century America, Smithsonian, 96. **CONTACT ADDRESS** English Dept, Emory Univ, 1380 Oxford Rd NE, Atlanta, GA, 30322-1950. **EMAIL** cmleven@emory.edu

LEVI, JUDITH N.
DISCIPLINE LINGUISTICS **EDUCATION** Univ Chicago, PhD. **CAREER** Prof, Northwestern Univ. **RESEARCH** Language and the Law; semantics; word formation. **SELECTED PUBLICATIONS** Auth, Review of Language and Law, Harlow, Essex: Longman, 94; What is Meaning in a Legal Text, A First Dialogue for Law and Linguistics,. Wash Univ Law Quart, 95; Language as Evidence: The Linguist as Expert Witness in North American Courts, Forensic Linguistics: The Int J Speech, Lang and the Law, 94; Language and Law: A Bibliographic Guide to Social Science Research in the USA, Chicago: Am Bar Asn, 94; Evaluating Jury Comprehension of Illinois Capital Sentencing Instructions, Am Speech, 93; coauth, Improving Decisions on Death by Revising and Testing Jury Instructions, Judicature, 96; Regulatory Variables and Statutory Interpretation, Wash Univ Law Quart, 1995; Bringing Linguistics into Judicial Decisionmaking: Semantic Analysis Submitted to the US Supreme Court, Forensic Ling: The Int J Speech, Lang, and the Law, 95; Plain Meaning and Hard Cases, Yale Law J, 94. **CONTACT ADDRESS** Dept of Linguistics, Northwestern Univ, 2016 Sheridan Rd, Evanston, IL, 60208-4090. **EMAIL** j-levi@nwu.edu

LEVIN, BETH
DISCIPLINE LINGUISTICS **EDUCATION** MIT, PhD. **CAREER** Prof, Northwestern Univ. **RESEARCH** Lexical semantics; syntax; morphology; language typology. **SELECTED PUBLICATIONS** Auth, Approaches to Lexical Semantic Representation, Automating the Lexicon I: Research and Practice in a Multilingual Environment, Oxford UP, 95; Coauth, Morphology and Lexical Semantics, Handbook of Morphology, Blackwell, Oxford, 98; Making Sense of Corpus Data: A Case Study of Verbs of Sound, Int J Corpus Ling, 97; Lexical Semantics and Syntactic Structure, The Handbook of Contemp Semantic Theory, Blackwell, Oxford, 96; Two Types of Derived Accomplishments, Proceedings of the First LFG Conf, 96; Building on a Corpus: A Linguistic and Lexicographical Look at Some Near-synonyms, Int J Lexicography, 95; Unaccusativity: At the Syntax-Lexical Semantics Interface, Linguistic Inquiry Monograph 26, MIT Press, Cambridge, Mass, 95; The Elasticity of Verb Meaning, Proceedings of the 10 Annual Conf Israel Asn for Theoret Ling and Workshop on the Syntax-Semantics Interface, 95. **CONTACT ADDRESS** Dept of Linguistics, Northwestern Univ, 2016 Sheridan Rd, Evanston, IL, 60208.

LEVIN, JULES FRED
PERSONAL Born 01/25/1940, Chicago, IL, m, 1967, 1 child **DISCIPLINE** LINGUISTICS **EDUCATION** Univ Calif, Los Angeles, BA, 61, MA, 64; PhD(Balto-Slavic ling), 71. **CAREER** Vis lectr Russ, Univ Calif, Santa Barbara, 68-69; acting asst prof Russ and ling, 69-71, asst prof, 71-77, ASSOC PROF RUSS AND LING, UNIV CALIF, RIVERSIDE, 77-. **MEMBERSHIPS** Ling Soc Am; Am Asn Teachers Slavic and EEurop Lang; Asn Advan Baltic Studies. **RESEARCH** Linguistics: historical and dialectology; Balto-Slavic linguistics: historical, dialectology, phonology. **SELECTED PUBLICATIONS** Auth, Semiotics of Inspired Illustration in a Molokan Sacred Text, Amer J Semiotics, Vol 0009, 92. **CONTACT ADDRESS** Dept of Lit and Lang, Univ of Cal, 900 University Ave, Riverside, CA, 92521-0001.

LEVIN, MAURICE IRWIN
PERSONAL Born 02/13/1931, Boston, MA, m, 1953, 2 children **DISCIPLINE** SLAVIC LINGUISTICS **EDUCATION** Boston Univ, BA, 53; Harvard Univ, MA, 58, PhD(Slavic), 64. **CAREER** Instr mod lang, Mass Inst Technol, 61-63; asst prof Russ, Bowdoin Col, 63-65; asst prof Slavic, Ind Univ, Bloomington, 65-68; assoc prof, 68-72, PROF SLAVIC, UNIV MASS, AMHERST, 72-. **MEMBERSHIPS** Am Asn Teachers Slavic and EEurop Lang; Am Coun Teachers Russ. **RESEARCH** Russian language; structure of Russian; pedagogy of Russian. **SELECTED PUBLICATIONS** The Stress Patterns of the Russian Verb, Russ lang J, 71; Variant Forms in Russian Conjugation, Slavic and EEurop J, 72; Some Uses of the Accusative Case in Time Expressions, 73 and Stress Notation in the Russian adjective, 75, Russian Lang J, 75; Irregularities in Imperfective Derivation, Slavic and EEurop J, 77; Russian Declension and Conjugation: a Structural Description with Exercises, Slavica Publ, 78; Stress Notation in Russian Declension, Folia Slavica, 78; On Predicting the Genitive Case of Pluralia Tantum Nouns, Russ Lang J, 80. **CONTACT ADDRESS** Dept of Slavic Lang and Lit, Univ of Mass, Amherst, MA, 01003.

LEVIN, THOMAS Y.
PERSONAL Born 09/14/1957, Cincinnati, OH, s **DISCIPLINE** GERMAN **EDUCATION** Yale Coll, BA, 79; Yale Univ, MA hist of art, 81; MA philosophy, 83; PhD, 89. **CAREER** Asst Prof, Princeton Univ, German Dept, 90-97; Assoc Prof 97-; Acting Chmn, Fall 98. **HONORS AND AWARDS** Fel, J. Paul Getty Ctr for Hist of Art and Humanities, 90-91; Fel, Inst for Advanced Studey/Collegium Budapest, Hungary, 94; Research Scholar, Int Forschungszentrum Kulturwissenschaften, 95; Pro Helvetia Found, Geneva, Switz, 97. **MEMBERSHIPS** MLA, AATG, IAPL, Society for Cinema Studies. **RESEARCH** Media and Cultural Theory; Frankfurt Sch; Aesthetics and Politics **SELECTED PUBLICATIONS** coed, Siegried Kracauer. Neue Interpretationen, Tubingen: Stauffenburg Verlag 90; auth, Musical Quarterly, Elements of a Radio Theory: Adorno and the Princeton Radio Research Project, Summer 94; auth, Technophonia: Essays in Sound 2, After the Beep: A Short History of Voice Mail, Contemporary Sound Arts, Darlinghurst, Australia, 95; auth, Meaning in the Visual Arts: Views from the Outside. A Centennial Commemoration of Erwin Panofsky (1892-1968), Iconology at the Movies: Panofsky's Film Theory, Inst for Adv Study, Princeton, 95; ed, Siegfried Kracauer, The Mass Ornament. Weimar Essays, Harvard Univ Press, 95; auth, Situacionistas: arte, politica, urbanismo/Situationist: art, politics, urbanism, Geopolitics of Hibernation: The Drift of Situationist Urbanism, Museu d'art contemporani, Barcelona, 96; **CONTACT ADDRESS** German Dept, Princeton Univ, 230 E Pyne, Princeton, NJ, 08544. **EMAIL** tylevin@princeton.edu

LEVINE, DANIEL
DISCIPLINE GREEK LITERATURE **EDUCATION** Univ Minn, BA, 75; Univ Cincinnati, PhD, 80. **CAREER** English and Lit, Univ Ark. **HONORS AND AWARDS** Excellence Tchng Classics; Burlington Northern Outstanding Fac-Scholar Tchng Award., Chair, Classical Studies Prog. **SELECTED PUBLICATIONS** Area: Greek epic, lyric, dramatic, and historical texts. **CONTACT ADDRESS** Univ Ark, Fayetteville, AR, 72701.

LEVINE, GEORGE L.
DISCIPLINE ENGLISH LANGUAGE AND LITERATURE **EDUCATION** NY Univ, BA; Univ Minn, MA; PhD. **CAREER** Kenneth Burke Prof Engl. **RESEARCH** Victorian literature and culture; novel and narrative; science and culture; Darwin. **SELECTED PUBLICATIONS** Auth, Darwin and the Novelists; auth, The Realistic Imagination; Lifebirds. **CONTACT ADDRESS** Dept of English, Rutgers Univ, 510 George St, Murray Hall, New Brunswick, NJ, 08901-1167. **EMAIL** gelevine@compuserve.com

LEVINSON, BERNARD M.
PERSONAL S Porcupine, ON, Canada **DISCIPLINE** NEAR EASTERN STUDIES **EDUCATION** York Univ, Toronto, BA, 74; McMaster Univ, Ontario, MA, 78; Brandeis Univ, PhD, 91. **CAREER** Vis lectr, Hebrew and relig stud, Middlebury Col, 83, 84; tchg fel, Brandeis Univ, 86-87; Stroum Fel Advanc Jewish Stud, Univ Wash, 87-88; instr relig, Penn State Univ, 88-90; asst prof Near Eastern Lang and Cult, adj asst prof Relig Stud, Jewish Stud, Indiana Univ, 90-97; Berman Family Chair Jewish Stud and Hebrew Bible, assoc prof Classical and Near Eastern Stud, Univ Minn, 97- . **HONORS AND AWARDS** First Class Honors, 74; dInt Sem on Bibl and Ancient Near Eastern Law, 92; fac res grant, Middle Eastern Stud Prof, 94; IU Summer Fac Fel, 95; Soc of Bibl Lit res grant, 96; Int Fel in Jewish Stud, memorial Found, 96; Littauer Found res grant, 96; Center for Judaic Stud, Univ Penn, sem, 97; Stanford Hum Ctr, 97; mem, Inst for Advanc Stud, Sch of Soc Sci, Princeton, 97. **MEMBERSHIPS** Am Acad Relig; Am Oriental Soc; Asn for Jewish Stud; Can Soc for Bibl Stud; Jewish Law Asn; Soc of Bibl Lit; World Union of Jewish Stud. **RESEARCH** Biblical and ancient Near Eastern law; religion; hermeneutics. **SELECTED PUBLICATIONS** Ed and contribur, Theory and Method in Biblical and Cuneiform Law: Revision, Interpolation and Development, Sheffield Academic, 94; auth, But You Shall Surely Kill Him! The Text-Critical and Neo-Assyrian Evidence for MT Deuteronomy 13:10, in Braulik, ed, Bundesdokument und Gesetz: Studien zum Deuteronomium, Herder, 95; auth, Deuteronomy and the Hermeneutics of Legal Innovation, Oxford, 97; co-ed, Gender and Law in the Hebrew Bible and the Ancient Near East, Sheffield Academic, 98. **CONTACT ADDRESS** Dept of Classical and Near Eastern Studies, Univ of Minnesota, 9 Pleasant St SE, Minneapolis, MN, 55455-0125. **EMAIL** levinson@tc.umn.edu

LEVITINE, EDA MEZER
PERSONAL Born 02/16/1927, Russia, m, 1944, 3 children **DISCIPLINE** FRENCH LITERATURE **EDUCATION** Boston Univ, AB, 50, MA, 52. **CAREER** From instr to asst prof French, Lesley Col, 57-64; asst prof, 64-69, ASSOC PROF FRENCH, TRINITY COL, 69-, CHMN DEPT, 70-. **MEMBERSHIPS** Am Asn Teachers Fr. **RESEARCH** French 19th century literature; Baudelaire, Flaubert; relationship between French literature and French art. **SELECTED PUBLICATIONS** Auth, Baudelaire, Charles Revisited, 19th-Century Fr Stud, Vol 0021, 93. **CONTACT ADDRESS** Dept of French, Trinity Col, 125 Michigan Ave N E, Washington, DC, 20017-1090.

LEVITT, JESSE
PERSONAL Born 06/15/1919, New York, NY, m, 1958, 2 children **DISCIPLINE** ROMANCE LANGUAGES & LINGUISTICS **EDUCATION** City Col New York, BA, 38; Columbia Univ, MA, 40, PhD(Romance philol), 63. **CAREER** Trans & later info specialist, Foreign Broadcast Information Service, 41-54; teacher high schs, Md, 55-56; teacher, Jr High Sch, NY, 56: teacher high sch, NY, 57-59; from instr to asst prof French & Span, Wash State Univ, 60-65; assoc prof French & Romance lang, 65-70, chm dept foreign lang, 75-81, prof For Lang, Univ Bridgeport, 70-89, Ed, Geolinguistics, Am Soc Geoling, 73- **HONORS AND AWARDS** Phi Beta Kappa; magna cum laude, 38. **MEMBERSHIPS** Am Soc Geoling (2nd vpres, 71-72, 1st vpres, 72-73, pres, 73-74, secy, 80-; MLA; Am Name Soc. **RESEARCH** French linguistics, 17th to 20th centuries; French literature of the 20th century; Spanish linguistics. **SELECTED PUBLICATIONS** Auth, The Grammaire des Grammaires of Girault-Duvivier: A Study of Nineteenth-Century French, Mouton, The Hague, 68; The Concept of Euphony in Traditional French Grammar, In: Studies in Honor of Mario A Pei, Univ NC, 72; The Agreement of the Past Participle in Modern French, Linguistics, 10/73; The Influence of English on Spanish, English Around World, 11/75 & 11/77; Names in Beckett's Theater: Irony and Mystification, 77 & Irony and Allusiveness in Gide's Onomastics, 76, Lit Onomastics; The Influence of Orthography on Phonology: A Comparative Study (English, French, Spanish, Italian, German), Linguistics, 78; From Literature to the Lexicon: Names of Authors, Books and Literary Characters as Vocabulary in the Romance Languages, Papers in Onomastics, Univ Mo-Rolla, 11/81; ed and contrib, Geolinguistic Perspectives, Proceedings of the 1985 Conf of the Am Soc of Geolinguistics, Univ Press of Am; co-ed and contribur, Justice, Interdisciplinary and Global Perspectives, Univ Press of Am, 88; ed and contrib, Language in Contemporary Society, Proceedings of the 1992 Conference of the American Society of Geolinguistics; ed and contrib, Language and Communication in the New Century, Cummings & Hathaway, 99. **CONTACT ADDRESS** 485 Brooklawn Ave, Fairfield, CT, 06432.

LEVY, DIANE WOLFE
PERSONAL Born 06/06/1944, Washington, DC, m, 1966, 1 child **DISCIPLINE** FRENCH LITERATURE, COMPARATIVE LITERATURE **EDUCATION** Barnard Col, BA, 66; Columbia Univ, MA, 69, PhD(French and Romance philol), 73. **CAREER** Asst prof French, Columbia Univ, 73-74; ASST PROF FRENCH, STATE UNIV NY, ALBANY, 74-80. **MEMBERSHIPS** MLA; Nat Asn Teachers Fr; Northeast Mod Lang Asn. **RESEARCH** Urban literature; narrative structure. **SELECTED PUBLICATIONS** Auth, History as art: Ironic parody in Anatole France's Les Sept Femmes de la Barbe-Bleue, Nineteenth-Century Fr Studies, spring 76; coauth, How to Use French Verbs, Barron's Educ Ser, 77; auth, Cityscapes: Towards a definition of urban literature, Mod Fiction Studies, spring 78; Ironic Techniques in the Short Stories of Anatole France, NC Ser Romance Lang and Lit (in press). **CONTACT ADDRESS** 9317 Ocala St, Silver Spring, MD, 20901.

LEVY, KAREN
DISCIPLINE FRENCH LITERATURE **EDUCATION** Univ Ky, PhD, 71. **CAREER** Prof. **RESEARCH** Twentieth century French fiction, poetry, and literary criticism. **SELECTED PUBLICATIONS** Auth, pubs on prose works of Michel Tournier, criticism of Jean Paulhan and Jacques Riviere, and later writings of Andre Malraux, and John Romeiser. **CONTACT ADDRESS** Dept of Romance Languages, Knoxville, TN, 37996.

LEVY, KURT LEOPOLD
PERSONAL Born 07/10/1917, Berlin, Germany, m, 1947, 5 children **DISCIPLINE** SPANISH **EDUCATION** Univ Toronto, BA, 45, MA, 46, PhD(Span), 54. **CAREER** Instr Span lang and lit, 45-50, lectr Span and Span Am lit, 50-55, from asst prof to assoc prof, 55-65, dir Latin Am studies and assoc chmn dept Hisp studies, 65-70, PROF HISP STUDIES, UNIV TORONTO, 65-, Chmn Dept Span and Port, 78-, Govt Columbia lectr, SAm, 55; Can Coun sr res fel, Columbia and Latin Am Univs, 65; external examr Span, Univ West Indies, 69-71; Rockefeller vis prof lit, Univ Valle, Columbia, 71-73; TREAS, INT FEDN INSTS TEACHING SPAN, 72-. **MEMBERSHIPS** Can Asn Latin Am Studies (pres, 69-71); MLA; Am Asn Teachers Span and Port; Inst Int Lit Iberoam (pres, 67-69); Am Coun Teaching Foreign Lang. **RESEARCH** Spanish American prose fiction,

specifically Colombian. **SELECTED PUBLICATIONS** Auth, Remembering Mead, Robert, G., Hispania-J Devoted tchg Span Port, Vol 0079, 96. **CONTACT ADDRESS** Univ Toronto, 11 Rathnelly Ave, Toronto, ON, M4V 2M2.

LEWIS, BART L.
DISCIPLINE LATIN AMERICAN LITERATURE **EDUCATION** Southern Methodist Univ, BA; Univ NM, MA, PhD. **CAREER** J William Fulbright prof, Lyon Col. **SELECTED PUBLICATIONS** Auth, Mexican Modernism in A Hist Mex Lit. **CONTACT ADDRESS** Dept of Mod Lang, Lyon Col, 300 Highland Rd, PO Box 2317, Batesville, AR, 72503.

LEWIS, DAVID WILFRID PAUL
PERSONAL Born 01/24/1932, Clacton-on-Sea, England, m, 1959, 4 children **DISCIPLINE** MODERN LANGUAGES **EDUCATION** Oxford Univ, BA, Hons, 53, MA, 68; Col Europe, dipl int relat, 57; Univ Paris, Dr, 73. **CAREER** Dean students, Col Europe, 57-58; Coun of Europe, Strasbourg, info off, 58-62, adminr educ prog, 62-65; secy, Europ Comt Conserv Nature and Natural Resources, 65-68; assoc prof mod lang, Lakehead Univ, 68-77, chmn dept, 68-70; PROF MOD LANG AND CHMN DEPT MOD FOREIGN LANG, LEHIGH UNIV, 77-, Vis prof, Univ Ottawa, 71, Univ Prince Edward Island, 74 and Univ Ottawa, 77; campus dir admin, Champlain Regional Col, St Lambert, Quebec, 75-76; transl consult, secy state, Govt Can, 76-77. **HONORS AND AWARDS** French Govt Award of Merit for Contrib to Europ Coop in Educ, 63; ODK Nat Honor Soc, 80. **MEMBERSHIPS** Int Arthurian Soc; Asn Int Etud Fr; Am Asn Teachers Fr; Asn Int Docteurs Univ Paris. **RESEARCH** Modern languages, especially 19th century French poetry and French for business and international affairs; international relations, especially European integration. **SELECTED PUBLICATIONS** Auth, Crossing the Text, 19th-Century Fr Stud, Vol 0021, 93; Expositions--Literature and Architecture in 19th-Century France, 19th-Century Fr Stud, Vol 0022, 93; Between the Sheets--the Perils of Courtship by Correspondence in Balzac La 'Femme Abandonnee', 19th-Century Fr Stud, Vol 0024, 96. **CONTACT ADDRESS** Dept of Mod Foreign Lang, Lehigh Univ, Bethlehem, PA, 18015.

LEWIS, GERTRUD JARON
PERSONAL Born 10/27/1931, Frankfurt-Main, Germany, m, 1960, 3 children **DISCIPLINE** MEDIEVAL GERMAN LITERATURE **EDUCATION** Univ Alta, MA, 67, PhD(Ger), 71. **CAREER** Instr Ger and French, Univ Redlands, 59-62; asst prof Ger, 72-78, ASSOC PROF GER, LAURENTIAN UNIV, 78-, Can Coun publ grant, 73; Laurentian Univ publ grant, 74; Soc Sci and Humanities Res Coun Can fel, 80; Soc Sci and Humanities grant, 82. **MEMBERSHIPS** MLA; Can Asn Univ Teachers Ger; Can Comp Lit Asn; Mediaeval Acad Am; Int Arthurian Soc. **RESEARCH** Middle high German epic; German women mystics of the Middle Ages. **SELECTED PUBLICATIONS** Auth, The Heart as the Center of Mystical Experience--Mysticism in Cistercian Convents in 13th-Century Helfta, Speculum-J Medieval Stud, Vol 0068, 93; In Search of Woman in the Middle Ages, Seminar-J Ger Stud, Vol 0029, 93; Tears and Saints, Arachne, Vol 0003, 96. **CONTACT ADDRESS** Dept of Mod Lang, Laurentian Univ, 935 Ramsey Lake Rd, Sudbury, ON, P3E 2C6.

LEWIS, MARVIN A.
PERSONAL Born 10/09/1942, VA, m, 2 children **DISCIPLINE** FOREIGN LANGUAGES **EDUCATION** Morgan State Univ, BA, 68; Purdue Univ, MA, 68-69; Univ Calif Berkeley, MA, 70; Univ Wash, PhD, 74. **CAREER** Asst prof, Univ Minn, 75-76; from asst to assoc prof to dir, Univ Ill, 76-89; dir, 86-89, prof 89-, Univ Mo. **HONORS AND AWARDS** NEH, 89; NEH Travel Grant, 90; Fulbright Grant, 89, 99; ACLS Grant 88, 91;, Martin Luther King Grant, Woodrow Wilson Found; Charles E. Kany Scholar, 69-70; NDEA Fel, 71-74. **MEMBERSHIPS** MLA; Afro-Latin/Am Res Asn. **RESEARCH** Afro Hispanic and Latin American Literature. **SELECTED PUBLICATIONS** Auth, From Lima to Leticia: The Peruvian Novels of Mario Vargas Llosa, 83; auth, Afro-Hispanic Poetry, 1940-1980: From Slavery to Negritud in South American Verse, 83; auth, Treading the Ebony Path: Ideology and Violence in Contemporary Afro-Colombian Prose Fiction, 87; auth, Ethnicity and Identity in Contemporary Afro-Venezuelan Literature: A Culturalist Approach, 92; auth, Diaspora, 96. **CONTACT ADDRESS** Dept of Romance Languages, Univ of Missouri, 143 Arts and Science Bldg, Columbia, MO, 65211.

LEWIS, PHILIP EUGENE
PERSONAL Born 09/08/1942, Kingsport, TN, m, 1966, 2 children **DISCIPLINE** FRENCH LITERATURE **EDUCATION** Davidson Col, BA, 64; Yale Univ, PhD(French), 69. **CAREER** Asst prof, 68-74, chm dept, 73-76, assoc prof, 74-79, ed, Diacritics, 76-81, chm dept, 78-80, Prof Romance Studies, 79- , dean Arts & Sciences, 95- , Cornell Univ. **RESEARCH** Seventeenth century French literature; Semiotics. **SELECTED PUBLICATIONS** Auth, La Rochefoucauld: The Art of Abstraction, Cornell Univ, 77; auth, Seeing Through the Mother Goose Tales, Stanford, 96. **CONTACT ADDRESS** College of Arts and Sciences, Cornell Univ, 147 Goldwin Smith, Ithaca, NY, 14853-3201.

LEWIS, TODD VERNON
PERSONAL Born 01/12/1949, Lynwood, CA, m **DISCIPLINE** SPEECH COMMUNICATION **EDUCATION** Biola Univ, BA, 72; Ohio State Univ, MA, 74; Louisiana State Univ, PhD, 80. **CAREER** Teaching asst speech, Ohio State Univ, Columbus, 73-74; teaching asst, Louisiana State Univ, Baton Rouge, 77-78; prof & chm, commun, Biola Univ, La Mirada, Calif, 74-. **HONORS AND AWARDS** AFA-NIET Distinguished Serv Award, 90 **MEMBERSHIPS** Speech Commun Assn; Am Forensics Assn; Relig Speech Commun Assn; Nat Forensics Assn. **RESEARCH** Religious communication (rhetoric); readers theatre; forensics; film history. **SELECTED PUBLICATIONS** Auth, Communicating Literature, 3rd ed, Kendall/Hunt Pub co, 99. **CONTACT ADDRESS** Dept of Communication, Biola Univ, 13800 Biola Ave, La Mirada, CA, 90639-0001. **EMAIL** todd_lewis@peter.biola.edu

LI, AUDREY
DISCIPLINE EAST ASIAN LANGUAGES AND CULTURES **EDUCATION** Univ Southern Calif, PhD, 85. **CAREER** Asso prof, Univ Southern Calif. **RESEARCH** Linguistics; English, Mandarin and Taiwanese language; language policies in Taiwan. **SELECTED PUBLICATIONS** Auth, New Horizons in Chinese Linguistics; Syntax of Scope; Order and Constituency in Mandarin Chinese. **CONTACT ADDRESS** East Asian Studies Center, Univ Southern Calif, University Park Campus, Los Angeles, CA, 90089.

LIBERMAN, ANATOLY
PERSONAL Born 03/10/1937, Leningrad, Russia, m, 1969, 1 child **DISCIPLINE** GERMANIC PHILOLOGY **EDUCATION** Hertzen Pedagogical Inst, BA, 59; Lenigrad Univ, candidate Philology, 65; Acad of Sci of the USSR, DrPhilol, 72. **CAREER** Tchr, Russia, 59-62; instr, Leningrad Polytech Inst, 62-65; res fel, Acad of Sci of the USSR, 65-75; assoc prof, Univ Minn, 75-78, prof, 78- . **HONORS AND AWARDS** Guggenheim fel, 82; Fulbright fel, 88; Bush fel, 95; England's best book of the year in folklore, 85; NEH sem, 80, 91. **MEMBERSHIPS** Soc for the Advan of Scandinavian Stud; Dict Soc of N Am; Soc for German Philol; Natl Assoc of Scholars; Assoc of Lit Scholars and Critics; PEN. **RESEARCH** Germanic and Slavic philology. **SELECTED PUBLICATIONS** Trans and auth, On the Heights of Creation: The Lyrics of Fedor Tyntchev, JAI, 93; auth, Word Heath, Il Calamo, 94; auth, Vrachevanie dukha (Healing of the Spirit), Effect, 95; co-ed, Literaturnyi vitrazh, Assoc of Russian-American Scholars in the USA, 97; auth numerous articles. **CONTACT ADDRESS** 312 Seymour Pl SE, Minneapolis, MN, 55414. **EMAIL** liber002@tc.umn.edu

LIDA, DENAH LEVY
PERSONAL Born 09/09/1923, New York, NY, m, 1955 **DISCIPLINE** SPANISH **EDUCATION** Hunter Col, BA, 43; Columbia Univ, MA, 44; Nat Univ Mex, Dr Let(Span), 52. **CAREER** From instr to asst prof Span, Smith Col, 45-53; asst prof mod lang, Sweet Briar Col, 54-55; from instr to assoc prof Span, 55-67, chmn dept Romance & comp lit, 64-66 & 74-77, Prof Span, Brandeis Univ, 67-, Assoc scholar, Radcliffe Inst Independent Study, 61-62, chmn, Joint Prog Lit Studies, 78-81, chmn, Hum Coun, 81-82. **MEMBERSHIPS** MLA; Renaissance Soc Am; Asoc Int Hispanistas; Asoc Int Galdositas. **RESEARCH** Comp lit, the Don Juan theme; Sephardic Spanish; 19th century Spanish lit. **SELECTED PUBLICATIONS** Ed, Pronunciation of Smyrnian Judeo-Spanish 52 & On Almudena and his speech, Nueva Rev Filol Hispanica, 61; El amigo manso, Oxford Univ, 63; Sobre el Krausismo de Galdos, Anales Galdosianos, 68; El crimen de la calle de Fuencarral, Homenaje a Casalduero, 72; Galdos entre cronica y novela, 73 & Galdos y sus santas modernas, 75, Anales Galdosianos; The Catalogues of Don Giovanni and Don Juan Tenorio, Hispano-Italic Studies, 79. **CONTACT ADDRESS** Dept of Romance & Comp Lit, Brandeis Univ, Waltham, MA, 02154.

LIEBERMAN, PHILIP
PERSONAL Born 10/25/1934, Brooklyn, NY, m, 1957, 2 children **DISCIPLINE** COGNITIVE SCIENCE **EDUCATION** Mass Inst Technol, BSEE & MSEE, 58, PhD(ling), 66. **CAREER** Res asst elec eng, Mass Inst Technol, 56-58; phys scientist speech, Air Force Comn Res Labs, 58-67; assoc prof ling & elec eng, Univ Conn, 67-69, prof ling, 69-74; prof ling, Brown Univ, 74-, guest, inst ling, Mass Inst Technol, 67-70; mem staff ling, Haskins Lab, New York, 67-74; prof, George Hazard Crooker Univ, 86-97; Fred M. Seed Prof of Cognitive and Linguistic Sci, 97-. **HONORS AND AWARDS** Fel Am Asn for Advan of Sci (AAAS), 82; Guggenheim Fel, 82; Visiting NATO Prof, 82; Max-Plank Institit fur Psycholinguistik, Neimegen Lectures, 90; Distinguished Lectr, Academia Sinica, Taipei, 91. **MEMBERSHIPS** Acoust Soc Am; Ling Soc Am; MLA; fel Am Anthrop Asn; fel Am Asn Phys Anthrop. **RESEARCH** Speech production and perception; innate mechanisms and linguistic ability; evolution of linguistic ability. **SELECTED PUBLICATIONS** Auth, Intonation, Perception and Language, Mass Inst Technol, 67; Speech of Primates, Mouton, The Hague, 72; Phonetic Ability and Related Anatomy of the Newborn and Adult Human, Neanderthal Man & the Chimpanzee, Am Anthrop, 6/72; On the Origins of Language, Macmillan, 75; Speech Physiology & Acoustic Phonetics, Macmillan, 76; Biology and Evolution of Language, Harvard, 84; Uniquely Human, Harvard, 91; Eve Spoke: Human Language and Human Evolution, Norton, 98; The Functional Language System of the Human Brain, Harvard, 99. **CONTACT ADDRESS** Dept of Cognitive and Ling Sci, Brown Univ, Providence, RI, 02912-1978. **EMAIL** Philip_Lieberman@Brown.edu

LIEBERMAN, STEPHEN JACOB
PERSONAL Born 03/21/1943, Minneapolis, MN **DISCIPLINE** ASSYRIOLOGY, LINGUISTICS **EDUCATION** Univ Minn, BA, 63; Harvard Univ, PhD(Near Eastern lang), 72. **CAREER** From asst prof to assoc prof Near Eastern studies, New York Univ, 71-75; res specialist, Sumerian Dict, Univ Mus, Univ Pa, 76-79; ASSOC PROF ASSYRIOL AND SEMITIC LING, DROPSIE UNIV, 82-, Fel Mesopotamian civilization, Baghdad Ctr Comt, Am Schs Orient Res, 70-71; Nat Endowment for Humanities fel, 75-76; Guggenheim fel, 79-80; Inaugural fel, Found for Mesopotamian Studies, 80- **MEMBERSHIPS** Am Orient Soc; AHA; Archaeol Inst Am; Ling Soc Am; NAm Conf Afro-Asiatic Ling. **RESEARCH** Sumerian and Akkadian languages and cultures; Semitic linguistics; Mesopotamian history. **SELECTED PUBLICATIONS** Auth, Bar Ilan Studies in Assyriology Dedicated to Artzi, Pinhas, J Amer Oriental Soc, Vol 0112, 92. **CONTACT ADDRESS** Dept Assyriol and Semitic Ling, Dropsie Univ, Philadelphia, PA, 19132.

LIGHTFOOT, D.
PERSONAL Born 02/10/1945, Loor, United Kingdom, m, 1982, 4 children **DISCIPLINE** LINGUISTICS **EDUCATION** Univ Mich, PhD, 71. **CAREER** Asst-assoc prof, McGill Univ, 70-78; prof, Univ Utrecht, 78-83; PROF, UNIV MD, 83- . **RESEARCH** Syntax, language change, language acquisition. **SELECTED PUBLICATIONS** Ed with N. Homstern, Explanation of Linguistics: The Logical Problem of Language Acquisition, 81; auth, The Language Lottery: Toward a Biology of Grammar, 82; auth, How to Get Parameters: Arguments from Language Change, 91; ed with N. Homstern, Verb Movement, 94; The Development of Language: Acqisition, Change or Evolution, 98. **CONTACT ADDRESS** Dept Linguist, Univ Md, College Park, MD, 20742. **EMAIL** dlight@deans.umd.edu

LIHANI, JOHN
PERSONAL Born 03/24/1927, Czechoslovakia, m, 1950, 3 children **DISCIPLINE** SPANISH LANGUAGE AND LITERATURE **EDUCATION** Case Western Reserve Univ, BS, 48; Ohio State Univ, MA, 50; Univ Tex, PhD(Romance lang), 54. **CAREER** Asst Span, Tulane Univ, 50-51; instr, Univ Tex, 53-54; from instr to asst prof, Yale Univ, 54-62; assoc prof Romance lang, Univ Pittsburgh, 62-69; PROF SPAN LING AND LIT, UNIV KY, 69-, Morse fel, 60-61; Fulbright prof, Inst Caro y Cuervo, Colombia, 65-66; ed, La Coronica, 72-73; assoc ed, Bull Comediantes, 73-; Int Res and Exchanges Bd res award, 74; Am Philos Soc res award, 77; Am Coun Learned Soc grant, 80. **MEMBERSHIPS** MLA; Am Asn Teachers Span and Port; SAtlantic Mod Lang Asn. **RESEARCH** Romance linguistics; Spanish medieval and classical literature; general linguistics. **SELECTED PUBLICATIONS** Auth, The Unrecognized Precursors of Montemayor 'Diana', Romance Quart, Vol 0040, 93; Polyglotism in the Theater of Lope De Vega, Bull Comediantes, Vol 0045, 93; Calderondelabarca,Pedro, El 'Mayor Monstruo Del Mundo', Bull Comediantes, Vol 0048, 96. **CONTACT ADDRESS** Dept Span and Ital, Univ of Ky, Lexington, KY, 40506.

LILES, BETTY Z.
DISCIPLINE COMMUNICATION SCIENCES **EDUCATION** Lady of the Lake Univ, MA, 68; Univ Minn, PhD, 73. **CAREER** Prof emer, Univ Conn; past Speech and Lang Consult, ACES, North Haven, CT. **RESEARCH** Normal and disordered child language. **SELECTED PUBLICATIONS** Auth, Narrative Discourse in Children with Language Disorders and Children with Normal Language: A Critical Review of the Literature, JSHR, 93; The Measurement of Narrative Discourse in Children with Language Disorders, JSHR, 95. **CONTACT ADDRESS** Dept of Communication Sci, Univ of Connecticut, 1097 Storrs Rd, Storrs, CT, 06269-1085.

LILLO-MARTIN, DIANE C.
DISCIPLINE LINGUISTICS **EDUCATION** Univ Calif, San Diego, PhD. **CAREER** Assoc prof, Univ Conn; dept ch. **RESEARCH** Language acquisition, structure of American Sign Language. **SELECTED PUBLICATIONS** Auth, Universal Grammar and American Sign Language: Setting the Null Argument Parameters, Dordrecht: Kluwer Acad Press, 91; Two Kinds of Null Arguments in American Sign Language, Natural Lang and Ling Theory 4, 86; coauth, Language and Cognition: The View from Sign Language and Deafness, Oxford, UK: Oxford UP, 97; Wh-Movement and the Position of SPEC CP: Evidence from American Sign Language, Lang 73, 97. **CONTACT ADDRESS** Dept of Linguistics, Univ of Connecticut, 1266 Storrs Rd, Storrs, CT, 06269-1085. **EMAIL** lillom@uconnvm.uconn.edu

LILLYMAN, WILLIAM J.
PERSONAL Born 04/17/1937, Sydney, Australia, m, 1962
DISCIPLINE GERMAN COMPARATIVE LITERATURE
EDUCATION Sydney Univ, BA, 59; Stanford Univ, PhD(-
Ger), 64. CAREER Asst prof Ger lit, Stanford Univ, 64-67;
from asst prof to assoc prof, Univ Calif, Santa Cruz, 67-72;
assoc prof and chmn dept, 72-73, PROF GER AND DEAN HU-
MANITIES, 73-82, VICE CHANCELLOR, UNIV CALIF, IR-
VINE, 82-, Humanities res fel, Univ Calif, Irvine, 73; dir, Goe-
the Res Prog, 81- MEMBERSHIPS MLA; Am Asn Teachers
Ger. RESEARCH Nineteenth century German and compara-
tive literature. SELECTED PUBLICATIONS Auth, Com-
plete Works and Letters-Historical Critical Edition, Vol 1,
Works, J Engl and Ger Philol, Vol 0093, 94; Complete Works
and Letters-Historical Critical Edition, Vol 2, Correspondence,
Accounts of Travels, Philological Writings, Das 'Kloster Net-
ley', Commentary by Contemporaries, J Engl and Ger Philol;
Tieck,Ludwig--an Annotated Guide to Research, J Engl and
Ger Philol, Vol 0094, 95. CONTACT ADDRESS Office of
Vice Chancellor, Univ of Calif, Irvine, CA, 92717.

LIMBRICK, ELAINE
DISCIPLINE SIXTEENTH; SEVENTEENTH CENTURY
FRENCH LITERATURE EDUCATION Univ Poitiers, PhD.
RESEARCH Montaigne's literary influence; relationship be-
tween literature and the arts. SELECTED PUBLICATIONS
Auth, Franciscus Sanches, That nothing is known, Cambridge
UP, 88; The use of the vernacular in the popularization of phi-
losophy: Descartes' case, History of European Ideas, Pergamon
Press, 91; Montaigne: metamorphose d'un philosophe en
theologien, Conclusion, Bibliographie, Montaigne Penseur et
Philosophe, Champion, 90; L'ocil du poete: vision ct perspec-
tive dans la poesie francaise de la Renaissance, Etudes lit-
teraires, 87. CONTACT ADDRESS Dept of French, Victoria
Univ, PO Box 3045 STN CSC, Victoria, BC, V8W 3P4.
EMAIL French@uvvm.uvic.ca

LINDSTROM, NAOMI E.
PERSONAL Born 11/21/1950, Chicago, IL DISCIPLINE
LATIN AMERICAN LITERATURE EDUCATION Univ
Chicago, AB, 71; Ariz State Univ, MA, 72, PhD(Span), 74.
CAREER Instr Span, Ariz State Univ, 74-75; asst prof 75-82,
from assoc prof to prof Span & Portuguese, Univ Tex, 82-90;
consult, Women & World Issues Study Group, Washington,
DC, 80-; lit ed, Rocky Mountain Rev Lang & Lit, 80-. MEM-
BERSHIPS Inst Int Lit Iberoam; Latin American Studies Assn;
Latin American Jewish Studies Assn, MLA; Am Asn Teachers
Span & Port. RESEARCH Argentine vanguard literature 1920-
1940; contemporary Argentine literature; ethnic studies. SE-
LECTED PUBLICATIONS Auth, Literary Expression in Ar-
gentina, Ariz State Univ, 77; Macedonio Fernandez and Jacques
Serrida: Co-Visionaries, Rev Ctr Inter Am Rels, 78; Narrative
Garble in Arlt: A study in the conventions of expressionism, Ky
Romance Quart, 79; La elaboracion de un discurso contracultur-
al en las Aguafertes de Arlt, Hisp J, 80; Feminist criticism of
Latin American literature, Latin Am Res Rev, 80; Macedonio
Fernandez, Studies in Span & Span-Am Authors, 81; Echever-
ria to Quiroga, In: The Latin American Short Story, Twayne
Publ, 82; Woman's Voice in Latin American Literature, Three
Continents Press, 89; The Social Conscience of Latin American
Writing, Univ of Texas Press, 98. CONTACT ADDRESS
Dept of Span & Port, Univ of Texas, Austin, TX, 78712-1026.
EMAIL iacfbl@asuvm.inre.asu.edu

LINN, MICHAEL D.
PERSONAL Born 03/07/1936, Aberdeen, SD, m, 1962, 1 child
DISCIPLINE LINGUISTICS, AMERICAN ENGLISH EDU-
CATION Univ Mont, BA, 60, MA, 62; Univ Minn, MA, 70,
PhD(commun), 74. CAREER Instr English, Lamara State Col
of Tech, 63-65; res asst ling, Univ Minn, 68-71 and Cent Midwest Regional Educ Lab, 71-72; from instr to asst prof English,
Va Commonwealth Univ, 72-77; asst prof, 77-80, ASSOC
PROF ENGLISH AND ANTHROP, UNIV MINN, DULUTH,
80-, Consult, Cent Midwest Regional Educ Lab, 72-73, Richmond Pub Sch, 74-75 and Va State Dept of Educ, 74-75; tape
collector, US Dialect Tape Depository, 75-78; reader and consult, Choice, 75-; lectr, Arrowhead Speaker Serv, 78-81; manuscript reader, Halcyon, 78-; res fel, Mass Inst of Technol, 78;
manuscript referee, J Teacher Educ, 79-81. MEMBERSHIPS
NCTE; Am Dialect Soc; MLA; Ling Soc Am; Asn Appl Ling.
RESEARCH American dialects; language variation; the teaching of writing. SELECTED PUBLICATIONS Auth, Papers
From the Special Session in Honor of Professor Sibata, Takesi--
Introduction, Amer Speech, Vol 0071, 96. CONTACT AD-
DRESS English Dept, Univ of Minn, 10 University Dr, Duluth,
MN, 55812-2496.

LINTZ, BERNADETTE C.
DISCIPLINE 19TH-CENTURY FRENCH LITERATURE,
FRENCH THEATER EDUCATION DUEL, License es Let-
tres Modernes, Maitrise d'Anglais Univ de Strasbourg; Rice
Univ, MA, 82, PhD, 84. CAREER Act ch, 95; dir, Dijon Study
Group, 86, 89, 94; instr, Univ IN, Univ Houston, Rice Univ;
assoc prof-. HONORS AND AWARDS Sr Picker research fel,
Colgate Univ, 90; travel grant, Am Coun Learned Societies, 85.
RESEARCH Victor Hugo, Romantic Drama, Emile Zola, nat-
uralism. SELECTED PUBLICATIONS Auth, Victor Hugo:

Oeuvres et critique, 81-83; co-auth, Minard, 92; co-ed, The
French Novel from Lafayette to Desvignes, New Paradigm
Press, 95; Nana: le savoir de l'alcove, The Fr Novel from Lafay-
ette to Desvignes, New Paradigm Press, 95; contrib, Critical
Bibliography of Fr Lit: The XIX Century (Syracuse UP, 91; ar-
ticles, Analecta Husserliana, The Fr Rev, Nineteenth-Century
Fr Studies, Symposium, Travaux de Litterature; rev(s), L'Esprit
Createur, Nineteenth-Century Fr Studies. CONTACT AD-
DRESS Dept of Romance Lang, Colgate Univ, 13 Oak Drive,
Hamilton, NY, 13346. EMAIL blintz@center.colgate.edu

LIPSCHUTZ, ILSE HEMPEL
PERSONAL Born 08/19/1923, Bonnigheim, Germany, m,
1952, 4 children DISCIPLINE FRENCH EDUCATION Inst
Prof Francais a l'Etranger, dipl, 43, Sorbonne, Lic es Let, 43,
dipl Etudes Super, 44; Univ Madrid, dipl Estud Hisp, 45; Har-
vard Univ, MA, 49, PhD, 58. CAREER Teaching fel French
and Span, Harvard Univ and Radcliffe Col, 47-51; instr, 51-58,
asst prof, 58-63, assoc prof, 63-72, prof French, 72-81, AN-
DREW W MELLON PROF HUMANITIES, VASSAR COL,
81-, Chmn Dept, 75-, Am Asn Univ Women fel, 50-51; Anne
Radcliffe fel, 50-51; Vassar Col fac fel, 60-61 and 66-67; US-
Spain Treatise of Friendship res fel, 79-80 and 81. MEMBER-
SHIPS MLA; AAUP; Am Asn Univ Women; Int Soc Fr
Studies; Soc Etudes Romantiques; Soc Theophile Gautier. SE-
LECTED PUBLICATIONS Auth, El despojo de obras de arte
durante la Guerra de Independencia, 61 & El pintor y las poetas,
Goya y los romanticos franceses, summer 68, Arte Espanol;
Spanish Painting and the French Romantics, Harvard Univ, 72,
Span ed, Taurus (Madrid), 88; Victor Hugo, Louis Boulanger,
Francisco de Goya: Amities, affinites, influences, Nineteenth-
Century Fr Studies, fall-winter 75-76; Theophile Gautier, su Es-
pana legendaria y los Caprichos de Goya, Revista de Occidente,
12/76; Theophile Gautier et son Espagne retrouvee dans
l'oeuvre grave de Goya, Bull Soc Theophile Gautier, 80; Ima-
genes y palabras, los franceses ante la pintura espanola, in La
Imagen Romantica de Espana, Madrid, 81; auth, Gautier,
Theophile, Life and Work, 19th-Century Fr Stud, Vol 0026, 97.
CONTACT ADDRESS 11 Park Ave, Poughkeepsie, NY,
12603.

LISKER, LEIGH
PERSONAL Born 12/07/1918, Philadelphia, PA, m, 1947, 3
children DISCIPLINE LINGUISTICS EDUCATION Univ
Pa, BA, 41, MA, 46, PhD(ling), 49. CAREER Asst instr Ger,
47-48; from instr to assoc prof ling and Dravidian ling, 48-64,
chmn dept, 76-80, PROF LING, UNIV PA, 64-, Am Coun
Learned Soc fel, 47-48; Fulbright grant, India, 51-52, 59-60;
RES CONSULT, HASKINS LABS, NY, 53-; vis lectr, Deccan
Col Post-Grad and Res Inst Poona, India, 59-60. MEMBER-
SHIPS Acoust Soc Am. RESEARCH Structural and Dravidian
linguistics; acoustic and physiological phonetics. SELECTED
PUBLICATIONS Auth, Auditory and Visual Cueing of the
Rounded Feature of Vowels, Lang and Speech, Vol 0035, 92;
Studies in General and English Phonetics--Essays in Honor of
Professor Oconnor, J.D., J Ling, Vol 0033, 97. CONTACT
ADDRESS Dept of Ling, Univ of Pa, Philadelphia, PA, 19104.

LITTLE, GRETA D.
PERSONAL Born 12/03/1943, Asheville, NC DISCIPLINE
LINGUISTICS, ENGLISH AS A FOREIGN LANGUAGE
EDUCATION Carleton Col, BA, 65; Univ NC, MA, 69, Ph-
D(ling), 74. CAREER Peace Corps teacher English, Haile Se-
lassie 1st Sch, Ethiopia, 65-67; teaching asst Swahili, Univ NC
and Duke Univ, 72; inst ling, Univ NC, 72-73; Fulbright lectr
English, Cyril and Methodius Univ, Skopje, 73-74; dir English
for Foreign Students, 77-79, ASST PROF ENGLISH AND
LING, UNIV SC, 74-, ASSOC ED, SOUTHEASTERN CONF
LING REV, 77-. MEMBERSHIPS Ling Soc Am; Ling Asn
Can and US; Southeastern Conf Ling; Southern Asn African-
ists; Teachers English to Speakers Other Lang. RESEARCH
Syntactic change; African languages. SELECTED PUBLICA-
TIONS Auth, Teaching and Research Language in African
Classrooms, Mod Lang J, Vol 0079, 95; Fern, Fanny, Legacy,
Vol 0012, 95; Dodge, Mary, Mapes, Legacy, Vol 0012, 95.
CONTACT ADDRESS English Dept, Univ of SC, Columbia,
SC, 29208.

LLOYD, CARYL
DISCIPLINE FRENCH LITERATURE EDUCATION Univ
Iowa, PhD. SELECTED PUBLICATIONS Auth, pubs on
eighteenth and nineteenth century literature, French women
writers, and Leona Queyrouze. CONTACT ADDRESS Dept
Foreign Languages and Literature, State Univ of West Georgia,
Carrollton, GA, 30118.

LLOYD, PAUL M.
PERSONAL Born 09/15/1929, Rochester, NY, m, 1952, 2
children DISCIPLINE ROMANCE PHILOLOGY EDUCA-
TION Oberlin Col, AB, 52; Brown Univ, AM, 54; Univ Calif,
Berkeley, PhD, 60. CAREER Teaching asst Span, Brown
Univ, 52-54 & Univ Calif, 54-58; instr, Dartmouth Col, 58-60
& Ling Sci Romance Lang, Sch Lang, Foreign Serv inst, 60-61;
from asst prof to assoc prof, 61-70, prof Romance Lang, Univ
PA, 70-, assoc ed, Hisp Rev, 65-; Fulbright lectr English, Univ
Deusto, Spain, 66-67. HONORS AND AWARDS John Fred-
erick Lewis Award from American Philosophical Society, 88.

MEMBERSHIPS Ling Soc Am; Am Asn Teachers Span &
Port; Soc Ling Romane; Ling Asn Can & US; Sci Fiction Res
Asn. RESEARCH Romance philology; general and Spanish
linguistics. SELECTED PUBLICATIONS Auth, Verb-
complement Compounds in Spanish, Max Niemeyer, Tubingen,
68; L'action du substrat et la structure linguistique, In: Actele
celui de-al XII-les Congres International de Linguistica si
Filologie Romanica, 1968, 71; Contribucion al estudio del tema
de Don Juan en las comedias de Tirso de Molina, In: Homenaje
al Prof William L Fichter, 71; coauth, A Graded Spanish Review Grammar with Composition, Prentice-Hall, 73; auth, La
metafonia vocalica y el sistema verbal romanico, In: Proceedings of the 14th International Congress of Romance Linguistics
and Philology, Amsterdam, Benjamins, 77; On the definition of
Vulgar Latin, Neuphilogische Mitteilungen, 79; From Latin to
Spanish, American Philosophical Society, 87, Spanish translation: Del Latin al espanol, 93. CONTACT ADDRESS Dept of
Romance Lang, Univ of Pennsylvania, Philadelphia, PA,
19104-6305.

LLOYD, ROSEMARY
DISCIPLINE FRENCH LITERATURE EDUCATION Cam-
bridge Univ, PhD, 78. CAREER Prof. SELECTED PUBLI-
CATIONS Auth, Baudelaire: The Prose Poems and La Fanfar-
lo, 91; The Lost Content of Childhood: Representations of
Children and Childhood in Nineteenth-Century France, 92;
George Sand: The Master Piper, 94; Closer and Closer Apart:
Jealousy in Literature, 95; Revolutions in Writing: Nineteenth-
Century French Prose, 96. CONTACT ADDRESS Dept of
French and Italian, Indiana Univ, Bloomington, 300 N Jordan
Ave, Bloomington, IN, 47405.

LO, CHIN-TANG
PERSONAL Born 07/27/1929, Lungsi, China, m, 1959 DIS-
CIPLINE CHINESE EDUCATION Nat Taiwan Univ, BA,
52, MA, 56, LittD, 61. CAREER Assoc prof, New Asian Col,
Chinese Univ Hong Kong, 60-61; lectr, Univ Hong Kong, 61-
66; assoc prof, 66-70, Prof Chinese, Univ Hawaii, Manoa, 71-;
Vis prof, Univ Hamburg, 72-73, Nat Taiwan Univ, 79-80; Chair
Prof of Tung-Hai Univ, 86-87. SELECTED PUBLICA-
TIONS Auth, An introduction to the literary value of Confucian
classics, 67; The development of Chinese fiction, 68; translr,
Early Chinese Literature, B Watson, 69; Clues leading to the
discovery of Hsi Yu Chi Ping-hua, 69; Popular stories of Wei
and Chin period, 71; Goethe and the novels of Ming Dynasty,
73; Chinese point of view to drama, 73; On Classical Chinese
drama, 77; Chinese Study and Sinology, 79; The Development
of Chinese Drama, 80. CONTACT ADDRESS Dept of East
Asian Lang & Lit, Univ of Hawaii, Manoa, 1890 E West Rd,
Honolulu, HI, 96822-2318.

LOCKE, JOHN
DISCIPLINE COMPARATIVE LITERATURE EDUCA-
TION Univ Iowa, PhD. CAREER English and Lit, Univ Ark.
HONORS AND AWARDS Dir, Comp Lit. SELECTED
PUBLICATIONS Transl, Nine Plays by Rainer Maria Rilke,
Ungar, 79. CONTACT ADDRESS Univ Ark, Fayetteville,
AR, 72701.

LOCKHART, PHILIP N.
PERSONAL Born 05/03/1928, Smicksburg, PA, m, 1959, 2
children DISCIPLINE CLASSICAL STUDIES EDUCA-
TION Univ Pa, BA, 50; Univ NC, MA, 51; Yale Univ, PhD(-
classical lang), 59. CAREER Teacher, Ezel Mission Sch, Ky,
51-52; instr class lang, Univ Mo, 54-56; instr class studies, Univ
Pa, 57-61, asst prof, 61-63; assoc prof class lang and chmn dept,
63-68, prof, 68-71, ASBURY J CLARKE PROF LATIN and
CHMN DEPT, DICKINSON COL, 71- Vis prof, Ohio State
Univ, 69-70. HONORS AND AWARDS Ganoe Award Teach-
ing, Dickinson Col, 69, 73. MEMBERSHIPS Am Philol Asn;
Archaeol Inst Am; Am Class League; Vergilian Soc Am. RE-
SEARCH Latin poetry; fourth century AD; Homeric back-
ground. SELECTED PUBLICATIONS Auth, Moser, Mary,
E. 1950-1996--in Memoriam, Class World, Vol 0089, 96.
CONTACT ADDRESS Dept of Class Lang, Dickinson Col,
Carlisle, PA, 17013.

LOEWEN, LYNN
DISCIPLINE SPANISH LANGUAGE EDUCATION Univ
Wis, BA, MA, PhD. CAREER Languages, Carthage Col. SE-
LECTED PUBLICATIONS Area: teaching English as a sec-
ond language. CONTACT ADDRESS Carthage Col, 2001 Al-
ford Dr., Kenosha, WI, 53140. EMAIL loewen@carthage.edu

LOFSTEDT, BENGT
PERSONAL Born 11/14/1931, Lund, Sweden, m, 1961, 4 chil-
dren DISCIPLINE LATIN EDUCATION Univ Uppsala, MA,
54, Phil lic, 57, PhD(Latin), 61. CAREER Asst prof Latin,
Univ Uppsala, 62-67; assoc prof, 67-68, PROF MEDIEVAL
LATIN, UNIV CALIF, LOS ANGELES, 68- Alexander von
Humbolt-Stiftung fel, 61-62; Univ Calif fel, Humanities Inst, 68
and 72; Am Coun Learned Soc grant, 72. MEMBERSHIPS
Am Philol Asn; Soc Etudes Latines; Indoger Ges. RESEARCH
History of the Latin language, with emphasis on the later peri-
ods; medieval Latin grammarians; patristics. SELECTED
PUBLICATIONS Auth, Notes on Archaic Latin, Maia-Rivista

Di Letterature Classiche, Vol 0044, 92; Gleanings .6. Miscellaneous Notes on Late Latin Grammar and Lexicography, Maia-Rivista Di Letterature Classiche, Vol 0045, 93; Latin Romance Noun + Verb Compounds and the Origin of Romance Verb Completion Compounds, Zeitschrift fur Romanische Philol, Vol 0110, 94; Late Antique and Early Medieval Latin, Latomus, Vol 0053, 94; Diversions of Galway--Papers on the History of Linguistics, Word-J Int Ling Asn, Vol 0046, 95; Lever,Firmin Latin-French Dictionary, Romance Philol, Vol 0049, 96; Etymology, Word-J Int Ling Asn, Vol 0047, 96; Notes on the Latest Edition of the 'Martyrologium' of Maurus, Rabanus, Aevum Rassegna Di Scienze Storiche Linguistiche E Filologiche, Vol 0071, 97; Vulgar Latin, Late Latin Iv--Proc 4th Int-Congress on Vulgar and Late Latin Caen, September 2-5 1994, Romance Philol, Vol 0051, 97; Problems in the 'Testamentum Porcelli' + Proposed Translations of Obscure Words in the Late Latin Parody, Aevum Rassegna Di Scienze Storiche Linguistiche E Filologiche, Vol 0071, 97. **CONTACT ADDRESS** Dept of Classics, Univ of Calif, 405 Hilgard Ave, Los Angeles, CA, 90024.

LOGAN, PAUL ELLIS
PERSONAL Born 10/05/1945, Washington, DC **DISCIPLINE** GERMAN LANGUAGE & LITERATURE **EDUCATION** Howard Univ, BA, 66; Univ Md, MA, 70, PhD(Ger), 74. **CAREER** Instr German, Univ Md, 69-73; assoc prof, Morgan State Univ, 73-77; chm dept Ger/Russian, Howard Univ, 77-, assoc dean humanities, Col of Arts and Sci, 91-. **HONORS AND AWARDS** Faculty res grant, Morgan State Univ, 76; Fulbright scholar, 76 & 82; German Acad Exchange Serv fel, 79 & 81; Distinguished Alumni Award from Nat Asn for Equal Opportunity in Educ. **MEMBERSHIPS** Col Lang Asn; Mod Lang Asn; Frobenius-Gesellschaft; Am Asn Teachers Ger; Afrika-Gesellschaft. **RESEARCH** German Africa travelogs of the 16th and 17th century; American Slavery as a theme in German literature of the 18th and 19th century. **SELECTED PUBLICATIONS** Auth, Gottfried Finckelthaus Rediscovered, CLA J, 75; Leo Frobenius and Negritude, Negro Hist Bull, 78; Leo Frobenius: The Demonic Child, CLA J, 78: transl, The Sign and the Sense(Le signe et le sens-Der Sinn und das Mittel), CLA J, 78; Leo Frobenius, Negritude and the Escape of Caliban, In: Festschrift for Leon-Gontran Damas, 79; The Image of the Black in J LE Kolb's Erzahlungen von den Sitten und Schicksalen der Negersklaven, Monatshefte, 81; J E Kolb's Der Neger Makandal, Negro Hist Bull, 81; A Howard Reader: An Intellectual and Cultural Quilt of the African-American Experience, Houghton Mifflin, 97. **CONTACT ADDRESS** Office of the Dean, Col of Arts and Sci, Howard Univ, 2400 6th St N W, Washington, DC, 20059-0002.

LOHRLI, ANNE
PERSONAL Born 02/09/1906, Bake Oven, OR **DISCIPLINE** ENGLISH LANGUAGE AND LITERATURE **EDUCATION** Occidental Col, AB, 27, AM, 28; Columbia Univ, AM, 32; Univ Southern Calif, PhD, 37. **CAREER** Res and collaboration, 27-37; teacher, Los Angeles City Schs, 38-45; prof, 45-65, EMER PROF ENGLISH, N MEX HIGHLANDS UNIV, 65-, Vis prof, Univ Trieste, 54. **MEMBERSHIPS** MLA. **RESEARCH** Victorian periodicals. **SELECTED PUBLICATIONS** Auth, Fresh Fields and Pastures New + Misquoting Milton Line From 'Lycidas', Notes and Queries, Vol 0041, 94; The Divine Williams--Query, Notes and Queries, Vol 0044, 97. **CONTACT ADDRESS** New Mexico Highlands Univ, 790 Baylor Ave, Claremont, CA, 91711.

LOMBA, ARTHUR J.
DISCIPLINE FRENCH **EDUCATION** Eastern Nazarene Col, BA; Am Univ, MA; Boston Univ, PhD. **CAREER** Eng Dept, Eastern Nazarene Col **RESEARCH** Cult and hist of the Cape Verde Islands; Cape Verde immigrants; Cape Verdean Crioulo (CVC) lang. **SELECTED PUBLICATIONS** Auth, Basic CVC Pedagogical Grammar. **CONTACT ADDRESS** Eastern Nazarene Col, 23 East Elm Ave, Quincy, MA, 02170-2999.

LOMBARDO, STANLEY
DISCIPLINE GREEK AND LATIN LITERATURE **EDUCATION** Loyola Univ, BA; Tulane Univ, MA; Univ TX, PhD, 76. **CAREER** Dept ch; prof, Univ KS. **HONORS AND AWARDS** Kemper tchg fel; Nat Transl Ctr award. **RESEARCH** Transl of Homer's Odyssey. **SELECTED PUBLICATIONS** Transl, Greek poetry, including Homer's Iliad, Hackett, 97; Hesiod's Works & Daysand Theogony, Hackett, 93; Aratus' Phaenomena, N Atlantic, 82; Parmenides and Empedocles, The Fragments in Verse Translation, Grey Fox, 79; Horace's Odes in Latin Lyric and Elegiac Poetry, Garland, 95; Tao Te Ching, Hackett, 93; co-transl, Callimachus' Hymns, Epigrams & Select Fragments, Johns Hopkins, 88. **CONTACT ADDRESS** Dept of Class, Univ Kansas, Admin Building, Lawrence, KS, 66045. **EMAIL** LOMBARDO@KUHUB.CC.UKANS.EDU

LONEY, GLENN MEREDITH
PERSONAL Born 12/24/1928, Sacramento, CA **DISCIPLINE** THEATRE & SPEECH **EDUCATION** Univ Calif, Berkeley, AB, 50; Univ Wis-Madison, MA, 51; Stanford Univ, PhD, 54. **CAREER** Instr, 55-56, San Francisco State Col; instr, 56, Univ Nev, Las Vegas; lectr, Europe, 56-59, Univ Md; instr, 59-61, Hofstra Univ; from asst prof to assoc prof, 61-70, prof, 70-, Brooklyn Col; prof, 70-, emeritus prof, 91, Grad Ctr, CUNY; hon fel, 60, Am Scand Found. **MEMBERSHIPS** Am Theatre Assn; Am Soc Theatre Res; Theatre Libr Assocs; Int Fed Theatre Res; Theatre Hist Soc; AAUP; Am Music Critics Assn, Am Theatre Critics Assn; Drama Desk; Outer Critics Circle; Muni Art Soc NY; Phi Beta Kappa; Alpha Mu Gamma, Phi Eta Sigma, Phi Delta Phi. **RESEARCH** Opera as theatre; preservation of historic theatres; dance theatre. **SELECTED PUBLICATIONS** Auth, Your Future in the Performing Arts, Rosen, 80; The House of Mirth-the Play of the Novel, Assoc Univ Presses, 81; auth, 20th Century Theatre, Facts on File, 82; auth, California Gold Rush Drama, Musical Theatre in America, 84; auth, Creating Careers in Music Theatre, 88; auth, Staging Shakespeare, 90; auth, Peter Brrok: Oxford To Orghast, 98; ed, Art Deco News & The Modernist, 81-94; chief corresp, New York Theatre - Wire, NY Museum Wire, online, 96. **CONTACT ADDRESS** 3 E 71st St, New York, NY, 10021.

LOPEZ, IGNACIO JAVIER
PERSONAL Born 02/25/1956, Galdakao, Spain, m, 1979, 3 children **DISCIPLINE** ROMANCE LANGUAGES **EDUCATION** Instituto Simancas, Madrid, Spain, Bachilerato, 73; Universidad Autonoma, Madrid, Spain, Licenciado, 79; Univ of Wi Madison, PhD, 84. **CAREER** Asst prof to assoc prof, Univ Va, 84-90; assoc prof to prof to dept chair, 90- . **HONORS AND AWARDS** Book rev ed, Hispanic Review, 90-97; gen ed, Hispanic Review, 97- ; Ed Bd, Siglo XIX, Univ Valladolid, Spain, Dialogos, Univ Amsterdam, Netherlands., Colaborador Universitario, Univ Autonoma, Madrid, Spain, 76; Knapp Fel, Univ Wi, 83-84. **MEMBERSHIPS** MLA; NEMLA; Asociacion Internacional de Hispanistas. **RESEARCH** Modern period; Spanish lit; hist of ideas; aesthetics; lit theory. **SELECTED PUBLICATIONS** Auth, Caballero de novela, Barcelona, 86; Realismo y ficcion, Barcelona, 89; Galdos y el arte de la prosa, Barcelona, 93; ed, La madre Naturaleza, Madrid, 92; Jardin cerrado, Malaga, 95; Dibujo de la muerte, Madrid, 98; Homenaje a Russell P. Sebold, Alicante, 99. **CONTACT ADDRESS** Dept of Romance Languages, Univ of Pa, Philadelphia, PA, 19104. **EMAIL** ijlopez@yahoo.com; ilopez@sas.upenn.edu

LORBE, RUTH ELISABETH
PERSONAL Born 05/02/1925, Nuremberg, Germany **DISCIPLINE** MODERN GERMAN LITERATURE **EDUCATION** Univ Erlangen, PhD, 52. **CAREER** Student Raetin Ger, hist and English, intermediate sch, Nuremberg, 52-54, 55-60 and 62-64; lectr Ger, Univ Col North Staffordshire, 54-55; from instr to assoc prof, 60-72, PROF GER, UNIV ILL, URBANA, 72-. **MEMBERSHIPS** MLA; Am Asn Teachers Ger; Am Comp Lit Asn; Hofmannsthal-Gesellschaft; Int Brecht Soc. **RESEARCH** Children's songs, especially nursery rhymes; modern German poetry; German literataure after 1850. **SELECTED PUBLICATIONS** Auth, Hofmannsthal or the Geometry of the Subject--Psychostructural and Iconographic Studies on the Prose Works, J Engl and Ger Philol, Vol 0092, 93; Morike Muses--Critical Essays on Morike, Eduard, Ger Rev, Vol 0069, 94; Carossa, Hans--13 Essays on his Works, J Engl and Ger Philol, Vol 0095, 96. **CONTACT ADDRESS** Dept of Ger Lang and Lit, Univ of Ill, Urbana, IL, 61801.

LORE, ANTHONY GEORGE
PERSONAL Born 02/21/1922, Cleveland, OH, m, 1 child **DISCIPLINE** ROMANCE LANGUAGES **EDUCATION** La State Univ, BA, 48, MA, 49; Univ NC, PhD(Romance lang), 65. **CAREER** ASSOC PROF SPAN AND METHODOL AND DIR LANG LAB, UNIV NC, CHAPEL HILL, 60-. **MEMBERSHIPS** Am Asn Teachers Span and Port; MLA; Nat Asn Lang Lab Dir, NEA; Nat Soc Prog Instr. **CONTACT ADDRESS** Univ of NC, 105 Dey Hall, Chapel Hill, NC, 27514.

LORENZI, PAOLA G.
DISCIPLINE ITALIAN LITERATURE **EDUCATION** Col Edu Univ Florence, PhD, 81;post grad studies, Art Ctr Col Design Pasadena, Calif. **CAREER** Asst prof, CA State Univ; vis asst prof, Texas A&M Univ; instr, Univ Houston, Col Arch; vis lectr, 89-. **RESEARCH** Hist of Italian Cinema **SELECTED PUBLICATIONS** Auth, Commercial Terminology for the Oil & Gas Industry, Agip Petroleum Company, Inc, 87; transl, The Rose of Yesterday, Alessandro Carrera, Rev Contemp Fiction, 92; The Prodigal Son, Alessandro Carrera, SW Lit Arts Coun, 88. **CONTACT ADDRESS** Dept of Commun, Pepperdine Univ, 24255 Pacific Coast Hwy, Malibu, CA, 90263. **EMAIL** plorenzi@pepperdine.edu

LOSEFF, LEV V.
DISCIPLINE RUSSIAN LANGUAGE **EDUCATION** Univ MI, PhD. **CAREER** Prof, Dartmouth Col. **RESEARCH** 19th and 20th century Russ prose and poetry. **SELECTED PUBLICATIONS** Auth, On the Beneficence of Censorship: Aesopian Language in Modern Russian Literature, Poetika Brodskogo, three collections of poetry in Rus; co-ed, Brodsky's Poetics and Aesthetics; A Sense of Place: Tsarskoe Selo and Its Poets. **CONTACT ADDRESS** Dartmouth Col, 44 N College St, #208, Hanover, NH, 03755-1801. **EMAIL** lev.loseff@dartmouth.edu

LOTT, ROBERT EUGENE
PERSONAL Born 11/30/1926, Miami, FL, m, 1954 **DISCIPLINE** SPANISH, ROMANCE STYLISTICS **EDUCATION** Athens Col, AB, 51; Univ Ala, MA, 52; Cath Univ Am, PhD, 58. **CAREER** Teaching asst, Univ Ala, 51-52; instr, Cath Univ Am, 52-56, teaching asst, 56-58; from asst prof to assoc prof Span, Univ Ga, 58-66; assoc prof mod Span, 66-68, assoc mem ctr advan studies, 72, PROF MOD SPAN LIT, UNIV ILL, URBANA, 68- **MEMBERSHIPS** MLA; Am Asn Teachers Span and Port; Midwest Mod Lang Asn. **RESEARCH** Modern and Contemporary Spanish literature; Romance stylistics; the modern novel. **SELECTED PUBLICATIONS** Auth, Wild about Sarah + Vaughn,Sarah Classic Interview, Down Beat, Vol 0064, 97. **CONTACT ADDRESS** Dept Foreign Lang, Univ of Ill, Urbana, IL, 61801.

LOUDEN, BRUCE
DISCIPLINE COMPARATIVE LITERATURE **EDUCATION** Univ Calif Berkeley, PhD, 90. **CAREER** Viss asst prof, Univ Wis Madison, 90-91; asst prof, Univ Tex El Paso, 91-97; assoc prof, Univ Tex El Paso, 97-. **MEMBERSHIPS** Am Philol Asn; Classical Asn of the Midwest and South. **RESEARCH** Epic Poetry; Greek Literature; Latin Literature; English Literature; Sanskrit Literature; Indo-European Linguistics and Poetics; Bible Studies. **SELECTED PUBLICATIONS** Auth, Categories of Homeric Wordplay, Transactions of the Am Philol asn, 95; Epeios, Odysseus, and the Inod-European Metaphor for Poet, J of Indo-European Studies, 96; A Narrative Technique in Beowulf and Homeric Epic, Oral Tradition, 96; Milton and the Appropriation of a Homeric narrative Technique, Classical and Modern Lit, 96; Eumaios, Alkinoos: The Audience and the Odyssey, Phoenix, 97; Bacchylides 17: Theseus and Indo-Iranian Apam Napat, J of Indo-European Studies, forthcoming; The Odyssey: Structure, Narration, and Meaning, 99. **CONTACT ADDRESS** Univ of Tex, 136 Liberal Arts, El Paso, TX, 79968-0531. **EMAIL** blouden@mail.utep.edu

LOUNSBURY, RICHARD CECIL
PERSONAL Born 01/03/1949, Yorkton, SK, Canada **DISCIPLINE** CLASSICAL LANGUAGES, CLASSICAL TRADITION, AMERICAN INTELLECTUAL HISTORY **EDUCATION** Univ Calgary, BA, 70; Univ Tex, Austin, MA, 72, PhD(classics), 79. **CAREER** Lectr classics, Univ Witwatersrand, 79-81; asst prof, Univ Victoria, 81-82; Prof Classics & Comp Lit, Brigham Young Univ, 82- **MEMBERSHIPS** Am Philol Asn; Class Asn Can; Am Comp Lit Asn; Int Soc Hist Rhetoric. **RESEARCH** Roman literature of the early Empire; classical rhetoric; intellectual history of the American South. **SELECTED PUBLICATIONS** Auth, The death of Domitius in the Pharsalia, Trans Am Philol Asn, 75; History and motive in book seven of Lucan's Pharsalia, Hermes, 76; Restoring the generous past: Recent books of rhetoric and criticism, Mich Quart Rev, 79; contribr, Intellectual Life in Antebellum Charleston, Tennessee, 86; auth, The Arts of Suetonius: An Introduction, peter Lang, 87; ed, Louisa S. McCord: Political and Social Essays, Univ Press of Virginia, 95; ed, Louisa S. McCord: Poems, Drama, Biography, Letters, Univ Press of Virginia, 96; ed, Louisa S. McCord: Selected Writings, Univ Press of Virginia, 97. **CONTACT ADDRESS** Dept of Humanities Classics & Comp Lit, Brigham Young Univ, 3010 Jhkb, Provo, UT, 84602-0002. **EMAIL** richard_lounsbury@byu.edu

LOVE, FREDERICK RUTAN
PERSONAL Born 02/20/1927, Brooklyn, NY **DISCIPLINE** GERMAN LANGUAGE AND LITERATURE **EDUCATION** Yale Univ, AB, 49, PhD, 58; Univ Calif, Berkeley, MA, 51. **CAREER** From instr to asst prof, 56-64, assoc prof, 64-80, PROF GER, BROWN UNIV, 80-. **MEMBERSHIPS** MLA; Am Asn Teachers Ger. **RESEARCH** Nineteenth and 20th century German literature, especially the drama; Nietzsche. **SELECTED PUBLICATIONS** Auth, Die 'Reise Nach Triest', World Lit Today, Vol 0066, 92; Grunes Grunes Grab, World Lit Today, Vol 0067, 93; Shalamuns Papiere, World Lit Today, Vol 0067, 93; Wessis in Weimar, Szenen Aus Einem Besetzten Land, World Lit Today, Vol 0068, 94; Julia Oder Der Weg Zur Macht, World Lit Today, Vol 0069, 95; Der 'Junge Mit Den Blutigen Schuhen', World Lit Today, Vol 0070, 96. **CONTACT ADDRESS** Dept of Ger, Brown Univ, Box E, Providence, RI, 02912.

LOVELADY, EDGAR JOHN
PERSONAL Born 11/12/1937, Grand Rapids, MI, m, 1958, 2 children **DISCIPLINE** ENGLISH, GREEK **EDUCATION** Toronto Bible Col, dipl bible, 58; Grace Col, BA, 60; Grace Theol Sem, MDiv, 63; St Francis Col, MA, 66; Purdue Univ, PhD(English), 74; Grace Theol Sem, ThM, 76. **CAREER** Teacher English, W Noble Sch Corp, 63-66; Prof English & Greek, Grace Col, 66-. **HONORS AND AWARDS** Alva J McClain Award, Grace Col, 75; Distinguished Alumnus, 75; Delta Epsilon Chi; Phi Kappa Phi; Int Who's Who in Educ. **MEMBERSHIPS** MLA; Ind Coun of Teachers of English. **RESEARCH** Old English grammar; Greek grammar. **SELECTED PUBLICATIONS** Auth, The Logos concept in John 1:1, Grace J, spring 63; The rise of Silas Lapham as problem novel, Ind English J, 73-74. **CONTACT ADDRESS** Grace Col, 200 Seminary Dr., Box 397, Winona Lake, IN, 46590-1294. **EMAIL** lovelaej@grace.edu

LOWELL MAXWELL, DAVID
DISCIPLINE ANATOMY AND PHYSIOLOGY OF SPEECH AND HEARING **EDUCATION** Southern IL Univ, BS, MS, PhD. **CAREER** Emerson Col. **MEMBERSHIPS** Boston Naval Hosp; Depart Behav Neurology Eunice Kennedy Shriver Ctr, Mass Gener Hospital; Craniofacial Study Gp; Harvard Med Sch; Boston Univ Medic Sch; Boston Univ Grad Sch Dental Med; Instit Correction Facial Deformities; Univ Hospital; New England Med Ctr; Cognitive Behav Assessment Unit Douglas Thom Clinic. **SELECTED PUBLICATIONS** Auth, Research and Statistical Meghods in Communication Disorders, Maxwell & Satake, 97; Theory of Probability for Clinical Diagnostic Testing, Satake & Maxwell, 93. **CONTACT ADDRESS** Emerson Col, 100 Beacon Street, Boston, MA, 02116-1596.

LOWENSTAM, STEVEN
PERSONAL Born 12/14/1945, Springfield, IL **DISCIPLINE** CLASSICAL LANGUAGES **EDUCATION** Univ Chicago, BA, 67; Harvard Univ, MA, 69, PhD(classics), 75. **CAREER** Asst prof, 75-81, ASSOC PROF CLASSICS, UNIV ORE, 81-. **MEMBERSHIPS** Am Philol Asn; Archaeol Inst Am; Philol Asn PACIFIC Coast. **RESEARCH** Archaic epic; literary criticism; glyptics. **SELECTED PUBLICATIONS** Auth, The Uses of Vase Depictions in Homeric Studies, Transactions of the Amer Philol Asn, Vol 0122, 92; The Dialogs of Plato, Vol 2, 'Symposium', Class World, Vol 0086, 92; The Arming of Achilleus on Early Greek Vases, Class Antiquity, Vol 0012, 93; Is Literary Criticism an Illegitimate Discipline--a Fallacious Argument in Plato 'Ion', Ramus Critical Studies in Greek and Roman Literature, Vol 0022, 93; The Pictures on Junos Temple in the 'Aeneid', Class World, Vol 0087, 93; Homer, the 'Odyssey', Class World, Vol 0088, 94; Sympotica, a Symposium on the Symposion, Class World, Vol 0087, 94; The 'Odyssey' of Homer, Class World, Vol 0088, 94; The 'Odyssey', an Epic of Return, Class World, Vol 0088, 94; Vatican 35617 and Iliad 16, Amer J Archaeol, Vol 0098, 94; The Bending of the Bow, Class World, Vol 0090, 97; Blood and Iron--Stories and Storytelling in Homer 'Odyssey', Class World, Vol 0090, 97. **CONTACT ADDRESS** Dept of Classics, Univ of Ore, Eugene, OR, 97403-1205.

LOWRIE, JOYCE OLIVER
PERSONAL Born 12/16/1936, Curitiba, Brazil, m, 1959, 1 child **DISCIPLINE** ROMANCE LANGUAGES **EDUCATION** Baylor Univ, BA, 57; Yale Univ, PhD, 66. **CAREER** Asst prof, 66-71, assoc prof, 71-77, PROF FRENCH, WESLEYAN UNIV, 77-. **MEMBERSHIPS** Am Asn Teachers Fr. **SELECTED PUBLICATIONS** Auth, The Mirror and the Flesh--Decadent Narcissism in Lorrain, Jean Le 'Crapaud', 19th-Century Fr Stud, Vol 0024, 95; The Art of Short Fiction According to Lorrain, Jean, 19th-Century Fr Stud, Vol 0025, 96. **CONTACT ADDRESS** Dept of Romance Lang, Wesleyan Univ, Middletown, CT, 06459.

LUCHTING, WOLFGANG ALEXANDER
PERSONAL Born 09/29/1927, Muenchen, Germany **DISCIPLINE** GERMAN, SPANISH **EDUCATION** Univ Munich, Dr phil(Am studies), 56. **CAREER** Lectr mod Ger lit, San Marcos Univ and Cath Univ, Lima, Peru, 61-62; asst prof Ger, Antioch Col, 62-64, Goethe-Inst, Radolfszell and Berlin, Ger, 64-65, asst prof Ger and Span, Univ Mo, St Louis, 65-66; assoc prof, 66-70, PROF SPAN AND GER, WASH STATE UNIV, 70-, Lectr, Inst Raul Porras Barrenechea, Lima, Peru, 65-, San Marcos Univ, Lima, 66, Oficina Difusion Cult Pres Chile, Santiago, 67, Galeria Cult y Libertad, Lima, 67, Univ Educ, Peru, 67, 68, Agrarian Univ, Peru, 68 and Inst Cult Las Condes, Santiago, Chile, 68; Soc Sci Res Coun grant, 70-71. **MEMBERSHIPS** Am Asn Teachers Span and Port; Inst Int lit Latino-am; MLA. **RESEARCH** American literature, especially North; modern Latin American literature; modern German literature. **SELECTED PUBLICATIONS** Auth, Bobby Estuvo Aqui, World Lit Today, Vol 0066, 92. **CONTACT ADDRESS** Dept of Foreign Lang and Lit, Wash State Univ, Pullman, WA, 99164.

LUCIANI, FREDERICK
DISCIPLINE LATIN AMERICAN LITERATURE OF THE COLONIAL PERIOD, NINETEENTH AND TWENTIETH **EDUCATION** Rutgers Univ, BA, 72-76; Yale Univ, MA, 76-77, PhD, 77-82. **CAREER** Dir, Vassar-Wesleyan-Colgate prog, Spain, 94; dept ch, 91-92, 94, 96-; ch, assoc prof-. **HONORS AND AWARDS** NEH fel, 95; res fel, Am Coun of Learned Soc, 84; summer res fel, Cornell Univ, 87; Picker res fel, 88., Res assoc, Ctr Latin Am Studies, Univ CA, Berkley, 91; ed bd, Latin Am Lit Rev, 90-96; Colonial Latin-Am Rev, 1995-. **MEMBERSHIPS** Mem, Mod Lang Assn Comm Prof Employment, 96-97. **SELECTED PUBLICATIONS** Auth, The Man in the Car/in the Trees/behind the Fence: From Cortazar's 'Blow-Up' to Stone's JFK, anthology of critical essays on Julio Cortazar, Cambridge UP, 97; Spanish American Theatre of the Colonial Period and Spanish American Theatre of the Eighteenth Century, The Cambridge History of Latin American Literature, vol 1, Cambridge UP, 96; articles, Colonial Latin Am rev, Discurso Literario, Latin American Lit Rev, Bulletin of Hisp Studies, Romance Quart, Revista Iberoamericana, Hisp Jour, Texto Cretico; rev(s), NY Times Bk Rev; Hispanofila; Colonial Latin Am Rev; Revista Iberoamericana, Boleten de la Biblioteca Menendez Pelayo. **CONTACT ADDRESS** Dept of Romance Lang, Colgate Univ, 13 Oak Drive, Hamilton, NY, 13346. **EMAIL** fluciani@center.colgate.edu

LUDWINOWSKI, RETT R.
PERSONAL Born 11/06/1943, Skawina, Poland, m, 1995, 2 children **DISCIPLINE** COMPARATIVE AND LITERATURE LAW **EDUCATION** Jagiellonian Univ, Cracow, Poland, MA (law), 66, D Phil (law), 71, grad studies in law, post of legal counsellor, 73, post doctorate degree in law, habiliation, 76; **CAREER** Asst to the chair of Hist of Political Ideas, Inst of Political Science, Jagiellonian Univ, 66-67, sr lect, 67-71, adjunct prof, 71-76, asst prof, 76-81, chmn, Div of Business, 76-81, chmn, Div of Law, 80-81, assoc prof of Law, 81, supervisor, chair of Hist of Legal and Political Ideas, 81, holder of chair of the Hist of Legal and Political Ideas, 81; sr fel, Marguerite Eyer Wilbur Found, 82; vis prof of Political Science, Elizabethtown Col, PA, spring 82; vis scholar, The Hoover Inst, Stanford Univ, 83; vis prof of Politics, Alfred Univ, fall 83; vis prof of Politics, Cath Univ Am, 84; vis prof Law, Cath Univ Am, 84-85; prof of Law, 85, tenured, 86, dir, Cath Univ of Am Int Business and Trade summer prog in Poland, dir, Comparative and International Law Institute, Cath Univ Am Law School, 87-; vis scholar, Max-Planck-Inst, fall 90; Sr Fulbright Scholar, Jagiellonian Univ, 97. **HONORS AND AWARDS** Sr fel, Marguerite Eyer Wilbur Found, residential; Hoover Inst grant as vis scholar, summer 82; vis prof with grant from Earhart Found, Cath Univ of Am, 84; res grants from the following: Earhart Found, 87, 88, 91-92; Wilbur Found, 87, 89; Rosenstiel Found, 89, 90; Bartory Found, 90; Bradley Found, 92; residential fel, Max-Planck-Inst, Hamburg, Ger, 90. **SELECTED PUBLICATIONS** Auth, The Beginning of the Constitutional Era, A Comparative Study of the First American and European Constitution, co-auth with William Fox Jr, CUA Press, 93; Constitution Making in the Countries of Former Soviet Dominance: Current Develoment, GA J of Int and Comparative Law, vol 23, no 2, 93; Fundamental Constitutional Rights in the New Constitution of Eastern and Central Europe, Cardozo J of Int and Comparative Law, vol 3, no 1, spring 95; Regulations of International Trade and Business, vol I, International Trade, ABC, 96, vol II, Business Transactions, co-auth and ed, ABC, winter 96; Constitution Making in the Countries of Former Soviet Dominance, Duke Univ Press, 96; numerous other publications. **CONTACT ADDRESS** Columbus School of Law, Catholic Univ of America, Washington, DC, 20064. **EMAIL** ludwikowski@law.cus.edu

LUIS, WILLIAM
PERSONAL Born 07/12/1948, New York, NY, m **DISCIPLINE** LATIN AMERICAN STUDIES **EDUCATION** SUNY at Binghamton, BA 1971; Univ of WI Madison, MA 1973; Cornell Univ, MA 1979, PhD 1980. **CAREER** Bd of Educ NYC, tchr 1971-72, tchr 1973-74; Handbook of Latin Amer Studies, contrib editor 1981-, consul 1981-; Latin Amer Literary Review, mem editorial bd 1985-; Natl Endowment for the Humanities, reader 1985; Natl Research Cncl/Ford Fndtn Fellowship Panel, 1986; Dartmouth Coll, asst prof of Latin Amer & Caribbean, assoc prof 1985-88; visiting assoc, Washington Univ, 1988; assoc prof, dir, Latin Amer and Caribbean Area Studies Prog, 1988-91; Vanderbilt Univ, assoc prof, 1991-96, prof, 1996-; Yale Univ, visting prof, 1998. **HONORS AND AWARDS** Deans List SUNY at Binghamton 1968-71; Vilas Fellowship UW 1972; Grad Sch Fellowship UW 1973; Grad Sch Fellowship CU 1974-76; Berkowitz Travel & Rsch Fellowship CU 1974-76; Sigma Delta Pi 1975; Latin Amer Studies Prog Travel Grant CU 1977; Edwin Gould Awd Aspira 1974-76-78; Tchng Asst CU 1976-78; Summer Rsch Fellowships CU 1975-79; Special Grad School Fellowships CU 1975-79; Amer Coun of Learned Society's, Fellowship, 1994; Directory of Amer Scholars 1982; ed Voices from Under, Black Narrative inLatin Amer & the Caribbean 1984; Literary Bondage and Slavery in Cuban Narratives, 1990; Modern Latin Amer Fiction Writers, Vols 1&2, 1992, 1994; Dance Between Two Cultures: Latino-Caribbean Literature Written in the US, 1997; and numerous lectures, publications, articles. **MEMBERSHIPS** Mem Modern Lang Assn; Assn of Caribbean Studies; Amer Assn of Tchrs of Spanish & Portuguese; mem adv bd Comm on Spec Educ Projects; mem Ad Hoc Comm to Study Hispanic Admissions & Recruitment; mem Minority Educ Council; mem Black Caucus; mem African Afro-Amer Studies Steering Comm; mem Literary Criticism Seminar; mem Latin Amer Literary Seminar; co-dir Latin Amer Literary Seminar; faculty advisor Phi Sigma Psi; mem African & Afro-Amer Studies Seminar; mem exec comm Assn of Caribbean Studies; mem Screening Comm for the Dir & Adjunct Curator of Film DC; mem Native Amer Studies Steering Comm; mem exec comm of the Faculty of DC; mem Agenda Subcomm of the Exec Comm of the Faculty of DC; mem Library Search Comm for the Humanities Bibliographer. **CONTACT ADDRESS** Latin American Literature, Vanderbilt Univ, Nashville, TN, 37235.

LUKACHER, NED
PERSONAL Born 09/03/1950, York, PA, m, 1978 **DISCIPLINE** ENGLISH LITERATURE, COMPARATIVE LITERATURE **EDUCATION** Dickinson Col, BA, 72; Univ Ariz, MA, 74; Duke Univ, PhD(English), 78. **CAREER** ASST PROF ENGLISH, UNIV ILL, CHICAGO, 80-. **SELECTED PUBLICATIONS** Auth, The 3rd Wound, Bowie, Malcolm, Brooks, Peter, and the Myth of Actaeon, Comp Lit, Vol 0048, 96. **CONTACT ADDRESS** Univ Illinois, Chicago, IL, 60680.

LUMPKINS, DAVID W.
PERSONAL Born 11/16/1944, Lafollette, TN, m, 1964 **DISCIPLINE** SLAVIC LANGUAGES **EDUCATION** Univ Tn, BA, 66; Vanderbilt Univ, PhD, 74. **CAREER** Prof, Univ South, 68- **MEMBERSHIPS** AME; Assoc of Teachers of Slavic & East-Eur Lang **RESEARCH** Nineteenth cent Russian lit **CONTACT ADDRESS** 735 University Ave, Sewanee, TN, 37383-1000. **EMAIL** dlumpkin@sewanee.edu

LUND, JEROME A.
PERSONAL Born 09/12/1948, Willmar, MN, m, 1988, 3 children **DISCIPLINE** ANCIENT SEMITIC LANGUAGES **EDUCATION** Hebrew Univ, PhD, 89; LA Baptist Theol Sem, MDiv, 73. **CAREER** Assoc res scholar, 90-, Hebrew Union College. **HONORS AND AWARDS** James Montgomery fel. **MEMBERSHIPS** AOS; SBL; IBR. **RESEARCH** Aramaic and Hebrew Languages; Ancient Bible Versions. **SELECTED PUBLICATIONS** The Old Testament in Syriac according to the Peshitta Version, Concordance to the Pentateuch, prepared by PG Borbone, J Cook, KD Jenner, DM Walter in collaboration with JA Lund and MP Weitzman, Leiden Brill, 97; Sepher Bereshit Jerusalem: Caspari Center, 94, a study book on the book of Genesis; The Third and Forth Oracles of Balaam in the Peshitta and Targums, in: Targum Studies 2: Targum and Peshitta, ed, Paul V Flesher, Atlanta, Scholars Press, 98; The Noun mattar Prison: A possible Ghost Word in the Lexicon of Middle Western Aramaic, Orientalia, 97. **CONTACT ADDRESS** 3101 Clifton Ave, Cincinnati, OH, 45220. **EMAIL** JLund@cn.huc.edu

LUNDELL, TORBORG LOVISA
PERSONAL Stockholm, Sweden **DISCIPLINE** COMPARATIVE LITERATURE, FOLKTALE **EDUCATION** Univ Calif, Berkeley, PhD(comp Lit), 73. **CAREER** Actg asst prof, 69-72, lectr, 72-73, asst prof, 73-77, ASSOC PROF SWED, UNIV CALIF, SANTA BARBARA, 77-. **MEMBERSHIPS** Soc Advan Scand Studies; MLA; Philol Asn PACIFIC Coast; Am Comp Lit Asn; C G Jung Found Anal Psychol. **RESEARCH** Modern Swedish Novel; film. **SELECTED PUBLICATIONS** Auth, Effects of Gender Linked Language Differences in Adults Written Discourse--Multivariate Tests of Language Effects, Lang and Commun, Vol 0014, 94. **CONTACT ADDRESS** Dept of Ger and Slavic Lang, Univ of Calif, 552 University Rd, Santa Barbara, CA, 93106-0001.

LUNT, HORACE GRAY
PERSONAL Born 09/12/1918, Colorado Springs, CO **DISCIPLINE** SLAVIC LINGUISTICS **EDUCATION** Harvard Univ, AB, 41; Univ Calif, AM, 42; Columbia Univ, PhD, 50. **CAREER** Teaching asst Slavic langs, Univ Calif, 46; lectr Serbocroatian, Columbia Univ, 48-49; from asst prof to assoc prof, 49-59; PROF SLAVIC LANG AND LIT, HARVARD UNIV, 59-, Guggenheim fel, 60-61. **MEMBERSHIPS** Ling Soc Am; Am Asn Advan Slavic Studies; MLA; Am Asn Teachers Slavic and East Europ Lang. **RESEARCH** Church Slavonic; comparative Slavic linguistics. **SELECTED PUBLICATIONS** Auth, Notes on Nationalist Attitudes in Slavic Studies, Can Slavonic Papers-Revue Canadienne Des Slavistes, Vol 0034, 92; The Slavonic Book of Esther--Translation From Hebrew Or Evidence for a Lost Greek Text, Harvard Theolog Rev, Vol 0087, 94; The Great Moravian-Empire--Reality Or Fiction--a New Interpretation of the Sources for the History of the Middle Danube Basin in the 9th-Century, Speculum-J Medieval Stud, Vol 0071, 96. **CONTACT ADDRESS** Dept of Slavic Lang, Harvard Univ, Cambridge, MA, 02138.

LUSTIG, MYRON W.
DISCIPLINE INTERPERSONAL COMMUNICATION **EDUCATION** Univ WI, PhD. **CAREER** Comm, San Diego St Univ. **HONORS AND AWARDS** Assoc ed, Commun Monogr; assoc ed, W Jour Commun. **SELECTED PUBLICATIONS** Auth, Intercultural Competence: Interpersonal Communication Across Cultures, 96. **CONTACT ADDRESS** Dept of Commun, San Diego State Univ, 5500 Campanile Dr, San Diego, CA, 92182. **EMAIL** rlustig@mail.sdsu.eduy

LUTCAVAGE, CHARLES
DISCIPLINE GERMAN **EDUCATION** La Salle Col; Lessing Kolleg in Marburg; Univ Vienna; Harvard Univ, PhD. **CAREER** Sr preceptor & coordr Ger Lang Instr; head crse, Ger A & Ger D. **HONORS AND AWARDS** Created interactive comput and video prog for Ger and Austrian Landeskunde. **RESEARCH** Language pedagogy; technology in language teaching; Austrian and Dutch history and literature. **SELECTED PUBLICATIONS** Publ on, methodology. **CONTACT ADDRESS** Dept of Germanic Languages and Literature, Harvard Univ, 8 Garden St, Cambridge, MA, 02138. **EMAIL** lutcavag@fas.harvard.edu

LUTHY, MELVIN JOSEPH
PERSONAL Born 11/15/1936, Logan, UT, m, 1965, 4 children **DISCIPLINE** LINGUISTICS, ENGLISH LANGUAGE **EDUCATION** UT State Univ, BS, 62; IN Univ, PhD, 67. **CAREER** Asst prof Eng & ling, Univ WI-Oshkosh, 69-71; assoc prof, 71-80, Prof Eng & Ling, Brigham Young Univ, 80. **MEMBERSHIPS** Ling Soc Am; Tchr(s) of Eng Speakers Other Lang; Phi

Kappa Phi; Soc for Advancement Scandinavian Studies. **RESEARCH** Mod grammars; lang pedag; Finnish lang and lit. **SELECTED PUBLICATIONS** Auth, Phonological and Lexical Aspects of Colloquial Finnish, Ind Univ, 73-, coauth, TICCIT Composition and Grammar Course, 74 & auth, Finnish Noun/Adjective/Verb Wheels, 76, Brigham Young Univ; Why transformational grammar fails in the classroom, Col Compos & Commun, 77; The case of Prufrock's grammar, Col English, 78; A comparative generative junction approach to Finnish morphosyntax, J Uralic & Altaic Studies, 82; Study in English Grammars, Brigham Young Univ Homestudy, 90. **CONTACT ADDRESS** Dept of Linguistics, Brigham Young Univ, 2129 Jkhb, Provo, UT, 84602-0002. **EMAIL** melvin_luthy@byu.edu

LUTKUS, ALAN
PERSONAL Born 09/28/1940, East Chicago, IN, m, 1966 **DISCIPLINE** ENGLISH, LINGUISTICS **EDUCATION** Harvard Univ, BA, 62; Ind Univ, MA, 66, PhD, 75. **CAREER** Ndea Lectr Ling, Trinity Col, Conn, 68; Instr Eng & ling, Northern IL Univ, 69-71; Assoc Prof Eng & Ling, State Univ NY Col Geneseo, 73-; Chief Ling Consul, Amer Inst Tech, vocab series Wordscape, 90; media consilt, NEH Amer radio Project, 96-97. **RESEARCH** Stylistics; compos. **SELECTED PUBLICATIONS** Coauth, Arts and Skills of English: Daybook, Grades 3-6, Holt, 72-73; auth, Troublespeaking the approach to public doublespeaking: Purism and our concept of language, Col English, 76; coauth, Spelling Matters, 77 & The World of Spelling, Grades 1-8, 78, Heath; coauth, Spelling Worlds, Grades 2-6, Ditto Master Series, Heath, 79; Buster Keaton, p265-272, Sir John Falstaff, p176-184, Touchstone, p466-470, in Fools and jesters in Literature, Art, and History: A Bio-Biographical Sourcebook, Greenwood Press, 98; Composition Theory Meet sPractice and They Pretty Well Get Along Twice, Journal of Teaching Writing, 3, 84; Literacy Reconsidered For Better and Worse, Review essay, Journal of Teaching Writing, 2, 83. **CONTACT ADDRESS** Dept of Eng, SUNY, Geneseo, 1 College Cir, Geneseo, NY, 14454-1401. **EMAIL** lutkus@uno.cc.genesco.edu

LUTZELER, PAUL MICHAEL
PERSONAL Born 11/04/1943, Germany, m, 1972, 2 children **DISCIPLINE** GERMAN AND COMPARATIVE LITERATURE; EUROPEAN STUDIES **EDUCATION** Indiana Univ, Bloomington, MA, 70, PhD, 72. **CAREER** Asst prof German, 73-77, assoc prof, 77-81, prof of German and Comparative Lit, 81-93, ROSA MAY DISTINGUISHED UNIV PROF IN THE HUMANITIES, WASHINGTON UNIV, ST. LOUIS, 93-. **HONORS AND AWARDS** Austrian Cross of Honor for Arts and Sciences, 1st Class, 87; Cross of Merit of the Federal Republic of Germany, 88; Outstanding Educator Award (Am Asn of Teachers of German), 92; Res Award of the Alexander von Humboldt Found, 98., Director, European Studies Prog, and Director, Center for Contemporary German Literature, Washington Univ. **MEMBERSHIPS** MLA; GSA; Council for European Studies; European Community Studies Asn; The Atlantic Council. **RESEARCH** German and English lit and culture, especially Post-Modernism, Multiculturalism, and Postcolonialism. **SELECTED PUBLICATIONS** Auth, The Symbolism in Broch,Hermann Works--Plato the 'Simile of the Cave' as a Subtext, Colloquia Germanica, Vol 0025, 92; Early Romanticism, Ger Quart, Vol 0066, 93; The Vanishing Subject--Early Psychology and Literary Modernism, J Engl and Ger Philol Vol 0092, 93; Modernity Reconstructed--Studies on German Literature After 1945--Literature, Culture, Society, Ger Quart, Vol 0066, 93; The Presence of History, Postmodern Constellations in Contemporary Narrative Literature, Neue Rundschau, Vol 0104, 93; Inscribing the Other, Ger Quart, Vol 0066, 93; Narrated Visibility--Studies on the Relationship Between Text and Image in Broch,Hermann Trilogy of Novels die 'Schlafwandler', Ger Quart, Vol 0067, 94; Ein 'Gott Der Frechheit', World Lit Today, Vol 0069, 95; The Track of Violence--History of the Element of Horror in Literature and the Theory of Literature, Ger Quart, Vol 0068, 95; The Postcolonial View--Writers From the German-Speaking Countries Report From the 3rd-World, World Lit Today, Vol 0069, 95; Multiculturalism in Contemporary German Literature--Introduction, World Lit Today, Vol 0069, 95; Novalis Or Napoleo--German Language Essays on the Problems of Europe, Neue Rundschau, Vol 0107, 96; Poeticization/Politicization--Images of Germany in Literature Before 1848, Ger Quart, Vol 0069, 96; The Joy of Reading--How Entertaining is Modern German Literature, Ger Quart, Vol 0069, 96; From a Postcolonial Viewpoint, Reports of German-Language Writers From the 3rd-World, Neue Rundschau, Vol 0107, 96; Autobiog and History, Ger Quarty, Vol 0070, 97. **CONTACT ADDRESS** German Dept., Washington Univ, One Brookings Dr., Campus Box 1104, St. Louis, MO, 63130-4899. **EMAIL** europe@artsci.wustl.edu

LUZBETAK, LOUIS JOSEPH
PERSONAL Born 09/19/1918, Joliet, IL **DISCIPLINE** LINGUISTIC ANALYSIS, CULTURAL ANTHROPOLOGY **EDUCATION** Divine Word Sem, BA, 42; Pontif Gregorian Univ, STL, 46, JCB, 47; Univ Fribourg, PhD(anthrop), 51. **CAREER** Prof anthrop, ling and missiology, Divine Word Sem, Ill, 51-52, 56-58; lectr and summer asst prof appl anthrop, Cath Univ Am, 60-65; exec dir, Ctr Appl Res in Apostolate, Washington, DC, 65-73; pres, Divine Word Col, Iowa, 73-78; ED, ANTHROPOS, INT REV ETHNOLOGY AND LING, 79-, Dir, Anthropos Inst, St Augustin bei Sieberg, WGer, 51-; Ford Found fel, 52-54; cult anthrop and ling field work, New Guinea, 52-56; lectr appl anthrop, Ctr Intercult Formation, Cuernavaca, Mex, 60-65; Ctr for Intercult Commun, Cath Univ PR, 60-65; rector, Divine Word Col, DC, 68-73; Walsh-Price fel, Ctr Mission Studies, Maryknoll, NY, 78-79. **HONORS AND AWARDS** Pierre Charles Award, Fordham Univ, 64. **MEMBERSHIPS** Fel Am Anthrop Asn; Cath Anthrop Asn (vpres, 61-62, pres, 62-69); Ling Soc Am; Soc Appl Anthrop; Am Soc Missiology (pres, 75-76). **SELECTED PUBLICATIONS** Auth, Schmidt, Wilhelm, an Ethnologist for All Seasons, Cath Hist Rev, Vol 0079, 93. **CONTACT ADDRESS** 5205 Sankt Augustin 1, 52045.

LYMAN-HAGER, MARY ANN
DISCIPLINE ITALIAN, FRENCH **EDUCATION** Univ Ariz, MA, 75; Univ Idaho, MEd, 81; PhD, 86. **CAREER** Asst prof, 87-90, Univ Mass, Amherst; asst, assoc, prof, Pa State Univ, 90-97; PROF, SAN DIEGO STATE UNIV, 97-. **CONTACT ADDRESS** Dept French, Italian, San Diego State Univ, San Diego, CA, 92182. **EMAIL** mlymanha@mail.sdsu.edu

LYONS, BRIDGET G.
PERSONAL Born 08/28/1932, Prague, Czechoslovakia, m, 1971 **DISCIPLINE** ENGLISH LANGUAGE AND LITERATURE **EDUCATION** Radcliffe Univ, BA; Oxford Univ, MA; Columbia, PhD. **CAREER** Prof. **RESEARCH** 16th-17th century English literature; European Renaissance. **SELECTED PUBLICATIONS** Auth, Orson Welles: Chimes at Midnight, Reading in an Age of Theory; ed, Voices of Melancholy. **CONTACT ADDRESS** Dept of English, Rutgers Univ, 510 George St, Murray Hall, New Brunswick, NJ, 08901-1167. **EMAIL** lyons@fas-english.rutgers.edu

LYONS, DECLAN P.
PERSONAL Born 12/03/1961, Galway, Ireland **DISCIPLINE** ANCIENT CLASSICS, FRENCH **EDUCATION** Nat Univ Ireland, BA; Univ Dublin, MLitt, 90; SUNY-Buffalo, PhD, 98. **CAREER** Tchg asst, SUNY-Buffalo, 88-92; res scholar, Univ de Geneve-Suisse, 92-93; asst prof Classics, Franciscan Univ, 94- . **HONORS AND AWARDS** Coun Euro res fel, Switz, 92-93; Ital Cult inst res awd, 98. **MEMBERSHIPS** APA; CAAS. **RESEARCH** Hellenistic Philosophy; Neronian Rome; SENECA; Hellenistic Poetry; Psychology and Classics. **CONTACT ADDRESS** Dept of Modern and Ancient Language, Franciscan Univ of Steubenville, Franciscan Way, Steuberville, OH, 43952. **EMAIL** lyons@fran.u.edu

LYOVIN, ANATOLE VLADIMIROVICH
PERSONAL Born 11/13/1938, Leskovats, Yugoslavia, m, 1963, 2 children **DISCIPLINE** CHINESE LINGUISTICS, PHONOLOGY **EDUCATION** Princeton Univ, AB, 64; Univ Calif, Berkeley, PhD(Ling), 72. **CAREER** Asst prof, 68-73, assoc prof Ling, Univ Hawaii, Manoa, 73-, co-prin investr, Northwest Lang Relationships Proj, Pac & Asian Ling inst, 72-73. **MEMBERSHIPS** Ling Soc Am. **RESEARCH** Phonological change; historical phonology of Chinese; Classical Tibetan. **SELECTED PUBLICATIONS** Auth, Notes on the addition of final stops in Maru, 6/68; A Chinese dialect dictionary on computer: Progress report, Proj Ling Anal Reports, 6/68; co-ed, CLIBOC: Chinese Linguistics Bibliography on Computer, Cambridge Univ, 70; auth, Sound change, homophony and lexical diffusion, Proj Ling Analy Reports, 11/71; Intro to the Languages of the world, Oxford, Univ, 97. **CONTACT ADDRESS** Dept of Ling, Univ of Hawaii, 1890 E West Rd, Honolulu, HI, 96822-2318. **EMAIL** lyovin@hawaii.edu

LYS, FRANZISKA
DISCIPLINE GERMAN **EDUCATION** Northwestern Univ, PhD. **CAREER** Col lectr; dir, Undergraduat Studies; ch, Coun Lang Instr. **HONORS AND AWARDS** Charles Deering McCormick Univ distinguished lectr, 97-98; Lieutenant Governor's Awd, Ill Coun Tchr(s) For Lang, 96; outstanding tchg Col Arts Sci(s), Northwestern Univ, 87-88; Fac Honor Roll Dept of German, Northwestern Univ, 84-87., Developer, CD-ROM multi-media software Drehort: Neubrandenburg Interaktiv and Azubi Interaktiv. **RESEARCH** Intermatik, an interactive German grammar on the internet and a new multi-media application for language teaching. **SELECTED PUBLICATIONS** Producer and auth educ documentaries, Drehort: Neubrandenburg; AZUBI; Drehort: Bern; Gesichter einer Stadt, Berne; Faces of a City. **CONTACT ADDRESS** Dept of German, Northwestern Univ, 1801 Hinman, Evanston, IL, 60208. **EMAIL** flys@nwu.edu

M

MA, JOHN
DISCIPLINE GREEK **EDUCATION** Oxford Univ, BA, 91; D Phil, 97. **CAREER** Dept Classics, Princeton Univ **RESEARCH** Greek history, especially Hellenistic. **SELECTED PUBLICATIONS** Articles on: Greek epigraphy and history. **CONTACT ADDRESS** Princeton Univ, 1 Nassau Hall, Princeton, NJ, 08544.

MAAZAOUI, ABBES
PERSONAL Born 03/01/1953, Tunisia, m, 1 child **DISCIPLINE** FRENCH **EDUCATION** Maitrise, Univ of Tunis, Tunisia, 78; Doctorat de 3e cycle, Univ Provence, France, 82. **CAREER** Asst prof, 82-87, assoc prof, Univ Tunis, Sousse, Tunisia, 87-89, co-dir, French Dept, 88, co-dir, Study Abroad Prog, CREDIF in Paris, France, spring 88; vis asst prof, Bowdoin Col, Brunswick, ME, 90-91; vis asst prof, Colby Col, Waterville, ME, 91-92; asst prof, Ramapo Col, Mahwah, NJ, 92-93, dir, Lang Lab, 92-93; ASST PROF FRENCH, LINCOLN UNIV, PA, 93-, academic dir, Int Inst for Public Policy Summer Lang Inst, 97-98 (co-founder), acting chair, Dept of Langs and Linguistics, 96-97, supervisor, Foreign Lang Teaching Assts, fall 95-spring 98, coord, Lang Placement Exam, 95-, dir, Lang Lab, 93-94. **HONORS AND AWARDS** Lincoln fac development grant, fall 98; Inst for Int Public Policy, 5 year grant, for a Summer Lang Inst at Lincoln Univ, summer 97; Who's Who Among America's Teachers, 96; Who's Who in the East, 95; numerous grants and scholarships from France and Tunisia. **MEMBERSHIPS** Northeast Modern lang Asn; Conseil Int d'Etudes Francophones; Am Asn of Teachers of French; Modern Lang Asn. **RESEARCH** French and Francophone lit and cultures; literary theories; Marcel Proust. **SELECTED PUBLICATIONS** Auth, Ethnicity, Race, and Gender: A Colonial Perspective in French Film, The Humanities Newsletter, Vol 1, no 3, summer 95; Steven Ungar, Scandal and Aftereffect: Blanchot and France since 1930, Univ MN Press, 95, forthcoming in Romance Quart; Representation et alterite dans les romans de Robbe-Grillet, the French Rev, Vol 68, no 3, 95; L'Enfant de sable et La Nuit sacree ou le corps tragique, the French Rev, Vol 69, no 1, 95; A World of Films: The International Film Series, The Humanities Newsletter, Vol 2, no 1, fall 96; A World of Films: The International Film Series (Part II), The Humanities Newsletter, vol 2, no 2, spring 97; The 1997-98 International Film Series, The Humanities Newsletter, Vol 3, no 1, fall 97; Les traces du terroir dans Talismano de Meddeb et Le Conclave des pleureuses de Mellah, in Tunisie Plurielle, Vol 1, ed Hedi Bouraoui, L'Or du temps, 97; Literary Theories and Minority Literature, the Humanities Newsletter, Vol 3, no 2, spring 98; L'Erotisme et le sacre: Ben Jelloun, Djebar, Mellah, Romance Notes, 38, no 2, winter 98; Poetique des marges et marges de la poetique, in Transgressing Boundaries: the Poetics of Marginality, spring 98; several other publications. **CONTACT ADDRESS** Dept of Langs and Linguistics, Lincoln Univ, Lincoln Univ, PA, 19352. **EMAIL** maazaoui@lu.lincoln.edu

MACARY, JEAN LOUIS
PERSONAL Born 01/26/1931, Paris, France, m, 1959, 3 children **DISCIPLINE** FRENCH LITERATURE **EDUCATION** Sorbonne, Lic Lett & dipl etudes super, 54, Agregation Lett, 62; Doctorat d'etat es Lettres, Pantheon-Sorbonne, 74. **CAREER** Asst French lit, Sorbonne, 65-68; lectr, Princeton Univ, 69-70, asst prof, 70-76; assoc prof, 76-80, Prof French Lit & Chmn Dept Fordham Univ, 80-. **MEMBERSHIPS** Am Soc 18th Century Studies; Int Soc Studies 18th Century; MLA. **RESEARCH** Seventeenth & 18th century French literature; history of ideas. **SELECTED PUBLICATIONS** Ed, Voltaire, Facetics, Presses Univ, France, 73; auth, Mas que et lumieres au XVIIIe: A-F2 des landes, citoyen et philosophe 1680-1757, Nijhoff, The Hague, 75; ed, Essays on the Age of Enlightenment, In Honor of Ira O Wade, Droz, Geneva, 77. **CONTACT ADDRESS** Dept of Mod Lang, Fordham Univ, 501 E Fordham Rd, Bronx, NY, 10458-5191. **EMAIL** voldid@aol.com

MACAULEY, BETH
DISCIPLINE CCC-SPEECH-LANGUAGE PATHOLOGY **EDUCATION** Univ Fla, BA, 87, MA, 89, PhD, 98. **CAREER** Assoc prof, Wash State Univ, 95-; grad tchg asst, Dept Commun Processes and Disorders, Univ Fla, 94-95 & grad res asst, 91-95; speech lang pathologist, Tacachale, 90-95, Res-Care cluster and group homes, 90-95. **SELECTED PUBLICATIONS** Coauth, Limb Apraxia Results From a Fractionation of Movement Representations I: Deficits in Spatial Planning, In Press - Brain, 94; Joint Coordination Deficits in Limb Apraxia. In Press - Brain, 94; Ecological Implications of Limb Apraxia: Evidence From Mealtime Behavior, In Press - J the Int Neuropsychological Soc, 94; Lateralized Hand Use in Gestural Communication, In Press - Brain & Cognition, 94 & Left Hemisphere Movement Control, Soc for Neuroscience Abstracts, vol 20, 94. **CONTACT ADDRESS** Dept of Speech and Hearing Sciences, Washington State Univ, 201 Daggy Hall, Pullman, WA, 99164-2420. **EMAIL** macauleyb@wsu.edu

MACDONALD, MARYELLEN
DISCIPLINE PSYCHOLOGY, LINGUISTICS, AND THE NEUROSCIENCE PROGRAM **EDUCATION** Univ Calif, Los Angeles, PhD, 86. **CAREER** Assoc prof, Univ Southern Calif. **RESEARCH** Human language comprehension; Speech production & its relationship to comprehension; role of working memory in language processing; decline of language processing abilities in patients with Alzheimer's Disease. **SELECTED PUBLICATIONS** Coauth, The lexical nature of syntactic ambiguity resolution, Psycholog Rev, 101, 94; ed, Lexical representations & sentence processing, Hove, Sussex, UK: Psychology Press, Publ simultaneously as Issues 2-3 jour Lang and Cognitive Processes, 97. **CONTACT ADDRESS** Dept of Linguistics, Univ Southern Calif, University Park Campus, Los Angeles, CA, 90089-2520. **EMAIL** mcm@gizmo.usc.edu

MACE, CARROLL E.
PERSONAL Born 12/05/1926, Neosho, MO **DISCIPLINE** SPANISH **EDUCATION** Drury Col, BA, 49; Tulane Univ, MA, 52, PhD(Span), 66. **CAREER** Asst prof, Univ SC, 60-63; instr Span, Tulane Univ, 63-65; asst prof, 65-67, assoc prof, 67-70, prof Span, Xavier Univ LA, 71-, chmn Dept Mod Lang, 72-; chmn Dept Mod Lang of Xavier 1970-90; retired, 98. **MEMBERSHIPS** Am Asn Teachers Span & Port; SCent Mod Lang Asn. **RESEARCH** Cervantes and the generation of 1898; folk literature of Guatemala. **SELECTED PUBLICATIONS** Auth, The Patzca dance of Rabinal, El Palacio, fall 61; translr, The day of the dead of 1836: Figaro in the cemetery by Larra, Shenandoah, Winter 65; auth, New information about dance-dramas of Rabinal and the Rabinal-Achi, Xavier Univ Studies, 2/67; Two Spanish-Quiche Dance-Dramas of Rabinal, Tulane Studies Romance Lang & Lit, 70; Charles Etienne Brasseur de Bourbourg, Handbk Mid Am Indians, 73; Los Negritos: A Maya Christmas comedy, Xavier Rev, 1/81; Algunos apuntes sobre los bailes de Guatemala y de Rabinal, Mesoamerica, 2/81; Bailes y Teatro Prehispanicos en Guatemala, in vol one, gen ed, Dr Jorge Lujan Munoz, 98. **CONTACT ADDRESS** Dept of Mod Lang, Xavier Univ, 7325 Palmetto St, New Orleans, LA, 70125-1098.

MACHONIS, PETER A.
DISCIPLINE FRENCH LITERATURE **EDUCATION** Pa State Univ, PhD, 82. **CAREER** Assoc prof. **HONORS AND AWARDS** Excellence Tchg Awd. **SELECTED PUBLICATIONS** Auth, The support verb make, 91. **CONTACT ADDRESS** Dept of Modern Languages, Florida State Univ, 11200 SW 8th St, Miami, FL, 33174. **EMAIL** machonis@fiu.edu

MACIAS, MANUEL JATO
PERSONAL Born 03/25/1929, Portland, OR **DISCIPLINE** SPANISH **EDUCATION** Univ Portland, AB, 51, AM, 52; Univ Madrid, DrPhil & Let, 56; Northwestern Univ, PhD, 63; Univ Coimbra, dipl, 70; Univ Portland, MA, 77. **CAREER** Instr mod lang, Marquette Univ, 55-57, asst prof Span, 57-58; from Asst Prof to Prof, 58-95, Prof Emeritus Span, Univ Portland, 95-, admin dir prog in Spain, Univ Navarre, 70-72, Chmn Dept For Lang, 72, Lectr, Portland State Col, 59; Fulbright exchange prof, Gt Brit, 59-60; vis assoc prof Span, Lewis & Clark Col, 68-69; lectr Span, Portland State Univ, 76-78. **MEMBERSHIPS** Am Asn Tchr(s) Span & Port; Philol Asn Pac Coast; AAUP; Pac Northwest Foreign Lang Conf (pres, 68-69); Am Coun For Lang Tchg. **RESEARCH** Nineteenth and twentieth century Span drama; mod Galician lit. **SELECTED PUBLICATIONS** Auth, La ensenanza del espanol en los EEUU de American, Ed Cult Hisp, 61. **CONTACT ADDRESS** Dept of Eng & Mod Lang, Univ of Portland, 5000 N Willamette, Portland, OR, 97203-5798. **EMAIL** macias@up.edu

MACKENDRICK, LOUIS KING
DISCIPLINE ENGLISH LANGUAGE; LITERATURE **EDUCATION** Western Ontario, BA, MA; Toronto, PhilM, PhD, 71. **CAREER** Prof **RESEARCH** Canadian short story. **SELECTED PUBLICATIONS** Auth, Robert Harlow and His Works; Al Purdy and His Works & Some Other Reality: Alice Munro's Something I've Been Meaning to Tell You; ed, Probable Fictions: Alice Munro's Narrative Acts & issue of Essays on Canadian Writing on Al Purdy. **CONTACT ADDRESS** Dept of English Language and Literature, Univ of Windsor, 401 Sunset Ave, Windsor, ON, N9B 3P4.

MACKENZIE, LOUIS A.
DISCIPLINE FRENCH LITERATURE **EDUCATION** Univ Notre Dame, BA, 69; Middlebury Col, MA, 72; Cornell Univ, PhD, 77. **CAREER** Assoc prof. **RESEARCH** 17th century literature. **SELECTED PUBLICATIONS** Auth, Strategies of Fragmentation in Pascal's Lettres provinciales. **CONTACT ADDRESS** Romance Languages and Literatures Dept, Univ of Notre Dame, Notre Dame, IN, 46556.

MACKEY, LOUIS HENRY
PERSONAL Born 09/24/1926, Sidney, OH, d, 4 children **DISCIPLINE** PHILOSOPHY, COMPARATIVE LITERATURE **EDUCATION** Capital Univ, BA, 48; Yale Univ, MA, 53, PhD(philos), 54. **CAREER** From instr to asst prof philos, Yale Univ, 53-59; from assoc prof to prof, Rice Univ, 59-67; vis prof, 67-68, prof Philos, Univ Tex, Austin, 68-, Morse fel, Yale Univ, 57-58; vis prof, Haverford Col, 71-72; Nat Endowment for Humanities res fel, 76-77; vis prof, Univ of Tulsa, 83. **HONORS AND AWARDS** President's Assoc Teaching Excellence Award, 91; Award for Outstanding Grad Teaching, 94. **MEMBERSHIPS** Amer Comparative Lit Assoc, Inter Assoc for Philo and Lit. **RESEARCH** Literary theory; medieval philosophy; Kierkegaard. **SELECTED PUBLICATIONS** Auth, Soren Kierkegaard, In: Existentialism, McGraw, 64; Kierkegaard: A Kind of Poet, Univ Pa, 71; The loss of the world in Kierkegaard's ethics, In: Kierkegaard: A Collection of Critical Essays, Doubleday, 72; Entreatments of God: Reflections on Aquinas' five ways, Franciscan Studies, 77; Anatomical curiosities: Northrop Frye's theory of criticism, Tex Studies in Lang & Lit, 81; Paranoia, Pynchon and preterition, Sub-Stance, 81; Redemptive subversions: The Christian discourse of St Bonaventure, In: The Autonomy of Religious Belief, Notre Dame, 81; A ram in the afternoon: Kierkegaard's discourse of the other, Psychiat & Humanities, Vol 5, 81; Theory and Practic in the Rhetoric of I A Richards, Rheoric Soc Quarterly, 97. **CONTACT ADDRESS** Univ of Texas, Austin, TX, 78712-1026.

MACKEY, WILLIAM FRANCIS
PERSONAL Born 01/26/1918, Winnipeg, MB, Canada, m, 1949, 2 children **DISCIPLINE** LINGUISTICS, BILINGUALISM **EDUCATION** Univ Man, BA, 40; Laval Univ, MA, 42; Harvard Univ, MA, 47; Univ Geneva, DLitt, 65. **CAREER** Sr lectr ling method, Univ London, 48-50; assoc prof English philol, 50-54, prof English philol and ling, 54-61, dir lang lab, 57-69, dir div lang didactics, 61-69, prof lang didactics, 61-71, exec dir, Int Ctr Res Bilingualism, 67-70, RES PROF, LAVAL UNIV, 71-, Consult, Comt Educ of Poles, English, 48; Commonwealth Off Educ, Australia, 49; Intergovt Comt Europ Migration, Geneva, 55-56; Dept Citizenship and Immigration, Can, 57-69; mem Humanities Res Coun Can, 60-70; US Dept Health, Educ and Welfare, 66-70; Royal Comn Bilingualism and Biculturalism, 66, consult, 66-68; mem acad senate, Can Coun, 67; mem Lang Attitudes Res Comt, Irish Govt, 71-; ed, Studies Bilingual Educ, 71-; fed comnr, Bilingual Districts Adv Bd, Can Govt, 72-; comnr, Kommission fur sprachpolitische Integrationsfragan europaischen Gerneinschaft, 75-; chmn, lang policy, Can Coun Develop Comt on Individual, Lang and Soc, 75-77, comnr, Fed Govt Comn Lang Training in Pub Serv Can, 75-77. **HONORS AND AWARDS** 1974 Jubilee Medal, Inst Ling, London, England, 75. **MEMBERSHIPS** Ling Soc Am; Can Ling Asn; Ling Soc Paris; Int Phonetic Asn; fel Royal Soc Can. **RESEARCH** Bilingualism; geolinguistics; lexicometrics. **SELECTED PUBLICATIONS** Auth, Literary Diglossia, Biculturalism and Cosmopolitanism in Literature, Visible Lang, Vol 0027, 93; The English Infinitive, Can J Ling-Revue Canadienne De Linguistique, Vol 0040, 95. **CONTACT ADDRESS** Int Ctr Language Management Re, Laval Univ, Quebec, PQ, G1K 7P4.

MACKSEY, RICHARD ALAN
PERSONAL Born 07/25/1931, Glen Ridge, NJ, m, 1956, 1 child **DISCIPLINE** COMPARATIVE LITERATURE, ENGLISH **EDUCATION** Johns Hopkins Univ, MA, 53, PhD, 57. **CAREER** Jr instr English, Johns Hopkins Univ, 53-55; from instr to asst prof, Loyola Col, 56-58; asst prof writing sem, 58-63, assoc prof humanistic studies, 64-73, Carnegie lectr sem hist ideas, 62-64, chmn sect lang, lit and cult, 66-72, actg dir humanities ctr, 68-69, PROF HUMANISTIC STUDIES AND CHMN HUMANITIES CTR, JOHNS HOPKINS UNIV, 73-, Chmn comt internal evidence, Bibliog Conf, 62; lectr, Baltimore Mus Art, 64-65; dir, Bollingen Poetry Festival, Turnbull lect, Theatre Hopkins, Center Stage, Tantamount Films, Carroll House and Levering Hall; moderator, Dialogue of the Arts, CBS; ed comp lit, Mod Lang Notes and Structure. **MEMBERSHIPS** MLA; Am Soc Aesthet; Renaissance Soc Am; Mediaeval Acad Am; Col English Asn. **RESEARCH** European and English novel; poetics, rhetoric, and theory of literature; interrelation of arts, comparative methodology and intellectual history. **SELECTED PUBLICATIONS** Auth, Mcclain, William ,H. 1917-1994--in Memoriam, Mln-Mod Lang Notes, Vol 0110, 95. **CONTACT ADDRESS** Ctr for Humanities, Johns Hopkins Univ, 3400 N Charles St, Baltimore, MD, 21218-2680.

MACLEISH, ANDREW
PERSONAL Born 08/30/1923, Philadelphia, PA, m, 1950, 3 children **DISCIPLINE** LINGUISTICS, PHILOLOGY **EDUCATION** Roosevelt Univ, AB, 50; Univ Chicago, MA, 51; Univ Wis, PhD(English philol), 61. **CAREER** Instr English, Valparaiso Univ, 51-53 and Rockford Col, 56-58; from asst prof to assoc prof, Northern Ill Univ, 58-67; assoc prof English, Univ Minn, Minneapolis, 67-68, assoc prof English and ling, 68-71, PROF ENGLISH AND LING, 71-80. Dir, US Off Educ English Proj, Curric Ctr Ling, 64-67; Peace Corps res grant, 65-67; consult, Hilo Lang Develop Proj, Hawaii, 65-68. **MEMBERSHIPS** Nat Coun Teachers English; Ling Soc Am; Midwest Mod Lang Asn. **RESEARCH** English in Southeast Asia; descriptive historical English linguistics; materials for teaching standard English in Hawaii. **SELECTED PUBLICATIONS** Auth, of Books and a Dedication, Western Humanities Rev, Vol 0051, 97. **CONTACT ADDRESS** 3709 Upton Ave, S Minneapolis, MN, 55410.

MACLEOD, ALISTAIR
DISCIPLINE ENGLISH LANGUAGE; LITERATURE **EDUCATION** St F X, BA, BEd; New Brunswick, MA; Univ Notre Dame, PhD; St F X, LLD, 69. **CAREER** Prof; fiction ed, The Windsor Review; tchr, advanced writing in the summer prog at, Banff; Can participant in the Can Scotland Writers-in-Residence Exchange Prog, 84-85. **RESEARCH** 19th-century literature; Creative Writing. **SELECTED PUBLICATIONS** Auth, The Lost Salt Gift of Blood, 76; As Birds Bring Forth the Sun, 86. **CONTACT ADDRESS** Dept of English Language and Literature, Univ of Windsor, 401 Sunset Ave, Windsor, ON, N9B 3P4.

MACPHAIL, ERIC
DISCIPLINE FRENCH LITERATURE **EDUCATION** Princeton Univ; PhD, 88. **CAREER** Assoc prof. **SELECTED PUBLICATIONS** Auth, The Voyage to Rome in French Renaissance Literature; pubs on Rabelais, Du Bellay, Montaigne, Cervantes, Cyrano, Prophecy, Astrology, and Antiquarianism. **CONTACT ADDRESS** Dept of French and Italian, Indiana Univ, Bloomington, 300 N Jordan Ave, Bloomington, IN, 47405.

MACRIS, PETER JOHN
PERSONAL Born 10/06/1931, Buffalo, NY, m, 1963, 3 children **DISCIPLINE** GERMAN LANGUAGE AND LITERATURE **EDUCATION** State Univ NY, Buffalo, BS, 56; Middlebury Col, MA, 63; NY Univ, PhD(Ger lang and lit), 68. **CAREER** From asst prof to assoc prof, 64-70, PROF GER LANG AND LIT, STATE UNIV NY, COL ONEONTA, 70-. **MEMBERSHIPS** AAUP; Am Asn Teachers Ger; Int Brecht Soc. **RESEARCH** Modern drama; Bertolt Brecht; literary texts used in music. **SELECTED PUBLICATIONS** Auth, Nitsch, Hermann Gruesome, Ritualistic Theater and the Hysteria of the Greeks--Sources and Traditions in the Viennese Image of Antiquity Since 1900, Mod Austrian Lit, Vol 0026, 93. **CONTACT ADDRESS** Dept of Foreign Lang, State Univ of New York Col, P O Box 4015, Oneonta, NY, 13820-4015.

MACRO, ANTHONY DAVID
PERSONAL Born 07/10/1938, London, England, m, 1967, 2 children **DISCIPLINE** CLASSICAL PHILOLOGY, ANCIENT HISTORY **EDUCATION** Oxford Univ, BA, 61, MA, 64; Johns Hopkins Univ, PhD, 69. **CAREER** Teaching assoc classics, Ind Univ, Bloomington, 61-62; instr, Univ Md, College Park, 65-67; jr instr, Johns Hopkins Univ, 67-69; asst prof classics, 69-75, assoc prof, 75-85, prof, 85-, Hobart Prof Class Lang, 92-, Trinity Col. **HONORS AND AWARDS** Leverhulme Commonwealth fel, Univ Wales, 75-76. **MEMBERSHIPS** Am Philol Asn; Soc Prom Hellenic Studies; Soc Prom Roman Studies. **RESEARCH** Greek epigraphy; Roman imperial history; comparative linguistics. **SELECTED PUBLICATIONS** Auth, Sophocles, Trachiniai, 112-21, American Journal of Philology, 73; Imperial provisions for Pergamum: OGIS 484, Greek, Roman & Byzantine Studies, 76; "A Confirmed Asiarch," American Journal of Philology, 79; The Cities of Asia Minor under the Roman imperium, Aufstieg und Niedergang der romischen Welt, Vol 2, No 7, Berlin, 80; Applied classics: Using Latin and Greek in the modern world, Class Outlook, 81; auth, "Asiarch Reconfirmed," American Journal of Philology, 85; auth, Prolegemena to the Study of Galatian-Celtic Name Formations, Celtic Connections, ACTA, 94. **CONTACT ADDRESS** Dept of Classics, Trinity Col, 300 Summit St, Hartford, CT, 06106-3186. **EMAIL** ad.macro@mail.trincoll.edu

MADDEN, DEIDRE
PERSONAL Born 01/08/1936, Washington, DC, m, 3 children **DISCIPLINE** SPEECH & LANGUAGE **EDUCATION** Ohio Univ, BA, 58; Western Reserve, MA, 67; Kent St, PhD, 82 **CAREER** Speech Pathol, 60-68, Parochial; Lect, 67-68, Com Col; Asst, Full Prof, 67-98, Baldwin-Wallace Col **HONORS AND AWARDS** Chair-Dept-BW; Co-Chair, Faculty-BW; Chair-Sexual Harrassment Com-BW **MEMBERSHIPS** ASHA; OSHA; ASTD **CONTACT ADDRESS** Medina, OH, 44256.

MADDOX, DONALD
DISCIPLINE FRENCH LITERATURE **EDUCATION** Duke Univ, PhD. **CAREER** Prof, Univ MA Amherst. **RESEARCH** Medieval lit; Old French discourse; semiotics; pre industrial cult(s). **SELECTED PUBLICATIONS** Auth, Voix et textualites du recit eschatalogique; The Arthurian Romances of Chretien de Troyes: Once and Future Fictions. **CONTACT ADDRESS** Dept of French and Italian Studies, Univ Massachusetts Amherst, Mass Ave, Amherst, MA, 01003. **EMAIL** maddox@frital.umass.edu

MADDOX, SARA STURM
DISCIPLINE FRENCH LITERATURE **EDUCATION** NC Univ, PhD. **CAREER** Prof, Univ MA Amherst. **RESEARCH** Medieval and Renaissance lit. **SELECTED PUBLICATIONS** Auth, Petrarch's Laurels; co-ed, Literary Aspects of Courtly Culture and Intergenres: Intergeneric Perspectives on Medieval French Literature. **CONTACT ADDRESS** Dept of French and Italian Studies, Univ Massachusetts Amherst, Mass Ave, Amherst, MA, 01003. **EMAIL** ssmaddox@frital.umass.edu

MADDUX, STEPHEN
DISCIPLINE MODERN LANGUAGE AND LITERATURE **EDUCATION** Univ Dallas, BA, 71; Univ Chicago, MA, 73; PhD, 79; addn stud, Univ Paris, 71-72; Univ Toronto, 75-76; Wilhelms Univ, 77-78. **CAREER** Assoc prof; hd, Fr prog. **RESEARCH** Montaigne, Pascal. **SELECTED PUBLICATIONS** Auth, The Fiction of the Livre in Robert de Boron's Merlin, Jour Rocky Mountain Medieval and Renaissance Assn, 85; Satan With and Without a Human Face in the Novels of Georges Bernanos, Claudel Studies, 86; Cocteau's Tristan and Iseut: A Case of Overmuch Respect, Tristan and Isolde: A Casebook New York: Garland, 95. **CONTACT ADDRESS** Dept of Mod Lang and Lit, Univ Dallas, 1845 E Northgate Dr, Irving, TX, 75062. **EMAIL** maddux@acad.udallas.edu

MADISON, CHARLES L.
DISCIPLINE CCC-SPEECH-LANGUAGE PATHOLOGY **EDUCATION** State Univ NY, BS, 66; Ohio Univ, MA, 67, PhD, 70. **CAREER** Prof, Wash State Univ, 70-. **HONORS AND AWARDS** Cert Clinical Competence in Speech Pathology, 71-; Wash Speech Lang Hearing Asn, 96. **MEMBERSHIPS** Amer Speech-Language-Hearing Asn; Int Asn for the Study of Child Lang; Int Soc Applied Psycholing; Wash Speech and Hearing Asn. **RESEARCH** Voice disorders, research methods, advanced speech and hearing sciences, and current literature. **SELECTED PUBLICATIONS** Auth, Attitudes Toward Mild Misarticulation Disordered Peers, Lang Speech and Hearing Services in Schools 23, 92; coauth, A Survey of Program Selection and Expectations of Current and Prospective Graduate Students, National Stud Speech-Lang-Hearing Asn J 20, 93. **CONTACT ADDRESS** Dept of Speech and Hearing Sciences, Washington State Univ, 201 Daggy Hall, Pullman, WA, 99164-2420. **EMAIL** madisonc@wsu.edu

MADLAND, HELGA STIPA
PERSONAL Born 00/00/1939, Klodnitz, Upper Silesai **DISCIPLINE** GERMAN LITERATURE AND LANGUAGE **EDUCATION** Idaho State Univ, BA, 74; Univ Wash, MA, 79, PhD(German and Span), 81. **CAREER** ASST PROF GERMAN, UNIV OKLA, 81-. **MEMBERSHIPS** MLA; SCent Mod Lang Asn; Lessing Soc; Am Asn Teachers German. **RESEARCH** Eighteenth century German literature; dramatic theory. **SELECTED PUBLICATIONS** Auth, The German Nachspiel in the 18th-Century, Ger Stud Rev, Vol 0016, 93; Madness and Lenz, 200 Years Later, Ger Quart, Vol 0066, 93; Women and Dramas in the 18th-Century, Ger Stud Rev, Vol 0016, 93; Action in Drama--its Theory and Practice According to Gottsched, J.C. and Lenz,J.M.R., J Engl and Ger Philol, Vol 0094, 95; Lenz, Jakob, Michael, Reinhold--Studies on his Complete Oeuvre, Seminar-J Ger Stud, Vol 0031, 95; The Taming of the Wild Soul--Literature and Passion in the Enlightenment, J Engl and Ger Philol, Vol 0096, 97. **CONTACT ADDRESS** Dept Mod Lang and Lit, Univ Okla, Norman, OK, 73019.

MAGLIOLA, ROBERT
PERSONAL NJ, 3 children **DISCIPLINE** COMPARATIVE LITERATURE, HERMENEUTICS CONCENTRATION **EDUCATION** Princeton Univ, PhD, 70. **CAREER** Asst prof of comparative lit, Purdue Univ, W Lafayette, IN, 70-73, assoc prof, 74-80, full prof, 81-84; Distinguished chair prof, National Taiwan Univ, Taipei, Taiwan, 90-93; distinguished prof of Philosophy and Religions, ABAC Univ, Bangkok, Thailand, 94-. **HONORS AND AWARDS** Resident NHC grantee, 79; NSC/Taiwan grants, 97. **MEMBERSHIPS** SPEP; IAPL; MLA; AAR; Centre Cultural International Cerisy-la-Salle, France. **RESEARCH** Hermeneutics (European and Asian); Buddism and Cathoicism in dialogue; Jacques Derrida. **SELECTED PUBLICATIONS** Auth, Phenomenology and Literature, Purdue Univ Press, 77; Derrida on the Mend, Purdue Univ Press, 84; On Deconstructing Life-Worlds: Buddhism, Christianity, Culture, Atlanta: Scholars Press, Am Academy of Relig, 97. **CONTACT ADDRESS** 100 Barbados Dr, Toms River, NJ, 08757-4024. **EMAIL** rmagliol@bellatlantic.net; jmagliola@lycos.com

MAHARG, JAMES
PERSONAL Born 05/12/1940, Glasgow, Scotland, m, 1967, 2 children **DISCIPLINE** SPANISH AMERICAN AND BRAZILIAN LITERATURES **EDUCATION** Univ Glasgow, MA, 67; Univ Ill, Urbana, PhD(Span-Am lit), 70. **CAREER** Asst prof, Univ Mich, Ann Arbor, 70-76; ASSOC PROF SPAN AND PORT, UNIV ILL, CHICAGO CIRCLE, 76-, Nat Endowment for Humanities res grant, 73; reader Span, Col Entrance Bd, 77. **RESEARCH** Reputation of Jose Ortega y Gasset in Latin America; modern Brazilian and Spanish American literatures; realism and naturalism in Brazil. **SELECTED PUBLICATIONS** Auth, Historiografia Indiana, Bull Hisp Stud, Vol 0071, 94; Ortegaygasset, a Humanist for Our Times, Bull Hisp Stud, Vol 0071, 94; The Armature of Conquest--Spanish Accounts of the Discovery of America, 1492-1589, Bull Hisp Stud, Vol 0072, 95; Spain and America Collide--Texts and Documents From Chroniclers of the Indies to Contemporary Writers 1492-1992, Bull Hisp Stud, Vol 0072, 95. **CONTACT ADDRESS** Dept Span Ital and Port, Univ of Ill, Chicago Circle, Chicago, IL, 60680.

MAHLENDORF, URSULA R.
PERSONAL Born 10/24/1929, Strehlen **DISCIPLINE** GERMAN LITERATURE **EDUCATION** Brown Univ, PhD, 58. **CAREER** Asst Ger, Brown Univ, 54-57; from instr to assoc prof, 57-77, PROF GER, UNIV CALIF, SANTA BARBARA, 77-, CHMN DEPT GER AND SLAVIC LANG, 80-, Assoc dir, Educ Abroad Prog, 68-71. **MEMBERSHIPS** MLA; Int Asn of Social Psychol; Am Asn of Social Psychiat; Asn Applied Psychoanal. **RESEARCH** Nineteenth and 20th century literature; psychology. **SELECTED PUBLICATIONS** Auth, Niedere Gangarten, World Lit Today, Vol 0066, 92; Unstete Leute, World Lit Today, Vol 0067, 93; Between the Past and the Future-Women Writers of the Gdr From an American Point-of View, Ger Quart, Vol 0069, 96. **CONTACT ADDRESS** Univ Calif, 399 Loma Media, Santa Barbara, CA, 93106.

MAIER, CAROL SMITH
PERSONAL Born 06/10/1943, Pittsburgh, PA, m, 1962, 2 children **DISCIPLINE** HISPANIC LITERATURE **EDUCATION** Douglass Col, BA, 68; Rutgers Univ, MA, 72, PhD(Span), 75. **CAREER** Asst prof, 76-80, ASSOC PROF SPAN, BRADLEY UNIV, 80-. **MEMBERSHIPS** MLA; Am Asn Teachers Span and Port; Am Lit Translr Asn; Women's Caucus Mod Lang; Asoc Int de Hispanistas. **RESEARCH** Ramon del Valle-Inclan; literary translation; women's studies. **SELECTED PUBLICATIONS** Auth, La aportacion cerrvantina a Yo soy aquel que ayer no mas decia, Mester, 5/66; Symbolist Aesthetics in Spanish: the concept of language in Valle-Inclan's La lampara maravillosa, Waiting for Pegasus, Studies of the Presence of Symbolism and Decadence in Hispanic Letters, Essays in Lit, 79; The poetry of Ana Castillo: a dialogue between poet and critic, Letras Femeninas, spring 80; Notas sobre melancolia y creacion en dos narradores valleinclanescos: El Marques de Brandomin y el poetta de La lampara marvillosa, Revista de Estudios Hispanicos, 1/81; Notas hacia una definicion del concepto de la historia en La lampara maravillosa, Explicacion de Textos Literarios, Vol IX, No 2; Xose Conde Corbal e a estetica do grabado: Una reforma do ollo por medio da deformacion da lina, Grial, Vol 70, 80; Transl, Imagination and (Un) academic Activity, Transl Rev, winter 80; Por tierras de Portugal y de Espana e Galicia: Unha rectificacion da perspectiva caztiza, planteada por Valle-Inclan, Grial, Vol 75, 82. **CONTACT ADDRESS** Dept of English and Foreign Lang, Bradley Univ, Peoria, IL, 61625.

MAIER, LINDA
DISCIPLINE SPANISH AMERICAN LITERATURE **EDUCATION** WA Univ, AB, 80; Univ VA, MA, 82 PhD, 87. **CAREER** Univ Ala **SELECTED PUBLICATIONS** Auth, Borges and the European Avant-garde, Lang, 96. **CONTACT ADDRESS** Univ AL, Huntsville, AL, 35899. **EMAIL** maierl@email.uah.edu

MAIERHOFER, WALTER
PERSONAL Burghausen, Germany **DISCIPLINE** GERMAN LITERATURE **EDUCATION** Univ Regensburg, Germany, MA, 85, PhD, 88. **CAREER** Lectr, 89-90, Univ Calif Santa Barbara; asst prof to assoc prof, 90-, Univ Iowa. **HONORS AND AWARDS** Alexander von Humboldt fel, 98. **MEMBERSHIPS** MLA; ASECS; N Amer Goethe Soc; Heine Soc. **RESEARCH** German literature, eighteenth & nineteenth century. **SELECTED PUBLICATIONS** Auth, Wilhelm Meisters Wanderjahre' und der Roman des Nebeneinander, 90; auth, Angelika Kauffman, dargestellt von Waltraud Maierhofer, 97; auth, Wahrheit und Dichtung, Historiographie und Fiktion im Erzahlwerk Ricarda Huchs, Euphorion, 94; auth, Krieg und Frieden in Gemalden und Briefen Angelika Kauffmanns, Jahrbuch des Vorarlberger Landesmuseumsvereins, 97; auth, Vetter Grune Goetherezeption in Julian Schuttings Zuhorerbehelligungen und Leserbelastigungen, Zeitschrift fur Deutsche Philologie, 97. **CONTACT ADDRESS** German Dept, Univ Iowa, Iowa City, IA, 52242-1323. **EMAIL** waltraud-maierhofer@uiowa.edu

MAIR, VICTOR H.
PERSONAL Born 03/25/1943, Canton, OH, m, 1970, 1 child **DISCIPLINE** CHINESE LANGUAGE AND LITERATURE **EDUCATION** Dartmouth Col, BA, 65; Univ London, BA, 72; Harvard Univ, MA, 73; PhD, 76; Univ London, M Phil, 84. **CAREER** Lectr, Tunghai Univ, 70-72; teaching fel and lectr, Harvard Univ, 73-77; asst prof, 77-79; asst prof, Univ Pa, 79-84; assoc prof, 84-88; prof, 89- ; vis prof, Duke Univ, 93-94; vis res prof, Kyoto Univ, 95-96. **HONORS AND AWARDS** Res grants from Alfred P. Slaon Found, Luce Found and Freeman Found; Nat Humanites Ctr fel, 91-92; Inst for Advan Study fel, 98. **MEMBERSHIPS** Asoc for Asian Studies; T'ang Studies Soc; Chinoper; Chinese Lang Soc of Hong Kong; World Hist Asoc. **RESEARCH** Popular Buddhist literature; vernauclar Sinitic lang; Sinitic etymology; origins of Chinese characters; Sino-Indian and Sino-Iranian cultural exchange; history of Chinese literature. **SELECTED PUBLICATIONS** Auth, Modern Chinese Writing, The World's Writing System, 96; auth, Ma Jianzhong and the Invention of Chinese Grammar, Studies on the History of Chines Syntax, 97; auth, The Prosimetirc Form in the Chinese Literary Tradition, Prosimetrum: Cross-Cultural Perspectives on Narrative in Prose and Verse, 97; ed, The Bronze Age and Early Iron Age Peoples of Eastern Central Asia, 98. **CONTACT ADDRESS** Dept. of Asian & ME Studies, Univ of Pennsylvania, Philadelphia, PA, 19104-6305. **EMAIL** vmair@sas.upenn.edu

MAIRE-CARLS, ALICE-CATHERINE
PERSONAL Born 06/14/1950, Mulhouse, France, m, 1977, 3 children **DISCIPLINE** HISTORY, POLISH LITERATURE **EDUCATION** Univ de Paris IV-Sorbonne, BA, 70, MA, 72, BA, 73, Doctorat de Troisieme Cycle, 76. **CAREER** Eastern Europ corresp, 81-98, ed adv, 98- , Center for Public Justice, Washington DC; from asst prof, history, to assoc prof, 92- , chemn Dept of Hist and Polit Sci, Univ Tenn, Martin. **HONORS AND AWARDS** Listed, Who's Who in America, Who's Who among Polish-Americans, Who's Who in American Education, Who's Who in Polish America, Who's Who in the World, Who's Who among America's Teachers, Who's Who in the South and Southwest, International Authors and Writers Who's Who, Who's Who of American Women; Int Scholar Award nominee, Univ Tenn, 95. **MEMBERSHIPS** Phi Kappa Phi; Phi Alpha Theta; Pi Delta Phi; Polish-Am Hist Asn; Polish Inst of Arts and Sci; Am Asn for Adv of Slavic Stud; AHA; Ctr for Public Justice; So Asn for Slavic Stud; So Hist Asn. **RESEARCH** Translation; Eastern European literature; history; twentieth-century Polish literature, history, society and politics. **SELECTED PUBLICATIONS** Transl, Echapper a ma tombe, by Jozef M. Rostocki, with intro, Editions Editiner, 95; transl, Jozef Wittlin, with intro, Poesie Premiere, 97; transl, Clarte, grace, humour: l'intellect de Wislawa Szymborska, by Anna Frajlich, Poesie Premiere, 97; transl, Polyphonic, equilibre, couleur: la poesie vitale de Awaikta, by Marilou Awiakta, with intro, Poesie premiere, 97; transl, Aleksander Wat, a contri-courant, with intro, Poesie Premiere, 98; transl, Devant l'autoportrait de Weimar, par Durer, Nocturnes, Devant Bonnard, Calligraphies, Les saules d'Alma-Ata, Nuit d'automne avec montagnes, oliviers et pleine lune, Poeme bucolique, by Aleksander Wat, with intro, le Journal des Poetes, Brusseld, 98; transl, Une mouche dans ma soupe, by Jozef M. Rostocki, Editions Editinter, 98; contribur, Encyclopedia of Modern East Europe, 1815-1989, Garland, forthcoming; auth, Jozef Wittlin's Passage Through France, in Proceedings of the Jozef Wittlin Conference, Columbia Univ, forthcoming. **CONTACT ADDRESS** 59 Lesa Dr, Jackson, TN, 38305. **EMAIL** accarls@utm.edu

MAJOR, JEAN-LOUIS
PERSONAL Born 07/16/1937, Cornwall, ON, Canada **DISCIPLINE** FRENCH LITERATURE **EDUCATION** Univ Ottawa, BA, BPh, 59, BA(Hon), LPh, 60, MA, 61, PhD, 65; Ecole Pratique des Hautes Etudes, Paris, 68-69. **CAREER** Prof, Col Bruyere d'Ottawa, 60-61; dept phil, Univ d'Ottawa, 61-65; prof adjoint, 65-67, prof agrege, 67-71, PROF TITULAIRE DEPT DE LETTRES FRANCAISES, UNIV D'OTTAWA, 71-, doyen associe a la recherche, faculte des arts, 91-97; vis prof, Univ Toronto, 70-71. **MEMBERSHIPS** Soc Royale Can **SELECTED PUBLICATIONS** Auth, Saint-Exupery, l'ecriture et la pensee, 68; auth, Leone de Jean Cocteau, 75; auth, Anne Hebert et le miracle de la parole, 76; auth, Radiguet, Cocteau, Les Joues en feu, 77; auth, La litterature francaise par les textes theoriques: XIX siecle, 77; auth, Paul-Marie Lapointe: la nuit incendiee, 78; auth, Le jeu en etoile, 78; auth, Entre l'ecriture et la parole, 84; auth, Henriette Dessaulles, Journal edition critique, 89; auth, Ringuet, Trente arpents edition critique, 91; ed, Autobiographies dans la revue Lettres quebecoises, 78-83; co-dir, Cahiers d'Inedits; dir, Bibliotheque du Nouveau Monde; coordr, Corpus d'Editions Critiques. **CONTACT ADDRESS** Dept de Lettres Francaises, Univ of Ottawa, Ottawa, ON, K1N 6N5.

MAJOR, JOHN STEPHEN
PERSONAL Born 10/05/1942, Englewood, NJ **DISCIPLINE** CHINESE INTELLECTUAL HISTORY, HISTORY OF SCIENCE **EDUCATION** Haverford Col, BA, 64; Harvard Univ, MA, 65, PhD(hist and EAsian lang), 73. **CAREER** Instr, 71-73, asst prof, 73-79, ASSOC PROF HIST, DARTMOUTH COL, 79-, Am Coun Learned Soc res grant Chinese hist, 74; vis fel, Cambridge Univ, 81-82. **MEMBERSHIPS** Asn Asian Studies; Soc Study Early China; Soc Study Chinese Relig; Am Orient Soc. **RESEARCH** Early Chinese religion and cosmology; theoretical foundations of Chinese science. **SELECTED PUBLICATIONS** Auth, The Rise of Early Modern Science--Islam, China, and the West, Isis, Vol 0085, 94. **CONTACT ADDRESS** Dept of Hist, Dartmouth Col, Hanover, NH, 03755.

MAKINO, YASUKO
PERSONAL Born 04/08/1937, Tokyo, Japan, m, 1963, 1 child **DISCIPLINE** LIBRARY SCIENCE; JAPANESE STUDIES **EDUCATION** Tokyo Women's Christian Univ, BA; Univ IL, MA, 70, MLS, 72. **CAREER** Univ IL, Urbana-Champaign, 72-91; Columbia Univ, 91-98; PRINCETON UNIV LIBRARY, 98-. **MEMBERSHIPS** ALA; Asn for Asian Studies. **RESEARCH** Japanese bibliography and reference works. **SELECTED PUBLICATIONS** Auth, Japan Through Children's Literature, Greenwood Press, 85; Student Guide to Japanese Sources in the Humanities, Center for Japanese Studies, Univ MI, 94; Japan and the Japanese: A Bibliographical Guide to Reference Sources, Greenwood Press, 96. **CONTACT ADDRESS** 7 Westwinds Dr., Princeton Junction, NJ, 08550. **EMAIL** ymakino@princeton.edu

MAKKAI, ADAM
PERSONAL Born 12/16/1935, Budapest, Hungary, m, 1966, 2 children **DISCIPLINE** LINGUISTICS **EDUCATION** Harvard Univ, BA, 58; Yale Univ, MA, 62, PhD(gen ling), 65. **CAREER** Asst prof English, Calif State Univ, Long Beach, 66-67; from asst prof to assoc prof ling, 67-74, PROF LING, UNIV ILL CHICAGO CIRCLE, 74-, Exec Dir and Dir Publ, Ling Asn Can and US, 74-, Paderewski Found grant ling, Univ Malaya, Kuala Lumpur, 63-64; Am Coun Learned Soc, Yale Univ, 64-65; NSF grant comput ling, Rand Corp, Santa Monica, Calif, 65-66; asst prof Russ, Occidental Col, 66-67; managing ed jour, Word, Int Ling Asn, 73-74; exec dir and dir publ and ed jour, Forum Ling, Ling Asn Can and US. **MEMBERSHIPS** Ling Soc Am; MLA; Int Ling Asn; Ling Asn Can and US. **RESEARCH** Idomaticity and English semantics; English lexicog-

raphy, poetry and translation; stratificational grammar. **SELECTED PUBLICATIONS** Auth, In Search of a Revolution--Discussion, Lang and Commun, Vol 0015, 95; Idiomatic Adaptive vs Literal Traditional Translation + Macleod, Ian Translation of Madach, Imre the 'Tragedy of Man', Hungarian Quart, Vol 0037, 96. **CONTACT ADDRESS** Dept of Ling, Univ Illinois, Chicago, IL, 60637.

MAKWARD, CHRISTIANE PERRIN
PERSONAL Born 01/06/1941, Hyeres, France, m, 1960, 2 children **DISCIPLINE** FRENCH LITERATURE, WOMEN'S STUDIES **EDUCATION** Sorbonne, Lic es Lett, 63, DLit(-French), 74; Univ Dakar, DES, 65. **CAREER** From asst lectr to lectr French lang & lit, Univ Ibadan, Nigeria, 62-67; lectr French lit, Univ Wis, 68-69 & 74-75; lectr, Univ Que-Rimouski, 76-77; asst prof, 77-80, assoc prof French, Pa State Univ, 80-96, prof French, 96-, Ed, Breff, Pa State Univ, 76-. **MEMBERSHIPS** MLA; Am Asn Teachers Fr; Women's Caucus Mod Lang; Asn Int Femmes Ecrivians; Asn Amis Cerisy-la-Salle. **RESEARCH** Contemporary French literature; psychoanalysis; stylistics. **SELECTED PUBLICATIONS** Auth, Mallarme and Ricardou: Echoes, 73, Claude Simon: Earth, Eros and Death, 74 & Interview with Helene Cixous, 76, Sub-Stance; La critique feminists: Elements d'une problematique, Revue Sci Humanies, Lille, 12/77; auth, Aspects of bisexuality in Claude Simon's works, In: Blinded Orion, Bucknell Univ (in press); Structures du silence/du delire: Marguerite Duras/Helene Cixous, Poetique, Paris (in press); Nouveau regard sur la crituque feministe, Revue de l'Univ d'Ottawa, Vol 50, No 1; Colette and signs, In: Colette, The Woman, The Writer, Pa State Univ Press, 81. **CONTACT ADDRESS** Dept of French, Pennsylvania State Univ, 316 Burrowes Bldg, University Park, PA, 16802-6203. **EMAIL** cjmg@psu.edu

MALANDRA, WILLIAM
DISCIPLINE CLASSICAL AND NEAR EASTERN STUDIES **EDUCATION** Haverford Col, BA, 64; Brown Univ, BA, 66; Univ Pa, PhD, 71. **CAREER** Assoc prof, Univ Minn, Twin Cities. **RESEARCH** Indo-Iranian philological studies. **SELECTED PUBLICATIONS** Auth, Avestan zanu-drajah: an Obscene Gesture, Indo-Iranian J 22, 80; An Introduction to Old Iranian Religion, Univ Minn Press, 83; Rasnu and the Office of Divine Judge: Comparative Reconstructions and the Varuna Problem, Festschrift for Ludo Rocher, Madras: Adyar Libr, 87. **CONTACT ADDRESS** Dept of Class and Near Eastern Stud, Univ Minn, Twin Cities, Minneapolis, MN, 55455.

MALBY, MARIA BOZICEVIC
PERSONAL Born 05/16/1937, Zagreb, Yugoslavia, d, 1 child **DISCIPLINE** RUSSIAN AND SERBO-CROATIAN LANGUAGES AND LITERATURES **EDUCATION** Fla State Univ, BA, 62; Harvard Univ, AM, 63, PhD(Slavic lang and lit), 70. **CAREER** Asst prof, Frostburg State Col, 66-70; assoc prof, 70-80, PROF GER AND RUSS, EAST CAROLINA UNIV, 80-. **MEMBERSHIPS** AAUP; MLA; SAtlantic Mod Lang Asn; Am Asn Teachers Slavic and East Europ Lang; Am Asn Slavic Scholars. **RESEARCH** Comparative Russian and Serbo-Croatian literature; German. **SELECTED PUBLICATIONS** Auth, Insel Bin Ich, Im Herzen Der Welt, World Lit Today, Vol 0069, 95; Die Schule Der Gottlosigkeit, World Lit Today, Vol 0069, 95. **CONTACT ADDRESS** Dept of Foreign Lang and Lit, East Carolina Univ, Greenville, NC, 27834.

MALKIEL, YAKOV
PERSONAL Born 07/22/1914, Kiev, Russia **DISCIPLINE** ROMANCE PHILOLOGY **EDUCATION** Univ Berlin, PhD, 38. **CAREER** Insts, Univ Wyo, 42; from lectr to asst prof Span and Port, 42-48, from assoc prof to prof Romance philol, 48-66, assoc dean, grad div, 63-66, PROF LING AND ROMANCE PHILOL, UNIV CALIF, BERKELEY, 66-, ED IN CHIEF, ROMANCE PHILOL, 47-; Guggenheim fels, 48-49, 59, 67; Intramural res fel humanities, 68-69; consult, Can Coun, 70 and Nat Endowment for Humanities, 77. **HONORS AND AWARDS** DHL, Univ Chicago, 69; LittD, Univ Ill, Urbana-Champaign, 76. **MEMBERSHIPS** MLA; Ling Soc Am (vpres, 55, pres, 65); Am Orient Soc; Philol Asn PACIFIC Coast (vpres, 63, pres, 65); Soc Ling Romane. **RESEARCH** General and Romance linguistics; theory of etymology; Hispanic lexicology. **SELECTED PUBLICATIONS** Auth, A Tribute to Devoto, Giacomo on the 10th-Anniversary of the 2-Day Seminar Held at Borzonasca in 1984, Italica, Vol 0069, 92; Latin and the Romance Languages in the Early Middle Ages, Stud in Lang, Vol 0016, 92; Writings on Philology and Linguistics, Italica, Vol 0069, 92; Levi,Ezio of Ancona, Italica, Vol 0069, 92; Judeo Romance Linguistics--a Bibliography, Latin, Italo Gallo Ibero, and Rhaeto Romance Except Castilian, Romance Philol, Vol 0046, 93; Michaelisdevasconcelos, Carolina 1851-1925, Romance Philol, Vol 0047, 93; Kahane,Henry + in Memoriam, Romance Philol, Vol 0046, 93; French Etymology--Introduction and Overview, Romance Philol, Vol 0046, 93; 3 Heirs to a Judeo-Latin Legacy--Judeo Ibero Romance, Yiddish and Rotwelsch, Romance Philol, Vol 0046, 93; Semantic Versus Formal Ingredients Distillable From Resistance to Language Shift, the Case of Spanish Dormir-Morir, Neophilologus, Vol 0077, 93; The Problem of the Old Spanish Sibilants, 3 Consecutive New Style Explanations, Bull Hisp Stud, Vol 0070, 93; Literary Language and its Public in Late Latin Antiquity and in the Middle Ages, Romance Philol, Vol 0048, 94; The Brothers Darmesteter and the Dawn of French Philosophy, Revue Des Etudes Juives, Vol 0153, 94. **CONTACT ADDRESS** Dept of Ling, Univ of Calif, 2321 Dwinelle Hall, Berkeley, CA, 94720.

MALL, LAURENCE
DISCIPLINE FRENCH LITERATURE **EDUCATION** Faculte des Lettres d'Avignon, France, BA, 80; Univ Pa, PhD, 90. **CAREER** Prof, Univ Ill Urbana Champaign. **RESEARCH** Rousseau; 18th century novel; 18th century history of ideas; narratology. **SELECTED PUBLICATIONS** Auth, Origines et retraites dans La Nouvelle, Peter Lang, 97; L'ethnotexte de la banlieue: Journal du dehors d'Annie Ernaux, 98. **CONTACT ADDRESS** French Dept, Univ Ill Urbana Champaign, 52 E Gregory Dr, Champaign, IL, 61820.

MALL, RITA SPARROW
PERSONAL New York, NY **DISCIPLINE** FRENCH LITERATURE **EDUCATION** Brooklyn Col, BA, 57; NY Univ, MA, 60; Univ Ill, Urbana, PhD(French), 69. **CAREER** Instr French, Univ Mass, Amherst, 60-62; asst prof, 68-76, ASSOC PROF FRENCH AND ASST DEAN ARTS AND SCI, LA SALLE COL, 76-, Asst French, NY Univ, 58-59 and Univ Ill, Urbana, 64-65 and 67-68. **MEMBERSHIPS** Am Asn Teachers Fr; AAUP. **RESEARCH** Nineteenth and twentieth century French novel. **SELECTED PUBLICATIONS** Auth, Tragic Muse--Rachel of the Comedie Francaise, 19th-Century Fr Stud, Vol 0024, 95. **CONTACT ADDRESS** Dept of Foreign Lang, La Salle Univ, 1900 W Olney Ave, Philadelphia, PA, 19141-1199.

MALONE, JOSEPH LAWRENCE
PERSONAL Born 07/02/1937, New York, NY, m, 1964, 2 children **DISCIPLINE** LINGUISTICS **EDUCATION** Univ Calif, Berkeley, BA, 63, PhD(ling), 67. **CAREER** From instr to assoc prof, 67-75, Prof Ling, Barnard Col, Columbia Univ, 75-, Chmn Dept, 67-, Contrib consult ling, Grolier Publ Co, NJ, 77-. **MEMBERSHIPS** Ling Soc Am; Am Orient Soc; North Am Conference on Afrnasiatic Lings. **RESEARCH** Linguistic theory; Semitic linguistics; translation. **SELECTED PUBLICATIONS** Auth, The Science and Linguistics in the Art of Translation, SUNY, Albany, 88; Tiberian Hebrew Phonology, Eisenbrauns, Winona Lake, 93; Carmina Gaiana, Linear Arts Books, NY, 97. **CONTACT ADDRESS** Dept of Ling Barnard Col, Columbia Univ, 3009 Broadway, New York, NY, 10027-6598. **EMAIL** jmalone@barnard.columbia.edu

MALONEY, ELLIOTT CHARLES
PERSONAL Born 04/17/1946, Pittsburgh, PA **DISCIPLINE** NEW TESTAMENT STUDIES, BIBLICAL LANGUAGES **EDUCATION** St Vincent Col, AB, 68; Pontifical Atheneum of St Anselm, Rome, STL, 72; Fordham Univ, PhD(New Testament), 79. **CAREER** Instr, 76-81, Asst Prof New Testament Studies & Bibl Lang, 81-92; Professor New Testament Studies & Bibl Lang, 92-, St Vincent Sem, 81-. **MEMBERSHIPS** Soc Bibl Lit; Cath Bibl Asn. **RESEARCH** Greek language of the New Testament; Gospel of Mark; Epistles of Paul. **SELECTED PUBLICATIONS** Auth, Semitic interference in Marcan Syntox, Soc Bibl Lit Dissertation Series, 81; transl, Epistles of James, 1-2 Peter, Jude, In: New American Bible, rev New Testament, 86. **CONTACT ADDRESS** St Vincent Col, 300 Fraser Purchase, Latrobe, PA, 15650-2690. **EMAIL** emaloney@stvincent.edu

MALPEZZI PRICE, PAOLA
DISCIPLINE ITALIAN AND FRENCH LITERATURE **EDUCATION** Univ Oregon, PhD. **CAREER** Assoc prof. **RESEARCH** Italian language and culture; French language, literature, and culture. **SELECTED PUBLICATIONS** Auth, pubs on French and Italian women writers. **CONTACT ADDRESS** Foreign Languages and Literature Dept, Colorado State Univ, Fort Collins, CO, 80523. **EMAIL** pmalpezziprice@vines.colostate.edu

MAMA, RAOUF
DISCIPLINE AFRICAN LITERATURE **EDUCATION** Univ MI, PhD. **CAREER** Eng Dept, Eastern Conn State Univ **SELECTED PUBLICATIONS** Tales in: Storytelling Mag; Parabola; CT Rev; Facts & Fiction. **CONTACT ADDRESS** Eastern Connecticut State Univ, 83 Windham Street, Willimantic, CT, 06226. **EMAIL** MAMA@ECSU.CTSTATEU.EDU

MANCA, FRANCO
PERSONAL Sardinia, Italy **DISCIPLINE** ITALIAN STUDIES **EDUCATION** Univ Calif, Berkeley, PhD. **CAREER** Assoc prof Ital, Univ Nev, Reno. **RESEARCH** Dante; the Italian renaissance. **SELECTED PUBLICATIONS** Published a number of articles on Dante and the Italian Renaissance; he has also published on contemporary Italian literature. **CONTACT ADDRESS** Univ Nev, Reno, Reno, NV, 89557. **EMAIL** unrug@unr.edu

MANIQUIS, ROBERT MANUEL
PERSONAL Born 09/04/1940, Newark, NY, m, 1961, 2 children **DISCIPLINE** ENGLISH LITERATURE, COMPARATIVE LITERATURE **EDUCATION** Rutgers Univ, BA, 62; Columbia Univ, MA, 63, PhD(English), 67. **CAREER** Asst prof English, 66-77, dir freshman English, 75-76, ASSOC PROF ENGLISH, UNIV CALIF, LOS ANGELES, 77-, Am Coun Learned Soc fel, 72-73. **MEMBERSHIPS** MLA; Philol Asn PACIFIC Coast. **RESEARCH** Nineteenth century Romanticism, English, French, and German; 19th century novel, English, French, and German. **SELECTED PUBLICATIONS** Auth, In the Theater of Romanticism--Coleridge, Nationalism, Women, Mod Lang Quart, Vol 0057, 96; Sacramental Commodities--Gift, Text and the Sublime in De-Quincey, Stud in Romanticism, Vol 0036, 97. **CONTACT ADDRESS** Dept of English, Univ of Calif, Los Angeles, CA, 90024.

MANLEY, FRANK
DISCIPLINE ENGLISH LANGUAGE AND LITERATURE **EDUCATION** Johns Hopkins Univ, PhD, 59. **CAREER** Charles Howard Candler Prof Ren Lit. **RESEARCH** Shakespeare; Donne; Renaissance drama and poetry. **SELECTED PUBLICATIONS** Ed/Trans, Epistola Ad Pomeranum; ed, All Fools; The Anniversaries; co-ed/trans, De Fructu qui ex Doctrina Percipitur. **CONTACT ADDRESS** English Dept, Emory Univ, 1380 Oxford Rd NE, Atlanta, GA, 30322-1950.

MANLEY, JOAN
PERSONAL England **DISCIPLINE** LINGUISTICS **EDUCATION** Univ Col, London, BA; Univ Tex at Austin, PhD. **CAREER** Past ch, ACTFL/Texas Proj; past pres, Tex For Lang Asn; undergrade stud adv; dept adv, over 20 yrs; actg dir, university's Acad Adv Ctr, 90-93; main tchr, Methods of For Lang Instruction. **MEMBERSHIPS** Bd, Southwest Conf Lang Tchg; bd, Amer Coun on the Teaching of For Languages. **RESEARCH** Renaissance theatre; preparation and certification of foreign language teachers; French language programs for beginners. **SELECTED PUBLICATIONS** Lead auth, 1st beginning Fr Prog, Qu'est-ce qu'on dit, Heinle and Heinle, 94; sec, Horizons, Heinle and Heinle, 98; **CONTACT ADDRESS** Dept of Languages and Linguistics, Univ of Texas, El Paso, 500 W University Ave, El Paso, TX, 79968. **EMAIL** jmanley@utep.edu

MANN, JOAN DEBBIE
PERSONAL Born 09/19/1955, Lakeland, FL, m, 1981, 1 child **DISCIPLINE** FRENCH **EDUCATION** Berry Col, BA, 76; Univ Fla, MA, 78, PhD, 87. **CAREER** From asst prof to assoc prof, Southern Ill Univ, 88-. **HONORS AND AWARDS** Phi Beta Kappa. **MEMBERSHIPS** MLA; AATF. **RESEARCH** 20th century French prose; francophone novel; short story genre. **SELECTED PUBLICATIONS** Auth, art, Andree Chedid, 95; auth, art, Andree Chedid Nouvelliste, 96. **CONTACT ADDRESS** Dept of Foreign Languages, Southern Illinois Univ Edwardsville, Box 1432, Edwardsville, IL, 62026-1432. **EMAIL** jmann@siue.edu

MANNING, ALAN
PERSONAL Born 11/12/1945, London, England, m, 1971, 2 children **DISCIPLINE** MEDIEVAL LITERATURE AND LANGUAGE **EDUCATION** Univ Wales, BA Hons, 69; Univ Wis-Milwaukee, MA, 72; Pa State Univ, PhD(French), 76. **CAREER** Asst prof transl, Laurentian Univ, 76-80; ASST PROF TRANSL, UNIV LAVAL, 80-, Can Coun res grant, Res Coun Can, 78. **RESEARCH** French Medieval treatises on heraldry; Medieval French literature and language. **SELECTED PUBLICATIONS** Auth, Articulation of the Text in English and French, Meta, Vol 0037, 92. **CONTACT ADDRESS** Dept of Transl, Univ of Laval, Quebec, PQ, G1K 7P4.

MANNING, SCOTT
DISCIPLINE FRENCH LITERATURE **EDUCATION** Wichita State Univ, BA, 86; Univ Kans, MA, 90, PhD, 97. **CAREER** French Dept, Susquehanna Univ **MEMBERSHIPS** Asn des Amis d'Andre Gide; Am Asn Tchr French. **SELECTED PUBLICATIONS** Auth, Understanding Eugene Ionesco (rev), 94. **CONTACT ADDRESS** Susquehanna Univ, 514 University Ave, Selinsgrove, PA. **EMAIL** manning@roo.susqu.edu

MANSOUR, GEORGE PHILLIP
PERSONAL Born 09/04/1939, Huntington, WV, m, 1961, 2 children **DISCIPLINE** SPANISH LITERATURE **EDUCATION** Marshall Univ, AB, 61; MI State Univ, MA, 62, PhD, 65. **CAREER** From instr to asst prof, 64-68, assoc prof, 68-77, assoc chairperson romance & class lang, 72-82, Prof Span, MI State Univ, 77. **MEMBERSHIPS** Am Asn Tchrs Span & Port; MLA. **RESEARCH** Nineteenth century Span lit; Don Juan theme; Span Romanticism. **SELECTED PUBLICATIONS** Auth, El convidado de piedra: A zarzuela by Rafael de Castillo, Hispania, 12/65; Time in the prose of J Echegaray, Ky Foreign Lang Quart, 68; Algunos Don Juanes olvidados del siglo XIX, Rev Estudios Hisp, 11/69; Concerning Rivas unexplained localization of Don Alvaro, Romance Notes, winter 78; Parallelism in Don Juan Tenorio, Hispania, 5/78; The poetization of experience, Hisp J, 81. **CONTACT ADDRESS** Dept of Romance Lang, Michigan State Univ, 161 Old Horticulture, East Lansing, MI, 48824-1112. **EMAIL** mansour@msu.edu

MANTEIGA, ROBERT CHARLES
PERSONAL Born 06/08/1947, Brooklyn, NY, m, 1970, 1 child **DISCIPLINE** SPANISH LETTERS & COMPARATIVE LITERATURE **EDUCATION** Univ Va, BA, 69, PhD(Span), 77; NY Univ, MA, 71. **CAREER** Instr Span, Univ Va, 72-73; instr, Univ RI, 73-75; lectr, Rutgers Univ, 75-76; asst prof, 76-80, Assoc Prof Span, Univ RI, 81-86, prof, 87-. **MEMBERSHIPS** MLA; Am Asn Teachers Span & Port; AAUP. **RESEARCH** Medieval lyric poetry; 20th century peninsular literature. **SELECTED PUBLICATIONS** Auth, Rafael Alberti,s Poetry: A visual Approach, Tamesis, London, 78; Emilio Prados, a Critical Biography in Dictionary of Literary Biographies, 94. **CONTACT ADDRESS** Dept of Lang, Univ of Rhode Island, Kingston, RI, 02881. **EMAIL** robert@uri2cc.uri.edu

MANTERO, MANUEL
PERSONAL Born 07/29/1930, Sevilla, Spain, m, 1963, 5 children **DISCIPLINE** MODERN HISPANIC POETRY **EDUCATION** Univ Seville, lic Derecho, 53; Univ Salamanca, Dr Derecho, 57. **CAREER** Prof, Univ Madrid, 60-69; from vis prof to prof, Western Mich Univ, 69-73; PROF SPAN, UNIV GA, 73-, Fels, Ital Govt and Coun Sci Res, Spain; mem, Coun Sci Res, Spain. **HONORS AND AWARDS** March Found Award, Spain; Nat Prize Lit, Spain, 60; Fastenrath Prize, Royal Span Acad Lang, 66. **MEMBERSHIPS** Am Asn Teachers and Span and Port; SAtlantic Mod Lang Asn. **RESEARCH** Twentieth century Spanish and Spanish-American poetry; modern Spanish literature. **SELECTED PUBLICATIONS** Auth, This Splendor, Lit Rev, Vol 0036, 93; The 'Art of Going Mad', Lit Rev, Vol 0036, 93; To Kronos, Or Words From a Drunk, Lit Rev, Vol 0036, 93; Cela, Camilo, Jose--the Rejection of the Ordinary, Ga Rev, Vol 0049, 95. **CONTACT ADDRESS** Dept Romance Lang, Univ Ga, Athens, GA, 30602.

MANUEL, SHARON Y.
DISCIPLINE PRODUCTION, ACOUSTICS, AND PERCEPTION OF SPEECH **EDUCATION** IA State Univ, BS; ID State Univ, MS; Yale Univ, Mphil, PhD. **CAREER** Speech, Emerson Col. **SELECTED PUBLICATIONS** Areas: variations among lang, speaking styles, and normal and disordered speech. **CONTACT ADDRESS** Emerson Col, 100 Beacon Street, Boston, MA, 02116-1596.

MAPA, MARINA VARGAS
PERSONAL Born 09/04/1925, Iloilo, Philippines **DISCIPLINE** SPANISH LANGUAGES & LITERATURE **EDUCATION** San Francisco Col Women, BA, 52, MA, 55; Stanford Univ, PhD(Span), 60. **CAREER** Instr Span & Latin, San Francisco Col Women, 56-61, from asst prof to assoc prof Span, 61-69, chmn dept, 63-69, lang lab dir, 65-69, registr, 66-68; Assoc Prof Span & Lang Lab Dir, Univ San Diego, 69- **MEMBERSHIPS** Nat Asn Lang Lab Dirs; Am Asn Teachers Span & Port; AAUP; Am Coun Teaching Foreign Lang. **RESEARCH** Methods of teaching Spanish. **CONTACT ADDRESS** Dept of Foreign Lang, Univ of San Diego, 5998 Alcala Park, San Diego, CA, 92110-2492. **EMAIL** mmapa@acusd.edu

MAPLES, ROBERT JOHN BARRIE
PERSONAL Born 05/01/1934, Rochester, NY, m, 1961, 1 child **DISCIPLINE** ROMANCE LANGUAGES **EDUCATION** Univ Rochester, AB, 56; Yale Univ, PhD(French), 65. **CAREER** Instr French, Univ Rochester, 62-65; asst prof, Univ Mich, Ann Arbor, 65-69; Assoc Prof French, Lycoming Col, 69-. **MEMBERSHIPS** Am Asn Teachers Fr. **RESEARCH** French Romantic literature. **SELECTED PUBLICATIONS** Auth, Individuation in Nodier's La fee aux miettes, Studies Romanticism, fall 68. **CONTACT ADDRESS** Dept of Foreign Lang & Lit, Lycoming Col, 700 College Pl, Williamsport, PA, 17701-5192. **EMAIL** maples@lycoming.edu

MARAHRENS, GERWIN
PERSONAL Born 12/12/1929, Breslau, Germany, m, 1962, 1 child **DISCIPLINE** GERMAN LANGUAGES AND LITERATURE **EDUCATION** Univ Freiburg, PhD, 58. **CAREER** Asst lectr Ger lang and lit, Univ Edinburgh, 58-61; from asst prof to assoc prof, 62-72, actg chmn dept, 70, PROF GER LANG, UNIV ALTA 72-, CHMN DEPT, 71-. **MEMBERSHIPS** Can Asn Univ Teachers Ger; Am Asn Teachers Ger; MLA; Am Soc 18th Century Studies. **RESEARCH** Eighteenth to 20th century literature; Goethe. **SELECTED PUBLICATIONS** Auth, Redefining Goethe Aphorisms, Goethe Jahrbuch, Vol 0110, 93; Goethe Other 'Faust'--the Drama, Part II, Seminar-J Ger Stud, Vol 0031, 95. **CONTACT ADDRESS** Dept of Ger Lang, Univ of Alta, 183 Quesnell Crescent, Edmonton, AB, T6G 2E1.

MARANTZ, ENID GOLDSTINE
PERSONAL Born 12/25/1923, Winnipeg, MB, Canada, m, 1961 **DISCIPLINE** FRENCH **EDUCATION** Univ Man, BA, 46; Univ Paris, DUniv, 49. **CAREER** Lectr, 51-52, 53-58, asst prof, 58-68, dep registr, 66-67, registr, Univ Col, 68-71, ASSOC PROF FRENCH, UNIV MAN, 68-, Vpres, Alliance Francaise de Winnipeg, 64-70; mem, Second Lang Curric Coun, Prov Man, 69-73; pres, Alliance Francaise, Man, 70-73; adv, Fed Alliances Francaises du Can, 71-; mem bd teacher educ and certification, Prov Man, 77-78; mem senate, Univ Man, 76-81, senate exec, 79-81. **MEMBERSHIPS** Asn Can Univ Teachers Fr; Can Comp Lit Asn; Soc des Amis de Marcel; Praust et des Amis de Cornbray; MLA. **RESEARCH** Comparative literature; Marcel Proust; 20th century novel and drama. **SELECTED PUBLICATIONS** Auth, The Infinite, the Uncompleted and the Ending in the Proustian Text--the Case of Mlle De Stermaria, Etudes Francaises, Vol 0030, 94. **CONTACT ADDRESS** Univ Man, 467 Univ Col, Winnipeg, MB, R3T 2N2.

MARCEAU, WILLIAM CHARLES
PERSONAL Born 02/23/1927, Rochester, NY **DISCIPLINE** FRENCH LITERATURE **EDUCATION** Univ Western Ont, BA, 52; Univ Laval, M-es-A, 64, PhD(French lit), 68; Sorbonne, dipl French lit, 69. **CAREER** Prof English, Sec Inst Sacre-Coeur, Annonay, France, 60-62; head dept lang, Aquinas Inst Rochester, 63-65; chmn dept lang, 68-72, ASSOC PROF FRENCH LIT, ST JOHN FISHER COL, 68-, COORDR FOREIGN STUDIES PROG, 80-, Fulbrigt prog adv, St John Fisher Col. **HONORS AND AWARDS** MA, Univ Laval, 75. **MEMBERSHIPS** AAUP; Am Asn Teachers Fr; Acad Salesienne; Am Coun Teaching Foreign Lang; N Am Soc 17th Century Fr Lit. **RESEARCH** History of modern French philosophy; history of French literature; French spirituality of the 17th century. **SELECTED PUBLICATIONS** Auth, an Approach to the 'Pensees' of Pascal, Fr Rev, Vol 0069, 95; 'Reflexions Sur Leloquence Des Predicateurs' 1695 by Arnauld,Antoine and 'Avertissement En Tete De Sa Traduction Des Sermons De Saint Augustin' 1694 by Dubois, Philippe, Goibaut, Fr Rev, Vol 0068, 95. **CONTACT ADDRESS** Dept of Mod Lang, St John Fisher Col, Rochester, NY, 14618.

MARCH, WALLACE EUGENE
PERSONAL Born 07/08/1935, Dallas, TX, m, 1957, 2 children **DISCIPLINE** THEOLOGY; ANCIENT LANGUAGES **EDUCATION** Austin Col, BA, 57; Austin Presby Theol Sem, BD, 60; Union Theol Sem, NY, PhD(Old Testament), 66. **CAREER** From instr to assoc prof, Austin Presby Theol Sem, 64-73, prof, 73-82; Arnold B Rhodes Prof Old Testament, Louisville Presby Theol Sem, 82-, Dean, 92-. **HONORS AND AWARDS** Rockefeller Schol, 64; Advanced Rel Study Fel, 66, 74; Asn Theol Schs Theol Scholar res grant, 80. **MEMBERSHIPS** Soc Bibl Lit; Am Schs Orient Res. **RESEARCH** Prophetic literature, particularly the sixth and eighth centuries; form criticism and literary criticism; Biblical theology. **SELECTED PUBLICATIONS** Contribr, Laken: its functions and meanings, In: Rhetorical Criticism, Pickwick, 74; Prophecy, In: Old Testament Form Criticism, Trinity Univ, 74; auth, Basic Bible Study, German Press, 78; Ed, Texts and Testaments: Critical Essays on the Bible and Early Church Fathers, Trinity Univ, 80; auth, Biblical Theology, authority and the Presbyterians, J Presby Hist, 81; Israel and the Politics of Land, John Knox Press, 94; Haggai, The New Interpreter's Bible, Abingdon Press, 96. **CONTACT ADDRESS** Louisville Presbyterian Theol Sem, 1044 Alta Vista Rd, Louisville, KY, 40205-1758. **EMAIL** emarch@lpts.edu

MARCHAND, JAMES WOODROW
PERSONAL Born 11/11/1926, Birmingham, AL, m, 3 children **DISCIPLINE** GERMANIC LANGUAGES **EDUCATION** George Peabody Col, BA, 50; Vanderbilt Univ, MA, 51; Univ Mich, PhD(Ger lang), 55. **CAREER** Asst prof mod lang, Cumberland Univ, 50-51; asst prof, Howard Col, 51-52; instr Ger, Wayne Univ, 53-54; instr, Univ Mich, 54-55; asst prof, Wash Univ, 55-58; assoc prof, Univ Calif, 58-60; prof, Vanderbilt Univ, 60-67; prof, Cornell Univ, 67-69; prof, univ, 69-71, PROF GER, CTR ADVAN STUDY, UNIV ILL, URBANA, 71-, Vis lectr, Harvard Univ, 57; Guggenheim fel, 58; researcher, Nat Endowment for Humanities, 76-77. **MEMBERSHIPS** MLA; Ling Soc Am; Soc Advan Scand Studies. **RESEARCH** Mediaeval literature; Ger linguistics; general linguistics. **SELECTED PUBLICATIONS** Auth, Singers of the Virgin in 13th-Century Spain + an Essay on Johannes Aegidii, Bull Hisp Stud, Vol 0071, 94; A Complete Concordance to Gottfried-Von-Strassburg 'Tristan', Ger Quart, Vol 0068, 95; The Computer in the Humanities, Friend Or Foe, J Aesth Educ, Vol 0030, 96. **CONTACT ADDRESS** Ctr for Advan Study, Univ of Ill, Urbana, IL, 61801.

MARCHIONE, MARGHERITA FRANCES
PERSONAL Born 02/19/1922, Little Ferry, NJ **DISCIPLINE** ROMANCE LANGUAGES; AMERICAN HISTORY **EDUCATION** Georgian Court Col, AB, 43; Columbia Univ, AM, 49, PhD(Ital), 60. **CAREER** Teacher parochial & private high schs, 43-54; instr lang, Villa Walsh Col, 54-67; assoc prof, 67-77, chmn dept lang, 67-68, Prof Ital, Fairleigh Dickinson Univ, Florham-Madison Campus, 77-, Res grants, Fairleigh Dickinson Univ, 68-69, 71-82; NDEA grant Ital inst undergrad, US Off Educ, 68; consult & rep, Gallery Mod Art, 68, 69; dir Ital Inst, Univ Salerno, 72, Tivoli, 73, Rome, 74; mem exec coun, Am Ital Hist Asn, 77-79; mem adv bd, NJ Cath Hist Rec Comn, 77-; NJ Hist Comn, 78-; Nat Hist Publ & Records Comn, 78, 79, 80 & 81; Nat Endowment for Humanities grant, 80-83. **HONORS AND AWARDS** Am-Ital Achievement Award in Educ, 71; UNICO Nat Rizzuto Award, 77; Star of Solidarity of Ital Repub, Pres Italy, 77. **MEMBERSHIPS** Am Asn Teachers Ital; MLA; Am Coun Teaching Foreign Lang; Am Inst Ital Studies (pres, 77-80); Am Ital Hist Asn. **RESEARCH** Contemporary Italian Culture and literature; Dante; the papers of Philip Mazzei. **SELECTED PUBLICATIONS** Transl & ed, Philip Mazzei: Jefferson's Zelous Whig, Am Inst Ital Studies, 75; ed, Lettere di Clemente Rebora, Ed di Storia e Letteratura, Rome, vol I, 76, vol II, 82; auth, Clemente Rebora, G K Hall, 78; ed, Philip Mazzei: My life and wanderings, Am Inst Ital Studies, 80; Philip Mazzei: The comprehensive microfilm edition of his papers, Kraus-Thomson Orgn Ltd, 82; Guiseppe Prezzolini: Un secodo, di attivita, Ruscovi Books, Milan, 82; Philip Mazzei: Selected Writings and Correspondence, 1730-1816, Ed di Storia a Letteratura, Rome, vol I, 82. **CONTACT ADDRESS** Col of Arts & Sci Fairleigh, Fairleigh Dickinson Univ, Madison, NJ, 07940.

MARCONE, ROSE MARIE
PERSONAL Born 11/05/1938, White Plains, NY **DISCIPLINE** SPANISH **EDUCATION** Mary Washington Col, BA, 60; Johns Hopkins Univ, PhD(Span), 64. **CAREER** Asst prof, 64-67, assoc prof, 67-74, PROF SPAN AND ITAL, UNIV RICHMOND, 74-, CHMN DEPT MOD FOREIGN LANG, 72-. **MEMBERSHIPS** MLA; AAUP; Am Asn Teachers Span and Port. **RESEARCH** Contemporary Spanish literature; Golden Age drama. **SELECTED PUBLICATIONS** Auth, The Role of Augusto-Perez + Unamuno--a Study of 'Niebla', Confluencia-Revista Hisp De Cultura Y Lit, Vol 0005, 89; an Approach to Unamuno 'Cuentos', Neophilologus, Vol 0078, 94. **CONTACT ADDRESS** Dept of Mod Foreign Lang, Univ of Richmond, 28 Westhampton Way, Richmond, VA, 23173-0002.

MARCUS, DAVID
PERSONAL Dublin, Ireland **DISCIPLINE** BIBLE AND ANCIENT SEMITIC LANGUAGES **EDUCATION** Cambridge Univ, BA; Columbia Univ, PhD. **CAREER** Fac, Columbia Univ; prof, chr, Bible and Ancient Semitic Languages, Jewish Theol Sem Am. **RESEARCH** Thc Bible and the Ancient Near East; presently working with an international team of scholars revising the critical edition of the Hebrew Bible. **SELECTED PUBLICATIONS** Auth, From Balaam to Jonah: Anti-prophetic Satire in the Hebrew Bible, Brown Judaic Studies series; numerous scholarly articles; two language manuals, Akkadian, the ancient language of Mesopotamia, Tthe Aramaic of the Babylonian Talmud. **CONTACT ADDRESS** Jewish Theol Sem of America, 3080 Broadway, New York, NY, 10027. **EMAIL** damarcus@jtsa.edu

MARCUS, MILICENT
DISCIPLINE ITALIAN STUDIES **EDUCATION** Cornell, BA, 68; Yale Univ, PhD, 74. **CAREER** Asst prof to prof, Univ Tx, 73-98; PROF, UNIV PA, 98-. **HONORS AND AWARDS** Phi Beta Kappa; Guggenheim fel; Getty grant; Fulbright fel; Marcus DiVito chair, Italian stud. **MEMBERSHIPS** MLA; AATI; AAIS; Am Boccaccio Asn. **RESEARCH** Medieval and mod Italian lit, Italian cinema. **SELECTED PUBLICATIONS** Auth, Filmmaking by the Book: Italian Cinema and Literary Adaptation, Johns Hopkins Univ Press, 93; auth, Italian Film in the Light of Neorealism, Princeton Univ Press, 86; auth, An Allegory of Form: Literary Self-Consciousness in the Decameron, in Stanford French and Italian Studies, 18, 79; auth, Liberating the Garden: Eden and the Fall from Paisa to Mediterraneo, in Italy and America, 1943-44, La Citta del Sole, 97; auth, I misteriosi fegatelli di Ginger e Fred Mystfest 1997, Mondadori, 97. **CONTACT ADDRESS** Dept of Romance Langs, Univ of Pennsylvania, Philadelphia, PA, 19104.

MARGOLIN, URI
PERSONAL Born 12/22/1942, Tel Aviv, Israel, m, 1968, 1 child **DISCIPLINE** COMPARATIVE LITERATURE, POETICS **EDUCATION** Hebrew Univ, Jerusalem, BA, 64; Cornell Univ, MA, 70, PhD(comp lit), 72. **CAREER** ASSOC PROF COMP LIT, UNIV ALTA, 72-, Alexander von Humboldt postdoctoral comp lit, W Ger, 76-77; Can Coun fel comp lit, Ottawa, 77. **MEMBERSHIPS** Int Comp Lit Asn; Can Comp Lit Asn. **RESEARCH** Poetics; theory of genres; literary methodology. **SELECTED PUBLICATIONS** Auth, How to De-Construct a Narrative World, Can Rev Comp Lit-Revue Canadienne De Litterature Comparee, Vol 0021, 94; Possible Worlds in Literary Theory, Style, Vol 0029, 95; Changing Individuals in Narrative--Science, Philos, Lit, Semiotica, Vol 0107, 95; Postmodern Characters--a Study of Characterization in British and American Postmodern Fiction, Semiotica, Vol 0106, 95. **CONTACT ADDRESS** Dept of Comp Lit, Univ of Alta, Edmonton, AB, T6G 2E1.

MARGOLIS, NADIA
PERSONAL Born 04/27/1949, Neuilly-sur-Seine, France **DISCIPLINE** MEDIEVAL LITERATURE, FRENCH POETRY **EDUCATION** Univ NH, AB, 71; Stanford Univ, PhD (French), 77. **CAREER** Ed asst, Speculum, Mediaeval Acad Am, 77-78; ASST PROF FRENCH, AMHERST COL, 78-, Attache res humanisme francais, Ctr Nat Res Sci, 73-; Nat Endowment for Humanities independent res fel, 81-82. **MEMBERSHIPS** MLA; Mediaeval Acad Am; Soc Rencesvals; Int Courtly Lit Soc. **RESEARCH** Fifteenth century France; French poetic theory; comparative Medieval literature. **SELECTED PUBLICATIONS** Auth, Christine De Pizan--a Bibliographical Guide, Supplement I, Speculum-J Medieval Stud, Vol 0072, 97; John of Salisbury 'Policraticus' 1372--Books I-III, Speculum-J Medieval Stud, Vol 0072, 97. **CONTACT ADDRESS** Dept of Romance Lang, Amherst Col, Amherst, MA, 01002.

MARICHAL, JUAN
PERSONAL Born 02/02/1922, Teneriffe, Spain, m, 1947, 2 children **DISCIPLINE** SPANISH **EDUCATION** Univ Algiers, bachelier, 41; Princeton Univ, MA, 48, PhD(Romance lang), 49. **CAREER** Instr Span, Princeton Univ, 46-48 and Johns Hopkins Univ, 48-49; asst prof Romance lang, Harvard Univ, 49-53; assoc prof Span, Bryn Mawr Col, 53-58; assoc prof Romance lang, 58-61, prof, 61-80, SMITH PROF ROMANCE LANG AND LIT, HARVARD UNIV, 80-, Guggenheim fel, 59 and 71-72; syndicator, Univ Press, Harvard Univ, 65-69; mem educ adv bd, Guggenheim Found, 67-. **HONORS AND AWARDS** Hon chair, San Marcos Univ, Lima, 65. **MEMBERSHIPS** Corresp mem Hisp Soc Am; MLA; Am Asn Teachers Span and Port. **RESEARCH** Spanish history, 1898-1936; Latin American intellectual history, 1810-1960. **SELECTED PUBLICATIONS** Auth, an Interview With Marichal, Juan, Insula Revista De Letras Y Ciencias Humanas, Vol 0051, 96. **CONTACT ADDRESS** Widener Libr, Harvard Univ, Cambridge, MA, 02138.

MARINONI, R. MAX
DISCIPLINE FRENCH LANGUAGE **EDUCATION** Univ Grenoble, BA, 61; Univ WA, MA, 65, Doctorate, 75. **CAREER** Instr, Seattle Univ. **MEMBERSHIPS** Northwest Asn Lang Lab; MLA; WAFLT; Puget Sound Alliance For FL. **SELECTED PUBLICATIONS** Transl, Paul Bleton, auth, Paralitterature and Serialization, Para-Doxa; Marc Richir, auth, Merleau Ponty and the Question of Phenomenological Architectonics in Patrick Burke and Jan Van Der Veke, eds, Merleau Ponty in Contemporary Perspective, Klower, 93. **CONTACT ADDRESS** Seattle Univ, Seattle, WA, 98122-4460. **EMAIL** marinoni@seattleu.edu

MARIOTTI, ARLEEN
DISCIPLINE READING, LANGUAGE ARTS AND EDUCATIONAL MEASUREMENT **EDUCATION** Univ FL, BA, 70, MEd, 71; Univ S FL, PhD, 82. **CAREER** Assoc prof, Univ of Tampa. **MEMBERSHIPS** Phi Delta Kappa; Kappa Delta Pi. **SELECTED PUBLICATIONS** Coauth, text Linking Reading Assessment to Instruction: An Application Worktext for Elementary Classroom Teachers, 2nd ed, 97. **CONTACT ADDRESS** Dept of Educ, Univ of Tampa, 401 W. Kennedy Blvd, Tampa, FL, 33606-1490.

MARKS, ELAINE
PERSONAL Born 11/13/1930, New York, NY, d **DISCIPLINE** FRENCH STUDIES **EDUCATION** Bryn Mawr Col, AB(magna cum laude with Honors in French), 52; Univ PA, MA, 53; New York Univ, PhD, 58. **CAREER** Graduate asst, NY Univ, 54-56, instr, 57-60, asst prof, 60-62; assoc prof, Univ WI-Milwaukee, 63-65; prof, Univ MA-Amherst, 65-66; prof, Univ WI-Madison, 66-68; vis prof, Univ MA-Amherst, 71, prof, 71-73; lect, Univ WI-Madison, 77, prof to Germaine Bree prof, Dept of French and Italian and Women's Studies Prog, Univ WI-Madison, 80-. **HONORS AND AWARDS** Fulbright fel to Paris, 56-57; NY Univ Alumnae Pin for Scholarship, 58; Johnson fel, Inst for Res in the Humanities of the Univ WI, 62-63; grants from the Ford Found, the Johnson Found, the Stackner Family, 79-84; YWCA Women of Distinction Award, 82; grad school res support (summer), 86, 88; WARF/Univ Houses professorship, 88; Vilas Assoc awarded and declined, 88; Univ WI Fac Development grant, 90; elected second vice pres, MLA, 91; John Simon Guggenheim Memorial Found fel, 92; Chancellor's Award for Excellence in Teaching, 93; pres, MLA, 93; NYU, Distinguished Alumni Award, 94; Officier dans l'Ordre des Palmes Academiques, 94; Hilldale Award in the Humanities, 95-96. **MEMBERSHIPS** MLA; MMLA; AATF; Nat Women's Studies Asn; Societe des Amis de Colette; Simone de Beauvoir Soc; Women in French. **RESEARCH** 19th and 20th Century French Lit; women writers. **SELECTED PUBLICATIONS** Auth, Marr and as Metaphor: the Jewish Presence in French Writing, Columbia Univ Press, 96. **CONTACT ADDRESS** Dept of French and Italian, Univ of Wisconsin, Madison, 618 Van Hize Hall, 1220 Linder Dr, Madison, WI, 53706. **EMAIL** emarks@marc.wisc.edu

MARMURA, MICHAEL ELIAS
PERSONAL Born 11/11/1929, Jerusalem, Palestine, m, 1962, 3 children **DISCIPLINE** ISLAMIC PHILOSOPHY, ARABIC **EDUCATION** Univ Wis, BA, 53; Univ Mich, MA, 55, PhD(Near Eastern studies), 59. **CAREER** Lectr Islamic philos and theol, 59-62, from asst prof to assoc prof, 62-69, assoc chmn dept Mid E and Islamic studies, 69-78, PROF ISLAMIC PHILOS AND THEOL, UNIV TORONTO, 69, CHMN DEPT MID E AND ISLAMIC STUDIES, 78-. **MEMBERSHIPS** Am Orient Soc; Can Philos Asn. **RESEARCH** Islamic theology. **SELECTED PUBLICATIONS** Auth, Ghazalian Causes and Intermediaries + Article Rev of Frank,Richard 'Creation and the Cosmic System', J Amer Oriental Soc, Vol 0115, 95; The Formation of Modern Arabic Scientific and Intellectual Vocabulary, Speculum-J Medieval Stud, Vol 0071, 96. **CONTACT ADDRESS** Dept of Mid E and Islamic Studies, Univ of Toronto, Toronto, ON, M5S 1A1.

MARQUESS, HARLAN EARL
PERSONAL Born 01/23/1931, Sheridan, WY, m, 1958, 3 children **DISCIPLINE** SLAVIC LINGUISTICS, RUSSIAN LANGUAGE **EDUCATION** Univ Calif, Berkeley, AB, 58, MA, 60, PhD, 66. **CAREER** From instr to prof, 64-98, prof emer Slavic Lang, Univ Wis, Madison, 98-. **MEMBERSHIPS** Ling Soc Am; Int Ling Asn; Am Asn Teachers Slavic & E Europ Lang; Am Asn Advan Slavic Studies. **RESEARCH** Structure of Russian; nonstandard Russian speech; morphology of Czech. **SELECTED PUBLICATIONS** Coauth, Soviet Prison Camp Speech, Univ Wis, 72. **CONTACT ADDRESS** Dept of Slavic Lang, Univ of Wis, 1220 Linden Drive, Madison, WI, 53706-1557. **EMAIL** hemarque@facstaff.wisc.edu

MARQUEZ, ANTONIO
DISCIPLINE AMERICAN AND COMPARATIVE LITERATURE **EDUCATION** Univ Nmex, PhD, 77. **CAREER** Instr, Univ NMex, 77-. **HONORS AND AWARDS** Fulbright scholar/lectr. **SELECTED PUBLICATIONS** Auth, Richard Rodriguez's Hunger of Memory and New Perspectives on Ethnic Autobiography, Tchg Am Ethnic Lit, UNM, 95. **CONTACT ADDRESS** Univ NMex, Albuquerque, NM, 87131.

MARQUEZ-VILLANUEVA, FRANCISCO
PERSONAL Born 03/21/1931, Seville, Spain, m, 1960, 3 children **DISCIPLINE** SPANISH LANGUAGE AND LITERATURE **EDUCATION** Univ Seville, Spain, PhD(lit), 58. **CAREER** Prof adj Span lit, Univ Seville, Spain, 55-59; instr Romance lang, Harvard Univ, 59-62; asst prof, Univ BC, 62-65 and Harvard Univ, 65-67; prof, Rutgers Univ, 67-68 and Grad Ctr, City Univ New York, 68-78; PROF SPAN, HARVARD UNIV, 78-. **MEMBERSHIPS** MLA; Int Asn Hispanists; Soc Span and Port Hist Studies. **RESEARCH** Mediaeval and Golden Age Spanish literature; intellectual and religious history; comparative literature. **SELECTED PUBLICATIONS** Auth, A Modest Tribute to Widener Library, Harvard Libr Bull, Vol 0006, 95. **CONTACT ADDRESS** Dept of Romance Lang, Harvard Univ, Boylston Hall, Cambridge, MA, 02138-3800.

MARRONE, NILA GUTIERREZ
PERSONAL La Paz, Bolivia **DISCIPLINE** SPANISH LINGUISTICS, SPANISH AMERICAN LITERATURE **EDUCATION** Columbia Univ, BA, 70, NY Univ, MA, 72, PhD(Span and ling), 75. **CAREER** Lectr Span, New York Univ, 72-73; assoc, Columbia Univ, 73-74; ASST PROF SPAN, UNIV CONN, 75-. **MEMBERSHIPS** Am Asn Teachers Span and Port; MLA. **RESEARCH** Descriptive Spanish linguistics; applied and sociolinguistics. **SELECTED PUBLICATIONS** Auth, Remembering Mead, Robert, G., Hispania-J Devoted tchg Span Port, Vol 0079, 96. **CONTACT ADDRESS** Dept of Span, Univ of Conn, Storrs, CT, 06268.

MARSHALL, GROVER EDWIN
PERSONAL Born 03/28/1930, Portland, ME, m, 1966, 1 child **DISCIPLINE** FRENCH; ITALIAN **EDUCATION** Bowdoin Col, BA, 51; Princeton Univ, MA, 54, PhD(French), 71. **CAREER** Instr French & Ital, Princeton Univ, 54-58; instr, Williams Col, 58-60, asst prof Romanic lang, 60-64, lectr, 64-65; Asst Prof, 65-90, Assoc Prof French & Ital, Univ NH, 95-, Chmn Dept, 73-80, 81-83, 88-91. **HONORS AND AWARDS** Phi Beta Kappa, 50. **MEMBERSHIPS** Am Asn Teachers Fr; NE Mod Lang Asn. **RESEARCH** Francophone Caribbean **CONTACT ADDRESS** Dept of French, Univ of New Hampshire, 15 Library Way, Durham, NH, 03824-3596. **EMAIL** groverm@christa.unh.edu

MARSHALL, PETER K.
PERSONAL Born 07/02/1934, Cardiff, Wales, d, 2 children **DISCIPLINE** CLASSICAL LANGUAGES, MEDIEVAL LITERATURE **EDUCATION** Univ SWales, BA, 54; Oxford Univ BA, 56, MA, 60. **CAREER** Instr classics, 59-61, asst prof, 62-68, assoc prof, 68-73, Prof Classics, Amherst Col, 73-, Asst lectr Latin & Greek, Univ Liverpool, England, 61-62. **HONORS AND AWARDS** ACLS fel, 76-77; Guggenheim fel, 80-81, MA, Amherst Col, 73. **MEMBERSHIPS** Class Asn Gt Brit; Am Philol Asn; Medieval Acad Am. **RESEARCH** The textual transmission of classical Latin authors; the Commentarii of Servius; the De Proprietatibus Rerum of Bartholomaeus Anglicus. **SELECTED PUBLICATIONS** Auth, Utopia, Sir Thomas More, Washington Sq Press, 65; ed, A Gellii Noctes Atticae, 2 vols, Oxford Univ Press, 68; auth, The Manuscript Tradition of Cornelius Nepos, Univ London, 77; ed, Cornelii Nepotis Vitae cum Fragmentis, Teubner, Leipzig, 77; Isidore, Etymologies Book II, Les Belles Lett, Paris, 82; coauth, Texts and Transmission, Clarendon Press, 83; auth, Servati Lupi Epistulae, Teubner, 84; Hyginus Fabulae, Teubner, 93; Servius and Commentary on Virgil, CEMERS, 97. **CONTACT ADDRESS** Dept of Classics, Amherst Col, Amherst, MA, 01002-5000. **EMAIL** pkmarshall@amherst.edu

MARSLAND, AMY
PERSONAL Born 03/23/1924, Saskatoon, Canada, m, 1951, 4 children **DISCIPLINE** LANGUAGES, ROMANCE & ENGLISH LITERATURE **EDUCATION** Univ Saskatchewan, MA, 44; Univ Mich, MA, 45, PhD, 50. **CAREER** Instr, Carleton Col, 50-51; lectr, SUNY Binghamton, 61-65; ed Chenango Am, 58-62; treas Twin Valley Publ, 65-86; Phi Beta Kappa; Phi Kappa Phi. **RESEARCH** Comparative Cultures. **SELECTED PUBLICATIONS** Venezuela Through Its History, 54; Cache-Cache, 80; Snow White, the Wolf and the Unicorn: Structural Origins of Western Culture, 81; A Classic Death, 85; Symbols in Art, 30,000 BC to the Present, http://members.aol.com/symartamym, 98. **CONTACT ADDRESS** 12 S Chenango St, Greene, NY, 13778. **EMAIL** MarslandSr@AOL

MARTEINSON, PETER
DISCIPLINE FRENCH LITERATURE **EDUCATION** Univ Toronto, BA; MA; PhD. **HONORS AND AWARDS** Ed, Applied Semiotics. **RESEARCH** Theatre; literary theory. **SELECTED PUBLICATIONS** Auth, pub(s) on eighteenth century theatre, Beaumarchais, and Marivaux. **CONTACT ADDRESS** Dept of French, Waterloo Univ, 200 University Ave W, Waterloo, ON, N2L 3G1. **EMAIL** marteinson@uwaterloo.ca

MARTIN, CHARLES EDWARD
PERSONAL Born 09/03/1930, Mantee, MS, m, 1953, 3 children **DISCIPLINE** MODERN LANGUAGES **EDUCATION** Miss Col, BA, 51; US Army Lang Sch, dipl, 52; Tulane Univ, MA, 58, PhD(Span), 65. **CAREER** Asst prof mod lang, 57-62, assoc prof, 62-67, head, Dept Foreign Lang, 66-69, PROF SPAN, MISS COL, 67-, VPRES ACAD AFFAIRS, 69-, Chmn, Southern Baptist Col Deans, 80 & Nat Deans' Conf, 81. **MEMBERSHIPS** Am Asn Teachers Span & Port. **RESEARCH** The generation of 1898 in Spain. **CONTACT ADDRESS** Dept of Foreign Lang, Mississippi Col, Clinton, MS, 39056.

MARTIN, DANIEL
PERSONAL Born 12/07/1932, Madrid, Spain, m, 1960, 1 child **DISCIPLINE** FRENCH RENAISSANCE LITERATURE **EDUCATION** Univ IL, Chicago Circle, BA, 69; Yale Univ, MPhil, 72, PhD, 73. **CAREER** Asst prof, 73-80, assoc prof, 80-84, PROF FRENCH, UNIV MA, AMHERST, 85-. **MEMBERSHIPS** Soc Amis Montaigne Paris; MLA; Renaissance Soc Am. **RESEARCH** Montaigne; structural criticism; the philos of chance and mnemonics. **SELECTED PUBLICATIONS** Ed, Michel de Montaigne, Essais 1580 avec une introduction et des notes sur les variantes, Libr Slatkine, Geneva, 76; auth, Montaigne et la Fortune: Essai sur le hasard et le language, Paris: Honore Champion, 77; ed, The Order of Montaigne's Essays, Amherst, MA: Herstia Press, 89; auth, L'Architecture des Essais de Montaigne: memoire artificielle et mythologie, Paris: Nizet, 92; ed, Montaigne and the Gods: The Mythological Key to the Essays, Amherst, MA: Hestia Press, 93; auth, Le Triptyque des Essais de Montaigne et l'heraldique des dieux greco-remains, Paris & Tours, Nizet, 96; Montaigne et son cheval ou les sept couleurs du discours De la servitude volontaire, Paris & Tours, Nizet, 98. **CONTACT ADDRESS** Dept of French & Ital, Univ Massachusetts, Amherst, MA, 01003-0002. **EMAIL** dmartin@frital.umass.edu

MARTIN, DELLITA LILLIAN
PERSONAL Born 10/27/1946, New Orleans, LA, m, 2 children **DISCIPLINE** SPANISH LITERATURE, COMPARATIVE LITERATURE **EDUCATION** La State Univ, BA, 68; Ohio State Univ, MA, 71, PhD(Romance lang & lit), 75. **CAREER** Instr Span & French, St Matthias Cath Sch, 76; asst prof, 76-82, ASSOC PROF SPAN & AM LIT, UNIV ALA, BIRMINGHAM, 82-, Univ Col fac res grant, Univ Ala, Birmingham, 78-79; secy, Comt Humanities Ala, 78-81. **MEMBERSHIPS** African Lit Asn; AAUP; Asn of Caribbean Studies; Col Lang Asn; MLA. **RESEARCH** Contemporary Latin American prose fiction and poetry; the Francophone writers of West Africa and the Caribbean; Afro-American and Afro-Hispanic literatures. **SELECTED PUBLICATIONS** Auth, Labe, Louise 'Elegies'--The Burden of Love and the Burden of Being a Writer, Etudes Lit, vol 0027, 94. **CONTACT ADDRESS** Dept of Foreign Lang Univ of Ala, Univ Sta, Birmingham, AL, 35294.

MARTIN, LAURA
DISCIPLINE LANGUAGES OF MESOAMERICA **EDUCATION** Degrees of BA (Spanish), MA, and PhD, (Linguistics) from the Univ of FL. **CAREER** Prof CSU fac in both Anthrop and Mod Lang since 71. **RESEARCH** Mayan lang **SELECTED PUBLICATIONS** Publ, Spanish Dialectology, Language, Culture, Second-lang Acquisition. **CONTACT ADDRESS** Dept of For Lang, Cleveland State Univ, 83 E 24th St, Cleveland, OH, 44115.

MARTIN, PHILIPPE JEAN
PERSONAL Born 01/04/1944, Brussels, Belgium **DISCIPLINE** LINGUISTICS, ACOUSTICS **EDUCATION** Free Univ Brussels, Ingenieur civil, 67, Dr(sci), 73; Univ Nancy, Dr 3rd cycle, 72. **CAREER** Res engr acoustics, 68-70, lectr phonetics, 70-72, asst prof, 72-75, assoc prof, 75-77, PROF PHONETICS, UNIV TORONTO, 81-, Res assoc, Royal Mus Cent Africa, Brussels, 71-; sr researcher, Inst Phonetics, Univ Bruxelles, 74-77; lectr phonetics, Univ Provence, 78-81. **RESEARCH** Syntax; intonation. **SELECTED PUBLICATIONS** Coauth, Prolegomenes a l'Etude des Structures Intonatives, Didier, Paris, 70; Classification Formelle Automatique et Industries Lithiques, Mus Tervuren, 72; auth, Analyse phonologique de la phrase Francaise, Linguistics, 75; Questions de phonosyntaxe et de phonosemantique en Francais, Linquisticae Investigationes, 78; coauth, Toronto English, Didier; auth, Vets une theo-

rie syntaxique de l'intonation, In: Intonation: de l'acoustique a la semantique, Klincksieck, Paus, 81; Pitch Analysis by Spectral Combination Method, Proc ICASSP, 82. **CONTACT ADDRESS** Exp Phonetics Lab, Univ Toronto, 39 Queen's Park Crescent E, Toronto, ON, M5S 1A1.

MARTIN, RICHARD PETER

PERSONAL Born 05/19/1954, Dorchester, MA **DISCIPLINE** GREEK AND LATIN: LANGUAGE COURSES **EDUCATION** Harvard, AB, 76, AM, 78; PhD, 81. **CAREER** The Boston Globe, gen assignment reporter, 74-78; Harvard, tchg fellow, 78-81; asst prof, 81-88, assoc prof, 89-94 Princeton Univ; Vis assoc prof, Univ Calif, 91; Prof, Princeton Univ, 94-. **HONORS AND AWARDS** Harvard, Bowdoin Prize, 79; Howard Behrman tchg fel, 96-00; Grants, Stanley Seeger fel res Cyclades,94; Stanley Seeger fel res, Ionian islands, 95; Onassis Found grant, fieldwork in oral tradition Crete, 96; Princeton 250th anniversary Award for Innovative Tchg, 97. **RESEARCH** Latin poetry; Hesiod; Greek hymns; Pindar. **SELECTED PUBLICATIONS** Auth, The Language of Heroes: Speech and Performance in the Iliad. Cornell Univ Press, 89; Bulfinch's Mythology, Harper Collins, 91; Similes in Performance; The Scythian Accent: Anacharsis and the Cynics, Univ Calif Press 97. **CONTACT ADDRESS** Princeton Univ, 1 Nassau Hall, Princeton, NJ, 08544. **EMAIL** rpmartin@princeton.edu

MARTIN, SAMUEL ELMO

PERSONAL Born 01/29/1924, Pittsburg, KS **DISCIPLINE** LINGUISTICS **EDUCATION** Univ Calif, AB, 47, AM, 49; Yale Univ, PhD, 50. **CAREER** From instr to asst prof Japanese & Korean, 50-58, assoc prof Far Eastern ling, 58-62, chmn dept East & South Asian lang, 63-65, chmn dept ling, 66-80, PROF FAR EASTERN LING, YALE UNIV, 62-, Vis prof, Georgetown Univ, 55, Univ Mich, 56, Univ Alta, 59 & Univ Wash, 62-63; secy, Comt Uralic & Altaic Studies, Am Coun Learned Soc, 58-64; vis prof ling & dir Pac & Asian ling inst, Univ Hawaii, 65-66. **MEMBERSHIPS** Ling Soc Am; Am Orient Soc; Asn Asian Studies. **RESEARCH** Phonemics, morphophonemics and historical phonology of Japanese, Korean and Chinese. **SELECTED PUBLICATIONS** Auth, On ohe Finite Forms of Old Japanese Verbs, J E Asian Ling, vol 0005, 96; How Did Korean Get--For Middle-Chinese Words Ending in + Articulation and Ling Change, J E Asian Ling, vol 0006, 97. **CONTACT ADDRESS** Dept of Ling Grad Sch, Yale Univ, New Haven, CT, 06520.

MARTIN-OGUNSOLA, DELLITA LILLIAN

PERSONAL Born 10/27/1946, New Orleans, Louisiana, m, 1979 **DISCIPLINE** SPANISH, FRENCH **EDUCATION** Louisiana State Univ, New Orleans, BA, 1968; Ohio State Univ, MA, 1971, PhD, 1975. **CAREER** St Mathias High School, instructor of Spanish/French, 1975-76; Univ of Alabama-Birmingham, asst prof of Spanish, 1976-82, assoc prof of Spanish, 1982-99; prof of Spanish, 1999-; chair of dept of foreign langs, 1993-. **HONORS AND AWARDS** Presidential Award for Excellence in Teaching, 1997; Outstanding Faculty-UAB Honors Program, 1998; Faculty Rep to the Bd of Trustees, Univ of Alabama System, 1994-95; Phi Beta Delta, Beta Nu Chapter, Charter Member Honor Soc for International Scholars, 1992; Alpha Lambda Delta, UAB Honorary Faculty Member, 1992; UAB-Univ College, Ingalls Finalist for Teaching Excellence, 1979-80, 1983, 1989; Sigma Delta Pi, Omicron Mu Chapter, UAB Faculty/Assoc Member, 1985. **MEMBERSHIPS** Afro-Hispanic Association, consulting and contributing editor, 1990-; Alabama Association of Teachers of Spanish, 1977-; Association of Caribbean Studies, liaison sec, 1979, 1982-84; College Language Association, 1977-; Hispanic Conf of Greater Birmingham, 1984-; Modern Language Association, 1976, sec 1977-78, chair Afro-Am ex com, 1979; South Atlantic Modern Lang Assn, 1979-; Alabama Humanities Foundation, sec exec sub-committee 1978-80, chair nominations sub-committee, 1979. **SELECTED PUBLICATIONS** Selected Poems of Langston Hughes and Nicolas Guillen, Doctoral Dissertation, Ohio State Univ, 1975; "West African & Hispanic Elements in NG's La cancion del bongo," South Atlantic Bulletin, 45:1, p 47-63, 1980; "Langston Hughes & the Musico-Poetry of the African Diaspora," in Langston Hughes Review, 5:1, p 1-17, 1986; "Translation as a Poetic Experience/Experiment: Short Fiction of Quince Duncan," Afro-Hispanic Review, 10:3, p 42-50, 1991; Las mejores historias de Quince Duncan/The Best Short Stories of Quince Duncan editorial, San Jose, Costa Rica, 1995; Female Characters in the Fiction of Quince Duncan, 1999. **CONTACT ADDRESS** Univ of Alabama at Birmingham, 900 S 13th St, Arts & Humanities Bldg Rm 407-B, Birmingham, AL, 35294-1260.

MARTIN-RODRIGUEZ, MANUEL M.

PERSONAL Born 09/26/1962, Sevilla, Spain **DISCIPLINE** HISPANIC LANGUAGE & LITERATURE **EDUCATION** Universidad de Sevilla, Spain, Licenciature en Filologia Hispanica, 85; Univ Houston, MA, 87; Univ Calif Santa Barbara, PhD, 90. **CAREER** Lectr, 90, Univ Calif Santa Barbara; asst prof, 90-96, Yale Univ; assoc prof, 96-98, Wayne St Univ; assoc prof, dir, 98-, Univ Wi Milwaukee. **HONORS AND AWARDS** Grad Scholar, 88-89; Special Regents Fel, 87-90; Samuel Wofsy Mem Prize for Outstanding PhD Stud, 90; Grad Dissertation Fel, 90; A Whitney Griswold Fac Award, 92; Morse Fel, 92-93, Hilles Publ Fund, 94; Summer Res Grant, 97; Humanities Center Fel, 97; Small Res Grant, 97. **SELECTED PUBLICATIONS** Auth, Rolando Hinojosa y su 'cronicon' chicana: Una novela del lector, Universidad de Sevilla, 93; auth, La voz urgente: Antologia de literature chicana en espanol, Fundamentos, 95; auth, Life in Search of Readers: Reading Chicano/ a Literature, Univ NM Press, 99; auth, La nueva novela de la tierra: conflicto cultural y fronterizo en la narrativa chicana de Texas, La Torre, 99. **CONTACT ADDRESS** Robert Hernandez Center, Univ Wi Milwaukee, PO Box 413, Milwaukee, WI, 53201. **EMAIL** mmartin@uwm.edu

MARTINEZ, ELIZABETH COONROD

DISCIPLINE LATIN AMERICAN LITERATURE **EDUCATION** Portland State Univ, 83 BA; NY Univ, MA, 91; Univ NM in Albuquerque, PhD, 95. **CAREER** Journalist; frn lng, Sonoma St Univ.. **SELECTED PUBLICATIONS** Auth, Henry Cisneros: Mexican-American Leader, 93; Sor Juana Ines de la Cruz: A Trail-blazing Thinker, 93; Edward James Olmos: Mexican-American Actor, 94; Coming to America: The Mexican-American Experience, 95. **CONTACT ADDRESS** Dept of For Lang, Sonoma State Univ, 1801 E. Cotati Ave., Rohnert Park, CA, 94928-3609. **EMAIL** elizabeth.martinez@sonoma.edu

MARTINEZ, ESTHER M.

DISCIPLINE SPANISH MEDIEVAL LITERATURE **EDUCATION** Univ Mich, PhD, 89. **CAREER** Assoc prof. **RESEARCH** Cuaderna via narrative poetry of the 13th century. **SELECTED PUBLICATIONS** Publ on, cohesion theory and 13th-century cuaderna via, several aspects of the Libro de Alexandre and the circular structure of the Libro de buen amor; Traditional material in the Poema de Yucuf, Perez de Guzm n's translation of Seneca's Epistulae, rhetoric in the Novelas ejemplares, and holymorphism in the poetry of Sor Juana Ines de la Cruz. **CONTACT ADDRESS** Dept of Language and Cultures, William Paterson Col, 300 Pompton Rd., Wayne, NJ, 07470.

MARTINEZ, H. SALVADOR

PERSONAL Born 03/31/1936, Leon, Spain **DISCIPLINE** MEDIEVAL SPANISH LITERATURE, PHILOSOPHY OF HISTORY **EDUCATION** Univ Rome, Dr Laurea, 60; Gregoriana Univ, Rome, Laurea, 68; Univ Toronto, PhD, 72. **CAREER** Prof Span lit & philos, Angelo State Univ, 72-76; Prof Medieval Span Lit, NY Univ, 76-. **MEMBERSHIPS** Soc Rencesvals; Asoc Int Hispanistas; Mediaeval Acad Am; MLA; Am Acad Res Historians Medieval Spain. **CONTACT ADDRESS** Dept of Span & Port, New York Univ, 19 University Pl, New York, NY, 10003-4556. **EMAIL** hsm1@is.nyu.edu

MARTINEZ, JOSE-LUIS

DISCIPLINE LATIN AMERICAN AND SPANISH CIVILIZATION **EDUCATION** Univ Puerto Rico, BA, 84; Univ Tex, MA, 87, PhD, 93. **CAREER** Tchg asst, asst instr, Univ Tex; Instr, Austin Comm Coll; Asst prof, Univ Central Ark, 92- . **RESEARCH** Spanish American literature and culture; Hispanic Caribbean literature and culture. **SELECTED PUBLICATIONS** Auth, El bolero y la guaracha en las novelas de Luis Rafael Sanchez, Revista Metafora; auth, Musica y literature: testimonio cultural de deferentes grupos raciales llegdos de Africa a las Antillas del Caribe hispano, Jour Afro-Latin Am Studies & Lit. **CONTACT ADDRESS** Univ Central Ark, 201 Donaghey Ave, Conway, AR, 72035-0001.

MARTINEZ, RONALD L.

DISCIPLINE COMPARATIVE MEDIEVAL AND RENAISSANCE (ITALIAN, ENGLISH, SPANISH AND FRENCH) **EDUCATION** Univ Calif, Santa Cruz, PhD. **CAREER** Instr, Univ Minn, Twin Cities. **RESEARCH** Dante studies. **SELECTED PUBLICATIONS** Auth, Time and the Crystal. **CONTACT ADDRESS** Univ Minn, Twin Cities, Minneapolis, MN, 55455.

MARTINEZ-BONATI, FELIX

PERSONAL Born 03/07/1929, Santiago, Chile, m, 1957, 2 children **DISCIPLINE** SPANISH & COMPARATIVE LITERATURE **EDUCATION** Univ Goettingen, DrPhil, 57; Univ Chile MPhil, 58. **CAREER** Prof Span, Univ Chile, 57-62; pres, Univ Austral Valdivia, 62-68; Alexander von Humboldt fel, 69-70; prof Span & comp lit, Univ Iowa, 71-77; prof Span, Univ IL, Chicago, 77-78; PROF SPAN, COLUMBIA UNIV, 78-; Vis prof philos, Univ Goettingen, 64-66; Vis prof Span, Princeton Univ, 83. **HONORS AND AWARDS** Dr honoris causa Univ Austral Chile, 74. **MEMBERSHIPS** MLA; Am Asn Teachers Span & Port. **RESEARCH** Theory of literature; intellectual history. **SELECTED PUBLICATIONS** Auth, La concepcion del lenguaje en la filosofia de Husserl, 60 & Las ideas esteticas de Schiller, Univ Chile, 60; La estructura de la obra literaria, Seix-Barral, Barcelona, 60, 72, 85; Fictive Discourse and the Structures of Literature, Cornell Univ Press, 82; Don Quixote and the Poetics of the Novel, Cornell Univ Press, 92; La ficcion narrativa, Univ Murcia, 92; El Quijote y la poetica de la novela, Madrid, 95. **CONTACT ADDRESS** Dept of Span, Columbia Univ, 2960 Broadway, Box 4348, New York, NY, 10027-6900.

MARTINSON, STEVEN D.

PERSONAL Born 08/10/1949, Puyallup, WA, m, 1975, 3 children **DISCIPLINE** GERMANIC STUDIES **EDUCATION** Univ of WA, PhD, 77, MA, 73; Seattle Pac Univ, BA, 71; Univ of Heidelberg, 69-70 **CAREER** Prof, 91-, Spec Asst, 96-98, Assoc Prof, 88-91, Univ of AZ; Asst Prof, 80-88, Univ of CA; Asst Prof, 77-80, Northwestern Univ **HONORS AND AWARDS** Alexander von Humboldt fel, 99; Choice awd, 97 **MEMBERSHIPS** The Lessing Soc; The German Studies Asn **RESEARCH** Modern Ger Lit **SELECTED PUBLICATIONS** Auth, Harmonious Tensions: The Writings of Friedrich Schiller, Associated Univ Presses, 96 **CONTACT ADDRESS** Dept of German Stud, Univ of Arizona, Tucson, AZ, 85721. **EMAIL** martinso@u.arizona.edu

MARULLO, THOMAS GAITON

DISCIPLINE SLAVIC LANGUAGES **EDUCATION** Col The Holy Cross, BA, 70; Cornell Univ, MA, 71, PhD, 75; Ind Univ, S Bend, MBA, 89. **CAREER** Instr, Ithaca Col, 73-75; asst prof, 75-81, ASSOC PROF, 81-, UNIV NOTRE DAME. **CONTACT ADDRESS** Dept of German, Russian Langs & Lit, Univ of Notre Dame, Notre Dame, IN, 46556. **EMAIL** Thomas.G.Marullo.1@nd.edu

MARX, LEONIE

DISCIPLINE GERMAN LITERATURE **EDUCATION** Univ IL, PhD. **CAREER** Instr, Univ Ger, Denmark; Univ WI; prof-. **RESEARCH** Ger and Danish lit and Ger-Scandinavian lit rel. **SELECTED PUBLICATIONS** Auth, pioneering analysis of the contemp Danish author Benny Andersen, Eng ed, 83; Danish ed, 8; comprehensive study of the Ger short story since the late nineteenth century, Metzler, 2nd, augmented ed, 97; pub(s), bk chapters, Der deutsche Frauenroman im 19. Jahrhundert, Handbuch des Romans; Thomas Mann und die Literaturen Skandinaviens, Thomas-Mann-Handbuch; Die deutsche Kurzgeschichte, Formen der Literatur. **CONTACT ADDRESS** Dept of Ger Lang and Lit, Univ Kansas, Admin Building, Lawrence, KS, 66045. **EMAIL** marx@kuhub.cc.ukans.edu

MASTERS, GEORGE MALLARY

PERSONAL Born 06/19/1936, Savannah, GA **DISCIPLINE** ROMANCE LANGUAGES **EDUCATION** Columbia Univ, BS, 60; Johns Hopkins Univ, MA, 62, PhD(Romance lang), 64. **CAREER** Asst prof French, Univ Mo, 64-66; asst prof Romance lang, State Univ NY, Binghamton, 66-69, assoc prof, 69-70; assoc prof, 70-78, PROF ROMANCE LANGS & LITS, UNIV NC, CHAPEL HILL, 78-, Univ Mo Res Coun Grants-in-aid, 64-66; State Univ NY Res Found grant-in-aid, 67-69, grant-in-aid & fel, 69-70; Am Coun Learned Soc fel, 76-77. **MEMBERSHIPS** SAtlantic Mod Lang Asn; Am Asn Teachers Fr; Renaissance Soc Am. **RESEARCH** French Renaissance; Rabelais; Jehan Thenaud. **SELECTED PUBLICATIONS** Auth, Heroic Virtue, Comic Infidelity--Reassessing Marguerite de Navarre 'Heptameron', Philos and Lit, vol 0019, 95. **CONTACT ADDRESS** PO Box 778, Chapel Hill, NC, 27514.

MASTRONARDE, DONALD JOHN

PERSONAL Born 11/13/1948, Hartford, CT, m, 1971, 2 children **DISCIPLINE** CLASSICAL PHILOLOGY **EDUCATION** Amherst Col, BA, 69; Oxford Univ, BA, 71; Univ Toronto, PhD(classical studies), 74. **CAREER** From Asst Prof to Assoc Prof, 73-84, Prof Classics, Univ Calif, Berkeley, 84-, Dept Chair, 93-99. **HONORS AND AWARDS** Am Coun Learned Soc, fel, 78-79, 96-97; Guggenheim Fel, 84-85; Charles J. Goodwin Award of Merit, Am Philol Asn, 97. **MEMBERSHIPS** Am Philol Asn. **RESEARCH** Greek tragedy; Greek and Latin poetry. **SELECTED PUBLICATIONS** Auth, Theocritus' Idyll 13: love and the hero, Trans Am Philol Asn, 99, 68; Seneca's Oedipus: the drama in the word, Trans Am Philol Asn 101, 70; Iconography and imagery in Euripides' Ion, Calif Studies in Class Antiquity 8, 75; Are Euripides' Phoinissai 1104-1140 interpolated?, Phoenix, Vol 32; Contact and Discontinuity: Some conventions of speech and action on the Greek tragic stage, Univ Calif Publ Class Studies, Vol 21, 79; P Strasbourg WG 307 re-examined (Eur Phoin 1499-1581, 1710-1736), Zeitschrift fuer Papyrologie und Epigraphik 38, 1; coauth, The Textual Tradition of Euripides' Phoinissai, Univ Calif Publ Class Studies, Vol 27, 82; auth, Euripides, Phoenissae, Teubner editon, 88; Introduction to Attic Greek, Univ Calif Press, 93; Euripides, Phoenissae, Cambridge Classical Texts and Commentaries, 29, 94. **CONTACT ADDRESS** Dept of Class, Univ of California, Berkeley, 7303 Dwinelle Hall, Berkeley, CA, 94720-2520. **EMAIL** pinax@socrates.berkeley.edu

MATANLE, STEPHEN

DISCIPLINE LANGUAGE AND LITERATURE **EDUCATION** Johns Hopkins Univ, MA; Am Univ, PhD. **CAREER** Assoc prof, Univ Baltimore; ch, Div Lang, Lit & Comm Design, 95-. **CONTACT ADDRESS** Commun Dept, Univ Baltimore, 1420 N. Charles Street, Baltimore, MD, 21201.

MATEJIC, MATEJA

PERSONAL Born 02/19/1924, Smederevo, Yugoslavia, m, 1949, 5 children **DISCIPLINE** SLAVIC LANGUAGES AND LITERATURES **EDUCATION** Theol Acad, Eboli, Italy, degree theol, 46; Wayne State Univ, BA, 63; Univ Mich, PhD(Slavic lang & lit), 67. **CAREER** Asst prof Slavic lang & lit, Case Western Reserve Univ, 67-68; PROF SLAVIC LANG & LIT, OHIO STATE UNIV, 68-, Priest, Monroe, Mich, 56-67 & Columbus, Ohio, 67-; ED, PATH OF ORTHODOXY; 68-; DIR, HILANDAR MICROFILMING PROJ, 70-. **MEMBERSHIPS** Am Asn Teachers Slavic & E Europ Lang; Am Asn Advan Slavic Studies. **RESEARCH** Medieval Slavic manuscripts; medieval Russian and Serbian literature; theology.Medieval Slavic manuscripts; medieval Russian and Serbian literature; theology. **SELECTED PUBLICATIONS** Auth, Zavicaj Smrti, World Lit Today, vol 0069, 95. **CONTACT ADDRESS** Dept Slavic Lang and Lit, Ohio State Univ, Columbus, OH, 43210.

MATHEWS, GARY
PERSONAL Born 09/15/1953, Owensboro, KY, s **DISCIPLINE** COMPARATIVE LITERATURE **EDUCATION** Univ Calif Berkeley, PhD, 92. **CAREER** Tchg asst, Dept Comp Lit & Dept Rhetoric, 83-85, instr, Dept Comp Lit & Dept Classics, 85-92, Univ Calif Berkeley; lectr, Dept Classics, 93, vis instr, Dept World & Comp Lit & Dept Classics, 93-95, lectr, Dept World & Comp Lit & Dept Hum & Dept Classics & NEXA Interdisciplinary Prog, 95-97, San Francisco State Univ; Hum tchr, Div gen studies, N Carolina Sschool or Arts, 97- . **MEMBERSHIPS** Mod Lang Asn; Am Comp Lit Asn; Am Philol Asn; N Carolina Class Asn; Am Class League; Womens Class Caucus; S Comp Lit Asn. **RESEARCH** Euripides; Latin elegy; Mythology. **SELECTED PUBLICATIONS** Auth, Finding What One Wants: Desire and Interpretation in Euripides' Iphigeneia at Aulis, Laetaberis, 94; Walter Benjamins Origin of German Tragic Drama and the Baroque World View of Euripedes and Thucydides, Mag, 95; Aristophanes High Lyrics Reconsidered, Maia, 97. **CONTACT ADDRESS** Gen Studies, No Carolina Sch of the Arts, 1533 S Main St., Winston-Salem, NC, 27117-2189. **EMAIL** mathewsg@ncsavx.ncarts.edu

MATHEWS, THOMAS J.
DISCIPLINE SPANISH **EDUCATION** Weber State Col, BA, 81; Middlebury Col, MA, 84; Univ Del, PhD, 92 **CAREER** Assoc prof, Weber State Univ, 96-; asst prof, Brigham Young Univ, 91-96. **MEMBERSHIPS** Amer Asn Teachers Span and Portuguese; Amer Coun for the Tchg For Lang; Golden Spike Empire Lang Alliance; Rocky Mt Mod Lang Asn; Southwest Conf on Lang Tchg; Utah For Lang Asn. **SELECTED PUBLICATIONS** Auth, The Acquisition of Sexist Language by Native and Non-Native Speakers of Spanish, Hisp, 98; A case for Increasing Negative Effect in Foreign Language Classes, Lang Learning J 13, 96; Avoiding Sexist Language in Composition: Complementary Solutions in Spanish and English, Mid-Atlan J For Lang Pedagogy, 95; rev, Aprendizaje: Tecnicas de composicion, In Hisp 81, 98. **CONTACT ADDRESS** Dept of Foreign Language and Literature, Weber State Univ, 1403 University Cir, Ogden, UT, 84408-1403. **EMAIL** tmathews@weber.edu

MATHIAS, GERALD BARTON
PERSONAL Born 07/09/1935, Berkeley, CA, m, 1959, 2 children **DISCIPLINE** JAPANESE LANGUAGE & LITERATURE, LINGUISTICS **EDUCATION** Univ Calif, Berkeley, AB, 61, MA, 65, PhD(Orient Lang), 68. **CAREER** From lectr to asst prof East Asian Lang & Lit, Ind Univ, 67-75; assoc prof Japanese, Univ Hawaii, Manoa, 75-. **MEMBERSHIPS** Asn Asian Studies; Asn Teachers Japanese; Ling Soc Am; Asn Computational Ling. **RESEARCH** Prehistory of Japanese language; semantic structure of language; mechanical parsing. **SELECTED PUBLICATIONS** Auth, Toward the semantics of -te-i- attachment, J Newslett Asn Teachers Japanese, 69; On the modification of certain reconstructions of proto-Korean-Japanese, 73 & Some problems with word meaning, 73, Papers Japanese Ling; Seven tales of Yamato, In: K'uei Hsing, Ind Univ, 74; Subject and topic in Korean, Japanese, and English, Korean Ling, 78. **CONTACT ADDRESS** Dept of East Asian Lang, Univ of Hawaii, 1890 E West Rd, Honolulu, HI, 96822-2318. **EMAIL** mathias@hawaii.edu

MATHIOT, MADELEINE
PERSONAL Born 06/11/1927, Saulxures-sur-Moselotte, France, m, 1960, 1 child **DISCIPLINE** LINGUISTICS, ANTHROPOLOGY **EDUCATION** Georgetown Univ, BS, 54, MS, 55; Cath Univ Am, PhD(anthrop), 66. **CAREER** Asst prof anthrop, Univ Calif, Los Angeles, 67-69; assoc prof ling, 69-74, Prof Ling & Anthrop, State Univ NY Buffalo, 74-, Dir, Ctr Studies Cult Transmission, 74- **MEMBERSHIPS** Am Anthrop Asn; Ling Soc Am; Semiotic Soc Am. **RESEARCH** Lexicology; ethnosemantics; face-to-face interaction. **SELECTED PUBLICATIONS** Auth, An Approach to the Cognitive Study of Language, 68 & A Papago Dictionary of Usage, vol 1, 73, vol 2, 78, Ind Univ; ed, Approaches to the Analysis of Face-to-Face Interaction, Semiotica, 78; Ethnolinguistics: Boas, Sapir, Whorf Revisited, Mouton, 79; A meaning based theory of face to face interaction, Int J Soc Ling (in prep). **CONTACT ADDRESS** Dept Ling, State Univ NY, Buffalo, NY, 14260.

MATILAL, BIMAL KRISHNA
PERSONAL Born 06/01/1935, Joynagar, India, m, 1958, 1 child **DISCIPLINE** INDIAN PHILOSOPHY AND LINGUISTICS **EDUCATION** Univ Calcutta, BA, 54, MA, 56; Harvard Univ, AM, 63, PhD(Indian logic), 65. **CAREER** Lectr Sanskrit lit, Govt Sanskrit Col, Univ Calcutta, 57-62; from asst prof to assoc prof, 65-71, PROF INDIAN PHILOS, UNIV TORONTO, 71-, Guest lectr, III Int Cong Orient, 67 ; Can Coun travel grant, 67; UNESCO Coun Humanities & Philos grant, 67; overseas res lei, Univ Toronto, 67; assoc prof, Univ Pa, 69-70; ed, J Indian Philos, Reidel, 70-; vis sr fel, Univ London, 71-72. **MEMBERSHIPS** Am Orient Soc; Soc Asian & Comp Philos (vpres, 73-). **RESEARCH** Indian logic and epistemology; theories of linguistics and semantics in ancient India; Sanskrit literature and literary criticism. **SELECTED PUBLICATIONS** Auth, Is Prasanga a Form of Deconstruction, J Indian Philos, vol 0020, 92; A Note on Samkara Theodicy, J Indian Philos, vol 0020, 92. **CONTACT ADDRESS** Dept of Sanskrit & Indian Studies, Univ of Toronto, Toronto, ON, M5S 1A1.

MATISOFF, JAMES ALAN
PERSONAL Born 07/14/1937, Boston, MA, m, 1962, 2 children **DISCIPLINE** LINGUISTICS, SOUTHEAST ASIAN STUDIES **EDUCATION** Harvard Univ, AB, 58, AM, 59; Univ Calif, Berkeley, PhD(ling), 67. **CAREER** From instr to asst prof, Columbia Univ, 66-70; assoc prof, 70-80, PROF LING, UNIV CALIF, BERKELEY, 80-, Am Coun Leanred Soc grant for res in Asia, 70; vis scholar, Summer Inst Ling Soc Am, Ann Arbor, Mich, 73. **MEMBERSHIPS** Ling Soc Am; Northern Thai Soc. **RESEARCH** Psycho-semantics. **SELECTED PUBLICATIONS** Auth, Selected Papers on Comparative Tai Studies, Lang, vol 0069, 93; Cross Cultural Pragmatics--The Semantics of Human Interaction, Lang, vol 0072, 96. **CONTACT ADDRESS** Dept of Ling, Univ of Calif, 2337 Dwinelle Hall, Berkeley, CA, 94720-2651.

MATLON, RONALD
DISCIPLINE LEGAL COMMUNICATION **EDUCATION** Purdue Univ PhD, 66. **CAREER** Instr, chp, dept Mass Commun and Commun Stud, Towson Univ. **SELECTED PUBLICATIONS** Auth, Communication in the Legal Process; Communication Strategies in the Practice of Lawyering; Opening Statements/Closing Arguments; Index to Journals in Communication Studies. **CONTACT ADDRESS** Towson Univ, Towson, MD, 21252-0001. **EMAIL** rmatlon@towson.edu

MATTEO, SANTE
DISCIPLINE ITALIAN **EDUCATION** Kenyon Col, BA; Miami Univ, MA; Johns Hopkins Univ, MA, PhD. **CAREER** Prof, Miami Univ **MEMBERSHIPS** Exec sec, Amer Asn Italian Stud, 87-93; MLA Div Exec Comt, Italian lit, 17th century-, 88-92; ed, Il Gonfaloniere, Newsl AAIS, 87-95; adv bd(s), Machiavelli Stud; Italian Cult & Italica. **RESEARCH** All periods of Italian literature, with an emphasis on the modern periods, as well as literary theory and Italian cinema. **SELECTED PUBLICATIONS** Auth, Textual Exile: The Reader in Sterne and Foscolo, Peter Lang, 85; co-ed, The Reasonable Romantic: Essays on Alessandro Manzoni, Peter Lang, 86 & Italian Echoes in the Rocky Mountains, AAIS, 90. **CONTACT ADDRESS** Dept of French and Italian, Miami Univ, Oxford, OH, 45056. **EMAIL** matteos@muohio.edu

MATTINGLY, IGNATIUS G.
DISCIPLINE LINGUISTICS **EDUCATION** Yale Univ, PhD. **CAREER** Prof emer, Univ Conn. **RESEARCH** Experimental phonetics, writing systems. **SELECTED PUBLICATIONS** Auth, Speech Cues and Sign Stimuli, Amer Scientist 60, 72; Reading, the Linguistic Process, and Linguistic Awareness, In Lang by Ear and by Eye, MIT Press, 72; Synthesis by Rule of General American English, Haskins Laboratories Status Report on Speech Res, Supp, 68; coauth, The Motor Theory of Speech Perception Revised, Cognition 21, 85. **CONTACT ADDRESS** Dept of Linguistics, Univ of Connecticut, 1266 Storrs Rd, Storrs, CT, 06269-1085. **EMAIL** ignatius@uconnvm.uconn.edu

MAURER, WARREN R.
DISCIPLINE GERMAN LITERATURE **EDUCATION** Franklin and Marshall Col, BA; Univ Chicago, MA; Univ CA at Berkeley, PhD. **CAREER** Prof, 68-, Univ KS. **HONORS AND AWARDS** Dept ch. **SELECTED PUBLICATIONS** Auth, bk(s) on Gerhart Hauptmann; a bk on Ger Naturalism; co-ed, anthology of articles on Rilke; pub(s), articles on Ger lit, folklore and lit onomastics. **CONTACT ADDRESS** Dept of Ger Lit and Lang, Univ Kansas, Admin Building, Lawrence, KS, 66045. **EMAIL** kufacts@ukans.edu

MAURIN, MARIO
PERSONAL Born 12/22/1928, France **DISCIPLINE** FRENCH **EDUCATION** Yale Univ, BA, 48, MA, 49, PhD, 51. **CAREER** From asst prof to assoc prof, 53-65, chmn dept, 59-67, Prof French, Bryn Mawr Col, 65-; Guggenheim fel, 59; columnist in Span, Agencia Latino Am, 75-81. **HONORS AND AWARDS** Prix de la Langue Francaise, Academic Francaise, 73. **MEMBERSHIPS** Am Asn Teachers Fr; Soc Fr Prof Am; MLA; ALS. **RESEARCH** Modern poetry and its background; French literature from 1880-1920. **SELECTED PUBLICATIONS** Auth, Leopardi, Seghers, 61; Henri de Regnier: Le Labyrinthe et le Double, Univ Montreal, 72. **CONTACT ADDRESS** Dept of French, Bryn Mawr Col, 101 N Merion Ave, Bryn Mawr, PA, 19010-2899. **EMAIL** mmaurin@brynmawr.edu

MAY, GEORGES
PERSONAL Born 10/07/1920, Paris, France, m, 1949, 2 children **DISCIPLINE** FRENCH LITERATURE **EDUCATION** Univ Paris, Lic es Lett, 41; Univ Montpellier, dipl, 41; Univ Ill, PhD, 47. **CAREER** Instr, 45-46, 47-48, from asst prof to prof, 48-71, dean, Yale Col, 63-71, chmn dept, 78-80, provost, 79-81, Sterling Prof French, Yale Univ, 71-, Guggenheim fel, 50-51; secy, 4th Int Cong on Enlightenment, 71-75. **HONORS AND AWARDS** Chevalier, Legion d'honneur, France, 71. **MEMBERSHIPS** MLA; Am Asn Teachers Fr; Soc Hist Lit France; Am Soc 18th Century Studies (vpres, 72-74); Am Acad Arts & Sci. **RESEARCH** Various parts of French literature. **SELECTED PUBLICATIONS** Auth, J J Rousseau par Lui-Meme, Ed Seuil, France, 61; Le Dilemme du Roman au XVIIIe Siecle, Presses Univs, France & Yale Univ, 63; L'unite de sang chez Racine, Rev Hist Litteraire, France, 72; co-ed, Diderot's La Religieuse and Preface, In: Diderot's Oeuvres Completes, Hermann, Paris, 75; auth, Autobiography and the eighteenth century, In: The Author in His Work, Yale Univ, 78; L'Autobiographie, Presses Univs France, Paris, 79; Biography, autobiography and the novel in 18th century France, In: Bibliography in the 18th Century, Garland Publ Co, 80; co-ed, Diderot's Sur Terence, In: Diderot's Oeuvres Completes, Paris: Hermann, 80. **CONTACT ADDRESS** 77 Everit St, New Haven, CT, 06511-1306. **EMAIL** georges.may@yale.edu

MAY, GITA
PERSONAL Born 09/16/1929, Brussels, Belgium, m, 1947 **DISCIPLINE** FRENCH **EDUCATION** Hunter Col, BA, 53; Columbia Univ, MA, 54, PhD, 57. **CAREER** From lectr to instr, 53-58, from asst prof to assoc prof, 58-68, Prof French Lit & Dept Rep French, Columbia Univ, 68-; US Educ Comn lectr, Gt Brit, 65-83; prof and ch, French Lit, Columbia Univ, 83-92. **HONORS AND AWARDS** Coun Res Humanities grants, 60, 67 & 69; Am Coun Learned Soc grant, 61; Hunter Col Award for Outstanding achievement, 63; Guggenheim fel & Fulbright grant, 64-65; Chevalier and Officier Palmes Academiques, 68, 81; Van Amringe Distinguished Bk Award, 71; Nat Endowment for Humanities sr fel, 71-72; Fac Award for Distinguished Teaching, Columbia Univ, 80; mem, Acad of Lit Studies, 86. **MEMBERSHIPS** Am Asn Teachers Fr; MLA (exec coun, 80-83); Soc Diderot; Rousseau Soc; NE Am Soc 18th Century Studies (vpres, 80-81, pres, 81-82); Fr Soc Studies 18th Century; Am Soc Fr Acad Palms. **RESEARCH** Aesthetics and history of ideas in the Age of Enlightenment; Diderot and Rousseau; Stendhal; women in history, literature and the arts. **SELECTED PUBLICATIONS** Auth, Diderot and Baudelaire, Art Critics, de Jean-Jacques Rousseau a Madame Roland; Diderot and Burke, PMLA, 12/60; Les pensees detachees sur la pointure de Diderot, Rev d'Hist Lit France, 1/70; Diderot et Roger de Piles, PMLA, 5/70; Madame Roland and the Age of Revolution, 70 & Stendhal and the Age of Revolution, 77, Columbia Univ; Les Confessions, Roman picaresque, Fritz Schalk Festschrift, 82; numerous other articles and reviews from 84-present. **CONTACT ADDRESS** Dept of French, Columbia Univ, 2960 Broadway, 516 Philos, New York, NY, 10027-6900. **EMAIL** gm9@columbia.edu

MAY, JAMES M.
DISCIPLINE GREEK AND ROMAN RHETORIC **EDUCATION** Kent State Univ, BS, 73; Univ NC, PhD, 77. **CAREER** Drama, St. Olaf Col. **SELECTED PUBLICATIONS** Auth, Trials of Character: The Eloquence of Ciceronian Ethos, Univ N Carolina Press, 88. **CONTACT ADDRESS** St Olaf Col, 1520 St Olaf Ave, Northfield, MN, 55057. **EMAIL** may@stolaf.edu

MAY, RACHEL
PERSONAL MA, m, 1996, 1 child **DISCIPLINE** SLAVIC LANGUAGES AND LITERATURE **EDUCATION** Stanford Univ, PhD, 90. **CAREER** Asst prof of Russian, SUNY Stony Brook, 90-92; asst prof, 92-97; assoc prof, Macalaster Coll, 97-. **HONORS AND AWARDS** NEH Fel, 98-99. **MEMBERSHIPS** MLA; AAASS; AAUP. **RESEARCH** Nature and Russian Culture; Translation Studies. **SELECTED PUBLICATIONS** Auth, The Translator in Text: On Reading Russian Literature in English, 94; Superego as Literary Subtext: Story and Structure in Mikhail Zoshchenko's Before Sunrise, Slavic Rev, 96; Sensible Elocution: How Translation Works in and upon Punctuation, The Translator, 97; The Power of Speech: Dialogue as History in the Russian Primary Chronicle, Dialogue and Critical Discourse, 97; Everywhere is Breadth and Distance, forthcoming; Is There a Russian Wilderness?, forthcoming. **CONTACT ADDRESS** 655 Allen St, Syracuse, NY, 13210. **EMAIL** may@macalester.edu

MAYBERRY, NANCY KENNINGTON
PERSONAL St. Thomas, ON, Canada, m, 1967, 2 children **DISCIPLINE** SPANISH DRAMA AND LITERATURE **EDUCATION** Univ Western Ont, BA, 61; Univ NC Chapel Hill, MA, 63, PhD(Span), 66. **CAREER** Asst prof Span & French, Univ NC, Greensboro, 65-66; asst prof Span, Univ Western Ont, 66-67; assoc prof Span & French, 67-75, assoc prof, 75-82, PROF SPAN & FRENCH, EAST CAROLINA UNIV, 82-. **RESEARCH** Spanish Golden Age drama; 19th century Spanish romanticism. **SELECTED PUBLICATIONS** Auth, 'Don Juan Tenorio' as the End Marker of Spanish Romanticism, Critica Hisp, vol 0018, 96. **CONTACT ADDRESS** Dept of Foreign Lang, East Carolina Univ, Greenville, NC, 27834.

MAYER, BRUCE HILLIS
PERSONAL Born 09/09/1945, Cumberland, MD **DISCIPLINE** FRENCH LITERATURE **EDUCATION** Wesleyan Univ, BA (Liberal Arts), 68; Univ TX, Austin, MA (French Lit), 70, PhD (French Lit), 79. **CAREER** Teaching asst, Univ TX, Austin, 72-74; Assistant de Langue vivante, Lycee Carnot, Paris, 70-71, Lycee Charlemagne, Paris, 74-75; Member of Foreign Lang Dept, Williston-Northhampton School, 76-82 (Director Intersession Prog in Paris, 76-82); asst prof of French and Italian, Tulane Univ, 82-84; asst prof French, 84-88, assoc prof French, 88-93, Chairperson Dept Foreign Langs and Lit, 92-97, PROF FRENCH, LYNCHBURG COL, 93-. **HONORS AND AWARDS** NDEA Title IV Fel, Univ TX, 68-72; Rotary Int Fel to France, 75-76; NEH Summer Seminar, Yale Univ, 89; Mednick Memorial Fel, VA Found for Independent Colleges, 92; CIBER Fel to CIEL de Strasbourg France, Ministry of Ed and French, San Diego State Univ, 94. **RESEARCH** French lit of the 18th century; French political hist; Ancien Regime; Italian lang. **SELECTED PUBLICATIONS** Auth, Machiavelli's Promise to the Citizen: Political Freedom?, in Machiavelli Studies, Vol 1, 87; The Strategy of Rehabilitation: Pierre Bayle on Machiavelli, in Studi Francesi, Anno 33, no 98, 89; bibliography prepared for Machiavelli Studies, Vols I, II, & III, 87-90; book review, Christopher Lasch, The True and Only Heaven: Progress and its Critics, in Utopian Studies, Vol 4, no 1, 93. **CONTACT ADDRESS** Dept of Foreign Langs and Lit, Lynchburg Col, Lynchburg, VA, 24501.

MAYER, SIGRID
DISCIPLINE GERMAN **EDUCATION** Univ UT, PhD, 73. **CAREER** Emer prof; Univ WY, 73. **RESEARCH** Contemp Ger lit. **SELECTED PUBLICATIONS** Publ, bk on the Golem legend, 2 vol(s) of graphic art and texts by Gunter Grass & an annotated biblog on Ernst Cassirer. **CONTACT ADDRESS** Dept of Mod and Class Lang(s), Univ WY, PO Box 3964, Laramie, WY, 82071-3964. **EMAIL** MAYERSIG@UWYO.EDU

MAYR, FRANZ KARL
PERSONAL Born 03/12/1932, Linz, Austria, m, 1968, 2 children **DISCIPLINE** PHILOSOPHY OF RELIGION & LANGUAGE; METAPHYSICS; LEGAL PHILOSOPHY **EDUCATION** Univ Innsbruck, LPh, 56, PhD(philos), 57, MLaw, 62. **CAREER** Asst prof philos, Univ Innsbruck, 63-64 & 65-68; asst prof relig & philos, 64-65, assoc prof, 68-76, PROF PHILOS, UNIV PORTLAND, OR, 76- . **RESEARCH** Political philosophy; Philosophy of religion. **SELECTED PUBLICATIONS** Coauth, Lexikon fur Theologie und Kirche, Herder, Freiburg, 63; auth, Geschichte der Philosophie Antike, 64; Genos und Geschlecht: Zum Problem der Metaphysik, 65 & Der Gott Hermes und die Hermeneutik, 68, Tijdschrift voor Filos, Louvain; Trinitaet und Familie in Augustinus De TrinitateXII: Reone des Etudes Augustimiemes, Paris, 72; Der Aristolelische Gottesbeweis in Lichte de Religious Grschichte, Feitschrift fur Religious und Geistes Gerschichte, Cologne, 72; Philosophische Implikationen Amerikanischer Linguistik, Feitschrift fur Philosophische Forschung, Stuttgart, 73; Language, Sacramentune Mundi, An Encyclopedia of Theology III, New York-London, 69; Philosophische Hermenentik und Dentsche Sprache, Tydschrift von Filosofie, Louvain, 86; Horen: Lexikon fur Antike und Christentum, Bonn, 90; Der Ausschluss der Weiblich-Mutterlichen Analogie fur Gott bei Thomas von Aquin, S.C.G. IV, Theologie und Glanbe, Paderborn, 73; Trinitetsche unde theologische Anthropologie, Feitschrift fur Theologie und Kirche, 70; Die Einseitigkeit der Traditionellen Gottesche Zum Verhilhims von Anthropologie und Tneumatologie, Erfehrung und Theolgie des Hl. Geistes, Munich, 74; Tatriachales Gottesverstanduis, Theologische Quartaloschrift, Tubingen, 72; Sprache, Sprachphilosophie, Herders Theologisches Taschenlevikon, 81; coauth, Existential Sacramentum mundi: International Theological Lexicon, Herder & Herder, 69; Simbolos, Mitos y Archetypos, Antropologia Vasca: Gram Encyclopedia Vasca, Bilbao, 80; El Matriarcalismo Vasco, Bilbao, 80; coauth, El Inconsciente Colectivo Vasco, San Sebastian, 82; coauth, Arquetipos y Simbolos Colectivos: Circulo Eranos I, Barcelona, 94; Lenguaje: Diccionario de Hermenentica, Univ de Densto Bilbao, 77. **CONTACT ADDRESS** Dept of Philosophy, Univ of Portland, 5000 N Willamette, Portland, OR, 97203-5798.

MAZZOCCO, ANGELO
PERSONAL Born 05/13/1936, Isernia, Italy, m, 2 children **DISCIPLINE** ROMANCE LANGUAGES & LITERATURES **EDUCATION** OH State Univ, BA & BSc, 59, MA, 63; Univ CA, Berkeley, PhD, 73. **CAREER** Instr Span, John Carroll Univ, 62-65; tchg asst Ital, Univ CA, Berkeley, 66-69; asst prof Ital, Northern IL Univ, 70-75; asst prof Ital & Span, 75-76, Assoc Prof Ital & Span, 76-83, Prof Ital & Span 83- Chmn Dept, 81-84, 93-96; Chmn Romance Lang(s) and Lit(s) 89-93; Assoc Columbia Univ Renaissance Seminar 81-90. **HONORS AND AWARDS** Univ CA Ital-Am Traveling fel, 69-70; Fel, Nat Endowment for Hum, 81; Grantee, Am Council of Learned Societies, 85; Res fel, Gladys Krieble Delmas Found, 93-94, 96-97; Grantee, Nat Endowment for the Hum/Nat Sci Found, 95-98; Fel in Residence, Inst for Advanced Studies, IN Univ, Bloomington, 98. **MEMBERSHIPS** MLA (NE Chpt exec com Medieval and Ren Ital Lit, 81-85, assembly del 85-87); Am Asn Tchr(s) Ital; Dante Soc Am (coun assoc 85-90, coun 94-97); Renaissance Soc Am; Med Academy; Int Asn Neo-Latin Studies; N Am Asn His Lang Soc; Asn Int Studi di Lingua e Letteratura Italiana; Int Soc Classical Tradition, Am Boccaccio Asn (vp 82-83); Nat Asn Scholars. **RESEARCH** Latin humanism; hist linguistics of Ital and Span, Dante antiq, intellectual hist. **SELECTED PUBLICATIONS** Auth, Linguistic Theories in Dante and the Humantists, 93; contbr numerous chpts in bks and many articles and review to profl jours. **CONTACT ADDRESS** Dept of Span & Ital, Mount Holyoke Col, 50 College St, South Hadley, MA, 01075-1461. **EMAIL** amazzocc@mlhc.mtholyoke.edu

MAZZOCCO, ELIZABETH H.
DISCIPLINE FRENCH LITERATURE **EDUCATION** Bryn Mawr Univ, PhD. **CAREER** Prof, Univ MA Amherst. **RESEARCH** Italian epic; Italian theater; for lang tech. **SELECTED PUBLICATIONS** Auth, pubs on Boiardo's Orlando Innamorato; Renaissance chivalry. **CONTACT ADDRESS** Dept of French and Italian Studies, Univ Massachusetts Amherst, Mass Ave, Amherst, MA, 01003. **EMAIL** mazzocco@frital.umass.edu

MAZZOLA, MICHAEL LEE
PERSONAL Born 01/19/1941, Frankfort, NY **DISCIPLINE** ROMANCE LINGUISTICS **EDUCATION** Le Moyne Col, NY, AB, 62; Middlebury Col, MA, 64; Cornell Univ, PhD, 67. **CAREER** Lectr French, Cornell Univ, 65-66, asst prof ling, 66-68; asst prof French & Ital, Ind Univ, Bloomington, 68-74; vis fel, Cornell Univ, 74-75; asst prof, 75-79, assoc prof French & Ital, Northern Ill Univ, 79-. **HONORS AND AWARDS** Grant, Summer Linguistics Inst at UCLA, Am Coun Learned Soc, 66; grant, NEH Summer Seminar, Harvard Univ, 82; grant, NEH, Folger Library, 84. **MEMBERSHIPS** Ling Soc Am; MLA. **RESEARCH** French and Italian dialectology; French phonology and syntax; general linguistics. **SELECTED PUBLICATIONS** Auth, Proto-Romance and Sicilian, Peter de Ridder, Lisse, Neth, 76; The Romance Stammbaum in the South, in Semasia, Vol V, 78; French Rhythm and French Segments, in Ling Perspectives on the Romance Lang: Selected Papers from the 21st LSRL, J. Benjamins, 93; Indirect Phonology & French Segments, in Generative French Phonology: Retrospective and Perspectives, Asn Fr Lang Studies & Europ Studies Res Inst, 94; Syntactic Constituency and Prosodic Phenomena, in Aspects of Romance Linguistics: Selected Papers from the LSRL XXIV, Georgetown Univ Press, 96; From Stress in Latin and Romance to Lexical Stress in Italian, in Certamen Phonologicum III, Turin, Rosenberg & Sellier, 97; Issues and Theory in Romance Linguistics: Selected Papers from the Linguistic Symposium on Romance Languages XXIII, Georgetown Univ Press, 94; author of numerous other articles and reviews. **CONTACT ADDRESS** Dept of Foreign Lang & Lit, No Illinois Univ, 1425 W Lincoln Hwy, De Kalb, IL, 60115-2825. **EMAIL** mlmazzola@niu.edu

MCALPIN, MARY
DISCIPLINE FRENCH LITERATURE **EDUCATION** Columbia Univ, PhD, 94. **CAREER** Asst prof. **SELECTED PUBLICATIONS** Auth, pubs on Rousseau's correspondence and Memoires de Mme Roland. **CONTACT ADDRESS** Dept of Romance Languages, Tennessee Univ, Knoxville, TN, 37996.

MCBRIDE, ANGELA BARRON
PERSONAL Born 01/16/1941, Baltimore, MD, m, 1965, 2 children **DISCIPLINE** NURSING; PSYCHIATRIC-MENTAL HEALTH NURSING; DEVELOPMENTAL PSYCHOLOGY/SOCIAL **EDUCATION** Georgetown Univ, BSN, 62; Yale Univ, MSN, 64; Purdue Univ, PhD, 78. **CAREER** Adjunt Assoc Prof, 81-present, Dept of Psychiatry, Indiana Univ Sch of Medicine; Adjunct Prof, 81-present, Dept of Psychology, Purdue Univ Sch of Sci at Indianapolis; Adjunct Prof, 88-present, Indiana Univ Women's Studies; Execu Assoc Dean for Research, 90-91, Interim Dean, 91-92, University Dean, 92-, Distinguish Prof of Nursing, 92-,Indiana Univ Sch of Nursing; Adjunct Prof, 95-, Philanthropic Studies Sch of Liberal Arts IUPUI, Senior Vice Pres for Academic Affairs Nursing, 97-present, Nursing/Patient Services Clarian Health Partners, Inc. **HONORS AND AWARDS** Distinguished Alumna Award, Yale Univ, 78, Purdue Univ; Distinguished Research Award of Midwest Nursing Res Soc, 85; Univ Medallion, Univ of San Francisco, 93; Mentor Award, Sigma Theta Tau Intl, 93; Outstanding Contribution to Nursing and Health Psychology Award, Amer Psychological Assoc Div 38, 95; named "Who's Who in Health care" by Indianapolis Business Journal, 95, 96, 98. **MEMBERSHIPS** Amer Acad of Nursing; Amer Psychological Assn; Indiana State Nurses' Assn; Intl Council on Women's Health Issues; Midwest Nursing Research Soc; Natl Council on Family Relations; Sigma Theta Tau Intl; Sigma Xi; Soc for Education and Research in Psychiatric Nursing; Soc for Research in Child Development. **RESEARCH** Experience of parents, health concerns of women, and functional assessment of the seriously mentally ill. **SELECTED PUBLICATIONS** coauth, Women's Health and Women's Health Care: Recommendations of the 1996 AAAN Expert Panel on Women's Health, Nursing Outlook, 97; Auth, Future of Nursing Scholarship, Image: Journal of Nursing Scholarship, 97; Attribution theory, Encyclopedia of nursing research, 98; Feminist methods, Encyclopedia of nursing research, 98; coauth, Feminist perspectives on policy and politics, in Policy and Politics in Nursing and Health Care, 98; Psychosocial care needs of parents of children with new-onset seizures, Journal of Neuroscience Nursing, 98; Legacy: Defining Nursing, in E.K. Herrman (ed), Virginia Avenel Henderson: Signature for nursing, 98; Women's health reseach, Enncyclopedia of nursing research, 98. **CONTACT ADDRESS** Sch of Nursing, Dept of Psychiatric/Mental Health , Indiana Univ-Purdue Univ, Indianapolis, Indianapolis, IN, 46223. **EMAIL** amcbride@iupui.edu

MCCANN, DAVID RICHARD
PERSONAL Born 07/01/1944, Lewiston, ME, m, 1968, 2 children **DISCIPLINE** KOREAN AND JAPANESE LITERATURE **EDUCATION** Amherst Col, BA, 66; Harvard Univ, MA, 71, PhD(Korean lit), 76. **CAREER** Asst prof, Cornell Univ, 76-77, asst prof Japanese lit, 78-79; staff writer, 79-80, ASST DIR FEDN RELS, UNIV DEVELOP, 80-. **HONORS AND AWARDS** Pushcart Prize, Pushcart Prize Anthology III, 78. **MEMBERSHIPS** Asn for Asian Studies; Asn Teachers of Japanese (secy, 78-); Poetry Soc of Am; Poets & Writers, Inc. **RESEARCH** Japanese and Korean verse literature; modern poetry. **SELECTED PUBLICATIONS** Auth, Fault Lines, Modern Korean Poetry, Chicago Rev, vol 0039, 93. **CONTACT ADDRESS** Cornell Univ, 726 University Ave Univ Develop, Ithaca, NY, 14853.

MCCARREN, VINCENT PAUL
PERSONAL Born 03/22/1939, New York, NY, m, 1968 **DISCIPLINE** CLASSICAL STUDIES, MEDIEVAL LITERATURE **EDUCATION** Fordham Univ, AB, 60; Columbia Univ, AM, 67; Univ Mich, PhD(class studies), 75. **CAREER** Lectr Greek & Latin, Brooklyn Col, 63-68; instr, Hunter Col, 68-69, class lang & lit, Herbert H Lehman Col, 69-70; lcctr Greek & Latin, 75-76, acad coun gen acad areas, 77-78, RESEARCHER, MIDDLE ENGLISH DICT, UNIV MICH, 79-. **MEMBERSHIPS** Am Soc Papyrologists; Am Philol Soc. **RESEARCH** Documentary papyrology; Greek and Latin etymological studies. **SELECTED PUBLICATIONS** Aith, The Tanner Bede--The Old English Version of Bede 'Historia Ecclesiastica', Oxford Bodleian Library Tanner 10, Together With the Mediaeval Binding Leaves, Oxford Bodleian Library 10, and the Domitian Extracts, London British Libra, Speculum; Bristol University Ms Dm 1, a Fragment of the 'Medulla Grammaticae'--an dd, Traditio Stud in Ancient and Medieval Hist Thought and Relig, vol 0048, 93. **CONTACT ADDRESS** Middle English Dict, Univ Michigan, 555 S Forest, Ann Arbor, MI, 48109.

MCCARTHY, DENNIS JOHN
PERSONAL Born 10/14/1924, Chicago, IL **DISCIPLINE** OLD TESTAMENT EXEGESIS, SEMITIC LANGUAGES **EDUCATION** St Louis Univ, MA, 51; Inst Cath, Paris, STD, 62; Pontifical Bibl Inst, Rome, SSL, 63. **CAREER** From asst prof to assoc prof Old Testament, St Louis Univ, 63-69; extraordinary prof, 69-74, PROF OLD TESTAMENT, PONTIFICAL BIBL INST, ROME, 74-, Assoc ed, Cath Bibl Quart, 68-76; ED, OLD TESTAMENT, BIBLICA, 79-. **MEMBERSHIPS** Soc Bibl Lit; Cath Bibl Asn Am. **RESEARCH** Old Testament historical books; folklore and literature. **SELECTED PUBLICATIONS** Society, personality and inspiration, Theol Studies, 63; II Samuel 7 and the structure of the Deuteronomic history, J Bibl Lit, 65; Der Gottesbund im Alten Testament, Katholisches Bibelwerk, Ger, 66; Prophetism, In: New Cath Encycl, 67; Kings and Prophets, Bruce, 68; Hosea, In: Jerome Commentary, Old Testament Covenant (in Ital), Blackwell & Marietti 72; Treaty and Covenant: A Study in Form in the Ancient Near Eastern Documents in the Old Testament, 2nd ed, Pontifical Bibl Inst, 78. **CONTACT ADDRESS** Via della Pilotta 25, Rome, ..

MCCARTHY, JOHN ALOYSIUS
PERSONAL Born 01/09/1942, St. Clair, MI, m, 1965, 2 children **DISCIPLINE** GERMAN **EDUCATION** Oakland Univ, BA, 64; State Univ NY Buffalo, MA, 67, PhD(Ger), 72. **CAREER** Instr Ger, Oakland Univ, 69-72; asst prof, 72-78, ASSOC PROF GER, UNIV PA, 79-, Ed, Ger Sect, ECCB, 77-80; undergrad chmn, Univ Pa, 73-75; Am Philos Soc grant, 77, Pa res found fel, 82. **HONORS AND AWARDS** AM, Univ Pa. 79. **MEMBERSHIPS** Am Leasing Soc; Am Asn 18th Century Studies; Am Asn Teachers Ger; MLA; Deutsche Schiller Gesellschaft. **RESEARCH** Eighteenth century German and European literature; Christoph Martin Wieland; eighteenth century reading habits. **SELECTED PUBLICATIONS** Auth, Fantasy and Reality: An Epistemological Approach to Wieland, Herbert Lang, Bern, 74; Wielands metamorphose?, Deutsche Vierteljahresschrift Litgesch, 75; Some aspects of imagery in Buchners Woyzeck, Mod Lang Notes, 76; Wieland as essayist, Leasing Yearbk, 76; Shaftesbury and Wieland: The question of enthusiasm, SECC, 77; Die republikanische Freiheit des Lesers Zum Lesepublikum von Schillers, In: Der Verbrecher aus verlorener Ehre, Wirkendes Wort, 78; C M Wieland, Twayne, 79; The poet as Jist and essayist, vol XII, No 1 & vol XIII, No 1, JIG. **CONTACT ADDRESS** Dept of Ger Lang, Univ of Pa, 745 Williams Hall, Philadelphia, PA, 19174.

MCCARTHY, MARY THERESA
PERSONAL Born 08/13/1927, Plainfield, NJ **DISCIPLINE** FRENCH LANGUAGE & LITERATURE **EDUCATION** Georgian Court Col, BA, 57; Laval Univ, MA, 65; Inst Cath Paris, dip d'Etudes Francaises, 67; Sorbonne, dipl cult Francaise contemp, 67; Ruigers Univ, PhD(French), 73. **CAREER** Teacher Latin, Mt St Mary Acad, North Plainfield, NJ, 45-46; teacher social studies, St Mary Sch, South Amboy, NJ, 47-49; teacher prim grades, Cathedral Grammar Sch, Trenton, 49-56; teacher mid grades, St Matthew Sch, Edison, 56-57; teacher Latin & French, Holy Spirit High Sch, Atlantic City, 57-59; instr French, 59-75, PROF FRENCH, 75-, DIR, FOREIGN STUDY, GEORGIAN COURT COL, 86-; Fulbright Scholar French, Univ Paris, 66-67; Nat Endowment Humanities fel comp lit, Univ Chicago, 75; reader, advan placement tests French lang, Educ Testing Serv, 76-81; Exxon Educ Found grant lang model workshop, Dartmouth Col, 77, Univ PA, 80; assoc Danforth Found, 78-84; Nat Endowment for Humanities fel French lit, Princeton Univ, 79, 87, Columbia Univ, 83, Univ CA Santa Cruz, 89, Radcliffe Col, 91; sr lang consult, Rassias Found, 79-; writer, Col Bd French Achievement Test, 80; consult, NJ Comt for Humanities, 80-81; Quebec gov grant, 90. **MEMBERSHIPS** Sisters of Mercy; MLA; Am Asn Teachers French; Am Transit Asn; Alliance Francaise; Am Coun for Quebec Studies. **RESEARCH** Modern French literature, especially the modern French novel, most especially Henri Bosco's dream novels. **SELECTED PUBLICATIONS** Contribr, The Adventures of Pascalet, Oxford Univ, 76; Historic Houses of New Jersey, William H Wise & Co, 77; Culotte the Donkey, Oxford Univ, 78; auth, Winter Idyl (poem), Poet Lore, spring 78; Today Never Came (poem), Revue de Louisiane/La Rev, fall 78; Autumn Passion (poem), NJ Poetry Monthly, 10/78; Faith on Easter Morn (poem), 4/81 & Autumn Air (poem), 10/78, Villager; Georgian Court-An Estate of the Gilded Age, Philadelphia Art Alliance Press, 82; Quebec's Ursline Foundation, Sisters Today, Jan 91; Being Irish (poem), Irish Echo, 3/25/92; Blackeyed (poem), The Cord, Dec 92; Anti-Nuclear Exposition (poem), Sisters Today, May 93; Climat d'ecoute #1, Alternative Physiognomy and Climat d'ecoute #2: Alternative Metaphysics (poems), Rev for Religions, Dec 94; Gabriel Redican: Early Days of Mercy Higher Education, The MAST J, summer 95; Prayers for All People, Doubleday, 95; Americanization of Art: Mere Maufils (1671-1702), Sisters Today, Nov 96; Une Autre Abbeville, Le Bull des Antiquaires de Picardie, Nov 96. **CONTACT ADDRESS** Georgian Court Col, 900 Lakewood Ave, Lakewood, NJ, 08701-2697. **EMAIL** mccarthy@georgian.edu

MCCASH, JUNE HALL
PERSONAL Born 06/08/1938, Newberry, SC, m, 1961, 2 children **DISCIPLINE** MEDIEVAL FRENCH & COMPARATIVE LITERATURE **EDUCATION** Agnes Scott Col, AB, 60; Emory Univ, MA, 63, PhD, 67. **CAREER** Instr French & humanities, Emory Univ, 64-67; from asst prof to assoc prof French, 67-75, dir hon prog, 73-80, Prof French, Mid Tenn State Univ, 75-, Chairperson, Dept Foreign Lang, 80-92; NEH younger humanist fel, 75, sem, 78. **HONORS AND AWARDS** Distinguished Res Award, MTSU Found, 96; Outstanding Alumnae Career Achievement Award, Agnes Scott Col, 96. **MEMBERSHIPS** MLA; SAtlantic Mod Lang Asn; Societe Rencesvals; Medieval Acad Am; Int Courtly Lit Soc. **RESEARCH** Medieval literature; epic, courtly romance; Jekyll Island. **SELECTED PUBLICATIONS** Auth, Love's Fools: Aucassin, Troilus, Calisto and the Parody of the Courtly Lover, Tamesis, London, 72; Scientia and Sapientia in the Chanson de Roland, Medievalia et Humanistica, 82; coauth, The Jekyll Island Club: Southern Haven for America's Millionaires, Univ Ga Press, 89; auth, The Cultural Patronage of Medieval Women, Univ Ga Press, 96; Images of Women in the Lais of Marie de France, Medieval Perspectives 11, 96; Amor in Marie de France's Equitan and Frene: The Failure of the Courtly Ideal, In: The Court and Cultural Diversity, Boydell and Brewer, 97; The Jekyll Island Cottage Colony, Univ Ga Press, 98; author of other journal articles. **CONTACT ADDRESS** Middle Tennessee State Univ, Box 79, Murfreesboro, TN, 37132-0001. **EMAIL** jmccash@mtsu.edu

MCCAULEY, REBECCA J.
DISCIPLINE COMMUNCATION SCIENCES **EDUCATION** Univ Chicago, PhD, 81. **CAREER** Dept Comm, Vermont Univ **MEMBERSHIPS** ASHA; VSHA; Acoust Soc Am. **RESEARCH** Normal and disordered speech; testing and measurement of speech and language. **SELECTED PUBLICATIONS** Auth, Familiar strangers: criterion-referenced measures in communication disorders, 96; Phonologic Disorders, 94; A comprehensive phonological approach to assessment and treatment of sound system disorders, 93; coauth, Intelligibility and analysis of phonetic contrast errors in speakers with amyotrophic lateral sclerosis, Jour Speech Hearing Res, 95. **CONTACT ADDRESS** Dept of Communication Sciences, Vermont Univ, 360 Waterman Bldg, Burlington, VT, 05405. **EMAIL** rmccaule@zoo.uvm.edu

MCCAWLEY, JAMES D.
PERSONAL Born 03/30/1938, Glasgow, Scotland **DISCIPLINE** LINGUISTICS **EDUCATION** Univ Chicago, MS, 58; Mass Inst Technol, PhD, 65. **CAREER** Asst prof ling, 64-70, Prof Ling, Univ Chicago, 70. **MEMBERSHIPS** Ling Soc Am; Soc Exact Philos; Asn Tchr(s) of Japan. **RESEARCH** Syntax; semantics; struct of Eng and Japan. **SELECTED PUBLICATIONS** Auth, The Phonological Component of a Grammar of Japanese, Mouton, The Hague, 68; Adverbs, Vowels, and Other Objects of Wonder, Univ Chicago Press, 79; Everything that Linguists have Always Wanted to Know About Logic, Univ Chicago Press, 82; Thirty Million Theories of Grammar, Croom Helm, 82; The Eater's Guide to Chinese Characters, Univ Chicago Press, 84; The Syntactic Phenomena of English, Univ Chicago Press, 88. **CONTACT ADDRESS** Dept of Ling, Univ of Chicago, 1010 E 59th St, Chicago, IL, 60637-1512. **EMAIL** jmccawle@midway.uchicago.edu

MCCLAIN, T. VAN
PERSONAL Born 06/10/1952, Dallas, TX, m, 1977, 3 children **DISCIPLINE** OLD TESTAMENT AND HEBREW **EDUCATION** SW Baptist Theol Sem, MDiv, 77, PhD, 85. **CAREER** Assoc Prof, Dir library serv, 89-, Mid-Amer Baptist Theol Sem. **MEMBERSHIPS** ETS; SBL. **RESEARCH** Old Testament and New Testament; Semitic Languages; Cults; Hermeneutics. **SELECTED PUBLICATIONS** Auth, The Use of Amos in the New Testament, Mid-America Theol J, 95; Hosea's Marriage to Gomer, Mid-Amer Theol J, 93; Introduction to the Book Of Isaiah, Mid-Amer Theol J, 91. **CONTACT ADDRESS** Northeast Branch, Mid-America Baptist Theol Sem, 2810 Curry Rd, Schenectady, NY, 12303. **EMAIL** VMcClain@mabtsne.edu

MCCLOSKEY, JAMES
DISCIPLINE LINGUISTICS **EDUCATION** Univ Coll, Dublin, BA; Univ Tex, Austin, PhD, 79. **CAREER** PROF, LING, UNIV CALIF, SANTA CRUZ. **RESEARCH** Theory of syntax. **SELECTED PUBLICATIONS** Auth, Clause Structure, Ellipsis and Proper Government in Irish, Lingua, 91; Resumptive Pronouns, A-Binding, and Levels of Representation in Irish, The Syntax of the Modern Celtic Languages, Acad Press, 90; co-auth, Control and A-Chains in Modern Irish, Natural Lang and Ling Theory, 88; Government, Barriers and Small Clauses in Modern Irish, Ling Inquiry, 87; On the Syntax of Person-Number Inflection in Modern Irish, Natural Lang and Ling Theory, 84. **CONTACT ADDRESS** Dept of Ling, Univ Calif, 1156 High St, Santa Cruz, CA, 95064.

MCCLURE, CHARLOTTE SWAIN
PERSONAL Born 07/30/1921, Newark, OH, m, 1945, 3 children **DISCIPLINE** AMERICAN AND COMPARATIVE LITERATURE **EDUCATION** Denison Univ, Ohio, BA, 44; Univ NMex, MA, 66, PhD(English), 73. **CAREER** Staff & feature writer state govt, Int News Serv, Columbus, 44-45; staff & feature writer local govt & gen news, J-Herald, Dayton, 46-47; instr English & chmn dept, Sandia Sch, Albuquerque, 66-68; from instr to asst prof, 69-75, dir honors prog admin, 75-79, asst prof for lang & comp lit, 78-82, ASSOC PROF COMP LIT, GA STATE UNIV, ATLANTA, 82-, Fac, Gerontology Ctr, Ga State Univ, 79-; Women's Educ Equity Act Prog grant, 79-82. **MEMBERSHIPS** MLA; SAtlantic Mod Lang Asn; Southern Comp Lit Asn; Western Lit Asn. **RESEARCH** Rediscovery of American writers, especially women of late 19th and early 20th centuries; comparison of types of literary characters portrayed in the literatures of the western world; comparative study of themes in western hemispheric literatures. **SELECTED PUBLICATIONS** Auth, The Adventures of the Woman Homesteader--The Life and Letters of Stewart, Elinore, Pruitt, Amer Lit, vol 0065, 93; Helen of the West Indies + Walcott, Derek and 'Omeros'--History or Poetry of a Caribbean Realm, Stud in the Lit Imagination, vol 0026, 93; California Daughter, Atherton, Gertrude and Her Times, Resources for Amer Lit Study, vol 0022, 96. **CONTACT ADDRESS** Georgia State Univ, 2674 Leslie Dr NE, Atlanta, GA, 30345.

MCCLURE, JOHN
DISCIPLINE ENGLISH LANGUAGE AND LITERATURE **EDUCATION** Tufts Univ, BA; Stanford, MA; PhD. **CAREER** Prof. **RESEARCH** Colonial cultural studies; religious cultural studies; contemporary fiction. **SELECTED PUBLICATIONS** Auth, Kipling and Conrad: The Colonial Fiction, Late Imperial Romance. **CONTACT ADDRESS** Dept of English, Rutgers Univ, 510 George St, Murray Hall, New Brunswick, NJ, 08901-1167. **EMAIL** jmcclure@rci.rutgers.edu

MCCONNELL, WINDER
PERSONAL Born 11/19/1945, Belfast, Ireland, m, 1973, 2 children **DISCIPLINE** GERMAN MEDIEVAL LITERATURE **EDUCATION** McGill Univ, BA, 67; Univ Kans, MA, 69, PhD(Ger), 73. **CAREER** Instr Ger, Univ Western Ont, 72-73; Ordinarius English, Hist & gemeinschaftskunde, Gym Munden, West Ger, 73-74; res & teaching fel Ger, Stanford Univ, 74-76; asst prof, Johns Hopkins Univ, 76-78; asst prof, 78-82, from assoc prof to prof German, Univ Calif, Davis, 82-88; vis prof, sum 90, UC Santa Barbara; vis prof, Univ Stirling, Scotland, 90-91. **HONORS AND AWARDS** Medal of Honor, Heinrich-Heine Univ, Dusseldorf, Ger. **MEMBERSHIPS** MLA; Med Assoc of the Pacific; Assoc Lit Scholars and Critics. **RESEARCH** Medieval German heroic epic; Jungian approaches to lit. **SELECTED PUBLICATIONS** Auth, Wate and Wada, MLN, 77; The Wate Figure in Medieval Tradition, Peter Lang Verlag, 78; Ritual and literary tradition: The brobdingnagian element in Dukus Horant, Mediaevalia, 81; Hagen and the otherworld in Kudrun, Res Publ Litterarum, 82; Kriemhild and Gerlind, Houston Ger Studies, 82; Marriage in the Nibelungenlied and Kudrun: A contrastive analysis, Festschrift for George F Jones, 83; The Nibelungenlied, Twayne's World Authors Series, 84; The Lament of the Nibelungen, Diu Chlage, 94; Companion to the Nibelungenlied, 98. **CONTACT ADDRESS** Dept of German, Univ of California, Davis, Davis, CA, 95616. **EMAIL** wamcconnell@ucdavis.edu.

MCCULLOH, WILLIAM EZRA
PERSONAL Born 09/08/1931, McPherson, KS, m, 1956, 2 children **DISCIPLINE** CLASSICAL LANGUAGES & LITERATURES **EDUCATION** Ohio Wesleyan Univ, AB, 53; Oxford Univ, BA, 56; Yale Univ, PhD, 62. **CAREER** Instr classics, Wesleyan Univ, 56-61; from instr to assoc prof, 61-68, prof classics, Kenyon Col, 68-. **HONORS AND AWARDS** Am Philological Assoc Award for Excellence in Teaching, 85; Nat Endowment for the Humanitites Fel for Col Teachers, 84-85; Ohio Prof of the Year, Carnegie Found for the Advancement of Teaching and Council for Advancement and Support of Educ, 95. **MEMBERSHIPS** Am Philol Asn; Class Asn Mid W & S; Soc Ancient Greek Philos; NAm Patristics Soc; Int Soc for Neoplatonic Studies. **RESEARCH** Greek poetry and philosophy; the ancient novel; Greek patristics. **SELECTED PUBLICATIONS** Auth, Introduction to Greek Lyric Poetry, Bantam, 62; Metaphysical solace in Greek tragedy, Class J, 12/63; Aristophanes seen whole, Sewanee Rev, fall 65; Longus, Twayne, 70. **CONTACT ADDRESS** Dept of Classics, Kenyon Col, Ascension Hall, Gambier, OH, 43022-9623. **EMAIL** mcculloh@kenyon.edu

MCCUMBER, JOHN
DISCIPLINE GERMAN **EDUCATION** Pomona Col, BA; Univ Toronto, MA, PhD. **CAREER** Prof, Northwestern Univ. **HONORS AND AWARDS** Koldyke prof tchg excellence, 94-96; Jean Gimbal Lane Humanities prof, 96-97. **RESEARCH** Include two manuscripts: Metaphysics and Oppression; Heidegger's Challange and The Capture of Time: Situation and Logos in Post-Kantian Philosophy. **SELECTED PUBLICATIONS** Auth, Poetic Interaction and The Company of Words; essays and articles on, philos from Aristotle to Derrida. **CONTACT ADDRESS** Dept of German, Northwestern Univ, 1801 Hinman, Evanston, IL, 60208. **EMAIL** jmcc@nwu.edu

MCDANIEL, THOMAS F.
PERSONAL Baltimore, MD, m **DISCIPLINE** OLD TESTAMENT STUDIES AND HEBREW **EDUCATION** Univ Richmond, BA; E Baptist Theol Sem, BD; Univ Pa, MA, 56; Johns Hopkins Univ, PhD, 66. **CAREER** Prof, E Baptist Theol Sem. **SELECTED PUBLICATIONS** Auth, rev, Deborah Never Sang: A Philol Commentary on Judges 5, Makor Press, Jerusalem, 83. **CONTACT ADDRESS** Eastern Baptist Theol Sem, 6 Lancaster Ave, Wynnewood, PA, 19096.

MCDONALD, WILLIAM CECIL
PERSONAL Born 01/26/1941, Mt Clemens, MI, m, 1968, 1 child **DISCIPLINE** MEDIEVAL GERMAN LITERATURE AND LANGUAGE **EDUCATION** Wayne State Univ, BE, 62, MA, 63; Ohio State Univ, PhD(Ger medieval studies), 72. **CAREER** Instr, Wayne State Univ, 62-64; teaching asst, Ohio State Univ, 65-68, instr, 68-71; asst prof, Va Polytech Inst, 71-75; asst prof, 75-80, ASSOC PROF GER, UNIV VA, 80-, Assoc ed, Semasia, 74-76 St Ger Quart, 76-77; exec coun, Southeastern Medieval Asn, 77-; vis prof, Ger Acad Exchange Serv, 77; bd rev ed, Tristania, 82- **MEMBERSHIPS** Int Courtly Lit Soc (Am pres, 80-82); South Atlantic Mod Lang Asn; MLA; Medieval Acad; Southeastern Medieval Ago. **RESEARCH** Medieval rhetoric; development of literary motifs; late medieval studies. **SELECTED PUBLICATIONS** Auth, Swiss Minnesang Poets, vol 1, Texts, J Engl and Ger Philol, vol 0092, 93; History, Fiction, Verisimilitude--Studies in the Poetics of Gottfried 'Tristan', Ger Quart, vol 0069, 96. **CONTACT ADDRESS** Dept of Ger Lang, Univ of Va, 1 Cocke Hall, Charlottesville, VA, 22903-3248.

MCDONOUGH, CHRISTOPHER MICHAEL
PERSONAL Born 12/28/1963, Boston, MA, m, 1990 **DISCIPLINE** CLASSICAL PHILOLOGY **EDUCATION** Tufts Univ, BA, 86; Univ North Carolina, MA, 91, PhD, 96. **CAREER** Adj prof, Univ North Carolina, Greensboro, 92-96; vis asst prof, Princeton Univ, 96-97; asst prof, Boston Col, 97- . **MEMBERSHIPS** APA; CAMWS; Am Soc of Lit Critics; Am Acad in Rome. **RESEARCH** Roman religion; social history. **CONTACT ADDRESS** Dept of Classics, Boston Col, 158 Carney, Chestnut Hill, MA, 02167. **EMAIL** mcdonoch@bc.edu

MCGAHA, MICHAEL DENNIS
PERSONAL Born 12/31/1941, Dallas, TX, m, 1964, 2 children **DISCIPLINE** SPANISH LANGUAGE & PENINSULAR LITERATURE, JEWISH STUDIES **EDUCATION** Univ Dallas, BA, 65; Univ Tex, Austin, PhD, 70. **CAREER** Instr Span, Univ Tex, Austin, 69-70; PROF ROMANCE LANGUAGES, POMONA COL, 70-. **HONORS AND AWARDS** Fulbright grant, 65-66; Woodrow Wilson fel, 66-67, NEH fel, 80-81. **MEMBERSHIPS** AATSP; Asociacion Internacional de Hispanistas; Asn Jewish Studies; Cervantes Soc Am; Middle East

Studies Asn. **RESEARCH** Cervantes; Spanish theatre of Golden Age; history and literature of Sephardic Jews. **SELECTED PUBLICATIONS** Auth, The Theatre in Madrid during the Second Republic, Grant & Cutler, 79; Ed, Cervantes and the Reanissance, Juan de la Cuesta, 80; Approaches to the Theater of Calderon, UP of Am, 82; Lope de Vega's La fabula de Perseo, Reichenberger, 85; Editing the Comedia, Mish Romance Studies, 85; transl, Lope de Amescua's Acting Is Believing, Trinity UP, 86; Antonio Mira de Amescua's The Devil's slave, Doehouse, 89; ed, Editing the Comedia II, Mich Romance Studies, 91; Antonio Enriquez Gomez's The Perfect King, Bilingual Rev/Press, 91; Calderon de la Barca's Suenos hay que verdad son, Reichenberger, 97; Auth, Coat of Many Cultures: The Story of Joseph in Spanish Literature, 1200-1492, Jewish Publ Soc, 97; The Story of Joseph in Spanish Golden Age Drama, Bucknell UP, 98; over 60 articles & book reviews. **CONTACT ADDRESS** Dept Romance Lang, Pomona Col, 550 N Harvard Ave, Claremont, CA, 91711-6369. **EMAIL** mmcgaha@pomona.edu

MCGARRELL, HEDY M.
DISCIPLINE LINGUISTICS **EDUCATION** Univ Concordia, BA; Univ Ottawa, MA, PhD. **CAREER** Assoc prof. **RESEARCH** Development of metalinguistic ability in first and second language acquisition. **SELECTED PUBLICATIONS** Auth, "Writing a Research Paper: Eight Steps to Keep on Track," Intl Jour for Tchrs Eng Wrtg Skills, Vol 1, No 1, 95; "Exchanging Superstitions for Writing Fluency," Virtual Connections: Online Act and Proj for Networking Lang Learners, Univ Hawaii, 95; "Pen Pals for Purpose, Practice and Product," Virtual Connections: Online Activities and Projects for Networking Language Learners, Honolulu, HI: Univ Hawaii, 95; "Self-Directed Learning Contracts to Individualize Language Learning in the Classroom," For Lang Annals 96, Vol 29, 96. **CONTACT ADDRESS** Humanities, Brock Univ, 500 Glenridge Ave, St Catharines, ON, L2S 3A1. **EMAIL** hmcgarre@spartan.ac.BrockU.CA

MCGLATHERY, JAMES MELVILLE
PERSONAL Born 11/22/1936, New Orleans, LA, m, 1963, 4 children **DISCIPLINE** GERMANIC LANGUAGES **EDUCATION** Princeton Univ, AB, 58; Yale Univ, AM, 59, PhD(Ger), 64. **CAREER** Instr Ger, Phillips Andover Acad, 59-60; instr, Harvard Univ, 63-65; from Asst Prof to Assoc Prof, 65-84, Prof Ger, Univ Ill, Urbana-Champaign, 84-, Dept Head, 85-95; Managing ed, J English & Ger Philol, 72-; Vis Prof, Univ Guttingen, Ger, 93-94. **MEMBERSHIPS** MLA; Am Asn Teachers Ger. **RESEARCH** Romanticism and the 19th century literature. **SELECTED PUBLICATIONS** Auth, The suicide motif in E. T.A. Hoffmann's Der goldne Topf, Monatshefte, 6/66; Kleist's sber das Marionetten-Theater, Ger Life & Lett, 7/67; Fear of perdition in Droste-Holshoff's Judenbuche, In: Lebendige Form: Festschrift fur Heinrich E K Henel, Wilhelm Fink, Munich, 70; Kleist's version of Moliere's Amphitryon: olympian cuckolding and unio mystica, In: Moliere and the Commonwealth of Letters, Univ Miss, 75; Der Himmel hangt ihm voller Geigen: E T A Hoffmann's Rat Krespel, Die Fermate, and Der Baron von B, Ger Quart, 3/78; Bald dein Fall ins-Ehebett?: A new reading of E T A Hoffmann's Goldner Topf, Ger Rev, No 3, 78; Demon love: E T A Hoffmann's Elixiere des Teufels, Colloquia Germanica, Nos 1/2, 79; Mysticism and Sexuality: E T A Hoffmann Part One: Hoffmann and His Sources, Peter Lang, Berne, 81; Desire's Sway: The Plays and Stories of Heinrich von Kleist, Wayne State Univ Press, 83; Mysticism and Sexuality: E T A Hoffmann Part Two: Interpretations of the Tales, Peter Lang, Berne, 85; Fairy Tale Romance: The Grimms, Basile, Perrault, Univ Ill Press, 91; Grimms' Fairy Tales: A History of Criticism on a Popular Classic, Literary Criticism in Perspective, Camden House, 93; E.T.A. Hoffmann, Twayne's World Author's Series, 868, Twayne Publishers, 97; Wagner's Operas and Desire, North American Studies in Nineteenth-Century German Literature, 22, Peter Lang, 98; author of numerous journal articles and other book contributions. **CONTACT ADDRESS** Dept of Ger Lang & Lit, Univ of Illinois, Urbana-Champaign, 707 S Mathews Ave, Urbana, IL, 61801-3675. **EMAIL** mcglath@staff.uiuc.edu

MCGRATH, MICHAEL J.
PERSONAL Born 08/19/1966, Holland, PA, m, 1998 **DISCIPLINE** SPANISH **EDUCATION** Univ of KY, PhD, 98; Middlebury Col, MA, 89; GA S Univ, BA, 88 **CAREER** Asst Prof, 97-, Kings Col **HONORS AND AWARDS** Sigma Delta Pi, 86 **MEMBERSHIPS** Am Classical League; Cervantes Soc of Am **RESEARCH** Modern Spanish lit **CONTACT ADDRESS** Dept of Foreign Lang, King's Col, Wilkes-Barre, PA, 18711. **EMAIL** mjmcgrat@kings.edu

MCGREGOR, JAMES H.
DISCIPLINE COMPARATIVE LITERATURE **EDUCATION** Princeton Univ, BA, 68, PhD, 75. **CAREER** ASSOC PROF, UNIV GA, 81-. **CONTACT ADDRESS** Dept of Comparative Lit, Univ of Georgia, Athens, GA, 30602. **EMAIL** mcgregor@arches.uga.edu

MCHUGH, MICHAEL P.
PERSONAL Born 06/07/1933, Lackawanna, NY, m, 1961, 4 children **DISCIPLINE** CLASSICAL PHILOLOGY, PATRISTIC STUDIES **EDUCATION** Cath Univ Am, AB, 55, MA, 56, PhD(classics), 65. **CAREER** From instr to asst prof classics & humanities, Howard Univ, 58-68; from asst prof to assoc prof, 68-77, PROF CLASSICS, UNIV CONN, STORRS, 77-. **MEMBERSHIPS** NAm Patristic Soc; Am Philol Asn; Vergilian Soc; Am Class League; Medieval Acad Am. **RESEARCH** St Ambrose; Prosper of Aquitaine; textual studies. **SELECTED PUBLICATIONS** Auth, Christianity and the Rhetoric of Empire--The Development of Christian Discourse, J Early Christian Stud, vol 0001, 93. **CONTACT ADDRESS** Univ of Conn, Box U-57, Storrs, CT, 06268.

MCINNIS, JUDY BREDESON
PERSONAL Born 09/22/1943, Roseau, MN, m, 1967, 2 children **DISCIPLINE** COMPARATIVE LITERATURE, SPANISH **EDUCATION** Bemidji State Col, BS, 64; Univ NC, Chapel Hell, PhD(compt lit), 74. **CAREER** Peace Corps vol English, US Govt, Santiago, Chile, 64-66; instr, 71-75, asst prof, 75-82, ASSOC PROF SPAND UNIV DEL, 82-. **MEMBERSHIPS** Am Comp Lit Asn; MLA; Am Asn Teachers Span & Port; Southern Comp Lit Asn. **RESEARCH** Spanish literary criticism 1400-1700; Spanish poetry 1400-1700; Federico Garcia Lorca. **SELECTED PUBLICATIONS** Auth, Approaches to the Study of Literature in Spanish, Mod Lang J, vol 0078, 94; Album, 2nd ed, Mod Lang J, vol 0078, 94; Poesia Cancioneril Castellana, Hispania-J Devoted Tchg Span and Port, vol 0078, 95; Mirtos Frescoes Y Deleito Sa Nave--The Poetry of Sotoderojas, Pedro, Hispania-J Devoted Tchg Span and Port, vol 0078, 95; El Gaucho Vegetariano and Other Plays for Students of Spanish, Mod Lang J, vol 0080, 96. **CONTACT ADDRESS** Dept of Lang & Lit, Univ of Del, Newark, DE, 19718.

MCINTOSH, ANNE
DISCIPLINE SPEECH COMMUNICATION **EDUCATION** UNC Chapel Hill, BA, 88; Univ of Mont Missoula, MA, 91; Univ of Tex Austin, PhD, 95. **CAREER** Res consult; instr. **HONORS AND AWARDS** Lucia Morgan Scholar, 88. **MEMBERSHIPS** Nat Commun Asn; Western States Commun Asn. **RESEARCH** Male-female communication; interpersonal communication; deafness; health communication. **SELECTED PUBLICATIONS** Auth, Getting Back into a Career Again, Hearing Health, 97; Putting ALDs on the Menu, Hearing Health, 97; And Now a Word on Auto Safety..., Hearing Health, 96; Semantic Mapping Across the Curriculum: Helping Students Discover Connections, Perspectives in Ed and Deafness, 95; In Memory of Steve Hodges: An Interview, Hearing Health, 95; Making Science Accessible to Deaf Students, Am Annals of the Deaf, 95. **CONTACT ADDRESS** PO Box 1961, Davidson, NC, 28036. **EMAIL** mcintosh@vnet.net

MCKAY, DOUGLAS R.
PERSONAL Born 11/12/1936, Salt Lake City, UT, m, 1989, 2 children **DISCIPLINE** LANGUAGE **EDUCATION** Univ Utah, BA, 62; Univ Oregon, MA, 64; Michigan State Univ, PhD, 68. **CAREER** From asst prof to prof, 68-99, chemn 68-75, 81, 97, Prof Emeritus, Dept of Lang and Cultures, 99- , Univ Colorado, Colorado Springs. **HONORS AND AWARDS** Hon Woodrow Wilson fel; NDEA fel; NEH Summer Sem grants; res and tchg awards; Civic Service Award, UCCS. **RESEARCH** Twentieth century Spanish peninsular drama; local and regional history. **CONTACT ADDRESS** 1116 Westmoor Dr, Colorado Springs, CO, 80904. **EMAIL** dmckay@mail.uccs.edu

MCKEEN, WILLIAM
PERSONAL Born 09/16/1954, Indianapolis, IN, d, 3 children **DISCIPLINE** HISTORY; MASS COMMUNICATION; EDUCATION **EDUCATION** Indiana Univ, BA, 74, MA, 77; Univ OK, PhD, 86. **CAREER** Educator, 77-; Prof and ch, jour dept, Univ Florida. **HONORS AND AWARDS** Various teaching Awds **MEMBERSHIPS** Pop culture asn; SO book critics cir; AJHA; asn for edu in journ and mass comm. **RESEARCH** Pop cult; journ hist; music. **SELECTED PUBLICATIONS** The Norton Book of Rock and Roll, 99; Good Stories, Well Told, 99; Tom Wolfe, 95; Bob Dylan: A Bio-Bibliography, 93; Hunter S Thompson, 91; The Beatles: A Bio-Bibliography, 90. **CONTACT ADDRESS** Univ Florida, 2089 Weimer Hall, Gainsville, FL, 32611. **EMAIL** wmckeen@jou.ufl.edu

MCKENNA, ANDREW JOSEPH
PERSONAL Born 11/29/1942, Massapequa, NY, m, 1964, 2 children **DISCIPLINE** FRENCH LITERATURE **EDUCATION** Col Holy Cross, AB, 64; Johns Hopkins Univ, MA, 66, PhD, 70. **CAREER** Instr French, Northwestern Univ, 67-70; asst prof, 71-80, assoc prof French, Loyola Univ, Chicago, 80-86. **RESEARCH** Nineteenth century French literature; 20th century French literature; critical theory. **SELECTED PUBLICATIONS** Auth, Violence and Difference: Girard, Perrida and Deconstruction, University of Illinois Press, 92; ed in chief, Contagion: Journal of Violence, Milnesis, and Culture, 96. **CONTACT ADDRESS** Loyola Univ, Chicago, 6525 N Sheridan Rd, Chicago, IL, 60626-5385. **EMAIL** 2mckenn@orion.it.luc.edu

MCKENNA, SHEILA
DISCIPLINE ENGLISH AS A SECOND LANGUAGE **EDUCATION** Columbia Univ, PhD. **CAREER** Asst prof, Long Island Univ, C.W. Post Campus. **SELECTED PUBLICATIONS** Auth, English Composition Organizational Patterns Influenced by Ethnocultural Backgrounds; Orientational Prepositions: Cross-Cultural Misinterpretations; Marge Piercy Poetry & Music. **CONTACT ADDRESS** Long Island Univ, C.W. Post, Brookville, NY, 11548-1300.

MCKEOWN, JAMES C.
DISCIPLINE CLASSICAL STUDIES **EDUCATION** Cambridge Univ, PhD, 78. **CAREER** Dept Classics, Wisc Univ **RESEARCH** Latin literature. **SELECTED PUBLICATIONS** Auth, pubs on Latin poetry, and Ovid's Amores. **CONTACT ADDRESS** Dept of Classics, Univ of Wisconsin, Madison, 500 Lincoln Drive, Madison, WI, 53706. **EMAIL** jmckeown@macc.wisc.edu

MCKINLEY, MARY B.
PERSONAL Born 05/15/1943, Pittsburgh, PA **DISCIPLINE** FRENCH RENAISSANCE LITERATURE **EDUCATION** Seton Hill Col, BA, 65; Univ Wis, MA, 66; Rutgers Univ, PhD(French), 74. **CAREER** Instr French, Albertus Magnus Col, 67-69; acad dir Ital, Exp Int Living, 72-73; asst prof, 74-80, Assoc Prof French, Univ Va, 80-, Mem Cent Exec Comt, Folger Inst Renaissance & 18th Century Studies, 76- **MEMBERSHIPS** MLA: Renaissance Soc Am; Am Asn Teachers Fr. **RESEARCH** Montaigne; history of rhetoric and language theory. **SELECTED PUBLICATIONS** Auth, Montaigne and Greece, 1588-1988, Fr Forum, vol 0018, 93; Rape and Writing in the 'Heptameron' of Marguerite of Navarre, Renaissance Quart, vol 0047, 94. **CONTACT ADDRESS** Dept of French, Univ of Va, 1 Cabell Hall, Charlottesville, VA, 22903.

MCKINNEY, MARK
DISCIPLINE FRENCH **EDUCATION** Univ Tex at Austin, BA; Cornell Univ, MA, PhD. **CAREER** Prof, Miami Univ **RESEARCH** Fiction from the North African diaspora in France; nationalism and identity; racism and gendered identities; popular culture and imperialism; North African literature; 20th-century French and francophone literatures and cultures. **SELECTED PUBLICATIONS** Auth, Haunting Figures in Contemporary Discourse and Popular Culture in France in Sites: The Journal of Twentieth-Century/Contemporary French Studies Vol 1, 97; co-ed, Post-Colonial Cultures in France, Routledge, 97. **CONTACT ADDRESS** Dept of French and Italian, Miami Univ, Oxford, OH, 45056. **EMAIL** mckinnm@muohio.edu

MCKULIK, BEN
DISCIPLINE COMPARATIVE LITERATURE **EDUCATION** Princeton Univ, AB; Univ SC, PhD. **CAREER** Prof; **SELECTED PUBLICATIONS** Areas: Jungian archetypes and a variety of critical approaches to international literature. **CONTACT ADDRESS** York Col, Pennsylvania, 441 Country Club Road, York, PA, 17403.

MCLEAN, HUGH
PERSONAL Born 02/05/1925, Denver, CO, m, 1957, 3 children **DISCIPLINE** SLAVIC LANGUAGES & LITERATURES **EDUCATION** Yale Univ, AB, 47; Columbia Univ, AM, 49; Harvard Univ, PhD(Slavic lang & lit), 56. **CAREER** From instr to asst prof Slavic Lang & Lit, Harvard Univ, 53-59; from assoc prof to prof Russ Lit, Univ Chicago, 59-68, chmn Dept Slavic Lang & Lit, 61-67; chmn Dept, 70-72, 74-76, dean Div Humanities, Col Lett & Sci, 76-81, actg provost & dean, 80-81, prof Slavic Lang & Lit, Univ Calif, Berkeley, 68-94; prof Emeritus, 94; Fulbright Award, UK, 58-59; Am Coun Learned Soc fel Humanities, 58-59; Guggenheim fel, 65-66; IREX fellowships to Russian Academy of Sciences, 83; 92. **MEMBERSHIPS** Am Asn Teachers Slavic & East Europ Lang; Am Asn Advan Slavic Studies. **RESEARCH** Russian literature of the 19th and 20th centuries. **SELECTED PUBLICATIONS** Auth, The development of modern Russian literature, Slavic Rev, 9/62; Nikolai Leskov: The Man and his Art, Harvard Univ, 77. **CONTACT ADDRESS** Dept of Slavic Lang & Lit, Univ of California, Berekely, 6210 Dwinelle Hall, Berkeley, CA, 94720-2979. **EMAIL** hmclean@uclink4.berkeley.edu

MCLENDON, WILL LOVING
PERSONAL Born 08/26/1925, Center, TX **DISCIPLINE** FRENCH **EDUCATION** Univ Tex, BS, 45; Middlebury Col, MA, 47; Univ Paris, DUniv, 52. **CAREER** Instr French, Tex Technol Col, 47-48; instr, Southern Methodist Univ, 50; from asst prof to assoc prof, 53-68, PROF FRENCH, UNIV HOUSTON, 68-, Chmn Dept, 77-. **HONORS AND AWARDS** Chevalier, Palmes Academiques, 65. **RESEARCH** The 20th century novel; the works of Jean Giraudoux; modern poetry. **SELECTED PUBLICATIONS** Auth, Barbeydaurevilly 100 Years Later 1889-1989, Fr Forum, vol 0017, 92; Neurosis and Narrative, the Decadent Short Fiction of Proust, Lorrain, and Rachilde, Romance Quart, vol 0042, 95. **CONTACT ADDRESS** Dept of French, Univ of Houston, Houston, TX, 77004.

MCLEOD, ALAN L.
PERSONAL Born 03/13/1928, Sydney, Australia, m, 1954, 2 children **DISCIPLINE** ENGLISH, SPEECH **EDUCATION** Univ Sydney, Australia, BA, 50, MA, 52, Dipl Ed, 51; Univ Melbourne, Australia, BEd, 56; Pa State Univ, PhD, 57. **CAREER** Lectr English & speech, Wagga State Teachers Col, Australia, 52; asst speech, Pa State Univ, 52-53 & 54-56; lectr English & speech, Balmain State Teachers Col, 56-57; from asst prof to assoc prof, State Univ Col Fredonia, 57-62; prof, Lock Haven State Col, 62-66; PROF ENGLISH & SPEECH, RIDER COL, 66-, State Univ NY res fel, 62. **MEMBERSHIPS** Speech Commun Asn; MLA; Book Collectors Soc, Australia. **RESEARCH** Seventeenth and eighteenth century poetry and drama; commonwealth literature; rhetorical criticism. **SELECTED PUBLICATIONS** Auth, It So Happen, World Lit Today, vol 0066, 92; South of the West--Postcolonialism and the Narrative Construction of Australia, World Lit Today, vol 0067, 93; One of Bens, a Tribe Transported, World Lit Today, vol 0068, 94; Divina Trace, World Lit Today, vol 0068, 94; Spirits in the Dark, World Lit Today, vol 0069, 95; The 'Longest Memory', World Lit Today, vol 0069, 95; The 'Assistant Professor', World Lit Today, vol 0071, 97; 'How Loud Can the Village Cock Crow' and Other Stories, World Lit Today, vol 0071, 97. **CONTACT ADDRESS** Dept of English, Rider Coll, Lawrenceville, NJ, 08648.

MCMAHON, JAMES VINCENT
PERSONAL Born 10/10/1937, Buffalo, NY, m, 1963, 3 children **DISCIPLINE** GERMAN LITERATURE & LANGUAGE **EDUCATION** St Bonaventure Univ, BA, 60; Univ Tex, PhD(Ger), 67. **CAREER** From instr to asst prof, 64-71, ASSOC PROF GER, EMORY UNIV, 71-, CHMN DEPT, 72-. **MEMBERSHIPS** MLA; Am Asn Teachers Ger; Mediaeval Acad Am; AAUP; Am Translators Asn. **RESEARCH** Medieval German textual criticism; Middle High German language and literature; music of minnesang. **SELECTED PUBLICATIONS** Auth, The Music of Early Minnesang, 90. **CONTACT ADDRESS** Emory Univ, German Studies Dept, Atlanta, GA, 30322-2280. **EMAIL** jvmcmah@emory.edu

MCMULLEN, WAYNE J.
PERSONAL Born 12/10/1954, Trenton, NJ **DISCIPLINE** SPEECH COMMUNICATION **EDUCATION** Penn State, PhD 89; Auburn Univ, MA 82; Temple Univ, BA 80. **CAREER** Penn State, asst prof, assoc prof, 91 to 98-; West Chester Univ, asst prof, inst, 88-91; Penn State, inst/res asst, 82-87. **HONORS AND AWARDS** Outstanding Tchr, 97 **MEMBERSHIPS** NCA; ORWC **RESEARCH** Rhetoric of Film **SELECTED PUBLICATIONS** Auth, Portrayals of Women's Friendships in Thelma and Louise, coauth, forthcoming; Sleep No More: Issues of Paranoia and Conformity in Invasion of the Body Snatchers, coauth, forthcoming; Reconstruction of the Frontier Myth in Witness, The SO Comm Jour, 96; Gender and the American Dream in Kramer vs Kramer, Women's Stud In comm, 96; Mythic Perspectives in Film Criticism, Jour of the NW Comm Assoc, 96; The China Syndrome: Corruption to the Core, Lit/Film Quart, 95; The Politics of Adaptation: Steven Speilberg's Appropriation of The Color Purple, coauth, Text and Perf Quart, 94. **CONTACT ADDRESS** Dept of Communication, Pennsylvania State Univ, Media, PA, 19063. **EMAIL** wjm11@psu.edu

MCNEILL, DAVID
PERSONAL Born 12/21/1933, Santa Rosa, CA, m, 1957, 2 children **DISCIPLINE** PSYCHOLINGUISTICS **EDUCATION** Univ Calif, Berkeley, AB, 53, PhD(psychol), 62. **CAREER** Res fel, Ctr Cognitive Studies, Harvard Univ, 63-65; from asst prof to assoc prof psychol, Univ Mich, 65-68; PROF BEHAV SCI & LING, UNIV CHICAGO, 69-, Guggenheim Found fel, 73-74; mem, Inst Advan Studies, 73-75. **MEMBERSHIPS** Ling Soc Arn; Am Asn Advan Sci. **RESEARCH** Psychological processes involved in the use of language; comparison of gestures for language; development of gesture in children. **SELECTED PUBLICATIONS** Auth, Abstract Deixis, Semiotica, vol 0095, 93. **CONTACT ADDRESS** Dept of Behav Sci, Univ of Chicago, Chicago, IL, 60637.

MCSHEA, WILLIAM PATRICK
PERSONAL Born 08/16/1930, Pittsburgh, PA, m, 1955, 3 children **DISCIPLINE** HISTORY, LATIN CLASSICS **EDUCATION** St Vincent Col, BA, 52; Duquesne Univ, MA, 54. **CAREER** From instr to assoc prof hist, Mt Mercy Col, 53-70; PROF & CHMN, DEPT HIST, CARLOW COL, 70-, DIR, PEACE STUDIES PROG, 76-, Prof, Comp Communism Consortia, var univs in Pa, 73-; mem adv coun, Int Poetry Forum, 77-. **MEMBERSHIPS** Int Soc Psycho Historians. **RESEARCH** Reformation; psycho history; recent American history. **SELECTED PUBLICATIONS** Auth, The Christian Tradition--Beyond Its European Captivity, J Ecumenical Stud, vol 0030, 93; Luther Legacy--Salvation and English Reformers 1525-1556, Theol Stud, vol 0056, 95; Lutheran Identity and Mission--Evangelical and Evangelistic, J Ecumenical Stud, vol 0032, 95; A Common Calling--The Witness of Our Reformation Churches in North America Today, J Ecumenical Stud, vol 0032, 95; Nothing Beyond the Necessary--Roman Catholicism and the Ecumenical Future, Theol Stud, vol 0057, 96; **CONTACT ADDRESS** Carlow Col, 3333 Fifth Ave, Pittsburgh, PA, 15213.

MEAD, GERALD
DISCIPLINE FRENCH **EDUCATION** Yale Univ, PhD. **CAREER** Assoc prof, Northestern Univ; past dir, CIC Summer Prog Univ Laval, Quebec; asst dean, Col Arts Sci. **HONORS AND AWARDS** E. Leroy Hall Award, 77; Excellence tchg, 97. **RESEARCH** Quebec literature; 19th century France; modernism; cultural studies. **SELECTED PUBLICATIONS** Auth, The Surrealist Image: A Stylistic Study and of articles on literary style and on writers Gabrielle Roy and Maupassant; The Representation of Solitude in Gabrielle Roy's Bonheur d'occasion, Quebec Studies, 88; The Representation of Fictional Character, Style, 90; Social Commentary and Sexuality in Maupassant's La Maison Tellier, 19th-Century Fr Studies, 96. **CONTACT ADDRESS** Dept of French, Northwestern Univ, 1801 Hinman, Evanston, IL, 60208.

MEADOWS, PATRICK
DISCIPLINE FRENCH LITERATURE **EDUCATION** Princeton Univ, PhD, 90. **CAREER** Asst prof. **SELECTED PUBLICATIONS** Auth, Le Thanh Khoi, Pham Van Ky et Pierre Do Dinh: Trois poetes vietnamiens face a la transition entre societe archaique et societe moderne, 97. **CONTACT ADDRESS** Dept of French and Italian, Indiana Univ, Bloomington, 300 N Jordan Ave, Bloomington, IN, 47405.

MEANS, JAMES
PERSONAL m **DISCIPLINE** PASTORAL MINISTRIES AND HOMILETICS **EDUCATION** Wheaton Col, BA; Denver Sem, BD; Univ Denver, MA, PhD. **CAREER** Prof, Denver Sem, 68-. **HONORS AND AWARDS** Gold Medallion Book Award winner., Sr pastor, S Gables Evangel Free Church; pastor, Evangel Free Churches in Loomis and Omaha, Nebr. **MEMBERSHIPS** Mem, Soc for Pastoral Theol; Assn of Practical Theol. **SELECTED PUBLICATIONS** Auth, Leadership in Christian Ministry; Effective Pastors for a New Century. **CONTACT ADDRESS** Denver Conservative Baptist Sem, PO Box 10000, Denver, CO, 80250. **EMAIL** jimm@densem.edu

MEANS, JOHN B.
PERSONAL Born 01/02/1939, Cincinnati, OH **DISCIPLINE** FOREIGN LANGUAGES **EDUCATION** Univ Ill Urbana, BA, 60, MA, 62, PhD, 68. **CAREER** Instr, Univ Ill, 64-67; from asst prof to assoc prof to prof, 68-, Temple Univ. **HONORS AND AWARDS** Exec dir, Nat Asn of Self Instructional Language Programs, 77-97; exec secy and treas, Nat Foreign Lang Ctr, 89. **MEMBERSHIPS** Nat Asn Self Instructional Lang Program; Brazilian Students Asn; Joint Nat Committee Lang. **RESEARCH** Second language acquisition for the less commonly taught languages. **SELECTED PUBLICATIONS** Ed, Essays on Brazilian Literature, 71. **CONTACT ADDRESS** PO Box 565, Yardley, PA, 19067-8565. **EMAIL** means@vm.temple.edu

MEDHURST, MARTIN J.
PERSONAL Born 10/15/1952, Alton, IL, m, 1989, 2 children **DISCIPLINE** SPEECH COMMUNICATION **EDUCATION** Wheaton Col, BA, 74; Northern Ill Univ, MA, 75; Penn State Univ, PhD, 80. **CAREER** Asst prof, 79-85, assoc prof, 85-88, Univ of Calif at Davis; ASSOC PROF, 88-91, PROF, 91-, TEXAS A&M UNIV; coordr, Prog in Presidential Rhetoric, Bush School of Gov and Public Service, 93-. **HONORS AND AWARDS** Nat Commun Asn Golden Anniversary Prize Fund Award, 82; Religious Speech Commun Asn Pub Award, 83; Marie Hochmuth Nichols Award for Outstanding Scholar in Public Address, 95 & 97; Naomi Lews Fac Fel in Liberal Arts, Tex A&M Univ, 93-94 & 94-95; Speech Commun Asn Anniversary Prize Fund Award, 82; Paul K. Crawford Award for Outstanding Graduate Student, Northern Ill Univ, 75. **MEMBERSHIPS** Nat Commun Asn; Southern Commun Asn; Western Commun Asn; Int Soc for the Hist of Rhetoric; Rhetoric Soc of Am; Soc for Historians of Am Foreign Relations. **RESEARCH** Cold War rhetoric; Presidential rhetoric; rhetoric of film. **SELECTED PUBLICATIONS** Ed, Beyond the Rhetorical Presidency, Tex A&M Univ Press, 96; ed, Eisenhower's War of Words: Rhetoric and Leadership, Mich State Univ Press, 94; auth, Martial Decision Making: MacArthur, Inchon, and the Dimensions of Rhetoric, in Rhetoric and Community: Studies in Unity and Fragmentation, Univ of South Carolina Press, 98; auth, A Tale of Two Constructs: The Rhetorical Presidency versus Presidential Rhetoric, Beyond the Rhetorical Presidency, Tex A&M Univ Press, 96; auth, Dwight D. Eisenhower, U.S. Presidents as Orators: A Bio-Critical Sourcebook, Greenwood Press, 95; auth, Eisenhower's Rhetorical Leadership: An Interprestation, Eisenhower's War of Words: Rhetoric and Leadership, Mich State Univ Press, 94; coauth, Rhetorical Reduplication in MTV's Rock the Vote Campaign, Commun Studies 49, 98; auth, The Rhetorical Renaissance: A Battlefield Report, Southern Commun Journal 64, 98; auth, Rhetorical Education in the 21st Century, Southern Commun Journal, 98. **CONTACT ADDRESS** Dept of Speech Commun, Texas A&M Univ, College Station, TX, 77843. **EMAIL** m-medhurst@tamu.edu

MEDINA, CINDY
DISCIPLINE FOREIGN LANGUAGES **EDUCATION** Pa State Univ, BA, PhD. **CAREER** Coor, foreign lang. **SELECTED PUBLICATIONS** Auth, Nuevos Destinos. **CONTACT ADDRESS** York Col, Pennsylvania, 441 Country Club Road, York, PA, 17403.

MEDINA, JEREMY TYLER
PERSONAL Born 08/01/1942, Orange, NJ, m, 1966, 3 children **DISCIPLINE** SPANISH, SPANISH LITERATURE **EDUCATION** Princeton Univ, AB, 64; Middlebury Span Sch, Spain, MA, 66; Univ Pa, PhD(Span), 70. **CAREER** Instr Span, Phillips Acad, Andover, Mass, 64-65; from instr to asst prof, 68-75, dir in residence, acad year in Spain, 74-75, 79-80, assoc prof, 75-82, prof Span, Hamilton Col, 82-; gen dir acad year in Spain, 74-. **MEMBERSHIPS** MLA; AAUP; Am Asn Teachers Span & Port. **RESEARCH** Nineteenth century Spanish realism; generations of 1898 and 1927 in Spain; Cervantes. **SELECTED PUBLICATIONS** Auth, Theme and Structure in Herrera's Cancion de Lepanto, 72 & Theme and Structure of Alarcon's El sombrero de tres picos, 73, Romance Notes; Introduction to Spanish Literature: An Analytical Approach, Harper 74, Krieger, 82; The Artistry of Blasco Ibanez' Canas y barro, Hispania, 77; Spanish Realism: The Theory and Practice of a Concept in the Nineteenth Century, Jose Porrua, 78; The Artistry of Blasco Ibanez' Flor de Mayo, Hispania, 82; Leopoldo Alas (Clarin), Vicente Blasco Ibanez, Benito Perez Galdos, and Emilia Pardo Bagan, In: Critical Survey of Long Fiction,-Salem Press , 84; Blasco Ibanez' Arroz y yartana, Hispanic J, 84; The Valencian Novels of Vincente Blasco Ibanez, Albatros, 84; The Psychological Novels of Vincente Blasco Ibanez, Albatross, 90; A Note on Narrative Structure, Don Quijote, Part II, Critica Hispanica, 90; Gibraltar Interlude: the Artistry of Blasco Ibanez' Luna Benamor, Hispania, 90; From Sermon to Art: the Thesis Novels of Vincente Blasco Ibanez, Albatross, 98; Narrative Framing and the Structure of Don Quijote, Part I, Confluencia, 98. **CONTACT ADDRESS** Dept of Romance Lang, Hamilton Col, 198 College Hill Rd, Clinton, NY, 13323-1292. **EMAIL** jmedina@hamilton.edu

MEGENNEY, WILLIAM WILBER
PERSONAL Born 04/13/1940, Langley AFB, VA, m, 1963, 3 children **DISCIPLINE** LATIN AMERICAN LINGUISTICS **EDUCATION** Rutgers Univ, BA, 62; Univ NMex, MA, 67, PhD, 69. **CAREER** Prof Span & Port, Univ Calif, Riverside, 69-. **MEMBERSHIPS** Am Asn Teachers Span & Port; Ling Soc Am; Caribbean Studies Asn; Asn Afro-Hisp & Cultural Studies. **RESEARCH** Latin American linguistics. **SELECTED PUBLICATIONS** Auth, A Bahian Heritage, Univ NC, 78; African en Venezuela: su herencia linguistica y su cultura literaria, In: Montalban series of Catholic University of Venezuela, 85; El palenquero: un lenguaje post-criollo de Columbia, Inst Caro y Cuervo, Bogota, Columbia, 86; Africa en Santo Domingo: su herencia linguistica, Museo del Hombre Dominicano and the Acad de Ciencias de la Republica Dominicana, 90; author of numerous articles. **CONTACT ADDRESS** Dept of Hispanic Studies, Univ of Calif, 900 University Ave, Riverside, CA, 92521-0001. **EMAIL** william.megenney@ucr.edu

MEIER, A.J.
PERSONAL Born 11/15/1952, IA **DISCIPLINE** LINGUISTICS **EDUCATION** Wartburg Coe, BA summa cum laude ; Univ Iowa, MA; Univ Vienna Austria, PhD. **CAREER** Univ Vienna, lectr, 81-92; Univ N Iowa, asst prof, assoc prof, 92 to 98-. **MEMBERSHIPS** TESOL; MIDTESOL; AAAL; IPra. **RESEARCH** Sociopragmatics, sociolinguistics; grammar in edu; politeness theory; apologies and conflict mgmt; intercultural communication. **SELECTED PUBLICATIONS** Auth, Apologies: What do we know?, Intl Jour of Applied Linguistics, forthcoming; Grammar in MA TESOL programs: Form function usage and application, Teacher Edu Interest Sec NL, forthcoming; Meeting the editors at Orlando, TESOL Matters, 97; What's the excuse: Image repair in Austrian German, The Mod Lang Jour, 97; Teaching the universals of politeness, Eng Lang Teach Jour, 97; Two cultures mirrored in repair work, Multilingua, 96; Hey-Lady, Dictionaries, 96; Passages of politeness, Jour of Pragmatics, 95. **CONTACT ADDRESS** Dept of English, No Iowa Univ, Cedar Falls, IA, 50613-0502. **EMAIL** aj.meier@uni.edu

MEIER, MARGA
PERSONAL Born 04/22/1922, Bad Kissingen, Germany **DISCIPLINE** LANGUAGES **EDUCATION** Univ Wurzburg, PhD, 44. **CAREER** Court interpreter, Nurnberg War Crimes Trials, 46-49 and US Court Appeals, Frankfurt, 49-52; ASSOC PROF GER, 55-76, PROF LANG, IND CENT UNIV, 76-. **MEMBERSHIPS** Am Asn Teachers Ger; Foreign Lang Teachers Asn. **SELECTED PUBLICATIONS** Auth, Maimonides School and the Rav, Trad J Orthodox Jewish Thought, Vol 31, 97. **CONTACT ADDRESS** Dept of Foreign Lang, Indiana Central Univ, Indianapolis, IN, 46227.

MEINHARDT, WARREN LEE
PERSONAL Born 03/30/1931, Lennox, CA, m, 1953, 4 children **DISCIPLINE** LATIN AMERICAN LITERATURE **EDUCATION** Pomona Col, BA, 53; Stanford Univ, MA, 55: Univ Calif Berkeley, PhD(Romance lang and lit), 65. **CAREER** Asst instr Span, Univ Ill, Urbana, 60-64; from instr to asst prof, 64-69; asst prof foreign lang, 69-73, ASSOC PROF FOREIGN LANG AND LIT, SOUTHERN ILL UNIV, CARBONDALE, 73-, Fac fel, Univ Ill, Urbana, 66; Univ Ill fac fel, 66 and 73; Nat Endowment for Humanities fels, summer 78 and 81. **MEMBERSHIPS** Am Asn Teachers Span and Port. **RESEARCH** Latin American prose fiction; the new Latin Ameri-

can novel; Chicano literature. **SELECTED PUBLICATIONS** Auth, Writers from Latin, Chasqui Revista Lit Latinoamericana, Vol 22, 93; Literary and Cultural Journeys--Selected Letters to Torresrioseco, Arturo, Chasqui Revista Lit Latinoamericana, Vol 26, 97; A Bibliography of Latin American and Caribbean Bibliographies, 1985-1989, Revista De Estudios Hispanicos, Vol 28, 94; Out of Context, Improbable but Textual Conversations Essays, With Rulfo, Juan, Girondo, Oliverio, Miller, Henry and for One Time Only Between Vangogh, Vincent and Kafka, Franz, Revista Iberoamericana, Vol 60, 94; Rulfo, Juan, From Heath to Hope, A Critical Reading of his Works, Revista De Estudios Hispanicos, Vol 27, 93; Spanish American Authors, The 20th Century, Chasqui Revista Lit Latinoamericana, Vol 22, 93; Rulfo, Juan, The Complete Works, Revista Iberoamericana, Vol 59, 93; Dictionary of Mexican Literature, Revista De Estudios Hispanicos, Vol 28, 94; Rulfo, Juan, Armed Autobiography, Explicacion De Textos Literarios, Vol 22, 93. **CONTACT ADDRESS** Dept of Foreign Lang and Lit, Southern Ill Univ, Carbondale, IL, 62901-4300.

MEININGER, ROBERT ALAN
PERSONAL Born 03/29/1938, Torrington, WY, m, 1962, 1 child **DISCIPLINE** ROMANCE LANGUAGES **EDUCATION** Univ Wyo, BA, 61; Univ Nebr, MA, 64, PhD(Romance lang), 70. **CAREER** Instr French, Univ Nebr, 68-70; asst prof, 70-72, assoc prof, 72-80, Prof French, Nebr Wesleyan Univ, 80-, Chm Dept, 72-, Chm, Humanities Div, 78-. **HONORS AND AWARDS** Phi Beta Kappa; Phi Beta Phi; Fulbright grants. **MEMBERSHIPS** Am Asn Teachers Fr; Am Asn Teachers Ger; Asn of Slavic Studies. **RESEARCH** French, Belgian cultural history; Russian history. **SELECTED PUBLICATIONS** Auth, Belgian culture, In: Encycl Am, Grolier, 68-98; translations from German and Russian for Am Hist Soc Ger/Rus. **CONTACT ADDRESS** Dept of Foreign Lang, Nebraska Wesleyan Univ, 5000 St Paul Ave, Lincoln, NE, 68504-2760. **EMAIL** ram@NebrWesleyan.edu

MEISEL, MARTIN
PERSONAL Born 03/22/1931, New York, NY, m, 1957, 3 children **DISCIPLINE** ENGLISH, COMPARATIVE LITERATURE **EDUCATION** Queens Col, NY, BA, 52; Princeton Univ, MA, 57, PhD(English), 60. **CAREER** Army, 54-56; instr English, Rutgers Univ, 57-58; from instr to assoc prof, Dartmouth Col, 59-65; prof, Univ WI, 65-68; vchm dept, 73-76, prof English, 68-86, chm dept English & comp lit, 80-83, vice pres arts and sciences, 86-87, 89-93, Brander Matthews prof of dramatic lit, Columbia Univ, 87-; Guggenheim fel, 63-64, 87-88; Am Coun Learned our Carribean Poets, Duluth: Poetry Harbor, 96; Lawrence Ferlinghetti, Gregory Corso and Gwendolyn Brooks, in Frank N Magill, ed, Cyclopedia of World Authors, Revised Edition, Pasadena, CA: Salem Press, 97; If Beale Street Could Talk, in Frank N Magill, ed, Masterplots II: Juvenile and Young Adult Literature Series, Supplement, 3 vols, Pasadena, CA: Salem Press, 97; The Wapshot Scandal, The Country Husband, and John Cheever, in David Peck, ed, Identities and Issues in Literature, 3 vols, Pasadena, CA: Salem Press, 97; The Beat Generation: A Bibliographical Teaching Guide, Lanham, MD: Scarecrow Press, 98. **CONTACT ADDRESS** Dept of English, Univ of Wisconsin, 2100 Main St, Stevens Point, WI, 54481-3897. **EMAIL** wlawlor@uwsp.edu

MELCHERT, H. CRAIG
PERSONAL Born 04/05/1945, Manhattan, KS **DISCIPLINE** LINGUISTICS **EDUCATION** Mich State Univ, BA, 67; Harvard Univ, PhD, 77. **CAREER** From asst prof to assoc prof to prof, 78-, distinguished prof, 93-96, Univ North Carolina, Chapel Hill; vis prof, Yale Univ, 90; vis prof, Harvard Univ, 96; vis prof, Cornell Univ, 97. **HONORS AND AWARDS** Nat Merit Scholar, 63-67; Woodrow Wilson Fel, 67-68; Whiting Fel, 67-77. **MEMBERSHIPS** Linguistic Soc Am; Indogermanische Gesellschaft; Am Oriental Soc. **RESEARCH** Indo-European linguistics; Hittite and Anatolian languages. **SELECTED PUBLICATIONS** Auth, Studies in Hittite Historical Phonology, 84; auth, Cuneiform Luvian Lexicon, 93; auth, Lycian Lexicon, 93; auth, Anatolian Historical Phonology, 94. **CONTACT ADDRESS** Dept of Linguistics CB, Univ North Carolina, Chapel Hill, CB 3155, Chapel Hill, NC, 27599-3155. **EMAIL** melchert@email.unc.edu

MELIA, DANIEL FREDERICK
PERSONAL Born 03/02/1944, Fall River, MA **DISCIPLINE** CELTIC LANGUAGES AND LITERATURE **EDUCATION** Harvard Col, BA, 66, Harvard Univ, MA, 70, PhD(Celtic lang and lit), 72. **CAREER** Asst prof, 72-78, ASSOC PROF RHETORIC, UNIV CALIF, BERKELEY, 78-, ASSOC DEAN, COL LETT AND SCI, 81-, Vis asst prof English, Univ Calif, Los Angeles, 73-74; Nat Endowment for Humanities jr res fel Celtic and Regents fac fel humanities, Univ Calif, 75. **MEMBERSHIPS** Celtic Studies Asn (secy treas, 77-79); fel Medieval Acad Ireland; MLA; Medieval Acad Am; Am Folklore Soc. **RESEARCH** Medieval Celtic literature; folklore and mythology; rhetoric and poetics. **SELECTED PUBLICATIONS** Auth, Celtic Languages and Literature See Vol III, The Irish Literary Tradition, Speculum J Medieval Stud, Vol 72, 97; The Irish Tradition in Old English Literature, Speculum J Medieval Stud, Vol 72, 97; From Scythia to Camelot--A Radical Reassessment of the Legends of King Arthur, The Knights of the Round

Table, and The Holy Grail, W Folklore, Vol 55, 96. **CONTACT ADDRESS** Dept of Rhetoric, Univ of Calif, 2125 Dwinelle Hall, Berkeley, CA, 94720-2671.

MELLOR, CHAUNCEY JEFFRIES
PERSONAL Born 11/10/1942, Pittsburgh, PA, m, 1977 **DISCIPLINE** GERMANIC PHILOLOGY **EDUCATION** Univ Chicago, BA, 65, MA, 67, PhD(Ger), 72. **CAREER** Instr, 70-72, ASST PROP GER, UNIV TENN, KNOXVILLE, 72-, ED, DER SPOTTVOGEL, AM ASN TEACHERS GER, 72- **MEMBERSHIPS** Am Asn Teachers Ger; Ling Soc Am; MLA. **RESEARCH** German lexicography. **SELECTED PUBLICATIONS** Auth, German Dictionary, 9th Edition, Colloquia Germ, Vol 26, 93; German Dictionary, 9th Edition, Colloquia Germ Vol 26, 93. **CONTACT ADDRESS** Dept of Ger and Slavic, Univ of Tenn, Knoxville, TN, 37916.

MELZI, ROBERT C.
PERSONAL Born 03/12/1915, Milano, Italy, m, 1948, 3 children **DISCIPLINE** ROMANCE LANGUAGES **EDUCATION** Univ Padua, D in L, 38; Univ Pa, MA, 53, PhD, 62. **CAREER** Asst instr Romance lang, Univ Pa, 50-53; interpreter French and Ital, US Dept Justice, 53-56; teacher French and Span, Plymouth Whitemarsh High Sch, 58-61; assoc prof, Millersville State Col, 62-63; assoc prof, 63-67, prof French and chmn dept mod lang, 67-80, PROF ROMANCE LANG, WIDENER COL, 67-, Vis lectr, Univ Pa, 68-69. **MEMBERSHIPS** MLA; Dante Soc Am; Renaissance Soc Am; Am Asn Teachers Ital. **RESEARCH** Italian Renaissance; Lodovico Castelvetro; bilingual lexicography. **SELECTED PUBLICATIONS** Auth The Giuliano Dalmati in Canada--Considerations and Imagery, Forum Italicum, Vol 29, 95; Scripts and Scenarios, 16th Century Jour, Vol 25, 94; Jewish Life in Renaissance Italy, 16th Century Jour, Vol 26, 95; The Giuliano Dalmati in Canada--Considerations and Imagery, Forum Italicum, Vol 29, 95; Viaggio Di Francia, Costumi E Qualita Di Quei Paesi 1664-1665, Italica, Vol 69, 92; The Isole Fortunate,16th Century Jour, Vol 27, 96; Tommaseo, Niccolo Il Dizionario Dei Sinonimi, Italica, Vol 69, 92; Jews and Marranos in Italian Renaissance Comedies , Sefarad, Vol 55, 95. **CONTACT ADDRESS** Dept of Mod Lang, Widener Col, Chester, PA, 19013.

MEMON, MUHAMMAD UMAR
PERSONAL Born 05/15/1939, Aligarh, India **DISCIPLINE** ISLAMIC STUDIES, URDU LANGUAGE & LITERATURE **EDUCATION** Karachi Univ, BA, 60, MA, 61; Harvard Univ, AM, 65; Univ Calif, Los Angeles, PhD, 71. **CAREER** Lectr Islamic hist, Sachal Sarmast Col, Pakistan, 62; lectr Arabic, Sind Univ, 62-64; instr Arabic, Persian & Urdu, 70-71, asst prof, 72-76, assoc prof Islamics, Persian & Urdu, Univ Wis-Madison, 76-; vis asst prof Urdu & Islamics, Dept SAsian Studies, Univ Minn, Minneapolis, 74-75; mem US adv comt, Berkeley Urdu Lang Prog in Pakistan, 75-; res grant, Grad Sch, Univ Wis-Madison, 77; SSRC, 84; assoc ed, SAsian Lit, 80-83; prof Islamic Studies, Persian & Urdu, Univ Wisc-Madison, 84-. **MEMBERSHIPS** Mid E Studies Assn N Am; Am Orient Soc; Assoc for Asian Studies. **RESEARCH** Islamic history and religion; Arabic and Urdu literature. **SELECTED PUBLICATIONS** Auth, The Seventh Door and Other Stories, Lynne Rienner, 89; auth, Hasan Manzar: A Requiem for the Earth, Oxford Univ Press, 98; auth, Abdullah Hussein: Storeis of Exile and Alienation, Oxford Univ Press, 98; auth, An Epic Unwritten: Penguin Book of Partition Stories, Penguin, 98. **CONTACT ADDRESS** Dept of South Asian Studies, Univ of Wisconsin, 1220 Linden Dr, Madison, WI, 53706-1557. **EMAIL** mumemon@facstaff.wisc.edu

MENTON, SEYMOUR
PERSONAL Born 03/06/1927, New York, NY **DISCIPLINE** SPANISH AMERICAN LITERATURE **EDUCATION** City Col NY, BA, 48; Nat Univ Mex, MA, 49; NY Univ, PhD(Span Am lit), 52. **CAREER** Teacher English and hist of Span lang, Inst Recapacitation, Mex, 48-49; teacher, Pub Schs, NY, 49-52; instr Span and Span Am lit, Dartmouth Col, 52-54; from asst prof to prof, Univ Kans, 54-65; chmn dept foreign lang, 65-70, PROF SPAN AND PORT, UNIV CALIF, IRVINE, 65-, Ed, Hispania, 63-65. **MEMBERSHIPS** Int Inst Span Am Lit; Am Asn Teachers Span and Port; MLA. **RESEARCH** Cuban prose fiction; Mexican novel; Spanish American short story. **SELECTED PUBLICATIONS** Auth Remembering Mead, Robert, G., Hispania J Devoted Teaching Span Portug, Vol 79, 96; A Tribute to Earle, Peter, G., Hisp Rev, Vol 61, 93; Magic Realism-Social Context and Discourse, Hisp Rev, Vol 65, 97; Conquest of the New World, Experimental Fiction and Translation in the America, Hispania J Devoted Teaching Span Portug, Vol 78, 95; Asturias, Miguel, Angel Archaeology of Return, Hisp Rev, Vol 63, 95; Vigilia Del Almirante, World Lit Today, Vol 68, 94; Conquest of the New World, Experimental Fiction and Translation in the America, Hispania J Devoted Teaching Span Portug, Vol 78, 95Falsas Cronicas Del Sur, World Lit Today, Vol 67, 93. **CONTACT ADDRESS** 2641 Basswood St, Newport Beach, CA, 92660.

MERCADO, JUAN CARLOS
DISCIPLINE CULTURAL STUDIES **EDUCATION** Univ Comahue, BS; Queens Col, MA; CUNY, PhD. **CAREER** Eastern Stroudsburg Univ PA **HONORS AND AWARDS** NEH

grant. **SELECTED PUBLICATIONS** Auth, Esteban Echeverrea: Building a Nation: The Case of Echeverrea. **CONTACT ADDRESS** East Stroudsburg Univ of Pennsylvania, 200 Prospect Street, E Stroudsburg, PA, 18301-2999.

MERCERON, JACQUES E.
DISCIPLINE FRENCH LITERATURE **EDUCATION** Univ Ca, PhD, 93. **CAREER** Asst prof. **SELECTED PUBLICATIONS** Auth, Le Message et sa fiction: la communication par messager dans la litterature francaise des XIIe et XIIIe siecles, 98; pubs on French and Celtic folklore, folklore and Old French prose Lancelot, communication and medieval messenger motifs in epic poetry. **CONTACT ADDRESS** Dept of French and Italian, Indiana Univ, Bloomington, 300 N Jordan Ave, Bloomington, IN, 47405.

MEREDITH, HUGH EDWIN
PERSONAL Born 10/07/1930, Muskogee, OK, 4 children **DISCIPLINE** GERMANIC LANGUAGES & LITERATURE **EDUCATION** Okla Baptist Univ, BA, 52; Int Baptist Theol Sem Ruschlikon, Zurich, Switz, cert, 53; Southwestern Baptist Theol Sem, BD, 55; Univ Tex, MA, 60, PhD, 63. **CAREER** Prof Ger & vpres acad afairs, Angelo State Univ, 67-74; pres, Sul Ross State Univ, 74-76; Prof Mod Lang, Sam Houston State Univ, 76- **MEMBERSHIPS** MLA; Am Asn Teachers Ger; Ling Soc Am. **RESEARCH** Eighteenth and 19th century German literature; Karl Philipp Moritz; Jeremias Gotthelf; German immigration to Texas. **CONTACT ADDRESS** Dept of English and Foreign Langs, Sam Houston Univ, PO Box 2147, Huntsville, TX, 77341-2147. **EMAIL** fol_hem@shsu.edu

MERIVALE, PATRICIA
PERSONAL Born 07/19/1934, Derby, England **DISCIPLINE** ENGLISH, COMPARATIVE LITERATURE **EDUCATION** Univ Calif, Berkeley, BA, 55; Oxford Univ, BA, 58, MA, 62; Harvard Univ, PhD(comp lit), 63. **CAREER** From instr to assoc prof, 62-70, PROF ENGLISH, UNIV BC, 70-, Can Coun fels, 69-70. **MEMBERSHIPS** Can Comp Lit Asn (secy-treas, 77-79); MLA; Asn Can Univ Teachers English; Am Comp Lit Asn. **RESEARCH** Artifice and the artist parable; thematics; narrative structure in contemporary fiction. **SELECTED PUBLICATIONS** Auth The Works of Auster, Paul--Approaches and Multiple Readings, Contemporary Lit, Vol 38, 97; The Telling of Lies and the Sea of Stories Haroun, Pinocchio and the Postcolonial Artist Parable, Ariel Rev Int Eng Lit, Vol 28, 97; Literature and the Body, Can Rev Comp Lit Revue Can Litterature Comparee, Vol 22, 95; Atwood, Margaret Fairy Tale Sexual Politics, Eng Stud Can, Vol 22, 96; Beyond the Red Notebook--Essays on Auster, Paul, Contemporary Lit, Vol 38, 97. **CONTACT ADDRESS** Dept of English, Univ of BC, Vancouver, BC, V6T 1W5.

MERKEN, KATHLEEN
DISCIPLINE EAST ASIAN STUDIES **EDUCATION** Univ British Columbia, PhD. **CAREER** Fac lectr. **RESEARCH** Mod nvels; literary translation. **SELECTED PUBLICATIONS** Trans, Night Fragrance, The Literary Rev, Japanese Writing, 87. **CONTACT ADDRESS** East Asian Studies Dept, McGill Univ, 845 Sherbrooke St, Montreal, PQ, H3A 2T5.

MERLER, GRAZIA
PERSONAL Born 06/16/1938, Trento, Italy **DISCIPLINE** FRENCH AND FRENCH CANADIAN LITERATURE **EDUCATION** Univ BC, BA, 59; Laval Univ, MA, 61, PhD(French), 67. **CAREER** Instr French and Ital, Univ Tex, 63-65; lectr Ital, Univ BC, 65-66; prof French, Col Ste-Foy, 67-69; asst prof, 69-76, chmn French, 75-77, ASSOC PROF FRENCH, DEPT MOD LANG, SIMON FRASER UNIV, 76-, Can Coun leave fel, 77-78. **MEMBERSHIPS** MLA; Can Semiotics Res Asn; Asn Can Studies; Asn Can Univ Teachers Fr. **RESEARCH** Literary theory; Canadian short story. **SELECTED PUBLICATIONS** Auth, Laughter, Smiles and Tears in the Works of Stendhal--A Poetic Initiation,19th Century Fr Stud, Vol 23, 94; Stendhal from the Point of View of Adler, Alfred, 19th Century Fr Stud, Vol 23, 94. **CONTACT ADDRESS** Dept of Lang Lit and Ling, Simon Fraser Univ, Burnaby, BC, V5A 1S6.

MERMALL, THOMAS
PERSONAL Born 09/20/1937, Czechoslovakia, m, 1977 **DISCIPLINE** ROMANCE LANGUAGES **EDUCATION** Ill Wesleyan Univ, BA, 61; Univ Conn, MA, 65, PhD(Span), 68. **CAREER** Asst prof Span, State Univ NY, Stony Brook, 68-72; asst prof, 73-75, assoc prof, 75-80, PROF SPAN, BROOKLYN COL, 80- **MEMBERSHIPS** MLA. **RESEARCH** Contemporary Spanish essay; history of ideas. **SELECTED PUBLICATIONS** Auth, En Torno al Casticismo and Unamuno Rhetorical Evolution, Anales Lit Esp Contemporanea, Vol 18, 93; Voices, Silences and Echoes, A Theory of the Essay and the Critical Reception of Naturalism in Spain, Bull Hisp Stud, Vol 71, 94; El Mudejarillo, Anales Lit Esp Contemporanea, Vol 19, 94; Crossfire, Philosophy and the Novel in Spain 1900-1934, Revista Estudios Hispanicos, Vol 29, 95; Ayala, Francisco, Theorist and Literary Critic, Hisp Rev, Vol 63, 95. **CONTACT ADDRESS** Dept of Mod Lang, Brooklyn Col, CUNY, 2901 Bedford Ave, Brooklyn, NY, 11210-2813.

MERRELL, F.
PERSONAL Born 11/16/1937, Virden, NM, m, 1964, 3 children **DISCIPLINE** LATIN AMERICAN STUDIES **EDUCATION** Univ of NMex, PhD. **CAREER** PROF, PURDUE UNIV, 73-. **MEMBERSHIPS** Semiotic Soc of Am; MLA. **RESEARCH** Latin American studies; theory; Spanish American prose. **SELECTED PUBLICATIONS** Auth, Semiosis in the Postmodern Age, Purdue Univ Press, 95; auth, Peirce's Semiotics Now: A Primer, Canadian Scholars' Press, 95; auth, Signs Grow: Semiosis and Life Processes, Univ of Toronto Press, 96; auth, Peirce, Signs, and Meaning, Univ of Torontop Press, 97; auth, Simplicity and Complexity: Pondering Literature, Science and Painting, Univ of Mich Press, 98; auth, Sensing Semiosis: Toward the Possibility of Completmentary Cultural Longics, St Martin's Press, 98; auth, Semiosis, Science, Silver Linings: And Finally Literature, Semiotica, 96; auth, The Writing of Forking Paths: Borges, Calvino and Postmodern Models of Writing, Variaciones Borges, 97; auth, Just Waiting (Or Looking Back on the Lines of His Face), Variaciones Borges, 97; auth, Does the Life of Signs Yield a Meaningful Universe?, Semiotica, 98. **CONTACT ADDRESS** Dept of Foreign Lang & Lit, Purdue Univ, West Lafayette, IN, 47907. **EMAIL** fmerrell@purdue.edu

MERRIAM, ALLEN H.
PERSONAL Born 07/28/1942, Orange, NJ, m, 1992, 2 children **DISCIPLINE** SPEECH COMMUNICATION **EDUCATION** Drew Univ, BA, 64; Ohio Univ, MA, 70, PhD, 72. **CAREER** Asst prof, The Col of NJ, 72-77; vis asst prof, Univ of Va, 77-78; asst pro, Va Tech, 78-82; assoc prof, Va Tech, 82-88; prof, Mo S State Col, 88-. **MEMBERSHIPS** Nat Commun Assoc; Assoc for Asian Studs. **RESEARCH** Intercultural rhetoric; history of oratory; third world studies. **SELECTED PUBLICATIONS** Ghandi v0s. Jinnah, The Debate over the Partition of India, 80; numerous articles. **CONTACT ADDRESS** 1419 Marzelle Ct, Joplin, MO, 64801. **EMAIL** merriam-a@mail.mssc.edu

MERRIFIELD, WILLIAM R.
PERSONAL Born 09/28/1932, Chicago, IL, m, 1952, 4 children **DISCIPLINE** LINGUISTICS, ANTHROPOLOGY **EDUCATION** Wheaton Col, Ill BA, 54; Cornell Univ, MA, 63, PhD(cult anthrop), 65. **CAREER** Ling consult in Mex, 62-74, coordr anthrop res in Mex, 65-69, coordr ling res in Mex, 65-59, 72-74, dir sch, Univ Okla, 74-77, INT COORDR ANTHROP AND COMMUN DEVELOP, SUMMER INST LING, 72-, Dir, MUS ANTHROP, TEX, 74-, Vis asst prof ling, Univ Wash, 65-72; vis prof anthrop, Wheaton Col, 71-72; ADJ PROF LING, UNIV TEX, ARLINGTON, 74-; adj prof anthrop, Univ Okla, 75-77, adj prof ling, 77. **MEMBERSHIPS** Am Anthrop Asn; Ling Soc Am; Am Sci Affiliation; Am Asn Mus; Ling Asn Can and US. **RESEARCH** Cultural and applied anthropology; social organization; theory of grammar. **SELECTED PUBLICATIONS** Auth, Linguistic Theory and Grammatical Description Joseph, Je, Lan, Vol 70, 94. **CONTACT ADDRESS** Summer Inst of Ling, 7500 Camp Wisdom Rd, Dallas, TX, 75236.

MERRILL, REED
PERSONAL Born 10/28/1929, Provo, UT, m, 1951 **DISCIPLINE** COMPARATIVE LITERATURE **EDUCATION** Univ Utah, BS, 61, MA, 65; Univ Colo, Boulder, PhD(comp lit), 70. **CAREER** Bus mgr, Univ Utah Comput Ctr, 64-65; asst ed, Rocky Mountain Mod Lang Asn Bull, Univ Colo, Boulder, 67-68; lectr, 69-70, asst prof, 70-74, ASSOC PROF ENGLISH, WESTERN WASH UNIV, 74- **MEMBERSHIPS** Fedn Int Lang Lit Mod; Int Comp Lit Asn; MLA; Am Comp Lit Asn. **RESEARCH** Modern novel; literary criticism and theory; history of ideas. **SELECTED PUBLICATIONS** Auth, The Tucker Review--A 1/2 Century After his Met Debut, Colleagues Voice Their Feelings About A Great American Tenor/, Opera News, Vol 59, 95 Faulknerian Tragedy, The Example of As I Lay Dying , Mississippi Quart, Vol 47, 94; Something and Nothingness--The Fiction of Updike, John and Fowles, John, Am Lit, Vol 64, 92; The American Roman Noir--Hammett, Cain, and Chandler, Am Lit, Vol 69, 97; Mailer Tough Guys Dont Dance and the Detective Traditions, Critique Stud Contemporary Fiction, Vol 34, 93; Writing the American Classics, Mod Philol, Vol 90, 93; Critical Edition , Opera News, Vol 59, 94; Writing the American Classics, Modern Philol, Vol 90, 93. **CONTACT ADDRESS** Dept of English, Western Washington Univ, Bellingham, WA, 98225.

MERRILL, SAMMY RAY
PERSONAL Born 09/06/1941, Morehead City, NC, m, 1962, 2 children **DISCIPLINE** FOREIGN LANGUAGE **EDUCATION** Wake Forest Univ, BA, 63; Duke Univ, MA, 66; Cornell Univ, PhD, 72. **CAREER** Instr, Wake Forest Univ, 67-69; asst prof, Cornell Univ, 72-73; assoc prof to prof, Mary Washington Col, 73- . **HONORS AND AWARDS** NDEA Title IV Grad Fel, 69-72; Simpson Award for Excellence in Undergrad Teaching, 93., German Acad Exchange Svc Fel, 66-67; NEH grant, 76. **MEMBERSHIPS** Amer Assoc of Teachers of German; Foreign Lang Assoc of Va. **RESEARCH** Nineteenth & twentieth cent German lit; German lang. **CONTACT ADDRESS** Dept of Modern Foreign Lang, Mary Washington Col, Fredericksburg, VA, 22401. **EMAIL** smerrill@mwc.edu

MERRON, JEFFREY L.
DISCIPLINE FOREIGN LANGUAGES **EDUCATION** Bennington Col, BA, 83; Univ Wis, MA, 85; Univ NC, PhD, 91. **CAREER** Prof. **MEMBERSHIPS** IABC; AEJMC. **SELECTED PUBLICATIONS** Auth, Duke has a wealth of advertising history, 92; Murrow on TV: See It Now, Person to Person, and the Making of a 'Masscult Personality', 88; Undoing Babel: J. Walter Thompson's International Expansion and the Issues of Translation and Pattern Advertising in the 1920s, 92. **CONTACT ADDRESS** Dept of Foreign Languages, State Univ W Ga, Carrollton, GA, 30118. **EMAIL** vpaa@westga.edu

MESTER, ARMIN
DISCIPLINE LINGUISTICS **EDUCATION** Univ Mass-Amherst, PhD, 86. **CAREER** PROF, LING, UNIV CALIF, SANTA CRUZ. **RESEARCH** Theoretical phonology. **SELECTED PUBLICATIONS** Auth, Patterns of Truncation, Ling Inquiry, 90; Dependent Tier Ordering and the OCP, Features, Segmental Structure, and Harmony Processes, Foris, 88; The Quantitative Trochee in Latin, Natural Lang and Ling Theory, 94; co-auth, Japanese Phonology, Handbook of Phonological Theory, Blackwell, 94; Feature Predictability and Underspecification: Palatal Prosody in Japanese Mimetics, Language, 89. **CONTACT ADDRESS** Dept of Ling, Univ Calif, 1156 High St, Santa Cruz, CA, 95064.

METCALF, ALLAN ALBERT
PERSONAL Born 04/18/1940, Clayton, MO, d, 4 children **DISCIPLINE** ENGLISH, LINGUISTICS **EDUCATION** Cornell Univ, BA, 61; Univ Calif, Berkeley, MA, 64, PhD(English), 66. **CAREER** Asst prof English, Univ Calif, Riverside, 66-73; assoc prof, 73-81, prof English & chmn dept, MacMurray Col, IL, 81-, exec sec, Am Dialect Soc, 81-. **HONORS AND AWARDS** Phi Beta Kappa, Cornell, 61. **MEMBERSHIPS** MLA; Ling Soc Am; Mediaeval Acad Am; Am Dialect Soc; NCTE. **RESEARCH** American English dialects and Lexicography; California dialects; medieval English literature. **SELECTED PUBLICATIONS** Auth, Sir Gawain andyou, Chaucer Rev, Winter 71; The Sopken Language of a Southern California Community, Univ Calif, Riverside, 71; Directions of change in Southern California English, J English Ling, 3/72; Poetic Diction in the Old English Meters of Boethius, Mouton, The Hague, 73; Silent Knight: Sum for Cortaysye? Archiv For das Studium der neueren Sprchen und Literaturen, 76; Chicano English, Ctr Appl Ling, 79; A guide to the California-Nevada field records of the linguistic atlas of the Pacific Coast, Univ Calif, Berkeley, 79; Gawain's number, In: Essays in the Numerical Analysis of Medieval Literature, Bucknell Univ Press, 80; Typography of the Century Dictionary, Dictionaries, v 17, 96; The South in the Dictionary of American Regional English, in: Language Variety in the South Revisited, Univ of Alabama Press, 97; America in So Many Words: Words that Have Shaped America, with David K Barnhart, Houghton Mifflin, 97. **CONTACT ADDRESS** Dept of English, MacMurray Col, 477 E College Ave, Jacksonville, IL, 62650-2510. **EMAIL** aallan@aol.com

METZGER, ERIKA ALMA
PERSONAL Born 04/08/1933, Berlin, Germany, m, 1958 **DISCIPLINE** GERMAN LANGUAGE & LITERATURE **EDUCATION** Teachers' Training Col, Gottingen, dipl, 54; Free Univ Berlin, dipl, 58; Cornell Univ, MA, 61; State Univ NY Buffalo, PhD(Ger), 67. **CAREER** Teaching asst Ger, Cornell Univ, 58-61; instr, Univ Ill, 61-63; instr, Millard Fillmore Col, 63-67; asst prof, 67-72, assoc prof, 72-79, Prof Ger, State Univ NY, Buffalo, 79. **MEMBERSHIPS** MLA; Am Asn Teachers Ger, Int Ver Ger Sprach-u Literaturwiss. **RESEARCH** Development of German lyric poetry; Baroque; 20th century. **SELECTED PUBLICATIONS** Coauth, Paul Klee, 67 & Clara and Robert Schumann, 67, Houghton; ed, H A von Abschatz, Werke, Herbert Lang, Bern, 70; co-ed, Neukirch-Anthologie, Vol III, IV, V, VII, Niemeyer, Tubingen, 70; coauth, Stefan George, Twayne, 72; ed, H A von Abschatz, Gedichte, Herbert Lang, Bern, 73; auth, Marc-Antoine e Saint-Amant und Hans ABmann von Abschatz, In: Europaische Tradition, Francke, Bern, 73; Diatonisch-Doppelt-Erfahrenes, Blaeschke, Darmstadt, 77; co-ed, A Albertinus: Hofschul, Lang, Bern, 78; auth, Reading Andreas Gryphius, Critical Trends 1664-1993, Camden, 94. **CONTACT ADDRESS** Dept of Mod Lang, Univ of NY, PO Box 604620, Buffalo, NY, 14260-4620. **EMAIL** eam3@acsu.buffalo.edu

METZGER, MICHAEL MOSES
PERSONAL Born 06/02/1935, Frankfurt, Germany, m, 1958 **DISCIPLINE** GERMAN LANGUAGE & LITERATURE **EDUCATION** Columbia Univ, BA, 56; Cornell Univ, PhD(-Ger lit), 62. **CAREER** Instr Ger, Univ Ill, Urbana, 61-63; from asst prof to assoc prof, 63-71, prof Ger, State Univ NY, Buffalo, 71-, guest prof Ger Lit, Univ Va, Charlottesville, 77. **MEMBERSHIPS** MLA; Am Asn Teachers Ger; Internationale Vereinigung fur Germanische; Sprach-und Literaturwissenschaft. **RESEARCH** German literature of the Enlightenment and 20th century; Lessing; the early 18th century. **SELECTED PUBLICATIONS** Auth, Lessing and the Language of Comedy, Mouton, The Hague, 66; coauth, Paul Klee, 67 & Clara und Robert Schumann, 67, Houghton; Der Hofmeister und die Gouvernante, de Gruyter, 69; Stefan George, Twayne, 72; co-ed, Aegidius Albertinus Hof-Schul, Lang, Bern, 78; Neukirch-Anthologie, Vol V, Niemeyer, Tubingen, 81; Fairy Tales as Ways of Knowing, Lang, Bern, 81; co auth Reading Andreas Gryphius, Camden, Columbis, SC, 95. **CONTACT ADDRESS** Dept of Mod Lang & Lit, Univ of New York, PO Box 604620, Buffalo, NY, 14260-4620. **EMAIL** mmetzger@acsu.buffalo.edu

METZIDAKIS, ANGELO
DISCIPLINE FRENCH LANGUAGE AND LITERATURE **EDUCATION** Yale Univ, BA; MA; MPhil; PhD. **CAREER** Prof, Sweet Briar Col. **RESEARCH** 19th-century French civilization; French romanticism; the 19th century French novel; Victor Hugo; stylistics; transl. **SELECTED PUBLICATIONS** Auth, publ(s) about Victor Hugo's Les Miserables. **CONTACT ADDRESS** Sweet Briar Col, Sweet Briar, VA, 24595. **EMAIL** pr@sbc.edu

MEWS, SIEGFRIED
PERSONAL Born 09/28/1933, Berlin, Germany **DISCIPLINE** GERMAN/COMPARATIVE LITERATURE **EDUCATION** Univ Hamburg, Staatsexamen, 61; Southern Ill Univ, MA, 63; Univ Ill, Urbanna, PhD(comp lit), 67. **CAREER** Instr Ger, Centre Col, 62-63; instr, Univ Ill, 66-67; from asst prof to assoc prof Ger, 67-77, ed, Studies Germanic Lang & Lit, 68-80, Prof Ger, Univ NC, Chapel Hill, 77- **MEMBERSHIPS** MLA; Am Asn Teachers Ger; AAUP; Am Comp Lit Asn; Int Brecht Soc. **RESEARCH** German and comparative literature of the 19th and 20th centuries. **SELECTED PUBLICATIONS** Ed, Studies in German Literature of the Nineteenth and Twentieth Centuries, Univ NC, 70, 2nd ed, 72; Carl Zuckmayer: Der Hauptmann von Koepenick, 72, 3rd ed, 82 & Zuckmayer: Des Teufels General, 73, 2nd ed, 79, Diesterweg; co-ed, Essays on Brecht: Theater and Politics, Univ NC, 74 & 79; ed, Bertolt Brecht: Herr Puntila und sein Knecht Matti, 75 & Brecht: Der Kaukasische, Kreidedreis, 80, Diesterweg; auth, Carl Zuckmayer, 81, Twayne; ed, The Fisherman and His Wife: Gunter Grass's The Flounder in Critical Perspective, AMS Press, 82. **CONTACT ADDRESS** Dept of Ger Lang, Univ of North Carolina, Chapel Hill, Chapel Hill, NC, 27514. **EMAIL** Mews@email.unc.edu

MEYER, DORIS
PERSONAL Born 01/02/1942, Summit, NJ, m **DISCIPLINE** SPANISH **EDUCATION** Harvard Univ, Radcliffe, BA, 63; Univ Va, MA, 64, PhD, 67. **CAREER** Asst prof, 67-69, Univ NC Wilmington; instr to asst prof to assoc prof to prof, 69-86, Brooklyn Col; vis prof to prof to Roman S & Tatiana Weller Prof, 86-98, Ct Col; vis scholar, 98-, Univ NM. **HONORS AND AWARDS** Phi Beta Kappa, 63; Spanish Embassy Fell, 61; Harvard Latin Amer Travel Fel, 62; Woodrow Wilson Fel, 63-64, 64-65; Fulbright Fel, 63-64; CUNY Faculty Res Awards, 73-74, 76-77, 77-78; Amer Philos Soc Grant, 76; NEH Fel, 77-78. **MEMBERSHIPS** PEN, Modern Lang Assoc; Amer Assoc of Teachers of Spanish & Portuguese; Latin Amer Stud Assoc; Feministas Unidas. **SELECTED PUBLICATIONS** Ed, Reinterpreting the Spanish American Essay: Women Writers of the 19th and 20th Centuries, Univ Tx Press, 95; ed, Rereading the Spanish American Essay: Translations of 19th and 20th Centuries Women's Essays, Univ Tx Press, 95; auth, Speaking for Themselves: Neomexicano Cultural Identity and the Spanish-Language Press, 1880-1920, Univ NM Press, 96; art, The Early (Feminist) Essays of Victoria Ocampo, Stud Twentieth Century Lit, 96; art, The Correspondence of Gabriela Mistral and Victoria Ocampo: Reflections on American Identity, J of Inst of Romance Stud, 96. **CONTACT ADDRESS** 68 Estes Dr, Santa Fe, NM, 87501.

MEYER, PAUL HUGO
PERSONAL Born 12/05/1920, Berlin, Germany, m, 1946, 3 children **DISCIPLINE** FRENCH **EDUCATION** McGill Univ, BA, 43, MA, 45; Columbia Univ, PhD (French), 54. **CAREER** Lectr French, Columbia Univ, 51-52; instr, Bryn Mawr Col, 52-54; instr, 54-57, asst prof, 57-62, assoc prof, 62-66, PROF FRENCH, UNIV CONN, 66-, Am Coun Learned Soc res grant-in-aid, 58; Fulbright res scholar in France, 61-62; mem nat selection comt, Inst Int Educ, 71-73. **MEMBERSHIPS** MLA; Am Asn Teachers Fr; Am Soc 18th Century Studies; Int Asn Fr Studies; Soc Fr Etud XVIIIe Siecle. **RESEARCH** French philosophers; 18th century French and comparative literature; history of ideas. **SELECTED PUBLICATIONS** Auth, Blueprint--A Study of Diderot and the Encyclopedie Plates, Fr Rev, Vol 68, 95. **CONTACT ADDRESS** Dept of Romance Lang, Univ of Conn Storrs, CT, 06268.

MEYER, RONALD
DISCIPLINE SLAVIC LANGUAGES **EDUCATION** Ind Univ, PhD, 86. **CAREER** Prof. **RESEARCH** 20th-century Russian prose and poetry; contemporary Russian literature; Russian women's literature. **SELECTED PUBLICATIONS** Ed, My Half Century. **CONTACT ADDRESS** Dept of Slavic Languages, Columbia Col, New York, 2960 Broadway, New York, NY, 10027-6902. **EMAIL** rm56@columbia.edu

MEYERS, CAROL L.
PERSONAL Born 11/26/1942, Wilkes-Barre, PA, m, 1964, 2 children **DISCIPLINE** NEAR EASTERN STUDIES/ BIBLICAL STUDIES & ARCHAEOLOGY **EDUCATION** Wellesley Col, AB, 64; Brandeis Univ, MA, 66; PhD, 75. **CAREER** Prof Religion, Duke Univ, 90-; dir Women's Studies Program, Duke Univ, 92; assoc dir Women's Studies Program, Duke Univ, 86-90, 92-; consultant, DreamWorks production of Prince of Egypt, forthcoming; Ntl Endowment Humanities Inst on Image & Reality of Women in Near East Soc, 95; vis fac, Univ Conn, 94-; Consultant, Lilith Publications Network, 94-; Consultant, "Mysteries of the Bible," for Cable TV, 93; Consultant, New Dominion Pictures, 92-93; Consultant, "Religion, Culture, and Family," Univ Chi Divinity School, 91-97; assoc prof, Duke Univ, 84-90; Res Fac, Duke Univ, 83-; co-dir, Duke Univ Summer Prog in Israel, 80-. **HONORS AND AWARDS** Intl Correspondence Fel, Bar Ilan Univ, 98; Frankfurt am Main Res Assoc, Johann Wolfgang Goethe Universitat, 95; Alumni Distinguished Undergraduate Tchg Award Nominee, 94; Severinghaus Award, Wellesley Col, 91; Princeton Univ Vis Fel, 90-91; Princeton Univ Res Member, 90-91; Ntl Endowment Humanities, 82-83, 90-91; Howard Found Fel, 85-86; Duke Univ Res Council, 83-84, 85-86, 87-88, 90-91, 92-93, 93-94; Oxford Univ Vis Res Fel, 82-83; Oxford Centre for Postgraduate Hebrew Studies Vis Scholar, 82-83; Duke Univ Fac Summer Fel, 82; Cooperative Program in Judaic Studies Publications Grant, 81. **MEMBERSHIPS** Amer Acad Relig; Amer Schools of Oriental Res; Archaeol Inst Amer; Archaeol Soc Jordan; Assoc Jewish Studies; British School of Archaeol in Jerusalem; Cath Bibl Assoc; Center for Cross-Cult Res on Women; Harvard Semitic Museum; Israel Exploration Soc; Palestine Exploration Soc; Soc Bibl Lit; Soc Values in Higher Ed; Wellesley Col Center for Res on Women; Women's Assoc of Ancient Near East Studies; Women's Caucus, Assoc for Jewish Studies. **RESEARCH** Syro-Palestinian Archaelogy; Hebrew Bible; Gender in the Biblical World **SELECTED PUBLICATIONS** Coauth, Families in Ancient Israel, Westminister/John Knox Pr, 97; coed, Sepphoris in Galilee: Cross-Currents of Culture, N Carolina Museum Art, 96; coauth, Zippori (Sepphoris) 1994, Excavations & Surveys in Israel, 97; "New Faces of Eve," Humanistic Judaism, 97-98. **CONTACT ADDRESS** Dept of Religion, Duke Univ, Box 90964, Durham, NC, 27708-0964. **EMAIL** carol@acpub.duke.edu

MEYERS, ERIC MARK
PERSONAL Born 06/05/1940, Norwich, CT, m, 1964, 2 children **DISCIPLINE** BIBLE AND JUDAIC STUDIES **EDUCATION** Dartmouth Col, BA, 62; Brandeis Univ, MA, 64; Harvard Univ, PhD (Jewish hist, Bible and archaeol), 69. **CAREER** Asst prof relig, 69-71, assoc prof, 71-79, PROF RELIG, DUKE UNIV, 79-, Dir joint exped to Khirbet Shema, Meiron and Gush Halav, Nabratein; Am Schs Orient Res, 70-82; VIS ASSOC PROF, UNIV NC, CHAPEL HILL, 72-; dir coop prof Judaic studies, Duke Univ-Univ NC, Chapel Hill, ed, Present Tense, 73-75; BIBL ARCHAEOLOGIST, 81-; FIRST VPRES PUBL, AM SCHS ORIENT RES, 82- **MEMBERSHIPS** Asn Jewish Studies; Am Acad Relig; Am Schs Orient Res; Soc Religh Higher Educ; Soc Bibl Lit. **RESEARCH** Jewish history; archaeology; Bible. **SELECTED PUBLICATIONS** Auth, Galilee in the Time of Jesus, Archaeol, Vol 47, 94; The Monastery of Martyrius at Maale Adummim, J Am Orient Soc, Vol 0117, 97; Zechariah 9 14 and Malachi--A Commentary, Interpretation J Bible Theology, Vol 51, 97; The Making of The Oxford Encyclopedia of Archaeology in he Near East, Biblical Archaeol, Vol 59, 96. **CONTACT ADDRESS** Dept of Religion, Duke Univ, PO Box 473, Durham, NC, 27706.

MEYERS, WALTER EARL
PERSONAL Born 07/01/1939, Pittsburgh, PA, m, 1961, 3 children **DISCIPLINE** SCIENCE FICTION, ENGLISH LINGUISTICS **EDUCATION** Duquesne Univ, BA, 64; Univ Fla, PhD(English), 67. **CAREER** From asst prof to assoc prof, 67-78, PROF ENGLISH, NC STATE UNIV, 78- **HONORS AND AWARDS** SAtlantic Mod Lang Asn Studies Award, 78. **MEMBERSHIPS** Am Dialect Soc; MLA; Sci Fiction Res Asn. **RESEARCH** Medieval drama; modern English usage. **SELECTED PUBLICATIONS** Auth, Linguistics in TextbooksA 40-Year Comparison, Am Speech, Vol 70, 95;The Work of Aldiss, Brian, W.--An Annotated Bibliography and Guide, Sci Fiction Stu, Vol 20, 93; The Grammarians Desk--Krankor, Sci Fiction Stud, Vol 24, 97. **CONTACT ADDRESS** Dept of English, No Carolina State Univ, Raleigh, NC, 27650.

MICHAEL, COLETTE VERGER
PERSONAL Marseille, France, 6 children **DISCIPLINE** FRENCH AND PHILOSOPHY **EDUCATION** Univ Wash Seattle, fr and philos, BA, 69; Univ Wash Seattle, romance lang, MA, 70; Univ Wisc Madison, hist of sci, MA, 75; Univ Wisc Madison, fr and minor philos, PhD, 73. **CAREER** Tchg asst, Fr and Ital Dept, Univ Wisc Madison, 9/73-12/73; lectr, extension dept, Univ Wisc Madison, 7/74-8/74; lectr, fr and ital dept, Univ Wisc Madison, 2/74-8/74; prof, humanities, Shimer Col, Mt Carroll, Ill, 75-77; asst prof, foreign lang and lit, Northern Ill Univ, 77-84; assoc prof, foreign lang and lit, Northern Ill Univ, 84-90; prof, foreign lang and lit, Northern Ill Univ, 90-. **HONORS AND AWARDS** Consulat General de France Svc Culturel, Subvention for Bulletin de la Soc Amer de Philos, Jan, 92; Facul Develop grant, Hist and Tech of Fr Cinema, Fall, 91; Deans fund for res in the humanities, Spring, 87; Deans' Fund for Res, Grad Sch, Northern Ill Univ, asst for res on Negritude, Fall, 85; Deans's Fund for Res, Grad Sch, Northern Ill Univ, asst for res on The Marquis de Sade: The Man, His Works and His Critics, Fall, 83; Res award from Dean of Grad Sch, Northern Ill Univ, Topic: Choderlos de Laclos, The Man, His Works, and His Critics, Jan 80-Jun 80; Grad Sch Summer grant, NIU Topic: The Marquis de Condorcet, His Work, His Ideology, His Influence, 78; Nat Endow for the Humanities Summer Fel for Col Tchrs, Univ Ill Univ, Champaign, Topic: The European Enlightenment in the Amer Revolution, Summer, 77; Ford Found Fel, Fr and Ital Dept, Univ Wisc Madison, 71, 72, 73; Nonresident scholar, The Grad Sch, Univ Wisc Madison, 71-72. **RESEARCH** Philosophy, 18th Century. **SELECTED PUBLICATIONS** Articles, Camus, Science and Metaphors, Bull de la Soc Amer de Philos de Lang Fr VIII, 2, 78-88, 96; A la recherche de l'absolu: le neant des ecrivains maudits, Actes du Congres Intl des Soc de Philos de lang Fr, Poitiers, Fr, 167-169, 96; L'audiovisuel et la litterature francophone, Rev Francophone, VIII, 2, 73-83, 95; Justine ou la vertu devant la violence, Actes de Ile Congres mondial sur la violence et la coexistence humaine, Montreal, Vol VII, 429-435, 95; Billy Budd: An Allegory on the Rights of Man, Allegory Old and New: Creativity and Continuity in Culture, Analecta Husserliana, XLII, 251-258, 94; Light and Darkness and the Phenomenon of Creation in Victor Hugo, Analecta Husserliana: The Elemental Dialectic of Light and Darkness, XXXVIII, 131-149; Les Lettres de Doleances: Un Genre de Cahiers, ou Cahiers d'un nouveau Genre? Lang de la Revolution 1770-1815, Inst Nat de la Lang Fr: Lexicometrie et textes polit, Paris, Klimcksieck, 251-264, 95. **CONTACT ADDRESS** 635 Joanne Ln., De Kalb, IL, 60115. **EMAIL** tc0cvm1@corn.cso.niu.edu

MICHAEL, WOLFGANG FRIEDRICH
PERSONAL Born 02/23/1909, Freiburg, Germany, m, 1952, 3 children **DISCIPLINE** GERMAN **EDUCATION** Univ Munich, Phd, 34. **CAREER** Instr Ger, Bryn Mawr Col, 39; asst prof, Chestnut Hill Col, 39-46; from asst prof to assoc prof, 46-61, PROF GER, UNIV TEX, AUSTIN, 61- **HONORS AND AWARDS** Verdienstkreuz der Bundesrepublik, Goethemedaille. **MEMBERSHIPS** MLA. **RESEARCH** Renaissance and Reformation; Thomas Mann. **SELECTED PUBLICATIONS** Auth, The Custom of the King and the Epiphany Plays from the Romance Speaking Sections of Freiburg Canton, Jahrbuch Volksliedforschung, Vol 36, 91; Texts and Melodies from the Erlauer Spiele, Jahrbuch Volksliedforschung, Vol 37, 92; Boltz,Valentin Die Bekehrung Pauli, Zeitschrift Deutsche Philol, Vol 0113, 94; The Volksschauspiel as Presented in Archival Documents--A Contribution to Bavarian Cultural History, Jahrbuch Volksliedforschung, Vol 38, 93. **CONTACT ADDRESS** Dept of Ger, Univ of Tex, Austin, TX, 78712.

MICHAELS, DAVID
DISCIPLINE LINGUISTICS **EDUCATION** Univ Mich, PhD. **CAREER** Prof, Univ Conn. **RESEARCH** Phonological theory. **SELECTED PUBLICATIONS** Auth, Natural and Unnatural Phonology, Phonologica, 88; Cambridge Univ Press, 92; Movement Rules in Phonology, In Certamen Phonologicum II, Rosenberg and Seiler, Torino, 91; Prosegments and Syllable Structure, Revista di Grammatica Generativa 14, 89. **CONTACT ADDRESS** Dept of Linguistics, Univ of Connecticut, 1266 Storrs Rd, Storrs, CT, 06269-1085. **EMAIL** michaels@uconnvm.uconn.edu

MICHALCZYK, JOHN JOSEPH
PERSONAL Born 06/26/1941, Scranton, PA, m, 3 children **DISCIPLINE** FRENCH LITERATURE, CINEMA **EDUCATION** Boston Col, BA, 66, MA, 67; Harvard Univ, PhD (French lit & cinema), 72; Weston Col, MDiv, 74. **CAREER** Instr & chmn French & cinema, Loyola High Sch, Towson, Md, 67-69; instr, int French through film, Harvard Univ, 71-71; instr, graduate summer program in French, Rivier Col (Nashua, NH), 72-76; asst prof French & cinema, 74-80, assoc prof Fine Arts Dept, Boston Col, 80-, dir of film studies, Boston Col, 84-, prof & chmn Fine Arts Dept, 96-. **HONORS AND AWARDS** 2 New England Emmy Nominations for films: "Of Stars and Shamrocks: Boston's Jews & Irish" and "In the Shadow of the Reich: Nazi Medicine"; Distinguished documentary award from TASH (The Asn for the Severely Handicapped) for "Nazi Medicine"; "Palmes Academiques" from French Government for 25 years of contributions to French culture; Directory of American Scholars; Contemporary Authors; Fulbright (Italy); Mellon (Costa-Gavras). **MEMBERSHIPS** Malraux Soc. **RESEARCH** Issues of Social Justice in art, literature, and film; documentary film production. **SELECTED PUBLICATIONS** Auth, Malraux, le cinema, et La Condition humaine, 1/74 & Le cinema polonais en '73, 4/74, Cinema '74; Camus/Malraux: A staged version of Le Temps du mepris, 10/76 & Robbe-Grillet, Michelet and Barthes: From La Sorciere to Glissements progressifs du plaisir, 12/77, Fr Rev; Andre Malraux's Film Espoir: The Propaganda/Art Film and the Spanish Civil War, Romance Monogr, 77; Ingmar Bergman: La, Passion d'etre homme aujourd'hue, Beauchesne, Paris, 77; Recurrent Imagery of the Labyrinth in Robbe-Grillet's Films, Stanford Fr Rev, spring 78; The French Literary Filmmakers, Asn Univ Press, 80; Costa-Gavras: The Political Fiction Film, Arts Alliance Press, 84; Italian Political Filmmakers, Fairleigh Dickinson Univ Press, 86; Medicine, Ethics, and the Third Reich: Historical and Contemporary Issues, Sheed and Ward, 94; The Resisters, the Rescuers, and the Refugees, Sheed and Ward, 97; and articles on film and its relation to literature and the arts in: American Soc Legion of Honor; Annali d'Iliansistica; Cineaste; Cinema (Paris); Cinema and Soc (Paris); Contemporary French Civ; Current Research in Film; French Review; Lit/Film Quart; Magill's Cinema Annual; Melanges Malraux Miscellany; Stanford French Review; Twentieth Century Lit. **CONTACT ADDRESS** Fine Arts Dept, Boston Col, 140 Commonwealth Ave, Chestnut Hill, MA, 02167-3800. **EMAIL** john.michalczyk@bc.edu

MICHALSKI, JOHN
PERSONAL Born 10/13/1934, Czernowitz, Rumania **DISCIPLINE** COMPARATIVE LITERATURE & LINGUISTICS **EDUCATION** Univ Toledo, BA, 53; Inst World Affairs, cert; Northwestern Univ, MA, 54. **CAREER** Asst Ger, Northwestern Univ, 53-55; lectr mod lang, Roosevelt Univ, 56-57; instr, Marquette Univ, 57-61; asst prof Europ lang, Univ Hawaii, 61-68; asst to dean educ serv, 70-71, chmn First Hawaiian Innovations Inst, 72-73, prof Ger, Speech -Commun, Ling & Chmn Div Lang Arts, Leeward Community Col, 68-, Consult export & import policies, 54-; co-dir int serv ctr, Chicago Machine Tool Expos, 55; ed, Hawaii Lang Teacher. **MEMBERSHIPS** MLA; Am Asn Teachers Ger; Am Anthrop Asn; Am Comp Lit Asn; Am Coun Teaching Foreign Lang. **RESEARCH** Language teaching; communications; creative writing. **SELECTED PUBLICATIONS** Contribr, Am Peoples Encycl, 56-57 & Encycl World Lit, 63-64; auth, Stefan Andres: Wir sind Utopia, Heath, 63; Deutsche Dichter und Denker, Blaisdall, 67; Ferdinant Raimund, Twayne, 68. **CONTACT ADDRESS** Div of Lang Arts, Leeward Community Col, 96-045 Ala Ike, Pearl City, HI, 96782-3393. **EMAIL** j-michalski@lccada.lcc.hawaii.edu

MICHEL, JOSEPH
PERSONAL Born 03/29/1922, Mexico, m, 1959 **DISCIPLINE** FOREIGN LANGUAGE EDUCATION, SPANISH **EDUCATION** De LaSalle Col, BA, 44; Nat Univ Mex, MA, 47; Univ NMex, PhD (Span lit), 61. **CAREER** Teacher, Bernalillo Elem, NMex, 42-43, Inst Regiomontano, Mex, 44-49, Cathedral High Sch, Tex, 49 and St Paul's, La, 50-52; prof foreign lang and chmn dept, Col Santa Fe, 52-59; dir foreign lang instr, State Dept Educ, N Mex, 59-61; assoc prof curric and instr and Romance lang, Col Educ and Col Arts and Sci, Univ Tex, Austin, 62-67, prof foreign lang educ, curric and instr, Col Educ and Humanities, 67-73, dir, Foreign Lang Educ Ctr, 63-73, prof humanities, 71-73; DEAN COL MULTIDISCIPLINARY STUDIES, UNIV TEX, SAN ANTONIO, 73-, Consult bilingual educ, Serv Ctr XIII, 70; univ res inst grant, Univ Tex, San Antonio, 73. **MEMBERSHIPS** Am Asn Teachers Span and Port; Am Coun Teaching Foreign Lang; MLA; Southern Conf Lang Teaching; Nat Fed Mod Lang Teachers Asn. **RESEARCH** A recorded survey of the language of the five year old Texas bilingual; teaching reading to the Spanish-English bilingual; reading content for the Spanish-English bilingual. **SELECTED PUBLICATIONS** Auth, Church Music Under the Nazi Regime--10 Essays, Musik Kirche, Vol 65, 95; Proofs of the Book--Reflections on Leclezio,J.M.G. Etoile Roman, Lettres Romanes, Vol 47, 93. **CONTACT ADDRESS** Off Multidisciplinary Studies, Univ of Tex, San Antonio, TX, 78285.

MICKEL, EMANUEL J.
DISCIPLINE FRENCH LITERATURE **EDUCATION** Univ NC, PhD, 65. **CAREER** Prof. **RESEARCH** Aesthetic relationship between nineteenth century painting and literature; Latin and Old French narrative in the 12th century. **SELECTED PUBLICATIONS** Auth, Eugene Fromentin, 82; Ganelon, Treason and the Chanson de Roland, 89; Jules Verne's Twenty Thousand Leagues Under the Sea, 91; ed, The Shaping of Text: Style, Imagery, and Structure in French Literature, 93. **CONTACT ADDRESS** Dept of French and Italian, Indiana Univ, Bloomington, 300 N Jordan Ave, Bloomington, IN, 47405.

MICKLESEN, LEW R.
PERSONAL Born 01/09/1921, Red Wing, MN, m, 1950, 3 children **DISCIPLINE** SLAVIC LINGUISTICS **EDUCATION** Univ Minn, BS, 42; Harvard Univ, PhD, 51. **CAREER** Instr Russ and Span, US Navel Acad, 45-46; sr instr Russ, Air Force Russ Prog, Syracuse Univ, 51-52; asst prof, Univ Ore, 52-53; asst prof Slavic ling, Univ Wash, 53-59; group mgr mech transl, Int Bus Machines Res Ctr, 59-63; assoc prof Slavic ling, Univ Colo, 63-64; prof, Univ Ill, 64-66; PROF SLAVIC LING, UNIV WASH, 66- **MEMBERSHIPS** Am Asn Teachers Slavic and EEurop Lang; Ling Soc Am; Int Ling Asn. **RESEARCH** Balto-Slavic accentology; Russian morphology; Russian syntax. **SELECTED PUBLICATIONS** Auth, The Accentual Patterns o te Slavic Languages, Elementa Jur Slavic Stud Comp Cult Semiotics, Vol 2, 95. **CONTACT ADDRESS** Dept of Slavic Lang and Lit, Univ of Wash, Seattle, WA, 98195.

MIGIEL, MARILYN
DISCIPLINE ITALIAN LITERATURE **EDUCATION** Cornell Univ, AB, 75; Yale Univ, PhD, 81. **CAREER** Assoc prof **HONORS AND AWARDS** Stephen and Margery Russell awd for Distinguished tchg, 95; Amer Coun of Learned Societies, Grant-in-Aid, $3000, 92; Mellon Postdoc res and tchg fel, Cornell Univ, 86-87; Phi Beta Kappa, 75; Lane Cooper Scholar-

ship, 74-75; scholarship, Cornell Branch Telluride Asn, 72-75. **RESEARCH** Italian literature. **SELECTED PUBLICATIONS** Auth, Gender and Genealogy in Tasso's, Gerusalemme Liberata, Lewiston, NY: Edwin Mellen Press, 93; Veronica Franco, In Italian Women Writers: A Bio-Bibliographical Sourcebook, Westport, CT: Greenwood Press, 94; Olimpia's Secret Weapon: Gender, War, and Hermeneutics in Ariosto's Orlando Furioso, Critical Matrix: The Princeton Journal of Women, Gender, and Culture 95; ed, Refiguring Woman: Perspectives on Gender and the Italian Renaissance, Ithaca: Cornell UP, 91. **CONTACT ADDRESS** Dept of Romance Studies, Cornell Univ, 293 Goldwin Smith Hall, Ithaca, NY, 14853. **EMAIL** mm55@cornell.edu

MIGNOLO, WALTER
PERSONAL Argentina, m, 2 children **DISCIPLINE** ROMANCE STUDIES **EDUCATION** Univ Nac Cordobe, Licenciatura,68; Ecole des Hautes Etudes, Doctorat de Troisieme Cycle, 74. **CAREER** Vis asst prof, Indiana Univ, 73-74; vis asst prof, Univ Mich, 74-75; from asst to assoc to prof, Univ Mich, 75-92; WILLIAM H. WANNAMAKER DIST PROF, DUKE UNIV, 93-. **HONORS AND AWARDS** Fel study abroad, 69; Katherine Singer Kovacs Award, MLA, 94. **MEMBERSHIPS** LASA, MLA, AAA, ASA. **RESEARCH** Globalization **CONTACT ADDRESS** Dept of Romance Studies, Duke Univ, 205 Language Bldg., Box 90257, Durham, NC, 27708-0257. **EMAIL** wmignolo@acpub.duke.edu

MIHAILESCU, CALIN ANDREI
DISCIPLINE FRENCH LITERATURE **EDUCATION** Univ Bucharest, BA; Univ Toronto, MA; PhD. **RESEARCH** Continental philosophy; postmodern trends; 17th century philosophy and theology; French thought. **SELECTED PUBLICATIONS** Auth, pub(s) on Pascal, St. John of the Cross, St. Teresa, Plato, Aristotle, Baltasar Gracian, Kant, Benjamin, Heidegger, Adorno, Huxley, T. Mann, utopian and dystopian discourses, semiotics of folklore and myth, and economic aspects of narrative. **CONTACT ADDRESS** Dept of Modern Languages, Western Ontario Univ, London, ON, N6A 5B8.

MIHAILOVICH, VASA D.
PERSONAL Born 08/12/1926, Prokuplje, Yugoslavia, m, 1957, 2 children **DISCIPLINE** SLAVIC LANGUAGES AND LITERATURES **EDUCATION** Wayne State Univ, BA, 56, MA, 57; Univ Calif, Berkeley, PhD(Ger), 66. **CAREER** Teaching asst Ger, Univ Calif, Berkeley, 57-61; instr Russ, 61-63, from asst prof to assoc prof, 63-75, PROF SLAVIC LANG AND LIT, UNIV NC, CHAPEL HILL, 75- **MEMBERSHIPS** MLA; Am Asn Teachers Slavic and EEurop Lang; Am Asn Advan Slavic Studies; Am Asn SSlavic Studies; NAm Soc Serbian Studies. **RESEARCH** Russian literature; Yugoslav literatures; comparative study of Russian and Yugoslav literature and German. **SELECTED PUBLICATIONS** Auth, Pakao za dnevnu upotrebu, World Lit Today, Vol 68, 94; Excursions---Essays on Russian and Serbian Literature, World Lit Today, Vol 71, 97; Raskrsca ili autoportret bivseg narodnog neprijatelja, World Lit Today, Vol 68, 94; Kruna od peska, World Lit Today, Vol 69, 95; The Horse has Six Legs--An Anthology of Serbian Poetry, World Lit Today, Vol 67, 93; Crveni Klobuk, World Lit Today, Vol 69, 95. Svet izvezen stihovima, World Lit Today, Vol 66, 92; Between Myth and Play--The Poet Andric, Ivo, World Lit Today, Vol 66, 92; Imagination of History--The Problem of Historical and Literary--Aesthetic Distance in Serbian Novels about World War I, World Lit Today, Vol 69, 95; The Historical Novel--Collected Articles, World Literature Today, Vol 71, 97; Poems About Childhood and Wars, World Lit Today, Vol 67, 93; Jevandjelje po Majku, World Lit Today, Vol 69, 95; Contemporary Macedonian Poetry, Slavic Rev, Vol 53, 94; Andric, Ivo Revisited--The Bridge Still Stands , World Lit Today, Vol 70, 96; Dama u Belim Rukavicama, World Lit Today, Vol 68, 94; Price iz Hada, World Lit Today, Vol 68, 94; Putevima i prostorima, World Lit Today, Vol 68, 94; The Quest for Roots--The Poetry of Popa, VaskoA/, Slavic Rev, Vol 54, 95; Plays, World Lit Today, Vol 70, 96; Igla i konac, World Lit Today, Vol 67, 93; Albion, Albion, World Lit Today, Vol 69, 95; Posvecenik ljepote, World Lit Today, Vol 70, 96; The Days of the Consuls, World Lit Today, Vol 68, 94; Book About Andric, Ivo, World Lit Today, Vol 68, 94; Na Prelomu, World Lit Today, Vol 71, 97; Gospod Nad Vojskama, World Lit Today, Vol 71, 97; Nakjuce, World Lit Today, Vol 70, 96; U Potpalublju, World Lit Today, Vol 70, 96; A Rest from History, World Lit Today, Vol 69, 95; Bog se brine za Iliju, World Lit Today, Vol 69, 95; Suppressed Poems--Contemporary Serbian Emigre Poets, World Lit Today, Vol 68, 94; Na Prelomu, World Lit Today, Vol 69, 95; Skladiste, World Lit Today, Vol 70, 96; Ispunio sam svoju sudbinu, World LitToday, Vol 67, 93; Ne dam se, ljubavi, World Lit Today, Vol 70, 96. **CONTACT ADDRESS** Dept Slavic Lang and Lit, Univ NC, Chapel Hill, NC, 27514.

MILEHAM, JAMES WARREN
PERSONAL Born 03/31/1943, Aruba, West Indies, m, 2 children **DISCIPLINE** FRENCH LITERATURE **EDUCATION** Lafayette Col, AB, 65; Univ Ala, MA, 69; Univ Wis- Madison, PhD(French), 75. **CAREER** Asst prof, 75-81, Assoc Prof French, Univ Wis-Milwaukee, 81-; ed, the U.S.A. bibliography in the Ann e Balzacienne, 95-. **RESEARCH** French novel. **SELECTED PUBLICATIONS** Auth, A web of conspiracy: Structure and metaphor in Balzac's novels, Ky Romance Quart, 79; Blazac's Seven of Probation, winter 80 & Numbers in the Comedie humaine, Vol XXII, No 1, Romance Notes; The Conspiracy Novel: Structure and Metaphor in Balzac's Comedic humaine, Fr Forum Publ, 82; Labyrinths in Balzac's Ferragus, Nineteenth Century Fr Studies, 23, 3 & 4, 95. **CONTACT ADDRESS** Dept of French, Ital, and Comp Lit, Univ of Wis, PO Box 413, Milwaukee, WI, 53201-0413. **EMAIL** jmile@uwm.edu

MILES, DAVID HOLMES
PERSONAL Born 05/25/1940, Bangor, ME **DISCIPLINE** GERMAN **EDUCATION** Univ Maine, Orono, BA, 62; Princeton Univ, PhD, 68. **CAREER** Asst prof Ger, Univ Mass, Boston, 67-72; assoc prof, Ohio State Univ, 72-75; chmn dept, 78-80, ASSOC PROF GER, UNIV VA, 75-, Alexander von Humboldt fel, Freiburg, Ger, 70-71; Guggenheim fel, 76-77; mem, Ctr Advan Study, Univ Va, 77-78. **HONORS AND AWARDS** PMLA Parker Prize, 79. **MEMBERSHIPS** MLA; Am Asn Teachers Ger. **RESEARCH** Modern German literature; comparative literature; literary theory and the visual arts. **SELECTED PUBLICATIONS** Auth, Up Close and In Motion, Volvo Invents Cubist TV, Jour Film Video, Vol 46, 95. **CONTACT ADDRESS** Dept of Ger, Univ of Va, Charlottesville, VA, 22903.

MILES, JOSEPHINE
PERSONAL Born 06/11/1911, Chicago, IL **DISCIPLINE** ENGLISH PHILOLOGY AND CRITICISM **EDUCATION** Univ Calif, Los Angeles, AB, 32; Univ Calif, AM, 34, PhD, 38. **CAREER** From instr to prof, 40-52, UNIV PROF ENGLISH, UNIV CALIF, BERKELEY, 52-, Am Asn Univ Women res fel, 39-40; Guggenheim fel, 48-49; Am Coun Learned Soc fel, 64-65; Nat Found Arts fel, 67-68 and 79-80. Shelley Award, 35; Nat Inst Arts and Lett Award, 56; Lowell Award, MLA, 75. **HONORS AND AWARDS** DLitt, Mills Col, 66. **MEMBERSHIPS** MLA; Am Soc Aesthet; Philol Asn Pac Coast; Am Acad Arts and Sci; fel Acad Am Poets. **RESEARCH** Literary history; linguistics; modern poetry. **SELECTED PUBLICATIONS** Auth, The Sound of Silence, Lingua Fr, Vol 7,94; What Makes God God Like, Parnassus Poetry Rev, Vol 19, 94. **CONTACT ADDRESS** Dept of English, Univ of Calif, Berkeley, CA, 94720.

MILIC, LOUIS TONKO
PERSONAL Born 09/05/1922, Split, Yugoslavia, m, 3 children **DISCIPLINE** ENGLISH, STYLISTICS **EDUCATION** Columbia Univ, AB, 48, MA, 50, PhD, 63. **CAREER** Instr English, Mont State Col, 52-54; lectr, Columbia Univ, 55-58, from instr to asst prof, 58-67, assoc prof, Teachers Col, 67-69; chmn dept, 69-78, PROF ENGLISH, CLEVELAND STATE UNIV, 69-, Rev ed, Comput and Humanities, 66-71; Am Coun Learned Soc/Int Bus Mach fel, 67-68; GEN ED, NEW HUMANISTIC RES SER, TEACHERS COL; CO-ED, THE GAMUT, 79-; Nat Endowment for Humanities fel, summer, 80. **MEMBERSHIPS** Int Asn Univ Professors English; Am Soc 18th Century Studies; Asn Comput in Humanities; Asn Appl Ling. **RESEARCH** Rhetoric; 18th century English literature; computer-assisted literary research. **SELECTED PUBLICATIONS** Auth, Quantitative Aspects of Genre in the Century of Prose Corpus, Style, Vol 28, 94; Words of Ones Own, Some Evidence Against Mens Use of Language as a Tool of Domination, Style, Vol 29, 95 A Comment on Finch, Alison Article, Style, Vol 29, 95; A Comment on Finch, Alison Article, Style, Vol 29, 95. **CONTACT ADDRESS** 3111 Chelsea Dr, Cleveland Heights, OH, 44118.

MILLEN, ROCHELLE L.
DISCIPLINE JEWISH STUDIES **EDUCATION** MacMurray Col, BA; Christian Theological Seminary, MDiv; Univ Chicago, MA, PhD. **CAREER** Prof, 88-; fac, Wexner Heritage Found; co-chair, Am acad Rel. **HONORS AND AWARDS** Grants: McMaster Univ; Stern Col Women; Yeshiva Univ, Res grants: Lilly Found; Evangelical Lutheran Church; Am Jewish Archives, Hebrew Union Col; NEH. **RESEARCH** Women in religion, phenomenology of religion, and modern Jewish thought.women's prayer and Talmud. **SELECTED PUBLICATIONS** Auth, Martin Buber, Joseph B. Soloveitchik, and the response literature on women and Kaddish. **CONTACT ADDRESS** Wittenberg Univ, Springfield, OH, 45501-0720.

MILLER, DAVID
PERSONAL Born 12/16/1932, Chicago, IL **DISCIPLINE** COMPARATIVE RELIGION **EDUCATION** Harvard Divinity Sch, BD, 57-60; Univ Ill, BA, 51-55; Harvard Univ, PhD, 60-68. **CAREER** Assoc prof, 74-; assoc prof, Sir George Williams Univ, 72-74; asst prof, Sir George Williams Univ, 70-72; asst prof, Case W Reserve Univ, 68-70; lectr, Case W Reserve Univ, 65-68; vis lectr, Oberlin Col, 69-70. **RESEARCH** Study of contemporary Hindu monastics and gurus. **SELECTED PUBLICATIONS** co-auth, Hindu Monastic Life: The Monks and Monastics of Bhubaneswar, McGill-Queens UP, 76; Hindu Monastic Life, reprinted, Manamohar Press, New Delhi, 96; The Spiritual Descent of the Divine: The Life Story of Svami Sivananda, Hindu Spirituality, Vol II, 97; "Modernity in Hindu Monasticism," Intl Jour of Comparative Rel and Phil, 96; "The Chariot and the Phallus in the Temple Architecture of Orissa," Jour of Vaisnava Stud, 95. **CONTACT ADDRESS** Dept of Rel, Concordia Univ, Montreal, 1455 de Maisonneuve W, Montreal, PQ, H3G 1M8.

MILLER, PAUL
PERSONAL Born 11/07/1959, Kansas City, MO, m, 1987, 1 child **DISCIPLINE** COMPARATIVE LITERATURE **EDUCATION** Univ Texas, PhD 89. **CAREER** Drary Col, asst prof, 89-91; Tex Tech Univ, asst prof, assoc prof, 91-98; Hamilton Col, vis prof, 96; Univ S Carolina, prof, dir comp lit, 98-. **HONORS AND AWARDS** Who's Who in Amer Tchrs. **MEMBERSHIPS** MLA; APA; CAMWS; WCC; ACLA; Renaissance Soc. **RESEARCH** Lyric poetry; Classical tradition; Gender studies; Literary theory. **SELECTED PUBLICATIONS** Auth, Lyric Texts and Lyric Consciousness: The Birth of a Genre from Archaic Greece to Augustan Rome, London, Routledge, 94; auth, French Feminism Across the Disciplines, co-ed, spec issue, Intertexts, 98; auth, Rethinking Sexuality: Foucault and Classical Antiquity, co-ed, Princeton Univ Press, 98; auth, Sex and Gender in Medieval and Renaissance Texts: The Latin Tradition, co-ed, Albany, SUNY Press, 97; auth, Recapturing the Renaissance: Perspectives on Humanism Dialogue and Tradition, co-ed, Knoxville TN, New Paradigm Press, 96; Russian Literature and the Classics, co-ed, NY, Harwood Press, 96; auth, The Suppression of the Negative in Foucault's History of Sexuality, Arcadia, 98; auth, Floating Uteruses and Phallic Gazes: Hippocratic Medicine in the Encycl, Intertexts, 98; auth, Persius Ref Guide to World Literature, London, St James Press, 95; rev, Allen Cameron, Callimachus and Critics, Rel Stud Rev, 98; auth, Thomas Wiedemann, Emperors and Gladiators, Classical Outlook, 94. **CONTACT ADDRESS** Program Comparative Literature, South Carolina Univ, J Welsh Humanities Bldg, Columbia, SC, 29208. **EMAIL** millerpa@garnet.cla.sc.edu

MILLER, R. BAXTER
PERSONAL Born 10/11/1948, Rocky Mount, NC, d, 1 child **DISCIPLINE** ENGLISH LANGUAGE **EDUCATION** NC Ctrl Univ, BA, 70; Brown Univ, AM, 72, PhD, 74. **CAREER** Asst prof English, Haverford Col, 74-76; assoc prof English, Univ Tenn, 77-81; prof English & dir Black Lit Prog, 82-92, Lindsay Young prof lib arts & English, 86-87, PROF ENGLISH & DIR AFT AM STUD, 92- , UNIV GEORGIA; Mellon prof Xavier Univ, 88; lectr, SUNY, 74; Irvine Found vis scholar, Univ San Fran, 91. **MEMBERSHIPS** Langston Hughes Soc; Mod Lang Asn. **RESEARCH** Modern poetry. **SELECTED PUBLICATIONS** Auth, Black American Poets Between Worlds, 1940-1960, 86; The Southern Trace in Black Critical Theory, Xavier Rev, 91; co-ed, Call and Response: African American Tradition in Literature, Houghton Mifflin, 97; ed The Critical Methods of Aftrican Americans: 1865-1988, 99. **CONTACT ADDRESS** African Am Stud, Univ of Georgia, Athens, GA, 30602. **EMAIL** rbmiller@arches.uga.edu

MILLER, VERNON D.
PERSONAL Born 02/26/1955, Houston, TX, d, 2 children **DISCIPLINE** ORGANIZATIONAL COMMUNICATION **EDUCATION** Baylor Univ, BA, 77, MA, 79; Univ Tx at Austin, PhD, 88. **CAREER** Univ Wis at Milwaukee, 86-90; Mich State Univ, 90-98. **MEMBERSHIPS** Int Commun Asn; Acad of Management; Nat Commun Asn. **RESEARCH** Organizational assimilation; employment interviewing; role leavening; role negotiation. **SELECTED PUBLICATIONS** Coauth, Antecedents to willingness to participate in a planned organizational change, J of Applied Commun, 94; The maternity leave as a role negotiation process: A conceptual framework, J of Managerial Issues, 96; The role of communication in managing reducations in work force, J of Applied Commun Res, 96; Toward a research agenda for the second employment interview, J of Applied Commun Res, 96; The role of a conference in integrating a contractual network of health services organizations, J of Business Commun, 96; An experimental study of newcomers' information seeking behaviors during organizational entry, Commun Studies, 96; Communicating and Connecting: The functions of human communication, Harcourt Brace Col Pub, 96; Testing two contrasting models of innovativeness in a contractual network, Human Commun Res, 97; Survivors' information seeking following a reduction in workforce, Commun Res, 97; Downsizing and structural holes: Their impact on layoff survivors' perceptions of organizational chaos and openess to change, Commun Res, 98; The case of the aggrieved expatriate case analysis: Miller analysis, Management Commun Quart, 98. **CONTACT ADDRESS** Dept of Commun, Michigan State Univ, East Lansing, MI, 48824-1212.

MILLER, WILLIAM IRVIN
PERSONAL Born 11/14/1942, Cincinnati, OH, m, 1970, 1 child **DISCIPLINE** SPANISH LANGUAGE & LINGUISTICS **EDUCATION** Wittenberg Univ, BA, 65; Univ Fla, PhD(Romance Lang), 70. **CAREER** Assoc prof Span, Univ Akron, 70-. **MEMBERSHIPS** Am Asn Teachers Span & Port; Am Coun Teachers Foreign Lang. **RESEARCH** Hispanic and Romance Linguistics; foreign language pedagogy. **CONTACT ADDRESS** Dept of Mod Lang, Univ of Akron, 302 Buchtel Mall, Akron, OH, 44325-1907. **EMAIL** wmiller@uakron.edu

MILLS, CARL RHETT
PERSONAL Born 05/05/1942, Hillsboro, OR, m, 1968, 2 children **DISCIPLINE** LINGUISTICS, ENGLISH LITERACY **EDUCATION** Cent Wash State Col, BA, 69; Univ Ore, DA, 72, PhD(English & ling), 75. **CAREER** Instr English, Ore State Correctional Inst, 71-73; teacher, Univ Ore, 74-75; instr ling, 75-76, chm English lang & ling comt, 75-82, asst prof ling, 76-81, assoc prof Ling, Univ Cincinnati, 81-, Vpres, Grad Student Coun, Univ Ore, 70-72; Fulbright lectr, Univ Tromso, Norway, 77-78 & Cairo Univ, Egypt, 82-83. **RESEARCH** Psycholinguistics; sociolinguistics; computer approaches to literacy research. **SELECTED PUBLICATIONS** Auth, Stylistic application of ethnosemantics, Lang & Style, 76; Perceptual economy and sound change, Lang Today, 76-77; contribr, Papers for the Fourth Scandinavian Conference of Linguistics, Odense Univ Press, 78; Language Use and the Uses of Language, Georgetown Univ Press, 80; auth, The sociolinguistics of the merger in Pacific Northwest English, Papers Ling, 80; Speech samples in analysis of language attitudes, J Psycholing Res, 81; American Grammar: Sound, Form and Meaning, Peter Lang, 90; author of numerous articles, reviews, and papers from 75-98. **CONTACT ADDRESS** Dept of English, Univ of Cincinnati, PO Box 210069, Cincinnati, OH, 45221-0069. **EMAIL** carl.mills@uc.edu

MILLS, DAVID OTIS
PERSONAL Born 05/06/1936, Chicago, IL, m, 1963, 2 children **DISCIPLINE** JAPANESE LANGUAGE & LITERATURE, LINGUISTICS & LANGUAGE **EDUCATION** Univ Tex, Austin, BA, 58; Univ Mich, Ann Arbor, MA, 66, PhD, 74. **CAREER** Instr, assoc prof Japanese, 77-, chmn dept E Asian Lang & Lit, Univ Pittsburgh, 77-91; dir, Tech Japanese Lang Proj, MIT 87-97; Ling Ed, 77-99, Coord Ed, 91-94, Jour of Assoc of Teachers of Japanese; Nat Sci Grants, MIT: Tech Jap Lang Proj, 87-90, Univ of Pittsburgh: Intl Sem on Teaching Tech Japanese, 94. **MEMBERSHIPS** Assn Teachers Japanese; Soc Study Japanese Lang; Soc Teaching Japanese as Foreign Lang; Assn Asian Studies. **RESEARCH** History of the Japanese language; teaching Japanese as a second language; Japanese literature. **SELECTED PUBLICATIONS** Auth, Proceedings of 1994 US-Japan Seminar: State of Teaching Japanese to Scientists and Engineers, 95; auth, Giving Scientists the Japanese They Need, in Eleanor Jorden Festschrift, 97; auth, Models of Instruction for a Technical Japanese Course in Japanese Language for Scientists and Engineers, Tsukuba University, 96. **CONTACT ADDRESS** Dept of Foreign Lang & Lit, Univ of Pittsburgh, 1501 Cathedral/Learn, Pittsburgh, PA, 15260-0001. **EMAIL** dom+@pitt.edu

MILOSKY, LINDA M.
DISCIPLINE COMMUNICATION SCIENCES AND DISORDERS **EDUCATION** Univ WI Madison, PhD, 86. **CAREER** Assoc prof CCC-SLP, Syracuse Univ. **RESEARCH** Lang acquisition and disorders with specific interest in cognitive, linguistic, and soc aspects of discourse processing in normal and clinical populations. **SELECTED PUBLICATIONS** Auth, Addressing Nonliteral Language Abilities: Seeing the Forest for the Trees in Language Learning Disabilities in School-age Children & Adolescents: Some Underlying Principles & Applications, Merrill, 94; Children Listening: the Role of World Knowledge in Discourse Comprehension in Child Talk: Processes in Language Acquisition, Mosby Yearbook, 92. **CONTACT ADDRESS** Syracuse Univ, Syracuse, NY, 13244.

MINER, ELLIS D.
PERSONAL Born 04/16/1937, Los Angeles, CA, m, 1961, 7 children **DISCIPLINE** GERMAN & PHYSICS **EDUCATION** Utah State Univ, BS, 61; Brigham Young Univ, PhD, 65. **CAREER** Space Sci, Jet Propulsion Lab (NASA & Calif Tech), 65-. **HONORS AND AWARDS** Sci Manager for Cassini Mission to Saturn. **MEMBERSHIPS** Am Astron Soc; AAS Div for Planetary Sci. **RESEARCH** Planetary eploration via robotic spacecraft. **SELECTED PUBLICATIONS** Auth, URANUS: the planet, rings, and satellites, 1s ed, 91, 2nd ed, 97; co-ed, URANUS, 92. **CONTACT ADDRESS** Jet Propulsion Lab, 4800 Oak Grove Dr, Pasadena, CA, 91109. **EMAIL** ellis.d.miner@jpl.nasa.gov

MING LEE, HUGH
PERSONAL Honolulu, HI **DISCIPLINE** GREEK AND LATIN **EDUCATION** St Mary's Col, BA; Stanford University, MA, PhD. **CAREER** Instr, IN Univ; Univ OH; Howard Univ; assoc prof-. **HONORS AND AWARDS** Res fel(s), Fullbright Found, Rome; NEH, Amer Coun of Learned Soc(s)., Prog coord, DC Soc Archaeol Inst Am; mem, Bd of Governors. **RESEARCH** Ancient Greek and Roman athletics. **SELECTED PUBLICATIONS** Auth, Running and the Stadium, Archaeol, 96; Yet Another Scoring System for the Ancient Pentathlon, Nikephoros 8, 96. **CONTACT ADDRESS** Dept of Class, Univ MD, 4229 Art-Sociology Building, College Park, MD, 20742-1335. **EMAIL** hlee@deans.umd.edu

MINKOFF, HARVEY
PERSONAL New York, NY **DISCIPLINE** LINGUISTICS, ENGLISH **EDUCATION** City Col New York, BA, 65, MA, 66, Grad Ctr, PhD, 70. **CAREER** Asst prof English, Iona Col, 67-71; assoc prof English & Ling, 71-90, prof Eng and Ling, Hunter Col, 90-. **MEMBERSHIPS** Ling Soc Am; MLA. **RESEARCH** Applications of linguistics to language teaching and learning; theory and practice of literary translation. **SELECTED PUBLICATIONS** Ed, Teaching English Linguistically: Five Experimental Curricula, 71 & auth, The English Verb System, 72; (N)ever write like(?) you talk: Teaching the syntax of reading & composition, English Record, 74; coauth, Mastering Prestige English, Villa Press, 75; auth, Teaching the Transition From Print to Script Analytically, Elementary English, 75; Some Stylistic Consequences of Aelfric's Theory of Translation, Studies in Philol, 76; coauth, Transitions: A key to mature reading and writing, In: Classroom Practices in Teaching English, NCTE, 77; coauth, Complete Course in College Writing, Kendall-Hunt, 84; coauth, Visions and Revisions, Prentice-Hall, 90; ed, Approaches to the Bible, 2 Vols, Bibl Arch Soc, 95; coauth, Exploring America, Harcourt, 95; auth, Mysteries of the Dead Sea Scrolls, Ottenhenmer, 98. **CONTACT ADDRESS** Dept of English, Hunter Col, CUNY, 695 Park Ave, New York, NY, 10021-5085.

MINKOVA, DONKA
PERSONAL Born 01/13/1944, Sofia, Bulgaria, 2 children **DISCIPLINE** ENGLISH LINGUISTICS **EDUCATION** Univ Sofia, Bulgaria, BA, MA (English and German), 66, PhD (English Linguistics), 82. **CAREER** Lect, Univ Sofia, 68-79, senior lect, 79-83; vis lect, Univ Edinburgh, Scotland, 80-81; asst prof, 83-89, assoc prof, 89-92, PROF, UCLA, 92-. **HONORS AND AWARDS** British Coun Res fel, 77-78; Honorary fel, Inst for Advanced Studies in the Humanities, Edinburgh, 80-81; Univ CA Res Fel in the Humanities, 94-95., Exec bd member, Soc for Germanic Philol, 98-; ed bd member, Diachronica, J of English Lang and Lings, Am J of Germanic Lings, J of English Lings, Annotated Bibliography of English Studies, Edinburgh Univ Press, Peter Lang Verlag. **MEMBERSHIPS** Ling Soc Am; Am Dialect Soc; Int Soc for Hist Ling; New Chaucer Soc; Soc for Germanic Philol. **RESEARCH** Hist of the English lang; hist phonology and metrics. **SELECTED PUBLICATIONS** Auth, The History of Final Vowels in English. The Sound of Muting, Topics in English Linguistics 4, Mouton de Gruyter, 91; with Robert Stockwell, Prosody, in A Beowulf Handbook, ed by Robert E. Bjork and John D. Niles, Univ NE Press and Exeter Univ Press, 97; The Credibility of Pseudo-Alfred: Prosodic Insights Into Post-Conquest Mongrel Meter, Modern Philol, Vol 94, no 4, May 97; Constraint Ranking in Middle English Stress-shifting, English Lang and Lings, CA Univ Press, Vol 1, no 1, 97; with Robert Stockwell, The Origins of Short-Long Allomorphy in English, in Advances in English Hist Lings, ed by Jacek Fisiak and Marcin Krygier, Mouton de Gruyter, 98; Velars and Palatals in Old English Alliteration, in Hist Lings 1997, ed by Monika Schmid, Jennifer Austin and Dieter Stein, John Benjamins, 98. **CONTACT ADDRESS** Dept of English, Univ of California, Los Angeles, Los Angeles, CA, 90095. **EMAIL** minkova@humnet.UCLA.edu

MIRAGLIA, ANNE MARIE
DISCIPLINE FRENCH LITERATURE **EDUCATION** Univ Toronto, BA; MA, PhD. **RESEARCH** Contemporary Quebecois novel; literary theory; semiotics; Francophone literatures of Africa and the Caribbean. **SELECTED PUBLICATIONS** Auth, L'Ecriture de l'Autre chez Jacques Poulin, Quebec, 93; pub(s) on Claude Simon, Jacques Poulin, and Dany Laferriere. **CONTACT ADDRESS** Dept of French, Waterloo Univ, 200 University Ave W, Waterloo, ON, N2L 3G1. **EMAIL** ammiragl@watarts.uwaterloo.ca

MISTACCO, VICKI
PERSONAL Born 11/18/1942, Brooklyn, NY **DISCIPLINE** FRENCH LANGUAGE & LITERATURE **EDUCATION** NY Univ, BA, 63; Middlebury Col, MA, 64; Yale Univ, M Phil, 68, PhD, 72. **CAREER** Instr, 68-72, asst prof, 72-78, chmn dept, 78-81, assoc prof, 78-84, Prof French, Wellesley Col, 84-. **HONORS AND AWARDS** Phi Beta Kappa, 62; Fulbright Fel, 63-64; Woodrow Wilson Fel, 64-65, 66-67; NEWH Fel, 83-84, 94-95; Dir, NEH special project, 80-81. **MEMBERSHIPS** MLA; AATF; NE Mod Lang Asn. **RESEARCH** Twentieth century French fiction; theories of reading; narratology; French women writers, Middle Ages to present; Eighteenth Century French fiction. **SELECTED PUBLICATIONS** Auth, Narcissus and the image: symbol and meaning in L'Immoraliste, Ky Romance Quart, 76; co-auth, Interview: Alain Robbe-Grillet, Diacritics, winter 76; auth, Robbe-Grillet's Topologie d'une cite fantome: The theory and practice of reading Nouveaux Romans, In: The Reader in the Text, Princeton Univ, 80; Reading The Immoralist: The relevance of narrative roles, Bucknell Rev, 81; ed, Breaking the Sequence: Women, Literature, and the Future, and transl, To Break the Sequence Inscribe Oneself in the Memory of the Future, In: Breaking the Sequence, Wellesley Col Center Res Women, 82; Le Noeud de Viperes ou les limites de la lisibilite, Cahiers Francois Mauriac, 86; Marguerite Duras, ou les lectures illimitees, Roman, 6/88; Nomadic Meanings: The Woman Effect in La Femme adultere, In: Albert Camus L'Exil et le Royaume: The Third Decade, Les Editions Paratexte, 88; Mama's Boy: Reading Woman in L'Etranger, In: Camus's L'Etranger: Fifty Years On, Macmillan, 92; Plus ca change ...: The Critical Reception of Emily L, French Rev, 10/92; rev, Prevost, Antoine, Histoire d'une Grecque moderne, Flammarion, 90, The Eighteenth Century: A Current Bibliography, 98; Sample Course Outline: Women and the Literary Tradition, Teacher's Guide to Advanced Placement Course in French Literature, Col Entrance Exam Bd and Educ Testing Serv, 94. **CONTACT ADDRESS** Dept of French, Wellesley Col, 106 Central St, Wellesley, MA, 02481-8204. **EMAIL** vmistacco@wellesley.edu

MITCHELL, CHRISTOPHER
PERSONAL Born 11/04/1957, Palo Alto, CA, m, 1977, 2 children **DISCIPLINE** HEBREW **EDUCATION** Univ of WI, BS, 78, MA, 80, PhD, 83 **CAREER** Ed, 89-pres, Concordia Publ Hse; Pastor, 87-89 **HONORS AND AWARDS** Phi Kappi Phi **MEMBERSHIPS** Soc of Bibl Lit **RESEARCH** Hebrew; Old Testament; New Testament; Lutheran Theology **SELECTED PUBLICATIONS** Auth, The Meaning of BRK "to Bless" in the Old Testament, Scholars Press, 87 **CONTACT ADDRESS** 8921 Westhaven Ct, St Louis, MO, 63126.

MITCHELL, DOUGLAS
DISCIPLINE LINGUISTICS, SANSKRIT **EDUCATION** Baylor, BA; Univ TX, PhD. **CAREER** Instr, Rice Univ. **SELECTED PUBLICATIONS** Auth, History of the Latin Language, Tex Educ Agency, 67; coed, Sprung from Some Common Source: Investigations into the Prehistory of Languages, Stanford UP, 91. **CONTACT ADDRESS** Rice Univ, PO Box 1892, Houston, TX, 77251-1892. **EMAIL** douglas@ruf.rice.edu

MOAYYAD, HESHMAT
PERSONAL Born 11/28/1927, Hamadan, Iran, m, 1958, 2 children **DISCIPLINE** ORIENTAL LANGUAGES **EDUCATION** Univ Teheran, LL, 49; Univ Frankfurt, PhD(Persian Lit, Ger), 58. **CAREER** Lectr Persian, Univ Frankfurt, 52-59; lectr, Univ Naples, 60-61, assoc prof, 64-65; lectr, Harvard Univ, 62-63; from asst prof to assoc prof, 65-74, prof Persian Lit, Univ Chicago, 74-. **MEMBERSHIPS** Am Orient Soc; MidE Studies Asn NAm. **RESEARCH** Persian literature and philology; German literature. **SELECTED PUBLICATIONS** Auth, Die Magamat des Gaznawi, Univ Frankfurt, 59; Zum Problemkreis und Stand der Perischen Lexikographie, 62, Nachtrag zum Deutsch-Persischen Worterbuch von Eilers, 62 & Eine Wiedergefundene Schrift uber Ahmad-E Gam und Seine Nachkommen, 64, Annali 1st Univ Napoli; Parvin's poems: A cry in wilderness, In: Festschrift for Prof F Meier, Wiesbaden, Steiner, 73; ed, Faraid-I Chianthi (Medieval text), Vol I & II, Bonyad-I Farhang-1, Iran, 77-78; Once a Dewdrop, Essays on the Poetry of Parvin E'tesami, Mazda Publishers, 94. **CONTACT ADDRESS** Dept of Near East Lang, Univ of Chicago, 1155 E 58th St, Chicago, IL, 60637-1540.

MODER, CAROL LYNN
DISCIPLINE PSYCHOLINGUISTICS AND MORPHOLOGY **EDUCATION** SUNY, Buffalo, PhD, 86. **CAREER** Assoc head, dept Engl, Okla State Univ. **SELECTED PUBLICATIONS** Areas: discourse analysis and language testing. **CONTACT ADDRESS** Oklahoma State Univ, 101 Whitehurst Hall, Stillwater, OK, 74078.

MOELLER, HANS-BERNHARD
PERSONAL Born 06/26/1935, Hannover, Germany, m, 1986, 1 child **DISCIPLINE** GERMAN LITERATURE, EUROPEAN STUDIES **EDUCATION** Knox Col, GA, 60; Univ Southern CA, MA, 62, PhD, 64. **CAREER** Instr, Northwestern Univ, 62-64; asst prof, Univ MD, College Park, 64-66; lectr, Inst Aleman Cult, Goethe Inst, Barcelona, Spain, 67-68; asst prof, Hofstra Univ, 69-70; asst prof, 70-72, Assoc Prof Ger, Univ Tex, Austin, 72-; vis prof, Univ Southern CA, Los Angeles, 74-75; vis prof, Univ Marburg, FRG, 88; Andrew Mellon fel, Univ Pittsburgh, 68-69. **HONORS AND AWARDS** Thyssen res grant, 86; FRG, Ausw Amt Grant f Sesquicentennial, 86; DFG & Thyssen grants for Symposium, 86; Goethe Ins grants, RMMLA, Ger Spec Session on German 20th Century Writers & the Idea of Europe, 90. **MEMBERSHIPS** Ger Studies Asn; Internationale Vereinigung fur germansche Sprach- und Literaturwissenschaft. **RESEARCH** 20th Century lit; exile lit incl Spanish & Slavic exiles in Latin Am; 20th Century novel; Lit in the new Ger cinema; Film hist & genre; comp media criticism. **SELECTED PUBLICATIONS** Auth, Perception, Word-Play and the Printed Page: Arno Schmidt and His Poe Novel, BA, 71; auth, Exilautoren als Drehbuchautoren, In: Die dt Exillit ab 1933 in Kalifornien, Francke, Bern, 73; Feuchtwanger's Rousseau, J Spalek; ed, Latin America and the Literature of Exile: A Comparative View of 20th Century European Refugee Writers in the New World, Heidelberg: Winter Verlag, 82; Der deutsche Film in amerikanischer Forschung und Lehre, Film und Fernsehen in Forschung und Lehre, 84; Fassbinders und Zwerenz im deutschen Aufstieg verlorene Ehe der Maria Braun: Interpretation, vergleichende Kritik und neuer filmishliterarischer Adaptionskontext, Literatur und Film, Franke, Bern, 84; Wirkungsaspekte der Exilliteratur und literarische Aneignung der Asylkultur am Beispiel Argentinien, In: Exil: Wirkung und Wertung (D Daviau, ed), Columbia, SC, 84; West German Women's Cinema: The Case of Margarethe von Trotta, In: Film Criticism, winter 84-85, reprint fall/winter 87; German Hollywood Presence and Parnassus: Central European Exiles and American Filmmaking, Rocky Mountain Rev, 85; Feuchtwanger und Brecht, In: Lion Feuchtwanger: fur die Vernunft (Walter Huder and Friedrich Knilli, ed), Publica, Berlin, 85;

The New German Cinema -- College Course File. Jour Film & Television, spring 86, Erratum, winter 87; The Films of Margarethe von Trotta: Domination, Violence, Solidarity, and Social Criticism, In: Women in German Yearbk, 86; Westdeutscher Film in amerikanischer Forschung und Lehre II, Film und Fernsehen in Foschung und Lehre, 86; Volker Schloendorffs neuere Literaturverfilmungen, In: Kontroversen, alte und neue (Thomas Koebner, Wolhelm Vobkamp and Eberhard Lammert, ed), Medium Film, das Ende der Literatur?, Niemeyer, Tubingen, 86; West German Women's Cinema: The Case of M von Trotta, Film Criticism 10th Anniversary Issue, 87; Der deutsche Film in amerikanischer forschung und Lehre III, FFFL, 88; Productive Filmmaking & Personal Partnership: v Schlondorff and M von Trotta, In: Women in Recent German Films, Special Issue Schatzkammer (Klaus Phillips, ed), 88; Introduction, Alexander Kluge, Case Histories, Holmes & Meier, 88; Deutsche Literatur zur Zeit des Faschismus, In: Geschichte der deutschen Literatur (Ehrhard Bahr, ed), Francke Verlag, Tuebingen, 88; Schlondorff's Adult Children in the Context of the New German Cinema's Portrait of Youth, Germanistische Medienwissenschaft, 89; Fassbinder's Use of Brechtian Aesthetics: The Marriage of Maria Braun, Veronika Voss, Lola, Jump Cut, 90; Co-auth, Frederic Morton, Die deutschsprachige Exilliteratur seit 1933 in New York (John M Spalek and Joseph Strelka, ed), Francke Verlag, Bern, 90; Der deutsche Film in amerikanischer forschung und Lehre IV, FFFL, 91; Frederic Morton, In: Deutschsprachige Exilliteratur (John M Spalek, Konrad Feilchenfeldt and Sandra hawrylchack, ed), Saur, Bern, 94; This Is to Be Seen Dialectically: Schlondorffs 1960er/70er Projekt des Brechtschen Films. Alte Welten - neue Welten, Akten des IX Internationalen Germanisten-Kongresses, Vancouver, Niemeyer, 1996; Literatur/filom-Beziehungen: Frischs Homo faber als Schlondorffs Film, In: Desde la actualidad (Oscar Caeiro and Beatriz Mayor, ed), Cordoba/Argentina: Comunic-Arte Editorial, 98. **CONTACT ADDRESS** Dept of Ger Studies, Univ of Texas, E P Schoch 3 102, Austin, TX, 78712-1026. **EMAIL** h-b.moeller@mail.utexas.edu

MOHLER, STEPHEN CHARLES
PERSONAL Born 11/28/1937, Washington, DC, m, 1959, 3 children **DISCIPLINE** SPANISH & PORTUGUESE LANGUAGES **EDUCATION** George Washington Univ, PhD(Romance lang & lit), 69. **CAREER** Teacher Span, George C Marshall High Sch, 62-70; asst prof Romance lang & lit, Univ NC, Greensboro, 70-76, chmn dept, 74-76; assoc prof, 76-81, PROF MOD FOREIGN LANG, UNIV TN, MARTIN, 82-, Chmn dept, 77-92. **MEMBERSHIPS** SCent Mod Lang Asn; Am Asn Teachers Span & Port. **RESEARCH** Teaching Spanish and Portuguese; Spanish American literature; language teaching methods. **SELECTED PUBLICATIONS** Auth, El Estilo Poetico de Leon de Greiff, Tercer Mundo, 75; coauth, Descubrir y Crear, Harper & Row, 76, 2nd ed, 81, 3rd ed, 86. **CONTACT ADDRESS** Dept of Mod Foreign Lang, Univ of TN, 554 University St, Martin, TN, 38238-0002. **EMAIL** smohler@utm.edu

MOHSEN, RAED
PERSONAL Born 12/15/1959, Lebanon, s **DISCIPLINE** INTERPERSONAL COMMUNICATION **EDUCATION** Bowling Green State Univ, BA 83, pub admin 84, PhD ; Gallaudet Univ, MSW 96. **CAREER** Gallaudet Univ, asst prof, assoc prof, 89-97; Lebanese American Univ, assoc prof, 97-. **HONORS AND AWARDS** Who's Who Among Amer Tchrs. **MEMBERSHIPS** NCA; NASW. **RESEARCH** Intimate Relationships; Communication Practices; Behavior of Deaf People. **SELECTED PUBLICATIONS** Auth, Out on Campus: A Challenging Public Speaking Experience, The Speech Comm Teacher, 93; auth, Communicating Like and Dislikes During the Intimate Encounters of Married Couples, FL Comm Jour, 93; Petitioning Governments for Redress of Grievances: A Communication Approach to Terrorism, Speech and Theater Assoc of MO Jour, 93; auth, Communication Issues in deaf/Hearing Intimate Relationships: Toward A Better Future, A Deaf Amer Mono, 93. **CONTACT ADDRESS** Dept of Communication, Lebanese American Univ, 475 Riverside Dr #1846, New York, NY, 10115-0065. **EMAIL** rmohsen@lau.edu.lb

MONGA, LUIGI
DISCIPLINE FRENCH **EDUCATION** Liceao Manzoni; SUNY Buffalo, MA, 70, PhD, 72. **CAREER** Asst prof, SUNY,Buffalo, 69-76; prof, Vanderbilt Univ, 76-. **CONTACT ADDRESS** 1903 Linden Ave, Nashville, TN, 37212.

MONTGOMERY, MICHAEL M.
DISCIPLINE LINGUISTICS **EDUCATION** Univ Florida, PhD, 79; Univ Tenn-Knoxville, MA, 75; Maryville Col, BA, 73. **CAREER** Univ Florida, asst prof, assoc prof, 86 to 91-; Memphis State Univ, asst prof, 79-81; Univ Arkansas LR, instr, 78-79. **HONORS AND AWARDS** TESOL Lifetime Achv Awd; Forum Res Lang Scot/Ulster Hon Pres. **MEMBERSHIPS** ADS; SCL; LSA; ASA; ACIS; USLS. **RESEARCH** American English Dialects; Appalachian English. **SELECTED PUBLICATIONS** Auth, The Dictionary of Smoky Mountain English, coauth, 98, forthcoming; auth, The Scots Language in Ulster, coauth, The History of Scots, ed, Charles Jones, Edinburgh, Edin U Press, 97; Language Variety in the South: A Retrospective and Assessment, Language Variety in the South Revisited, eds, Cynthia Bernstein, Thomas Nunnally, Robin Sabino, U of Alabama Press, 97; auth, The Rediscovery of Ulster Scots, Englishes Around the World: Festschrift for Manfred Gorlach, ed, Edgar W Schneider, Amsterdam, Benjamins, 97; auth, The Scotch-Irish Influence on Appalachian English: How Broad? How Deep?, Ulster and N Amer: Transatlantic Perspectives on the Scotch-Irish, ed, Curtis Wood, Tyler Blethen, Tuscaloosa, U of Alabama Press, 97; auth, How Scotch-Irish is Your English?, Jour of E Tenn Hist, 96; auth, The Linguistic Value of Ulster Emigrant Letters, Ulster Folklife, 95. **CONTACT ADDRESS** Dept of English, Columbia, SC, 29208. **EMAIL** n270053@univscvm.edu

MONYE, LAURENT
DISCIPLINE FRENCH LANGUAGE AND LITERATURE **EDUCATION** Universite de Nancy II, PhD. **CAREER** Assoc prof Fr; coord Fr prog. **MEMBERSHIPS** CLA; AATF. **SELECTED PUBLICATIONS** Auth, Les Oeuvres de SembFne Ousmane. **CONTACT ADDRESS** Clark Atlanta Univ, 223 James P Brawley Dr, SW, Atlanta, GA, 30314.

MOORE, RAY A.
PERSONAL Born 11/14/1933, Waco, Tex, m, 1957, 2 children **DISCIPLINE** JAPANESE & EAST ASIAN HISTORY **EDUCATION** Univ Mich, AB, 58, MA, 60, PhD(hist), 67. **CAREER** From asst prof to prof, 65-76, dir, Ctr for East Asian Studies, 75-80, chmn dept, 79-80, PROF HIST, AMHERST COL, 76-, Trustee-fac fel, Amherst Col, 68-69; Nat Endowment for Humanities fel, 72-73; Fulbright res fel, Japan, 80-81. **HONORS AND AWARDS** MA, Amherst Col, 76. **MEMBERSHIPS** AHA; Asn Asian Studies. **RESEARCH** Early modern social history of Japan; postwar Japanese intellectual history; American-Japanese relations, 1945-55. **SELECTED PUBLICATIONS** Auth, Reflections on the Occupation of Japan, J Asian Studies, 8/79; The Occupation of Japan as history, Monumenta Nipponica, autumn 81; ed, Religion and Culture in Japanese-American Relations: Essays on Uchimura Kanzo, Univ Mich Ctr for Japanese Studies, 81; The Emperor and the Bible, Kodansha, 82; transl, The Birth of Japan's Postwar Constitution, Westview, 97; co-ed, The Japanese Constitution: A Documentary of it's Framing and Adoption, 1945-1947, Princeton Univ, 98. **CONTACT ADDRESS** Dept of Hist, Amherst Col, Amherst, MA, 01002-5003.

MORAN, THOMAS MORAN
DISCIPLINE CHINESE **EDUCATION** Syracuse Univ, BA, 80; Cornell Univ, MA, 88, PhD, 84. **CAREER** Asst prof, Middlebury Col **RESEARCH** Modern and contemporary Chinese literary. **SELECTED PUBLICATIONS** Transl, The Leader's Demise, In Chinese Lit: The Modern Tradition, Columbia UP, 95; First Person, In Chem Mao Would Not Be Amused: Fiction from Today's China, Grove Press, 95; rev, Modernism and the Nativist Resistance: Contemporary Chinese Fiction from Taiwan by Yvonne Sung-sheng Chang, Australian J Chinese Aff, 95 **CONTACT ADDRESS** Dept of Chinese, Middlebury Col, Middlebury, VT, 05753. **EMAIL** tmoran@middlebury.edu

MORAVCSIK, EDITH ANDREA
PERSONAL Born 05/02/1939, Budapest, Hungary **DISCIPLINE** LINGUISTICS **EDUCATION** Univ Budapest, Hungary, DrDipl(classics), 63; Ind Univ, MA, 68, PhD(ling), 71. **CAREER** Instr classics, Univ Debrecen, Hungary, 63-64 & Vassar Col, 64-66; teaching asst & lectr Hungarian, Ind Univ, 66-68; coordr, Lang Universals Proj, Stanford Univ, 68-72; actg asst prof ling, Univ Calif Los Angeles, 72-74; coordr, Lang Universals Proj, Stanford Univ, 75-76; from asst prof toProf Ling, Univ Wis-Milwaukee, 76-, Ed, Working Papers Lang Universals, 68-76; vis prof ling, Univ Vienna, 74 & 80; consult, Proj Lang Typology & Syntactic Fieldwork, NSF, 76-78; assoc ed, Lang, 81-. **MEMBERSHIPS** Ling Soc Am. **RESEARCH** Language universals; language typology; syntax. **SELECTED PUBLICATIONS** Auth, Agreement, Working Papers Lang Universals, 71; Borrowed verbs, Wiener Ling Gazette, 75; Necessary and possible universals about temporal constituent relations in language, Ind Ling Club, 77; Universals of language contact, Vol I & On the case-marking of objects, Vol IV, In: Universals of Human Language, Stanford Univ Press, 78; co-ed, Universals of Human Language, Vol I-IV, Stanford Univ Press, 78; auth, On the distribution of ergative and accusative patterns, Lingua, 78; co-ed, Current Approaches to Syntax, Acad Press, 80. **CONTACT ADDRESS** Dept of Ling, Univ of Wisconsin, PO Box 413, Milwaukee, WI, 53201-0413. **EMAIL** edith@uwm.edu

MOREY, JAMES
DISCIPLINE ENGLISH LANGUAGE AND LITERATURE **EDUCATION** Hamilton Univ, AB, 83; Cornell Univ, MA, 87; PhD, 90. **CAREER** Fac, Tex Tech Univ; assoc prof/dir undergrad studies, Emory Univ, 94-. **HONORS AND AWARDS** Fulbright scholar, 87-88. **RESEARCH** Old and Middle English, including Chaucer; Old French and Old Norse literature; Renaissance literature with a concentration on religious literature and the vernacular Bible. **SELECTED PUBLICATIONS** Auth, articles in Speculum, JEGP, Studies in Philol, Chaucer Rev, Spenser Studies, and Shakespeare Quart. **CONTACT ADDRESS** English Dept, Emory Univ, 1380 Oxford Rd NE, Atlanta, GA, 30322-1950. **EMAIL** jmorey@emory.edu

MORFORD, JILL P.
DISCIPLINE PSYCHOLINGUISTICS, LANGUAGE ACQUISITION, HOMESIGN SYSTEMS AND SIGNED LANGUA **EDUCATION** Univ Chicago, PhD. **CAREER** Instr, Univ NMex. **RESEARCH** Constituent order in picture pointing sequences produced by speaking children using AAC. **SELECTED PUBLICATIONS** Auth, How to hunt an iguana: The gestured narratives of non-signing deaf children, in H Bos & T Schermer, eds, Sign Language Research 1994: Proc of the 4th Europ Cong on Sign Lang Res in Munich, Signum Press, 95; Insights to language from the study of gesture: A review of research on the gestural communication of non-signing deaf people, Lang and Commun, 16 (2), 96; coauth, The genesis of language: How much time is needed to generate arbitrary symbols in a sign system?, in K Emmorey & J Reilly, eds, Language, Gesture and Space, Lawrence Erlbaum Assoc, 95; From homesign to ASL: Identifying the influences of a self-generated childhood gesture system upon language proficiency in adulthood, in D MacLaughlin & S McEwen, eds, Proc of the 19th Boston Univ Conf on Lang Develop, Cascadilla Press, 95; From here and now to there and then: The development of displaced reference in homesign and English, Child Develop, 68 (3), 97. **CONTACT ADDRESS** Univ NMex, Albuquerque, NM, 87131. **EMAIL** morford@unm.edu

MORGAN, JERRY LEE
PERSONAL Born 06/04/1939, Mt Clemens, MI **DISCIPLINE** LINGUISTICS **EDUCATION** Ind Univ, AB, 66; Univ Chicago, PhD(ling), 73. **CAREER** From instr to asst prof, 70-76, Assoc Prof Ling, Univ Ill, 76-. **RESEARCH** Linguistic theory; pragmatics; computational linguistics. **SELECTED PUBLICATIONS** Co-ed, Speech Acts, In: Vol 3, Syntax and Semantics, Acad Press, 75; auth, Conversational postulate revisited, Language, 77; Two types of convention in indirect speech acts, In: Syntax and Semantics, Vol 9, Acad Press, 78; Auxiliary Inversions And The Notion Default Specification, J Of Linguistics, Vol 0032, 1996. **CONTACT ADDRESS** Dept of Ling, Univ Ill, 707 S Mathews Ave, Urbana, IL, 61801-3625.

MORGAN, LESLIE ZURKER
PERSONAL Born 02/03/1954, Norfolk, VA, m, 1978 **DISCIPLINE** MODERN LANGUAGE & LITERATURE **EDUCATION** Mt Holyoke Col, AB, 74; Middlebury Col, MA, 75; Yale Univ, MA, 77, MPhil, 79, PhD, 83. **CAREER** Lectr to asst prof, 82-89, St Univ NY Stony Brook; asst prof to assoc prof, 89-, Loyola Col Md. **MEMBERSHIPS** AAIS; AATF; AATI; ACH; CALICO; Dante Soc of Amer; IAHS; ICLS; MLA; Societe Rencevals. **RESEARCH** Romance epic; computational philol; computer assisted lang learning. **SELECTED PUBLICATIONS** Coed, The Foreign Language Classroom: Bridging Theory and Practice; Garland Educ Series, 95; ed, Dante: Summa Medioevalis, Filalibrary, 95; auth, Berta ai piedi grandi: Historical Figure and Literary Symbol, Olifant, 94-95; auth, Bovo d'Antona in the Geste Francor: Unity of Composition and Clan Destiny, Italian Culture, 99. **CONTACT ADDRESS** Dept of Modern Lang & Lit, Loyola Col, 4501 N Charles St, Baltimore, MD, 21210-2699. **EMAIL** morgan@vax.loyola.edu

MORGAN, TERRELL A.
DISCIPLINE SPANISH **EDUCATION** Col Wm & Mary, BA, 79; Univ NC, Chapel Hill, MA, 83; Univ Tex, Austin, PhD. 84. **CAREER** Assoc prof, Ohio State Univ, 90-; vis assoc prof, Mich State Univ, 91; asst prof, Ohio State Univ, 84-90; asst instr, Univ Tex, 81-83; teach asst, Univ NC, 79-81; act dhair, dept Span, Port, Ohio State Univ, 91, 94; dir, Ohio State Univ summer sems abroad, 91-. **CONTACT ADDRESS** Dept of Span, Port, Ohio State Univ, 1841 Millikin Rd, Columbus, OH, 43210-1229. **EMAIL** morgan.3@osu.edu

MORITA, JAMES R.
PERSONAL Born 06/13/1931, Salem, OR, 2 children **DISCIPLINE** JAPANESE LITERATURE **EDUCATION** Univ Mich, MA, 59, MA, 60; Univ Chicago, PhD(Far Eastern lang & civilizations), 68. **CAREER** Instr Japanese, Univ Chicago, 66-68, asst prof Japanese lit, 68-69, Japanese librn, Far Eastern libr, 67-69; asst prof Japanese lit, Univ Ore, 69-72; Assoc Prof E Asian Lang & Lit, Ohio State Univ, 72-, Am Coun Learned Soc & Soc Sci Res Coun fel, 70; Japan Found prof fel, 77-78. **MEMBERSHIPS** Asn Teachers Japanese; MLA; Asn Asian Studies. **RESEARCH** Modern Japanese literature, especially poetry. **SELECTED PUBLICATIONS** Auth, Shigaramizoshi, 69, Garakuta bunko, 69 & Shimazaki Toson's four collections of poems, 70, Monumenta Nipponica; Poems of Kaneko Mitsuharu, Lit E & W, 73; The Jojoshi, JAsn Teachers Japanese, 75; Haru to shuts, In: Miyazawa Kenji Kenkyu Sosho, Vol 4, Gakuge Shorin, 75; Soseki no eishi-shiyakn shiron, 1077-178, Hon'yaku no Sekai; Kaneko Mitsuharu, Twayne Pub, 80; 'Shirobamba' - Inoue,Y, World Literature Today, Vol 0066, 1992; 'Naked' - English, Japanese - Tanikawa,S, Elliott,Wi, Kawamura,K, World Literature Today, Vol 0071, 1997; An Anthology Of Contemporary Japanese Poetry - Morton,L, World Literature Today, Vol 0068, 1994; 'Right Under The Big Sky, I Dont Wear A Hat' - The Haiku And Prose Of Hosai,Ozaki - Hosai,O, World Literature Today, Vol 0068, 1994; Like Underground Water - The Poetry Of Mid-20th Century Japan - Koriyama,N, Lueders,E, World Literature Today, Vol 0070, 1996. **CONTACT ADDRESS** Dept of Asian Lang & Lit, Ohio State Univ, Columbus, OH, 43210.

MORNIN, EDWARD
PERSONAL Born 11/27/1938, Greenock, Scotland, m, 1963, 2 children **DISCIPLINE** MODERN GERMAN LITERATURE **EDUCATION** Univ Glasgow, MA, 61, PhD(Ger), 69. **CAREER** Lectr English, Univ Cologne, Ger, 63-64; instr Ger, 65-68, asst prof, 68-77, Assoc Prof Ger, Univ BC, 77-. **MEMBERSHIPS** Can Asn Univ Teachers Ger; Can Comp Lit Asn; MacKay- Gesellschaft. **RESEARCH** German Romanticism19th century; JH Mackay. **SELECTED PUBLICATIONS** Ed, Die Schone Magelone, Reclam, 75; transIr, Outpourings of an Art-Loving Friar, 75 & contribr, Three Eerie Tales From 19th Century German, 75, Ungar; auth, Some patriotic novels and tales by La Motte Fouque, Seminar, 75; Taking games seriously: observations on the German sports-novel, Ger Rev, 76; Art and alienation, In: Franz Sternbald, Mod Lang Notes, 79; Tieck's revision of Franz Sternbald, Seminar, 79; Drinking in Joseph Roth's novels and tales, Int Fiction Rev, 79; Holderlin,Friedrich And Early German Romanticism - German - Roth,S, German Studies Review, Vol 0018, 1995; Wie-Verzweifelnd- Die-Indianer-Pflegen - American-Indians In Chamissos Poetry, Seminar-A J Of Germanic Studies, Vol 0033, 1997. **CONTACT ADDRESS** Dept of Ger Studies, Univ of BC, Vancouver, BC, V6T 1W5.

MORRIS, MARCIA A.
DISCIPLINE RUSSIAN LITERATURE **EDUCATION** Georgetown Univ, BS, 74, MS, 77, MS, 78; Columbia Univ, PhD, 87. **CAREER** Asst prof, 87-93, ASSOC PROF, 93-, GEORGETOWN UNIV. **CONTACT ADDRESS** Dept of Slavic Langs, Georgetown Univ, Washington, DC, 20057-1050. **EMAIL** morrisma@gunet.georgetown.edu

MORRIS, MARGARET LINDSAY
PERSONAL Born 12/23/1950, Princess Anne Co, VA, m, 1984 **DISCIPLINE** SPANISH **EDUCATION** Norfolk State U, BA 1973; Iberian Am Univ Mexico City, 1975; Univ of IL Urbana-Champaign, MA 1974, PhD 1979; Univ of Madrid, summer 1982; Michigan State Univ, summer, 1991. **CAREER** Lincoln U, asst prof of Spanish 1980-; Central State Univ Wilberforce OH, language lab dir 1980; Livingstone Coll Salisbury NC, asst prof 1981-85; Portsmouth City Schools, teacher 1986-; Hampton University, asst prof of Spanish. **HONORS AND AWARDS** Fellowship Univ of IL 1973-74; Fellowship Grad Coll Univ of IL 1975; 1st Black to Receive PhD in Spanish Univ of IL 1979; wrote proposal entitled "Personalizing Instruction in Modern Foreign Langugages" 1982-84; Ford Foundation Fellowship, 1992. **MEMBERSHIPS** Mem Am Assn of Tchr of Spanish & Portuguese 1976-80; mem Am Assn of Univ Prof 1976-80; mem Coll Language Assn 1980; life mem Alpha Kappa Mu Honor Soc 1972-; life mem Sigma Delta Pi Spanish Hon Soc 1974-; life mem Alpha Gamma Mu Spanish Hon Soc 1972-; mem Alpha Kappa Alpha Sor 1983-. **CONTACT ADDRESS** Hampton Univ, Hampton, VA, 23668.

MORRIS, MARSHALL
PERSONAL Born 04/08/1942, Altus, OK **DISCIPLINE** TRANSLATION, SOCIAL ANTHROPOLOGY **EDUCATION** Univ Tex, Austin, BA, 65, MA, 70; Oxford Univ, dipl(social anthrop), 74. **CAREER** Assoc dir honors prog, 72-73, Asst Prof Transl, Univ PR, Rio Piedras, 70-, Asst ed, Rev Interam, 76-. **MEMBERSHIPS** Fel, Royal Anthrop Inst; MLA; Am Translr Asn. **RESEARCH** Sociology of language. **SELECTED PUBLICATIONS** Translr, Jorge Enjoto's On Translation in Three Lectures on Translation, Univ PR, Rio Piedras, 72; Maria de los Angeles Castro de Davila's The Place of San Juan de Puerto Rico Among Hispanic American Cities, Rev Interam, summer 76, San Juan Star, 10977; Amador Cobas' Commentary on Dr Wigner's Article, Rev Interam, winter 76-77; Ismael Rodriquez Bou's Education and Social Change in Puerto Rico: The Role of Education in Puerto Rico, or The Path to Equality of Educational Opportunity, Proc 18th Int Conf Social Welfare, Columbia Univ, 77; Alfonso Garcia Martinez's Prologue, In: The Common Law Zone in Panama: A Case Study in Reception, Inter-Am Univ, 77; Eduardo Forastieri's Garcilaso: Translation and tradition (on some Vergilian texts in the Ecolgue I), in Problems in Translation, 78 & Valentin Garca Yebra's Three Spanish Translations of Voyelles in Problems in Translation, 78, Unv PR, Rio Piedras; Creating A Nation - Grimshaw,P, Lake,M, Mcgrath,A, Quartly,M, Meanjin, Vol 0053, 1994. **CONTACT ADDRESS** MA Prof in Translation, Univ of PR, Box 22613, San Juan, PR, 00931.

MORRIS, WALTER D.
PERSONAL Born 06/24/1929, Austin, TX, m, 1956, 4 children **DISCIPLINE** GERMANIC LANGUAGES & LITERATURES **EDUCATION** Univ Calif, Los Angeles, BA, 49; Univ Tex, Austin, MA, 55, PhD(Ger), 59. **CAREER** Assoc prof Ger, Birmingham-Southern Col, 58-62; assoc prof, Bowling Green State Univ, 62-70; Prof Ger, Iowa State Univ, 70-. **MEMBERSHIPS** MLA; Am Asn Teachers Ger. **RESEARCH** German literature of the 19th century, especially Conrad Ferdinand Meyer; Norwegian literature, especially Ibsen and post World War II. **SELECTED PUBLICATIONS** Auth, The image of America in modern Norwegian literature, Am Scand Rev, fall 68; A forum for the new Norwegian writing, Bks Abroad, fall 68; Tarjei Vesaas, In: Encycl of World Lit, Vol III, 71; Ibsen and ethics of self-realization, Ger Notes, summer 74; Thomas Mann and teachers, Univ Dayton Rev, spring 76; Jens Bjorneboe & Solveig Christov, In: Encycl of World Lit, Vol 1, 2nd ed, 81; coauth (with A T David), Chance, In: Encycl of Statist Sci, Vol 1, 82; 'Fortaering' - Norwegian - Ulven,T, World Literature Today, Vol 0066, 1992; 'Eks Og Sett' - Herbjornsrud,H, World Literature Today, Vol 0067, 1993; 'Tiden' - Hofmo,G, World Literature Today, Vol 0067, 1993; A Circle Of Ice - Norwegian - Vold,Je, World Literature Today, Vol 0068, 1994; 'Han Som Kommer' - Johanssen,T, World Literature Today, Vol 0068, 1994; Collected Poems 1973-1994 - Norwegian - Aamodt,B, World Literature Today, Vol 0070, 1996; 'En Liten Kvast Med Tusenfryd Og Fire Rare Lok' - Unknown Poems And Prose, 1925-1993 - Norwegian - Jacobsen,R, World Literature Today, Vol 0071, 1997; 'Denne Gangen Horer Du Deg Selv', Vol 2, 'Pasjonene' 'Minnetapet' - Norwegian - Kiosterud,E, World Literature Today, Vol 0071, 1997. **CONTACT ADDRESS** Dept of Foreign Lang, Iowa State Univ, Ames, IA, 50010.

MORTIMER, ARMINE KOTIN
PERSONAL Born 05/13/1943, Detroit, MI **DISCIPLINE** FRENCH LITERATURE & CRITICISM **EDUCATION** Radcliffe Col, BA, 64; UCLA, MA, 70; Yale Univ, MPhil, 73, & PhD, 74. **CAREER** From Asst Prof to Assoc Prof, 74-88, Prof French, Univ IL, Urbana-Champaign, 88-; Fel, 77, Assoc, Ctr Advan Study, Univ IL, 99. **MEMBERSHIPS** MLA. **RESEARCH** Analysis of narrative; interpretive theory; 19th & 20th century French lit. **SELECTED PUBLICATIONS** Auth, Pantagruel: language vs communication, Mod Lang Notes, 77; The Narrative Imagination: Comic Tales by Philippe de Vigneulles, Univ Ky, 77; La Maison Nucingen, ou le recit financier, Romanic Rev, 1/78; La lecture de la mort: Le Scarabee d'or d'Edgar Allan Poe, Litterature, 80; Problems of Closure in Balzac's Stories, Fr Forum, 85; La Cluture narrative, Corti, 85; The Gentlest Law: Roland Barthes's The Pleasure of the Text, Lang, 89; Plotting to Kill, Lang, 91; The Devious Second Story-in Kleist's Die Marquise von O, The Ger Quart, 94; Le corset de La Vieille Fille de Balzac, In: L'oeuvre d'identit¤: Essais sur le romantisme de Nodier Baudelaire, Paragraphes 13, Univ Montreal, 96; Dialogues of the Deaf: The Failure of Consolation in Les Liaisons dangereuses, MLN, 96; Naive and Devious: La religieuse, Romanic Rev, 97; Romantic Fever: The Second Story as Illegitimate Daughter in Wharton's Roman Fever, Narrative, 98; auth of numerous other articles and publ. **CONTACT ADDRESS** Dept of French, Univ of Illinois, 707 S Mathews Ave, Urbana, IL, 61801-3625. **EMAIL** armine@uiuc.edu

MOSELEY, MERRITT
PERSONAL m, 4 children **DISCIPLINE** ENGLISH LITERATURE AND LANGUAGE **EDUCATION** Huntingdon Col, BA; Univ NC, Chapel Hill, MA, PhD. **CAREER** Prof, dean, fac develop, Univ NC, Asheville. **SELECTED PUBLICATIONS** Auth, Understanding Julian Barnes, Univ SC Press, 97. **CONTACT ADDRESS** Univ N. Carolina, Asheville, Karpen Hall, Asheville, NC, 28804-8510. **EMAIL** MOSELEY@unca.edu

MOSER, CHARLES A.
PERSONAL Born 01/06/1935, Knoxville, TN **DISCIPLINE** SLAVIC LANGUAGE & LITERATURE **EDUCATION** Yale Univ, BA, 56; Russian Inst, Columbia Univ, MA, 58, PhD, 62. **CAREER** Instr Russ, Yale Univ, 60-63; asst prof Slavic lang, 63-67; assoc prof, 67-77, chmn dept Slavic lang, 69-74, prof Slavic, 77-, chmn Dept, 80-, George Washington Univ. **MEMBERSHIPS** Am Asn Teachers Slavic & East Europ Lang; Am Asn Advan Slavic Studies; Bulgarian Studies Asn (pres, 73-78). **RESEARCH** Russian literature of the 18th century; Russian literature of the 1860's; modern Bulgarian literature. **SELECTED PUBLICATIONS** Ed, the Russian Short Story: A Critical History, Twayne, 86; auth, Esthetics as Nightmare, Princeton, 89; ed, The Cambridge History of Russian Literature, Cambridge, 89, 2d ed, 92. **CONTACT ADDRESS** Pl Narodno subranie 12, Sofia, ..

MOSHI, LIOBA
DISCIPLINE LINGUISTICS **EDUCATION** Univ Dar Es Salaam, Tanzania, BA, 73, MS, 77; Univ York, England, MPhil, 81; Univ Calif, Los Angeles, PhD, 85. **CAREER** Instr, Marangu Teachers Col, Tanzania, 73-74; instr, dept head, Kigoma Sec Sch, Tanzania, 74-75; Instr, Tanzania Civil Svc, Secretarial Col, 75-78; asst res, Univ Dar Es Salaam, Tanzania, 78-79; Instr, Univ York, England, 79-81; teach assoc, Univ Calif, 81-85; res assoc, Ctr Stud Lang, Info, Standord Univ, 86-92; vis lectr, Univ Calif, Berkeley, 85-87; lectr, Stanford Univ, 85-88; asst prof anthropol, 88-91, asst prof, comp lit, 91-94; ASSOC PROF, COMP LIT, 94-, UNIV GA. **CONTACT ADDRESS** African Studies Prog, Univ of Georgia, Athens, GA, 30602.

MOSKOS, GEORGE
PERSONAL Born 10/16/1948, Charleston, SC, d **DISCIPLINE** FRENCH LITERATURE **EDUCATION** Davidson Col, BA, 70; Univ Wis-Madison, MA, 73, PhD(French), 75. **CAREER** Teaching asst, Univ Wis, 73-75; Asst Prof French, Swarthmore Col, 75- **RESEARCH** Flaubert; Stendhal; romanticism. **SELECTED PUBLICATIONS** Auth, Mythe, ecriture et revolution, In: Espagne erivains: Guerre civile, Pantheon Press, Paris, France, 75; coauth, Saint Oedipus: Psychocritical Approaches to Flaubert's Art, Cornell Univ Press, 82; Engendering Power In Hugo,Victor 'Hernani', Neophilologus, Vol 0078, 1994. **CONTACT ADDRESS** Dept Mod Lang & Lit, Swarthmore Col, 500 College Ave, Swarthmore, PA, 19081-1306.

MOSSER, KURT
DISCIPLINE PHILOSOPHY OF LOGIC AND LANGUAGE **EDUCATION** Univ Chicago, PhD, 90. **CAREER** Dept Philos, Univ Dayton **RESEARCH** Kant, epistemology and metaphysics. **SELECTED PUBLICATIONS** Auth, Stoff and Nonsense in Kant's First Critique, Hist Philos Quart, 93; Was Wittgenstein a neo-Kantian? A Response to Prof Haller, Grazer Philos Stud, 93; Kant's Critical Model of the Experiencing Subject, Idealistic Stud, 95. **CONTACT ADDRESS** Dept of Philos, Univ Dayton, 300 Col Park, Dayton, OH, 75062. **EMAIL** mosser@checkov.hm.udayton.edu

MOST, GLENN WARREN
PERSONAL Born 06/12/1952, Miami, FL **DISCIPLINE** COMPARATIVE LITERATURE, CLASSICAL LANGUAGES **EDUCATION** Harvard Univ, AB, 72; Yale Univ, MPhil, 78, PhD(comp lit), 80; Tubingen, WGer, DPhil, 80. **CAREER** Teaching asst philos, Yale Univ, 75, teaching asst lit, 76; teaching asst Latin, Univ Tubingen, 77-78; vis lectr lit theory, Yale Univ, 78-79; teaching asst classics, Univ Heidelberg, 79-80; Mellon Asst Prof Classics, Princeton Univ, 80-, Mellon fel, Am Acad Rome, 82-83. **RESEARCH** Literature; literary theory; philosophy. **SELECTED PUBLICATIONS** Auth, Principled reading, Diacritics, 79; Sappho Fr 16 6-7 LP, Class Quart, 81; Callimachus and Herophilus, Hermes, 81; On the arrangement of Catullus' Carmina Maiora, 81 & Neues Zur Geschichte des Terminus Epyllion, 82, Philologus; contribr, Geschichtsbewusstsein und Rationalitat: Zum Problem der Geschichtlichkeit in der Theoriebildung, Klett-Cotta Verlag, West Ger, 82; Ancient Writers: Greece and Rome, Charles Scribner's Sons, 82; co-ed, G W Leibniz, Specimen Dynamicum, Felix Meiner Verlag, Hamburg, West Ger, 82; Professionalizing Politics, Politicizing The Profession + Differences Between The Current State Of Classics In America And Europe, Transactions Of The American Philological Association, Vol 0122, 1992; A Seminar Held At The International Scholarly Forum In Heidelberg %June 16-18, 1995; On The Theme Of The Theory And History Of The Collection Of Literary Fragments, Organized By Most,Glen,W., Gnomon-Kritische Zeitschrift Fur Die Gesamte Klassische Al Schlegel,Friedrich, Schlegel,August,Wilhelm And The Birth Of The Tragic Paradigm, Poetica-Zeitschrift Fur Sprach-Und Literaturwissenschaft, Vol 0025, 1993; Reading Raphael - The 'School Of Athens' And Its Pre-Text, Critical Inquiry, Vol 0023, 1996. **CONTACT ADDRESS** Dept of Classics, Princeton Univ, Princeton, NJ, 08544.

MOUTSOS, DEMETRIUS GEORGE
PERSONAL Born 11/06/1934 **DISCIPLINE** LINGUISTICS **EDUCATION** Univ Athens, dipl classics, 56; Univ Chicago, AM, 60, PhD(ling), 63. **CAREER** From instr to assoc prof, 63-77, Prof Ling, Univ Rochester, 77-. **MEMBERSHIPS** Ling Soc Am; Am Name Soc. **SELECTED PUBLICATIONS** Auth, The origin of a Balkanism, Z Balkanologie, 69; Romanisn stapin and OChCl stopans, Z Vergleichende Sprachforsch, 70; The origin of a Balkan pastoral term, Sprache, 72; Byzantion, Zietschrift fur Balkanologie, Z Vergleichende Sprachforschung Akten des internationalen Kolloquicuims, Innsbruck, 72; Gothic Puggs And Middle-Greek Poungion, Indogermanische Forschungen, Vol 0098, 1993. **CONTACT ADDRESS** Dept of Foreign Lang Lit & Ling, Univ of Rochester, Rochester, NY, 14627.

MOWRY, HUA-YUAN LI
DISCIPLINE ASIAN AND MIDDLE EASTERN LANGUAGES AND LITERATURES **EDUCATION** Tunghai Univ, BA; Univ Calif Berkeley, MA, PhD. **CAREER** Chr and assoc prof, Dartmouth Col. **HONORS AND AWARDS** EDUCOM Software Awd, 91., Proj dir, Byrne Dictionary; res dir, Dartmouth-at-BNU Prog, 82, 84, 87, 90, 92, and 94. **SELECTED PUBLICATIONS** Auth, Chinese Love Stories from Ch'ing-shih; Yan-pan His--New Theater in China; Hanzi Assistant. **CONTACT ADDRESS** Dartmouth Col, 3529 N Main St, #207, Hanover, NH, 03755.

MOYSEY, ROBERT ALLEN
PERSONAL Born 06/27/1949, Richmond, IN **DISCIPLINE** CLASSICAL LANGUAGES, ANCIENT HISTORY **EDUCATION** Univ Cincinnati, BA, 71; Princeton Univ, MA, 73, PhD(class), 75. **CAREER** Teaching asst class, Princeton Univ, 73-75; vis asst prof, Hamilton Col, 77-78; vis asst prof hist, Univ Del, 79-80; asst prof class, 80-85, assoc prof class, 85-90, prof class, 90-, chair and prof class, Univ Miss, 93-. **HONORS AND AWARDS** Phi Beta Kappa; Charles McMicken Honors Prize. **MEMBERSHIPS** Archaeol Inst Am; Am Philol Asn; Asn Ancient Historians; Am Numis Soc. **RESEARCH** Greek & Persian history, 4th century BC; Greek epigraphy; Greek numismatics. **SELECTED PUBLICATIONS** Auth, The Date of the Strato of Sidon Decree, Am J of Ancient Hist, 76; The Thirty and the Pnyx, Am J of Archaeol, 81; Greek Funerary Monuments in Mississippi, Zeitschrift fur Papyrologie und Epigraphik, 88; Three Fragmentary Attic Inscriptions, Zeitschrift

fur Papyrologie und Epigraphik, 89; Observations on the Numismatic Evidence relating to the Great Satrapal Refolt of 362/1 BC, Revue des Etudes Anciennes, 89; Thucydides, Kimon and the Peace of Kallias, Ancient His Bulletin, 91; Diodoros, the Satraps and the Decline of the Persian Empire: A Book Review of Michael Weiskopf's The So-Called Great Satrapal Revolt 366-360 BC, Ancient Hist Bulletin, 91; A Brief History of Olynthus, Olynthus: An Overview, Univ Miss, 92; Plutarch, Nepos and the Satrapal Revolt of 362/1 BC, Historia, 92. **CONTACT ADDRESS** Dept of Classics, Univ of Mississippi, University, MS, 38677-9999. **EMAIL** clmoysey@olemiss.edu

MOZEJKO, EDWARD
PERSONAL Born 07/15/1932, Czemierniki, Poland, m, 1968, 1 child **DISCIPLINE** COMPARATIVE LITERATURE **EDUCATION** Jagiellonian Univ, MA, 56, PhD(Slavic lit), 64. **CAREER** Asst prof Slavic lit, Jagiellonian Univ, 57-65; lectr, Polish lang & lit, 69-71, assoc prof Russ & comp lit, 71-76, Prof Slavic Lang, Univ Alta, 76-, Alexander von Humboldt fel, Univ Munich, 71-72. **MEMBERSHIPS** Can Asn Slavists; Int Comp Lit Asn. **RESEARCH** Avant-garde trends; theory of literature; eastern-western literary relations in Europe. **SELECTED PUBLICATIONS** Auth, Sztuka pisarska Jordana Jovkova, Polish Acad Sci, 64; Ivan Vazov, Wiedza Pawszech, Warsaw, 67; Expressionism In The Works Of Stefanyk,V. - Ukrainian - Chernenko,O, Canadian Slavonic Papers-Revue Canadienne Des Slavistes, Vol 0035, 1993; Socialist Realism - An Impossible Aesthetic - Robin,R, World Literature Today, Vol 0068, 1994; Die 'Ratte' - Zaniewski,A, Matwinbuschmann,R, World Literature Today, Vol 0069, 1995; Emigration And Tamizdat - Polish - Suchanek,L, Canadian Slavonic Papers-Revue Canadienne Des Slavistes, Vol 0036, 1994; 'Clay And Star' - Contemporary Bulgarian Poets - Sapinkopf,L, Belev,G, World Literature Today, Vol 0068, 1994; 'Szczur' - Zaniewski,A, World Literature Today, Vol 0069, 1995; Poetry - Ukrainian Translation With Preface And Notes By Zujewskyj,Oleh - Ukrainian - Mallarme,S, Canadian Review Of Comparative Literature-Revue Canadienne De Litterature Comparee, Vol 0022, 1995. **CONTACT ADDRESS** Dept of Comp Lit, Univ of Alberta, Edmonton, AB, T6G 2G2.

MUDIMBE, VALENTINE
DISCIPLINE FRENCH AND COMPARATIVE LITERATURE AND LANGUAGE **EDUCATION** BA, 66; Louvain Univ, DPhil, 70. **CAREER** Prof, Stanford Univ. **RESEARCH** Indo-European langs and lits. **SELECTED PUBLICATIONS** Auth, Fables and Parables, 91; Shaba Deux, Paris Presence Africaine, 89; The Invention of Africa, 88. **CONTACT ADDRESS** Stanford Univ, Bldg 20, Main Quad, Stanford, CA, 94305.

MULLEN, KAREN A.
PERSONAL Born 07/05/1941 **DISCIPLINE** ENGLISH, LINGUISTICS **EDUCATION** Grinnell Col, BA, 63; Univ Iowa, MA, 66, PhD(English), 73. **CAREER** Asst rhet, 66-70, asst ling, 70-73, from instr to asst prof ling, 74-75, coord English as foreign lang prog, 75-77, assoc dir, Intensive English Prog, Univ Iowa, 76-78; Assoc Prof & Dir Intensive English, Univ Louisville, 78-, Ed, News lett for spec interest group lang anal & studies humanities, Asn Comput Mach, 71-75; consult ed, Comput & Humanities, 72-75. **MEMBERSHIPS** Asn Teachers English to Speakers Other Lang; Ling Soc Am; MLA; Nat Asn Foreign Student Affairs; Asn Comput Mach. **RESEARCH** Cloze-passage test; relationship between second-language proficiency and intelligence. **SELECTED PUBLICATIONS** Auth, In-core PLI sort and search procedures for lexical data, Siglash Newslett, 73; The Wanderer: Considered again, Neophilologus, 74; Rater reliability and oral proficiency evaluations, Occas Papers Ling, 77; Using rater judgments in the evaluation of writing proficiency for non-native speakers of English, Teaching & Learning English as 2nd Lang: Trends Res & Pract, 77; Direct evaluation of second language proficiency, Lang Learning, 79; More on Cloze tests, Concepts Lang Testing 79; An alternative to the Cloze test, TESOL, 79; Evaluating writing in ESL, chap 15 & Rater reliability and oral proficiency evaluations, chap 8, In: Research in Language Testing, Newbury House, 80; Making Progress In English - Furey,Pr, Menasche,L, Modern Language J, Vol 0077, 1993. **CONTACT ADDRESS** Dept of English, Univ of Louisville, Louisville, KY, 40208.

MULLER, MARCEL
PERSONAL Born 06/02/1926, Forty Fort, PA **DISCIPLINE** FRENCH **EDUCATION** Athenee Royal de Charleroi, Belgium, BA, 44; Univ Liege, MA, 51; Univ Wis, MA, 54, PhD(French), 65. **CAREER** Instr French & Latin, Ill Col, 54-56; teaching asst, Univ Wis, 57-58; instr French & Ger, Lawrence Univ, 58-59; from instr to asst prof French, 61-66; assoc prof, 66-76, Prof French, Univ Mich, Ann Arbor, 76-, mem fac, French School, Middlebury, 72; Nat Endowment for Humanities summer grant, 79; mem, Inst Res in Humanities, Wis, 79-80. **MEMBERSHIPS** Am Asn Teachers French; MLA; Soc Amis Marcel Proust; Int Asn Fr Studies. **RESEARCH** Proust; Valery; structuralism. **SELECTED PUBLICATIONS** Auth, Paul Valery lecteur de Leon Bloy, Romanic Rev, 59; Romananfang und Romanschluss bei Marcel Proust, In: Romananfange: Versuch zu einer Poetik des Romans, Literarisches Colloquium, Berlin, 65; Les voix narratives dans La Recherche du temps perdu, Droz, 65; La naturalisation de Charlus, Poetique, fall 71; Charlus dans le metro, Etudes proustiennes, 78; Ancien Testament et Noveau Testament dans 'A la Recherche du Temps Perdu, French Forum Monogr, 79; La Dialectique De L'ouvert Et Du Ferme Chez Paul Valery, Mich Romance Studies, 80; 1492-1992, Conquest And The Gospel In Latin-America, Questions For Contemporary Europe, French, Etudes Theologiques Et Religieuses, Vol 0068, 1993 **CONTACT ADDRESS** Dept of Romance Lang, Univ of Mich, Ann Arbor, MI, 48109.

MULLER-SIEVERS, HELMUT
DISCIPLINE GERMAN **EDUCATION** Stanford Univ, PhD. **CAREER** Assoc prof, Northwestern Univ. **RESEARCH** Monograph on Georg B chner's physiological writings and an investigation into the aporia of orientation. **SELECTED PUBLICATIONS** Auth, Epigenesis: Naturphilosophie im Sprachdenken Wilhelm von Humboldts; Self-Generation: Biology, Philosophy, and Literature Around 1800; essays on, the history of hermeneutics; Latin and German poetry and poetics; the relation of the natural sciences to philosophy and literature; the hermeneutics of American football. **CONTACT ADDRESS** Dept of German, Northwestern Univ, 1801 Hinman, Evanston, IL, 60208. **EMAIL** hms@nwu.edu

MUMBY, DENNIS K.
DISCIPLINE ORGANIZATIONAL COMMUNICATION, PHILOSOPHY OF COMMUNICATION **EDUCATION** Southern Ill Univ, PhD, 84. **CAREER** Assoc prof, Purdue Univ. **SELECTED PUBLICATIONS** Auth, The Political Function of Narrative in Organizations, Commun Monogr, 87; Communication & Power in Organizations, Ablex, 88; ed, Narrative & Social Control, Sage, 93. **CONTACT ADDRESS** Dept of Commun, Purdue Univ, 1080 Schleman Hall, West Lafayette, IN, 47907-1080. **EMAIL** dmumby@purdue.edu

MUNDT, HANNELORE
DISCIPLINE GERMAN **EDUCATION** Univ CA, Irvine, PhD, 84. **CAREER** Assoc prof; Univ WY, 96-. **RESEARCH** Contemp Ger lit. **SELECTED PUBLICATIONS** Publ on, questions of intertextuality in lit. **CONTACT ADDRESS** Dept of Mod and Class Lang(s), Univ WY, PO Box 3964, Laramie, WY, 82071-3964. **EMAIL** HMUNDT@UWYO.EDU

MUNIR, FAREED Z.
DISCIPLINE ISLAMIC STUDIES **EDUCATION** Univ PA, BA 81; Temple Univ, MA, 88, PhD, 93. **CAREER** Tchg asst, Temple Univ, 88-92; instr, Rowan Col, 91-92; lectr, Thomas Jefferson, Univ Philadelphia, 91-92; instr, Commun Col, 90-92; Philadelphia Hea Counr, 80-92; Camden VCh & mem, City Plan Bd, 82-90; VChp, Human Rights Comt, 96-; mem, Human Rights Comt, 93-, Bd Instr, 94-96, Multicultural Comt, 95-, Search Comt app Dean of the Arts Div, 94-95 & Search Comt app Dir Multicultural Aff, 95-95; internal Rd, Self Stud Report Marketing and Managing Dept, 95; fac adv, Higher Educ Opportunity Prog, 93-, Black and Latino Stud Union, 93- & Freshman stud Arts Div. **MEMBERSHIPS** Am Acad Rel; Islam in Am Conf; Am Coun for the Study of Islamic Soc(s); Muslim Stud Asn of Can & Namerica; Nat Asn Self-Instral Lang Prog; Bonfils Sem. **SELECTED PUBLICATIONS** Auth, Malcolm Xes Religious Pilgrimage: An African American Muslim Transition from Black Separation to Universalism, Westminster John Knox Press, 96; rev, The Muslim Almanac: A Reference Work on the History,Faith, Culture, and Peoples of Islam, Multicultural Rev, 96; other, Martin and Malcolm: Two Sides of the Same Coin, The Times Union, 95. **CONTACT ADDRESS** Dept of Relig Studies, Siena Col, 515 Loudon Rd., Loudonville, NY, 12211-1462.

MUNOZ, WILLY OSCAR
PERSONAL Born 04/06/1949, Cochabamba, Bolivia **DISCIPLINE** LATIN-AMERICAN & SPANISH LITERATURE **EDUCATION** Loras Col, BA, 72; Univ Iowa, MA, 74, PhD(Span), 79. **CAREER** Teaching asst Span, Univ Iowa, 72-76; instr, St Ambrose Col, 76-77; instr English, Centro Boliviano Am, 77; instr Span, Clarke Col, 78-79; lectr Latin Am lit, Inst Idiomas Maryknoll, 79-80; secy, Univ Coun, San Simon, 80; Asst Prof Span, Center Col KY, 81-, Nat Endowment for Humanities fel, 82. **MEMBERSHIPS** Union Nac Poetas Escritores, Bolivia. **RESEARCH** Disintegration in Latin-American fiction: Alejo Carpentier, Julio Cortazar, Jose Donoso; concept of modernity in Latin- American literature; critical studies of Bolivian plays. **SELECTED PUBLICATIONS** Auth, Tecnica narrative de Hijo de opa, Los Tiempos, 178; Medio siglo de milagros, Letras Bolivianas, 1279; Los invasores o el resurgimiento de los espectros del hambre, Los Tiempos, 380; Precursores del teatro boliviano, Presencia, 580; El monje de Potosi de Guillermo Francovich, 580 & Redescubrimiento de Sergio Suarez Figueroa, 580, Facetas, Los Tiempos; La autopista del sur o la epica de la humanidad, Los Tiempos, 980; Teatro boliviano contemporaneo, Casa Municipal Cult Franz Tamayo, 81; Teatro-De-Los-Andes, In Search Of A New Bolivian Theater, Latin American Theater Review, Vol 0027, 1993. **CONTACT ADDRESS** Centre Col, Box 735, Danville, KY, 40422.

MURATORE, MARY JO
PERSONAL Born 08/16/1950, OH **DISCIPLINE** ROMANCE LANGUAGES **EDUCATION** Kent St Univ, 72, MA, 74, Univ Calif David, PhD, 80. **CAREER** Vis asst prof, 79-80, Va Polytechnic Inst, Va St Univ; vis asst prof, 80-83, Purdue Univ; asst prof to assoc prof to prof, 83-, Univ Mo Columbia. **HONORS AND AWARDS** Univ Mo, Kemper Fellow for excellence in teaching & res, 91, Purple Chalk Teaching Award, 84, Prof Develop Award for Discipline Assessment, 90., BA, MA, PhD with honors; Univ Calif Davis Outstanding Doctoral Student Award, 79, Regent's Fel, 79, 80, Patton Res Award, 76. **MEMBERSHIPS** MLA. **RESEARCH** Seventeenth century French literature. **SELECTED PUBLICATIONS** Auth, Mimesis and Metatextuality in the Neo-Classical Text, Droz, 94; auth, The Gender of Truth: Rhetorical Privilege in Tristan's Mariane, Papers on French Seventeenth Century Literature, 97; auth, Stategies of Containement: Repetition as Ideology in Horace, Ramanische Forschungen, 97. **CONTACT ADDRESS** Dept of Romance Languages, Univ of Mo, 143 Arts & Science Bldg, Columbia, MO, 65211. **EMAIL** muratoreM@missouri.edu

MURDICK, WILLIAM
DISCIPLINE RHETORIC AND LINGUISTICS **EDUCATION** SUNY, Albany, BA; Univ IA, MFA; IN Univ PA, PhD. **CAREER** Instr, CA State Univ PA. **SELECTED PUBLICATIONS** Auth, What English Teachers Need to Know about Grammar, Eng J, Nov 96; coauth, Evolution of a Writing Center, Writing Ctr J, 91; Placing Whole Language in a Workshop Setting, Eng Leadership Quart, Dec 91; Art, Writing, and Politics, Art Educ, Sept 92; Journal Writing and Active Learning, Eng Leadership Quart, Oct 93. **CONTACT ADDRESS** California Univ of Pennsylvania, California, PA, 15419s. **EMAIL** murdick@cup.edu

MURDOCH, ADLAI H.
DISCIPLINE FRENCH LITERATURE **EDUCATION** Univ W Indies, BA; Howard Univ, MA; Cornell Univ, PhD. **CAREER** Asst prof, Univ Ill Urbana Champaign. **RESEARCH** French Literature; postcolonial studies; with a special interest in the narratives of the Francophone Caribbean and Francophone West Africa **SELECTED PUBLICATIONS** Auth, pubs on French literature and postcolonial studies, and narratives of Francophone Caribbean and Francophone West Africa. **CONTACT ADDRESS** French Dept, Univ Ill Urbana Champaign, 52 E Gregory Dr, Champaign, IL, 61820. **EMAIL** hmurdoch@uiuc.edu

MURPHY, JOSEPH ANTHONY
PERSONAL Born 03/27/1937, Philadelphia, PA **DISCIPLINE** FOREIGN LANGUAGE EDUCATION, ROMANCE LANGUAGES **EDUCATION** LaSalle Col, BA, 58; Ohio State Univ, PhD(foreign lang educ), 68. **CAREER** Asst prof French, Mich State Univ, 68-70; assoc prof, Lycoming Col, 70-72; Assoc Prof French & Lang Educ, W VA Univ, 72-. **MEMBERSHIPS** Am Asn Teachers Fr; Am Coun Teaching Foreign Lang; Teachers English to Speakers Other Lang. **RESEARCH** Foreign culture and English as second language library reference materials; language teaching methodology; French and English as second language culture reader production. **SELECTED PUBLICATIONS** Coauth, The use of the language laboratory to teach the reading lesson, Mod Lang J, 68; auth, MLA cooperative FL proficiency tests, 7th Mental Measurements Yearbk, 72; A mini- course in problem solving, Foreign Lang Annals, 73; contribr, How to do library research on a foreign culture, Eric Doc, 75; auth, Advanced placement in French literature St national teacher examinations: French, 8th Mental Measurements Yearbk, 78; French Review index of non-literary articles: 1960-79, Fr Rev, 380; ed, Proc Conf Southern Grad Schs, 80-82; auth, Cadres Culturels, Heinle & Heinle (in prep); Quebec Literary Bibliography - A Library Acquisitions Approach, French Review, Vol 0067, 1994; Kaleidoscope - Grammar In Context - French - Hadley,A, Chamberlain,J, Coulonthenderson,F, Chevillot,F, Harbour,L, Modern Language J, Vol 0079, 1995. **CONTACT ADDRESS** Dept of Foreign Lang, W VA Univ, Morgantown, WV, 26506.

MURPHY, LAURENCE LYONS
PERSONAL Born 08/23/1948, New York, NY **DISCIPLINE** COMPARATIVE LITERATURE, PHILOSOPHY **EDUCATION** Rugers Univ, PhD, 90 **CAREER** Asst prof Intellectual Heritage, Philos, Temple Univ, Tyler Sch Art, 91- . **HONORS AND AWARDS** Merit Hons; Violet Keters awd for disting Srv and tchg. **MEMBERSHIPS** Amer Philos Asn **RESEARCH** Phenomenology, Hermeneutics. **SELECTED PUBLICATIONS** Exec ed, Ellipses, Jour Arts and Ideas. **CONTACT ADDRESS** Dept of Art, Temple Univ, 7900 Old York Rd, No 308A, Elkins Park, PA, 19027. **EMAIL** lmurphy@erols.com

MURSTEIN, NELLY KASHY
PERSONAL Born 04/13/1932, Bagdad, Iraq, m, 1954, 2 children **DISCIPLINE** FRENCH **EDUCATION** Univ Paris, BA, 49; Univ Tex, BA, 53; Rice Univ, MA, 53, PhD, 60. **CAREER** Lectr French, Univ Portland, 59-60; instr, Reed Col, 61-62; from instr to assoc prof, 62-76, chmn dept French & Ital, 70-74 & 80-82, Prof French, Conn Col, 76-. **MEMBERSHIPS** Am Asn Teachers French; Am Asn Dept Foreign Lang. **RE-**

SEARCH Contemporary theatre and poetry. **SELECTED PUBLICATIONS** Auth, Jean Giraudoux: A passing fad?, New Theater Mag, summer 69; Une entrevue avec Eugene Ionesco, French Rev, 2/72; L'Etrange Electra de J Giraudoux, Rice Univ Studies, summer 73. **CONTACT ADDRESS** Dept of French & Ital, Connecticut Col, 270 Mohegan Ave, Box 1503, New London, CT, 06320-4125. **EMAIL** nkmur@conncoll.edu

MUSA, MARK
DISCIPLINE ITALIAN LITERATURE **EDUCATION** Johns Hopkins Univ, PhD, 61. **CAREER** Prof. **HONORS AND AWARDS** Distinguished Tchg Mentoring Awd. **RESEARCH** Dante and Medieval literature. **SELECTED PUBLICATIONS** Ed, The Divine Comedy, Petrarch's Canzoniere, Pirandello's Six Characters in Search of an Author. **CONTACT ADDRESS** Dept of French and Italian, Indiana Univ, Bloomington, 300 N Jordan Ave, Bloomington, IN, 47405.

MUST, GUSTAV
PERSONAL Born 02/02/1908, Estonia, m, 1939 **DISCIPLINE** GERMANIC PHILOLOGY, COMPARATIVE LINGUISTICS **EDUCATION** Tartu State Univ, PhM, 38; Univ Gottingen, PhD, 49. **CAREER** Teacher Ger & Estonia, col, Estonia, 34-44; asst prof Ger philol, Baltic Univ, Ger, 46-49; res assoc mod lang, Cornell Univ, 52; asst prof Ger, Baldwin-Wallace Col, 56-57; from asst prof to assoc prof, Augustana Col, Ill, 57-60, head dept, 57-60; assoc prof, Univ Conn, 60-62; assoc Prof, 62-68, res, prof, 67- 70, prof, 68-78, Emer Prof Ger, Valparaiso Univ, 78-, Am Coun Learned Soc fel, 50-51. **MEMBERSHIPS** MLA; Ling Soc Am. **RESEARCH** Germanic and other Indo-European languages; West Finnic languages; comparative philology. **SELECTED PUBLICATIONS** Auth, The origin of the Germanic dental preterit, Language, 51, 52; The problem of the inscription on helmet B of Negau, Harvard Studies Class Philol, 57; The origin of the German word Ehre, PMLA, 6 1; The spelling or Proto-Germanic f in Old High German, Language, Vol 43; Das St Galler Paternoster, Akten des V Int Germanisten-Kongresses Cambridge 1975, 76; Das ST Galler Credo, Fruhmittelalterliche Studien 15, 81; The Origins of The Word Deutsch, German, Indogermanische Forschungen, Vol 0097, 1992. **CONTACT ADDRESS** 1953 Lawndale Dr, Valparaiso, IN, 46383.

MUYSKENS, JUDITH ANN
PERSONAL Born 06/05/1948, Holland, MI **DISCIPLINE** FOREIGN LANGUAGE EDUCATION, FRENCH CIVILIZATION **EDUCATION** Cent Col, BA, 70; Ohio State Univ, MA, 73, PhD(lang educ), 77. **CAREER** Instr French & educ, Va Polytech Inst & State Univ, 76-77, asst prof, 77-79; Asst Prof French, Univ Cincinnati, 78- **MEMBERSHIPS** MLA; Am Asn Teachers Fr; Am Coun Teaching For Lang; Am Asn Univ Supervisors & Coordrs Foreign Lang Prog. **SELECTED PUBLICATIONS** Coauth, French women in language textbooks: The fiction and the reality, Contemp Fr Civilization, fall 77; A personalized approach to the teaching of literature at the elementary and intermediate levels of instruction, For Lang Ann, 280; Rendez- vous: An Invitation to French, 81 & Rendez-vous: Anthologic Litteraire, 82, Random House; University and secondary school articulation: Four steps for creating a resource network, In: ESL and the Foreign Language Teacher, Nat Textbook Co, 82; Priorities For Intermediate-level Language Instruction, Modern Language J, Vol 0078, 1994. **CONTACT ADDRESS** Dept of Romance Lang & Lit, Univ of Cincinnati, P O Box 210377, Cincinnati, OH, 45221-0377.

MYERS, EUNICE DOMAN
PERSONAL Born 12/01/1948, Lexington, NC, m, 1969, 1 child **DISCIPLINE** SPANISH LITERATURE & LANGUAGE **EDUCATION** Univ NC, Chapel Hill, BA, 71, MA, 73, PhD(Romance lang), 77. **CAREER** Teaching asst Span, Univ NC, Chapel Hill, 71-76; vis instr, NC State Univ, 76-77, asst prof, 77-81; Asst Prof Span, Wichita State Univ, 81-, Consult & reviewer, Eirik Borve Inc, 77- & Scott Foresman, 78- **MEMBERSHIPS** Am Asn Teachers Span & Port; MLA; Asoc Pensamiento Hisp. **RESEARCH** Modern Spanish novel; modern women authors from Spain especially Rosa Chacel; Ramon Perez de Ayala's essays. **SELECTED PUBLICATIONS** Auth, Tradition and modernity in Perez de Ayalas literary theories, Critica Hisp, Vol II, No 1; contribr, Sentimental Club: Un cuento filos ofico de Ramon Perez de Ayala, In: Simposio Int Ramon Perez de Ayala, Imprenta Flores, Gijon, 81; La 'Perla Del Oriente' - Ordaz,j, Hispania-a J Devoted to The Teaching of Spanish And Portuguese, Vol 0078, 1995; El 'Corazon Inmovil' - Spanish - Egido,lg, Hispania-a J Devoted to The Teaching of Spanish And Portuguese, Vol 0080, 1997; The 'Maravillas District' - Spanish - Chacel,r, Demers,da, Hispania-a J Devoted to The Teaching of Spanish And Portuguese, Vol 0078, 1995; The Canon - Meditations on Its Literary And Theatrical Reception Perezdeayala With Regard to Benavente - Spanish - Gonzalezdelvalle,lt, Hispania-a J Devoted to The Teaching of Spanish And Portuguese, Vol 0078, 1995; The Canon - Meditations on Its Literary And Theatrical Reception Perezdeayala With Regard to Benavente - Spanish - Gonzalezdelvalle,lt, Hispania-a J Devoted to The Teaching of Spanish And Portuguese, Vol 0078, 1995; El 'Corazon Inmovil' - Spanish - Egido,lg, Hispania-a J Devoted to The Teaching of Spanish And Portuguese, Vol 0080, 1997. **CONTACT ADDRESS** Dept of Romance Lang, Wichita State Univ, Wichita, KS, 67208.

N

NABARRA, ALAIN
DISCIPLINE FRENCH LANGUAGE **EDUCATION** Univ Sorbonne, Paris, MLit, DES, LL. **CAREER** Assoc prof, 68-. **SELECTED PUBLICATIONS** Auth, Dictionnaire de la presse de langue francaise 1600-1784, Oxford and Paris, 91; Women Intellectuals of the French Eighteenth Century, NY, 94; La lettre au XVIIIe siecle, Toronto, 96. **CONTACT ADDRESS** Dept of Lang, Lakehead Univ, 955 Oliver Rd, Thunder Bay, ON, P7B 5E1. **EMAIL** ANABARRA@Mist.Lakeheadu.Ca

NAESS, HARALD S.
PERSONAL Born 12/27/1925, Oddernes, Norway, m, 1950, 3 children **DISCIPLINE** SCANDINAVIAN STUDIES **EDUCATION** Univ Oslo, Cand Phil, 52. **CAREER** Lector Norweg, King's Col, Univ Durham, 53-58, lectr, 58- 59; vis lectr, 59-61, assoc prof, 61-67, Torger Thompson Prof Scand Studies, Univ Wis-Madison, 67-, Fulbright scholar, 59-61; mem ed comt, Nordic Trans Serv, Univ Wis, 64-; ed, Scand Studies, 73-77. **MEMBERSHIPS** Soc Advan Scand Studies; Norweg-Am Hist Soc. **RESEARCH** Scandinavian, particularly Norwegian, eighteenth and nineteenth century literature; American-Norwegian Immigration history. **SELECTED PUBLICATIONS** Auth, Knut Hamsuns brevveksling med postmaster Frydenlund (1862-1947), 59 & Forsok over Vesaas' prosastil, 62, Edda; Knut Hamsun og Amerika, Gyldendal, 69; ed, Norway number, Lit Rev, 69; co-ed, Americana-Norvegica III, 71 & auth, Norsk litteraturhistorisk bibliografi, 75, Universitetsforlaget; Norwegian Influence on the Upper Midwest, Univ Minn, 76; Denmark - Miller,ke, Scandinavian Studies, Vol 0065, 1993; Sweden - Sather,lb, Swanson,a, Scandinavian Studies, Vol 0065, 1993; a Bright Flash of Light - Abel,niels,henrik And His Times - Norwegian - Stubhaug,a, Scandinavica, Vol 0036, 1997. **CONTACT ADDRESS** Dept of Scand Studies, Univ Wis, Madison, WI, 53706.

NAFF, WILLIAM E.
PERSONAL Born 02/14/1929, Wenatchee, WA, m, 1957 **DISCIPLINE** JAPANESE **EDUCATION** Univ Wash, MA, PhD(Japanese lang), 66. **CAREER** Asst Japanese, Univ Calif, Los Angeles, 58-59; lectr, Stanford Univ, 59-60; from asst prof to assoc prof, Univ Ore, 62-69; assoc prof, 69-80, Prof Asian Studies & Chmn Prog, Univ Mass, Amherst, 80-, Dir ctr Japanese studies, Univ Ore, 65-66 & 67-68. **MEMBERSHIPS** Asn Asian Studies; Asn Teachers Japanese. **RESEARCH** Japanese language; history of Japanese literature; modern Japanese literature. **SELECTED PUBLICATIONS** Auth, Shimazaki Toson, an introduction, Univ Wash; Toson The 'Three' + Translating Shimazaki,toson 'Sannin', Literary Review, Vol 0039, 1996. **CONTACT ADDRESS** Asian Studies Prog, Univ of Massachusetts, Amherst, MA, 01002.

NAGEL, ALAN FREDERICK
PERSONAL Born 03/09/1941, Beverly, MA, m, 1973 **DISCIPLINE** COMPARATIVE LITERATURE, ENGLISH **EDUCATION** Harvard Col, BA, 63; Cornell Univ, MA, 65, PhD(comp lit), 69. **CAREER** Asst prof, 69-72, chmn, Grad Prog, 71-75, assoc prof, 72- 80, Prof English & Comp Lit, Univ Iowa, 80-, Chmn, BA Lett, Univ Iowa, 71-81, chmn, Interdiscipline Prog Lit, Sci & Arts; vis prof, Univ Paul Valery, Montpelier, France, fall, 82. **MEMBERSHIPS** MLA; Am Comp Lit Asn; Midwest Mod Lang Asn. **RESEARCH** Poetics; Renaissance literature, literary theory. **SELECTED PUBLICATIONS** Co-ed, The Three Crowns of Florence: Humanist Assessments of Dante, Petrarca, Boccaccio, Harper, 72; auth, Lies and the limitable inane Contradiction in More's Utopia, Renaissance Quart, 73; Literary and historical context in Ronsard's Sonnets pour Helene, Pub Mod Lang Asn, 79; Rhetoric, value and action in Alberti, Mod Lang Notes, 80; 'Mastro Don Gesualdo', Gender, Dialect, And The Body, Stanford Italian Review, Vol 0011, 1992; Countercurrents - on The Primacy of Texts in Literary-criticism - Prier,ra, Comparative Literature Studies, Vol 0031, 1994. **CONTACT ADDRESS** Dept of Comp Lit, Univ of Iowa, 308 English Phil Bld, Iowa City, IA, 52242-1492.

NAGELE, RAINER
PERSONAL Born 08/02/1943, Triesen, Liechtenstein, m, 1971 **DISCIPLINE** GERMAN LITERATURE, LITERARY THEORY **EDUCATION** Univ Calif, Santa Barbara, PhD, 71. **CAREER** Asst prof Ger, Univ Iowa, 71-74; assoc prof Ger lit, Ohio State Univ, 75-77; Assoc Prof Ger Lit, Johns Hopkins Univ, 77-. **MEMBERSHIPS** MLA; Am Asn Teachers Ger. **RESEARCH** German literature of the 20th century; German literature from 1700 to present; literary theory and aesthetics. **SELECTED PUBLICATIONS** Auth, Zwischen Erinnerung und Erwartung: Gesellschaftskritik u Utopie bei M Walser, Basis, 72; Theater und keqn Gutes: Theatersymbolik u Rollenpsychologie in Heinrich Mann, Colloquia Germanica, 73; Die Vermittelte Welt Fiktion u Wirklichkeit, JDeutschen Schillergesellsch, 75; Hermetik u Offentlichkeit, Holderlix J1920, 75-77; Heinrich Boll Einfuhrung in das Werk u Forschung, Fischer-Athenaum, Frankfurt, 76; Literatur u Utopie Versuche zu Holderlin, Lothar Stiehm, Heidelberg, 78; Peter Handke, Beck, Munchen, 78; Freud und die Topologie des Testes, Mod Lang Notes, 78; The Poetic Ground Laid Bare Benjamin Reading Baudelaire, Diacritics-a Review of Contemporary Criticism, Vol 0022, 1992. **CONTACT ADDRESS** Dept of Ger, Johns Hopkins Univ, 3400 N Charles St, Baltimore, MD, 21218-2680.

NAGEM, MONIQUE F.
PERSONAL Born 05/24/1941, Paris, France, m, 1964 **DISCIPLINE** COMPARATIVE LITERATURE **EDUCATION** Univ Tex at Austin, PhD, 86. **CAREER** Prof, McNeese State Univ, 81-. **MEMBERSHIPS** Am Translators Asn; Am Lit Translators Asn; Women in French; Am Asn of Tchrs of French. **RESEARCH** Translation. **SELECTED PUBLICATIONS** Auth, Chantal Chawaf: en quete des origines, d'un lieu mythique, Mythes dans litterature contemporaine d'expression francaise, Univ Ottawa, 94; auth, Chantal Chawaf's Redemptive Literature, Continental, Latin American and Francophone Women Writers, Vol IV, Wichita State Univ, 97. **CONTACT ADDRESS** Dept of Languages, McNeese State Univ, Lake Charles, LA, 70609-2655. **EMAIL** mnagem@mail.mcneese.edu

NAGLE, BETTY ROSE
DISCIPLINE CLASSICAL STUDIES **EDUCATION** Univ Pa, BA, 70; Univ Ind, PhD, 75. **CAREER** Prof. **SELECTED PUBLICATIONS** Auth, Ovid's Fasti: Roman Holidays, Ind Univ, 95; Ovid: Fasti V, Bryn Mawr, 96. **CONTACT ADDRESS** Dept of Classical Studies, Indiana Univ, Bloomington, 300 N Jordan Ave, Bloomington, IN, 47405.

NAGLER, MICHAEL NICHOLAS
PERSONAL Born 01/20/1937, New York, NY, m, 1959, 2 children **DISCIPLINE** CLASSICAL LITERATURE AND SOCIETY **EDUCATION** NY Univ, BA, 60; Univ Calif, Berkeley, MA, 62, PhD(comp lit), 66. **CAREER** Instr foreign lang, San Francisco State Col, 63-65; asst prof, 65-73, humanities res fel, 68-69, Assoc Prof Classics & Comp Lit, Univ Calif, Berkeley, 73-, Am Coun Learned Soc study grant, Sanskrit lang & lit, 71-72. **MEMBERSHIPS** Am Philol Asn; Int Comp Lit Asn. **RESEARCH** Oral poetry, chiefly Homer, Old English and Sanskirt; myth and religion; peace and conflict studies. **SELECTED PUBLICATIONS** Auth, Towards a generative view of the Homeric formula, Trans Am Philol Asn, 67; Oral poetry and the question of originality in literature, Proc Vth Cong Int Comp Lit Asn, 67; Spontaneity and Tradition: A Study of Homer's Oral Art, Univ Calif, 74; Dread goddess endowed with speech, Archaeol News, 77; Mysticism: A hardheaded definition for a romantic age, Study Mystica, 78; Peace as a paradigm shift, Bull Atom Scientists, 81; America Without Violence, Island Press, 82; Epic Singers And Oral Tradition - Lord,ab, Classical J, Vol 0087, 1992; Discourse And Conflict Hesiod - Eris And The Erides, Ramus- critical Studies in Greek And Roman Literature, Vol 0021, 1992; Penelope Male Hand - Gender And Violence in The 'Odyssey', Colby Quarterly, Vol 0029, 1993. **CONTACT ADDRESS** Dept of Classics, Univ of Calif, Berkeley, CA, 94720.

NAGY, EDWARD
PERSONAL Born 09/27/1921, Yugoslavia, m **DISCIPLINE** ROMANCE LANGUAGES **EDUCATION** Univ Zagreb, Can Zwv, 45; Univ Madrid, Lic, 50, PhD, 52. **CAREER** Instr Span & Ital, 56-60, from asst prof to assoc prof Span, 60-67, dir Span grad prog, 67-81, Prof Span, Rutgers Univ, New Brunswick, 67-. **MEMBERSHIPS** MLA; Am Asn Teachers Span & Port; Cervantes Soc Am. **RESEARCH** Picaresque novel and drama of the Spanish Golden Age. **SELECTED PUBLICATIONS** Auth, Rodrigo Fernandez de Ribera, El meson de mundo, 63, Miguel de Cervantes, Pedro de Urdemalas, 65, Las Americas; Lope de Vega y la Celestina, Univ Veracruzana, Mex, 68; El anhelo del Guzman de Aleman de conocer su sangre, Ky Romance Quart, 69; La parodia y la satira en El alcaide de si mismo de Pedro Calderon de la Barea, Romanische Forschungen, 71; El Prodigo ye el Picaro, Ed Sever-Cuesta, Valladolid, 74; El galeote de Lepanto de Luis Velez de Guevara: la diversion en vez del escarmiento, Bull of Comediantes, 77; ed, Miguel de Cervantes, El Rufian Dichoso, Ediciones Catedra, Madrid, 77; La picardia castrense en Flandes y su utilizacion por Lope de Vega, Lope de Vega y los origenes del Teatro Espanol, Actas del I Congreso Internacional sobre Lope de Vega, Patronato Archipreste de Hita, Madrid, 81; The Relationship Between Royalty And Craftiness in El 'Principe Don Carlos' of Jimenezdeenciso,diego + The Picaresque Philosophy of Tejoletas And Its Influence on Don-carlos, Bulletin of The Comediantes, Vol 0046, 1994. **CONTACT ADDRESS** Dept of Span & Port, Rutgers Univ, New Brunswick, NJ, 08903.

NAGY, GREGORY JOHN
PERSONAL Born 10/22/1942, Budapest, Hungary **DISCIPLINE** CLASSICS, LINGUISTICS **EDUCATION** Ind Univ, AB, 62; Harvard Univ, PhD(classics), 66. **CAREER** Instr classics & ling, Harvard Univ, 66-69, asst prof classics, 69-73; from assoc prof to prof, Johns Hopkins Univ, 73-75; Prof Classics, Harvard Univ, 75- **MEMBERSHIPS** Am Philol Asn; Ling Soc Am. **RESEARCH** Greek literature; Indo-European linguistics; poetics. **SELECTED PUBLICATIONS** Auth, Observations on the sign-grouping and vocabulary of linear A, Am J Archaeol, 65; On dialectal anomalies in Pylian texts, Atti Memorie

1st Cong Int Micenologia, 68; Greek Dialects and the Transformation of an Indo-European Process, Harvard Univ, 70; coauth, Greek: A Survey of Recent Work, Mouton, The Hague: 73; auth, Phaethon, Sappho's Phaon, and the White Rock of Leukas, Harvard Studies Class Philol, 73; Comparative Studies in Greek and Indic Meter, Harvard Univ, 74. **CONTACT ADDRESS** Dept of Classics, Harvard Univ, 204 Boylston Hall, Cambridge, MA, 02138-3800. **EMAIL** gnagy@fas.harvard.edu

NAGY, MOSES MELCHIOR
PERSONAL Born 01/05/1927, Hadikfalva, Romania **DISCIPLINE** ROMANCE LANGUAGES **EDUCATION** Marquette Univ, MA, 56; Laval Univ, PhD(French), 60; Sorbonne, dipl French lang & lit, 66. **CAREER** Chmn dept, 65-76, Prof French, Univ Dallas, 65-, Pres, Cercle Francais, Dallas, 70; vp, Alliance Francaise, Dallas, 72; ed-in-chief, Claudel Studies, 72- **MEMBERSHIPS** MLA; Am Asn Teachers French; SCent Mod Lang Asn; Paul Claudel Soc Am. **RESEARCH** French Catholicism and literature; surrealism; La Joie dans l'oeuvre de Claudel. **SELECTED PUBLICATIONS** Auth, Claudel's Immortal Heroes, Am Benedictine Rev, 672; Report on rencontres internationales Claudeliennes de Branques, Claudel Studies, spring 73; Claudel: From the Absurd of Death to the Joy of Life, Rev Nat Lit, fall 73; International-colloquium on Claudel,paul Les 'Odes' + Toronto, October 22-23, 1993, Claudel Studies, Vol 0020, 1993; The Marvels of Tragic Life - Zaza-mabille %Lacoin And Claudel, Claudel Studies, Vol 0022, 1995; The Franco-german Conflict Seen by Lacoin,zaza Elizabeth 1928-1929, Claudel Studies, Vol 0023, 1996; La 'Crise' - Diplomatic Correspondence - America, 1927-1932 - French - Claudel,p, Claudel Studies, Vol 0021, 1994; 2 Experiences of Spiritual Pilgrimage, 'Israel' And The 'Apocalypse', Claudel Studies, Vol 0021, 1994; Claudel,paul 'Partage De Midi' - French - Antoine,g, Claudel Studies, Vol 0021, 1994; Understanding French Poetry, Essays For a New Millennium - Metzidakis,s, Claudel Studies, Vol 0023, 1996; Claudel,paul Silent Dialog With The 3rd-repubic of France, Claudel Studies, Vol 0024, 1997; Great Readers And Readings of Claudel - Introduction, Claudel Studies, Vol 0024, 1997. **CONTACT ADDRESS** Dept of Languages, Univ of Dallas, PO Box 1330, Irving, TX, 75060.

NAHRGANG, WILBUR LEE
PERSONAL Born 06/06/1939, Iowa Park, TX, m, 1964 **DISCIPLINE** MODERN GERMAN LITERATURE **EDUCATION** Texas Christian Univ, BA, 60; Univ Kans, MA, 63, PhD, 66. **CAREER** From instr to assoc prof, 65-69, Assoc Prof Ger, North Tex State Univ, 69-, Co-ed, Schatzkammer, 77-. **MEMBERSHIPS** Am Asn Teachers Ger; Am Coun Teaching Foreign Lang; MLA Western Asn Ger Studies. **RESEARCH** Heinrich Boll and his works; German novels of World War II. **SELECTED PUBLICATIONS** Heinrich Boll's war books: A study in changing literary purpose, Mod Lang Notes, 10/73. **CONTACT ADDRESS** Dept of Foreign Lang & Lit, No Texas State Univ, P O Box 311127, Denton, TX, 76203-1127. **EMAIL** nahrgang@unt.edu

NAHSON, DANIEL L.
DISCIPLINE SPANISH **EDUCATION** Hebrew Univ Jerusalem, BA, 85, Columbia Univ, MA, 90; Mphil, 92; PhD, 95. **CAREER** Vis asst prof, Williams Col, 98. **HONORS AND AWARDS** Span Embassy Dissertation res grant, 93; Jewish Theol Sem Am Res Asst Scholar, 90. **RESEARCH** Spanish language and culture; contemporary Latin American literature. **SELECTED PUBLICATIONS** Auth, Fray Luis de Leon's translation and interpretation of the Song of Songs: Subversive didacticism in the vernacular, in Criticon and presented at the IV Congreso de la Asociacion Int del Siglo de Oro, 96. **CONTACT ADDRESS** Center for Foreign Languages, Literatures and Cult, Williams Col, Williamstown, MA, 01267. **EMAIL** Daniel.H.Nahson@williams.edu

NAIM, CHOUDHRI MOHAMMED
PERSONAL Born 06/03/1936, Bara Banki, India, 2 children **DISCIPLINE** URDU LANGUAGE & LITERATURE **EDUCATION** Univ Lucknow, BA, 54, MA, 55; Univ CA, Berkeley, MA, 61. **CAREER** From instr to asst prof, 63-71, Assoc Prof Urdu, Univ Chicago, 71-; Co-ed, J South Asian Lit, 63-78; reader Urdu, Aligarh Muslim Univ, India, 71-72. **MEMBERSHIPS** Asn Asian Studies. **RESEARCH** Cultl hist of Muslim South Asia; Muslim society in India, Pakistan and Bangladesh. **SELECTED PUBLICATIONS** Ed, Readings in Urdu: Prose and Poetry, East-West, Honolulu, 65; auth, The consequences of Indo-Pakistani war for Urdu language and literature, J Asian Studies, 69; Arabic orthography and some non-Semitic languages, In: Islam and Its Cultural Divergence, Univ Ill, 71; Yes, the poem itself, Lit East & West, 72; Muslim contribution to literature in India: The Medieval period, Encycl Brittanica, 15th ed, 74; Muslim press in India and the Bangladesh crisis, Quest, 75; Introductory Urdu (2 vols), Cosas, 75. **CONTACT ADDRESS** Dept of S Asian Lang, Univ of Chicago, 1130 E 59th St, Chicago, IL, 60637-1539. **EMAIL** naim@midway.uchicago.edu

NAKAYAMA, MINEHARU
PERSONAL Born 12/11/1958, Nagano, Japan, m, 1992 **DISCIPLINE** LINGUISTICS **EDUCATION** Waseda Univ, Tokyo, Japan, BA, 83; Univ Ct, MA, 86, PhD, 88. **CAREER** Lectr, Univ Ct, 84-86; vis instr, Ct Col, 85-88; asst prof to assoc prof, Oh St Univ, 94- . **HONORS AND AWARDS** Waseda Univ Centennial Celebration Awards for Study Papers, 82; Rotary Found Award, 83; Extraordinary Expenses Award, Res Found, Univ Ct, 87; Off of Int Educ Outstanding Int Faculty Award, Oh St Univ, 98. **MEMBERSHIPS** Assoc for Asian Stud; Assoc of Teachers of Japanese; Ling Soc of Amer; Lake Erie Teachers of Japanese. **RESEARCH** Psycholinguistics; syntax; learnability; lang teaching. **SELECTED PUBLICATIONS** Auth, Acquisition of Japanese Empty Categories, Kuroshio Publ, 96; Empty categories and argument structures, in Formal Approaches to Japanese Ling, MIT Working Papers in Ling, 96; Numeral Classifier Systems: The Case of Japanese by Pamela Downing, Modern Lang J, 97; An Introduction to Japanese Ling by Natsuko Tsujimura, Modern Lang J, 98; Sentence processing, in A Handbook of Japanese Linguistics, Blackwell, 99. **CONTACT ADDRESS** Dept of East Asian Lang & Lit, Ohio State Univ, 204 Cunz Hall, 1841 Millikin Rd, Columbus, OH, 43210. **EMAIL** nakayama.1@osu.edu

NAKHIMOVSKY, ALICE
PERSONAL m **DISCIPLINE** MODERN RUSSIAN LITERATURE **EDUCATION** Cornell Univ, Ab, PhD, 75. **CAREER** Prof, Colgate Univ, dept ch. **RESEARCH** Russ 20th century fiction, mod Jewish fiction and Western Traditions. **SELECTED PUBLICATIONS** Auth, Russian-Jewish Literature and Identity, Johns Hopkins, 92); Witness to History: The photographs of Yevgeny Khaldei, Aperture, 97. **CONTACT ADDRESS** Dept of Russ Stud, Colgate Univ, 13 Oak Drive, Hamilton, NY, 13346.

NAKUMA, CONSTANCIO
DISCIPLINE FRENCH LITERATURE **EDUCATION** Sorbonne Nouvelle, PhD, 90. **CAREER** Asst prof. **SELECTED PUBLICATIONS** Auth, pubs on Dagaare phonology. **CONTACT ADDRESS** Dept of Romance Languages, Knoxville, TN, 37996.

NALBANTIAN, SUZANNE
DISCIPLINE COMPARATIVE LITERATURE, CRITICAL THEORY **EDUCATION** Columbia Univ, PhD. **CAREER** Prof, Long Island Univ, C.W. Post Campus. **SELECTED PUBLICATIONS** Auth, Aesthetic Autobiography; The Symbol of the Soul from Holderlin to Yeats: A Study in Metonymy; Seeds of Decadence in the Late Nineteenth-Century Novel. **CONTACT ADDRESS** Long Island Univ, C.W. Post, Brookville, NY, 11548-1300.

NANFITO, JACQUELINE C.
DISCIPLINE SPANISH AND COMPARATIVE LITERATURE **EDUCATION** Saint Mary's Col Notre Dame, BA, 79; Univ Mich, MA, 82; UCLA, PhD, 87. **CAREER** English, Case Western Reserve Univ. **HONORS AND AWARDS** Nancy Wing Award Outstanding Performance Doctoral Qualifying Exams; Alpha Chi Nat Honor Soc Outstanding Prof Award; Fac Appreciation Award Student Senate; Phi Gamma Outstanding Fac Mem Award; Tex Educ Agency Grant; Prof Develop Grant; Flora Stone Mather Alumnae Asn Grant. **SELECTED PUBLICATIONS** Articles, Latin American and Spanish Peninsular literature. **CONTACT ADDRESS** Case Western Reserve Univ, 10900 Euclid Ave, Cleveland, OH, 44106. **EMAIL** jcn@po.cwru.edu

NANJI, AZIM A
PERSONAL Nairobi, Kenya **DISCIPLINE** ISLAMIC, AFRICAN STUDIES **EDUCATION** Makerere Univ, Uganda, BA, 68; McGill Univ, MA, 70, PhD(Islamic studies), 72. **CAREER** Res fel Islamic studies, Inst Islamic Studies, McGill Univ, 72-73; Chmn Dept Humanities, Okla State Univ 73-, Killam fel relig, Dalhousie Univ, 74-76. **HONORS AND AWARDS** Can Coun Pub Award, 77. **MEMBERSHIPS** Mid E Studies Asn; Am Orient Soc. **RESEARCH** Ismaili studies; Medieval Muslim history; modernization and change in religion. **SELECTED PUBLICATIONS** Auth, Modernization and change in the Nizari Ismaili community in East Africa, J Relig Africa, 74; The Ginan tradition among the Nizari Ismailis, Actes du XIX Congr Int des Orientalistes, 75; A theory of learning in the Rasail Ikhwan Al Safa, Muslim World, 76; contribr, An Ismaili theory of Walayah, In: Essays on Islamic Civilization Presented to N Berkes, E JBrill, 76; The Ismailis in history, In: Ismaili Contributions to Islamic Culture, Imperial Iranian Acad Philos, 77; auth, The Nizari Ismaili Tradition in the Indo-Pakistan Subcontinent, Caravan Bks, 78; The Just Ruler Al-sultan Al-adil in Shiite Islam - The Comprehensive Authority of The Jurist in Imami Jurisprudence - Sachedina,AA, J of The American Academy of Religion, Vol 0062, 1994; The 'Bujh Niranjan' - an Ismaili Mystical Poem - Asani,as, J of The American Oriental Society, Vol 0117, 1997. **CONTACT ADDRESS** Univ Florida, Gainesville, FL, 32611.

NAPPA, CHRISTOPHER
DISCIPLINE CLASSICAL STUDIES **EDUCATION** Univ Tex, BA, 90; Univ Va, MA, 92, PhD, 96. **CAREER** Instr. **SELECTED PUBLICATIONS** Auth, Agamemnon 717-36: The Parable of the Lion Cub, 94; Catullan Provocations (rev), Univ Ca, 93; Virgil, New Haven, 91. **CONTACT ADDRESS** Dept of Classics, Knoxville, TN, 37996.

NARO, ANTHONY JULIUS
PERSONAL Born 11/12/1942, Nashville, TN, m, 1966, 2 children **DISCIPLINE** LINGUISTICS **EDUCATION** Polytech Inst NY, BSc, 63; Mass Inst Technol, PhD(ling), 68. **CAREER** Asst prof ling & philol, Univ Chicago, 68-74; prof ling, Fed Univ & prof lett, Pontif Cath Univ, Rio de Janeiro, 74-79; Res Prof Ling, Nat Coun Res & Sci Develop, Brazil, 79-, Researcher, Univ Coimbra, 68; Angola Sci Res Inst, 70-72; vis prof, Fed Univ Rio de Janeiro, 72; researcher, Ctr Philol Res, Lisbon, 73; res dir, Brazilian Literacy Found & Brazilian Found Res. **MEMBERSHIPS** Ling Soc Am; Asn Brasileira Ling; Asn Lit & Ling Comput; Asn Comput Ling. **RESEARCH** Historical linguistics; Pidgins and Creoles; romance linguistics. **SELECTED PUBLICATIONS** Auth, Da metrica medieval galaico-portuguesa, Ocidente, Lisbon, 402: 227-236; On f h in Castilian and western Romance, Z romanische Philol, 88: 435-447; ed, Tendencias Atuais da Linguistics e da Filologia no Brasil, Livraria Francisco Alves, Rio de Janeiro, 76; auth, The Genesis of the Reflexive Impersonal in Portuguese, 76 & A Study on the Origins of Pidginiation, 78, Language, coauth, Competencias Basicas do Portugues, Fundacao Mobral, 78; Portuguese in Brazil, In: Trends in Romance Linguistics and Philology, Mouton Pub, 82; The social and structural dimensions of a syntactic change, Language, 63- 98; Arguing About Arguin + a Reply to Clements,j.clancy on The Origins of Pidgin Portuguese, J of Pidgin And Creole Languages, Vol 0008, 1993. **CONTACT ADDRESS** 191 Waverly Pl, New York, NY, 10014.

NASH, STANLEY
DISCIPLINE HEBREW LITERATURE **EDUCATION** Columbia Univ, PhD, 72. **CAREER** Prof, HUC-JIR/NY; ordained, Jewish Theol Sem, 67. **SELECTED PUBLICATIONS** Pub(s), Hebrew literacy figures and trends. **CONTACT ADDRESS** Hebrew Union College-Jewish Institute of Religion, Univ Southern Calif, University Park Campus, Los Angeles, CA, 90089.

NATALICIO, DIANA
PERSONAL Born 08/25/1939, St Louis, MO **DISCIPLINE** LINGUISTICS, ENGLISH AS SECOND LANGUAGE **EDUCATION** St, Louis Univ, BS, 61; Univ Tex, Austin, MA, 64, PhD (ling), 69. **CAREER** Res assoc eval res, Ctr Commun Res, 70-71; asst prof ling & mod lang, 71-73, chmn mod lang & assoc prof, 73-77, assoc dean lib arts, 77-79, Prof Ling & Mod Lang, Univ Tex, El Paso, 77- & Dean Lib Arts, 80-84, vp, acad aff, 84-88, pres, 88-. **HONORS AND AWARDS** Harold W. McGraw Jr. Prize in Educ; Torch of Liberty Awd; Conquistador Awd for Outstand Svc to Citizens of El Paso; El Paso Women's Hall of Fame; Humanitarian Awd. **MEMBERSHIPS** Nat Sci Bd; NASA Adv Cnl; US-Mexico Comm for Educ and Cultural Exchange; Nat Act Cnl for Minorities in Engineering **RESEARCH** Language acquisition; bilingualism; language testing. **SELECTED PUBLICATIONS** Coauth, A comparative study of English pluralization by native and non-native English speakers, Child Develop, 71; auth, Sentence repetition as a language assessment technique: Some issues and applications, Bilingual Rev/La Rev Bilingue, 77; coauth, The Sounds of Children, Prentice-Hall, 77 & 81; contribr, Theory & Practice or Early Reading, Lawrence Earlbaum Assoc, 79; auth, Repetition and dictation as language testing techniques, Mod Lang J, 79; contribr, Festschrift in Honor of Jacob Ornstein: Studies in General and Sociolinguistics, Newbury House, 80; coauth, Some characteristics of word classification in a second language, Mod Lang J, 82. **CONTACT ADDRESS** Off of President, Univ of Tex, El Paso, TX, 79968-0500. **EMAIL** dnatliclo@utep.edu

NATALLE, ELIZABETH
DISCIPLINE INTERPERSONAL COMMUNICATION, COMMUNICATION THEORY **EDUCATION** FL State Univ, MA, PhD. **CAREER** Assoc prof, dir, intercultural commun exchange prog, Univ NC, Greensboro. **HONORS AND AWARDS** Woman of Distinction Award, Univ NC, Greensboro, 96. **RESEARCH** Gender and interpersonal process; feminist criticism; women's commun networks. **SELECTED PUBLICATIONS** Auth, Gender and communication theory, Commun Educ, 40, 91; Gendered issues in the workplace, in J.T. Wood, ed, Gendered relationships, Mayfield Press, 96; coauth, Deconstructing gender differences in persuasibility: A bricolage, Women's Stud in Commun, 16, 93; Feminist philosophy and the transformation of organizational communication, in B. Kovacic, ed, New approaches to organizational communication, SUNY Press, 94; Sex differences, organizational level, and superiors' evaluation of managerial leadership, Mgt Commun Quart, 10, 97. **CONTACT ADDRESS** Univ N. Carolina, Greensboro, Greensboro, NC, 27412-5001. **EMAIL** ej_natalle@uncg.edu

NATHAN, GEOFFREY STEVEN
PERSONAL Born 10/18/1949, Hove, England **DISCIPLINE** LINGUISTICS **EDUCATION** Univ Toronto, BA, 71; Univ Hawaii, MA, 72, PhD(ling), 78. **CAREER** Vis asst prof, Univ Mont, 77-78 & Univ Hawaii, 78-80; vis asst prof, 80-82, asst prof, 82-88, assoc prof, 89-, Southern Ill Univ. **MEMBERSHIPS** Ling Soc Am; Acoustic Soc Am. **RESEARCH** English as a second language; phonology; syntax. **SELECTED PUBLICATIONS** Auth, Nauruan in the Austronesian language family, Oceanic Ling, Vol XII, No 1-2; Towards a literate level

of language, Elements: Chicago Ling Soc Parasession, 78; Theoretical And Practical Phonetics - Rogers,h, Phonetica, Vol 0050, 1993; coauth, Negative polarity and romance syntax, Ling Symp Romance Lang, Vol XII, Ben J Amin (in press); Quantity Adjustment - Vowel Lengthening And Shortening in Early-middle-english -Ritt,n, Language, Vol 0073, 1997 **CONTACT ADDRESS** Dept of Ling, Southern IL Univ, Carbondale, IL, 62901-4300. **EMAIL** geoffn@siu.edu

NAUDIN, MARIE
PERSONAL Born 06/18/1926, Auxerre, France, 1 child **DISCIPLINE** ROMANCE LANGUAGES **EDUCATION** Sorbonne, BA, 46; Univ Pittsburgh, MA, 62, PhD, 66. **CAREER** From instr to asst prof French, Univ Mich, 64-67; asst prof, 67-71, Assoc Prof French, Univ Conn, 71-. **MEMBERSHIPS** Am Asn Teachers Fr; MLA; Soc Fr Prof Am. **RESEARCH** Relation between music and French poetry; 19th century French literature. **SELECTED PUBLICATIONS** Auth, La chanson francaise contemporaine, Fr Rev, 67; Evolution Parallele de la Poesie et de la Musique en France, Nizet, Paris, 68; Les 'Jours Ne Sen Vont Pas Lomgtemps' - French - Rinaldi,a, French Review, Vol 0068, 1995; Djaout,tahar + Assassinated Algerian Writer - The Metaphorical Landscape of Algeria, French Review, Vol 0070, 1996; L'incendie De La Sainte- victoire' - French - Fauconnier,b, French Review, Vol 0070, 1996. **CONTACT ADDRESS** Dept of Romance & Class Lang, Univ of Conn, Storrs, CT, 06268.

NAUGHTON, JOHN
DISCIPLINE 19TH AND 20TH CENTURY FRENCH POETRY, THE CONTEMPORARY FRENCH NOVEL **EDUCATION** Stanford Univ, BA, MA; Univ CA, Santa Cruz, MA, PhD. **CAREER** Former instr, Univ Tours, France; Univ CA; consult, Univ Chicago Press, 87; dir, Dijon Study Group, 95; prof. **HONORS AND AWARDS** Picker sr fac grant, Colgate Univ, 87; medal, Col de France, Paris, 91; hon(s), Phi Eta Sigma., Nominee, Colgate prof yr, 91, 97. **SELECTED PUBLICATIONS** Transl, In the Shadows Light, Univ Chicago Press, 91; auth, Louis-Rene des Forets, Rodopi, 93; Yves Bonnefoy: New and Selected Poems, Univ Chicago Press and Carcanet Press, London, 95; articles, L'Esprit Createur; Sud; Temenos; Studies in 20th Century Literature; Dalhousie Fr Studies; transl(s), New Lit Hist; Critical Inquiry; Yale Fr Studies; Fr-Brit Studies; Poetry Rev; Tel-Aviv Rev; Graham House Rev; Mod Poetry in Translation; rev(s), World Lit Today; S Hum Rev; L'Esprit Createur; Fr Forum. **CONTACT ADDRESS** Dept of Romance Lang, Colgate Univ, 13 Oak Drive, Hamilton, NY, 13346. **EMAIL** jnaughton@center.colgate.edu

NAYLOR, ERIC WOODFIN
PERSONAL Born 12/06/1936, Union City, TN **DISCIPLINE** ROMANCE LANGUAGES **EDUCATION** Univ of the South, BA, 58; Univ Wis, MA, 59, PhD(Span), 63. **CAREER** From instr to assoc prof, 62-76, Prof Span, Univ of the South, 76-, Fulbright res grant, 64-65; lectr, Escuela de Investigacion Linguistica, Madrid, 70. **MEMBERSHIPS** Mediaeval Acad Am; Am Asn Teachers Span & Port; MLA; S Am Mod Lang Asn. **RESEARCH** Medieval Spanish literature; Golden Age literature. **SELECTED PUBLICATIONS** Coauth, Libro de Buen Amor, Consejo Super Invest Cientificas, 65; auth, La encomienda del Capitan Conreras, Rev Span Philol, 70; coauth, Glosario del Libro de Buen Amor, Soc Espanola de Reimpresiones y Edicones, SA ,Barcelona, 73; Libro de buen amor: Edicion critica y artistica, Ed Aguilar, 76; Libro de Buen Amor, Facsimil, Introduccion y Transcripcion del Codice de Toledo (2 vols), Espasa Calpe, Madrid, 77; The 'Book of Tales by A.b.c.' - Sanchezdevercial,c, Hispania-a J Devoted to The Teaching of Spanish And Portuguese, Vol 0077, 1994; Aesop Fables, With a Life of Aesop - Keller,je, Keating,lc, Translators, Hispania-a J Devoted to The Teaching of Spanish And Portuguese, Vol 0077, 1994; The Sanctification of Don-quixote - From Hidalgo to Priest - Ziolkowski,e, Sewanee Review, Vol 0102, 1994; Spanish Poetry of The 20th-century - Modernity And Beyond - Debicki,ap, Sewanee Review, Vol 0104, 1996. **CONTACT ADDRESS** Dept of Span, Univ of the South, Sewanee, TN, 37375.

NEEDLER, HOWARD
PERSONAL Born 07/22/1937, Manchester, England, m, 1963, 3 children **DISCIPLINE** ITALIAN LITERATURE **EDUCATION** Yale Univ, BS, 58; Oxford Univ, BA, 60, MA, 65; Columbia Univ, PhD, 65. **CAREER** Instr Ital, Barnard Col, Columbia Univ, 63-64; lectr, Yale Univ, 64-65; lectr, Hebrew Univ, 65-66; asst prof, Univ Colo, 67-69; asst prof, 69-72, assoc prof, 73-80, PROF, 81-, WESLEYAN UNIV. **HONORS AND AWARDS** Phi Beta Kappa; Rhodes scholarship; ACLS fel. **RESEARCH** Medieval literature, especially Dante; modern poetry; Jewish history, especially in medieval Italy. **CONTACT ADDRESS** Col of Lett, Wesleyan Univ, Middletown, CT, 06457. **EMAIL** hneedler@wesleyan.edu

NEGUS, KENNETH GEORGE
PERSONAL Born 12/23/1927, Council Bluffs, IA, w, 3 children **DISCIPLINE** GERMAN **EDUCATION** Princeton Univ, BA, 52, MA, 54, PhD, 57. **CAREER** Asst instr Ger, Princeton Univ, 53-54; instr, Northwestern Univ, 55-57; instr, Harvard Univ, 57-59; asst prof, Princeton Univ, 59-61; from asst prof to assoc prof, 61-66, Prof Ger, Rutgers Univ, 66- **MEMBERSHIPS** MLA; Am Asn Teachers Ger; ETA Hoffmann Ges; Am Soc Ger Lit of 16th & 17th Cent. **RESEARCH** Symbolism of the occult; German Romanticism; German Baroque literature. **SELECTED PUBLICATIONS** Auth, ETA Hoffmann's Other World, Univ Pa, 65; Paul Heyse's Novellentheorie: A Revaluation, Ger Rev, 65; Grimmelshausen, World Authors Series, Twayne, 74. **CONTACT ADDRESS** 175 S Harrison St, Princeton, NJ, 08540. **EMAIL** kennegus@aol.com

NEHRING, WOLFGANG
PERSONAL Born 11/15/1938, Oppeln, Germany, m, 1964 **DISCIPLINE** GERMAN LITERATURE **EDUCATION** Univ Bonn, PhD, 65. **CAREER** Sci asst Ger Lit, Univ Bonn, 65-66; asst prof, Boston Col, 66-67; from asst prof to assoc prof, 67-78, Prof Ger Lit, Univ Calif, Los Angeles, 78-, Co-ed, Kritische Hofmannsthal-Ausgabe, Arbeitsstelle Basel, 71-73; adv bd, Hugo von Hofmannsthal Ges, 76-. **MEMBERSHIPS** Am Asn Teachers Ger; Int Arthur Schnitzler Res Asn; Hugo von Hofmannsthal Ges (secy, 71-74); Int Asn Ger Studies; Schiller Ges. **RESEARCH** German Romanticism; JahrhundertwendeModerne; Austrian literature, especially Hofmannsthal and Schnitzler. **SELECTED PUBLICATIONS** Ed, E T A Hoffmann, Prinzessin Brambilla, 71 & WackenroderTieck, Phantasien uber die Kunst, 73, Reclam, Stuttgart; auth, Hofmannsthal und der Wiener Impressionismus, 75 & E T A Hoffmanns Erzahlwerk, Ein Modell und seine Variationen, 76, Z Deut Philol; Eichendorff und der Leser, Aurora, 77; Die Buhne als Tribunal Der zweite Weltkrieg im dokumentarischen Theater, In: GegenwartslitDrittes Reich, Reclam, Stuttgart, 77; Der Beginn der Moderne, In: Handbuch der deutschen Erzahlung Bagel, Duusseldorf, 81; E T A Hoffmann: Die Elixiere des Teufels, In: Romane und Erzahlungen der deutschen Romantik, Reclam, Stuttgart, 81; Schnitzler,arthur And The French- revolution, Modern Austrian Literature, Vol 0025, 1992; Ich- mochte-mir-flugelwunschen - Schlegel,dorothea Life - German - Stern,c, Michigan Germanic Studies, Vol 0018, 1992; Ich-mochte- mir-flugelwunschen - Schlegel,dorothea Life - German - Stern,c, Michigan Germanic Studies, Vol 0018, 1992; The Rediscovered Poet - Schreyvogl,friedrich Novel About Grillparzer And The Present- day Reception of Grillparzer Works, Modern Austrian Literature, Vol 0028, 1995. **CONTACT ADDRESS** Dept of Ger Lang, Univ Calif, Los Angeles, CA, 90024.

NELSON, ARDIS L.
PERSONAL Born 08/14/1942, Auburn, NY **DISCIPLINE** HISPANIC CINEMA, CUBAN LITERATURE **EDUCATION** Oberlin Col, Ba, 65; Middlebury Col, Madrid, MA, 72; IN Univ, Bloomington, PhD, 80 **CAREER** Prof, 94-99, E TN St Univ; Assoc Prof, 85-94, Asst prof, 81-85, FL St Univ; Inst, 79-81, Dickinson Col; Lect, 77-78, Gettysburg Col; Assoc Inst, 72-77, IN Univ; Second Sch Tchr, 65-71, Rochester, NY **MEMBERSHIPS** Am Asn of Tchrs of Spanish and portugese; Feministas Unidas **SELECTED PUBLICATIONS** Auth, Cabrera Infante in the Menippean Tradition, Newark, Delaware: Juan de la Cuesta Hispanic monographs, 83; Guillermo Cabrera Infante: Assays, Essays, and other Arts, Twayne-Simon & Schuster Macmillian, 99 **CONTACT ADDRESS** Dept of Foreign Lang, East Tennessee State Univ, Johnson City, TN, 37614-0312. **EMAIL** nelsona@etsu.edu

NELSON, DEBORAH HUBBARD
PERSONAL Born 07/19/1940, Springfield, OH, m, 1963, 2 children **DISCIPLINE** MEDIEVAL FRENCH & PROVENCAL LANGUAGE & LITERATURE **EDUCATION** Wittenberg Univ, BS, 60; Univ Grenoble, Certificat d'Etudes Francaises, 61; Ohio State Univ, MA, 64, PhD(Romance lang), 70. **CAREER** Asst Prof, Western Col, 70-74; asst prof, 74-81, Assoc Prof French, Rich Univ, 81-, Res grant, Rice Univ, 75. **MEMBERSHIPS** MLA; S Cent Mod Lang Asn; Int Courtly Lit Soc; Soc Rencesvals. **RESEARCH** Twelfth and thirteenth century French and Provencal poetry; teaching of modern French language. **SELECTED PUBLICATIONS** Auth, Animal imagery in Marcabru's poetry, Studies in Medieval Culture XI, 77; Bird imagery in Marcabru's poetry, Round Table, 1077; Yonec: A religious and chivalric fantasy, Univ S Fla Lang Quart, spring 78; The implications of love and sacrifice in Fresne and Eliduc, S Cent Bull, winter 78; Eliduc's saluation, Fr Rev, 1O81; The Pubic & private images of chiges, Fenice Reading Medieval Studies, Vol VII, 81; Gillebert-de- berneville, Les 'Poesies' - Fresco,k, Editor, Romance Philology, Vol 0046, 1992; Gillebert-de-berneville, Les 'Poesies' - Fresco,k, Editor, Romance Philology, Vol 0046, 1992. **CONTACT ADDRESS** Dept Fr & Ital, Rice Univ, Houston, TX.

NELSON, ROBERT J. AMES
PERSONAL Born 03/29/1925, Woodside, NY, m, 1947, 2 children **DISCIPLINE** FRENCH **EDUCATION** Columbia Univ, BA, 49, MA, 50, PhD, 55. **CAREER** Instr French, Columbia CoL, 53-55; instr, Yale Univ, 55-58; asst prof, Univ Mich, 58-59; from assoc prof to prof Romance lang, Univ Pa, 59-69; Prof French & Comp Lit, Univ Ill, Urbana, 69, Head Dept, 73-, Morse fel, Yale Univ, 57-58; grant-in-aid fels, Am Coun Learned Soc, 60 & 65; Am Philos Soc, 63; dir Northeast Conf Teaching Foreign Lang, 64-68; Guggenheim fel, 66- 67; assoc, Ctr for Adv Study, Univ Ill, 76. **HONORS AND AWARDS** Chevalier, Palmes Academiques, 72. **MEMBERSHIPS** MLA; Am Asn Teachers Fr. **RESEARCH** Pascal; world theater; French civilization. **SELECTED PUBLICATIONS** Auth, Play Within a Play: The Dramatist's Conception of His Art--Shakespeare to Anouilh, Yale Univ, 58; Corneille: His Heroes and Their Worlds, Univ Pa, 63; Immanence and Transcendence: The Theater of Jean Rotrou (1609-1650), Ohio Univ, 69; Bipolarity of French classicism, Essays Fr Lit, 71; Classicism: The Crises of the Baroque, Esprit Createur, 71; The fiction of John Williams, Denver Quart, 73; France, Impressed And Suppressed Voices in French Literature From The 'Song of Roland' to 'Waiting For Godot', J of Aesthetic Education, Vol 0030, 1996; The Tragedy of Origins - Corneille,pierre And Historical-perspective - Lyons,jd, French Forum, Vol 0022, 1997. **CONTACT ADDRESS** Dept of French, Univ of Ill, Urbana, IL, 61822.

NELSON, WILLIAM B.
DISCIPLINE NEAR EASTERN LANGUAGES AND CIVILIZATIONS **EDUCATION** Harvard Univ, PhD, 91. **CAREER** Assoc prof, 86-; chaplain, US Air Force Reserves, 93-; asst pastor, First Baptist Church, 92. **HONORS AND AWARDS** Tchr yr, 90. **RESEARCH** Biblical lang; Old Testament hist; Old Testament theol. **SELECTED PUBLICATIONS** Auth, Revelation; Eschatology; Jebusites; Melchizedek; Promised Land; Rechabites, in Oxford Companion to the Bible, 93. **CONTACT ADDRESS** Dept of Rel, Westmont Col, 955 La Paz Rd, Santa Barbara, CA, 93108-1099.

NEPAULSINGH, COLBERT IVOR
PERSONAL Born 05/10/1943, Sangre Grande, Trinidad, m, 1966, 3 children **DISCIPLINE** SPANISH LANGUAGE AND LITERATURE **EDUCATION** Univ BC, BA, 66, MA, 67; Univ Toronto, PhD(Span lang & lit), 73. **CAREER** Assoc VP Acad Aff, Univ Albany, 88-91; Prof Span, State Univ NY Albany, 86- **HONORS AND AWARDS** Guggenheim fel, 96; Excel in Teaching; Excel in Acad Serv. **MEMBERSHIPS** MLA; Medieval Acad Am; Int Asn Hispanists. **RESEARCH** Medieval Spanish literature; Spanish literature of the Golden Age. **SELECTED PUBLICATIONS** Auth, La poesia de Micer Francisco Imperial, Clasicos Castellanos; Towards a History of Literary Composition in Medieval Spain, Univ Toronto; auth, Apples of Gold in Filigrees of Silver, Holmes and Meier. **CONTACT ADDRESS** Dept of Latin Am and Carib Stu, 55250C, SUNY, Albany, 1400 Washington Ave, Albany, NY, 12222-1000.

NERSESSIAN, NANCY
DISCIPLINE COGNITIVE SCIENCES **EDUCATION** Case Western Reserve Univ, PhD. **CAREER** Prof, Ga Inst of Technol; ser ed, Sci and Philos bk ser, Kluwer Acad Publ. **MEMBERSHIPS** Gov bd, Philos of Sci Asn. **RESEARCH** The role of imagery, analogy, and thought experimenting in conceptual change. **SELECTED PUBLICATIONS** Auth, Faraday to Einstein: Constructing Meaning in Scientific Theories, Kluwer Acad Publ, 84, 90; How do scientists think? Capturing the dynamics of conceptual change in science, in Cognitive Models of Science, R Giere, ed, Minn Stud in Philos of Sci 15, Univ Minn Press,91; Constructing and Instructing: The role of 'abstraction techniques' in developing and teaching scientific theories, in Philosophy of Science, Cognitive Science, and Educational Theory and Practice, R Duschl & R Hamilton, eds, SUNY Press, 92; In the theoretician's laboratory: thought experimenting as mental modeling, PSA 92, Vol 2, D Hull, M Forbes, K Okruhlik, eds, 93. **CONTACT ADDRESS** Sch of Lit, Commun, & Cult, Georgia Inst of Tech, Skiles Cla, Atlanta, GA, 30332. **EMAIL** nancyn@cc.gatech.edu

NEUSE, ERNA KRITSCH
PERSONAL Born 08/07/1923, Austria **DISCIPLINE** GERMAN LANGUAGE & LITERATURE **EDUCATION** Univ Vienna, Austria, PhD, 47. **CAREER** Prof German, Rutgers Univ, New Brunswick, 54-, Dir, Grad Prog, Rutgers Univ, New Brunswick. **MEMBERSHIPS** MLA; Am Asn Teachers Ger. **RESEARCH** Modern German literature; methods of teaching German. **SELECTED PUBLICATIONS** Auth, Modernes Deutsch, 60, Moderne Erzahlungen, 64, Neue deutsche Prosa, 68 & Modern German, 70, Prenticc-Hall; Buchners Lenz-zur Struktur der Novelle, Ger Quart, 3/70; Deutsch fur Anfanger, Prentice-Hall, 71; Die Funktion von Motiven und Stereotypen Wendungen in Schnitzlers Reigen, Monatshefte, winter 72; Das Rhetorische in Durrenmatts Der Besuch der alten Dame, Zur Funktion des Dialogs im Drama, Seminar, 2/75; Die deutsche Kurzgeschichte, Bouvier, Bonn, 80;Der Erzahler in der deutschen Kurzgeschichte, Camden House, 91. **CONTACT ADDRESS** 7 Cobb Rd, New Brunswick, NJ, 08901.

NEVIN, THOMAS
PERSONAL Born 10/27/1944, m, 1977, 4 children **DISCIPLINE** LANGUAGES **EDUCATION** Univ of CO, BA, 66; Univ of WI, MA, 68, PhD, 73 **CAREER** Asst Prof, 80-88, Assoc Prof, 88-95, Prof, 95-, John Carroll Univ **HONORS AND AWARDS** Phi Beta Kappa; Woodrow Wilson Fel **MEMBERSHIPS** Am Philol Asn; Dante Soc of Am **RESEARCH** Dante **SELECTED PUBLICATIONS** Auth, Ernst Junger and Germany: Into the Abyss, 1914-1945, Duke Univ Press, 96, London: Constable, 97; Simone Weil: Portrait of a Self-Exiled

Jew, Chapel Hill, Univ of NC Press, 91 **CONTACT ADDRESS** Dept of Lang, John Carroll Univ, 20700 N Park Blvd, University Heights, OH, 44118. **EMAIL** tnevin@jcu.vaxa.edu

NEWMAN, GAIL M.
DISCIPLINE GERMAN **EDUCATION** Northwestern Univ, BA, 76; Univ Minn, PhD, 84. **CAREER** Assoc prof, Williams Col, 83-; fac coordr for Williams Writing Prog with Theodore Roosevelt High Sch Bronx, NY,95-. **RESEARCH** German romanticism; psychoanalytic theory; turn of the century and 20th-century Austria. **SELECTED PUBLICATIONS** Auth, Du bist nicht anders als ich:' Kleist's Correspondence with Wilhelmine von Zenge, Ger Life and Letters, 89; The Status of the Subject in Novalis's Heinrich von Ofterdingen and Kleist's Die Marquise von O., Ger Quart, 90; Family Violence in Kleist's Der Findling, Colloquia Germanica, 96; Locating the Romantic Subject: Novalis with Winnicott, Wayne State Univ Press, 97; Narrating the Asymbolic Subject in Hoffman's Der Sandmann, Sem, 97. **CONTACT ADDRESS** Center for Foreign Languages, Literatures and Cult, Williams Col, Williamstown, MA, 01267. **EMAIL** Gail.M.Newman@williams.edu

NEWMAN, JOHN KEVIN
PERSONAL Born 08/17/1928, Yorkshire, England, m, 1970, 3 children **DISCIPLINE** CLASSICAL PHILOLOGY, COMPARATIVE LITERATURE **EDUCATION** Oxford Univ, BA (Lit Humaniores), 50, BA(Russ), 52, MA, 53; Bristol Univ, PhD (Classics), 67. **CAREER** Master classics, Downside Sch, Bath, England, 55-69; assoc prof, 70-80, prof Classics, Univ Ill, Urbana, 80-, chmn dept, 81-85, Ed, Ill Class Studies, 81-87. **HONORS AND AWARDS** Awards, Vatican Int Latin Poetry Competition, 60, 63, 66, 97; Certamen Capitolinum, 68 & 80; assoc mem. **RESEARCH** Greek and Latin poetic traditions. **SELECTED PUBLICATIONS** Auth, Augustus and the new poetry, 67 & The concept of Vates in Augustan poetry, 67, Collection Latomus; Pushkin's Bronze horseman and the epic tradition, Comp Lit Studies, 72; co-ed, Serta Turyniana, 74; Univ Ill; Latin Compositions, 76, Golden Violence, 76 & Dislocated: An American Carnival, 77, Ex Aedibus, Urbana, Ill; De Novo Galli Fragmento in Nubia Eruto, Latinitas, 80. **CONTACT ADDRESS** 707 S Mathews Ave, Urbana, IL, 61801-3625. **EMAIL** j-newman@uiuc.edu

NEWMAN, JUDITH H.
PERSONAL Born 02/01/1961, Alexandria, VA, m, 1987, 2 children **DISCIPLINE** NEAR EASTERN LANGUAGES AND CIVILIZATIONS **EDUCATION** Princeton, AB, 83; Yale Divinity School, MAR, 88; Harvard Univ, 96. **CAREER** Asst prof, General Theol Sem, 98-. **HONORS AND AWARDS** Episcopal church Found fel, 92-95. **MEMBERSHIPS** SBL; CBA. **RESEARCH** History of Biblical interpretation; second temple Judaism; history of Jewish and Christian Liturgy. **SELECTED PUBLICATIONS** Auth, Praying By the Book: the Scripturalization of Prayer in Second Temple Judaism, EJL Series, Atlanta: Scholars, 98. **CONTACT ADDRESS** General Theol Sem, 175 Ninth Ave, New York, NY, 10011-4977. **EMAIL** newman@gts.edu

NEWMARK, LEONARD
PERSONAL Born 04/08/1929, Attica, IN, m, 1951, 2 children **DISCIPLINE** LINGUISTICS **EDUCATION** Univ Chicago, AB, 47; IN Univ, MA, 51, PhD, 55. **CAREER** Instr to assoc prof, OH State Univ, 54-61; vis asst prof, Univ MI, 61; assoc prof, IN Univ, 62; prof, Univ CA, San Diego, 63-92, prof Emeritus, 93-. **HONORS AND AWARDS** ACLS; NEH; Office of Education. **MEMBERSHIPS** Linguistics Soc of Am; Dictionary Soc of North Am. **RESEARCH** Albanian language. **SELECTED PUBLICATIONS** Auth, Introduction to the Linguistic History of English, 63; Using American English, 64; Standard Albanian: A Reference Grammar, 82; Spoken Albanian, 97; Oxford Albanian-English Dictionary, 98. **CONTACT ADDRESS** 2643 St Tropez Place, La Jolla, CA, 92037. **EMAIL** ldnewmark@ucsd.edu

NEWTON, ROBERT PARR
PERSONAL Born 07/31/1929, San Antonio, TX, m, 1959, 2 children **DISCIPLINE** MODERN GERMAN LITERATURE, STYLISTICS **EDUCATION** Rice Univ, BA, 50, MA, 58; Johns Hopkins Univ, PhD(Ger), 64. **CAREER** From instr to asst prof Ger, Univ Pa, 62-70; assoc prof, 70-76, prof Ger, 76-94, prof emer, 94- , Univ NC, Greensboro; vis lectr Ger, Swarthmore Col, 65-70. **MEMBERSHIPS** MLA; SAtlantic Mod Lang Asn; Am Asn Teachers Ger; AAUP. **RESEARCH** Linguistic metrics, German poetry, modern German drama. **SELECTED PUBLICATIONS** Auth, Dada, Expressionism and Some Modern Modes, Rice Univ Studies, summer 69; The First Voice: Vowel Configuration in the German lyric, J English & Ger Philol, 10/69; Vokallange und Vokalgleichklang als Rhythmische Antriebs-und Gestaltungsmomente, LiLi: Z Ling und Lit, 9/71; Form in the Menschheitsdammerung, The Hague, 71; Ditonic Rhythmemes: Formal Elements of Rhythmic Patterning, Poetics: Int Rev Theory Lit, 74; Trochaic and Iambic, Lang & Style, Int J, spring 75; Vowel Undersong: Studies of Vocalic Timbre and Chroneme Patterning in German Lyric Poetry, The Hague, 81; Eye Imagery in Else Lasker-Schuer, Mod Lang Notes, 3/82. **CONTACT ADDRESS** Univ N. Carolina, Greensboro, NC, 27412. **EMAIL** Robert Newton@compuserve.com

NEY, JAMES WALTER
PERSONAL Born 07/28/1932, Nakuru, Kenya, m, 1954, 3 children **DISCIPLINE** ENGLISH, LINGUISTICS **EDUCATION** Wheaton Col, Ill, AB, 55, AM, 58; Univ Mich, EdD(English), 63. **CAREER** English specialist, Dade County Pub Schs, Fla, 61-62 & Univ Ryukyus, 62-64; asst prof, Mich State Univ, 65-69; assoc prof, 69-75, Prof English, Ariz State Univ, 75-, Res grant, NCTE, 76, chmn comt to evaluate ling, 77-80. **MEMBERSHIPS** Can Ling Soc; Nat Asn Foreign Student Affairs; Teaching English to Speakers Other Lang; Ling Soc Am; MLA. **RESEARCH** Teaching English as a second language; teaching of written composition to native speakers of English. Coauth, Readings on American Society, 69, Readings from Samuel Clemens, 69, Blaisdell; Adventures in English, Laidlaw Bros, 72; Marckwardt, 72; Two apparent fallacies in current grammatical thought, Gen Ling, 74; Linguistics, Language Teaching and Composition in the Grades, Mouton, The Hague, 75; The modals in English: A floating Semantic feature analysis, JEnglish Ling, 76; Sexism in the English language: A biased view in a biased society, ETC, 76; Semantic Structures, Mouton, The Hague, 81; Generativity, The History of a Notion That Never Was, Historiographia Linguistica, Vol 0020, 1993; Letters - Resource Books For Teachers - Burbidge,n, Gray,p, Levy,s, Rinvolucri,m, Modern Language J, Vol 0081, 1997. **CONTACT ADDRESS** Dept of English, Arizona State Univ, Tempe, Tempe, AZ, 85281.

NGUYEN, DINH-HOA
PERSONAL Born 01/17/1924, Hanoi, Vietnam, m, 1952, 4 children **DISCIPLINE** LINGUISTICS, LITERATURE **EDUCATION** Union Col, BA, 50; NY Univ, MA, 52, PhD(English educ), 56. **CAREER** Lectr Vietnamese, Columbia Univ, 53-57; from asst prof to prof English & ling, Univ Saigon, 57-65, dean fac lett, 57-58, chmn dept, 57-65; Prof Ling & Foreign Lang, Southern Ill Univ, Carbondale & Dir Ctr Vietnamese Studies, 69-, Dir cult affairs, Ministry of Educ, Saigon, Vietnam, 62-65; secy-gen, Vietnam Nat Comm, Unesco, 62-65; vis prof, Univ Wash, 65-66; cult counr, Embassy of Vietnam, Washington, DC, 66-69; Fulbright prof ling & English, Rabat, Morocco, 81-82; two res grants, Nat Endowment for Humanities, 77-82; Fulbright grant ling, Morocco, 81-82. **MEMBERSHIPS** Ling Soc Am; Am Orient Soc; Asn Asian Studies; Dict Soc NAm; Am Coun Teachers Uncommonly-Taught Asian Lang (pres, 76-77 & 77-78). **RESEARCH** Students' review grammar of Vietnamese; English-Vietnamese dictionary; outline of Vietnamese culture. **SELECTED PUBLICATIONS** Auth, Read Vietnamese, 66 & Hoa's Vietnamese-English Dictionary, 66 Tuttle; Vietnamese-English Student Dictionary, 71 & Colloquial Vietnamese, 74, Southern Ill Univ; Beginning English for Vietnamese Speakers & Intermediate English for Vietnamese Speakers, Tuttle, 76; 201 Vietnamese Verbs, Barron's 79; Language in Vietnamese Society, 80 & Essential English- Vietnamese Dictionary, 80, Asia Bks; 'Nuoc Chay Qua Cau' - Tran,tbg, World Literature Today, Vol 0067, 1993; Ca Lon' - Dao- khanh, World Literature Today, Vol 0067, 1993; 'Dam Khuya' - Hoang,tdt, World Literature Today, Vol 0067, 1993; Les 'Enfants De Thai Binh,' Vol 1, 'Nostalgies Provinciales' - Duyenanh, World Literature Today, Vol 0068, 1994; Tuyen-tap Vantho Van But Nam Hoa-ky' - Nguyen,vs, World Literature Today, Vol 0069, 1995; Bao-ninh The 'Sorrow of War' - a Novel of North-vietnam - Palmos,f, Hao,pt, World Literature Today, Vol 0069, 1995; 'Two Shores Deux Rives' - English, French - Vuongriddick,t, World Literature Today, Vol 0070, 1996; The 'Stone Boy' And Other Stories - Thich,nh, World Literature Today, Vol 0071, 1997; The 'Other Side of Heaven' - Postwar Fiction by Vietnamese And American Writers - Karlin,w, World Literature Today, Vol 0071, 1997; 'Hoa Dia-nguc' - The 'Flowers of Hell' - English, Vietnamese - Nguyen,ct, Nguyen,nb, World Literature Today, Vol 0071, 1997; an Anthology of Vietnamese Poems - From The 11th Through The 20th Centuries - Huynh,st, World Literature Today, Vol 0071, 1997; b Vietnam - a Travelers Literary Companion - Balaban,j, Nguyen,qd, World Literature Today, Vol 0071, 1997. **CONTACT ADDRESS** Dept of Ling, Southern Ill Univ, Carbondale, IL, 62901.

NI, W.J.
PERSONAL Born 10/21/1954, China, m, 1985, 1 child **DISCIPLINE** LINGUISTICS **EDUCATION** Univ Conn, PhD, 91. **CAREER** Res assoc, Univ Conn, 91-93; res assoc, Haskins Lab, New Haven, Conn; res assoc, Yale Univ Sch of Med, 96- . **MEMBERSHIPS** Ling Soc Am; Acad of Aphasia. **RESEARCH** Language comprehension and production in normal and abnormal populations. **SELECTED PUBLICATIONS** Coauth, Learning, Parsing and Modularity, in Frazier, ed, Perspectives on Sentence Processing, Lawrence Erlbaum, 94; coauth, Syntactic Complexity and Working Memory in Explaining Comprehension Difficulties, Brain and Lang, 95; coauth, Production in Broca's Aphasia: A Case of Syntactic and Phonetic Aspects, Brain and Lang, 96; coauth, Tasks and Timing in the Perception of Linguistic Anomaly, J of Psycholinguistic Res, 96; coauth, Meaning, Memory and Modularity, MIT Occas Papers in Ling, 96; coauth, Individual Differences in Working Memory and Eye-Movement Patterns in Reading Relative Clauses, Univ Conn Working Papers in Ling, 96; coauth, Sidestepping Garden Paths: Assessing the Contributions of Syntax, Semantics and Plausibility in Resolving Ambiguities, Lang and Cognitive Proc, 96; coauth, Production and Comprehension of Relative Clause Syntax in Nonfluent Aphasia: A Coordinated Study, Brain and Lang, 97; coauth, Anomaly Detection: Eye-Movement Patterns, J of Psycholinguistic Res, 98. **CONTACT ADDRESS** 831 Rail Fence Rd, Orange, CT, 06477. **EMAIL** weijia.ni@yale.edu

NIANG, SADA
DISCIPLINE AFRICAN; CARIBBEAN LITERATURES **EDUCATION** Univ York, PhD. **RESEARCH** African cinema. **SELECTED PUBLICATIONS** Coauth, Elsewhere in Africa, Hatier, Paris,78; African Continuities/L'heritage africain, erebi, Toronto, 89; auth, Litterature et cinema en Afrique francophone, L'Harmattan, Paris, 96. **CONTACT ADDRESS** Dept of French, Victoria Univ, PO Box 3045 STN CSC, Victoria, BC, V8W 3P4. **EMAIL** sniang@uvic.ca

NICASTRO, ANTHONY J.
DISCIPLINE ROMANCE LANGUAGES **EDUCATION** NY Univ, BA, 64; Columbia Univ, PhD, 71. **CAREER** Vis prof, Williams Col, 83-; prof, N Adams State Col. **HONORS AND AWARDS** NEH, Wayne State Univ, 82; NEH, Yale Univ, 85; NEH, Univ Miss Ctr for the Stud of Southern Cult, 95. **RESEARCH** Foreign-language acquisition and pedagogy with emphasis on teaching strictly in the target language at all levels; history of the romance languages; Flamenco history; Flamenco guitar technique; Flamenco as literature; Flamenco as compared with Blues. **SELECTED PUBLICATIONS** Auth, Modernidad y reminiscencias de la literatura francesa en Concierto barroco de Alejo Carpentier, Confluencia, Univ Northern Colorado. **CONTACT ADDRESS** Center for Foreign Languages, Literatures and Cult, Williams Col, Williamstown, MA, 01267. **EMAIL** anicastro@nasc.mass.edu

NICCOLI, GABRIEL
DISCIPLINE ITALIAN; FRENCH STUDIES **EDUCATION** Univ British Columbia, BA, 70; MA, 73; PhD, 83. **CAREER** Assoc prof **RESEARCH** 16th century pastoral drama in Italy and France; literate women of the Italian renaissance. **SELECTED PUBLICATIONS** Auth, Autobiography and Fiction in Veronica Franco's Epistolary Narrative; Eros and the Art of Self-Promotion in Veronica Franco's Terze rime; Teoria e prassi: note sulla questione della tragicommedia pastorale: in Italia e in Francia; The God of Love in Pastor Fido: Blindness in Arcadia; Cupid Satyr and the Golden Age: Pastoral Dramatic Scenes of the Late Renaissance. **CONTACT ADDRESS** Dept of Italian and French Studies, St. Jerome's Univ, Waterloo, ON, N2L 3G3. **EMAIL** ganiccol@watarts.uwaterloo.ca

NICHOLAS, ROBERT LEON
PERSONAL Born 12/10/1937, Lebanon, OR, m, 1967, 2 children **DISCIPLINE** MODERN SPANISH LITERATURE **EDUCATION** Univ Ore, BA, 59, MA, 63, PhD(romance lang), 67. **CAREER** From instr to assoc prof, 65-76, chmn dept Span & Port, 79- 82, Prof Span, Univ Wis-Madison, 76-, Dir study prog, Madrid, 72-73. **MEMBERSHIPS** Am Asn Teachers Span & Port; MLA. **RESEARCH** Modern Spanish Theater; modern Spanish novel; generation of 1898. **SELECTED PUBLICATIONS** Contribr, The history plays: Buero Vallejo's experiment in dramatic expression, Rev Estud Hispanicos, 1169; auth, El Mundo de Hoy, Scott, 71; The Tragic Stages of Antonio Buero Vallejo, Estud Hispanofila, Univ NC, 72; coauth, En Camino!, Adelante! & Churros y Chocolate!, Scott, 77; La historia de historia de una escalera, Estreno, spring 79; En Camino! Adelante! Scott, 2nd ed, 81; El proceso de creacion en Abel Sanchez, Homenaje a Antonio Sanchez-Barbudo: Ensayos de literature espanola moderna, Univ Wis-Madison, 81; La camisa, entre el sainete y el melodrama, Primer Acto, 82; coauth, En camino: motivos de conversacion, Scott (in prep); Benavente, Buerovallejo And The 20th-century, Estreno-cuadernos Del Teatro Espanol Contemporaneo, Vol 0020, 1994; The Madrid Stage Between 1918 And 1926 - Spanish - Dougherty,d, Vilches,mf, Hispanic Review, Vol 0061, 1993; a Letter For Olmo,lauro - In-memoriam, Estreno- cuadernos Del Teatro Espanol Contemporaneo, Vol 0022, 1996. **CONTACT ADDRESS** Dept of Span & Port, Univ Wis, Room 1038 Van Hise Hall, Madison, WI, 53706.

NICHOLLS, JAMES C.
DISCIPLINE INTERMEDIATE FRENCH, INTRODUCTION TO FRENCH LITERATURE **EDUCATION** BA, Univ WI, 51, MA, 52, PhD, 62. **CAREER** Assoc dean, Colgate Univ, 80-82; ch, Fr Achievement Test Comm, 87-90; prof. **HONORS AND AWARDS** Fulbright scholar, Univ Dijon, 57-58. **RESEARCH** Eighteenth-century french lit, Diderot. **SELECTED PUBLICATIONS** Auth, Grading the Advanced Placement Examination in French Literature, 81; Grading the Advanced Placement Examination in French Language, 81; Toward a Chronology of Jacques le Fataliste, Studies on Voltaire and the Eighteenth Century, 93. **CONTACT ADDRESS** Dept of Romance Lang, Colgate Univ, 13 Oak Drive, Hamilton, NY, 13346.

NICHOLLS, MARIA
DISCIPLINE FRENCH LITERATURE **EDUCATION** SUNY-Morrisville, BA, 81; SUNY-Binghamton, MA, 84, PhD, 91. **CAREER** Soc dir, NDEA Summer Inst, 64, 65; dir, Lang

Lab, 72-87; spec instr, Neglected Language Prog, Portugese; lectr, 87-91; asst prof-. **SELECTED PUBLICATIONS** Auth, Lady Dedlock's Sin, The Dickensian, 93. **CONTACT ADDRESS** Dept of Romance Lang, Colgate Univ, 13 Oak Drive, Hamilton, NY, 13346. **EMAIL** mnicholls@center.colgate.edu

NICHOLLS, ROGER ARCHIBALD
PERSONAL Born 05/24/1922, London, England, m, 1955 **DISCIPLINE** GERMAN **EDUCATION** Oxford Univ, BA, 49; Univ Calif, PhD, 53. **CAREER** Instr Ger, Univ Toronto, 52-54; asst prof, Univ Chicago, 54-61; assoc prof, Reed Col, 61-63; asst prof, 63-65, Prof Ger, Univ ORE, 65-. **MEMBERSHIPS** MLA; Am Asn Teachers Ger; Philol Asn Pac Coast (pres, 67- 68). **RESEARCH** Nineteenth century drama; literary movements at the end of the nineteenth century; Thomas Mann. **SELECTED PUBLICATIONS** Auth, Nietzsche in the Early Work of Thomas Mann, Univ Calif, 55; The Dramas of CD Grabbe, Mouton, 68; Kleist Aristocratic Heritage And Das 'Katchen Von Heilbronn' - Reeve,wc, Colloquia Germanica, Vol 0025, 1992; Kleist Aristocratic Heritage And Das 'Katchen Von Heilbronn' - Reeve,wc, Colloquia Germanica, Vol 0025, 1992; The Author, Art, And The Market - Rereading The History of Aesthetics - Woodmansee,m, Comparative Literature, Vol 0048, 1996. **CONTACT ADDRESS** 2840 Elinor St, Eugene, OR, 97403.

NICHOLS, ANN
DISCIPLINE LINGUISTICS **EDUCATION** St. Mary's Col , BA; Univ Wash, MA, 58, PhD, 64. **CAREER** Prof; **HONORS AND AWARDS** NEH grant, 95. **RESEARCH** Text and image in late medieval culture; indexing all illustrations in English manuscripts 1377-1508.. **SELECTED PUBLICATIONS** Auth, Seeable Signs: The Iconography of the Seven Sacraments 1350-1544 **CONTACT ADDRESS** Winona State Univ, PO Box 5838, Winona, MN, 55987-5838.

NICHOLS, FRED JOSEPH
PERSONAL Born 03/24/1939, Staten Island, NY, 1 child **DISCIPLINE** COMPARATIVE LITERATURE **EDUCATION** Georgetown Univ, AB, 61; NY Univ, MA, 66, PhD(comp lit), 67. **CAREER** From instr to asst prof English, Yale Univ, 67-76; from assoc prof to PROF COMP LIT, GRAD CTR, CITY UNIV NEW YORK, 76-. **MEMBERSHIPS** MLA; Renaissance Soc Am; Am Comp Lit Asn; Am Asn Neth Studies. **RESEARCH** Renaissance literature; Netherlandic literature; Latin literature. **SELECTED PUBLICATIONS** An Anthology of Neo-Latin Poetry, Yale Univ Press, 79. **CONTACT ADDRESS** Dept of Comp Lit, Graduate Sch and Univ Ctr, CUNY, New York, NY, 10036.

NICHOLS, PATRICIA CAUSEY
PERSONAL Born 12/29/1938, Conway, SC, m, 1959, 2 children **DISCIPLINE** ENGLISH, LINGUISTICS **EDUCATION** Winthrop Col, BA, 58; Univ Minn, MA, 66; San Jose State Univ, MA, 72; Stanford Univ, PhD(ling), 76. **CAREER** Teacher, Hampton Pub Schs, Va, 58-60; Lectr English, Ling & Educ, San Jose State Univ, 76-, Co-ed, Women & Lang News, 76; vis asst prof English, Univ SC, 80-81; vis instr, Univ Calif, Santa Barbara, 82. **MEMBERSHIPS** MLA; Ling Soc Am; Am Dialect Soc. **RESEARCH** Gullah; gender and sex differences in speech; American dialects. **SELECTED PUBLICATIONS** Auth, A sociolinguistic perspective on reading and black children, Lang Arts, 54: 150-157; Ethnic consciousness in the British Isles, Lang Problems & Lang Planning, 1: 10-31; Black women in the rural south: Conservative and innovative, Int J Social Lang, Vol 17, 78; Planning for language change, San Jose Studies, 6: 18-25; Variation among Gullah speakers in rural South Carolina, In: Language Use and the Uses of Language, Georgetown Univ Press, 80; Women in their speech communities, In: Women and Language In Literature and Society, Praeger Pub, 80; Creoles in the USA, In: Language in the USA, Cambridge Univ Press, 81; Linguistic options and choices for black women in the rural South, In: Language, Gender and Society, Newbury House Pub (in press); a Syntactic Analysis of Sea-island Creole - Cunningham,iae, J of Pidgin And Creole Languages, Vol 0009, 1994. **CONTACT ADDRESS** 1430 Westmont Ave, Campbell, CA, 95008.

NICKERSON, CATHERINE ROSS
DISCIPLINE ENGLISH LANGUAGE AND LITERATURE **EDUCATION** Yale Univ, PhD, 91. **CAREER** Dir undergrad studies/assoc prof Grad Inst Lib Arts/dept Engl. **RESEARCH** Detective fiction; Lizzie Borden; narrative and the representation of mystery, crime, and violence; Asian American literature. **SELECTED PUBLICATIONS** Auth, 'The Cunning of Her Sex:' The Rhetoric of Guilt, Innocence, and Gender in the Trial of Lizzie Borden in Violence and American History, NY UP; Murder as Social Criticism, Am Lit Hist, 97; Serial Detection and Serial Killers in Twin Peaks, Lit/Film Quart, 93. **CONTACT ADDRESS** Grad Inst Lib Arts, Emory Univ, 1380 Oxford Rd NE, Atlanta, GA, 30322-1950. **EMAIL** cnicker@emory.edu

NICOLAI, ELKE
DISCIPLINE GERMAN **EDUCATION** Univ-Gh- Siegen, Ger, PhD. **CAREER** Asst prof. **MEMBERSHIPS** MLA; Amer Coun Teaching For Languages; Ger Stud Asn & Women in Ger Asn. **RESEARCH** Literature of the 19th and 20th centuries. **SELECTED PUBLICATIONS** Auth, bk on Klaus Mann and his literary contemporaries in the mid-twenties and early thirties; bibliog of the int lit of the Spanish Civil War 36-39. **CONTACT ADDRESS** Dept of German, Hunter Col, CUNY, 695 Park Ave, New York, NY, 10021.

NIEBYLSKI, DIANNA
DISCIPLINE COMPARATIVE LITERATURE **EDUCATION** Univ Nevada, BA, 79; Brandeis Univ, MA, 83, PhD, 88. **CAREER** Vis assoc prof, Univ Chicago, 95-96, 98-99; ASSOC PROF, SPAN, COMP LIT, EARLHAM COL, 85-. **CONTACT ADDRESS** Dept of Langs, Lit, Earlham Col, Richmond, IN, 47374.

NIEMAN, NANCY DALE
PERSONAL Born 05/10/1939, St. Paul, MN **DISCIPLINE** ROMANCE LANGUAGES **EDUCATION** Beloit Col, BA, 61; Middlebury Col, Vt, MA, 62; Inst Phonetique, Univ Paris, dipl, 65; Univ Madrid, Dr Philos & Lett(Span), 66; Inst Brasil-Estados Unidos, cert, 74. **CAREER** Instr Span, Wayne State Col, 62-64; from instr to asst prof, Beloit Col, 64-71, assoc prof Mod Lang, 71-79; sr lectr, Univ Southern Calif, 79-81; prof Mod Lang, Santa Monica Col, 81-; Univ So Calif Madrid Cen, res dir, 89; Int Inst Foundation of Spain, res dir, 90-91; chmn, Dept Modern Languages, Santa Monica Coll, 94-98; coord, Overseas Progs, SMC, 95-97. **MEMBERSHIPS** Am Asn Teachers Span & Port; MLA; AAUP; Am Asn Advan Humanities. **RESEARCH** Contemporary Spanish literature, especially theater and novel. **SELECTED PUBLICATIONS** Auth, El mundo poetico de Alejandro Casona, Rev Univ Madrid, 10/66; The festival of the dove, Beloit Daily News, 3/23/73; Feast of the Holy Name, The Garden of Your Delights, translations of two poems by Ana Rossetti, RE:AL, 97. **CONTACT ADDRESS** Dept Spanish, Santa Monica Col, 1900 Pico Blvd, Santa Monica, CA, 90405-1644. **EMAIL** nieman_nancy@smc.edu

NILSEN, ALLEEN PACE
PERSONAL Born 10/10/1936, Phoenix, AZ, m, 1958, 3 children **DISCIPLINE** LINGUISTICS **EDUCATION** Brigham Young Univ, BA, 58; Am Univ, MEd, 61; Univ Iowa, PhD(English, ling), 73. **CAREER** Instr English, Eastern Mich Univ, 66-67; teacher, Am Int Sch Kabul, Afghanistan, 67-69: instr English, Eastern Mich Univ, 69-71; asst prof educ, Univ Northern Iowa, 71-73; assoc prof, 73-80, Prof English, Ariz State Univ, 80- **HONORS AND AWARDS** Rewey Belle Inglis Award, Natl Coun of Tchrs of English, 90. **MEMBERSHIPS** Nat Coun Teachers English; Am Libr Asn; Rocky Mountain Mod Lang Asn. **RESEARCH** Sexism as shown in language; children's and adolescent literature; humor scholarship. **SELECTED PUBLICATIONS** Coauth, Pronunciation Contrasts in English, Simon & Schuster, 71; auth, Sexism in English: A feminist view, In: Female Studies VI: Closer to the Ground, Feminist Press, 72; coauth, Semantic Theory: A Linguistic Perspective, Newbury House, 75; ed & coauth, Sexism and Language, Nat Coun Teachers English, 77; Five factors contributing to the unequal treatment of females in picture books, Top News, spring 78; coauth, Language Play: An Introduction to Linguistics, Newbury House, 78; coauth, Literature for Today's Young Adults, 6th ed, Longman, 99; auth, Living Language, Allyn & Bacon, 99; co-auth, Encyclopedia of Humor and Research, Oryx, 99. **CONTACT ADDRESS** Dept of English, Arizona State Univ, Tempe, PO Box 870302, Tempe, AZ, 85287-0302. **EMAIL** Alleen.Nilsen@asu.edu

NILSEN, DON LEE FRED
PERSONAL Born 10/19/1934, Spanish Fork, UT, m, 1958, 3 children **DISCIPLINE** ENGLISH LINGUISTICS **EDUCATION** Brigham Young Univ, BA, 58; Am Univ, MA, 61; Univ Mich, Ann Arbor, PhD(ling), 71. **CAREER** Asst prof English ling, State Univ NY Oswego, 64-66; specialist compos, Teachers Col, Columbia Univ, 67-69; dir sect ling & teaching English as foreign lang, Univ Northern Iowa, 71- 73; assoc prof, 73-77, Prof English Ling, Ariz State Univ, 78- **MEMBERSHIPS** Ling Soc Am; MLA; NCTE; Am Dialect Soc; Workshop Libr World Humour. **RESEARCH** Componential analysis; language deviation; linguistic humor. **SELECTED PUBLICATIONS** Coauth, English Conversational Practices, Univ Mich, 68; auth, Toward a Semantic Specification of Deep Case, 72, English Adverbials, 72 & The Instrumental Case in English, 73, Mouton, The Hague; Pronunciation Contrasts in English, Regents, 2nd ed, 73; coauth, Semantic Theory: A Linguistic Perspective, 75 & Language Play: A Intro to Linguistics, 78, Newbury House; Cruel And Unusual Puns - Hauptman,d, Humor-international J of Humor Research, Vol 0006, 1993; The Great Eskimo Vocabulary Hoax And Other Irreverent Essays on The Study of Language - Pullum,gk, Thalia-studies in Literary Humor, Vol 0013, 1993; Conversational Joking - Humor in Everyday Talk - Norrick,nr, Thalia-studies in Literary Humor, Vol 0013, 1993; France Through Literary Eyes, Thalia-studies in Literary Humor, Vol 0014, 1994; The Appeal of Bloopers - a Reader-response Interpretation, Humor-international J of Humor Research, Vol 0007, 1994; Anatomy of Humor - Berger,aa, Humor-international J of Humor Research, Vol 0007, 1994; Humor in The News, Humor-international J of Humor Research, Vol 0008, 1995. **CONTACT ADDRESS** 1884 E Alameda Dr, Tempe, AZ, 85282.

NISETICH, FRANK
PERSONAL Born 05/29/1942, Sacramento, CA, 2 children **DISCIPLINE** CLASSICAL PHILOLOGY **EDUCATION** Univ Calif, Berkeley, BA, 65, MA, 67; Harvard Univ, PhD(class philol), 73. **CAREER** From instr to asst prof, 71-78, fac growth grant, 77, assoc to prof and chmn Classics, Univ Mass, Boston, 78-, vis asst classics, Yale Univ, 73-74. **HONORS AND AWARDS** Translation Award, 78; Chancellor's Distinguished Scholar Award, 81. **MEMBERSHIPS** Am Philol Asn. **RESEARCH** Classical philology; ancient Greek lyric poetry; tragedy; Callimachus. **SELECTED PUBLICATIONS** Auth, Olympian 1.8-11: An Epinician Metaphor, Harvard Studies Class Philol, 75; The Leaves of Triumph and Mortality, Trans Am Philol Asn, 77; Convention and Occasion in Isthm.2, Calif Studies in Class Antiquity, 77; Pindar's Victory Songs, Johns Hopkins Univ, 80; Immortality in Heragas, Class Philol, 88; Euripides, Orestes, Oxford Univ, 95. **CONTACT ADDRESS** Dept of Classics, Univ of Mass, 100 Morrissey Blvd, Boston, MA, 02125-3300. **EMAIL** Nisetich@umbsky.cc.umb.edu

NIXON, ROB
DISCIPLINE AFRICAN AND BRITISH LITERATURES **EDUCATION** Rhodes Univ, S Africa, BA, 77; Univ Iowa, MA, 82; Columbia Univ, PhD, 89. **CAREER** Assoc prof. **SELECTED PUBLICATIONS** Auth, London Calling: VS Naipaul, Post-Colonial Mandarin, Oxford UP, 92; Homelands, Harlem, Hollywood: South African Culture and the World Beyond, Routledge, 94; auth, ninety essays and rev, New Yorker; Critical Inquiry; NY Times; TLS; London Rev of Bks; The Village Voice; S Atlantic Quart; Grand St; Nat; Black Renaissance/Renaissance Noire; Transition; The Independent. **CONTACT ADDRESS** Dept of Eng, Columbia Col, New York, 2960 Broadway, New York, NY, 10027-6902.

NNAEMEKA, OBIOMA G.
PERSONAL Agulu, Nigeria, 2 children **DISCIPLINE** FRENCH **EDUCATION** Univ Dakar, Diplome d'etudes francaises, 71; Univ Nigeria, BA, 72; Univ Minn, MA, 77, PhD, 78. **CAREER** Jr. Res Fel, 72-74, Lectr, Univ Nigeria, 82-88; Asst Prof, Concordia Col, 88-89; Asst Prof, Univ Minn, 90-91; Asst Prof, Metro State Univ, 91; Asst Prof, Col Wooster, 89-91; Assoc Prof, Ind Univ, 91-. **HONORS AND AWARDS** Queen's Merit Award, Queen's Sch, 65; Bus & Professional Women's Asn Schol, 63-65; East Central State (Nigeria) Govt Schol, 66-67, 70-72; Fr Govt Schol, 70-72; Jr. Res Fel, Univ Nigeria, 72-78; Fed Govt Nigeria Schol, 74-80; Colonial Dames Fel, 79-80, 80-81; Altrusa Found Fel, 80-81; Business and Professional Women's Asn Merit Award, 86; Edith Kreeger Wolf Distinguished Vis Prof, Northwestern Univ, 92; Rockefeller Humanist-in-Residence, Ctr Advanced Feminist Studies, Univ Minn, 91-92; Nigerian Achiever of the Year in Leadership Award, Network Africa, 94; Teaching Excellence Recognition Award, Ind Univ, 97; Fac Achievement Award, Ind Univ, 97; Black Schol in Residence, Col Wooster, 98; Outstanding Fac Award, Ind Univ, 98; recipient of numerous grants. **MEMBERSHIPS** African Lit Asn; African Studies Asn; Am Asn Teachers Fr; Am Asn Univ Women; Ind For Lang Teachers Asn; Lit Soc Nigeria. **SELECTED PUBLICATIONS** Auth, Black Women Writers, Women's Studies Quart, 97; Development, Cultural Forces, and Women's Achievement in Africa, Law & Pol, 97; Fighting on All Fronts: Gendered Spaces, Ethnic Boundaries, and the Nigerian Civil War, Dialectical Anthropol 22, 97; ed, The Politics of (M)Othering: Womanhood, Identity, and Resistance in African Literature, Routledge, 97; Sisterhood, Feminisms, and Power: From Africa to the Diaspora, African World Press, 98; author of numerous other publications. **CONTACT ADDRESS** Indiana Univ-Purdue Univ, Indianapolis, Indianapolis, IN, 46202. **EMAIL** nnaemeka@iupui.edu

NOAKES, SUSAN
DISCIPLINE THE MEDIEVAL AND RENAISSANCE PERIODS IN FRENCH AND ITALIAN **EDUCATION** Yale Univ, PhD. **CAREER** Instr, Univ Minn, Twin Cities. **RESEARCH** Economics and gender in the Decameron. **SELECTED PUBLICATIONS** Auth, Timely Reading: Between Exegesis and Interpretaion, Cornell, 88; coed, Tommaseo Schifaldo, De indagationibus grammaticis, Humanistica Lovaniensia, 82; The Comparative Perspective on Literature, Cornell, 88. **CONTACT ADDRESS** Univ Minn, Twin Cities, Minneapolis, MN, 55455.

NOBLE, DOUGLAS
DISCIPLINE COMPUTERS IN ARCHITECTURE, DESIGN, DESIGN THEORIES AND METHODS **EDUCATION** CA State Polytech Univ, Pomona, BS, 81, BA, 82; Univ CA, Berkeley, MA, 83, PhD, 91. **CAREER** Asst prof, USC, 91-; lectr, Univ CA, Berkeley, 84-91; Kenneth S Wing & Assoc, Arch, 85-86; CHCG Arch, 78-84. **HONORS AND AWARDS** William Van Alen Memorial Prize, 94; ACSA AIAS New Fac Tchg Awd, 94; PhD Comt Prize, UC Berkeley, 89; Distinguished Tchg Asst Awd, 87; Pasadena/Foothill AIA Design Awd, 83; 1st Prize-AISC Stud Design Competition, 80. **MEMBERSHIPS** Asn for Comput Aided Design in Arch; Am Inst Arch; Asn Collegiate Schools Arch. **RESEARCH** Design theories and methods; site analysis through digital photography. **SELECTED PUBLICATIONS** Auth, Issues Regarding Architectural Records of the Future: Planning for Change in Libraries,

94; Mission, Method, Madness; Computer Supported Design in Architecture, ACADIA, 92; Software for Architects: A Guide to Software for the Architectural Profession, 92; Issues in the Design of Tall Buildings, 91; User's Guide to Berkeley Architecture, Daily Calif, 90; coauth, Computer Aided Architectural Design, Univ Calif, Berkeley, 90; Shading Mask: A Teaching Tool for Sun Shading Devices, 95-96; Student Initiated Explorations in the Design Studio, ACADIA, 94; Issues Regarding Architectural Records of the Future: Planning for Change in Libraries, Architronic: Elec J Arch, 94; The Sorcerers Apprentice, Computer Graphics World, 90. **CONTACT ADDRESS** School of Archit, Univ of Southern California, University Park Campus, Los Angeles, CA, 90089. **EMAIL** dnoble@mizar.usc.edu

NOEGEL, SCOTT
PERSONAL Born 05/29/1962, Richfield, WI, m, 1995 **DISCIPLINE** SEMITIC LANGUAGES AND LITERATURES. **EDUCATION** Univ of WI, BA, 89; Cornell Univ, MA, 93, PhD, 95. **CAREER** Graduate research asst, 89-90, graduate teaching asst, 90-93, lectr, 93-94, Cornell Univ; lectr, 94, Ithaca Col; Consultant: Discovery channel, 94-95; Hazel Cole Fel in Jewish Studies, 95-96; vis lectr, 96, vis lectr, University WA; vis asst prof, 96-97, Rice University; high school instructor, 97-98, Jewish Federation of Greater Seattle; acting asst prof, 97-98, asst prof, 98, University WA. **HONORS AND AWARDS** NY State Council on the Arts Technical Asst Grant, 95; Electronic Media and Film Program Grant, 95-96; Hazel Cole Fel in Jewish Studies at the Univ WA, 95-96; NY State Council on the Arts Technical Asst Grant, 96-97; Rockefeller Found Natl Fil/Video/Multimedia Fel Nominee for Interactive/Digital Work, 97-98; Natl Endowment for the Arts, 98-99. **MEMBERSHIPS** Amer Acad of Religion; Amer Oriental Soc; Amer Schs of Oriental Research; Assn for Jewish Studies; Phi Beta Kappa; Phi Kappa Phi; Soc of Biblical Lit. **RESEARCH** Hebrew Bible; Assyriology, Egyptology languages, literatures, history, culture, archaeology and linguistics. **SELECTED PUBLICATIONS** Auth, A Slip of the Reader and Not the Reed: (Infinitive Absolutes with Divergent Finite Forms). Part II, Jewish Bible Quarterly, 98; auth, The Aegean Ogygos of Boeotia and the Biblical Og of Bashan: Reflections of the Same Myth, Zeitschrift fur die alttestamentliche Wissenschaft, 98, in press; auth, A Crux and a Taunt: Night-Time Then Sunset in Genesis 15, The World of Genesis: Persons, Places, Perspectives, Sheffield, 98; auth, The Book of Genesis, Reader's Guide to Judaism, 99, in press; Babylonia, Reader's Guide to Judaism, 99, in press; auth, Ancient Near East, Reader's Guide to Judaism, Fitzroy, 99, in press; auth, Hermeneutic, Reader's Guide to Judaism, 99, Fitroy, in press; auth, Canaanites, Reader's Guide to Judaism, 99, Fitzroy, in press. **CONTACT ADDRESS** Dept of Near East Languages and Civilizations, Univ Washington, 229 Denny Hall, Seattle, WA, 98195-3120. **EMAIL** snoegel@u.washington.edu

NOEL, ROGER A.
PERSONAL Born 11/22/1942, Wanne, Belgium, m, 1969, 2 children **DISCIPLINE** FRENCH LANGUAGE AND LITERATURE **EDUCATION** Univ Liege, Belgium, Licence, 65; Univ Mo, Columbia, MA, 66; Washington Univ, St Louis, PhD, 84. **CAREER** Instr to lectr, Univ Mo, St Louis, 70-86; asst prof to chair to assoc prof, Monmouth Col, Monmouth, Il, 86-; assoc prof to prof, GC&SU, Milledgeville, Ga, 92-. **HONORS AND AWARDS** NEH Inst, Transatlantic Encounters, Newberry Libr, 88., Assoc ed, J of Baltic Stud, 91-. **MEMBERSHIPS** AAUP; MLA; Int Arthurian Soc; AATF; AATG-GA; Il Coun Teaching of Foreign Lang; ACTFL, Center Belgian Culture; Ga Classical Assoc; Foreign Lang Assoc of Ga; Old Capital Hist Soc; Heart of Ga Acad Alliance; Amer Assoc of French Acad Palms; SAMLA; Allied Arts; Alpha Mu Gamma; Smithsonian; Nat Assoc of Scholars, S Poverty Law Center; The Carter Center. **SELECTED PUBLICATIONS** Coauth, An Introduction to An Academic Vocabulary, Lanham: UPA, 89; auth, A Thesaurus of Word Roots of the English Language, Lanham: UPA, 92; auth, A Thesaurus of Medical Word Roots, Imprimis, 96; auth, Discover It!, Imprimis, 96; coed, The Independence of the Baltic States: Origins, Causes, and Consequences, 96. **CONTACT ADDRESS** 3624 Sussex Dr NE, Milledgeville, GA, 31061. **EMAIL** rnoel@mail.gcsu.edu

NOICE, HELGA
PERSONAL Born 12/26/1939, Pyritz, Germany, m, 1970 **DISCIPLINE** COGNITIVE PSYCHOLOGY **EDUCATION** PhD, Rutgers Univ, 88. **CAREER** Res asst, Fla Atlantic Univ, 82-84; tchg asst, Rutgers Univ, 84-88; instr, Rutgers Univ, summers, 85-88, visiting asst prof, Fla Atlantic Univ, fall 88-summer 89; asst prof, Augustana Col, 89-96; assoc prof, Augustana Col, 96-. **HONORS AND AWARDS** Who's Who in Sci and Eng, 96; Phi Kappa Phi; Sigma X1. **MEMBERSHIPS** Cognitive Sci Soc; Psychonomics; Amer Psychol Soc; Midwestern Psychol Asn; Intl Asn for the Empirical Study of Lit; Soc for Text and Discourse; Soc of Appl Res in Mem and Cognition. **RESEARCH** Mental representation; Expertise (professional actors); Text comprehension; Cognition and emotion; Memory training for older adults. **SELECTED PUBLICATIONS** Auth, with T. Noice, Expertise of professional actors: A cognitive view, Hillsdale, NJ, Lawrence Erlbaum Assoc, 97; with T. Noice, Verbatim retention of theatrical scripts by means of character analysis, ed S. Toetoesy de Zepetnek & Irene Sywenky, The systemic and empirical approach to literature and culture as theory and application, pp 485-504, Edmonton, Alberta, Univ Alberta, 97; with T. Noice, The mental processes of professional actors as examined through self report, experimental investigation and think-aloud protocol, ed R. J. Kreuz & M. S. MacNealey, Empirical Approaches to Literature and Aesthetics, vol 52, pp 361-377, Norwood, NJ, Ablex Publ; jour, with T. Noice, Effort and active experiencing as factors in verbatim recall, Discourse Proc, 23, 51-69, 97; with T. Noice, Long-term memory for verbal material as a result of accompanying non-literal action events, Proceedings of the Nineteenth Annual Conference of the Cognitive Science Society, Hillsdale, NJ, Lawrence Erlbaum, 97; with T. Noice, Two approaches to learning a theatrical script, Memory, 4, 1-17, 96; with T. Noice, Analyzing the role preparation of a professional actor, Discourse Proc, 18, 345-369, 94; Psychology and the Pew Science Program in undergraduate education, Coun on Undergrad Res Quart, 14, 4, 190-192, 94. **CONTACT ADDRESS** Dept. of Psychology, Augustana Col, 639 38th St., Rock Island, IL, 61202. **EMAIL** psnoice@augustana.edu

NOLAND, CARRIE J.
DISCIPLINE FRENCH LANGUAGE **EDUCATION** Harvard Univ, PhD. **CAREER** ASST PROF, FR, UNIV CALIF, IRVINE. **SELECTED PUBLICATIONS** Auth, The Poetics of Motherhood: Yves Bonnefoy and Julia Kristeva; "What's in a Name? Yves Bonnefoy and the Creation of Douve"; "Allegories of Temporality: Philippe Jaccottet, Francis Ponge and the Poetics of the Notebook." **CONTACT ADDRESS** Dept of Fr and Ital, Univ Calif, Irvine, CA, 92697.

NOLLENDORFS, VALTERS
PERSONAL Born 03/22/1931, Riga, Latvia, m, 1955, 6 children **DISCIPLINE** GERMAN & LATVIAN LITERATURE **EDUCATION** Univ Nebr, BSc in Ed, 54, MA, 55; Univ Mich, PhD, 62. **CAREER** Teaching asst, Univ Nebr, 54-55; instr Ger, Univ Mich 59- 61; from instr to assoc prof, 61-74, Prof Ger, Univ Wis, Madison, 74-, Chmn Dept, 75-, Ed, Monatshefte, 72-; mem exec bd, Asn Advan Baltic Studies, 74, pres, 76-78; mem exec comt, div 18th & early 19th century Ger Lit, MLA. **MEMBERSHIPS** MLA; Am Asn Teachers Ger; Asn Advan Baltic Studies. **RESEARCH** Age of Goethe; Goethe's Faust; contemporary Latvian literature. **SELECTED PUBLICATIONS** Auth, Der Steit um den Urfaust, Mouton, The Hague, 67; The rite of life: A theme and its variations in the poetry of Soviet Latvia, Mosaic, 73; Time and experience in Goethe's Trilogie der Leidenschaft, In: Husbanding the Golden Grain, Studies in Honor of Henry Nordmeyer, Ann Arbor, 73; The demythologization of Latvian literature, Books Abroad, 73; Partial rhyme in contemporary Latvian poetry, Baltic Lit & Ling, 73; The voices of one calling: The mastering of the Latvian legacy in Bels and Rungis, J Baltic Studies, 75; co-ed, Ger Studies in the United States: Assessment and Outlook, Univ Wis, 76; auth, Latvian literature, In: Reader's Adviser, Bowker, 77; for Poems Are Forever Spirals Without End - a Meditative Letter to Ivask,ivar 1927-1992 on His Baltic-elegies, J of Baltic Studies, Vol 0026, 1995. **CONTACT ADDRESS** Dept of Ger, Univ of Wis, Madison, WI, 53706.

NORDLING, JOHN G.
PERSONAL Born 03/17/1957, Portland, OR, m, 1985 **DISCIPLINE** CLASSICS AND LATIN LITERATURE **EDUCATION** Univ Wisc Madison, PhD, 91. **CAREER** Asst prof, dept foreign lang & lit, Valparaiso Univ, 94-. **MEMBERSHIPS** Amer Philol Asn; Soc of Bibl Lit; Archaeol Inst of Amer. **RESEARCH** Ancient epistelography; Paul - life and theology; Ancient slavery. **SELECTED PUBLICATIONS** Rev, G. Clark, Augustine Confessions: Books I-IV, Concordia Theol Quart, 61, 318-319, 97; rev, D. E. Goatley, Were You There?: Godforsakenness in Slave Religion, Concordia Jour, 23, 265-266, 97; rev, C. Hill, The Scriptures Jesus Knew, Concordia Jour, 22, 70-71, 97; rev, T. Cahill, How the Irish Saved Civilization, Concordia Jour, 22, 121-122, 96; rev, D. W. J. Gill and C. Gempf, The Book of Acts in its First Century Setting. Volume 2: Greco-Roman Setting, Logia4, 68-70, 95; rev, Robert Grant, Heresy and Criticism, Logia3, 65-66, 94; rev, Wayne Meeks, The First Urban Christians, Condordia Jour, 19, 277-80, 93; article, Christ Leavens Culture: St. Paul on Slavery, Concordia Jour, 24, 43-52, 98; article, Onesimus Fugitivus: a Defense of the Runaway Slave Hypothesis in Philemon, Jour for the Study of the New Testament, 41, 97-119, 91. **CONTACT ADDRESS** Valparaiso Univ, 108 Meier Hall, Valparaiso, IN, 46383. **EMAIL** jnorfdling@exodus.valpo.edu

NORMAND, GUESSLER
PERSONAL Born 02/24/1937, 2 children **DISCIPLINE** FRENCH LITERATURE, FOREIGN LANGUAGE EDUCATION **EDUCATION** Univ Aix-Marseille, dipl Fr, 63; Univ Ky, MA, 67, PhD(French), 70. **CAREER** Instr French, Southern Univ, 61-62 & 63-64, Univ Akron, 68-70; Asst Prof French, Univ Toledo, 70-, Fac res fel, Univ Toldeo, summer, 79. **MEMBERSHIPS** Am Asn Teachers Fr; AAUP; Am Coun Teaching Foreign Lang. **RESEARCH** Twentieth century French literature; the literature of commitment. **SELECTED PUBLICATIONS** Henri Barbusse and his Monde (1928-1935): Progeny of the Clarte Movement and the Rev Clarte, J Contemp Hist, 7/76; Henri Barbusse and his Monde (1928-1935): Precursors to the Litterature Engagee Movement, Ky Romance Quart, Vol XXIV, No 4, 449-460; Meeting individual needs in the college foreign language classroom, Foreign Lang Ann, 2/79; Toward better articulation between high school and college foreign language teachers, ADFL Bull, 3/80; Motivating with media: The use of video in the foreign language classroom, Can Mod Lang Rev, 10/80. **CONTACT ADDRESS** 2801 W Bancroft St, Toledo, OH, 43606-3390.

NORTH, HELEN FLORENCE
PERSONAL Born 01/31/1921, Utica, NY **DISCIPLINE** CLASSICAL LITERATURE, RHETORIC **EDUCATION** Cornell Univ, AB, 42, AM, 43, PhD(classics), 45. **CAREER** Sibley fel, 45-46; instr class lang, Rosary Col, 46-48; asst prof Greek & Latin, 48-53, assoc prof, 53-62, William J Kenan prof, 73-78, Prof Classics, Swarthmore Col, 62-, Chmn Dept, 59-, Centennial Prof, 78-, Ford & Fulbright fels, Rome, 53-54; vis assoc prof, Barnard Col, Columbia Univ, 54-55; Guggenheim fel, Rome, 58-59; secy adv coun, Sch Class Studies, Am Acad Rome, 60-62 & 64, mem bd trustees, 72-75 & 77-91; Asn Univ Women res fel, Rome, 62-63; Nat Endowment for Hum sr fel, Rome, 67-68; chmn, Cath Comn on Intellectual & Cult Affairs, 68-69; mem bd dir, King's Col, Pa, 69-71 & 73-75; Am Coun Learned Soc fel, Rome, 71-72; Martin class lectr, Oberlin Col, 72; mem bd trustees, La Salle Col, 73-; Guggenheim fel, 75-76. **HONORS AND AWARDS** Harbison Tchg Prize, Danforth Found, 69; Charles A Goodwin Award for Sophrosyne, Am Philol Asn, 69. **MEMBERSHIPS** Am Philol Asn (2nd vpres, 74, pres, 76); Class Asn Atlantic States; Class Soc Am Acad Rome (pres, 60-61); AAAS. **RESEARCH** Concept of Sophrosyne in Greek lit; Plato's rhetoric; Roman rhetoric. **SELECTED PUBLICATIONS** Trans Milton's Second Defence of the English people, In: Vol IV, Complete Prose Works of John Milton, Yale Univ, 66; Sophrosyne: Self-Knowledge and Self-Restraint in Greek Literature, 66 & coed, Of Eloquence; Studies in Ancient and Mediaeval Rhetoric, Cornell Univ, 70; auth, Ancient Salt: The New Rhetoric and the Old, J Hist Ideas, 74; ed, Interpretations of Plato: A Swarthmore Symposium, Brill, 77; auth, The Yoke of necessity: Aulis and beyond, Class World, 77; From Myth to Icon, Cornell Univ, 79; auth, Opening Socrates, Ill Class Stud, 94; auth, The Dacian Walls Speak, Festschrift fur Paul MacKendrick, 98. **CONTACT ADDRESS** 604 Ogden Ave, Swarthmore, PA, 19081.

NORTON, GLYN P.
DISCIPLINE ROMANCE LANGUAGES **EDUCATION** Univ Mich, AB, 63; AM, 65; PhD, 68. **CAREER** Willcox B. & Harriet M. Adsit prof, Williams Col, 88-; asst prof, Dartmouth Col, 68-71; prof, Pa State Univ, 71-88; dir, Ctr For Lang(s), Lit(s) & Cult(s), Williams Col, 90-92. **HONORS AND AWARDS** Sr fel, NEH, 73-74; La Medaille de Melun, Fr, 85; The Pa State Univ Scholar Medal for Outstanding Achievement in the Arts and Humanities, 86; Guggenheim fel, Paris, 86-87; Distinguished PhD Recipient, Hon by Rackham Sch of Grad Stud, Univ Mich, 88. **RESEARCH** French and Italian literature and criticism of the renaissance; the theory and practice of translation. **SELECTED PUBLICATIONS** Auth, Montaigne and the Introspective Mind, 75; The Ideology and Language of Translation in Renaissance France and their Humanist Antecedents, 84; Literary Translation in the Continuum of Renaissance Thought: A Conceptual Overview, Die literarische ubersetzung: Stand u Perspektiven ihrer Erforschung, 88; Du Bellay and the Emblematics of Regret, Writing the Renaissance: Essays on Fr Renaissance Lit Presented to Floyd Gray, 92; Image and Introspective Imagination in Montaigne's Essais, Collections of Criticism on Montaigne, 95. **CONTACT ADDRESS** Center for Foreign Languages, Literatures and Cult, Williams Col, Williamstown, MA, 01267. **EMAIL** Glyn.P.Norton@williams.edu

NORTON, ROBERT E.
DISCIPLINE GERMAN, RUSSIAN **EDUCATION** Univ Calif, Santa Barbara, BA, 82; Princeton Univ, MA, 85, PhD, 88. **CAREER** Vis asst prof, Mount Holyoke Col, 88-89; asst prof, 89-93, assoc prof, 93-97, prof, 97-98, Vassar Col; PROF, UNIV NOTRE DAME, 98. **CONTACT ADDRESS** Dept of German & Russian, Univ of Notre Dame, Notre Dame, IN, 46556. **EMAIL** norton.15@nd.edu

NOSTRAND, HOWARD LEE
PERSONAL Born 11/16/1910, New York, NY, m, 1933, 3 children **DISCIPLINE** FRENCH CULTURE **EDUCATION** Amherst Col, AB, 32; Harvard Univ, AM, 33; Univ Paris, D Univ, 34. **CAREER** Instr, Univ Buffalo, 34-36 & US Naval Acad, 36-38; asst prof French, Brown Univ, 38-39; chmn dept, 39-64, prof, 39-80, Emer Prof Romance Lang, Univ Wash, 80-, Romance ed, Mod Lang Quart, 40-45; cult relat attache, US Embassy, Peru, 44-47; El sol del Peru, 47; Guggenheim fel, 53-54; mem adv comt, New Media Prog, US Off Educ, 58-61; dir NDEA Inst Lang Teachers, Univ Wash, 59-60, proj, dir, res in culturography, 62-63; mem Nat Comn Teacher Educ & Prof Standards, Nat Educ Asn, 63-67, chmn, 66-67; mem ERIC adv Bd, MLA, 66-71; mem conn Ethnography, Am Asn Teachers French, 74-; vis prof Col France, 75; Stepladder prog, Am Coun Teaching Foreign Lang, 81-; vis prof, Simon Fraser Univ, 82. **HONORS AND AWARDS** Palmes Academiques, 50; Chevalier, Legion d'honneur, 62; Leadership Award, Northeast Conf Teaching Foreign Lang, 78; Northeast Conf Award, 78; Officier dans l'Ordre des Arts et des Letters, 79. **MEMBERSHIPS** Am

Asn Teachers Fr(vp, 56-58, pres, 60-62); MLA. **RESEARCH** Modern French literature; history of ideas; description of literate cultures. **SELECTED PUBLICATIONS** Auth, Ortega y Gasset's Mission of the University, Princeton Univ; The Cultural Attache, The Hazen Found; coauth, Research on Language Teaching: An Annotated International Bibliography for 1945-64, 65; Background Data for Teaching French, 67; Honored by Festschrift, Essays on the Teaching of Culture, Advancement Press, Am, 74; How to Discover a Culture in its Literature - Examples from Steinbeck, Saroyan, and Pagnol, Foreign Language Annals, Vol 0029, 1996. **CONTACT ADDRESS** Dept of Romance Lang, Univ of Wash, GN-60, Seattle, WA, 98195.

NUESSEL, FRANK
PERSONAL Born 01/22/1943, Evergreen Park, IL **DISCIPLINE** SPANISH LINGUISTICS **EDUCATION** Ind Univ, AB, 65; Mich State Univ, MA, 67; Univ Ill, PhD, 73 **CAREER** Instr, Northern Ill Univ, 67-70; asst prof, Ind State Univ, 73-75; prof, Univ Louisville, 75- **HONORS AND AWARDS** Oppenheimer Fel, 85-86; Univ Louisville President's Award, 97 **MEMBERSHIPS** Amer Assoc of Teachers of Spanish & Portuguese; Amer Assoc of Teachers of Italian; Gerontological Soc Amer; Amer Assoc of Teachers of Esperanto **RESEARCH** Hispanic Linguistics; Italian Studies; Esperantic Studies; Semiotics; Gerontology **SELECTED PUBLICATIONS** Auth, The Esperanto Language, Legas, 99; Coauth, The Imaginative Basis of Thought and Culture: Contemporary Perspectives on Giambattista Vico, Canadian Scholars, 94; auth, The Semiotics of Ageism, Univ Toronto, 92 **CONTACT ADDRESS** Modern Languages, Univ Louisville, Louisville, KY, 40292-0001. **EMAIL** fhnues01@ulkyvm.lousville.edu

NUGENT, PAULINE
PERSONAL Born 06/28/1938, Ireland **DISCIPLINE** CLASSICAL STUDIES **EDUCATION** Univ Incarnate Word, BA, 64; Univ Tex Austin, MA, 71, PhD 92. **CAREER** Instr, Incarnate Word Col, 75-79; asst prof, Southwest Mo State Univ, 92-97; assoc prof, 98-. **MEMBERSHIPS** Am Philol Asn; Class Asn of Middle West and South; North Am Patristic Soc; Vergilian Soc of Am; Am Asn of Teachers of French; Int Soc for the Class Traditions. **RESEARCH** Patristics; Classical studies; Antiquity; Biblical Hebrew. **SELECTED PUBLICATIONS** Auth, "Prefaces for Profit Without Prophets" in Studia Patristica, 97. **CONTACT ADDRESS** 1830 S Fremont Ave, Springfield, MO, 65804. **EMAIL** PAN851F@mail.smsu.edu

NUSSBAUM, ALAN
PERSONAL Born 12/17/1947, New York, NY, m, 1987, 3 children **DISCIPLINE** LINGUISTICS **EDUCATION** Washington Sq Coll of NYU, BA, 69; Oxford Univ, diploma, 74; Harvard Univ, PhD, 76. **CAREER** Instr, 75-85, asst prof, 76, assoc prof, 81, Yale Univ; prof/assoc prof, Cornell Univ, 85-. **MEMBERSHIPS** Amer Philological Assoc (APA) **RESEARCH** Indo-European linguistics, Greek and Latin historical grammar **SELECTED PUBLICATIONS** Auth, Head and Horn in Indo-European, 86; coauth, Black Athena Revisited, Word Games: The linguistic evidence in Black Athena, Chapel Hill, 96; auth, Sound Law and Analogy: Papers in honor of R. S.P. Beekes, The Saussure Effect in Latin and Italic, Amsterdam-Atlanta, 97; Mir Curad: Studies in honor of Calvert Watkins, Severe Problems, Innsbruck, 98. **CONTACT ADDRESS** Classics Dept, Cornell Univ, 120 Goldwin Smith Hall, Ithaca, NY, 14853-3201. **EMAIL** ajn8@cornell.edu

NYE, JEAN C.
PERSONAL Born 03/16/1932, New Sewickley Twp, PA, m, 1955 **DISCIPLINE** ROMANCE LANGUAGES **EDUCATION** Geneva Col, BA, 53; Univ Pittsburgh, MLitt, 57; Univ Toledo, PhD, 72. **CAREER** Teacher English & French, Zelienople High Sch, 53-59; from asst prof to assoc prof, 59-72, prof Span & French, Findlay Col, 72-, Spanish transl, Centrex Corp; mem bd dirs, Cent States Conf Teaching Foreign Lang; asst vpres Instit Advancement. **MEMBERSHIPS** Teachers English to Speakers Other Lang; MLA; Am Asn Teachers Span & Port; founder Int Cen for Lang & Resource Development. **RESEARCH** Teaching of English in the junior high schools in Puerto Rico; billingual, bicultural education. **SELECTED PUBLICATIONS** Auth, Christmas as portrayed in Spanish art, 12/66 & Easter as protrayed in Spanish art, 3/70, Church Advocate. **CONTACT ADDRESS** Dept of Mod Lang, Univ of Findlay, 1000 N Main St, Findlay, OH, 45840-3695. **EMAIL** nye@lucy.findlay.edu

O

O'CONNELL, JOANNA
DISCIPLINE SPANISH AND PORTUGUESE LITERATURE **EDUCATION** Univ Calif Berkeley, BA, 79; MA, 82; PhD, 88. **RESEARCH** Latin American literature and culture; feminism and feminist theory; issues of colonialism, race, and nationalism; indigenous revitalization movements and writing; African and Caribbean writing in French and English. **SELECTED PUBLICATIONS** Auth, Prospero's Daughter: The Prose of Rosario Castellanos, Univ Tex, 95; Pre-Columbian Literatures in Mexico, Manual Mex Lit, 94; co-ed, Post-Colonial, Emergent, and Indigenous Feministms, J Women Cult Soc, 95. **CONTACT ADDRESS** Spanish and Portuguese Dept, Univ of Minnesota, Twin Cities, 34 Folwell Hall, 9 Pleasant St SE, Minneapolis, MN, 55455. **EMAIL** oconn001@maroon.tc.umn.edu

O'CONNOR, MICHAEL PATRICK
PERSONAL Born 04/07/1950, Lackawanna, NY **DISCIPLINE** ANCIENT NEAR EASTERN LANGUAGES; LITERATURE **EDUCATION** Univ Michigan, PhD 78, AM 74; Univ of British Columbia, MA 72; Univ Notre Dame, BA 70. **CAREER** Catholic Univ of Amer, assoc prof 97-; Union Theol Sem, assoc prof 95-97; Univ St Thomas St Paul Sem, asst prof 92-95; Editing 80-93; Eisenbrauns IN, Sr consul editor 85-; Boston Univ Med Sch, neuro consul 85-89; The Anchor Bible, DoubleDay & Co NY, asst gen editor 77-80. **MEMBERSHIPS** AOS; CBA; SBL; Biblical Colloquium. **RESEARCH** Poetry **SELECTED PUBLICATIONS** Auth, Hebrew Verse Structure, Winona Lake IN, Eisenbrauns, 80, 2nd print, 97; auth, An Introduction to Biblical Hebrew Syntax, coauth, Winona Lake IN, Eisenbrauns, 90, 6th print 97. **CONTACT ADDRESS** Languages and Literatures, The Catholic Univ of America, Washington, DC, 20064. **EMAIL** oconnorm@cua.edu

O'CONNOR, PATRICIA W.
PERSONAL Born 04/26/1931, Memphis, TN, m, 1953, 2 children **DISCIPLINE** ROMANCE LANGUAGES **EDUCATION** Univ Fla, BAE, 53, MA, 54, PhD(Span & French), 62. **CAREER** From Instr to Prof Span, 62-96, Charles Phelps Taft Prof Span Lang & Lit, Univ Cincinnati, 96-. **HONORS AND AWARDS** Taft res grant, Spain, 65, 72, 75, 79 & 81; Rieveschl Award for creative & scholarly works, 82; Correspondiente of the Royal Span Acad of Lang, 90; Distinguished Res Prof of the Year, 90; Alumna of Achievement, Univ Fla, 97. **MEMBERSHIPS** Am Asn Teachers Span & Port; MLA; Midwest Mod Lang Asn; AAUP. **RESEARCH** Contemporary Spanish theater; post-war Spanish novel; sexism in literature. **SELECTED PUBLICATIONS** Auth, Women in the Theater of Gregorio Martinez Sierra, American, 67; Gregorio and Maria Martinez Sierra, Twayne, 77; Contemporary Spanish Theater, Scribner's, 80; transl & ed, Plays of Protest from the Franco Era, Madrid, 81; auth, Contemporary Spanish Theater: The Social Comedies, Madrid, SGEL, 83; Dramturgas espa?olas de hoy: una introducc?on, Madrid, Fundamentos, 89; Plays of the New Dramatic Spain (1975-1990), Univ Press Am, 92; Julia Maura: Lark in a Hostile Garden, In: Studies in Honor at Geogina Sabat-Rivers, Madrid, Castalia, 92; Julia Maura, In: Spanish Women Writers, Greenwood Press, 93; Antonio Buero Vallejo en sus espejos, Fundamentos, 96; Piezas Breves de mujeres sobre mujeres/ Short Spanish Plays By Women About Women (Bilingual ed), Madrid, Fundamentos, 98; author of numerous journal articles. **CONTACT ADDRESS** Dept of Romance Lang & Lit, Univ of Cincinnati, PO Box 210377, Cincinnati, OH, 45221-0377. **EMAIL** pat.oconnor@uc.edu

O'CONNOR, THOMAS
DISCIPLINE SPANISH LANGUAGE AND LITERATURE **EDUCATION** SUNY Albany, PhD. **CAREER** Prof, SUNY Binghamton. **RESEARCH** Span lit of the Golden Age, particularly Calderonian theater; myth studies; and the relationship of theatrical discourse to soc practice. **SELECTED PUBLICATIONS** Auth, Myth and Mythology in the Theater of Calderon, 88; auth/ed, El encanto es la hermosura/La segunda Celestina, 94; ed, Spanish Classical Texts, Pegasus; co-ed, Spanish Golden Age Theater, Bilingual. **CONTACT ADDRESS** SUNY Binghamton, PO Box 6000, Binghamton, NY, 13902-6000. **EMAIL** toconnor@binghamton.edu

O'DONNELL, MABRY MILLER
PERSONAL Born 07/18/1945, Huntsville, AL, m, 1972, 3 children **DISCIPLINE** SPEECH COMMUNICATION, GENDER STUDIES **EDUCATION** La State Univ, BA, 67; Univ Ala, MA, 69; Bowling Green State Univ, PhD(interpersonal and public commun), 77. **CAREER** Instr to assoc prof, 69-88, PROF SPEECH, MARIETTA COL, 88-, Forensics Coach, 69-. **HONORS AND AWARDS** Outstanding Fac Award, 88, 97; Alpha Lambda Delta Fac Award, 89, 90; Outstanding Fac Mem in Continuing Educ, 91; Harness Fel, 92-95; McCoy Prof, 94-98; Speech Commun Asn of Ohio's 1994 Col Teacher of the Year; William R. and Marie Adamson Flescher Prof of Humanities, 95-99; Pi Kappa Delta Coaches Hon Roll, 95, 97; E.R. Nichols Award, Outstanding Forensics Instr in the Nation, presented by Pi Kappa Delta, 96. **MEMBERSHIPS** Nat Commun Asn; Ohio Acad of Hist; Ohio Forensic Asn; Alpha Epsilon Rho; Alpha Lambda Delta; Delta Gamma; Omicron Delta Kappa; Order of Omega; Phi Alpha Theta; Pi Kappa Delta. **RESEARCH** Frances Wright; forensics; public address. **SELECTED PUBLICATIONS** Auth, Effective Interviewing or How to Get Your Client to Tell You What You Need to Know, Proc of Small Bus Inst Dir Asn, 2/94; Interpersonal Communication, In: Ready for the Real World. **CONTACT ADDRESS** 215 5th St., Marietta, OH, 45750-4025. **EMAIL** odonnelm@marietta.edu

O'DONNELL, VICTORIA
PERSONAL Born 02/12/1939, Greensburg, PA, m, 1993, 2 children **DISCIPLINE** SPEECH COMMUNICATION **EDUCATION** Pa St Univ, BA 59, MA, 62, PhD, 68. **CAREER** Asst prof to prof, Dept of Commun/Pub Address, Univ of N Tex, 67-89; Dept Ch, 81-89, Dept of Commun/Pub Address, Univ of N Tex; Dept Ch, Dept of Speech Commun, Ore State Univ, 89-91; Prof, Dept of Speech Commun, Mo State Univ-Bozeman, 91-93; Dir, Univ Honors Prog, Mo State Univ-Bozeman, 93-. **HONORS AND AWARDS** Honors prof, Univ of N Tex, 76; Mortar Board Top Prof, 79, 86; Mo State Univ Alum Assoc & Bozeman Chamber of Com Excellence Award, 97. **MEMBERSHIPS** Nat Commun Assoc; Int Commun Assoc; Western States Commun Assoc; Nat Col Honors Coun. **RESEARCH** Television criticism; propaganda & persuasion; env commun; documentary filmmaker. **SELECTED PUBLICATIONS** Coauth, Persuasion and Propaganda, Sage, 86, 92, 93, 98; auth, Introduction to Public Communication, Kendall-Hunt, 92, 93; auth, Collective Memory and the End of the Cold War, The National Honors Report, 95. **CONTACT ADDRESS** Univ Honors Prog, Montana State Univ, PO Box 172140, Bozeman, MT, 59717-2140. **EMAIL** vodonnel@montana.edu

O'FLAHERTY, JAMES CARNEAL
PERSONAL Born 04/28/1914, Henrico Co, VA, m, 1936, 1 child **DISCIPLINE** GERMAN **EDUCATION** Georgetown Col, BA, 39; Univ Ky, MA, 41; Univ Chicago, PhD, 50. **CAREER** Instr hist & relig, Georgetown Col, 39-41; from instr to assoc prof, 47-58, chmn dept, 61-69, Prof Ger, Wake Forest Univ, 58-, Am Philos Soc res grant, Ger, 58; Beecher lectr, Amherst Col, 58; Fulbright res fel, Ger, 60-61; lectr Kulterelles Wort Ser, Sudwestfunk, Baden-Baden, Ger, 61; mem adv comt, Fulbright Awards, 62, chmn, 63; lectr, 4th Int Cong Germanists, Princeton Univ, 70; lectr, 1st Int Hamann-Colloquium, Luneburg, Ger, 76. **HONORS AND AWARDS** Friendship Award, Fed Rep Germany, 83 **MEMBERSHIPS** S Atlantic Mod Lang Asn; Am Asn Teachers Ger; NAm Nietzsche Soc. **RESEARCH** Johann Georg Hamann; Nietzsche; philosophy of language. **SELECTED PUBLICATIONS** Auth, Unity and Language: A Study in the philosophy of Johann Georg Hamann, Univ NC, Chapel Hill, 52, Ams Press, 66; Max Planck and Adolf Hitler, AAUP Bull, 56; Hamann's Socratic Memorabilia, Johns Hopkins Univ, 67; co-auth, Raabe's Else von der Tanne, Univ Ala Press, 72; auth, The Quiarrel of Reason with Itself: Essays on Hamann, Michaelis, Lessing, Camden House, 88; East and West in the thought of Hamann, Ger Rev, 68; Eros and creativity in Nietzsche's Birth of Tragedy, In: Studies in German Literature of the Nineteenth and Twentieth Centuries, Univ NC, 70; The Concept of knowledge in Hamann's Sokratische Denkwurdigkeiten and Nietzsche's Geburt der Gragodie, Monatshefte, 4/72; co-ed & contribr, Studies in Nietzsche and the Classical Tradition, Univ NC, Chapel Hill, 76; auth, Johann Georg Hamann, G K Hall, 79; auth, Werner Heisenberg on the Nazi Revolution: Three Hitherto Unpublished Letters, J Hist Ideas, Oct 92; Johann Georg Hamann, Dictionary of Literary Biography, 90. **CONTACT ADDRESS** 2164 Faculty Dr, Winston-Salem, NC, 27106. **EMAIL** jcof@erols.com

O'HARA, JAMES J.
DISCIPLINE AUGUSTAN POETRY **EDUCATION** Col Holy Cross, AB; Univ Mich, PhD. **CAREER** Vis asst prof, 86-87; asst prof, 87-92; assoc prof, 92-97; Professor, 97-. **HONORS AND AWARDS** Holy Cross, Nat Merit Scholar; Henry Bean four-year full-tuition Classics Sch; Philip A. Conniff Clas Prize; Valedictorian Mich: Sci & Arts First-year Fel; dept Clas Studies, Dissertatoion fel, Horace H. Rackham Predoctoral Fel. Nat Endowment Hum Rome Prize fel, Proj grants. **SELECTED PUBLICATIONS** Auth, Death and the Optimistic Prophecy in Vergil's Aeneid, Princeton, 90. **CONTACT ADDRESS** Wesleyan Univ, Middletown, CT, 06459. **EMAIL** johara@wesleyan.edu

O'HEARN, CAROLYN
DISCIPLINE ENGLISH LINGUISTICS AND LITERATURE **EDUCATION** Univ Mo, BS; Ariz State Univ, MA, PhD; **CAREER** Assoc prof. **RESEARCH** Medieval literature, technical writing. **SELECTED PUBLICATIONS** Auth, Writing, Grammar and Usage, 89; articles on ling and lit. **CONTACT ADDRESS** Dept of Eng, Pittsburg State Univ, 1701 S Broadway St, Pittsburg, KS, 66762. **EMAIL** cohearn@pittstate.edu

OATES, MICHAEL DAVID
PERSONAL Born 09/23/1939, Derby, CT, m, 1963, 2 children **DISCIPLINE** FRENCH LINGUISTICS & METHODOLOGY **EDUCATION** Fairfield Univ, AB, 61; Assumption Col, MAT, 63; Georgetown Univ, PhD(French ling), 70. **CAREER** Intern French, Framingham High Sch, Mass, 61-62; teacher, Malden High Sch, 62-65; assoc prof, 67-75, Prof French, Univ Northern Iowa, 75-, Pres, Study Ed Asn Conn, 60-61; honors intern, Assumption Col, 61-62; Univ Northern Iowa study grant, Univ Besancon, 72. **MEMBERSHIPS** Am Coun Teachers Foreign Lang; Am Asn Teachers Fr. **RESEARCH** French linguistics; language teaching research. **SELECTED PUBLICATIONS** Auth, A Syntactic Classification of French Verbs as a Basis for a Monostructural Presentation at the Beginning Level, Current Issues in Teaching French, 472; Principles and Techniques for Stimulating Foreign-Language Conversation, Foreign Lang Annals, 1-72; Grass Roots Efforts to Encourage the Study of French, 476 & Commentetre francais, 1178, AATF Nat Bull;

A Non-Intensive FLES Program in French, Fr Rev, 380; Oral Translation: An Old Horse for the New Frontier, In: The Report of the 1980 Central States Conference on the Teaching of Foreign Languages, New Frontiers in Foreign Lang Educ, 80; Cooperative Grouping in French Conversation and Composition, In: Proceedings of the Second National Conference on Individualized Instruction in Foreign Languages, Ohio State Univ, 81; Keys to Study Abroad Programs, Alberta Mod Lang J, spring 81; Representing Things Foreign And Teaching Foreign-languages - French - Zarate,g, Modern Language J, Vol 0079, 1995; 2nd-language Practice - Classroom Strategies For Developing Communicative Competence - Duquette,g, Modern Language J, Vol 0080, 1996. **CONTACT ADDRESS** Dept of Foreign Lang, Univ of Northern Iowa, Cedar Falls, IA, 50613.

OBERHELMAN, HARLEY DEAN
PERSONAL Born 06/30/1928, Clay Center, KS, m, 1954, 2 children **DISCIPLINE** SPANISH LANGUAGE & LITERATURE **EDUCATION** Univ Kans, BSEd, 50, MA, 52, PhD(romance lang), 58. **CAREER** Teaching asst Span, Univ Kans, 50-56; dir foreign lang, Lawrence Pub Schs, Kans, 56-58; from asst prof to assoc prof foreign lang, 58-64, chmn dept, 63-70, prof Class & Romance Lang, Tex Tech Univ, 64-, lectr Span methodology, Univ Wis, 55, Univ NMex, 56, Eastern Mont Col, 59 & Univ Kans, 60; Fulbright lectr, Nat Univ Tucuman, 61; State of Tex res study grant, Uruguay, 61 & Colombia, 77; assoc ed, Hispania, 62-66; chmn Latin Am area studies, Tex Tech Univ, 69-77. **MEMBERSHIPS** Am Asn Teachers Span & Port. **RESEARCH** Spanish American literature; methodology of second language teaching; River Plate literature. **SELECTED PUBLICATIONS** Auth, Sobre la vida y las ficciones de Ernesto Sabato, In: Obras de Ficcion, Losada, Buenos Aires, 67; Ernesto Sabato, Twayne, 70; coauth, Espanol Moderno, Merrill, 70; auth, Jose Donoso and the Nueva Narrativa, Revista de Estudios Hispanicos, 1/75; Garcia Marquez and the American South, Chasqui, 11/75; Education and History of Knowledge, In: Cien Anos de Soledad, Studies by SCMLA, 4/75; Myth and Structure in Sabato's Abaddon, Am Hispanist, 3/76; The Presence of Faulkner in the Writings of Garcia Marquez, Tex Tech Press, 80; auth, Gabriel Garcia Marquez, A Study of the Short Fiction, Twayne, 80; The Presence of Hemingway in the Short Fiction of Gabriel Garcia Marquez, York, 94; Garcia Marquez and Cuba, York, 95; ed, Alone Against the Sea, Poetry from Cuba, York, 98. **CONTACT ADDRESS** Dept of Class & Modern Lang, Tex Tech Univ, Lubbock, TX, 79409-2071. **EMAIL** pvobe@ttacs.ttu.edu

OCAMPO, FRANCISCO
DISCIPLINE SPANISH AND PORTUGUESE LITERATURE **EDUCATION** State Univ NY Buffalo, MA, 82; Univ SC, PhD, 89. **RESEARCH** Relationship between syntax, cognition and discourse; word order in spoken Spanish; language variation; conversation analysis; language and ideology. **SELECTED PUBLICATIONS** Auth, Pragmatic factors on word order: constructions with a verb and an adverb in spoken Spanish, Probus, 95; The word order of two-constituent constructions in Spoken Spanish, John Benjamins, 95; The word order of constructions with a verb, a subject, and a direct object in spoken Spanish, John Benjamins, 94; co-auth, Spanish OV/VO word order variationin Spanish/Quechua bilingual speakers, Georgetown Univ, 95. **CONTACT ADDRESS** Spanish and Portuguese Dept, Univ of Minnesota, Twin Cities, 34 Folwell Hall, 9 Pleasant St SE, Minneapolis, MN, 55455. **EMAIL** Francisco.A.Ocampo-1@tc.umn.edu

ODEN, ROBERT A., JR.
PERSONAL Born 09/11/1946, SD, m, 1967, 2 children **DISCIPLINE** NEAR EASTERN LANGUAGES **EDUCATION** Harvard Col, AB, 69; Cambridge Univ, BA, MA, 71; Harvard Univ, PhD, 75. **CAREER** Asst, assoc, full prof Relig, Dartmouth Col, 75-89; headmaster, Hotchkiss sch, 89-95; Pres, Kenyon Col, 95- . **HONORS AND AWARDS** Dartmouth Col disting tchg awd, first recipient, 79. **MEMBERSHIPS** Soc Biblical Lit **RESEARCH** Ancient Near Eastern languages and literatures. **SELECTED PUBLICATIONS** Auth, The Bible Without Theology, Harper, 87; The Phoenician History, 83. **CONTACT ADDRESS** Office of the President, Kenyon Col, Ransom Hall, Gambier, OH, 43022. **EMAIL** odenr@kenyon.edu

OETTING, JANNA B.
PERSONAL Born 01/15/1964, Seward, NE, m, 1991, 2 children **DISCIPLINE** CHILD LANGUAGE **EDUCATION** Augustana Col, BA, 86; Univ Kans, MA, 88, PhD, 92. **CAREER** Asst Prof, 92-98, Assoc Prof, La State Univ, 98-. **HONORS AND AWARDS** Nat Asn Am Bus Clubs Student Schol, 87; Colmery O'Neil Veteran's Admin Student Traineeship, 87; Sertoma Student Schol, 87; Dept Speech-Lang-Hearing Grad Clinician Award, Univ Kans, 88; Kappa Kappa Gamma Student Rehab Schol, Nat Office, 88; Dept Speech-Lang-Hearing Grad Res Award, Univ Kans, 89; Scheifelbush Grad Student Res Award, Univ Kans, 92; recipient of numerous research grants and student training grants. **MEMBERSHIPS** Omicron Delta Kappa; Phi Kappa Phi; Am Speech-Lang-Hearing Asn, 88; Soc Res Child Development; Sigma Xi; Int Asn Study Child Lang; La Speech-Lang-Hearing Asn; Int Clinical Phonetics and Ling Asn; Coun Exceptional Children. **RESEARCH** Child language acquisition; language impairments in children; linguistic diversity/dialect. **SELECTED PUBLICATIONS** Coauth, Frequency of input effects on SLI children's Word Comprehension, J Speech & Hearing Res, 94; Quick incidental learning (QUIL) of words by school-age children with and without a language impairment, J Speech & Hearing Res, 95; Past tense marking by children with and without specific language impairment, J Speech, Lang, & Hearing Res, 97; Identifying language impairmentin the context of dialect, Clinical Ling & Phonetics (in press). **CONTACT ADDRESS** Louisiana State Univ, M&DA Bldg, Rm 163, Baton Rouge, LA, 70803-2606. **EMAIL** cdjanna@lsuvm.sncc.lsu.edu

OGLES, ROBERT M.
DISCIPLINE SOCIAL PSYCHOLOGICAL EFFECTS OF MASS COMMUNICATION CONTENT, HISTORY OF MASS **EDUCATION** Univ Wis, PhD, 87. **CAREER** Assoc prof, Purdue Univ. **RESEARCH** History of mass communications. **SELECTED PUBLICATIONS** Auth, Getting Research Out of the Classroom and Into the Newspaper, Col Media Rev, 91; MTV: Music Television in R.G. Picard (ed), The Cable Network Handbk, 93; coauth, Question Specificity in Studies of Television's Contributions to Viewers' Fear and Perceived Probability of Criminal Victimization", Mass Commun Rev, 93. **CONTACT ADDRESS** Dept of Commun, Purdue Univ, 1080 Schleman Hall, West Lafayette, IN, 47907-1080. **EMAIL** rogles@sla.purdue.edu

OHALA, JOHN JEROME
PERSONAL Born 07/19/1941, Chicago, IL, m, 1969 **DISCIPLINE** LINGUISTICS **EDUCATION** Univ Notre Dame, BA, 63; Univ Calif, Los Angeles, MA, 66, PhD(ling), 69. **CAREER** Nat Sci Found fel, Res Inst Logopedics & Phoniatrics, Fac Med, Univ Tokyo, 69-70; asst prof, 70-72, assoc prof, 72-77, Prof Ling, Univ Calif, Berkeley, 77-, Vis lector, Inst Fonetik, Copenhagen Univ, 73. **MEMBERSHIPS** Ling Soc Am; AAAS; Acoust Soc Am. **RESEARCH** Physiology of speech; sound change; phonology. **SELECTED PUBLICATIONS** Auth, Aspects of the Control and Production of Speech, Univ Calif, 70; Physical Models in Phonology, Proc Cong Phonetic Sci, 72; contribr, Experimental historical phonology, In: Historical Linguistics II, North Holland, 74; Production of tone, In: Tone: A Linguistic Survey, Acad Press, 78; Coarticulation And Phonology, Language And Speech, Vol 0036, 1993; Listeners Normalization of Vowel Quality Is Influenced by Restored Consonantal Context, Phonetica, Vol 0051, 1994; A Probable Case of Clicks Influencing The Sound Patterns of Some European Languages, Phonetica, Vol 0052, 1995. **CONTACT ADDRESS** Dept of Ling, Univ of Calif, 2337 Dwinelle Hall, Berkeley, CA, 94720-2651.

OHNUMA, REIKO
PERSONAL Born 04/10/1963, New Haven, CT, m, 1993, 1 child **DISCIPLINE** ASIAN STUDIES, BUDDHIST STUDIES **EDUCATION** Univ of Michigan, Ann Arbor, PhD, 97. **CAREER** Vis lectr, 96-98, Univ of TX, Austin; Asst Prof, 98-99, Univ of AL, Tuscaloosa. **HONORS AND AWARDS** Charlotte Newcombe Doctoral Dissertation Fellowship. **MEMBERSHIPS** Intl Assoc of Buddhist Stud; Amer Acad of Rel. **RESEARCH** Indian Buddhist Literature, especially narrative literature; Women and Literature. **SELECTED PUBLICATIONS** Auth, The Gift of the Body and the Gift of Dharma, History of Religions, 98. **CONTACT ADDRESS** 11 Dubois Terrace, Tuscaloosa, AL, 35401. **EMAIL** rohnuma@bama.ua.edu

OINAS, FELIX JOHANNES
PERSONAL Born 03/06/1911, Estonia, m, 1937, 2 children **DISCIPLINE** SLAVIC & FINNO-UGRIC LINGUISTICS **EDUCATION** Tartu Univ, MA, 37; Ind Univ, PhD(ling), 52. **CAREER** Lectr Finno-Ugric, Pazmany Peter Univ, Budapest, 38-40; vis lectr Estonian, Baltic Univ, Ger, 46-48; lectr Slavic lang & lit, 51-52, from instr to assoc prof, 52-65, actg chmn Uralic & Altaic prog, 60-61, Prof Slavic Lang & Lit & Uralic & Altaic Studies, Ind Univ, Bloomington, 65-, Fulbright scholar, Finland, 61-62; Guggenheim scholar, Finland, 61-62 & 66-67; Fulbright- Hays grant, Yugoslavia, 64-65; Nat Endowment for Humanities grant, 74; fel, Folklore Inst, Ind Univ Commemorative Medal, Finnish Govt, 68; vis prof folklore, Univ Calif, Berkeley, 76. **HONORS AND AWARDS** Cultural Award, Found Estonian Arts & Lett, 78; First Prize, Arthur Puksow Found, 80. **MEMBERSHIPS** MLA; corresp mem Finnish Lit Soc; Asn Advan Baltic Studies (vp, 72-73); fel Am Folklore Soc; Finnish Acad Sci. **RESEARCH** Slavic and Finno-Ugric linguistics and folklore. **SELECTED PUBLICATIONS** Estonian General Reader, 63 & Basic Course in Estonian, 66, Mouton; Studies in Finnic-Slavic Folklore Relations, Finnish Acad Sci, 69; co-ed, The Study of Russian Folklore, Mouton, 75; ed, Folklore, Nationalism, and Politics, Slavica, 78; Heroic Epic and Saga: An Introduction to the World's Great Folk Epics, Ind Univ, 78; Kalevipoeg kutkeis, Mans, 79; ed, European Folklore, Trickster Press, 81; Shamanism - Soviet Studies of Traditional Religion in Siberia And Central-asia - Balzer,mm, J of Folklore Research, Vol 0029, 1992; Couvade in Estonia + Transferring The Mothers Birth Pangs to Her Husband, Slavic And East European J, Vol 0037, 1993; The Great Bear, a Thematic Anthology of Oral Poetry in Finno-ugrian Languages - Honko,l, Timonen,s, Branch,m, J of Folklore Research, Vol 0032, 1995. **CONTACT ADDRESS** 2513 E Eighth St, Bloomington, IN, 47401.

OLCOTT, ANTHONY
PERSONAL m **DISCIPLINE** MODERN RUSSIAN-LANGUAGE AND LITERATURE **EDUCATION** Stanford Univ, PhD, 76. **CAREER** Instr, Univ VA, Hamilton Col, SUNY Oswego, Phillips Acad; instr, 86-. **HONORS AND AWARDS** Asst dir, Colgate Univ, Moscow Study Group, 97. **RESEARCH** Crime genre in Russ. **SELECTED PUBLICATIONS** Auth, Murder at the Red October; May Day in Magadan. **CONTACT ADDRESS** Dept of Russ Stud, Colgate Univ, 13 Oak Drive, Hamilton, NY, 13346.

OLDCORN, ANTHONY
PERSONAL Born 06/20/1935, Longridge, England, m, 1960, 2 children **DISCIPLINE** ITALIAN LANGUAGE AND LITERATURE **EDUCATION** Oxford Univ, BA, 58; Univ Virginia, MA, 61; Harvard Univ, PhD, 70. **CAREER** Instr French & Ital, Boston Col, 60-62; teaching fel, Harvard Univ, 62-65; from instr to asst prof Ital, Wellesley Col, 66-71, acting chmn dept, 69-70; asst prof, 71-76; assoc prof, 76-80, Prof Ital Studies, Brown Univ, 80-, Nat Endowment for Humanities fel, 78-79; vis prof Ital, Vassar Col, 80-81, Dante Antolini chair, 81-; Ital field ed, Twayne World Authors Series, 81. **HONORS AND AWARDS** MA, Brown Univ, 77. **MEMBERSHIPS** Am Asn Tchr(s) Ital; Am Comt Hist 2nd World War; Dante Soc Am; MLA. **RESEARCH** Medieval, Renaissance, baroque and mod Italian lit; textual criticism; rhetoric and lit stylistics. **SELECTED PUBLICATIONS** Auth, A Recensio of the Sources of the Gerusalemme Conquistata: Notes for a New Edition, Forum Italicum, 75; Virgilio Giotti (poems) (Transl), Copper Beech Press, 75; Pirandello o del candore?, Mod Lang Notes, 76; The Textual Problems of Tasso's Gerusalemme Conquistata, Longo, 76; Tasso's Epic Theory, Italica, 77. **CONTACT ADDRESS** Italian Stu Dept, Brown Univ, PO Box 1942, Providence, RI, 02912-9127. **EMAIL** anthony_oldcorn@brown.edu

OLENIK, JOHN KENNETH
PERSONAL Born 05/07/1941, Cleveland, OH, m **DISCIPLINE** MODERN CHINESE HISTORY AND LITERATURE **EDUCATION** John Carroll Univ, BSS, 63; Seton Hall Univ, MA, 66; Cornell Univ, MA, 70, PhD(hist China), 73. **CAREER** Asst prof, 71-78, Assoc Prof Hist E Asia, Montclair State Col, 78-, Am Coun Learned SocNat Endowment for Humanities lang & res fel, Japan, 76-77; vis scholar, Fac Law, Keio Univ, Japan, 76-77. **MEMBERSHIPS** AHA; Asn Asian Studies. **RESEARCH** China, Repubican Period; China, political parties and movements; China, poetry of the Six Dynasties Period. **SELECTED PUBLICATIONS** Mountain Fires - The Red-army 3-year War in South China, 1934-1938 - Benton,g, J of Asian History, Vol 0028, 1994; Mountain Fires - The Red-army 3-year War in South China, 1934- 1938 - Benton,g, J of Asian History, Vol 0028, 1994. **CONTACT ADDRESS** 1 Normal Ave, Montclair, NJ, 07043-1699.

OLIVER, MARY BETH
DISCIPLINE PSYCHOLOGICAL AND SOCIAL EFFECTS MASS MEDIA **EDUCATION** VA Polytech Inst & State Univ, BA, 86; Univ WI, MA, 88, PhD, 91. **CAREER** Assoc Prof, , 96; Asst Prof, VA Polytech Inst & State Univ, 91-96. **HONORS AND AWARDS** Second-ranked student paper, Interpersonal div, Int Comm Asn, 89; Outstanding Grad Student Tchr Award, 90; Grad Student Tchg Excellence, 90; Top student paper, Mass Comm, Int Comm Asn, 90; Elizabeth Warner Risser fel, 90; Top Three paper in the Mass Comm Div, Speech Comm Asn, 95; Certificate Tchg Excellence Award, Va, Tech, 95; Alumni Tchg Award, 96; Mem, Acad Tchg Excellence, 96; Member, Acad Tchg, VA Tech, 96-; COTA Fel, 96-. **MEMBERSHIPS** Adv, 45 Undergraduates each semester; Fac dir, Supervisor, Fac Adv; Mem, VA Small Grants Comt, Scholar Comt, Comm studies search comt, Comm studies grad comt; Freshman Fac Conversation gp; Comput liaison; VA Tech; Mem, Women's hist month comt. **SELECTED PUBLICATIONS** Auth, Review On television: The violence factor, Jour Hist, 98; Rev Measuring psychol responses medial, Jour Broadcasting & Electronic Media, 98. **CONTACT ADDRESS** Virginia Polytech Inst & State Univ, Blacksburg, VA, 24061. **EMAIL** olivermb@vt.edu

OLIVERA WILLIAMS, MARIA ROSA
DISCIPLINE SPANISH LITERATURE **EDUCATION** Univ Toledo, BAS, 76; Ohio State Univ, MA, 78, PhD, 83. **CAREER** Assoc prof. **RESEARCH** Spanish American literature of the 19th and 20th centuries; feminist criticism; contemporary women authors. **SELECTED PUBLICATIONS** Auth, La poesia gauchesca de Hidalgo a Hernandez; pubs on Uruguayan literature in exile, Mario Benedetti, Armonia Somers, Cristina Peri-Ross, Juan Gelman and Jose Emilio Pacheco. **CONTACT ADDRESS** Romance Languages and Literatures Dept, Univ of Notre Dame, Notre Dame, IN, 46556.

OLIVIA, LEONORA
DISCIPLINE GREEK AND LATIN LANGUAGES AND LITERATURES **EDUCATION** Brown Univ, PhD. **CAREER**

Dept Classics, Millsaps Col **SELECTED PUBLICATIONS** Publ on, comp lit. **CONTACT ADDRESS** Dept of Classics, Millsaps Col, 1701 N State St, Jackson, MS, 39210. **EMAIL** olivil@okra.millsaps.edu

OLLER, JOHN WILLIAM
PERSONAL Born 10/22/1943, Las Vegas, NV, m, 1976, 4 children **DISCIPLINE** LINGUISTICS **EDUCATION** Fresno State Col, BA, 65; Univ Rochester, NY, MA, 68, PhD, 69. **CAREER** Assoc prof, Dept of English, UCLA, 69-72; prof, Dept of Linguistics, Univ NM, 72-96; prof and head, Dept of Communicative Disorders, Univ South-Western LA, Lafayette, LA, 97-. **HONORS AND AWARDS** MLA Middleberger Medal, 83 (best book on foreign language teaching); NDEA Fel, Univ Rochester, 66-69. **MEMBERSHIPS** Linguistic Soc Am; Am Speech Language Hearing Asn. **RESEARCH** Language and intelligence, autism. **SELECTED PUBLICATIONS** Auth, Coding Information in Natural Languages, Mouton, 71; ed with Jack C Richards, Focus on the Learner: Pragmatic Perspectives for the Language Teacher, Newbury House, 73; ed with Kyle Perkins, Language in Health Education: Testing the Tests, Newbury House, 78; auth, Language Tests at School: A Pragmatic Approach, Longman, 79, Japanese trans, Longman, 94; ed with Kyle Perkins, Research in Language Testing, Newbury House, 80; ed, Issues in Language Testing Research, Newbury House, 83; ed with Patricia Richard-Amato, Methods That Work: A Smorgasbord of Ideas for Language Teachers, Newbury House, 83; ed, Language and Experience: Classic Pragmatism, Univ Press Am, 89; auth with J. Robert Scott and S Chesarek, Language and Bilingualism: More Tests of Tests, Bucknell Univ Press, 91; auth with Saowalak Rattanavich and R F Walker, Teaching All the Children to Read, Open Univ Press, 92; ed, Methods That Work: Ideas for Literacy and Language Teachers, Heinle and Heinle Pubs, 93; auth with Jon Jonz, Cloze and Coherence, Bucknell Univ Press, 94. **CONTACT ADDRESS** Dept of Communicative Disorders, Univ of Southwestern Louisiana, PO Box 43170, Lafayette, LA, 70504-3170. **EMAIL** joller@usl.edu

OLLIVIER, LOUIS L.
DISCIPLINE SPANISH **EDUCATION** St Mary's Col Calif, BA, 64; Middlebury Col, MA, 66; Univ NMex, PhD, 73. **CAREER** Asst prof, 96-; **HONORS AND AWARDS** NDEA Title VI fel, Univ NMex, 70; Org Am States res fel, Porto Alegre, Brazil, 71. **SELECTED PUBLICATIONS** Auth, Cien anos de soledad: Existence is the Word, Latin Am Lit Rev, 75; O Tempo e o Vento: Universality of Yesterday, Chasqui, revista de lit latinoamericana, 74; rev, Graciliano Ramos by Richard Mazarra,Twayne Publ(s) Inc, 74. **CONTACT ADDRESS** Dept of For Lang, Western New Mexico Univ, 1000 West College Ave., Silver City, NM, 88061. **EMAIL** cowlingl@cs.wnmu.edu

OLMSTED, JANE
DISCIPLINE AMERICAN LITERATURE, MULTICULTURALISM **EDUCATION** Bowling Green State Univ, BFA; Univ Louisville, MA; Univ Minn, PhD. **CAREER** Prof **RESEARCH** Women Writers. **SELECTED PUBLICATIONS** Auth, The Pull to Memory and the Language of Place in Paule Marshall's The Chosen Place, The Timeless People, and Praisesong for the Widow, African Am Rev, 97. **CONTACT ADDRESS** Western Kentucky Univ, 1526 Big Red Way Street, Bowling Green, KY, 42101. **EMAIL** jane.olmsted@wku.edu

OLSEN, SOLVEIG
PERSONAL Born 08/23/1940, Hamburg, Germany **DISCIPLINE** GERMAN LANGUAGE & LITERATURE **EDUCATION** Univ Oslo, Cand Mag, 63, Cand Phil, 64; Pedag Sem, Oslo, Norway, teaching cert, 65; Rice Univ, Phd(Ger), 68. **CAREER** AdJGer, English & Norweg, Manglerud Komb Sk, Oslo, Norway, 60-64, lector, 64-65; asst prof, 68-74, Assoc Prof Ger & Chairperson Dept Foreign Lang & Lit, NTex State Univ, 74-, Res grant NTex State Univ, 76; Danforth fel, Danforth Found, 77-. **MEMBERSHIPS** MLA; AAUP; Am Asn Teachers Ger; Int Arbeitskreis fur Barockliteratur; Am Coun Teaching Foreign Lang. **SELECTED PUBLICATIONS** Auth, Der Anfang der Weltlichen Kantate in Deutschland, Lang Quart, Univ SFla, 72; Chr Hch Postels Beitrag zur Deutschen Literatur: Versuch einer Darstellung, Rodopi, Amsterdam, 73; Diesuche - Das-andere-lehrwerk-fur-deutsch-als-fremdsprache - German - Eismann,v, Enzenberger,hm, Vaneunen,k, Helmling,b, Kast,b, Mummert,i, Thurmair,m, Modern Language J, Vol 0080, 1996; Tapescript to Accompany Alles-gute - Basic German For Communication, 4th Edition- Briggs,j, Modern Language J, Vol 0081, 1997; Instructors Resource Kit to Accompany Alles-gute - Basic German For Communication, 4th Edition - Briggs,j, Modern Language J, Vol 0081, 1997; Alles-gute - Basic German For Communication 4th Edition- Briggs,j, Crean,je, Strasser,gf, Modern Language J, Vol 0081, 1997; Laboratory Manual to Accompany Alles-gute - Basic German For Communication 4 Edition - Briggs,j, Modern Language J, Vol 0081, 1997; Audiocassette Program to Accompany Alles-gute - Basic German For Communication 4th Edition - Briggs,j, Modern Language J, Vol 0081, 1997. **CONTACT ADDRESS** Dept of Foreign Lang & Lit, No Texas State Univ, PO Box 311127, Denton, TX, 76203-1127.

OLSON, PAUL RICHARD
PERSONAL Born 11/02/1925, Rockford, IL, m, 1953, 4 children **DISCIPLINE** ROMANCE LANGUAGES **EDUCATION** Univ Ill, AB, 48, AM, 50; Harvard Univ, PhD, 59. **CAREER** From instr to asst prof Span, Dartmouth Col, 56-61; from asst prof to assoc prof, 61-68, Prof Span, Johns Hopkins Univ, 68-, Guggenheim fel, 64-65; Fulbright Award, Spain, 64-65. **MEMBERSHIPS** MLA; Asoc Int Hispanistas. **RESEARCH** Spanish literature. **SELECTED PUBLICATIONS** Auth, Circle of Paradox: Time and Essence in the Poetry of Juan Ramon Jimenez, Johns Hopkins Press, 67; Galdos and history, MLN, 70; Unamuno's lacquered boxes, RHM, 74; Unamuno's Niebla, Ga Rev, 75; ed, Miguel de Unamuno: Como se nace una novela, Ediciones Guadarrama, Madrid, 77; contribr, Dos metafisicas del texto poetico, Asn Int Hisp, Toronto, 78. **CONTACT ADDRESS** 100 W University Pkwy, #4F, Baltimore, MD, 21210.

OLSON, STUART DOUGLAS
PERSONAL 2 children **DISCIPLINE** GREEK **EDUCATION** Bryn Mawr Coll, PhD, 87. **CAREER** Lectr, 87-90, Howard Univ; Asst Prof to Assoc Prof, 90-97, Univ of IL; Assoc Prof, 97-, Univ of Minnesota. **HONORS AND AWARDS** Whiting Fellowship in Hum, 86-87; James Rignall Wheeler Fellow; ASCSA; Outstanding Faculty Member; LAS Coll Award for Excellence; Alpha Epsilon Delta Outstanding Tchr Award. **MEMBERSHIPS** APA, Classical Assoc of the Middle West of South. **RESEARCH** Greek Poetry. **SELECTED PUBLICATIONS** Auth, Blood and Iron: Stories and Storytelling in Homer's Odyssey, Mnemosyne Supplement 148, Leiden, 95; Aristophanes: Peace, forthcoming Oxford University Press, 98; co-auth, Archestratos of Gela, Text, Translation and Commentary, forthcoming Oxford University Press; Politics and Poetry in Aristophanes Wasp, 96; Studies in the Later Manuscript Tradition of Aristophanes Peace, 98; Was Carcinus I a Tragic Playwright?, A Response, CP97. **CONTACT ADDRESS** Dept of Classical & Near Eastern Studies, Univ of Minn, 9 Pleasant St SE, Minneapolis, MN, 55455-0125. **EMAIL** sdolson@tc.umn.edu

OMAGGIO HADLEY, ALICE
DISCIPLINE FRENCH LITERATURE **EDUCATION** Pa State Univ, BS, 69; Ohio State Univ, MA, 72; PhD, 77. **CAREER** Prof, Univ Ill Urbana Champaign. **RESEARCH** Foreign language education; teacher education; second language learning. **SELECTED PUBLICATIONS** Auth, Teaching Language in Context: Proficiency-Oriented Instruction, Heinle, 86; Making Reading Comprehensible, For Lang Annals, 84; Proficiency-Based Instruction: Implications for Methodology, 88; co-auth, Bonjour ca va?, McGraw Hill, 87; Kalidoscope: Grammaire en contexte, Random, 88; Rendezvous: An Invitation to French, McGraw-Hill, 90; co-ed, Research in Language Learning: Principles, Processes and Prospects, 93. **CONTACT ADDRESS** French Dept, Univ Ill Urbana Champaign, 52 E Gregory Dr, Champaign, IL, 61820. **EMAIL** acoh@uiuc.edu

ONG, RORY J.
DISCIPLINE ASIAN AMERICAN LITERATURE AND RHETORIC AND COMPOSITION **EDUCATION** Miami, PhD. **CAREER** Asst prof, Washington State Univ. **RESEARCH** Ethnic studies, cultural studies, discourse theory. **CONTACT ADDRESS** Dept of English, Washington State Univ, 1 SE Stadium Way, PO Box 645020, Pullman, WA, 99164-5020. **EMAIL** rjong@wsuvm1.csc.wsu.edu

OPPENHEIMER, FRED E.
PERSONAL Born 02/22/1929, Berlin, Germany, d, 2 children **DISCIPLINE** GERMAN LANGUAGE & LITERATURE **EDUCATION** Cent MI Col, BA, 51; Univ WI, MA, 57, PhD, 61. **CAREER** From instr to asst prof Ger, Purdue Univ, 61-65; asst prof, Colo Col, 65-71; assoc prof Ger, 71-88, PROF GERMAN, MILLERSVILLE STATE COL, 88-98, CHMN, DEPT OF FOREIGN LANG, 79-98, RETIRED 8/21/98; Dir Jr Year Abroad, 72-. **MEMBERSHIPS** Am Asn Teachers Ger; MLA. **RESEARCH** Literature of German Classicism; the German novelle; literary allusion in the novels of Theodor Fontane. **CONTACT ADDRESS** Dept of Foreign Lang, Millersville Univ, Pennsylvania, PO Box 1002, Millersville, PA, 17551-0302.

ORDONEZ, ELIZABETH JANE
PERSONAL Born 07/27/1945, Los Angeles, CA **DISCIPLINE** SPANISH LITERATURE **EDUCATION** Univ Calif, Los Angeles, BA, 66, MA, 69; Univ Calif, Irvine, PhD(Span lit), 76. **CAREER** Asst prof Span, Ripon Col, 74-79; Assoc Prof Span, Univ Tex, Arlington, 79-, Span Govt grant, Ministerio de Asuntos Exteriores, 77. **MEMBERSHIPS** MLA; Am Asn Teachers Span & Port; Asoc Lit Femenina Hisp; Sch Latin Am; Am Asoc Advan Humanities. **RESEARCH** Spanish feminist literary theory and practice; film; Chicana literature. **SELECTED PUBLICATIONS** Auth, Forms of alienation in Matute's La Trampa, JSpan Studies: 20th Century, winter 76; Symbolic vision in Clarice Lispector's The Applie in the Dark, Letras Femeninas, spring 76; Nada: initiation into bourgeois patriarchy, In: The Analysis of Hispanic Texts: Current Trends in Methodology, Bilingual Press, 77; Mitificacion e imagen de la mujer en La Enferma de Elena Quiroga, Letras Femeninas, fall 77; The decoding and encoding of sex roles in Carmen Martin Gaite's Retahilas, Ky Romance Quart, 80; The female quest pattern in Concha Alos, Os habla Electra, Revista de estudios hispanicos, 80; Untold Sisters - Hispanic Nuns in Their Own Works - Arenal,e, Schlau,s, Tulsa Studies in Womens Literature, Vol 0010, 1991; The Garden Across The Border - Rodoreda,merce Fiction - Mcnerney,k, Vosburg,n, Anales De La Literatura Espanola Contemporanea, Vol 0021, 1996. **CONTACT ADDRESS** Dept Foreign Lang & Ling, Univ of Tex, Arlington, TX, 76019.

ORDONEZ, FRANCISCO
DISCIPLINE SPANISH LITERATURE **EDUCATION** City Univ NY, M.Phil, PhD, 97. **CAREER** Asst prof, Univ Ill Urbana Champaign. **RESEARCH** Syntax; comparative syntax; dialectology. **SELECTED PUBLICATIONS** Auth, The inversion construction in interrogatives in Spanish and Catalan, John Benjamins, 98; Post-verbal asymmetries in Spanish, Natural Lang Ling Theory, 98. **CONTACT ADDRESS** Spanish, Italian, and Portuguese Dept, Univ Ill Urbana Champaign, 52 E Gregory Dr, Champaign, IL, 61820. **EMAIL** fordonez@uiuc.edu

OREL, HAROLD
PERSONAL Born 03/31/1926, Boston, MA, m, 1951, 2 children **DISCIPLINE** ENGLISH LANGUAGE AND LIT **EDUCATION** UNH, BA, 48; Univ Mich, MA, 49, PhD, 52. **CAREER** Instr, Univ MD, Col Pk, 52-56; Info Spec, GE, Evendale OH, 56-57; Assoc prof, Univ Kansas, 57-62, prof, 63-97, dist prof, 74-. **HONORS AND AWARDS** Orator Poets Corner West Minster Abbey, 78, 86; Am Comm on Irish stud, Pres, 70-72; Thomas Hardy Soc, Eng, VP, 68-; Royal Soc Lit, Eng, fel, 86-; Higuchi Res Achmt Awd, 90. **RESEARCH** 19th and 20th C, Brit and Am Lit. **SELECTED PUBLICATIONS** The Brontes: Interviews and Recollections, ed, London, Macmillan, Iowa, Univ Iowa press, 97; The Historical Novel from Scott to Sabatini, London, Macmillan, 95; Critical Essays on Thomas Hardy's Poetry, ed, NY, G K Hall, 95; Critical Essays on Sir Arthur Conan Doyle, NY, G K Hall, 92; numerous other books and articles. **CONTACT ADDRESS** Dept English, Univ Kansas, Lawrence, KS, 66045-2115.

ORLANDO, VALERIE
DISCIPLINE FRENCH LANGUAGE **EDUCATION** Brown Univ, PhD. **CAREER** Vis asst prof Fr, Purdue Univ. **RESEARCH** 19th century French Literature; Francophone Literature of North Africa; 20th century French Literature and Philosophy. **SELECTED PUBLICATIONS** Auth, Assia Djebar's Vaste est la prison: Platform for a New Space of Agency and Feminine Enunciation in Algeria, Paroles GelSes, Vol 16. 97; Who's Covering Who in the Postmodern 90s: Subverting the Orientalist Image, Contemporary North African Francophone Text, Romance Lang Annual, Vol.8, 97; The Algerian Family Code: A Product of Falsified History and the Subversion of Political Literalism, Women, Politics and Law: A Code of Shame, Leeds Univ Press, 97; Women, War, Autobiography and the Historical Metafictional Text: Unveiling the Veiled Feminine Identity in Assia Djebar's L'Amour, la fantasia, in Spoils of War: Women, Cultures and Revolutions, Rowman & Littlefield, 97; Beyond Postcolonial Discourse: The Problematic of Feminine Identity in Contemporary Francophone Literature of the Maghred, Ohio Univ Press, 98. **CONTACT ADDRESS** Dept of For Lang and Lit, Purdue Univ, 1080 Schleman Hall, West Lafayette, IN, 47907-1080. **EMAIL** orlandov@omni.cc.purdue.edu

ORMAND, KIRK
PERSONAL Born 11/05/1962, Traverse City, MI, m, 1984, 1 child **DISCIPLINE** CLASSICAL STUDIES **EDUCATION** Stanford Univ, PhD, 92. **CAREER** Vis Asst Prof, Oberlin Col, 92-93; Asst Prof, Loyola Univ Chicago, 93-97. **HONORS AND AWARDS** John J. Winkler Memorial Prize, 91; Gildersleeve Prize, Am J Philol, 96; Solmsen Fel, Inst Res Humanities, 98-99. **MEMBERSHIPS** Am Philol Asn; Women's Classical Caucus; Lesbian Gay and Bisexual Classical Caucus. **RESEARCH** Ancient Greek literature and culture; modern critical theory. **SELECTED PUBLICATIONS** Auth, Trachiniae 1055ff: More Wedding Imagery, Mnemosyne 67, 93; Lucan's auctor vix fidelis, Classical Antiquity, 94; Silent by Convention? Sophocles' Tekmessa, AJP, 96; Exchange and the Maiden: Marriage in Sophoclean Tragedy, Univ Tex Press (forthcoming 99). **CONTACT ADDRESS** Washburn Observatory, Univ Wisconsin Madison, 1401 Observatory Dr., Madison, WI, 53706. **EMAIL** kormand@facstaff.wisc.edu

ORRINGER, NELSON ROBERT
PERSONAL Born 11/09/1940, Pittsburgh, PA, m, 1965, 3 children **DISCIPLINE** HISPANIC PHILOSOPHY & LITERATURE **EDUCATION** Dartmouth Col, AB, 62; Brown Univ, AM, 65, PhD(Hisp lett), 69. **CAREER** Lectr Span, Williams Col, 69-70, asst prof Romanic lang, 70-74; assoc prof, 74-81, Prof Span, Univ Conn, 81-, Res grant, Coun Int Exchange Scholars, 81; vis prof Span, Univ Mich, Ann Arbor, 81; Brown Univ Alumni scholar, 81; Univ Granada Inaugural speaker philos, 81. **MEMBERSHIPS** MLA;; Asoc Int de Hispanistas; Asoc de Pensamiento Hispanico. **RESEARCH** Twentieth century Spanish literature; history of philosophy; comparative literature. **SELECTED PUBLICATIONS** Auth, Responsabilidad

y evasion en La cabeza del cordero de Francisco Ayala, Hispanofila, 174; Nobles in La rebelion de las masas: Ortega's Source, Am Hispan, 176; Depth perception in Ortega and Jaensch, Comp Lit Studies, Muertes de perro de Ayala: Critica del Estado, Hispania, 977; Ortega y sus fuentes germanicas, Gredos, Madrid, 79; Ser y no-ser en Platon, Hartmann y Ortega, Nueva Revista de Filologia Hispanica, 80; Foreword, The Artist & the City by Eugenio Trias, Columbia Univ Press, 82; Sobre la teologia protestante liberal en Del sentimiento tragico de la vida, Cuadernos Salmantinos de Filosofia, 82; Medicus- hispaniae + Lainentralgo,pedro as Healer of The National Ills of Spain, Arbor-ciencia Pensamiento Y Cultura, Vol 0143, 1992.; Unamuno And The Dialogic Thought - Unamuno,miguel,de And Bakhtin,m. - Spanish - Zavala,im, Anales De La Literatura Espanola Contemporanea, Vol 0018, 1993. **CONTACT ADDRESS** Dept of Romance Class, Univ of Conn, Storrs, CT, 06268.

OSSAR, MICHAEL LEE
PERSONAL Born 03/31/1938, Bryn Mawr, PA, m, 1963, 2 children **DISCIPLINE** GERMAN LITERATURE **EDUCATION** Cornell Univ, AB, 61; Univ Pa, MS, 63, MA, 67, PhD(Ger lit), 73. **CAREER** Res fel physics, Univ Pa, 61-61, teaching fel Ger, 63-67; lektor English, Univ Freiburg, Ger, 67-68; instr Ger, Sweet Briar Col, 68-71; from Asst Prof to Assoc Prof, 71-88, Prof Ger, Kans State Univ, 88-, Dept Head, 95-; Vis lectr, Swarthmore Col, 66; ed, Studies in Twentieth Century Lit, 78-; vis prof, Giessen Univ, 88. **HONORS AND AWARDS** Nat Endowment for Humanities grant, 76, 77 & 81. **MEMBERSHIPS** MLA; Am Asn Teachers Ger. **RESEARCH** Expressionism; post-war German literature; politics and literature; Adolf Muschg; Celan. **SELECTED PUBLICATIONS** Auth, Das Erdbeben in Chili und Die Marquise von O--, Revue des Langues Vivantes, 68; Die Kunstlergestalt in Goethes Tasso und Grillparzers Sappho, Ger Quart, 72; Note on relativity theory in Der Zauberberg, PMLA, 73; Ernst Toller's Masse-Mensch, Germanic Rev, 76; Anarchism in the Dramas of Ernst Toller, Suny Press, 80; Der eigebildete Kranke bei Adolf Muschg, Neophilogus, 82; Muschg's Ein Glockenspiel, Transl Rev; Individual & Type in Schuitzler's Liebeler, Mod Austrian Lit; Toller: Life and Works, In: Dictionary of Literary Biography; Malevolent God in Celan's Tenebrae, Deutsche Viertolja hisschrift; Kafa's Forschuugen eiues Huudes, Colloquia Germanica; Frischmuth's Amy oder die Metamorphose, In: The Writer as I. **CONTACT ADDRESS** Dept of Mod Lang, Kansas State Univ, 104 Eisenhower Hall, Manhattan, KS, 66506-1003. **EMAIL** mlo@ksu.edu

OSTER, JUDITH
DISCIPLINE COMPOSITION AND ENGLISH AS A SECOND LANGUAGE TEACHING **EDUCATION** Case Western Reserve Univ, BA, MA, PhD. **CAREER** English, Case Western Reserve Univ. **HONORS AND AWARDS** Dir, Writing Ctr. **SELECTED PUBLICATIONS** Auth or ed, Toward Robert Frost: The Reader and the Poet; From Reading to Writing: A Rhetoric and Reader. **CONTACT ADDRESS** Case Western Reserve Univ, 10900 Euclid Ave, Cleveland, OH, 44106.

OSTERLE, HEINZ D.
PERSONAL Born 08/29/1932, Ulm, Germany, m, 1960, 3 children **DISCIPLINE** GERMAN LITERATURE **EDUCATION** Univ Freiburg, MA, 57; Brown Univ, PhD(Ger), 64. **CAREER** From asst prof to assoc prof Ger, George Washington Univ, 60-65; asst prof, NY Univ, 65-67 & Yale Univ, 67-72; dir div Ger & classics, 73-74, assoc prof, 72-82, Prof Ger, Northern Ill Univ, 82-, Mem screening comt Ger lit, Int Educ & Cult Exchange Prog, 69-72, chmn comt, 71-72. **HONORS AND AWARDS** Am Asn Teachers Ger Award for Best Article in Unterrichts praxis, 81. **MEMBERSHIPS** MLA; Am Asn Teachers Ger. **RESEARCH** Twentieth-Century German literature; German literature in exile 1933-45; American-German literary relations. **SELECTED PUBLICATIONS** Auth, The other Germany: Resistance to the Third Reich in German literature, Ger Quart, 68; Alfred Doblin's Revolutionstrilogie November 1918, Monatshefte, spring 70; Hermann Broch, Die Schlafwandler: Kritik der Zentralen Metapher, Deutsche Vierteljahrsschrift Literaturwissenschaft und Geistesgeschichte, summer 70; Hermann Broch, Die Schlafwandler: Revolution and Apocalypse, PMLA, 71; Uwe Johnson, Jahrestage: Das Bild der USA, Ger Quart, 75; Denkbilder uber die USA: Gunter Kunerts Reisebuch Der andere Plante, In: Basis: Jahrbuch fur deutsche Literatur der Gegenwart, Frankfurt Suhrkamp, 77; Alfred Doblins Revolutionsroman, postscript to Alfred Doblin, November 1918, (4 vols), Munich, 78; coauth, German studies in America, In: German Studies Notes Ser, Inst Ger Studies, Ind Univ, Bloomington, 78; The lost utopia: New images of America in German literature, Ger Quart, 81; Johnson,uwe 'Undine Geht' - The Novels Background - German - Paulsen,w, German Quarterly, Vol 0068, 1995; German History And German Identity - Johnson,uwe 'Jahrestage' - Bond,dg, German Quarterly, Vol 0068, 1995; German History And German Identity - Johnson,uwe 'Jahrestage' - Bond,dg, German Quarterly, Vol 0068, 1995; Understanding Weiss,peter - Cohen,r, German Quarterly, Vol 0069, 1996; Aus Alter Und Neuer Welt' - Essays And Poems - German - Steiner,c, German Quarterly, Vol 0070, 1997; Johnson,uwe Between Pre- modernism And Postmodernism - International-symposium on Johnson,uwe, September 22-24, 1994 - German - Gansel,c, Riedel,n, German Quarterly, Vol 0070, 1997. **CONTACT ADDRESS** Dept of Foreign Lang, No Illinois Univ, 1425 W Lincoln Hwy, De Kalb, IL, 60115-2825.

OSTRIKER, ALICIA
DISCIPLINE ENGLISH LANGUAGE AND LITERATURE **EDUCATION** Brandeis, BA; Univ Wis, PhD. **CAREER** Prof Eng, Ctr for the Stud of Jewish Life, Rutgers, The State Univ NJ, Univ Col-Camden. **RESEARCH** Poetry; feminism; religion. **SELECTED PUBLICATIONS** Auth, Stealing the Language: the Emergence of Women's Poetry in America; The Nakedness of the Fathers: Biblical Visions and Revisions; The Mother/Child Papers; The Imaginary Lover; Green Age, The Crack in Everything. **CONTACT ADDRESS** Dept of Lit in Eng, Rutgers, The State Univ New Jersey, Univ Col-Camde, Murray Hall 203B, New Brunswick, NJ, 08903. **EMAIL** ostriker@rci.rutgers.edu

OSTWALD, MARTIN
PERSONAL Born 01/15/1922, Dortmund, Germany, m, 1948, 2 children **DISCIPLINE** CLASSICAL PHILOLOGY **EDUCATION** Univ Toronto, BA 46; Univ Chicago, AM, 48; Columbia Univ, PhD, 52. **CAREER** Instr class philol, 50-51, Wesleyan Univ; lectr & assoc Greek & Latin, 51-54, Columbia Univ; asst prof, 54-58, assoc prof, 58-66, prof classics, 66-92, Swarthmore Col; prof class studies, 68-92, prof emeritus, 92- Univ Pa; Fulbright res fel, Greece, 61-62; Am Coun Learned Soc res fel, 65-66; NEH sr fel, 70-71; vis fel, 70-71, Balliol Col Oxford Univ; mem, Inst Adv Study, 74-75 & 81-82, Princeton Univ; dir, NEH fel-in-residence in classics, 76-77; Guggenheim fel, 77-78. **HONORS AND AWARDS** Goodwin award of Merit of Amer Philol Assn, 90; fel, Amer acad of Arts & Sci, 91; Amer Philos Soc, 93; hon mem, Soc for Promotion of Hellenic Stud, 95; Dr Honuris Causa, Fribourg, Suisse, 95. **MEMBERSHIPS** Soc Prom Hellenic Studies; Am Philol Assn; Class Assn Can; Archaeol Inst Am. **RESEARCH** Greek social and political thought and institutions; Greek history, philosophy and literature. **SELECTED PUBLICATIONS** Auth, Autonomia: Its Genesis and Early History, Scholars, 82; auth, From Popular Sovereignty to the Sovereignty of Law, Univ Calif Press, 86. **CONTACT ADDRESS** 408 Walnut Ln, Swarthmore, PA, 19081. **EMAIL** mostwal1@swarthmore.edu

OTERO, JOSE
PERSONAL Born 07/18/1932, Ecuador, m, 1957, 2 children **DISCIPLINE** HISPANIC AMERICAN LITERATURE **EDUCATION** Univ NM, BA, 62, MA; 64, PhD(Span), 69. **CAREER** Teaching asst Span, Univ NM, 64-68; asst prof, 68-73, Assoc Prof Span, Colo State Univ, 73- **MEMBERSHIPS** Rocky Mountain Mod Lang Asn; Am Asn Teachers Span & Port; Casa Cult Am, Filial de Guayaquil. **RESEARCH** Hispanish American poetry and novel. **SELECTED PUBLICATIONS** Auth, Los Pajaros en la Poesia de Jorge Carrera Andrade, El Comercio, Quito, 67; El tiempo en la poesia de Jose Asuncion Silva, Bull Rocky Mountain Mod Lang Asn, 70; Nuevas voces del reino de Strossner, Nueva Narrativa Hispanoam, 71; La estetica del doble en Aura de Carlos Fuentes, Explicacion de Textos Lit, 76; Hispanic Colorado, Centenial, 76; H G Wells y E Anderson Imbert: The Truth About Pyecraft y El leve Pedro, Hispanofila, 79; El misticismo poetico de Pablo, Explicacion de Textos Literarios, 80-81; Delmira Agustini: Erotismo poetico o misticismo erotico?, In: In Honor of Boyd G Carter, Univ Wyo, 81; Contemporary Spanish-american Poets - a Bibliography of Primary And Secondary Sources - Sefami,j, Chasqui-revista De Literatura Latinoamericana, Vol 0021, 1992; 'Querido Diego, The Abraza Quiela', Destruction And Reconstruction of The Personality - Language, Structure And Symbols, Confluencia- revista Hispanica De Cultura Y Literatura, Vol 0007, 1992; Writing in Cuba, Interviews With Cuban Writers 1979-1989 - Spanish - Bejel,e, Chasqui-revista De Literatura Latinoamericana, Vol 0022, 1993. **CONTACT ADDRESS** Dept of Foreign Lang, Colorado State Univ, Ft Collins, CO, 80523.

OTT, BRIAN L.
PERSONAL Born 03/22/1969, Erie, PA **DISCIPLINE** SPEECH COMMUNICATION **EDUCATION** PA State Univ, PhD, 97. **CAREER** Asst prof of Media Studies, CO State Univ, 98-. **HONORS AND AWARDS** Col of Liberal Arts Outstanding Teaching Award, PA State, 96. **MEMBERSHIPS** Nat Commun Asn; Int Commun Asn. **RESEARCH** Critical media studies; television criticism; cultural studies. **SELECTED PUBLICATIONS** Auth, Memorializing the Holocaust: Schindler's List and Public Memory, The Rev of Ed/Pedagogy/Cultural Studies, 18, 96. **CONTACT ADDRESS** Dept of Speech Commun, Colorado State Univ, 202 Eddy Hall, Fort Collins, CO, 80523. **EMAIL** Bott@vines.colostate.edu

OTTENHOFF, JOHN
DISCIPLINE RHETORIC, LINGUISTICS AND BRITISH LITERATURE **EDUCATION** Univ Chicago, PhD. **CAREER** Prof, adv, Sigma Tau Delta, Alma Col. **HONORS AND AWARDS** Outstanding Fac Mem in Hum Award. **RESEARCH** Shakespeare; Shakespeare on film. **SELECTED PUBLICATIONS** Publications in his specialty, Renaissance devotional poetry. **CONTACT ADDRESS** Alma Col, Alma, MI, 48801.

OUIMETTE, VICTOR
PERSONAL Born 04/21/1944, Calgary, AB, Canada, m, 1967 **DISCIPLINE** SPANISH LITERATURE **EDUCATION** McGill Univ, BA, 65; Yale Univ, PhD(Span), 68. **CAREER** Asst prof, 68-73, Assoc Prof Span, McGill Univ, 73-. **MEMBERSHIPS** MLA; Am Asn Teachers Span & Port; Can Asn Hispanists; Northeast Mod Lang Asn; Asoc Pensamiento Hisp. **RESEARCH** The generation of 1898; the realist novel in Spain and France; modern Spanish currents of ideas. **SELECTED PUBLICATIONS** Auth, Reason aflame: Unamuno and the Heroic Will, Yale Univ, 74; Unamuno, Blasco Ibanez and Espana con Honra, Bull Hisp Studies, 1076; The liberalism of Baroja and the second RePubic, Hispia, 377; Unamuno and Le Quotidien, Rev Can Estudios Hispan, 1077; Jose Ortega y Gasset, G K Hall, 82; Marias,julian, The 1st 80-years, Hispania-a J Devoted to The Teaching of Spanish And Portuguese, Vol 0077, 1994; Crossfire - Philosophy And The Novel in Spain, 1900-1934 - Johnson,r, Hispanic Review, Vol 0064, 1996. **CONTACT ADDRESS** Dept of Hisp Studies, McGill Univ, Montreal, PQ, H3A 1G5.

OVERFIELD, DENISE
DISCIPLINE LINGUISTICS **EDUCATION** Univ Pittsburgh, MA, PhD. **RESEARCH** Community based language learning. **SELECTED PUBLICATIONS** Auth, pubs on community-based language learning. **CONTACT ADDRESS** Dept Foreign Languages and Literature, State Univ of West Georgia, Carrollton, GA, 30118.

OWEN, DAVID I.
PERSONAL Born 10/28/1940, Boston, MA, m, 1964, 2 children **DISCIPLINE** ASSYRIOLOGY, ARCHEOLOGY **EDUCATION** Boston Univ, AB, 62; Brandeis Univ, MA, 63, PhD, 69. **CAREER** Res asst archaeol, Univ Mus, Univ PA, 64-65, asst cur archaeol, 69-71, res assoc Assyriol, 71-75; asst prof Ancient Near Eastern studies, Dropsie Univ, 71-74; asst prof, 74-77, assoc prof, 77-82, chmn dept, 75-79, prof ancient near eastern hist & archaeol, dept dept near eastern studies, Cornell Univ, 83, Fulbright scholar, Ankara Univ, 66-68; adj prof Ancient Near Eastern Studies, Inst Nautical Archaeol, TX A&M Univ. **HONORS AND AWARDS** NEH Sr Fel, Am Sch Oriental Res, Jerusalem, 88-89. **MEMBERSHIPS** Archaeol Inst Am; Am Orient Soc; Israel Exploration Soc; Fondation assyriologique George Dossin. **RESEARCH** Assyriology; hist and archaeol of the Ancient Near East. **SELECTED PUBLICATIONS** Auth, The John Frederick Lewis Collection: Texts from the Third Millennium in the Free Library of Philadelphia, Materiali per il Vocabolario Neosumerico, Multigrafica Editrice, Rome, 75; A Sumerian letter from an angry housewife(?), In: The Bible World, Studies in Honor of Cyrus H Gordon, KTAV, New York, 80; Widows's rights in Ur III Sumer, In: Zeitschrift for Assyriologie, Berlin, 80; An Akkadian letter from Ugarit at Tel Aphek, In: Tel Aviv, Tel Aviv, 81; Of birds, eggs and turtles, In: Zeitschrift for Assyriologie, Berlin, 81; co-ed (with M A Morrison), Studies on the Civilization and Culture of Nuzi and the Hurrians in Honor of Ernest R Lacheman, 81 &; Neo-Sumerian Archival Texts Primarily from Nippur in the University Museum, the Oriental Institute and the Iraq Museum, 82, Eisenbrauns; Selected Ur III Texts from the Harvard Semitic Museum, Materiali per il Vocabolario Neosumerico, Vol 11, Multigrafica Editrice, Rome, 82. **CONTACT ADDRESS** Dept of Near Eastern Studies, Cornell Univ, Rockefeller Hall, Ithaca, NY, 14853-2502. **EMAIL** dio1@cornell.edu

OWENS, JOHN BINGNER
PERSONAL Born 02/26/1944, Baltimore, MD, m, 1966, 3 children **DISCIPLINE** SPANISH & RENAISSANCE HISTORY **EDUCATION** Oberlin Col, BA, 66; Univ Wis-Madison, MA, 68, PhD(hist), 72. **CAREER** From instr to asst prof hist, NY Univ, 71-73; asst prof, Lehigh Univ, 73-75; asst prof, 75-80, Assoc Prof Hist, Idaho State Univ, 80-, Consult Span hist, Libr Cong, 72-73; Joint US- Span Comt Educ & Cult Affairs fel, Spain, 78-79; head labor hist res group, Inst Murcian Studies, 78-80. **MEMBERSHIPS** Rocky Mountain Medieval & Renaissance Asn; Renaissance Soc Am; Soc Span & Port Hist Studies; Soc Reformation Res; Historians Early Mod Europe. **RESEARCH** Cultural and social history of Spain, 1450-1650. **SELECTED PUBLICATIONS** Auth, Diana at the Bar: Hunting, aristocrats and the law in Renaissance Castile, Sixteenth Century J, 77; The conception of absolute royal power in sixteenth century Castile, II Pensiero politico, 77; A city for the King: The impact of a rural revolt on Talavera during the Communidades of Castile, Societas, 78; Spanish Euro communism and the communist party organization in Murcia, Iberian Studies, 79; Rebelion, monarquia y oligarquia murciana en la epoca de Carlos V, Univ de Murcia, Spain, 80; Los regidores y jurados de Murcia, 1500-1650: Una guia, Anales de Univ de Murcia, 81; Posicion social y poder politico en Murcia, 1490-1570, Vol 5, 81 & La oliguarquia en defensa de su posicion, 1570-1650, Vol 6, 82, Historia de Murcia; Isabel The Queen, Life And Times - Liss,pk, Americas, Vol 0051, 1994; Inventing America, Spanish Historiography And The Formation of Eurocentrism - Rabasa,j, Americas, Vol 0051, 1994; 2 Hearts, One Soul - The Correspondence of The Galve,condesa,de, 1688-96 - Dodge,md, Hendricks,r, Hispanic American Historical Review, Vol 0074, 1994; The Castilian Crisis of The 17th-century - New Perspectives on The Economic And Social-history of The 17th- century Spain - Thompson,iaa, Sixteenth Century J,

Vol 0027, 1996; The 2 Faces of Janus - Monarchy, City And The Individual - Murcia, 1588-1648 - Spanish - Ruizibanez,jj, Sixteenth Century J, Vol 0028, 1997; Spain, Europe, And The Spanish-miracle, 1700- 1900 - Ringrose,d, American Historical Review, Vol 0102, 1997; The Village And The Outside World in Golden-age Castile - Mobility And Migration in Everyday Rural Life - Vassberg,de, J of Interdisciplinary History, Vol 0028, 1997. **CONTACT ADDRESS** Dept of Hist, Idaho State Univ, 921 S 8th Ave, Pocatello, ID, 83209-0001.

OWOMOYELA, OYEKAN
PERSONAL Born 04/22/1938, Ifon, Nigeria, m, 1975 **DISCIPLINE** AFRICAN LITERATURE **EDUCATION** Univ London, BA, 63; Univ Calif, Los Angeles, MFA, 66, PhD(theater hist), 70. **CAREER** Lectr audio visuals, Univ Ibadan, Nigeria, 68-71; asst prof, 72-75, assoc prof, 75-81, Prof Lit & Drama, Univ Nebr- Lincoln, 81-, Sr consult, Ctr Mgt Develop, Nigerian, 75. **MEMBERSHIPS** African Studies Asn; African Lit Asn; Am Folklore Soc. **RESEARCH** Sociology of African literature; Yoruba folklore and society. **SELECTED PUBLICATIONS** Auth, Folklore and Yoruba theater, Res in African Lit, fall 71; The Sociology of sex and crudity in Yorbua Proverbs, Proverbium: Bull d'information sur les recherches paremiologiques, 20: 751-758; coauth (with Bernth Lindfors), Yoruba Proverbs: Translations and Annotations, Ohio Univ Ctr Int Studies, 73; auth, Western humanism and African usage: A critical survey of non-African responses to African literature, Issue: A Quart J Opinion IV, winter 74; African Literatures: An Introduction, Crossroads Press, 79; Obotunde Ijimere, the phantom of Nigerian theater, 79 & Dissidence and the African writer: Commitment or dependency, 381, Studies Rev; The pragmatic humanism of Yoruba culture, J African Studies, fall 81; an Enchanting Darkness - The American Vision of Africa in The 20th-century - Hickey,d, Wylie,kc, African American Review, Vol 0029, 1995; African Philosophy in Search of Identity - Masolo,da, Research in African Literatures, Vol 0027, 1996; The Hermeneutics of African Philosophy - Horizon And Discourse - Serequeberhan,t, Research in African Literatures, Vol 0027, 1996; The Idea of Africa - Mudimbe,vy, Research in African Literatures, Vol 0027, 1996; The Wisdom of Many - Essays of The Proverb - Mieder,w, Dundes,a, Research in African Literatures, Vol 0027, 1996. **CONTACT ADDRESS** Dept of English, Univ Nebr, P O Box 880333, Lincoln, NE, 68588-0333.

OXENHANDLER, NEAL
PERSONAL Born 02/03/1926, St. Louis, MO, 3 children **DISCIPLINE** FRENCH **EDUCATION** Univ Chicago, AB, 48; Columbia Univ, MA, 50; Yale Univ, PhD, 55. **CAREER** Instr French, Yale Univ, 53-57; from asst prof to assoc prof, Univ CA, Los Angeles, 57-66; prof French lit, Cowell Col, Univ CA, Santa Cruz, 66-69; Prof French Lit, 69-87, Edward Tuck Prof French, Dartmouth Col, 87-94, Prof Emeritus, 94-, Ch, Dept Fr & Ital, 87-91, Fac, Semester at Sea, 95. **HONORS AND AWARDS** Fulbright fel, 53; Guggenheim fel, 61-62; cross disciplinary fel, 66 & 67; dir, Nat Endowment for Hum sem, 81. **MEMBERSHIPS** MLA. **RESEARCH** French lit of the 19th and 20th centuries; psychoanalysis and lit; French cinema. **SELECTED PUBLICATIONS** Auth, Scandal and Parade, Rutgers Univ, 57; coauth, Aspects of French Literature, Appleton, 61; auth, A Change of Gods, Harcourt, 62; Max Jacob and Les Feux de Paris, Univ Calif, 64; French Literary Criticism, Prentice-Hall, 66; Quest for pure consciousness in Husserl and Mallarme, In: Quest for Imagination, Case-Western Reserve, 71; Literature as perception in the work of Merleau-Ponty, In: Modern French Criticism, Univ Chicago Press, 72; Intimacy and Distance in the Cinema of Jean-Luc Godard, Symp, 73; The Man with Shoes of Wind, In: The Gadamer-Derrida Encounter, SUNY Press, 89; Listening to Burroughs' Voice, In: Burroughs at the Front: Critical Reception 1959-1989, 91; coauth, Looking for Heroes in Postwar France, Univ Press New England, 96; auth, Cocteau on Video, Bucknell Rev, 97. **CONTACT ADDRESS** Dept of French & Ital, Dartmouth Col, 6087 Dartmouth Hall, Hanover, NH, 03755-3511. **EMAIL** neal.oxenhandler@dartmouth.edu

OXENHANDLER, NEAL
PERSONAL Born 02/03/1926, St. Louis, MO, 3 children **DISCIPLINE** FRENCH **EDUCATION** Univ Chicago, AB, 48; Columbia Univ, MA, 50; Yale Univ, PhD(French), 55. **CAREER** Instr French, Yale Univ, 53-57; from asst prof to assoc prof, Univ CA, Los Angeles, 57-66; prof French lit, Cowell Col, Univ CA, Santa Cruz, 66-69; Prof French Lit, Dartmouth Col, 69-86, EDWARD TUCK PROF FRENCH, 87-; Fulbright fel, 53; Guggenheim fel, 61-62; cross disciplinary fel, 66 & 67; dir, Nat Endowment for Humanities sem, 81. **MEMBERSHIPS** MLA; Am Asn Teachers Fr; Am Comp Lit Asn. **RESEARCH** French literature of the 19th and 20th centuries; psychoanalysis and literature; French cinema. **SELECTED PUBLICATIONS** Auth, Scandal and Parade, Rutgers Univ, 57; coauth, Aspects of French Literature, Appleton, 61; auth, A Change of Gods, Harcourt, 62; Max Jacob and Les Feux de Paris, Univ CA, 64; French Literary Criticism, Prentice-Hall, 66; Quest for Pure Consciousness in Husserl and Mallarme, In: Quest for Imagination, Case-Western Reserve, 71; Literature as Perception in the Work of Merleau-Ponty, In: Modern French Criticism, Univ Chicago Press, 72; Intimacy and Distance in the Cinema of Jean-Luc Godard, Symp, 73. **CONTACT ADDRESS** Dept of French & Ital, Dartmouth Col, 6087 Dartmouth Hall, Hanover, NH, 03755-3511. **EMAIL** neal.oxenhandler@dartmouth.edu

P

PACHMUSS, TEMIRA
DISCIPLINE RUSSIAN LITERATURE & LANGUAGE **EDUCATION** Univ Melbourne, BA, 54, MA, 55; Univ Wash, PhD, 59. **CAREER** Court interpreter, US Mil Govt Court, Ger, 45-49; instr Russ, Univ Melbourne, 52-54, teacher, Univ High Sch, 54-55; teaching assoc Russ, Univ Wash, 55-58; instr, Russ lang, Univ Mich, 58-59; instr Russ lang & lit, Univ Colo, 59-60; from instr to assoc prof, 60-68, Prof Russ Lit, Univ Ill, Urbana, 68-. **HONORS AND AWARDS** Phi Kappa Phi; Nat Slavic Honor Soc "Dobro Slovo"; Estonian Learned Soc Am. **MEMBERSHIPS** Estonian Learned Soc Am. **RESEARCH** Works of Dostoevsky and Zinaida Hippius; women writers in Russian modernism; Russian literature in exile 1921-1939. **SELECTED PUBLICATIONS** Auth, D.S. Merezhkovsky in Exile: The Master of the Genre of Biographie Romancee, Peter Lang, 90; co-ed, Vadim Gardner: At the Bay of Finland, Granite, 90; ed, D.S. Merezhkovsky, Reformatory: Luther, Calvin, Pascal, Foyer Oriental Chretiens and La Presse Libre, 90; ed, D.S. Merezhkovsky/Z.N. Hippius, Dante. Boris Godunov, Gnosis Press, 90; auth, A Moving River of Tears: Russia's Experience in Finland, Peter Lang, 91. **CONTACT ADDRESS** Dept of Slavic Lang & Lit, Univ of Ill, 707 S Mathews Ave, Urbana, IL, 61801-3625. **EMAIL** tpachmus@uiuc.edu

PACHOW, WANG
PERSONAL Born 06/01/1918, Chungking, China, m, 1956, 1 child **DISCIPLINE** ASIAN CIVILIZATION, BUDDHIST STUDIES **EDUCATION** Mengtsang Col, BA, 36; Visva-Bharati Univ, MA, 42; Univ Bombay, PhD(Buddhist studies), 48. **CAREER** Lectr Chinese, Visva-Bharati Univ, 41-47; lect & head dept, Univ Allahabad, 47-53; sr lectr Buddhist & Chinese studies, Univ Ceylon, 54-65, reader Pali & Buddhist civilization, 66-68; assoc prof world relig, 68-75, Prof World Relig, Sch Relig, Univ Iowa, 75-, Res fel, Yale Univ, 61; Acad Hospitality Award, Univ London, 61-62; vis prof, Visva-Bharati Univ, 62; hon consult for the Humanities, Washington, 77; external examr, Univ Delhi, India, 78- **MEMBERSHIPS** Am Acad Relig; Am Orient Soc; Asn Asian Studies; Maha-Bodhi Soc; Soc Study Chinese Relig. **RESEARCH** Chinese thought and literature; Sino-India culture. **SELECTED PUBLICATIONS** Auth, A Comparative Study of Pratimoksa, On the Basis of Its Chinese, Tibetan, Sanskrit and Pali Versions, Comp Sino- Indian Cult Soc, 55; A study of the Dotted Record, J Am Orient Soc, 7-965; Tripitaka, Encycl Britannica, 68; Gautama Buddha: Man or superman?, In: Malalasekera Commemoration Volume, Colombo, Ceylon, 76; The controversy over the immortality of the soul in Chinese Buddhism, J Orient Studies, Univ Hong Kong, 1278; A Study of the Twenty-Two Dialogues on Mahayana Buddhism, The Chinese Culture, 79; Chinese Buddhism: Aspects of Interaction and Reinterpretation, Univ Am Press, 80; Arahant, Bhavacakra, Paticcasamuppada, In: Abingdon Dict of Living Religions, 81; Tan,yun-shan And Cultural-relations Between China And India, Indian Horizons, Vol 0043, 1994; Tan,yun-shan And Cultural-relations Between China And India, Indian Horizons, Vol 0043, 1994. **CONTACT ADDRESS** Sch of Relig, Univ of Iowa, Iowa City, IA, 52242.

PADEN, WILLIAM D.
PERSONAL Born 06/20/1941, Lawrence, TX, m, 1973, 2 children **DISCIPLINE** COMPARATIVE LITERATURE **EDUCATION** Yale, PhD, 71. **CAREER** Prof, Northwestern Univ, 68- . **HONORS AND AWARDS** NEH sen fel, 76-77; 87-88. **MEMBERSHIPS** MLA, Societe Guillaume IX; AATF. **RESEARCH** Medieval poetry. **SELECTED PUBLICATIONS** Auth, De Monachis rithmos facientibus: Helinant de Froidmont, Bertran de Born, and the Cistercian General Chapter of 1199, Speculum 55, 80; Europe from Latin to Vernacular in Epic, Lyric, Romance, Performance in Lit in Hist Perspectives, ed D. W. Thompson, 83; Tenebrism in the Song of Roland, Modern Philology 86, 89; Rape in the Pastourelle, Romanic Rev 80, 89; The Troubadours and the Albigensian Crusade: A Long View, Romance Philology 49, 95; The Chronology of Genres in Medieval Galician-Portuguese Lyric Poetry, La Coronica 26.1, 97; Introduction to Old Occitan, Introductions to Older Languages, MLA, 98; coauth, The Troubadour's Lady: Her Marital Status and Social Rank, Studies in Philology 72, 75; The Poems of the Trobairitz Na Castelloza, Romance Philology 35, 81; ed, The Medieval Pastourelle, 2 vols, 87; The Voice of Trobairitz: Perspectives on the Women Troubadours, 89; The Future of the Middle Ages: Medieval Literature in the 1990s, 94; coed, The Poems of the Troubadour Bertran de Born, 86; De Tradicione Guenonis: An Edion with Translation, Traditio 44, 88. **CONTACT ADDRESS** Dept of French and Italian, Northwestern Univ, Evanston, IL, 60208-2204. **EMAIL** wpaden@nwu.edu

PADGETT, JAYE
DISCIPLINE LINGUISTICS **EDUCATION** Univ Md, BA; Univ Mass-Amherst, PhD, 91. **CAREER** ASST PROF, LING, UNIV CALIF, SANTA CRUZ. **RESEARCH** Slavic phonology. **SELECTED PUBLICATIONS** Auth, "OCP Subsidiary Features," Proc of the Northeast Ling Soc 22, 92. **CONTACT ADDRESS** Univ Calif, 1156 High St, Santa Cruz, CA, 95064.

PAGAN, SAMUEL
PERSONAL Born 07/29/1950, San Juan, PR, m, 1973, 2 children **DISCIPLINE** HEBREW LITERATURE; HEBREW BIBLE **EDUCATION** The Jewish Theol Sem, Doctor in Hebrew Lit, 88. **CAREER** Regional coordinator, Translation of the Bible Dept, United Bible Societies, 85-95; PRES, EVANGELICAL SEM OF PUERTO RICO, 95-. **RESEARCH** Translation of the Bible and sociological exegesis. **SELECTED PUBLICATIONS** Auth, Ester, Nehemias Ester, Miami: Editorial caribe, 93; Palama viva, Miami: Editorial Caribe, 96; Obadiah, NIB, Nashville: Alsing Conn Press, 97; Isaias, Miami: Editorial Caribe, 97; Yose quien soy, San Juan: Pulsicaciones Puertorri guertas, 97; Ester, Dallas: Univ Dallas, 99. **CONTACT ADDRESS** 776 Ponce de Leon, San Juan, PR, 00925. **EMAIL** drspagan@icepr.com

PAGANINI, MARIA
DISCIPLINE 19TH- AND 20TH-CENTURY NARRATIVE IN FRENCH LITERATURE **EDUCATION** Zurich Univ, PhD. **CAREER** Instr, Univ Minn, Twin Cities. **RESEARCH** The relation of literature to the law. **SELECTED PUBLICATIONS** Auth, Flaubert: La Presence de l'ecrivain dans l'oeuvre, Juris Verlag, 74; Reading Proust: In Search of the Wolffish, Univ Minn Press. **CONTACT ADDRESS** Univ Minn, Twin Cities, Minneapolis, MN, 55455.

PALENCIA-ROTH, MICHAEL
PERSONAL Born 06/26/1946, Girardot, Colombia, m, 1968, 2 children **DISCIPLINE** COMPARATIVE LITERATURE **EDUCATION** Vanderbilt Univ, BA, 68; Harvard Univ, MA, 71, PhD(comp lit), 76. **CAREER** Tutor comp lit, Harvard Univ, 71-73; from instr to asst prof, Univ Mich, Dearborn, 74-77; from Asst Prof to Assoc Prof, 77-87, Prof Comp Lit, Univ Ill, 87-, Dir Undergrad Studies Comp Lit, 78-80, 81-87, Dir, Program Comp Lit, 88-94; Assoc ed, Philos & Lit, 75-77; asst ed, Comp Lit Studies, 77-; Dir, Univ of Michigan-Dearborn, at the Universitat Wien, Vienna, Summer 77; permanent academic consultant and distinguished extra-mural professor for the Escuela de Estudios Literarios and the Facultad de Humanidades, Universidad del Valle, Columbia. **HONORS AND AWARDS** Univ Schol, 64-68; Merrill Moore Award, Vanderbilt, 67; Phi Beta Kappa, Magna Cum Laude, Honors in English & Philos, 68; Woodrow Wilson Fel, 68; DAAD Fel to Harvard, 69-73; Grad Prize Fel to Harvard, 69-73; Grad Prize Dissertation Fel, 73-74; Res Assistance Grants, Univ Ill, 78-79, 81-82, 83-84, 88-89; Nat Endowment for Humanities fel, 80-81; Exploratory Grant, Ill, for research in Mexico City, 83; Newberry Libr Fel in Paleography, 84; Herman Dunlap Smith Fel in the Hist of Cartog, Newberry Libr, 85; recipient of numerous other grants, awards, and fellowships. **MEMBERSHIPS** MLA; Am Comp Lit Asn; Int Soc Comp Study Civilizations; Inst Int de Lit Iberoamericana. **RESEARCH** The Faustiansensibility; philosophical and psychoanalytic approaches to literature. **SELECTED PUBLICATIONS** Auth, Thomas Mann's non relationship to James Joyce, Mod Lang Notes, 76; The anti-faustian ethos of Die Blechtrommel, J Europ Studies, 79; Faust and the cultural stages of Wagner's Ring, The Opera J, 79; The Contexts of Busoni's Doktor Faust, Science/Technology and the Humanities, 79; Mothers, fathers and the life of reason in Mill's Autobiography, Comp Civilizations Rev, 80; Albrecht Durer's Melecolia I and Thomas Mann's Doktor Faustus, Ger Studies Rev, 80; La imagen del Urboros: el incesto en Cien anos de soledad, Caudernos Americanos, 81; ed, Perspectives on Faust, Alpha Academic, 83; auth, Gabriel Garcia Marquez: La linea, el circulo y las metamorfosis del mito, Editorial Gredos, 84; ed, The New World, the New Man, and Latin America, special Latin American Issue of Comp Civilizations Rev, no 12, 85; auth, Myth and the Modern Novel, Garland Publ Co, 87; co-ed, Comparative Literature in the Nineties, Am Comp Lit Asn, special double issue of the ACLA Bulletin, 24, no 2, 93; author of numerous journal articles and reviews. **CONTACT ADDRESS** Prog in Comp Lit, Univ of Illinois, Urbana-Champaign, 707 S Mathews Ave, Urbana, IL, 61801-3625. **EMAIL** palencia@uiuc.edu

PALIYENKO, ADRIANNA M.
PERSONAL Born 02/17/1956, Kingston, ON, Canada, m, 1986, 3 children **DISCIPLINE** FRENCH **EDUCATION** Univ NC Chapel Hill, MA, 77, PhD, 87; Boston Univ, MA, 82. **CAREER** Assoc prof, 89-, Colby Col. **HONORS AND AWARDS** Fulbright-Hays Scholar, 82-83; Phi Beta Kappa, Phi Eta Sigma, French Gov Award, 75-76. **MEMBERSHIPS** MLA; NE Modern Lang Assoc; S Atlantic Modern Lang Assoc; Amer Assoc of Teachers of French; Women in French. **RESEARCH** Francophone women poets; 19th cent French poetry; Surrealism: 20th cent French theatre; feminist & psychoanalytic approaches to creativity; gender & poetry; artistic relations. **SELECTED PUBLICATIONS** Auth, Mis-Reading the Creative Impulse: The Poetic Subject in Rimbaud and Claudel, Restaged, S Il Univ Press, 97; contr, A Feminist Companion to French Literature, 98; art, Postmodern Turns Against the Cartesian Subject: Descartes' "I", Lacan's Other, Feminist Interpretations of Descartes, Pa St Univ Press, 99; art, Is a Woman Poet Born or

Made?: Discourse of Maternity in Louise Ackermann and Louisa Siefert, Esprit Createur, 99. **CONTACT ADDRESS** Dept of French, Colby Col, 4670 Mayflower Hill, Waterville, ME, 04901-8846. **EMAIL** ampaliye@colby.edu

PALLEY, JULIAN
PERSONAL Born 09/16/1925, Atlantic City, NJ, m, 1950, 4 children **DISCIPLINE** ROMANCE LANGUAGES **EDUCATION** Mexico City Col, BA, 50; Univ Ariz, MA, 52; Univ NM, PhD, 58. **CAREER** Asst Romance lang, Univ NM, 52-55; instr, Rutgers Univ, 56- 59; asst prof Span, Ariz State Univ, 59-62; assoc prof, Univ Ore, 62-66; assoc prof Span, 66-73, chmn dept Span & Port, 70- 73, Prof Span & Port, Univ Calif, Irvine, 73-. **MEMBERSHIPS** MLA; Am Asn Teachers Span & Port. **RESEARCH** Contemporary Spanish literature; Pedro Salinas; modern Spanish novel. **SELECTED PUBLICATIONS** Auth, La Luz no Usada: La Poesia de Pedro Salinas, Studium, Mex, 66; ed, Jorge Guillen: Affirmation, A Bilingual Anthology, 1919-1966, Univ Okla, 68; auth, Spinoza's Stone and Other Poems, JNR Pub, 76; El Laberinto y la Esfera: Cien Anos de la novela Espanola, Insula, Madrid, 78; Metatheater in The Work of Garcialorca,federico - Spanish - Vitale,r, Estrenocuadernos Del Teatro Espanol Contemporaneo, Vol 0019, 1993. **CONTACT ADDRESS** Dept of Span & Port, Univ of Calif, Irvine, CA, 92717.

PALLISTER, JANIS LOUISE
PERSONAL Born 01/12/1926, Rochester, MN **DISCIPLINE** ROMANCE LANGUAGES **EDUCATION** Univ Minn, BA, 46, MA, 48, PhD(French), 64. **CAREER** Instr French, Span & English, Black Hills Teachers Col, 48- 50; teaching asst French, Univ Wis, 51-52; teaching asst, Univ Minn, 54-59; instr, Colby Col, 59-61; from instr to assoc prof, 61-71, prof French, 71-79, Univ Prof, Bowling Green State Univ, 79-. **HONORS AND AWARDS** OEA Human Rels Comn Award, 79. **MEMBERSHIPS** Am Asn Teachers Fr; MLA; AAUP; Renaissance Soc Am; Mediaeval Acad Am. **RESEARCH** French medieval language and literature; French Renaissance and baroque literature; lyric poetry. **SELECTED PUBLICATIONS** Auth, Beroalde de Verville's Stances de la Mort and Soupirs Amoureux, Nottingham French Studies, 70; Presentation motifs in the prologue of Claudel's L'Annonce Faite a Marie, Romance Notes, 72; coauth, En attendant Godot, tragedy or comedy?, Esprit Createur, fall 71; auth, The World View of Beroalde de Verville, Vrin, Paris, 71; translr, Bolamba's Esanzo, 77; coauth, Waiting for Death: The Philosophical Significance of Beckett's En Attendant Godot, Univ Ala, 79; The Bruised Reed, Naaman, 78; On Monsters and Marvels, Univ Chicago, 82; b Duras,marguerite - Fascinating Vision And Narrative Cure - Glassman,dn, J of Popular Film And Television, Vol 0020, 1992; Review of 'Aime Cesaire' - Authors Reply, French Review, Vol 0068, 1994; Sampling The Book - Renaissance Prologues And The French Conteurs - Losse,dn, French Review, Vol 0070, 1996; The Apotheosis of Orpheus - Aesthetics of The Ode in France in The 16th-century From Sebillet to Scaliger 1548-1561- French - Rouget,f, French Review, Vol 0070, 1996; Social And Political- change in Literature And Film - Chapple,rl, J of Popular Film And Television, Vol 0024, 1996; Gold, Currency, And Exchange in Renaissance Culture - French - Tournon,a, Perouse,ga, French Review, Vol 0070, 1997. **CONTACT ADDRESS** Dept of Romance Lang, Bowling Green State Univ, Bowling Green, OH, 43402.

PALMERTON, PATRICIA R.
DISCIPLINE ORAL COMMUNICATION **EDUCATION** Macalester Col, BA, 72; Univ MN, MA, 79, PhD, 84. **CAREER** Prof, dir Oral Commun, Hamline Univ. **RESEARCH** Commun and rhetorical theory. **SELECTED PUBLICATIONS** Publ in rhetoric, soc change, curriculum develop, commun educ, and instructional commun. **CONTACT ADDRESS** Hamline Univ, 1666 Robbins, St Paul, MN. **EMAIL** ppalmert@piper.hamline.edu

PAN, DA'AN
DISCIPLINE COMPARATIVE LITERATURE **EDUCATION** Rohester Univ, PhD, 91. **CAREER** Asst prof, Univ IL Urbana Champaign. **RESEARCH** Class Chinese poetry and painting; comp poetics; interartistic semiotics. **SELECTED PUBLICATIONS** Auth, Decoding the Textual Other-Deconstructive Subtext in Shitao's Landscape; Decoding Sharawadgi-Taoist Influence on the Chinese Landscape Garden; A Compendium of Basic Learning from the Collegiate Chinese Program. **CONTACT ADDRESS** Comp Lit Dept, Univ Illinois Urbana Champaign, E Gregory Drive, PO Box 52, Champaign, IL, 61820.

PANCRAZIO, JAMES
DISCIPLINE SPANISH AMERICAN LITERATURE **EDUCATION** Ill State Univ, BA, 87; Univ Ill, MA, 91, PhD, 95. **CAREER** English and Lit, Univ Ark **SELECTED PUBLICATIONS** Auth, Columbus: Beyond the Myth: Teaching the Encounter of Two Worlds in High School and College Classrooms, Urbana-Champaign, Ill, 92; Rethinking Carpentier's Baroque, Monographic Rev, 94. **CONTACT ADDRESS** Univ Ark Little Rock, 2801 S University Ave., Little Rock, AR, 72204-1099. **EMAIL** jjpancrazio@ualr.edu

PANTHEL, HANS WALTER
PERSONAL Born 00/00/1935, m, 2 children **DISCIPLINE** MODERN GERMAN LITERATURE **EDUCATION** Univ Waterloo, BA, 62, PhD (Ger & Fr lit), 70; Univ Cincinnati, MA, 64. **CAREER** Asst & lectr Ger, Univ Cincinnati, 62-64; lectr, 66-70, asst prof, 70-74, Assoc Prof Ger Lit, Univ Waterloo, 74-, Can Coun grants, 71-73; Univ Waterloo res grant, 72. **MEMBERSHIPS** Asn Can Univ Teachers Ger; Rilke-Ges; Ger Ethnic Cult Asn (pres, 73-). **RESEARCH** German literature form 1890- 1930; French-German literary relations; German literature of the 18th century. **SELECTED PUBLICATIONS** Ed, M Maeterlinck's Pelleas und Melisande, Reclam, Stuttgart, 72; auth, R M Rilke und Maurice Maeterlinck, E Schmidt, Berlin, 73; Zu Rilkes Gedichtzyklus Les Fenetres, Etudis Germaniques, Vol 24, No 1; JStillings Weltendzeit und Zar Alexander I, Germano-Slavica, 74; Rilke's Lettres a une Amie Venitienne, Studi Germanici, 77; JH J-Stilling, Briefe an Freunde, Verwandte u Fremde von 1787-1816, H A Gerstenberg, Hildesheim, 78; Germany 1945-1949 - a Sourcebook - Manfred,m, Germanic Notes And Reviews, Vol 0025, 1994. **CONTACT ADDRESS** Dept of Ger & Slavic Lang, Univ of Waterloo, Waterloo, ON, N2L 3G1.

PAOLINI, GILBERTO
PERSONAL Born 12/22/1928, L'Aquila, Italy, m, 1960, 2 children **DISCIPLINE** ROMANCE LANGUAGES & LITERATURE **EDUCATION** Univ Buffalo, BA, 57, MA, 59; Univ Minn, PhD (Span), 65. **CAREER** Instr Ital & Latin lit, Univ Mass, 58-60; from instr to asst prof Span & Ital, Syracuse Univ, 62-67; assoc prof, 67-76, Prof Span Lit, Tulane Univ, 76-, Reader, Educ Testing Serv, Princeton, 79; exec bd, Southeastern Am Soc 18th Cent Studies, 79-82. **HONORS AND AWARDS** Distinguished Service Award, Soc Espanola, 79. **MEMBERSHIPS** MLA; Am Asn Teachers Span & Port; Asn Int Hispanistas; Am Soc 18th Century Study; AAUP. **RESEARCH** Nineteenth century Spanish and Italian novel; naturalism; Galdos. **SELECTED PUBLICATIONS** Auth, Bartolome Soler, novelista: Procedimientos estilisticos, Ed Juventud, 63; An aspect of spiritualistic naturalism in the novels of B P Galdos: Charity, Las Americas, 69; Galdos and Verga: A rapprochement, Rev Letras, 970; Voluntad y el ideario galdosiano, Estudios Escenicos, 74; La psicopatologia en la literatura italoespanola: D'Annunzio y Palacio Valdes, The Two Hesperias, 78; Tipos Psicopaticos en Declaracion de un vencido de Alejandro Sawa, Critica Hispanica, 179; ed, La Chispa '81: Selected Proceedings, New Orleans, 81; auth, The Confluence of the Mythic, Artistic and Psychic Creation in Valera's Dona Luz, Rev Estudios Hispanicos, 82; The Theater in 19th-century Spain - Gies,dt, Hispania-a J Devoted to The Teaching of Spanish And Portuguese, Vol 0079, 1996. **CONTACT ADDRESS** Dept of Span & Port, Tulane Univ, New Orleans, LA, 70118.

PAPER, HERBERT HARRY
PERSONAL Born 01/11/1925, Baltimore, MD, m, 1949, 2 children **DISCIPLINE** LINGUISTICS **EDUCATION** Univ Colo, BA, 43; Univ Chicago, MA, 48, PhD (Assyriology), 51. **CAREER** Res asst, Orient Inst, Univ Chicago, 49-51; res assoc, Div Mod Lang, Cornell Univ, 52-53; from asst prof to assoc prof Near Eastern lang & ling, Univ Mich, Ann Arbor, 53-62, prof ling, 62- 76, chmn Dept, 63-68; Prof Ling & Dean Grad Studies, Hebrew Union Col, 77-, Fulbright fel, Iran, 51-52; Am Coun Learned Soc fel, Cambridge, 59-60; mem comt lang prog, Am Coun Learned Soc, 59-, chmn, 61-63; mem comt, Near & Mid East Studies, Am Coun Learned Soc-Social Sci Res Coun, 62-63; Nat Sci Found res grant, 68-70; res prof, Ben-Zvi Inst, Hebrew Univ, Jerusalem, 68-69; trustee, Ctr Appl Ling, 73-75; NEH fel, 75-76; vis prof Hebrew Univ, Jerusalem, 75-76. **MEMBERSHIPS** Ling Soc Am; Am Orient Soc; Am Asn Jewish Studies. **RESEARCH** Indo-Iranian linguistics; modern Persian including Judeo- Persian; Elamite. **SELECTED PUBLICATIONS** Coauth, English for Iranians, 55 & The Writing System of Modern Persian, 55, Am Coun Learned Soc; auth, The Phonology and Morphology of Royal Achaemenid Elamite, Univ Mich, 55; ed, Jewish Languages: Theme & Variations, Am Asn Jewish Studies, 70; auth, A Judeo-Persian Pentateuch, Ben-Zvi Inst, Hebrew Univ Jerusalem, 72; Biblia Judaeo-Persica: Editio Variorum, Univ Microfilms, 73; ed, Language and Texts, Univ Mich, 75; coauth, The Song of Songs in Judeo-Persian, Royal Danish Acad, 77; Elamite Dictionary, Vol 1, A-h, Vol 2, I-z - German - Hinz,w, Koch,h, J of The American Oriental Society, Vol 0112, 1992; The Judeo-persian Poet Emrani And His 'Book of Treasure' - Emrani 'Ganj-name', a Versified Commentary on The Mishnaic Tractate 'Abot' - Yeroushalmi,d, J of The American Oriental Society, Vol 0117, 1997. **CONTACT ADDRESS** Sch of Grad Studies, Hebrew Union Col, Cincinnati, OH, 45220.

PAREDES, LILIANA
DISCIPLINE LANGUAGE **EDUCATION** Univ S Calif, PhD, 96. **CAREER** Asst prof, Univ NC-Greensboro, 97-. **HONORS AND AWARDS** New Fac Grant/Res, UNC; Summer Excellency Award, UNC. **MEMBERSHIPS** LSA, MLA, ALFAL. **RESEARCH** Bilingualism; languages in contact; sociolinguistics. **SELECTED PUBLICATIONS** Coauth, art, Null Objects In Bilingual Andean Spanish, 97; coauth, art, The genitive clitic and the genitive construction in Andean Spanish, 97. **CONTACT ADDRESS** Dept of Romance Languages, Univ of North Carolina, 321 McIver, Greensboro, NC, 27402. **EMAIL** l_parede@uncg.edu

PARENT, DAVID J.
PERSONAL Born 05/31/1931, Hamlin, ME, m, 1971, 2 children **DISCIPLINE** GERMAN LANGUAGE & LITERATURE **EDUCATION** Marist Col, BA, 53; Univ Heidelberg, cert, 57; Univ Cincinnati, MA, 65, PhD (Ger), 67. **CAREER** Instr Ger & Russ, Col Mt St Joseph, 63-66; from instr to asst prof Ger, Boston Col, 66-68; Assoc Prof Ger, Ill State Univ, 68-, Ed, Appl Lit Press, 76-; ed assoc, Telos, 78-. **MEMBERSHIPS** MLA; Am Asn Teachers Ger **RESEARCH** Modern German literature. **SELECTED PUBLICATIONS** Transl, Michael Landmann's Reform of the Hebrew Alphabet, 76; Juan Garcia Ponce's Modern Literature and Reality, 76; Jorge Millas' The Intellectual and Moral Challenge of Mass Society, 77; Michael Landmann's Philosophy: Its Mission and its Disciplines, 77; Alienatory Reason, 78; Gustav Landauer's For Socialism, 78; Michael Landmann's De Homine: Man in the Mirror of his Thought, 79; auth, Franz Kafka, and ETA Hoffmann, In: Critical Survey of Short Fiction, 81; Hebbel Dramatic Fantasy - a Categorial Analysis - German - Nolle,v, German Quarterly, Vol 0067, 1994. **CONTACT ADDRESS** Dept of Foreign Lang, Illinois State Univ, Normal, IL, 61761.

PARENTE, JR, JAMES A.
DISCIPLINE MEDIEVAL AND EARLY MODERN GERMAN, SCANDINAVIAN, AND NETHERLANDIC LITERATURE **EDUCATION** Yale Univ, PhD. **CAREER** Prof, Univ Minn, Twin Cities. **SELECTED PUBLICATIONS** Auth, Religious Drama and the Humanist Tradition: Christian Theatre in Germany and the Netherlands, 87; ed, Socio-Historical Approaches to Early Modern German Literature, 93; coed, Literary Culture in the Holy Roman Empire, 1580-1720, 93; Studies in German and Scandinavian Literature after 1500, 93. **CONTACT ADDRESS** Dept of Ger, Scand & Dutch, Univ Minn, Twin Cities, 216 Folwel, Minneapolis, MN, 55455. **EMAIL** paren001@tc.umn.edu

PARISH, CHARLES
PERSONAL Born 05/11/1927, Shreveport, LA, m, 1965, 3 children **DISCIPLINE** LINGUISTICS, ENGLISH AS FOREIGN LANGUAGE **EDUCATION** Brooklyn Col, BA, 52; Univ NM, MA, 55, PhD (English ling), 58. **CAREER** Instr English, Univ Wichita, 56-57, asst prof, 58-59; asst prof English & ling, Southern Ill Univ, Alton, 59-63; assoc prof, 65-71, Prof Ling, Southern Ill Univ, Carbondale, 71-, Fulbright lectr, Univ Mandalay, 61-62 & Univ Rome, 62-64, 68-69; Coun Am Study Rome, 63-65; consult, Univ Rome, 79. **MEMBERSHIPS** Ling Soc Am; MLA; Teachers English to Speakers Other Lang. **RESEARCH** English as a foreign language teacher-training; second- language acquisition. **SELECTED PUBLICATIONS** Ed, Corso d'Inglese Parlato, Vol 3, 65 & coauth, Vol 4, 68, Harcourt; auth, Some phonetic problems for Burmese speakers of English, Lang Learning, 64; Tristram Shandy Notes, Cliff's Notes, 68; Agenbite of Agendath Netaim, James Joyce Quart, spring 69; The Shandy Bull vindicated, Mod Lang Quart, 370; ESL practice-teaching utilizing videotape, 76 & A practical philosophy of pronunciation, 77, TESOL Quart. **CONTACT ADDRESS** Dept of Ling, Southern Ill Univ, Carbondale, IL, 62901.

PARK, JIN Y.
PERSONAL Born 05/31/1962, Seoul, Korea, m, 1996 **DISCIPLINE** COMPARATIVE STUDIES **EDUCATION** SUNY Stony Brook, PhD, 98. **CAREER** Yonsei Univ Seoul, lectr, 87; SUNY Stony Brook, tchg asst, adj lect, 93-. **HONORS AND AWARDS** Yonsei Univ, Grad & Undergrad Fel, NY Lit Young Writers Award, Buddhist Grant. **MEMBERSHIPS** AAR, APA, AAS, IAPL, KWAA, KWWA, KNA, MLA, NAKA, SACP, SPEP. **RESEARCH** Asian and comparative thought; deconstruction and Buddhism; Korean and E Asian Zen Buddhism; contemp continental philosophy. **SELECTED PUBLICATIONS** Auth, Hwadu and Hwaom in Chinul - A Postmodern Perspective, Jour Buddhist Stud, 98; auth, Ch'an Language: the Case of Chinul's Hwadu, Jour Korean Thought, 98; auth, The Doctrine of the Mean and Its Theory of the Inner Revolution, Modern Buddhism, 94; translations, Hwadu and Freedom: Pojo Chinul's Treaties on Resolving Doubts about Hwadu Mediation, Jour of Korean Thought, 98; auth, Mother and Dove: Korean-American poetry Anthology, co-trans, Flushing: Institute for Korean-American Culture, Printing & AD Express Inc, 97; auth, Buddhist Enlightenment and Hegelian Teleology, by Bockja Kim, Modern Buddhism, 95. **CONTACT ADDRESS** Dept of Comparative Studies, SUNY, Stony Brook Univ, 500 High Point Dr, Apt PH12, Hartsdale, NY, 10530. **EMAIL** jypark@prodigy.net

PARKER, MARGARET
PERSONAL Born 11/10/1941, Lubbock, TX, 1 child **DISCIPLINE** SPANISH **EDUCATION** Tex Tech Univ, BA, 63, MA, 64; Ind Univ, PhD, 69. **CAREER** Instr Span, Odessa Col, 64-65; instr, 68-69, asst prof, 69-78; assoc prof, prof Spanish, La State Univ, Baton Rouge, 79-. **MEMBERSHIPS** MLA; Am Asn Teachers Span & Port; SCent Mod Lang Asn. **RESEARCH** Spanish medieval literature; Women in Hispanic literature. **SELECTED PUBLICATIONS** Auth, The Didactic Structure and Content of El libro de Calila e Digna, Ed Universal, 78; auth The Story of a Story: The Case of the Concella Teodor. Tamesis, 96. **CONTACT ADDRESS** Dept Foreign Lang, Louisiana State Univ, Baton Rouge, LA, 70803-5306. **EMAIL** mparker@unixl.sncc.lsu.edu

PARKER, SIMON B.
PERSONAL Born 02/23/1940, Manchester, England, m, 1961, 2 children **DISCIPLINE** ANCIENT NEAR EASTERN STUDIES, SEMITIC LANGUAGES, HEBREW BIBLE **EDUCATION** Univ Manchester, BA, 60; Asbury Theol Sem, BD, 63; Johns Hopkins Univ, PhD, 67. **CAREER** Asst prof of Humanities and Relig, Reed Col, 67-75; asst to the Pres, Boston Univ, 77-78, asst provost, 78-81, assoc dean and assoc prof, Boston Univ School of Theol, 81-88, assoc prof of Hebrew Bible, 88-97, prof of Hebrew Bible, Boston Univ School of Theol, 97-. **HONORS AND AWARDS** Graves Award, 72; Named First Harrell F Beck Scholar of Hebrew Scripture, Boston Univ. **MEMBERSHIPS** Am Oriental Soc; Am Schools of Oriental Res; Soc of Biblical Lit; Soc for Old Testament Study, UK. **RESEARCH** Continuities and discontinuities in the lit and relig of ancient Israel; Canaan Israelite culture and social hist. **SELECTED PUBLICATIONS** Auth, The Pre-Biblical Narrative Tradition: Essays on the Ugaritic Poems Keret and Aqhat, Resources for Biblical Study 24, Scholar Press, 89; Official Attitudes Toward Prophecy at Mari and in Israel, Vetus Testamentum 45, 93; The Beginning of the Reign of God--Psalm 82 an Myth and Liturgy, Revue Biblique 102, 95; Stories in Scripture and Inscriptions, Oxford Univ Press, 97; ed and trans, Ugaritic Narrative poetry, Writings From the Ancient World, Scholars Press, 97; gen ed since 1994 of Writings From the Ancient World, Scholars Press; numerous scholarly articles in books and journals. **CONTACT ADDRESS** School of Theology, Boston Univ, 745 Commonwealth Ave, Boston, MA, 02215. **EMAIL** sbparker@bu.edu

PARKER, STEPHEN JAN
PERSONAL Born 08/05/1939, Brooklyn, NY, m, 1965, 2 children **DISCIPLINE** RUSSIAN & COMPARATIVE LITERATURE **EDUCATION** Cornell Univ, BA, 60, MA, 62, PhD (Russ & comp lit), 69. **CAREER** Asst prof Russ, Univ Okla, 66-67; asst prof, 67-73, Assoc Prof Russ, Univ Kans, 73-, Assoc Chmn & Dir Grad Studies, 78-; mem nat selection comt, Coun Int Educ Exchange, Russ Lang Prof, 77; ed, The Nabokovian, 78-. **HONORS AND AWARDS** Nat Endowment for Humanities younger humanist fel, 70-71. **MEMBERSHIPS** MLA; Am Asn Advan Slavic Lang; Am Asn Teachers Slavic & East Europ Lang; Vladimir Nabokov Soc. **RESEARCH** Russian prose fiction of the 19th and 20th centuries; Europan and American modern novel; writings of Vladimir Nabokov. **SELECTED PUBLICATIONS** Coauth, Russia on Canvas: Ily a Repin, Pa State Univ Press, 81; co-ed, The Achievements of Vladimir Nabokov, Cornell Univ, 85; auth, Understanding Vladimir Nabokov, 89; author of numerous articles and reviews. **CONTACT ADDRESS** Dept of Slavic Lang & Lit, Univ of Kans, Lawrence, KS, 66045-0001. **EMAIL** sjparker@kuhub.cc.ukans.edu

PARSELL, DAVID BEATTY
PERSONAL Born 12/04/1941, Charleston, SC, m, 1967, 2 children **DISCIPLINE** FRENCH **EDUCATION** Hamilton Col, AB, 63; Vanderbilt Univ, MA, 68, PhD(French), 70. **CAREER** Instr French, Grinnell Col, 67-69; from instr to assoc prof, 69-86, Prof Mod Foreign Lang, Furman Univ, 86-. **MEMBERSHIPS** Am Asn Teachers Fr; Southern Comp Lit Asn. **RESEARCH** Georges Neveux; French theatre 1930-1960; surrealism. **SELECTED PUBLICATIONS** Auth, Le Voyageur Sans Bagage and the case against tragedy, Fr Rev, 3/77; Sign and Image in Peret and Magritte, Univ SC Fr Lit Set, Vol 5, 78; Aspects of Comedy in Camus' Le Malentendu, Symposium, Winter 83-84; Louis Auchincloss, Twayne, 86; Michel de Ghelderode, Twayne, 94. **CONTACT ADDRESS** Dept of Mod Foreign Lang, Furman Univ, 3300 Poinsett Hwy, Greenville, SC, 29613-0002. **EMAIL** david.parsell@furman.edu

PARSONS, ROBERT A.
PERSONAL Born 04/08/1948, Ft. Benning, GA, m, 1970, 2 children **DISCIPLINE** SPANISH **EDUCATION** WV Univ, BA, 70, MA, 72; OH Univ, MA, 76; Penn St Univ, PhD, 82 **CAREER** Asst prof, 79-83, Assoc prof, 84-91; Prof, 91-, Univ of Scranton **HONORS AND AWARDS** NEH, 84 **MEMBERSHIPS** AATSP, LASA **RESEARCH** Latin Am lit, satire **CONTACT ADDRESS** Dept of Foreign Lang, Univ of Scranton, Scranton, PA, 18510. **EMAIL** parsonsrl@uofs.edu

PARTEE, BARBARA H.
DISCIPLINE LINGUISTICS **EDUCATION** Univ Swarthmore, BA, 61; Univ Mass, PhD, 65. **CAREER** Prof. **RESEARCH** Semantics; semantics relation to syntax, pragmatics, logic, philosophy of language, and cognitive and representational theories of language. **SELECTED PUBLICATIONS** Auth, Noun Phrase Interpretation and Type-shifting Principles, Dordrecht, 87; Possible Worlds in Model-Theoretic Semantics: A Linguistic Perspective, de Gruyter, 89; Nominal and Temporal Anaphora, Ling Philos, 84; co-auth, Mathematical Methods in Linguistics, Kluwer, 90; co-ed, Topic, Focus, and Quantification, Kluwer, 95. **CONTACT ADDRESS** Linguistics Dept, Univ of Massachusetts, Amherst, S College 222, Amherst, MA, 01003. **EMAIL** partee@linguist.umass.edu

PARTSCH, CORNELIUS
DISCIPLINE GERMAN **EDUCATION** Oberlin Col, BA; Brown Univ, Ma, PhD. **CAREER** Instr, Hamilton Col; vis asst prof-, Colby Col. **SELECTED PUBLICATIONS** Publ, pop cult, lit, music, second lang acquisition. **CONTACT ADDRESS** Dept of Ger, Colby Col, 4000 Mayflower Hill, Watereville, ME, 04901-8840.

PASCAL, CECIL BENNETT
PERSONAL Born 05/04/1926, Chicago, IL, m, 1959, 1 child **DISCIPLINE** CLASSICAL PHILOLOGY **EDUCATION** Univ Calif, Los Angeles, AB, 48, MA, 50; Harvard Univ, MA, 53, PhD, 56. **CAREER** Instr classics, Univ Ill, 55-56; instr, Cornell Univ, 57- 60; asst prof classic lang, 60-65, head dept classics, Chinese & Japanese, 65-67 & 72-73, assoc prof, 65-76, Prof Classics, Univ Ore, 76-, Head Dept Classics, 78-, William Amory Gardner traveling fel, Harvard Univ, 56-57; Fulbright-Hays res fel, Univ Rome, 67-68. **MEMBERSHIPS** Am Philol Asn; Philol Asn Pac Coast; Classic Asn Pac Northwest; Archaeol Inst Arn; AAUP. **RESEARCH** Latin and Greek literature; Roman religion. **SELECTED PUBLICATIONS** Auth, Horatian Chiaroscuro, In: Hommages a Marcel Renard, Latomus, 69; Rex Nemorensis, Numen, 76; October Horse, Harvard State Col Philol, 81; The Dubious Devotion of Turnus + Vergil 'Aeneid', Book-11, Transactions of The American Philological Association, Vol 0120, 1990. **CONTACT ADDRESS** Dept of Classics, Univ of Ore, Eugene, OR, 97403.

PASCAL, PAUL
PERSONAL Born 03/26/1925, New York, NY, m, 1948, 2 children **DISCIPLINE** CLASSICS, MEDIEVAL LATIN **EDUCATION** Univ VT, BA, 48; Univ NC, PHD(classics), 53. **CAREER** Prof Classics, Univ Wash, 53-. **MEMBERSHIPS** Am Philol Asn. **RESEARCH** Mediaeval Latin literature. **SELECTED PUBLICATIONS** Coauth, The Institutionum Disciplinae of Isidore of Seville, Traditio, 57; Notes on Missus Sum in Vineam of Walter of Chatillon, Studies in Honor of B L Ullman, Rome, 64; The Conclusion of the Pervigilium Veneris, Neophilologus, 65; The Julius Exclusus of Erasmus, Ind Univ, 68; The Poetry of Boethius - Odaly,g, Classical J, Vol 0087, 1992. **CONTACT ADDRESS** Dept of Classics, Univ of Wash, Seattle, WA, 98105.

PASLICK, ROBERT H.
PERSONAL Born 02/11/1930, Denver, CO, m, 1958, 3 children **DISCIPLINE** GERMAN LITERATURE **EDUCATION** Univ Louisville, AB, 52; Ind Univ, MA, 58, PhD(Ger), 62. **CAREER** From instr to assoc prof, 61-74, Assoc Prof Ger, Univ Mich, Ann Arbor, 74-. **HONORS AND AWARDS** Sinclair Counseling Award, 68. **RESEARCH** European 20th century prose. **SELECTED PUBLICATIONS** Auth, Dialectic and non-attachment: The structure of Hermann Hesse's Siddhartha, Symp, 73; The tempter: Bergengruen's Grande Prince and the Hermetic tradition, Neophilologus, 73; Narrowing the distance: Siegfried Lenz's Deutschstunde, Ger Quart, 73; From Nothingness to Nothingness - The Nature And Destiny of The Self in Boehme And Nishitani, Eastern Buddhist, Vol 0030, 1997. **CONTACT ADDRESS** Dept of Ger Lang & Lit, Univ Mich, Ann Arbor, MI, 48104.

PASTOR, LESLIE P.
PERSONAL Born 05/08/1925, 2 children **DISCIPLINE** EUROPEAN HISTORY, GERMAN **EDUCATION** Educ: Seton Hall Univ, AB, 56; Columbia Univ, MA, 59, PhD, 67; Inst E Cent Europe, cert, 60. **CAREER** Instr Seton Hall Prep Sch, 56-60; from instr to asst prof, 60-68, Assoc Prof Ger, Seton Hall Univ, 68-. **MEMBERSHIPS** Am Asn Advan Slavic Studies; Am Asn Tchr(s) Ger; Am Asn for Study Hungarian Hist. **RESEARCH** Ger lang and lit; 18th and 19th century Hungarian hist; hist of East Central Europe; mod East Europ hist. **CONTACT ADDRESS** Dept of Mod Lang, Seton Hall Univ, 400 S Orange Ave, South Orange, NJ, 07079-2697. **EMAIL** pastorle@shu.edu

PASTORE PASSARO, MARIA C.
DISCIPLINE ITALIAN LANGUAGE AND LITERATURE **EDUCATION** SUNY Univ Ctr, PhD, 87. **CAREER** Assoc prof. **HONORS AND AWARDS** Acad Honors,NEH, Agnelli Found, NIAF, Fulbright; Excel Tchg Awd, Central Conn State Univ, 94; grant, Yale/Mellon, 96-97. **RESEARCH** Middle Ages and Renaissance. **SELECTED PUBLICATIONS** Auth, several short plays; trans, Longfellow's Michael Angelo, Tusiani's Gente Mia and Other Poems, Rind and All, The Fifth Season; trans, Tasso's King Torrismondo, Fordham Univ Press, 97. **CONTACT ADDRESS** Central Connecticut State Univ, 1615 Stanley St, New Britain, CT, 06050.

PATERNOST, JOSEPH
PERSONAL Born 03/17/1931, Yugoslavia, m, 1960 **DISCIPLINE** LANGUAGES **EDUCATION** Ohio Univ, BA, 55; Ind Univ, MA, 56, PhD(Slavic ling), 63. **CAREER** From instr to asst prof Russ, 60-68, assoc prof Slavic lang, 68-77 Prof Salvic Lang, PA State Univ, University Park, 77-, Nat Defense Foreign Lang fel, 59-60. **MEMBERSHIPS** Am Asn Teachers Slavic & E Europ Lang; Am Asn Advan Slavic Studies; MLA; Am Asn Southeast Europ Studies; Soc Slovene Studies. **RESEARCH** Slovenian; Russian; theory and practice of translation. **SELECTED PUBLICATIONS** Auth, Russian-English Glossary of Linguistic Terms, 65 & Slovenian-English Glossary of Linguistic Terms, 66, PA State Univ; From English to Slovenian: Problems in Translation Equivalence, PA State Univ, 70; The Adequacy of Translations from English into Slovenian from the Point of View of Formal and Dynamic Equivalence & Three-Level Theory of Translation (both written in Slovenian), Prostor in cas, Ljubljana, Yugoslavia, 72; Slovenian lanugage on Minnesota's iron range: Some sociolinguistic aspects of language maintenance and language shift, Gen Ling, 76; a Basic Reference Grammar of Slovene - Derbyshire,ww, Slavic Review, Vol 0054, 1995. **CONTACT ADDRESS** State Univ, N-438 Burrowes, University Park, PA, 16802.

PATERSON, JANET M.
PERSONAL Berne, Switzerland **DISCIPLINE** FRENCH LITERATURE **EDUCATION** Univ Toronto, BA, 64, MA, 75, PhD, 81. **CAREER** Lang tchr, Reform Sch for Girls, 65-70; lectr, 70-74, PROF FRENCH, UNIV TORONTO 81-, chair grad stud, 91-95. **HONORS AND AWARDS** Gabrielle Roy Prize, 90. **MEMBERSHIPS** Asn Can Que Lit; Asn Can Stud. **SELECTED PUBLICATIONS** Auth, Anne Hebert: architexture romanesque, 85; auth, Postmodernism and the Quebec Novel, 94; co-ed, Challenges, Projects, Texts, 93. **CONTACT ADDRESS** Faculty Arts & Sciences, Univ Toronto, 100 St. George St, Toronto, ON, M5S 3G3. **EMAIL** jpaters@chass.utoronto.ca

PATTERSON, WILLIAM TAYLOR
PERSONAL Born 10/25/1931, Hattiesburg, MS **DISCIPLINE** FRENCH, ROMANCE LANGUAGES **EDUCATION** Univ Kans, BA, 54; Univ Montpellier, cert, 55; Pa State Univ, University Park ,MEd, 61; Stanford Univ, PhD(Ling), 67. **CAREER** Asst prof French, 61-64, assoc prof French & Romance Ling 68-74, prof French & Romance Ling, Tex Tech Univ, 74-, vis prof, Univ Nebr, 62, Stillman Col, 64, Colo State Univ, 65 & Emory Univ, 66; mem, Nat Fullbright Selection Comt for France, 79-80. **HONORS AND AWARDS** Phi Beta Kappa, 53; Fulbright Scholarship, Univ of Montpellier, France, 54-55; NDEA Fel, Stanford Univ, 64-67; Mortar Board-Omicron Delta Kappa Outstanding Teaching Award, 93. **MEMBERSHIPS** Am Asn Teachers Fr; Am Asn Teachers Span & Port; MLA; SCent Mod Lang Asn. **RESEARCH** Romance lexicology; Old French; Occitan. **SELECTED PUBLICATIONS** Auth, On the genealogical structure of the Spanish vocabulary, Festschrift Martinet, 4/68; The Spanish lexicon: a genealogical and functional correlation, Hisp, 4/73; A genealogical classification of Spanish words, Ling, 10/73; The Spanish lexicon: a genealogical and physical correlation, Revista de Estudios Hisp, 74; The lexical Structure of Spanish, Mouton, The Hague, 75; A genealogical classification of French words, Can Mod Lang Rev, Winter 82; The Spanish Lexicon: A Correlation of Basic Word Properties, Univ Press Am, 82; Lexical Borrowings in Spanish: Function, Length, Genealogy, and Chronology, Canadian Modern Language Review, 86. **CONTACT ADDRESS** Dept of Classical & Mod Lang, Texas Tech Univ, Lubbock, TX, 79409-2071.

PATTY, JAMES SINGLETON
PERSONAL Born 07/17/1925, Florence, AL **DISCIPLINE** FRENCH **EDUCATION** Univ NC, AB, 45, MA, 47, PhD, 53. **CAREER** Instr French, Univ NC, 46-53; instr French St Span, Univ Colo, 53-54; from asst prof to assoc prof French, Univ Tenn, 54-60; assoc prof, Washington & Lee Univ, 60-64; assoc prof, 64-69, Prof French, PROF FRENCH EMER, 88- , Vanderbilt Univ, 69-, Co-ed, Bull Baudelairien; foreign corresp, Soc Hist Lit France; ed bd, Romance Quart; Phi Beta Kappa, 45. **HONORS AND AWARDS** Outstanding Chap Treas Am Asn Tchrs Fr, 81 **MEMBERSHIPS** Am Asn Teachers Fr; MLA; Am Comp Lit Asn; Soc Etudes Romantiques. **RESEARCH** Nineteenth century French literature; Baudelaire; Romanticism. **SELECTED PUBLICATIONS** Auth, Baudelaire's knowledge and use of Dante, Studies Philol, 10/56; Baudelaire and Bossuet on laughter, Publ Mod Lang Asn Am, 9/65; ed, Jean Giraudoux's Electre, Appleton, 65; auth, Baudelaire et Hippolyte Babou, Rev Hist Lit France, 4-6/67; co-ed, Hommage a W T Bandy, La Baconniere, 73; coed Hommage a Claude Pichois, La Baconniete, 85; Durer in French Letters, Honore Champion-Slatkine, 89. **CONTACT ADDRESS** Vanderbilt Univ, Station B, Box 1630, Nashville, TN, 37235.

PAULSEN, WOLFGANG
PERSONAL Born 09/21/1910, Dusseldorf, Germany, m, 1938, 1 child **DISCIPLINE** GERMAN LITERATURE **EDUCATION** Univ Berne, PhD, 34. **CAREER** Asst lectr Ger, Univ Durham, 35-37; asst lectr, Univ Reading & asst, Westfield Col, London, 37-38; asst prof mod lang, Southwestern Col, 38-43; asst prof Ger, State Univ IA, 43-47; assoc prof, Smith Col, 47-53; assoc prof, NY State Col for Teachers, Albany, 53-54; asst prof, Univ CT, 54-61, prof, 61-66; chmn dept, 66-71, Prof Ger, Univ MA, Amherst, 66-. **MEMBERSHIPS** MLA; Schiller Ges. **RESEARCH** Eighteenth to twentieth century German literature; modern German drama. **SELECTED PUBLICATIONS** Auth, Georg Kaiser, Die Perspektiven seines Werkes, 60 & Die Ahnfrau, Zu Grillparzers fruher Dramatik, 62, Niemeyer, Tubingen; Versuch uber Rolf Bongs, Blaschke, Darmstadt, 74; Chr M Wieland, Der Mensch und sein Werk, 75, Eichendorff und sein Taugenichts, 76 & Johann Elias Schlegel und die Komodie, 77, Francke, Bern; Der Expressionismus in der deutschen Literatur, Peter Lang, Bern, 82. **CONTACT ADDRESS** Dept of Ger Lang & Lit, Univ of Massachusetts, Amherst, MA, 01002.

PAULSON, MICHAEL G.
PERSONAL Born 09/27/1945, Pittsburgh, PA, m, 1972 **DISCIPLINE** FRENCH, SPANISH **EDUCATION** Kutztown Univ, BS, 67; Fla State Univ, MA, 68, PhD, 73; Univ Central Ark, MA, 83. **CAREER** Asst prof of Foreign Langs, South Dakota State Univ, 73-76; lectr of Foreign Langs & English, Univ Central Ark, 76-85; adjunct prof of Foreign Langs, Northampton Community Col, 85-86; asst prof of Foreign Langs, Muhlenburg Col, 86-87; assoc prof, 87-89, PROF OF FOREIGN LANGS, KUTZTOWN UNIV, 93-. **HONORS AND AWARDS** Roubey Romance Lang Award, 67; AAUP Grad Student Award, 67; NDEA Fel, 68-69 & 71-72. **MEMBERSHIPS** South Central MLA; Mountain Interstate Foreign Lang Conf. **RESEARCH** 17th Century French literature; Golden Age Spanish literature; urban literature. **SELECTED PUBLICATIONS** Auth, Kings, Queens, and Splendor: A Critical Analysis of La Princesse de Cleves as a Royal Exemplary Novel, The Edwin Mellen Press, 91; The Youth and the Beach: A Comparative Study of Thomas Mann's A Death in Venice and Reinaldo Arenas' Otra vez el mar, Ediciones Universal, 93; Madame de La Fayette's The Princess of Cleves: A New Translation, Univ Press of Am, 95; Facets of a Princess: Multiple Readings of Madam de La Fayette's La Princesse de Cleves, Peter Lang, 98. **CONTACT ADDRESS** Dept of Foreign Langs, Kutztown Univ, Pennsylvania, Kutztown, PA, 19530.

PAULSTON, CHRISTINA BRATT
PERSONAL Stockholm, Sweden, m, 1963, 2 children **DISCIPLINE** LINGUISTICS, LANGUAGE TEACHING **EDUCATION** Carleton Col, BA, 53; Univ Minn, Minneapolis, MA, 55; Columbia Univ, EdD(ling), 66. **CAREER** Teacher English, Pub High Schs, Clara City & Pinc Island, Minn, 55-60; teacher English & French, Am Sch Tangier, 60-62; teacher, Katrineholm Hogre Allmanna Laroverk, Sweden, 62-63; instr, Teachers Col, Columbia Univ, 64-66; AID spec, Punjab Univ, India, 66 & Cath Univ Peru, 66-67; consult lang teaching, Inst Ling Verano, Peru, 67-68; from asst prof to assoc prof, 69- 76, asst dir English Lang Inst, 69-70, Prof Ling, Univ Pittsburgh, 76-, Dir, English Lang Inst, 70, NDEA & Nat Endowment for Humanities grant & prog dir, Quechua-Aymara Inst, 72. **MEMBERSHIPS** Teachers English to Speakers Other Lang (2nd vp, 71-72, pres, 75-76); Ling Soc Am; Int Asn Teachers English as Foreign Lang; Am Coun Teaching Foreign Lang; MLA. **RESEARCH** Sociolinguistics; language policy. **SELECTED PUBLICATIONS** Coauth, Controlled Composition, Regents, 73; From Substitution to Substance: A Handbook of Structural Pattern Drills, Newbury House, 73; auth, Implications of language learning theory for language planning, Ctr Appl Ling, 75; coauth, Developing Communicative Competence: Roleplays in English as a Second Language, Univ Pittsburgh, 75; Procedures & Techniques in Teaching English as a Second Language, Winthrop, 76; Individualizing the Language Classroom: Learning & Teaching in a Communicative Context, Jacaranda, 76; auth, Bilingual Education: Issues and Theories, Newbury House, 80; English as a Second Language, Nat Educ Asn, 80; Language Planning - Focusschrift in Honor of Fishman,joshua,a., Vol 3 - Marshall,df, Language in Society, Vol 0022, 1993; European Models of Bilingual Education - Beardsmore,hb, Language in Society, Vol 0024, 1995; Language Use in Rural-development - an African Perspective - Robinson,cdw, Applied Linguistics, Vol 0018, 1997. **CONTACT ADDRESS** Dept of Gen Ling, Univ of Pittsburgh, Pittsburgh, PA, 15213.

PAUTROT, JEAN-LOUIS
DISCIPLINE FRENCH **EDUCATION** Washington Univ, PhD, 92 **CAREER** Asst prof, St. Louis Univ, 91-95; assoc prof, St. Louis Univ, 95- **HONORS AND AWARDS** Egilrud Fel Humanities, Washington Univ, 88-89 **MEMBERSHIPS** Mod Lang Assoc; Consei Int des Etudes Francophones; Missouri Philoi Soc; 20-Century Fr Studies; Amer Assoc Teachers Fr; Int Assoc Word Music Studies **RESEARCH** Interrelations between Music and Literature; French Literature and Cinema 1945 to Present; Cultural Stereotypes **SELECTED PUBLICATIONS** "Opera." Fr Rev, 98-99; "The Battle of the Somme, 1916: Historiography and Annotated Bibliography." Fr Rev, 98-99; "Les sept noms du peintre." Fr Rev, 98 **CONTACT ADDRESS** Dept Modern & Classical Lang, St Louis Univ, 221 N Grand Blvd., St Louis, MO, 63103. **EMAIL** pautropj@slu.edu

PAUWELS, HEIDI
PERSONAL Belgium **DISCIPLINE** ASIAN STUDIES **EDUCATION** Univ Washington, PhD, 94. **CAREER** Lectr, School of Oriental and African Studies, 94-97; Asst Prof, Univ Washington, 97-. **HONORS AND AWARDS** Fulbright to study at Univ Wash; Grant from Belgian Embassy for 1 yr field work in India. **MEMBERSHIPS** AAR; AOS; AAS **RESEARCH** Hinduism (Bhakti/Hagiography/Reworking of Scripture); Gender issues; Hindi Lit. **SELECTED PUBLICATIONS** Auth, Krishna's Round Dance Reconsidered **CONTACT ADDRESS** Dept Asian Language & Literature, Univ of Washington, Seattle, WA, 98195-3521.

PAXMAN, DAVID B.
PERSONAL Born 12/31/1946, Salt Lake City, UT, m, 1996, 10 children **DISCIPLINE** ENGLISH LANGUAGE; LITERATURE **EDUCATION** Univ Chicago, PhD 82, MA 72; Brigham Young Univ, BA 71. **CAREER** Brigham Young Univ, assoc prof, 88-; Brigham Young Univ HI, asst prof, assoc prof, 76-83. **MEMBERSHIPS** ASECS; WSECS. **RESEARCH** Eighteenth-century British Literature; Intellectual History. **SELECTED PUBLICATIONS** Auth, Samuel Johnson Life's Incompleteness and the Limits of Representation, Lit and Belief, 98; auth, Failure as Authority: Poetic Voices and the Muse of Grace in William Cowper's The Task, 1650-1850, Ideas Aesthetics and Inquiries in the Early Modern Era, 98; auth, Writing about the Arts and Humanities, coauth, Needham Hts MA, Simon and Schuster Custom, 96; auth, Adam in a Strange Country: Locke's Language Theory and Travel Literature, Modern Philos, 95; auth, Oral and Literate Discourse in Aphra Behn's Oroonoko, Restoration: Studies in English Literary Culture, 1600-1700, 94; auth, A New Comer's Guide to Honolulu, Mutual Pub, 93. **CONTACT ADDRESS** Dept of Literature, Brigham Young Univ, 3136 JKHB, Provo, UT, 84602. **EMAIL** david_paxman@byu.edu

PAZ, FRANCIS XAVIER
PERSONAL Born 11/05/1931, Chicago, IL, m, 1973, 1 child **DISCIPLINE** COMPARATIVE LITERATURE, ORIENTAL STUDIES **EDUCATION** Univ Chicago, BA, 52, MA, 57; Columbia Univ, PhD(Orient studies), 72. **CAREER** Lectr humanities, Bishop Col, 56-57; lectr Orient humanities, Columbia Univ, 63-65; Prof English & Comp Lit, State Univ NY, New Paltz, 66, Univ fel Arabic lit, Columbia Univ, 77-. **MEMBERSHIPS** MLA; Am Orient Soc; Mideast Studies Asn. **RESEARCH** Modern American and Arabic fiction. **SELECTED PUBLICATIONS** Translr, The Assemblies of Al-Hamadhani, State Univ NY, (in press); The Monument - Art, Vulgarity And Responsibility in Iraq - Alkhalil,s, J of The American Oriental Society, Vol 0113, 1993. **CONTACT ADDRESS** Dept Lit, State Univ Col, New Paltz, NY, 12562.

PEARCE, JAMES
DISCIPLINE GREEK AND LATIN LANGUAGE AND LITERATURE **EDUCATION** Baylor Univ, BA; Univ TX-Austin, MA, PhD. **CAREER** Prof,68-, Trinity Univ. **RESEARCH** Pastoral poetry. **SELECTED PUBLICATIONS** Auth, The Eclogues of Calpurnius Siculus, 90; The Eclogues of Nemesian and the Einsiedeln Manuscript, 92. **CONTACT ADDRESS** Dept of Class, Trinity Univ, 715 Stadium Dr, San Antonio, TX, 78212.

PEARSON, LON
DISCIPLINE SPANISH LANGUAGE AND LITERATURE **EDUCATION** Univ Utah, BA, magna cum laude, 65; UCLA, MA, 68, CPhil, 69, PhD, 73. **CAREER** Tchg fel, Univ Utah, 65-66; assoc, UCLA, 69-70; instr, Univ Mo, Rolla, 70-73; asst prof, 73-77, hd, Lang Sect, 74, 77, 79, grad fac, 76-91, assoc prof, 77-87, doctoral fac, 77-91, prof, Univ Mo, Rolla, 87-91; vis prof, Brigham Young Univ, 82-83; grad fac, 91-, grad fel, 92-, prof, 91, ch, dept Mod Lang, Univ Nebr, Kearney, 91-; ed, Mo For Lang J, 73-78; ed, 79-93, assoc ed/bk rev ed, Chasqui, J of Lat Am Lit, 93-; consult ed, Stud in Contemp Satire, 94-. **HONORS AND AWARDS** Phi Eta Sigma, 63; Phi Kappa Phi, 65; Phi Beta Kappa, 66; Sigma Delta Pi, 66; fac res fel Univ Mo, Rolla, 71, 73, 81, 85; NEH Yr Fel in Residence, Johns Hopkins Univ, 75-76; NEH-Exxon grant, 79; Scouting Award of Merit, Ozark Coun of Boy Scouts of Am, 81; Weldon Springs grant, Chile, 81; NEH summer sem, Yeshiva Univ, 81. **MEMBERSHIPS** Am Asn of Tchr of Span & Port, 68-; Int Inst of Iberoamerican Lit, 69-; MLA, 69-85; exec bd, 73-80, exec secy, For Lang Asn Mo, 78-79; Rocky Mt Coun on Lat Am Stud, 83-90; Mo Philol Asn. **SELECTED PUBLICATIONS** Auth, La novela de la generacion de 1938 de Chile y su herencia poetica: Influencia de la novela espanola y el poema en prosa francesa, La hora actual de la novela hispanica, ed, Eduardo Godoy Gallardo, Ediciones Universitarias de Valparaiso de la Universidad Catolica de Valparaiso, 94; An Overview of Computers and How They Can Aid Translations, Platte Vly Rev, 23:2, 95. **CONTACT ADDRESS** Univ Nebr, Kearney, Kearney, NE, 68849.

PEAVLER, TERRY J.
PERSONAL Born 10/25/1942, Seminole, OK, 2 children **DISCIPLINE** SPANISH **EDUCATION** Univ Colo, Boulder, BA, 65, MA, 67; Univ Calif, Berkeley, PhD(comp lit), 73. **CAREER** Asst prof, 71-79, Assoc Prof, 79-88, PROF SPAN & COMP LIT, PA STATE UNIV, UNIV PARK, 88- . **HONORS AND AWARDS** Nat Sci Found Inst grant, 73-74. **MEMBERSHIPS** MLA; Am Asn Teachers Span & Port. **RESEARCH** Latin American novel; Cuban, Mexican, Argentine literature; narrative theory. **SELECTED PUBLICATIONS** Auth, The source for the archetype in Los Pasos Perdidos, Romance Notes, 74; A new novel by Alejo Carpentier, Latin Am Lit Rev, 76; Prose fiction criticism and theory in Cuban journals, Cuban Studies, 77; Edmundo Desnoes and Cuba's lost generation, Latin Am Res Rev, 77; Guillermo Cabrera Infante's Debt to Ernest Hemingway, Hispania, 79; Blow-Up: A reconsideration of Antonioni's Infidelity to Cortazar, PLMA, 79; Teaching film and literature: A few principles, J Gen Educ, 80; Alejo Carpentier and the humanization of Spanish American fiction, Hispanofila, 82; auth, Individuations: The Novel as Dissent, Univ Press Am, 87; auth, El texto en llamas: al arte narrativo de Juan Rulfo, Lang, 88; auth, Julio Cortazar, Twayne, 90; auth, Structures of Power: Essays on Spanish American Fiction, State Univ NY, 96. **CONTACT ADDRESS** Dept of Span Ital & Port, Pennsylvania State Univ, 352 N Burrowes Bldg, University Park, PA, 16802. **EMAIL** tjp@psu.edu

PECK, JEFFREY MARC
PERSONAL Born 01/05/1950, Pittsburgh, PA **DISCIPLINE** GERMAN & COMPARATIVE LITERATURE **EDUCATION** Mich State Univ, BA, 72; Univ Chicago, MA, 74; Univ Calif, Berkeley, PhD(comp lit & Ger), 79. **CAREER** Actg instr world lit & comp, Univ Calif, Berkeley, 78; Asst Prof Germanics & Comp Lit, Univ Washington, 79- **MEMBERSHIPS** MLA; Am Comp Lit Asn; Int Verein Germanistik; Am Asn Teachers Ger; Philol Asn Pac Coast. **RESEARCH** Literary criticism and theory, especially hermeneutics; 19th and 20th century German literature; academic institutionalization of literature and criticism. **SELECTED PUBLICATIONS** Auth, Comparative historiography: Canonization and perodization in German, French and English literary histories, Proc Int Ger Studies Conf, Peter Lang, 80; The policies of reading and the poetics of reading: The Hermeneutic Text-- Heinrich von Kleist's Die Marquise von O, Cahiers roumains etudes litteraires, 82; Hermes Disguised: Literary Hermeneutics and the Interpretation of Literature, Kleist, Grillparzer, Fontane, Peter Lang (in press). **CONTACT ADDRESS** Dept of Germanics, Univ of Wash, Denny Hall DH-30, Seattle, WA, 98195.

PEDERSON, LEE
DISCIPLINE ENGLISH LANGUAGE AND LITERATURE **EDUCATION** Univ Chicago, PhD, 64. **CAREER** Charles Howard Candler Prof. **RESEARCH** Linguistics. **SELECTED PUBLICATIONS** Auth, East Tennessee Folk Speech; An Annotated Bibliography of Southern Speech; Pronunciation of English in Metropolitan Chicago; co-auth, A Manual for Dialect Research in the Southern States; ed, The Linguistic Atlas of the Gulf States, (v 1-4). **CONTACT ADDRESS** English Dept, Emory Univ, 1380 Oxford Rd NE, Atlanta, GA, 30322-1950.

PEDRONI, PETER
DISCIPLINE ITALIAN **EDUCATION** Yale Univ, BA; Middlebury, MA; Rutgers, PhD. **CAREER** Prof; Int Stud Assoc, Miami Univ **SELECTED PUBLICATIONS** Auth, Existence as Theme in Carlo Cassola's Fiction, NY: Peter Lang, 85; The Anti-Naturalist Experience: Federigo Tozzi, Tallahassee: De Soto, 89; transl and introd, Last Act in Urbino, NY: Italica, 95; articles on, Cassola, Tozzi, Volponi, Moravia & Verga in Italica, Forum Italica, Italian Cult, Can J Italian Stud, Italian Criticism: Lit and Cult. **CONTACT ADDRESS** Dept of French and Italian, Miami Univ, Oxford, OH, 45056. **EMAIL** pedronpn@muohio.edu

PEER, LARRY HOWARD
PERSONAL Born 01/02/1942, Ogden, UT, m, 1967, 9 children **DISCIPLINE** COMPARATIVE LITERATURE **EDUCATION** Brigham Young Univ, BA, 63, MA, 65; Univ Md, PhD, 69. **CAREER** Instr Ger, Univ Md, 67-68; from asst prof to assoc prof comp lit, Univ Ga, 68-75, acting head dept, 73-74; assoc prof, 75-78, dir hon prog, 77-78, chmn dept 78-81, Prof Comp Lit, Brigham Young Univ, 78-, Pres, Western Regional Hon Coun, 78-80; Exec Dir, Am Conf on Romanticism; Ed, Prism(s): Essays in Romanticism. **HONORS AND AWARDS** Alcuin Prof of General Educ, Brigham Young Univ. **MEMBERSHIPS** Int Comp Lit Asn; Am Comp Lit Asn; MLA; Am Soc Aesthet; Am Conf Romanticism; Int Byron Soc. **RESEARCH** Literary theory; Romanticism. **SELECTED PUBLICATIONS** Auth, Pushkin and Goethe again: Lensky's character, Papers on Lang & Lit, summer 69; Schlegel, Christianity and history: Manzoni's theory of the novel, Comp Lit Studies, fall 62; Friedrich Schelgel's Theory of the Novel, Colloquia Germanica, 76. **CONTACT ADDRESS** Dept of Comp Lit, Brigham Young Univ, 3010 JHKB, Provo, UT, 84602-6047. **EMAIL** lhp@email.byu.edu

PEISCHL, MARGARET THERESA
PERSONAL Born 02/05/1933, Pottsville, PA **DISCIPLINE** GERMAN LANGUAGE AND LITERATURE **EDUCATION** PA State Univ, BA, 55; Univ Southern Calif, MA, 74, PhD(-Ger), 81. **CAREER** Head, English Dept, John Burroughs Jr High Sch, 67-71; instr Ger, El Camino Col, 72-80; asst prof, Old Dominion Univ, 80-81; Asst Prof Ger, VA Commonwealth Univ, 81-. **MEMBERSHIPS** MLA; Am Asn Teacher Ger; Theodor-Storm Soc. **RESEARCH** Theodor Storm; 19th century Novella German literature. **SELECTED PUBLICATIONS** Auth, Das Damonische im Werk Theodor Storms, Peter Lang, Verlag, Ger, 82; Buchner 'Lenz' - a Study of Madness, Germanic Notes And Reviews, Vol 0027, 1996. **CONTACT ADDRESS** 666 Elgin Terrace, Richmond, VA, 23225.

PELLER HALLETT, JUDITH
DISCIPLINE LATIN LANGUAGE AND LITERATURE **EDUCATION** Wellesley Col, AB; Harvard Univ, MA, PhD; postdoc stud, Am Acad, Rome; Inst Classical Stud, Univ London. **HONORS AND AWARDS** Distinguished scholar-tchr, 92-93; award for excellence tchg, Col of Arts and Hum. **RESEARCH** Women, sexuality and the family in class antiquity. **SELECTED PUBLICATIONS** Auth, Fathers and Daughters in Roman Society: Women and the Elite Family, Princeton 84;

co-ed, Compromising Traditions: the Personal Voice in Classical Scholarship, Routledge, 96. **CONTACT ADDRESS** Dept of Class, Univ MD, 4229 Art-Sociology Building, College Park, MD, 20742-1335. **EMAIL** jh10@umail.umd.edu

PELLI, MOSHE
PERSONAL Born 05/19/1936, Haifa, Israel, m, 1961, 2 children **DISCIPLINE** HEBREW LITERATURE & LANGUAGE **EDUCATION** NY Univ, BS, 61; Dropsie Univ, PhD(Hebrew lit), 67. **CAREER** Ed, Niv, Hebrew Lang & Cult Asn, 57-66: asst prof Hebrew lit, Univ Tex, Austin, 67-71, coordr Hebrew study prog, 69; sr lectr Hebrew lit, Univ of the Negev, Israel, 71-74; assoc prof hebrew lit, Cornell Univ, 74-78, Hebrew Lang prog, 75-77, grad field rep, 75-77; Assoc Prof Mod Hebrew Lit, Yeshiva Univ, NY, 78-, Ed, Lamishpaha, 64-66; vis lectr Jewish studies, Rice Univ, spring 70 & 71; vis sr lectr Hebrew lit, Hebrew Univ Jerusalem, 71-72; vis prof Middle Eastern studies, Melbourne Univ, Australia, summer, 77 & 78; Am Coun Learned Soc travel grant, 77; Oxford Ctr for Postgrad Hebrew Studies res fel, 79; vis prof Hebrew lang & lit, Brooklyn Col, 79 & 80. **HONORS AND AWARDS** Short Story Prize, Haboker, Daily, Tel Aviv, 55. **MEMBERSHIPS** Asn Jewish Studies; World Union Jewish Studies; Nat Asn Professors Hebrew; Am Acad Jewish Res; Am Soc 18th Century Studies. **RESEARCH** The Hebrew Enlightenment: literature and religious, social and cultural thought; contemporary Hebrew literature; Holocaust literature. **SELECTED PUBLICATIONS** Auth, Moses Mendelssohn: Bonds of Tradition, Alef, Tel Aviv, 72; Introduction to Modern Hebrew Literature in 18th and 19th Centuries, Hebrew Univ, Akademon, Jersualem, 72; Isaac Euchel: Tradition and change in the first generation Haskalah, J Jewish Studies, 75 & 76; Saul Berlin's Ktav Yosher: The beginning of satire in modern Hebrew literature, 75 & 77 & The beginning of the epistolary genre in Hebrew Enlightenment literature in Germany: The affinity between lettres persanes and Igrot Meshulam, 79, Leo Baeck Inst Yearbook; The Age of Haskalah-Studies in Hebrew Literature of the Enlightenment in Germany, E J Brill, Leiden, 79; Berlin,saul Ktav-yosher - The Beginning of Satire in Hebrew Enlightenment in Germany, Hebrew Union College Annual, Vol 0064, 1994. **CONTACT ADDRESS** 134 Graham Rd 1-B4, Ithaca, NY, 14850.

PENCE, ELLSWORTH DEAN
PERSONAL Born 03/18/1938, Carbon Hill, OH, 4 children **DISCIPLINE** FRENCH LANGUAGE & LITERATURE, LATIN **EDUCATION** Ohio Univ, BA, 59; Univ Wis, MA, 64, PhD, 71. **CAREER** Teacher French & English, Bettsville High Sch, Ohio, 59-60; instr French, Univ Wis, Ctr-Manitowoc, 67-68; asst prof, Univ Wis, Manitowoc & Green Bay, 68-73; prof French, Humboldt State Univ, 73-, resident dir, int prog, Aix-en-Provence, France, 82-83. **MEMBERSHIPS** Am Asn Teachers French; CLTH; Am Names Soc. **RESEARCH** French romantic fiction; French prose poem; 19th century French novel; French place names. **SELECTED PUBLICATIONS** French Place Names in California. **CONTACT ADDRESS** Dept of Modern Lang, Humboldt State Univ, 1 Harpst St, Arcata, CA, 95521-8299. **EMAIL** edp1@axe.humboldt.edu

PENZL, HERBERT
PERSONAL Born 09/02/1910, Neufelden, Austria, m, 1950 **DISCIPLINE** LINGUISTICS **EDUCATION** Univ Vienna, PhD, 35. **CAREER** Ed asst, Ling Atlas of US, Brown Univ, 32-34; asst prof Ger, Rockford Col, 36-38; assoc, Univ Ill, 38-39, asst prof, 39- 49; assoc prof, Univ Mich, 50-53, prof, 53-63; Prof Ger Philol, Univ Calif, Berkeley, 63-, Smith-Mundt vis prof, Kabul Univ, Afghanistan, 58-59; John S Guggenheim Mem Found fel, 67; vis prof, Univ Vienna, Austria, 80 & Univ Regensburg, 81. **HONORS AND AWARDS** Austrian Cross of Honour Sci & Arts, 80; Berkeley Citation, 80. **MEMBERSHIPS** Am Asn Teachers Ger; MLA; Ling Soc Am; Am Dialect Soc; Am Name Soc. **RESEARCH** German, Germanic and general linguistics. **SELECTED PUBLICATIONS** Auth, A Grammar of Pashto: A Descriptive Study of the Dialect of Kandahar, Afghanistan, Am Coun Learned Soc, 55; A Reader of Pashto, Univ Mich, 65; Geschichtliche deutsche Lautlehre, 69 & Lautsystem und Lautwandel in den althochdeutschen Dialekten, 71, Max Hueber, Munich; Methoden der germanischen Linguistik, 72 & contribr, Toward a Grammar of Proto-Germanic, 72, Max Niemeyer, Tubingen; coauth, Probleme der historischen Phonologie, Wiesbaden, Steiner Verlag, 74; auth, Vom Urgermanischen zum Neuhochdeutscheneine historische Phonologie, Erich Schmidt Verlag, Berlin, 75; Johann Christian Gottscheds Deutsche Sprachkunst, de Gruyter, Berlin, 80; Fuhneuhochdeutsch: Eine Einfuhrung in die Sprache, P Lang Verlag, Bern, 82; The Cambridge History of The English-language, Vol 1, The Beginnings to 1066 - Hogg,rm, Language, Vol 0070, 1994; German Loanwords in English, an Historical Dictionary - Pfeffer,ja, Cannon,g, American Speech, Vol 0070, 1995; Methods of Lyric Analysis - a Rejoinder to Davis,william,s. Subjectivity And Exteriority in Goethe 'Dauer Im Wechsel', German Quarterly, Vol 0068, 1995; The Cambridge History of The English-language, Vol 1, The Beginnings to 1066, Vol 2, 1066-1476 - Blake,n, Studies in Language, Vol 0019, 1995; The I-umlaut in Old-high- german Dialects, Folia Linguistica Historica, Vol 0016, 1995. **CONTACT ADDRESS** Dept of German, Univ of Calif, Berkeley, CA, 94720.

PERCIVAL, WALTER KEITH
PERSONAL Born 02/24/1930, Leeds, England, m, 1968 **DISCIPLINE** LINGUISTICS **EDUCATION** Leeds Univ, BA, 51; Yale Univ, MA, 59, PhD(ling), 64. **CAREER** Lectr ling, Brandeis Univ, 62-63; from asst prof to assoc prof, Univ Wis-Milwaukee, 64-69, chmn dept, 64-69; assoc prof, 69-74, Prof Ling, Univ Kans, 74-, Am Philos Soc res grant, 72-. **MEMBERSHIPS** Ling Soc Am; Renaissance Soc Am; Mediaeval Acad Am; Soc Ling Europaea; Int Soc Hist Rhetoric. **RESEARCH** History of linguistics; Austronesian languages; Medieval and Renaissance grammar, rhetoric and logic. **SELECTED PUBLICATIONS** Auth, On the Non-Existence of Cartesian Linguistics, In: Cartesian Studies, 72; contribr, The Grammatical Tradition and the Rise of the Vernaculars, In: Current Trends in Linguistics, 75; Deep and Surface Structure Concepts in Syntactic Theory, In: History of Linguistic Thought and Contemporary Linguistics, 76; auth, The Applicability of Kuhn's Paradigms to the History of Linguistics, Language, 76; The Artis Grammaticae Opusculum of Bartolomeo Sulmonese, Renaissance Quart, 78; Ferdinand de Saussure and the History of Semiotics, In: Semiotic Themes, 81; A Grammar of the Urbanised Toba-Batak of Medan, Canberra, The Australian Nat Univ, 81; The Saussurean Paradigm: Fact or Fantasy? Semiotica, 81; Nebrija Syntactic Theory in Its Historical Setting, Historiographia Linguistica, Vol 0024, 1997. **CONTACT ADDRESS** Dept of Ling, Univ of Kans, Lawrence, KS, 66045.

PEREZ STANSFIELD, MARIA PILAR
DISCIPLINE SPANISH LITERATURE **EDUCATION** Univ Colo, PhD. **CAREER** Assoc prof. **SELECTED PUBLICATIONS** Auth, pubs on avant-garde theatre, and feminist and minorities literature. **CONTACT ADDRESS** Foreign Languages and Literature Dept, Colorado State Univ, Fort Collins, CO, 80523. **EMAIL** pperez-stansfield@vines.colostate.edu

PEREZ-LOPEZ, RENE
PERSONAL Born 05/12/1945, Santa Clara, Cuba, m, 1971, 2 children **DISCIPLINE** LATIN AMERICAN STUDIES **EDUCATION** SUNY, BA, 67, MLS, 71; Case Western Reserve Univ, MA, 69. **CAREER** Coordr, Norfolk Public Libr, 71-86; libr dir, 86-, adj, 88-, vp, 95-, Va Wesleyan Col. **HONORS AND AWARDS** Red Cross, 97. **MEMBERSHIPS** ALA; Am Translators Asn; VLA. **RESEARCH** Cuban Stud **SELECTED PUBLICATIONS** Auth, An Index to the First 25 Years of Cuban Studies, 97; auth, Recent Work in Cuban Stud, 98. **CONTACT ADDRESS** 6429 Newport Ave, Norfolk, VA, 23505. **EMAIL** reneperezlopez@vwc.edu

PEREZ-PISONERO, ARTURO
DISCIPLINE SPANISH **EDUCATION** Our Lady Lake Col, BA, 66; Univ Okla, PhD, 70. **CAREER** From asst prof, 70-76 to assoc prof , 76-, Univ Tex at El Paso. **HONORS AND AWARDS** Symposium of the Asociacion Internacional de Teatro Espanol y Novohispano en los Siglos de Oro, 92; grants for the Golden Age Spanish Drama Symp, 81-; grants from, Univ Tex at El paso, Univ Tex at Austin, Tex Endowment for the Humanities and URI. **MEMBERSHIPS** Dir and founder of TEXTO Y ESPECTACULO. Golden Age Drama Symposium, 80-91; VP Asn Int de Teatro Espanol y Novohispano, 92; Comt for Premio Nacional de Literatura Jose Fuentes Mares, 91; bd dir, Centro de Estudios Alarconianos, 89; Siglo de Oro Drama Festival. **RESEARCH** Latin American literature. **SELECTED PUBLICATIONS** Auth, El texto literario y sus multiples lecturas, 8 estrategias de cretica literaria, Cuestionario y temas de composicion; Nicolas Guillen y la intrahistoria cubana, Afro-Hisp Rev; Norte y Frontera: Dicotomea y simbiosis en la novela de Ricardo Elizondo Setenta veces 7. Actas del IV Encuentro Nacional de Escritores en la Frontera Norte; Las luces del mundo, Entorno; Jesusa Palancares, esperpento femenino, Mujer y Literatura, Mexicana y Chicana; La novela Chicana: Un pueblo en busca de su historia, Romanische Forschungen. **CONTACT ADDRESS** Dept of Languages and Linguistics, Univ of Texas, El Paso, 500 W University Ave, El Paso, TX, 79968. **EMAIL** aperez@utep.edu

PERISSINOTTO, GIORGIO
PERSONAL Born 06/13/1942, Trieste, Italy, m, 1968 **DISCIPLINE** HISPANIC LINGUISTICS **EDUCATION** Syracuse Univ, BA, 65; Columbia Univ, MA, 66, PhD(Span), 71. **CAREER** Instr Span, State Univ NY Stony Brook, 68-72, asst prof, 72-75; asst prof, Univ Tex, San Antonio, 75-76; Assoc Prof Span, Univ Calif, Santa Barbara, 76-, Vis prof ling, Inst Invest Integracion Social Estado Oaxaca, 72-73. **RESEARCH** Hispanic linguistics. **SELECTED PUBLICATIONS** Auth, Education reform and government intervention in Mexico, Current Hist, Vol 66, 74; Fonologia del espanol hablado en la ciudad de Mexico, Colegio Mex, 75; La Reconquista en el Poema del Cid: Una nueva lectura, Hispanofila, Vol 65, 79; A proposito de Ins versos 793 y 794 de las Mocedades de Rodrigo, Cult Neolatina, Vol 39, 79; From Gachupin to Criollo or How The Spanish Assimilated Into America - Spanish - Alberro,s, Revista De Estudios Hispanicos, Vol 0028, 1994. **CONTACT ADDRESS** 5220 Calle Cristobal, Santa Barbara, CA, 93111.

PERKINS, ALLAN KYLE
PERSONAL Born 11/14/1947, Corbin, KY, m, 1978, 2 children **DISCIPLINE** APPLIED & THEORETICAL LINGUISTICS **EDUCATION** Union Col, Ky, BA, 69; Southern Ill Univ, MA, 71; Univ Mich, PhD(ling), 76. **CAREER** Instr, 75-76, asst prof, 76-80, Assoc Prof Ling, Southern Ill Univ, 80-, Vis assoc prof, English Lang Inst, Am Univ Cairo, 82-83; prof, Ling, SIU, 85. **MEMBERSHIPS** Teachers English Speakers Other Lang; Midwest Mod Lang Asn. **RESEARCH** Language testing; second language testing methodology; theoretical syntax. **SELECTED PUBLICATIONS** Coauth, Language in Education: Testing the Tests, 78 & Research in Language Testing, 80, Newbury House Publ Inc; co-ed, On Tesol 79: The Learner in Focus, Teachers English Other Langs, 79; auth, Using objective methods of attained writing proficiency, Teacher English Speaker Other Langs Quart, 80; Determining coreferentiality by sight and sound, Regional English Lang Ctr J, 81; On predicate complements, Int Rev Appl Ling, 81; coauth, Discourse analysis and the art of coherence, Col English, 82; Test of ability to subordinate: Predictive and concurrent validity, Proc Fourth Int Lang Testing Symp, 82. **CONTACT ADDRESS** Acad Affairs, Southern Illinois Univ, Carbondale, IL, 62901-4305. **EMAIL** kperkins@siu.edu

PERKINS, GEORGE W.
PERSONAL Born 07/11/1937, m, 1961, 6 children **DISCIPLINE** JAPANESE LITERATURE & LANGUAGE **EDUCATION** Brigham Young Univ, BA, 62; Stanford Univ, MA, 67, PhD, 77. **CAREER** Lectr Japanese, Stanford Univ, 69-70; lectr, Auckland Univ, 71-74; asst prof Japanese, Brigham Young Univ, 75-. **MEMBERSHIPS** Asn Asian Studies; Asn Teachers Japanese. **RESEARCH** Pre-modern Japanese literature; the modern Japanese novel. **CONTACT ADDRESS** Dept of Asian & Slavic Lang, Brigham Young Univ, 4052 Jkhb, Provo, UT, 84602-0002.

PERKOWSKI, JAN LOUIS
PERSONAL Born 12/29/1936, Perth Amboy, NJ, m, 1989, 3 children **DISCIPLINE** SLAVIC LANGUAGES **EDUCATION** Harvard Univ, AB, 59, AM, 60, PhD(Slavic lang & lit), 65. **CAREER** Asst prof Russ, Univ CA, Santa Barbara, 64-65; from asst prof to assoc prof slavic lang, Univ TX, Austin, 65-74, chm dept, 66-68 & 73-74; prof Slavic lang, univ VA, 74-, chm dept Slavic lang & lit, 76-83, 96-98. **HONORS AND AWARDS** Over 30 fellowships and grants. **MEMBERSHIPS** Am Asn Advan Slavic Studies; Am Comt Slavists; Am Asn Southeast European Studies. **RESEARCH** Balkan religious syncretism and South Slavic demonology. **SELECTED PUBLICATIONS** Auth, A Kashubian Idiolect in the United States, Lang Sci Monogr, IN Univ, 69; Vampires, Dwarves and Witches Among the Ontario Kashubs, Mercury Set 1, Nat Mus of Man, Ottwa, 72; Vampires of the Slavs, Slavica, 76; Linguistic Change in Texas Czech, Studies in Czechoslovak Hist, 76; Gusle and Ganga among the Hercegovinians of Toronto, Ann Arbor, 78; The Darkling: A Treatise on Slavic Vampirism, Slavica, 89; Slavic Soothsayers in Numinous Settings, Zeitschrift fur Balkanologie, Wiesbaden, 95; Ethnic and Religious Identity in Balkan Oral Tradition: The Case of Hercegovinia's Croats and Serbs, The South Slav J, London, 98; author of a total of five books and 60 articles. **CONTACT ADDRESS** Dept Slavic Lang & Lit, Univ Virginia, 109 Cabell Hall, Charlottesville, VA, 22903-3125. **EMAIL** slavic@virginia.edu

PERL, JEFFERY MICHAEL
PERSONAL Born 05/30/1952, Minneapolis, MN **DISCIPLINE** COMPARATIVE LITERATURE **EDUCATION** Stanford Univ, AB, 74; Oxford Univ, BA philos, 76; Princeton Univ, MA, 79, PhD, 80. **CAREER** Asst Prof, eng comp, Columbia Univ, 80-87; Assoc Prof, Columbia Univ, 87-89; Prog of Humanities, Univ Texas at Dallas, 89-98; Fulbright, vis, Hebrew Univ, Jerusalem, 98-99; Founding Editor, Common Knowledge, 92-. **HONORS AND AWARDS** NEH, 83; vis fel, Mansfield Col, Oxford, 83; Rockefeller fel, 84-85; Guggenheim fel, 88-89; Fulbright Sr Scholar, 98-99. **MEMBERSHIPS** MLA, Am Comp Lit Asn. **RESEARCH** Modernizing History of Aesthetics **SELECTED PUBLICATIONS** Auth, Skepticism and Modern Enmity, Johns Hopkins Univ, 89; The Tradition of Return: The Implicit History of Modern Literature, Princeton, 84; pubs in TLS, Partisan Rev, Sewanee Rev, S Rev, Philos East and West. **CONTACT ADDRESS** Hebrew Univ, Dept English, TX, 95105. **EMAIL** perl@utdallas.edu

PEROZO, JAIME J.
DISCIPLINE SPANISH **EDUCATION** Univ Central de Venezuela, BA, 71; Tex A&I Univ, BA, 75; WA State Univ, MA Sociol, 79, MA Span & Span Am Lit, 86; Univ OR, PhD Sociol, 84; Univ WA, PhD Span & Span Am Lit, 94. **CAREER** Res asst, Univ OR & WA State Univ. **MEMBERSHIPS** Am Sociol Asn; MLA. **SELECTED PUBLICATIONS** Auth, The Sociopolitical Cosmovision in the Work of Miguel Otero Silva, Univ WA, 94; The role of Oil in Shaping Mexico and Venezuela as Semi peripheral Countries, Univ OR, 84; The Impact of Petroleum on the Human Carrying Capacity of Venezuela, WA State Univ, 79; Mahor Educ Community Res Proj, Dominican Repub Proj, Seattle, WA, 93; rev, Entre amigos, Houghton & Mifflin Co, 93. **CONTACT ADDRESS** Dept of For Lang, Seattle Univ, 900 Broadway, Seattle, WA, 98122-4460. **EMAIL** jperozo@seattleu.edu

PERRIN WILCOX, PHYLLIS
DISCIPLINE AMERICAN SIGN LANGUAGE, INTERPRETING THEORY AND PRACTICE **EDUCATION** Univ NMex, PhD. **CAREER** Instr, Univ NMex. **SELECTED PUBLICATIONS** Auth, Dual Interpretation and Discourse Effectiveness in Legal Settings, Spec Issue: The Bilingual-Bimodal Courtroom, J of Interp, 7(1), 95; Deontic and Epistemic Modals in ASL: A Discourse Analysis, in A Goldberg, ed,Conceptual Structure,Discourse and Language, Ctr Stud Lang and Infor,Stanford, 96; coauth, Gestural Expression of Modals in American Sign Language, in J Bybee & S Fleischman, eds,Modality in Grammar and Discourse, John Benjamins, 95; Learning to See: American Sign Language as a Second Language, Gallaudet UP. **CONTACT ADDRESS** Univ NMex, Albuquerque, NM, 87131. **EMAIL** pwilcox@unm.edu

PERRY, CATHERINE
DISCIPLINE FRENCH LITERATURE **EDUCATION** Indiana Univ, BA, 87, MA, 91; Princeton Univ, PhD, 95. **CAREER** Asst prof. **RESEARCH** French literature of the 19th and early 20th centuries; intellectual history; literary theory; gender studies; artistic relations between France and the Maghreb. **SELECTED PUBLICATIONS** Auth, pubs on Ronsard, Stendhal, Balzac, Barres and Wagner, Anna de Noailles, Gerard d'Houville, Valery, and Nicole Brossard. **CONTACT ADDRESS** Romance Languages and Literatures Dept, Univ of Notre Dame, Notre Dame, IN, 46556.

PESCA-CUPOLO, CARMELA
DISCIPLINE ITALIAN LANGUAGE AND LITERATURE **EDUCATION** Univ Salerno, Laurea; Univ Conn, PhD. **CAREER** Fac, Univ Conn, Trinity Col Hartford; Central Conn State Univ, 95-. **RESEARCH** Medieval and Renaissance Italian literature; interdisciplicinary pedagogy and collaboration. **SELECTED PUBLICATIONS** Auth, articles of literary criticism on Medieval and Renaissance authors. **CONTACT ADDRESS** Central Connecticut State Univ, 1615 Stanley St, New Britain, CT, 06050.

PETERS, ANN MARIE
PERSONAL Born 07/31/1938, Pasadena, CA **DISCIPLINE** LINGUISTICS **EDUCATION** Bryn Mawr Col, BA, 59; Univ Wis-Madison, MA, 61, PhD(ling), 66. **CAREER** Assoc Researcher Ling, Univ Hawaii, Manoa, 71-. **MEMBERSHIPS** Ling Soc Am. **RESEARCH** Child language acquisition; phonological rule testing; African tone languages. **SELECTED PUBLICATIONS** Auth, Algorithms for processing phonological rule schemata, Prof Fourth Int Conf Syst Sci, 71; A new formalization of downdrift, Studies African Ling, 73; Language learning strategies, Lang, 77; False Starts And Filler Syllables - Ways to Learn Grammatical Morphemes, Language, Vol 0069, 1993. **CONTACT ADDRESS** Dept of Ling, Univ of Hawaii at Manoa, 1890 E West Rd, Honolulu, HI, 96822-2318.

PETERS, FRANCIS EDWARD
PERSONAL Born 06/23/1927, New York, NY, m, 1957, 1 child **DISCIPLINE** CLASSICS, ISLAMIC STUDIES **EDUCATION** St Louis Univ, AB, 50, MA, 52; Princeton Univ, PhD(Orient studies), 61. **CAREER** Instr English, Latin & Greek, Canisius High Sch, Buffalo, NY, 52-54; instr English, Scarborough Country Day Sch, NY, 55- 56; from asst prof to assoc prof classics, 61-69, Prof Hist & Near Eastern Lang & Lit & Chmn Dept Near Eastern Lang & Lit, New York Univ, 70-. **MEMBERSHIPS** Am Orient Soc; Mid E Studies Asn. **RESEARCH** Social and intellectual history of Late Antiquity and Early Islam; Near Eastern urbanism. **SELECTED PUBLICATIONS** Auth, Greek Philosophical Terms, 67 & Aristotle and the Arabs, 68, New York Univ; Aristoteles Arabus, Brill, 68; The Harvest of Hellenism, 71 & Allah's Commonwealth, 74, Simon & Schuster; Ours, R Mareck, 81; The Children of Abraham: Judaism, Christianity, Islam, Princeton Univ Press, 82; Jesus And Muhammad - a Historians Reflections, Muslim World, Vol 0086, 1996; Ritual, Politics And The City in Fatimid Cairo, Sanders,p, Speculum-a J of Medieval Studies, Vol 0071, 1996; Ritual, Politics And The City in Fatimid Cairo, Sanders,p, Speculum-a J of Medieval Studies, Vol 0071, 1996; Abraham, Sign of Hope For Jews, Christians And Muslims - Kuschel,kj, J of Religion, Vol 0077, 1997. **CONTACT ADDRESS** Dept of Near Eastern Lang & Lit, New York Univ, New York, NY, 10003.

PETERSEN, KLAUS
PERSONAL Born 10/13/1937, Hamburg, Germany **DISCIPLINE** GERMAN LITERATURE **EDUCATION** Univ Hamburg, Staatsexamen, 63; Univ BC, PhD(Ger), 74. **CAREER** Asst prof Ger, Univ Winnipeg, 74-76; asst prof, 76-80, Assoc Prof Ger, Univ BC, 80-. **MEMBERSHIPS** Asn Can Univ Teachers Ger; West Asn Ger Studies. **RESEARCH** Expressionism; literature of the nineteen-twenties; literary theory. **SELECTED PUBLICATIONS** Auth, Georg Kaiser: Kunstlerbild und Kunstlerfigur, Herbert Lang, 76; Ludwig Rubiner: Eine Einfuhrung mit Textauswahl und Bibliographie, Bouvier Verlag, 80; Die Gruppe 1925: Geschichte und Soziologie einer Schriftstellervereinigung, Carl Winter, 81; The Harmful Pubications Young Persons Act of 1926 - Literary Censorship And The Politics of Morality in The Weimar-republic, German Studies Review, Vol 0015, 1992; Dancing on The Volcano - Essays on The Culture of The Weimar-republic - Kniesche,t, Brockmann,s, Seminar-a J of Germanic Studies, Vol 0031, 1995. **CONTACT ADDRESS** Dept of Ger Studies, Univ of BC, Vancouver, BC, V6T 1W5.

PETERSON, BRENT O.
DISCIPLINE 19TH AND 20TH-CENTURY GERMAN LITERATURE **EDUCATION** Johns Hopkins Univ, BA; Univ IA, MA; Univ MN, PhD. **CAREER** Assoc prof, Ripon Col; instr, Humboldt Univ, Berlin. **HONORS AND AWARDS** NEH grants. **SELECTED PUBLICATIONS** Wrote a book on 19th-century Ger-Am(s). **CONTACT ADDRESS** Ripon Col, Ripon, WI. **EMAIL** PetersonB@mac.ripon.edu

PETERSON, PHILIP LESLIE
PERSONAL Born 03/12/1937, San Francisco, CA, m, 1967, 2 children **DISCIPLINE** PHILOSOPHY, LINGUISTICS **EDUCATION** Col William & Mary, AB, 59; Duke Univ, PhD (philos), 63. **CAREER** From asst prof to assoc prof, 63-76, Prof Philos, Syracuse Univ, 76-, Res assoc, Century Res Corp, 59-63, consult, 63-; Woodrow Wilson fel, 60-63; proj leader ling, Info Processing Systs Res, US Air Force Contracts, 66-71; partic, Early Mod Philos Inst, R Williams Col, 74. **MEMBERSHIPS** Am Philos Asn; AAAS; AAUP; Ling Soc Am. **RESEARCH** Philosophy of language; semantics; epistemology. **SELECTED PUBLICATIONS** Auth, Concepts and Language, Mouton, The Hague, 73; An abuse of terminology, Found Lang, 76; On specific reference, Semantikos, 76; How to infer belief from knowledge, Philos Studies, 77; On representing event reference, In: Presupposition, Acad Press, 79; On the logic of few, many, and most, Notre Dame J Formal Logic, 79; What causes effects?, Philos Studies, 81; Philosophy of Language, Social Res, 81. **CONTACT ADDRESS** 222 Buckingham Ave, Syracuse, NY, 13210.

PETERSON, TARLA RAI
DISCIPLINE ENVIRONMENTAL COMMUNICATION **EDUCATION** Wash State Univ, PhD. **CAREER** Assoc prof, Texas A&M Univ. **SELECTED PUBLICATIONS** Auth, Sharing the World: The Rhetoric of Sustainable Development; co-ed, Communication and the Culture of Technology; Contribur, Transforming Visions:Feminist Critiques in Speech Communication & A Voice of Their Own: The Woman Suffrage Press, 1840-1910; assoc ed, Quart J Speech; bk rev ed, Quart J Speech. **CONTACT ADDRESS** Dept of Speech Communication, Texas A&M Univ, College Station, TX, 77843-4234.

PETRAGLIA-BAHRI, DEEPIKA
DISCIPLINE ENGLISH LANGUAGE AND LITERATURE **EDUCATION** Bowling Green Univ, PhD, 92. **CAREER** Fac, Ga Inst Tech, 94; fac, Bowling Green Univ, 92-94; asst prof, Emory Univ, 95. **RESEARCH** Postcolonial literature and theory; technology, culture, and postcolonialism. **SELECTED PUBLICATIONS** Auth, Terms of Engagement: Postcolonialism, Transnationalism, and Composition Studies, Exploring Borderlands: Postcolonial and Composition Studies, Jour Comp Theory,, 98; Marginally Off-Center: Postcolonialism in the Teaching Machine, Col Engl, 97; Once more with Feeling: What is Postcolonialism?" ARIEL: Rev Int Engl Lit, 95; Disembodying the Corpus: Postcolonial Pathology in Tsitsi Dangarembga's Nervous Conditions, Postmod Cult: An Elec Jour Interdisc Crit, 94; Boethius and Sir Thomas Browne: The Common Ground, Mythes, Croyances et Religion dans le monde Anglo-Saxon, 92; The Reader's Guide to P.G. Wodehouse's America, Studies Am Humor, 89; coauth, "Swallowing for Twenty Years/the American Mind and Body:" An Interview with G. S. Sharat Chandra, Jour Commonwealth Postcolonial Studies, 97; co-ed, Between the Lines: South Asians and Postcoloniality, Temple UP, 96. **CONTACT ADDRESS** English Dept, Emory Univ, 1380 Oxford Rd NE, Atlanta, GA, 30322-1950. **EMAIL** dpetrag@emory.edu

PETRAGLIA-BAHRI, JOSEPH
DISCIPLINE RHETORIC AND COGNITIVE SCIENCE **EDUCATION** Carnegie Mellon Univ, PhD, 91. **CAREER** Asst prof, Ga Inst of Technol. **RESEARCH** The rhetoric of inquiry. **SELECTED PUBLICATIONS** Ed, Reconceiving Writing, Rethinking Writing Instruction, Lawrence Erlbaum, 95. **CONTACT ADDRESS** Sch of Lit, Commun, & Cult, Georgia Inst of Tech, Skiles Cla, Atlanta, GA, 30332. **EMAIL** joseph.petraglia@lcc.gatech.edu

PETRESS, KENNETH C.
PERSONAL Born 11/01/1939, Chicago, IL **DISCIPLINE** SPEECH COMMUNICATION **EDUCATION** Northern IL Univ, BS Ed, 77, MA, 79, CAS, 80; LA State Univ, PhD, 88. **CAREER** Instr, Northern IL Univ, 80-83; vis prof, Xi Dian Univ, Xian, China, 83-84; lect, Empora State Univ, 84-86; prof, Univ ME at Presque Isle, 88-. **MEMBERSHIPS** Nat Commun Asn; Southern States Commun Asn; Yale-China Asn. **RESEARCH** Rhetoriaty of political symbols. **SELECTED PUBLICATIONS** Auth, Coping with a New Educational Environment: Chinese Students' Imagined Interactions Before Beginning Studies in the US, J of Instr Psychol, 22 (1), 95; A Partial Solution to the University Journal Subscription Problem, J of Instr Psychol, 22 (3), 95; with Keith L Madore, College Faculty Absences Need to Be Treated More Seriously, College Student J, 29 (3), 95; Olympic Participation By Children: Is There A Dark Side?, ME Scholar, 8, 95; Questions of Obligation, Cost Effectiveness, and Efficiency: University Remedial Programs, Education, 116 (1), 95; The Multiple Roles of An Undergraduate's Academic Advisor, Education, 117 (1), 96; The Dilema of University Undergraduate Student Attendance Policies: To Require Class Attendance or Not, Col Student J 30 (3), 96; Broasdcasting in China, in Alan Wells, ed, World Broadcasting: A Comparative View, Ablex, 96; with Kurt O Hofmann, The Community Review Board Offers Students Fairness in Administrative Decision Appeals, Education, 118 (1), 97. **CONTACT ADDRESS** 181 Main St, Presque, ME, 04769-2888. **EMAIL** petress@polaris.umpi.maine.edu

PETREY, SANDY
PERSONAL Born 08/29/1941 **DISCIPLINE** FRENCH LITERATURE **EDUCATION** Emory Univ, BA, 62; Yale Univ, PhD, 66. **CAREER** Prof, 82-. **SELECTED PUBLICATIONS** Auth, History in the Text: Quatrevingt-Treize and the French Revolution, Purdue, 80; Realism and Revolution: Balzac, Stendhal, Zola, and the Performances of History, Cornell, 88; Speech Acts and Literary Theory, Routledge, 90; ed, French Studies/Cultural Studies: Reciprocal Invigoration or Mutual Destruction?, 95; Anna-Nana-Nana: Identite sexuelle, ecriture naturaliste, lectures lesbiennes, 95; Men in Love, Saint-Simonism, Indiana, 95; Identite et alterite sous la Monarchie de juillet, 96. **CONTACT ADDRESS** English Dept, SUNY Stony Brook, Stony Brook, NY, 11794. **EMAIL** mbishop@notes.cc.sunysb.edu

PETROVIC, NJEGOS M.
PERSONAL Born 05/20/1933, Vucitrn, Yugoslavia, m, 1960, 3 children **DISCIPLINE** SERBO & FRENCH LANGUAGE & LITERATURE **EDUCATION** Univ Belgrade, BA, 53, super dipl, 57; Univ Montreal, MA, 62, PhD, 67. **CAREER** Instr mod lang, Class Col, Belgrade, 56-57; instr, Univ Paris, 58-61; asst prof French, Class Col St Jean, 61-64; asst prof, Royal Mil Col, Que, 64-65; asst prof Nebr Wesleyan Univ, 65-67; assoc prof, 67-74, Prof French, Univ Scranton, 74-; chmn, Concert & Theater Scr, 69-92; art adv, Pa Coun Arts, 73-76. **MEMBERSHIPS** Humanities Assn Can; MLA; AAUP. **RESEARCH** French, Serb and Russian language and literature of 19th and 20th centuries. **SELECTED PUBLICATIONS** Auth, Tisina Kamenja (poems), Prosveta, Belgrade, 54; art, Reve de bonheur, Provinces, Paris, 12/59; Carillon, 5/65 & Les Faubourgs, 6/65; auth, Ivo Andric, l'homme et l'oeuvre, Les Ed Lemeac, Montreal, 69; ed, Everhart Museum Catalog, Art Print Co, Scranton, Pa, 74. **CONTACT ADDRESS** 800 Linden St, Scranton, PA, 18510-4501.

PETTEY, JOHN CARSON
DISCIPLINE GERMAN LANGUAGE, LITERATURE, AND CULTURE **EDUCATION** Wash Univ, PhD. **CAREER** Instr, Wash Univ; assoc prof Ger, Univ Nev, Reno. **SELECTED PUBLICATIONS** Published on the the female aphorism, as well as one on Nietzsche and Garcea Marquez. **CONTACT ADDRESS** Univ Nev, Reno, Reno, NV, 89557. **EMAIL** unrug@unr.edu

PFOHL, RUSSELL
DISCIPLINE FRENCH LITERATURE **EDUCATION** Johns Hopkins Univ, PhD, 67. **CAREER** Assoc prof. **SELECTED PUBLICATIONS** Auth, Racine's "Iphigenie": Literary Rehearsal and Tragic Recognition, 74; articles on Italo Svevo, Proust, French and Italian literature. **CONTACT ADDRESS** Dept of French and Italian, Indiana Univ, Bloomington, 300 N Jordan Ave, Bloomington, IN, 47405.

PHILIPPIDES, MARIOS
PERSONAL Born 08/05/1950, Athens, Greece, m, 1973 **DISCIPLINE** GREEK, LATIN **EDUCATION** Queens Col, BA, 73; State Univ NY Buffalo, MA, 76, PhD(classics), 78. **CAREER** Asst prof, Union Col, 77-78; Asst Prof Classics, Univ Mass, Amherst, 78- **MEMBERSHIPS** Am Philol Asn; Class Asn New England; Modern Greek Studies Asn; Am Inst Archaeol; Am Class League. **RESEARCH** Palaeologan period of the Byzantine empire; ancient Greek religion and Mediterranean ritual and myth; the ancient novel. **SELECTED PUBLICATIONS** Auth, A note on Longus' Lesbiaka, The Class World, 78; The foundation of Taras and the Spartan partheniai, The Ancient World, 79; The Fall of the Byzantine Empire, Univ Mass Press, 80; The digressive aitia in Longus, The Class World, 80; The characters in Freedom or Death, The Charioteer, 80; The pronunciation of Greek, Phone, 81; The fall of Constantinople 1453, Greek, Roman & Byzantine Studies, 81; the prooemium in Lorgus, The Class Bull, 82; Late 15th-century Euboea - the Economy, Population, and Registers of 1474 - French - Balta,e, Speculum-a J of Medieval Studies, Vol 0068, 1993; Byzantium Last Imperial Offensive in Asia-minor - the Documentary Evidence for and Hagiographical Lore about John-iii-ducas-vatatzes Crusade Against the Turks, Ad-1222 or 1225 to 1231 - Langdon,js, Speculum-a J of Medieval Studies, Vol 0069, 1994; Byzantium and the Bulgars 7th-century to the 10th-century - a Study of Byzantine Foreign-policy - Greek and German - Kyriakis,ek, Speculum-a J of Medieval Studies, Vol 0070, 1995; Nicephorus-ii- phocas 63-69, His Reforms as Military Commander and Emperor - German - Kolias,tg, Specu-

lum-a J of Medieval Studies, Vol 0070, 1995; the Church and Social-reform - the Policies of the Patriarch Athanasios-of-constantinople - Boojamra,jl, Speculum-a J of Medieval Studies, Vol 0071, 1996; Greeks, Westerners and Turks from Ad1054 to 1453 - 4 Centuries of History and International-relations - French - Spiridonakis,bg, Catholic Historical Review, Vol 0082, 1996; Church and Social-reform - the Policies of the Patriarch Athanasios-of-constantinople - Boojamra,jl, Speculum-a J of Medieval Studies, Vol 0071, 1996; the Last Centuries of Byzantium, Ad 1261-1453 - Nicol,dm, Speculum-a J of Medieval Studies, Vol 0071, 1996; Church and Society in Byzantium under the Comneni, 1081-1261 - Angold,m, Speculum-a J of Medieval Studies, Vol 0072, 1997. **CONTACT ADDRESS** Dept of Classics, Univ Mass, Amherst, MA, 01003-0002.

PHILLIPS, JOANNE HIGGINS
PERSONAL Born 08/26/1946, Boston, MA **DISCIPLINE** CLASSICAL PHILOLOGY **EDUCATION** Boston Univ, AB, 68; Harvard Univ, MA, 71, PhD(class philol), 77. **CAREER** Assoc Prof Classics, Tufts Univ, 77-. **MEMBERSHIPS** Am Philol Asn; Am Asn Hist Med. **RESEARCH** History of Greek and Roman medicine. **SELECTED PUBLICATIONS** Auth, The boneless one in Hesiod, Phiologus, 80; Early Greek medicine and poetry of Solon, Clio Medica, 80; The emergence of the Greek medical profession in the Roman Republic, Trans and Studies of Col of Physicians Philadelphia, 80; Juxtaposed medical traditions: Pliny NH 27 106 131, 81 & Lucretius on the inefficacy of the medical art: 6 1179 and 6 1226-1238, 82, Class Philol; The Hippocratic physician and astronomy, Proc of the IVth Int Colloquium on Hippocratic Med, Lausanne, Switz, 81, 82. **CONTACT ADDRESS** Dept of Classics, Tufts Univ, 318 Eaton Hall, Medford, MA, 02155-0000. **EMAIL** jphillip@emerald.tufts.edu

PHILLIPS, KENDALL R.
PERSONAL Born 05/12/1969, San Antonio, TX, m, 1994 **DISCIPLINE** SPEECH COMMUNICATION **EDUCATION** Southwest Baptist Univ, BS, 90; Cent Mo State Univ, MA, 92; Pa State Univ, PhD, 95. **CAREER** Asst prof, Cent Mo State Univ, 95-. **HONORS AND AWARDS** Kathryn DeBoer Distinguished Teaching award; Top Paper, Rhetoric & Pub addres, E Commun Assoc. **MEMBERSHIPS** Nat Commun Assoc; Rhet Soc of Am; Am Forensics Assoc. **RESEARCH** Rhetorical theory/criticism; continental philosophy. **SELECTED PUBLICATIONS** Co-auth, Self-monitoring and argumentativeness: Using argument as impression management, Argument in Controversy, Speech Commun Assoc, 193-196, 91; co-auth, Impact and implications of parliamentary debate format on American debate, Advanced debate: Readings in theory, practice, and teaching, Net Textbook Co, 94-104, 92; co-auth, Cyberphobia and Education, Commun Law & Policy Newsletter, vol 7, no 1, 3, 96; auth, The spaces of public dissension: Reconsidering the public sphere, Commun monographs, vol 63, 231-248, 96; auth, Interpretive controversy and The Silence of the Lambs, Rhet Soc Quart, vol, 28, 33-47, 98; auth, Rhetoric, resistance and criticism: A response to Sloop and Ono, Philos & Rhet, (in press); auth, Tactical apologies: The American Nursing Association and assisted suicide, South Commun J, (in press). **CONTACT ADDRESS** Dept of Commun, Central Missouri State Univ, 136 Martin Hall, Warrensburg, MO, 64093. **EMAIL** phillips@cmsuvmb.cmsu.edu

PHILLIPS, KLAUS
DISCIPLINE NEW GERMAN CINEMA **EDUCATION** Univ AR, BA, MA; Univ TX, Austin, PhD, 84. **CAREER** Instr, Univ IL, VA Mil Inst; vis prof, Sweet Briar Col; prof Ger and Film, ch, dept Ger & Russ, Hollins Col. **SELECTED PUBLICATIONS** Auth, Rainer Maria Rilke: Nine Plays; Women in Recent German Films; New German Filmmakers: From Oberhausen Through the 1970's. **CONTACT ADDRESS** Hollins Col, Roanoke, VA, 24020.

PICARD, ANNE MARIE
DISCIPLINE FRENCH LITERATURE **EDUCATION** Univ Haute Normandie, BA; Dalhousie Univ, MA; Univ Toronto, PhD. **RESEARCH** Lacanian psychoanalysis; theories of the body; theories of reading; 19th and 20th century French literature; history of criticism; existentialism; narratology; Saussurian linguistics; semantics. **SELECTED PUBLICATIONS** Auth, Le Corps et la lettre: psychanalyse et metacritique, Nuit Blanche, 95; ed, Mises-en-scenes du regard, Dalhousie, 95. **CONTACT ADDRESS** Dept of French, Western Ontario Univ, London, ON, N6A 5B8.

PICERNO, RICHARD A.
DISCIPLINE SPANISH LANGUAGE AND LITERATURE **EDUCATION** Providence Col, BA, 61; Boston Col, MA, 64; Univ Conn, PhD, 69. **CAREER** Fac, Univ Conn, Storrs, Suffolk Univ and Boston Univ; prof mod langs, 66-. **HONORS AND AWARDS** Fulbright Scholar, Universidad de Madrid, 61-62. **SELECTED PUBLICATIONS** Auth, Lope de Vega's: Lo que pasa en une tarde, Univ NC Press, 71; La Estrella de Sevilla, Ediciones Universal, 83; Medieval Spanish Ejempla, A Study of Selected Tales from Calila y Dimna, El libro de los engaos, Libro de los exemplos por ABC, Ediciones Universal, 88. **CONTACT ADDRESS** Central Connecticut State Univ, 1615 Stanley St, New Britain, CT, 06050.

PICHERIT, JEAN-LOUIS
DISCIPLINE FRENCH **EDUCATION** Univ NC at Chapel Hill, PhD, 71. **CAREER** Prof; Univ WY, 76-; coord exchange progr, UW & Univ Tours and Strasbourg. **HONORS AND AWARDS** Arts & Sci Seibold Professorship. **RESEARCH** French medieval epic; study of med metaphors in French medieval lit; Middle-French lit. **SELECTED PUBLICATIONS** Ed & transl, medieval epic. **CONTACT ADDRESS** Dept of Mod and Class Lang(s), Univ WY, PO Box 3964, Laramie, WY, 82071-3964. **EMAIL** PICHERIT@UWYO.EDU

PICHOIS, CLAUDE
PERSONAL Born 07/21/1925, Paris, France, m, 1961 **DISCIPLINE** FRENCH LITERATURE, COMPARATIVE LITERATURE **EDUCATION** Hautes Etudes Commerciales, Paris, Dipl, 48; Sorbonne, Doctorat d'Etat, 63. **CAREER** Assoc prof French lit, Faculte des Lettres d'Aix-en- Provence, France, 56, assoc prof comp lit, 58-61; prof French lit, Faculte d'Hist et de Philos, Basel, Switz, 61-70; prof, 70- 73, Distinguished Prof French Lit, Vanderbilt Univ, 73-, CO-ed, Revue d'Hist litteraire de la France, Armand Colin, Paris, 50-, Etudes baudelairiennes, La Baconniere, Switz, 69- & Bull baudelairien, Vanderbilt Univ, 70-; gen ed, Litterature francaise, Arthaud, Paris, 68-80; vis res prof, Inst Res Humanities, Madison, Wis, 68; John Simon Guggenheim Mem Found fel, 78. **MEMBERSHIPS** MLA; Soc d'Hist litteraire France. **SELECTED PUBLICATIONS** AUth, L'Image de Jean-Paul Richter dans les lettres francaises, 63 & Philarete Chasles et la vie litteraire au temps du romantisme, 65, Jose Corti, Paris; Litterature et Progres: Vitesse et vision du monde, La Baconniere, 73; ed, Baudelaire's Correspondence, 2 vols, 73 & Baudelaire's Complete Works, 2 vols, 75-76, Bibliot de la Pleiade, Paris; Baudelaire and Nadar + a Recent Exhibition at the Metropolitan-museum-of-art of the Latters Photographic Interpretation of the Formers Work/, Nineteenth-century French Studies, Vol 0023, 1995; Memory in the Service of Homage + Morot-sir,edouard - In-memoriam/, Romance Notes, Vol 0035, 1995. **CONTACT ADDRESS** Vanderbilt Univ, Box 6203 Sta B, Nashville, TN, 37235.

PICKENS, GEORGE F.
PERSONAL Born 02/26/1958, Parkersburg, WV, m, 1980, 2 children **DISCIPLINE** INTERCULTURAL STUDIES, MISSION STUDIES **EDUCATION** Ky Christian Col, BA, 80; Ohio Univ, MA, 84; Univ Birmingham, Eng, PhD, 97. **CAREER** Lectr, Daystar Univ, Nairobi, Kenya; prof Intercult Studs, Ky Christian Col, 97- . **HONORS AND AWARDS** Overseas Studs Res Scheme, UK, 94-97, Neville Chamberlain prize, Univ Birmingham, UK, 94-95. **MEMBERSHIPS** Amer Acad Rel; Amer Soc Missiology. **RESEARCH** Oral history; African religion and Historical studies. **CONTACT ADDRESS** Dept of Intercultural Studies, Kentucky Christian Col, 100 Academic Pkwy, PO Box 2050, Grayson, KY, 41143-2205. **EMAIL** gpickens@email.kcc.edu

PICKETT, TERRY H.
PERSONAL Born 04/19/1941, Washington, GA, m, 1961, 2 children **DISCIPLINE** GERMAN LITERATURE & HISTORY **EDUCATION** Univ GA, AB, 66; Vanderbilt Univ, PhD(-Ger lit), 70. **CAREER** Asst prof, 70-79, Prof Ger, Univ Ala, 80-, Chmn Dept Ger & Russ, 78-, Fulbright-Exchange Teacher, Hans-Sachs-Gym & Univ of Erlangen-Nurnberg, 72-73. **MEMBERSHIPS** MLA; Southeastern Mod Lang Asn; Am Asn Teaciers Ger. **RESEARCH** Nineteenth century German literature; Tenacious literature 1800-1850; Varnhagen von Ense. **SELECTED PUBLICATIONS** Auth, Varnhagen's mistaken identity in two recent works, Germanic Notes, 71; Heinrich Boll's plea for civilization, Southern Humanities Rev, 73; Varnhagen von Ense & his mistaken identity, Ger Life & Lett, 4/74; coauth, Varnhagen von Ense and the reception of Russian literature in Germany, Germano-Slavica, fall 74;Masters and Lords - Mid-19th-century United-states Planters and Prussian Junkers - Bowman,sd, Germanic Notes and Reviews, Vol 0025, 1994; the Biedermeier Novel and the Corporatist Order Crisis - Studies on Literary Conservatism - German - Brandmeyer,r, Germanic Notes and Reviews, Vol 0025, 1994; the Faces of Physiognomy - Interdisciplinary Approaches to Lavater,johann,caspar - Shookman,e, Germanic Notes and Reviews, Vol 0026, 1995; Terrible Sociability - the Text of Manners in Laclos, Goethe, and James - Winnett,s, Germanic Notes and Reviews, Vol 0028, 1997; a Grand Illusion - an Essay on Europe - Judt,t/, Germanic Notes and Reviews, Vol 0028, 1997; Fascist Italy and Nazi Germany - the Fascist Style of Rule - Degrand,aj/, Germanic Notes and Reviews, Vol 0028, 1997; Terrible Sociability - the Text of Manners in Laclos, Goethe, and James - Winnett,s, Germanic Notes and Reviews, Vol 0028, 1997. **CONTACT ADDRESS** Dept of Ger, Univ of Ala, University, AL, 35486.

PIEDMONT, FERDINAND
PERSONAL Born 11/19/1926, Trier, Germany **DISCIPLINE** GERMAN **EDUCATION** Univ Bonn, MA, 53, PhD, 54. **CAREER** Studienrat Ger & English, Schiller Gym, Cologne, 58-63; from asst to assoc prof, 63-76, Prof Ger, Ind Univ, Bloomington, 76-, Fulbright vis lectr, 60-61. **MEMBERSHIPS** MLA; Am Asn Teachers Ger; Am Lessing Soc. **RESEARCH** Late 18th and early 19th century literature; drama and Theater; teaching methodology. **SELECTED PUBLICATIONS** Auth, Textsammlung Moderner Kurzgeschichten, Diesterweg, Ger, 59; Coauth, Kurz belichtet (German Literature Reader), Rinehart, 73; auth, Zur Rolle des Erzahlers in der Kurzgeschichte, Z Deut Philol, 11/73; Tendenzen moderner Schiller-Auffuehrungen 1965-1975, Jb Deut Schillerges, 77; Wittkowski,w. Review of Piedmont Book on Staging Schiller Dramas 1946-1985 - a Reply/, German Quarterly, Vol 0065, 1992; Reisst- die-mauern-ein - Schiller 'Wilhelm Tell' on the Stage in the Year of the German Revolution, 1989/, German Studies Review, Vol 0018, 1995; Schiller Dramas - Idealism and Skepticism - German - Guthke,ks/, Colloquia Germanica, Vol 0029, 1996. **CONTACT ADDRESS** Dept of Ger, Indiana Univ, Bloomington, Bloomington, IN, 47401.

PIEDRA, JOSE
DISCIPLINE SPANISH LITERATURE **EDUCATION** Yale Univ, PhD. **CAREER** Assoc prof and co-founder and first dir, Prog of Hisp-Amer Stud, Cornell Univ; art curator. **RESEARCH** Early modern images and contributions of blacks in Spanish and Spanish American cultures. **SELECTED PUBLICATIONS** Auth, In Search of the Black Stud, in Pre-Modern Sexualities, Routledge, 97; Nationalizing Sissies, in Entiendes, Queer Readings, Hisp Writings, Duke, 97. **CONTACT ADDRESS** Dept of Romance Studies, Cornell Univ, 283 Goldwin Smith Hall, Ithaca, NY, 14853.

PIERCE, GLENN
PERSONAL San Diego, CA **DISCIPLINE** ITALIAN **EDUCATION** UCLA, PhD, 77 **CAREER** Asst prof, UVA, 78-84; assoc prof, MU, 85-. **HONORS AND AWARDS** Golden Key Honor Soc, Georgetown Univ; Scholar, Johns Hopkins Bologna Ctr. **MEMBERSHIPS** MLA; AAIS; AATI. **RESEARCH** Italian Baroque. **SELECTED PUBLICATIONS** Auth, art, What is Tragic About Torrismondo, 91; auth, art, Tecniche teatrali ne I promessi sposi, 95; auth, art, A bacchic dithyramb in the Ottocento?, 95; auth, Alessandro Manzoni and the Aesthetics of the Lombard Seicento: Finding the arts in the narra **CONTACT ADDRESS** Dept of Romance Lang, Univ of Missouri, A/S 123, Columbia, MO, 65211. **EMAIL** pierceg@missouri.edu

PIERREHUMBERT, JANET
DISCIPLINE LINGUISTICS **EDUCATION** MIT, PhD. **CAREER** Prof, Northwestern Univ. **RESEARCH** Phonetics; phonology; prosody and intonation. **SELECTED PUBLICATIONS** Auth, Syllable Structure and Word Structure, Papers in Lab Phonology, Cambridge Univ Press, 94; Lenition of /h/ and glottal stop, Papers in Lab Phonology, Cambridge Univ Press, 91; On ichlaut, achlaut, and structure preservation, Phonol, 91; On Attributing Grammars to Dynamical Systems, J. Phonetics, 90; Categories of Tonal Alignment in English, Phonetica, 90; The Timing of Prenuclear High Accents in English, Papers in Lab Phonology I, Cambridge UP, 90; Japanese Tone Structure, Linguistic Inquiry Monograph 15, MIT Press, Cambridge, 88; Prosodic Effects on Glottal Allophones in Vocal Fold Physiology 8, Singular Press, 94; rev, Autosegmental and Metrical Phonology, J Phonetics, 94. **CONTACT ADDRESS** Dept of Linguistics, Northwestern Univ, 2016 Sheridan Rd, Evanston, IL, 60208.

PILUSO, ROBERT VINCENT
PERSONAL Born 04/05/1937, Yonkers, NY, m, 1967, 3 children **DISCIPLINE** ROMANCE LANGUAGES **EDUCATION** Fordham Univ, AB, 58, AM, 60; NY Univ, PhD, 65. **CAREER** Instr Span & French, St Peter's Col, 59-60; tchr Span & Latin, Tuckahoe High Sch, 60-63; instr Span & French, Manhattan Col, 63-65; instr Span, Hunter Col, 65-67; assoc prof, 67-72, Prof Romance Lang, State Univ NY Col New Paltz, 72. **HONORS AND AWARDS** Who's Who Among Italian Am, 93; Directory of Ital Am Scholars, 92; Lectured at the Congresses of the Intl Hispanists, Salamanca Spain, 71, Bordeaux France, 74, Toronto Ontario, 77, Venice Italy, 80, Brown Univ Rhode Island, 83; Directory of Am Scholars, 69; Fulbright Grant to Burgos Spain, 65; Founders Day Award, NY Univ, 65; Span tchg Fel, Fordham Univ, 58. **MEMBERSHIPS** Am Assoc Tchrs Span & Port, Tchrs of Italian, Tchrs of French; MLA; Assoc Int Hispanists; Nat Italian Am Federation; Am Classical League; Classical Assoc of the Atlantic States; Alliance Francaise de Westchester. **RESEARCH** Cervantes and Golden Age prose; Golden Age drama; contemp theater, espec Span; Garcia-Loca. **SELECTED PUBLICATIONS** Auth, La fuerza de la sangre: Un analisis estructural, Hispania, 64; Amor, matrimonio y honra en Cervantes, Las Americas, 67; Analisis de El infamador, Duquesne Hisp Rev, 68; Honor in Valdivielso and Cervantes, Ky Romance Quart, 70; Co ed, Jose de Valdivielso: Teatro completo, volumen I and II, Madrid: editorial Isla, 75 and 81; Italian Fundamentals, Barron's Edu series, 92; Italian on Location, eng ver, Barron's Edu series, 92. **CONTACT ADDRESS** Dept Span State, Univ NY Col, 75 S Manheim Blvd, New Paltz, NY, 12561-2400. **EMAIL** rpiluso@worldnet.att.net

PINKUS, KAREN
DISCIPLINE FRENCH AND ITALIAN AND COMPARATIVE LITERATURE **EDUCATION** City Univ NY, PhD. **CAREER** Prof, Univ Southern Calif. **RESEARCH** Cultural history of Italy in the 1950s. **SELECTED PUBLICATIONS** Auth, Bodily Regimes: Italian Advertising under Fascism, Univ Minn

Press, 95; Picturing Silence: Emblem, Language, Counter-Reformation Materiality, Univ Mich Press; The Body, in Theory ser, 96. **CONTACT ADDRESS** Col Letters, Arts & Sciences, Univ Southern Calif, University Park Campus, Los Angeles, CA, 90089.

PIPER, ANSON CONANT
PERSONAL Born 08/14/1918, Newton, MA, m, 1945, 4 children **DISCIPLINE** ROMANCE LANGUAGES **EDUCATION** Williams Col, Mass, BA, 40; Univ Wis, MA, 47, PhD(Span), 53, U.S. Navy, 42-46. **CAREER** From instr to prof Romanic lang, 49-68, chmn dept, 61-71, William Dwight Whitney Prof Romanic Lang, Williams Col, 68- . **MEMBERSHIPS** Am Asn Teachers Span & Port; Phi Beta Kappa. **RESEARCH** Portuguese literature; Spanish literature, especially 19th century novel; Romance linguisitics. **SELECTED PUBLICATIONS** Auth, Asi es la vida, Norton, 58; coauth, Fundamental Portuguese Vocabulary, Univ Louvain, 68. **CONTACT ADDRESS** 70 Baxter Rd, Williamstown, MA, 01267.

PIREDDU, NICOLETTA
DISCIPLINE LANGUAGE **EDUCATION** Universita degli Studi di Verona, Italy, Laurea, 89; Univ Calif Los Angeles, MA, 91, PhD, 96; Universita degli Studi de Venezia, Ci' Foscari, Italy, Dottorato, 97. **CAREER** Vis asst prof, Duke Univ, 96-97; asst prof, Univ Houston, 97-98; asst prof, Georgetown Univ, 98- . **HONORS AND AWARDS** Doctoral res fel, Universita degli Studi di Venezia, Calif' Foscari; Dissertation Year Fel, Univ Calif Los Angeles; Paris Prog in Critical Theory & Borchard Found Fel; Laurea in Lingue e Letterature Straniere, summa cum laude. **MEMBERSHIPS** Modern Lang Assoc of Amer; S Atlantic Modern Lang Assoc of Amer; Soc for Critical Exchange; Contemporary Women's Writing Network. **RESEARCH** Nineteenth-& twentieth-century Italian, English, French lit & culture; decadence, modernism, postmodernism in lit & the visual arts; literary theory; theories of the novel & of romance; anthropological approaches to lit; relations between lit & sci. **SELECTED PUBLICATIONS** Rev, Walter Pater, Lover of Strange Souls, Rivista di Studi Vittoriani, 97; auth, CaRterbury Tales: Romances of Disenchantment in Geoffrey Chaucer and Angela Carter, Comparatist, 97; 'Il divino pregio del dono': Andrea Sperelli's economy of pleasures, Annali d'italianistica, 97; critical intro, The Importance of Being Earnest, Loffredo Editore, 99; rev, La crise de la volonte ou le romanesque en question: Borgese, Green, Perutz, Pirandello, Kafka, Canadian Rev of Comparative Lit, 99. **CONTACT ADDRESS** Dept of Italian, Georgetown Univ, ICC 307, 37th and O Sts, Washington, DC, 20057. **EMAIL** pireddun@gusun.georgetown.edu

PIROG, GERALD
PERSONAL Born 01/12/1948, NJ **DISCIPLINE** SLAVIC LANGUAGES AND LITERATURES **EDUCATION** Rutgers Univ, AB, 69; Yale Univ, MPhil, 72, PhD(Slavic), 75. **CAREER** Instr Russ, William Patterson Col NJ, 73-75; asst prof, 75- 80, Prof Russ & Polish, Rutgers Univ, 80-. **MEMBERSHIPS** Am Asn Advan Slavic Studies; Am Asn Teachers Slavic & E Europ Lang & Lit; MLA. **RESEARCH** Russian symbolist poetry, particularly Aleksandr Blok; early period of Soviet Cinema; Slavic literary theory. **SELECTED PUBLICATIONS** Auth, The city, the woman, the Madonna: Metaphorical inference in Blok's Ital janskie stixi, Forum Iowa Russ Lit, 12/77; Blok's Blagovescenie: A study in iconological transformation, Vol VII, 79 & Blok's Ravenna: The city as sign, Vol VII, 80, Russ Lit; Iconicity & narrative: The Eisenstein- Vertor controversy, Semiotica (in press); Aleksandr Blok's Italjanski Stikhi: Confrontations and disillusionment, Slavica Pub (in press); Brodsky,joseph and the Creation of Exile - Bethea,dm/, Slavic Review, Vol 0054, 1995; Borderline Culture - the Politics of Identity in 4 20th-century Slavic Novels - Longinovic,tz/, Slavic Review, Vol 0053, 1994. **CONTACT ADDRESS** Dept of Slavic, Rutgers Univ, P O Box 5062, New Brunswick, NJ, 08903-5062.

PITT, DAVID
DISCIPLINE PHILOSOPHY OF LANGUAGE, FORMAL SEMANTICS, AND THE PHILOSOPHY OF MIND **EDUCATION** CUNY, PhD, 94. **CAREER** Vis asst prof, Univ Nebr, Lincoln. **SELECTED PUBLICATIONS** Published in music and the philosophy of mind. **CONTACT ADDRESS** Univ Nebr, Lincoln, Lincoln, NE, 68588-0417.

PIZER, JOHN
DISCIPLINE 18TH-20TH CENTURY GERMAN LITERATURE, GERMAN LANGUAGE, COMP LIT **EDUCATION** Univ Wash, PhD, 85. **CAREER** Assoc prof Ger and Comp Lit, sect hd, Ger, recycling comt, Rally Day coordr for Ger prog, univ fac senate, Col Arts & Sci fac senate, La State Univ. **RESEARCH** 18th-20th Century German Literature; Hermeneutics; Critical Theory. **SELECTED PUBLICATIONS** Auth, The Historical Perspective in German Genre Theory: Its Development from Gottsched to Hegel, 85; Toward a Theory of Radical Origin: Essays on Modern German Thought, 95. **CONTACT ADDRESS** Dept of For Lang and Lit, Louisiana State Univ, 145 B Prescott Hall, Baton Rouge, LA, 70803. **EMAIL** pizer@homer.forlang.lsu.edu

PLANT, HELMUT R.
PERSONAL Born 01/15/1932, Munich, Germany, m, 1957, 1 child **DISCIPLINE** GERMAN **EDUCATION** Fairmont State Col, AB, 57; Univ Cincinnati, MA, 61, PhD(Ger), 64. **CAREER** Instr Ger, Cornell Univ, 63-65, asst prof, 65-66; wiss asst, Aachen Tech, Ger, 66-67; asst prof, 67-71, assoc prof Ger, Univ Ore, 71-. **MEMBERSHIPS** Am Asn Teachers Ger; Ling Soc Europe. **RESEARCH** German grammar; audiovisual instruction. **SELECTED PUBLICATIONS** Auth Syntaktische Studien zu den Monseer Fragmenten, Mouton, The Hague, 69; Syntactic devices in the teaching of manuscript Middle High German, Folia Ling, Vol II, Nos 1-2; coauth, Guten Tag at Oregon: an audiovisual experiment, Unterrichtspraxis, Vol VI, No 1; coed Die sogenannte Mainauer Naturlehre, der Basler Hs B VIII 27, Abbildung, Transkription, Kommentar Herausgegeben von Helmut R Plant, Marie Rowlands und Rolf Burkhart, Verlag Alfred Kummerle, Goppingen, 72. **CONTACT ADDRESS** Dept of German, Univ of Oregon, Eugene, OR, 97403-1205. **EMAIL** hplant@oregon.uoregon.edu

PLATER, EDWARD M.V.
PERSONAL Saginaw, MI **DISCIPLINE** GERMAN **EDUCATION** Univ Mich, AB, 60, MA, 62, PhD(Ger), 68. **CAREER** Instr Ger, Univ Mich, 66-67; instr, 67-68, asst prof, 68-80, Assoc Prof Ger, Miami Univ, 68-, Nat Endowment for Humanities summer sem, 78. **MEMBERSHIPS** Am Asn Teachers Ger. **RESEARCH** Conrad Ferdinand Meyer; 19th century German literature. **SELECTED PUBLICATIONS** Auth, The Banquet of Life: Conrad Ferdinand Meyer's Die Versuchung des Pescara, Seminar, 6/72; The figure of Dante in Die Hochzeit des Momchs, Mod Lang Notes, 75; Der schone Leib in the prose of C F Meyer, Seminar, spring 79; The symbolism in Ferdinand von Saar's Norelle, Marianne, Sem, spring 82; Kautner,helmut Film Adaptation of Des Taufels General Literature-film Quarterly, Vol 0022, 1994. **CONTACT ADDRESS** Dept of Foreign Lang, Miami Univ, 500 E High St, Oxford, OH, 45056-1602.

PLOTTEL, JEANINE PARISIER
PERSONAL Born 09/21/1934, Paris, France, m, 1956, 3 children **DISCIPLINE** LANGUAGES **EDUCATION** Columbia Univ, BA, 54, MA, 55, PhD, 59. **CAREER** Lectr French, Columbia Univ, 55-59; res assoc, MLA, 59-60; asst prof French, Juilliard Sch Music, 60-65; from asst prof to assoc prof Romance lang, 65-81, Prof French, Hunter Col, 82-, Lectr, City Col New York, 59-60, French Embassy, 59- & Ecole Libre des Hautes Etudes, 59; City Univ New York res grant, 72- 73; ed, New York Lit Forum, 77-; Nat Endowment for Humanities fel, 79-80; fac res fel, City Univ New York, 81. **MEMBERSHIPS** Asn Int Etudes Fr; Soc Paul Valery; MLA; Am Asn Teachers Fr; Am Comp Lit Asn. **RESEARCH** Nineteenth and twentieth century French literature; comparative literature. **SELECTED PUBLICATIONS** Auth, Les Dialogues de Paul Valery, Presses Univ France, 60; Structures and counter-structures in Raymond Roussel's Impressions of Africa, Dada/Surrealism, 75; Anamorphose d'un coute, Sub-Stance, 76; Rhetoric of chance, Dada/Surrealism, 77; Anamorphosis in painting & literature, Yearbk Gen & Comp Lit, 79; The mathematics of Surrealism, Romantic Rev, 80; The poetics of autobiography in Paul Valery, L'Eprit Createur, Prevost, Laclos & Constant, Scribner's (in press); Colette Love Triangles/, Esprit Createur, Vol 0034, 1994. **CONTACT ADDRESS** Hunter Col, CUNY, New York, NY, 10036.

POAG, JAMES F.
PERSONAL Born 08/07/1934, IL, m, 1960, 2 children **DISCIPLINE** GERMAN PHILOLOGY **EDUCATION** Univ Ill, BA, 56, MA, 58, PhD, 61. **CAREER** From instr to assoc prof Ger, Ind Univ, Bloomington, 61-76; Prof Ger & Chmn Dept, Wash Univ, 76-, Fulbright & Humbold res grants, Univ Gottingen, 63-64. **MEMBERSHIPS** MLA; Am Asn Teachers Ger. **RESEARCH** Mediaeval German literature. **SELECTED PUBLICATIONS** Forms of Incitative Speech in Eckhart,meister - Studies on the Literary Concept of German Sermons - German - Hasebrink,B, J of English and Germanic Philology, Vol 0093, 1994; Forms of Incitative Speech in Eckhart,meister - Studies on the Literary Concept of German Sermons - German - Hasebrink,b, J of English and Germanic Philology, Vol 0093, 1994; German Mysticism from Hildegard-of-Bingen to Wittgenstein,Ludwig - a Literary and Intellectual History - Weeks,A, German Quarterly, Vol 0068, 1995; Romancing the Grail - Genre, Science, and Quest in Wolfram 'Parzival' - Groos,A, J of English and Germanic Philology, Vol 0096, 1997; The Knowledge of Childhood in the German Middle- ages, 1100-1350 - Schultz,J, J of English and Germanic Philology, Vol 0096, 1997. **CONTACT ADDRESS** Dept of Ger, Wash Univ, 1 Brookings Dr, Saint Louis, MO, 63130-4899.

PODUSKA, DONALD MILES
PERSONAL Born 12/02/1934, Chicago, IL, m, 1958, 3 children **DISCIPLINE** CLASSICAL LANGUAGES **EDUCATION** Loyola Univ, Ill, AB, 56; Univ Ky, MA, 57; Ohio State Univ, PhD, 63. **CAREER** From instr to assoc prof, 60-73, prof class lang, John Carroll Univ, 73-; vis assoc prof class lang, 70-71, vis prof class lang, 85-86, Rome Ctr, Loyola Univ, Ill. **MEMBERSHIPS** Am Philol Assn; Am Class League; Vergilian Soc; Class Assn Mid W & S. **RESEARCH** Roman comedy; Roman historians; Vergil. **CONTACT ADDRESS** Dept of Class Lang, John Carroll Univ, 20700 N Park Blvd, Cleveland, OH, 44118-4581. **EMAIL** poduska@jcvaxa.jcu.edu

POE, JOE PARK
DISCIPLINE GREEK AND LATIN LITERATURE **CAREER** Instr, NY Univ, 60-62; lectr, Brooklyn Col, 62; instr, Univ TX, 62-64; act asst prof, Univ CA-Barkeley, 64-65; asst prof, 65-70; assoc prof, 70-89; prof, 89-; dept ch, 71-74, 77-88. **RESEARCH** Theatrical antiquities. **SELECTED PUBLICATIONS** The Determination of Episodes in Greek Tragedy, Amer Jour Philol 114, 93; The Periaktoi and Actors' Entrances, Hermes 121, 93; Pollux and the Klision, Philologus 138, 94; The Supposed Conventional Meanings of Dramatic Masks: A Re-examination of Pollux 4. 133-54, Philologus 140, 96. **CONTACT ADDRESS** Dept of Class Stud, Tulane Univ, 6823 St Charles Ave, New Orleans, LA, 70118. **EMAIL** jpoe@mailhost.tcs.tulane.edu

POLACHEK, DORA
DISCIPLINE FRENCH LANGUAGE AND LITERATURE **EDUCATION** Barnard Col, BA; NY Univ, MA; Univ NC Chapel Hill, PhD. **CAREER** Fac. SUNY Binghamton. **RESEARCH** French Renaissance lit. **SELECTED PUBLICATIONS** Auth, publ about Marguerite de Navarre and Montaigne, French Renaissance theater, and issues relating to gender and power in the early mod period. **CONTACT ADDRESS** SUNY Binghamton, PO Box 6000, Binghamton, NY, 13902-6000. **EMAIL** dpolachk@binghamton.edu

POLAKIEWICZ, LEONARD A.
DISCIPLINE SLAVIC LANGUAGES & LITERATURE **EDUCATION** Univ Minn, BS, BA, 64; Univ Wis, Madison, 68, PhD, 78; Maria Curie-Sklodowska Univ, Poland, Diploma, 81. **CAREER** Teac asst, Univ Minn, 64, 69-70; instr, Univ MInn, 78-90; asst prof, 78-90, ASSOC PROF, SLAVIC LANGS, LITS, UNIV MINN, 90-; vis prof,Sch Slavonic, E European Stud, Univ London, 84; assoc chair, dept Russian, E European Stud, 83-85, dir grad stud, 87- 89, dir Polish stud, 85-88, Univ Minn; dir, instr, Lublin Prog, Maria Curie-Sklodowsha Univ, Poland, 84-89(summers). **CONTACT ADDRESS** Inst Ling, Asian & Slavic Langs, Univ of Minnesota, 192 Klaeber Ct, Minneapolis, MN, 55455. **EMAIL** polak001@maroon.tc.umn.edu

POLANSKY, SUSAN
DISCIPLINE SPANISH **EDUCATION** Boston Col, PhD. **CAREER** Languages, Carnegie Mellon Univ. **SELECTED PUBLICATIONS** Auth, Narrators and Fragmentation in Cela's Mrs. Caldwell habla con su hijo, Revista de Estudios Hispanicos, 88; Provocation to Audience Response: Narrators in the Plays of Antonio Buero Vallejo, Letras Peninsulares, 88; Textual Coherence in the Duke of Rivas's El desenga-o en un sue-o: The Dramaturgy of Destiny, Mod Lang Studies, 89; Irony, Allusion, and the Nature of Tyranny in Pedro Salinas's Judit y el tirano, Revista de Estudios Hispanicos, R'o Piedras, 90; Puntos de vista Lectura. Heinle and Heinle, 94. **CONTACT ADDRESS** Carnegie Mellon Univ, 5000 Forbes Ave, Pittsburgh, PA, 15213.

POLASKY, JANET
DISCIPLINE COMPARATIVE EUROPEAN, EARLY MODERN AND MODERN FRENCH HISTORY, EUROPEAN WOME **EDUCATION** Stanford Univ, PhD. **CAREER** Prof, Univ NH, 80-. **HONORS AND AWARDS** Prize in Arts and Lett, Belgian Royal Acad, 84; UNH Bk Prize, 85; Fulbright, 85-86, 96-97; NEH, 88; Pierlot Prize in Contemp Hist, 93; Lindberg Award, 96; Gustavson fel, 97. **RESEARCH** Social Planning in Britain, France and Belgium, 1869-1914. **SELECTED PUBLICATIONS** Auth, Revolution in Brussels, 1787-1793, 86; Le Patron du Parti ourier belge, 94; The Democratic Socialism of Emile Vandervelde, Between Reform and Revolution, 94. **CONTACT ADDRESS** Univ NH, Durham, NH, 03824. **EMAIL** jpolasky@christa.unh.edu

POLLACK, GLORIA W.
DISCIPLINE HEBREW LITERATURE **EDUCATION** Yeshiva Univ, Stern Col, BA, 67; NY Univ, MA, 68; Columbia Univ, MPhil, 78, PhD, 81. **CAREER** ASST PROF HEBREW, COORD HEBREW PROG, KINGSBOROUGH COMMUNITY COL, CUNY, 94-. **CONTACT ADDRESS** 333 Meehan Ave, Far Rockaway, NY, 11691. **EMAIL** glorpol@earthling

POLLITT, JEROME J.
PERSONAL Born 11/26/1934, Fair Lawn, NJ **DISCIPLINE** HISTORY OF ART, CLASSICAL PHILOLOGY **EDUCATION** Yale Univ, BA, 57; Columbia Univ, PhD(hist of art), 63. **CAREER** Instr classics, 62-65, from asst prof to assoc prof class art & archaeol, 65-73, chmn, Dept Classics, 75-77, PROF CLASS ARCHAEOL & HIST OF ART, YALE UNIV, 73-, Chmn, Dept Hist of Art, 81-, Dean, 86-91; Morse fel, 67-68; ed, Am J Archaeol, 73-77. **MEMBERSHIPS** Archaeol Inst Am **RESEARCH** Greek art and archaeology; art criticism. **SELECTED PUBLICATIONS** Auth, The Art of Greece: 1400-31 BC, 65 & The Art of Rome: c 753 BC-337 AD, 66, Prentice-

Hall; Art and Experience in Classical Greece, Cambridge Univ, 72; The Ancient View of Greek Art, Yale Univ, 74; The impact of Greek art on Rome, Trans Am Philol Asn, 78; Kernoi from the Athenian Agora, Hesperia, 79; Art in the Hellenistic Age, Cambridge Univ, 86; The Art of Greece, Sources and Documents, Cambridge Univ, 90; Personal Styles in Greek Sculpture, Cambridge Univ, 96. **CONTACT ADDRESS** Dept of Classics, Yale Univ, PO Box 208272, New Haven, CT, 06520-8272. **EMAIL** jerome.pollitt@yale.edu

POLLY, LYLE R.
PERSONAL Born 02/13/1940, Cornwall, NY, m, 1962, 3 children **DISCIPLINE** FRENCH LANGUAGE AND LITERATURE **EDUCATION** Geneva Col, BA, 61; Univ Wis, MA, 62; State Univ NY Buffalo, PhD(French), 72. **CAREER** Teacher French, Span & Latin, Ardsley High Sch, 62-64; asst prof French & Span, Geneva Col, 64-67; asst prof French, State Univ NY Geneseo, 70-72; Assoc Prof French & Span, Southwest MO State Univ, 72-. **MEMBERSHIPS** Am Asn Teachers French; Soc Amis Romania; Am Coun Teaching Foreign Lang; Soc Rencesvals; Nat Fedn Mod Lang Teachers Asn. **RESEARCH** Medieval literature; pedagogy. **SELECTED PUBLICATIONS** Coauth, Meusault on trial: multi-skills activities for teaching L'Etranger, Can Mod Lang Rev, 1078; auth, A note on the rhyme Henrilit and the dating of the Chanson de Toile Bele Siglentine, Orbis, 27: 31-32; Three Fifteen-Minute Activities for Beginning Foreign Language Students: Reading, Writing, and Arithmetic, NALLD J, 79; Two Visuals to Accompany Albert Valdman's Langue et Culture, 80 & coauth, Communicative Competence and Ancillary Cources in French, 281, Foreign Lang Annals; The Chanson de Toile an the Chanson de Geste: Reconsidering some Considerations, Romance Notes, 81; Aw-3.0 to French Conversion Program - Lurot,d, French Review, Vol 0066, 1993. **CONTACT ADDRESS** Dept of Foreign Lang, Southwest MO State Univ, 901 S National, Springfield, MO, 65802.

POLOME, EDGAR C.
PERSONAL Born 07/31/1920, Brussels, Belgium, m, 1991, 2 children **DISCIPLINE** GERMANIC LANGUAGES; INDO-EUROPEAN STUDIES **EDUCATION** Univ Brussels, PhD, 49 **CAREER** Prof, Univ Tx, 61-98; dir, Ford Found Survey of Lang & Educ of E Africa, 69-70; prof, Univ Belgian Congo, 56-60. **HONORS AND AWARDS** First Prize of Univ Umea, Sweden, in Sociolinguistics Studies; Hon Member, Soc of Germantic Linguistics. **MEMBERSHIPS** Belgian Assoc of Celtic Studies; Amer Oriental Soc; Linguistic Soc of Amer; Amer Anthrop Assoc; Societe de Linguistique de Paris. **RESEARCH** Indo-European Historico-Comparative Linguistics; Comparative Religion; Pre-Christian Era; Old Germantic Dialects; Classical Languages. **SELECTED PUBLICATIONS** Asst ed of Angela della Volpe, Proceedings of the Seventh UCLA Indo-European Conference, Los Angeles 1995, Inst for Study of Man, 98; Thoughts about the Celtic religious vocabulary, in Scrbthair a ainm n-ogaim: Scritti in memoria di Enrico Campanile, 98; Fremdes und Heimisches im Wortschatz von Haus und Hof, in Haus und Hof in ur-und fruhgeschichtlicher Zeit. Gedenkschrift H. Jankuihn, Vandenhoeck & Ruprecht, 98; Some considerations on Dutch erg, etc," in Mir Curad: Studies in honor of Calvert Watkins, 98. **CONTACT ADDRESS** Texas Univ, 2701 Rock Terrace Dr, Austin, TX, 78704-3843. **EMAIL** polome@flash.net

POLT, JOHN H.R.
PERSONAL Born 08/20/1929, Usti nad Labem, Czechoslovakia, m, 1953 **DISCIPLINE** FOREIGN LANGUAGES **EDUCATION** Princeton Univ, AB, 49; Univ Calif, MA, 50, PhD (Romance lang & lit), 56. **CAREER** From instr to assoc prof, 56-70, Prof Span, Univ Calif, Berkeley, 70-, Am Philos Soc grant, 59-60; assoc dir, Univ Calif Studies Ctr, Madrid, 64-65, dir, 68-70; vis assoc prof, Univ Calif, Santa Barbara, 65-66; Am Coun Learned Soc fel, 73; Guggenheim Mem Found fel, 74. **MEMBERSHIPS** Am Asn Teachers Span & Port; Philol Asn Pac Coast. **RESEARCH** Spanish literature, 18th to 20th century. **SELECTED PUBLICATIONS** Auth, The Writings of Eduardo Mallea, Univ Calif, 59; Jovellanos and His English Sources, Am Philos Soc, 64; ed, Fortier, Los Gramaticos, Univ Calif & Ed Castalia, 70; auth, Gaspar Melchor de Jovellanos, Twayne, 71; ed, Poesia del siglo XVIII, Ed Castalia, 75; co-ed, Juan Melendez Valdes, Poesias Selectas: La Liba de marfil, Ed Castalia, 81; Melendez Valdes, Obras en verso, Catedra Feijoo, 81; Melendezvaldes,juan Translations from the Latin, Diecioho-hispanic Enlightenment, Vol 0016, 1993. **CONTACT ADDRESS** Dept of Span & Port, Univ of Calif, Berkeley, CA, 94720.

POMEROY, SARAH B.
PERSONAL Born 03/13/1938, New York, NY, 3 children **DISCIPLINE** CLASSICAL PHILOLOGY **EDUCATION** Barnard Col, BA, 57; Columbia Univ, MA, 59, PhD, 61. **CAREER** Instr class lang, Univ Tex, 61-62; lectr classics, 63-68, asst prof, 68-75, Assoc Prof Classics, 75-97, distinguished prof, 97- , Hunter Col; Coordr, Women's Studies Prog, 75-, Lectr classics, Brooklyn Col, 66-67; Am Coun Learned Soc grant-in-aid, 73-74; Nat Endowment for Humanities summer stipend, 73; fel, 81-82; Ford Found fel, 74-75; res grant, Fac Res Award Prog, City Univ New York, 75-79 & 82-83; Danforth assoc, 76-

HONORS AND AWARDS ACLS grant, 73, 74; NEH summer stipend, 73; Hunter Col grant, 73-74; Ford Found fel, 74-75; fac res award CUNY 75-77, 82-83, 85-86; NEH fel 76; Danforth Assoc, 76-82; NEH grant, 79-81; NEH fel, 81-82; NEH, dir, Hum Inst on Women in Classical Antiquity, 83; fel, Hum Res Ctr, Australian Natl Univ, 86; NEH, dir, Summer Sem, 87, 89; NEH sr fel, 87-88; Scholars Incentive Award, CUNY, 87; Pres Award for Excellence in Scholarship, 95; Guggenheim fel, 99. **MEMBERSHIPS** Am Philol Asn; Archaeol Inst Am; Am Soc Papryologists; Friends Ancient Hist; Asn Ancient Historians. **RESEARCH** Greek literature; women in classical antiquity; social history. **SELECTED PUBLICATIONS** Auth, Women in hellenistic Egypt from Alexander to Cleopatra, Wayne State Univ, reissue, 90; ed, Women's History and Ancient History, Univ North Carolina, 91; auth, Goddesses, Whores, Wives, and Slaves: Women in Classical Antiquity, Schocken, reissue 94; coauth, Women in the Classical World: Image and Text, Oxford, 94; auth, Xenophon Oeconomicus: A Social and Historical Commentary, Oxford, 94; coauth, Women's Realities, Women's Choices: An Introduction to Women's Studies, 2d ed, Oxford, 95; auth, Families in Classical and Hellenistic Greece: Representations and Realities, Oxford, 97; coauth, Ancient Greece, Oxford, 98. **CONTACT ADDRESS** Dept of Classics, Hunter Col, CUNY, 695 Park Ave, New York, NY, 10021-5085.

POPESCU, NICOLAE
DISCIPLINE FRENCH LITERATURE **EDUCATION** McGill Univ, BA, 87; MA, 89; Yale Univ, MA, 91; PhD, 93. **CAREER** Prof, Univ Ill Urbana Champaign. **SELECTED PUBLICATIONS** Auth, Le sentier de la tanisre, Libert¤ 92; Le catafalque de Cioran, Libert¤ 92; L'exil permanent, Liberte, 91; La mortelle condition de M. Kundera, Libert¤ 90; La quitude de Carver, Libert, 90; La trs orthodoxe demeure d'A. Tarkovski, Libert¤, 89; Les yeux de Buster Keaton, Libert, 89. **CONTACT ADDRESS** French Dept, Univ Ill Urbana Champaign, 52 E Gregory Dr, Champaign, IL, 61820. **EMAIL** npopescu@uiuc.edu

POPLACK, SHANA
PERSONAL Detroit, MI **DISCIPLINE** LINGUISTICS **EDUCATION** Queens Col, BA, 68; NY Univ, MA, 71; Univ Pa, PhD(ling), 79. **CAREER** Res assoc ling, Ctr Puetro Rican Studies, CUNY, 77-81; asst prof, 81-82, Assoc Prof Ling, Univ Ottawa, 82-, Vis asst prof, NY Univ, 78-79. **MEMBERSHIPS** Ling Soc Am; Can Ling Asn. **RESEARCH** Sociolinguistics; bilingualism; Hispanic and French dialectology. **SELECTED PUBLICATIONS** Auth, Dialect acquisition among Puerto Rican bilinguals, Lang & Soc, 7: 89-103; Deletion and disambiguation in Puerto Rican Spanish, Language, 56.2: 371-385; Sometimes I'll start a sentence in Spanish y termino in Espanol: Toward a typology of code-switching, Linguistics, 18: 7-8; coauth (with D Sankoff), A formal grammar for code-switching, Papers in Ling, 14:2:3-46; auth, Syntactic structure and social function of code-switching, In: Latino Discourse and Communicative Behavior, Ablex Pub Corp, 81; Bilingualism and the vernacular, In: Issues in International Bilingual Education: The role of the Vernacular, Plenum Pub Corp, 82; coauth, Competing influences on gender assignment: Variable process, stable outcome, Lingua, 56: 139-166; -S or Nothing, Marking the Plural in the African-American Diaspora, American Speech, Vol 0069, 1994; Plural Marking Patterns in Nigerian Pidgin English, J of Pidgin and Creole Languages, Vol 0012, 1997. **CONTACT ADDRESS** Dept of Ling, Univ of Ottawa, Ottawa, ON, K1N 6N5.

PORTER, ABIOSEH MICHAEL
DISCIPLINE COMPARATIVE LITERATURE **EDUCATION** Univ Alberta, PhD, 84. **CAREER** Assoc prof, 86-91, asst prof, 91-, Drexel Univ. **SELECTED PUBLICATIONS** Auth, They Were There Too: Women and the Civil War(s) in Emecheta's Destination Biafra, Africa World, 96; An Afrocentric View of Religion in Baldwin's Go Tell it on the Mountain and Jumbam's The White Man of God (rev), 93. **CONTACT ADDRESS** Dept of Hum and Commun, Drexel Univ, Chestnut St, PO Box 3141, Philadelphia, PA, 19104. **EMAIL** abiosehp@dunx1.ocs.drexel.edu

PORTER, CHARLES ALLEN
PERSONAL Born 05/31/1932, Chicago, IL, m, 1956 **DISCIPLINE** FRENCH LANGUAGE & LITERATURE **EDUCATION** Northwestern Univ, BS, 53, MA, 54; Yale Univ, PhD, 62. **CAREER** From instr to assoc prof, 60-75, Dir Summer Lang Inst, Yale Univ, 71-, Prof French, 75-, Chmn Dept, 80-, Lect, Univ Lyons, 55-56. **MEMBERSHIPS** MLA; Am Asn Teachers Fr. **RESEARCH** Restif de la Bretonne; Chateaubriand; French roman personnel. **SELECTED PUBLICATIONS** Auth, Restif's Novels, or an Autobiography in Search of an Author, Yale Univ, 67; Chateaubriand: Composition, Imagination, and Poetry, ANMA Libri, 78; Delphine', Vol 2, the Avant-text - French - Stael,ALG, Omacini,L, French Review, Vol 0067, 1994; the Land of Lost Content - Children and Childhood in 19th- century French Literature - Lloyd,R, French Review, Vol 0067, 1994; Chateaubriand, the Exile and the Glory - from the Familial Novel to the Identite-litteraire in the Oeuvre of Chateaubriand - French - Roulin,jm, Nineteenth-century French Studies, Vol 0023, 1995; the Thought and Art of Joubert,Joseph 1754-1824- Kinloch,dp, French Review, Vol 0068, 1995. **CONTACT ADDRESS** Yale Univ, P O Box 208251, New Haven, CT, 06520-8251.

PORTER, DENNIS
DISCIPLINE FRENCH LITERATURE **EDUCATION** Univ CA, PhD. **CAREER** Prof, Univ MA Amherst. **RESEARCH** French lit and cult hist from the late 18th century to the present; French intellectuals; contemp literary theory; mass cult genres; French film. **SELECTED PUBLICATIONS** Auth, Rousseau's Legacy: Emergence and Eclipse of the Writer in France; Haunted Journeys; The Pursuit of Crime. **CONTACT ADDRESS** Dept of French and Italian Studies, Univ Massachusetts Amherst, Mass Ave, Amherst, MA, 01003. **EMAIL** dporter@frital.umass.edu

PORTER, J.I.
DISCIPLINE COMPARATIVE LITERATURE (GREEK, LATIN, GERMAN) **EDUCATION** Univ CA, Berkeley, PhD, 86. **CAREER** Asst and assoc prof, Dept of Classical Studies and Prog in Comparative Lit, Univ MI, 86-. **HONORS AND AWARDS** NEH, 89; fel, Stanford Humanities Center, 95, 96; Humboldt fel, 97, 98. **MEMBERSHIPS** APA. **RESEARCH** Cultural and literary history. **SELECTED PUBLICATIONS** Auth, Nietzsche and the Philosophy of the Future, Stanford, forthcoming; The Invention of Dionysus, Stanford, forthcoming; ed, Construction of the Classical Body, Univ MI press, 99; articles on Greek philos and poetics. **CONTACT ADDRESS** Dept of Classical Studies, Univ of Michigan, Ann Arbor, Ann Arbor, MI, 48109. **EMAIL** jport@umich.edu

PORTER, LAURENCE M.
PERSONAL Born 01/17/1936, Ossining, NY, m, 1993, 3 children **DISCIPLINE** FRENCH & COMPARATIVE LITERATURE **EDUCATION** Harvard Univ, AB, 57, AM, 59, PhD(French lit), 65. **CAREER** Instr French, 63-65, from asst prof to assoc prof, 65-73, Prof French & Comp Lit, Mich State Univ, 73-, Co-dir, Nat Colloquium 19th Century Fr Studies, 78; vis Andrew W Mellon disting prof comp lit, Univ Pittsburgh, 80. **MEMBERSHIPS** MLA; AAUP; Am Comp Lit Asn; Int Comp Lit Asn. **RESEARCH** Romanticism; French poetry; literature and psychology. **SELECTED PUBLICATIONS** Co-ed, Aging in Literature, Internation Book Publisher, 84; The Interpretation of Dreams; Freud's Theories Revisited, Twayne, 87; The Crisis of French Symbolism, Cornell, 90; co-ed, Approaches to teaching Flaubert's Madame Bovary, MLA, 95; Vitor Hugo, Twayne, 99; ed, Approaches to teaching Baudelaire's Fleurs du Mal, MLA, 99. **CONTACT ADDRESS** Dept of Romance & Class Lang, Michigan State Univ, 161 Old Horticulture, East Lansing, MI, 48824-1112. **EMAIL** porter@pilot.msu.edu

PORTER, MICHAEL
PERSONAL Born 02/26/1942, New Haven, CT **DISCIPLINE** COMPARATIVE & GERMAN LITERATURE **EDUCATION** Yale Univ, BA, 65; Cornell Univ, PhD(comp lit), 70. **CAREER** Lectr Ger, Rutgers Univ, 69-70, asst prof, 70-73; asst prof, Tulane Univ, 73-80. **MEMBERSHIPS** MLA; Am Comp Lit Asn; Hugo von Hofmannsthal Ges; Int Arthur Schnitzler Res Asn. **RESEARCH** Post-Romantic Lyric Poetry; Theory Of Literature; Modern German Literature. **SELECTED PUBLICATIONS** Auth, Hugo Von Hofmannsthal's Der Tor Und Der Tod: The Poet As Fool, Mod Austrian Lit, 72; Leitchsanleicht And Schwer In The Poetry Of Hugo Von Hofmannsthal, Monatshefte, 73; The Presence Of Whales, Western Amn Literature, Vol 31, 96; Religion In Australia - A History, Australian Hist Studies, Vol 27, 96. **CONTACT ADDRESS** 2035 Jenn, New Orleans, LA, 70115.

PORTUGES, CATHERINE
DISCIPLINE FRENCH LITERATURE **EDUCATION** UCLA Univ, PhD. **CAREER** Prof, Univ MA Amherst. **RESEARCH** French women writers; autobiog lit. **SELECTED PUBLICATIONS** Auth, Screen Memories: The Hungarian Cinema of Marta Meszaros. **CONTACT ADDRESS** Dept of French and Italian Studies, Univ Massachusetts Amherst, Mass Ave, Amherst, MA, 01003. **EMAIL** portuges@complit.umass.edu

POUWELS, JOEL
DISCIPLINE HISPANIC LITERATURE AND CULTURE **EDUCATION** Mich State Univ, PhD, 72. **CAREER** Prof, Univ Central Ark. **HONORS AND AWARDS** NEH grant. **MEMBERSHIPS** UCA's Latin Am Studies Comt. **RESEARCH** Contemporary Spanish American novel. **SELECTED PUBLICATIONS** Auth, Luis Spota Revisited, Revista de Estudio Hispanicos, 94; Mexican Presidential Futurology, Studies Latin Am Popul Cult, 97. **CONTACT ADDRESS** Univ Central Ark, 201 Donaghey Ave, Conway, AR, 72035-0001.

POWERS, JOHN H.
PERSONAL Born 10/07/1947, Valparaiso, IN, m, 1987, 1 child **DISCIPLINE** SPEECH COMMUNICATION THEORY **EDUCATION** Milligan Col, BA, 69; Univ Denver, MA, 74,

PhD, 77. **CAREER** Asst prof, TX A&M Univ, 77-83, assoc prof, 83-93; assoc prof, Hong Kong Baptist Univ, 93-. **MEMBERSHIPS** Nat Commun Asn; Int Commun Asn; World Commun Asn. **RESEARCH** Communication theory; language and commun; public/political commun. **SELECTED PUBLICATIONS** Auth, Public Speaking: The Lively Art, Harper Collins, 94; On the Intellectual Structure of the Human Communication Discipline, Communication Education, 44, 95; Conflict Genres and Management Strategies During China's Ten Years of Turmoil, Intercultural Commun Studies, 7, 97; ed with Randy Kluver, Civic Discourse, Civil Society and the Chinese World, Ablex, in press. **CONTACT ADDRESS** Comm Studies Dept, Hong Kong Baptist Univ, Kowloon, .. **EMAIL** JPowers@hkbu.edu.hk

PRATS, JORGE
PERSONAL Born 08/01/1932, Barcelona, Spain, m, 1961, 3 children **DISCIPLINE** SPANISH **EDUCATION** Univ Ill, BA, 60, MA, 62, PhD(Span), 68. **CAREER** Instr, 62-64, asst prof, 68-73, Assoc Prof Span, Knox Col, Ill, 73-,80, prof, 80-; Dir, Jr Year Abroad, Barcelona, Spain, 71-72, 77-79, 82-84, 87, 91-94, 96-99. **MEMBERSHIPS** MLA; Am Asn Teachers Span & Port; Am Coun Teaching Foreign Lang. **SELECTED PUBLICATIONS** Coauth, Contribucion a una bibliografia de dialectologia espanola y americana, 67 & auth, America poetica-JMG, 68, Real Acad Espanola. **CONTACT ADDRESS** Dept of Lang, Knox Col, 2 E South St, Galesburg, IL, 61401-4938. **EMAIL** 106101.573@compuserve.com

PRATT, L.
PERSONAL Born 11/24/1960, New York, NY, m, 1988, 1 child **DISCIPLINE** CLASSICAL STUDIES **EDUCATION** Williams Col, BA 82; Univ Michigan, AM 84, PhD 88. **CAREER** Bowdoin Col, vis asst prof, 88-89; Emory Univ, asst prof, assoc prof, 89 to 95-. **HONORS AND AWARDS** OBK **MEMBERSHIPS** APA; CA of Midwest and S; WCC; GCA; ACL. **RESEARCH** Ancient Greek and Roman Lang; Literature and Culture. **SELECTED PUBLICATIONS** Auth, Lying and Poetry for Homer to Pindar: Falsehood and Deception in Archaic Greek Poetics, Univ Mich Press, 93; auth, Odyssey: On the Interpretations of Dreams and Signs in Homer, Classical Philos, 94; auth, The Seal of Theognis Writing and the Oral Poetry, Amer Jour of Philos, 95. **CONTACT ADDRESS** Dept of Classics, Emory Univ, 404 D Callaway Cen North, Atlanta, GA, 30322. **EMAIL** lpratt@emory.edu

PRATT, MARY LOUISE
DISCIPLINE COMPARATIVE LITERATURE **EDUCATION** Univ Toronto, BA; Univ IL, MA; Stanford Univ, PhD. **CAREER** Dept Comp Lit, Stanford Univ **RESEARCH** Latin Am lit; cult theory; postcolonial theory. **SELECTED PUBLICATIONS** Auth, Toward a Speech Act Theory of Literary Discourse; Imperial Eyes: Travel Writing and Transculturation; coauth, Linguistics for Students of Literature and Women, Culture and Politics in Latin America. **CONTACT ADDRESS** Dept Comp Lit, Stanford Univ, Pigott Hall, Stanford, CA, 94305-2031.

PRECKSHOT, JUDITH
DISCIPLINE 20TH-CENTURY FRENCH POETRY, FEMINISM, AND FRANCOPHONE LITERATURE **EDUCATION** Univ Calif, Irvine, PhD. **CAREER** Instr, Univ Minn, Twin Cities. **RESEARCH** African women's autobiographies and novels. **SELECTED PUBLICATIONS** Published on the use of prose poetry (Ponge Michaux), the relation of the text to image (Breton, Apollinaire), and the role of the woman writer in Surrealism (Mansour). **CONTACT ADDRESS** Univ Minn, Twin Cities, Minneapolis, MN, 55455.

PREDMORE, MICHAEL P.
PERSONAL Born 02/05/1938, New Brunswick, NJ **DISCIPLINE** SPANISH LANGUAGE & LITERATURE **EDUCATION** Swarthmore Col, BA, 59; Univ Wis, MA, 61, PhD(Span), 65. **CAREER** From asst prof to assoc prof, 65-74, Prof Span, Univ Wash, 74-, Jr fel, Inst Res Humanities, Univ Wis, 68-69; Guggenheim Mem Found fel, 75-76; Coun Int Exchange Scholars grant, Spain, 82. **MEMBERSHIPS** Am Asn Teachers Span & Port; MLA. **RESEARCH** Nineteenth and 20th century Spanish peninsular literature; aesthetics. **SELECTED PUBLICATIONS** Auth, La Obra En Prosa De J R Jimenez, Gredos, 66; The Structure Of Platero Y Yo, PMLA, 70; A Stylistic Analysis Of Lo Fatal, Hisp Rev, 71; The Structure Of The Dario De Un Poeta Reciencasado, Contemp Lit, 72; La Poesia Hermetica De Juan Ramon Jimenez, Gredos, 73; Teoria De La Expresion Poetica And Twentieth Century Spanish Lyric Poetry, Mod Lang Notes, 74; Una Espana Joven En La Poesia De Antonio Machado, Insula, 81; Ed, Platero Y Yo, 6th Ed, Catedra, 82; Dario,Ruben, An Anthology Of Poetry, Hispanic Rev, Vol 64, 96. **CONTACT ADDRESS** Dept of Romance Lang, Univ of Wash, Seattle, WA, 98195.

PRELL, RIV-ELLEN
DISCIPLINE JEWISH STUDIES AND WOMEN'S STUDIES **EDUCATION** Univ Chicago, PhD. **CAREER** Assoc prof, Univ Minn, Twin Cities. **RESEARCH** Religion and ritual and ethnicity. **SELECTED PUBLICATIONS** Auth,

Prayer and Community: The Hauura in American Judaism; coed, Interpreting Women's Lives: Personal Narratives and Feminist Theory. **CONTACT ADDRESS** Univ Minn, Twin Cities, Minneapolis, MN, 55455. **EMAIL** prell001@maroon.tc.umn.edu

PRELOCK, PATRICIA A.
PERSONAL Born 05/31/1954, Youngstown, OH, m, 1976, 1 child **DISCIPLINE** SPEECH-LANGUAGE PATHOLOGY **EDUCATION** Kent State Univ, BS, 76, MA, 77; Univ of Pittsburgh, PhD, 83. **CAREER** Grad, res and teaching asst, Kent State Univ, 76-79; speech-lang pathologist, 76-79; instr, Univ of Pittsburgh, 81-82; transdisciplinary team mem/lang consult, Children's Hosp of Pittsburgh, 82-83; dir of clinical assessment and vpres of res & assessment serv, Transact Health Systems, Monroeville, Penn, 84-85; clinical supvr/researcher, Univ of Pittsburgh, 85-86; asst prof, Col of St Rose, 86-87; transdisciplinary team mem/lang consult, Cincinatti Ctr for Developmental Disorders, 88-90; adj, vis and res asst prof, Univ of Cincinnati, 88-94; assoc prof, Univ of Vermont, 94-. **HONORS AND AWARDS** Alpha Lambda Delta, Kent State Univ, 73; City of Akron Panhellic Scholar, 74; Who's Who in Cols and Univs, 74-76; Mortar Bd, Kent State Univ, 75; Pierce Mem Award for Speech, Kent State Univ, 75; Magna Cum Laude, Kent State Univ, 76; Doctoral Fel, Univ of Pittsburgh, 80-82; Delta Epsilon Sigma, Col of St Rose, 87; ASHA Award for Continuing Educ, 88, 94; Who's Who Among Human Service Professionals, 88-89; Nat Distinguished Serv Registry: Speech, Lang & Hearing, 90; SWOSHA Honors of the Asn, 94; Who's Who Among Educ Professionals, 94-96; Friends Award, Vermont Parent Infor Ctr, 98. **MEMBERSHIPS** Autism Soc of Am; Coun of Supvrs in Speech-Lang Pathology & Audiology; Vermont Asn for Supv & Curric Develop; Nat Asn for Supv & Curric Develop; Vermont Speech & Hearing Asn; Coun for Exceptional Children; Int Clinical Phonetics & Ling Asn; Am Speech, Lang and Hearing Asn. **RESEARCH** Child language, especially assessment and intervention; phonological intervention; efficacy of service delivery models; autism. **SELECTED PUBLICATIONS** Auth, A proactive approach for managing the language/learning needs of the communication-impaired preScher, in Clinics in Commun Disorders 3, 93; Communication Science Resource Manual, 94; Rethinking collaboration: A speech-language pathology perspective, in J of Educational and Psychological Consultation 6, 95; Assessment of young children: Making connections for families, in HEARSAY 10, 96; Language-based curriculum analysis: A collaborative assessment and intervention process, in J of Childhood Commun Disorders 19, 97; Where are associations going as the millennium approaches?, in ASHA Spec Interest Div 1 Lang, Learning & Educ Newsletter 5, 98; coauth, Metapragmatic awareness of explanation adequacy: Developing skills for academic success from a collaborative communications skills unit, in Lang, Speech, Hearing Servs in Schs 25, 94; Teacher Perceptions of Communication-Impaired Students, in Lang, Speech, Hearing Servs in Schs 25, 94; Collaboration in supervision: The First Year, in J of Childhood Commun Disorders 16, 95; Language regression in children with autism, in J of Autism 25, 95; Effects of collaboration on language performance, in J of Childhood Commun Disorders 17, 95; Collaborative partnerships in a language in the classroom program, in Lang, Speech, Hearing Servs in Schs 26, 95; Prosodic analysis of child speech, in Topics in Lang Disorders 17, 97; Foreword, in Topics in Lang Disorders 17, 97; Maintenance of Metapragmatic Awareness of Explanation Adequacy Six Months Following Intervention, in Lang, Speech Hearing Servs in Schs 28, 97; rev, Communication skills in children with Down syndrome: A book review, in Down Syndrome Quart 2, 97; ed, Special Interest Division 1 Newsletter, Language Learning & Education, 96, 97, 98; coed, Topics in Language Disorders, 97; Language, Speech, Hearing Services in Schs, 98-01. **CONTACT ADDRESS** Dept of Communication Sciences, Univ of Vermont, 489 Main St, 407 Pomeroy Hall, Burlington, VT, 05405-0024. **EMAIL** pprelock@zoo.uvm.edu

PRESBERG, CHARLES D.
PERSONAL Born 05/03/1956, Evanston, IL, m, 1992, 3 children **DISCIPLINE** ROMANTIC LANGUAGES **EDUCATION** Harvard Univ, PhD, 94. **CAREER** Asst prof, Univ S Calif, 92-95; asst prof, Univ Mo Columbia, 95-. **RESEARCH** Cervantes Spanish literature of renaissance & baroque periods. **SELECTED PUBLICATIONS** Auth, Deliverance in the Prison-House: Paradoxes of Self, Culture and Language in the Writings of Quevedo, Hispania, 95; auth, This is Not a Prologue: Paradoxes of Historical and Poetic Discourse in the Prologue to Don Quixote, 95; auth, Precious Exchanges: The Poetics of Desire, Power and Reciprocity in Cervantes' La gitanilla, Cervantes, 98; auth, Transfiguring Form: The Poetics of Self, Contradiction and Silence in San Juan de la Cruz, Laberinto, 98; auth, Making a Liar of Truth: The 'Play' of Society, Fiction and Deceit in Cervantes, El viejo celoso, Revista de Estudios Hispanicos, 99. **CONTACT ADDRESS** Dept of Romance Languages, Univ Mo, 143 Arts & Science, Columbia, MO, 65211.

PREUSS, MARY
PERSONAL PA, m **DISCIPLINE** FOREIGN LANGUAGES **EDUCATION** Univ Pittsburgh, PhD, MED, BA **CAREER** Assoc Prof, 89-, PA St Univ at mcKeesport; Assoc Prof, 81-89, Geneva Col; Lect, 79-81, Carlow Col; Lect, 78-80 Chatham Col

HONORS AND AWARDS Acad Exc Awd; Scholar of the yr awd, Pres, LAILA/ALILA **MEMBERSHIPS** AATSP; LAILA/ALILA; MLA **RESEARCH** Mayan lit **SELECTED PUBLICATIONS** Ed, Beyond Indigenous voices, Lancaster, CA: Labyrinthos, 96; Messages and Meanings, Lancaster, CA: Labyrinthos, 97 **CONTACT ADDRESS** Pittsburgh, PA, 15229-1058. **EMAIL** mhp1@psu.edu

PRIBIC, RADO
PERSONAL Born 02/04/1947, Dorfen, Germany **DISCIPLINE** INTERNATIONAL AFFAIRS, GERMAN & RUSSIAN LITERATURES & SOCIETIES **EDUCATION** Fla State Univ, BA, 68; Vanderbilt Univ, MA, 70, PhD(Ger), 72. **CAREER** Teacher Ger, Russ, Latin & World Lit, Webb Sch, Bell Buckle, Tenn, 69-71; prof Foreign Lang & Lit; chmn Int Affairs Prog, Lafayette Col, 71-. **HONORS AND AWARDS** Linback, Jones, Morgan's Teaching Awards; Fulbright; NEH. **MEMBERSHIPS** Am Asn Teachers Ger; SAtlantic Mod Lang Asn; MLA; Int Dostoevsky Soc; Southern Comp Lit Asn. **RESEARCH** Germano-Slavic literary relations; South German regional literature; 19th century European literature. **SELECTED PUBLICATIONS** Auth, Bonaventura's Nachtwachen and Dostoevsky's Notes From the Underground: A Comparison in Nihilism, Otto Sagner, Munich, 74; Alienation in Nachtwachen by Bonaventura and Dostoevskij's Notes From the Underground, Germano-Slavica, 75; America's image in Mayakovski and Essenin, Sci Technol & Humanities, 78; Keyserling's Schwule Tage and Turgenev's First Love, In: Festschrift for Andre von Gronicka, 78; The Importance of German for the Science Student, Die Unterrisfts Praxis, 80; Young people's literature in the Federal Republic of Germany Today, J Reading, 81; The German Public and the Persecution of Jews, 1933-1945, No One Participated, No One Knew It, ed Jorg Wollenber, ed, trans Rado Pribic, Atlantic Highlands, NJ, Humanities Press, 96; Die Carpetbaggers in den Neuen Bundeslandern, In Schreiben im heutigen Deutschland, Die literarische Szene nach der Wende, ed Ursula E Beitter, New York, Peter Lang Publishing, 97. **CONTACT ADDRESS** Dept of Languages, Lafayette Col, Easton, PA, 18042-1798. **EMAIL** pribicr@lafayette.edu

PRIDEAUX, GARY DEAN
PERSONAL Born 04/21/1939, Muskogee, OK, m, 1963 **DISCIPLINE** LINGUISTICS **EDUCATION** Rice Univ, BA, 61; Univ Tex, PhD(ling), 66. **CAREER** Asst prof, 66-71, Assoc Prof Ling, Univ Alta, 71-, Chmn Dept, 75-, Fulbright-Hays exchange grant, Japan, 67-68; co-ed, Can J Ling; Experimental Ling, 76. **MEMBERSHIPS** Ling Soc Am; Can Ling Asn. **RESEARCH** Psycholinguistics; linguistic theory, syntax and semantics. **SELECTED PUBLICATIONS** Auth, The Syntax Of Japanese Honorifics, Mouton, The Hague, 70; On The Notion Linguistically Significant Gerneralization, Lingua, 71; Coauth, Grammatical Properties Of Sentences As A Basis For Concept Formation, J Psycholing Res, 73; Auth, A Functional Analysis Of English Questions, J Child Lang, 76; Lexical Restructuring Is Rule Addition, In: Festschrift W P Lehmann, 77; Les Types De Contraintes Sur Les Descriptions Grammaticales, Psycholing Experimentale Et Theorique, 77; Co-Ed, Experimental Linguistics, Scientia; Rethinking Context--Language As An Interactive Phenomenon, Canadian J Of Linguistics-Revue Canadienne De Linguistique, Vol 39, 94; Understanding Utterances--An Introduction To Pragmatics, Word-J Of The Int Linguistic Asn, Vol 46, 95; Markedness As A Discourse Management Device, The Role Of Alternative Adverbial Clause Orders, Word-J Of The Int Linguistic Association, Vol 44, 93. **CONTACT ADDRESS** Dept of Ling, Univ of Alta, Edmonton, AB, T6G 2H1.

PRIEVE, BETH A.
DISCIPLINE COMMUNICATION SCIENCES AND DISORDERS **EDUCATION** Univ OH, PhD, 89. **CAREER** Asst prof CCC-A, Syracuse Univ. **RESEARCH** Physiological auditory functions and their clinical applications; evoked otoacoustic emissions, electrocochleography and auditory brainstem responses; diagnostic audiology; identification of hearing loss in infants and children. **SELECTED PUBLICATIONS** Auth, COAEs and SSOAEs in Adults with Increased Age, Ear and Hearing, 95;. Otoacoustic Emissions in Infants and Children: Basic Characteristics and Clinical Applications, Sem Hearing, 92; coauth, Analysis of Transient-evoked Otoacoustic Emissions in Normal-hearing and Hearing-impaired Ears, Jour Acoustical Soc Am, 93. **CONTACT ADDRESS** Syracuse Univ, Syracuse, NY, 13244.

PRINCE, GERALD
PERSONAL Born 11/07/1942, Alexandria, Egypt, m, 1967 **DISCIPLINE** ROMANCE LANGUAGES **EDUCATION** Brooklyn Col, BA (magna cum laude), 63; Univ of Fla, MA, 63; Brown Univ, PhD, 68. **CAREER** Vis prof, Trent Univ, 95; vist prof, Emory Univ, 90; vis prof, Johns Hopkins Univ, 86, vis prof, Univ of Alberta at Edmonton, 86, vis prof Univ of Queensland, 83; INSTR, 67-68, PROF OF ROMANCE LANG, 81-, LOIS & JERRY MAGNIN FAMILY TERM PROF, UNIV OF PA, 93-98. **HONORS AND AWARDS** Phi Beta Kappa, 63; Lindback Awd for Excellence in Tchg, 74; Awd of Honor, Brooklyn Col, 78. **MEMBERSHIPS** AATF; ACLA; AAUP; MLA. **RESEARCH** Narrative theory; modern French Lit; Twentieth-Century French fiction. **SELECTED PUBLICA-**

TIONS Auth, Metaphysique et technique dans l'oeuvre romaneque de Sartre, 68; A Grammer of Stories, 73; Narratology: The Form and Functioning of Narrative, 82; A Dictionary of Narratology, 87; Narrative as Theme: Studies in French Fiction, 92. **CONTACT ADDRESS** Univ of Pennsylvania, 521 Williams Hall, Philadelphia, PA, 19104-6305. **EMAIL** gerry@babel.ling.upen.edu

PRITCHETT, KAY
PERSONAL Born 09/10/1946, Greenville, MS, m, 1988 **DISCIPLINE** SPANISH **EDUCATION** Univ NC, PhD, 79. **CAREER** Prof of Spanish, Univ Arkansas, 82-; Fulbright-Hays fel. **RESEARCH** Contemporary poetry and fiction; Psychoanalytic theory; Feminism; Spanish literature of 20th Century. **SELECTED PUBLICATIONS** Auth Four Postmodern Poets of Spain: A Critical Study with Translations of the Poems, 91; transl Jonah and the Pink Whale, 91; In the Land of Silence, 94. **CONTACT ADDRESS** 523 N Willow Ave, Fayetteville, AR, 72701. **EMAIL** pritche@comp.vark.edu

PROFIT, VERA BARBARA
DISCIPLINE FRENCH & GERMAN LITERATURE **EDUCATION** Alverno Col, BA, 67; Univ Rochester, MA, 69, PhD(comp lit), 74. **CAREER** Instr Ger, St Olaf Col, 74-75; asst prof, 75-81, assoc prof, German & comp lit, 81-96, prof Ger & comp lit, Univ Notre Dame, 96-; vis scholar, Harvard Univ, 79-80; vis scholar, Northwestern Univ, 84. **HONORS AND AWARDS** NDEA Title IV fel. **MEMBERSHIPS** MLA; Am Asn Teachers Ger. **RESEARCH** Poetry and novel of the German-speaking countries, written after 1945; 20th century French and German prose and poetry. **SELECTED PUBLICATIONS** Auth, Interpretations of Iwan Goll's Late Poetry with a Comprehensive and Annotated Bibliography of the Writings by and about Iwan Goll, Peter Lang, Bern, Switz, 77; Ein Portrat meiner Selbst: Karl Krolow's Autobiographical Poems (1945-1958) and Their French Sources, Peter Lang, Bern, Switz, 91; Menschlich: Gesprache mit Karl Krolow, Peter Lang, Bern Switz, 96. **CONTACT ADDRESS** Dept Ger, Russian Lang & Lit, Univ Notre Dame, 318 Oshaugnessy Hall, Notre Dame, IN, 46556. **EMAIL** Vera.B.Profit.1@nd.edu

PUCCI, JOSEPH M.
PERSONAL Born 09/25/1957, Cleveland, OH, m, 1982, 1 child **DISCIPLINE** COMPARATIVE LITERATURE **EDUCATION** John Carroll Univ, BA, 79; Univ Chicago, MA, 82, PhD, 87. **CAREER** Asst Prof, Assoc Prof, 89 to 97-, Brown Univ; Asst Prof 87-89, Univ Kentucky. **HONORS AND AWARDS** Dist Teach Awd; Dist Adv Awd. **MEMBERSHIPS** APA; MLA; MLANA. **RESEARCH** Later and Medieval Latin, language and literature. **SELECTED PUBLICATIONS** Auth, Medieval Latin, 2nd edition, U of Chicago Press, 97; Full Knowing Reader: Allusion and the Power of the Reader in the Western Lit Tradition, Yale, 98. **CONTACT ADDRESS** Dept Classics, Brown Univ, Box 1856, Providence, RI, 02912. **EMAIL** joseph_pucci@brown.edu

PUGH, ANTHONY ROY
PERSONAL Born 08/16/1931, Liverpool, England, m, 1962, 3 children **DISCIPLINE** FRENCH LITERATURE **EDUCATION** Cambridge Univ, BA, 53, MA, 56, PhD(French), 59. **CAREER** Asst lectr French, King's Col, Univ London, 56-59; lectr, Queen's Univ Belfast, 59-69; chmn dept Romance lang, 73-75, Prof French, Univ NB, Fredericton, 69-, Vis prof, Univ NB, 68. **MEMBERSHIPS** MLA. **RESEARCH** Balzac; Pascal; form and meaning in French literature. **SELECTED PUBLICATIONS** Auth, Le Mariage De Figaro, Macmillan, 68; The Genesis Of Cesar Birotteau, Fr Studies, 1/68; The Unity Of Theophile's La Solitude, Fr Rev, Fall 71; Coed, Studies In Balzac And Nineteenth Century, Leicester Univ, 72; Balzac's Recurring Characters, Univ Toronto, 74; Butor On Beethoven, Int Fiction Rev, 76; The Autonomy Of Belzac's Une Fille d'Eve, Romance Rev, 78; The Ambiguity Of Cesar Birotteau, 19th Century Fr Studies, 80; The Art Of Persuasion In The 'Pensees' Of Pascal, French Rev, Vol 67, 94; From Pascal To Voltaire--The Role Of Pascal 'Pensees' In The Hist Of Ideas Between 1670 And 1734, French Rev, Vol 66, 93. **CONTACT ADDRESS** Dept of Fr, Univ of NB, Fredericton, NB, E3B 5A3.

PUGLIESE, OLGA
PERSONAL Toronto, ON, Canada **DISCIPLINE** ITALIAN STUDIES **EDUCATION** Univ Toronto, BA, 63, MA, 64, PhD, 69. **CAREER** Fac mem to PROF ITALIAN STUDS, UNIV TORONTO, 67-, fel, Victoria Col, 78-. **MEMBERSHIPS** Can Soc Renaissance Studs; Renaissance Soc Am; Can Soc Ital Studs; Am Asn Tchrs Ital. **SELECTED PUBLICATIONS** Auth, Il discoro labirintico del dialogo rinascimentale, 95; ed/transl, Lorenzo Valla, The Profession of the Religious and Selections from the Donation of Constantine, 85; ed/transl, Lorenzo Valla, La falsa donazione di Constantino, 94. **CONTACT ADDRESS** Dept of Italian Studies, Univ Toronto, Toronto, ON, M5S 1A1. **EMAIL** pugliese@chass.utoronto.ca

PULLEYBLANK, EDWIN GEORGE
PERSONAL Born 08/07/1922, Calgary, AB, Canada, m, 3 children **DISCIPLINE** CHINESE LANGUAGE & HISTORY **EDUCATION** Univ Alta, BA, 42; Univ London, PhD(Chinese), 51; Cambridge Univ, MA, 53. **CAREER** Lectr class Chinese, Univ London, 48-52, lectr Chinese hist, 52-53; prof Chinese, Cambridge Univ, 53-66; head dept Asian studies, 68-75, Prof Chinese, Univ BC, 66-, Fel, Downing Col, Cambridge Univ, 55-66. **MEMBERSHIPS** Asn Asian Studies; Am Orient Soc; Ling Soc Am; Can Soc Asian Studies (pres, 71-74); fel Royal Soc Can. **RESEARCH** Chinese history; historical phonology and grammar of classical Chinese. **SELECTED PUBLICATIONS** Auth, The Old-Chinese Origin Of Type-A And Type-B Syllables, J Of Chinese Linguistics, Vol 22, 94; Old-Chinese Phonology--A Rev Article, J Of Chinese Linguistics, Vol 21, 93; Old-Chinese Phonology--A Rev Article, J Of Chinese Linguistics, Vol 21, 93; The Old-Chinese Origin Of Type-A And Type-B Syllables, J Of Chinese Linguistics, Vol 22, 94; Old Chinese Phonology--Reply To William Baxter, J Of Chinese Linguistics, Vol 22, 94; Prosody Or Pharyngealization In Old Chinese--The Origin Of The Distinction Between Type-A And Type-B Syllables, J Of The Am Oriental Society, Vol 116, 96; How Do We Reconstruct Old Chinese, J Of The Am Oriental Society, Vol 112, 92; The Cambridge Hist Of China, Vol 6, Alien Regimes And Border States, 907-1368, Int Hist Rev, Vol 18, 96. **CONTACT ADDRESS** Dept of Asian Studies, Univ of BC, Vancouver, BC, V6T 1W5.

PULLUM, GEOFFREY K.
DISCIPLINE GENERAL LINGUISTIC THEORY AND THE SYNTAX OF ENGLISH **EDUCATION** Univ York, BA; Univ London, PhD, 76. **CAREER** PROF, LING, UNIV CALIF, SANTA CRUZ. **RESEARCH** Interface between syntax and phonology, phonetics, and philosophy of linguistics. **SELECTED PUBLICATIONS** Auth, English Nominal Gerund Phrases as Noun Phrases with Verb Phrase Heads, Ling, 91; "The Origins of the Cyclic Principle," CLS 28, vol 2: Papers from the Parasession on the Cycle, Ling Theory; co-auth, "Condition Duplication, Paradigm Homonymy, and Transconstructional Constraints," Proc of the Seventeenth Annual Meeting of the Berkeley Ling Soc, 91; A Theory of Command Relations, Ling and Philos, 90; The X-bar Theory of Phrase Structure, Lang, 90. **CONTACT ADDRESS** Dept of Ling, Univ Calif, 1156 High St, Santa Cruz, CA, 95064.

PURCELL, JOHN MARSHALL
PERSONAL Born 11/25/1932, Pittsburgh, PA **DISCIPLINE** FOREIGN LANGUAGE EDUCATION, SPANISH **EDUCATION** Univ Cincinnati, BA, 54, BEd, 55; Middlebury Col, MA, 62; Ohio State Univ, PhD(foreign lang educ), 69. **CAREER** Teacher Span & chmn dept, Hughes High Sch, Cincinnati, Ohio, 59-62 & Aiken Sr High Sch, Cincinnati, Ohio, 62-70; asst prof, 70-73, Assoc Prof Span & Foreign Lang Educ, Cleveland State Univ, 73-, Consult, NDEA title III workships, Ohio, 68-70 & Cleveland Pub Schs Biling-Bicult Prog, 75-79. **MEMBERSHIPS** Am Asn Teachers Span & Port; Am Coun Teaching Foreign Lang; Cent States Conf Foreign Lang Teaching. **RESEARCH** Foreign language methodology. **SELECTED PUBLICATIONS** Auth, A Liberal Education In The United States, J Gen Educ, 71; How To Help Your Student Teacher, 10/72 & Teaching The Short Story, Winter 74, Am Foreign Lang Teacher; Simulation And Success In Business Spanish, Accent Am Coun Teaching Foreign Lang, 1/75; Co-Ed, Personalizing Foreign Language Instruction, Nat Txtbk Co, 77; Auth, Teaching Novels And Plays, In: Filling And Fulfilling The Advanced Foreign Language Class & Co-Ed, Filling And Fulfilling The Advanced Foreign Language Class, 81, Heinle & Heinle; Auth, The Preparation Of Modern Language Teachers In Latin America, The Modern Lang J, 81; Livelier Fles-Asterisk Lessons Through Role-Play + In The Primary And Middle School Spanish-Language Classroom, Hispania-A J Devoted To The Teaching Of Spanish And Portuguese, Vol 76, 93. **CONTACT ADDRESS** Dept of Mod Lang, Cleveland State Univ, Euclid Ave at 24th st, Cleveland, OH, 44115.

PURCZINSKY, JULIUS O.
PERSONAL Born 01/06/1925, Levi, TX **DISCIPLINE** MEDIEVAL PHILOLOGY, STRUCTURAL LINGUISTICS **EDUCATION** Baylor Univ, BA, 49; Univ Tex, Austin, MA, 53, PhD, 57. **CAREER** Asst prof Span, Baylor Univ, 57-58; Fulbright lectr English, Nat Univ Athens, 58-59; assoc prof Ger, French & Span, Univ Southwestern La, 59-61; asst prof Span, Kans State Univ, 61-63; assoc prof Span & French, Univ Nev, 63-65; asst prof, 65-72, Assoc Prof Romance Ling, Hunter Col, 72- **MEMBERSHIPS** Int Ling Asn; Mediaeval Acad Am. **SELECTED PUBLICATIONS** Auth, Additional Frankish superstratum in Old French, 64 & Germanic influence in the Sainte Eulalie, 65, Romance Philol; auth, A Neo-Schushardtian Theory of General Romance Diphthongization, 70. **CONTACT ADDRESS** Dept of Romance Lang, Hunter Col, CUNY, 695 Park Ave, New York, NY, 10021-5085.

PURDY, ANTHONY
DISCIPLINE FRENCH LITERATURE **EDUCATION** Cambridge Univ, BA; Western Univ, MA; Queen's Univ, PhD. **RESEARCH** Collecting; cultural memory; literature and modernity; narrative theory; interarts; migration of concepts across disciplines. **SELECTED PUBLICATIONS** Auth, A Certain Difficulty of Being: Essays on the Quebec Novel, McGill-Queen's, 90; co-auth, Peter Greenaway: Architecture and Allegory, Acad, 97; ed, Writing Quebec, Alberta, 88; Problems of Literary Reception, Alberta, 88; Prefaces and Literary Manifestoes, Alberta, 90; Literature and the Body, Rodopi, 92; Literature and Money, Rodopi, 93; Literature and Science, Rodopi, 94. **CONTACT ADDRESS** Dept of French, Western Ontario Univ, London, ON, N6A 5B8.

Q

QIAN, NANXIU
DISCIPLINE LINGUISTICS, CHINESE LITERATURE **EDUCATION** Nanjing Univ, China, MA, 82; Yale Univ, PhD, 94. **CAREER** Instr, Nanjing Univ, China; instr, Univ MN, 92-93; asst prof, Rice Univ, 93-. **MEMBERSHIPS** Asn for Asian Stud; Am Orient Soc. **RESEARCH** The Shih-shuo hsin-yu in the Chinese literary tradition. **SELECTED PUBLICATIONS** Ed, A Guide to Chinese Culture; transl, A Selected Translation of the Shih-shuo hsin-yu, with Annotations and An Introduction. **CONTACT ADDRESS** Rice Univ, PO Box 1892, Houston, TX, 77251-1892. **EMAIL** nanxiuq@owlnet.rice.edu

QUACKENBUSH, LOUIS HOWARD
PERSONAL Born 11/28/1939, Bellingham, WA, m, 1963, 7 children **DISCIPLINE** LATIN AMERICAN LITERATURE **EDUCATION** Brigham Young Univ, BA, 65, MA, 67; Univ Ill, Urbana, PhD(Span), 70. **CAREER** Teacher, teacher suprv & counr Span lang training, Lang Training Mission, 63-67, Assoc Prof Span, Brigham Young Univ, 70 **MEMBERSHIPS** MLA; Rocky Mountain Mod Lang Asn; Am Asn Teachers Span & Port. **RESEARCH** Spanish American drama; Brazilian drama; Spanish American poetry. **SELECTED PUBLICATIONS** Auth, The Other Pastorelas Of Spanish American Drama, Latin Am Theatre Rev, Spring 73; The Auto In Contemporary Mexican Drama, Ky Romance Quart, 74; Theatre Of The Absurd, Reality And Carlos Maggi, J Span Studies: 20th Century, Spring 75; La Desavenencia Religiosa: Una Clave A El Tuerto Es Rey De Carlos Fuentes, Explicacion De Textos Literarios, 75/76; The Contemporary Latin American Short Story, 79; The Legacy Of Albee's Who's Afraid Of Virginia Woolf? In The Spanish American Absurdist Theatre, Spring 79 & Pablo Nervda: Sus Versos Finales Y Ultimos Comienzos, Summer 80, Revista/Rev Interamericana; Pugilism As Mirror And Metafiction In Life And In Contemporary Spanish-American Drama, Latin American Theatre Rev, Vol 26, 92; Reality Behind Reality, The Numinous In Gonzalo Rojas, Chasqui-Revista De Literatura Latinoamericana, Vol 22, 93. **CONTACT ADDRESS** Dept of Span, Brigham Young Univ, Provo, UT, 84601.

QUALLS, BARRY V.
DISCIPLINE ENGLISH LANGUAGE AND LITERATURE **EDUCATION** Fla State Univ, BA; Northwestern Univ, MA; PhD. **CAREER** Assoc Dean Hum. **RESEARCH** Victorian literature; Biblical literature; poetry. **SELECTED PUBLICATIONS** Auth, The Secular Pilgrims of Victorian Fiction: the Novel as Book of Life. **CONTACT ADDRESS** Dept of English, Rutgers Univ, 510 George St, Murray Hall, New Brunswick, NJ, 08901-1167.

QUINSEY, KATHERINE M.
DISCIPLINE ENGLISH LANGUAGE; LITERATURE **EDUCATION** Trent, BA; London, PhD, 89. **CAREER** Assoc prof **HONORS AND AWARDS** SSHRCC grant, 93-96. **RESEARCH** Pope, Dryden, print culture; seventeenth-century and Restoration rhetoric and linguistic philosophy; feminism 1600-1800. **SELECTED PUBLICATIONS** Ed, Broken Boundaries: Women and Feminism in Restoration Drama, 96. **CONTACT ADDRESS** Dept of English Language and Literature, Univ of Windsor, 401 Sunset Ave, Windsor, ON, N9B 3P4. **EMAIL** kateq4@uwindsor.ca

QUINTERO, RUBEN
PERSONAL Born 05/05/1949, Montebello, CA, m, 1973, 4 children **DISCIPLINE** ENGLISH; AMERICAN LITERATURE; LANGUAGE **EDUCATION** CSULA, BA, 78, 80; Harvard Univ, AM, 83, PhD, 88. **CAREER** ASSOC PROF, CSULA; Phi Kappa Phi. **HONORS AND AWARDS** Univ DE Press Manuscript Award 18th Century Studies, 90. **MEMBERSHIPS** ASECS; ASLSC; Int Soc Hist Rhet **RESEARCH** Restoration and eighteenth-century British literature. **SELECTED PUBLICATIONS** Literate Culture: Pope's Rhetorical Art, 82. **CONTACT ADDRESS** Dept of English, California State Univ, Los Angeles, 5151 State Univ Dr, Los Angeles, CA, 90032-8110. **EMAIL** rquint@calstatela.edu

QUIRK, RONALD JOSEPH
PERSONAL Born 03/22/1942, Bristol, CT, m, 1967, 4 children **DISCIPLINE** SPANISH LANGUAGE & LITERATURE **EDUCATION** Trinity Col, BA, 64; Brown Univ, MA, 66, PhD(Span), 71. **CAREER** Instr Span, RI Col, 68-69; from instr to asst prof, Trinity Col, 69-72; asst prof, 72-74, assoc prof, 74-80, prof Span, Quinnipiac Col, 80-. **MEMBERSHIPS** Am Asn Teachers Span & Port; Northeast Mod Lang Asn. **RESEARCH** Nineteenth century Spanish literature; linguistics and literature of Puerto Rico. **SELECTED PUBLICATIONS** Auth, Glosario Borinqueno, Trinity Col, 70; On the extent and origin of

questions in the formque tu tienes?, Hispania, 5/72; The authorship of La gruta azul: Juan Valera or Serafin Estebanez Calderon, Romance Notes, spring 74; El problema del habla regional en Los Pazos de Ulloa, Inti, 10/75; Nueve cartas de Estebanez Calderon, Rev de Archivos, Bibliot y Museos, 1-3/76; Temporal adverbs in Puerto Rican Spanish, Hispania, 5/76; The Cebre Cycle: Emilia Pardo Bazan and Galician reform, Am Hispanist, 5/77; Basic Spanish for Legal Personnel, Collegium Bks, 79; Serafin Estebanez Calderon: Bajo la Corteza de su Obra, Peter Lang Pub, 92; Literature as Introspection: Spain Confronts Trafalgar, Peter Lang Pub, 98. **CONTACT ADDRESS** Dept of Mod Foreign Lang, Quinnipiac Col, 275 Mt Carmel Ave, Hamden, CT, 06518-1908. **EMAIL** quirk@quinnipiac.edu

R

RABASSA, GREGORY
PERSONAL Born 03/09/1922, Yonkers, NY, m, 1966, 2 children **DISCIPLINE** SPANISH; PORTUGUESE **EDUCATION** Dartmouth Col, AB, 45; Columbia Univ, MA, 47, PhD(Port), 54. **CAREER** Instr Span, columbia Univ, 47-52, assoc, 52-58, asst prof, 58-63, assoc prof Span & Port, 63-68; Prof Romance Lang, DISTINGUISHED PROF, QUEENS COL, NY, 68-, Assoc ed, Odyssey Rev, 61-64, Fulbright-Hays fel, Brazil, 65-66; Nat Endowment for Humanities fel, 79-80. **HONORS AND AWARDS** Nat Bk Award for transl, 67; Transl Prize, Pen Am Ctr, 77; Am Transl Asn Gode Medal, 80; PEN Transl Medal, 82., LittD, Dartmouth Col, 82. **MEMBERSHIPS** Renaissance Soc Am; MLA; Am Asn Teachers Span & Port; Latin Am Studies Asn; PEN Club. **RESEARCH** Brazilian literature; Spanish American literature; modern Spanish literature. **SELECTED PUBLICATIONS** Auth, O Negro na ficcao Brasileira, Tempo Brasileiro Rio, 65; The Negro in Brazilian literature, African Forum, spring 67; If this be treason: Translation, Am Scholar, winter 74/75. **CONTACT ADDRESS** 140 East 72 St, Apt 10B, New York, NY, 10021.

RABBITT, KARA
DISCIPLINE FRENCH LITERATURE AND LINGUISTICS **EDUCATION** Cornell Univ, PhD, 96. **CAREER** Asst prof. **RESEARCH** 19th-century French literature and contemporary Francophone literature. **SELECTED PUBLICATIONS** Publ on the works of, Charles Baudelaire, Aime Cesaire, CLR. James, Arthur Rimbaud, Stendhal & Quebecois and Caribbean artistic movements. **CONTACT ADDRESS** Dept of Language and Cultures, William Paterson Col, 300 Pompton Rd., Wayne, NJ, 07470.

RABINE, LESLIE W.
DISCIPLINE FRENCH LANGUAGE **EDUCATION** Stanford Univ, PhD. **CAREER** PROF, FR, UNIV CALIF, IRVINE. **SELECTED PUBLICATIONS** Auth, Reading the Romantic Heroine: Text, History, Ideology; Rebel Daughters: Women and the French Revolution; Dominion, Socialism, and French Romanticism. **CONTACT ADDRESS** Dept of Fr and Ital, Univ Calif, Irvine, CA, 92697.

RABINOWITZ, PETER JACOB
PERSONAL Born 02/18/1944, Brooklyn, NY, m, 2 children **DISCIPLINE** COMPARATIVE LITERATURE **EDUCATION** Univ Chicago, BA, 65, MA, 67, PhD(comp lit), 72. **CAREER** Asst prof humanities, City Col Chicago, 68-74; asst prof lit, Kirkland Col, 74-78; asst prof comp lit, 78-81, assoc prof Comp Lit, Hamilton Col, 81-, Chm, 79-84, 86-87, 94-98, Panelist, Music Prog, NY State Coun on Arts, 82-85; Fanfare, contrib ed, 89-; co-ed, Series on Theory and Interpretation of Narrative, Ohio State Univ Press, 91-; Narrative, Advisory Editor, 92-; ACLA Advisory Board, 93-97; PMLA Editorial Board, 93-95. **MEMBERSHIPS** MLA; Am Comp Lit Asn; Asn Recorded Sound Collections. **RESEARCH** Literary theory; literature and music. **SELECTED PUBLICATIONS** Auth, Before Reading: Narrative Conventions and the Politics of Interpretation, Cornell Univ Press, 87, reprint, Ohio State Univ Press, 98; co-ed, Understanding Narrative, Ohio State Univ Press, 94; coauth, Authorizing Readers: Resistance and Respect in the Teaching of Literature, Teachers Col Press, 98; author of numerous articles in PMLA, Critical Inquiry, 19th Century Music, Modern Philology, and other journals. **CONTACT ADDRESS** Dept of Comp Lit, Hamilton Col, 198 College Hill Rd., Clinton, NY, 13323-1292.

RAGSDALE, J. DONALD
DISCIPLINE COMMUNICATION THEORY, INTERPERSONAL COMMUNICATION, FILM **EDUCATION** Samford Univ, BA, 61; Univ Ill, MA, PhD. **CAREER** Prof, La State Univ. **MEMBERSHIPS** Pres, Southern States Commun Asn. **RESEARCH** Marital communication. **SELECTED PUBLICATIONS** Author of numerous scholarly articles and book chapters in communication theory, interpersonal communication, film, and marital communication. **CONTACT ADDRESS** Dept of Speech Commun, Louisiana State Univ, Baton Rouge, LA, 70803.

RAINER, ULRIKE
DISCIPLINE GERMAN LANGUAGE **EDUCATION** Harvard Univ, PhD, 85. **CAREER** Assoc prof, Darmouth Col. **RESEARCH** Age of Goethe to the 20th century, centering on poetry and narrative fiction and the interrelation of lit and film. **SELECTED PUBLICATIONS** Auth, publ studies on Fontane, Elfriede Jelinek, Christine Lavant, Schiller, and Trakl. **CONTACT ADDRESS** Dartmouth Col, 3529 N Main St, #207, Hanover, NH, 03755.

RAJAGOPAL, ARVIND
DISCIPLINE CULTURAL STUDIES, MASS MEDIA, POSTCOLONIAL STUDIES **EDUCATION** UCLA, Berkeley, PhD, 92. **CAREER** Asst prof, Purdue Univ. **SELECTED PUBLICATIONS** Auth, And the Poor Get Gassed: Multinational-aided Development and the State: The Case of Bhopal, 87; The Rise of National Programming: The Case of Indian Television, Media, Cult, and Soc, 93; coauth, Mapping Hegemony: Television News and Industrial Conflict, Ablex, 91. **CONTACT ADDRESS** Dept of Commun, Purdue Univ, 1080 Schleman Hall, West Lafayette, IN, 47907-1080. **EMAIL** arvind@purdue.edu

RAMBALDO, ANA M.
PERSONAL Galvez, Argentina **DISCIPLINE** SPANISH, SPANISH COMMUNITY RELATIONS **EDUCATION** Southern Methodist Univ, BA, 50; NY Univ, MA, 67, PhD(Span), 71. **CAREER** Asst prof, 67-80, prof Span, Montclair State Col, 80-; retired, 98. **MEMBERSHIPS** MLA. **RESEARCH** Spanish medieval theater; Renaissance. **SELECTED PUBLICATIONS** Auth, El Cancionero de Juan del Encina Dentro de so Ambito Historico y Literario, Castellvi, Arg, 72; Obras Completas de Juan del Encina, Clasicos Castellanos (4 vols), Espasa-Calpe, Madrid, 78-82. **CONTACT ADDRESS** Dept of Span, Montclair State Univ, 1 Normal Ave, Montclair, NJ, 07043-1699.

RAMBUSS, RICHARD
DISCIPLINE ENGLISH LANGUAGE AND LITERATURE **EDUCATION** Johns Hopkins Univ, PhD. **CAREER** Assoc prof, 96. **RESEARCH** Renaissance literaure and culture; cultural criticism; film; history of sexuality. **SELECTED PUBLICATIONS** Auth, Closet Devotions, Duke UP, 98; Spenser's Secret Career, Cambridge UP, 93; Spenser's Lives, Spenser's Careers in Spenser and the Subject of Biography, U Mass P, 97; Devotion and Defilement: The Haigiographics of Chaucer's 'Prioress' Tale' in Textual Bodies, SUNY P, 97; Homodevotion in Cruising the Performative, Indiana UP, 95; and Christ's Ganymede, Yale Jour Law Hum, 95. **CONTACT ADDRESS** English Dept, Emory Univ, 1380 Oxford Rd NE, Atlanta, GA, 30322-1950. **EMAIL** rrambus@emory.edu

RAMEH, CLEA ABDON
PERSONAL Born 01/09/1927, Recife, Brazil **DISCIPLINE** LINGUISTICS; PORTUGUESE LANGUAGE **EDUCATION** Univ Sao Paulo, BA, 47, Lic Anglo-Ger lang, 48, Especialization Anglo-Ger lang, 55; Georgetown Univ, MS, 62, PhD, 70. **CAREER** Teacher English State Schs Sao Paulo, Brazil, 51-63 & Regional Ctr Educ Res, Univ Sao Paulo, 63-65; linguist, Res Proj Port, US Naval Acad, 68-69; from instr to asst prof, 69-75, ASSOC PROF PORT, GEORGETOWN UNIV, 75- ; Chmn Dept, 79-87 & 91-94; Consult, Port Res Proj, US Naval Inst, 69-72; chmn, Georgetown Univ Round Table Lang & Ling, 76; Guggenheim Found grant, 80, 81; Fulbright, 59; Phi Beta Kappa, 69. **HONORS AND AWARDS** GWATFL Distinguished Educ Award, 85. **MEMBERSHIPS** Ling Soc Am; MLA; Am Coun Teaching Foreign Lang; Am Asn Teachers Span & Port; Asoc Ling y Filol Am Latina. **RESEARCH** Sociolinguistic implications of Portuguese linguistics; use of computer for language research applied to Portuguese; teaching of foreign languages. **SELECTED PUBLICATIONS** Coauth Portugues Contemporaneo, Vol I, 66, 67, 69, 71, 72 & 75 & Vol II, 67, 69, 71, 73 & 77; auth Toward a computerized syntactic analysis of Portuguese, Comput & Humanities, 9/71; auth, O preparo de material para analise do Portugues em computador, Construtura, 74; ed, Gurt 1976 Semantics: Theory and Application, Georgetown Univ, 76; auth, The Portuguese-English language contact in US, In: The Third Lacus Forum, Hornbeam, 76; Cecilia Meireles: Viagem e Solombra--uma analise linguistics, Rev Brasileira Ling, 77; O Vocabulo Portugues e o Computador, In: SENARA-Revista de filoloxia, Vol II, Colexio Univ, Spain, 80; Aspectos da Lingua Portuguesa nos Estados Unidos da America do Norte, In: From Linguistics to Literature: Romance Studies offered to Francis M Rogers, John Benjamins B V, Holland, 81. **CONTACT ADDRESS** Dept of Spanish & Port, Georgetown Univ, 37th & O St NW, Washington, DC, 22057. **EMAIL** ramehc@GU.NET.georgetown.edu

RAMESH, CLOSPETH N.
DISCIPLINE INTERPERSONAL, INTERCULTURAL, AND MASS COMMUNICATION **EDUCATION** Bangalore Univ, India, BA, 77; Univ S MS, MS, 87; MI State Univ, PhD, 92. **CAREER** Assoc prof, 91-, Truman State Univ. **HONORS AND AWARDS** Kulapati award, Bharatiya Vidya Bhavan, India, 85; grad stud award for tchg excellence, Intl Commun Assn, 91. **MEMBERSHIPS** Mem, Nat Commun Assn; Consult Comm on Indic Traditions and Conflict Mgt, Columbia Univ. **RESEARCH** Asian Indians in the US, and hostage negotiations. **SELECTED PUBLICATIONS** Pub(s), Commun Res; Intl Jourf Gp Tensions; Media Devel; Jour Intl Commun. **CONTACT ADDRESS** Dept of Commun, Truman State Univ, 100 E Normal St, Kirksville, MO, 63501-4221. **EMAIL** LL88@Truman.edu

RAMIACUTEREZ, MARIACUTEA-ESTHER D.
DISCIPLINE SPANISH CIVILIZATION AND CULTURE, SPANISH GRAMMAR, SPANISH COMPOSITION AND **EDUCATION** Univ Madrid, Spain, PhD, 87. **CAREER** Instr Span, mem, undergrad curric comt, 90-; Span textbk sel comt, 93-, La State Univ. **RESEARCH** Social history of the Hispanic groups in different historical periods; acquisition of grammatical and discourse competence. **SELECTED PUBLICATIONS** Auth, San Antonio, Texas, En La Epoca Colonial (1718-1821), Eds de Cult Hispacutenica, 89. **CONTACT ADDRESS** Dept of For Lang and Lit, Louisiana State Univ, 124 B Prescott Hall, Baton Rouge, LA, 70803. **EMAIL** insandy@unix1.sncc.lsu.edu

RAMIREZ, ARNULFO G.
DISCIPLINE APPLIED PSYCHOLINGUISTICS, SOCIOLINGUISTICS, SECOND LANGUAGE ACQUISITION **EDUCATION** Stanford Univ, PhD, 74. **CAREER** Prof Hisp Ling, hd, Span sect, dept ch, 89-95; core fac mem, Ling prog, 89-; adj fac mem, Comp Lit prog, 90; mem, the Int Bus Ctr Adv Coun, 93-, La State Univ. **RESEARCH** Bilingualism, language attrition, linguistic approaches to literature. **SELECTED PUBLICATIONS** Auth, El Espantildeol De Los Estados Unidos, Mapfre, 92; Creating Contexts For Second Language Acquisition, Longman, 95. **CONTACT ADDRESS** Dept of For Lang and Lit, Louisiana State Univ, 217 A Prescott Hall, Baton Rouge, LA, 70803. **EMAIL** ramirez@homer.forlang.lsu.edu

RAMOS-GARCIA, LUIS A.
DISCIPLINE SPANISH AND PORTUGUESE LITERATURE **EDUCATION** Univ Tex Austin, BA, 72; MA, 75; PhD, 85. **SELECTED PUBLICATIONS** Auth, A Corrected and Annotated Edition of Pedro Montengon's Frioleras Eruditas, Edwin Mellen, 97; Bilingual Anthology of Contemporary Spanish Poetry: Circa 1970-1990, Edwin Mellen, 97; From the Threshold: Contemporary Peruvian Fiction in Translation, Hisp Studies, 87; ed, Sociolinguistics of the Spanish Speaking World: Iberia, Latin America, and United States, Bilingual Rev, 91. **CONTACT ADDRESS** Spanish and Portuguese Dept, Univ of Minnesota, Twin Cities, 34 Folwell Hall, 9 Pleasant St SE, Minneapolis, MN, 55455. **EMAIL** laramosg@maroon.tc.umn.edu

RANEY, GEORGE WILLIAM
PERSONAL Born 05/05/1938, Haverhill, MA, m, 1968, 4 children **DISCIPLINE** APPLIED LINGUISTICS, ENGLISH AS A SECOND LANGUAGE, WORLD ENGLISHES **EDUCATION** Loyola Univ Los Angeles, BA, 61; Univ Southern Calif, MA, 66, PhD, 72. **CAREER** Lang coordr, Tagalog, Peace Corps, Philippines, 66 & Univ Hawaii, Hilo, 66; Fulbright lectr teaching English as foreign lang, Adam Mickiewicz Univ, Poznan, 67-68; lectr English as second lang, Univ Southern Calif, 68-69; asst prof, 69-74, dir English Am Inst, 72-77, fac develop fel, 76, Assoc Prof Ling, Calif State Univ, Fresno, 74-, Dept Chair, 96-2000; Consult, Bur Indian Affairs, 67; ed, Calif Ling Newslett, 73-76. **MEMBERSHIPS** Teachers English to Speakers Other Lang; Ling Soc Am; AAUP. **RESEARCH** English grammar; applied linguistics; world Englishes. **SELECTED PUBLICATIONS** Auth, Using the National Observer in the ESOL classroom, Teachers English to Speakers Other Lang Newslett, 4/76; On using the National Observer as an ESOL teaching device, Calif Asn of Teachers English to Speakers Other Lang, fall, 76. **CONTACT ADDRESS** Dept of Ling, California State Univ, Fresno, 5245 N Backer Ave, M/S 92, Fresno, CA, 93740-8001. **EMAIL** george_raney@csufresno.edu

RANWEZ, ALAIN DANIEL
PERSONAL Born 06/25/1944, Paris, France, m, 1968, 2 children **DISCIPLINE** FRENCH LITERATURE **EDUCATION** Montclair State Col, BA, 67; Univ MO, Columbia, PHD(French, Ital), 74. **CAREER** Asst prof French, Northern State Col, 71-72; asst prof, 72-80, Assoc Prof French, Metrop State Col, 80-, Nat Endowment for Humanities fel comp lit, Univ Chicago, 75; mem bibliog staff foreign lang, Am Coun Teachers Foreign Lang, 78-; Nat Endowment for Humanities fel, Wash Univ, 80. **MEMBERSHIPS** MLA; Am Coun Teachers Foreign Lang; Rocky Mountain Mod Lang Asn; Am Asn Teachers Fr. **RESEARCH** Post World War II French novel; French feminine writing. **SELECTED PUBLICATIONS** Auth, Baudelaire's Une Charogne, Explicator, Summer 77; Sartre's Les Temps Modernes, Whitston, 79; L Homme-Au-Baton, French Rev, Vol 67, 94; L Ami Du Genre Humain, French Rev, Vol 68, 95; Chemin Decole, French Rev, Vol 70, 96. **CONTACT ADDRESS** Dept of French, Metropolitan State Col, Denver, Denver, CO, 80204.

RAO, NAGESH
DISCIPLINE INTERCULTURAL COMMUNICATION **EDUCATION** MI State Univ, PhD, 94. **CAREER** Asst prof, Univ MD . **RESEARCH** Role of cult appropriateness in designing effective health campaigns. **SELECTED PUBLICATIONS** Co-auth, Communication and Community in a City Under Seige: The AIDS Epidemic in San Francisco, Commun Res 22, 95. **CONTACT ADDRESS** Dept of Commun, Univ MD, 4229 Art-Sociology Building, College Park, MD, 20742-1335. **EMAIL** nr35@umail.umd.edu

RAOUL, VALERIE
PERSONAL Shrewsbury, England **DISCIPLINE** FRENCH/ WOMEN'S STUDIES **EDUCATION** Girton Col, Univ Cambridge, BA, 63, MA, 68; London Sch Econ, Dip Social Admin, 64; McMaster Univ, MA, 71, PhD, 78. **CAREER** Tchr, McMaster Univ, Univ Toronto, Ryerson Polytechnic Univ, 70-79; dept Fr, 79-, head dept, 91-96, PROF UNIV BRITISH COLUMBIA 92-, dir, Ctr Res Women's Studs & Gender Rels 96-. **MEMBERSHIPS** Asn Prof Fr Can Univs; Asn Can Que Lits; CFH; Asn Chs Fr Depts Can Univs; **SELECTED PUBLICATIONS** Auth, The French Fictional Journal: Fictional Narcissism/Narcissistic Fiction, 79; auth, Distinctly Narcissistic: Diary Fiction in Quebec, 94; co-ed, The Anatomy of Gender: Women's Struggle for the Body, 88. **CONTACT ADDRESS** Dept of French, Univ of BC, Vancouver, BC, V6T 1Z1. **EMAIL** valraoul@unixg.ubc.ca

RASCH, WILLIAM
PERSONAL Born 10/25/1949, m, 1977, 1 child **DISCIPLINE** GERMAN STUDIES **EDUCATION** Univ Wash, PhD. **CAREER** Lect, 87-90, Univ Mo; vis asst prof, 90-94, asst prof,94-, Ind Univ, **MEMBERSHIPS** MLA; AATG; GSA; Int Brecht Soc. **RESEARCH** German philos tradition; social theory; Brecht and theater. **SELECTED PUBLICATIONS** Auth, Theories of Complexity, Complexities of Theory: Habermas, Luhmann, and the Study of Social Systems, Ger Stud Rev, 14, 91; auth, Injecting Noise Into the System: Hermeneutics and the Necessity of Misunderstanding, Substance: A Review of Theory and Literary Criticism 21, 92; auth, Chastising Reflection: Fichte's Suspicion of Language, Monatshefte 84, 92; auth, Mensch, Burger, Weib: Gender and the Limitations of Late 18th-Century Neohumanist Discourse, The German Quart 66.1, 93; auth, In Search of the Lyotard Archipelago, Or, How to Live with Paradox and Learn to Like It, New Ger Critique 61, 94, rep, Postmodern Literary Theory: An Anthology, Blackwell, 99; auth, Immanent Systems, Transcendental Temptations, and the Limits of Ethics, Cultural Critique 30, 95; The Limit of Modernity: Luhmann and Lyotard on Exclusion, Soziale Systeme 3.2, 97. **CONTACT ADDRESS** Dept of Germanic Studies, Indiana Univ, Bloomington, BH644, Bloomington, IN, 47405. **EMAIL** wrasch@indiana.edu

RASHKOW, ILONA N.
DISCIPLINE COMPARATIVE LITERATURE **EDUCATION** Cath Univ Am, BM, 71; Univ Md, MA, 84, PhD, 88. **CAREER** Assoc prof. **MEMBERSHIPS** Soc Bibl Lit; Am Acad Relig; MLA; Am Comp Lit Asn; World Union Jewish Studies; Asn Jewish Studies. **SELECTED PUBLICATIONS** Auth, The Phallacy of Genesis: A Feminist-Psychoanalytic Approach, Westminster/John Knox, 93; Upon the Dark Places: Sexism and Anti-Semitism in English Renaissance Biblical Translation, Sheffield, 90; Seeking Ezekiel (rev), Jour Am Acad Relig, 96; Countertraditions in the Bible: A Feminist Approach by Ilana Pardes (rev), Bible Rev, 95. **CONTACT ADDRESS** English Dept, SUNY Stony Brook, Stony Brook, NY, 11794. **EMAIL** irashkow@ccmail.sunysb.edu

RASTALSKY, HARTMUT
DISCIPLINE COMPARATIVE LITERATURE **EDUCATION** Princeton Univ, BA (Mathematics), 86; Univ Mich, MA (Mathematics), 88, MA (Comp Lit), 90, PhD (Comp Lit), 97. **CAREER** LANG PROG DIR, ASST PROF, GER, UNIV MICH, 97-. **CONTACT ADDRESS** Dept of Germanic Lang & Lit, Univ Michigan, 812 E Washington, Ann Arbor, MI, 48109-1275. **EMAIL** hmr@umich.edu

RATLIFF, GERALD LEE
PERSONAL Born 10/23/1944, Middletown, OH **DISCIPLINE** ENGLISH; COMMUNICATION **EDUCATION** Georgetown Col, BA, 67; Univ Cincinnati, MA, 70; Bowling Green St Univ, PhD, 75. **HONORS AND AWARDS** Medallion of Honor, Theta Alpha Phi, 89; Silver Medal of Honor, Int Biog Centere, 98; Teaching Fel, East Commun Assoc, 98; Man of Year, Amer Biog Inst, 998; Deputy Gen Dir Int Biog Centre, 99., Theta Alpha Phi Nat Theatre Honorary, 90; Fulbright Scholar, 90; Fel, Int Schools of Theatre Assoc, 91; US Delegate John F. Kennedy Center for Perf Arts, Int Scholar Exchange Prog, 91; Outstanding Graduate Alumni Award, Bowling Green St Univ, 94; Fel, Nat Fulbright Assoc, 97. **MEMBERSHIPS** E Commun Assoc; Nat Commun Assoc, NY Col English Assoc; Fulbright Assoc. **RESEARCH** Dramatic imagery in Mamet & O'Neill; Reader's Theatre approaches to visualization; literary themes in contemporary drama & poetry **SELECTED PUBLICATIONS** Coauth, An Introduction to Theatre, Rosen Press, 88; auth, The Politics of Machiavelli's The Prince, Barron's Publ Ltd, 86; A Sourcebook for Playing Scenes, Meriwether Publ Ltd, 93; Contemporary Scene Study, Meriwether Publ Ltd, 96; The Theatre Handbook, Meriwether Publ Ltd, 98. **CONTACT ADDRESS** English/Commun Dept, SUNY Potsdam, Potsdam, NY, 13676. **EMAIL** ratlifgl@potsdam.edu

READ, CHARLES
PERSONAL Born 07/10/1940, Clinton, IA, m, 1967, 2 children **DISCIPLINE** LINGUISTICS, PSYCHOLINGUISTICS **EDUCATION** Haverford, Col, AB, 61; Harvard Univ, MAT, 63, PhD , 71. **CAREER** Prof Eng and Ling, Univ WI-Madison, 80-, Ed, Harvard Educ Rev, 65-67; vis scholar sci ling, MA Inst Techool, 73-74; vis scholar ling, Univ Nijmegen, Netherlands, 78-79; chmn dept ling, Univ WI-Madison, 79-82; vis scholar ling, Beijing Normal Univ, 82-83; dean , Sch of Edu, 95. **MEMBERSHIPS** Ling Soc Am. **RESEARCH** Ling Found of reading and writing. **SELECTED PUBLICATIONS** Auth, Preschool children's knowledge of English phonology, Harvard Educ Rev, 71; Children's Categorization of Speech Sounds in English, Nat Coun Teachers English, 75; Children's awareness of language, with emphasis on sound systems, In: The Child's Conception of Language, Springer, 78; Creative spelling by young children, In: Standards and dialects in English, Winthrop, 80; Why short subjects are harder to find than long ones, In: Language Acquisition: The State of the Art, Cambridge, 82; Childrens Creative Spelling, Rutledge, 86; The Acoustic Analysis of Speech, Singular, 91. **CONTACT ADDRESS** Deans Office, Univ of Wisconsin, 100 Bascom Mall, Madison, WI, 53706.

REBAY, LUCIANO
PERSONAL Born 04/23/1928, Milan, Italy **DISCIPLINE** ITALIAN LITERATURE **EDUCATION** Univ Aix Marseille, Lic es Let, 51; Columbia Univ, PhD(Ital), 60. **CAREER** Lectr Ital, Ecole Norm, Ajaccio, France, 48-49, Ecole Norm, Nice, 49-50; prof, Lycee Francais, London, England, 52-55, Lycee Francais, New York, 55-56; from instr to assoc prof, Columbia Univ, 57-63, prof Ital, 65-72; GIUSEPPE UNGARETTI PROF ITAL LIT, 73-; Chamberlain fel, 62-63; Guggenheim fel, 66-67; Am Coun Learned Soc fel, 70-71; fel, Ctr Humanities, Wesleyan Univ, 71; vis prof Ital lit, Univ Calif, Berkeley, spring, 74; vis Mellon prof mod lang, Univ Pittsburgh, fall, 74; Nat Endowment for Humanities fel, 80-81. **MEMBERSHIPS** Am Asn Teachers Ital; MLA. **RESEARCH** Contemporary Italian literature; Italian lyric poetry; Franco-Italian comparative literature. **SELECTED PUBLICATIONS** Auth, Le origini della poesia di Giuseppe Ungaretti, Ed Storia e Lett, 62; I diaspori di Montale, Italica, 69; Invitation to Italian Poetry, Dover, 69; Alberto Moravia, Columbia Univ, 70; La rete a strascico di Montale, Forum Italicum, 71; co-ed, Giuseppe Ungaretti, Saggi e interventi, Mondadori, Milan, 74; Sull autobiografismo di Montale, Olschki, Florence 76; Ungaretti: Gli Scritti Egiziani 1909-1912, Forum Italicum, 80. **CONTACT ADDRESS** Columbia Univ, 513 Hamilton Hall, New York, NY, 10017.

RECK, RIMA DRELL
PERSONAL Born 09/29/1933, New York, NY, m, 1956 **DISCIPLINE** COMPARATIVE LITERATURE **EDUCATION** Brandeis Univ, BA, 54; Yale Univ, PhD(Romance lang), 60. **CAREER** Instr French, Tulane Univ, 58-61; from asst prof to assoc prof French & comp lit, 61-68, res coun grant, 64, Prof Comp Lit, Univ New Orleans, 68-, Am Philos Soc res grants, 62, 64; assoc ed, Southern Rev, 63-; Am Coun Learned Soc res grant, 68; Guggenheim fel, 72-73. **MEMBERSHIPS** MLA; Am Asn Teachers Fr; SCent Mod Lang Asn; Am Comp Lit Asn; Soc Amis Marcel Proust. **RESEARCH** French novel of the 20th century; the novel and its relation to other arts; 19th century Russian literature. **SELECTED PUBLICATIONS** Coauth, Studies in Comparative Literature, 62, ed, Explorations of Literatue, 66 & auth, Literature and Responsibility: The French Novelist in the Twentieth Century, 69, La State Univ; Old and new in the French new novel, Southern Rev, 10/65; Celine and the Aural Novel, Bks Abroad, 65; coauth, Bernanos, Confrontations, Minard, Paris, 66 & The New Orleans Cookbook, 74; auth, The crises of French nationalism in the twentieth century, In: The Cry of Home, Univ Tenn, 72; Guide To The Courtauld-Institute Galleries At Somerset-House, French Rev, Vol 67, 94; Fauve Painting--The Making Of Cultural Politics, French Rev, Vol 68, 94. **CONTACT ADDRESS** Dept of Foreign Lang, Univ of New Orleans, New Orleans, LA, 70122.

REED, GERVAIS EYER
PERSONAL Born 08/06/1931, Greeley, CO, m, 1960, 2 children **DISCIPLINE** FRENCH **EDUCATION** Princeton Univ, AB, 54; Brown Univ, MA, 62, PhD(French), 64. **CAREER** Asst prof, 64-70, assoc prof, 70-81, Prof French, Lawrence Univ, 81- **MEMBERSHIPS** MLA; Am Asn Teachers French. **RESEARCH** French 17th century literature and bibliography. **SELECTED PUBLICATIONS** Auth, Claude Barbin, libraire de Paris sous le regne de Louis XIV, Droz, Geneva; Moliere's Privilege of 18 March 1671, The Library, 65; Stylistic and thematic parallels in Corneille's Theatre and his imitation de Jesus Christ, Symposium, XXXIII: 263-87; L Amour Nomade, French Rev, Vol 66, 93; Le Rire De Mandrin, French Rev, Vol 68, 94; Huit Petites Etudes Sur Le Desir De Voir, French Rev, Vol 66, 93. **CONTACT ADDRESS** Dept of French, Lawrence Univ, Appleton, WI, 54911.

REED, WALTER
DISCIPLINE ENGLISH LANGUAGE AND LITERATURE **EDUCATION** Yale Univ, BA, PhD. **CAREER** Fac, Yale Univ; fac, Univ Tex Austin; prof/chemn dept, Emory Univ, 87-. **HONORS AND AWARDS** Guggenheim fel, 77-78., Co-dir, NEH summer sem col tchrs, 95. **RESEARCH** British Romanticism; comparative literature. **SELECTED PUBLICATIONS** Auth, pubs on the Romantic hero in 19th century fiction, on the Quixotic and picaresque traditions in the history of the novel, and on the Bible as literature from a Bakhtinian perspective. **CONTACT ADDRESS** English Dept, Emory Univ, 1380 Oxford Rd NE, Atlanta, GA, 30322-1950. **EMAIL** wlreed@emory.edu

REEDER, HEIDI M.
DISCIPLINE INTERPERSONAL COMMUNICATION, RELATIONAL COMMUNICATION **EDUCATION** Univ OR, BS, summa cum laude, 91; Stanford Univ, MA, 93; AZ State Univ, PhD, 96. **CAREER** Dept Comm, Univ NC **RESEARCH** Interpersonal commun; male-female relationships. **SELECTED PUBLICATIONS** Auth, The subjective experience of love through adult life, Int J of Aging and Human Develop, 43, 96; coauth, Unwanted escalation of sexual intimacy: Male and female perceptions of connotations and relational consequences of resistance messages, Commun Monogr, 62, 95; Disclosure of sexual abuse by children and adolescents, J of Appl Commun, 24, 96. **CONTACT ADDRESS** Dept of Commun Stud, Univ N. Carolina, Greensboro, 102 Fergus, Greensboro, NC, 27412-5001. **EMAIL** hmreeder@hamlet.uncg.edu

REFAI, SHAHID
PERSONAL Born 12/17/1936, Baroda, India, m, 1998, 3 children **DISCIPLINE** ASIAN STUDIES **EDUCATION** Baroda Univ, MA, 61; Cambridge Univ, PhD, 68. **CAREER** Asst librn, British Museum Lib, 68-69; vis lectr, Univ Calif, Los Angeles, 69-70; vis lectr, Univ Calif, Berkeley, 71; asst prof, 71-77, assoc prof, 77-83, Central Washington Univ; prof Hist, Col of Saint Rose, 84- . **HONORS AND AWARDS** Summa cum laude, 61; Cambridge Soc Scholar, 64-68; Lady Mountbatton Scholar, 67-68; Col of Saint Rose teaching awards. **MEMBERSHIPS** Exec Bd, NY Conf on Asian Stud; Asn for Asian Stud; Soc for Sci Study of Relig. **RESEARCH** Educational and social activism of American women missionaries in India in the nineteenth and twentieth centuries. **SELECTED PUBLICATIONS** Rev of Cynthia Hoehler-Fatton's Women of Fire and Spirit, Rev of Relig Res, 97; rev of Omar Khalidi's Indian Muslims Since Independence, Rev of Relig Res, 98. **CONTACT ADDRESS** Col of Saint Rose, PO Box 123, Albany, NY, 12203. **EMAIL** refais@rosnet.strose.edu

REGALADO, NANCY FREEMAN
PERSONAL Born 06/08/1935, Boston, MA, 2 children **DISCIPLINE** ROMANCE LANGUAGES **EDUCATION** Wellesley Col, BA, 57; Yale Univ, PhD, 66. **CAREER** Asst instr French, Yale Univ, 58-62, actg instr, 62-65; from instr to asst prof, Wesleyan Univ, 65-67; from asst prof to assoc prof, 68-77, prof French, 77-, NY Univ; NEH fel, 79-80; Am Coun Learned Soc grant, 79. **HONORS AND AWARDS** ACLS fel, 88; NEH fel, 79-80, 92; Officier de l'Ordre des Palmes Academiques, 92; Guggenheim fel, 93-94. **MEMBERSHIPS** MLA; Mediaeval Acad Am. **RESEARCH** Medieval French literature. **SELECTED PUBLICATIONS** Coauth, Feste: The Account of the 1313 Celebration of the Knighting of the Three Sons of Philip the Fair in the Chronique Metrique of in BN Ms Fr. 146, City and Spectacle in Medieval Europe, Minnesota, 94; contribur, Garland Encyclopedia of Medieval Literature, Garland, 95; auth, Speaking in Script: The Construction of Voice, Presence, and Perspective in Villon's TestamentOral Tradition in the Middle Ages, CEMERS, 95; auth, Staging the Roman de Renart: Medieval Theater and the Diffusion of Political Concerns into Popular Culture, Mediaevalia, 95; auth, Le Porcher au palais; Kalila et Dimna, Le Roman de Fauvel, Machaut, et Boccace, Etudes Litteraires, 98; auth, The Chronique Metrique and the Moral Design of Paris: Feasts of Good and Evil, Fauvel Studies, Oxford, 98. **CONTACT ADDRESS** Dept of French, New York Univ, 100 Bleeker St, New York, NY, 10012. **EMAIL** nancy.regalado@nyu.edu

REGOSIN, RICHARD L.
DISCIPLINE FRENCH LANGUAGE **EDUCATION** Johns Hopkins Univ, PhD. **CAREER** PROF, FR, UNIV CALIF, IRVINE. **SELECTED PUBLICATIONS** Auth, Agrippa d'Aubigne's 'Les Tragiques'; The Poetry of Inspiration; The Matter of My Book: Montaigne's 'Essais' as the Book of the Self; Montaigne's Unruly Brood: Textual Engendering & the Challenge to Paternal Authority; pub(s), articles on sixteenth-century Fr lit. **CONTACT ADDRESS** Dept of Fr and Ital, Univ Calif, Irvine, CA, 92697. **EMAIL** uci-cwis-support@uci.edu

REGUEIRO, JOSE MIGUEL
PERSONAL Born 12/20/1930, Cordoba, Argentina **DISCIPLINE** SPANISH LITERATURE **EDUCATION** Univ Pa, PhD(Span), 72. **CAREER** From instr to asst prof, 70-78, Assoc Prof Span, Univ PA, 78- **MEMBERSHIPS** Renaissance Soc Am; MLA; Am Asn Teachers Span & Port; AAUP. **RESEARCH** Spanish medieval and Renaissance theater; Spanish Golden Age literature. **SELECTED PUBLICATIONS** Auth,

A catalogue of the Comedia collection at the University of Pennsylvania Libraries, 71; coauth, Dramatic Manuscripts in the Hispanic Society of America, 78; contrib reviews and articles to literary publications; A Tribute To Peter G. Earle, Hispanic Rev, Vol 61, 93; The Spanish Drama Collection At The Ohio-State-University-Library - A Descriptive Catalog, Bullet Of The Comediantes, Vol 48, 96. **CONTACT ADDRESS** Dept of Romance Lang, Univ of Pa, 34th and Spruce St, Philadelphia, PA, 19104.

REID, LAWRENCE ANDREW

PERSONAL Born 06/02/1934, New Zealand, 4 children **DISCIPLINE** LINGUISTICS **EDUCATION** Univ Hawaii, MA, 64, PhD, 66. **CAREER** Instr phonetics & grammar, Summer Inst Ling, Australia, 58-59; field researcher Bontok, Summer Inst Ling, Philippines, 59-63; field researcher Ivatan & Austronesian lang, Philippines & Taiwan, 65; instr ling, Univ Hawaii, 66; asst dir, Summer Inst Ling, Univ Auckland, 67; field researcher, Philippines, 68; chief ling consult, Summer Inst Ling, Philippines, 69; from asst linguist to assoc linguist, Pac & Asian Ling Inst, Univ Hawaii, Manoa, 70-77; RESEARCHER LING, SOC SCI RES INST & DEPT LING, UNIV HAWAII, 77-; Vis prof, Univ Auckland, 78; ed, Filipinas, 82-85; vis res prof, Institute for the Study of the Languages and Cultures of Asia and Africa, Tokyo Univ of Foreign Studies, 91-92, 98-99. **HONORS AND AWARDS** E-W Center Fel, 64; E-W Center Excellence in Scholarship Award, 66; Nat Science Found Grant, 70, 93; UH Intramural Research Award, 72, 73; UH Summer Research Initiation Award, 72; UH Research Travel Award, 72; Ford Found Asia Prog Res Fel, 74; NEH Grant, 74; Uh Res Travel Grant, 76, 80, 82, 85, 87, 88, 95; Pacific Area Lang Materials devel Center Office of Bilingual Ed Title VII Grant, 79; Am Coun of Learned Soc Travel Grant, 85; Computers for Pacific Lang Res Database--UH Vice-Pres for Res Grant, 86; Optical Character Scanner for the Pacific Lang Res Database--UH Res Relations Fund Grant, 87; UH Res Initiation Grant, 87; Wenner-Gren Found Res Grant, 90; Res Grant--Tokyo Univ Foreign Studies, 91; UH CSEAS Conference Travel Grant, 94, 95, 98; Anonymous Grant--Tasaday Res, 94-97; UH Res Relations Travel Grant, 97. **MEMBERSHIPS** Ling Soc NZ; Ling Soc Philippines; Ling Soc Am; Polynesian Soc; Asn Asian Studies. **RESEARCH** Philippine and aboriginal Formosan descriptive and comparative linguistics; ethnography of Northern Luzon; discourse analysis; the Austric hypothesis. **SELECTED PUBLICATIONS** Auth, A Guinaang Wedding Ceremony, Philippine Sociol Rev, 61; An Ivatan Syntax, Univ Hawaii, 66; ed, Philippine Minor Languages: Word Lists and Phonologies, Univ Hawaii, 72; auth, Central Bontoc: Discourse, Paragraph and Sentence Structures, Summer Inst Ling, 72; Diachronic Typology of Philippine Vowel Systems, In: Current Trends in Linguistics, Vol XI, Mouton, The Hague, 73; Bontoc-English Dictionary and Finder List, Pac Ling Ser C, 74; The Problem *R and *1 Reflexes in Kankanay, In: Festschrift in Honor of Cecilio Lopez, Ling Soc Philippines, 74; The State of the Art of Philippine Linguistics, 1970-1980, In: Philippine Studies: Political Science, Economics, and Linguistics, Occas Papers Ctr for Southeast Asian Studies, No 8, Northern IL Univ, 81; auth, Benedict's Austro-Tai Hypothesis, Asian Perspectives, 26, 84-85; The Early Switch Hypothesis: Linguistic Evidence for Contact Between Negritos and Austronesians, Man and Culture in Oceania 3, 87; Guinaang Bontok Texts, Institute for the Study of the Languages and Cultures of Asia and Africa, Monograph Series, Tokyo Univ Foreign Studies, 92; Unraveling the Linguistic Histories of Philippine Negritos, in T. E. Dutton and D. T. Tryon, eds, Language Contact and Change in the Austronesian World, Berlin: Mouton de Gruyter, 94; The Current State of Linguistic Research on the Relatedness of the Language Families of East and Southeast Asia, in Ian C. Glover and Peter Bellwood, ed co-ordinators, Indo-Pacific Prehistory: The Chiang Mai Papers, vol 2, Bulletin of the Indo-Pacific Prehistory Asn 15, Canberra: Australian Nat Univ, 96; Archaeological Linguistics: Tracking Down the Tasaday Language, in Robert Blench, ed, Proceedings of the 3rd World Congress of Archaeologists, New Delhi, India, 97; and numerous other articles, papers, and research projects. **CONTACT ADDRESS** Dept of Ling, Univ of Hawaii, 1890 E West Rd, Honolulu, HI, 96822-2318. **EMAIL** reid@hawaii.edu

REIDEL-SCHREWE, URSULA

PERSONAL Hamburg, Germany **DISCIPLINE** GERMAN LANGUAGE, LITERATURE AND CULTURE **EDUCATION** Harvard Univ, MA, PhD. **CAREER** Assoc prof, Colby Col. **SELECTED PUBLICATIONS** Publ, Bk, articles, narrative theory and early 20th-century Ger lit. **CONTACT ADDRESS** Dept of Ger, Colby Col, 4000 Mayflower Hill, Watereville, ME, 04901-8840.

REILLY, LINDA

DISCIPLINE CLASSICAL STUDIES **EDUCATION** Vassar Col, AB, 65; Johns Hopkins Univ, MA, 66, PhD, 69. **CAREER** Assoc prof, 74-; ch, 92-95; asst prof, 69-74; assoc provest, 81-86 & dean Undergrad Progr and asst VP for Acad Aff, Col William and Mary; Abby Leach fel, low, Amer Sch Class Stud, Athens, Greece, 66-67; Ctr Hellenistic Stud, Wash, 74-75; sr res assoc, Amer Sch Class Stud, Athens, Greece, 86-87 & 95-96. **RESEARCH** Ancient dogs; Ancient city; Neoclassical traditions in North America. **SELECTED PUBLICATIONS** Auth, Slaves in Ancient Greece, Ares Publishers, 78, repr, 84; The Dogs from the Hunting Frieze at Vergina, J Hellenic Stud, Vol 113, 93; A Greek Inscription at Williamsburg, Amer J Archaeol, 74; New Inscriptions from Echinos, Amer J Philol, 71; Who Stole the Sphinx's Nose, Mediter Soc Am, Richmond, 96; participant and guest lecturer, La State Semr for High Sch Humanities Teachers, Northwestern State Univ, Natchidoches, 93; A Protogemometric Naiskos From Crete CAMWS, Boulder, 97; Neo-Classical Achitecture in Williamsburg, VA, CAMWS-SS, Richmond, 92; Kerberos and Orthos: Two Monstrous Brothers, given at CAMWS in Austin, 92; Rumpus: One of A Kind, Dog World, 86 & Rumpus: A Full Life for a Deaf Corgi, Dog World, 90. **CONTACT ADDRESS** Dept of Classical Studies, Col of William and Mary, Morton Hall, Williamsburg, VA, 23187-8795. **EMAIL** lcreil@morton.wm.edu

REINER, ERICA

PERSONAL Budapest, Hungary **DISCIPLINE** ASSYRIOLOGY **EDUCATION** Sorbonne, Dipl Assyriol, 51; Univ Chicago, PhD(Assyriol), 55. **CAREER** From res asst to res assoc Assyriol, 52-56, from asst prof to prof, 56-73, John A. Wilson Prof Assyriol, Univ Chicago, 73-, Distinguished Serv Prof, 83-; Assoc ed, Assyrian Dictionary, Orient Inst, Univ Chicago, 57-62, ed, 62-, ed-in-charge, 73-96. **HONORS AND AWARDS** Guggenheim fel, 74. **MEMBERSHIPS** Am Orient Soc; Ling Soc Am; Am Philos Soc; fel Am Acad Arts & Sci. **RESEARCH** Linguistics; Babylonian literature. **SELECTED PUBLICATIONS** Auth, Surpu: A Collection of Sumerian and Akkadian Incantations, Weidner, Graz, 58; A Linguistic Analysis of Akkadian, Mouton, The Hague, 66; Elamite language, In: Handbuch der Orientalistik, Brill, Leiden, 69; Akkadian, In: Current Trends in Linguistics, Mouton, The Hague, 69; Babylonian Planetary Omens: Parts 1 & 2, Undena, 75 & 81; Astral Magic in Babylonia, Transactions Am Philos Soc, 85/4, 95. **CONTACT ADDRESS** Orient Inst, Univ of Chicago, 1155 E 58th St, Chicago, IL, 60637-1540.

REINHARTZ, DENNIS PAUL

PERSONAL Born 04/29/1944, Irvington, NJ, m, 1966 **DISCIPLINE** RUSSIAN & EAST EUROPEAN HISTORY **EDUCATION** Rutgers Univ, AB, 66, AM, 67; NY Univ, PhD, 70. **CAREER** Instr hist, Newark Col Eng, 68-70; from asst prof to assoc prof, Madison Col, 70-73; from asst prof to assoc prof, 73-98, asst dean lib arts, 76-79, prof hist & Russ, Univ Tex, Arlington, 98-; Reviewer, NEH, 74-; assoc ed, Red River Valley Hist J, 75-. **HONORS AND AWARDS** NY Univ Founders Day Award for Acad Schol Achievement, 70; Col Lib Arts Constituency Coun Award for Excellence in Teaching, 76; Notable NJ Author Citation for Milovan Djilas, 83; Presidio La Bahia Award for The Mapping of the American Southwest, 87; The Adele Mellen Prize for The Cartographer and the Literati, Friends of the UTA Libr Fac Award, 96; Fort Worth Country Day Sch Mack Family Schol; recipient of numerous grants and fellowships. **MEMBERSHIPS** Southwestern Asn Slavic Studies(pres, 76-77); AHA; Am Asn Advan Slavic Studies; Hist Film Comt; Southern Conf Slavic Studies. **RESEARCH** Pre-Marxist 19th century Russian intellectual history; the Yugoslav Revolution; 20th century Balkan history. **SELECTED PUBLICATIONS** Auth, Milovan Djilas: A Revolutionary as a Writer, Columbia Univ Press, 81; coauth, Teach-Practice-Apply: The TPA Instructional Model, Nat Educ Asn, 88; Geography Across the School Curriculum, Nat Educ Asn, 90; Tabula Terra Nova, The Somesuch Press, 92; auth, The Cartographer and the Literati: Herman Moll and his Intellectual Circle, The Edwin Mellen Press, 97; author of numerous journal articles, book essays, reviews, and other scholarly publications. **CONTACT ADDRESS** Dept of Hist, Univ of Tex, Arlington, TX, 76019. **EMAIL** dprein@utarlg.uta.edu

REINKING, VICTOR

DISCIPLINE FRENCH **EDUCATION** Univ CO, BA, 70; Univ WA, MA, 86, PhD, 93. **CAREER** Languages, Seattle Univ. **SELECTED PUBLICATIONS** Auth, Riddle on the Way to the Bottom: Morroccan Summer, poetry, Greensboro, NC: Int Poetry Rev, 90; Rousseau's Bliss: Jouissance, Oxford Univ, Voltaire Found: Stud on Voltaire and the 18th Century, 95; Associate editor's Perspective on Critical Approaches, Seattle and Nantes, France: Para*doxa, 95; rev(s), in A Vietnam War Filmography, NY: MacFarlan, 93, contrib 7 rev(s) & commentaries on films depict/facultying US involvement in Vietnam War; transl, Suns Under Arrest & other poems by Abdellatif Laabi: Greensboro, NC: Int Poetry Rev, 91; Phenomenology and Ontology: Hannah Arrendt and Maurice Merleau-Ponty, article included Contemp Perspectives on Merleau-Ponty, Brussels, Kluver, 93; For a Poetics of Paraliterature, Part I: Paraliterature and the Oral Tradition, Seattle and Nantes, France: Para*doxa, 95; For a poetics of Paraliterature, Part II: Paraliterature and Rhetoric, Seattle and Nantes, France: Para*doxa, 95. **CONTACT ADDRESS** Dept of For Lang, Seattle Univ, 900 Broadway, Seattle, WA, 98122-4460. **EMAIL** vicr@seattleu.edu

REISS, CHARLES

DISCIPLINE PHONOLOGY **EDUCATION** Swarthmore Col, BA, 85;Harvard Univ, MA, 90, PhD, 95. **CAREER** Asst prof, dir, 95-; adj res prof, Carleton Univ, 98-; tchr, 5th Cent Europ Summer Sch in Generative Ling, Debrecen, Hungary, 98; vis res, Umea Univ, 97; adj asst prof, McGill Univ, 96; lectr, Harvard Univ Summer Sch, 95; res assoc, Harvard Univ, 95; preceptor, Harvard Univ, 95; lectr, Boston Univ, 94-95; asst Hd Tutor, Harvard Univ, 89-94; tchg fel, Harvard Univ, 89-94; lectr, Brandeis Univ, 93. **HONORS AND AWARDS** Res coun grants, Can Soc Sci and Hum, 95-96, 96-97; summer research travel grant, Concordia Univ, 97; Affinity MasterCard award, Concordia Univ, 96-97; Eva and Einar Haugen award, Scandinavian Forum, 94; Hoopes prize, Harvard Univ, 94; wrtg fel, Harvard Univ, 93; Howard Osborn scholar, Swarthmore Col, 84., Manuscript ref, Ling Inquiry, Can Jour Ling; abstract rev, E States Conf Ling, 97, Yale Univ, 97. **MEMBERSHIPS** Mem, Ling Soc Am, SIGPHON. **RESEARCH** Historical Linguistics. **SELECTED PUBLICATIONS** Rev,Review of John Archibald, Phonological theory and phonological acquisition, Lang, 97; Review of Iggy Roca, Derivations and Constraints in Phonology, Jour Ling, 97; coauth, "Phonological Underspecification & the Subset Principle," Proc of the W Conf on Ling, UC-Santa Cruz, 98. **CONTACT ADDRESS** Dept of Classics, Mod Lang and Ling, Concordia Univ, Montreal, 1455 de Maisonneuve W, Montreal, PQ, H3G 1M8. **EMAIL** reiss@alcor.concordia.ca

REITZ, RICHARD ALLEN

PERSONAL Born 09/14/1937, Clay Center, KS, m, 1966, 1 child **DISCIPLINE** SPANISH **EDUCATION** Univ KS, BA, 59, MA, 61; Univ KY, PhD, 70. **CAREER** Instr Span, VA Mil Inst, 59-60; asst, Univ KS, 60-61; assoc prof, 63-74, Prof Span, Catawba Col, 74, Dept Ch, 97-; Asst prof, Univ KY, 67-68; **HONORS AND AWARDS** Nat Endowment for the Hum Sem fel, Univ Pittsburgh, 75. **MEMBERSHIPS** Am Asn Tchr(s) Span & Port. **RESEARCH** Span Am lit; Brazilian lit; Faulkerian influences on Gabriel Garcia Marquez, Paper delivered, 1976. **SELECTED PUBLICATIONS** Translr, Noticias Secretas, R & D Bks, Salisbury, NC, 78. **CONTACT ADDRESS** Dept of Mod Lang, Catawba Col, 2300 W Innes St, Salisbury, NC, 28144-2488. **EMAIL** dreitz@catawba.edu

REMAK, HENRY HEYMANN HERMAN

PERSONAL Born 07/27/1916, Berlin, Germany, m, 1946, 4 children **DISCIPLINE** GERMAN, COMPARATIVE LITERATURE **EDUCATION** Univ Montpellier, lic es let, 36; Ind Univ, AM, 37; Univ Chicago, PhD, 47. **CAREER** Instr Ger & Span, Indianapolis Exten Ctr, Ind Univ, 39-43; from instr to prof Ger, 46-64, chmn W Europ studies, 66-69, vchancellor & dean fac, 69-74, Prof Ger & Comp Lit, Ind Univ, 64-, Dir Ger summer sch, 67-71; assoc ed, Ger Quart, 58-62; assoc ed, Yearbk Compt & Gen Lit, 61-66, ed, 66-78; Fulbright lectr comp & Ger lit, Univ Hamburg, 67; Guggenheim fel, 67-68; Nat Endowment for Humanities fel, 77-78; dir summer & yr-long seminars, Nat Endowmen for Humanities, 77 & 78-79; pres, Coordr Comt Comp Hist Lit in Europ Langs, Int Comp Lit Asn, 77-. **HONORS AND AWARDS** Litt D, Univ Lille, 73. **MEMBERSHIPS** Corresp mem Acad Sci, Arts & Lett, Marseilles. **RESEARCH** Franco-German literary relations; modern German literature; general comparative literature. **SELECTED PUBLICATIONS** Contribr, Comparative Literature: Method and Perspective, Southern Ill Univ, 71; auth, Der Rahmen in der deutschen Novelle, Delp, Munich, 72; Exoticism in Romanticism, Comp Lit Studies, 3/78; Der Weg zur Weltliteratur: Fontanes bret harteentwurf, 80; The Users of Comparative Literature, Value Judgment, 81; Die novelle in der Klassik uhd, Romanttik, 82; Literary-History And Comparative Literary-History--The Odds For And Against It In Scholarship, Neohelicon, Vol 20, 93. **CONTACT ADDRESS** Dept of Lit, Indiana Univ, Bloomington, Bloomington, IN, 47401.

RENEHAN, ROBERT

DISCIPLINE GREEK AND LATIN LITERATURE **EDUCATION** Harvard Univ, PhD, 63. **CAREER** PROF, UNIV CALIF, SANTA BARBARA. **RESEARCH** Ancient medicine; philos; hist of class scholar; textual criticism; lexicography. **SELECTED PUBLICATIONS** Auth, Greek Textual Criticism, Harvard Univ Press, 69; Leo Medicus, De Natura Hominis, Akademie Verlag, Berlin, 69; Greek Lexicographical Notes I and II, Gottingen, 75, 82; Studies in Greek Texts, Gottingen, 76; The Staunching of Odysseus' Blood: The Healing Power of Magic, AJP 92; "Some Special Problems in the Editing of Aristotle," SIFC, 3rd series, 92; "Plato, Apology 27A-B," CP 88, 93; "Of Mice and Men in Aristotle," CP 89, 94; "Polus, Plato, and Aristotle," CQ 45, 95; "On Some Genitives and a Few Accusatives in Aristotle: A Study in Style," Hermes 125, 97; rev(s), The New Oxford Sophocles, CP 87, 92; "Avotins, On the Greek of the Novels of Justinian," Phoenix 49, 95. **CONTACT ADDRESS** Dept of Classics, Univ Calif, Santa Barbara, CA, 93106-7150. **EMAIL** renehan@humanitas.ucsb.edu

RENNERT, HELLMUT HAL

PERSONAL Born 11/29/1939, Weimar, Germany, m, 1963, 1 child **DISCIPLINE** GERMAN & COMPARATIVE LITERATURE **EDUCATION** Wichita State Univ, BA, 66, MA, 69; Univ Wash, PhD(comp lit), 75. **CAREER** Instr, Wichita State Univ 73-74; asst prof, Carnegie-Mellon Univ, 76-79; ASST PROF GERMAN, UNIV FLA, 79-; Pres, Asn Prof Transl, 78-79. **MEMBERSHIPS** MLA; Am Asn Teachers German; Deutsche Schillergesellschaft; Am Comp Lit Asn; Am Transl Asn **RESEARCH** Contemporary German literature; German area studies; early 19th century German literature. **SELECTED**

PUBLICATIONS Auth, A comparison of two translations of Eduard Morikes poem auf eine Lampe, Univ South Fla Lang Quat, 72; Transformations: Thoughts regarding film title translations, Post Scripts, 81; Affinities in Romanticism: Kleist and Keats, Heinrich von Kleist Studies, AMS press and E Schmidt Verlag, 82; The threat of the invisible: The portrait of the physicist in modern German drama, Comp Drama Papers, 82; Deutsche Firmen, Deutsche Sprache in Florida, Unterrichtspraxis, 82. **CONTACT ADDRESS** Dept Germanic & Slavic Lang & Lit, Univ Fla, PO Box 117430, Gainesville, FL, 32611-7430. **EMAIL** rennert@nervm.nerdc.ufl.edu

RESLER, W. MICHAEL
PERSONAL Born 07/07/1948, FL, s **DISCIPLINE** GERMAN **EDUCATION** Harvard Univ, AM, 73, PhD, 76; Johannes-Gutenberg-Univ, 71; Col of William & Mary, AB, 70 **CAREER** Prof, 91-, Boston Col; Lect, 78-94, Harvard Univ; Assoc Prof, 87-91, Adj Assoc Prof, 82-87, Adj Assist Prof, 80-82; Asst Prof, 76-80, Boston Col; Lect, 74, New England Conserv of Music **HONORS AND AWARDS** Phi Beta Kappa Tch awd **MEMBERSHIPS** Am Asn of Tchrs **RESEARCH** Germanic philol **SELECTED PUBLICATIONS** Auth, Der Stricker, Daniel von dem bluhenden Tal, Niemeyer, 95 **CONTACT ADDRESS** Dept of German, Boston Col, Chestnut Hill, MA, 02467-3804. **EMAIL** resler@bc.edu

REY, WILLIAM HENRY
PERSONAL Born 04/07/1911, Frankfurt-am-Main, Germany, m, 1954, 1 child **DISCIPLINE** GERMAN LITERATURE **EDUCATION** Univ Frankfurt, PhD, 37. **CAREER** Instr, Ohio State Univ, 47-48; asst prof, Grinnell Col, 48-50; from asst prof to assoc prof, 50-59, exec off dept, 60-73, Prof Ger, Univ Wash, 59- **MEMBERSHIPS** MLA. **RESEARCH** Modern German and Austrian literature; contemporary poetry. **SELECTED PUBLICATIONS** Auth, Weltentzweiung und Weltversohnung in Hofmannsthals Griechischen Dramen, Univ Pa, 62; Arthur Schnitzler: Die spate Prosa als Gipfelseines Schaffens, Schmidt, Berlin, 68; Arthur Schnitzler: Professor Bernhardi, Fink, Munche, 71; Poesie der Antipoesie, Moderne Lyrik: Genesis, Theorie, Struktur, Stiehm, Heidelberg, 78; Revolutionstropodie und Mysteriesnspiel, Peter Lang, Bern; Misused Femininity--Ambivalent Reflections On Mann,Thomas Depiction Of The Relation Between Joseph And Mut-Em-Enet In His Joseph Tetralogy, Orbis Litterarum, Vol 51, 96. **CONTACT ADDRESS** Dept of Ger Lang & Lit, Univ of Wash, Seattle, WA, 98195.

REYFMAN, IRINA
DISCIPLINE SLAVIC LANGUAGES **EDUCATION** Stanford Univ, PhD, 86. **CAREER** Assoc prof. **RESEARCH** Eighteenth and early nineteenth-century Russian literature; cultural history; semiotics of culture. **SELECTED PUBLICATIONS** Auth, Imagery of Time and Eternity in Eighteenth Century Russian Poetry: Mikhail Murav'ev and Semen Bobrov, Ind Slavic Papers, 96; The Emergence of the Duel of Honor in Russia: Corporal Punishment and the Honor Code, Russian Rev, 95; Poetic Justice and Injustice: Autobiographical Echoes in Pushkin's The Captain Daughter, Slavic E Europ Jour, 94. **CONTACT ADDRESS** Dept of Slavic Languages, Columbia Col, New York, 2960 Broadway, New York, NY, 10027-6902. **EMAIL** IR2@columbia.edu

RHOADES, DUANE
DISCIPLINE SPANISH **EDUCATION** Univ IL, PhD, 76. **CAREER** Assoc prof; Univ WY, 82; past exec dir, Partners of the Am exchange-state Goias in Brazil & state coordr, Nat Span Exam. **HONORS AND AWARDS** UW's John P Ellbogen awd, 86. **RESEARCH** Dramatic lit in Span, Portuguese and related lang(s). **SELECTED PUBLICATIONS** Auth, bk on monotheatre in Lat Am, 86; publ on, Lat Am poetry, prose fiction,theater & Peninsular drama. **CONTACT ADDRESS** Dept of Mod and Class Lang(s), Univ WY, PO Box 3964, Laramie, WY, 82071-3964. **EMAIL** DRHOADES@UWYO.EDU

RICAPITO, JOSEPH V.
PERSONAL Born 10/30/1933, Giovinazzo, Italy, m, 1958, 2 children **DISCIPLINE** ROMANCE LANGUAGES **EDUCATION** Brooklyn Col, BA, 55; State Univ IA, MA, 56; Univ CA, Los Angeles, PhD(Romance lang), 66. **CAREER** Assoc Span, Univ CA, Los Angeles, 61-62; from instr to asst prof Span & Ital, Pomona Col, 62-70; assoc prof Span, 70-78, prof Span & comp lit, IN Univ, 78-80; prof Span & chemn dept, LA State Univ, Baton Rouge, 80-85, dir, program in comp lit, LSU, 94-; Ford Found & Pomona Col fel, 68-69. **MEMBERSHIPS** MLA; Am Comp Lit Asn; Renaissance Soc Am. **RESEARCH** Italian Renaissance; Spanish Golden Age; comparative literature. **SELECTED PUBLICATIONS** Auth, Lazarillo de Tormes y Machiavelli & El contorno picaresco del Conde Lucanor, 72, Romanische Forsch; Americo Castro y la novela picaresca, Insula, 73; La vida de Lazarillo de Tormes, Madrid, Catedra, 10th ed, 76; Bibliografia razonada y anotada ... Madrid, Castalia, 80. **CONTACT ADDRESS** Dept Span & Port, Louisiana State Univ, Baton Rouge, LA, 70803-0001. **EMAIL** ricapito@homer.forlang.lsu.edu

RICARD, FRANCOIS
PERSONAL Born 06/04/1947, Shawinigan, PQ, Canada **DISCIPLINE** FRENCH AND QUEBEC LITERATURE **EDUCATION** Univ Laval, BA, 66; McGill Univ, MA, 68; Univ-d'Aix-Marseille (France), PhD, 71. **CAREER** Prof French & Quebec literature, McGill Univ, 71-. **HONORS AND AWARDS** Gov Gen Award Non-fiction (Fr lang), 86; Killam Res Fel, 88-90. **MEMBERSHIPS** Royal Soc Can **SELECTED PUBLICATIONS** Auth, Gabrielle Roy, 75; auth, Le Prince et la tenebre, 80; auth, L'incroyable odyssee, 81; auth, La litterature contre elle-meme, 85; auth, La generation lyrique, 92; auth, Gabrielle Roy, Une vie, 96; co-auth, Histoire du Quebec contemporain, 86. **CONTACT ADDRESS** Dept of French, McGill Univ, 3460 McTavish St, Montreal, PQ, H3A 1X9.

RICE, LAURA
DISCIPLINE COMPARATIVE LITERATURE **EDUCATION** Ohio State Univ, BA, 68; Kent State Univ, MA, 71; Univ Wash, PhD, 76. **CAREER** Engl, Oregon St Univ. **SELECTED PUBLICATIONS** Auth, The Camera Always Lies, Review Essay of Trinh T. Minh-ha, The Framer Framed in The Women's Review of Books X, 93; Departures: Translations of and Essays on Isabelle Eberhardt, City Lights Press, 94. **CONTACT ADDRESS** Oregon State Univ, Corvallis, OR, 97331-4501. **EMAIL** lrice@orst.edu

RICH, JOHN STANLEY
PERSONAL Born 03/05/1943, Birmingham, AL **DISCIPLINE** DIALECTOLOGY **EDUCATION** Univ Ala, BA, 66, PhD(English), 79; Univ Pa, MS, 68. **CAREER** Instr English, Stillman Col, 68-73; teaching asst, Univ Ala, 73-79; from Asst Prof to Prof English, Univ SC, Aiken, 79- **HONORS AND AWARDS** Fulbright Lect Award to Poland, 93-94. **MEMBERSHIPS** MLA; Nat Coun Teachers English; Am Dialect Soc; Am Name Soc. **RESEARCH** American place names; English composition and rhetoric. **SELECTED PUBLICATIONS** Auth, Some South Carolina names transferred to West Alabama, Names in SC, 10/82; numerous articles in: Secol Rev, SAtl Rev, Folklore Quart, Names. **CONTACT ADDRESS** 171 University Pky, PO Box 2582, Aiken, SC, 29801-6309. **EMAIL** stanr@aiken.sc.edu

RICHARDSON, HORST FUCHS
PERSONAL Born 06/11/1941, Nuremberg, Germany, m, 1967, 2 children **DISCIPLINE** GERMAN LANGUAGE & LITERATURE **EDUCATION** Univ CA, Riverside, BA, 63, MA, 66; Univ CT, PhD, 76. **CAREER** From instr to asst prof Ger, 65-77, Assoc Prof Ger, CO Col, 77. **MEMBERSHIPS** Am Asn Tchr() Ger; MLA; Asn Depts For Lang. **RESEARCH** Ger drama and theatre. **SELECTED PUBLICATIONS** Auth, The teaching of college German under a modular system, Mod Lang J, 73; A playwrite's experiment in third-yeard German, 73 & German play productions in US and Canadian colleges and universities since 1959, 74, Unterrichtspraxis; Sieg Heil: War letters of tank gunner Karl Fuchs, 1937-1941, Archon Books, 87. **CONTACT ADDRESS** Dept of Ger & Russ, Colorado Col, 14 E Cache La Poudre, CO Springs, CO, 80903-3294. **EMAIL** hrichardson@cc.colorado.edu

RICHARDSON, SCOTT D.
PERSONAL Born 11/27/1956, St. Paul, MN, m, 1976, 2 children **DISCIPLINE** COMPARATIVE LITERATURE **EDUCATION** Harvard, BA, 78; Stanford, MA, 80, PhD, 84. **CAREER** Asst Prof, Assoc Prof, Prof, 84-, St John's Univ, Collegeville, MN. **HONORS AND AWARDS** Teacher of the Yr, 89; Advisor of the Yr, 93; NEH Summer Stipend, 89. **MEMBERSHIPS** APA, Class Assoc of MN. **RESEARCH** Humor; James Joyce; Thomas Pynchon. **SELECTED PUBLICATIONS** Auth, Truth in the Tales of the Odessy, Mnemosyne, 96; The Homeric Narrator, Nashville, Vanderbilt Univ Press, 90; co-auth, Euripdes Iphegenia at Aulis, adaptation for the stage, Lanham, Maryland, Univ Press of Amer, 88. **CONTACT ADDRESS** Dept Modern & Class Languages, St John's Univ, Collegeville, MN, 56321. **EMAIL** SRichardson@csbsju.edu

RICHMAN, STEPHEN
DISCIPLINE ROMANCE LANGUAGES **EDUCATION** Univ Pa, BA, 57, MS, 59, PhD, 65. **CAREER** PROF SPAN, (TRENTON JR COL)MERCER COUNTY COL, 65-; COORD, FOR LANGS, MERCER COUNTY COL, 85-; chair hum, Mmercer, 10 yrs. **CONTACT ADDRESS** Lib Arts Div, Mercer County Comm Col, 1200 Old Trenton Rd., Trenton, NJ, 08690.

RICKER-ABDERHALDEN, JUDITH
DISCIPLINE CONTEMPORARY GERMAN **EDUCATION** Univ Nebr, BA, 72, MA, 74, PhD, 80. **CAREER** English and Lit, Univ Ark. **HONORS AND AWARDS** Fulbright Col Master Tchr Award; Certificate Merit Outstanding Achievements. **MEMBERSHIPS** Am Asn Tchrs German; German Studies Asn. **SELECTED PUBLICATIONS** Areas: contemporary German, Austrian, and Swiss literature and civilization, foreign language pedagogy, and dialects. **CONTACT ADDRESS** Univ Ark, Fayetteville, AR, 72701.

RIEBER, STEVEN
DISCIPLINE PHILOSOPHY OF LANGUAGE, PHILOSOPHY OF MIND, METAPHYSICS, EPISTEMOLOGY, ETHI **EDUCATION** Princeton Univ, PhD, 91. **CAREER** Assoc prof, Ga State Univ. **SELECTED PUBLICATIONS** Author of eight recent articles in journals such as Analysis, Nous and Philos Stud. **CONTACT ADDRESS** Georgia State Univ, Atlanta, GA, 30303. **EMAIL** phlsdr@panther.gsu.edu

RIEDEL, WALTER ERWIN
PERSONAL Born 08/03/1936, Germany, m, 1963 **DISCIPLINE** GERMAN **EDUCATION** Univ Alta, BEd, 60, MA, 63; McGill Univ, PhD(Ger), 66. **CAREER** Teacher high sch, Edmonton, 60-61; instr French & Ger, 62-64, asst prof, 66-70, Assoc Prof Ger, Univ Victoria, BC, 70- **MEMBERSHIPS** Can Asn Univ Teachers Ger; Can Comp Lit Asn. **RESEARCH** Expressionism; translation; German and Canadian literary relations. **SELECTED PUBLICATIONS** Coauth, Kanadische Erzahler der Gegenwart, Manesse, 67; Modern Canadian Short Stories, Max Hueber, Munchen, 69; Der Neue Mensch Mythos und Wirklichkeit, Bouvier, Bonn, 70; Moderne Erzahler der Welt Kanada, Erdmann, Tubingen, 76; Das Literarische Kamadabild, Bourier, Bonn, 80; German Canadiana--A Bibliography, Seminar-A Journal Of Germanic Studies, Vol 29, 93. **CONTACT ADDRESS** Dept of Ger lang & Lit, Univ Victoria, Victoria, BC, V8W 2Y2.

RIESE HUBERT, RENEE
DISCIPLINE FRENCH AND COMPARATIVE LITERATURE **EDUCATION** Columbia Univ, PhD. **CAREER** PROF EMER, FR AND COMPAR LIT, UNIV CALIF, IRVINE. **SELECTED PUBLICATIONS** Auth, Surrealism and the Book; Magnifying Mirrors: Women, Surrealism, and Partnership. **CONTACT ADDRESS** Dept of Fr and Ital, Univ Calif, Irvine, CA, 92697.

RIGSBY, KENT JEFFERSON
PERSONAL Born 02/25/1945, Tulsa, OK, m, 1969, 2 children **DISCIPLINE** CLASSICAL LANGUAGES, ANCIENT HISTORY **EDUCATION** Yale Univ, BA, 66; Univ Toronto, MA, 68. **CAREER** Asst prof, 71-77, Assoc Prof Classics, Duke Univ, 77-, Asst ed, Greek, Roman & Byzantine Studies, 72-77, assoc ed, 77-79, Roman ed, 79 & sr ed, 80- **MEMBERSHIPS** Am Philol Asn. **RESEARCH** Greek epigraphy; Hellenistic history; ancient religion. **SELECTED PUBLICATIONS** Auth, Cnossus and Capua, Trans Am Philol Asn, 76; Sacred Ephebie games at Oxyrhynchus, Chronique D'Egypte, 77; The era of the Province of Asia, Phoenix, 79; Seleucid Notes, Trans Am Philol Asn, 80; Missing Places + Confused And Erroneous Readings Of Toponyms In Greek And Coptic Texts/, Classical Philology, Vol 91, 96; Greek And Latin Inscriptions In The Manisa-Museum, Vienna, Am J Of Philology, Vol 117, 96; Missing Places + Confused And Erroneous Readings Of Toponyms In Greek And Coptic Texts, Classical Philology, Vol 91, 96. **CONTACT ADDRESS** Dept Class Studies, Duke Univ, Durham, NC, 27706.

RINDISBACHER, HANS J.
PERSONAL m, 2 children **DISCIPLINE** GERMAN LANGUAGE AND LITERATURE **EDUCATION** Univ Bern, Switz, Lisc Phil 83; Stanford Univ, PhD, 89. **CAREER** Asst prof, 93-; asst prof, 93-95, Swarthmore Col; instr, 92, Univ La Verne, 92; visiting asst, 89-91, Reed Col; tchg asst, 84-88, Stanford Univ; asst, 83-84, Univ Bern, Switzerland. . **HONORS AND AWARDS** Third Prize DAAD Ger Studies Syllabus Contest, 94; MLA Award, 93; NEH Summer Seminar, Univ Wash, 92; fel(s), Stanford Univ, 85-89. **SELECTED PUBLICATIONS** Auth, bk publ by independent scholar; publ, numerous articles. **CONTACT ADDRESS** Dept of Ger, Pomona Col, 333 N College Way, Claremont, CA, 91711.

RINGEN, CATHERINE OLESON
PERSONAL Born 06/03/1943, Brooklyn, NY, m, 1969 **DISCIPLINE** LINGUISTICS **EDUCATION** Ind Univ, BA, 70, MA, 72, PhD(Ling), 75. **CAREER** Vis lectr Ling, Univ Minn, 73-74; asst prof, 75-79, from assoc prof Ling, 80-88; chmn, 87-93; act chmn, Fall, 96; Univ Iowa, 79-, Fulbright prof, Univ Trondheim, Norway, 80; Adam Nickiewicz Univ, Poznan, Poland, 94-95. **MEMBERSHIPS** Ling Soc Am; AAAS. **RESEARCH** Phonological theory; philosophy of linguistics; phonetics. **SELECTED PUBLICATIONS** Auth, On arguments for rule ordering, Found Lang, 8, 72; coauth, Rule reordering and the history of High German vowel length, Papers from Ninth Regional Meeting of Chicago Ling Soc, 73, auth, Obligatory-optional precedence, Found Lang, 74; contribr, Rule Order and Obligatory Rules, Proc of Eleventh Int Congress Ling, 75; Vowel Harmony: Implications for the Alternation Condition, Phonologica, 77; auth, Another view of the theoretical implications of Hungarian vowel harmony, Ling Inquiry, 78; Uralic and Altaic vowel harmony: A problem for Natural Generative Phonology, J Ling, 80; contribr, A concrete analysis of Hungarian vowel harmony, Issues in Vowel Harmony, 80; Catherine O Ringen and Robert Vago, A Constraints based analysis of Hungarian vowel harmony, in Approaches to Hungarian, Vol 5: Levels and Structures, Istvan Kenesei, ed, 95; Catherine O Ringen and Robert Vago, Hungarian roundness harmony in Optimality Theory, Approaches to Hungarian, Vol 6, Casper de

Groot, ed, 98. **CONTACT ADDRESS** Dept of Linguistics, Univ of Iowa, 570 English Phil Bldg, Iowa City, IA, 52242-1408. **EMAIL** catherine-ringen@viowa.edu

RINKEVICH, THOMAS E.
DISCIPLINE GREEK AND LATIN LANGUAGES, GREEK AND LATIN POETRY, EGYPTIAN LANGUAGE, ANCIE **EDUCATION** Xavier Univ, BA, 64; Ohio State Univ, MA, 66, PhD, 73. **CAREER** Instr, 67-73, asst prof, 73-96, assoc prof, 96-, actg ch, Classics, Univ Nebr, Lincoln. **MEMBERSHIPS** APA, (CAMWS, ACL, CML); MAM. **SELECTED PUBLICATIONS** Auth, A KWIC Concordance to Lucretius, De Rerum Natura. **CONTACT ADDRESS** Univ Nebr, Lincoln, Lincoln, NE, 68588-0417. **EMAIL** rgorman@unlinfo.unl.edu

RINKUS, JEROME JOSEPH
PERSONAL Born 09/11/1938, Baltimore, MD **DISCIPLINE** RUSSIAN LITERATURE **EDUCATION** Middlebury Col, AB, 60; Brown Univ, AM, 62, PhD, 71. **CAREER** Teaching asst Russ lang, Brown Univ, 62-64 & 67-68; asst linguist, Intensive Lang Training Ctr, Ind Univ, 65-66; asst prof Russ lang & lit, Bucknell Univ, 68-73; asst prof, 73-79, assoc prof Russ lang & lit & coordr Russ prog, Pomona Col, 79-. **HONORS AND AWARDS** NEH fel, 75 & grant, 78; consult, Nat Endowment for Humanities, 77-78; NEH grant, 87, Irex grant,88; ACTFL grant, 90; MLA grant, 90. **MEMBERSHIPS** Am Assn Advan Slavic Studies; Am Assn Teachers Slavic & East Europ Lang; MLA; Am Coun Teaching Foreign Lang; ACTR Amer Coun of Tchrs of Russi. **RESEARCH** Nineteenth century Russian literature; the novel; methodology of Russian language teaching. **SELECTED PUBLICATIONS** Auth, Pushkin's The Queen of Sages, Encyclopedia of Literary Characters II, Salem Press, 90, art, Sergei Timofeevich Alsakov, The Modern Encyclopedia of Russia and The Soviet Union, MERSU, Academic International Press, 90. **CONTACT ADDRESS** Dept of Mod Lang & Lit, Pomona Col, 333 N College Way, Claremont, CA, 91711-6319. **EMAIL** jrinkus@pomona.edu

RIPPLEY, LA VERN J.
PERSONAL Born 03/02/1935, Waumandee, WI, m, 1960, 2 children **DISCIPLINE** GERMAN ROMANTICISM & IMMIGRATION HISTORY **EDUCATION** Col Holy Cross, BA, 56; Univ Wis, BS, 58; Kent State Univ, MA, 61; Ohio State Univ, PhD(Ger), 65. **CAREER** Teacher, River Falls Sr High Sch, 58-60; teaching asst, Ohio State Univ, 61-63; asst prof Ger, Ohio Wesleyan Univ, 64-67; assoc prof, 67-71, chmn dept, 67-74, Prof Ger, St Olaf Col, 71-, Ed, Newsletter Soc Ger-Am Studies; Fulbright fel, 63-64 & Deutscher Akademischer Austauschdienst Fulbright, 82. **MEMBERSHIPS** Cent States Mod Lang Asn; MLA; Am Asn Teachers Ger; Am Hist Soc Ger from Russia; Norweg Am Hist Asn. **RESEARCH** German-Americana; German Romanticism; modern German literature. **SELECTED PUBLICATIONS** Transit, Excursion through America, R.R. Donnelley, 73; auth, The German-Americans, Twayne, 74; Germans from Russia, In: Harvard Encycl of American Ethnic Groups, Harvard Univ Press, 80; Immigrant Wisconsin, Twayne, 85; German Place Names in Minnesota / Deutsche Ortsnamen in Minnesota, St. Olaf Col / Rainer Schmeissner, 89; co-transl, The German Colonies on the Lower Volga, Their Origin and Early Development, Am Hist Soc of Germans from Russia, 91; auth, The Whoopee John Wilfahrt Dance Band. His Bohemian-German Roots, Northfield, 92; coauth, The German-American Experience, Ind-Purdue Univ at Indianapolis, 93; auth, German-Bohemians: The Quiet Immigrants, Northfield, 93; co-ed, Emigration and Settlement Patterns of German Communities in North America, Ind-Purdue Univ at Indianapolis, 95; Noble Women, Restless Men. The Rippley (Rieple, Ripley, Ripli, Rippli) Family in Wisconsin, North Dakota, Minnesota and Montana, St. Olaf Col Press, 96; author of numerous articles. **CONTACT ADDRESS** 1520 St Olaf Ave, Northfield, MN, 55057-1098. **EMAIL** rippleyl@stolaf.edu

RISCO, ANTONIO
PERSONAL Born 05/30/1926, Allariz, Spain, m, 1964 **DISCIPLINE** SPANISH LITERATURE **EDUCATION** Univ Santiago, Spain, BA, 45; Univ Madrid, MA, 61, PhD, 66. **CAREER** Prof, Col San Jose, Orense, 60-61; lectr, Col Enseignement Gen Fabre, Toulouse, France, 61-64; instr, Univ Ore, 64-66; asst, Mt Allison Univ, 66-69; from asst prof to assoc prof, 69-76, Prof Span Lit, Laval Univ: 76-, Dir Div, 76-, Vis prof, Univ Calif, Irvine, 72 & Carleton Univ, Ottawa, 77. **MEMBERSHIPS** Can Asn Hispanists; Int Asn Hispanists. **RESEARCH** Spanish literature of the 19th and 20th centuries; comparative Spanish and French literatures; the fantastic in literature. **SELECTED PUBLICATIONS** Auth, El Caballero de las Botas Azules, de Rosalia, una obra abierta, Papeles de Son Armadaus, Palma Mallorca, 75; La novela de Azorin y el Nouveau Roman Frances, Rev Can Estud Hispanicos, 76; El Demiurgo y su Mundo: Hacia un Nuevo Enfoque de la obra de Valle-Inclan, Gredos, Madrid, 77; La lucha por la vida de Baroja en la evolucion de la novelistica espanola, Rev Can Estud Hispanicos, 78; Azorin y la ruptura con la novela tradicional, Alhambra, Madrid, 80; Literatura y figuracion, Gredos, Madrid, 82; Literatura y fantasia, Taurus, Madrid, 82; El caso (novel), Akal, Madrid, 82; A Specter Is Haunting Europe: A Sociohistorical Approach To The Fantastic, Hispanic Rev, Vol 61, 93; The Postmodernist Movement In Latin-America, Etudes Litteraires, Vol 27, 94. **CONTACT ADDRESS** Dept of Lit, Laval Univ, Quebec, PQ, G1K 7P4.

RITTERSON, MICHAEL
DISCIPLINE GERMAN LANGUAGE AND LITERATURE **EDUCATION** Franklin and Marshall Col, AB, 62; Harvard Univ, PhD, 73. **CAREER** Instr Ger, Northeastern Univ, 66-67; instr, 68-74, Asst Prof Ger, Gettysburg Col, 74. **MEMBERSHIPS** Am Asn Tchr(s) Ger; MLA; Lessing Soc; Goethe Soc NAm; Raabe-Gesellschaft. **RESEARCH** Wilhelm Raabe; Ger lit in the Weimar Republic; eighteenth-century studies. **SELECTED PUBLICATIONS** Auth, Ruckwendung, Vorausdeutung und Erzahlablauf in Wilhelm Raabes Das Odfeld und Hastenbeck, Jahrbuch Raabe-Gesellschaft, 76; Waiting for Synthesis: Kurt Tucholsky Views America, 1925-1935, Occasional Papers Soc Ger-Am Studies, 81; Irony in Enlightenment Novel and 19th -c German Realism, Oeuvers and Critiques, 85. **CONTACT ADDRESS** Dept of Ger & Russ, Gettysburg Col, 300 N Washington St, Gettysburg, PA, 17325-1486. **EMAIL** mritters@gettysberg.edu

RIVERA RODAS, OSCAR
DISCIPLINE SPANISH LITERATURE **EDUCATION** Univ Ca, PhD, 80. **CAREER** Prof. **SELECTED PUBLICATIONS** Auth, pubs on Latin American texts. **CONTACT ADDRESS** Dept of Romance Languages, Knoxville, TN, 37996.

RIVERO, ELIANA SUAREZ
PERSONAL Born 11/07/1942, Artemisa, Cuba **DISCIPLINE** SPANISH, LATIN AMERICAN & U S LATINO LITERATURES **EDUCATION** Univ Miami, BA, 64, PhD(Span), 68. **CAREER** From asst prof to assoc prof, 67-78, PROF SPAN & PORT DEPT, UNIV ARIZ, 78-. **HONORS AND AWARDS** NEH res grant, 84; Rockefeller grant, 96. **MEMBERSHIPS** MLA; Am Asn Teachers Span & Port; Inst Int Lit Iberoam; Latin Am Studies Asn **RESEARCH** Poetry of Pablo Neruda; poetry of the 20th century; Latin American women writers; U S Latino writers **SELECTED PUBLICATIONS** Auth, El Gran Amor de Pablo Neruda, Plaza Mayor Ed, 71; Simbolismo tematico y titular de Las manos del dia, Mester, spring 74; La estetica esencial en una oda nerudiana, In: Simposio Pablo Neruda, Las Americas, 75; Analisis de perspectivas y significacion en La Rosa Separada, Rev Iberoam, 76; Dialectica de la Persona poetica en la obra de Julia de Burgos, Rev Critics Lit Latinoam, fall 76; Vision social y feminista en la obra lirica de Rosario Castellanos, In: Estudios de Hispanofila, Univ NC, 79; Reflexiones pars una Nueva Poetica, Actas Asoc int de Hispanistas, Toronto, 80; Hacia una Lectura Feminista de Tres Tristes Tigres, Feminist Literary Criticism: Theory and Practice, Bilingual Press, 82; Relectura de Ismaelillo, Estudios Martianos, 84; Hispanic literature in the U S, Revista Chicano-Reguena, 85; From immigrants to ethnics: Cuban women writers in the U S, In: Breaking Boundaries, UMass Press, 89; Eva Luna and women storytellers, Splintering Darkness, Latin Am Lit Rev Press, 90; Testimonial literature as literary discourse, latin American Perspectives, 91; (Re)writing sugarcane memories: Cuban Americans and literature, Am Rev, 91; co-ed, Infinite Divisions: An Anthology of Chicana Literature, Univ Ariz Press, 93; Border islander, In: Bridges to Cuba, Univ Mich Press, 95; Flores ocultas de previa cubana, Homenaje a Luis Monguio, Juan de la Cuesta, 98; Creative writing (poetry) in: Siete poetas, 77; Woman of her work, 83; Nosotias, 86; Veinte anos de literature cubanoameriana, 88, Daughters of the fifth sun, 95; Floricanto si, An Anthology of Latina Poetry, Penguin 98. **CONTACT ADDRESS** Dept of Span & Port, Univ of Ariz, PO Box 210067, Tucson, AZ, 85721-0067. **EMAIL** eliana@u.arizona.edu

RIVERO, MARIA LUISA
PERSONAL Born 02/01/1943, Madrid, Spain, m, 1964, 2 children **DISCIPLINE** LINGUISTICS **EDUCATION** Univ Rochester, MA, 64, PhD(ling), 70. **CAREER** Asst prof, 70-75, assoc prof, 75-82, Prof Ling, Univ Ottawa, 82-, Res grant, Can Coun, 71-82. **MEMBERSHIPS** Ling Soc Am; Can Ling Asn; Soc Espanola de Ling; Asn Can de Hispanistas. **RESEARCH** Romance syntax and semantics; generative grammar; history of logic and linguistics. **SELECTED PUBLICATIONS** Auth, On left dislocation and topicalization in Spanish, Linguistic Inquiry, 80; Theoretical implications of the syntax of left-branch modifiers in Spanish, Ling Analysis, 80; coauth, Catalan restrictive relatives: Core and periphery, Lang, 81; Bulgarian And Serbo-Croatian Yes-No Questions--V0-Raising To -Li Versus -Li Hopping, Linguistic Inquiry, Vol 24, 93; Long Head Movement Vs V2, And Null Subjects In Old Romance, Lingua, Vol 89, 93; Imperatives, V-Movement And Logical Mood, J Of Linguistics, Vol 31, 95; Clitic Auxiliaries And Incorporation In Polish, Natural Language & Linguistic Theory, Vol 12, 94; On Indirect Questions, Commands, And Spanish Quotative Que, Linguistic Inquiry, Vol 25, 94. **CONTACT ADDRESS** Dept of Ling, Univ of Ottawa, Ottawa, ON, K1N 6N5.

RIVERS, ELIAS LYNCH
PERSONAL Born 09/19/1924, Charleston, SC, m, 1945, 3 children **DISCIPLINE** SPANISH **EDUCATION** **EDUCATION** Yale Univ, AB, 48, MA, 50, PhD(Span), 52. **CAREER** Instr Span, Yale Univ, 51-52; from instr to asst prof, Dartmouth Uol, 52-62; prof, Ohio State Univ, 62-64; prof, Johns Hopkins Univ, 64-78; Prof Span & Comp Lit, State Univ NY, 78-, Howard fel, 56-57; Guggenheim fel, 59-60; Fulbright res grant, Madrid, 64-65; Nat Endowment for Humanities res grant, 67-68, 70-71 & 81-82, sem dir, 75-76. **HONORS AND AWARDS** MA, Dartmouth Col, 62. **MEMBERSHIPS** MLA; Am Asn Teachers Span & Port; Asoc Int Hispanistas (secy-gen, 62-80). **RESEARCH** Renaissance poetry in Spain; oral and written styles of composition. **SELECTED PUBLICATIONS** Auth, 17th-Century Spanish Poetry, The Power Of Artifice, Mln-Modern Language Notes, Vol 110, 95; Gongora,Luis,De, Selected, Hispanic Rev, Vol 61, 93; The Works Of Boscan Updated And Compiled In 3 Volumes, Hispanic Rev, Vol 63, 95; 6 Masters Of The Spanish Sonnet, Hispanic Rev, Vol 62, 94; 17th-Century Spanish Poetry, The Power Of Artifice, Mln-Modern Language Notes, Vol 110, 95. **CONTACT ADDRESS** Dept of Hisp Studies, State Univ NY, Stony Brook, NY, 11794.

RIVERS, WILGA MARIE
PERSONAL Melbourne, Australia **DISCIPLINE** FRENCH, FOREIGN LANGUAGE EDUCATION **EDUCATION** Univ Melbourne, dipl educ, BA, 40, MA, 48; Univ Lille, dipl French studies, 50; Univs Lille & Montpellier, Lic es Lett, 52; Univ Ill, Urbana-Champaign, PhD(educ & French), 62. **CAREER** Sr teacher French & English, Australian high & prep schs, 40-59; asst prof French, Northern Ill Univ, 62-64; from lectr to assoc prof, Monash Univ, Australia, 64-69; vis prof, Teachers Col, Columbia Univ, 70-71; prof, Univ Ill, Urbana-Champaign, 71-74; Prof Romance Lang & Lang Coordr, Harvard Univ, 74-, Teacher English Lycee Jeune Filles, Douai, & Norm Sch, Montpellier, 49-52; participant, Can UNESCO sem biling, 67; vis scholar, French govt, 68; consult, Rockefeller Found English teaching proj, Bangkok, 71; prof ling, Mid East Ling Inst, Cairo, 74 & Ling Soc Am, Ling Inst, Oswego, NY, 76; consult, Nat Endowment for Humanities, 75-76; JACET sem, Tokyo, 79. **HONORS AND AWARDS** Florence Steiner Award, Am Coun Teachers Foreign Lang, 77. **MEMBERSHIPS** Am Asn Appl Ling (pres, 77-78); Ling Soc Am; Am Coun Teaching Foreign Lang; Am Asn Teachers Fr; Teachers English to Speakers Other Lang. **RESEARCH** Language teaching; psycholinguistics; college curriculum. **SELECTED PUBLICATIONS** Auth, The Psychologist and the Foreign Language Teacher, 64 & Teaching Foreign Language Skills, 68 & 81, Univ Chicago; Speaking in Many Tongues, 72, 76 & co-ed, Changing Patterns in Foreign Language Programs, 72, Newbury House; auth, Practical Guide to the Teaching of French, 75, coauth, Practical Guide to the Teaching of German, 75, Practical Guide to the Teaching of Spanish, 76 & Practical Guide to the Teaching of English SL, 78, Oxford Univ; Cultures, Languages And The International Smorgasbord--Musings For A New Millennium, Canadian Modern Language Review-Revue Canadienne Des Langues Vivantes, Vol 50, 93. **CONTACT ADDRESS** Dept of Romance Lang & Lit, Harvard Univ, 206 Boylston Hall, Cambridge, MA, 02138.

RIZZUTO, ANTHONY
PERSONAL Born 03/25/1937, Brooklyn, NY, m, 1966, 2 children **DISCIPLINE** FRENCH LANGUAGE; LITERATURE **EDUCATION** Columbia Univ, PhD 66, MA 60; Columbia Col, BA 58. **CAREER** SUNY Stony Brook, assoc prof, 68-; Tufts Univ, asst prof, 66-68; Columbia Col, inst, 61-66. **HONORS AND AWARDS** Fulbright fel; NEH. **MEMBERSHIPS** MLA; ALSC; AATF; SEC. **RESEARCH** 19th and 20th Century French lit. **SELECTED PUBLICATIONS** Auth, Camus: Love and Sexuality, U of FL Press, 98. **CONTACT ADDRESS** Dept of French, Stony Brook Col-SUNY, PO Box 48, Miller Place, NY, 11764.

ROBB, JAMES WILLIS
PERSONAL Born 06/27/1918, Jamaica, NY **DISCIPLINE** ROMANCE LANGUAGES & LITERATURES **EDUCATION** Colgate Univ, AB, 39; Middlebury Col, AM, 50; Cath Univ Am, PhD, 58. **CAREER** Instr, 46-50, Norwich Univ; from asst prof to assoc prof, 50-66, prof romance lang, 66-88, prof emeritus, 88-, George Washington Univ. **HONORS AND AWARDS** Alfonso Reyes Int Lit Prize, Mexico, 78. **MEMBERSHIPS** MLA; Am Assn Teachers Span & Port; Inst Int Lit Iberoam. **RESEARCH** The works of Alfonso Reyes; modern Spanish American literature; Mexican & Colombian literature. **SELECTED PUBLICATIONS** Auth, Por Loscaminos de Alfonso Reyes, INBA/Univ Valle Mex, 81; auth, Variedades de ensayismo en A Reyes y German Arciniegas, 81; auth, La cena de A Reyes, cuento onirico: Surrealismo o realismo magico?, 81; auth, Caminos cruzados en el epistolario de M Toussaint y A Reyes, A Reyes: Homenaje de la Facultad de Filosofia y Letras, Univ Nac Autonoma Mex, Mex, 81. **CONTACT ADDRESS** Dept of Romance Lang, George Washington Univ, Washington, DC, 20052.

ROBB, MICHAEL P.
DISCIPLINE COMMUNICATION SCIENCES **EDUCATION** Western Mich Univ, BS, 79; Syracuse Univ, MS, 83, PhD, 88. **CAREER** Assoc prof, Univ Conn; instr, Univ Hawaii. **RESEARCH** Acoustic and phonetic characteristics of vocal development among infants and toddlers. **SELECTED PUBLICATIONS** Coauth, Formant Frequency Fluctuation in Stutterers and Nonstutterers, J Fluency Disorders 23, 98; How Steady are Vowel Steady-States, Clinical Ling and Phonetics 12, 98; A Note on Vowel Centralization in Stuttering and Nonstuttering Individuals, J Speech, Lang, and Hearing Res 41, 98; Vocal Tract Resonance Characteristics of Adults Wth Obstruc-

tive Sleep apnea, Acta Otolaryngologica 117, 97; Formant Frequency and Bandwidth Development in Infants and Toddlers, Folia Phoniatrica 49, 97; Formant Frequency Development: 15-36 months, J Voice 11, 97; An Acoustic Template of Normal Newborn Cry, Folia Phoniatrica 49, 97; An Acoustic Template of Normal and At-Risk Infant Crying, Biology of the Neonate 71, 97; Analysis of F2 Transitions in the Speech of Stutterers and Nonstutterers, J Fluency Disorders 22, 97; An Acoustic Examination of Naturalistic Modal and Falsetto Voice Registers, Logopedics, Phoniatrics and Vocology 22, 97; A Note on Prespeech Early Speech Coarticulation, Logopedics, Phoniatrics and Vocology 22, 97. **CONTACT ADDRESS** Dept of Communication Sci, Univ of Connecticut, 850 Bolton Rd, Storrs, CT, 06269-1085. **EMAIL** mrobb@uconnvm.uconn.edu

ROBBINS, JILL
DISCIPLINE COMPARATIVE LITERATURE **EDUCATION** Cornell Univ, BA; Yale Univ, PhD. **CAREER** Assoc prof, SUNY Buffalo. **RESEARCH** Bibl and philosophical hermeneutics; the Bible as lit; lit theory; ethical thought of Emmanuel Levinas; Levinas' philos in its rel to lit. **SELECTED PUBLICATIONS** Auth, Prodigal Son/Elder Brother: Interpretation and Alterity in Augustine, Petrarch, Kafka, Levinas, Univ Chicago P, 91; The Writing of the Holocaust: Claude Lanzmann's Shoah; Visage, Figure: Reading Levinas' Totality and Infinity; An Inscribed Responsibility: Levinas' Difficult Freedom. **CONTACT ADDRESS** Dept Comp Lit, SUNY Buffalo, 639 Clemens Hall, Buffalo, NY, 14260.

ROBERTS, ANNA
DISCIPLINE FRENCH **EDUCATION** Brown, MA, PhD. **CAREER** Asst prof; Medieval Stud Comt, Women's Stud Prog & Ling Comt, Miami Univ. **HONORS AND AWARDS** Co-organized, Brown University's Grad Conf in Fr Stud. **RESEARCH** Medieval and Renaissance literature, especially on women's studies and on the history of art and technology. **SELECTED PUBLICATIONS** Auth, Violence against Women in Medieval Texts, UP Fla, 98; controb, Les propos spectacle: Etudes de pragmatique theatrale, 96. **CONTACT ADDRESS** Dept of French and Italian, Miami Univ, Oxford, OH, 45056.

ROBERTS, JULIE
DISCIPLINE COMMUNCATION SCIENCES **EDUCATION** Univ Pa, PhD, 94. **CAREER** Dept Comm, Vermont Univ **MEMBERSHIPS** Ling Soc Am; Am Dialect Soc; Int Asn Study Child Lang; Am Speech Lang Hearing Asn. **SELECTED PUBLICATIONS** Auth, Learning to talk Philadelphian; Acquisition of shot a by preschool children, 95; Late talkers at two: Outcome at age three, Jour Speech Hearing Res, 97. **CONTACT ADDRESS** Dept of Communication Sciences, Vermont Univ, 360 Waterman Bldg, Burlington, VT, 05405. **EMAIL** jroberts@polyglot.uvm.edu

ROBEY, DAVID H.
DISCIPLINE SPEECH COMMUNICATION **EDUCATION** Pillsbury Col, BA, 70; Bob Jones Univ, MA, 72; Union Inst, PhD. **CAREER** Prof, Tennessee Temple Univ, 72-81; Prof, Cedarville Col, 81-. **SELECTED PUBLICATIONS** Auth, Two for Missions, Lillenas Publ Co, Kansas City, Miss, 88. **CONTACT ADDRESS** Cedarville Col, PO Box 601, Cedarville, OH, 45314.

ROBINS, GAY
PERSONAL Born 06/28/1951, Fleet, England, m, 1980 **DISCIPLINE** EGYPTOLOGY **EDUCATION** Univ Durham, BA (honors), 75; Univ Oxford, DPhil, 81. **CAREER** Lady Wallis Budge Fellow in Egyptology, Christ's College, Cambridge, 79-83; honorary research fel, Univ Coll London, 84-88; asst prof, 88-94, assoc prof, 94-98, prof, 98-, Art History Dept, curator of Egyptian art, 88-94, faculty curator of ancient Egyptian art, 94-98, faculty consult for ancient Egyptian art, 98-, Michael C. Carlos Museum, Emory Univ. **HONORS AND AWARDS** Thomas Mulvey Fund grant, H.M. Chadwick Fund grant, Univ Cambridge, 85; Suzette Taylor Travelling Fellow, Lady Margaret Hall, Oxford, 85-86; Wainwright Near Eastern Archeol Fund grant, 87; Natl Endowment for the Humanities grant, 92; Univ Research Comm grant, Emory Univ, 95-96. **MEMBERSHIPS** Amer Res Center in Egypt; Coll Art Assn; Egyptian Exploration Soc; Egyptological Seminar of New York; Intl Assn of Egyptologists; Soc Study Egyptian Antiquities. **RESEARCH** The content and function of ancient Egyptian art; use of the squared grid and changes in the proportions of figures in ancient Egyptian art; the Amarna grid system; composition of whole scenes in ancient Egyptian art; hierarchies in ancient Egyptian art; status of women in ancient Egypt. **SELECTED PUBLICATIONS** Coauth, Egyptian Painting and Relief, 86; coauth, The Rhind Mathematical Papyrus, 87, reprinted, 90, 98; auth, Women in Ancient Egypt, 93, reprinted, 96; auth, Proportion and Style in Ancient Egyptian Art, 94; auth, The Art of Ancient Egypt, 97. **CONTACT ADDRESS** Art History Dept, Emory Univ, Carlos Hall, Atlanta, GA, 30322. **EMAIL** grobins@emory.edu

ROBINSON, DANIEL N.
PERSONAL Born 03/09/1937, New York, NY, m, 1967, 2 children **DISCIPLINE** NEUROPSYCHOLOGY **EDUCATION** Colgate Univ, BA, 58; Hofstra Univ, MA, 60; CUNY, PhD, 65. **CAREER** Res psychologist, Columbia Univ Sch Engineer & Applied Sci, 60-68; asst prof, Amherst Coll, 68-70; assoc prof, Psych, Amherst Coll, 70-71; vis lectr, Philos, Univ Oxford, 91-; prof, Psych, Georgetown Univ, 74-98; DISTINGUISH RES PROF, GEORGETOWN UNIV, 98-. **MEMBERSHIPS** Am Psychol Asn **RESEARCH** History & Philosophical Psychology; Intellect history; Philosophy of mind; Mind/Brain relations. **SELECTED PUBLICATIONS** "Wild Beasts and Idle Humours: Legal Insanity and the Finding of Fault," Philosophy, Psychiatry, and Psychology, Cambridge Univ Press, 95; "On the Laws of History," Psychological Inquiry, 95; "The Logic of Reductionistic Models," New Ideas in Psychology, 95; "On the Primacy of Duties," Philosophy, 95; "Radical Ontologies," Int Jour for the Philos of Sci, 95; "Therapy as Theory and Civics," Theory & Psychol, 97; "Studies of Hysteria a Century Later," Amer Jour of Clinical Hypnosis, 96; An Intellectual History of Psychology, Univ Wis, 95; Wild Beasts and Idle Humours: The Insanity Defense from Antiquity to the Present," Harvard Univ Press, 96; The Mind: An Oxford Reader, Oxford Univ Press, 98. **CONTACT ADDRESS** Dept Psychol, Georgetown Univ, Washington, DC, 20007. **EMAIL** robinsdn@gunet.georgetown.edu

ROBINSON, FRED C.
DISCIPLINE LANGUAGE **EDUCATION** Birmingham Southern Col, BA, 53; MA, 54, PhD, 61, Univ N Carolina; Williams Col, DLit (honorary), 85; Yale Univ, MA (honorary), 89. **CAREER** Instr and Asst Prof, 60-65, Assoc Prof/Prof, 67-72, Stanford Univ; Asst and Assoc Prof, Cornell Univ, 65-67; Visiting Prof, Harvard Univ, 82; Prof, 72-83, Douglas Tracy Smith Prof, 83-, Yale Univ. **CONTACT ADDRESS** Dept of English, Yale Univ, PO Box 208302, New Haven, CT, 06520-8302.

ROBINSON, IRA
PERSONAL Born 05/02/1951, Boston, MA, m, 1976, 2 children **DISCIPLINE** NEAR EASTERN LANGUAGES AND CIVILIZATIONS **EDUCATION** Harvard Univ, PhD, 80. **CAREER** Prof, relig, Concordia Univ, 79-. **HONORS AND AWARDS** Toronto Jewish Book award, 97; Kenneth B. Smilen book prize, Jewish Mus, 86. **MEMBERSHIPS** Asn for Can Jewish Studies; Asn for Jewish Studies; Soc Quebecois pour lietude de la religion; Amer Jewish Hist Soc. **RESEARCH** Canadian Jewry; Orthodox Judaism in North America. **SELECTED PUBLICATIONS** Rev, Pseudo-Rabad Commentary to Sifre Deuteronomy, Studies in Relig, 97; auth, Cyrus Adler: President of the Jewish Theological Seminary, 1915-1940, Tradition Renewed: a History of the Jewish Theological Seminary, Jewish Theol Sem of Amer, 97; rev, The Kiss of God: Spiritual and Mystical Death in Judaism, AJS Rev, 96; rev, Jewish Learning in American Universities: the First Century, Amer Jewish Hist, 96; auth, The Foundation Documents of the Jewish Community Council of Montreal, Jewish Polit Studies Rev, 96; ed, Renewing Our Days: Montreal Jews in the Twentieth Century, Vehicule Press, 95; auth, An Identification and a Correction, Amer Jewish Archives, 95; foreward, A Selected Bibliography of Research on Canadian Jewry, 1900-1980, Amer Jewish Archiv, v, 95; auth, The Zaddik as Hero in Hasidic Hagiography, Crisis and Reaction: the Hero in Jewish History, Creighton Univ Press, 95; rev, Commentary on the Book of Job, Studies in Relig, 94; rev, Habad: the Hasidism of Rabbi Shneur Zalman of Lyadi, AJS Rev, 19, 94; rev, New York's Jewish Jews: the Orthodox Community in the Interwar Years, Jewish Quart Rev, 94; auth, The Diffusion of Scientific Knowledge Among Eastern European Jews in the Nineteenth Century: the Writings of Hayyim Selig Slonimsky, The Interaction of Scientific and Jewish Cultures in Modern Times, Edwin Mellen Press, 94; auth, Toward a History of Kashrut in Montreal: the Fight Over Municipal Bylaw 828 (1922-1924), Renewing Our Days: Montreal Jews in the Twentieth Century, 95; auth, Two North American Kehillot and Their Structure: Philadelphia and Montreal, Proceedings of the Eleventh World Congress of Jewish Studies, Division B The History of the Jewish People, vol III, Modern Times 94; auth, The Invention of American Jewish History, Amer Jewish Hist, 94; co-ed, The Interaction of Scientific and Jewish Cultures In Modern Times, Edwin Mellen Press, 94; auth, Moses Cordovero's Introduction to Kabbala: An Annotated Translation of His Or Ne'Erav, Yeshiva Univ Press, 94. **CONTACT ADDRESS** Dept. of Religion, Concordia Univ, Montreal, 1455 Maisonneuve Blvd. W, Montreal, PQ, H3G 1M8. **EMAIL** robinso@vax2.concordia.ca

ROBINSON, KELLY A.
DISCIPLINE ACQUIRED NEUROGENIC DISORDERS OF COMMUNICATION **EDUCATION** SUNY, BA, MA; Emerson Col, PhD. **CAREER** Emerson Col. **SELECTED PUBLICATIONS** Area: affect acquired brain injury has on attention, memory, and lang(s). **CONTACT ADDRESS** Emerson Col, 100 Beacon Street, Boston, MA, 02116-1596.

ROBISON, R.E.
PERSONAL Born 10/21/1950, Kansas City, MO, m, 1971, 10 children **DISCIPLINE** LINGUISTICS **EDUCATION** Univ Cal LA, PhD 93, MA 85; Gordon-Conwell Theological Sem, Mdiv 76; Massachusetts Inst of Technology, SB 72. **CAREER** Azusa Pacific Univ, prof 97-, assoc prof 91-97; Univ Cal LA, tchg fel 87-92; Glendale Community Col, inst 86-91; Univ Cal LA, tchg assoc 82-86. **HONORS AND AWARDS** Phi Beta Kappa; Eugene Nida Awd. **MEMBERSHIPS** Teachers of Eng to Speakers of Other Lang; Cal Tchrs of Eng to Speaks of Other Lang **RESEARCH** Verb morphology in interlanguage; interlanguage analysis. **SELECTED PUBLICATIONS** Auth, Verb inflections in native speaker speech: Do the mean what we think?, in: The development of morphological systematicity: A cross-linguistic perspective, eds H. Pishwa and K. Maroldt, Tubingen, Gunter Narr, 95; The aspect hypothesis revisited: A cross sectional study of tense and aspect marking in interlanguage, Applied Ling, 95; Aspectual marking in English interlanguage, Stud in Sec Lang Acquis, 90. **CONTACT ADDRESS** Dept of Global Studies, Azusa Pacific Univ, 901 East Alosta Av, Azusa, CA, 91702-7000. **EMAIL** rrobison@apu.edu

ROCKLAND, MICHAEL AARON
PERSONAL Born 07/14/1935, New York, NY, m, 5 children **DISCIPLINE** AMERICAN & LATIN AMERICAN STUDIES **EDUCATION** Hunter Col, BA, 55; Univ Minn, MA, 60, PhD(Am studies), 68. **CAREER** Teaching asst Am studies, Univ Minn, 57-59, instr, 60-61, counsel, Col Arts & Sci, 59-61; asst cult attache, Am Embassy, Buenos Aires, 62-63, asst cult attache & dir, Casa Am Cult Ctr, Am Embassy, Madrid, 63-67; exec asst to chancellor, NJ State Dept Higher Educ, 68-69; asst prof, 69-71, asst dean col, 69-72, assoc prof, 72-81, Prof Am Studies, Douglass Col, Rutgers Univ, 81-, Chm Dept, 69-; Lectr, Univ Santa Fe, Arg, 63; guest lectr, Span Univ Syst, 64-67; publ subventions, Rutgers Univ & Arg Embassy, 70; fac chm contemporary Am sem returning foreign serv officers, US Info Agency, 72-73, mem bd, Int Inst Women Studies, 72-; contrib ed, NJ Monthly, 77-; contrib reporter, NJ Nightly News, 78-. **HONORS AND AWARDS** Alumni Hall of Fame, Hunter Col, 73; NJ Pres Assoc Award, 80; Pulitzer Prize nominee, 80; First Prize for Feature Journalism, Am Soc of Jour, 92; The Nat Am Studies Prize for Distinguished Teaching, 97; The Warren Susman Award for Distinguished Teaching, 97; Teacher of the Year Award, Rutgers Col, 98. **MEMBERSHIPS** Am Studies Asn (pres, 71-72); Orgn Am Historians; hon mem Inst Sarmiento, Arg. **RESEARCH** Foreign commentators on the United States; ethnic affairs in the United States, especially the relationship between Jews and the other ethnic groups; mobility in America; Am Aesthetics. **SELECTED PUBLICATIONS** Auth, Sarmiento's Travels in the United States in 1847, Princeton Univ, 70; ed, America in the Fifties and Sixties: Julian Marias on the United States, Pa State Univ, 72; coauth, Three Days on Big City Waters (film), Nat Educ TV, 74; auth, The American Jewish Experience in Literature, Haifa Univ, 75; Homes on Wheels, Rutgers Univ Pres, 80; A Bliss Case, Coffee House Press, 89; coauth, Looking for America on the New Jersey Turnpike, Rutgers Univ Press, 80; auth, Snowshoeing Through Sewers, Rutgers Univ Press, 94. **CONTACT ADDRESS** Dept of Am Studies, Rutgers Univ, PO Box 270, New Brunswick, NJ, 08903-0270. **EMAIL** rockland@rci.rutgers.edu

ROCKMORE, SYLVIE
DISCIPLINE FRENCH AND FRANCOPHONE CULTURES **EDUCATION** Vanderbilt Univ, PhD. **CAREER** Languages, Carnegie Mellon Univ. **MEMBERSHIPS** Alliance francaise; Am Asn Tchrs French **SELECTED PUBLICATIONS** Auth, De Leuk-le lievre a Brer Rabbit : transformations d'un conte. Presentation, 88; Organized the Conference on Simone de Beauvoir: Beauvoir at 90: A Reevaluation, Carnegie Mellon Univ, 98; Quelques idees pour celebrer la negritude. AATF Nat Bull, 96. **CONTACT ADDRESS** Carnegie Mellon Univ, 5000 Forbes Ave, Pittsburgh, PA, 15213.

RODGERS, JOSEPH JAMES, JR.
PERSONAL Born 11/22/1939, Hopewell, VI **DISCIPLINE** LINGUISTICS **EDUCATION** Morehouse Coll, BA 1962; Univ de Grenoble France, Cert d'etudes 1960; Univ of WI, MA 1965; Univ of So CA, PhD 1969. **CAREER** Los Angeles City Coll, lecturer 1966-67; Univ of So CA, instr 1968-69; Occidental Coll, asst prof 1968-73; VA State Coll, prof & chmn 1970-71; Intl Curriculum Devel Program Phelps-Stokes Fund, reg coord 1975-; Carib-Amer School to Dominican Republic, 1975; LINCOLN UNIV, CHMN, PROF 1973-; CENTER FOR CRITICAL CARE LANGUAGES, DIR, 1990-; AMERICAN UNIV OF UZES, FRANCE, PRES, 1990-. **HONORS AND AWARDS** Merrill Travel Study Group to Europe 1959-60; W Wilson Fellowship to Harvard 1962-63; NDEA & Oakley Fellow Univ of So CA 1965-69; numerous articles in Maghreb Digest 1966-67; Distinguished Teaching 1974; Lindback Awd Pi Delta Phi Frat Honor Soc; Alpha Mu Gamma Natl Foreign Language Honor Soc; Honored Nominee, CASE Professor of the Year 1989; Distinguished Faculty Award for Scholarship Lincoln Univ, 1989. **MEMBERSHIPS** Pr tutor Stanley Kramer's son 1966-67; mem African Ethnic Herit Sem 1974, 1975. **SELECTED PUBLICATIONS** "African Leadership Ideology" (w/Ukandi Damachi) Praeger 1976; "Sacrificing Qual Lang Learn for Pol Exped" 1977. **CONTACT ADDRESS** Dept of Languages/Linguistics, Lincoln University, PA, 19352.

RODINI, ROBERT JOSEPH
PERSONAL Born 08/02/1936, Albany, CA, m, 1962, 2 children **DISCIPLINE** ROMANCE LANGUAGES **EDUCATION** Univ Calif, Berkeley, MA, 60, PhD, 67. **CAREER** From

instr to assoc prof, 65-76, prof Ital, 76-87, PROF EMERITUS, UNIV WI-MADISON, 87-, Dir, Ind Univ- Univ Wis jr year, Bologna, Italy, 71-72; Am Coun Learned Soc fel, 76. **MEMBERSHIPS** MLA; Am Asn Teachers Ital; Renaissance Soc Am. **RESEARCH** Renaissance drama, especially Italian, 16th century; the Italian baroque. **SELECTED PUBLICATIONS** Auth, Antonfrancesco Grazzini: Poet, Dramatist and Novelliere, Univ Wis- Madison, 70; contribr, A Renaissance Alphabet, Univ Wis, 71; ed, Opere di Dio, Houghton, 76; Medieval and renaissance spectacle and theatre, Vol XIV, No 3, Forum Italium, 80. **CONTACT ADDRESS** Dept of French, Univ Wis, 1220 Linden Drive, Madison, WI, 53706-1557. **EMAIL** rjrodini@macc.wisc.edu

RODRIGO, VICTORIA
DISCIPLINE SECOND LANGUAGE ACQUISITION, METHODOLOGY, PEDAGOGY **EDUCATION** Univ Southern Calif, PhD, 95. **CAREER** Asst prof Span, undergrad comt, La State Univ. **RESEARCH** Reading and listening as ways to promote language acquisition. **SELECTED PUBLICATIONS** Coauth, La aplicacion del Argumento de la Audicion Enfocada en el Aula de Clase, Granada Eng Tchg Asn, Univ Granada, Spain; A Reading Din in the Head: Evidence of Involuntary Mental Rehearsal in Second Language Readers, in For Lang Ann, 95; Free Voluntary Reading and Vocabulary Knowledge in Native Speakers of Spanish, Perceptual and Motor Skills, 96. **CONTACT ADDRESS** Dept of For Lang and Lit, Louisiana State Univ, 245B Prescott Hall, Baton Rouge, LA, 70803. **EMAIL** rodrigo@homer.forlang.lsu.edu

RODRIQUEZ - LUIS, JULIO
PERSONAL Born 10/09/1937, Cuba, m, 1968 **DISCIPLINE** SPANISH & COMPARATIVE LIT **EDUCATION** Univ Puerto Rico, BA, 59; Brown Univ, MA, 60; Princeton Univ, PhD, 66. **CAREER** Asst prof, 67-70, Wesleyan Univ; assoc prof, 70-81, prof, 81-93, SUNY Binghamton; prof, 93-, Univ Wisc - Milwaukee. **RESEARCH** Spanish Amer lit; Cervantes; Soc in lit. **CONTACT ADDRESS** Dept of Spanish and Portuguese, Univ of Wisconsin, PO Box 413, Milwaukee, WI, 53201. **EMAIL** jrluis@csd.uwm.edu

ROEPER, THOMAS
DISCIPLINE LINGUISTICS **EDUCATION** Reed Univ, BA, 65; Harvard Univ, PhD, 73. **CAREER** Prof. **RESEARCH** Theoretical approaches to language acquisition and morphology. **SELECTED PUBLICATIONS** Auth, Compound Syntax and Head Movement, Foris, 88; co-auth, On the Ergative and Middle Constructions in English, Ling Inquiry, 84; Implicit Arguments and the Head-Complement Relation, Ling Inquiry, 87; Deductive Parameters and the Growth of Language, Reidel, 87. **CONTACT ADDRESS** Linguistics Dept, Univ of Massachusetts, Amherst, S College 218, Amherst, MA, 01003. **EMAIL** roeper@linguist.umass.edu

ROETHKE, GISELA
DISCIPLINE 19TH AND 20TH CENTURY GERMAN LITERATURE **EDUCATION** Wash State Univ, MA; Harvard Univ, PhD, 88. **CAREER** Instr, 85-; coord, women's studies, 95-96; chp-. **RESEARCH** Modern women authors **SELECTED PUBLICATIONS** Publ, on Christa Wolf and Barbara Frischmuth. **CONTACT ADDRESS** Dept of Ger, Dickinson Col, PO Box 1773, Carlisle, PA, 17013-2896. **EMAIL** roethke@dickinson.edu

ROGERS, JACK E.
PERSONAL Born 12/13/1957, Stillwater, OK, m, 1991, 4 children **DISCIPLINE** SPEECH COMMUNICATION, SOCIOLOGY **EDUCATION** La State Univ, PhD, 94. **CAREER** Assoc prof, Southern Univ, 86-95; ASST PROF, UNIV OF TX AT TYLER, 96-. **HONORS AND AWARDS** Pres, Int Debat Asn. **MEMBERSHIPS** NCA, SSCA, CEDA, IPDA. **RESEARCH** Debate; forensics. **SELECTED PUBLICATIONS** Auth, A Community of Unequals: An Analysis of Dominant and Subdominant Culturally Linked Perceptions of Participation and Success within Intercollegiate Competitive Debate, Contemporary Argumentations & Debate: The J of the Cross-Examination Debate Asn, 97; A Critique of the Lexis/Nexis Debate: What's Missing Here?, The Southern J of Forensics, 96; Interrogating the Myth of Multiculturalism: Toward Significant Membership and Participation of Afrian Americans in Forensics, The Forensic of Pi Kappa Delta, 95; The Minority Perspective: Toward the Future Forensics Participation of Historically Black College and Universities, Proceedings from the Pi Kappa Delta Development Conf, 95; Constructing the Deconstruction: Toward the Empowerment of Women and Minorities in Forensics, Pi Kappa Delta Nat Development Conf, 95; What do they have that I haven't got? Comparison Survey Data of the Resources and Support Systems of Top CEDA Programs and Directors, CEDA Yearbook, 91. **CONTACT ADDRESS** Univ Texas at Tyler, 3900 University Blvd, Tyler, TX, 75799.

ROGERS, KENNETH HALL
PERSONAL Born 06/01/1939, Needham, MA, m, 1963, 2 children **DISCIPLINE** ROMANCE LINGUISTICS, FRENCH **EDUCATION** Boston Univ, BA, 61; Columbia Univ, MA, 63, PhD (Romance Philol), 70. **CAREER** Instr French, 68-70, Asst Prof French & Romance Ling, Univ RI, 70-. **MEMBERSHIPS** MLA; Ling Soc Am; Int Ling Asn; Am Asn Teachers Fr; Am Soc Geoling (pres, 77-78). **RESEARCH** Romance linguistics-phonology and morphology; sociolinguistics and linguistic nationlism. **SELECTED PUBLICATIONS** Auth, Vocalic Alternation in the Surselvan Romansh Verb, In: Studies in Honor of Mario A Pei, 72; Romance Philology and the Sociology of Language: A Pedagogical Perspective, Yearbk 1975 Pedagog Sem Romance Philol, MLA, 75; La Situation Diglossique dan les Grisons, Cahier Groupe Recherches Diglossie, Univ Montpellier, 76; Rheto-Romance: Dialect and Geography in Southeastern Switzerland, Geoling Ill, 77; Studies on linguistic nationalism in the Romance languages, In: Trends in Romance Philology and Linguistics, Vol 2, Mouton, The Hague, 81; Selected recent studies in linguistic nationalism in the Romance languages, Rev Can Etudes sur Nationalisme VIII, Fall 81; Languages and language policies in the USSR, Geolinguistics, VII, 81. **CONTACT ADDRESS** Dept of Languages, Univ of Rhode Island, Kingston, RI, 02881. **EMAIL** rog101@urikcc.uri.edu

ROGERS, LAWRENCE WILLIAM
PERSONAL Oakland, CA, 2 children **DISCIPLINE** JAPANESE LITERATURE AND LANGUAGE **EDUCATION** Univ CA, Berkeley, BA, 61, MA, 66, PhD (oriental lang), 75. **CAREER** Actg instr Japanese, Univ CA, Berkeley, 72-74; actg asst prof, Univ CA, Los Angeles, 74-75; asst prof, 76- 82, assoc prof, 82-89, prof Japanese, Univ Hawaii, Hilo, 89-; vis fac, Univ BC, summer 78 & Int Christian Univ, Tokyo, summers 81 & 82. **HONORS AND AWARDS** Various travel grants. **MEMBERSHIPS** Asn for Asian Studies; Asn Teachers Japanese; Soc Writers, Ed & Transl. **RESEARCH** Modern Japanese poetry and fiction; the haibun essay. **SELECTED PUBLICATIONS** Auth, Rags and Tatters: The Uzuragoromo of Yokoi Yayu, Monumenta Nipponica, autumn 79; She Loves Me, She Loves Me Not, Shinju and Shikido okagami, Monumenta Nipponica, spring 94; transl, Citadel in Spring (novel), Kodansha Int, 90; various short story translations. **CONTACT ADDRESS** Dept Lang, Univ Hawaii, Hilo, 200 W Kawili St, Hilo, HI, 96720-4091. **EMAIL** rogers@hawaii.edu

ROGERS, THOMAS FRANKLYN
PERSONAL Born 04/12/1933, Salt Lake City, UT, m, 1958, 7 children **DISCIPLINE** RUSSIAN LITERATURE **EDUCATION** Univ UT, BA, 55; Yale Univ, MA, 62; Georgetown Univ, PhD, 68. **CAREER** Instr Ger, Russ & humanities, Howard Univ, 62-66; asst prof Russ, Univ UT, 66-69; assoc prof, 69-76, Prof Russ, Brigham Young Univ, 76-, Dir hon prog, Brigham Young Univ, 74-77; ed, Encyclia, J of the UT Academy, 91-93; Russian Enterprises Development, Inc (REDI), member, bd of dirs, 96-. **HONORS AND AWARDS** Emeritus Member, Playwrights' Circle; Distinguished Service Award, BYU Honors Prog, 77; Drama Prize, Asn of Mormon Letters, 83; Col of Humanities Award for Academic Distinction, BYU, 84; Distinguished Teacher Award, FORSCOM, 91; 2nd place Short Story Prize, Dialogue Magazine, 91; Lifetime Service Award, Mormon Festival of the Arts, St George, UT, 98. **MEMBERSHIPS** Am Asn Teachers Slavic & East Europ Lang; Rocky Mountain Mod Lang Asn; Am Coun Teachers of Russian, member, bd of dirs, 97-. **RESEARCH** Soviet literature; drama; playwrighting. **SELECTED PUBLICATIONS** Auth, Trends in Soviet Prose of the Thaw Period, Rocky Mountain Mod Lang Asn J, winter 69; The Ironic Mode in Soviet Russian Prose, 69 & The Implications of Christ's Passion in Doctor Zhivago, Vol XVIII, No 4, 384-391, Slavic & East Europ J; transl, S Panchev, Turbulence and Random Functions, Pergamon Press, 71; Superflous Men and the Post-Stalin Thaw, The Hague: Mouton, 72; Ethical Idealism in Post-Stalin Fiction, Rocky Mountain Soc Sci J, 4/75; Hedonism and humanitas: The Pushkin Perplex, The Need Beyond Research, and Other Essays, Brigham Young Univ Press, 76; The Sacred in Literature, Lit & Belief, 81; The Suffering Christ in Grotowski's Apokalypsis cum Figuris, Relig & Theatre; God's Fools: Four Plays by Thomas F. Rogers, Midvale, UT: Edan Hill, 83; Myth and Symbol in Soviet Fiction, San Francisco: Mellon Research Univ Press, 92; Huebner and Other Plays, Provo, UT: Poor Robert's Pubs, 92; Twentieth Century Pioneers: Mormons in Russia, Provo, UT: BYU Studies, forthcoming; numerous articles and reviews. **CONTACT ADDRESS** Dept of Germanic & Slavic Lang, Brigham Young Univ, 4094 Jkhb, Provo, UT, 84602-0002. **EMAIL** thomas_rogers@byu.edu

ROHINSKY, MARIE-CLAIRE
DISCIPLINE MODERN LANGUAGES **EDUCATION** Univ Caen, PhD. **CAREER** Asst prof, Fr/Span/Women's Studies. **HONORS AND AWARDS** Coord, W Europ Studies/Int Studies Prog, Central Conn State Univ; coord, Lang Across Curr proj, Central Conn State Univ; organizer/co-dir French Summer Study Abroad Prog, Central Conn State Univ. **RESEARCH** 19th-century French poetry and music, 18th-century French theatre, and French Women Writers and World War II. **SELECTED PUBLICATIONS** Auth, The Singer's Debussy, Rosen, 87. **CONTACT ADDRESS** Central Connecticut State Univ, 1615 Stanley St, New Britain, CT, 06050.

ROHRBACHER, BERNHARD
DISCIPLINE LINGUISTICS **EDUCATION** Univ Mass Amherst, PhD. **CAREER** Prof, Northwestern Univ. **RESEARCH** What is the source for crosslinguistic variation, and how do young children acquire a first language. **SELECTED PUBLICATIONS** Auth, Explaining the Syntactic Consequences of Rich Agreement Morphology, On the Licensing of V-to-AgrS Raising and pro, Proceedings of the 13th West Coast Conf on Formal Ling, 95; Notes on the Antisymmetry of Syntax, Univ Pa Working Papers in Ling 1, 94; English Main Verbs Move Never, The Penn Rev Ling 18, 94; coauth, Features and Projections: Arguments for the Full Competence Hypothesis, Talk given at the 21th Annual Boston Univ Conf on Lang Develop, 96; Functional Projections, Markedness, and Root Infinitives in Early Child Greek, Talk given at the Workshop on Current Trends in Modern Greek Syntax at the 17th GLOW Conf, 96; Null Subjects in Russian Inverted Constructions, Proceedings of the 4th Annual Workshop on Formal Approaches to Slavic Ling, 96; On German Verb Syntax under Age 2, Proceedings of the 19th Annual Boston Univ Conf on Lang Develop 95; Null Subjects in Early Child English and the Theory of Economy of Projection, Univ Pa Working Papers in Ling 2, 95. **CONTACT ADDRESS** Dept of Linguistics, Northwestern Univ, 1801 Hinman, Evanston, IL, 60208.

ROJAS, CARLOS
PERSONAL Born 08/12/1928, Barcelona, Spain, m, 1966, 2 children **DISCIPLINE** SPANISH LITERATURE, HISTORY **EDUCATION** Barcelona Univ, MA, 51; Univ Cent, Madrid, PhD(Span lit), 55. **CAREER** Asst prof Romance lang, Rollins Col, 57-60; from asst prof to assoc prof, 60-68, prof, 68-80, Charles Howard Candler Prof Romance Lang, 80-, emeritus, Emory Univ. **HONORS AND AWARDS** Nat Prize for Lit, Govt Spain, 68; Planeta Prize, Ed Planeta, 73; Ateneo de Sevilla Prize, 77; Nadal Prize, 80. **MEMBERSHIPS** MLA; SAtlantic Mod Lang Asn. **RESEARCH** Contemporary Spanish; art history. **SELECTED PUBLICATIONS** Auth, Dialogos Para Otra Espana, Ariel, 66; Auto de Fe, Guadarrama, 68; Diez Figuras Ante la Guerra Civil, Nauta, 73; Azana, 73, La Guerra Civil Vista por los Exiliados, 75, Retratos Antifranquistas, 77 & Memorias Ineditas, 78, Planeta; El Ingenioso Hidalgo y Poeta Federico Garcia Lorca Asciende a los Infiernos, 80, La Barcelonade Picasso, 81. **CONTACT ADDRESS** Dept of Romance Lang, Emory Univ, Atlanta, GA, 30322.

ROJAS, J. NELSON
PERSONAL Chile **DISCIPLINE** ROMANCE AND SPANISH LINGUISTICS, CONTEMPORARY LATIN AMERICAN POETRY, SPANIS **EDUCATION** Univ Wash, PhD. **CAREER** Prof Span, Univ Nev, Reno. **RESEARCH** Linguistic approaches to the poetry of Gabriela Mistral. **SELECTED PUBLICATIONS** Published widely in the areas of linguistics and Latin American poetry. **CONTACT ADDRESS** Univ Nev, Reno, Reno, NV, 89557. **EMAIL** rojas@unr.edu

ROJAS, LOURDES
DISCIPLINE LATIN AMERICAN CONTEMPORARY NOVEL **EDUCATION** Univ CA, La Jolla, BA, 70; SUNY, MA, 74, PhD, 85. **CAREER** Instr, SUNY Old Westbury, Hamilton Col; dir, Vassar-Wesleyan-Colgate prog, Madrid, 97-98; assoc prof; dir, Africana and Latin Am Studies prog. **HONORS AND AWARDS** Ford Found grant; Picker fel; res fel Latin Am Studies, Cornell Univ. **SELECTED PUBLICATIONS** Auth, La mujer, desmitificacion y novela,90; Women Essayists of the Caribbean, 98; Women and Sexuality in Latin America, Trends in Hist; At the Crossroads: Latina's Affirmation of Life, Breaking Boundaries; La obra de Carlos Fuentes, Theorizing About Essays, Anthology of Latin Am Lit of Exile, 93. **CONTACT ADDRESS** Dept of Romance Lang, Colgate Univ, 13 Oak Drive, Hamilton, NY, 13346. **EMAIL** lrojas@center.colgate.edu

ROLFE, OLIVER WILLIS
PERSONAL Born 01/20/1938, Alamosa, CO, m, 1968, 2 children **DISCIPLINE** FRENCH LANGUAGE, LINGUISTICS **EDUCATION** Washburn Univ, Topeka, AB, 60; Stanford Univ, AM, 64, PhD, 67. **CAREER** Tchr & tutor, Menninger Found, Topeka, KS, 58-60; tchg asst French, Stanford Univ, 61-63, actg instr ling, 63-65, instr tchg Eng as a second lang, 65-66; asst prof Romance ling, Univ WA, 66-70; assoc prof, 70-76, Prof Foreign Lang, Univ MT, 76-, Res asst, Stanford Comput Ctr, 61-63; instr French, San Jose State Col, spring 64. **MEMBERSHIPS** Am Asn Tchr(s) Fr; Am Coun Tchg For Lang; AAUP. **RESEARCH** French and Romance linguistics; lang tchg methodology. **SELECTED PUBLICATIONS** Co-ed, Linguistic Studies Present to Andre Martinet on the Occassion of His 60th Birthday, Ling Circle of NY, 72; autb, Grammatical frequency and language teaching: Verbal categories in French and Spanish, In: Linguistic Studies Presented to Andre Martinet, 72; Morphological Frequency: French & Spanish Verbal Themes, In: Papers on Linguistics & Child Language, Hague, Mouton, 78. **CONTACT ADDRESS** Dept of For Lang, Univ MT, Missoula, MT, 59812-1015. **EMAIL** olivier@selway.umt.edu

ROMANOWSKI, SYLVIE
DISCIPLINE FRENCH **EDUCATION** Yale Univ, PhD. **CAREER** Assoc prof; dir, Women's Studies Prog, Northwestern Univ; lect, Modern Lang Asn; North Am Asn for French 17th-Century Lit; Am Soc for 18th-Century Studies; Univ Tex, Aus-

tin; Univ Kans; Ohio State Univ. **RESEARCH** Literature of the 17th and 18th centuries; theater; feminism. **SELECTED PUBLICATIONS** Auth, La qu te du savoir dans les Lettres persanes, 18th-Century Fiction, 91; Satire and its Context in the Bourgeois gentilhomme, Papers on French 17th- Century Lit, 90; Language and Space in Tartuffe, Approaches to Teaching Moliere's Tartuffe and Other Plays, MLA Publication. **CONTACT ADDRESS** Dept of French, Northwestern Univ, 1801 Hinman, Evanston, IL, 60208.

ROMEISER, JOHN B.
DISCIPLINE SPANISH LITERATURE **EDUCATION** Vanderbilt Univ, PhD, 75. **CAREER** Prof. **SELECTED PUBLICATIONS** Auth, pubs on Spanish Civil War. **CONTACT ADDRESS** Dept of Romance Languages, Knoxville, TN, 37996.

RONNICK, MICHELE VALERIE
DISCIPLINE CLASSICS, GREEK, LATIN **EDUCATION** Boston Univ, PhD, 90. **CAREER** ASSOC PROF, DEPT OF CLASSICS, WAYNE STATE UNIV. **HONORS AND AWARDS** Award For Teaching Excellence, APA, 97; Award for Outstanding State VP, Classical Asn of the Middle West and South, 96; Award for the Most Significant Project, Vanderbilt Univ, 96; Incentive Award for Younger Scholars, Classical and Modern Literature, 94. **MEMBERSHIPS** Int Soc for the Classical Tradition; APA; Classical Asn of the Middle West and South; Classical Asn of the Atlantic States; Am Asn of Neo-Latin Studies. **RESEARCH** Latin literature; Classical tradition; Classical studies & people of African descent. **SELECTED PUBLICATIONS** Auth, Substructural Elements of Architectonic Rhetoric and Philosophical Thought in Fronto's Epistles, Roman Persuasion, 97; Aratus, Dictionary of Literary Biography: Ancient Greek Authors, Gale Research Co, 97; Cicero's Paradoxa Stoicorum: A Commentary, an Interpretation, and a Study of Its Influence, 91; referee, Bos, Fur, Sus, atque Sacerdoes: Additional Light on Kaiser's Solution of a Minor Mystery, Proceedings of the Mass Hist Sco, 95; Concerning the Dramatic Elements in Milton's Defensiones: Theater Without a Stage, Classical and Modern Lit, 95; Seneca's Medea and Ultima Thule in Poe's Dream-land, Poe Studies/Dark Romanticism, 94; David Paul Brown's Sertorius or The Roman Patriot (1830): Another Influence on John Wilkes Booth, J of Am Culture, 96; Seneca's Epistle 12 and Emerson's Circles, Emerson Soc Papers, 96; Further Evidence Concerning the Origin of Cromwell's Title Lord Protector: Milton's Pro Se Defensio, Cromwelliana, 97; After Lefkowitz and Bernal: Research Opportunities in Classica Africana, The Negro Hist Bull, 97. **CONTACT ADDRESS** Dept of Classics, Wayne State Univ, 431 Manoogian Hall, Detroit, MI, 48202.

ROOD, DAVID STANLEY
PERSONAL Born 09/14/1940, Albany, NY, 1 child **DISCIPLINE** LINGUISTICS **EDUCATION** Cornell Univ, BA, 63; Univ Calif, Berkeley, MA, 65, PhD, 69. **CAREER** Instr Ger & ling, 67-69, asst prof ling, 69-77, assoc prof, 77-82, Prof Ling, Univ Colo, Boulder, 82-; NSF grants, 77-96; Nat Endowment for Humanities grants, 77-96; ed, Int J Am Ling, 81-. **MEMBERSHIPS** Ling Soc Am; Am Anthrop Asn; Teachers of English to Speakers of Other Lang. **RESEARCH** Applied linguistics in second language teaching; American Indian languages; linguistic theory and semantic-based grammar. **SELECTED PUBLICATIONS** Auth, Agent and Object in Wichita, Lingua, 71; Aspects of subordination in Lakhota and Wichita, In: You Take the High Node and I'll Take the Low Node, Chicago Ling Asn, 73; Implications of Wichita phonology, Language, 75; Wichita Grammar, Garland, 76; coauth, Beginning Lakhota, Univ Colo, Ling Dept, 76; contribr, Siouan, In: The Languages of Native America, Univ Tex, 79; auth, Locative Expressions in Siouan and Caddoan, Colo Res Ling, 79; User's Handbook for the Siouan Languages Archive, Univ Colo, Dept Ling, 81. **CONTACT ADDRESS** Dept of Ling, Univ of Colorado, Box 295, Boulder, CO, 80309-0295.

ROSA, WILLIAM
DISCIPLINE LATIN AMERICAN LITERATURE **EDUCATION** PhD **CAREER** Assoc prof & dept chp. **RESEARCH** 19th century novel and short story of the Caribbean basin. **SELECTED PUBLICATIONS** Auth bk on, Alfredo Collado Martell, Inst de Culturea Puertorriquena. **CONTACT ADDRESS** Dept of Language and Cultures, William Paterson Col, 300 Pompton Rd., Wayne, NJ, 07470.

ROSE, MARILYN GADDIS
PERSONAL Born 04/02/1930, Fayette, MO, m, 1968, 1 child **DISCIPLINE** COMPARATIVE LITERATURE **EDUCATION** Cent Methodist Col, BA, 52; Univ SC, MA, 55; Univ Mo, PhD, 58. **CAREER** Asst French, Univ SC, 54-55; instr, Univ Mo, 55-58; assoc prof comp lit, Stephens Col, 58-68; assoc prof French & comp lit, 68-73, chmn dept, 71-78, prof comp lit, 73-90, Distinguished Service Prof, comp lit, 91-, dir, Transl Prog, 73-, SUNY, Binghamton. **HONORS AND AWARDS** Alexander Gode Medal, Am Transl Asn, 88; ATA Special Service Award, 95. **MEMBERSHIPS** MLA; Northeast Mod Lang Asn; Am Transl Asn; Am Lit Transl Asn. **RESEARCH** Anglo-Irish literature; French-American literary relations; translating; tanslation theory and pedagogy. **SELECTED PUBLICATIONS** Transl, Villiers de l'Isle-Adam, Eve of the Future Eden, Coronado; transl, Louise Colet, Lui, 87; transl, Sainte-Beuve, Volupte, 96; auth, Translation and Literary Criticism, 97. **CONTACT ADDRESS** CRIT/TRIP, SUNY, Binghamton, PO Box 6000, Binghamton, NY, 13902-6000. **EMAIL** mgrose@binghamton.edu

ROSE, SHARON
DISCIPLINE PHONOLOGY **EDUCATION** Univ Toronto, BA; Univ du Quebec a Montreal, MA; McGill Univ, PhD. **CAREER** ASST PROF, LING, UNIV CALIF, SAN DIEGO. **RESEARCH** Ethiopian Semitic languages. **SELECTED PUBLICATIONS** Auth, Ethio-Semitic Inflectional Affix Order: A Phonological Solution, Langues Orientales Anciennes, Philol et Ling, 95; Allomorphy and Morphological Categories in Muher, Essays in Gurage Language and Culture, Wiesbaden: Harrassowitz Verlag, 96; Variable Laryngeals and Vowel Lowering, Phonology 13, 96; Inflectional Affix Order, Ethio-Semitic, Stud in AfroAsiatic Grammar, The Hague: Holland Academic Graphics, 96; Book Notice of Wolf Leslau: Reference Grammar of Amharic, Lang 72, 96; Featural Morphology and Dialect Variation: the Contribution of Historical Change, Variation, Change and Phonological Theory, Current Issues, Ling Theory 146, Amsterdam: John Benjamins, 97; Theoretical Issues, Comparative Ethio-Semitic Phonology and Morphology, 97. **CONTACT ADDRESS** Dept of Ling, Univ Calif, San Diego, 9500 Gilman Dr, La Jolla, CA, 92093. **EMAIL** rose@ling.ucsd.edu

ROSE, STANLEY LUDWIG
PERSONAL Born 02/03/1936, Richmond, IN, m, 1958, 2 children **DISCIPLINE** LUSO--BRAZILIAN & SPANISH LANGUAGE & LITERATURES **EDUCATION** Univ AZ, BA, 58; Univ WI-Madison, MA, 60, PhD, 69. **CAREER** Actg asst Span & Port, Univ OR, 65-69, asst prof, 69-72; asst prof Port, NDEA Inst Port, Vanderbilt Univ, 68; asst prof, 72-75, Assoc Prof Span & Port, Univ MT, 75. **MEMBERSHIPS** Am Asn Tchr(s) Span & Port. **RESEARCH** Medieval Portuguese lang and lit; mod Brazilian lit. **SELECTED PUBLICATIONS** Auth, Alberto de Oliveira, In: Encycl World Lit 20th Century, Ungar, 70; translr, Carta de Doacoa and Foral of Duarte Coelho, In: A Documentary History of Brazil, Knopf, 71; auth, Ancedotal narrative in Fernao Lopes' Cronica de D Pedro I, Luso-Brazilian Rev, 71; The land and the peasant in the novel of the Brazilian Northeast, J Rocky Mt Coun Latin Am Studies, 12/75. **CONTACT ADDRESS** Dept of For Lang & Lit, Univ of MT, Missoula, MT, 59812-0001. **EMAIL** slrose@selway.umt.edu

ROSENBERG, JOEL WILLIAM
PERSONAL Born 04/13/1943, Los Angeles, CA **DISCIPLINE** HEBREW & COMPARATIVE LITERATURE **EDUCATION** Univ CA, Berkeley, BA, 65; Hebrew Union Col, BHL, 68; Univ CA, Santa Cruz, PhD, 78. **CAREER** Vis lectr relig, Univ CA, Davis, 73-74; vis lectr, Wesleyan Univ, 76-78, vis asst prof, 78-79; Asst prof, 80-84, assoc prof, Judaic Studies & World lit, Tufts Univ, 84, Lee S McCollester Assoc Prof, Bibl Lit, 92. **HONORS AND AWARDS** Phi Beta Kappa, 64; H W Hill Scholarship, Univ Calif Berkeley, 64; Fac Award in Scholarship, Hebrew Unon Col-Jewish Inst of Relig, Regent's fel, Univ Calif, Santa Cruz, 71-72; Nat Defense Educ Act fel, Columbia Univ and Univ Calif, Berkeley, 66, 71; Poet-in-Residence, Del State Arts Counc/NEA, 4/79; Mellon Found Grant-in-Aid, Fac Develop, Tufts Univ, summer 82; NEH fel, 96. **MEMBERSHIPS** MLA; Asn Jewish Studies; Soc Bibl Lit; Am Acad Relig. **RESEARCH** Bibl lit; hist of bibl interpretation; comp lit; film hist and theory. **SELECTED PUBLICATIONS** Auth, Agnon's World, Genesis 2, 3/70; The Jew as Poet, In: The New Jews (James A Sleeper and Alan L Mintz, ed), Vintage Books/Random House, 71; Contemporary Religious Questing, Judaism, winter 71; Jonah and the Prophetic Vocation, Response, summer 74; Meanings, Morals and Mysteries--Literary Approaches to Torah, Response, summer 75; The Feminine through a (Male) Glass Darkly--Preface to a Demythologizing, Response, winter 75-76; The Next Jewish Book, Shma: Jour of Jewish Responsibility, 12/76; Bringing Fire Down to Earth, Genesis 2, 3/79; At the Edge of the Garden--Understanding Jewish Mysticism, Baltimore Jewish Times, 9/79; A Brief History of the Terms for Jew, The Origins of the Hebrew Letters, Ten Jewish Classics, and Metamorphoses of a Trett: Ten Jewish Symbols, In: The Jewish Almanac (Richard Siegel and Carl Rheins, ed), Bantam Books, 80; From Generation to Degeneration: Christopher Lasch on the Family, The Melton Jour, fall 80; Enacting Our Texts, Review of Elizabeth Swados The Haggaday Cantata, Moment, 6/80; Second Avenue's Second Life: The Reincarnation of Jewish Theater, Moment, 11/80; The Garden Story Forward and Backward: The Non-Narrative Dimension of Genesis 2-3, Prooftexts: Jour of Jewish Lit Hist, Johns Hopkins Univ, 1/81; The Violin Tree, and The First Wedding in the World, poems, In: Voices Within the Ark: The Modern Jewish Poets (Howard Schwartz, ed), Avon Books, 81; Jacob at the River, In: Gates to the New City: Jewish Legends and Tales (Howard Schwartz, ed), Avon Books, 82; Some Notes on Traditional Prayer, Response, spring 83; John Le Carre's Mideast, Moment, 7/83; Xeroxosis? On Woody Allen's Zelig, Moment, 12/83; Biblical Narrative, In: Back to the Sources: Reading the Classic Jewish Texts (Barry W Holtz, ed), Summit Books/Simon & Schuster, 84; Dual Vocations: The Biblical Storyteller and the Biblical Scholar, Prooftexts: Jour Jewish Lit Hist, 9/85; Biblical Traditions: Literature and Spirit in Ancient Israel, In: Jewish Spirituality from the Bible through the Middle Ages (Arthur Green, ed), Crossroad, 86; King and Kin: Political Allegory in the Hebrew Bible, Ind Univ Pres, 86; Creation, Firmament, Seth, Tubal-Cain, Noah, Rainbow, Babel, Lot, Terphim, Elders, Eldad, Kibbroth-Hattaavah, Jonah, and Hulda, In: Harper's Bible Dictionary (Paul J Achtemeier, ed), Harper & Row/Soc for Biblical Lit, 86; This Way and That: The Politics of the Field in the Davidic History, Shofar: An Interdisciplinary Quart in Jewish Studies, fall 86; The Institutional Matrix of Treachery in 2 Samuel 11, Semeia: An Experimental Jour in Biblical Lit, 87; 1 and 2 Samuel, and Jeremiah and Ezekial, In: The Literary Guide to the Bible (Robert Alter and Frank Kermode, ed), Harvard Univ Press/The Belknap Press, 87, and Collins, London, 87; Jonah and the Nakedness of Deeds, Tikkun: A Bi-Monthly Critique of Politics, Culture and Soc, 9/87; Confederation and Kingdom: An Important Polarity in Biblical History, Proceedings of the Distinguished Leader Ins, Brandeis Univ, 89; Midrash on the Ten Commandments (transl), In: Rabbinic Fantasies (David Stern and Mark Mirsky, ed), JPS, 90, and Yale Univ Press, 98; Grammer with a Small g, Review of Lewis Glinert A Grammar of Modern Hebrew, Prooftexts: Jour of Jewish Lit Hist, 5/91; Genesis: A Commentary, In: The Harper Collins Study Bible (Wayne A Meeks, ed), Harper Collins, 93; Kol Haneshamah: The Reconstructionist Sabbath and Festival Prayer Book (transl), vol 1 (David A Teutsch, ed), Reconstructionist Press, 90, and vol 2, 93; Alternate Roads to Integrity: On Old Age in the Hebrew Bible, Melton Jour, 5/94; Jewish Experience on Film: An American Overview, Am Jewish Yearbk, 96; Shylock's Revenge: The Doubly Vanished Jew in Ernst Lubitsch's To Be or Not to Be, Prooftexts, 96; What the Bible and Old Movies Have in Common, Biblical Interpretation, 98; Kol Haneshamah: The Reconstructionist Daily Prayer Book ; Kol Haneshamah: The Reconstructionist High Holiday Prayer Book; Incarnation and Disguise: Jewish Experience on Film, 1920-1947. **CONTACT ADDRESS** Dept of Ger & Russ, Tufts Univ, 520 Boston Ave, Medford, MA, 02155-5555. **EMAIL** jrosenb1@emerald.tufts.edu

ROSENBERG, JUSTUS
PERSONAL Born 01/23/1931, Danzig, Poland **DISCIPLINE** APPLIED LINGUISTICS **EDUCATION** Sorbonne, BA, 46; Univ Calif, Los Angeles, MA, 48; Univ Cincinnati, PhD(comp lit), 50. **CAREER** Assoc prof foreign lang, Univ Dayton, 46-56 & Swarthmore Col, 56-62; Prof Foreign Lang, Bard Col, 62-, vis prof, Univ Cincinnati, 51-56 & New Sch Social Res, 60-; fel, Columbia Univ, 65-66; vis prof, Nanyang Univ, 66-68; fel lit, Univ Belgrade, 72. **HONORS AND AWARDS** Lecturer, N. Y. S. Coun for the Humanities. **MEMBERSHIPS** AAUP; MLA; Am Acad Polit & Soc Sci. **RESEARCH** Political commitment in the literature of the 20th century; methodology for teaching of English as a second language. **SELECTED PUBLICATIONS** Auth, Constant Factors in Translation, Princeton Univ, 56; Sound and Structure, D Moore, 68. **CONTACT ADDRESS** Dept of Foreign Lang, Bard Col, PO Box 5000, Annandale, NY, 12504-5000. **EMAIL** rosenber@bard.edu

ROSENBERG, SAMUEL N.
DISCIPLINE FRENCH LITERATURE **EDUCATION** Johns Hopkins Univ, PhD, 65. **CAREER** Prof. **RESEARCH** Medieval language and literature; historical and modern syntax. **SELECTED PUBLICATIONS** Co-auth, Harper's Grammar of French, 83; ed, French Secular Compositions of the Fourteenth Century, 73; Chanter m'estuet: Songs of the Trouveres, 81; The Lyrics and Melodies of Gace Brule, 85; The Monophonic Songs in the Roman de Fauvel, 91; Chansons des trouveres, 95; Songs of the Troubadors and Trouveres, 97. **CONTACT ADDRESS** Dept of French and Italian, Indiana Univ, Bloomington, 300 N Jordan Ave, Bloomington, IN, 47405.

ROSENTHAL, MARGARET F.
DISCIPLINE ITALIAN RENAISSANCE ITALIAN LITERATURE **EDUCATION** Yale Univ, PhD. **CAREER** Asso prof, Univ Southern Calif. **RESEARCH** Women writers in early-modern Venice; social, cultural, political forces in Venice in the 16th century. **SELECTED PUBLICATIONS** Auth, The Honest Courtesan, Veronica Franco, Citizen and Writer in Sixteenth-Century Venice, 92. **CONTACT ADDRESS** Col Letters, Arts & Sciences, Univ Southern Calif, University Park Campus, Los Angeles, CA, 90089.

ROSES, LORRAINE ELENA
PERSONAL New York, NY, m, 1981, 4 children **DISCIPLINE** SPANISH **EDUCATION** Mt Holyoke Col, BA, 65; Harvard Univ, MA, 66, PhD, 74. **CAREER** Lectr English & Span, Tel Aviv Univ, 69-71; instr Span, Mt Holyoke Col, 71-74, asst prof, 74-75; asst prof, Boston Univ, 75-77; asst prof, 77-81, assoc prof, 81-87, PROF SPAN, WELLESLEY COL 87-, co-dir, Latin Am Studies, 92-, vis res scholar, Center for Res Women; affiliate in residence, Bunting Inst, Radcliffe Col, 98-99. **HONORS AND AWARDS** Woodrow Wilson Nat fel, 65; Radcliffe Inst travel fel, 68; Mount Holyoke Col fac grant, 71; Boston Univ fac grant, 87; Summer fac res grants, Wellesley, 81-; Ford Commitment Fund Grant, summer 82; Mellon grant, 85; Phelps Fund, Center for Res Women, Wellesley, 85 & 86; NEH summer stipend, 87; Ford Found training stipend, 88; Pew grant, Wellesley, 89; NEH Summer Inst, 89; Pew grant, Wellesley Col, summer 91; NEH summer inst, lead scholar,

Middlesex Comm Col, 92; Am Coun Learned Soc fel, 98-99. **MEMBERSHIPS** MLA; Am Asn Teacher Span & Port. **RESEARCH** Spanish American and African American literature. **SELECTED PUBLICATIONS** Auth, Lino Novas Calvo: A sense of the preternatural, Symp, fall 75; Myth montage in a contemporary Puerto Rican tragedy, Latin Am Lit Rev, fall-winter 75; El realismo magico en la critica hispanoamericana, J Span Studies: 20th Century, Vol 4, No 3; La epoca espanola de Lino Novas Calvo: 1936-1939, Chasqui, 5/77; Affirmation of black heritage in Arrivi's Mascara puertorriquena, Studies Afro-Hisp Lit, Vol I, 77; co-auth, Harlem Renaissance and Beyond: Literary Biographies of 100 Black Women Writers, 1900-1945, G K Hall, 90; Las esperanzas de Pandora: prototipos femeninos en la obra de Rosario Ferre, Revista Iberoamericana, 1-6/93; Introduction and Selection, Selected Works of Edythe Mae Gordon, in African American Women Writers, 1910-1940, G K Hall, 96; ed, Harlem's Glory: Black Women Writing, 1900-1945, Harvard Univ Press, 96. **CONTACT ADDRESS** Span Dept, Wellesley Col, 106 Central St, Wellesley, MA, 02481-8204. **EMAIL** lroses@wellesley.edu

ROSIVACH, VINCENT JOHN
PERSONAL Born 05/08/1940, Jersey City, NJ **DISCIPLINE** CLASSICAL PHILOLOGY **EDUCATION** Fordham Univ, AB, 61, MA, 64, PhD(classics), 66. **CAREER** Adj instr Latin, Sch Educ, Fordham Univ, 63-64; from instr to assoc prof, 65-76, Prof Classics, Fairfield Univ, 76-. **MEMBERSHIPS** Am Philol Asn; Class Asn New Eng. **RESEARCH** Greek and Roman drama; Greek history. **SELECTED PUBLICATIONS** Auth, Plautine stage settings, Trans & Proc Am Philol Soc, 70; Manuscripts of Matthias Corvinus in the Barberini Collection, Manuscripta, 71; Terence, Adelphoe 155-9, Class Quart, 73, Terence, Adelphoe 60 63, Class Philol, 75; The first stasimon of the Hecuba, Am J Philol, 75; Sophocles' Ajax, Class J, 76; Hector in the Rhesus, Hermes, 77; Earthborns and Olympians: The parodos of the Ion, Class Quart, 77; The System of Public Sacrifice in Fourth Century Athens, Scholars Press, 94; When a Young Man Falls in Love: The Sexual Exploitation of Women in New Comedy, Routledge, 98. **CONTACT ADDRESS** Greek and Roman Studies, Fairfield Univ, 1073 N Benson Rd, Fairfield, CT, 06430-5195. **EMAIL** Rosivach@fair1.fairfield.edu

ROSS, CLAUDIA
DISCIPLINE CHINESE **EDUCATION** Barnard Col, Columbia Univ, BA, 71; Univ Mich, MA, 73, PhD, 78. **CAREER** Assoc prof; dir, Int Stud; coordr, Chinese Sect & Asian Stud fac mem. **RESEARCH** Linguistics: Lexical and semantic structure; Chinese language teaching; Teacher training. **SELECTED PUBLICATIONS** Temporal and Aspectual Reference in Mandarin Chinese, J Chinese Ling 23 1, 95. **CONTACT ADDRESS** Dept of Modern Languages and Literatures, Col of the Holy Cross, 1 College St, PO Box 11A, Worcester, MA, 01610-2395. **EMAIL** cross@holycross.edu

ROSS, MARILYN A.
PERSONAL Born 09/06/1946, New York, NY, s **DISCIPLINE** CLASSICAL PHILOLOGY **EDUCATION** Cornell Univ, PhD, 73. **CAREER** Assoc prof and assoc dean of the col, Wells Col; assoc prof and asst to the pres, Sweet Briar Col; pres, Ross Associates. **HONORS AND AWARDS** Phi Beta Kappa. **MEMBERSHIPS** Am Philol Asoc. **CONTACT ADDRESS** 6324 Burning Tree Terrace, Fayettevielle, PA, 17222. **EMAIL** maross@mail.cvn.net

ROSS, MARY ELLEN
DISCIPLINE EIGHTEENTH CENTURY FRENCH LITERATURE **EDUCATION** Univ Toronto, PhD. **RESEARCH** Contemporary literature of Quebec. **SELECTED PUBLICATIONS** Auth, Amazones et sauvagesses: roles feminins et societes exotiques dans le theatre de la Foire, Studies on Voltaire and the Eighteenth Century 319, 94; Le Deuil et le probleme du paraitre chez la veuve comique de debut du dix-huitieme siecle, Nophilologus 76, 92; Que le diable l'emporte: realisme merveilleux et religion dans La Chaise du marechal ferrant, Can Lit 142/143, 94; Realisme merveilleux et autorepresentation dans L'Amelanchier de Jacques Ferron, Voix et images 49, 91. **CONTACT ADDRESS** Dept of French, Victoria Univ, PO Box 3045 STN CSC, Victoria, BC, V8W 3P4. **EMAIL** meross@uvic.ca

ROTH, LANE
PERSONAL Born 00/00/1943, New York, NY **DISCIPLINE** CINEMA, COMMUNICATIONS **EDUCATION** NY Univ, BA, 64; Fla State Univ, MA, 74, PhD, 76. **CAREER** Asst prof, Univ Evansville, 76-78; assoc prof, 78-82; ASSOC PROF, COMMUN, LAMAR UNIV, 82-. **HONORS AND AWARDS** National German Honors, 64; Regents' Merit Award for Teaching Excellence, Lamar Univ, 80. **MEMBERSHIPS** Intl Asn for the Fantastic in Arts, Bd, Mental Health Asn Jefferson Cty; pres of the bd, 1997- **RESEARCH** Jungian psychol, literary criticism, philos. **SELECTED PUBLICATIONS** Auth, Humanity, Technology and Comedy in Microbi, a Hungarian Animated Science Fiction Television Series, World Communication, 93; Co-auth, G. M. Broncho Billy" Anderson: The First Movie Cowboy Hero, in Back in the Saddle: Essays on Western Film and Television Actors, McFarland Publ, 98. **CONTACT ADDRESS** Communications Dept, Lamar Univ, PO Box 10050, Beaumont, TX, 77710-0050.

ROTHENBERG, MOLLY
DISCIPLINE COMPARATIVE LITERATURE **EDUCATION** Yale Univ, BA, 74; Univ CA at Irvine, PhD, 85. **CAREER** Instr, 88, Tulane Univ. **SELECTED PUBLICATIONS** Auth, Para-Siting America: The Radical Function of Heterogeneity in Paine's Early Writing, Eighteenth Century Stud, 93; co-auth, Fashionable Theory and Fashionable Women, Critical Inquiry, 95. **CONTACT ADDRESS** Dept of Eng, Tulane Univ, 6823 St Charles Ave, New Orleans, LA, 70118. **EMAIL** mollyr@mailhost.tcs.tulane.edu

ROTHSTEIN, MARIAN
DISCIPLINE FRENCH LANGUAGE, LITERATURE **EDUCATION** Univ Wisc, BA, MA PhD. **CAREER** Vis asst prof, Grinnell Col; Vis asst prof, Univ Wisc. **HONORS AND AWARDS** Newberry Library Resident fel, Nat Endowment Humanities grant. **SELECTED PUBLICATIONS** Articles: Bibliotheque d'Humanisme et Renaissance; Renaissance Quart; Studies Philol. **CONTACT ADDRESS** Carthage Col, 2001 Alford Dr., Kenosha, WI, 53140. **EMAIL** rothst1@carthage.edu

ROUHI, LEYLA
DISCIPLINE SPANISH **EDUCATION** Oxford Univ, BA, 87; Harvard Univ, MA, 88; PhD, 95. **CAREER** Asst prof, Williams Col, 93-. **RESEARCH** Cultural and intellectual exchange in the middle ages; Cervantes; relationship between medieval and modern literary theory. **SELECTED PUBLICATIONS** Auth, A Definition of Medieval Woman's Work, Celestinesca, 98. **CONTACT ADDRESS** Center for Foreign Languages, Literatures and Cult, Williams Col, Williamstown, MA, 01267. **EMAIL** Leyla.Rouhi@williams.edu

ROULIN, JEAN-MARIE
PERSONAL Born 12/13/1960, Alexandria, Egypt, s **DISCIPLINE** ROMANCE LANGUAGES **EDUCATION** Univ Lausanne, Licence es Lettres, 83, Doctorat es Lettres, 92. **CAREER** Charge de cours, 83-84, Maitre-asst, 94-97, Univ Lausanne; asst & charge de cours, 84-89, res asst, 86-89, Univ Zurich; vis prof, Univ Neuchatel, 96-97; ASST PROF, UNIV PENN, 97- . **HONORS AND AWARDS** Fel Fonds Nat Suisse de la Recherche Sci Paris, 89-91 & 91-94; Award of Res Found, Univ Penn, 98. **MEMBERSHIPS** Soc Chateaubriand. **RESEARCH** French literature XIX Century; Romanticism epic in XVIII Century; Swiss literature. **SELECTED PUBLICATIONS** Auth, L'Exil et la Gloire. Du roman familial a l'identite litteraire dans l'oeuvre de Chateaubriand, Champion, 94; Ma Vie de Benjamin Constant: malaise dans la communication, Annales Benjamin Constant, 95; Le Grand Siecle au futur: Voltaire, de la prophetie epique a l'ecriture de l'histoire, Revue d'Histoire litteraire de la France, 96; Alexandre Vinet Histoire de la litterature en Suisse romande, Payot, 97; co-auth, Entre Humanisme et reverie. Etudes sur les litteratures francaise et italienne de la Renaissance au Romantisme, Champion, 98; La Reflexion sur l'epopee en Suisse au dix-huitieme siecle, Reconceptualizing Nature, Science and Aesthetics, UCLA, 98; La Grandeur chex Ramuz: une notion'passerelle', Revue des Lettres modernes, Ramuz, 98; Les travail de la negation dans les Memoires d'Outre-Tombe, Chateaubriand e i 'Memoires d'Outre-Tombe, ETS/Slatkine, 98. **CONTACT ADDRESS** Dept Romance Lang, Univ Pennsylvania, 521 Williams Hall, Philadelphia, PA, 19104-6305. **EMAIL** jmroulin@sas.upenn.edu

ROULSTON, CHRISTINE
DISCIPLINE FRENCH LITERATURE **EDUCATION** Univ Southampton, MA; Univ Toronto, PhD. **RESEARCH** Feminist theory; post-structuralist theory; subjectivity and the 18th century novel. **SELECTED PUBLICATIONS** Auth, Virtue, Gender and the Authentic Self in Eighteenth Century Fiction, Fla Univ, 98. **CONTACT ADDRESS** Dept of French, Western Ontario Univ, London, ON, N6A 5B8.

ROUMAN, JOHN CHRIST
PERSONAL Born 05/01/1916, Tomahawk, WI **DISCIPLINE** CLASSICS, LINGUISTICS **EDUCATION** Carleton Col, BA, 50; Columbia Univ, MA, 51; Univ WI-Madison, PhD, 65. **CAREER** Tchr, Seton Hall Prep Sch, NJ, 54-56 & Malverne High Sch, NY, 57-59; res asst Greek epigraphy, Inst Advan Study, Princeton Univ, 62-63; asst prof, 65-71, chmn dept Span & class, 72-76, assoc prof, 71-91, prof class, Univ NH, 91-, Chair classics, 87-98, Coord classics, 98-; Pres, Strafford Cty Greco-Roman Found, Bd mem, Phi Kappa Theta Nat Found. **HONORS AND AWARDS** Noyse Prize for Greek, Carleton Col, 50; Fulbright Scholar, Univ Kiel, WGer, 56-57; UNH Alumni Asn, Distinguished Tchg Award, 85; Barlow-Beach Award for Serv, Cause of Class, Class Asn of New Engl, 91; Am Philol Asn Nat Award for Excellence in Tchg, Class, 91; AHEPA and Daughters of Penelope, Pericles Award, 93. **MEMBERSHIPS** Am Philol Asn; Medieval Acad Am; Mod Greek Studies Asn; Class Asn New Engl. **RESEARCH** Class philol, espec Pindar and Homer; mod Greek studies; Byzantine hist. **SELECTED PUBLICATIONS** Auth, Nominal-Compound Epithets in Pindar: A Linguistic Analysis, Univ Microfilms, 67; coauth, More still on the Trojan Horse, Class J, 4-5/72. **CONTACT ADDRESS** Dept of Langs, Lit and Cult, Univ of NH, 125 Technology Dr, Durham, NH, 03824-4724. **EMAIL** jcrouman@christa.unh.edu

ROWAN, KATHERINE E.
PERSONAL Born 02/17/1954, Alexandra, VA **DISCIPLINE** ENGLISH, RHETORIC AND COMPOSITION, SPEECH COMMUNICATION **EDUCATION** George Mason Univ, Fairfax, VA, BA (English Lit), 75; Univ IL, Urbana-Champaign, MA (Speech Commun), 78; Purdue Univ, PhD (English), 85. **CAREER** Teaching asst, Dept of Speech Commun, Univ IL, Urbana, 76-79; lect, English div, Parkland Col, Champaign, Il, 78-79; lect, Dept of Rhetoric & Commun, SUNY, Albany, 79-81; lect, Master's in Managrment Prog, Col of St Rose, Albany, NY, 80; lect, Dept of English (evening div), Russell Sage Col, Troy, NY, 80-81; teaching asst, Dept of English, Purdue Univ, 82-84; graduate instr, 84-85, asst prof, 85-91, assoc prof, 91-95, prof, Dept of Commun, Purdue Univ, West Lafayette, IN, 96-. **HONORS AND AWARDS** Graduated magna cum laude, George Mason Univ, 75; listed, Who's Who Among American Colleges and Universities; Phi Kappa Phi, Purdue Univ, 83; David Ross Summer res fel, Dept of English, Purdue Univ, 84; Gannett Foun Teaching fel, IN Univ, Bloomington, 87; Poynter Inst Teaching fel, Poynter Inst for Media Studies, St Petersburg, FL, 88; X-L Summer res grant, Purdue Univ, 86, 90; Outstanding Young Teacher Award, Central States Commun Asn, 90; Purdue Univ School of Liberal Arts Educational Excellence Award, 91; Top 3 Paper, Public Relations Interest Group, Int Commun Asn, 92; directed two master's theses which won the Outstanding Master's Thesis Award, Health Commun Div of the Nat Commun Asn and Int Commun Asn (Rose G Campbell, 94, and Susan L Smith, 96). **MEMBERSHIPS** Asn for Ed in Journalism and Mass Commun; Int Commun Asn; Nat Commun Asn; Nat Coun of Teachers of English; Phi Kappa Phi; Soc of Professional Journalists. **SELECTED PUBLICATIONS** Auth, review of Psycholinguistics of Readable Writing, by Alice S Horning, Commun Theory, 4, 94; Why Rules for Risk Communication Fail: A Problem-Solving Approach to Risk Communication, Risk Analysis, 14, 94; The Technical and Democratic Approaches to Risk Situations: Their Appeal, Limitations, and Rhetorical Alternative, Argumentation, 8, 94; Expository Writing, in A C Purves, ed, Encyclopedia of English Studies and Language Arts, vol 1, Scholastic, Inc, 94; with M R Dennis, R A Feinberg, R Widdows, and R E Crable, Corporate Civil Disobedience in the Consumer Interest: The Case of Kellogg's Catalytic Defiance of FDA Health Claim Laws, Advancing the Consumer Interest, 6, 94; with D M Hoover, Communicating Risk to Patients: Detecting, Diagnosing, and Overcoming Lay Theories, Communicating Risk to Patients, US Pharmacopeial Convention, 94; What Risk Communicators Need to Know: An Agenda for Research, in B R Burleson, ed, Communication Yearbook, 18, Sage, 95; A New Pedagogy for Explanatory Speaking: Why Arrangement Should Not Substitute for Invention, Conmmunication Education, 44, 95; Exposition, in T Enos, ed, Encyclopedia of Rhetoric and Composition: Communication from Ancient Times to the Information Age, Garland Pub, 96; numerous other publications. **CONTACT ADDRESS** Dept of Commun, Purdue Univ, West Lafayette, IN, 47907. **EMAIL** rowan@purdue.edu

ROY, GEORGE ROSS
PERSONAL Born 08/20/1924, Montreal, PQ, Canada, m, 1954, 1 child **DISCIPLINE** ENGLISH, COMPARATIVE LITERATURE **EDUCATION** Concordia Univ, BA, 50; Univ Montreal, MA, 51, PhD(English), 59; Univ Strasbourg, dipl, 54; Univ Paris, DUniv(comp lit), 58. **CAREER** Lectr English, Royal Mil Col, St Jean, 54-56; asst prof, Univ Ala, 58-61; from asst prof to assoc prof, Univ Montreal, 61-63; prof, Tex Technol Univ, 63-65; prof English & Comp Lit, Univ SC, 65-90; Huntington Libr grant, 62; Can Coun & Am Philos Soc grant, 63; founding mem bd gov & chmn libr comt, Am-Scottish Found, NY, 66-; founding ed, Studies in Scottish Lit, 63- ; gen ed, Scottish Poetry Reprints, Quarto Press, London & Dept English Bibliog Ser, Univ SC. **HONORS AND AWARDS** Founding vice-pres, Asn for Scottish Lit Stud; fel, Soc of Antiq of Scotland; hon life pres, Robert Burns Federation; Robert Burce Award, Old Dominion Univ; distinguished prof Univ S Carolina, 89. **MEMBERSHIPS** Int Comp Lit Asn; Am Comp Lit Asn; MLA; S Atlantic MLA; Edinburgh Bibl Soc; Thomas Carlyle Soc; James Boswell Soc. **RESEARCH** Comparative literature; Scottish literature; Robert Burns. **SELECTED PUBLICATIONS** Auth, Editing the Makars in the Eighteenth and Early Nineteenth Centuries, in Strauss, ed, Scottish Language and Literature, Medieval and Renaissance, Frankfurt am Main, 86; auth, The Bible in Burns and Scott, in Wright, ed, The Bible in Scottish Literature, Edinburgh, 88; auth, Scottish Poets and the French Revolution, Etudes Ecossaises, 92, auth, Editing Burns' Letters in the Twentieth Century, in Carnie, ed, Robert Burns: Some Twentieth-Century Perspectives, Calgary, 93; auth, Editing Robert Burns in the Nineteenth Century, in Simpson, ed, Burns Now, Edinburgh, 94. **CONTACT ADDRESS** Dept of English, Univ of SC, Columbia, SC, 29208.

ROZBICKI, MICHAEL J.
PERSONAL Born 06/24/1946, Gdynia, m, 1991, 1 child **DISCIPLINE** ENGLISH LITERATURE/HISTORY **EDUCATION** Warsaw Univ, Poland, MA, 70, PhD, 84; Maria Curie-Sklodowska Univ, Poland, 75. **CAREER** Asst prof to assoc prof, 76-92, Warsaw Univ; asst prof to assoc prof, 92-, St Louis Univ. **HONORS AND AWARDS** Free Univ Berlin Fel, 82, 89; Oxford Univ Fel, 84; Rockefeller Found Fel, 90; John Carter

Brown Libr Fel, 86; Huntington Libr Fel, 91; Amer Coun of Learned Soc Fel, 79-80. **MEMBERSHIPS** AAUP; Org Amer Hist. **RESEARCH** Cultural hist of colonial British Amer **SELECTED PUBLICATIONS** Auth, Transformation of English Cultural Ethos in Colonial America: Maryland 1634-1720, Univ Press Amer, 88; auth, The Birth of a Nation: History of the United States of American to 1860, Interim Publ House, Warsaw, 91; art, Between East-Central Europe and Britain: Reformation, Science, and the Emergence of Intellectual Networks in Mid-Seventeenth Century, E Europe Quart, 96; art, The Curse of Provincialism: Negative Perceptions of Colonial American Plantation Gentry, J S Hist, 97; auth, A Bridge to a Barrier to American Identity? The Uses of European Taste among Eighteenth-Century Plantation Gentry in British America, Amerikastudien, Heidelberg, 98; auth, The Complete Colonial Gentleman: Cultural Legitimacy in Plantation America, Univ Press Va, 98. **CONTACT ADDRESS** Dept of History, St. Louis Univ, 3800 Lindell Blvd, PO Box 56907, St. Louis, MO, 63156-0907. **EMAIL** rozbicmj@slu.edu

RUBIN, MORDECAI S.
PERSONAL Born 06/20/1930, Brooklyn, NY, m, 1953, 3 children **DISCIPLINE** FOREIGN LANGUAGES **EDUCATION** Rutgers Univ, AB, 52; Univ Md, PhD, 61. **CAREER** Instr Span, French & Ital, Gannon Col, 56-59: asst prof Spanish & French, Wash Col, 59-62; asst prof Romance lang, Clark Univ, 62-65; assoc prof, 65-69, Prof Span, Teachers Col, Columbia Univ, 69-, Lang educ consult, UN, Peace Corps & Teacher Corps. **HONORS AND AWARDS** Elected Spanish Royal Academy, Madrid, 95; Elected Iberian American Academy of Poetry, 96. **MEMBERSHIPS** Am Asn Teachers Span & Port; MLA. **RESEARCH** Bilingual education, Spanish poetry, Distance learning. **SELECTED PUBLICATIONS** Translr, Cargo loss prevention, Int Insurance Monitor, 63; auth, Una poetica moderns, Univ Ala & Nat Univ Mex, 66; The image of the language teacher, J English As Second Lang, 68; Toward a modern methodology for teaching Chinese, J Am Asn Teachers Chinese, 68; Considerations home dialect and English teaching Spanish bilinguals, In: Anthology, Louisville Linguistics Conference 1977, Georgetown Univ, 3/78. **CONTACT ADDRESS** Dept Span Teachers Col, Columbia Univ, 525 W 120th St, New York, NY, 10027-6670. **EMAIL** MRubin@aol.com

RUBIN, REBECCA B.
PERSONAL Born 12/11/1948, York, PA, m **DISCIPLINE** SPEECH COMMUNICATION **EDUCATION** Penn St Univ, BA, 70, MA, 71; Univ IL UC, PhD, 75 **CAREER** Instr, 71-72, Messiah Col PA; tchng/res asst, Dept of Speech and Drama, 72-75, Univ of IL; asst prof, 75-76, Georgia Southern Col; instr, Dept of Drama & Speech, 76-77, Univ of NC; asst prof, Communication Discipline, 77-81, Univ of WI; asst prof, Dept of Communication, 81-82, Cleveland St Univ; assoc prof, School of Speech Comm, prof, School for Communication Stud, 88-, Kent St Univ. **HONORS AND AWARDS** Who's Who in the Media and Communications; Women in Communication a Biographical Sourcebook; Outstanding Merit Award Speech Comm Asn, 95; Kent St Univ Pres Honor Roll, 92; Phi Beta Delta Honor Soc for Intl Scholars, 92. **MEMBERSHIPS** Natl Comm Asn; Intl Comm Asn. **RESEARCH** Interpersonal communication; communication competence. **SELECTED PUBLICATIONS** Coauth, Communication Research Strategies and Sources, Wadsworth, 93; auth, Communication Competency Assessment Instrument High School Edition, Spectra Inc, 94; auth, Communication Competency Assessment Instrument, Spectra, 94; auth, SCA Summer Conference Proceedings and Prepared Remarks, Speech Comm Asn, 94; coauth, Communication Research Measures: A Sourcebook, Guilford, 94; coauth, Communication Research Strategies and Sources, Wadsworth, 96; coauth, Media Education Assessment Handbook, Erlbaum, 97; coauth, Preparing Competent College Graduates Setting New and Higher Expectations for Student Learning, 97; coauth, Communication and Personality Trait perspectives, Hampton Press, 98; coauth, Test of a Self-Efficacy Model of Interpersonal Communication Competence, Comm Quart 41, 93; coauth, The Role of Self-Disclosure and Self-Awareness in Affinity-Seeking Competence, Comm Res Reports 10, 93; coauth, Development of a Communication Flexibility Measure, South Comm Jour 59, 94; coauth, Development of a Measure of Interpersonal Communication Competence, Comm Res Reports 11, 94; coauth, Organizational Entry: An Investigation of Newcomer Communication Behavior and Uncertainty, Comm Res 22, 95; coauth, A New Measure of Cognitive Flexibility, Psychol Reports 76, 95; coauth, Performance Based Assessment of High School Speech Instruction, Comm Ed 44, 95; coauth, Effects of Instruction on Communication Apprehension and Communication Competence, Comm Ed 46, 97; coauth, Affinity-Seeking in Initial Interactions, South Jour of Comm, 98. **CONTACT ADDRESS** Kent State Univ, PO Box 5190, Kent, OH, 44242-0001. **EMAIL** rrubin@kent.edu

RUBINCAM, CATHERINE I.
PERSONAL Born 08/23/1943, Belfast, Northern Ireland, m, 1974, 4 children **DISCIPLINE** CLASSICAL STUDIES **EDUCATION** Univ Toronto, BA, 64; Oxford Univ, BA, 66; Harvard Univ, PhD, 69. **CAREER** Asst prof then assoc prof, classics, Erindale Col, Univ Toronto, 69- . **MEMBERSHIPS** Am Philol Asn. **RESEARCH** Ancient Greek history and historiography; history of classical tradition; history of women in the professoriate. **SELECTED PUBLICATIONS** Auth, Mary White and Women Professors of Classics in Canadian Universities, Class World, 96-97; auth, The Organization of Material in Graeco-Roman World Histories, in, Pre-Modern Encyclopedic Texts: Proceedings of the Second COMERS Congress, 97; auth, Did Diodorus Siculus Take Over Cross-References from His Sources? Am J of Philol, 98; auth, How Many Books Did Diodorus Siculus Originally Intend to Write? Class Q, 98. **CONTACT ADDRESS** Dept of Classics, Univ of Toronto, Mississauga, ON, L5L 1C6. **EMAIL** rubincam@chass.utoronto.ca

RUCK, CARL ANTON PAUL
PERSONAL Born 12/08/1935, Bridgeport, CT **DISCIPLINE** GREEK LANGUAGE & LITERATURE **EDUCATION** Yale Univ, BA, 58; Univ Mich, Ann Arbor, MA, 59; Harvard Univ, PhD(classics), 65. **CAREER** From instr to assoc prof, 64-76, PROF CLASSICS, BOSTON UNIV, 76-. **MEMBERSHIPS** Am Philol Asn. **RESEARCH** Greek tragedy and comedy; Greek mythology; teaching methods for Greek and Latin; ethnobotany; ethnopharmacology; clinical mythologist. **SELECTED PUBLICATIONS** Auth, IG II 2323: The List of Victors in Comedy at the Dionysia, Brill, 67; coauth, Pindar: Selected Odes (transl & essays), Univ Mich, 68; auth, Ancient Greek: A New Approach, Mass Inst Technol, 68, 72 & 79; On the Sacred Names of Iamos and Ion: Ethnobotanical Referents in the Hero's Parentage, Class J, 76; Duality and the Madness of Herakles, Arethusa, 76; coauth, The Road to Eleusis: Unveiling the Secret of the Mysteries, Harcourt, 78 (later translated into Spanish, Italian, Greek, and German); Mushrooms and Philosophers, 81 & The Wild and the Cultivated: Wine in Euripides' Bacchae, 82, J Ethnopharmacology; auth, Marginalia Pindarica I-VI, Hermes, 68-72; Euripides' Mother: Vegetables and the Phallos in Aristophanes, Arion, 75; coauth, A Mythic Search for Identity in a Male to Female Transsexual, J of Analytical Psch, 79; coauth, Strategies in Teaching Greek and Latin: Two Decades of Experimentation(Reading Greek), Scholars press, 91; coauth, On Nature (The Wild and the Cultivated in Greek religion), Notre Dame, 84; coauth, Persephone's Quest: Entheogens and the Origins of Religion, Yale, 86; auth, Latin: A Concise Structural Course, Univ Press Am, 87; coauth, The Sacred Mushroom Seeker (Mr Wasson and the Greeks), Dioscorides, 90; coauth, The World of Classical Myth: Gods and Godesses, Heroines and Heros, Carolina Academic Press, 94; coauth, Ethnobotany: Evolution of a Discipline (Gods and Plants in the Classical World), Dioscorides, 95; auth, Intensive Latin: First Year and Review (with computer tutorial Vade Mecum), Carolina Academic Press, 97; coauth, Mistletoe, Centaurs, and Datura, Eleusis n s 1.2, 98; auth, entry on Myth in the Blackwell Dictionary of Anthropology. **CONTACT ADDRESS** Dept of Classics, Boston Univ, 745 Commonwealth Ave, Boston, MA, 02215-1401. **EMAIL** bacchus@bu.edu

RUDD, JILL
DISCIPLINE INTERPERSONAL COMMUNICATION, GROUP COMMUNICATION **EDUCATION** Kent State Univ, BA, MA, PhD. **CAREER** Comm, Cleveland St Univ. **SELECTED PUBLICATIONS** Auth, Divorce Mediation: One Step Forward Two Steps Back?, Communication and the Disenfranchised,L. Erlbaum Assoc, 96. **CONTACT ADDRESS** Commun Dept, Cleveland State Univ, 83 E 24th St, Cleveland, OH, 44115. **EMAIL** j.rudd@csuohio.edu

RUDNYTZKY, LEONID
PERSONAL Born 09/08/1935, Lviv, Ukraine, m, 1964, 3 children **DISCIPLINE** GERMAN & SLAVIC LITERATURE **EDUCATION** La Salle Col, BA, 58; Univ Pa, MA, 60; Ukrainian Free Univ, Munich, PhD, 65. **CAREER** Prof foreign lang, 63-75, prof Slavic & Ger Lit, La Salle Col, 75-; consult, Cath Renascence Soc, 65-68,; prof, Ukrainian Free Univ, 75; ethic heritage studies grants, 80, 81; NEH grant, 82. **HONORS AND AWARDS** Lindback Award for Distinguished Teaching, La Salle College, Philadelphia, 66; Doctor Habil; St. Clement Pope Ukrainian Catholic Univ, Rome, 76; Hon Dr, Holy Family Col, Philadelphia, 91; Ivan Franko Prize for Ukrainian Lit, The Writers' Union of Ukraine, Kiev, 92; Elected Pres of the World Council of The Shevchenko Scientific Soc, Lviv, Ukraine, 92. **MEMBERSHIPS** Shevchenko Sci Soc; MLA; Am Assn Teachers Ger; Am Assn Teachers Slavic & E Europ Lang; St. Sophia Rel Soc Assoc of Ukrainian Catholics-Exec Sec; Intl PEN Club. **RESEARCH** Comparative literature; history of Easten churches and Eastern spirituality; the Ukrainian Catholic Church. **SELECTED PUBLICATIONS** Auth, Research Guide to European Historial Biography 1450 - Present, Beachan Publishing, Washington, DC, 93; ed, Faith and Hope, The Dyivan Church in Communion with Rome: 1596-1996, Philadelphia, Washington, Toronto, 97. **CONTACT ADDRESS** Dept of Foreign Lang & Lit, La Salle Univ, 1900 W Olney Ave, Philadelphia, PA, 19141-1199. **EMAIL** rudnytzk@alpha.lasalle.edu

RUEBEL, JAMES
PERSONAL Born 08/18/1945, Cincinnati, OH, m, 1966, 2 children **DISCIPLINE** ANCIENT ROMAN HISTORY, CLASSICAL LANGUAGES **EDUCATION** Yale Univ, BA, 67; Univ Cincinnati, MA, 70, PhD, 72. **CAREER** Instr Greek & Latin, Classics Dept, Univ Cincinnati, 72-73; asst prof, Classics Dept, Univ MN, 73-78; asst prof, 78-81, Assoc Prof, 81-93, PROF CLASSICS, FOR LANG & LIT, IA STATE UNIV, 93-. **MEMBERSHIPS** Am Philol Asn; Asn Ancient Historians; Class Asn Midwest & South; Am Class League; Archaeol Inst Am. **RESEARCH** Roman republican history; Roman culture from Hannibal to Horace. **CONTACT ADDRESS** Dept of For Lang & Lit, Iowa State Univ, Ames, IA, 50011-2205. **EMAIL** jsruebel@iastate.edu

RUESCHMANN, EVA
DISCIPLINE COMPARATIVE LITERATURE AND CULTURAL STUDIES **EDUCATION** Univ Heidelberg, Ger, BA; Univ MA, Amherst, PhD. **CAREER** Vis asst prof, Hampshire Col. **SELECTED PUBLICATIONS** Publ articles on Senegalese novelist Mariama Ba, African American writers Jessie Fauset and Dorothy West, filmmakers Alan Rudolph and Margarethe von Trotta, and psychoanalytic and cultural readings of sister relationships in contemp world cinema. **CONTACT ADDRESS** Hampshire Col, Amherst, MA, 01002.

RUGG, MARILYN D.
DISCIPLINE SPANISH LITERATURE **EDUCATION** Cornell Univ, BA, 75, MA, 78; The Johns Hopkins Univ, PhD, 85; Marawood Col, MSW, 89. **CAREER** Assoc prof-, Colgate Univ. **HONORS AND AWARDS** Hon(s), Phi Eta Sigma., Nominee, Colgate Univ prof yr, 90, 91, 95. **RESEARCH** 19th and early 20th-century Span lit. **SELECTED PUBLICATIONS** Auth, Self and Text in Unamuno's Amor y pedagogea, ALEC, 17, 92; The Figure of the Author in Gomez de la Serna's El novelista, ALEC, 14, 89; Dona Berta: Claren's Allegory of Signification, MLN, 103, 88. **CONTACT ADDRESS** Dept of Romance Lang, Colgate Univ, 13 Oak Drive, Hamilton, NY, 13346. **EMAIL** MRugg@center.colgate.edu

RUNDELL, RICHARD JASON
PERSONAL Born 12/15/1939, Chicago, IL, m, 1969, 2 children **DISCIPLINE** GERMAN LITERATURE & LINGUISTICS **EDUCATION** Colo Col, BA, 61; Middlebury Col, MA, 62; Univ Colo, PhD, 72. **CAREER** Instr Ger, St Lawrence Univ, 62-65 & Univ Colo, 69-71; asst prof, Emporia Kans State Col, 71-72; lectr English, Univ Regensburg, W Ger, 72-75; asst prof, 75-80, assoc prof, 80-86, PROF GER, NMEX STATE UNIV, 86-. **MEMBERSHIPS** Am Asn Teachers Ger; Int Brecht Soc; MLA; Ger Studies Asn. **RESEARCH** Twentieth century German literature; Brecht; East German literature; German film; German theater. **SELECTED PUBLICATIONS** Auth, Duerer year 1971, Ger Postal Spec, 71; The Brechtian influence and German Dem Repub poetry of political, criticism, Weber & Heinen: Bertolt Brecht, Polit Theory & Lit Pract, 78; Ragtime, bicentennial: Nostalgia, Gulliver, Deutschenglische Jahrbk, 78; Keller's Kleider machen leute as novelle and film, Unterrichtspraxis 13, 80; guest ed, Liedermacher issue of Dimension, vol 19, 1, 91; Liedermacher im Zeichen der Wende, in Literatur fur leser, 3/96. **CONTACT ADDRESS** Dept of Langs & Lings, New Mexico State Univ, MSC 3L, Las Cruces, NM, 88003-8001. **EMAIL** rrundell@nmsu.edu

RUNNING, LEONA GLIDDEN
PERSONAL Born 08/24/1916, Mt Morris, MI **DISCIPLINE** SEMITIC LANGUAGES **EDUCATION** Emmanuel Missionary Col, BA, 37; Seventh-Day Adventist Theol Sem, MA, 55; Johns Hopkins Univ, PhD, 64. **CAREER** Teacher Lang, Laurelwood Acad, Ore, 37-41; lang secy, Voice of Prophecy Radio Broadcast, 44-48; ed secy, Gen Conf Seventh-Day Adventists, 50-54; from instr to assoc prof, 55-69, prof, 69-81, Emer Prof Bibl Lang, Andrews Univ, 81- **HONORS AND AWARDS** Weniger and Andrews medals; Medallion of Distinction, Gen Conf Dept Educ. **MEMBERSHIPS** Soc Bibl Lit; Chi Soc Bibl Res. **RESEARCH** The Syriac manuscripts of Isaiah. **SELECTED PUBLICATIONS** Auth, An investigation of the Syriac version of Isaiah, 7/65, 1/66 & 7/66 & Syriac variants in Isaiah 26, 1/67, Andrews Univ Sem Studies; coauth, William Foxwell Albright, A Twentieth-Century Genius, Andrews Univ Press, 91. **CONTACT ADDRESS** Theol Sem, Andrews Univ, Berrien Springs, MI, 49104-0001.

RUNYON, RANDOLPH PAUL
PERSONAL Born 02/13/1947, Maysville, KY, 2 children **DISCIPLINE** FRENCH LITERATURE, AMERICAN STUDIES **EDUCATION** Johns Hopkins Univ, PhD(French), 73. **CAREER** Asst prof, Case Western Reserve Univ, 74-76; asst prof to assoc prof, 77-84, Prof French, Miami Univ, 84-. **MEMBERSHIPS** MLA; Soc des Amis de Montaigne; Am Studies Asn; SAtlantic Mod Lang Asn; Robert Penn Warren Circle. **RESEARCH** Sixteenth century French literature; 20th century French literature; literary criticism; 20th century American literature. **SELECTED PUBLICATIONS** Auth, Deliverance: Souffrir non souffrir, Mod Lang Notes, 5/73; La Parole genee: Genese et palinodie, Change, 11/73; The errors of desire, Diacritics, fall 74; Sceve's Aultre Troye, Mod Lang Notes, 5/75; Fragments of an amorous discourse: Canon in U-bis, Visible Lang, fall 77; Montaigne his, In: Resnaissance et Nouvelle Critique, State Univ NY, Albany, 78; Fowles, Irving, Barthes: Canonical Variations on an Apocryphal Theme, Ohio State Univ Press, 81; The Braided Dream: Robert Penn Warren's Late Poetry, Univ Press of Ky, 90; The Taciturn Text: The Fiction of Robert Penn Warren, Ohio State Univ Press, 90; Reading Raymond Carver, Syracuse Univ Press, 92; Delia Webster and

the Underground Railroad, Univ Press of Ky, 96. **CONTACT ADDRESS** Dept of French & Ital, Miami Univ, Oxford, OH, 45056-1602. **EMAIL** runyonr@muohio.edu

RUNYON, RANDY
DISCIPLINE FRENCH **EDUCATION** Johns Hopkins Univ, PhD. **CAREER** Prof, Miami Univ **RESEARCH** 16th-century French literature; interdisciplinary studies in music and literature; American studies. **SELECTED PUBLICATIONS** Auth, Fowles/Irving/Barthes: Canonical Variations on an Apocryphal Theme; The Braided Dream: Robert Penn Warren; Reading Raymond Carver; Delia Webster and the Underground Railroad. **CONTACT ADDRESS** Dept of French and Italian, Miami Univ, Oxford, OH, 45056. **EMAIL** runyonr@muohio.edu

RUSSELL, CHARLES
PERSONAL Born 12/16/1944, New York, NY, m, 1990 **DISCIPLINE** COMPARATIVE LITERATURE **EDUCATION** Wesleyan Univ, AB, 66; Cornell Univ, PhD, 72. **CAREER** Asst prof, Univ Va, 72-76; asst prof, 77-83, assoc dean arts scis, 85-87, assoc provost, 88-94, ASSOC PROF ENGLISH, 83-, RUTGERS UNIV, NEWARK. **HONORS AND AWARDS** Fulbright lect Univ Augsburg, 80 **MEMBERSHIPS** MLA; CAA. **RESEARCH** Contemporary lit and art **SELECTED PUBLICATIONS** Auth, Poets, Prophets and Revolutionaires: The Literary Avant-garde from Rimbaud through Postmodernism, Oxford Univ Press, 85; auth, The Avant-garde Today, Univ Ill Press, 81. **CONTACT ADDRESS** English Dept, Rutgers Univ, Newark, NJ, 07102. **EMAIL** crr@andromeda.rutgers.edu

RUSSELL, DELBERT
DISCIPLINE FRENCH LITERATURE **EDUCATION** Univ Toronto, BA; MA; PhD. **RESEARCH** French-Canadian literature; medieval French language and literature; bibliography. **SELECTED PUBLICATIONS** Auth, An Annotated Bibliography (rev), 87; Le Legendier apostolique anglo-normand, Montreal, 89; La Vie S. Richard, Bishop Chichester, 95. **CONTACT ADDRESS** Waterloo Univ, 200 University Ave W, Waterloo, ON, N2L 3G1. **EMAIL** drussell@watarts.uwaterloo.ca

RUSSELL, RINALDINA
PERSONAL Ancona, Italy **DISCIPLINE** ITALIAN LITERATURE **EDUCATION** Columbia Univ, PhD, 71. **CAREER** Instr Ital lang & lit, Barnard Col, Columbia Univ, 69-71; asst prof romance lang, 71-76, assoc prof romance lang, 76-85, prof European lang & lit, 85-, Queens Col, NY, 76-. **MEMBERSHIPS** MLA; Dante Soc Am; Renaissance Soc Am; Am Asn Teachers Ital; Am Asn Ital Studies. **SELECTED PUBLICATIONS** Auth, Tre versanti delta poesia stilnovistica: Guinizzelli, Cavalcanti e Dante, Adriatica Editrice, Bari, 73; Generi poetici medievali, Modelli c funzioni letterarie, Societa Editrice Napoletana, Naples, 82; ed, Italian Women Writers, Greenwood, 94; The Feminist Encyclopedia of Italian Literature, Greenwood, 97; co-ed Tullia d' Aragona, Dialogue on the Infinity of Love, Univ Chicago, 97. **CONTACT ADDRESS** Dept of European Lang & Lit, Queens Col, CUNY, 6530 Kissena Blvd, Flushing, NY, 11367-1597.

RUTHERFORD, WILLIAM E.
DISCIPLINE LINGUISTICS **EDUCATION** UCLA, PhD. **CAREER** Prof, Univ Southern Calif. **RESEARCH** Second language acquisiton and grammatical theory. **SELECTED PUBLICATIONS** Co-gen ed ser, Language Acquisition and Language Disorders. **CONTACT ADDRESS** Dept of Linguistics, Univ Southern Calif, University Park Campus, Los Angeles, CA, 90089. **EMAIL** rthrford@vm.usc.edu

RYAN, JUDITH
DISCIPLINE GERMAN AND COMPARATIVE LITERATURE **EDUCATION** Sydney Univ, Australia, BA; Univ Mnnster, Ger, PhD. **CAREER** Harvard Col prof & Robert K. and Dale J. Weary prof; dir, Grad Stud; taught at, Smith Col. **RESEARCH** 19th and 20th century literature, especially poetry and the novel. **SELECTED PUBLICATIONS** Auth, Umschlag und Verwandlung; The Uncompleted Past & The Vanishing Subject; articles on, Franz Kafka, Paul Celan, Christa Wolf & Gnnter Grass. **CONTACT ADDRESS** Dept of Germanic Languages and Literature, Harvard Univ, 8 Garden St, Cambridge, MA, 02138. **EMAIL** jryan@fas.harvard.edu

RYAN, ROBERT
DISCIPLINE FRENCH LITERATURE **EDUCATION** Dalhousie Univ, BA; MA; Aix en Provence Univ, PhD. **RESEARCH** Acadian speech of Atlantic Canada. **SELECTED PUBLICATIONS** Auth, pub(s) on phonology and verb morphology of a Nova Scotian Acadian dialect. **CONTACT ADDRESS** Dept of French, Waterloo Univ, 200 University Ave W, Waterloo, ON, N2L 3G1. **EMAIL** rbauer@watarts.uwaterloo.ca

RZHEVSKY, NICHOLAS
PERSONAL Born 11/08/1943, Linz, Austria, m, 1966, 2 children **DISCIPLINE** RUSSIAN LITERATURE **EDUCATION** Rutgers Univ, BA, 64; Princeton Univ, MA, 68, PhD, 72. **CAREER** Oberlin Col; Rutgers Univ; Livingston Col; Univ Ill; SUNY Stony Brook. **HONORS AND AWARDS** Four Fulbright-Hays awards; three IREX grants; one NEH grant; one DOE grant. **MEMBERSHIPS** AATSEEL; AAASS; Phi Beta Kappa. **RESEARCH** Literature; theater; culture; ideology. **SELECTED PUBLICATIONS** Co-ed, Dramaturgics and Dramaturgy, Slavic and East Europ Arts, Stony Brook, 86; auth, Russian Literature and Ideology: Herzen, Dostoevsky, Tolstoy, Leontiev, Fadeyev, Univ Ill, 83; ed, An Anthology of Russian Literature from Earliest Writings to Modern Fiction: Introduction to A Culture, M.E. Sharpe, 96; transl and ed, Alexander Pushkin's Boris Godunov, M.E. Sharpe, 98; ed, Cambridge Companion to Modern Russian Culture, Cambridge, 98. **CONTACT ADDRESS** Dept of European Languages, Literatures and Cultures, SUNY Stony Brook, Stony Brook, NY, 11794. **EMAIL** Nicholas.Rzhevsky@sunysb.edu

S

SAA, ORLAND
DISCIPLINE SPANISH LANGUAGE AND LITERATURE AND LATIN LANGUAGE **EDUCATION** Tulane Univ, PhD, 73. **CAREER** Prof, William Paterson Univ, 74-; VP, Circulo de Cult Panamericano, Chap NJ. **SELECTED PUBLICATIONS** Auth, La serenidad en las obras de Eugenio Florit, 73; De una anguistia por destino, 86; El teatro escolar de los jesuitas en Espana; 90. **CONTACT ADDRESS** Dept of Language and Cultures, William Paterson Col, 300 Pompton Rd., Wayne, NJ, 07470.

SACKETT, THEODORE ALAN
DISCIPLINE SPANISH **EDUCATION** Univ Ariz, PhD. **CAREER** Prof Span, ch, dept For Lang and Lit, Univ Nev, Reno; ed, J Hispania, 84-92. **RESEARCH** Spanish literature of the 19th and 20th centures. **SELECTED PUBLICATIONS** Published extensively on the narratives and theatre of Perez Galdos, as well as on Pereda, Blasco Ibanez, Ortega y Gasset, Sastre, Delibes, and the Ecuadorian novelist Jorge Icaza. **CONTACT ADDRESS** Univ Nev, Reno, Reno, NV, 89557. **EMAIL** sackett@unr.edu

SADDLEMYER, ANN
PERSONAL Born 11/28/1932, Prince Albert, SK, Canada **DISCIPLINE** DRAMA/COMPARATIVE LITERATURE **EDUCATION** Univ Sask, BA, 53(Eng & Psychol), 55(Eng Hons); Queen's Univ, MA, 56; Bedford Col, Univ London, PhD, 61. **CAREER** Lectr, 56-57, instr, Victoria (BC) Col, 60; asst prof, 62, assoc prof, 65, prof, Univ Victoria, 68-71; prof, 71-95, dir, grad drama ctr, 72-77, acting dir, 85-86, PROF EMER ENGLISH, GRAD CTR FOR STUD DRAMA, COMPARATIVE LITERATURE, 95-; vis prof Berg Ch, NY Univ, 75; sr fel, 75-88, master 88-95, MASTER EMER, MASSEY COL, 95-; **HONORS AND AWARDS** Guggenheim fel, 65, 77; Connaught sr res fel, 86; Distinguished Serv Award, Prov Ont, 85; Univ Toronto Alumni Award, 90; off, Order Can, 95; LLD(hon), Queen's Univ, 77; DLitt(hon), Univ Victoria, 89; DLitt(hon), McGill Univ, 89; DLitt(hon), Univ Windsor, 90. **MEMBERSHIPS** Int Asn Stud Anglo-Irish Lit (past chmn); Asn Can Theatre Res (founding pres); Can Asn Irish Stud. **RESEARCH** Anglo-Irish literature; theatre history **SELECTED PUBLICATIONS** Auth, In Defence of Lady Gregory, Playwright, 66; auth, The Plays of J.M. Synge, Books One and Two, 68; auth, Synge and Modern Comedy, 68; auth, The Plays of Lady Gregory, 70; auth, A Selection of Letters from J.M. Synge to W.B. Yeats and Lady Gregory, 71; auth, Letters to Molly: J.M. Synge to Maire O'Neill, 71; auth, Theatre Business, The Correspondence of the First Abbey Theatre Directors, 82; auth, The Collected Letters of J.M. Synge, vol I 83, vol II 84; coauth, The World of W.B. Yeats, 65; Lady Gregory Fifty Years After, 87; ed, Early Stages: Essays on Theatre in Ontario 1800-1914, 90; Later Stages: Essays on Theatre in Ontario World War I to the 1970s, 97; co-ed, The World's Classics J.M. Synge, 95; co-ed, Theatre Hist Can, 79-86; ed bd, Irish Univ Rev; ed bd, Can J Irish Stud; ed bd, The Shaw Rev. **CONTACT ADDRESS** Massey Col, Univ of Toronto, 4 Devonshire Pl, Toronto, ON, M5S 2E1. **EMAIL** saddlemy@chass.utoronto.ca

SAG, IVAN ANDREW
PERSONAL Born 11/09/1949, Alliance, OH **DISCIPLINE** THEORETICAL & COMPUTATIONAL LINGUISTICS **EDUCATION** Univ Rochester, BA, 71; Univ Pa, MA, 73; Mass Inst Technol, PhD(ling), 76. **CAREER** Asst prof ling, Univ Pa, 76-79; Asst Prof Ling, Stanfrod Univ, 79-, A Mellon fel, Stanford Univ, 78-79; vist asst prof, Univ Tex, Austin, 79, Univ Calif, Berkeley, 80 & Ling Inst, Univ Md, 82; consult, Hewlett-Packard Labs, 81- **MEMBERSHIPS** Ling Soc Am; Asn Comput Ling. **RESEARCH** Natural language syntax and semantics; natural language processing. **SELECTED PUBLICATIONS** Auth, English Relative Clause Constructions/, J Of Linguistics, Vol 0033, 1997; French Clitic Movement Without Clitics Or Movement/, Natural Lang & Linguistic Theory, Vol 0015, 1997. **CONTACT ADDRESS** Dept of Ling, Stanford Univ, Stanford, CA, 97305.

SAHA, PROSANTA KUMAR
PERSONAL Born 12/04/1932, Calcutta, India, m, 1958, 2 children **DISCIPLINE** ENGLISH, LINGUISTICS **EDUCATION** Univ Calcutta, BA, 56; Oberlin Col, MA 57; Western Reserve Univ, PhD(English), 66. **CAREER** Teacher, Hawken Sch, 57-62; instr English, 62-64, asst prof English & ling, 66-72, Assoc Prof English & Ling & Chmn Ling & Undergrad Humanities Prog, Case Western Reserve Univ, 72- **HONORS AND AWARDS** Carl F Wittke Award, Case Western Reserve Univ, 71. **MEMBERSHIPS** Ling Soc Am. **RESEARCH** English literature and linguistics; computer analysis of literature, especially stylistics; Bengali literature and linguistics. **SELECTED PUBLICATIONS** Auth, Reflexive Revisited + English Pronouns/, Am Speech, Vol 0068, 1993. **CONTACT ADDRESS** Dept of English, Case Western Reserve Univ, Clark Hall Rm 103 Case, Cleveland, OH, 44106.

SAHNI, CHAMAN LALL
PERSONAL Born 06/10/1933, Thatta, India, m, 1960, 2 children **DISCIPLINE** ENGLISH, FAR EASTERN LINGUISTICS **EDUCATION** Agra Univ, India, BA, 54; Lucknow Univ, India, MA, 56; Univ RI, MA, 68; Wayne State Univ, PhD, 74. **CAREER** Lectr Eng, Bareilly Col, India, 56-59; head dept, Seth Motilal Col, 59-60; lectr, S D Col, India, 60-62 & Kurukshetra Univ, 62-67; from instr to asst prof, Wayne State Univ, 71-75; asst prof, 75-78, assoc prof, 78-81, prof eng, Boise State Univ, 81. **MEMBERSHIPS** MLA; SAsian Lit Asn **RESEARCH** Mod Brit fiction. **SELECTED PUBLICATIONS** Ed with introd & notes, Chaucer: The Prologue, 66 & Milton's Samson Agonistes, 67, Kitab Ghar, India; auth, The Marabar Caves in the light of Indian thought, In: Focus on Forster's A Passage to India, Humanities, 76; ed with introd & notes, Shelley's Adonais, 7th ed, 93, coauth, Advanced Literary Essays, 16th ed, 94 & auth, Principles and History of Literary Criticism, 3rd ed, 77, Bareilly U P, India; Forster's A Passage to India: The Religious Dimension, Arnold-Heinemann, India, 81, and Humanities Press 81; Gandhi and Tagore, SAsian Rev, 7/81; E M Forster's A Passage to India: The Islamic Dimension, South Asian Rev, 83, and Cahiers Victoriens & Edouardiens, 83; Indian Writers of English Fiction, Advanced Lit Essays, Prakash Book Depot, India, 85; Indian Poetry in English, Advanced Lit Essays, Prakash Book Depot, India, 85; The Images of Mahatma Gandhi in Indo-English Fiction, Advanced Lit Essays, Prakash Book Depot, India, 85; Rabindranath Tagor: Sidelights, Contemporary Authors, Gale Res Co, 87; Steppenwolf and Indian Thought, South Asian Rev, 88; Raja Rao: The Serpent and the Rope, Kamala Markandaya: Nectar in a Sieve, and Anita Desai: Fire on the Mountain, In: Cyclopedia of Literary Characters II, Salem Press, 90; R K Narayan, E M Forester, and Bharati Mukherjee, In: Critical Survey of Short Fiction, rev ed, Salem Press, 93; Sasthi Brata, In: Writers of the Indian Diaspora: A Bio-Bibliographical Source Book, Greenwood Press, 93; Donald Duk by Frank Chin, and Jasmine by Bharati Mukherjee, In: Masterplots II: American Fiction, supplement, Salem Press, 94; Krishna Janamashtami, Lala Hardayal, Gayatri Chakravorti Spivak, and Bharati Mukherjee, In: Asian American Encyclopedia, Marshall Cavendish, 95; Wife by Bharati Mukherjee, In: Masterplots II: Women's Literature, Marshall Cavendish, 95; Anita Desai, In: Magill's Survey of World Literature, Supplement, Salem Press, 95; Siddhartha by Hermann Hesse, In: Masterplots: Revised Second Edition, Salem Press; 96; Jasmine by Bharati Mukherjee, In: Masterplots II: Short Story, Supplement, Salem Press, 96; Kamala Markandaya and Anita Desai, In: Cyclopedia of World Authors, rev ed, Salem Press, 97. **CONTACT ADDRESS** Dept of Eng, Boise State Univ, 1910 University Dr, Boise, ID, 83725-0399. **EMAIL** csahni@bsu.idbsu.edu

SAIGAL, M.
PERSONAL Born 10/26/1938, Paris, France, m, 1972, 2 children **DISCIPLINE** FRENCH; SPANISH **EDUCATION** Lycee Laude Debussy, Paris; BA, MA, PhD, UCLA. **CAREER** Teaching asst, 62-65, Univ CA; instr, 65-70, asst prof, 70-75, assoc prof 76-84, Prof, 84-, Pomona Coll, **HONORS AND AWARDS** Wig award for Exceellent Teaching **MEMBERSHIPS** MLA; Assn of French Teachers, Women in French. **RESEARCH** 20th century writings **SELECTED PUBLICATIONS** Auth, Chantal Chawaf, Thirty Voices in the Feminine, 96;Recyclage urbain chez Annie Ernaux, Foreign Literature Series, 97; book reviews, Jeanne Hyvrard: Theorist of the Modern World by Jennifer Waelti-Walters, in The French Review, Feb 98; au presage de la mienne de Jeanne Hyvrard, in The French Review, May 98. **CONTACT ADDRESS** Dept of Romance Lang & Lit, Pomona Col, 550 Harvard Ave, Claremont, CA, 91711. **EMAIL** msaigal@pomona.edu

SAINE, THOMAS PRICE
PERSONAL Born 03/08/1941, Brooklyn, NY **DISCIPLINE** GERMAN LITERATURE **EDUCATION** Yale Univ, BA, 62, MPh, 67, PhD(Ger), 68. **CAREER** From instr to assoc prof Ger, Yale Univ, 68-75; assoc prof, 75-76, Prof Ger, Univ Calif, Irvine, 76-, Vis prof Ger, Univ Cincinnati, 73-74; assoc ed, Ger Quart, 78-81; ed, Goethe Yearbk, 82-; Am Coun Learned Soc fel, 82-83; Guggenheim fel, 83. **MEMBERSHIPS** MLA; Lessing Soc; Am Asn Teachers Ger; Am Soc 18th Century Studies; Goethe Soc NAm. **RESEARCH** German 18th century literature; 18th century European intellectual history; Goethe and German classicism. **SELECTED PUBLICATIONS** Auth,

Revolution And Reform In Goethe Political Historical Thought And In His Activities As A Government Official 1790-1800/, Goethe Jahrbuch, Vol 0110, 1993. **CONTACT ADDRESS** Dept of Ger, Univ of Calif, Irvine, CA, 92717.

SAINT-JACQUES, BERNARD
PERSONAL Born 04/26/1928, Montreal, PQ, Canada **DISCIPLINE** LINGUISTICS **EDUCATION** Univ Montreal, BA, 49, Licence, 54; Sophia Univ (Tokyo), MA, 62; Georgetown Univ, MS, 64; Univ Paris, PhD, 66, DL, 75. **CAREER** Asst prof, Sophia Univ, 66-67; instr to assoc prof, 66-78, prof ling, 78-89, PROF EMER, UNIV BC, 89-; PROF & DIR, INST LANGUAGE & CULTURE, INTERCULTURAL COMMUNICATION GRADUATE PROGRAM, AICHI SHUKUTOKU UNIV (JAPAN), 90-; **HONORS AND AWARDS** Mem, Royal Soc Can. **MEMBERSHIPS** Ling Soc Am; Asn Tchrs Japanese; Can Soc Asian Stud; BC Asn Transl Interp (founding mem); Ibunkakan Kyoikukai (Int Soc Japan). **SELECTED PUBLICATIONS** Auth, Analyse structurale de la syntaxe du japonais moderne, 66; auth, Structural analysis of Modern Japanese, 71; auth, Aspects sociolinguistiques du bilinguisme canadien, 76; auth, Studies in Language and Culture, 95; coauth, Aspects of Bilingualism, 78; coauth, The Languages of Immigrants, 79; coauth, Atipa revisite, 89; coauth, Langue et Identite, 90; ed, Language and Ethnic Relations, 79; ed, Japanese Studies in Canada, 85. **CONTACT ADDRESS** Dept of Linguistics, Univ BC, Vancouver, BC, V6T 1Z1. **EMAIL** saintj@asu.aasa.ac.jp

SAITZ, ROBERT LEONARD
PERSONAL Born 07/09/1928, Boston, MA, m, 1962 **DISCIPLINE** ENGLISH AS SECOND LANGUAGE, LINGUISTICS **EDUCATION** Boston Univ, BA, 49; Univ Iowa, MA, 50; Univ Wis, PhD(English ling), 55. **CAREER** Instr English, Univ Wis, 57-59; asst prof, Southern Ill Univ, 59-60; coord, English as second lang, Fulbright grant, Colombia Univ, 60-62; from asst prof to assoc prof, 62-72, Prof Ling & English As Second Lang, Boston Univ, 72-, Consult English as second lang, Boston & New Bedford schs, 67; Fulbright lectr, Univ Seville, 69-70. **MEMBERSHIPS** Ling Soc Am; Nat Asn Foreign Student Affairs; Teachers English to Speakers Other Langs. **RESEARCH** Old English syntax; second language learning; kinesics. **SELECTED PUBLICATIONS** Coauth, Selected Readings in English, Winthrop, 72; Handbook of Gestures, Mouton, The Hague, 72; Ideas in English, Winthrop, 74; Advanced Reading & Writing, Holt, 78; Challenge, Winthrop, 78; Stimulus, Little Brown, 83; Contemporary Perspectives, Little Brown, 84; Points Wkbks, Addison-Wesley, 86; Milestones, Little Brown, 87; Short Takes, Addison-Wesley, 93, Workout in English, Prentic-Halle, 98. **CONTACT ADDRESS** Dept of English, Boston Univ, 236 Bay State Rd, Boston, MA, 02215-1403.

SALEM, PHILIP
PERSONAL Born 08/07/1945, Sioux City, IA, d, 1 child **DISCIPLINE** COMMUNICATION STUDIES; SPEECH COMMUNICATION **EDUCATION** Northern State Col, BS, 68; Univ S Dakota, 80; Univ Denver, MA, 72; Univ Denver, PhD, 74 **CAREER** Radio Announcer, KABR Aberdeen, S Dak, 66-69; TV Newsman, KXAB Aberdeen S Dak, 68; Teacher, Webster Independent School District, S Dak, 69-71; Radio Announcer, KADX, 71-74; Graduate Teaching Asst, Univ Denver, 73-74; prof, Southwest Tex St Univ, 74- **HONORS AND AWARDS** Dir, "Organizational Communication and Change: Challenges in the Next Century," 96; President's Award Res, nominee to the SWTSU President, 84, 85, 88, 92, 95, 97; President's Award Teaching, nominee to the SWTSU President, 84, 95; Southwest Bus Syposium Award, 94; Fund for Improvement of Postsecondary Education Grant, 94 **MEMBERSHIPS** Tex Speech Comm Assoc; Western States Comm Assoc; Conflict Resolution Education Network; Acad Management; Ntl Comm Assoc; ;Int Comm Assoc **RESEARCH** Communication Theory; Organizational Communication; Interpersonal Communication; Information Systems; Communication and Technology; Communication and Conflict Management **SELECTED PUBLICATIONS** Ed, Organizational communication and change, Hampton Pr, forthcoming; Institutional factors influencing the success of Drug Abuse Education and Prevention Programs, US Dept Education, 91; Organizational communication and higher education, Amer Assoc Education, 81 **CONTACT ADDRESS** Dept Speech Comm, Southwest Tex St Univ, San Marcos, TX, 78666. **EMAIL** ps05@swt.edu

SALGADO, MARIA ANTONIA
PERSONAL Born 01/15/1933, Canary Islands, Spain, m, 1954, 2 children **DISCIPLINE** ROMANCE LANGUAGES **EDUCATION** Fla State Univ, BA, 58; Univ NC, MA, 60; Univ Md, PhD, 66. **CAREER** Asst prof, 62, Univ Md; instr, 63-67; from asst prof to assoc prof, 67-77, prof Span AM Lit, 77-, Univ NC, Chapel Hill. **MEMBERSHIPS** MLA; Am Assn Teachers Span & Port; Assn Int Hispanistas; Inst Int Lit Iberoam. **RESEARCH** The art of caricature in literature; contemporary Spanish and Spanish-American poetry; literary portrait and autobiography. **SELECTED PUBLICATIONS** Auth, UT Pictura Poesis y el Autorretrato de Olmedo, Dieciocho, 96; auth, Pio Cid soy yo: Mito/auto/bio/grafia de Angel Ganivet, RILCE, 97; auth, Mi Esposa es de Mi Tierra; Mi Querida de Paris, el Espanolismo de Ruben Dario, Anthropos, 97; auth, Converfencias y divergencias de la Representacion Femenina, Estudios en Honor de Janet Perez, Scripta Humanistica, 98. **CONTACT ADDRESS** Dept of Romance Lang, Univ of North Carolina, Chapel Hill, Box 3170, Chapel Hill, NC, 27599-3170. **EMAIL** masal@email.unc.edu

SALLUSTIO, ANTHONY THOMAS
PERSONAL Born 06/26/1936, Flushing, NY, m, 1960 **DISCIPLINE** ROMANCE LANGUAGES **EDUCATION** Iona Col, AB, 58; St John's Univ, MA, 60; Fordham Univ, PhD, 73. **CAREER** Instr Mod lang, Iona Col, 60-63; from asst prof to assoc prof, 63-78, Prof Foreign Lang, Pace Univ, NY, 78-, Chmn Dept, 68-79, 85-93. **HONORS AND AWARDS** Kenan Award for Teaching Excellence, Pace, 87; NEH Summer Seminars, Columbia, 83, Princeton, 867, Duke, 94. **MEMBERSHIPS** MLA; Am Asn Teachers of French; Am Asn Teachers Span & Port; Sixteenth Century Studies Conference. **RESEARCH** The works of Jean-Pierre Camus; early 17th century fictional prose in France; Hispanic and Italian literary influences on 17th century French letters. **CONTACT ADDRESS** Dept of Foreign Lang, Pace Univ, 1 Pace Plaza, New York, NY, 10038-1598. **EMAIL** asallustio@fsmail.pace.edu

SALMON, JOHN HEARSEY MCMILLAN
PERSONAL Born 12/02/1925, Thames, New Zealand **DISCIPLINE** EARLY MODERN HISTORY, FRENCH LITERATURE **EDUCATION** Victoria Univ Wellington, BA, 50, MA, 52, LittD(hist), 70; MLitt, Cambridge Univ, 57. **CAREER** Approved lectr hist, Cambridge Univ, 55-57; lectr, Victoria Univ Wellington, 57-60; prof, Univ NSW, 60-65 & Univ Waikato, NZ, 65-69; prof, 69-71, MARJORIE WALTER GOODHART PROF HIST, BRYN MAWR COL, 71-, Fr Hist Studies, Sixteenth Century J & J Mod Hist. **MEMBERSHIPS** AHA; fel Royal Hist Soc; Soc Fr Hist Studies. **RESEARCH** Early modern French history; French literature in the early modern period; French political theory. **SELECTED PUBLICATIONS** Auth, Soc And Institutions In Early-Modern France - Holt,Mp, Editor/, Renaissance Quart, Vol 0046, 1993; Constitutions, Old And New, Henriondepansey Before And After The Fr-Revolution/, Hist J, Vol 0038, 1995; The Legacy Of Bodin,Jean - Absolutism, Populism Or Constitutionalism/, Hist Of Pol Thought, Vol 0017, 1996; The Inside Of Hist - Merledaubigne,Jean,Henri And Romantic Historiography - Roney,Jb/, Sixteenth Century J, Vol 0027, 1996; The Making Of The Fr Episcopate 1589-1661 - Bergin,J/, Sixteenth Century J, Vol 0028, 1997; Civic Agendas And Religion Passion - Chalons-Sur-Marne During The Fr Wars Of Reigion - Konnert,Mw/, Sixteenth Century J, Vol 0028, 1997; State And Status - The Rise Of The State And Aristocratic Power In Western-Europe - Clark,S/, Am Hist Rev, Vol 0102, 1997; The Afterlife Of Henry-Of-Navarre + A Look At How Subsequent Generations Portrayed France Very Human 16th-Century Ruler/, Hist Today, Vol 0047, 1997. **CONTACT ADDRESS** Dept of Hist, Bryn Mawr Col, Bryn Mawr, PA, 19010.

SALTARELLI, MARIO
DISCIPLINE HISPANIC LINGUISTIC **EDUCATION** Univ Ill, PhD. **CAREER** Prof, Univ Southern Calif. **RESEARCH** Romance languages and its dialects, with particular attention to Spanish and Italian, Latin and Basque. **SELECTED PUBLICATIONS** Publ on, Phonology of Italian in a Generative Grammar; La Grammatica Generativa Trasformazionale, and Most Recently Basque; Romance and Latin Phonology; Morphology; and Syntax; Italian; Spanish; Southern Italian Dialects; Chicano Spanish; Catalan; Development and Maintenance of Spanish and Italian as Emigrant Languages; co-ed, Diachronic Studies in Romance Linguistics; ed, vol(s) on applied ling. **CONTACT ADDRESS** Dept of Spanish and Portuguese, Univ Southern Calif, University Park Campus, Los Angeles, CA, 90089. **EMAIL** saltarel@usc.edu

SAMARIN, WILLIAM J.
PERSONAL Born 02/07/1926, Los Angeles, CA, m, 1947, 2 children **DISCIPLINE** LINGUISTICS, ANTHROPOLOGY **EDUCATION** Bible Theol Sem Los Angeles, BTh, 48; Univ Calif, Berkeley, BA, 50, PhD(ling), 62. **CAREER** Missionary linguist, Foreign Missionary Soc, Brethren Church, 51-60; from asst prof to prof ling, Hartford Sem Found, 61-68, dir Sango grammar & dict proj, US Dept Health, Educ & Welfare, 62-68; assoc prof, 68-71, Prof Anthrop & Ling, Univ Toronto, 71-, Nat Sci Found travel gant, WAfrican Lang Surv Congr, Dakar, Senegal, 62; Am Coun Learned Soc travel grant, int colloquium on multilingualism in Africa, Brazzaville, Congo Repub, 62; consult, Africa educ, studies-math proj, Educ Serv Inc, 62; NCTE proj sec sch textbooks for teaching English as a second lang, Africa ed, 62-64; consult nat literacy prog, Repub of Mali, Agency Int Develop, 63; travel grant, chair ling session, African Studies Asn, San Francisco, Calif, 63; vis prof, Univ Leiden, 66-67; res grants, Can Coun, lang alternation among new Canadians, 70-71, Am Philos Soc, emergence of Sango as lingua franca, 72-73; mem ed bd, Lang in Soc, 72- **MEMBERSHIPS** Can Ling Asn; Ling Soc Am; African Studies Asn; Am Anthrop Asn; WAfrican Ling Soc. **RESEARCH** African languages; sociolinguistics; marginal linguistic phenomena. **SELECTED PUBLICATIONS** Auth, Soc Motivations For Codeswitching - Evidence From Africa - In The Series Oxford Studies In Language Contact - Myersscotton,C/, Can Jl Of Linguistics-Revue Canadienne De Linguistique, Vol 0040, 1995; Interlanguage Pragmatics - Requests, Complaints And Apologies - Trosborg,A/, Can J Of Linguistics-Revue Canadienne De Linguistique, Vol 0041, 1996; Sociolinguistic Theory - Linguistic Variation And Its Soc Significance - Chambers,Jk/, Jl Of Pidgin And Creole Languages, Vol 0012, 1997. **CONTACT ADDRESS** 24 Candleigh Ave, Toronto, ON, M4R 1T2.

SAMMONS, JEFFREY L.
PERSONAL Born 11/09/1936, Cleveland, OH, m, 1967, 4 children **DISCIPLINE** GERMAN LANGUAGE **EDUCATION** Yale Univ, BA, 58, PhD, 62. **CAREER** Instr to asst prof, 61-64, Brown Univ; instr, 62, Univ RI; asst prof to assoc prof to prof, dir, chair, 64-, Yale Univ. **HONORS AND AWARDS** Woodrow Wilson fel, 58-60; Lewis-Farmington Fel, 60-61; Morse Fel, 66-67; Guggenheim Fel, 72-73; Amer Coun of Learned Soc Fel, 77-78; Leavenworth Professorship, 79-; Charles Phelps Taft Lectr, Univ Cincinnati, 79; Amer Coun of Learned Soc Travel Grant, 83; Adoptive Stipendiary, Duke August Lib, Wolfenbuttel, 83; Humphrey Fel, Ben Gurion Univ, Beer Sheva, 90; Harold Jantz Mem Lectr, Oberlin Col, 94. **MEMBERSHIPS** Modern Lang Assoc; Amer Assoc of Teachers of German; German Stud Assoc; N Amer Heine Soc; Kleist-Gesellschaft: Schiller-Gesellschaft; Raabe-Gesellschaft, Goethe Soc of N Amer. **RESEARCH** Nineteenth century German **SELECTED PUBLICATIONS** Auth, Heinrich Heine, Metzler, Stuttgart, 91; auth, The Shifting Fortunes of Wilhelm Raabe: A History of Criticism as a Cautionary Tale, Camden House, 92; auth, Ideology, Mimesis, Fantasy: Charles Sealsfield, Friedrich Gerstacker, Karl May, and Other German Novelists of America, Univ NC Press, 98. **CONTACT ADDRESS** Dept of German, Yale Univ, PO Box 208210, New Haven, CT, 06520-8210. **EMAIL** jeffrey.sammons@yale.edu

SAMMONS, JEFFREY LEONARD
PERSONAL Born 11/09/1936, Cleveland, OH, 4 children **DISCIPLINE** GERMANIC LANGUAGES & LITERATURES. **EDUCATION** Yale Univ, BA, 58, PhD(Ger), 62. **CAREER** From instr to asst prof of German, brown Univ, 61-64; asst prof to assoc prof, Yale Univ, 64-69, prof German to Leavenworth prof of German, Yale Univ, 69-; Guggenheim fel, 72-73: Am Coun Learned Socs fel, 77-78. **MEMBERSHIPS** MLA; Am Asn Teachers Ger; Lessing Soc; Heinrich-Heine-Gesellschaft, North Am Goethe Soc. **RESEARCH** Nineteenth century German literature; literary sociology. **SELECTED PUBLICATIONS** Auth, The Nachtwachen von Bonaventura, Mouton, The Hague, 65: Angelus Silesius, Twayne, 67; Heinrich Heine, The Elusive Poet, Yale Univ, 69; co-ed, Lebendige Form: Festschrift fur Heinrich E K Henel, Fink, Munich, 70; auth, Six Essays on the Young German Novel, Univ NC, 72; Literary Sociology and Practical Criticism: An Inquiry, IN Univ, 77; Heinrich Heine: A Modern Biography, Princeton Univ, 79; A Selected Critical Bibliography 1956-1980, Garland, 82; Wilhelm Raabe: The Fiction of the Alternative Community, Princeton Univ, 87; Heinrich Heine, Metzler, Stuttgart, 91; The Shifting Fortunes of Wilhelm Raabe: A History of Criticism as a Cautionary Tale, Camden House, Columbia, SC, 91; Ideology, Mimesis, Fantasy: Charles Sealsfield, Friedrich Gestacker, Karl May, and Other German Novelists of America, Univ NC, 98; ed, Die Protokolle der Weisen von Zion, Die Grundlage des modernen Antisemitismus--eine Falschung, Text und Kommentary, Wallstein, Gottingen, 98. **CONTACT ADDRESS** Dept German, Yale Univ, PO Box 208210, New Haven, CT, 06520-8210. **EMAIL** jeffrey.sammons@yale.edu

SAMPON-NICOLAS, ANNETTE
DISCIPLINE TWENTIETH-CENTURY FRENCH LITERATURE AND CONTEMPORARY POETRY **EDUCATION** Univ WI, Madison, PhD. **CAREER** Instr, 85, ch, dept Fr, Hollins Col. **RESEARCH** The relationship between lit and the visual arts. **SELECTED PUBLICATIONS** Auth, Francis Ponge: La Poetique du figural. **CONTACT ADDRESS** Hollins Col, Roanoke, VA, 24020.

SAMTER, WENDY
DISCIPLINE INTERPERSONAL COMMUNICATION **EDUCATION** LaSalle Univ, BA, 81; Purdue Univ, MA, 83; PhD, 89. **CAREER** Tchg asst, Purdue Univ, 81-88; res asst, Purdue Univ; asst dir, Purdue Univ, 83-86; asst prof, 89-. **HONORS AND AWARDS** Univ fel, Purdue Univ, 81-82; David Ross Found summer dissertation res grant, Purdue Univ, 84; Intl Commun Assn award for outstanding grad stud tchr, 85; Bruce Kendall Award for excellence in tchg, Purdue Univ, 85; David Ross res fel, Purdue Univ, 84-85; Alan H Monroe scholar, Purdue Univ, 88-89; intl travel grant, 90; supplemental funds grant, 90, 91; award for distinguished achievement field of commun, Commun Dept, Lasalle Univ, 93., Pres, Tri-State Commun Assn, 1993 **MEMBERSHIPS** Mem, Intl Commun Assn; Speech Commun Assn; Tri-State Commun Assn. **RESEARCH** Individual differences in social cognition. **SELECTED PUBLICATIONS** Co-auth, Cognitive and Motivational Influences on Spontaneous Comforting Behavior, Brown & Benchmark, 93; A Social Skills Analysis of Relationship Maintenance: How Individual Differences in Communication Skills Affect the Achievement of Relationship Ffunctions, Communication and Relational Maintenance, Acad Press, 94; auth, Unsupportive Relationships: Deficiencies in the Support-giving Skills of the

Lonely Pperson's Friends, Communication of Social Support: Messages, Interactions, Relationships, and Community, Sage, 94. **CONTACT ADDRESS** Dept of Commun, Univ Delaware, 162 Ctr Mall, Newark, DE, 19716.

SANCHEZ, MONICA E.
DISCIPLINE LINGUISTICS **EDUCATION** Univ Toronto, BA, 88, MA, 89; Univ Brit Columbia, PhD, 96. **CAREER** Asst prof. **RESEARCH** Syntactic theory, acquired language disorders. **SELECTED PUBLICATIONS** Auth, Language Breakdown: Implications for the Theory of Functional Categories, Working Papers of the Ling Circle of the Univ Victoria, 95; Nominal and Verbal Extended Projections in Agrammatism, Proc of the 95 Can Ling Assn Annual Conf, 95; Categorial, Agreement and Case Features in Agrammatism, Proc 96 Northwestern Ling Conf, Univ Wash, 96; Categorial and Agreement/ Case Features are Different: Evidence from Language Disorders, Proc 96 Can Ling Assn Annual Conf, 96. **CONTACT ADDRESS** Dept of Applied Lang Stud, Brock Univ, 500 Glenridge Ave, St Catharines, ON, L2S 3A1. **EMAIL** msanchez@spartan.ac.BrockU.CA

SANCHEZ SILVA, ARLYN
DISCIPLINE CONTEMPORARY SPANISH-AMERICAN LITERATURE **EDUCATION** Univ Puerto Rico, BA; Harvard Univ, MA, PhD. **CAREER** Lit, Emmanuel Col. **MEMBERSHIPS** MLA; Am Asn Tchrs Span & Portuguese; Sine Nomine. **SELECTED PUBLICATIONS** Coauth, Davis Grant proposal for assessment of the tech needs in for lang pedag. **CONTACT ADDRESS** Emmanuel Col, Massachusetts, 400 The Fenway, Boston, MA, 02115. **EMAIL** silva@emmanuel.eduv

SANDERS, IVAN
PERSONAL Born 01/24/1944, Budapest, Hungary, m, 1968, 2 children **DISCIPLINE** COMPARATIVE LITERATURE, EAST EUROPEAN FICTION **EDUCATION** Brooklyn Col, BA, 65, MA, 67; NY Univ, PhD(comp lit), 72. **CAREER** Prof English, Suffolk County Community Col, 68-, vis assoc prof, Sch Continuing Educ, Columbia Univ, 78-79. **HONORS AND AWARDS** Irex fel, Hungarian Acad Sci, Inst Lit Res, Budapest, 79; sr fel, Inst ECent Europe, Columbia Univ, 82; Fulbright fel, 89. **MEMBERSHIPS** MLA; Am Hungarian Educ Asn; Am Fed Teachers. **RESEARCH** Contemporary American fiction; contemporary East European fiction and film; Hungarian literature. **SELECTED PUBLICATIONS** Auth, Engaol'd tongue?: Notes on the Language of Hungarian Americans, Valosag, Budapest, Vol XVI, No 5; The Gifts of Strangeness: Alienation and Creation in Jerzy Kosinski's Fiction, Polish Rev, Vol XIX, No 3-4; Human Dialogues are Born, Nation, 4/23/77; trans, George Konrad's The City Builder, Harcourt Brace Jovanavich, 77; auth, Simple Elements and Violent Combinations: Reflections on the Fiction of Amos Oz, Judaism, Vol XXVII, No 1; The Possibilities of Fiction: On Recent American Novels, Valosag, Vol XXI, No 1, 78; trans, George Konrad's The Loser, Harcourt Brace Jovanavich, 82; co-ed, Essays on World War I: Total War and Peacemaking, A Case Study on Trianon, Columbia Univ Press, 82; auth, The Other Europeans, The Nation, 87; trans, Milan Fust, The Story of My Wife, PAJ, 87; auth, Budapest Letter: New Themes, New Writers, NY Times Book Rev, 88; co-trans, Peter Nadas, A Book of Memories, Farrar STraus & Giroux, 97. **CONTACT ADDRESS** 4 Coed Ln, Stony Brook, NY, 11790.

SANDERS, MARK
DISCIPLINE ENGLISH LANGUAGE AND LITERATURE **EDUCATION** Brown Univ, PhD, 92. **CAREER** Assoc prof **RESEARCH** African-American literature; 20th-century American literature. **SELECTED PUBLICATIONS** Ed, A Son's Return: Selected Essays of Sterling A. Brown. **CONTACT ADDRESS** English Dept, Emory Univ, 1380 Oxford Rd NE, Atlanta, GA, 30322-1950.

SANDERS, ROBERT E.
DISCIPLINE INTERPERSONAL COMMUNICATION **EDUCATION** PhD. **CAREER** Univ Albany - SUNY **SELECTED PUBLICATIONS** Auth, Cognitive Foundations of Calculated Speech, 87; The role of mass communication processes in the social upheavals in the Soviet Union, Eastern Europe, and China, SUNY Press, 92; Cognition, computation, and conversation, Human Comm Res, 92; Culture, communication, and preferences for directness in the expression of directives, Comm Theory, 94; A retrospective essay on the consequentiality of communication, Lawrence Erlbaum, 95; A neo-rhetorical perspective: The enactment of role-identities as interactive and strategic, Lawrence Erlbaum, 95; The sequential-inferential theories of Sanders and Gottman, SUNY Press, 95; An impersonal basis for shared interpretations of messages in context, Context Press , 97; The production of symbolic objects as components of larger wholes , Lawrence Erlbaum, 97; Children's neo-rhetorical participation in peer interactions, Falmer , 97; Find your partner and do-si-do: The formation of personal relationships between social beings, Jour Soc & Personal Relationships, 97. **CONTACT ADDRESS** Univ Albany-SUNY, 1400 Washington Ave, Albany, NY, 12222. **EMAIL** RES72@cnsvax.albany.edu

SANDLER, SAMUEL
PERSONAL Born 10/25/1925, Lodz, Poland, m, 1948, 1 child **DISCIPLINE** POLISH LITERATURE **EDUCATION** Wroclaw Univ, MA, 50, PhD(Polish philol), 51 **CAREER** Instr Polish lit, Wroclaw Univ, 50-51; asst prof, Inst Lit Res, Polish Acad Sci, 51-57, 62-69; asst prof, Univ Warsaw, 54-57 & Univ Lodz, 55-62; assoc prof, Tel-Aviv Univ, 69-72; Prof Polish Lit, Univ Chicago, 72-, Co-ed & co-dir, Ed Polish & For Lit Classics Ser, Nat Libr, Ossolineum, 51-69; mem comt lit, Polish Acad Sci, 60-69; vis prof Polish lit, Univ Lodz, 64-69; vis assoc prof, Univ Ill, Chicago Circle, 70-72. **MEMBERSHIPS** Polish Inst Arts & Sci Am; MLA; Am Asn Teachers Slavic & E Europ Lang. **RESEARCH** Polish literature of the 19th and 20th century; literary criticism; sociology of literature. **SELECTED PUBLICATIONS** Auth, A Laboratory Of Impure Forms - The Plays Of Rozewicz,Tadeusz - Filipowicz,H/, Slavic Rev, Vol 0053, 1994. **CONTACT ADDRESS** 1465 E 55th Place, Chicago, IL, 60637.

SANDRO, PAUL DENNEY
PERSONAL Born 11/10/1944, Marshfield, WI, m, 1967, 1 child **DISCIPLINE** FRENCH LANGUAGE & LITERATURE **EDUCATION** Beloit Col, BA, 66; Univ Wis-Madison, MA, 67; Cornell Univ, PhD, 74. **CAREER** From asst to assoc prof, 74-90, prof French, 91-, Miami Univ, Ohio. **RESEARCH** Film theory and criticism; 20th century French literature. **SELECTED PUBLICATIONS** Art, Textuality of the subject in Belle de Jour, Substance, No 26, 80; art, The Management of Destiny in Narrative Form, Cine-tracts, spring 81; auth, Diversions of Pleasure: Luis Bunuel and the Crises of Desire, Ohio State, 87. **CONTACT ADDRESS** Dept of French & Ital, Miami Univ, 500 E High St, Oxford, OH, 45056-1602. **EMAIL** sandrop@muohio.edu

SANDSTROEM, YVONNE LUTTROPP
PERSONAL Born 08/10/1933, Vasteras, Sweden, m, 1954, 2 children **DISCIPLINE** ENGLISH & SCANDINAVIAN LITERATURE **EDUCATION** Brown Univ, AM, 66, PhD(English), 70. **CAREER** Asst prof, 69-75, ASSOC PROF ENGLISH, SOUTHEASTERN MASS UNIV, 75- **MEMBERSHIPS** MLA; Soc Advan Scand Studies; Renaissance Soc Am; Am Literary Translr Asn. **RESEARCH** Seventeenth century English literature; modern Scandinavian literature; translations of Swedish literature. **SELECTED PUBLICATIONS** Auth Ett 'Andetag Djupt Ar Livet' - Swedish - Andersson,P/, World Literature Today, Vol 0066, 1992. **CONTACT ADDRESS** Dept of English, Southeastern Mass Univ, North Dartmouth, MA, 02747.

SANKOVITCH, TILDE
DISCIPLINE FRENCH **EDUCATION** Northwestern Univ, PhD. **CAREER** Prof, Northwestern Univ; ed bd, Simone de Beauvoir Studies; Exec Comt, Newberry Library Center for Renaissance Studies; Harold H and Virginia Anderson Ch Col Arts Sci, Northwestern Univ; dir, Women's Studies; plenary address, 7th Annual Meeting of the Illinois Medieval Asn; lect, Renaissance Soc Am Int Renaissance Colloquium, Amherst; Newberry Library, Chicago; Nat Mus Women in the Arts, Wash, DC. **HONORS AND AWARDS** Alumnae distinguished tchg awd, Col Arts Sci distinguished tchg awd; chevalier, Ordre des palmes Acad miques. **RESEARCH** Theater and women's writing; early women authors and Montaigne. **SELECTED PUBLICATIONS** Auth, The Body and its Figures: Textual Strategies in the Writings of the Dames des Roches, Women Writers in Pre-Revolutionary France, Garland Press, 97; Un travail fort n cessaire: the 1724 Edition of Montaigne's Essais, Montaigne Studies, 95; Catherine des Roches and Claudian's 'Le ravissement de Proserpine: A Humanist, Feminist Translation, Fr/Am Perspectives on Fr Renaissance Women Writers: Texts and Context, Wayne State Univ Press, 93; Jodelle et la cr ation du masque: Etude structurale et normative de l'Eug ne; French Women Writers; Myths of Access and Desire; co-ed, The Poems of the Troubadour Bertran de Born. **CONTACT ADDRESS** Dept of French, Northwestern Univ, 1801 Hinman, Evanston, IL, 60208.

SANTANA, JORGE ARMANDO
PERSONAL Born 11/21/1944, Rosarito, Mexico, m, 1969, 1 child **DISCIPLINE** LATIN AMERICAN LITERATURE, CHICANO STUDIES **EDUCATION** San Diego Univ, AB, 67, MA 70; Univ Madrid, PhD(Span), 72. **CAREER** Instr Span, San Diego State Univ, 69-70; chmn dept Span & Port, 76-79, Assoc Prof, Calif State Univ, Sacramento, 72-, Ed, Explicacion Textos Literarios. **RESEARCH** The Mexican revolution novel; Chicano literature and culture. **SELECTED PUBLICATIONS** Auth, The Riddle Throughout 500-Years of Hisp Cult + Spain And Latin-America/, Explicacion de Textos Literarios, Vol 0021, 1992. **CONTACT ADDRESS** Dept of Span & Port, California State Univ, Sacramento, 6000 J St, Sacramento, CA, 95819-2694.

SAPORTA, SOL
PERSONAL Born 03/12/1925, New York, NY, m, 1952, 3 children **DISCIPLINE** SPANISH, LINGUISTICS **EDUCATION** Brooklyn Col, BA, 44; Univ Ill, MA, 52, PhD, 55. **CAREER** Asst prof Span & ling, end Univ, 55-60; chmn dept ling, 62-77, assoc prof, 60-79, Prof Romance Lang & Ling, Univ Wash, 80- **MEMBERSHIPS** Am Asn Teachers Span & Port; Ling Soc Am. **RESEARCH** Structural linguistics; psycholinguistics; Spanish linguistics. **SELECTED PUBLICATIONS** Auth, Expressions For Sexual Harassment - A Semantic Hole/, Verbatim, Vol 0021, 1995. **CONTACT ADDRESS** Dept of Ling, Univ of Wash, Seattle, WA, 98105.

SARA, SOLOMON ISHU
PERSONAL Born 05/01/1930 **DISCIPLINE** THEORETICAL LINGUISTICS & PHONOLOGY **EDUCATION** Boston Col, BA, 56, MA, 57; Weston Col, STB, 64; Georgetown Univ, PhD(ling), 69; Cleveland Inst Electronics, dipl, 76. **CAREER** Asst prof, 69-80, Assoc Prof Ling, Georgetown Univ, 80- **MEMBERSHIPS** Ling Soc Am; Int Ling Asn; Int Phonetic Asn; Am Asn Adv Sci. **RESEARCH** Instrumental phonetics; linguistic theory; comparative semitics. **SELECTED PUBLICATIONS** Auth, Islamic Dawah In The W - Muslim Missionary Activity And The Dynamics Of Conversion To Islam - Poston,L/, Theol Studies, Vol 0054, 1993; The Nearest In Affection - Towards A Christian Understanding Of Islam - Brown,S/, Theol Studies, Vol 0056, 1995. **CONTACT ADDRESS** Sch of Lang & Ling, Georgetown Univ, 1421 37th St N W, Washington, DC, 20057-0001.

SARDKODIE-MENSAH, KWASI
PERSONAL Born 06/13/1955, Ejisu, Ghana, m, 1980, 3 children **DISCIPLINE** FRENCH/SPANISH/LIBRARY AND INFORMATION SCIENCE **EDUCATION** Univ of IL, PhD, 98; Clarion Univ, MSLS, 83; Univ of Ghana, BA, 79 **CAREER** Mgr, 92-, Adj Facul, Chief Ref Librn, Boston Col; Ghanaian Lang consultant, 92-, State and Fed Govrnmts; Libr Coord, 89-92, NE Univ **HONORS AND AWARDS** Bill Day awd for dedicat and exc cont; Beta Phi Mu, 90-; Infor Sci Fel, 87 **MEMBERSHIPS** ARCL/IS; LIRT **RESEARCH** Libr svcs for int students **SELECTED PUBLICATIONS** Auth, Using Humor for Effective Library Instruction Sessions, Catholic Library World, 98; The Human Side of Reference in an Era of Technology, The Reference Librarian, 97; Nigerian-Americans, Gayle Encyclopedia, 95 **CONTACT ADDRESS** Winchester, MA, 01890-1121. **EMAIL** sarkodik@bc.edu

SARGENT, STUART H.
DISCIPLINE CHINESE LITERATURE **EDUCATION** Stanford Univ, PhD. **CAREER** Assoc prof. **RESEARCH** Chinese poetrt of the late 17th century. **SELECTED PUBLICATIONS** Auth, pubs on literary theory and poetry. **CONTACT ADDRESS** Foreign Languages and Literature Dept, Colorado State Univ, Fort Collins, CO, 80523. **EMAIL** Ssargent@vines.colostate.edu

SARLES, HARVEY BURTON
PERSONAL Born 07/12/1933, Buffalo, NY, m, 1956, 2 children **DISCIPLINE** LINGUISTICS **EDUCATION** Univ Buffalo, BA, 54, MA, 59; Univ Chicago, PhD(Anthrop) 66. **CAREER** Mathematician, Cornell Aeronaut Lab, 55-56; res asst Ling, Univ Chicago, 60-61; asst prof Anthrop & Ling, Sch Med, Univ Pittsburgh, 62-66; assoc prof, 66-80, prof Anthrop, Univ Minn, Minneapolis, 80-88, Leverhulme vis fel ethnoling, Univ Sussex, 70-71; consult, Allegheny County Ment Health/Ment Retardation, 73-74; vis prof Ling, State Univ NY, Buffalo, 74. **MEMBERSHIPS** Am Anthrop Asn; Animal Behav Soc; Ling Soc Am; MLS. **RESEARCH** Behavioral linguistics; human ethology; non-verbal communication. **SELECTED PUBLICATIONS** Auth, The study of intelligiblity, Linguistics, 8/67; The study of language and communication across species, Current Anthrop, 4-6/69; Facial expression and body movement, In: Current Trends in Linguistics, Mouton, The Hague, 74; After Metaphysics, Peter de Ridder, 78, 80-86; Teaching As Dialogue, Univ Press of America, 93; Toward an Anthropology of the Ordinary: Seeing with New Lenses, In Ethics and Cultural Diversity, ed, L Olive, Univ Nacional Autonoma de Mexico, publishing in Spanish, 95; Is Life But a Dream? The World as Text or Text as the World, Religious Humanism: vol XXX, nos 1-2, 96; The Emergent University, Humanism Today, vol 11, 97. **CONTACT ADDRESS** Cultural Studies & Comp Lit, Univ of Minnesota, 9 Pleasant St SE, Minneapolis, MN, 55455-0194. **EMAIL** sarle001@tc.umn.edu

SASKOVA-PIERCE, MILA
DISCIPLINE SLAVIC LANGUAGES AND LINGUISTICS **EDUCATION** Univ Kans, MA, 80, PhD, 86. **CAREER** Asst prof Czech and Russ, Univ Nebr, Lincoln, 89. **RESEARCH** Teaching methodology; Slavic linguistics. **SELECTED PUBLICATIONS** Published several articles on Teaching Methodology, on Czech settlements in the USA, and a textbook of Czech Language. **CONTACT ADDRESS** Univ Nebr, Lincoln, Lincoln, NE, 68588-0417.

SASSON, JACK MURAD
PERSONAL Born 10/01/1941, Aleppo, Syria **DISCIPLINE** FOREIGN LANGUAGES, HISTORY **EDUCATION** Brooklyn Col, BA, 62; Brandeis Univ, MA, 63, PhD, 66. **CAREER** From asst prof to assoc prof, 66-77, Prof Relig, Univ NC, Chapel Hill, 77-, Soc Relig Higher Educ fel, 69-70; assoc ed, J Am Orient Soc, 77. **MEMBERSHIPS** Soc Bibl Lit; Am Orient Soc; Israel Explor Soc; Dutch Orient Soc. **RESEARCH** An-

cient Near Eastern societies. **SELECTED PUBLICATIONS** Auth, Albright As An Orientalist + Albright,William,Foxwell And Palestinian Archaeol/, Bibl Archaeol, Vol 0056, 1993; Jonah - A Commentary - Limburg,J/, Interpretation-A J Of Bible And Theol, Vol 0049, 1995. **CONTACT ADDRESS** Dept of Relig, Univ of NC, Chapel Hill, NC, 27514.

SAUER, ANGELIKA
PERSONAL Erlanger, Germany **DISCIPLINE** GERMAN CANADIAN STUDIES **EDUCATION** Univ Augsburg, MA, 86; Carleton Univ, MA, 88; Univ Waterloo, PhD, 94. **CAREER** CHAIR GERMAN CAN STUDS, UNIV WINNIPEG, 94-. **HONORS AND AWARDS** Beaverbrook Prize, Carleton Univ, 87; Award Foreign Nats, Gov Can, 88-92. **MEMBERSHIPS** Can Inst Int Affairs; Comt Hist Second World War; Org Stud Nat Hist Can. **SELECTED PUBLICATIONS** Auth, A Matter of Domestic Policy? Canadian Immigration Policy and the Admission of Germans, 1945-50, in Can Hist Rev 74 2, 93; auth, Christian Charity, Government Policy and German Immigration to Canada and Australia, 1947 to 1952, in Immigration and Ethnicity in Canada, 96; auth, Hopes of Lasting Peace: Canada and Post-Hostilities Germany, 1945, in 1945 in Canada and Germany: The Past Viewed Through the Present, 96. **CONTACT ADDRESS** Dept of German Canadian Studies, Univ Winnipeg, Winnipeg, MB, R3B 2E9.

SAUR, PAMELA S.
PERSONAL New York, NY, m, 1969, 2 children **DISCIPLINE** FOREIGN LANGUAGE; LITERATURE **EDUCATION** Univ Iowa, BA 70, MA 72, PhD 82; Univ Mass, MEd 84. **CAREER** Auburn Univ, asst prof 84-88; Lamar Univ, asst prof, assoc prof, 89 to 95-. **HONORS AND AWARDS** Schtzkammer Ch Ed; TFLAB Ed. **RESEARCH** Modern Austrian Literature; Lang and Lit; Pedagogy; Comparative Lit. **SELECTED PUBLICATIONS** Auth, The Place of Asian Literature in Translation, in Amer Univ's, CLA Jour, 98; Barbara Frischmuth's Use of Mythology in Her Demeter Triology, Out from the shadows: Essays on Contemporary Aust Women Writers and Filmmakers, Margarette Lamb-Faffelbeger, ed, Riverside CA, Ariadne Press, 97; Real and Imaginary Journeys In Barbara Frischmuth's Writings, Ger Notes and Rev, 97; Amer Lit and Aust Lit, Two Histories, Geschichte der osterreichischen Lit, Teil I, Donald G. Daviau, Herbert Arlt, eds, St Ingbert, Rohrig Univ, 96; Regional dramas of Karl Schonherr and the Nazi Stigma, Ger Notes and Rev, 96; Property Wealth and the Amer Dream, in: Barn Burning, Teaching Faulkner, Cen for Faulkner Stud, MO State U, 95; Captain Anthony Forthcoming; Lucas: An Austrian Pioneer, Austrian Info, 95. **CONTACT ADDRESS** Dept of Literature, Lamar Univ, PO Box 10023, Beaumont, TX, 77710. **EMAIL** saurps@hal.lamar.edu

SAUTERMAISTER, GERT
PERSONAL Ulm, Germany **DISCIPLINE** GERMAN **EDUCATION** Univ Munich, PhD, 71. **CAREER** Prof Ger, Univ Bremen; vis prof, Univ Munich, Ger; Univ Aarhus, Denmark; Univ Nizza, Fr; Univ Zix-Marseille, Fr; Max Kade distinguished vis prof-. **RESEARCH** Gottfried Keller and exile lit. **SELECTED PUBLICATIONS** Auth, monographs on Friedrich Schiller, Georg Christoph Lichtenberg, and Thomas Mann; articles on Ger lit from the period of the Enlightenment until the present. **CONTACT ADDRESS** Dept of Ger Lang and Lit, Univ Kansas, Admin Building, Lawrence, KS, 66045. **EMAIL** kufacts@ukans.edu

SAVVAS, MINAS
PERSONAL Born 04/02/1939, Athens, Greece **DISCIPLINE** COMPARATIVE LITERATURE, CREATIVE WRITING **EDUCATION** Univ Ill, BA, 64, MA, 65; Univ Calif, Santa Barbara, PhD(English), 71. **CAREER** Asst prof English, Univ Calif, Santa Barbara, 65-68; assoc prof, 68-74, Prof English, San Diego State Univ, 74- **MEMBERSHIPS** MLA; Mod Greek Studies Asn; Hellenic Cult Soc. **RESEARCH** Modern Greek literature; continental novel; translation. **SELECTED PUBLICATIONS** Auth, Remembering Ritsos,Yannis + Poet/, Literary Review, Vol 0036, 1993; The 'Fourth Dimension' - Ritsos,Y, Green,P, Translator, Bardsley,B, Translator/, World Lit Today, Vol 0068, 1994; The Oldest Dead White Europ Males And Other Reflections On The Classics - Knox,B/, J Of Modern Greek Studies, Vol 0012, 1994; 'Vreghmeno Rouho' - Bramos,G/, World Lit Today, Vol 0068, 1994; 'Mavra Litharia' - Ganas,M/, World Lit Today, Vol 0068, 1994; I 'Mihani Ton Mistikon' - Siotis,D/, World Lit Today, Vol 0068, 1994; The Poetry And Poetics Of Cavafy,Constantine,P - Aesthetic Visions Of Sensual Reality - Anton,Jp/, World Lit Today, Vol 0070, 1996; 'Oudheteri Zoni' - Greek - Kariotis,M/, World Lit Today, Vol 0070, 1996; To 'Taxidi 1963-1992' - Greek - Tsaloumas,D/, World Lit Today, Vol 0070, 1996. **CONTACT ADDRESS** Sch of Lit, San Diego State Univ, San Diego, CA, 92115.

SAYLOR, CHARLES F.
DISCIPLINE LATIN LITERATURE **EDUCATION** Univ Wash, BA, MA; Univ Calif Berkeley, PhD. **CAREER** Prof & supv Grad tchg assistants; past dir, Undergrad Study & Grad Study & 3 terms, ch; Univ Mo, 68-; thaught at, St Mary's Col, Calif, UC Davis & San Diego State Univ. **RESEARCH** Roman Comedy; silver Latin literature. **SELECTED PUBLICATIONS** Publ on, Propertius, Plautus, Terence, Vergil, Lucan, Pliny, Horace, Lucretius & Petronius. **CONTACT ADDRESS** Dept of Classical Studies, Univ of Missouri-Columbia, 309 University Hall, Columbia, MO, 65211.

SAYWARD, CHARLES
DISCIPLINE PHILOSOPHY OF LOGIC, PHILOSOPHY OF LANGUAGE, AND POLITICAL PHILOSOPHY **EDUCATION** Cornell Univ, PhD, 64. **CAREER** Prof, Univ Nebr, Lincoln. **RESEARCH** The philosophy of mathematics. **SELECTED PUBLICATIONS** Auth, Definite Descriptions, Negation and Necessitation, Russell 13, 93; coauth, Two Concepts of Truth, Philos Stud 70, 93; The Internal/External Question, Grazer Philosophische Studien 47, 94; Intentionality and truth: an essay on the philosophy of Arthur Prior. **CONTACT ADDRESS** Univ Nebr, Lincoln, Lincoln, NE, 68588-0417.

SAZ, SARA M.
DISCIPLINE SPANISH LITERATURE **EDUCATION** Univ Southampton, PhD. **CAREER** Prof. **SELECTED PUBLICATIONS** Auth, pubs on English as a Second Language, Argentinian poetry and prose, Spanish and Latin American literature and film. **CONTACT ADDRESS** Foreign Languages and Literature Dept, Colorado State Univ, Fort Collins, CO, 80523. **EMAIL** ssaz@vines.colostate.edu

SAZAKI, KRISTINA R.
DISCIPLINE GERMAN **EDUCATION** Calif State Univ, Sacramento,BA, 80, MA, 82; Univ Calif, Los Angeles, PhD, 88. **CAREER** Asst Prof. **RESEARCH** Berthold Auerbach; Annette von Droste-Hulshoff; Amerikabild; German-Jewish literary history 1800-1945; technology in the classroom. **SELECTED PUBLICATIONS** Auth, Mimicking Theater: Charlotte Birch-Pfeiffer's Dorf und Stadt in Relation to Berthold Auerbach's Die Frau Professorin, Thalia's Daughters: German Women Dramatists from the Eighteenth Century to the Present, Tubingen: Franke, 96 & Franz Grillparzer's and Lion Feuchtwanger's Die Judin von Toledo, Was nutzt der Glaube ohne Werke Studien zu Franz Grillparzer anlasslich seines 200. Geburtstages, Otago Ger Stud 7, Dunedin: Univ Otago, 92. **CONTACT ADDRESS** Dept of Modern Languages and Literatures, Col of the Holy Cross, 1 College St, PO Box 189A, Worcester, MA, 01610-2395. **EMAIL** ksazaki@holycross.edu

SBROCCHI, LEONARD G.
DISCIPLINE ITALIAN LANGUAGE AND LITERATURE **EDUCATION** Univ Toronto, BA, PhD; Univ Wash, MA. **CAREER** Prof, Univ Ottawa. **HONORS AND AWARDS** Ed, monogr series Biblioteca di Quaderni d'Italianistica, Ottawa: CSIS, 84-; assoc ed, Il Forneri; ed, Legas. **RESEARCH** Renaissance, 18th and 20th century Italian literature. **SELECTED PUBLICATIONS** Auth, Stilistica nella narrativa Pavesiana, Casamari, 67; Renato Fucini, L'uomo e l'opera, D'Anna, 77; I verbi italiani, et leurs equivalents francais-and their English Equivalents, LEGAS, 89; co-ed, transl, The Comedies of Ariosto, Univ, Chicago Press, 75; Aretino's Marescalco, Dovehouse Editions, 86; Pirandello's Tonight We Improvise, Can Soc Ital Stud, 87; Leonora addio! Can Soc Ital Stud, 87; ed, Renato Fucini, Napoli a occhio nudo, Einaudi, 76; co-ed, L'enigma Pirandello, Can Soc Ital Stud, 88; L2 and Beyond, Legas, 93; Moral and Political Philosophies in the Middle Ages, Legas, 95. **CONTACT ADDRESS** Dept of Modern Languages and Literature, Univ Ottawa, 70 Laurier Ave, PO Box 450, Ottawa, ON, K1N 6N5.

SCALES, MANDERLINE ELIZABETH
PERSONAL Born 03/14/1927, Winston-Salem, North Carolina, m, 1955 **DISCIPLINE** SPANISH **EDUCATION** Spelman Coll, AB 1949; Univ Pittsburgh, MEd; Univ of Valencia, Spain; Univ of NC at Greensboro, doctorate. **CAREER** Winston-Salem State U, prof Soc Sci Spanish; The Winston-Salem Forsyth Co Schs Forsyth Tech Inst, tchr; Assn of Classroom Tchrs, past Pres; Dist & State Levels of Foreign Lang Tchrs In NCTA, chmn; Forsyth PTA Enrich Proj, chmn; Forsyth Co YWCA, dir on bd; Winston-Salem Natl Council of Negro Women. **HONORS AND AWARDS** Recip Outstanding Woman in Civic & Comm Winston-Salem 1974; hon by 1972 class of Winston-Salem State U; Commandress of Yr Nat Organ of Daughters of Isis; Com on the Forsyth County Hall of Justice in Winston-Salem; Relationships of Members and Non-Members of Fraternities & Sororities, l982. **MEMBERSHIPS** Past Loyal Lady Ruler Golden Circ, past Commandress Daughters of Isis; mem OES; Delta Sigma Theta Sor; The Delta Fine Arts Proj bd of dirs; trust Shiloh Bapt Ch; pres Union RJ Reynolds Flwshp to study in Spain; dir, Shilohian St Peter's Corp Family Center 1984-98; pres, Top Ladies of Distinction, Inc, 1986-89; natl pres, Nation Women of Achievement Inc. **CONTACT ADDRESS** Past Assistant Vice-Chancellor for Student Affairs/ Devt, Winston-Salem State Univ, 601 Martin Luther King Jr Dr, Winston-Salem, NC, 27101.

SCANLAN, TIMOTHY MICHAEL
PERSONAL Born 08/31/1946, Akron, OH, m, 1969, 1 child **DISCIPLINE** FRENCH LITERATURE **EDUCATION** Univ Akron, BA, 66; Case Western Reserve Univ, MA, 68, PhD(-French), 71. **CAREER** From instr to asst prof, 70-75, assoc prof, 75-80, Prof French, Univ Toledo, 80- **MEMBERSHIPS** MLA; Am Asn Teachers Fr; Am Soc 18th Century Studies; Am Coun Teaching Foreign Lang; NAm Soc 17th Century Fr Lit. **RESEARCH** Foreign language pedagogy; 17th and 18th century French literature. **SELECTED PUBLICATIONS** Auth, The Portrayal Of Columbus,Christopher And The Natives Of San-Salvador In Rousseau La 'Decouverte Du Nouveau Monde'/, Orbis Litterarum, Vol 0051, 1996. **CONTACT ADDRESS** Dept of Foreign Lang, Univ of Toledo, 2801 W Bancroft St, Toledo, OH, 43606-3390.

SCANLON, THOMAS FRANCIS
PERSONAL Born 09/26/1951, Pittsburgh, PA **DISCIPLINE** CLASSICAL LANGUAGES **EDUCATION** Duquesne Univ, BA, 72; Ohio State Univ, MA, 75, PhD(classics), 78. **CAREER** Asst prof classics, Univ Md, College Park, 79-80 & Univ Calif, Los Angeles, 80-81; Asst Prof Classics, Univ Calif, Riverside, 81-, Scholar, Univ Vienna, Austria, 78-79; Fulbright fel, Austrian Fulbright-Hays Prog, 78-79. **MEMBERSHIPS** Am Philol Asn. **RESEARCH** Greek and Roman historical writing, athletics and linguistics. **SELECTED PUBLICATIONS** Auth, Echoes Of Herodotus In Thucydides - Self-Sufficiency, Admiration, And Law/, Historia-Zeitschrift Fur Alte Geschichte, Vol 0043, 1994; Games For Girls/, Archaeol, Vol 0049, 1996. **CONTACT ADDRESS** Dept of Lit & Lang, Univ of Calif, 900 University Ave, Riverside, CA, 92521-0001.

SCATTON, ERNEST ALDEN
PERSONAL Born 09/04/1942, Hazleton, PA, m, 1964, 2 children **DISCIPLINE** SLAVIC LINGUISTICS **EDUCATION** Univ PA, BA, 64; Harvard Univ, MA, 67, PhD(Slavic lang & lit), 70. **CAREER** From lectr to asst prof Slavic lang, IN Univ, 70-72; asst prof, Univ VA, 72-76; assoc dean, Humanities & Fine Arts, 77-79, assoc prof Slavic lang, to dist service prof, SUNY, Albany, 76-97, chemn Slavic lang & lit, 80-, assoc dir, Slavic Workshop, IN Univ, 71. **HONORS AND AWARDS** Dir, Philol Sciences (honoris causae), Sofia Univ, 96. **MEMBERSHIPS** Bulgarian Studies Asn; Am Asn Teachers Slavic & East Europ Lang. **RESEARCH** Phonology of Slavic languages, especially Russian, Bulgarian & Serbo-Croatian; Balkan linguistics; general phonology. **SELECTED PUBLICATIONS** Auth, Bulgarian Phonology, Slavica, 75; co-ed, A Festschrift for Horace G Lunt, Slavica, 78; Reference Grammar of Modern Bulgarian, Slavica, 83. **CONTACT ADDRESS** Languages, Literatures, Cultures, Univ Albany (SUNY), 1400 Washington Ave, Albany, NY, 12222-1000.

SCHADE, GEORGE D.
PERSONAL Born 07/16/1923, Portland, OR, m, 2 children **DISCIPLINE** SPANISH, ROMANCE LANGUAGES **EDUCATION** Univ Ore, BA, 45, MA, 47; Univ Calif, Berkeley, PhD, 53. **CAREER** Instr Romance lang, Univ Ore, 46-47; lectr Span, Univ Calif, 53-54; instr, Univ NMex, 54-55; from instr to assoc prof, 55-66, Prof Span, Univ Tex, Austin, 66-98, PROF EMER, UNIV TEX, AUSTIN, 98-; Fulbright-Hays Advan Res grant, 67-68 & 79-80. **MEMBERSHIPS** MLA; Am Asn Teachers Span & Port Chile, Mexico, and Argentina. **SELECTED PUBLICATIONS** Auth, Augury in Al filo del agua, Tex Studies in Lit & Lang, spring 60; Juan Jose Arreola, Confabulario and Other Inventions, translated with critical introd, 64, Juan Rulfo, The Burning Plain and Other Stories, transl with critical introd, 67, co-ed, Ruben Dario Centennial Studies, 70 & contrib, Introduction to The Decapitated Chicken and Other Stories by Horacio Quiroga, 76, Univ Tex, Austin; co-ed, Literatura espanola contemporanea, Antologia, Introduccion, notas, Charles Scribner's Sons, 65; El arte narrativo de Garcia Marquez en su novels corta La increible y triste historia de la candida Erendira y de su abuela desalmada, Thesaurus, Mayoagosto, 77; Costumbrismo y novela sentimental, Literatura en imagenes, 79; Le segunda generacion modernista, Literatura en imagenes, 79; Sight, Sense and Sound: Seaweed, Onions and Oranges: Notes on Translating Neruda, Symposium, spring 84; Encyclopedia of Latin American Writers (articles on Alberto Blest Gana, Eugenio Cambaceres, Horacio Quiroga, and Pablo Neruda; El llano en llamas: mundo poetico y monstruoso, Homenaje a Ricard Gullon, 95; tranls with introduction, Pablo Neruda, Fify Odes, 96. **CONTACT ADDRESS** Dept of Span & Port, Univ of Tex, Austin, TX, 78712-1026. **EMAIL** schade@mail.utex.edu

SCHAEFFER, PETER MORITZ-FRIEDRICH
PERSONAL Born 05/14/1930, Breslau, Ger, m, 1968 **DISCIPLINE** GERMANIC STUDIES, COMPARATIVE LITERATURE **EDUCATION** Univ Ottawa, Lic Theol, 59; Princeton Univ, PhD(Germanic studies), 71. **CAREER** From lectr to asst prof Germanic studies, Princeton Univ, 70-74; vis lectr Ger & comp lit, Univ Calif, Berkeley, 74-76; Assoc prof to prof Ger, Univ Calif, Davis, 76-. **MEMBERSHIPS** ALSC; Renaissance Soc Am **RESEARCH** Renaissance; Neo-Latin literature; Classical tradition **SELECTED PUBLICATIONS** Auth, Joachim Vadianus, De poetica, Text, Translation & Commentary, Wilhelm Fink, Munich, 73; auth, Hoffmannswaldau De Studiorum, Peter Lang, 91; auth, Japidus Consolator, Annuaire de Selestat, 96. **CONTACT ADDRESS** German Dept., Univ Cal Davis, 1 Shields Ave., Davis, CA, 95616-8702. **EMAIL** pmschaeffer@ucdavis@ucdavis.edu

SCHAEFFER, PETER MORITZ-FRIEDRICH
PERSONAL Born 05/14/1930, Breslau, Germany, m, 1968 **DISCIPLINE** GERMANIC STUDIES, CLASSICS, RELIGIOUS STUDIES. **EDUCATION** Univ Ottawa, Lic Theol, 59; Princeton Univ, PhD(Germanic studies), 71. **CAREER** From lectr to asst prof Germanic studies, Princeton Univ, 70-74; vis lectr Ger & comp lit, Univ CA, Berkeley, 74-76; ASSOC PROF TO PROF GER, UNIV CA, DAVIS, 76-. **MEMBERSHIPS** ALSC; Renaissance Soc Am; Erasmus Soc; Tyndale Soc. **RESEARCH** Renaissance; Neo-Latin literature; Classical tradition. **SELECTED PUBLICATIONS** Auth, Joachim Vadianus, De poetica, Text, Translation & Commentary, Wilhelm Fink, Munich, 73; Hoffmannswaldau, De curriculo studiorum, Peter Lano, Bern, 91; Sapidus Consulator, Annvaire de Selestat, 96. **CONTACT ADDRESS** German Dept, Univ of California, Davis, One Shields Ave, Davis, CA, 95616-5200. **EMAIL** pmschaeffer@ucdavis.edu

SCHAMSCHULA, WALTER
PERSONAL Born 12/23/1929, Prague, Czechoslovakia, m, 1958, 1 child **DISCIPLINE** SLAVIC LANGUAGES & LITERATURES **EDUCATION** Univ Frankfurt, PhD(Slavic lang & lit), 60, Habil, 70. **CAREER** Asst Slavic lang & lit, Univ Frankfurt, 58-60, lectr Czech, 60-70, privatdocent Slavic lang & lit, 70-72; Prof Slavic Lang & Lit, Univ Calif, Berkeley, 72-, Vis lectr, Univ Calif, Berkeley, 70-71; Univ Calif humanities res fel, 76. **MEMBERSHIPS** Asn Slavicists Fed Repub Ger. **RESEARCH** Russian historical novel; Pushkin; Czech literature. **SELECTED PUBLICATIONS** Auth, Aspects Of Cultural Integration - A Festschrift In Honor Of Mestan,Antonin - Ger, Czech, Russian - Macha,K, Drews,P, Editors/, Rlc-Revue De Litterature Comparee, Vol 0068, 1994; Division And Its Consequences - A Trend In Czech Literature 1969-1989 - Ger - Bock,I/, Slavic And E Europ J, Vol 0039, 1995; Questions Of Identity - Czech And Slovak Ideas Of Nationality And Personality - Pynsent,Rp/, Zeitschrift Fur Slavische Philologie, Vol 0055, 1995; Origins Of The Czech National Renascence - Agnew,Hl/, Jahrbucher Fur Geschichte Osteuropas, Vol 0044, 1996. **CONTACT ADDRESS** Dept of Slavic Lang & Lit, Univ of Calif, Berkeley, CA, 94720.

SCHEIN, BARRY
DISCIPLINE LINGUISTICS **EDUCATION** MIT, PhD. **CAREER** Assoc prof & ch, Univ Southern Calif. **RESEARCH** Semantics; syntax of logical form. **SELECTED PUBLICATIONS** Auth, Plurals and Events, MIT Press, 94; coauth, Plurals, NELS, 89. **CONTACT ADDRESS** Dept of Linguistics, Univ Southern Calif, University Park Campus, Los Angeles, CA, 90089. **EMAIL** schein@usc.edu

SCHEINDLIN, RAYMOND PAUL
PERSONAL Born 05/13/1940, Philadelphia, PA, 2 children **DISCIPLINE** ARABIC & HEBREW LITERATURE **EDUCATION** Gratz Col, Cert, 59; Univ Pa, BA, 61; Jewish Theol Sem Am, MHL, 63, Rabbi, 65; Columbia Univ, PhD, 71. **CAREER** Asst prof Hebrew, McGill Univ, 69-72; asst prof Hebrew & Arabic, Cornell Univ, 72-74; Assoc Prof, 74-85, Prof Medieval Hebrew Lit, Jewish Theol Sem Am, 85-, Provost, 84-89; Dir, Shalom Spiegel Inst Medieval Hebrew Poetry, 96. **HONORS AND AWARDS** Guggenheim Fel, 98. **MEMBERSHIPS** Asn Jewish Studies; Rabbinical Assembly Am; Am Acad Jewish Res; Soc Judeo-Arabic Studies; World Union Jewish Studies. **RESEARCH** Medieval Arabic and Hebrew poetry; Judeo-Arabic lit and civilization. **SELECTED PUBLICATIONS** Transl, Of Bygone Days, In: A Stetl and Other Yiddish Novellas, 73; auth, Form and Structure in the Poetry of al-Mu'Tamid Ibn 'Abbad, De Goeje Fund, 74; 201 Arabic Verbs, Barrons Educ Series, 78; Wine, Women, and Death: Medieval Hebrew Poems on the Good Life, Jewish Publ Soc, 86; The Gazelle: Medieval Hebrew Poetry on God, Israel, and the Soul, Jewish Publ Soc, 86; transl, Jewish Liturgy in Its Historical Development, Jewish Publ Soc, 93; Chapter from Voyage to the End of the Millenium, Mod Hebrew Lit NS 19, 97; auth, The Book of Job translated, introduced, and annotated, W.W. Norton, 98; auth of numerous articles. **CONTACT ADDRESS** Jewish Theol Sem of America, 3080 Broadway, New York, NY, 10027-4650. **EMAIL** rascheindlin@jtsa.edu

SCHER, STEVEN PAUL
PERSONAL Born 03/02/1936, Budapest, Hungary **DISCIPLINE** GERMANIC STUDIES **EDUCATION** Yale Univ BA, 60, MA, 63, PhD, 65. **CAREER** Instr, 65-67, Columbia Univ; asst to assoc prof, 67-74, Yale Univ; chmn, German dept, 74-80, 93-96, prof, 74-, Dartmouth Col. **HONORS AND AWARDS** DAAD Grant, 64-65; Morse fel, 69-70; Humboldt fel, 72-73; Geisel Third Century Prof, Humanities, 84-89; dir, NEH Sum Sem, 86, 89, 94. **MEMBERSHIPS** MLA; Am Comp Lit Assn; Am Assn Tchrs Ger; Intl Assn of Work & Music Stud. **RESEARCH** Romanticism; 19th & 20th century lit, lit & music. **SELECTED PUBLICATIONS** Auth, Verbal Music in German Literature, Yale Univ, 68; co-ed, Postwar German Culture: An Anthology, Dutton, 74, Ind Univ, 80; ed, Interpretationen zu ETA Hoffmann, Klett, 81; co-ed, Literature and the Other Arts, Univ Innsbruck, 81; ed, Literature und Musik, Ein Handbuch zur Theorie und Praxis eines Komparatistischen Grenzgebietes, E Schmidt, Berlin, 84; Music and Text: Critical Inquiries, Cambridge Univ, 92. **CONTACT ADDRESS** Dept of German Stud, Dartmouth Col, 6084 Dartmouth Hall, Hanover, NH, 03755-3511. **EMAIL** Steven.P.Scher@Dartmouth.edu

SCHERER, WILLIAM F.
PERSONAL Born 08/05/1939, Eureka, IL, m, 1968 **DISCIPLINE** GERMAN LITERATURE **EDUCATION** Univ Colo, AB, 61; Univ Southern Calif, MA, 62, PhD(Ger), 67. **CAREER** Asst prof Ger, Univ Calif, Berkeley, 65-68; asst prof, 68-72, curric develop grant, 69-70, chmn Ger div, 75-77, Assoc Prof Ger & Europ Lit, Univ Hawaii, Manoa, 72-, Grad Chmn Ger Studies, 75-, Consult, Am Coun Educ, 69; Univ Hawaii Found grant, Wash, 70; guest lectr, Mich State Univ, 72; 15th Congr Australasian Univs Lang & Lit Asn, Univ New South Wales, 73; Am Philos Soc res fel, Stuttgart, Ger, 74-75. **MEMBERSHIPS** Am Asn Teachers Ger; Philol Asn Pac Coast; Rocky Mtn Mod Lang Asn; Pac Northwest Conf Foreign Lang; Australasian Univs Lang & Lit Asn. **RESEARCH** Sixteenth and 17th century German literature; medieval European lyric; history of Western consciousness and European civilization. **SELECTED PUBLICATIONS** Auth, Trial Of Strength, Furtwangler,Wilhelm In The Third-Reich - Prieberg,Fk/, Biog-An Interdisciplinary Quart, Vol 0018, 1995. **CONTACT ADDRESS** Dept Europ Lang & Lit, Univ of Hawaii, 1890 E West Rd, Honolulu, HI, 96822-2362.

SCHERR, BARRY P.
PERSONAL Born 05/20/1945, Hartford, CT, m, 1974, 2 children **DISCIPLINE** FOREIGN LANGUAGES **EDUCATION** Harvard Univ, AB, 66; Univ Chicago, AM, 67, PhD, 73. **CAREER** From acting asst prof to asst prof, 70-74, Univ WA; from asst prof to assoc prof to prof, 74-, Mandel Family prof, 97-, chair, Dept Russ, 81-90, 96-97, assoc dean, 97-, Dartmouth Col. **HONORS AND AWARDS** NDEA Title VI Fel, 66-69; IREX grants, 69-70, 93, 94, 98; NEH Summer Stipend, 85; NEH Grants for conferences, 87, 89; Phi Beta Kappa, 96., Pres, AATSEEL, 87-88; co-org, Int Conferences on Russian Verse Theory, 87, Anna Akmatova and the Poets of Tsarskoe Selo, 89, and on Sergei Eisenstein, 98. **MEMBERSHIPS** MLA; Am Asn Adv Slavic Stud; Am Asn Tchrs Slavic East European Lang. **RESEARCH** Russian prose (primarily late 19th and early 20th centuries); Russian poetry (early 20th century); Russian verse theory; Russian film. **SELECTED PUBLICATIONS** Auth, Russian Poetry: Meter, Rhythm, and Rhyme, Univ CA Press, 86; coauth, "To and From Autumn: Pasternak's Translations of Keats," in Essays in the Art and Theory of Translation, Edwin Mellen Press, 97; coauth, "Searching for the Ur-Text: Gorky's English Mother," Russ Lang Jour, 97; auth, "Synagogues, Synchrony and the Sea: Babel's Odessa," in And Meaning for a Life Entire: Festschift for Charles A. Moser on the Occasion of His Sixtieth Birthday, Slavica, 98; "Cherubina de Gabriak," in Russ Women Writers, Garland, 99. **CONTACT ADDRESS** Dept of Russian, Dartmouth Col, 44 N College St, Hanover, NH, 03755-1801. **EMAIL** b.scherr@dartmouth.edu

SCHIFFMAN, LAWRENCE H.
PERSONAL Born 05/04/1948, New York, NY, m, 1970, 3 children **DISCIPLINE** HEBREW & JUDAIC STUDIES **EDUCATION** Brandeis Univ, BA & MA, 70, PhD(Near Eastern & Judaic studies), 74. **CAREER** Instr in Hebrew, Univ Minn, 71-72; from instr to Hebrew to asst prof Hebrew, 72-77, Assoc Prof Hebrew & Judaic Studies, New York Univ, 77-, Lectr, Hebrew Union Col, 75-; ed consult, KTAV Publ House, 76-; grants, Am Coun Learned Socs & Am Philos Soc. **MEMBERSHIPS** Asn Jewish Studies; Soc Bibl Lit; Am Orient Soc; World Union Jewish Studies; Israel Explor Soc. **RESEARCH** Dead Sea Scrolls; Judaism in late antiquity; Jewish law. **SELECTED PUBLICATIONS** Auth, Eschatology In The Theodicies Of 2-Baruch And 4-Ezra - Wilett,Tw/, Jewish Quart Rev, Vol 0083, 1992; The Greek Minor-Prophets-Scroll From Nahal-Hever - The Seiyal-Collection - Tov,E, Kraft,Ra, Parsons,Pj/, J Of Bibl Lit, Vol 0111, 1992; Origin And Early Hist Of The Qumran Sect/, Biblical Archaeol, Vol 0058, 1995. **CONTACT ADDRESS** Kevorkian Ctr Near Eastern Studies, New York Univ, New York, NY, 10003.

SCHINE, ROBERT S.
DISCIPLINE JEWISH STUDIES AND BIBLICAL HEBREW **EDUCATION** Kenyon Col, AB; Univ Freiburg, MA; Jewish Theol Sem Am, PhD. **CAREER** Prof, Relig dept & Class dept; coordr, annual Hannah A. Quint Lect in Jewish Stud; Middlebury Col, 85-. **RESEARCH** 19th- and 20th-century European Jewish thought. **SELECTED PUBLICATIONS** Auth, Jewish Thought Adrift: Max Wiener 1882-1950. **CONTACT ADDRESS** Dept of Religion, Middlebury Col, Middlebury, VT, 05753.

SCHLANT, ERNESTINE
PERSONAL Born 08/14/1935, Passau, Germany, m, 2 children **DISCIPLINE** GERMAN, COMPARATIVE LITERATURE **EDUCATION** Emory Univ, PhD(compt lit), 65. **CAREER** Instr French, Spelman Col, 63-65; asst prof Ger, State Univ NY Stony Brook, 65-69; asst producer films, Cinema Arts Inc, 69-71; assoc prof, 71-80, PROF GER, MONTCLAIR STATE COL, 81-. **HONORS AND AWARDS** Phi Beta Kappa; fel, Woodrow Wilson Int le... for scholars. **MEMBERSHIPS** AAUP; MLA; AATG. **SELECTED PUBLICATIONS** Coauth, various Ger textbks for Holt, 69,71 & 73; auth, Die Philosophie Hermann Brochs, Francke, Bern, 71; Hermann Broch, Twayne, 78; co-ed, Legacies and Ambiguities: Postwar Fiction and Culture in West Germany and Japan, Washington, DC: Woodrow Wilson le... Press and Baltimore: Johns Hopkins Univ Press, 91. **CONTACT ADDRESS** Dept of Ger, Montclair State Univ, Upper Montclair, NJ, 07043.

SCHLATTER, FREDRIC WILLIAM
PERSONAL Born 06/16/1926, Tacoma, WA **DISCIPLINE** CLASSICAL LANGUAGES, HISTORY **EDUCATION** Gonzaga Univ, AB, 49, MA, 50; Alma Col, Calif, STL, 57; Princeton Univ, PhD(classics), 60. **CAREER** Instr classics, Gonzaga Prep, 50-52; instr, St Francis Xavier Div, 52-53, from asst prof to assoc prof, 61-74, dean, 62-65, Prof Classics, Gonzaga Univ, 74-, Chmn Dept Class Lang, 68-, Prof Hist, 76- **MEMBERSHIPS** Am Philol Asn; Archaeol Inst Am; Asn Ancient Historians. **RESEARCH** Justin's Epitome of Pompeius Trogus. **SELECTED PUBLICATIONS** Auth, A Mosaic Interpretation Of Jerome, 'In Hiezechielem'/, Vigiliae Christianae, Vol 0049, 1995; The 2 Women In The Mosaic Of Santa-Pudenziana + Exploring The Exegetical, Apologetic, And Illustrative Significance Of Roman Theodosian Classicism/, J Of Early Christian Studies, Vol 0003, 1995; The Clash Of Gods - A Reinterpretation Of Early-Christian Art - Mathews,Tf/, Heythrop J-A Quart Rev Of Philos And Theol, Vol 0037, 1996. **CONTACT ADDRESS** Dept of Class Lang, Gonzaga Univ, 502 E Boone Ave, Spokane, WA, 99258-0001.

SCHLEINER, WINFRIED H.
PERSONAL Born 10/19/1938, Mannheim, Germany, m, 1968, 2 children **DISCIPLINE** ENGLISH & COMPARITIVE LITERATURE **EDUCATION** Univ Kiel, Staatsexamen, 64; Brown Univ, MA, 65, PhD, 68. **CAREER** Asst master & schoolmaster Eng & French, Max-Planck-Schule, Kiel, Ger, 68-70; asst prof Eng, RI Col, 70-73; asst prof, 73-75, assoc prof eng, Univ CA, Davis, 75. **HONORS AND AWARDS** UC Pres Fel Hum; Neh; Foreign Lib; Wolfenbuttel Biblothek fel. **MEMBERSHIPS** MLA; 16th Century Conf; Renaissance Soc Am; Am soc Hist of Med. **RESEARCH** Renaissance lit; comp lit; linguistics; hist med; gender studies. **SELECTED PUBLICATIONS** Auth, The Imagery of John Donne's Sermons, Brown Univ, 70; Aeneas' flight from Troy, Comp Lit, 75; Franklin and the infant Hercules, 18th Century Studies, 76-77; coauth, New material from the Grimm-Emerson correspondence, Harvard Libr Bull, 77; The Imagery of John Donnes Sermons, Brown Univ Press, 70; Melancholy Genius and Utopia in the Renaissance, Harrassowitz, 91; Medical Ethics in the Renaissance, Georgetown Univ Press, 95; A plot to his mose and cares cutt of: Schoppe as seen by the Archbishop of Canterbury, Renaissance and Reformation, 95; Cross-Dressing, Gender Errors and Sexual Taboos in Renaissance Literature in: Gender Reversals and Gender Cultures, London, 96. **CONTACT ADDRESS** Dept of Eng, Univ of California, Davis, CA, 95616-5200. **EMAIL** whschleiner@ucdavis.edu

SCHLOSSMAN, BERYL
DISCIPLINE FRENCH **EDUCATION** John Hopkins Univ, PhD. **CAREER** Languages, Carnegie Mellon Univ. **SELECTED PUBLICATIONS** Auth, Joyce's Catholic Comedy of Language, Univ Wisc Press, 85; The Orient of Style: Modernist Allegories of Conversion, Duke Univ Press, 91; Baudelaire: Liberte, Libertinage, and Modernite. Sub-Stance, 93. **CONTACT ADDRESS** Carnegie Mellon Univ, 5000 Forbes Ave, Pittsburgh, PA, 15213.

SCHLUNK, JUERGEN ECKART
PERSONAL Born 05/26/1944, Marburg, Germany, 1 child **DISCIPLINE** GERMAN LANGUAGE & LITERATURE **EDUCATION** Univ NH, MA, 68; Philipps-Univ Marburg, PhD(Am drama), 70. **CAREER** Dir & resident adv Ger, Jr Year Abroad Prog, Davidson Col, 72-73; asst prof, Franklin & Marshall Col, 73-74; asst prof, 74-80, assoc prof Ger, WVa Univ, 80-, Dramatist, Theater tri-buehne, Stuttgart, Ger, 76-77 & 80-81. **HONORS AND AWARDS** Outstanding Teacher Award, W VA Univ, 91. **MEMBERSHIPS** Am Asn Teachers Ger; MLA. **RESEARCH** Theater; film. **SELECTED PUBLICATIONS** Auth, Foreign language exposure beyond the classroom: How to import theater, Die Unterrichtspraxis, 78; The image of America in German literature and in the new German cinema: Wim Wenders' The American Friend, Lit/Film Quart, Vol 7, No 3. **CONTACT ADDRESS** Dept of Foreign Lang, West Virginia Univ, PO Box 6298, Morgantown, WV, 26506-6298. **EMAIL** jschlunk@wvu.edu

SCHMALSTIEG, WILLIAM RIEGEL
PERSONAL Born 10/03/1929, Sayre, PA, m, 1952, 2 children **DISCIPLINE** SLAVIC LINGUISTICS **EDUCATION** Univ Minn, BA, 50; Univ Pa, MA, 51, PhD, 56. **CAREER** Asst prof Russ, Univ Ky, 56-59; asst prof Russ & French, Lafayette Col, 59-63; assoc prof Slavic ling, Univ Minn, 63-64; assoc prof, 64-67, Prof Slavic Lang, PA State Univ, University Park, 67-, Head Dept, 69-91, Ed, Gen Ling, 71-82; consult, ling div, MLA Bibliog, 72-73; Nat Endowment for Humanities fel, 78. **HONORS AND AWARDS** Fulbright Schol on exchange with Lithuanian Acad Sci, 86; Distinguished Alumnus, Breck Sch, 90; Friend of Lithuania Award, 90; PhD (honoris causa), Univ Vil-

nius, 94. **MEMBERSHIPS** Am Asn Teachers Slavic & EEurop Lang; Ling Soc Am. **RESEARCH** Historical linguistics; comparative Balto-Slavic linguistics. **SELECTED PUBLICATIONS** Coauth, Introduction to Modern Lithuanian, Franciscan Fathers Press, 66, 5th ed, 93; Lithuanian Reader for Self-Instruction, Franciscan Fathers Press, 67; Janis Endzelins' Comparative Phonology and Morphology of the Baltic Languages, Mouton, The Hague, 71; auth, Die Entwicklung der a-Deklination im Slavischen, Z Slavische Philol, 72; An Old Prussian Grammar, 74 & Studies in Old Prussian, 76, Pa State Univ; An Introduction to Old Church Slavic, Slavica, 76, 2nd ed, 83; Indo-European Linguistics, Penn State Univ Press, 80; Lithuanian Historical Syntax, Slavica Press, 88; coauth, Beginning Hittite, Slavica Press, 88; auth, An Introduction to Old Russian, J Indo-Europ Studies, Monograph Fifteen, 95; A Student Guide to the Genitive of Agent in the Indo-European Languages, J Indo-Europ Studies, Monograph 14, 95. **CONTACT ADDRESS** Sch of Lang, Pennsylvania State Univ, 302A Burrowes Bldg, University Park, PA, 16802-6204. **EMAIL** wxsl@psu.edu

SCHMIDT, DARYL DEAN
PERSONAL Born 08/12/1944, Sioux Falls, SD, m, 1977 **DISCIPLINE** NEW TESTAMENT STUDIES, LINGUISTICS **EDUCATION** Bethel Col, BA, 66; Assoc Mennonite Bibl Sem, MDiv, 70; Grad Theol Union, PhD(bibl studies), 79. **CAREER** Instr New Testament, Pac Sch Relig, 77-78; Asst Prof Relig, Tex Christian Univ, 79- **MEMBERSHIPS** Soc Bibl Lit. **RESEARCH** Synoptic gospels; Hellenistic Greek syntax; second language acquisition. **SELECTED PUBLICATIONS** Auth, A Morphology Of New-Testament Greek - A Rev And Reference Grammar - Brooks,Ja, Winbery,Cl/, J Of Bibl Lit, Vol 0115, 1996. **CONTACT ADDRESS** Dept of Relig Studies, Tex Christian Univ, Fort Worth, TX, 76129-0002.

SCHMIDT, HANNS-PETER
PERSONAL Born 07/30/1930, Berlin, Germany **DISCIPLINE** INDO-IRANIAN STUDIES **EDUCATION** Univ Hamburg, PhD(Indo-Iranian studies), 57. **CAREER** Asst prof Indo-Iranian studies, Univ Saugar, 59-61; asst Indology, Univ Tubingen, 61-64, dozent, 65-67; from asst prof to assoc prof, 67-70, Prof Indo-Iranian Studies, Univ Calif, Los Angeles, 70-, Res fel, Deccan Col Post-Grad & Res Inst, Poona, India, 57-59 & Ger Res Asn, 61; prof Sanskrit, Rijksuniversiteit te Leiden, Netherlands, 74-76. **MEMBERSHIPS** Am Orient Soc; Ger Orient Soc. **RESEARCH** Sanskrit; Avesta; Middle Persian. **SELECTED PUBLICATIONS** Auth, Erbedestan - An Avesta-Pahlavi Text - Humbach,H, Editor/Translator/, Indo-Iranian J, Vol 0036, 1993. **CONTACT ADDRESS** Dept of Near Eastern Lang & Cult, Univ of Calif, Los Angeles, CA, 90024.

SCHMIEDEL, DONALD EMERSON
PERSONAL Born 11/21/1939, Kent, OH, m, 1965 **DISCIPLINE** SPANISH **EDUCATION** Kent State Univ, AB, 61; Univ Southern CA, AM, 63, PhD, 66. **CAREER** From lectr to asst prof, 65-73, Assoc Prof Span, Univ Nev, Las Vegas, 73 **MEMBERSHIPS** Asn Tchr(s) Span & Port. **RESEARCH** Span Golden Age drama. **SELECTED PUBLICATIONS** Auth, El Conde de Sex (Antonio Coello), a critical edition and study, Plaza Mayor, 72; Coello's debt to Gongora, Bull Comediantes, fall 73. **CONTACT ADDRESS** Dept of Span, Univ of NV, PO Box 455047, Las Vegas, NV, 89154-5047.

SCHMIESING, ANN
PERSONAL Born 10/14/1969, Minneapolis, MN, m, 1997 **DISCIPLINE** GERMANIC LANGUAGES & LITERATURE, SLAVIC LANGUAGES **EDUCATION** Willamette Univ, BA, 89; Univ of WA, MA, 91; Cambridge Univ, PhD, 96 **CAREER** Inst, 95-96, Asst Prof, 96-, Univ of Co **HONORS AND AWARDS** Jr Facul Develop Awd, 98; Tiarks Res Grant, 93 **MEMBERSHIPS** Am Asn of Tchrs of German **RESEARCH** Lessing and the Enlightenment; German drama; Scandinavian lit **SELECTED PUBLICATIONS** Auth, Remembering and Forgetting in Miss Sara Sampson, Lessing Yearbook, 95; Showing versus Telling: Johan Falkberget and the Interpretation of Scripture in Den fjerde nattevakt, Scandinavica, 37:1, 98 **CONTACT ADDRESS** Dept of Germanic and Slavic Langs, Univ of Colorado, Boulder, CO, 80309-0276.

SCHNAUBER, CORNELIUS
PERSONAL Born 04/18/1939, Freital, Germany, m, 1966, 2 children **DISCIPLINE** GERMAN **EDUCATION** Univ of Hamburg, PhD, 65 **CAREER** Asst Prof, 66-67, Univ ND; Asst Prof, 68-72, Univ So CA; Chmn, 75-84, USC; Dir, 84-, Max Kade Inst; Diction Coach, 92-, Los Angeles Opera **HONORS AND AWARDS** Cross of the Order of Merit of the Fed Rep of Ger, 86 **MEMBERSHIPS** PEN Center London; Soc of Phonetic Sci **RESEARCH** Music theory; opera **SELECTED PUBLICATIONS** Auth, Placido Domingo. Boston: Northeastern Univ Press, 97; Placido Domingo. London: jerome Robson, 97; Die Hausmanns. Eine Hollywood-Chronik, Munchen: ECON, 98 **CONTACT ADDRESS** Max Kade Inst, Univ of So California, Los Angeles, CA, 90089-0351.

SCHNEIDER, CHRISTIAN IMMO
PERSONAL Born 01/27/1935, Dresden, Germany, m, 1964, 1 child **DISCIPLINE** MODERN GERMAN LITERATURE **EDUCATION** Univ Calif, Santa Barbara, PhD, 68; Cent Wash Univ, MA, 78. **CAREER** Asst Ger, Antioch Univ, 64-65; assoc, Univ Calif, Santa Barbara, 65-68; from Asst Prof to Prof Ger, 68-91, EWU Distinguished Prof, Cent Wash Univ, 91-. **MEMBERSHIPS** Am Asn Teachers Ger. **RESEARCH** German literature of the 20th century; Hermann Hesse research, concert organist and composer. **SELECTED PUBLICATIONS** Auth, Das Todesproblem bei Hermann Hesse, NG Elwert, Marlburg, 73; Hermann Hesse (monography), C.H. Beck, 91; Twelve Short Organ Pieces, Augsberg Fortress, 91. **CONTACT ADDRESS** Dept of Foreign Lang, Central Washington Univ, Ellensburg, WA, 98926-7502.

SCHNEIDER, GERD KLAUS
PERSONAL Born 04/01/1931, Berlin, Germany, m, 1967, 1 child **DISCIPLINE** GERMAN, LINGUISTICS **EDUCATION** Univ BC, BA, 62; Univ Wash, MA, 63, PhD(Ger), 68. **CAREER** Asst prof, 66-71, chmn dept Ger, 74-77, dir doctor of arts prog foreign fang, 77-80, Assoc Prof Ger Lit, Syracuse Univ, 71-, Deutsche Sommerschule, Middlebury Col, 73. **MEMBERSHIPS** Am Asn Teachers Ger; MLA; Int Arthur Schnitzler Res Asn; Am Coun Studies Austrian Lit; Am Coun Teaching Foreign Lang. **RESEARCH** Modern German literature; applied German linguistics. **SELECTED PUBLICATIONS** Auth, Metamorphosis Or The Aging Process As Alienation In Amery,Jean/, Modern Austrian Lit, Vol 0028, 1995; Und-Dennoch-Sagt-Der-Viel-Der-Heimat-Sagt - Turrini Views On Austria And The Austria Soul/, Modern Austrian Lit, Vol 0029, 1996; Time And Script - Austrian Lit After 1945 - Ger - Auckenthaler,Kf/, Modern Austrian Lit, Vol 0029, 1996; 'Abschied Von Jerusalem' - Ger - Mitgutsch,A/, Modern Austrian Lit, Vol 0029, 1996; Dostoevski And Russian Lit In Austria Since 1900 - Ger - Belobratov,Av, Zherebin,Ai/, Modern Austrian Lit, Vol 0029, 1996. **CONTACT ADDRESS** Dept of Ger, Syracuse Univ, Syracuse, NY, 13210.

SCHNEIDER, MARSHALL JERROLD
PERSONAL Born 09/21/1942, Bronx, NY **DISCIPLINE** SPANISH LITERATURE **EDUCATION** City Col New York, BA, 62; Univ Conn, MA, 67, PhD, 69. **CAREER** From Asst Prof to Assoc Prof, 67-91, Prof Span, Baruch Col, 91-, Chair, Dept Mod Lang & Comp Lit, 96-; Consult, Holt, Rinehart & Winston & Harper & Row, 70-75, Encycl World Lit 20th Century, 79- & Al-Anon, 81-. **MEMBERSHIPS** Am Asn Teachers Span & Port; AAUP; MLA. **RESEARCH** Novels of Ramon J Sender; studies in literary structure and theory. **SELECTED PUBLICATIONS** Auth, articles on Blasco Ibanez, Buero Vallejo, Casona, Garcia Lorca, Jimenez, In: Encycl of World Literature in the 20th Century, Vols I & II, 81-82; co-ed, Modern Spanish and Portuguese Literature (Libr of Criticism Series), Continum, 88; author of several chapters in: Contexts and Comparisons: A Student Guide to the Great Works Courses, Kendall/Hunt, 91; author of numerous other articles. **CONTACT ADDRESS** Dept of Mod Lang & Comp Lit, Baruch Col, CUNY, 17 Lexington Ave, New York, NY, 10010-5518. **EMAIL** marshall_schneider@baruch.cuny.edu

SCHNEIDER, VALERIE LOIS
PERSONAL Born 02/12/1941, Chicago, IL **DISCIPLINE** SPEECH & COMMUNICATION **EDUCATION** Carrol l Col, BA, 63; Univ WI, Madison, MA, 66; Univ FL, PhD(speech), 69; Appalachian State Univ, cert, 81. **CAREER** Interim asst prof speech, Univ FL, 69-70; asst prof, Edinboro State Col, 70-71; assoc prof, 71-75, prof speech, 75-97, prof emeritus, speech & commun, E TN State Univ, 98-; Danforth assoc, 77. **HONORS AND AWARDS** Best Article Award, Relig Speech Commun Asn, 76; Finalist, Money Magazine Best Personal Finance Manager in America contest, 94. **MEMBERSHIPS** Speech Commun Asn; Southern Speech Commun Asn; Relig Speech Commun Asn. **RESEARCH** Persuasion; rhetorical criticism; study skills. **SELECTED PUBLICATIONS** Auth, Informal Persuasion Analysis, Speech Teacher, 1/71; Hugh Blair's Theories of Style and Taste, NC J Speech, 12/71; Role-playing and your Local Newspaper, Speech Teacher, 9/71; Parker's Assessment of Webster: Argumentative Synthesis through the Tragic Metaphor, Quart J Speech, 10/78; Mainlining the Handicapped: An Analysis of Butterflies are Free, J Humanics, 12/78; A Process for Self-mastery for Study Habits, J Develop & Remedial Educ, winter 79; Experimental Course Formats, Nat Asn Pub Continuing & Adult Educ Exchange, winter 80; Two Courses for the Price of One: A Study Skills Component for a Speech Communications Course, J Develop & Remedial Educ, spring 82; and various other articles in Speech Communication Teacher, 88-94; writer of Video Visions column, Kingsport Times-News, 84-86; ed, ETSY Evening and Off-Campus newsletter, 86-93. **CONTACT ADDRESS** East Tennesee State Univ, PO Box 23098, Johnson City, TN, 37614-0001.

SCHNIEDEWIND, WILLIAM M.
PERSONAL Born 09/05/1962, New York, NY, m, 1990, 2 children **DISCIPLINE** NEAR EASTERN STUDIES **EDUCATION** Brandeis Univ, PhD 92. **CAREER** UCLA, asst prof, 94-. **MEMBERSHIPS** ASOR; SBL. **RESEARCH** Social History of Israel; Early Biblical Interpretation. **SELECTED PUBLICATIONS** Auth, Society and the Promise to David: The Reception History of the 2 Samuel 7:1-17, Oxford Univ Press, forthcoming; A Social History of the Hebrew Language: From Its Origins to the Rabbinic Period, in progress; auth, The Word of God in Transition: From Prophet to Exegete in the Second Temple Period, Jour Stud Old Testament, Sheffield, JSOT Press, 95; auth, Qumran Hebrew as an Antilanguage, Jour of Biblical stud, forthcoming; The Davidic Dynasty and Biblical Interpretation in the Qumran Community, proceedings of Intl Congress on Dead Sea Scrolls, Jerusalem, Israel, forthcoming; Manasseh King, in: Encycl of the Dead Sea Scrolls, Oxford Univ Press, forthcoming; auth, The Dialect of the Elisha-Elijah Narratives: A Case Study in Northern Hebrew, coauth, Jewish Quart Rev, 97; The Problem With Kings: Recent Study of the Deuteronomistic History, Rel Stud Rev, 96; auth, Are We His People?, Biblical Interpretation During Crisis, Biblica, 95; auth, History and Interpretation: The Religion of Ahab and Manasseh in the Book of Kings, Cath Biblical Quart, 93. **CONTACT ADDRESS** Univ of California, Los Angeles, 405 Hilgard, Los Angeles, CA, 90095-1511. **EMAIL** williams@ucla.edu

SCHNITZER, M.L.
PERSONAL Born 10/10/1947, New York, NY, m, 1981, 2 children **DISCIPLINE** LINGUISTICS **EDUCATION** Univ Rochester, PhD, 71 **CAREER** Asst prof, Pa State Univ, 71-76; vis fel, Institut de Linguistique, Univ Catholique de Louvain, 73-74; assoc prof, Univ de Puerto Rico, 77-83; assoc prof, 79-83, chmn, grad prog, 87-89, 93-94, interim asst dean grad stud, 91-92, PROF ENG, LING, UNIV PUERTO RICO, 83-. **HONORS AND AWARDS** Fulbright-Hays fel, 73-74; fdn Francisco Carvajal res grant, 94; acad excellence, Univ Puerto Rico, 97. **MEMBERSHIPS** Ling Soc Am; Am Asn Teachers Span, Port; Am Speech-Lang- Hearing Asn; Org Puertorriquena Path de Habla, Lang, y Audiologia. **RESEARCH** Neurolinguistics; psycholinguistics; language acquisition; applied ling. **SELECTED PUBLICATIONS** Auth, The Pragmatic Basis of Aphasia: A Neurolinguistic Study of Morphosyntax Among Bilinguals, Lawrence Erlbaum Assoc, 89; auth, Fonologia contrastiva: espanol-ingles/Spanish-English Contrastive Phonology, Piedras Press, 97; auth, Steady as a Rock: Does the steady state represent cognitive fossilization? J Psycholinguistic Res 22, 93; co-auth, The Development of Segmental Phonological Production in a Bilingual Child, J Child Lang 21, 94; auth, The Regression Hypothesis: Communicative Continuum vs Parametrically Defined Grammars, Brain & Lang 48, 95; co-auth, The Development of Segmental Phonological Production in a Bilingual Child: A Contrasting Second Case, J Child Lang 23, 96; auth, Knowledge and Acquisition of the Spanish Verbal Paradigm in Five Communities, Hispania 79, 96; auth, Adquisicion y conocimiento del paradigma verbal en Buenos Aires, Magisterio del Rio de la Plata, 12:2, 97. **CONTACT ADDRESS** PO Box 23356, San Juan, PR, 00931-3356. **EMAIL** esniqui@coqui.net

SCHOEPS, KARL H.
PERSONAL Born 12/08/1935, Dinslaken, West Germany, m, 1965 **DISCIPLINE** GERMAN COMPARATIVE LITERATURE **EDUCATION** Bonn Univ, Staatsexam, 62; Univ Wis-Madison, PhD(Ger), 71. **CAREER** Teacher English, Gymnasium Wipperfurth & Wuppertal, Ger, 64-67; teaching asst Ger, Univ Kans, 63-64 & Univ Wis, 67-71; asst prof, Univ Il, 71-76 & Mt Holyoke Col, 77; Assoc Prof Ger, Univ Ill, 77- **MEMBERSHIPS** MLA; Am Asn Teachers Ger; Int Brecht Soc. **RESEARCH** Modern German drama; East German literature; Anglo-American and German literary relations. **SELECTED PUBLICATIONS** Co-ed, DDR: Literatur im Tanwetter, Lang, 85; auth, Bertolt Brecht: Life, Work, and Criticism, York, 89; co-ed, Neue Interpretationen von der Aufularung zur Moderne, Lang, 91; auth, Literatur im Dritten Reich, Lang, 92; auth, Intellectuals, unification and Political Change 1990: The Case of Christa Wolf, 1870-71 - 1989-90, German Unifications, 93; auth, Der Lohndrucker Revisited, Miller, 95; auth, Brecht and the Weimar Republic, Brecht Unbound, 95; auth, Brecht's Lehrstudie, in Bertolt Brecht Reference Companion, 97. **CONTACT ADDRESS** Dept of Ger Lang & Lit, Univ of Ill, 707 S Mathews Ave, Urbana, IL, 61801-3625. **EMAIL** schoeps@uiuc.edu

SCHOLES, ROBERT
PERSONAL Born 05/19/1929, Brooklyn, NY **DISCIPLINE** ENGLISH, COMPARATIVE LITERATURE **EDUCATION** Yale Univ, AB, 50; Cornell Univ, MA, 56, PhD, 59. **CAREER** From instr to asst prof English, Univ Va, 59-63; from assoc prof to prof, Univ Iowa, 64-70; PROF ENGLISH, BROWN UNIV, 70-; Jr fel, Inst Res Humanities, Univ Wis, 63-64; Guggenheim Found fel, 77-78. **HONORS AND AWARDS** Am Acad Arts & Sci, 98. **MEMBERSHIPS** MLA; NCTE; PEN; Acad Lit Studies; Science Fiction Res Asn. **RESEARCH** Semiotics; composition; modern literature. **SELECTED PUBLICATIONS** Coauth, The Nature of Narrative, 66 & auth, The Fabulators, 67, Oxford Univ; auth, Structuralism in Literature, Yale Univ, 74; coauth, Science Fiction: History, Science, Vision, 77 & Elements of Literature, 78, Oxford Univ; auth, Fabulation and Metafiction, Univ Ill, 79; coauth, The Practice of Writing, St Martin's, 81; auth, Semiotics and Interpretation, Yale Univ, 82; auth, Textual Power, Yale Univ, 85; auth, Protocols of Reading, Yale Univ, 89; co-auth, Hemingway's Genders, Yale Univ, 94; auth, The Rise and Fall of English, Yale

Univ, 98. **CONTACT ADDRESS** ENGLISH, Brown Univ, MCM Box 1957, Providence, RI, 02912-9127. **EMAIL** Robert_Scholes@brown.edu

SCHOLES, ROBERT JAMES

PERSONAL Born 08/15/1932, Ft Wayne, IN, m, 1962, 2 children **DISCIPLINE** LINGUISTICS **EDUCATION** Ind Univ, AB, 57, PhD(ling), 64. **CAREER** Teacher high sch, Ind, 57-59; from instr to asst prof ling, Ind Univ, 61-66; from asst prof speech to assoc prof speech & ling, 67-76, Prof Speech & Ling, Univ Fla, 76-, Mem res staff speech synthesis, Int Bus Machines Res Lab, Calif, 63-65. **MEMBERSHIPS** Ling Soc Am; Ling Circle NY; Asn Machine Transl & Computational Ling. **RESEARCH** Language production and perception in children and adults; psycholinguistics. **SELECTED PUBLICATIONS** Auth, The Descent Of Lang - Writing In Praise Of Babel - Mengham,R/, Applied Linguistics, Vol 0016, 1995. **CONTACT ADDRESS** Dept of Speech & Ling, Univ of Fla, 335 J Manning Dauer, Gainesville, FL, 32611-9500.

SCHONBERGER, VINCENT L.

DISCIPLINE FRENCH LANGUAGE AND LITERATURE **EDUCATION** Univ Ottawa, PhD. **CAREER** Assoc prof, 86-. **HONORS AND AWARDS** Legal interpreter, Min of the Atty Gen of On. **MEMBERSHIPS** Mem, Aesthetics Soc of Can. **RESEARCH** French-Canadian novel, literary works of Gabrielle Roy. **SELECTED PUBLICATIONS** Auth, "The Problem of Language and the Difficulty of Writing in the Literary Works of Gabrielle Roy," Stud in Can Lit, 89; "Tentatives d'evasion dans Huis clos," Proc of the Sartre Soc of Can, 90; Alexandre Chenevert: Un recit pluricodique, Portes de communication, Etudes discursives et stylistiques de l'oeuvre de Gabrielle Roy, Pres de l'Univ Laval, 95; Strategies de demythification du discours ideologique dans Alexandre Chenevert, Actes du Colloque Intl Gabrielle Roy, Pres Univ de Saint-Boniface, 96. **CONTACT ADDRESS** Dept of Lang, Lakehead Univ, 955 Oliver Rd, Thunder Bay, ON, P7B 5E1. **EMAIL** VLSCHONB@Mist.Lakeheadu.Ca

SCHOOLFIELD, GEORGE C.

PERSONAL Born 08/14/1925, Charleston, WV, m, 1949 **DISCIPLINE** GERMANIC LANGUAGES & LITERATURES **EDUCATION** Univ Cincinnati, BA, 46, MA, 47; Princeton Univ, PhD(Ger), 49. **CAREER** Instr Ger, 49-52, tutor hist & lit, Harvard Univ, 50-52; from asst prof to assoc prof Ger lang, Univ Buffalo, 52-59; assoc prof Ger, Duke Univ, 59-61; prof Ger & Scand & head dept, Univ Cincinnati, 61-64; prof Ger lang & lit, Univ Pa, 64-69; Prof Ger & Scand Lit, Yale Univ, 69-, Fulbright res fel, Austria, 52-53, Finland, 67-68, US Educ Found, Finland, 72; Guggenheim fcl, Sweden, 55-56; managing ed, Scand Studies, 69-73, rev ed, 73-; vis prof Ger lit, Univ Fla, 71; grad ctr, City Univ New York, 71-72. **MEMBERSHIPS** Rilke Soc; Acad Lit Studies; Am Coun Studies Austrian Lit; MLA; Am Asn Teachers Ger. **RESEARCH** German Scandinavian literary relations; recent German and Scandinavian literature. **SELECTED PUBLICATIONS** Auth, 'Ditt Hjarta Fargar Din Ros' - A Novel About Almqvist,Carl,Jonas,Love And His Times - Swedish - Stigsjoo,S/, World Lit Today, Vol 0066, 1992; 'Hid' - Agren,G/, World Lit Today, Vol 0067, 1993; 'Berattelser Om Mig Och Andra' - Hulden,L/, World Lit Today, Vol 0067, 1993; 'Sormenjalkia Tyhjassa' - Holappa,P/, World Lite Today, Vol 0067, 1993; 'Psalmer For Trolosa Kristna' - Hulden,L/, World Lit Today, Vol 0067, 1993; 'Arnaia Kastad I Havet' - Tikkanen,M/, World Lit Today, Vol 0067, 1993; A Lexicon Of Rhetoric - Norwegian - Eide,T/, Ger Notes And Rev, Vol 0025, 1994; 'I Det Sedda' - Swedish - Carpelan,B/, World Lit Today, Vol 0070, 1996; 'Tanten Och Krokodilen' - Swedish - Mazzarella,M/, World Lit Today, Vol 0070, 1996; Rilke,Rainer,Maria Correspondence With Key,Ellen - Ger - Fiedler,T, Rilke,Rm/, Scandinavian Studies, Vol 0068, 1996; Collected Poems, Vols 1 And 2 - Swedish - Columbus,S/, Scandinavian Studies, Vol 0069, 1997; Olsson,Hagar And Growing Melancholia - Her Life And Writings 1945-1978 - Swedish - Holmstrom,R/, Ger Notes And Revs, Vol 0028, 1997. **CONTACT ADDRESS** Dept of Ger Lang & Lit, Yale Univ, New Haven, CT, 06520.

SCHOTT-DESROSIERS, NICOLE

DISCIPLINE FRENCH **EDUCATION** Mt Holyoke, MA, 68; Univ de Clermont-Ferrand, MA, 70; Univ Mass, PhD, 80. **CAREER** Lectr, Williams Col, 75-; tchr, Lenox Memorial High Sch; coordr, high sch stud exchange prog. **HONORS AND AWARDS** Founding mem, For Acad Alliance in Berkshire County, 88-. **RESEARCH** Translation; composition; teaching of culture; computers use in teaching foreign languages; High school student exchange program. **SELECTED PUBLICATIONS** Auth, En Direct: A French Activity Workbook and Teacher's Manual. **CONTACT ADDRESS** Center for Foreign Languages, Literatures and Cult, Williams Col, Williamstown, MA, 01267.

SCHOVILLE, KEITH NORMAN

PERSONAL Born 03/03/1928, Soldiers Grove, WI, 5 children **DISCIPLINE** HEBREW, BIBLICAL STUDIES **EDUCATION** Milligan Col, BA, 56; Univ Wis-Madison, MA, 66, PhD(Hebrew & Semitic studies), 69. **CAREER** From instr to asst prof, 68-74, assoc prof, 74-81, chmn dept, 77-82, Prof Hebrew & Semitic Studies, Univ Wis-Madison, 81-, Ed, Hebrew Studies. **MEMBERSHIPS** Am Orient Soc; Soc Biblical Lit; Am Schs Orient Res; Nat Asn Prof Hebrew (secy); Archaeol Inst Am. **RESEARCH** The human factor in archaeology; literary and historical illumination of biblical literature; the Intertestamental Period. **SELECTED PUBLICATIONS** Auth, Bab-Edh-Dhra - Excavations In The Cemetery Directed By Lapp,Paul,W 1965-67 - Schaub,Rt, Rast,Pw/, J Of The Am Oriental Soc, Vol 0112, 1992. **CONTACT ADDRESS** Hebrew & Semitic Studies, Univ Wis, Madison, WI, 53706.

SCHOW, WAYNE

DISCIPLINE COMPARATIVE LITERATURE **EDUCATION** Univ Iowa, PhD, 70. **CAREER** Prof. **RESEARCH** Scandinavian literature; literature and religion. **SELECTED PUBLICATIONS** Auth, Remembering Brad: On the Loss of a Son to AIDS; co-ed, Peculiar People: Mormons and Same Sex Orientation. **CONTACT ADDRESS** Dept of English and Philosophy, Idaho State Univ, Pocatello, ID, 83209. **EMAIL** schowayn@isu.edu

SCHRADER, DOROTHY LYNNE

PERSONAL Born 08/13/1947, Pensacola, FL, 1 child **DISCIPLINE** FRENCH **EDUCATION** Agnes Scott Col, BA, 69; Middlebury Col, MA, 71; Univ Paris III, lic es lett, 74; Fla State Univ, PhD(Fr), 76. **CAREER** Asst prof French, Southern Ill Univ, Edwardsville, 76-77; asst prof, 77-82, assoc Prof French, Okla State Univ, 82-, lectr English, Ecole Nat Admin, Paris & Inst Nat Agronomique, Paris, 72-74. **MEMBERSHIPS** MLA; Societe Rencesvals; Mid-America Medieval Asn; Southeastern Medieval Asn. **RESEARCH** Women protagonists in the French Medieval epics; Parise la Duchesse, critical edition; Le Dit de l'Unicorne, critical edition. **SELECTED PUBLICATIONS** Coauth, Teaching the Basics in the Foreign Language Classroom: Options and Strategies, Nat Textbk Co, 79. **CONTACT ADDRESS** Dept of Foreign Lang, Oklahoma State Univ, Stillwater, OK, 74078-0002. **EMAIL** schrade@okway.okstate.edu

SCHRAIBMAN, JOSEPH

PERSONAL Born 09/29/1935, Havana, Cuba, m, 1963 **DISCIPLINE** FOREIGN LANGUAGES & LITERATURES **EDUCATION** Brooklyn Col, BA, 55; Univ Ill, MA, 56, PhD, 59. **CAREER** From instr to asst prof Romance lang, Princeton Univ, 59-65, bicentennial preceptor, 63-65; assoc prof Span & Port, Ind Univ, Bloomington, 65-69; chmn dept, 72-78, Prof Romance Lang, Wash Univ, 69-, Am Coun Learned Soc grant-in-aid, 62-63; Fulbright res grant, Spain 62-63; consult, Educ Testing Serv Advan Placement Exam; chmn, Comt Advan Placement & consult cd, Xerox Publ Co, 65-; Danforth teaching assoc, 68; mem exec comt, Bks Abroad, 71-74; Mellon fel, Univ Pittsburgh-, 75- **MEMBERSHIPS** MLA; Am Asn Teachers Span & Port; Am Asn Teachers Fr. **RESEARCH** Stylistics; Galdos; Clarin. **SELECTED PUBLICATIONS** Auth, Sephardim, The Jews Of Spain - Diazmas,P/, Revista De Estudios Hispanicos, Vol 0028, 1994; 'Match Ball' - Skarmeta,A/, Revista Iberoamericana, Vol 0060, 1994; The Origins And Sociology Of The So-Called Celestinesco Theme - Spa - Marquezvillanueva,F/, Revista De Estudios Hispanicos, Vol 0029, 1995; Life Of The Hyphen, The Cuban-American Way - Perezfirmat,G/, Revista De Estudios Hispanicos, Vol 0030, 1996; Creation In Sephardic Language - Spa - Romero,E/, Revista De Estudios Hispanicos, Vol 0030, 1996; Popular Sephardic Cancionero And Spa Tradition - Spa - Jimenezbenitez,Ae/, Revista De Estudios Hispanicos, Vol 0030, 1996. **CONTACT ADDRESS** 10 Pricewoods Lane, St Louis, MO, 63132.

SCHRIBER, MARY SUZANNE

PERSONAL Born 09/22/1938, Muskegon, MI **DISCIPLINE** COMPARATIVE LITERATURE **EDUCATION** Mich State Univ, BS, 60, MA, 63, PhD, 67. **CAREER** From Asst Prof to Prof, 67-96, Distinguished Teaching Prof English, Northern Ill Univ, 96-. **MEMBERSHIPS** MLA; Midwest Mod Lang Asn; Edith Wharton Soc; ALA. **RESEARCH** Edith Wharton; 19th century American literature; feminist criticism; travel writing by women. **SELECTED PUBLICATIONS** Auth, Isabel Archer and Victorian manners, Studies Novel, winter 76; Anderson in France: 1919-1939, Twentieth Century Lit, 2/77; Bringing chaos to order: The novel tradition and Kurt Vonnegut, Genre, summer 77; Darwin, Wharton, and the descent of man: Blueprints of American society, Studies in Short Fiction, winter 80; Edith Wharton and the French critics, 1906-1937, Am Lit Realism, spring 80; Toward Daisy Miller: Cooper's idea of the American girl, Studies in the Novel, fall 81; Justice to Zenobia, New England Quart, 3/82; Gender and the Writer's Imagination, 87; Telling Travels, 95; Writing Home: American Women Abroad, 1830-1920, 97. **CONTACT ADDRESS** Dept of English, No Illinois Univ, De Kalb, IL, 60115-2825. **EMAIL** mschriber@niu.edu

SCHUBERT, VIRGINIA ANN

PERSONAL Born 10/15/1935, St. Paul, MN **DISCIPLINE** FRENCH LANGUAGE & LITERATURE **EDUCATION** Col St Catherine, St Paul, Minn, BA, 57; Univ Minn, Minneapolis, MA, 63, PhD(French), 74. **CAREER** Instr French, Col St Catherine, 58-60; teacher, Alexander Ramsey High Sch, Roseville, 61-65; Prof French, Ch, Macalester Col, 65- **HONORS AND AWARDS** Chevalier Ordre des Palmes Academiques, French govt, 75; Officer Ordre des Palmes Academiques, Fr Govt, 94. **MEMBERSHIPS** MLA; Am Asn Teachers French; Am Coun Teachers Foreign Lang. **RESEARCH** Nineteenth century French literature; humanities, especially nineteenth century France. **SELECTED PUBLICATIONS** Coauth, Le Nouveau Passe-Muraille, Prentice-Hall, 70. **CONTACT ADDRESS** Dept of French, Macalester Col, 1600 Grand Ave, Saint Paul, MN, 55105-1899. **EMAIL** schubert@macalester.edu

SCHUCHARD, W. RONALD

DISCIPLINE ENGLISH LANGUAGE AND LITERATURE **EDUCATION** Univ Tex Austin, PhD, 69. **CAREER** Fac, 69; dir Emory Univ Brit Studies Prog Univ Col, Oxford Univ, present; Goodrich C. White Prof, concurrent. **RESEARCH** Modern British and Irish literature; T. S. Eliot and W. B. Yeats. **SELECTED PUBLICATIONS** Ed, T. S. Eliot's Clark and Turnbull Lectures, The Varieties of Metaphysical Poetry, Faber, 93; rptd Harcourt, 94; rptd Harvest, 96; co-ed, The Collected Letters of W. B. Yeats (v 3), Oxford UP, 94. **CONTACT ADDRESS** English Dept, Emory Univ, 1380 Oxford Rd NE, Atlanta, GA, 30322-1950. **EMAIL** engrs@emory.edu

SCHUELER, HEINZ JUERGEN

PERSONAL Born 07/15/1933, Mbeya, Tanzania, m, 1957, 2 children **DISCIPLINE** GERMAN LANGUAGE & LITERATURE **EDUCATION** Univ Toronto, BA, 59, MA, 61, PhD(Ger), 65. **CAREER** Lectr & asst prof Ger, Univ Western Ont, 64-66; asst prof, Univ Guelph, 66-68; asst prof, 68-70, assoc prof, 70-78, Prof Ger, York Univ, 78-, Can Coun res grants & fels, 68, 69, 73-74, 77 & 79-80. **MEMBERSHIPS** Internationale Vereinigung fur Germanische Sprach- und Literaturwissenschaft; Am Asn Teachers Ger; MLA; Can Asn Univ Teachers Ger. **RESEARCH** Late 18th, 19th and 20th century German literature; archetypal criticism; genre criticsm. **SELECTED PUBLICATIONS** Auth, Shortly Before The Curtain Fell - Theater In The Gdr - Ger - Flood,Jl/, Seminar-A J Of Ger Studies, Vol 0029, 1993; Remarks On The Needed Reform Of Ger Studies In The United-States - Vancleve,J, Willson,Al/, Seminar-A J Of Ger Studies, Vol 0031, 1995. **CONTACT ADDRESS** Dept of Lang Lit & Ling, York Univ, 4700 Keele St, Downsview, ON, M3J 1P3.

SCHULTZ, JOSEPH P.

PERSONAL Born 12/02/1928, Chicago, IL, m, 1955, 3 children **DISCIPLINE** JEWISH STUDIES, RELIGION **EDUCATION** Yeshiva Univ, BA, 51; Jewish Theol Sem, MHL, 55; Brandeis Univ, PhD, 62. **CAREER** Lectr foreign lang, Boston Univ, 63-64, instr foreign lang, 64-68, asst prof relig, 68-73; assoc prof hist, 73-78, OPPENSTEIN BROS DISTINGUISHED PROF JUDAIC STUDIES, UNIV MO-KANSAS CITY, 78-, DIR JUDAIC STUDIES PROG, 73-, dir Center for Relig Studies, 95; Res grant, Grad Sch Arts & Sci, Boston Univ, 71-72. **HONORS AND AWARDS** Hyman G Enelow Award, Jewish Theol Sem, 76. **MEMBERSHIPS** Asn Jewish Studies; Am Acad Relig. **RESEARCH** Comparative religion; Jewish studies. **SELECTED PUBLICATIONS** Auth, Angelic opposition to the ascension of Moses and the revelation of the law, Jewish Quart Rev, 71; The religious psychology of Jonathan Edwards and the Hasidic Masters of Habad, J Ecumenical Studies, 73; The Lurianic strand in Jonathan Edwards' Concept of Progress, Judaica, 74; Reciprocity in confucian and Rabbinic ethics, J Relig Ethics, 74; contribr, Studies and Texts in Honor of Nahum Glatzer, Brill, 75; auth, From My Father's Vineyard, Vile-Goller, 78; co-ed, From Destruction to Rebirth: The Holocaust and the State of Israel, Univ Am, 78; auth, Judaism and The Gentile Faiths; Comparative Studies in Religion, Fairleigh Dickinson Univ, 78; Mid-America's Promise: A Profile of Kansas City Jewry, Am Jewish Hist Soc, 82; ed, Ze'enah U-Re'enah: Book of Genesis, Dropsie Col, 85; Sinai and Olympus: A Comarative Study with Lois S. Spatz, Univ Press of Am, 95. **CONTACT ADDRESS** Danciger Judaic Studies Prog, Univ of Mo, 5100 Rockhill Rd, Kansas City, MO, 64110-2499.

SCHULZ, RENATE A.

PERSONAL Born 02/24/1940, Lohr/Main, Germany, d, 1 child **DISCIPLINE** FOREIGN LANGUAGES **EDUCATION** Mankato State Coll, BS, 62; Univ Co, MA, 67; Oh State Univ, PhD, 74. **CAREER** Asst prof, Otterbein Col, 74-76; asst prof, SUNY, Buffalo, 76-77; asst, assoc prof, Univ AR, 77-81; prof Univ AZ, 81-. **HONORS AND AWARDS** Creative Tchg Award, 84 Univ Az; ACTFL's Florence Steiner Award, 93; Verdienstkreuz erster Klasse, 90, Federal Republic Germany; J. William Fulbright Fel, 97. **MEMBERSHIPS** AAAL; AATG; ACTFL; MLA; ATTF; AATSP; TESOL; Az Foreign Lang Asn. **RESEARCH** Second language acquisition; foreign language learning and teaching; testing and evaluation; foreign language teacher development. **SELECTED PUBLICATIONS** Co-auth, Lesen, Lachen, Lernen, Holt, Rinehart, and Winston, 78; auth, "Second Language Acquistion Theories and Teaching Practice: How Do They Fit?," Modern Lang Jour, 91; "Profile of the Profession: Results of the 1992 AATG Membership Survey," Unterrichtspraxis, 93; co-auth, "Beer, Fast Cars, and . . .: Stereotypes Held by US College-Level Students of German," Unterrichtspraxis, 95; auth, "Focus on Form in the Foreign Language Classroom: Students and Teachers Views on Error Correction and the Role of Grammar," For Lang Annals,

96. **CONTACT ADDRESS** Dept of German Studies, Univ of Arizona, Tucson, AZ, 85721-0067. **EMAIL** schulzr@u.arizona.edu

SCHURLKNIGHT, DONALD E.
DISCIPLINE ROMANCE LANGUAGES; LITERATURE **EDUCATION** Duke Univ, BA, 69; Univ Pa, MA, 71, PhD, 75. **CAREER** Lectr, Rosemont Col, 72-76; assoc prof, Wayne St Univ, 76- . **HONORS AND AWARDS** Fulbright Fel, Coun for Int Exchange of Scholars; Amer Philos Soc Grant. **MEMBERSHIPS** AATSP; MLA. **RESEARCH** Spanish romanticism; Spanish eighteenth & nineteenth centuries lit. **SELECTED PUBLICATIONS** Auth, Some Forgotten Poetry by Larra, Romance Notes, 89; Romantic Literary Theory as Seen Through Post-Fernandine Periodicals: El Correo de las Damas, Rivista de Estudios Hispanicos, 91; Spanish Romanticism and Mannerism: Pedro de Madrazo, Critica Hispanica, 92; La conjuracion de Venecia , Revista de Estudios Hispanicos, 98; Spanish romanticism in Context: Of Subversion, Contradiction and Politics, Univ Press Amer, 98. **CONTACT ADDRESS** Dept of Romance Lang & Lit, Wayne St Univ, 487 Manoogian Hall, Detroit, MI, 48202. **EMAIL** D.Schurlknight@wayne.edu

SCHUSTER, MARILYN R.
PERSONAL Born 09/22/1943, Washington, DC **DISCIPLINE** FRENCH, WOMEN'S STUDIES **EDUCATION** Mills Coll, BA, Fr, 65; Yale Univ, PhD, Fr Lang & Lit, 73. **CAREER** Instr, Sonoma Sate Coll, 67; tchg assoc, Yale Univ, 67068; instr, Yale Summer Lang Inst, 70; instr, Fordham Univ-Lincoln Center, 70-71; dean, Smith Coll, 81-83; dir, Women's Stud Prog, Smith Coll, 86-87; assoc dean of faculty, Smith Coll, 87-90; ch, Fr dept, 92-95; PROF, FR & WOMEN'S STUD, 87- **MEMBERSHIPS** MLA; NE Mod Lang Asn. **RESEARCH** 20th century women's fiction in France & England; gay/lesbian/queer studies **SELECTED PUBLICATIONS** Marguerite Duras Revisited, MacMillan publ, 93; co-edr, Women's Place in the Academy: Transforming the Liberal Arts Curriculum, Rowman & Allanheld, 85; "The Gendered Politics of Knowledge: Lessons from the US," Asian Women, 96; "Inscribing a Lesbian Reader, Projecting a Lesbian Subject: A Jane Rule Diptych," The Jour of Homosexuality, Gay & Lesbian Lit Since World War II: His & Memory, 98. **CONTACT ADDRESS** Neilson Libr, Smith Coll, Northampton, MA, 01063. **EMAIL** mschuste@sophia.smith.edu

SCHUTZ, ALBERT J.
PERSONAL Born 08/09/1936, Mishawaka, IN **DISCIPLINE** LINGUISTICS **EDUCATION** Purdue Univ, BS, 58; Cornell Univ, PhD, 62. **CAREER** From asst prof to assoc prof, 62-72, prof Ling, Univ Hawaii, Manoa, 72-, prin investr, NSF Grant, Nguna, New Hebrides Lexicography, 69-70; dir, Fijian Dictionary Proj, 71-79; prin investr, Nat Endowment for Humanities res grant, 78-80. **MEMBERSHIPS** Ling Soc Am; Polynesian Soc. **RESEARCH** Malayo-Polynesian linguistics; lexicography. **SELECTED PUBLICATIONS** Coauth, Spoken Fijian, Univ Hawaii, 71; auth, The Languages of Fiji, Clarendon, Oxford, 72; Say it in Fijian, Pac Publ, Sydney, 72; ed, The Diaries and Correspondence of David Cargill, 1832-1843, Australian Nat Univ, 77; auth, Suva: A History and Guide, Pac Publ, 78; ed, Fijian Language Studies: Borrowing and Pidginization, Fiji Mus, 78; auth, Fijian Grammar for Teachers of Fijian, Univ SPac, Suva, 79; co-ed, David Cargill's Fijian Grammar, Fiji Mus, 80; The Fijian Language, Univ Hawaii, 85; The Voices of Eden: A History of Hawaiian Language Studies, Univ Hawaii, 94; All about Hawaiian, Univ Hawaii, 95; Things Hawaiian: A Pocket Guide to the Hawaiian Language, Island Heritage, 97; Hawaiianisch, Abera, 98. **CONTACT ADDRESS** Dept of Linguistics, Univ of Hawaii, Manoa, 1890 E West Rd, Honolulu, HI, 96822-2318. **EMAIL** schultz@hawaii.edu

SCHUTZ, HERBERT
PERSONAL Born 02/25/1937 **DISCIPLINE** GERMAN LANGUAGE & LITERATURE **EDUCATION** Univ Toronto, BA, MA, 65, PhD(Ger), 68. **CAREER** Teacher sec sch French, Ger, hist & music, Toronto Bd of Educ, 61-65; asst head dept moderns, 65-66; asst prof, 68-71, Assoc Prof Ger, Brock Univ, 71- **MEMBERSHIPS** Can Asn Teachers Ger; Am Asn Teachers Ger; Leasing Soc; Am Soc Eighteenth Century Studies. **RESEARCH** Eighteenth century German literature and thought; German cultural history; language teaching methodology. **SELECTED PUBLICATIONS** Auth, Natures Hidden Terror, Violent Nature Imagery In 18th-Century Germany - Brown,Rh/, Seminar-A J Of Ger Studies, Vol 0029, 1993; The Subject As Child - The Invention Of Childhood In The 18th-Century Novel - Ger - Schindler,Sk/, Seminar-A J Of Ger Studies, Vol 0031, 1995. **CONTACT ADDRESS** Dept of Germanic & Slavic Studies, Brock Univ, St Catharines, ON, L2S 3A1.

SCHWARTZWALD, ROBERT
DISCIPLINE FRENCH LITERATURE **EDUCATION** Laval Univ, PhD. **CAREER** Prof, Univ MA Amherst. **RESEARCH** Lit and cult of Quebec; cult studies, espec issues of nationalism, gender, and identity in France; francophone world. **SELECTED PUBLICATIONS** Auth, Fictions de l'identitaire au Quebec; The Brown Plague, Travels in Late Weimar and Early Nazi Germany (rev); ed, Quebec Studies. **CONTACT ADDRESS** Dept of French and Italian Studies, Univ Massachusetts Amherst, Mass Ave, Amherst, MA, 01003. **EMAIL** rss@frital.umass.edu

SCHWARZ, E.
PERSONAL Born 08/08/1922, Vienna, Austria, m, 1950, 3 children **DISCIPLINE** GERMAN LITERATURE **EDUCATION** Univ Wash, Seattle. **CAREER** Harvard Univ, 54-61; Wash Univ, 61-93; prof emer, Rosa May Distinguished Univ. **HONORS AND AWARDS** Joseph von Eucludorf medal; Austrian medal of art und science; honorary dr of philos, Univ Vienna; Humboldt Scholar prize. **MEMBERSHIPS** Modern Lang Asn; Amer Asn of Tchrs of Ger; Austrian Asn of Ger. **RESEARCH** European literature; History of Jews in modern times. **SELECTED PUBLICATIONS** Literatur aus vier Kulturer: Essays und Bespreslusyer, Vandenhoech & Ruprecht Gotinger, 87; Veine Jeit fur Eichlendorff: Chronik unfreiusliger Wanderjerher, Buchergilde Gutenberg Frankfurt, 92; Dratung, Kulik, Geschilte, Essays aur Literatur 1900-1950, Vandenhoech & Ruprecht Gotinger, 83; Poetry and Politics in the Works of Rainer Maria Rolke, Unger, NY, 81; Das Verschluchte Schluchten: Poesic und Politik bir Rainer Maria Rilke, 72; Joseph von Eichendorff, Twayne, 72; Hofrueniusthal und Calderon, Harvard Univ Press, 62. **CONTACT ADDRESS** 1036 Oakland Av., St. Louis, MO, 63122.

SCHWEITZER, CHRISTOPH EUGEN
PERSONAL Born 07/11/1922, Berlin, Germany, m, 1949 **DISCIPLINE** GERMAN **EDUCATION** Univ Wis, MA(-Span), 49, MA(Ger), 50; Yale Univ, PhD(Ger), 54. **CAREER** From instr to asst prof Ger, Yale Univ, 53-59; from assoc prof to prof, Bryn Mawr Col, 59-70; chmn dept, 70-75, Prof Ger Lang, Univ NC, Chapel Hill, 70-, Vis prof, Yale Univ, spring 80. **MEMBERSHIPS** MLA; Am Asn Teachers Ger; Goethe Ges; Lessing Soc; Soc for Ger-Am Studies. **RESEARCH** German baroque and classical literature; early German-American literature. **SELECTED PUBLICATIONS** Auth, Schiller,Friedrich - Drama, Thought And Politics - Sharpe,L/, J Of English And Ger Philol, Vol 0092, 1993; Gottsched,Johann,Christoph 1700-1766- Harbinger Of Ger Classicism - Mitchell,Pm/, Colloquia Germanica, Vol 0028, 1995; Goethe Mignon And Her Sisters - Interpretations And Reception - Ger - Hoffmeister,G/, Ger Rev, Vol 0070, 1995; The Origin Of Poetry - Ger - Eibl,K/, J Of English And Ger Philol, Vol 0096, 1997. **CONTACT ADDRESS** Dept of Ger Lang, Univ of NC, Chapel Hill, NC, 27514.

SCHWEIZER, NIKLAUS R.
PERSONAL Born 08/24/1939, Zurich, Switzerland **DISCIPLINE** GERMAN **EDUCATION** Univ Calif, Davis, MA, 66, PhD, 68. **CAREER** Teacher Ger, Punahou Sch, Honolulu, 68-70; Prof Ger, Univ Hawaii, 70-. **MEMBERSHIPS** AAUP; Am Asn Teachers Ger. **RESEARCH** Eighteenth century German literature; Germans in the Pacific. **SELECTED PUBLICATIONS** Auth, The Ut Pictura Poesis Controversy in Eighteenth-Century England and Germany, Lang, 72; The Germans in old Hawaii, Ethnologische Zeitschrift Zurich, 72; A Poet among Explorers: Chamisso in the South Seas, Lang, 73; Introduction to Hildebrand Jacob of the sister arts: An essay, London, 1734, Augustan Reprint Soc, 74; The Swiss in Hawaii, Newslett Swiss Am Hist Soc, 76; Hawaii two centuries later, Swiss Rev World Affairs, 78; Hawai'i und die deutschsprachigen Volker, Lang, 82; Hawai'i and the German Speaking Peoples, Topgallant, 82; His Hawaiian Excellency, Lang 87/94; ed, By Royal Command, Hui Hanai, 88. **CONTACT ADDRESS** Dept of Europ Lang & Lit, Univ of Hawaii, 1890 E West Rd, Honolulu, HI, 96822-2362.

SCOTT, CHARLES THOMAS
PERSONAL Born 10/21/1932, New York, NY, m, 1957, 4 children **DISCIPLINE** LINGUISTICS **EDUCATION** St John's Univ, NY, BA, 54; NY Univ, MA, 58; Univ Tex, PhD(ling), 63. **CAREER** Specialist comp lit, Teachers Col, Columbia Univ-Int Coop Admin, Afghanistan Proj, 58-60; from asst prof to assoc prof English, 63-68, chmn dept, 70-74, Prof English, Univ Wis-Madison, 68-; Consult for Japan Soc, Inc to English lang Educ Coun, Tokyo, 65-66; mem, US Info Agency English Teaching Adv Panel, 67-73; Nat Adv Coun on Teaching English as Foreign Lang, 67-70; chmn, Comt on Inst Coop Panel in English Lang Teaching, 68-70; Comt Int Exchange Persons Screening Panel, Ling & Teaching English as Foreign Lang, 73-76. **MEMBERSHIPS** Ling Soc Am; aal; MLA; AAUP. **RESEARCH** Formal criteria for definition of literary folkloristic genres; contemporary English linguistics; application of linguistics to literary theory. **SELECTED PUBLICATIONS** Auth, Persian and Arabic Riddles: A Language-Centered Approach to Genre Definition, Ind Univ, 65; Preliminaries to English Teaching, English Lang Educ Coun, Tokyo, 66; Linguistics basis for development of reading skill, Mod Lang J, 66; co-ed, Approaches in Linguistic Methodology, Univ Wis, 67; Readings for the History of the English Language, Allyn & Bacon, 68; auth, Transformational grammar and English as a second language /dialect, Georgetown Monogr Ser, 68; Literary history at Wisconsin, New Lit Hist, 73; co-ed w/T W Machan, English in its Social Contexts, Oxford Univ Press, 92. **CONTACT ADDRESS** Dept of English, Univ of Wisconsin, 600 North Park St, Madison, WI, 53706-1403. **EMAIL** ctscott@facstaff.wisc.edu

SCOTT, DANIEL MARCELLUS
PERSONAL Born 10/13/1960, Gardena, CA, s **DISCIPLINE** COMPARATIVE LITERATURE **EDUCATION** Univ IL Urbana, PhD 72. **CAREER** Univ N Carolina Chapel Hill, postdoc fel, 92-94; Rhode Island Col, asst prof, 94-. **MEMBERSHIPS** MLA; MELUS; NCTE. **RESEARCH** Colonial and Post Colonial; African American Studies. **SELECTED PUBLICATIONS** Auth, Fossil and Psyche, Issues and Identities in Lit, Pasadena CA, Salem Press, forthcoming; Womb of Space, Issues and Identities in Lit, Pasadena CA, Salem Press, forthcoming; Theodore Wilson Harris, Issues and Identities In Lit, Pasadena CA, Salem Press, forthcoming; John Francisco Rechy, Issues and Identities In Lit, Pasadena CA, Salem Press, forthcoming; Marlon Riggs, The African American Encycl Supplement, Marshall Cavendish NY, 96; auth, Walter Mosley, The African American Encycl, Supplement, Marshall Cavendish NY, 93; auth, From Myth to Ritual: Jung Soyinka and the Modern World, World Lit Written In English, 96; auth, Interrogating Identity: Appropriation and Transformation in Middle Passage, Afri Amer Rev, 95; Dreaming the Other: Breton Cesaire and the Problematics of Influence, Romance Quart, 95; auth, Cahier d'un retour au pays natal: la poetique de la vilonce, Romance Notes, 93. **CONTACT ADDRESS** Dept of English, Rhode Island Col, 600 Mt Pleasant Ave, Providence, RI, 02908. **EMAIL** dscott@grog.ric.edu

SCOTT, LINDY
PERSONAL Born 12/26/1951, Columbus, OH, m, 1978, 3 children **DISCIPLINE** FOREIGN LANGUAGES **EDUCATION** Ohio Univ, BA, 73; Trinity Evang Div Sch, MA, 75, Mdiv, 76; Northwestern Univ, PhD, 91 **CAREER** Assoc Prof, 95-, Wheaton Col; Dean, Prof, 90-95, Comunidad Teologica de mexico; Prof, 82-84, 88-92, Centro de Estudios Superiores de Integracion Cristiana; Prof, 80-82, Universidad nacional Autonoma de Mexico **HONORS AND AWARDS** Christian Writer of the Year Awd, 95, Cum Laude or with Honors in all graduate work **MEMBERSHIPS** FTL **RESEARCH** Christianity in Latin Am **CONTACT ADDRESS** Foreign Lang Dept, Wheaton Col, Wheaton, IL, 60187. **EMAIL** Lindy.scott@wheaton.edu

SCOTT, NINA MARGARET
PERSONAL Born 09/04/1937, Hamburg, Germany, m, 1961, 3 children **DISCIPLINE** MODERN SPANISH LITERATURE, SPANISH CIVILIZATION **EDUCATION** Wellesley Col, BA, 59; Stanford Univ, MA, 61, PhD(Span), 68. **CAREER** Teachers Ger, Am Sch in Switz, 63-64; asst prof, 68-74, Assoc Prof Span & Port, Univ Mass, Amherst, 74-, Fac Growth grant for teaching, Univ Mass, Amherst, 75; Mary Elvira Stevens Travelling fel, Wellesley Col, 76-77. **MEMBERSHIPS** Am Asn Univ Women; Am Asn Teachers Span & Port; MLA; Northeast Mod Lang Asn; Int Inst, Spain. **RESEARCH** Contemporary Spanish literature; comparative North/South American literature; art and literature. **SELECTED PUBLICATIONS** Auth, Between 2 Waters - Narratives Of Transculturation In Latin-America - Spitta,S/, Modern Fiction Studies, Vol 0043, 1997. **CONTACT ADDRESS** Dept of Span & Port, Univ of Mass, Amherst, MA, 01003-0002.

SCROGGINS, DANIEL COY
PERSONAL Born 06/19/1937, Compton, AR, m, 1961, 1 child **DISCIPLINE** HISPANIC LITERATURE **EDUCATION** Univ Ark, BA, 58, MA, 61; Univ Mich, PhD(Span), 66. **CAREER** Asst prof Span, Univ Miami, 63-65, Ind Univ, Bloomington, 66-69; asst prof, 69-71, Assoc Prof Span, Univ Mo-Columbia, 71- **MEMBERSHIPS** MLA; Am Asn Teachers Span & Port; Latin Am Studies Asn. **RESEARCH** Argentine literature; colonial Latin American literature; the essay. **SELECTED PUBLICATIONS** Auth, Telluric Poetry Of Northwestern Argentina - Spa - Arancibia,Ja/, Chasqui-Revista De Literatura Latinoamericana, Vol 0023, 1994. **CONTACT ADDRESS** Dept of Romance Lang, Univ of Mo, Columbia, MO, 65201.

SCULLY, STEPHEN P.
PERSONAL Born 06/04/1947, m, 3 children **DISCIPLINE** CLASSICAL STUDIES **EDUCATION** NY Univ, BA, 71; U NC Chapel Hill, MA, 75; Brown Univ, PhD, 78. **CAREER** Mellen Fellow, 78-80, John Hopkins Univ; Assoc Prof, 80-, Boston Univ. **HONORS AND AWARDS** NEH Summer Stipend; Jasper Whiting Fellowship; Honor and the Sacred City; Best Acad Books, Choice. **MEMBERSHIPS** Amer Philos Assoc; New England Class Assoc. **RESEARCH** Epic; Tragedy; Near Eastern Lit; Renaissance Stud. **SELECTED PUBLICATIONS** Coauth, Arion, 3rd Series, 3.1 and 4.1, Special Issue, The Chorus in Greek Tragedy and Culture, 96 & 96; auth, Homer and The Sacred City, Ithaca, NY, Cornell Univ, 90; coauth, Euripides Suppliant Women, Oxford, Oxford Univ Press, 95. **CONTACT ADDRESS** Dept Classics, Boston Univ, Boston, MA, 02215. **EMAIL** sscully@bu.edu

SEARLES, GEORGE J.
PERSONAL Born 11/10/1944, Bayonne, NJ **DISCIPLINE** MODERN LANGUAGE **EDUCATION** Marist Col, BA, 68; SUNY New Paltz, MA, 71; Binghamton Univ, PhD, 79. **CAREER** Adj instr, 76, NY Inst of Tech; adj instr, Utica Col, 80-81, Syracuse Univ; adj instr, 91-92, SUNY Inst of Technology;

adj grad faculty, 91-92, New Sch for Soc Res; prof, 76-, Mohawk Valley Commun Col. **HONORS AND AWARDS** St Univ NY Chancellor's Medal for Excellence in Teaching, 85; Mohawk Valley Commun Col Award for Excellence in Svc, 85; keynote address, SUNY Librns, Assoc Convention, 91., Listed in Poets & Writers, Inc's Dir of Amer Poets & Fiction Writers; selected for inclusion in NY Coun for the Humanities speakers prog, 90-92; chosen poet to read at 83 NE Modern Lang Assoc conv. **MEMBERSHIPS** MLA; NE Modern Lang Assoc; Classical Assoc of Empire St; NCTE. **RESEARCH** Contemporary poetry & fiction; popular culture; tech writing. **SELECTED PUBLICATIONS** Auth, A Casebook on Ken Kesey's One Flew Over the Cuckoo's Nest, Univ NM Press, 92; auth, Conversations With Philip Roth, Univ Press Miss, 92; auth, Workplace Communications: The Basics, Allyn & Bacon, 99. **CONTACT ADDRESS** Humanities Dept, Mohawk Valley Commun Col, 1101 Sherman Dr, Utica, NY, 13501.

SEARS, DIANNE
DISCIPLINE FRENCH LITERATURE **EDUCATION** Yale Univ, PhD. **CAREER** Prof, Univ MA Amherst. **RESEARCH** Poetry; 20th-century lit; contemp lit of Quebec; literary theory. **SELECTED PUBLICATIONS** Auth, pubs on art criticism and metatextuality in Ponge's work; female leads in the works of Queneau and Vian; transgression in Blais' work; language in Lalonde's work. **CONTACT ADDRESS** Dept of French and Italian Studies, Univ Massachusetts Amherst, Mass Ave, Amherst, MA, 01003. **EMAIL** dsears@frital.umass.edu

SEATON, SHIRLEY SMITH
PERSONAL Cleveland, OH, m, 1965 **DISCIPLINE** MULTICULTURAL AFFAIRS **EDUCATION** Howard Univ, Washington DC, BA, 1947, MA, 1948; Case Western Reserve Univ, Cleveland OH, MA, 1956; Institute Universitario di Studi Europei, Turin, Italy, cert. advanced study, 1959; Univ of Akron, Akron OH, PhD, 1981; Beijing Normal Univ, Beijing, China, 1982; postdoctorate. **CAREER** Cleveland Board of Education, teacher, 1950-58, asst principal, 1959-65, principal, 1966-76; US Government, Department of Education, educational specialist, 1965; WEWS-TV, Cleveland OH, teacher, 1963-67; Cleveland State Univ, adjunct prof, 1977-85; Basics and Beyond Education Consultants, dir; JOHN CARROLL UNIVERSITY, ASSOC DIR, MULTICULTURAL AFFAIRS, 1989-. **HONORS AND AWARDS** Fulbright grant to Italy, 1959, and to China, 1982; Martin Luther King Outstanding Educator Award, 1989; Outstanding Educator Awards, Cleveland City Cncl and Ohio State Legislature; Governor of Ohio, Martin Luther King Humanitarian Award, 1992. **MEMBERSHIPS** National Alliance of Black School Educators, National Council for Social Studies, National Association of Secondary School Principals, Association for Supervision & Curriculum Development; pres, Metropolitan Cleveland Alliance of Black School Educators 1981-; Coalition of 100 Black Women 1991-; Phi Delta Kappa 1979-; Fulbright Association; board member, Western Reserve Historical Society; board member, Retired and Senior Volunteer Program. **CONTACT ADDRESS** Multicultural Affairs, John Carroll Univ, 20700 N Park Blvd, University Heights, OH, 44118.

SEBESTA, JUDITH LYNN
PERSONAL Chicago, IL **DISCIPLINE** CLASSICAL LANGUAGES AND LITERATURE, ANCIENT HISTORY, WOMEN IN ANTIQUITY **EDUCATION** Univ Chicago, AB, 68; Stanford Univ, PhD, 72. **CAREER** From instr to asst prof, 72-77, Assoc Prof Classics, Univ S Dak, 77-, Dir, Integrated Humanities Prof, Univ SDak, 81, Dir Classics, 81, Chair, Dept Hist, 97-. **HONORS AND AWARDS** Phi Beta Kappa, 67; Harrington Lectr, Col Arts & Sci, 94. **MEMBERSHIPS** Am Philol Asn; Class Asn Midwest & South; Am Classical League. **RESEARCH** The Roman army; provinces of the Roman empire; classical philology. **SELECTED PUBLICATIONS** Auth, Carl Orff Carmina Burana, Bolchazy-Carducci Publ, 84, 96; Mantles of the Gods and Catullus 64, Syllectu Classica 5, 93; coauth, The World of Roman Costume, Univ Wis Press, 94; auth, Women's Costume and Feminine Civic Morality in Augustan Rome, Gender & Hist 9, 97; Aliquid Sem per Novi: New Challenges & New Approaches, in Latin for the 21st Century, Addison-Wesley, 97. **CONTACT ADDRESS** Dept of Hist, Univ of SDak, 414 E Clark St, Vermillion, SD, 57069-2390. **EMAIL** jsebesta@sunbird.usd.edu

SEBOLD, RUSSELL PERRY
PERSONAL Born 08/20/1928, Dayton, OH, m, 1955, 2 children **DISCIPLINE** SPANISH **EDUCATION** Ind Univ, BA, 49; Princeton Univ, MA, 51, PhD, 53. **CAREER** Instr Span, Duke Univ, 55-56; from instr to assoc prof, Univ Wis, Madison, 56-66; prof foreign lang & chmn dept, Univ Md, 66-68; chmn dept, 68-78, Prof Romance Lang, Univ Pa, 68-, Guggenheim fel, 62-63; co-ed, Hisp Rev, 68-73, gen ed, 73-; Am Philos Soc grant-in-aid, 71, 76 & 82; Am Coun Learned Soc fel, 79-80. **MEMBERSHIPS** MLA; Am Asn Teachers Span & Port; Hisp Soc Am; Centro de Estudios del Siglo XVIII (Oviedo, Spain). **RESEARCH** Eighteenth century Spanish literature; Spanish Romanticism; aesthetics and poetics. **SELECTED PUBLICATIONS** Auth, A Tribute To Peter,G./, Hisp Rev, Vol 0061, 1993; Zorrilla In His 'Orientales' - Historical Sense And Art/, Insula-Revista De Letras Y Ciencias Humanas, Vol 0048, 1993; In Between Centuries, Baroque And Neoclassicism + An Approach To The Spa Poetry Of The Late 17th-Century And Early 18th-Century/, Dieciocho-Hisp Enlightenment, Vol 0016, 1993; On Campoamor And His Lessons In Reality/, Insula-Revista De Letras Y Ciencias Humanas, Vol 0049, 1994; The 'Rima V' Of Becquer In The Second-Person/, Boletin De La Real Academia Espanola, Vol 0075, 1995; The Poetics Of Religious Doubt In The Poetry Of Bermudez-De-Castro/, Critica Hispanica, Vol 0018, 1996; Tears And Heroes In 'Sancho Saldana'/, Hisp Rev, Vol 0064, 1996; Tuberculosis And Mysticism In El 'Senor De Bembibre' + Gilycarrasco,Enrique/, Hisp Rev, Vol 0064, 1996. **CONTACT ADDRESS** Dept of Romance Lang, Univ of Pa, 34th and Spruce St, Philadelphia, PA, 19104.

SEEBA, HINRICH CLAASSEN
PERSONAL Born 02/05/1940, Hannover, Germany **DISCIPLINE** GERMAN LITERATURE **EDUCATION** Univ Tubingen, DPhil(Ger & Greek), 67. **CAREER** From Instr to assoc prof, 68-76, chmn dept, 77-81, Prof Ger, Univ Calif, Berkeley, 76-, Studienstiftung des deutschen Volkes fel, 63-68; Guggenheim Found fel, 70-71. **MEMBERSHIPS** MLA; Am Asn Teachers Ger; Philol Asn Pac Coast; Am Lessing Soc; Am Asn Advan Humanities. **RESEARCH** Eighteenth to 20th century German literature; hermeneutics; methods of literary criticism. **SELECTED PUBLICATIONS** Auth, Intercultural Perspectives - Beginnings Of Comparative Cultural Criticism In Lamprecht,Karl And In The Writings Of Exiled Germanists/, Ger Studies Rev, Vol 0016, 1993; Germany, A Literary Concept - The Myth Of National Lit/, Ger Studies Rev, Vol 0017, 1994; Grillparzer And Heine - Historiographical Aspects Of Their Encounter/, Modern Austrian Lit, Vol 0028, 1995; Cultural Versus Linguistic Competence - Bilingualism, Language In Exile, And The Future Of Ger Studies/, Ger Quart, Vol 0069, 1996. **CONTACT ADDRESS** Dept of Ger, Univ of Calif, 5315 Dwinelle Hall, Berkeley, CA, 94720-3244.

SEELIG, HARRY E.
PERSONAL Born 03/13/1937, New York, NY, m, 1967, 2 children **DISCIPLINE** GERMAN LITERATURE, MUSIC **EDUCATION** Oberlin Col, AB, 59, Conserv, BM, 61; Univ Kans, MA, 64, PhD(German), 69. **CAREER** Instr, Univ Kans, 66-67; instr, 67-69, asst prof, 69-80, assoc prof German, Univ Mass, 80-, vis lectr, Univ Kent, 78-79; res dir, UMass Baden-Wuerttemberg Exchange Prog, 85-86m 86-97. **HONORS AND AWARDS** NDEA Fell, 961-65; German Govt Grant, Dankstipendium, 63-64; Newberry Library Grant in Aid, 67; Pi Kappa Lambola; Delta Phi Alpha. **MEMBERSHIPS** MLA; Am Asn Teachers German. **RESEARCH** German literature since Goethe; poetry and music; translation of contemporary German poetry. **SELECTED PUBLICATIONS** Transl, Rolf Bongs, Insel-Ile-Island, Guido Hildebrandt Verlag Duisburg, WGermany, 73; Rolf Bongs, Aufstieg zum Kilimandscharo, The Literary Rev, 74; auth, Schuberts Beitrag zu besserem Verstadnis' von Goethes Suleika-Gestalt: Eine literarischmuskalische studie der Suleika-Lieder, Beitrage zur Musikwissenschaft, 75; transl, Rolf Bongs, Oberwelt, 76 & Ralph Glockler's, Ich Sehe Dichnoch und andere lyrik, 76, Dimension; The Literary Context: Goethe as Source and Catalyst, in: German Lieder of the Nineteenth Century, New York: Macmillan, G Schirmer Books, 96. **CONTACT ADDRESS** German Dept, Univ of Massachusetts, Herter Hall, Amherst, MA, 01003-0002. **EMAIL** seelig@german.umass.edu

SEGAL, MARILYN
PERSONAL Born 08/09/1927, Utica, NY, d, 5 children **DISCIPLINE** DEVELOPMENTAL PSYCHOLOGY **EDUCATION** Wellesley Col, BA; McGill Univ , BSc soc wk; Nova Univ, PhD, psychol. **CAREER** Boston City Hosp, casewkr, 50-51; Dir pre-sch and hd start cen, 65-70; Nova Southeastern Univ, asst prof, assoc prof, prof, dean, 70-98-. **HONORS AND AWARDS** Sentin Pub Awd winner, 97; Spirit of excell Awd; NSU outstand alumni; Chief Awd, FL Indep Col; Woman of the Year Awd. **MEMBERSHIPS** APA; FL Psychol Asn; Zero to Three; Nat Cen for Infants Toddlers and Family. **RESEARCH** Devel of play in typical children with autism; social interaction in yng childrn; infant toddler interactive play; play assment. **SELECTED PUBLICATIONS** Non-Structured Play Observations: Guidelines, benefits, caveats, M Segal N Webber in: New Visions for the Delvel Assess of Infants and Young Children, ed S Meisels E Fenichel, Zero to Three, Washington DC, 96; Creative Beginnings, Addison Wellesley Alt, Pub, CA, 95; Play Together Grow Together, Nova Univ, 93; several other pub and articles. **CONTACT ADDRESS** Family Center, Nova Southeastern Univ, 3301 College Ave, Fort Lauderdale, FL, 33314. **EMAIL** segal@nsu.nova.edu

SEGEL, HAROLD BERNARD
PERSONAL Born 09/13/1930, Boston, MA **DISCIPLINE** SLAVIC LANGUAGES & LITERATURES **EDUCATION** Boston Col, BS, 51; Harvard Univ, PhD, 55. **CAREER** Asst prof Slavic lang & lit, Univ Fla, 55-59; from asst prof to assoc prof Slavic Lit, Columbia Univ, 59-69, prof, 69-80. **HONORS AND AWARDS** Polish Ministry of Cult Award, 75. **MEMBERSHIPS** Am Asn Advan Slavic Studies; Am Soc 18th Century Studies. **RESEARCH** Slavic literatures; drama and theatre; Polish literature. **SELECTED PUBLICATIONS** Auth, Monumenta-Polonica, The 1st 4 Centuries Of Polish Poetry - A Bilingual Anthology - Carpenter,B/, Slavic Rev, Vol 0052, 1993; National Theater In Northern And Eastern-Europe, 1746-1900 - Senelick,L/, Slavic And East Europ J, Vol 0037, 1993; Russian Theater Art, 1910-1936 - Ger - Lesak,B/, Slavic Rev, Vol 0053, 1994; The 'Adventures Of Mr. Nicholas Wisdom' - Krasicki,I, Hoisington,Th, Ed-Translator/, Slavic And East Europ J, Vol 0038, 1994; A Journey Through Other Spaces - Essays And Manifestos, 1944-1990 - Kantor,T/, Slavic Rev, Vol 0054, 1995. **CONTACT ADDRESS** 700 Columbus Ave, New York, NY, 10025.

SEIDEN, MORTON IRVING
PERSONAL Born 07/29/1921, New York, NY **DISCIPLINE** ENGLISH, COMPARATIVE LITERATURE **EDUCATION** NY Univ, BS, 43; Columbia Univ, MA, 44, PhD, 52. **CAREER** Instr English, City Col New York, 45-46, NY Univ, 46-49, Smith Col, 49-52 & Queens Col, NY, 52-53; from instr to assoc prof, 53-70, PROF ENGLISH, BROOKLYN COL, 70-; Lectr, Columbia Univ Grad Sch, 48-49. **HONORS AND AWARDS** Brooklyn Col Excellence in Teaching Award, 67. **MEMBERSHIPS** MLA; Mod Humanities Res Asn; English Inst. **RESEARCH** Nineteenth and Twentieth Century English literature; English, Irish Renaissance; Comparative Literature. **SELECTED PUBLICATIONS** Auth, A psychoanalytical essay on William Butler Yeats, Accent, spring 46; Myth in the Poetry of William Butler Yeats, Am Imago, 12/48; W B Yeats as a playwright, Western Humanities Rev, winter 49; William Butler Yeats: The Poet as a Mythmaker-- 1865-19339, Mich State Univ, 62; The Paradox of Hate: A Study in Ritual Murder, Yoseloff, 68; coauth, Ivan Goncharov's Oblomov: A study of the anti-Faust as a Christian saint, Can Slavic Studies, spring 69. **CONTACT ADDRESS** Dept of English, Brooklyn Col, CUNY, 2901 Bedford Ave, Brooklyn, NY, 11210-2813.

SEIDENBERG, MARK
DISCIPLINE PSYCHOLOGY, LINGUISTICS, COMPUTER SCIENCE **EDUCATION** Columbia Univ, PhD, 80. **CAREER** Prof, Univ Southern Calif. **RESEARCH** Psycholinguistics, Neurolinguistics. **SELECTED PUBLICATIONS** Auth, Language Acquisition and Use: Learning and Applying Probabilistic Constraints, Sci, 275, 97; coauth, Evaluating Behavioral and Neuroimaging Data on Past Tense Processing, Language, 74, 98; Category Specific Semantic Deficits in Focal and Widespread Brain Damage: A Computational Account, J Cognitive Neuroscience 10, 98; Learning to Segment Speech Using Multiple Cues: A Connectionist Model, Language and Cognitive Processes 13, 98; On the Nature and Scope of Featural Representations of Word Meaning, J Experimental Psychology: Gen 126, 97; On the basis of Two Subtypes of Developmental Dyslexia, Cognition 58, 96. **CONTACT ADDRESS** Dept of Linguistics, Univ Southern Calif, University Park Campus, Los Angeles, CA, 90089. **EMAIL** marks@gizmo.usc.edu

SEIDLER, INGO
PERSONAL Born 10/08/1928, Graz, Austria, m, 1958, 3 children **DISCIPLINE** GERMAN & COMPARATIVE LITERATURE **EDUCATION** Cornell Univ, BA 51; Univ Vienna, Dr Phil, 53. **CAREER** From instr to assoc prof, 57-68, Prof Ger, Univ Mich, Ann Arbor, 68-, H Rackham res fel, 60, 66 & 77; Am Coun Learned Soc travel grant, 65; vis prof, Washington Univ, 69, Univ Freidburg & res dir, jr year, 71-72 & Northwestern Univ, 82; res grant, Deutscher Akademisher Austauschdienst, 77; reader, Adv Placement Prog, 78; mem, Nat Endowment for Humanities transl proj, 79. **MEMBERSHIPS** Brecht Soc; Int Ver Germanisten; Am Nietzsche Soc; MLA. **RESEARCH** Nineteenth and 20th century literature, especially poetry and drama; criticism; theory of literature. **SELECTED PUBLICATIONS** Auth, The Fin-De-Siecle Cult Of Adolescence - Neubauer,J/, Mich Ger Studies, Vol 0019, 1993. **CONTACT ADDRESS** Dept of Ger, Univ Mich, Ann Arbor, MI, 48109.

SEILER, WILLIAM JOHN
PERSONAL Born 10/17/1942, Milwaukee, WI, m, 1966, 1 child **DISCIPLINE** SPEECH COMMUNICATION **EDUCATION** Univ Wis, Whitewater, BEd, 65; Kans State Univ, MA, 67; Purdue Univ, West Lafayette, PhD(speech), 71. **CAREER** Asst prof speech, Purdue Univ, Calumet Campus, 70-72; assoc prof speech commun, Univ Nebr, Lincoln, 75-83, prof, 84-, dept chmn, 90-, dir undergrad studies, 82-86, Courtesy Appt-Teachers College 3/10/80. **HONORS AND AWARDS** Outstanding Young Alumni, Univ of Wisc-Whitewater, 74; Outstanding Young Col Teacher, Nebr Speech Commun Asn, 75; Outstanding Educators of America, 76; International Who's Who in Education, 77; Distinguished Alumni Award, Univ of Wisc-Whitewater, 89; UNL Parent's Recognition Award, 90. **MEMBERSHIPS** Am Educ Res Asn; Nat Commun Asn; Int Commun Asn; Cent States Commun Asn. **RESEARCH** Classroom communication; organizational communication; communication apprehension. **SELECTED PUBLICATIONS** Auth, Audiovisual Materials in Classroom Instruction: A Theoretical Approach, 72 & coauth, Performance-Based Teacher Education Program in Speech and Drama, 75, Speech Teacher; The Effects of Talking Apprehension on Student Academic Achievement: Three Empirical Investigations in Communication-Restricted and Traditional Laboratory Classes in the Life Sciences, Int Commun Yearbk I, 77; Communication Apprehension and Teaching Assistants, J Chem Educ, 78; Effects of Communica-

tion Apprehension on Student Learning in College Science Classes, J Col Sci Teaching, 78; Learners Cognitive Style and Levels of Learning in TV & Print Instruction for Use in Open Learning: An Exploratory Study, Int & Nat J Instr Media, 81; Communications in Business & Professional Organizations, Addison-Wesley, 82; auth, PSI: An Attractive Alternative for the Basic Speech Communication Course, Commun Educ, Jan 83; Developing the Personalized System of Instruction for the Basic Speech Communication Course, with Marilyn Fuss-Reincki, Commm Ed, April 86; The Temporal Organization of Classrooms as an Interactional Accomplishment, with Drew McGukin, Journal of Thought, winter 87; The Comparative Effectiveness of Systematic Desensitation and Visualization Therapy Treatments in Treating Public Speaking Anxiety, with Ana Rossi, Imagination, Cognition, and Personality, 89; What We Know About the Basic Course: What has the Research Told Us?, with Drew McGukin, Basic Course Annual, 89; An Investigation Into the Communication Needs and Concerns of asian Students in Speech Performance Classes, with Ester Yook, Basic Course Annual, 90; The Nebraska Department of Communication Story: There are Happy Endings that Go Beyond Football and a Good Crop Year. JACA, 95; Learning Style Preferences and Academic Achievement within the Basic Communication Course, with Chuck Lubbers, Basic Course Annual, 98; and many publications, textbooks, and other materials. **CONTACT ADDRESS** Dept of Commun Studies, Univ of Nebr, PO Box 880329, Lincoln, NE, 68588-0329. **EMAIL** bseiler@unl.edu

SELIGER, HELFRIED WERNER
PERSONAL Born 08/09/1939, Vienna, Austria **DISCIPLINE** GERMAN LITERATURE **EDUCATION** Univ Alta, BA, 62; McGill Univ, MA, 64, PhD(Ger), 72. **CAREER** Asst prof, 72-75, Assoc Prof Ger, Victoria Col, Univ Toronto, 75- **MEMBERSHIPS** MLA; Am Asn Teachers Ger; Can Asn Univ Teachers Ger (secy-treas, 73-75); Int Brecht Soc; Can Comp Int Asn. **RESEARCH** German Romanticism; German-Spanish literary relations; 20th century German literature. **SELECTED PUBLICATIONS** Auth, Heimat In The Novel - Burden Or Pleasure - Transformations Of A Genre In Austrian Postwar Lit - Ger - Kunne,A/, Seminar-A J Of Ger Studies, Vol 0032, 1996. **CONTACT ADDRESS** Dept of Ger, Univ Toronto, Toronto, ON, M5S 1A1.

SELKIRK, ELISABETH
DISCIPLINE LINGUISTICS **EDUCATION** Univ Calif Berkeley, BA, MAss Inst Tech, PhD, 72. **CAREER** Prof. **RESEARCH** Phonological theory; interfaces of phonology with other components of grammar; prosodic phrasing in English. **SELECTED PUBLICATIONS** Auth, The Syntax of Words, MIT, 82; The Role of Prosodic Categories in English Word Stress, Ling Inquiry, 80; Phonology and Syntax: The Relation between Sound and Structure, MIT, 84; The Major Class Features and Syllable Theory, MIT, 85; Derived Domains in Sentence Phonology, 86; co-auth, Government and Tonal Phrasing in Papago, 87. **CONTACT ADDRESS** Linguistics Dept, Univ of Massachusetts, Amherst, S College 231, Amherst, MA, 01003. **EMAIL** selkirk@linguist.umass.edu

SELVIDGE, MARLA J.
PERSONAL Born 11/11/1948, Gross Pt, MI, m, 1982 **DISCIPLINE** BIBLICAL LANGUAGES AND LITERATURE **EDUCATION** Taylor Univ, BA, 70; Wheaton Col, MA, 73; St. Louis Univ, PhD, 80. **CAREER** Asst prof, John Wesley Col, 73-74; pers dir, Thalhimers, 74-76; res asst, Cts for Reformation Res, 76-77; dir evening div, St Louis Univ, 77-80; lect, St. Louis Univ, 78-80; asst prof, Carthage Col, 80-81; ast prof, Univ Dayton, 81-84; asst prof, Converse Col, 84-87; chemn Relig and Philos, Converse Col, 84-85; coordr grant writing, Cheshire Public Sch, 87-89; asst prof, Marist Col, 89-90; dir, assoc prof, Central Missouri St Univ, 90-94; prof, dir, Center for Relig Stud, Central Missouri St Univ, 94- . **HONORS AND AWARDS** Tenney Awd, Best Thesis, 73; Fac of the Year, 74; nominated Outstanding Women in America, 80; res grant, William R. Kenan Fund and Natl Endowment for the Hum, 84-87; res grant CMSU, 91-92; Missouri Hum Council Grant, 92-94. **MEMBERSHIPS** Soc Bibl Lit; Am Acad Relig; Missouri St Tchr Asn. **SELECTED PUBLICATIONS** Auth, "Chautauqua Revival Brings to Life Religious Figures," Relig Stud News, 93; "Mennonites and Amish," Women in American Religious History, Kathryn Kuhlman, Missouri Chautauqua, 93; "Magic and Menses," Explorations, 93; "Discovering Women," Teacher Created Materials, 95; "Notorious Voices," Continuum, 96; "Reflections on Violence and Pornography," A Feminist Companion to the Bible, Sheffield, 96; The New Testament, PrenticeHall, 98. **CONTACT ADDRESS** Center For Religious Studies, Central Missouri State Univ, Martin 118, Warrensburg, MO, 64093.

SENN, HARRY
DISCIPLINE FRENCH LANGUAGE AND LITERATURE **EDUCATION** Univ Minn, BA, MA; Univ Calif, Berkeley, PhD. **CAREER** Prof, 70-. **MEMBERSHIPS** Mem, S Calif Mediation Assn. **RESEARCH** Folklore, folk mythology, personal mythology in literature and psychology. **SELECTED PUBLICATIONS** Auth, The Shamanic Narrative in the Post-Modern Era, The Humanistic Psychologist, 95; Jungian Shamanism, Jour of Psychoactive Drugs, 91; Marcel Proust and Melusine: From Fairy Magic to Personal Mythology, Southern Folklore Quart, 84. **CONTACT ADDRESS** Dept of Lang, Pitzer Col, 1050 N. Mills Ave., Claremont, CA, 91711-6101. **EMAIL** harry_senn@email.pitzer.edu

SEPULVEDA-PULVENTINI, EMMA
PERSONAL Chile **DISCIPLINE** SPANISH **EDUCATION** Univ Calif, Davis, PhD. **CAREER** Assoc prof Span, Univ Nev, Reno. **RESEARCH** Contemporary Latin American and Spanish poetry and testimonial literature. **SELECTED PUBLICATIONS** Recently edited two collections--personal testimonies of the Chilean arpilleristas and essays on female testimonial writings. **CONTACT ADDRESS** Univ Nev, Reno, Reno, NV, 89557. **EMAIL** sepulveda@unr.edu

SERRANO, RICHARD
DISCIPLINE COMPARATIVE LITERATURE, FRENCH **EDUCATION** Stanford Univ, BA, 88; Univ of Calif, MA, 91, PhD, 96. **CAREER** ASST PROF OF FRENCH AND COMPARATIVE LIT, RUTGERS UNIV, 98-. **HONORS AND AWARDS** Mellon Tchg fel, Columbia Univ Soc of Fels in the Humanities, 96-98. **MEMBERSHIPS** Rutgers Univ Prog in Middle Eastern Studies; Rutgers Univ African Studies Coord Comt; Middle Eastern Studies Asn; African Lit Asn; Modern Lang Asn. **RESEARCH** Lyric poetry; Francophone lit; Classical Arabic lit; Classical Chinese lit. **SELECTED PUBLICATIONS** Auth, Translation and the Interlingual Text in the Novels of Rachid Boudjedra, Critical Perspectives on Maghrebian Lit, Lynn Rienner, 99; Fans, Silks, and Ptyx: Mallarme and Classical Chinese Poetry, Comparative Lit, 98; Lacan's Oriental Language of the Unconscious, SubStance, 97; Al-Buhturi's Poetics of Persian Abodes, J of Arabic Lit, 97; Al-Sharif Al-Taliq, Jacques Lacan, and the Poetics of Abbreviation, Homoeroticism in Classical Arabic Writing, Columbia Univ Press, 97; No Place for a Lady in the Chanson de Roland, pacific Coast Philology, 92. **CONTACT ADDRESS** Dept of French, Rutgers Univ, 131 George St, New Brunswick, NJ, 08903-0270. **EMAIL** rserrano@rci.rutgers.edu

SETTLE, PETER
DISCIPLINE ORGANIZATIONAL AND INTERPERSONAL COMMUNICATION **EDUCATION** Marquette Univ, MA; Bowling Green Univ, PhD. **CAREER** Law, Caroll Col. **HONORS AND AWARDS** Andrew T. Weaver Award; Alumnus Award -- Wisconsin Gamma of Pi Kappa Delta. **SELECTED PUBLICATIONS** Articles, Asn Comm Administration Jour, Wis Comm Asn Jour. **CONTACT ADDRESS** Carroll Col, Wisconsin, 100 N East Ave, Waukesha, WI, 53186.

SEVERINO, ROBERTO
PERSONAL Born 07/19/1940, Catania, Italy, d, 1 child **DISCIPLINE** ITALIAN LITERATURE **EDUCATION** Columbia Union Col, BA, 67; Univ Il Urbana, MA, 69, PhD, 73. **CAREER** Prof, chair, Georgetown Univ. **HONORS AND AWARDS** Who's Who; Gold Medal & Diploma First-Class, by decree of Pres of Italy; Marranzano d'argento, Acireale, 89; Commendatore dell'Ordine al Merito della Repubblica Italiana, by decree of Pres of Italy, 90; Georgetown Univ Vicennial Medal, 94; Premio Telamone, Agrigento, 95. **SELECTED PUBLICATIONS** Auth, ed, A Carte Scoperte: Manzoniana e Altri Saggi Filologici e Critici sulla Cultura Italiana in America, Roma, 90; auth, The Battle for Humanism, Washington DC, 94; auth, Alessandro Dumas: Mariano Stabile, Sindaco di Palermo, Valverde, 94; coauth, coed, Preserving and Promoting Italian Language and Culture in North America, Toronto, 97; auth, Italian Verbs At a Glance, Falls Church Va, 98. **CONTACT ADDRESS** Georgetown Univ, 307 ICC, Washington, DC, 20007. **EMAIL** severiro@gunet.georgetown.edu

SEYMOUR, HARRY N.
DISCIPLINE LINGUISTICS **EDUCATION** Ohio State Univ, PhD, 71. **CAREER** Adj prof. **RESEARCH** Child language disorders. **SELECTED PUBLICATIONS** Auth, Clinical intervention strategies for language disorders among nonstandard English speaking children, Hil, 86; co-auth, Black English and Standard American English Contrasts in Consonantal Development of Four and Five year old Children, J Speech Hearing Disorders, 81; A minority perspective in diagnosis of child language disorders, 91; Speech and language assessment of preschool children, 92. **CONTACT ADDRESS** Linguistics Dept, Univ of Massachusetts, Amherst, 720 Massachusetts Ave, Amherst, MA, 01003. **EMAIL** hseymour@comdis.umass.edu

SEYMOUR, RICHARD KELLOGG
PERSONAL Born 06/21/1930, Hinsdale, IL, m, 1951, 2 children **DISCIPLINE** GERMAN **EDUCATION** Univ Mich, BA, 51, MA, 52; Univ Pa, PhD(Ger philol), 56. **CAREER** Asst instr Ger, Univ Pa, 52-54; instr Ger & ling, Princeton Univ, 54-58; asst prof, Duke Univ, 58-63, assoc prof, 63-67; prof Ger & chmn dept Europ lang, Univ Hawaii, Manoa, 67-75; vis prof English, Univ Cologne, Ger, 75; prof Ger, Pennsylvania State Univ, 75-77; Prof Ger, Univ Hawaii, 77-, Actg Dean, Lang, Ling & Lit, Arts & Sci 81-, Assoc ed, Unterrichtspraxis, 69-80; Fulbright travel grant, 81. **MEMBERSHIPS** Am Asn Teachers Ger; Ling Soc Am; Int Ling Asn; SAtlantic Mod Lang Asn (secy-treas, 62-67); Nat Ger Hon Soc (secy-treas, 68-). **RESEARCH** German dialectology; German word formation; collegiate slang. **SELECTED PUBLICATIONS** Auth, Glossary Of Middle High Ger Lexicographic Word Origins - Ger - Gartner,K, Ed/, Speculum-A J Of Medieval Studies, Vol 0069, 1994; Glossary Of Middle High Ger Lexicographic Word Origins - Ger - Gartner,K, Ed/, Speculum-A J Of Medieval Studies, Vol 0069, 1994; Which-Way-Is-East Revisited + Honolulu Compass Directions/, Am Speech, Vol 0070, 1995. **CONTACT ADDRESS** Dept of German, Univ Hawaii at Manoa, Honolulu, HI, 96822.

SHANE, ALEX MICHAEL
PERSONAL Born 07/16/1933, San Francisco, CA, m, 1957, 2 children **DISCIPLINE** SLAVIC LANGUAGES & LITERATURES **EDUCATION** Univ Chicago, BA, 53, MA, 55; Univ CA, Berkeley, PhD, 65. **CAREER** Instr Russ, Princeton Univ, 58-60; from asst prof to assoc prof, Univ CA, Davis, 63-71; chmn dept, 71-80, PROF & DIR, SLAVIC LANG & LIT, STATE UNIV NY ALBANY, 71-; Dir Off Int Prog, 81-, Am Coun Learned Soc grant-in-aid, 66; Humanities inst grant, Univ CA, 67; vis assoc prof Russ lit, Stanford Univ, 69-70; fel, NEH Independent Study & Res, 77-78; State Univ NY-Moscow State Univ exchange scholar, 82, 84. **MEMBERSHIPS** Am Asn Teachers Slavic & East Europ Lang (pres, 77, 78); Am Asn Advan Slavic Studies. **RESEARCH** Nineteenth and 20th century Russian prose fiction. **SELECTED PUBLICATIONS** Auth, The Life and Works of Evgenij Zamjatin, Univ Calif, 68; Russian literary periodicals (1901-1916) at the Helsinki University Library, Slavic Rev, 3/69; An evaluation of the existing college norms for the MLA-Cooperative Russian Test, Mod Lang J, 2/71; A prisoner of fate: Remizov's short fiction, Russ Lit Triquart, 5/72; An introduction to Alexei Remizov, Triquart, spring 73; American and Canadian doctoral dissertations in Slavic and East European Languages and literatures, 1961-1972, Slavic and EEurop J, summer 73; The slavic workforce in the United States and Canada: Survey and commentary, Slavic & EEurop J, fall 78; contrib, Columbia Dictionary of Modern European Literature, ed by Jean-Albert Bede and William B. Edgerton, 2nd ed, NY: Columbia Univ Press, 80; auth, Individualized, self-paced instruction: Alternative to the traditional classroom? ADFL Bull, 4/81; contrib, Encyclopedia of World Literature of the 20th Century, vol 4, ed by Leonard S. Klein, rev ed, NY: Frederic Ungar Pub Co, 84; contrib, Handbook of Russian Literature, ed by Victor Terras, New Haven, CT: Yale Univ Press, 85; auth, Rhythm Without Rhyme: The Poetry of Aleksej Remizov, Aleksej Reminov: Approaches to a Protean Writer, ed by Greta Slobin, Columbus: Slavica Pubs, 87; contrib, European Writers: The Twentieth Century, vol 10, ed by George Stade, NY: Charles Scribner's Sons, 90. **CONTACT ADDRESS** Int Programs, LI-66, State Univ of NY, 1400 Washington Ave, Albany, NY, 12222-1000. **EMAIL** ashane@csc.albany.edu

SHAPIRO, LEWIS P.
DISCIPLINE PSYCHOLINGUISTICS **EDUCATION** Brandeis Univ, PhD, 87. **CAREER** Dir, Lang Processes Lab; ERP Lab Doctoral Program Executive Comt. **RESEARCH** Adult lang disorders. **SELECTED PUBLICATIONS** Auth, An introduction to syntax, Jour of Speech, Lang, and Hearing Res 40, 97; co-auth, Context effects re-visited, Sentence Processing: A Cross-Linguistic Perspective, Acad Press; How to milk a coat: The effects of semantic and acoustic information on phoneme categorization, Jour Acoustical Soc Am 103, 98; On-line examination of language performance in normal and neurologically-impaired adults, Amer Jour Speech-Lang Pathol, 98; Training wh-question productions in agrammatic aphasia: An analysis of lexical and syntactic properties, Brain and Lang, 98. **CONTACT ADDRESS** Dept of Commun Disorders, San Diego State Univ, 5500 Campanile Dr, San Diego, CA, 92182. **EMAIL** shapiro@mail.sdsu.edu

SHAPIRO, MICHAEL C.
DISCIPLINE ASIAN LANGUAGE; LITERATURE **EDUCATION** Queens Col, BA, 67; Univ Chicago, MA, 70, PhD, 74. **CAREER** Prof. **RESEARCH** Hindi language; linguistics and literature; Indo-Aryan linguistics; historical and comparative linguistics. **SELECTED PUBLICATIONS** Auth, A Primer of Modern Standard Hindi; Current Trends in Hindi Syntax: A Bibliographic Survey; coauth, Language and Society in South Asia. **CONTACT ADDRESS** Washington Univ, 5001 25th Ave NE, Seattle, WA, 98105. **EMAIL** hindimcs@u.washington.edu

SHARP, FRANCIS MICHAEL
PERSONAL Born 02/10/1941, Troy, KS, m, 1968, 1 child **DISCIPLINE** GERMAN LITEARTURE **EDUCATION** Univ Mo, BA, 64; Univ Calif, Berkeley, MA, 69, PhD(German lang & lit), 74. **CAREER** Asst prof German lang & lit, Princeton Univ, 73-79; Asst Prof German Lang & Lit, Univ of the Pac, 79- **MEMBERSHIPS** MLA; Am Asn Teachers German. **RESEARCH** Modern German poetry; contemporary German prose; literature and psychology. **SELECTED PUBLICATIONS** Auth, The Art Of Living - Fromm,Erich Life And Works - Knapp,Gp/, Ger Studies Rev, Vol 0015, 1992; Love In Expressionism - A Study Of Poetry Published In The Periodicals Die 'Aktion' And Der 'Sturm' From 1910 To 1914 - Ger

- Froelich,J/, Ger Studies Rev, Vol 0015, 1992; 'Tristan Island' - Skwara,Ew/, World Lit Today, Vol 0067, 1993; 'Uber Die Dunkle Flache' - Poems 1986-1993 - Ger - Hein,Mp/, World Lit Today, Vol 0068, 1994; 'Nachtspur' - Poetry And Prose 1987-1992 - Ger - Czechowski,H/, World Lit Today, Vol 0068, 1994; Der 'Burgwart Der Wartburg' - Buch,Hc/, World Lit Today, Vol 0069, 1995; Understanding Werfel,Franz - Wagener,H/, Ger Quart, Vol 0068, 1995; 'Mein Hund, Meine Sau, Mein Leben' - Stadler,A/, World Lit Today, Vol 0069, 1995; Poetic Process - Kudszus,Wg/, Modern Austrian Lit, Vol 0029, 1996; Die 'Heimlichen Konige' - Skwara,Ew/, World Lit Today, Vol 0070, 1996; 'Traum Am Fruhen Morgen' - Ger - Buch,Hc/, World Lit Today, Vol 0071, 1997; 'Galilei Vermisst Dantes Holle Und Bleibt An Den Massen Hangen' - Essays 1989-1995 - Ger - Grunbein,D/, World Lit Today, Vol 0071, 1997. **CONTACT ADDRESS** Dept of Mod Lang & Lit, Univ of the Pacific, Stockton, CA, 95211.

SHARPE, PEGGY
DISCIPLINE PORTUGUESE LITERATURE **EDUCATION** Univ NY, MA; Univ NMex, PhD, 81. **CAREER** Assoc prof, Univ Ill Urbana Champaign. **RESEARCH** Luso-Brazilian literature; Brazilian women writers of the XIXth and XXth centuries; feminist theory. **SELECTED PUBLICATIONS** Auth, A Tropical Utopia: The Brazilian Fairy Tales of Marina Colasanti, 98; A politica maternalista da obra liter ria de Jlia Lopes de Almeida, Lisboa, 95; Fragmented Identities and the Process of Metamorphosis in Works by Lygia Fagundes Telles, Greenwood, 95; ed, Entre resistir e identificar-se: Para uma teoria da pr tica da narrativa barasileira de autoria feminina, 97. **CONTACT ADDRESS** Spanish, Italian, and Portuguese Dept, Univ Ill Urbana Champaign, 52 E Gregory Dr, Champaign, IL, 61820. **EMAIL** psharpe@uiuc.edu

SHAW, BRADLEY ALAN
PERSONAL Born 12/23/1945, Tremonton, UT, m, 1969, 2 children **DISCIPLINE** SPANISH LANGUAGE, HISPANIC LITERATURE, TRANSLATION **EDUCATION** Lewis & Clark Col, BA, 68; Northwestern Univ, Evanston, MA, 69; Univ NM, PhD, 74. **CAREER** From instr to asst prof Span, Va Commonwealth Univ, 72-74; asst prof, 74-80, Assoc Prof Span & Dir, Secondary Maj Prog Latin Am Studies, Kans State Univ, 80-, Assoc Dir, Tri-Univ Ctr Latin Am Studies, 76-; assoc ed, Studies in Twentieth Century Lit; head, dept modern lang, 88-95; dir intl and area studies, coll of atrs and sci, 95. **MEMBERSHIPS** MLA; ACTFL; Am Transl(s) Assoc. **RESEARCH** Contemp Peruvian lit; Latin Am novel; Latin Am theater. **SELECTED PUBLICATIONS** Auth, Latin American Literature in English Translation: An Annotated Bibliography, New York Univ, 76; coauth, Hispanic Writers in French Journals: An Annotated Bibliography, Soc of Span & Span-Am Studies, 78; The new Spanish American narrative, Pac Quart, 78; auth, Latin American Literature in English: 1975-1978, suppl to Rev, 4/79; coauth, Luis Romero, Twayne, 79; translr, Mogollon (transl, Augusto Higa Oshiro, El equipito de Mogollon, In: Between Fire and Love: Contemporary Peruvian Writing, Miss Mud Press, 80; The Indigenista Novel in Peru After Arguedas: The Case of Mauel Scorza, Selecta, 82; The Overt Narrator in Scorzas Redoble Por Rancas, Discurso Literario, 86; Narrative Distance in Arguedas, La Agonia de Rasu-Niti, 86, Manue Scorza: Su Vision de la Realidad Mitica del Peru, 91. **CONTACT ADDRESS** Dept of Mod Lang, Kansas State Univ, 104 Eisenhower Hall, Manhattan, KS, 66506-2800. **EMAIL** bradshaw@ksu.edu

SHAW, WAYNE EUGENE
PERSONAL Born 05/23/1932, Covington, IN, m, 1957, 3 children **DISCIPLINE** HOMILETICS, SPEECH **EDUCATION** Lincoln Christian Col, AB, 54; Christian Theol Sem, BD, 60; Butler Univ, MS, 63; Ind Univ, PhD, 69. **CAREER** Prof preaching, Lincoln Christian Sem, 66-, acad dean, 74-, Mem chaplaincy endorsement comn, Christian Churches & Churches of Christ, 74- **MEMBERSHIPS** Acad Homiletics **RESEARCH** Preaching; communication; Biblical studies. **SELECTED PUBLICATIONS** Auth, The historian's treatment of the Cane Ridge Revival, Filson Quart, 62; contribr, The Seer, The Savior, The Saved, Col Press, 63; coauth, Birth of a Revolution: How the Church Can Change the World, Standard, 74; auth, Designing the Sermon, Bicentennial Comt, 75; Love in the midst of crises, Christian Standard, 77. **CONTACT ADDRESS** 100 Campus View Dr, Lincoln, IL, 62656-2111. **EMAIL** wshaw@lccs.edu

SHEA, GEORGE W.
PERSONAL Born 10/07/1934, Paterson, NJ, m, 1956, 3 children **DISCIPLINE** CLASSICAL LANGUAGES **EDUCATION** Fordham Univ, BA, 56; Columbia Univ, MA, 60, PhD(classics), 66. **CAREER** Asst prof Latin & Greek, St John's Univ, NY, 61-65; asst prof classics, asst dean, Fordham Col & dir jr year abroad prog, 67-70, assoc prof classics & dean Col at Lincoln Ctr, Fordham Univ, 70-. **MEMBERSHIPS** Am Philol Asn; Am Conf Acad Deans. **RESEARCH** Latin epic poetry and Roman history; Iohannis of Flavius Cresconius Corippus. **SELECTED PUBLICATIONS** Auth, The Poems of Alcimus Avitus, MRTS, 97; The Iohannis of Flavius Crescorius Corippus, Mellon, 98; Delia and Nemesis, UPA, 98. **CONTACT ADDRESS** Classics Dept, Fordham Univ, 113 W 60th St, New York, NY, 10023-7484.

SHEA, KERRY
DISCIPLINE MIDDLE HIGH GERMAN AND OLD NORSE LITERATURE **EDUCATION** Cornell Univ, PhD. **CAREER** Eng, St. Michaels Col. **SELECTED PUBLICATIONS** Auth, Engendering Romance: Women and European Medieval Romance. **CONTACT ADDRESS** St. Michael's Col, Winooski Park, Colchester, VT, 05439. **EMAIL** kshea@smcvt.edu

SHEETS, GEORGE ARCHIBALD
PERSONAL Born 08/18/1947, Buenos Aires, Argentina, m, 1969, 2 children **DISCIPLINE** CLASSICAL LANGUAGES, HISTORICAL LINGUISTICS **EDUCATION** Univ NC, BA, 70; Duke Univ, PhD(class studies), 74; JD W. Mitchell Col of Law, 90. **CAREER** Instr classics, Univ TX, Austin, 74-75; Mellon fel classics, Bryn Mawr Col, 76-77; asst prof, 77-82, ASSOC PROF CLASSICS, UNIV MN, MINNEAPOLIS, 82-. **MEMBERSHIPS** Am Philol Asn; Class Asn Mid West & South; Minnesota State Bar. **RESEARCH** Historical linguistics; Roman literature; legal history. **SELECTED PUBLICATIONS** Auth, Palatalization in Greek, Indoger Forsch, 75; Secondary midvowels in Greek, Am J Philol, 79; The dialect gloss, Hellenistic poetics and Livius Andronicus, 81, Am J Philol; Grammatical commentary to Book I of the Histories of Herodotus, Bryn Mawr Commentaries, 81; Ennius Lyricus, 8 IL Class Studies; Plautus and early Roman Tragedy, 8 Ill Class Studies, Rome Prize, Am Academy, 85; Conceptualizing International Law in Thucydides, 115, Am J Philol. **CONTACT ADDRESS** Classical and NE Studies, Univ of MN, 9 Pleasant St S E, 330 Folwel, Minneapolis, MN, 55455-0194. **EMAIL** gasheets@umn.edu

SHELDON, RICHARD
PERSONAL Born 07/12/1932, Kansas City, KS, m, 1964, 4 children **DISCIPLINE** SLAVIC LANGUAGE & LITERATURE **EDUCATION** Univ Ks, BA, 54; Univ Mich, JD, 60, MA, 62, PhD, 66. **CAREER** Asst prof, 65-66, Grinnell Col; vis prof, 68, Univ Calif Berkeley; vis prof, 74, Stanford Univ; asst prof to prof, 66-, chair, 70-81, 90-00, dept of Russian lang & lit, assoc dean, 84-89, Dartmouth Col. **HONORS AND AWARDS** Phi Beta Kappa, 54; Nat Defense Act Fel, 61-64; Center for Adv Stud Fel, 69-70; Amer Coun of Learned Soc Grant, 70; Sr Assoc Member, St Antony's Col, Oxford, 83-84. **MEMBERSHIPS** AAASS; AATSEEL. **RESEARCH** Twentieth-century Russian lit **SELECTED PUBLICATIONS** Coed Soviet Society and Culture, Westview Press, 88; auth, The Transformations of Babi Yar, Soviet Society and Culture, Westview Press, 88; art, Problems in the English Translation of Anna Karenina, Essays in the Art and Theory of Translation, Edwin Mellen Press, 97; coauth, Westward Flows the Don: The Translation and the Text, Slavic & E Europ J, 98. **CONTACT ADDRESS** 86 S Main, Hanover, NM, 03755-2089. **EMAIL** Richard.Sheldon@Dartmouth.edu

SHELMERDINE, SUSAN C.
PERSONAL Born 04/21/1954, Boston, MA, s **DISCIPLINE** CLASSICAL STUDIES **EDUCATION** Smith Col, BA, 76; Univ Mich, MA, 77, PhD, 81. **CAREER** Lect, Univ N Carolina, 81-82, ast prof, 82-88; vis asoc prof, Univ Mich, 88-89; asoc prof, Univ N Carolina, 88- , dept head, 89-92, asoc dean, 92-95. **HONORS AND AWARDS** Jr fel, Ctr Hellenic Stud, Washington DC, 95-86; NEH Fel, 96-97. **MEMBERSHIPS** APA; Class Asn Middle West & South. **RESEARCH** Greek poetry; language pedagogy. **SELECTED PUBLICATIONS** Co-auth, Greek for Reading, Univ Mich, 94; auth, The Homeric Hymns, Focus Information Grp, 95; contribur, HarperCollins Dictionary of Religion, HarperCollins, 95; auth, "Greek Studies Today," Class Jrnl, 96 **CONTACT ADDRESS** Dept of Classical Studies, Univ of North Carolina Greensboro, PO Box 26170, Greensboro, NC, 27402-6170. **EMAIL** shelmerd@uncg.edu

SHERMAN, CAROL LYNN
PERSONAL Fairfield, IA **DISCIPLINE** EIGHTEENTH-CCENTURY FRENCH LITERATURE **EDUCATION** Parsons Col, BS, 61; Northwestern Univ, Evanston, MA, 68; Univ Chicago, PhD(French), 72. **CAREER** Asst prof, 72-77, Assoc Prof French Lit, Univ NC, Chapel Hill, 77-, Ed, Romance Notes. **MEMBERSHIPS** Am Soc 18th Century Studies; Soc Int 18th Century Studies; SAtlantic Mod Lang Asn; MLA. **RESEARCH** Denis Diderot; rococo structures; Voltaire and narratology. **SELECTED PUBLICATIONS** Auth, The Nomadic Self - Transparency And Transcodification In Graffigny 'Lettres Dune Peruvienne'/, Romance Notes, Vol 0035, 1995. **CONTACT ADDRESS** Dept of Romance Lang, Univ of NC, Chapel Hill, NC, 27514.

SHERWIN, BYRON LEE
PERSONAL Born 02/18/1946, New York, NY, m, 1972, 1 child **DISCIPLINE** JEWISH STUDIES, CULTURAL HISTORY **EDUCATION** Columbia Univ, BS, 66; Jewish Theol Sem Am, BHL, 66, MHL, 68; New York Univ, MA, 69; Univ Chicago, PhD, 78. **CAREER** Prof Judaica, Spertus Col Judaica, 70-, Proj dir holocaust studies, Nat Endowment for Hum, 76-78. **HONORS AND AWARDS** Presidential Medal, Repub of Poland, 95; Doctor of Hebrew Letters, Honoris Causa, 96. **MEMBERSHIPS** Rabbinical Assembly Am; Am Acad Relig; Relig Educ Asn; Authors Guild; Am Philos Soc. **RESEARCH** Mysticism; Holocaust studies. **SELECTED PUBLICATIONS** Auth, How to Be a Jew: Ethical Teachings of Judaism, Jason Aronson Press, 92; The Spiritual Heritage of Polish Jewry (in Polish), Voratio Press, 95; Sparks Amidst the Ashes: The Spiritual Legacy of Polish Jewry, Oxford Univ Press, 97; Crafting the Soul, Inner Traditions, 98; Why Be Good?, Daybreak Books, 98; Jewish Ethics Today, Syracuse Univ Press, 99; John Paul II and Interreligious Dialogue, Orbis Books, 99. **CONTACT ADDRESS** Spertus Col of Judaica, 618 S Michigan Ave, Chicago, IL, 60605-1901. **EMAIL** sijs@spertus.edu

SHETTER, WILLIAM ZEIDERS
PERSONAL Born 08/17/1927, Allentown, PA **DISCIPLINE** GERMANIC LANGUAGES & LINGUISTICS **EDUCATION** Univ Pa, AB, 51; Univ Calif, MA, 53, PhD(Ger), 55. **CAREER** Teaching asst, Univ Calif, 51-55; instr Ger, Univ Wis, 56-59, asst prof, 59-61; from asst prof to assoc prof Ger, Bryn Mawr Col, 62-65, assoc prof Ger lang, 65-71, Prof Ger Lang, Ind Univ, 71-, Fulbright fel, State Univ Leiden, 55-56; res grant ling, State Univ Groningen, 61-62. **MEMBERSHIPS** Ling Soc Am; MLA; Maatschappij der Nederlandse Taal - en Letterkunde; Int Vereniging voor Nederlandistiek. **RESEARCH** Linguistics; civilization of the Netherlands; medieval literature. **SELECTED PUBLICATIONS** Auth, The Value Of An Early Education - A Study On The Implications Of Literacy On The Lives Of The Inhabitants Of Eindhoven And Surrounding Communities, 1800-1920 - Boonstra,Owa/, J Of Interdisciplinary Hist, Vol 0026, 1995. **CONTACT ADDRESS** Dept Ger Lang, Indiana Univ, Bloomington, Bloomington, IN, 47401.

SHIELDS, JOHN CHARLES
PERSONAL Born 10/29/1944, Phoenix, AZ **DISCIPLINE** AMERICAN & CLASSICAL LITERATURES **EDUCATION** Univ Tenn, Knoxville, BA, 67, MACT, 79, PhD(English), 78; George Peabody Col Teachers, EdS, 75. **CAREER** Teacher English & art hist, Sevier County High Sch, Sevierville, Tenn, 67-68; head dept English & teacher Latin, Battle Ground Acad, Franklin, Tenn, 67-68; dir acad, Brentwood Acad, Tenn, 71-73; Instr English, Columbia State Community Col, 75-76; ASST PROF ENGLISH, ILL STATE UNIV, 80-, Instr English & dir writing lab, Univ Tenn, Nashville, 71-74; fac res grant, Ill State Univ, summers 80 & 81. **MEMBERSHIPS** MLA; Medieval Acad Am; Soc Cinema Studies. **SELECTED PUBLICATIONS** Auth, Wheatley,Phillis Subversion Of Classical Stylistics/, Style, Vol 0027, 1993; African-Am Poetics - Introd/, Style, Vol 0027, 1993; Wheatley,Phillis Subversive Pastoral/, Eighteenth-Century Studies, Vol 0027, 1994. **CONTACT ADDRESS** English Dept, Illinois State Univ, Normal, IL, 61761.

SHIPLEY, WILLIAM F.
DISCIPLINE LINGUISTICS **EDUCATION** Univ Calif, Berkeley, PhD, 59. **CAREER** PROF EMER, UNIV CALIF, SANTA CRUZ. **RESEARCH** Language and culture of the Maidu Indians. **SELECTED PUBLICATIONS** Auth, Maidu Texts and Dictionary, Univ Calif Publ in Ling, vol 33, 63; Maidu Grammar, Univ Calif Publ in Ling, vol 41, 64; The Maidu Indian Myths and Stories of Hancibyjin, Heyday Press, 91; co-auth, Nisenan Texts and Dictionary, Univ Calif Publ in Ling, vol 46, 66; Proto-Maidun Stress and Vowel Length: Reconstruction of One, Two, Three, and Four, Intl Jour of Amer Ling, 79. **CONTACT ADDRESS** Dept of Ling, Univ Calif, 1156 High St, Santa Cruz, CA, 95064.

SHIRINIAN, LORNE
DISCIPLINE ARMENIAN-NORTH AMERICAN LITERATURE **EDUCATION** Univ of Montreal, PhD. **RESEARCH** Armenian-North American Lit; multiculturism; film noir, hard-boiled fiction, cinema and the cinematic adaptation of literary works. **SELECTED PUBLICATIONS** Auth, In a Dark Light: David Goodis and Film Noir; auth, Writing Memory: The Search for Home in Armenian Diaspora Literature and Film; auth, Survivor Memoirs and Photographs of the Armenian's Genocide. **CONTACT ADDRESS** Dept of English, Royal Military Col Canada, 323 Massey Bldg., PO Box 17000, Kingston, ON, K7K 7B4. **EMAIL** shirinian-l@rmc.ca

SHIRLEY, PAULA
DISCIPLINE COMPARATIVE LITERATURE **EDUCATION** Univ SC, Ba, 67, MA, 69, PhD, 76. **CAREER** Prof, 78. **RESEARCH** US Hispanic Literature. **SELECTED PUBLICATIONS** Co-auth, Understanding Chicano Literature, Univ SC Press, 88. **CONTACT ADDRESS** Dept of Mod Lang and Lit, Columbia Col, So Carolina, 1301 Columbia Col Dr, Columbia, SC, 29203. **EMAIL** pshirley@colacoll.edu

SHIVERS, GEORGE ROBERT
PERSONAL Born 09/09/1943, Salisbury, MD, m, 1 child **DISCIPLINE** SPANISH LAGUAGE & LITERATURE **EDUCATION** Am Univ, BA, 65; Univ Md, MA, 69, PhD(Span), 72. **CAREER** From Asst Prof to Assoc Prof, 69-86, Prof Span, Washington Col, 86-. **HONORS AND AWARDS** NEH Summer Inst 86; Fulbright Summer Study in Brazil, 87; NEH Summer Fel, 92. **MEMBERSHIPS** Am Asn Teachers Span & Port; NEMLA; Brazilian Studies Asn; Am Lit Transl Asn. **RESEARCH** Contemporary Spanish American literature and culture; literary translation; Brazilian literature and culture. **SELECTED PUBLICATIONS** Auth, La historicidad de El

Cerco de Numancia de Milguel de Cervantes Saavedra, Hispanofila, 70; La vision magico-mesianica en tres relatos de Garcia Marquez, 6/75, El tema del hombre y su destino en Borges y Cortazar, 12/76 & La dualidad y unidad en La Casa Verde de Vargas Llosa, 6/77, Arbor; contribr, La unidad dramatica en la Cisma de Inglaterra de Calderon de la Barca, In: Perspectivas de la Comedia, Estudios de Hispanofila, 78; auth, The Other Without and the Other Within in Works by Julio Cortzar and Gabriel Garcia Marquez, In: In Retrospect: Essays on Latin American Literature, Span Lit Asn Publ, 87; transl, The Last Song of Manuel Sendero, Viking Press, 87; Trademark Territory, Index on Censorship, 5/88; My House is on Fire, Viking Press, 90; Hard Rain, Readers Int, 90; Some Write to the Future, Duke Univ Press, 91. **CONTACT ADDRESS** Dept of For Lang, Lit, and Cult, Washington Col, 300 Washington Ave, Chestertown, MD, 21620-1197. **EMAIL** george.shivers@washcoll.edu

SHOCKEY, GARY C.
PERSONAL Born 11/07/1959, New London, CT **DISCIPLINE** FOREIGN LANGUAGES **EDUCATION** Hartwick Col, BA, 81; Middlebury Col, MA, 82; Univ Calif, PhD, 98. **CAREER** Vis asst prof, John Carroll Univ, 97-. **MEMBERSHIPS** MLA; ALSC; AATG; MAP. **RESEARCH** Post-classical courtly romances of the 13th century; medieval law political discourse; status of peasantry in medieval courtly romance; Minnesang. **CONTACT ADDRESS** John Carroll Univ, 20700 N Park Blvd, OC 142, University Heights, OH, 44118. **EMAIL** gshockey@jcu.edu

SHOOKMAN, ELLIS
DISCIPLINE GERMAN LANGUAGE **EDUCATION** Yale Univ, PhD, 87. **CAREER** Assoc prof, Dartmouth Col. **RESEARCH** 18th and 20th-century narratives and in subj such as fictionality and physiognomy **SELECTED PUBLICATIONS** Auth, publ(s) on Brecht, Fallada, Puckler-Muskau, Arno Schmidt, and Wieland; ed, study of Lavater and an anthology of 18th-century Ger prose. **CONTACT ADDRESS** Dartmouth Col, 3529 N Main St, #207, Hanover, NH, 03755.

SHORES, DAVID LEE
PERSONAL Born 01/28/1933, Tangier, VA, m, 1956, 2 children **DISCIPLINE** ENGLISH, LINGUISTICS **EDUCATION** Randolph-Macon Col, BA, 55; George Peabody Col, MA, 56, EdS, 64, PhD(English), 66. **CAREER** Instr English & Ger, Richard Bland Col, Col William & Mary, 61-62; from asst prof to assoc prof, 66-70, dir freshman English, 70-73, grad prog dir English, 73-75, chmn dept, 75-80, PROF ENGLISH, OLD DOMINION UNIV, 70-, Instr & assoc dir, US Off Educ Inst Col English Instr Black Cols, 70-73; consult, Nat Teachers Exam, Educ Testing Serv, 72-73. **MEMBERSHIPS** MLA; SAtlantic Mod Lang Asn; NCTE; Am Dialect Soc; Southeast Conf Ling. **RESEARCH** Old and Middle English language and literature; Chaucer; English linguistics. **SELECTED PUBLICATIONS** Auth, More On Porchmouth + Va Tidewater Pronunciation/, Am Speech, Vol 0069, 1994. **CONTACT ADDRESS** Dept of English, Old Dominion Univ, Norfolk, VA, 23508.

SHOWALTER, ENGLISH
PERSONAL Born 05/14/1935, Roanoke, VA, m, 1962, 2 children **DISCIPLINE** FRENCH **EDUCATION** Yale Univ, BA, 57, PhD, 64. **CAREER** Instr, Haverford Col, 61-64; Asst Prof, Univ Calif, Davis, 64-66; Asst Prof, Princeton Univ, 66-74; Assoc Prof, Prof, Prof II, Rutgers Univ, 74-. **HONORS AND AWARDS** NEH Fellow, 77-78; John Simon Guggenhiem Found Fellow, 82-83; Warren L Susman Award for Excellence in Tchng, 86; NEH Collaborative Proj Grant, 97-98. **MEMBERSHIPS** MLA (Exec Dir, 83-85); ASECS; AATF; AAUP; Societe d'etudes francaises du dix-huitieme siecle, Societe Diderot. **RESEARCH** French 18th century, especially fiction, epistolary literature, social history. **SELECTED PUBLICATIONS** Co-ed, La Correspondance complete de Madame de Graffigny, The Voltaire Foundation, vols 1-5, 85-97; ed & translator, My Night at Maud's, Rutger's univ Press, 93; auth, Modernities, Eighteenth Cent Fiction, 7, 325-28, 95; auth, Graffigny at Cirey: A Fraud Esposed, French Forum, 21:1, 29-44, 1/96; auth, various entries in Dictionnaire de Jean-Jacques Rousseau, Honore Champion, 386-87, 679, 871-72, 892, 96; auth, Prose Fiction: France, The Cambridge Hist of Lit Criticism, vol 4, Cambridge Univ Press, 210 -237, 97. **CONTACT ADDRESS** Dept French, Rutgers Univ, Armitage Hall, Camden, NJ, 08102-1405. **EMAIL** showalte@crab.rutgers.edu

SHUFORD, WILLIAM HARRIS
PERSONAL Born 10/28/1932, Lincolnton, NC **DISCIPLINE** ROMANCE LANGUAGES **EDUCATION** Lenoir-Rhyne Col, AB, 54; Univ Fla, MA, 56; Univ NC, PhD(Romance lang), 63. **CAREER** Asst prof Span, Lenoir-Rhyne Col, 61-64, assoc prof, 64-67; assoc prof, Furman Univ, 67-69; chm dept mod & class lang, 69-, prof Span, Lenoir-Rhyne Col, 69-. **MEMBERSHIPS** MLA; SAtlantic Mod Lang Asn; Am Asn Teachers Span & Port. **CONTACT ADDRESS** Dept of Mod & Class Lang, Lenoir-Rhyne Col, 743 6th St. NE, Hickory, NC, 28601-3976. **EMAIL** shufordw@lrc.edu

SHUMWAY, ERIC BRANDON
PERSONAL Born 11/08/1939, Holbrook, AZ, m, 1963, 7 children **DISCIPLINE** ENGLISH LITERATURE & POLYNESIAN LANGUAGES **EDUCATION** Brigham Young Univ, BA, 64, MA, 66; Univ VA, PhD, 73. **CAREER** From instr to assoc prof, 66-78, prof eng, Brigham Young Univ, HI, 78. **RESEARCH** Browning's love poetry; love in 19th century lit; the Tongan oral tradition. **SELECTED PUBLICATIONS** Auth, Intensive Course in Tongan, Univ HI, 71, rev, Inst of Polynesian Studies, with tapes, 88; Coe Ta'ane: A Royal Marriage (video doc), fall 76 & The Punake of Tonga (video doc), fall 77, Brigham Young Univ-HI; The eulogistic function of the Tongan poet, Pac Studies, fall 77; Tonga Saints: Legacy of Fartl, Inst for Polynesian Studies, 91; Koe Fakapangai: In the Circle of the Sovereign, 93 (video doc). **CONTACT ADDRESS** 55-220 Kulanui St, Laie, HI, 96762-1294. **EMAIL** shumwaye@byuh.edu

SHUY, ROGER W.
PERSONAL Born 01/05/1931, Akron, OH, m, 1952, 3 children **DISCIPLINE** LINGUISTICS **EDUCATION** Wheaton Col, IL, AB, 52; Kent State Univ, MA, 54; Western Reserve Univ, PhD, 62. **CAREER** Tchr lang arts, Kenmore Jr & Sr High Sch, Akron, OH, 56-58; from instr to asst prof Eng & ling, Wheaton Col, Ill, 58-64; assoc prof, MI State Univ, 64-67; dir sociolinguistics prog, Ctr Appl Ling, 67-70; dir Nat Sci Found grant to estabish prog in socioling, 70-73, Prof Ling & Dir Socioling Prog, Georgetown Univ, 70-87, Am Coun Learned Soc grant, 57; Univ Chicago res grant, 62; dir, Detroit Dialect Studies, 66-67; Carnegie Corp NY & Nat Inst Ment Health grants, Ctr Appl Ling, 67-; ling adv, Xerox Intermediate Dictionary, 72; mem eval panel, early childhood educ, Nat educ, Nat Inst Educ, 72; comt socioling, Soc Sci Res Coun, 72-; assoc dir, Ctr Appl Ling, 74-; res award on acquistion of children's use of lang functions, Carnegie Corp of NY, 75; ch liguistics, 87-90; distinguished res prof, 96-98; prof Emeritus, 98. **MEMBERSHIPS** Int Reading Asn; Ling Soc Am; AAAS; Am Asn Appl Ling (pres, 78); NCTE. **RESEARCH** Ling and educ; sociolinguistics; the Eng lang. **SELECTED PUBLICATIONS** Auth, Discovering American Dialects, NCTE, 67; Field Techniques in an Urban Language Study, Ctr Appl Ling, 68; co-ed, New Ways of Analyzing Variation in Englihs, 73, Language Attitudes, 73 & ed, Sociolinguistics: Current Trends and Prospects, 73, Georgetown Univ; co-ed, Dialect Differences: Do They Interfere?, Int Reading Asn, 73; ed, Linguistic Theory: What Does it Have to Say About Reading, Int Reading Asn, 77; Studies in Language Variation, Georgetown Univ, 77; ed, The Relation of Theoretical and Applied Linguistics, Plenum, 87; co auth, Dialogue Journal Communication, Ablcx, 88; auth, Language Crimes, Blackwell, 96; auth, The Language of Confession, Interrogation and Deception, Sage, 98; auth, Bereaucratic Language, Geargetown Press, 98. **CONTACT ADDRESS** Socioling Prog, 629 Beverly Ave, Missouls, MT, 59801. **EMAIL** shuyr@gusun.georgetown.edu

SICES, DAVID
PERSONAL Born 06/10/1933, New York, NY, m, 1956, 4 children **DISCIPLINE** FRENCH LANGUAGE & LITERATURE **EDUCATION** Dartmouth Col, BA, 54; Yale Univ, PhD, 62. **CAREER** From instr to asst prof French, 57-66, assoc prof French & Ital, 66-71, chmn dept Romance lang & lit, 70-79, Prof French & Ital, 71-95, PROF EMER FRENCH & ITALIAN, 95- , DARTMOUTH COL, 71- ; Am Coun Learned Soc fel, Paris, 69-70; asst ed, French Rev, 80-; Nat Screening Comt, Inst Int Educ, 80- . **HONORS AND AWARDS** MA, Dartmouth Col, 71. **MEMBERSHIPS** Am Asn Teachers Fr; Am Asn Teachers Ital; Am Asn Univ Professors Ital. **RESEARCH** Theater of Musset and the Romantics; 19th century French poetry and novel; translation of French and Italian drama. **SELECTED PUBLICATIONS** Auth, Music and the Musician in Jean-Christopher, Yale Univ, 68; Theater of Solitude: The Drama of Alfred de Musset, New England Univ, 74; 2001 French and English Idioms, Barron's, 96. **CONTACT ADDRESS** Dept of French & Italian, Dartmouth Col, Hanover, NH, 03755. **EMAIL** David.Sices@Dartmouth.edu

SIEKHAUS, ELISABETH
DISCIPLINE GERMAN STUDIES **EDUCATION** Univ Calif, Berkeley, BA, 65, MA, 67, PhD, 72. **CAREER** Prof; Mills Col, 77. **RESEARCH** German culture and literature; German poetry and music; Age of Goethe and the 19th century; interdisciplinary studies. **SELECTED PUBLICATIONS** Auth, Die lyrischen Sonette der Catharina Regina von Greiffenberg, Berner Beitraege zur Barockgermanistik: Peter Lang, Bern/ Frankfurt, 82; Europaeische Hochschulschriften: Peter Lang, Bern/ Frankfurt, 82 double-publ; Six Hundred Years of German Women's Poetry; introduced and ed, articles by Mills Col Ger majors, 92-94, 95; Strategies to Enhance the Foreign Language Learning Experience of Adult Beginners, In: The Canberra Linguist, Vol XVIII, 89. **CONTACT ADDRESS** Dept of German Studies, Mills Col, 5000 MacArthur Blvd, Oakland, CA, 94613-1301. **EMAIL** siekhaus@mills.edu

SIGALOV, PAVEL S.
DISCIPLINE RUSSIAN AND SLAVIC LINGUISTICS **EDUCATION** Leningrad Univ, PhD, 63. **CAREER** Prof, Univ WY, 83-; vis prof, Harvard Univ, 89-91. **SELECTED PUBLICATIONS** Coauth, comp grammar of the Slavic lang; publ over 60 academic articles on Slavic ling & Russ lit. **CONTACT ADDRESS** Dept of Mod and Class Lang(s), Univ WY, PO Box 3964, Laramie, WY, 82071-3964. **EMAIL** PSIGALOV@UWYO.EDU

SIHLER, ANDREW L.
PERSONAL Born 02/25/1941, Seattle, WA **DISCIPLINE** LINGUISTICS **EDUCATION** Harvard Univ, BA, 62; Yale Univ, MA, 65, PhD, 67. **CAREER** From asst prof to assoc prof ling, 67-78, prof ling, Univ Wis-Madison, 78-. **MEMBERSHIPS** Am Orient Soc; Ling Soc Am. **SELECTED PUBLICATIONS** Auth, New Comparative Grammar of Greek and Latin, Oxford, 95. **CONTACT ADDRESS** Dept of Ling, Univ of Wisconsin, 1220 Linden Dr, Madison, WI, 53706-1557. **EMAIL** asihl@macc.wisc.edu

SILBAJORIS, RIMVYDAS
PERSONAL Born 01/06/1926, Kretinga, Lithuania, m, 1955, 2 children **DISCIPLINE** RUSSIAN AND LITHUANIAN LITERATURES **EDUCATION** Antioch Col, BA, 53; Columbia Univ, MA, 55, PhD, 62. **CAREER** Instr to Asst Prof, Oberlin Col, 57-63; Assoc Prof to Prof, 67-91, Prof Emeritus Slavic & East Europ Langs, Ohio State Univ, 91-; Special Instr in Scientific Russ, Case Inst Technol, 57-58; Vis Prof, The Vytautas Magnus Univ, Lithuania, 92, 94; Vis Prof, Vilnius Pedagogical Univ, Lithuania, 97; Vis Prof, Univ NC, 95; Vis Prof, Northwestern Univ, 96. **HONORS AND AWARDS** Antioch Col For Students Scholarship, 49-53; Inter-University Travel Grant, 63-64; Lithuanian Community Achievement Award for Publications on Lithuanian Literature in English, 82; Lithuanian Med Asn Achievement Award for contributions to Lithuanian cultural activities abroad, 85; The Vilis Vitols Prize for contribution to the J Baltic Studies in the 1989 publication year; recipient of numerous grants and fellowships. **MEMBERSHIPS** Am Asn Teachers Slavic & East Europ Langs; Am Asn Advancement Slavic Studies; Baltiska Inst, Stockholm Univ; Asn Advancement Baltic Studies; Am Asn Univ Prof; Inst Lithuanian Studies; Asn Russ-Am Schol USA. **RESEARCH** Russian poetry and prose, particularly Tolstoy; Lithuanian literature. **SELECTED PUBLICATIONS** Ed, Tolstoy and the Teachers. Essays on War and Peace, Ohio State Univ Slavic Papers, 85; auth, Tolstoy's Aesthetics and His Art, Slavica Publ, 91; Netekties zenklai (Signs of Dispossession), Vaga Publ house, 92; War and Peace. Tolstoy's Mirror of the World, Twayne Publ, 95; author of numerous journal articles and other publications. **CONTACT ADDRESS** Slavic Languages Dept, Ohio State Univ, Columbus, OH, 43210. **EMAIL** Silbajoris.1@osu.edu

SILBER, CATHY L.
DISCIPLINE CHINESE **EDUCATION** Univ Iowa, BA, 80, MA, 84; Univ Mich, Ann Arbor, PhD, 95. **CAREER** Asst prof & coordr, Chinese Lang and Lit Prog, Williams Col, 97-; asst prof, Iowa State Univ, Ames, 95-97. **RESEARCH** Chinese language, literature, and culture; gender studies. **SELECTED PUBLICATIONS** Auth, Wang Meng, A Winter's Topic, The Stubborn Porridge and Other Stories, NY: George Braziller, 94; cotransl & co-ed, Ding Xiaoqi, Maidenhome, Melbourne: Hyland House in assoc with Monash Asia Inst, 93; San Francisco: Aunt Lute Bk(s), 94; co-ed, From Daughter to Daughter-in-law, Women's Script of Southern Hunan, Engendering China: Women, Culture, and the State, Harvard Univ Press, 94; transl(s) of 25 poems and 3 critical biographies, An Anthology of Chinese Women Poets from Ancient Times to 1911, Stanford Univ Press, 98. **CONTACT ADDRESS** Center for Foreign Languages, Literatures and Cult, Williams Col, Williamstown, MA, 01267. **EMAIL** csilber@williams.edu

SILBERMAN, M.
PERSONAL Born 04/08/1948, Minneapolis, MN, m, 1981 **DISCIPLINE** GERMAN **EDUCATION** Univ Minn, BA cum laude 69; Indiana Univ, MA 72, PhD 75. **CAREER** Univ Texas SA, asst, assoc prof 75-88; Univ Wisconsin Madison, assoc prof, prof, 88 to 98-; UCLA, guest prof 89; Free Univ of Berlin, guest prof, 95 & 99. **MEMBERSHIPS** MLA; ATG; IBS; SCS; GSA. **RESEARCH** German lit, cult, theater and cinema in 20th century. **SELECTED PUBLICATIONS** Auth, German Cinema: Texts in Context, Detroit, WSU Press, 95; Contentious Memories: Looking Back at the GDR, co-ed, NY Peter Lang, 98; drive b: Brecht 100, Berlin, Theater der Zelt Intl Brecht Soc, 97. **CONTACT ADDRESS** German Dept, Univ of Wisconsin, Madison, 818 Van Hise Hall, Madison, WI, 53706. **EMAIL** mdsilber@facstaff.wisc.edu

SILENIEKS, JURIS
PERSONAL Born 05/29/1925, Riga, Latvia, m, 1952, 2 children **DISCIPLINE** FRENCH LITERATURE **EDUCATION** Univ Nebr, BA, 55, MA, 57, PhD, 63. **CAREER** Instr French, Univ Nebr, 57-60; from instr to assoc prof, 61-76, head dept, 68-79, Prof Mod Lang, Carnegie-Mellon Univ, 71-, Dir Prog Mod Lang, 79- **MEMBERSHIPS** MLA; Am Asn Teachers Fr; Asn Advan Baltic Studies. **RESEARCH** Black writers of French expression; contemporary French theater; Latvian literature. **SELECTED PUBLICATIONS** Auth, 'Bille' - Belsevica,V/, World Lit Today, Vol 0067, 1993; 'Advente 1986-1989' - Rancane,A/, World Lite Today, Vol 0067, 1993; 'Tutepatas' - Ziedonis,I/, World Lit Today, Vol 0067, 1993; 'Dzives

Pieredze Un Ziepju Burbuli' - Ziedonis,R/, World Lit Today, Vol 0067, 1993; Le 'Maitre-Piece' - Radford,D/, World Lit Today, Vol 0068, 1994; 'Vardojums, Licu Loki' - Ivaska,A/, World Lit Today, Vol 0068, 1994; 'Dveselu Pulcesana' - Paternal Ancestry - Latvian - Vanaga,M/, World Lit Today, Vol 0068, 1994; 'Mamzelle Libellule' - Confiant,R/, World Lit Today, Vol 0069, 1995; Complete Poems - Fr - Glissant,E/, World Lit Today, Vol 0069, 1995; 'Saulesmasa' - Liepa,A/, World Lit Today, Vol 0069, 1995; 'Puka Ola' - Collected Short-Stories - Latvian - Ezera,R/, World Lit Today, Vol 0070, 1996; 2 Poems - 'Somnambulists' And 'Stikla Sieviete' - Latvian - Kraujiete,A/, World Lit Today, Vol 0070, 1996. **CONTACT ADDRESS** Dept of Mod Lang, Carnegie Mellon Univ, Schenley Park, Pittsburgh, PA, 15213.

SILVA, EURIDICE
DISCIPLINE PORTUGUESE LITERATURE **EDUCATION** Univ NC, PhD, 94. **CAREER** Asst prof. **RESEARCH** Post modernism in Brazil; literary theory; popular culture; foreign language acquisition. **SELECTED PUBLICATIONS** Auth, pubs on Brazilian theater. **CONTACT ADDRESS** Dept of Romance Languages, Knoxville, TN, 37996.

SILVA-CORVALAN, CARMEN M.
PERSONAL Chile **DISCIPLINE** LINGUISTICS **EDUCATION** Univ Chile, BA, 70; Univ London, MA, 73; Univ Calif, Los Angeles, MA, 77, PhD(Ling), 79. **CAREER** Assoc prof Appl Ling, Univ Chile, 73-78; prof Span Ling, Univ Southern Calif, 79-. **HONORS AND AWARDS** NSF grants 83, 88; Ford Found Fell, 75-79; Brit Council Scholarship, 71-73. **MEMBERSHIPS** Ling Soc Am; MLA; Am Asn Teachers Span & Port; Asn Ling y Filol America Latina. **RESEARCH** Sociolinguistics; language change; Spanish syntax and semantics; bilingualism; discourse analysis. **SELECTED PUBLICATIONS** Auth, La funcion pragmatica de la duplicacion de pronombres cliticos, Boletin Filologia, Vol XXXI, 80; The diffusion of object verb agreement in Spanish, Papers in Romance, 12/81; contribr, Spanish in the United States: Sociolinguistics Aspects, Cambridge Univ Press, 82; On the interaction of word order and intonation, In: Discourse Perspectives on Syntax, Acad Press, 82; Sociolinguistica: Teoria y analisis, Alhambra, 89; Language Contact and Change: Spanish in Los Angeles, Clarendon, 94; Invariant meanings and contextbound functions of tense in Spanish, In: The Function of Tense in Texts, North-Holland, 91; The gradual Loss of Mood Distinctions in Los Angeles Spanish, Lang Variation and Change, 94; Contextual Conditions for the interpretation of poder and deber in Spanish, In: Modality in Grammar and Discourse, Benjamins, 95; On Borrowing as a Mechanism of Syntactic Change, in: Romance Linguistics: Theoretical Perspectives, J Benjamins, 98. **CONTACT ADDRESS** Dept of Spanish & Portuguese, Univ of Southern California, 3501 Trousdale Pky, Los Angeles, CA, 90089-0008. **EMAIL** csilva@usc.edu

SILVER, PHILIP WARNOCK
PERSONAL Born 11/12/1932, Bryn Mawr, PA, m, 1958, 3 children **DISCIPLINE** ROMANCE LANGUAGES **EDUCATION** Haverford Col, BA, 54; Middlebury Col, MA, 55; Princeton Univ, MA, 60, PhD, 63. **CAREER** Instr Span, Rutgers Univ, 61-63; asst prof, Oberlin Col, 63-66, assoc prof, 67-71; vis prof, 71-72, chmn dept, 73-76, Prof Span & Port, Columbia Univ, 72-, Guggenheim fel, 66; Nat Endowment for Humanities fel, 76. **MEMBERSHIPS** MLA; Am Transl Am. **RESEARCH** Modern Spa poetry & novel; philosophy and esthetics of Oretga y Gasset. **SELECTED PUBLICATIONS** Auth, Towards A Revisionary Theory Of Spa Romanticism/, Revista De Estudios Hispanicos, Vol 0028, 1994; The Politics Of Spa Romanticism/, Critica Hispanica, Vol 0018, 1996. **CONTACT ADDRESS** Dept Span & Port, Columbia Univ, 2960 Broadway, New York, NY, 10027-6900.

SILVERBERG, JOANN C.
PERSONAL Born 05/19/1940, New York, NY, 1 child **DISCIPLINE** CLASSICAL PHILOLOGY **EDUCATION** Barnard, AB, 60; Radcliffe, AM, 62; Harvard, PhD, 67. **CAREER** Sweet Brian Col, 64-65; from asst prof to assoc prof, 67-, Conn Col. **HONORS AND AWARDS** Phi Beta Kappa; Woodrow Wilson Fel; Mellon, Fulbright, Dartmouth-Dana, NYS Regents Grants. **MEMBERSHIPS** APA; CANE. **RESEARCH** Latin and Greek language and literature; historiography comedy and love poetry; linguistics, gender and women's studies. **SELECTED PUBLICATIONS** Auth, for, A Feminist Classicist Reflects on Athena; auth, rev, The Chilly Classroom Climate: A Guide to Improve the Education of Women, 98. **CONTACT ADDRESS** Connecticut Col, 270 Mohegan Ave, Box 5551, New London, CT, 06320. **EMAIL** jcsil@conncoll.edu

SILVERMAN, DANIEL
PERSONAL Born 03/09/1963, s **DISCIPLINE** LINGUISTICS **EDUCATION** Univ of Pensylvania, BA, 85; UCLA, PhD, 95. **CAREER** Asst Prof, 97-, UIUC. **RESEARCH** Phonology. **SELECTED PUBLICATIONS** Auth, Reduplication in Kihehe The Asymmetrical Enforcement of Phonological and Morphological Principles, Ling Jour of Korea, 93; CoAuth, Aerodynamic Evidence for Articulatory Overlap in Korean, Phonetica, 94; CoAuth, Phonetic Structures in Jalapa Mazatec, Anthropological Ling, 95; Auth, Optional Conditional and Obligatory Prenasalization in Bafanji, Jour of W African Lang, 95; Phonology at the Interface of Morphology and Phonetics Root-Final Laryngeals in Chong Korean and Sanskrit, Jour of E Asian Ling, 96; Tone Sandhi in Comaltepec Chinantec, Language, 97; Laryngeal complexity in Otomanguean vowels, Phonology, 97. **CONTACT ADDRESS** 212 W Healey #203, Champaign, IL, 81820. **EMAIL** daniel@cogsci.uiuc.edu

SILVERMAN, MALCOLM NOEL
PERSONAL Born 04/18/1946, New York, NY, m, 1974, 2 children **DISCIPLINE** PORTUGUESE & SPANISH LANGUAGES **EDUCATION** Queens Col, NY, BA, 67: Univ Ill, MA, 68, PhD, 71. **CAREER** Asst prof Port & Span, Univ Kans, 70-73, dir jr year abroad, Costa Rica, 73; sr lectr Port, Univ Witwatersrand, 74-75; lectr, 75-77, asst prof, 77-79, assoc prof, 79-82, prof Port & Span, San Diego State Univ, 82-; vis prof Port, Univ Costa Rica, 73. **MEMBERSHIPS** Am Asn Teachers Span & Port. **RESEARCH** Contemporary Brazilian prose fiction; Luso-Brazilian literature; 20th Century Portuguese novel. **SELECTED PUBLICATIONS** Auth, Moderna Ficcao, Brasileira, Vol I, 78 & Vol II, 81, Civilizacao Brasileira/MEC; O Novo Conto Brasileiro, Nova Fronteira; A Satira na Prosa Brasileira Pos-1964, Codecri; Imagens Jornalisticas Brasileiras, McGraw-Hill; Protesto c o Novo Romance Brasileiro, Civilizacao Brasileira. **CONTACT ADDRESS** Dept Span & Port, San Diego State Univ, 5500 Campanile Dr, San Diego, CA, 92182-7703. **EMAIL** silverma@mail.sdsu.edu

SIMMONS, DONALD B.
DISCIPLINE PUBLIC ADDRESS; COMMUNICATION. **EDUCATION** Ohio Univ, PhD, 81. **CAREER** Prof Commun Asbury Col, 81-. **HONORS AND AWARDS** Mem Advisory Coun Documentary Channel, 98. **MEMBERSHIPS** Nat Commun Asn. **RESEARCH** Public speaking; speech criticism. **SELECTED PUBLICATIONS** Auth, The Golden Rule Philosophy of Samuel M. Jones, Proceedings of the Ky Commun Asn, 9/98. **CONTACT ADDRESS** Communication Arts Dept, Asbury Col, 1 Macklem Dr., Wilmore, KY, 40390. **EMAIL** don.simmons@asbury.edu

SIMON, ECKEHARD
PERSONAL Born 01/05/1939, Schneidemuhl, Germany, m, 1959, 4 children **DISCIPLINE** MEDIEVAL GERMAN LITERATURE, PHILOLOGY, CULTURAL HISTORY **EDUCATION** Columbia Col, AB, 60; Harvard Univ, AM, 61, PhD, 64. **CAREER** From Instr to Prof Ger, 64-96, Victor S. Thomas Prof Ger Lang, Harvard Univ, 96-, Chmn Dept Ger Lang & Lit, 76-82, 85-86, 96-99; asst ed, Speculum, J Medieval Studies. **HONORS AND AWARDS** Nat Endowment for Hum younger scholar fel, 69; Guggenheim Mem Found fel, 69; Nat Endowment for Hum fel for Independent study and res, 77; Fulbright sr res grant, Cologne, 83. **MEMBERSHIPS** Medieval Acad Am; MLA; Am Asn Tchr(s). **RESEARCH** Middle High Ger song poetry; Medieval German drama; Editing; codicology. **SELECTED PUBLICATIONS** Auth, Neidhart von Reuental: Geschichte der Forschung und Bibliographie, Harvard Germanic Studies 4, Harvard Univ Press, 68; Neidhart von Reuental, Twayne's World Authors ser, 364, Twayne, G K Hall, 75; The Torkenkalender (1454) Attributed to Gutenberg and the Strasbourg Lunation Tracts, Speculum Anniversary Monographs 16, The Medieval Acad Am, 88; ed, The Theatre of Medieval Europe. New Research in Early Drama, Cambridge Studies in Medieval Lit 9, Cambridge Univ Press, 91; Die Anfunge des weltlichen deutschen Schauspiels, 1370-1520 (in progress); The Carnival of Nuremberg (in progress); author of numerous articles and rev. **CONTACT ADDRESS** Harvard Univ, Barker Ctr 345, Cambridge, MA, 02138-3879. **EMAIL** simon2@fas.harvard.edu

SIMON, ROLAND HENRI
PERSONAL Born 10/07/1940, Haiphong, North Vietnam **DISCIPLINE** LITERARY SEMIOTICS, FRENCH CIVILIZATION **EDUCATION** Univ Wis, MA, 67 Stanford Univ, PhD(French & humanities), 76. **CAREER** Instr French, Middlebury Col, 72-75, dean French sch, 73-76, asst prof, 75-76; Asst Prof French, Univ VA, 76-. **MEMBERSHIPS** MLA; Am Asn Teachers French; NEastern Mod Lang Asn; SAtlantic Mod Lang Asn. **RESEARCH** Theory of literature; autobiography; French civilization. **SELECTED PUBLICATIONS** Auth, The Course Of Fr Hist - Goubert,P/, Fr Rev, Vol 0066, 1993; La 'Lectrice, 6 Characters In Search Of An Author' - Reply/, Fr Rev, Vol 0068, 1994. **CONTACT ADDRESS** Dept of French & Gen Ling, Univ of Va, 1 Cabell Hall, Charlottesville, VA, 22903-3125.

SIMONS, JOHN DONALD
PERSONAL Born 10/05/1935, Lone Oak, TX, m, 1962 **DISCIPLINE** GERMAN & COMPARATIVE LITERATURE **EDUCATION** Univ TX, BA, 59, MA, 6 1; Rice Univ PhD, 66. **CAREER** Instr English, Berlitz Sch Lang, Paris, 59-61; instr Ger, TX Southern Univ, 62-66; asst prof, Univ IA, 66-70; ASSOC PROF GER & COMP LIT, FL STATE UNIV, 70-. **HONORS AND AWARDS** Fulbright Teacher Exchange, Bremen, GER, 87-88. **MEMBERSHIPS** MLA; Am Asn Teachers Ger; AAUP; Int Dostoevsky Soc. **RESEARCH** Eighteenth and 20th century German literature. **SELECTED PUBLICATIONS** Auth, The Nature of Oppression in Don Carlos, Mod Lang Notes, 4/69; Myth of Progress in Schiller and Dostoevsky, Comp lit, 4/72; Hermann Hesse's Steppenwolf. A Critical Commentary, 72, Gunter Grass' The Tin Drum, 73, Thomas Mann's Death in Venice, 74, Dostoevsky's Crime and Punishment, 76 & The Brothers Karamazov, 76, Simon & Schuster; Friedrich Schiller, Twayne, 81; Literature and Film in the Historical Dimension, Univ Press FL, 94; and numerous articles on German literature. **CONTACT ADDRESS** Dept of Mod Lang, Florida State Univ, 600 W College Ave, Tallahassee, FL, 32306-1096. **EMAIL** jsimons@mailer.fsu.edu

SIMPSON, ETHEL C.
PERSONAL Born 07/22/1937, Opelouasas, LA, w, 1959, 2 children **DISCIPLINE** COMPARATIVE LIT **EDUCATION** Univ Arkansas PhD, 77. **CAREER** Univ MD, Instr eng stud, 60-64; Southeastern LA Univ, asst prof eng, 65-69; Univ Arkansas, various, 74-, prof, librarian, hd of arch and manuscripts, special col, 87-. **RESEARCH** Arkansas and regional stud **SELECTED PUBLICATIONS** Simkinsville and Vicinity: Arkansas Stories of Ruth McEnery Stuart, Fayetteville, Univ AR Press, 83; Tulip Evermore: Emma Butler and William Paisley, Their Lives in Letters, 1857-1887, with Eliz Paisley Huckaby, Fayet, Univ AR Press, 85; Arkansas in Short Fiction, with William M Baker, Little Rock, August House, 86; Image and Reflection: Pictorial Hist of Univ AR, Fayet, Univ AR Press, 90; The Selected Letters of John Gould Fletcher, with Leighton Rudolph, Fayet, Univ AR Press, 96. **CONTACT ADDRESS** Univ Arkansas, Special Collections, Mullins Library, Fayetteville, AR, 72701. **EMAIL** csimpson@comp.uark.edu

SIMPSON, MICHAEL
DISCIPLINE CLASSICAL STUDIES **EDUCATION** Yale Univ, PhD, 64. **CAREER** Prof. **SELECTED PUBLICATIONS** Auth, Gods and Heroes of the Greeks: The Library of Apollodorus, Univ Mass, 95; Manners as Morals: Hospitality in the Odyssey, Art Inst, 92; Artistry in Mood: Iliad 3.204-224, Class Jour, 88; Cosmologies and Myths, Charles Scribner's Sons, 88. **CONTACT ADDRESS** Dept of Classics, Richardson, TX, 75083-0688. **EMAIL** msimpson@utdallas.edu

SIMS, EDNA N.
PERSONAL Joliet, IL **DISCIPLINE** ROMANCE LANGUAGES **EDUCATION** Univ Ill, Urbana, BAT, 62, MA, 63; Cath Univ Am, PhD(Romance Lang), 70. **CAREER** Instr Span & French, Howard Univ, 63-69; Prof Span & French, DC Teachers Col, 70-, Vis prof Span, Inter-Am Univ PR, San German, 70; mem foreign lang comt, US Dept Agr Grad Sch, 70-; vis prof Span, Univ Panama, 71. **MEMBERSHIPS** Am Coun Teachers Foreign Lang; Am Asn Teachers Span & Port; Hisp Rev Suc; Col Lang Asn. **RESEARCH** Spanish language; Spanish literature. **SELECTED PUBLICATIONS** Auth, Poet, Mystic, Modern-Hero - Rielopardal,Fernando - Brooks,Zi/, Revista De Estudios Hispanicos, Vol 0026, 1992; Ideas + The Use Of Electronic Equipment In Learning A Foreign-Lang - A Cult Excursion With A Tape-Recorder/, Hispania-A J Devoted To The Teaching Of Spa And Port, Vol 0078, 1995. **CONTACT ADDRESS** Dept of Foreign Lang, Univ of DC, Washington, DC, 20009.

SIMS, ROBERT LEWIS
PERSONAL Born 10/26/1943, Petoskey, MI **DISCIPLINE** FRENCH & SPANISH **EDUCATION** Univ Mich, BA, 66; Univ Wis, MA, 68, PhD(French), 73. **CAREER** Asst prof French & Span, Colby Col, 73-74; asst prof, Pa State Univ, 74-76; Asst Prof French & Span, VA Commonwealth Univ, 76-. **HONORS AND AWARDS** Best Article Award, Am Asn Teachers Span & Port, 77. **MEMBERSHIPS** Am Asn Teachers Fr; Am Asn Teachers Span & Port. **RESEARCH** Twentieth century French literature; myth and novel; modern Latin American novel. **SELECTED PUBLICATIONS** Auth, From Fictional To Factual Narrative, Contemporary Critical Heteroglossia, Garciamarquez,Gabriel Journalism And Bigeneric Writing/, Studies In The Literary Imagination, Vol 0025, 1992. **CONTACT ADDRESS** Dept of Foreign Lang, Va Commonwealth Univ, B0x 2021, Richmond, VA, 23284-9004.

SINGERMAN, ALAN J.
DISCIPLINE FRENCH LANGUAGE AND LITERATURE **EDUCATION** OH Univ, BA, 64; IN Univ, MA, 66; PhD, 70. **CAREER** French, Davidson Col. **HONORS AND AWARDS** Dir, study abroad progs in Pau, Rennes, Montpellier; dir, study abroad progs Paris, Tour 95-96. **RESEARCH** 18th-century French novel and film adaptations. **SELECTED PUBLICATIONS** Auth, articles on French lit and film; monograph on the novels of the Abbe Prevost, L'Abbe Prevost: l'amour et la morale. Droz, 87; ed, crit ed Prevost's Histoire d'une Grecque moderne, Flammarion, 90; Toward A New Integration of Language and Culture, NE Conf Rpts, 88; Acquiring Cross-Cultural Competence: Four Stages For Students of French, Nat Textbook, 96. **CONTACT ADDRESS** Davidson Col, 102 N Main St, PO Box 1719, Davidson, NC, 28036.

SINKA, MARGIT M.
PERSONAL Debrecen, Hungary **DISCIPLINE** GERMAN LITERATURE & LANGUAGE **EDUCATION** Baldwin-Wallace Col, BA, 64; Middlebury Col, MA, 65; Univ NC, Ph-

D(German), 74. **CAREER** Jr instr German, Univ Va, 65-66 St Univ NC, 67-71; instr, Ill State Univ, 66-67; asst prof German & Span, Mars Hill Col, 71-74; asst prof, 74-79, Assoc Prof German & Span, Clemson Univ, 79-, Nat Endowment for Humanities grant, Ind Univ, summer 77 & Fordham Univ, summer 81; Fulbright grant modern cult, Germany, summer 78; Clemson Univ grant medieval lit, summer 79. **MEMBERSHIPS** Am Asn Ger Teachers; SAtlantic Mod Lang Asn; MLA. **RESEARCH** German medieval literature, epics and mysticism; 19th and 20th century German prose, genre studies and symbolism; pedagogy. **SELECTED PUBLICATIONS** Auth, Happiness, Death, And The Moment - Realism And Utopia In The Works Of Wellershoff,Dieter - Ger - Tschierske,U/, Colloquia Germanica, Vol 0025, 1992. **CONTACT ADDRESS** Lang Dept, Clemson Univ, Clemson, SC, 29631.

SIRACUSA, JOSEPH
PERSONAL Born 07/30/1929, Siculiana, Italy **DISCIPLINE** ROMANCE LINGUISTICS **EDUCATION** Univ Rochester, AB, 58; Univ Ill, MA, 59, PhD, 62. **CAREER** Asst prof Span & Ital, Rice Univ, 62-65; assoc prof, Del Mar Col, 65-67; Prof Span & Ital, State Univ NY Col, Brockport, 67-, NDEA lang inst, vis prof Ital ling, Cent Conn State Col, 60 & Span ling, Knox Col, 61, 62; prof, Univ NC, 63; assoc dir & prof Span ling, Rice Univ, 64, 65, vis prof, San Lorenzo de El Escorial, Spain, 67; mem test develop comt, Am Asn Teachers Span & Port Nat Span Exam, 66-76. **RESEARCH** Spanish and Italian historical linguistics; literary relations between Italy and the Hispanic world; Italian dialectology. **SELECTED PUBLICATIONS** Auth, Master The Basics - Italian 2nd Edition - Danesi,M/, Modern Lang J, Vol 0081, 1997. **CONTACT ADDRESS** Dept of Foreign Lang, State Univ of NY, 350 New Campus Dr, Brockport, NY, 14420-2914.

SITTER, JOHN
DISCIPLINE ENGLISH LANGUAGE AND LITERATURE **EDUCATION** Harvard Univ, BA, 66; Univ Minn, PhD, 69. **CAREER** Fac, Univ Mass Amherst; fac, Univ Kent Canterbury; fac, Emory Univ, 80-; Charles Howard Candler Prof, present. **RESEARCH** 18th-century literature; satire and poetry; literary criticism; Restoration literature; contemporary poetry. **SELECTED PUBLICATIONS** Auth, The Poetry of Pope's "Dunciad"; Literary Loneliness in Mid-Eighteenth-Century England; Arguments of Augustan Wit; and articles on Restoration and 18th-century literature and on contemporary poetry. **CONTACT ADDRESS** English Dept, Emory Univ, 1380 Oxford Rd NE, Atlanta, GA, 30322-1950. **EMAIL** engjs@emory.edu

SIVERT, EILEEN
DISCIPLINE FRENCH LITERATURE **EDUCATION** Univ Calif, Riverside, PhD. **CAREER** Instr, Univ Minn, Twin Cities. **RESEARCH** Narrative theory and feminist criticism. **SELECTED PUBLICATIONS** Published on various aspects of 19th-century French writing, on political and labor writings in the 19th century, and on 19th- and 20th century autobiographical writing by women. **CONTACT ADDRESS** Univ Minn, Twin Cities, Minneapolis, MN, 55455.

SJOBERG, ANDREE FRANCES
PERSONAL Born 01/19/1924, Jamaica, NY, m, 1947 **DISCIPLINE** LINGUISTICS **EDUCATION** Univ NMex, BS, 47; Univ Tex, MA, 51, PhD, 57. **CAREER** Spec insts, 60-63, asst prof ling, 63-76, Assoc Prof Orient & African Lang & Lit, Ctr Asian Studies, Univ Tex, Austin, 76-, Grants, US Off Educ & Am Coun Learned Soc, 60-62; Ctr Appl Ling, Washington, DC, fall 62; assoc, Current Anthrop; NDEA-Fulbright-Hays res award, SIndia, 65-66; US Off Educ, 68-69. **MEMBERSHIPS** Ling Soc Am; Am Anthrop Asn; Am Orient Soc; Ling Soc India; Asn Asian Studies. **RESEARCH** Structure of Dravidian languages, especially Telugu; structure of Turkic languages, especially Uzbek; writing systems and literacy. **SELECTED PUBLICATIONS** Auth, Lang Planning And National-Development - The Uzbek Experience - Fierman,W/, Lang In Soc, Vol 0023, 1994. **CONTACT ADDRESS** Ctr for Asian Studies, Univ Tex, 0 Univ of Texas, Austin, TX, 78712-1026.

SKALITZKY, RACHEL IRENE
PERSONAL Born 02/07/1937, Waterloo, WI **DISCIPLINE** COMPARATIVE LITERATURE, MEDIEVAL STUDIES **EDUCATION** Mt Mary Col, BA, 62; Fordham Univ, MA, 66, PhD(class lang & lit), 68. **CAREER** Teacher 6th grade, St Boniface Sch, Milwaukee, 58-62; teacher Latin & music, St Anthony High Sch, Detroit, 62-63; instr classics, Mt Mary Col, 68-69, asst prof & chmn, 69-72; lectr classics, 72-73, asst prof, 73-76, Assoc Prof Comp Lit, Univ WI-Milwaukee, 76-, Coordr Women's Studies, 75-. **MEMBERSHIPS** Am Comp Lit Asn; Am Philol Asn; Nat Women's Studies Asn; MLA; Am Asn Univ Women. **RESEARCH** Classical philology; literary criticism; patristic lit. **SELECTED PUBLICATIONS** Auth, Good wine in a new vase, Horace, Epistles 1.2, Trans & Proc Am Philol Asn, 68; Annianus of Celeda: His Text of Chrysostom's Homilies on Matthew, Aevum, 71; Horace on travel, Epistles 1.11, Class J, 73; Plotinian Echoes in Peri Hypsous 7.2 and 9.7-10, Class Bull, 2/77. **CONTACT ADDRESS** Dept of Comp Lit, Univ of Wisconsin, Po Box 413, Milwaukee, WI, 53201-0413. **EMAIL** rachelsk@uwm.edu

SKITTER, HANS GUNTER
PERSONAL Born 07/26/1936, Bad Kreuznach, Germany, m, 1970, 2 children **DISCIPLINE** GERMAN & AMERICAN LITERATURE **EDUCATION** Univ Freiburg, PhD, 68. **CAREER** Asst teacher Ger, Queen Elizabeth's Sch Girls, London, 59-60; asst English, Univ Freiburg, 64-67; asst prof Ger, Shippensburg State Col, 68-69; asst prof, 69-71, dir jr yr abroad, 70-72, assoc prof Ger, 71-97, PROF AND CHAIR, DEPT OF FOREIGN LANG, MILLERSVILLE UNIV, 98-; Dir Jr Yr Abroad, Marburg, 73-. **MEMBERSHIPS** Am Asn Teachers Ger; MLA; Deut Shakespeare Ges; Nat His Soc. **RESEARCH** Twentieth century German and American literature; language teaching. **SELECTED PUBLICATIONS** Auth, Die drie Letzten Romane F Scott Fitzgeralds, Gouvier, Bonn, 68. **CONTACT ADDRESS** Dept of Foreign Lang, Millersville Univ, Pennsylvania, PO Box 1002, Millersville, PA, 17551-0302.

SKLAR, ROBERT ANTHONY
PERSONAL Born 12/03/1936, New Brunswick, NJ, m, 1958, 2 children **DISCIPLINE** CINEMA STUDIES, CULTURAL HISTORY **EDUCATION** Princeton Univ, AB, 58; Harvard Univ, PhD, 65. **CAREER** From asst prof to prof hist, Univ Mich, Ann Arbor, 65-76; PROF CINEMA STUDIES & CHMN DEPT, NY UNIV, 77-, Rackham fel, 67; Fulbright lectr, USEC, Japan, 71; distinguished vis prof, Bard Col, 75-76; Rockefeller Found humanities fel, 76-77; contribr ed, Am Film Mag, 77-. **HONORS AND AWARDS** Theatre Libr Asn Award, 75. **MEMBERSHIPS** Am Studies Asn (vpres, 71); Soc Cinema Studies; Nat Film Preserv Bd; New York Film Fest Selec Cmt; Mich Am Stu Asn; ed bd, Am Qrt. **RESEARCH** American movies and television; twentieth century American culture and society. **SELECTED PUBLICATIONS** Auth, F Scott Fitzgerald, Oxford Univ, 67; ed, The Plastic Age: 1917-1930, Braziller, 70; auth, Movie-Made America: A Cultural History of American Movies, Random House, 75; auth, Prime Time America: Life On and Behind the Television Screen, Random House, 82; co-ed, Resisting Images: Essays on Cinema and History, Temple Univ, 90; auth, City Boys: Cagney, Bogart, Garfield, Princeton Univ, 92; auth, Film: An International History of the Medium, Prentice Hall, 93; auth, Movie-Made AmericaL A Cultural History of American Movies, Vintage Bks, 94; co-ed, Frank Capra: Authorship and the Studio System, Temple Univ, 98. **CONTACT ADDRESS** Dept of Cinema Studies, New York Univ, 721 Broadway, Rm 600, New York, NY, 10003-6807. **EMAIL** rs9@is2.nyu.edu

SKOUSEN, ROYAL JON
PERSONAL Born 08/05/1945, Cleveland, OH, m, 1968, 7 children **DISCIPLINE** LINGUISTICS **EDUCATION** Brigham Young Univ, BA, 69; Univ Ill, Urbana, MA, 71, PhD, 72. **CAREER** Prof ling, Univ Tex, Austin, 72-79; Prof English, Brigham Young Univ, 79-; Vis prof, Univ Calif, San Diego, 81; Fulbright lectr, Univ Tampere, Finland, 82. **HONORS AND AWARDS** Barker lectureship, BYU, 85-86. **MEMBERSHIPS** Int Soc Quantitative Ling; Nat Asn Schol; Asn Lit Schol and Critics. **RESEARCH** Linguistics; textual criticism; analogical modeling of language. **SELECTED PUBLICATIONS** Auth, On capturing regularities, Papers Eighth Regional Meeting Chicago Ling Soc, 72; On limiting the number of phonological descriptions, Glossa (vol 7), 73; An explanatory theory of morphology, Papers Chicago Ling Soc, 74; Substantive Evidence in Phonology, Mouton, 75; On the nature of morphophoemic alternation, TG Paradigm & Mod Ling Theory, John Benjamins, 75; Empirical restrictions on the power of transformational grammars, in Formal Aspects of Cognitive Processes, Springer, 75; Analogical sources of abstractness, Phonology in the 1970's, Story-Scientia, 81; English spelling and phonemic representation, Visible Language, 82; Analogical Modeling of Language, Kluwer, 89; Analogy and Structure, Kluwer, 92; The Book of Mormon: The Original Manuscript (in press); The Book of Mormon: The Printer's Manuscript (in press). **CONTACT ADDRESS** Col Humanities, Brigham Young Univ, 2054 JKHB, Provo, UT, 84602. **EMAIL** royal_skousen@byu.edu

SKRUPSKELIS, VIKTORIA
PERSONAL Born 12/01/1935, Kaunas, Lithuania **DISCIPLINE** ROMANCE LANGUAGES, FRENCH **EDUCATION** St Joseph Col, Conn, BA, 55; Fordham Univ, MA, 59; Univ Ill, PhD(French), 66. **CAREER** Instr French, Univ Ill, 62-63; asst prof, Univ Chicago, 63-67; asst prof, 67-76, Assoc Prof French, Oberlin Col, 76- **SELECTED PUBLICATIONS** Auth, 'Come Into My Time' - Lithuania In Prose-Fiction, 1970-90 - Kelertas,V/, World Lit Today, Vol 0067, 1993. **CONTACT ADDRESS** Dept of Romance Lang, Oberlin Col, Oberlin, OH, 44074.

SLADE, CAROLE
PERSONAL CA **DISCIPLINE** COMPARATIVE LITERATURE, ENGLISH **EDUCATION** Pomona Col, BA, 65; Univ Wis, MA, 66; New York Univ, PhD(comp lit), 73. **CAREER** Lectr English, Bronx Community Col, City Univ New York, 71-74, asst prof, 74-78; asst prof, Baylor Univ, 78-80; Asst Prof English & Comp Lit, Columbia Univ, 80- **MEMBERSHIPS** MLA; Northeast Mod Lang Asn; Am Comp Lit Asn; Dante Soc Am; NCTE. **SELECTED PUBLICATIONS** Auth, Body And Soul - Essays On Medieval Women And Mysticism - Petroff,Ea/, Rel & Lit, Vol 0027, 1995; Kempe,Margery Dissenting Fictions - Staley,L/, Rel & Lit, Vol 0027, 1995; Julian-Of-Norwich 'Showings' - From Vision To Book - Baker,Dn/, Rel & Lit, Vol 0027, 1995; From Madrid To Purgatory - The Art And Craft Of Dying In 16th-Century Spain - Eire,Cmn/, J Of Rel, Vol 0077, 1997. **CONTACT ADDRESS** Dept of English, Columbia Univ, New York, NY, 10027.

SLAGLE, JUDITH BAILY
PERSONAL Born 11/20/1949, Kingsport, TN, m, 1969 **DISCIPLINE** CLASSICAL LITERATURE **EDUCATION** East Tenn State Univ, MA, 85; Univ Tenn, PhD, 91. **CAREER** Asst Prof, Middle Tenn State Univ, 93-97; Chr Humanities, Roane State Col, 97-. **HONORS AND AWARDS** Honorary Research Fel, Univ of Edinburgh Inst for Advanced Studies in the Humanities, 96. **MEMBERSHIPS** Amer Soc for Eighteenth Century Studies; Eighteenth Century Scottish Studies Soc. **RESEARCH** Thomas Shadwell (Restoration Dramatist); Joanna Baillie (Scottish playwright) **SELECTED PUBLICATIONS** Auth, The Collected Letters of Joanna Baillie, 99. **CONTACT ADDRESS** 907 Pintail Rd, Knoxville, TN, 37922. **EMAIL** slagle_jb@a1.rscc.cc.tn.us

SLATKIN, LAURA M.
DISCIPLINE CLASSICAL PHILOLOGY **EDUCATION** Radcliffe Col, BA, 68; Cambridge Univ, MA, 70; Harvard Univ, PhD, 79. **CAREER** Asst prof, Univ Calif, 76-80; Vis Asst Prof, Yale Univ, 80-81; Lectr, Columbia Univ, 81-83; Asst prof to Assoc prof, Columbia Univ, Colubia Univ, 83-90; Assoc prof, Univ Chicago, 93- . **HONORS AND AWARDS** NEH Fel; Columbia Univ Coun Res Hum Fel; Mellon Fel; ACLS Fel; Am Asn Univ Women Fel. **SELECTED PUBLICATIONS** Auth, Oedipus at Colonus: Exile and Integration, Univ Calif Press, 86; The Wrath of Thetis, TAPA, 86; Genre and Generation in the Odyssey, METIS, 87; Univ Calif Press, 92; auth, The Power of Thetis: Allusion and Interpretation in the Iliad, Univ Calif Press, 92; auth, Myth in Homer, Leiden, 95; Composition by Theme and the Metis of the Odyssey, Princeton Univ Press, 96; auth, the Poetics of Exchange in the Iliad, The Iliad and Its Contexts, 97; auth, Measure and mortality in Hesiod's Works and Days, Metis, 97. **CONTACT ADDRESS** Dept of Classics, Univ Chicago, 1050 E 59th St, Chicago, IL, 60637.

SLAVUTYCH, YAR
PERSONAL Born 01/11/1918, Blahodatne, Ukraine **DISCIPLINE** UKRAINIAN LANGUAGE & LITERATURE **EDUCATION** Pedagogic Inst Zaporizhia, dipl 40; Univ Pa, MA, 54, PhD, 55. **CAREER** Sr instr, US Army Lang Sch, 55-60; asst prof to prof, 60-83, PROF EMER, UNIV ALTA, 83-; mgr, Slavuta Publs, 60-. **HONORS AND AWARDS** Ukrainian Poet Laureate Abroad; Shevchenko Gold Medal; Can Coun res award; Ukrainian Can Centennial Medal. **MEMBERSHIPS** Can Soc Stud Names; Ukrainian Shakespeare Soc; W Can br, Shevchenko Sci Soc. **SELECTED PUBLICATIONS** Auth, Conversational Ukrainian, 59, 5th ed, 87; auth, Ukrainian for Beginners, 62, 8th ed, 93; auth, Zhyvi smoloskypy, 83, 2nd ed, 92; auth, Standard Ukrainian Grammar, 87, 2nd ed, 90; auth, Ukrains'ka literatura v Kanadi, 92; auth, Rozstriliana muza, 92; auth, Shabli topol, 92; auth, Tvory v dvokh tomakh, 94; auth, Tvory v piaty tomakh, 98; comp & ed, Collected Papers on Ukrainian Settlers in Western Canada, 2 vols, 73, 75; comp & ed, An Annotated Bibliography of Ukrainian Literature in Canada, 84, 86, 87; comp & ed, Ukrainian Shakespeariana in the West, 2 vols, 87, 90; bibliogr, MLA Int Bibliog, 68-. **CONTACT ADDRESS** 72 Westbrook Dr, Edmonton, AB, T6J 2E1.

SLAWEK, STEPHEN
DISCIPLINE MUSIC AND ASIAN STUDIES **EDUCATION** Univ IL at Urbana-Champaign, PhD. **CAREER** Assoc prof & div & head; Univ TX at Austin, 83-; dir, N Indian Class Music Ensemble. **RESEARCH** Musical traditions of South Asia. **SELECTED PUBLICATIONS** Auth, Sitar Technique in Nibaddh Forms, Delhi, Motilal Banarsidass, 87; coauth, Musical Instruments of North India: Eighteenth century Portraits by Baltazard Solvyns, Delhi, Manohar Publ, 97. **CONTACT ADDRESS** School of Music, Univ of Texas at Austin, 2613 Wichita St, Austin, TX, 78705.

SLOANE, DAVID A.
PERSONAL Born 01/29/1946, New York, NY, m, 1968, 1 child **DISCIPLINE** RUSSIAN LITERATURE AND LANGUAGE **EDUCATION** Williams Coll, BA, 68; Harvard Univ, MA, 73, PhD, 79. **CAREER** Instr, Williams Coll, 69-71; instr, Middlebury Coll, summers 73-76, 90-91; asst prof to assoc prof, Tufts Univ, 79- **MEMBERSHIPS** Amer Assn Teachers Slavic and East European Languages; Amer Assn Advancement Slavic Studies; New England Slavic Assn; Assn Literary Scholars and Critics. **RESEARCH** Russian poetry; Tolstoy; Aleksandr Blok. **SELECTED PUBLICATIONS** Auth, "The Dynamics of Space and Time in Karolina Pavlova's Lyric Cycle Phantamagories," Russian Literature, Oct 93; auth, "The Linkage of Time: Problems of Continuity in Russian Literature at the End of the 19- Beginning of the 20th Centuries," Slavic Review, vol 54, no 3, 95; auth, "The Poetry in War and Peace," Slavic and East European Journal, spring 96; auth, book review, Tolstoy and the Genesis of War and Peace, Tolstoy Studies Journal, vol 9, 97; auth, "Aleksandr Blok," The Encyclopedia of the Essay,

97. **CONTACT ADDRESS** Dept of German, Russian and Asian Languages, Tufts Univ, Medford, MA, 02155. **EMAIL** dsloane@emerald.tufts.edu

SLOBIN, DAN ISAAC
PERSONAL Born 05/07/1939, Detroit, MI, d, 2 children **DISCIPLINE** PSYCHOLINGUISTICS **EDUCATION** Univ Mich, Ann Arbor, BA, 60; Harvard Univ, MA, 62, PhD(social psychol), 64. **CAREER** From asst prof to assoc prof, 64-72, Prof Psychol, Univ Calif, Berkeley, 72- ; res psychologist, Inst of Cognitive Stud and Inst of Human Develop; mem, 90- , chemn, 94- , Sci Council Max-Planck-Inst for Psycholinguistics. **HONORS AND AWARDS** Ed, Soviet Psychol, 62-70; mem comt on cognition, Soc Sci Res Coun, 71-75; Guggenheim fel, 84-85; NY Acad Sci award in behavioral sci, 86. **MEMBERSHIPS** Asn for Ling Typology; Int Asn of Cross-Cultural Psychol; Int Asn for Study of Child Lang; Int Cognitive Ling Asn; Ling Soc of Am; Int Pragmatics Asn; Soc for Study of Child Development; Turkish Stud Asn.. **RESEARCH** Language and cognitive development in the child; linguistics; sign language. **SELECTED PUBLICATIONS** Auth, Psycholinguistics, Scott, Foresman, 71, 2nd ed, 79; auth, Cognitive Prerequisites for the Development of Grammar, in, Ferguson, ed, Studies of Child Language Development, Holt, Rinehart & Winston, 73; auth, Crosslinguistic Evidence for the Language-Making Capacity, in Slobin, ed, The Crosslinguistic Study of Language Acquisition, vol, 2, Lawrence Erlbaum, 85; coauth, Relating Events in narrative: A Crosslinguistic Developmental Study, Lawrence Erlbaum, 94; coauth, Reference to Movement in Spoken and Signed Languages: Typological Considerations, Proc of Twentieth Annual Meeting of the Berkeley Ling Soc, 94; auth, From Thought and Language to Thinking for Speaking, in Gumperz, ed, Rethinking Linguistic Relativity, Cambridge, 96. **CONTACT ADDRESS** Dept of Psychology, Univ of Calif, 3210 Tolman Hall, Berkeley, CA, 94720-1650. **EMAIL** slobin@cogsci.berkeley.edu

SLOTKIN, ALAN ROBERT
PERSONAL Born 11/07/1943, Brooklyn, NY **DISCIPLINE** ENGLISH LINGUISTICS, AMERICAN LITERATURE **EDUCATION** Univ Miami, AB, 65; Univ SC, MA, 70, PhD(English), 71. **CAREER** Asst prof, 70-80, Assoc Prof English, Tenn Technol Univ, 80-, Ed, Tenn Ling. **MEMBERSHIPS** Am Dialect Soc; Ling Soc Am; Southeastern Conf Ling; SAtlantic Mod Lang Asn. **RESEARCH** American dialects; American dialect literature; modern drama. **SELECTED PUBLICATIONS** Auth, A Back-To-The-Future-Formation Plus Back-Formation And The Etymology Of Contraption/, Am Speech, Vol 0068, 1993; Improvography + Dance Terminology - A Contradiction In Terms/, Am Speech, Vol 0068, 1993; 2 New Obscenities, The Acceptability Of Taboo Words In The Media/, Am Speech, Vol 0069, 1994. **CONTACT ADDRESS** Dept English, Tenn Technol Univ, Cookville, TN, 38501.

SMEDICK, LOIS KATHERINE
DISCIPLINE ENGLISH LANGUAGE; LITERATURE **EDUCATION** Wilson, BA; Toronto, MSL; Bryn Mawr, PhD,-63. **CAREER** Prof **RESEARCH** Chaucer and his contemporaries; chivalric romance; and Middle English prose style. **SELECTED PUBLICATIONS** Pub (s), medieval devotional prose; Form of Living of Richard Rolle; Latin stylistic device, the cursus. **CONTACT ADDRESS** Dept of English Language and Literature, Univ of Windsor, 401 Sunset Ave, Windsor, ON, N9B 3P4. **EMAIL** smedick@uwindsor.ca

SMITH, BARDWELL L.
DISCIPLINE RELIGIOUS TRADITIONS OF ASIA **EDUCATION** Yale Univ, BA, BD, PhD. **CAREER** Religion, Carleton Univ. **SELECTED PUBLICATIONS** Auth, Ed, The City as a Sacred Complex, 87, Warlords, Artists; Commoners: Japan in the Sixteenth Century. **CONTACT ADDRESS** Carleton Col, 100 S College St., Northfield, MN, 55057-4016.

SMITH, CARLOTA S.
PERSONAL Born 05/21/1934, New York, NY, d, 2 children **DISCIPLINE** LINGUISTICS, PSYCHOLINGUISTICS **EDUCATION** Radcliffe Col, BA, 55; Univ Pa, MA, 62; PhD(ling), 67. **CAREER** Res asst ling, Univ Pa, 59-60 & 61-63 & Mass Inst Technol, 60-61; asst prof English, Univ Pa, 67-69; fac assoc ling, 69-71, asst prof, 71-72, assoc prof, 73-80, Prof & Chmn Ling, Univ Tex, Austin, 80- **MEMBERSHIPS** Ling Soc Am; Int Ling Asn. **RESEARCH** Syntax and semantics; language acquisition; text structure. **SELECTED PUBLICATIONS** Auth, Aspectual Viewpoint And Situation Type In Mandarian Chinese/, J Of E Asian Linguistics, Vol 0003, 1994. **CONTACT ADDRESS** Dept Ling, Univ Tex, 0 Univ of Texas, Austin, TX, 78712-1026.

SMITH, DAVID RICHARD
PERSONAL Born 04/24/1942, Jersey City, NJ, m, 1989, 5 children **DISCIPLINE** CLASSICAL STUDIES **EDUCATION** David Lipscomb Col, BA, 64; Vanderbilt Univ, MA, 66; Univ PA, PhD(class studies), 68. **CAREER** Asst prof classics, Univ CA, Riverside, 68-70; asst prof, 70-75, assoc prof, 75-80, prof hist, CA State Polytech Univ Pomona, 80-; assoc ed, Helios J Class Asn Southwest, 75-77. **MEMBERSHIPS** Class Asn Southwest; Am Philol Asn; AHA; WHA. **RESEARCH** Greek history, religion and philosophy of history; world history and teaching methodologies. **SELECTED PUBLICATIONS** Auth, Hieropoioi and Hierothytai on Rhodes, L'Antiquite Classique, 72; The Hieropoioi on Kos, Numen, 73; The Coan Festival of Zeus Polieus, Class J, 10/73; Review of G S Kirk, Myth: Its Meaning and Function in Ancient and Other Cultures, Helios, 5/76; The Poetic Focus in Horace, Odes 3.13, Latomus, 76; Teaching Religion in the Medieval Period, World Hist Bull, 90-91; Teaching and Assessing the Doing World History Method in the World History Survey, Aspen World Hist Handbook, vol 2, 97; Technology in the World History Survey, Aspen World Hist Handbook, vol 2, 97. **CONTACT ADDRESS** Dept Hist, California State Polytech Univ, 3801 W Temple Ave, Pomona, CA, 91768-4001. **EMAIL** drsmith2@csupomona.edu

SMITH, DAVID W.
PERSONAL Born 11/14/1932, Loughborough, England **DISCIPLINE** FRENCH **EDUCATION** Univ Leeds, BA, 53, PhD, 61. **CAREER** Asst prof, Memorial Univ Nfld, 60-63; asst prof, 63-67, assoc prof, 67-71, PROF FRENCH, VICTORIA UNIV IN UNIV TORONTO, 71-. **HONORS AND AWARDS** Killam res fel, 80-81; Connaught res fel, 85-86; Guggenheim res fel, 86-87. **MEMBERSHIPS** Can Soc 18th Century Stud (founder & 1st pres); Int Soc 18th Century Stud (vice pres, 87-95). **SELECTED PUBLICATIONS** Auth, Helvetius: A Study in Persecution, 65, repr 82; ed, Helvetius Correspondance generale, vol I 81, vol II 84, vol III 91, vol IV 98; transl, The American Dream in Nineteenth Century Quebec, 96; adv comt ed, Voltaire's Complete Works; ed bd, Studies on Voltaire. **CONTACT ADDRESS** Victoria Univ, Univ of Toronto, Toronto, ON, M5S 1K7.

SMITH, DIANE E.
PERSONAL Born 02/27/1959, Grand Rapids, MI, m, 1981, 4 children **DISCIPLINE** CLASSICS, LATIN **EDUCATION** Villanova Univ, MA 86; Univ of Michigan, BA, 80; Richmond Coll, 76-77; Intercollegiate Center for Classical Stud, Rome, 79-80; Amer School of Classical Stud, Athens, 82. **CAREER** Tchr, 86-88, School of the Holy Child, Rye NY; Scholar and Typesetter, in Greek, Latin, Linguistics and Modern Lang, 88-, Teacher, 87-, Waco Christian Sem, Waco, TX. **HONORS AND AWARDS** Graduate Fellowship, Villanova Univ. **MEMBERSHIPS** Classical Assoc of Midwest and South; Amer Classical League. **SELECTED PUBLICATIONS** Typesetting in the following; Bolchazy-Carducci, Schemling, Gareth and Jon D. Mikalson, eds, Qui Miscuit Utile Dulci, Festschrift Essays for Paul Lachlan MacKendrick, 98; L & L Enterprises/Bolchazy-Carducci, DuBose, Gaylan, Farrago, 97; Franz Steiner Verlag, Linderski, J., Ed, Imperium Sine Fine, Festschrift for T.R.S. Broughton, Historia-Einzelschrift, 105, 96; Rowmand and Littlefield, Edmunds, Lowell, Oedipus at Colonus, 96; Oxford University Press, Battye, Adriand and Ian Roberts, eds, Clause Structure and Language Change, 95; Longman Publishing Group, Davis, Sally, Review and Test Preparation Guide for the beginning Latin Student, 94. **CONTACT ADDRESS** 5801 Fairview Dr, Waco, TX, 76710.

SMITH, GAYLE LEPPIN
PERSONAL Born 07/05/1946, New York, NY **DISCIPLINE** AMERICAN LITERATURE, STYLISTICS **EDUCATION** Univ Denver, BA, 68; Univ Mass, MA, 72, PhD(English), 77. **CAREER** Teaching asst compos, Univ Mass, 68-70, instr Am lit, 72 & 73; instr lang & lit, Holyoke Community Col, 75; ASST PROF ENGLISH, PA STATE UNIV, 77- **MEMBERSHIPS** MLA; NCTE; Conf Col Compos & Commun; Northeast Mod Lang Asn. **RESEARCH** Emerson studies; style studies; composition and rhetoric. **SELECTED PUBLICATIONS** Auth, Transformational theory and developmental compositon, Exercise Exchange, spring 80; When students grade themselves: What we teach and what we learn, Pa Coun Teachers English Bull, 5/81; Style and vision in Emerson's experience, ESQ: J Am Renaissance, spring 81; The language of transcendence in S O Jewett's A White Heron, Colby Libr Quart (in prep); From graveyard to classroom: Thinking about data, Teaching English Two-Yr Col; contribr, Revising: New Essays for Writing Teachers, NCTE; Reading Song Of Myself--Assuming What Whitman Assumes, Am Transcendental Quart, Vol 06, 92. **CONTACT ADDRESS** Dept of English, Pennsylvania State Univ, 120 Ridgeview Dr, Dunmore, PA, 18512-1602.

SMITH, KAREN A.
PERSONAL Born 11/30/1965, Brooklyn, NY, s **DISCIPLINE** SPEECH COMMUNICATION **EDUCATION** CUNY, BA, 89; SUNY, MA, 92; S IL Univ, Carbondale, Speech Commun, 96 **CAREER** Lect, 96-97, SIU-Carbondale; Asst Prof, 97-, Col of St Rose **MEMBERSHIPS** Nat Commun Asn **RESEARCH** Methods, Critical Pedagogy **CONTACT ADDRESS** Col of Saint Rose, Albany, NY, 12203. **EMAIL** ksmith@rosnet.strose.edu

SMITH, NIGEL
DISCIPLINE FRENCH LITERATURE **EDUCATION** Univ NC Chapel Hill, MA, PhD. **RESEARCH** Romanticism; fantastic literature; gender studies. **SELECTED PUBLICATIONS** Auth, pubs on nineteenth and seventeenth century French literature. **CONTACT ADDRESS** Dept Foreign Languages and Literature, State Univ of West Georgia, Carrollton, GA, 30118.

SMITH, RICHARD J.
DISCIPLINE HISTORY, CHINESE CULTURE **EDUCATION** Univ CA, Davis, PhD, 72. **CAREER** Master, Hanszen Col, 82-87; adj prof, Univ TX, Austin; prof, 73-, dir, Asian Stud, Rice Univ. **HONORS AND AWARDS** Piper Professorship, 87; George R. Brown Cert of Highest Merit, 92; Sarofim Distinguished Tchg Professorship, 94-96; Nicolas Salgo Distinguished Tchg Prize, 96. **MEMBERSHIPS** Pres, TX Found for China Stud; pres, Southwest Conf of the Asn for Asian Stud. **RESEARCH** Contemp Chinese cult. **SELECTED PUBLICATIONS** Auth, China's Cultural Heritage: The Qing Dynasty, 1644-1912, 83; Fortune-tellers and Philosophers: Divination in Traditional Chinese Society, 91; Chinese Almanacs, 92; Chinese Maps: Images of All Under Heaven, 96; coauth, Robert Hart and China's Early Modernization, 91; H.B. Morse, Customs Commissioner and Historian of China, 95; coed, Cosmology, Ontology, and Human Efficacy: Essays in Chinese Thought, 93. **CONTACT ADDRESS** Rice Univ, PO Box 1892, Houston, TX, 77251-1892. **EMAIL** smithrj@ruf.rice.edu

SMITH, RILEY BLAKE
PERSONAL Born 07/07/1930, Mexico, MO **DISCIPLINE** ENGLISH, LINGUISTICS **EDUCATION** Univ Tex, Austin, BA, 58, PhD, 73. **CAREER** Asst prof English, Tex A&M Univ, 68-70; actg asst prof, Univ Calif, Los Angeles, 70-72; lectr Anglistics, Univ Duisburg, Ger, 74-76 & Univ Wuppertal, Ger, 76-77; asst prof, 77-81, Assoc Prof English, Bloomsburg Univ, 81-; Fulbright lectr, Leningrad Polytech Inst, USSR, 81. **HONORS AND AWARDS** Nat Endowment for Humanities fel, summer sem, Univ Pa, 80; Fulbright Grantee, USSR, 81. **MEMBERSHIPS** Ling Soc Am; Am Dialect Soc; Teachers English to Speakers Other Lang; Ling Asn Can & US; Int Sociol Asn. **RESEARCH** American dialects; language attitudes; language policy. **SELECTED PUBLICATIONS** Auth, Interrelatedness of certain deviant grammatical structures of Negro nonstandard dialects, 3/69 & Hyperformation and basilect reconstruction, 3/74, J English Ling; Black English: Books for English education, English educ, 4-5/75; Research perspectives on American Black English: A brief historical sketch, Am Speech, 76; Interference in phonological research in nonstandard dialects: its implication for teaching, In: Soziolinguistik, Hochschulverlag, Stuttgart, 78; coauth, Standard and disparate varieties of English in the United States: Educational and sociopolitical implications, Int J Sociol Lang, 79. **CONTACT ADDRESS** Dept of English, Bloomsburg Univ of Pennsylvania, 400 E 2nd St, Bloomsburg, PA, 17815-1399.

SMITH, ROBERT P., JR.
PERSONAL Born 10/12/1923, New Orleans, Louisiana, m, 1954 **DISCIPLINE** LANGUAGES **EDUCATION** Howard Univ, BA 1948; Univ of Chicago, MA 1950; DEU Univ of Bordeaux, France l953; Univ of PA, PhD 1969. **CAREER** Talladega Coll, instructor French Spanish German 1953-54; Fisk Univ, asst prof French & Spanish 1954-58; Rutgers Univ, instructor, asst prof, assoc prof, chmn of French Dept 1965-73; assoc dean for academic affairs 1973-79; full prof 1984-89; emeritus l987-. **HONORS AND AWARDS** Fulbright Fellowship to France DEU CEF Universite de Bordeaux France 1952-53; John Hay Whitney Found Fellowship 1958-59; NEH Summer Grant l981. **MEMBERSHIPS** Mem Alpha Phi Alpha, Amer Assn of Univ Profs, Amer Assn of Teachers of French, Mod Lang Assn, African Lit Assoc; published articles in French Review, College Lang Assn Journal, Langston Hughes Review, Le Petit Courier, Celacef Bulletin, World Literature Today, Celfan Review; treasurer, College Language Assn, 1986-.

SMITH, ROCH CHARLES
PERSONAL Born 04/01/1941, Sturgeon Falls, ON, Canada, m, 1962, 3 children **DISCIPLINE** FRENCH LITERATURE, SPANISH **EDUCATION** Univ Fla, AB, 62, MAT, 65; Emory Univ, MA, 70, PhD, 71. **CAREER** Instr French & Span, Palm Beach Com Col, 65-67, teaching assoc French, Emory Univ, 69-70; from lectr to assoc prof Romance lang, 70-82, assoc prof Romance Lang, Univ NC, Greensboro, 82-, head, Dept Romance Lang, Univ NC, Greensboro, 81-85, assoc Dean, Col of Arts and Sciences, 85-87, assoc Vice-Chancellor, Academic Affairs, 88-90. **MEMBERSHIPS** MLA; Am Asn Teachers Fr; SAtlantic Mod Lang Asn; Malraux Soc; New Novel Assoc. **RESEARCH** Andre Malraux; Gaston Bachelard; Alain Robbe-Grillet. **SELECTED PUBLICATIONS** Auth, Le Meurtrier et la vision tragique: Essai sur les romans d'Andre Malraux, Didier, 75; Orphic Motifs in Malraux's last novels, 76 & Gaston Bachelard and the Power of Poetic Being, 77, Fr Lit Ser; Malraux's Miroir des Limbes and the Orphic Temptation, Symp, 78; French Canadian Literature: A Not-So-Anonymous Impertinence, Sci, Technol & Humanities, 79; Gaston Bachelard, Critical Bibliog Fr Lit, 80; Gaston Bachelard and Critical Discourse: The Philosopher of Science as Reader, Stanford Fr Rev, 81; Gaston Bachelard, Twayne, 82. Auth, Tchen's Sacred Isolation: Preludr to Malroux's Fraternal Humanism, Twentieth Century Lit, 82; Naming the M/inotaur: Beckett's Trilogy and the Clown of Illusion in the Trilogy, Philological Papers, 83; Bachelard's Logosphere and Derrida'a Logocentrism: Is There a Difference?, French Forum, 85; Generating the Erotic Dream Machine: Robbe-Grillet's L'Eden et Apres and La Belle Captive, French Review, 90; Open Narrative in Robbe-Grillet's Glissements progressifs du plaisir and Wim Weuders' Paris, Texas, Lit/Film Quart, 95; The Erotic Dream Machine: Inter-

views with Alain Robbe-Grillet on his Films, Southern Ill Univ Press, 92, 95; The Image as Generative Narrator in L'Annee derniere a Marienbad amd L'Immortelle, New Novel Review, 96; Gaston Bachelard, The Encyclopedia of Aesthetics, 98. **CONTACT ADDRESS** Dept of Romance Lang, Univ of N. Carolina at Greensboro, Greensboro, NC, 27402-6170. **EMAIL** rcsmith2@hamlet.uncg.edu

SMITH, VONCILE MARSHALL
PERSONAL Born 03/17/1931, Ft Myers, FL, m, 1951, 5 children **DISCIPLINE** SPEECH COMMUNICATION, COMMUNICATION THEORY **EDUCATION** Univ Fla, BAEd, 60, MA, 64, PhD(speech), 66. **CAREER** Asst prof speech, 60-70, assoc prof, 70-78, prof Commun, Fla Atlantic Univ, 78-, Chm Dept Commun, 73-82, 94-98, ed, Fla Speech Commun J, 78-81; ed, J Int Listening Asn, 86-88. **HONORS AND AWARDS** Phi Kappa Phi. **MEMBERSHIPS** Nat Commun Asn; Southern States Commun Asn; Asn for Commun Admin; Fla Commun Asn. **RESEARCH** Studies in listening; interpersonal communication; communication theory. **SELECTED PUBLICATIONS** Coauth, Communication for Health Professionals, Lippincott, 79. **CONTACT ADDRESS** Dept of Commun, Col of Arts and Letters, Florida Atlantic Univ, PO Box 3091, Boca Raton, FL, 33431-0991. **EMAIL** vsmith@acc.fau.edu

SMITH MCKOY, SHEILA
DISCIPLINE AMERICAN LITERATURE, AFRICAN LITERATURE, AFRICAN-AMERICAN LITERATURE, AFRO- **EDUCATION** Duke Univ, PhD. **CAREER** Instr, Vanderbilt Univ. **RESEARCH** South African literature and culture; diaspora oral traditions. **SELECTED PUBLICATIONS** Contribu, Oxford Companion to Women's Writing in the United States. **CONTACT ADDRESS** Vanderbilt Univ, Nashville, TN, 37203-1727.

SMITH-SOTO, MARK
PERSONAL Born 05/29/1948, Washington, DC, m **DISCIPLINE** FOREIGN LANGUAGES **EDUCATION** Univ Md, BA, 70; Univ Calif at Berkeley, MA, 72, PhD, 75. **CAREER** Teach asst, Univ Calif, Berkeley, 74; instr of Spanish to asst prof to assoc prof to PROF, SPANISH, 75-, head, dept of Romance Languages, 86-94, UNIV NC, GREENSBORO. **HONORS AND AWARDS** Danforth fel, 70-74; Woodrow Wilson fel, 70; Acad Am Poets Prize, Univ Calif at Berkeley, Hon Men, 72; Nimrod Pablo Neruda Poetry Competition, Finalist, 86; Plum Review Int Poetry Contest, Finalist, 95; Salmon Run Press Nat Poetry Bk Award, Finalist and Hon Men, 96; Randall Jarrell Poetry Contest, finalist, 97; Univ NC, Greensboro's Sen Alumni Teach Excellence Award, 97. **MEMBERSHIPS** NC Writers' Network; NC Poetry Soc; Mod Lang Asn; Asoc Int de Hispanistas. **RESEARCH** Spanish-American modernismo; 19th and 20th -century Spanish- American poetry. **SELECTED PUBLICATIONS** Auth, Jose Asuncion Silva: contexto y estructura de su obra, Editorial Tercer Mundo, 81; auth, "See It on Video," The Sun 232, 95; "Latino," The Plum Review 9, 96; "My Tongue Finds Itself," The Sun, 96; "The Parting," Poetry East 42, 96; "Why I am Afraid of Physical Harm," and "Frieze," The Chattahoocheee Rev XVI, 4, 96; "Caf of Mirrors," Q West, 97; "How It Happened," The Sun, 98; "Jose Asuncion Silva y el 'sadismo intelectual," Thesaurus, XLIX, 98. **CONTACT ADDRESS** Dept of Romance Languages, Univ N. Carolina, Greensboro, Greensboro, NC, 27402-6170. **EMAIL** smithsom@uncg.edu

SNAPPER, JOHAN PIETER
PERSONAL Born 06/04/1935, Naaldwijk, Netherlands, m, 1959, 3 children **DISCIPLINE** GERMANIC LANGUAGES **EDUCATION** Calvin Col, BA, 58; Univ Chicago, MA, 62; Univ Calif, Los Angeles, PhD(Ger), 67. **CAREER** Instr Ger, Univ Calif, Los Angeles, 64-66; asst prof Ger & Dutch, 66-73, Princess Beatrix prof Dutch lang, lit & cult, 71, assoc prof, 73-82, Queen Beatrix Prof Ger & Dutch, Univ Calif, Berkeley, 82-, Dir Dutch Studies, 73- **MEMBERSHIPS** MLA; Philol Asn Pac Coast; Am Asn Teachers Ger; Int Asn Netherlandists. **RESEARCH** German literature, Aufklarung, Sturm und Drang, classicism; 20th century Dutch literature. **SELECTED PUBLICATIONS** Auth, Nederlands in het buitenland: heeft het nog zin?, Ons Erfdeel, 1/77; Teeth on edge: The child in the modern Dutch short story, Rev Nat Lit, 77; From Cronus to Janus: The problem of time in the works of G K Reve, Dutch Studies, 77; coauth, Mariken Van Nieumeghen--A Bilingual Edition In Medieval Texts And Translations--Middle-Dutch And English, Daphnis-Zeitschrift Fur Mittlere Deutsche Literatur, Vol 24, 95; Something Understood, Studies In Anglo-Dutch Literary-Translation, Modern Philology, Vol 91, 93; Something Understood, Studies In Anglo-Dutch Literary-Translation, Modern Philology, Vol 91, 93. **CONTACT ADDRESS** Dept of Ger, Univ of Calif, 5315 Dwinelle Hall, Berkeley, CA, 94720-3244.

SNELL, DANIEL C.
PERSONAL Born 10/01/1947, Jackson, MI, m, 1986, 2 children **DISCIPLINE** NEAR EASTERN LANGUAGES & CIVILIZATIONS **EDUCATION** Stanford, MA, 71; Yale Univ, PhD, 75. **CAREER** Instr, Near Eastern Languages, 75-76, Univ Wash; Mellon fel, CUNY, 76-77; vis asst prof, Near Eastern Studies, Univ Mich, 77; asst prof, Religious Studies, Conn Col, 77-78; asst prof, Religious Studies, Barnard Col, 78-80; NEH fel, 80-81; asst prof Religion, Gustavus Aadolphus Col, 81-82; Fulbright res Syria, 82-83; from asst prof, 83-87, to assoc prof, 87-92, to prof of history, 92-, Univ of Okla, 83-. **HONORS AND AWARDS** Edinburgh Ctr Advan Studies Hum, 97; Oregon Hum Ctr Summer fel, 96; Hum Res Ctr fel, 90; Nat Hum Ctr fel, 89-90. **MEMBERSHIPS** Amer Orient Soc; Amer Hist Asn; Soc Bibl Lit **RESEARCH** Ancient Near Eastern social and economic history; Money and prices; Slavery; Biblical Book of Proverbs **SELECTED PUBLICATIONS** Auth, Taxes and Taxation. Tax Office. Trade and Commerce in the Ancient Near East, Anchor Bible Dictionary, Doubleday, 92; Ancient Israelite and Neo-Assyrian Societies and Economics, The Tablet and The Scroll, Near Eastern Studies in Homor of William W Hallo, CDL Press, 93; Twice-Told Proverbs and the Composition of the Book of Proverbs, Eisenbrauns, 93; A Neo-Babylonian Colophon, Revue d Assyriologie, 94; Methods of Exchange and Coinage, Civilizations of the Ancient Near East, Scribners, 95; Life in the Ancient Near East 3100-332 BC, Yale Univ Press, 97. **CONTACT ADDRESS** Dept of History, Univ of Okla, 455 W Lindsey, Norman, OK, 73019. **EMAIL** dcsnell@ou.edu

SNYDER, WILLIAM
DISCIPLINE LINGUISTICS **EDUCATION** Mass Inst Tech, PhD. **CAREER** Asst prof, Univ Conn. **MEMBERSHIPS** American Association for the Advancement of Science;International Association ,Child Language; Linguistic Society of America; Sigma Xi Scientific Research Society. **RESEARCH** Language acquisition comparative syntax, syntax-semantics interface. **SELECTED PUBLICATIONS** Auth, The Acquisitional Role of the Syntax-Morphology Interface: Morphological Compounds and Syntactic Complex Predicates, In Proceedings of the 20th Annual Boston Univ Conf on Lang Develop. Somerville, MA: Cascadilla Press, 96; A Neo-Davidsonian Approach to Resultatives, Particles, and Datives, Proceedings of the North East Linguistics Society 25, Amherst: GLSA, 95; coauth, Romance Auxiliary Selection with Reflexive Clitics: Evidence for Early Knowledge of Unaccusativity, In Proceedings of the Twenty-sixth Annual Child Language Research Forum, Stanford, CA: CSLI, 95; The Syntactic Representation of Degree and Quantity: Perspectives from Japanese and Child English, In Proceedings of the West Coast Conference on Formal Linguistics XIII, CSLI, 95. **CONTACT ADDRESS** Dept of Linguistics, Univ of Connecticut, 1266 Storrs Rd, Storrs, CT, 06269-1085. **EMAIL** wsnyder@sp.uconn.edu

SO, SUFUMI
DISCIPLINE JAPANESE **EDUCATION** Univ Toronto, PhD. **CAREER** Languages, Carnegie Mellon Univ. **SELECTED PUBLICATIONS** Coauth, Comparing writing process and product across two languages: A study of 6 Singaporean university student writers, Jour Sec Lang Writing, 93;Tutoring second language text revision: Does the approach to instruction or the language of communication make a difference, Jour Sec Lang Writing, 96; Learning to do research on language teaching and learning: Graduate apprenticeships, 97; The teaching of English-as-a-second-language writing in the Asia-Pacific region: a cross-coutry comparison, RELC Jour, 97; To be a reflective teacher, The Canadian Mod Lang Rev, 97. **CONTACT ADDRESS** Carnegie Mellon Univ, 5000 Forbes Ave, Pittsburgh, PA, 15213.

SOBIN, NICHOLAS
DISCIPLINE LINGUISTICS **EDUCATION** Univ Tex, PhD. **CAREER** English and Lit, Univ Ark **SELECTED PUBLICATIONS** Auth, Agreement, Default Rules, and Grammatical Viruses, Linguistic Inquiry; Case Assignment in Ukrainian Morphological Passive Constructions, Linguistic Inquiry; The Variable Status of COMP-trace Phenomena, Natural Language & Linguistic Theory; An Acceptable Ungrammatical Construction, The Reality of Linguistic Rules; On the Syntax of English Echo Questions; Lingua; Agreement in CP; Gapping as Evidence of Distinct L2 Acquisition, Spanish in the U.S. Setting. **CONTACT ADDRESS** Univ Ark Little Rock, 2801 S University Ave., Little Rock, AR, 72204-1099. **EMAIL** njsobin@ualr.edu

SOCHA, DONALD
DISCIPLINE SPANISH LITERATURE **EDUCATION** Univ Va, PhD. **CAREER** Dept For Lang, Wisc Univ **MEMBERSHIPS** Spanish Nat Honor Soc. **RESEARCH** Foreign language teaching. **SELECTED PUBLICATIONS** Auth, pubs on Garcia Lorca, Calderon de la Barca and Miguel de Cervantes. **CONTACT ADDRESS** Dept of Foreign Languages, Univ of Wisconsin, La Crosse, 1725 State St, La Crosse, WI, 54601. **EMAIL** socha@mail.uwlax.edu

SOCKEN, PAUL
DISCIPLINE FRENCH LITERATURE **EDUCATION** Univ Toronto, BA; Univ Iowa, MA; Univ Toronto, PhD. **CAREER** Prof **RESEARCH** Thematic and stylistic aspects of Gabrielle Roy. **SELECTED PUBLICATIONS** Auth, Gabrielle Roy's Bonheur d'Occasion; Myth and Morality in Alexandre Chenevert; The Myth of the Lost Paradise in the Novels of Jacques Poulin, Fairleigh Dickinson, 93; pub(s) in area of mythology and French-Canadian literature. **CONTACT ADDRESS** Dept of French, Waterloo Univ, 200 University Ave W, Waterloo, ON, N2L 3G1. **EMAIL** psocken@watarts.uwaterloo.ca

SOKEL, WALTER H.
PERSONAL Born 12/17/1917, Vienna, Austria, m, 1961, 1 child **DISCIPLINE** GERMAN LANGUAGE & LITERATURE **EDUCATION** Rutgers Univ, AB, 41, MA, 44; Columbia Univ, PhD(Ger), 53. **CAREER** Instr Ger, OH State Univ, 46-47; instr, Temple Univ, 47-53; from instr to assoc prof Ger & hum, Columbia Univ, 53-64; prof Ger, Stanford Univ, 64-73; Commonwealth Prof Ger & Eng Lit, Ctr Advan Studies, 73-94, Commonwealth Prof Emeritus, Ger and Eng Lit, 94- , Univ VA; Am Coun Learned Soc grant-in-aid, 62; exchange prof, Univ Hamburg, 65; Nat Endowment for Hum sr fel, 71-72; vis prof Ger, Harvard Univ, 78-79; exch prof, Univ Freiburg, Ger, 85; guest prof, Univ Graz, Austria, 88, 90, 92. **HONORS AND AWARDS** Alex von Humboldt Res Prize, Fed Repub Ger, 82; Cross of Honor First Class for Sci and Art, Rep of Austria, 97; hon doc, Univ Graz, Austria, 98. **MEMBERSHIPS** Int Brecht Soc (vpres, 74-); MLA; Am Asn Tchrs Ger; Am Comp Lit Asn; Am Kafka Soc, hon pres; Leo Baeck Inst, mem bd; Int Robert-Musil-Soc; Int Pen Club. **RESEARCH** Mod Ger lit; the existentialist tradition; intellectual hist and lit. **SELECTED PUBLICATIONS** Auth, The Writer in Extremis, Stanford Univ, 59; ed, An Anthology of German Expressionist Drama, Anchor Bks, 63; auth, Franz Kafka: Tragik und Ironie, Langen-Muller, Munich, 64; Franz Kafka, Columbia Univ, 66; Brecht's concept of character, Comp Drama, 71; Demaskierung und Untergang wilh Reprasentaz, In: Herkomen und Erneuerung, Max Niemeyer Verlag, 76; Perspectives and truth in The Judgment, In: The Problem of The Judgment, 77 & The three endings of Josef K, In: The Kafka Debate, 77, Gordian; auth, The Myth of Power and the Self, Wayne State Univ, 99. **CONTACT ADDRESS** 5764 E Camino del Celador, Tucson, AZ, 85750-1825.

SOKOL, ELENA
DISCIPLINE RUSSIAN LITERATURE **EDUCATION** Colo Univ, BA, 65; Univ Calif-Berkeley, MA, 67, PhD, 74. **CAREER** Assoc prof. **RESEARCH** Contemporary Czech fiction. **SELECTED PUBLICATIONS** Transl story by Prochazkova, Artful Dodge, a lit mag published at Wooster. **CONTACT ADDRESS** Dept of Russ, Col of Wooster, Wooster, OH, 44691. **EMAIL** esokol@acs.wooster.edu

SOLAN, LAWRENCE
PERSONAL Born 05/07/1952, New York, NY, m, 1982, 2 children **DISCIPLINE** LAW, LINGUISTICS **EDUCATION** Brandeis Univ, BA, 74; Univ Massachusetts, PhD Linguistics, 78; Harvard Law School, JD, 82. **CAREER** Law Clerk, Supreme Ct of NJ, 83-86; assoc, Orans, Elsen & Lupert, 83-86; partner, Orans, Elsen & Lupert, 89-96; Assoc Prof, Brooklyn Law School ol, 96-. **HONORS AND AWARDS** Bd Dir, Int Acad of Law and Mental health, 98-. **MEMBERSHIPS** Ling Soc of Am; Asn of the Bar of the City of New York; Law and Soc Asn; Int Asn of Forensic Ling; Int Acad of Law and Mental Health. **RESEARCH** Law; Language; Cognition. **SELECTED PUBLICATIONS** Auth, The Language of Judges, 993; When Judges Use the Dictionary, Am Speech, 93; Chomsku and Cardozo: Linguistics and the Law, 94; When All is Lost: Why it is Difficult for Judges to Write About Concepts, Graven Images, 94; Judicial Decision and Linguistic Analysis: Is There a Linguist in the Court?, Wash Univ, 95; Learning Our Limits: The Decline of Textualism in Statutory Cases, Wisconsin L Rev, 97; rev, Making Sense in Law, Forensic Ling, 97; Law, Language, and Lenity, William & Mary Rev, forthcoming; coauth, Linguists on the Witness Stand: law, Language and Cognition, forthcoming. **CONTACT ADDRESS** Brooklyn Law Sch, 250 Joralemon St, Brooklyn, NY, 11201. **EMAIL** lsolan@brooklaw.edu

SOLE, CARLOS A.
PERSONAL Born 09/09/1937, Panama, m, 1964, 1 child **DISCIPLINE** HISPANIC LINGUISTICS **EDUCATION** Georgetown Univ, PhD, 66. **CAREER** Asst prof, Harvard Univ; assoc prof and prof, Univ Texas, Austin. **HONORS AND AWARDS** Academico de Numero; Academia Norteamericana de la Lengua; Sociedad Argentina de la Lengua. **MEMBERSHIPS** MLA; FIATSP; PILEI; ALFAL. **RESEARCH** Spanish grammar; Spanish linguistics; historical spanish sociolinguistics. **SELECTED PUBLICATIONS** Gen ed, Latin American Writers, 2 v; auth, Foundation Course in Spanish, 98. **CONTACT ADDRESS** Dept of Spanish and Portuguese, Univ of Texas at Austin, Austin, TX, 78712.

SOLOMON, JANIS VIRGINIA LITTLE
PERSONAL Born 06/09/1938, Ranger, TX, m, 1978, 1 child **DISCIPLINE** GERMAN LITERATURE **EDUCATION** Univ Tex, Austin, BA, 60; Yale Univ, MA, 64, PhD(Ger lit), 65. **CAREER** From instr to assoc prof, 65-78, Prof Ger, Conn Col, 81-, actg chmn dept, 67-71, chmn dept Ger, 71-79, 81-82, & 92-, dir mod Europ studies, 74- 79, dir film studies, 84-. **HONORS AND AWARDS** Alexander von Humboldt-Stiftung fel, 72-73; Yale fac fel, 75. **MEMBERSHIPS** MLA; Am Asn Teachers Ger. **RESEARCH** Baroque lyric; modern drama; expressionism; film studies. **SELECTED PUBLICATIONS** Auth, Liebesgedichte & Lebensgeschichte bei Martin Opitz, Deut Vierteljahrsschrift Fur Literaturgeschichte, Vol 42, 161-181; contribr, Lebendige Form (Henelfestschrift), Fink, Munich, 70; Europaische Tradition & deutsche Barockliteratur, Francke, Bern, 73; auth, Die weltliche Lyrik des Martin Opitz, Francke,

Bern & Munich, 73; Buchner's Dantons Tod: History as theatre, Ger Rev, Vol 54, 9-19; Further Dutch Sources Used by Martin Opitz, Neophilologus, Vol 53, 157-175; contribr, Arbeit als Thema in der deutschen Literatur vom Mittelalter bis zur Gegenwart, Athenaum, Konigstein, 79; auth, Die Kriegsdramen Reinhard Goerings, Francke, Bern & Munich, 85; Martin Opitz: Ihr Himmel trieffetdoch, Daphnis 11, 55-63; contribr, German Baroque Literature: The European Perspective, Ungar, 83. **CONTACT ADDRESS** Dept of Ger, Connecticut Col, 270 Mohegan Ave, New London, CT, 06320-4196. **EMAIL** jlsol@conncoll.edu

SONNENFELD, ALBERT
PERSONAL Born 07/22/1934, Berlin, Germany, m, 1987, 2 children **DISCIPLINE** COMPARATIVE LITERATURE **EDUCATION** Oberlin Col, BA, 55; Princeton Univ, MA, 57, PhD, 58. **CAREER** Asst prof, 60-64, assoc prof, French, 64-68, prof French and Comp Lit, 68-86, chemn 78-84, Princeton Univ; M.F. Chevalier Prof of French and Comp Lit, 87- , chemn 86-98, Univ So Calif; Nat Bd of Dir, Am Inst of Wine and Food, 88- . **HONORS AND AWARDS** Officer des Palmes academiques & Officer des Arts et lettres, French Republic; Bicentennial preceptorship, Princeton Univ, 62-64; Raubenheimer Prize, Univ S Carolina, 92; Fulbright lectr; Fulbright fel, NEH St Fel; ACLS grants; Am Philos Soc grants; Princeton Hum Res grants. **RESEARCH** Culinary history; modern European literature; Proust; Joyce. **SELECTED PUBLICATIONS** Ed, Thirty-Six French Poems, 60; auth, O'Oeuvre poetique de Tristan Corbiere, 61; coauth, Temoins de l'Homme, 65; auth, Crossroads: Essays on the Catholic Novelists, 82; ed, Food: a Culinary History from Antiquity to the Present, 2000. **CONTACT ADDRESS** Univ of So California, University Park, Los Angeles, CA, 90089-0359. **EMAIL** Albertsonn@aol.com

SONNENFELD, MARION WILMA
PERSONAL Born 02/13/1928, Berlin, Germany **DISCIPLINE** GERMAN **EDUCATION** Swarthmore Col, BA, 50; Yale Univ, MA, 51, PhD, 56. **CAREER** From instr to asst prof Ger, Smith Col, 54-62; assoc prof, Wells Col, 62-67, chmn dept, 65-67; from assoc prof to prof, 67-77, Distinguished Teaching Prof Ger, 77-93, DISTINGUISHED TEACHING PROF EMER, STATE UNIV NY COL FREDONIA, 93-; Mem fac, Middlebury Col Ger Sch, 61-63; asst dir, Wells Col Summer Sch Ger, 64, dir, 65-67; actg dean arts & humanities, 80-81; actg dir, Int Educ, 80-81; coordr, Stefan Zweig Symp, Fredonia, 81; mem Nat Screening Comt,Fulbright grants, 89-91. **HONORS AND AWARDS** State Univ NY Summer Award, 80; Fund for the Improvement of Post Secondary Educ grant, mem comt assessment, 88-90. **MEMBERSHIPS** MLA; Int Germanisten Ver; Am Asn Teachers Ger. **RESEARCH** Novelle; Kafka; the German drama. **SELECTED PUBLICATIONS** Auth, An etymological interpretation of the Hagen figure, Neophilologus, 57; Paralleles in Novelle und Verwandlung, Symp, 59; Amerika und Prozess als Bildungsromanfragmente, Ger Quart, 62; transl, Kleist's Amphitryon, Ungar, 62; ed, Wert und Wort, Wells Col, 65; ed, Gepragte Form, Fredonia, 75; transl, Three Plays by Hebbel, 74 & co-transl, The Narrative Prose of C F Meyer, 76, Bucknell Univ. **CONTACT ADDRESS** Dept of Foreign Lang & Lit, State Univ NY, Fredonia, NY, 14063-1143. **EMAIL** marionw@netsync.net

SOONS, C. ALAN
PERSONAL Born 02/09/1925, Grantham, England, m, 3 children **DISCIPLINE** SPANISH LITERATURE **EDUCATION** Univ Sheffield, BA, 51, MA, 53; Harvard Univ, PhD(Romance lang & lit), 71. **CAREER** Asst lectr Span, Univ St Andrews, 55-57; from lectr to sr lectr, Univ W Indies, Jamaica, Barbados & Trinidad, 57-68; vis assoc prof Romance lang, Univ Mass, Amherst, 68-70; vis assoc prof Span, Rice Univ, 71-72; assoc prof, 72-81, Prof Span, State Univ NY Buffalo, 81-, Vis fel, St Catherine's Col, Oxford, 80. **MEMBERSHIPS** Asoc Int Hispanistas; Soc Saint-Simon. **RESEARCH** Late medieval and Renaissance literature; Spanish-American literature of the colonial period; folk-narrative. **SELECTED PUBLICATIONS** Auth, Ficcion y comedia en el Siglo de Oro, Madrid, 67; The patterning of La gitanilla, Romanistisches Jahrbuch, 75; Alonso Ramirez in an enchanted and a disenchanted world, Bull Hisp Studies, 76; Haz y enves del cuento risible en el Siglo de Oro, Tamesis, London, 76; contribr, Enxyklopadie des Marchens, Gottingen, 76; ed, Esteban Terralla Landa Lima por dentro y fuera, Exeter: Exeter Hisp Texts, 78; auth, Alonso de Castillo Solorzano, Twayne, 78; Juan de Mariana, Twayne, 82; Theaters And Theater Life In Tudela, 1563-1750--Studies And Documents, Bulletin Of The Comediantes, Vol 45, 93. **CONTACT ADDRESS** Dept Mod Lang, State Univ of NY, Buffalo, NY, 14260.

SORIA, REGINA
PERSONAL Born 05/17/1911, Rome, Italy, m, 1936 **DISCIPLINE** ROMANCE LANGUAGES, AMERICAN ART **EDUCATION** Univ Rome, LittD, 33. **CAREER** From instr to assoc prof foreign lang, 42-61, prof Ital, 61-76, Emer Prof Mod Lang, Col Notre Dame, MD, 76. Instr Span, McCoy Col, 50-52; field researcher, Arch Am Art, 60-63, archivist, Rome Off, 63-64. **MEMBERSHIPS** MLA; Am Studies Asn; Am Asn Teachers Ital; AAUP. **RESEARCH** Biography and catalogue of the works of Elihu Vedder-American painter; American artists in Italy, 1760-1914; Italian participation in the visual arts of 18th and 19th century America. **SELECTED PUBLICATIONS** Auth, Washington Allston's lectures on art, the first American art treatise, J Aesthet & Art Criticism, 3/60; Some background for Elihu Vedder's Cumean Sibyl and Young Marysays, spring 60 & Elihu Vedder's mythical creatures, summer 63; Art Quart; Mark Twain and Vedder's Medusa, Am Quart, winter 64; Life of Elihu Vedder & spring, 76; Elihu Vedder, American Old Master, Ga Mus Art Bull, spring 76; Hendrik Andersen: American Sculptor, Ny Rev Of Books, Vol 40, 93. **CONTACT ADDRESS** 1609 Ramblewood Rd, Baltimore, MD, 21239.

SORKIN, ADAM J.
PERSONAL Born 08/09/1943, New York, NY, m, 1964, 2 children **DISCIPLINE** AMERICAN LITERATURE PROSE FICTION, TRANSLATION OF CONTEMPORARY ROMANIAN LIT **EDUCATION** Cornell Univ, AB, 64, MA, 65; Univ NC, PhD, 72. **CAREER** Instr Eng, Univ IL, Chicago Circle, 65-66; instr Eng & Am lit, Univ NC, Chapel Hill, 70-71; instr, Stockton State Col, 71-73; instr, Drexel Univ & Community Col Philadelphia, 73; asst prof Eng & Am lit, Bluefield State Col, 74-78; from Asst Prof to Prof Eng, PA State Univ, 78-; Fulbright lectr, Univ Bucharest, Romania, 80-81. **HONORS AND AWARDS** NEH Summer Seminar, 75; IREX Fel, 91; Rockefeller Found Residency, Study and Conf Ctr, Italy, 95; Recommended Transl, Poetry Bk Soc, for The Sky Behind the Forest, 96-97; Crossing Boundaries Translation Award, Int Quart, for The Europ Mechanism, Fall 97; Story Short Short Competition winner, 14th place, for The Telephone, 97. **MEMBERSHIPS** MLA; SAtlantic Mod Lang Asn; Northeast Mod Lang Asn; Am Lit Translr(s) Asn. **RESEARCH** Am lit; prose fiction; mod lit. **SELECTED PUBLICATIONS** Ed, Politics and the Muse: Studies in the Politics of Recent American Literature, Bowling Green State Univ Popular Press, 89; Conversations with Joseph Heller, Literary Conversations Series, Univ Press MS, 93; auth, Marin Sorescu: Comedian of Antiheroic Resistance, Romanian Civilization, Summer 92; Half in Flight Half in Chains: The Paradoxical Vision of Iona Ieronim's Poetry, Conn Rev, Fall 95; Petre Stoica's Tiananmen Square II: Anger, Protest, and an Angel with a Crow's Wings, Romanian Civilization, Winter 95-96; Liliana Ursu's Poetry, Delos: A J Transl & World Lit 18, 96; The Forbidden World and Hidden Words: Steadfast Illumination in Marin Sorescu's Poems Selected by Censorship, Romanian Civilization, Fall 96; Postmodernism in Romanian Poetry: The Abnormally Normal, Romania & Western Civilization / Romania si civilizatia occidentala, Iasi: The Ctr for Romanian Studies, 97; On The Circle by Martin Sorescu, Two Lines: A J of Transl, Spring 97; I Was of Three Minds: Some Notes on Translating, Metamorphoses, April 98; author and translator of numerous other articles, poems, and short stories. **CONTACT ADDRESS** Eng Dept, Pennsylvania State Univ, 25 Yearsley Mill Rd, Media, PA, 19063-5596. **EMAIL** ajs2@psu.edu

SOSSAMAN, STEPHEN
DISCIPLINE CREATIVE WRITING, WORLD LITERATURE, MODERN AMERICAN LITERATURE **EDUCATION** Columbia Univ, BA; State Univ NY, MA; NYU, PhD. **CAREER** Bus wrtg consult. **SELECTED PUBLICATIONS** Publ, Paris Rev, Centennial Rev, Southern Hum Rev. **CONTACT ADDRESS** Dept of Engl, Westfield State Col, 577 Western Ave., Westfield, MA, 01085.

SOUSA, RONALD W.
PERSONAL Born 08/14/1943, Santa Cruz, CA, m, 1968, 2 children **DISCIPLINE** LANGUAGE **EDUCATION** Univ Calif Berkeley, BA, 66, MA, 68, PhD, 73. **CAREER** Asst prof, 71-74, Univ Tx Austin; asst prof to assoc prof to prof, 74-93, 94-, Univ Mn Minneapolis; vis prof, 77, Univ Calif Berkeley; prof, 94-, Univ Il Champaign-Urbana. **HONORS AND AWARDS** Nat Endow for the Humanities Summer Stipend, 76, 86; Grant-in-Aid Amer Philos Soc, 76-77; Putnam Dana MacMillan Fel, 79; Bolsa de Estudos, Fundacao Calouste Gulbenkian, 80; **RESEARCH** Portuguese lit; lit & hist; theory of hist; lit theory. **SELECTED PUBLICATIONS** Auth, The Rediscoverers: Major Figures in the Portuguese Literature of National Regeneration, Pa St Univ Press, 81; art, Vos outros tambem cantai por vosso uso acostumade..., Literature Among Discourses: The Spanish Golden Age, Univ Mn Press, 87; coauth, Reading the Harper: On A Portuguese Immigrant Poem, California, 1901, Gavea-Brown, 96; art, Pessoa Criticism and the Antagonistic Literary Institutionality of the Estado Novo, J of Hispanic Lit, 96; art, Cannibal, Cartographer, Soldier, Spy: The Peirai of Mendes Pinto's Peregrinacao, The Project of Prose in Early Modern Europe and the New World, Cambridge Univ Press, 97. **CONTACT ADDRESS** 1807 Bentbrook Dr, Campaign, IL, 61822. **EMAIL** r-sousa@uiuc.edu

SOUTHERLAND, RONALD HAMILTON
PERSONAL Born 03/07/1942, Wilmington, NC **DISCIPLINE** LINGUISTICS, GERMAN **EDUCATION** Univ NC, AB, 65, MA, 67; Univ Pa, PhD(ling), 70. **CAREER** Asst prof ling & Ger, Duquesne Univ, 70-71; asst prof ling, 71-76, Assoc Prof Ling, Univ Calgary, 76- **MEMBERSHIPS** Ling Soc Am; Ling Soc Europe. **RESEARCH** Sociolinguistics; social and situational differentiation of speech; historical linguistics. **SELECTED PUBLICATIONS** Ed, Readings on Language in Canada, 73 & auth, The linguistic mix in French Canada, In: Readings on Language in Canada, 73, Univ Calgary; Comparative and typological perspectives on the reconstruction of the PIE Gutturals, Calgary Working Papers Ling, 78; Derivatives In Pre-, A Persuasive Morphological Resource, Am Speech, Vol 69, 94; Modern American English, American Speech, Vol 69, 94. **CONTACT ADDRESS** Dept of Ling, Univ of Calgary, Calgary, AB, T2N 1N4.

SOUZA, RAYMOND D.
PERSONAL Born 03/11/1936, Attleboro, MA, m, 1966, 2 children **DISCIPLINE** SPANISH **EDUCATION** Drury Col, BA, 58; Univ Mo, MA, 60, PhD(Span), 64. **CAREER** Teacher high sch, Mo, 58-59; instr Span, Kent State Univ, 61-62; from asst prof to assoc prof, 63-73, chmn dept Span & Port, 68-74, prof Span, Univ Kans, 73-, Am Philos Soc Johnson Fund fel, 68; Exxon inter-univ vis prof ling & philos, 81-82; Tinker Found fel, Costa Rica, 82. **MEMBERSHIPS** Am Asn Teachers Span & Port; Inst Int Lit Iberoam; MLA; Assoc of North American Colombianists, Pres, 87-89. **RESEARCH** Spanish American prose fiction and poetry; Cuban literature; Colombian literature, film. **SELECTED PUBLICATIONS** Auth, Language vs Structure in the contemporary Spanish American Novel, Hispania, 12/69;Time and Terror in the Stories of Lino Novas Calvo, Symposium, winter 75; Time and Space Configurations in Two Poems of Octavio Paz, J Span Studies: Twentieth Century, fall 76; Major Cuban Novelists: Innovation & Tradition, Univ Mo, Columbia 76, London 76; ; Lino Novas Calvo, G K Hall, 81; The Poetic Fiction of Jose Lezama Lima, Univ Mo, Columbia, 83; Novel and Context in Costa Rica and Nicaragua, Romance Quart, April 86; Yes, We Have No Havana(s): Requiem for a Lost City, World Lit Today, April 87; La Historia en la novela hispanoamericana moderna, Tercer Mundo, Bogota, 88; Columbus in the Novel of the Americas: Alejo Carpentier, Abel Posse, & Stephen Marlowe, in Raymond Williams ed, Reading the Americas, Univ Colorado, Boulder, 92; Guillermo Cadrera Infante: Two Islands, Many Worlds, Univ Tx, Austin, 96. **CONTACT ADDRESS** Dept of Span & Port, Univ of Kans, Lawrence, KS, 66045-0001. **EMAIL** rdsouza@falcon.cc.ukans.edu

SPACCARELLI, THOMAS DEAN
PERSONAL Born 09/25/1947, Chicago, IL, m, 1970 **DISCIPLINE** SPANISH LINGUISTIC, MEDIEVAL SPANISH LITERATURE **EDUCATION** Univ Ill, Chicago Circle, AB, 69; Univ Wis-Madison, MA, 71, PhD(Span), 75. **CAREER** Lectr Span, Univ Ill Chicago Circle, 73-74; instr, 74-75, Asst Prof Span, Univ Of The South, 75-, Mem, Span Joint Comt, Educ & Cult Affairs, 80-81. **MEMBERSHIPS** Am Asn Teachers of Span & Port; MLA; Mediaeval Acad Am. **RESEARCH** Spanish lexicography; medieval romance. **SELECTED PUBLICATIONS** Ed, Complete Concordances and Texts of the Fourteenth-Century Aragonese Manuscripts of Jaun Fernandez de heredia, Hisp Sem of Medieval Studies, Ltd, 82; The Emergence Of The Erotic In Don Juan Tenorio, Romance Notes, Vol 34, 93. **CONTACT ADDRESS** Dept of Span, Univ of the South, Sewanee, TN, 37375.

SPAHR, BLAKE LEE
PERSONAL Born 07/11/1924, Carlisle, PA, m, 1957, 1 child **DISCIPLINE** GERMAN & COMPARATIVE LITERATURE **EDUCATION** Dickinson Col, BA, 47; Yale Univ, MA, 48, PhD, 51. **CAREER** Instr Ger, Dickinson Col, 46-47; instr, Yale Univ, 50-53; from asst prof to assoc prof, 54-64, chmn dept Ger, 65-70; chmn dept comp lit, 72-80, Prof Ger & Comp Lit, Univ Calif, Berkeley, 64-, Morse res fel, Yale Univ, 52-53; Guggenheim fel, 62. **MEMBERSHIPS** Mediaeval Acad Am; MLA; Int Arthurian Soc; Pegnesischer Blumenorden. **RESEARCH** German literature of the Middle Ages and the 17th century; Comparative Arthurian literature. **SELECTED PUBLICATIONS** Auth, The Legacy Of Curt Vonfaberdufaur To The United-States, Colloquia Germanica, Vol 25, 92; The German Poetry Of Paul Fleming--Studies In Genre And Hist, Daphnis-Zeitschrift Fur Mittlere Deutsche Literatur, Vol 21, 92; Reading Gryphius,Andreas--Critical Trends, 1664-1993, Daphnis-Zeitschrift Fur Mittlere Deutsche Literatur, Vol 24, 95; Zuckmayer,Carl Criticism--Tracing Endangered Fame, Seminar-A J Of Germanic Studies, Vol 33, 97; The Adventures Of Simplicius Simplicissimus, Daphnis-Zeitschrift Fur Mittlere Deutsche Literatur, Vol 23, 94; Boehme--An Intellectual Biography Of The 17th-Century Philosopher And Mystic, Daphnis-Zeitschrift Fur Mittlere Deutsche Literatur, Vol 21, 92; German Poetry Of Fleming,Paul, Daphnis-Zeitschrift Fur Mittlere Deutsche Literatur, Vol 23, 94; Love And The Butchers Son, Or Opitz,Martin And His Critics, Daphnis-Zeitschrift Fur Mittlere Deutsche Literatur, Vol 24, 95; The Heroism Of Love In Hoffmannswaldau Heldenbriefe, Daphnis-Zeitschrift Fur Mittlere Deutsche Literatur, Vol 23, 94. **CONTACT ADDRESS** Dept of Ger, Univ of Calif, Berkeley, CA, 94720.

SPANOS, ANTHONY
DISCIPLINE SPANISH **EDUCATION** Weber State Col, BA, 68; Univ Nev-Reno, MA, 73; Univ Utah, PhD, 88. **CAREER** Prof, Weber State Univ. **HONORS AND AWARDS** Acad Resources and Comput Grant, 90; Hemingway Fac Develop Awd, 91 and 92; Res, Schol and Prof Growth Grant, 92; Fac Awd for Exemplary Tchg, 92; Hemingway Fac Vitality Awd, 95 and 96;

Int Mission-Related Grant, 95; Exemplary Collab Awd, 95; Utah Higher Educ Technol Initiative Grant, 95; Cert Distance Learning Proficiency, 95. **RESEARCH** Contemporary Latin American literature, Latin American culture and civilization, writing across the curriculum, speaking excellence across the curriculum, ACTFL Oral, computer based technology (CBT). **SELECTED PUBLICATIONS** Auth, Confinement, Confusion and Creation in Como agua para chocolate, Chiricu, Vol 7, 95 & The Paradoxical Metaphors of the Kitchen in Laura Esquivel's Like Water for Chocolate, Letras Femeninas 21, 95; coauth, Antonia y Demasiado amor: el Bildungsroman: su estrategia y definicion en la experiencia mexicana femenina, Confluencia, 97. **CONTACT ADDRESS** Dept of Foreign Language and Literature, Weber State Univ, 1403 University Cir, Ogden, UT, 84408-1403. **EMAIL** tspanos@weber.edu

SPARKS, KIMBERLY
PERSONAL Born 10/02/1930, Baltimore, MD, m, 1952, 3 children **DISCIPLINE** GERMANIC LANGUAGES **EDUCATION** Princeton Univ, AB, 56, MA, 59, PhD(Ger), 63. **CAREER** From instr to foreign lang, 66-71, chmn comt, 73-76, Charles A Dana Prof Ger, Middlebury Col, 71-, Chmn exam comt, Ger Achievement Test, 66-68; dir, Northeast Conf Teaching Foreign Lang, 68-72; mem nat bd consults, Nat Endowment for Humanities, 77- **MEMBERSHIPS** MLA. **RESEARCH** Novels of Hermann Broch; language teaching. **SELECTED PUBLICATIONS** Auth, Korfs Uhr, In: Perspective der Forschung; Drei Schwarze Kaninchen Z Deut Philol, 65; coauth, Der Web zum Lesen, 67, German in Review, 67, Modern German, 71, S ist es, 71 & Thomas Manns Tonio Kroger als Weg zur Literatur, 74, Harcout; auth, The radicalization of space in Kafka, In: On Kafka, Elek, London, 77; Schnitzler The 'Dead Are Silent--Introduction, New England Review-Middlebury Series, Vol 18, 1997. **CONTACT ADDRESS** Dept of Ger, Middlebury Col, Middlebury, VT, 05753.

SPEAS, MARGARET
DISCIPLINE LINGUISTICS **EDUCATION** Wash Univ, BA, 73; Univ Ariz, MA, 81; Univ Mass, PhD, 86. **CAREER** Assoc prof. **SELECTED PUBLICATIONS** Auth, Optimality in Syntax: Control and Null Arguments, Blackwell, 97; Null Arguments in a Theory of Economy of Projection, 94; Functional Heads and Inflectional Morphemes, ling rev, 91; Phrase Structure in Natural Language, Kluwer, 90. **CONTACT ADDRESS** Linguistics Dept, Univ of Massachusetts, Amherst, S College 220, Amherst, MA, 01003. **EMAIL** pspeas@linguist.umass.edu

SPECK, OLIVER C.
DISCIPLINE GERMAN **EDUCATION** Univ Waterloo, MA, 90; Univ Mannheim, PhD, 96. **CAREER** Adj lectr, Northwestern Univ. **RESEARCH** German, English and French Literature; Film; Film and media theory; literary theory; cultural studies. **SELECTED PUBLICATIONS** Auth, Lemmy Caution als Bildner der Ich-Funktion: Intermedialit t in Godards Alphaville, in: Volker Roloff und Scarlett Winter, Hrsg Godard Intermedial; Tubingen: Stauffenberg Verlag, 97. **CONTACT ADDRESS** Dept of German, Northwestern Univ, 1801 Hinman, Evanston Der unter-sagte, IL, 60208. **EMAIL** ocspeck@nwu.edu

SPELLMAN, JOHN WILLARD
PERSONAL Born 07/27/1934, Tewksbury, MA **DISCIPLINE** HISTORY, ASIAN STUDIES **EDUCATION** Northeastern Univ, BA, 56; Univ London, PhD(Indian hist), 60. **CAREER** Vis asst prof hist, Wesleyan Univ, 61-62; vis lectr Indian polit, Univ Kerala, 62-64; asst prof, Univ Wash, 64-67; head dept, 67-79, PROF ASIAN STUDIES, 67-, Ford Found Non-Western study grant, 64-66; consult, Peace Corps Training Prog, India, 64-68; Can Univ Serv Overseas, 66-68; consult & regional field dir, Asia Develop, Madras India, Can Univ Serv Overseas, 82. **MEMBERSHIPS** Fel Royal Asiatic Soc; Am Orient Soc; Asn Asian Studies; Indian Polit Sci Asn; Can Soc Asian Studies. **RESEARCH** Religion and society in ancient India; Indian cultural values; Indian healing and witchcraft. **SELECTED PUBLICATIONS** Auth, Political Theory of Ancient India, Oxford Univ, 64; An analysis of the 1963 Trivandrum II by-election, Polit Sci Rev, Rajasthan, 65; The Beautiful Blue Jay and Other Tales of India, Little, 67; An annotated bibliography of ancient Indian politics, Motilal Banarsidass, New Delhi; Symbolic significance of the number twelve in ancient India, J Asian Studies, Vol XXII, No 1; The Construction Of Religious Boundaries--Culture, Identity And Diversity In The Sikh Tradition, Studies In Religion-Sciences Religieuses, Vol 25, 96. **CONTACT ADDRESS** Dept of Asian Studies, Univ of Windsor, Windsor, ON, N9B 3P4.

SPENCER, JANINE
DISCIPLINE FRENCH **EDUCATION** Northwestern Univ, PhD. **CAREER** Sr lectr; coordr, second-yr Fr, Northwestern Univ; trained, ACTFL oral proficiency tester; dir,Multi-Media Learning Center. **RESEARCH** Material development for oral and written communication, instructional technology in foreign language instruction and alternate models of instruction. **SELECTED PUBLICATIONS** Coauth, Et votre avis, Holt, Rinehart and Winston, 90. **CONTACT ADDRESS** Dept of French, Northwestern Univ, 1801 Hinman, Evanston, IL, 60208.

SPENCER, SAMIA ISKANDER
PERSONAL Born 07/04/1943, Alexandria, Egypt, m, 1969, 2 children **DISCIPLINE** FRENCH **EDUCATION** Alexandria Univ, Egypt, BA, 64; Univ Ill, Urbana, MA, 69, PhD(French), 75. **CAREER** Secy & gen asst, US Info Serv, Egypt 65-67; secy, World Health Orgn, Egypt, 67 & UN Develop Prog, NY, 68; teaching asst French, Univ Ill, Urbana, 68-72; instr, 72-75, asst prof, 75-80, Assoc Prof French, Auburn Univ, 80-, Res grant-in-aid, Auburn Univ, 75; Ala Comt Humanities & Pub Policy grant, 76; grant, Govt of Quebec, 82. **MEMBERSHIPS** Am Asn Teachers Fr (secy-treas, 81-); Am Soc 18th Century Studies; MLA. **RESEARCH** The eighteenth century French novel; women in eighteenth century French literature; the teaching of foreign languages. **SELECTED PUBLICATIONS** Coauth, French and American Women in the Feminine Press: A Cross Cultural Look, Contemp Fr Civilization, winter 81; auth, The Xy Of Masculine Identity--French, French Rev, Vol 68, 95; The Droit-De-Cuissage--France 1860-1930, French Rev, Vol 70, 97; Flesh, The Devil And The Confessor, French Rev, Vol 70, 96; Fathers And Sons, French Rev, Vol 67, 94; Historical Dictionary Of The French-Language, French Rev, Vol 68, 95; This Male Self-Assurance, French Rev, Vol 69, 96. **CONTACT ADDRESS** Dept of Foreign Lang, Auburn Univ, Auburn, AL, 36830.

SPILKA, MARK
PERSONAL Born 08/06/1925, Cleveland, OH, m, 7 children **DISCIPLINE** ENGLISH, COMPARATIVE LITERATURE **EDUCATION** Brown Univ, BA, 49; Ind Univ, MA, 53, PhD(comp lit), 56. **CAREER** Ed asst, Am Mercury, 49-51; instr English lit, Univ Mich, 54-58, asst prof, English, 58-63; assoc prof, 63-67, chmn, Dept English, 68-73, PROF ENGLISH LIT, BROWN UNIV, 67-, Fel, Ind Sch Lett, 61; managing ed, Novel: A Forum on Fiction, Brown Univ, 67-77, ed, 78-; Guggenheim fel, 67-68; Nat Endowment for Humanitites fel independent study & res, 78-79; vis prof, Ind Univ, summer, 76. **MEMBERSHIPS** MLA **RESEARCH** English and American novel, especially 19th and 20th centuries; comparative literature; modern literary criticism. **SELECTED PUBLICATIONS** Auth, Love Ethic of D H Lawrence, 55 & Dickens and Kafka: A Mutual Interpretation, 63, Ind Univ; ed, D H Lawrence: A Collection of Critical Essays, Prentice-Hall, 63; Towards a Poetics of Fiction, Ind Univ, 77; auth, Virginia Woolf's Quarrel with Grieving, Univ Nebr Press, 80; auth, Renewing the Normative D. H. Lawrence: A Personal Progress, Missouri, 92; auth, Eight Lessons in Love: A Domestic Violence Reader, Missouri, 97. **CONTACT ADDRESS** 294 Doyle Ave, Providence, RI, 02906. **EMAIL** mark.spilka@brown.edu

SPIRES, ROBERT CECIL
PERSONAL Born 12/01/1936, Missouri Valley, IA, m, 1963, 2 children **DISCIPLINE** CONTEMPORARY SPANISH LITERATURE **EDUCATION** Univ Iowa, BA, 59, MA, 63, PhD(Span), 68. **CAREER** From instr to asst prof Span, Ohio Univ, 67-69; asst prof, 69-74, assoc prof, 74-78, Prof Span, Univ Kans, 78-. **HONORS AND AWARDS** Univ Kans Mortar Bd Award, 77; NEH Fel for Independent Study and Res, 81-82; U. S.-Spanish Joint Comm Fel for Res in Spain, 85-86; Chancellor's Teaching Award, Univ of Kans, 88-89; Spain's Ministry of Culture and United States' Universities Fel for Res in Spain, Spring 92. **MEMBERSHIPS** MLA; Am Asn Teachers Span & Port. **RESEARCH** Contemporary Hispanic novel; contemporary Spanish drama; contemporary Spanish poetry. **SELECTED PUBLICATIONS** Auth, Tecnica y tema en La familia de Pascual Duarte, Insula, 9/71; Systematic doubt: The moral art of La familia de Pascual Duarte, Hisp Rev, summer 72; Cela's La colmena: The creative process as message, Hispania, 12/72; contribr, Novelistas Epanoles de Postguerra, Taurus, Madrid, 76; auth, Linguistic codes and dramatic action in La casa de Bernarda Alba, Am Hispanist, 1/78; La Novela Espanola de Postguerra: Creacion Artistica y Experiencia Personal, Editorial Planeta/Universidad, Madrid, 78; Latrines, whirlpools and voids: The metafictional mode of Juan sin Tierra, Hisp Rev, spring 80; La colera de Aguiles: Un texto producto del lector, Revista Iberoamericana, Julio-Dic, 81; Beyond the Metafictional Mode: Direction in the Modern Spanish Novel, Univ Press of Ky, 84; Transparent Simulacra: Spanish Fiction 1902-1926, Univ of Mo Press, 88; Post-Totalitarian Spanish Fiction, Univ of Mo Press, 96. **CONTACT ADDRESS** Dept of Span & Port, Univ of Kans, Lawrence, KS, 66045-0001. **EMAIL** rspires@kuhub.cc.ukans.edu

SPIVAK, GAYATRI CHAKRAVORTY
PERSONAL Born 02/24/1942, Calcutta, India **DISCIPLINE** COMPARATIVE LITERATURE **EDUCATION** Univ Calcutta, BA, 59; Univ Calcutta, MA, 62; Cornell Univ, PhD, 67 **CAREER** Avalon prof Humanities, Cornell Univ, 91- **HONORS AND AWARDS** Fel, Nat Humanities Inst; Fel, Center for the Humanities Wesleyan; Fel, Humanities Res Center at Australian National Univ; Kent Fel; Guggenheim Fel; Tagore Fel Maharaja Sayajirao Univ Baroda, India; Translation Prize Sahitya Akademi, 1997 **RESEARCH** Nineteenth Century Literature; Marxism; Feminism; Deconstruction; Poststructuralism **SELECTED PUBLICATIONS** Auth, Murti, Seagull, 98; auth, A Critique of Postcolonial Reason, Harvard Univ, 99; auth, The Breast Stories, Seagull, 97; auth, The Spivak Reader, Routledge, 95; **CONTACT ADDRESS** Dept English, Columbia Univ, 602 Philosophy Hall, New York, NY, 10027.

SPRAUVE, GILBERT A.
PERSONAL Born 06/09/1937, St Thomas, Virgin Islands, d **DISCIPLINE** MODERN LANGUAGES **EDUCATION** Brooklyn Coll, BA 1960; Univ of So CA, MA 1965; Princeton U, PhD 1974. **CAREER** Coll of the VI, assoc prof modern langs 1967-; LA City Schs CA, French, Spanish tchr 1963-67; Albert Acad Sierra Leone, French, Spanish tchr 1961-63; Lyce Donka Guinea, Span, Engl tchr 1960-61; Third Constitutional Conv of VI, del 1977; 14th Leg of Virgin Islands, senator at-large, vp; candidate for it gov on the runner-up Bryan/Sprauve ticket in 1986 general elections; Univ of Virgin Islands, prof of modern langs; Smithsonian Institution, Festival of American Folklife, Virgin Islands Section, general advisor & research, 1990; Smithsonian Institution, Office of Folklife Programs, senior visiting scholar, 1991 . **HONORS AND AWARDS** Del Pres Conf on Libraries 1979; principal role Derek Walcott's "Marie La Veau" a world premiere workshop at Coll VI 1979; authorship of numerous articles and monographs on Virgin Islands language and cultural history. **MEMBERSHIPS** Mem VI Bd of Educ 1978-; adv bd mem Caribbean Fishery Mgmt Council 1979-; Rockefeller Foun Fellowship Grad Black Studies 1971-74. **SELECTED PUBLICATIONS** Pub "The Queue" The Literary Review 1974; **CONTACT ADDRESS** Professor, Univ of the Virgin Islands, St Thomas, 00801.

SPROUL, BARBARA CHAMBERLAIN
PERSONAL Born 06/18/1945, New York, NY, 2 children **DISCIPLINE** COMPARATIVE RELIGION, HUMAN RIGHTS **EDUCATION** Sarah Lawrence Col, BA, 66; Columbia Univ, MA, 68, PhD, 72. **CAREER** Asst prof, 72-77, assoc prof, 77-79, prof relig, 79, chmn prog in relig, 73-, Hunter Col; mem exec comt human rights, Amnesty Int USA, 70, gen secy, 78-. **MEMBERSHIPS** Am Acad Relig. **RESEARCH** Creation mythology; human rights. **SELECTED PUBLICATIONS** Ed, Primal Myths, Harper & Row, 79. **CONTACT ADDRESS** Dept of Relig, Hunter Col, CUNY, 695 Park Ave, New York, NY, 10021-5085.

SPURLOCK, JOHN HOWARD
PERSONAL Born 10/22/1939, Huntington, WV, m, 1962, 1 child **DISCIPLINE** LINGUISTICS, AMERICAN LITERATURE **EDUCATION** WVa Univ, BA, 62; Univ Louisville, MA, 64, PhD, 86. **CAREER** Instr English, Western Ky Univ, 64-69 & Louisville Country Day Sch, 69-70; assoc prof, 71-86, prof English, Western Ky Univ, 86-. **HONORS AND AWARDS** Award for Editorial Excellence, Jesse Stuart Found, 96. **MEMBERSHIPS** Appalachian Writers Asn; Jesse Stuart Found (ed and mem bd dir); Ky Speakers' Bureau. **RESEARCH** Sociolinguistics; Appalachian literature; Kentucky literature. **SELECTED PUBLICATIONS** Auth, He Sings For Us--A Sociolinguistic Analysis of the Appalachian Subculture and of Jesse Stuart as a Major American Author, Univ Press of Am, 80 & 82; Appalachian--Appalachia/strange man--strange land, In: Speechways of American Subcultures, Univ Press of Ky, 82; ed, Jesse Stuart's Daughter of the Legend, Jesse Stuart Found, 94; Jesse Stuart's Beyond Dark Hills, Jesse Stuart Found, 96. **CONTACT ADDRESS** 1 Big Red Way St, Box 495, Bowling Green, KY, 42101-3576.

SRIDHAR, S.N.
PERSONAL Born 05/26/1950, Shimoga, India, m, 1974 **DISCIPLINE** LINGUISTICS, FOREIGN LANGUAGES & LITERATURES **EDUCATION** Bangalore Univ, India, BA Hons, 69, MA, 71; Univ Ill, MA, 75, PhD(ling), 80. **CAREER** Res assoc, Teachers English to Speakers Other Lang, Cent Inst English & Lang, Hyderabad, India, 71-72, lectr ling, 72-73; res asst ling, Univ, Ill, Urbana,, 73-79; Asst Prof Ling, State Univ NY, Stony Brook, 80-,Consult, Dict Int Varieties of English, 78- & Univ Wash, Seattle, 79; secy, NY State Coun Ling, 81-82. **MEMBERSHIPS** Ling Soc Am; Teachers English to Speakers Other Lang; Ling Soc India; Dravidian Ling Asn; Am Asn Applied Ling. **RESEARCH** Dravidian linguistics; psycholinguistic aspects of sentence production, bilingualism and second language acquisition; teaching English as a second language. **SELECTED PUBLICATIONS** Co-ed, Language Through Literature, Vol II, Oxford Univ Press, 75; coauth, Clause-union and relational grammar, Ling Inquiry, 77; co-ed, Aspects of sociolinguistics in South Asia, Int J Sociol Lang, 78; auth, Dative subjects and the notion of subjective, Lingua, 79; Contrastive analysis, error analysis and interlanguage, In: Readings in English as a Second Language, Winthrop, 2nd ed, 80; coauth, Syntax & psycholinguistics of bilingual code mixing, Can J Psychol, 80; auth, Kannada: A Descriptive Grammar, North Holland Publ Co, 82; Language teaching and litercy in South Asia, In: Annual Review of Applied Linguistics, Newbury House, 82; A Reality Check For Sla Theories, Tesol Quart, Vol 28, 94. **CONTACT ADDRESS** Prog in Ling State, Univ NY, 100 Nicolls Rd, Stony Brook, NY, 11794-0002.

ST. CLAIR LESMAN, ANN
DISCIPLINE SPANISH LANGUAGE **EDUCATION** Rollins Col, BA; Duke Univ, MEd; Univ MD, MA, PhD. **CAREER** Prof, Shenandoah Univ. **HONORS AND AWARDS** Award for Excellence in For Lang Educ, For Lang Asn VA, 80; outstanding fac mem, Alumni Fedn Fac of the Yr Award, Shenandoah Univ, 96; Fulbright-Hayes fel, 96. **MEMBERSHIPS** Pres, For Lang Asn VA, 89-90 **SELECTED PUBLICATIONS** Wrote articles on the tchg of conversational skills. **CONTACT ADDRESS** Shenandoah Univ, Winchester, VA, 22601.

ST. OMER, GARTH
DISCIPLINE AMERICAN AND CARIBBEAN LITERATURE **EDUCATION** Princeton Univ, PhD, 75. **CAREER** PROF, ENG, UNIV CALIF, SANTA BARBARA. **RESEARCH** Fiction; creat writing. **SELECTED PUBLICATIONS** Auth, A Room on the Hill, Faber and Faber, 68; Shades of Grey, Faber and Faber, 68; Nor Any Country, Faber and Faber, 69; Black Bam and the Masqueraders, Faber and Faber, 72. **CONTACT ADDRESS** Dept of Eng, Univ Calif, Santa Barbara, CA, 93106-7150.

STAAL, ARIE
PERSONAL Born 09/27/1933, Grand Rapids, MI, m, 1963, 2 children **DISCIPLINE** AMERICAN & NETHERLANDIC LITERATURE **EDUCATION** Calvin Col, BA, 63; Univ Mich, MA, 64, PhD(English), 70. **CAREER** Instr, Calvin Col, 64-65 & Eastern Mich Univ, 68-70; lectr, Univ Helsinki, 70-71; asst prof, 71-76, assoc prof, 76-82, PROF ENGLISH, EASTERN MICH UNIV, 82-, Lectr, Bur of Sch Serv, Univ Mich, 68-70; Fulbright lectr, US Govt, 70. **MEMBERSHIPS** Can Asn Advan Netherlandic Studies; AAUP; Fine Arts Soc; Conf Christianity & Lit. **RESEARCH** Narrative techiques in traditional American fiction; narrative techniques in twentieth-century Netherlandic fiction; experimentation in twentieth-century Netherlandic poetry. **SELECTED PUBLICATIONS** Auth, Het Hotel, World Lit Today, Vol 69, 95; Cellojaren, World Lit Today, Vol 70, 96; The Following Story, World Lit Today, Vol 70, 96; Een Goede Zaak, World Lit Today, Vol 70, 96; De Zoektocht, World Lit Today, Vol 67, 93; Omhelzingen, World Lit Today, Vol 68, 94; Poems 1948-1993, World Lit Today, Vol 69, 95; Jazz, World Lit Today, Vol 67, 93; Okokas Wonderpark, World Lit Today, Vol 69, 95; Eclips, World Lit Today, Vol 68, 94; De Vriendschap, World Lit Today, Vol 70, 96; Het Woeden Der Gehele Wereld, World Lit Today, Vol 69, 95; Groenten Uit Balen, World Lit Today, Vol 68, 94; Respyt, World Lit Today, Vol 68, 94; Ontroeringen, World Lit Today, Vol 66, 92. **CONTACT ADDRESS** English Dept, Eastern Michigan Univ, 612 Pray Harrold, Ypsilanti, MI, 48197-2201.

STADLER, EVA MARIA
PERSONAL Born 03/28/1931, Prague, Czechoslovakia, m, 1957 **DISCIPLINE** COMPARATIVE LITERATURE, FILM STUDIES **EDUCATION** Barnard Col, AB, 52; Columbia Univ, PhD(French), 67. **CAREER** Lectr French, Columbia Univ, 53-57; instr French & Ger, Wash Col, 57-58; instr French, Douglass Col, Rutgers Univ, 58-64; asst prof French & Ger, 65-67, assoc prof, Manhattan Community Col, 67-68; assoc prof Comp Lit, French & Film Studies, 68-95, chair Humanities div, 73-79, dir Media Studies, 88-95, ASSOC PROF ENGLISH COMMUN & MEDIA STUDIES, FORDHAM UNIV, LINCOLN CENTER, 95-. **MEMBERSHIPS** MLA; ACLA; Soc 18th Century Studies; ACLA Nat Cmt on Undergraduate prog, 71-75 & 78-82; Colloquium fel in Comp Lit, NYU, 72-92; Juror, Am Film Festival 80 & 81 **RESEARCH** History and theory of the novel; fiction and film; French film and film theory; 18th Century literature. **SELECTED PUBLICATIONS** Coauth, Premiers textes litteraires, Blaisdell, 66, Wiley, 75; auth, Rameau's Nephew by Diderot: Un film de Michael Snow, In: Interpeter Diderot Au-jourd'hui, Le Sycomore, 84; Espace acoustique et cinema moderne: l'exemple de Rovert Bresson, In: Bulletin de la SPFFA, 86-87; The Red Dress of Oriane de Guermantes, In: Reading Proust Now, Lang, 90; Diderot et le cinema: Les paradoxes de l'adaptation, Francographies, 92; Defining the Female Body within Social Space; The Function of Clothes in Some 18th Century Novels, Proceedings of the XIIth Congress of the ICLA, 90; Francophonie et cinema: l'exemple de deux cineastes senegalais, Francographies, 93; Addressing Social Boundaries: Dressing the Female Body in Early Realist Fiction, In: Reconfigured Spheres: Feminist Explorations of Literary Space, Univ Mass Press, 94; Une femme douce de Robert Bresson: Le cinema et ses pre-textes, Francographies, 95 **CONTACT ADDRESS** Dept of English, Fordham Univ, 113 W 60th St, New York, NY, 10023. **EMAIL** evastadler@aol.com

STADTER, PHILIP AUSTIN
PERSONAL Born 11/29/1936, Cleveland, OH, m, 1963, 3 children **DISCIPLINE** CLASSICAL LITERATURE **EDUCATION** Princeton Univ, AB, 58; Harvard Univ, MA, 59, PhD, 63. **CAREER** From instr to assoc prof, 62-71, PROF CLASSICS, 71- , EUGENE FALK PROF OF HUMANITIES, 91- , UNIV NC, CHAPEL HILL, 71- ; Chmn Dept, 76-86, Guggenheim fel, 67-68; Nat Endowment for Humanities sr fel, 74-75; Am Coun-Learned Soc fel, 82-83; Nat Hum Ctr fel, 89-90. **MEMBERSHIPS** Am Philol Asn; Class Asn Midwest & South; Asn Ancient Historians. **RESEARCH** Plutarch, Arrian, Greek in Renaissance; Greek historiograph **SELECTED PUBLICATIONS** Auth, Plutarch's Historical Methods, Harvard Univ, 65; Flavius Arrianus: The new Xenophon, Greek, Roman & Byzantine Studies, 67; The structure of Livy's history, Historia, 72; coauth, The Public Library of Renaissance Florence, Antenore, Italy, 72; ed, The Speeches of Thucydides, Univ NC, 73; auth, Pace, Planudes, and Plutarch, Ital Medioevale e Umanistica, 73; Arrianus, Flavius, In: Catalogus Translationum et Commentariorum, Vol III, Cath Univ Am, 76; Arrian of Nicomedia, Univ NC, 80; A Commentary on Plutarch's Pericles, Univ NC, 89; ed Plutarch and the Historical Tradition, Routledge, Eng, 92. **CONTACT ADDRESS** Dept of Classics, Univ of N. Carolina, Chapel Hill, NC, 27514. **EMAIL** stadter@unc.edu

STALKER, JAMES CURTIS
PERSONAL Born 06/23/1940, Louisville, KY, m, 1964, 2 children **DISCIPLINE** APPLIED ENGLISH LINGUISTICS **EDUCATION** Univ NC, Chapel Hill, BA, 62; Univ Louisville, MA, 64; Univ WI-Madison, PhD, 70. **CAREER** Instr English ling, Univ Wis-Exten, 67-69; asst prof, 69-74, assoc prof, 74-82, prof English, Mi State Univ, 82-, dir English Lang Ctr, 80-90; dir MA TESOL Prog, Mi State Univ, 78-90; dir MA TESOL Prog, Billent Univ, Ankara, Turkey, 90-92. **HONORS AND AWARDS** Phi Beta Kappa, Phi Eta Sigma, Fulbright Scholar, Ankara, Turkey, 90-92. **MEMBERSHIPS** NCTE; TESOL; Am Asn Appl Ling. **RESEARCH** Slang, Language variation, International English, Pedogical linguistics, Stylistics. **SELECTED PUBLICATIONS** Auth, The poetic dialect: Syntactic ambiquity, Mich English Teacher, 5/77; A linguist's view of the composing process, CEA Critic, 5/78; Introduction to American dialects, Bridging the Gap, Mich State Univ, 79; Reader expectations and the poetic line, Resources Educ, 3/79; Reading is non-linear, Reading, Mich Coun Teachers English, 80; Propriety and dogma, Linguistics and the University Education, Mich State Univ, 80; Usage: Or back to basics: An old saw resharpened, ERIC, 8/81; Review: Crowley, Robert, ed, Proper English: Readings in Language, History and Cultural Identity, World Englishes, 94; Review of Trudgill, Peter and Chambers, J K, 91; Dialects of English: Studies in Grammatical Variation, London:Longman, World Englishes, 95; Idioma, Cognicion y cultura: Conexiones culturales y politicas, Las Lenguas Extanjeras en la Ensenanza: Lengua y Cultura, Montevideo, Uruguay: Alianza Cultural Uruguay-Estados Unidos, 96; Slang is Not Novel, ERIC Document Repro Serv, 96; Language Variation and Cultural Identity: Reader and Writer Conflicts in Language Use, Approaches to Teaching Non-Native English Speakers Across the Curriculum, New Directions for Teaching and Learning, No 70, San Francisco: Jossey-Bass Publ, 97; Some comments on dude, Comments on Etymology, 27, 16-18, 97. **CONTACT ADDRESS** Dept of English, Michigan State Univ, 201 Morrill Hall, East Lansing, MI, 48824-1036. **EMAIL** stalker@pilot.msu.edu

STAMELMAN, RICHARD
DISCIPLINE ROMANCE LANGUAGES **EDUCATION** Hamilton Col, BA, 63; Duke Univ, PhD, 68. **CAREER** Prof, Williams Col, 93-; -William R Kenan, Jr, prof, Humanities, Wesleyan Univ, 83-92; dean, Humanities, Wesleyan Univ, 86-89; ch, Dept Fr & Italian, Univ Colorado, 91-92. **HONORS AND AWARDS** La medaille du College de Fr, 93; Chevalier dans l'Ordre des Palmes Academiques, 93. **RESEARCH** 19th and 20th-century French poetry; relationship of art and literature; French cultural studies: fashion and perfume; literary theory. **SELECTED PUBLICATIONS** Auth, The Drama of Self in Guillaume Apollinaire's Alcools, 76; Lost beyond Telling: Representations of Death and Absence in Modern French Poetry, 90; ed, Ecrire, le livre: Authour d'Edmond Jabes. Colloque de Cerisy la Salle, 89; guest ed, French Poetry Since the War: The Poetics of Presence and Passage, L'Esprit createur, 92; transl & ed, The Lure and the Truth of Painting. Selected Essays of Yves Bonnefoy on Art, 95. **CONTACT ADDRESS** Center for Foreign Languages, Literatures and Cult, Williams Col, Williamstown, MA, 01267. **EMAIL** Richard.H.Stamelman@williams.edu

STAMPINO, MARIA GALLI
PERSONAL Born 12/18/1964, Gallarate, Italy, m, 1993 **DISCIPLINE** ITALIAN, FRENCH **EDUCATION** Universita Cattolica, Milan, Italy, laurea, For Lang & Lit, 88; Univ Kansas, MA, Am Stud, 90; Stanford Univ, Ital & Compar Lit, MA, 92, PhD, 96. **CAREER** Tchg asst, Univ Kansas, Ital, 88-90; tchg asst, Stanford Univ, Ital, 90-93; lectr, Wash Univ, Ital, 96; asst prof, Univ Miami, Ital & French, 96-98; VIS ASST PROF, ST LOUIS UNIV, ITAL & FRENCH, 98-. **MEMBERSHIPS** MLA; Am Asn Tchrs of Ital; Nat Commun Asn; Renaissance Soc Am; Am Soc Theater Res; Asn Theater in High Educ **RESEARCH** European Renaissance; Lyric poetry; Theater; Baroque. **SELECTED PUBLICATIONS** "Bodily Boundaries Represented: The Petrarchan, the Burlesque, and the Arcimboldo's Example," Quaderni d'Italianistica, 95; "The Space of the Performance: Aminta, the Court, and the Theater," Romance Review, 96; "Epideictic Pastoral: Rhetorical Tensions in the Staging of Torquato Tasso's Aminta," Theater Symposium: Drama as Rhetoric/Rhetoric as Drama, 97; "Performance, text, and Canon: The Case of Aminta," RLA, 98. **CONTACT ADDRESS** St. Louis Univ, 314 Clara Ave, Apt 35, St Louis, MO, 63112. **EMAIL** mgstampino@miami.edu

STANLEY, PATRICIA H.
PERSONAL New Bedford, MA **DISCIPLINE** GERMAN HUMANITIES **EDUCATION** Univ Louisville, AB, 64, MA, 69; Univ Va, PhD(Ger), 75. **CAREER** Asst prof Ger, Univ Va, 76-77; asst prof, 77-80, Prof Ger, Fla State Univ, 94-. **MEMBERSHIPS** Am Asn Teachers Ger; MLA; S Atlantic Mod Lang Asn; Am Lit Translators Asn; Kafka Soc Am. **RESEARCH** Literature of the absurd; women's issues; literary theory. **SELECTED PUBLICATIONS** Auth, Wolfgang Hildesheimer's Das Opfer Helena: Another Triumph of the "They", In: University of Florida Drama Conference Papers, II, 83; Hoffman's Phantasiestcke in Callots Manier in Light of Friedrich Schlegel's Theory of the Arabesque, Ger Studies Rev, VIII, October 85; Wolfgang Hildesheimer, biographical entry in Dictionary of Literary Biography, 69, Contemp Ger Fiction Writers, 88; Walter Kempowski, biographical entry in Dictionary of Literary Biography, 75, Contemp Ger Fiction Writers, 88; The Realm of Possibilities. Wolfgang Hildesheimer's Non-Traditional Non-Fictional Prose, Univ Press of Am, 88; More than a Misspelling: (Con)Textual Differences in Woyzeck/Wozzeck, In: Theoretically Speaking, 7, 92; Gunter Herberger, Wolfgang Hildesheimer, biographical entries in Dictionary of Literary Biography, 124, Twentieth-Century German Dramatists, 1919-1992, 92; Wolfgang Hildesheimer and His Critics, Camden House, 93; Sum, ergo spero?, Wolfgang Hildesheimer's Tentative Absurd Hope, Seminar, 2/95; A Thousand Thanks. Dr. Albert Schweitzer's Correspondence with Dr. Antonia Brico, Johns Hopkins Press (forthcoming), auth of several other books and articles. **CONTACT ADDRESS** Dept of Mod Lang, Florida State Univ, Tallahassee, FL, 32306-1540. **EMAIL** pstanley@mailer.fsu.edu

STANTON, EDWARD F.
PERSONAL Born 10/29/1942, Colorado Springs, CO, m, 1996, 2 children **DISCIPLINE** HISPANIC LANGUAGES & LITERATURE **EDUCATION** Univ Calif, Los Angeles, PhD, 72. **CAREER** Asst Prof, 72-78, Assoc Prof, 79-89, Prof, 89-, Univ Ky. **HONORS AND AWARDS** Sr Fulbright Lecturer, 90; Vis Prof, Universidad Autonoma, Madrid Spain, 96; NEH Summer Stipend, 81; ACLS Travel Grant, 84. **MEMBERSHIPS** Hemingway Soc; Friends of Camino de Santiago; Garcia Lorca Foundation. **RESEARCH** Hispanic poetry, film, & popular culture; compariative lit. **SELECTED PUBLICATIONS** Auth, Road of Stars to Santiago, Univ Press of Ky, 94; auth, Hemingway y El Pais Vasco, Inst Vasco de las Artes l y las Letras, 97; auth, Handbook of Spanish Popular Culture, Greenwood Press, 99. **CONTACT ADDRESS** Dept of Spanish & Italian, Univ Ky, Lexington, KY, 40506. **EMAIL** stanton@ukcc.uky.edu

STANTON, LEONARD J.
DISCIPLINE RUSSIAN LANGUAGE, 19TH AND 20TH CENTURY LITERATURE, CULTURE AND INTERDISCIP **EDUCATION** Univ Kans, PhD, 84. **CAREER** Assoc prof Russ, comt on acad plan and prog eval, La State Univ. **RESEARCH** Religious literature; iconography; hypertext. **SELECTED PUBLICATIONS** Auth, Three Levels of Authorship in the Way of a Pilgrim, in St Vladimir's Theol Quart, 33, 89; The Optina Pustyn Monastery in the Russian Literary Imagination, Peter Lang, 95. **CONTACT ADDRESS** Dept of For Lang and Lit, Louisiana State Univ, 153 B Prescott Hall, Baton Rouge, LA, 70803. **EMAIL** stanton@homer.forlang.lsu.edu

STANTON, MARGARET
DISCIPLINE SPANISH LANGUAGE AND LITERATURE **EDUCATION** Mt Mercy Col, BA; Univ WI Madison, PhD. **CAREER** Assoc prof; coord, Latin Am Studies Prog. **RESEARCH** Latin Am lit. **SELECTED PUBLICATIONS** Auth, transl of Latin Am short stories. **CONTACT ADDRESS** Sweet Briar Col, Sweet Briar, VA, 24595.

STARK, JAMES
DISCIPLINE GERMAN **EDUCATION** Portland Univ, BA, 64; Univ WA, BA, 64, PhD, 72. **CAREER** Languages, Seattle Univ. **MEMBERSHIPS** AATG, Europ Stud Asn; Asn for Interdisciplinary Stud of Arts; NEMLA; MLA; ISSEI. **SELECTED PUBLICATIONS** Auth, Wolfgang Burchert's Germany: Reflections of the Third Reich, UP Amer, Baltimore, 96; cotransl, Outside in Front of the Door; Crossing Subtle Borders in the Works of German Immigrant Writers; E Pluribus Unum: Literary Reflections of a New German Identity; Wolfgang Borchert's 'Die Kuechenluhr' and 'Das Brot' Love Among the Ruins; Der Staendebaum' and 'Das Schaukelbrett: Two Symbols of Oppression; Symbolic Gender Transformation: A Comparison of Brecht and Grimmelshausen; **CONTACT ADDRESS** Dept of For Lang, Seattle Univ, 900 Broadway, Seattle, WA, 98122-4460. **EMAIL** jstark@seattleu.edu

STAROSTA, WILLIAM J.
PERSONAL Born 05/23/1946, Oconomowoc, WI, m, 1967, 1 child **DISCIPLINE** INTERCULTURAL COMMUNICATION **EDUCATION** Indiana Univ, AM, 70, PhD, 73. **CAREER** Univ of Va, asst prof, 72-78; Howard Univ, grad prof, 78-. **HONORS AND AWARDS** Fulbright diss. fel; Am Inst of Indian Studies fel; Wis-Berkeley Year-in-India scholar., Held professional office in regional and national socs. **MEMBERSHIPS** Nat Commun Asn; Eastern Commun Asn; World Commun Asn; Intl. Commun Asn. **RESEARCH** Ethnic conflict; Third Culture; Multiculturalism; Interethnic and intercultural communication; Culture and rhetoric. **SELECTED PUBLICATIONS** Coauth, Foundations of Intercultural Communication; ed, The Howard Jour of Communs. **CONTACT ADDRESS** Dept of Human Communication Studies, Howard Univ, 3015 Rosemoor Ln., Fairfax, VA, 22031. **EMAIL** wstarosta@fac.howard.edu

STARR, PETER
DISCIPLINE FRENCH AND COMPARATIVE LITERATURE **EDUCATION** Johns Hopkins Univ, PhD. **CAREER** Assoc prof, Univ Southern Calif. **RESEARCH** Vicissitudes of paranoia in modern and postmodern literature, film, and theory **SELECTED PUBLICATIONS** Auth, Logics of Failed Revolt: French Theory After May '68, 95; **CONTACT ADDRESS** Col Letters, Arts & Sciences, Univ Southern Calif, University Park Campus, Los Angeles, CA, 90089. **EMAIL** pstarr@usc.edu

STARR, RAYMOND JAMES
PERSONAL Born 05/17/1952, Grand Rapids, MI, m, 1975 **DISCIPLINE** CLASSICAL LANGUAGES **EDUCATION** Univ Mich, BA, 74; Princeton Univ, MA, 76, PhD(class), 78. **CAREER** Lectr class, Princeton Univ, 78-79; Asst Prof Greek & Latin, Wellesley Col, 79-, Fel, Am Coun Learned Soc, 82-83. **MEMBERSHIPS** Am Philol Asn; Class Asn Can; Class Asn New England. **RESEARCH** Social context of ancient literature; Roman historiography; comedy. **SELECTED PUBLICATIONS** VERGIL 'SEVENTH ECLOGUE' AND ITS READERS - BIOGRAPHICAL ALLEGORY AS AN INTERPRETATIVE STRATEGY IN ANTIQUITY AND LATE-ANTIQUITY/, CLASSICAL PHILOLOGY, Vol 0090, 1995 **CONTACT ADDRESS** Dept of Greek & Latin, Wellesley Col, 106 Central St, Wellesley, MA, 02181-8204.

STATHATOS, CONSTANTINE CHRISTOPHER
PERSONAL Born 04/12/1939, Athens, Greece **DISCIPLINE** SPANISH **EDUCATION** Eastern Ore Col, BA, 63; Univ Ore, MA, 66, PhD(Span), 70. **CAREER** Asst prof, 70-75, assoc prof Span, Univ Wis-Parkside,75-, prof, 86-. **RESEARCH** Spanish drama of the Siglo de Oro; Oil Vicente; translation. **SELECTED PUBLICATIONS** Ed, A Critical Edition with Introduction and Notes of Gil Vicente's Floresta de Enganos, Univ NC, 72; auth, Antecendents of Gil Vicente's Floresta de Enganos, Luso-Brazilian Rev, 72; co-ed, En onda, Norton, 75; A bibliography of translations of Gil Vicente's works since 1940, Vortice, 75; French contributions to the study of Gil Vicente (1942-1975), Luso-Brazilian Rev, 78; Another Look at Mira de Amescua's Don Alvaro de Luna, Segismundo, 78-80; A Gil Vicente Bibliography (1940-1975), Grant & Cutler, 80; Lazarillo de Tormes in Current English: Two Notes, Hispanofila, 82, Ed, A Critical Edition of Gil Vicente's Auto da India, Puvill, 97, A Gil Vicente Bibliography, 75-95, Leigh UP, 97. **CONTACT ADDRESS** Mod Lang Dept, Univ of Wisconsin, Parkside, Box 2000, Kenosha, WI, 53141-2000. **EMAIL** constantin.stathatos@uwp.edu

STAVAN, HENRY-ANTHONY
PERSONAL Born 06/13/1925, Ostrava, Czechoslovakia **DISCIPLINE** FRENCH **EDUCATION** San Francisco State Col, BA, 56; Univ Calif, Berkeley, MA, 60, PhD(Romance lit), 63. **CAREER** Instr Span, Sacramento State Col, 61-62; asst prof French, Univ Wyo, 63-64; asst prof, Univ Minn, 64-66; assoc prof, 66-75, Prof French, Univ Colo, Boulder, 75-, Foe fel, Colo Univ, 69-70 & 74-75; vis prof, Univ of Tubingen, Ger, 78-79. **MEMBERSHIPS** Fr Soc 18th Century Studies. **RESEARCH** Eighteenth century French literature. **SELECTED PUBLICATIONS** Auth, Un roman sentimental entre Rousseau et Bernardin de Saint-Pierrc, Rev Univ Ottawa, 72; Quelques aspects de lyrisme dans la poesie du XVIIIe siecle, Rev Sci Huamaines, 73; coauth, Editing The Complete Works of Voltaire, Voltaire Found, Banbury, Oxfordshire, UK, 73-75; auth, Le lyrisme dans la poesie francaise de 1760 a 1820, Mouton, The Hague, 76; The Ugly Americans of 1780, Stanford Fr Studies, 78; Voltaire und Kurfurst Karl Theodor von der Pfalz, Gesellschaft der Freunde Mannheims, 78; Voltaire et la Duchesse de Gotha, Studies Voltaire, 80; Herzogin Louise Dorothee von Sachsen-Gotha und Voltaire, Jahrbuch Coburger Landesstiftung, 80; French Adaptation Of L Alcade De Zalamea At The End Of The 18th-Century, Revue D Histoire Du Theatre, Vol 44, 92; French Adaptation Of Calderondelabarca,Pedro, Revue D Histoire Du Theatre, Vol 44, 92. **CONTACT ADDRESS** Dept of French, Univ of Colo, Boulder, CO, 80302.

STECKLINE, C. TURNER
PERSONAL Born 12/28/1954, Sanborn, NY **DISCIPLINE** SPEECH COMMUNICATION, DRAMTIC ARTS, PERFORMANCE STUDIES **EDUCATION** Univ of Northern Colo, BA, 75; Univ of Iowa, MA, 78; Southern Ill Univ at Carbondale, PhD, 97. **CAREER** Chair, dept of speech commun, Univ of Dubuque, 79-82; asst prof of speech commun, Loras Col, 82-87; instr/asst dir of forensics, Iowa State Univ, 88-89; dir of forensics, 89-91, asst prof, 91-95, Univ of Wis-Platteville; ASST PROF OF SPEECH COMMUN AND THEATRE ARTS, NORTHEAST LA UNIV, 97-. **HONORS AND AWARDS** Marion Kleinau Theatre Award, Southern Ill Univ, 95; Kleinau Theatre Production Assistantship, 95 & 96; Graduate Teaching Assistantship, Southern Ill Unive, 92-95, 97; initiating honors sequence: Vision, Language & Reality, Univ of Wis-Platteville, 91-92; adjunct fac appointment, 80-82, teaching Excellence, Loras Col, 86; grad teaching asst, The Rhetoric Prog, Univ of Iowa, 76-79. **MEMBERSHIPS** Nat Commun Asn; Southern States Commun Asn; La Commun Asn; Nat Coun for Teachers of English; Nat Women's Studies Asn; Nat Storytelling Asn. **RESEARCH** Whistleblowing/ethical resistances; diffusion; response theory & bearing witness; disability and family communication; performance of ethnography/ethnography of performance. **SELECTED PUBLICATIONS** Auth, Ideas and Images of Performed Witnessing: A Cross-Genre Analysis, Southern Ill Univ at Carbondale, 97; auth, Books in Review: Ecological Feminism, Ecological Literary Criticism: Romantic Imagining and the Biology of the Mind, Text and Performance Quarterly, 96. **CONTACT ADDRESS** Dept of Speech Commun & Theatre, Northeast Louisiana Univ, Monroe, LA, 71203. **EMAIL** coyote@hc3.com

STEELE, MARTA N.
PERSONAL Born 05/20/1949, Trenton, NJ, d, 1 child **DISCIPLINE** CLASSICAL PHILOLOGY **EDUCATION** Wellesley Col, BA, 71; Univ CA, Los Angelos, MA, 73; Boston Univ, PhD candidate, 80-. **CAREER** Full-time and freelance newspaper reporter, 83-85; adjunct instr, English composition, res and exposition, business writing, Rider Col Dept of English, 84-85; copy chief, NJ Network, Trenton, NJ, 85; freelance manuscript ed, indexer, and proofreader, 87-91; freelance trans/author, 95-97; manuscript ed, series ed, Princeton Univ Press, 91-. **HONORS AND AWARDS** Listed in Who's Who in the East and Int Who's Who of Professionals; honored at Royal Danish Embassy, Washington, DC, and Princeton Univ Press, 5/98, for completeion of the 25 text volumes of the Kierkegaard's Writings series. **MEMBERSHIPS** Am Philol Asn; Am Classical League. **RESEARCH** Homeric philology (PhD thesis topic); poetics, epic in general; computer programs to facilitate various aspects of Classics editing and indexing. **SELECTED PUBLICATIONS** Editor, R Rehm, Marriage to Death: The Conflagation of Wedding and Funeral Rituals in Greek Tragedy, 94; P C Miller, Dreams in Late Antiquity: Studies in the Imagination of a Culture, 94; D J Furley and A Nehamas, eds, Aristotle's Rhetoric: Philosophical Essays, 94; G Vlastos, ed by D Graham, Studies in Greek Philosophy: Volume 1: The Presocratics; Volume II, Socrates, Plato, and Their Tradition, 95; M W Gleason, Making Men: Sophists and Self-Presentation in Ancient Rome, 95; N Loraux, trans Paula Wissing, The Experiences of Tiresias: The Feminine and the Greek Man, 95; E Stehle, Performance and Gender in Ancient Greece, 96; S Schein, Reading the Odyssey: Selected Interpretive Essays, 96; J Ober and C Hendrick, eds, Demokratia: A Conversation on Democracies, Ancient and Modern, 96; D Lyons, Gender and Immortality: Heroines in Ancient Greek Myth and Cult, 97; Patricia Curd, The Legacy of Parmenides: Eleatic Monism and Later Presocratic Thought, 98; Johanna Prins (Yopi), Victorian Sappho, forthcoming 99; Sidney Alexander, trans and commentator, The Complete Odes and Satires of Horace, forthcoming 99; editor of numerous other publications. **CONTACT ADDRESS** Univ Press, Princeton Univ, 41 William St, Princeton, NJ, 08540. **EMAIL** marta_steele@pupress.princeton.edu

STEETS, CHERYL
PERSONAL Born 10/02/1954, Warwick, RI, m, 1992 **DISCIPLINE** INDO-IRANIAN STUDIES **EDUCATION** Univ RI, BA, 77; UCLA, PhD, 93. **CAREER** Tchg asst, tchg fel, UCLA, 84-91. **HONORS AND AWARDS** Univ Calif Fel, 89; Mabel Wilson Richards Found Scholar, 91. **MEMBERSHIPS** Am Oriental Soc, APA. **RESEARCH** Comparative mythology and Indo-European literature; Indo-Iranian studies; Indo-Iranian linguistics. **SELECTED PUBLICATIONS** Auth, "Sun Maiden's Wedding," UMI, 93 (diss); "Ajahad u dva mithuna," Studies in Honor of Jean Puhvel, pt 1, Ancient Languages; Institute for the Study of Man, 97. **CONTACT ADDRESS** 6755 Mira Mesa Blvd, #123-168, San Diego, CA, 92121. **EMAIL** nad@earthlink.net

STEFANOVSKA, MALINA
PERSONAL Born 12/30/1952, Yugoslavia, m, 1997, 1 child **DISCIPLINE** FRENCH LITERATURE **EDUCATION** Univ Grenoble, BA, 73; Univ Oregon, MA, 84; Johns Hopkins Univ, PhD, 90. **CAREER** Assoc prof, Univ Calif Los Angeles, 90-. **HONORS AND AWARDS** UCLA Career Develop Award, 93, 95; Acad Senate Res Grant, 90-97; Gilman fel, 84-90; selected to teach at Ecole Normale Superieure, Fontenay/Saint-Cloud, 97-98, through the Education Abroad Program. **RESEARCH** Memoirs and historiography; seventeenth century studies; cultural studies. **SELECTED PUBLICATIONS** Auth, Histoire ou historiette: le portrait du prince par Tellemant des Reaux et Saint-Simon, Papers on French Seventeenth-Century Lit, 93; auth, Saint-Simon: un moraliste dans le reel, Dalhousie French Stud, 94; auth, Strolling through the Galleries, Hiding in A Cabinet: Clio at the French Absolutist Court, Eighteenth Century: Theory and Interpretation, 94; auth, Un solipe absolu: le portrait de Louis XIV par Saint-Simon, Actes de Lexington, Papers on Seventeenth-Century French Lit, 95; auth, Le corps de la nation selon l'opposition novilaire a Louis XIV, Biblio 17, Papers on French Seventeenth-Century Lit, 95; auth, A Well-staged Coup de theatre: The Royal Lit de Justice in 1718, Sub/Stance, 96; auth, A Monumental Triptych: The Parallel of the First Three Bourbon Kings by Saint-Simon, Fr Hist Stud, 96; auth, Saint-Simon, Un Historien Dans Les Marges, Paris, Honore Champion, 98. **CONTACT ADDRESS** Univ of California, Los Angeles, CA, 90024. **EMAIL** stefanov@humnet.ucla.edu

STEINBERG, THEODORE LOUIS
PERSONAL Born 01/08/1947, Baltimore, MD, m, 3 children **DISCIPLINE** MEDIEVAL ENGLISH; JEWISH LITERATURE **EDUCATION** Johns Hopkins Univ, BA, 68; Univ Ill, AM, 69, PhD(English), 71. **CAREER** Asst prof, 71-75, assoc prof, 75-79, prof English, State Univ NY Col Fredonia, 79- **HONORS AND AWARDS** Chancellor's Award for Excellence in Teaching, 96; **MEMBERSHIPS** Medieval Acad Am; Am Asn Prof Yiddish; Spenser Soc. **RESEARCH** Medieval and Renaissance literature; Jewish literature. **SELECTED PUBLICATIONS** Auth, Spenser's Shepherdes Calender and EK's, Mod Lang Studies, winter 73; The schoolmaster: Teaching sixteenth century literature, English Rec, 73; I B Singer: Responses to catastrophe, Yiddish, 75; The anatomy of Euphues, Studies English Lit, 77; Mendele Mocher Seforim, G K Hall, 77; The humanities and the Holocaust, Humanist Educators, 80; Poetry and the perpendicular style, J Aesthet & Art Criticism, 81; Piers Plowman and Prophecy, Garland, 91. **CONTACT ADDRESS** Dept of English, SUNY, Fredonia, Fredonia, NY, 14063-1143. **EMAIL** steinberg@fredonia.edu

STEINER, CARL
PERSONAL Born 08/05/1927, Vienna, Austria, m, 1954, 3 children **DISCIPLINE** GERMAN LANGUAGE & LITERATURE **EDUCATION** George Washington Univ, BA, 58, MA, 62, PhD(Ger), 66. **CAREER** From instr to asst prof, 64-68, assoc prof, 68-78, chmn dept Ger lang & lit, 70-82, Prof Ger, George Washington Univ, 78-, Recording secy, Am Goethe Soc, 67; consult, Can Coun, 76-77. **MEMBERSHIPS** SAtlantic Mod Lang Asn; Am Asn Teachers Ger; Am Goethe Soc (pres, 81-). **RESEARCH** German emigre literature; 19th century German realism; 20th century German literature; German socio-critical literature. **SELECTED PUBLICATIONS** Auth, Uber Gottfried Kellers Verhaltnis zur Demokratie, Vol LX, No 4 & Die Goethe- Gesellschaft von Washington, Vol LX, No 4, Monatsh, Univ Wis; Frankreichbild und Katholizismus bei Joseph Roth, Ger Quart, 1/73; Moliere und die Kleistische Komodie Versuch einer Deutung, In: Moliere and the Commonwealth of Letters, Univ Miss, 75; Kafkas Amerika Illusion oder Wirklichkeit?, In: Franz Kafka-Symposium, Agora Verlag, Berlin, 78; Georg Kaiser, Ein Moderner Mythenmacher, In: Georg Kaiser, Agora Verlag, Berlin, 80; Franz Werfel Novel Jeremias Horet Die Stimme, A Confession Of Jewish Faith, Modern Austrian Literature, Vol 27, 94; Storm,Theodor, German Studies Rev, Vol 16, 93. **CONTACT ADDRESS** Dept of Ger Lang & Lit, George Washington Univ, Washington, DC, 20052.

STEINER, THOMAS ROBERT
PERSONAL Born 08/18/1934, Budapest, Hungary, m, 1966, 2 children **DISCIPLINE** ENGLISH, COMPARATIVE LITERATURE **EDUCATION** Cornell Univ, BA, 55; Columbia Univ, MA, 60 PhD(English), 67. **CAREER** Lectr, Hunter Col, 61-64 & Brooklyn Col, 64-66; asst prof, 66-74, ASSOC PROF ENGLISH, UNIV CALIF, SANTA BARBARA, 74-, Fel, Calif Humanities Inst, 69-70; consult-reader, PMLA, 71; consult, Harcourt Brace Jovanovich, Inc, 72; vis assoc prof English, Univ Ill, Urbana-Champaign, 74-75; reader, J English & Ger Philol, 74; consult, Calif Coun for Humanities Pub Policy, 77-79. **HONORS AND AWARDS** Nathanael West Essay Contest Prize, Southern Rev, 70. **RESEARCH** Eighteenth century English literature; literary theory; detective fiction. **SELECTED PUBLICATIONS** Auth, Precursors to Dryden, Comp Lit Studies, 3/70; West's Lemuel and the American dream, Southern Rev, 10/71; English Translation Theory, 1650-1800, Van Gorcum, 75; The heroic ape: Teaching pope, Eighteenth Century Life, spring 79; The Origin Of Raymond Chandler: Mean-Streets, Anq-A Quart J Of Short Articles Notes And Reviews, Vol 7, 94. **CONTACT ADDRESS** Dept of English, Univ of Calif, Santa Barbara, CA, 93106.

STENSON, NANCY JEAN
PERSONAL Born 08/07/1945, San Mateo, CA, m, 1976, 1 child **DISCIPLINE** LINGUISTICS **EDUCATION** Pomona Col, BA, 67; Univ Calif, San Diego, MA, 70, PhD(ling), 76. **CAREER** English as second lang specialist, Lang Res Found, 71-72; Assoc Prof Ling, Univ Minn, Minneapolis, 78-, Dublin Inst for Advan Studies scholar, 76-77; consult, Havasupai & Hualapai Bilingual Ed Prog, 75-76. **MEMBERSHIPS** Ling Soc Am; Am Asn Applied Ling; N Am ASN Celtic Lang Teachers. **RESEARCH** Syntax; Irish language; language contact; code switching. **SELECTED PUBLICATIONS** Auth, Overlapping systems in the Irish comparative construction, Word, 77: Plural formation in Rath Cairn Eigse: J Irish Studies, 78; Questions on the accessibility hierarchy, Elements, Chicago Ling Soc, 79; Studies in Irish syntax, Gunter Narr Verlag, 81; On short term language change: Developments in Irish Morphology, Proc 5th Int Cong Hist Ling, 82; Irish Autonomous Impersonal, Natural Lang & Ling Theory, 7, 89; Prepositional pronouns in a transitional dialect, Celtica, 21, 90; Patterns of initial mutation in Irish loanwords, Eigse, 24, 90; Phrase structure congruence, government & Irish English code switching, Syntaxt Semantics, 23, 90; Code Switching vs. Borrowing in Modern Irish, In: Language Contact in the British Isles, 91; coauth, Learner-controlled listening materials using a commercial videodisk, CAELL J, 2, 91; The effectiveness of computer-assisted pronunciation training, Calico J, 9, 92; auth, English Influence on Irish: the last 100 Years, J Celtic Ling, 2, 93; Patterns of variation in Irish loan phonology, Principles & Predictions:

the Analysis of Natural Language, 93; Language Contact & the development of Irish directional phrase idioms, D un de Oide, 97; video in the Irish language classroom, Teinga, 16, 96. **CONTACT ADDRESS** Dept of Ling, Univ of Minnesota, 320 16th Ave SE, Minneapolis, MN, 55455-0143. **EMAIL** stenson@tc.unm.edu

STERN, GUY
PERSONAL Born 01/14/1922, Germany, m **DISCIPLINE** GERMAN, COMPARITIVE LITERATURE **EDUCATION** Hofstra Col, BA, 48; Columbia Univ, MA, 50, PhD, 54. **CAREER** Instr Ger, Columbia Univ, 48-54; assoc prof mod lang, Denison Univ, 54-64; prof Ger lang & lit & chmn dept Ger, Univ Cincinnati, 64-75, univ dean grad educ & res, 73-75; prof Ger & Slavic lang & lit & chmn dept, Univ MD, College Park, 75-78; provost & sr vpres, 78-81, Distinguished Prof Romance Lang & Ger, Wayne State Univ, 81-; Dir, Int Exchange, Div Arts & Humanities, 78-, Adv ed, Dover Publ, 58-; Fulbright res grant, 61-62; Leo Baeck fel, 61-; Bollingen res fel, 62-63; chmn, Fulbright Screening Comt Germanistics, 67-72; consult, Col Entrance Exam Bd, 68-72; secy, Am Coun Ger Studies, 68-; Ger Acad Exchange Serv res fel, 81; guest prof, univ Potsdam, 98. **HONORS AND AWARDS** Distinguished Graduate Faculty Award, 97-98; Honor PhD, Hofstra univ, 98. **MEMBERSHIPS** SAtlantic Mod Lang Asn; Am Asn Tchr(s) Ger (pres, 70-72); Lessing Soc (pres, 74-76); MLA. **RESEARCH** Class and mod Ger lit; Eng-Ger comp lit. **SELECTED PUBLICATIONS** Auth, Saint or hypocrite: A study of Wieland's Jacinte episode, Ger Rev, 53; Hugo v Hofmannsthal and the Speiers, PMLA, 1/57; Konstellationen, 1914/25, Deut Verlangs-Anstalt, Stuttgart, 64; Efraim Frisch: Zum Verstandnis des Geistigen, Lambert Schneider, Heidelberg, 64; Prolegomena zu einer Geschichte der deutschen Nachkriegsprose, Colloquia Germanica, 11/67; War, Weimar and Literature: The Story of the Neue Merkur, Pa State Univ, 71; Exile literature: Designation or misnomer, Colloquia Germanica, 1/72; Science and literature: Arno Reinfrank as a poet of facts, In: Festschrift Andre von Gronicka, Bouvier, Bonn, 78; ed, Alfred Neumann, Steiner, Wiesbaden, 79; Literarissche Kultur im Exil, Dresdin univ Press, 98. **CONTACT ADDRESS** Dept of Foreign Lang, Wayne State Univ, 409 Manoogian, Detroit, MI, 48202-3919.

STERN, IRWIN
PERSONAL Born 07/28/1946, Brooklyn, NY **DISCIPLINE** LUSO-BRAZILIAN LANGUAGE & LITERATURE **EDUCATION** Queens Col, NY, BA, 67, MA, 69; City Univ New York, PhD(Port), 72. **CAREER** Instr Romance lang, Univ Nebr-Lincoln, 69-71; adj lectr, City Col New York, 71-72, asst prof Port & Span, 72-76. Grad fac comp lit, City Univ New York, 75-76; adj asst prof Span & Port, New York Univ, 77-; lectr Port, Columbia Univ, 79-; vis asst prof, Adelphi Univ, spring, 76; vis prof, Univ Pittsburgh, 78; vis asst prof, Queens Col, 79. **HONORS AND AWARDS** PEN Club Transl Prize, 81. **MEMBERSHIPS** Am Asn Teachers Span & Port; MLA; Am-Port Soc; Int Conf Group Mod Port. **RESEARCH** Nineteenth century Portuguese literature; 19th and 20th centuries Luso-Brazilian fiction; Spanish fiction. **SELECTED PUBLICATIONS** Auth, Julio Dinis e o romance portugues, Porto: Lello & Irmao, Editores, 72; Suppressed Portuguese Fiction: 1926-1974, Bks Abroad, winter 76; Jane Austen e Julio Dinis, 3/76 & Ecade Queiroz e Pinhero Chagas, 5/80, Coloquio/ Letras; Luandino Vieira's Short Fiction: Decolonization in the Third Register, When the Drumbeat Changes, Three Continents, 81; Continuing the Marvelous Journes, Review, 1-4/81; Violeta E A Noite--Portuguese, World Lit Today, Vol 66, 92. **CONTACT ADDRESS** 380 Riverside Dr Apt 5-M, New York, NY, 10025.

STERNBACH, NANCY SAPORTA
PERSONAL Born 04/05/1945, New York, NY, 2 children **DISCIPLINE** LANGUAGE **EDUCATION** Univ Wi, BA, 71, Middlebury Col, MA, 73; Univ Az, PhD, 84. **CAREER** Assoc prof, Chair, Smith Col **HONORS AND AWARDS** Nat Endow for the Humanities, 97 **MEMBERSHIPS** MLA **RESEARCH** Latina writers **SELECTED PUBLICATIONS** Auth, Engendering the Future: Cenizas de Izalco and the Making of a Writer, in Claribel Alegria and Central American Literature: Critical Essays, Oh Univ Center for Latin Amer Stud, 94; coauth, Latin American Women Essayists: Intruders and Usurpers, in The Politics of the Essay: A Feminist Perspective, Univ Ind Press, 94; auth, Mejorar la condicion de mi secso: The Essays of Rosa Guerra, in Reinterpreting the Spanish-American Essay, Univ Tx Press, 95; coauth, Rehearsing in front of the Mirror: Marga Gomez' Lesbian Subjectivity as a Work-in-progress, in women and Performance, 96; coed, Puro Teatro: An Anthology of Latina Theatre, Performance and Testimonio, Univ Az Press, 99. **CONTACT ADDRESS** Smith Col, Hatfield Hall, Northampton, MA, 01063. **EMAIL** nsternba@sophia.smith.edu

STEVENS, LIZBETH JANE
PERSONAL Born 10/31/1949, Angola, IN, m, 1968, 3 children **DISCIPLINE** SPEECH PATHOLOGY **EDUCATION** Univ of Mich, BA, 74, MS, 76; Wayne St Univ, PhD, 92. **CAREER** Tchr of speech and lang impaired, 78-98, Warren Woods School District; adj instr, 97-98, Wayne St Univ; asst prof, 98-, Eastern Mich Univ. **HONORS AND AWARDS** Awards for Cont Ed, Amer Speech-Lang-Hearing Assoc, 98, 96, 93, 90, 87, 83; Clara B. Stoddard, Wayne St Univ, 86; James B Angell Scholar, 75. **MEMBERSHIPS** Amer Speech-Lang-Hearing Assoc; MI Speech-Lang-Hearing Assoc; Macomb/St Clair Speech-Lang-Hearing Assoc; ISAAC; Us Soc for AAC. **RESEARCH** Augmentative/alternative comm, child language **SELECTED PUBLICATIONS** Cauth, , Conflict Resolution Abilities of Children with Specific Language Impairment and Normal Language, J of Speech and Hearing Res, 95; art, Comparison of Two Measures of Receptive Vocabulary, Mich Speech-Lang-Hearing Assoc J, 87. **CONTACT ADDRESS** Dept of Scpecial Ed, Eastern Michigan Univ, 122 Rackham, Ypsilanti, MI, 48197. **EMAIL** Lizbeth.Stevens@emich.edu

STEVENS-ARROYO, ANTONIO M.
DISCIPLINE COMPARATIVE RELIGION **EDUCATION** Passionist Monastic Sem, BA, 64; St Michael's Col, MA, 68; NY Univ, MA, 75; Fordham Univ, PhD, 81. **CAREER** Dept Puerto Rican Stud, PROF, 89-, CUNY, BROOKLYN COL; fel, teach, Ctr Stud Am Rel, Woodrow Wilson Ctr, Princeton Univ, Union Theol Sem, Fordham Univ, Rutgers Univ, Ctr Adv Stud Puerto Rico and Caribbean, San Juan, Univ La Laguna, Spain; assoc ed, Encyclopedia Cont Religion, Macmillian Ref Libr; ed bd, Latino Studies Journal. **CONTACT ADDRESS** RISC, Brooklyn Col, CUNY, 2900 Bedford Ave, Brooklyn, NY, 11210. **EMAIL** astevens@brooklyn.cuny.edu

STEVENSON, WALT
PERSONAL Born 08/03/1961, Philadelphia, PA, m, 1989, 2 children **DISCIPLINE** CLASSICAL PHILOLOGY **EDUCATION** Carleton Col, BA (classical philol), 83; Brown Univ, PhD (classical philol), 90. **CAREER** Lect, Univ RI, 88-89; instr, Dickinson Col, 89-90; vis prof, L'rivskaj Derzhavni Universitet/L'rivska Bohoslorska Akademia, 97-98; assoc prof, Univ Richmond, 90-. **HONORS AND AWARDS** Fulbright fel, 97-98. **MEMBERSHIPS** Am Philol Asn; Classical Asn of the Midwest and South. **RESEARCH** Greek and Latin lit; Roman Imperial Social History. **SELECTED PUBLICATIONS** Auth, Plato's Symposium 190d7, Phoenix 47, 93; The Rise of Eunuchs in Greco-Roman Antiquity, J of the Hist of Sexuality 5, 95; De Italia: Italy Goes Multimedia, New England Classical Newsletter & J 23, 95; Professional Poets and Poetic Heroes in Homeric Greece, Usna Epika: Etnichni Tradytsii ta Vykonavstvo II, Kiev, 97. **CONTACT ADDRESS** Dept of Classics, Univ of Richmond, Richmond, VA, 23173. **EMAIL** wstevens@richmond.edu

STEWART, JOAN HINDE
PERSONAL New York, NY, m, 1970, 2 children **DISCIPLINE** FRENCH LITERATURE **EDUCATION** St Joseph's Col, BA, 65; Yale Univ, PhD(romance lang), 70. **CAREER** From instr to asst prof French, Wellesley Col, 70-72; asst prof, 73-77, assoc prof, 77-81, Prof French, NC State Univ, 81-, Fel, Nat Humanities Ctr, 82-83. **HONORS AND AWARDS** NC State Univ Outstanding Teacher Award, 77. **MEMBERSHIPS** MLA; SAtlantic Mod Lang Asn; Southeast Am Soc for 18th Century Studies; Southern Comp Lit Asn; Am Asn Teachers of Fr. **RESEARCH** Eighteenth-century fiction; women wirters; Colette. **SELECTED PUBLICATIONS** Auth, The Novels of Madame Riccoboni, NC Studies Romance Lang & Lit, 76; Some aspects of verb use in Aucassin et Nicolette, Fr Rev, 77; Sensibility with irony: Mme de Montolieu at the end of an era, Ky Romance Quart, 78; Colette: The Mirror Image, Fr Forum, 78; Colette and the hallowing of age, Romance Notes, 79-80; Colette's Gynaeceum: Regression and Renewal, Fr Rev, 80; The School and the Home, Women's Studies, 81; Colette, G K Hall; The Correspondence Of Graffigny, Vol 2, June 19th 1739 To September 24th 1740, French Rev, Vol 67, 94; Writing Love--Letters, Women, And The Novel In France, 1605-1776, French Forum, Vol 22, 97. **CONTACT ADDRESS** 6 Logging Trial, Durham, NC, 27707.

STEWART, PAMELA DAWES
PERSONAL Born 01/23/1934, Montreal, PQ, Canada **DISCIPLINE** ITALIAN, COMPARATIVE LITERATURE **EDUCATION** Univ Montreal, BA, 59; McGill Univ, MA, 61. **CAREER** Lectr, 63-65, asst prof, 65-69, assoc prof, 69-80, Prof Ital Studies, McGill Univ, 80-, Chmn Dept Ital, 77-, Assoc dir, McGill Ctr for Continuing Educ, 68-; mem comt aid to publ, Can Fedn for Humanities, 77- **MEMBERSHIPS** MLA; Can Soc Ital Studies; Am Asn Ital; Can Soc Renaissance Studies. **RESEARCH** Boccaccio; Italian Renaissance theatre; the reception of Machiavelli in France. **SELECTED PUBLICATIONS** Auth, Innocent Gentillet e la sua Polemica Antimachiavellica, La Nuova Italia, Firenze, 69; contribr, Dizionario Critico Della Letteratura Francese, UTET, Torino, 72; auth, An unknown edition of the Praxis aurea by J P De Ferrariis, Yearbk Ital Studies 1971, 72; co-ed, Discours contre Machiavcl, Casalini Libri, Firenze, 74; auth, La novella di Madonna Oretta e le due parti del Decameron, Yearbk Ital Studies 1973-75, 77; Boccaccio e lat tradizione retoriaca: La definizione della novella come genere letterario, Stanford Ital Rev, Vol I, No 1, 79; Il testo teatrale e la questions del doppio destinatario: L'eoempio della Calandria, Quaderri d'i'talianistica, Vol I, 80; Goldoni As Librettist--Theatrical Reform And The Drammi-Giocosi, Quaderni D Italianistica, Vol 14, 93; Almanacco Delle Donne, Quaderni D Italianistica, Vol 14, 93. **CONTACT ADDRESS** Dept of Ital, McGill Univ, Montreal, PQ, H3A IG5.

STEWART, WALTER K
PERSONAL Los Angeles, CA **DISCIPLINE** GERMAN LITERATURE **EDUCATION** Calif State Univ, Northridge, BA, 68; Univ Calif, Los Angeles, MA, 70, PhD(Ger lit), 75. **CAREER** Scholar Ger, Univ Calif, Los Angeles, 78-79; Asst Prof Ger & Chmn Dept, Calif Lutheran Col, 79- **MEMBERSHIPS** MLA; Am Asn Teachers Ger; Philol Asn Pac Coast. **RESEARCH** Goethe period literature; dramatic theory; Thomas Mann. **SELECTED PUBLICATIONS** Auth, Hans Carossa, In: Encycl Hebraica, 77; Der Tod in Venedig: The path to insight, Ger Rev; Time Structure in Drama: Goethe's Sturm und Drang Plays, Amsterdamer Publikationen Rodopi Verlag; Wilhelm Meisters Travels--Translation Of The 1st Edition By Thomas Carlyle With An Introduction By James Hardin, Colloquia Germanica, Vol 25, 92. **CONTACT ADDRESS** Dept of German, California Lutheran Univ, 60 Olsen Rd, Thousand Oaks, CA, 91360-2700.

STHELE, EVA
DISCIPLINE GREEK AND ROMAN LITERATURE **EDUCATION** Univ Cincinnati, PhD. **CAREER** Instr, Wheaton Col; prof-. **HONORS AND AWARDS** Coord, dept's Latin Day. **RESEARCH** Ancient relig(s). **SELECTED PUBLICATIONS** Auth, Performance and Gender in Ancient Greece: Nondramatic Poetry in its Setting, Princeton UP, 96; Women Looking at Women: Women's Ritual and Temple Sculpture, Sexuality in Ancient Art, Cambridge UP, 96; Help Me to Sing, Muse, of Plataia, The New Simonides, Arethusa 29, 96. **CONTACT ADDRESS** Dept of Class, Univ MD, 4229 Art-Sociology Building, College Park, MD, 20742-1335. **EMAIL** es39@umail.umd.edu

STICCA, SANDRO
DISCIPLINE FRENCH LANGUAGE AND LITERATURE **EDUCATION** Columbia Univ, PhD. **CAREER** Prof/Dir grad studies, SUNY Binghamton. **HONORS AND AWARDS** Ed-in-chief, Mediaevalia. **RESEARCH** Romance Philology; medieval lit (Latin, French and Italian); medieval drama and lyric; the Renaissance; mod French and Italian lit and comp lit. **SELECTED PUBLICATIONS** Auth, The Latin Passion Play, 70; The Planctus Mariae in the Dramatic Tradition of the Middle Ages, 89; Il Convento di S Maria del Paradiso, 89; Studio Iconografico-Storico, 86; La poetica del tempo sacramentale, 66; ed, Medieval Drama, 72; Arte ed esistenza in Gennaro Manna, 93; Studies in Hagiography, 96. **CONTACT ADDRESS** SUNY Binghamton, PO Box 6000, Binghamton, NY, 13902-6000. **EMAIL** cstiner@binghamton.edu

STILLMAN, NORMAN ARTHUR
PERSONAL Born 07/06/1945, New York, NY, m, 1967, 2 children **DISCIPLINE** ORIENTAL STUDIES, MIDDLE EASTERN HISTORY **EDUCATION** Univ Pa, BA, 67, PhD(Orient studies), 70. **CAREER** Asst prof Near Eastern lang & lit, NY Univ, 70-73; ASSOC PROF HIST & ARABIC, STATE UNIV NY BINGHAMTON, 73-, Jewish Theol Sem fel, 70-71; consult, Soc Sci Res Coun, 72-77 & Nat Geog Soc, 79-80; vis assoc prof Mid Eastern & Jewish hist, Haifa Univ, 79-80. **MEMBERSHIPS** Am Orient Soc; Mid East Studies Asn NAm; Asn Jewish Studies; Conf Jewish Social Studies; Societe de l'histoire du Maroc. **RESEARCH** History of the Jews under Islam; North African history; semitic languages and literatures. **SELECTED PUBLICATIONS** Auth, The story of Cain and Abel in the Qur'an and the Muslim commentators: Some observations, J Semitic Studies, autumn 74; A new source for eighteenth-century Moroccan history in the John Rylands University Library of Manchester: The Dombay Papers, Bull John Rylands Univ Libr Manchester, spring 75; Charity and social service in Medieval Islam, Societas, spring 75; New attitudes toward the Jew in the Arab world, Jewish Social Studies, summer-fall 75; coauth, The art of a Moroccan folk poetess, ZDMG, 78; auth, The Jews of Arab Lands, Jewish Publ Soc Am, 79; co-ed, Studies in Judaism and Islam, 81 & asst ed, Studies in Geniza and Sepharad: Heritage, 81, Magnes Press; Sephardi Entrepreneurs In Eretz Israel--The Amzalak Family 1816-1918, Am Hist Rev, Vol 97, 92. **CONTACT ADDRESS** Dept of Hist, State Univ NY, Binghamton, NY, 13901.

STILLMAN, YEDIDA KALFON
PERSONAL Born 04/08/1946, Fez, Morocco, m, 1967, 2 children **DISCIPLINE** MIDDLE EASTERN ETHNOGRAPHY & LITERATURE **EDUCATION** Univ Pa, MA, 68, PhD(Oriental studies), 72. **CAREER** Asst prof, 73-79, Assoc Prof Class & Near Eastern Studies, State Univ NY, Binghamton, 79-, Consult, Int Folk Art Found, 72-, Cult Res & Commun, Inc, 78-79 & Irth Cult Heritage Found, 80-; vis sr lectr, Haifa Univ, 79-80. **HONORS AND AWARDS** Chancellor's Award for Excellence in Teaching, State Univ NY, 78. **MEMBERSHIPS** Am Oriental Soc; Asn Jewish Studies. **RESEARCH** Middle Eastern costume history; middle Eastern folk literature. **SELECTED PUBLICATIONS** Auth, The three magic objects: A Yemanite folktale: (Analysis and parallels), Fabula, Vol XIV, 73; The importance of the Cairo Geniza manuscripts for the history of medieval female attire, Int J Middle East Studies, Vol VII, 76 coauth, The art of a Moroccan folk poetess, Zeitschrift der Deutschen Morganla6ndischen Gesellschaft, Vol 128, 78; auth, New data on Islamic textiles from the Geniza, Textile Hist, Vol X, 79; Palestinian Costume and Jewelry, Univ NMex Pres, 79;

The costume of the Moroccan Jewish woman, Studies in Jewish Folklore, 80; Attitudes toward women in traditional Near Eastern societies, Studies in Judaism & Islam, Magnes Press, Jerusalem, 81; From Southern Morocco to Northern Israel: Material Culture in Shelomi, Haifa Univ Press, Haifa, 82; Jewish Life In Muslim Libya--Rivals And Relatives, Jewish Quart Rev, Vol 84, 94. **CONTACT ADDRESS** Dept Class & Near Eastern Studies, State Univ NY, Binghamton, NY, 13901.

STIMILLI, DAVIDE
DISCIPLINE FRENCH **EDUCATION** Yale Univ, PhD. **CAREER** Asst prof; Northwestern Univ, 97-; lect, Brit Soc for 18th-Century Studies, Conf Int Soc Study Europ Ideas, Johns Hopkins Humanities Center, Univ Chicago, MLA. **RESEARCH** History and theory of physiognomy, Italian literature, intellectual history. **SELECTED PUBLICATIONS** Auth, Kafka e la musica, Il bianco e il nero, 97; Italics vs Blackletter: The Triestine Typography, Atenea, 96; Character and Caricature, Schede umanistiche, 96; ber Schamhaftigkeit: Ein Beitrag zur historischen Semantik einiger physiognomischer Begriffe, Geschichten der Physiognomik, 95; Was Kafka a Saint, Litteraria Pragensia, 94; articles on, Bruno; Kafka; Svevo; Saba. **CONTACT ADDRESS** Dept of French, Northwestern Univ, 1801 Hinman, Evanston, IL, 60208.

STIMSON, HUGH MCBIRNEY
PERSONAL Born 12/05/1931, Port Chester, NY **DISCIPLINE** LINGUISTICS, PHILOLOGY **EDUCATION** Yale Univ, BA, 53, MA, 57, PhD, 59. **CAREER** Sci linguist, Foreign Serv Inst, US Dept State, 59; suprvy instr Chinese, Chinese Lang Sch, China, 59-60; from asst prof to assoc prof, 60-69, assoc prof Chinese lang & ling, 69-74, Prof Chinese Ling, Yale Univ, 74. **MEMBERSHIPS** MLA; Ling Soc Am; Am Orient Soc(secy-treas, 69-76); Asn Asian Studies. **RESEARCH** Chinese historical phonology; Chinese grammar espec class and mod; Chinese poetics. **SELECTED PUBLICATIONS** Auth, The Jong-yuan in yunn: A Study of Early Mandarin Phonology, Far Eastern Publ, 66; The sound of a Tarng poem: Grieving about Green Slope by Duh-Fuu, 69 & Sheir, Shwu 'who? whom?' and moh 'none' in old Chinese, 71, J Am Orient Soc; More on Peking archaisms, T'oung Pao, 72; T'ang Poetic Vocabulary, 76, Fifty-Five T'ang Poems, 76 & coauth, Spoken Standard Chinese Vols 1 & 2, 76 & 78 & Written Standard Chinese, Vol I, 80, Far Eastern Publ. **CONTACT ADDRESS** Dept of East Asian Lang & Lit, Yale Univ, PO Box 208308, New Haven, CT, 06520-8308.

STINE, PHILIP C.
PERSONAL Born 08/30/1943, Harrisburg, IL, m, 1976, 2 children **DISCIPLINE** LINGUISTICS **EDUCATION** Univ Mich, PhD 68, MA 65; Asbury Col, BA 64. **CAREER** United Bible Societies, Dir trans, prod dist, 68-98; Executive and Management Consultancy, 98-. **MEMBERSHIPS** LSA; SBL; AAA. **RESEARCH** Translation **SELECTED PUBLICATIONS** Auth, A Handbook on Jeremiah, coauth, NY, United Bible Soc, forthcoming; Facing the Third Millennium: Bible Societies and the Long View, Reading UK, UBS Bull, 97; Doke, Clement Martyn, Smith, Edwin Williams, van Bulck, Gaaston, Westerman, Diedrich Hermann, Articles in: Biographical Dictionary of Christian Missions, ed, Gerald H. Anderson, Simon and Schuster, 97; auth, The Training of Missiologists to Develop Local Bible Translators, Missiological Edu for the 21st Century: The Book the Circle and the Sandals, eds, J. Dudley Woodberry, Charles van Engen, Edgar J. Elliston, NY, Orbis Books, 96; auth, Trends in Translation, in: The Bible Translator, 95; auth, Relating to Others: Facing the Facts, The Bible Distributor, 95; Managing the Publishing Process, The Bible Distributor, 95. **CONTACT ADDRESS** USIS/USEU Brussels, PSC 82, PO Box 002, APO, AE, 09710. **EMAIL** pcstine@compuserve.com

STIVALE, CHARLES J.
PERSONAL Born 12/13/1949, Glen Ridge, NJ, m, 1981 **DISCIPLINE** ROMANCE LANGUAGES; LITERATURE **EDUCATION** Knox Col, BA, 71; Sorbonne Paris-IV, MA, 73, Maitrise, 74; Univ Il Urbana-Champaign, PhD, 81. **CAREER** Inst, W Mich Univ, 80-81; res dir, Univ of Haute Bretagne, Rennes, France, 81-82; asst prof, Franklin & Marshall Col, 82-86; asst prof, Tulane Univ, 86-90; assoc prof to prof & chair, Wayne St Univ, 90- . **MEMBERSHIPS** Modern Lang Assoc; Midwest Modern Lang Assoc, Amer Assoc of Teachers of French; Alliance Francaise. **RESEARCH** Nineteenth-century French lit; twentieth-century critical theory; French cultural stud; cybercriticism; deleuze & Guattari. **SELECTED PUBLICATIONS** Auth, The Art of Rupture, Narrative Desire and Duplicity in the Tales of Guy de Maupassant, Univ Mich Press, 94; Comments on a Meeting With Gilles Deleuze, Nth Dimension, 96; 'help manners', Cyber-democracy and Its Vicissitudes, Enculturation, 97; On Cultural Lessons, French and Other, Contemporary French Stud, 97; The Two-Fold Thought of Deleuze and Guattari: Intersections and Animations. Guilford Publ, 98. **CONTACT ADDRESS** Dept of Romance Lang & Lit, Wayne St Univ, 487 Manoogian Hall, Detroit, MI, 48202. **EMAIL** C_Stivale@wayne.edu

STOCKMAN, IDA J.
PERSONAL Born 09/06/1942, Sumner, Mississippi, m, 1969 **DISCIPLINE** AUDIOLOGY AND SPEECH SCIENCES **EDUCATION** Jackson State Univ, Jackson, MS, BS, 1962; University of Iowa, Iowa City, IA, MA, 1965; Pennsylvania State Univ, State College, PA, PhD, 1971. **CAREER** Jackson State University, Jackson, MS, instructor, 1965-66; Rehabilitation Center, Binghamton, NY, speech/language pathologist, 1966-67; Kantonsspital St Gallen, St Gallen, Switzerland, research assoc, 1972-76 summers; Howard University, Washington, DC, asst/prof assoc, 1971-79; Center for Applied Linguistic, Washington, DC, research assoc, 1980-82; Michigan State University, East Lansing, MI, assoc prof, 1982-. **HONORS AND AWARDS** Information Exchange Scholar, World Rehabilitation Fund Inc, 1985; Research Grant Award, National Science Foundation, 1985; Research Grant Award, National Institute of Education, 1980; Outstanding Woman Achiever, Michigan State University, 1986; Phi Delta Kappa Professional Honor Society, 1981. **MEMBERSHIPS** Board of directors, National Association Black Speech, Language & Hearing, 1989-; board of directors, Michigan Association-Deaf, Speech and Hearing Services, 1989-; editorial board, Howard Journal of Communication; Howard University, Washington, DC, 1988-; editorial board, Journal of Linguistics and Education, 1988-; educational standards board, The American Speech, Language, Hearing Association, 1990-. **CONTACT ADDRESS** Dept of Audiology and Speech Sciences, Michigan State Univ, 371 Communication Arts & Sciences Bldg, East Lansing, MI, 48824.

STOCKWELL, ROBERT PAUL
PERSONAL Born 06/12/1925, OK, m, 1946, 1 child **DISCIPLINE** ENGLISH LANGUAGE & LINGUISTICS **EDUCATION** Univ VA, BA, 46, MA, 49, PhD(English philol & ling), 52. **CAREER** Instr English, Univ Okla City, 46-48; dir English for foreigners proj Nashville Auto-Diesel Col, 52; from instr to assoc prof ling, Foreign Serv Inst, US Dept State, 52-56, chmn Latin-Am lang & area prog, 53-56; asst prof English, 56-58, from assoc prof to prof, 58-66, chmn dept, 66-73, Prof Ling, Univ Calif, Los Angeles, 66-, Chmn Dept, 79-, Vis prof, Philippines, 59 & 60 & Ling Inst, Univ Tex, 61; Am Coun Learned Soc fel, 63-64; vis prof, Univ Mich, 65. **HONORS AND AWARDS** Distinguished Teaching Award, Univ Calif, Los Angeles, 68. **MEMBERSHIPS** MLA; Ling Soc Am; Philol Soc, England. **RESEARCH** English and Spanish language; history of English phonology and syntax; general linguistic theory. **SELECTED PUBLICATIONS** Coauth, Patterns of Spanish Pronunciation, 60, Sounds of English and Spanish, 65 & Grammatical Structure of English and Spanish, 65, Univ Chicago; co-ed, Linguistic Change and Generative Theory, Ind Univ 72; coauth, Major Syntactic Structures of English, Holt, 73; auth, Foundations of Syntactic Theory, Prentice-Hall, 77; A History of Old-English Meter, Language, Vol 71, 95; Dwight,L Bolinger, Language, Vol 69, 93; The Cambridge Hist of the English-Language, Vol 2 1066-1476, J Of Linguistics, Vol 30, 94. **CONTACT ADDRESS** Dept of Ling, Univ of Calif, Los Angeles, CA, 90024.

STOHL, CYNTHIA B.
DISCIPLINE ORGANIZATIONAL COMMUNICATION, SOCIAL NETWORKS **EDUCATION** Univ Purdue, PhD, 82. **CAREER** Prof, Purdue Univ. **RESEARCH** Participatory processes in multicultural/international organizations. **SELECTED PUBLICATIONS** Auth, European Managers Interpretations of Participation: a semantic network analysis, Human Commun Res, 93; Participating and Participation, Commun Monogr, 93; Organizational Communication: Connectedness in Action, Sage, 95; Paradoxes of Participation, Orgn and Commun, 95. **CONTACT ADDRESS** Dept of Commun, Purdue Univ, 1080 Schleman Hall, West Lafayette, IN, 47907-1080. **EMAIL** cstohl@purdue.edu

STOKKER, KATHLEEN MARIE
PERSONAL Born 10/10/1946, St. Paul, MN **DISCIPLINE** NORWEGIAN LANGUAGE & LITERATURE **EDUCATION** St Olaf Col, Minn, BA, 68; Univ Wis-Madison, MA, 71, PhD(Scand), 78. **CAREER** Instr Norweg, Moorhead State Univ, 73-77 & St Olaf Col, 77-78; asst prof, 78-82, assoc prof Norweg, 82-87, prof, 87-, Luther Col, Iowa, 82-, res fel, Am Scand Found, 72-73 & Nat Endowment for Humanities, 81-82; trustee Norweg-Am Cult Inst, 78-. **MEMBERSHIPS** Soc Advan Scand Study; Norweg Am Hist Asn; Am Scand Found; Norweg Am Cult Inst; Ibsen Soc Am. **RESEARCH** Norwegian folklore, folkbelief and legends, study of cultural historical background and function of folktales; Norwegian literary and cultural periodicals pre-1900; foreign language pedagogy; humor, World War II. **SELECTED PUBLICATIONS** Auth, J E Sars and Nyt Norsk Tidsskrift: Their Influence on the Modern Breakthrough in Norway, Norweg Scholarly Res Asn, 78; coauth, Norsk, nordmenn og Norge, Univ Wis Press, 81; Norsk, nordmenn og Norge: Antologi, Univ Wis Press, 93; Folklore Fights the Nazis: Humor in Occupied Norway 1940-45, Univ Wis Press, 96. **CONTACT ADDRESS** Dept of Norweg, Luther Col, 700 College Dr, Decorah, IA, 52101-1045. **EMAIL** Stokkeka@Luther.edu

STOKOE, WILLIAM CLARENCE
PERSONAL Born 07/21/1919, Lancaster, NH, m, 1942, 2 children **DISCIPLINE** LINGUISTICS **EDUCATION** Cornell Univ, AB, 42, PhD, 46. **CAREER** From asst to actg instr, Cornell Univ, 43-46; from asst prof to assoc prof, Wells Col, 46-55, chmn dept, 50-52; prof English & chmn dept, 55-68, prof ling & English, 68-81, Ling Res Prof, Gallaudet Col, 57- & Dir, Ling Res Lab, 71-, Assoc ed, Am Ann Deaf, 56-57; adj prof ling, Gallaudet Col, 81-; NSF grants, 60-63, 71-78; ed, Sign Lang Studies, 72- & Lingtok Press, Inc, 78-; vis fel Claire Hall, Univ Cambridge, 77. **MEMBERSHIPS** MLA; fel Am Anthrop Asn; fel AAAS. **RESEARCH** Sign language of the American deaf; linguistics theory and structure; language origins. **SELECTED PUBLICATIONS** Auth, Hand And Mind--What Gestures Reveal About Thought, Semiotica, Vol 104, 95; Language And Human-Behavior, Semiotica, Vol 113, 97; Do You See What I Mean--Plains Indian Sign Talk And The Embodiment Of Action, Semiotica, Vol 114, 97. **CONTACT ADDRESS** Ling Res Lab, Gallaudet Univ, Washington, DC, 20002.

STOLL, ANITA K.
DISCIPLINE SPANISH AND LATIN AMERICAN LITERATURE **EDUCATION** Case Western Reserve Univ, PhD. **CAREER** Prof, Cleveland State Univ, chp. **SELECTED PUBLICATIONS** Publ, Spanish Golden Age Drama, Twentieth-century Mexican literature. **CONTACT ADDRESS** Dept of For Lang, Cleveland State Univ, 83 E 24th St, Cleveland, OH, 44115.

STOLZ, BENJAMIN ARMOND
PERSONAL Born 03/28/1934, Lansing, MI, m, 1962, 2 children **DISCIPLINE** SLAVIC LANGUAGES **EDUCATION** Univ Mich, AB, 55; Univ Brussels, cert Polish, 56; Harvard Univ, AM, 57, PhD(Slavic), 65. **CAREER** Lectr, 63, from asst prof to assoc prof, 64-73, Prof Slavic Lang & Lit, Univ Mich, Ann Arbor, 73-, Chmn Dept, 71-, Fulbright-Hays fel, Eng & Yugoslavia, 70-71. **MEMBERSHIPS** Am Asn Advan Slavic Studies; Am Asn Teachers Slavic & EEurop Lang; Ling Soc Am; MLA; Midwest Mod Lang Asn (pres, 76-77). **RESEARCH** Slavic linguistics and folklore. **SELECTED PUBLICATIONS** Auth, Nikac and Hamza: multiformity in the Serbo-Croatian heroic epic, J Folklore Inst, 69; On the history of the Serbo-Croatian diplomatic language and its role in the formation of the contemporary standard, In: American Contributions to the Seventh International Congress of Slavists, Vol I, 73 & Serbo-Croatian in the works of Bartholomaeus Georgievits (Bartol Durdevic): a reappraisal, In: Konstantin Mihailovic, Memoirs of a Janissary, 75 & ed, Papers in Slavic Philology, Vol I & IV, 77, Mich Slavic Publ; co-ed, Oral Literature and the Formula, Ctr Coord Ancient & Mod Studies, 77; On the language of Kanstantin Mihailovic's Kronilca turecka, Am Contribr 8th Int Congr Slavists, Vol I, 78; Kopitar and Vuk: An assessment of their roles in the rise of the new Serbian literary language, Vol II, 82; The Origins Of Slavs--A Linguists View, Slavic And East European J, Vol 38, 94; Karadzic,Vuk In The European Context--Proceedings Of An Int Scientific Symposium Of The Vuk-Karadzic-Jacob-Grimm-Gesellschaft, Slavic Rev, Vol 55, 96. **CONTACT ADDRESS** Dept of Slavic Lang & Lit, Univ of Mich, 812 E Washington St, Ann Arbor, MI, 48109-1275.

STONE, CYNTHIA
DISCIPLINE SPANISH **EDUCATION** Williams Col, BA, 83; Columbia Univ, MA, 86; Univ Mich, PhD, 92. **CAREER** Asst prof. **RESEARCH** Compilations of indigenous traditions; films set in Colonial Spanish America. **SELECTED PUBLICATIONS** Auth, The Filming of Colonial Spanish America, Colonial Latin Amer Rev 5 2, 96; Multiple Authorship in the Relacion de Michoacan, Hacia un nuevo canon literario, New Hampshire: Ediciones del Norte, 95; Rewriting Indigenous Traditions: The Burial Ceremony of the Cazonci, Colonial Latin Amer Rev 3 1-2, 94 & El lector implecito de Rayuela y los blancos de la narracion, Los ochenta mundos de Cortazar: ensayos, Madrid: Edi-6, 87. **CONTACT ADDRESS** Dept of Modern Languages and Literatures, Col of the Holy Cross, 1 College St, PO Box 10A, Worcester, MA, 01610-2395. **EMAIL** cstone@holycross.edu

STONE, JENNIFER
DISCIPLINE FRENCH LITERATURE **EDUCATION** London Univ, PhD. **CAREER** Prof, Univ MA Amherst. **MEMBERSHIPS** Soc Pirandello Studies. **RESEARCH** Freudian psychoanalytic theory with application to contemp French and Italian lit and film. **SELECTED PUBLICATIONS** Auth, Pirandello's Naked Prompt: The Structure of Repetition in Modernism. **CONTACT ADDRESS** Dept of French and Italian Studies, Univ Massachusetts Amherst, Mass Ave, Amherst, MA, 01003. **EMAIL** Jastonephd@aol.com

STOUT, JOSEPH ALLEN
PERSONAL Born 05/27/1939, Sioux City, IA, m, 1975, 2 children **DISCIPLINE** SPANISH, HISTORY **EDUCATION** PhD, Hist Oklahoma State Univ, 71; MA, Hist, TX A&M Univ, 68; BA, Angelo State Col, 67. **CAREER** San Angelo TX Public Sachools, Inst Hist, 68-69; Missouri Southern State College Asst Prof, 71-72; Oklahoma State Univ, Asst to Prof, 72-.

HONORS AND AWARDS Phi Kappa Phi; Phi Alpha Theta. **MEMBERSHIPS** Conf of US-Mexican Historians; TX State Hist Assoc; Southwest council of Latin Am Area Studies. **RESEARCH** US Mexican Frontier; US Mexican Military; Mexican Revolutionary period. **SELECTED PUBLICATIONS** The United States and the Native Americans in John A Carroll, and Colin Baxter; The American Military Tradition from Colonial Times to the Present, Wilmington, Delaware, Scholarly Resources Inc, 96; Historiography and Sources in Mexico for Frontier History, in Jaime E Rodriguez and Virginia Guedea, Cinco Siglos en las Historia de Mexico, 2 vols, Mexico, D F, Instituto Mora and Irvine CA, Univ of CA, Irvine, 92; Deadly Crossings: Carrancistas, Villistas, and the Punitive Expedition, 1915-1920, in press, Texas Christian Univ Press, 99. **CONTACT ADDRESS** Dept Hist, Oklahoma State Univ, Stillwater, OK, 74074. **EMAIL** JAS1624@OKWAY.OKSTATE.EDU

STOWE, WILLIAM W.
PERSONAL Born 12/07/1946, New Haven, CT, m, 1976 **DISCIPLINE** COMPARATIVE LIT **EDUCATION** Princeton BA, 68, Yale MPhil, 76, Yale PhD, 78. **CAREER** Wesleyan Univ, asst prof, 78-84, assoc prof, 84-90, prof eng, 90-, Benjamin L Waite Prof eng, 97-. **HONORS AND AWARDS** Fulbright Fellowship (declined) 68; Yale Univ Fellowship 73-76; Edgar Nomination, Det Writers of Am, 84. **MEMBERSHIPS** MLA; SSNL; ASLE. **RESEARCH** 19 century US Lit and Environ; Travel Writing. **SELECTED PUBLICATIONS** Balzac, James and the Realistic Novel, Princ 83; The Poetics of Murder, ed with Glenn W Most, Harcourt B Jovanovich, 83; Going Abroad: Euro Trav in 19 Cen American Cult, Princ 94; James', Elusive Wings in Jonathan Freedman, ed Cambridge Comp to Henry James, Cambr 98. **CONTACT ADDRESS** Wesleyan Univ, Dept Eng, Middletown, CT, 06457. **EMAIL** wstowe@wesleyan.edu

STRAUS, BARRIE RUTH
DISCIPLINE ENGLISH LANGUAGE; LITERATURE **EDUCATION** Oregon Univ, BA; Iowa Univ, MA, PhD, 90. **CAREER** Prof **RESEARCH** Medieval literature; contemporary critical theory; women's studies; modern narrative. **SELECTED PUBLICATIONS** Auth, Catholic Church & Skirting the Texts. **CONTACT ADDRESS** Dept of English Language and Literature, Univ of Windsor, 401 Sunset Ave, Windsor, ON, N9B 3P4.

STRAUSS, JONATHAN
DISCIPLINE FRENCH **CAREER** Asst prof & actg ch, Miami Univ **RESEARCH** 19th- and 20th-century French literature; Romanticism; philosophy and literature; poetry; theory; visual arts. **SELECTED PUBLICATIONS** Auth, Nerval's 'Le Christ aux oliviers': The Subject Writes After His Own Death, in Romanic Rev, 97; Death-Based Subjectivity in the Creation of Nerval's Lyric Self, in Death in French Literature and Film, L'Esprit Createur, 95; The Inverted Icarus, in Yale Fr Stud, 78; transl, Helmut Federle, The line which I have chosen, Painting: Current Territories, Valence: Editions de l'Ecole de Beaux Arts de Valence, 97; Gilles Deleuze, Material Coils, in Yale Fr Stud, 80 & Georges Bataille, Hegel, Death, and Sacrifice, in Yale Fr Stud, 78. **CONTACT ADDRESS** Dept of French and Italian, Miami Univ, Oxford, OH, 45056. **EMAIL** strausja@muohio.edu

STRAUSS, WALTER ADOLF
PERSONAL Born 05/14/1923, Mannheim, Germany, m, 5 children **DISCIPLINE** ROMANCE LANGUAGES **EDUCATION** Emory Univ, BA, 44; Harvard Univ, MA, 48, PhD, 51. **CAREER** Instr Romance lang & gen educ, Harvard Univ, 51-54; from asst prof to prof Romance lang, Emory Univ, 54-70, dir div humanities prog, 65-70; Treuhaft Prof Humanities, Case Western Reserve Univ, 70-, Chmn Dept Mod Lang, 79-, Guggenheim & Bollingen fels, 62-63; NDEA summer fel, 77. **MEMBERSHIPS** MLA; Dante Soc; Midwest Mod Lang Asn; Kafka Soc; Beckett Soc. **RESEARCH** Contemporary French literature; comparative literature, 19th and 20th centuries. **SELECTED PUBLICATIONS** Auth, Proust and literature: The novelist as a critic; Twelve unpublished letters of Marcel Proust, Harvard Libr Bull; Dante's Belacqua and Beckett's tramps, Comp Lit, 59; Descent and Return: The Orphic Theme in Modern Literature, Harvard Univ, 71; All Is True--The Claims And Strategies Of Realist Fiction, Germanic Rev, Vol 72, 97; The Architecture And Music Of Thinking--Proust And The Stones Of Combray, Romance Notes, Vol 35, 95; The Fiction Of Relationship, Comparative Literature Studies, Vol 31, 94. **CONTACT ADDRESS** Dept of Mod Lang & Lit, Case Western Reserve Univ, Cleveland, OH, 44106.

STRAUSS CLAY, JENNY
DISCIPLINE CLASSICAL STUDIES **EDUCATION** Univ Wash, PhD. **CAREER** Prof. **SELECTED PUBLICATIONS** Auth, Wrath of Athena, Princeton, 83; The Politics of Olympus, Princeton, 89; pubs on Greek and Roman poetry. **CONTACT ADDRESS** Dept of Classics, Virginia Univ, Charlottesville, VA, 22903. **EMAIL** jsc2t@virginia.edu

STREET, JACK DAVID
PERSONAL Born 04/17/1929, Lafayette, AL, m, 1955, 2 children **DISCIPLINE** FOREIGN LANGUAGES **EDUCATION** Jacksonville State Col, AB & BS, 50; Univ Ala, MA, 52; State Univ Iowa, PhD(French), 64 Univ of Florence, dipl(Ital lang, lit & cult), 75; Scuola Dante Alighieri, dipl(Ital lang, lit & cult), 77. **CAREER** Teacher French & English, Tuscaloosa High Sch, 51-52; asst prof mod lang, NCent Col, 58-61; from asst prof to assoc prof, 61-72, prof mod lang, 72-97, chmn dept of mod lang & lit, 75-97, HARRY C MOORE PROF MOD LANG, BELOIT COL, 97-. **MEMBERSHIPS** Am Asn Teachers Fr; Am Coun Teaching Foreign Lang; AAUP **RESEARCH** Marcel Proust; Chateaubriand; Montherlant; French in the Valley d'Aosta, Italy. **SELECTED PUBLICATIONS** Auth, Seminar in France, 1959: An appraisal, 2/60 & A statistical study of the vocabulary of Les aventures du dernier Abencerage by Chateaubriand, 10/68, Fr Rev; 8 articles on French in the Valley d'Aosta, Italy, in: Contemporary French Civilization and French Rev. **CONTACT ADDRESS** Dept of Mod Lang, Beloit Col, 700 College St, Beloit, WI, 53511-5595. **EMAIL** streetj@beloit.edu

STREETER, DONALD
PERSONAL Born 04/24/1911, Huron, SD, d, 2 children **DISCIPLINE** ENGLISH, SPEECH **EDUCATION** Univ of Minn, BEd, 33; Univ of Iowa, MA, 38, PhD, 48. **CAREER** High school instr, 33-38; teaching fel, Univ of Iowa, 38-41 & 46-48; prof & chair, Univ of Memphis, 48-57; prof & chair emeritus, Univ of Houston, 57-76; adjunct, Tx A&M, Alvin Col, & Galveston Col, 76-96. **HONORS AND AWARDS** Outstanding Achievement, Galveston Col, 96; Educator of the Year, Rotary Int, 97. **MEMBERSHIPS** Tx Speech Commun; Speech Asn of Am. **SELECTED PUBLICATIONS** Auth, 50 Years of the Texas Speech Association; major public addreses of LQC Lamar, autobiography. **CONTACT ADDRESS** 6210 Sea Isle, Galveston, TX, 77554-9600.

STRELKA, JOSEPH PETER
PERSONAL Born 05/03/1927, Wiener Neustadt, Austria, m, 1963, 1 child **DISCIPLINE** GERMAN LITERATURE, THEORY OF LITERATURE **EDUCATION** Univ Vienna, PhD(Ger lit), 50. **CAREER** Assoc prof Ger lit, Univ Southern Calif, 64, dir Vienna prog, Univ Vienna, 65; prof Ger, Pa State Univ, University Park, 66-71; Prof Ger & Comp Lit, State Univ NY Albany, 71-; Theodor Koerner Found award, 55-57; City of Vienna award, 58; Austrian Govt res fel, Austrian Inst Cult Affairs Paris, 58-59; ed, Yearbook of Comparative Criticism Ser, 68 & Penn State Series in German literature, 71-; exchange scholar, State Univ NY, 75; Inst Humanistic Studies fel, 77; New Yorker Beitrage zur Vergleichenden Literaturwissenschaft, 82-; New Yorker Studien zur Neueren Deutschen Literaturgeschichte, 82- **HONORS AND AWARDS** Austrian Cross of Honor for the Arts and Sci First Class, Republic of Austria, 78. **MEMBERSHIPS** Pen Club; Int Asn Ger Studies, Int Comp Lit Asn; MLA; Humboldt-Gesellschaft. **RESEARCH** LIterary theory; literature of the Renaissance; German literature of the 20th century. **SELECTED PUBLICATIONS** Auth, War In Goethe Writings--Representation And Assessment, German Quarterly, Vol 66, 93; Im Reich Des Wurstels. Ein Alpentraum In 17 Phasen, Modern Austrian Literature, Vol 30, 97; Das 'Ausbleiben'--Poems--German--Lubomirski,K/, Modern Austrian Literature, Vol 28, 95; Paul Celan, A Biography Of His Youth, Colloquia Germanica, Vol 26, 93; Rhodes And Helios--Myth, Topos And Cultural-Development, Modern Austrian Lit, Vol 30, 97; Hexeneinmaleins, Modern Austrian Lit, Vol 28, 95; Limbo/Zwischenwelt--Italian And German, Modern Austrian Lit, Vol 29, 96; Poetry--Italian And German, Modern Austrian Lit, Vol 29, 96; The Object Of Poetry--A Study Based On Shakespeare Hamlet, Holderlin 'Abendphantasie and Dostoevski Crime And Punishment, Colloquia Germanica, Vol 25, 92; Kampflaufer Oder Charly Und Die Modlinger--German, Modern Austrian Lit, Vol 26, 93; Licht Der Freiheit--Novel Of A Freemason, Modern Austrian Lit, Vol 27, 94. **CONTACT ADDRESS** Dept of Ger, State Univ of NY, Albany, NY, 12222.

STROLLE, JON M
PERSONAL Born 04/21/1940, Gaylord, MI, m, 1987, 2 children **DISCIPLINE** LANGUAGES **EDUCATION** Oberlin Col, Ba, 62; Univ Wisc, Madison, MA, 64, PhD, 68. **CAREER** Asst prof, 67-74, Ind Univ; asst prof, 74-76, SUNY Brockport; dean, Spanish Schl, 76-80, Middlebury Col; fel, US dept of Ed, 80-81, Wash, DC; 81-85, dean, 85-, SAGE Jr Col, Albany; dean, grad schl of lang & ed ling, assoc provost, Monterey Inst of Intl Stud. **RESEARCH** Language policy, Spanish in the US. **CONTACT ADDRESS** Monterey Inst of Intl Studies, Van Buren St, Monterey, CA, 93940. **EMAIL** jstrolle@miis.edu

STROUD, MATTHEW DAVID
PERSONAL Born 10/04/1950, Hillsboro, TX **DISCIPLINE** SPANISH **EDUCATION** Univ Tex, Austin, BA, 71; Univ Southern Calif, MA, 74, PhD(Span), 77. **CAREER** Asst Prof Span, Trinity Univ, 77- **MEMBERSHIPS** MLA; SCent Mod Lang Asn; Am Asn Teachers Span & Port; AAUP; Asoc Int Hisp; Cervantes Soc Am. **RESEARCH** Seventeenth century Spanish dramas de honor; principles of dramatic irony and stagecraft; poetics. **SELECTED PUBLICATIONS** Auth, Stylistic considerations of Calderon's opera Librettos, Critica Hisp,

82; The resocializaiton of the Muher Varonil in three plays by Velez, In: Antiguidad y actualidad de Luis Velez de Guevara: Estudios Criticos, Purdue Univ Press, 82; The Desiring Subject And The Promise Of Salvation, A Lacanian Study Of Juana-Ines-De-La-Cruz El Divino Narciso, Hispania-A J Devoted To The Teaching Of Spanish And Portuguese, Vol 76, 93; The Play Of Power, Mythological Court Dramas Of Calderondelabarca, Hispania-A J Devoted To The Teaching Of Spanish And Portuguese, Vol 76, 93. **CONTACT ADDRESS** Dept of Span, Trinity Univ, San Antonio, TX, 78284.

STRUC, ROMAN SVIATOSLAV
PERSONAL Born 10/18/1927, Ukraine **DISCIPLINE** GERMAN & SLAVIC LITERATURE **EDUCATION** Univ Wash, MA, 57, PhD(comp lit, Ger, Russ), 62. **CAREER** Teaching asst Ger, Univ Washington, 58-60, instr, 60-62; from asst prof to assoc prof Ger & Russ, Washington Univ, 62-66; assoc prof Ger & comp lit, Univ Wash, 66-70; prof Ger & Russ & head, Dept Ger & Slavic Studies, 70-80, Prof Ger, Univ Calgary, 80- Can Coun res grant, 74. **MEMBERSHIPS** MLA; Ukrainian Acad Arts & Sci in US; Can Asn Slavists. **RESEARCH** Modern German literature; 19th century German-Slavic literary relations. **SELECTED PUBLICATIONS** Coauth, Dialogue on Poetry and Literary Aphorisms, Pa State Univ, 68; Zwei Erzahlungen von E T A Hoffmann und Franz Kafka, Rev Langues Vivantes, 68; Categories of the grotesque: Gogol and Kafka, Comp Lit Symp, 70; Petty demons and beauty: Gogol, Dostoevsky, Sologub, In: Essays on European Literature, Washington Univ, 72; contribr, Die Slawische Welt im Werke Joseph Roths, In: Joseph Roth und die Tradition, Agora, Darmstadt, 75; Zu einigen Gestalten in Effi Briest und Buddenbrooks, 81; Man And World In Dostoevski Works--A Contribution To Poetic Anthropology, Slavic Rev, Vol 54, 95. **CONTACT ADDRESS** Dept of Ger & Slavic Studies, Univ of Calgary, Calgary, AB, T2N 1N4.

STRUVE, WALTER
PERSONAL Born 05/06/1935, Somers Point, NJ, m, 1959 **DISCIPLINE** EUROPEAN HISTORY, GERMAN STUDIES **EDUCATION** Lafayette Col, AB, 55; Yale Univ, MA, 57, PhD(mod Europ hist), 63. **CAREER** Instr hist, Princeton Univ, 61-64; from instr to assoc prof, 64-82, PROF HIST, CITY COL NEW YORK, 82-, Res grants, City Univ New York, 67, 71, 73-76 & 81, Am Philos Soc, 68-69, Ger Acad Exchange Serv, 78, Fulbright, Ger, 78-79 & Fritz Thyssen Found, 79-80. **MEMBERSHIPS** Conf Group Cent Europ Hist; AHA; Immigration Hist Soc; Conf Group Int Labor & Working-Class Hist; Soc Ger-Am Studies. **RESEARCH** German history; US immigration; history of white-collar unionism. **SELECTED PUBLICATIONS** Auth, Elites Against Democracy: Leadership Ideals in Bourgeois Political Thought in Germany, 1890-1933, Princeton Univ, 73; The Republic of Texas, Bremen, and the Hildesheim District: A Contribution to the History of Emigration, Commerce, and Social Change in the Nineteenth Century, August Lax, Hildesheim, Ger, 82; Jews And The German State--The Political-History Of A Minority, 1848-1933, German Studies Rev, Vol 19, 96; Emigrant Agencies And Emigrant Associations In The 19th-Century And 20th-Century, German Studies Rev, Vol 16, ; The German Communists And The Rise Of Nazism, German Studies Rev, Vol 15, 92. **CONTACT ADDRESS** 2727 Palisade Ave, Bronx, NY, 10463.

STUART, DOUGLAS KEITH
PERSONAL Born 02/08/1943, Concord, MA, m, 1971, 8 children **DISCIPLINE** OLD TESTAMENT, NEAR EASTERN LANGUAGES **EDUCATION** Harvard Univ, BA, 64, PhD, 71. **CAREER** Instr Near East hist, 68-69, Gordon Col; asst prof, 71-77, assoc prof, 78-81, prof Old Testament, 81-, Gordon-Conwell Theol Sem; pres, 74-, Boston area chap, Huxley Inst Biosocial Res; co-chmn, 75-, Boston Theol Inst; trustee, 80-, Mass Bible Soc; trustee, Boxford Acad, 96-. **MEMBERSHIPS** Am Schs Orient Res; Inst Bibl Res; Evangel Theol Soc; Soc Bibl Lit; Bibl Archeol Soc. **RESEARCH** Hebrew meter; minor prophets; exegesis techniques. **SELECTED PUBLICATIONS** Coauth, How to Read the Bible for All Its Worth, Zondervan Publ House, 82; auth, Hosea-Jonah, Word Biblical Comm, 87; auth, Hosea-Jonah, Word Biblical Themes, 88; auth, Favorite Old Testament Passages, Westminster Press, 89; auth, Malachi, Baker Bk House, 98. **CONTACT ADDRESS** Gordon-Conwell Theol Sem, 130 Essex St, South Hamilton, MA, 01982-2395.

STURM-MADDOX, SARA
PERSONAL Born 12/22/1938, Nashville, TN, m, 2 children **DISCIPLINE** ROMANCE LANGUAGES; MEDIEVAL LITERATURE **EDUCATION** Univ MN, BA, 63, MA, 65; Univ NC, PhD(Romance philol), 67. **CAREER** Asst prof French, Queens Col, NC, 66-67; asst prof Ital, Univ KY, 67-69; Prof French & Ital, Univ MA, Amherst, 75-, Am Coun Learned Soc. **HONORS AND AWARDS** Foundation Camargo, NEH **MEMBERSHIPS** MLA, Dante Soc Am; Int Arthurian Soc; Soc Rencesvals; Am Asn Tchrs; Int Courtly Lit Soc. **RESEARCH** Medieval French romance, epic and lyric; Dante; Renaissance Italian. **SELECTED PUBLICATIONS** Auth, The Lay of Guingamor: A Study, Univ NC, 68; Lorenzo de'Medici, Twayne, 74; Petrarch's Metamorphoses, Univ MO, 85; Petrarch's Laurels, Penn State Univ, 92; co-ed, Literary Aspects

of Courtly Culture, Boydell & Brewer, 94; Transtextualities, MRTS, 96; Melusine of Lusignan, Univ of GA, 96; Froissart Across the Genres, Univ of FL, 98. **CONTACT ADDRESS** Dept of French & Ital, Univ of MA, Amherst, MA, 01003. **EMAIL** smadox@frital.umass.edu

SUAREZ GARCIA, JOSE LUIS
DISCIPLINE SPANISH LITERATURE **EDUCATION** Univ Ill Urbana-Champaign, PhD. **CAREER** Assoc prof. **SELECTED PUBLICATIONS** Auth, pubs on Spanish Golden Age, medieval bibliography, poetic and dramatic theory, and contemporary theater. **CONTACT ADDRESS** Foreign Languages and Literature Dept, Colorado State Univ, Fort Collins, CO, 80523. **EMAIL** jsuarez-garcia@vines.colostate.edu

SUAREZ-GALBAN, EUGENIO
DISCIPLINE LATIN AMERICAN NARRATIVE, COMPARATIVE LITERATURE, SPANISH GOLDEN AGE, ANGLO **EDUCATION** BA, Boston Col, 61; NYU, MA, 65, PhD, 67. **CAREER** Vis prof, Colgate Univ. **HONORS AND AWARDS** PhD with hon(s), NYU, 67; Sesamo prize, 82 ;tchg award, Hamilton Col, 91; medal, Inst De Cult Puertorriquena, 97., Selected for Anthol Poesia Espanola E Hispanoamericana, Madrid, 96. **CONTACT ADDRESS** Dept of Romance Lang, Colgate Univ, 13 Oak Drive, Hamilton, NY, 13346.

SUGIMOTO, NAOMI
PERSONAL Tokyo, Japan, s **DISCIPLINE** SPEECH COMMUNICATION **EDUCATION** Int Christian Univ, Japan, BA, 88; Univ Ill at Urbana-Champaign, MA, 90m, PhD, 95. **CAREER** Grad teaching/res asst, Univ Ill at Urbana-Champaign, 88-94; lecturer, Kanda Univ of Int Studs, Japan, 95-96; lecturer, Ferris Univ Japan, 96-98; asst prof, 98-. **HONORS AND AWARDS** Univ Fellowship, Univ Ill at Urbana-Champaign, 93; Rotary Int Scholar, 87-88; ICU Scholar, Int Christian Univ, 84-85. **MEMBERSHIPS** Nat Commun Assoc; Int Commun Assoc; Commun Assoc Japan; Soc for Int Educ, Training, Res, Japan; Int Assoc of Cross-Cultural Psychology; Pac Commun Assoc; Int Assoc for Intercultural Commun Studs; The Japan Soc for Corp Commun Studs. **RESEARCH** Intercultural communication; apology; comunication education; communation research methods. **SELECTED PUBLICATIONS** Auth, Impromptu Fortune-telling exercise, Speech Commun Teacher, 8(1), 5, 93; A Comparison of conceptualizations of apology in English and Japanese, Intercultural Commun Studs, vol 8, 143-167, 96; auth, A Japan-US, comparison of apology styles, Commun Res, 24 (4), 349-269, 97; auth, Apology Research: Past, present, and a future-a case of Japan and the US, Ferris Studs, vol 33, 27-43, 98. **CONTACT ADDRESS** 3-6-8 Kugenuma-Kaigan, Fujisawa, Kanagawa, ., 251-0037. **EMAIL** naomi.@city.fujisawa.kanagawa.jp

SUITS, THOMAS ALLAN
PERSONAL Born 04/05/1933, Milwaukee, WI, m, 1955, 2 children **DISCIPLINE** CLASSICAL PHILOLOGY **EDUCATION** Yale Univ, AB, 55, MA, 56, PhD(classics), 58. **CAREER** From instr to asst prof Greek & Latin, Columbia Univ, 58-66; assoc prof classics, 66-72, Prof Classics, Univ Conn, 72-Mem class jury, Am Acad in Rome, 77-79. **MEMBERSHIPS** Am Philol Asn; Class Asn New England (pres, 80-81). **RESEARCH** Latin literature, especially Elegy; Propertius. **SELECTED PUBLICATIONS** Coauth, Latin Selections, Bantam, 61; auth, Mythology, address, and structure in Propertius 2.8, 65 & The Vertumnus elegy of Propertids, 69, Trans & Proc Am Philol Asn; ed, Macrobius: The Saturnalia, Columbia Univ, 69; auth, The structure of Livy's 32nd book, Philologus, 74; The knee and the shin: Seneca, Apocolocyntosis 10.3, Class Philol, 75; The iambic character of Propertius 1.4, Philologus, 76; Tibullus, Elegies Ii--With Introduction And Commentary, Am J Of Philology, Vol 117, 96. **CONTACT ADDRESS** 12 Hillyndale Rd, Storrs, CT, 06268.

SULEIMAN, SUSAN RUBIN
PERSONAL Budapest, Hungary, m, 1966, 2 children **DISCIPLINE** FRENCH & COMPARATIVE LITERATURE **EDUCATION** Columbia Univ, BA, 60; Harvard Univ, MA, 64, PhD(Romance lang & lit), 69. **CAREER** Asst prof French, Columbia Univ, 69-76; from asst prof to assoc prof, Occidental Col, 76-81; Assoc Prof Romance Lang & Lit, Harvard Univ, 81-, Vis asst prof, Univ Calif, Los Angeles, 76. **MEMBERSHIPS** MLA; Am Asn Teachers French; Am Comp Lit Asn. **RESEARCH** Twentieth century French fiction; theory of narrative; feminist theory. **SELECTED PUBLICATIONS** Auth, Le recit exemplaire: Parabole, fable, roman a these, Poetique, 11/77; co-ed & contribr, The Reader in the Text: Essays on Audience and Interpretation, Princeton Univ Press, 80; contribr, What is Criticism?, Ind Univ Press, 81; The question of readability in Avant-Garde fiction, Studies in Twentieth Century Lit, 82; Comparative Literature And The Amn-University and Introduction--Three Papers From the 97 Acla Annual-Meeting, Comparative Lit, Vol 49, 97; Introduction--On Signposts, Travelers, Outsiders, And Backward Glances, Poetics Today, Vol 17, 96. **CONTACT ADDRESS** Dept of Romance Lang & Lit, Harvard Univ, Boylston Hall, Cambridge, MA, 02138-3800.

SULLIVAN, CONSTANCE
DISCIPLINE SPANISH AND PORTUGUESE LITERATURE **EDUCATION** Univ Rochester, BA, 60; Univ Ill, MA, 62; PhD, 68. **RESEARCH** Spanish literature and culture of the 18th, 19th, and 20th centuries; women writers of Spain; feminist theories. **SELECTED PUBLICATIONS** Auth, Gender, Text, and Cross-Dressing: The Case of 'Beatriz Cienfuegos' and La Pensadora Gaditana, Dieciocho, 95; The Quiet Feminism of Josefa Amar y Borbon's Book on the Education of Women, Ind J Hisp Lit, 93; The Boundary-Crossing Essays of Carmen Martin Gaite, Univ Ind, 93; Josefa Amar y Borbon (1749-1833), Greenwood, 93; 'Dinos, dinos quien eres': The Poetic Identity of Maria Gertrudis Hore (1742-1801), Mich Romance Studies, 92; Josefa Amar y Borbon and the Royal Aragonese Economic Society, Dieciocho, 92. **CONTACT ADDRESS** Spanish and Portuguese Dept, Univ of Minnesota, Twin Cities, 34 Folwell Hall, 9 Pleasant St SE, Minneapolis, MN, 55455. **EMAIL** sulli002@maroon.tc.umn.edu

SULLIVAN, DENIS
DISCIPLINE GREEK, LATIN, CLASSICAL PHILOLOGY AND ANCIENT HISTORY **EDUCATION** Tufts Univ, AB, 66; Univ NC Chapel Hill, PhD, 72; Cath Univ, MS, 75. **CAREER** Libr staff, Univ Md, 75-78; asst dean, Univ Md, Univ Col, 78-82; asst prof, Univ Md Col Pk, 82-88; assoc prof, Univ Md Col Pk, 88-. **HONORS AND AWARDS** Phi Beta Kappa; NDEA Title IV Fel; Woodrow Wilson Dissertation Fel; Dumbarton Oaks Byzantine Fel, 91-92 and 98-99. **MEMBERSHIPS** Amer Philol Asn; Ctr for Byzantine Studies; US Nat Comt on Byzantine Studies. **RESEARCH** Byzantine studies; Textual criticism. **SELECTED PUBLICATIONS** Auth, The Life of St. Ioannikios in Byzantine Defenders of Images, ed A. M. Talbot, Dumbarton Oaks, Wash, DC, 243-351, 98; Tenth Century Byzantine Offensive Siege Warfare: Instructional Prescriptions and Historical Practice, Byzantium at War, Athens, Nat Hellenic Res Foun, 179-200, 97; Was Constantine VI Iassoed at Markellai?, Greek, Roman and Byzantine Studies, 35, 3, 287-291, 94; Legal Opinion of Eustathios (Romaios) the Magistros, A. Laiou, Consent and Coercion to Sex and Marriage in Ancient and Medieval Societies, Wash, 175-175, 93; The Life of Saint Nikon: Text, Translation and Commentary, Brookline, Ma, Hellenic Col Press, 87; The Versions of the Vita Niconis, Dumbarton Oaks Papers, 32, 157-173, 78. **CONTACT ADDRESS** Dumbarton Oaks, 1703 32nd St. Northwest, Washington, DC, 20007-2961. **EMAIL** ds77@umail.umd.edu

SULLIVAN, JOHN P.
PERSONAL Born 07/13/1930, Liverpool, England **DISCIPLINE** FOREIGN LANGUAGES **EDUCATION** Cambridge Univ, BA, 53, MA, 57; Ozford Univ, MA, 57. **CAREER** Teacher classics, Clare & Magdalene Cols, Cambridge Univ, 52-53; teacher philos & classics, Hertford & Lincoln Cols, Oxford Univ & Queens' Col, Cambridge Univ, 53-55; fel & tutor classics, Lincoln Col, Oxford Univ, 55-62, dean, 60-61; vis prof class lang, Univ Tex, Austin, 61-62, assoc prof, 62-63, prof class lang, 63-69, actg chmn dept classics, 62-63, chmn dept, 63-65, Univ Res Inst grants, 61, 62, Bromberg award, 62; provost, State Univ NY, Buffalo, 72-75, fac profarts & lett, 69-78; Prof Classics, Univ Calif, Santa Barbara, 78-, Lectr, Oxford Univ, 56-60; co-ed, Arion, 61-69; Am Coun Learned Soc grant, 63; Nat Endowment Humanities sr fel, 67-68; ed, Arethusa, 71-; vis fel classics, Clare Hall, Cambridge Univ, 75-76; Martin lectr Neronian lit, Oberlin Col, 76; vis prof classics, Univ Hawaii, Manoa, 77; Gray lectr Martial, Cambridge Univ, 78; vis fel, Wolfson Col, Oxford Univ, 81; vis Hill prof, Univ Minn, 82. **MEMBERSHIPS** Am Philol Asn; Hellenic Soc. **RESEARCH** Latin literature; comparative literature. **SELECTED PUBLICATIONS** Coauth, Critical Essays in Roman Literature (2 vols), Routledge & Kegan Paul, 62 & 63; auth, The Satyricon of Petronius: A Literary Study, Faber, 68; ed, Ezra Pound: A Critical Anthology, Penguin, 72; Politics and literature in the Augustan Age, 72, Women in classical antiquity, 72 & Psychoanalysis and the classics, 74, Arethusa; auth, Propertius: A Critical Introduction, Cambridge Univ, 76; auth, & translr, Petronius: The Satyricon & Seneca: The Apocolocyntosis, Penguin, rev ed, 77; The Poems Of Petronius--English And Latin, Classical J, Vol 87, 92. **CONTACT ADDRESS** Classics Dept, Univ of Calif, Santa Barbara, CA, 93010.

SULLIVAN, SHIRLEY DARCUS
PERSONAL Vancouver, BC, Canada **DISCIPLINE** CLASSICAL LANGUAGES, EARLY GREEK PHILOSOPHY **EDUCATION** Univ BC, BA, 66, MA, 68; Univ Toronto, PhD(class), 73. **CAREER** Assoc Prof Class, Univ BC, 72-**MEMBERSHIPS** Am Philol Asn; Class Asn Can; Soc Ancient Greek Philos; Class Asn Pac NW; Class Asn Can West. **RESEARCH** Presocratic philosophers; Greek lyric poets; Homer. **SELECTED PUBLICATIONS** Auth, Daimon parallels the Holy Phren in Empedocles, Phronesis, 77; Noos precedes Phren in Greek lyric poetry, L'Antiquite Classique, 77; Thumos and Psyche in Heraclitus B 85, Rivista di Studi Classici, 77; The Phren of the Noos in Xenophane's God, Symbolae Osloenses, 78; What death brings in Heraclitus, Gymnasium, 78; A Person's Relation to Psyche in Homer, Hesiod and the Greek Lyric Poets, 79 & How a Person Relates to Noos in Homer, Hesiod and the Greek Lyric Poets, 80, Glotta; A Strand of Thought in Pindar, Olympians 7, TAPA, 82; THE WORD-FIELD SEELE-GEIST IN THE VOCABULARY OF HOMER, PHOENIX-THE J OF THE CLASSICAL Assn OF CANADA, Vol 45, 91. **CONTACT ADDRESS** Dept of Class, Univ of BC, Vancouver, BC, V6T 1W5.

SUNER, MARGARITA
PERSONAL Buenos Aires, Argentina, 2 children **DISCIPLINE** THEORETICAL SYNTAX, HISPANIC LINGUISTICS **EDUCATION** Univ del Salvador, EFL, 65; Univ Kans, MA, 68; Ind Univ, MA, 70, PhD(Span ling), 73. **CAREER** Asst prof, 73-79, Assoc Prof, 79-86, prof ling, 86- , Cornell Univ. **HONORS AND AWARDS** Humanities fac res grants, Cornell Univ; Fulbright-Hays Fac Res Grant, 93; ACLS Travel Grant, 93. **MEMBERSHIPS** Ling Soc Am; Am Asn Teachers Span & Port; Asn Ling y Filologia de America Latina; Glow. **RESEARCH** General and Spanish syntax; clause structure; indirect questions; relative clauses; clitics; agreement. **SELECTED PUBLICATIONS** Auth, Subject Clitics in the Northern Italian Vernaculars and the Matching Hypothesis, in Natural Language and Linguistic Theory, 92; auth, About Indirect Questions and Semi-Questions, Linguistics and Philosophy, 93; auth, Verb-movement and the Licensing of Argumental Wh-phrases in Spanish, Natural Language and Linguistic Theory, 94; co-ed, Syntactic Theory and First Language Acquisition: Crosslinguistic Perspectives, v 1: Heads, Projections, and Learnability, Lawrence Erlbaum Assoc, 94; auth, Neg-elements, island Effects, and Resumptive No, The Ling Rev, 95; auth, Resumptive Restrictive Relative Clauses: A Crosslinguistic Perspective, Language, 98; coauth, Gramatica Expanola: Analisis Linguistico y Practica, McGraw-Hill, 98. **CONTACT ADDRESS** Dept of Linguistics, Cornell Univ, Morrill Hall, Ithaca, NY, 14853-4701. **EMAIL** ms24@cornell.edu

SUNGDAI, CHO
PERSONAL Born 01/25/1958, Seoul, Korea, m, 1989, 2 children **DISCIPLINE** LINGUISTICS **EDUCATION** Univ Hawaii, PhD, 95. **CAREER** Korean Prog Coordr, Univ Michigan, Ann Arbor, 93-96; Korean Prog Coordr, Stanford Univ, 96-. **MEMBERSHIPS** LSA; AAS; AATK; TESOL; ACFEL. **RESEARCH** Syntax and morphology; language pedagogy. **SELECTED PUBLICATIONS** Auth, On The Potential Middle Constructions in Korean, Lang Res, 93; auth, Review for Korean Textbooks for English Speakers: Grammar, Culture and Task/Function, Jour Am Asn of Tchrs of Korean, 98; auth, Passive and Middle Constructions in Korean, Jour of the Int Circle of Korean Ling, 98; auth, An Optimality-Theoretic Account of Korean Nominal Inflection: Selected Papers from the 11th International Conference on Korean Linguistics, Univ Hawaii, 98. **CONTACT ADDRESS** Dept of Asian Languages, Stanford Univ, Stanford, CA, 94305. **EMAIL** sundy@leland.stanford.edu

SUNGOLOWSKY, JOSEPH
PERSONAL Born 12/21/1931, Charleroi, Belgium, m, 1967, 2 children **DISCIPLINE** FRENCH LITERATURE **EDUCATION** Yeshiva Univ, BA, 55; NY Univ, MA, 58; Yale Univ, PhD, 63. **CAREER** Asst instr French, Yale Univ, 57-59, instr, 59-62; from instr to asst prof, Vassar Col, 62-65; asst prof, 65-72, Assoc Prof French Lit, Queens Col, NY, 72-. **HONORS AND AWARDS** Chevalier dans l'Ordre des Palmes Academiques (Knight in the Order of the Academic Palms by French govt. **MEMBERSHIPS** Societe des Professeurs Francais et Francophones en Amerique **RESEARCH** Beaumarchais; contemporary French Jewish literature; 18th and 19th centuries in France. **SELECTED PUBLICATIONS** Auth, Alfred de Vigny et le dix-huitieme siecle, Nizet, Paris, 68; Vue sur Germinal apres une lecture de La peste, Cahiers Naturalistes, 70; Du cote de Beaumarchais, Les Nouveaux Cahiers, 71: Beaumarchais, Twayne, 74; I B Singer and Tshuvah, Midstream, 94; Flaubert a-t-il prevu l'univers concentrationnaire, Guerres Moddiales & Conflits Contemporains, 97. **CONTACT ADDRESS** Dept of European Langs, Queens Col, CUNY, 6530 Kissena Blvd, Flushing, NY, 11367-1597. **EMAIL** jsuqc@qcvaxa.acc.qc.edu

SURRIDGE, MARIE
PERSONAL London, England **DISCIPLINE** FRENCH STUDIES **EDUCATION** Oxford Univ, BA, 53, MA, 57, PhD, 62. **CAREER** Tchr, part-time, Oxford Univ, 55-67; asst prof, 70-77, assoc prof, 77-87, head Fr dept, 83-93, PROF, QUEEN'S UNIV, 87-. **SELECTED PUBLICATIONS** Auth, Le ou la? The Gender of French Nouns, 95. **CONTACT ADDRESS** Dept of French Studies, Queen's Univ, Kingston, ON, K7L 3N6.

SUSSMAN, HENRY
DISCIPLINE COMPARATIVE LITERATURE **EDUCATION** Brandeis Univ, BA; Johns Hopkins Univ, PhD. **CAREER** Fac hum ctr, Johns Hopkins Univ; Julian Park Prof Comp Lit, SUNY Buffalo, present. **RESEARCH** The sublime and the grandiose in lit and psychol; Kafka's The Trial. **SELECTED PUBLICATIONS** Auth, Afterimages of Modernity 90; High Resolution: Critical Theory and the Problem of Literacy, 89; The Hegelian Aftermath, 82; Franz Kafka: Geometrician of Metaphor, 79; The Aesthetic Contract: Statutes of Art and Intellectual Work in Modernity, Stanford, 97, Psyche and Text: The Sublime and the Grandiose in Literature, Psychopathology, and Culture, 93; The Trial: Kafka's Unholy Trinity, 93; co-ed,

Psychoanalysis And... . **CONTACT ADDRESS** Dept Comp Lit, SUNY Buffalo, 639 Clemens Hall, Buffalo, NY, 14260. **EMAIL** hsussman@acsu.buffalo.edu

SUTTON, HOMER B.
PERSONAL m, 2 children **DISCIPLINE** FRENCH LANGUAGE AND LITERATURE **EDUCATION** Davidson Col, BA, 71; IN Univ, MA and PhD, 79. **CAREER** Fac, Sorbonne Nouvelle, 77-79; fac, Davidson Col, 81-; coord study abroad progs, 83-94; interim dean admissions, 91-92; res dir Fr prog, present. **RESEARCH** French lang, lit, and civilization; hist of France and French soc since 1945. **SELECTED PUBLICATIONS** Auth, publ articles on French univ reform, changes in the FM band in France in the early 80's when Mitterrand liberalized the airwaves, and "harkis" allied with French during the Algerian struggle for independence. **CONTACT ADDRESS** Davidson Col, 102 N Main St, PO Box 1719, Davidson, NC, 28036.

SUTTPN, DANA F.
DISCIPLINE CLASSICAL STUDIES, PHILOLOGY **EDUCATION** New School for Social Research, BA, 65; Univ Wisc, MA, 66, PhD, 70. **CAREER** Lectr, CUNY, Herbert Lehman Coll, 69-72; asst prof, Univ Ill, 75-79; asst to assoc to PROF, UNIV CALIF, IRVINE, 79-. **HONORS AND AWARDS** Guggenheim fel, 75; Adele Mellon Prize, disting scholarship, 96. **RESEARCH** Greek, Latin, Neolatin poetry and drama. **SELECTED PUBLICATIONS** Auth, Sophocles' Inachus, in Beitrage zur klassischen Philologie, Verlag Anton Hain, Meisenheim am Glan, 79; auth, The Greek Satyr Play, in Beitrage zur klassischen Philologie, Verlag Anton Hain, Meisenheim am Glan, 80; auth, Self and Society in ARitsophanes, Univ Press Am, 80; auth, The Dramaturgy of the Octavia, in Beitrage zur klassischen Philologie, Verlag Anton Hain, Konigstein/Taunus, 83; auth, The Lost Sophocles, Univ Press Am, 84; auth, The Satyr Play, in Cambridge History of Classical Literature I, 85; auth, Seneca on the Stage, in Mnemosyne, E. J. Brill, 86; auth, The Greek Dithyrambographers, Georg Olms Verlag, 89; auth, Thomas Legge: The Complete Plays, Peter Lang Verlag, 93; auth, Ancient Comedy: The Conflict of the Generations, in Twaynes' Literary Genres and Themes Series, Macmillan, 93; auth, The Catharsis of Comedy, in Greek Studies: Interdisciplinary Approaches, Rowman and Littlefield, 94; auth, William Gager: The Complete Works, Garland Press, 94; auth, Oxford Poetry by Richard Eedes and George Peele, Garland Press, 95; auth, The COmplete Works of Thomas Watson (1556-1592), Edwin Mellen Press, 96; auth, Homer in the Papyri, hypertext version, http://eee/uci.edu/üpapyri, 97; Matthew Gwinne's tragedy Nero, hypertext, http://eee/uci/edu/üpapyri/Nero, 97; Edward Forsett's comedy Pedantius, hypertext, http://eee/uci.edu/üpapyri.forsett, 98; Geroge Ruggle's comedy Ignoramus, hypertext, http://eee/uci.edu/üpapyri.ruggle, 98; William Alabaster's tragedy Roxana, hypertext, http://eee/uci.edu/üpapyri.alabaster, 98; auth, The Complete Latin Poetry of William Savage Landor, Edwin Mellen Press, forthcoming. **CONTACT ADDRESS** Dept of Classics, Univ of California, Irvine, 120 HOB II, Irvine, CA, 97692-2000. **EMAIL** DanaS64562@aol.com

SWAFFAR, JANET KING
PERSONAL Born 04/28/1935, Minneapolis, MN, m, 1964, 2 children **DISCIPLINE** GERMAN LITERATURE, FOREIGN LANGUAGE PEDAGOGY **EDUCATION** Mankato State Teachers Col, BA, 56; Univ Wis, MA, 59, PbD, 65. **CAREER** From instr to asst prof, 65-71, assoc prof, 71-82, prof German, Univ Tex, Austin, 82-, dir, Nat Endowment for Humanities Prog grant, Univ Tex, 77-80. **HONORS AND AWARDS** Paul Pimsleur Award, Am Coun Teaching Foreign Lang, 80; Guest FRG, 85; Univ Tex Centennial Teaching Award, 87; Secy Navy Fel, 90; Pres Assoc Teaching Excellence Award Univ Tx, 94. **MEMBERSHIPS** MLA; Am Asn Teachers Ger; Am Coun Teaching Foreign Lang. **RESEARCH** Modern Germany (east-west), foreign language acquistion, reading history. **SELECTED PUBLICATIONS** Coauth, Imitation and correction in foreign language learning, Mod Lang J, 12/71 & Educ Digest, 72; Literarische Zeitschriften 1945-70, Sammlung, Stuttgart, 74; Lenz viewed sane, Ger Rev, 74; The Ethics of Exploitation: Brecht's Der gute Mensch von Sezuan, University of Dayton Review, spring 79; Foreign Languages in the University: The Case for a Content Orientation for the Discipline, Monatshefte, Vol 73, 271-288; Reading in the Foreign Language Classroom: Focus on Process, Unterrichtspraxis, Vol 14, 176-194; (with Arens & Morgan), Teacher classroom practices: Redefining method as task hierarchy, Mod Lang J, Vol 66, 24-33; Using Foreign Languages to Learn: Rethinking the College Foreign Language Curriculum, Reflecting on Proficiency for the Classroom Perspective, Nat Textbook Co, 93; Reading and Listening Comprehension: Perspectives on Research and Implications for the Classroom, Research in Language Learning Principles, Processes, and Prospects, Nat Textbook Co, 93; Aesthetics and Gender: Anna Seghers as a Case Study, Monatshefte 87, 95; Institutional Mission and Academic Disciplines: Rethinking Accountability, J Gen Educ, 95; Instructor's Resource Manual for Treffpunkt Deutsch, 2 ed, Prentice Hall, 96; A Sequential Model for Video Viewing in the Foreigh Language Curriculum, Mod Lang J, 97; Language on Line: Research and Pedagogy in ESL and L2, Daedalus Grp, 98. **CONTACT ADDRESS** Dept of German Lang, Univ Tex, Austin, TX, 78712-1026. **EMAIL** jswaffar@mail.utexas.edu

SWANSON, ROY ARTHUR
PERSONAL Born 04/07/1925, St. Paul, MN, m, 1946, 4 children **DISCIPLINE** CLASSICS, COMPARATIVE LITERATURE **EDUCATION** Univ Minn, BA, 48, BS, 49, MA, 51; Univ Ill, PhD, 54. **CAREER** Instr educ, Univ Ill, 52-53; instr classics, Ind Univ, 54-57; from asst prof to prof classics & humanities, Univ Minn, 57-65, chm dept comp lit, 64-65; prof English, Macalester Col, 65-67, coordr humanities, 66-67; chm dept classics, 67-70, 86-89; chm dept comp lit, 69-73, 76-82, Prof Classics & Comp Lit, Univ Wis-Milwaukee, 67-, Chm Dept Comp Lit, 76-, Fulbright scholar, Rome, 53; fel, Univ Ill, 54; ed, Minn Rev, 64-67; Lilly Found fel, Stockholm, 65-66; ed, Class J, 68-73. **HONORS AND AWARDS** Distinguished Teacher Award, Univ Minn, 62 & Univ Wis- Milwaukee, 74, 91; grad sch res grant, 68-69, 74 & 81. **MEMBERSHIPS** Am Philol Asn; MLA; Am Comp Lit Asn; Int Comp Lit Asn; Southern Comp Lit Asn. **RESEARCH** Lyric poetry, especially Greek and Roman; mediaeval studies; literary criticism. **SELECTED PUBLICATIONS** Auth, Odi et Amo: the complete poetry of Catullus, Lib Arts Press, 59; Heart of reason: Introductory essays in modern-world humanities, Denison, 63; The humor of Don Quixote, Romanic Rev, 10/63; Evil and love in Lagerkvist's crucifixion cycle, Scand Studies, 11/66; Pindar's odes, Bobbs, 74; Love is the function of death: Forster, Lagerkvist, and Zamyatin, Can Rev Comp Lit, 76; Deceptive symmetry: Classical echoes in the poetry of Richard Emil Braun, Mod Poetry Studies, 76; Ionesco's classical absurdity, In: The Two Faces of Ionesco, Whitston, 78; Pur Lager-Kvist: Five Early Works, Lewiston, 89; De nuptis metamorphoseon et mechanicorum quantorum, Stone Soup (London), 97. **CONTACT ADDRESS** Depts of Fr, Ital, & Comp Lit, For Lang and Li, Univ of Wis, PO Box 413, Milwaukee, WI, 53201-0413. **EMAIL** rexcy@uwm.edu

SWART, PAULA
PERSONAL The Hague, Netherlands **DISCIPLINE** ASIAN STUDIES **EDUCATION** Lang Inst, Beijing, Chinese Lang, 78; Univ Leiden, BA, 79; Univ Nanjing, China, 79; Univ Amsterdam, MA, 82. **CAREER** Participant, res proj Witte Leeuw, 79-81; res asst, Montreal Mus Fine Arts, 83-89; CURATOR, ASIAN STUDIES, VANCOUVER MUSEUM, 89-. **HONORS AND AWARDS** Undergrad Scholar, 74-77; Holland China Exchange Scholar, 77-78; Grad Scholar, 79-81, Dutch Gov. **MEMBERSHIPS** Japan Sword Appreciation Soc; Can Soc Asian Art; Am Museum Asn. **SELECTED PUBLICATIONS** Auth, Bronze Carriages from the Tomb of China's First Emperor, in Archaeol, Vol 37, 84; auth, Art from the Roof of the World: Tibet, 89; coauth, In Search of Old Nanking, 82; coauth, Chinese Jade Stone for the Emperors, 86. **CONTACT ADDRESS** Curator Asian Studies, Vancouver Museum, 1100 Chestnut St, Vancouver, BC, V6J 3J9.

SWEETSER, MARIE-ODILE
PERSONAL Born 12/28/1925, Verdun, France, m, 1955, 1 child **DISCIPLINE** FRENCH LANGUAGE & LITERATURE **EDUCATION** Univ Nancy, Lic es Let, 44, dipl, 45; Bryn Mawr Col, MA, 50; Univ Pa, PhD, 56. **CAREER** Lectr French, McGill Univ, 50-52; asst instr, Univ Pa, 52-56; instr, Cedar Crest Col, 56-57 & Mills Col, 57-60; from instr to asst prof, City Coll New York, 60-69; assoc prof, 69-79, Prof French, Univ Ill, Chicago Circle, 79-, Chmn, Fourth Conf 17th Century French Lit, Corneille Symp, 72; exec comt MLA div French 17th century lit, 71-78; Nat Endowment for Humanities panelist, 80 & 81; consult, La Bd of Regents, 82. **MEMBERSHIPS** MLA; Am Asn Teachers Fr; Soc Prof Fr Am; Int Asn Fr Studies. **RESEARCH** French literature of the 17th century; theater, novel, literary criticism poetry; classical tradition in French literature. **SELECTED PUBLICATIONS** Auth, A Pact With Silence--Art and Thought In the Fables of Jean De Lafontaine, French Rev, Vol 66, 93; Moliere, Proceedings Of The Nottingham Moliere Confr, December-17-18, 93, Esprit Createur, Vol 36, 96; Jean De Lafontaine: Fables, French Rev, Vol 69, 96; Literature And Anthropology--Human-Nature And Character In The Classical-Age--French-, French Rev, Vol 69, 96; Madame De Sevigne and the Love Letter, French Rev, Vol 67, 94; The Commedia-Dellarte In Paris 1644-1697, French Rev, Vol 66, 93; Henriette-Dangleterre, Duchess Of Orleans, French Rev, Vol 70, 96; The Pastoral Masquerade--Disguise And Identity In L Astree, French Rev, Vol 68, 95. **CONTACT ADDRESS** Dept French, Univ Ill, Chicago, IL, 60680.

SWITTEN, MARGARET L.
PERSONAL m, 1950 **DISCIPLINE** FRENCH & PROVENCIAL LANGUAGE & LITERATURE **EDUCATION** Westminster Choir Col, BMus, 47; Barnard Col, BA, 48; Bryn Mawr Col, MA, 49, PhD(Fr), 52. **CAREER** From asst prof to assoc prof Music & French, Hampton Inst, 52-62, prof French, 62-63; Class of 1926 prof French, 63-; from asst prof to assoc prof, chmn dept, 69-76 & 82-83, prof French, Mt Holyoke Col, 63-, chmn dept, 82-, lectr, Smith Col, 66 & 68. **HONORS AND AWARDS** Fulbright Post-Doctoral Research Award to Paris, 56-7; American Council of Learned Societies Fellowship, 69-70; Officier dans l'Ordre des Palmes Académiques. **MEMBERSHIPS** Am Asn Teachers Fr; Medieval Acad Am; MLA; Mod Humanities Res Am; Int Courtly Lit Asn. **RESEARCH** The poetry and the music of the Old Provencal troubadours; literature and society in 12th century France; medieval music. **SELECTED PUBLICATIONS** Auth, Diderot's theory of language as the medium of literature, 44: 185-196, L'Histoire and La Poesie in Diderot's writings on the novel, 47: 259-269 & Metrical and musical structure in the Songs of Peirol, 51: 241-255, Romanic Rev; Text and melody in Peirol's Cansos, Publ Mod Lang Asn, 86: 320-325; Raimon de Miraval's Be m'agrada and the unrhymed refrain in troubadour poetry, Romance Philol, 11: 432-448; The CanSos of Raimon de Miraval: A Study of Poems and Melodies, Med Acad Am; 85; Of the Comtessa and the Vilana: Women in Troubadour Song, forthcoming in Women and Music: A Journal of Gender and Culture, Fall, 98; Music and Versification: Fetz Marcabrus los mots e i so, in The Troubadours: An Introduction, forthcoming, Spring, 99. **CONTACT ADDRESS** 50 College St, South Hadley, MA, 01075-1461. **EMAIL** mswitten@mtholyoke.edu

SYPHER, FRANCIS JACQUES
PERSONAL Born 11/04/1941, Hackensack, NJ, d, 1 child **DISCIPLINE** ENGLISH, COMPARATIVE LITERATURE **EDUCATION** Columbia Univ, AB, 63, MA, 64, PhD, 68. **CAREER** Precep, Eng, 65-68, Columbia Univ; asst prof, Eng, 68-75, SUNY, Albany; ed consul, 75-81, R.R. Bowker, NYU Press, & other publ; Fulbright Sr lectr, Amer lit, 81-83, Univ du Benin, W Africa; asst to pres, 83-85, NY Schl of Inter Design, concurrent, adj prof, Eng, NY Univ; dir, 85-86, Amer Eng Lang Prog, Amer Cult Ctr, US Info Svc, Dakar Senegal, W Africa; Fulbright Sr Lectr, 86-88, Amer Lit, Univ Omar Bongo, Libreville Gabon C Africa, writer, ed consul, 88-, NY. **HONORS AND AWARDS** NY St Regents Fel, 63-65; SUNY Res Found Award, 74; Fulbright Sr Lectr, 81-83, 86-88; Pres Bronze Medal, 93, St Nicholas Soc NY. **MEMBERSHIPS** Art Stud League of NY; NY Genealogical and Biographical Soc; Friends of the Columbia Univ Lib. **RESEARCH** English & comparative lit; life and works of Letitia Elizabeth Landon, 1802-1838; NY history & biography. **SELECTED PUBLICATIONS** Auth, Ethel Churchill, 92; auth, Critical Writings, 96; auth, The Vow of the Peacock, 97; auth, Romance and Reality, 98; coauth, ed, The Saint Nicholas Society, A 150 Year Record, 93; ed & trans, The Iskenius Letters from Germany to New York 1726-1737, 94; ed, The Image of Irelande, Derricke, 98; art, Victorian Poetry; art, Harvard Lib Bull; art, Quart Jour of the Lib of Cong; art, NY Genealogical & Biographical Record; art, Proceedings of Amer Antiquarian Soc; art, Annales de l'Universite du Benin, Colloque sur les Etudes Americaines 5-8, avril 83, Univ de Dakar; art, New Orleans Rev; art, NY History; art, Columbia Lib Col; art, Annals of Scholar; art, Connotations; art, Furn Hist; art, Trinity per Saecula; art, Review; art, Amer Natl Biography. **CONTACT ADDRESS** FDR Station, PO Box 1125, New York, NY, 10150-1125.

SZARYCZ, IRENEUSZ
DISCIPLINE RUSSIAN LITERATURE **EDUCATION** Kazan State Univ, BA; Univ Poznan, MA; Univ Ottawa, PhD. **CAREER** Assoc prof **MEMBERSHIPS** Waterloo Fac Assn. **RESEARCH** Contemporary Russian literature; Russian folklore. **SELECTED PUBLICATIONS** Auth, Obraz nochi i vselennoi v tvorchestve Rainera Marii Rilke i Borisa L. Pasternaka, 95; Zatovarennaja bochkotara Vasiliia Aksenova: Stilisticheskii analiz odnogo abzatsa, Poznan, 95; Symbols of the National Past: Nibelungenlied and Slovo o polku Igoreve, 97. **CONTACT ADDRESS** Dept of German and Slavic Literature, Waterloo Univ, 200 University Ave W, Waterloo, ON, N2L 3G1. **EMAIL** iszarycz@artshh.watstar.uwaterloo.ca

SZPEK, HEIDI M.
PERSONAL Born 09/27/1958, Milwaukee, WI, m, 1984, 2 children **DISCIPLINE** HEBREW STUDIES **EDUCATION** Univ of Wis, BA, 80, MA, 83, MA, 88, PhD, 91. **CAREER** Lectr, 80-84, 87-93, Concordia Univ Wis; Asst lect Milwaukee, 93-97, Guest Lectr, Madison, Univ of Wis; adj fac, 98-, Pima Comm Coll W, Tucson. **HONORS AND AWARDS** Grad Fel Univ Wis; Honor Soc Phi Beta Kappa; Liakon Awd. **MEMBERSHIPS** SBL, AAR, Phi Beta Kappa. **RESEARCH** Women in the bible, Peshitta studies, Job. **SELECTED PUBLICATIONS** Auth, Translation Technique in the Peshitta to Job, A Model for Evaluating a Text with Documentation from the Peshitta to Job, in: J of Biblical Lit Dissertation Series, Scholars Press, 92; co-ed, Women in the Hebrew Bible, A Literary Approach, Papers delivered at the 98 Midwest Regional SBL Meeting, Andres Univ Press, forthcoming; art, The Peshitta on Job 7:6, My days are swifter than an arg, in: JBL, 94; On the Influence of the Targum on the Peshittato Job, USF Stud in the Hist of Judaism, Atlanta GA, Scholars Press 98; An Observation of the Peshitta's Translation of Shaddai in Job, VT, 97; On the Influence of the Septuagint on the Peshitta to Job, CBQ, forthcoming 99. **CONTACT ADDRESS** 5522 E Burns St, Tucson, AZ, 85711. **EMAIL** hszpek@aol.com

T

TAHARA, MILDRED MACHIKO
PERSONAL Born 05/15/1941, Hilo, HI **DISCIPLINE** CLASSICAL & MODERN JAPANESE LITERATURE **EDUCATION** Univ Hawaii, Manoa, BA, 63, MA, 65; Columbia Univ, PhD(Japanese Lit), 69. **CAREER** Asst prof, 69-76, Assoc Prof Japanese Lit, Univ Hawaii, Manoa, 76-. **MEMBERSHIPS** Asn

Asian Studies; Asn Teachers Japanese; Mod Lang Assoc. **RESEARCH** Heian literature; modern and contemporary novels and short stories; classical poetry; image and text. **SELECTED PUBLICATIONS** Auth, Heichu, As Seen in Yamato Monogatari, 71 & Yamato Monogatari: A Poem-tale of Heian Japan, 72, Monumenta Nopponica; Genji monogatari: Heian loves, Orientations, 12/72; The ink stick (short story), Japan Quart, Vol 22, No 4; Fujiwara Michinaga, In: Great Historical Figures of Japan, Japan Cult Inst, 78; auth & transl, Tales of Yamato, Univ Hawaii Press, 80; transl, Ariyoshi Sawako, The River Ki, Kodansha Int, 80, trans, Ariyoshi Sawako, The Twilight Years, Kodansha Int, 84. **CONTACT ADDRESS** Dept of East Asian Lit, Univ of Hawaii, Manoa, 1890 E West Rd, Honolulu, HI, 96822-2318. **EMAIL** tahara@hawaii.edu

TALBOT, EMILE
PERSONAL Born 04/12/1941, Brunswick, ME, m, 1966, 2 children **DISCIPLINE** FRENCH **EDUCATION** St Francis Col, BA, 63; Brown Univ, MA, 65, PhD(French), 68. **CAREER** From instr to asst prof, 67-73, assoc prof French, Univ Ill, Urbana, 73-86; prof French and Comparative Literature, 86-; head dept French, 88-94. **HONORS AND AWARDS** Fel, Ctr Advan Studies, Univ Ill, 73; Nat Endowment for Humanities younger humanist fel, 73-74; Camargo Found fel, 77; distinguished vis prof, Eastern Ill Univ, Summer, 81; recipient, Palmes academiques from French government, 98. **MEMBERSHIPS** MLA; Am Asn Teachers Fr; Asn for Can Studies US; American Council for Quebec Studies, vp 95-97, pres, 97-99. **RESEARCH** 19th Century French; criticism; French Canadian literature. **SELECTED PUBLICATIONS** Auth, Considerations sur la definition stendbalienne du romantisme, 69, Remarques sur la mort de Madame de Renal, 73 & Stendhal, le beau et le laid: Autour de quelques problemes esthetiques, 78, Stendhal-Club; Style and the Self: Some Notes on La Chartreuse de Parme, Lang & Style, 72; Stendhal, the Artist, and Society, Studies in Romanticism, 74; Author and Audience: A Perspective on Stendhal's Concept of Literature, Nineteenth-Century Fr Studies, 74; La crituque Stendhalienne de Balzac a Zola, Fr Lit Publ, 79; Les Incarnations d'un texte nationaliste: Hemon, Savard, Carrier, Presence Francophone, 80. **CONTACT ADDRESS** Dept of French, Univ of Illinois, Urbana-Champaign, 707 S Mathews Ave, Urbana, IL, 61801-3625. **EMAIL** ejtalbot@uiuc.edu

TANDY, DAVID
PERSONAL Born 04/19/1950, New York, NY, 2 children **DISCIPLINE** CLASSICAL PHILOLOGY **EDUCATION** Yale, PhD, 79 **CAREER** Distinguished Prof in Humanities, Univ TN, 98-; Asst Prof, 80-pres, Univ of TN **MEMBERSHIPS** Am Philol Assoc; Econ Hist Assoc; Karl Polanyi Inst of Polit Econ **RESEARCH** Forms of Domination & Resistance in the Classical World; Social & Economic History of Ancient Greece & Rome **SELECTED PUBLICATIONS** Auth, Warriors into Traders, Univ of CA, 97 **CONTACT ADDRESS** Dept of Classics, Univ of TN, Knoxville, TN, 37996-0413. **EMAIL** dtandy@utk.edu

TANNEN, DEBORAH F.
PERSONAL Brooklyn, NY **DISCIPLINE** LINGUISTICS, MODERN GREEK LITERATURE **EDUCATION** State Univ NY, Binghamton, BA, 66; Wayne State Univ, MA, 70; Univ Calif, Berkeley, MA, 76, PhD, 79. **CAREER** Instr English, Mercer County Community Col, 70-71; lectr acad skills, Lehman Col, City Univ New York, 71-74; asst prof Ling, 79-85, univ prof, 91-, Georgetown Univ, Rockefeller Humanities fel, Rockefeller Foundation, 82-83. **MEMBERSHIPS** Ling Soc Am; Mod Greek Studies Asn; Am Anthrop Asn; MLA; Am Asn App Ling; Intl Pragmatics Asn. **RESEARCH** Discourse analysis; cross-cultural communication. **SELECTED PUBLICATIONS** Auth, The Argument Culture: Moving from Debate to Dialogue, Random House, 98; Talking from 9 to 5: Women and Men in the Workplace: Language, Sex, and Power, Avon, 95; Gender & Discourse, Oxford, 94; You Just Don't Understand: Women and Men in Conversation, Ballantine, 90; ed, Framing in Discourse, Oxford, 93; Gender and Conversational Interaction, Oxford, 93; Linguistics in Context: Connecting Observation and Understanding, Ablex, 88. **CONTACT ADDRESS** Linguistics Dept, Georgetown Univ, Box 571051, Washington, DC, 20057-1051. **EMAIL** robinsda@gunet.georgetown.edu

TAPIA, ELENA
DISCIPLINE SECOND LANGUAGE ACQUISITION **EDUCATION** IN Univ, PhD. **CAREER** Eng Dept, Eastern Conn State Univ **SELECTED PUBLICATIONS** Areas: cognitive demand and writing assessment, second lang learners acquiring conceptual metaphors, psycholinguistic factors influencing second lang writers. **CONTACT ADDRESS** Eastern Connecticut State Univ, 83 Windham Street, Willimantic, CT, 06226. **EMAIL** TAPIAE@ECSU.CTSTATEU.EDU

TAPPY, RON E.
DISCIPLINE NEAR EASTERN LANGUAGES AND CIVILIZATIONS **EDUCATION** Harvard Univ, PhD, 90. **CAREER** Res assoc, Harvard Univ, 90-91; vis asst prof, Univ Mich, 90-92; assoc prof, Westmont Col, 92-. **RESEARCH** Archaeology of Ancient Syria-Palestine; Biblical Archaeology **SELECTED PUBLICATIONS** Auth, Samaria, Encycl Near Eastern Archaeol, Oxford UP, 96; Review of Ancient Jerusalem Revealed, Jour of Near Eastern Stud, 96; Did the Dead Ever Die in Biblical Judah, Bulletin of the Amer Sch of Oriental Res, 95; Psalm 23: Symbolism and Structure, The Cath Bibl Quart, 95; Ahab, Hazor, Megiddo, The Oxford Companion to the Bible, Oxford UP, 93. **CONTACT ADDRESS** Dept of Rel, Westmont Col, 955 La Paz Rd, Santa Barbara, CA, 93108-1099.

TARICA, RALPH
PERSONAL Born 09/09/1932, Atlanta, GA, m, 1964, 2 children **DISCIPLINE** FRENCH LITERATURE **EDUCATION** Emory Univ, BA, 54, MA, 58; Harvard Univ, PhD(Romance lang), 66. **CAREER** Instr mod lang, Ga Inst Technol, 58-60; from instr to asst prof French, Brandeis Univ, 63-69; from assoc prof to prof French, Univ MD, College Park, 69-. **HONORS AND AWARDS** Phi Beta Kappa chap pres, 93-95; French Academic Palmes, 94. **MEMBERSHIPS** MLA; S Atlantic Mod Lang Asn. **RESEARCH** Modern French literature; the novel; stylistics. **SELECTED PUBLICATIONS** Contrib, Image and Theme in Modern French Fiction, Harvard Univ, 69; auth, The Child Motif in Malraux's fiction, Malraux Miscellany, 78; Imagery in the Novels of Andr¤ Malraux, Fairleigh Dickinson, 80; Les signes de l'anxiete dans les romans de Malraux, Berenice, 83; contribr, Witnessing Andr¤ Malraux: Visions and Re-Visions, Wesleyan Univ, 84; Antoine de Saint-Exupery, Scribner's, 90. **CONTACT ADDRESS** Dept of French and Ital, Univ of Md, College Park, MD, 20742-4821. **EMAIL** rt2@umail.umd.edu

TARKOW, THEODORE A.
DISCIPLINE CLASSICAL STUDIES **EDUCATION** Oberlin Col, AB, 66; Univ Mich, MA, 67; Univ Mich, PhD, 71. **CAREER** Asst prof to prof, class studies, Univ Mo Columbia, 70-; assoc dean, col of arts and sci; Univ Mo Columbia, 82-. **HONORS AND AWARDS** Woodrow Wilson fel, 67; Amer Philos Asn award for excellence in teaching of the classics, 81; pres, Class Asn of Middlewest & South, 87. **MEMBERSHIPS** Amer Philol Asn; Archaeol Inst of Amer; Class Asn of Middlewest & South. **RESEARCH** Greek comedy & tragedy; Greek lyric poetry. **SELECTED PUBLICATIONS** Auth, Scan of Orestes, Rheinisches Mus fur Philol, 124; auth, Ainthes & the ghost of Aeschylus in Aristophanes Frogs, Traditio, 38; auth, Tyrtaeus 9D, L'antiquite Classique, 52; auth, Sight & Seeing in the Prometheus Board, Eranus, 89. **CONTACT ADDRESS** Univ of Missouri, 317 Lowry Hall, Columbia, MO, 65211. **EMAIL** tarkowt@missouri.edu

TATAR, MARIA
PERSONAL Born 05/13/1945, m, 2 children **DISCIPLINE** GERMAN LITERATURE **EDUCATION** Denison Univ, BA, 67; Princeton Univ, MA, 69, PhD(Ger), 71. **CAREER** Asst prof, 71-77, assoc prof, 77-79, Prof Ger, Harvard Univ, 79-. **HONORS AND AWARDS** Res fel lit, Nat Endowment for Humanities, 74-75 & Radcliffe Inst Independent Study, 77-79; Humboldt Fel, 85-86; Ger Studies Book Award, 92. **MEMBERSHIPS** MLA; Am Asn Teachers Ger. **RESEARCH** Weimar Germany; cultural studies; folklore; children's literature. **SELECTED PUBLICATIONS** Auth, Mesmerism, madness, and death in E T A Hoffmann's Der goldne Topf, Studies Romanticism, 75; Spellbound: Studies on Mesmerism and Literature, Princeton Univ, 78; Deracination and alienation in Ludwig Tieck's Der Runenberg, Ger Quart, 78; Reflections and romantic irony: E T A Hoffmann's Der Sandmann, Mod Lang Notes, 80; The art of biography in Wackenroder's Herzensergiessungen eines kunstliebenden Klosterbruders and phantasien ubet die kunst, Studies Romanticism, 80; The houses of fiction: Toward a definition of the uncanny, Comp Lit, 81; Folkloristic phantasies: Grimms' fairy tales and Freud's family romance, In: Fairy Tales as Ways of Knowing, 81; Spellbound: Studies on Mesmerism in Literature, Princeton Univ, 78; The Hard Facts of Grimm's Fairy Tales, Princeton Univ, 87; Off With Their Heads: Fairy Tales and the Culture of Childhood, Princeton Univ, 92; Neverending Stories, Princeton Univ, 95; Lustmord: Sexual Murder in Weimar German, Princeton Univ, 97. **CONTACT ADDRESS** Dept of German, Harvard Univ, 353 Barker Ctr., Cambridge, MA, 02138-3800. **EMAIL** tatar@fas.harvard.edu

TATE, PAUL DEAN
PERSONAL Born 11/22/1945, Fort Worth, TX, m, 1976 **DISCIPLINE** PHILOSOPHY, SANSKRIT **EDUCATION** Univ Tex, Austin, BA, 67; Yale Univ, MPhil, 74, PhD, 76. **CAREER** Dean of Grad Studies, Idaho State Univ **MEMBERSHIPS** Am Philos Assn. **RESEARCH** The philosophy of Martin Heidegger; the nature of language; Indian philosophy. **SELECTED PUBLICATIONS** Auth, His Holiness Gives an Example, Kite Bks, 73; auth, The Agivtic Hotel, Latitude Press, 87. **CONTACT ADDRESS** Idaho State Univ, 921 S 8th Ave, Box 8399, Pocatello, ID, 83209-0001. **EMAIL** tatepaul@isu.edu

TATLOCK, LYNN
DISCIPLINE GERMAN LITERATURE **EDUCATION** Ind Univ, BA, 71, MA, 75, PhD, 81. **CAREER** Asst prof, 81-87, assoc prof, 87-94, PROF, 94-, DEPT CHAIR, 92-97, WASH UNIV. **CONTACT ADDRESS** Washington Univ, 1 Brookings Dr, Box 1104, St. Louis, MO, 63130. **EMAIL** ltatlock@artsci.wustl.edu

TAVERA RIVERA, MARGARITA
DISCIPLINE LATIN AMERICAN AND CHICANO LITERATURE **EDUCATION** Univ Ore, BA; Stanford Univ, MA, PhD; Univ Calif, MA; Humboldt State Univ, MA. **CAREER** English, Carthage Col. **SELECTED PUBLICATIONS** Articles: New Chicano Writing; Maize, El Tecolote Literary Magazine; El Chicano. **CONTACT ADDRESS** Carthage Col, 2001 Alford Dr., Kenosha, WI, 53140.

TAYLOR, ALLAN ROSS
PERSONAL Born 12/24/1931, Palisade, CO, m, 1958, 5 children **DISCIPLINE** LINGUISTICS **EDUCATION** Univ Colo, Boulder, BA, 53; Univ Calif, Berkeley, PhD(ling), 69. **CAREER** Teaching assoc Russ, Univ Calif, Berkeley, 58-61, lectr, 61-62; from instr to assoc profling, 64-77, PROF LING, UNIV COLO, BOULDER, 77-, Consult, MLA, 65-66; mem Russ listening comprehension comt, Col Entrance Exam Bd, Educ Testing Serv, Princeton, NJ, 66-71; dir Lakhota proj, Nat Endowment for Humanities grant, 72-75; asst dir, Siouan Lang Archives, Nat Endowment for the Humanities, 78; dir, Gros Ventre Dict, Nat Endowment for Humanities grants, 80. **MEMBERSHIPS** Ling Soc Am; Am Anthrop Asn. **RESEARCH** American Indian languages; applied linguistics. **SELECTED PUBLICATIONS** Auth, An English-Dakota Dictionary, Great Plains Quart, Vol 14, 94; Some New Old Word Lists, Int J Am Ling, Vol 58, 92; Traditional Narratives of the Arikara Indians, Int J Am Ling, Vol 60, 94. **CONTACT ADDRESS** Dept of Ling, Univ of Colo, Boulder, CO, 80309.

TAYLOR, DANIEL JENNINGS
PERSONAL Born 09/01/1941, Covington, KY, m, 1966, 2 children **DISCIPLINE** CLASSICS, LINGUISTICS **EDUCATION** Lawrence Col, BA, 63; Univ Wash, MA, 65, PhD(classics), 70. **CAREER** From instr to asst prof classics, Univ Ill, Urbana, 68-74; asst prof, 74-78, ASSOC PROF CLASSICS, LAWRENCE UNIV, 78-, Chmn Dept, 75-, Actg vpres & dean for Campus life, Lawrence Univ, 77-78, 79-80; Nat Endowment for Humanities fel, 80-81. **MEMBERSHIPS** Am Philol Asn; Am Class League; Archaeological Inst Am. **RESEARCH** Syntax of Greek and Latin; history of linguistics; Varro. **SELECTED PUBLICATIONS** Auth, Studies on the Text of Suetonius 'De Grammaticis Et Rhetoribus', Hist Ling, Vol 21, 94; Desperately Seeking Syntax--Rewriting the History of Syntactic Theory in Greece and Rome, Lang Commun, Vol 13, 93; Theories of the Sign in Classical Antiquity, Hist Ling, Vol 21, 94. **CONTACT ADDRESS** 115 S Drew St, Appleton, WI, 54911-5798.

TAYLOR, RICHARD A.
PERSONAL Born 03/25/1944, Sikeston, MO, m, 1969, 2 children **DISCIPLINE** SEMITIC LANGUAGES **EDUCATION** Cath Univ Am, PhD, 90. **CAREER** Prof of Old Testament Studiesm, Dallas Theol Sem, 89-. **MEMBERSHIPS** Am Orient Soc; Soc Bibl Lit; Int Orgn Septuagint & Cognate Studies; Int Asn Coptic Studies; Evangelical Theol Soc; Inst Bibl Res; Nat Asn Prof Hebrew. **RESEARCH** Text criticism of Hebrew Bible; Ancient versions of the Bible; Syriac patristics; Semitic philology. **SELECTED PUBLICATIONS** Auth, The Peshitta of Daniel, Monographs of the Peshitta Institute, 94. **CONTACT ADDRESS** Dept of Old Testament Studies, Dallas Theol Sem, 3909 Swiss Ave., Dallas, TX, 75204. **EMAIL** Rick_taylor@dts.edu

TAYLOR, STEVEN MILLEN
PERSONAL Born 06/13/1941, Detroit, MI, m, 1973, 1 child **DISCIPLINE** FRENCH MEDIEVAL LITERATURE **EDUCATION** Wayne State Univ, PhD(French), 76. **CAREER** Asst prof French & Russian, Univ Tex, El Paso, 77-78; Asst Prof Medieval French, Marquette Univ, 78- **MEMBERSHIPS** MLA; Am Asn Teachers Fr; Medieval Acad Am; Soc Rencesvals; Soc Prof Francais en Am. **RESEARCH** French didactic literature of the 13th-15th centuries; French comic literature of the 13th-15th centuries; 19th century French and Russian literature. **SELECTED PUBLICATIONS** Auth, The Vices of the Villeins--The Transformation of the Deadly Sins and Cardinal Virtues in the Works of Alain Chartier, Moyen Age, Vol 0102, 96. **CONTACT ADDRESS** Dept For Lang & Lit, Marquette Univ, Milwaukee, WI, 53233.

TAYLOR, TALBOT
PERSONAL Born 07/23/1952, New York, NY, m, 1975 **DISCIPLINE** FRENCH, LINGUISTICS **EDUCATION** Tufts Univ, BA (French), 74, MA, 75; Oxford Univ, M Litt, 79, D Phil (linguistics), 82. **CAREER** Asst prof, 82-88, assoc prof, 89-95, L G T Cooley prof of English and Linguistics, Col of William and Mary, 96-. **HONORS AND AWARDS** Guggenheim fel, 94-95. **MEMBERSHIPS** North Am Asn for Hist of Lang Sciences. **RESEARCH** Linguistic theory; philos of lang; hist of linguistics. **SELECTED PUBLICATIONS** Auth, Mutual Understanding, Duke Univ Press, 92; Theorizing Language, Pergamm Press, 97; Apes, Language & Human Mind, with S Savage-Rumbayh & S Shantr, Oxford Univ Press, 98. **CONTACT ADDRESS** Col of William and Mary, 706 College Terrace, Williamsburg, VA, 23187. **EMAIL** txtayl@mail.wm.edu

TCHUDI, STEPHEN
PERSONAL m, 4 children **DISCIPLINE** ENGLISH LANGUAGE AND LITERATURE **EDUCATION** Hamilton Col, BA, 63; Northwestern Univ, MAT, 64, PhD, 67. **CAREER** Instr, Mich State Univ; prof, 90-, ch, dept Eng, Univ Nev, Reno; ed, Eng J; ed, Silver Sage. **HONORS AND AWARDS** Distinguished Fac Award, Mich State Univ, 90; Mousel-Felter Award, Univ Nev, Reno, 97. **MEMBERSHIPS** Past pres, NCTE; past pres, Nev State Coun of Tchr of Eng. **SELECTED PUBLICATIONS** Auth, Lock & Key: The Secrets of Locking Things Up, In, and Out, Scribner's, 93; The Interdisciplinary Teachers' Handbook with Stephen Lafer, Heinemann/Boynton Cook, 96; Science, Technology, and the American West, Halcyon, 97; coauth, The New Literacy, Jossey Bass, 96. **CONTACT ADDRESS** Dept of Eng, Univ Nev, Reno, Reno, NV, 89557. **EMAIL** stuchu@powernet.net

TEISER, STEPHEN F.
DISCIPLINE RELIGIOUS STUDIES; EAST ASIAN STUDIES **EDUCATION** Oberlin Col, AB, 78; Princeton Univ, MA, 83; PhD, 86. **CAREER** Vis asst prof, Middlebury Col, 86-87; asst prof, Univ S Ccalif, 87-88; prof dept of religion, Princrton Univ, 88- ; **HONORS AND AWARDS** ACLS Award Best Book Hist Relig, 88; AAS Joseph Levenson Award Best Book Chinese Studies, 94. **MEMBERSHIPS** Asn Asian Studies; Am Acad Relig; Soc Study Chinese Relig; Am Asn Study Relig. **RESEARCH** Chinese Buddhism; manuscripts from Dunhuang. **SELECTED PUBLICATIONS** Auth, The Growth in Purgatory, Religion and Society in T'ang and Sung China, Univ Hawaii Press, 93; The Scripture on the Ten Kings and the Making of Purgatory in Medieval Chinese Buddhism, Univ Hawaii, 94; Popular Religion, Chinese Religion: The State of the Field, Jour Asian Studies, 95; Introduction: The Spirits of Chinese Religion, Religions of China in Practice, Princeton Univ Press, 96; The Ghost Festival in Medieval China, Princeton Univ Press 88. **CONTACT ADDRESS** Dept of Religion, Princeton Univ, Seventy-Nine Hall, Princeton, NJ, 08544-1006. **EMAIL** sfteiser@princeton.edu

TENG, TONY
DISCIPLINE EAST ASIAN HISTORY, MODERN CHINA AND JAPAN **EDUCATION** Tunghai Univ, Taiwan, BA; Occidental Col, MA; Univ WI, Madison, PhD. **CAREER** Instr, RI Col. **RESEARCH** Mod Chinese diplomatic hist. **SELECTED PUBLICATIONS** Publ entries in National Dictionary of Revolutionary China, 1838-1926 and Nationalism in East Asia, an Encyclopdia Study. **CONTACT ADDRESS** Rhode Island Col, Providence, RI, 02908.

TERNES, HANS
PERSONAL Born 09/10/1937, Kogolniceanu, Romania, m, 1962, 2 children **DISCIPLINE** GERMAN LITERATURE, AESTHETICS **EDUCATION** Univ Il, BA, 61, MA, 63; Univ Pa, PhD, 68. **CAREER** Lectr English, Univ Freiburg, Ger, 65-66; instr Ger, Univ Pa, 66-68; asst prof, 68-75, assoc prof Ger, Lawrence Univ, 76-. **MEMBERSHIPS** Am Asn Teachers Ger; MLA. **RESEARCH** Twentieth century German literature, primarily Thomas Mann, Friedrich Durrenmatt, Franz Kafka; problems in aesthetics, the grotesque; genre studies, nature poetry. **SELECTED PUBLICATIONS** Auth, Das Problem der Gerechtigkeit in Durrenmatts Die Panne, Germanic Notes, 75; Das Groteske in den Werken Thomas Manns, Stuttgarter Arbeiten zur Germanistik, 75; Anmerkungen zur Zeitblomgestalt, Germanic Notes, 76; co-ed, Probleme der Komparatistik & Interpretation, Festschrift for Prof Andre von Gronicka, Bouvier Vlg, Bonn, 78; contribr, Franz Kafka's Hunter Gracchus: an interpretation, Festschrift for Prof Andre von Gronicka, 78; Das Bild des Helden in DDR Roman, Rocky Mtn Rev, 83; The fantastic in the works of Franz Kafha, The Scope of the Fantastic, Greenwood, Inc, 85; Wolfgang Ammon Ein Deutsch-Brasilianischer Schriftsteller, Hans Staden-Jahrbuch, Sao Paulo, 86; Franz Xaver Kroetz, Magill's Critical Survey of Drama: Foreign Languages, Salem Press Ca, 86. **CONTACT ADDRESS** Dept of German, Lawrence Univ, 115 S Drew St, Appleton, WI, 54911-5798. **EMAIL** Hans.Ternes@Lawrence.edu

TERRAS, RITA
PERSONAL Germany, m, 1951, 1 child **DISCIPLINE** GERMAN LANGUAGE & LITERATURE **EDUCATION** Univ Ill, Urbana, BA, 61, MA, 66; Univ Wis-Madison, PhD(Ger), 69. **CAREER** Lectr Ger, Univ Wis, 69-70; asst prof, Univ RI, 71-72; asst prof, 72-76, ASSOC PROF GER, CONN COL, 76-, Vis fac fel, Yale Univ, 78-79; vis assoc prof Ger, Brown Univ, 81-82. **MEMBERSHIPS** MLA; Am Asn Teachers Ger; Lessing Soc; Am Soc 18th Century Studies. **RESEARCH** German Classicism & Romanticism; the contemporary German novel; contemporary poetry. **SELECTED PUBLICATIONS** Auth, Ein 'Stein Aus Davids Hirtentasche', World Lit Today, Vol 67, 93; 'Landlaufiges Wunder', World Lit Today, Vol 70, 96; 'Epikurs Garten', World Lit Today, Vol 70, 96; 'Veritas'--Lyric Poetry and Prose 1950-1992, World Lit Today, Vol 68, 94; 'Staub Von Stadten'--Selected Poems, World Lit Today, Vol 70, 96; 'Von Der Grammatik Des Heutigen Tages', World Lit Today, Vol 67, 93; 'Erlkonigs Tochter', World Lit Today, Vol 67, 93; 'Wiese Und Macht', World Lit Today, Vol 68, 94. **CONTACT ADDRESS** Dept of Ger, Connecticut Col, 270 Mohegan Ave, Box 1586, New London, CT, 06320.

TERRAS, VICTOR
PERSONAL Born 01/21/1921, Estonia, m, 1951, 1 child **DISCIPLINE** SLAVIC LANGUAGES & LITERATURE **EDUCATION** Univ Estonia, Cand Phil, 41, Mag Phil, 42; Univ Chicago, PhD(Russ lit), 63. **CAREER** From instr to assoc prof Russ, Univ IL, 59-65, prof Slavic lang & lit, 65-66; prof Slavic lang, Univ WI-Madison, 66-70; chmn dept, 72-76, Prof Slavic Lang, Brown Univ, 70-89, Prof emer, Brown Univ, 1989-. **RESEARCH** Comp Slavic linguistics; Russ lit. **SELECTED PUBLICATIONS** Auth, The Young Dostoevsky, 1846-1849: A Critical Study, Mouton, The Hague & Paris, 69; Belinskij and Russian Literary Criticism, Univ WI-Madison, 73; A Karamazov Companion: Commentary on the Genesis, Language, and Style of Dostoevsky's Novel, Univ Wis-Madison, 81; Aleksis Rannit: Luhimonograafia, Lund, 75, Vladimir Maiakovsky, Twayne Publishers, 83; A Handbook of Russian Literature, Yale Univ Press, 85; The Idiot: An Interpretation, Twayne Publishers, 90; A History of Russian Literature, Yale Univ Press, 91; Poetry of the Silver Age: The Various Voice of Russian Modernism, Dresden Univ Press, 98. **CONTACT ADDRESS** Dept of Slavic Lang, Brown Univ, Providence, RI, 02912.

TERRILL, ROSS
PERSONAL Melbourne, Australia **DISCIPLINE** ASIAN STUDIES **EDUCATION** Weley Col Melbourne, 56; BA, First Class Hon, Univ of Melbourne, 62; PhD, Polit Sci, Harvard Univ, 70; **CAREER** Austalian Army, 57-58; Tutor in Polit Sci, Univ of Melbourne, 62-63; Staff Sec Australian Student Christian Movement, 62, 64-65; Res Fel Asia Sic, 68-70, Lectr on Govt, 70-74, Dir Student Prog in Intl Affairs, 74-77, Assoc Prof Govt, Harvard Univ, 74-78; Vis Prof, Monash Univ, 96-98; Res Assoc, Fairbank Center for East Asian Res, Harvard Univ 70-. **HONORS AND AWARDS** Natl Mag Award for Reporting Excellence, 72; George Polk Memoria Award for Outstanding Mag Reporting, 72; Summer Prize for PhD Thesis, Harvard Univ, 70; Exhibition in Polit Sci, Univ of Melbourne, 57; Frank Knox Memorial Fellowship, Harvard Univ, 65-66. **SELECTED PUBLICATIONS** China in Our Time, Simon & Schuster, 92; The Australians, Simon & Schuster, 87; The White-Boned Demon: A Biography of Madame Mao Zedong, William Morrow, 84; Mao in History, The Natl Interest, 98; China Under Deng, Foreign Affairs, Vol 73 No 5, 94; United States-China Relations, Australian Journal of Chinese Affairs, No 3, 80; China Quarterly, No 139, 94; Journal of Asian Studies, Vol 48, No 4, 89; Bulletin of Australian Political Studies Associations, Vol 8 No 2, Political Sci Quarterly, No 40, 69. **CONTACT ADDRESS** Fairbank Center for East Asian Res, Harvard Univ, Cambridge, MA, 02138. **EMAIL** terr@compuserve.com

TERRY, ROBERT MEREDITH
PERSONAL Born 12/16/1939, Danville, VA, m, 1965, 3 children **DISCIPLINE** ROMANCE LANGUAGES **EDUCATION** Randolph-Macon Col, BA, 62; Duke Univ, PhD(Romance lang), 66. **CAREER** Instr French, Duke Univ, 63-64, 65-66; asst prof, Univ Fla, 66-68; ASSOC PROF FRENCH, UNIV RICHMOND, 68-, Ed, Les Nouvelles. **MEMBERSHIPS** Am Asn Teachers Fr; Am Coun Teaching For Lang. **RESEARCH** Contemporary French language; foreign language methodology. **SELECTED PUBLICATIONS** Auth, Untitled, For Lang, Vol 27, 94; Evaluation, Modern Lang J, Vol 77, 93; The Dynamics of Language Program Direction, Modern Lang J, Vol 78, 94. **CONTACT ADDRESS** Dept of Mod Foreign Lang, Univ Richmond, 28 Westhampton Way, Richmond, VA, 23173-0002.

TESCHNER, RICHARD VINCENT
PERSONAL Born 07/19/1942, Madison, WI **DISCIPLINE** SPANISH, LINGUISTICS **EDUCATION** Stanford Univ, AB, 65; Middlebury Col, MA, 66; Univ Wis-Madison, PhD(Span), 72. **CAREER** From instr to asst prof Span, Univ Wis-Parkside, 70-74; asst prof, Univ Iowa, 74-76; asst prof, 76-88; prof Span Ling, Univ Tex, El Paso, 88-; Dir, Nat Endowment for the Humanities sponsored Surv of Res Tool Needs in the Hisp Lang and Lit, 77-78. **MEMBERSHIPS** Ling Soc Am; MLA; Am Asn Teachers Span & Port; Ling Asn Southwest. **RESEARCH** Spanish morphosyntaxis, Spanish phonetics/phenology. **SELECTED PUBLICATIONS** coauth, Spanish and English of United States Hispanos: A Critical, Annotated, Linguistic Bibliography, Ctr Appl Ling, 75; Espanol escrito: curso para hispano-hablantes bilingues, Charles Scribner's Sons, 78, 4th ed, Prentice Hall, 98; Festschrift for Jacob Ornstein, Newbury House, 80; Historical-psychological portraits as complements to sociolinguistic studies in relational bilingualism, Bilingual Review, 81. **CONTACT ADDRESS** Dept of Lit & Lang, Univ of Texas, 500 W University Ave, El Paso, TX, 79968-0531. **EMAIL** teschner@mail.utep.edu

TETEL, MARCEL
PERSONAL Born 10/11/1932, Paris, France, m, 1957, 1 child **DISCIPLINE** ROMANCE LANGUAGES **EDUCATION** Univ Chattanooga, BA, 54; Emory Univ, MA, 56; Univ Wis, PhD, 62. **CAREER** From asst prof to assoc prof, 60-68, PROF ROMANCE LANG, DUKE UNIV, 68-, Am Coun Learned Soc grant-in-aid, 63; Fulbright res grant, Florence, 66-67; Guggenheim fel, 70; Am Philos Soc grant, 73. **MEMBERSHIPS** Int Asn Fr Studies; Am Asn Teachers Fr; Am Asn Teachers Ital; MLA; SAtlantic Mod Lang Asn. **RESEARCH** French and Italian Renaissance. **SELECTED PUBLICATIONS** Co-auth, Comedy in the Epoque of Henri-II and Charles-IX, French Rev, Vol 70, 96. **CONTACT ADDRESS** Dept of Romance Lang, Duke Univ, Durham, NC, 27706.

TETZLAFF, OTTO W.
PERSONAL Born 08/26/1930, Noerenberg, Germany, m, 1958, 3 children **DISCIPLINE** FOREIGN LANGUAGE **EDUCATION** N Ill Univ, BA, 62; Univ Ill, MA, 63; Univ Tex, PhD, 68. **CAREER** Instr, N Ill Univ, 63-65; asst prof, Va Polytechnical Univ, 68-69; from assoc prof to prof, 69-, Angelo State Univ. **HONORS AND AWARDS** NDEA Fel Title VI, 66-68; Nat Endowment Humanities, 72; Fulbright Post-doctoral Fel, 89; Minnie Stevens Piper Professorship, 91. **MEMBERSHIPS** AATG; MLA; TFLA; Schoperhauer Gesellshaft. **RESEARCH** Medieval Latin drama; 19th century literature. **SELECTED PUBLICATIONS** Auth, art, Johannes Urzidil, 80; auth, art, A Glimpse at the Stonemasons, 87; auth, art, The Best Kept Secret in the West, 92; auth, art, Public Education, The Brethren of the Common Life, and Their Theatrical Endeavor, 92; auth, The Handbook of Texas, 96. **CONTACT ADDRESS** Dept of Modern Languages, Angelo State Univ, San Angelo, TX, 76909. **EMAIL** otto.tetzlaff@angelo.edu

THAMELING, CARL L.
DISCIPLINE SPEECH COMMUNICATION **EDUCATION** Univ Louisville, BA, 79; Ind Univ, Bloomington, MA, 84, PhD, 90. **CAREER** Asst prof, Univ Col Cape Breton, 88-91; asst prof, Miami Univ, Ohio, 91-98; ASST PROF, NORTHEAST LA UNIV, 88-. **CONTACT ADDRESS** 322 Woodale Dr, #59, Monroe, LA, 71203. **EMAIL** CNThameling@alpha.nlu.edu

THIHER, OTTAH ALLEN
PERSONAL Born 04/04/1941, Fort Worth, TX, m, 1997 **DISCIPLINE** ROMANCE LANGUAGES, FRENCH **EDUCATION** Univ of Tx, BA, 63; Univ of Wis, PhD, 68. **CAREER** Asst prof, Duke Univ, 67-69; asst prof, Middlebury Col, 69-75; ASSOC PROF, 82-, Middlebush Prof of Romance Languages, 85-89, Curators' Prof, 90-, Univ Missouri. **HONORS AND AWARDS** Phi Beta Kappa, Univ of Tx; Univ Fels, 63-66, Univ of Wis; Fulbright Scholar, France, 66-67; fac res grant, Middlebury Col, 71; Shell Found grant for fac development, 73; Guggenheim Fel, Berlin, 76-77; travel grant, 79, 81, & 85; Chancellor's Award for Outstanding Res in the Humanities and the Arts, 81; summer res fel, 78 & 85; res leave, Univ of Mo, 83-84, 87-88, & 95-96; fel, Camargo Found, 88. **MEMBERSHIPS** Am Asn of Teachers of French; Les Amis de Valentin Bru (Soc for Raymond Queneau studies); Soc for Lit and Sci; MLA. **RESEARCH** Development of modern French fiction. **SELECTED PUBLICATIONS** Auth, Celine: The Novel as Delirium, Rutgers Univ Press, 72; auth, The Cinematic Muse: Critical Studies in the History of French Cinema, Univ of Mo Press, 79; auth, Words in Reflections: Modern Language Theory and Postmodern Fiction, Univ of Chicago Press, 84 & 87; auth, Raymond Queneau, G.K. Hall, 85; auth, The Short Stories of Franz Kafka, G.K. Hall, 89; auth, The Power of Tautology: The Roots of Literary Theory, Assoc Univ Presses, 97; auth, Revels in Madness: Insanity in Medicine and Literature, Univ of Mich Press, in press; auth, Lacan, Madness and Women's Fiction in France, Postmodern Studies, 94; auth, Jerome Klinkowitz: Structuring the Void, Postmodern Studies: Narrative Turns and Minor Genres in Postmodernism, 94; auth, The Tautological Thinking of Historicism, Tx Studies in Lit and Language, 97; auth, The Legacy of Kafka's Short Fiction: Knowledge of the Impossibility of Knowledge, The Legacy of Kafka in Austrian Lit, Adriadne Press, 97; auth, A Skeptical Critique of the Lacanian Approach to Literary Theory, to appear in Romance Quarterly. **CONTACT ADDRESS** Dept of Romance Languages, Univ of Missouri, 143 Arts & Science Bldg., Columbia, MO, 65211.

THOMAS, GARY CRAIG
PERSONAL Born 11/20/1944, Long Beach, CA **DISCIPLINE** GERMAN LITERATURE, MUSICOLOGY **EDUCATION** Univ Calif, Los Angeles, AB, 66; Harvard Univ, MA, 70, PhD, 73. **CAREER** Asst prof, Humanities & Ger, 71-91, ASSOC PROF CULTURAL STUDIES & GER, UNIV MINN, MINNEAPOLIS, 91-. **MEMBERSHIPS** MLA; Am Soc Study 16th & 17th Century Ger Lit; Renaissance Soc Am; Am Guild Organists. **RESEARCH** Gay studies; musical-literary relations; cultural studies. **SELECTED PUBLICATIONS** Auth, Philipp von Zesen's German Madrigals, Argenis, 78; Zesen, Rinckart and the Musical Origins of the Dactyl, Argenis, 78; Dance Music and the Origins of the Dactylic Meter, in Daphnis, Zeitschrift fur Mittlere Deutsche Literatur, 87; Die Aelbianische Musen-Lust, Peter Lang, 91; Musical Rhetoric and Politics in the Early German Lied, in Music and German Literature: Their Relationship since the Middle Ages, Camden House, 92; Philipp von Zesen's German Madrigals, in Daphnis: Zeitschrift fur Mittlere Deutsche Literatur, 92; co-ed, Queering the Pitch: The New Gay and Lesbian Musicology, Routledge, 93; Was George Frideric Handel Gay? - On Closet Questions and Cultural Politics, in Queering the Pitch: The New Gay and Lesbian Musicology, Routledge, 94. **CONTACT ADDRESS** Dept of Cultural Studies & Comp Lit, Univ of Minn, 9 Pleasant St SE, Minneapolis, MN, 55455-0194. **EMAIL** thoma002@tc.umn.edu

THOMAS, GERALD
PERSONAL Born 12/29/1940, Porthcawl, Wales, m, 1981, 5 children **DISCIPLINE** FOLKLORE, FRENCH **EDUCATION** Univ Wales, BA, 63; Mem Univ Nfld, MA, 70, PhD(folklore), 77. **CAREER** Lectr Fr, 64-67, asst prof, 67-74, assoc prof, 74-77, ASSOC PROF FR & FOLKLORE, MEM UNIV NFLD, 78-, Dir, Centre D'etudes Franco-Terreneuviennes, 75-, Mem, Fel Comt, Social Sci & Humanities Res Coun Can, 79-81. **MEMBERSHIPS** Folklore Studies Asn Can (pres, 78-79); Am Folklore Soc; Can Folk Music Soc. **RESEARCH** Folk narrative; folklore of French cultures, especially Newfoundland French; traditional aesthetics. **SELECTED PUBLICATIONS** Auth, Saying Isnt Believing--Conversation, Narrative and the Discourse of Belief in a French Newfoundland Community, Rev Hist Am Francaise, Vol 46, 92. **CONTACT ADDRESS** Dept of French, Memorial Univ of Newfoundland, St John's, NF, A1B 3X9.

THOMAS, JOHN WESLEY
PERSONAL Born 05/24/1916, Thomas, OK, m, 1948, 3 children **DISCIPLINE** GERMAN **EDUCATION** Houghton Col, AB, 37; Pa State Col, AM, 39, PhD, 42. **CAREER** Instr, Cent Jr Col, 37-38, Roberts Col, 41-42, Washington & Jefferson Coll, 42-44 & Univ Mich, 46-47; from assoc prof to prof Ger, Univ Ark, 47-69; PROF GER, UNIV KY, 69-, Fulbright res scholar, Luxembourg, 49-50; guest prof, Univ Hamburg, 55-56 & Univ Tubingen, 59-60. **MEMBERSHIPS** MLA; SAtlantic Mod Lang Asn. **RESEARCH** German. **SELECTED PUBLICATIONS** Auth, Domestic Tragedy in Works of the German High-Middle-Ages, Germanic Notes Rev, vol 0028, 97; The Other Kingdom in the Arthurian Romances of Medieval Germany and the Motif of Departure and Return, Germanic Notes Rev, Vol 25, 94; The Other Kingdom in the Arthurian Romances of Medieval Germany and the Motif of Departure and Return, Germanic Notes Rev, Vol 25, 94; Hartmann-Von-Aue Humor, Neuphilologische Mitteilungen, Vol 94, 93; Invisibility in the Narratives of the German High-Middle-Ages, Germanic Notes Rev, Vol 27, 96. **CONTACT ADDRESS** Dept of Ger, Univ of Ky, Lexington, KY, 40506.

THOMAS, MARGARET
PERSONAL Born 04/05/1952, Woodbury, NJ, m, 3 children **DISCIPLINE** LINGUISTICS **EDUCATION** Yale Univ, BA, 74; Boston Univ, MEd, 83; Harvard Univ, AM, 85, PhD, 91. **CAREER** Asst Prof, 91-96, Assoc Prof, Boston Col, 96-. **HONORS AND AWARDS** Sumitomo Travel-Study Fel, 74-75; Dokkyo Univ Int Cooperation Res Fel, 89; Spencer Post-doctoral Fel, 95-96. **MEMBERSHIPS** LSA; AAAL; MLA; NAHoLS **RESEARCH** Language acquisition & linguistic theory; history of linguistics. **SELECTED PUBLICATIONS** Auth, The interpretation of English reflexive pronouns by non-native speakers, Studies in 2nd Lang Acquisition 11, 89; Universal grammar and the interpretation of reflexives in a second language, Lang 67, 91; Knowledge of Reflexives in a Second Language, John Benjamins Press, 93; Linguistic variation in Spike Lee's School Daze, Col English, 94; Acquisition of the Japanese reflexive zibun and movement of anaphors in Logical Form, 2nd Lang Res, 95; Medieval and modern views of Universal Grammar and the nature of second language learning, Mod Lang J, 95. **CONTACT ADDRESS** Slavic & Eastern Lang Dept, Boston Col, Chestnut Hill, MA, 02167. **EMAIL** thomasm@bc.edu

THOMAS, ROGER K.
PERSONAL Born 12/18/1953, Spanish Ford, UT, m, 1984, 1 child **DISCIPLINE** JAPANESE LITERATURE **EDUCATION** Ind Univ, PhD, 91 **CAREER** ASSOC PROF, ILL STATE UNIV, 90-. **MEMBERSHIPS** Asn Asian Studies, Asn Teachers of Japanese, Asn Japanese Lit Studies. **RESEARCH** Waka poetry and poetics of Tokugawa period, Tokugawa aesthetics. **SELECTED PUBLICATIONS** Auth, "Macroscopic vs. Microscopic: Spatial Sensibilities in Waka of the Bakumatsu Period," Harvard Jour of Asiatic Studies, Winter 98; auth, "Okuma Kotomichi and the Re-Visioning of Kokinshu Elegance," PMAJLS, Summer 97; auth, "Akera Kanko no 'tenko' to kaikaku-go no kyoka," in Uta no hibiki, monogatari no yokubo, 96, Shinwasha; auth, "Kawatake Mokuami as Lyricist," PMAJLS, Summer 95; auth, "High vs. Low: The Fude no Saga Controversy and Bakumatsu Poetics," Monumenta Nipponica, Winter 94. **CONTACT ADDRESS** Dept For Lang, Illinois State Univ, Box 4300, Normal, IL, 61790. **EMAIL** rkthoma@ilstu.edu

THOMAS, RUTH PAULA
PERSONAL Born 11/09/1935, New York, NY, m, 1974, 2 children **DISCIPLINE** FRENCH **EDUCATION** Bryn Mawr Col, BA, 57; Yale Univ, MA, 58, PhD(French), 64. **CAREER** Instr French, Simmons Col, 61-63; asst prof, 64-73, ASSOC PROF FRENCH, TEMPLE UNIV, 73- **MEMBERSHIPS** Am Asn Teachers Fr; MLA; Am Soc Eighteenth Century Studies. **RESEARCH** Eighteenth and 17th century French novel. **SELECTED PUBLICATIONS** Auth, Essays on the 'Neveu De Rameau' of Diderot, French Rev, Vol 66, 93; Eroticism and the Body-Politic, French Rev, Vol 67, 94. **CONTACT ADDRESS** 1530 Locust St Apt 5F, Philadelphia, PA, 19012.

THOMPSON, EWA MAJEWSKA
PERSONAL Kaunas, Lithuania, m **DISCIPLINE** COMPARATIVE LITERATURE **EDUCATION** Vanderbilt Univ, PhD, Comp Lit, 67. **CAREER** Tchr, Vanderbilt Univ; Ind State Univ; Ind Univ; Univ Va, PROF, RICE UNIV, 79-. **MEMBERSHIPS** Am Asn Advancement Slavic Stud; Am Asn Tchrs of Slavic and East Europ Lang **RESEARCH** Colonialism in Russian literature; Russian & Polish culture & politics **SELECTED PUBLICATIONS** "Why the Conservative Tradition Is an Important Philosophical Option in Polish Intellectual Life," Periphery, 97; "Thomas Venclovas Aleksander Wat," The Chesterton Rev, 97; "Aleksandr Solzhenitsyn's Cancer Ward and the Russian Colonialist Experience," Slavia Orientalis, 97; "Nationalism, Imperialism, Identity: Second Thoughts, Modern Age,98; Understanding Russia: The Holy Fool in Russian Culture, Oxford Univ Press, 95. **CONTACT ADDRESS** Dept German & Slavic Stud, Rice Univ, 6100 S Main St, Houston, TX, 77005-1892.

THOMPSON, LAURENCE G.
PERSONAL Born 07/09/1920, Ichowfu, China, m, 1943, 5 children **DISCIPLINE** ASIAN STUDIES, SINOLOGY **EDUCATION** Univ Calif, Los Angeles, BA, 42; US Navy Japanese Lang Sch, dipl, 43; Claremont Grad Sch, MA, 47, PhD(Orient studies), 54. **CAREER** Teacher pub & pvt schs, Calif & Colo, 46-51; cult attache, Am Embassy, Taipei, 51-53; staff off, US Foreign Serv Tokyo, Singapore, Manila & Hong Kong, 54-56; rep Asian Found, Korea, 56-58 & Taiwan, 58-59; prof music, Taiwan Norm Univ, 59-62; asst prof Chinese lang & lit, Pomona Col, 62-65; from asst prof to assoc prof, 65-70, dir East Asian Studies Ctr, 72-74, chmn dept East Asian lang & cult, 68-70 & 72-76, PROF EAST ASIAN LANG & CULT, UNIV SOUTHERN CALIF, 70- **MEMBERSHIPS** Am Orient Soc; Royal Asiatic Soc; Asn Asian Studies; Am Acad Relig; Soc Study Chinese Relig. **RESEARCH** Chinese thought and religion; history of Taiwan. **SELECTED PUBLICATIONS** Auth, A Gods Own Tale--The 'Book Of Transformations' of Wenchang, the Divine Lord of Zitong, J Am Oriental Hist, Vol 0115, 95. **CONTACT ADDRESS** Dept of E Asian Lang & Cult, Univ of Southern Calif, Los Angeles, CA, 90007.

THOMPSON, ROGER MARK
PERSONAL Born 07/15/1942, Oakland, CA, m, 1967, 10 children **DISCIPLINE** LINGUISTIC, SOCIOLINGUISTICS, TESL **EDUCATION** Brigham Young Univ, BA, 66, MA, 68; Univ Tex, Austin, PhD(Ling), 71. **CAREER** Prog specialist teaching English as Foreign Lang, Int Off, Univ Tex, Austin, 68-71; asst prof, 71-76, assoc prof English & Ling, Univ Fla, 76-, ed, Southern Folklore Quart, 72-75; vis prof Universidad de las Americas, Cholula, Puebla, Mexico, 82-83. **HONORS AND AWARDS** Fulbright Travel Grant/Hungary, 90; Fulbright Scholar, Philippine Depart of Ed, Culture and Sports, 96-97. **MEMBERSHIPS** Ling Soc Am; Am Dialect Soc; Teachers of English to Speakers of Other Lang; Am Asn Applied Ling. **RESEARCH** Bilingualism; second language acquisition; English as a second language. **SELECTED PUBLICATIONS** Coauth, Cakchiquel Basic Course, Brigham Young Univ, Vol I, 69; auth, Mexican American language loyalty and the validity of the 1970 census, Int J Sociol Lang, 74; The decline of Cedar Key: Mormon stories in North Florida and their social function, Southern Folklore Quart, 75; Mexican-American English: Social correlates of regional pronunciation, Am Speech, 75; Language planning in frontier America, Lang Problems & Lang Planning, 82; Linguistics Studies in Honor of Bohdan Saciuk, West Lafayett IN: Learning Systems, 97; Why can't they take a hint? The negative in spoken English, ACELT Journal, 97. **CONTACT ADDRESS** Dept of English, Univ of Florida, PO Box 117310, Gainesville, FL, 32611-7310. **EMAIL** rthompson@english.ufl.edu

THOMSON, CLIVE
DISCIPLINE FRENCH LITERATURE **EDUCATION** Univ Toronto, BA; MA; PhD. **RESEARCH** Late 19th century French literature; women writers; interdisciplinary discourses on homosexuality in France between 1880-1900; literary and cultural theories of Mikhail Bakhtin; critical reception of work by the Bakhtin Circle. **SELECTED PUBLICATIONS** Co-ed, Le singe a la porte, Peter Lang, 84; Dire la parodie: colloque de Cerisy, Peter Lang, 89; Dialogism and Cultural Criticism, Mestengo, 95; Scientific Discourse as Prejudice Carrier, Mestengo, 98. **CONTACT ADDRESS** Dept of French, Western Ontario Univ, London, ON, N6A 5B8.

THOMSON, ROBERT WILLIAM
PERSONAL Born 03/24/1934, Chearn, England, m, 1963 **DISCIPLINE** NEAR EASTERN LANGUAGES **EDUCATION** Cambridge Univ, BA, 55, dipl Orient lang, 57, MA, 59, PhD(theol), 62; Univ Louvain, lic Orient Lang, 62. **CAREER** Instr class Armenian, 63-65, asst prof, 65-69, chmn, Dept Near Eastern Lang, 73-78, Prof Armenian Studies, Harvard Univ, 69- **HONORS AND AWARDS** MA, Harvard Univ, 69. **RESEARCH** Armenian; patristic studies. **SELECTED PUBLICATIONS** Koriwn Biography of Mesrop-Mastoc in Translation and Commentary, Cath Hist Rev, Vol 0082, 96; Critical Editions of the Works of Gregory-Nazianzenus in The Armenian Version, Vol 1 in Orations-Ii,Ix,Xii, J Theol Studies, Vol 0046, 95; Armenia and the Bible in Papers Presented to the International Symposium Held at Heidelberg, July-16-19,1990, J Theol Studies, Vol 0045, 94; Commentary on the Divine Liturgy in Anjewaci, J Theol Studies, Vol 0044, 93; The Armenian Version of Daniel, J Theol Studies, Vol 0044, 93. **CONTACT ADDRESS** Dept of Near Eastern Lang, Harvard Univ, 6 Divinity Ave, Cambridge, MA, 02138.

THORBURN, CAROLYN COLES
PERSONAL Born 12/20/1941, Newark, New Jersey **DISCIPLINE** SPANISH **EDUCATION** Douglass Coll, BA Spanish 1962; Rutgers Univ, MA Spanish 1964, PhD Spanish 1972; PhD, nutrition, 1987. **CAREER** Barringer HS, Spanish teacher 1964-66; Rutgers Univ, teaching asst Spanish 1966-67; Upsala Coll, prof of Spanish/coord of black studies 1967-95; Union County College, adjunct prof of Spanish, 1992-; Seton Hall Univ and E. Orange School District, educational consultant, 1995-. **HONORS AND AWARDS** Romance Language Honor Soc Phi Sigma Iota 1972. **MEMBERSHIPS** Mem Modern Language Assoc, Natl Council of Black Studies, Amer Assoc of Univ Profs, Amer Assoc of the Teachers of Spanish & Portuguese. **SELECTED PUBLICATIONS** Author, Mastery of Conversational Spanish, 1992; author, Complete Mastery of Spanish, 1993; author, Complete Mastery of Spanish Workbook, 1994; speaks Spanish. **CONTACT ADDRESS** Prof of Spanish, Educational Research Center Language School, 75 Central Avenue, East Orange, NJ, 07018.

THORN, ARLINE ROUSH
PERSONAL Born 11/22/1946, New Haven, WV, d, 1 child **DISCIPLINE** COMPARATIVE & ENGLISH LITERATURE **EDUCATION** Marshall Univ, AB, 67; Univ IL, Urbana, MA, 68, PhD, 71. **CAREER** From Instr to Assoc Prof, 71-79, prof eng, WVA State Col, 79-, Ch, Dept Eng, 86-94; Adj prof Eng, Marshall Univ Grad Col, 75-; mem, State Col System Bd Dir, 94-97. **HONORS AND AWARDS** Woodrow Wilson Inst on Interpreting Hum, 86; Citation as Outstanding Fac Mem, WVA Legislature, 89; Fulbright Seminar in Brazil, 93; First Prize, WVA Writers statewide competition, poetry, 96, 98. **MEMBERSHIPS** Am Comp Lit Asn; MLA; Asn for Integrative Studies. **RESEARCH** Women's studies; hist and theory of the novel; Holocaust Studies. **SELECTED PUBLICATIONS** Coauth, The veluminous word: McLuhan-D H Lawrence, Midwest Monogr, 71; The pivotal character in Dickens' novels, Papers WV a Asn Col Eng Tchr(s), spring 72; Shelley's Cenci as Tragedy, Costerus: Essays Eng Lit & Lang, 12/73; Harriette Arnow's mountain women, Bull WVA Asn Col Eng Tchr(s), 77; Feminine time in Dorothy Richardson's Pilgrimage, Int J Women's Studies, 78; How I became a historian, Kanawha Rev, 80; A mighty maze: Ulysses, Perspectives Contemp Lit, 80; co-ed, Origins: Texts for an Inquiry, Tapestry Press, 91; author of poems in Pikeville Rev, Southern Humanities Rev, and various anthologies. **CONTACT ADDRESS** Dept of Eng, West Virginia State Col, PO Box 1000, Institute, WV, 25112-1000. **EMAIL** athorn@wvsvax.wvnet.edu

THORSEN, KRISTINE
DISCIPLINE GERMAN **EDUCATION** Cornell Univ, AB; Univ Chicago, AM; Northwestern Univ, MA, PhD. **CAREER** Dir,first yr German. **RESEARCH** German literature; contemprary poetry and novels by women, pedagogy and methodology. **SELECTED PUBLICATIONS** Auth, Poetry by American Women: A Bibliography; Gertrud v. le Fort's Recollections of an Era in Imperial Germany. **CONTACT ADDRESS** Dept of German, Northwestern Univ, 1801 Hinman, Evanston, IL, 60208. **EMAIL** kat162@nwu.edu

THORSON, HELGA
DISCIPLINE GERMAN AND AUSTRIAN WOMEN WRITERS **EDUCATION** Earlham Col, BA, 87; Univ Minn, MA, 90, PhD, 96. **CAREER** English and Lit, Univ Ark **SELECTED PUBLICATIONS** Coauth, Schriftbilder, Independence Press, 89; Writing Theory and Practice in the Second Language Classroom: A Selected Annotated Bibliography, Univ Minn, 95; Using Intensive Writing-to-Learn Activities in the Foreign Language Classroom, Univ Minn, 96. **CONTACT ADDRESS** Univ Ark Little Rock, 2801 S University Ave., Little Rock, AR, 72204-1099. **EMAIL** hmthorson@ualr.edu

THREATTE, LESLIE LEE
PERSONAL Born 02/01/1943, Miami, FL **DISCIPLINE** CLASSICAL PHILOLOGY **EDUCATION** Oberlin Col, BA Harvard Univ, PhD(Class Philol), 69. **CAREER** Asst prof Class, Cornell Univ, 68-70; asst prof 70-75; assoc prof Class, 75-80; Univ Calif, Berkeley. **MEMBERSHIPS** Am Philol Assn. **SELECTED PUBLICATIONS** Auth, The Grammar of Attic Inscriptions I, de Gruyter, Berlin, 79, II, 96. **CONTACT ADDRESS** Dept of Classcs, Univ of California, Berkeley, 7211 Dwinelle Hall, Berkeley, CA, 94720-2520.

THUENTE, MARY HELEN
PERSONAL Born 03/21/1946, Chicago, IL, m, 1967, 2 children **DISCIPLINE** ENGLISH, IRISH LIT **EDUCATION** Clarke Col, BA, 67; Univ Kans, MA, 69, PhD, 73. **CAREER** Asst prof, 75-80, assoc prof to prof Eng, 80-, Ind Univ/Purdue Univ. **MEMBERSHIPS** MLA; Am Comt Irish Studies; Can Assn Irish Studies; Int Assn Study Irish Lit. **RESEARCH** Irish

literature, hist. **SELECTED PUBLICATIONS** Auth, The Harp Re-Strung, 94. **CONTACT ADDRESS** Dept of English, Indiana Univ-Purdue Univ, Fort Wayne, 2101 Coliseum Blvd E, Ft. Wayne, IN, 46805-1445. **EMAIL** thuentem@ipfw.edu

THUNDY, ZACHARIAS PONTIAN
PERSONAL Born 09/28/1936, Changanacherry, India **DISCIPLINE** ENGLISH, LINGUISTICS **EDUCATION** Pontif Athenaeum, India, BPh, 58, LPh, 59, BTh, 61, STL, 63; DePaul Univ, MA, 66; Univ Notre Dame, PhD(English), 69. **CAREER** Instr philos, Dharmaram Col, Bangalore, India, 63-64; from asst prof to assoc prof, 68-77, prof English, Northern Mich Univ, 77-, Am Inst Indian Studies sr fel, 74-75. **HONORS AND AWARDS** Citation & Medal, Mich Acad Sci, Arts & Lett, 77. **MEMBERSHIPS** MLA; Int Arthurian Soc; Midwest Mod Lang Asn; Ling Soc Am; AAUP. **RESEARCH** Anthropological linguistics; American dialect survey; feminism in the Middle Ages. **SELECTED PUBLICATIONS** Auth, Circumstance, circumference, and center, Hartford Studies Lit, 71; Oaths in Germanic folklore, Folklore, 71; Covenant in Anglo-Saxon Thought, Macmillan, 72; co-ed, Language and Culture, Northern Mich Univ, 73; auth, Beowulf and Jus diaboli, Christian Scholar's Rev, 73; co-ed, Chaucerian Problems and Perspectives, Univ Notre Dame, 78. **CONTACT ADDRESS** Dept of English, No Michigan Univ, 1401 Presque Isle Ave, Marquette, MI, 49855-5301. **EMAIL** zthundy@nmu.edu

TIKKU, GIRDHARI
DISCIPLINE COMPARATIVE LITERATURE **EDUCATION** Tehran Univ, PhD, 61. **CAREER** Prof, Univ IL Urbana Champaign. **HONORS AND AWARDS** Jammu and Kashmir Cult Acad Awd. **RESEARCH** Indo Iranian cult; Persian lit; East West encounters; Inter Asian rel(s); comp mystical poetry; Asian responses to the West; transl theory. **SELECTED PUBLICATIONS** Auth, Persian Poetry in Kashmir; Islam and its Cultural Divergence; Mysticism in Kashmir; pubs on Persian poetry, Indian and Iranian Islam, Tagore, fiction, and poetry from Persian. **CONTACT ADDRESS** Comp Lit Dept, Univ Illinois Urbana Champaign, E Gregory Drive, PO Box 52, Champaign, IL, 61820.

TIMPE, EUGENE FRANK
PERSONAL Born 09/24/1926, Tacoma, WA, m, 1950, 3 children **DISCIPLINE** COMPARATIVE LITERATURE **EDUCATION** Occidental Col, BA, 48; Univ Southern Calif, MA, 52, PhD(comp lit), 60. **CAREER** Instr English, El Camino Col, 53-66; assoc prof Ger & comp lit, PA State Univ, University Park, 66-72; chmn dept foreign lang & lit, 72-81, prof Ger & Comp Lit, Southern Ill Univ, Carbondale, 72-; lectr, Univ Md, Munich, 63-64; vis prof, Univ Neuchatel, Switz, 70-71. **HONORS AND AWARDS** Fulbright grants, Vienna, 58-59, Rome 60-61, Ger, 85; Am Philos Soc grant, 70; NEH grant, 83; US Dept Educ Title VI A grant, 87-90, 92-94; US Dept Educ Title VI B grant, 89-91. **MEMBERSHIPS** MLA; Am Comp Lit Asn; Int Ver Ger Sprach-u Literaturwiss; Am Lessing Soc; Asn Dept Foreign Lang (pres, 77). **RESEARCH** 18th century; literary theory. **SELECTED PUBLICATIONS** Auth, American Literature in Germany, 1861-1872, Chapel Hill, 64; Hesse's Siddhartha and the Bhagavad Gita, Comp lit, 70; The Spatial Dimension: A Stylistic Typology, In: Yearbook of Comparative Criticism, Vol III, 71; ed & contribr, Thoreau Abroad, Archon Bks, 71; auth, Infernal space: Structure and Context, Ital Quart, 72; Wieland's Singspiele and the Rebirth of German Opera, Seminar, 77; Memory and Literary Structures, J Mind & Behav, 81; Metastasio and Austrian Rococo Literature, Ital Quart, 118, 92. **CONTACT ADDRESS** Dept of Foreign Lang & Lit, Southern Ill Univ, Carbondale, IL, 62901-4300. **EMAIL** etimpe@siu.edu

TITTLER, JONATHAN PAUL
PERSONAL Born 04/19/1945, Brooklyn, NY, m, 1978 **DISCIPLINE** LATIN AMERICAN NOVEL, CONTEMPORARY LITERARY CRITICISM **EDUCATION** Hamilton Col, AB, 67; Cornell Univ, PhD(Span lit), 74. **CAREER** Asst prof Span, Hamilton Col, 74-75; Bates Col, 75-76; vis asst prof, Hamilton Col, 76-77; vis asst prof, 77-78, asst prof, 78-82, Assoc Prof Span, Cornell Univ, 82-90; prof Romance Stud, 90-97, Prince of Asturias Chair, Univ Auckland, NZ; Juror Premico Novela Jorge Isaacs, Calif, Colombia, 82. **HONORS AND AWARDS** Fulbright St Scholar, 91; Pedro Morales Pino Medal for Honor in Arts and Culture, 98. **MEMBERSHIPS** MLA: Am Asn Teachers Span & Port; Northeast Mod Lang Asn. **RESEARCH** Afro-Latin-American novel; popular culture; semiotics; translation studies. **SELECTED PUBLICATIONS** Auth, Intratextual distance in Tres tristes tigres, Mod Lang Notes, 3/78; Interview with Carlos Fuentes, Diacritics, 9/80; Interview with Gustavo Alvarez Gardeazabal, Chasqui, 11/81; Latia Julia (historia) y el escribidor (ficcion), Actas en honeuaje a Slejo Carpentier, Monte Avila, 6/82; The Esthetics of Fragmentation in La Vida a Plazos de don Jacobo Lerner, Taller Literario, 6/82; transl, Abalberto Ortiz, Juyungo, Three Continents Press, 6/82; auth, Order, Chaos, and Re-order: The Novels of Manuel Prig, Ky Romance Quart; Approximately Irony, Mod Lang Studies; auth, Narrative irony in the Contemporary Spanish American Novel, Cornell, 84; auth, Manuel Puig, G.K. Hall, 93. **CONTACT ADDRESS** Dept of Spanish, Univ Auckland, Private Bag 92019, Auckland, .. **EMAIL** j.tittler@auckland.ac.nz

TOBIN, RONALD WILLIAM FRANCIS
PERSONAL Born 06/19/1936, New York, NY, m, 1960, 1 child **DISCIPLINE** FRENCH LANGUAGE & LITERATURE **EDUCATION** St Peter's Col, AB, 57; Princeton Univ, MA, 59, PhD(Romance lang), 62. **CAREER** Instr French Lang & Lit, Williams Col, 62-63; from asst prof to assoc prof French, Univ Kans, 63-69, chmn Dept French & Ital, 67-69; chmn Dept French & Ital, 69-71, chmn Dept French & Ital, 75-80, prof French, Univ Calif, Santa Barbara, 69-, asst, Princeton Univ, 60-61; Am Philos Soc res grant, 63; mem univ adv coun, Am Coun Life Insurance, 70-; mem bd trustees, Baudry Franco-Am Found, 77-; Am Coun Learned Soc grant, 78 & 80; sr fel Monterey Inst of Inter Studies, 78-84; mem Higher Ed Adv Council for Apple Computer, Inc, 90-91. **HONORS AND AWARDS** Chevalier, Palmes Academiques, 72; Order of Merit, 84; Orders of Arts and letters, 98. **MEMBERSHIPS** Mod Humanities Res Asn; MLA; Am Asn Teachers Fr; Soc Etude XVIIe Siecle. **RESEARCH** Seventeenth century French tragedy; Racine; Mythology in literature. **SELECTED PUBLICATIONS** Auth, Racine and Seneca, Univ NC, 71; coauth, Paths to Freedom: Studies in French Classicism in Honor of E B O Borgerhoff, L'Esprit Createur, 71; auth, Trends in Racinian Criticism, Fr Rev, 72; ed, Myth and Mythology in 17th Century French Literature, L'Esprit Createur, 76; Esthetique et Societe au 17e Siecle, Papers on French 17th Century Literature, No 6, 76; Theme et Thematique de la Tragedia, Papers French 17th Century Lit, 79; Papers on 17th-Century Fr Lit, 1995; Moliere a tavola, Bulzoni, 98; Jean Racine Revisited, Simon & Schuster, 99. **CONTACT ADDRESS** Dept of French, Univ of California, Santa Barbara, 552 University Rd, Santa Barbara, CA, 93106-0001. **EMAIL** rwtobin@humanitas.ucsb.edu

TOLLEFSON, JAMES WILLIAM
PERSONAL Born 02/19/1950, WA, m, 1990, 2 children **DISCIPLINE** LINGUISTICS **EDUCATION** Stanford Univ, PhD, 78. **CAREER** Lect, 79-80, San Jose St Univ; asst prof, 80-84, assoc prof, 84-90, prof, 90-, Univ Wash. **HONORS AND AWARDS** Fulbright-Hays Lect, 76-77; Fulbright-Hays Sr Researcher, 80. **MEMBERSHIPS** Am Asn for Applied Linguistics; Mod Lang Asn; Nat Coun of Tchrs of Eng; Soc for Slovene Stud; Tchrs of Eng to Speakers of Other Lang. **RESEARCH** Language policy; language aquisition; language ed; pacifism and war resistance. **SELECTED PUBLICATIONS** Auth, Planning Language, Planning Inequality: Language Policy in the Community, Longman, 91; auth, Language Policy and Migration in the United States, Lit, Cult & Ethnic, Ljubljana: Filozofska fakulteta, 92; auth, The Strength Not to Fight: An Oral History of the Conscientious Objectors of the Vietnam War, Little, Brown, 93; auth, Conscientous Objection to Military Service, in Peace and Conflict Resolution, Ohio St Univ Mershon Ctr, 94; auth, Conscientous Objection to the Vietnam War, Mag of Hist, vol 8, no 3, 94; auth, Power and Inequality in Language Education, Cambridge Univ Press, 95; auth, Language Policy and Changing Patterns of Migration, Ethnic Lit & Cult in the USA, Canada, & Australia, Peter Lang, 96; auth, Language Policy in Independent Slovenia, Int J of the Sociology of Lang, no 126, 97; auth, Draft Resistance and Evasion, Oxford Comp to Am Mil Hist, Oxford Univ Press. **CONTACT ADDRESS** Dept of English, Univ of Washington, Seattle, WA, 98195. **EMAIL** tollefso@u.washington.edu

TOLLIVER, JOYCE
DISCIPLINE SPANISH LITERATURE **EDUCATION** Univ Southern Calif, PhD, 87. **CAREER** Assoc prof, Univ Ill Urbana Champaign. **SELECTED PUBLICATIONS** Auth, From Labov and Waletsky to 'Contextualist Narratology': 1967-1997, J Narrative Life Hist, 97; El encaje roto y otros cuentos de Emilia Pardo Baz n., 96; 'Sor Aparicion' and the Gaze: Pardo Baz n's Gendered Reply to the Romantic Don Juan, Hisp, 94; Script Theory, Perspective and Message in Narrative: The Case of 'Mi suicidio', Univ Ala, 94. **CONTACT ADDRESS** Spanish, Italian, and Portuguese Dept, Univ Ill Urbana Champaign, 52 E Gregory Dr, Champaign, IL, 61820. **EMAIL** joycet@uiuc.edu

TOLO, KHAMA-BASILLI
DISCIPLINE FRENCH **EDUCATION** Vanderbilt Univ, PhD, 90. **CAREER** Assoc prof; Univ WY, 90-. **RESEARCH** 19th-century French; 19th- and 20th- century Francophone lit(s). **SELECTED PUBLICATIONS** Publ, short stories and poems, articles on lit criticism. **CONTACT ADDRESS** Dept of Mod and Class Lang(s), Univ WY, PO Box 3964, Laramie, WY, 82071-3964. **EMAIL** KBTOLO@UWYO.EDU

TOLTON, CAMERON DAVID EDWARD
PERSONAL Born 08/15/1936, Toronto, ON, Canada **DISCIPLINE** ROMANCE LANGUAGES AND LITERATURES, CINEMA **EDUCATION** Univ Toronto, BA, 58; Harvard Univ, AM, 59, PhD(Romance lang and lit), 65. **CAREER** From lectr to asst prof, 64-69, ASSOC PROF FRENCH, VICTORIA COL, UNIV TORONTO, 69-, MEM, ADV ACAD PANEL, SOC SCI AND HUMANITIES RES COUN OF CAN, 79- **MEMBERSHIPS** MLA; Asn Can Univ Teachers Fr; Can Comp Lit Asn; Film Studies Asn Can. **RESEARCH** Andre Gide; the French novel, 1800-1950; French autobiography. **SELECTED PUBLICATIONS** Auth, Image-Conveying Abstractions in the Works of Andre Gide in Image and Theme: Studies in Modern French Fiction, Harvard Univ, 69; Andre Gide and the Art of Autobiography, Macmillan, Can, 75; The Revirement: A Structural Key to the Novels of Francois Mauriac, Aus J Fr Studies, 1-4/75; Andre Gide and Christopher Isherwood: Two Worlds of Counterfeiters, Comp Lit, spring 78; Le Mottheme Attente et l'Ironie Gidienne, Bull Des Amis D'Andre Gide, 1/82; A Lost Screenplay Unearthed, Mod Lang Rev, Vol 0088, 93; Symbolism And Irony--A New Reading Of Gide 'Traite De Narcisse,' Studi Francesi, Vol 0040, 96. **CONTACT ADDRESS** Dept of French Victoria Col, Univ of Toronto, Toronto, ON, M5S 1K7.

TOMAYKO, JAMES EDWARD
PERSONAL Born 07/08/1949, Charleroi, PA, m, 1972 **DISCIPLINE** CHINESE LANGUAGE, HISTORY OF TECHNOLOGY **EDUCATION** Carnegie-Mellon Univ, BA, 71, DA, 80; Univ Pittsburgh, MA, 72. **CAREER** Headmaster, Self-Directed Learning Ctr, 75-80; instr hist, Garden City Community Col, 80-81; tech pub specialist, NCR Corp, 81; ASST PROF COMP SCI, HIST AND CHINESE, WICHITA STATE UNIV, 82- **MEMBERSHIPS** Soc for the Hist of Technol; Asn Comput Mach; Chinese Lang Teachers Asn; Am Asn Artificial Intelligence; Asn Comput Ling. **RESEARCH** History of computing; Chinese natural language processing. **SELECTED PUBLICATIONS** Auth, The Ditch Irrigation Boom in Southwest Kansas, J West, fall 82; A Simple, Comprehensive Input/Output System for Chinese Natural Language Processing, Comp Sci Dept, Wichita State Univ, 5/82; The Relationship Between the N-BU-N and V-BU-V Constructions in Chinese, Proc of the Mid-Am Ling Conf, 82; Memories of Turing, Alan in Annals of the History of Computing, Vol 0015, 93. **CONTACT ADDRESS** 828 S Holyoke, Wichita, KS, 67218.

TONG, DIANE
PERSONAL Born 06/19/1943, New York, NY **DISCIPLINE** LINGUISTICS **EDUCATION** Queens Col, BA 69; NYU, MA 82. **CAREER** Author **MEMBERSHIPS** Authors Guild **RESEARCH** Gypsy Studies; Photography. **SELECTED PUBLICATIONS** Auth, Gypsies: An Interdisciplinary reader, NY, Garland Pub, 98; Jour of Mediterranean Studies, ed, Gypsies and Gypsy Cultures in the Mediterranean, 97; Gypsies: A Multidisciplinary Annotated Bibliography, NY, Garland Pub, 95; Gypsy Folktales, San Diego, Harcourt Brace Jovanovich, 89; Milano, 90 and Madrid, 97. **CONTACT ADDRESS** 67 Park Av Apt 5D, New York, NY, 1006 2557. **EMAIL** dianetong@delphi.com

TORUNO, RHINA
PERSONAL San Salvador, El Salvador **DISCIPLINE** SPANISH **EDUCATION** Nat Univ El Salvador, BA, 71; Cath Univ Louvain Belgium, MA, 73; Nat Univ Paris-Sorbonne, MA, 76; Cath Univ Louvain Belgium, PhD, 78; IN Univ, Bloomington, PhD, 94. **CAREER** Asst prof, Univ TX Permian Basin, Odessa, 95-; vis asst prof, FL State Univ, Tallahassee, 94-95; part timr lectr, IN Univ,Bloomington, 90-93; vis prof, Collegium Pro Am Lat, Louvain, Belgium, 89; assoc instr, IN Univ, Bloomington, 83-89; tchg asst, Univ CA, Irvine, 82-83; vis scholar, Stanford Univ, 81-82; prof, Nat Univ El Salvador, 76-81. **HONORS AND AWARDS** Elected chp, session Mex lit for, Nat Conf 98, 78 Nat Conf Am Asn Tchrs Span & Port, Inc, Orlando, 96; keynote speaker, Hisp Grad Ceremony, Univ TX of Permain Basin, 96; Awd for Educ Res & publ, Pan Amer Round Table Odessa, 96; key-note speaker, 3rd Coloquio Bi-Annual Span & Span-Am Lit, AZ State Univ, 96; nominated, Honor Mem Ecologic Mex Club, Monterrey, 96; inducted as 1st female mem, Salvadoran Acad Span Lang, 95. **MEMBERSHIPS** Asoc de Ling y Filologia de la America Latina; Amer Asn Tchr(s) Span & Port, Inc; Asociacion de Lit Femenina Hispanica; Asn des Amis d'Emmanuel Mounier, Fr; Asociacion de Mujeres Univ de El Salvador; Club Ecologico Novaterra, Monterrey, Mex; Feministas Unidas, USA; Inst Int de Literatura Iberoamericana; Lat Amer Stud Asn; Midland Hisp Chamber Commerce; MLA; Southwest Coun Lat Am Stud; S Atl Mod Lang Asn; S Ctr Mod Lang Asn; Royal Acad Span Lang Spain; Salvadoran Acad Lang; Salvadoran Acad Arts & Sci. **RESEARCH** 20th century Spain and Latin Am narrative; poetry; drama and literary theory; educ exchange with Mexico. **SELECTED PUBLICATIONS** Auth, Tiempo, Destino Y Opresion El La Obra De Elena Garro, Time, Destiny and Oppression in the Work of Elena Garro, NY, Mellen UP, 96; Del realismo magico de Los recuerdos del porvenir al realismo social de Y Matarazo no llamo, From the Magical Realism of Recollection of Things to Come to the Social Realism of And Matarazo didn't call, Deslinde Nuevo Leon, Mexico, UP, 95; Y Matarazo no llamo Novela poletica y la ltima escrita por Elena Garro, And Matarazo didn't call, Analysis of the Political Novel and the Most Recent Work by Elena Garro, Letras Informa, Ano II, U, San Carlos, Guatemala, 94; Distintos referentes y afines significantes en La muerte de Artemio Cruz y El siglo de las luces, Distinct References and Related Significance in the Death of Artemio Cruz, and The Century of Light, Arts 3, San Salvador, 93; Protesta contra la opresion: categoreas medulares en la obra narrativa y dramatica de Elena Garro, Protest Against Oppression: Central Categories in the Narrative and Drama Work of Elena Garro, Deslinde Nuevo Leon, Mex UP, 92; Sobre la vida desgarradora de Elena Garro, Concerning the Shattered Life of Elena Garro, El Diario, Las Prensa, New York Times, NY, 96; Dialogo con Elena Garro sobre sus tecnicas literarias, Dialog with Elena

Garro about her literary style, Diario Latino, Lit Supplement, 96; coauth, La cenicienta en una fiesta de medianoche en el paes de la sonrisa, Despues de Medianoche, Cinderella in the Midnight Ball in the Country of Smile in After Midnight by David Escobar Galindo, Drama in Obras teatrales de un solo acto de dramaturgos latinoamericanos, Drama Works of One Act by Latin-American Dramatists, Univ de Antioquia, Colombia, 96. **CONTACT ADDRESS** Dept of Mod Lang, Univ of Texas of the Permian Basin, Odessa, TX, 79762. **EMAIL** toruno_r@utpb.edu

TOUMAYAN, ALAIN P.
DISCIPLINE FRENCH LITERATURE **EDUCATION** Univ of Penn, BA, 76; Yale Univ, MA, 78, Mphil, 80, PhD, 82. **CAREER** Assoc prof. **RESEARCH** 19th and 20th century French literature. **SELECTED PUBLICATIONS** Auth, pubs on the problem of evil in 19th century texts, 19th and 20th century subjects, and Festschrift on literary generations. **CONTACT ADDRESS** Romance Languages and Literatures Dept, Univ of Notre Dame, Notre Dame, IN, 46556.

TOURNIER, CLAUDE
DISCIPLINE FRENCH **EDUCATION** Northwestern Univ, PhD. **CAREER** Sr lectr; prog coordr, first-yr Fr and tchg asst supvr Northwestern Univ; lect, ACTFL, Central States, IFLTA; trained as, ACTFL oral proficiency tester. **RESEARCH** Cooperative learning, curriculum design, development of materials for a communicative approach to teaching, and the use of technology in the classroom. **SELECTED PUBLICATIONS** Coauth, Voil, Heinle & Heinle. **CONTACT ADDRESS** Dept of French, Northwestern Univ, 1801 Hinman, Evanston, IL, 60208.

TOWNER, WAYNE SIBLEY
PERSONAL Born 01/10/1933, Scottsbluff, NE, m, 1956, 2 children **DISCIPLINE** RELIGION, PHILOLOGY **EDUCATION** Yale Univ, BA, 54, BD, 60, MA, 61, PhD, 65. **CAREER** Eng tchr, Gerard Inst, Sidon, Lebanon, 54-57; instr Old Testament, Princeton Theol Sem, 63-64; lectr, divinity sch, Yale Univ, 64-65, asst prof 65-69, assoc prof Old Testament, 69-71; prof & dean Theol Sem, Univ Dubuque, 71-75; Prof Old Testament, Union Theol Sem, Richmond, Va, 75-, Dean, 85-88. **HONORS AND AWARDS** First Prize, Theology Category, Harper Collins Annual Best Sermons Award, 87; Second Prize, Christian Ministry, Alfred P Klausner Sermon Award, 97. **MEMBERSHIPS** Soc Bibl Lit. **RESEARCH** Old Testament; rabbinnic lit. **SELECTED PUBLICATIONS** Auth, The Rabbinic Enumeration of Scriptural Examples, Brill, Leiden, 73; How God Deals with Evil, Westminster, 76; Daniel, Westminster John Knox, 84. **CONTACT ADDRESS** 3401 Brook Rd, Richmond, VA, 23227-4514. **EMAIL** stowner@utsva.edu

TOWNSEND, CHARLES EDWARD
PERSONAL Born 09/29/1932, New Rochelle, NY, m, 1957, 3 children **DISCIPLINE** SLAVIC LANGUAGES AND LINGUISTICS **EDUCATION** Yale Univ, AB, 54; Harvard Univ, MA, 60, PhD, 62. **CAREER** Instr Slavic long and lit, Harvard Univ, 62-65, asst prof Slavic long, 65-66; asst prof Slavic long, 66-68, assoc prof Slavic Lang and Lit, 68-71, bicentennial preceptor, 66-68, dir, Critical Lang Prog, 68-70, Prof Slavic Lang and Lit, Princeton Univ, 71-, Chmn Dept, 70-, Clark Fund grant, Harvard Found Advan Studies and Res, 63, 65; Inter-Univ Cmt travel grant, Czech and res fel, Inst Lang and Lit, Czech Acad Sci, 68, Int Res and Exchanges Bd res fel, CZECH LANG INST, 71; MEM ADV BD, RUSS LANG J, 73- AND ED BD, FOLIA SLAVICA, 77- **MEMBERSHIPS** Am Asn Teachers Slavic and East Europ Lang; Ling Soc Am; Am Coun Teachers Russ. **RESEARCH** Russian language and linguistics; Czech language and linguistics; Slavic linguistics. **SELECTED PUBLICATIONS** Introduction to the Study of Slavic Languages, Slavic E Europ J, Vol 37, 93; Introduction to the Study of Slavic Languages, Slavic E Europ J, Vol 37, 93; Czech as It Is--Czech, Slavic E Europ J, Vol 38, 94; Dutch Contributions to the 11th Internstional-Congress of Slavists, Bratislava--Linguistics, Slavic Rev, Vol 54, 95; 'Dita Saxova,' Slavic Rev, Vol 54, 95; The Prague School of Structural and Functional Linguistics--A Short introduction, Slavic Rev, Vol 54, 95; Semantics of the Preverb U- in Czech and Russian--Negative and Positive Modality, Welt der Slaven-Halbjahresschrift fur Slavistik, Vol 42, 97; The Dawn of Slavic--An introduction to Slavic Philology, Slavic Rev, Vol 56, 97; The Russian Language in the 20th-Century, Mod Lang J, Vol 81, 97. **CONTACT ADDRESS** 145 Hickory Ct, Princeton, NJ, 08540.

TRAHAN, ELIZABETH WELT
PERSONAL Born 11/19/1924, Berlin, Germany, d, 1 child **DISCIPLINE** COMPARATIVE LITERATURE **EDUCATION** Sarah Lawrence Col, BA, 51; Cornell Univ, MA, 53; Yale Univ, PhD, 57. **CAREER** Instr, German and Russian, Univ Mass, 56-60; asst prof, Univ Pitt, 60-64; assoc prof, 64-66; assoc prof Humanities,Monterey Inst of For and Internatl Stud, 68-75, ch, Dept of Translation & Interpretation, 68-74, prof Humanities, 75-88, act dean, 76-77; vis prof Amherst Col, 85-92. **MEMBERSHIPS** MLA; Nat Coalition of Independent Scholars. **RESEARCH** Comparative literature of the nineteenth and twentieth centuries; literary translation; Holocaust studies. **SELECTED PUBLICATIONS** Auth, Crime and Punishment: A Basic Approach, Univ Mass, 59; ed, Gogol's Overcoat: Critical Essays, Ardis, 82; trans, Leo Tolstoy: The Divine and the Human, Delos, 90; auth, The Door is Always Open: The Ironic Subtexts of Kafka's Before the Law and Dygat's Usher of the Helios Movie Theatre, in Comparatist, 93; auth, George Bendemann's Path to the Judgment, in Approaches to Teaching: Kafka's Short Fiction, MLA, 95; auth, The Possessed as Dostoevskij's Homage to Gogol: An Essay in Traditional Criticism, in Russian Lit, 96; auth, Geisterbeschworung: Eine Judische Jugend im Wien der Kriegsjahre, Picus Verlag, 96; auth, Walking with Ghosts: A Jewish Childhood in Wartime Vienna, Peter Lang, 98. **CONTACT ADDRESS** 222 North East St, Apt. 1, Amherst, MA, 01002.

TRAILL, DAVID ANGUS
PERSONAL Born 01/28/1942, Helensburgh, Scotland **DISCIPLINE** LATIN, GREEK **EDUCATION** Univ St Andrews, MA, 64; Univ Calif, Berkeley, PhD(classics), 71. **CAREER** Asst prof, 70-78, ASSOC PROF CLASSICS, UNIV CALIF, DAVIS, 78- **MEMBERSHIPS** Am Philol Asn; Medieval Asn Pac; Am Inst Archaeol. **RESEARCH** Classical and medieval Latin poetry; Schliemann. **SELECTED PUBLICATIONS** Auth, Ovid, 'Tristia' 2.8, 2.296, and 2.507--Happier Solutions, Hermes-Zeitschrift Fur Klassische Philologie, Vol 120, 92; The Text of Catullus 64.24, Class Philol, Vol 87, 92; The Text of Catullus 64.24, Class Philol, Vol 87, 92; Frazer,J.G.--His Life and Work, Class J, Vol 87, 92; Between Scylla and Charybdis at 'Aeneid' 3.684-86--A Smoother Passage, Am J Philology, Vol 114, 93; Horace 'Carmen 1,30'--Glyceras Problem, Class Philol, Vol 88, 93; Horace 'Carmen 1,30'--Glyceras Problem, Class Philol, Vol 88, 93; Propertius 'Elegy Book-1, Number-21'--The Sister, The Bones, and The Wayfarer, Am J Philology, Vol 115, 94; Troia--Bridge Between East and West, Am J Archaeol, Vol 98, 94; The Spoken Language of Orazio, Class World, Vol 90, 97. **CONTACT ADDRESS** Dept Classics, Univ of Calif, Davis, CA, 95616.

TRAPNELL, WILLIAM HOLMES
PERSONAL Born 09/16/1931, Richmond, VA, m, 1958 **DISCIPLINE** FRENCH LITERATURE **EDUCATION** Hampden-Sydney Col, BA, 54; Middlebury Col, MA, 62; Univ Pittsburgh, PhD (French lit), 67. **CAREER** Instr French, Hampden-Sydney Col, 59-60; instr, Rollins Col, 60-63; asst instr, Univ Pittsburgh, 66-67; asst prof, Brown Univ, 67-69; asst prof, 69-73, ASSOC PROF FRENCH, IND UNIV, BLOOMINGTON, 73- **MEMBERSHIPS** Am Soc Eighteenth Century Studies; Mod Humanities Res Asn. **RESEARCH** Eighteenth century French literature; Marivaux; Voltaire. **SELECTED PUBLICATIONS** Auth, The philosophical Implications of Marivaux's Dispute and Voltaire's Manuscripts and Collective Edition--Studies on Voltaire and the Eighteenth Century, 70; Marivaux's Unfinished Novels, Fr Studies, 7/70; Voltaire and His Portable Dictionary, Analecta Romanica, 72; Voltaire and the Eucharist in Studies on Voltaire and the Eighteenth Century, 81; Christ and His Associates in Voltairian Polemic in Stanford French and Italian Studies, 82; DeLambert, Madame And Her Milieu, Mod Lang Rev, Vol 89, 94; Studies on Voltaire and the 18th-Century, Mod Lang Rev, Vol 89, 94. **CONTACT ADDRESS** Dept of French and Ital, Indiana Univ, Bloomington, Bloomington, IN, 47401.

TRAUGOTT, ELIZABETH CLOSS
PERSONAL Born 04/09/1939, Bristol, England, m, 1967 **DISCIPLINE** LINGUISTICS **EDUCATION** Oxford Univ, BA, 60, MA, 64; Univ Calif, Berkeley, PhD(English lang), 64. **CAREER** Asst prof English, Univ Calif, Berkeley, 64-68; lectr ling, 68-71, assoc prof, 71-76, PROF LING AND ENGLISH, STANFORD UNIV, 76-, Mem, Joint Inst/Ministry Educ Lang and Lit Panel, Dar es Salaam, Tanzania, 65-66; vis lectr ling, Univ EAfrica, 65-66 and Univ York, England, 66-67; Am Coun Learned Soc fel, 75-76. **MEMBERSHIPS** Ling Soc Am; Int Ling Asn; Ling Asn Gt Brit; Am Asn Univ Women. **RESEARCH** Language change; structure and history of the English language; linguistics and literature. **SELECTED PUBLICATIONS** Auth, Tense and Narrativity--from Medieval Performance to Modern Fiction, Style, Vol 26, 92; How to Set Parameters--Arguments from Language Change, J Ling, Vol 29, 93; Tense and Narrativity--From Medieval Performance to Modern Fiction, Style, Vol 26, 92; Internal and External Factors in Syntactic Change, Studies Lang, Vol 18, 94; Principles of Linguistic Change, Vol 1, Internal Factors, Studies Lang, Vol 21, 97; Thoughts on Grammaticalization, J Ling, Vol 33, 97. **CONTACT ADDRESS** Dept of Ling, Stanford Univ, Stanford, CA, 94305-1926.

TRAUPMAN, JOHN CHARLES
PERSONAL Born 01/02/1923, Nazareth, PA, m, 1949, 1 child **DISCIPLINE** CLASSICAL LANGUAGES **EDUCATION** Moravian Col, BA, 48; Princeton Univ, MA, 51, PhD(classics), 56. **CAREER** From instr to assoc prof, 51-61, Prof Classics, 61-89, chemn 57-89, St Joseph's Univ; Assoc ed, Scribner Bantam English Dictionary, 77. **HONORS AND AWARDS** Magna cum laude, 48; Schulze Greek Award, 48; Robbins Scholar, Princeton Univ, 50-51; Faculty Merit Award for Research, 82; St Joseph's Univ Col Tchg Award, 86; Award of the Class Asn of the Atlantic States, 90; Special Award of the Class Asn of the Atlantic States, 96. **MEMBERSHIPS** Am Philol Asn; Archaeol Inst Am; Am Class League. **RESEARCH** Archaeology; Latin lexicography. **SELECTED PUBLICATIONS** Auth, New Collegiate Latin and English Dictionary, Bantam, 66, rev ed, 95; The New College Latin and English Dictionary, Amsco 68; ed, German-English Dictionary, Bantam, 82; auth, latin is Fun,, book I, Amsco, 88, book II, Amsco, 94; assoc ed, Scribner English Dictionary, Scribner, 77; auth, German Fundamentals, Barron's, 92; auth, Conversational latin for Oral Proficiency, 2d ed, Bolchazy-Carducci, 97; auth, Lingua Latina, book I, Amsco, 98. **CONTACT ADDRESS** Dept of Classics, St. Joseph's Univ, Philadelphia, PA, 19131. **EMAIL** traupman@sju.edu

TROIANO, JAMES J.
PERSONAL Born 12/17/1944, Elizabeth, NJ, m, 1972 **DISCIPLINE** SPANISH **EDUCATION** Rutgers Col, AB, 66; State Univ NY, Buffalo, AM, 68, PhD(Span), 73. **CAREER** From instr to asst prof Span, Canisius Col, 70-75; instr, 75-76, asst prof, 76-80, ASSOC PROF SPAN, UNIV MAINE, ORONO, 80-, Consult, Libr J, 73-; ed, Revista Entre Nosotros, 75-76; Seville Ctr Policy Comt, Coun Int Educ Exchange, 78- **MEMBERSHIPS** MLA; Am Asn Teachers Span and Port; Nat Educ Asn. **RESEARCH** Contemporary Latin American theater and short story. **SELECTED PUBLICATIONS** Auth, Love and Madness in Arlt La 'Juerga De Los Polichinelas, Confluencia-Rev Hisp de Cult y Lit, Vol 0006, 90. **CONTACT ADDRESS** Dept of Foreign Lang and Classics, Univ of Maine, Orono, ME, 04473.

TROMMLER, FRANK ALFRED
PERSONAL Born 05/11/1939, Zwickau, Germany, m, 2 children **DISCIPLINE** GERMAN LITERATURE **EDUCATION** Univ Munich, Dr phil (Ger lit), 64. **CAREER** Vis lectr Ger Lit, Harvard Univ, 67-69; prof Ger Lit, Univ Pa, 70-, vis prof, Princeton Univ, 78, Johns Hopkins Univ, 80, chmn Ger Dept, 80-86, 95-97; dir Humanities Prog, Am Inst for Contemp Ger Studies, 95. **HONORS AND AWARDS** Dir NEH Summer Sem, 83; Guggenheim Fellow 84-85; Dir DAAD Summer Sem 88, 90; Certificate of Merit AATG/Goethe Inst, 91. **MEMBERSHIPS** MLA Exec Council 95-98; AATG chp Philadephia Pres 86-90, German Studies Assoc Vice Pres, 88-90; Pres 90-92. **RESEARCH** German literature of the 19th and 20th centuries; modernism and Technology, Ger-Am cultural relations. **SELECTED PUBLICATIONS** Auth, Roman und Wirklichkeit, Kohihammer, 66; Der Nullpunkt 1945, Basis 1, 70; Der zocgernde Nachwuchs: Entwicklungsprobleme der Nachkriegsliteratur, Tendenzen der deutschen Literatur seit 1945, Kroner, 71; Sozialistische Literatur in Deutschland, Kroner, 76; coauth, die Kultur der Weimarer Republik, Nymphenburger, 78; co-ed, Jahrhundertwende Deutsche Literatur VIII, Rowohlt, 82; Literatur und sozialismus Neues Handbuch 20, Athenaioh, 82; Kulturpolitik der Nachkmegszeit Kulturpolitisches Woerterbuch, Metzler, 82; co ed, American and the Germans, Univ of Pa Press, 85; Der Mythos Jugend, Suhrkamp, 85; ed Thematics Reconsidered Rodopi, 95; co ed Revisiting Zero Hour, 1945, AICGS Washington, 96. **CONTACT ADDRESS** Dept of German, Univ of Pennsylvania, 255 S 36th St, Philadelphia, PA, 19104-6305. **EMAIL** trommler@ccat.sas.upenn.edu

TSAI, SHIH-SHAN HENRY
DISCIPLINE ASIAN STUDIES **EDUCATION** Nat Taiwan Normal Univ, BA, 62; Univ Ore, MA, 67, PhD, 70. **CAREER** Vis assoc prof, Nat Taiwan Univ, 70-71; vis assoc prof, Univ Calif, Los Angeles, 79; vis assoc prof, Univ Calif, Berkely, 81; PROF, DIR ASIAN STUDIES, UNIV ARK, 83-. **SELECTED PUBLICATIONS** Auth, Organizing Asian-American Labor--The Pacific Coast Canned-Salmon Industry, 1870-1942, Jour Amer Hist, Vol 0082, 95; Margins and Mainstreams--Asians in American History and Culture, Pacific Hist Rev, Vol 0064, 95; The Asian-American Movement, Pacific Hist Rev, Vol 0064, 95; In Search of Equality--The Chinese Struggle Against Discrimination in 19th-Century America, Pacific Hist Rev, Vol 0065, 96. **CONTACT ADDRESS** 2105 Austin Dr, Fayetteville, AR, 72703. **EMAIL** HTSAI@comp.uark.edu

TSIAPERA, MARIA
PERSONAL Born 07/26/1932, Cyprus **DISCIPLINE** LINGUISTICS, ARABIC **EDUCATION** Univ Tex, BA, 57, MA, 58, PhD(ling), 63. **CAREER** Asst prof ling, Fresno State Col, 64-66; from asst prof to assoc prof, 66-68, from actg chmn dept to chmn dept, 67-73, PROF LING, UNIV NC, CHAPEL HILL, 72-, Fel, Univ Tex, 63-64; NSF travel grant, 77; res grant, Univ NC, 77. **MEMBERSHIPS** Ling Soc Am; Southeastern Conf Ling (vpres, 70-71, pres, 71-72); SAlantic Mod Lang Asn; Am Orient Soc; Am Asn Teachers Arabic. **RESEARCH** History and philosophy of linguistics; Greek historical dialectology; Arabic dialectology. **SELECTED PUBLICATIONS** Auth, Aristotle and the Grammaire Generale et Raisonee, Folia Ling Hist, Vol 0011, 92. **CONTACT ADDRESS** Dept of Linguistics, Univ of North Carolina, Chapel Hill, NC, 27514.

TSUKIMURA, REIKO
PERSONAL Born 02/13/1930, Tokyo, Japan **DISCIPLINE** JAPANESE LITERATURE, COMPARATIVE LITERATURE **EDUCATION** Japan Women's Univ, BA, 51; Univ Sask, MA, 62; Ind Univ, PhD(comp lit), 67. **CAREER** Instr English, Japan Women's Univ, 59-60; instr Japanese, Univ BC, 62-63; from

instr to assoc prof, Univ Minn, Minneapolis, 66-74; assoc prof, 74-79, PROF JAPANESE LIT, UNIV TORONTO, 79-, Vis lectr, Harvard Univ, 68-69; Soc Sci Res Coun/Am Coun Learned Soc res grant Japanese studies, 73-74; Japan Found prof fel, 80-81. **MEMBERSHIPS** Asn Teachers Japanese; Can Asian Studies Asn. **RESEARCH** Japanese literature, especially poetry; comparative literature, especially Western and Oriental literary relationships. **SELECTED PUBLICATIONS** Auth, An Anthology of Contemporary Japanese Poetry, Monumenta Nipponica, Vol 0050, 95. **CONTACT ADDRESS** Dept of EA-sian Studies, Univ of Toronto, Toronto, ON, M5S 1A5.

TU, CHING-I
PERSONAL Born 05/13/1935, Nanking, China, m, 1970, 2 children **DISCIPLINE** FOREIGN LANGUAGE **EDUCATION** Nat Taiwan Univ, BA, 58; Univ Wash, PhD, 67. **CAREER** Asst prof to assoc prof to prof to chemn, 66-, Rutgers Univ; vis assoc prof, Univ Hawaii, 71-72; vis prof, Nat Taiwan Univ, 74-75. **HONORS AND AWARDS** Res grant, US Dept Educ; res grant, Chiang Ching-Kuo Found; grants, Korean Found., Found dir, Chinese Prog, found chair, dept E Asian lang and cultures, Rutgers Univ. **MEMBERSHIPS** Asn Asian Stud; Am Asn Chinese Stud; MLA. **RESEARCH** Chinese literary criticism; Chinese intellectual history; cultural changes in Asia. **SELECTED PUBLICATIONS** Auth, Anthology of Chinese Literature, 72-; auth, Readings in Classical Chinese Literature, 81; auth, Tradition and Creativity: Essays on East Asian Civilization, 88; auth, Essays on East Asian Humanities; 91; auth, Classics and Interpretations: The Hermeneutic Traditions in Chinese Culture, 99. **CONTACT ADDRESS** Dept of Asian Lang and Cultures, Rutgers Univ, New Brunswick, NJ, 08903. **EMAIL** citu@rci.rutgers.edu

TUCKER, CYNTHIA GRANT
PERSONAL Born 06/17/1941, New York, NY, m, 1966, 2 children **DISCIPLINE** COMPARATIVE LITERATURE, ENGLISH **EDUCATION** Denison Univ, BA, 63; Univ Iowa, PhD(comp lit), 67. **CAREER** Asst prof English, 67-75, dir prog Comp Lit, 72-75, assoc prof, 75-82, prof English, Univ Memphis, 82-, Nat Endowment for Humanities prog grants, 78-81 & fel col teachers, 82. **HONORS AND AWARDS** Disting Res Award nom, 80-87; Disting Teaching Award nom, 73, 96. **MEMBERSHIPS** MLA; Women's Caucus Mod Lang. **RESEARCH** Biography, Humor, Women's Studies, Women in Religion, Journals Diary Lit. **SELECTED PUBLICATIONS** Auth, Meredith's broken laurel: Modern Love and the Renaissance sonnet tradition, Victorian Poetry, 72; The Rilkean poet-lover and his laurel, Philol Quart, 74; Translation as resurrection: Rilke and Louise Labe, Mod Lang Notes, 74; Petrarchizing into the horrible: Baudelaire's Grotesque, Fr Rev, 75; Kate Freeman Clark: A Painter Rediscovered, Univ Press Miss, 81; Spirited Threads: The Writing and Art of Patricia Roberts Cline, Portland, OR, Sibyl Publications, Fall, 97. **CONTACT ADDRESS** Dept of English, Memphis State Univ, 3706 Alumni St, Memphis, TN, 38152-0001. **EMAIL** cgtucker@cc.memphis.edu

TUCKER, JANET
DISCIPLINE NINETEENTH AND TWENTIETH-CENTURY RUSSIAN WRITERS **EDUCATION** Indiana Univ, BA, 63, MA, 65, PhD, 73. **CAREER** English and Lit, Univ Ark. **HONORS AND AWARDS** Fulbright Col Res Incentive Grant, 91. **SELECTED PUBLICATIONS** Areas: the Russian poet Innokentij Annenskij, Anatolij Gladilin. **CONTACT ADDRESS** Univ Ark, Fayetteville, AR, 72701.

TUCKER, JOHN J.
DISCIPLINE OLD ICELANDI; OLD ENGLISH LITERATURE **EDUCATION** Univ Toronto, BA, MA, PhD; Univ Oxford, BLitt. **CAREER** Prof; dept ch. **RESEARCH** History of the language; the historical film; hagiography. **SELECTED PUBLICATIONS** Ed, Sagas of the Icelanders: A Book of Essays, Garland, 89; coauth, Islensk-ensk ordabok, Idunn, 89; Glossary to the Poetic Edda, 92; transl, Saga and Society, Odense, 94. **CONTACT ADDRESS** Dept of English, Victoria Univ, PO Box 3070, Victoria, BC, V8W 3W1. **EMAIL** jtucker@uvic.ca

TUCKER, RICHARD
DISCIPLINE APPLIED LINGUISTICS **EDUCATION** McGill Univ, PhD. **CAREER** Languages, Carnegie Mellon Univ. **HONORS AND AWARDS** Dept head. **MEMBERSHIPS** Eng Lang Progs Advisory Panel; Discipline Advisory Comt; TEFL/Applied Linguistics Fulbright prog, Board Dirs Consortium Soc Sci Asns; Exec Comt Nat Ctr Res Cult Diversity & Sec Lang Learning. **SELECTED PUBLICATIONS** Auth, Language learning for the 21st century: Challenges of the North American Free Trade Agreement, Canadian Mod Lang Rev; 93; Policy and practice in the education of culturally and linguistically diverse students. Alexandria, VA: TESOL, 94; Concluding thoughts: Language planning issues for the coming decade, Annual Rev Applied Linguistics, Cambridge Univ Press, 94; Coauth, A multiple perspectives analysis of a Japanese FLES program. For Lang Annals, 95. **CONTACT ADDRESS** Carnegie Mellon Univ, 5000 Forbes Ave, Pittsburgh, PA, 15213.

TUCKER, ROBERT ASKEW
PERSONAL Born 03/23/1930, Atlanta, GA **DISCIPLINE** LATIN, GREEK **EDUCATION** Emory Univ, BBA, 51, MAT, 62; Johns Hopkins Univ, PhD(classics), 67. **CAREER** Teacher Latin, Cross Keys High Sch, DeKalb County, Ga, 62-65; asst prof classics, 67-72, ASSOC PROF CLASSICS, UNIV GA, 72-. **MEMBERSHIPS** Class Asn Mid W and S (secy-treas, 71-73); Am Philol Asn; Vergilian Soc Am; Am Archaeol Inst; Am Class League. **RESEARCH** Roman epic, especially Lucan. **SELECTED PUBLICATIONS** Auth, Vergil, Class Bulletin, Vol 0070, 94. **CONTACT ADDRESS** Dept of Classics, Univ of Georgia, Athens, GA, 30602.

TURK, EDWARD BARON
PERSONAL Born 09/29/1946, New York, NY **DISCIPLINE** FRENCH LITERATURE AND FILM **EDUCATION** Brooklyn Col, BA, 67; Yale Univ, MPh, 71, PhD(French), 73. **CAREER** Asst prof and dir undergrad studies, Yale Univ, 72-78; ASSOC PROF FRENCH AND HUMANITIES, MASS INST TECHNOL, 78-, Morse fel humanities, Yale Univ, 75-76; Nat Endowment for Humanities grant, 81. **MEMBERSHIPS** MLA; Am Asn Teachers Fr; NAm Soc Seventeenth-Century French Lit; Am Film Inst. **RESEARCH** Seventeenth century French literature; French film history. **SELECTED PUBLICATIONS** Auth, The Cine Goes to Town--French Cinema 1896-1914, Fr Rev, Vol 0069, 95. **CONTACT ADDRESS** Dept of Humanities, Massachusetts Inst of Tech, 77 Massachusetts Ave, Cambridge, MA, 02139-4307.

TURNER, DORIS J.
PERSONAL St Louis, Missouri **DISCIPLINE** LATIN AMERICAN STUDIES **EDUCATION** Stowe Coll St Louis, BA 1953; Universidade da Bahia Salvador Bahia Brazil, 1963; St Louis U, PhD 1967. **CAREER** Kent State Univ, asso prof & coordinator, Latin American Studies, currently. **HONORS AND AWARDS** Fulbright Fellowship Brazil 1962-64; Research Grant to Brazil, Kent State Univ 1976; Danforth Assn 1976; NEH Summer Fellwshp Brown Univ 1979; Postdoctoral Fellowship, Ford Foundation, 1987-88; Outstanding Teaching Award, College of Arts & Sciences, Kent State Univ, 1986. **MEMBERSHIPS** Field reader US Ofc of Educ (HEW) 1976-77, 79; elected mem & past chmn Nat Ofc Steering & Com of Consortium of Latin Am Studies Prog 1973-76. **CONTACT ADDRESS** Romance Languages & Literatures, Kent State Univ, 101 Satterfield Hall, Kent, OH, 44242.

TURNER, JAMES HILTON
PERSONAL Born 04/19/1918, Woodville, ON, Canada, m, 1945, 3 children **DISCIPLINE** CLASSICAL LANGUAGES **EDUCATION** Univ Toronto, BA, 40; Univ Cincinnati, PhD, 44. **CAREER** Mem fac, Bishop's Col Sch, 44-45 McCallie Sch, 45-47; from instr to asst prof class lang, Univ Vt, 47-51; asst prof, Heidelberg Col, 51-52; from asst prof to assoc prof, 52-57, chmn dept lang, 53-62, PROF CLASS LANG, WESTMINSTER COL, 57-, Assoc ed, Class World, 57-60. **MEMBERSHIPS** Class Asn Atlantic States; Am Class League (vpres, 58-59); AAUP. **RESEARCH** Aristophanes. **SELECTED PUBLICATIONS** Auth, Aristophanes, Lysistrata, Class World, Vol 0086, 93; Introduction to Attic Greek, Class World, Vol 0089, 96. **CONTACT ADDRESS** Dept of Foreign Languages, Westminster Col, New Wilmington, PA, 16142.

TURNER, JOAN
DISCIPLINE NINETEENTH AND TWENTIETH-CENTURY RUSSIAN WRITERS **EDUCATION** Brown Univ, BA, 67, MAT, 69; Ohio State Univ, PhD, 88. **CAREER** English and Lit, Univ Ark. **SELECTED PUBLICATIONS** Areas: TA training/supervision and language learning disabilities. **CONTACT ADDRESS** Univ Ark, Fayetteville, AR, 72701.

TURNER, STEPHEN
PERSONAL Born 03/01/1951, Chicago, IL, m, 1990, 2 children **DISCIPLINE** SOCIOLOGY; PHILOSOPHY **EDUCATION** AB, 71, AM, 71, AM, 72, PhD, 75, Univ Missouri-Columbia. **CAREER** Visiting prof, 82, Notre Dame; Visiting Prof, 85, Virginia Poytech Inst; Visiting Prof, 87, Boston Univ; Asst Prof, 75-, Univ South Florida. **HONORS AND AWARDS** NEH Fel, 91-92; Fel, Swedish Collegium for Advanced Studies in the Social Sciences, 92 & 98; Honorary Visiting Prof, Univ Manchester, 96. **RESEARCH** History of social thought; philosophy of social science; science studies **SELECTED PUBLICATIONS** Auth, The Search for a Methodology of Social Science: Durkheim, Weber, and the Nineteenth Century Problem of Cause, Probability, and Action, Boston Studies in Philosophy of Science, 86; Coauth, The Impossible Science: An Institutional Analysis of American Sociology, 90; Max Weber: The Lawyer as a Social Thinker, 94; Auth, The Social Theory of Practices: Tradition, Tacit Knowledge, and Presuppositions, 94. **CONTACT ADDRESS** Dept of Philosophy, Univ South Florida, Tampa, FL, 33620. **EMAIL** turner@chuma.cas.usf.edu

TUSIANI, JOSEPH
PERSONAL Born 01/14/1924, San Marco in Lamis, Italy **DISCIPLINE** ITALIAN LANGUAGE AND LITERATURE **EDUCATION** Univ Naples, Dott in Lettere, 47. **CAREER** Instr Ital, Col New Rochelle, 48-51; asst prof Ital, 51-60; from assoc prof to prof, Col Mt St Vincent, 60-71; PROF, LEHMAN COL CITY UNIV, NEW YORK, 71-, Vis prof, New York Univ, 58-63, Cent Conn State Col, 64, Fairleigh Dickinson Univ, 68, Rutgers Univ, 70 and Fordham Univ, 80. **HONORS AND AWARDS** Greenwood Prize, Poetry Soc England, 56; Di Castagnola Award, Poetry Soc Am, 68; Spirit Gold Medal, Cath Poetry Soc Am, 69., LittD, Col Mt St Vincent, 71. **MEMBERSHIPS** Dante Soc Am; Am Asn Teachers Ital; Poetry Soc Am (vpres, 57-69); Am Pen. **RESEARCH** Verse translation of Pulci's Morgante. **SELECTED PUBLICATIONS** Auth, The Contingent Word--Avant-Garde and Experimentalism in 20th-Century Italian--Italian, World Lit Today, Vol 0067, 93. **CONTACT ADDRESS** 2140 Tomlinson Ave, Bronx, NY, 10461.

TUTTLE, EDWARD FOWLER
PERSONAL Born 03/08/1942, Los Angeles, CA, m, 1962, 2 children **DISCIPLINE** ROMANCE LINGUISTICS **EDUCATION** Univ Calif, Los Angeles, BA, 65, MA, 67; Univ Calif, Berkeley, PhD(Romance philol), 72. **CAREER** Assoc prof Ital and chmn Romance ling, 71-81, PROF ITAL AND ROMANCE LING, UNIV CALIF, LOS ANGELES, 81-. **MEMBERSHIPS** Ling Soc Am; Mediaeval Acad Am. **RESEARCH** Comparative Romance linguistics; Italian dialectology and philology. **SELECTED PUBLICATIONS** Auth, On Placing Northern Italian Noun Singulars from Plurals of the Type Amis-Friend Within a Theory of Optimality and Markedness, Romance Philol, Vol 0048, 95. **CONTACT ADDRESS** Dept of Italian, Univ of Calif, Los Angeles, CA, 90024.

U

UDWIN, VICTOR
PERSONAL Born 01/19/1953, Bedford, England, m, 1973, 4 children **DISCIPLINE** COMPARATIVE LITERATURE **EDUCATION** Univ Calif, Berkeley, BA, 76, MA, 80, PhD, 85. **CAREER** Vis lectr, rhet, UC Berkeley, 85-86; vis prof, inst for Geistes-and Sozialwissenschaften, univ-Gesamthochschule-Siegen, Ger, 86-87; vis prof, Graduierten Kolleg, Siegen, Ger, 87; dir, Fifth Col writing prog, UC San Diego, 88-89; lectr, Ger, UC San Diego, 89-90; asst prof, 90-98, assoc prof, Ger and comp lit, Univ Tulsa, 98- . **HONORS AND AWARDS** Univ Tulsa fac develop fel, 91, 93, 95, 96, 97; UC Berkeley Comp Lit dept citation, 76; Phi Beta Kappa, 76; UC Berkeley BA with high hon, 76; Regents fel, UC Berkeley 83-84; women's studs course develop grant, 92; Okla Arts and human counc grant, 93; Okla State Senate citation for outstanding svc, 95. **MEMBERSHIPS** ACLA; APA; AATG; AAH; OFLTA; MMSA. **RESEARCH** Epic (German and Greek); Medieval studies; literary and cultural theory; Languages and literature: German, Classic Greek, Old English. **SELECTED PUBLICATIONS** Auth, Reading and Writing--the Rhetoric of Reversal, Reader 17, 87, 5-16; Reading the Red Ball--A Phenomenology of Narrative Processes, in Papers in Comp Lit 5, 88, 115-126; Der materiale Signifikant, in Materialitat der Kommunikation, Frankfurt, Suhrkamp, 88; Autopoiesis and Poetry, in Textuality and Subjectivity, Columbia, S.C., Camden House, 91; Between Two Armies, Leiden, Brill, 98. **CONTACT ADDRESS** Dept of Languages, Tulsa Univ, 600 S College Ave, Tulsa, OK, 74104. **EMAIL** udwinvm@centum.utulsa.edu

UGARTE, MICHAEL
PERSONAL Born 02/16/1949, Hanover, MA, m, 2 children **DISCIPLINE** SPANISH LITERATURE **EDUCATION** Cornell Univ, PhD, 78. **CAREER** Full Prof-writer, Univ of Missouri, 79-present. **HONORS AND AWARDS** Gugganheim Fellowship, Catherine P. Middlehash Prof, Univ of MO, Columbia, 95-99. **MEMBERSHIPS** MLA; AATSP. **RESEARCH** Modern Pennsular Lit, Cultural Studies. **CONTACT ADDRESS** Dept of Romance Languages, Univ of Missouri, Columbia, MO, 65201. **EMAIL** langmike@showme.missouri.edu

UITTI, KARL DAVID
PERSONAL Born 12/10/1933, Calumet, MI, m, 1974, 1 child **DISCIPLINE** FRENCH LITERATURE AND PHILOLOGY **EDUCATION** Univ Calif, Berkeley, BA and MA, 52, PhD, 59. **CAREER** From instr to assoc prof, 59-68, preceptor, 63-66, chmn dept, 72-78, PROF ROMANCE LANG, PRINCETON UNIV, 68-, Guggenheim Mem fel, 63-64; consult, Nat Endowment for Humanities, 76-78. **MEMBERSHIPS** Mediaeval Acad Am; MLA. **RESEARCH** Old French and Romance philology; Medieval poetics; linguistics and literary theory. **SELECTED PUBLICATIONS** Auth, An Annotated-Bibliography and Guide to Alexis Studies La Vie De Saint Alexis, Romance Philol, Vol 0046, 92; Rutebeuf, Complete Works, Vol 1, Romance Philol, Vol 0046, 93; Vernacularization and Translation--Textual Fidelity in the Romance Vernaculars--Italian, Speculum-Jour Medieval Stud, Vol 0069, 94; Villon le Grand Testament and the Poetics of Marginality, Mod Philol, Vol 0093, 95; Alexis, Roland, and French Poesie-Nationale, Comparative Lit Stud, Vol 0032, 95. **CONTACT ADDRESS** Dept of Romance Lang, Princeton Univ, Princeton, NJ, 08540.

ULATOWSKA, HANNA K.
PERSONAL Born 03/14/1933, Krynica-Zdroj, Poland **DISCIPLINE** LINGUISTICS **EDUCATION** Univ Warsaw, MA, 55; Univ Edinburgh, dipl, 59, PhD(ling), 6 1. **CAREER** Lectr English, Univ Warsaw, 55-58; res scientist ling, Georgetown Univ, 62-63; lectr, Witwatersrand Univ, 63-65; res scientist, Ling Res Ctr, Univ Tex, Austin, 65-67; comput syst analyst, Div Comput Res and Technol, NIH, 67-70, sr staff fel, 70-71; assoc prof, Univ Tex, Arlington, 71; via prof, Southern Methodist Univ, 71-72; ASSOC PROF OF LING, UNIV TEX, DALLAS, 73-, Assoc prof dept neurol, Univ Tex Health Sci Ctr, Dallas, 71. **MEMBERSHIPS** Acad Aphasia; Soc Neurosci; Ling Soc Am; MLA. **RESEARCH** Neurolinguistics. **SELECTED PUBLICATIONS** Auth, Narrative Discourse in Aphasia on the Example of Aesop Fables, Pamietnik Literacki, Vol 0085, 94. **CONTACT ADDRESS** 4422 Wildwood Rd, Dallas, TX, 75208.

ULLMAN, PIERRE LIONI
PERSONAL Born 10/31/1929, Nice, France, m, 1956, 2 children **DISCIPLINE** SPANISH **EDUCATION** Yale Univ, BA, 52; Columbia Univ, MA, 56; Princeton Univ, PhD, 62. **CAREER** Master French and Span, Choate Sch, Wallingford, Conn, 56-57; master French, Latin and Span, St Bernard's Sch, Gladstone, NJ, 57-58; asst French and Span, Princeton Univ, 58-61; instr Rutgers Univ, 61-63; asst prof Span, Univ Calif, Davis, 63-65; assoc prof, 65-48, chmn dept, 66-67, PROF SPAN, UNIV WIS-MILWAUKEE, 68- Adv ed, Papers on Lang and Lit, 66-; vis prof Span, Univ Minn, Minneapolis, 70-71; adv ed, Estudos Ibero-Americanos, Brazil, 75-; vis prof, Univ Mich, summer 75; adv ed, Los Ensayistas, 77- **MEMBERSHIPS** Am Asn Teachers Span and Port; MLA; Am Asn Teachers Esperanto; Midwest Mod Lang Asn; Universal Esperanto Asn; Esperanto League NAm. **RESEARCH** Spanish literature; contemporary Esperanto poetry. **SELECTED PUBLICATIONS** Auth, Utopia and Counterutopia in the Quixote, Hispania-Jour Devoted to the Tchg of Span and Port, Vol 0076, 93; Voices, Silences, and Echoes, a Theory of the Essays and the Critical Reception of Naturalism in Spain, Hispania-Jour Devoted to the Tchg of Span and Port, Vol 0077, 94; Psyche-Machines--Spanish, Critica Hispanica, Vol 0017, 95; Cervantes and the Burlesque Sonnet, Critica Hispanica, Vol 0017, 95; Another Fivefold Polysemous Approach to Don Juan Tenorio, Critica Hispanica, Vol 0018, 96. **CONTACT ADDRESS** Dept of Spanish and Portuguese, Univ of Wisconsin, Milwaukee, WI, 53201.

UNGAR, STEVEN RONALD
PERSONAL Born 09/08/1945, Chicago, IL, m, 1968, 2 children **DISCIPLINE** FRENCH LITERATURE **EDUCATION** Univ Wis-Madison, BA, 66, MA, 68; Cornell Univ, PhD(-French), 73. **CAREER** Asst prof French, Case Western Reserve Univ, 72-76; asst prof to assoc prof, 76-85, Prof French & Comp Lit, Univ Iowa, 85-; Lectr English, Lycee Technique d'Etat, Rennes, France, 68-69; res fel, Camargo Found, Cassis, France, 81. **MEMBERSHIPS** MLA; Asn Study of Dada & Surrealism. **RESEARCH** Modern literature and philosophical disciplines; literary criticism; applied and theoretical. **SELECTED PUBLICATIONS** Auth, Ponge, Sartre, and the ghost of Husserl, Sub-stance, 4/74; Waiting for Blanchot, Diacritics, 5/75; Parts and holes: Heraclitus, Nietzsche, Blanchot, Sub-stance, 9/76; RB: the third degree, Diacritics, 3/77; Night Moves: Spatial Perception & the Place of Blanchot's Early Fiction, 4/79 & The Professor of Desire, 6/82, Yale Fr Studies; Roland Barthes: The Professor of Desire, Univ Nebr Press, 83; co-ed, Signs in Culture: Roland Barthes Today, Univ Iowa Press, 89; auth, Scandal and Aftereffect: Maurice Blauchot and France Since 1930, Univ Minn Press, 95; co-ed, Identity Papers: Contested Nationhood in Twentieth-Century France, Univ Minn Press, 96. **CONTACT ADDRESS** Dept of French & Ital, Univ of Iowa, 555 Phillips Hall, Iowa City, IA, 52242-1409. **EMAIL** steven-ungar@uiowa.edu

UNGER, JAMES MARSHALL
PERSONAL Born 05/28/1947, Cleveland, OH **DISCIPLINE** JAPANESE LANGUAGE, LINGUISTICS **EDUCATION** Univ Chicago, BA, 69, MA, 71; Yale Univ, MA, 73, PhD(ling), 75. **CAREER** Sr lectr Japanese, Univ Canterbury, NZ, 75-76; ASST PROF JAPANESE, UNIV HAWAII, MANOA, 77- **MEMBERSHIPS** Ling Soc Am; Asn Asian Studies; Kokugo Gakkai, Japan; Asn Teachers Japanese. **RESEARCH** Historical linguistics. **SELECTED PUBLICATIONS** Auth, Chinese Script and the Diversity of Writing Systems, Ling, Vol 0032, 94. **CONTACT ADDRESS** Dept of East Asian Lang, Univ of Hawaii, Manna Honolulu, HI, 96822.

URBAIN, HENRI
PERSONAL Born 05/24/1927, Hanoi, Indochina, m, 1962, 3 children **DISCIPLINE** FRENCH LITERATURE **EDUCATION** Univ Calif, Berkeley, AB, 56, MA, 57, PhD(Romance lang & lit), 70. **CAREER** Teaching asst, Univ Calif, Berkeley, 57-61; assoc, Univ Calif, Santa Barbara, 61-63; asst prof French, San Diego State Col, 63-64 & Mills Col, 65-66; prof French, Salem State Col, 68-. **MEMBERSHIPS** MLA; Soc d'Etudes du XVIIeme siecle. **RESEARCH** Seventeenth century French literature; Franco-Spanish literary relations in the 17th century. **CONTACT ADDRESS** Dept of Foreign Lang, Salem State Col, 352 Lafayette St, Salem, MA, 01970-5353.

UZGALIS, WILLIAM
DISCIPLINE PHILOSOPHIES OF CHINA **EDUCATION** Univ Calif, Irving, BA; Calif State Univ, Long Beach, MA; Stanford Univ, PhD. **CAREER** Philos, Oregon St Univ. **SELECTED PUBLICATIONS** Auth, The Anti-Essential Locke and Natural Kinds; The Same Tyrannical Principle: The Lockean Legacy on Slavery. **CONTACT ADDRESS** Dept Philos, Oregon State Univ, Corvallis, OR, 97331-4501. **EMAIL** wuzgalis@orst.edu

V

VAHLKAMP, CHARLES G.
PERSONAL m **DISCIPLINE** FRENCH LANGUAGE AND LITERATURE **EDUCATION** Vanderbilt Univ, BA; MA; Phd. **CAREER** Fac, 67; Hazelrigg Prof Hum. **HONORS AND AWARDS** Exec Comm Fac Athletics Reps Asn, NCAA. **RESEARCH** Voltaire and the 18th century; film history and criticism. **SELECTED PUBLICATIONS** Auth, scholarly studies on Voltaire and the 18th century published in Romance Notes. **CONTACT ADDRESS** Centre Col, 600 W Walnut St, Danville, KY, 40422. **EMAIL** vahlkamp@centre.edu

VAILAKIS, IVAN GORDON
PERSONAL Quito, Ecuador **DISCIPLINE** LATIN AMERICA LITERATURE **EDUCATION** Univ Calf Irvine, PhD, **CAREER** Prof, Univ Redlands. **RESEARCH** Contemporary Latin American Poetry. **SELECTED PUBLICATIONS** Auth, Colibries en el exilio, 97; Nuestrario, 87; pubs on Gabriela Mistral, Alicia Y nez Cossio, Sandra Cisneros, and Helen Maria Viramontes. **CONTACT ADDRESS** History Dept, Univ Redlands, 1200 E Colton Ave, Box 3090, Redlands, CA, 92373-0999.

VAILLANCOURT, DANIEL
DISCIPLINE FRENCH LITERATURE **EDUCATION** Univ Quebec, BA; PhD. **RESEARCH** Semiotics; narrative theory; mystical discourse; theories of reading; travel narratives; Quebec literature. **SELECTED PUBLICATIONS** Auth, Figures and Seriation: A Semiotic Theory of Reading. **CONTACT ADDRESS** Dept of French, Western Ontario Univ, London, ON, N6A 5B8.

VALBUENA-BRIONES, ANGEL JULIAN
PERSONAL Born 01/11/1928, Madrid, Spain, m, 1957, 2 children **DISCIPLINE** HISPANIC LITERATURE **EDUCATION** Univ Murcia, MA, 49; Univ Madrid, PhD, 52. **CAREER** Lectr Span & Span-Am lit, Oxford Univ, 53-55; asst prof Span lit, Univ Madrid, 55-56; vis lectr Span-Am lit, Univ Wis, 56-58; asst prof Span lit, Yale Univ, 58-60; Elias Ahuja Prof Span Lit, Univ Del, 60- ; post-doctoral fel; Consejo Super Invest Ciient , Madrid, 70-71; vis prof, Univ Madrid, 70-71; vis prof, Inst Caro y Cuervo, Columbia, summer 80; Nat Screening bd, Fulbright-Hays Comt, Spain & Port, 80-84 & 89-91; chmn, div 16th & 17th century Span Lit, MLA, 77; Sigma Delta Pi, 56; Phi Kappa Phi, 75; UD Excellence Tchg Award, 88; Col Arts & Sci Outstanding Scholar Award, 96. **MEMBERSHIPS** Asn Teachers Span & Port; MLA; Renaissance Soc Am; Am Asn Univ Prof, Int Asn Hispanist; Asn Lit Scholars & Critics; Inst Int de Lit Iberoamericana; Anglo-Ger Asn Calderonists. **RESEARCH** Spanish Golden Age literature; Latin American literary currents; history of the Spanish languauge; history of the Spanish language. **SELECTED PUBLICATIONS** Auth, Obras completas de Calderon, Aguilar, Madrid, Vols I & II, 56, 59; Literatura Hispanoamericana, Gustavo Gili, Barcelona, 62, 4th ed, 69; Perspectiva critica de Ins dramas de Calderon, Rialp, Madrid, 65; Ideas y palabras, Eliseo Torres, 68; ed, Calderon's El alcalde de Zalamea, Anaya, Madrid, 71; Primera parte de las comedias de Calderon, Vol I, 74, Vol II, 81, Consejo Superior de Investigaciones Cientificas, Madrid; La dama duende de Calderon, 76 & El alcalde de Zalamea, Calderon, 77 Catedra, 77; auth, Calderon y la comedia nueva, Espasa-Calpe, 77; El mayor monstruo del mundo de Calderan, Juan de la Cuesta, 95; Teatro Espanol del Siglo de Oro, CD-ROM, 98. **CONTACT ADDRESS** 203 Nottingham Rd, Newark, DE, 19711. **EMAIL** 18402@udel.edu

VALDES, MARIO JAMES
PERSONAL Born 01/28/1934, Chicago, IL, m, 1955, 2 children **DISCIPLINE** SPANISH LITERATURE **EDUCATION** Univ Ill, BA, 57, MA, 59, PhD(Span), 62. **CAREER** Instr Span, Univ Mich, 62-63; from asst prof to assoc prof, 63-70, PROF SPAN AND COMP LIT, UNIV TORONTO, 70-, Dir Comp Lit, 78-, Can Coun fels, 65, 66, 67 and grant, 72-73; Victoria Col, Univ Toronto sr fel, 75; head dept Span, Ital and Port, Univ Ill, Chicago Circle, 76-78; ed, Revista Canadiense Estud Hisp, 76-; co-ed, Monogr Set Comp Lit, 78- **MEMBERSHIPS** MLA; Asn Int Hispanistas; Int Asn Comp Lit; Can Asn Comp Lit. **RESEARCH** Theory of literature; literary and philosophical studies of Unamuno; 20th century Spanish novel. **SELECTED PUBLICATIONS** Auth, Requiem For Augusto-Perez, Alterity, Alienation and Identity--Unamuno Niebla, Rev Estud Hisp, Vol 0029, 95; From Geography to Poetry--A Braudelian Comparative Literary-History of Latin-America, Can Rev Comp Lit-Rev Can Lit Comp, Vol 0023, 96; Liminaire--Constructing the Imagination, Can Rev Comp Lit-Rev Can Lit Comp, Vol 0023, 96; Forum--Interdisciplinarity in Literary-Studies-Perspectives from Particular Fields, Pmla-Pub(s) Mod Lang Assn Am, Vol 0111, 96; The Configuration of the Filmic Subject, Semiotica, Vol 0112, 96. **CONTACT ADDRESS** Dept of Comp Lit, Univ of Toronto, Toronto, ON, M5S 1A1.

VALDMAN, ALBERT
DISCIPLINE FRENCH LITERATURE **EDUCATION** Cornell Univ, PhD, 60. **CAREER** Prof. **HONORS AND AWARDS** Pres, AATF. **RESEARCH** Phonology; dialectology; sociolinguistics; applied linguistics. **SELECTED PUBLICATIONS** Co-auth, Chez Nous, Prentice Hall, 97; ed, Theoretical Orientations in Creole Studies, 80; Historicity and Variation in Creole Studies, 81; Issues in International Bilingual Education, 82); Haiti Today and Tomorrow: An Interdisciplinary Study, 84. **CONTACT ADDRESS** Dept of French and Italian, Indiana Univ, Bloomington, 300 N Jordan Ave, Bloomington, IN, 47405.

VALETTE, REBECCA MARIANNE
PERSONAL Born 12/21/1938, New York, NY, m, 1959, 3 children **DISCIPLINE** FRENCH, FOREIGN LANGUAGE EDUCATION **EDUCATION** Mt Holyoke Col, BA, 59; Univ Colo, PhD(French), 63. **CAREER** Instr and examr French and Ger, Univ SFla, 61-63; res assoc phonetics, Supreme Hq Allied Powers Europe Educ Off, Paris, 63-64; instr French, Wellesley Col, 64-65; from asst prof to assoc prof French, 65-73, PROF FRENCH, BOSTON COL, 73-, Dir Lang Lab, 65-, Fulbright Comn sr lectr, Ger, 73-74; fel acad admin, Am Coun Educ, 76-77; mem, MLA Task Force on Commonly Taught Languages. **HONORS AND AWARDS** LHD, Mt Holyoke Col, 74. **MEMBERSHIPS** Am Conn Teaching Foreign Lang; MLA; Am Asn Teachers Fr (vpres, 80-82); Am Asn Teachers Ger; Am Asn Teachers Span and Port. **RESEARCH** Modern language testing and methodology. **SELECTED PUBLICATIONS** Auth, The Challenge of the Future--Teaching Students to Speak Fluently and Accurately, Can Mod Lang Rev-Rev Can Lang Vivantes, Vol 0050, 93. **CONTACT ADDRESS** 140 Commonwealth Ave, Chestnut Hill, MA, 02167-3800.

VALIS, NOEL M.
PERSONAL Born 12/24/1945, Lakewood, NJ, d, 1 child **DISCIPLINE** SPANISH/FRENCH STUDIES **EDUCATION** Douglas College, BA, summa cum laude, 68; Bryn Mawr, MA, 75, PhD, 75. **CAREER** Prof, Ch, 91-, John Hopkins Univ; vis Prof, 95, NY Univ; vis Prof, 93, Bryn Mawr College; Prof, 86-91, Univ Michigan; vis Prof, 85-86, Univ Penn; Asst Prof, Assoc Prof, 77-85, Univ Georgia; Lectr, 71-72,76-77, Rosemont College. **HONORS AND AWARDS** Phi Beta Kappa; Woodrow Wilson Fel; NDEA Grad Fel; NEH Fel; US Spain Friend/Treaty Res Fel. **MEMBERSHIPS** MLA; AIH; AIG; FUCL. **RESEARCH** 19th & 20th Century Literature and Culture; Gender Studies; Translation. **SELECTED PUBLICATIONS** Auth, Poetry of Julia Uceda, intro, trans, NY, Peter Lang, 95; Prelude to Pleasure, by Pedro, trans, intro, Lewisburg, Bucknell UP, 93; Confesion y cuerpo en Insolacion, de Emilia Pardo Bazan, Estudios sobre Emilia Pardo Bazan, ed, JMG Herran, Santiago de Compostela, Santiago Univ, 97; Aspects of an Improper Birth: Clarin's La Rengenta, New Hispanisms Li Culture Theory, ed PJ Smith, Mark Millington, Ottawa, Dovehouse, 94; La autoridad en Galdos, Insuls, 93; auth, Fabricating Culture in Galdos's Canovas, MLN, 92; books in progress: Metaphor and Identity in Modern Spain; Body Sacraments; Hispanic Narratives of Authority and Revelation. **CONTACT ADDRESS** Dept of Hispanic and Italian Studies, Johns Hopkins Univ, 3400 N Charles St, Baltimore, MD, 21218. **EMAIL** valis@jhuvms.hcf.jhu.edu

VALLEY, DAVID B.
PERSONAL Born 09/12/1944, Rock Island, IL, m, 1990, 3 children **DISCIPLINE** SPEECH COMMUNICATIONS **EDUCATION** Univ of IL, PhD; IL St Univ, MS; Blackhawk Cmnty Col, AS **CAREER** 82-, Prof, S IL Univ **HONORS AND AWARDS** Tch Recog awd, 93 **MEMBERSHIPS** Nat Commun Asn; Cent Sts Speech Asn **RESEARCH** Parent-child conversation **SELECTED PUBLICATIONS** Auth, A History and Analysis of Democratic Presidential Nomination Acceptance Speeches to 1968, Univ Press of America, 88 **CONTACT ADDRESS** Dept of Speech Commun, So Illinois Univ, Edwardsville, IL, 62026-1772. **EMAIL** dvalley@siue.edu

VALLONE, RALPH, JR.
PERSONAL Born 04/15/1947, Philadelphia, PA **DISCIPLINE** ROMANCE LITERATURE **EDUCATION** Yale Univ, BA, 66, MPhil; Harvard Law Sch, LLD. **CAREER** Prof law, Interamericana Univ, PR, 71-72; atty at law to present; exec dir New San Juan Health Ctr. **MEMBERSHIPS** Am Bar Asn; Hispanic Bar Asn; Am Soc Law and Medicine. **RESEARCH** History; Egyptology; science; mathematics; chess; behavioral sciences. **SELECTED PUBLICATIONS** Auth, Second Vision, Dutton, 95. **CONTACT ADDRESS** 16 Carrion Ct, San Juan, PR, 00911.

VAN, THOMAS A.
PERSONAL Born 05/22/1938, New York, NY, m, 1963 **DISCIPLINE** ENGLISH, LINGUISTICS **EDUCATION** City Col New York, BA, 60; Duke Univ, MA, 63, PhD(English), 66. **CAREER** Instr English, Univ NC, Chapel Hill, 65-66; asst prof, Univ Ky, 66-70; ASSOS PROF ENGLISH, UNIV LOUISVILLE, 70-, CHMN DEPT, 80-. **MEMBERSHIPS** MLA; NCTE; Mediaeval Acad Am; fel NDEA. **RESEARCH** Dante; Chaucer; Shakespeare. **SELECTED PUBLICATIONS** Auth, False Texts and Disappearing Women in the Wife of Baths Prologue and Tale--An Analysis of the Thematic Development of Contradiction and Anomaly Between Teller and Tale in the Canterbury Tales of Chaucer, Geoffrey, Chaucer Rev, Vol 0029, 94. **CONTACT ADDRESS** Dept of English, Univ of Louisville, Louisville, KY, 40208.

VAN BAELEN, JACQUELINE
DISCIPLINE FRENCH LANGUAGE AND LITERATURE **EDUCATION** Vassar Univ, BA; MA; UCLA, PhD. **CAREER** Prof emer, SUNY Binghamton. **RESEARCH** 17th Century French lit; feminist lit and criticism. **SELECTED PUBLICATIONS** Auth, publ in 17th xentury French lit. **CONTACT ADDRESS** SUNY Binghamton, PO Box 6000, Binghamton, NY, 13902-6000. **EMAIL** frances@binghamton.edu

VAN DEN HOVEN, ADRIAN
DISCIPLINE FRENCH **CAREER** Prof & dir, 3rd Yr Nice prog; co-ed, Sartre Stud Int. **MEMBERSHIPS** Conseil d'Administration of the Groupe d'etudes sartriennes. **SELECTED PUBLICATIONS** Pub (s), Sartre, de Beauvoir and Camus; transl, Truth and Existence and of Hope Now, The Sartre-Benny Levy Interviews, 80; co-ed, Sartre Alive. **CONTACT ADDRESS** Dept of French Language and Literature, Univ of Windsor, 401 Sunset Ave, Windsor, ON, N9B 3P4. **EMAIL** vdhoven@uwindsor.ca

VAN SETERS, JOHN
PERSONAL Born 05/02/1935, Hamilton, ON, Canada, m, 1960, 2 children **DISCIPLINE** OLD TESTAMENT, NEAR EASTERN STUDIES **EDUCATION** Univ Toronto, BA, 58; Yale Univ, MA, 59, PhD(Near Eastern studies), 65; Princeton Theol Sem, BD, 62. **CAREER** Asst prof Near Eastern studies, Waterloo Lutheran Univ, 65-67; assoc prof Old Testament, Andover Newton Theol Sch, 67-70; assoc prof Near Eastern studies, Univ Toronto, 70-76, prof Near Eastern studies, 76-77; James A Gray Prof Bibl Lit, Dept Of Relig, Univ NC, Chapel Hill, 77- & Chmn Dept, 80-88, 93-95. **HONORS AND AWARDS** Woodrow Wilson fel, 58; Princeton fel Old Testament, 62; Obermann fel Yale, 62, 63; Agusta-Hazard Fel, 64; Canada Council res grant, 73; Guggenheim Mem Award; 79-80; NEH sem, 84, 89; NEH res fel, 85-86; ACLS res fel, 91-92; sen res fel, Katholiek Univ Leuven, 97; AHA Breasted Prize, 85; Am Acad Rel bok award, 86; Canadian Hist Asn Ferguson Prize, hon men, 86., Assoc dir Wadi Tumilat archaeol expedition to Tell el Maskhuta, Egypt, 78,81. **MEMBERSHIPS** Am Schs Orient Res; Soc Bibl Lit; Soc Study Egyptian Antiq; Am Orient Soc. **RESEARCH** Book of Genesis; Pentateuch; historical books: Joshua to II Kings. **SELECTED PUBLICATIONS** Auth, The Hyksos: A New Investigation, Yale Univ, 66; The conquest of Sihon's kingdom: A literary examination, J Bibl Lit, 72; The terms Amorite and Hittite in the Old Testament, 72 & Confessional reformulation in the exilic period, 72, Vetus Testamentum; Abraham in History and Tradition, Yale Univ, 75; Recent studies on the Pentateuch: A crisis in method, J Am Orient Soc, 79; The religion of the patriarchs in Genesis, Biblica, 80; Histories and historians of the Ancient Near East: The Israelite, Orientalia, 81; auth, Prologue to History: The Yahwist as Historian in Genesis, Westminster/John Knox Press and Theologischer Verlag (Zurich), 92; auth, The Life of Moses: The Yawhist as Historian in Exodus-Numbers, Westminster/John Knox Press and Kok-Pharos:Lampen, Netherlands, 94; auth, From Faithful Prophet to Villain: Observations on the Tradition History of the Balaam Story, in a Biblical Itinerary: In Search of Method, Form and Content. Essays in Honor of George W. Coats, 97; auth, Solomon's Temple: Fact and Ideology in Biblical and Near Eastern Historiography, Catholic Bibl Q 59, 97; auth, The Deuteronomistic Redaction of the Pentateuch: The CAse Against it. in Deuteronomy and Deuteronomic Literature: Festscrift for C Brekelmans, Leuven Univ Press, 97; auth, The Pentateuch, in The Hebrew Bible Today, Westminster/John Knox Press, 98; scholarly revs in Lutheran World, J Am Oriental Soc, J Bibl Lit, Biblio Orientalis, J Egyptian Archaeol, Orientalistische Literaturzeitung. **CONTACT ADDRESS** Dept of Relig, Univ of North Carolina, Chapel Hill, 101 Saunders Hall, Box 3225, Chapel Hill, NC, 27599. **EMAIL** jvanset@email.unc.edu

VAN VLIET, EDWARD R.
DISCIPLINE LINGUISTICS **EDUCATION** Bowdoin Col, AB, 65; Brown Univ, AM, 67, PhD, 73. **CAREER** Adj, Brown Univ, Univ RI, 65-77; asst prof, Salve Regina Univ, 69-71; asst prof, 71-74, chair, dept mod lang, 72-78, assoc prof, 74-80, Elizabethtown Col; instr, Interlangues, Paris, vic lectr, Univ Paris, 77-78; headmaster, Cellucam Int Sch, Cameroon, 78-79; assoc, SUNY, 80-92; postgrad stud, Syracuse Univ, 91-92; prof, Kansai Gaidai Univ, Osaka, 94-97; ASSOC PROF, SUNY, GENESCO, 80-. **CONTACT ADDRESS** 2051 Livonia Ctr Rd, Lima, NY, 14485-0269. **EMAIL** vanvliet@uno.cc.genesco.edu

VANCE, BARBARA
DISCIPLINE FRENCH LITERATURE **EDUCATION** Cornell Univ, PhD, 89. **CAREER** Assoc prof. **SELECTED PUBLICATIONS** Auth, Syntactic Change in Medieval French, 97; articles on the syntax of Old, Middle, and Modern French. **CONTACT ADDRESS** Dept of French and Italian, Indiana Univ, Bloomington, 300 N Jordan Ave, Bloomington, IN, 47405.

VANCE, TIMOTHY
PERSONAL Born 08/25/1951, Minneapolis, MN **DISCIPLINE** JAPANESE LANGUAGE **EDUCATION** WA Univ, BA, 73; Univ Chicago, MA, 76, PhD, 79. **CAREER** Lectr, Univ IL, 79-80; asst prof, Univ FL, 81-86; asst prof, 86-88; assoc prof, Univ HI, 88-93; assoc prof, 93-94; prof, CT Col, 94-. **HONORS AND AWARDS** Am Oriental Soc; Asn Asian Studies: Asn Tchr Japanese; Int Phonetic Asn; Ling Soc Am. **RESEARCH** Phonology; Japanese linguistics. **SELECTED PUBLICATIONS** Auth, An Introduction to Japanese Phonology, Univ NY, 87; Instant Vocabulary through Prefixes and Suffixes, Kodansha Int, 90; Final Accent vs. No Accent: Utterance Final Neutralization in Tokyo Japanese, Jour Phonetics, 95; Sequential Voicing in Sino-Japanese, Jour Asn Tchr Japanese, 96; **CONTACT ADDRESS** Connecticut Col, Mohegan Ave, PO Box 270, New London, CT, 06320. **EMAIL** tjvan@conncoll.edu

VANDELOISE, CLAUDE
DISCIPLINE FRENCH LINGUISTICS, COGNITIVE LINGUISTICS **EDUCATION** Univ Calif, PhD, 84. **CAREER** Prof, La State Univ. **SELECTED PUBLICATIONS** Auth, Spatial Prepositions, A Case Study in French, 91; S?mantique cognitive, in Commun, 91; La couleur des pr?positions, 93. **CONTACT ADDRESS** Dept of Fr Grad Stud, Louisiana State Univ, Baton Rouge, LA, 70803.

VANN, ROBERTA JEANNE
PERSONAL Born 12/17/1947, Indianapolis, IN, 1 child **DISCIPLINE** TEACHING ENGLISH AS A FOREIGN LANGUAGE, APPLIED LINGUISTICS **EDUCATION** Ind Univ, AB, 70, MS, 73, PhD(English educ), 78. **CAREER** Instr teaching English as for lang, Haile Selaissie I Univ, Gondar, Ethiopia, 70-71; Fulbright lectr, Univ Gdansk, Poland, 74-76; asst prof English, 78-83, assoc prof, 83-91, prof 81-, dir intensive English & orientation prog, Iowa State Univ, 80-, Lang consult, US, Int Info Agency, 75-95. **MEMBERSHIPS** NCTE; Teaching English to Speakers Other Lang. **RESEARCH** Second language learning. **SELECTED PUBLICATIONS** Auth, Bilingual education today: The unresolved issues, Lang Arts, 2/78; Oral and written syntactic relationships in second language learning, In: On TESOL '79: The Learner in Focus, TESOL, 79; co-ed, Connections and Contrasts: Exploring Speaking and Writing Relationships & auth, Bridging the gap between oral and written communication in EFL, In: Connections and Contrasts, NCTE, 81. **CONTACT ADDRESS** English Dept, Iowa State Univ, Ames, IA, 50011-0002. **EMAIL** rvann@iastnte.edu

VANPATTEN, BILL
DISCIPLINE SPANISH LITERATURE **EDUCATION** Univ Tex, PhD, 83. **CAREER** Prof, Univ Ill Urbana-Champaign. **RESEARCH** Second language acquisition theory and research; input processing; psycholinguistics of focus on form. **SELECTED PUBLICATIONS** Auth, On the Relevance of Input Processing to Second Language Acquisition Theory and Second Language Instruction, Cascadilla, 97; Input Processing and Grammar Instruction: Theory and Research, Norwood, 95; coauth, The Effects of Intrasentential Context on Second Language Sentence Processing, Spanish Applied Ling, 98; On Input and Output Practice in Second Language Acquisition: a Response to Salaberry, Can Modern Lang Rev, 98; Acoustic Salience: Testing Location, Stress and the Boundedness of Grammatical Form in Second Language Acquisition Input Perception, Cascadilla, 97; Making Communicative Language Teaching Happen, McGraw-Hill, 95. **CONTACT ADDRESS** Spanish, Italian, and Portuguese Dept, Univ Ill Urbana Champaign, 52 E Gregory Dr, Champaign, IL, 61820. **EMAIL** bvp@uiuc.edu

VARALLO, SHARON
DISCIPLINE INTERPERSONAL COM, FAMILY AND GENDER COMMUNICATION **EDUCATION** PhD, OH State Univ, MA, Univ of NC, Chapel Hill, BA, Col of William and Mary. **CAREER** Comm, Cleveland St Univ. **SELECTED PUBLICATIONS** Co-auth, Dialectic of Difference: A Thematic Analysis of Intimates' Meanings for Differences, Interpretive Approaches to Interpersonal Communication, 94; auth, Family Photos: A Generic Critique, Rhetorical Criticism: Exploration and Practice, 96. **CONTACT ADDRESS** Commun Dept, Cleveland State Univ, 83 E 24th St, Cleveland, OH, 44115.

VARGAS, MARGARITA
PERSONAL Born 05/20/1956, El Paso, TX, m, 1984, 3 children **DISCIPLINE** SPANISH LITERATURE **EDUCATION** Univ Kansas, PhD 85, MA 82; Yale Univ BA 79. **CAREER** SUNY Buffalo, vis prof, asst prof, assoc prof, 85 to 98-. **HONORS AND AWARDS** Elected to MLA Del Assem Org Comm; Chancellor's Awd; Sigma Delta Pi; Yale Cum laude; Bildner Prize; DeForest Prize. **MEMBERSHIPS** MLA; AATSP; FU **RESEARCH** Questions of Identity in Span/Amer Theater; Post modernism and feminism; Translation. **SELECTED PUBLICATIONS** Auth, Power and Resistance in De noche vienes, by Elena Poniatowska, Hispanic Jour, 95; Mexican Romanticism, Mexican Literature: A History, ed, David William Foster, trans, David E Johnson, Austin, U of TX Press, 94; Bio-bibliographic entries in: Dictionary of Mexican Literature, ed, Eladio Cortes, 13 entries, Westport CT and London, Greenwood, 92; Women Writing Women: An Anthology of Spanish-American Theater og the 1980's, co-trans, Albany, SUNY Press, 97; The House on the Beach, by Juan Garcia Ponce, co-trans, Austin, U of TX Press, 94. **CONTACT ADDRESS** Dept of Modern Languages and Literature, SUNY Buffalo, 910 Clemens Hall, Buffalo, NY, 14260. **EMAIL** mvargas@acsu.buffalo.edu

VARTABEDIAN, ROBERT A.
PERSONAL Born 08/27/1952, Fresno, CA, m, 1978, 2 children **DISCIPLINE** SPEECH COMMUNICATION **EDUCATION** CA State Univ, Fresno, BA (speech commun, magna cum laude), 74, CA Teaching Credential, 75; Wichita State Univ, MA (speech commun), 80; Univ OK, PhD (Commun), 81. **CAREER** Graduate asst, part-time instr, CA State Univ, Fresno, 74-75, 77; res asst, Wichita State Univ, 77-78; grad asst, Univ OK, 78-80; asst prof, East Central OK State Univ, 80-81; Dir of forensics, 81-86, head, div of rhetoric and commun, 85-88, coord, grad studies in commun, 86-87, asst dean of graduate studies, Wichita State Univ, 87-88; head, dept of Art, Commun, & Theatre, 88-93, assoc prof, 88-92, prof, West TX A&M Univ, 92-. **HONORS AND AWARDS** Outstanding Teaching award, Univ OK, 80; Outstanding Dir of Forensics Award, Univ UT, 83; President's Award, Nat Intercollegiate Cross Examination Debate Asn, 86; Mortar Board Teaching Award, Wichita State Univ, 88; Dean's nominee for Outstanding Graduate Fac Award, WTAMU, 91, 93; Carnegie Found Prof of the Year, WTAMU, 94; Greek Council, Outstanding Fac Member Award, WTAMU, 96; Univ Teaching Excellence Award, WTAMU, 96; Univ Piper Professorship, WTAMU, 97. **MEMBERSHIPS** Am Forensic Asn; Central States Commun Asn; Cross Examination Debate Asn; Int Commun Asn; TX Speech Commun Asn; Nat Forensic Asn; Nat Commun Asn; West TX Speech Commun Asn. **RESEARCH** Presidential rhetoric; political communication; rhetorical criticism. **SELECTED PUBLICATIONS** Co-auth, with L K Vartabedian, Humor in the Workplace: A Communication Challenge, in Resources in Ed, 93; auth, Recruitment and Retention of Graduate Faculty at the Non-Doctoral Graduate Program, in Resources in Ed, 93; with J M Burger, Self-Disclosure and Decreased Persuasiveness of Political Speakers, in Resources in Ed, 94; auth, the Loud, Clear, and Transporting Voice of Oral Interpretation, in Resources in Ed, 95; with J M Burger, Self-Disclosure and Decreased Persuasiveness of Political Speakers, Speech Commun Annual, 10, 96; auth, Scholarly vs Non-Scholarly Print Sources, in L W Hugenberg and B S Moyer, eds, Teaching Ideas for the Basic Communication Course, in press; Audience Analysis, in L W Hugenberg and B S Moyer, eds, Teaching Ideas for the Basic Communication Course, in press; with R A Knight, Jones v. Clinton and the Apologetic Imperative, Speaker and Gavel, in press; numerous other publications. **CONTACT ADDRESS** 95 Jynteewood Dr, Canyon, TX, 79015. **EMAIL** robert.vartabedian@wtamu.edu

VASVARI, LOUISE O.
PERSONAL Born 05/13/1943, Budapest, Hungary **DISCIPLINE** COMPARATIVE LITERATURE **EDUCATION** Montclair State Univ, BA, 63; Univ Ca, MA, 66, PhD, 69. **CAREER** Prof, 84-. **HONORS AND AWARDS** John K. Walsh Prize, 94. **MEMBERSHIPS** Am Comp Lit Asn; MLA; Ling Soc Am; Boccaccio Soc; Int Lings Asn; Asn Int de Hispanistas; Asn Hispanica de Literatura Medieval; Medieval Acad; Hungarian-Am Educr Asn. **SELECTED PUBLICATIONS** Auth, Festive Phallic Discourse in the Libro del Arcipreste, 94; The usignuolo in gabbia in the Decameron: Popular Tradition and Pornographic Parody, 94; Joseph on the Margin in the Merode Mousetrap, 95; Don Huron Trickster: Un arquetipo psicofolklorico, 95; Multiple Transparencia Semantica de los Nombres de la Alcahueta en el Libro del Arcipreste, 95; Nouns and Countability: Towards A Contrastive Teaching Grammar of English and Spanish, 95. **CONTACT ADDRESS** English Dept, SUNY Stony Brook, Stony Brook, NY, 11794. **EMAIL** LVasvari@ccmail.sunysb.edu

VAUTIER, MARIE
DISCIPLINE COMPARATIVE CANADIAN LITERATURE **EDUCATION** Univ Toronto, PhD. **RESEARCH** Literary theory; Quebecois literature; stylistics and translation. **SELECTED PUBLICATIONS** Auth, New World Myth: Postmodernism and Postcolonialism in Canadian Fiction, McGill-Queen's UP, 98; Comparative Postcolonialism and the Amerindian in English-speaking Canada and Quebec, Can Ethnic Stud, 96; Les metarecits, le postmodernisme et le mythe postcolonial au Quebec, Etudes litteraires, 94; Postmodern Myth, Post-European History, and the Figure of the Amerindian: Francois Barcelo, George Bowering, and Jacques Poulin, Can Lit 141, 94. **CONTACT ADDRESS** Dept of French, Victoria Univ, PO Box 3045 STN CSC, Victoria, BC, V8W 3P4. **EMAIL** mvautier@uvic.ca

VELEZ, JOSEPH FRANCISCO
PERSONAL Born 01/29/1928, Puebla, Mexico, m, 1969, 6 children **DISCIPLINE** ROMANCE LANGUAGES, THEOLOGY **EDUCATION** Howard Payne Univ, BA, 62; Univ Okla, MA, 68, PhD(romance lang), 69. **CAREER** Instr Span, Univ Okla, 65-68; from asst prof to assoc prof Span and French, Western Ky Univ, 68-71; co-chmn dept Span, 76-77, ASSOC PROF SPAN, BAYLOR UNIV, 71-, DIR LATIN AM STUDIES, 77-, Interim pastor for Span speaking congregation, First Baptist Church, Marlin, Tex, 81. **MEMBERSHIPS** MLA; SCent Mod Lang Asn; Nat Asn Chicano Studies; Am Asn Teachers Span and Port; AAUP. **RESEARCH** Latin American literature. **SELECTED PUBLICATIONS** Auth, Paradise-Lost or Gained, the Literature of Hispanic Exile, Hispania-Jour Devoted Tchg Span and Port, Vol 0076, 93. **CONTACT ADDRESS** Dept of Spanish, Baylor Univ, Waco, TX, 76798.

VENA, MICHAEL
PERSONAL Born 07/04/1941, Jelsi, Italy **DISCIPLINE** FOREIGN LANGUAGES **EDUCATION** Univ Bridgeport, BA, 65; Yale Univ, MA, 67, PhD(Ital), 72; Univ Rome, dipl Ital, 72. **CAREER** Lectr Ital, Yale Univ, 69-70; assoc prof, 70-80, PROF ITAL, SOUTHERN CONN STATE COL, 80-, CHMN DEPT FOREIGN LANG, 76-. **MEMBERSHIPS** MLA; Am Asn Teachers Ital. **RESEARCH** Renaissance literature and language; modern theatre. **SELECTED PUBLICATIONS** Auth, The Grotteschi Revisited--20th-Century Grotesque Theater, Forum Italicum, Vol 0031, 97. **CONTACT ADDRESS** Dept of Ital, Southern Conn State Col, 501 Crescent St, New Haven, CT, 06515-1330.

VENCLOVA, TOMAS ANDRIUS
PERSONAL Born 09/11/1937, Klaipeda, Lithuania, m, 1990, 2 children **DISCIPLINE** SLAVIC & LITHUANIAN LITERATURES **EDUCATION** Univ Vilnius, dipl, 60; Yale Univ, PhD, 85. **CAREER** Lectr lit, Univ Vilnius, 66-73; jr fel semiotics, Acad Sci, Lithuania, 74-76; Regents prof semiotics art, Univ Calif, Berkeley, 77; lectr semiotics art, Univ Calif, Los Angeles, 77-80; Lectr Russ Lit, 80-85, Asst prof Slavic Lit, 85-90, Assoc prof Slavic Lit, 90-93, PROF SLAVIC LIT, 93- ,YALE UNIV, 80- ; Lit consult, Siauliai Drama Theater, Lithuania, 74-76. **HONORS AND AWARDS** Int Lit Prize Vilenica, 90; Dr Hon Causa, Univ Dublin, 91. **MEMBERSHIPS** PEN Club; Am Asn Advan Slavic Studies; Am Asn Tchr Slavic E Europ Lang; Asn Advan Baltic Stud (pres, 89-91). **RESEARCH** Slavic literatures; Lithuanian literature; semiotics of art. **SELECTED PUBLICATIONS** Auth, Unstable Equilibrium: Eight Rusden Poetic Texts, Yale Ctr Int & Area Stud, 86; Aleksender Wat: Life and Art of an Iconoclast, Yale Univ Press, 96; Participants in the Feast, Baltos Lankos, 97. **CONTACT ADDRESS** Dept of Slavic Lang & Lit, Yale Univ, PO Box 208236, New Haven, CT, 06520-8236. **EMAIL** tomas.venclova@yale.edu

VERANI, HUGO JUAN
PERSONAL Born 04/04/1941, Montevideo, Uruguay, m, 1964, 2 children **DISCIPLINE** LATIN AMERICAN LITERATURE **EDUCATION** Phillips Univ, AB, 66; Univ Wis-Madison, MA, 67, PhD(Span), 73. **CAREER** From instr to asst prof, Mt Holyoke Col, 70-74; asst prof, 74-78, assoc prof, 78-82, PROF SPAN, UNIV CALIF, DAVIS, 82-. **MEMBERSHIPS** MLA; Am Asn Teachers Span and Port; Inst Int Lit Iberam; Asn Int Hispanistas; Philol Asn Pac Coast. **RESEARCH** Contemporary Spanish American literature; 20th century fiction; literary theory. **SELECTED PUBLICATIONS** Auth, Onetti, Juan, Carlos 1909-1994--In-Memoriam, Rev Iberoamericana, Vol 0060, 94. **CONTACT ADDRESS** Dept of Spanish, Univ of Calif, Davis, CA, 95616.

VERDESIO, GUSTAVO
DISCIPLINE LATIN AMERICAN COLONIAL LITERATURE, LITERARY THEORY, 19TH CENTURY LATIN AME **EDUCATION** Northwestern Univ, PhD, 92. **CAREER** Asst prof Span, undergrad adv, Span, grad comt for Span grad prog, dept travel comt, La State Univ. **RESEARCH** Latin American colonial literature; literary theory. **SELECTED PUBLICATIONS** Auth, Escritura e identidad cultural en el Uruguay colonial, in Letterature d' America: Revista Trimestrale, Univ Roma, l3, 49, 93; Una ausencia en el canon: Los discursos coloniales sobre el Uruguay en el marco de la historiografia literaria uruguaya y los estudios coloniales latinoamericanos, Revista Iberoamericana, 60, 95. **CONTACT ADDRESS** Dept of For Lang and Lit, Louisiana State Univ, 141 B Prescott Hall, Baton Rouge, LA, 70803. **EMAIL** verdesio@homer.forlang.lsu.edu

VERENE, DONALD PHILLIP
DISCIPLINE GERMAN IDEALISM **EDUCATION** WA Univ, PhD, 64. **CAREER** Philos, Emory Univ. **HONORS AND AWARDS** Vis fel, Pembroke Col, Oxford Univ, 88; Dir seminar "Barbarism, Memory, and Rhetoric", Folger Inst, 94. **SELECTED PUBLICATIONS** Auth, Vico's Science of Imagination; Hegel's Recollection: A Study of Images in the Phenomenology of Spirit; The New Art of Autobiography: An Essay on the "Life of Giambattista Vico, Written by Himself"; Ed, Hegel's Social and Political Thought; Symbol, Myth, and Culture: Essays and Lectures of Ernst Cassirer 1935-45; Vico and Joyce; Coed, Giambattista Vico's Science of Humanity. **CONTACT ADDRESS** Emory Univ, Atlanta, GA, 30322-1950.

VERGNAUD, JEAN-ROGER
DISCIPLINE LINGUISTICS **EDUCATION** MIT, PhD. **CAREER** Prof, Univ Southern Calif. **RESEARCH** Syntax; Phonology; Morphology. **SELECTED PUBLICATIONS** Auth, Dependances et niveaux de representation en syntaxe, John Benjamins BV, 85; coauth, An Essay on Stress, MIT Press, 87. **CONTACT ADDRESS** Dept of Linguistics, Univ Southern Calif, University Park Campus, Los Angeles, CA, 90089. **EMAIL** vergnaud@usc.edu

VERMETTE, ROSALIE ANN
PERSONAL Born 05/10/1946, Lewiston, ME, m, 1982 **DISCIPLINE** FRENCH LANGUAGE & LITERATURE **EDUCATION** Univ Maine, Orono, AB, 68; Univ Iowa, MA, 70, PhD(French), 75. **CAREER** Lectr English, Univ Poitiers, France, 72-73; from instr to asst prof French, Univ Iowa, 74-76; from assoc prof to prof French, Ind Univ/Purdue Univ, Indianapolis, 76-. **HONORS AND AWARDS** Phi Beta Kappa, 68. **MEMBERSHIPS** Mediaeval Acad Am; Int Arthurian Soc; MLA; Am Asn Teachers Fr; Midwest Mod Lang Asn. **RESEARCH** Medieval French hagiographic textual studies; medieval French romance studies; textual criticism. **SELECTED PUBLICATIONS** Auth, The Huit Beatitudes in old French prose, Manuscripta, 74; coauth, Un manuscit inconnu de Bartolomeo Visconti: les Dialogi de Gregoire le grand, Scriptorium, 78; auth, An Unrecorded Fragment of Richart d'Irlande's Propheties de Merlin, Romance Philol, 81; Some Dim Notion, the World Viewed Through Old French Saints' Lives, Romance Lanugages Annual, 94. **CONTACT ADDRESS** Dept of French, Indiana Univ-Purdue Univ, Indianapolis, 425 University Blvd, Indianapolis, IN, 46202-5148. **EMAIL** ruermette@iupui.edu

VERNIER, RICHARD
PERSONAL Born 02/01/1929, Clermont-Ferrand, France, m, 1962, 3 children **DISCIPLINE** FRENCH LITERATURE **EDUCATION** Univ Calif, Berkeley, AB, 58, PhD(Romance lang), 65. **CAREER** Lectr French, City Col New York, 62-63; asst prof, San Diego State Col, 63-66 and Univ Wash, 66-72; assoc prof, State Univ NY Fredonia, 72-73; ASSOC PROF FRENCH, WAYNE STATE UNIV, DETROIT, 73-, Vis assoc prof, Scripps Col, 75-76. **HONORS AND AWARDS** Palmes Academiques, Fr Govt, 81. **MEMBERSHIPS** MLA; Am Asn Teachers Fr. **RESEARCH** Modern poetry and poetics; French culture and civilization; Swiss-French literature. **SELECTED PUBLICATIONS** Auth, In the Time of Talking Animals--Folkloric Influences in Milosz, O.V.Del. Works, Europe-Rev Lit Mensuelle, Vol 0073, 95. **CONTACT ADDRESS** 1706 Oxford, Berkley, MI, 48072.

VERNOFF, CHARLES ELLIOTT
PERSONAL Born 02/11/1942, Miami, FL **DISCIPLINE** COMPARATIVE PHILOSOPHY OF RELIGION **EDUCATION** Univ Chicago, BA, 63; Univ Calif, Santa Barbara, MA, 72, PhD(relig studies), 79. **CAREER** Prof Relig, Cornell Col, 78-. **MEMBERSHIPS** Am Acad Relig; Asn Jewish Studies. **RESEARCH** Theory and method in the study of religion; modern Jewish thought; Holocaust studies. **SELECTED PUBLICATIONS** Auth, Towards a transnatural Judaic theology of Halakhah, In: Jewish Essays and Studies, Vol II, Reconstructionist Rabbinical Col Press, 81. **CONTACT ADDRESS** Dept of Relig, Cornell Col, 600 First St W, Mount Vernon, IA, 52314-1098.

VESSELY, THOMAS RICHARD
PERSONAL Born 11/06/1944, San Marcos, TX, m, 1978, 1 child **DISCIPLINE** FRENCH LITERATURE **EDUCATION** Ind Univ, PhD, 79. **CAREER** Asst Prof French, Univ Tex, Austin, 79-. **MEMBERSHIPS** MLA; Am Asn Teachers Fr; Soc 18th Century Studies. **RESEARCH** The French fairy tale; short prose fiction. **SELECTED PUBLICATIONS** Auth, Innocence and impotence: The scenario of initiation in L'Ecumoire and in the literary fairy tale, 18th Century Life, 82. **CONTACT ADDRESS** Dept Fr & Ital, Univ Tex, Austin, TX, 78712-1026. **EMAIL** trv@mail.utexas.edu

VETRANO, ANTHONY JOSEPH
PERSONAL Born 02/03/1931, Endicott, NY, m, 1964, 2 children **DISCIPLINE** ROMANCE LANGUAGES **EDUCATION** State Univ NY Binghamton, BA, 55; Univ Rochester, MA, 56; Syracuse Univ, PhD(Romance lang), 66. **CAREER** From instr to assoc prof, 59-74, prof mod lang, Le Moyne Col, 74-, chemn dept, 62-86; fac res grants, Le Moyne Col, 67-68 & 73-74. **MEMBERSHIPS** AAUP; MLA; Am Asn Teachers Span & Port. **RESEARCH** Twentieth century Spanish American novel, especially the Ecuadorian novel of social protest; modern Spanish Peninsular literature; Italian Trecento. **SELECTED PUBLICATIONS** Auth, Imagery in Two of Jorge Icaza's Novels: Huasipungo and Huairapamushcas, Rev Estudios Hisp, 5/72; La problematica Psico-social y su correlacion linguistica en las novelas de Jorge Icaza, Ed Universal, 74; Jorge Icaza and the Spanish-American Indianist Novel: Some Observations on Huasipungo, In: Studies in Romance Languages and Literature, State Univ NY Binghamton, 79. **CONTACT ADDRESS** Dept of For Lang & Lit, LeMoyne Col, 1419 Salt Springs Rd, Syracuse, NY, 13214-1300. **EMAIL** vetrano@maple.lemoyne.edu

VICKERS, NANCY
DISCIPLINE FRENCH AND ITALIAN COMPARATIVE LITERATURE **EDUCATION** Yale Univ, PhD. **CAREER** Prof, Univ Southern Calif. **RESEARCH** Poetic and the plastic arts of early modern culture. **SELECTED PUBLICATIONS** Publ on, Petrarch; Marot; Labe; Cellini & Shakespeare; co-ed, Rewriting the Renaissance: The Discourses of Sexual Difference in Early Modern Europe, 86. **CONTACT ADDRESS** Col Letters, Arts & Sciences, Univ Southern Calif, University Park Campus, Los Angeles, CA, 90089. **EMAIL** vickers@usc.edu

VICKERY, WALTER
PERSONAL Born 09/14/1921, London, England, m, 6 children **DISCIPLINE** SLAVIC LANGUAGE AND LITERATURE **EDUCATION** Oxford Univ, BA, 48, MA, 52; Harvard Univ, PhD, 58. **CAREER** Lectr Russ, Oxford Univ, 48-53; from asst prof to assoc prof Slavic lang and lit, Ind Univ, Bloomington, 58-64; prof, Univ Colo, 64-69; PROF SLAVIC LANG AND LIT, UNIV NC, CHAPEL HILL, 69-, Ind Univ fac fel, Oxford Univ, 63; Fulbright-Hays fel, Italy, 65; Am Coun Learned Soc fel, Leningrad, 67-68; Univ Colo fac fel, Italy, 68; mem screening comt, Int Asn Exchange of Persons, 72-; vis prof Yale Univ, 75; exchange scholar, Am Coun Learned Soc, Soviet Acad, 1-6/76. **MEMBERSHIPS** Am Asn Advan Slavic Studies. **RESEARCH** Soviet literary problems; Pushkin; Russian versification. **SELECTED PUBLICATIONS** Auth, A History of Russian Poetry, Russ Rev, Vol 0053, 94. **CONTACT ADDRESS** Dept of Slavic Lang, Univ of NC, Chapel Hill, NC, 27514.

VICKREY, JOHN FREDERICK
PERSONAL Born 08/24/1924, Chicago, IL, m, 1966 **DISCIPLINE** ENGLISH LINGUISTICS AND PHILOLOGY **EDUCATION** Univ Chicago, PhB, 49, MA, 52; Ind Univ, PhD(English), 60. **CAREER** Instr English, Rutgers Univ, 57-61; from asst prof to assoc prof, 61-74, PROF ENGLISH LIT, LEHIGH UNIV, 74-. **MEMBERSHIPS** MLA; Mediaeval Acad Am. **RESEARCH** Old English, Old Saxon and Middle English language and literature. **SELECTED PUBLICATIONS** Auth, The Seafarer 111-15--Old-English Poem by Gordon,II, Papers on Lang and Lit, Vol 0028, 92; On the Eorth Compounds in the Old-English Finn-Stories--The Finn Episode in Beowulf, Stud Neophilol, Vol 0065, 93; Inferno VII--Dante-Alighieri Divina Commedia--Deathstyles of the Rich and Famous, Neophilologus, Vol 0079, 95; The Seafarer 97-102--Dives and the Burial of Treasure, Jour Eng and Ger Philol, Vol 0094, 95. **CONTACT ADDRESS** Dept of English, Lehigh Univ, Bethlehem, PA, 18015.

VIDAL, HERNAN
PERSONAL Born 04/18/1937, Villa Alemana, Chile, m, 1962, 3 children **DISCIPLINE** SPANISH AMERICAN LITERATURE **EDUCATION** Univ Iowa, PhD(Span), 67. **CAREER** Instr English, Univ Chile, Temuco, 62-64; instr Span, Univ Iowa, 66-67; asst prof, Univ Va, 67-72; assoc prof, 72-80, PROF SPAN AND PORT AND DIR GRAD STUDIES, UNIV MINN, MINNEAPOLIS, 80-. **MEMBERSHIPS** Am Asn Teachers Span and Port; MLA. **RESEARCH** Spanish American novel and drama. **SELECTED PUBLICATIONS** Auth, Postmodernism, Postleftism, Neo-Avant-Gardism, the Case of Chiles Revista-De-Critica-Cultural, Boundary 2-Intl Jour Lit and Cult, Vol 0020, 93. **CONTACT ADDRESS** Dept of Span and Port, Univ of Minn, 9 Pleasant St S E, Minneapolis, MN, 55455-0194.

VIEHMEYER, L. ALLEN
PERSONAL Born 07/30/1942, Peoria, IL, m, 1967, 2 children **DISCIPLINE** GERMAN LITERATURE & LINGUISTICS **EDUCATION** Western Ill Univ, BSEd, 64; Univ Ill, Urbana-Champaign, AM, 67, PhD, 71. **CAREER** Instr Ger, Wartburg Col, 69-71; asst prof, 71-78, assoc prof Ger, 78-85; prof Ger, 85-, Youngstown State Univ. **MEMBERSHIPS** Am Assn Teachers Ger. **RESEARCH** Pennsylvania German literature 1683-1830; German-American hymnology 1683-1830. **SELECTED PUBLICATIONS** Auth, An Index to Hymns and Hymn Tunes of the Ephrata Cloister 1730-1766, Ephrata Cloister Associates, Ephrata, PA, 95. **CONTACT ADDRESS** Dept of Foreign Lang & Lit, Youngstown State Univ, One University Plz., Youngstown, OH, 44555-0002. **EMAIL** laviehme@cc.ysu.edu

VIERA, DAVID JOHN
PERSONAL Born 06/09/1943, Providence, RI, m, 1980 **DISCIPLINE** MEDIEVAL HISPANIC LITERATURE **EDUCATION** Providence Col, BA, 65; Cath Univ of Am, MA, 69, PhD(Iberian studies), 72. **CAREER** Asst prof, State Univ Col Geneseo, NY, 75-77; ASSOC PROF SPANISH, TENN TECH UNIV, 77-, Asst prof Spanish, Tenn Tech Univ, 72-74. **HONORS AND AWARDS** Ferran Soldevila Award, Fundacio Salvador Vives Casajuana, 79. **MEMBERSHIPS** Medieval Acad Am; MLA; South Atlantic Mod Lang Asn; Am Asn Teachers Spanish and Portuguese; NAm Catalan Soc. **RESEARCH** Francesc Eiximenis; Antero de Quental. **SELECTED PUBLICATIONS** Auth, Eiximenis, Francesc Dissension with the Royal House of Aragon, Jour Medieval Hist, Vol 0022, 96. **CONTACT ADDRESS** Dept of Foreign Lang, Tenn Technol Univ, Cookeville, TN, 38501.

VINCENT, JON S.
PERSONAL Born 02/28/1938, Denver, CO, m, 1962, 2 children **DISCIPLINE** BRAZILIAN LITERATURE, PORTUGUESE **EDUCATION** Univ NMex, BA, 61, PhD(Ibero-Am studies), 70. **CAREER** Instr, Univ N Mex, 63-64; asst prof, 67-74, assoc prof Span & Port & assoc chmn dept, 74-78, prof & chmn dept Univ Kans, 79-82, Encargado de Catedra Port, Univ Costa Rica, 72, Co-director, Center of Latin American Studies, 87-89, Director, Center of Latin American Studies, 89-92. **HONORS AND AWARDS** New York Univ Scholarship, Universidade Federal da Bahia, 59-60; Title VI Fellow, Univ NMex, 61-65; Fulbright Fellow, Univerdidade de Lisboa, 62-63; Title VI Fellow, Univ NMex, 66; Title VI Fulbright-Hays Fellow, Brazil, 66-67. **MEMBERSHIPS** MLA; Latin Am Studies Asn; Am Asn Teachers of Span & Port. **RESEARCH** Modern Brazilian prose fiction, Brazilian poetry, Spanish-American fiction. **SELECTED PUBLICATIONS** Auth, The Brazilian Novel: Some Paradoxes of Popularity, J Interam Studies & World Affairs, 72; Gracifiano Ramos: The Dialectics of Defeat, Ind Univ, 76; Corpo de Baile, Luso-Brazilian Rev, 77; Jose Marti: Surrealist or Seer?, Latin Am Res Rev, 78; Jorge Amado, Jorge Desprezado, Luso Brazilian Rev, summer 78; Gran Serton: El imperative critico, Texto Critico, summer 78; Joao Guimaraes Rosa, Twayne, 78; Guimaraes Rosa's Sagarana, American Hispanist, 78; Graciliano Ramos, Encyclopedia of Worl Lit of the 20th Century, 84; Jose Lins do Rego, Ency of World Lit of the 20th Century, 84; Several entries in asterplots II, 1986; Jose Lins do Rego, Dict of Brazilian Lit, 88; Jorge Amado, Latin American Writers (Scribners), 89; Jorge Amado and Joao Guimaraes Rosa, Cyclopedia of World Authors II, 89; Joao Guimaraes Rosa, Modern Latin-American Fiction Writers, 92; Jose Lins do Rego, Encyclopedia of Latin American History and Culture, 96. **CONTACT ADDRESS** Dept of Span & Port, Univ Kans, Lawrence, KS, 66045-0001. **EMAIL** vicente@falcon.cc.ukans.edu

VISSON, LYNN
PERSONAL Born 04/26/1945, New York, NY **DISCIPLINE** RUSSIAN LANGUAGE AND LITERATURE **EDUCATION** Radcliffe Col, BA, 66; Columbia Univ, MA, 67; Harvard Univ, PhD (Slavic lang and lit), 72. **CAREER** Instr and assoc Russ, Barnard Col, Columbia Univ, 69-70, from instr to asst prof, 71-76; asst prof, Bryn Mawr Col, 76-78; asst prof Russ, Hunter Col, 78-79; INTERPRETER, UN, 81-; Mem fac exchange with Soviet Union, Moscow State Univ, 70-71; Am Coun Learned Soc grant in Soviet Studies, 76. **MEMBERSHIPS** Am Asn Teachers Slavic and East Europ Lang; Am Coun Teachers Russ. **RESEARCH** Soviet poetry; Esenin; Russian language. **SELECTED PUBLICATIONS** Auth, Classic Russian Cooking in Molokhovets, Elena, A Gift to Young Housewives, Slavic Rev, Vol 54, 95. **CONTACT ADDRESS** 60 Riverside Dr Apt 7H, New York, NY, 10024.

VITELLO, RALPH MICHAEL
PERSONAL Born 12/26/1949, Buffalo, NY **DISCIPLINE** FRENCH RENAISSANCE LITERATURE **EDUCATION** State Univ NY Buffalo, BA, 71; Yale Univ, MPhil, 77, PhD (French), 78. **CAREER** Actg instr French, Yale Univ, 75-77; lectr, Univ Calif, Los Angeles, 77-78; ASST PROF FRENCH, YALE UNIV, 78-. **MEMBERSHIPS** Soc Amis Montaigne; MLA; Am Asn Teachers Fr. **RESEARCH** Literature of ideas in the Renaissance; French and American modern poetry. **SELECTED PUBLICATIONS** Auth, Montaigne Unruly Brood in Textual Engendering and the Challenge to Paternal Authority, Sixteenth Century J, Vol 28, 97. **CONTACT ADDRESS** Dept of French, Yale Univ, New Haven, CT, 06520.

VITZ, EVELYN BIRGE
PERSONAL Born 10/16/1941, Indianapolis, IN, m, 1969, 3 children **DISCIPLINE** FRENCH MEDIEVAL AND FRENCH RENAISSANCE LITERATURE **EDUCATION** Smith Col, BA, 63; Yale Univ, PhD (French), 68. **CAREER** From instr to asst prof, 68-74, ASSOC PROF FRENCH, DEPT FRENCH AND ITAL, NEW YORK UNIV, 74-; Nat Endowment for Humanities younger humanist fel, 74-75. **MEMBERSHIPS** MLA; Medieval Acad Am. **RESEARCH** Medieval narrative; modern narrative theory; medieval and Renaissance lyric poetry. **SELECTED PUBLICATIONS** Auth, Pretentious, Preposterous, Pathetic in a Response to Henking, Susan and to Daly, Mary on Psychology and Religion, J Psychol Theol, Vol 21, 93; The Stripping of the Altars in Traditional Religion in England 1400-1580, Theol Studies, Vol 54, 93; Commentary on the Testament of Villon in Octets I-XIV and Octets LXXVIII-LXXXIV, J Medieval Studies, Vol 69, 94; The Art of Medieval French Narrative, French Forum, Vol , 94; Rereading Rape in Medieval Literature, Partisan Rev, Vol 63, 96. **CONTACT ADDRESS** Dept of French, New York Univ, University Pl, New York, NY, 10003-4556.

VLASOPOLOS, ANCA
PERSONAL Born 10/14/1948, Bucharest, Romania, m, 1972, 1 child **DISCIPLINE** COMPARATIVE LITERATURE, WOMEN'S STUDIES **EDUCATION** Wayne State Univ, BA, 70; Univ Mich, MA, 71, PhD(Comp Lit), 77. **CAREER** Instr, 74-77, asst prof English, Wayne State Univ, 77-83; assoc prof, 83-95; prof, 95-; asst ed, Corridors, 81-. **MEMBERSHIPS** MLA; Wordsworth-Coleridge Asn. **RESEARCH** Romantic poetry; comparative drama. **SELECTED PUBLICATIONS** Auth, The ritual of midsummer: A pattern for A Midsummer Night's Dream, Renaissance Quart, 78; The rime of The Ancient Mariners as Romantic quest, Wordsworth Circle, 79; Kenn Russell's Clouds of Glory: The ruling passion as key to the artist, Lit & Film Quart, 80; Mary Wollstonecraft's Mask of Reason in A Virdication of the Rights of Woman, Dalhousie Rev, 80; Thematic contexts in Yeast's theatre, Mod Drama, 81; Through the Straits, At Large (Ridgeway Press, 97; Chapters: Free-Floating Marginals in the Paris and London of the Mid and Late-Nineteenth Century, 98. **CONTACT ADDRESS** Dept of English, Wayne State Univ, 51 W Warren, State Hall, Detroit, MI, 48202-1308. **EMAIL** ab1165@wayne.edu

VOGELEY, NANCY JEANNE
PERSONAL Born 06/19/1937, San Pedro, CA **DISCIPLINE** LATIN AMERICAN AND SPANISH LITERATURE **EDUCATION** Pa State Univ, BA, 58, MA, 62; Univ Madrid, dipl Span, 60; Stanford Univ, PhD(Span), 80. **CAREER** Instr Span, Allegheny Col, 62-63, Ithaca Col, 63-64 & Col San Mateo, 65-66; instr, 66-70, asst prof, 70-81, Assoc Prof Span, 81-86, prof Span, Univ San Francisco, 86-. Instr Span, Univ San Francisco, Valencia, Spain, summer, 69. **MEMBERSHIPS** Am Asn Teachers Span & Port; MLA; Philol Asn Pac Coast; Am Soc 18th Century Studies; Latin Am Studies Asn. **RESEARCH** Jose Joaquin Fernandez de Lizardi and the period of Mexican Independence; Alfonso Sastre and contemporary Spanish theater. **SELECTED PUBLICATIONS** Auth, Jose Joaquin Fernandez Lizardi and the Inquisition, Dieciocho, fall 80; Alfonso Sastre on Alfonso Sastre (interview), Hispania, 9/81; Blacks in Peru: The poetry of Nicomedes Santa Cruz, Phylon 43, No 1, 82; The figure of the Black Payador in Martin Fierro, CLA Jour 26, 34-48, 9/82; Mexican Newspaper Culture on the Eve of Mexican Independence, Ideologies and Literature, 4 Second Cycle, 358-377, 9-10/82; The Concept of the People in El Periquillo Sarnieto, Hispania 70, 457-467, 9/87; Defining the Colonial Reader: El Periquillo Sarniento, PMLA 102, 784-800, 10/87, reprinted in Nineteenth-Century Literature Criticism, NCLC 30, Gale Res, 79-88, 91; Updating the Picaresque Tradition: Alfonso Sastre's Lumpen Marginacion U Herigonca, Ideologies and Literature 2 New Series, 25-42, 87, reprinted in Alfonso Sastre, Murcia: Universidad de Murcia, 65-80, 93; Questioning Authority: Lizardi's Noches tristes y dia alegre, Dispositio 15, 53-70, 90; Testamento de Napoleon Bonaparte-A Manuscript by Jose Joaquin Fernandez de Lizardi?, Dieciocho 13, 84-89, 90; Intertextuality and Nineteenth-Century Nationalism: Perucho: Nieto de Periquillo, Bul of Hispanic Stu 71, 485-497, 94; Colonial Discourse in a Post-Colonial Latin American Review 2, 189-212, 93; Formacion cultural despues de la independencia: Una revista mexicana de literatura, 1826, Estudios (Caracas) 5, 79-90, 95; El Amor Republicano: una novela del Mexico poscolonial, Revista Iberoamericana 61. 663-374, 95; Italian Opera in Early National Mexico, Modern Language Quarterly 57, 279-288, 96; Turks and Indians: Orientalist Discourse in Post-Colonial Mexico, Diacrtitcs, 25, 3-20, 95; China and the American Indies: A Sixteenth-Century History, Colonial Latin Am Rev 6, 165-184, 97; Eva Forest, Women Writers of Spain, Greenwood, 114-115, 86; Bernice Zamora, Chicano Writers First Series, Dictionary of Literary Biography, Gale Res, 289-294, 89; Jose Joaquin Fernandez de Lizardi, Latin American Writers, Vol 1, Scribners, 119-128, 89; The Discoure of Colonial Loyalty: Mexico, 1808m Nacropolitics of Nineteenth-Century Liturature: Nationalism, Exoticism, Imperialism, Univ of Penn, 37-55, 91, reprinted, Duke Univ, 95; Discurso colonial en un contexto post-colonial: Mesico, Siglo XIX, Critica y descolonizacion: El sujeto colonial en la cultura latinoamericana, Academia Nacional del al Historia, 607-624, 92; Heredia y el escribir de la historia, La imaginacion historica en el siglo XIX, UNR Editora, 39-56, 96; La figuracion de la mujer: Mexico en el momento de la Independencia, Mujer en la Colonia hispanoamericana, Biblioteca de America, instituto Internacional de Literatira Ieroamericana, 307-326, 96; Death and its Challenge to Decolonization: Jose Joaquin Fernandez de Lizardi's Last Will and Testament, Pos-Colonialismo e Identiadade, Edicoes Univ Fernando, 98. **CONTACT ADDRESS** Dept of Modern Lang, Univ of San Francisco, 2130 Fulton St, San Francisco, CA, 94117-1050. **EMAIL** vogeleyn@usfca.edu

VOGLER, FREDERICK WRIGHT
PERSONAL Born 05/27/1931, Burlington, VT, m, 1965 **DISCIPLINE** ROMANCE LANGUAGES **EDUCATION** Univ NC, Chapel Hill, AB, 53, MA, 55, PhD (Romance lang), 61. **CAREER** Instr French, Univ NC, Chapel Hill, 61-62; asst prof, Univ Iowa, 62-63; From asst prof to assoc prof, 63-78, PROF FRENCH, UNIV NC, CHAPEL HILL, 78-; ASSOC DEAN COL ARTS AND SCI, 76-; Mem French achievement comt, Col Entrance Exam Bd, 67-70. **MEMBERSHIPS** MLA; SAtlantic Mod Lang Asn; Am Asn Teachers French. **RESEARCH** Early 17th century French novel; French classical doctrine and practice. **SELECTED PUBLICATIONS** Auth, Venceslas, Fr Rev, Vol 66, 93; Audiguier, Vital,De and Lennox, Charlotte in Baroque Studies, Womens Stud, Lit Resurrection, Romance Notes, Vol 36, 96. **CONTACT ADDRESS** Dept of Romance Lang, Univ of NC, Chapel Hill, NC, 27514.

VOIGTS, LINDA EHRSAM
PERSONAL Born 05/09/1942, Abilene, KS, m, 1963, 1 child **DISCIPLINE** OLD AND MIDDLE ENGLISH, HISTORY OF MEDICINE **EDUCATION** William Jewell Col, BA, 63; Univ Mo-Kansas City, MA, 66; Univ Mo-Columbia, PhD (English), 73. **CAREER** Teacher Ger and English, North Kansas City High Sch, 63-65; instr English, William Jewell Col, 65-69; instr compos, Univ Mo-Columbia, 72; vis asst prof English, William Jewell Col, 73-74 and Univ Mo-Columbia, 74-75; asst prof, 75-79, ASSOC PROF ENGLISH, UNIV MO-KANSAS CITY, 79-; Am Coun Learned Soc grant-in-aid, 75; Andrew W Mellon fac fel humanities, Harvard Univ, 78-79; vis instr, Harvard Univ, summer, 80. **HONORS AND AWARDS** Zeitlin-VerBrugge Prize, Hist of Sci Soc, 81. **MEMBERSHIPS** Mediaeval Acad Am; MLA; Hist of Sci Soc; Am Asn Hist Med; New Chaucer Soc. **RESEARCH** Old English; Middle English. **SELECTED PUBLICATIONS** Auth, Memorials of the Book Trade in Medieval London in the Archives of Old London Bridge, Anglia Zeitschrift fur Englische Philologie, Vol 111, 93; The Authorship of the Equatorie of the Planetis, Isis, Vol 86, 95; Anglo-Saxon Medicine, Isis, Vol 86, 95; What's the Word and the Vernacularization of Science and Medicine in England from 1375 To 1475, Bilingualism in Late Medieval England, Speculum J Medieval Stud, Vol 71, 96. **CONTACT ADDRESS** Dept of English, Univ of Mo, 5100 Rockhill Rd, Kansas City, MO, 64110-2499.

VOLPE, GERALD CARMINE
PERSONAL Born 05/27/1931, Fitchburg, MA **DISCIPLINE** ROMANCE LANGUAGES **EDUCATION** Holy Cross Col, BA, 54; Fordham Univ, MA, 56; Princeton Univ, PhD (Romance lang), 63. **CAREER** From instr to asst prof French and Ital, Brandeis Univ, 60-66; asst prof, 66-72, acting chmn dept Ital, 73-74, chmn dept, 74-75, ASSOC PROF FRENCH AND ITAL, UNIV MASS, BOSTON, 72-. **MEMBERSHIPS** MLA; AAUP; Am Asn Teachers Fr; Am Asn Teachers Ital; Dante Soc. **RESEARCH** French Renaissance; Dante; Ethnic studies. **SELECTED PUBLICATIONS** Auth, Le Gout De La Catastrophe, Fr Rev, Vol 66, 93; Charles, Fr Rev, Vol 68, 95; La Folie Du Moment, Fr Rev, Vol 70, 97. **CONTACT ADDRESS** Dept of French and Ital, Univ of Mass, Boston, MA, 02116.

VON DASSANOWSKY, ROBERT
PERSONAL New York, NY **DISCIPLINE** GERMANIC STUDIES; POLITICAL SCIENCE; FILM **EDUCATION** Am Acad of Dramatic Arts, 78; AFI Conservatory Prog, 81; Univ Calif, LA, BA, 85, MA, 88, PhD, 92. **CAREER** Vis Asst Prof German, UCLA, 92-93; Asst Prof of German & Fil Stud, Univ Colo, 93-; Head of German Prog, 93-; Dir, Film Studies, 97-. **HONORS AND AWARDS** Residency Award, Michael Karolyi Mem Fnd, France, 79; Julie Harris/BHTG Playwriting Award, 84; Accademico Honoris Causa, Italy, 89; LA Cultural Aff Off Grant, 90-92; Univ Colo CRCW Grant, 94, 95, 97; Univ Colo Pres Fund for the Hum Grant, 96; Outstanding Fac Award, Univ Colo, 98. **MEMBERSHIPS** Found pres, PEN Colo Chapt; Bd Member, PEN USA/W Ctr, LA; VP, Austrian Am Film Asn; VP, Int Alexander Lernet-Holenia Soc; Women's Issues Leadership Council; Proeuropa; MLA; Soc for Cinema Stud; Screen Actors Guild; AATG; Dramatists Guild; Authors League; Ed Bd Member for various publications. **RESEARCH** 19th/20th century Austrian & Germanic literature & culture; fin-de-siecle & interwar European artistic movements; fascism; Anglo/American, Central European, & Italian film; popular culture of the 1960s; feminist & women's literature & film; postmodernism. **SELECTED PUBLICATIONS** auth, The Southern Journey: Candy and The Magic Christian as Cinematic Picaresques, Stud in Popular Culture, XV:1, 93; auth, Finding the Words: Literary-Historical Revisionism in Christine Bruckner's Wenn du geredet hattest, Desdemona, Seminar: A J of Germanic Stud, 9/95; auth, Phantom Empires: The Novels of Alexander Lernet-Holenia and the Question of Postempirial Austrian Identity, Ariadne, 96; Verses of a Marriage: translation of Strophen einer Ehe by Hans Raimund, Event Horizon, 96; co-ed, Filmkunst, no 54, 97; Telegrams from the Metropole: Selected Poetry 1980-97, Univ Salzburg Press, 99; auth, Mars in Aries: translation of Mars im Widder by Alexander Lernet-Holenia, Sun & Moon, 99. **CONTACT ADDRESS** Dept of Lang & Cultures, Univ Colo, Colorado Springs, CO, 80933.

VON DER EMDE, SILKE
DISCIPLINE GERMAN **EDUCATION** Ind Univ, Bloomington, PhD, 94. **CAREER** Asst prof; prof, Dartmouth Col. **RESEARCH** Contemporary German literature, especially East German women writers; women in German film; women studies; literary theory. **SELECTED PUBLICATIONS** Publ on research interest. **CONTACT ADDRESS** Classics Dept, Vassar Col, 124 Raymond Ave., Poughkeepsie, NY, 12604. **EMAIL** vonderemde@vassar.edu

VON SCHNEIDEMESSER, LUANNE
PERSONAL Born 02/28/1945, San Diego, CA, m, 1972, 2 children **DISCIPLINE** GERMAN/LINGUISTICS AND PHILOLOGY **EDUCATION** Kansas State Univ, BA, 68; MA, 70, PhD, 79, Univ Wisconsin, Madison. **CAREER** Ed, 78-88, sr ed, 88- , Dictionary of American Regional English, lector, Dept of German, 91, Univ of Wisc, Madison. **HONORS AND AWARDS** Seaton Awd, Kansas Q, 91; prof dev grant, 86-87; featured paper, Methods VIII: Int Conf on Dialectology, 93. **MEMBERSHIPS** Dictionary Soc N Am; Am Dialect Soc; Soc of German-American Stud; Am Coun of Learned Soc Conf of

Admin Off. **RESEARCH** Lexicography; sociolinguistics; dialect geography; American English; German. **SELECTED PUBLICATIONS** Auth, Introduction, to An Index by Region, Usage, and Etymology to the Dictionary of American Regional English, 93; auth, DARE's Completion A Beginning?, in Zeitschrift fur Dialektologenkongresses, 93; auth, More German Loanwords from the Dictionary of American Regional English, in The German Lang in Am, 93; auth, Gesundheit!, in Soc for German Am Stud Newsl, 95; auth, Terms Used for Children's Games: Comparing DARE's Findings with Usage of Today's Youth, in Varieties of English around the World: Focus on the USA, 96; auth, Soda or Pop?, in J of Eng Ling, 96; auth, Expletives and Euphemisms in DARE: An Initial Look, in Language Variety in the South Revisited, 97; auth, Regional Labels in DARE, in Dictionaries, 97; auth, An Index by Region, Usage and Etymology to the Dictionary of American Regional English, v 3,Am Dialect Soc, 99. **CONTACT ADDRESS** Dictionary of American Regional English, Univ of Wisconsin, Madison, 600 N Park St, Madison, WI, 53706. **EMAIL** lvonschn@facstaff.wisc.edu

VOS, MORRIS
PERSONAL Born 12/10/1944, Mahaska Co, Iowa, m, 1966, 2 children **DISCIPLINE** GERMAN LITERATURE & LANGUAGE **EDUCATION** Calvin Col, BA, 66; Ind Univ, Bloomington, MA, 67, PhD(Ger), 75. **CAREER** Assoc instr Ger, Ind Univ, Bloomington, 70-71; asst prof, 71-79, Assoc Prof Ger, 79-91, prof, Western Ill Univ, 91- Western Ill Univ Res Coun award, 78; Ger Acad Exchange Serv study visit, 80. **MEMBERSHIPS** Midwest Mod Lang Asn; Am Asn Teachers Ger; Am Coun Teaching Foreign Lang; Conf Christianity & Lit. **RESEARCH** German narration theory of the 18th century; religion and literature; foreign language pedagogy. **SELECTED PUBLICATIONS** Auth, The concept of dramatic narration, In: Jahrbuch fur Internationale Germanistik, Band 4, 79; co-ed, Shaping the Future of Foreign Language Education, 88; auth, Dramatic Narration: The Speech Criterion in Seventeenth Cenutry German Narration Theory, Neophilious, 91. **CONTACT ADDRESS** Foreign Lang & Lit, Western Illinois Univ, 1 University Cir, Macomb, IL, 61455-1390. **EMAIL** mvoss@wiu.edu

W

WACHAL, ROBERT STANLEY
PERSONAL Born 03/13/1929, Omaha, NE, m, 1968 **DISCIPLINE** NEUROLINGUISTICS, APPLIED LINGUISTICS **EDUCATION** Univ Minn, Minneapolis, BA, 52; Univ Wis-Madison, MS, 59, PhD (English, ling), 66. **CAREER** From asst prof to assoc prof, 70-75, PROF LING, UNIV IOWA, 75-; Coordr English lang prog, US Educ Found, Greece, 66-67. **MEMBERSHIPS** Ling Soc Am; Acad Aphasia; Teachers of English to Speakers of Other Lang. **RESEARCH** Language pathology; style and statistics; sociolinguistics. **SELECTED PUBLICATIONS** Auth, Social Stylistics in Syntactic Variation in British Newspapers, Am Speech, Vol 69, 94; Heartland English, Variation and Tradition in the American Midwest, Am Speech, Vol 70, 95. **CONTACT ADDRESS** Dept of Ling, Univ of Iowa, Iowa City, IA, 52242.

WAELTI-WALTERS, JENNIFER
PERSONAL England **DISCIPLINE** FRENCH/WOMEN'S STUDIES **EDUCATION** Univ London, BA, 64, PhD, 68. **CAREER** Instr, Univ de Paris, 67-68; PROF FRENCH, UNIV VICTORIA, 68-, ch Fr dept, 79-84, instr, 79-, dir women's studs, 88-95. **HONORS AND AWARDS** Prize Best Work Pub French, Asn Profs de Francais des Univs Can, 89; Community Award, Univ Victoria, 93. **MEMBERSHIPS** Can Fedn Hum; Hum Asn Can; Can Res Inst Advan Women; Can Asn Women's Studs; Sr Women Acad Admins Can. **SELECTED PUBLICATIONS** Auth, Fairytales and the Female Imagination, 82; auth, Jeanne Hyrvrard: Theorist of the Modern World, 96; coauth, Feminisms of the Belle Epoque, 94. **CONTACT ADDRESS** Women's Studies, Univ Victoria, Victoria, BC, V8W 3P4.

WAGENER, GUY
DISCIPLINE FRENCH LANGUAGE, LITERATURE, AND CULTURE **EDUCATION** Univ Calif, Irvine, PhD, **CAREER** Assoc prof Fr, Univ Nev, Reno. **RESEARCH** Epicurus, Diderot, and Michel Serres; women's access to culture as reflected in Moliere's theatre. **SELECTED PUBLICATIONS** Published on Diderot. **CONTACT ADDRESS** Univ Nev, Reno, Reno, NV, 89557. **EMAIL** unrug@unr.edu

WAGENER, HANS
PERSONAL Born 07/27/1940, Lage, West Germany **DISCIPLINE** GERMAN LITERATURE **EDUCATION** Univ Freiburg, BA, 63; Univ Calif, Los Angeles, MA, 65, PhD (Ger), 67. **CAREER** Asst prof Ger, Univ Southern Calif, 67-68; From asst prof to assoc prof, 68-75, chmn dept, 77-81, PROF GER, UNIV CALIF, LOS ANGELES, 75-. **MEMBERSHIPS** MLA; Am Asn Teachers Ger. **RESEARCH** Modern German literature; 17th and 18th century German literature. **SELECTED PUBLICATIONS** Auth, Fantasy and Politics in Visions of the Future in the Weimar Republic, J Engl Ger Phil, Vol 92, 93; Christiani Gryphii Gedachtnisschriften in Reprint of the 1702 Leipzig Edition, Colloquia Germanica, Vol 26, 93; Philological Practice, Vol 1, Experiences and Reflections, Jahrbuch Fur internationale Germanistik, Vol 25, 93; Herrn Von Hoffmannswaldau und Anderer Deutschen Auserlesener und Bissher Ungedruckter Gedichte Siebender theil in a New Edition Based On the 1727 Printing, Colloquia Germanica, Vol 26, 93; Christiani Gryphii Gedachtnisschriften in Reprint of the 1702 Leipzig Edition, Colloquia Germanica, Vol 26, 93; The Self in the Mirror of Language in autobiographical Writings in 20th Century German Literature, Ger Quart, Vol 66, 93; Hellwig, Johann in a Descriptive Bibliography, Colloquia Germanica, Vol 27, 94; Germany, 2000 Years, Vol 3, from the Nazi Era to German Unification, Ger Quart, Vol 67, 94; German and international Perspectives on the Spanish Civil War in the Aesthetics of Partiality, Ger Quart, Vol 67, 94; Germany, 2000 Years, Vol 3, from the Nazi Era to German Unification, Ger Quart, Vol 67, 94: Idea of Empire and Ethics of Love in a Reconstruction of Lohenstein arminius Novel, Colloquia Germanica, Vol 27, 94; Hellwig, Johann Die 'Nymphe Noris' 1650 in a Critical Edition, Colloquia Germanica, Vol 27, 94; Werfel, Franz and the Critics, Mod Austrian Lit, Vol 28, 95; Wefel, Franz in His Way to the Novel, Ger Quart, Vol 69, 96; The Zeitroman of the Late Weimar Republic, Ger Quart, Vol 70, 97. **CONTACT ADDRESS** Dept of Ger Lang, Univ of Calif, Los Angeles, CA, 90024.

WAILES, STEPHEN L
PERSONAL Born 05/28/1937, Summit, NJ, m, 1964 **DISCIPLINE** GERMANIC LANGUAGES **EDUCATION** Harvard Univ, AB, 60, PhD (Ger), 68. **CAREER** Asst prof, 68-72, assoc prof, 72-80, Prof Ger, Ind Univ, Bloomington, 80-; Assoc Dean Fac, 78-; Soc for Values in Higher Educ fel, 72; Alexander von Humboldt-Stiftung fel, 76. **RESEARCH** Medieval theological and didactic literature. **SELECTED PUBLICATIONS** Auth, Early German Novella Art, J Eng Ger Phil, Vol 92, 93; The Envy of Angels in Cathedral Schools and Social Ideals in Medieval Europe, 950-1200, J Eng Ger Phil, Vol 95, 96. **CONTACT ADDRESS** 1710 Devon Lane, Bloomington, IN, 47401.

WAKEFIELD, RAY MILAN
PERSONAL Born 01/30/1942, Fremont, MI, m, 1964, 2 children **DISCIPLINE** PHILOLOGY, NETHERLANDIC LITERATURE **EDUCATION** Dartmouth Col, BA, 64; Ind Univ, Bloomington, MA, 66, PhD(Ger, dutch & Scand), 72. **CAREER** From Instr to Asst Prof, 69-87, Assoc Prof Ger & Dutch, Univ Minn, Minneapolis, 87-. **HONORS AND AWARDS** Officer in the Order of Oranje-Nassau, by Her Majesty Queen Beatrix of the Netherlands, 91. **MEMBERSHIPS** MLA; Am Asn Teachers Ger; Int Ver Ned. **RESEARCH** Comparative Germanic prosody; courtly Romance; second language acquisition; medieval Dutch literature. **SELECTED PUBLICATIONS** Auth, Nibelungen Prosody, Mouton, 76; Hadewijch: A Formalist's Dream, Dutch Crossings, 79; The Early Dutch-German Poetic Tradition, Amsterdammer, Bertragezur Alteren Germanistik, 79; coauth, Kreise, Heinle & Heinle, 92; auth, Heinsiusund Opitz: Germanic Prosody Revisited, PAANS, 94; Excalibur: Film Reception vs Political Distance, Politics in Ger Lit, 98. **CONTACT ADDRESS** Dept of Ger, Scandinavian, & Dutch, Univ of Minnesota, 205 Folwell Hall, Minneapolis, MN, 55455-0194. **EMAIL** wakef001@tc.umn.edu

WALDAUER, JOSEPH
DISCIPLINE 18TH-CENTURY FRENCH LITERATURE **EDUCATION** Columbia Univ, PhD. **CAREER** Instr, Univ Minn, Twin Cities. **SELECTED PUBLICATIONS** Published on Diderot, Rousseau, and Stendhal. **CONTACT ADDRESS** Univ Minn, Twin Cities, Minneapolis, MN, 55455.

WALDINGER, RENEE
PERSONAL Born 08/26/1927, m, 1948, 2 children **DISCIPLINE** FRENCH LANGUAGE AND LITERATURE **EDUCATION** Hunter Col, BA, 48; Columbia Univ, MA, PhD (French), 53. **CAREER** Lectr French, Queens Col, NY, 54-55; From instr to assoc prof, 57-70, chmn dept Romance lang, 70-76, PROF FRENCH, GRAD SCH AND UNIV CTR, CITY UNIV OF NEW YORK, 72-; EXEC OFF, 81-; Nat Endowment for Humanities grant, Inst Contemp Cult, 82. **HONORS AND AWARDS** Chevalier, Ordre Palmes Acad, 80. **MEMBERSHIPS** MLA; Am Asn Teachers Fr; Am Asn 18th Century Studies; AAUP. **RESEARCH** French literature of the 18th century; pedagogy; French contemporary culture. **SELECTED PUBLICATIONS** Auth, Writings on the Body from Descartes to Laclos, Fr Rev, Vol 67, 93; Histoire Dune Grecque Moderne, Fr Rev, Vol 66, 93; Between Melting Pot and Mosaic in african Americans and Puerto Ricans in the New York Political Economy, J Am Ethnic Hist, Vol 15, 96; Newcomers in the Workplace in Immigrants and the Restructuring of The Us Economy - Lamphere,L, Stepick,A, Grenier,G, J American Ethnic History, Vol 15, 96. **CONTACT ADDRESS** Romance Lang Dept, Graduate Sch and Univ Ctr, CUNY, New York, NY, 10036.

WALDMAN, GLENYS A.
DISCIPLINE GERMAN LANGUAGES **EDUCATION** Oberlin Col, BA, 67; Univ Pa, MA, 70, PhD, 75; Drexel Univ, MSLS, 78. **CAREER** Assoc/actg librn, Hist Soc Pa, 84-87; asst librn, Grand Lodge F & AM of Pa Libr, 87-89; asst libr, cur, Masonic Libr & Mus Pa, 90-95; LIBR, CUR, MASONIC LIBR, MUS PA, 96-. **CONTACT ADDRESS** Masonic Libr/Mus of Pa, 1 N Broad St, Philadelphia, PA, 19107-2520. **EMAIL** gwaldman@fast.net

WALDRON, WILLIAM S.
DISCIPLINE ASIAN RELIGIOUS TRADITIONS **EDUCATION** Univ Wis, BA, PhD. **CAREER** Prof; Middlebury Col, 96-. **RESEARCH** Indigenous psychological systems of Indian Buddhism and their dialogue with modern psychology. **SELECTED PUBLICATIONS** Publ on, res interest. **CONTACT ADDRESS** Dept of Religion, Middlebury Col, Middlebury, VT, 05753.

WALKER, HALLAM
PERSONAL Born 05/23/1921, Newark, NJ, m, 1949, 2 children **DISCIPLINE** ROMANCE LANGUAGES **EDUCATION** Princeton Univ, AB, 43, MA, 50, PhD (Romance lang), 52. **CAREER** Instr French, Pa State Univ, 49-51; instr, Washington and Lee Univ, 53-54; asst prof, Duke Univ, 54-65; assoc prof, 65-72, PROF FRENCH AND CHMN DEPT, DAVIDSON COL, 72-. **MEMBERSHIPS** MLA; Am Asn Teachers Fr; SAtlantic Mod Lang Asn. **RESEARCH** Classical French theater; nineteenth and twentieth centuries French novel and poetry. **SELECTED PUBLICATIONS** Auth, JAPANESE VENTURE and THE NEWLY FORMED BALLET-DEPARTMENT AT THE SHOWA-ACADEMIA-MUSICAE IN TOKYO, DANCING TIMES, Vol 87, 97. **CONTACT ADDRESS** Dept of French, Davidson Col, Davidson, NC, 28036.

WALKER, JANET ANDERSON
PERSONAL Milwaukee, WI, m, 1967 **DISCIPLINE** COMPARATIVE AND ASIAN LITERATURE **EDUCATION** Univ Wis, Madison, BA, 65; Harvard Univ, AM, 68, PhD (comp lit), 74. **CAREER** Asst prof, 71-77, ASSOC PROF COMP LIT, RUTGERS UNIV, 77-; Japan Found Short-term fel, 82-83. **MEMBERSHIPS** Am Comp Lit Asn; Int Comp Lit Asn; Int Courtly Lit Soc; Asn Asian Studies; Asn Teachers Japanese. **RESEARCH** Japanese-Western literary relations; narrative East and West; courtly literature in Japan and Western Europe. **SELECTED PUBLICATIONS** Auth, the Artistry of Aeschylus and Zeami in a Comparative Study of Greek Tragedy and No, Comp Lit, Vol 45, 93; Staging Depth in Oneill, Eugene and the Politics of Psychological Discourse, Theatre J, Vol 48, 96. **CONTACT ADDRESS** Dept of Com Lit, Rutgers Univ, Ac Hlth Sc Ctr-Cn, New Brunswick, NJ, 08903.

WALKER, JANET L.
PERSONAL London, England **DISCIPLINE** FRENCH **EDUCATION** Bryn Mawr Col, PhD, 74, MA, 69; Chatham Col, BA, 67, BA, 93 **CAREER** Prof, 70-, Chatham Col **HONORS AND AWARDS** Phi Beta Kappa; NDEA Title IV Fel **MEMBERSHIPS** ASECS **RESEARCH** Diderot **CONTACT ADDRESS** Chatham Col, Pittsburgh, PA, 15232. **EMAIL** walker@chatham.edu

WALKER, RICHARD ERNEST
PERSONAL Born 01/31/1941, Cedar Grove, WV, m, 1970, 2 children **DISCIPLINE** GERMANIC LANGUAGES & LIT AND GERMAN & RUSSIAN LANGUAGE AND LIT **EDUCATION** Univ WV, BA, 66; WV Univ, MA, 68; PhD, Univ Chicago, PhD, 73. **CAREER** Asst prof, Dept of Ger & Russ, Mich State Univ, 72-77; asst prof, Dept of Ger & Russ; Univ Fla, 77-78; asst prof, Dept of Germ & Slavic Lang & Lit, Univ Md Col Pk, 79-84; anal/transl, Libr of Congress, Fed Res Div, Wash, DC, 85-86; Soviet anal, Army Intelligence Agency, 86-87; assoc prof, Dept of Ger and Russ, Howard Univ, 87-92; chair, Dept of Ger & Russ, Howard Univ, 90-92; assoc prof, Dept of Ger & Slavic Lang & Lit, Univ Md Col Pk, 92-; acting chair, Dept of Ger & Slavic Lang & Lit, 93-94; chair, Dept of Ger Studies, 94-97. **HONORS AND AWARDS** Symposium grant, Austrian lit & culture, Ger Studies, Col of Arts & Humanities, Univ Md Col Pk, fall 97; travel grant, Embassy of Austria, summer 97; res grant, Herzog Aug Bibliothek, Wolfenbuttel, Ger, jun 97; grant, Fulbright, summer sem, Ger, 95; grant/organizer, Sumposium: Diversity in a Europ context, Afro-Ger/Afro-Russ, Univ Md Col Pk, 95; grant, Symposium: Cultural Diversity in Ger: Hist Perspectives, Univ Md Col Pk, 95; res grant, Herzog Aug Bibliothek, Wolfenbuttel, Ger, summer 94; GRB Summer Res Grant, Univ Md Col Pk, summer 94. **MEMBERSHIPS** Amer Medieval Acad; Sixteenth Century Studies Asn; Amer Asn of Tchrs of Ger. **RESEARCH** Medieval narrative; Medieval German literature; Early modern historiography; Folklore & folk literature; 16th century Catholic Polemic. **SELECTED PUBLICATIONS** Articles, Johannes Nas, Encyl of the Reformation, Oxford, NY, Oxford Univ Press, 94; Michel Stifel, Encyl of the Reformation, Oxford, NY, Oxford Univ Press, 94; Pamphilus Gengenbach, Encycl of the Reformation, Oxford, NY, Oxford Univ Press, 94; Thomas Murner, Encycl of the Reformation, Oxford, NY, Oxford Univ Press, 94; paper, Manisfestations of Otherness in Early Modern Germany: Women, Children and the Poor, Dept of Foreign Lang, St Mary's Col, St Marys, Md, apr 96. **CONTACT ADDRESS** Dept. of Germanic Studies, Univ of Maryland, 3224 Jimenez Hall, College Park, MD, 27042. **EMAIL** rw87@umail.umd.edu

WALKER, ROBERT JEFFERSON
PERSONAL Born 04/22/1922, Gooding, ID, m, 1946, 2 children **DISCIPLINE** SPEECH, COMMUNICATION **EDUCATION** Univ Ill, BSEd, 46; Northwestern Univ, MA, 48; Wayne State Univ, PhD (mass commun), 66. **CAREER** Instr English and Speech, Kennedy-King Col, 46-48; asst prof speech and theatre, Chicago Teachers Col, 50-61; PROF SPEECH, NORTHEASTERN ILL UNIV, 61-. **MEMBERSHIPS** Int Commun Asn; Speech Commun Asn; Int Listening Asn. **RESEARCH** Interpersonal communication; mass media; organizational communication. **SELECTED PUBLICATIONS** Auth, A Contest of Faiths in Missionary Women and Pluralism in the American Southwest, Church Hist, Vol 65, 96; Presbyterian Missions and Cultural Interaction in The Far Southwest 1850-1950, Church Hist, Vol 65, 96; Winning the West for Christ in Jackson, Sheldon and Presbyterianism on the Rocky-Mountain Frontier, 1869-1880, NMex Histl Rev, Vol 72, 97. **CONTACT ADDRESS** Dept of Speech and Performing Arts, Northeastern Illinois Univ, Chicago, IL, 60625.

WALKER, STEVEN FRIEMEL
PERSONAL Born 03/28/1944, Washington, DC, m, 1966 **DISCIPLINE** COMPARATIVE LITERATURE **EDUCATION** Univ Wis-Madison, BA, 65; Harvard Univ, MA, 66, PhD (comp lit), 73. **CAREER** Asst prof, 71-79, ASSOC PROF COMP LIT, RUTGERS UNIV, 79-. **MEMBERSHIPS** Am Comp Lit Asn; MLA; Asn Asian Studies. **RESEARCH** Renaissance love poetry; th century literature; pastoral poetry. **SELECTED PUBLICATIONS** Auth, the Possible Role of Asymmetric Laryngeal Innervation in Language Lateralization in Points For and Against, Brain Lang, Vol 46, 94; Integrity In Depth, Zygon, Vol 30, 95. **CONTACT ADDRESS** 77 Lincoln Ave, Highland Park, NJ, 08904.

WALKER, WILLARD
PERSONAL Born 07/29/1926, Boston, MA, m, 1952, 2 children **DISCIPLINE** ANTHROPOLOGY, LINGUISTICS **EDUCATION** Harvard Univ, AB, 50; Univ Ariz, MA, 53; Cornell Univ, PhD (gen ling), 64. **CAREER** Res assoc, Univ Chicago Carnegie Cross-Cult Educ Proj, Tahlequah, Okla, 64-66; From asst prof to assoc prof anthrop, 66-77, PROF ANTHROP, WESLEYAN UNIV, 77-. **MEMBERSHIPS** Am Anthrop Asn; Ling Soc Am; Soc Appl Anthrop; Am Ethnol Soc; Am Soc Ethnohist. **RESEARCH** North American Indian languages; ethnology of North America; native writing systems. **SELECTED PUBLICATIONS** Auth, the Early History of the Cherokee Syllabary, Ethnohistory, Vol 40, 93; Pamela and Skepticism, Eighteenth Century Life, Vol 16, 92; Deadlock, Or, the Two Titles, Parnassus Poetry Rev, Vol 18, 93; As A Man Grows Older and Svevo Senilita in Translation, NY Rev Books, Vol 41, 94; The Way Home, Parnassus Poetry Rev, Vol 20, 95; Tlooth, Parnassus Poetry Rev, Vol 20, 95; Cigarettes, Parnassus Poetry Rev, Vol 20, 95; Singular Pleasures, Parnassus Poetry Rev, Vol 20, 95; Out of Bounds, Parnassus Poetry Rev, Vol 20, 95; Armenian Papers in Poems 1954-1984, Parnassus Poetry Rev, Vol 20, 95; Machiavellian Rhetoric in from the Counterreformation To Milton, Philos Lit, Vol , 95; The Sinking of the Odradek Stadium and Other Novels, Parnassus Poetry Rev, Vol 20, 95; Immeasurable Distances, Parnassus Poetry Rev, Vol 20, 95; 20 Lines A Day, Parnassus Poetry Rev, Vol 20, 95; Selected Declarations of Dependence, Parnassus Poetry Rev, Vol 20, 95; The Jist, Parnassus Poetry Rev, Vol 20, 95; Mikmaq Hieroglyphic Prayers in Readings in North America First Indigenous Script, Am Indian Cult Res J, Vol 20, 96; The Determination of Locke, Hume and Fielding, Eighteenth Century Life, Vol 20, 96; Professional Correctness in Literary Studies and Political Change, Philos Lit, Vol 20, 96; Reason and Rhetoric in the Philosophy of Hobbes, Philos Lit, Vol 21, 97; Fair New World, Int Fiction Rev, Vol 24, 97. **CONTACT ADDRESS** Dept of Anthrop, Wesleyan Univ, Middletown, CT, 06457.

WALLACE, KAREN SMYLEY
PERSONAL Born 12/11/1943, New Orleans, Louisiana, m **DISCIPLINE** ROMANCE LANGUAGES **EDUCATION** Hunter Coll NY, BA 1965; Middlebury Grad Sch, MA 1967; City Univ of NY, PhD 1977. **CAREER** SUNY Stony Brook, instructor 1967-71; Univ of MD, instructor 1972-75; Howard Univ Washington, assoc prof 1975-. **HONORS AND AWARDS** Fulbright Hayes Study Abroad 1965-67; Ford Found Dissertation Grant 1971; Phelps Stokes Teacher Exchange 1979; AW Mellon Rsch Grant 1984. **MEMBERSHIPS** Chair of educ comm Mayor's Intl Advisory Council 1980-. **CONTACT ADDRESS** Dept of Romance Languages, Howard Univ, Room 350, Locke Hall, Washington, VT, 20059.

WALLACH, GERALDINE P.
DISCIPLINE SPEECH-LANGUAGE PATHOLOGY **EDUCATION** Long Island Univ, BA; NY Univ, MA; CUNY, PhD. **CAREER** Speech, Emerson Col. **HONORS AND AWARDS** Fel, ASHA. **SELECTED PUBLICATIONS** Coed, Language Learning Disabilities of School-Age Children and Language Intervention Strategies and Academic Success. **CONTACT ADDRESS** Emerson Col, 100 Beacon Street, Boston, MA, 02116-1596.

WALLACH, LUITPOLD
PERSONAL Born 02/06/1910, Munich, Germany, m, 1970 **DISCIPLINE** CLASSICS, MEDIEVAL LATIN **EDUCATION** Univ Tuebingen, DPhil(hist), 32; Cornell Univ, PhD (classics), 47. **CAREER** Asst prof classics, Hamilton Col, 51-52; asst prof hist, Univ Ore, 53; asst prof classics, Cornell Univ, 53-55; asst prof, Univ Okla, 55-57; asst prof, Harpur Col, 57-62; prof, Marquette Univ, 62-67; prof, 67-78, EMER PROF CLASSICS, UNIV ILL, URBANA, 78-; Fund Advan Educ fel, 52; Am Coun Learned Soc grant, 60; mem bd, Grad Sch, Marquette Univ, 63-67, fac fel, 67; Leo Baeck Inst fel, 67; assoc, Ctr Advan Studies, Univ Ill, 69-70. **HONORS AND AWARDS** Festschrift: Beitraege Luitpold Wallach Gewidmet, Hiersemann, Stuttgart, 75. **MEMBERSHIPS** Am Philol Asn; AHA; Mediaeval Acad Am. **RESEARCH** Philology; mediaeval Latin and history. **SELECTED PUBLICATIONS** Auth, Coercive Uses of Mandatory Reporting in Therapeutic Relationships, Behavioral Scis Law, Vol 11, 93. **CONTACT ADDRESS** Dept of Classics, Univ of Ill, Urbana, IL, 61801.

WALLACH, MARTHA K.
DISCIPLINE GERMAN LANGUAGE AND LITERATURE **EDUCATION** Univ Wash, PhD, 72. **CAREER** Fac, Univ Wisc Green Bay; fac, Central Conn State Univ, 88; prof Ger and chr Mod Lang Dept, 97-. **HONORS AND AWARDS** Bd dirs, N Am Heine Soc; ed database and mem dir, Women in Ger. **MEMBERSHIPS** N Am Heine Soc; Women in Ger. **RESEARCH** German literature; Heirich Heine; Therese Albertine Luise von Jakob Robinson; Barbara Frischmuth. **SELECTED PUBLICATIONS** Auth, pubs about Heinrich Heine and Therese Albertine Luise von Jakob Robinson, on mother-daughter relationships in German literature, and the image of Poles in German literature; trans, works of Barbara Frischmuth. **CONTACT ADDRESS** Central Connecticut State Univ, 1615 Stanley St, New Britain, CT, 06050.

WALLACKER, BENJAMIN E
PERSONAL Born 11/27/1926, San Francisco, CA **DISCIPLINE** EAST ASIAN PHILOLOGY **EDUCATION** Univ Calif, Berkeley, AB, 50, MA, 54, PhD (Orient lang), 60. **CAREER** Instr Chinese, Univ Kans, 59-60, from asst prof to assoc prof Orient lang, 60-64; assoc prof, 64-69; PROF ORIENT LANG, UNIV CALIF, DAVIS, 70-. **MEMBERSHIPS** Am Orient Soc; Asn Asian Studies. **RESEARCH** The art of war in traditional China; the growth of imperial institutions in Former Han; the development of law in early China. **SELECTED PUBLICATIONS** Auth, Fairbank Remembered, J Asian Hist, Vol 27, 93; The Common-Law System in Chinese Context in Hong Kong in Transition, J Asian Hist, Vol 27, 93; Law and Legality in China in The Testament of a China Watcher, J Asian Hist, Vol 28, 94; The Textual History of the Huai Nan Tzu, J Asian Hist, Vol 28, 94; Law and Morality in ancient China in The Silk Manuscripts of Huang Lao, J Asian Hist, Vol 28, 94; Policing and Punishment in China in from Patriarchy to the People, J Asian Hist, Vol 28, 94; Chinese Loan Agreements from Discoveries at Turfan in a Study of the History of Chinese Civil Law, J Asian Hist, Vol 28, 94; Law and Order in Sung China, J Asian Hist, Vol 28, 94; Law and Morality in ancient China in The Silk Manuscripts of Huang Lao, J Asian Hist, Vol 28, 94; Policing and Punishment in China in from Patriarchy to the People, J Asian Hist, Vol 28, 94; The Textual History of The Huai Nan Tzu, J Asian Hist, Vol 28, 94; Heaven and Earth in Early Han Thought in Chapters 3, 4 and 5 of Huainanzi, J Asian Hist, Vol 28, 94; Law and Order in Sung China, J Asian Hist, Vol 28, 94; Autocratic Tradition and Chinese Politics, J Asian Hist, Vol 29, 95; Civil Law in Qing and Republican China, J Asian Hist, Vol 29, 95; To Steal a Book is an Elegant offense in Intellectual Property Law in Chinese Civilization, J Asian Hist, Vol 30, 96; Law and Local Society in Late Imperial China in Northern Taiwan in The 19Th Century, J Asian Hist, Vol 30, 96; Negotiating Daily Life in Traditional China in How Ordinary People Used Contracts, 600-1400, J Asian Hist, Vol 31, 97; Scarlet Memorial in Tales of Cannibalism in Modern China, J Asian Hist, Vol 31, 97. **CONTACT ADDRESS** Dept of Anthrop, Univ of Calif, Davis, CA, 95616.

WALLER, MARGUERITE R.
PERSONAL Born 03/16/1948, Nyack, NY **DISCIPLINE** COMPARATIVE LITERATURE **EDUCATION** Cornell Univ, BA, 69; Yale Univ, M Phil, 72, PhD, 78. **CAREER** Asst, assoc, full prof English, Amherst Col, 74-90; prof English and Women's Studies, Univ CA, Riverside, 90-. **HONORS AND AWARDS** Phi Beta Kappa; Fulbrights: Italy, France, Hungary; Woodrow Wilson Fac Development grant; NEH Summer fel. **MEMBERSHIPS** MLA; Am Asn of Italian Studies; Am Studies Asn; Am Women's Studies Asn. **RESEARCH** Film and visual culture; global feminism; new media; cultural studies. **SELECTED PUBLICATIONS** Auth, The Voice of Woman in Contemporary Society: Hillary Rodham Clinton, Reden: The J of the North Am Studies Center, Alcala, Spain, spring 94; The Art of Miscegenation in an Age of Electronic Communication, Romance Languages Annual, Purdue Res Found, 94; Hungarian Film Week, 1994, The Am Historical Rev, vol 99, no 4, Oct 94; Border Boda or Divorce Fronterizo, Negotiating Performance in Latin(o) America, ed Diana Taylor and Juan Villegas, Duke Univ Press, 94; Signifying the Holocaust: Liliana Cavani's Portiere di notte, Feminisms in the Cinema, ed Laura Pietropaolo and Ada Testaferri, IN Univ Press, 95; If 'Reality is the Best Metaphor,' It Must be Virtual?, Diacritics, 97; New Media in Old Film Cans: Maurizio Nichetti's Multi-Media Cinema, in Romance Languages Annual, Purdue Res Found, 98; Declonizing the Screen: From Ladri di biciclette to Ladri di saponette, in Designing Italy: Italy in Asia, Africa, the Americas, and Europe, ed Beverly Allen and Mary Russo, Univ MN Press, 98; Pocha or Porkchop?: Introduction to and Interview with Laura Esparza, in Latinas on Stage: Practice and Theory, ed Alicia Arrizon and Lilian Manzor Coats, Berkeley: Third Woman Press, forthcoming; nunmerous other publications, videos and exhibitions. **CONTACT ADDRESS** Dept of English, Univ of California, Riverside, Riverside, CA, 92521. **EMAIL** marguerite.waller@ucr.edu

WALSH, JOHN KEVIN
PERSONAL Born 08/10/1939, New York, NY **DISCIPLINE** MEDIEVAL SPANISH LITERATURE, SPANISH LINGUISTICS **EDUCATION** Univ Notre Dame, AB, 61; Univ Madrid, dipl, 62; Columbia Univ, MA, 64; Univ Va, PhD (Span), 67. **CAREER** From instr to asst prof Span, Univ Va, 66-69; asst prof, 69-75, assoc prof, 75-78, PROF SPAN, UNIV CALIF, BERKELEY, 78-. **MEMBERSHIPS** MLA; Am Asn Teachers Span and Port. **RESEARCH** Hispanic linguistics; Garcia Lorca. **SELECTED PUBLICATIONS** Auth, the Poem Within the Trance, On John of the Cross, Romance Philol, Vol 46, 93. **CONTACT ADDRESS** Dept of Span and Port, Univ of Calif, Berkeley, CA, 94720.

WALSH, JONATHAN D.
DISCIPLINE 17TH AND 18TH CENTURY FRENCH THEATER AND PROSE **EDUCATION** Univ Calif, Santa Barbara, PhD. **CAREER** Fr, Wheaton Col. **RESEARCH** Psychoanalysis and literature; jealousy and symbolic exchange in the French novel; French moralists and philosophes. **SELECTED PUBLICATIONS** Publ, on Abbo Provost, Marcel Proust and Enlightenment authors appear in Romance Quart and Esprit Createur. **CONTACT ADDRESS** Dept of Fr, Wheaton Col, 26 East Main St, Norton, MA, 02766.

WALTER, RENEE
PERSONAL Born 01/15/1930, Senta, Yugoslavia **DISCIPLINE** SPANISH AND HISPANO-AMERICAN LITERATURE **EDUCATION** Univ of the Repub, Uruguay, BABS, 56; Brooklyn Col, BA, 62; Univ Poitiers, dipl, 65; NY Univ, MA, 65, PhD (Span lang and lit), 69. **CAREER** Instr Span lang and lit, Brooklyn Col, 63-65; Fulbright scholar, Spain, 66-68; asst prof, 68-73, ASSOC PROF SPAN AND HISP AM LIT, GUSTAVUS ADOLPHUS COL, 73-. **MEMBERSHIPS** MLA; Asn Span Writers. **RESEARCH** Spanish Golden Age; 16th century European history; Reformation and counterreformation. **SELECTED PUBLICATIONS** Auth, In Memoriam Anton Bruckner fur Orgel Op91, Musik Und Kirche, Vol 65, 95; Missa in Labore Requies for 24 Voices, Mus Kirche, Vol 65, 95; Marranos in Madrid 1600-1670, Historische Zeitschrift, Vol 264, 97. **CONTACT ADDRESS** Dept of Spanish, Gustavus Adolphus Col, St Peter, MN, 56082.

WANG, AIHE
DISCIPLINE HISTORY; LANGUAGE **EDUCATION** Higher Education Examination Committee, P.R.C., BA, 83; Chinese Acad of Social Sciences, MA, 86; MA, 90, PhD, Harvard Univ **CAREER** Asst prof, Purdue Univ, 95-. **CONTACT ADDRESS** Dept of History, Purdue Univ, 1358 University Hall, West Lafayette, IN, 47907-1358. **EMAIL** aihewang@purdue.edu

WANG, JOAN PARSONS
PERSONAL Born 10/21/1925, Cincinnait, OH, w, 2 children **DISCIPLINE** ENGLISH, COMPARATIVE LITERATURE **EDUCATION** Radcliffe Col, AB, 47; Brown Univ, MA, 49; Ind Univ, PhD (comp lit), 64. **CAREER** Asst prof, 66-80, ASSOC PROF ENGLISH, INDEPENDENT STUDIES DIV, SCH CONTINUING STUDIES, IND UNIV, BLOOMINGTON, 80-. **HONORS AND AWARDS** Cert Merit, Nat Univ Exten Asn, 71 and 81. **MEMBERSHIPS** Nat Univ Exten Asn. **RESEARCH** Writing syllabi for indePENdent study courses in English and world literature; modern European drama; women's studies. **SELECTED PUBLICATIONS** Auth, the Muslim Protest in China and An Analysis of the Marxist in Islamic Confrontations, Temenos, Vol 32, 96. **CONTACT ADDRESS** Dept of English, Indiana Univ, Bloomington, Bloomington, IN, 47401.

WANG, MASON YU-HENG
PERSONAL Born 05/07/1936, China, m, 1963, 3 children **DISCIPLINE** SHAKESPEARE, COMPARATIVE LITERATURE **EDUCATION** Nat Taiwan Univ, BA, 59; IN Univ, MA, 65, PhD(English), 72. **CAREER** Instr English, Cent MO State Col, 65-68; from instr to asst prof, 69-76, chmn dept, 74-78, assoc prof, 76-83, PROF ENGLISH SAGINAW VALLEY STATE UNIV, 83-. **MEMBERSHIPS** Shakespeare Asn Am. **RESEARCH** Shakespeare; comparative literature; Chinese literature. **SELECTED PUBLICATIONS** Auth, Burlesque and Irony in The Two Gentlemen of Verona, Shakespeare Newslett, 9/72; Review of Ten Poems and Lyrics by Mao Tse-tung, Green River Rev, 76; ed, Perspectives in Contemporary Chinese Liter-

ature, Green River Press, 83; tr & ed, Zhang Siyang, Hamlet's Melancholy, and Zhang Xiaoyang, Shakespeare and the Idea of Nature in the Renaissance, Shakespeare and the Triple Play, ed Sidney Homan, Bucknell Univ Press, 88; contrib & ed, Meng Xianqiang. A Historical .Survey of Shakespeare in China, Shakespeare Res Center of NE Normal Univ, 96. **CONTACT ADDRESS** Dept of English, Saginaw Valley State Univ, 7400 Bay Rd, University Center, MI, 48710-0001. **EMAIL** mywang@tardis.svsu.edu

WANG, WILLIAM S.Y.
PERSONAL Born 08/14/1933, Shanghai, China, m, 1973, 4 children **DISCIPLINE** LINGUISTICS **EDUCATION** Columbia Col, AB, 55; Univ Mich, MA, 56, PhD (ling), 60. **CAREER** Mem staff, Res Lab Electronics, Mass Inst Technol, 60; instr commun sci and res assoc, Commun Sci Lab, Univ Mich, 60-61; mem staff, Int Bus Machines Res Ctr, 61; asst prof ling and chmn dept Eastern Asian lang and lit, Ohio State Univ, 61-63, assoc prof ling, 62-65, chmn div, 62-65; PROF LING, UNIV CALIF, BERKELEY, 65-; Nat Sci Found rea grant, 61; Ohio State Univ grant to establish ling res lab, 62; fel ling, Ctr Advan Studies Behav Sci, 69-70; Fulbright prof ling, Sweden, 71-72; ED, J CHINESE LING, 73-; Guggenheim fel, 78. **MEMBERSHIPS** Charter mem Am Asn Phonetic Sci; Ling Soc Am; MLA; Acoust Soc Am. **RESEARCH** Languages; speech. **SELECTED PUBLICATIONS** Auth, Lexical Diffusion in Semantic Change with Special Reference to Universal Changes, Folia Ling Hist, Vol 16, 95; Bai Ma Si, A Case of Folk Etymology and The Name of the Temple Comes from the Sanskrit Word Padma, Which Means Lotus, J Chinese Ling, Vol 24, 96. **CONTACT ADDRESS** Dept of Ling, Univ of California, Berkeley, CA, 94720.

WANNER, ADRIAN J.
PERSONAL Born 01/26/1960, Besh, Switzerland, m, 1989, 2 children **DISCIPLINE** RUSSIAN LANGUAGE **EDUCATION** Columbia Univ, PhD, 92. **CAREER** Asst prof, 92-96, Univ Evansville; asst prof to assoc prof, 96-, Penn St. **HONORS AND AWARDS** Poetry Prize, Columbia Univ, 90; AAASS Nat Award for best Slavic Papers, 92. **MEMBERSHIPS** MLA; AAASS; AATSEEL; ALTA. **RESEARCH** Russian symbolism; comparative literature. **SELECTED PUBLICATIONS** Auth, Alexander Blok: Gedichte, Suhrkamp Verlage, 90; auth, Baudelaire in Russia, Univ Press Fl, 96; art, From Subversion to Affirmation: The Prose Poem as a Russian Genre, Slavic Review, 97; auth, Innokentij Annenskij: Die Schwarze Silhouette, Pano Verlag, 98; art, Aleksei Remizov's Dreams: Surrealism Avant la Lettre?, Russian Review, 99. **CONTACT ADDRESS** Dept of Germanic & Slavic Lang, 315 Burrowes Bldg, University Park, PA, 16801. **EMAIL** ajw3@psu.edu

WARD, DOROTHY COX
PERSONAL Born 07/14/1925, Birmingham, AL, m, 1949, 4 children **DISCIPLINE** GERMANIC STUDIES **EDUCATION** Birmingham-Southern Col, AB, 45, BM, 50; Columbia Univ, MA, 54, PhD, 76. **CAREER** Instr Ger and French, Birmingham-Southern Col, 46-49; instr Ger, Univ Ala, 49-50; instr Ger and French, Birmingham-Southern Coll, 50-52; instr Ger, Sch Gen Studies, Columbia Univ, 52-54; asst prof Ger and French, Birmingham-Southern Col, 54-56; instr English and French, Walddorfer Schule, Hamburg, Ger, 56-57; From asst prof to assoc prof Ger and French, 57-76, PROF GER AND FRENCH AND CHMN DEPT MOD FOREIGN LANG, BIRMINGHAM-SOUTHERN COL, 76-; CHAIRPERSON DIV HUMANITIES, 80-. **MEMBERSHIPS** Am Asn Teachers Ger; SAtlantic Mod Lang Asn, Southern Conf on Foreign Lang Teaching. **RESEARCH** Modern German literature; Hermann Hesse. **SELECTED PUBLICATIONS** Auth, Adams, John in a Life, Penn Mag Hist Biog, Vol 118, 94; The Cultivation of Hatred in the Bourgeois Experience in Victoria to Freud, J Mil Hist, Vol 58, 94; Portia in the World of Adams, Abigail, Penn Mag Hist Biog, Vol 118, 94; Victorian America and the Civil War, Civil War Hist, Vol 40, 94; The Letters of Bryant, William, Cullen, Vol 5, 1865-1871, Vol 6, 1872-1978, New York Hist, Vol 76, 95; The Book of American Diaries in from Heart and Mind to PEN and Paper in Day by Day Personal Accounts Through the Centuries, Penn Mag Hist Biog, Vol 120, 96; Mavericks Progress in an Autobiography, Penn Mag Hist Biog, Vol 120, 96; The Information, Virginia Quart Rev, Vol 72, 96; Look to the Earth, Historical Archaeology and the American Civil War, Civil War Hist, Vol 42, 96; Love Again in Larkin and Obscenity, Sewanee Rev, Vol 105, 97. **CONTACT ADDRESS** Dept of Mod Foreign Lang, Birmingham-So Col, Birmingham, AL, 35204.

WARD, GREGORY
PERSONAL Born 10/08/1955, Northridge, CA, m, 1992 **DISCIPLINE** LINGUISTICS **EDUCATION** Univ CA, Berkeley, BA (Linguistics, with honors, and Comparative lit), 78; Univ PA, PhD (Linguistics), 85. **CAREER** Lect, Dept of Linguistics, Univ PA, 83-84; lect, Dept of Linguistics, San Diego State Univ, 85-86; asst prof, 86-91, assoc prof, 91-97, prof, Dept of Linguistics, Northwestern Univ, 97-; consult, AT & T Labs-Res, 86-97; vis prof, LSA Linguistic Inst, OH State Univ, 93; vis prof, UFR Angellier, Universite Charles de Gaulle-Lille 3, 96; vis prof, LSA Linguistic Inst, Cornell Univ, 97. **HONORS AND AWARDS** Phi Beta Kappa; graduated with Great Distinction in General Scholarship from the College of Letters and Sciences, Univ CA, Berkeley, 78; Meritorious Performance and Professional Promise Award, Col of Arts and Letters, San Diego State Univ, 86; Northwestern Univ grant for Ed Excellence, 91; Northwestern Univ Res grant, 91-93; Co-PI, Nat Inst on Deafness and Other Communication Disorders, Dept of Health and Human Services, 91-96; fel, Center for Advanced Study in the Behavioral Sciences, to be arranged. **MEMBERSHIPS** Int Pragmatics Asn; Am Asn of Artificial Intelligence; Asn for Computational Linguistics; Linguistic Soc of Am; ed bd, Computational Linguistics, 95-97; adv ed, Current Res in the Semantics/Pragmatics Interface, 97-. **SELECTED PUBLICATIONS** Auth, The Semantics and Pragmatics of Preposing, Outstanding Dissertations in Linguistics series, Garland, 88; with Gail McKoon and Roger Ratcliff, Testing Theories of Language Processing: An Empirical Investigation of the On-Line Lexical Decision Task, in J of Experimental Psychology: Learning, Memory, and Cognition, 94; with Julia Hirschberg, The Interpretation of the High-Rise Question Contour in English, in J of Pragmatics, 95; with Betty J Birner, Definiteness and the English Existential, in Language, 95; From Discourse Process to Grammatical Construction: On Left-Dislocation in English (1992), by Ronald Geluykens, invited review, Language, 95; with Betty J Birner, A Crosslinguistic Study of Postposing in Discourse, in Language and Speech: Special Issue on Discourse, Syntax, and Information, 96; with Betty J Birner, on the Discourse Function of Rightward Movement in English, in Conceptual Structure, Discourse and Language, ed by Adele Goldberg, Stanford: Center for the Study of Language and Information, 96; auth, The Battle Over Anaphoric Islands: Syntax vs Pragmatics, in Directions in Functional Linguistics, ed by Akio Kamio, John Benjamins, 97; with Betty J Birner, Response to Abbott, in Language, 97; with Betty J Birner, Information Status and Noncanonical Word Order in English, John Benjamins, 98; with Laurence R Horn, Phatic Communication and Pragmatic Theory: A Reply, in J of Linguistics, forthcoming; Word's Out: Gay Men's English (1996), by William Leap, invited review in J of the Hist of Sexuality, forthcoming; numerous other book reviews, chapters, articles, papers, and other publications. **CONTACT ADDRESS** Dept of Linguistics, Northwestern Univ, 2016 Sheridan Rd, Evanston, IL, 60208-4090. **EMAIL** gw@nwu.edu

WARD, PATRICIA ANN
PERSONAL Born 08/26/1940, Warren, PA **DISCIPLINE** COMPARATIVE LITERATURE AND FRENCH **EDUCATION** Eastern Nazarene Col, BA, 62; Univ Wis, MA, 64, PhD (comp lit), 68. **CAREER** Asst prof comp lit, State Univ NY Albany, 68-72; asst prof, 72-75, actg head, dept French, 80-81, assoc prof, 75-82, PROF FRENCH AND COMP LIT, PA STATE UNIV, UNIVERSITY PARK, 82-; State Univ NY Res Found grant-in-aid, 71; res initiation grant, Pa State Univ, 73-74; fel Inst Arts and Humanistic Studies, Pa State Univ, 79; ASSOC ED, CHRISTIAN SCHOLAR'S REV, 81-; vis prof comp lit, Baylor Univ, 82. **MEMBERSHIPS** MLA; Am Comp Lit Asn; Conf Christianity and Lit (treas, 72-74, vpres, 78-80); Am Asn Teachers Fr; Alliance Fr. **RESEARCH** Literary criticism; th-century French literature; European Romanticism. **SELECTED PUBLICATIONS** Auth, Getting it Right in Language, Literature, and Ethics, Relig Lit, Vol 25, 93;The Sublime and Revolutionary Oratory in Themes and Myths of the Restoration and the July Monarchy, Nineteenth Century Fr Stud, Vol 22, 93; Getting it Right in Language, Literature, and Ethics, Religion Lit, Vol 25, 93; Contemporary Literary Theory in a Christian Appraisal, Religion Lit, Vol 25, 93; The Culture of Redemption, Phil Lit, Vol 17, 93; The Ethics of Criticism, Religion Lit, Vol 25, 93; The Thought and Art of Joubert, Joseph 1754-1824, Rev D Hist Lit De La France, Vol 94, 94; A Southern Story, New Orleans Rev, Vol 23, 97; Dictionary for Les Miserables in an Encyclopedic Dictionary of Hugo, Victor Novel Created Using the Latest Technologies, Nineteenth-Century Fr Stud, Vol 25, 97;. **CONTACT ADDRESS** Dept of French, Pennsylvania State Univ, University Park, PA, 16802.

WARD, SETH
PERSONAL Born 12/15/1952, New York, NY, m, 1978, 4 children **DISCIPLINE** NEAR EASTERN LANGUAGES **EDUCATION** Yale Univ, BA, 74, MA, 78, PhD, 84. **CAREER** Instr, 84-85, Yale Univ; lectr, 85-88, Univ Haifa; guest lectr, 89, Ben Gurion Univ, Negev; lectr, 89-91, Israel Inst Techn; asst prof, 91-, Univ Denver. **RESEARCH** Jewish-Muslim relationship; Jews of Islamic lands; Egypt; land of Israel; crypto-Jews. **SELECTED PUBLICATIONS** Art, Taqi al-Din al-Subki on Construction, Continuance and Repair of Churches and Synagogues in Islamic Law, Stud in Islamic & Judaic Traditions II, Scholars Press, 89; art, Expel the Jews and Christians from the Arabian Peninsula, Bull of Schl of African & Oriental Stud, 53, 90; art, Dhimmi Women and Mourning, Islamic Legal Interpretation: Muftis and the Fatwas, Harvard Univ Press, 96; art, Sepphoris in the Arab Period, Sepphoris in Gallilee: Crosscurrents of Culture, NC Museum of Art, 96; art, Sepphoris in Sacred Geography, Galilee, Confluence of Cultures, Winona Lake Ind, 99; art, Tsippori be-tekufah ha-aravit (Sepphoris in the Arabic Period) Yerushalayim ve-Eretz Yisrael I, Bar-Ilan Univ Press, 99; art, Ibn Rifa on the Churches and Synagogues of Cairo, Avoda & Ibada, Lit & Rit in Islamic and Judaic Soc, Mediaeval Encounters: Jewish Christian and Muslim Culture in Confluence and Dialogue, 99; ed, Avoda and Ibada, Liturgy and Ritual in Islamic and Judaic Societies, Mediaeval Encounters: Jewish Christian and Muslim Culture in Confluence and Dialogue, 99. **CONTACT ADDRESS** Center for Judaic Studies, Univ of Denver, Denver, CO, 80208. **EMAIL** sward@du.edu

WARGA JR., RICHARD G.
DISCIPLINE GREEK, LATIN, MYTHOLOGY, SCIENTIFIC TERMINOLOGY **EDUCATION** Univ Ill, Urbana-Champaign, PhD, 88. **CAREER** Instr Classics, coordr, elem Lat crse, La State Univ. **RESEARCH** Epigraphy; papyrology; Coptic studies. **SELECTED PUBLICATIONS** Auth, A Coptic-Greek Stele from Memphis, Tennessee, in Chronique d'Egypte LXVI, 91; A Repayment of a Loan, in Zeitschrift f(r Papyrologie und Epigraphik 100, 94. **CONTACT ADDRESS** Dept of For Lang and Lit, Louisiana State Univ, 122 A Prescott Hall, Baton Rouge, LA, 70803. **EMAIL** warga@homer.forlang.lsu.edu

WARNER, NICHOLAS OLIVER
PERSONAL Born 02/11/1950, San Francisco, CA, m, 3 children **DISCIPLINE** COMPARATIVE ; ENGLISH & AMERICAN LITERATURE **EDUCATION** Stanford Univ, BA, 72; Univ Calif, Berkeley, PhD, 77. **CAREER** Vis asst prof Eng, Oberlin Col, 78-80; asst prof Lit, Claremont McKenna Col, 80-86; assoc prof, Claremont McKenna Col, 86-94; full prof, Claremont McKenna Col, 94-. **HONORS AND AWARDS** Huntton Award for Superior Tchg, 83, 84, 88, 90; Graves fel in the Humanities. **MEMBERSHIPS** MLA; Am Asn Advan Slavic Studies; Am Studies Assoc. **RESEARCH** Literature and visual arts; 19th century British, Am & Russ lit. **SELECTED PUBLICATIONS** Auth, Blakes Moon-Ark symbolism, Blake Quart, fall 80; Spirits of America: Intoxication in 19th Century American Literature, Univ Oklahoma, 97; The theme of travel in Russian and English Romanticism, Russian Lit Triquart (in press); In search of literary science! The Russian formalist tradition, Pac Coast Philol (in press). **CONTACT ADDRESS** Dept of Literature, Claremont McKenna Col, 500 E 9th St, Claremont, CA, 91711-6400. **EMAIL** nwarner@mckenna.edu

WARREN, EDWARD W.
PERSONAL Born 01/20/1929, San Francisco, CA, m, 1955, 3 children **DISCIPLINE** PHILOSOPHY, GREEK **EDUCATION** Stanford Univ, BA, 50; Johns Hopkins Univ, PhD (philos), 61. **CAREER** Asst prof philos, Syracuse Univ, 59-63; From asst prof to prof, 63-70, PROF CLASSICS AND PHILOS, SAN DIEGO STATE UNIV, 70-. **MEMBERSHIPS** Am Philol Asn; Soc Greek Philos; AAUP; Int Soc Neo-Platonic Studies. **RESEARCH** Greek philosophy; Plotinus; metaphysics. **SELECTED PUBLICATIONS** Auth, More Good Than Harm in a First Principle for Environmental Agencies and Reving Courts, Ecology Law Quart, Vol 20, 93; Science, Environment, and the Law in Discussion, Ecol Law Quart, Vol 21, 94. **CONTACT ADDRESS** Dept of Class and Orient Lang and Lit, San Diego State Univ, San Diego, CA, 92182.

WARRIN, DONALD OGDEN
PERSONAL Born 04/17/1933, Montclair, NJ, d, 4 children **DISCIPLINE** PORTUGUESE **EDUCATION** Univ Southern Calif, BA, 60; NY Univ, MA, 66, PhD(Port), 73. **CAREER** Assoc Prof Port, Calif State Univ, Hayward, 69-; PROF EMER, Calif State Univ, Hayward. **HONORS AND AWARDS** Causa Portuguesa, Poruguese Union of the State of Calif (UPEC), 87. **MEMBERSHIPS** Immigration Hist Soc; Hist Inst of Terceira, Azores; Nantucket Hist Asn; Nev Hist Soc; Western Hist Asn **RESEARCH** Portuguese immigrant history and literature **SELECTED PUBLICATIONS** Coauth, Bibliography of Instructional Materials for the Teaching of Portuguese, Calif Dept Educ, 76; auth, A literature do imigrante portugues na California, Horizontes, 3-4/77; On the function of the poetic sign in Alvares de Azevedo, Luso-Brazilian Rev, summer 1980; Alfred Lewis--Romance e poesia em dois idiamas, Arquipelago, 1/81; ed, Cem Anos de Poesia Portuguesa na California, Porto, Portugal, 86; Aguarelas Florentinas e Outras Poesias, Angra do Heroismo, Portugal, 86; Portuguese Pioneers in Early Nevada, nev Hist Soc Quart, spring 92; co-auth, Portuguese Women on the American Frontier, O Rosto Feminino da Expansao Pourtuguesa, Lisbon, 95; An Immigrant Path to Social Mobility: Portuguese Atlantic Islanders in the California Sheep Industry, Calif Hist, winter 77/98; The Portuguese in Nevada: A Visual History, hist photograph exhibit, Nev State Libr and Archives, 95; Cowboys, Miners, and Sheepherders: Portuguese in the Old West, hist photograph exhibit, Univ Mass, Dartmouth, 96. **CONTACT ADDRESS** Dept of Foreign Lang, California State Univ, Hayward, 25800 Carlos Bee Bvd, Hayward, CA, 94542-3001. **EMAIL** dwarrin@csuhayward.edu

WARWICK, JACK
PERSONAL Born 10/09/1930, Huddersfield, England, m, 1954, 3 children **DISCIPLINE** ROMANCE LANGUAGES **EDUCATION** Oxford Univ, BA, 53, MA, 59; Univ Western Ont, PhD (French), 63. **CAREER** Instr French, Huron Col, 59-60; From instr to asst prof French and Span, Univ Western Ont, 60-68; assoc prof French, McMaster Univ, 68-70; ASSOC PROF FRENCH LIT AND SOC SCI, YORK UNIV, 70-; Can Coun sr fel, 66-67; vis prof, Laval Univ, 72. **MEMBERSHIPS** Int Asn Fr Studies; Asn Can Univ Teachers Fr; MLA; Asn Prof

de Francais des Univ Can (pres, 76-78). **RESEARCH** French-Canadian literature; seventeenth century French nature concepts particularly early happy savages; sociological methodology in literature. **SELECTED PUBLICATIONS** Auth, Literary Life in Quebec, Vol 2, the National Project of Canadians, 1806-1839, Univ Toronto Quart, Vol 64, 94. **CONTACT ADDRESS** Atkinson Col, York Univ, 4700 Keele St, Toronto, ON, M3j 1P3.

WASHBURN, DENNIS
DISCIPLINE ASIAN AND MIDDLE EASTERN LANGUAGES AND LITERATURES **EDUCATION** Harvard Univ, BA; Oxford Univ, MA; Yale Univ, MPhil, PhD. **CAREER** Asst prof, Dartmouth Col. **HONORS AND AWARDS** Monbusho Scholar, Japanese Min Educ. **RESEARCH** Transition from Edo to Meiji lit; transl of moral categories in Meiji fiction. **SELECTED PUBLICATIONS** Auth, The Dilemma of the Modern in Japanese Fiction, Yale UP, 95; articles on var works by Mori Ogai, Ueda Akinari, Miyazawa Kenji, Mishima Yukio, and Ooka Shohei. **CONTACT ADDRESS** Dartmouth Col, 3529 N Main St, #207, Hanover, NH, 03755.

WASHBURN, YULAN M.
DISCIPLINE PORTUGUESE LITERATURE **EDUCATION** Univ NC, PhD, 67. **CAREER** Prof. **SELECTED PUBLICATIONS** Auth, pubs on secularized culture. **CONTACT ADDRESS** Dept of Romance Languages, Knoxville, TN, 37996.

WASHINGTON, IDA HARRISON
PERSONAL Port Washington, NY, m, 1948, 6 children **DISCIPLINE** GERMAN LITERATURE **EDUCATION** Wellesley Col, AB, 46; Middlebury Col, AM, 50; Columbia Univ, PhD, 62. **CAREER** Instr Ger, Univ Minn, 61-62; instr, Drew Univ, 64; instr, NY Univ, 64-65; lectr, Seton Hall Univ, 65-66; asst prof, 66-72, assoc prof mod lang, 72-77, PROF MOD LANG, SOUTHEASTERN MASS UNIV, 77-; EXEC SECY, NORTHEAST MOD LANG ASN, 80-. **MEMBERSHIPS** Am Asn Teachers Ger; MLA; Northeast Mod Lang Asn; Soc Ger-Am Studies. **RESEARCH** Poetic realism. **SELECTED PUBLICATIONS** Auth, the Fortunes of German Writers in america in Studies in Literary Reception, J Eng Ger Philol, Vol 92, 93. **CONTACT ADDRESS** Dept of Mod Lang, Southeastern Mass Univ, North Dartmouth, MA, 02747.

WASIOLEK, EDWARD
PERSONAL Born 04/27/1924, Camden, NJ, m, 1948, 3 children **DISCIPLINE** COMPARATIVE LITERATURE **EDUCATION** Rutgers Univ, BA, 49; Harvard Univ, MA, 50, PhD, 55. **CAREER** Res assoc, Russ Res Ctr, Harvard Univ, 51-53, teaching fel English, 53-54; instr English & humanities, Ohio Wesleyan Univ, 54-55; asst prof English, 55-59, assoc prof English, Slavic lang & lit, 59-64, chmn dept, 70-76, prof Comp Lit, English & Slavic Lang & Lit, Univ Chicago, 64-, chmn Dept Comp Lit, 65-, mem adv bd, Encycl Brittanica, 73. **RESEARCH** Modern novel; especially technique and comparative aspects; theory of criticism. **SELECTED PUBLICATIONS** Soviet Portraits, Mass Inst Technol, 55; Croce and contextualist criticism, Mod Philol, 8-59; Tolstoy's The Death of Ivan Ilych, and James' fictional imperatives, Mod Fiction Studies, winter 61; ed, Crime and Punishment and the Critics, Wadsworth, 61; Aut Caesar, aut Nihil, a study of Dostoevsky's moral dialectic, PMLA, 3/63; auth, Dostoevsky: The Major Fiction, Mass Inst Technol, 64; The Brothers Karamazov and the Critics, Wadsworth, 67; The Notebooks for Crime and Punishment, 67, The Notebooks for the Idiot, 68, The Notebooks for the Possessed, 68, ed & transl, The Notebooks for the Brothers Karamazov, 71 & ed, The Gambler and Paulina Suslova's diary, 72, Univ Chicago; auth, Tolstoy's Major Fiction, Univ Chicago, 78; Fathers and Sons: Russia at the Crossroads, Twayne, 93. **CONTACT ADDRESS** Dept of Slavic Language & Literature, Univ Chicago, 1130 E 59th St, Chicago, IL, 60637-1539. **EMAIL** e-wasiolek@uchicago.edu

WASOW, THOMAS ALEXANDER
PERSONAL Born 12/14/1945, New Rochelle, NY, m, 1971, 2 children **DISCIPLINE** THEORETICAL LINGUISTICS **EDUCATION** Reed Col, BA, 67; Mass Inst Technol, PhD (ling), 72. **CAREER** Asst prof ling, Hampshire Col, 72-73; asst prof, 74-78, ASSOC PROF LING AND PHILOS, STANFORD UNIV, 78-; Vis prof, Ling Soc Am Summer Inst, 79; co-ed, Squibs and Discussion Sect, Ling Inquiry, 79-81; CONSULT, HEWLETT-PACKARD CORP, 81-. **MEMBERSHIPS** Ling Soc Am; Asn Comput Ling. **RESEARCH** Syntactic theory; computational and mathematical linguistics; mental representation of linguistic knowledge. **SELECTED PUBLICATIONS** Auth, Syntactic Variation and Change in Progress in Loss of the Verbal Coda in Topic Restricting as Far as Constructions, Lang, Vol 71, 95. **CONTACT ADDRESS** Dept of Ling, Stanford Univ, Stanford, CA, 94305.

WATERS, HAROLD A.
PERSONAL Born 11/08/1926, Wilmington, NC, m, 1952, 3 children **DISCIPLINE** FRENCH **EDUCATION** Harvard Univ, AB, 49; Univ Paris, dipl & cert, 51; Univ WA, MA, 54, PhD(Romance lang), 56. **CAREER** From instr to asst prof mod lang, Col William & Mary, 55-60; asst prof Romance lang, Carleton Col, 60-62; from asst prof to assoc prof French, 62-69, Prof French, 69- , prof emeritus, Univ RI; Founder & coordr, Claudel Newslett, 68-72; assoc ed, Claudel Studies, 72-. **HONORS AND AWARDS** Betsy Colquitt Award for Poetry, 98. **MEMBERSHIPS** Am Asn Tchrs Fr; AAUP; Northeast Mod Lang Asn. **RESEARCH** Black French lit; French soc theater; Claudel. **SELECTED PUBLICATIONS** Auth, Philosophic progression in Anouilh's plays, Symposium, summer 62; A propos de la seconde version de l'Echange, Rev Lett Mod annual Paul Claudel issue, 65; Paul Claudel, Twayne, 70; The heroic years of French Social Theater, Mod Lang Studies, spring 75; Black Theater in French: A Guide, Editions Naaman, 78; coauth, Today's English, Hatier-Nouvelles Editions Africaines, 79; auth, Theatre Noir, Three Continents, 88. **CONTACT ADDRESS** Box 233, Saunderstown, RI, 02874. **EMAIL** hawaters@uriacc.uri.edu

WATKINS, CALVERT WARD
PERSONAL Born 03/13/1933, Pittsburgh, PA, m, 1980, 4 children **DISCIPLINE** LINGUISTICS **EDUCATION** Harvard Univ, BA, 54, PhD(ling), 59. **CAREER** From instr to assoc prof, 59-66, chmn dept ling, 63-66, 69-70 & 71 72, Prof Ling & Classics, 66-89, Victor S. Thomas Prof Linguistics & Classics, 89- ,Harvard Univ; Vis prof, Sch Celtic Studies, Dublin Inst Advan Studies, 61-62 & 81; Ctr Advan Study Behav Sci fel, 66-67; overseas fel, Churchill Col, Cambridge, 70-71; Ling Soc Am Collita Prof, Salzburg, 79; vis prof Ecole Normale, Univ Sorbonne, 83; NEH fel, 84-85; Guggenheim fel, 91-92. **HONORS AND AWARDS** Hon mem Royal Irish Acad, 68; fel, Am Acad Arts & Sci, 73; mem, Am Philos Soc, 75; corresp fel, British Acad, 87; corresp etranger, Acad des Inscriptions et Belles-Lettres, 90; festschrift, 98; Goodwin Award, Am Philol Asn, 98. **MEMBERSHIPS** Ling Soc Am; Am Orient Soc; Philol Soc; hon mem Royal Irish Acad; Am Philol Soc; Soc Ling Paris. **RESEARCH** Indo-European; linguistics and poetics; Hittite. **SELECTED PUBLICATIONS** Auth, American Heritage Dictionary of Indo-European Roots, Houghton Mifflin, 85; ed, Studies in memory of Warner Cowgill, 1929-1985, de Gruyter, 87; ed, C. Watkins, Selected Writings, 2 v, Innsbrucker Beitrage zur Sprachwissenschaft, 94; auth, How to Kill a Dragon: Aspects of Indo-European Poetics, Oxford, 95. **CONTACT ADDRESS** Dept of Ling Sci, Harvard Univ, Boylston 314, Cambridge, MA, 02138. **EMAIL** watkins@fas.harvard.edu

WATSON, JOHN A.
PERSONAL Born 07/08/1920, Greenville, SC, d, 2 children **DISCIPLINE** ROMANCE LANGUAGES **EDUCATION** Howard Univ, AB, 42; Univ Paris, cert French, 46; Columbia Univ, MA, 50; Cath Univ Am, PhD, 76. **CAREER** Instr Span & French, Va Union Univ, 48-50; instr, Howard Univ, 53; asst prof, 54-57, assoc prof, 59-76, prof Span & French, VA Union Univ, 76-, Danforth spec award, 57-58; assoc prof Span & French, Va State Col, 59-61. **MEMBERSHIPS** NEA; MLA; Am Asn Teachers Span & Port; Nat Asn Lang Lab Dir. **RESEARCH** Gongorism: Luis de Gongora, sixteenth century Spanish poet; metaphorical procedure of Gongora and Calderon. **CONTACT ADDRESS** Dept of Mod Lang, Va Union Univ, 1500 N Lombardy St, Richmond, VA, 23220-1711.

WATSON, JOHN W.
PERSONAL Born 11/09/1917, Blacksburg, VA, m, 1941, 3 children **DISCIPLINE** LINGUISTICS, STATISTICS **EDUCATION** Va Polytech Inst, BS, 37; Univ Va, MA, 39, PhD (English philol), 41. **CAREER** Asst prof English, Tulane Univ, 45-46; analyst, US Dept Navy, 46-49; analyst, Armed Forces Security Agency, Nat Security Agency, 49-6 1; staff engr and scientist, Radio Corp Am, 61-64; MEM TECH STAFF, MITRE CORP, 64-; Lectr, George Washington Univ, 46-58; consult, Govt Employees Ins Co, 52-54; mem, Architectural Bd Rev, Alexandria, Va, 54-57; lectr, Univ Vs Ext, 54-60. **MEMBERSHIPS** Old English phonology; statistical inference; computer simulation. **SELECTED PUBLICATIONS** Auth, Leadership Secrets of Attila the Hun, Mil Law Rev, Vol 145, 94; Unabsorbed Overhead Costs and the Eichleay Formula, Mil Law Rev, Vol 147, 95. **CONTACT ADDRESS** 8131 Saxony Dr, Annandale, VA, 22003.

WATT, JONATHAN M.
PERSONAL Born 05/16/1957, Sydney, Australia, m, 1977, 4 children **DISCIPLINE** LINGUSTICS **EDUCATION** Univ Pittsburgh, PhD. **CAREER** Instr, Geneva Col; instr, Reformed Presby Theol Sem; pastor, Reformed Presby Church of North Am. **MEMBERSHIPS** Soc of Bibl Lit; Evangelical Theol Soc. **RESEARCH** Sociolingistics of Biblical literature. **SELECTED PUBLICATIONS** Auth, Code-Switching in Luke and Acts, 97. **CONTACT ADDRESS** 510 32nd St., Beaver Falls, PA, 15010. **EMAIL** jwatt@geneva.edu

WATT, WILLIAM CARNELL
PERSONAL Born 04/23/1932, Philadelphia, PA, m, 1980, 4 children **DISCIPLINE** SEMIOTICS, LINGUISTICS **EDUCATION** Univ NC, AB, 54; Georgetown Univ, MSL, 59; Univ Pa, PhD(ling), 67. **CAREER** Systems analysis, Nat Bureau of Standards, 63-66; asst prof comput sci, Carnegie-Mellon Univ, 67-70; assoc prof, 70-80, Prof Ling & Semiotics, Univ Calif, Irvine, 80-, Consult, Bunker-Ramo Corp, 69-70, Nat Bureau of Standards, 69- & Tech Operations Res, 70-72. **MEMBERSHIPS** Semiotic Soc Am; AAAS; Soc Archit Historians. **RESEARCH** Cognitive semiotics; cognitive linguistics. **SELECTED PUBLICATIONS** Auth, Competing economy critera, Prob actuels en psycholinguistique, CNRS, Paris, 74; The indiscreteness with which impenetrables are penetrated, Lingua, 75; What is the proper characterization of the alphabet?, I: Desiderata, Visible Lang, 75 Iconic perspectives on linguistic explanation, Perspectives on Experimental Ling, John Benjamins BV, 79; Against evolution, Ling & Philos, 79; Iconic equilibrium, Semiotica, 79; What is the proper characterization of the alphabet?, II: Composition, 80 & What is the proper characterization of the alphabet?, III: Appearance, 81, Ars Semiotica; Signification And Its Discontents, Semiotica, Vol 0097, 1993; Critique Of Evolutionary Accounts Of Writing - Pettersson,Js, Semiotica, Vol 0098, 1994; Before Writing, Vol 1, From Counting To Cuneiform - Schmandtbesserat,D/, Semiotica, Vol 0099, 1994. **CONTACT ADDRESS** Sch Social Sci, Univ Calif, Irvine, CA, 92717.

WAUGH, LINDA RUTH
PERSONAL Born 11/02/1942, Boston, MA **DISCIPLINE** LINGUISTICS, FRENCH **EDUCATION** Tufts Univ, BA, 64; Stanford Univ, MA, 65; Ind Univ, PhD(ling), 70. **CAREER** Asst prof, 71-76, assoc prof, 76-82, Prof Ling, Cornell Univ, 82-, Ford Found fel, 77; vis assoc prof ling, Yale Univ, 78; Nat Endowment foı Humanities fel, 79-80. **MEMBERSHIPS** Ling Soc Am; Am Asn Teachers French; Semiotic Soc Am; Int Ling Asn. **RESEARCH** Semantics; structure of French; semiotics. **SELECTED PUBLICATIONS** Auth, Lexical meaning: The prepositions en and dans in French, Lingua, 76; Roman Jakobson's Science of Language, Peter de Ridder, 76; A Semantic Analysis of Word Order: Adjective Position in French, Brill, Leiden, Holland, 77; coauth, Basic Course in Susu/Susu: Cours de base, Ind Univ (in press); The context-sensitive meaning of the French subjunctive, In: Cornell Linguistic Contributions, Grammatical Studies, 79; coauth, The Sound Shape of Language, Ind Univ, 79; co-ed, The Melody of Language, Univ Pk Press, 80; Contributions to Historical Linguistics, Brill, 80; Marks Sign's Poems: Semiotics, Linguistics, Poetics, Toronto Semiotic Circle, 82; Degrees Of Iconicity In The Lexicon/, Journal Of Pragmatics, Vol 0022, 1994. **CONTACT ADDRESS** Dept of Mod Lang & Lit, Cornell Univ, 203 Morrill Hall, Ithaca, NY, 14853-4701.

WAYMAN, ALEX
PERSONAL Born 01/11/1921, Chicago, IL, m, 1956 **DISCIPLINE** SANSKRIT & TIBETAN LANGUAGES **EDUCATION** Univ Calif, Los Angeles, BA, 48, MA, 49; Univ Calif, Berkeley, PhD (Sanskrit), 59. **CAREER** Vis lectr Buddhism & Sanskrit, Univ Mich, 60-6 1; from asst prof to assoc prof Buddhism, Univ Wis-Madison, 61-66; vis assoc prof, 66-67, Prof Sanskrit, Columbia Univ, 67-, Am Inst Indian Studies res grant, India, 63-64 & 76-77; Soc Sci Res Coun res grant, Japan, 76, Switz, 77. **MEMBERSHIPS** Am Orient Soc; Asn Asian Studies; Am Soc Study Relig; Soc Asian & Comp Philos; Int Asn Buddhist Studies. **RESEARCH** Sanskrit and Tibetan Buddhism; Indian philosophy; Tantrism. **SELECTED PUBLICATIONS** Auth, Analysis of the Sravakabhumi manuscript, Vol 17, In: University of California Publications in Classical Philology, Univ Calif, 61; coauth, Mkhas grub rje's Fundamentals of the Buddhist Tantras, Vol VIII, In: Indo-Iranian Monographs, Mouton, The Hague, 68; auth, Buddhism, In: Historia Religionum, Vol II, E J Brill, Leiden, 71; The Buddhist Tantras: Light on Indo-Tibetan Esotericism, Weiser, 73; coauth, The Lion's Roar of Queen Srimala: A Buddhist Scripture on the Tathagatagarbha Theory, Columbia Univ, 74; auth, Yoga of the Guhyasamajatantra: The Arcane Lore of Forty Verses, Motilal Banarsidass, Delhi, 77; Who Understands the four alternatives of the Buddhist texts?, Philos E & W, 1/77; Mind Only - A Philosophical And Doctrinal Analysis Of The 'Vijnanavada' - Wood,Te/, Journal Of The American Oriental Society, Vol 0112, 1992; Response To Tatz,Mark Review Of 'Ethics Of Tibet' - Bodhisattva-Section Of Tsong-Kha-Pa 'Lam Rim Chen Mo'/, Philosophy East & West, Vol 0044, 1994; Calming the Mind and Discerning the Real: Buddhist Meditation and the Middle View, from the Tibetan of Tson-kha-pa's Lam rim Chen mo, Columbia Univ, 78; The Realm Of Awakening - Chapter-10 Of Asanga 'Mahayanasangraha' - Griffiths,Pj, Hakamaya,N, Keenan,Jp, Swanson,Pl, Journal Of The American Oriental Society, Vol 0112, 1992; A Defense Of Yogacara Buddhism/, Philosophy East & West, Vol 0046, 1996. **CONTACT ADDRESS** Dept of Mid, Columbia Univ, E Lang Kent Hall, New York, NY, 10027.

WEAVER, ELISSA B.
PERSONAL Born 04/11/1940, Springfield, IL **DISCIPLINE** ROMANCE LANGUAGES **EDUCATION** Univ Ill, Urbana, BS, 61; UCLA, MA, 65, PhD, 75. **CAREER** Instr, 68-72, Rutgers Univ; asst prof, 72-77, assoc prof, 77-89, prof, 89-, chmn, dept romance lang & lit, 94- Univ Chicago. **RESEARCH** Italian lit & lang in early modern period, women's lit. **CONTACT ADDRESS** 1419 E 56th St, #2, Chicago, IL, 60637. **EMAIL** c-weaver@uchicago.edu

WEBB, EUGENE
PERSONAL Born 11/10/1938, Santa Monica, CA, m, 1964 **DISCIPLINE** COMPARATIVE LITERATURE, RELIGION **EDUCATION** Univ Calif, Los Angeles, BA, 60; Columbia Univ, MA, 26, PhD(comp lit), 65. **CAREER** Asst prof English, Simon Fraser Univ, 65-66; asst prof, 66-76, Prof Comp Relig & Comp Lit, Univ Wash, 76-. **MEMBERSHIPS** Am Acad Relig. **RESEARCH** Twentieth century English, German and French literature; 18th century English; philosophy of history. **SELECTED PUBLICATIONS** Auth, Samuel Beckett: A Study of His Novels, 70 & The Plays of Samuel Beckett, 72 Univ Wash; Peter Owen, London; The New Social-Psychology Of France + Girard,Rene - The Girardian-School, Religion, Vol 0023, 1993; The Dark Dove: The Sacred and Secular in Modern Lit, 75 & Eric Voegelin: Philosopher of History, 81, Univ Wash; Consciousness And Transcendence - The Theology Of Voegelin,Eric - Morrissey,Mp, Journal Of Religion, Vol 0075, 1995; In Search Of The Classic - Reconsidering The Greco-Roman Tradition, Homer To Valery And Beyond - Shankman,S, Comparative Literature, Vol 0048, 1996. **CONTACT ADDRESS** Dept of English, Univ of Washington, Seattle, WA, 98195.

WEBB, GISELA
PERSONAL Born 07/15/1949, San Juan, Puerto Rico, m, 2 children **DISCIPLINE** ISLAMIC STUDIES, COMPARATIVE RELIGION STUDIES, PHILOSOPHY OF MYSTICISM **EDUCATION** Temple Univ, PhD, 89. **CAREER** Assoc prof Dept Relig Stud, Seton Hall Univ, 89-; Phi Beta Kappa; NEH award. **MEMBERSHIPS** AAR; MESA; ACSIS. **RESEARCH** Medieval and contemporary developments of mysticism, esp Sufism womens studies. **SELECTED PUBLICATIONS** Tradition and Innovation in Contemporary American Islamic Spirituality, Muslim Communities in North America, SUNY Press, 94; Islam, Sufism, & Subud, Am Alternative Relig, SUNY Press, 95. **CONTACT ADDRESS** 125 Union Ave, Bala Cynwyd, PA, 19004. **EMAIL** webbgise@shu.edu

WEBB JR, RALPH
DISCIPLINE INTERPERSONAL COMMUNICATION **EDUCATION** Univ Wis, PhD, 65. **CAREER** Prof, Purdue Univ. **RESEARCH** Language; gender; intercultural communication; communication theory. **SELECTED PUBLICATIONS** Auth, Interpersonal Speech Communication: Principles and Practices, 75; Graduate Education in Speech Communication: Current Status and Future Directions, Commun Educ, 79. **CONTACT ADDRESS** Dept of Commun, Purdue Univ, 1080 Schleman Hall, West Lafayette, IN, 47907-1080.

WEBBER, PHILIP ELLSWORTH
PERSONAL Born 12/02/1944, Akron, OH, m, 1966, 3 children **DISCIPLINE** GERMANIC PHILOLOGY **EDUCATION** Earlham Col, AB, 67; Univ Chicago, MA, 68; Bryn Mawr Col, PhD(Ger philol), 72. **CAREER** Instr English community col, Reutlingen, Ger, 70-71; asst prof Ger, ling & educ, Widener Col, 72-76; prof Ger, Ling & Dutch, Central Col, IA, 76-; Res counr, Shipley Sch, Bryn Mawr, 71-72; prog coordr Ger, Alternative Schs Proj, 71-72; instr Ger, Bryn Mawr Col, 72. **HONORS AND AWARDS** Mellon, 80, 81; Exxon, 85; NEH Fellowship, 77, 87; Outstanding Faculty Award, 84, 87; numerous IA Humanities Board grants. **MEMBERSHIPS** Int Ver Ned; Am Asn Teachers Ger; Maatschappij der Nederlandse Letterkunde. **RESEARCH** Mediaeval Netherlandic manuscripts; ethnic sociolinguistics. **SELECTED PUBLICATIONS** Auth, Pella Dutch: The Portrait of a Language and its Use in one of Iowa's Ethnic Communities, Ames, IA: IA State Univ Press, 88; A Late Medieval Devotional Anthology from Salzburg, Nonnberg Passion: Huntington Library HM 195, Commentary and Edition, Goppingen, GER: Kummerle, 90; chief coauth, Medieval Netherlandic Manuscripts in the Pierpont Morgan Library, New York, Brussels: Archief-en Bibliotheekwezen in Belgie, 91; Kolonie-Deutsch: Life and Language in Amana, Ames, IA: IA State Univ Press, 93. **CONTACT ADDRESS** Dept of Ger, Central Col, Iowa, 812 University St, Pella, IA, 50219-1999.

WEDBERG, LLOYD W.
DISCIPLINE MODERN GERMAN AND ENGLISH WRITING **EDUCATION** Univ Mich, BA, MA, PhD. **CAREER** Prof, 61-. **HONORS AND AWARDS** Grant, Exxon Edu Found. **SELECTED PUBLICATIONS** Pub(s), 19th Century German Novelle; connections between the German Narrenschiff and Katherine Anne Porter's Ship of Fools. **CONTACT ADDRESS** Dept of Eng, Univ Detroit Mercy, 4001 W McNichols Rd, PO BOX 19900, Detroit, MI, 48219-0900.

WEDEL, ALFRED R.
PERSONAL Born 10/31/1934, Sevilla, Spain, m, 1961, 2 children **DISCIPLINE** GERMAN & SPANISH PHILOLOGY **EDUCATION** Univ Madrid, BA, 60; Univ Pa, MA, 65, PhD(-Ger philol), 70. **CAREER** Instr Ger & English, Mangold Inst, Madrid, 60-61; instr Ger, Span & French, Marple Newtown High Schs, Pa, 61-65; asst prof, 65-74, Assoc Prof Ger & Span, Univ Del, 74-, Assoc Chmn, 80-, Res grant, 76; fac adv, Medieval Soc, Univ Del. **HONORS AND AWARDS** Excellence in Teaching Award, Univ Del, 75. **MEMBERSHIPS** MLA; Am Asn Teachers Ger. **RESEARCH** German literature; Germanic philology; comparative literature. **SELECTED PUBLICATIONS** Auth, Ortega y Gassett y su concepto de una facultad de cultural, Rev Occidente, 73; The verbal aspects of the prefixed and unprefixed verbal forms: Stantan, sizzan, sezzan, lickan, leckan in the Old High German Benedictine rule, J English & Ger Philol, 74; Subjective and Objective aspect: The preterit in the Old High German Isidor, Linguistics, 74; Der Konflikt von Aspekt/Zeitstufe und Aktionsart in der althochdeutschen Ubersetzung der Benediktinerregel, Neuphilologische Mitteilungen, 76; Die Gauchfigur und er Cornuto in Moscheroschs Bearbeitung der Traumvisionen des Spaniers Quevedo, In: Problemeer Komparatistik und der Interpretation, Festschrift fur A von Gronicka, 77. **CONTACT ADDRESS** Dept of Lang & Lit, Univ of Del, Newark, DE, 19711. **EMAIL** fredy@udel.edu

WEIGER, JOHN GEORGE
PERSONAL Born 02/06/1933, Dresden, Germany, m, 1955, 3 children **DISCIPLINE** ROMANCE LANGUAGES **EDUCATION** Middlebury Col, BA, 55; Univ Colo, MA, 57; Ind Univ, PhD(Span), 66. **CAREER** Instr Span, Univ Colo, 55-57 & Lawrence Col, 57-58; from instr to assoc prof, 58-73, from asst dean to dean, Col Arts & Sci, 68-76, Prof Span, Univ VT, 73-, Consult, Eirikk Borue, Inc; vis lectr, Univ Bologna, Italy, 78. **MEMBERSHIPS** Renaissance Soc Am; MLA; Am Asn Teachers Span & Port; Comediantes; Asoc Int Hisp. **RESEARCH** Spanish comedia; Cervantes; linguistics. **SELECTED PUBLICATIONS** Auth, The Valencian Dramatists of Spain's Golden Age, 76 & Cristobal de Virues, 78, Twayne; Initial and extended speech in the theater of Guillen de Castro, In: Studies in Honor of Gerald E Wade, 78; La supercheria esta descubierta: Don Quijote and Gines de Pasamonte, Philol Quart, spring 78; The Individuated Self: Cervantes and the Emergence of the Individual, Univ Ohio, 79; Hacia la comedia: De los valencianos a lope, Cupsa, Madrid, 78; Las Hazanas del cid, Puvill, Barcelona, 80; The curious pertinence of Eugenio's tale in Don Quixote, Mod Lang Notes, 81; **CONTACT ADDRESS** Dept of Romance Lang, Univ of Vermont, Waterman Bldg, Burlington, VT, 05405-0001.

WEINER, JACK
PERSONAL Born 01/13/1934, Baltimore, MD, m, 1968, 1 child **DISCIPLINE** SPANISH, RUSSIAN **EDUCATION** Univ Md, BA, 56; Middlebury Col, MA, 59 & 63; Ind Univ, PhD(Span, Russ), 68. **CAREER** Asst prof Span, Univ Kans, 66-70; assoc prof, 70-77, Prof Span, Northern Ill Univ, 77-**MEMBERSHIPS** Am Asn Teachers Span & Port; MLA; Int Asn Hispanists; Renaissance Soc Am. **RESEARCH** Spanish Golden Age literature, especially the comedia and prose; Hispano-Russian literary and cultural relations. **SELECTED PUBLICATIONS** Auth, Mantillas in Moscovy: The Spanish Golden Age Theater in Tsarist Russia: 1672-1917, Humanities Ser, Univ Kans, 70; El Diario Espanol de Alexander Veselovskii, Cuadernos Hispanoamericanos, 70; Cancionero de Sebastian de Horozco, Utah Studies in Lit & Ling, 75; El escudero y las prostitutas: Lazaro y el escuder en el rio, Rev Signos, Vol IV, No 2 & Romance Notes, Vol XIII, No 2; coauth, Turgenev's Fathers and Sons and Galdos' Dona Perfecta, PMLA, LXXXVI: 19-23; Cervantes La 'Numancia' And The Covenant Between God And Israel, Neophilologus, Vol 0081, 1997; Cervantes La 'Numancia' And The Covenant Between God And Israel, Neophilologus, Vol 0081, 1997; Los 'Ninos Y Los Locos Dizen Las Verdades', An Anti-Clerical Folktale By Horozco,Sebastian,De 1510-1580, Revista De Filologia Espanola, Vol 0076, 1996. **CONTACT ADDRESS** Dept of Foreign Lang & Lit, No Illinois Univ, 1425 W Lincoln Hwy, De Kalb, IL, 60115-2825.

WEINER, JACK
PERSONAL Born 01/13/1934, Baltimore, MD, m, 1968, 1 child **DISCIPLINE** SPANISH, RUSSIAN **EDUCATION** Univ Md, BA, 56; Middlebury Col, MA, 59 & 63; Ind Univ, PhD, 68. **CAREER** Asst prof Span, Univ Kans, 66-70; assoc prof, 70-77, prof Spanish, Northern Ill Univ, 77-. **MEMBERSHIPS** Am Asn Teachers Span & Port; MLA; Int Asn Hispanists; Renaissance Soc Am. **RESEARCH** Spanish Golden Age literature, especially the comedia and prose; Hispano-Russian literary and cultural relations. **SELECTED PUBLICATIONS** Auth, Mantillas in Moscovy: The Spanish Golden Age Theater in Tsarist Russia: 1672-1917, Humanities Ser, Univ Kans, 70; El Diario Espanol de Alexander Veselovskii, Cuadernos Hispanoamericanos, 70; Cancionero de Sebastian de Horozco, Utah Studies in Lit & Ling, 75; El escudero y las prostitutas: Lazaro y el escuder en el rio, Rev Signos, Vol IV, No 2 & Romance Notes, Vol XIII, No 2; coauth, Turgenev's Fathers and Sons and Galdos' Dona Perfecta, PMLA, LXXXVI: 19-23. **CONTACT ADDRESS** Dept of Foreign Lang & Lit, No Illinois Univ, 1425 W Lincoln Hwy, De Kalb, IL, 60115-2825.

WEING, SIEGFRIED
DISCIPLINE GERMAN **EDUCATION** Vanderbilt Univ, PhD. **CAREER** Dept head, Mod lang. **SELECTED PUBLICATIONS** Author 2 bk(s) & articles on, Ger novella; German Review Grammar, second-yr Ger textbk. **CONTACT ADDRESS** Dept of Modern Languages, Virginia Military Inst, Lexington, VA, 24450.

WEINSTEIN, STANLEY
PERSONAL Born 11/13/1929, Brooklyn, NY, m, 1952, 1 child **DISCIPLINE** BUDDHIST & EAST ASIAN STUDIES **EDUCATION** Komazawa Univ, Japan, BA, 58; Univ Tokyo, MA, 60; Harvard Univ, PhD(Far Eastern lang), 66. **CAREER** Lectr Far Eastern Buddhism, Univ London, 62-68; assoc prof Buddhist studies, 68-74, PROF BUDDHIST STUDIES, YALE UNIV, 74-; NEH sr fel, 74-75. **MEMBERSHIPS** Am Orient Soc; Asn Asian Studies **RESEARCH** Buddhist studies; East Asian languages and history. **SELECTED PUBLICATIONS** Auth, The Kanjin kakumusho: A Compendium of the Teachings of the Hosso Sect, Komazawa Daigaku Kenkyu Kiyo, 60; contr ed, Japanese-English Buddhist Dictionary, Tokyo, 65; Buddhism, In: The Cambridge Encyclopedia of China, Cambridge Univ Press, 82; 38 medium length and 82 short articles In: The Encylcopedia of Japan, Kodansha, Tokyo, 82; Alayavijnana and Buddhism, Schools of: Chinese Buddhism, In: The Encyclopedia of Religion, Macmillang Publ Co, 87; Buddhism Under the T'ang, Cambridge Univ Press, 87; Nihon Bukkyo to ichi Amerikajin Bukkyo kenkyuka no setten: Todai no Bukkyo no hakkan ni chinande, Komazawa Daigaku Bukkyo gakubu ronshu, 88; tangdae Pulgyo chongp'a hyongsong e issoso hwangsil ui huwon (in Korean)(Imperial Patronage in the Formation of the Tang Buddhist Schools), Chonggyo wa munhwa (Relgion and Culture), 12/95; Rennyo shiso ni okeru renzokusei to henka (Continuity and Change the Thought of Rennyo Shonin ¤1415-1499|, In: rennyo no sekai (The World of Rennyo), Bun'eido, Kyoto, Japan, 98. **CONTACT ADDRESS** Dept of Relig Studies, Yale Univ, PO Box 208287, New Haven, CT, 06520-8287. **EMAIL** stanley.weinstein@yale.edu

WEISBERG, DAVID B.
PERSONAL Born 11/15/1938, New York, NY, M, 1958, 4 children **DISCIPLINE** ASSYRIOLOGY **EDUCATION** Columbia Col, AB, 60; Jewish Theol Sem Am, BHL, 60; Yale Univ, PhD, 65. **CAREER** Res Assoc Assyriol, Orient Inst, Univ Chicago, 65-67; from asst prof to assoc prof, 67-71, Prof Bible & Semitic Lang, Hebrew Union Col, Ohio, 71- **MEMBERSHIPS** Am Orient Soc; Soc Bibl Lit. **RESEARCH** Bible; Assyriology. **SELECTED PUBLICATIONS** Auth, Guild Structure and Political Allegiance in Early Achaemenid Mesopotamia, Near Eastern Res, No. 1, Yale Univ, 67; A neo-Babylonian temple report, J Am Orient Soc, 67; Rare accents of the 21 books, Jewish Quart Rev, 67; Texts from the Time of Nebuchadnezzar, Yale, Vol 17, 80; Uruk - Late Babylonian Economic Texts From The Eanna Archive, Pt 1, Texts Of Varied Contents - German And Akkadian - Gehlken,E, Journal Of Near Eastern Studies, Vol 0055, 1996; Uruk - Late Babylonian Economic Texts From The Eanna Archive, Pt 1, Texts Of Varied Contents - German And Akkadian - Gehlken,E, Journal Of Near Eastern Studies, Vol 0055, 1996; Images Of Nebuchadnezzar - The Emergence Of A Legend - Sack,Rh, Journal Of Near Eastern Studies, Vol 0055, 1996; Images Of Nebuchadnezzar - The Emergence Of A Legend - Sack,Rh, Journal Of Near Eastern Studies, Vol 0055, 1996. **CONTACT ADDRESS** Dept of Bible & Semitic Lang, Hebrew Union Col, Cincinnati, OH, 45220.

WEISS, BENO
PERSONAL Born 08/07/1933, Fiume, Italy, m, 2 children **DISCIPLINE** ITALIAN LITERATURE **EDUCATION** NY Univ, BA, 63, MA, 65, PhD, 71. **CAREER** Instr Ital, NY Univ, 66-69; asst prof Ital, Pa State Univ, 69-76; assoc prof Ital, Pa State Univ, 76-88; prof Ital, Pa State, 88 -; Inst Arts & Humanistic Studies res fel, Italy, 72, 74, 81, 91; Am Philos Soc fel, 78, 85, 91. **HONORS AND AWARDS** Tchg Award, Col Lib Arts, Pa State Univ, 77; Kagey Award; Cervantes Medal, NY Univ. **MEMBERSHIPS** MLA; Am Asn Tchrs Ital; Am Ital Hist Asn; Am Soc of Sephardic Studies; Am Asn Tchrs Spanish; Am Asn Italian Studies, Sons of Italy. **RESEARCH** 19th and 20th Century Italian lit., espec Italo Svevo, Pirandello and Calvino. **SELECTED PUBLICATIONS** Auth, Svevo's Inferiorita, Mod Fiction Studies, spring 72; Translation of a husband: a play in three acts by Italo Svevo, Mod Int Drama, fall 72; An Annotated Bibliography on the Theater of Italo Svevo, Pa State Univ, 74; Federico Garcia Lorca in Italy, Garcia Lorca Rev, spring-fall, 75; Italo Svevo, Boston:Twayne World, 87; Maria de Zayas y Sotomayor: El castigo de la miseria y La inocencia castigada, Valencia: Albatros ediciones, 90; Understanding Italo Calvino, Univ of South Carolina, 93; coauth, Beginnings and Discoveries. Polydore Vergil's De Inventoribus rerum. An Unabridged Translation and Edition with Introduction, Notes and Glossary, Nieuwkoop: De Graaf, 97; Drama Across the Centuries: A Style Guide, Penn State Univ, 81. **CONTACT ADDRESS** Dept of Span, Ital, and Port, Pennsylvania State Univ, 352 N Burrowes Bldg, University Park, PA, 16802-6203. **EMAIL** BXW@PSU.EDU

WEISS, HERMANN FRIEDRICH
PERSONAL Born 06/17/1937, Beuel, Germany, m, 1997 **DISCIPLINE** GERMAN LANGUAGE & LITERATURE **EDUCATION** Univ Bonn, Staatsexamen, 63; Princeton Univ, MA, 67, PhD(Ger lit), 68. **CAREER** Lektor Ger, Univ St Andrews, 63-64; instr, Univ Ore, 64-65; from asst prof to assoc prof, 68-82, Prof Ger, Univ Mich, Ann Arbor, 82-; Book Review Ed, Mich Germanic Studies, 92-. **MEMBERSHIPS** MLA; Am Asn Teachers Ger; AAUP. **RESEARCH** Achim von Arnim; fiction from the 18th to the 19th century; 18th and 19th century drama;

Heinrich von Kleist; Novalis. **SELECTED PUBLICATIONS** Auth, Achim von Arnims Metamorphosen der Gesellschaft, Zeitschrift fur Deut Philol, 72; Unveroffentlichte prosaentwurfe A von Arnim's zur Zeitkritik (um 1810), Jahrbuch des Hochstifts, 77; Vorspiel zur Revolution. Die Bewertung der Demut in den vierziger Jahren des 19 Jahrhunderts, Zeitschrift fur Deut Philol, 78; Ein unbekannter brief Heinrichs von Kleist an Marie von Kleist, Jahrbuch der Deutachen Schillergesellschaft, 78; Funde und Studien zu Heinrich von Kleist, T?ingen: Niemeyer, 84; ed, Unbekannte B riefe von und an Achim von Arnim aus der Sammlung Varnhagen und anderen Bestanden, Berlin: Duncker & Humblot, 86; co-ed, Achim von Arnim, Werke, vol 6, Deutscher Klassiker Verlag, 92; author of numerous other journal articles. **CONTACT ADDRESS** Dept of Ger, Univ of Mich, 812 E Washington St, Ann Arbor, MI, 48109-1275. **EMAIL** hfweiss@umich.edu

WEISSENBERGER, KLAUS
PERSONAL Born 11/15/1939, Sydney, Australia, m, 1974 **DISCIPLINE** GERMAN LITERATURE **EDUCATION** Univ Hamburg, Staatsexamen, 65; Univ Southern Calif, PhD(Ger), 67. **CAREER** From asst prof to assoc prof, 67-77, chmn dept, 72-79, Prof Ger, Rice Univ, 77- **MEMBERSHIPS** Am Asn Teachers Ger; MLA; Int Asn Ger Studies; SCent Mod Lang Asn. **RESEARCH** Lyric poetry as a genre; German exile literature; development of lyric poetry from Rilke to Celan. **SELECTED PUBLICATIONS** Auth, Formen der Elegie von Goethe bis Celan, 69, Die Elegie bei Paul Celan, 69 & Zwischen Stein und Stern, Mystische Formgebung in der Dichtung von Else Lasker-Schuler, Nelly Sachs und Paul Celan, 74, Franke, Bern; Dissonanzen und neugestimmte Saiten--eine Typologie der Exillyrik, Literaturwissenschaftliches Jahrbuch, Vol 17, 76; Mythopoesis in German literary criticism, Lit & Myth, Vol 9, 79; Eine systematische Stiltypologie als Antwort auf einen dichtungsfrmeden Systemzwang, Jahrbuch fur Int Germanistik, Vol 12, 80; ed, Die deutsche Lyrik von 1945 bis 1975, Zwischen Botschaft und Spiel, 81; The Resonance Of Exile - Successful And Failed Reception Of German-Speaking Exile Authors - German - Sevin,D, German Quarterly, Vol 0067, 1994; Between Reality And Dream - The Austrian Quality In Literature - German - Strelka,Jp, Journal Of English And Germanic Philology, Vol 0095, 1996; 'Schicksalsreise' - German - Doblin,A, German Quarterly, Vol 0068, 1995; Idioms Of Uncertainty - Goethe And The Essay - Burgard,Pj, German Quarterly, Vol 0070, 1997. **CONTACT ADDRESS** Dept of Ger, Rice Univ, Houston, TX, 77001.

WEISSTEIN, ULRICH
PERSONAL Born 11/14/1925, Breslau, Germany, m, 1952, 4 children **DISCIPLINE** COMPARATIVE LITERATURE, GERMAN **EDUCATION** Ind Univ, MA, 53, PhD(comp lit), 54. **CAREER** From instr to asst prof Ger & fine arts, Lehigh Univ, 54-58; from asst prof to assoc prof English & comp lit, 59-66, Prof Ger & Comp Lit, Ind Univ, Bloomington, 66-, Vis prof comp lit, Univ Wis-Madison, 66, Univ Vienna, 76 & Stanford Univ, 78, vis prof Ger, Deut Sommerschule, Middlebury Col, 70, Univ Hamburg, 71 & 82; Guggenheim Found fel, 73; dir, Ind Purdue Studienprogramm, Hamburg, 81-82. **MEMBERSHIPS** Am Asn Teachers Ger; MLA; Am Comp Lit Asn; Int Comp Lit Asn. **RESEARCH** Anglo-German and Franco-German relations; literature and the arts; German literature, especially since 1870. **SELECTED PUBLICATIONS** Auth, The Essence of Opera, Free Press, 64; Max Frisch, Twayne, 67; Einfuhrung in die vergleichende Literaturwissenschaft, Kohlhammer, Stuttgart, 68; ed, Expressionism as an International Literary Phenomenon, Akad Kiado, Budapest & Didier, Paris, 73; co-ed, Texte and Kontexte: Festschrift fur Norbert fuerst zum 65 Geburstag, Francke, Bern, 73; auth, Comparative Literature and Literary Theory: Survey and Introduction, Ind Univ, Bloomington, 73; ed, Literature and the other arts, Vol III, Proc IXth ICLA Cong, Innsbruck, 81; Vergleichende Literaturwissenschaft: Ein Forschungsbericht 1968-1977, Lang, Berne, 82; Dance And Death In Art And Literature - German - Link,F, Aaa-Arbeiten Aus Anglistik Und Amerikanistik, Vol 0019, 1994; Approaches To Mozart,Wolfgang,Amadeus - German - Knepler,G, German Quarterly, Vol 0067, 1994. **CONTACT ADDRESS** 2204 Queens Way, Bloomington, IN, 47401.

WEITZMAN, RAYMOND STANLEY
PERSONAL Born 06/23/1938, Los Angeles, CA, 1 child **DISCIPLINE** LINGUISTICS, JAPANESE LANGUAGE **EDUCATION** Univ Calif, Los Angeles, AB, 64; Univ Southern Calif, MA, 66, PhD(ling), 69. **CAREER** From asst prof to assoc prof, 71-76, chmn dept, 79-82, prof ling, Calif State Univ, Fresno, 77-, Proj dir grant, Nat Sci Found Instr Sci Equip Prog, 70-72. **MEMBERSHIPS** Ling Soc Am; Asn of Behavior Analysis; Phonetic Soc Japan; Acoust Soc Am. **RESEARCH** Acoustic phonetic properties of speech; the structure of the Japanese language; language acquisition. **SELECTED PUBLICATIONS** Auth, Lacuna in Generative Phonology: Contrast and Free Variation, Papers Ling, 72; coauth, Devoiced and Whispered Vowels in Japanese, Ann Bull Res Inst Logopedics & Phoniatrics, 76; Rehabilitation of a Patient with Complete Mandibulectomy and Partial Glossectomy, Am J of Otolaryngology, 80; Vowel Categorization and the Critical Band, Language and Speech, Vol 35 (1,2), pp 115-126; The Relative Perceptual Salience of Spectral and Durational Differences, in Proceedings of the 2nd International Conference on Spoken Language Processing, Banff, Alberta, Can, pp 1095-1098; How to Get the Horse to Open Its Mouth: Using the Concept Formation Paradigm in Speech Perception Research, in In Honor of Frederick Brengelman on the Occasion of the 25th Anniversary of the Linguistics Department at California State University, Fresno, pp 141-149. **CONTACT ADDRESS** Dept of Ling, California State Univ, Fresno, 5245 N Baker, Fresno, CA, 93740-8001. **EMAIL** raymondw@csufresno.edu

WELDON, JAMES
DISCIPLINE OLD; MIDDLE ENGLISH LITERATURE **EDUCATION** New Brunswick, BA, MA; Queen's, PhD. **CAREER** Assoc Prof **SELECTED PUBLICATIONS** Auth, Decorative Reading: Some Implications of Ordinatio in Piers Plowman; Ordinatio and Genre in MS CCC 201: Piers Plowman; Gesture of Perception: The Pattern of Kneeling in Piers Plowman B.18-19; The Structure of Dream Visions in Piers Plowman; The Infernal Present: Auden's Use of Inferno III in The Chimeras. **CONTACT ADDRESS** Dept of English, Wilfrid Laurier Univ, 75 University Ave W, Waterloo, ON, N2L 3C5. **EMAIL** jweldon@mach1.wlu.ca

WELLES, MARCIA LOUISE
PERSONAL Born 06/17/1943, Bridgeport, CT, m, 1967, 2 children **DISCIPLINE** SPANISH LITERATURE **EDUCATION** Columbia Univ, AB, 65, PhD(Span), 71; Middlebury Col, MA, 66. **CAREER** Asst Prof Span, Barnard Col, Columbia Univ, 70-. **MEMBERSHIPS** MLA; Am Asn Teachers Span & Port. **RESEARCH** Seventeenth century Spanish prose; feminist studies in Spain and Latin America. **SELECTED PUBLICATIONS** Zayas,Maria,De - The Dynamics Of Discourse - Williamsen,Ar, Whitenack,Ja, Revista De Estudios Hispanicos, Vol 0030, 1996; The Anxiety Of Gender, The Transformation Of Tamar In Tirso La 'Venganza De Tamar' And Calderon Los 'Cabellos De Absalon', Bulletin Of The Comediantes, Vol 0047, 1995; White Ink, Essays On 20th-Century Feminine Fiction In Spain And Latin-America - Hart,Sm, Bulletin Of Hispanic Studies, Vol 0072, 1995. **CONTACT ADDRESS** Dept of Span Barnard Col, Columbia Univ, New York, NY, 10028.

WELLIVER, GLENN EDWIN
PERSONAL Born 02/20/1933, Baltimore, MD, m, 1958, 1 child **DISCIPLINE** GERMAN LANGUAGE & LITERATURE **EDUCATION** Dickinson Col, AB, 55; Northwestern Univ, Evanston, MA, 56, PhD0, 64. **CAREER** From instr to assoc prof Ger, 61-76, PROF GER, DEPAUW UNIV, 76-, chmn, Dept Ger & Russ, 82-98. **HONORS AND AWARDS** Phi Beta Kappa. **MEMBERSHIPS** MLA; Midwest Mod Lang Asn; AATG; Soc Ger Am Studies. **RESEARCH** Modern drama; German cultural history. **CONTACT ADDRESS** Dept Ger & Russ, DePauw Univ, 400 S Locust St, Greencastle, IN, 46135.

WELLS, COLIN
DISCIPLINE CLASSICAL STUDIES **EDUCATION** Univ Oxford, BA, MA, PhD. **CAREER** Instr, Univ Ottawa; T Frank Murchison distinguished prof, 87-; dept ch. **HONORS AND AWARDS** Dir, Sec Can Team excavations, Carthage, Tunisia, 76-86; dir, Trinity Univ excavations, 90-. **RESEARCH** Roman frontier studies. **SELECTED PUBLICATIONS** Auth, The German Policy of Augustus, 72; The Roman Empire, Harvard UP, 95. **CONTACT ADDRESS** Dept of Class, Trinity Univ, 715 Stadium Dr, San Antonio, TX, 78212.

WELLS, MARIA XENIA ZEVELCHI
DISCIPLINE COMPARATIVE LANG & LITS **EDUCATION** Univ Pisa, PhD, 59. **CAREER** Teacher, AM High School and Univ MD, Pisa; lectr, Univ Tx, Austin, 62-72; curator, Harry Ransom Hum Res Ctr, Univ Tx, Austin, 73-97; ADJ PROF FRENCH, ITAL, RANSOM CTR, 97. **MEMBERSHIPS** Am Asn Ital Stud; AISLLI; Am Trans Asn; Fulbright Asn; Minerva Hist Asn, Trieste; Soc Ital Hist Stud; Nat Ital Am Fdn. **SELECTED PUBLICATIONS** Aldine Press Books at the Harry Ransom Humanties Research Center: A Descriptive Catalogue, UT Press; Memoriale di Paolo Volponi: l'uom e la Fabbrica, esame della varianti nel manoscritto, AISILLI, Torino, 94; Il manoscritto di Cristo si e' fermato e Eboli, lettura su piano storico e critico, Anma Libri, 97; I Paladini di Sicilia, in FMR april 95; Fuochi d'Artificio: manoscritto del 1500, in FMR april 95. **CONTACT ADDRESS** Harry Ransom Hum Res Ctr, Univ Texas, Austin, Austin, TX. **EMAIL** mxwells@nora.hrc.utexas.edu

WENDLAND, ERNST R.
PERSONAL Born 10/14/1944, Washington, IA, m, 1971, 4 children **DISCIPLINE** AFRICAN LANGUAGES AND LITERATURE **EDUCATION** NW Col, BA, 68; Univ Wisc, MA, 75, PhD, 79. **CAREER** Instr, Lutheran Sem (Lusaka, Zambia), 68-; Lang coordr publ, Lutheran Church Cent Africa, 71-; transl adv, 75-96, transl consult, united bible soc, 96-. **MEMBERSHIPS** New Testament Soc S Africa; Old Testament Soc S Africa **RESEARCH** Discourse, stylistic, and rhetorical analysis of Biblical and Bantu language texts, especially poetry, prophecy, and preaching. **SELECTED PUBLICATIONS** Ed, Discourse Perspectives on Hebrew Poetry in the Scriptures, United Bible Soc, 94; auth, The Discourse Analysis of Hebrew Prophetic Literature, Mellen Bibl Press, 95; Buku Loyera: An Introduction to the New Chichewa Bible Translation, Kachere Books, 98; Analyzing the Psalms, Summer Inst Ling, 98. **CONTACT ADDRESS** American Embassy Lusaka, DOS, Washington, DC, 20521-2310. **EMAIL** wendland@zamnet.zm

WENSINGER, ARTHUR STEVENS
PERSONAL Born 03/09/1926, Grosse Pointe, Mich **DISCIPLINE** GERMAN LITERATURE & LANGUAGE **EDUCATION** Dartmouth Col, AB, 48; Univ Mich, AM, 50, PhD, 58. **CAREER** From instr to prof, 55-77, Marcus Taff Prof Ger & Humanities, Wesleyan Univ, 77-, Sr Tutor, Col Lett, 63-, Chmn Dept Ger, 70-73, 77-, Danforth grant, 59; Ford Found fel, 70-71; Wesleyan Ctr Humanities fel, 74; Int Nationes grantee, 79. **MEMBERSHIPS** MLA; Am Asn Teachers Ger; Heinrich von Kleist Ges; Am translr Asn; Kafka Soc Am. **RESEARCH** Heinrich von Kleist; translations from German; Thomas Mann & Franz Kafka. **SELECTED PUBLICATIONS** Transl, Ger sect, Language of Love (short story anthology), 64 & ed, Ger & Austrian sect, Modern European Poetry, 66, Bantam; co-transl & co-ed, Chapliande, Mass Rev, Vol VI, No 3, Methusalem or the Eternal Bouregois, In: Plays for a New Theater, New Directions, 66; The Immortals, Malahat Rev, Univ Victoria, 10/67; ed & transl, Hogarth on High Life, The Lichtenberg Commentaries, Wesleyan Univ Press, 71, ed & coauth, Peter et amicorum· Memorial Anthology for Novelist P S Boynton, Gehenna, 72; ed, Stone Island, Harcourt, 73; ed & transl, Paula Modersohn-Becker in Letters and Journals, Taplinger Publ Co, 82. **CONTACT ADDRESS** Dept Ger Lang & lit, Wesleyan Univ, Middletown, CT, 06457.

WENTE, EDWARD FRANK
PERSONAL Born 10/07/1930, New York, NY, m, 1970 **DISCIPLINE** EGYPTOLOGY **EDUCATION** Univ Chicago, AB, 51, PhD(Egyptol), 59. **CAREER** Dir Egyptol, Am Res Ctr Egypt, 57-58; res assoc, 59-63, from asst prof to assoc prof, 63-70, chmn, Dept Near Eastern Lang & Civilization, 75-79, Prof Egyptol; Orient Inst, Univ Chicago, 70-, Mem, Am Res Ctr Egypt, 57-; field dir epigraphic surv, Orient Inst, Luxor, Egypt, 72-73; mem archeol adv coun, Smithsonian Inst, 79-82. **RESEARCH** Epigraphy; Egyptian philology; history of the Egyptian New Kingdom. **SELECTED PUBLICATIONS** Coauth, Medinet Habu, Vol VI, 63, Vol VII, 64; auth, Late Ramesside Letters, 67 & coauth, The Beit el-Wali Temple of Ramesses II 67, Univ Chicago; The Literature of Ancient Egypt, Yale Univ, 72; A chronology of the New Kingdom, In: Studies in Honor of George R Hughes, Univ Chicago, 76; The Temple of Khonsu, Vol I, 79, Vol II 81; The Tomb of Kheruef, 80; co-ed, An X-Ray Atlas of the Royal Mummies, Univ Chicago, 80; Egyptian Historical Inscriptions Of The 20th-Dynasty - Peden,Aj, Journal Of The American Oriental Society, Vol 0116, 1996. **CONTACT ADDRESS** Orient Inst, Univ of Chicago, 1155 E 58th St, Chicago, IL, 60637.

WENZEL, JOSEPH WILFRED
PERSONAL Born 11/30/1933, Elkhart, IN, m, 1959, 2 children **DISCIPLINE** SPEECH; COMMUNICATION **EDUCATION** Univ Ill, BS, 57, PhD(speech), 63; Northwestern Univ, MA, 58. **CAREER** Lectr speech, Hunter Col, City Univ NY, 60-63; from Asst Prof to Assoc Prof, 63-93, PROF SPEECH COMM, UNIV ILL, URBANA, 94-. **HONORS AND AWARDS** Am Forensic Asn Res Award. **MEMBERSHIPS** Nat Commun Asn; Am Forensic Asn; Int Soc Hist Rhetoric; Int Soc Study of Argumentation. **RESEARCH** Argumentation; rhetorical theory. **CONTACT ADDRESS** Dept of Speech Commun, Univ of Illinois, Urbana-Champaign, 702 S Wright, #244, Urbana, IL, 61801-3631. **EMAIL** jwengel@uiuc.edu

WERTZ, CHRISTOPHER ALLEN
PERSONAL Born 06/13/1941, Lakewood, OH **DISCIPLINE** SLAVIC & GENERAL LINGUISTICS **EDUCATION** Columbia Univ, BA, 63; Univ Michigan, Ann Arbor, PhD(Slavic), 71. **CAREER** Asst prof Russ & ling, Washington Univ, St louis, 71-75 & Univ Wyo, Laramie, 75-77; asst prof, 77- 80, Assoc Prof Russian, Univ Iowa, Iowa City, 81-. **RESEARCH** Russian morphology; Polish morphology; interlinguistics. **SELECTED PUBLICATIONS** Auth, The number of genders in Polish, Can Slavonic Papers, Vol 19, No 1; entry on Baudouin de Courtenay, Mod Encycl Russ & Soviet Lit, Vol 2, 78; An alternate way of teaching verbs of motion in Russian, Russ Lang J, Vol 32, No 116; coauth, entry on Ferdinand de Saussure, Mod Encycl Russ & Soviet Lit, Vol 5, 81; auth, Some proposals regarding the creation of an international auxiliary language, Brit J Lang Teaching, Vol 19, No 3; The Pedagogical Case For Predicatives In Russian, Slavic And East European Journal, Vol 0038, 1994. **CONTACT ADDRESS** Dept of Russ, Univ of Iowa, 230 Jessup Hall, Iowa City, IA, 52242-1316.

WESCOTT, ROGER WILLIAMS
PERSONAL Born 04/28/1925, Philadelphia, PA, m, 2 children **DISCIPLINE** LINGUISTIC ANTHROPOLOGY **EDUCATION** Princeton Univ, AB, 44 & 45, MA, 47, PhD(ling sci), 48; Oxford Univ, BLitt, 52. **CAREER** Ed & interviewer, Gallup Poll, 52; asst prof hist & human rels, Mass Inst Technol & Boston Univ, 53-57; assoc prof English & soc sci, Mich State Univ,

57-62, dir African lang prog, 59-62; prof anthrop & hist & chmn, Div Soc Sci, Southern Conn State Col, 62-63; lectr sociol & anthrop, Wilson Col, 64-66; co-dir behav studies prog, 73-76, Prof Anthrop & Ling & Chmn Dept Anthrop, Drew Univ, 66-, Ford fel, Univ Ibadan, Nigeria, 55-56; foreign lang consult, US Off Educ, 61; West African Ling Surv grant, Ibadan, 61-62; consult ed, J African Lang, 62-; poetry ed, The Interpreter, 62-; ling fieldworker, Sierra Leone, 63; linguist, Bur Appl Social Res, Columbia Univ, 63-64; rev ed, Int Soc Studies Comp Civilizations, 73-; pres prof humanities & soc sci, Colo Sch Mines, 80-81. **MEMBERSHIPS** Fel African Studies Asn; fel Am Anthrop Asn; fel AAAS; Int Ling Asn; Int Soc Comp Study of Civilizations. **SELECTED PUBLICATIONS** Auth, The Divine Animal: An Exploration of Human Potentiality, Funk, 69; coauth, A Pre-Conference Volume on Cultural Futurology, Am Anthrop Asn, 70; Human Futuristics, Univ Hawaii, 71; The Experimental Symposium on Comparative Futurology, Univ Minn, 71; auth, Traditional Greek conceptions of the future, In: The Experimental Symposium on Comparative Futurology, Univ Minn, 71; coauth, The Highest State of Consciousness, Anchor Bks, 72; auth, Seven Bini charms, Folklore Forum, 10/72; Metaphones in Bini and English, In: Studies in Linguistics in Honor of George L Trager, Mouton, The Hague, 73; Sound and Sense, Jupiter Press, 80; Toward A More Concise Inventory Of Proto-Indo-European Roots, Word-Journal Of The International Linguistic Association, Vol 0044, 1993. **CONTACT ADDRESS** Dept of Anthropology, Drew Univ, Madison, NJ, 07940.

WEST, CORNEL
PERSONAL Born 06/02/1953, Tulsa, Oklahoma, d **DISCIPLINE** NEAR EASTERN LANGUAGES **EDUCATION** Harvard University, bachelor's degree (magna cum laude), Near Eastern languages and literature; Princeton Univeristy, PhD work. **CAREER** Yale University Divinty School, professor, 1984; Le Monde Diplomatique, American correspondent; University of Paris, educator, one semester; Princeton University, Dept of Religion, professor, Dept of Afro-American Studies, director; Harvard University, African American studies, currently. **HONORS AND AWARDS** Harvard University, Du Bois Fellow. **SELECTED PUBLICATIONS** Author: Race Matters, Beacon Press, 1993; co-author with bell hooks, Breaking Bread: Insurgent Black Intellectual Life, South End Press, 1992; Prophesy Deliverance! An Afro-American Revolutionary Christianity, Westminster/John Knox Press; The American Evasion of Philosophy: A Genealogy of Pragamatism, University of Wisconsin Press. **CONTACT ADDRESS** African American Studies, Harvard Univ, 12 Quincy St., Cambridge, MA, 02138.

WEST, LARRY E.
PERSONAL Born 05/09/1942, Canada, KY, m, 1963, 2 children **DISCIPLINE** LANGUAGE; LITERATURE **EDUCATION** Berea Col, BA 64; Vanderbilt Univ, PhD, 69. **CAREER** Asst Prof, West Georgia Col, 67-69; Asst Prof, Assoc Prof, Prof, 69-, Wake Forest Univ. **HONORS AND AWARDS** Fullbright Grant for Study at Goethe Inst, 70; Amer Phil Soc Grant for Research, 80; Lower Division Advising Award, Wake Forest Univ, 95. **RESEARCH** Medieval German literature; The German Passion Play of Late Middle Ages **SELECTED PUBLICATIONS** Auth, The Alsfield Passion Play (Translated with an Introduction, 97. **CONTACT ADDRESS** Dept of German and Russian, Wake Forest Univ, Winston-Salem, NC, 27109. **EMAIL** westle@wfu.edu

WETSEL, WILLIAM DAVID
PERSONAL Sweetwater, TX, s **DISCIPLINE** FRENCH **EDUCATION** Univ Texas, BA, 71; Brandeis Univ, MA, 74, PhD, 78; The Divinity School, Univ Chicago, MA, 88. **CAREER** Vis asst prof, Dept Fr & Ital, Univ Mass-Amherst, 78-79; Andrew Mellon fel, Dept Fr & Ital, Univ Pitts, 80-81; vis asst prof, Dept Fr & Ital, Univ Texas-Austin, 81-85; asst prof, Dept For Lang, Centenary Col Louisiana, 85-86; asst prof, Univ Hon Prog, Dept For Lang, Portland State Univ, 88-89; asst prof, 89-92, assoc prof, 92-95, PROF, DEPT LANG & LIT, ARIZON STATE UNIV, 95- . **HONORS AND AWARDS** Fulbright Tchg Asst, 71-72; Woodrow Wilson Fel, 72-73; Gilbert Chinard Scholar, 80; res grant, Am Coun Learned Soc, 80; Fulbright Scholar Univ Paris, 82; Phi Beta Kappa. **MEMBERSHIPS** N Am Soc Fr 17th Century Lit. **RESEARCH** 17th Century French literature: Pascal/Port-Royal. **SELECTED PUBLICATIONS** Auth, Pascal's Pensees and Recent Critical Theory: Illumination or Deformation of the Text?, Papers on French Seventeenth-Century Literature, 93; La religion de Mahomet: Pascal and the Tradition of Anti-Islamic Polemics, Papers on French Seventeenth-Century Lit, 93; Pascal and Mitton: Theological Objections to l'honnetete in the Pensees in French Studies, 93; Pascal's Attack on Deism: the Pensees and the Quatrains du Deiste, Papers on French Seventeenth-Century Literature, 94; Copi: His Theater and Novels, Latin American Gay Literature: A Biographical and Critical Sourcebook, Greenwood Press, 94; Pascal and the Polemics of Christian Orthodoxy, Papers on French Seventeenth Century Literature, 95; auth, Pascal and Disbelief: Catechesis and Conversion in the Pensees, Cath Univ Am Press, 95; Pascal: Moralist or Theologian in De la morale a l'economie politique: dialogue francoamericain sur les moralistes francais, Publ de l'Univ de Pau, 96; Pascal on Death, Papers on French Seventeenth Century Literature, 99; La Mothe le Vayer and the Subversion of Christian Belief, Seventeenth-Century French Studies, 99. **CONTACT ADDRESS** Dept of Lang & Lit, Arizona State Univ, Tempe, PO Box 870202, Tempe, AZ, 85287-0202. **EMAIL** David.Wetsel@asu.edu

WETZEL, HEINZ
PERSONAL Born 05/11/1935, Ziesar, Germany, m, 1957, 3 children **DISCIPLINE** GERMAN LANGUAGE & LITERATURE **EDUCATION** Univ Gottingen, DrPhil, 67. **CAREER** Lectr Ger lang & lit, Univ Lille, 60-64; vis instr, Univ Wis-Madison, 64-65; asst prof, Queen's Univ, Ont, 65-69; assoc prof, 69-72, Prof Ger Lang & Lit, Univ Toronto, 72-, Vis prof, Univ Calif, San Diego, spring 73 & Technische Univ Braunschweig, Ger, fall 73; ed, Seminar: A Journal of Germanic Studies, 80. **MEMBERSHIPS** MLA; Can Asn Univ Teachers. **RESEARCH** German literature of the 19th and 20th centuries; comparative literature. **SELECTED PUBLICATIONS** Auth, Klang und Bild inden dichtungen Georg Trakls, Vandenhoeck & Ruprecht, Fottingen, 68, 2nd rev & enlarged ed, 72; Konkordanz zu den Dichtungen Georg Trakis, Otto Muller, Salburg, 72; Banale Vitalitat and lahmenes Erkennen, Drei vergleichende Studien u T S Eliiots The Waste Land, Herbert Lang, Bern & Frankfurt, 74; Dantons Tod und das Erwachen von Buechners sozialem Selbstverstandis, Deut Vierteljahrsschritt, 76; Bildungsprivileg und Vereinsamung in Buchners Lenz und Dostojewskis Damonen, Arcadia 78; ElektrasKult der Tat - freilicb mit Ironie behandelt, Jahrbuch des Freien Deutschen Hochstifts 80; Die Entwicklung Woyecks in Buchners Entwurfen, Euphorion 80; Georg Buchner und ein polnischer General: Zwischen politischem Engagement und ironischer Distan, Jahrbuch der Deutschen Schillergesellschaft, 81; Trakl,Georg - A Biography With Pictures, Texts, And Documents - German - Weichselbaum,H, Seminar-A Journal Of Germanic Studies, Vol 0032, 1996; Works, Journals, Letters - German - Muller,W, Seminar-A Journal Of Germanic Studies, Vol 0032, 1996. **CONTACT ADDRESS** Dept of Ger Univ Col, Univ of Toronto, Toronto, ON, M5S 1A1.

WHALEY, LINDSAY
DISCIPLINE LINGUISTICS AND CLASSICS **EDUCATION** SUNY Buffalo, PhD, 93. **CAREER** Asst prof, Dartmouth Col. **RESEARCH** Lang typology; syntactic theory; word order variability; Bantu linguistics; Tungus linguistics. **SELECTED PUBLICATIONS** Auth, An Introduction to Language Typology: The Unity and Diversity of Language, Sage, 97; Manchu-Tungus languages, Encyclopedia Britannica, 97; The Effect of Non-Surface Grammatical Relations on the Genitive Absolute in Koine Greek in Grammatical Relations: A Cross Theoretical Perspective, CSLI, 90;coauth, Endangered Languages: Current Issues and Future Prospects, Int Jour Soc Lang, 96; Kinyarwanda Multiple Applicatives and the 2-AEX in Papers from the 28th Regional Meeting of the Chicago Linguistic Society, Univ Chicago, 93; Locatives vs. Instrumentals in Kinyarwanda in Proceedings of the 17th Annual Meeting of the Berkeley Linguistic Society: Special Session on African Language Structure, 91. **CONTACT ADDRESS** Dartmouth Col, 3529 N Main St, #207, Hanover, NH, 03755. **EMAIL** lindsay.j.whaley@dartmouth.edu

WHATLEY, ERIC GORDON
PERSONAL Born 07/16/1944, Blackburn, England, m, 1980, 2 children **DISCIPLINE** ENGLISH LITERATURE, LANGUAGE **EDUCATION** Oxford Univ, BA, 66; Harvard Univ, PhD(English), 73. **CAREER** Asst prof English, Lake Forest Col, 72-78, asst dean fac, 76-79; asst prof English, 80-84, assoc prof, 85-92, prof, Queens Col, NY, 93-; CUNY Grad Center, 89-. **HONORS AND AWARDS** Dir & fac fel, Newberry Libr Humanities Prog, Assoc Cols Midwest, 75-76; Nat Endowment for Humanities independent study fel, 79-80; Am Phil S oc grants, 75, 83; Nat Endowment for Humanities Res Tools grant (dir Paul Szarmach), 90-92; PSC-CUNY Res awards, 82-83, 85-87, 93, 97-98. **MEMBERSHIPS** Mediaeval Acad Am; Int Soc Anglo-Saxonists; Hagiography Soc N Am; Friends of the Saints. **RESEARCH** Old and Middle English hagiography; Medieval Latin hagiography. **SELECTED PUBLICATIONS** Auth, Cynewulf and Troy: A note on Cynewulf's Elene, Notes & Queries, 73; Bread and stone: Cynewulf's Elene 611-618, Neuphilol Mitteilungen, 75; Old English monastics and narrative art: Elene 1062, Mod Philol, 75; The Figure of Constantine the Great in Cynewulf's Elene, Traditio 37; The Middle English St Erkenwald in its liturgical context, Mediaevalia, 82; Opus dei, opus mundi: Patterns of Conflict in a Twelfth-century Miracle Collection, in Michael Sargent, ed, De cello in seculum, 89; The Saint of London: the Life and Miracles of St Erkenwald, 89; Acta Sanctorum, in Sources of Anglo-Saxon Literary Culture: A Trial Version, ed F Biggs et al, 90; Hagiography in Anglo-Saxon England: A Preliminary View from SASLC, Old English Newsletter, 90; with Jo Ann McNamara & John E Halborg, Sainted Women of the Dark Ages, 92; An Early Literary Quotation from the Inventio S. Crucis: a Note on Baudonivia's Vita S. Radegundis (BHL 7049), Analecta Bollandiana, 93; Late Old English Hagiography, ca 950-1150, in Hagiographies, ed Guy Philippart, 96; A Introduction to the Study of Old English Prose Hagiography: Sources and Resources, in Holy Men and Holy Women: Old English Prose Saints' Lives and Their Contexts, ed Paul E Szarmach, 96; Lost in Translation: Some Episodes in Old English Prose Saints' Lives, Anglo-Saxon England, 97. **CONTACT ADDRESS** Dept of English, Queens Col, CUNY, 6530 Kissena Blvd, Flushing, NY, 11367-1597.

WHITE, PETER
PERSONAL Born 09/24/1941, Washington, DC, m, 1968, 2 children **DISCIPLINE** CLASSICAL PHILOLOGY **EDUCATION** Boston Col, BA, 63; Harvard Univ, PhD, 72. **CAREER** Asst prof, 68-74, assoc prof, 74-92, prof 93-, chmn dept classics, 80-83, 97-98, Assoc Prof Classics, Univ Chicago, 74-, Ed, Classical Philology, 74-78; Am Coun Learned Soc fel, 78-79; chmn comt publ, vice pres publ, 85-87, Am Philol Asn, 82-84,natl endow human fel, 94-95. **HONORS AND AWARDS** Goodwin award merit, Am Philol Asn, 95. **MEMBERSHIPS** Am Philol Asn. **RESEARCH** Latin lit of the early Empire; Greek and Roman historiography. **SELECTED PUBLICATIONS** Auth, The authorship of the Historia Augusta, J Roman Studies, 67; Vibius Maximus the friend of Statius, Historia, 73; The presentation and dedication of the Silvae and the Epigrams, J Roman Studies, 74; The friends of Martial, Statius and Pliny, Harvard Studies in Class Philol, 75; Amicitia and the profession of poetry in early Imperial Rome, J Roman Studies, 78; Julius Caesar in Rome, Pheonix, 88; Maecenas Retirement, univ press, 91; Promised Verse: Poets in the Society of Augustan Rome, harvard univ press, 93; Julius Caesar and the Publication of Acta in Late Republican rome, chiron, 97. **CONTACT ADDRESS** Dept of Class, Univ of Chicago, 1010 E 59th St, Chicago, IL, 60637-1512. **EMAIL** pwhi@midway.uchicago.edu

WHITENACK, JUDITH A.
PERSONAL Born 10/29/1944, Milwaukee, WI **DISCIPLINE** SPANISH LITERATURE **EDUCATION** Univ Wis, BS, 66, MA, 70, PhD(Span), 80. **CAREER** Lectr, Univ Wis, 78-79; Asst Prof Span, Univ Nev, Reno, 79-. **MEMBERSHIPS** MLA; Medieval Asn Pac; Philol Asn Pac Coast; Rocky Mountain Mod Lang Asn; Am Asn Teachers of Span & Port. **RESEARCH** Goldn age Spanish prose and poetry; Medieval Spanish poetry; Judaeo-Spanish poetry. **SELECTED PUBLICATIONS** Auth, The destruction of confession in Guzman de Alfarache, Revista de Estudios Hispanicos (in press); Cada dia notables afientas: Time and the protagonist in Guzman de Alfarache, Am Hispanis (in press); A new look at autobiography and confession, Forum (in press); Autobiography As Burla In The 'Guzman De Alfarache' - Davis,Nc, Journal Of Hispanic Philology, Vol 0016, 1992; A Lost 17th-Century Voice, Meneses,Leonor,De And El 'Desdenado Mas Firme', Journal Of Hispanic Philology, Vol 0017, 1992. **CONTACT ADDRESS** 1530 Hillside Dr, Reno, NV, 89503.

WHITLARK, JAMES S.
DISCIPLINE WORLD LITERATURE **EDUCATION** Univ Chicago, PhD, 76. **CAREER** Prof, TX Tech Univ. **RESEARCH** Relig in lit. **SELECTED PUBLICATIONS** Auth, Illuminated Fantasy: From Blake's Visions to Recent Graphic Fiction, Assoc UP, 88; Behind the Great Wall: A Post-Jungian Approach to Kafkaesque Literature, Assoc UP, 91; coed, The Literature of Emigration and Exile, TX Tech, 92. **CONTACT ADDRESS** Texas Tech Univ, Lubbock, TX, 79409-5015. **EMAIL** ditjw@ttacs.ttu.edu

WICKHAM, CHRISTOPHER J.
PERSONAL Born 05/26/1950, Reading, England, m **DISCIPLINE** GERMAN LITERATURE **EDUCATION** Univ of Reading, BA, 72, MPhil, 74; Univ Wisc, PhD, 82. **CAREER** Lec English, Univ Regensburg, Ger, 73-76; asst prof, Allegheny Col, 82-85; asst prof, Univ of Ill, Chicago, 85-91; asst prof,Univ Texas, San Antonio, 91-97, assoc prof, 97- . **MEMBERSHIPS** MLA; Am Assoc Tchrs Ger; Ger Stud Assoc; Soc for Lit and Sci; Int Dialect Inst. **RESEARCH** German language, literature and culture; Bavaria; explorers and travel writing; German painters in the Americas. **SELECTED PUBLICATIONS** Ed, Framing the Past: The Historiography of German Cinema and Television, Southern Ill, 92; auth, The Business of Survival: Aspects of Economy in Pevny/Turrini's Alpensaga, in Mod Lang Stud, 94; auth, Postmodern Mundart: Zum Schnubiglbaierisch des Felix Hoerburger, in Im Gefuge der Sprachen, 94; auth, Oil and Water: The Development of the Portrayal of Native Americans by 19th Century German Painters, in Yearbk of German-Am Stud, 96; auth, Wohin und Zuruck: Perspectives on Axel Corti's Jewish Trilogy, in Crossing Cultural Bounds in Contemporary Austrian Literature and Cinema, forthcoming. **CONTACT ADDRESS** Div of Foreign Languages, Univ of Texas at San Antonio, San Antonio, TX, 78249-0644. **EMAIL** cwickham@lonestar.utsa.edu

WIEMANN, JOHN M.
PERSONAL Born 07/11/1947, New Orleans, LA, m, 1969, 2 children **DISCIPLINE** INTERPERSONAL COMMUNICATION **EDUCATION** Loyola Univ (La), AB, 69; Purdue Univ, MS, 73, PhD(commun), 75. **CAREER** Employee rels specialist, Int Bus Machines Corp, 69-71; grad instr commun, Purdue Univ, 71-75; asst prof human commun, Rutgers Univ, 75-77; Asst Prof Commun Studies, Univ Calif, Santa Barbara, 77-, Res Assoc, Instrnl Develop, Measurement & Res Ctr, Purdue Univ, 73-74; vis scholar, Col Commun, Univ Tex, Austin, fall 80; W K Kellogg Found nat fel, 80-83. **HONORS AND AWARDS** Industry Award Outstanding Applied Res, Orgn Commun Div, Int Commun Asn, 74; Outstanding Res Report, Interpersonal

Commun Div, Int Commun Asn, 76. **MEMBERSHIPS** Int Commun Asn; Speech Commun Asn; AAAS; Am Educ Res Asn; Am Psychol Asn. **RESEARCH** Effective interpersonal communication; nonverbal communication; organizational communication & development. **SELECTED PUBLICATIONS** Coauth, Turn-taking in conversations, J Commun, 75; auth, Explication & test of a model of communicative competence, Human Commun Res, 77; Needed research & training in speaking & listening literacy, Commun Educ, 78; coauth, Nonverbal communication: Issues and appraisal, Human Commun Res, 78; Current theory & research in Communicative competence, Rev Educ Res, 80; Pragmatics of Interpersonal Competence, Rigor & Imagination, Praeger Press, 81; auth, Effects of laboratory videotaping procedures on selected conversation behaviors, Human Commun Rec, 81; co-ed, Nonverbal Communication, Sage, 83; The Dark Side Of Interpersonal-Communication - Cupach,Wr, Spitzberg,Bh, Journal Of Language And Social Psychology, Vol 0013, 1994. **CONTACT ADDRESS** Commun Studies Prog, Univ of Calif, 552 University Rd, Santa Barbara, CA, 93106-0001.

WIGNALL, DENNIS L.
PERSONAL Born 05/31/1943, Salt Lake City, UT, m, 3 children **DISCIPLINE** HUMAN COMMUNICATION **EDUCATION** Univ of Denver, PhD, 93. **CAREER** 31 years as adjunct faculty at: Univ of CO-Denver, Metro State Col of Denver, Regis Univ, Front Range Community Col, Univ of Northern CO, Int Univ, Univ of Denver. **HONORS AND AWARDS** Recipient of multiple awards: teaching excellence. **MEMBERSHIPS** Nat Commun Asn (life member); Int Commun Asn (assoc member); Western States Commun Asn (assoc member); CO Speed Commun Asn (member). **RESEARCH** Human commun and the influence of ....and the internet. **CONTACT ADDRESS** 5063 W Radcliffe Ave, Denver, CO, 80236. **EMAIL** dwignall@csn.net

WILCOX, JOHN CHAPMAN
PERSONAL Born 04/20/1943, Liverpool, England, m, 1967 **DISCIPLINE** SPANISH LITERATURE, POETRY **EDUCATION** Univ Bristol, BA, 65; Univ Tx Austin, PhD, 76. **CAREER** Teaching asst, Univ Tex Austin, 66-70; lects, Queens Col, 70-75; fel, Univ Cincinnati, 77-78, asst prof, 78-79; asst prof Span, 79-85, assoc prof Spanish, 85-96, prof Spanish, 96-, Dir Grad Studies dept Spanish, Italian and Portugues, 88-92, Int head: Dept of Spanish, Italian and Portuguese, 92-94, Univ Ill-Urbana, 79; Resident Dir-Educ Abroad Prog Univ Ca and Il, 86-88 and 94-96. **HONORS AND AWARDS** Charles Phelps Taft Postdoctoral Fel, Univ Cincinnati, 77-78; Fel Ctr Advan Study, Univ Il-Urbana, 84; LAS Coun Award, 87-88. **MEMBERSHIPS** MLA; Am Asn Teachers Span & Port; Asoc Int de Hispanistas; Twentieth Century Span Assoc Am; Assoc de Literatura Femenina Hispanica; Sigma Delta Pi Span Hon Soc. **RESEARCH** The poetry of Juan Ramon Jimenez; Spanish poetry of the 20th Century: Women poets of Spain. **SELECTED PUBLICATIONS** Auth, Juan Ramon Jimenez: transformacion y evolucion poetica de cuatro temas fundamentales de su obra, Cuadernos Hispanoamericas CXXV, 81; Arbol arraigado y pleamar: respuesta a la transformacion de la decadencia y la estetica en Juan Ramon y Nietzsche, La Torre, 81; Naked versus Pure Poetry in Juan Ramon Jimenez, with Remarks on the Impact of W B Yeats, Hispania, 83; At Home and Beyond: New Essays on Spanish Poets of the Twenties, Soc Span and Span-Am Studies, 83; Self and Image in Juan Ramon Jimenez (Modern and Post-Modern Readings, Univ Ill, 87; After the War: Essays on Recent Spanish Poetry, Soc Span and Span-Am Studies, 88; Anales de la literatura espanola contemporanea, 91; Anales de la literatura espanola contemporanea, 93; Women Poets of Spain, 1860-1990: Toward a Gynocentric Vision, Univ Ill, 97. **CONTACT ADDRESS** Dept of Spanish, Italian and Portoguese, Univ Ill, 707 S Mathews Ave, Urbana, IL, 61801-3625. **EMAIL** j-wilcox@uiuc.edu

WILCOX, SHERMAN E.
DISCIPLINE SIGNED LANGUAGE LINGUISTICS, LANGUAGE EVOLUTION **EDUCATION** Univ NMex, PhD. **CAREER** Prof, Univ NMex. **SELECTED PUBLICATIONS** Auth, The Multimedia Dictionary of American Sign Language, Proc of ASSETS Conf, Asn Comput Machinists, 94; Struggling for a Voice: An Interactionist Approach to Literacy in Deaf Education, in V John-Steiner, C Panofsky, & L Smith, eds, Interactionist Approaches to Language and Literacy, Cambridge UP, 94; Representation of the Dynamic Elements of Signs: Issues in the Development of the Multimedia Dictionary of American Sign Language, J of Contemp Legal Issues, Vol 6, 95; The Gestural Expression of Modals in American Sign Language, in S Fleischman & J Bybee, eds, Modality in Grammar and Discourse, John Benjamins, 95; coauth, Signs of the Origins of Syntax, Current Anthrop, 94; The Gestural Expression of Modality in ASL, in J Bybee & S Fleischman, eds, Modality in Grammar and Discourse, John Benjamins, 95; Gesture and the Nature of Language, Cambridge UP, 95; Learning to See: American Sign Language as a Second Language, 2nd ed, Gallaudet UP, 96. **CONTACT ADDRESS** Univ NMex, Albuquerque, NM, 87131. **EMAIL** wilcox@unm.edu

WILDNER-BASSETT, MARY E.
PERSONAL Born 10/26/1952, Billings, MT, m, 1978, 3 children **DISCIPLINE** FOREIGN LANGUAGES **EDUCATION** E IL Univ, BA, 74; Univ Wis, Madison, MA, 78; Ruhr Univ, Bochum, Germany, PhD, 83. **CAREER** Asst prof, Univ Hamburg, 83-86; asst prof, 86-93, assoc prof, 93-, fac, 91-, Univ AZ. **HONORS AND AWARDS** Small Grant, 90-91, Diversity Action Coun Award, 94-95, Hum Tchg Initiative Award, 96-97, Univ AZ; Fulbright Sen Res full maintenance Award, 93-94; Burlington Fac Excellence Tchg Award, 93; Instructional Computing Grant, 94-95; Award to attend Wakonse Tchg Conference, 95. **MEMBERSHIPS** AATG; ACTFL; AAUSC. **RESEARCH** Second language acquistion and teaching; interlanguage pragmatics; pragmatics of multiple literacies. **SELECTED PUBLICATIONS** Auth, Improving Pragmatic Aspects of Learners' Interlanguage, Gunter Narr Verlag, 84; Gesprachsroutinen und -strategien fur Deutsch als Alltags- und Wirtschaftssprache, Goethe Institut, 85; "Intercultural Pragmatics and Proficiency: Polite Noises for Cultural Appropriateness," Int Rev of Applied Ling, 94; "The Language Discovery Environment in the German Classroom of the 21st Century," Die Unterrichtspraxis, 94; "Intercultural Pragmatics and Metapragmatic Knowledge: Tapping the Source Using the Pragmatic Differential," Jour of Intensive Eng Studies, 97. **CONTACT ADDRESS** Dept of German Studies, Univ of Arizona, ML 571, Tucson, AZ, 85721. **EMAIL** wildnerb@u.arizona.edu

WILEY, RAYMOND A.
PERSONAL Born 10/30/1923, New York, NY, m, 1948, 8 children **DISCIPLINE** GERMAN, MYTHOLOGY & CLASSICAL LITERATURE **EDUCATION** Fordham Univ, AB, 46, MA, 48; Goethe Inst, Munich, cert, 56; Syracuse Univ, PhD(humanities), 66. **CAREER** Instr Ger & English, Boston Col, 47-48; from instr to assoc prof Ger, 48-71, dir lang lab, 70-77, actg chm dept mod lang, 76, actg chm dept classics, 76-78, Prof, 71-89, Adjunct Prof Emeritus Foreign Lang & Lit, Le Moyne Col, 89-, chm, Dept For Lang & Lit, 86-89. **HONORS AND AWARDS** Fordharn Univ Encaenia award, 56; Fulbright Summer Teachers Award to Germany, 56; NEH Summer Seminar, Stanford Univ, 80. **MEMBERSHIPS** Am Asn Teachers Ger. **RESEARCH** The Correspondence between John Mitchell Kemble and Jakob Grimm, 1832-52; 19th century German-English literary relations; Teutonic mythology. **SELECTED PUBLICATIONS** Auth, Four unpublished letters of Jacob Grimm to John Mitchell Kemble, 1832-40, J English & Ger Philol, 7/68; ed, John Mitchell Kemble and Jacob Grimm, a Correspondence: 1832-1852, Brill, Leiden, 71; auth, From letters to life, Heights Mag, Le Moyne Col, fall 71; The German-American verse of Dr Franz Lahmeyer, Ger-Am Studies, spring 74; ed, Austausch, Cent NY Chap Am Asn Teachers Ger Newslett, Vols 1-5, 70-74; auth, Dear Harriet: Fanny Kemble's View of Centennial America, Pa Gazette, 7/76; Anglo-Saxon Kemble, The Life and Works of John Mitchell Kemble 1807-57: Philologist, Historian, Archaeologist, Brit Archaeol Rec, No 72: Anglo-Saxon Studies Archaeol & Hist, I: 165-273; ed, John Mitchell Kemble's Review of Jacob Grimm's Deutsche Grammatik, State Univ NY Ctr Medieval & Early Renaissance Studies, 81; transl, On the Origin of Language, Leiden, Brill, 84; auth, Tints and Texts, A Comparison of the Nibelungenlied's MS Illustrations with Its Narrative, Acta, X, 86; Grimm's Grammar Gains Ground in England, In: The Grimm Brothers & The Germanic Past, J. Benjamins, 90. **CONTACT ADDRESS** Dept of Foreign Lang, LeMoyne Col, 1419 Salt Springs Rd., Syracuse, NY, 13214-1300.

WILHELM, JAMES JEROME
PERSONAL Born 02/02/1932, Youngstown, OH **DISCIPLINE** COMPARATIVE LITERATURE **EDUCATION** Yale Univ, BA, 54, PhD(comp lit), 61; Columbia Univ, MA, 58. **CAREER** From instr to asst prof English, Queens Col, 61-65; PROF COMP LIT, RUTGERS UNIV, NEW BRUNSWICK, 65-, Gen Ed, Garland Libr of Medieval Lit. **MEMBERSHIPS** MLA; Dante Soc; Mediaeval Acad Am; Am Comp Lit Asn. **SELECTED PUBLICATIONS** Auth, The Cruelest Month: Spring, Nature & Love in Classical & Medieval Lyrics, Yale Univ, 65; Seven Troubadours, Pa State Univ, 70; Medieval Song, Dutton, 71 & Allen & Unwin, 72; Dante and Pound: The Epic of Judgement, Univ Maine, 74; Arnaut Daniel's Legacy to Dante and to Pound, Italian Lit: Roots & Branches, Yale Univ, 76; The Later Cantos of Ezra Pound, Walker, 77; The Poetry of Arnaut Daniel, Garland, 81; IE Miglior Fabbro: The Cult of the Difficult in Daniel, Dante, and Pound, Maine, 82; In The Haunt Of The Priestess Of The Hidden Nest - A Tribute To Rudge,Olga, Paideuma-A Journal Devoted To Ezra Pound Scholarship, Vol 0026, 1997. **CONTACT ADDRESS** 165 E 35 St 3 E, New York, NY, 10016.

WILLEM, LINDA M.
PERSONAL Born 06/06/1949, Chicago, IL, m, 1991, 1 child **DISCIPLINE** SPANISH LITERATURE **EDUCATION** Univ Wi Milwaukee, BS, 71, MA, 77; Univ Calif Los Angeles, PhD, 88. **CAREER** Teaching asst, Univ Wi Milwaukee, 75-76; instr, 77-80, Alverno Col; teaching fel to teaching assoc, 80-86, Univ of Calif Los Angeles; instr to asst prof to assoc prof to dept head, 87-, Butler Univ. **HONORS AND AWARDS** Butler Academic Grants for archival res, Filmoteca Nacional, Madrid, 97-98; Nat Endowment, Humanities Summer Seminar for Col Teachers: Rhetorical Theory of Narrative, 95; Butler Academic Grants, archival res, Casa-Museo Perez Galdos, Las Palmas, Biblioteca Nacional, Madrid, 93-94; Del Amo Endowment Dissertation Fel, 86-87; Nancy N Wing Award, Outstanding Performance, Doctoral Qualifying Exams, 85; James A Phillips Award, Outstanding Article Published by a UCLA Student, 85; Nat Endowment, Humanities Summer Seminar, College Teachers: Case History & Fiction, 79. **MEMBERSHIPS** Int Assoc of Galdosian Scholars; Int Assoc of Hispanists, Amer Assoc of Teachers of Spanish & Portuguese; Soc for Study of Narrative Lit; Modern Lang Assoc; Soc for Cinema Stud; Sigma Delta Pi; Phi Sigma Iota; Phi Kappa Phi. **RESEARCH** 19th century Spanish lit & Spanish cinema **SELECTED PUBLICATIONS** Ed, A Sesquicentennial Tribute to Galdos 1843/1993, Newark, De, 93; auth, Test and Intertext: James Whale's Frankenstein in El espiritu de la colmena, Romance Lang Annual, 98; art, Almodovar on the Verge of Cocteau's La Voix humaine, Kterature/Film Quart, 98; art, Linearity and Circularity in Carlos Saura's Peppermint Frappe, Romance Lang Annual, 99; auth, Galdos's Segunda Manera: Thetorical Strategies and Affective Response, Univ of N Calif, 99. **CONTACT ADDRESS** Dept of Modern Foreign Lang, Butler Univ, 4600 Sunset Ave, Indianapolis, IN, 46208. **EMAIL** lwillem@thomas.butler.edu

WILLIAMS, BRUCE
DISCIPLINE HISPANIC LANGUAGES AND LITERATURES **EDUCATION** Univ Calif-Los Angeles, PhD, 86. **CAREER** Asst prof. **RESEARCH** Film theory and cinema history and aesthetics. **SELECTED PUBLICATIONS** Publ on res interest. **CONTACT ADDRESS** Dept of Language and Cultures, William Paterson Col, 300 Pompton Rd., Wayne, NJ, 07470.

WILLIAMS, CHARLES GARFIELD SINGER
PERSONAL Born 05/17/1939, Mt Vernon, OH **DISCIPLINE** FRENCH LITERATURE, COMPARATIVE LITERATURE **EDUCATION** Kenyon Col, AB, 63; Oxford Univ, BA, 65; Yale Univ, MPhil, 69; Oxford Univ, MA, 70; Yale Univ, PhD(-Fr), 70. **CAREER** From instr to asst prof, 68-74, assoc prof French, 74-88, Prof, OH State Univ, 89-, chair, 89-95; Contrib ed, French 17, 79-. **MEMBERSHIPS** MLA; Mod Humanities Res Asn; Am Asn Teacher Fr; Am Soc 18th Century Studies; Fr Hist Soc. **RESEARCH** Sevigne; Valincour; 17th century French prose and academic eloquence. **SELECTED PUBLICATIONS** Auth, Valincour's life of guise, In: Literature and History in the Age of Ideas, OH State Univ, 75; ed, Literature and History in the Age of Ideas, OH State Univ, 75; Madame de Sevigne, G K Hall, 81; Memorialists, Historiography & History of Science and Medicine, In: Cabeen Bibliography, Suppl III, 82; Valincour, 91. **CONTACT ADDRESS** Dept of French, Ohio State Univ, 1841 Millikin Rd, Columbus, OH, 43210-1229.

WILLIAMS, DANIEL ANTHONY
PERSONAL Born 05/08/1942, Frederick, MD, m, 1963, 2 children **DISCIPLINE** SPANISH LANGUAGE & LITERATURE **EDUCATION** Univ Md, College Park, AB, 64; Johns Hopkins Univ, MA, 67, PhD, 72. **CAREER** Instr Span, Villa Julie Col, 66-67 & Sweet Briar Col, 67-71; asst prof, Va Wesleyan Col, 69; asst prof, 72-79, ASSOC PROF & CHMN, WESTERN MD COL, 79-. **RESEARCH** Contemporary Latin American narrative; comparative studies; 20th century Spanish poetry. **SELECTED PUBLICATIONS** Auth, Phantoms of the Afternoon (poem), Delta, 5/60; translr, War (poem), Brambler, 5/68 & Numbers (poem), Inlet, 5/72. **CONTACT ADDRESS** Dept of Foreign Langs, Western Maryland Col, 2 College Hill, Westminster, MD, 21157-4390. **EMAIL** dwilliam@wmdc.edu

WILLIAMS, EDWIN W.
PERSONAL Born 06/22/1936, Belzoni, MS, m, 1997, 2 children **DISCIPLINE** LANGUAGES **EDUCATION** Millsaps Col, BA, 58; Duke Univ, MDiv, 62; Univ NC Chapel Hill, PhD, 72. **CAREER** Asst prof, 65-67, Bibl Stud, Brevard Col; asst prof, 72-78, asst dean, 78-79, assoc prof, 78-85, prof, engl, 85-, E Tenn St Univ. **RESEARCH** James Joyce, Irish Stud, Victorian period. **CONTACT ADDRESS** Dept of English, East Tennesee State Univ, PO Box 70683, Johnson City, TN, 37614. **EMAIL** williaew@Access.ETSU.Edu

WILLIAMS, GERHILD SCHOLZ
PERSONAL Born 09/18/1942, Perleberg, Germany, m, 1974, 1 child **DISCIPLINE** MEDIEVAL STUDIES, LINGUISTICS **EDUCATION** Univ Wash, BA, 69, MA, 71, PhD(comp lit), 74. **CAREER** Asst prof, 75-81, Assoc Prof Ger, Washington Univ 81-. **MEMBERSHIPS** Medieval Acad Am; MLA, Am Asn Teachers Ger; Foreign Lang Teachers Asn; Midwestern Mod Lang Asn. **RESEARCH** French, German, Latin literature of the early and later Middle Ages. **SELECTED PUBLICATIONS** Auth, The vision of death, A study of the memento mori expressions in some Latin, German and French Didactic texts of the 11th and 12th centuries, Kummerle Goppingen W Ger, 10/76; Against court and school: Heinrich of Melk and Helinant of Froidmont as critics of Twelfth Century Society, Neophilolgus, 7/78; Against church and state: Heinrich von Melk und Helinant de Froidmont as critics of 12th century society, Neophilologus, 62: 513-526; Sozio-Semiotik als rekonstruktion, Zur interpretation mittelalterlicher literature Germanistiche Linguistik, 1-2: 217-236; coauth (with Alexander Schwarz), Das Uberetzen aus dem mittelalterlichen Deutsch,

Sprachspiegel, 9/80; auth, The arthurian model in Emperor Maximilian's autobiographic writings Weisskunig & Theuerdannk, Sixteenth Century J, 11, 4: 2-23; Es war einmal, ist und wird einmal sein: Geschichte und Geschichten in Gunter Grass Der Butt, In: deutsche Literatur in der Bundesrepuseit 1965, Konigstein/Ts Athenaum, 80; Annotated Bibliography of Maximilian I, his literary activities and the impact on the culture of his day, Sixteenth Century Bibliog, Vol 21, 82; 'Melusine', Experiential Realism In The Novel Of The Early Modern-Age + 'Melusine' By Jean-Darras And Thuring-Von-Ringoltingen, Lili-Zeitschrift Fur Literaturwissenschaft Und Linguistik, Vol 0023, 1993; Faustus On Trial - The Origins Of Spies,Johann 'Historia' In An Age Of Witch Hunting - Baron,F, German Quarterly, Vol 0068, 1995; Faustus On Trial - The Origins Of Spies,Johann 'Historia' In An Age Of Witch Hunting - Baron,F, German Quarterly, Vol 0068, 1995; Fearless Wives And Frightened Shrews - The Construction Of The Witch In Early-Modern Germany - Brauner,S, German Quarterly, Vol 0070, 1997; The Literary Body Of Saints - Lifes And Vitae Of Christina-Von-Stommeln 1242-1312 - German - Ruhrberg,C, German Quarterly, Vol 0070, 1997; Female Virginity In Verse Epics Of The 12th And 13th-Century - German - Muller,Me, German Quarterly, Vol 0070, 1997. **CONTACT ADDRESS** Dept of Ger, Washington Univ, St Louis, MO, 63130.

WILLIAMS, JOHN HOWARD
PERSONAL Born 11/19/1946, Louisville, KY, m, 1969, 2 children **DISCIPLINE** FRENCH LANGUAGES & LITERATURE, CLASSICS. **EDUCATION** David Lipscomb Col, BA, 67; Univ Wis-Madison, MA, 68, PhD(French), 72. **CAREER** Instr French, Tenn Technol Univ, 68-69; Fulbright advan teaching fel Am lit, Univ Besancon, 71-72; asst prof French, Eastern Ky Univ, 72-74; asst prof, 74-76, assoc prof, 76-82, Prof French & Chmn Dept, Abilene Christian Univ, 82-. **MEMBERSHIPS** MLA; Am Asn Teachers Fr. **RESEARCH** Contemporary French culture; 16th century French Poetry. **CONTACT ADDRESS** Abilene Christian Univ, Station Box 824, Abilene, TX, 79601.

WILLIAMS, JOSEPH M.
PERSONAL Born 08/18/1933, Cleveland, OH, m, 1960, 2 children **DISCIPLINE** ENGLISH, LINGUISTICS **EDUCATION** Miami Univ, BA, 55, MA, 60; Univ Wis, PhD(English), 66. **CAREER** Instr English, Miami Univ, 59-60; from instr to assoc prof, 65-76, Prof English, Univ Chicago, 76-, Consult med writing, Am Med Asn, 66. **MEMBERSHIPS** MLA; Lang Soc Am; Col English Asn. **RESEARCH** Stylistics; rhetoric; generative grammars. **SELECTED PUBLICATIONS** Auth, the source of Spenser's Labryde, Mod Lang Notes, 61; Caliban and Ariel meet Trager & Smith, Col English, 62. **CONTACT ADDRESS** Dept of English, Univ of Chicago, 5845 Ellis Av, Chicago, IL, 60637-1476.

WILLIAMS, PHILIP F.C.
PERSONAL AR, m, 1990, 1 child **DISCIPLINE** CHINESE LITERATURE **EDUCATION** UCLA, MA, 81, PhD, 85. **CAREER** Vis asst prof, Chinese, 86, UCLA; contract escort, Chinese interpreter, 86-96, US Dept of St, Office of Language Svcs; asst prof, Chinese, 86-92, Ariz St Univ; post doc res fel, 90-91, Fairbank Center for East Asian Research, Harvard Univ; asst prof, 91-92 Univ of Vermont; assoc prof, Chinese Literature and Interdisciplinary Humanities, 93-, Ariz St Univ. **HONORS AND AWARDS** Phi Beta Kappa, 78; UCLA Alumni Asn Award for Academic Achievement, 81; Humanities Res Award, AZ St Univ, 89; Svc Award, AZ St Univ, 97; Pres Southwest Conf on Asian Stud, 96-97. **MEMBERSHIPS** Council of Conf Member of the Asn for Asian Stud; Exec Bd Mem of the Southwest Conf on Asian Stud; Exec Comm of the Amer Asn for Chinese Comparative Lit; AZ Beta Chapter of the Phi Beta Kappa Honorary Soc. **RESEARCH** Chinese literature and society, esp in 20th century; Chinese language and cultural history. **SELECTED PUBLICATIONS** Auth, Village Echoes: The Fiction of Wa Zuxiang, Westview Press, 93; auth, Chinese the Easy Way, Hauppauge, NY Barron's Ed Series, 99; auth, Selected Papers of the 1997 Southwest Conference on Asian Studies, Tempe: Southwest Conf on Asian Stud, 98. **CONTACT ADDRESS** Dept of Languages and Lit, Arizona State Univ, Tempe, PO Box 870202, Tempe, AZ, 85287-0202. **EMAIL** phil.williams@asu.edu

WILLIAMS, QUEEN J.
PERSONAL Born 12/16/1946, Pembroke, KY, m, 1965, 3 children **DISCIPLINE** LANGUAGE **EDUCATION** Univ Louisville, BA, 69; Murray St Univ, MA, 78. **CAREER** Lang specialist, 69-71, Louisville Bd of Ed; ABE instr, 80-82, Kirkwood Col; paideia instr, 88-, Luther Col. **RESEARCH** African-Amer women's hist. **CONTACT ADDRESS** 601 West Water St, Decorah, IA, 52101. **EMAIL** williaqu@luther.edu

WILLIAMSON, KEITH
DISCIPLINE INTERPERSONAL COMMUNICATION, COMMUNICATION THEORY **EDUCATION** Temple Univ, PhD. **CAREER** Asst prof, Director of the Basic Course. Chair Depart Speech Commun,Wichita State Univ. **SELECTED PUBLICATIONS** Publ, Communication Education; co-auth, Leading Interpersonal Communication Textbook. **CONTACT ADDRESS** Wichita State Univ, 1845 Fairmont, Wichita, KS, 67260-0062. **EMAIL** williamson@elliott.es.twsu.edu

WILLIS, WILLIAM HAILEY
PERSONAL Born 04/29/1916, Meridian, MS, m, 1943, 4 children **DISCIPLINE** CLASSICAL PHILOLOGY **EDUCATION** Miss Col, AB, 36; Columbia Univ, AM, 37; Yale Univ, PhD(Greck), 40. **CAREER** Instr classics, Yale Univ, 40-42; assoc prof Greek & Latin, Univ Miss, 46-47; prof Greek & Latin & chmn dept classics, 47-63; PROF GREEK, DUKE UNIV, 63-, Fund Advan Educ fac fel, Harvard Univ, 52-53; mem managing comt, Am Sch Class Studies Athens, 53-, vchmn, 79-81; vis prof class lang, Univ Tex, 57-58; vis prof classics, Univ NC, 59, 63-64, 66; fac fel theol, Church Divinity Sch Pac, 59; sr ed, Greek, Roman & Byzantine Studies, 59-79; vis scholar, Fac of Relig, Oxford Univ, 61-62, vis mem, Brasenose & Queen's Cols, 61-62; Am Philos Soc Penrose Fund res grant, 62; Am Coun Learned Soc fac res grant, 62; corresp mem, Inst Antiquity & Christianity, 68-; Guggenheim fel, 80-81. **MEMBERSHIPS** Archaeol Inst Am; Am Philol Asn (pres, 72-73); Southern Class Asn (pres, 58-60); Southern Humanities Conf (secy, 56-58); Class Asn Mid W & S (pres, 66-67). **RESEARCH** Greek philology; papyrology; Coptic studies. **SELECTED PUBLICATIONS** Auth, Comoedia Dukiana + Fragment of Greek Comedy among Duke University Papyri, Greek Roman and Byzantine Stud, Vol 0032, 91; Dow, Sterling--19 Nov 1903 9 Jan 1995, Greek Roman and Byzantine Stud, Vol 0036, 95. **CONTACT ADDRESS** Duke Station, Box 4715, Durham, NC, 27706.

WILSON, DON
DISCIPLINE FRENCH LITERATURE **EDUCATION** Trinity Col, MA; PhD. **RESEARCH** Twentieth century literature; contemporary novel. **SELECTED PUBLICATIONS** Auth, pub(s) on Andre Gide, critical theory and contemporary criticism. **CONTACT ADDRESS** Dept of French, Waterloo Univ, 200 University Ave W, Waterloo, ON, N2L 3G1. **EMAIL** wdwilson@watarts.uwaterloo.ca

WILSON, DONNA M.
DISCIPLINE SPANISH **EDUCATION** Ohio State Univ, BA, 73, MA, 76; Univ Salamanca, Spain, Univ Wash, doctoral studies. **CAREER** Prof, 86-98, chair for lang, 90-94, chair arts & hum, 94-98, Highline Col; ASSOC DEAN ACAD AFF, GREENFIELD COMMUNITY COL, 98-. **CONTACT ADDRESS** Greenfield Comm Col, 1 College Dr, Greenfield, MA, 01301. **EMAIL** wilsond@gcc.mass.edu

WILSON, JOSEPH BENJAMIN
PERSONAL Born 10/11/1928, Houston, TX, m, 1947, 4 children **DISCIPLINE** GERMANIC LANGUAGES AND LITERATURE **EDUCATION** Rice Univ, BA, 50, MA, 53; Stanford Univ, PhD, 60. **CAREER** From instr to asst prof, 54-63, ASSOC PROF GER, RICE UNIV, 63-, Humboldt Found fel, Univ Kiel, 65-66 & Univ Marburg, 79. **MEMBERSHIPS** MLA; AAUP; Am Asn Teachers Ger; Soc Advan Scand Studies; Soc Am Archaeol. **RESEARCH** Germanic philology; computerized lexicography; Paleo-Indian archaeology. **SELECTED PUBLICATIONS** Auth, A conjecture on the second Merseburg charm, Rice Univ Studies, 69; Unusual German lexical items from Lee-Fayette County, In: Texas Studies in Bilingualism, de Gruyter, Berlin, 70; Probleme der Wortindexarbeit, In: Literatur und Datenverarbeitung, Niemeyer, Tubingen, 72; Extended Rime in Otfrid, Rice Univ Studies, 76; ed, Texas and Germany: Crosscurrents, Rice Univ, 77; English of German Americans in Texas, In: Languages in Conflict, Univ Nebr Press, 81; A prelim report on a Clovis-Plainview site, Bull Tex Archeol Soc, 80; Earliest Anglicisms in Texas German, Yearbk Ger-Am Studies, 81. **CONTACT ADDRESS** Dept of German, Rice Univ, Houston, TX, 77001.

WILSON, JOSEPH P.
DISCIPLINE FOREIGN LANGUAGES AND LITERATURES **EDUCATION** Univ Toledo, BA; Univ IA, PhD. **CAREER** Assoc prof, Univ of Scranton. **RESEARCH** Greek and Latin poetry; Greek tragedy; 20th-century Italian Women's Writing; Roman hist; Roman law. **SELECTED PUBLICATIONS** Auth, Defending an Unwed Stepmother: Catullus 64. 402, The Death of Lucan: Suicide and Execution in Tacitus, The Hero and the City: An Interpretation of Sophocles' Oedipus at Colonus. **CONTACT ADDRESS** Dept of For Lang(s) and Lit(s), Univ of Scranton, Scranton, PA, 18510.

WILSON, WILLIAM ALBERT
PERSONAL Born 09/23/1933, Tremonton, UT, m, 1957, 4 children **DISCIPLINE** FOLKLORE, FINNISH LITERATURE **EDUCATION** Brigham Young Univ, BA, 58, MA, 62; Ind Univ, PhD(folklore), 74. **CAREER** Instr English, Bountiful High Sch, 59-60; instr, Brigham Young Univ, 60-62, prof English & folklore, 67-78; instr English & folklore, Ind Univ, Ft Wayne, 66; PROF FOLKLORE, UTAH STATE UNIV, 78-, Vis prof, Univ Calif, Los Angeles, 68; bk rev ed, Western Folklore, 72-78, ed, 78-; dir, Utah State Univ Folklore Prog, 78-; Folk Arts panel mem, Nat Endowment for Arts, 80-. **HONORS AND AWARDS** Gustave O Arlt Humanities Award, Coun Grad Schs US, 77. **MEMBERSHIPS** MLA; Am Folklore Soc; Mormon Hist Asn; Finnish Lit Soc. **RESEARCH** Finnish folklore; Mormon folklore; the history of folklore scholarship. **SELECTED PUBLICATIONS** Auth, Folklore and history: Fact amid the legends, Utah Hist Quart, 73; Herder, folklore and romantic nationalism, J Popular Cult, 73; The Kalevala and Finnish politics, J Folklore Inst, 75; Folklore and Nationalism in Modern Finland, Ind Univ Press, 76; The paradox of Mormon folklore, Brigham Young Univ Studies, 76; ed, Mormon folklore, Utah Hist Quart, Spec issue No 4, 76; auth, The evolutionary method in folklore theory and the Finnish method, Western Folklore, 76; On being human: The folklore of Mormon missionaries, Utah State Univ Press, 81. **CONTACT ADDRESS** 1140 E 50 South, Logan, UT, 85321.

WILTROUT, ANN ELIZABETH
PERSONAL Born 08/03/1939, Elkhart, IN **DISCIPLINE** SPANISH **EDUCATION** Hanover Col, BA, 61; Ind Univ, MA, 64, PhD, 68. **CAREER** Vis asst prof Span, Ind Univ, Bloomington, 68-69; asst prof foreign lang, 69-71, Assoc Prof Foreign Lang, Miss State Univ, 71-87; prof of For Lng, 87-; Nat Endowment for Humanities fel-in-residence for col teachers, 77-78. **HONORS AND AWARDS** Distinguished Alumni, Hanover College, 74. **MEMBERSHIPS** MLA; Am Asn Teachers Span & Port; SCent Mod Lang Asn; SAtlantic Mod Lang Asn; AAUP. **RESEARCH** Spanish Renaissance and Golden Age literature. **SELECTED PUBLICATIONS** Auth, A Patron and a Playwright in Renaissance Spain: The House of Feria and Diego Sanchez de Badajoz, LindonL Tameses, 87; auth, The Lazarillo de Tormes and Erasmus Opulentia Sordida, Romanische Forschungen, Vol 69; Hacia algunas interpretaciones dramaticas de la leyenda de Santa Barbara, Filologia, Vol 15; Women in the Works of Antonio de Gueriara, Neophilologus, Vol 60; Quien espere desespera: El suicidio en el teatro de Juan del Encina, Hispanofila, Vol 72; Gines de Pasamonte: The Picaro and his Art, Anales Cervantinos, Vol 17; Gomez Suarez de Figueroa, Patron od Diego Sanchez de Badajoz's Recopilacion en metro, Bull Comediantes, Vol 31; auth, Role Playing and Rites of Passage: La ilustre fregona and La gitanilla, Hispania, Vol 64; auth, El Villano del Danubio: Foreign Policy and Literary Structure, Critica Hispanica, Vol 3. **CONTACT ADDRESS** Dept of Foreign Languages Drawer FL, Mississippi State Univ, Box F1, Mississippi State, MS, 39762-5720. **EMAIL** wiltrout@ra.msstate.edu

WIMMER, ALBERT K.
DISCIPLINE GERMAN **EDUCATION** Univ Notre Dame, MA, 64, MA, 67; Indiana Univ, PhD, 75. **CAREER** Dir, Innsbruck Prog, 70-73, 78-80; act chair, 97-98, PROF GER, PRESENTLY, UNIV NOTRE DAME. **CONTACT ADDRESS** 317 O'Shaughnessy Hall, Notre Dame, IN, 46556. **EMAIL** wimmer.7@nd.edu

WINCHATZ, MICHAELA R.
PERSONAL Born 01/04/1967, Summit, NJ, m, 1992 **DISCIPLINE** SPEECH COMMUNICATION AND PSYCHOLINGUISTICS **EDUCATION** Rutgers Col, BA, 88; Ludwig-Maximilians Univ, Germany, MA, 92; Univ of Washington, PhD, 97. **CAREER** Asst Prof, 97-, Southern Illinois University-Carbondale. **HONORS AND AWARDS** Alice Schlimmbach Alumnae Soc Scholar stud in Germany, Rutgers Univ, 86; Class of 1920 Merit Scholar, Rutgers Univ, 88; Fulbright Full Grant, 90-91, renewal grant, 91-92; DAAD Annual Grant to Germany, 95-96; Humanities Dissertation Fel, Univ of Washington, 96; Joint Womens Stud and Univ Womens Prof Advancement Juried Comp Res Awd, 97., Ed Asst, Quarterly Jour of Speech, 97. **MEMBERSHIPS** NCA, WSCA **RESEARCH** Ethnography of communication; intercultural communication; interpersonal communication; conversations analysis. **SELECTED PUBLICATIONS** CoAuth, Reading Ella CaraDelorias Waterlily for Cultured Speech, Iowa Jour of Comm, 97; CoAuth, Acting Out Our Minds Incorporating Behavior into Models of Stereotype Based Expectancies for Cross Cultural Interactions, Comm Mono, 97. **CONTACT ADDRESS** Southern Illinois Univ, Dept of Speech Communication, Mailcode 6605, Carbondale, IL, 62901-6605. **EMAIL** winchatz@siu.edu

WINDFUHR, GERNOT LUDWIG
PERSONAL Born 08/02/1938, Essen, Germany, m, 1965, 2 children **DISCIPLINE** IRANISTICS **EDUCATION** Univ Hamburg, Dr Phil, 65. **CAREER** Acad asst ling, Univ Kiel, 65-66; from asst prof to assoc prof, 66-73, Prof Iranian Lang & Ling, Univ Mich, Ann Arbor, 73-, Chmn Dept Near Eastern Studies, 77-. **MEMBERSHIPS** Ling Soc Am; Ling Soc Europe; MidE Studies Asn NAm; Am Orient Soc. **RESEARCH** Linguistics; literary theory; Zoroastrianism. **SELECTED PUBLICATIONS** Auth, Verbalmorpheme in Sangesari, privately publ, 65; Diacritic and Distinctive Features in Avestan: Some Avestan Rules and Their Signs, J Am Orient Soc, 71 & 72; coauth, A Dictionary of Sangesari with a Grammatical Outline, Franklin BK, Tehran, 72; A Linguist's Criticism of Persian Literature, In: Neue Methodologia in der Iranistik, Harrassowitz, Wiesbaden, 74; Isoglosses: A Sketch on Persians and Parthians, Kurds and Medes, Acts Iranica, V, 75; Vohu Manah: A Key to the Zoroastrain World Formula, Studies in Honor of GG Cameron, Ann Arbor, 76; Linguistics: The Study of the Middle East: Research and Scholarship in the Humanities and Social Sciences, John Wiley, NY, 76; Auth, Persian Grammar: History and State of Research, In: Jauna Linguarum Series Critica, Mouton, The Hague, 79. **CONTACT ADDRESS** Dept of Near Eastern Studies, Univ of Michigan, Ann Arbor, 2068 Frieze Bldg, Ann Arbor, MI, 48109-1285.

WINKLER, CAROL
DISCIPLINE SPEECH COMMUNICATION **EDUCATION** Univ Md, PhD, 87. **CAREER** Assoc prof, ch, dept Commun, Ga State Univ, 94-. **HONORS AND AWARDS** Mortarboard Distinguished Prof Award. **MEMBERSHIPS** Exec Comt, Southern Speech Commun Asn; Legis Coun, Speech Commun Asn. **RESEARCH** Visual communication. **SELECTED PUBLICATIONS** Wrote three books and published more than forty articles in political debates, visual communication, and presidential foreign policy rhetoric. **CONTACT ADDRESS** Georgia State Univ, Atlanta, GA, 30303. **EMAIL** cwinkler@gsu.edu

WINN, COLETTE HENRIETTE
PERSONAL Born 12/10/1951, La Grand-Combe, France, m, 1974 **DISCIPLINE** FRENCH LITERATURE AND LANGUAGE **EDUCATION** Universite Paul Valery Montpellier, Fr, Lic D'Anglais, 73; Univ Mo, MA, 76, PhD(Fr lang & lit), 80. **CAREER** Teaching asst Fr, Winslow Pub Sch, England, 71-72 & Univ Mo-Columbia, 75-79; ASST PROF FRENCH, WASHINGTON UNIV, ST LOUIS, 80-, Instr Fr, Univ Mo-Columbia, 78-79. **MEMBERSHIPS** MLA; Am Asn Teachers Fr. **RESEARCH** French poetry, particularly sixteenth and twentieth centuries; women poets and writers of the sixteenth century; Marguerite de Navarre. **SELECTED PUBLICATIONS** Auth, Sponde's Sonnet de la Mort II: A Semantic analysis, Lang & Style (in press); Le symbolisme des mains dans la poesi de Paul Eluard, Romanische Forschungen (in press). **CONTACT ADDRESS** 15975 Deer Trail, Chesterfield, MO, 63017.

WINNER, ANTHONY
PERSONAL Born 08/17/1931, New York, NY, m, 1964, 1 child **DISCIPLINE** ENGLISH, COMPARATIVE LITERATURE **EDUCATION** Harvard Univ, AB, 53, PhD, 62; Columbia Univ, MA, 54. **CAREER** Instr English, Univ Pa, 61-63 & Hunter Col, 63-65; asst prof, 65-68, ASSOC PROF ENGLISH, UNIV VA, 68-. **MEMBERSHIPS** MLA **RESEARCH** The novel; realism; character in fiction. **SELECTED PUBLICATIONS** Auth, Malouf, David 'Childs Play', Narrative Traditions in a Postmodern Game, Southerly, Vol 0054, 94; Disorders of Reading Short Novels and Perplexities, Kenyon Rev, Vol 0018, 96; Imagining Argentina, Kenyon Rev, Vol 0019, 97; On the Valuing of Narratives + Excerpt from a Set of Studies to be Entitled the 'Borderlines of Narrative', Va Quart Rev, Vol 0073, 97; One Hundred Years of Solitude, Kenyon Rev, Vol 0019, 97; See Under, Love, Kenyon Rev, Vol 0019, 97; Midnights Children, Kenyon Rev, Vol 0019, 97. **CONTACT ADDRESS** Dept of English, Univ of Va, 219 Bryan Hall, Charlottesville, VA, 22903.

WINSTON, JANE
DISCIPLINE FRENCH **EDUCATION** Duke Univ, PhD. **CAREER** Asst prof, Alice Berline Kaplan Center fel, Northwestern Univ fel; lectr, Twentieth-Century Colloquium, Fr; Francophone Studies, Stanford and Amherst; Fr Feminist Theory Conf; Dalhousie Univ, Nova Scotia; Univ Va. **HONORS AND AWARDS** Gerald Kahane Scholar's Prize, 96 **RESEARCH** Southeast Asian postcolonial theory and literature; cross-cultural feminist and gender studies; literary and cultural studies. **SELECTED PUBLICATIONS** Auth, Gender and Sexual Identity in the Modern French Novel, Cambridge Companion to the Modern Fr Novel, 97; Marguerite Duras: Marxism, Feminism, Writing, Theatre J, 95; Autour de la rue Saint-Benoit: An interview with Dionys Mascolo, Contemp Fr Civilization, 94; Forever Feminine: Marguerite Duras and Her Critics, New Lit Hist, 93. **CONTACT ADDRESS** Dept of French, Northwestern Univ, 1801 Hinman, Evanston, IL, 60208.

WINSTON, KRISHNA
PERSONAL Born 06/07/1944, Greenfield, MA, d, 1 child **DISCIPLINE** GERMAN LANGUAGE; LITERATURE **EDUCATION** Smith Col, BA, 61; Yale Univ, MPhil, 69, PhD, 74. **CAREER** Instr to asst prof to assoc prof to prof, acting dean, 70-, Wesleyan Univ. **HONORS AND AWARDS** Schlegel-Tieck Translation Prize; DAAD Fel, 73-74., Summa cum laude, Phi Beta Kappa, Smith Col. **MEMBERSHIPS** MLA; AATG; ALTA. **RESEARCH** Literary translation; exile literature **SELECTED PUBLICATIONS** Auth, Peter Handke, Essay on the Jukebox, Farrar Straus Giroux, 94; auth, Robert Menasse, excerpt from Happy Times, Brittle World, Fiction, 94; auth, Peter Handke, My Year in the No-Man's-Bay, Farrar Straus Giroux, 98; auth, Gunter Grass, Too Far Afield, Harcourt Brace, 2000. **CONTACT ADDRESS** Dept of German Stud, Wesleyan Univ, 262 High St, Middletown, CT, 06459-0040. **EMAIL** kwinston@wesleyan.edu

WINTER, IAN JAMES
PERSONAL Born 05/21/1927, Penang, Malaya, m, 1958 **DISCIPLINE** FRENCH LANGUAGE AND LITERATURE **EDUCATION** Univ Lyon, dipl, 50; Univ Edinburgh, MA, 51, dipl educ, 54; Wash Univ, PhD(French), 70. **CAREER** Instr French, Moray House Teachers Col, Edinburgh, 56-58; instr French & Span, Fettes Col, Edinburgh, 58-63 & Principia Col, 63-66; asst prof French, Millikin Univ, 67-70; asst prof, 70-76, ASSOC PROF FRENCH, UNIV WIS-MILWAUKEE, 76-, CHMN DEPT FRENCH & ITAL, 77-. **MEMBERSHIPS** Am Asn Teachers French; Mod Humanities Res Asn; La Societe des amis de Montaigne; Bibliog Soc, Renaissance Soc Am. **RESEARCH** Montaigne; 16th century French literature. **SELECTED PUBLICATIONS** Auth, Mon livre et moi: Montaigne's deepening evaluation of his own work, Renaissance Quart, 3/72; From self-concept to self-knowledge: Death and nature in Montaigne's de la phisionomie, In: French Renaissance Studies in Honor of Isidore Silver & Ky Romance Quart, Vol 21, 74; Montaigne's self-portrait and its influences in France, 1580-1630, French Forum, Lexington, 76; Montaigne's self-portraiture: Contemporary and societal reaction, Ky Romance Quart, Vol 23, 76; Concordances to Montaigne's J De Voyage, Lettres and Ephemerides, Hist Sem Medieval Studies, 81. **CONTACT ADDRESS** Dept of French and Italian, Univ of Wisconsin Downer & Kenwood, Milwaukee, WI, 53201.

WINTER, WERNER
PERSONAL Born 10/25/1923, Haselau, Germany, m, 1952, 1 child **DISCIPLINE** LINGUISTICS **EDUCATION** Univ Berne, PhD, 49. **CAREER** Instr ling, Univ Hamburg, 50-53; asst prof Russ & Ger, Univ Kans, 53-57; from assoc prof to prof ling, Ger & Russ, Univ Tex, Austin, 57-65; PROF LING, UNIV KIEL, 64-, Res grants, Univs Kans & Tex, 54-63; vis prof, Univ Kiel, 58; res sci & consult mech transl prof, Austin, 59-63; Am Coun Learned Soc fel, 60-61, deleg to USSR, 63; vis prof, Univ Hamburg, 63-64; Collitz prof, Ling Inst, Univ Calif, Los Angeles, 66; vis prof, Univ Copenhagen 66, Yale Univ, 67, Univ Calif, Berkeley, 69, Stanford Univ, 73 & Poznan, 77, 80, 81; Rose Morgan vis prof ling, Univ Kans, 73; ed, Ars Linguistica, Tuebingen, 78-; dir, Linguistic Survey of Nepal, 81- **HONORS AND AWARDS** Medal of Merit, Univ Poznan, 82. **MEMBERSHIPS** Ling Soc Am; Am Orient Soc; Ling Soc Paris; Ling Soc India; Ling Soc Europe (secy, 66-). **RESEARCH** Indo-European linguistics; Central Asian studies; American Indian languages. **SELECTED PUBLICATIONS** Auth, Sociolinguistics, Zeitschrift fur Dialektologie und Linguistik, Vol 0059, 92; Proto Indo European, J Indo Europ Stud, Vol 0022, 94. **CONTACT ADDRESS** Univ Kiel, Von Liliencronstr 2 D 2308 Preetz.

WISHARD, ARMIN
DISCIPLINE GERMAN LITERATURE **EDUCATION** Univ Ca, BA, 65, MA, 66; Univ Oregon, PhD, 70. **CAREER** Prof. **RESEARCH** Medieval literature; Romantic German literature. **SELECTED PUBLICATIONS** Auth, Salman und Morolf; pubs on German literature and teaching methodology. **CONTACT ADDRESS** German Dept, Columbia Col, New York, 14 E Cache La Poudre St, Colorado Springs, CO, 80903. **EMAIL** awishard@cc.colorado.edu

WITMER, DIANE F.
PERSONAL Born 01/20/0000, Pasadena, CA, d, 1 child **DISCIPLINE** COMMUNICATION ARTS & SCIENCES **EDUCATION** Univ of La Verne, BS, 80; Univ S Cal, MS, 89, MA, 93, PhD, 94. **CAREER** Instr, 90, Univ of La Verne; Instr, 90-91 & 92-94, dept of comm, Cal State Univ, Fullerton; researcher, 92, Nat Acad of Sci, Wash DC; Asst Lectr, 91-94, Univ S Cal, LA; Asst Prof, Communication, 94-97, Purdue Univ, IN; Assoc Prof, 97-, Cal State Univ, Fullerton. **HONORS AND AWARDS** Dept Honors 4.0/4.0 gpa, Univ La Verne, 2 Protos Awds, Top Four Paper Awd, Who's Who in; of Amer Women, in America, in the West & in the Midwest. **MEMBERSHIPS** CIOR, ICA, NCA, PRSA, WSCA. **RESEARCH** Computer-mediated communications, organizational communications & public relations. **SELECTED PUBLICATIONS** Auth, Understanding the Human Communication Process, Study Guide, Englewood CO, Jones Intl Ltd, 98; Public Relations, Study Guide, Englewood CO, Jones Intl Ltd, 97; Human Communications, Study Guide, Englewood CO, Jones Intl Ltd, 97; co-auth, From Paper-and-Pencil to Screen-and-Keyboard, Toward a Methodology for Survey Research on the Internet, in: Doing Internet Research, ed, S Jones, forthcoming; Practicing Safe Computing, Why People engage in Risky Computer-mediated Communication, in: Network and Netplay, Virtual Groups on the Internet, eds, F Sudweeks, M L McLaughlin & S Rafaeli, Menlo Park CA, AAAI/MIT Press, 98; Risky Business, Do People Feel Safe in Sexually Explicit Online Communication? in: J of Computer-Mediated Communication, 97. **CONTACT ADDRESS** Dept of Communications, California State Univ, Fullerton, Box 6846, Fullerton, CA, 92834-6846. **EMAIL** dwitmer@fullerton.edu

WITT, MARY A.
PERSONAL Born 11/30/1937, Urbana, IL, m **DISCIPLINE** COMPARATIVE LITERATURE **EDUCATION** Harvard Univ, PhD, 68. **CAREER** Asst prof, Wellesley Coll, 69-70; asst prof, NC Central Univ, 72-76; asst prof, NC State Univ, 77-85; asst to assoc to PROF, FRENCH, ITALIAN, NC STATE UNIV. 85-. **RESEARCH** Modern French, Italian lit. Drama theory. **SELECTED PUBLICATIONS** Auth, Modes of Narration in Pirandello's Sei Personaggi, in Luigi Pirandello: Poetica e Presenza, Bulzoni, 88; auth, La Figliastra di Pirandello e la creazione artistica, Prometeo 7 (28), fall 87; Towards a Theater of Immobility: Henry IV, The Condemned of Altona, and the Balcony, Comparative Drama, vol 24, summer 90; Pirandello's Sicilian COmedies and the Comic Tradition, in Pirandello and the Commedia dell'Arte, PUblication of the Pirandello Society of America, vol VI, 90; Mothers or Women? Feminine Conditions in Pirandello, in A Companion to Pirandello Studies, Greenwood Press, 91; Il Linguaggio femminile nel teatro di Pirandello, in Pirandello e la lingua, Mursia, 94; Authority and Contructions of Actress in the Drama of Pirandello and Genet, Comparative Literature Studies, vol 32, no 1, spring 95; Pirandellian dislocation or the dying dramatic author, in Ars dramatica, Lang, 97. **CONTACT ADDRESS** Dept For Lang & Lit, N Carolina State Univ, Raleigh, NC, 22695-8106. **EMAIL** witt@social.chass.ndsu.edu

WITT, MARY A.
PERSONAL Born 11/30/1937, Urbana, IL, m, 1965, 3 children **DISCIPLINE** COMPARATIVE LITERATURE **EDUCATION** Harvard Univ, PhD, 68 **CAREER** Asst prof, Wellesley Col, 69-70; asst prof, NC Central Univ, 72-76; from asst prof to prof, NC State Univ, 77-. **HONORS AND AWARDS** Fulbright Scholar, 85-86; Outstanding Book Award, NCSU Hums and Soc Scis, 87; Hums Ctr Fel, Univ of Utah, 96-97. **MEMBERSHIPS** ACLA; SCLA; MLA **RESEARCH** Modern French and Italian literatyre; drama theory. **SELECTED PUBLICATIONS** Auth, The Humanities: Cultural Roots and Continuities with Instructor's Guide, 80; Existential Prisons: Confinement in Mid-Twentieth Century French Literature, 85; Murder as Sign and Cycle in Les Negres, in Proceedings of the Am Semiotic Soc, 90; Towards a Theater of Immobility: Henry IV, The Condemned of Altona, and The Balcony, in Comparative Drama, 24, 90; Pirandello's Sicilian Comedies and the Comic Tradition, in Pirandello and the Commedia dell'Arte, vol. VI, 90; Mothers or Women? Feminine Conditions in Pirandello, in A Companion to Pirandello Studies, 91; Pirandellian Theater and Fascist Discourse, in South Atlantic Quart, 92; Pirandello's 'La Patente': mode, genre, narrative, in Aesthetics and the Text, 92; Reading Modern Drama: Voice in the Didascaliae, in Studies in the Literary Imagination, vol.25, no.1, 92; Fascist Aesthetics and Theatre under the Occupation: The Case of Anouilh, in J of European Studies xxiii, 93; Il linguaggio femminile nel teatro di Pirandello, in Pirandello e la lingua, 94; Authority and Constructions of Actress in the Drama of Pirandello and Genet, in Comparative Literature Studies, vol.32, no.1, 95; Pirandellian dislocation or the dying dramatic author, in Ars dramatica, 97; rev, Edward Said, Culture and Imperialism, in The Comparatist , 94; Richard Golson, ed. Fascism and Culture, in The Minnesota Review, 95; Harold Bloom, The Western Canon, in The Comparatist, 96. **CONTACT ADDRESS** Dept of Foreign Languages & Literature, No Carolina State Univ, Raleigh, NC, 27695-8106. **EMAIL** witt@social.chass.ncsu.edu

WITTKOWSKI, WOLFGANG
PERSONAL Born 08/15/1925, Halle, Germany, m, 1954, 4 children **DISCIPLINE** GERMAN LITERATURE **EDUCATION** Univ Frankfurt, PhD(Ger), 54. **CAREER** Asst Ger, Univ Frankfurt, 50-53; studienrat, gymnasium, Bad Nauheim, Ger, 56-63; from assoc prof to prof, Ohio State Univ, 63-77; PROF GER, STATE UNIV NY, ALBANY 78-, Vis prof Ger, State Univ NY, Albany, 77-78. **MEMBERSHIPS** MLA; Am Asn Teachers Ger. **RESEARCH** Classical and 19th century German literature; Kleist; ETA Hoffmann. **SELECTED PUBLICATIONS** Auth, Schiller, Friedrich, Ger Quart, Vol 0066, 93; Fathers and Daughters in a Middle Class Drama, or, Did 'Miss Sara Sampson' Really Not Happen + Lessing, G.E., J Engl and Ger Philol, Vol 0092, 93; The Modern Parable, J Engl and Ger Philol, Vol 0092, 93; Schiller, Seminar-J Ger Stud, Vol 0030, 94; Dare to be Happy, J Engl and Ger Philol, Vol 0094, 95; The Motif and Structural Principle of a Threshold in Grillparzer die 'Judin Von Toledo', Mod Austrian Lit, Vol 0028, 95; The Heimat is Not Enough, Mod Austrian Lit, Vol 0029, 96. **CONTACT ADDRESS** State Univ NY, Hu 209 1400 Washington Ave, Albany, NY, 12222.

WITTROCK, MERLIN CARL
PERSONAL Born 01/03/1931, Twin Falls, ID, m, 1953, 3 children **DISCIPLINE** EDUCATIONAL PSYCHOLOGY **EDUCATION** Univ of Mo, BS, 53; MEd, 56; Univ of Ill, PhD. 60. **CAREER** Asst prof, Univ of Calif, LA, 60-64; assoc prof, 64-67; PROF, 67-. **HONORS AND AWARDS** Outstanding Teacher of the Univ, Univ of Calif, LA, 90; UCLA Thorndike Award for Outstanding Res. **MEMBERSHIPS** Am Psychol Asn; Am Educ Res Asn. **RESEARCH** Cognition; Learning; Teaching of reading, science, and math. **SELECTED PUBLICATIONS** auth, Handbook of Research and Teaching; auth, The Human Brain; auth, The Brain and Psychology; auth, Testing and Cognition; auth, The Evaluation of Instruction. **CONTACT ADDRESS** Grad Sch of Educ, Univ of Calif, Louisiana, 3339 Moore Hall, Los Angeles, CA, 90095. **EMAIL** wittrock@ucla.edu

WOLFE, ETHYLE RENEE
PERSONAL Born 03/14/1919, Burlington, VT, m, 1954 **DISCIPLINE** CLASSICAL LANGUAGES AND LITERATURE **EDUCATION** Univ Vt, BA, 40, MA, 42; NY Univ, PhD, 50. **CAREER** Lectr classics, eve session, 47-49, from instr to assoc prof, 49-67, acting chmn dept classics & comp lit, 62-63, chmn, 67-72, PROF CLASSICS, BROOKLYN COL, 68-, Dean Sch Humanities, 71-, Assoc ed, Class World, 65-70; co-ed, Am

Class Rev, 70-. **MEMBERSHIPS** Am Philol Asn; Archaeol Inst Am; Am Soc Papyrologists. **RESEARCH** Latin poetry; Greek tragedy; papyrology. **SELECTED PUBLICATIONS** Auth, The Brooklyn College Core Curriculum, Arethusa, Vol 0027, 94; Cicero 'De Oratore' and the Liberal Arts Tradition in America, Class World, Vol 0088, 95. **CONTACT ADDRESS** Brooklyn Col, CUNY, Brooklyn, NY, 11210.

WOLFF, FLORENCE I.
PERSONAL Pittsburgh, PA, 7 children **DISCIPLINE** SPEECH COMMUNICATION **EDUCATION** Temple Univ, BS, 41; Duquesne Univ, MA, 67; Univ Pittsburgh, PhD, 69. **CAREER** Sec tchr bus educ & Eng, Charleroi Sr High Sch, 41-46, Pub & Pvt High Schs, 56-60 & Cent Dist Cath High Sch, 61-69; from Instr to Prof Speech Commun, 70-89, Prof Emeritus Commun, Univ Dayton, 89; Dir, Wolff Innovative Training System - conducts management training seminars for corporations, the military, and law enforcement. **HONORS AND AWARDS** Inductee, Int Listening Asn Hall of Fame. **MEMBERSHIPS** Relig Speech Commun Asn (exec secy, 78-81, 2nd vpres, 82, 1st vpres, 83); Int Listening Asn; Speech Commun Asn; hon mem Nat Forensic League. **RESEARCH** Listening; oral interpretation; public address. **SELECTED PUBLICATIONS** Auth, A survey of evaluative criteria for faculty promotion in college and university speech departments, Speech Teacher, 11/71; A teacher oriented eclectic review of recent interpersonal and small group communication research, Speech Asn Minn J, 5/75; Student evaluation of college and university speech communication courses and faculty: A survey, Speech Teacher, 9/75; A 1977 Survey: General insights into the status of listening course offerings in selected colleges and universities, NC J Speech Commun, winter 79; A lector's nightmare: Professional tips for proclaiming the word, Today's Parish, 9/80; A unique synthesized motivational evaluation strategy for assessing high school students' speech performance: An instructional unit, Ohio Speech J, 80; Re-creative bible reading, Relig Commun Today, 9/80; Perceptive Listening, Holt, Rinehart & Winston, 2nd ed, 93. **CONTACT ADDRESS** Dept of Commun, Univ of Dayton, 300 College Park, Dayton, OH, 45469-0000.

WOLFF, JOHN ULRICH
PERSONAL Born 11/01/1932, Berlin, Germany, m, 1963, 4 children **DISCIPLINE** GENERAL AND MALAYO-POLYNESIAN LINGUISTICS **EDUCATION** Cornell Univ, BA, 54, MA, 55; Yale Univ, PhD(ling), 64. **CAREER** Assoc prof, 63-80, PROF MOD LANG & LING, CORNELL UNIV, 80-. **MEMBERSHIPS** Ling Soc Am; Am Orient Soc; Asn Asian Studies. **SELECTED PUBLICATIONS** Auth, The Polynesians, J Amer Oriental Soc, Vol 0112, 92; Everyday Malay, Mod Lang J, Vol 0079, 95; Comparative Austronesian Dictionary, Language, Vol 0073, 97. **CONTACT ADDRESS** Cornell Univ, 203 Morrill Hall, Ithaca, NY, 14853-4701.

WOLFF, RONALD A.
DISCIPLINE GERMAN LITERATURE **EDUCATION** Univ Wis, PhD. **CAREER** Assoc prof. **RESEARCH** German pedagogy; contemporary German socio-linguistics. **CONTACT ADDRESS** Foreign Languages and Literature Dept, Colorado State Univ, Fort Collins, CO, 80523. **EMAIL** rwolff@vines.colostate.edu

WOLSEY, MARY LOU MORRIS
PERSONAL Born 02/21/1936, Baltimore, MD, m, 1965, 2 children **DISCIPLINE** MEDIEVAL FRENCH LANGUAGE & LITERATURE **EDUCATION** Mary Washington Col, BA, 58; Univ Kans, MA, 61; Univ Besancon, cert etudes super, 64; Univ Minn, PhD(French), 72. **CAREER** Asst instr French, Univ Kans, 58-61; instr, Mary Washington Col, 61-63; asst English, Teachers Col, Besancon, France, 63-64; teaching assoc French, Univ Pa, 64-65 & Univ Minn, 65-67; instr, Macalester Col, 67-68, adj prof, 72-78; part-time asst prof, 76-81, Asst Prof French, Col St Thomas, 81-, Vis prof, Univ Bristol, England, 78-79. **MEMBERSHIPS** Am Asn Teachers French; Am Coun Teaching Foreign Lang; Mediaeval Acad Am; Alliance Francaise; Midwest Mod Lang Asn Am. **RESEARCH** Medieval French romance; the French novel; computer research in French. **SELECTED PUBLICATIONS** Auth, The Eracle of Gautier d'Arras: A critical study, Diss Abstr Int, 10/72. **CONTACT ADDRESS** 2115 Summit Ave, St. Paul, MN, 55105-1096. **EMAIL** mpwopsey@stthomas.edu

WOLVIN, ANDREW D.
DISCIPLINE ORGANIZATIONAL COMMUNICATION AND COMMUNICATION EDUCATION **EDUCATION** Purdue Univ, PhD, 68. **CAREER** Dir undergrad stud; prof, Univ MD. **RESEARCH** The study of listening behavior. **SELECTED PUBLICATIONS** Co-auth, Listening, 5th edn, Brown, 96; Communicating: A Social and Career Focus, 7th edn, Houghton-Mifflin, 98. **CONTACT ADDRESS** Dept of Commun, Univ MD, 4229 Art-Sociology Building, College Park, MD, 20742-1335. **EMAIL** aw30@umail.umd.edu

WONG, JEAN
PERSONAL Born 05/05/1951, Boston, MA, m, 1978, 2 children **DISCIPLINE** APPLIED LINGUISTICS **EDUCATION** Connecticut Col, BA (summa cum laude and with honors), 73; UCLA, MA, 85, PhD, 94. **CAREER** Asst prof, The Col of New Jersey, 77-. **HONORS AND AWARDS** Phi Beta Kappa; recipient of a Thomas Watson Found fel; UCLA, Faculty Woman's Club fel. **MEMBERSHIPS** TESOL; AAAL; IRA; NCA; ICA. **RESEARCH** Discourse and conversation analysis; sociolinguistics. **SELECTED PUBLICATIONS** Auth, The Token 'Year' in Narrative Speaker English Comminication, forthcoming. **CONTACT ADDRESS** Dept of Lang and Commun Sciences, PO Box 7718, Ewing, NJ, 08628. **EMAIL** jwonng@tenj.edu

WONG, TIMOTHY C.
PERSONAL Born 01/24/1941, Hong Kong, China, m, 1970, 3 children **DISCIPLINE** CHINESE LITERATURE **EDUCATION** St Mary's Col, BA, 63; Univ Hawaii, MA, 68; Stanford Univ, PhD, 75. **CAREER** Asst prof, 74-79, assoc prof, 79-85, prof, 95-, Arizona St Univ; assoc prof, 85-95, Ohio St Univ. **RESEARCH** Traditional Chinese fiction and narratology **CONTACT ADDRESS** Center for Asian Studies, Arizona State Univ, Tempe, PO Box 871702, Tempe, AZ, 85287-1702. **EMAIL** timothy.wong@asu.edu

WOOD, BRYANT G.
PERSONAL Born 10/07/1936, Endicott, NY, m, 1958, 4 children **DISCIPLINE** NEAR EASTERN STUDIES, BIBLICAL HISTORY, AND SYRO-PALESTINIAN ARCHAEOLOGY **EDUCATION** Univ Mich, MA, 74; Univ Toronto, PhD, 85. **CAREER** Visitng Prof, Dept of Near Eastern Studies, Univ Toronto, 89-90; Res Analysit, 90-94, DIR, ASSOC FOR BIBLICAL RES, 95-. **HONORS AND AWARDS** Endowment for Biblical Res Grant, 81; Travel Grant, 81, Summer Stipend, Nat Endowment for the Humanities, 92. **MEMBERSHIPS** Near East Archaeol Soc; Inst for Biblical Res. **RESEARCH** Archaeology of the Bronze Age and Iron Age Periods in Palestine. **SELECTED PUBLICATIONS** Auth, Pottery Making in Bible Times, By the Sweat of Thy Brow: Labor and Laborers in the Biblical World, Sheffield Academic Press, forthcoming; Cisterns and Reservoirs, Encyclo of the Dead Sea Scrolls, Oxford Univ Press, forthcoming; Water Systems, Encyclo of the Dead Sea Scrolls, Oxford Univ Press, forthcoming; The Role of Shechem in the Conquest of Canaan, To Understand the Scriptures: Essays in Honor of William H. Shea, Inst of Archeaol/Siegfried H. Horn Archaeol Museum, Andrews Univ, 97; Kh. Nisya, 94, Israel Exploration J, 95; Biblical Archaeology's Greatest Achievement, Failure and Challenge, Biblical Archaeol Rev, 95; Rev of Excavations at Tell Deir Alla, Bullet of the Am Schools of Oriental Res, 94; coauth, Kh. Nisya, 93, Israel Exploration J, 94. **CONTACT ADDRESS** Associates for Biblical Res, 4328 Crestview Rd., Harrisburg, PA, 17112-2005.

WOOD, PAUL WILLIAM
PERSONAL Born 03/24/1933, Cincinnati, OH, m, 1960, 4 children **DISCIPLINE** FRENCH LANGUAGE & LITERATURE **EDUCATION** Athenaeum of Ohio, BA, 54; Univ of Cincinnati, MA, 60; Northwestern Univ, Evanston, PhD(French), 70. **CAREER** High sch teacher French & Latin, Forest Hills Sch Dist, Ohio, 60-62; instr French, Loyola Univ Chicago, 62-67; asst prof, Univ Akron, 67-71; asst prof, 71-76, assoc prof French, St Bonaventure Univ, 76-88, chmn dept mod lang & lit, 77-83, prof, St. Bonaventure Univ, 88-. **HONORS AND AWARDS** Ferdinand Di Bartholo NY State Distinguished Leadership Award, 86. **MEMBERSHIPS** MLA; Am Asn Teachers Fr; Am Coun Teaching Foreign Lang; AAUP. **RESEARCH** Modern French theatre; Moliere. **SELECTED PUBLICATIONS** Auth, How to Conduct a Language Fair (Filmstrip), NY State Asn Foreign Lang Teachers, 77; coauth, Student Motivation: Try a Foreign Language Day, Foreign Lang Annals/Accent on Am Coun Teachers For Lang, 2/78; Creating an Environment for Second Language Aquisition, ed, NY State Asn of Foreign Lang Teachers, 88. **CONTACT ADDRESS** Dept of Modern Lang & Lit, St Bonaventure Univ, St Bonas, NY, 14778-9999. **EMAIL** pswood@sbu.edu

WOOD, PHILIP R.
DISCIPLINE FRENCH **EDUCATION** English Univ Cape Town, BA, 70-74; Univ York, MA, 78-80; Yale Univ, PhD, 82-88. **CAREER** Assoc prof, Rice Univ, 92-; asst prof, Rice Univ, 90-92; asst prof, Purdue Univ, 88-90; vis asst prof Univ Wash Seattle, 86-88; asst prof, Universidade de Coimbra Portugal, 80-82. **HONORS AND AWARDS** Amer Council Learned Soc Fel, 91; XL Summer Res Grant, Purdue Univ, 90; Yale Univ Lurcy Fel, 84-85; Yale Univ Fel, 82-86; FR Leavis Award, Univ York, 79. **SELECTED PUBLICATIONS** Co-ed, Terror and Consensus: Vicissitudes of French Thought, Stanford Univ Pr, 98; Introduction, in Terror and Consensus: a French Debate, Stanford Univ Pr, 98;"Apotheosis and Demise of the Philosophy of the Subject: Hegel, Sartre, Heidegger, Structuralism and Poststructuralism, Sartre Revisited, St Martin's Pr, 97; Heidegger Debates, Ethics in Poststructuralism, the 'Death' of the Subject and the Future of the Earth," Contemporary French Civilization, 95. **CONTACT ADDRESS** Dept of French Studies, Rice Univ, Box 1892, Houston, TX, 77251. **EMAIL** prw@ruf.rice.edu

WOODARD, ROGER
DISCIPLINE LINGUISTICS **EDUCATION** Univ NC, PhD. **CAREER** Assoc prof, joint app with Classics, Univ Southern Calif. **RESEARCH** Language change. **SELECTED PUBLICATIONS** Auth, In On Interpreting Morphological Change, 90. **CONTACT ADDRESS** Dept of Linguistics, Univ Southern Calif, University Park Campus, Los Angeles, CA, 90089. **EMAIL** woodard@usc.edu

WOODBRIDGE, HENSLEY CHARLES
PERSONAL Born 02/06/1923, Champaign, IL, m, 1953, 1 child **DISCIPLINE** SPANISH **EDUCATION** Col William & Mary, AB, 43; Harvard Univ, MA, 46; Univ Ill, PhD(Span), 50, MSLS, 51; Lincoln Mem Univ, Tenn, DA, 76. **CAREER** Instr French & Span, Univ Richmond, 46-47; teaching asst Span, Univ Ill, 48-50; ref librn, Ala Polytech Inst, 51-53; head librn, Murray State Col, 53-63; assoc prof foreign lang, 65-71, bibliogr Latin Am, 65-74, PROF FOREIGN LANG, SOUTHERN ILL UNIV, CARBONDALE, 71-, Assoc ed, Hispania, 67-81; contrib ed, Am Bk Collector; ed, Jack London Newslett. **MEMBERSHIPS** Am Asn Teachers Span & Port; MLA; Medieval Acad Am. **RESEARCH** Spanish nautical terms; Jack London; Ruben Dario. **SELECTED PUBLICATIONS** Auth, Contemporary Spanish American Poets, Hispania-J Devoted Tchg Spanand Port, Vol 0076, 93; Mistral, Gabriela and the Critics, Chasqui-Revista de Lit Latinoamericana, Vol 0024, 95. **CONTACT ADDRESS** Dept of Foreign Lang, Southern Ill Univ, Carbondale, IL, 62901.

WOODWARD, PAULINE
DISCIPLINE ENGLISH LANGUAGE AND LITERATURE **EDUCATION** Boston Univ, AB; Univ Hartford, MA; Tufts Univ, PhD. **CAREER** Eng Dept, Endicott Col **RESEARCH** 20th century traditions in Am Lit, concentrating on the works of Asian Am, Native Am, black Am, and Chicanos. **SELECTED PUBLICATIONS** Auth, study of Louise Erdich's fiction in American Writers: Supplement IV, Scribner's/Macmillan. **CONTACT ADDRESS** Endicott Col, 376 Hale St, Beverly, MA, 01915.

WOOLDRIDGE, JOHN B.
DISCIPLINE SPANISH **EDUCATION** Univ Richmond, BA; Univ MD, MA, PhD. **CAREER** Adj prof; pres, Potomac Chap, Am Asn Tchr(s) Span & Port, 82-86 & pres, For Lang Asn of VA, 83-84. **HONORS AND AWARDS** Awd Excellence in For Lang Educ, 83 & campus's Alumni Fedn Fac of the Yr Awd, 97. **SELECTED PUBLICATIONS** Auth, critical edition of Lope de Vega's El amor enamorado, Spain, 78, subsequent res on, Span Golden Age drama, has produced some 20 articles and rev(s) in scholarly jour both in this country and abroad. **CONTACT ADDRESS** Dept of Span, Shenandoah Univ, 1460 University Dr., Winchester, VA, 22601.

WOOLEY, ALLAN D.
PERSONAL Born 01/01/1936, Rumford, ME **DISCIPLINE** CLASSICAL PHILOLOGY **EDUCATION** Bowdoin Col, BA, 58; Princteon Univ, PhD, 62. **CAREER** Asst prof, Duke Univ, 62-67; dept chair, Gould Acad, 67-68; instr, Greek and Latin, Phillips Exeter Acad, 68-84; instr and coord, acad computing, Phillips Exeter Acad, 84-89; dept chair, Phillips Exeter Acad, 91-96; Bradbury Longfellow Gilley prof, Greek, Phillips Exeter Acad, 96-. **MEMBERSHIPS** Class Asn of New England; Amer Class League; Amer Philol Asn. **RESEARCH** Classical philology. **SELECTED PUBLICATIONS** Article, Ideographic Imagery in Aeneid and Vergil's Philosophizing, New Eng Class Jour, may, 98. **CONTACT ADDRESS** Phillips Exeter Acad, 20 Main St., MSC 81420, Exeter, NH, 03833. **EMAIL** awooley@exeter.edu

WOOLFORD, ELLEN
DISCIPLINE LINGUISTICS **EDUCATION** Rice Univ, BA, 71; Duke Univ, PhD, 77. **CAREER** Prof. **SELECTED PUBLICATIONS** Auth, VP Internal Subjects in VSO and Non-Configurational Languages, Ling Inquiry, 93; Symmetric and Asymmetric Passives, Natural Lang Ling Theory, 94; Why Passive Can Block Object Marking, 95; Object Agreement in Palauan: Specificity, Humanness, Economy, and Optimality, Univ Mass, 97; Four-Way Case Systems: Ergative, Nominative, Objective and Accusative, Natural Lang Ling Theory. **CONTACT ADDRESS** Linguistics Dept, Univ of Massachusetts, Amherst, S College 131, Amherst, MA, 01003. **EMAIL** woolford@linguist.umass.edu

WORTH, DEAN STODDARD
PERSONAL Born 09/30/1927, Brooklyn, NY, m, 1953, 1 child **DISCIPLINE** SLAVIC LINGUISTICS **EDUCATION** Dartmouth Col, AB, 49; Ecole Langues Orient, Paris, dipl, 52; Sorbonne, cert, 52; Harvard Univ, AM, 53, PhD, 56. **CAREER** Res fel, Russ Res Ctr, Harvard Univ, 56-57; from asst prof to assoc prof Slavic lang, 57-65, PROF SLAVIC LANG, UNIV CALIF, LOS ANGELES, 65-, SECY, AM COMT SLAVISTS, 60-, CHMN, 78-; Guggenheim fel, 63-64; fel, Konnan Inst Advan Russ Studies (Wilson Ctr), 78-79. **MEMBERSHIPS** Am Asn Advan Slavic Studies; Ling Soc Am; Medieval Acad Am; Am Asn Teachers Slavic & East Europ Lang; Ling Soc Europe. **RESEARCH** Paleosiberian languages; Old Russian liter-

ature. **SELECTED PUBLICATIONS** Auth, In Honor of Professor Levin, Victor, Slavic Rev, Vol 0052, 93; The Hagiography of Kievan Rus, Slavic Rev, Vol 0054, 95; Comprehensive Index to the Contents of Russian Philological JS and Series, Slavic Rev, Vol 0054, 95; The Distribution of Metrical Fillers in the Russian Folk Lament, Elementa-J Slavic Studies and Comp Cultural Semiotics, Vol 0002, 96. **CONTACT ADDRESS** Univ Calif, Los Angeles, CA, 90024.

WORTH, FABIENNE ANDRE
PERSONAL Born 05/24/1944, Lyon, France, m, 1967, 2 children **DISCIPLINE** FRENCH LITERATURE, CINEMA **EDUCATION** Univ NC, Chapel Hill, BA, 70, MA, 73, PhD(comp lit), 79. **CAREER** Vis lectr, 78-79, VIS LECTR FRENCH LIT, DUKE UNIV, 80-, Instr, French Cinema Arts Sch, Carrboro, NC, 80. **MEMBERSHIPS** MLA; Am Asn Teachers Fr; Am Comp Lit Asn. **RESEARCH** History and the novel; authorship in the cinema. **SELECTED PUBLICATIONS** Auth, Le Sacre Et Le Sida--Representations of Sexuality and Their Contradictions in France, 1971-1996, a Perspective from Across the Atlantic, Temps Modernes, Vol 0052, 97. **CONTACT ADDRESS** 209 Pritchard Ave, Chapel Hill, NC, 27514.

WRAGE, WILLIAM
PERSONAL Born 01/10/1936, Lincoln, IL, m, 1959, 2 children **DISCIPLINE** FRENCH **EDUCATION** Wash Univ, BA, 57; Univ Wis-Madison, MA, 60, PhD, 64. **CAREER** From instr to asst prof French, Miami Univ, 63-69, adv studies abroad, 66-69; assoc prof, 69-73, grad chmn mod lang, 70-72 & 77-80, chmn dept mod lang, 72-77, grad chmn mod lang, 77-80, Prof French, Ohio Univ, 73-. **MEMBERSHIPS** Am Asn Teachers Fr. **RESEARCH** French civilization; 18th century French literature. **CONTACT ADDRESS** Dept of Mod Lang, Ohio Univ, Athens, OH, 45701-2979.

WRAY, DAVID L.
PERSONAL Born 05/25/1959, Atlanta, GA, m, 1997 **DISCIPLINE** CLASSICAL PHILOLOGY **EDUCATION** Emory Univ, BA, 80; Harvard Univ, PhD, 96. **CAREER** Asst prof, class lang and lit, Univ Chicago, 97-. **MEMBERSHIPS** Am Philol Asn; Am Class League. **RESEARCH** Latin poetry; Hellenistic poetry; literary criticism. **SELECTED PUBLICATIONS** Auth, Catullus: Sexual Personae and Invective Tradition, Cambridge, forthcoming; auth, Lucretius, in Briggs, ed, Roman Authors vol of Dictionary of Literary Biography, Bruccoli Clark Layman, forthcoming; auth, Apollonius Masterplot: A Reading of Argonautical in Harder, ed, Apollonius Rhodius: Hellenistica Groningana IV, Groningen, forthcoming. **CONTACT ADDRESS** Dept of Classics, Univ of Chicago, 1010 E 59th St, Chicago, IL, 60637. **EMAIL** d_wray@uchicago.edu

WRIGHT, JOHN
DISCIPLINE LATIN LANGUAGE AND LITERATURE **EDUCATION** Swarthmore, BA, 62; Ind Univ, MA, 64; Am Acad Rome, FAAR, 68; Ind Univ, PhD, 71. **SELECTED PUBLICATIONS** Auth, Dancing in Chains, Rome, 74; The Life of Cola di Rienzo, Toronto, 75; rev, Homeric Greek: A Book for Beginners, Okla, 85; rev, ed, Plautus' Curculio, Okla, 93. **CONTACT ADDRESS** Dept of Classics, Northwestern Univ, 1801 Hinma, Evanston, IL, 60208.

WRIGHT, ROBERT L.
DISCIPLINE THOUGHT AND LANGUAGE **EDUCATION** Defiance, BA, 43; Univ Minn, MA, 47; Columbia's Teachers Col, EdD, 55; postdoc study, Stockholm, 57-58. **CAREER** Emer Prof Thought and Language, Mich State Univ. **HONORS AND AWARDS** Mich State Univ Book Award. **RESEARCH** Ballads and songs, emigrant ballads. **CONTACT ADDRESS** 274 Oakland Dr., East Lansing, MI, 48823.

WU, JOSEPH SEN
PERSONAL Born 09/10/1934, Canton, China, m, 1982, 3 children **DISCIPLINE** PHILOSOPHY, CHINESE CLASSICS **EDUCATION** Taiwan Norm Univ, BA, 59; Wash Univ, MA, 62; Southern Ill Univ, PhD(philos), 67. **CAREER** From instr to asst prof philos Univ Mo-St Louis, 63-67; asst prof, Northern Ill Univ, 67-70; assoc prof, 70-73, prof philos, Calif State Univ Sacramento 73-, vis prof, Loyola Univ, Ill, 69-70 & Nat Taiwan Univ, 76-77. **MEMBERSHIPS** Am Philos Asn; Soc Comp & Asian Philos. **RESEARCH** American philosophy; Far Eastern philosophy; philosophy of culture. **SELECTED PUBLICATIONS** Auth, Contemporary Western Philosophy from an Eastern viewpoint, Int Philos Quart, 68; The Paradoxical Situation of Western Philosophy and the Search for Chinese Wisdom, Inquiry, 71; Understanding Maoism, Studies Soviet Thought, 74; Comparative Philosophy and Culture (in Chinese), Tung Ta, Taiwan, 78; Clarification and Enlightenment: Essays in Comparative Philosophy, Univ Am, 78; many articles in contemporary philosophy and comparative philosophy in 1980's and 1990's. **CONTACT ADDRESS** Dept of Philos, California State Univ, Sacramento, 6000 J St, Sacramento, CA, 95819-6033.

WU, PEI-YI
PERSONAL Born 12/03/1927, Nanking, China **DISCIPLINE** CHINESE LITERATURE, INTELLECTUAL HISTORY **EDUCATION** Nat Cent Univ, Nanking, AB, 50; Boston Univ, MA, 52; Columbia Univ, PhD(Chinese lit), 69. **CAREER** Ibstr Chinese, Army Lang Sch, 53-58; res linguist, Univ Calif, Berkeley, 58-59; preceptor, Columbia Univ, 62-63; instr, 63-66, lectr, 66-67; vis assoc prof, 67-69, Assoc Prof Chinese, Queens Col, 69-, Mem univ fac senate, City Univ New York, 71-74; VIS ASSOC PROF, COLUMBIA UNIV, 72-; Nat Endowment for Humanities fel, 74. **MEMBERSHIPS** Am Orient Soc; Asn Asian Studies. **RESEARCH** Chinese autobiography and myth. **SELECTED PUBLICATIONS** Auth, Memories of Kai-Feng--Meng,Yuan-Lao Description of the City in Tung-Ching Meng Hua Lu, New Lit Hist, Vol 0025, 94. **CONTACT ADDRESS** Dept of Class & Orient Lang, Queens Col, CUNY, 6530 Kissena Blvd, Flushing, NY, 11367.

WULFF, DONALD H.
PERSONAL Born 08/05/1944, Billings, MT, d, 2 children **DISCIPLINE** SPEECH COMMUNICATION **EDUCATION** Univ Mont, MA, 75; Univ Wash, PhD, 85. **CAREER** Instruct Develop Specialist, 85-88; asst dir, 99-92, assoc dir, Center for Instruct Develop and Res, Univ Wash Seattle, 92-. **HONORS AND AWARDS** Distinguished tchg Award, Univ Wash, 84; Univ Wash Tchg Acad, 98-. **MEMBERSHIPS** Nat Commun Asn; Prof Orgn Develop network; Am Asn for Higher Educ; Am Educ Res Asn. **RESEARCH** Teaching Effectiveness/ Student Learning; The evelopment of graduate teaching assistants as Future professors. **SELECTED PUBLICATIONS** Auth, The Case of worrisome workload, Learning from students: Early term student feedback in higher education, 94; coauth, Working Effectively with Graduate Assistants, 96; Professional development for consultants at the University Washington's Center for Instructional Development and Research, Practically speaking: A sourcebook for instructional consultants in higher education, 97; Engaging students in learning in the communication classroom, forthcoming. **CONTACT ADDRESS** Center for Instructional Development and Research, Univ of Wash, Box 351725, Seattle, WA, 98195-1725. **EMAIL** wulff@cidr.washington.edu

WYLIE, HAL
PERSONAL Born 09/16/1935, New York, NY, m, 1956, 5 children **DISCIPLINE** FRENCH LITERATURE **EDUCATION** Univ Ariz, BA, 57; Stanford Univ, MA, 61, PhD(French & humanities), 65. **CAREER** Asst ed, Agr Experiment Station, Univ Ariz, 57-59; ASST PROF FRENCH, UNIV TEX, AUSTIN, 64-. **MEMBERSHIPS** African Lit Asn; South Cent Mod Lang Asn; Am Asn Teachers Fr. **RESEARCH** Caribbean and African literature. **SELECTED PUBLICATIONS** Auth, Choutoumounou, World Lit Today, Vol 0070, 96; Le Songe Dune Photo Denfance, World Lit Today, Vol 0068, 94; La Vierge du Grand Retour, World Lit Today, Vol 0071, 97; Creole Letters--West-Indian and French Elements in the Literatures of Haiti, Guadeloupe, Martinique and Guiana, 1635-1975-French, World Lit Today, Vol 0066, 92; Louis Vortex, World Lit Today, Vol 0066, 92; La Colonie du Nouveau Monde, World Lit Today, Vol 0068, 94; Chemin-D Ecole, World Lit Today, Vol 0069, 95; Tambour-Babel, World Lit Today, Vol 0071, 97; The Fictional Works of Alexis, Jacques, Stephen--A Poetic Corpus, a Political Involvement--French, World Lit Today, Vol 0067, 93; Haiti--Literature and Being-French, World Lit Today, Vol 0067, 93; Krik Krak, World Lit Today, Vol 0070, 96; L'ile et Une Nuit, World Lit Today, Vol 0070, 96; Les Urnes Scellees, World Lit Today, Vol 0070, 96; James Wait et Les Lunettes Noires, World Lit Today, Vol 0070, 96; Ravines du Devant-Jour, World Lit Today, Vol 0068, 94; Passages, World Lit Today, Vol 0069, 95; The Cosmopolitan Conde, or Unscrambling the Worlds, World Lit Today, Vol 0067, 93. **CONTACT ADDRESS** Dept of French, Univ of Tex, Austin, TX, 78712.

Y

YALDEN, JANICE
PERSONAL Kingston, Jamaica **DISCIPLINE** LINGUISTICS **EDUCATION** Univ Toronto, BA, 52; Univ Michigan, MA, 56. **CAREER** Lectr, 69-83, founding dir, Ctr Applied Lang Studs, 81-84, PROF LINGUISTICS, CARLTON UNIV 83-, dean arts, 87-92, ch, dept Ling & Applied Lang Studs, 94-. **MEMBERSHIPS** Ont Mod Lang Tchr Asn; Can Asn Applied Ling; Maurice Price Found; Soc Educ Visits & Exchanges Can. **SELECTED PUBLICATIONS** Auth, Communicative Language Teaching: Principles and Practice, 81; auth, The Communicative Syllabus: Evolution, Design and Implementation, 83; auth, Principles of Course Design for Language Teaching, 87; auth, Second Language Teaching at the Post-Secondary Level, in Bull Can Asn Applied Ling, 84. **CONTACT ADDRESS** Dept Ling & Applied Lang Studies, Carleton Univ, 1125 Colonel By Dr, Ottawa, ON, K1S 5B6. **EMAIL** jyalden@ccs.carleton.ca

YAMADA, REIKO
DISCIPLINE JAPANESE **EDUCATION** Portland State Univ, BA, 78; Cornell Univ, MA, 82; PhD, 88. **CAREER** Assoc prof & coordr, Japanese Lang Prog, Williams Col, 86; assoc prof, Hokkaido Tokai Univ; vis asst prof, , Meiji Gakuin Univ. **HONORS AND AWARDS** Tokai Univ env res grants; Heiwa Nakajima Found grant; Clark Awd, excellence in tchg, Cornell Univ. **RESEARCH** Japanese language pedagogy; linguistics; intercultural communication. **SELECTED PUBLICATIONS** Auth, Pragmatics and Sociolinguistics of -tara and -(r)eba in Japanese Conversational Discourse, Univ Microfilms Int, 88. **CONTACT ADDRESS** Center for Foreign Languages, Literatures and Cult, Williams Col, Williamstown, MA, 01267. **EMAIL** Reiko.Yamada@williams.edu

YAMAMOTO, TRAISE
DISCIPLINE ASIAN AMERICAN LITERATURE AND CULTURE **EDUCATION** San Jose State Univ, BA; Univ Wash, MFA, MA, PhD. **CAREER** PROF, UNIV CALIF, RIVERSIDE, 94-. **HONORS AND AWARDS** Exec bd, Assn Asian Amer Stud; assoc dir, Ctr Asian Pacific Am. **RESEARCH** Poetry, race and gender theory, autobiography studies, and British and American Modernism. **SELECTED PUBLICATIONS** Auth, Between the Lines; "Different Silences: The Poetics and Politics of Location," The Intimate Critique, Duke Univ Press, 93. **CONTACT ADDRESS** Dept of Eng, Univ Calif, 1156 Hinderaker Hall, Riverside, CA, 92521-0209.

YAMAUCHI, EDWIN MASAO
PERSONAL Born 02/01/1937, Hilo, HI, m, 1962, 2 children **DISCIPLINE** ANCIENT HISTORY, SEMITIC LANGUAGES **EDUCATION** Shelton Col, BA, 60; Brandeis Univ, MA, 62, PhD(Mediter studies), 64. **CAREER** Asst prof ancient hist, Rutgers Univ, New Brunswick, 64-69; assoc prof, 69-73, dir grad studies, Hist Dept, 78-82, prof Hist, Miami Univ, 73-, Nat Endowment for Humanities fel, 68; Am Philos Soc grant, 70; consult ed hist, J Am Sci Affiliation, 70-; sr ed, Christianity Today, 92-94. **MEMBERSHIPS** Am Sci Affil (pres, 83); Archaeol Inst Am; Conf Faith & Hist (pres, 74-76); Near E Archaeol Soc (vpres, 78); Inst Bibl Res (pres, 87-89). **RESEARCH** Gnosticism; ancient magic; Old and New Testaments. **SELECTED PUBLICATIONS** Auth, Greece and Babylon, Baker Bk, 67; Mandaic incantation texts, Am Orient Soc, 67; Gnostic Ethics and Mandaean Origins, Harvard Univ, 70; The Stones and the Scriptures, Lippincott, 72; Pre-Christian Gnosticism, Tyndale Press, London & Eerdmans, 73; The Archaeology of New Testament Cities in Western Asia Minor, Baker Bk, 80; The Scriptures and Archaeology, Western Conserv Baptist Sem, 80; World of the New Testament, Harper & Row, 81; Foes from the Northern Frontier, Baker Bk, 82; coeditor, Chronos, Kairos, Christos, Eisenbrauns, 89; Persia and the Bible, Baker Bk, 90; coauth, The Two Kingdoms, Moody, 93; coed, Peoples of the Old Testament World, Baker, 94. **CONTACT ADDRESS** Dept of History, Miami Univ, 500 E High St, Oxford, OH, 45056-1602. **EMAIL** Yamauce@casmail.muohio.edu

YAMAUCHI, JOANNE
DISCIPLINE CULTURAL DIVERSITY AND ASIAN PACIFIC AMERICAN ISSUES **EDUCATION** Goucher Col, BA; Columbia Col, MA, Northwestern Univ, PhD. **CAREER** Asst prof, Am Univ; consult, U.S. Govt Agencies, corp business. **HONORS AND AWARDS** Excellence Educ 2000; U.S. Pan Asian Chamber Com; Excellence Tchg; Multicultural Affairs Office, Am Univ., Assoc ed, Int & Intercultural Comm annual, Int Jour Intercultural Rels, Jour Applied Comm. **MEMBERSHIPS** AT&T; NASA; Procter & Gamble; Am Coun Educ; Soc Intercultural Educa; Intercultural & Int comm commission Speech Comm Asn. **SELECTED PUBLICATIONS** Auth, Making a Difference Through ValuingDifferences; Asian Americans and the Glass Ceiling; Prejudice, Promotion,and Power in the Newsroom: A Survey of Asian American Broadcasters; Ass ed, International and Intercultural Commun Annual. **CONTACT ADDRESS** American Univ, 4400 Massachusetts Ave, Washington, DC, 20016.

YANDELL, CATHY
DISCIPLINE FRENCH RENAISSANCE PROSE **EDUCATION** Univ Calif, PhD. **CAREER** Literature, Carleton Col. **HONORS AND AWARDS** David & Marian Adams Bryn-Jones Distinguished Tchg Prof Hum. **SELECTED PUBLICATIONS** Articles, Tyard, Montaigne, Louise Labe and Pernette du Guillet **CONTACT ADDRESS** Carleton Col, 100 S College St., Northfield, MN, 55057-4016.

YANG, FENGGANG
PERSONAL Born 06/28/1962, Cangzhou, China, m, 1988, 2 children **DISCIPLINE** SOCIOLOGY; RELIGION; ETHNICITY **EDUCATION** Hebei Normal Univ, Shijiazhuang, China, BA, 82; Nankai Univ, Tianjin, China; MA, 92, PhD, 97, Catholic Univ of Amer. **CAREER** Lectr, Cangzhou Education Col, Hebei, China, 82-84; Asst Prof, People's Univ of China, 87-89; Research Assoc, Center for Immigration Research, Univ Houston, 97-. **HONORS AND AWARDS** Thomas V. Moore Doctoral Scholarship, 89-92; Research Award for the Scientific Study of Religion, 93; Outstanding Graduate Student, Catholic Univ of Amer, 93 & 95; Teaching and Research Fel, People's Univ China, 94; Dissertation Fel, Univ of Illinois at Chicago, 94-95; Dissertation Fel, Louisville Inst of Protestantism and

American Culture, 95-96; Postdoctoral Fel, Center for Immigration Research, 97-98; Research Fel, Center for Immigration Research, 99. **MEMBERSHIPS** Amer Sociological Assoc; Assoc for Sociology of Religion; Soc for the Scientific Study of Religion; Assoc for Asian Amer Studies; Assoc for Asian Studies; Amer Acad of Religion. **RESEARCH** Chinese American religions and cultures; Chinese religions and cultures; Diasporic identities; Immigrant assimilation and ethnic groups. **SELECTED PUBLICATIONS** Auth, Decree and Covenant: Different Notions of Law in Chinese and Western Societies, Cultural China, 96; A Sociological Comparison of Christianity and the Chinese Traditional Value System, Christian Culture Review, 96; Tension and the Healthy Development of Society, Economic Ethics and Chinese Culture, 97; Tenacious Unity in a Contentious Community: Cultural and Religious Dynamics in a Chinese Christian Church, Gatherings in Diaspora: Religious Communities and the New Immigration, 98; Chinese Conversion to Evangelical Christianity: The Importance of Social and Cultural Contexts, Sociology of Relgion: A Quarterly Review, 98; The Chinese Gospel Church: Sinofication of Christianity, Modernity, Nationalism and Traditional Culture: Challenges to Christianity in China, Deconstruction and Reconstruction: Perspectives on the Renewal of Chinese Culture, 98; The Religious Mosaic: The Diversity of Immigrant Congregations, 99; Hsi Nan Buddhist Temple: Seeking to Americanize, The Religious Mosaic: The Diversity of Immigrant Congregations, 99; PRC Immigrants in the US: A Demographic Profile and an Assessment of their Integration in the Chinese American Community, The Chines Triangle of Mainland-Taiwan-Hong Kong: Comparate Institutional Analyses, 99; ABC and XYZ: Religious, Ethnic and Racial Identities of the New Second Generation Chinese in Christian Churches, Amerasia Journal, 99; Chinese Christians in America: Conversion, Assimilation, and Adhesive Identities, 99. **CONTACT ADDRESS** Dept of Sociology, Univ of Houston, Houston, TX, 77204-3474. **EMAIL** fyang@uh.edu

YANG, INSUN
DISCIPLINE LINGUISTICS, KOREAN LANGUAGE **EDUCATION** Ehwa Woman's Univ, Korea, BA; PA State Univ, MA; Rice Univ, PhD. **CAREER** Instr, 93-, dir, Korean Stud, Rice Univ. **RESEARCH** Korean and other Ural-Altaic dative markers. **SELECTED PUBLICATIONS** Publ articles in the J of Korean-Am Educ and the J of the Ling Asn of Can and the US. **CONTACT ADDRESS** Rice Univ, PO Box 1892, Houston, TX, 77251-1892. **EMAIL** iyang@rice.edu

YANG, MIMI
DISCIPLINE SPANISH LANGUAGE AND LITERATURE **EDUCATION** Beijing, BA; Univ Ariz, MA PhD. **CAREER** English, Carthage Col. **HONORS AND AWARDS** Vis Asst Prof, Ill Weslyean Univ. **SELECTED PUBLICATIONS** Auth, To be Human: Is the Rassias Method the Rassias Madness?, Ram's Horn, 95; Una mirada oriental a las letras perunas, Lundero, 89. **CONTACT ADDRESS** Carthage Col, 2001 Alford Dr., Kenosha, WI, 53140. **EMAIL** yang@carthage.edu

YANG, PETER JIANHUA
DISCIPLINE GERMAN, CHINESE, COMPARATIVE LIT **EDUCATION** Univ Utah, PhD, 96. **CAREER** Translator, Central Trnslating & Editing Ctr, Beijing, 75- 79; res, interpreter, Ministry For Econ Relations, Trade, Beijing, 82-89; instr, 90-94, LANG LAB DIR, 94-, JESSE HAWK SHERO ASST PROF GERMAN, CHINESE, COMP LIT, 96-. **CONTACT ADDRESS** 10900 Euclid Ave, Bldg 7118, Cleveland, OH, 44106-7118. **EMAIL** pjyz@po.cwra.edu

YANG, WINSTON L.
PERSONAL Born 06/01/1935, Nanking, China, m, 1964, 2 children **DISCIPLINE** ASIAN STUDIES **EDUCATION** National Taiwan Univ, BA, 58; Stanford Univ, PhD, 70. **CAREER** Prof and chemn, Dept of Asian Stud, Seton Hall Univ, 84- . **HONORS AND AWARDS** Royal Asiatic Soc of Gt Brit and Ireland. **MEMBERSHIPS** Asn for Asian Stud. **RESEARCH** Modern China and Taiwan. **SELECTED PUBLICATIONS** Auth, Tianammon: China's Struggle for Democracy, Univ Maryland, 90; auth, The Political Journey of Lian Chan, Business Weekly, 96. **CONTACT ADDRESS** 3 Waldeck Ct, West Orange, NJ, 07052.

YARRISON, BETSY
DISCIPLINE COMPARATIVE LITERATURE **EDUCATION** Univ Wisc, PhD. **CAREER** Asst prof, Univ Baltimore. **RESEARCH** Dramatic theory; language behavior; professional writing. **CONTACT ADDRESS** Commun Dept, Univ Baltimore, 1420 N. Charles Street, Baltimore, MD, 21201.

YARUSS, J. SCOTT
PERSONAL Born 12/01/1967, Downey, CA, m, 1989, 2 children **DISCIPLINE** SPEECH-LANGUAGE PATHOLOGY **EDUCATION** Syracuse Univ, MS, 91, PhD, 94. **CAREER** Co-dir, Stuttering Center Western Pa; asst prof, Northwestern Univ, 94-98; asst prof, Univ Pa, 98-. **HONORS AND AWARDS** Carol Prutting Editor's Award, Amer Speech Lang Hearing Assn. **MEMBERSHIPS** Amer Speech Lang Hearing Assn. **RESEARCH** Stuttering; fluency disorders; child phenology. **CONTACT ADDRESS** 4033 Forbes Tower, Pittsburgh, PA, 15260. **EMAIL** jsyaruss@csd.upmc.edu

YATES, DONALD ALFRED
PERSONAL Born 04/11/1930, Ayer, MA, m, 1951, 3 children **DISCIPLINE** FOREIGN LANGUAGES **EDUCATION** Univ Mich, BA, 51, MA, 54, PhD(Span), 61. **CAREER** Teaching asst Span, Univ Mich, 53-57; all-univ res grant to Mex, 58 & 61, PROF SPAN, MICH STATE UNIV, 57-, Fulbright res award, Arg 62-63; gen ed, Macmillan Mod Span Am Lit Ser, 62-; Fulbright lectr, Arg, 67-68 & 70; lectr Am lit, Univ Buenos Aires & Univ La Plata; vis prof, Ctr 20th Century Studies, Univ Wis-Milwaukee, 74; vis prof, San Francisco State Univ, 81. **HONORS AND AWARDS** Silver Medallion for Contrib to Field of Latin Am Lit, Instituto de Cultura Hisp, Madrid, Spain, 75. **MEMBERSHIPS** Am Asn Teachers Span & Port; MLA; Inst Int Lit Iberoam; Latin Am Studies Asn; Asoc Int Hispanistas. **RESEARCH** Spanish American literature of fantasy and imagination; Argentine literature; writings of Jorge Luis Borges. **SELECTED PUBLICATIONS** Auth, Borges Craft of Fiction--Selected Essays on His Writing, World Lit Today, Vol 0067, 93; A Tribute to Earle, Peter,G., Hisp Rev, Vol 0061, 93. **CONTACT ADDRESS** Michigan State Univ, 537 Wells Hall, East Lansing, MI, 48824.

YATES, ROBIN D.S.
DISCIPLINE EAST ASIAN STUDIES **EDUCATION** Harvard Univ, PhD. **CAREER** Prof. **RESEARCH** Early and traditional Chinese history; historical theory; archaeology of China; newly discovered ancient texts; Chinese science and technology; traditional popular culture; Chinese poetry. **SELECTED PUBLICATIONS** Auth, Science and Civilisation in China, Cambridge, 94; auth, An Introduction to and a Partial Reconstruction of the Yin Yang Texts from Yinqueshan: Notes on their Significance in Relation to HuangLao Daoism, 94; auth, Body, Space, Time, and Bureaucracy: Boundary Creation and Control Mechanisms in Early China, Reaktion Bk, 94. **CONTACT ADDRESS** East Asian Studies Dept, McGill Univ, 845 Sherbrooke St, Montreal, PQ, H3A 2T5.

YERKES, DAVID
DISCIPLINE ANGLO-SAXON LANGUAGE AND LITERATURE **EDUCATION** Yale Univ, 71; Oxford Univ, BA, 73 Dphil, 76. **CAREER** Prof, 77-. **MEMBERSHIPS** Mem, London Medieval Soc; Medieval Acad; Soc Text Scholar. **SELECTED PUBLICATIONS** Auth, An Old English Thesaurus; Syntax and Style in Old English; The Old English Life of Machutus. **CONTACT ADDRESS** Dept of Eng, Columbia Col, New York, 2960 Broadway, New York, NY, 10027-6902.

YETIV, ISAAC
PERSONAL Born 03/13/1929, Nabeul, Tunisia, m, 1953, 3 children **DISCIPLINE** FRENCH AND HEBREW LANGUAGE AND LITERATURE **EDUCATION** Hebrew Univ Jerusalem, BA, 67; Univ Wis- Madison, PhD(French lit, Hebrew), 70. **CAREER** Teacher math, physics & lang, Safed High Sch, Israel, 50-54; teacher math & physics, Reali Lyceum, Haifa, 54-67; teaching asst Hebrew, Univ Wis-Madison, 67-69; from asst prof to assoc prof French & Hebrew, Univ Hartford, 69-75; PROF FRENCH & HEBREW & HEAD DEPT MOD LANG, UNIV AKRON, 75-, Dir English Lang Inst, 76-, Lectr Hebrew, Univ Conn, 70-71. **MEMBERSHIPS** MLA; Nat Asn Prof Hebrew. **RESEARCH** Twentieth century French and Hebrew literature; Black African and North African literature in French; alienation of the marginal man in world literature. **SELECTED PUBLICATIONS** Auth, Judeo-Maghrebian Literature Written in French--French, Res African Lit, Vol 0023, 92. **CONTACT ADDRESS** 2078 Wyndham Rd, Akron, OH, 44313.

YETMAN, MICHAEL G
PERSONAL Born 08/16/1939, New York, NY, m, 1963, 3 children **DISCIPLINE** ROMANTIC AND VICTORIAN LITERATURE **EDUCATION** St Peter's Col, NJ, BS, 61; Univ Notre Dame, MA, 62, PhD(English), 67. **CAREER** Instr English, St Mary's Col, Ind, 65-68; asst prof, 68-73, ASSOC PROF ENGLISH, PURDUE UNIV, WEST LAFAYETTE, 73- **MEMBERSHIPS** MLA **RESEARCH** Modern literature. **SELECTED PUBLICATIONS** Auth, In Xanadu, Mass Rev, Vol 0035, 94. **CONTACT ADDRESS** Dept of English, Purdue Univ, West Lafayette, IN, 47907-1968.

YETUNDE FAELARIN SCHLEICHER, ANTONIA
DISCIPLINE AFRICAN LITERATURE **EDUCATION** Univ Kans, PhD. **CAREER** Dept African Lang, Wisc Univ **MEMBERSHIPS** African Lang Tchr Asn. **RESEARCH** Interface between phonology and morphology; experimental phonetics; foreign language learning and teaching; Yoruba culture. **SELECTED PUBLICATIONS** Auth, Je K'A Sae Yoruba, Yale, 93. **CONTACT ADDRESS** Dept of African Languages and Literature, Univ of Wisconsin, Madison, 500 Lincoln Drive, Madison, WI, 53706. **EMAIL** ayschlei@facstaff.wisc.edu

YINGLING, JULIE
PERSONAL Born 02/19/1948, Washington, DC **DISCIPLINE** SPEECH COMMUNICATION **EDUCATION** Univ Denver, PhD, 81. **CAREER** Asst prof, Univ WI, 81-85; assoc prof, Univ Northern CO, 85-88; vis assoc prof, Univ IA, 93-94; prof, Humboldt State Univ, 88-98. **MEMBERSHIPS** Int Network on Personal Relationships; Nat Commun Asn; Western States Commun Asn. **RESEARCH** Commun development in children; relational commun. **SELECTED PUBLICATIONS** Auth, Does That Mean No? Negotiating Protoconversations in Infany-Caregiver Pairs, Res on Lang and Social Interaction, vol 24, 91; Childhood: Talking the Mind Into Existence, in D R Vocate, ed, Intrapersonal Communication: Different Voice, Different Minds, Lawrence Erlbaum Assocs, 94; Constituting Friendship in Talk and Metatalk, J of Social and Personal Relationships, 11 (3), 94; Development as the Context of Student Assessment, in S Morreale & M Brooks, eds, 1994 SCA summer conference: Proceedings and prepared remarks, The Speech Commun Asn, 94; The First Relationship: Infant-Parent Communication, in T J Socha & G H Stamp, eds, Parents, Children and Communication: Frontiers of Theory and Research, Lawrence Erlbaum Assocs, 95; Resource review of Children Communication: The First 5 Years, by B B Haslett & W Samter, and Normal Conversation Aquisition: An Animated Database of Behaviors, Version 1-0 for Macintosh and Windows by K S Retherford, in Communication Education, in press. **CONTACT ADDRESS** 1850 Lime Ave, McKinleyville, CA, 95519. **EMAIL** jmy2@axe.humboldt.edu

YODER, DON
PERSONAL Mediapolis, IA **DISCIPLINE** ORGANIZATIONAL COMMUNICATION **EDUCATION** Iowa State Univ, BA, 73; Univ Nebr, MA, 75; Ohio State Univ, PhD, 82. **CAREER** Instr, Iowa State Univ; asst, assoc prof, Creighton Univ; assoc prof, chp, Univ Dayton, 89. **RESEARCH** Motivation in communications; conflict management; communnication education. **SELECTED PUBLICATIONS** Co-author, Creating Competent Communication. **CONTACT ADDRESS** Dept of Commun, Univ Dayton, 300 Col Park, Dayton, OH, 75062. **EMAIL** Yoder@udayton.edu

YODER, LAUREN WAYNE
PERSONAL Born 03/09/1943, Newport News, VA, m, 1964, 2 children **DISCIPLINE** FRENCH LANGUAGE AND LITERATURE **EDUCATION** Eastern Mennonite Col, BA, 64; Univ Iowa, MA, 69, PhD(French), 73. **CAREER** Teacher physics, Ecole Pedag Protestante, Kikwit, Zaire, 66-68; vis asst prof English, Univ Paris, 71-72; asst prof, 73-80, ASSOC PROF FRENCH, DAVIDSON COL, 80- **MEMBERSHIPS** MLA; Am Asn Teachers Fr; African Lit Asn; Southern Asn Africanists. **RESEARCH** Medieval French tale; African novel. **SELECTED PUBLICATIONS** Auth, Magume, Ou Les Ombres Du Sentier, Fr Rev, Vol 0070, 96. **CONTACT ADDRESS** Davidson Col, Po Box 1719, Davidson, NC, 28036-1719.

YOKEN, MEL B.
PERSONAL Born 06/25/1939, Fall River, MA, m, 1976, 3 children **DISCIPLINE** FRENCH LANGUAGE & LITERATURE **EDUCATION** Univ Mass, Amherst, BA, 60; Brown Univ, MAT, 61; Five-Col Prog, Univ Mass, Amherst Col, Smith Col, Mt Holyoke Col & Hampshire Col, PhD(French), 72. **CAREER** From instr to asst prof, 66-76, assoc prof, 76-81, Prof French, Southeastern Mass Univ, 82-, Res fel, Quebec Studies, 81. **MEMBERSHIPS** MLA; Am Asn Teachers Fr; Am Conn Teaching Foreign Lang; New England Foreign Lang Asn. **RESEARCH** The French novel; French literature of the 19th century; French literature of the 20th century. **SELECTED PUBLICATIONS** Auth, Paleneo, Mass Foreign Lang Bull, fall 73; Wise guy Solomon, Outlook 3/74; Claude Tillier, Twayne, 76; Speech is Plurality, Univ Press of Am, 78; Claude Tillier: Fame and fortune in his novelistic work, Fairleigh Dickinson Univ, 78; France's Shakespeare: Moliere, Cambridge Univ Press. **CONTACT ADDRESS** Dept of Modern Lang, Southeastern Massachusetts Univ, 285 Old Westport Rd, North Dartmouth, MA, 02747-2300.

YOON, WON Z.
PERSONAL Born 10/15/1932, Pyongyang, Korea, m, 1957, 3 children **DISCIPLINE** EAST ASIAN & SOUTHEAST ASIAN STUDIES **EDUCATION** Friends Univ, BA, 59; Wichita State Univ, MA, 61; NY Univ, PhD(Hist), 71. **CAREER** Asst prof Hist, State Univ NY Col Geneseo, 63-71; coordr, vis Asian prof proj, 67, assoc prof, 71-74, prof Hist, Siena Col, 74-, vis fel, inst SE Asian Studies, Singapore, 78. **MEMBERSHIPS** Asn Asian Studies; AAUP. **RESEARCH** Japanese military administration in Burma, 1942-43; Japan's occupation of Burma, 1941-45. **SELECTED PUBLICATIONS** Transl, Burma: Japanese Military Administration, Selected Documents, 1941-1945, Univ Pa Press, 71; auth, Japan's scheme for the liberation of Burma and the role of the Minami Kikan and the Thirty Comrades, Ohio Univ, 73; Military Expediency--A Determining Factor in the Japanese Policy Regarding Burmese Independence, 78. **CONTACT ADDRESS** Dept of History, Siena Col, 515 Loudonville Rd, Loudonville, NY, 12211-1462. **EMAIL** yoon@siena.edu

YOUNG, DOLLY J.
DISCIPLINE SPANISH LITERATURE **EDUCATION** Univ Tex, PhD, 85. **CAREER** Assoc prof. **RESEARCH** Language acquisition; psycholinguistics; foreign language education. **SELECTED PUBLICATIONS** Auth, pubs on foreign language reading, language anxiety, the analysis of Spanish language textbooks, and teacher training. **CONTACT ADDRESS** Dept of Romance Languages, Knoxville, TN, 37996.

YOUNG, DWIGHT WAYNE
PERSONAL Born 12/15/1925, Lambert, OK, m, 1946, 2 children **DISCIPLINE** SEMITIC PHILOLOGY **EDUCATION** Hardin Simmons Univ, BA, 49, ThM(Semitics), 56; Dropsie Col, PhD(Egyptol), 55. **CAREER** Asst prof Semitic lang, Dallas Theol Sem, 54-58; asst prof, Brandeis Univ, 58-63, assoc prof Mediterranean studies, 63-67; vis prof Coptic, Hebrew Univ, Israel, 65; vis prof Semitic lang, Cornell Univ, 67-69; assoc prof Semitic lang, 69-72, PROF ANCIENT NEAR EAST CIVILIZATION, BRANDIES UNIV, 72-, NDEA fel, 60; mem, Am Res Ctr Egypt. **HONORS AND AWARDS** Solomon Award, Dallas Theol Sem, 51. **MEMBERSHIPS** Am Orient Soc; Soc Bibl Lit; Am Res Ctr Egypt. **RESEARCH** Comparative Semitic grammar; ancient history; Egyptology. **SELECTED PUBLICATIONS** Auth, Cuneiform Mathematical Texts as a Reflection of Everyday Life in Mesopotamia, Jour Near East Stud, Vol 0055, 96. **CONTACT ADDRESS** Dept of Near East Studies, Brandeis Univ, Waltham, MA, 02154.

YOUNG, HOWARD THOMAS
PERSONAL Born 03/24/1926, Cumberland, MD **DISCIPLINE** SPANISH, FRENCH **EDUCATION** Columbia Univ, BS, 50, MA, 52, PhD(Span), 56. **CAREER** Lectr, Columbia Col, Columbia Univ, 53-54; prof Romance Lang, Pomona Col, 54-, chmn Dept Mod Lang, 77-, Fulbright lectr, Spain, 67-68; independent study & res, Nat Endowment for Humanities, 75-76; chmn Span Lang Develop Comt, Educ Testing Serv, Princeton, NJ, 77-81. **MEMBERSHIPS** MLA; Am Asn Teachers Span & Port; Am Comp Lit Asn; Asn Dept For Lang. **RESEARCH** Contemporary Spanish poetry; comparative study of modern Spanish and English poetry. **SELECTED PUBLICATIONS** Auth, Mexico-a revolution gone bankrupt, New Repub, 4/60; Pedro Salinas y los Estados Unidos, Cuadernos Hispanoam, 62; The Victorious Expression, Univ Wis, 64; Juan Ramon Jimenez, Columbia Univ, 67; Anglo-American poetry in the correspondence of Luisa and Juan Ramon Jimenez, Hispanic Rev, 76; On using foreign service institute tests and standards on campuses, In: Measuring Spoken Language Proficiency, Georgetown Univ, 80; The Line in the Margin: Juan Ramon Jimenez and His Readings in Blake, Shelley, and Yeats, Univ Wis, 80; The exact names, Modern Lang Notes, 81; Rereading and Rewriting the Poem: Juan Ramon Jimenez and Jorge Guillen, Guillen at McGill, Essays for a Centenary, ed, K M Sibbald, Ottowa: Dovehouse Editions, 96; In Loving Translation: Zenobia and Juan Ramon, Revista Hispanica Moderna, 96. **CONTACT ADDRESS** Pomona Col, 333 N College Way, Claremont, CA, 91711-6319. **EMAIL** htyoung@pomona.edu

YOUNG, MARY
DISCIPLINE AFRICAN-AMERICAN AND ASIAN-AMERICAN LITERATURE **EDUCATION** St Louis Univ, BA, 63, MA, 71; Univ Tex, MA; St Louis Univ, PhD, 90. **CAREER** Asst prof. **SELECTED PUBLICATIONS** Auth, Mules and Dragons: Popular Culture Images, Selected Writings of African-American and Chinese-American Women Writers. **CONTACT ADDRESS** Dept of Eng, Col of Wooster, Wooster, OH, 44691.

YOUNG, RICHARD
PERSONAL Born 10/15/1948, London, England, m, 1983, 2 children **DISCIPLINE** EDUCATIONAL LINGUISTICS **EDUCATION** Univ Pa, PhD, 89. **CAREER** Asst prof, Southern Ill Univ at Carbondale 90-93; asst prof, Univ Wis-Madisonm 93-95; assoc prof, 95- . **MEMBERSHIPS** Am Asoc for Applied Ling; Ling Soc of Am; Teachers of English to Speakers of Other Lang. **RESEARCH** Applied linguistics; second language acquisition; English as a second language. **SELECTED PUBLICATIONS** Auth, Form-function Relations in Articles in English Interlanguage, Second Language Acquisition and Linguistic Variation, 96; auth with M.D. Shermis, K. Perkins, and S.R. Brutten, From Conventional to Computer-Adaptive Testing of ESL Reading Comprehension, System, 96; auth with G.B. Hallek, Let Them Eat Cake! Or How to Avoid Losing your Head in Cross-Cultural Conversations, Talking and Testing: Discourse Approaches to the Assessment of Oral Proficiency, 98; Auth with A.W. He, Language Proficiency Interviews: A Discourse Approach, Talking and Testing: Discourse Approaches to the Assessment of Oral Proficiency, 98; co-ed with A.W. He, Talking and Testing: Discourse Approaches to the Assessment fo Oral Proficiency, 98. **CONTACT ADDRESS** English Dept, Univ of Wisconsin, 600 N. Park St., Madison, WI, 53706. **EMAIL** rfyoung@facstaff.wisc.edu

YOUNG, ROBERT VAUGHAN
PERSONAL Born 06/20/1947, Marianna, FL, m, 1968, 5 children **DISCIPLINE** RENAISSANCE ENGLISH, COMPARATIVE LITERATURE **EDUCATION** Rollins Col, BA, 68; Yale Univ, 71, PhD(English), 72. **CAREER** Asst prof, 72-79, ASSOC PROF ENGLISH, NC STATE UNIV, 80-, Fel, Southestern Inst Medieval & Renaissance Studies, summer, 78; prof English & social theory, Kairos Inst, El Escorial Spain, summer, 79; vis prof & actg chmn English, Christendom Col, 79-80; Fulbright res fel, Cath Univ Louvain & Free Univ Brussels, winter, 83. **MEMBERSHIPS** MLA; SAtlantic Mod Lang Asn; Soc Christian Cult; Fel Cath Scholars. **RESEARCH** Comparative literature of Baroque Age, especially English, Latin and Spanish; neo-Latin rhetorical studies, especially Justus Lipsius; contemporary moral & social issues. **SELECTED PUBLICATIONS** Auth, The Wit of 17th-Century Poetry, Renaissance and Reformation, Vol 0020, 96; Herbert and the Real Presence, Renascence-Essays on Values in Lit, Vol 0045, 93; Donne, John, Pseudo-Martyr, Renaissance Quart, Vol 0049, 96. **CONTACT ADDRESS** Dept of English, No Carolina State Univ, Raleigh, NC, 27650.

YOUNG, THEODORE ROBERT
DISCIPLINE SPANISH AND PORTUGUESE LITERATURE **EDUCATION** Harvard Univ, PhD, 93. **CAREER** Asst prof. **SELECTED PUBLICATIONS** Auth, O Questionamento da Historia em O Tempo e o Vento de Erico Verissimo, 97; Um Realismo M gico no Brasil?: Um Levantamento, 95; A Fabricat o de um Sonho: A Recriat o do Processo Sonhador em Sinais de Fogo de Jorge de Sena, 95; Subvers o da Imagem do Estado Paternalista em O Tempo e o Vento, 95. **CONTACT ADDRESS** Dept of Modern Languages, Florida State Univ, 11200 SW 8th St, Miami, FL, 33174. **EMAIL** youngtr@servax.fiu.edu

YOUNG-EISENDRATH, POLLY
PERSONAL Born 02/04/1947, Akron, OH, m, 1985, 3 children **DISCIPLINE** PSYCHOLOGY: DEVELOPMENTAL & CLINICAL **EDUCATION** Ohio Univ, AB, 65-69; Goddard College, MA, 72-74; Washington Univ, MSW, 76; diploma in Jungian Analysis, Inter-Regional Soc of Jungian Analysts, 78-86; Washington Univ, PhD, 80. **CAREER** Asst prof, 80-86, Visit lectr 86-89, Advisor for Doc dissertations 86-94, Bryn Mawr College; Adv for Doc dissertations Union Grad Inst and Fielding Inst, 94-; Jungian psychoanalyst, private practice, 94-; Clinical assoc prof Medical Coll of the Univ Vermont, 96-.. **HONORS AND AWARDS** Phi Beta Kappa; Mortar Board; Phi Kappa Phi; Teaching Fel and Assistantships; Research Assistantships; Washington Univ Graduate Tuition Awards; Goddard Coll Graduate Fel; Madge Miller Award for Faculty Research, Bryn Mawr Coll; Junior Faculty Research Award, Bryn Mawr Coll. **MEMBERSHIPS** Intl Assn for Analytical Psychology; Amer Psychological Assn, member of Divisions 24, 29, 35 and 39; Vermont Psychological Assn; NY Assn for Analytical Psychology; Philadelphia Assc of Jungian Analysts (founding member); C.G. Jung Inst of Pittsburgh; Independent Soc for Analytical Psychology (founding member). **SELECTED PUBLICATIONS** coauth, Jung's Self Psychology: A constructivist Perspective, 91; auth, You're Not What I Expected: Learning to Love the Opposite Sex, 93; The Cambridge Companion to Jung, 97; The Resilient Spirit: Transforming Suffering Into Insight, Compassion and Renewal, 97; Gender and Desire: Uncursing Pandora, 97; auth, Contrasexuality and the Dialect of Desire, in The Post-Jungians Today, 98; Jungian Constructivism and the Value of Uncertainty, The Journal of Analytical Psychology, 97; The Self in Analysis, Journal of Analytical Psychology, 97. **CONTACT ADDRESS** 166 Battery St., Burlington, VT, 05401.

YU, ANTHONY C.
PERSONAL Born 10/06/1938, Hong Kong, m, 1963, 1 child **DISCIPLINE** RELIGION, WESTERN & CHINESE LITERATURE **EDUCATION** Houghton Col, BA, 60; Fuller Theol Sem, STB, 63; Univ Chicago, PhD(relig & lit), 69. **CAREER** Instr English, Univ Ill Chicago Circle, 67-68; from instr to asst prof relig & lit, 68-74, assoc prof, 74-78, Prof Relig & Lit, Divinity Sch & Prof Dept Far Eastern Lang & Civilizations, Comt Social Thought, English & Comp Lit, Univ Chicago, 78-90, Asst ed, J Asian Studies, 75-77, co-ed, Monogr Ser, 77-; Guggenheim Mem Found fel Chinese Lit, 76-77; Nat Endowment for Humanities special grant, 77-80 & 81-82; co-ed, J Relig, 80-90; Carl Darling Buck Distinguished Service Prof Humanities, 90; Sr Fel, Am Coun of Learned Soc, 86-87; Master Texts Study Grant, Seminar for Public Sch Teachers, NEH, 92; **HONORS AND AWARDS** Gordon J Laing Prize, Univ of Chicago Press, 83. **MEMBERSHIPS** Asn Asian Studies, Elec Mem, China & Inner Asia Coun, 79-82; Am Acad Relig; Milton Soc of Am, Life Mem; MLA, Elec Mem, Exec Council, 98-01; Mem, Board of Dir, Illinois Hum Coun, 95-98. **RESEARCH** Religious approaches to classical literatures, western and non-western; comparative literature; translation. **SELECTED PUBLICATIONS** Auth, New Gods and old order: Tragic theology in the Prometheus Bound, J Am Acad Relig, 71; ed, Parnasus Revisited: Modern Criticism and The Epic Tradition, Am Libr Asn, 73; auth, Problems and prospects in Chinese-Western literary relations, In: Yearbook of General and Comparative Literature, 74; Chapter nine and the problem of narrative structure, J Asian Studies, 75; On translating the Hsi-yu chi, In: The Art and Profession of Translation, Hong Kong Transl Soc, 76; transl & ed, The Journey to the West, Vol I, Univ Chicago, 77; Self and family in the Hung-lou meng, Chinese Lit: Essays, Articles, Rev, 80; Life in the garden: Freedom and the image of God in Paradise Lost, J Relig, 80; Order of Temptations in Paradis Regained, in Perspectives on Christology, ed, Marguerite Shuster & Richard Muller, Zondervan, 91; Rereading the Stone: Desire and the Making of Fiction in Hongloumeng, Princeton, 97. **CONTACT ADDRESS** Divinity Sch, Univ of Chicago, 1025-35 E 58th St, Chicago, IL, 60637-1577. **EMAIL** acyu@midway.uchicago.edu

YU, CLARA
DISCIPLINE CHINESE **EDUCATION** Nat Taiwan Univ, Taipei, BA, 71; Univ Ill, Urbana, MA, 73, PhD, 78. **CAREER** Cornelius V. Starr prof Ling and Lang & dir, Proj 2001, opp 97; asst, assoc & prof, Middlebury Col, 87-; asst prof, Univ Md, Col Park, 79-83; exec VP, Middlebury Col, 96; VP, Lang & dir, Lang Sch(s), Middlebury College, 93-96; dir, Mellon Initiative in Teaching Languages with Technol, 94-97. **RESEARCH** Second Language Acquisition; Artificial Intelligence; Comparative literature; Chinese literature; Chinese Culture. **CONTACT ADDRESS** Dept of Chinese, Middlebury Col, Middlebury, VT, 05753.

YUDIN, FLORENCE L.
PERSONAL Born 01/26/1937, Brooklyn, NY **DISCIPLINE** SPANISH, LITERATURE **EDUCATION** Brooklyn Col, BA, 58; Univ IL, Urbana, MA, 60, PhD, 64. **CAREER** From instr to asst prof Span, Univ MI, Ann Arbor, 64-69; asst prof, Dartmouth Col, 69-71; assoc prof, 71-74, chmn dept mod lang, 71-76, Prof Span, FL Int Univ, 74-98, Publ subsidy, FL Int Univ Found, 74. **HONORS AND AWARDS** Fla Int Univ Found, Publ Subvention, 74; Excellence in Tchg Award, FL Int Univ, 87; Acad Affairs Res Competition, Summer A, 90; Latin Am and Caribbean Affairs Center, Res Support, fall 90, spring 91; Excellence in Res Award, FL Int Univ, 95; Latin Am and Caribbean Center: Publ Subvention, 97. **MEMBERSHIPS** MLA; Midwest Mod Lang Asn. **RESEARCH** Contemp Span poetry; contemp Eng poetry; 17th & 20th century Span lit. **SELECTED PUBLICATIONS** Auth, The novela corta as comedia: Lope's Las Fortunas de Diana, Bull Hisp Studies, 68; Theory and practice of the novela comdiesca, Romanishche Forsch, 69; Earth words, 74 & Whose House of books, 74, Caribbean Rev; The Vibrant Silence in Jorge Guillen's Aire Nuestro, Univ NC, 74; The dark silence in Lorca's poetry, Garcia Lorca Rev, 78; The Yes and the No of Lorca's Ocean, The World of Nature in the Works of Federico Garcia Lorca, 80; Lawrence Durrell's Songs to Syntax, Lang and Style, 83; The Dialectical Failiure in Neruda's Las furias y las penas, Hispania, 3/85; The Poetry of Jorge Guillen, In: Contemporary World Writers, St James Press, 86; The Dark Canticles in Jorge Guillen's Y otros poemas, Hispania, 12/87; From Synthesis to Continuity: Jorge Guillen's Y otros poemas, In: Jorge Guillen Aire nuestro, Anthropos, 10/91; Rozando el paraiso (Poety in Spanish), Thesaurus, Brazil, 95; Nightglow: Borges' Poetics of Blindness, Catedra de Poetica Fray Luis de Leon, Salamanca, Spain, 97. **CONTACT ADDRESS** Dept of Mod Lang, Florida Intl Univ, 1 F I U Univ Park Campus, Miami, FL, 33199.

Z

ZACHAU, REINHARD KONRAD
PERSONAL Born 05/04/1948, Lubeck, Germany, m, 1975, 1 child **DISCIPLINE** GERMAN LITERATURE **EDUCATION** Univ Hamburg, Staatsexamen, 74; Univ Pittsburgh, PhD(Ger lit), 78. **CAREER** Instr Ger for foreigners, Christian-Albrechts Univ, 77; ASST PROF GER, UNIV OF THE SOUTH, 78-**MEMBERSHIPS** MLA; Am Asn Teacher's German; SAtlantic Mod Lang Asn; Northeast Mod Lang Asn. **RESEARCH** East German literature; exile literature; modern West German literature. **SELECTED PUBLICATIONS** Auth, The Narrative Fiction of Boll, Heinrich--Social Conscience and Literary Achievement, Ger Quart, Vol 0070, 97; German Literature in Exile in the Netherlands 1933-1940--German, Seminar-Jour Ger Stud, Vol 0032, 96; Understanding Hein, Christoph, Ger Stud Rev, Vol 0019, 96; Mann, Erika--A Biography--German, Ger Quart, Vol 0068, 95; A Chronicler Without a Message--Hein, Christoph--A Workbook, Materials, Notes, Bibliography--German, Ger Quart, Vol 0066, 93. **CONTACT ADDRESS** SPO 1199, Sewanee, TN, 37375.

ZAHAREAS, ANTHONY
DISCIPLINE SPANISH AND PORTUGUESE LITERATURE **EDUCATION** Ohio State Univ, BA, 56; MA, 58; PhD, 62. **SELECTED PUBLICATIONS** Auth, Le Funcion Historica delHumor en Don Quiiote, Tulane Univ, 93; Cervantes, Shakespeare and Calderon: Theater and Society, Baton Rouge, 95; Primera Memoria como Realidad y Metafora, Compas de Letras, 94; Modernidad y Experimentalismo Revista de Filologia y Linguistica, Univ Costa Rica, 96. **CONTACT ADDRESS** Spanish and Portuguese Dept, Univ of Minnesota, Twin Cities, 34 Folwell Hall, 9 Pleasant St SE, Minneapolis, MN, 55455. **EMAIL** zahar001@maroon.tc.umn.edu

ZAHNISER, A. H. MATHIAS
PERSONAL Born 01/01/1938, Washington, DC, m, 1959, 3 children **DISCIPLINE** ISLAMIC STUDIES **EDUCATION** Greenville Col, IL, BA, 60; Am Univ, MA, 62; Asbury Theol Sem, M Div, 65; Johns Hopkins Univ, PhD, 73. **CAREER** Asst to assoc prof, relig stud, 71-78, Cent Mich Univ; prof, 78-83 Greenville Col; assoc prof, 83-86, Mission Asbury Theol Sem; John Wesley Beeson Prof Of Christian Mission, 86-, Asbury Theol Sem **HONORS AND AWARDS** Univ Achievement Award, Cent Mich Univ, 73. **MEMBERSHIPS** Am Soc of Missiology; AAR. **RESEARCH** Literary analysis of the Quran; use of symbols and ritual in Christian nurture and forma-

tion. **SELECTED PUBLICATIONS** Auth, Symbol and Ceremony: Making Disciples Across Cultures, MARC Pubs, 77; auth, Ritual Process and Christian Discipling: Contextualizing a Buddhist Rite of Passage, Missiology, XIX, no 1, 91; auth, The Word of God and the Apostleship of Isa: A Narrative Analysis of Al Imran, J of Semitic Studies, XXXVIII, no 1, 91; auth, Close Encounters of the Venerable Kind: Christian Dialogical Proclamation Among Muslims, Asbury Theol J, XLIX, no 1, 94; auth, Sura as Guidance and Exhortation: The Composition of Surat al-Nisa, Humanism, Culture, and Language in the Near East: Studies in Honor of Georg Krotkoff, Eisenbrauns, 97; co-ed, Humanism, Culture, and Language in the Near East: Studies in Honor of Georg Krotkoff, Eisenbrauns, 97. **CONTACT ADDRESS** Asbury Theol Sem, Wilmore, KY, 40390. **EMAIL** mathias_zahniser@ats.wilmore.ky.us

ZAHORSKI, KENNETH
PERSONAL Born 10/23/1939, Cedarville, IN, m, 1962, 2 children **DISCIPLINE** ENGLISH, SPEECH **EDUCATION** Univ Wis-River Falls, BS, 61; Ariz State Univ, MA, 63; Univ Wis, PhD(English), 67. **CAREER** Asst prof English, Univ Wis-Eau Claire, 67-69; asst prof, 69-71, asoc prof, 71-80, prof English, St Norbert Col, 80-, consult, Choice, 72-; sr assoc, CIC, 94-. **HONORS AND AWARDS** Outstanding Teacher of the Year Award, St Norbert Col, 74; Outstanding Alumnus Award, Univ Wis-River Falls, 75; Distinguished Scholar Award, St Norbert Col, 87; Sears Roebuck Found, Teaching Excellence and Campus Leadership Award, 91. **MEMBERSHIPS** MLA; NCTE; AAUP; Col English Asn. **RESEARCH** Renaissance Drama; modern drama; Fantasy literature. **SELECTED PUBLICATIONS** Co-ed, Visions of Wonder: An Anthology of Christian Fantasy, Avon Bks, 81; Fantasists on Fantasy, Avon, 84; Visions and Imaginings, Acad Chicago Pubs, 92; auth, Peter S Beagle, Starmont Press, 88; The Sabbatical Mentor, Anker Pub Co, 94. **CONTACT ADDRESS** Dept of English, St. Norbert Col, 100 Grant St, De Pere, WI, 54115-2099. **EMAIL** zahokj@sncac.snc.edu

ZALACAIN, DANIEL
PERSONAL Born 12/15/1948, Havana, Cuba, m, 1976, 1 child **DISCIPLINE** LATIN AMERICAN LITERATURE & THEATRE **EDUCATION** Wake Forrest Univ, BA, 71; Univ NC, Chapel Hill, MA, 72, PhD, 76. **CAREER** Asst prof Span lang & lit & bus Span, Northern IL Univ, 77-80; Asst Prof Span Lang & Lit & Bus Span, Seton Hall Univ, 80. **MEMBERSHIPS** Am Asn Tchr(s) Span & Port; MLA. **RESEARCH** Latin Am theatre of the absurd; Span for business careers; Latin Am myths. **SELECTED PUBLICATIONS** Auth, Rene Marques, del absurdo a la realidad, Latin Am Theatre Rev, fall 78; El arte dramatico en Cuculcan, Explicacion textos lit, 78; Calabar: O elogio da traicao, Chasqui: Rev Lit Latinoam, 2/79; Falsa alarma: Vanguardia del absurdo, Romance Notes, 80; El tiempo, tema fundamental en la obra de Rene Marques, Ky Romance Quart, 80; El personae fuera del juego en el teatro de Griselda Gambaro, Rev Estudios Hispanicos, 5/80; Los recursos dramaticos en Soluna, Latin Am Theatre Rev, spring 81; La Antigona de Sanchez: Recreacion puertorriquena del mito, Explicacion Textos Lit, 81. **CONTACT ADDRESS** Dept of Mod Lang, Seton Hall Univ, 400 S Orange Ave, South Orange, NJ, 07079-2697.

ZAMORA, JUAN C.
PERSONAL Born 05/14/1930, New York, NY, m, 1953, 2 children **DISCIPLINE** HISPANIC LINGUISTICS & HISTORY OF LINGUISTICS **EDUCATION** Univ Havana, JD, 52, Lic Soc Sc, 60; State Univ NY Buffalo, MA, 66, PhD(Span), 71. **CAREER** Prof law, Univ Popular, Havana, 47-57; adv, Ministry Educ & chief of chancellery, Ministry Foreign Affairs, Cuba, 59-60; teacher English, Dade County pub schs, 62-63; from instr to lectr Span, State Univ NY Buffalo, 63-70; asst prof, Cent Conn State Col, 70-71; asst prof to assoc prof ,Span, Univ Mass, Amherst, 71-83, prof Span, Univ Mass, Amherst, 83-, grad prog dir,80-82, dept chair, 87-93, Dept Span & Port, Univ Mass, Amherst. **MEMBERSHIPS** MLA; Am Asn Teachers Span & Port; Ling Soc Am; Int Ling Asn; Caribbean Stds Asn, Soc Espanola Hist Ling. **RESEARCH** Spanish American Dialectology: Bilingualism and Language Contact; Language Aquisition; History of Linguistics. **SELECTED PUBLICATIONS** Auth, Indigenismos en la lengua de los conquistadores, Univ of PR, 76; coauth, Dialectologia hispanoamericana, 2nd ed, Col de Esp, Spain, 88; coauth, Fundamentos de Linguistica hispanica, Playor, Spain, 88; Historiografia linguistica: Edad Media y Renacimiento, Col de Esp, Spain, 93; articles in prof journals and books pub in Mexico, PR, Spain, U.K., and U.S. **CONTACT ADDRESS** Dept of Span & Port, Univ of Mass, Amherst, MA, 01003-0002. **EMAIL** zamora@spanport.umass.edu

ZANTOP, SUSANNE
DISCIPLINE GERMAN AND COMPARATIVE LITERATURE **EDUCATION** Harvard Univ, PhD, 84. **CAREER** Fac, Santiago de Compostela (Spain); chr and prof, Darmouth Col. **RESEARCH** 18th and 19th century fiction and the hist of ideas. **SELECTED PUBLICATIONS** Auth, publ(s) about Julchen Gruumlnthal, Heinrich Heine, Frederike Unger, and topics concerning Ger colonialist fictions and the French Revolution; ed, a study of Heine and an anthology of Ger women writers. **CONTACT ADDRESS** Dartmouth Col, 3529 N Main St, #207, Hanover, NH, 03755.

ZANTS, EMILY
PERSONAL Born 08/03/1937, Tulsa, OK **DISCIPLINE** FRENCH LITERATURE **EDUCATION** Stanford Univ, BA, 58; Columbia Univ, MA, 61, PhD(French), 65. **CAREER** Instr French, Brooklyn Col, 65-67; asst prof, Univ Calif, Davis, 67-72; assoc prof, 72-80, PROF FRENCH LANG & LIT, UNIV HAWAII, MANOA, 80- **HONORS AND AWARDS** Mabelle McLeod Lewis Award, Stanford Univ, 72. **MEMBERSHIPS** MLA; Am Soc 18th Century Studies; Am Asn Teachers Fr; Am Inst Architects. **RESEARCH** The novel; Flaubert; Proust. **SELECTED PUBLICATIONS** Auth, Mon Oncle--Tati, Jacques, Fr Rev, Vol 0069, 95. **CONTACT ADDRESS** Dept of Europ Lang, Univ of Hawaii, at Manoa, Honolulu, HI, 96822.

ZAYAS-BAZAN, EDUARDO
PERSONAL Born 11/17/1935, Camaguay, Cuba, m, 1959, 2 children **DISCIPLINE** HISPANIC CULTURE AND LITERATURE **EDUCATION** Nat Univ Jose Marti, Havana, JD, 58; Kans State Teachers Col, MA, 66. **CAREER** Teacher Span, Plattsmouth High Sch, Nebr, 64-65 & Topeka West High Sch, Kans, 65-66; instr, Appalachian State Univ, 66-68; asst prof, 68-73, assoc prof, 73-79, Prof Span Foreign Lang Dept, East Tenn State Univ, 79-, Chmn Dept, 73-93. **HONORS AND AWARDS** Distinguished Faculty award, 78. **MEMBERSHIPS** Am Asn Teachers Span & Port; MLA; Am Coun on the Tchg of For Lang; Tenn Foreign Lang Tchg Asn; Nat Asn Cuban-Am Educ; Sigma Delta Phi. **RESEARCH** Bilingual education. **SELECTED PUBLICATIONS** Co-ed, Del amor a la revolucion, Norton, 75; auth, "Hemingway: His Cuban Friends Remember," Fitzgerald/Hemingway Annual, 75; co-ed, MIFC Selected Proceedings; coauth, De aqui y de alla, D C Heath & Co, 80; Secret Report on the Cuban Revolution, Trans, 81; coauth, Como dominar la redaccion, 89; coauth, Como aumentar su vocabulario 3, Como escribir cartas eficaces, 89; coauth, Nuestro mundo, 90; coauth, Arriba!, 93; coauth, No se equivoque con el ingles, 93; auth, El ingles que usted no sabe que sabe, 93. **CONTACT ADDRESS** Dept of Foreign Lang, East Tennessee State Univ, PO Box 10001, Johnson City, TN, 37614-0001. **EMAIL** Zayasbae@etsu.edu

ZEGURA, ELIZABETH CHESNEY
PERSONAL Born 09/07/1949, Knoxville, TN, m, 1983, 1 child **DISCIPLINE** RENAISSANCE LITERATURE, FRENCH, ITALIAN **EDUCATION** Bryn Mawr Col, AB, 71; Duke Univ, MA, 74, PhD, 76. **CAREER** Instr, Davidson Col, 75-76; asst prof, DePauw Univ, 81-82; VISTING ASST PROF, 78-80, LECTR, 85, 87-88, 89-, UNIV OF ARIZ. **HONORS AND AWARDS** AB (magna cum laude), Bryn Mawr, 71; NDEA Fel, Duke Univ. **MEMBERSHIPS** Renaissance Soc of Am. **RESEARCH** Renaissance Literature: Rabelais, Ariosto, Marguerite de Navarre. **SELECTED PUBLICATIONS** Auth, The Countervoyage of Rabelais and Ariosto: A Comparative Reading of Two Renaissance Mock Epics, Duke Univ Press, 82; coauth, Rabelais Revisited, MacMillan/Twayne, 93. **CONTACT ADDRESS** Dept of French and Italian, Univ of Ariz, Tucson, AZ, 85721. **EMAIL** zeguras@u.arizona.edu

ZEITLIN, FROMA I.
DISCIPLINE GREEK LANGUAGE AND LITERATURE. **EDUCATION** Radcliffe Col, AB, 54; Catholic Univ, MA, 65; Columbia Univ, PhD, 70. **CAREER** Prof, Princeton Univ. **RESEARCH** Mythology; Greek tragedy and lyric poetry; poetics; Religion; Gender Studies. **SELECTED PUBLICATIONS** Auth, Under the Sign of the Shield: Semiotics and Aeschylus' Seven Against Thebes; Nothing to Do with Dionysos?; Playing the other: Gender and Society in Classicl Greek Literature. **CONTACT ADDRESS** Princeton Univ, 1 Nassau Hall, Princeton, NJ, 08544. **EMAIL** fiz@princeton.edu

ZEITZ, EILEEN
DISCIPLINE SPANISH AMERICAN LITERATURE EDUCATION Univ Ill, Urbana-Champaign, PhD. **CAREER** Instr, Univ Minn, Duluth. **RESEARCH** Spanish American prose fiction. **SELECTED PUBLICATIONS** Published critical articles on a variety of Spanish American prose fiction writers, and a critical book on the novels of the Uruguayan writer Mario Benedetti; she also has published two books of creative fiction--short stories and poetry--in Spanish. **CONTACT ADDRESS** Univ Minn, Duluth, Duluth, MN, 55812-2496.

ZEKULIN, NICHOLAS GLEB
PERSONAL Born 01/23/1946, Prague, Czechoslovakia, m, 1968, 3 children **DISCIPLINE** RUSSIAN LITERATURE **EDUCATION** McGill Univ, BA, 66; Yale Univ, MPhil, 69, PhD(Slavic), 74. **CAREER** Asst prof, 71-79, ASSOC PROF RUSS LANG & LIT, UNIV CALGARY, 79- **MEMBERSHIPS** Can Asn Slavists (secy-treas, 79-82, vpres, 82-83); Am Asn Advan Slavic Studies; Asn des Amis d'Ivan Tourgueniev, Pauline Viardot, Maria Malibran. **RESEARCH** Ivan Turgenev and era; A I Solzhenitsyn; literature and music links. **SELECTED PUBLICATIONS** Auth, Changing Perspectives, the Prose of Baranskaya, Natalya, Can Slavonic Papers-Rev Can Slavistes, Vol 0035, 94; Literature and Politics--Studies in Honor of Goetzstankiewicz, Marketa, Seminar-Jour Ger Stud, Vol 0031, 95; Beginning Russian Computer Exercises for Dos, Slavic and E Europ Jour, Vol 0041, 97. **CONTACT ADDRESS** Dept of Ger & Slavic Studies, Univ of Calgary, Calgary, AB, T2N 1N4.

ZEPS, VALDIS JURIS
PERSONAL Born 05/29/1932, Daugavpils, Latvia, m, 1957, 4 children **DISCIPLINE** LINGUISTICS **EDUCATION** Miami Univ, AB, 53; Ind Univ, PhD, 61. **CAREER** Sci linguist, Off Geog, US Dept Interior, 61-62; vis asst prof Slavic lang, 62, from asst prof to assoc prof ling, 63-68, PROF LING, UNIV WIS-MADISON, 68-, Nat Sci Found fel, Ctr Advan Studies Behav Sci, 60-61; Soc Sci Res Coun- Am Coun Learned Soc, Univ Wis, 63; managing ed, Slavic & EEurop Lang; Asn Advan Baltic Studies. **RESEARCH** Linguistic theory; East European languages; East Latvian History. **SELECTED PUBLICATIONS** Auth, Historical Maps of Latvia-Latvian, Jour Baltic Stud, Vol 0023, 92; An Atlas of Latvian Streets, 1940--German, Jour Baltic Stud, Vol 0024, 93; Latvian Sun Song Index--Latvian and English, Jour Baltic Stud, Vol 0024, 93; Latvian Highway Atlas--Latvian, Jour Baltic Stud, Vol 0026, 95; Latgalian Literature in Exile, Jour Baltic Stud, Vol 0026, 95; Pre-Latgalian Hydronyms in East Latvia, Jour Baltic Stud, Vol 0026, 95. **CONTACT ADDRESS** Dept of Ling, Univ of Wis, Madison, WI, 53706.

ZEVELECHI WELLS, MARIA XENIA
DISCIPLINE FRENCH; ITALIAN **EDUCATION** Univ of Pisa, Italy, PhD, 59. **CAREER** Teacher, Am High Sch, Pisa, Italy and asst prof, Univ of Pisa, Italy, 57-62; lectr, Univ of Tex, 62-72; cur of Ital Collections, H. Ransom Hums Res Ctr, Univ or Tex, 73-97; adj prof, H. Ransom Ctr, Univ of Tex, 97-. **HONORS AND AWARDS** Fulbright Scholar, 54-55; Inst of Am Studies in Rome Scholar, 56; App to the Libr Servs and Construct Act Adv Coun, 86, 89; App to attend the Conv of Ital Lang and Cult in Rome, Italy, Ital Ministry of Foreign Affairs, 87; J.R. Dougherty Jr. Found Grant, 87; Ital Private Found Grant, 89; Fulbright Res Grant, 91; App to the Fulbright Campus Screening Comt, 92; App mem fo the Am Comt for the Medici Arch Proj Inc. Florence and NY, 96 TIL Coun, the Soerette Diehl Fraser Transl Award Adv Coun, 97. **MEMBERSHIPS** Am Asn for Ital Studies; Associazione Internazionale di Studi di Lingua e Letteratura Italiana; Am Translators Asn; Fulbright Asn; Minerva Hist Asn; Nat Fulbright Alumni Asn; Soc for Ital Hist Studies; Nat Ital Am Found. **RESEARCH** Carlo Levi **SELECTED PUBLICATIONS** Auth, The Ranuzzi Manuscripts, in exhibit catalog, H. Ransom Hums Res Ctr Publs, 80; Annibale Ranuzzi e La Repubblica del Texas, 1842, in Il Carrobbio 10, 84; Una Biblioteca Italiana nel Texas, in Biblioteche Oggi, vol VII-n.1, 89; Libraries and Cultures, issue on the history of Italian libraries, twelve essays, vol 25/no. 3, 90; Italian Post-1600 Manuscripts and Family Archives in North American Libraries, 92; The Italian Collections Across the Centuries: Literature, Art, and Theatre, exhibit catalog as double issue of The Libr Chronicle, vol 21, nos. 2/3, 93; Fuochi d'Artificio: manoscritto del 1500, in FMR aprile, 95; I Paladini di Sicilia, in FMR dicembre, 95; Il manoscritto di Cristo si e' fermato a Eboli, lettura su piano storico e critico, in Stanford French and Ital Studies, 97; Memoriale di Paolo Volponi: L'uomo e la Fabbrica, esame delle varianti nel manoscritto, in selected procs of the Conf: Letteratura e Industria, AISILLI, 94; Aldine Press Books at the Harry Ransom Humanities Research Center: A descriptive catalogue, in H. Ransom Spec Publs, September, 98. **CONTACT ADDRESS** Harry Ransom Humanities Research Center, Univ of Texas, Austin, Austin, TX, 78713-7219. **EMAIL** mxwells@nora.hrc.utexas.edu

ZEVIT, ZIONY
PERSONAL Born 02/13/1942, Winnipeg, MB, Canada **DISCIPLINE** FOREIGN LANGUAGES **EDUCATION** Univ Calif, PhD, 73. **CAREER** Prof, Univ Judaism, 74-; vis prof, Univ Calif, 98; vis prof, Univ Penn Ctr Judaic Studies, 97; vis prof, W.F. Albright Inst, 94; vis prof, Hebrew Univ, 94; vis prof, Univ Calif LA, 91-92; vis prof, Claremont Grad Sch, 92. **HONORS AND AWARDS** Univ Penn Ctr Judaic Studies Fel, 97; John Simon Guggenheim Mem Found, 94; Abraham Biran Fel Bibl Archeol, 87. **MEMBERSHIPS** ASOR; AOS; AJS; CBA; NAPH; NACAAL; SBL. **RESEARCH** Near Eastern languages; semitic philology; Bible; ancient Near Eastern history and archeology. **SELECTED PUBLICATIONS** Auth, Solving Riddles and Untying Knots: Biblical, Epigraphic and Semitic Studies Presented to Jonas C. Greenfield, 95; auth, Philology, Archeology, and a Terminus a Quo for P's Hatta't Legislation, Pomegranates and Golden Bells: Studies in Bibl, Jewish, and Near Eastern Ritual, Law, and Lit in Honor of Jacob Milgrom, 95; auth, The Earthen Altar Laws of Exod 20:24-26 and Related Sacrificial Restrictions in their Cultural Context, Texts, Temples, and Traditions: A Tribute to Menahem Haran, 96; auth, The Israelite Ethos in which Deuteronomy Developed, Shnaton: An Annual for Bibl and Ancient Near Eastern Studies, 97; auth, The Gerizim-Samarian Community In and Between Texts and Times: An Experimental Study, The Quest for Context and Meaning: Studies in Bibl Intertextuality in Honor of James A. Sanders, 97; auth, Proclamations to the Fruitful Tree and the Spiritualization of Androgyny, The Echoes of Many Texts: Reflections on Jewish and Christian Traditions, Essays in Honor of Lou H. Silberman, 97; auth, The Anterior Construction in Ancient Hebrew, 98. **CONTACT ADDRESS** Dept of Near Eastern Languages, Judaism Univ, 15600 Mulholland Dr., Los Angeles, CA, 90077.

ZGUSTA, LADISLAV
PERSONAL Born 03/20/1924, Bohemia, Czechoslovakia, m, 2 children **DISCIPLINE** PHILOLOGY **EDUCATION** Prague Univ, PhD, 49, DSc, 64. **CAREER** Hd, lexicographic teams, Czech Acad Sci, 58-70; prof, linguistics and classics, 71-95, dir, Ctr for Advan Stud, 87-95, prof emer, 95- , Univ of Ill. **HONORS AND AWARDS** Res grant, Am Coun Learned Soc, 73; Guggenheim Found fel, 77, 84; mem, Austrian Acad Sci, 83; NEH res grant, 89. **MEMBERSHIPS** Am Acad Sci; Ling Soc Am; Dict Soc N Am; European Lixicographic Asn; Am Name Soc; Indogermanische Ges. **RESEARCH** Theory and practice of lexicography; Indo-European linguistics; name studies. **SELECTED PUBLICATIONS** Auth, Kleinasiatische Ortsnamen, Carl Winter, 84; auth, The Old Ossetic Inscription from the River Zelencuk, Verlag der Osterreichischen Akademie der Wissenschaften, 87; auth, Lexicography Today: An Annotated bibliography of the Theory of Lexicography, Max Niemeyer, 88; ed, International Encyclopedia of Lexicography, de Gruyter, 89; auth, Name Studies: An International Handbook of Onomastics, de Gruyter, 95; auth of numerous articles and book reviews. **CONTACT ADDRESS** 115 W. Michigan Ave., Urbana, IL, 61801. **EMAIL** l-zgusta@uiuc.edu

ZHOLKOVSKY, ALEXANDER
DISCIPLINE SLAVIC LANGUAGES AND LITERATURES **EDUCATION** Moscow Univ, MGU, USSR, PhD. **CAREER** Prof, Univ Southern Calif. **RESEARCH** Aesopian language; dystopian writing; avantgardist debasement of classical hypograms; 20th-century appropriation of the earlier tradition. **SELECTED PUBLICATIONS** Auth, Themes and Texts, 84; Bluzhdaiushchie sny, Wandering Dreams, 92, 94; Text Counter Text: Rereadings in Russian Literary History, 94; Inventsii, Inventions, 95; NRZB, UNRDBL, 91; coauth, Poetics of Expressiveness, 87; Isaak, Babel, 94. **CONTACT ADDRESS** Col Letters, Arts & Sciences, Univ Southern Calif, University Park Campus, Los Angeles, CA, 90089. **EMAIL** alik@usc.edu

ZIADEH, FARHAT JACOB
PERSONAL Born 04/08/1917, Palestine, m, 1949, 5 children **DISCIPLINE** ARABIC, ISLAMICS **EDUCATION** Am Univ Beirut, BA, 37; Univ London, LLB, 40. **CAREER** Magistrate, Govt of Palestine, 47-48; from lectr to assoc prof Orient studies, Princeton Univ, 48-66; PROF NEAR EASTERN STUDIES, UNIV WASH, 66-, Gov Am Res Ctr, Egypt, 70-78, fel, 71-72 & 77. **MEMBERSHIPS** Am Orient Soc; Mid East Studies Asn NAm (pres, 80). **RESEARCH** Arabic language and literature; Islamic law; Islamic institutions. **SELECTED PUBLICATIONS** Auth, The Reliance of the Traveler--A Classical Manual of Islamic Sacred Law by Ibnnaqibalmisri, Ahmad D. 769/1368--In Arabic with Facing English Text, Commentary and Appendixes, Jour Amer Oriental Soc, Vol 0115, 95. **CONTACT ADDRESS** Dept of Near Eastern Lang & Lit, Univ of Wash, Seattle, WA, 98195.

ZIEFLE, HELMUT WILHELM
PERSONAL Born 04/02/1939, Heilbronn-Sontheim, Germany, m, 1965, 2 children **DISCIPLINE** GERMAN LITERATURE, MODERN GERMAN HISTORY **EDUCATION** State Univ NY Albany, BA, 64, MA, 66; Univ Ill, PhD, 73. **CAREER** Teacher Ger, Bethlehem Cent High, 65-67; from instr to assoc prof, 67-82, Prof Ger, Wheaton Col, 82-, Dir, Wheaton in Ger, 77-; pres, Ger Evening Sch, Wheaton, 78-80; scholar in residence, Ger Dept, Circle Campus, fall, 79; pres, AATG Northern Ill Chapter, 89-91. **HONORS AND AWARDS** AATG/Goethe House Certificate of Merit Award, 92. **MEMBERSHIPS** Am Asn Teachers Ger; ICTFL; NACFLA. **RESEARCH** Early German baroque literature; modern German literature: Hesse, Mann and postwar German literature; history of the Third Reich especially German opposition to Hitler. **SELECTED PUBLICATIONS** Auth, Sibylle Schwarz: Life and work, in Studies in German, English and Comparative Literature, Bouvier, Bonn, 75; Opitz' influence on poetry of Sibylle Schwarz, Vol 4, 76 & Occupation of Greifswald during Thirty Years War, Vol 2, 77, Pommern; A Christian family resists Hitler, Christianity Today, Vol 6, 78; The long shadow of Hitler, The Christian Reader, 79, 2-5; ed, Sibylle Schwarz: German poetic poems, in Middle German Literature, Lang, Bern, 80; auth, One Woman Against the Reich, Bethany House Publ, 81; Dict of Modern Theological German, Baker Bk House, 82; ed, Hermann Hesse und das Christentum, R. Brockhaus Verlag, 94; auth, Modern Theological German: A Reader and Dictionary, Baker Book House, 97. **CONTACT ADDRESS** 501 College Ave, Wheaton, IL, 60187. **EMAIL** helmut w ziefle@wheaton.edu

ZIEFTE, HELMUT W.
PERSONAL Born 04/02/1939, Heilbron, Germany, m, 1965, 3 children **DISCIPLINE** LANGUAGES **EDUCATION** SUNY, BA, 64, MA, 66; Univ ILL, PhD, 73. **CAREER** Tchr, German, 65-67, Bethlehem Cent High Schl; instr, 67-72, asst prof, 72-77, assoc prof, 77-82, prof, 82-, Wheaton Col. **RESEARCH** Hermann Hesse, German theology, German hist. **CONTACT ADDRESS** ON460 Fanchon St, Wheaton, IL, 60187.

ZIEGLER, VICKIE L.
DISCIPLINE GERMAN, MEDIEVAL STUDIES **EDUCATION** MacMurray Col, BA, 64; Univ Vienna, study, 65; Yale Univ, PhD, 70. **CAREER** Asst prof, 70-76, ASSOC PROF, GERMAN, PA STATE UNIV, 76-, DIR, CENTER FOR MEDIEVAL STUDIES, 92-. **HONORS AND AWARDS** Class of 1933 Univ Humanities Award, 91; Faculty Res Fellowships, Inst for Arts and Humanistic Studies. **MEMBERSHIPS** Medieval Academy of Am; Int Vereinigung der Germanisten. **RESEARCH** Medieval German lang and lit; minnesang; trials by combat. **SELECTED PUBLICATIONS** Auth, The Physician and the Artist: Psychological Issues in E. T. A. Hoffmann's Work, Hist of Psychiatry, Royal Col of Psychiatrists, Vol 5, 94; Arnims Amazonen, Grenzgange: Studien zu L. Achim von Arnim, ed Michael Andermatt, Bonn, Germany, 94; A Burning Issue: Isolde's Ordeal by Fire, in The Germanic Mosaic: Cultural and Linguistic Diversity in Society, London, 94; ed with Robert Edwards, Matrons and Marginal Women in the Middle Ages, Cambridge, England, 95; Geneluns Prozess : das alte und das neue Recht in den mittelhochdeutschen Karlsepen, in The Medieval Translator, 6: Proceedings of the Int Conference of Gottingen, 22-25, July 96, eds Roger Ellis, Rene Tixier and Bernd Weitemeier, Brussels, Belgium, 98; numerous other publications. **CONTACT ADDRESS** Pennsylvania State Univ, S409 Burrowes, University Park, PA, 16802. **EMAIL** vlz1@psu.edu

ZIEGLER, VICKIE LYNNE
PERSONAL Rock Island, Ill **DISCIPLINE** GERMAN **EDUCATION** MacMurray Col, BA, 64; Yale Univ, PhD(Ger), 70. **CAREER** Asst prof Ger, Pa State Univ, University Park, 76-, dir, Ctr for Medieval Stu, 93-. **MEMBERSHIPS** Mediaeval Acad Am; Int Vereinigung fu germanische Sprachen und Literaturwissenschaft. **RESEARCH** Medieval German lyric; Medieval German romance; romantic Rahmennovelle. **SELECTED PUBLICATIONS** Auth, The Leitword in Minnesang, Ger ser, Pa State Univ, 74; Justice in Brentano's 'Die Schactel mit der Friedenspuppe', Ger Rev, fall 78; auth, Goethe and the French ActressL How Clarion became Antonelli, Monatshefte 76, 84; auth, Bending the Frame in the German Cyclical Narrative: Achim von Arnim's Der Wintergarten and E.T.A. Hoffman's Die Serapionsbruder, Catholic Univ of Am, 91; auth, Arnims Amazonen, Grenzgange: Studien zu L. Achim von Arnim, Bonn, 94; auth, A Burning Issue: Isolde's Ordeal by Fire, The Germanic MosaicL Cultural and Linguistic Diversity in Society, Westport, 94. **CONTACT ADDRESS** Dept of German, Pa State Univ, University Park, PA, 16802-1014.

ZILCOSKY, JOHN
DISCIPLINE GERMAN **EDUCATION** Harvard Univ, AB, 87; Temple Univ, MA, 92; Univ Pa, PhD, 98. **CAREER** Vis asst prof, Williams Col, 98-99. **HONORS AND AWARDS** Sch of Arts and Sci Dissertation fel, Univ Pa, 97-98; Fulbright Scholar, 96-97; DAAD res grant, 95. **RESEARCH** 19th and 20th century German, Austrian, and American literature; literary theory and philosophy; psychoanalysis and the history of psychoanalysis; German film; modern central European history; creative writing and translation. **SELECTED PUBLICATIONS** Auth, Of Sugar Barons and Banana Kings: Franz Kafka, Imperialism, and Schaffsteins Grune Bandchen, J of the Kafka Soc of Amer, 90. **CONTACT ADDRESS** Center for Foreign Languages, Literatures and Cult, Williams Col, Williamstown, MA, 01267. **EMAIL** John.Zilcosky@williams.edu

ZIMMERMAN, ZORA DEVRNJA
PERSONAL Born 05/12/1945, Marienbad, Czechoslovakia, m, 1976, 2 children **DISCIPLINE** COMPARATIVE LITERATURE, FOLKLORE **EDUCATION** State Univ NY, BA, 67, PhD, 74. **CAREER** Asst prof, 74-79, assoc prof, 80-84, PROF ENGLISH, IOWA STATE UNIV, 85-. **HONORS AND AWARDS** NEH summer fel. **MEMBERSHIPS** AAASS; Am Folklore Soc; H"lderlin Ges; CCAS; Nat Asn Ethnic Studies. **RESEARCH** Serbian traditional narrative and lyric; dynamics of change and persistence in folklore; English and European Romanticism. **SELECTED PUBLICATIONS** Co-ed, The Arc from Now (poems), Iowa State Univ, 78; auth, Moral vision in the Serbian folk epic: The foundation sacrifice of Skadas, Slavic & East Europ J, Vol 23, 79; The changing roles of the Vila in Serbian traditional literature, J of Folklore Inst, Vol 26, 79; Metrics of passion: The poetry of Carl Dennis, Poet & Critic, Vol 12, 80; transl & ed, Serbian Folk Poetry: The Oldest Epics, Kosovo Publ Co, 82; Teaching folklore in Iowa, in Teaching Folklore, Am Folklore Soc Inc, 84, rev ed, 89; Traditiona and change in a ritual feast: The Serbian Krsna Slava in America, Great Lakes Rev, fall 85; Serbian Folk Poetry: Ancient Legends, Romantic Songs, Kasovo Publ Co, 86; On the hermeneutics of oral poetry: The Uosovo Mythos, Serbian Studies, fall 90; The building of Skadar, in The Walled-Up Wife Casebook, Univ Wisc Press, 96. **CONTACT ADDRESS** Col of Lib Arts & Sci, Iowa State Univ, Ames, IA, 50011-0002. **EMAIL** zdzimme@iastate.edu

ZINNI, HANNAH CASE
PERSONAL Born 10/01/1944, Cincinnati, OH, m, 1977, 3 children **DISCIPLINE** FRENCH LANGUAGE & LITERATURE **EDUCATION** Oberlin Col, BA, 66; Northwestern Univ, MA, 67, PhD, 71. **CAREER** Asst prof, 70-75, assoc prof, 75-81, prof French, 81-, Slippery Rock Univ. **HONORS AND AWARDS** Phi Beta Kappa, Oberlin College, 66. **MEMBERSHIPS** Am Assn Teachers French; MLA; PSMLA. **RESEARCH** Art and the artist in the works of Samuel Beckett; the couple in Samuel Beckett's works; the Louisiana French; Franco-American history; the French in America. **SELECTED PUBLICATIONS** Auth, Art and the Artist in the Works of Samuel Beckett, Mouton, 75; art, The couples in Comment C'est, Samuel Beckett: The Art of Rhetoric, Univ NC, 76; art, Bibliog for Andre DuBouchet, Andre Frenaud & Philippe Soupault, Critical Bibliography of French Literature of the Twentieth Century, 80. **CONTACT ADDRESS** Dept of Mod Lang & Cult, Slippery Rock Univ, 14 Maltby Dr, Slippery Rock, PA, 16057-1326. **EMAIL** hannah.zinni@sru.edu

ZIOLKOWSKI, JOHN EDMUND
PERSONAL Born 06/19/1938, Montevallo, AL, m, 1958, 2 children **DISCIPLINE** CLASSICAL LANGUAGES **EDUCATION** Duke Univ, AB, 58; Univ NC, PhD(classics), 63. **CAREER** Instr Latin, Univ NC, 62-64; asst prof classics, Randolph-Macon Woman's Col, 64-67; asst prof, 67-72, ASSOC PROF CLASSICS, GEORGE WASHINGTON UNIV, 72-, CHMN DEPT 71-. **MEMBERSHIPS** Am Philol Asn; Am Inst Archeol. **RESEARCH** Greek and Roman literature; Renaissance Latin; Classical influence on Washington DC. **SELECTED PUBLICATIONS** Auth, The Parthenon Stone in the Washington Monument, Prologue-Quart Nat Archv, Vol 0025, 93; A Commentary on Thucydides, Vol 1, Books-1-3, Class World, Vol 0086, 93; City-States in Classical Antiquity and Medieval Italy, Class World, Vol 0087, 94; The Classics in American Theater of the 1960s and Early 1970s, Class World, Vol 0088, 95; Shakespeare and Classical Comedy--The Influence of Plautus and Terence, Class World, Vol 0090, 97; Sacred Geography of the Ancient Greeks--Astrological Symbolism in Art, Architecture, Class World, Vol 0090, 97. **CONTACT ADDRESS** Dept of Classics, George Washington Univ, 2035 H St N W, Washington, DC, 20052-0001.

ZLOTCHEW, CLARK M.
PERSONAL Born 10/14/1932, Jersey City, NJ, m, 3 children **DISCIPLINE** SPANISH LANGUAGE, SPANISH & SPANISH-AMERICAN LITERATURE **EDUCATION** New York Univ, BS, 57; Middlebury Col, MA, 66; State Univ NY Binghamton, PhD, 74. **CAREER** Sales/Production liason, Schenley Int Corp, New York, 55-62; Teacher Span, Dumont High Sch, NJ, 62-66; Asst Prof Span, Norwich Univ, 66-68; Tchg Asst Span, State Univ NY-Binghamton, 68-70; Instr, State Univ NY-Geneseo, 70-74; Proj Coordr, migrant educ, Genesee-WY Bd of Coop Educ Serv, 74-75; from Asst Prof to Assoc Prof, 75-82, Prof Span & Ling, State Univ NY Fredonia, 82. **HONORS AND AWARDS** Nat Endowment for Hum grant, 78, 87; SUNY President's Award for Excellence in Tchg, 88; Kasling Lectr, for scholarship, 92; Fac Exchange Schol of SUNY, 87; Faculty Grant for the Improvement of Undergraduate Instruction from SUNY Central Awards, Summer 89. **MEMBERSHIPS** Am Asn Tchr(s) Span & Port; Northeastern Mod Lang Asn; MLA; Am Lit Transl Asn; Academia Portena del Lunfardo (U.S. Correspondent, 82-); NY Int Asn Torch Clubs; State Coun Ling (Secy 79); Instituto Literario y Cultural Hisp; Int Asn Torch Clubs; Circulo de Cultura Panamericano. **RESEARCH** Nineteenth-century Peninsular lit; comtemp Latin-Am lit; Hispanic linguistics. **SELECTED PUBLICATIONS** Auth, Libido into Literature: The Primera Epoca of Benito Perez Galdos, Borgo Press, 93; Voices of the River Plate: Interviews With Writers of Argentina and Uruguay, Borgo Press, 95; transl, Seven Conversations with Jorge Luis Borges, Whitston Publ Co, 82; Falling Through the Cracks: Short Stories of Julio Ricci, White Pine Press, 89; co-transl, The House at Isla Negra, White Pine Press, 88; The House in the Sand: Prose Poems by Pablo Neruda, Milkweed Editions, 90; auth and transl of numerous articles and other publ. **CONTACT ADDRESS** Dept of For Lang, State Univ of NY-Fredonia, Fredonia, NY, 14063-1143. **EMAIL** Zlotchew@Fredonia.edu

ZOHN, HARRY
PERSONAL Born 11/21/1923, Vienna, Austria, m, 1962, 2 children **DISCIPLINE** GERMAN **EDUCATION** Suffolk Univ, BA, 46; Clark Univ, MA Ed, 47; Harvard Univ, AM, 49, PhD(Ger lang & lit), 52. **CAREER** From instr to assoc prof, 51-67, PROF GER, BRANDEIS UNIV, 67-, Trustee, Suffolk Univ, 78-81; chmn grad prog lit studies, 81- **HONORS AND AWARDS** LittD, Suffolk Univ, 76. **MEMBERSHIPS** Am Transl Asn; Am Asn Teachers Ger; MLA; PEN Club; Int Arthur Schnitzler Res Asn (vpres, 77-). **RESEARCH** Problems of translation; Austrian literature; German-Jewish writers. **SELECTED PUBLICATIONS** Auth, Das Verschwinden des Blicks--German, World Lit Today, Vol 0066, 92; Benjamin,Walter, Colloquia Ger, Vol 0025, 92; Heine,Heinrich, Ger Stud Rev, Vol 0016, 93; Professions of a Lucky Jew, Mod Austrian Lit, Vol 0026, 93; Die Fliegenpein, World Lit Today, Vol 0067, 93; Laughter Unlimited--Essays on Humor, Satire, and the Comic, Ger Quart, Vol 0066, 93; Wir Heimatlosen, 1989-1992, World Lit Today, Vol 0067, 93; 3 Late Plays--the Sisters, or Casanova in Spa, Seduction Comedy, the Way to the Pond, World Lit Today, Vol 0068, 94; Second Land, World Lit Today, Vol 0068, 94; The Jewish Reception of Heine, Heinrich, Jour Eng and Ger Philol, Vol 0093, 94; Plague in Siena, World Lit

Today, Vol 0068, 94; The Jewish Reception of Heine,Heinrich, Jour Eng and Ger Philol, Vol 0093, 94; Professor Bernhardi and Other Plays, World Lit Today, Vol 0068, 94; Inventory of the Zweig, Stefan Collection in Reed Library, Mod Austrian Lit, Vol 0028, 95; Saturn auf der Sonne, World Lit Today, Vol 0069, 95; Beerhofmann,Richard--Self-Awareness of Viennese Jews at the Turn-of-the-20th-Century--German, Mod Austrian Lit, Vol 0028, 95; Hier Kocht der Wirt, World Lit Today, Vol 0070, 96; Criminal-Law and Satire in Kraus, Karl Work-- German, Mod Austrian Lit, Vol 0029, 96; Kraus Contra George--Commentaries on the Translation of Shakespeare Son- nets--German, Mod Austrian Lit, Vol 0029, 96; Absterbende Gemutlichkeit--12 Stories from the Center of the World-- German, World Lit Today, Vol 0071, 97; The Good Life- German, World Lit Today, Vol 0071, 97. **CONTACT ADDRESS** Dept of Ger, Brandeis Univ, Waltham, MA, 02154.

ZOLBROD, PAUL GEYER
PERSONAL Born 12/10/1932, Pittsburgh, PA, m, 1967, 2 chil- dren **DISCIPLINE** LITERARY CRITICISM, LINGUISTICS **EDUCATION** Univ Pittsburgh, BA, 58, MA, 62, PhD(En- glish), 67. **CAREER** Instr English, Univ Pittsburgh, Titusville, 63-64; from instr to assoc prof 64-77, PROF ENGLISH, ALLE- GHENY COL, MEADVILLE, 77-, Fel, Univ NMex, 71-72; consult, Public Broadcasting Northwest Pa, 76-78; Res fel, Nat Endowment Humanities, 78-79. **MEMBERSHIPS** MLA; AAUP; NCTE; Northwest Mod Lang Asn; Soc Am Indian Studies. **RESEARCH** Renaissance literature; ethnopoetics; lin- guistics. **SELECTED PUBLICATIONS** Auth, The Wind in a Jar, Amer Indian Cult and Res Jour, Vol 0018, 94; Saanii- Dahataal--The Women Are Singing, Amer Indian Cult and Res Jour, Vol 0018, 94. **CONTACT ADDRESS** Dept of English, Allegheny Col, Park Ave, Meadville, PA, 16335.

ZORITA, C. ANGEL
DISCIPLINE SPANISH LANGUAGE, LITERATURE, AND CIVILIZATION **EDUCATION** Gregorian Univ, Rome, AD; Univ Madrid, MA; Univ Seville, PhD. **CAREER** Former instr, Univ Madrid; W VA Univ; prof. **RESEARCH** Old Span song books. **SELECTED PUBLICATIONS** Publ, Spanish Litera- ture. **CONTACT ADDRESS** Dept of For Lang, Cleveland State Univ, 83 E 24th St, Cleveland, OH, 44115.

ZOU, KE
PERSONAL Born 10/30/1956, Nanchang, China, m, 1985 **DISCIPLINE** LINGUISTICS **EDUCATION** Jiangxi Normal Univ, Nanchang, BA, 82; Guangzhou For Lang Inst, MA, 85; Ohio State Univ, MA, 89; Univ So Calif, Los Angeles, MA, 91, PhD, 95. **CAREER** Instr, Eng Dept, 82-83, instr, ling, 85-86, Jiangxi Normal Univ; instr ling, Ohio State Univ, 88-89; lectr, Eng Dept, Calif State Univ, Dominguez Hills, 90-97; lectr, Eng Dept, El Camino Col, 96-97; lectr, Eng Dept, Chapman Univ, 98; asst prof, Eng Dept, Calif State Univ, Hayward, 98-. **HON- ORS AND AWARDS** Hum Dean's Fel, 89-90, 94-95, Out- standing Academic Achievement Award, 91; Hum Grad Fel, 90-94, Univ So Calif; res grant award, 92-94, travel award, 94- 97, internationalization award, 97, Affirmative Action Fac Dev Award, 97, Calif State Univ, Dominguez Hills; **MEMBER- SHIPS** Ling Soc Am; Int Asn of Chinese Ling. **RESEARCH** Syntax; morphology; Chinese linguistics. **SELECTED PUB- LICATIONS** Auth, Preverbal and Postverbal Objects in the Chinese BA-construction, Proc of the 23rd W Conf on Ling, 93; auth, The Syntax of the Chinese BA-construction, Linguistics, 93; auth, Resultative V-V Compounds, Proc of MIT Morpholo- gy-Syntax Connection Workshop, 94; auth, Directional Verb- compounds, Proc of 30th Conf of Chicago Ling Soc, 94; auth, The Negation of the Chinese BA-Construction, Proc of the 4th Int Conf on Chinese, 95; auth, The Syntax of the Chinese BA- Construction: A Minimalist Approach, Proc of the 25th W Conf on Ling, 95; auth, Resultative Verb Compounds and Non- Personal Subjects, Proc of the 8th N Am Conf on Chinese Ling, 96; auth, Unergative and Unaccusative Verb Compounds, Proc of the 31st Mid-Am Ling Conf, 96; auth, Alienable and Inalien- able Objects in the Passive Construction, Proc of the 9th N Am Conf on Chinese Ling, 97; auth, The Chinese BA-construction: A Morpho-syntactic Analysis, Symp Ser of the Inst of Hist and Philol: Morphology and Lexicon, 97; auth, Directional Verb Movement in Chinese; Proc of the 10th N Am Conf on Chinese Ling, 98. **CONTACT ADDRESS** English Dept, California State Univ, Hayward, Hayward, CA, 94542-3037. **EMAIL** kzou@csuhayward.edu

ZUBIZARRETA, ARMANDO F.
DISCIPLINE 20TH CENTURY SPANISH LITERATURE **EDUCATION** Pontificia Universidad Catolica del Peru, MA, 59; Universidad de Salamanca, PhD, 59. **CAREER** English, Case Western Reserve Univ. **HONORS AND AWARDS** Pre- mio Extraordinario, 59; Premio Nacional de Critica Literaria Manuel Gonzalez Prada, 68. **SELECTED PUBLICATIONS** Auth, Perfil Y Entrana De "El Caballero Carmelo", 68; Cuando Mas Ardea El Fuego. **CONTACT ADDRESS** Case Western Reserve Univ, 10900 Euclid Ave, Cleveland, OH, 44106. **EMAIL** afz@po.cwru.edu

ZUBIZARRETA, MARIA LUISA
DISCIPLINE LINGUISTICS **EDUCATION** MIT, PhD. **CA- REER** Assoc prof, Univ Southern Calif. **RESEARCH** Syntax;

representation of the Lexicon. **SELECTED PUBLICATIONS** Auth, The Relation Between Morphophonology and Morpho- syntax: The Case of Romance Causatives, Ling Inquiry, MIT Press, 85; Levels of Representation in the Lexicon and in the Syntax, Foris Publ, 87; coauth, The Definite Determiner and the Inalienable Constructions in French and in English, in Ling In- quiry, MIT Press, 92. **CONTACT ADDRESS** Dept of Linguis- tics, Univ Southern Calif, University Park Campus, Los Ange- les, CA, 90089. **EMAIL** zubizarr@usc.edu

ZUCKERMAN, BRUCE
PERSONAL Born 07/31/1947, Los Angeles, CA, m, 1975, 3 children **DISCIPLINE** NEAR EASTERN STUDIES **EDUCA- TION** Princeton Univ, BA, 69; Yale Univ, PhD, 80. **CAREER** Dir, Univ So Calif Archaeol Res Col, 81- ; dir, West Semitic Res Proj, 83- , assoc prof, relig, 88- , Univ So Calif, 83- . **MEM- BERSHIPS** Am Oriental Soc; Am Res Ctr in Egypt; Nat Asn of Prof of Hebrew; Soc of Bibl Lit. **RESEARCH** Bible; An- cient Near East; Northwest Semitic epigraphy and philology. **SELECTED PUBLICATIONS** Co-ed, Facsimile Edition of the Leningrad Codex; auth, Job the Silent: A Study in Historical Counterpoint. **CONTACT ADDRESS** School of Religion, Univ of So California, Univ Park, Los Angeles, CA, 90089- 0355. **EMAIL** bzuckerm@bcf.usc.edu

ZURAKOWSKI, MICHELE M.
PERSONAL Born 03/06/1960, Bay City, MI, m, 1982, 1 child **DISCIPLINE** SPEECH COMMUNICATION **EDUCATION** Univ Minn, PhD, 92. **CAREER** Asst Prof Speech Commun, Col St. Catherine, 94-, Dept Chair, 94-. **MEMBERSHIPS** NCA; CSCA; CTAM. **RESEARCH** Women and public ad- dress; birth control rhetoric. **SELECTED PUBLICATIONS** Auth, "Interiors" as Interdisciplinary Text: A Case Analysis Using Film to Integrate Classroom Discussion of Interpersonal and Mass Mediated Meanings, Mich Asn Speech Commun J, 94; From Doctors and Lawyers to Wives and Mothers: Enacting "Feminine Style" and Changing Abortion Rights Arguments, Women's Studies in Communication, Spring 94; Ti-Grace At- kinson, Women Public Speakers in the United States, 1925- 1993: A Bio-Critical Sourcebook, Greenwood Press, 94; Mod- eling Rhetorical Criticism, The Speech Commun Teacher 11, 97. **CONTACT ADDRESS** Speech Communication Dept, Col of St. Catherine, 2004 Randolph Ave., St. Paul, MN, 55105. **EMAIL** mmzurakowski@stkate.edu

ZWEERS, ALEXANDER FREDERIK
PERSONAL Born 06/11/1931, Amsterdam, Netherlands, m, 1963, 2 children **DISCIPLINE** RUSSIAN LITERATURE **ED- UCATION** Univ Amsterdam, Drs, 59; Univ Groningen, Hol- land, PhD(Russ lit), 71. **CAREER** Instr, Univ BC, 62-67; asst prof, 67-73, ASSOC PROF RUSS & CHURCH SLAVONIC, UNIV WATERLOO, 73-, Can Coun res grants, 71, 72, 74 & 77; partic, Exchange Prog Can & Soviet Scholars, 74. **MEM- BERSHIPS** Can Asn Slavists; Can Asn Advan Netherlandic Studies. **RESEARCH** L N Tolstoy; I A Bunin; Russian-Dutch literary relations. **SELECTED PUBLICATIONS** Auth, Auto- biographical Statements in 20th-Century Russian Literature, Ger-Slavica, Vol 0007, 91; An Autobiography, Is an Autobiog- raphy, Is an Autobiography--Genre in Russian Literature, Can Slavonic Papers-Rev Can Slavistes, Vol 0034, 92. **CONTACT ADDRESS** 116 Keats Way Pl, Waterloo, ON, N2L 5H3.

ZYLA, WOLODYMYR T.
PERSONAL Born 06/25/1919, Zbaraz, Ukraine, m, 1945, 3 children **DISCIPLINE** SLAVIC PHILOLOGY **EDUCATION** Univ Man, BS, 59, MA, 62; Ukrainian Free Univ, Munich, PhD(Slavic philol), 67. **CAREER** Assoc prof Russ & Ger lang & Russ lit, 63-74, PROF SLAVIC LANG & LIT, TEX TECH UNIV, 74-, Ed, Proc Comp Lit Symp, Vol I-IV, 68-71, coed, Vol V-X, 72-77; chmn, Interdept Comt Comp Lit, Tex Tech Univ, 69-76; Nat Endowment for Humanities grant, 75. **HON- ORS AND AWARDS** Lett & Cert, Am Revolution Bicentenni- al Admin, 76. **MEMBERSHIPS** Multi-Ethnic Lit US; Am Asn Teachers Slavic & East Europ Lang; Am Name Soc; Shevcheko Sci Soc; Am Comp Lit Asn. **RESEARCH** Ukrainian literature, 16th and 17th centuries; literary criticism of modern literature; comparative literature. **SELECTED PUBLICATIONS** Auth, 3 Narratives and 6 Poems, World Lit Today, Vol 0067, 93; Ukrainian Literature in Canada--Ukrainian, World Lit Today, Vol 0067, 93; Poems, World Lit Today, Vol 0067, 93; Mech I Pero, World Lit Today, Vol 0069, 95 Literary Lvov, 1939- 1944--Ukrainian, World Lit Today, Vol 0070, 96; Garden of Verse, World Lit Today, Vol 0067, 97. **CONTACT AD- DRESS** 5220 29th St, Lubbock, TX, 79407.

Geographic Index

ALABAMA

Athens
Laubenthal, Penne J.

Auburn
Billiams, Lynn Barstis
Spencer, Samia Iskander

Birmingham
Allgood, Myralyn Frizzelle
Carter, William Causey
Leffel, Katherine
Martin, Dellita Lillian
Martin-Ogunsola, Dellita Lillian
Ward, Dorothy Cox

Huntsville
Maier, Linda

Maxwell AFB
Kline, John A.

Mobile
Lally, Tim Douglas Patrick

Montgomery
Crowley, Joseph P.

Tuscaloosa
Galli, Barbara E.
Ohnuma, Reiko

University
Latimer, Dan Raymond
Pickett, Terry H.

ALASKA

Anchorage
Haley, Michael
Katasse, Conny

Fairbanks
Hollerbach, Wolf
Krauss, Michael

ARIZONA

Glendale
Griggs, John W.

Phoenix
Foster, David William

Tempe
Croft, Lee B.
Curran, Mark Joseph
Friedman, Edward Herbert
Gruzinska, Aleksandra
Guntermann, Gail
Horan, Elizabeth R.
Horwath, Peter
Ney, James Walter

Nilsen, Alleen Pace
Nilsen, Don Lee Fred
Wetsel, William David
Williams, Philip F.C.
Wong, Timothy C.

Tucson
Adamec, Ludwig W
Arnett, Carlee
Chandola, Anoop Chandra
Chisholm, David
Classen, Albrecht
Demers, Richard Arthur
Fuchs, Esther
Kinkade, Richard Paisley
Kosta, Barbara
Kovach, Thomas A.
Langendoen, Donald Terence
Martinson, Steven D.
Rivero, Eliana Suarez
Schulz, Renate A.
Sokel, Walter H.
Szpek, Heidi M.
Wildner-Bassett, Mary E.
Zegura, Elizabeth Chesney

ARKANSAS

Batesville
Bordeau, Catherine
Lewis, Bart L.

Conway
Bailey, Phillip
Brodman, Marian
Langston, Dwight E.
Martinez, Jose-Luis
Pouwels, Joel

Fayetteville
Amason, Patricia
Bell, Steven
Brady, Robert M.
Christiansen, Hope
Cory, Mark
Davis, James
Duval, John
Eichmann, Raymond
Ford, James
Ford, James Francis
Hanlin, Todd
Haydar, Adnan
Kahf, Mohja
Levine, Daniel
Locke, John
Pritchett, Kay
Ricker-Abderhalden, Judith
Simpson, Ethel C.
Tsai, Shih-shan Henry
Tucker, Janet
Turner, Joan

Little Rock
Garnett, Mary Anne
Pancrazio, James
Sobin, Nicholas
Thorson, Helga

Searcy
Goss, Noble T.

State University
Bayless, Ovid Lyndal

CALIFORNIA

Arcata
Pence, Ellsworth Dean

Azusa
Robison, R.E.

Berkeley
Alter, Robert
Azevedo, Milton M.
Botterill, Steven
Brinner, William Michael
Cascardi, Anthony Joseph
Clader, Linda
Clubb, Louise George
Duggan, Joseph John
Emeneau, Murray Barnson
Faulhaber, Charles Bailey
Fleischman, Suzanne
Grossman, Joan Delaney
Gumperz, John J.
Heinze, Ruth-Inge
Hillen, Gerd
Holub, Renate
Holub, Robert C.
Jaini, Padmanabh S.
Johnson, Leonard Wilkie
Karlinsky, Simon
Kudszus, Winfried
Malkiel, Yakov
Mastronarde, Donald John
Matisoff, James Alan
McLean, Hugh
Melia, Daniel Frederick
Miles, Josephine
Nagler, Michael Nicholas
Ohala, John Jerome
Penzl, Herbert
Polt, John H.R.
Schamschula, Walter
Seeba, Hinrich Claassen
Slobin, Dan Isaac
Snapper, Johan Pieter
Spahr, Blake Lee
Threatte, Leslie Lee
Walsh, John Kevin
Wang, William S.Y.

Campbell
Nichols, Patricia Causey

Chico
Brown, James Lorin

Claremont
Adler, Sara Maria
Atlas, Jay David
Lohrli, Anne
McGaha, Michael Dennis
Rindisbacher, Hans J.
Rinkus, Jerome Joseph

Saigal, M.
Senn, Harry
Warner, Nicholas Oliver
Young, Howard Thomas

Davis
Bernd, Clifford Albrecht
Bowsky, Martha Welborn
Fetzer, John Francis
Kusch, Manfred
McConnell, Winder
Schaeffer, Peter Moritz-Friedrich
Schaeffer, Peter Moritz-Friedrich
Schleiner, Winfried H.
Traill, David Angus
Verani, Hugo Juan
Wallacker, Benjamin E

El Dorado Hills
Albada-Jelgersma, Jill Elizabeth

Fresno
Adams, Katherine L.
Bochin, Hal William
Carmichael, Carl W.
Freeman, David
Freeman, Yvonne
Golston, Chris
Raney, George William
Weitzman, Raymond Stanley

Fullerton
Kaye, Alan Stewart
Witmer, Diane F.

Hayward
Warrin, Donald Ogden
Zou, Ke

Irvine
Carroll, David
Chiampi, James T.
Fuller, M.A.
Gearhart, Suzzane
Guthrie, Elizabeth M.
Hart, Gail K.
Huang, J.
Hubert, Judd D.
Hubert, Renee Riese
Laborde, Alice M.
Lehnert, Herbert Hermann
Lillyman, William J.
Noland, Carrie J.
Palley, Julian
Rabine, Leslie W.
Regosin, Richard L.
Riese Hubert, Renee
Saine, Thomas Price
Suttpn, Dana F.
Watt, William Carnell

La Jolla
Cancel, Robert
Dijkstra, Bram
Friedman, Richard Elliott
Humphries, Tom
Kirkpatrick, Susan
Klima, Edward Stephens
Langacker, Ronald Wayne
Newmark, Leonard

Rose, Sharon

La Mirada
Lewis, Todd Vernon

Los Angeles
Andersen, Elaine
Ando, Clifford
Aoun, Joseph
Babcock, Arthur Edward
Bahr, Ehrhard
Barnouw, Dagmar
Bauer, George Howard
Bauml, Franz H.
Bergren, Ann L.T.
Birge, Bettine
Birnbaum, Henrik
Blumberg, Sherry H.
Bonebakker, Seeger A.
Borer, Hagit
Bruneau, Marie Florine
Carnicke, Sharon Marie
Chambers, Mortimer Hardin
Cheung, Dominic C.N.
Chrzanowski, Joseph
Clausing, Gerhard
Cuenca, Jose Ramon Araluce
Cutter, William
Diaz, Roberto Ignacio
Eekman, Thomas
Ehret, Christopher
Finegan, Edward J.
Frakes, Jerold C.
Frischer, Bernard
Fromkin, Victoria A
Fulco, William J.
Georges, Robert A.
Gonzalez, Alfonso
Han, Mieko
Hawkins, John A.
Hayden, George A.
Hoji, Hajime
Ilie, Paul
Ivanov, Vyacheslav V.
Johnson, Carroll B.
Jun, Sun-Ah
Kamuf, Peggy
Kaplan, Robert B.
Kerr, Lucille
Kim, Nam-Kil
King, Katherine Callen
Komar, Kathleen Lenore
Ladefoged, Peter
Li, Audrey
Lofstedt, Bengt
MacDonald, Maryellen
Maniquis, Robert Manuel
Minkova, Donka
Nash, Stanley
Nehring, Wolfgang
Noble, Douglas
Pinkus, Karen
Quintero, Ruben
Rosenthal, Margaret F.
Rutherford, William E.
Saltarelli, Mario
Schein, Barry
Schmidt, Hanns-Peter
Schnauber, Cornelius
Schniedewind, William M.
Seidenberg, Mark

Silva-Corvalan, Carmen M.
Sonnenfeld, Albert
Starr, Peter
Stefanovska, Malina
Stockwell, Robert Paul
Thompson, Laurence G.
Tuttle, Edward Fowler
Vergnaud, Jean-Roger
Vickers, Nancy
Wagener, Hans
Wittrock, Merlin Carl
Woodard, Roger
Worth, Dean Stoddard
Zevit, Ziony
Zholkovsky, Alexander
Zubizarreta, Maria Luisa
Zuckerman, Bruce

Malibu
Casmir, Fred L.
Durham, Ken R.
Lorenzi, Paola G.

McKinleyville
Yingling, Julie

Monterey
Cooper, Danielle Chavy
Strolle, Jon M

Moraga
Dawson Boyd, Candy

Newport Beach
Menton, Seymour

Northridge
Bjork, Robert Eric
Ford, Alvin Earle
Gariano, Carmelo
Hussain, Amir

Oakland
Adisa, Opal Palmer
Caufield, Carlota
Cavallari, Hector Mario
Siekhaus, Elisabeth

Orange
Axelrod, Mark R.
Deck, Allan F.

Pasadena
Barber, Elizabeth J. Wayland
Barber, Paul Thomas
Bogen, Joseph E.
Miner, Ellis D.

Pomona
Smith, David Richard

Redlands
Vailakis, Ivan Gordon

Riverside
Barricelli, Jean-Pierre
Chen, Jingsong
Daviau, Donald G.
Fagundo, Ana Maria
Ganim, John Michael
Gericke, Philip Otto
Levin, Jules Fred
Megenney, William Wilber
Scanlon, Thomas Francis
Waller, Marguerite R.
Yamamoto, Traise

Rohnert Park
Haslam, Gerald William
Martinez, Elizabeth Coonrod

Sacramento
Dennis, Harry Joe
Giles, Mary E.
Santana, Jorge Armando
Wu, Joseph Sen

San Diego
Case, Thomas Edward
Dukas, Vytas
Farber, Gerald Howard
Jackson, Elizabeth R.
Lustig, Myron W.
Lyman-Hager, Mary Ann
Mapa, Marina Vargas
Savvas, Minas
Shapiro, Lewis P.

Silverman, Malcolm Noel
Steets, Cheryl
Warren, Edward W.

San Francisco
Chinosole
Kolbert, Jack
Vogeley, Nancy Jeanne

San Jose
Leung, Kai-Cheong

Santa Barbara
Acimovic Wallace, Vesna
Athanassakis, Apostolos N.
Blackwood-Collier, Mary
Chandler Mcentyre, Marilyn
Docter, Mary K.
Dunn, F.M.
Exner, Richard
Hernadi, Paul
Hoffmeister, Gerhart
Jackman, Jarrell C.
Johnson, Donald Barton
Leal, Luis
Lundell, Torborg Lovisa
Mahlendorf, Ursula R.
Nelson, William B.
Perissinotto, Giorgio
Renehan, Robert
St. Omer, Garth
Steiner, Thomas Robert
Sullivan, John P.
Tappy, Ron E.
Tobin, Ronald William Francis
Wiemann, John M.

Santa Clara
Jimenez, Francisco

Santa Cruz
Aissen, Judith
Chung, Sandra
Farkas, Donka F.
Foley, Mary Kathleen
Hankamer, Jorge
Henton, Caroline G.
Ito, Junko
Ladusaw, William A.
Mccloskey, James
Mester, Armin
Padgett, Jaye
Pullum, Geoffrey K.
Shipley, William F.

Santa Monica
Nieman, Nancy Dale

Stanford
Clark, Eve Vivienne
Cohn, Robert G.
Hester, Ralph M.
Hilton, Ronald
Mudimbe, Valentine
Pratt, Mary Louise
Sag, Ivan Andrew
Sungdai, Cho
Traugott, Elizabeth Closs
Wasow, Thomas Alexander

Stockton
Sharp, Francis Michael

Sun Valley
Barrick, William D.

Thousand Oaks
Stewart, Walter K

Van Nuys
Garber, Zev Warren

Venice
Heidsieck, Arnold

COLORADO

Boulder
Barchilon, Jacques
Frajzyngier, Zygmunt
Geary, John Steven
Jensen, Frede
Kopff, Edward Christian
Kroll, Paul William
Lee, Charles Nicholas

Lester, Robert Carlton
Rood, David Stanley
Schmiesing, Ann
Stavan, Henry-Anthony
Taylor, Allan Ross

Colorado Springs
Koc, Richard
McKay, Douglas R.
Richardson, Horst Fuchs
von Dassanowsky, Robert
Wishard, Armin

Denver
Furness, Edna Lue
Gilroy, James Paul
Ishimatsu, Ginette
Means, James
Ranwez, Alain Daniel
Ward, Seth
Wignall, Dennis L.

Evergreen
Gibson, Todd

Fort Collins
Bodine, Jay F.
Castro, Amanda
Crabtree, Loren William
Fowler, Carolyn A.
Gilmore, Roger H.
Hoffmann, Klaus D.
Hunt, Irmgard E.
Jones, Tobin H.
Malpezzi Price, Paola
Otero, Jose
Ott, Brian L.
Perez Stansfield, Maria Pilar
Sargent, Stuart H.
Saz, Sara M.
Suarez Garcia, Jose Luis
Wolff, Ronald A.

Greeley
Arneson, Pat
George, Hermon, Jr.
Keaten, James A.

Louisville
Del Caro, Adrian

Pueblo
Griffin, John R.

CONNECTICUT

Bethel
Dobsevage, Alvin P

Fairfield
Campos, Javier F.
Leeber, Victor F.
Levitt, Jesse
Rosivach, Vincent John

Hamden
Quirk, Ronald Joseph

Hartford
BiJlefeld, Willem A.
Lee, Sonia M.
Macro, Anthony David

Middletown
Dunn, Peter Norman
Gonzalez, Bernardo Antonio
Katz, Marilyn A.
Lowrie, Joyce Oliver
Needler, Howard
O'Hara, James J.
Stowe, William W.
Walker, Willard
Wensinger, Arthur Stevens
Winston, Krishna

New Britain
Auld, Louis
Iannace, Gaetano Antonio
Pastore Passaro, Maria C.
Pesca-Cupolo, Carmela
Picerno, Richard A.
Rohinsky, Marie-Claire
Wallach, Martha K.

New Haven
Anderson, Michael John
Brooks, Peter Preston
Erlich, Victor
Ferguson, Margaret Williams
Foster, Benjamin Read
Hein, Norvin
Hubert, Marie Louise
Insler, Stanley
Jackson, Robert Louis
Lee, Ta-ling
Martin, Samuel Elmo
May, Georges
Pollitt, Jerome J.
Porter, Charles Allen
Robinson, Fred C.
Sammons, Jeffrey L.
Sammons, Jeffrey Leonard
Schoolfield, George C.
Stimson, Hugh McBirney
Vena, Michael
Venclova, Tomas Andrius
Vitello, Ralph Michael
Weinstein, Stanley

New London
Murstein, Nelly Kashy
Silverberg, Joann C.
Solomon, Janis Virginia Little
Terras, Rita
Vance, Timothy

Orange
Ni, W.J.

Stamford
Frank, Yakira H

Storrs
Abramson, Arthur Seymour
Beck, Sigrid
Boskovic, Zeljko
Calabrese, Andrea
Coelho, Carl
Crosby, Donald H.
Gilbert, Harvey R.
Higonnet, Margaret Randolph
Lasnik, Howard
Lederer, Herbert
Liles, Betty Z.
Lillo-Martin, Diane C.
Marrone, Nila Gutierrez
Mattingly, Ignatius G.
Mchugh, Michael P.
Michaels, David
Naudin, Marie
Orringer, Nelson Robert
Robb, Michael P.
Snyder, William
Suits, Thomas Allan

West Haven
Emma, Ronald David

Willimantic
Mama, Raouf
Tapia, Elena

DELAWARE

Newark
Afifi, Walid A.
Bergstrom, Anna
Braun, Theodore Edward Daniel
Courtright, John A.
Haslett, Betty J.
Mcinnis, Judy Bredeson
Samter, Wendy
Valbuena-Briones, Angel Julian
Wedel, Alfred R.

DISTRICT OF COLUMBIA

Washington
Bedini, Silvio A.
Bensky, Roger Daniel
Betz, Dorothy
Brown, John Lackey
Captain, Yvonne
Damiani, Bruno Mario
Fernandes, James
Fitzgerald, Aloysius

Frank, Richard Macdonough
Frey, John Andrew
Gerli, Edmondo Michael
Gignac, Francis Thomas
Ginsberg, Ellen Sutor
Guieu, Jean-Max
Halton, Thomas
Jamme, Albert W.F.
Lesko Baker, Deborah
Levitine, Eda Mezer
Logan, Paul Ellis
Ludwinowski, Rett R.
Morris, Marcia A.
O'Connor, Michael Patrick
Pireddu, Nicoletta
Rameh, Clea Abdon
Robb, James Willis
Robinson, Daniel N.
Sara, Solomon Ishu
Severino, Roberto
Sims, Edna N.
Steiner, Carl
Stokoe, William Clarence
Sullivan, Denis
Tannen, Deborah F.
Wendland, Ernst R.
Yamauchi, Joanne
Ziolkowski, John Edmund

FLORIDA

Boca Raton
Abramson, Henry
Kramer, Phyllis S.
Smith, Voncile Marshall

Dunedin
Hyers, M. Conrad

Fort Lauderdale
Segal, Marilyn

Gainesville
Baker, Susan Read
Cailler, Bernadette Anne
Casagrande, Jean
Chu, Chauncey Cheng-Hsi
Der-Houssikian, Haig
Diller, George Theodore
Gay-Crosier, Raymond
Johnston, Otto William
Katritzky, Linde
McKeen, William
Nanji, Azim A
Rennert, Hellmut Hal
Scholes, Robert James
Thompson, Roger Mark

Lutz
Brulotte, Gaetan

Miami
Cadely, Jean Robert Joseph
Camayd Freixas, Erik
Castellanos, Isabel
Castells, Ricardo
Gorman, John
Jensen, John Barry
Lee, Joseph Patrick
Machonis, Peter A.
Young, Theodore Robert
Yudin, Florence L.

Pensacola
Josephs, Allen

St. Petersburg
Carter, Albert Howard

Tallahassee
Allaire, Joseph Leo
Darst, David High
Gerato, Erasmo Gabriele
Hemmingway, Beulah S.
Simons, John Donald
Stanley, Patricia H.

Tampa
Mariotti, Arleen
Turner, Stephen

Content

West Lafayette
Beer, Jeanette Mary Ayres
Burleson, Brant R.
Garfinkel, Alan
Hart, Patricia
Hatasa, Kazumi
Haywood, Richard Mowbray
Keck, Christiane Elisabeth
Kirby, John T.
Merrell, F.
Mumby, Dennis K.
Ogles, Robert M.
Orlando, Valerie
Rajagopal, Arvind
Rowan, Katherine E.
Stohl, Cynthia B.
Wang, Aihe
Webb, Ralph, Jr.
Yetman, Michael G

Winona Lake
Lovelady, Edgar John

IOWA

Ames
Courteau, Joanna
Dow, James Raymond
Morris, Walter D.
Ruebel, James
Vann, Roberta Jeanne
Zimmerman, Zora Devrnja

Cedar Falls
Meier, A.J.
Oates, Michael David

Decorah
Gibbs, Virginia
Kath, Ruth R.
Kemp, Henrietta J.
Kurth, William Charles
Stokker, Kathleen Marie
Williams, Queen J.

Des Moines
Beynen, Gijsbertus Koolemans

Grinnell
Kaiser, Daniel Hugh

Indianola
Gieber, Robert L.

Iowa City
Aikin, Judith Popovich
Altman, Charles Frederick
Balderston, Daniel
Coblin, Weldon South
Diaz-Duque, Ozzie Francis
Douglass, R. Thomas
Ertl, Wolfgang
Hahn, Oscar
Ke, C.R.
Kuenzli, Rudolf Ernst
Maierhofer, Walter
Nagel, Alan Frederick
Pachow, Wang
Ringen, Catherine Oleson
Ungar, Steven Ronald
Wachal, Robert Stanley
Wertz, Christopher Allen

Mount Vernon
Vernoff, Charles Elliott

Pella
Webber, Philip Ellsworth

KANSAS

Emporia
Clamurro, William

Hays
Firestone, Ruth H.

Lawrence
Anderson, Danny L.
Baron, Frank
Blue, William Robert
Boon, Jean-Pierre
Brushwood, John Stubbs

Chamberlin, V.A.
Conrad, Joseph Lawrence
Corbeill, Anthony
Debicki, Andrew Peter
Dick, Ernst S.
Dinneen, David A.
Doudoroff, Michael John
Fourny, Diane
Freeman, Bryant C.
Galton, Herbert
Greenberg, Marc L.
Hartman, James Walter
Herzfeld, Anita
Ingemann, Frances
Jewers, Caroline
Keel, William D.
Kelly, Van
Kozma, Janice M.
Lombardo, Stanley
Marx, Leonie
Maurer, Warren R.
Orel, Harold
Parker, Stephen Jan
Percival, Walter Keith
Sautermaister, Gert
Souza, Raymond D.
Spires, Robert Cecil
Vincent, Jon S.

Manhattan
Benson, Douglas Keith
Dehon, Claire L.
Hedrick, Donald Keith
Kolonosky, Walter F.
Ossar, Michael Lee
Shaw, Bradley Alan

Pittsburg
Drew, Shirley K.
O'Hearn, Carolyn

Wichita
Hawkins, Kate
Myers, Eunice Doman
Tomayko, James Edward
Williamson, Keith

KENTUCKY

Bowling Green
Baldwin, Thomas Pratt
Olmsted, Jane
Spurlock, John Howard

Danville
Ciholas, Karin Nordenhaug
Finch, Patricia S.
Keffer, Charles K., Jr.
Munoz, Willy Oscar
Vahlkamp, Charles G.

Grayson
Pickens, George F.

Lexington
Dendle, Brian John
Fiedler, Theodore
Jones, Margaret E.W.
Keller, John Esten
Kratz, Bernd
Lihani, John
Stanton, Edward F.
Thomas, John Wesley

Louisville
Berrong, Richard Michael
Byers, Lori
Gouverneur, Gray Henry
March, Wallace Eugene
Mullen, Karen A.
Nuessel, Frank
Van, Thomas A.

Murray
Keller, Howard Hughes

Owensboro
Browne, Maureen

Wilmore
Simmons, Donald B.
Zahniser, A. H. Mathias

LOUISIANA

Baton Rouge
Bradford, Clinton W.
Brind'Amour, Lucie
Brody, Jules
Curry, Corrada
Di Maio, Irene Stocksieker
Di Napoli, Thomas John
Dupuy, Beatrice
Durmelat, Sylvie
Edgeworth, Robert J.
Erickson, John David
Gellrich, Michelle
Hart, Pierre Romaine
Honeycutt, James M.
Humphries, John J.
Lafayette, Robert
Oetting, Janna B.
Parker, Margaret
Pizer, John
Ragsdale, J. Donald
Ramiacuterez, Mariacutea-Esther D.
Ramirez, Arnulfo G.
Ricapito, Joseph V.
Rodrigo, Victoria
Stanton, Leonard J.
Vandeloise, Claude
Verdesio, Gustavo
Warga, Richard G., Jr.

Hammond
Gaines, James Frederick

Lafayette
Arehole, S.
Berkeley, Istvan S.N.
Oller, John William

Lake Charles
Nagem, Monique F.

Monroe
Steckline, C. Turner
Thameling, Carl L.

New Orleans
Baron, John H.
Berlin, Netta
Brumfield, William Craft
Carroll, Linda Louise
Frank, Elfrieda
Hallock, Ann Hayes
Hasselbach, Ingrid Tiesler
Hasselbach, Karl Heinz
Heiple, Daniel L
Mace, Carroll E.
Paolini, Gilberto
Poe, Joe Park
Porter, Michael
Reck, Rima Drell
Rothenberg, Molly

MAINE

Brunswick
Boyd, Barbara Weiden
Cerf, Steven Roy

New Vineyard
Bliss, Francis Royster

Orono
French, Paulette
Troiano, James J.

Portland
Dietrich, Craig

Presque Isle
Petress, Kenneth C.

Waterville
Paliyenko, Adrianna M.
Partsch, Cornelius
Reidel-Schrewe, Ursula

MARYLAND

Adelphi
Fuegi, John B.

Annapolis
Culham, Phyllis

Baltimore
Baumgarten, Joseph M.
Chaffee-Sorace, Diane
Colombat, Andre P.
Cooper, Jerrold Stephen
Goedicke, Hans
Hillers, Delbert Roy
Krotkoff, Georg
Macksey, Richard Alan
Matanle, Stephen
Morgan, Leslie Zurker
Nagele, Rainer
Olson, Paul Richard
Soria, Regina
Valis, Noel M.
Yarrison, Betsy

Bethesda
Bates, Margaret Jane
Fink, Beatrice

Chestertown
Shivers, George Robert

College Park
Best, Otto Ferdinand
Doherty, Lillian E.
Fleck, Jere
Hallett, Judith P.
Igel, Regina
Lightfoot, D.
Ming Lee, Hugh
Peller Hallett, Judith
Rao, Nagesh
Sthele, Eva
Tarica, Ralph
Walker, Richard Ernest
Wolvin, Andrew D.

Darnestown
Knox, Bernard MacGregor Walker

Emmitsburg
Hamel, Mary

Lanham
Bormanshinov, Arash

Silver Spring
Levy, Diane Wolfe

Towson
Giro, Jorge A.
Matlon, Ronald

Westminster
Cobb, Eulalia Benejam
Williams, Daniel Anthony

MASSACHUSETTS

Amherst
Bach, Emmon
Bauschinger, Sigrid Elisabeth
Berwald, Jean-Pierre
Boudreau, Harold Laverne
Busi, Frederick
Carre, Marie-Rose
Cassirer, Thomas
Cathey, James E.
Cheney, Donald
Cohen, Alvin Philip
Duckert, Audrey Rosalind
Frazier, Lyn
Garaud, Christian
Green, Lisa
Greenfield, Sumner M.
Higgins, Roger F.
Hodder, Alan
Holland, Norman
Johnson, Kyle B.
Kingston, John
Kitchell, Kenneth F.
Kratzer, Angelika
Lawall, Sarah Nesbit
Levin, Maurice Irwin
Maddox, Donald
Maddox, Sara Sturm
Margolis, Nadia
Marshall, Peter K.
Martin, Daniel
Mazzocco, Elizabeth H.

Moore, Ray A.
Naff, William E.
Partee, Barbara H.
Paulsen, Wolfgang
Philippides, Marios
Porter, Dennis
Portuges, Catherine
Roeper, Thomas
Rueschmann, Eva
Schwartzwald, Robert
Scott, Nina Margaret
Sears, Dianne
Seelig, Harry E.
Selkirk, Elisabeth
Seymour, Harry N.
Speas, Margaret
Stone, Jennifer
Sturm-Maddox, Sara
Trahan, Elizabeth Welt
Woolford, Ellen
Zamora, Juan C.

Auburndale
Breines, Joseph

Babson Park
Bruner, M. Lane

Belmont
Fairley, Irene R.

Beverly
Woodward, Pauline

Boston
Aram, Dorothy M.
Bartlett, Cynthia L.
Bashir, Anthony S.
Burgin, Diana Lewis
Crannell, Kenneth C.
Hoddie, James Henry
Horsley, Ritta Jo
Kline, Thomas Jefferson
Lowell Maxwell, David
Manuel, Sharon Y.
Nisetich, Frank
Parker, Simon B.
Robinson, Kelly A.
Ruck, Carl Anton Paul
Saitz, Robert Leonard
Sanchez Silva, Arlyn
Scully, Stephen P.
Volpe, Gerald Carmine
Wallach, Geraldine P.

Cambridge
Berlin, Charles
Chomsky, Noam
Chvany, Catherine Vakar
Cohn, Dorrit
Cranston, Edwin Augustus
Crecelius, Kathryn June
Donaldson, Peter Samuel
Dyck, Martin
Fanger, Donald Lee
Fernandezcifuentes, L.
Flier, Michael S.
Francke, Kuno
Frye, Richard Nelson
Graham, William A.
Guthke, Karl Siegfried
Halle, Morris
Hanan, Patrick Dewes
Iliescu, Nicolae
Kuno, Susumu
Lunt, Horace Gray
Lutcavage, Charles
Marichal, Juan
Marquez-Villanueva, Francisco
Nagy, Gregory John
Rivers, Wilga Marie
Ryan, Judith
Simon, Eckehard
Suleiman, Susan Rubin
Tatar, Maria
Terrill, Ross
Thomson, Robert William
Turk, Edward Baron
Watkins, Calvert Ward
West, Cornel

Chestnut Hill
Araujo, Norman
Eykman, Christoph Wolfgang
McDonough, Christopher Michael
Michalczyk, John Joseph
Resler, W. Michael
Thomas, Margaret

Valette, Rebecca Marianne

Concord
Berthoff, Ann Evans

Greenfield
Wilson, Donna M.

Lexington
Gendzier, Stephen J.

Medford
Gittleman, Sol
Phillips, Joanne Higgins
Rosenberg, Joel William
Sloane, David A.

Nahant
Butler, Thomas J.

North Dartmouth
Sandstroem, Yvonne Luttropp
Washington, Ida Harrison
Yoken, Mel B.

Northampton
Ball, D.
Banerjee, Maria Nemcova
Berkman, Leonard
Clemente, Alice Rodrigues
Graf, Eric
Schuster, Marilyn R.
Sternbach, Nancy Saporta

Norton
Anderson, Kirk
Gallagher, Edward J.
Gallaher, Edward J.
Letts, Janet Taylor
Walsh, Jonathan D.

Quincy
Lomba, Arthur J.

Roslindale
Figurito, Joseph

Salem
Urbain, Henri

South Hadley
Farnham, Anthony Edward
Gelfand, Elissa Deborah
Mazzocco, Angelo
Switten, Margaret L.

South Hamilton
Cooley, Robert E.
Stuart, Douglas Keith

Waltham
Engelberg, Edward
Harth, Erica
Jackendoff, Ray Saul
Johnston, Patricia Ann
Kaplan, Edward Kivie
Lansing, Richard Hewson
Lida, Denah Levy
Young, Dwight Wayne
Zohn, Harry

Wayland
Clogan, Paul Maurice

Wellesley
Galand, Rene
Hansen, Thomas S.
Mistacco, Vicki
Roses, Lorraine Elena
Starr, Raymond James

Westfield
Fellbaum, Christiane
Kane, Leslie
Sossaman, Stephen

Williamstown
Bell-Villada, Gene Harold
Chang, Cecilia
Druxes, Helga
Dunn, Susan
Gagliardi, Frank M.
Gimenez, Antonio
Ishikawa, Minako
Katarzyna, Olga B.
Kieffer, Bruce
Kubler, Cornelius C.

Nahson, Daniel L.
Newman, Gail M.
Nicastro, Anthony J.
Norton, Glyn P.
Piper, Anson Conant
Rouhi, Leyla
Schott-Desrosiers, Nicole
Silber, Cathy L.
Stamelman, Richard
Yamada, Reiko
Zilcosky, John

Winchester
Sardkodie-Mensah, Kwasi

Worcester
Alvarez Borland, Isabel
Arend, Jutta
Bernstein, Eckhard Richard
Cull, John T.
DeHoratius, Edmund F.
Ferguson, William Rotch
Fraser, Theodore
Freear Roberts, Helen
Hamilton, John Daniel Burgoyne
Kom, Ambroise
Lamoureux, Normand J.
Lavery, Gerard B.
Ross, Claudia
Sazaki, Kristina R.
Stone, Cynthia

MICHIGAN

Adrian
Elardo, Ronald Joseph

Albion
Baumgartner, Ingeborg Hogh

Allendale
Franklin, Ursula

Alma
Ottenhoff, John

Ann Arbor
Becker, Alton Lewis
Bellamy, James Andrew
Billick, David Joseph
Brend, Ruth Margaret
Burling, Robbins
Casa, Frank Paul
Cowen, Roy C.
Danly, Robert Lyons
Fabian, Hans Joachim
Field, Norma
Freedman, David Noel
Frier, Bruce Woodward
George, Emery Edward
Goic, Cedomil
Gray, Floyd Francis
Hafter, Monroe Z.
Johnson, Mayumi Yuki
Koenen, Ludwig
McCarren, Vincent Paul
Muller, Marcel
Paslick, Robert H.
Porter, J.I.
Rastalsky, Hartmut
Seidler, Ingo
Stolz, Benjamin Armond
Weiss, Hermann Friedrich
Windfuhr, Gernot Ludwig

Berkley
Vernier, Richard

Berrien Springs
Economou, Elly Helen
Running, Leona Glidden

Detroit
Chauderlot, Fabienne Sophie
Cobbs, Alfred Leon
Dubruck, Edelgard E.
Gutierrez, Jesus
Kibler, Louis Wayne
Koontz, Christian
Latta, Susan M.
Lauer, Janice M
Ronnick, Michele Valerie
Schurlknight, Donald E.
Stern, Guy
Stivale, Charles J.
Vlasopolos, Anca

Wedberg, Lloyd W.

East Lansing
Abbott, B.
Compitello, Malcolm Alan
Dulai, Surjit Singh
Falk, Julia Sableski
Fiore, Robert L.
Goodson, Alfred Clement
Gray, Eugene Francis
Hughes, William Nolin
Imamura, Shigeo
Josephs, Herbert
Juntune, Thomas William
Koppisch, Michael Seibert
Kronegger, Maria Elisabeth
Mansour, George Phillip
Miller, Vernon D.
Porter, Laurence M.
Stalker, James Curtis
Stockman, Ida J.
Wright, Robert L.
Yates, Donald Alfred

Grand Rapids
Fetzer, Glenn W.

Kalamazoo
Earhart, Harry Byron
Gibson, Melissa K.

Lansing
Harrison, Ann Tukey
Kissling, Paul J.

Marquette
Thundy, Zacharias Pontian

Rochester
Coppola, Carlo

University Center
Clark, Basil Alfred
Wang, Mason Yu-Heng

Ypsilanti
Daigle-Williamson, Marsha A.
Kauffman, Janet
Keller, Gary D.
Staal, Arie
Stevens, Lizbeth Jane

MINNESOTA

Collegeville
Haile, Getatchew
Richardson, Scott D.

Duluth
Conant, Jonathan Brendan
Hellenbrand, Harold
Jankofsky, Klaus J.
Linn, Michael D.
Zeitz, Eileen

Gorham
Cowart, Wayne
Fouchereaux, Jean

Minneapolis
Akehurst, F.R.P.
Arenas, Fernando
Barnes, Betsy
Bashiri, Iraj
Brewer, Maria Minich
Clayton, Tom
Erickson, Gerald M.
Ferran, Ofelia
Firchow, Evelyn Scherabon
Fullerton, Gerald Lee
Grimstad, Kaaren
Gumpel, Liselotte
Gundel, J.K.
Hirschbach, Frank Donald
Jahn, Gary Robert
Jara, Rene
Jensen, J. Vernon
Klee, Carol
Krevans, Nita
Lardinois, Andre P.M.H.
Levinson, Bernard M.
Liberman, Anatoly
Malandra, William
Martinez, Ronald L.
Noakes, Susan

O'Connell, Joanna
Ocampo, Francisco
Olson, Stuart Douglas
Paganini, Maria
Parente, James A., Jr.
Polakiewicz, Leonard A.
Preckshot, Judith
Prell, Riv-Ellen
Ramos-Garcia, Luis A.
Sarles, Harvey Burton
Sheets, George Archibald
Sivert, Eileen
Stenson, Nancy Jean
Sullivan, Constance
Thomas, Gary Craig
Vidal, Hernan
Wakefield, Ray Milan
Waldauer, Joseph
Zahareas, Anthony

Moorhead
Kaplan, James Maurice

Northfield
Achberger, Karen Ripp
Allen, Wendy
Buckstead, Richard C.
Cisar, Mary
Dust, Patrick
Fink, Karl J.
Groton, Anne H.
Ignashev, Diane M. Nemec
Kaga, Mariko
May, James M.
Rippley, La Vern J.
Smith, Bardwell L.
Yandell, Cathy

South Minneapolis
MacLeish, Andrew

St. Paul
Chew, Kristina
Dye, Robert Ellis
Hensley, Carl Wayne
Palmerton, Patricia R.
Schubert, Virginia Ann
Wolsey, Mary Lou Morris
Zurakowski, Michele M.

St. Peter
Flory, Stewart Gilman
Walter, Renee

Winona
Nichols, Ann

MISSISSIPPI

Clinton
Martin, Charles Edward

Jackson
Freis, Catherine R.
Freis, Richard
Gleason, Michael
Harvey, Maria-Luisa Alvarez
Krabbe, Judith
Olivia, Leonora

Mississippi State
Blaney, Benjamin
Chatham, James Ray
Emplaincourt, Edmond Arthur
Wiltrout, Ann Elizabeth

University
Moysey, Robert Allen

MISSOURI

Bolivar
Derryberry, Bob R.

Chesterfield
Winn, Colette Henriette

Columbia
Barabtarlo, Gennady
Braun, Ernst
Cavigioli, Rita C.
Curtis, James Malcolm
Estevez, Victor A.

Glenn, Pierce
Hooley, Daniel M.
Kuizenga, Donna
Lago, Mary Mcclelland
Lance, Donald M.
Lewis, Marvin A.
Muratore, Mary Jo
Pierce, Glenn
Presberg, Charles D.
Saylor, Charles F.
Scroggins, Daniel Coy
Tarkow, Theodore A.
Thiher, Ottah Allen
Ugarte, Michael

Fayette
Burres, Kenneth Lee
Geist, Joseph E.

Hannibal
Bergen, Robert D.

Joplin
Merriam, Allen H.

Kansas City
Andrews, Stephen J.
Brodsky, Patricia Pollock
Schultz, Joseph P.
Voigts, Linda Ehrsam

Kirksville
Barnes, Jim Weaver
Ramesh, Clospeth N.

Springfield
Nugent, Pauline
Polly, Lyle R.

St. Louis
Cargas, Harry James
Danker, Frederick W.
Hegel, Robert Earl
Herron, Robert Deupree
Lutzeler, Paul Michael
Mitchell, Christopher
Pautrot, Jean-Louis
Poag, James F.
Rozbicki, Michael J.
Schraibman, Joseph
Schwarz, E.
Stampino, Maria Galli
Tatlock, Lynn
Williams, Gerhild Scholz

Warrensburg
Doyle, Ruth Lestha
Phillips, Kendall R.
Selvidge, Marla J.

MONTANA

Billings
Jensen, Theodore Wayne

Bozeman
Coffey, Jerome Edward
Jelinski, Jack Bernard
O'Donnell, Victoria

Missoula
Acker, Robert
Arens, Hiltrud
Kanevskaya, Marina
Rolfe, Oliver Willis
Rose, Stanley Ludwig
Shuy, Roger W.

NEBRASKA

Kearney
Pearson, Lon

Lincoln
Balasubramanian, Radha
Becker, Edward
Bormann, Dennis Robert
Crawford, Dan
Crawford, Sidnie White
Karch, Dieter
Meininger, Robert Alan
Owomoyela, Oyekan
Pitt, David

Rinkevich, Thomas E.
Saskova-Pierce, Mila
Sayward, Charles
Seiler, William John

Omaha
Conner, Maurice Wayne
Irvin, Deborah M.
Lafontant, Julien J.

NEVADA

Las Vegas
Clark, Thomas L.
Engberg, Norma J.
Healey, William C.
Hilgar, Marie-France
Irsfeld, John Henry
Koester, Rudolf Alfred
Kyle Higgins, Amanda
Schmiedel, Donald Emerson

Reno
De Rafols, Wifredo
Lange, Horst
Manca, Franco
Pettey, John Carson
Rojas, J. Nelson
Sackett, Theodore Alan
Sepulveda-Pulventini, Emma
Tchudi, Stephen
Wagener, Guy
Whitenack, Judith A.

NEW HAMPSHIRE

Bradford
Jacobsen, Thorkild

Dublin
Germain, Edward B.

Durham
Callan, Richard Jerome
Clark, Mary Morris
Jacoby, Sally
Marshall, Grover Edwin
Polasky, Janet
Rouman, John Christ

Exeter
Wooley, Allan D.

Hanover
Allan, Sarah
Beasley, Faith E.
Chitoran, Ioanaa
Dorsey, James
Duncan, Bruce
Garretson, Deborah
Gemunden, Gerd
Glinert, Lewis
Grenoble, Lenore A.
Higgins, Lynn Anthony
Hirsch, Marianne
Hoffmeister, Werner
Kacandes, Irene
Kenkel, Konrad
Kogan, Vivian
Loseff, Lev V.
Major, John Stephen
Mowry, Hua-yuan Li
Oxenhandler, Neal
Oxenhandler, Neal
Rainer, Ulrike
Scher, Steven Paul
Scherr, Barry P.
Shookman, Ellis
Sices, David
Washburn, Dennis
Whaley, Lindsay
Zantop, Susanne

Portsmouth
Howard, Joan E.

NEW JERSEY

Bloomfield
Figueredo, Danilo H.
Fuller, Clarence

Camden
Showalter, English

East Orange
Thorburn, Carolyn Coles

Ewing
Wong, Jean

Highland Park
Walker, Steven Friemel

Lakewood
McCarthy, Mary Theresa

Lawrenceville
Finello, Dominick Louis
Mcleod, Alan L.

Madison
Becker, Lucille Frackman
Kopp, Richard L.
Lenz, John Richard
Marchione, Margherita Frances
Wescott, Roger Williams

Montclair
Kelly, David H.
Olenik, John Kenneth
Rambaldo, Ana M.

Morristown
Hahn, Hannelore

New Brunswick
Attridge, Derek
Belton, John
Chandler, Daniel Ross
Crane, Susan
DeKoven, Marianne
Derbyshire, William W.
Dowling, William C.
Epstein, Richard
Fizer, John
Galperin, William
George, Kearns
Guetti, James L.
Harris, Daniel A.
Jehlin, Myra
Levine, George L.
Lyons, Bridget G.
McClure, John
Nagy, Edward
Neuse, Erna Kritsch
Ostriker, Alicia
Pirog, Gerald
Qualls, Barry V.
Rockland, Michael Aaron
Serrano, Richard
Tu, Ching-I
Walker, Janet Anderson

Newark
Russell, Charles

Piscataway
Dauster, Frank Nicholas

Princeton
Bing, Janet Mueller
Clinton, Jerome Wright
Corngold, Stanley Alan
Curschmann, Michael
Ermolaev, Herman
Fagles, Robert
Hinderer, Walter
Hollander, Robert
Isaac, Ephraim
Kaster, Robert A.
Levin, Thomas Y.
Ma, John
Martin, Richard Peter
Most, Glenn Warren
Negus, Kenneth George
Steele, Marta N.
Teiser, Stephen F.
Townsend, Charles Edward
Uitti, Karl David
Zeitlin, Froma I.

Princeton Junction
Makino, Yasuko

Somerset
Azzi, Marie-Denise Boros

South Orange
Pastor, Leslie P.
Zalacain, Daniel

Toms River
Magliola, Robert

Trenton
Richman, Stephen

Upper Montclair
Schlant, Ernestine

Wayne
Aguirre, Angela M.
Keumsil, Kim Yoon
Lesikin, Joan
Martinez, Esther M.
Rabbitt, Kara
Rosa, William
Saa, Orland
Williams, Bruce

West Orange
Yang, Winston L.

NEW MEXICO

Albuquerque
Axelrod, Melissa
Beene, LynnDianne
Bills, Garland D.
Bybee, Joan L.
Gillette Sturm, Fred
Hall, Linda
Isham, William P.
John-Steiner, Vera P.
Marquez, Antonio
Morford, Jill P.
Perrin Wilcox, Phyllis
Wilcox, Sherman E.

Hanover
Sheldon, Richard

Las Cruces
Rundell, Richard Jason

Santa Fe
Meyer, Doris

Silver City
Ollivier, Louis L.

University Park
Dubois, Betty Lou

NEW YORK

Albany
Baran, Henryk
Elam, Helen Regueiro
Frank, Francine
Greene, Robert William
Hartman, C.
Kanes, Martin
Lawrence, Samuel G.
Nepaulsingh, Colbert Ivor
Refai, Shahid
Sanders, Robert E.
Scatton, Ernest Alden
Shane, Alex Michael
Smith, Karen A.
Strelka, Joseph Peter
Wittkowski, Wolfgang

Annandale
Rosenberg, Justus

Binghamton
Bernardo, Aldo Sisto
Block, Haskell M.
Coates, Carrol F.
Cocozzella, Peter
Cypess, Sandra Messinger
Fischler, Alexander

LaValva, Rosemarie
O'Connor, Thomas
Polachek, Dora
Rose, Marilyn Gaddis
Sticca, Sandro
Stillman, Norman Arthur
Stillman, Yedida Kalfon
Van Baelen, Jacqueline

Brockport
Siracusa, Joseph

Bronx
Bullaro, Grace Russo
Clark, John Richard
Dimler, George Richard
Kabakoff, Jacob
Kligerman, Jack
Macary, Jean Louis
Struve, Walter
Tusiani, Joseph

Brooklyn
Ashley, Leonard R.N.
Black, Nancy BreMiller
Clayman, Dee Lesser
Doron, Pinchas
Filer, Malva Esther
Fogel, Herbert
Gerber, Barbara Leslie
Jofen, Jean
Koch, Ernst
Langley, Stephen G.
Mermall, Thomas
Seiden, Morton Irving
Solan, Lawrence
Stevens-Arroyo, Antonio M.
Wolfe, Ethyle Renee

Brookville
McKenna, Sheila
Nalbantian, Suzanne

Buffalo
Aubery, Pierre
Bachman, Charles Roger
Bucher, Gerard C.
Camurati, Mireya Beatriz
Coffta, David J.
Copjec, Joan
Dudley, Edward J.
Feal, Carlos
Feal, Gisele C.
Feal, Rosemary Geisdorfer
Federman, Raymond
Fradin, Joseph I.
Gasche, Rodolphe
Grosz, Elizabeth
Guitart, Jorge Miguel
Hewitt, Andrew
Iggers, Wilma Abeles
Jacobs, Carol F.
Koekkoek, Byron J.
Mathiot, Madeleine
Metzger, Erika Alma
Metzger, Michael Moses
Robbins, Jill
Soons, C. Alan
Sussman, Henry
Vargas, Margarita

Canton
Goldberg, Rita Maria

Clinton
Medina, Jeremy Tyler
Rabinowitz, Peter Jacob

Fairport
Carlton, Charles Merritt

Far Rockaway
Pollack, Gloria W.

Flushing
Brown, Royal Scott
Epstein, Edmund Lloyd
Fichtner, Edward G.
Haller, Hermann Walter
Russell, Rinaldina
Sungolowsky, Joseph
Whatley, Eric Gordon
Wu, Pei-Yi

Fredonia
Goetz, Thomas Henry
Sonnenfeld, Marion Wilma
Steinberg, Theodore Louis

Zlotchew, Clark M.

Garden City
Friedman, Eva Mary

Geneseo
Lutkus, Alan

Greene
Marsland, Amy

Hamilton
Bien, Gloria
Gallucci, John
Hathaway, Robert L.
Johnson, Anita L.
Julien, Helene
Kepnes, Steven D.
Lintz, Bernadette C.
Luciani, Frederick
Nakhimovsky, Alice
Naughton, John
Nicholls, James C.
Nicholls, Maria
Olcott, Anthony
Rojas, Lourdes
Rugg, Marilyn D.
Suarez-Galban, Eugenio

Hartsdale
Park, Jin Y.

Hempstead
Keener, Frederick M.

Ithaca
Arroyo, Ciriaco
Babby, Leonard Harvey
Bereaud, Jacques
Cohen, Walter Isaac
Colby-Hall, Alice Mary
Deinert, Herbert
Gair, James Wells
Gibian, George
Grossvogel, David I.
Hohendahl, Peter U.
Kaplan, Jane Payne
Kaske, Robert Earl
Kennedy, William John
Kirkwood, Gordon Macdonald
Kronik, John William
Lewis, Philip Eugene
McCann, David Richard
Migiel, Marilyn
Nussbaum, Alan
Owen, David I.
Pelli, Moshe
Piedra, Jose
Suner, Margarita
Waugh, Linda Ruth
Wolff, John Ulrich

Lima
Van Vliet, Edward R.

Loudonville
Munir, Fareed Z.
Yoon, Won C.

Miller Place
Rizzuto, Anthony

New Paltz
Paz, Francis Xavier
Piluso, Robert Vincent

New Rochelle
Colaneri, John Nunzio

New York
Affron, Charles M.
Alexander, Aley E.
Bacon, Helen Hazard
Bagnall, Roger Shaler
Balakian, Anna
Barolini, Teodolinda
Beardsley, Theodore S., Jr.
Belknap, Robert Lamont
Bentley, Eric
Brown, Steven M.
Brush, Craig Balcombe
Cachia, Pierre J.E.
Cameron, Alan
Carrubba, Robert W.
Carson, Katharine Whitman
Cavallo, JoAnn
Caws, Mary Ann
Chelkowski, Peter Jan

Toledo
Abu-Absi, Samir
Boening, John
Gregory, Elmer Richard
Hottell, Ruth A.
Normand, Guessler
Scanlan, Timothy Michael

University Heights
Gyekenyesi Gatto, Katherine
Nevin, Thomas
Seaton, Shirley Smith
Shockey, Gary C.

Wooster
Christianson, Paul
Durham, Carolyn Ann
Falkner, Thomas M.
Gabriele, John P.
Gaylord, Inez K.
Sokol, Elena
Young, Mary

Youngstown
Viehmeyer, L. Allen

OKLAHOMA

Bethany
Jennings, Lawrence Charles

Enid
Green, Virginia M.

Norman
Byre, Calvin S.
Gross, David Stuart
Madland, Helga Stipa
Snell, Daniel C.

Stillwater
Brown, Robert
Converse, Hyla Stuntz
Fitz, Brewster
Halleck, Gene B.
Jewsbury, George Frederick
Moder, Carol Lynn
Schrader, Dorothy Lynne
Stout, Joseph Allen

Tulsa
Udwin, Victor

Weatherford
Lackey, Robert Sam

OREGON

Corvallis
Carroll, Carleton Warren
Kesler, Linc
Rice, Laura
Uzgalis, William

Eugene
Desroches, Richard Henry
Epple, Juan Armando
Gontrum, Peter B.
Hart, Thomas Roy
Kohl, Stephen William
Lowenstam, Steven
Nicholls, Roger Archibald
Pascal, Cecil Bennett
Plant, Helmut R.

Portland
Engelhardt, Klaus Heinrich
Macias, Manuel Jato
Mayr, Franz Karl

PENNSYLVANIA

Abington
Cintas, Pierre Francois Diego

Allentown
Kipa, Albert Alexander

Ardmore
Abdelrahim-Soboleva, Valentina

Bala-Cynwyd
Webb, Gisela

Beaver Falls
Watt, Jonathan M.

Bethlehem
Fifer, Elizabeth
Lewis, David Wilfrid Paul
Vickrey, John Frederick

Bloomsburg
Bertelsen, Dale A.
Brasch, Walter Milton
Fuller, Lawrence Benedict
Smith, Riley Blake

Bryn Mawr
Banziger, Hans
Dersofi, Nancy
Dickerson, Gregory Weimer
Dorian, Nancy Currier
Gaisser, Julia Haig
Hamilton, Richard
Lang, Mabel Louise
Maurin, Mario
Salmon, John Hearsey Mcmillan

California
Murdick, William

Carlisle
Beverley Driver, Eddy
Lockhart, Philip N.
Roethke, Gisela

Chester
Melzi, Robert C.

Collegeville
Clark, Hugh R.
Clouser, Robin A.

Doylestown
Corbett, Janice

Dunmore
Daniels, Marilyn
Smith, Gayle Leppin

East Stroudsburg
Ahumada, Alfredo
Mercado, Juan Carlos

Easton
Cap, Jean-Pierre
Pribic, Rado

Elkins Park
Murphy, Laurence Lyons

Fayetteville
Ross, Marilyn A.

Gettysburg
Crowner, David L.
Ritterson, Michael

Harrisburg
Wood, Bryant G.

Haverford
Anyinefa, Koffi

Huntingdon
Doyle, Esther M.

Immaculata
Bonfini, Marie Roseanne IHM

Kutztown
Craig, Charlotte Marie
Paulson, Michael G.

Lancaster
Farber, Jay Joel
Jeannet, Angela Maria

Latrobe
Maloney, Elliott Charles

Lewisburg
Beard, Robert Earl
Huffines, Marion Lois

Lincoln University
Maazaoui, Abbes
Rodgers, Joseph James, Jr.

Malvern
Kelley, Kathleen Alita

Meadville
Zolbrod, Paul Geyer

Media
McMullen, Wayne J.
Sorkin, Adam J.

Millersville
Hopkins, Leroy Taft, Jr.
Oppenheimer, Fred E.
Skitter, Hans Gunter

New Wilmington
Botzenhart-Viehe, Verena
Bove, Carol Mastrangelo
Turner, James Hilton

Philadelphia
Allen, Roger Michael Ashley
Bender, Ernest
Benson, Morton
Blumenthal, Bernhardt George
Bodde, Derk
Bowman, Frank Paul
Brevart, Francis B.
Burch, Francis Floyd
Cardona, George
Donahue, Thomas John
Earle, Peter G.
Enns, Peter
Freeman, Donald Cary
Gaeffke, Peter
Garr, W. Randall
Herz, Julius Michael
Hiz, Henry
Hoenigswald, Henry M.
Lebofsky, Dennis Stanley
Leichty, Erle Verdun
Lieberman, Stephen Jacob
Lisker, Leigh
Lloyd, Paul M.
Lopez, Ignacio Javier
Mair, Victor H.
Mall, Rita Sparrow
Marcus, Milicent
McCarthy, John Aloysius
Porter, Abioseh Michael
Prince, Gerald
Regueiro, Jose Miguel
Roulin, Jean-Marie
Rudnytzky, Leonid
Sebold, Russell Perry
Thomas, Ruth Paula
Traupman, John Charles
Trommler, Frank Alfred
Waldman, Glenys A.

Pittsburgh
Al-Kasey, Tamara
Ashliman, D.L.
Bart, Benjamin Franklin
Colecchia, Frances
Dana, Marie Immaculee
Dekeyser, R.M.
Dworkin y Mendez, Kenya C.
Feldman, Heidi M.
Freed, Barbara
Frey, Herschel J.
Green, Anne
Groch, John R.
Hallstein, Christian W.
Harris, Jane Gary
Hart, John Augustine
Hopper, Paul
Jonas, Klaus Werner
Jones, Christopher M.
Jones, Nicholas Francis
Juffs, Alan
Koch, Philip
Koda, Keiko
Mcshea, William Patrick
Mills, David Otis
Paulston, Christina Bratt
Polansky, Susan
Preuss, Mary
Rockmore, Sylvie
Schlossman, Beryl
Silenieks, Juris
So, Sufumi
Tucker, Richard
Walker, Janet L.

Yaruss, J. Scott

Radnor
Halpern, Cynthia L.
Halpern, Cynthia Leone

Rosemont
Glass, Erlis

Saint Davids
Boehne, Patricia Jeanne

Scranton
Kamla, Thomas A.
Ledford-Miller, Linda
Parsons, Robert A.
Petrovic, Njegos M.
Wilson, Joseph P.

Selinsgrove
Manning, Scott

Slippery Rock
Zinni, Hannah Case

State College
Betlyon, John Wilson

Swarthmore
Avery, George Costas
Moskos, George
North, Helen Florence
Ostwald, Martin

University Park
Brault, Gerard Joseph
Browning, Barton W.
Fitz, Earl Eugene
Fleming, Raymond Richard
Frautschi, Richard Lane
Gentry, F.G.
Greenberg, Wendy
Grossman, Kathryn Marie
Hale, Thomas Albert
Halsey, Martha T.
Knight, Alan Edgar
Lacy, Norris J.
Makward, Christiane Perrin
Paternost, Joseph
Peavler, Terry J.
Schmalstieg, William Riegel
Wanner, Adrian J.
Ward, Patricia Ann
Weiss, Beno
Ziegler, Vickie L.
Ziegler, Vickie Lynne

Villanova
Helmetag, Charles Hugh

West Chester
Gutwirth, Madelyn

Wilkes-Barre
Corgan, Margaret M.
Krawczeniuk, Joseph V.
McGrath, Michael J.

Williamsport
Maples, Robert John Barrie

Wynnewood
McDaniel, Thomas F.

Yardley
Means, John B.

York
Barr, Jeanine R.
McKulik, Ben
Medina, Cindy

RHODE ISLAND

Kingston
Culatta, Barbara
Hutton, Lewis J.
Ketrow, Sandra M.
Kovarsky, Dana
Manteiga, Robert Charles
Rogers, Kenneth Hall

Providence
Ahearn, Edward J.
Blumstein, Sheila Ellen

Chaika, Elaine Ostrach
Coons, Dix Scott
Crossgrove, William Charles
Durand, Frank
Fido, Franco
Francis, Winthrop Nelson
Kucera, Henry
Lesko, Leonard Henry
Lieberman, Philip
Love, Frederick Rutan
Oldcorn, Anthony
Pucci, Joseph M.
Scholes, Robert
Scott, Daniel Marcellus
Spilka, Mark
Teng, Tony
Terras, Victor

Saunderstown
Waters, Harold A.

SOUTH CAROLINA

Aiken
Rich, John Stanley

Clemson
Sinka, Margit M.

Columbia
Elfe, Wolfgang Dieter
French, Harold Wendell
Fryer, T. Bruce
Hardin, James Neal
Henry, Freeman George
Little, Greta D.
Miller, Paul
Montgomery, Michael M.
Roy, George Ross
Shirley, Paula

Florence
Harding, George E.

Greenville
Cherry, Charles Maurice
Cox, Jerry Lynn
Lawson, Darren P.
Parsell, David Beatty

Hartsville
Doubles, Malcolm Carroll

Spartanburg
Bullard, John Moore

SOUTH DAKOTA

Vermillion
Klein, Dennis Allan
Sebesta, Judith Lynn

Yankton
Kessler, Ann Verona

TENNESSEE

Bristol
Jordan, Greogory D.

Cleveland
Kailing, Joel

Cookeville
Campana, Phillip Joseph
Slotkin, Alan Robert
Viera, David John

Jackson
Maire-Carls, Alice-Catherine

Johnson City
Harrington, Karen A.
Nelson, Ardis H.
Schneider, Valerie Lois
Williams, Edwin W.
Zayas-Bazan, Eduardo

Contreras, Heles
Eastman, Carol M.
Ellrich, Robert John
Gray, Richard T.
Hertling, Gunter H.
Klausenburger, Jurgen
Kramer, Karl D.
Marinoni, R. Max
Micklesen, Lew R.
Noegel, Scott
Nostrand, Howard Lee
Pascal, Paul
Pauwels, Heidi
Peck, Jeffrey Marc
Perozo, Jaime J.
Predmore, Michael P.
Reinking, Victor
Rey, William Henry
Saporta, Sol
Shapiro, Michael C.
Stark, James
Tollefson, James William
Webb, Eugene
Wulff, Donald H.
Ziadeh, Farhat Jacob

Spokane
Cook, Susan L.
Hazel, Harry Charles
Schlatter, Fredric William

Tacoma
Curley, Michael Joseph

Walla Walla
Hashimoto, I.Y.

WEST VIRGINIA

Institute
Thorn, Arline Roush

Morgantown
Bruner, Jeffrey
Conner, Patrick Wayne
Murphy, Joseph Anthony
Schlunk, Juergen Eckart

Wheeling
Laker, Joseph Alphonse

WISCONSIN

Appleton
Reed, Gervais Eyer
Taylor, Daniel Jennings
Ternes, Hans

Beloit
Freeman, Thomas Parry
Street, Jack David

De Pere
Zahorski, Kenneth

Green Bay
Fleurant, Ken

Kenosha
Dean, Dennis Richard
Loewen, Lynn
Rothstein, Marian
Stathatos, Constantine Christopher
Tavera Rivera, Margarita
Yang, Mimi

La Crosse
Socha, Donald

Madison
Bender, Todd K.
Berghahn, Klaus L
Cassidy, Frederic Gomes
Ciplijauskaite, Birute
Cunliffe, William Gordon
Grittner, Frank Merton
Gross, Sabine
Hanrez, Marc
Hermand, Jost
Hunter, Linda
Ingwersen, Niels
Kleinhenz, Christopher
LeMoine, Fannie J.

Marks, Elaine
Marquess, Harlan Earl
McKeown, James C.
Memon, Muhammad Umar
Naess, Harald S.
Nicholas, Robert Leon
Nollendorfs, Valters
Ormand, Kirk
Read, Charles
Rodini, Robert Joseph
Schoville, Keith Norman
Scott, Charles Thomas
Sihler, Andrew L.
Silberman, M.
Von Schneidemesser, Luanne
Yetunde Faelarin Schleicher, Antonia
Young, Richard
Zeps, Valdis Juris

Manitowoc
Bjerke, Robert Alan

Milwaukee
Benda, Gisela
Blau, Herbert
Corre, Alan David
Downing, Pamela A.
Filips-Juswigg, Katherina P.
Friedman, Melvin Jack
Grossfeld, Bernard
Hubbard, Carol P.
Jones, Robert Alston
Martin-Rodriguez, Manuel M.
Mileham, James Warren
Moravcsik, Edith Andrea
Rodriquez - Luis, Julio
Skalitzky, Rachel Irene
Swanson, Roy Arthur
Taylor, Steven Millen
Ullman, Pierre Lioni
Winter, Ian James

Ripon
Peterson, Brent O.

Stevens Point
Meisel, Martin

Waukesha
Dailey, Joseph
Settle, Peter

Whitewater
Adams, George Roy

WYOMING

Laramie
Bagby, Lewis
Bangerter, Lowell A.
Durer, Christopher
Hanson, Klaus D.
Langlois, Walter G.
Larsen, Kevin
Mayer, Sigrid
Mundt, Hannelore
Picherit, Jean-Louis
Rhoades, Duane
Sigalov, Pavel S.
Tolo, Khama-Basilli

PUERTO RICO

San Juan
Guerro, Maria C.M. de
Morris, Marshall
Pagan, Samuel
Schnitzer, M.L.
Vallone, Ralph, Jr.

VIRGIN ISLANDS

St. Thomas
Cooper, Vincent O'Mahony
Sprauve, Gilbert A.

CANADA

ALBERTA

Calgary
Cook, Eung-Do
Southerland, Ronald Hamilton
Struc, Roman Sviatoslav
Zekulin, Nicholas Gleb

Edmonton
Blodgett, Edward D.
Dimic, Milan Velimir
Dryer, Matthew S.
Egert, Eugene
Forcadas, Alberto M.
Grant, Raymond James Shepherd
Marahrens, Gerwin
Margolin, Uri
Mozejko, Edward
Prideaux, Gary Dean
Slavutych, Yar

BRITISH COLUMBIA

Burnaby
Davison, Rosena
Merler, Grazia

Vancouver
Batts, Michael S.
Bongie, Laurence
Frose, Victor
Goetz-Stankiewicz, Marketa
Hamlin, Frank Rodway
Knutson, Harold Christian
Merivale, Patricia
Mornin, Edward
Petersen, Klaus
Pulleyblank, Edwin George
Raoul, Valerie
Saint-Jacques, Bernard
Sullivan, Shirley Darcus
Swart, Paula

Victoria
Archibald, Elizabeth F.
Bradley, Keith Richard
Carlin, Claire L.
Edwards, Anthony S.G.
Fitch, J.G.
Hadley, Michael Llewellyn
Herique, Emmanuel
Holmberg, I.E.
Howard, Lloyd H.
Hsieh, Yvonne Y.
Limbrick, Elaine
Niang, Sada
Riedel, Walter Erwin
Ross, Mary Ellen
Tucker, John J.
Vautier, Marie
Waelti-Walters, Jennifer

MANITOBA

Winnipeg
Cooper, Craig
Doerksen, Victor Gerard
Gordon, Alexander Lobban
Harvey, Carol
Heidenreich, Rosmarin
Joubert, Andre
Klostermaier, Klaus Konrad
Marantz, Enid Goldstine
Sauer, Angelika

NEW BRUNSWICK

Fredericton
Edwards, Viviane
Pugh, Anthony Roy

Moncton
Gallant, Christel

NEWFOUNDLAND

St. John's
Hewson, John
Thomas, Gerald

NOVA SCOTIA

Halifax
Bishop, Michael
Chavy, Paul
Gesner, B. Edward

Wolfville
Best, Janice
Fink, Robert J.

ONTARIO

Downsview
Bar-Lewaw, Itzhak I.
Corbett, Noel L.
Cotnam, Jacques
Schueler, Heinz Juergen

Guelph
Benson, Renate

Hamilton
Cro, Stelio
Lee, Alvin A

Kingston
Bessette, Gerard
Bly, Peter Anthony
Shirinian, Lorne
Surridge, Marie

London
Baguley, David
Cozea, Angela
de Looze, Laurence
Mihailescu, Calin Andrei
Picard, Anne Marie
Purdy, Anthony
Roulston, Christine
Thomson, Clive
Vaillancourt, Daniel

Mississauga
Rubincam, Catherine I.

Montreal
Bircher, Martin

North York
Brown, Michael G.
Embleton, Sheila

Ottawa
Clayton, John Douglas
Delisle, Jean
Dionne, Rene
Elbaz, Andre Elie
Eldredge, Laurence Milton
Goheen, Jutta
Grise, Yolande
Gualtieri, Antonio Roberto
Imbert, Patrick L.
Jensen, John T.
Jurado, Jose
Kelly, Louis G.
Koerner, Ernst F.K.
Lapierre, Andre
Le Moine, Roger
Major, Jean-Louis
Poplack, Shana
Rivero, Maria Luisa
Sbrocchi, Leonard G.
Yalden, Janice

Rockwood
Eichner, Hans

St. Catharines
McGarrell, Hedy M.
Sanchez, Monica E.
Schutz, Herbert

Sudbury
Colilli, Paul
Lewis, Gertrud Jaron

Thunder Bay
Nabarra, Alain
Schonberger, Vincent L.

Toronto
Burke, James F.
Case, Fredrick I.
Chambers, J.K.
Chandler, Stanley Bernard
Ching, Julia
Clarke, Ernest George
Clivio, Gianrenzo Pietro
Cloutier, Cecile
Curtis, Alexander Ross
Dainard, James A.
Danesi, Marcel
Dolezel, Lubomir
Dolezvelova-Velingerova, Milena
Ellis, Keith A.A.
Fitch, Brian T.
Genno, Charles N.
Grayson, Albert K.
Gulsoy, J.
Hayne, David Mackness
Heinemann, Edward Arthur
Hutcheon, Linda
Iannucci, Amilcare Alfredo
Joyce, Dougals A.
Kushner, Eva
Latta, Alan Dennis
Lehouck, Emile
Leland, Charles Wallace
Leon, Pedro
Leon, Pierre R.A.
Levy, Kurt Leopold
Marmura, Michael Elias
Martin, Philippe Jean
Matilal, Bimal Krishna
Paterson, Janet M.
Pugliese, Olga
Saddlemyer, Ann
Samarin, William J.
Seliger, Helfried Werner
Smith, David W.
Tolton, Cameron David Edward
Tsukimura, Reiko
Valdes, Mario James
Warwick, Jack
Wetzel, Heinz

Waterloo
Abbott, Carmeta
Ages, Arnold
Castricano, Jodey
Dube, Pierre
Forsyth, Phyllis
Fournier, Hannah
Grubisic, Vinko
Hoefert, Sigfrid
John, David Gethin
Kuxdorf, Manfred
Marteinson, Peter
Miraglia, Anne Marie
Niccoli, Gabriel
Panthel, Hans Walter
Russell, Delbert
Ryan, Robert
Socken, Paul
Szarycz, Ireneusz
Weldon, James
Wilson, Don
Zweers, Alexander Frederik

West Hill
Franceschetti, Antonio

Windsor
Atkinson, Colin B.
Bebout, Linda J.
Ditsky, John M.
Halford, Peter W.
Harder, Bernhard D.
Herendeen, Wyman H.
Janzen, Henry David
Kingstone, Basil D.
Mackendrick, Louis King
MacLeod, Alistair
Quinsey, Katherine M.
Smedick, Lois Katherine
Spellman, John Willard
Straus, Barrie Ruth
van den Hoven, Adrian

QUEBEC

Hull
L'Allier, Louis

Lennoxville
Kuepper, Karl Josef

Montreal
Austin, Paul Murray
Bernier, Paul
Bertrand de Munoz, Maryse
Clarke, Murray
Clas, Andre
Culter, Suzanne
D'Andrea, Antonio
Dean, Kenneth
Domaradzki, Theodore F.
Dorsinville, Max

Duquette, Jean-Pierre
Fong, Grace
Gallati, Ernst
Germain, Claude
Godin, Jean Cleo
Gopnik, Myrna
Haberl, Franz P.
Hale, Mark
Hanna, Blake Thompson
LaMarre, Thomas
Merken, Kathleen
Miller, David
Ouimette, Victor
Reiss, Charles
Ricard, Francois
Robinson, Ira
Stewart, Pamela Dawes
Yates, Robin D.S.

Quebec
Desautels, Jacques
Desautels, Jacques
Hirtle, Walter Heal
Mackey, William Francis
Manning, Alan
Risco, Antonio

Sherbrooke
Forest, Jean

OTHER COUNTRIES

BULGARIA
Moser, Charles A.

FRANCE
Benichou, Paul
Issacharoff, Michael

GERMANY
Krois, John Michael

HONG KONG
Powers, John H.

ISRAEL
Greenberg, Moshe
Greenfield, Jonas Carl

ITALY
McCarthy, Dennis John

JAPAN
Sugimoto, Naomi
Bruce, James C.

NEW ZEALAND
Tittler, Jonathan Paul

SWITZERLAND
Jost, Dominik

TAIWAN
Chen, Shih-Shin